New Standard Encyclopedia
Dictionary

Webster Illustrated
Contemporary
Dictionary
New Standard Encyclopedia Edition

Standard Educational Corporation

CHICAGO

Pro·crus·tes (prō·krus′tēz) *Gk. Myth.* A giant who tied travelers to an iron bed and amputated or stretched their limbs until they fitted it.

proc·tol·o·gy (prok·tol′ə·jē) *n.* The branch of medicine which deals with diseases of the lower colon, rectum, and anus. [< Gk. *proktos* anus + -LOGY] —**proc·to·log·i·cal** (prok′tə·loj′i·kəl) *adj.* —**proc·tol′o·gist** *n.*

proc·tor (prok′tər) *n.* **1** An agent acting for another; proxy. **2** A university or college official charged with maintaining order, supervising examinations, etc. —*v.t.* & *v.i.* To supervise (an examination). [< PROCURATOR] —**proc·to·ri·al** (prok·tôr′ē·əl, -tō′rē-) *adj.*

proc·to·scope (prok′tə·skōp) *n.* A surgical instrument for examining the interior of the rectum. —**proc·tos·co·py** (prok·tos′kə·pē) *n.*

pro·cum·bent (prō·kum′bənt) *adj.* **1** *Bot.* Lying on the ground; trailing. **2** Lying face down; prone. [< L *pro-* forward + *cubare* lie down]

proc·u·ra·tor (prok′yə·rā′tər) *n.* **1** A person authorized to manage the affairs of another. **2** In ancient Rome, one in charge of imperial revenues, esp. in a province. —**proc′u·ra·to′ri·al** (-rə·tôr′ē·əl, -tō′rē-) *adj.*

pro·cure (prō·kyŏŏr′) *v.* **·cured**, **·cur·ing** *v.t.* **1** To obtain by some effort or means; acquire. **2** To bring about; cause. **3** To obtain for the sexual gratification of others. —*v.i.* **4** To obtain women for prostitution. [< L *procurare* look after] —**pro·cur′a·ble** *adj.* —**pro·cure′ment, pro·cur′er** *n.*

Pro·cy·on (prō′sē·on) *n.* The most conspicuous star in the constellation Canis Minor. [< Gk. *pro-* before + *kyōn* dog]

prod (prod) *v.t.* **prod·ded, prod·ding** **1** To punch or poke with or as with a pointed instrument. **2** To arouse mentally; urge; goad. —*n.* **1** Any pointed instrument used for prodding. **2** Something that incites one to action. [?] —**prod′der** *n.*

prod. produce; produced; product.

prod·i·gal (prod′ə·gəl) *adj.* **1** Wastefully extravagant, as of money, time, etc. **2** Yielding in profusion; bountiful. **3** Lavish; profuse. —*n.* One who is wastefully extravagant; a spendthrift. [< L *prodigus* wasteful] —**prod′i·gal′i·ty** (-gal′ə·tē) *n.* —**prod′i·gal·ly** *adv.*

pro·dig·ious (prə·dij′əs, prō-) *adj.* **1** Enormous or extraordinary in size, quantity, or degree. **2** Marvelous; amazing. —**pro·dig′ious·ly** *adv.* —**pro·dig′ious·ness** *n.*

prod·i·gy (prod′ə·jē) *n. pl.* **·gies** **1** Something extraordinary or awe-inspiring. **2** An exceptionally gifted child. **3** A monstrosity of nature. [< L *prodigium*]

pro·duce (prə·dyōōs′) *v.* **·duced, ·duc·ing** *v.t.* **1** To bring forth or bear; yield. **2** To bring forth by mental effort; compose, write, etc. **3** To cause to happen or be: His words *produced* a violent reaction. **4** To bring to view; exhibit; show: to *produce* evidence. **5** To manufacture; make. **6** To bring to performance before the public, as a play. **7** To extend or lengthen, as a line. **8** *Econ.* To create (anything with exchangeable value). —*v.i.* **9** To yield or generate an appropriate product or result. —*n.* (prod′yōōs, prō′dyōōs) That which is produced, esp. farm products collectively. [< L *pro-* forward + *ducere* to lead] —**pro·duc′i·ble** *adj.*

pro·duc·er (prə·dyōō′sər) *n.* **1** One who or that which produces. **2** One who makes things for sale and use. **3** One in charge of the production of a public presentation, as of a play, motion picture, etc.

prod·uct (prod′əkt, -ukt) *n.* **1** Anything produced or obtained as a result of some operation or work. **2** *Math.* The result obtained by multiplication. **3** *Chem.* Any substance resulting from chemical change.

pro·duc·tion (prə·duk′shən) *n.* **1** The act or process of producing. **2** The amount produced. **3** Something produced, esp. an artistic work, as a play, motion picture, etc. **4** In political economy, a producing of goods or services.

pro·duc·tive (prə·duk′tiv) *adj.* **1** Producing easily or abundantly. **2** Characterized by fruitful work and accomplishment: a *productive* meeting. **3** Causing; resulting in: with *of.* —**pro·duc′tive·ly** *adv.* —**pro·duc·tiv·i·ty** (prō′duk·tiv′ə·tē), **pro·duc′tive·ness** *n.*

pro·em (prō′əm) *n.* A preface; prelude. [< Gk. *pro-* before + *oimē* song] —**pro·e·mi·al** (prō·ē′mē·əl) *adj.*

prof (prof) *n. Informal* PROFESSOR.

Prof. Professor. • See PROFESSOR.

prof·a·na·tion (prof′ə·nā′shən, prō·fə-) *n.* The act of profaning or the condition of being profaned.

pro·fane (prō·fān′, prə-) *v.t.* **·faned, ·fan·ing** **1** To treat (something sacred) with irreverence or abuse; desecrate. **2** To put to an unworthy or degrading use; debase. —*adj.* **1** Manifesting irreverence or disrespect toward sacred things. **2** Not sacred or religious in theme, content, use, etc.; secular. **3** Not esoteric; ordinary. **4** Vulgar. [< L *pro-* before + *fanum* temple] —**pro·fan·a·to·ry** (prō·fan′ə·tôr′ē, -tō′rē, prə-) *adj.* —**pro·fane′ly** *adv.* —**pro·fan′er** *n.*

pro·fan·i·ty (prō·fan′ə·tē, prə-) *n. pl.* **·ties** **1** The state of being profane. **2** Profane speech or action. Also **pro·fane′ness** (-fān′nis).

pro·fess (prə·fes′, prō-) *v.t.* **1** To declare openly; avow; affirm. **2** To assert, usu. insincerely; make a pretense of: to *profess* remorse. **3** To declare or affirm faith in. **4** To have as one's profession: to *profess* the law. **5** To receive into a religious order. —*v.i.* **6** To make open declaration; avow; offer public affirmation. **7** To take the vows of a religious order. [< L *professus,* pp. of *profiteri* avow, confess] —**pro·fessed′** *adj.* —**pro·fess′ed·ly** (-fes′id·lē) *adv.*

pro·fes·sion (prə·fesh′ən) *n.* **1** An occupation that involves a higher education or its equivalent, and mental rather than manual labor, as law, medicine, teaching, etc. **2** The collective body of those following such an occupation. **3** Any calling or occupation requiring special skills, talents, etc.: the acting *profession.* **4** Any occupation. **5** The act of professing or declaring: *professions* of good will. **6** That which is avowed or professed.

pro·fes·sion·al (prə·fesh′ən·əl) *adj.* **1** Connected with, preparing for, engaged in, appropriate, or conforming to a profession: *professional* courtesy; *professional* skill. **2** Performing or doing for pay an activity often engaged in only for pleasure or recreation: a *professional* golfer. **3** Engaged in by performers, players, etc., who are paid: *professional* hockey. **4** Single-minded and zealous, often excessively so: a *professional* do-gooder. —*n.* **1** One who practices any profession or engages in any activity for pay. **2** One who is exceptionally skilled in some activity. —**pro·fes′sion·al·ism′** *n.* —**pro·fes′sion·al·ly** *adv.*

pro·fes·sion·al·ize (prə·fesh′ən·əl·īz′) *v.t.* **·ized, ·iz·ing** To make professional in character or quality: to *professionalize* tourism. —**pro·fes′sion·al·i·za′tion** *n.*

pro·fes·sor (prə·fes′ər) *n.* **1** A teacher of the highest grade in a university or college. **2** One who professes skill and offers instruction in some sport or art: a *professor* of gymnastics. **3** One who makes open declaration of his opinions, religious faith, etc. —**pro·fes·so·ri·al** (prō′fə·sôr′ē·əl, -sō′rē-, prof′ə-) *adj.* —**pro′fes·so′ri·al·ly** *adv.* —**pro′fes·so′ri·ate** (-it), **pro·fes′sor·ship** *n.* • In writing to a college or university professor, one may use either *Professor* or *Prof.* if the name is written in full or if the initials are used with the last name: *Professor Alfred Kern; Prof. C. E. Young.* If only the last name is used, *Professor* is spelled out.

prof·fer (prof′ər) *v.t.* To offer for acceptance. —*n.* The act of proffering, or that which is proffered. [< L *pro-* in behalf of + *offerre* to offer] —**prof′fer·er** *n.*

pro·fi·cien·cy (prə·fish′ən·sē) *n. pl.* **·cies** The fact or quality of being proficient; skill; competence; expertness.

pro·fi·cient (prə·fish′ənt) *adj.* Thoroughly competent; skilled; expert. —*n.* An expert. [< L *proficere* make progress, go forward] —**pro·fi′cient·ly** *adv.*

pro·file (prō′fīl, *esp. Brit.* prō′fēl) *n.* **1** A human head or face, as viewed from the side; also, a drawing of such a side view. **2** A drawing or view of something in outline or contour. **3** A somewhat brief biographical sketch. **4** Degree of exposure to public attention; public image: The army generals who seized control maintained a very low *profile.* **5** A vertical section of stratified soil or rock. —*v.t.* **·filed, ·fil·ing** **1** To draw a profile of; outline. **2** To write a profile of. [< Ital. *proffilare* draw in outline]

Profile *def. 1*

prof·it (prof′it) n. 1 Any benefit, advantage, or return. 2 *Often pl.* Excess of returns over outlay or expenditure. 3 *Often pl.* The gain obtained from invested capital; also, the ratio of gain to the amount of capital invested. 4 Income gained from property, stocks, etc. —v.i. 1 To be of advantage or benefit. 2 To derive gain or benefit. —v.t. 3 To be of profit or advantage to. [< L *profectus*, p.p. of *proficere* go forward] —**prof′it·less** *adj.*

prof·it·a·ble (prof′it·ə·bəl) *adj.* Bringing profit or gain. —**prof·it·a·bil·i·ty** (prof′ə·tə·bil′ə·tē), **prof′it·a·ble·ness** n. —**prof′it·a·bly** *adv.* —**Syn.** advantageous, beneficial, desirable, expedient, gainful, lucrative, productive, useful, worthwhile.

prof·i·teer (prof′ə·tir′) v.i. To seek or obtain excessive profits. —n. One who makes excessive profits, esp. to the detriment of others. —**prof′i·teer′ing** n.

profit sharing A system by which employees are given a percentage of the net profits of a business.

prof·li·ga·cy (prof′lə·gə·sē) n. The condition or quality of being profligate.

prof·li·gate (prof′lə·git, -gāt) *adj.* 1 Extremely immoral or dissipated; dissolute. 2 Recklessly extravagant. —n. A profligate person. [< L *profligare* strike to the ground, destroy] —**prof′li·gate·ly** *adv.*

pro·found (prə·found′, prō-) *adj.* 1 Intellectually deep or exhaustive: *profound* learning. 2 Reaching to, arising from, or affecting the depth of one's being: a *profound* look; *profound* respect. 3 Reaching far below the surface; deep: a *profound* chasm. 4 Complete; total: a *profound* revision of the book. [< L *pro-* very + *fundus* deep] —**pro·found′ly** *adv.* —**pro·found′ness** n.

pro·fun·di·ty (prə·fun′də·tē, prō-) n. pl. ·ties 1 The state or quality of being profound. 2 A deep place. 3 A profound statement, theory, etc.

pro·fuse (prə·fyōōs′, prō-) *adj.* 1 Giving or given forth lavishly; extravagantly generous. 2 Copious; abundant: *profuse* vegetation. [< L *profusus*, pp. of *profundere* pour forth] —**pro·fuse′ly** *adv.* —**pro·fuse′ness** n.

pro·fu·sion (prə·fyōō′zhən, prō-) n. 1 A lavish supply or condition: a *profusion* of ornaments. 2 The act of pouring forth or supplying in great abundance; prodigality.

prog. progress; progressive.

pro·gen·i·tor (prō·jen′ə·tər) n. 1 A forefather or parent. 2 The originator or source of something. [< L *progignere* beget] —**pro·gen′i·tor·ship′** n.

prog·e·ny (proj′ə·nē) n. pl. ·nies Offspring; descendants. [< L *progignere* beget]

pro·ges·ter·one (prō·jes′tə·rōn) n. An ovarian hormone active in preparing the uterus for reception of the fertilized ovum. Also **pro·ges′tin** (-tin). [< PRO-¹ + GE(STATION) + STER(OL) + -ONE]

prog·na·thous (prog′nə·thəs, prog·nā′-) *adj.* Having projecting jaws. Also **prog·nath·ic** (prog·nath′ik). [< PRO-² + Gk. *gnathos* jaw] —**prog·na·thism** (prog′nə·thiz′əm) n.

prog·no·sis (prog·nō′sis) n. pl. ·ses (-sēz) A prediction or forecast, esp. as to the future course of a disease. [< Gk. *pro-* before + *gignōskein* know]

prog·nos·tic (prog·nos′tik) *adj.* 1 Predictive. 2 Of or useful in a prognosis. —n. 1 A sign of some future occurrence. 2 A basis for a prognosis.

prog·nos·ti·cate (prog·nos′tə·kāt) v.t. ·cat·ed, ·cat·ing 1 To foretell by present indcations. 2 To indicate beforehand; foreshadow. —**prog·nos′ti·ca′tion, prog·nos′ti·ca′tor** n. —**prog·nos′ti·ca′tive** (-kā′tiv) *adj.*

pro·gram (prō′gram, -grəm) n. 1 A printed list giving in order the items, selections, etc., making up an entertainment; also, the selections, etc., collectively. 2 A printed list of the cast of characters, the performers, the acts or scenes, etc., in a play, opera, or the like. 3 A radio or television show. 4 Any prearranged plan or course of proceedings. 5 A sequence of instructions to be executed by a computer in solving a problem, usu. with means for automatically modifying the sequence depending on conditions that arise. *Brit. sp.* ·**gramme.** —v.t. ·**gramed,** ·**grammed,** ·**gram·ing** or ·**gram·ming** 1 To arrange a program of or for: to *program* one's day. 2 To schedule (an act, performer, etc.) for a program. 3 To furnish a program for (a computer). 4 To feed (information, instructions, etc.) into a computer. [< LL *programma* public announcement]

—**pro·gram·mat·ic** (prō′grə·mat′ik) *adj.* —**pro′gram·er, pro′·gram·mer** n.

programed instruction Instruction in which the learner responds to a prearranged series of questions, items, or statements, using various printed texts, audiovisual means, or a teaching machine. Also **programmed instruction.**

program music Music intended to suggest moods, scenes, or incidents.

prog·ress (prog′res, *esp. Brit.* prō′gres) n. 1 A moving forward in space, as toward a destination. 2 Advancement toward something better; improvement. —v.i. (prə·gres′) 1 To move forward or onward. 2 To advance toward completion or improvement. [< L *progressus*, pp. of *progredi* go forward]

pro·gres·sion (prə·gresh′ən) n. 1 The act of progressing. 2 A successive series of events, happenings, etc. 3 *Math.* A sequence of numbers or elements each of which is derived from the preceding by rule. 4 *Music* a An advance from one tone or chord to another. b A sequence or succession of tones or chords. 5 Course or lapse of time; passage. —**pro·gres′sion·al** *adj.* —**pro·gres′sion·ism** n.

pro·gres·sive (prə·gres′iv) *adj.* 1 Moving forward in space; advancing. 2 Increasing by successive stages: a *progressive* deterioration. 3 Aiming at or characterized by progress toward something better: a *progressive* country. 4 Favoring or characterized by reform, new techniques, etc.: a *progressive* party, jazz, etc. 5 Increasing in severity: said of a disease. 6 *Gram.* Designating an aspect of the verb which expresses continuing action: formed with any tense of the auxiliary *be* and the present participle; as, He *is speaking;* he *had been speaking.* —n. One who favors or promotes reforms or changes, as in politics. —**pro·gres′·sive·ly** *adv.* —**pro·gres′sive·ness** n.

pro·hib·it (prō·hib′it, prə-) v.t. 1 To forbid, esp. by authority or law; interdict. 2 To prevent or hinder. [< L *prohibere*] —**pro·hib′it·er** n. —**Syn.** 1 disallow, ban, deny, bar, debar. 2 impede, restrict, constrain, check, block, obstruct.

pro·hi·bi·tion (prō′ə·bish′ən) n. 1 A prohibiting or being prohibited. 2 A decree or order forbidding anything. 3 *Often cap.* The forbidding of the manufacture, transportation, and sale of alcoholic liquors as beverages. —**pro′hi·bi′tion·ist** n.

pro·hib·i·tive (prō·hib′ə·tiv, prə-) *adj.* Prohibiting or tending to prohibit. Also **pro·hib′i·to′ry** (-tôr′ē, -tō′rē). —**pro·hib′i·tive·ly** *adv.*

proj·ect (proj′ekt) n. 1 A course of action; a plan. 2 An organized, usu. rather extensive undertaking: a research *project.* 3 A group of single dwellings or of apartment houses forming a residential complex. —v.t. (prə·jekt′) 1 To cause to extend forward or out. 2 To throw forth or forward, as missiles. 3 To cause (an image, shadow, etc.) to fall on a surface. 4 To plan or estimate something in the future: to *project* living expenses. 5 To create or invent in the mind: to *project* an image of one's destiny. 6 To cause (one's voice) to be heard at a distance. 7 To have the ability to communicate (a dramatic role, one's personality, ideas, etc.) effectively, as to an audience. 8 *Psychol.* To ascribe or impute (one's own ideas, feelings, etc.) to another person, group, or object. 9 To make a projection (def. 4) of. —v.i. 10 To extend out; protrude. 11 To cause one's voice to be heard at a distance. 12 To communicate effectively, as to an audience. 13 *Psychol.* To impute one's own ideas, feelings, etc., to another person, group, or object. [< L *pro-* before + *jacere* throw]

pro·jec·tile (prə·jek′təl, -tīl) *adj.* 1 Projecting, or impelling forward. 2 Capable of being or intended to be projected or shot forth. —n. 1 A body projected or thrown forth by force. 2 A missile for discharge from a gun, cannon, etc.

pro·jec·tion (prə·jek′shən) n. 1 The act of projecting. 2 That which projects. 3 A prediction or estimation of something in the future based on current information, data, etc. 4 A system of lines drawn on a given fixed plane, as on a map, which represents, point for point, a given terrestrial or celestial surface. 5 *Psychol.* The process or an instance of projecting. 6 The exhibiting of pictures upon a screen. —**pro·jec′tive** *adj.* —**pro·jec′tive·ly** *adv.*

pro·jec·tion·ist (prə·jek′shən·ist) *n.* The operator of a motion-picture or slide projector.

pro·jec·tor (prə·jek′tər) *n.* One who or that which projects, esp. an apparatus for throwing images on a screen: a motion-picture *projector*.

pro·lapse (prō·laps′) *v.i.* **·lapsed, ·laps·ing** *Med.* To fall out of place, as an organ or part. —*n. Med.* (*also* prō′laps) Displacement of a part, esp. toward a natural orifice. [< L *pro-* forward + *labi* glide, fall]

pro·late (prō′lāt) *adj.* **1** Extended lengthwise. **2** Lengthened toward the poles. [< L *prolatus*]

prole (prōl) *n. & adj. Informal* PROLETARIAN.

pro·le·tar·i·an (prō′lə·târ′ē·ən) *adj.* Of the proletariat. —*n.* A member of the proletariat. [< L *proletarius* a Roman citizen of a class that, lacking property, served the state only by having children < *proles* offspring] —**pro′le·tar′i·an·ism** *n.*

pro·le·tar·i·at (prō′lə·târ′ē·ət) *n.* **1** Formerly, the lower classes. **2** The laboring class, esp. industrial wage earners.

pro·lif·er·ate (prō·lif′ə·rāt, prə-) *v.t. & v.i.* **·at·ed, ·at·ing** To create or reproduce in rapid succession. [< L *proles* offspring + *ferre* bear] —**pro·lif′er·a′tion** *n.* —**pro·lif′er·a′tive, pro·lif′er·ous** *adj.*

pro·lif·ic (prō·lif′ik, prə-) *adj.* **1** Producing abundantly, as offspring or fruit. **2** Producing creative or intellectual products abundantly: a *prolific* writer. [< L *proles* offspring + *facere* make] —**pro·lif′i·ca·cy** (-i·kə·sē), **pro·lif′ic·ness** *n.* —**pro·lif′i·cal·ly** *adv.*

pro·lix (prō′liks, prō·liks′) *adj.* **1** Unduly long and wordy. **2** Indulging in long and wordy discourse. [< L *prolixus* extended] —**pro·lix·i·ty** (prō·lik′sə·tē), **pro′lix·ness** *n.* —**pro′·lix·ly** *adv.*

pro·logue (prō′lôg, -log) *n.* **1** A preface, esp. an introduction, often in verse, spoken or sung by an actor before a play or opera. **2** Any anticipatory act or event. —*v.t.* To introduce with a prologue or preface. Also **pro′log.** [< Gk. *pro-* before + *logos* discourse]

pro·long (prə·lông′, -long′) *v.t.* To extend in time or space; continue; lengthen. Also **pro·lon′gate** (-lông′gāt, -long′-). [< L *pro-* forth + *longus* long] —**pro′lon·ga′tion, pro·long′ment, pro·long′er** *n.*

prom (prom) *n. Informal* A formal college or school dance or ball. [Short for PROMENADE]

prom. promenade; promontory.

prom·e·nade (prom′ə·nād′, -näd′) *n.* **1** A leisurely walk taken for pleasure. **2** A place for promenading. **3** A concert or ball opened with a formal march. —*v.* **·nad·ed, ·nad·ing** *v.i.* **1** To take a promenade. —*v.t.* **2** To take a promenade through or along. **3** To take or exhibit on or as on a promenade; parade. [< L *prominare* drive forward] —**prom′e·nad′er** *n.*

Pro·me·theus (prə·mē′thē·əs) *Gk. Myth.* A Titan who stole fire from heaven for mankind and as a punishment was chained to a rock, where an eagle daily devoured his liver. —**Pro·me′the·an** *adj.*

pro·me·thi·um (prə·mē′thē·əm) *n.* A radioactive element (symbol Pm) produced by uranium fission and belonging to the lanthanide series. [< PROMETHEUS]

prom·i·nence (prom′ə·nəns) *n.* **1** The state of being prominent; conspicuousness. **2** Something that extends forth or protrudes. **3** *Astron.* One of the great luminous clouds arising from the sun's surface, seen during total eclipses: also **solar prominence.** Also **prom′i·nen·cy.**

prom·i·nent (prom′ə·nənt) *adj.* **1** Jutting out; projecting; protuberant. **2** Conspicuous. **3** Very well known; eminent: a *prominent* lawyer. [< L *prominere* to project] —**prom′i·nent·ly** *adv.* —**Syn. 3** famous, noted, renowned, celebrated, popular, honored, outstanding.

prom·is·cu·i·ty (prom′is·kyōō′ə·tē, prō′mis-) *n. pl.* **·ties** The state, quality, or an instance of being promiscuous, esp. in sexual relations.

pro·mis·cu·ous (prə·mis′kyōō·əs) *adj.* **1** Composed of persons or things confusedly mingled. **2** Indiscriminate; esp., having sexual relations indiscriminately or casually with various persons. **3** Casual; irregular. [< L *promiscuus* mixed] —**pro·mis′cu·ous·ly** *adv.* —**pro·mis′cu·ous·ness** *n.*

prom·ise (prom′is) *n.* **1** An assurance given that a specified action will or will not be taken. **2** Reasonable ground for hope or expectation of future excellence, satisfaction, etc. **3** Something promised. —*v.* **·ised, ·is·ing** *v.t.* **1** To engage or pledge by a promise: He *promised* to do it. **2** To make a promise of (something) to someone. **3** To give reason for expecting. **4** *Informal* To assure (someone). —*v.i.* **5** To make a promise. **6** To give reason for expectation: often with *well* or *fair*. [< L *promissum*, pp. of *promittere* send forward] —**prom′is·er** *n.*

Promised Land 1 Canaan, promised to Abraham by God. *Gen.* 15:18. **2** Any longed-for place of happiness or improvement.

prom·is·ing (prom′is·ing) *adj.* Giving promise of good results or development. —**prom′is·ing·ly** *adv.*

prom·is·so·ry (prom′ə·sôr′ē, -sō′rē) *adj.* Containing or of the nature of a promise.

promissory note A written promise by one person to pay another unconditionally a certain sum of money at a specified time.

pro·mo (prō′mō) *Slang n.* PROMOTION (def. 3). —*adj.* Of, for, or relating to promotion (def. 3); promotional.

prom·on·to·ry (prom′ən·tôr′ē, -tō′rē) *n. pl.* **·ries** A high point of land extending into a body of water; headland. [< L *promunturium*]

pro·mote (prə·mōt′) *v.t.* **·mot·ed, ·mot·ing 1** To contribute to the progress, development, or growth of; further; encourage. **2** To advance to a higher position, grade, or rank. **3** To advocate actively. **4** To publicize (a person, product, event, etc.), as by advertising, public appearances, etc. [< L *pro-* forward + *movere* to move] —**pro·mot′a·ble** *adj.*

pro·mot·er (prə·mō′tər) *n.* One who or that which promotes, esp. one who assists, by securing capital, etc., in promoting some enterprise, as a sports event, commercial venture, etc.

pro·mo·tion (prə·mō′shən) *n.* **1** Advancement in dignity, rank, grade, etc. **2** Furtherance or development, as of a cause. **3** Anything, as advertising, public appearances, etc., done to publicize a person, product, event, etc. —**pro·mo′tion·al** *adj.*

pro·mo·tive (prə·mō′tiv) *adj.* Tending to promote.

prompt (prompt) *v.t.* **1** To incite to action; instigate. **2** To suggest or inspire (an act, thought, etc.). **3** To remind of what has been forgotten or of what comes next; give a cue to. —*v.i.* **4** To give help or suggestions. —*adj.* **1** Quick to act, respond, etc.; ready. **2** Taking place at the appointed time; punctual. [< L *promptus* brought forth, hence, at hand] —**promp′ti·tude, prompt′ness** *n.* —**prompt′ly** *adv.*

prompt·er (promp′tər) **1** In a theater, one who follows the lines and prompts the actors. **2** One who or that which prompts.

prom·ul·gate (prom′əl·gāt, prō·mul′gāt) *v.t.* **·gat·ed, ·gat·ing 1** To make known or announce officially, as a law, dogma, etc. **2** To make known or effective over a wide area or extent. [< L *promulgare* make known] —**prom·ul·ga·tion** (prom′əl·gā′shən, prō′mul-), **prom′ul·gat·or** *n.*

pron. pronoun; pronounced; pronunciation.

prone (prōn) *adj.* **1** Lying flat, esp. with the face, front, or palm downward; prostrate. **2** Leaning forward or downward. **3** Mentally inclined or predisposed: with *to*. [< L *pronus*] —**prone′ly** *adv.* —**prone′ness** *n.*

prong (prông, prong) *n.* **1** A pointed end of a fork. **2** Any pointed and projecting part, as the end of an antler, etc. —*v.t.* To prick or stab with a prong. [ME *pronge*] —**pronged** *adj.*

prong·horn (prông′hôrn′, prong′-) *n. pl.* **·horns** *or* **·horn** A small, deerlike mammal of w North America.

pro·nom·i·nal (prō·nom′ə·nəl) *adj.* Of, pertaining to, like, or having the nature of a pronoun. —**pro·nom′i·nal·ly** *adv.*

pro·noun (prō′noun) *n.* A word used as a substitute for a noun, as *he, she, that*. [< L *pro-* in place of + *nomen* name, noun]

Pronghorn

pro·nounce (prə·nouns′) *v.*

·nounced, ·nounc·ing *v.t.* **1** To utter or deliver officially or solemnly; proclaim. **2** To assert; declare, esp. as one's judgment: The judge *pronounced* her guilty. **3** To give utterance to; articulate (words, etc.). **4** To articulate in a prescribed manner: hard to *pronounce* his name. **5** To indicate the sound of (a word) by phonetic symbols. —*v.i.* **6** To make a pronouncement or assertion. **7** To articulate words; speak. [< L *pronuntiare* proclaim < *pro-* forth + *nuntiare* announce] **—pro·nounce′a·ble** *adj.* **—pro·nounc′er** *n.*

pro·nounced (prə·nounst′) *adj.* Clearly noticeable; decided. **—pro·nounc·ed·ly** (prə·noun′sid·lē) *adv.*

pro·nounce·ment (prə·nouns′mənt) *n.* **1** The act of pronouncing. **2** A formal declaration or announcement.

pron·to (pron′tō) *adv.* *Slang* Quickly; promptly; instantly. [< L *promptus*]

pro·nun·ci·a·men·to (prə·nun′sē·ə·men′tō) *n. pl.* **·tos** A public announcement; proclamation; manifesto. [< L *pronuntiare* pronounce]

pro·nun·ci·a·tion (prə·nun′sē·ā′shən) *n.* The act or manner of pronouncing words.

proof (proof) *n.* **1** The act or process of proving; esp., the establishment of a fact by evidence or a truth by other truths. **2** A trial of strength, truth, fact, or excellence, etc.; a test. **3** Evidence and argument sufficient to induce belief. **4** *Law* Anything that serves to convince the mind of the truth or falsity of a fact or proposition. **5** The state or quality of having successfully undergone a proof or test. **6** The standard of strength of alcoholic liquors: see PROOF SPIRIT. **7** *Printing* A printed trial sheet showing the contents or condition of matter in type. **8** In engraving and etching, a trial impression taken from an engraved plate, stone, or block. **9** *Phot.* A trial print from a negative. **10** *Math.* A procedure that shows that a proposition is true. **11** Anything proved true; experience. **12** In philately, an experimental printing of a stamp. —*adj.* **1** Employed in or connected with proving or correcting. **2** Capable of resisting successfully; firm: with *against*: *proof* against bribes. **3** Of standard alcoholic strength, as liquors. —*v.t.* **1** To make a test or proof of. **2** To protect or make impervious: to *proof* a garment against stains. **3** PROOFREAD. [< L *probare* PROVE]

-proof *combining form* **1** Impervious to; not damaged by: *waterproof*. **2** Protected against: *mothproof*. **3** As strong as: *armorproof*. **4** Resisting; showing no effects of: *panicproof*.

proof·read (proof′rēd′) *v.t. & v.i.* **·read** (-red′), **·read·ing** (-rē′ding) To read and correct (printers' proofs). **—proof′read′er** *n.*

prop[1] (prop) *v.t.* **propped, prop·ping** **1** To support or keep from falling by or as by means of a prop. **2** To lean or place: usu. with *against*. **3** To support; sustain. —*n.* A support. [< MDu. *proppe* a vine prop]

prop[2] (prop) *n.* PROPERTY (def. 5).

prop[3] (prop) *n.* *Informal* PROPELLER.

prop. proper; properly; property; proposition; proprietor.

prop·a·gan·da (prop′ə·gan′də) *n.* **1** Any widespread scheme or effort to spread or promote an idea, opinion, or course of action in order to help or do damage to a cause, person, etc. **2** The ideas, opinions, etc., so spread or promoted: now often used disparagingly because of the deceitful or distorted character of much propaganda. [< NL *(congregatio de) propaganda (fide)* (the congregation for) propagating (the faith)]

prop·a·gan·dism (prop′ə·gan′diz·əm) *n.* The art, practice, or system of using propaganda. **—prop′a·gan′dist** *adj., n.* **—prop′a·gan·dis′tic** *adj.* **—prop′a·gan·dis′ti·cal·ly** *adv.*

prop·a·gan·dize (prop′ə·gan′dīz) *v.* **·dized, ·diz·ing** *v.t.* **1** To subject to propaganda. **2** To spread by means of propaganda. —*v.i.* **3** To carry on or spread propaganda.

prop·a·gate (prop′ə·gāt) *v.* **·gat·ed, ·gat·ing** *v.t.* **1** To cause (animals, plants, etc.) to multiply by natural reproduction; breed. **2** To reproduce (itself). **3** To spread abroad or from person to person; disseminate. **4** *Physics* To transmit (a form of energy) through space. —*v.i.* **5** To multiply by natural reproduction; breed. **6** *Physics* To pass or spread through space, as waves, heat, etc. [< L *propago* a slip for transplanting] **—prop′a·ga′tion, prop′a·ga′tor** *n.* **—prop′a·ga′tive** *adj.*

pro·pane (prō′pān) *n.* A gaseous hydrocarbon of the paraffin series. [< PROP(YL) + (METH)ANE]

pro·pel (prə·pel′) *v.t.* **·pelled, ·pel·ling** To cause to move forward or ahead; drive or urge forward. [< L *pro-* forward + *pellere* drive]

pro·pel·lant (prə·pel′ənt) *n.* That which propels, esp. an explosive or fuel that propels a projectile, rocket, etc.

pro·pel·lent (prə·pel′ənt) *adj.* Propelling; able to propel.

pro·pel·ler (prə·pel′ər) *n.* **1** One who or that which propels. **2** Any device for propelling a craft through water or air; esp., a set of rotating vanes operating like a screw. Also **pro·pel′lor.**

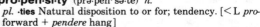
Propeller

pro·pen·si·ty (prə·pen′sə·tē) *n. pl.* **·ties** Natural disposition to or for; tendency. [< L *pro-* forward + *pendere* hang]

---

proof spirit An alcoholic liquor of a standard strength, in the U.S., containing ethyl alcohol in the amount of 50 percent of its volume, equal to 100 proof.

prop·er (prop′ər) *adj.* **1** Having special fitness; specially suited; appropriate. **2** Conforming to a standard; correct: the *proper* pronunciation. **3** Seemly; right; fitting: the *proper* outfit. **4** Genteel and respectable, often excessively so. **5** Understood in the most correct or strict sense: usu. following the noun modified: Boston *proper.* **6** Naturally belonging to a person or thing: with *to: Snow is proper to winter. —n. Often cap.* That portion of the breviary or missal containing the prayers and collects suitable to special occasions. [< L *proprius* one's own] **—prop′er·ly** *adv.* **—prop′er·ness** *n.*

proper fraction A fraction in which the denominator exceeds the numerator.

proper noun A noun designating a specific person, place, or thing, always capitalized in English, as *John, Mount Everest, Apollo II.*

proper subset Any subset not identical with the entire set.

prop·er·tied (prop′ər·tēd) *adj.* Owning property.

prop·er·ty (prop′ər·tē) *n. pl.* **·ties 1** Any object that a person may lawfully acquire and own; any possession, esp. land or real estate. **2** A specific piece of land or real estate. **3** The legal right to the possession, use, and disposal of a thing. **4** An inherent quality or characteristic. **5** In the theater, movies, television, ballet, etc., any portable article, except scenery and costumes, used by the performers while performing. [< L *proprius* one's own]

proph·e·cy (prof′ə·sē) *n. pl.* **·cies 1** A prediction made under divine influence. **2** Any prediction. [< Gk. *pro-* before + *phanai* speak]

proph·e·sy (prof′ə·sī) *v.* **·sied, ·sy·ing** *v.t.* **1** To utter or foretell with or as with divine inspiration. **2** To predict (a future event). **3** To point out beforehand. —*v.i.* **4** To speak by divine influence. **5** To foretell the future. [< PROPHECY] **—proph′e·si′er** *n.*

proph·et (prof′it) *n.* **1** One who delivers divine messages or interprets the divine will. **2** One who foretells the future. **3** A religious leader. **4** An interpreter or spokesman for any cause. **—the Prophet** According to Islam, Mohammed. **—the Prophets** The Old Testament books written by the prophets. [< Gk. *pro-* before + *phanai* speak] **—proph′et·ess** *n. Fem.* **—proph′et·hood** (-hŏŏd) *n.*

pro·phet·ic (prə·fet′ik) *adj.* **1** Of or pertaining to a prophet or prophecy. **2** Predicting or foreshadowing a future event. Also **pro·phet′i·cal. —pro·phet′i·cal·ly** *adv.*

pro·phy·lac·tic (prō′fə·lak′tik, prof′ə-) *adj.* Pertaining to prophylaxis. —*n.* **1** A prophylactic medicine or appliance. **2** A condom.

pro·phy·lax·is (prō′fə·lak′sis, prof′ə-) *n.* Preventive treatment for disease. [< Gk. *pro-* before + *phylaxis* a guarding]

pro·pin·qui·ty (prō·ping′kwə·tē) *n.* **1** Nearness in place or time. **2** Kinship. [< L *propinquus* near]

pro·pi·ti·ate (prō·pish′ē·āt) *v.t.* **·at·ed, ·at·ing** To cause to be favorably disposed; appease; conciliate. [< L *propitiare* render favorable, appease] **—pro·pi·ti·a·ble** (prō·pish′ē·ə·bəl), **pro·pi′ti·a′tive, pro·pi′ti·a·to′ry** *adj.* **—pro·pi·ti·a·tion** (prō-pish′ē·ā′shən), **pro·pi′ti·a′tor** *n.* **—Syn.** pacify, placate, mollify, reconcile.

pro·pi·tious (prō·pish′əs) *adj.* **1** Kindly disposed; gracious. **2** Attended by favorable circumstances; auspicious. [< L *propitius* favorable] **—pro·pi′tious·ly** *adv.* **—pro·pi′· tious·ness** *n.* **—Syn. 2** timely, fortunate, lucky, providential, happy, felicitous.

pro·po·nent (prə·pō′nənt) *n.* **1** One who makes a proposal or puts forward a proposition. **2** *Law* One who presents a will for probate. **3** One who advocates or supports a cause or doctrine. [< L *pro-* forth + *ponere* put]

pro·por·tion (prə·pôr′shən, -pōr′-) *n.* **1** Relative magnitude, number, or degree, as existing between parts, a part and a whole, or different things. **2** Balance and harmony; symmetry. **3** A proportionate or proper share. **4** *pl.* Size; dimensions. **5** An equality or identity between ratios. **6** *Math.* An identity or equation involving a pair of fractions, in the general form $4/2 = 8/4$. —*v.t.* **1** To adjust properly as to relative magnitude, amount, or degree. **2** To form with a harmonious relation of parts. [< L *pro-* before + *portio* a share] **—pro·por′tion·a·ble** *adj.* **—pro·por′tion·a·bly** *adv.* **—pro·por′tion·er** *n.*

pro·por·tion·al (prə·pôr′shən·əl, -pōr′-) *adj.* **1** Of, pertaining to, or being in proportion. **2** *Math.* Being the product of a given function or variable and a constant: The area of a circle is *proportional* to the square of the radius. **—pro·por′tion·al·ly** *adv.* **—pro·por′tion·al′i·ty** (-al′ə·tē) *n.*

pro·por·tion·ate (prə·pôr′shən·it, -pōr′-) *adj.* Being in due proportion; proportional. —*v.t.* (-āt) **·at·ed, ·at·ing** To make proportionate. **—pro·por′tion·ate·ly** *adv.* **—pro·por′· tion·ate·ness** *n.*

pro·po·sal (prə·pō′zəl) *n.* **1** An offer proposing something to be accepted or adopted. **2** An offer of marriage. **3** Something proposed.

pro·pose (prə·pōz′) *v.* **·posed, ·pos·ing** *v.t.* **1** To put forward for acceptance or consideration. **2** To nominate, as for admission or appointment. **3** To intend; purpose. **4** To suggest the drinking of (a toast or health). —*v.i.* **5** To form or announce a plan or design. **6** To make an offer, as of marriage. [< OF *pro-* forth + *poser* put] **—pro·pos′er** *n.*

prop·o·si·tion (prop′ə·zish′ən) *n.* **1** A scheme or proposal offered for consideration or acceptance. **2** *Informal* Any matter or person to be dealt with: a tough *proposition.* **3** *Informal* A proposal for illicit sexual intercourse. **4** A subject or statement presented for discussion. **5** *Logic* A statement in which the subject is affirmed or denied by the predicate. **6** *Math.* A statement whose truth is assumed or demonstrated. —*v.t.* *Informal* To make a proposal to (someone) to have illicit sexual intercourse. **—prop′o·si′· tion·al** *adj.* **—prop′o·si′tion·al·ly** *adv.*

pro·pound (prə·pound′) *v.t.* To put forward for consideration, solution, etc. [< L *proponere* set forth] **—pro·pound′· er** *n.*

pro·pri·e·tar·y (prə·prī′ə·ter′ē) *adj.* **1** Pertaining to a proprietor. **2** Protected as to name, composition, or process of manufacture by copyright, patent, etc. —*n. pl.* **·tar· ies 1** A proprietor or proprietors collectively. **2** Proprietorship. [< LL *proprietas* property]

pro·pri·e·tor (prə·prī′ə·tər) *n.* A person having the exclusive title to anything; owner. **—pro·pri′e·tor·ship′** *n.* **—pro· pri′e·tress** *n. Fem.*

pro·pri·e·ty (prə·prī′ə·tē) *n. pl.* **·ties** The character or quality of being proper; esp., accordance with recognized usage, custom, or principles. **—the proprieties** The standards of good social behavior. [< L *proprius* one's own]

pro·pul·sion (prə·pul′shən) *n.* **1** A propelling or being propelled. **2** Something that propels. [< L *propulsus,* pp. of *propellere* propel] **—pro·pul′sive** (-siv) *adj.*

pro·pyl (prō′pil) *n.* The univalent radical derived from propane.

pro ra·ta (prō rā′tə, rat′ə, rä′tə) Proportionate or proportionately: The loss was shared *pro rata.* [< L *pro rata (parte)* according to the calculated (share)]

pro·rate (prō·rāt′, prō′rāt′) *v.t. & v.i.* **·rat·ed, ·rat·ing** To distribute or divide proportionately. [< PRO RATA] **—pro· rat′a·ble** *adj.* **—pro·ra′tion** *n.*

pro·rogue (prō·rōg′) *v.t.* **·rogued, ·ro·guing** To discontinue a session of (an assembly, esp. the British Parliament). [< L *pro-* forth + *rogare* ask] **—pro·ro·ga·tion** (prō′rō·gā′shən) *n.*

pro·sa·ic (prō·zā′ik) *adj.* **1** Unimaginative; commonplace; dull. **2** Of or like prose. [< L *prosa* prose] **—pro·sa′i· cal·ly** *adv.* **—pro·sa′ic·ness** *n.*

pro·sce·ni·um (prō·sē′nē·əm) *n. pl.* **·ni·ums** or **·ni·a** (-nē·ə) **1** In a modern theater, that part of the stage between the curtain and the orchestra, sometimes including the curtain and its arch (**proscenium arch**). **2** In the ancient Greek or Roman theater, the stage. [< Gk. *proskēnion* < *pro-* before + *skēnē* a stage, orig. a tent]

pro·sciut·to (prō·shŏŏ′tō) *n. pl.* **·ti** (-tē) or **·tos** A spicy, dry-cured ham, usu. sliced very thin. [Ital.]

pro·scribe (prō·skrīb′) *v.t.* **·scribed, ·scrib·ing 1** To denounce or condemn; prohibit; interdict. **2** To outlaw or banish. **3** In ancient Rome, to publish the name of (one condemned or exiled). [< L *pro-* before + *scribere* write] **— pro·scrib′er, pro·scrip′tion** (-skrip′shən) *n.* **—pro·scrip′tive** *adj.* **—pro·scrip′tive·ly** *adv.*

prose (prōz) *n.* 1 Speech or writing as found in ordinary conversation, letters, newspapers, etc. 2 Writing, esp. in literature, distinguished from poetry by the lack of conscious rhyme and usu. by rhythms suggesting ordinary speech or by a presentation in the form of a series of sentences with the initial letters capitalized. 3 Commonplace or tedious talk, style, quality, etc. —*adj.* 1 Of or in prose. 2 Tedious. —*v.t. & v.i.* prosed, pros·ing To write or speak in prose. [<L *prosa (oratio)* straight-forward (discourse)]

pros·e·cute (pros′ə-kyōōt) *v.* ·cut·ed, ·cut·ing *v.t.* 1 To go on with so as to complete; pursue to the end: to *prosecute* an inquiry. 2 To carry on or engage in, as a trade. 3 *Law* a To bring suit against for redress of wrong or punishment of crime. b To seek to enforce or obtain, as a claim or right, by legal process. —*v.i.* 4 To begin and carry on a legal proceeding. [<L *prosequi* pursue]

prosecuting attorney The attorney empowered to act in behalf of the government, whether state, county, or national, in prosecuting for penal offenses.

pros·e·cu·tion (pros′ə-kyōō′shən) *n.* 1 The act or process of prosecuting. 2 *Law* a The instituting and carrying forward of a judicial or criminal proceeding. b The party instituting and conducting it.

pros·e·cu·tor (pros′ə-kyōō′tər) *n.* 1 One who prosecutes. 2 *Law* a One who institutes and carries on a suit, esp. a criminal suit. b PROSECUTING ATTORNEY.

pros·e·lyte (pros′ə-līt) *n.* One who has been converted to any opinion, belief, sect, or party. —*v.t. & v.i.* ·lyt·ed, ·lyt·ing PROSELYTIZE. [<Gk. *proselytos* a convert to Judaism] —pros′e·lyt·ism (-līt′iz·əm, -lə·tiz′əm), pros′e·lyt·ist *n.*

pros·e·lyt·ize (pros′ə·lə·tīz′) *v.t. & v.i.* ·ized, ·iz·ing To convert or try to convert (a person) to one's religion, opinions, party, etc. —pros′e·ly·tiz′er *n.*

pro·sit (prō′sit) *interj.* A toast used in drinking health. [L, lit., may it benefit (you)]

pros·o·dy (pros′ə·dē, proz′-) *n.* The study of poetical forms, including meter, rhyme schemes, structural analysis, etc. [<Gk. *prosōidia* a song sung to music] —pro·sod·ic (prə·sod′ik, -zod′-) or ·i·cal *adj.* —pros′o·dist *n.*

pros·pect (pros′pekt) *n.* 1 A future probability or something anticipated. 2 *Usu. pl.* Chances, as for success. 3 A scene; an extended view. 4 The direction in which anything faces; an exposure; outlook. 5 A potential buyer, candidate, etc. 6 The act of observing or examining; survey. 7 *Mining* a A place having signs of the presence of mineral ore. b The sample of mineral obtained by washing a small portion of ore or dirt. —*v.t. & v.i.* To explore (a region) for gold, oil, etc. [<L *pro-* forward + *specere* look]

pro·spec·tive (prə·spek′tiv) *adj.* 1 Anticipated; expected. 2 Looking toward the future; anticipatory. —pro·spec′tive·ly *adv.*

pros·pec·tor (pros′pek·tər) *n.* One who prospects for mineral deposits, oil, etc.

pro·spec·tus (prə·spek′təs) *n.* 1 A paper containing information of a proposed literary or business undertaking. 2 A summary; outline. [L, a look-out, prospect]

pros·per (pros′pər) *v.i.* 1 To thrive; flourish. —*v.t.* 2 To render prosperous. [<OF<L favorable]

pros·per·i·ty (pros·per′ə·tē) *n.* The state of being prosperous; esp., wealth or success.

pros·per·ous (pros′pər·əs) *adj.* 1 Successful; flourishing. 2 Wealthy; well-to-do. 3 Promising; favorable [<L *prosper* favorable] —pros′per·ous·ly *adv.* —pros′per·ous·ness *n.*

pros·ta·gland·in (pros′tə·glan′din) *n.* A fatty acid, found in many body tissues, including the prostate gland, that regulates many bodily functions.

pros·tate (pros′tāt) *adj.* Of the prostate gland. —*n.* PROSTATE GLAND. [<Gk. *prostatēs* one who stands before]

prostate gland A partly muscular gland at the base of the bladder around the urethra in male mammals.

pros·the·sis (pros·thē′sis, pros′thə-) *n. pl.* ·the·ses (-thē′sēz) 1 Replacement of a missing part of the body with an artificial substitute. 2 A device used in prosthesis, as an artificial leg, eye, etc. [<Gk. *pros-* toward, besides + *tithenai* place, put] —pros·thet·ic (pros·thet′ik) *adj.*

pros·ti·tute (pros′tə·t^yōōt) *n.* 1 A woman who engages in sexual intercourse for money. 2 A person who engages in sexual acts for money: a male *prostitute.* 3 A person who uses his talents or gifts for unworthy or corrupt purposes. —*v.t.* ·tut·ed, ·tut·ing 1 To put to base or unworthy purposes. 2 To offer (oneself or another) for lewd purposes, esp. for hire. [<L *prostituere* expose publicly, prostitute] —pros′ti·tu′tion, pros′ti·tu′tor *n.*

pros·trate (pros′trāt) *adj.* 1 Lying prone, or with the face to the ground. 2 Brought low in mind or body, as from grief, exhaustion, etc. 3 Lying at the mercy of another; defenseless. 4 *Bot.* Trailing along the ground. —*v.t.* ·trat·ed, ·trat·ing 1 To bow or cast (oneself) down, as in adoration or pleading. 2 To throw flat; lay on the ground. 3 To overthrow or overcome; reduce to helplessness. [<L *prostratus*, pp. of *prosternere* lay flat] —pros·tra′tion *n.*

pros·y (prō′zē) *adj.* pros·i·er, pros·i·est 1 Like prose. 2 Dull; commonplace. —pros′i·ly *adv.* —pros′i·ness *n.*

Prot. Protestant.

pro·tac·tin·i·um (prō′tak·tin′ē·əm) *n.* A radioactive element (symbol Pa) occurring in small amounts in uranium ores. [<PROT(O)- + ACTINIUM]

pro·tag·o·nist (prō·tag′ə·nist) *n.* 1 The actor who played the chief part in a Greek drama. 2 A leader in any enterprise or contest. [<Gk. *prōtos* first + *agōnistēs* a contestant, an actor]

pro·te·an (prō′tē·ən, prō·tē′ən) *adj.* Readily assuming different forms or aspects; changeable. [<PROTEUS]

pro·tect (prə·tekt′) *v.t.* 1 To shield or defend from attack, harm, or injury; guard; defend. 2 *Econ.* To assist (domestic industry) by protective tariffs. 3 In commerce, to provide funds to guarantee payment of (a draft, etc.). [<L *pro-* before + *tegere* to cover] —pro·tec′tive *adj.* —pro·tec′tive·ly *adv.* —pro·tec′tive·ness, pro·tec′tor *n.*

pro·tec·tion (prə·tek′shən) *n.* 1 The act of protecting or the state of being protected. 2 That which protects: Our dog is a great *protection.* 3 A system aiming to protect the industries of a country, as by imposing duties. 4 A safe-conduct pass. 5 *Slang* Security purchased under threat of violence from racketeers; also, the money so paid.

pro·tec·tion·ism (prə·tek′shən·iz′əm) *n.* The economic doctrine or system of protection. —pro·tec′tion·ist *adj., n.*

protective coloration Any natural coloration of a plant or animal that tends to disguise or conceal it from its enemies.

protective tariff A tariff that is intended to insure protection of domestic industries against foreign competition.

pro·tec·tor·ate (prə·tek′tər·it) *n.* 1 A relation of protection and partial control by a strong nation over a weaker power. 2 A country or region so protected.

pro·té·gé (prō′tə·zhā, prō·tə·zhā′) *n.* One aided, esp. in promoting a career, by another who is older or more powerful. [F, pp. of *protéger* protect] —pro′té·gée *n. Fem.*

pro·tein (prō′tēn, -tē·in) *n.* Any of a class of complex nitrogenous compounds found in all living matter and forming an essential part of the diet of animals. —*adj.* Composed of protein.

pro tem·po·re (prō tem′pə·rē) For the time being; temporary: usu. shortened to **pro tem.** [L]

Prot·er·o·zo·ic (prot′ər·ə·zō′ik, prō′tər-) *adj., n.* • See GEOLOGY. [<Gk. *proteros* former + *zōion* animal]

pro·test (prō′test) *n.* 1 An objection, complaint, or declaration of disapproval. 2 A public expression of dissent, esp. if organized. 3 A formal certificate attesting the fact that a note or bill of exchange has not been paid. —*adj.* Of or relating to public protest: *protest* demonstrations. —*v.* (prə·test′) *v.t.* 1 To assert earnestly or positively; state formally, esp. against opposition or doubt. 2 To make a protest against; object to. 3 To declare formally that payment of (a promissory note, etc.) has been duly submitted and refused. —*v.i.* 4 To make solemn affirmation. 5 To make a protest; object. [<L *pro-* forth + *testari* affirm] —pro·test′er, pro·test′or *n.*

Prot·es·tant (prot′is·tənt) *n.* Any Christian who is not a member of the Roman Catholic or Eastern Orthodox Churches. —*adj.* Pertaining to Protestants or Protestantism. —Prot′es·tant·ism *n.*

Protestant Episcopal Church A religious body in the U.S. which is descended from the Church of England.

prot·es·ta·tion (prot′is·tā′shən, prō′tes-) *n.* 1 The act of protesting. **2** That which is protested. **3** Any protest or objection.

Pro·te·us (prō'tē·əs, -tyōōs) *Gk. Myth.* A sea god who had the power of assuming different forms. **—Pro'te·an** *adj.*

proto- *combining form* **1** First in rank or time; chief; typical: *protozoan.* **2** Primitive; original: *prototype.* Also **prot-.** [< Gk. *prōtos* first]

pro·to·col (prō'tə·kol) *n.* **1** The preliminary draft of an official document, as a treaty. **2** The preliminary draft or report of the negotiations and conclusions arrived at by a diplomatic conference, having the force of a treaty when ratified. **3** The rules of diplomatic and state etiquette and ceremony. **—***v.i.* To write or form protocols. [< LGk. *prōtokollon* the first glued sheet of a papyrus roll]

pro·ton (prō'ton) *n.* A stable, positively charged subatomic particle found typically in atomic nuclei, having a charge equal in magnitude to that of an electron and a mass of about 1.672×10^{-24} gram. [< Gk. *prōtos* first]

pro·to·plasm (prō'tə·plaz'əm) *n.* The basic living substance of plant and animal cells. [< Gk. *prōtos* first + PLASMA] **—pro'to·plas'mic** *adj.*

pro·to·type (prō'tə·tīp) *n.* A first or original model; an archetype. **—pro'to·typ'al** (-tī'pəl), **pro'to·typ'ic** (-tip'ik), **pro'to·typ'i·cal** *adj.*

pro·to·zo·an (prō'tə·zō'ən) *n. pl.* **·zo·a** (-zō'ə) Any of a phylum of single-celled animals, including free-living, aquatic forms and pathogenic parasites. Also **pro'to·zo'·on.** **—***adj.* Pertaining or belonging to the phylum of protozoans: also **pro'to·zo'·ic.** [< PROTO- + Gk. *zōion* animal]

pro·tract (prō·trakt', prə-) *v.t.* **1** To extend in time; prolong. **2** In surveying, to draw or map by means of a scale and protractor; plot. **3** *Zool.* To protrude or extend. [< L *protractus,* pp. of *protrahere* extend] **—pro·trac'tion** *n.* **—pro·tract'i·ble, pro·trac'tive** *adj.*

pro·tract·ed (prō·trak'tid, prə-) *adj.* Unduly or unusually extended or prolonged. **—pro·tract'ed·ly** *adv.* **—pro·tract'ed·ness** *n.*

pro·trac·tile (prō·trak'til) *adj.* Capable of being protracted or protruded; protrusile.

pro·trac·tor (prō·trak'tər) *n.* **1** An instrument for measuring and laying off angles. **2** One who or that which protracts.

pro·trude (prō·trōōd', prə-) *v.t. & v.i.* **·trud·ed, ·trud·ing** To push or thrust out; project outward. [< L *pro-* forward + *trudere* thrust] **—pro·tru'dent** *adj.* **—pro·tru'sion** (-trōō'·zhən) *n.*

pro·tru·sile (prō·trōō'sil) *adj.* Adapted to being thrust out, as a tentacle, etc. Also **pro·tru'si·ble.**

pro·tru·sive (prō·trōō'siv) *adj.* **1** Tending to protrude. **2** Pushing or driving forward. **—pro·tru'sive·ly** *adv.* **—pro·tru'sive·ness** *n.*

pro·tu·ber·ance (prō·t'yōō'bər·əns) *n.* **1** Something that protrudes; a knob; prominence. **2** The state of being protuberant. Also **pro·tu'ber·an·cy.** [< LL *protuberare* bulge out] **—pro·tu'ber·ant** *adj.* **—pro·tu'ber·ant·ly** *adv.*

proud (proud) *adj.* **1** Moved by, having, or exhibiting a due sense of pride; self-respecting. **2** Characterized by excessive or immoderate pride. **3** Being a cause of honorable pride: a *proud* occasion. **4** Appreciative of an honor; glad: *proud* of his heritage. **5** High-mettled, as a horse; spirited. [< OE *prūd*] **—proud'ly** *adv.* **—Syn. 2** arrogant, haughty, supercilious, disdainful.

proud flesh An excessive growth of tissue at a healing wound or ulcer.

Prov, Prov. Proverbs.

prov. province; provincial; provisional; provost.

prove (prōōv) *v.* **proved, proved** or **prov·en** (prōō'vən), **prov·ing** *v.t.* **1** To show to be true or genuine, as by evidence or argument. **2** To determine the quality or genuineness of; test. **3** To establish the authenticity or validity of, as a will. **4** *Math.* To verify the accuracy of by an independent process. **5** *Printing* To take a proof of or from. **6** *Archaic* To learn by experience. **—***v.i.* **7** To turn out to be: His hopes *proved* vain. [< L *probare* to test, try] **—prov'a·ble** *adj.* **—prov'er** *n.*

prov·e·nance (prov'ə·nəns) *n.* Origin or source, as of an

archeological find or an object of art. [F< *provenant,* pr.p. of *provenir* come forth]

Pro·ven·çal (prō'vən·säl', *Fr.* prō·vän·sàl') *n.* **1** The Romance language of Provence, France. **2** A native or resident of Provence. **—***adj.* Of or pertaining to Provence, its inhabitants, or their language.

prov·en·der (prov'ən·dər) *n.* **1** Dry food for cattle, as hay. **2** Provisions. [< OF *provende* an allowance of food]

pro·ve·ni·ence (prō·vē'nē·əns, -vēn'yəns) *n.* PROVENANCE.

prov·erb (prov'ərb) *n.* **1** A terse expression of a popularly accepted piece of wisdom. **2** Something proverbial; a typical example; byword. [< L *pro-* before + *verbum* a word] **—Syn. 1** adage, aphorism, maxim, motto, saying, truism.

pro·ver·bi·al (prə·vûr'bē·əl) *adj.* **1** Of the nature of or pertaining to a proverb. **2** Generally known or remarked. **—pro·ver'bi·al·ly** *adv.*

Prov·erbs (prov'ərbz) *n.pl. (construed as sing.)* A book of the Old Testament consisting of moral sayings.

pro·vide (prə·vīd') *v.* **·vid·ed, ·vid·ing** *v.t.* **1** To acquire for or supply; furnish. **2** To afford; yield: to *provide* pleasure. **3** To set down as a condition; stipulate. **—***v.i.* **4** To take measures in advance: with *for* or *against.* **5** To furnish means of subsistence: usu. with *for.* **6** To make a stipulation. [< L *providere* foresee] **—pro·vid'er** *n.*

pro·vid·ed (prə·vī'did) *conj.* On condition that.

prov·i·dence (prov'ə·dəns) *n.* **1** *Often cap.* The care exercised by nature or God's will over the universe. **2** Care exercised for the future; foresight. [< L *providentia* < *providens,* pr.p. of *providere* foresee]

Prov·i·dence (prov'ə·dəns) *n.* God; the Deity.

prov·i·dent (prov'ə·dənt) *adj.* **1** Anticipating and preparing for future wants or emergencies; exercising foresight. **2** Economical; thrifty. **—prov'i·dent·ly** *adv.*

prov·i·den·tial (prov'ə·den'shəl) *adj.* **1** Resulting from or revealing the action of God's providence. **2** As if caused by divine intervention; wonderful. **—prov'i·den'tial·ly** *adv.*

pro·vid·ing (prə·vī'ding) *conj.* Provided; in case that.

prov·ince (prov'ins) *n.* **1** An administrative division within a country: the *provinces* of Canada. **2** A region or country ruled by the Roman Empire. **3** *pl.* Those regions that lie at a distance from the capital or major cities. **4** A sphere of knowledge or activity: the *province* of chemistry. **5** Proper concern or compass, as of responsibilities or duties: The *province* of the judge is to apply the laws. [< L *provincia* an official duty or charge, a province]

pro·vin·cial (prə·vin'shəl) *adj.* **1** Of or characteristic of a province. **2** Confined to a province; rustic. **3** Narrow; unsophisticated; uninformed. **—***n.* **1** A native or inhabitant of a province. **2** One who is provincial. **—pro·vin'ci·al'i·ty** (-shē·al'ə·tē) *n.* **—pro·vin'cial·ly** *adv.*

pro·vin·cial·ism (prə·vin'shəl·iz'əm) *n.* **1** The quality of being provincial. **2** Provincial peculiarity, esp. of speech.

pro·vi·sion (prə·vizh'ən) *n.* **1** A measure taken in advance, as against future need. **2** *pl.* Food or a supply of food; victuals. **3** Something provided or prepared in anticipation of need. **4** A stipulation or requirement. **—***v.t.* To provide with food or provisions. [< L *provisus,* p.p. of *providere* foresee] **—pro·vi'sion·er** *n.*

pro·vi·sion·al (prə·vizh'ən·əl) *adj.* Provided for a present service or temporary necessity: a *provisional* army. Also **pro·vi'sion·ar'y** (-er'ē). **—pro·vi'sion·al·ly** *adv.*

pro·vi·so (prə·vī'zō) *n. pl.* **·sos** or **·soes** **1** A conditional stipulation. **2** A clause, as in a contract or statute, limiting, modifying, or rendering conditional its operation. [< Med. L *proviso (quod)* it being provided (that)]

pro·vi·so·ry (prə·vī'zər·ē) *adj.* **1** Conditional. **2** Provisional. **—pro·vi'so·ri·ly** *adv.*

pro·vo (prō'vō) *n. pl.* **·vos** A youthful member of any of various groups committed to violent political action. [Du. < F *provocateur*]

prov·o·ca·tion (prov'ə·kā'shən) *n.* **1** The act of provoking. **2** Something that provokes or incites; esp., something that provokes anger or annoyance.

pro·voc·a·tive (prə·vok'ə·tiv) *adj.* Serving to provoke or excite; stimulating: a *provocative* theory. **—***n.* That which provokes or tends to provoke. **—pro·voc′a·tive·ly** adv. — **pro·voc′a·tive·ness** n.

pro·voke (prə·vōk′) v.t. **·voked**, **·vok·ing** 1 To stir to anger or resentment; irritate; vex. 2 To arouse or stimulate to some action. 3 To stir up or bring about: to *provoke* a quarrel. [< L *pro-* forth + *vocare* to call]

prov·ost (prō′vōst, prō′vəst, prov′əst) n. 1 A person having charge or authority over others. 2 The chief magistrate of a Scottish burgh. 3 An administrative official in some English and American colleges. 4 *Eccl.* The head of a collegiate chapter or a cathedral; a dean. [< L *praepositus* a prefect] **—prov′ost·ship** n.

pro·vost marshal (prō′vō) A military officer commanding a company of military police (**provost guard**).

prow (prou) n. 1 The forward part of a ship; the bow. 2 Any pointed projection, as of an airplane. [< Gk. *prōira*]

prow·ess (prou′is) n. 1 Strength, skill, and courage, esp. in battle. 2 Formidable skill; expertise. [< OF *prou* brave]

prowl (proul) v.t. & v.i. To roam about stealthily, as in search of prey or plunder. —n. The act of prowling. [ME *prollen*] **—prowl′er** n.

prowl car SQUAD CAR.

prox·i·mal (prok′sə·məl) adj. 1 Relatively nearer the center of the body or point of origin. 2 PROXIMATE. [< L *proximus* nearest] **—prox′i·mal·ly** adv.

Prow of a ship

prox·i·mate (prok′sə·mit) adj. Being in immediate relation with something else; next; near. [< L *proximus* nearest, superl. of *prope* near] **—prox′i·mate·ly** adv.

prox·im·i·ty (prok·sim′ə·tē) n. The state or fact of being near; nearness. [< L *proximus* nearest]

prox·i·mo (prok′sə·mō) adv. In or of the next or coming month. [< L *proximo (mense)* in the next (month)]

prox·y (prok′sē) n. pl. **prox·ies** 1 A person empowered by another to act for him. 2 The means or agency of one so empowered: to vote by *proxy*. 3 The office or right to act for another. 4 A document conferring the authority to act for another. [< L *procurare* procure]

pr.p. present participle.

prude (prōōd) n. One who displays an exaggerated devotion to modesty and propriety, esp. in sexual matters. [F < *prudefemme* an excellent woman] **—prud′ish** adj. — **prud′ish·ly** adv. **—prud′ish·ness** n.

pru·dence (prōōd′ns) n. 1 The exercise of thoughtful care, sound judgment, or discretion; cautious wisdom. 2 Economy; thrift. **—pru·den′tial** (prōō·den′shəl) adj.

pru·dent (prōōd′nt) adj. 1 Habitually careful to avoid errors and to follow the most reasonable or practical course; politic. 2 Exercising sound judgment; wise; judicious. 3 Characterized by discretion; cautious in manner. 4 Frugal; provident. [< L *prudens* knowing, skilled] **—pru′dent·ly** adv. **—Syn.** 1 shrewd. 2 sensible, sagacious, thoughtful. 3 circumspect.

prud·er·y (prōō′dər·ē) n. pl. **·er·ies** 1 Exaggerated devotion to modesty and propriety, esp. in sexual matters. 2 An action characteristic of a prude.

prune¹ (prōōn) n. 1 The dried fruit of any of several varieties of plum. 2 *Slang* A stupid or disagreeable person. [< Gk. *prounon* a plum]

prune² (prōōn) v.t. & v.i. **pruned**, **prun·ing** 1 To trim or cut superfluous branches or parts (from). 2 To cut off (superfluous branches or parts). [< OF *proignier*] **—prun′er** n.

pru·ri·ent (prŏŏr′ē·ənt) adj. 1 Tending to excite lustful thoughts or desires; lewd. 2 Characterized by or having lustful thoughts or desires: *prurient* interest. [< L *prurire* itch, long for] **—pru′ri·ence**, **pru′ri·en·cy** n. **—pru′ri·ent·ly** adv.

Prussian blue 1 A dark blue pigment or dye composed of various cyanogen compounds of iron. 2 A strong, blue color.

prussic acid HYDROCYANIC ACID.

pry¹ (prī) v.i. **pried**, **pry·ing** To look or peer carefully, curiously, or slyly; snoop. [ME *prien*]

pry² (prī) v.t. **pried**, **pry·ing** 1 To raise, move, or open by means of a lever. 2 To obtain by effort. —n. 1 A lever, as a bar, stick, or beam. 2 Leverage. [< PRIZE²]

pry·er (prī′ər) n. PRIER.

P.S. public school.

P.S., p.s. postscript.

Ps, Ps., Psa. Psalms.

psalm (säm) n. A sacred song or lyric, esp. one contained in the Old Testament Book of Psalms; a hymn. [< Gk. *psalmos* a song sung to the harp]

psalm·ist (sä′mist) n. A composer of psalms. **—the Psalmist** King David, the traditional author of many of the Scriptural psalms.

psalm·o·dy (sä′mə·dē, sal′-) n. pl. **·dies** 1 The singing of psalms in divine worship. 2 A collection of psalms. [< Gk. *psalmos* a psalm + *ōidē* a song] **—psalm′o·dist** n.

Psalms (sämz) n.pl. (construed as sing.) A lyrical book of the Old Testament, containing 150 hymns. Also **Book of Psalms.**

psal·ter (sôl′tər) n. A version of the Book of Psalms used in religious services. [< L *psalterium* a psaltery]

Psal·ter (sôl′tər) n. The Book of Psalms. Also **Psal′ter·y.**

psal·ter·y (sôl′tər·ē) n. pl. **·ter·ies** An ancient stringed musical instrument played by plucking. [< Gk. *psaltērion* < *psallein* to twitch, twang]

pseud. pseudonym.

pseu·do (sōō′dō) adj. Pretended; sham; false.

pseudo- combining form 1 False; pretended: *pseudonym*. 2 Closely resembling; serving or functioning as: *pseudopodium*. Also **pseud-.** [< Gk. *pseudēs* false]

Psaltery

pseu·do·nym (sōō′də·nim) n. A fictitious name; pen name. [< Gk. *pseudēs* false + *onyma* a name] **—pseu·don·y·mous** (sōō·don′ə·məs) adj. **—pseu·don′y·mous·ly** adv. **— pseu·do·nym′i·ty** (sōō′də·nim′ə·tē) n.

pseu·do·po·di·um (sōō′də·pō′dē·əm) n. pl. **·di·a** (-dē·ə) A temporary extension of the protoplasm of a cell or unicellular organism, serving for taking in food, locomotion, etc. Also **pseu′do·pod** (-pod). [< PSEUDO- + Gk. *podion* little foot] **—pseu′do·po′di·al, pseu·dop′o·dal** (sōō·dop′ə·dəl) adj.

psf, p.s.f. pounds per square foot.

pshaw (shô) interj. & n. An exclamation of annoyance, disgust, or impatience.

psi (sī, psī, psē) n. The twenty-third letter of the Greek alphabet (Ψ, ψ).

psi, p.s.i. pounds per square inch.

psi·lo·cy·bin (sī′lə·sī′bin) n. A hallucinogenic drug derived from a Mexican mushroom. [< *Psilocybe,* generic name of the mushroom + -IN]

psit·ta·co·sis (sit′ə·kō′sis) n. A viral infection affecting parrots, pigeons, etc., and sometimes humans, in whom it causes pneumonia, fever, etc. [< Gk. *psittakos* a parrot + -OSIS]

pso·ri·a·sis (sə·rī′ə·sis) n. A chronic skin condition characterized by reddish patches and white scales. [< Gk. *psōra* an itch] **—pso·ri·at·ic** (sôr′ē·at′ik, sō′rē-) adj.

PST, P.S.T., P.s.t. Pacific standard time.

psych (sīk) v.t. **psyched, psych·ing** *Slang* 1 To make mentally ready, as by inducing alertness or tension; key up: often with *up.* 2 To cause to lose self-assurance, esp. in order to place at a competitive disadvantage; demoralize: often with *out*: to *psych* rivals. 3 To manipulate by the use of psychology; esp., to outwit: often with *out: psyched* him into giving me a loan. 4 To understand: with *out*: couldn't *psych* it out. Also **psyche.** **—Syn.** 2 intimidate, distress, put off, disconcert, discountenance.

psych., psychol. psychologist; psychology.

psy·che (sī′kē) n. 1 The human soul. 2 The mind. [< Gk. *psychē* the soul < *psychein* breathe, blow]

Psy·che (sī′kē) *Gk. & Rom. Myth.* A maiden beloved by Cupid and regarded as a personification of the soul.

psy·che·de·li·a (sī′kə·dē′lē·ə, -dēl′yə) n. Psychedelic drugs and accessories, or things associated with them.

psy·che·del·ic (sī′kə·del′ik) adj. Causing or having to do with abnormal alterations of consciousness or perception: *psychedelic* drugs. [< Gk. *psychē* soul + *del(os)* manifest + -IC] **—psy′che·del′i·cal·ly** adv.

psy·chi·a·trist (sĭ·kī'ə·trist) *n.* A medical doctor specializing in the practice of psychiatry.

psy·chi·a·try (sĭ·kī'ə·trē) *n.* The branch of medicine concerned with mental and emotional disorders. [< PSYCH(O)- + Gk. *iatros* healer] —**psy·chi·at·ric** (sī'kē·at'rik) or ·ri·cal *adj.* —**psy'chi·at'ri·cal·ly** *adv.*

psy·chic (sī'kik) *adj.* 1 Of or pertaining to the psyche or mind. 2 Inexplicable with reference to present knowledge or scientific theory: *psychic* phenomena. 3 Sensitive or responsive to phenomena apparently independent of normal sensory stimuli: a *psychic* person. Also **psy'chi·cal.** — *n.* 1 A psychic person. 2 A spiritualistic medium. [< Gk. *psychē* soul] —**psy'chi·cal·ly** *adv.*

psy·cho (sī'kō) *n. pl.* ·chos *Slang* A mentally disturbed person; a neurotic or psychopath. —*adj.* 1 Psychologically disturbed. 2 Psychological or psychiatric. [< PSYCHO(NEUROTIC)]

psycho- *combining form* Mind; soul; spirit: *psychosomatic.* Also **psych-.** [< Gk. *psychē* spirit, soul]

psy·cho·ac·tive (sī'kō·ak'tiv) *adj.* Having an effect on the mind or on behavior.

psy·cho·a·nal·y·sis (sī'kō·ə·nal'ə·sis) *n.* 1 A method of psychotherapeutic treatment developed by Sigmund Freud and others, which seeks to alleviate certain mental and emotional disorders. 2 The theory or practice of such treatment. —**psy'cho·an'a·lyt'ic** (-an'ə·lit'ik) or ·i·cal *adj.* — **psy'cho·an'a·lyt'i·cal·ly** *adv.*

psy·cho·an·a·lyst (sī'kō·an'ə·list) *n.* One who practices psychoanalysis.

psy·cho·an·a·lyze (sī'kō·an'ə·līz) *v.t.* ·lyzed, ·lyz·ing To treat by psychoanalysis. *Brit. sp.* ·lyse.

psy·cho·dra·ma (sī'kō·drä'mə, -dram'ə) *n.* A form of psychotherapy in which the patient acts out, occasionally before an audience, situations involving his problems. — **psy'cho·dra·mat'ic** *adj.*

psy·cho·gen·ic (sī'kō·jen'ik) *adj.* Originating in the mind; caused by a mental or emotional condition. —**psy'·cho·gen'i·cal·ly** *adv.*

psy·cho·log·i·cal (sī'kə·loj'i·kəl) *adj.* 1 Of or pertaining to psychology. 2 Of or in the mind. 3 Suitable for affecting the mind: the *psychological* moment. Also **psy'cho·log'ic.** —**psy'cho·log'i·cal·ly** *adv.*

psy·chol·o·gist (sī·kol'ə·jist) *n.* A specialist in psychology.

psy·chol·o·gize (sī·kol'ə·jīz) *v.* ·gized, ·giz·ing *v.i.* 1 To theorize psychologically. —*v.t.* 2 To interpret psychologically.

psy·chol·o·gy (sī·kol'ə·jē) *n.* 1 The science of the mind in any of its aspects. 2 The systematic investigation of human or animal learning, behavior, etc. 3 The pattern of mental processes characteristic of an individual or type.

psy·cho·neu·ro·sis (sī'kō·nyŏŏ·rō'sis) *n. pl.* ·ses (-sēz) NEUROSIS. —**psy'cho·neu·rot'ic** (-rot'ik) *adj., n.*

psy·cho·path (sī'kō·path) *n.* One exhibiting severely deranged behavior. —**psy'cho·path'ic** *adj.*

psy·cho·pa·thol·o·gy (sī'kō·pə·thol'ə·jē) *n.* The pathology of the mind. —**psy'cho·path'o·log'i·cal** (-path'ə·loj'i·kəl) *adj.* —**psy'cho·pa·thol'o·gist** *n.*

psy·chop·a·thy (sī·kop'ə·thē) *n.* Mental disorder.

psy·cho·sis (sī·kō'sis) *n. pl.* ·ses (-sēz) A severe mental disorder marked by disorganization of the personality. [< Gk. *psychōsis* a giving of life]

psy·cho·so·mat·ic (sī'kō·sō·mat'ik) *adj.* 1 Of or pertaining to the interrelationships of mind and body, esp. with reference to disease. 2 Designating a physical ailment caused or influenced by emotional stress. [< PSYCHO- + SOMATIC]

psy·cho·sur·ger·y (sī'kō·sûr'jər·ē) *n.* Brain surgery performed to treat a mental disorder or alter behavior. — **psy'cho·sur'geon** (-sûr'jən) *n.* —**psy'cho·sur'gi·cal** *adj.*

psy·cho·ther·a·py (sī'kō·ther'ə·pē) *n.* The treatment of certain nervous and mental disorders by psychological techniques such as counseling, psychoanalysis, etc. Also **psy'cho·ther'a·peu'tics** (-ther'ə·pyŏŏ'tiks). —**psy'cho·ther'·a·peu'tic** *adj.* —**psy'cho·ther'a·pist** *n.*

psy·chot·ic (sī·kot'ik) *n.* One suffering from a psychosis. —*adj.* Of psychosis or a psychotic. —**psy·chot'i·cal·ly** *adv.*

Pt platinum.

pt. (*pl.* **pts.**) part; payment; pint; point; port; preterit.

p.t. past tense; for the time being (L *pro tempore*).

PTA, P.T.A. Parent-Teacher Association.

ptar·mi·gan (tär'mə·gən) *n. pl.* ·gans or ·gan Any of various species of grouse of northern regions, usu. having white winter plumage. [< Scot. Gaelic *tarmachan*]

PT boat (pē'tē') A high-speed, easily maneuverable motorboat equipped with torpedoes and, usu. machine guns and depth charges. [< *p(atrol) t(orpedo)*]

pter·i·do·phyte (ter'i·dō·fīt') *n.* Any of a division of flowerless plants comprising the ferns, horsetails, and related plants with vascular stems, roots, and leaves. [< Gk. *pteris, pteridos* a fern + *phyton* a plant] —**pter'i·do·phyt'ic** (-fit'ik), **pter'i·doph'y·tous** (-dof'ə·təs) *adj.*

ptero- *combining form* Wing; feather; plume; resembling wings: *pterodactyl.* Also **pter-.** [< Gk. *pteron* wing]

pter·o·dac·tyl (ter'ə·dak'til) *n.* PTEROSAUR. [< Gk. *pteron* a wing + *daktylos* a finger]

pter·o·saur (ter'ə·sôr') *n.* Any of various fossil reptiles having batlike wings. [< Gk. *pteros* wing + *sauros* lizard] —**pter'o·saur'i·an** *adj.*

-pterous *combining form* Having a specified number or kind of wings: *dipterous.* [< Gk. *pteron* wing]

ptg. printing.

Ptol·e·ma·ic (tol'ə·mā'ik) *adj.* Of or pertaining to Ptolemy, the astronomer who lived in the second century A.D., or to the Ptolemies who ruled Egypt.

Ptolemaic system The astronomical system of Ptolemy, which assumed that the earth was the central body around which the sun, planets, stars, etc., moved.

pto·maine (tō'mān, tō·mān') *n.* Any of a class of usu. nontoxic compounds derived from decomposing protein. Also **pto'main.** [< Gk. *ptōma* a corpse]

ptomaine poisoning FOOD POISONING. • The term is based upon the erroneous idea that ptomaines usually cause food poisoning.

pty. proprietary.

pty·a·lin (tī'ə·lin) *n.* A digestive enzyme converting starch into dextrin and maltose. [< Gk. *ptyalon* saliva + -IN]

Pu plutonium.

pub (pub) *n. Brit.* A tavern or bar. [< PUB(LIC) (HOUSE)]

pub. public; publication; published; publisher.

pu·ber·ty (pyŏŏ'bər·tē) *n.* 1 The state in an individual's development when he or she is physically capable of sexual reproduction. 2 The age at which puberty begins, usu. fixed legally at 14 years in boys and 12 in girls. [< L *pubes, puberis* an adult]

pu·bes (pyŏŏ'bēz) *n.* 1 The hair that appears on the body at puberty. 2 The genital area that is covered with hair in the adult. [L, pubic hair]

pu·bes·cent (pyŏŏ·bes'ənt) *adj.* 1 Arriving or having arrived at puberty. 2 *Biol.* Covered with fine hair or down, as leaves, etc. [< L *pubescere* attain puberty] —**pu·bes'·cence** *n.*

pu·bic (pyŏŏ'bik) *adj.* Of or pertaining to the region in the lower part of the abdomen.

pu·bis (pyŏŏ'bis) *n. pl.* ·bes (-bēz) Either of the two bones which join to form the front arch of the pelvis. [< L *(os) pubis* pubic (bone)]

publ. publication; published; publisher.

pub·lic (pub'lik) *adj.* 1 Of, pertaining to, or affecting the people at large. 2 Of or relating to the community as distinguished from private or personal matters. 3 For the use of or open to all; maintained by or for the community: *public* parks. 4 Well-known; open: a *public* scandal. 5 Occupying an official position. 6 Acting before or for the community: a *public* speaker. —*n.* 1 The people collectively. 2 A group of people sharing some attribute or purpose: the church-going *public.* [< L *publicus*] —**pub'lic·ly** *adv.* —**pub'lic·ness** *n.*

pub·li·can (pub'lə·kən) *n.* 1 In England, the keeper of a public house. 2 In ancient Rome, one who collected the public revenues. [< L *publicanus* a tax gatherer]

---

add, āce, câre, pälm; end, ēven; it, īce; odd, ōpen, ôrder; tŏŏk, pōōl; up, bûrn; ə = *a* in *above, u* in *focus;* yōō = *u* in *fuse;* oil; pout; check; go; ring; thin; this; zh, *vision.* < derived from; ? origin uncertain or unknown.

pub·li·ca·tion (pub′lə·kā′shən) *n.* **1** The act of publishing. **2** That which is published; any printed work placed on sale or otherwise distributed.

public domain 1 Lands owned by a government. **2** The condition of being freely available for unrestricted use and not protected by copyright or patent.

public house 1 An inn, tavern, or hotel. **2** *Brit.* A saloon or bar.

pub·li·cist (pub′lə·sist) *n.* **1** One who publicizes, as an activity, a person, etc. **2** A writer on international law.

pub·lic·i·ty (pub·lis′ə·tē) *n.* **1** The state of being public. **2** Information, news, or promotional material intended to elicit public interest in some person, product, cause, etc.; also the work or business of preparing and releasing such material. **3** The attention or interest of the public.

pub·li·cize (pub′lə·sīz) *v.t.* **·cized, ·ciz·ing** To give publicity to; promote. *Brit. sp.* **pub·li·cise.**

public opinion The prevailing ideas, beliefs, or attitudes of a community.

public relations The business of representing and promoting the interests or reputation of a person or an organization in its relations with the public.

public school 1 A school maintained by public funds for the free education of the children of the community, usu. covering elementary and secondary grades. **2** In England, a private, endowed boarding school preparing students for the universities.

public servant A government official.

pub·lic-spir·it·ed (pub′lik-spir′it·id) *adj.* Showing an enlightened interest in the welfare of the community.

public utility A business organization which performs some public service, as the supplying of water or electric power, and is subject to governmental regulations.

public works Works built with public money, as post offices, roads, etc.

pub·lish (pub′lish) *v.t.* **1** To print and issue (a book, magazine, etc.) to the public. **2** To make known or announce publicly. **3** To print and issue the work of. —*v.i.* **4** To engage in the business of publishing books, magazines, newspapers, etc. **5** To have one's work printed and issued. [< L *publicare* make public] **—pub′lish·a·ble** *adj.* **—Syn. 2** promulgate, proclaim, declare, advertise.

pub·lish·er (pub′lish·ər) *n.* One who makes a business of publishing books, periodicals, etc.

puce (pyo͞os) *n.* Dark purplish brown. —*adj.* Of this color. [F, lit., flea < L *pulex*]

puck[1] (puk) *n.* A mischievous sprite or hobgoblin. [< OE *pūca* a goblin] **—puck′ish** *adj.* **—puck′ish·ly** *adv.* **—puck′ish·ness** *n.*

puck[2] (puk) *n.* A hard rubber disk used in playing hockey. [? var. of POKE[1]]

puck·a (puk′ə) *adj.* PUKKA.

puck·er (puk′ər) *v.t. & v.i.* To gather or draw up into small folds or wrinkles. —*n.* A wrinkle. [?< POKE[2]]

pud·ding (po͝od′ing) *n.* **1** A sweetened and flavored dessert of soft food. **2** A sausage stuffed with seasoned, minced meat, blood, etc. [ME *poding*]

pud·dle (pud′l) *n.* **1** A small pool of water or other liquid. **2** A pasty mixture of clay and water. —*v.t.* **·dled, ·dling 1** To convert (molten pig iron) into wrought iron by melting and stirring in the presence of oxidizing agents. **2** To mix (clay, etc.) with water to obtain a watertight paste. **3** To line, as canal banks, with such a mixture. **4** To make muddy; stir up. [ME < OE *pudd* a ditch] **—pud′dler** *n.*

pud·dling (pud′ling) *n.* The operation of making wrought iron from pig iron by agitation in a molten state with oxidizing agents present.

pu·den·dum (pyo͞o·den′dəm) *n. pl.* **·da** (-də) **1** The vulva. **2** *pl.* The external genitals of either sex. [L, neut. of *pudendus* (something) to be ashamed of] **—pu·den′dal** *adj.*

pudg·y (puj′ē) *adj.* **pudg·i·er, pudg·i·est** Short and thick; fat. [< Scot. *pud* belly] **—pudg′i·ly** *adv.* **—pudg′i·ness** *n.*

pueb·lo (pweb′lō *for*

Hopi Indian pueblo

def. 1, pwä′blō *for def. 2*) *n. pl.* **·los 1** A communal adobe or stone building or group of buildings of the Indians of the sw U.S. **2** A town or village of Indians or Spanish Americans, as in Mexico. [Sp., a town, people < L *populus*]

Pueb·lo (pweb′lō) *n.* A member of one of the Indian tribes of Mexico and the sw U.S.

pu·er·ile (pyo͞o′ər·il, pwer′il, -īl) *adj.* Childish; immature; silly. [< L *puer* boy] **—pu′er·ile·ly** *adv.* **—pu·er·il′i·ty, pu′er·ile·ness** *n.*

pu·er·per·al (pyo͞o·ûr′pər·əl) *adj.* Pertaining to or resulting from childbirth. [< L *puer* boy + *parere* bring forth]

Puer·to Ri·co (pwer·tə rē′kō, pôr-) An island commonwealth of the West Indies, a part of the U.S., 3,423 sq. mi., cap. San Juan. •See map at DOMINICAN REPUBLIC. **—Puer′to Ri′can** *adj., n.*

puff (puf) *n.* **1** A short, mild explosive force or emission, as a gust of air or expelled breath. **2** The sound of such a force. **3** The air, breath, etc., so felt or emitted: a small *puff* of smoke. **4** The act of sucking in and exhaling in the course of smoking a cigarette, etc. **5** A light, air-filled piece of pastry. **6** A pad for dusting powder on the skin. **7** A small protuberance or swelling. **8** A loose roll of hair. **9** A quilted bed coverlet. **10** A part of a fabric gathered at the edges. **11** A public expression of fulsome praise. —*v.i.* **1** To blow in puffs, as the wind. **2** To breathe hard, as after violent exertion. **3** To emit smoke, steam, etc., in puffs. **4** To smoke a cigarette, etc., with puffs. **5** To move, act, or exert oneself while emitting puffs: with *away, up,* etc. **6** To swell, as with air or pride; dilate: often with *up.* —*v.t.* **7** To send forth or emit with short puffs or breaths. **8** To move, impel, or stir up with or in puffs. **9** To smoke, as a cigarette or pipe, with puffs. **10** To swell or distend. **11** To praise fulsomely. **12** To arrange (the hair) in a puff. [< OE *pyffan*] **—puff′i·ly** *adv.* **—puff′i·ness** *n.* **—puff′y** *adj.* **(·i·er, ·i·est)**

puff adder 1 A large African viper that puffs and hisses when disturbed. **2** HOGNOSE.

puff·ball (puf′bôl′) *n.* A globular fungus that puffs out dustlike spores if broken open when ripe.

puff·er (puf′ər) *n.* **1** One who puffs. **2** Any of various fishes that can inflate themselves with air or water.

puff·er·y (puf′ər·ē) *n.* Excessive praise, esp. to obtain publicity.

puf·fin (puf′in) *n.* Any of various northern sea birds with a chunky body and a large, triangular bill. [ME *poffin*]

Puffin

pug[1] (pug) *v.t.* **pugged, pug·ging 1** To work (clay) with water in molding pottery or making bricks. **2** To fill in or cover with mortar, clay, felt, etc., to deaden sound. —*n.* A mixture of clay worked with water for brick-making, etc. [< dial. E]

pug[2] (pug) *n.* **1** A short-haired dog with a square body, upturned nose and curled tail. **2** PUG NOSE. [?]

pug[3] (pug) *n.* *Slang* A professional prizefighter. [Short for PUGILIST]

pu·gi·lism (pyo͞o′jə·liz′əm) *n.* BOXING. [< L *pugil* a boxer] **—pu′gi·list** *n.* **—pu′gi·lis′tic** *adj.* **—pu′gi·lis′ti·cal·ly** *adv.*

pug·na·cious (pug·nā′shəs) *adj.* Disposed or inclined to fight; quarrelsome. [< L *pugnus* fist] **—pug·na′cious·ly** *adv.* **—pug·nac·i·ty** (-nas′ə·tē), **pug·na′cious·ness** *n.*

pug nose A thick, short, upturned nose. [< PUG[2] + NOSE] **—pug′-nosed′** *adj.*

pu·is·sant (pyo͞o′ə·sənt, pyo͞o·is′ənt, pwis′ənt) *adj.* Powerful; mighty. [< L *posse* be able] **—pu′is·sance** *n.* **—pu′is·sant·ly** *adv.*

puke (pyo͞ok) *v.t. & v.i.* **puked, puk·ing,** *n. Informal* VOMIT. [?]

puk·ka (puk′ə) *adj.* Genuine; sound. [< Hind. *pakkā* cooked, ripe]

pul·chri·tude (pul′krə·t^yo͞od) *n.* Beauty; grace. [< L *pulcher* beautiful] **—pul·chri·tu·di·nous** (-t^yo͞o′də·nəs) *adj.*

pule (pyo͞ol) *v.i.* **puled, pul·ing** To cry plaintively, as a child; whimper; whine. [< MF *pioler* chirp] **—pul′er** *n.*

Pul·it·zer Prize (pŏol′it·sər, pyŏo′lit-) Any of several annual awards for outstanding work in American journalism, literature, drama, and music, established by Joseph Pulitzer, 1847–1911, U.S. journalist.

pull (pŏol) *v.t.* **1** To apply force to so as to cause motion toward or after the person or thing exerting force; drag; tug. **2** To draw or remove from a natural or fixed place: to *pull* a tooth or plug. **3** To give a pull or tug to. **4** To pluck, as a fowl. **5** To draw asunder; tear; rend: with *to pieces, apart,* etc. **6** To strain so as to cause injury: to *pull* a ligament. **7** In sports, to strike (the ball) so as to cause it to curve obliquely from the direction in which the striker faces. **8** *Informal* To put into effect; carry out: to *pull* off a robbery. **9** *Informal* To make a raid on; arrest. **10** *Informal* To draw out so as to use: to *pull* a knife. **11** To make or obtain by impression from type: to *pull* a proof. **12** In boxing, to deliver (a punch, etc.) with less than full strength. **13** In horse-racing, to restrain (a horse) so as to prevent its winning. **14** To operate (an oar) by drawing toward one. —*v.i.* **15** To use force in hauling, dragging, moving, etc. **16** To move: with *out, in, away, ahead,* etc. **17** To drink or inhale deeply. **18** *Informal* To attract attention or customers: an ad that *pulls.* **19** To row. —**pull for 1** To strive in behalf of. **2** *Informal* To declare one's allegiance to. —**pull oneself together** To regain one's composure. —**pull through** To survive in spite of illness, etc. —**pull up** To come to a halt. —*n.* **1** The act or process of pulling. **2** Something that is pulled, as a handle. **3** A long swallow or a deep puff. **4** The drawing of an oar in rowing. **5** A steady, continuous effort, as in climbing: a long *pull* to the top. **6** *Informal* Influence, esp. with those in power: political *pull.* **7** An attractive force: the *pull* of gravity. [< OE *pullian* pluck] —**pull′er** *n.*

pull·back (pŏol′bak′) *n.* A withdrawal, as of troops.

pul·let (pŏol′it) *n.* A young hen, usu. less than a year old. [< L *pullus* chicken]

pul·ley (pŏol′ē) *n.* **1** A wheel or wheels grooved to receive a rope, usu. mounted in a block, used singly to reverse the direction of force applied, as in lifting a weight, and in various combinations to increase force at the expense of distance. **2** A flat or flanged wheel driving, carrying, or being driven by a flat belt, used to transmit power. [< Gk. *polos* a pivot, axis]

Pull·man (pŏol′mən) *n.* A railroad car with compartments for sleeping or other special accommodations. Also **Pullman car.** [< George M. *Pullman,* 1831–97, U.S. inventor]

Pulleys
a. single fixed. b.
fixed and runner.

pull·out (pŏol′out′) *n.* **1** A withdrawal or removal, as of troops. **2** Something to be pulled out, as an oversize leaf folded into a magazine.

pull·o·ver (pŏol′ō′vər) *adj.* Put on by being drawn over the head. —*n.* A garment put on in such a way, as a sweater.

pul·mo·nar·y (pŏol′mə·ner′ē, pul′-) *adj.* **1** Pertaining to or affecting the lungs. **2** Having lunglike organs. **3** Designating the blood vessels carrying blood between the lungs and heart. Also **pul·mon·ic** (pŏol·mon′ik, pul-). [< L *pulmo, pulmonis* lung] • See HEART.

Pul·mo·tor (pŏol′mō′tər, pul′-) *n.* A machine for applying artificial respiration: a trade name.

pulp (pulp) *n.* **1** A moist, soft, slightly cohering mass, as the soft, succulent part of fruit. **2** A mixture of wood fibers or rags, made semifluid and forming the basis from which paper is made. **3** *pl.* Magazines printed on rough, unglazed, wood-pulp paper, and usu. having contents of a sensational nature. **4** Powdered ore mixed with water. **5** The soft tissue of vessels and nerves that fills the central part of a tooth. • See TOOTH. —*v.t.* **1** To reduce to pulp. **2** To remove the pulp from. —*v.i.* **3** To be or become pulp. [< L *pulpa* flesh, pulp] —**pulp′i·ness** *n.* —**pulp′y** *adj.*

pul·pit (pŏol′pit, pul′-) *n.* **1** An elevated stand or desk for preaching in a church. **2** The office or work of preaching. **3** The clergy. [< L *pulpitum* platform]

pulp·wood (pulp′wŏod′) *n.* Soft wood used in the manufacture of paper.

pul·que (pul′kē, pŏol′-; *Sp.* pŏol′kä) *n.* A fermented Mexican drink made from agave. [Sp.]

pul·sar (pul′sär) *n.* An astronomical object that emits radio waves in pulses whose repetition rate is extremely stable. [< *puls(ating)* + *(st)ar*]

pul·sate (pul′sāt) *v.i.* **·sat·ed, ·sat·ing 1** To move or throb with rhythmical impulses, as the pulse or heart. **2** To vibrate; quiver. [< L *pulsare,* freq. of *pellere* beat] —**pul·sa′tion, pul′sa·tor** *n.* —**pul′sa·tive** (-sə-tiv), **pul′sa·to′ry** *adj.*

pulse[1] (puls) *n.* **1** The rhythmic pressure in the arteries due to the beating of the heart. **2** Any short, regular throbbing; pulsation. **3** A brief surge of energy, esp. electrical or electromagnetic energy. **4** Feelings and attitudes sensitively perceived as belonging to a group or community; also, an indication of such feelings. —*v.i.* **pulsed, puls·ing** To manifest a pulse; pulsate; throb. [< L *pulsus* p.p. of *pellere* beat]

pulse[2] (puls) *n.* Leguminous plants collectively, as peas, beans, etc., or their edible seeds. [< L *puls* pottage]

pulse·jet (puls′jet′) *n.* A jet engine that operates intermittently and produces power in rapid bursts.

pul·ver·ize (pul′və·rīz) *v.* **·ized, ·iz·ing** *v.t.* **1** To reduce to powder or dust, as by grinding or crushing. **2** To demolish; annihilate. —*v.i.* **3** To become reduced to powder or dust. *Brit. sp.* **·ise.** [< L *pulvis, pulveris* a powder, dust] —**pul′ver·iz′a·ble, pul·ver·a·ble** (pul′və·rə·bəl) *adj.* —**pul′ver·i·za′tion, pul′ver·iz′er** *n.*

pu·ma (pyŏo′mə) *n.* MOUNTAIN LION. [< Quechua]

pum·ice (pum′is) *n.* Porous volcanic lava, used as an abrasive and polisher, esp. when powdered. Also **pumice stone.** —*v.t.* **·iced, ·ic·ing** To smooth, polish, or clean with pumice. [< L *pumex*] —**pu·mi·ceous** (pyŏo·mish′əs) *adj.*

pum·mel (pum′əl) *v.t.* **·meled** or **·melled, ·mel·ing** or **·mel·ling** POMMEL.

pump[1] (pump) *n.* A device using suction or pressure to raise, circulate, exhaust, or compress a liquid or gas. —*v.t.* **1** To raise (a liquid) with a pump. **2** To remove the water, etc., from. **3** To inflate with air by means of a pump. **4** To propel, discharge, force, etc., from or as if from a pump. **5** To cause to operate in the manner of a pump. **6** To question persistently or subtly. **7** To obtain (information) in such a manner. —*v.i.* **8** To work a pump. **9** To raise water or other liquid with a pump. **10** To move up and down like a pump or pump handle. [< MDu. *pompe*] —**pump′er** *n.*

pump[2] (pump) *n.* A low-cut shoe without a fastening, worn esp. by women. [?]

pum·per·nick·el (pum′pər·nik′əl) *n.* A coarse, dark bread made with rye flour. [G]

pump·kin (pump′kin, pum′-, pung′-) *n.* **1** A coarse trailing vine with gourdlike fruit. **2** Its large, edible, orange-yellow fruit. [< Gk. *pepōn* a melon]

pun (pun) *n.* The humorous use of two words having the same or similar sounds but different meanings, or of a word having two more or less incongruous meanings. —*v.i.* **punned, pun·ning** To make a pun or puns. [? < Ital. *puntiglio* a fine point]

punch[1] (punch) *n.* **1** A tool for perforating or indenting, or for driving an object into a hole. **2** A machine for impressing a design or stamping a die. —*v.t.* To perforate, shape, indent, etc., with a punch. [ME *punchon puncheon*]

punch[2] (punch) *v.t.* **1** To strike sharply, esp. with the fist. **2** To poke with a stick; prod. **3** To drive (cattle). —*n.* **1** A swift blow with the fist. **2** A thrust or nudge. **3** *Informal* Vitality; effectiveness; force. —**punch in** (or **out**) To activate a time clock and record the hour at the start (or completion) of a period of work. [ME *punchen*] —**punch′er** *n.* —**Syn. 1** hit, pound, pommel, box.

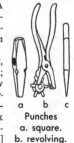

a   b   c
Punches
a. square.
b. revolving.
c. stamping.

punch[3] (punch) *n.* A hot or cold beverage made with fruit juices, spices, and other ingredients, as tea or soda water, and often mixed with alcoholic spirits. [< Skt. *pañchan* five; from the five original ingredients]

Punch (punch) *n.* The quarrelsome, grotesque hero of a comic puppet show, **Punch and Judy. —pleased as Punch** Extremely pleased; highly gratified. [Short for PUNCHINELLO]

punch card In data processing, a card having an arrangement of positions into which holes may be punched for the storage of information. Also **punched card.**

pun·cheon (pun′chən) *n.* **1** An upright supporting timber. **2** A punch or perforating tool. **3** A broad, heavy piece of roughly dressed timber, having one flat, hewed side. **4** A liquor cask of variable capacity, from 72 to 120 gallons. **5** The amount held by such a cask. [< OF *poinçon, poinchon* a punch]

pun·chi·nel·lo (pun′chə·nel′ō) *n. pl.* **·los** or **·loes 1** *Usu. cap.* A character in an Italian puppet show, the original of the English Punch. **2** A grotesque character; buffoon. [< dial. Ital. *Polcenella*]

punching bag An inflated or stuffed ball, usu. suspended, that is punched for exercise.

punch press A machine equipped with dies for cutting or forming metal.

punch·y (pun′chē) *adj.* **punch·i·er, punch·i·est** *Informal* **1** Dazed or confused, as from having been struck on the head: also **punch-drunk** (punch′drungk′). **2** Lively; snappy. —**punch′i·ly** *adv.* —**punch′i·ness** *n.*

punc·til·i·o (pungk·til′ē·ō) *n. pl.* **·til·i·os 1** A fine point of etiquette. **2** Preciseness in the observance of etiquette. [< L *punctum* a point]

punc·til·i·ous (pungk·til′ē·əs) *adj.* Very exacting in observing rules or conventions. [< Ital. *puntiglio* small point] —**punc·til′i·ous·ly** *adv.* —**punc·til′i·ous·ness** *n.*

punc·tu·al (pungk′chōō·əl) *adj.* **1** Arriving on time; prompt. **2** Habitually exact as to appointed time. **3** Consisting of or confined to a point. [< L *punctus* a point] —**punc′tu·al′i·ty** *n.* —**punc′tu·al·ly** *adv.*

punc·tu·ate (pungk′chōō·āt) *v.* **·at·ed, ·at·ing** *v.t.* **1** To divide or mark with punctuation. **2** To interrupt at intervals. **3** To emphasize. —*v.i.* **4** To use punctuation. [< L *punctus* a point] —**punc′tu·a′tor** *n.*

punc·tu·a·tion (pungk′chōō·ā′shən) *n.* **1** The use of points or marks in written or printed matter to aid in the better comprehension of the meaning and grammatical relation of the words. **2** The marks so used.

punctuation mark Any of the marks used in punctuating, as the period or comma.

punc·ture (pungk′chər) *v.* **·tured, ·tur·ing** *v.t.* **1** To pierce with a sharp point. **2** To make by pricking, as a hole. **3** To cause to collapse: to *puncture* a cherished illusion. —*v.i.* **4** To be pierced or punctured. —*n.* **1** A small hole, as one made by piercing. **2** The act of puncturing. [< L *punctus,* p.p. of *pungere* prick]

pun·dit (pun′dit) *n.* **1** One who is or assumes the part of an expert in making pronouncements, criticisms, predictions, etc. **2** In India, a Brahmin versed in Sanskrit lore, Hindu religion, etc. [< Skt. *paṇḍita* learned] —**pun′dit·ry** (-rē) *n.*

pun·gent (pun′jənt) *adj.* **1** Causing a sharp pricking, stinging, piercing, or acrid sensation. **2** Affecting the mind or feelings so as to cause pain; piercing; sharp. **3** Caustic; keen; cutting: *pungent* sarcasm. **4** Telling; pointed. [< L *pungere* prick] —**pun′gen·cy** *n.* —**pun′gent·ly** *adv.*

Pu·nic (pyōō′nik) *adj.* Of or pertaining to ancient Carthage or the Carthaginians.

pun·ish (pun′ish) *v.t.* **1** To subject (a person) to pain, confinement, or other penalty for a crime or fault. **2** To subject the perpetrator of (an offense) to a penalty. **3** To treat roughly; injure; hurt. [< L *punire*] —**pun′ish·a·ble** *adj.* —**pun′ish·a·bil′i·ty, pun′ish·er** *n.*

pun·ish·ing (pun′ish·ing) *adj.* Requiring exhausting effort; taxing; demanding: a *punishing* schedule.

pun·ish·ment (pun′ish·mənt) *n.* **1** Penalty imposed, as for a violation of law. **2** Any pain or loss inflicted in response to wrongdoing. **3** The act of punishing. **4** Physical damage or abuse.

pu·ni·tive (pyōō′nə·tiv) *adj.* Pertaining to or inflicting punishment. —**pu′ni·tive·ly** *adv.* —**pu′ni·tive·ness** *n.*

punk¹ (pungk) *n.* **1** Decayed wood, used as tinder. **2** Any substance that smolders when ignited. [< Algon.]

punk² (pungk) *Slang n.* **1** Rubbish; nonsense; anything worthless. **2** A petty hoodlum. **3** An inexperienced youth, esp. a young man: usu. contemptuous. —*adj.* Worthless; useless. [?]

pun·ky (pung′kē) *n. pl.* **·kies** Any of various tiny, bloodsucking insects. Also **pun′key, pun′kie.** [< PUNK¹]

pun·ster (pun′stər) *n.* One who enjoys making puns. Also **pun′ner.**

punt¹ (punt) *n.* A flat-bottomed, square-ended boat for use in shallow waters, and propelled with a pole. —*v.t.* **1** To propel (a boat) by pushing with a pole against the bottom of a shallow stream, lake, etc. **2** To convey in a punt. —*v.i.* **3** To go or hunt in a punt. [< L *ponto*] —**punt′er** *n.*

Punt

punt² (punt) *v.i.* To gamble or bet in certain card games, esp. against the banker. [< L *punctum* a point]

punt³ (punt) *n.* In football, a kick made by dropping the ball from the hands and kicking it before it strikes the ground. —*v.t.* **1** To propel (a football) with a punt. —*v.i.* **2** In football, to make a punt. [?] —**punt′er** *n.*

pu·ny (pyōō′nē) *adj.* **·ni·er, ·ni·est** Small or inferior, as in power, significance, etc. [< OF *puisne* born afterward] —**pu′ni·ly** *adv.* —**pu′ni·ness** *n.* —**Syn.** slight, minor, unimportant, frail.

pup (pup) *n.* The young of certain animals, as a dog, wolf, fox, seal, whale, etc. —*v.i.* **pupped, pup·ping** To bring forth pups. [Short for PUPPY]

pu·pa (pyōō′pə) *n. pl.* **·pae** (-pē) or **·pas** A quiescent stage between larva and adult in the metamorphosis of certain insects. [L, a girl, puppet] —**pu′pal** *adj.*

pu·pate (pyōō′pāt) *v.i.* **·pat·ed, ·pat·ing** To enter upon or undergo the pupal condition. —**pu·pa′tion** *n.*

pu·pil¹ (pyōō′pəl) *n.* A person under the care of a teacher, as in a school. [< L *pupillus* and *pupilla,* dim. of *pupus* boy and *pupa* girl] —**pu′pil·age, pu′pil·lage** *n.* —**Syn.** student, disciple, scholar, learner.

Pupa of a butterfly

pu·pil² (pyōō′pəl) *n.* The circular opening in the iris of the eye, through which light reaches the retina. [< L *pupilla* pupil of the eye] • See EYE.

pup·pet (pup′it) *n.* **1** A small figure, as of a person or animal, manipulated usu. by the hands, or by pulling strings or wires attached to its jointed parts. **2** A person controlled by the will or whim of another. **3** A doll. —*adj.* **1** Of puppets. **2** Performing the will of an unseen power; not autonomous: a *puppet* state or government. [< L *pupa* a girl, doll, puppet] —**pup′pet·ry** (-rē) *n.*

pup·pet·eer (pup′i·tir′) *n.* One who manipulates puppets.

pup·py (pup′ē) *n. pl.* **·pies** A young dog. [< L *pupa* a girl, doll]

puppy love Temporary affection or love that a boy and girl feel for each other.

pup tent A small tent providing shelter for one or two people.

pur (pûr) *n. & v.* PURR.

pur·blind (pûr′blīnd′) *adj.* **1** Partly blind. **2** Having little or no insight. **3** *Obs.* Totally blind. [< ME *pur* totally + *blind* blind] —**pur′blind·ly** *adv.* —**pur′blind′ness** *n.*

pur·chase (pûr′chəs) *v.t.* **·chased, ·chas·ing 1** To acquire by paying money or its equivalent; buy. **2** To obtain by exertion, sacrifice, flattery, etc. **3** To move, hoist, or hold by a mechanical purchase. —*n.* **1** The act of purchasing. **2** That which is purchased. **3** A mechanical hold or grip. **4** A device that gives a mechanical advantage, as a tackle or lever. [OF *porchacier* seek for] —**pur′chas·er** *n.* —**Syn.** 1, 2 get, obtain, procure, secure.

pur·dah (pûr′də) *n.* **1** A curtain or screen used to seclude Muslim and Hindu women, esp. in India. **2** The state of seclusion so secured. [< Pers. *pardah* a veil]

pure (pyŏŏr) *adj.* **pur·er, pur·est 1** Free from mixture or contact with that which weakens, impairs, or pollutes. **2** Free from adulteration; clear; clean: *pure* water. **3** Faultless; righteous: *pure* motives. **4** Chaste; innocent. **5** Concerned with fundamental research, as distinguished from practical application: *pure* science. **6** Bred from stock having no admixture for many generations. **7** Nothing but; sheer: *pure* luck. [< L *purus* clean, pure] —**pure′ness** *n.*

pu·rée (pyo͞o·rā′, pyo͞or′ā) *n.* **1** A thick pulp, usu. of vegetables, boiled and strained. **2** A thick soup so prepared. — *v.t.* **·réed, ·ree·ing** To put (cooked or soft food) through a sieve, blender, etc. Also **pu·ree′.** [F< OF *purer* strain< L *purus* pure]

pure·ly (pyo͞or′lē) *adv.* **1** So as to be free from admixture, taint, or any harmful substance. **2** Chastely; innocently. **3** Merely; only: *purely* as a hobby. **4** Completely: *purely* up to him.

pur·ga·tive (pûr′gə·tiv) *adj.* Purging; cathartic. —*n.* A medication used in purging; cathartic.

pur·ga·to·ry (pûr′gə·tôr′ē, -tō′rē) *n. pl.* **·ries 1** In Roman Catholic theology, a state or place where the souls of those who have died penitent are made fit for paradise by expiating venial sins. **2** Any place or state of temporary banishment, suffering, or punishment. [< AF < L *purgare* cleanse] —**pur′ga·to′ri·al** *adj.*

purge (pûrj) *v.* **purged, purg·ing** *v.t.* **1** To cleanse of what is impure or extraneous; purify. **2** To remove (impurities, etc.) in cleansing: with *away, off,* or *out.* **3** To rid (a group, nation, etc.) of individuals regarded as undesirable. **4** To remove or kill such individuals. **5** To cleanse or rid of sin, fault, or defilement. **6** *Med.* **a** To cause evacuation of (the bowels, etc.). **b** To induce evacuation of the bowels of.—*v.i.* **7** To become clean or pure. **8** *Med.* To have or induce evacuation of the bowels. —*n.* **1** The action of an organization, esp. a government, in removing from office or positions of power individuals regarded as undesirable. **2** The act of purging. **3** That which purges; a cathartic. [< L *purgare* cleanse] —**pur·ga·tion** (pûr·gā′shən), **purg′er** *n.*

pu·ri·fy (pyo͞or′ə·fī) *v.* **·fied, ·fy·ing** *v.t.* **1** To make pure or clean; rid of extraneous or noxious matter. **2** To free from sin or defilement. **3** To free of debasing elements. —*v.i.* **4** To become pure or clean. [< L *purus* pure + *facere* make] —**pu·ri·fi·ca·to·ry** (pyo͞o·rif′ə·kə·tôr′ē, -tō′rē) *adj.* —**pu·ri·fi·ca·tion** (pyo͞or′ə·fə·kā′shən), **pu′ri·fi′er** *n.*

Pu·rim (pyo͞or′im; *Hebrew* po͞o·rēm′) *n.* A Jewish festival commemorating the defeat of Haman's plot to massacre the Jews. *Esth.* 9:26.

pur·ism (pyo͞or′iz·əm) *n.* **1** Strong endorsement of a strict compliance with standards, rules, or conventions considered correct or pure, as in language. **2** Strict compliance with rules of correctness. **3** An instance of such compliance. —**pur′ist** *n.* —**pu·ris′tic, pu·ris′ti·cal** *adj.* —**pu·ris′ti·cal·ly** *adv.*

pu·ri·tan (pyo͞or′ə·tən) *n.* One who is unusually or excessively strict regarding adherence to morality or religious practice. —*adj.* Of or characteristic of puritans. [< LL *puritas* purity] —**pu′ri·tan′ic** or **·i·cal** *adj.* —**pu′ri·tan′i·cal·ly** *adv.* —**pu′ri·tan′i·cal·ness, pu′ri·tan·ism** *n.*

Pu·ri·tan (pyo͞or′ə·tən) *n.* One of a group of English Protestants of the 16th and 17th centuries, many of whom emigrated to the American colonies, who advocated simpler forms of creed and ritual in the Church of England. —*adj.* Of or relating to the Puritans. —**Pu′ri·tan′ic** or **·i·cal** *adj.* —**Pu′ri·tan·ism** *n.*

pu·ri·ty (pyo͞or′ə·tē) *n.* **1** The character or state of being pure. **2** Absence of admixture or adulteration. **3** Innocence; blamelessness. **4** Degree of absence of white; saturation: said of a color.

purl[1] (pûrl) *v.i.* **1** To whirl; turn. **2** To flow with a bubbling sound. **3** To move in eddies. —*n.* **1** A circling movement of water; an eddy. **2** A gentle murmur, as of a rippling stream. [< Norw. *purla*]

purl[2] (pûrl) *v.t.* **1** To decorate, as with a border. **2** In knitting, to make (a stitch) backward. **3** To edge with lace, embroidery, etc. —*v.i.* **4** To do edging with lace, etc. —*n.* **1** An edge of lace, embroidery, etc. **2** In lacework, a spiral of gold or silver wire. **3** In knitting, the inversion of the knit stitch. [Earlier *pyrle*]

pur·lieu (pûr′lo͞o) *n.* **1** *pl.* Outlying districts; outskirts. **2**

A place habitually visited; a haunt. **3** *pl.* Bounds. [< OF *puraler* go through]

pur·lin (pûr′lin) *n.* One of several horizontal timbers supporting rafters. Also **pur′line** (-lin). [ME *purlyn*]

pur·loin (pûr·loin′) *v.t. & v.i.* To steal; filch. [< AF *purloignier* remove, put far off] —**pur·loin′er** *n.*

pur·ple (pûr′pəl) *n.* **1** A color of mingled red and blue, between crimson and violet. **2** Cloth or a garment of this color, an emblem of royalty. **3** Royal power or dignity. **4** Preeminence in rank. —*adj.* **1** Of the color of purple. **2** Imperial; regal. **3** Conspicuously fanciful or ornate: *purple* prose.—*v.t. & v.i.* **·pled, ·pling** To make or become purple. [< Gk. *porphyra* purple dye] —**pur′plish** *adj.*

Purple Heart A U.S. military decoration of honor awarded to members of the armed forces wounded in action.

pur·port (pər·pôrt′, -pōrt′, pûr′pôrt, -pōrt) *v.t.* **1** To have or bear as its meaning; signify; imply. **2** To claim or profess (to be), esp. falsely. —*n.* (pûr′pôrt, -pōrt) **1** That which is conveyed or suggested as the meaning. **2** The substance of a statement, etc., given in other than the exact words. [< L < *pro-* forth + *portare* carry] —**Syn.** *n.* **1** import, significance. **2** gist, meaning. —**pur·port′ed·ly** *adv.*

pur·pose (pûr′pəs) *n.* **1** An end of effort or action; something to be attained; plan; design; aim. **2** Settled resolution; determination. —**on purpose** Intentionally. —*v.t. & v.i.* **·posed, ·pos·ing** To intend to do or accomplish; aim. [< OF *porposer*] —**pur′pose·less** *adj.* —**pur′pose·less·ly** *adv.* —**pur′pose·less·ness** *n.*

pur·pose·ful (pûr′pəs·fəl) *adj.* Having, or marked by, purpose; intentional. —**pur′pose·ful·ly** *adv.* —**pur′pose·ful·ness** *n.*

pur·pose·ly (pûr′pəs·lē) *adv.* Intentionally; deliberately; on purpose.

purr (pûr) *n.* An intermittent murmuring sound, such as a cat makes when pleased. —*v.i.* **1** To make such a sound. —*v.t.* **2** To express by purring. [Imit.]

purse (pûrs) *n.* **1** A small bag or pouch for money. **2** A receptacle carried usu. by women for holding personal articles, as a wallet, cosmetics, etc.; pocketbook. **3** Resources or means; a treasury. **4** A sum of money offered as a prize or gift. —*v.t.* **pursed, purs·ing** To contract into wrinkles or folds; pucker. [< Gk. *byrsa* a skin]

purs·er (pûr′sər) *n.* A ship's officer having charge of the accounts, records, payroll, etc.

purs·lane (pûrs′lin, -lān) *n.* Any of various prostrate, weedy plants with fleshy leaves and reddish stems. [< L *porcilaca,* var. of *portulaca*]

pur·su·ance (pər·so͞o′əns) *n.* The act of pursuing; a following after or following through: in *pursuance* of the truth.

pur·su·ant (pər·so͞o′ənt) *adj.* Pursuing. —**pursuant to** In accordance with; by reason of.

pur·sue (pər·so͞o′) *v.* **·sued, ·su·ing** *v.t.* **1** To follow in an attempt to overtake or capture; chase. **2** To seek to attain or gain: to *pursue* fame. **3** To advance along the course of, as a path or plan. **4** To apply one's energies to or have as one's profession. **5** To follow persistently; harass; worry. —*v.i.* **6** To follow. **7** To continue. [< L *pro-* forth + *sequi* follow] —**pur·su′er** *n.*

pur·suit (pər·so͞ot′) *n.* **1** The act of pursuing. **2** A continued employment, vocation, or preoccupation.

pur·sui·vant (pûr′swi·vənt) *n.* **1** An attendant upon a herald. **2** A follower; esp., a military attendant. [< OF *porsievre* pursue]

purs·y (pûr′sē) *adj.* **purs·i·er, purs·i·est 1** Short-breathed. **2** Fat. [< OF *polser* pant, gasp] —**purs′i·ness** *n.*

pu·ru·lent (pyo͞or′ə·lənt, -yə·lənt) *adj.* Consisting of or secreting pus; suppurating. [< L *pus, puris* pus] —**pu′ru·lence** or **·len·cy** *n.* —**pu′ru·lent·ly** *adv.*

pur·vey (pər·vā′) *v.t. & v.i.* To furnish or provide, as provisions. [< L *providere* foresee] —**pur·vey′or** *n.*

pur·vey·ance (pər·vā′əns) *n.* **1** The act of purveying. **2** Provisions.

pur·view (pûr′vyo͞o) *n.* **1** Extent or scope of anything, as of official authority. **2** Range of view, experience, or under-

---

add, āce, câre, pälm; end, ēven; it, īce; odd, ōpen, ôrder; to͞ok, po͞ol; up, bûrn; ə = *a* in *above, u* in *focus;* yo͞o = *u* in *fuse;* oil; pout; check; go; ring; thin; this; zh, *vision.* < derived from; ? origin uncertain or unknown.

standing; outlook. **3** *Law* The body or the scope or limit of a statute. [< OF *porveier* purvey]

pus (pus) *n.* A viscid, usu. yellowish fluid consisting of bacteria, leukocytes, serum, and dead cells from inflamed tissue.

push (pŏŏsh) *v.t.* **1** To exert force upon or against (an object) for the purpose of moving. **2** To force (one's way), as through a crowd. **3** To develop, advocate, or promote vigorously and persistently: to *push* a new product. **4** To bear hard upon; press: to be *pushed* for time. **5** *Informal* To approach or come close to: He's *pushing* fifty. **6** *Slang* To sell (narcotic or other drugs) illegally. —*v.i.* **7** To exert pressure against something so as to move it. **8** To move or advance vigorously or persistently. **9** To exert great effort. —*n.* **1** The act of pushing; a propelling or thrusting pressure. **2** Anything pushed to cause action. **3** Determined activity; energy; drive. **4** A vigorous and persistent advance or effort. **5** An emergency; exigency. [< L *pulsare* to push, beat] —**Syn.** *v.* **1** shove, thrust, press, propel, drive.

push button A button or knob which, on being pushed, opens or closes an electric switch. —**push′-but′ton** *adj.*

push·cart (pŏŏsh′kärt′) *n.* A wheeled cart pushed by hand.

push·er (pŏŏsh′ər) *n.* **1** One who or that which pushes; esp., an active, energetic person. **2** *Slang* One who sells narcotic or other drugs illegally.

push·ing (pŏŏsh′ing) *adj.* **1** Enterprising; energetic. **2** Too aggressive; impertinent. —**push′ing·ly** *adv.*

push·o·ver (pŏŏsh′ō′vər) *n. Slang* **1** Anything that can be done with little or no effort. **2** Someone easily defeated, overcome, outwitted, etc.; one who represents no challenge to one's aims.

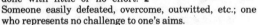

Supermarket pushcart

push·y (pŏŏsh′ē) *adj.* **·i·er**, **·i·est** Unpleasantly aggressive and persistent. —**push′i·ly** *adv.* —**push′i·ness** *n.*

pu·sil·lan·i·mous (pyōō′sə·lan′ə·məs) *adj.* Weak or cowardly in spirit; lacking strength of mind or courage. [< L *pusillus* very little + *animus* mind] —**pu′sil·la·nim′i·ty** (-lə·nim′ə·tē), **pu′sil·lan′i·mous·ness** *n.* —**pu′sil·lan′i·mous·ly** *adv.*

puss¹ (pŏŏs) *n.* **1** A cat. **2** A young girl: a term of affection. [?]

puss² (pŏŏs) *n. Slang* The mouth; face. [< Ir. *pus* mouth, lips]

pus·sy¹ (pŏŏs′ē) *n. pl.* **·sies 1** PUSS¹. **2** A fuzzy catkin, as of a willow.

pus·sy² (pus′ē) *adj.* **pus·si·er**, **pus·si·est** Full of or like pus. —**pus′si·ness** *n.*

pus·sy·foot (pŏŏs′ē·fŏŏt′) *v.i.* **1** To move softly and stealthily, as a cat does. **2** To act or proceed warily or tentatively, so as to be able to withdraw or change course before one's intentions are apparent. —**pus′sy·foot′er** *n.*

pus·sy willow (pŏŏs′ē) A small North American willow bearing velvety catkins in early spring.

pus·tu·late (pus′chŏŏ·lāt) *v.t.* & *v.i.* **·lat·ed**, **·lat·ing** To form into or become pustules. —*adj.* (-lāt, -lit) Covered with pustules. —**pus′tu·la′tion** *n.*

pus·tule (pus′chŏŏl) *n.* **1** A small, circumscribed elevation of the skin with an inflamed base containing pus. **2** Any elevation resembling a pimple or a blister. [< L *pustula*] —**pus′tu·lar**, **pus′tu·lous** *adj.*

put (pŏŏt) *v.* **put**, **put·ting** *v.t.* **1** To bring into or set in a specified or implied place or position; lay: *Put* the dishes in the sink. **2** To bring into a specified state, condition, or relation: to *put* someone to work; to *put* merchandise on sale. **3** To order or bring about the establishment or placement of: to *put* a new store in Dallas; to *put* a man on the moon. **4** To send or direct, as by projecting or thrusting: to *put* a dart in the bull's-eye. **5** To throw with a pushing motion: to *put* the shot. **6** To bring to bear; apply: They *put* pressure on her. **7** To impose: to *put* a tax on air travel. **8** To effect; carry out: I'll *put* a stop to that. **9** To express; state:

Pussy willow

to *put* it simply. **10** To subject: to *put* his loyalty to the test. **11** To incite; prompt: Who *put* him up to it? **12** To ascribe or attribute: to *put* the wrong interpretation on a remark. **13** To propose for debate, consideration, etc.: to *put* the question. **14** To estimate: to *put* the time at five o'clock. **15** To establish; fix, as a price. **16** To risk; bet: to *put* money on a horse. —*v.i.* **17** To go; proceed: to *put* to sea. —**put about 1** *Naut.* To change to the opposite tack. **2** To change direction. —**put across 1** To carry out successfully. **2** To manage to be understood. **3** To bring about through deceit. —**put aside** (or **by**) **1** To place in reserve; save. **2** To thrust aside; discard. —**put away 1** PUT ASIDE. **2** *Informal* To eat or drink. **3** *Informal* To kill, as an injured or sick animal. —**put down 1** To repress; crush. **2** To degrade; demote. **3** To write. **4** *Slang* To humble or deflate. **5** To preserve or can. —**put forth 1** To grow, as shoots or buds. **2** To set out; leave port. **3** To proffer; suggest. **4** To publish. **5** To exert. —**put forward** To advance; advocate, as a proposal. —**put in 1** To submit or advance, as a claim or application. **2** To interject; interpolate. **3** *Naut.* To enter a harbor. **4** *Informal* To devote; expend, as time. —**put off 1** To delay; postpone. **2** To discard. **3** To make uneasy or uncomfortable; disconcert. —**put on 1** To clothe oneself in; don. **2** To bring into operation; effectuate: to *put on* a light. **3** To add: to *put on* weight. **4** To stage, as a play. **5** To simulate; pretend: to *put on* a sad face. **6** *Slang* To fool or deceive mischievously. —**put out 1** To extinguish, as a flame. **2** To expel; eject. **3** To disconcert; embarrass. **4** To inconvenience. **5** PUT FORTH. **6** In baseball, to retire (a batter or base runner). **7** To publish or manufacture, as a book or magazine. **8** *Slang* To use extra effort; exert oneself. —**put over 1** To delay; postpone. **2** To carry out successfully. **3** To bring about through deceit. —**put through 1** To bring to successful completion. **2** To cause to perform. **3** To establish a telephone connection for. —**put up 1** To erect; build. **2** To provide (money, capital, etc.). **3** To preserve or can. **4** To sheathe, as a weapon. **5** To nominate as a candidate. **6** To provide accommodations for. **7** *Informal* To incite. —**put up with** To endure; tolerate. —*n.* The act of putting or casting, esp. the shot. —*adj. Informal* Settled in place; fixed: My hat won't stay *put.* [< OE *putian* place] —**put′ter** *n.*

pu·ta·tive (pyōō′tə·tiv) *adj.* Supposed; reported; reputed. [< L *putare* think] —**pu′ta·tive·ly** *adv.*

put-down (pŏŏt′doun′) *n. Slang* Something that humbles or deflates, as a cutting remark.

put-on (pŏŏt′on′) *n. Slang* A hoax; deception.

put-out (pŏŏt′out′) *n.* In baseball, the act of causing an out, as of a batter or base runner.

pu·tre·fac·tion (pyōō′trə·fak′shən) *n.* **1** The process of rotting or decomposing, as by bacterial action. **2** The state of being putrefied. —**pu′tre·fac′tive** *adj.*

pu·tre·fy (pyōō′trə·fī) *v.t.* & *v.i.* **·fied**, **·fy·ing** To decay or cause to decay; rot. [< L *puter* rotten + *facere* make] —**pu′tre·fi′er** *n.*

pu·tres·cent (pyōō·tres′ənt) *adj.* **1** Becoming putrid. **2** Pertaining to putrefaction. [< L *putrescere* grow rotten] —**pu·tres′cence** *n.*

pu·trid (pyōō′trid) *adj.* **1** Being in a state of putrefaction; rotten. **2** Indicating or produced by putrefaction: a *putrid* smell. **3** Corrupt. [< L *putridus*] —**pu·trid·i·ty** (pyōō·trid′ə·tē), **pu′trid·ness** *n.*

putsch (pŏŏch) *n. Often cap.* An outbreak or rebellion; an attempted coup d'état. [G]

putt (put) *n.* In golf, a light stroke made on a putting green to place the ball in or near the hole. —*v.t.* & *v.i.* To strike (the ball) with such a stroke. [Var. of PUT]

put·tee (put′ē, pu·tē′) *n.* A strip of cloth or leather gaiter fastened about the leg from knee to ankle. [< Skt. *paṭṭa* a strip of cloth]

put·ter¹ (put′ər) *n.* **1** One who putts. **2** A golf club used in putting. • See GOLF.

put·ter² (put′ər) *v.i.* **1** To act, work, or proceed in a dawdling or ineffective manner. —*v.t.* **2** To waste or spend (time, etc.) in dawdling or puttering. [< OE *potion* push, kick]

put·ting green (put′ing) In golf, a smooth area of closely mown grass in which the hole is situated.

put·ty (put′ē) *n.* **1** A doughy mixture of clay and linseed oil, used to cement panes in windows, fill cracks, etc. **2** Any substance similar in properties or uses. —*v.t.* **·tied,** **·ty·ing** To fill, stop, fasten, etc., with putty. [< OF *potee* calcined tin, lit., a potful] **—put'ti·er** *n.*

put-up (po͝ot'up') *adj. Informal* Prearranged or contrived; staged: a *put-up* job.

put-up·on (po͝ot'ə·pon') *adj.* Beset or harassed, as by impositions; abused.

puz·zle (puz'əl) *v.* **·zled, ·zling** *v.t.* **1** To confuse or perplex; mystify. **2** To solve by investigation and study, as something perplexing: with *out.* —*v.i.* **3** To be perplexed or confused. **—puzzle over** To attempt to understand or solve. —*n.* **1** Something difficult to understand or explain; an enigma or problem. **2** A device, as a toy, or a problem designed for recreation and requiring ingenuity to solve. **3** The state of being puzzled; perplexity. [?] **—puz'zle·ment,** **puz'zler** *n.*

Pvt. Private.

PW prisoner of war.

pwt. pennyweight.

PX post exchange.

py·e·mi·a (pī·ē'mē·ə) *n.* Septicemia caused by pus-producing microorganisms. Also **py·ae'mi·a.** [< Gk. *pyon* pus + *haima* blood] **—py·e'mic** *adj.*

pyg·my (pig'mē) *adj.* Diminutive; dwarfish. —*n. pl.* **·mies** **1** Someone of no importance. **2** A dwarfish person or animal.

Pyg·my (pig'mē) *n. pl.* **·mies** A member of a Negroid people of equatorial Africa, ranging in height from four to five feet. [< Gk. *pygmalos* a dwarf]

py·ja·mas (pə·jä'məz, -jam'əz) *n.pl. Brit.* PAJAMAS.

py·lon (pī'lon) *n.* **1** *Archit.* A monumental gateway, as to an Egyptian temple or other large edifice. **2** A tall, mastlike structure, as for supporting high-tension wires or for marking a course for aircraft. [< Gk. *pylōn* a gateway]

py·lo·rus (pī·lôr'əs, -lō'rəs, pi-) *n. pl.* **·ri** (-rī) The muscularly controlled opening between the stomach and the duodenum. [< Gk. *pylōros* a gatekeeper] **—py·lor'ic** (-lôr'ik, -lor'ik) *adj.*

py·or·rhe·a (pī'ə·rē'ə) *n.* A discharge of pus; esp., inflammation and pus discharge affecting the gums and tooth sockets. Also **py'or·rhoe'a.** [< Gk. *pys, pyos* pus + *rheein* flow] **—py'or·rhe'al** *adj.*

pyr·a·mid (pir'ə·mid) *n.* **1** A solid structure of masonry with a square base and triangular sides meeting in an apex, such as those constructed by the ancient Egyptians as royal tombs. **2** Something having the form

Egyptian pyramids

of a pyramid. **3** *Geom.* A solid having a polygonal base and triangular sides that meet in a common vertex. —*v.i.* **1** To increase in a series of steps; escalate. **2** To buy or sell stock with paper profits used as margin to finance succeeding transactions. —*v.t.* **3** To increase by steps. **4** To buy and sell (stock) with paper profits used as margin to

finance succeeding transactions. [< Gk. *pyramis*] **—py·ram·i·dal** (pi·ram'ə·dəl, pir'ə·mid'əl), **pyr'a·mid'ic** or **·i·cal** *adj.* **—pyr'a·mid'i·cal·ly** *adv.*

pyre (pīr) *n.* A heap of combustibles arranged for burning a dead body as a funeral rite. [< Gk. *pyr* a fire]

py·reth·rum (pī·reth'rəm, -rē'thrəm) *n.* **1** A species of chrysanthemum. **2** An insecticide prepared from the powdered flowers of certain chrysanthemums. [L, feverfew]

Py·rex (pī'reks) *n.* A type of heat-resistant glass: a trade name.

pyr·i·dox·ine (pir'ə·dok'sēn, -sin) *n.* A constituent of the vitamin B complex. [< Gk. *pyr* fire + -ID(E) + OX(Y)- + -INE]

py·rite (pī'rīt) *n.* A lustrous, pale yellow, mineral sulfide of iron. [< Gk. *pyritēs* flint]

py·ri·tes (pī·rī'tēz, pī'rīts) *n. pl.* **py·ri·tes** (pī·rī'tēz) Any of various mineral sulfides with a metallic sheen, including pyrite: copper *pyrites.* **—py·rit'ic** (-rit'ik) or **·i·cal** *adj.*

pyro- *combining form* Fire; heat: *pyromania.* Also **pyr-.** [< Gk. *pyr* fire]

py·ro·ma·ni·a (pī'rə·mā'nē·ə, -mān'yə) *n.* A compulsion to commit arson. **—py'ro·ma'ni·ac** (-ak) *adj., n.* **—py'ro·ma·ni·a·cal** (pī'rō·mə·nī'ə·kəl) *adj.*

py·rom·e·ter (pī·rom'ə·tər) *n.* A thermometer designed to measure high temperatures. **—py·ro·met·ric** (pī'rə·met'rik) or **·ri·cal** *adj.* **—py·rom'e·try** *n.*

py·ro·tech·nics (pī'rə·tek'niks) *n. pl. (construed as sing. in def. 1)* **1** The art of making or using fireworks. **2** A display of fireworks. **3** An ostentatious display, as of oratory; virtuosity. [< PYRO- + Gk. *technē* an art] **—py'ro·tech'nic** or **·ni·cal** *adj.*

py·rox·y·lin (pī·rok'sə·lin) *n.* A nitrocellulose that is more stable than guncotton, used in making quick-drying lacquers, etc. Also **py·rox'y·line** (-lēn, -lin). [< Gk. *pyr, pyros* fire + *xylon* wood + -INE]

Pyr·rhic victory (pir'ik) A victory gained at a ruinous cost, such as that of Pyrrhus over the Romans in 279 B.C.

Py·thag·o·re·an theorem (pi·thag'ə·rē'ən) *Math.* The theorem that the sum of the squares of the two sides of a right triangle is equal to the square of the hypotenuse. [< *Pythagoras,* c. 500 B.C., Greek philosopher]

Pyth·i·as (pith'ē·əs) See DAMON AND PYTHIAS.

py·thon (pī'thon, -thən) *n.* A large, nonvenomous snake that crushes its prey. [< Gk. *Pythōn* a serpent slain by Apollo]

Python

py·tho·ness (pī'thə·nis, pith'ə-) *n.* **1** The priestess of the Delphic oracle. **2** Any woman supposed to be possessed of the spirit of prophecy; a witch. [< Gk. *Pytho* a familiar spirit, orig. Delphi]

pyx (piks) *n.* A container for keeping the consecrated wafer of the Eucharist or for carrying it to the sick. [< L *pyxis* a box]

pyx·is (pik'sis) *n. pl.* **pyx·i·des** (pik'sə·dēz) *Bot.* A dehiscent seed vessel with the upper portion separating as a lid. Also **pyx·id·i·um** (pik·sid'ē·əm). [< L, a box]

Q

Q, q (kyōō) *n. pl.* **Q's, q's** or **Qs, qs** (kyōōz) **1** The 17th letter of the English alphabet. **2** Any spoken sound representing the letter *Q* or *q*. **3** Something shaped like a Q. —*adj.* Shaped like a Q.

Q queen (chess).

Q. Quebec.

q. quart; quarter; quarterly; quarto; quasi; queen; query; question

Qa·tar (kä′tär) *n.* A British protected sheikdom on the w coast of the Persian Gulf, 8,500 sq. mi., cap. Doha. • See map at SAUDI ARABIA.

qb., q.b. quarterback.

Q.C. Quartermaster Corps; Queen's Counsel.

q.e. which is (L *quod est*).

Q.E.D. which was to be demonstrated (L *quod erat demonstrandum*).

Q.E.F. which was to be done (L *quod erat faciendum*).

QM, Q.M. Quartermaster.

QMC, Q.M.C. Quartermaster Corps.

QMG, Q.M.G., Q.M.Gen. Quartermaster General.

Qq. quartos.

qq.v. which see (L *quos vide*).

qr. quarter; quarterly; quire.

q.s. as much as suffices (L *quantum sufficit*).

qt. quart; quantity.

q.t. *Slang* quiet, esp. **on the q.t.** in secret.

qto. quarto.

qts, qts. quarts.

qu. quart; quarter; queen; query; question.

quack¹ (kwak) *v.i.* To utter a harsh, croaking cry, as a duck. —*n.* The sound made by a duck, or a similar croaking noise [Imit.]

quack² (kwak) *n.* **1** A pretender to medical knowledge or skill. **2** A charlatan. —*adj.* Of or pertaining to quacks or quackery. —*v.i.* To play the quack. [Short for QUACKSALVER] —**quack′ish** *adj.* —**quack′ish·ly** *adv.*

quack·er·y (kwak′ər·ē) *n. pl.* ·**er·ies** The deceitful practices of a quack.

quack·sal·ver (kwak′sal′vər) *n.* QUACK². [< MDu. *quacsalven* use home remedies]

quad¹ (kwod) *n. Informal.* A quadrangle, as of a college or prison.

quad² (kwod) *n. Printing* A piece of type metal lower than the letters, used for spacing. [ME *quadrat*, a square instrument]

quad³ (kwod) *adj.* QUADRAPHONIC.

quad. quadrangle; quadrant; quadrat; quadruple.

Quad·ra·ges·i·ma (kwod′rə·jes′ə·mə) *n.* The first Sunday in Lent. Also **Quadragesima Sunday.** [L, fortieth]

quad·ran·gle (kwod′rang·gəl) *n.* **1** *Geom.* A plane figure having four sides and four angles. **2** An area shaped like a quadrangle, esp. when it is enclosed by buildings. **3** The buildings that enclose such an area. [< L *quattuor* four + *angulus* angle] —**quad·ran′gu·lar** *adj.*

quad·rant (kwod′rənt) *n.* **1** A quarter part of a circle; also, its circumference, having an arc of 90°. **2** An instrument having a graduated arc of 90°, with a movable radius for measuring angles on it. [< L *quattuor* four] —**quad·ran·tal** (kwod·ran′təl) *adj.*

quad·ra·phon·ic (kwod′rə·fon′ik) *adj.* Of, pertaining to, or employing a system of sound reproduction that uses four transmission channels and loudspeakers. [< QUADR(I)- + PHONIC]

Quadrant

quad·rat (kwod′rət) *n.* QUAD².

quad·rate (kwod′rāt, -rit) *adj.* Square; four-sided. —*v.* (-rāt) ·**rat·ed, ·rat·ing** *v.i.* **1** To correspond or agree: with *with.* —*v.t.* **2** To cause to conform; bring in accordance with. [< L *quadrare* to square < *quattuor* four]

quad·rat·ic (kwod·rat′ik) *adj.* **1** Pertaining to or resem-

bling a square. **2** Of or designating a quadratic equation. —*n. Math.* A quadratic equation.

quadratic equation An equation of the general form $ax^2 + bx + c = 0$, where a, b, c are constants.

quad·ra·ture (kwod′rə·chər) *n.* **1** The act or process of squaring. **2** The determining of the area of any surface.

quad·ren·ni·al (kwod·ren′ē·əl) *adj.* **1** Occurring once in four years. **2** Comprising four years. —*n.* A quadrennial period or event. [< QUADR(I)- + L *annus* year]

quadri- *combining form* Four: *quadrilateral.* Also **quadr-.** [< L *quattuor* four]

quad·ri·lat·er·al (kwod′rə·lat′ər·əl) *adj.* Formed or bounded by four lines; four-sided. —*n.* **1** *Geom.* A polygon of four sides. **2** A space or area defended by four enclosing fortresses. [< QUADRI- + L *latus, lateris* side]

qua·drille (kwə·dril′) *n.* **1** A square dance for four couples. **2** Music for such a dance. [< L *quattuor* four]

quad·ril·lion (kwod·ril′yən) *n. & adj.* See NUMBER. [< F *quatre* four + *(m)illion* million]

quad·ri·ple·gi·a (kwod′rə·plē′jē·ə) *n.* Paralysis of the arms and legs.

quad·ri·va·lent (kwod′rə·vā′lənt) *adj. Chem.* Having a valence of four. [< QUADRI- + L *valere* be worth]

quad·roon (kwod·rōōn′) *n.* A person having one Negro and three white grandparents. [< Sp. *cuarto* fourth]

quad·ru·ped (kwod′rōō·ped) *n.* A four-footed animal, esp. a mammal. —*adj.* Having four feet. [< L *quattuor* four + *pes* foot] —**quad·ru·pe·dal** (kwod·rōō′pə·dəl, kwod′·rōō·ped′l) *adj.*

quad·ru·ple (kwod·rōō′pəl, -rū′-, kwod′rōō·pəl) *adj.* **1** Four times as great or as many. **2** Having four parts or members. **3** Marked by four beats to the measure. —*n.* A number or sum four times as great as another. —*v.t. & v.i.* ·**pled, ·pling** To multiply by four. —*adv.* Fourfold. [< L *quadruplus*]

quad·ru·plet (kwod·rōō′plit, -rū′-, kwod′rōō-) *n.* A combination of four objects. **2** One of four offspring born of the same mother at one birth.

quad·ru·pli·cate (kwod·rōō′plə·kit, -kāt) *adj.* **1** FOURFOLD. **2** Raised to the fourth power. —*v.t.* (-kāt) ·**cat·ed, ·cat·ing** To multiply by four; quadruple. —*n.* The fourth of four like things: to file a *quadruplicate.* —**in quadruplicate** In four identical copies. —**quad·ru′pli·ca′tion** *n.*

quaes·tor (kwes′tər, kwēs′-) *n.* Any of a number of public officials in ancient Rome. Also **ques′tor.** [L < *quaerere* seek, inqure] —**quaes′to′ri·al** *adj.* —**quaes′tor·ship** *n.*

quaff (kwaf, kwof, kwôf) *v.t. & v.i.* To drink, esp. copiously or with relish. —*n.* The act of quaffing; also, that which is quaffed. [?] —**quaff′er** *n.*

quag·gy (kwag′ē, kwog′ē) *adj.* ·**gi·er, ·gi·est 1** Yielding to or quaking under the foot, as soft, wet earth; boggy. **2** Soft; yielding; flabby. [< QUAGMIRE]

quag·mire (kwag′mīr′, kwog′-) *n.* **1** Marshy ground that gives way under the foot; bog. **2** A difficult situation. [? < earlier *quab*- wetness + MIRE] —**quag′mired′** *adj.*

qua·haug (kwô′hôg, -hog, kwə·hôg′, -hog′) *n.* An edible, thick-shelled clam of the Atlantic coast of North America. Also **qua′hog.** [< Algon.]

quail¹ (kwāl) *n.* **1** Any of various small game birds related to the partridge. **2** BOBWHITE. [< OF *quaille*]

quail² (kwāl) *v.i.* To shrink with fear; lose heart or courage. [ME *quailen*]

quaint (kwānt) *adj.* **1** Pleasingly different, fanciful, or old-fashioned. **2** Unusual; odd; curious. [< L *cognitus* known] —**quaint′ly** *adv.* —**quaint′ness** *n.*

quake (kwāk) *v.i.* **quaked, quak·ing 1** To shake, as with violent

Quail

emotion or cold; shudder; shiver. **2** To shake or tremble, as earth during an earthquake. —*n.* **1** A shaking or shuddering. **2** EARTHQUAKE. [< OE *cwacian* shake]

Quak·er (kwā′kər) *n.* A member of the Society of Friends: originally a term of derision, and still not used within the society. See SOCIETY OF FRIENDS. [< QUAKE, *v.;* with ref. to their founder's admonition to them to tremble at the word of the Lord] —**Quak′er·ish** *adj.* —**Quak′er·ism′** *n.*

quak·y (kwā′kē) *adj.* **quak·i·er, quak·i·est** Shaky; tremulous. —**quak′i·ly** *adv.* —**quak′i·ness** *n.*

qual·i·fi·ca·tion (kwol′ə·fə·kā′shən) *n.* **1** The act of qualifying, or the state of being qualified. **2** That which fits a person or thing for something. **3** A restriction; modification.

qual·i·fied (kwol′ə·fīd) *adj.* **1** Competent or eligible, as for public office. **2** Restricted or modified in some way. —**qual′i·fied′ly** *adv.*

qual·i·fy (kwol′ə·fī) *v.* **·fied, ·fy·ing** *v.t.* **1** To make fit or capable, as for an office, occupation, or privilege. **2** To make legally capable, as by the administration of an oath. **3** To limit, restrict, or lessen somewhat: He *qualified* his enthusiasm with a few criticisms. **4** To attribute a quality to; describe; characterize or name. **5** To make less strong or extreme; soften; moderate. **6** To change the strength or flavor of. **7** *Gram.* To modify. —*v.i.* **8** To be or become qualified. [< L *qualis* of such a kind + *facere* make] —**qual′i·fi′a·ble** *adj.* —**qual′i·fi′er** *n.*

qual·i·ta·tive (kwol′ə·tā′tiv) *adj.* Of or pertaining to quality. —**qual′i·ta′tive·ly** *adv.*

qualitative analysis The chemical identification of the elements or components in a compound or mixture.

qual·i·ty (kwol′ə·tē) *n. pl.* **·ties 1** That which makes a being or thing such as it is: a distinguishing element or characteristic: a *quality* of gases. **2** The basic nature or character of something: the *quality* of a summer's day. **3** Excellence: striving for *quality.* **4** Degree of excellence; relative goodness; grade: high *quality* of fabric. **5** A personal attribute, trait or characteristic: a woman with good and bad *qualities.* **6** *Archaic* Social rank; also, persons of rank, collectively. **7** *Music* That which distinguishes one tone from another, aside from pitch or loudness; timbre. —*adj.* Characterized by or having to do with quality: a *quality* product. [< L *qualis* of such a kind]

qualm (kwäm, kwôm) *n.* **1** A twinge of conscience; moral scruple. **2** A sensation of fear or misgiving. **3** A feeling of sickness. [? < OE *cwealm* death] —**qualm′ish, qualm′y** *adj.* —**qualm′ish·ly** *adv.* —**qualm′ish·ness** *n.*

quan·da·ry (kwon′dər·ē, -drē) *n. pl.* **·da·ries** A state of hesitation or perplexity; predicament. [?]

quan·ti·ta·tive (kwon′tə·tā′tiv) *adj.* **1** Of or pertaining to quantity. **2** Capable of being measured. —**quan′ti·ta′tive·ly** *adv.* —**quan′ti·ta′tive·ness** *n.*

quantitative analysis The precise determination of the relative amount of each chemical component in a compound or mixture.

quan·ti·ty (kwon′tə·tē) *n. pl.* **·ties 1** A definite or indefinite amount or number. **2** *pl.* Large amounts or numbers: *quantities* of food and drink. **3** That property of a thing which admits of exact measurement and numerical statement. **4** In prosody and phonetics, the relative period of time required to produce a given sound. [< L *quantus* how much, how large]

quan·tum (kwon′təm) *n. pl.* **·ta** (-tə) *Physics* A fundamental unit of energy or action as described in the quantum theory. [< L *quantus* how much]

quantum theory *Physics* A physical theory including as one of its essential features the postulate that energy is not continuous but divided into discrete packets, or quanta.

quar·an·tine (kwôr′ən·tēn, kwor′-) *n.* **1** A period of time fixed for the isolation and observation of persons, animals, or plants suspected of harboring an infectious disease. **2** A place for such isolation. **3** The isolation of subjects exposed to or infected with a communicable disease. —*v.t.* **·tined, ·tin·ing** To retain in quarantine. [< L *quadraginta* forty; a ref. to the original 40-day quarantine]

quark (kwärk) *n. Physics* Any of a group of three types of hypothetical fundamental particles proposed as the entities of which all other strongly interacting particles are composed. [Coined by M. Gell-Mann, born 1929, U.S. physicist]

quar·rel[1] (kwôr′əl, kwor′-) *n.* **1** An unfriendly, angry, or violent dispute. **2** A falling out or contention; breach of friendly relations: a lover's *quarrel.* **3** The cause for dispute. —*v.i.* **·reled** or **·relled, ·rel·ing** or **·rel·ling 1** To engage in a quarrel; dispute; contend; fight: to *quarrel* about money. **2** To break off a mutual friendship; fall out; disagree. **3** To find fault; cavil. [< L *querela* complaint] —**quar′rel·er** or **quar′rel·ler** *n.* —**Syn.** *n.* **1** altercation, bickering, brawl, controversy, feud, fracas, fray. **2** disagreement, fuss, misunderstanding, scene.

quar·rel[2] (kwôr′əl, kwor′-) *n.* **1** A dart or arrow with a four-edged head, formerly used with a crossbow. **2** A stonemason's chisel, glazier's diamond, or other tool having a several-edged point. [< L *quattuor* four]

quar·rel·some (kwôr′əl·səm, kwor′-) *adj.* Inclined to quarrel. —**quar′rel·some·ly** *adv.* —**quar′rel·some·ness** *n.*

quar·ri·er (kwôr′ē·ər, kwor′-) *n.* A workman in a stone quarry.

quar·ry[1] (kwôr′ē, kwor′ē) *n. pl.* **·ries 1** An animal being hunted down; game; prey. **2** Anything hunted, slaughtered, or eagerly pursued. [< L *corium* hide]

quar·ry[2] (kwôr′ē, kwor′ē) *n. pl.* **·ries** An excavation from which stone is taken by cutting, blasting, or the like. —*v.t.* **·ried, ·ry·ing 1** To cut, dig, or take from or as from a quarry. **2** To establish a quarry in. [< LL *quadraria* place for squaring stone]

Quarrels
def. 1

quart (kwôrt) *n.* **1 a** A U.S. measure of dry capacity equal to 2 pints or 1.10 liters. **b** A U.S. measure of fluid capacity equal to 2 pints or 0.946 liter. **2** A vessel of such capacity. [< L *quartus* fourth]

quar·ter (kwôr′tər) *n.* **1** One of four equal parts of something; a fourth. **2** Fifteen minutes or the fourth of an hour, or the moment with which it begins or ends. **3** A fourth of a year or three months. **4** A limb of a quadruped with the adjacent parts. **5** In the U.S. and Canada, a coin of the value of 25 cents. **6** *Astron.* **a** The time it takes the moon to make one fourth of its revolution around the earth. **b** Either of the phases of the moon between new moon and full moon. **7** *Nav.* One of the four principal points of the compass or divisions of the horizon; also, a point or direction of the compass. **8** A person, persons, or place, esp. as a source or origin of something: gossip coming from all *quarters.* **9** A particular division or district, as of a city. **10** *Usu. pl.* Proper or assigned station, position, or place, as of officers and crew on a warship. **11** *pl.* A place of lodging or residence. **12** *Naut.* The part of a vessel's after side, between the aftermost mast and the stern. **13** *Her.* Any of four equal divisions into which a shield is divided, or a figure or device occupying such a division. **14** Mercy shown to a vanquished foe by sparing his life; clemency. **15** One of the four periods into which a game, as football, is divided. —**at close quarters** Close by; at close range. —*adj.* **1** Consisting of a quarter. **2** Equal to a quarter. —*v.t.* **1** To divide into four equal parts. **2** To divide into a number of parts or pieces. **3** To cut the body of (an executed person) into four parts: He was hanged, drawn, and *quartered.* **4** To range from one side to the other of (a field, etc.) while advancing: The dogs *quartered* the field. **5** To furnish with quarters or shelter; lodge, station, or billet. **6** *Her.* **a** To divide (a shield) into quarters by vertical and horizontal lines. **b** To bear or arrange (different coats of arms) upon the quarters of a shield or escutcheon. —*v.i.* **7** To be stationed or lodged. **8** To range from side to side of an area, as dogs in hunting. **9** *Naut.* To blow on a ship's quarter: said of the wind. [< L *quartus* fourth]

quar·ter·back (kwôr′tər·bak′) *n.* In football, one of the backfield, who calls the signals and directs the offensive play of his team.

---

quarter day A day that begins a new quarter of the year, when quarterly payments, as of rent, etc., are due.

quar·ter-deck (kwôr′tər-dek′) *n. Naut.* The rear part of a ship's upper deck, reserved for officers.

quar·tered (kwôr′tərd) *adj.* 1 Divided into quarters. 2 Having quarters or lodgings. 3 Quartersawed.

quar·ter·ly (kwôr′tər-lē) *adj.* 1 Containing or being a quarter. 2 Occurring at intervals of three months. —*n. pl.* ·lies A publication issued once every three months. —*adv.* 1 Once in a quarter of a year. 2 In or by quarters.

quar·ter·mas·ter (kwôr′tər-mas′tər, -mäs′-) *n.* 1 The officer on an army post who is responsible for the supply of food, clothing, etc. 2 On shipboard, a petty officer who assists the master or navigator.

quar·tern (kwôr′tərn) *n. Chiefly Brit.* A fourth part, as of certain measures or weights. [< L *quartus* fourth]

quarter note *Music* A note with one fourth the time value of a whole note. • See NOTE.

quar·ter·saw (kwôr′tər-sô′) *v.t.* ·sawed, ·sawed or ·sawn, ·saw·ing To saw (a log) lengthwise into quarters and then into planks or boards, in order to show the wood grain advantageously.

quar·ter-sec·tion (kwôr′tər-sek′shən) *n.* A tract of land half a mile square, containing one fourth of a square mile; 160 acres.

quar·ter-ses·sions (kwôr′tər-sesh′ənz) *n.* 1 In the U.S., any of various courts with criminal jurisdiction and, sometimes, administrative functions. 2 In England, a local court held quarterly that has limited criminal and civil jurisdiction and, often, administrative functions.

quar·ter·staff (kwôr′tər-staf′, -stäf′) *n. pl.* ·staves (-stāvz′) A stout, iron-tipped staff about 6½ feet long, formerly used in England as a weapon.

quar·tet (kwôr-tet′) *n.* 1 A composition for four voices or instruments. 2 The four persons who render such a composition. 3 Any group of four persons or things. Also **quar·tette′.** [< Ital. *quarto* fourth]

quar·to (kwôr′tō) *adj.* Having four leaves or eight pages to the sheet: a *quarto* book. —*n. pl.* ·tos 1 The size of a piece of paper obtained by folding a sheet into four leaves. 2 Paper of this size; also, a page of this size. 3 A book made of pages of this size. [< L *(in) quarto* (in) fourth]

quartz (kwôrts) *n.* A hard mineral form of silicon dioxide occurring in many varieties, some of which are valued as gems. [< G *Quarz*]

qua·sar (kwā′zär, -sär) *n. Astron.* QUASI-STELLAR OBJECT. [< QUAS(I) - (STELL)AR RADIO SOURCE]

quash¹ (kwosh) *v.t. Law* To make void or set aside, as an indictment; annul. [< LL *cassare* to empty]

quash² (kwosh) *v.t.* To put down or suppress forcibly or summarily. [< L *quassare*, freq. of *quatere* shake]

qua·si (kwā′zī, -sī; kwä′zē, -sē) *adj.* More in resemblance than in fact: a *quasi* scholar. [L, as if]

quasi- *combining form* Resembling but not quite; in some ways or to some extent: *quasi-legal, quasi-official.* [< L *quasi* as if]

qua·si-stel·lar object (kwā′zī-stel′ər, -sī-, kwä′zē-, -sē-) Any of various starlike objects emitting vast amounts of radiation over a broad spectrum and having large red shifts. Also **quasi-stellar radio source.**

quas·si·a (kwosh′ē-ə, kwosh′ə) *n.* 1 Any of several tropical trees having bitter wood and bark. 2 A bitter extract obtained from a quassia tree, used to allay fever. 3 An insecticide obtained from the wood of a certain quassia tree. [< Graman *Quassi*, a Surinam Negro who discovered its use in 1730]

qua·ter·na·ry (kwot′ər·ner′ē, kwə·tûr′nə·rē) *adj.* Consisting of four. [< L *quaterni* by fours]

Qua·ter·na·ry (kwot′ər·ner′ē, kwə·tûr′nə·rē) *adj. & n.* See GEOLOGY.

quat·rain (kwot′rān, kwot-rān′) *n.* A stanza of four lines. [< F *quatre* four]

quat·re·foil (kat′ər·foil′, kat′·rə-) *n.* 1 *Bot.* A leaf or flower with four leaflets or petals. 2 *Archit.* An ornament with four foils or lobes. [< OF *quatre* four + *foil* leaf]

Quatrefoil window

quat·tro·cen·to (kwät′trō·chen′tō) *n.* The 15th century, esp. in connection with Italian art and literature. —*adj.* Of or pertaining to the quattrocento. [< Ital., four hundred < *quattro* four + *cento* hundred]

qua·ver (kwā′vər) *v.i.* 1 To tremble or shake: said usu. of the voice. 2 To produce trills or quavers in singing or in playing a musical instrument. —*v.t.* 3 To utter or sing in a tremulous voice. —*n.* 1 A trembling or shaking, as in the voice. 2 A shake or trill, as in singing. 3 An eighth note. [< ME *cwafian* tremble] —**qua′ver·y** *adj.*

quay (kē) *n.* A wharf or artificial landing place where vessels load and unload. [F]

Que. Quebec.

quean (kwēn) *n.* A brazen woman; harlot; prostitute. [< OE *cwene* woman]

quea·sy (kwē′zē) *adj.* ·si·er, ·si·est 1 Feeling or causing nausea. 2 Easily nauseated; squeamish. 3 Causing or feeling uneasiness or discomfort. [ME *coysy*] —**quea′si·ly** *adv.* —**quea′si·ness** *n.*

Quech·ua (kech′wä) *n.* 1 One of a tribe of South American Indians which dominated the Inca empire prior to the Spanish conquest. 2 The language of the Quechuas. — **Quech′uan** *adj., n.*

queen (kwēn) *n.* 1 The wife of a king. 2 A female sovereign or monarch. 3 A woman preeminent in a given activity, accomplishment, etc. 4 A place or thing of great beauty, excellence, etc. 5 The most powerful piece in chess, capable of moving any number of squares in a straight or diagonal line. 6 A playing card bearing a conventional picture of a queen in her robes. 7 An egg-producing female in a colony of social insects, as bees, ants, etc. —*v.t.* 1 To make a queen of. —*v.i.* 2 To reign as or play the part of a queen: often with *it.* [< OE *cwēn* woman, queen] —**queen′ly** *adj., adv.* —**queen′li·ness** *n.*

Queen Anne's lace The wild carrot, having filmy white flowers resembling lace.

queen consort The wife of a reigning king.

queen dowager The widow of a king.

queen mother A queen dowager who is mother of a reigning sovereign.

queer (kwir) *adj.* 1 Different from the usual; strange; odd. 2 Of questionable character; open to suspicion; mysterious. 3 *Slang* Counterfeit. 4 Mentally unbalanced or eccentric. 5 Queasy or giddy. 6 *Slang* Homosexual: a contemptuous term. —*n. Slang* 1 Counterfeit money. 2 A homosexual, esp. a male homosexual: a contemptuous term. —*v.t. Slang* 1 To jeopardize or spoil. 2 To put into an unfavorable or embarrassing position. [< G *quer* oblique] —**queer′ly** *adv.* —**queer′ness** *n.* —**Syn.** *adj.* 1 bizarre, curious, droll, fantastic, grotesque, peculiar, singular. 2 suspect, suspicious. 4 peculiar, odd, deranged.

quell (kwel) *v.t.* 1 To put down or suppress by force; extinguish. 2 To quiet; allay, as pain. [< OE *cwellan* kill] — **quell′er** *n.*

quench (kwench) *v.t.* 1 To put out or extinguish, as a fire. 2 To slake or satisfy (thirst). 3 To suppress or repress, as emotions. 4 To cool, as heated iron or steel, by thrusting into water or other liquid. [ME *cwenken*] —**quench′a·ble** *adj.* —**quench′er** *n.*

quench·less (kwench′lis) *adj.* Incapable of being quenched; insatiable; irrepressible. —**quench′less·ly** *adv.* —**quench′less·ness** *n.*

quer·u·lous (kwer′ə·ləs, -yə·ləs) *adj.* 1 Disposed to complain or be fretful; faultfinding. 2 Indicating or expressing a complaint. [< L *queri* complain] —**quer′u·lous·ly** *adv.* —**quer′u·lous·ness** *n.* —**Syn.** 1 carping, captious, disparaging, critical, censorious.

que·ry (kwir′ē) *v.t.* ·ried, ·ry·ing 1 To inquire into; ask about. 2 To ask questions of; interrogate. 3 To express doubt concerning the correctness or truth of, esp., as in printing, by marking with a question mark. —*n. pl.* ·ries 1 An inquiry; question. 2 A doubt. 3 A question mark. [< L *quaerere* ask]

ques. question.

quest (kwest) *n.* 1 The act of seeking; a looking for something. 2 A search, as an adventure or expedition in medieval romance; also, the person or persons making the search. —*v.i.* To go on a quest. [< L *quaerere* ask, seek] — **quest′er** *n.*

ques·tion (kwes′chən) *n.* **1** An inquiry, esp. to obtain information, test knowledge, etc. **2** A written or vocal expression of such an inquiry; an interrogative sentence, clause, or expression. **3** A subject of debate or dispute. **4** An issue or problem: It's not a *question* of time. **5** A doubt or uncertainty: There is no *question* of his skill. —**out of the question** Not to be considered as a possibility. —*v.t.* **1** To put a question or questions to; interrogate. **2** To be uncertain of; doubt. **3** To make objection to; challenge; dispute. —*v.i.* **4** To ask a question or questions. [< L *quaerere* ask] —**ques′tion·er** *n.*

ques·tion·a·ble (kwes′chən-ə-bəl) *adj.* **1** Open to question; debatable. **2** Dubious or suspect, as regards morality, integrity, respectability, etc.: *questionable* motives. —**ques′tion·a·bil′i·ty, ques′tion·a·ble·ness** *n.* —**ques′tion·a·bly** *adv.*

question mark A punctuation mark (?) indicating that the sentence it closes is a direct question. A question mark is also used to denote that a fact, statement, etc., is uncertain or doubtful.

ques·tion·naire (kwes′chə-nâr′) *n.* A written or printed form comprising a series of questions submitted to one or more persons in order to obtain data, as for a survey or report. [F]

quet·zal (ket·säl′) *n. pl.* **·zals** or **·zal·es** (-sä′läs) A crested bird of Central America having long, upper tail feathers in the male. **2** The monetary unit of Guatemala. Also **que·zal** (kä·säl′). [< Nahuatl]

queue (kyōō) *n.* **1** A braid of hair hanging from the back of the head; a pigtail. **2** A line of persons or vehicles waiting in the order of their arrival. —*v.i.* **queued, queu·ing** To form such a line: usu. with *up.* [< L *cauda* a tail]

quib·ble (kwib′əl) *n.* **1** An evasion of a point or question; an equivocation. **2** A minor objection; cavil. —*v.i.* **·bled, ·bling** To use quibbles. [< L *quibus,* ablative pl. of *qui* who, which] —**quib′bler** *n.*

quiche (kēsh) *n.* Any of various non-dessert, custardlike pies, having meat, cheese, vegetables, etc., as principal ingredients. [F]

quick (kwik) *adj.* **1** Done or occurring in a short time; expeditious; brisk; prompt; speedy: a *quick* answer. **2** Characterized by rapidity or readiness of movement or action; nimble; rapid; swift: a *quick* pace. **3** Alert; sensitive; perceptive: a *quick* ear; *quick* wit. **4** Responding readily; excitable; hasty: *quick-tempered.* **5** Lasting only a short time: a *quick* lunch. —*n.* **1** That which has life; those who are alive: chiefly in the phrase **the quick and the dead. 2** The living flesh; esp., the tender flesh under a nail. **3** The most sensitive feelings: hurt to the *quick.* —*adv.* Quickly; rapidly. [< OE *cwic* alive]

Quetzal

quick bread Any bread, biscuits, etc., whose leavening agent makes immediate baking possible.

quick·en (kwik′ən) *v.t.* **1** To cause to move more rapidly; hasten or accelerate. **2** To make alive or quick; give or restore life to. **3** To excite or arouse; stimulate: to *quicken* the appetite. —*v.i.* **4** To move or act more quickly. **5** To come or return to life; revive. —**quick′en·er** *n.*

quick-freeze (kwik′frēz′) *v.t.* **-froze, -fro·zen, -freez·ing** To preserve by freezing rapidly and storing at a low temperature. —**quick′-fro′zen** *adj.*

quick·ie (kwik′ē) *n. Slang* Anything done hastily, as by short cuts or makeshift methods.

quick·lime (kwik′līm′) *n.* Unslaked lime.

quick·ly (kwik′lē) *adv.* In a quick manner; rapidly; soon.

quick·sand (kwik′sand′) *n.* A deep, wet bed of sand subjected to pressure by water below it and usu. incapable of supporting the weight of a person or animal.

quick·set (kwik′set′) *n.* **1** A slip, as of hawthorn, ready for planting. **2** A hedge made of such slips. —*adj.* Composed of quickset.

quick·sil·ver (kwik′sil′vər) *n.* Elemental mercury.

quick·step (kwik′step′) *n.* **1** A lively tune, esp. one in the rhythm of quick time. **2** A lively dance step, or a combination of such steps.

quick-tem·pered (kwik′tem′pərd) *adj.* Easily angered.

quick time A marching step of 120 paces a minute, each pace of 30 inches.

quick-wit·ted (kwik′wit′id) *adj.* Having a ready wit or quick discernment; keen; alert. —**quick′-wit′ted·ly** *adv.* —**quick′-wit′ted·ness** *n.*

quid[1] (kwid) *n.* A small portion, as of tobacco, to be chewed but not swallowed. [Var. of CUD]

quid[2] (kwid) *n. Brit. Slang* In England, a pound sterling, or a sovereign. [?]

quid·di·ty (kwid′ə·tē) *n. pl.* **·ties 1** The essence of a thing. **2** A quibble; cavil. [< L *quid* which, what]

quid·nunc (kwid′nungk′) *n.* A gossip; busybody. [< L *quid nunc* what now]

quid pro quo (kwid′ prō kwō′) A thing given or received for another thing. [L, lit., something for something]

qui·es·cent (kwī·es′ənt, kwē-) *adj.* Being in a state of repose or inaction; quiet; still. [< L *quiescere* be quiet] —**qui·es′cence** *n.* —**qui·es′cent·ly** *adv.*

qui·et (kwī′ət) *adj.* **1** Being in a state of repose; still; calm; motionless. **2** Free from turmoil, strife, or busyness; tranquil; peaceful. **3** Having or making little or no noise; silent. **4** Gentle or mild, as of disposition. **5** Undisturbed by din or bustle; secluded. **6** Not showy or obtrusive, as dress. —*n.* The condition or quality of being free from motion, disturbance, noise, etc.; peace; calm. —*v.t. & v.i.* To make or become quiet: often with *down.* —*adv.* In a quiet or peaceful manner. [< L *quies* rest, repose] —**qui′et·ly** *adv.* —**qui′et·ness** *n.*

qui·et·en (kwī′ə·tən) *v.t. & v.i. Brit. or Regional* To make or become quiet: often with *down.*

qui·e·tude (kwī′ə·tyōōd) *n.* A state or condition of calm or tranquillity; repose; rest.

qui·e·tus (kwī·ē′təs) *n.* **1** A final discharge or settlement, as of a debt. **2** A release from or extinction of activity or life; death. **3** Something that silences or suppresses. **4** Something that kills. [< L *quietus (est)* (he is) quiet]

quill (kwil) *n.* **1** A large, strong, wing or tail feather. **2** The hollow, horny stem of a feather. **3** Something made from this, as a pen or a plectrum. **4** A spine of a porcupine or hedgehog. [ME *quil*]

quilt (kwilt) *n.* **1** A bedcover made by stitching together two layers of cloth with a soft padding between them. **2** Any bedcover, esp. if thick. **3** A quilted skirt or other quilted article. —*v.t.* **1** To stitch together (two pieces of material) with a soft substance between. **2** To stitch in ornamental patterns or crossing lines. —*v.i.* **3** To make a quilt or quilted work. [< L *culcita* mattress] —**quilt′work′** *n.*

Quill

quilt·ing (kwil′ting) *n.* **1** The act or process of making a quilt, or of stitching as in making a quilt. **2** Material for quiltwork. **3** A quilting bee or party.

quilting bee A social gathering of the women of a community for working on a quilt or quilts. Also **quilting party.**

quince (kwins) *n.* **1** A hard, acid, yellowish fruit, used for preserves. **2** The small tree, related to the apple, which bears quinces. [ME < Gk. *Kydōnia,* a town in Crete]

qui·nine (kwī′nīn, *esp. Brit.* kwi·nēn′) *n.* **1** A bitter alkaloid obtained from cinchona. **2** A medicinal compound of quinine, used to relieve the symptoms of malaria. [< Sp. *quina* cinchona bark + -INE]

Quin·qua·ges·i·ma (kwin′kwə·jes′ə·mə) *n.* The Sunday before Lent. Also **Quinquagesima Sunday.** [< L *quinquagesimus* fiftieth]

quin·sy (kwin′zē) *n.* An acute infection of the throat, esp. when suppurative. [< Gk. *kyōn* dog + *anchein* to choke]

quint (kwint) *n. Informal* A quintuplet. [< L *quinque* five]

quin·tal (kwin′təl) *n.* **1** A hundredweight. **2** In the metric system, 100 kilograms. [< Ar. *qintar*]

quin·tes·sence (kwin·tes′əns) *n.* **1** The essence of anything, esp. in its most pure, concentrated form. **2** The perfect manifestation or embodiment of anything. [<L *quinta essentia* fifth essence] —**quin·tes·sen·tial** (kwin′tə·sen′shəl) *adj.*

quin·tet (kwin·tet′) *n.* **1** A musical composition for five voices or instruments. **2** The five performers of such a composition. **3** Any group of five persons or things. Also **quin·tette′**. [<Ital. *quinto* fifth]

quin·til·lion (kwin·til′yən) *n. & adj.* See NUMBER. [<L *quintus* fifth + MILLION] —**quin·til′lionth** (-yənth) *adj., n.*

quin·tu·ple (kwin·t^yōō′pəl, -tup′əl, kwin′t^yōō·pəl) *v.t. & v.i.* **·pled, ·pling** To multiply by five; make or become five times as large. —*adj.* **1** Consisting of five. **2** Being five times as much or as many. —*n.* A number or an amount five times as great as another. [<L *quintus* fifth + *-plex* -fold]

quin·tu·plet (kwin·tup′lit, -t^yōō′plit, -t^yōō′-, kwint′əp·lit) *n.* **1** Five things of a kind considered together. **2** One of five offspring born of the same mother at one birth.

quip (kwip) *n.* **1** A witty or sarcastic remark or retort; gibe. **2** A quibble. **3** An odd, fantastic action or object. —*v.i.* **quipped, quip·ping** To make a quip or quips. [<L *quippe* indeed] —**quip′pish** *adj.* —**quip′ster** *n.*

quire (kwīr) *n.* A set of 24 (or 25) sheets of paper of the same size and quality. [<L *quaterni* by fours]

Quir·i·nal (kwir′ə·nəl) *n.* One of the seven hills on which Rome stands, containing the **Quirinal palace,** formerly a papal residence, after 1870 the royal residence, now the residence of the president of Italy. —*adj.* Pertaining to or situated on the Quirinal.

quirk (kwûrk) *n.* **1** A peculiar mannerism or trait; idiosyncracy. **2** An evasion; quibble. **3** A witticism; quip. **4** An abrupt curve or twist, as a flourish in writing. [?]

quirk·y (kwûrk′ē) *adj.* **quirk·i·er, quirk·i·est** Peculiar, unpredictable, and idiosyncratic: a *quirky* individual. —**quirk′i·ly** *adv.* —**quirk′i·ness** *n.*

quirt (kwûrt) *n.* A short-handled riding whip with a braided rawhide lash. —*v.t.* To strike with a quirt. [?]

quis·ling (kwiz′ling) *n.* One who betrays his country to the enemy and is then given political power by the conquerors. [< Vidkun *Quisling*, 1887–1945, Norwegian politician] —**quis′ling·ism** *n.*

quit (kwit) *v.* **quit** or **quit·ted, quit·ting** *v.t.* **1** To cease or desist from; discontinue. **2** To give up; renounce; relinquish: to *quit* a job. **3** To go away from; leave. **4** To let go of (something held). **5** To free; release. **6** To discharge; pay back. —*v.i.* **7** To resign from a position, etc. **8** To stop; cease; discontinue. **9** To leave; depart. —*adj.* Released, relieved, or absolved from something, as a duty, obligation, encumbrance, or debt; clear; free; rid. —*n.* The act of quitting. [<L *quies* rest, repose]

quit·claim (kwit′klām′) *n. Law* **1** The giving up of a claim, right, title, or interest. **2** An instrument by which one person gives up to another a claim or title to an estate. —*v.t.* To relinquish or give up claim or title to; release from a claim. [<QUIT + CLAIM]

quite (kwīt) *adv.* **1** Completely; fully; totally: not *quite* finished. **2** To a great or considerable extent; very: *quite* ill. **3** Positively; really: *quite* certain. [ME, rid of]

quit·tance (kwit′ns) *n.* **1** Discharge or release, as from a debt or obligation. **2** A document in evidence of this; receipt. **3** Something given or tendered by way of repayment. [<F *quiter* quit]

quit·ter (kwit′ər) *n.* One who quits needlessly; a shirker; slacker; coward.

quiv·er¹ (kwiv′ər) *v.i.* To shake with a slight, tremulous motion; vibrate; tremble. —*n.* The act or fact of quivering; a trembling or shaking. [?<QUAVER]

quiv·er² (kwiv′ər) *n.* A portable case or sheath for arrows; also, its contents. [<AF *quiveir*]

Quiver
of arrows

qui vive? (kē vēv′) "Who goes there?": used by French sentinels. —**be on the qui vive** To be on the look-out; be wide-awake. [F, who lives?]

quix·ot·ic (kwik·sot′ik) *adj.* **1** Pertaining to or like Don Quixote, the hero of a Spanish romance ridiculing knighterrantry. **2** Ridiculously chivalrous or romantic; having high but impractical sentiments, aims, etc. —**quix·ot′i·cal·ly** *adv.* —**quix·ot·ism** (kwik′sə·tiz′əm) *n.*

quiz (kwiz) *n. pl.* **quiz·zes** **1** The act of questioning; specifically, a brief oral or written examination. **2** A person given to ridicule or practical jokes. **3** A hoax; practical joke. —*v.t.* **quizzed, quiz·zing** **1** To examine by asking questions; question. **2** To make fun of; ridicule. [?] —**quiz′zer** *n.*

quiz program A television or radio program in which selected contestants or a panel of experts compete in answering questions.

quiz·zi·cal (kwiz′i·kəl) *adj.* **1** Mocking; teasing. **2** Perplexed; puzzled. **3** Queer; odd. —**quiz′zi·cal·ly** *adv.*

quod (kwod) *n. Brit. Slang* A prison. [?]

quoin (koin, kwoin) *n.* **1** An external angle of a building. **2** A large square stone forming such an angle. **3** A wedge-shaped stone, etc., as the keystone of an arch. [Var. of COIN]

Quoins *def.* 2

quoit (kwoit, *esp. Brit.* koit) *n.* **1** A ring of iron or other material to be thrown over a stake, used in the game of quoits. **2** *pl.* A game played by throwing these disks at a short stake.

quon·dam (kwon′dəm) *adj.* Having been formerly; former. [L]

Quon·set hut (kwon′sit) A prefabricated metal structure in the form of half a cylinder resting lengthwise on its flat surface: a trade name.

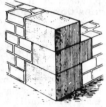
Quonset hut

quo·rum (kwôr′əm, kwō′rəm) *n.* The number of members of any deliberative or corporate body that is necessary for the legal transaction of business, usu., a majority. [L, of whom]

quot. quotation.

quo·ta (kwō′tə) *n.* A proportional part or share given to or required from a person, group, etc. [<L *quotus* how great]

quo·ta·tion (kwō·tā′shən) *n.* **1** The act of quoting. **2** The words quoted. **3** A price quoted or current, as of securities, etc. —**quo·ta′tion·al** *adj.* —**quo·ta′tion·al·ly** *adv.*

quotation mark One of a pair of marks (" " or ' ') placed at the beginning and end of a quoted word or passage, the single marks usu. being used to set off a quotation within a quotation.

quote (kwōt) *v.* **quot·ed, quot·ing** *v.t.* **1** To repeat or reproduce the words of. **2** To repeat or cite (a rule, author, etc.), as for authority or illustration. **3** In commerce: **a** To state (a price). **b** To give the current or market price of. —*v.i.* **4** To make a quotation, as from a book. —*n.* **1** QUOTATION. **2** QUOTATION MARK. [<Med. L *quotare* distinguish by number <L *quot* how many] —**quot′a·bil′i·ty, quot′er** *n.* —**quot′a·ble** *adj.*

quoth (kwōth) *v.t. Archaic* Said or spoke; uttered: used only in the first and third persons, the subject always following the verb, as *quoth* he. [<OE *cwethan* say]

quo·tid·i·an (kwō·tid′ē·ən) *adj.* Recurring or occurring every day. —*n.* Something that returns every day, as a fever. [<L *quotidianus* daily]

quo·tient (kwō′shənt) *n. Math.* The result obtained by division; a factor by which a given number must be multiplied to produce a given product. [<L *quotiens* how often]

q.v. which see (L *quod vide*).

qy. query.

R

R, r (är) *n. pl.* **R's, r's, Rs, rs** (ärz) **1** The 18th letter of the English alphabet. **2** Any spoken sound representing the letter *R* or *r*. **3** Something shaped like an R. —**the three R's** Reading, writing, and arithmetic (regarded humorously as spelled *reading, 'riting,* and *'rithmetic*); the essential elements of a primary education. —*adj.* Shaped like an R.

R radical; ratio; Republican; rook (chess); registered (trademark).

R., r. rabbi; railroad; river; road; ruble; rupee.

r roentgen(s); radius.

r. range; rare; received; residence; retired; radius.

Ra (rä) The supreme Egyptian deity, the sun-god.

Ra radium.

rab·bet (rab′it) *n.* **1** A recess or groove in or near the edge of one piece of wood or other material to receive the edge of another piece. **2** A joint so made. —*v.t.* **1** To cut a rectangular groove in. **2** To unite in a rabbet. —*v.i.* **3** To be jointed by a rabbet. [< OF *rabattre* beat down]

rab·bi (rab′ī) *n. pl.* **·bis 1** A Jew authorized to teach or expound Jewish law. **2** The official head of a Jewish congregation. [< Heb. *rabbī* my master]

rab·bin·i·cal (rə·bin′i·kəl) *adj.* Of or pertaining to the rabbis or to their opinions, languages, writings, etc. Also **rab·bin′ic.** —**rab·bin′i·cal·ly** *adv.*

rab·bit (rab′it) *n.* **1** Any of numerous small, herbivorous mammals having soft fur, long legs and ears, and a short tail. **2** HARE. **3** The pelt of a rabbit or hare. —*v.i.* To hunt rabbits. [ME *rabette*] —**rab′bit·er** *n.*

rabbit fever TULAREMIA.

rabbit foot The left hind foot of a rabbit carried as a good-luck charm. Also **rabbit's foot.**

rab·ble (rab′əl) *n.* A disorderly crowd; mob. —**the rabble** The common people: a contemptuous term. [?]

rab·ble-rous·er (rab′əl·rou′zər) *n.* One who tries to incite mobs by arousing prejudices and passions. —**Syn.** demagogue, instigator, agitator.

Rab·e·lai·si·an (rab′ə·lā′zē·ən, -zhən) *adj.* **1** Of, pertaining to, or like Rabelais or his works. **2** Humorously coarse and boisterous; bawdy. —**Rab′e·lai′si·an·ism** *n.*

rab·id (rab′id) *adj.* **1** Affected with, arising from, or pertaining to rabies; mad. **2** Unreasonably zealous; fanatical. **3** Furious; raging. [< L *rabere* be mad] —**ra·bid·i·ty** (rə·bid′- ə·tē), **rab′id·ness** —**rab′id·ly** *adv.*

ra·bies (rā′bēz) *n. pl.* **·bies** An acute viral disease affecting the central nervous system of dogs, bats, and other warm-blooded animals and transmissible to man by the bite of an infected animal. [< L *rabere* rave]

rac·coon (ra·kōōn′) *n.* **1** A North American nocturnal, tree-climbing mammal with a black face mask, long gray-brown fur, and a bushy, black-ringed tail. **2** The fur of this animal. Also **ra·coon′.** [< Algon.]

Raccoon

race¹ (rās) *n.* **1** A subdivision of mankind having a relatively constant set of physical traits, such as color of skin and eyes, stature, texture of hair, etc. **2** Any grouping of peoples according to geography, nation, etc. **3** A genealogical or family stock; clan: the *race* of MacGregor. **4** Any class of people having similar activities, interests, etc.: the *race* of lawyers. **5** *Biol.* A group of plants or animals within a species with distinct, inheritable characteristics; a variety. [< Ital. *razza*]

race² (rās) *n.* **1** A contest to determine the relative speed of the persons or animals which are in competition. **2** *pl.* A series of such contests, as for horses. **3** Any contest. **4** Duration of life; course; career. **5** A swift current of water or its channel. **6** A swift current or heavy sea. **7** A sluice or channel by which to conduct water to or from a waterwheel or around a dam. **8** Any guide or channel along which some part of a machine moves. **9** SLIPSTREAM. —*v.* **raced, rac·ing** *v.i.* **1** To take part in a race. **2** To move at great or top speed. **3** To move at an accelerated or too great speed, as an engine. —*v.t.* **4** To contend against in a race. **5** To cause to race. [< ON *rās*]

race·course (rās′kôrs′, -kōrs′) *n.* A course or track for racing.

ra·ceme (rā·sēm′, rə-) *n. Bot.* A flower cluster having flowers on short stalks arranged at intervals along a central stalk. [< L *racemus* cluster] —**rac·e·mose** (ras′ə·mōs) *adj.* —**rac′e·mose·ly** *adv.*

rac·er (rā′sər) *n.* **1** One who races. **2** Anything having unusually rapid speed, as a car, yacht, etc. **3** Any of a genus of large, agile snakes of North America.

race riot A riot caused by racial hostility, as between two groups of different races.

race·track (rās′trak′) *n.* A course or track for racing, esp. one for horse or dog racing.

Ra·chel (rā′chəl) In the Bible, the wife of Jacob and mother of Joseph.

ra·chi·tis (rə·kī′tis) *n.* RICKETS. [< Gk. *rhachitis* spinal inflammation] —**ra·chit′ic** (-kit′ik) *adj.*

ra·cial (rā′shəl) *adj.* **1** Of, pertaining to, characteristic of a race. **2** Existing between races: *racial* brotherhood. —**ra′cial·ly** *adv.*

ra·cial·ism (rā′shəl·iz′əm) *n.* **1** The belief in or practice of racial superiority. **2** RACISM.

ra·cism (rā′siz·əm) *n.* **1** An excessive and irrational belief in the superiority of one's own racial group. **2** A doctrine, program, or practice based on such belief. —**ra′cist** *adj., n.*

rack¹ (rak) *n.* **1** Something on which various articles can be hung, stored, or canned. **2** A triangular frame for arranging the balls on a billiard table. **3** *Mech.* A bar having teeth that engage those of a gearwheel or pinion. **4** A machine for stretching or making tense; esp., an instrument of torture which stretches the limbs of victims. **5** Intense mental or physical suffering or its cause. **6** A wrenching or straining, as from a storm. —**on the rack** In great physical or mental pain. —*v.t.* **1** To place or arrange in or on a rack. **2** To torture on the rack. **3** To torment. **4** To strain, as with the effort of thinking: to *rack* one's brains. **5** To raise (rents) excessively. —**rack up** *Informal* To gain or achieve: to *rack up* a good score. [Prob. < MDu. *recken* to stretch] —**rack′er** *n.*

Rack *def. 3* and pinion

rack² (rak) *n.* SINGLE FOOT. —*v.i.* To proceed or move with this gait. [? Var. of ROCK²]

rack³ (rak) *n.* Thin, flying, or broken clouds. [< Scand.]

rack⁴ (rak) *n.* Destruction: obsolete except in the phrase **go to rack and ruin.** [Var. of WRACK]

rack·et¹ (rak′it) *n.* **1** A bat consisting of an oval, wooden or metal hoop strung with catgut, nylon, etc., and having a handle, used in playing tennis, etc. **2** *pl. (construed as sing.)* A game resembling court tennis, played in a court with four walls: also **rac·quets** (rak′its). [< Ar. *rāha* palm of the hand]

rack·et² (rak′it) *n.* **1** A loud, clattering or confused noise. **2** *Informal* A scheme for getting money or other benefits by fraud, intimidation, or other illegitimate means. **3**

---

add, āce, câre, pälm; end, ēven; it, īce; odd, ōpen, ôrder; tŏŏk, pōōl; up, bûrn; ə = *a* in *above, u* in *focus;* yōō = *u* in *fuse;* oil; pout; check; go; ring; thin; this; zh, *vision.* < derived from; ? origin uncertain or unknown.

Slang Any business or occupation. —*v.i.* To make a loud, clattering noise. [?] —**rack'et·y** *adj.*

rack·et·eer (rak'ə·tir') *n.* One who gets money or other benefits by fraud, intimidation, or other illegitimate means. —**rack'et·eer'ing** *n.*

rac·on·teur (rak'on·tûr', *Fr.* rȧ·kôṅ·tœr') *n.* A skilled storyteller. [F]

rac·y (rā'sē) *adj.* **rac·i·er, rac·i·est 1** Full of spirit and vigor: a *racy* style. **2** Slightly immodest or risqué. **3** Spicy; piquant. [< RACE¹] —**rac'i·ly** *adv.* —**rac'i·ness** *n.*

rad (rad) *n.* A unit of absorbed radiation equivalent to 100 ergs of absorbed energy per gram of absorbing material. [< R(ADIATION) + A(BSORBED) + D(OSE)]

rad radian.

ra·dar (rā'där) *n. Electronics* A device which detects, locates, and indicates the speed and approximate nature of aircraft, ships, objects, etc., by means of reflected microwaves. [< RA(DIO) D(ETECTING) A(ND) R(ANGING)]

ra·di·al (rā'dē·əl) *adj.* **1** Pertaining to, consisting of, or resembling a ray or radius. **2** Extending from a center like rays. **3** *Anat.* Of, pertaining to, or near the radius or forearm. **4** Developing uniformly on all sides. —*n.* **1** A radiating part. **2** RADIAL TIRE. —**ra'di·al·ly** *adv.*

radial tire A pneumatic tire with plies of fabric laid at right angles to the direction of the tread. Also **ra·di·al·ply tire** (rā'dē·əl·plī').

ra·di·an (rā'dē·ən) *n.* The angle subtended by an arc equal in length to the radius of the circle of which it is a part: a unit of measure. [< RADIUS]

ra·di·ance (rā'dē·əns) *n.* The quality or state of being radiant. Also **ra'di·an·cy, ra'di·ant·ness.**

ra·di·ant (rā'dē·ənt) *adj.* **1** Emitting rays of light or heat. **2** Beaming with brightness: a *radiant* smile. **3** Resembling rays. **4** Consisting of or transmitted by radiation: *radiant* heat. [< L *radiare* emit rays] —**ra'di·ant·ly** *adv.*

radiant energy *Physics* Energy transmitted by radiation, as electromagnetic waves.

ra·di·ate (rā'dē·āt) *v.* **·at·ed, ·at·ing** *v.i.* **1** To emit rays or radiation; be radiant. **2** To issue forth in rays. **3** To spread out from a center, as the spokes of a wheel. —*v.t.* **4** To send out or emit in rays. **5** To spread or show (joy, love, etc.) as if from a center. —*adj.* (-dē·it) Divided or separated into rays; having rays; radiating. [< L *radiare* emit rays] —**ra'di·a·tive** *adj.*

ra·di·a·tion (rā'dē·ā'shən) *n.* **1** The act or process of radiating or the state of being radiated. **2** That which is radiated, as energy in the form of particles or waves.

radiation sickness Sickness resulting from exposure to X-rays, nuclear explosions, etc.

ra·di·a·tor (rā'dē·ā'tər) *n.* **1** That which radiates. **2** A device for distributing heat, partly by radiation, as in heating or cooling systems.

rad·i·cal (rad'i·kəl) *adj.* **1** Thoroughgoing; extreme: *radical* measures. **2** Of, pertaining to, or professing policies and practices of extreme change, as in government. **3** Of or pertaining to the root or foundation; essential; basic. —*n.* **1** One who holds radical or extreme convictions. **2** In politics, one who advocates extreme governmental changes. **3** The primitive or underived part of a word; root. **4** *Math.* An indicated root of a number, expression, etc. **5** *Chem.* A group of atoms that act as a unit in a compound and remain together during a chemical reaction. [< L *radix, radicis* root] —**rad'i·cal·ly** *adv.* —**rad'i·cal·ness** *n.*

rad·i·cal·ism (rad'i·kəl·iz'əm) *n.* **1** The state of being radical. **2** Advocacy of radical or extreme measures.

rad·i·cal·ize (rad'i·kə·līz') *v.t.* **·ized, ·iz·ing** To make radical, as in politics. —**rad'i·cal·i·za·tion** (rad'i·kə·lə·zā'shən) *n.*

radical sign *Math.* The symbol √ placed around a number or expression to indicate that its root is to be taken. A number above it, not written where equal to 2, shows what root is to be taken; thus ⁿ√a stands for the *n*th root of *a*.

rad·i·cle (rad'i·kəl) *n. Bot.* The embryonic root of a sprouting seed. [< L *radix, radicis* root]

ra·di·o (rā'dē·ō) *n. pl.* **·os 1** The technology and process of communicating by means of radio waves. **2** A transmitter or receiver used in such communication. **3** The process, business, or industry of producing programs to be communicated in this way. —*adj.* Of, pertaining to, designat-ing, employing, or produced by radiant energy, esp. electromagnetic waves: a *radio* beam. —*v.t. & v.i.* **·di·oed, ·di·o·ing 1** To transmit (a message, etc.) by radio. **2** To communicate with (someone) by radio. [< RADIO(TELEGRAPHY)]

radio- *combining form* Radiation: *radioscopy.* [< L *radius* a ray]

ra·di·o·ac·tive (rā'dē·ō·ak'tiv) *adj.* Of, pertaining to, exhibiting, caused by, or characteristic of radioactivity.

ra·di·o·ac·tiv·i·ty (rā'dē·ō·ak·tiv'ə·tē) *n. Physics* The spontaneous disintegration of nuclei of certain elements and isotopes, with the emission of particles or rays.

radio astronomy The branch of astronomy which studies celestial phenomena by means of radio waves received from stars and other objects in space.

radio beacon A stationary radio transmitter which sends out signals for the guidance of ships and aircraft.

radio beam 1 A steady flow of radio signals concentrated along a given course or direction. **2** The narrow zone marked out for the guidance of aircraft by radio beacons.

ra·di·o·broad·cast (rā'dē·ō·brôd'kast', -käst') *v.t. & v.i.* **·cast** or **·cast·ed, ·cast·ing** To broadcast by radio. —*n.* BROADCAST. —**ra'di·o·broad'cast'er** *n.* —**ra'di·o·broad'cast'ing** *n.*

ra·di·o·car·bon (rā'dē·ō·kär'bən) *n.* CARBON 14.

radio frequency Any wave frequency from about 10 kilohertz to about 30,000 megahertz.

ra·di·o·gram (rā'dē·ō·gram') *n.* **1** A message sent by wireless telegraphy. **2** RADIOGRAPH.

ra·di·o·graph (rā'dē·ō·graf', -gräf') *n.* An image made by means of X-rays or the products of radioactivity. —*v.t.* To make a radiograph of. —**ra·di·og·ra·pher** (-og'rə·fər), **ra·di·og'ra·phy** *n.* —**ra'di·o·graph'ic** or **·i·cal** *adj.*

ra·di·o·i·so·tope (rā'dē·ō·ī'sə·tōp) *n.* A radioactive isotope, usu. one of an element having also a stable isotope.

ra·di·ol·o·gy (rā'dē·ol'ə·jē) *n.* That branch of science concerned with radioactivity, X-rays, etc., esp. in diagnostic and therapeutic applications. —**ra·di·o·log·i·cal** (rā'dē·ə·loj'i·kəl) or **ra'di·o·log'ic** *adj.* —**ra'di·ol'o·gist** *n.*

ra·di·om·e·ter (rā'dē·om'ə·tər) *n.* An instrument for detecting and measuring radiant energy by noting the speed of rotation of blackened disks suspended in a partially evacuated chamber.

ra·di·o·phone (rā'dē·ō·fōn') *n.* RADIO-TELEPHONE.

ra·di·o·pho·to (rā'dē·ō·fō'tō) *n.* A photograph or image transmitted by radio. Also **ra'di·o·pho'to·graph.**

ra·di·o·scope (rā'dē·ō·skōp') *n.* An apparatus for detecting radioactivity or X-rays.

Radiometer

ra·di·os·co·py (rā'dē·os'kə·pē) *n.* Examination of bodies opaque to light by X-rays or other penetrating radiation. —**ra'di·o·scop'ic** (-skop'ik) or **·i·cal** *adj.*

ra·di·o·sonde (rā'dē·ō·sond') *n. Meteorol.* A device, usu. attached to a small balloon and sent aloft, which measures the pressure, temperature, and humidity of the upper air and radios the data to the ground. [< RADIO + F *sonde* sounding]

radio star A star that emits a sizable part of its energy as radio waves.

ra·di·o·tel·e·gram (rā'dē·ō·tel'ə·gram) *n.* A message sent by radiotelegraphy.

ra·di·o·te·leg·ra·phy (rā'dē·ō·tə·leg'rə·fē) *n.* Telegraphic communication by means of radio waves. Also **ra'di·o·tel'e·graph** (-tel'ə·graf, -gräf). —**ra'di·o·tel'e·graph'ic** *adj.*

ra·di·o·tel·e·phone (rā'dē·ō·tel'ə·fōn') *n.* A telephone set that uses radio waves to carry messages. —**ra'di·o·te·leph'o·ny** (-tə·lef'ə·nē) *n.*

radio telescope A sensitive radio receiver designed to receive radio waves from space.

Radiosonde

ra·di·o·ther·a·py (rā'dē·ō·ther'ə·pē) *n.* The use of X-rays and radioactivity in the treatment of disease.

radio wave Any electromagnetic wave of radio frequency.

rad·ish (rad′ish) *n.* **1** A tall, branching herb of the mustard family. **2** Its pungent, edible root, commonly eaten raw. [< L *radix, radicis* root]

ra·di·um (rā′dē·əm) *n.* A radioactive metallic element (symbol Ra) found in pitchblende as a disintegration product of uranium. [< L *radius* ray]

radium therapy The treatment of disease, esp. cancer, by means of radium.

ra·di·us (rā′dē·əs) *n. pl.* **·di·i** (-dē·ī) or **·di·us·es** **1** A straight line segment joining the surface of a sphere or circumference of a circle with its center. **2** *Anat.* The shorter of the two bones of the forearm. **3** *Zool.* A corresponding bone in the forelimb of other vertebrates. **4** *Bot.* A ray floret of a composite flower. **5** A raylike part, as a wheel spoke. **6** A circular area or boundary measured by its radius. **7** Sphere, scope, or limit, as of activity. **8** A fixed or circumscribed area or distance of travel. [L, spoke of a wheel, ray]

radius vector *pl.* **radius vectors** or **ra·di·i vec·to·res** (rā′dē·ī vek·tôr′ēz, -tō′rēz) *Math.* The distance in an indicated direction from a fixed origin to any point.

Radius def. 2

ra·dix (rā′diks) *n. pl.* **rad·i·ces** (rad′ə·sēz, rā′də-) or **ra·dix·es** *Math.* A number or symbol used as the base of a system of numeration. [L, root]

ra·dome (rā′dōm) *n.* A housing, transparent to microwaves, for a radar assembly. [< RA(DAR) + DOME]

ra·don (rā′don) *n.* A gaseous, radioactive element (symbol Rn) resulting from the decay of radium and having a half-life of about four days. [< RAD(IUM) + (NE)ON]

RAF, R.A.F. Royal Air Force.

raf·fi·a (raf′e·ə) *n.* **1** A cultivated palm of Madagascar. **2** Fiber made from the leaves of this palm, used for weaving baskets, etc. [< Malagasy *rafia*]

raff·ish (raf′ish) *adj.* **1** Tawdry; gaudy; vulgar. **2** Disreputable. [< ME *raf* rubbish + -ISH]

raf·fle (raf′əl) *n.* A form of lottery in which a number of people buy chances on an object. —*v.* **·fled, ·fling** *v.t.* **1** To dispose of by a raffle: often with *off.* —*v.i.* **2** To take part in a raffle. [< OF *rafle* a game of dice] —**raf′fler** *n.*

raft[1] (raft, räft) *n.* **1** A float of logs, planks, etc., fastened together for transportation by water. **2** A flat, often inflatable object, as of rubber, that floats on water. —*v.t.* **1** To transport on a raft. **2** To form into a raft. —*v.i.* **3** To travel by or work on a raft. [< ON *raptr* log] —**rafts′man** *n.*

raft[2] (raft, räft) *n. Informal* A large number or an indiscriminate collection of any kind. [< ME *raf* rubbish]

raft·er (raf′tər, räf′-) *n.* A timber or beam giving form, slope, and support to a roof. [< OE *ræfter*]

rag[1] (rag) *v.t.* **ragged, rag·ging** *Slang* **1** To tease or irritate. **2** To scold. —*n. Brit.* A prank. [?]

rag[2] (rag) *n.* **1** A waste, usu. torn piece of cloth. **2** A fragment of anything. **3** *pl.* Tattered or shabby clothing. **4** *pl.* Any clothing: a jocular use. **5** *Slang* A newspaper. —**chew the rag** *Slang* To talk or argue at length. —**glad rags** *Slang* One's best clothes. [< ON *rögg* tuft or strip of fur]

rag[3] (rag) *n.* RAGTIME. —*v.t.* **ragged, rag·ging** To compose or play in ragtime.

ra·ga (rä′gə) *n.* One of a large number of traditional melodic patterns, used by Hindu musicians as the basis for improvisation. [< Skt. *rāga* (musical) color]

rag·a·muf·fin (rag′ə·muf′in) *n.* Anyone, esp. a child, wearing very ragged clothes. [< *Ragamoffyn*, demon in *Piers Plowman* (1393), a long allegorical poem]

rag-bag (rag′bag′) *n.* **1** A bag in which rags or scraps of cloth are kept. **2** A miscellaneous collection; potpourri.

rage (rāj) *n.* **1** Violent anger; wrath; fury. **2** Any great violence or intensity, as of a fever or a storm. **3** Extreme eagerness or emotion. **4** Something that arouses great enthusiasm; craze; vogue. —*v.i.* **raged, rag·ing** **1** To feel or show violent anger. **2** To act or proceed with great vio-

lence. **3** To spread or prevail uncontrolled, as an epidemic. [< L *rabies* madness]

rag·ged (rag′id) *adj.* **1** Torn or worn into rags; frayed. **2** Wearing worn, frayed, or shabby garments. **3** Of rough or uneven character or aspect: a *ragged* performance. **4** Naturally of a rough or shabby appearance. —**rag′ged·ly** *adv.* —**rag′ged·ness** *n.*

rag·ged·y (rag′id·ē) *adj.* Ragged in appearance.

rag·lan (rag′lən) *n.* An overcoat or topcoat, the sleeves of which extend in one piece up to the collar. —*adj.* Of or designating such a sleeve or a garment with such sleeves. [< Lord Fitzroy *Raglan*, 1788–1855, Eng. field marshal]

rag·man (rag′man′, -mən) *n. pl.* **·men** (-men′, -mən) One who buys and sells old rags and other waste; a ragpicker.

ra·gout (ra·gōō′) *n.* A highly seasoned dish of stewed meat and vegetables. —*v.t.* **ra·gouted** (-gōōd′), **ra·gout·ing** (-gōō′-ing) To make into a ragout. [< F *ragoûter* revive the appetite]

rag·pick·er (rag′pik′ər) *n.* One who picks up and sells rags and other junk for a livelihood.

rag·time (rag′tīm′) *n.* **1** A kind of American dance music, popular 1890 to 1920, highly syncopated and in quick tempo. **2** The rhythm of this dance. [< *ragged time*]

rag·weed (rag′wēd′) *n.* Any of a genus of coarse, composite plants having pollen that often induces hay fever.

rag·wort (rag′wûrt′) *n.* GROUNDSEL (def. 1).

rah (rä) *interj.* Hurrah!: a cheer used esp. in school yells.

raid (rād) *n.* **1** A hostile or predatory attack, as by a rapidly moving body of troops. **2** AIR RAID. **3** Any sudden breaking into, invasion, or capture, as by the police. **4** A manipulative attempt to make stock prices fall by concerted selling. —*v.t.* **1** To make a raid on. —*v.i.* **2** To participate in a raid. [< OE *rād* a ride] —**raid′er** *n.*

rail[1] (rāl) *n.* **1** A bar, usu. of wood or metal, resting on supports, as in a fence, at the side of a stairway or roadway, or capping the bulwarks of a ship; a railing. **2** One of a series of parallel bars, of iron or steel, resting upon cross-ties, forming a support and guide for wheels, as of a railway. **3** A railroad: to ship by *rail.* —*v.t.* To furnish or shut in with rails; fence. [< L *regula* ruler]

rail[2] (rāl) *n.* Any of various small marsh and shore birds having short wings and tail. [< OF *raale, ralle*]

rail[3] (rāl) *v.i.* To use scornful, insolent, or abusive language: with *at* or *against.* [< MF *railler* to mock]

rail·ing (rā′ling) *n.* **1** A series of rails; a balustrade. **2** Rails or material from which rails are made.

rail·ler·y (rā′lər·ē) *n. pl.* **·ler·ies** Merry jesting or teasing. [< F *raillerie* jesting]

Rail

rail·road (rāl′rōd′) *n.* **1** A graded road, having metal rails supported by ties, for the passage of trains or other rolling stock drawn by locomotives. **2** The system of tracks, stations, etc., used in transportation by rail. **3** The corporation or persons owning or operating such a system. —*v.t.* **1** To transport by railroad. **2** *Informal* To rush or force with great speed or without deliberation: to *railroad* a bill through Congress. **3** *Slang* To cause to be imprisoned on false charges or without fair trial. —*v.i.* **4** To work on a railroad. —**rail′road′er** *n.*

railroad flat An apartment having rooms arranged one after another in a straight line without hallways.

rail-split·ter (rāl′split′ər) *n.* One who splits logs into fence rails.

rail·way (rāl′wā′) *n.* **1** A railroad, esp. one using comparatively light vehicles. **2** *Brit.* RAILROAD. **3** Any track having rails for wheeled equipment.

rai·ment (rā′mənt) *n.* Wearing apparel; clothing; garb. [< ARRAY + -MENT]

rain (rān) *n.* **1** The condensed water vapor of the atmosphere falling in drops. **2** The fall of such drops. **3** A fall or shower of anything in the manner of rain. **4** A rainstorm; shower. **5** *pl.* The rainy season in a tropical country. —*v.i.* **1** To fall from the clouds in drops of water. **2** To fall like rain. **3** To send or pour down rain. —*v.t.* **4** To send down like rain; shower. [<OE *regn*]

rain·bow (rān'bō') *n.* **1** An arch of light formed in the sky opposite the sun and exhibiting the colors of the spectrum. It is caused by refraction, reflection, and dispersion of sunlight in raindrops or mist. **2** Any brilliant display of color. **3** Any unfounded hope.

rain check 1 The stub of a ticket to an outdoor event entitling the holder to future admission if for any reason the event is called off. **2** Any postponed invitation.

rain·coat (rān'kōt') *n.* A water-resistant coat giving protection against rain.

rain·drop (rān'drop') *n.* A drop of rain.

rain·fall (rān'fôl') *n.* **1** A fall of rain. **2** *Meteorol.* The amount of water precipitated in a given region over a stated time.

rain gauge An instrument for measuring rainfall.

rain·proof (rān'prōōf') *adj.* Shedding rain. —*v.t.* To make rainproof.

rain·storm (rān'stôrm') *n.* A storm accompanied by heavy rain.

rain·wa·ter (rān'wô'tər, -wot'ər) *n.* Water that falls or has fallen as rain.

rain·y (rā'nē) *adj.* **rain·i·er, rain·i·est** Of, abounding in, or bringing rain. —**rain'i·ly** *adv.* —**rain'i·ness** *n.*

rainy day A time of need; hard times.

raise (rāz) *v.* **raised, rais·ing** *v.t.* **1** To cause to move upward or to a higher level; lift; elevate. **2** To place erect; set up. **3** To construct or build; erect. **4** To make greater in amount, size, or value: to *raise* the price of corn. **5** To advance or elevate in rank, estimation, etc. **6** To increase the strength, intensity, or degree of. **7** To breed; grow: to *raise* chickens or tomatoes. **8** To rear (children, a family, etc.). **9** To cause to be heard: to *raise* a hue and cry. **10** To cause; occasion, as a smile or laugh. **11** To stir to action or emotion; arouse. **12** To waken; animate or reanimate: to *raise* the dead. **13** To obtain or collect, as an army, capital, etc. **14** To bring up for consideration, as a question. **15** To cause to swell or become lighter; leaven. **16** To put an end to, as a siege. **17** In card games, to bid or bet more than. **18** *Naut.* To cause to appear above the horizon, as land or a ship, by approaching nearer. —*v.i.* **19** *Regional* To rise or arise. **20** In card games, to increase a bid or bet. —**raise Cain** (or **the devil, the dickens, a rumpus,** etc.) *Informal* To make a great disturbance; stir up confusion. —*n.* **1** The act of raising. **2** An increase, as of wages or a bet. [<ON *reisa* lift, set up]

raised (rāzd) *adj.* **1** Elevated in low relief. **2** Made with yeast or leaven.

rai·sin (rā'zən) *n.* A grape of a special sort dried in the sun or in an oven. [<L *racemus* bunch of grapes]

rai·son d'ê·tre (re·zôn' de'tr') *French* A reason or excuse for existing.

raj (räj) *n.* In India, sovereignty; rule [<Hind. *rāj*]

ra·ja (rä'jə) *n.* **1** A prince or chief of India. **2** A Malay or Javanese ruler. Also **ra'jah.** [<Skt. *rājan* king]

rake¹ (rāk) *n.* A long-handled, toothed implement for drawing together loose material, making a surface smooth, etc. — *v.* **raked, rak·ing** *v.t.* **1** To gather together with or as with a rake. **2** To smooth, clean, or prepare with a rake. **3** To gather by diligent effort. **4** To search or examine carefully. **5** To direct heavy gunfire along the length of. —*v.i.* **6** To use a rake. **7** To scrape or pass roughly or violently: with *across, over,* etc. **8** To make a search. —**rake in** *Informal* To earn or acquire (money, etc.) in large quantities. —**rake up** *Informal* To make public or bring to light: to *rake up* old gossip. [<OE *raca*]

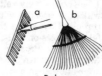

Rakes
a. garden. b. broom.

rake² (rāk) *v.* **raked, rak·ing** *v.i.* **1** To lean from the perpendicular, as a ship's masts. —*v.t.* **2** To cause to lean; incline. —*n.* Inclination from the perpendicular or horizontal, as the edge of a cutting tool. [?] —**raked** *adj.*

rake³ (rāk) *n.* A dissolute, lewd man. [Orig. *rakehell* < ME *rakel* rash, wild] —**Syn.** roué, libertine, lecher, profligate.

rake-off (rāk'ôf', -of') *n. Slang* A percentage, as of profits; commission or rebate, usu. illegitimate.

rak·ish¹ (rā'kish) *adj.* **1** Dashing; jaunty. **2** *Naut.* Having the masts unusually inclined, usu. connoting speed. [<RAKE²] —**rak'ish·ly** *adv.* —**rak'ish·ness** *n.*

rak·ish² (rā'kish) *adj.* Like a rake; dissolute. —**rak'ish·ly** *adv.* —**rak'ish·ness** *n.*

ral·len·tan·do (ral'ən·tan'dō, *Ital.* räl'len·tän'dō) *adj.* & *adv. Music* Gradually slower. [Ital., pr.p. of *rallentare* slow down]

ral·ly¹ (ral'ē) *v.* **·lied, ·ly·ing** *v.t.* **1** To bring together and restore to effective discipline: to *rally* fleeing troops. **2** To summon up or revive: to *rally* one's spirits. **3** To bring together for common action. —*v.i.* **4** To return to effective discipline or action: The enemy *rallied.* **5** To unite for common action. **6** To make a partial or complete return to a normal condition. **7** In tennis, badminton, etc. to engage in a rally. —*n. pl.* **·lies 1** An assembly of people, esp. to arouse enthusiasm. **2** A quick recovery or improvement, as of health, spirits, vigor, etc. **3** A reassembling, as of scattered troops. **4** In tennis, badminton, etc., an exchange of several strokes before one side wins the point. **5** A competition for automobiles that emphasizes driving and navigational skills rather than speed. [<F *re-* again + *allier* join]

ral·ly² (ral'ē) *v.t.* & *v.i.* To tease or ridicule; banter. [<F *railler* banter]

ram (ram) *n.* **1** A male sheep. **2** BATTERING-RAM. **3** Any device for forcing or thrusting, as by heavy blows. **4** A device for raising water by pressure of its own flow; a hydraulic ram. —*v.t.* **rammed, ram·ming 1** To strike with or as with a ram; dash against. **2** To drive or force down or into something. **3** To cram; stuff. [<OE]

Ram (ram) *n.* ARIES.

RAM Random access memory, a kind of computer memory in which information may be stored and/or erased repeatedly.

ram·ble (ram'bəl) *v.i.* **·bled, ·bling 1** To walk about freely and aimlessly; roam. **2** To write or talk aimlessly or without sequence of ideas. **3** To proceed with turns and twists; meander. —*n.* **1** The act of rambling. **2** A meandering path; maze. [?]

ram·bler (ram'blər) *n.* **1** One who or that which rambles. **2** Any of several varieties of climbing roses.

ram·bunc·tious (ram·bungk'shəs) *adj. Informal* Difficult to control or manage; unruly. [?]

ram·e·kin (ram'ə·kin) *n.* **1** Any of various food mixtures, usu. containing cheese, baked and served in individual dishes. **2** Any small or individual baking dish. Also **ram'e·quin.** [<F *ramequin*]

ram·i·fi·ca·tion (ram'ə·fə·kā'shən) *n.* **1** The act or process of ramifying. **2** An offshoot or branch. **3** A result or consequence; outgrowth, as of an action.

ram·i·fy (ram'ə·fī) *v.t.* & *v.i.* **·fied, ·fy·ing** To divide or spread out into or as into branches. [<L *ramus* branch + *facere* make]

ram·jet (ram'jet') *n.* A type of jet engine consisting of a duct whose forward motion provides compressed air which mixes with fuel that burns and provides an exhaust velocity high enough to create thrust.

ra·mose (rā'mōs, rə·mōs') *adj.* **1** Branching. **2** Consisting of or having branches. [<L *ramus* branch]

ramp¹ (ramp) *n.* **1** An inclined passageway or roadway that connects different levels. **2** A movable stairway or passageway for entering or leaving an airplane. **3** *Archit.* A concave part at the top or cap of a railing, wall, or coping. [<F *ramper* to climb]

ramp² (ramp) *v.i.* **1** To rear up on the hind legs and stretch out the forepaws. **2** To act in a violent or threatening manner. —*n.* The act of ramping. [<OF *ramper* to climb]

ram·page (ram'pāj) *n.* An outbreak of boisterous or angry agitation or violence. —*v.i.* (ram·pāj') **·paged, ·pag·ing** To rush or act violently; storm; rage [Orig. Scot.,? < RAMP²]

Rampant lion

ram·pant (ram'pənt) *adj.* **1** Exceeding all bounds; unrestrained; wild. **2** Widespread; unchecked, as an erroneous belief. **3** Standing on the hind legs; rearing: said of a quadruped. **4** *Her.* Standing on the hind legs, with both forelegs elevated. [<OF *ramper* to climb] —**ram'pan·cy** *n.* —**ram'pant·ly** *adv.*

ram·part (ram'pärt, -pərt) *n.* **1** The embankment surrounding a fort, on which the parapet is raised. **2** A bulwark or defense. —*v.t.* To supply with or as with ramparts; fortify. [< OF *re-* again + *emparer* prepare]

ram·pike (ram'pīk') *n. Can.* A bare, dead tree, esp. one destroyed by fire. [?]

ram·rod (ram'rod') *n.* **1** A rod used to compact the charge of a muzzleloading firearm. **2** A similar rod used for cleaning the barrel of a rifle, etc.

ram·shack·le (ram'shak'əl) *adj.* About to go to pieces from age and neglect. [?] —**Syn.** dilapidated, unsteady, shaky, battered.

ran (ran) *p.t.* of RUN.

ranch (ranch) *n.* **1** An establishment for rearing or grazing cattle, sheep, horses, etc., in large herds. **2** The buildings, personnel, and lands connected with it. **3** A large farm. —*v.i.* To manage or work on a ranch. [< Sp. *rancho* group eating together, mess] —**ranch'er, ranch'man** *n.*

ranch house 1 A long, one-story residence having a low-pitched roof. **2** The main house on a ranch.

ran·cid (ran'sid) *adj.* Having the bad taste or smell of spoiled fats. [< L *rancere* be rancid] —**ran·cid·i·ty** (ran·sid'ə·tē), **ran'cid·ness** *n.*

ran·cor (rang'kər) *n.* Bitter and vindictive enmity. *Brit. sp.* **ran·cour.** [< L *rancere* be rank] —**ran'cor·ous** *adj.* —**ran'cor·ous·ly** *adv.* —**ran'cor·ous·ness** *n.* —**Syn.** malice, spite, hatred, hostility.

ran·dom (ran'dəm) *n.* Lack of definite purpose or intention: now chiefly in the phrase **at random,** without careful thought, planning, intent, etc.; haphazardly. —*adj.* **1** Done or chosen without deliberation or plan; chance; casual. **2** Chosen, determined, or varying without pattern, rule, or bias. [< OF *randonner, rander* move rapidly, gallop] —**ran'dom·ly** *adv.* —**ran'dom·ness** *n.*

ra·nee (rä'nē) *n.* RANI.

rang (rang) *p.t.* of RING[2].

range (rānj) *n.* **1** The area over which anything moves, operates, or is distributed. **2** An extensive tract of land over which cattle, sheep, etc., roam and graze. **3** Extent or scope: the whole *range* of political influence. **4** The extent of variation of anything: the temperature *range.* **5** A line, row, or series, as of mountains. **6** The horizontal distance between a gun and its target. **7** The horizontal distance covered by a projectile. **8** The maximum distance for which an airplane, ship, vehicle, etc., can be fueled. **9** The maximum effective distance, as of a weapon. **10** *Math.* The entire set of possible values of a dependent variable. **11** A place for shooting at a mark: a rifle *range.* **12** A large cooking stove. —*adj.* Of or pertaining to a range. —*v.* **ranged, rang·ing** *v.t.* **1** To place or arrange in definite order, as in rows. **2** To assign to a class, division, or category; classify. **3** To move about or over (a region, etc.), as in exploration. **4** To put (cattle) to graze on a range. **5** To adjust or train, as a telescope or gun. —*v.i.* **6** To move over an area in a thorough, systematic manner. **7** To rove; roam. **8** To occur; extend; be found: forests *ranging* to the east. **9** To vary within specified limits. **10** To lie in the same direction, line, etc. **11** To have a specified range. [< OF *ranger* arrange < *renc* row]

rang·er (rān'jər) *n.* **1** One who or that which ranges. **2** One of a group of mounted troops that protect large tracts of country. **3** One of a herd of cattle that feeds on a range. **4** A warden employed in patrolling forest tracts. **5** *Brit.* A government official in charge of a royal forest or park. **6** One of a group of soldiers trained esp. for raiding and close combat.

rang·y (rān'jē) *adj.* **rang·i·er, rang·i·est 1** Disposed to roam, or adapted for roving, as cattle. **2** Having long, slender limbs. **3** Roomy; spacious.

ra·ni (rä'nē) *n.* **1** The wife of a raja or prince. **2** A reigning Hindu queen or princess.

rank[1] (rangk) *n.* **1** A series of objects ranged in a line or row. **2** A degree of official standing: the *rank* of colonel. **3** A line of soldiers side by side in close order. **4** *pl.* An army; also, the common body of soldiers: to rise from the *ranks.* **5** Relative position in a scale; degree; grade: a writer of low *rank.* **6** A social class or stratum: from all *ranks* of life. **7** High degree or position: a lady of *rank.* —*v.t.* **1** To place or arrange in a rank or ranks. **2** To assign to a position or classification. **3** To outrank: Sergeants *rank* corporals. —*v.i.* **4** To hold a specified place or rank. **5** To have the highest rank or grade. [< OF *ranc, renc*]

rank[2] (rangk) *adj.* **1** Flourishing and luxuriant in growth: *rank* weeds. **2** Strong and disagreeable to the taste or smell. **3** Utter; total: *rank* injustice. **4** Indecent; gross; vulgar. [< OE *ranc* strong] —**rank'ly** *adv.* —**rank'ness** *n.*

rank and file 1 The common soldiers of an army. **2** Those who form the main body of any organization, as distinguished from its leaders.

rank·ing (rangk'ing) *adj.* Taking precedence (over others): a *ranking* senator, officer, etc. —**Syn.** superior, senior.

ran·kle (rang'kəl) *v.* **·kled, ·kling** *v.i.* **1** To cause continued resentment, sense of injury, etc. **2** To become irritated or inflamed. —*v.t.* **3** To irritate; embitter. [< OF *rancler*]

ran·sack (ran'sak) *v.t.* **1** To search through every part of. **2** To search for plunder; pillage. [< ON *rann* house + *sækja* seek] —**ran'sack·er** *n.*

ran·som (ran'səm) *v.t.* **1** To secure the release of (a person, property, etc.) for a required price, as from captivity or detention. **2** To set free on payment of ransom. —*n.* **1** The price paid to ransom a person or property. **2** Release purchased, as from captivity. [< L *redimere* redeem] —**ran'som·er** *n.*

rant (rant) *v.i.* **1** To speak in loud, violent, or extravagant language. —*v.t.* **2** To exclaim or utter in a ranting manner. —*n.* Declamatory and bombastic talk. [< MDu. *ranten*] —**rant'er** *n.* —**rant'ing·ly** *adv.*

rap[1] (rap) *v.* **rapped, rap·ping** *v.t.* **1** To strike sharply and quickly; hit. **2** To utter in a sharp manner: with *out.* **3** *Slang* To criticize severely. —*v.i.* **4** To strike sharp, quick blows. **5** *Slang* To have a frank discussion; talk. —*n.* **1** A sharp blow. **2** A sound caused by or as by knocking. **3** *Slang* A severe criticism. **4** *Slang* Blame or punishment, as for wrongdoing: to take the *rap.* **5** *Slang* A prison sentence. **6** *Slang* A talk; discussion. —*adj. Slang* Marked by frank discussion: a *rap* session. [Imit.] —**rap'per** *n.*

rap[2] (rap) *n. Informal* The least bit: I don't care a *rap.* [?]

ra·pa·cious (rə·pā'shəs) *adj.* **1** Given to plunder or rapine. **2** Greedy; grasping. **3** Subsisting on prey seized alive, as hawks, etc. [< L *rapere* seize] —**ra·pa'cious·ly** *adv.* —**ra·pac·i·ty** (rə·pas'ə·tē), **ra·pa'cious·ness** *n.*

rape[1] (rāp) *v.* **raped, rap·ing** *v.t.* **1** To commit rape on. **2** To plunder or sack (a city, etc.). —*v.i.* To commit rape. —*n.* **1** The act of a man who has sexual intercourse with a woman against her will or (called **statutory rape**) with a girl below the age of consent. **2** Any unlawful sexual intercourse or sexual connection by force or threat: homosexual *rape* in prison. **3** The plundering or sacking of a city, etc. **4** Any gross violation, assault, or abuse: the *rape* of natural forests. [< L *rapere* seize] —**rap'ist** *n.*

rape[2] (rāp) *n.* A plant related to mustard, grown for forage. [< L *rapum* turnip]

rape oil An oil obtained from seeds of the rape, used as a lubricant, etc. Also **rape·seed oil** (rāp'sēd').

rap·id (rap'id) *adj.* **1** Having or done with great speed; swift; fast. **2** Marked or characterized by rapidity. —*n. Usu. pl.* A swift-flowing descent in a river. [< L *rapidus* < *rapere* seize, rush] —**ra·pid·i·ty** (rə·pid'ə·tē), **rap'id·ness** *n.* —**rap'id·ly** *adv.*

rap·id-fire (rap'id·fīr') *adj.* **1** Firing or designed to fire shots rapidly. **2** Characterized by speed: *rapid-fire* repartee. Also **rap'id-fir'ing.**

rapid transit An urban passenger railway system.

ra·pi·er (rā'pē·ər, rāp'yər) *n.* **1** A long, pointed, two-edged sword with a large cup hilt, used in dueling, chiefly for thrusting. **2** A shorter straight sword without cutting edge and therefore used for thrusting only. [< F *rapière*]

Rapier

rap·ine (rap′in) *n.* The taking of property by force, as in war. [<L *rapere* seize] **—Syn.** plunder, pillage, looting, spoiling.

rap·pel (ra·pel′) *n.* A way of lowering oneself down a vertical surface, using a rope attached at the top and to the climber's body. **—v.i.** To lower oneself using a rappel. [<F]

rap·port (rə·pôr′, -pōr′, *Fr.* rȧ·pôr′) *n.* Harmonious, sympathetic relationship; accord. **—en rapport** (äṅ rȧ·pôr′) *French* In close accord. [<F *rapporter* refer, bring back]

rap·proche·ment (rȧ·prôsh·män′) *n.* A state of harmony or reconciliation; restoration of cordial relations. [F]

rap·scal·lion (rap·skal′yən) *n.* A scamp; rascal. [Earlier *rascallion*<RASCAL]

rapt (rapt) *adj.* **1** Carried away with lofty emotion; enraptured; transported. **2** Deeply engrossed or intent. [<L *raptus,* pp. of *rapere* seize]

rap·to·ri·al (rap·tôr′ē·əl, -tō′rē-) *adj.* **1** Seizing and devouring living prey; predatory. **2** Having talons adapted for seizing prey: said esp. of hawks, vultures, eagles, owls, etc. [<L *raptus,* pp. of *rapere* seize]

rap·ture (rap′chər) *n.* **1** The state of being rapt or transported; ecstatic joy; ecstasy. **2** An expression of excessive delight. **—v.t.** **·tured, ·tur·ing** To enrapture; transport with ecstasy. **—rap′tur·ous** *adj.* **—rap′tur·ous·ly** *adv.*

rare[1] (râr) *adj.* **rar·er, rar·est** **1** Occurring infrequently; not common, usual, or ordinary. **2** Excellent in quality, merit, etc. **3** Rarefied: now said chiefly of the atmosphere. [<L *rarus*] **—Syn. 2** extraordinary, distinctive, fine, choice.

rare[2] (râr) *adj.* **rar·er, rar·est** Not thoroughly cooked, as roasted or broiled meat retaining its redness and juices. [<OE *hrēre* lightly boiled]

rare·bit (râr′bit) *n.* WELSH RABBIT. [Alter. of (WELSH) RABBIT]

rare earth Any of the oxides of the rare-earth elements.

rare-earth elements The series of metallic elements comprising atomic numbers 57 through 71. See PERIODIC TABLE OF ELEMENTS. Also **rare-earth metals.**

rar·e·fy (râr′ə·fī) *v.t. & v.i.* **·fied, ·fy·ing** **1** To make or become rare, thin, or less dense. **2** To make or become more refined, pure, subtle, etc. [<L *rarus* rare + *facere* make] **—rar′e·fac′tion** (-fak′shən) *n.* **—rar′e·fac′tive** *adj.*

rare·ly (râr′lē) *adv.* **1** Not often; infrequently. **2** With unusual excellence or effect; finely. **3** Exceptionally; extremely.

rar·ing (râr′ing) *adj. Informal* Full of enthusiasm; intensely desirous; eager: used with an infinitive: *raring* to go. [<dial. E, var. of REAR[2], to raise]

rar·i·ty (râr′ə·tē) *n. pl.* **·ties** **1** The quality or state of being rare, uncommon, or infrequent. **2** That which is exceptionally valued because scarce. **3** Thinness; tenuousness.

ras·cal (ras′kəl) *n.* **1** An unscrupulous person; scoundrel. **2** A mischievous person; tease; scamp. [<OF *rasque* filth, shavings] **—ras·cal′i·ty** (-kal′ə·tē) *n.* **—ras′cal·ly** *adj. & adv.*

rash[1] (rash) *adj.* **1** Acting without due caution or regard of consequences; reckless. **2** Exhibiting recklessness or precipitancy. [ME *rasch*] **—rash′ly** *adv.* **—rash′ness** *n.*

rash[2] (rash) *n.* A patch of redness, itchiness, or other usu. temporary skin lesion.

rash·er (rash′ər) *n.* **1** A thin slice of meat, esp. of bacon. **2** A serving of several such slices.[?]

rasp (rasp, räsp) *n.* **1** A filelike tool having coarse, pointed projections. **2** The act or sound of rasping. **—v.t.** **1** To scrape with or as with a rasp. **2** To affect unpleasantly; irritate. **3** To utter in a rough voice. **—v.i.** **4** To grate; scrape. **5** To make a harsh, grating sound. [<OF *rasper* to scrape] **—rasp′er** *n.* **—rasp′y** *adj.* (**·i·er, ·i·est**)

rasp·ber·ry (raz′ber′ē, -bər·ē, räz′-) *n. pl.* **·ries** **1** A sweet, edible fruit, composed of drupelets clustered around a fleshy receptacle. **2** Any of a genus of brambles yielding this fruit. **3** *Slang* BRONX CHEER. [Earlier *rasp, raspis* raspberry + BERRY]

rat (rat) *n.* **1** Any of a genus of long-tailed rodents of worldwide distribution, larger and more aggressive than the mouse. **2** Any of various similar animals. **3** *Slang* A contemptible person, esp. one who deserts or betrays his associates. **4** A pad over which a woman's hair is combed to give more fullness. **—v.i.** **rat·ted, rat·ting** **1** To hunt rats. **2**

Slang To desert one's party, companions, etc. **3** *Slang* To betray or inform: with *on.* [<OE *ræt*]

rat·a·ble (rā′tə·bəl) *adj.* That may be rated or valued. Also **rate′a·ble. —rat′a·bil′i·ty** *n.* **—rat′a·bly** *adv.*

ra·tan (ra·tan′) *n.* RATTAN.

ratch·et (rach′it) *n.* **1** A mechanism consisting of a notched wheel, the teeth of which engage with a pawl, permitting relative motion in one direction only. **2** The pawl or the wheel thus used. Also **ratchet wheel.** [< Ital. *rochetto* bobbin]

a. ratchet.
b. pawl.

rate[1] (rāt) *n.* **1** The quantity, quality, degree, etc., of a thing in relation to units of something else: a typing *rate* of 50 words per minute. **2** A price or value, esp. the unit cost of a commodity or service: the *rate* for electricity. **3** Rank or class: to be of the first *rate.* **4** A fixed ratio: the *rate* of exchange. **5** *Brit.* A local tax on property. **—at any rate** In any case; anyhow. **—v.** **rat·ed, rat·ing** *v.t.* **1** To estimate the value or worth of; appraise. **2** To place in a certain rank or grade. **3** To consider; regard: He is *rated* as a great statesman. **4** To fix the rate for the transportation of (goods), as by rail, water, or air. **—v.i.** **5** To have rank, rating, or value. [<L *ratus,* pp. of *reri* reckon] **—rat′er** *n.*

rate[2] (rāt) *v.t. & v.i.* **rat·ed, rat·ing** To reprove with vehemence; scold.[?]

rath·er (rath′ər, rä′thər) *adv.* **1** More willingly; preferably. **2** With more reason, justice, wisdom, etc.: We, *rather* than they, should leave first. **3** More accurately or precisely: my teacher, or *rather* my friend. **4** Somewhat; to a certain extent: *rather* tired. **5** On the contrary. **—interj.** *Chiefly Brit.* (ra′thūr′, rä′-) Most assuredly; absolutely. [<OE *hrathor* sooner]

raths·kel·ler (rath′skel·ər, räts′kel·ər) *n.* A beer hall or restaurant, often located below the street level. [<G *Rat* town hall + *Keller* cellar]

rat·i·fy (rat′ə·fī) *v.t.* **·fied, ·fy·ing** To give sanction to, esp. official sanction. [<L *ratus* fixed, reckoned + *facere* make] **—rat′i·fi·ca′tion, rat′i·fi′er** *n.* **—Syn.** confirm, approve, endorse, validate.

rat·ing (rā′ting) *n.* **1** A classification or evaluation based on a standard; grade; rank. **2** An evaluation of the financial standing of a business firm or an individual. **3** A classification of men in the armed services based on their specialties. **4** In radio and television, the popularity of a program as determined by polling public opinion. **5** Any of several classifications given a motion picture regarding the content or treatment of its subject matter.

ra·tio (rā′shō, -shē·ō) *n. pl.* **·tios** **1** Relation of degree, number, etc., between two similar things; proportion; rate. **2** A fraction or indicated quotient, esp. one used to compare the magnitudes of numbers. [L, computation<*reri* think]

ra·ti·oc·i·nate (rash′ē·ōs′ə·nāt, -os′-, rat′ē-) *v.i.* **·nat·ed, ·nat·ing** To make a deduction from premises; reason. [<L *ratiocinari* calculate, deliberate] **—ra′ti·oc′i·na′tion, ra′ti·oc′i·na′tor** *n.* **—ra′ti·oc′i·na′tive** *adj.*

ra·tion (rash′ən, rā′shən) *n.* **1** A portion; share. **2** A fixed allowance or portion of food or provisions, as alloted daily to a soldier, etc. **3** *pl.* Food or provisions, as for an army, expedition, etc. **—v.t.** **1** To issue rations to, as an army. **2** To give out or allot in rations. [<L *ratio* computation]

ra·tion·al (rash′ən·əl) *adj.* **1** Of, pertaining to, or attained by reasoning. **2** Able to reason; mentally sound; sane. **3** Sensible; judicious. **4** *Math.* **a** Of or being a rational number. **b** Denoting an algebraic expression, as $\sqrt{x^2 - y^2}$, containing a radical that can be solved. [<L *ratio* reckoning] **—ra′tion·al′i·ty** (-al′ə·tē) *n.* **—ra′tion·al·ly** *adv.*

ra·tion·ale (rash′ən·al′) *n.* **1** A logical basis or reason for something. **2** A rational exposition of principles.

ra·tion·al·ism (rash′ən·əl·iz′əm) *n.* **1** The formation of opinions by relying upon reason alone. **2** *Philos.* The theory that truth and knowledge are attainable through reason alone rather than through experience or sense perception. **—ra′tion·al·ist** *adj., n.* **—ra′tion·al·is′tic** *adj.*

ra·tion·al·ize (rash′ən·əl·īz′) *v.* **·ized, ·iz·ing** *v.t.* **1** To explain (one's behavior) plausibly without recognizing the actual motives. **2** To explain or treat from a rationalistic point of view. **3** To make rational or reasonable. **4** *Math.*

To solve the radicals of (an expression or equation containing variables). —*v.i.* **5** To think in a rational or rationalistic manner. **6** To rationalize one's behavior. —**ra′tion·al·i·za′tion** (-ə-zā′shən, -ī·zā′shən) *n.*

rational number A number expressible as a quotient of two integers; a fraction.

rat·ite (rat′īt) *adj.* Designating any of various large, flightless birds, as ostriches, kiwis, emus, etc. [< L *ratis* raft, in ref. to lack of a keel on the sternum]

rat·line (rat′lin) *n. Naut.* One of the small ropes fastened across the shrouds of a ship, used as a ladder for going aloft or descending. Also **rat′lin** (-lin), **rat′ling** (-ling). [?]

rat race *Slang* Frantic, usu. competitive activity or strife.

rats·bane (rats′bān′) *n.* Rat poison.

rat·tan (ra·tan′) *n.* **1** The long, tough, flexible stem of various climbing palms, used in wickerwork, etc. **2** Any of these palms. [< Malay *rotan*]

Ratlines

rat·ter (rat′ər) *n.* **1** A dog or cat that catches rats. **2** *Slang* A deserter or traitor.

rat·tle (rat′l) *v.* **·tled, ·tling** *v.i.* **1** To make a series of sharp noises in rapid succession. **2** To move or act with such noises. **3** To talk rapidly and foolishly; chatter. —*v.t.* **4** To cause to rattle. **5** To utter or perform rapidly or noisily. **6** *Informal* To confuse; disconcert. —*n.* **1** A series of short, sharp sounds in rapid succession. **2** A plaything, implement, etc., adapted to produce a rattling noise. **3** The series of jointed horny rings in the tail of a rattlesnake, or one of these. **4** Rapid and noisy talk; chatter. **5** A sound caused by the passage of air through mucus in the throat. [< ME *ratelen*]

rat·tle·brain (rat′l·brān′) *n.* A talkative, flighty person; foolish chatterer. Also **rat′tle·head′** (-hed′), **rat′tle·pate′** (-pāt′). —**rat′tle·brained′** *adj.*

rat·tler (rat′lər) *n.* **1** RATTLESNAKE. **2** One who or that which rattles.

rat·tle·snake (rat′l·snāk′) *n.* Any of various venomous American snakes with a tail ending in a series of horny rings that rattle when the tail is vibrated.

rat·tle·trap (rat′l·trap′) *n.* Any rickety, clattering, or worn-out vehicle or article.

rat·ty (rat′ē) *adj.* **·ti·er, ·ti·est** **1** Ratlike, or abounding in rats. **2** *Slang* Disreputable; treacherous. **3** *Slang* Rundown; shabby. —**rat′ti·ness** *n.*

rau·cous (rô′kəs) *adj.* **1** Rough in sound; hoarse; harsh. **2** Noisy and rowdy. [< L *raucus*] —**rau′cous·ly** *adv.* —**rau′·cous·ness** *n.*

raunch·y (rôn′chē, rän′-) *adj. Slang* **raunch·i·er, raunch·i·est** **1** Sloppy; slovenly. **2** Sexually vulgar; lewd. **3** Lustful. [?] —**raunch′i·ly** *adv.* —**raunch′i·ness** *n.*

rav·age (rav′ij) *v.* **·aged, ·ag·ing** *v.t.* **1** To lay waste, as by pillaging or burning; despoil; ruin. —*v.i.* **2** To wreak havoc; be destructive. —*n.* Violent and destructive action, or its result; ruin. [< F *ravir* ravish] —**rav′ag·er** *n.*

rave (rāv) *v.* **raved, rav·ing** *v.i.* **1** To speak wildly or incoherently. **2** To speak with extravagant enthusiasm. **3** To make a wild, roaring sound; rage. —*v.t.* **4** To utter wildly or incoherently. —*n.* **1** The act or state of raving. **2** *Informal* A highly favorable review. —*adj. Informal* Extravagantly enthusiastic: *rave* reviews. [< L *rabere* to rage] — Syn. **1** babble, rant, gibber.

rav·el (rav′əl) *v.* **·eled** or **·elled, ·el·ing** or **·el·ling** *v.t.* **1** To separate the threads or fibers of; unravel. **2** To make clear or plain; explain: often with *out.* —*v.i.* **3** To become separated, as threads or fibers; unravel; fray. —*n.* A raveled part or thread; a raveling. [? < MDu. *ravelen* to tangle] — **rav′el·er** or **rav′el·ler** *n.*

rav·el·ing (rav′əl·ing) *n.* A thread or threads raveled from a fabric. Also **rav′el·ling.**

ra·ven (rā′vən) *n.* A large, crowlike bird. —*adj.* Black and shining. [< OE *hræfn*]

rav·en·ing (rav′ən·ing) *adj.* **1** Seeking eagerly for prey; rapacious. **2** Mad. [< OF *raviner* ravage]

rav·en·ous (rav′ən·əs) *adj.* **1** Violently hungry; voracious. **2** Extremely eager; greedy; grasping: *ravenous* for praise. [< OF *ravine* rapine] —**rav′en·ous·ly** *adv.* —**rav′en·ous·ness** *n.*

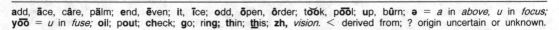

Raven

ra·vine (rə·vēn′) *n.* A deep gorge or gully, esp. one worn by a flow of water. [F, small gully or torrent]

rav·ing (rā′ving) *adj.* **1** Furious; delirious; frenzied. **2** *Informal* Extraordinary; remarkable: a *raving* beauty. —*n.* Frenzied or irrational speech.

ra·vi·o·li (rä·vyō′lē, rä′vē·ō′lē, rav′ē-) *n.pl. (usu. construed as sing.)* Little envelopes of dough encasing meat, cheese, etc., which are boiled in broth and sauced. [Ital.]

rav·ish (rav′ish) *v.t.* **1** To fill with strong emotion, esp. delight; enrapture. **2** To rape. **3** To carry off by force. [< L *rapere* seize] —**rav′ish·er, rav′ish·ment** *n.*

rav·ish·ing (rav′ish·ing) *adj.* Very attractive, pleasing, etc. —**rav′ish·ing·ly** *adv.*

raw (rô) *adj.* **1** Not changed or prepared by cooking; uncooked. **2** In its original state or condition; not refined, processed, etc.: *raw* wool; *raw* sugar. **3** Having the skin torn or abraded: a *raw* wound. **4** Bleak; chilling: a *raw* wind. **5** Newly done; fresh: *raw* paint; *raw* work. **6** Inexperienced; undisciplined: a *raw* recruit. **7** Vulgar; off-color: a *raw* joke. **8** *Informal* Brutally harsh or unfair: a *raw* deal. —*n.* A sore or abraded spot. —**in the raw** **1** In a raw, unspoiled, or unrefined state. **2** *Informal* Nude. [< OE *hrēaw*] —**raw′ly** *adv.* —**raw′ness** *n.*

raw-boned (rô′bōnd′) *adj.* Bony; gaunt.

raw·hide (rô′hīd′) *n.* **1** An untanned cattle hide. **2** A whip made of such hide.

ray¹ (rā) *n.* **1** A narrow beam of light. **2** Any of several lines radiating from an object. **3** *Geom.* A straight line emerging from a point and extending in one direction only. **4** A slight amount or indication: a *ray* of hope. **5** *Zool.* **a** A supporting spine of a fish's fin. **b** Any of numerous parts radiating from a common center, as the arms of a starfish. **6** *Bot.* **a** RAY FLOWER. **b** One of the flower stalks of an umbel. **7** *Physics* A stream of particles or waves. —*v.i.* **1** To emit rays; shine. **2** To radiate. —*v.t.* **3** To send forth as rays. **4** To mark with rays or radiating lines. [< L *radius*]

ray² (rā) *n.* Any of an order of marine fishes having a cartilaginous skeleton and a horizontally flattened body, dorsally placed eyes, and a thin, usu. long tail. [< L *raia*]

ray flower *Bot.* Any of the straplike flowers encircling certain composite flower heads, as in the daisy or sunflower. Also **ray floret.**

Ray

ray·on (rā′on) *n.* **1** A synthetic fiber made from a cellulose solution that is forced through spinnerets to produce solidified filaments. **2** A fabric made from these fibers. [F, ray; in ref. to its sheen]

raze (rāz) *v.t.* **razed, raz·ing** **1** To tear down; demolish. **2** To scrape or shave off. [< L *rasum*, pp. of *radere* scrape]

ra·zor (rā′zər) *n.* A sharp cutting implement used for shaving off the beard or hair. [< OF *raser* to scrape]

ra·zor·back (rā′zər·bak′) *n.* **1** FINBACK WHALE. **2** A lean half-wild hog of SE U.S. **3** A sharp ridge. —**ra′zor-backed′** *adj.*

razz (raz) *n. Slang* BRONX CHEER. —*v.t.* To heckle; deride. [< RASPBERRY]

raz·zle-daz·zle (raz′əl·daz′əl) *n. Slang* Any bewildering, exciting, or dazzling activity or performance. [Varied reduplication of DAZZLE]

Rb rubidium.

RBI, rbi, r.b.i. run(s) batted in.

R.C. Red Cross; Roman Catholic.

RCAF, R.C.A.F. Royal Canadian Air Force.
RCMP, R.C.M.P. Royal Canadian Mounted Police.
RCN, R.C.N. Royal Canadian Navy.
RCP, R.C.P. Royal College of Physicians.
RCS, R.C.S. Royal College of Surgeons
R.D. Rural Delivery.
R & D, R. & D., R and D research and development.
re[1] (rä) *n. Music* In solmization, the second tone of a diatonic scale. [< L *re(sonare)* resound. See GAMUT.]
re[2] (rē, rä) *prep.* Concerning; about; in the matter of: used in business letters, etc. [L, ablative of *res* thing.]
re- *prefix* **1** Back: *remit* (to send back). **2** Again; anew; again and again: *regenerate.* [< L *re-, red-* back, again] • In the list of words below, *re-* is used solely to mean *again, anew, again and again.* These words are for the most part written solid. A hyphen, however, is sometimes used: **a** To prevent confusion with a similarly spelled word having a different meaning, as in *retreat* (to go back) and *re-treat* (to treat again). **b** In the formation of nonce words, as "We *reread* the contract and then *re-reread* it." Formerly, a hyphen was the rule before words beginning with *e,* as *re-edit,* but such words are now often written solid.

reabsorb	recharter	redraw
reabsorption	recheck	redrive
reaccess	rechoose	reecho
reaccommodate	rechristen	reedit
reaccredit	reclose	reelect
reaccuse	reclothe	reelection
readapt	recoin	reelevate
readdict	recoinage	reembark
readdress	recolonize	reembarkation
readjourn	recolor	reemerge
readjournment	recombination	reemergence
readjust	recombine	reemit
readjustment	recommence	reemphasize
readopt	recommission	reenact
readorn	recompose	reenaction
readvance	recompute	reenactment
readvertise	reconcentrate	reencourage
reaffirm	recondensation	reencouragement
realign	recondense	reendow
realignment	reconfirm	reengage
reanoint	reconjoin	reengagement
reappear	reconquer	reengrave
reappearance	reconquest	reenjoy
reapply	reconsecrate	reenjoyment
reappoint	reconsecration	reenlist
reappointment	reconsign	reenlistment
reapportion	reconsolidate	reenslave
reapportionment	reconsolidation	reenslavement
reargue	reconvene	reenter
reargument	reconvey	reenthrone
rearrest	recopy	reenthronement
reascend	recross	reentrance
reascension	recrystallization	reequip
reascent	recrystallize	reestablish
reassemblage	recultivate	reestablishment
reassemble	recultivation	reevaluate
reassert	redecorate	reevaluation
reassertion	rededicate	reexamination
reassign	rededication	reexamine
reassignment	redefine	reexchange
reassimilate	redeliberate	reexhibit
reassimilation	redeliver	reexpel
reassociate	redemand	reexperience
reattach	redemonstrate	reexport
reattachment	redeposit	reexportation
reattempt	redescend	reexpulsion
reavow	redescent	reface
reawake	redesign	refashion
reawakening	redesignate	refasten
rebaptism	redetermine	refertilize
rebaptize	redial	refind
rebid	redigest	reflavor
rebill	redirect	reflight
rebind	rediscover	reflorescence
rebloom	rediscovery	reflourish
reblossom	redissolve	reflow
reboil	redistill	reflower
reborn	redistribute	refluctuation
rebottle	redistribution	refold
rebuild	redivide	reformulate
recalibrate	redo	refortification
recapitalize	redraft	refortify
recharge		refreeze

refuel	reload	resegregate
refurbish	reloan	reseize
refurnish	relocate	reseizure
regalvanize	relocation	resell
regather	reman	resensitize
regerminate	remarriage	reseparate
regermination	remarry	re-serve
regild	remast	reset
regrade	remaster	resettle
regraft	remeasure	resettlement
regrant	remelt	reshape
regroup	remigrate	resharpen
rehandle	remigration	reshoot
rehang	remilitarize	reshuffle
rehearing	remix	re-sign
reheat	remold	resite
reheel	rename	resolder
rehire	renationalize	resole
rehybridize	renavigate	re-solve
rehydrate	renegotiate	re-sound
reimplant	renominate	resow
reimport	renomination	respeak
reimportation	renumber	respell
reimpose	renumerate	restart
reimposition	reobtain	restock
reimpress	reoccupation	restoke
reimprison	reoccupy	re-store
reinaugurate	reopen	restrengthen
reincorporate	reoppose	restress
reincur	reordain	restrike
reinduce	reorder	resubject
reinfect	reordination	resubjection
reinfection	reorient	resubjugate
reinflame	reorientation	resubmit
reinform	reossify	resummon
reinfuse	repacify	resummons
reingratiate	repack	resupply
reinhabit	repackage	resurprise
reinjure	repaint	resurvey
reinoculate	repartition	retake
reinoculation	repass	retarget
reinscribe	repassage	retell
reinsert	repeople	retool
reinsertion	rephrase	retrace
reinspect	replant	retrain
reinspection	replantation	re-treat
reinspire	replaster	retrial
reinstall	repledge	retrim
reinstruct	replunge	retry
reinsure	repolish	retune
reintegrate	repoll	re-turn
reintegration	repopulate	reunification
reinter	repopulation	reunify
reinterment	repossess	reurge
reintroduce	repour	reuse
reintroduction	re-press	reutilize
reinvest	reprocess	reutter
reinvestigate	reprogram	revaccinate
reinvestment	repropose	revaccination
reinvigorate	re-prove	revaluation
reinvigoration	republish	revalue
reinvitation	repurchase	revarnish
reinvite	repurify	revest
reinvolve	reread	re-view
reinvolvement	re-record	revindication
reissue	re-refer	revisit
rekindle	re-release	reweave
reknit	resail	reweigh
reland	resale	rewin
relaunch	resalute	rewind
relet	re-search	rewire
reliquidate	reseat	reword
reliquidation	reschool	rework

Re rhenium.
reach (rēch) *v.t.* **1** To stretch out or forth, as the hand. **2** To present or deliver; hand over. **3** To touch, grasp, or extend as far as: Can you *reach* the top shelf? **4** To arrive at or come to by motion or progress. **5** To achieve communication with; gain access to. **6** To amount to; total. **7** To have an influence on; affect. —*v.i.* **8** To stretch the hand, foot, etc., out or forth. **9** To attempt to touch or obtain something: He *reached* for his wallet. **10** To have extent in space, time, amount, influence, etc.: The ladder *reached* to the ceiling. **11** *Naut.* To sail on a tack with the wind on or forward of the beam. —*n.* **1** The act or power of reaching. **2** The distance one is able to reach, as with

the hand, an instrument, or missile. **3** An extent or result attained by thought, influence, etc.; scope; range. **4** An unbroken stretch, as of a stream; a vista or expanse. **5** *Naut.* The sailing, or the distance sailed, by a vessel on one tack. [< OE *ræcan*] —**reach′er** *n.*

re·act (rē·akt′) *v.i.* **1** To act in response, as to a stimulus. **2** To act in a manner contrary to some preceding act. **3** To be affected by a circumstance, influence, act, etc. **4** *Chem.* To undergo chemical change.

re·act (rē′akt′) *v.t.* To act again.

re·ac·tance (rē·ak′təns) *n. Electr.* The component of impedance that results from the presence of capacitance or inductance.

re·ac·tion (rē·ak′shən) *n.* **1** Any response, as to a stimulus, event, influence, etc. **2** A trend or tendency toward a former state of things; esp., a trend toward an earlier, usu. outmoded social, political, or economic policy or condition. **3** Any change in an organism effected by an agent, as a drug, food, allergen, etc., or an environmental condition, as heat, cold, etc. **4** *Physics* The force exerted on an agent by the body acted upon. **5** Any process involving a change in the composition or structure of an atomic nucleus, as fission, fusion, or radioactive decay. **6** *Chem.* A molecular change undergone by two or more substances in contact. —**re·ac′tion·al** *adj.* —**re·ac′tion·al·ly** *adv.*

re·ac·tion·ar·y (rē·ak′shən·er′ē) *adj.* Of, relating to, favoring, or characterized by reaction (def. 2). —*n. pl.* ·**ar·ies** One who generally opposes change or liberalism in political or social matters. Also **re·ac′tion·ist.**

re·ac·ti·vate (rē·ak′tə·vāt) *v.t.* ·**vat·ed,** ·**vat·ing** To make active or effective again. —**re·ac′ti·va′tion** *n.*

re·ac·tive (rē·ak′tiv) *adj.* **1** Tending to react, or resulting from reaction. **2** Responsive to a stimulus. —**re·ac′tive·ly** *adv.* —**re·ac′tiv′i·ty, re·ac′tive·ness** *n.*

re·ac·tor (rē·ak′tər) *n.* **1** One who or that which reacts. **2** An assembly of fissionable material, moderator, coolant, shielding, and other accessories, designed to control and utilize the energy released by atomic fission.

read (rēd) *v.* **read** (red), **read·ing** (rē′ding) *v.t.* **1** To apprehend the meaning of (a book, writing, etc.) by perceiving the form and relation of the printed or written characters. **2** To utter aloud (something printed or written). **3** To understand the significance of as if by reading: to *read* the sky. **4** To apprehend the meaning of something printed or written in (a foreign language). **5** To make a study of: to *read* law. **6** To discover the nature or significance of (a person, character, etc.) by observation or scrutiny. **7** To interpret (something read) in a specified manner. **8** To take as the meaning of something read. **9** To have or exhibit as the wording: The passage *reads* "principal," not "principle." **10** To indicate or register: The meter *reads* zero. **11** To extract (data) from storage: said of a computer or other information-retrieval system. **12** To bring into a specified condition by reading: I *read* her to sleep. —*v.i.* **13** To apprehend the characters of a book, musical score, etc. **14** To utter aloud the words or contents of a book, etc. **15** To gain information by reading: with *of* or *about.* **16** To learn by means of books; study. **17** To have a specified wording: The contract *reads* as follows. **18** To admit of being read in a specified manner. **19** To give a public reading or recital. —**read between the lines** To perceive or infer what is not expressed or obvious. —**read into** To discern (implicit meanings or implications) in a statement or position. —**read out** To expel from a religious body, political party, etc., by proclamation or concerted action. —**read up** (or **up on**) To learn by reading. —*adj.* (red) Informed by or acquainted with books or literature: *well-read.* [< OE *rædan* advise, read]

read·a·ble (rē′də·bəl) *adj.* **1** That can be read; legible. **2** Easy and pleasant to read. **3** MACHINE-READABLE. —**read′a·bil′i·ty, read′a·ble·ness** *n.* —**read′a·bly** *adv.*

read·er (rē′dər) *n.* **1** One who reads. **2** Any of various devices that provide readable images, as by projection on a screen, of material or microfilm, microcards, etc. **3** One who reads and criticizes manuscripts offered to publishers. **4** PROOFREADER. **5** A layman authorized to read the lesson in church services. **6** A professional reciter. **7** A textbook containing matter for exercises in reading.

read·ing (rē′ding) *n.* **1** The act or practice of one who reads. **2** The public recital of literary works. **3** Matter that is read or is designed to be read. **4** The datum indicated by an instrument, as a thermometer. **5** The form in which any passage or word appears in any copy of a work. **6** An interpretation, as of a musical composition. —*adj.* **1** Pertaining to or suitable for reading. **2** Inclined to read.

read·out (rēd′out′) *n.* **1** A display in intelligible form of specific items of information derived from data that have been recorded automatically or processed by computer. **2** The information so displayed.

read·y (red′ē) *adj.* **read·i·er, read·i·est 1** Prepared for use or action. **2** Prepared in mind; willing. **3** Likely or liable: with *to: ready* to sink. **4** Quick to act, follow, occur, or appear; prompt. **5** Immediately available; convenient; handy. **6** Designating the standard position in which a rifle is held just before aiming. **7** Quick to understand; alert; quick; facile: a *ready* wit. —*n.* The position in which a rifle is held before aiming. —*v.t.* **read·ied, read·y·ing** To make ready; prepare. [< OE *ræde, geræde*] —**read′i·ly** *adv.* —**read′i·ness** *n.*

read·y-made (red′ē·mād′) *adj.* **1** Not made to order: *ready-made* clothing. **2** Not impromptu or original: *ready-made* opinions.

re·a·gent (rē·ā′jənt) *n.* Any substance used to induce a chemical reaction. [< RE- + AGENT]

re·al[1] (rē′əl, rēl) *adj.* **1** Having existence or actuality as a thing or state; not imaginary: a *real* event. **2** Not artificial or counterfeit; genuine. **3** Representing the true or actual, as opposed to the apparent or ostensible: the *real* reason. **4** Unaffected; unpretentious: a *real* person. **5** *Philos.* Having actual existence, and not merely possible, apparent, or imaginary. **6** *Law* Of or pertaining to things permanent and immovable: *real* property. **7** *Math.* Of or being a real number. —*n.* That which is real. —*adv. Informal* Very; extremely: to be *real* glad. [< Med. L *realis* < L *res* thing] —**re′al·ness** *n.*

re·al[2] (rē′əl, *Sp.* rä·äl′) *n. pl.* **re·als** or **re·a·les** (rā·ä′läs) **1** A former small silver coin of Spain. **2** *pl.* **reis** (rās) A former Portuguese and Brazilian coin; one thousandth of a milreis. [Sp., lit., royal]

real estate Land, including whatever is made part of or attached to it by man or nature, as trees, houses, etc. —**re′al·es·tate′** *adj.*

re·al·ism (rē′əl·iz′əm) *n.* **1** A disposition to deal solely with facts and reality and to reject the impractical or visionary. **2** In literature and art, the principle of depicting persons and scenes as they actually exist, without any idealization. **3** *Philos.* **a** The doctrine that universals or abstract concepts have actual, objective existence. **b** The doctrine that things have reality apart from the conscious perception of them. —**re′al·ist** *adj., n.* —**re′al·is′tic** *adj.* —**re′al·is′ti·cal·ly** *adv.*

re·al·i·ty (rē·al′ə·tē) *n. pl.* ·**ties 1** The fact, state, or quality of being real, genuine, or true to life. **2** That which is real; an actual thing, situation, or event. **3** *Philos.* The absolute or the ultimate.

re·al·ize (rē′əl·īz) *v.* ·**ized,** ·**iz·ing** *v.t.* **1** To understand or appreciate fully. **2** To make real or concrete. **3** To cause to appear real. **4** To obtain as a profit or return. **5** To obtain money in return for: He *realized* his holdings for a profit. —*v.i.* **6** To sell property for cash. —**re′al·iz′a·ble** *adj.* —**re′al·i·za′tion, re′al·iz′er** *n.*

re·al·ly (rē′ə·lē, rē′lē) *adv.* **1** In reality; actually. **2** Truly; genuinely: a *really* fine play. —*interj.* Oh: used to express surprise, doubt, etc.

realm (relm) *n.* **1** A kingdom. **2** Domain; sphere: the *realm* of imagination. [< L *regalis* royal]

real number A number whose square is greater than or equal to zero.

re·al·tor (rē′əl·tər, -tôr) *n.* **1** A person engaged in the real-estate business. **2** *Usu. cap.* A member of the National Association of Real Estate Boards: a trade name.

re·al·ty (rē′əl·tē) *n. pl.* ·**ties** REAL ESTATE.

---

ream[1] (rēm) n. 1 A quantity of paper equal to 20 quires and consisting of 480, 500, or 516 sheets. 2 pl. Informal A prodigious amount. [< Ar. rizmah packet]

ream[2] (rēm) v.t. 1 To increase the size of (a hole), as with a rotating cutter or reamer. 2 To get rid of (a defect) by reaming. [< OE rēman enlarge, make room]

ream·er (rē′mər) n. 1 One who or that which reams. 2 A rotary tool with cutting edges for reaming. 3 A device with a ridged cone for extracting juice from cit-rus fruits.

Reamers

re·an·i·mate (rē·an′ə·māt) v.t. ·mat·ed, ·mat·ing 1 To bring back to life; resuscitate. 2 To revive; encourage. —re′an·i·ma′tion n.

reap (rēp) v.t. 1 To cut and gather (grain) with a scythe, reaper, etc. 2 To harvest a crop from: to reap a field. 3 To obtain as the result of action or effort. —v.i. 4 To harvest grain, etc. 5 To receive a return or result. [< OE repan] —reap′a·ble adj. —reap′ing n.

reap·er (rē′pər) n. 1 One who reaps. 2 A machine for reaping grain.

rear[1] (rir) n. 1 The back or hind part. 2 A place or position at the back of or behind anything. 3 That division of a military force which is farthest from the front. —adj. Being in the rear. [< ARREAR]

rear[2] (rir) v.t. 1 To place upright; raise. 2 To build; erect. 3 To care for and bring to maturity. 4 To breed or grow. —v.i. 5 To rise upon its hind legs, as a horse. 6 To rise high; tower, as a mountain. [< OE ræran set upright] —rear′er n.

rear admiral See GRADE.

rear guard A body of troops to protect the rear of an army.

re·arm (rē·ärm′) v.t. & v.i. 1 To arm again. 2 To arm with more modern weapons. —re·ar′ma·ment n.

rear·most (rir′mōst′) adj. Coming or stationed last.

re·ar·range (rē′ə·ranj′) v.t. & v.i. ·ranged, ·rang·ing To ar-range again or in some new way. —re·ar·range′ment n. — Syn. reorder, redispose, reorganize, readjust.

rear·ward (rir′wərd) adj. Coming last or toward the rear; hindward. —adv. Toward or at the rear; backward: also rear′wards. —n. The rear; end.

rea·son (rē′zən) n. 1 A motive or basis for an action, opin-ion, etc. 2 A statement which explains or accounts for an action, belief, etc. 3 The ability to think logically and rationally. 4 Sound thinking or judgment; common sense. 5 Sanity. —by reason of Because of. —in (or within) reason Within reasonable limits or bounds. —it stands to reason It is logical. —with reason Justifiably. —v.i. 1 To think logically; obtain inferences or conclusions from known or presumed facts. 2 To talk or argue logically. — v.t. 3 To think out carefully and logically; analyze: with out. 4 To influence or persuade by means of reason. 5 To argue; debate. [< L ratio computation] —rea′son·er n.

rea·son·a·ble (rē′zən·ə·bəl, rēz′nə-) adj. 1 Conformable to reason. 2 Having the faculty of reason; rational. 3 Gov-erned by reason. 4 Not extreme or excessive; moderate. — rea′son·a·bil′i·ty, rea′son·a·ble·ness n. —rea′son·a·bly adv.

rea·son·ing (rē′zən·ing) n. 1 The act or process of using one's rational faculties to draw conclusions from known or assumed facts. 2 The reasons or proofs resulting from this process.

re·as·sure (rē′ə·shŏŏr′) v.t. ·sured, ·sur·ing 1 To restore to courage or confidence. 2 To assure again. 3 To reinsure. — re′as·sur′ance n. —re′as·sur′ing·ly adv.

re·bate (rē′bāt, ri·bāt′) v.t. ·bat·ed, ·bat·ing 1 To allow as a deduc-tion. 2 To make a deduction from. —n. A deduction from a gross amount; discount: also re·bate′·ment. [< OF rabattre beat down] —re′bat·er n.

re·bec (rē′bek) n. A medieval bowed instrument, somewhat like a violin. Also re′beck. [< Ar. rabāb]

Rebec

Re·bec·ca (ri·bek′ə) In the Bible, wife of Isaac and mother of Esau and Jacob.

re·bel (ri·bel′) v.i. ·belled, ·bel·ling 1 To resist or fight against any authority, established custom, etc. 2 To react with violent aversion: usu. with at. —n. (reb′əl) One who rebels. —adj. (reb′əl) 1 Rebellious; refractory. 2 Of rebels. [< L re- again + bellare make war]

re·bel·lion (ri·bel′yən) n. 1 The act of rebelling. 2 Organ-ized resistance to a government or to any lawful au-thority.

re·bel·lious (ri·bel′yəs) adj. 1 Being in a state of rebel-lion; insubordinate. 2 Of or pertaining to a rebel or rebel-lion. 3 Resisting control; refractory: a rebellious temper. —re·bel′lious·ly adv. —re·bel′lious·ness n.

re·birth (rē·bûrth′, rē′bûrth′) n. 1 A new birth. 2 A revival or renaissance.

re·bound (ri·bound′) v.i. 1 To bounce or spring back after or as after hitting something. 2 To recover, as from a difficulty. 3 To reecho. —v.t. 4 To cause to rebound. —n. (rē′bound′, ri·bound′) 1 A bounding back; recoil. 2 Some-thing that rebounds, as a basketball from a backboard. 3 Reaction after a disappointment: to fall in love on the rebound. [< F re- back + bondir bound]

re·broad·cast (rē·brôd′kast′, -käst′) v.t. ·cast or ·cast·ed, ·cast·ing To broadcast (the same program) again. —n. A program so transmitted.

re·buff (ri·buf′) v.t. 1 To reject or refuse abruptly or rudely. 2 To drive or beat back; repel. —n. 1 A sudden repulse; curt denial. 2 A sudden check; defeat. 3 A beating back. [< Ital. ribuffare]

re·buke (ri·byōōk′) v.t. ·buked, ·buk·ing To reprove sharply; reprimand. —n. A strong expression of disap-proval. [< OF re- back + bucher beat] —re·buk′er n.

re·bus (rē′bəs) n. A representation of a word, phrase, or sentence by letters, numerals, pictures, etc., whose names sug-gest the same sounds as the words or phrases they represent. [L, ablative pl. of res thing]

Rebus meaning
I can see.

re·but (ri·but′) v.t. ·but·ted, ·but-ting To dispute or show the falsity of, as by argument or by contrary evidence. [< OF re- back + bouter push, strike] —re·but′ter n. —Syn. disprove, refute, contradict.

re·but·tal (ri·but′l) n. The act of rebutting; refutation.

rec. receipt; recipe; record; recording.

re·cal·ci·trant (ri·kal′sə·trənt) adj. Not complying; obsti-nate; rebellious; refractory. —n. One who is recalcitrant. [< L re- back + calcitrare to kick] —re·cal′ci·trance, re·cal′-ci·tran·cy n.

re·call (ri·kôl′) v.t. 1 To call back; order or summon to return. 2 To summon back in awareness or attention. 3 To recollect; remember. 4 To take back; revoke; counter-mand. —n. (ri·kôl′, rē′kôl′) 1 A calling back. 2 An ability to remember. 3 Revocation, as of an order. 4 A system whereby public officials may be removed from office by popular vote.

re·cant (ri·kant′) v.t. 1 To withdraw formally one's belief in (something previously believed or maintained). —v.i. 2 To disavow an opinion or belief previously held. [< L re- again + cantare sing] —re·can·ta·tion (rē′kan·tā′shən), re·cant′er n.

re·cap[1] (rē′kap′, rē·kap′) v.t. ·capped, ·cap·ping 1 To pro-vide (a worn pneumatic tire) with a tread of new rubber. 2 To replace a cap on. —n. (rē′kap′) A tire which has been so treated. [< RE- + CAP]

re·cap[2] (rē′kap′) v.t. & v.i. ·capped, ·cap·ping RECAPITU-LATE. —n. RECAPITULATION (def. 2).

re·ca·pit·u·late (rē′kə·pich′ōō·lāt) v.t. & v.i. ·lat·ed, ·lat-ing To restate or review briefly; sum up. [< LL re- again + capitulare draw up in chapters]

re·ca·pit·u·la·tion (rē′kə·pich′ōō·lā′shən) n. 1 The act of recapitulating. 2 A brief summary. —re′ca·pit′u·la′tive, re′-ca·pit′u·la·to·ry (-lə·tôr′ē, -tō′rē) adj.

re·cap·ture (rē·kap′chər) v.t. ·tured, ·tur·ing 1 To capture again. 2 To recall; remember. —n. The act of recapturing or the state of being recaptured.

re·cast (rē·kast′, -käst′) v.t. ·cast, ·cast·ing 1 To form anew; cast again. 2 To fashion anew by changing style, arrangement, etc., as a sentence. 3 To calculate anew. — n. (rē′kast′, -käst′) Something which has been recast.

recd. received.

re·cede (ri·sēd′) v.i. ·ced·ed, ·ced·ing 1 To move back; withdraw, as flood waters. 2 To withdraw, as from an assertion, position, agreement, etc. 3 To slope backward: a *receding* forehead. 4 To become more distant or smaller. [< L *re-* back + *cedere* go]

re·cede (rē′sēd′) v.t. ·ced·ed, ·ced·ing To cede back; grant or yield to a former owner.

re·ceipt (ri·sēt′) n. 1 The act or state of receiving anything: to be in *receipt* of good news. 2 *Usu. pl.* That which is received: cash *receipts.* 3 A written acknowledgment of the payment of money, of the delivery of goods, etc. 4 RECIPE. —v.t. 1 To give a receipt for the payment of. 2 To write acknowledgment of payment on, as a bill. —v.i. 3 To give a receipt, as for money paid. [< L *receptus,* pp. of *recipere* take back, receive]

re·ceiv·a·ble (ri·sē′və·bəl) adj. 1 Capable of being received; fit to be received, as legal tender. 2 Due to be paid. —n. pl. Outstanding accounts listed as business assets.

re·ceive (ri·sēv′) v. ·ceived, ·ceiv·ing v.t. 1 To take into one's hand or possession (something given, offered, delivered, etc.). 2 To gain knowledge or information of. 3 To take from another by hearing or listening. 4 To bear; support. 5 To experience; meet with: to *receive* abuse. 6 To undergo; suffer: He *received* a wound in his arm. 7 To contain; hold. 8 To allow entrance to; admit; greet. 9 To perceive mentally: to *receive* a bad impression. 10 To regard in a specified way: The play was well *received.* —v.i. 11 To be a recipient. 12 To welcome visitors or callers. 13 *Telecom.* To convert incoming signals, as radio waves, into intelligible sounds or shapes, as in a radio or television set. [< L *re-* back + *capere* take]

re·ceived (ri·sēvd′) adj. *Chiefly Brit.* Accepted by established opinion or authority; standard.

re·ceiv·er (ri·sē′vər) n. 1 One who receives; a recipient. 2 An official assigned to receive money due. 3 *Law* A person appointed by a court to take into his custody the property or funds of another pending litigation. 4 One who knowingly buys or receives stolen goods. 5 Something which receives; a receptacle. 6 *Telecom.* An instrument designed to receive electric or electromagnetic signals and process them or transmit them to another stage.

re·ceiv·er·ship (ri·sē′vər·ship) n. 1 The office and functions pertaining to a receiver. 2 *Law* The state of being in the hands of a receiver.

re·cent (rē′sənt) adj. 1 Of or pertaining to a time not long past. 2 Occurring, formed, or characterized by association with a time not long past; modern; fresh; new. [< L *recens*] —re′cent·ly adv. —re′cen·cy, re′cent·ness n.

Re·cent (rē′sənt) adj. & n. See GEOLOGY.

re·cep·ta·cle (ri·sep′tə·kəl) n. 1 Anything that serves to contain or hold other things. 2 *Bot.* The base on which the parts of a flower grow. 3 An electric outlet. [< L *receptare,* freq. of *recipere* receive]

re·cep·tion (ri·sep′shən) n. 1 The act of receiving, or the state of being received. 2 A formal social entertainment of guests: a wedding *reception.* 3 The manner of receiving a person or persons: a warm *reception.* 4 *Telecom.* The act or process of receiving or, esp., the quality of reproduction achieved: poor radio *reception.*

re·cep·tion·ist (ri·sep′shən·ist) n. A person employed to receive callers, etc., as in a place of business.

re·cep·tive (ri·sep′tiv) adj. 1 Able or inclined to receive favorably; receptive to new ideas. 2 Able to contain or hold. —re·cep′tive·ly adv. —re·cep·tiv·i·ty (rē′sep·tiv′ə·tē), re·cep′tive·ness n.

re·cep·tor (ri·sep′tər) n. A sensory nerve ending adapted to receiving stimuli. [L, receiver]

re·cess (rē′ses, ri·ses′) n. 1 A depression or indentation in any otherwise continuous line or surface, esp. in a wall; niche. 2 A time of cessation from employment or occupation. 3 *Usu. pl.* A quiet and secluded spot; withdrawn or inner place: the *recesses* of the mind. —v. (usu. ri·ses′) v.t. 1 To place in or as in a recess. 2 To make a recess in. 3 To interrupt for a recess. —v.i. 4 To take a recess. [< L *recessus,* pp. of *recedere* go back]

re·ces·sion (ri·sesh′ən) n. 1 The act of receding; a withdrawal. 2 The procession of the clergy, choir, etc., as they leave the chancel after a church service. 3 A temporary economic setback occurring during a period of generally rising prosperity.

re·ces·sion (rē′sesh′ən) n. The act of ceding back, as to a former owner.

re·ces·sion·al (ri·sesh′ən·əl) adj. Of or pertaining to recession. —n. A hymn sung as the choir or clergy leave the chancel.

re·ces·sive (ri·ses′iv) adj. 1 Having a tendency to recede or go back. 2 *Genetics* Designating a hereditary factor that remains latent unless it is present in both members of a pair of chromosomes. —n. *Genetics* 1 A recessive factor or trait. 2 An organism having such factors or traits. —re·ces′sive·ly adv. —re·ces′sive·ness n.

re·cher·ché (rə·sher·shā′) adj. 1 Much sought after; choice; rare. 2 Elegant or refined, usu. to an excessive degree. [F]

re·cid·i·vism (rə·sid′ə·viz′əm) n. A tendency to relapse into a former state or condition, esp. into crime. [< L *recidivus* falling back] —re·cid′i·vist adj., n. —re·cid′i·vis′tic, re·cid′i·vous adj.

rec·i·pe (res′ə·pē) n. 1 A list of ingredients and directions for combining them, as in cooking, pharmacy, etc. 2 The means prescribed for attaining an end. [< L, imperative of *recipere* take]

re·cip·i·ent (ri·sip′ē·ənt) adj. Receiving or ready to receive; receptive. —n. One who or that which receives. —re·cip′i·ence, re·cip′i·en·cy n.

re·cip·ro·cal (ri·sip′rə·kəl) adj. 1 Done or given by each of two to the other; mutual. 2 Mutually interchangeable. 3 Related or corresponding, but in an inverse manner; opposite. 4 *Gram.* Expressive of mutual relationship or action: *One another* is a *reciprocal* phrase. 5 *Math.* Having a product of 1, as a pair of numbers. —n. 1 That which is reciprocal. 2 *Math.* Either of a pair of numbers having 1 as their product. [< L *reciprocus*] —re·cip′ro·cal·ly adv.

re·cip·ro·cate (ri·sip′rə·kāt) v. ·cat·ed, ·cat·ing v.t. 1 To cause to move backward and forward alternately. 2 To give and receive mutually; interchange. 3 To give, feel, do, etc., in return. —v.i. 4 To move backward and forward. 5 To make a return in kind. 6 To give and receive favors, gifts, etc., mutually. [< L *reciprocare* move to and fro] —re·cip′ro·ca′tion, re·cip′ro·ca′tor n. —re·cip′ro·ca′tive, re·cip′ro·ca·to·ry (-kə·tôr′ē, -kə·tō′rē) adj.

rec·i·proc·i·ty (res′ə·pros′ə·tē) n. 1 Reciprocal obligation, action, or relation. 2 A trade relation between two countries by which each makes concessions favoring the importation of the products of the other.

re·cit·al (ri·sīt′l) n. 1 A retelling in detail of an event, etc.; a narration; also, that which is retold. 2 A public delivery of something memorized. 3 A musical or dance program by a single performer or by a small group.

rec·i·ta·tion (res′ə·tā′shən) n. 1 The act of publicly reciting something that has been memorized. 2 That which is recited. 3 The reciting of a lesson in school or the time during a class when this takes place.

rec·i·ta·tive (res′ə·tə·tēv′, rə·sit′ə·tiv) n. *Music* 1 A style of singing that approaches ordinary speech in its rhythms and lack of melodic variation, used in opera and oratorio. 2 A passage so sung. Also *Italian* **re·ci·ta·ti·vo** (rā′chē·tä·tē′vō) —adj. Having the character of a recitative. [< Ital. *recitativo*]

re·cite (ri·sīt′) v. ·cit·ed, ·cit·ing v.t. 1 To declaim or say from memory, esp. formally, as in public or in a class. 2 To tell in particular detail; relate. 3 To enumerate. —v.i. 4 To declaim or speak something from memory. 5 To repeat or be examined in a lesson or part of a lesson in class. [< L *re-* again + *citare* cite] —re·cit′er n.

reck (rek) v.t. & v.i. *Archaic* 1 To heed; mind. 2 To be of concern or interest (to). [< OE *rēccan*]

reck·less (rek′lis) adj. 1 Foolishly heedless of danger; rash. 2 Careless; irresponsible. [< OE *recceleās*] —reck′less·ly adv. —reck′less·ness n.

reck·on (rek′ən) v.t. 1 To count; compute; calculate. 2 To look upon as being; regard. **3** *Regional* To suppose or guess; expect. —*v.i.* **4** To make computation; count up. **5** To rely or depend: with *on* or *upon.* —**reckon with 1** To settle accounts with. **2** To take into consideration; consider. [< OE *recenian* explain] —**reck′on·er** *n.*

reck·on·ing (rek′ən·ing) *n.* **1** The act of counting; computation. **2** A settlement of accounts. **3** Account; bill, as at a hotel. **4** An appraisal or estimate. **5** *Naut.* The calculation of a ship's position.

re·claim (ri·klām′) *v.t.* **1** To bring (a swamp, desert, etc.) into a condition to support cultivation or life, as by draining or irrigating. **2** To obtain (a substance) from used or waste products. **3** To cause to reform. —*n.* The act of reclaiming or state of being reclaimed. [< L *re-* against + *clamare* cry out] —**re·claim′a·ble** *adj.* —**re·claim′er, re·claim′ant** *n.*

re-claim (rē′klām′) *v.t.* To claim again.

rec·la·ma·tion (rek′lə·mā′shən) *n.* **1** The act of reclaiming. **2** Restoration, as to ownership, usefulness, etc.

re·cline (ri·klīn′) *v.t. & v.i.* **·clined, ·clin·ing** To assume or cause to assume a recumbent position; lie or lay down or back. [< L *re-* back + *clinare* lean] —**rec·li·na·tion** (rek′lə·nā′shən), **re·clin′er** *n.*

rec·luse (rek′lōōs, ri·klōōs′) *n.* One who lives in solitude and seclusion; hermit. —*adj.* Secluded or retired from the world. [< L *recludere* shut off] —**re·clu′sion** *n.* —**re·clu′sive** *adj.*

rec·og·ni·tion (rek′əg·nish′ən) *n.* **1** The act of recognizing or the condition of being recognized. **2** Special notice or acknowledgment; attention: His work has received much *recognition.* **3** Acknowledgment and acceptance on the part of one government of the independence and validity of another. —**re·cog·ni·to·ry** (ri·kog′nə·tôr′ē, -tō′rē), **re·cog′ni·tive** *adj.*

re·cog·ni·zance (ri·kog′nə·zəns, -kon′ə-) *n.* *Law* **1** An acknowledgment or obligation of record, with condition to do some particular act, as to appear and answer. **2** A sum of money deposited as surety for fulfillment of such act or obligation, and forfeited by its nonperformance. [< L *recognoscere* call to mind] —**re·cog′ni·zant** *adj.*

rec·og·nize (rek′əg·nīz) *v.t.* **·nized, ·niz·ing 1** To perceive as identical with someone or something previously known. **2** To identify or know, as by previous experience or knowledge: I *recognize* the symptoms. **3** To perceive as true; realize: I *recognize* my error. **4** To acknowledge the independence and validity of, as a newly constituted government. **5** To indicate appreciation or approval of. **6** To regard as valid or genuine: to *recognize* a claim. **7** To give (someone) permission to speak, as in a legislative body. **8** To admit the acquaintance of; greet. [Back formation < RECOGNIZANCE] —**rec·og·niz·a·ble** (rek′əg·nīz′ə·bəl) *adj.* —**rec′og·niz′a·bly** *adv.* —**rec′og·niz′er** *n.* —**Syn. 3** acknowledge, admit, allow.

re·coil (ri·koil′) *v.i.* **1** To start back, as in fear or loathing; shrink. **2** To spring back, as from force of discharge or impact. **3** To return to the source; react: with *on* or *upon.* **4** To move; retreat. —*n.* (rē′koil′) **1** A backward movement or impulse, as of a gun at the moment of firing. **2** A shrinking. [< OF *reculer*] —**re·coil′er** *n.*

re-coil (rē′koil′) *v.t. & v.i.* To coil again.

rec·ol·lect (rek′ə·lekt′) *v.t.* **1** To call back to the mind; remember. —*v.i.* **2** To have a recollection of something. [< L *recollectus,* pp. of *recolligere* gather together again]

re-col·lect (rē′kə·lekt′) *v.t.* **1** To collect again, as things scattered. **2** To collect or recover (one's thoughts, strength, etc.). **3** To compose (oneself). Also, for defs. 2 & 3, **rec·ol·lect** (rek′ə·lekt′). —**re′-col·lec′tion** *n.*

rec·ol·lec·tion (rek′ə·lek′shən) *n.* **1** The act or power of recollecting. **2** Something remembered. —**rec′ol·lec′tive** *adj.* —**rec′ol·lec′tive·ly** *adv.* —**rec′ol·lec′tive·ness** *n.*

rec·om·mend (rek′ə·mend′) *v.t.* **1** To commend or praise as desirable, worthy, etc. **2** To make attractive or acceptable. **3** To advise; urge. **4** To give in charge; commend. —**rec′om·mend′a·ble, rec′om·men·da·to·ry** (-də·tôr′ē, -tōr′ē) *adj.* —**rec′om·mend′er** *n.*

rec·om·men·da·tion (rek′ə·mən·dā′shən, -men-) *n.* **1** The act of recommending. **2** Something that recommends, as a letter or statement.

re·com·mit (rē′kə·mit′) *v.t.* **·mit·ted, ·mit·ting 1** To commit

again. **2** To refer back to a committee, as a bill. —**re′com·mit′ment, re′com·mit′tal** *n.*

rec·om·pense (rek′əm·pens) *v.t.* **·pensed, ·pens·ing 1** To give compensation to; pay or repay; reward. **2** To give compensation for, as a loss. —*n.* An equivalent for anything given, done, or suffered; payment; compensation; reward. [< L *re-* again + *compensare* compensate]

rec·on·cil·a·ble (rek′ən·sī′lə·bəl, rek′ən·sī′-) *adj.* Capable of being reconciled, adjusted, or harmonized. —**rec′on·cil′a·bil′i·ty, rec′on·cil′a·ble·ness** *n.* —**rec′on·cil′a·bly** *adv.*

rec·on·cile (rek′ən·sīl) *v.t.* **·ciled, ·cil·ing 1** To bring back to friendship after estrangement. **2** To settle or adjust, as a quarrel. **3** To bring to acquiescence, content, or submission. **4** To make or show to be consistent or congruous; harmonize. [< L *re-* again + *conciliare* unite] —**rec′on·cile′ment, rec′on·cil·er, rec·on·cil·i·a·tion** (rek′ən·sil′ē·ā′shən) *n.* —**rec′on·cil′i·a·to·ry** (-sil′ē·ə·tôr′ē, -tō′rē) *adj.*

rec·on·dite (rek′ən·dīt, ri·kon′dīt) *adj.* **1** Beyond ordinary or easy understanding or perception; abstruse. **2** Dealing in difficult matters. **3** Hidden; obscure. [< L *recondere* put away, hide] —**rec′on·dite′ly** *adv.* —**rec′on·dite′-ness** *n.*

re·con·di·tion (rē′kən·dish′ən) *v.t.* To put back into good or working condition, as by making repairs.

re·con·nais·sance (ri·kon′ə·səns, -säns) *n.* **1** An exploratory examination or survey, as of territory. **2** *Mil.* The act of obtaining information regarding the position, strength, and movement of enemy forces. [F]

re·con·noi·ter (rē′kə·noi′tər, rek′ə-) *v.t.* **1** To examine or survey, as for military, engineering, or geological purposes. —*v.i.* **2** To make a reconnaissance. *Brit. sp.* **·noi′tre.** [< OF *reconoistre*] —**re′con·noi′ter·er, re′con·noi′trer** *n.*

re·con·sid·er (rē′kən·sid′ər) *v.t. & v.i.* To consider again, esp. with a view to a reversal of a previous action. —**re′·con·sid′er·a′tion** *n.*

re·con·sti·tute (rē·kon′stə·tyōōt) *v.t.* **·tut·ed, ·tut·ing** To constitute again, esp. to add water to a dehydrated or condensed substance. —**re·con′sti·tu′tion** *n.*

re·con·struct (rē′kən·strukt′) *v.t.* To construct again. — **Syn.** rebuild, refashion, reestablish, remodel.

re·con·struc·tion (rē′kən·struk′shən) *n.* **1** The act of reconstructing. **2** Something reconstructed. **3** *Usu. cap.* **a** The restoration of the seceded s States as members of the Union after the American Civil War. **b** The period of this restoration, from 1867–1877. —**re′con·struc′tive** *adj.*

re·con·vert (rē′kən·vûrt′) *v.t.* To change back, as to a former condition, form, religion, etc. —**re′con·ver′sion** (-vûr′zhən) *n.*

rec·ord (rek′ərd) *n.* **1** An account in written or other permanent form serving as evidence of a fact or event. **2** Something on which such an account is made, as a monument. **3** Information preserved and handed down: the heaviest rainfall on *record.* **4** The known career or performance of a person, animal, organization, etc. **5** The best listed achievement, as in a competitive sport. **6** *Law* **a** A written account of an act, statement, or transaction made by an officer acting under authority of law. **b** An official written account of a judicial or legislative proceeding. **7** A disk or cylinder, grooved so as to reproduce sounds that have been registered on its surface. —**go on record** To state publically or officially. —**off the record** Not for quotation or publication. — *adj.* Surpassing any previously recorded achievement or performance of its kind. — **re·cord** (ri·kôrd′) *v.t.* **1** To write down or otherwise inscribe, as for preservation, evidence, etc. **2** To indicate; register. **3** To offer evidence of. **4** To register and make permanently reproducible, as on tape, a phonograph record, etc. —*v.i.* **5** To record something. [< L *recordari* call to mind]

re·cord·er (ri·kôr′dər) *n.* **1** One who records. **2** A magistrate having criminal jurisdiction in a city or borough. **3** A type of flute blown at one end. **4** A device that records, as a tape recorder.

Recorder
def. 3

re·cord·ing (ri·kôr′ding) *n.* **1** The act or process of making a representation from which sound, video, data, etc., can be reproduced. **2** The material so represented.

record player A machine for reproducing sound from a record (def. 7).

re·count[1] (ri·kount′) v.t. **1** To relate the particulars of; narrate in detail. **2** To enumerate; recite. [< OF *reconter* relate] —**re·count′er** n.

re·count[2] (rē′kount′) v.t. To count again. —n. (rē′kount′) An additional count, esp. a second count of votes cast.

re·count·al (ri·koun′təl) n. A detailed narrative.

re·coup (ri·kōōp′) v.t. **1** To recover or make up for, as a loss. **2** To regain, as health. **3** To repay or reimburse. —n. The act of recouping. [< F *re-* again + *couper* to cut] —**re·coup′a·ble** adj. —**re·coup′ment** n.

re·course (rē′kôrs, -kōrs, ri·kôrs′, -kōrs′) n. **1** Resort to or application for help or security in trouble. **2** The person or thing resorted to. [< L *recursus* a running back]

re·cov·er (ri·kuv′ər) v.t. **1** To obtain again, as after losing; regain. **2** To make up for; retrieve, as a loss. **3** To restore (oneself) to natural balance, health, etc. **4** To reclaim, as land. **5** *Law* To gain or regain in judicial proceedings. —v.i. **6** To regain health, composure, etc. **7** *Law* To succeed in a lawsuit. [< L *recuperare*] —**re·cov′er·a·ble** adj.

re·cov·er (rē′kuv′ər) v.t. To cover again.

re·cov·er·y (ri·kuv′ər·ē) n. pl. **·er·ies** **1** The act, process, or an instance of recovering. **2** The duration of recovering. **3** Restoration from sickness or from any undesirable or abnormal condition. **4** The extraction of usable substances and materials from byproducts, waste, etc. **5** The retrieval of a flying object, as a balloon, space vehicle, meteorite, etc., after it has fallen to earth.

rec·re·ant (rek′rē·ənt) adj. **1** Unfaithful to a cause or pledge; false. **2** Craven; cowardly. —n. A cowardly or faithless person; also, a deserter. [< L *re-* back + *credere* believe] —**rec′re·ance, rec′re·an·cy** n. —**rec′re·ant·ly** adv.

rec·re·ate[1] (rek′rē·āt) v. **·at·ed, ·at·ing** v.t. **1** To impart fresh vigor to; refresh, esp. after toil. —v.i. **2** To take recreation. [< L *recreare* create anew] —**rec′re·a′tive** adj.

re·cre·ate[2] (rē′krē·āt′) v.t. **·at·ed, ·at·ing** To create anew. —**re′cre·a′tion** n.

rec·re·a·tion (rek′rē·ā′shən) n. **1** Refreshment of body or mind, esp. after work; diversion; amusement. **2** Any pleasurable exercise or occupation. —**rec′re·a′tion·al** adj.

re·crim·i·nate (ri·krim′ə·nāt) v. **·nat·ed, ·nat·ing** v.t. **1** To accuse in return. —v.i. **2** To repel one accusation by making another in return. [< L *re-* again + *criminare* accuse] —**re·crim′i·na′tor** n. —**re·crim′i·na′tive, re·crim·i·na·to·ry** (ri·krim′ə·nə·tôr′ē, -tō′rē) adj.

re·crim·i·na·tion (ri·krim′ə·nā′shən) n. **1** The act of recriminating. **2** An accusation made in response to another.

re·cru·desce (rē′krōō·des′) v.i. **·desced, ·desc·ing** To reappear after lying dormant. [< L *re-* again + *crudescere* become harsh, break out] —**re′cru·des′cence** n. —**re′cru·des′cent** adj.

re·cruit (ri·krōōt′) v.t. **1** To enlist (men or women) for service, as in a military organization or a police force. **2** To muster; raise, as an army, by enlistment. **3** To enlist the aid, services, or support of: to *recruit* new members for a political party. **4** To replenish. —v.i. **5** To enlist new personnel for service, as in an army or other organization. **6** To gain or raise new supplies of anything lost or needed. —n. **1** A newly enlisted person, as a soldier or sailor. **2** Any new adherent of a cause, organization, or the like. [< F *recrute*] —**re·cruit′er, re·cruit′ment** n.

rec. sec. recording secretary.

rect. receipt; rectangle; rector; rectory.

rec·tal (rek′təl) adj. Pertaining to, for, or in the region of the rectum.

rec·tan·gle (rek′tang′gəl) n. A parallelogram with all angles right angles. [< L *rectus* straight + *angulus* angle] • See PARALLELOGRAM.

rec·tan·gu·lar (rek·tang′gyə·lər) adj. **1** Having right angles. **2** Resembling a rectangle. —**rec·tan′gu·lar′i·ty** (-lar′ə·tē) n. —**rec·tan′gu·lar·ly** adv.

recti- *combining form* Straight: *rectilinear*. [< L *rectus* straight]

rec·ti·fi·er (rek′tə·fī′ər) n. **1** One who or that which rectifies. **2** *Electr.* A device that conducts in only one direction.

rec·ti·fy (rek′tə·fī) v.t. **·fied, ·fy·ing** **1** To make right; correct; amend. **2** *Chem.* To refine or purify, as a liquid, by distillation. **3** *Electr.* To change (an alternating current) into a direct current. **4** To allow for errors or inaccuracies in, as a compass reading. [< L *rectus* right + *facere* make] —**rec′ti·fi′a·ble** adj. —**rec′ti·fi·ca′tion** (-tə·fə·kā′shən) n.

rec·ti·lin·e·ar (rek′tə·lin′ē·ər) adj. Pertaining to, consisting of, moving in, or bounded by a straight line or lines; straight. Also **rec′ti·lin′e·al.** —**rec′ti·lin′e·ar·ly** adv.

rec·ti·tude (rek′tə·t^yōōd) n. **1** Uprightness in principles and conduct. **2** Correctness of judgment, method, etc. [< L *rectus* right]

rec·tor (rek′tər) n. **1** In the Church of England, a priest who has full charge of a parish. **2** In the Protestant Episcopal Church, a priest in charge of a parish. **3** In the Roman Catholic Church: **a** A priest in charge of a congregation or church. **b** The head of a seminary or university. **4** In certain universities, colleges, and schools, the headmaster or principal. [< L *rectus*, pp. of *regere* rule] —**rec′tor·ate** (-it) n. —**rec·to·ri·al** (rek·tôr′ē·əl, -tō′rē-) adj.

rec·to·ry (rek′tər·ē) n. pl. **·ries** **1** A rector's dwelling. **2** In England, a parish domain with its buildings, revenue, etc.

rec·tum (rek′təm) n. pl. **·tums** or **·ta** (-tə) The terminal part of the large intestine ending at the anus. [< NL *rectum (intestinum)* straight (intestine)]

re·cum·bent (ri·kum′bənt) adj. **1** Lying down, wholly or partly. **2** Resting; inactive. [< L *re-* back + *cumbere* lie] —**re·cum′bence, re·cum′ben·cy** n.

re·cu·per·ate (ri·k^yōō′pə·rāt) v. **·at·ed, ·at·ing** v.i. **1** To regain health or strength. **2** To recover from loss, as of money. —v.t. **3** To obtain again after loss; recover. **4** To restore to vigor and health. [< L *recuperare*] —**re·cu′per·a′tion, re·cu′per·a′tor** n. —**re·cu′per·a′tive** adj.

re·cur (ri·kûr′) v.i. **·curred, ·cur·ring** **1** To happen again or repeatedly. **2** To come back or return, as to the memory, in conversation, etc. [< L *re-* back + *currere* run]

re·cur·rent (ri·kûr′ənt) adj. **1** Happening or appearing again or repeatedly; recurring. **2** Turning back toward the source, as certain arteries and nerves. —**re·cur′rence, re·cur′ren·cy** n. —**re·cur′rent·ly** adv.

re·curve (ri·kûrv′) v.t. & v.i. **·curved, ·curv·ing** To curve or bend backward. [< L *re-* back + *curvus* curved] —**re·cur′·vate** (-kûr′vit, -vāt) adj.

re·cy·cle (rē·sī′kəl) v.t. **·cy·cled, ·cy·cling** To reclaim (waste materials, as used newsprint, glass bottles, etc.) by using in the manufacture of new products. —**re·cy′cla·ble** adj.

red (red) adj. **red·der, red·dest** **1** Having or being of a bright color resembling blood. **2** Of a hue approximating red: *red* hair. **3** Ultraradical in politics, esp. communistic. —n. **1** One of the primary colors, occurring at the opposite end of the spectrum from violet; the color of fresh human blood. **2** A hue or tint that approximates primary red. **3** Any pigment or dye having or giving this color. **4** A red animal or object. **5** *Often cap.* An ultraradical or revolutionary in politics, esp. a communist: from the red banner of revolution. —**in the red** *Informal* Operating at a loss; owing money. —**see red** To be very angry. [< OE *rēad*] —**red′dish** adj. —**red′ly** adv. —**red′ness** n.

red. reduce; reduction.

re·dact (ri·dakt′) v.t. **1** To prepare, as for publication; edit; revise. **2** To draw up or frame, as a message or edict. [< L *redactus*, pp. of *redigere* lead back, restore] —**re·dac′tion, re·dac′tor** n.

red algae A class of marine algae having predominantly red pigment and usu. mosslike growth.

red·bait (red′bāt′) v.t. To denounce as being communist. —**red′bait′er** n.

red·bird (red′bûrd′) n. Any of various birds with red plumage in the male, as cardinals, certain tanagers, etc.

red-blood·ed (red′blud′id) adj. Having vitality and vigor. —**red′-blood′ed·ness** n.

red·breast (red′brest′) n. A robin.

red·cap (red′kap′) n. A porter, as in a railroad or airline terminal.

---

add, āce, câre, pälm; end, ēven; it, īce; odd, ōpen, ôrder; tŏŏk, pōōl; up, bûrn; ə = a in *above*, u in *focus*; yōō = u in *fuse*; oil; pout; check; go; ring; thin; this; zh, *vision*. < derived from; ? origin uncertain or unknown.

red carpet A long red carpet traditionally used for important guests to walk on. —**red′-car′pet** *adj.*

Red China *Informal* The People's Republic of China.

red·coat (red′kōt′) *n.* **1** A British soldier during the American Revolution and the War of 1812. **2** *Can.* MOUNTIE.

red corpuscle ERYTHROCYTE.

Red Cross 1 An international society for bringing aid to victims of a war or disaster. **2** Any national branch of this society. **3** Their emblem, a red Greek cross on a white ground, symbol of neutrality.

red deer 1 A common deer of Europe and Asia. **2** The white-tailed deer in its summer coat.

red·den (red′n) *v.t.* **1** To make red. —*v.i.* **2** To grow red, esp. to blush.

re·deem (ri·dēm′) *v.t.* **1** To regain possession of by paying a price. **2** To pay off, as a promissory note. **3** To convert into cash or a premium: to *redeem* stocks or trading stamps. **4** To set free; ransom. **5** *Theol.* To rescue from sin and its penalties. **6** To fulfill, as an oath or promise. **7** To make worthwhile. [< L *re-* back + *emere* buy] —**re·deem′a·ble, re·demp′ti·ble** (-demp′tə·bəl) *adj.*

re·deem·er (ri·dē′mər) *n.* One who redeems. —**the Redeemer** Jesus Christ.

re·demp·tion (ri·demp′shən) *n.* **1** The act of redeeming, or the state of being redeemed. **2** The recovery of what is mortgaged or pawned. **3** The payment of a debt or obligation, esp. the paying of the value of its notes, warrants, etc., by a government. **4** Deliverance or rescue, as by paying a ransom. —**re·demp′tive, re·demp′to·ry** *adj.*

re·de·ploy (rē′di·ploi′) *v.t.* To transfer (troops) from one zone of combat to another. —**re′de·ploy′ment** *n.*

re·de·vel·op (rē′di·vel′əp) *v.t.* **1** To develop again. **2** To rebuild, as a slum area. **3** *Phot.* To intensify with chemicals and put through a second developing process. —*v.i.* **4** To develop again. —**re′de·vel′op·er, re′de·vel′op·ment** *n.*

red·eye (red′ī′) *n. Slang* Inferior whiskey.

red-hand·ed (red′han′did) *adj.* **1** Having just committed any crime. **2** Caught in the act of doing some particular thing. —**red′-hand′ed·ly** *adv.* —**red′-hand′ed·ness** *n.*

red·head (red′hed′) *n.* **1** A person with red hair. **2** A North American duck, the male of which has a red head. —**red′head′ed** *adj.*

redheaded woodpecker A North American woodpecker having a red head and neck.

red herring 1 Smoked herring. **2** An irrelevant topic introduced in order to divert attention from the main point under discussion.

red-hot (red′hot′) *adj.* **1** Heated to redness. **2** New; fresh. **3** Marked by excitement, agitation, or enthusiasm.

red·in·gote (red′ing·gōt) *n.* An outer coat with long full skirts. [F< E *riding coat*]

re·dis·trict (rē′dis′trikt) *v.t.* To redraw the district boundaries of.

red lead (led) An oxide of lead, used as a red pigment.

red-let·ter (red′let′ər) *adj.* Happy or memorable: from the use on calendars of red letters to indicate holidays.

red light A traffic signal light meaning stop.

red-light district (red′līt′) That part of a city or town in which brothels are numerous: from the former use of red lights to mark brothels.

red man An American Indian.

red·neck (red′nek′) *n.* A white, usu. uneducated laborer of the South: a disparaging term. Also **red′-neck′.**

red·o·lent (red′ə·lənt) *adj.* **1** Fragrant; odorous. **2** Smelling: with *of:* a swamp *redolent* of decay. **3** Evocative: with *of: redolent* of the past. [< L *redolere* emit a smell] —**red′o·lence, red′o·len·cy** *n.* —**red′o·lent·ly** *adv.*

re·doub·le (rē·dub′əl) *v.t. & v.i.* **·led, ·ling 1** To make or become double. **2** To increase greatly. **3** To echo or re-echo. **4** To fold or double back again. **5** In bridge, to double (an opponent's double).

re·doubt (ri·dout′) *n.* **1** A temporary fortification, as to defend a pass, a hilltop, etc. **2** Any place providing protection; stronghold. [< Med. L *reductus*, lit., a refuge]

re·doubt·a·ble (ri·dou′tə·bəl) *adj.* **1** Inspiring fear; formidable. **2** Deserving respect or deference. Also **re·doubt′·ed.** [< L *re-* thoroughly + *dubitare* doubt] —**re·doubt′a·ble·ness** *n.* —**re·doubt′a·bly** *adv.*

re·dound (ri·dound′) *v.i.* **1** To have an effect or result. **2** To return; reflect. —*n.* A return by way of consequence; result. [< L *redundare* to overflow]

red pepper 1 Any of various capsicums having fruit that is red when ripe. **2** Such a fruit, or a condiment made from it, as cayenne, pimiento, etc.

red·poll (red′pōl′) *n.* A small finch of northern regions, having a reddish crown.

re·dress (ri·dres′) *v.t.* **1** To set right or make reparation for, as a wrong, by compensation or by punishment. **2** To make reparation to; compensate. **3** To remedy; correct. —*n.* (rē′dres, ri·dres′) **1** Satisfaction for wrong done; reparation; amends. **2** A restoration; correction. [< F *redresser* straighten] —**re·dress′er** or **re·dres′sor** *n.*

red shift *Astron.* Displacement toward the red or low-frequency end of the spectrum of light or radio waves from a celestial body that is receding at high velocity.

red snapper Any of various reddish, marine fish highly esteemed as food.

red·start (red′stärt′) *n.* Any of various small warblers having red markings. [< RED + obs. *start* tail]

Red snapper

red tape Rigid official regulations, forms, or procedure involving delay or inaction: from the former practice of tying public documents with red tape.

red·top (red′top′) *n.* Any of certain grasses used for lawns and pasturage.

re·duce (ri·dyo̅o̅s′) *v.* **·duced, ·duc·ing** *v.t.* **1** To make less in size, amount, number, intensity, etc.; diminish. **2** To bring into a certain system or order; classify. **3** To bring to a lower condition; degrade. **4** To bring to submission; subdue; conquer. **5** To bring to a specified condition or state: with *to:* to *reduce* rock to powder; *reduced* to tears. **6** To thin (paint, etc.) with oil or turpentine. **7** *Math.* To change (an expression) to a more elementary form. **8** *Chem.* **a** To remove oxygen from (a compound). **b** To add electrons to (an atom). **c** To decrease the positive valence of (an atom). **9** *Phot.* To diminish the density of (a photographic negative). —*v.i.* **10** To become less in any way. **11** To decrease one's weight, as by dieting. [< L *re-* back + *ducere* lead] —**re·duc′er, re·duc′i·bil′i·ty** *n.* —**re·duc′i·ble** *adj.* —**re·duc′i·bly** *adv.*

reducing agent *Chem.* Any substance that reduces another substance and is thereby oxidized in a chemical reaction.

re·duc·ti·o ad ab·sur·dum (ri·duk′tē·ō ad ab·sûr′dəm, -shē·ō) Disproof of a proposition by showing that it is self-contradictory. [L, lit., reduction to absurdity]

re·duc·tion (ri·duk′shən) *n.* **1** The act or process of reducing. **2** Something that results from reducing. **3** The amount by which something is reduced. —**re·duc′tion·al, re·duc′tive** *adj.*

re·dun·dan·cy (ri·dun′dən·sē) *n. pl.* **·cies 1** The condition or quality of being redundant. **2** Something redundant, esp. unnecessary repetition. **3** Excess; surplus. **4** In information theory, repeated information in a message, used to lessen the probability of error. Also **re·dun′dance.**

re·dun·dant (ri·dun′dənt) *adj.* **1** Being more than is required; constituting an excess. **2** Unnecessarily repetitive or verbose. [< L *redundare* to overflow] —**re·dun′dant·ly** *adv.* —*Syn.* **1** superfluous, excessive, inordinate, undue. **2** repetitious, iterative, reiterative, wordy.

re·du·pli·cate (ri·dyo̅o̅′plə·kāt) *v.* **·cat·ed, ·cat·ing** *v.t.* **1** To repeat again and again; copy; iterate. **2** *Ling.* To affix a reduplication to. —*v.i.* **3** To undergo reduplication. —*adj.* (-kit) Repeated again and again; duplicated. —**re·du′pli·ca′tive** *adj.*

re·du·pli·ca·tion (ri·dyo̅o̅′plə·kā′shən) *n.* **1** The act of reduplicating, or the state of being reduplicated; a redoubling. **2** *Ling.* **a** The repetition of an initial element or elements in a word. **b** The doubling of all or part of a word, often with vowel or consonant change, as in *fiddle-faddle.*

red·wing (red′wing′) *n.* **1** A North American blackbird with red and yellow wing patches in the male: also **red-winged blackbird. 2** An Old World thrush with reddish orange on its wings.

red·wood (red′wo̅o̅d′) *n.* **1** SEQUOIA. **2** Its wood.

reed (rēd) n. 1 The slender, frequently jointed stem of certain tall grasses growing in wet places; also, the grasses themselves. 2 *Music* a A thin, elastic plate of reed, wood, or metal nearly closing an opening, as in a pipe, used in reed organs, reed pipes of pipe organs, and some woodwind instruments, to produce a musical tone when vibrated by air. b An instrument having such a reed or reeds. 3 A crude musical pipe made of the hollow stem of a plant. 4 *Archit.* REEDING. 5 A comblike device on a loom that keeps the warp yarns evenly separated. —v.t. 1 To fashion into or decorate with reeds. 2 To thatch with reeds. —adj. *Music* Equipped with a reed or reeds. [< OE *hrēod*]

reed·ing (rē'ding) n. *Archit.* 1 Small, convex molding. 2 Parallel ornamentation using such molding.

reed organ A keyboard musical instrument sounding by means of reeds that vibrate freely in response to air currents.

re·ed·u·cate (rē·ej'oō·kāt) v.t. ·cat·ed, ·cat·ing 1 To educate again. 2 To rehabilitate, as a criminal, by education. —re'ed·u·ca'tion n.

reed·y (rē'dē) adj. reed·i·er, reed·i·est 1 Full of reeds. 2 Like a reed. 3 Having a tone like that of a reed instrument. —reed'i·ness n.

reef[1] (rēf) n. 1 A ridge of sand or rocks, or esp. of coral, at or near the surface of the water. 2 A lode, vein, or ledge. [< ON *rif* rib, reef] —reef'y adj. • See ATOLL.

reef[2] (rēf) *Naut.* n. 1 The part of a sail that is folded and secured or untied and let out in regulating its size on the mast. 2 The tuck taken in a sail when reefed. —v.t. 1 To reduce (a sail) by folding a part and tying it to a yard or boom. 2 To shorten or lower, as a topmast, by taking part of it in. [Prob. < ON *rif* rib]

reef·er[1] (rē'fər) n. 1 One who reefs. 2 A short, double-breasted coat or jacket.

reef·er[2] (rē'fər) n. *Slang* A marihuana cigarette. [?]

reef knot SQUARE KNOT.

reek (rēk) v.i. 1 To give off smoke, vapor, etc. 2 To give off a strong, offensive smell. 3 To be pervaded with anything offensive. —v.t. 4 To expose to smoke or its action. 5 To give off; emit. [< OE *rēocan*] —reek'er n. —reek'y adj. (·i·er, ·i·est)

reel[1] (rēl) n. 1 A rotatory device or frame for winding rope, cord, photographic film, or other flexible substance. 2 Such a device attached to a fishing rod. 3 The length of wire, film, thread, etc., wound on one reel. —v.t. 1 To wind on a reel or bobbin, as a line. 2 To draw in by reeling a line: with *in:* to *reel* a fish in. 3 To say, do, etc., easily and fluently: with *off.* [< OE *hrēol*] —reel'a·ble adj. —reel'er n.

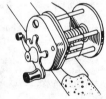

Fishing reel

reel[2] (rēl) v.i. 1 To stagger, sway, or lurch, as when giddy or drunk. 2 To whirl round and round. 3 To have a sensation of giddiness or whirling: My head *reels.* 4 To waver or fall back, as attacking troops. —v.t. 5 To cause to reel. —n. A staggering motion; giddiness. [< REEL[1]] —reel'er n.

reel[3] (rēl) n. 1 A lively Scottish dance. 2 The music for such a dance. [?< REEL[1]]

re·en·force (rē'in·fôrs', -en-, -fōrs') v. ·forced, ·forc·ing REINFORCE.

re·en·try (rē·en'trē) n. 1 The act of entering again. 2 In whist and bridge, a card by which a player can regain the lead. 3 The return into the atmosphere of an object launched into space from the earth.

reeve[1] (rēv) v.t. reeved or rove (for p.p. also rov·en), reev·ing *Naut.* 1 To pass, as a rope or rod, through a hole, block, or aperture. 2 To fasten in such manner. 3 To pass a rope, etc., through (a block or pulley). [?< Du. *reven* reef a sail]

reeve[2] (rēv) n. In Canada, an elected official who presides over the council in certain villages and townships. [< OE *gerēfa* steward]

ref. referee; reference; referred; refining; reformed.

re·fec·tion (ri·fek'shən) n. 1 Refreshment by food and drink. 2 A light meal. [< L *refectus,* pp. of *reficere* remake, refresh]

re·fec·to·ry (ri·fek'tər·ē) n. pl. ·ries A room for eating, esp. in a monastery, convent, or college. [< Med. L *refectorium*]

re·fer (ri·fûr') v. ·ferred, ·fer·ring v.t. 1 To direct or send for information or other purpose. 2 To hand over for consideration, settlement, etc. 3 To assign or attribute to a source, cause, group, class, etc. —v.i. 4 To make reference; allude. 5 To turn, as for information, help, or authority. [< L *re*- back + *ferre* bear, carry] —ref·er·a·ble (ref'ər·ə·bəl, ri·fûr'-), re·fer'ra·ble or re·fer'ri·ble adj. —re·fer'rer n.

ref·er·ee (ref'ə·rē') n. 1 A person to whom a thing is referred for judgment or decision. 2 An official who sees that the rules of certain sports events are observed. —v.t. & v.i. To judge as a referee.

ref·er·ence (ref'ər·əns, ref'rəns) n. 1 The act of referring. 2 An incidental allusion or direction of the attention. 3 A note or other indication in a book, referring to some other book or passage. 4 One who or that which is or may be referred to. 5 A book or other source intended to be referred to for information, as a dictionary. 6 Relation: in *reference* to your inquiry. 7 A person to whom an employer may refer for information about a potential employee. 8 A written statement or testimonial referring to character or dependability. —ref·er·en·tial (-ər·en'shəl) adj. —ref'er·en'tial·ly adv.

ref·er·en·dum (ref'ə·ren'dəm) n. pl. ·dums or ·da (-də) 1 The submission of a proposed public measure or law, which has been passed upon by a legislature or convention, to a vote of the people for ratification or rejection. 2 The vote itself. [L, gerund of *referre* refer]

ref·er·ent (ref'ər·ənt) n. Something referred to, esp. the thing to which reference is made in any verbal statement.

re·fer·ral (ri·fûr'əl) n. 1 The act of referring or the condition of being referred. 2 One who has been referred.

re·fill (rē·fil') v.t. & v.i. To fill or become filled again. —n. (rē'fil') Any commodity packaged to fit and fill a container originally containing that commodity. —re·fill'a·ble adj.

re·fine (ri·fīn') v. ·fined, ·fin·ing v.t. 1 To make fine or pure. 2 To make more elegant, polished, etc. 3 To improve or perfect. —v.i. 4 To become fine or pure. 5 To become more polished or cultured. 6 To make fine distinctions; use subtlety in thought or speech. [< RE- + FINE[1], v.] —re·fin'er n.

re·fined (ri·fīnd') adj. 1 Characterized by refinement or polish. 2 Free from impurity. 3 Exceedingly precise or exact; subtle.

re·fine·ment (ri·fīn'mənt) n. 1 The act or process of refining. 2 The result of refining, esp. an improvement. 3 Fineness of thought, taste, language, etc.; freedom from coarseness or vulgarity. 4 A nice distinction; subtlety.

re·fin·er·y (ri·fī'nər·ē) n. pl. ·er·ies A plant for extracting useful products from raw material, as metal from ore, etc.

re·fit (rē·fit') v.t. & v.i. ·fit·ted, ·fit·ting To make or be made fit or ready again, as by making or obtaining repairs, replacing equipment, etc. —n. The repair of damages or wear, esp. of a ship.

refl. reflection; reflex; reflexive.

re·flect (ri·flekt') v.t. 1 To turn or throw back, as rays of light, heat, or sound. 2 To produce a symmetrically reversed image of, as a mirror. 3 To cause or bring as a result: with *on:* He *reflects* credit on his teacher. 4 To show or manifest: His writings *reflect* great imagination. —v.i. 5 To send back rays, as of light or heat. 6 To return in rays. 7 To give back an image; also, to be mirrored. 8 To think carefully; ponder. 9 To bring blame, discredit, etc.: with *on* or *upon.* [< L *re*- back + *flectere* bend]

re·flec·tion (ri·flek'shən) n. 1 The act of reflecting, or the state of being reflected. 2 *Physics* The throwing off or back (from a surface) of impinging light, heat, sound, or any form of radiant energy. 3 Reflected rays or an image thrown by reflection. 4 Careful, serious thought or consideration. 5 The result of such thought. 6 Censure; discredit; also, a remark or action tending to discredit. —re·flec'tion·al adj.

re·flec·tive (re·flek'tiv) adj. 1 Given to reflection or thought; meditative. **2** Of or caused by reflection. **3** That reflects. —**re·flec′tive·ly** *adv.* —**re·flec′tive·ness, re′flec·tiv′i·ty** *n.*

re·flec·tor (ri·flek′tər) *n.* One who or that which reflects, esp. a device for reflecting light, heat, sound, etc.

re·flex (rē′fleks) *adj.* **1** Turned, bent, directed, or thrown backward. **2** *Physiol.* Of, pertaining to, or produced by an involuntary action or response. —*n.* **1** Reflection, as of light, or an image produced by reflection. **2** *Physiol.* An involuntary response to a stimulus: also **reflex action. 3** A habitual or automatic reaction. [< L *reflexus* reflected, pp. of *reflectere* bend back]

re·flex·ive (ri·flek′siv) *adj.* **1** REFLEX. **2** *Gram.* **a** Designating a verb whose object is identical with its subject, as "dresses" in "He dresses himself." **b** Designating a pronoun which is the direct object of a reflexive verb. —*n.* A reflexive verb or pronoun. —**re·flex′ive·ly** *adv.* —**re·flex′ive·ness, re·flex·iv·i·ty** (rē′flek·siv′ə·tē) *n.*

ref·lu·ent (ref′lŏŏ·ənt) *adj.* Flowing back; ebbing, as the tide. [< L *re-* back + *fluere* flow] —**ref′lu·ence, ref′lu·en·cy** *n.*

re·flux (rē′fluks′) *n.* A flowing back; ebb; return. [< L *refluxus,* pp. of *refluere* flow back]

re·for·est (rē·fôr′ist, -for′-) *v.t. & v.i.* To replant (an area) with trees. —**re′for·es·ta′tion** *n.*

re·form (ri·fôrm′) *v.t.* **1** To make better by removing abuses, malpractice, etc. **2** To make better morally; persuade or educate from a sinful to a moral life. **3** To put an end to; stop (an abuse, malpractice, etc.). —*v.i.* **4** To give up sin or error; become better. —*n.* A correction or improvement of social or personal evils or errors. [< L *re-* again + *formare* to form] —**re·form′a·tive** *adj.* —**re·form′er** *n.* —**re·form′ist** *adj., n.*

re-form (rē′fôrm′) *v.t. & v.i.* To form again. —**re′-for·ma′tion** *n.*

ref·or·ma·tion (ref′ər·mā′shən) *n.* **1** The act of reforming. **2** The state of being reformed.

Ref·or·ma·tion (ref′ər·mā′shən) *n.* The religious revolution of the 16th century that began by trying to reform Catholicism and ended with the establishment of Protestantism.

re·form·a·to·ry (ri·fôr′mə·tôr′ē, -tō′rē) *adj.* Tending or aiming to reform. —*n. pl.* **·ries** An institution for the reformation and instruction of juvenile offenders: also **reform school.**

re·fract (ri·frakt′) *v.t.* **1** To deflect (a ray) by refraction. **2** *Optics* To determine the degree of refraction of (an eye or lens). [< L *refractus,* pp. of *refringere* turn aside]

re·frac·tion (ri·frak′shən) *n.* *Physics* The change of direction of a ray, as of light or heat, in oblique passage between media of different densities. —**re·frac′tive** *adj.* —**re·frac′tive·ness, re·frac·tiv·i·ty** (rē′frak·tiv′ə·tē), re·frac′tor *n.*

re·frac·to·ry (ri·frak′tər·ē) *adj.* **1** Hard to control; stubborn; obstinate. **2** Resisting heat. **3** Resisting treatment, as a disease. —*n. pl.* **·ries 1** A refractory or obstinate person or thing. **2** Any of various highly heat-resistant materials. [< L *refractarius*] —**re·frac′to·ri·ly** *adv.* —**re·frac′to·ri·ness** *n.*

Light refraction **a. air. b.** glass prism.

re·frain¹ (ri·frān′) *v.i.* To hold oneself back. [< L *refrenare* curb] —**re·frain′er** *n.* —**Syn.** abstain, forbear, forgo, renounce.

re·frain² (ri·frān′) *n.* **1** A phrase or verse repeated at intervals in a poem or a song. **2** The music for a refrain. [< OF *refraindre* to check, repeat]

re·fran·gi·ble (ri·fran′jə·bəl) *adj.* Capable of being refracted, as light. [< RE- + L *frangere* to break] —**re·fran′gi·bil′i·ty, re·fran′gi·ble·ness** *n.*

re·fresh (ri·fresh′) *v.t.* **1** To revive (a person), as with food or rest. **2** To make fresh, clean, cool, etc. **3** To stimulate, as the memory. **4** To renew or replenish with or as with new supplies. —*v.i.* **5** To become fresh again; revive. **6** To take refreshment. —**re·fresh′er** *n.*

refresher course A course for reviewing and learning of recent developments in a profession or field of study.

re·fresh·ing (ri·fresh′ing) *adj.* **1** Serving to refresh. **2** Pleasing because new or unusual. —**re·fresh′ing·ly** *adv.*

re·fresh·ment (ri·fresh′mənt) *n.* **1** The act of refreshing, or the state of being refreshed. **2** That which refreshes. **3** *pl.* Food, or food and drink, served as a light meal.

re·frig·er·ant (ri·frij′ər·ənt) *adj.* **1** Cooling or freezing. **2** Allaying heat or fever. —*n.* **1** Any medicine or material that reduces fever. **2** A substance used to produce refrigeration.

re·frig·er·ate (ri·frij′ə·rāt) *v.t.* **·at·ed, ·at·ing 1** To keep or cause to become cold; cool. **2** To freeze or chill for preservative purposes, as foodstuffs. [< L *re-* thoroughly + *frigerare* to cool] —**re·frig′er·a′tion** *n.* —**re·frig′er·a′tive** *adj., n.* —**re·frig′er·a·to′ry** *adj.*

re·frig·er·a·tor (ri·frij′ə·rā′tər) *n.* A box, cabinet, room, railroad car, etc., equipped with a cooling apparatus for preserving the freshness of perishable foods, etc.

ref·uge (ref′yŏŏj) *n.* **1** Shelter or protection, as from danger or distress. **2** A safe place; asylum. **3** Something that brings relief, lessens difficulties, etc. [< L *refugere* to retreat]

ref·u·gee (ref′yŏŏ·jē′, ref′yŏŏ·jē′) *n.* One who flees to find refuge in another land or place, as from persecution or political danger.

re·ful·gent (ri·ful′jənt) *adj.* Shining; radiant; resplendent. [< L *refulgere* reflect light] —**re·ful′gence, re·ful′gen·cy** *n.* —**re·ful′gent·ly** *adv.*

re·fund¹ (ri·fund′) *v.t.* **1** To give or pay back (money, etc.). **2** To repay (a person). —*v.i.* **3** To make repayment. —*n.* (rē′fund) A repayment; refunding; also, the amount repaid. [< L *refundere* pour back] —**re·fund′er, re·fund′ment** *n.*

re·fund² (rē′fund′) *v.t.* To fund anew.

re·fus·al (ri·fyŏŏ′zəl) *n.* **1** The act of refusing. **2** The privilege or opportunity of accepting or rejecting before others.

re·fuse¹ (ri·fyŏŏz′) *v.* **·fused, ·fus·ing** *v.t.* **1** To decline to do, permit, take, or yield. **2** To decline to fulfill the request or desire of (a person). **3** To balk at jumping over (a ditch, hedge, etc.): said of a horse. —*v.i.* **4** To decline to do, permit, take, or yield something. [< L *refusus,* pp. of *refundere* pour back] —**re·fus′er** *n.*

ref·use² (ref′yŏŏs) *n.* Anything worthless; rubbish. [< OF *refus* refused]

re·fute (ri·fyŏŏt′) *v.t.* **·fut·ed, ·fut·ing 1** To prove the incorrectness or falsity of (a statement). **2** To prove (a person) to be in error; confute. [< L *refutare*] —**re·fut′a·ble** *adj.* —**re·fut′a·bly** *adv.* —**ref·u·ta·tion** (ref′yə·tā′shən), re·fu′tal, re·fut′er *n.*

reg. regiment; region; register; registered; regular; regulation.

re·gain (ri·gān′) *v.t.* **1** To get possession of again. **2** To reach again; get back to. —**re·gain′er** *n.*

re·gal (rē′gəl) *adj.* Belonging to or fit for a king; royal, stately, magnificent, etc. [< L *rex, regis* king] —**re·gal·i·ty** (ri·gal′ə·tē) *n.* —**re′gal·ly** *adv.*

re·gale (ri·gāl′) *v.* **·galed, ·gal·ing** *v.t.* **1** To give unusual pleasure to; delight. **2** To entertain royally or sumptuously; feast. —*v.i.* **3** To feast. [< F *régaler*] —**re·gale′ment** *n.*

re·ga·li·a (ri·gā′lē·ə, -gāl′yə) *n. pl.* **1** The insignia and emblems of royalty, as the crown, scepter, etc. **2** The distinctive symbols, insignia, etc., of any society, order, or rank. **3** Fine clothes; fancy trappings.

re·gard (ri·gärd′) *v.t.* **1** To look at or observe attentively. **2** To look on or think of in a certain way. **3** To take into account; consider. **4** To have relevance to. —*v.i.* **5** To pay attention. **6** To gaze or look. —*n.* **1** A look; gaze. **2** Careful attention; consideration. **3** Respect; esteem. **4** *Usu. pl.* Greetings; good wishes. **5** Reference; relation: with *regard* to your letter. [< OF *regarder* look at]

re·gard·ful (ri·gärd′fəl) *adj.* **1** Having or showing regard; heedful. **2** Respectful. —**re·gard′ful·ly** *adv.* —**re·gard′ful·ness** *n.*

re·gard·ing (ri·gär′ding) *prep.* In reference to; with regard to.

re·gard·less (ri·gärd′lis) *adj.* Having no regard or consideration; heedless; negligent. —*adv. Informal* In spite of everything. —**re·gard′less·ly** *adv.*

re·gat·ta (ri·gat′ə, -gä′tə) *n.* A boat race, or a series of such races. [Ital.]

re·gen·cy (rē′jən·sē) *n. pl.* **·cies 1** The government or office of a regent or body of regents. **2** The period during which a regent or body of regents governs. **3** A body of regents. **4** The district under the rule of a regent. Also **re′gent·ship.**

re·gen·er·ate (ri·jen′ə·rāt) *v.* **·at·ed, ·at·ing** *v.t.* **1** To cause moral and spiritual reformation in. **2** To produce or form anew; reestablish; recreate. **3** *Biol.* To replace (a lost organ or tissue) with new growth. —*v.i.* **4** To form anew; be reproduced. **5** To become spiritually regenerate. **6** To effect regeneration. —*adj.* (ri·jen′ər·it) **1** Having new life; restored. **2** Spiritually renewed; regenerated. —**re·gen′er·a·cy** (-ər·ə·sē), **re·gen′er·a′tion, re·gen′er·a′tor** *n.*

re·gent (rē′jənt) *n.* **1** One who rules in the name and place of a sovereign. **2** One of various officers having charge of education, as of a university or state. [<L *regens,* pr.p. of *regere* rule]

reg·gae (reg′ā, rā′gā) *n.* A popular music of West Indian origin having a rhythm that suggests both blues and rock.

reg·i·cide (rej′ə·sīd) *n.* **1** The killing of a king. **2** The killer of a king. [<L *rex, regis* king + -CIDE] —**reg′i·ci′dal** *adj.*

re·gime (ri·zhēm′) *n.* **1** System of government or administration. **2** A particular government or its duration of rule. **3** A social system. **4** REGIMEN. Also **ré·gime** (rā·zhēm′). [< F<L *regimen*]

reg·i·men (rej′ə·mən) *n.* A system of diet, exercise, etc., used for therapeutic purposes. [<L *regimen<regere* to rule]

reg·i·ment (rej′ə·mənt) *n.* A military unit larger than a battalion and smaller than a division. —*v.t.* **1** To form into a regiment or regiments; organize. **2** To assign to a regiment. **3** To form into well-defined or specific units or groups; systematize. **4** To make uniform. [<LL *regimentum<L regere* to rule] —**reg′i·men′tal** *adj.* —**reg′i·men·ta′-tion** *n.*

reg·i·men·tals (rej′ə·men′təlz) *n. pl.* **1** Military uniform. **2** The uniform worn by the men and officers of a regiment.

re·gion (rē′jən) *n.* **1** An indefinite, usu. large portion of territory or space. **2** A specific area or place. **3** A specified area of activity, interest, etc.: the *region* of art. **4** A portion of the body. [<L *regio<regere* to rule]

re·gion·al (rē′jən·əl) *adj.* **1** Of or pertaining to a particular region; sectional; local: *regional* planning. **2** Of or pertaining to an entire region or section. —**re′gion·al·ly** *adv.*
• In this dictionary the label *Regional* is applied to terms used chiefly or exclusively within a particular region of the U.S., and constituting a part of that region's distinctive variety of speech or dialect. A user of regional speech should be aware that terms so labeled may be misunderstood or considered odd or illiterate in other parts of the country.

reg·is·ter (rej′is·tər) *n.* **1** An official record, as of names, events, transactions, etc. **2** The book containing such a record. **3** An item in such a record. **4** Any of various devices for adding or recording: a cash *register.* **5** REGISTRAR. **6** A device for regulating the admission of heated air to a room. **7** *Music* **a** The range or compass of a voice or instrument. **b** A series of tones of a particular quality or belonging to a particular portion of the compass of a voice or instrument. **8** *Printing* **a** Exact correspondence of the lines and margins on the opposite sides of a printed sheet. **b** Correct imposition of the colors in color printing. —*v.t.* **1** To enter in or as in a register; enroll or record officially. **2** To indicate on a scale. **3** To express or indicate: His face *registered* disapproval. **4** *Printing* To effect exact correspondence or imposition of. **5** To cause (mail) to be recorded, on payment of a fee, so as to insure delivery. —*v.i.* **6** To enter one's name in a register, poll, etc. **7** To have effect; make an impression. **8** *Printing* To be in register. [<L *regestus,* pp. of *regerere* register] —**reg·is·tra·ble** (rej′is·trə·bəl) *adj.* —**reg′is·trant** (-trənt) *n.*

reg·is·tered (rej′is·tərd) *adj.* **1** Recorded, as a birth, a voter, an animal's pedigree, etc. **2** Officially or formally qualified.

reg·is·trar (rej′is·trär) *n.* An authorized keeper of a register or of records, esp. of a college or court.

reg·is·tra·tion (rej′is·trā′shən) *n.* **1** The act of register-ing, as of voters, students, etc. **2** The number of persons registered. **3** An entry in a register.

reg·is·try (rej′is·trē) *n. pl.* **·tries 1** REGISTRATION. **2** A register, or the place where it is kept. **3** The nationality of a ship as entered in a register.

reg·nant (reg′nənt) *adj.* **1** Reigning in one's own right. **2** Predominant. **3** Widespread. [<L *regnum* reign]

re·gress (ri·gres′) *v.i.* **1** To go back; move backward; return. —*n.* (rē′gres) **1** A going back; return. **2** A return to a less perfect or lower state; retrogression. [<L *regressus,* pp. of *regredi* go back] —**re·gres′sive** *adj.* —**re·gres′sive·ly** *adv.* —**re·gres′sor** *n.*

re·gres·sion (ri·gresh′ən) *n.* **1** The act of regressing. **2** A return to a less perfect or lower state; retrogression. **3** *Psychoanal.* A retreat to earlier or infantile behavior.

re·gret (ri·gret′) *v.t.* **·gret·ted, ·gret·ting 1** To look back upon with a feeling of distress or loss. **2** To feel sorrow or grief concerning. —*n.* **1** Distress of mind in recalling some past event, act, loss, etc. **2** Remorseful sorrow; compunction. **3** *pl.* A polite refusal in response to an invitation. [< OF *regreter*] —**re·gret′ter** *n.*

re·gret·ful (ri·gret′fəl) *adj.* Feeling, expressive of, or full of regret. —**re·gret′ful·ly** *adv.* —**re·gret′ful·ness** *n.* —**Syn.** sorry, remorseful, contrite, apologetic.

re·gret·ta·ble (ri·gret′ə·bəl) *adj.* Deserving regret; unfortunate. —**re·gret′ta·bly** *adv.*

regt. regiment.

reg·u·lar (reg′yə·lər) *adj.* **1** Made, formed, or arranged according to a rule, standard, or type; symmetrical; normal. **2** Methodical; orderly: *regular* habits. **3** Conforming to a fixed or proper procedure or principle. **4** Customary; habitual: his *regular* breakfast. **5** Officially authorized. **6** Without variation or abnormality: His pulse is *regular.* **7** Thorough; unmitigated: a *regular* bore. **8** *Informal* Pleasant, good, honest, etc.: a *regular* guy. **9** *Gram.* Undergoing the inflection that is normal or most common. **10** *Bot.* Having all similar parts or organs of the same shape and size: said mainly of flowers. **11** *Eccl.* Belonging to a religious order: the *regular* clergy. **12** *Mil.* Pertaining or belonging to the permanent army. **13** In politics, designating, nominated by, or loyal to the official party organization or platform. **14** *Geom.* Having equal sides and angles. **15** *Math.* Controlled or formed by one law or operation throughout. —*n.* **1** A soldier belonging to a permanent or standing army. **2** In sports, a starting member of a team. **3** An habitual customer, patron, etc. **4** A clothing size for those of average height and weight. **5** *Eccl.* A member of a religious order. **6** A person loyal to a certain political party. [<L *regula* rule] —**reg·u·lar′i·ty** *n.* —**reg′u·lar·ly** *adv.*

reg·u·lar·ize (reg′yə·lə·rīz′) *v.t.* **·ized, ·iz·ing** To make regular. —**reg′u·lar·i·za′tion** *n.*

reg·u·late (reg′yə·lāt) *v.t.* **·lat·ed, ·lat·ing 1** To direct, manage, or control according to certain rules, principles, etc. **2** To adjust according to a standard, degree, etc.: to *regulate* currency. **3** To adjust to accurate operation. **4** To put in order; set right. [<L *regula* a rule<*regere* rule, lead straight] —**reg′u·la·tive, reg′u·la·to′ry** (-lə·tôr′ē, -tō′rē) *adj.*

reg·u·la·tion (reg′yə·lā′shən) *n.* **1** The act of regulating, or the state of being regulated. **2** A prescribed rule of conduct or procedure. —*adj.* **1** Required by rule or regulation. **2** Normal; customary.

reg·u·la·tor (reg′yə·lā′tər) *n.* **1** One who or that which regulates. **2** A device for regulating the speed of a watch. **3** A contrivance for controlling motion, flow, voltage, etc.

re·gur·gi·tate (rē·gûr′jə·tāt) *v.* **·tat·ed, ·tat·ing** *v.i.* **1** To flow backward. —*v.t.* **2** To cause to surge back, as partially digested food to the mouth from the stomach. [<LL *re-* back + *gurgitare* flood, engulf] —**re·gur′gi·tant** *adj.* —**re·gur′gi·ta′tion** *n.*

re·ha·bil·i·tate (rē′hə·bil′ə·tāt, rē′ə-) *v.t.* **·tat·ed, ·tat·ing 1** To restore to a former state, capacity, privilege, rank, etc.; reinstate. **2** To restore to health or normal activity. [< Med. L *rehabilitare*] —**re′ha·bil′i·ta′tion** *n.*

re·hash (rē·hash′) *v.t.* To work into a new form; go over again. —*n.* (rē′hash′) The act or result of rehashing.

re·hears·al (ri·hûr′səl) n. 1 The act of rehearsing, as for a play. 2 The act of reciting or telling over again.

re·hearse (ri·hûrs′) v. **·hearsed**, **·hears·ing** v.t. 1 To practice privately in preparation for public performance, as a play or song. 2 To instruct or direct (a person) by way of preparation. 3 To say over again; repeat aloud; recite. 4 To give an account of; relate. —v.i. 5 To rehearse a play, song, dance, etc. [< OF *reherser* harrow over, repeat] —**re·hears′er** n.

Reich (rīk, *Ger.* rīkh) n. Formerly, Germany, the German government, or its territory. —**Third Reich** The Nazi state under Adolf Hitler, 1933–45. [G]

reichs·mark (rīks′märk′, *Ger.* rīkhs′-) n. pl. **·marks** or **·mark** A monetary unit of Germany from 1924–48.

Reichs·tag (rīks′täg′, *Ger.* rīkhs′täkh′) n. The former legislative assembly of Germany.

reign (rān) n. 1 Sovereign power or rule; sovereignty. 2 The time or duration of a sovereign's rule. 3 Domination; sway: the *reign* of rationalism. —v.i. 1 To hold and exercise sovereign power. 2 To hold sway; prevail: Winter *reigns*. [< L *regnum* rule]

Reign of Terror The period of the French Revolution from May, 1793, to August, 1794, during which Louis XVI, Marie Antoinette, and thousands of others were guillotined.

re·im·burse (rē′im·bûrs′) v.t. **·bursed**, **·burs·ing** 1 To pay back (a person) an equivalent for what has been spent or lost; recompense. 2 To pay back; refund. [< RE- + < L *in-* in + *bursa* purse] —**re′im·burs′a·ble** adj. —**re′im·burse′ment** n.

rein (rān) n. 1 *Usu. pl.* A strap attached to each end of a bit to control a horse or other draft animal. 2 Any means of restraint or control. —v.t. 1 To guide, check, or halt with or as with reins. —v.i. 2 To check or halt a horse by means of reins: with *in* or *up*. [< OF *resne*]

re·in·car·nate (rē′in·kär′nāt) v.t. **·nat·ed**, **·nat·ing** To cause to undergo reincarnation.

re·in·car·na·tion (rē′in·kär·nā′shən) n. 1 The rebirth of a soul in a new body. 2 The Hindu doctrine that the soul, upon the death of the body, returns to earth in another body or a new form.

rein·deer (rān′dir′) n. pl. **·deer** A European form of caribou, often domesticated. [< ON *hreinn* reindeer + *dyr* deer]

re·in·force (rē′in·fôrs′, -fōrs′) v.t. **·forced**, **·forc·ing** 1 To give new force or strength to. 2 *Mil.* To strengthen with more troops or ships. 3 To add some strengthening part or material to. 4 To increase the number of. [< RE- + *inforce*, var. of ENFORCE]

reinforced concrete Concrete containing metal bars, rods, or netting to increase its strength and durability.

re·in·force·ment (rē′in·fôrs′mənt, -fōrs′-) n. 1 The act of reinforcing. 2 Something that reinforces. 3 *Often pl. Mil.* A fresh body of troops or additional vessels.

re·in·state (rē′in·stāt′) v.t. **·stat·ed**, **·stat·ing** To restore to a former state, position, etc. —**re′in·state′ment** n.

reis (rās) n.pl. of REAL[2] (def. 2).

re·it·er·ate (rē·it′ə·rāt) v.t. **·at·ed**, **·at·ing** To say or do again and again. [< L *re-* again + *iterare* say] —**re·it′er·a′tion** n. —**re·it′er·a′tive** adj. —**re·it′er·a′tive·ly** adv. —**Syn.** iterate, repeat, retell, recapitulate.

re·ject (ri·jekt′) v.t. 1 To refuse to accept, recognize, believe, etc. 2 To refuse to grant; deny, as a petition. 3 To refuse (a person) recognition, acceptance, etc. 4 To expel; react against physiologically. 5 To cast away as worthless; discard. —n. (rē′jekt) A person or thing that has been rejected. [< L *re-* back + *jacere* to throw] —**re·ject′er** or **re·jec′tor**, **re·jec′tion** n.

re·joice (ri·jois′) v. **·joiced**, **·joic·ing** v.i. 1 To feel joyful; be glad. —v.t. 2 To fill with joy; gladden. [< L *re-* again + *ex-* thoroughly + *gaudere* be joyous] —**re·joic′er**, **re·joic′ing** n. —**re·joic′ing·ly** adv.

re·join[1] (ri·join′) v.t. 1 To say in reply; answer. —v.i. 2 To answer. [< F *rejoindre*]

re·join[2] (rē′join′) v.t. 1 To come again into company with. 2 To join together again; reunite. —v.i. 3 To come together again.

re·join·der (ri·join′dər) n. 1 An answer to a reply. 2 Any reply or retort. [< F *rejoindre* to answer, reply]

re·ju·ve·nate (ri·jōō′və·nāt) v.t. **·nat·ed**, **·nat·ing** To make young; give new vigor or youthfulness to. [< RE- again + L *juvenis* young + -ATE] —**re·ju′ve·na′tion** n.

rel. relating; relative; released; religion; religious.

re·lapse (ri·laps′) v.i. **·lapsed**, **·laps·ing** 1 To lapse back, as into disease after partial recovery. 2 To return to bad habits or sin; backslide. —n. (*also* rē′laps) 1 The act or an instance of relapsing. 2 The return of an illness after apparent recovery. [< L *relapsus*, pp. of *relabi* slide back] —**re·laps′er** n.

re·late (ri·lāt′) v. **·lat·ed**, **·lat·ing** v.t. 1 To tell the events or the particulars of; narrate. 2 To bring into connection or relation. —v.i. 3 To have relation: with *to*. 4 To have reference: with *to*. [< L *relatus*, pp. of *referre* to carry back] —**re·lat′er** n.

re·lat·ed (ri·lā′tid) adj. 1 Standing in relation; connected. 2 Of common ancestry; connected by blood or marriage; akin. 3 Narrated. —**re·lat′ed·ly** adv. —**re·lat′ed·ness** n.

re·la·tion (ri·lā′shən) n. 1 The fact or condition of being related or connected: the *relation* between poverty and disease. 2 Connection by blood or marriage; kinship. 3 A person connected by blood or marriage; a relative. 4 Reference; regard; allusion: in *relation* to your request. 5 *pl.* The contacts or dealings between or among individuals, groups, nations, etc.: race *relations;* political *relations*. 6 The act of relating or narrating; also, that which is related or told. —**re·la′tion·al** adj.

re·la·tion·ship (ri·lā′shən·ship) n. 1 The state or quality of being related; connection. 2 Kinship. 3 The kind or quality of association between people: a healthy *relationship*.

rel·a·tive (rel′ə·tiv) adj. 1 Having connection; pertinent: an inquiry *relative* to one's health. 2 Resulting from or depending upon a relation to or comparison with something else; comparative: a *relative* truth. 3 Intelligible only in relation to something else; not absolute. 4 *Gram.* Referring to or qualifying an antecedent: a *relative* pronoun. —n. 1 One who is related; a kinsman. 2 A relative word or term. —**rel′a·tive·ly** adv. —**rel′a·tive·ness** n.

relative clause *Gram.* A dependent clause introduced by a relative pronoun.

relative humidity At any given temperature, the percentage of the maximum possible water vapor content actually present in the air.

relative pronoun *Gram.* A pronoun that refers to an antecedent and introduces a dependent clause, as *who* in *We who knew him admired him.*

rel·a·tiv·i·ty (rel′ə·tiv′ə·tē) n. 1 The quality or condition of being relative; relativeness. 2 *Philos.* Existence viewed only as an object of, or in relation to, a thinking mind. 3 A condition of dependence or of close relation of one thing on or to another. 4 *Physics* The principle of the interdependence of matter, energy, space, and time, as mathematically formulated by Albert Einstein. The **special theory of relativity** states that the speed of light is the same in all frames of reference and that the same laws of physics hold in all frames of reference that are not accelerated. The **general theory of relativity** extends these principles to accelerated frames of reference and gravitational phenomena.

re·lax (ri·laks′) v.t. 1 To make lax or loose; make less tight or firm. 2 To make less stringent or severe, as discipline. 3 To abate; slacken, as efforts. 4 To relieve from strain or effort. —v.i. 5 To become lax or loose; loosen. 6 To become less stringent or severe. 7 To rest. 8 To unbend; become less formal. [< L *re-* again + *laxare* loosen] —**re·lax′a·ble** adj. —**re′lax·a′tion**, **re·lax′er** n.

re·lax·ant (ri·laks′ənt) adj. Pertaining to or causing relaxation. —n. A drug or other agent that reduces tension, esp. of muscles.

re·lay[1] (rē′lā) n. 1 A fresh set, as of men, horses, or dogs, to replace or relieve a tired set. 2 A supply of anything kept in store for anticipated use or need. 3 A relay race, or one of its laps or legs. 4 *Electr.* An electronically controlled switch. —v.t. (*also* ri·lā′) **·layed**, **·lay·ing** 1 To send onward by or as by relays. 2 To provide with relays. 3 *Telecom.* To retransmit (a message or signal). [< Ital. *rilasciare* leave behind]

re·lay[2] (rē′lā) v.t. **·laid**, **·lay·ing** To lay again.

re·lay race (rē′lā) A race between teams, each runner of which runs only a set part of the course and is relieved by a teammate.

re·lease (ri·lēs′) v.t. ·leased, ·leas·ing 1 To set free; liberate. 2 To deliver from worry, pain, obligation, etc. 3 To free from something that holds, binds, etc. 4 To permit the circulation, sale, performance, etc., of, as a motion picture, phonograph record, or news item. —n. 1 The act of releasing or setting free, or the state of being released. 2 A discharge from responsibility or penalty; also, a document authorizing this. 3 *Law* An instrument of conveyance by which one person surrenders and relinquishes all claims or rights to another person. 4 The releasing of something to the public; also, that which is released, as a news item, motion picture, etc. 5 *Mech.* Any catch or device to hold and release something. [< L *relaxare* relax] — **re·leas′er** n.

re-lease (rē′lēs′) v.t. ·leased, ·leas·ing To lease again.

rel·e·gate (rel′ə·gāt) v.t. ·gat·ed, ·gat·ing 1 To send off or consign, as to an obscure position or place. 2 To assign, as to a particular class or sphere. 3 To refer (a matter) to someone for decision, action, etc. 4 To banish; exile. [< L *re-* away, back + *legare* send] —**rel′e·ga′tion** n.

re·lent (ri·lent′) v.i. To soften in temper; become more gentle or compassionate. [< L *relentescere* grow soft]

re·lent·less (ri·lent′lis) adj. 1 Unremitting; continuous. 2 Not relenting; pitiless. —**re·lent′less·ly** adv. —**re·lent′less·ness** n.

rel·e·vant (rel′ə·vənt) adj. Fitting; pertinent; applicable. [< Med. L *relevare* bear upon] —**rel′e·vance, rel′e·van·cy** n. —**rel′e·vant·ly** adv.

re·li·a·ble (ri·lī′ə·bəl) adj. That may be relied upon; worthy of confidence. —**re·li′a·bil′i·ty, re·li′a·ble·ness** n. —**re·li′a·bly** adv. —Syn. trustworthy, dependable, loyal, constant.

re·li·ance (ri·lī′əns) n. 1 The act of relying. 2 Confidence; trust; dependence. 3 That upon which one relies.

re·li·ant (ri·lī′ənt) adj. 1 Having or manifesting reliance. 2 Dependent: with on. —**re·li′ant·ly** adv.

rel·ic (rel′ik) n. 1 Some remaining portion or fragment of that which has vanished or is destroyed. 2 A custom, habit, etc., from the past. 3 A keepsake or memento. 4 The body or part of the body of a saint, or any sacred memento. 5 pl. A corpse; remains. [< L *reliquiae* remains < *relinquere* leave]

re·lief (ri·lēf′) n. 1 The act of relieving, or the state of being relieved. 2 That which relieves. 3 Charitable aid, as money or food. 4 Release, as from a post or duty; also, the person or persons who take over for those released. 5 In architecture and sculpture, the projection of a figure, ornament, etc., from a surface; also, any such figure. 6 In painting, the apparent projection of forms and masses. 7 *Geog.* **a** The unevenness of land surface, as caused by mountains, hills, etc. **b** The parts of a map which portray such unevenness.

Relief *def. 5*

re·lieve (ri·lēv′) v.t. ·lieved, ·liev·ing 1 To free wholly or partly from pain, stress, pressure, etc. 2 To lessen or alleviate, as pain or pressure. 3 To give aid or assistance to. 4 To free from obligation, injustice, etc. 5 To release from duty by providing a substitute. 6 To make less monotonous, harsh, or unpleasant; vary. 7 To bring into prominence; display by contrast. [< L *relevare* lift up] —**re·liev′a·ble** adj. —**re·liev′er** n.

re·li·gion (ri·lij′ən) n. 1 A belief in a divine or superhuman power or principle, usu. thought of as the creator of all things. 2 The manifestation of such a belief in worship, ritual, conduct, etc. 3 Any system of religious faith or practice: the Jewish *religion*. 4 The religious or monastic life: to enter *religion*. 5 Anything that elicits devotion, zeal, dedication, etc.: Politics is his *religion*. [< L *religio*]

re·li·gi·os·i·ty (ri·lij′ē·os′ə·tē) n. The state or quality of being religious, esp. excessively or affectedly so.

re·li·gious (ri·lij′əs) adj. 1 Feeling and manifesting religion; devout; pious. 2 Of or pertaining to religion: a *religious* teacher. 3 Faithful and strict in performance; conscientious: a *religious* loyalty. 4 Belonging to the monastic life. —n. pl. ·ious A monk or nun. —**re·lig′ious·ly** adv. —**re·lig′ious·ness** n.

re·lin·quish (ri·ling′kwish) v.t. 1 To give up; abandon. 2 To renounce: to *relinquish* a claim. 3 To let go (a hold or something held). [< L *re-* back, from + *linquere* leave] — **re·lin′quish·er, re·lin′quish·ment** n.

rel·i·quar·y (rel′ə·kwer′ē) n. pl. ·quar·ies A casket, shrine, or other repository for relics. [< L *reliquiae* remains]

rel·ish (rel′ish) n. 1 Appetite; appreciation; liking. 2 The flavor, esp. when agreeable, in food and drink. 3 The quality in anything that lends spice or zest: Danger gives *relish* to adventure. 4 A savory food or condiment served with other food to lend it flavor or zest. 5 A hint, trace, or suggestion of some quality or characteristic. —v.t. 1 To like; enjoy: to *relish* a dinner or a joke. —v.i. 2 To have an agreeable flavor; afford gratification. [< OF *relaisser* leave behind] —**rel′ish·a·ble** adj.

re·live (rē·liv′) v.t. ·lived, ·liv·ing To experience again, as in one's memory.

re·luc·tance (ri·luk′təns) n. 1 The state of being reluctant; unwillingness. 2 *Electr.* Capacity for opposing magnetic induction. Also **re·luc′tan·cy.**

re·luc·tant (ri·luk′tənt) adj. 1 Disinclined; unwilling. 2 Marked by unwillingness. [< L *reluctari* fight back] —**re·luc′tant·ly** adv.

re·ly (ri·lī′) v.i. ·lied, ·ly·ing To place trust or confidence: with *on* or *upon*. [< L *re-* again + *ligare* to bind] —Syn. lean, depend, count, bank (all with *on* or *upon*).

re·main (ri·mān′) v.i. 1 To stay or be left behind after the removal, departure, or destruction of other persons or things. 2 To continue in one place, condition, or character. 3 To be left as something to be done, dealt with, etc. 4 To endure or last; abide. [< L *re-* back + *manere* stay, remain]

re·main·der (ri·mān′dər) n. 1 That which remains; something left over. 2 *Math.* **a** The result of subtraction; difference. **b** The difference of the product of the quotient and divisor subtracted from the dividend in division. 3 *Law* An estate in expectancy, but not in actual possession and enjoyment. 4 A copy or copies of a book remaining with a publisher after sales have fallen off or ceased. —adj. Left over; remaining. —v.t. To sell as a remainder (def. 4).

re·mains (ri·mānz′) n. pl. 1 That which is left after a part has been removed or destroyed; remnants. 2 A corpse. 3 Unpublished writings at the time of an author's death. 4 Survivals of the past, as fossils, monuments, etc.

re·make (rē·māk′) v.t. ·made, ·mak·ing To make again or in a different form: to *remake* a silent film. —n. (rē′māk) Something that is remade, esp. a motion picture.

re·mand (ri·mand′, -mänd′) v.t. 1 To order or send back. 2 *Law* **a** To recommit to custody, as an accused person after a preliminary examination. **b** To send (a case) back to a lower court. —n. The act of remanding or the state of being remanded. [< L *re-* back + *mandare* to order] — **re·mand′ment** n.

re·mark (ri·märk′) n. 1 A comment or saying; casual observation. 2 The act of noticing, observing, or perceiving. —v.t. 1 To say or write by way of comment. 2 To take particular notice of. —v.i. 3 To make remarks: with *on* or *upon*. [< F *re-* again + *marquer* to mark] —**re·mark′er** n.

re·mark·a·ble (ri·mär′kə·bəl) adj. 1 Worthy of special notice. 2 Extraordinary; unusual. —**re·mark′a·ble·ness** n. —**re·mark′a·bly** adv.

re·me·di·a·ble (ri·mē′dē·ə·bəl) adj. Capable of being cured or remedied. —**re·me′di·a·bly** adv.

re·me·di·al (ri·mē′dē·əl) adj. Of the nature of or adapted to be used as a remedy: *remedial* measures. —**re·me′di·al·ly** adv.

rem·e·dy (rem′ə·dē) v.t. ·died, ·dy·ing 1 To cure or heal, as by medicinal treatment. 2 To make right; repair; correct. 3 To overcome or remove (an evil or defect). —n. pl. ·dies 1 A medicine or remedial treatment. 2 A means of correcting an evil, fault, etc. 3 *Law* A legal mode for enforcing a right or redressing or preventing a wrong. [< L *re-* thoroughly + *mederi* heal, restore]

re·mem·ber (ri·mem′bər) *v.t.* 1 To bring back or present again to the mind or memory; recall. 2 To keep in mind carefully, as for a purpose. 3 To bear in mind with affection, respect, awe, etc. 4 To reward (someone) with a gift, legacy, tip, etc. —*v.i.* 5 To bring something back to or keep something in the mind. 6 To have or use one's memory. —**remember (one) to** To inform a person of the regard of: *Remember* me *to* your wife. [< L *re-* again + *memorare* bring to mind] —**re·mem′ber·er** *n.*

re·mem·brance (ri·mem′brəns) *n.* 1 The act or power of remembering or the state of being remembered. 2 The period within which one can remember. 3 That which is remembered. 4 A gift, memento, or keepsake. 5 An observance in commemoration.

re·mind (ri·mīnd′) *v.t.* To bring to (someone's) mind; cause to remember. —**re·mind′er** *n.* —**re·mind′ful** *adj.*

rem·i·nisce (rem′ə·nis′) *v.i.* ·nisced, ·nisc·ing To recall incidents or events of the past; indulge in reminiscences. [Back formation < REMINISCENCE]

rem·i·nis·cence (rem′ə·nis′əns) *n.* 1 The recalling to mind of past incidents and events. 2 A written or oral account of past experiences. 3 Anything that serves as a reminder of something else. [< L *reminisci* recollect] —**rem′i·nis′cent** *adj.* —**rem′i·nis′cent·ly** *adv.*

re·miss (ri·mis′) *adj.* Lax or careless in matters requiring attention; negligent. [< L *remittere* send back, slacken] —**re·miss′ness** *n.*

re·mis·si·ble (ri·mis′ə·bəl) *adj.* Capable of being remitted or pardoned, as sins. —**re·mis′si·bil′i·ty** *n.*

re·mis·sion (ri·mish′ən) *n.* 1 The act of remitting, or the state of being remitted. 2 Pardon, as of sins or a crime. 3 Release from a debt, penalty, or obligation. 4 Temporary abatement, as of pain, symptoms, etc.

re·mit (ri·mit′) *v.* ·mit·ted, ·mit·ting *v.t.* 1 To send, as money in payment for goods; transmit. 2 To refrain from exacting or inflicting, as a penalty. 3 To pardon; forgive. 4 To slacken; relax, as vigilance. 5 To restore; replace. 6 To put off; postpone. 7 *Law* To refer (a legal proceeding) to a lower court for further consideration. —*v.i.* 8 To send money, as in payment. 9 To diminish; abate. [< L *re-* back + *mittere* send] —**re·mit′ter** or **re·mit′tor** *n.*

re·mit·tal (ri·mit′l) *n.* REMISSION.

re·mit·tance (ri·mit′ns) *n.* 1 The act of remitting money or credit. 2 That which is remitted, as money.

re·mit·tent (ri·mit′nt) *adj.* Having temporary abatements: a *remittent* fever. —*n.* A remittent fever. [< L *remittere* remit] —**re·mit′tent·ly** *adv.*

rem·nant (rem′nənt) *n.* 1 That which remains of anything. 2 A piece of cloth, etc., left over after the last cutting. 3 A remaining trace or survival of anything: a *remnant* of faith. 4 A small remaining number or quantity, as of people. —*adj.* Remaining. [< OF *remaindre* remain]

re·mod·el (rē·mod′l) *v.t.* ·eled or ·elled, ·el·ing or ·el·ling 1 To model again. 2 To make over or anew.

re·mon·e·tize (rē·mon′ə·tīz) *v.t.* ·tized, ·tiz·ing To reinstate, esp. silver, as lawful money. [< RE- + L *moneta* money + -IZE] —**re·mon′e·ti·za′tion** *n.*

re·mon·strance (ri·mon′strəns) *n.* The act or an instance of remonstrating; protest.

re·mon·strant (ri·mon′strənt) *adj.* Protesting or opposing; expostulatory. —*n.* One who remonstrates.

re·mon·strate (ri·mon′strāt) *v.* ·strat·ed, ·strat·ing *v.t.* 1 To say or plead in protest or opposition. —*v.i.* 2 To protest; object. [< L *re-* again + *monstrare* show] —**re·mon·stra·tion** (rē′mon·strā′shən, rem′ən-), **re·mon′stra′tor** *n.* —**re·mon′stra·tive** (-strə·tiv) *adj.*

re·morse (ri·môrs′) *n.* The keen or hopeless anguish caused by a sense of guilt; distressing self-reproach. [< LL *remorsus* a biting back] —**re·morse′ful** *adj.* —**re·morse′ful·ly** *adv.* —**re·morse′ful·ness** *n.*

re·morse·less (ri·môrs′lis) *adj.* Having no remorse or compassion. —**re·morse′less·ly** *adv.* —**re·morse′less·ness** *n.* —**Syn.** pitiless, cruel, merciless, ruthless.

re·mote (ri·mōt′) *adj.* 1 Located far from a specified place. 2 Removed far from present time. 3 Having slight bearing on or connection with: a problem *remote* from our discussion. 4 Distant in relation: a *remote* cousin. 5 Not

obvious; faint; slight: a *remote* likeness. 6 Cold; aloof: a *remote* manner. [< L *remotus,* p.p. of *removere* remove] —**re·mote′ly** *adv.* —**re·mote′ness** *n.*

remote control Control from a distance, as of a machine, apparatus, aircraft, etc.

re·mount (rē·mount′) *v.t.* & *v.i.* To mount again or anew. —*n.* (rē′mount′) 1 A new setting or framing. 2 A fresh riding horse.

re·mov·a·ble (ri·mōō′və·bəl) *adj.* Capable of being removed. —**re·mov′a·bil′i·ty, re·mov′a·ble·ness** *n.*

re·mov·al (ri·mōō′vəl) *n.* 1 The act of removing or the state of being removed. 2 Dismissal, as from office. 3 Changing of place, esp. of habitation.

re·move (ri·mōōv′) *v.* ·moved, ·mov·ing *v.t.* 1 To take or move away or from one place to another. 2 To take off. 3 To get rid of; do away with: to *remove* abuses. 4 To kill. 5 To displace or dismiss, as from office. 6 To take out; extract: with *from.* —*v.i.* 7 To change one's place of residence or business. 8 To go away; depart. —*n.* 1 The act of removing. 2 The distance or degree of difference between things: He is only one *remove* from a fool. [< L *re-* again + *movere* move] —**re·mov′er** *n.*

re·moved (ri·mōōvd′) *adj.* Separated, as by intervening space, time, or relationship, or by difference in kind: a cousin twice *removed.* —**re·mov·ed·ness** (ri·mōō′vid·nis) *n.*

re·mu·ner·ate (ri·myōō′nə·rāt) *v.t.* ·at·ed, ·at·ing 1 To pay (a person) for something, as for services, losses, etc. 2 To compensate or reward for (work, diligence, etc.). [< L *remunerari*] —**re·mu′ner·a′tion, re·mu′ner·a′tor** *n.* —**re·mu′ner·a·tive** (-nər·ə·tiv, -nə·rā′tiv) *adj.* —**re·mu′ner·a·tive·ly** *adv.*

Re·mus (rē′məs) *Rom. Myth.* The twin brother of Romulus, by whom he was killed.

ren·ais·sance (ren′ə·säns′, -zäns′, ri·nā′səns) *n.* A new birth; resurrection; renascence. [F< *renaître* be reborn]

Ren·ais·sance (ren′ə·säns′, -zäns′, ri·nā′səns) *n.* 1 The revival of letters and art in Europe, marking the transition from the medieval to the modern world. 2 The period of this revival, from the 14th to the 16th century. 3 The style of art, literature, etc., marked by a classical influence, that was developed in and characteristic of this period. —*adj.* 1 Of, pertaining to, or characteristic of the Renaissance. 2 Pertaining to a style of architecture originating in Italy in the 15th century and based on the classical Roman style.

re·nal (rē′nəl) *adj.* Of or situated near the kidneys. [< L *renes* kidneys]

re·nas·cence (ri·nās′əns, -nas′-) *n.* A rebirth; revival. [< L *re-* again + *nasci* be born] —**re·nas′cent** *adj.*

Re·nas·cence (ri·nās′əns, -nas′-) *n.* RENAISSANCE.

rend (rend) *v.* **rent** or **rend·ed, rend·ing** *v.t.* 1 To tear apart forcibly. 2 To pull or remove forcibly: with *away, from, off,* etc. 3 To pass through (the air) violently and noisily. 4 To distress (the heart, etc.), as with grief or despair. —*v.i.* 5 To split; part. [< OE *rendan* tear, cut down] —**rend′er** *n.*

ren·der (ren′dər) *v.t.* 1 To give, present, or submit for action, approval, payment, etc. 2 To provide or furnish; give: to *render* aid. 3 To give as due: to *render* obedience. 4 To perform; do: to *render* great service. 5 To give or state formally. 6 To give by way of requital or retribution: to *render* good for evil. 7 To represent or depict, as in music or painting. 8 To cause to be: to *render* someone helpless. 9 To express in another language; translate. 10 To melt and clarify, as lard. 11 To give back; return: often with *back.* 12 To surrender; give up. [< L *reddere* give back] —**ren′der·a·ble** *adj.* —**ren′der·er** *n.*

ren·dez·vous (rän′dā·vōō, -də-) *n. pl.* **·vous** (-vōōz) 1 An appointed place of meeting. 2 A meeting or an appointment to meet. —*v.t.* & *v.i.* **·voused** (-vōōd), **·vous·ing** (-vōō′ing) To assemble or cause to assemble at a certain place or time. [< F *rendez-vous,* lit., betake yourself]

ren·di·tion (ren·dish′ən) *n.* 1 A version or interpretation of a text. 2 A performance or interpretation, as of a musical composition, role, etc. 3 The act of rendering. [< OF *rendre* render]

ren·e·gade (ren′ə·gād) *n.* 1 One who abandons a previous loyalty, as to a religion, political party, etc. 2 One who gives up conventional or lawful behavior. —*adj.* Traitorous. [< Sp. *renegar* deny]

re·nege (ri·nig′, -neg′, -nēg′) v.i. ·neged, ·neg·ing 1 In card games, to fail to follow suit when able or required by rule to do so. 2 To fail to fulfill a promise. [< L *re-* again + *negare* deny] —**re·neg′er** *n.*

re·new (ri·nyo͞o′) v.t. 1 To make new or as if new again. 2 To begin again; resume. 3 To repeat: to *renew* an oath. 4 To regain (vigor, strength, etc.). 5 To cause to continue in effect; extend: to *renew* a subscription. 6 To revive; reestablish. 7 To replenish or replace, as provisions. —v.i. 8 To become new again. 9 To begin or commence again. [< RE- + NEW] —**re·new′a·ble** *adj.* —**re·new′al, re·new′er** *n.* —**re·new′ed·ly** *adv.*

ren·i·form (ren′ə·fôrm, rē′nə-) *adj.* Kidney-shaped. [< L *renes* kidneys + -FORM]

ren·net (ren′it) *n.* 1 The mucous membrane lining the fourth stomach of a suckling calf or lamb. 2 An extract of this, used to curdle milk in making cheese, etc. 3 RENNIN. [< OE *rinnan* run together, coagulate]

ren·nin (ren′in) *n.* 1 A milk-curdling enzyme present in gastric juice. 2 This enzyme in partially purified form obtained from rennet.

re·nounce (ri·nouns′) v.t. ·nounced, ·nounc·ing 1 To give up, esp. by formal statement. 2 To disown; repudiate. [< L *renuntiare* protest against] —**re·nounce′ment, re·nounc′er** *n.* —**Syn.** 1 abjure, disavow, disclaim, forswear.

ren·o·vate (ren′ə·vāt) v.t. ·vat·ed, ·vat·ing 1 To make as good as new, as by repairing, cleaning, etc. 2 To renew; refresh; reinvigorate. [< L *re-* again + *novare* make new] —**ren′o·va′tion, ren′o·va′tor** *n.*

re·nown (ri·noun′) *n.* The state of being widely known for great achievements; fame. [< L *re-* again + *nominare* to name] —**re·nowned′** *adj.*

rent[1] (rent) *n.* Compensation, esp. payment in money, made by a tenant to a landlord or owner for the use of property, as land, a house, etc., usu. due at specified intervals. —**for rent** Available in return for a rent. —v.t. 1 To obtain the temporary possession and use of in return for paying rent. 2 To grant the temporary use of for a rent. —v.i. 3 To be let for rent. [< L *reddita* what is given back or paid] —**rent′a·ble** *adj.* —**rent′er** *n.*

rent[2] (rent) A *p.t.* & *p.p.* of REND. —*n.* 1 A hole or slit made by rending or tearing. 2 A violent separation; schism.

rent·al (ren′təl) *n.* 1 An amount paid or due to be paid as rent. 2 The revenue derived from rented property. 3 The act of renting. —*adj.* 1 Of or pertaining to rent. 2 Engaged in the business of renting or supervising rents.

re·nun·ci·a·tion (ri·nun′sē·ā′shən, -shē-) *n.* 1 The act of renouncing; repudiation. 2 A declaration in which something is renounced. —**re·nun′ci·a′tive** (-sē·ā′tiv), **re·nun′ci·a·to′ry** *adj.*

re·o·pen (rē·ō′pən) v.t. & v.i. 1 To open again. 2 To begin again; resume.

re·or·gan·i·za·tion (rē′ôr·gən·ə·zā′shən, -ī·zā′-) *n.* 1 The act of reorganizing. 2 The legal reconstruction of a corporation, usu. to avert a failure.

re·or·gan·ize (rē·ôr′gən·īz) v.t. & v.i. ·ized, ·iz·ing To organize anew. —**re·or′gan·iz′er** *n.*

rep[1] (rep) *n.* A silk, cotton, rayon, or wool fabric having a crosswise rib. [< F *reps*]

rep[2] (rep) *n. Slang* 1 REPERTORY. 2 REPRESENTATIVE. 3 REPUTATION.

Rep. Representative; Republic; Republican.

re·pair[1] (ri·pâr′) v.t. 1 To restore to sound or good condition after damage, injury, decay, etc. 2 To make up, as a loss; compensate for. —*n.* 1 The act or instance of repairing. 2 Condition after use or after repairing: in good *repair.* [< L *re-* again + *parare* prepare] —**re·pair′er** *n.*

re·pair[2] (ri·pâr′) v.i. To betake oneself; go: to *repair* to the garden. [< LL *repatriare* repatriate]

re·pair·man (ri·pâr′man′, -mən) *n. pl.* ·men (-men′, -mən) A man whose work is to make repairs.

rep·a·ra·ble (rep′ər·ə·bəl) *adj.* Capable of being repaired. —**rep′a·ra·bly** *adv.*

rep·a·ra·tion (rep′ə·rā′shən) *n.* 1 The act of making amends; atonement. 2 That which is done or paid by way of making amends. 3 *pl.* Indemnities paid by defeated countries for acts of war. 4 The act of repairing, or the state of being repaired. —**re·par·a·tive** (ri·par′ə·tiv) *adj.*

rep·ar·tee (rep′är·tē′, -ər-, -tā′) *n.* 1 Conversation marked by quick and witty replies. 2 Skill in such conversation. 3 A witty reply. [< F *re-* again + *partir* depart]

re·past (ri·past′, -päst′, rē′past) *n.* Food taken at a meal; a meal. [< LL *repascere* feed again]

re·pa·tri·ate (rē·pā′trē·āt) v.t. & v.i. ·at·ed, ·at·ing To send back to the country of birth, citizenship, or allegiance, as prisoners of war. —*n.* (rē·pā′trē·it) A person who has been repatriated. [< L *re-* again + *patria* native land] —**re·pa′tri·a′tion** *n.*

re·pay (ri·pā′) v. ·paid, ·pay·ing v.t. 1 To pay back; refund. 2 To pay back or refund something to. 3 To make compensation or retaliation for. —v.i. 4 To make repayment or requital. —**re·pay′ment** *n.*

re·peal (ri·pēl′) v.t. To withdraw the authority to effect; rescind; revoke. —*n.* The act of repealing; revocation. [< OF *rapeler* recall] —**re·peal′a·ble** *adj.* —**re·peal′er** *n.*

re·peat (ri·pēt′) v.t. 1 To say again; reiterate. 2 To recite

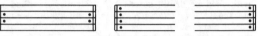

Repeats *def. 2a*

from memory. 3 To say (what another has just said). 4 To tell, as a secret, to another. 5 To do, make, or experience again. —v.i. 6 To say or do something again. 7 To vote more than once at the same election. —*n.* 1 The act of repeating. 2 *Music* **a** A sign indicating that a passage is to be repeated. **b** A passage meant to be repeated. [< L *repetere* do or say again] —**re·peat′a·ble** *adj.*

re·peat·ed (ri·pē′tid) *adj.* Occurring or spoken again and again. —**re·peat′ed·ly** *adv.*

re·peat·er (ri·pē′tər) *n.* 1 One who or that which repeats. 2 A firearm that can discharge several shots without being reloaded. 3 One who illegally votes more than once at the same election. 4 One who has been repeatedly imprisoned for criminal offenses.

re·pel (ri·pel′) v. ·pelled, ·pel·ling v.t. 1 To force or drive back; repulse. 2 To reject; refuse, as a suggestion. 3 To cause to feel distaste or aversion. 4 To fail to mix with or adhere to. —v.i. 5 To act so as to drive something back or away. 6 To cause distaste or aversion. [< L *re-* back + *pellere* drive] —**re·pel′ler** *n.*

re·pel·lent (ri·pel′ənt) *adj.* 1 Serving, tending, or having power to repel. 2 Exciting disgust; repugnant; repulsive. —*n.* Something that repels, as a substance that repels water, insects, etc. —**re·pel′len·cy, re·pel′lence** *n.*

re·pent (ri·pent′) v.i. 1 To feel remorse or regret, as for something done or undone; be contrite. 2 To change one's mind concerning past action: with *of.* —v.t. 3 To feel remorse or regret for (an action, sin, etc.). [< L *re-* again + *poenitere* cause to repent] —**re·pent′er** *n.*

re·pen·tance (ri·pen′təns) *n.* The act of repenting; sorrow for having done wrong. —**re·pen′tant** *adj.* —**re·pen′tant·ly** *adv.*

re·per·cus·sion (rē′pər·kush′ən) *n.* 1 *Usu. pl.* A long-range or unpredictable result, as of an event; aftereffect. 2 A reverberation; echo. [< L *repercussus,* p.p. of *repercutere* rebound] —**re′per·cus′sive** *adj.*

rep·er·toire (rep′ər·twär) *n.* 1 A list of works, as of music or drama, that a company or person is prepared to perform. 2 Such works collectively. 3 The aggregate of devices, methods, etc., used in a particular line of activity: the teacher's *repertoire* of visual aids. [< LL *repertorium* inventory]

rep·er·to·ry (rep′ər·tôr′ē, -tō′rē) *n. pl.* ·ries 1 A theatrical group having a repertoire of productions: also **repertory company, repertory theater.** 2 REPERTOIRE. 3 A place where things are gathered in readiness for use. [< L *repertus,* p.p. of *reperire* find, discover]

rep·e·ti·tion (rep′ə·tish′ən) *n.* 1 The doing, making, or saying of something again. 2 That which is repeated; a copy. —**re·pet·i·tive** (ri·pet′ə·tiv) *adj.* —**re·pet′i·tive·ly** *adv.*

rep·e·ti·tious (rep′ə·tish′əs) *adj.* Characterized by or

containing repetition, esp. useless or tedious repetition. —
rep′e·ti′tious·ly adv. —**rep′e·ti′tious·ness** n.

re·pine (ri·pīn′) v.i. ·pined, ·pin·ing To be discontented or
fretful. [< RE- + PINE²] —**re·pin′er** n.

re·place (ri·plās′) v.t. ·placed, ·plac·ing 1 To put back in
place. 2 To take or fill the place of; supersede. 3 To refund;
repay. —**re·place′a·ble** adj. —**re·plac′er** n.

re·place·ment (ri·plās′mənt) n. 1 The act of replacing,
or the state of being replaced. 2 Something used to replace, as a substitute.

re·play (rē·plā′) v.t. 1 To play again. 2 To show a replay
of. —n. (rē′plā′) 1 The act of playing again. 2 The playing
of a television tape, often in slow motion and usu. immediately following the live occurrence of the action shown. 3
The action shown in such a replay.

re·plen·ish (ri·plen′ish) v.t. 1 To fill again. 2 To bring
back to fullness or completeness, as diminished supplies.
[< L re- again + plenus full] —**re·plen′ish·er, re·plen′ish·
ment** n.

re·plete (ri·plēt′) adj. 1 Full to the uttermost. 2 Gorged
with food or drink; sated. 3 Abundantly supplied or
stocked. [< L repletus, p.p. of replere fill again] —**re·ple′·
tion, re·plete′ness** n.

rep·li·ca (rep′lə·kə) n. 1 A duplicate, as of a picture, executed by the original artist. 2 Any close copy or reproduction. [< L replicare to reply]

rep·li·cate (rep′lə·kāt) v.t. ·cat·ed, ·cat·ing 1 To make an
indeterminate number of copies of; duplicate. 2 To fold
over. —**rep′li·ca′tion** n.

re·ply (ri·plī′) v. ·plied, ·ply·ing v.i. 1 To give an answer. 2
To respond by some act, gesture, etc. 3 To echo. 4 Law To
file a pleading in answer to the statement of the defense.
—v.t. 5 To say in answer: She replied that she would do
it. —n. pl. ·plies Something said, written, or done by way
of answer. [< L replicare fold back, make a reply] —**re·
pli′er** n.

re·port (ri·pôrt′, -pōrt′) v.t. 1 To make or give an account
of; relate, as information obtained by investigation. 2 To
bear back or repeat to another, as an answer. 3 To complain about, esp. to the authorities. 4 To state the result
of consideration concerning: The committee reported the
bill. —v.i. 5 To make a report. 6 To act as a reporter. 7 To
present oneself, as for duty. —n. 1 That which is reported.
2 A formal statement of the result of an investigation. 3
Common talk; rumor. 4 Fame, reputation, or character. 5
A record of the transactions of a deliberative body. 6 An
account prepared for publication in the press. 7 An explosive sound: the report of a gun. [< L re- back + portare
carry] —**re·port′a·ble** adj. —**Syn** v. 1 describe, record, transcribe. n. 1, 2, 5, 6 account, statement, announcement. 3
gossip, hearsay.

re·port·age (ri·pôr′tij, -pōr′-, rep′ôr·täzh′) n. 1 The act
or art of reporting, as for publication. 2 Reports that deal
with events in a journalistic style. [F]

report card A periodic statement of a pupil's scholastic
record.

re·port·ed·ly (ri·pôr′tid·lē, -pōr′-) adv. According to report.

re·port·er (ri·pôr′tər, -pōr′-) n. 1 One who reports. 2 One
employed to gather and report news for publication or
broadcasting. —**rep·or·to·ri·al** (rep′ər·tôr′ē·əl, -tō′rē-) adj.

re·pose¹ (ri·pōz′) n. 1 The state of being at rest. 2 Sleep.
3 Freedom from excitement or anxiety; composure. 4 Dignified calmness; serenity; peacefulness. —v. ·posed, ·pos·
ing v.t. 1 To lay or place in a position of rest. —v.i. 2 To lie
at rest. 3 To lie in death. 4 To rely; depend: with on, upon,
or in. [< LL re- again + pausare to pause]—**re·pose′ful** adj.
—**re·pose′ful·ly** adv.

re·pose² (ri·pōz′) v.t. ·posed, ·pos·ing To place, as confidence or hope: with in. [< L repositus, p.p. of reponere put
back]

re·pos·i·to·ry (ri·poz′ə·tôr′ē, -tō′rē) n. pl. ·ries 1 A place
in which goods may be stored; a depository. 2 Anything
considered as a place of storage or assembly: a repository
of Indian lore. 3 A person to whom a secret is entrusted.
[< L repositorium]

re·pos·sess (rē′pə·zes′) v.t. To regain possession of, esp.
as a result of the default of payments due. —**re′pos·ses′·
sion** n.

rep·re·hend (rep′ri·hend′) v.t. To criticize sharply; find
fault with. [< L re- back + prehendere hold] —**rep′re·hen′·
sion** n. —**rep′re·hen′sive** adj. —**rep′re·hen′sive·ly** adv.

rep·re·hen·si·ble (rep′ri·hen′sə·bəl) adj. Deserving
blame or censure. —**rep′re·hen′si·bil′i·ty, rep′re·hen′si·ble·
ness** n. —**rep′re·hen′si·bly** adv.

rep·re·sent (rep′ri·zent′) v.t. 1 To serve as the symbol,
expression, or designation of; symbolize: The dove represents peace. 2 To serve as an example, specimen, type, etc.,
of; typify: They represent the best in America. 3 To set
forth a likeness or image of; depict; portray. 4 To serve as
or be the delegate, agent, etc., of, as by legal authority or
by election. 5 To act the part of; impersonate. 6 To bring
before the mind; present clearly: Goya etchings that
represent the horrors of war. 7 To set forth in words, esp.
in a forceful and persuasive manner. 8 To describe as
being of a specified character or condition: to represent a
signature as authentic. [< L re- again + praesentare to
present]

rep·re·sen·ta·tion (rep′ri·zen·tā′shən) n. 1 The act of
representing, or the state of being represented. 2 A likeness or model. 3 A statement usu. purporting to be descriptive that represents a point of view and is intended
to influence judgment. 4 A dramatic performance. 5 Representatives collectively.

rep·re·sen·ta·tive (rep′ri·zen′tə·tiv) adj. 1 Typifying a
group or class. 2 Acting or having the power to act as an
agent. 3 Made up of representatives. 4 Based on the political principle of representation. 5 Presenting, portraying,
or representing. —n. 1 One who or that which is typical
of a group or class. 2 One who is authorized as an agent
or delegate. 3 Often cap. A member of a legislative body,
esp., in the U.S., a member of the lower house of Congress
or of a state legislature. —**rep′re·sen′ta·tive·ly** adv. —**rep′re·
sen′ta·tive·ness** n.

re·press (ri·pres′) v.t. 1 To keep under restraint or control. 2 To block the expression of: to repress a groan. 3 To
put down; quell, as a rebellion. [< L repressus, p.p. of re-
primere press back] —**re·press′er, re·pres′sive·ness** n. —**re·
press′i·ble, re·pres′sive** adj. —**re·pres′sive·ly** adv. —**Syn.** 1
curb, rein. 2 suppress, hold in.

re·pres·sion (ri·presh′ən) n. 1 The act of repressing, or
the condition of being repressed. 2 Psychoanal. The exclusion from consciousness of painful desires, memories, etc.,
and consequent manifestation through the unconscious.

re·prieve (ri·prēv′) v.t. ·prieved, ·priev·ing 1 To suspend
temporarily the execution of a sentence upon. 2 To relieve
for a time from suffering or trouble. —n. 1 The temporary
suspension of a sentence. 2 Temporary relief or cessation
of pain; respite. [< F reprendre take back]

rep·ri·mand (rep′rə·mand) v.t. To reprove sharply or formally. —n. Severe reproof or formal censure. [< L re-
primendus to be repressed]

re·print (rē′print′) n. A printing that is an exact copy of
a work already printed. —v.t. (rē·print′) To print again,
esp. without alteration. —**re·print′er** n.

re·pri·sal (ri·prī′zəl) n. Any action done in retaliation for
harm or injuries received, esp. an action involving the use
of force and sanctioned by a government or political
group. [< OF reprendre take back]

re·proach (ri·prōch′) v.t. To charge with or blame for
something wrong; rebuke. —n. 1 The act of or an expression of reproaching; censure; reproof. 2 A cause of blame
or disgrace. 3 Disgrace; discredit. [< OF reprochier] —**re·
proach′ful** adj. —**re·proach′ful·ly** adv. —**re·proach′ful·ness** n.

rep·ro·bate (rep′rə·bāt) adj. 1 Utterly depraved; profligate; corrupt. 2 Theol. Abandoned in sin; condemned. —n.
One who is reprobate. —v.t. ·bat·ed, ·bat·ing 1 To disap-
prove of heartily; condemn. 2 Theol. To abandon to dam-
nation. [< LL reprobare reprove] —**rep′ro·ba′tion** n. —**rep′·
ro·ba′tive** adj.

re·pro·duce (rē′prə·dyoōs′) v. ·duced, ·duc·ing v.t. 1 To
make a copy or image of. 2 To bring (offspring) into existence by sexual or asexual generation. 3 To replace (a lost
part or organ) by regeneration. 4 To cause the reproduction of (plant life, etc.). 5 To produce again. 6 To recall to
the mind; recreate mentally. —v.i. 7 To produce offspring.
8 To undergo copying, reproduction, etc. —**re′pro·duc′er** n.
—**re′pro·duc′i·ble** adj.

re·pro·duc·tion (rē′prə·duk′shən) n. **1** The act or process of reproducing. **2** Any process by which animals or plants give rise to new organisms. **3** Something reproduced, as a photocopy. —**re′pro·duc′tive** adj. —**re′pro·duc′. tive·ly** adv. —**re′pro·duc′tive·ness** n.

re·prog·ra·phy (rē·prog′rə·fē) n. The reproduction of graphic material, esp. by electronic devices.

re·proof (ri·proof′) n. The act or an expression of reproving; censure.

re·prove (ri·proov′) v.t. **·proved, ·prov·ing 1** To censure, as for a fault; rebuke. **2** To express disapproval of (an act). [< L re- again + probare to test]—**re·prov′er** n.—**re·prov′ing·ly** adv. —**Syn. 1** admonish, chasten, chide, reproach, scold.

rep·tile (rep′tīl, -til) n. **1** Any of a class of cold-blooded, air-breathing vertebrates having a scaly skin, as crocodiles, lizards, snakes, turtles, etc. **2** A groveling, abject person. —adj. **1** Of, like, or characteristic of a reptile. **2** Groveling, sly, base, etc. [< L reptus, p.p. of repere creep] —**rep·til·i·an** (rep·til′ē·ən) adj., n.

Reptile (crocodile)

re·pub·lic (ri·pub′lik) n. **1** A state in which the sovereignty resides in the people entitled to vote for officers who represent them in governing. **2** This form of government. [< L res thing + publicus public]

re·pub·li·can (ri·pub′li·kən) adj. Pertaining to, of the nature of, or suitable for a republic. —n. An advocate of a republican form of government. —**re·pub′li·can·ism** n.

Re·pub·li·can (ri·pub′li·kən) n. A member of the Republican Party in the U.S. —**Re·pub′li·can·ism** n.

Republican Party One of the two major political parties in the U.S.

re·pu·di·ate (re·pyoo′dē·āt) v.t. **·at·ed, ·at·ing 1** To refuse to accept as valid, true, or authorized; reject. **2** To refuse to acknowledge or pay. **3** To cast off; disown, as a son. [< L repudium divorce] —**re·pu′di·a′tion, re·pu′di·a′tor** n.

re·pug·nance (ri·pug′nəns) n. **1** A feeling of strong distaste or aversion. **2** Contradiction; inconsistency.

re·pug·nant (ri·pug′nənt) adj. **1** Offensive to taste or feeling; exciting aversion. **2** Contradictory; inconsistent. [< L re back + pugnare to fight] —**re·pug′nant·ly** adv.

re·pulse (ri·puls′) v.t. **·pulsed, ·puls·ing 1** To drive back; repel, as an attacking force. **2** To repel by coldness, discourtesy, etc.; rebuff. **3** To excite disgust in. —n. **1** The act of repulsing, or the state of being repulsed. **2** Rejection; refusal. [< L repulsus, p.p. of repellere repel] —**re·puls′er** n.

re·pul·sion (ri·pul′shən) n. **1** The act of repelling, or the state of being repelled. **2** Aversion; repugnance. **3** Physics The mutual action of two bodies that tends to drive them apart.

re·pul·sive (ri·pul′siv) adj. **1** Exciting strong feelings of dislike or disgust; offensive. **2** Such as to discourage approach; forbidding. **3** Acting to repulse. —**re·pul′sive·ly** adv. —**re·pul′sive·ness** n.

rep·u·ta·ble (rep′yə·tə·bəl) adj. **1** Having a good reputation; estimable; honorable. **2** Complying with the usage of the best writers. —**rep′u·ta·bil′i·ty** n. —**rep′u·ta·bly** adv.

rep·u·ta·tion (rep′yə·tā′shən) n. **1** The general estimation in which a person or thing is held by others, either good or bad. **2** High regard or esteem. **3** A particular credit ascribed to a person or thing: a reputation for honesty. [< L reputare be reputed.]

re·pute (ri·pyoot′) v.t. **·put·ed, ·put·ing** To regard or consider: usu. in the passive: reputed to be clever. —n. REPUTATION (defs. 1 & 2). [< L re- again + putare think, count]

re·put·ed (ri·pyoo′tid) adj. Generally thought or supposed. —**re·put′ed·ly** adv.

re·quest (ri·kwest′) v.t. **1** To express a desire for, esp. politely. **2** To ask a favor of. —n. **1** The act of requesting; entreaty; petition. **2** That which is requested, as a favor. **3** The state of being requested: in request. [< L requisitus, p.p. of requirere seek again]

re·qui·em (rek′wē·əm, rē′kwē-) n. **1** Often cap. Any musical composition or service for the dead. **2** Often cap. A musical setting for such a service. [< L Requiem rest, the first word of a Roman Catholic mass for the dead]

req·ui·es·cat (rek′wē·es′kat) n. A prayer for the repose of the dead. [L, may he (or she) rest]

re·quire (ri·kwīr′) v. **·quired, ·quir·ing** v.t. **1** To have need of; find necessary. **2** To call for, demand: Hunting requires patience. **3** To insist upon: to require absolute silence. **4** To command; order. —v.i. **5** To make a demand or request. [< L re- again + quaerere ask, seek] —**re·quir′er** n.

re·quire·ment (ri·kwīr′mənt) n. **1** That which is required, as to satisfy a condition; a requisite. **2** A need or necessity.

req·ui·site (rek′wə·zit) adj. Required by the nature of things or by circumstances; indispensable. —n. That which cannot be dispensed with. —**req′ui·site·ly** adv. —**req′ui·site·ness** n.

req·ui·si·tion (rek′wə·zish′ən) n. **1** A formal request, as for supplies or equipment. **2** The act of requiring or demanding, as that something be supplied. **3** The state of being required. —v.t. To make a requisition for or to.

re·qui·tal (ri·kwīt′l) n. **1** The act of requiting. **2** Adequate return for good or ill; reward, compensation, or retaliation.

re·quite (ri·kwīt′) v.t. **·quit·ed, ·quit·ing 1** To make equivalent return for, as kindness, service, or injury. **2** To compensate or repay in kind. [< RE- + quite, obs. var. of QUIT] —**re·quit′er** n.

rere·dos (rir′ə dos, rer′ə-, rir′dos) n. An ornamental screen behind an altar. [< OF arere at the back + dos back]

re·run (rē′run′) n. A running over again, esp. a showing of a film of videotape after the initial showing. —v.t. (rē·run′) **·ran, ·run·ning** To run again.

res. research; reserve; residence; resolution.

re·scind (ri·sind′) v.t. To cancel or make void, as an order or an act. [< L re- back + scindere to cut]—**re·scind′ment, re·scind′er** n.

re·scis·sion (ri·sizh′ən) n. The act of rescinding. —**re·scis′si·ble, re·scis′so·ry** adj.

res·cue (res′kyoo) v.t. **·cued, ·cu·ing 1** To save or free from danger, captivity, evil, etc. **2** Law To take or remove forcibly from the custody of the law. —n. The act of rescuing. [< L re- again + excutere shake off] —**res′cu·er** n.

re·search (ri·sûrch′, rē′sûrch) n. Studious, systematic investigation or inquiry to ascertain, uncover, or assemble facts, used as a basis for conclusions or the formulation of theory. —v.t. **1** To do research on or for: to research an article. —v.i. **2** To do research; investigate. [< F recherche] —**re·search′er** n.

re·sect (ri·sekt′) v.t. To perform a resection on. [< L re- back + secare cut, amputate]

re·sec·tion (ri·sek′shən) n. The surgical removal of a part of a bone, organ, etc.

re·sem·blance (ri·zem′bləns) n. **1** The quality of similarlity in nature, appearance, etc.; likeness. **2** A point or degree of similarity. **3** That which resembles a person or thing; semblance.

re·sem·ble (ri·zem′bəl) v.t. **·bled, ·bling** To be similar to in appearance, quality, or character. [< OF re- again + sembler seem]

re·sent (ri·zent′) v.t. To be indignant at, as an injury or insult. [< L re- again + sentire feel] —**re·sent′ful** adj. —**re·sent′ful·ly** adv. —**re·sent′ful·ness** n.

re·sent·ment (ri·zent′mənt) n. Anger and ill will caused by a feeling of injury or mistreatment.

res·er·va·tion (rez′ər·vā′shən) n. **1** A feeling of doubt or skepticism, expressed or unexpressed. **2** A qualification; condition; limitation. **3** An agreement to hold something back, as a hotel room, restaurant table, etc., for use at a particular time; also, a record of such an agreement. **4** The act of reserving. **5** A tract of public land set aside for some special purpose, as for the use of Indians or for the preservation of wildlife.

re·serve (ri·zûrv′) v.t. **·served, ·serv·ing, 1** To hold back or set aside for special or future use. **2** To arrange for ahead of time; have set aside for one's use. **3** To hold back or delay the determination or disclosure of: to *reserve* judgment. **4** To keep as one's own; retain: to *reserve* the right to quit. —*n.* **1** Something stored up for future use or set aside for a particular purpose. **2** A restrained quality of character or manner; reluctance to divulge one's feelings, thoughts, etc. **3** *Usu. pl.* **a** A military force held back from active duty to meet possible emergencies. **b** Members or units of such a force. **4** A substitute player on an athletic team. **5** Funds held back from investment, as in a bank, to meet regular demands. **6** The act of reserving; stint; qualification: without *reserve*. —**in reserve** Subject to or held for future use when needed. —*adj.* Constituting a reserve: a *reserve* supply. [< L *re-* back + *servare* keep] — **re·serv′er** *n.* —**Syn.** *n.* **2** reticence, diffidence, aloofness, modesty, restraint.

reserve clause In professional sports, the stipulation in a contract that commits a player to work for a particular team until released or traded by the employer or until retirement.

re·served (ri·zûrvd′) *adj.* **1** Showing or characterized by reserve of manner; undemonstrative. **2** Kept in reserve; held ready for use. —**re·serv·ed·ly** (ri·zûr′vid·lē) *adv.* —**re·serv′ed·ness** *n.*

re·serv·ist (ri·zûr′vist) *n.* A member of a military reserve.

res·er·voir (rez′ər·vwär, -vwôr -vôr) *n.* **1** A place where some material is stored for use, esp. a lake, usu. artificial, for collecting and storing water. **2** A receptacle for a fluid. **3** An extra supply; store.

re·shape (rē·shāp′) *v.t.* **·shaped**, **·shap·ing** To give new form to; reorder the elements or structure of.

re·side (ri·zīd′) *v.i.* **·sid·ed**, **·sid·ing** **1** To dwell for a considerable time; live. **2** To exist as an attribute or quality: with *in*. **3** To be vested: with *in*. [< L *residere* sit back]

res·i·dence (rez′ə·dəns) *n.* **1** The place or the house where one resides. **2** The act of residing. **3** The length of time one resides in a place. **4** The act or fact of residing. **5** The condition of residing in a particular place to perform certain duties or to pursue studies, often for a specified length of time.

res·i·den·cy (rez′ə·dən·sē) *n. pl.* **·cies** **1** RESIDENCE. **2** A period of advanced training in a hospital, usu. in a medical specialty.

res·i·dent (rez′ə·dənt) *n.* **1** One who resides or dwells in a place. **2** A physician engaged in residency. **3** A diplomatic representative residing at a foreign seat of government. —*adj.* **1** Having a residence; residing. **2** Living in a place in connection with one's official work. **3** Not migratory: said of certain birds.

res·i·den·tial (rez′ə·den′shəl) *adj.* **1** Of, characteristic of, or suitable for residences. **2** Used by residents.

re·sid·u·al (ri·zij′o͞o·əl) *adj.* **1** Pertaining to or having the nature of a residue or remainder. **2** Left over as a residue. —*n.* **1** That which is left over from a total, as after subtraction. **2** *Often pl.* A payment made to a performer for each rerun of taped or filmed TV material in which he or she has appeared. —**re·sid′u·al·ly** *adv.*

re·sid·u·ar·y (ri·zij′o͞o·er′ē) *adj.* Entitled to receive the residue of an estate.

res·i·due (rez′ə·d(y)o͞o) *n.* **1** A remainder after a part has been separated or removed. **2** *Chem.* Matter left unaffected after combustion, distillation, evaporation, etc. **3** *Law* That portion of an estate which remains after all charges, debts, and particular bequests have been satisfied. [< L *residuus* remaining]

res·id·u·um (ri·zij′o͞o·əm) *n. pl.* **·sid·u·a** (-zij′o͞o·ə) **1** RESIDUAL (def. 1). **2** RESIDUE (def. 3). [L]

re·sign (ri·zīn′) *v.t.* **1** To give up, as a position, office, or trust. **2** To relinquish (a privilege, claim, etc.). **3** To give over (oneself, one's mind, etc.), as to fate or domination. —*v.i.* **4** To resign a position, etc. [< OF< L *re-* back + *signare* to sign] —**re·sign′er** *n.*

res·ig·na·tion (rez′ig·nā′shən) *n.* **1** The act of resigning. **2** A formal notice of resigning. **3** The quality of being submissive; unresisting acquiescence.

re·signed (ri·zīnd′) *adj.* Characterized by resignation; submissive. —**re·sign·ed·ly** (ri·zī′nid·lē) *adv.* —**re·sign′ed·ness** *n.*

re·sil·ience (ri·zil′yəns) *n.* **1** The quality of being resilient; elasticity. **2** Cheerful buoyancy. Also **re·sil′ien·cy.**

re·sil·ient (ri·zil′yənt) *adj.* **1** Springing back to a former shape or position after being bent, compressed, etc. **2** Able to recover quickly; buoyant. [< L *resilire* to rebound] — **re·sil′ient·ly** *adv.*

res·in (rez′in) *n.* **1** A solid or semisolid, usu. translucent substance exuded from certain plants, used in varnishes, plastics, etc. **2** Any of various substances resembling this made by chemical synthesis. **3** ROSIN. —*v.t.* To apply resin to. [< Gk. *rhētinē*] —**res·i·na·ceous** (rez′ə·nā′shəs), **res′in·ous** *adj.*

re·sist (ri·zist′) *v.t.* **1** To stay the effect of; withstand; hold off: Steel *resists* corrosion. **2** To fight or struggle against; seek to foil or frustrate: to *resist* arrest; to *resist* temptation. —*v.i.* **3** To offer opposition. [< L *re-* back + *sistere*, causative of *stare* stand] —**re·sist′er, re·sist′i·bil′i·ty** *n.* —**re·sist′i·ble, re·sis′tive** *adj.* —**re·sist′i·bly** *adv.*

re·sis·tance (ri·zis′təns) *n.* **1** The act of resisting. **2** Any force tending to hinder motion. **3** The capacity of an organism to ward off the effects of potentially harmful substances, as toxins. **4** *Electr.* The opposition of a body to the passage through it of an electric current. **5** The underground and guerrilla movement in a conquered country opposing the occupying power. —**re·sis′tant** *adj.*

re·sis·tor (ri·zis′tər) *n. Electr.* A device whose principal property is resistance.

res·o·lute (rez′ə·lo͞ot) *adj.* Having a fixed purpose; determined. [< L *resolutus*, p.p. of *resolvere* to resolve] —**res′o·lute·ly** *adv.* —**res′o·lute·ness** *n.* —**Syn.** steady, constant, firm, decisive.

res·o·lu·tion (rez′ə·lo͞o′shən) *n.* **1** The act of resolving or of reducing to a simpler form. **2** The making of a resolve. **3** The purpose or course resolved upon. **4** Firmness of purpose. **5** An outcome or result that serves to settle a problem, uncertainty, or conflict. **6** A statement expressing the intention or judgment of an assembly or group. **7** *Music* **a** The conventional replacement of a dissonant tone, chord, etc., by one that is consonant. **b** The tone or chord replacing the dissonant one. **8** The capacity of a telescope, microscope, etc., to give separate images of objects close together.

re·solve (ri·zolv′) *v.* **·solved**, **·solv·ing** *v.t.* **1** To decide; determine (to do something). **2** To cause to decide or determine. **3** To separate or break down into constituent parts; analyze. **4** To clear away or settle, as a problem, uncertainty, or conflict; explain or solve. **5** To state or decide by vote. **6** *Music* To cause (a dissonant tone, chord, etc.) to undergo resolution. **7** To make distinguishable, as with a telescope or microscope. —*v.i.* **8** To make up one's mind: with *on* or *upon*. **9** To become separated into constituent parts. **10** *Music* To undergo resolution. —*n.* **1** Fixity of purpose; determination. **2** Something resolved upon; a decision. **3** A formal expression of the intention or judgment of an assembly or group. [< L *resolvere* loosen again] —**re·solv′a·ble** *adj.* —**re·solv′er** *n.*

res·o·nance (rez′ə·nəns) *n.* **1** The state or quality of being resonant; resonant sound. **2** Prolongation and amplification of a sound or tone by reverberation. **3** *Physics* A property of oscillatory systems whereby excitation at certain frequencies produces response of greater amplitude than at other frequencies.

res·o·nant (rez′ə·nənt) *adj.* **1** Having the quality of prolonging and amplifying sound by reverberation; producing resonance. **2** Resounding; displaying resonance. **3** Full of or characterized by resonance: a *resonant* voice. [< L *resonare* resound, echo] —**res′o·nant·ly** *adv.*

res·o·nate (rez′ə·nāt) *v.i.* **·nat·ed**, **·nat·ing** To exhibit or produce resonance.

res·o·na·tor (rez′ə·nā′tər) *n.* Any device used to produce resonance or to increase sound by resonance.

re·sor·cin·ol (ri·zôr′sin·ōl, -ol) *n.* A derivative of phenol, used as an antiseptic and in making dyes, plastics, etc. Also **re·sor′cin.** [< RES(IN) + *orcinol* a phenol]

re·sort (ri·zôrt′) *v.i.* **1** To go frequently or habitually; repair. **2** To have recourse: with *to*. —*n.* **1** A hotel or other place that provides recreational facilities and sometimes entertainment, esp. for those on vacation. **2** The use of something as a means; a recourse; refuge. **3** A person looked to for help. **4** A place frequented regularly. [< OF *re-* again + *sortir* go out] —**re·sort′er** *n.*

re·sound (ri·zound′) *v.i.* **1** To be filled with sound; echo; reverberate. **2** To make a loud, prolonged, or echoing sound. **3** To ring; echo. **4** To be famed or extolled. —*v.t.* **5** To give back (a sound, etc.); re-echo. **6** To celebrate; extol. [< L *resonare*]

re·source (rē′sôrs, -sōrs, -zôrs, -zōrs, ri·sôrs′, -sōrs′, -zôrs′, -zōrs′) *n.* **1** *Usu. pl.* That which can be drawn upon as a means of help or support. **2** *Usu. pl.* Natural advantages, esp. of a country, as forests, oil deposits, etc. **3** *pl.* Available wealth or property. **4** Skill or ingenuity in meeting any situation. **5** Any way or method of coping with a difficult situation. [< L *re-* back + *surgere* to rise, surge]

re·source·ful (ri·sôrs′fəl, -sōrs′-, -zôrs′, -zōrs′) *adj.* Having the ability to meet the demands of any situation; ingenious. —**re·source′ful·ly** *adv.* —**re·source′ful·ness** *n.*

re·spect (ri·spekt′) *v.t.* **1** To have deferential regard for; esteem. **2** To treat with propriety or consideration. **3** To avoid intruding upon; regard as inviolable. **4** To have reference to; concern. —*n.* **1** A high regard for and appreciation of worth; esteem. **2** Due regard or consideration: *respect* for the law. **3** *pl.* Expressions of consideration; compliments: to pay one's *respects.* **4** The condition of being honored or respected. **5** A specific aspect or detail: In some *respects* the plan is impractical. **6** Reference or relation: usu. with *to:* with *respect* to profits. [< L *respectus,* p.p. of *respicere* look back, consider] —**re·spect′er** *n.*

re·spect·a·ble (ri·spek′tə·bəl) *adj.* **1** Deserving of respect. **2** Conventionally correct; socially acceptable. **3** Having a good appearance; presentable. **4** Moderate in quality, size, or amount; fair: a *respectable* talent. —**re·spect′a·bil′i·ty, re·spect′a·ble·ness** *n.* —**re·spect′a·bly** *adv.*

re·spect·ful (ri·spekt′fəl) *adj.* Characterized by or showing respect. —**re·spect′ful·ly** *adv.* —**re·spect′ful·ness** *n.*

re·spect·ing (ri·spek′ting) *prep.* In relation to.

re·spec·tive (ri·spek′tiv) *adj.* Relating separately to each of those under consideration; several.

re·spec·tive·ly (ri·spek′tiv·lē) *adv.* Singly in the order designated: to describe the duties of the judge and jury *respectively.*

res·pi·ra·tion (res′pə·rā′shən) *n.* **1** The act of inhaling air and expelling it; breathing. **2** The process by which an organism takes in and uses oxygen and gives off carbon dioxide and other waste products. —**re·spir·a·to·ry** (res′pər·ə·tôr′ē, ri·spīr′ə·tôr′ē) *adj.*

res·pi·ra·tor (res′pə·rā′tər) *n.* **1** A screen, as of fine gauze, worn over the mouth or nose, as a protection against dust, etc. **2** An apparatus for artificial respiration.

re·spire (ri·spīr′) *v.* **·spired, ·spir·ing** *v.i.* **1** To inhale and exhale air; breathe. —*v.t.* **2** To breathe. [< L *re-* again + *spirare* breathe]

res·pite (res′pit) *n.* **1** Postponement; delay. **2** Temporary relief from labor or effort; an interval of rest. [< Med. L *respectus* delay]

re·splen·dent (ri·splen′dənt) *adj.* Shining with brilliant luster; splendid; gorgeous. [< L *re-* again + *splendere* to shine] —**re·splen′dence, re·splen′den·cy** *n.* —**re·splen′dent·ly** *adv.*

re·spond (ri·spond′) *v.i.* **1** To give an answer; reply. **2** To act in reply or return. **3** To react favorably: to *respond* to treatment. —*v.t.* **4** To say in answer; reply. [< L *re-* back + *spondere* to pledge] —**re·spond′er** *n.*

re·spon·dent (ri·spon′dənt) *n.* **1** One who responds or answers. **2** *Law* The party called upon to answer an appeal or petition; a defendant. —**re·spon′dence, re·spon′den·cy** *n.*

re·sponse (ri·spons′) *n.* **1** Words or acts called forth as a reaction; an answer or reply. **2** *Eccl.* A portion of a church service said or sung by the congregation in reply to the officiating priest. **3** *Biol.* Any reaction resulting from a stimulus. **4** The action of a physical system when energized or disturbed.

re·spon·si·bil·i·ty (ri·spon′sə·bil′ə·tē) *n. pl.* **·ties 1** The state of being responsible or accountable. **2** That for which one is responsible; a duty or trust. Also **re·spon′si·ble·ness.**

re·spon·si·ble (ri·spon′sə·bəl) *adj.* **1** Subject to being called upon to account or answer for something; accountable. **2** Able to discriminate between right and wrong. **3** Able to account or answer for something; able to meet one's obligations. **4** Being the cause: Rain was *responsible* for the delay. —**re·spon′si·bly** *adv.*

re·spon·sive (ri·spon′siv) *adj.* **1** Constituting a response. **2** Inclined to react with sympathy or understanding. **3** Containing responses. —**re·spon′sive·ly** *adv.* —**re·spon′sive·ness[1]** *n.*

rest[1] (rest) *v.i.* **1** To cease working or exerting oneself for

Rests *def. 8b*
a. whole. b. half. c. quarter. d. eighth. e. sixteenth.
f. thirty-second. g. sixty-fourth.

a time; cease activity. **2** To obtain ease or refreshment by lying down, sleeping, etc. **3** To sleep. **4** To be still or quiet; cease all motion. **5** To be dead. **6** To be or lie in a specified place: The blame *rests* with me. **7** To be supported; stand, lean, lie, or sit: The rifle *rested* on the mantel. **8** To be founded or based: That *rests* on the assumption of his innocence. **9** To be directed, as the eyes. —*v.t.* **10** To give rest to; refresh by rest. **11** To put, lay, lean, etc., as for support or rest. **12** To found; base. **13** To direct (the gaze, eyes, etc.). **14** *Law* To cease presenting evidence in (a case). —*n.* **1** The act or state of resting. **2** A period of resting. **3** Freedom from disturbance or disquiet; peace; tranquility. **4** Sleep. **5** Death. **6** That on which anything rests; a support; basis. **7** A place for stopping or resting. **8** *Music* **a** A measured interval of silence. **b** A character representing this. —**at rest** In a state of rest; motionless, peaceful, asleep, or dead. [< OE *restan*] —**rest′er** *n.* —**Syn.** *n.* **1** repose, quiet, inactivity, relaxation. **2** respite. **3** serenity, peacefulness, calmness. **6** base, foundation.

rest[2] (rest) *n.* That which remains or is left over. —**the rest** That or those which remain; the remainder; the others. —*v.i.* To be and remain: *Rest* content. [< L *restare* stop, stand]

re·state (rē·stāt′) *v.t.* **·stat·ed, ·stat·ing** To state again or in a new way. —**re·state′ment** *n.*

res·tau·rant (res′tə·ränt, -tränt, -tər·ənt) *n.* A place where meals are prepared for sale and served on the premises. [F, lit., restoring]

res·tau·ra·teur (res′tər·ə·tûr′) *n.* The proprietor of a restaurant. [F]

rest·ful (rest′fəl) *adj.* **1** Full of or giving rest. **2** Being at rest; quiet. —**rest′ful·ly** *adv.* —**rest′ful·ness** *n.*

res·ti·tu·tion (res′tə·tyōō′shən) *n.* **1** The act of restoring something that has been taken away or lost. **2** Restoration or return to a rightful owner. **3** The act of making good for injury or loss. [< L *restituere* restore]

res·tive (res′tiv) *adj.* **1** Restless; fidgety: The audience grew *restive.* **2** Unwilling to submit to control; unruly; balky. [< F *rester* remain, balk] —**res′tive·ly** *adv.* —**res′·tive·ness** *n.*

rest·less (rest′lis) *adj.* **1** Affording no rest or little rest; disturbed: a *restless* sleep. **2** Uneasy; impatient; unquiet: to feel *restless.* **3** Never resting; unending: the *restless* waves. **4** Constantly seeking change or activity; unable or unwilling to rest. —**rest′less·ly** *adv.* —**rest′less·ness** *n.*

res·to·ra·tion (res′tə·rā′shən) *n.* **1** The act of restoring, or the state of being restored. **2** The bringing back to an original or earlier condition, as a work of art or a building; also, the object so restored. —**the Restoration 1** The return of Charles II to the English throne in 1660. **2** The period following his return up to the revolution in 1688.

re·stor·a·tive (ri·stôr′ə·tiv, -stō′rə-) *adj.* Tending or able to restore consciousness, strength, health, etc. —*n.* A restorative substance. —**re·sto′ra·tive·ly** *adv.* —**re·sto′ra·tive·ness** *n.*

re·store (ri·stôr′, -stōr′) *v.t.* **·stored, ·stor·ing 1** To bring into existence or effect again: to *restore* peace. **2** To bring back to a former or original condition, as a work of art or a building. **3** To put back in a former place or position; reinstate. **4** To bring back to health and vigor. **5** To give back (something lost or taken away); return. [< L *restaurare*] —**re·stor′er** *n.*

re·strain (ri·strān′) *v.t.* **1** To hold back from acting, proceeding, or advancing. **2** To restrict or limit. **3** To deprive of liberty, as by placing in a prison. [< L *re-* back + *stringere* draw tight] —**re·strain′ed·ly** (-strān′id·lē) *adv.* —**re·strain′er** *n.*

re·straint (ri·strānt′) *n.* **1** The act of restraining, or the state of being restrained. **2** Something that restrains, as a harness or similar device. **3** A restriction on conduct; stricture. **4** Control over the display of one's emotions, opinions, etc.; self-control.

re·strict (ri·strikt′) *v.t.* To hold or keep within limits or bounds; confine. [< L *re-* back + *stringere* draw tight]

re·strict·ed (ri·strik′tid) *adj.* **1** Limited or confined. **2** Available for use by certain persons or groups; also, excluding certain persons or groups.

re·stric·tion (ri·strik′shən) *n.* **1** The act of restricting, or the state of being restricted. **2** That which restricts; a limitation or restraint.

re·stric·tive (ri·strik′tiv) *adj.* **1** Serving, tending, or operating to restrict. **2** *Gram.* Limiting: a *restrictive* clause. —**re·stric′tive·ly** *adv.* • In *Will the man who spoke just now please stand up, who spoke just now* is a restrictive clause because it limits the application of *man*, which it modifies. It is not set off by commas, and is to be distinguished from a nonrestrictive clause, as in *The president, who will be 60 years old tomorrow, held a press conference today.*

rest room In a public building, a room or rooms provided with toilet facilities.

re·struc·ture (rē·struk′chər) *v.t.* **·tured, ·tur·ing** To reorganize on a different basis or into a new pattern.

re·sult (ri·zult′) *n.* **1** The outcome of an action, course, or process. **2** A quantity or value derived by calculation. —*v.i.* **1** To be a result or outcome; follow: with *from.* **2** To have as a consequence; end: with *in.* [< L *resultare* spring back]

re·sul·tant (ri·zul′tənt) *adj.* Arising or following as a result. —*n.* **1** That which results; a consequence. **2** *Physics* A vector representing the sum of two or more other vectors.

re·sume (ri·zo͞om′) *v.* **·sumed, ·sum·ing** *v.t.* **1** To begin again after an interruption. **2** To take or occupy again: *Resume your places.* —*v.i.* **3** To continue after an interruption. [< L *resumere* take up again] —**re·sum′er** *n.*

rés·u·mé (rez′o͝o·mā, rez′o͞o·mā′) *n.* A summary, as of one's employment record, education, etc., used in applying for a new position. Also **res·u·mé′, res·u·me′.** [F]

re·sump·tion (ri·zump′shən) *n.* The act of resuming; a beginning again.

re·sur·face (rē·sûr′fis) *v.t.* **·faced, ·fac·ing 1** To provide with a new surface. —*v.i.* **2** To come into view again; become evident.

re·sur·gence (ri·sûr′jəns) *n.* A rising again, as from death, inactivity, or defeat; a surging back. Also **re·sur′· gen·cy.** —**re·sur′gent** *adj.*

res·ur·rect (rez′ə·rekt′) *v.t.* **1** To bring back to life. **2** To bring back into use or to notice.

res·ur·rec·tion (rez′ə·rek′shən) *n.* **1** Any revival or renewal, as of a practice or custom. **2** *Theol.* **a** A rising from the dead. **b** The state of those who have risen from the dead. —**the Resurrection 1** The rising of Christ from the dead. **2** The rising again of all the dead at the day of final judgment. [< L *resurrectus*, p.p. of *resurgere* < *re-* again + *surgere* rise] —**res′ur·rec′tion·al** *adj.*

re·sus·ci·tate (ri·sus′ə·tāt) *v.t. & v.i.* **·tat·ed, ·tat·ing** To revive from unconsciousness or apparent death. [< L *re-* again + *suscitare* revive] —**re·sus′ci·ta′tion, re·sus′ci·ta′tor** *n.* —**re·sus′ci·ta′tive** *adj.*

ret (ret) *v.t.* **ret·ted, ret·ting** To steep or soak, as flax, to separate the fibers. [ME *reten*]

ret. retired.

re·tail (rē′tāl) *n.* The selling of goods in small quantities directly to the consumer. —**at retail 1** In small quantities to the consumer. **2** At retail prices. —*adj.* Of, pertaining

to, or engaged in the sale of goods at retail. —*adv.* AT RETAIL. —*v.t.* **1** To sell in small quantities directly to the consumer. **2** (ri·tāl′) To repeat, as gossip. —*v.i.* **3** To be sold at retail. [< OF *retailler* cut up] —**re′tail·er** *n.*

re·tain (ri·tān′) *v.t.* **1** To keep in one's possession; hold. **2** To maintain in use, practice, etc.: to *retain* one's standards. **3** To keep in a fixed condition or place. **4** To keep in mind; remember. **5** To hire or engage, as an attorney. [< L *re-* back + *tenere* to hold]

re·tain·er[1] (ri·tā′nər) *n.* **1** One employed in the service of a person of rank; servant. **2** One who or that which retains.

re·tain·er[2] (ri·tā′nər) *n.* **1** The fee paid to retain the services of an attorney or other adviser. **2** The act of retaining the services of an attorney, etc. [< OF *retenir* hold back]

retaining wall A wall to prevent a side of an embankment or cut from sliding.

re·tal·i·ate (ri·tal′ē·āt) *v.* **·at·ed, ·at·ing** *v.i.* **1** To return like for like; esp., to repay evil with evil. —*v.t.* **2** To repay (an injury, wrong, etc.) in kind; revenge. [< L *re-* back + *talio* punishment in kind] —**re·tal′i·a′tion** *n.* —**re·tal′i·a·tive, re·tal′i·a·to·ry** *adj.*

re·tard (ri·tärd′) *v.t.* **1** To hinder the advance or course of; impede; delay. —*v.i.* **2** To be delayed. —*n.* Delay; retardation. [< L *re-* back + *tardus* slow] —**re′tar·da′tion, re·tard′er** *n.* —**re·tard′a·tive** *adj.*

re·tard·ant (ri·tär′dənt) *n.* Something that retards: a fire *retardant.* —*adj.* Tending to retard.

re·tar·date (ri·tär′dāt) *n.* A mentally retarded person.

re·tard·ed (ri·tärd′id) *adj.* Abnormally slow in development, esp. mental development.

retch (rech) *v.i.* To make an effort to vomit; strain; heave. [< OE *hræcan* bring up (blood or phlegm)]

retd. retained; returned; retired.

re·ten·tion (ri·ten′shən) *n.* **1** The act of retaining, or the state of being retained. **2** The ability to retain data, images, etc., in the mind subject to later recall. **3** *Med.* A retaining within the body of materials normally excreted.

re·ten·tive (ri·ten′tiv) *adj.* Having the power or tendency to retain, esp. to retain in the mind: a *retentive* memory. —**re·ten′tive·ly** *adv.* —**re·ten′tive·ness, re·ten·tiv′i·ty** *n.*

re·think (rē·thingk′) *v.t.* **·thought** (-thôt), **·think·ing** To think about again, esp. in order to reassess; reconsider.

ret·i·cent (ret′ə·sənt) *adj.* **1** Reluctant to speak or speak freely; habitually silent; reserved. **2** Subdued or restrained; shunning bold statement: *reticent* prose. [< L *re-* again + *tacere* be silent] —**ret′i·cence, ret′i·cen·cy** *n.* —**ret′i·cent·ly** *adv.*

re·tic·u·lar (ri·tik′yə·lər) *adj.* **1** Like a net. **2** Intricate. **3** Of or pertaining to a reticulum. [< L *reticulum* network]

re·tic·u·late (ri·tik′yə·lāt) *v.* **·lat·ed, ·lat·ing** *v.t.* **1** To make a network of. **2** To cover with or as with lines of network. —*v.i.* **3** To form a network. —*adj.* (-lit, -lāt) Having the form or appearance of a network: also **re·tic′u·lat′ed.** —**re·tic′u·late·ly** *adv.* —**re·tic′u·la′tion** *n.*

ret·i·cule (ret′ə·kyo͞ol) *n.* A small handbag closed with a drawstring, formerly used by women. [< L *reticulum* network]

re·tic·u·lum (ri·tik′yə·ləm) *n. pl.* **·lums** or **·la** (-lə) The second stomach of a ruminant. [L, dim. of *rete* net]

ret·i·na (ret′ə·nə, ret′nə) *n. pl.* **·nas** or **·nae** (-nē) The light-sensitive membrane lining the back of the eyeball at the distal end of the optic nerve. [< L *rete* net] —**ret′i·nal** *adj.*

ret·i·nue (ret′ə·nyo͞o) *n.* The group of retainers attending a person of rank. [< F *retenir* retain]

re·tire (ri·tīr′) *v.* **·tired, ·tir·ing** *v.i.* **1** To withdraw oneself from business, public life, or active service. **2** To go away or withdraw, as for privacy, shelter, or rest. **3** To go to bed. **4** To fall back; retreat. **5** To move back; recede. —*v.t.* **6** To remove from active service. **7** To pay off and withdraw from circulation: to *retire* bonds. **8** To withdraw (troops, etc.) from action. **9** In baseball, to put out, as a batter. [< F *re-* back + *tirer* draw]

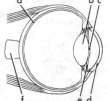

a. retina. b. lens. c. pupil. d. cornea. e. iris. f. optic nerve.

re·tired (ri·tīrd') *adj.* **1** Withdrawn from business, public life, or active service; esp., no longer actively engaged in one's occupation or profession because of having reached a certain age. **2** Of or for those in retirement. **3** Withdrawn from public view; secluded.

re·tir·ee (ri·tīr'ē') *n.* A person who is retired.

re·tire·ment (ri·tīr'mənt) *n.* **1** The act of retiring, or the state of being retired. **2** A withdrawal from active engagement in one's occupation or profession, esp. because of age. **3** An age or date at which retirement is planned. **4** A secluded place.

re·tir·ing (ri·tīr'ing) *adj.* Shy; modest; reserved. **—re·tir'· ing·ly** *adv.*

re·tort[1] (ri·tôrt') *v.t.* **1** To direct (a word or deed) back upon the originator. **2** To reply to, as an accusation or argument, by a similar one. **3** To say in reply. **—v.i.** **4** To answer, esp. sharply. **5** To respond to an accusation, etc., in kind. **—n.** A sharp or witty reply that turns back a previously expressed accusation, insult, etc., upon its originator. [<L *retorquere* twist back] **—re·tort'er** *n.* **—Syn.** *n.* rejoinder, riposte, comeback.

re·tort[2] (ri·tôrt') *n.* A stoppered vessel with a side tube, for heating or distilling substances. [<L *retortus* bent back]

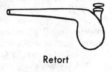
Retort

re·touch (rē·tuch') *v.t.* **1** To modify by changing details; touch up, as a painting. **2** To change or improve, as a photographic print, by a hand process. **—n.** (also rē'· tuch') A retouching, as of a picture. **—re·touch'er** *n.*

re·tract (ri·trakt') *v.t. & v.i.* **1** To take back (an assertion, accusation, admission, etc.); disavow. **2** To draw back or in, as the claws of a cat. [<F<L *retractare* draw back] **—re· tract'a·ble, re·trac'tive** *adj.* **—re·trac'tion, re·trac'tor** *n.*

re·trac·tile (ri·trak'til) *adj. Zool.* Capable of being drawn back or in. **—re·trac·til·i·ty** (rē'trak·til'ə·tē) *n.*

re·tread (rē'tred') *n.* A tire furnished with a new tread to replace a worn one. **—v.t.** (rē·tred') To fit or furnish (a tire) with a new tread.

re·treat (ri·trēt') *v.i.* **1** To go back or backward; withdraw. **2** To curve or slope backward. **—n.** **1** The act of retreating or drawing back, as from danger or conflict. **2** The retirement of an armed force from a position of danger. **3** In the armed forces, a signal, as by bugle, for the lowering of the flag at sunset. **4** A place of retirement or security; a refuge. **5** A period of religious contemplation and prayer by a group withdrawn from regular society. [<L *re-* again + *trahere* draw]

re·trench (ri·trench') *v.t.* **1** To cut down or curtail (expenditures). **2** To cut off or away. **—v.i.** **3** To economize. [<MF *re-* back + *trencher* to cut] **—re·trench'er, re·trench'ment** *n.*

ret·ri·bu·tion (ret'rə·byoo'shən) *n.* **1** The impartial infliction of punishment, as for evil done. **2** That which is done or given in requital, as a reward or, esp., a punishment. [<L *re-* back + *tribuere* to pay] **—re·trib·u·tive** (ri·trib'yə· tiv), **re·trib'u·to·ry** *adj.* **—re·trib'u·tive·ly** *adv.*

re·triev·al (ri·trē'vəl) *n.* **1** The act or process of retrieving. **2** The power to restore or retrieve.

re·trieve (ri·trēv') *v.* **·trieved, ·triev·ing** *v.t.* **1** To get back; regain. **2** To restore; revive, as flagging spirits. **3** To make up for; remedy the consequences of. **4** To call to mind; remember. **5** To locate and provide access to (data) in computer storage. **6** In tennis, etc., to return (a ball, etc.) after a run. **7** To find and bring in (wounded or dead game): said of dogs. **—v.i.** **8** To retrieve game. **—n.** The act of retrieving; recovery. [<OF *re-* again + *trouver* find] **—re·triev·a·bil'i·ty** *n.* **—re·triev'a·ble** *adj.*

re·triev·er (ri·trē'vər) *n.* **1** Any of various breeds of dog usu. trained to retrieve game. **2** A person who retrieves.

retro- *prefix* Back; backward: retrograde. [<L *retro* backward]

ret·ro·ac·tive (ret'rō·ak'tiv, rē'trō-) *adj.* Effective or applicable to a period prior to the time of enactment: a *retroactive* ruling granting wage increases as of last May. **—ret'ro·ac'tive·ly** *adv.* **—ret'ro·ac·tiv'i·ty** *n.*

ret·ro·grade (ret'rə·grād) *adj.* **1** Going, moving, or tend-

ing backward. **2** Declining toward a worse state or character. **3** Inverted in order. **—v.** **·grad·ed, ·grad·ing** *v.i.* **1** To move or appear to move backward. **2** To grow worse; decline; degenerate. [<L *retrogradus* a step backward] **— ret'ro·gra·da'tion** (-grā·dā'shən) *n.*

ret·ro·gress (ret'rə·gres) *v.i.* To go back to a more primitive or worse condition. [<L *retro-* backward + *gradi* walk] **—ret'ro·gres'sion** *n.* **—ret'ro·gres'sive** *adj.*

ret·ro·rock·et (ret'rō·rok'it) *n.* An auxiliary rocket that provides a backward thrust, as for reducing speed.

ret·ro·spect (ret'rə·spekt) *n.* A looking back on things past. **—in retrospect** In recalling or reviewing the past. [<L<*retro-* back + *specere* look] **—ret'ro·spec'tion** *n.*

ret·ro·spec·tive (ret'rə·spek'tiv) *adj.* **1** Looking back on the past. **2** RETROACTIVE. **—n.** An exhibition of works representing the entire period of an artist's productivity. **—ret'ro·spec'tive·ly** *adv.*

ret·ro·vi·rus (ret'rō·vī'rəs) *n.* A member of a family of viruses that contain RNA instead of DNA.

re·turn (ri·tûrn') *v.i.* **1** To come or go back, as to or toward a former place or condition. **2** To come back or revert in thought or speech. **3** To revert to a former owner. **4** To answer; respond. **—v.t.** **5** To bring, carry, send, or put back; restore; replace. **6** To give in return, esp. with an equivalent: to *return* a favor. **7** To yield or produce, as a profit. **8** To send back; reflect, as light or sound. **9** To render (a verdict, etc.). **10** In sports, to throw, hit, or carry back (a ball). **11** In card games, to lead (a suit previously led by one's partner). **—n.** **1** The act of bringing back or restoring something to a former place or condition; restoration or replacement. **2** An appearing again; recurrence. **3** Something given or sent back, esp. in kind or as an equivalent; repayment. **4** Something, as an article of merchandise, returned for exchange or reimbursement. **5** *Often pl.* Profit or revenue; yield. **6** A response; answer; retort. **7** A formal or official report: a tax *return.* **8** *pl.* A report of the tabulated votes of an election. **9** In sports, the act of returning a ball. **—in return** In repayment; as an equivalent **—adj.** **1** Of or for a return: a *return* ticket. **2** Constituting a return or recurrence: a *return* engagement. **3** Returning. **4** Used for return: a *return* address. [<OF] **—re·turn'er** *n.*

re·un·ion (rē·yoon'yən) *n.* **1** The act of reuniting. **2** A social gathering of persons who have been separated.

re·u·nite (rē'yoo·nīt') *v.t. & v.i.* **·nit·ed, ·nit·ing** To bring or come together after separation. **—re'u·nit'er** *n.*

rev (rev) *Informal n.* A revolution, as of a motor. **—v.t.** **revved, rev·ving** **1** To increase the speed of (an engine, motor, etc.,): often with *up.* **2** To increase in tempo or intensity with *up.* **3** To stimulate or excite: with *up.* **—v.i.** **4** To increase the speed of an engine, etc.: often with *up.* **5** To become stimulated or excited: with *up.*

Rev, Rev. Revelation; Reverend.

rev. revenue; reverse; review; revised; revision; revolution.

re·vamp (rē·vamp') *v.t.* To make over or renovate.

re·vanch·ism (ri·vänsh'iz'əm) *n.* The revengeful desire to reacquire the land and power lost by a nation through war. [<F *revanche* revenge + -ISM] **—re·vanch'ist** *adj., n.*

re·veal (ri·vēl') *v.t.* **1** To make known; disclose; divulge. **2** To make visible; expose to view. [<L *revelare* unveil]

rev·eil·le (rev'i·lē) *n.* A morning signal by drum or bugle, notifying soldiers or sailors to rise. [<F *reveillez-vous,* imperative of *se reveiller* wake up]

rev·el (rev'əl) *v.i.* **·eled** or **·elled, ·el·ing** or **·el·ling** **1** to take delight: with *in:* He *revels* in his freedom. **2** To make merry; engage in boisterous festivities. **—n.** **1** A boisterous festivity; celebration. **2** Merrymaking. [<OF<L *rebellare* to rebel] **—rev'el·er** or **rev'el·ler** *n.*

rev·e·la·tion (rev'ə·lā'shən) *n.* **1** The act of revealing. **2** That which is revealed, esp. news of a surprising nature. **3** *Theol.* **a** The act of revealing divine truth. **b** That which is so revealed.

Rev·e·la·tion (rev'ə·lā'shən) *n.* The Book of Revelation, the last book of the New Testament; the Apocalypse. Also **Rev'e·la'tions.**

rev·el·ry (rev′əl·rē) *n. pl.* **·ries** Noisy or boisterous merriment.

re·venge (ri·venj′) *n.* **1** The act of returning injury for injury to obtain satisfaction. **2** A means of avenging oneself or others. **3** The desire for vengeance. **4** An opportunity to obtain satisfaction, esp. to make up for a prior defeat, humiliation, etc. —*v.t.* **venged, veng·ing 1** To inflict punishment, injury, or loss in return for. **2** To take or seek vengeance in behalf of. [MF < L *re-* again + *vindicare* vindicate] —**re·venge′ful** *adj.* —**re·venge′ful·ly** *adv.* —**re·veng′er** *n.*

rev·e·nue (rev′ə·nyōō) *n.* **1** Total current income of a government. **2** Income from any property or investment. **3** A source or an item of income. [< F *revenir* to return]

re·ver·ber·ate (ri·vûr′bə·rāt) *v.* **·at·ed, ·at·ing** *v.i.* **1** To resound or reecho. **2** To be reflected or repelled. **3** To rebound or recoil. —*v.t.* **4** To echo back (a sound); reecho. **5** To reflect. [< L *reverberare* strike back, cause to rebound < *re-* back + *verberare* to beat] —**re·ver′ber·ant** *adj.* —**re·ver′ber·a·tor** *n.*

re·ver·ber·a·tion (ri·vûr′bə·rā′shən) *n.* **1** The act of reverberating, or the state of being reverberated. **2** The rebound or reflection of light, heat, or sound waves. —**re·ver′ber·a′tive, re·ver·ber·a·to′ry** *adj.*

re·vere (ri·vir′) *v.t.* **·vered, ·ver·ing** To regard with profound respect and awe; venerate. [< L *re-* again and again + *vereri* to fear] —**re·ver′er** *n.*

rev·er·ence (rev′ər·əns) *n.* **1** A feeling of profound respect often mingled with awe and affection. **2** An act of respect; an obeisance, as a bow or curtsy. **3** The state of being revered. **4** A reverend person: used as a title. —*v.t.* **·enced, ·enc·ing** To regard with reverence. —**Syn.** *n.* **1** adoration, awe, homage, honor, veneration.

rev·er·end (rev′ər·ənd) *adj.* **1** Worthy of reverence. **2** *Usu. cap.* Being a clergyman: used as a title. **3** Of or pertaining to the clergy. —*n.* A clergyman. • In formal usage, *Reverend* follows *the* and precedes the clergyman's full name or title of address and last name: *the Reverend Donald Smith; the Rev. Mr.* (or *Dr.*) *Smith.* Less formally, *Reverend* is used as a title of address: *Reverend Smith.* The use of *reverend* as a noun should be avoided, esp. in writing: *The reverend's sermon was much admired.*

rev·er·ent (rev′ər·ənt) *adj.* Feeling or expressing reverence. —**rev′er·ent·ly** *adv.*

rev·er·en·tial (rev′ə·ren′shəl) *adj.* Proceeding from or expressing reverence. —**rev′er·en′tial·ly** *adv.*

rev·er·ie (rev′ər·ē) *n. pl.* **·er·ies 1** Abstracted musing; daydreaming. **2** DAYDREAM. Also **rev′er·y.** [< F *rêver* dream]

re·vers (rə·vir′, -vâr′) *n. pl.* **·vers** (-virz′, -vârz′) A part of a garment folded over to show the inside, as the lapel of a coat. [< OF]

re·ver·sal (ri·vûr′səl) *n.* **1** The act of reversing. **2** A change to an opposite direction or course.

re·verse (ri·vûrs′) *adj.* **1** Turned backward; contrary or opposite in direction, order, etc. **2** Having the other side or back in view. **3** Causing backward motion. —*n.* **1** That which is directly opposite or contrary. **2** The back, rear, or secondary side or surface. **3** A change to an opposite position, direction, or state; reversal. **4** A change for the worse; a misfortune. **5** *Mech.* A gear that causes reverse motion. —*v.* **·versed, ·vers·ing** *v.t.* **1** To turn upside down or inside out. **2** To turn in an opposite direction. **3** To transpose; exchange. **4** To change completely or into something opposite: to *reverse* one's stand. **5** To set aside; annul: The higher court *reversed* the decision. **6** To apply (the charges for a telephone call) to the party receiving the call. **7** *Mech.* To cause to have an opposite motion or effect. —*v.i.* **8** To move or turn in the opposite direction. **9** To reverse its action: said of engines, etc. [< L *reversus*, p.p. of *revertere* turn around] —**re·verse′ly** *adv.* —**re·vers′er** *n.*

re·vers·i·ble (ri·vûr′sə·bəl) *adj.* **1** Capable of being worn or used with either side open to view, as a fabric, coat, rug, etc. **2** Capable of being reversed, as a chemical reaction. —*n.* A reversible coat, fabric, etc. —**re·vers′i·bil′i·ty** *n.* —**re·vers′i·bly** *adv.*

re·ver·sion (ri·vûr′zhən, -shən) *n.* **1** A return to some former condition or practice. **2** The act of reversing, or the state of being reversed. **3** *Biol.* The recurrence of ancestral characteristics; atavism. **4** *Law* The return of an estate to the grantor or his heirs after the expiration of the grant. —**re·ver′sion·ar′y, re·ver′sion·al** *adj.*

re·vert (ri·vûrt′) *v.i.* **1** To go or turn back to a former place, condition, attitude, topic, etc. **2** *Biol.* To return to or show characteristics of an earlier, primitive type. [< L *re-* back + *vertere* to turn]

re·vet·ment (ri·vet′mənt) *n.* A facing or retaining wall, as of masonry, for protecting earthworks, river banks, etc. [< F *revêtement*]

re·view (ri·vyōō′) *v.t.* **1** To go over or examine again: to *review* a lesson. **2** To look back upon, as in memory. **3** To study carefully; survey or evaluate: to *review* test scores. **4** To write or make a critical evaluation of, as a new book or film. **5** *Law* To examine (something done or adjudged by a lower court) so as to determine its legality or correctness. —*v.i.* **6** To go over material again. **7** To review books, films, etc. —*n.* **1** An examination or study of something; a retrospective survey. **2** A lesson studied again. **3** A careful study or survey. **4** A critical evaluation, as of a new book or film. **5** A periodical featuring critical reviews. **6** A formal inspection, as of troops. **7** *Law* The process by which the proceedings of a lower court are reexamined by a higher court. [< MF < L *re-* again + *videre* see] —**re·view′a·ble** *adj.* —**re·view′er** *n.*

re·vile (ri·vīl′) *v.* **·viled, ·vil·ing** *v.t.* **1** To assail with abusive language; attack verbally. —*v.i.* **2** To use abusive language. [< OF *reviler* treat as vile] —**re·vile′ment, re·vil′er** *n.* —**Syn.** abuse, vilify, malign, slander, defame.

re·vise (ri·vīz′) *v.t.* **·vised, ·vis·ing 1** To look over so as to correct errors, make changes, etc. **2** To change; alter: to *revise* one's opinion. —*n.* **1** An instance of revising. **2** A corrected proof after having been revised. [< L *revisere* look back, see again] —**re·vis′er** or **re·vi′sor** *n.*

re·vi·sion (ri·vizh′ən) *n.* **1** The act or process of revising. **2** A revised version or edition. —**re·vi′sion·ar′y, re·vi′sion·al** *adj.*

re·vi·sion·ist (ri·vizh′ən·ist) *n.* **1** One who proposes a course of action regarded as a deviation from accepted ideas or established policy, as of a Communist state. **2** One who advocates revision. —*adj.* Of or characteristic of a revisionist. —**re·vi′sion·ism** *n.* —**re·vi′sion·is′tic** *adj.*

re·vi·tal·ize (rē·vī′təl·īz) *v.t.* **·ized, ·iz·ing** To restore vitality to; revive. —**re·vi′tal·i·za′tion** *n.*

re·viv·al (ri·vī′vəl) *n.* **1** The act of reviving, or the state of being revived. **2** A restoration or renewal after neglect or obscurity: the *revival* of radio drama. **3** An awakening of interest in religion. **4** A series of often emotional evangelical meetings.

re·viv·al·ist (ri·vī′vəl·ist) *n.* A preacher or leader of religious revivals. —**re·vi′val·ism** *n.* —**re·vi′val·is′tic** *adj.*

re·vive (ri·vīv′) *v.* **·vived, ·viv·ing** *v.t.* **1** To bring to life or consciousness again. **2** To give new vigor, health, etc., to. **3** To bring back into use or currency, as after a period of neglect or obscurity: to *revive* an old play. **4** To renew in the mind or memory. —*v.i.* **5** To return to consciousness or life. **6** To assume new vigor, health, etc. **7** To come back into use or currency. [< F < L *revivere* < *re-* again + *vivere* live] —**re·viv′er** *n.*

re·viv·i·fy (ri·viv′ə·fī) *v.t.* **·fied, ·fy·ing** To give new life or spirit to. [< L *re-* again + *vivificare* vivify] —**re·viv′i·fi·ca′tion, re·viv′i·fi·er** *n.*

rev·o·ca·ble (rev′ə·kə·bəl) *adj.* Capable of being revoked. —**rev′o·ca·bil′i·ty** *n.* —**rev′o·ca·bly** *adv.*

rev·o·ca·tion (rev′ə·kā′shən) *n.* The act of revoking, or the state of being revoked; repeal.

re·voke (ri·vōk′) *v.* **·voked, ·vok·ing** *v.t.* **1** To annul or make void; rescind. —*v.i.* **2** In card games, to fail to follow suit when possible and required by the rules. —*n.* In card games, neglect to follow suit. [< L *re-* back + *vocare* call] —**re·vok′er** *n.*

re·volt (ri·vōlt′) *n.* **1** An uprising against authority, esp. a government; a rebellion or insurrection. **2** An act of protest or refusal. —*v.i.* **1** To rise in rebellion against constituted authority. **2** To turn away in disgust or abhorrence. —*v.t.* **3** To cause to feel disgust or revulsion; repel. [< L *revolutus*, p.p. of *revolvere* revolve] —**re·volt′er** *n.*

re·volt·ing (ri·vōl′ting) *adj.* Abhorrent; loathsome; nauseating. —**re·volt′ing·ly** *adv.*

rev·o·lu·tion (rev′ə·lōō′shən) *n.* **1** The act or state of revolving. **2** A motion in a closed curve around a center, or a complete or apparent circuit made by a body in such a course. **3** Any turning, winding, or rotation about an axis. **4** A round or cycle of successive events or changes. **5** The period of space or time occupied by a cycle. **6** The overthrow and replacement of a government or political system by those governed. **7** Any extensive or drastic change.

rev·o·lu·tion·ar·y (rev′ə·lōō′shən·er′ē) *adj.* **1** Pertaining to or of the nature of revolution. **2** Causing or tending to produce a revolution. —*n. pl.* **·ies** One who advocates or takes part in a revolution: also **rev′o·lu′tion·ist**.

Revolutionary War AMERICAN REVOLUTION.

rev·o·lu·tion·ize (rev′ə·lōō′shən·īz) *v.t.* **·ized, ·iz·ing** To bring about a radical or complete change in.

re·volve (ri·volv′) *v.* **·volved, ·volv·ing** *v.i.* **1** To move in a circle or closed path about a center. **2** To rotate. **3** To recur periodically. —*v.t.* **4** To cause to move in a circle or closed path. **5** To cause to rotate. **6** To turn over mentally. [< L *re-* back + *volvere* roll, turn]

re·volv·er (ri·vol′vər) *n.* A handgun with a cylinder that revolves to make possible successive discharges without reloading.

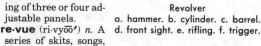

Revolver
a. hammer. b. cylinder. c. barrel. d. front sight. e. rifling. f. trigger.

revolving door A door rotating like a turnstile and consisting of three or four adjustable panels.

re·vue (ri·vyōō′) *n.* A series of skits, songs, dances, etc., often comical or satirical in nature. [F, revue]

re·vul·sion (ri·vul′shən) *n.* **1** A sudden change of feeling; a strong reaction. **2** Complete disgust or aversion; loathing. [< L *revulsus,* p.p. of *revellere* pluck away] —**re·vul′sive** *adj.*

re·ward (ri·wôrd′) *n.* **1** Something given or done in return, esp. to acknowledge and encourage merit, service, or achievement. **2** Money offered, as for the return of lost goods. —*v.t.* To give a reward to or for; recompense. [< AF *rewarder* look at] —**re·ward′er** *n.*

re·ward·ing (ri·wôrd′ing) *adj.* Yielding intangible rewards; satisfying: a *rewarding* career.

re·write (rē·rīt′) *v.t.* **·wrote, ·writ·ten, ·writ·ing 1** To write over again. **2** To revise or put into publishable form, as for a newspaper. —*n.* (rē′rīt′) A news item rewritten for publication.

RF, R.F., r.f. radio frequency.

RFD, R.F.D. Rural Free Delivery.

RH, R.H., r.h. right hand.

R.H. Royal Highness.

Rh rhodium.

r.h. relative humidity.

rhap·so·dize (rap′sə·dīz) *v.t. & v.i.* **·dized, ·diz·ing** To express or recite with exaggerated sentiment and enthusiasm. —**rhap′so·dist** *n.*

rhap·so·dy (rap′sə·dē) *n. pl.* **·dies 1** Any rapturous or highly enthusiastic utterance or writing. **2** *Music* An instrumental composition of free form. [< Gk. *rhaptein* stitch together + *ōidē* song] —**rhap·sod′ic** (rap·sod′ik) or **·i·cal** *adj.* —**rhap·sod′i·cal·ly** *adv.*

rhe·a (rē′ə) *n.* A ratite bird of South America, resembling but smaller than an ostrich, and having three toes. [NL]

rhe·ni·um (rē′nē·əm) *n.* A rare metallic element (symbol Re). [< L *Rhenus* Rhine]

rhe·o·stat (rē′ə·stat) *n. Electr.* A variable resistor used to control or limit current. [< Gk. *rheos* current + *statos* standing]

rhe·sus (rē′səs) *n.* A small macaque of India, widely used in research. Also **rhesus monkey.** [NL]

Rhe·sus factor (rē′səs) RH FACTOR.

rhet·o·ric (ret′ə·rik) *n.* **1** Skill in the use

Rhesus

of language, as in writing or speech. **2** The pretentious use of language. [< Gk. *rhētorikē (technē)* rhetorical (art)]

rhe·tor·i·cal (ri·tôr′i·kəl, -tor′-) *adj.* **1** Of the nature of rhetoric. **2** Designed for showy oratorical effect. —**rhe·tor′i·cal·ly** *adv.* —**rhe·tor′i·cal·ness** *n.*

rhetorical question A question put only for effect, the answer being implied in the question.

rhet·o·ri·cian (ret′ə·rish′ən) *n.* A master or teacher of rhetoric.

rheum (rōōm) *n.* **1** A watery discharge from the nose or eyes. **2** A cold in the head. [< Gk. *rheuma* a flow] —**rheum′y** *adj.* **(·i·er, ·i·est)**

rheu·mat·ic (rōō·mat′ik) *adj.* Of, causing, or affected with rheumatism. —*n.* One affected with rheumatism.

rheumatic fever A disease chiefly affecting young persons following streptococcal infection, characterized by swollen joints and fever.

rheu·ma·tism (rōō′mə·tiz′əm) *n.* Any of various painful disorders of the joints. [< Gk. *rheuma* rheum] —**rheu′ma·toid** (-toid) *adj.*

rheumatoid arthritis A chronic, crippling disease of the joints.

Rh factor (är′āch′) A genetically transmitted substance in the blood of most individuals (**Rh positive**) and which may cause hemolytic reactions under certain conditions, as during pregnancy, or following transfusions with blood lacking this factor (**Rh negative**). [< RH(ESUS) monkey, the laboratory animal used in discovering this substance]

rhine·stone (rīn′stōn′) *n.* A highly refractive, colorless glass or paste, used as an imitation gemstone.

Rhine wine (rīn) A light, dry, white wine produced in the region of the Rhine River in w. CEN. Europe.

rhi·ni·tis (rī·nī′tis) *n.* Inflammation of the mucous membrane of the nose. [< Gk. *rhis, rhinos* nose + -ITIS]

rhi·no (rī′nō) *n. pl.* **·nos** *Informal* A rhinoceros.

rhi·noc·e·ros (rī·nos′ər·əs) *n. pl.* **·ros·es** or **·ros** Any of various large, herbivorous, three-toed mammals of Africa and Asia, with one or two horns on the snout and a thick hide. [< Gk. *rhis, rhinos* nose + *keras* horn]

Indian rhinoceros

rhi·zome (rī′zōm) *n.* A specialized trailing or underground stem, producing roots from its lower surface and leaves or shoots from its upper surface or upturned tip. [< Gk. *rhizōma* mass of roots] —**rhi·zom·a·tous** (rī·zom′ə·təs, -zō′mə-) *adj.*

rho (rō) *n.* The 17th letter in the Greek alphabet (P,ρ).

Rhode Island Red (rōd) An American breed of chicken having reddish brown feathers.

Rho·de·sia (rō·dē′zhə, -zhē·ə) *n.* A British colony in CEN. Africa; unilaterally declared independence in 1965; 150,333 sq. mi., cap. Salisbury. —**Rho·de′sian** *adj., n.* • See map at AFRICA.

rho·di·um (rō′dē·əm) *n.* A hard, silvery metallic element (symbol Rh). [< Gk. *rhodon* rose; from the color of its salts]

Rhizome of bearded iris

rho·do·den·dron (rō′də·den′drən) *n.* Any of a genus of usu. evergreen shrubs or small trees with profuse clusters of flowers. [< Gk. *rhodon* rose + *dendron* tree]

rhom·boid (rom′boid) *n. Geom.* A parallelogram, esp. one with oblique angles, having unequal adjacent sides. —*adj.* Having the shape of a rhomboid or rhombus: also **rhom·boi′dal.** • See PARALLELOGRAM.

rhom·bus (rom′bəs) *n. pl.* **·bus·es** or **·bi** (-bī) *Geom.* An equilateral parallelogram, esp. one with oblique angles. [< Gk. *rhombos* spinning top, rhombus] —**rhom′bic** *adj.* • See PARALLELOGRAM.

rhu·barb (rōō′bärb) *n.* **1** Any of a genus of large-leaved perennial herbs. **2** The fleshy stalks of a species of rhubarb used in cooking. **3** *Slang* A heated argument or quarrel. [< Gk. *rha* rhubarb + *barbaron* foreign]

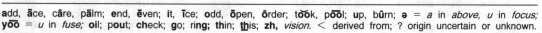

rhum·ba (rum′bə) *n. & v.* RUMBA.

rhyme (rīm) *n.* 1 A similarity of sounds of two or more words, esp. at the ends of lines of poetry. 2 A word wholly or partly similar in sound to another word. 3 A poem or verse employing such words, esp. at the ends of lines. 4 Poetry or verse in general. —*v.* **rhymed, rhy·ming** *v.i.* 1 To make rhymes or verses. 2 To be a rhyme. 3 To end in rhymes: said of verses. —*v.t.* 4 To write in rhyme. 5 To use as a rhyme. 6 To cause to be a rhyme or rhymes. [< Gk. *rhythmos* rhythm] —**rhym′er** *n.*

rhyme·ster (rīm′stər) *n.* A writer of light or inferior verse.

rhythm (rith′əm) *n.* 1 Movement or process characterized by the regular or harmonious recurrence of a beat, sound, action, development, etc.: the *rhythm* of the pulse; the *rhythm* of the seasons; the *rhythms* of speech. 2 a The property of music that arises from comparison of the relative duration and accents of sounds. b A particular arrangement of durations and accents: a dance *rhythm.* 3 In literature, drama, etc., a forward-moving or compelling development toward a particular end, effect, etc.: The *rhythm* of the play was all off. 4 In art, the regular or harmonious recurrence of colors, forms, etc. 5 In prosody: a The cadenced flow of sound as determined by the succession of accented and unaccented syllables. b A particular arrangement of such syllables: iambic *rhythm.* [< Gk. *rhythmos* < *rheein* flow] —**rhyth′mic** or **·mi·cal** *adj.* —**rhyth′mi·cal·ly** *adv.* —**rhyth′mist** *n.*

rhythm method A method of birth control that consists of sexual abstinence during the woman's monthly period of ovulation.

RI Rhode Island (P.O. abbr.).

R.I. King and Emperor (L *Rex et Imperator*); Queen and Empress (L *Regina et Imperatrix*); Rhode Island.

ri·al (rī′al) *n.* A silver coin, the basic monetary unit of Iran. [< OF *rial, real* royal]

ri·al·to (rē·al′tō) *n. pl.* **·tos** A market or place of exchange. [< *Rialto*, an island of Venice]

rib (rib) *n.* 1 *Anat.* One of the series of curved bones attached to the spine of most vertebrates, and enclosing the chest cavity. 2 Something, as a structural element, likened to a rib: the *rib* of an umbrella. 3 The curved piece of an arch; also, one of the intersecting arches in vaulting. 4 A curved side timber bending away from the keel in a boat or ship. 5 A raised wale or stripe in cloth or knit goods. 6 A vein or nerve of a leaf or insect's wing. 7 A cut of meat including one or more ribs. 8 A wife: in jocular allusion to the creation of Eve from Adam's rib. *Gen.* 2:22. 9 *Slang* A practical joke. —*v.t.* **ribbed, rib·bing** 1 To make with ridges: to *rib* a piece of knitting. 2 To strengthen by or enclose within ribs. 3 *Slang* To make fun of; tease. [< OE *ribb*]

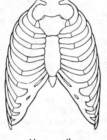
Human ribs

rib·ald (rib′əld) *adj.* Of or indulging in coarse, vulgar language or jokes. —*n.* A ribald person. [< OF *ribauld*] —**Syn.** *adj.* improper, unseemly, gross, obscene, impure.

rib·ald·ry (rib′əl·drē) *n. pl.* **·ries** Ribald language or jokes.

rib·bing (rib′ing) *n.* An arrangement of ribs, as in ribbed cloth, etc.

rib·bon (rib′ən) *n.* 1 A narrow strip of fabric made in a variety of weaves, used as trimming, for tying, etc. 2 Something shaped like or suggesting a ribbon. 3 *pl.* A narrow strip; a shred: torn to *ribbons.* 4 An ink-bearing strip of cloth in a typewriter. 5 A colored strip of cloth worn to signify the award of a prize, etc. 6 *Mil.* A strip of cloth worn to indicate campaigns served in, medals won, etc. —*v.t.* 1 To ornament with ribbons. 2 To tear into ribbons. [< OF *riban*]

ri·bo·fla·vin (rī′bō·flā′vin) *n.* A vitamin of the B complex found in many foods and essential for normal growth.

ri·bo·nu·cle·ic acid (rī′bō·nᵧoō·klē′ik, -klā′ik) A substance that controls various processes within living cells, esp. the synthesis of proteins.

rice (rīs) *n.* 1 A cereal grass widely cultivated on wet land in warm climates. 2 The edible, starchy seeds of this plant. —*v.t.* **riced, ric·ing** To reduce (a food) to ricelike grains. [< Gk. *oryza*]

rice paper 1 A thin paper made from rice straw. 2 A similar paper made from the pith of a Chinese shrub, the **rice-paper plant.**

ric·er (rī′sər) *n.* A utensil consisting of a perforated container through which cooked potatoes, etc., are pressed.

rich (rich) *adj.* 1 Having large possessions, as of money, goods, or lands; wealthy. 2 Abundantly supplied: with *in* or *with.* 3 Yielding abundant returns; plentiful: a *rich* source of oil. 4 Of precious materials, fine workmanship, etc.: *rich* fabrics. 5 Luxuriant; sumptuous. 6 Having many choice ingredients, as butter, cream, etc.: a *rich* dessert. 7 Pleasingly full and resonant: a *rich* tone. 8 Deep; intense: a *rich* color. 9 Very fragrant; pungent: a *rich* perfume. 10 Containing a high percentage of fuel to air: said of fuel mixtures. 11 Abounding in desirable qualities: *rich* soil. 12 *Informal* Very funny: a *rich* joke. [< OE *rīce*] —**rich′ly** *adv.* —**rich′ness** *n.*

rich·es (rich′iz) *n. pl.* 1 Abundant possessions; wealth. 2 Abundance of whatever is precious.

Rich·ter scale (rik′tər) A logarithmic measure of the estimated energy released by earthquakes according to which 1 represents an imperceptible tremor and 10 a theoretical maximum about one thousand times greater than any recorded earthquake. [< Charles R. *Richter*, born 1900, U.S. seismologist]

rick (rik) *n.* A stack, as of hay, having the top rounded and thatched to protect the interior from rain. —*v.t.* To pile in ricks. [< OE *hrēac*]

rick·ets (rik′its) *n. pl. (construed as sing.)* A children's disease in which the bones do not harden normally, usu. due to vitamin D deficiency. [?]

rick·ett·si·a (rik·et′sē·ə) *n. pl.* **·si·ae** (-sĭ·ē) Any of a genus of pathogenic bacterialike organisms parasitic in certain ticks and lice and transmissible to other animals and man. [< H. T. *Ricketts*, 1871–1910, U.S. pathologist] —**rick·ett′si·al** *adj.*

rick·et·y (rik′it·ē) *adj.* 1 Ready to fall; tottering. 2 Affected with rickets. 3 Feeble; infirm. —**rick′et·i·ly** *adv.* —**rick′et·i·ness** *n.*

rick·ey (rik′ē) *n. pl.* **rick·eys** A drink consisting of liquor, usu. gin, sweetened lime juice, and carbonated water. [?]

rick·rack (rik′rak′) *n.* Flat braid in zigzag form, used as trimming. [Reduplication of RACK¹]

rick·shaw (rik′shô) *n.* JINRIKISHA. Also **rick′sha.**

ric·o·chet (rik′ə·shā′, *esp. Brit.* -shet′) *v.i.* **·cheted** (-shād′) or **·chet·ted** (-shet′id), **·chet·ing** (-shā′ing) or **·chet·ting** (-shet′ing) To glance or rebound obliquely from a surface. —*n.* 1 A ricocheting. 2 Something that ricochets. [< OF]

ri·cot·ta (ri·kot′ə; *Ital.* rē·kôt′tä) *n.* An unripened cheese, Italian in origin and similar to cottage cheese but smoother. [< L *recoquere* to cook again]

rid (rid) *v.t.* **rid** or **rid·ded, rid·ding** To free, as from a burden or annoyance: usu. with *of.* —*adj.* Free; clear; quit: with *of:* We are well *rid* of him. [< ON *rythja* clear (land) of trees]

rid·dance (rid′ns) *n.* 1 A removal of something undesirable. 2 The state of being rid.

rid·den (rid′n) *p.p.* of RIDE.

rid·dle¹ (rid′l) *v.t.* **·dled, ·dling** 1 To perforate in numerous places, as with shot. 2 To sift through a coarse sieve. 3 To damage, injure, refute, etc., as if by perforating: to *riddle* a theory. —*n.* A coarse sieve. [< OE *hriddel* sieve] —**rid′· dler** *n.*

rid·dle² (rid′l) *n.* 1 A puzzling question or conundrum. 2 Any mysterious object or person. —*v.* **·dled, ·dling** *v.t.* 1 To solve; explain. —*v.i.* 2 To utter or solve riddles; speak in riddles. [< OE *rǣdels*]

ride (rīd) *v.* **rode** (*Regional* **rid**), **rid·den** (*Regional* **rid**), **rid·ing** *v.i.* 1 To sit on and be borne along by a horse or other animal. 2 To be borne along as if on horseback. 3 To travel or be carried on or in a vehicle or other conveyance. 4 To be supported in moving: The wheel *rides* on a shaft. 5 To float; be borne: The ship *rides* on the waves. 6 To carry a rider, etc., in a specified manner: This car *rides* well. 7 To seem to float in space, as a star. 8 To lie at anchor, as a ship. 9 To overlap or overlie, as broken bones. 10 To depend: with *on*: Everything *rides* on him. **11** To be a bet: with *on*: They let their money *ride* on the filly. **12** *Informal* To continue unchanged: Let it *ride*. —*v.t.* **13** To sit on and control the motion of (a horse, bicycle, etc.). **14** To be borne or supported upon. **15** To overlap or overlie. **16** To travel or traverse (an area, certain distance, etc.) on a horse, in an automobile, etc. **17** To harass or bother oppressively: usu. in the past participle: *ridden* with shame. **18** To accomplish by riding: to *ride* a race. **19** To convey. **20** *Informal* To tease or torment by ridicule, criticisms, etc. **21** To keep somewhat engaged, usu. unnecessarily: to *ride* the brake. —**ride for a fall** To be headed for trouble, failure, etc. —**ride herd on** To control or supervise closely. — **ride out** To survive; endure successfully. —**ride up** To move upward out of place, as clothing. —*n.* **1** An excursion by any means of conveyance. **2** A means of transportation: to ask for a *ride*. **3** A manner of riding: a smooth *ride*. **4** A mechanical contrivance for riding, as at an amusement park. —**take for a ride** *Slang* **1** To remove (a person) to a place with the intent to murder. **2** To cheat; swindle. [< OE *rīdan*] —**rid′a·ble** *adj.*

rid·er (rī′dər) *n.* **1** One who or that which rides. **2** A piece of writing added to a document, contract, etc. **3** An addition to a legislative bill.

rid·er·less (rī′dər·lis) *adj.* Without a rider.

ridge (rij) *n.* **1** A raised mass of land long in proportion to its width and height. **2** A long, raised or top part of something, as the backbone of an animal, crest of a wave or mountain, ribbed part of a fabric, etc. **3** That part of a roof where the rafters meet the ridgepole. —*v.* ridged, ridg·ing *v.t.* **1** To mark with ridges. **2** To form into ridges. —*v.i.* **3** To form ridges. [< OE *hrycg* spine, ridge]

ridge·pole (rij′pōl′) *n.* A horizontal timber at the ridge of a roof. Also **ridge′beam′, ridge′· piece′, ridge′plate′.**

rid·i·cule (rid′ə·kyool) *n.* Language or actions expressing amused contempt or scorn; derision; mockery. —*v.t.* ·culed, ·cul· ing To make fun of; hold up as a laughingstock; deride. [< L *ridiculum* a jest] —**rid′i·cul′er** *n.* —

Ridgepole

Syn. *v.* banter, chaff, jeer, mock, taunt, satirize, scoff.

ri·dic·u·lous (ri·dik′yə·ləs) *adj.* **1** Absurdly comical: a *ridiculous* costume. **2** Unworthy of consideration; preposterous. —**ri·dic′u·lous·ly** *adv.* —**ri·dic′u·lous·ness** *n.* —**Syn. 1** droll, funny, grotesque, laughable. **2** absurd, nonsensical, foolish, stupid, asinine, senseless.

rid·ing[1] (rī′ding) *n.* The act of one who rides. —*adj.* **1** Suitable for riding: a *riding* horse. **2** To be used while riding: *riding* boots.

rid·ing[2] (rī′ding) *n.* **1** One of the three administrative divisions of Yorkshire, England. **2** Any similar administrative or electoral division, as in Canada, New Zealand, etc. [< OE *thrithing* the third part (of a county)]

rife (rīf) *adj.* **1** Prevalent; widespread. **2** Plentiful; abundant. **3** Containing in abundance: with *with*. [< OE *rīfe*]

riff (rif) *n.* In jazz music, a melodic phrase or motif played repeatedly as background or used as the main theme. — *v.i.* To perform a riff. [? Alter. of REFRAIN]

rif·fle (rif′əl) *n.* **1** A shoal or rocky obstruction lying beneath the surface of a stream and causing a stretch of choppy water. **2** Such a stretch of water. **3** A way of shuffling cards. —*v.t.* & *v.i.* ·fled, ·fling **1** To cause or form a riffle. **2** To shuffle (cards) by bending up adjacent corners of two halves of the pack, and permitting the cards to slip together as they are released. **3** To thumb through (the pages of a book). [?]

riff·raff (rif′raf′) *n.* **1** Low, disreputable persons; rabble. **2** Miscellaneous rubbish. [< OF *rif et raf* every bit]

ri·fle[1] (rī′fəl) *n.* **1** A firearm having spiral grooves on the surface of the bore for imparting rotation to the projectile. **2** Such a weapon fired from the shoulder. **3** *pl.* A

Automatic rifle (M-14)

body of soldiers equipped with rifles. —*v.t.* ·fled, ·fling To cut a spirally grooved bore in (a firearm, etc.). [< OF *rifler* to scratch]

ri·fle[2] (rī′fəl) *v.t.* ·fled, ·fling **1** To search through and rob, as a safe. **2** To search and rob (a person). **3** To take away by force. [< OF *rifler* to scratch, plunder] —**ri′fler** *n.*

ri·fle·man (rī′fəl·mən) *n. pl.* ·men (-mən) One armed or skilled with the rifle.

ri·fling (rī′fling) *n.* **1** The operation of forming the grooves in a rifle. **2** Such grooves collectively. • See REVOLVER.

rift (rift) *n.* **1** An opening made by splitting; a cleft; fissure. **2** A break in friendly relations. —*v.t.* & *v.i.* To rive; burst open; split. [< Scand.]

rig[1] (rig) *v.t.* rigged, rig·ging **1** To fit out; equip. **2** *Naut.* **a** To fit, as a ship, with rigging. **b** To fit (sails, stays, etc.) to masts, yards, etc. **3** *Informal* To dress; clothe, esp. in finery: usu. with *out*. **4** To construct hurriedly or by makeshifts: often with *up*. **5** To prepare or arrange for special operation: controls *rigged* for the left hand only. —*n.* **1** The arrangement of sails, spars, etc., on a vessel. **2** *Informal* Dress or costume. **3** Gear, machinery, or equipment: an oil-well *rig*. **4** A carriage and its horse or horses. [< Scand.]

rig[2] (rig) *v.t.* rigged, rig·ging To control fraudulently: manipulate: to *rig* an election. [?]

rig·ger (rig′ər) *n.* One who rigs, esp. one who fits the rigging of ships, assembles lifting or hoisting gear, etc.

rig·ging (rig′ing) *n.* **1** *Naut.* The entire cordage system of a vessel. **2** Equipment or gear used in lifting, hauling, etc.

right (rīt) *adj.* **1** In accordance with some moral, just, or equitable law or standard; virtuous; upright. **2** Conformable to truth or fact; correct; accurate. **3** Proper; fitting; suitable. **4** Most desirable or preferable: to go to the *right* parties. **5** In an orderly or satisfactory state or condition: to put things *right*. **6** Sound; healthy; normal, as in mind or body. **7 a** Designating, being, or closest to that side of the body which is toward the south when one faces the sunrise. **b** Designating a corresponding side of anything. **8** Designating that surface or part of something designed to be worn outward or, when used, to be seen. **9** Politically conservative or reactionary. **10** *Geom.* Formed by lines, segments, or planes perpendicular to a base. —*adv.* **1** According to some moral, just, or equitable law or standard. **2** Correctly; accurately. **3** In a straight line; directly: Go *right* home. **4** Precisely: He stood *right* in the doorway. **5** Suitably; properly: I can't fix it *right*. **6** Completely: burned *right* to the ground. **7** Thoroughly: He felt *right* at home. **8** Immediately: *right* after the storm. **9** Very: used regionally or in certain titles: a *right* nice day; the *Right* Reverend. **10** On or toward the right: to go *right*. —*n.* **1** That which is right, good, just, true, proper, etc. **2** *Often pl.* Any power or privilege to which a person has a moral, legal, or just claim: the *right* to vote. **3** *pl.* A claim or title to, or interest in, anything that is enforceable by law or custom: *rights* to property; fishing *rights*. **4** Something a person feels belongs justly or properly to him: a *right* to leave. **5** The correct or factual report or interpretation of something. **6** The right hand or side of a person or thing. **7** A direction to or a location on the right. **8** Something adapted for right-hand use or position. **9** In boxing: **a** A blow delivered with the right hand. **b** The right hand. **10** *Often cap.* In politics, a conservative or reactionary position, or a party or group advocating such a position, so designated because of the views of the party occupying seats on the right side of the presiding officer in certain European legislative bodies. —**by right** (or **rights**) Justly; properly. —**to rights** *Informal* Into a proper or orderly condition. —*v.t.* **1** To restore to an upright or normal position. **2** To put in order; set right. **3** To make correct or in accord with facts. **4** To make reparation for; redress or avenge: to *right* a wrong. **5** To make reparation to (a person); do justice to. —*v.i.* **6** To regain an upright or normal position. —*interj.* I agree! I understand! —**right on** *Informal* An interjectory phrase expressing enthusiastic agreement or encouragement: also used adjectivally: He was *right on* in that speech. [< OE *riht*]

right·a·bout (rīt′ə·bout′) n. A turning in or to the opposite direction, physically or mentally: also **right′a·bout′-face′** (-fās′).

right angle An angle with a measure of 90°. —**right′-an′-gled** adj. • See ANGLE.

right·eous (rī′chəs) adj. 1 Morally right and just. 2 Virtuous; blameless: a righteous man. 3 Justifiable; defensible: righteous anger. [< OE riht right + wīs wise] —**right′-eous·ly** adv. —**right′eous·ness** n.

right·ful (rīt′fəl) adj. 1 Owned or held by just or legal claim: rightful heritage. 2 Having a just or legal claim: the rightful heir. 3 Fair; upright; just. 4 Proper; suitable. —**right′ful·ly** adv. —**right′ful·ness** n.

right-hand (rīt′hand′) adj. 1 Of, pertaining to, or situated on the right side. 2 Of or for the right hand. 3 Most dependable or helpful: He was my right-hand man.

right-hand·ed (rīt′han′did) adj. 1 Using the right hand habitually or more easily than the left. 2 Done with the right hand. 3 Turning or moving from left to right, as the hands of a clock. 4 Adapted for use by the right hand, as a tool. —**right′-hand′ed·ness** n.

right·ism (rī′tiz·əm) n. Politically conservative or reactionary policies or principles. —**right′ist** adj., n.

right·ly (rīt′lē) adv. 1 Correctly. 2 Honestly; uprightly. 3 Properly; aptly.

right-mind·ed (rīt′mīn′did) adj. Having feelings or opinions that are right or sound.

right·ness (rīt′nis) n. The quality or condition of being right.

right of search 1 In international law, the right of a belligerent vessel in time of war to verify the nationality of a vessel and to ascertain, if neutral, whether it carries contraband goods. 2 A similar right in time of peace exercised to prevent piracy or to enforce revenue laws.

right of way 1 Law a The right, general or special, of a person to pass over the land of another. b The land over which such passage is made. 2 The strip of land over which a railroad, public highway, or high-tension power line is built. 3 The legal or customary precedence which allows one vehicle to cross in front of another. 4 Any right of precedence. Also **right′-of-way′.**

right triangle A triangle containing one right angle. • See TRIANGLE.

right whale Any of various large-headed, toothless whales that feed by straining water through whalebone plates in the mouth.

right wing 1 A political party or group advocating conservative or reactionary policies. 2 That part of any group advocating such policies. Also **Right Wing.** —**right′-wing′** adj. —**right′-wing′er** n.

rig·id (rij′id) adj. 1 Resisting change of form; stiff. 2 Rigorous; inflexible; severe; strict. 3 Precise; exact, as reasoning. [< L rigere be stiff] —**rig′id·ly** adv. —**ri·gid′i·ty, rig′id·ness** n.

rig·ma·role (rig′mə·rōl, rig′ə·mə-) n. Incoherent or uselessly complicated talk, writing, procedures, etc. [Alter. of ragman roll catalog, long list]

rig·or (rig′ər) n. 1 Harshness; strictness; severity, as of opinions, methods, temperament, etc. 2 Severe hardship, discomfort, etc. 3 Inclemency, as of the weather. 4 Exactitude; precision. 5 The condition of being stiff or rigid. Brit. sp. **rig′our.** [< L rigere be stiff] —**rig′or·is′tic** adj.

rig·or mor·tis (rig′ər môr′tis, rī′gər) The muscular stiffening that ensues within a few hours after death. [L, stiffness of death]

rig·or·ous (rig′ər·əs) adj. 1 Marked by or acting with rigor; severe. 2 Rigidly accurate; exact; strict. 3 Extremely difficult, arduous, or demanding. 4 Extremely variable, as weather; inclement. —**rig′or·ous·ly** adv. —**rig′or·ous·ness** n.

rile (rīl) v.t. Informal 1 To vex; irritate. 2 To roil; make muddy. [Var. of ROIL]

rill (ril) n. A small stream; rivulet. [< Du. ril or G rille]

rim (rim) n. 1 The edge or border of an object, usu. of a circular object. 2 The circumference of a wheel, esp., on an automobile wheel, the detachable, metal band over which the tire is fitted. —v.t. **rimmed, rim·ming** 1 To provide with or serve as a rim; border. 2 In sports, to roll around the edge of (the basket, cup, etc.) without falling in. [< OE rima]

rime¹ (rīm) n., v. **rimed, rim·ing** RHYME.

rime² (rīm) n. HOARFROST. —v.t. & v.i. **rimed, rim·ing** To cover with rime. [< OE hrīm frost] —**rim′y** adj.

rind (rīnd) n. The skin or outer coat that may be peeled or taken off, as of fruit, cheese, bacon, plants, etc. [< OE rind bark, crust]

ring¹ (ring) n. 1 Any object, line, or figure having the form of a circle or similar closed curve. 2 A rim or border of something circular. 3 A circular band of precious metal, worn on a finger. 4 Any metal or wooden band used for holding or carrying something: a napkin ring. 5 A group of persons or things in a circle. 6 A group of persons engaged in some common, often corrupt activity, business, etc.: a dope ring. 7 A place where the bark has been cut away around a branch or tree trunk. 8 A concentric layer of wood formed during a single year's growth in most trees and shrubs: also **annual ring.** 9 An area or arena, usu. circular, for exhibitions, etc.: a circus ring. 10 a A square area, usu. bordered with ropes, for boxing or wrestling matches. b The sport of prizefighting: with the. 11 Any field of competition or rivalry: He tossed his hat into the ring. —v. **ringed, ring·ing** v.t. 1 To surround with a ring; encircle. 2 To form into a ring or rings. 3 To provide or decorate with a ring or rings. 4 To cut a ring of bark from (a branch or tree); girdle. 5 To put a ring in the nose of (a pig, bull, etc.). 6 To hem in (cattle, etc.) by riding in a circle around them. 7 In certain games, to cast a ring over (a peg or pin). —v.i. 8 To form a ring or rings. 9 To move or fly in rings or spirals; circle. [< OE hring]

ring² (ring) v. **rang, rung, ring·ing** v.i. 1 To give forth a resonant sound, as a bell when struck. 2 To sound loudly or be filled with sound or resonance; reverberate; resound. 3 To cause a bell or bells to sound, as in summoning a servant. 4 To have or suggest, as by sounding, a specified quality: His story rings true. 5 To have a continued sensation of ringing or buzzing: My ears ring. —v.t. 6 To cause to ring, as a bell. 7 To produce, as a sound, by or as by ringing. 8 To announce or proclaim by ringing: to ring the hour. 9 To summon, escort, usher, etc., by or as by ringing: with in or out: to ring out the old year. 10 To strike (coins, etc.) on something so as to test their quality. 11 To call on the telephone: often with up. —n. 1 The sound produced by a bell. 2 A sound suggesting this: the ring of laughter. 3 Any loud, reverberating sound. 4 A telephone call. 5 A sound that is characteristic or indicative: with of: His words have the ring of truth. [< OE hringan] —**Syn.** v. 1 clang, resound, peal, toll, chime.

ring bolt A bolt having a ring through an eye in its head.

ringed (ringd) adj. 1 Wearing a ring or rings. 2 Encircled or marked by a ring or rings. 3 Composed of rings.

ring·er¹ (ring′ər) n. 1 One who or that which rings a bell, chime, etc. 2 Slang An athlete, horse, etc., illegally entered in a sports competition. 3 Slang A person who bears a marked resemblance to another.

ring·er² (ring′ər) n. 1 One who or that which rings or encircles. 2 A quoit or horseshoe that falls around one of the posts.

ring·lead·er (ring′lē′dər) n. A leader of any undertaking, esp. of an unlawful one.

ring·let (ring′lit) n. A long, spiral lock of hair; a curl.

ring·mas·ter (ring′mas′tər, -mäs′-) n. One who has charge of a circus ring and of the performances in it.

ring·side (ring′sīd′) n. 1 The space or seats immediately surrounding a ring, as at a prize fight. 2 Any area for close viewing.

ring·worm (ring′wûrm′) n. A contagious skin disease caused by certain fungi and marked by itchy lesions that spread ringlike from the site of infection.

rink (ringk) n. 1 A smooth surface of ice, used for sports, as ice-skating, hockey, curling, etc. 2 A smooth floor, used for roller-skating. 3 A building containing a surface for ice-skating or roller-skating. [< OF renc row, rank]

rinse (rins) v.t. **rinsed, rins·ing** 1 To remove soap, dirt, impurities, etc., from by immersing in or flooding with clear water. 2 To remove (soap, dirt, etc.) in this manner. 3 To wash lightly: often with out. 4 To use a rinse on (the hair). —n. 1 The act of rinsing. 2 A solution used for coloring the hair. [? < L recens recent, fresh] —**rins′er** n.

rins·ing (rin′sing) n. 1 A rinse. 2 Usu. pl. a The liquid in which anything is rinsed. **b** That which is removed by rinsing; dregs.

ri·ot (rī′ət) *n.* **1** A violent or tumultuous public disturbance by a large number of persons; uproar; tumult. **2** Any boisterous outburst: a *riot* of laughter. **3** A vivid show or display: a *riot* of color. **4** *Informal* An uproariously amusing person, thing, or performance. **—run riot 1** To act or move wildly and without restraint. **2** To grow profusely, as vines. **—***v.i.* **1** To take part in a riot. **2** To live a life of unrestrained revelry. **—***v.t.* **3** To spend (time, money, etc.) in riot or revelry. [< OF *riote*] **—ri′ot·er** *n.*

riot act Any forceful or vigorous warning or reprimand. **—read the riot act to** To reprimand bluntly and severely.

ri·ot·ous (rī′ət·əs) *adj.* **1** Of, pertaining to, like, or engaged in a riot. **2** Loud; boisterous. **3** Profligate: *riotous* spending. **—ri′ot·ous·ly** *adv.* **—ri′ot·ous·ness** *n.*

rip[1] (rip) *v.* ripped, rip·ping *v.t.* **1** To tear or cut apart, often roughly or violently. **2** To tear or cut from something else, often in a rough or violent manner: with *off, away, out,* etc. **3** To saw or split (wood) in the direction of the grain. **—***v.i.* **4** To be torn or cut apart; split. **5** *Informal* To rush headlong. **—rip into** *Informal* To attack violently, as with blows or words. **—rip off** *Slang* **1** To steal or steal from. **2** To cheat, swindle, or dupe. **—rip out** *Informal* To utter with vehemence. **—***n.* **1** A tear or split. **2** The act of ripping. [ME *rippen*] **—rip′per** *n.*

rip[2] (rip) *n.* **1** A ripple; a rapid in a river. **2** A riptide.

R.I.P. may he (she, or they) rest in peace (L *requiescat in pace*)

ri·par·i·an (ri·pâr′ē·ən, rī-) *adj.* Pertaining to, growing, or located on the banks of a river or other watercourse. [< L *ripa* bank of a river]

rip·cord (rip′kôrd′) *n.* The cord by which the canopy of a parachute is released from its pack.

ripe (rīp) *adj.* rip·er, rip·est **1** Grown to maturity and fit for food, as fruit or grain. **2** Brought to a condition for use: *ripe* cheese. **3** Fully developed; matured; also, advanced, as in years. **4** In full readiness to do or try; prepared; ready: *ripe* for mutiny. **5** Resembling ripe fruit; rosy; luscious. **6** Ready for surgical treatment, as an abscess. [< OE *rīpe* ready for reaping] **—ripe′ly** *adv.* **—ripe′ness** *n.*

rip·en (rī′pən) *v.t. & v.i.* To make or become ripe; mature. **—rip′en·er** *n.*

rip-off (rip′ôf′, -of′) *n. Slang* **1** The act of ripping off; an act of stealing or cheating. **2** Anything dishonest, illegal, or exploitative.

ri·poste (ri·pōst′) *n.* **1** A return thrust, as in fencing. **2** A quick, clever reply or retort. Also **ri·post′.** [< L *responderi* to answer]

rip·ping (rip′ing) *adj. Brit. Slang* Splendid; excellent.

rip·ple (rip′əl) *v.* ·pled, ·pling *v.i.* **1** To become slightly agitated on the surface, as water. **2** To flow with small waves or undulations. **3** To make a sound like water flowing in small waves. **—***v.t.* **4** To cause to form ripples. **—***n.* **1** A small wave or undulation on the surface of water. **2** Anything suggesting this in appearance. **3** Any sound like that made by rippling. [?] **—rip′pler** *n.* **—rip′pling** *adj.* **—rip′pling·ly** *adv.*

rip-roar·ing (rip′rôr′ing, -rōr′-) *adj. Slang* Excellent; exciting; boisterous.

rip·saw (rip′sô′) *n.* A saw designed for cutting wood in the direction of the grain.

rip·tide (rip′tīd′) *n.* Water violently agitated by conflicting tides or currents.

rise (rīz) *v.* rose, ris·en, ris·ing *v.i.*
1 To move upward; go from a lower to a higher position. **2** To slope gradually upward: The ground *rises* here. **3** To have height or elevation; extend upward: The city *rises* above the plain. **4** To gain elevation in rank, status, fortune, or reputation. **5** To swell up: Dough *rises*. **6** To become greater in force, intensity, height, etc. **7** To become greater in amount, value, etc. **8** To become elated or more optimistic: Their spirits *rose*. **9** To become erect after lying down, sitting, etc.;

Ripsaw

stand up. **10** To get out of bed. **11** To return to life. **12** To revolt; rebel: The people *rose* against the tyrant. **13** To adjourn: The House passed the bill before *rising*. **14** To appear above the horizon: The sun *rose*. **15** To come to the surface, as a fish after a lure. **16** To have origin; begin. **17** To become perceptible to the mind or senses: The scene *rose* in his mind. **18** To occur; happen. **19** To be able to cope with an emergency, danger, etc.: Will he *rise* to the occasion? **—***v.t.* **20** To cause to rise. **—rise above** To prove superior to; show oneself indifferent to. **—***n.* **1** A moving or sloping upward; ascent. **2** An elevated place, as a small hill. **3** Appearance above the horizon. **4** The height of a stair step or of a flight of stairs. **5** Advance, as in rank, status, prosperity, etc. **6** Increase, as in price, volume, intensity, etc. **7** An origin, source, or beginning. **8** *Informal* An emotional reaction; a response or retort, esp. in the phrase **get a rise out of** (someone). **9** *Brit.* An increase in salary. [< OE *rīsan*]

ris·er (rī′zər) *n.* **1** One who rises or gets up, as from bed: an early *riser*. **2** The vertical part of a step or stair.

ris·i·bil·i·ty (riz′ə·bil′ə·tē) *n. pl.* ·ties **1** A tendency to laughter. **2** *Usu. pl.* Appreciation of what seems laughable or ridiculous.

ris·i·ble (riz′ə·bəl) *adj.* **1** Having the power of laughing. **2** Of a nature to excite laughter. **3** Pertaining to laughter. [< L *risus,* p.p. of *ridere* to laugh] **—ris′i·bly** *adv.*

ris·ing (rī′zing) *adj.* **1** Increasing in wealth, rank, fame, etc. **2** Ascending: the *rising* moon. **3** Sloping upward: a *rising* hill. **4** Advancing to adult years; maturing: the *rising* generation. **—***n.* **1** The act of one who or that which rises. **2** That which rises. **3** An uprising or revolt.

risk (risk) *n.* **1** A chance of encountering harm or loss; hazard; danger. **2** In insurance: **a** Chance of loss. **b** Degree of exposure to loss or injury. **c** An applicant for an insurance policy considered with regard to the hazard of insuring him. **—***v.t.* **1** To expose to a chance of injury or loss; hazard. **2** To incur the risk of. [< Ital. *risicare* to dare] **—risk′er** *n.*

risk·y (ris′kē) *adj.* risk·i·er, risk·i·est Attended with risk; hazardous; dangerous. **—Syn.** perilous, ticklish, unsafe, uncertain, critical.

ris·qué (ris·kā′) *adj.* Bordering on or suggesting impropriety; somewhat daring or improper. [F] **—Syn.** indelicate, lewd, smutty, dirty, unseemly, unbecoming.

ri·tar·dan·do (rē′tär·dän′dō) *adj. & adv. Music* In a gradually slower tempo. [< Ital. *ritardare* to delay]

rite (rīt) *n.* **1** A solemn ceremony performed in a prescribed manner. **2** The words or acts accompanying such a ceremony. **3** Any formal practice or custom. [< L *ritus*]

rit·u·al (rich′ōō·əl) *n.* **1** A prescribed form or method for the performance of a rite. **2** The use or performing of such rites. **3** A book setting forth such a system of rites or observances. **4** Any act, observance, or custom performed somewhat regularly or formally. **—***adj.* Of, pertaining to, or consisting of a rite or rites. **—rit′u·al·ly** *adv.*

rit·u·al·ism (rich′ōō·əl·iz′əm) *n.* **1** The use or performance of ritual. **2** Slavish devotion to ritual. **—rit′u·al·ist** *n.* **—rit′u·al·is′tic** *adj.* **—rit′u·al·is′ti·cal·ly** *adv.*

ritz·y (rit′sē) *adj.* ritz·i·er, ritz·i·est *Slang* Smart; elegant; luxurious. [< C. *Ritz,* 1850–1918, Swiss hotelier] **—Syn.** classy, posh, swank, chic.

ri·val (rī′vəl) *n.* **1** One who strives to equal or excel another; a competitor. **2** A person or thing equaling or nearly equaling another, in any respect. **—***v.t.* ·valed or ·valled, ·val·ing or ·val·ling **1** To strive to equal or excel; compete with. **2** To be the equal of or a match for. **—***adj.* Being a rival or rivals; competing. [< L *rivalis*]

ri·val·ry (rī′vəl·rē) *n. pl.* ·ries **1** The act of rivaling. **2** The state of being a rival or rivals; competition.

rive (rīv) *v.* rived, rived or riv·en, riv·ing *v.t.* **1** To split asunder by force; cleave. **2** To break (the heart, etc.). **—***v.i.* **3** To become split. [< ON *rifa* tear, rend] **—riv·er** (rī′vər) *n.*

riv·er (riv′ər) *n.* **1** A large, natural stream of water, usu. fed by converging tributaries along its course and discharging into a larger body of water. **2** A large stream of any kind; copious flow. **—sell down the river** To betray;

deceive. —**send up the river** *Slang* To send to a penitentiary. [<L *riparius*]

river basin An area of land drained by a river and its branches.

riv·er·side (riv′ər·sīd′) *n.* The land adjacent to a river.

riv·et (riv′it) *n.* A metal bolt, having a head on one end, used to join objects, as metal plates, by passing the shank through holes and forming a head by flattening out the plain end. —*v.t.* 1 To fasten with or as with a rivet. 2 To fasten firmly. 3 To engross or attract (the eyes, attention, etc.). [<OF *river* to clench] —**riv′et·er** *n.*

riv·u·let (riv′yə·lit) *n.* A small stream or brook. [<L *rivus* brook]

RM, R.M., RM., r.m. Reichsmark(s).

rm. ream; room.

rms. reams; rooms.

R.N. registered nurse; Royal Navy.

Rn radon.

RNA ribonucleic acid.

R.N.R. Royal Naval Reserve.

R.N.W.M.P. Royal Northwest Mounted Police.

roach[1] (rōch) *n.* 1 A European freshwater fish of the carp family. 2 One of other related fishes, as the American freshwater sunfish. [<OF *roche*]

roach[2] (rōch) *n.* 1 COCKROACH. 2 *Slang* The butt of a marihuana cigarette.

road (rōd) *n.* 1 An open way for public passage; a highway. 2 Any course followed in a journey or a project. 3 A railroad. —**on the road** 1 On tour: said of circuses, theatrical companies, athletic teams, etc. 2 Traveling, as a canvasser or salesman. [<OE *rād* a ride, a riding]

road·bed (rōd′bed′) *n.* The foundation of a railroad track or of a road.

road·block (rōd′blok′) *n.* 1 An obstruction, as of men or materials, for blocking passage, as along a road. 2 Any obstacle to progress or advancement.

road·house (rōd′hous′) *n.* A restaurant, bar, etc., located at the side of a suburban or rural road.

road·metal Broken stone or the like, used for making or repairing roads.

road·run·ner (rōd′run′ər) *n.* A long-tailed, very agile, crested ground cuckoo of SW North America.

road·stead (rōd′sted) *n. Naut.* A place of anchorage offshore, less sheltered than a harbor.

road·ster (rōd′stər) *n.* A light, open automobile having seats for two persons.

road·way (rōd′wā′) *n.* A road, esp. that part over which vehicles pass.

Roadrunner

roam (rōm) *v.i.* 1 To move about purposelessly from place to place; wander; rove. —*v.t.* 2 To wander over; range: to *roam* the fields. —*n.* The act of roaming. [ME *romen*] —**roam′er** *n.*

roan (rōn) *adj.* Of a color consisting of brown, reddish brown, black, or gray thickly interspersed with white hairs, as a horse. —*n.* 1 A roan color. 2 An animal of a roan color. [<Sp. *roano*]

roar (rôr, rōr) *v.i.* 1 To utter a deep, prolonged cry, as of rage or distress. 2 To make a loud noise or din, as a cannon. 3 To laugh loudly. 4 To move, proceed, or act noisily. —*v.t.* 5 To utter or express by roaring: The crowd *roared* its disapproval. —*n.* 1 A full, deep, resonant cry. 2 Any loud, prolonged sound, as of wind or waves. 3 Loud, boisterous laughter. [<OE *rārian*] —**roar′er** *n.*

roast (rōst) *v.t.* 1 To cook by subjecting to the action of heat, as in an oven or by placing in hot ashes, embers, etc. 2 To heat to an extreme degree. 3 To dry and parch: to *roast* coffee. 4 *Informal* To criticize or ridicule severely. —*v.i.* 5 To roast food in an oven, etc. 6 To be cooked or prepared by this method. 7 To be uncomfortably hot. —*n.* 1 Something prepared for roasting, or that is roasted. 2 A social gathering where food is roasted: a corn *roast*. 3 *Informal* Severe criticism or ridicule. —*adj.* Roasted. [<OHG *rösten*]

roast·er (rōs′tər) *n.* 1 A person who roasts. 2 A pan for roasting. 3 Something suitable for roasting, as a chicken.

rob (rob) *v.* **robbed, rob·bing** *v.t.* 1 To seize and carry off the property of by unlawful violence or threat of violence. 2 To deprive (a person) of something belonging, necessary, due, etc.: *robbed* him of his honor. 3 To take something unlawfully from: to *rob* a store. 4 To steal: to *rob* gold. —*v.i.* 5 To commit robbery. [<OHG *roubon*] —**rob′ber** *n.*

rob·ber·y (rob′ər·ē) *n. pl.* **·ber·ies** The act of robbing, esp. the taking away of the property of another unlawfully by using force or intimidation.

robe (rōb) *n.* 1 A long, loose, flowing, outer garment. 2 *pl.* Such a garment worn as a badge of office or rank. 3 A bathrobe or dressing gown. 4 A blanket or covering: lap *robe.* —*v.* **robed, rob·ing** *v.t.* 1 To put a robe upon; clothe; dress. —*v.i.* 2 To put on robes. [<OHG *roub* robbery]

rob·in (rob′in) *n.* 1 A large North American thrush with reddish brown breast and underparts. 2 A small European songbird with cheeks and breast yellowish red. [Dim. of *Robert*]

Robin Hood A legendary, English outlaw of great skill in archery, who robbed the rich to relieve the poor.

rob·in's-egg blue (rob′inz·eg′) A pale greenish blue.

Rob·in·son Cru·soe (rob′in·sən krōō′sō) The hero of Daniel Defoe's *Robinson Crusoe* (1719), a sailor shipwrecked on a tropical island.

American robin

ro·bot (rō′bət, ·bot) *n.* 1 A machine designed to resemble a person and perform human tasks. 2 Any mechanical device that performs complex, often humanlike actions automatically or by remote control. 3 A person who lives or works mechanically, without spontaneity, etc. [<Czech *robota* work, compulsory service]

robot bomb An early form of jet-powered guided missile having an explosive charge.

ro·bot·ics (rō·bot′iks) *n.* The science of robots, their design, manufacture, and purposes.

ro·bust (rō·bust′, rō′bust) *adj.* 1 Possessing or characterized by great strength or endurance. 2 Requiring strength. 3 Boisterous; rude: *robust* humor. 4 Rich, as in flavor: a *robust* soup. [<L *robur, roboris,* a hard variety of oak, strength] —**ro·bust′ly** *adv.* —**ro·bust′ness** *n.*

roc (rok) *n.* In Arabian and Persian legend, an enormous and powerful bird of prey.

Ro·chelle salt (rō·shel′) A potassium and sodium salt of tartaric acid, used as a cathartic, etc. [<La *Rochelle,* France]

rock[1] (rok) *n.* 1 A large mass of stone or stony matter, often forming a peak or cliff. 2 A piece of stone of any size. 3 *Geol.* Solid mineral matter, such as that forming an essential part of the earth's crust. 4 Any strong, solid person or thing, often acting as a support, refuge, defense, etc. 5 *Slang* A precious gem, esp. a diamond. —**on the rocks** *Informal* 1 In a ruined or disastrous condition. 2 Bankrupt; destitute. 3 Served with ice cubes: said of an alcoholic beverage. —*adj.* Made or composed of rock; hard; stony. [<OF *roque*]

rock[2] (rok) *v.i.* 1 To move backward and forward or from side to side; sway. 2 To sway, reel, or stagger, as from a blow. —*v.t.* 3 To move backward and forward or from side to side, esp. so as to soothe or put to sleep. 4 To cause to sway or reel. —*n.* 1 The act of rocking or a rocking motion. 2 A type of popular music whose origins lie in jazz, country music, and blues, characterized by a strong, persistent rhythm, simple, often repeated melodies, and usu. performed by small, electronically amplified instrumental-singing groups: also **rock and roll, rock-and-roll, rock'n' roll.** [<OE *roccian*]

rock·a·by (rok′ə·bī) *interj.* Go to sleep: used to lull a child to slumber. Also **rock′a-bye, rock′-a-bye.**

rock bottom 1 The very bottom; the lowest possible level. 2 The basis of any issue. —**rock′-bot′tom** *adj.*

rock-bound (rok′bound′) *adj.* Encircled by or bordered with rocks.

rock candy Sugar candied in hard, clear crystals.

rock crystal Colorless transparent quartz.

rock·er (rok′ər) *n.* 1 One who or that which rocks. 2 One of the curved pieces on which a rocking chair or a cradle rocks. **3** ROCKING CHAIR.

rock·et (rok′it) *n.* **1 a** A usu. cylindrical firework, projectile, missile, or other device propelled by the reaction of ejected matter. **b** An engine that develops thrust by ejecting matter. **2** A vehicle propelled by rockets and designed for space travel. —*v.i.* & *v.t.* **1** To move or cause to move rapidly, as a rocket. **2** To rise or cause to rise rapidly: Her career *rocketed.* [< Ital. *rocchetta* spool]

rock·et·ry (rok′it·rē) *n.* The science and technology of rocket flight, design, and construction.

rock garden A garden with flowers and plants growing in rocky ground or among rocks arranged to imitate this.

rocking chair A chair having the legs set on rockers.

rocking horse A toy horse mounted on rockers.

rock 'n' roll (rok′ən·rōl′) ROCK² *n.* (def. 2).

rock-ribbed (rok′ribd′) *adj.* **1** Surrounded or edged by rocks. **2** Inflexible; unchangeable.

rock salt Salt found in large, rocklike masses; halite.

Rocking horse

rock·y¹ (rok′ē) *adj.* **rock·i·er, rock·i·est 1** Consisting of, abounding in, or resembling rocks. **2** Marked by difficulties, obstacles, etc. **3** Tough; unfeeling; hard. —**rock′i·ness** *n.*

rock·y² (rok′ē) *adj.* **rock·i·er, rock·i·est 1** Not firm; shaky; wobbly. **2** *Informal* Unsteady; dizzy. —**rock′i·ness** *n.*

Rocky Mountain goat MOUNTAIN GOAT.

ro·co·co (rə·kō′kō, rō′kə·kō′) *n.* **1** A style of decoration and architecture distinguished by profuse, elaborate, and delicately executed ornament, esp. prevalent during the 18th century. **2** Anything sometimes considered overly elaborate or delicate, as in literature, music, etc. —*adj.* **1** Having, or built in, the style of rococo. **2** Overelaborate; florid. [< F *rocaille* shellwork]

rod (rod) *n.* **1** A straight, usu. slim piece of wood, metal, etc. **2** A stick used to inflict punishment; also, the punishment itself. **3** A staff, wand, or scepter used as a badge of office, rank, rule, etc. **4** Dominion; rule; power, esp. if harsh. **5** FISHING ROD. **6** LIGHTNING ROD. **7** A measure of length, equal to 5.5 yards or 16.5 feet, or 5.03 meters. **8** A measuring rule. **9** One of the rodlike bodies of the retina sensitive to faint light. **10** *Slang* A pistol. [< OE *rod.*]

rode (rōd) *p.t.* of RIDE.

ro·dent (rōd′nt) *n.* Any of an order of gnawing mammals having incisors that grow continually, as a squirrel, beaver, or rat. —*adj.* **1** Gnawing. **2** Pertaining to the rodents. [< L *rodere* gnaw]

ro·de·o (rō′dē·ō, rō·dā′ō) *n. pl.* **·de·os 1** A roundup of cattle. **2** A public performance in which the riding of broncos or bulls, roping of calves, lariat-throwing, etc., are presented. [< Sp. *rodear* go around]

rod·o·mon·tade (rod′ə·mon·tād′, rō′də-, -täd′) *n.* Vain boasting; bluster. —*adj.* Bragging. [< Ital. *rodomontata*]

roe¹ (rō) *n.* A mass of eggs of fish or of certain crustaceans, as lobsters. [< MDu. *roge*]

roe² (rō) *n.* A small, graceful deer of Europe and W Asia. Also **roe deer.** [< OE *rā*]

roe·buck (rō′buk′) *n.* The male of the roe deer.

Roent·gen ray (rent′gən, runt′-, ren′chən) X-RAY. [< W. K. *Roentgen,* 1845–1923, German physicist]

Ro·ga·tion days (rō·gā′shən) *Eccl.* The three days immediately preceding Ascension Day, observed by litanies, processions, etc. [< L *rogare* ask]

rog·er (roj′ər) *interj.* **1** *Often cap.* Message received: a code signal used in radiotelephone communication. **2** *Informal* All right; O.K. [< *Roger,* code word for *r* used in telecommunication]

rogue (rōg) *n.* **1** A dishonest and unprincipled person; scoundrel. **2** One who is innocently mischievous or playful. **3** A dangerous animal separated from the herd: also used adjectively: a *rogue* elephant. —*v.* **rogued, ro·guing** *v.t.* **1** To practice roguery upon; defraud. —*v.i.* **2** To live or act like a rogue. [?] —**Syn.** ne'er-do-well, dastard, good-fornothing, scamp, knave, rascal.

ro·guer·y (rō′gər·ē) *n. pl.* **·guer·ies 1** Knavery, cheating, or dishonesty. **2** Playful mischievousness.

rogues' gallery A collection of photographs of criminals taken to aid the police in their future identification.

ro·guish (rō′gish) *adj.* **1** Playfully mischievous. **2** Knavish; dishonest. —**ro′guish·ly** *adv.* —**ro′guish·ness** *n.*

roil (roil) *v.t.* **1** To make muddy, as a liquid, by stirring up sediment. **2** To irritate or anger. [?< F *rouiller* rust, make muddy] —**roil′y** *adj.*

roist·er (rois′tər) *v.i.* **1** To act in a blustery manner; swagger. **2** To engage in revelry. [< L *rusticus* rustic] —**roist′·er·er** *n.* —**roist′er·ing** *adj.*

ROK Republic of (South) Korea.

role (rōl) *n.* **1** A part or character taken by an actor. **2** Any assumed office or function. **3** A specific or acceptable pattern of behavior expected from those in a certain social status, profession, etc. Also **rôle.** [< F < Med. L *rotulus* roll of parchment]

roll (rōl) *v.i.* **1** To move upon a surface by turning round and round, as a wheel. **2** To move, be moved, travel about, etc., on or as on wheels. **3** To rotate wholly or partially: Her eyes *rolled.* **4** To assume the shape of a ball or cylinder by turning over and over upon itself. **5** To move or appear to move in undulations or swells, as waves or plains. **6** To sway or move from side to side, as a ship. **7** To rotate on a front-to-rear axis, as a projectile. **8** To walk with a swaying motion. **9** To make a sound as of heavy, rolling wheels; rumble: Thunder *rolled* across the sky. **10** To become spread or flat because of pressure applied by a roller, etc. **11** To perform a periodic revolution, as the sun. **12** To move ahead; progress. —*v.t.* **13** To cause to move by turning round and round or turning on an axis: to *roll* a ball; to *roll* a log. **14** To move, push forward, etc., on wheels or rollers. **15** To impel or cause to move onward with a steady, surging motion. **16** To begin to operate: *Roll* the presses. **17** To rotate, as the eyes. **18** To impart a swaying motion to. **19** To spread or make flat by means of a roller. **20** To wrap round and round upon itself. **21** To cause to assume the shape of a ball or cylinder by means of rotation and pressure: to *roll* a cigarette. **22** To wrap or envelop in or as in a covering. **23** To utter with a trilling sound: to *roll* one's r's. **24** To emit in a full and swelling manner, as musical sounds. **25** To beat a roll upon, as a drum. **26** To cast (dice) in the game of craps. **27** *Slang* To rob (a drunk or unconscious person). —**roll back** To cause (prices, wages, etc.) to return to a previous, lower level, as by government order. —**roll in 1** To arrive, usu. in large amounts: Money *rolled in.* **2** *Informal* To have large amounts of: *rolling in* money. —**roll out 1** To unroll. **2** *Informal* To get out of (bed, etc.). **3** To flatten by means of rollers. —**roll up 1** To assume or cause to assume the shape of a ball or cylinder by turning over and over upon itself. **2** To accumulate; amass: to *roll up* large profits. **3** To arrive, as in an automobile. —*n.* **1** The act or an instance of rolling. **2** Anything rolled up. **3** A list of names, a register of items, etc.: an honor roll. **4** A long strip of something rolled upon itself: a *roll* of carpet. **5** Any food rolled up in preparation for eating or cooking, esp. small, variously shaped pieces of baked bread dough. **6** A roller. **7** A rolling gait or movement. **8** A rotation on an axis from front to rear, as of an aircraft. **9** A reverberation, as of thunder. **10** A trill. **11** A rapid beating of a drum. **12** An undulation or swell, as of waves or land. **13** *Slang* A wad of paper money; also, money in general. [< L *rota* wheel]

roll·a·way (rōl′ə·wā′) *adj.* Mounted on rollers for easy movement into storage.

roll·back (rōl′bak′) *n.* A return, esp. by government order, to a lower level, as of prices, wages, or rents.

roll call 1 The act of calling out a list of names to ascertain who is present. **2** The time of or signal for this.

roll·er (rō′lər) *n.* **1** One who or that which rolls anything. **2** Any cylindrical device that rolls, as for smoothing, crushing, imprinting, etc. **3** The wheel of a caster or roller skate. **4** A rod on which something is rolled up, as a curtain, map, hair, etc. **5** One of a series of long, swelling waves which break on a coast.

---

add, āce, câre, pălm; end, ēven; it, īce; odd, ōpen, ôrder; tŏŏk, pōōl; up, bûrn; ə = *a* in *above, u* in *focus;*
yōō = *u* in *fuse;* oil; pout; check; go; ring; thin; this; zh, *vision.* < derived from; ? origin uncertain or unknown.

roller bearing A bearing employing rollers to lessen friction between parts.

roller coaster A railway having many steep inclines and sharp curves over which open cars run, as at an amusement park.

roller derby A race between two teams on roller skates, in which points are scored when a player overtakes opponents after skating around a track within a given time.

roll·er-skate (rōl'lər-skāt') v.i. -skat·ed, -skat·ing To go on roller skates. —**roller skater**

roller skate A metal frame on wheels, designed to be clamped to a shoe, or a shoe with wheels attached, for skating over a sidewalk, a wood floor, etc.

rol·lick·ing (rol'ik·ing) adj. Carelessly gay and frolicsome. Also **rol'lick·some** -(səm). [< earlier rollick, blend of ROMP and FROLIC]

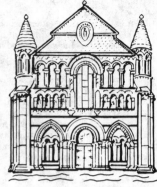
Roller skate

rolling mill A machine or factory in which metal is rolled into sheets, bars, etc.

rolling pin A cylindrical roller of wood, glass, etc., for rolling out dough, etc.

rolling stock The wheeled transport equipment of a railroad.

roll·top (rōl'top') adj. Having a flexible cover which slides back: a rolltop desk.

ro·ly-po·ly (rōl'lē-pō'lē) adj. Short and fat; pudgy; dumpy. —n. 1 Brit. A pudding made of a sheet of pastry dough spread with fruit, preserves, etc., rolled up and cooked. 2 A pudgy person.

ROM Read-only memory, a kind of computer memory from which information may only be read, not altered or erased.

Ro·ma·ic (rō·mā'ik) adj. Pertaining to the language or people of modern Greece. —n. Modern Greek. [< Gk. Rhōmaikos Roman]

ro·maine (rō·mān') n. A variety of lettuce having long leaves clustered in a head. [F, fem. of romain Roman]

ro·man (rō'mən) adj. Printing Designating a much-used style of type having serifs, and upright strokes thicker than horizontal strokes. —n. Roman type.

Ro·man (rō'mən) adj. 1 Of, pertaining to, or characteristic of Rome or its people. 2 Of the Roman Catholic Church. 3 LATIN. 4 Having a prominent, aquiline bridge: a Roman nose. —n. 1 A native, resident, or citizen of modern Rome or a citizen of ancient Rome. 2 A Roman Catholic.

ro·man à clef (rō·män' ä·klä') n. pl. romans à clef (-manz-) French A novel in which real persons or events appear under disguise; literally, novel with a key.

Roman calendar A calendar used by the ancient Romans. The day of the new moon (the calends), the full moon (the ides), and the ninth day before the ides (the nones) provided the bases for reckoning the day of the month.

Roman candle A tubular firework which discharges colored balls and sparks of fire.

Roman Catholic 1 A member of the Roman Catholic Church. 2 Of the Roman Catholic Church.

Roman Catholic Church The Christian church which recognizes the Pope as its supreme head on earth.

ro·mance (rō·mans', rō'mans) n. 1 Adventurous, fascinating, or picturesque nature or appeal: the romance of faraway places. 2 A disposition to delight in the mysterious, adventurous, sentimental, etc.: a child of romance. 3 A love affair. 4 A long narrative from medieval legend, usu. involving heroes in strange adventures and affairs of love. 5 Any fictitious narrative embodying adventure, love affairs, etc. 6 The class of literature consisting of romances (defs. 4 and 5). 7 An extravagant falsehood. —v. (rō·mans') ·manced, ·manc·ing v.i. 1 To tell romances. 2 To think or act in a romantic manner. 3 Informal To make love. —v.t. 4 Informal To make love to; woo. [< OF romans a story written in French] —ro·manc'er n.

Ro·mance languages (rō·mans') The languages developed from the vulgar Latin speech, including French, Italian, Spanish, Portuguese, and Rumanian.

Roman Empire The empire of ancient Rome, established in 27 B.C. and continuing until A.D. 395.

Ro·man·esque (rō'mən·esk') adj. Of, pertaining to, or designating the style of architecture prevalent from the 5th to 12th centuries and characterized by the use of rounded arches and general massiveness. —n. Romanesque architecture.

Roman holiday Enjoyment or profit derived from the sufferings of others. [< gladiatorial contests of ancient Rome]

Ro·ma·nia (rō·mā'nē·ə, -mān'yə) n. RUMANIA. —Ro·man'ian adj. n.

Romanesque façade

Ro·man·ic (rō·man'ik) adj. 1 Roman. 2 Of or pertaining to the Romance languages.

Ro·man·ism (rō'mən·iz'əm) n. The dogmas, forms, etc., of the Roman Catholic Church: a term used chiefly in disparagement. —Ro'man·ist adj., n.

Ro·man·ize (rō'mən·īz) v.t. & v.i. ·ized, ·iz·ing 1 To make or become Roman or Roman Catholic. 2 To write or speak in a Latinized style. —Ro'man·i·za'tion n.

Roman numerals The letters used until the tenth century as symbols in arithmetical notation. The basic letters are I (1), V (5), X (10), L (50), C (100), D (500), and M (1000). Intermediate and higher numbers are formed according to the following rules: Any symbol following another of equal or greater value adds to its value, as II = 2, XI = 11; any symbol preceding one of greater value subtracts from its value, as IV = 4, IX = 9, XC = 90; when a symbol stands between two of greater value, it is subtracted from the second and the remainder added to the first, as XIV = 14, LIX = 59.

ro·man·tic (rō·man'tik) adj. 1 Of, like, characterized or influenced by romance. 2 Given to feelings or thoughts of romance, adventure, idealism, etc. 3 Characterized by or conducive to love or amorousness. 4 Visionary; fantastic; impractical: a romantic scheme. 5 Strangely wild or picturesque: romantic scenery. 6 Of, pertaining to, or characteristic of romanticism (def. 1). —n. 1 An adherent of romanticism; a romanticist. 2 A romantic person. [< F romance romance, novel] —ro·man'ti·cal·ly adv.

ro·man·ti·cism (rō·man'tə·siz'əm) n. 1 Often cap. In the late 18th and early 19th centuries, a social and esthetic movement, beginning as a reaction to neo-classicism, and characterized, in art, literature, music, etc., by freedom of form, spontaneity of feeling, flights of lyricism and imagination, and a fascination with the remote past, nature, the strange and picturesque, etc. 2 The quality or characteristic of being romantic. —ro·man'ti·cist n.

ro·man·ti·cize (rō·man'tə·sīz) v.t. ·cized, ·ciz·ing To regard or interpret in a romantic manner.

Romantic Movement ROMANTICISM (def. 1).

Rom·a·ny (rom'ə·nē) n. pl. ·nies 1 GYPSY. 2 The Indic language of the Gypsies. [< Romany romani < rom man]

Ro·me·o (rō'mē·ō) n. 1 In Shakespeare's tragedy Romeo and Juliet, the hero of the play. 2 Any ardent male lover.

romp (romp) v.i. 1 To play boisterously. 2 To win easily. —n. 1 One, esp. a girl, who romps. 2 Noisy, exciting frolic or play. 3 An easy victory. [Var. of RAMP[2]]

romp·er (rom'pər) n. 1 One who romps. 2 pl. A combination of waist and bloomers, as worn by young children.

Rom·u·lus (rom'yə·ləs) Rom. Myth. The founder of Rome, who, with his twin brother Remus, was reared by a she-wolf.

ron·do (ron'dō, ron·dō') n. pl. ·dos Music A composition or movement having a main theme that is repeated after each of several subordinate themes. [Ital., round]

rood (rood) n. 1 A cross or crucifix. 2 A square land measure, equivalent to one fourth of an acre, or 40 square rods. [< OE rōd rod]

roof (roof, roof) n. 1 The exterior upper covering of a building. 2 Any top covering, as of the mouth, a car, etc. 3 A house; home. **4** The most elevated part of anything; top; summit. —*v.t.* To cover with or as with a roof. [< OE *hrōf*] —**roof′er** *n.*

roof garden 1 A garden on the roof of a building. **2** A gardenlike space on a roof used for a nightclub, restaurant, etc.

roof·ing (rōō′fing, rŏŏf′ing) *n.* **1** Roofs collectively. **2** Material for roofs. **3** The act of covering with a roof.

rook¹ (rŏŏk) *n.* **1** An Old World bird similar to a crow. **2** A sharper; cheat; trickster. —*v.t. & v.i.* To cheat; defraud. [< OE *hrōc*]

rook² (rŏŏk) *n.* One of a pair of castle-shaped chessmen; a castle. [< Pers. *rukh*]

rook·er·y (rŏŏk′ər·ē) *n. pl.* **·er·ies 1** A place where rooks flock together and breed. **2** A breeding place of sea birds, seals, etc.

rook·ie (rŏŏk′ē) *n. Slang* **1** A raw recruit in the army, police, or any other service. **2** A first-year player in a major professional sport. [Prob. alter. of RECRUIT]

room (rōōm, rŏŏm) *n.* **1 a** A space for occupancy or use enclosed on all sides, as in a building. **b** The people in a room. **2** Space available or sufficient for some specified purpose: *room* to park. **3** Suitable or warrantable occasion; opportunity: *room* for doubt. **4** *pl.* Lodgings. —*v.i.* To occupy a room; lodge. [< OE *rūm* space]

room·er (rōō′mər, rŏŏm′ər) *n.* A lodger.

room·ette (rōō·met′, rŏŏm·et′) *n.* A compartment with a single bed in some railroad sleeping-cars.

room·ful (rōōm′fŏŏl′, rŏŏm′-) *n.* **1** As many or as much as a room will hold. **2** The number of persons in a room.

rooming house A house for roomers.

room·mate (rōōm′māt′, rŏŏm′-) *n.* One who occupies a room with another or others.

room·y (rōō′mē, rŏŏm′ē) *adj.* **room·i·er, room·i·est** Having abundant room; spacious. —**room′i·ly** *adv.* —**room′i·ness** *n.*

roor·back (rŏŏr′bak) *n. U.S.* A fictitious report circulated for political purposes. [< *Roorback,* purported author of a (nonexistent) book of travel]

roost (rōōst) *n.* **1 a** A perch upon which fowls rest at night. **b** Any place where birds resort to spend the night. **2** Any temporary resting place. —*v.i.* **1** To sit or perch upon a roost. **2** To come to rest; settle. [< OE *hrōst*]

roost·er (rōōs′tər) *n.* The male of the chicken; cock. [< ROOST + -ER¹]

root¹ (rōōt, rŏŏt) *n.* **1** The descending axis of a plant, usu. growing underground, providing support and absorbing moisture from the soil. **2** Any underground growth, as a tuber or bulb. **3** Some rootlike part of an organ or structure: the *root* of a tooth, hair, nerve, etc. • See TOOTH. **4** That from which something derives its origin, growth, life, etc.: Money is the *root* of all evil. **5.** *pl.* A mental or emotional attachment to some place or people, as through birth, childhood, etc. **6** The essence or basic part: the *root* of the problem. **7** *Ling.* A word or word part serving as the basic constituent element of a related group of words, as *know* in *unknown, knowledge, knowable,* and *knowingly.* **8** *Math.* A number or element that, taken a specified number of times as a factor, will produce a given number or element. **9** *Music* The principal tone of a chord. —*v.i.* **1** To put forth roots and begin to grow. **2** To be or become firmly fixed or established. —*v.t.* **3** To fix or implant by or as by roots. **4** To pull, dig, or tear up by or as by the roots; extirpate; eradicate: with *up* or *out.* [< OE *rōt*] —**root′y** *adj.*

Rooster

root² (rōōt, rŏŏt) *v.t.* **1** To turn up or dig with the snout or nose, as swine. —*v.i.* **2** To turn up the earth with the snout. **3** To search for something; rummage. **4** To work hard; toil. [< OE *wrōtan* root up] —**root′er** *n.*

root³ (rōōt, rŏŏt) *v.i. Informal* To give one's moral support to a contestant, team, cause, etc.: with *for.* [? < ROOT²] —**root′er** *n.*

root beer A carbonated beverage flavored with the extracts of several roots.

root hair Any of numerous minute outgrowths on plant roots, having an absorbent function.

root·less (rōōt′lis, rŏŏt′-) *adj.* **1** Without roots. **2** Having no permanent or secure emotional attachment to a place, community, or culture. —**root′less·ness** *n.*

root·let (rōōt′lit, rŏŏt′-) *n.* A small root.

root·stock (rōōt′stok′, rŏŏt′-) *n.* RHIZOME.

rope (rōp) *n.* **1** An assembly of intertwined strands of fiber, wire, plastic, etc., forming a thick cord. **2** A collection of things plaited or united in a line. **3** A sticky or glutinous filament or thread of something, as of beaten egg yolks. **4 a** A cord or halter used in hanging. **b** Death by hanging. **5** LASSO. —*v.t.* **roped, rop·ing 1** To tie or fasten with or as with rope. **2** To enclose, border, or divide with a rope: usu. with *off:* He *roped* off the arena. **3** To catch with a lasso. **4** *Informal* To deceive: with *in.* [< OE *rāp*]

rop·y (rō′pē) *adj.* **rop·i·er, rop·i·est 1** That may be drawn into threads, as a glutinous substance; stringy. **2** Resembling ropes or cordage. —**rop′i·ly** *adv.* —**rop′i·ness** *n.*

Roque·fort cheese (rōk′fərt, *Fr.* rôk·fôr′) A strong cheese with a blue mold, made from ewe's and goat's milk. [< *Roquefort,* France, where first made]

ror·qual (rôr′kwəl) *n.* Any of various whales having a dorsal fin and marked lengthwise creases at the throat. [< Norw. *röyrkval*]

Rorqual

Ror·schach test (rôr′shäk, -shäkh, rôr′-) A psychological test based on the subject's interpretation of inkblot patterns. [< H. *Rorschach,* 1884–1922, Swiss psychiatrist]

ro·sa·ceous (rō·zā′shəs) *adj.* **1** Of, pertaining to, or designating the rose and related plants, as apple, hawthorn, etc. **2** Resembling a rose; rosy.

ro·sa·ry (rō′zə·rē) *n. pl.* **·ries** *Eccl.* **1** A string of beads for keeping count of a series of prayers, used esp. in Roman Catholicism. **2** The prayers. [< LL *rosarium* a rose garden]

rose¹ (rōz) *n.* **1** Any of a genus of hardy, erect or climbing shrubs with prickly stems and flowers of pink, red, white, yellow, etc. **2** The flower. **3** Any of various other plants or flowers having a likeness to the true rose. **4** A pinkish or purplish red color. **5** An ornamental knot, as of ribbon or lace; a rosette. **6** A form in which gems, esp. diamonds, are often cut. —*adj.* **1** Of, containing, or used for roses. **2** Of the color rose. **3** Rose-scented. [< L *rosa* < Gk. *rhodon*]

rose² (rōz) *p.t.* of RISE.

ro·se·ate (rō′zē·it, -āt) *adj.* **1** Of a rose color. **2** Optimistic; rosy. —**ro′se·ate·ly** *adv.*

rose·bud (rōz′bud′) *n.* The bud of a rose.

rose·bush (rōz′bŏŏsh′) *n.* A rose-bearing shrub.

rose chafer A hairy, fawn-colored beetle that feeds on the blossoms of roses and related plants. Also **rose beetle.**

rose fever A kind of hay fever that occurs in early summer when roses are in bloom. Also **rose cold.**

rose·mar·y (rōz′mâr′ē) *n. pl.* **·mar·ies 1** An evergreen, fragrant shrub related to mint. **2** Its leaves, used for their taste and aroma in cooking, perfumery, etc. [< L *ros* dew + *marinus* marine; infl. by *rose, Mary*]

rose of Sharon 1 In the Bible, an unidentified flower. **2** A species of hibiscus; althea. **3** A species of St. Johnswort.

ro·se·o·la (rō·zē·ō′lə, -zē′ə·lə) *n.* **1** A pink rash occurring as a symptom of various diseases. **2** A mild disease of infants, marked by fever and a pink rash. [< L *roseus* rosy]

Ro·set·ta stone (rō·zet′ə) A tablet containing an inscription in Egyptian hieroglyphics and in Greek, found near Rosetta, Egypt, in 1799. It supplied the key to the ancient inscriptions of Egypt.

ro·sette (rō·zet′) *n.* **1** A painted or sculptured architectural ornament with parts circularly arranged. **2** A ribbon badge shaped like a rose and worn to indicate possession of a certain military decoration. **3** Any flowerlike cluster as of leaves, markings, etc. [F, little rose]

---

rose water An aqueous extract of rose petals, used in perfumery and cooking. —**rose′-wa′ter** *adj.*

rose window A circular window filled with tracery that radiates from the center.

rose·wood (rōz′wŏŏd′) *n.* **1** The hard, dense, dark-colored wood of various tropical leguminous trees, valued for cabinet work. **2** Any tree yielding such a wood.

Rosh Ha·sha·na (rosh hə·shä′nə, rōsh) The Jewish New Year, celebrated in September or early October. Also **Rosh Ha·sho′nah** (-shō′-). [< Hebrew *rōsh* head of + *hash-shānāh* the year]

Rose window

ros·in (roz′in) *n.* A hard, usu. amber-colored resin obtained from turpentine. —*v.t.* To apply rosin to. [Var. of RESIN] —**ros′in·y** *adj.*

ros·ter (ros′tər) *n.* **1** A list of officers and men enrolled for duty. **2** Any list of names. [< Du. *rooster* list]

ros·trum (ros′trəm) *n. pl.* **·trums** or **·tra** (-trə) **1** A stage or platform for public speaking. **2** Those speaking publically on a rostrum. **3** *pl.* **ros·tra** The orators' platform in the Roman forum. **4** A beak or snout. **5** One of various beak-like parts, as the prow of an ancient war galley. [< L *rostrum* beak]

ros·y (rō′zē) *adj.* **ros·i·er, ros·i·est 1** Like a rose in color. **2** Blushing. **3** Fresh and blooming. **4** Favorable; optimistic. —**ros′i·ly** *adv.* —**ros′i·ness** *n.*

rot (rot) *v.* **rot·ted, rot·ting** *v.i.* **1** To undergo decomposition. **2** To fall or pass by decaying: with *away, off,* etc. **3** To become morally rotten. —*v.t.* **4** To cause to decompose; decay. —*n.* **1** The process of rotting or the state of being rotten. **2** Any of various plant and animal diseases characterized by destruction of tissue. **3** *Informal* Nonsense; bosh. —*interj.* Nonsense. [< OE *rotian*]

rot. rotating; rotation.

ro·ta·ry (rō′tər·ē) *adj.* **1** Turning on an axis, as a wheel. **2** Having some part that so turns: a *rotary* press. [< L *rota* wheel]

rotary engine An engine, as a turbine, in which rotary motion is directly produced without reciprocating parts.

ro·tate (rō′tāt, rō·tāt′) *v.t. & v.i.* **·tat·ed, ·tat·ing 1** To turn or cause to turn on or as on its axis. **2** To alternate in a definite order or succession. [< L *rota* wheel] —**ro·tat′a·ble, ro′ta·tive** (-tə·tiv) *adj.* —**ro′ta·tor** *n.*

ro·ta·tion (rō·tā′shən) *n.* **1** The act or state of rotating. **2** Alternation or succession in some fixed order. **3** *Agric.* The practice of planting a field with a series of various crops to preserve the fertility of the field: also **crop rotation.** —**ro·ta′tion·al** *adj.*

ro·ta·to·ry (rō′tə·tôr′ē, -tō′rē) *adj.* **1** Of, pertaining to, or producing rotation. **2** Alternating or recurring.

ROTC, R.O.T.C. Reserve Officers' Training Corps.

rote (rōt) *n.* A routine, mechanical way of doing something. —**by rote** Mechanically; without intelligent attention: to learn *by rote.* [ME]

ro·ti·fer (rō′tə·fər) *n.* Any of numerous many-celled, aquatic microorganisms having rows of cilia at one end, which in motion resemble revolving wheels. [< L *rota* wheel + *ferre* to bear] —**ro·tif·er·al** (rō·tif′ər·əl), **ro·tif′er·ous** *adj.*

ro·tis·se·rie (rō·tis′ə·rē) *n.* **1** An establishment where meat is roasted and sold. **2** A device for roasting meat by rotating it on a spit before or over a source of heat. [< F *rôtir* to roast]

Rotifer

ro·to·gra·vure (rō′tə·grə·vyŏŏr′) *n.* **1** A printing process in which an impression is produced by rotating cylinders which have been etched from photographic plates. **2** Something printed by this process. [< L *rota* wheel + GRAVURE]

ro·tor (rō′tər) *n.* **1** A rotary part of a machine. **2** *Aeron.* The horizontally rotating airfoil assembly of a helicopter. [Contraction of ROTATOR]

rot·ten (rot′n) *adj.* **1** Decomposed; spoiled. **2** Smelling of decomposition or decay; putrid. **3** Untrustworthy; dishonest. **4** Weak or unsound, as if decayed. **5** *Informal* Disa-greeable or very bad: a *rotten* disposition; a *rotten* movie. [< ON *rotinn*] —**rot′ten·ly** *adv.* —**rot′ten·ness** *n.*

rot·ter (rot′ər) *n. Chiefly Brit. Slang* A worthless or objectionable person.

ro·tund (rō·tund′) *adj.* **1** Rounded out, spherical, or plump. **2** Full-toned, as a voice or utterance. [< L *rota* wheel] —**ro·tun′di·ty** *n.* —**ro·tund′ly** *adv.*

ro·tun·da (rō·tun′də) *n.* A circular building, room, hall, etc., esp. one with a dome. [< L *rotundus* round]

rou·ble (rōō′bəl) *n.* RUBLE.

rouche (rōōsh) *n.* RUCHE.

rou·é (rōō·ā′) *n.* A dissolute man; sensualist. [< F *rouer* break on the wheel]

Rotunda

rouge¹ (rōōzh) *n.* **1** Any cosmetic used for coloring the cheeks or lips. **2** A red powder, mainly ferric oxide, used in polishing. —*v.* **rouged, roug·ing** *v.t. & v.i.* To color with or apply rouge. [< L *rubeus* ruby]

rouge² (rōōzh) *n. Can.* A member of the Liberal party in Quebec. —*adj.* Of or pertaining to the Liberal party in Quebec.

rough (ruf) *adj.* **1** Having an uneven surface: a *rough* pavement. **2** Coarse in texture; shaggy: a *rough* tweed. **3** Disordered or ragged: a *rough* shock of hair. **4** Characterized by rude or violent action: *rough* sports. **5** Agitated; stormy: a *rough* passage. **6** Rude; coarse: a *rough* manner. **7** Lacking finish and polish; crude: a *rough* gem. **8** Done or made hastily and without attention to details: a *rough* sketch. **9** *Phonet.* Uttered with an aspiration, or *h* sound. **10** Harsh to the senses: *rough* sounds. **11** Without comforts or conveniences: the *rough* life of the poor. **12** Requiring physical strength: *rough* work. **13** *Informal* Difficult; trying: It's been a *rough* day. —**in the rough** In an unpolished or crude condition. —*n.* **1** Any rough ground. **2** A crude, incomplete, or unpolished object, material, or condition. **3** Any part of a golf course on which tall grass, bushes, etc., grow. **4** *Chiefly Brit.* A rude or violent person; ruffian. —*v.t.* **1** To make rough; roughen. **2** To treat roughly: often with *up.* **3** To make, cut, or sketch roughly: to *rough* in the details of a plan. —*v.i.* **4** To become rough. **5** To behave roughly. —**rough it** To live under or endure conditions that are hard, rustic, inconvenient, etc. —*adv.* In a rude manner. [< OE *rūh*] —**rough′ly** *adv.* —**rough′ness** *n.* —**Syn.** *adj.* **3** unkempt. **6** boorish, uncultivated.

rough·age (ruf′ij) *n.* Food containing bulky, indigestible constituents that stimulate peristalsis.

rough-and-read·y (ruf′ən·red′ē) *adj.* Crude or rough in quality but effective for a particular purpose.

rough-and-tum·ble (ruf′ən·tum′bəl) *adj.* Disregarding all rules of fighting; disorderly and violent. —*n.* A fight in which anything goes; a brawl.

rough·cast (ruf′kast′, -käst′) *v.t.* **·cast, ·cast·ing 1** To shape or prepare in a preliminary or incomplete form. **2** To coat, as a wall, with coarse plaster. —*n.* **1** Very coarse plaster for the outside of buildings. **2** A rude model of a thing in its first rough stage. —**rough′-cast′er** *n.*

rough-dry (ruf′drī′) *v.t.* **-dried, -dry·ing** To dry (laundry) without ironing it afterward. —*adj.* Washed and dried but unironed.

rough·en (ruf′ən) *v.t. & v.i.* To make or become rough.

rough-hew (ruf′hyōō′) *v.t.* **-hewed, -hewed** or **-hewn, -hew·ing 1** To hew or shape roughly without smoothing. **2** To make crudely.

rough·house (ruf′hous′) *Slang n.* A noisy, boisterous disturbance; rough play. —*v.* (ruf′hous′, -houz′) **·housed, ·hous·ing** *v.i.* **1** To engage in roughhouse. —*v.t.* **2** To handle or treat roughly, usu. without hostile intent.

rough·neck (ruf′nek′) *n. Slang* A rowdy.

rough·rid·er (ruf′rī′dər) *n.* One skilled in breaking horses for riding, or accustomed to hard, rough riding.

Rough Riders The 1st U.S. Volunteer Cavalry in the Spanish-American War of 1898, commanded by Theodore Roosevelt.

rough-shod (ruf′shod′) *adj.* Shod with rough shoes to prevent slipping, as a horse. —**ride rough-shod (over)** To treat harshly and without consideration.

rou·lette (rōō·let′) *n.* 1 A gambling game in which participants place bets on which compartment of a rotating shallow bowl a small ball will fall into. 2 A toothed wheel for making marks or holes, as the tiny slits in a sheet of postage stamps. —*v.t.* ·let·ted, ·let·ting To use a roulette upon. [< L *rota* wheel]

Rou·ma·ni·a (rōō·mā′nē-ə, -mān′yə) *n.* RUMANIA. —**Rou·ma′ni·an** *adj., n.*

round (round) *adj.* 1 Having a shape like a ball, ring, or cylinder; spherical, circular, or cylindrical. 2 Semicircular: a *round* arch. 3 Plump. 4 Formed or moving in rotation or a circle: a *round* dance. 5 Approximate to the nearest ten, hundred, thousand, etc., as a number. 6 Pronounced with the lips forming a circle, as the vowel *o.* 7 Full; complete: a *round* dozen. 8 Large; ample; liberal: a good *round* fee. 9 Full in tone or resonance. 10 Free and easy; brisk: a *round* pace. —*n.* 1 Something round, as a globe, ring, or cylinder. 2 *Often pl.* A circular course or range; circuit; beat: to make one's *rounds.* 3 Motion in a circular path. 4 A series of recurrent actions; a routine: the daily *round* of life. 5 An outburst, as of applause. 6 In some sports and games, a division based on action or time. 7 A short canon for several voices. 8 A single shot fired by a weapon or by each of a number of weapons. 9 The ammunition used for such a shot. 10 ROUND DANCE (def. 1). 11 The state of being carved out on all sides: opposed to *relief.* 12 The state or condition of being circular; roundness. 13 A portion of a hind leg of beef, between the rump and lower leg. 14 A rung of a chair or ladder. —**go the rounds** To pass from person to person, as gossip, a rumor, etc. —*v.t.* 1 To make round or plump. 2 *Phonet.* To utter (a vowel) with the lips in a rounded position. 3 To travel or go around; make a circuit of. —*v.i.* 4 To become round or plump. 5 To make a circuit; travel a circular course. 6 To turn around. —**round off** (or **out**) 1 To make or become round. 2 To bring to perfection or completion. —**round up** 1 To collect (cattle, etc.) in a herd, as for driving to market. 2 *Informal* To gather together; assemble. —*adv.* 1 On all sides; in such a manner as to encircle: A crowd gathered *round.* 2 In a circular path, or with a circular motion: The plane circled *round;* The wheel turns *round.* 3 To each of a number, one after the other: provisions enough to go *round.* 4 In circumference: a log three feet *round.* 5 From one position to another; here and there. 6 In the vicinity: to loiter *round.* 7 So as to complete a period of time: Will spring ever come *round* again? 8 In a circuitous or indirect way: Come *round* by way of the shopping center. 9 In the opposite direction: to turn *round.* —*prep.* 1 Enclosing; encircling: a belt *round* his waist. 2 On every side of; surrounding. 3 Toward every side of; about: He peered *round* him. 4 In the vicinity of: farms *round* the town. 5 To all or many parts of: driving friends *round* the city. 6 Here and there in: to look *round* a room. 7 So as to get to the other side of: walking *round* the corner. 8 In a group or mass surrounding: a rich socialite with hangers-on *round* him. [< L *rotundus*] —**round′ness** *n.*

round·a·bout (round′ə·bout′) *adj.* 1 Circuitous; indirect. 2 Encircling. —*n.* 1 A short, tight-fitting jacket for men and boys. 2 *Brit.* A merry-go-round.

round dance 1 A country dance in which the dancers form or move in a circle. 2 A dance with revolving or circular movements, as a waltz or polka, performed by two persons.

roun·de·lay (roun′də·lā) *n.* A simple song with a recurrent refrain. [< OF *rond* round]

round·er (roun′dər) *n.* 1 *Informal* A dissolute person; wastrel. 2 A tool for rounding a surface or edge.

Round·head (round′hed′) *n.* A member of the Parliamentary party in England in the civil war of 1642–49.

round·house (round′hous′) *n.* 1 A cabin on the after part of the quarter-deck of a vessel. 2 A round building with a turntable in the center, used for housing and repairing locomotives.

round·ly (round′lē) *adv.* 1 In a round manner or form. 2 Severely; vigorously; bluntly. 3 Thoroughly; completely.

round robin 1 A petition, protest, etc., on which signa-

tures are written in a circle to avoid revealing the order of signing. 2 A tournament, as in tennis or chess, in which each player is matched with every other player.

round-shoul·dered (round′shōl′dərd) *adj.* Having the back rounded or the shoulders stooping.

round table 1 A group of persons meeting for a discussion. 2 Such a discussion. —**round′-ta′ble** *adj.*

Round Table 1 The table of King Arthur, made exactly circular so as to avoid any question of precedence among his knights. 2 King Arthur and his body of knights.

round trip A trip to a place and back again. —**round′-trip′** *adj.*

round·up (round′up′) *n.* 1 The bringing together of cattle scattered over a range for inspection, branding, etc. 2 The cowboys, horses, etc., employed in this work. 3 A bringing together, as of persons or things: a *roundup* of hobos.

round·worm (round′wûrm′) *n.* Any of a large phylum of worms with thin, cylindrical, unsegmented bodies; nematode worm.

rouse (rouz) *v.* roused, rous·ing *v.t.* 1 To cause to awaken from slumber, repose, unconsciousness, etc. 2 To excite to vigorous thought or action; stir up. 3 To startle or drive (game) from cover. —*v.i.* 4 To awaken from sleep or unconsciousness. 5 To become active. 6 To start from cover: said of game. —*n.* The act of rousing. [?] —**rous′er** *n.* —**Syn.** *v.* 2 animate, incite, arouse, stimulate.

rous·ing (rou′zing) *adj.* 1 Able to rouse or excite: a *rousing* speech. 2 Lively; vigorous: a *rousing* trade. 3 Exceptional; remarkable: a *rousing* success. —**rous′ing·ly** *adv.*

roust·a·bout (roust′tə·bout′) *n.* 1 A deck hand or dock worker. 2 An unskilled, semiskilled, or transient worker, as on an oil field or ranch. 3 A worker at a circus who helps to set up and dismantle tents, etc. [< *roust,* blend of ROUSE and ROUT]

rout¹ (rout) *n.* 1 A disorderly retreat or flight. 2 A boisterous and disorderly crowd; rabble. 3 An overwhelming defeat; debacle. —*v.t.* 1 To defeat disastrously. 2 To put to flight. [< L *ruptus,* p.p. of *rumpere* to break]

rout² (rout) *v.i.* 1 To turn up the earth with the snout, as swine. 2 To search; rummage. —*v.t.* 3 To dig or turn up with the snout. 4 To disclose to view; turn up as if with the snout: with *out.* 5 To hollow, gouge, or scrape, as with a scoop. 6 To drive or force out. [Var. of ROOT²]

route (rōōt, rout) *n.* 1 A course or way taken in passing from one point to another. 2 A road; highway. 3 The established passage which is regularly traveled by a person who delivers mail, milk, etc. 4 A way or means of approach: the *route* to success. —*v.t.* rout·ed, rout·ing 1 To send by a certain way, as passengers, goods, etc. 2 To arrange an itinerary for. [< L *rupta (via)* broken (road)] —**rout′er** *n.*

rou·tine (rōō·tēn′) *n.* 1 A detailed method of procedure, prescribed or regularly followed. 2 Anything that has become customary or habitual. —*adj.* 1 Customary; habitual. 2 Uninspired; dull: a *routine* performance. [< F *route* way, road] —**rou·tine′ly** *adv.*

rove¹ (rōv) *v.* roved, rov·ing *v.i.* 1 To go from place to place without any definite destination. —*v.t.* 2 To roam over, through, or about. —*n.* The act of roving or roaming. [? < Du. *rooven* rob] —**Syn.** 1 ramble, roam, wander.

rove² (rōv) A *p.t.* & *p.p.* of REEVE².

row¹ (rō) *n.* An arrangement or series of persons or things in a continued line, as a street lined with buildings on both sides, or a line of seats in a theater. —**a long row to hoe** A hard task or undertaking. —*v.t.* To arrange in a row: with *up.* [< OE *rāw* line]

row² (rō) *v.i.* 1 To use oars, sweeps, etc., in propelling a boat. 2 To be propelled by or as if by oars. —*v.t.* 3 To propel across the surface of the water with oars, as a boat. 4 To transport by rowing. 5 To be propelled by (a specific number of oars): said of boats. 6 To take part in (a rowing race). 7 To row against in a race. —*n.* 1 A trip in a rowboat; also, the distance covered. 2 The act of rowing, or an instance of it. [< OE *rōwan*]

row³ (rou) *n.* A noisy disturbance or quarrel; dispute; brawl; clamor. —*v.t.* & *v.i.* To engage in a row. [?]

row·an (rō′ən, rou′-) *n.* **1** Any of various related trees having compound pinnate leaves, white flowers and red berries, as the European or American mountain ash. **2** The fruit of these trees: also **row′an·ber′ry.** [< Scand.]

row·boat (rō′bōt′) *n.* A boat propelled by oars.

row·dy (rou′dē) *n. pl.* **·dies** One inclined to create disturbances or engage in rows; a rough, quarrelsome person. — *adj.* **·di·er, ·di·est** Rough and loud; disorderly. [?] —**row′di·ly** *adv.* —**row′di·ness, row′dy·ism** *n.* —**row′dy·ish** *adj.*

row·el (rou′əl) *n.* A spiked or toothed wheel, as on a spur. —*v.t.* **·eled** or **·elled, ·el·ing** or **·el·ling** To prick with a rowel; spur. [< L *rota* wheel]

row·lock (rō′lok′) *n. Brit.* OARLOCK.

roy. royal.

roy·al (roi′əl) *adj.* **1** Of, pertaining to, or being a king, queen, or other sovereign. **2** Of, pertaining to, or under the patronage or authority of a sovereign. **3** Like or suitable for a sovereign. **4** Of superior quality or size: *royal* octavo. —*n.* A small sail or mast next above the topgallant. [< L *regalis* kingly] —**roy′al·ly** *adv.* —**Syn.** *adj.* **3** imperial, kingly, noble, regal, stately.

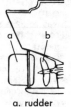

Rowel of spur

royal blue A vivid purplish or reddish blue.

roy·al·ist (roi′əl·ist) *n.* A supporter of a king, queen, or other sovereign. —**roy′al·ism** *n.*

roy·al·ty (roi′əl·tē) *n. pl.* **·ties 1** The rank, status, or authority of a sovereign. **2** A royal personage; also, royal persons collectively. **3** Royal nature or quality. **4** A share of proceeds paid to a proprietor, author, inventor, etc.

rpm, r.p.m. revolutions per minute.

rps, r.p.s. revolutions per second.

rpt. report.

R.R. railroad; Right Reverend.

R.S. Recording Secretary; Reformed Spelling; Revised Statutes.

R.S.F.S.R. Russian Soviet Federated Socialist Republic.

RSV Revised Standard Version (of the Bible).

R.S.V.P., r.s.v.p. please reply (F *répondez s'il vous plaît*).

Rt. Hon. Right Honorable.

Rt. Rev. Right Reverend.

Rts. rights.

Ru ruthenium.

rub (rub) *v.* **rubbed, rub·bing** *v.t.* **1** To move or pass over the surface of with pressure and friction. **2** To cause (something) to move or pass with friction. **3** To cause to become frayed, worn, or sore from friction: This collar *rubs* my neck. **4** To clean, shine, dry, etc., by means of pressure and friction, or by means of a substance applied thus. **5** To apply or spread with pressure and friction: to *rub* polish on a table. **6** To force by rubbing: with *in* or *into:* to *rub* oil into wood. **7** To remove or erase by friction: with *off* or *out.* —*v.i.* **8** To move along a surface with friction; scrape. **9** To exert pressure and friction. **10** To become frayed, worn, or sore from friction; chafe. **11** To undergo rubbing or removal by rubbing: with *off, out,* etc. —**rub down** To massage. —**rub it in** *Slang* To harp on someone's errors, faults, etc. —**rub out** *Slang* To kill. —**rub the wrong way** To irritate; annoy. —*n.* **1** A subjection to frictional pressure; rubbing: Give it a *rub.* **2** A hindrance or doubt: There's the *rub.* **3** Something that injures the feelings; a sarcasm. [ME *rubben*]

ru·ba·to (rōō·bä′tō) *Music adj. & adv.* With certain notes lengthened or shortened at the performer's discretion. —*n. pl.* **·tos** A rubato passage or manner of playing [Ital.]

rub·ber[1] (rub′ər) *n.* **1** A tough, resilient, elastic material made from the latex of certain tropical plants, or synthesized from coal, petroleum, etc. **2** An article made of this material, as: **a** A rubber overshoe. **b** A condom. **3** One who or that which rubs. —*adj.* Made of rubber. [< RUB] —**rub′ber·y** *adj.*

rub·ber[2] (rub′ər) *n.* **1** In bridge, whist, and other card games, a series of games (3, 5, or 7) played by the same partners against the same adversaries, terminated when one side has won a majority (2 out of 3, etc.). **2** The odd game which breaks a tie between the players. [?]

rubber band A continuous elastic band of rubber, stretched to encircle and bind articles, etc.

rub·ber·ize (rub′ər·īz) *v.t.* **·ized, ·iz·ing** To coat, impregnate, or cover with rubber or a rubber solution.

rub·ber·neck (rub′ər·nek′) *n. Slang* One who is extremely curious or inquisitive, as a tourist. —*v.i.* To look or listen with great curiosity.

rubber plant 1 Any of several plants yielding latex. **2** An Asian tree related to the fig, with oblong, leathery leaves, often kept as a house plant.

rub·ber-stamp (rub′ər·stamp′) *v.t.* **1** To endorse, initial, or approve with the mark made by a rubber stamping device. **2** *Informal* To pass or approve as a matter of course or routine.

rubber stamp 1 A stamp made of rubber which, when coated with ink, is used to print names, dates, etc. **2** A person or group of persons that approves something, as a policy or program, with little or no discussion, debate, etc. **3** Any routine approval.

rub·bish (rub′ish) *n.* **1** Waste refuse; garbage; trash. **2** Silly or worthless ideas, talk, etc.; nonsense. [?] —**rub′bish·y** *adj.* —**Syn. 1** debris, litter. **2** absurdity, foolishness.

rub·ble (rub′əl) *n.* **1** Rough, irregular pieces of broken stone, brick, etc. **2** The debris to which buildings of brick, stone, etc., have been reduced by destruction or decay. **3** Masonry composed of irregular or broken stone: also **rub′ble·work′.**

rub·down (rub′doun′) *n.* A massage.

rube (rōōb) *n. Slang* An unsophisticated country person; rustic. [Abbr. of *Reuben*]

ru·bel·la (rōō·bel′ə) *n.* A contagious viral disease benign in children but linked to birth defects of children born of women infected in early pregnancy; German measles. [< L *rubellus* reddish, dim. of *ruber* red]

ru·be·o·la (rōō′bē·ō′lə, rōō·bē′ə·lə) *n.* A contagious viral disease usu. affecting children, marked by catarrh, fever, and a rash that persists for about a week; measles. [< L *rubeus* red] —**ru·be′o·lar** *adj.*

Ru·bi·con (rōō′bi·kon) *n.* A river in N CEN. Italy that formed the boundary separating Julius Caesar's province of Gaul from Italy; by crossing it under arms he committed himself to a civil war. —**cross the Rubicon** To commit oneself irrevocably to some course of action.

ru·bi·cund (rōō′bə·kənd) *adj.* Red, or inclined to redness; ruddy. [< L *rubicundus*] —**ru′bi·cun′di·ty** *n.*

ru·bid·i·um (rōō·bid′ē·əm) *n.* A soft, rare, metallic element (symbol Rb) resembling potassium. [< L *rubidus* red]

ru·ble (rōō′bəl) *n.* The basic monetary unit of the Soviet Union.

ru·bric (rōō′brik) *n.* **1** In early manuscripts and books, the heading of a chapter, an initial letter, etc., that appears in red, or in some distinctive type. **2** Any heading or title, as that of a statute. **3** A direction or rule as in a prayer book, missal, or breviary. [< L *ruber* red] —**ru′bri·cal** *adj.* —**ru′bri·cal·ly** *adv.*

ru·by (rōō′bē) *n. pl.* **·bies 1** A translucent gemstone of a deep red color, a variety of corundum. **2** A rich red color like that of a ruby. —*adj.* Deep red. [< L *rubeus* red]

ruche (rōōsh) *n.* A pleated or gathered strip of fine fabric, worn about the neck or wrists of a woman's costume. [F< Med. L *rusca* tree bark]

ruch·ing (rōō′shing) *n.* **1** Material for ruches. **2** Ruches collectively.

ruck·sack (ruk′sak′, rōōk′-) *n.* KNAPSACK. [G, lit., back sack]

ruck·us (ruk′əs) *n. Slang* An uproar; commotion. [? blend of RUMPUS and *ruction,* alter. of INSURRECTION]

rud·der (rud′ər) *n.* **1** *Naut.* A broad, flat device hinged vertically at the stern of a vessel to direct its course. **2** Anything that guides or directs a course. **3** *Aeron.* A hinged or pivoted surface, used to turn an aircraft about its vertical axis. [< OE *rōthor* oar, scull] —**rud′der·less** *adj.*

rud·dy (rud′ē) *adj.* **·di·er, ·di·est 1** Red or tinged with red. **2** Having a healthy glow; rosy: a *ruddy* complexion. [< OE *rudig*] —**rud′di·ly** *adv.* —**rud′di·ness** *n.*

rude (rōōd) *adj.* **rud·er, rud·est 1** Offensively blunt or uncivil; impolite. **2** Characterized by lack of polish or refinement; uncouth. **3** Unskilfully made or done; crude. **4** Characterized by robust vigor; strong: *rude* health. **5** Barbarous; savage. **6**

a. rudder
def. 1.
b. screw.

Jarring to the ear; harsh; discordant. **7** Lacking skill, training, accuracy, etc. [< L *rudis* rough] —**rude′ly** *adv.* —**rude′ness** *n.* —**Syn. 1** discourteous, impertinent. **2** boorish, uncultivated. **5** uncivilized.

ru·di·ment (roo′də·mənt) *n.* **1** A first step, stage, or condition. **2** That which is undeveloped or partially developed. [< L *rudis* rough]

ru·di·men·ta·ry (roo′də·men′tər·ē) *adj.* **1** Introductory; elementary: *rudimentary* knowledge. **2** Being in an imperfectly developed state; undeveloped. **3** Vestigial. Also **ru′di·men′tal.** —**ru′di·men′ta·ri·ly** *adv.* —**ru′di·men′ta·ri·ness** *n.*

rue[1] (roo) *v.* **rued, ru·ing** *v.t.* **1** To feel sorrow or remorse for; regret extremely. —*v.i.* **2** To feel sorrow or remorse. —*n. Archaic* Sorrowful remembrance; regret. [< OE *hrēowan* be sorry] —**ru′er** *n.*

rue[2] (roo) *n.* **1** A small, pungent shrub with bitter, evergreen leaves. **2** An infusion of rue leaves. [< Gk. *rhytē*]

rue·ful (roo′fəl) *adj.* **1** Feeling or expressing sorrow, regret, or pity. **2** Causing sympathy or pity; pitiable. —**rue′·ful·ly** *adv.* —**rue′ful·ness** *n.*

ruff[1] (ruf) *n.* **1** A pleated, round, heavily starched collar popular in the 16th century. **2** A natural collar of projecting feathers or hair around the neck of a bird or mammal. **3** The male of a European species of sandpiper, which has a large ruff in the breeding season. [Short for RUFFLE[1]] —**ruffed** *adj.*

ruff[2] (ruf) *n.* In a card game, the act of trumping. —*v.t. & v.i.* To trump. [< OF *roffle*]

ruffed grouse (ruft) A North American grouse having in the male a fan-shaped tail and a black ruff.

Ruff

ruf·fi·an (ruf′ē·ən, ruf′yən) *n.* A lawless, brutal person. —*adj.* Lawlessly or recklessly brutal or cruel. [< MF *rufian*] —**ruf′fi·an·ism** *n.* —**ruf′fi·an·ly** *adj.*

ruf·fle[1] (ruf′əl) *n.* **1** A pleated strip; frill, as for trim or ornament. **2** Anything resembling this, as a bird's ruff. **3** A disturbance; discomposure. **4** A ripple. —*v.* **·fled, ·fling** *v.t.* **1** To disturb or destroy the smoothness or regularity of: The wind *ruffles* the lake. **2** To draw into folds or ruffles; gather. **3** To furnish with ruffles. **4** To erect (the feathers) in a ruff, as a bird when frightened. **5** To disturb or irritate; upset. **6 a** To shuffle (the pages of a book). **b** To shuffle (cards). —*v.i.* **7** To be or become rumpled or disordered. **8** To become disturbed or irritated. [ME *ruffelen* to ruffle]

ruf·fle[2] (ruf′əl) *n.* A low, continuous beat of a drum, not as loud as a roll. —*v.t.* **·fled, ·fling** To beat a ruffle upon, as a drum. [?]

rug (rug) *n.* **1** A covering for all or part of a floor, made of some heavy, durable fabric, strips of rag, animal skins, etc. **2** A warm covering, as of cloth, fur, etc., for the lap and feet.

rug·by (rug′bē) *n. Often cap.* A form of football. [< *Rugby* School, Rugby, England, where first played]

rug·ged (rug′id) *adj.* **1** Having a surface that is rough or uneven. **2** Rough; harsh: a *rugged* life. **3** Furrowed and irregular: *rugged* features. **4** Lacking polish and refinement. **5** Tempestuous; stormy: *rugged* weather. **6** Robust; sturdy: *rugged* health. [< Scand.] —**rug′ged·ly** *adv.* —**rug′ged·ness** *n.*

ru·in (roo′in) *n.* **1** Destruction, downfall, or decay. **2** A person or thing that has decayed, fallen, or been destroyed. **3** *Usu. pl.* That which remains of something that has decayed or been destroyed: the *ruins* of Dresden. **4** That which causes destruction, downfall, or decay: Gambling was his *ruin.* **5** The state of being destroyed, fallen, decayed, etc: to fall into *ruin.* —*v.t.* **1** To bring to ruin; destroy. **2** To bring to disgrace or bankruptcy. **3** To deprive of chastity; seduce. —*v.i.* **4** To fall into ruin. [< L *ruere* to fall] —**ru′in·er** *n.* —**Syn.** *n.* **1** collapse, devastation, dilapidation. *v.* **1** demolish, ravage, raze.

ru·in·a·tion (roo′in·ā′shən) *n.* **1** The act of ruining. **2** The state of being ruined. **3** Something that ruins.

ru·in·ous (roo′in·əs) *adj.* **1** Causing or tending to ruin. **2** Falling to ruin. —**ru′in·ous·ly** *adv.* —**ru′in·ous·ness** *n.*

rule (rool) *n.* **1** Controlling power, or its possession and exercise; government; reign; also, the period of time during which a ruler or government is in power. **2** A method or principle of action; regular course of procedure: I make early rising my *rule.* **3** An authoritative direction or regulation about something to do or the way of doing it. **4** The body of directions laid down by or for a religious order: the *rule* of St. Francis. **5** A procedure or formula for solving a given class of mathematical problems. **6** An established usage fixing the form of words: as a *rule* for forming the plural. **7** Something in the ordinary course of events or condition of things: In some communities illiteracy is the *rule.* **8** *Law* A judicial decision on some specific question or point of law. **9** A straight-edged instrument for use in measuring, or as a guide in drawing lines; a ruler. **10** *Printing* A strip of type-high metal for printing a rule or line. —**as a rule** Ordinarily; usually. —*v.* **ruled, rul·ing** *v.t.* **1** To have authority or control over; govern. **2** To influence greatly; dominate. **3** To decide judicially or authoritatively. **4** To restrain; keep in check. **5** To mark lines on, as with a ruler. —*v.i.* **6** To have authority or control. **7** To form and express a decision: The judge *ruled* on that point. —**rule out 1** To eliminate or exclude. **2** To preclude; prevent. [< L *regula* ruler, rule]

rule of thumb 1 A rule based on experience or common sense instead of scientific knowledge. **2** A method of procedure that is practical but not precise.

rul·er (roo′lər) *n.* **1** One who rules or governs, as a sovereign. **2** A straight-edged strip of wood, metal, etc., used in drawing lines and in measuring.

rul·ing (roo′ling) *adj.* **1** Exercising control. **2** Prevalent; predominant. —*n.* A decision, as of a judge or chairman.

rum[1] (rum) *n.* **1** An alcoholic liquor distilled from fermented molasses. **2** Any alcoholic liquor. [?]

rum[2] (rum) *adj. Brit. Slang* Queer; strange. [?]

Rum. Rumania; Rumanian.

Ru·ma·ni·a (roo·mā′nē·ə, -mān′yə) *n.* A republic of SE Europe, 91,671 sq. mi., cap. Bucharest. • See map at BALKAN STATES.

Ru·ma·ni·an (roo·mā′nē·ən, -mān′yən) *adj.* Of or pertaining to Rumania, its people, or their language. —*n.* **1** A native or citizen of Rumania. **2** The Romance language of the Rumanians.

rum·ba (rum′bə, Sp. room′bä) *n.* **1** A dance originated by Cuban Negroes. **2** A ballroom dance based on this. **3** Music for such a dance. —*v.i.* To dance the rumba. [Sp.]

rum·ble (rum′bəl) *v.* **·bled, ·bling** *v.i.* **1** To make a low, heavy, rolling sound, as thunder. **2** To move or proceed with such a sound. —*v.t.* **3** To cause to make a low, heavy, rolling sound. **4** To utter with such a sound. —*n.* **1** A continuous low, heavy, rolling sound; a muffled roar. **2** A seat or baggage compartment in the rear of an automobile or carriage: also **rumble seat. 3** *Slang* A street fight involving a group, usu. deliberately provoked. [< MDu. *rommelen*]

ru·men (roo′men) *n. pl.* **ru·mi·na** (roo′mə·nə) or **ru·mens** The first chamber of the stomach of a ruminant. [L, throat]

ru·mi·nant (roo′mə·nənt) *n.* Any of a division of even-toed ungulates, as a deer, sheep, cow, etc., that graze and chew the cud, which is temporarily stored in the first of the four chambers of the stomach. —*adj.* **1** Chewing the cud. **2** Of or pertaining to ruminants. **3** Meditative or thoughtful. [< L *ruminare* chew the cud, think over]

ru·mi·nate (roo′mə·nāt) *v.t. & v.i.* **·nat·ed, ·nat·ing 1** To chew (food previously swallowed and regurgitated) over again; chew (the cud). **2** To meditate or reflect (upon). —**ru′mi·nat′ing·ly, ru′mi·na′tive·ly** *adv.* —**ru′mi·na′tion, ru′mi·na′tor** *n.* —**Syn. 2** brood, consider, contemplate, muse.

rum·mage (rum′ij) *v.* **·maged, ·mag·ing** *v.t.* **1** To search through (a place, box, etc.) by turning over and disarranging the contents; ransack. **2** To find or bring out by searching: with *out* or *up.* —*v.i.* **3** To make a thorough search. —*n.* **1** Any act of rummaging. esp., disarranging things by searching thoroughly. **2** Odds and ends. [< MF *arrumer* pack or arrange cargo] —**rum′mag·er** *n.*

---

add, āce, câre, pälm; end, ēven; it, īce; odd, ōpen, ôrder; tŏŏk, pōōl; up, bûrn; ə = a in above, u in focus; yōō = u in fuse; oil; pout; check; go; ring; thin; this; zh, vision. < derived from; ? origin uncertain or unknown.

rummage sale A sale of donated miscellaneous objects to raise money, as for some charity.

rum·my[1] (rum'ē) *n.* Any of several card games the object of which is to match cards into sets of three or four of the same denomination or into sequences in the same suit. [?]

rum·my[2] (rum'ē) *n. pl.* **·mies** *Slang* A drunkard. —*adj.* Of, pertaining to, or affected by rum.

ru·mor (rōō'mər) *n.* **1** A story or report circulating without known foundation or authority. **2** Common gossip; hearsay. —*v.t.* To tell or spread as a rumor; report abroad. *Brit. sp.* **ru'mour.** [L, noise]

rump (rump) *n.* **1** The upper part of the hindquarters of an animal. **2** A cut of beef from this part. **3** The buttocks. **4** A last, often unimportant or undesirable part.

rum·ple (rum'pəl) *v.t. & v.i.* **·pled, ·pling** To form into creases or folds; wrinkle. —*n.* An irregular fold or crease; wrinkle. [< MDu. *rumpelen*]

rum·pus (rum'pəs) *n. Informal* A usu. noisy disturbance or commotion. [?]

rumpus room A room used for recreation, games, etc.

rum·run·ner (rum'run'ər) *n.* A person or ship involved in smuggling alcoholic liquor ashore or across a border.

run (run) *v.* **ran, run, run·ning** *v.i.* **1** To move by rapid steps, faster than walking. **2** To move rapidly; go swiftly. **3** To flee; take flight. **4** To make a brief or rapid journey: *We ran over to Staten Island last night.* **5** To make regular trips: *This steamer runs between New York and Liverpool.* **6 a** To take part in a race. **b** To be a candidate or contestant: *to run for dogcatcher.* **7** To finish a race in a specified position: *I ran a poor last.* **8** To move or pass easily: *The rope runs through the pulley.* **9** To pass or flow rapidly: *watching the tide run out.* **10** To proceed in direction or extent: *This road runs north.* **11** To flow: *His nose runs.* **12** To become liquid and flow, as wax; also, to spread or mingle confusedly, as colors when wet. **13** To move or roam about freely and easily: *to run around town with friends.* **14** To pass into a specified condition: *to run to seed.* **15** To unravel, as a fabric. **16** To give forth a discharge or flow. **17** To leak. **18** To continue or proceed without restraint: *The conversation ran on and on.* **19** To be operative; work: *Will the engine run?* **20** To continue or extend, as in time or space: *Our property runs down to the sea.* **21** To be reported or expressed: *The story runs as follows.* **22** To migrate, as salmon from the sea to spawn. **23** To occur or return to the mind: *An idea ran through his head.* **24** To occur with specified variation of size, quality, etc.: *The corn is running small this year.* **25** To be performed or repeated in continuous succession: *The play ran for forty nights.* **26** To pass or spread, as from mouth to mouth or point to point: *rumors running wild.* **27** To creep or climb, as a vine. —*v.t.* **28** To run or proceed along, as a route or path. **29** To make one's way over, through, or past: *to run rapids.* **30** To perform or accomplish by or as by running: *to run a race or an errand.* **31** To compete against in or as in a race. **32** To become subject to; incur: *to run the risk of failure.* **33** To present and support as a candidate. **34** To hunt or chase, as game. **35** To bring to a specified condition by or as by running: *to run oneself out of breath.* **36** To drive or force: with *out of, off, into, through,* etc. **37** To cause to move, as in some manner or direction: *They ran the ship into port.* **38** To move (the eye, hand, etc.) quickly or lightly: *He ran his hand over the table.* **39** To cause to move, slide, etc., as into a specified position: *to run up a flag.* **40** To transport or convey in a vessel or vehicle. **41** To smuggle. **42** To cause to flow: *to run water into a pot.* **43** To trace back: *trying to run a bit of gossip to its source.* **44** To mold, as from melted metal; found. **45** To sew (cloth) in a continuous line, usu. by taking a number of stitches with the needle at a time. **46** To control the motion or operation of; operate: *to run an engine.* **47** To direct or control; manage. **48** To allow to continue or mount up, as a bill. **49** In games, to make (a number of points, strokes, etc.) successively. **50** To publish in a magazine or newspaper: *to run an ad.* **51** To mark, set down, or trace, as a boundary line. **52** To suffer from (a fever, etc.). —**run across** To meet by chance. —**run down 1** To pursue and overtake, as a fugitive. **2** To strike down while moving. **3** To exhaust or damage, as by abuse or overwork. **4** To speak of disparagingly. —**run for it** To run to avoid something, to escape, seek safety, etc. —**run in 1** To insert; include. **2** *Slang* To arrest and place in confinement. — **run into 1** To meet by chance. **2** To collide with. —**run off 1** To produce on a typewriter, printing press, etc. **2** To decide (a tied race, game, etc.) by the outcome of another, subsequent race, game, etc. —**run out** To be exhausted, as supplies. —**run out of** To exhaust one's supply of. — **run over 1** To ride or drive over; run down. **2** To overflow. **3** To go over, examine, or rehearse. —**run through 1** To squander. **2** To stab or pierce. **3** To rehearse quickly. — **run up** To make hurriedly, as on a sewing machine. —*n.* **1** The act, or an act, of running or going rapidly. **2** A running pace: *to break into a run.* **3** Flow; movement; sweep: *the run of the tide.* **4** A distance covered by running. **5** A journey or passage, esp. between two points, made by a vessel, train, etc. **6** A rapid journey or excursion: *take a run into town.* **7** A swift stream or brook. **8** A migration of fish, esp. to up-river spawning grounds; also, the fish that so migrate. **9** A grazing or feeding ground for animals: *a sheep run.* **10** The regular trail or path of certain animals: *an elephant run.* **11** The privilege of free use or access: *to have the run of the place.* **12** A runway. **13** *Music* A rapid succession of tones. **14** A series, sequence, or succession. **15** A trend or tendency: *the general run of the market.* **16** A continuous spell (of some condition): *a run of luck.* **17** A surge of demands, as those made upon a bank or treasury to meet its obligations. **18** A period of continuous performance, occurrence, popularity, etc.: *a play with a long run.* **19** Class or type; also, the usual or general class or type. **20** A period of operation of a machine or device: *an experimental run.* **21** The output during such a period. **22** A period during which a liquid is allowed to run. **23** The amount of liquid allowed to flow at one time. **24** A narrow, lengthwise ravel, as in a sheer stocking. **25** An approach to a target made by a bombing plane. **26** In baseball, a score made by a player who completes a circuit of the bases from home plate before three outs are made. **27** An unbroken series of successful shots, strokes, etc., as in billiards. —**in the long run** As the ultimate outcome of any train of circumstances. —**on the run 1** Hastily: *to eat on the run.* **2** Running, running away, or retreating. —*adj.* **1** Made liquid; melted. **2** That has been melted or cast: *run metal.* [< OE *rinnan* to flow]

run·a·bout (run'ə·bout') *n.* **1** A light, open automobile. **2** A light, open wagon. **3** A small motorboat. **4** A person who wanders or runs about from place to place; gadabout.

run·a·round (run'ə·round') *n. Informal* Evasive or deceptive action or treatment: *to get the runaround from someone.*

run·a·way (run'ə·wā') *adj.* **1** Escaping or escaped from restraint or control. **2** Brought about by running away: *a runaway marriage.* **3** Easily won, as a horse race. —*n.* **1** One who or that which runs away or flees, as a fugitive or deserter, or a horse of which the driver has lost control. **2** An act of running away.

run·down (run'doun') *n.* **1** A summary; resumé. **2** In baseball, a play attempting to put out a base runner who is trapped between two bases.

run-down (run'doun') *adj.* **1** Debilitated; tired out. **2** Dilapidated; shabby. **3** Stopped because not wound, as a watch. —**Syn.** 1 exhausted, weary. 2 decayed, ruined.

rune (rōōn) *n.* **1** A character of an ancient Germanic alphabet. **2** A Finnish or Old Norse poem; also, one of the sections of such a poem. **3** An obscure or mystic mark, song, poem, verse, or saying. [< ON *rūn* mystery, rune] —**ru'nic** *adj.*

Runes from an 11th-century tomb

rung[1] (rung) *n.* **1** A round crosspiece of a ladder or chair. **2** A spoke of a wheel. [< OE *hrung* crossbar]

rung[2] (rung) *p.p.* of RING[2].

run-in (run'in') *n.* **1** A quarrel; bicker. **2** *Printing* Inserted or added matter. —*adj.* (run'in') *Printing* That is inserted or added.

run·nel (run'əl) *n.* A little stream; a brook. Also **run'let** (-lit). [< OE *rinnan* to run]

run·ner (run'ər) *n.* **1** One who or that which runs. **2** One who operates or manages anything. **3** One who runs errands or goes about on any kind of business, as a messenger. **4** That part on which an object runs or slides: the *runner* of a skate. **5** *Bot.* A slender horizontal stem that takes root at the nodes to produce new plants, as in the strawberry. **6** A smuggler. **7** A long, narrow rug or carpeting, used in hallways, etc. **8** A narrow strip of cloth, usu. of fine quality, used on tables, dressers, etc.

run·ner-up (run′ər-up′) *n. pl.* **·ners-up** or **·ner-ups** A contestant or team finishing second in a contest.

run·ning (run′ing) *adj.* **1** Inclined or trained to a running gait, as certain horses. **2** Done in or started with a run: a *running* jump. **3** Following one another without intermission; successive: He talked for three hours *running.* **4** Continuous: a *running* battle. **5** Characterized by easy flowing curves; cursive: a *running* hand. **6** Discharging, as pus from a sore. **7** Fluid or flowing. **8** In operation, as an engine. **9** Measured in a straight line: the cost per *running* foot. —*n.* **1** The act or movement of one who or that which runs. **2** That which runs or flows. —**in the running** Having a chance to win. —**out of the running** Having no chance to win.

running board A footboard, as on the side of a locomotive, certain automobiles, etc.

running head A heading or title at the top of each page or of every other page of a book, etc.: also **running title.**

running knot A knot made so as to slip along a noose and tighten when pulled upon.

running mate A candidate running with another but for a lesser position, as one seeking to be vice-president.

run·ny (run′ē) *adj.* **·ni·er, ·ni·est** Having a tendency to discharge: a *runny* nose. —**run′ni·ness** *n.*

run·off (run′ôf′ -of′) *n.* **1** Rainfall that drains from a particular area rather than soaking into the soil. **2** A final, deciding contest, game, etc.

run-of-the-mill (run′əv·thə-mil′) *adj.* Average; ordinary.

run-on (run′on′, -ôn′) *Printing n.* Appended or added matter. —*adj.* That is appended or added.

runt (runt) *n.* **1** A stunted animal, esp. the smallest of a litter. **2** A small or stunted person. [?] —**runt′i·ness** *n.* — **runt′y** *adj.* **(·i·er, ·i·est)**

run-through (run′thrōō′) *n.* A rapid reading through or rehearsal, as of a musical composition or a dramatic work.

run·way (run′wā′) *n.* **1** A way on, in, along, or over which something runs. **2** The path over which animals pass to and from their places of feeding or watering. **3** An enclosed place, as for chickens. **4** A strip of surfaced ground used for the takeoff and landing of airplanes. **5** A long, narrow platform extending from a stage into an auditorium.

ru·pee (rōō-pē′, rōō′pe) *n.* The basic monetary unit of India, Pakistan, and Sri Lanka. [< Skt. *rūpya* silver]

ru·pi·ah (rōō-pē′ä) *n.* The basic monetary unit of Indonesia.

rup·ture (rup′chər) *n.* **1** The act of breaking apart or the state of being broken apart. **2** HERNIA. **3** Breach of peace and agreement between individuals or nations. —*v.t.* & *v.i.* **·tured, ·tur·ing 1** To break apart. **2** To affect with or suffer a rupture. [< L *ruptus,* p.p. of *rumpere* to break]

ru·ral (rōōr′əl) *adj.* Of or pertaining to the country, country people, country life, or agriculture. [< L *rus, ruris* country] —**ru′ral·ism, ru′ral·ist, ru′ral·ness** *n.* —**ru′ral·ly** *adv.*

rural free delivery Free mail delivery by carrier in rural districts.

ru·ral·ize (rōōr′əl·īz) *v.* **·ized, ·iz·ing** *v.t.* To make rural. — *v.i.* To go into or live in the country; rusticate. —**ru′ral·i·za′tion** *n.*

Rus., Russ. Russia; Russian.

ruse (rōōs, rōōz) *n.* An action intended to mislead or deceive; a stratagem; trick. [< F *ruser* dodge, detour]

rush[1] (rush) *v.i.* **1** To move or go swiftly, impetuously, forcefully, or violently. **2** To make an attack; charge: with *on* or *upon.* **3** To proceed recklessly or rashly; plunge: with *in* or *into.* **4** To come, go, pass, act, etc. with suddenness or haste: Ideas kept *rushing* to her mind. **5** To advance a football in a running play. —*v.t.* **6** To move, push, drive,

etc. with haste, impetuosity, or violence. **7** To do, perform, deliver, etc. hastily or hurriedly: to *rush* one's work. **8** To make a sudden assault upon. **9** *Slang* To seek the favor of with assiduous attentions. **10** To advance (a football) in a running play. —*n.* **1** The act of rushing; a sudden turbulent movement, drive, surge, etc. **2** Frantic activity; haste: the *rush* of city life. **3** A sudden pressing demand; a run: a *rush* on foreign bonds. **4** A sudden exigency; urgent pressure: a *rush* of business. **5** A sudden flocking of people, as to some new location. **6** A general contest or scrimmage between students from different classes. **7** In football, an attempt to take the ball through the opposing linemen and toward the goal. **8** *Usu. pl.* In motion pictures, the first film prints of a scene or series of scenes, before editing or selection. —**with a rush** Suddenly and hastily. — *adj.* Requiring urgency or haste: a *rush* order. [< AF *russher* to push] —**rush′er** *n.* —**Syn.** *v.* **1** dash, hasten, hurry.

rush[2] (rush) *n.* **1** Any of various grasslike plants common in marshy ground. **2** The pliant stem of certain rush plants, used for mats, basketry, etc. [< OE *rysc*] —**rush′y** *adj.* **(·i·er, ·i·est)**

rush hour A time when large numbers of people are traveling, as to or from work. —**rush′-hour′** *adj.*

rush·light (rush′līt′) *n.* A candle made by dipping a rush in tallow: also **rush light, rush candle.**

rusk (rusk) *n.* **1** Plain or sweet bread that is sliced after baking and then toasted or baked a second time until it is brown and crisp. **2** A light, soft, sweet biscuit. [< Sp. *rosca,* twisted loaf of bread]

rus·set (rus′it) *n.* **1** Reddish brown or yellowish brown. **2** A coarse homespun cloth, russet in color, formerly used by country people. **3** A winter apple of russet color. —*adj.* **1** Reddish brown or yellowish brown. **2** Made of russet. [< L *russus* reddish] —**rus′set·y** *adj.*

Rus·sia (rush′ə) *n.* **1** Loosely, the Union of Soviet Socialist Republics. **2** The Russian Soviet Federated Socialist Republic.

Rus·sian (rush′ən) *n.* **1** Loosely, a citizen or native of the Union of Soviet Socialist Republics. **2** A citizen or native of Russia. **3** The language of Russia and the official language of the Union of Soviet Socialist Republics. —*adj.* **1** Loosely, of or pertaining to the Union of Soviet Socialist Republics. **2** Of or pertaining to Russia or its people. **3** Of or pertaining to Russian, the language.

Russian dressing Mayonnaise combined with chili sauce, chopped pickles, etc.

Rus·sian·ize (rush′ən·īz) *v.t.* **·ized, ·iz·ing** To make Russian. —**Rus′sian·i·za′tion** *n.*

Russian leather A smooth, well-tanned, high-grade leather, often dark red, of calfskin or light cattle hide, dressed with birch oil and having a characteristic odor.

Russian Orthodox Church An autonomous branch of the Eastern Orthodox Church.

Russian Revolution The uprising of 1917 that resulted in the overthrow of the czarist regime. The revolution had two phases: first, the establishment of a moderate, provisional government under Kerensky (the **February Revolution**), and, second, the seizure of power by the Bolsheviks (Communists) under Lenin (the **October Revolution**).

Russian thistle A large tumbleweed common on the central plains of North America.

Russian wolfhound BORZOI.

Russo- *combining form* **1** Russia. **2** Russian and: *Russo-*Egyptian.

rust (rust) *n.* **1** A reddish or yellow coating on iron or iron alloys due to spontaneous oxidation. **2** A corroded spot or film of oxide on any metal. **3** Any of various parasitic fungi living on higher plants. **4** A plant disease caused by such fungi, which form spots on stems and leaves. **5** Any spot or film resembling rust on metal. **6** Any of several shades of reddish brown. —*v.t.* & *v.i.* **1** To become or cause to become coated with rust. **2** To contract or cause to contract the plant disease rust. **3** To become or cause to become weakened because of disuse. [< OE *rūst*]

rus·tic (rus′tik) *adj.* **1** Of or pertaining to the country;

---

add, āce, câre, pălm; end, ēven; it, īce; odd, ōpen, ôrder; tŏŏk, pōōl; up, bûrn; ə = a in *above, u* in *focus;* yōō = u in *fuse;* oil; pout; check; go; ring; thin; this; zh, *vision.* < derived from; ? origin uncertain or unknown.

rural. **2** Uncultured; rude; awkward. **3** Unsophisticated; artless. **4** Made of the rough limbs of trees with the bark on them: *rustic* furniture. —*n.* **1** One who lives in the country. **2** An unsophisticated, coarse, or ignorant person, esp. one from a rural area. [< L *rus* country] —**rus′ti·cal·ly** *adv.*

rus·ti·cate (rus′tə·kāt) *v.* **·cat·ed, ·cat·ing** *v.i.* **1** To go to or live in the country. —*v.t.* **2** To send or banish to the country. **3** *Brit.* To suspend (a student) temporarily from a college for punishment. —**rus′ti·ca′tion, rus′ti·ca′tor** *n.*

rus·tic·i·ty (rus·tis′ə·tē) *n. pl.* **·ties 1** The condition or quality of being rustic. **2** A rustic trait or peculiarity.

rus·tle[1] (rus′əl) *v.t. & v.i.* **·tled, ·tling** To move or cause to move with a quick succession of small, light, rubbing sounds, as dry leaves or sheets of paper. —*n.* A rustling sound. [ME *rustelen*] —**rus′tler** *n.* —**rus′tling·ly** *adv.*

rus·tle[2] (rus′əl) *v.t. & v.i.* **·tled, ·tling 1** *Informal* To act with or obtain by energetic or vigorous action. **2** *Informal* To steal (cattle, etc.). [? Blend of RUSH and HUSTLE]

rus·tler (rus′lər) *n.* **1** *Slang* A person who is active and bustling. **2** *Informal* A cattle thief.

rust·y (rus′tē) *adj.* **rust·i·er, rust·i·est 1** Covered or affected with rust. **2** Consisting of or produced by rust. **3** Having the color or appearance of rust; discolored; faded, etc. **4** Not working well or freely; lacking nimbleness; stiff. **5** Impaired or deficient by neglect or want of practice: *rusty* in math. —**rust′i·ly** *adv.* —**rust′i·ness** *n.*

rut[1] (rut) *n.* **1** A sunken track worn by a wheel, as in a road. **2** A groove, furrow, etc., in which something runs. **3** A settled and tedious routine. —*v.t.* **rut·ted, rut·ting** To wear or make a rut or ruts in. [? Var. of ROUTE] —**rut′ti·ness** *n.* —**rut′ty** *adj.* **(·i·er, ·i·est)**

rut[2] (rut) *n.* The sexual excitement of various animals, esp. the male deer; also, the period during which it lasts. —*v.i.* **rut·ted, rut·ting** To be in rut. [< L *rugire* to roar]

ru·ta·ba·ga (rōō′tə·bā′gə) *n.* A variety of turnip having a large, yellowish root. [< dial. Sw. *rotabagge*]

ruth (rōōth) *n.* **1** Compassion; pity, mercy. **2** Grief; sorrow; remorse. [< OE *hrēow* sad]

Ruth (rōōth) In the Bible, a widow from Moab who left her people to live with her mother-in-law, Naomi. —*n.* The Old Testament book that tells her story.

ru·the·ni·um (rōō·thē′nē·əm) *n.* A rare metallic element (symbol Ru). [< *Ruthenia,* a region in the Ukraine]

ruth·less (rōōth′lis) *adj.* Having no compassion; merciless. —**ruth′less·ly** *adv.* —**ruth′less·ness** *n.*

R.V. Revised Version (of the Bible).

R.W. Right Worshipful; Right Worthy.

Rwan·da (rwän′də) *n.* A republic of CEN. Africa, 10,169 sq. mi., cap. Kigali. • See map at AFRICA.

Rx *symbol Med.* Take: the conventional heading for a prescription or formula. [Abbr. of L *recipe* take]

-ry Var. of -ERY.

Ry., ry. railway.

rye (rī) *n.* **1** A hardy, cultivated cereal grass. **2** The seeds of this grass. **3** Flour made from these seeds. **4** Whiskey consisting of a blend of bourbon and neutral spirits: also **rye whiskey.** [< OE *ryge*]

rye·grass (rī′gras′, -gräs′) *n.* A weedy grass sometimes cultivated for forage.

S

S, s (es) *n. pl.* **S's, s's, Ss, ss** (es′iz) **1** The 19th letter of the English alphabet. **2** Any spoken sound representing the letter *S* or *s.* **3** Something shaped like an S. —*adj.* Shaped like an S.

S Seaman; sulfur.

S. Sabbath; Saturday; Saxon; Senate; September; Signor; Sunday.

S., s. saint; school; senate; south; southern.

s. second; section; shilling; semi; series; shilling; son; southern; steamer; substantive; sun; surplus.

SA Seaman Apprentice.

S.A. Salvation Army; South Africa; South America.

Sab. Sabbath.

Sab·bath (sab′əth) *n.* **1** The seventh day of the week, a day of rest observed in Judaism and some Christian sects; Saturday. **2** The first day of the week as observed as a day of rest by Christians; Sunday. [< Heb. *shābath* to rest]

sab·bat·i·cal (sə·bat′i·kəl) *adj. Often cap.* Of the nature of or suitable for the Sabbath: also **sab·bat′ic.** —*n.* SABBATICAL YEAR (def. 2).

sabbatical year 1 In the ancient Jewish economy, every seventh year, in which the people were required to refrain from tillage. **2** In the U.S., a year of leave, or a shorter period, to be used for study and travel with full or partial salary, awarded to college faculty members, usu. every seven years: also **sabbatical leave.**

sa·ber (sā′bər) *n.* A heavy one-edged cavalry sword, often curved. —*v.t.* **·bered** or **·bred, ·ber·ing** or **·bring** To strike, wound, kill, or arm with a saber. Also, and *Brit. sp.,* **sa′bre.** [< MHG *sabel*]

Sa·bine (sā′bīn) *n.* A member of an ancient people of CEN. Italy, conquered and absorbed by Rome in 290 B.C. —*adj.* Of or pertaining to the Sabines.

sa·ble (sā′bəl) *n.* **1** A N Eurasian species of marten bearing costly fur. **2** The dressed fur of a sable. **3** *pl.* Garments made wholly or partly of this fur. **4** The color black. —*adj.* **1** Black; dark. **2** Made of sable fur. [< Med. L *sabelum*]

Saber

sa·bot (sab′ō, *Fr.* sȧ·bō′) *n.* **1** A wooden shoe, as of a French peasant. **2** A shoe having a wooden sole but flexible shank. [F]

sab·o·tage (sab′ə·täzh) *n.* **1** A wasting of materials or damage to machinery, tools, etc., by workmen to make management comply with their demands. **2** The destruction of bridges, railroads, supply depots, etc., either by enemy agents or by underground resisters. **3** Any deliberate effort to obstruct plans or aims. —*v.t. & v.i.* **·taged, ·tag·ing** To engage in, damage, or destroy by sabotage. [F < *saboter* work badly, damage]

sab·o·teur (sab′ə·tûr′, *Fr.* sȧ·bô·tœr′) *n.* One who engages in sabotage. [F]

sa·bra (sä′brə) *n. Often cap.* An Israeli born in Israel. [< Heb.]

sac (sak) *n.* A membranous pouch or cavity, often fluid-filled, in a plant or animal. [< L *saccus*]

SAC (sak) Strategic Air Command.

sac·cha·rin (sak′ər·in) *n.* A sweet compound derived from coal tar, used as a substitute for sugar. [< Gk. *sakcharon* sugar]

sac·cha·rine (sak′ər·in, -ə·rīn′, -ə·rēn′) *adj.* **1** Very sweet. **2** Cloyingly sweet: a *saccharine* voice. —*n.* SACCHARIN. —**sac′cha·rine·ly** *adv.* —**sac′cha·rin′i·ty** *n.*

sac·er·do·tal (sas′ər·dōt′l, sak′-) *adj.* Pertaining to a priest or priesthood; priestly. [< L *sacerdos* priest] —**sac′er·do′tal·ism** (-iz·əm) *n.* —**sac′er·do′tal·ly** *adv.*

sa·chem (sā′chəm) *n.* A North American Indian hereditary chief. [< Algon.]

sa·chet (sa·shā′) *n.* **1** A small bag for perfumed powder, used to scent closets, dresser drawers, etc. **2** The perfumed powder so used. [< L *saccus* a sack]

sack[1] (sak) *n.* **1** A large bag for holding heavy articles. **2** Such a bag and its contents: a *sack* of potatoes. **3** A measure or weight of varying amount. **4** A loosely hanging dress without a waistline, often worn without a belt: also **sack dress. 5** A short, loosely fitting coatlike garment worn by women and children. **6** *Slang* Dismissal, esp. in the phrases **get the sack, give (someone) the sack. 7** In baseball slang, a base. **8** *Slang* A bed; mattress. —**hit the sack** *Slang* To go to bed; retire for the night. —*v.t.* **1** To put into a sack or sacks. **2** *Slang* To dismiss, as an employee. [< Gk. *sakkos* < Heb. *saq* sackcloth]

sack² (sak) *v.t.* To plunder or pillage (a town or city) after capturing. —*n.* The pillaging of a captured town or city. [< L *saccus* a sack (for carrying off plunder)] —**sack′er** *n.*

sack³ (sak) *n.* Any of several strong, light-colored, dry Spanish wines, esp. sherry. [< L *siccus* dry]

sack·but (sak′but) *n.* **1** An early instrument resembling the trombone. **2** In the Bible, a stringed instrument. [< OF *saquer* to pull + *bouter* to push]

sack·cloth (sak′klôth′, -kloth′) *n.* **1** A coarse cloth used for making sacks. **2** Coarse cloth or haircloth worn in penance or mourning.

sack coat A man's short, loose-fitting coat with no waist seam, for informal wear.

sack·ful (sak′fŏŏl′) *n. pl.* **·fuls** Enough to fill a sack.

sack·ing (sak′ing) *n.* A coarse cloth made of hemp or flax and used for sacks.

sacque (sak) *n.* A jacket for a baby.

sac·ra·ment (sak′rə·mənt) *n.* **1** A rite ordained by Christ or by the church as an outward sign of grace, as baptism, confirmation, marriage, etc. **2** *Often cap.* **a** The Eucharist. **b** The consecrated bread and wine of the Eucharist: often with *the.* **3** Any solemn covenant or pledge. **4** Anything considered to have sacred significance. [< L *sacramentum* oath, pledge] —**sac′ra·men′tal** *adj.* —**sac′ra·men′tal·ly** *adv.*

sa·cred (sā′krid) *adj.* **1** Dedicated to religious use; hallowed. **2** Pertaining or related to religion: *sacred* books. **3** Consecrated by love or reverence: *sacred* to the memory of his father. **4** Dedicated to a person or purpose: a memorial *sacred* to those killed in battle. **5** Not to be profaned; inviolable: a *sacred* promise. [< L *sacer* holy] —**sa′cred·ly** *adv.* —**sa′cred·ness** *n.*

Sacred College COLLEGE OF CARDINALS.

sac·ri·fice (sak′rə·fīs) *n.* **1** The act of making an offering to a deity. **2** That which is sacrificed; a victim. **3** A giving up of something cherished or desired. **4** Loss incurred or suffered without return. **5** A reduction of price that leaves little profit or involves loss. **6** In baseball, a hit by which the batter is put out, but the base runner is advanced: also **sacrifice hit.** —*v.* **·ficed**, **·fic·ing** *v.t.* **1** To give up (something valued) for the sake of something else: to *sacrifice* one's principles for expediency. **2** To sell or part with at a loss. **3** To make an offering, as to a god. **4** In baseball, to advance (one or more runners) by means of a sacrifice. —*v.i.* **5** To make a sacrifice. [< L *sacer* holy + *facere* to make] —**sac′ri·fic′er** *n.* —**sac′ri·fic′ing·ly** *adv.*

sac·ri·fi·cial (sak′rə·fish′əl) *adj.* Pertaining to, performing, or of the nature of a sacrifice. —**sac′ri·fi′cial·ly** *adv.*

sac·ri·lege (sak′rə·lij) *n.* The act of violating or profaning anything sacred. [< L *sacer* holy + *legere* to plunder]

sac·ri·le·gious (sak′rə·lij′əs, -lē′jəs) *adj.* Disrespectful or injurious to sacred persons or things. —**sac′ri·le′gious·ly** *adv.* —**sac′ri·le′gious·ness** *n.* —**Syn.** blasphemous, godless, impious, irreligious, profane.

sac·ris·tan (sak′ris·tən) *n.* A church official having charge of a sacristy and its contents. Also **sa′crist** (sā′-krist). [< L *sacer* sacred]

sac·ris·ty (sak′ris·tē) *n. pl.* **·ties** A room in a church for the sacred vessels and vestments; a vestry. [< Med. L *sacrista* sacristan]

sac·ro·il·i·ac (sak′rō·il′ē·ak) *adj.* Pertaining to the sacrum and the ilium and the joint between them.

sac·ro·sanct (sak′rō·sangkt) *adj.* Exceedingly sacred; inviolable: sometimes used ironically. [< L *sacer* holy + *sanctus* made holy] —**sac′ro·sanc′ti·ty** *n.*

sa·crum (sā′krəm, sak′rəm) *n. pl.* **·cra** (-krə) A triangular bone formed of fused vertebrae at the lower end of the spinal column and articulating with the hip bone. [< L (*os*) *sacrum* sacred (bone); from its being offered in sacrifices] • See PELVIS.

sad (sad) *adj.* **sad·der**, **sad·dest** **1** Sorrowful or depressed in spirits; mournful. **2** Causing sorrow or pity; distressing. **3** *Informal* Very bad; awful: a *sad* situation. **4** Dark-hued; somber. [< OE *sæd* sated] —**sad′ly** *adv.* —**sad′ness** *n.* —**Syn. 1** dejected, despondent, disconsolate, miserable, un-

happy, depressed. **2** deplorable, grievous, lamentable, pitiful.

sad·den (sad′n) *v.t. & v.i.* To make or become sad.

sad·dle (sad′l) *n.* **1** A seat or pad for a rider, as on the back of a horse, bicycle, motorcycle, etc. **2** A padded cushion for a horse's back, as part of a harness or to support a pack, etc. **3.** The two hindquarters and part of the backbone of a carcass, as of mutton, venison, etc. **4** Some part or object like or likened to a saddle, as in form or position. —**in the saddle** In a position of control. —*v.t.* **·died**, **·dling** **1** To put a saddle on. **2** To load, as with a burden. **3** To place (a burden or responsibility) on a person. [< OE *sadol*]

American stock saddle
a. pommel or saddle
horn. b. cinches.
c. stirrup.

sad·dle·bag (sad′l·bag′) *n.* A large pouch, usu. one of a pair connected by a strap or band and slung over an animal's back behind the saddle.

saddle block A form of anesthesia used esp. during childbirth, in which the patient is injected in the lower spinal cord.

sad·dle·bow (sad′l·bō′) *n.* The arched front upper part of a saddle.

sad·dle·cloth (sad′l·klôth′, -kloth′) *n.* A thick cloth laid on an animal's back under a saddle.

saddle horse A horse used or trained for riding.

sad·dler (sad′lər) *n.* A maker of saddles, harness, etc.

sad·dler·y (sad′lər·ē) *n. pl.* **·dler·ies** **1** Saddles, harness, and fittings, collectively. **2** A shop or the work of a saddler.

saddle shoe A white sport shoe with a dark band of leather across the instep.

saddle soap A softening and preserving soap for leather, containing neat's-foot oil.

Sad·du·cee (saj′ŏŏ·sē, sad′yŏŏ·sē) *n.* A member of an ancient Jewish sect, which during the time of Jesus rejected doctrines of the oral tradition, as resurrection, and adhered strictly to the Mosaic law. —**Sad′du·ce′an, Sad′du·cae′an** *adj.* —**Sad′du·cee′ism** *n.*

sad-i-ron (sad′ī′ərn) *n.* A heavy flatiron pointed at each end. [< SAD, in obs. sense "heavy" + IRON]

sad·ism (sā′diz·əm, sad′iz·əm) *n.* **1** The obtaining of sexual gratification by inflicting pain. **2** A morbid delight in cruelty. [< Comte Donatien de *Sade*, 1740–1814, French writer] —**sad·ist** (sā′dist, sad′ist) *n., adj.* —**sa·dis·tic** (sə·dis′tik, sā-) *adj.* —**sa·dis′ti·cal·ly** *adv.*

sad·o·mas·o·chism (sā′dō·mas′ə·kiz′m, sad′ō-, -maz′-) *n.* A tendency in one individual to be both a sadist and a masochist. [< SAD (ISM) + -O- + MASOCHISM] —**sad′o·mas′o·chist** *n.* —**sad′o·mas′o·chis′tic** *adj.*

sad sack *Slang* A well-meaning but bungling person, esp. a soldier.

sa·fa·ri (sə·fä′rē) *n. pl.* **·ris** A hunting expedition or journey, esp. in E Africa. [< Ar. *safara* travel]

safe (sāf) *adj.* **saf·er**, **saf·est** **1** Free or freed from danger. **2** Having escaped injury or damage. **3** Not involving risk or loss: a *safe* investment. **4** Not likely to disappoint: It is *safe* to promise. **5** Not likely to cause or do harm or injury: Is this ladder *safe?* **6** No longer in a position to do harm: a burglar *safe* in jail. **7** In baseball, having reached base without being retired. —*n.* **1** A strong iron-and-steel receptacle, usu. fireproof, for protecting valuables. **2** Any place of safe storage. [< L *salvus* whole, healthy] —**safe′ly** *adv.* —**safe′ness** *n.* —**Syn. 1** secure. **2** unharmed, unscathed. **3** dependable, reliable.

safe-con·duct (sāf′kon′dukt) *n.* **1** Permission to travel in foreign or enemy territories without risking arrest or injury. **2** An official document assuring such protection.

safe-crack·er (sāf′krak′ər) *n.* One who breaks into safes to rob them. —**safe′crack′ing** *n.*

safe-de·pos·it box (sāf′di·poz′it) A box, safe, or drawer, usu. fireproof, for valuable jewelry, papers, etc., generally located in a bank. Also **safe′ty-de·pos′it box.**

---

add, āce, câre, pälm; end, ēven; it, īce; odd, ōpen, ôrder; tŏŏk, pōōl; up, bûrn; ə = a in *above*, u in *focus*;
yŏŏ = u in *fuse*; oil; pout; check; go; ring; thin; this; zh, *vision*. < derived from; ? origin uncertain or unknown.

safe·guard (sāf'gärd') *n.* **1** One who or that which guards or keeps in safety. **2** A mechanical device designed to prevent accident or injury. —*v.t.* To defend; guard.

safe·keep·ing (sāf'kē'ping) *n.* The act or state of keeping or being kept in safety; protection.

safe·ty (sāf'tē) *n. pl.* **·ties 1** Freedom from danger or risk. **2** Freedom from injury. **3** A device or catch designed as a safeguard. **4** In football, the touching of the ball to the ground behind the player's own goal line when the ball was propelled over the goal line by a member of his own team, scoring two points for the opposing team. **5** In baseball, a fair hit by which the batter reaches first base: also **base hit.** —*adj.* Providing protection.

safety belt 1 A strap that gives a workman needed freedom of movement and protection against falling. **2** SEAT BELT.

safety glass Glass strengthened by any of various methods to reduce the likelihood of its shattering upon impact.

safety match A match that ignites only if struck on a chemically prepared surface.

safety pin 1 A pin whose point springs into place within a protecting sheath. • See PIN. **2** A pin which prevents the premature detonation of a hand grenade.

safety razor A razor in which the blade is fixed and provided with a guard to reduce the risk of cuts.

safety valve 1 *Mech.* A valve for automatically relieving excessive pressure. **2** Any outlet for pent-up energy or emotion.

saf·flow·er (saf'lou'ər) *n.* A thistlelike herb with composite orange-red flowers and seeds that yield edible **safflower oil.** [< Ital. *saffiore* saffron]

saf·fron (saf'rən) *n.* **1** A species of crocus with orange stigmas. **2** The dried stigmas, used in cookery. **3** A deep yellow orange: also **saffron yellow.** —*adj.* Of the color or flavor of saffron. [< Ar. *za'farān*]

S. Afr. South Africa; South African.

sag (sag) *v.* **sagged, sag·ging** *v.i.* **1** To droop from weight or pressure, esp. in the middle. **2** To hang unevenly. **3** To lose firmness; weaken, as from exhaustion, age, etc. **4** To decline, as in price or value. —*v.t.* **5** To cause to sag. —*n.* **1** A sagging. **2** A depressed or sagging place: a *sag* in a roof. [ME *saggen*] —**sag'ging·ly** *adv.*

sa·ga (sä'gə) *n.* **1** A medieval Scandinavian narrative dealing with legendary and heroic exploits. **2** A story having the saga form or manner. [ON, history, narrative]

sa·ga·cious (sə-gā'shəs) *adj.* **1** Ready and apt to apprehend and to decide on a course; intelligent. **2** Shrewd and practical. [< L *sagax* wise] —**sa·ga'cious·ly** *adv.* —**sa·ga'cious·ness** *n.* —**Syn. 1** acute, discerning, clear-sighted, keen, perspicacious.

sa·gac·i·ty (sə-gas'ə-tē) *n. pl.* **·ties** The quality or an instance of being sagacious; discernment or shrewdness.

sag·a·more (sag'ə-môr, -mōr) *n.* A lesser chief among the Algonquian Indians of North America. [< Algon.]

sage¹ (sāj) *n.* A venerable man of profound wisdom, experience, and foresight. —*adj.* **1** Characterized by or proceeding from calm, far-seeing wisdom and prudence: a *sage* observation. **2** Profound; learned; wise. [< L *sapere* be wise] —**sage'ly** *adv.* —**sage'ness** *n.*

sage² (sāj) *n.* **1** A plant of the mint family with aromatic, gray-green leaves that are used for flavoring meats, etc. **2** Any of various related plants. **3** SAGEBRUSH. [< L *salvia*]

sage·brush (sāj'brush') *n.* Any of various small, aromatic shrubs with composite flowers, native to the w U.S.

sage grouse A large grouse of the plains of the w U.S.

sage hen The sage grouse, esp. the female.

Sag·it·ta·ri·us (saj'ə-târ'ē-əs) *n.* A constellation and the ninth sign of the zodiac; the Archer. • See ZODIAC.

sag·it·tate (saj'ə-tāt) *adj.* Shaped like an arrowhead, as certain leaves. [< L *sagitta* an arrow] • See LEAF.

sa·go (sā'gō) *n. pl.* **·gos 1** Any of several varieties of East Indian palm. **2** The powdered pith of this palm, used as a thickening agent in puddings, etc. [< Malay *sāgū*]

sa·gua·ro (sə-gwä'rō, -wä'-) *n. pl.* **·ros** A giant cactus of the sw U.S.: also **sa·hua·ro** (-wä'-). [< Sp.]

sa·hib (sä'ib) *n.* Master; lord; Mr.; sir: formerly used in India by natives in speaking of or addressing Europeans. Also **sa'heb.** [< Ar. *sāhib* a friend]

said (sed) *p.t. & p.p.* of SAY. —*adj. Law* Previously mentioned.

sail (sāl) *n.* **1** *Naut.* A piece of canvas, etc., attached to a mast, spread to catch the wind, and thus to propel a craft through the water. **2** Sails collectively. **3** *pl.* **sail** A sailing vessel or craft. **4** A trip in any watercraft. **5** Anything resembling a sail in form or use, as a windmill arm. —**set sail** To begin a voyage. —**take in sail** To lower the sails of a craft. —**under sail** With sails spread and driven by the wind. —*v.i.* **1** To move across the surface of water by the action of wind or steam. **2** To travel over water in a ship or boat. **3** To begin a voyage. **4** To manage a sailing craft: Can you *sail?* **5** To move, glide, or float in the air; soar. **6** To move along in a stately or dignified manner: She *sailed* by haughtily. **7** *Informal* To pass rapidly. **8** *Informal* To proceed boldly into action: with *in.* —*v.t.* **9** To move or travel across the surface of (a body of water) in a ship or boat. **10** To navigate. —**sail into 1** To begin with energy. **2** To attack violently. [< OE *segl*]

sail·boat (sāl'bōt') *n.* A small boat propelled by a sail or sails.

sail·cloth (sāl'klôth', -kloth') *n.* A very strong, firmly woven, cotton canvas suitable for sails.

sail·fish (sāl'fish') *n. pl.* **·fish** or **·fish·es** Any of a genus of marine fishes allied to the swordfish, having a large dorsal fin likened to a sail.

sail·or (sā'lər) *n.* **1** An enlisted man in any navy. **2** One whose work is sailing. **3** One

Sailfish

who works on a ship. **4** One skilled in sailing. **5** A passenger on a ship or boat, esp. in reference to seasickness: a good *sailor.* **6** A low-crowned, flat-topped hat with a brim. —**sail'or·ly** *adj.*

sail·plane (sāl'plān') *n.* A light maneuverable glider used for soaring. —*v.i.* **·planed, ·plan·ing** To fly a sailplane.

saint (sānt) *n.* **1** A holy or sanctified person. **2** Such a person who has died and been canonized by certain churches, as the Roman Catholic. **3** *Often cap.* A member of any of certain religious sects calling themselves saints. **4** A very patient, unselfish person. —*v.t.* To canonize; venerate as a saint. —*adj.* Holy; canonized. [< L *sanctus* holy, consecrated] —**saint'hood** *n.*

Saint Ber·nard (bər-närd') A working dog of great size and strength, originally bred in Switzerland to rescue travelers in the Swiss Alps.

saint·ed (sān'tid) *adj.* **1** Canonized. **2** Of holy character; saintly.

saint·ly (sānt'lē) *adj.* **·li·er, ·li·est 1** Like a saint; godly; holy. **2** Unusually good, kind, etc. —**saint'li·ness** *n.* —**Syn. 1** pious, sacred, blessed. **2** benevolent, charitable, kindly, righteous.

saith (seth, sā'ith) *Archaic* Present indicative third person singular of SAY.

sake¹ (sāk) *n.* **1** Purpose; motive; end: for the *sake* of peace and quiet. **2** Interest, regard, or consideration: for the *sake* of your children. [< OE *saccu* a (legal) case]

sa·ke² (sä'kē) *n.* A Japanese fermented alcoholic liquor made from rice: also **sa'ki.**

sal (sal) *n.* Salt: used esp. as a pharmaceutical term. [L]

sa·laam (sə-läm') *n.* **1** An Oriental salutation resembling a low bow, the palm of the right hand being held to the forehead. **2** A respectful or ceremonious greeting. —*v.t. & v.i.* To make a salaam. [< Ar. *salām* peace]

sal·a·ble (sā'lə-bəl) *adj.* Such as can be sold; marketable. —**sal'a·bil'i·ty, sal'a·ble·ness** *n.* —**sal'a·bly** *adv.*

sa·la·cious (sə-lā'shəs) *adj.* Lascivious; lustful; lecherous. [< L *salire* to leap] —**sa·la'cious·ly** *adv.* —**sa·la'cious·ness, sa·lac'i·ty** (-las'ə-te) *n.*

sal·ad (sal'əd) *n.* **1** A dish of vegetables such as lettuce, cucumbers, tomatoes, etc., usu. uncooked and served with a dressing, sometimes mixed with chopped cold meat, fish, hard-boiled eggs, etc. **2** Any green vegetable that can be eaten raw. [< L *salare* to salt]

salad days Days of youth and inexperience.

salad dressing A sauce used on salads, as mayonnaise, oil and vinegar, etc.

sal·a·man·der (sal′ə·man′dər) n. 1 Any of an order of tailed amphibians having a smooth, moist skin. 2 A fabled reptile purportedly able to live in fire. [< L *salamandra*] —**sal′a·man′drine** (-drin) *adj.*

Salamander

sa·la·mi (sə·lä′mē) n. pl. ·**mis** A salted, spiced sausage, originally Italian. [< L *sal* salt]

sal ammoniac AMMONIUM CHLORIDE. [L]

sal·a·ried (sal′ər·ēd) *adj.* 1 In receipt of a salary. 2 Yielding a salary.

sal·a·ry (sal′ər·ē) n. pl. ·**ries** A periodic payment as compensation for official or professional services. —v.t. ·**ried**, ·**ry·ing** To pay or allot a salary to. [< L *salarium* money paid Roman soldiers for their salt]

sale (sāl) n. 1 The exchange or transfer of property for money or its equivalent. 2 A selling of merchandise at prices lower than usual. 3 An auction. 4 Opportunity of selling; market: Stocks find no *sale*. 5 *Usu. pl.* The amount sold: last year's *sales*. —**for sale** Offered or ready for sale. —**on sale** For sale at bargain rates. [< OE *sala*]

sale·a·ble (sāl′lə·bəl) *adj.* SALABLE.

sal·e·ra·tus (sal′ə·rā′təs) n. BAKING SODA. [< NL *sal aëratus* aerated salt]

sales·girl (sālz′gûrl′) n. A woman or girl hired to sell merchandise, esp. in a store.

sales·la·dy (sālz′lā′dē) n. pl. ·**dies** *Informal* A woman or girl hired to sell merchandise, esp. in a store.

sales·man (sālz′mən) n. pl. ·**men** (-mən) A man hired to sell goods, stock, etc., in a store or by canvassing.

sales·man·ship (sālz′mən·ship) n. 1 The work of a salesman. 2 Skill in selling.

sales·peo·ple (sālz′pē′pəl) *n.pl.* Salespersons.

sales·per·son (sālz′pûr′sən) n. A person hired to sell merchandise, esp. in a store: also **sales′clerk′** (-klûrk′).

sales resistance A resistance on the part of a potential customer to buying certain goods.

sales·room (sālz′rōōm′, -rōōm′) n. A room where merchandise is displayed for sale.

sales tax A tax on money received from sales of goods, usu. passed on to the buyer.

sales·wom·an (sālz′wōōm′ən) n. pl. ·**wom·en** (-wim′in) A woman or girl hired to sell merchandise, esp. in a store.

Sal·ic (sal′ik) *adj.* Characterizing a law (the **Salic Law**) derived from Germanic sources in the fifth century, and providing that males only could inherit lands: later applied to the succession to the French and Spanish thrones.

sa·lic·y·late (sə·lis′ə·lāt, sal′ə·sil′āt) n. A salt or ester of salicylic acid.

sal·i·cyl·ic acid (sal′ə·sil′ik) A crystalline organic compound used in making aspirin and various analgesics. [< L *salix* willow]

sa·li·ent (sā′lē·ənt) *adj.* 1 Standing out prominently: a *salient* feature. 2 Extending outward; projecting: a *salient* angle. 3 Leaping; springing. —n. An extension, as of a fortification or a military line protruding toward the enemy. [< L *salire* to leap] —**sa′li·ence, sa′li·en·cy** n. —**sa′·li·ent·ly** *adv.* —**Syn.** 1 conspicuous, noticeable, significant. 2 jutting.

sa·line (sā′lēn, sā′līn) *adj.* Constituting, consisting of, or characteristic of salt; salty. —n. 1 A metallic salt, esp. a salt of one of the alkalis or of magnesium. 2 A solution of sodium chloride or other salt. 3 A natural deposit of salt. [< L *sal* salt] —**sa·lin·i·ty** (sə·lin′ə·tē) n.

Salis·bur·y steak (sôlz′ber·ē, -brē) Ground beef mixed with bread crumbs, onion, seasoning, etc., cooked as patties and usu. served with gravy. [< J. H. *Salisbury*, 19th-century English physician]

Sa·lish (sā′lish) n. 1 A family of Indian languages of the NW U.S. and SW Canada. 2 A member of a tribe speaking any of these languages. —*adj.* Of or pertaining to the Salish languages or the people speaking them. Also **Sa′·lish·an** (-ən).

sa·li·va (sə·lī′və) n. A mixture of mucus and fluid secreted by glands in the cheeks and lower jaw. [L] —**sal·i·var·y** (sal′ə·ver′ē) *adj.*

sal·i·vate (sal′ə·vāt) v. ·**vat·ed**, ·**vat·ing** v.i. 1 To secrete saliva. —v.t. 2 To cause to secrete saliva, esp. excessively. —**sal′i·va′tion** n.

sal·low (sal′ō) *adj.* Of an unhealthy yellowish color or complexion. —v.t. To make sallow. [< OE *salo*] —**sal′low·ness** n.

sal·ly (sal′ē) v.i. ·**lied**, ·**ly·ing** 1 To rush out suddenly. 2 To set out energetically. 3 To go out, as from a room or building. —n. pl. ·**lies** 1 A rushing forth, as of besieged troops against besiegers; sortie. 2 A going forth, as on a walk. 3 A witticism or bantering remark. [< L *salire* to leap]

sal·ma·gun·di (sal′mə·gun′dē) n. 1 A dish of chopped meat, anchovies, eggs, onions, etc., mixed and seasoned. 2 Any medley or miscellany. [?< Ital. *salami conditi* pickled meats]

salm·on (sam′ən) n. 1 Any of various anadromous food and game fishes inhabiting cool ocean waters and certain landlocked lakes. 2 The pinkish orange color of the flesh of certain salmon: also **salm′on-pink′**. —*adj.* Having the color salmon: also **salm′on-pink′**. [< L *salmo*]

Salmon

sal·mo·nel·la (sal′mō·nel′ə) n. pl. ·**lae** (lē) or ·**las** Any of a genus of aerobic bacteria that cause food poisoning and some diseases, including typhoid fever. [< D. E. *Salmon*, U.S. pathologist, 1850–1914]

salmon trout Any of various salmonlike fish, as the European sea trout, the namaycush, etc.

Sa·lo·me (sə·lō′mē, sal·ə·mä′) The daughter of Herodias, who asked from Herod the head of John the Baptist in return for her dancing.

sa·lon (sə·lon′, sal′on, Fr. sá·lôn′) n. 1 A room in which guests are received; a drawing-room. 2 The periodic gathering of noted persons, under the auspices of some distinguished personage. 3 A hall or gallery used for exhibiting works of art. 4 An establishment devoted to some specific purpose: a beauty *salon*. [< Ital. *sala* a room, hall]

sa·loon (sə·lōōn′) n. 1 A place where alcoholic drinks are sold; a bar. 2 A large room for public use, as on a passenger ship: a dining *saloon*. [< F *salon* salon] • In the U.S., *saloon* (def. 1) is now used mainly in historical contexts dealing with the American western frontier or as a rough equivalent of *dive* in describing a squalid bar.

sa·loon-keep·er (sə·lōōn′kē′pər) n. One who keeps a saloon (def. 1).

sal·si·fy (sal′sə·fē, ·fī) n. A plant with purple, composite flowers and a white, edible root of an oysterlike flavor. [< F *salsifis*]

sal soda Sodium carbonate; washing soda.

salt (sôlt) n. 1 A white, soluble, crystalline compound of sodium and chlorine, widely distributed in nature and found in all living organisms: also **table salt, common salt**. 2 *Chem.* Any compound derived from an acid by replacement of all or part of the hydrogen by an electropositive radical or a metal. 3 *pl.* Any of various mineral compounds in common use, as Epsom salts, smelling salts, etc. 4 Piquant humor; dry wit. 5 That which preserves, corrects, or purifies: the *salt* of criticism. 6 A sailor. 7 A saltcellar. —**salt of the earth** A person or persons regarded as being fine, honest, kindly, etc. —**take with a grain of salt** To allow for exaggeration; have doubts about. —**worth one's salt** Worth one's pay or keep; hardworking. —*adj.* 1 Seasoned with salt; salty. 2 Cured or preserved with salt. 3 Containing, or growing or living in or near, salt water. —v.t. 1 To season with salt. 2 To preserve or cure with salt. 3 To furnish with salt: to *salt* cattle. 4 To add zest or piquancy to. 5 To add something to so as fraudulently to increase the value: to *salt* a mine with gold. —**salt away** 1 To pack in salt for preserving. 2 *Informal* To store up; save. [< OE *sealt*] —**salt′er** n.

SALT, S.A.L.T. (sôlt) Strategic Arms Limitation Talks.

salt·cel·lar (sôlt′sel′ər) n. A small receptacle for table salt. [< ME *salt saler* < *salt* salt + *saler* saltcellar < OF *saliere*; form infl. by CELLAR]

salt chuck *Can. Regional* The sea.

salt·ed (sôlt'tid) *adj.* **1** Treated or preserved with salt. **2** *Informal* Experienced or expert.

salting out The injection of a saline solution into the amniotic fluid to terminate a pregnancy.

salt lick A place to which animals go to lick salt from superficial natural deposits.

salt marsh Low coastal land frequently overflowed by the tide, usu. covered with coarse grass: also **salt meadow.**

salt·pe·ter (sôlt'pē'tər) *n.* **1** POTASSIUM NITRATE. **2** CHILE SALTPETER. Also **salt'pe'tre.** [< L *sal* salt + *petra* rock]

salt·shak·er (sôlt'shā'kər) *n.* A container with small apertures for sprinkling table salt.

salt·wa·ter (sôlt'wô'tər, -wot'ər) *adj.* Of, composed of, or living in salt water.

salt·works (sôlt'wûrks') *n. pl.* **·works** An establishment where salt is made commercially.

salt·wort (sôlt'wûrt') *n.* Any of a genus of weedy plants adapted to saline soils.

salt·y (sôlt'tē) *adj.* **salt·i·er, salt·i·est 1** Tasting of or containing salt. **2** Piquant; sharp, as speech, etc. —**salt'i·ly** *adv.* — **salt'i·ness** *n.*

sa·lu·bri·ous (sə·lōō'brē·əs) *adj.* Conducive to health; healthful; wholesome. [< L *salus* health] —**sa·lu'bri·ous·ly** *adv.* —**sa·lu'bri·ty, sa·lu'bri·ous·ness** *n.*

sal·u·tar·y (sal'yə·ter'ē) *adj.* **1** Beneficial. **2** Wholesome; healthful. [< L *salus* health] —**sal'u·tar'i·ly** *adv.* —**sal'u·tar'i·ness** *n.*

sal·u·ta·tion (sal'yə·tā'shən) *n.* **1** The act of saluting. **2** Any form of greeting. **3** The opening words of a letter, as *Dear Sir* or *Dear Madam.*

sa·lu·ta·to·ri·an (sə·lōō'tə·tôr'ē·ən, -tō'rē-) *n.* In colleges and schools, the graduating student who delivers the salutatory at commencement.

sa·lu·ta·to·ry (sə·lōō'tə·tôr'ē, -tō'rē) *n. pl.* **·ries** An opening oration, as at a college commencement. —*adj.* Of or relating to a salutatory address. [< L *salutare*]

sa·lute (sə·lōōt') *v.* **·lut·ed, ·lut·ing** *v.t.* **1** To greet with an expression or sign of welcome, respect, etc.; welcome. **2** To honor in some prescribed way, as by raising the hand to the cap, presenting arms, firing cannon, etc. —*v.i.* **3** To make a salute. —*n.* **1** An act of saluting; a greeting, show of respect, etc. **2** The attitude assumed in giving a military hand salute. [< L *salutare* < *salus* health] —**sa·lut'er** *n.*

Sal·va·dor (sal'və·dôr', *Sp.* säl'vä·th̪ôr') *n.* EL SALVADOR.

Sal·va·do·ri·an (sal'və·dôr'ē·ən, -dō'rē-) *n.* A citizen or native of El Salvador. —*adj.* Of or pertaining to El Salvador or its people: also **Sal'va·do'ran.**

sal·vage (sal'vij) *v.t.* **·vaged, ·vag·ing 1** To save, as a ship or its cargo, from wreck, capture, etc. **2** To save (material) from something damaged or discarded for reuse: to *salvage* aluminum. —*n.* **1** The saving of a ship, cargo, etc., from loss. **2** Any act of saving property. **3** The compensation allowed to persons by whose exertions a vessel, its cargo, or the lives of those sailing on it are saved from loss. **4** That which is saved from a wrecked or abandoned vessel or from or after a fire. **5** Anything saved from destruction. [< OF *salver* to save] —**sal'vag·er** *n.*

sal·va·tion (sal·vā'shən) *n.* **1** The process or state of being saved. **2** A person or thing that delivers from evil, danger, or ruin. **3** *Theol.* Deliverance from sin and penalty; redemption. [< LL *salvare* to save]

Salvation Army A religious and charitable organization founded on semimilitary lines by William Booth in England in 1865. —**Sal·va'tion·ist** *n.*

salve[1] (sav, säv) *n.* **1** An emollient preparation for burns, cuts, etc. **2** Anything that heals, soothes, or mollifies. — *v.t.* **salved, salv·ing 1** To dress with salve or ointment. **2** To soothe; appease, as conscience, pride, etc. [< OE *sealf*]

salve[2] (salv) *v.t.* **salved, salv·ing** To save from loss; salvage. [Back formation < SALVAGE]

sal·ver (sal'vər) *n.* A tray, as of silver. [< Sp. *salva,* orig. the foretasting of food, as for a king]

sal·vi·a (sal'vē·ə) *n.* **1** An ornamental species of sage with red flowers. **2** Any plant of the sage genus. [L]

sal·vo (sal'vō) *n. pl.* **·vos** or **·voes 1** A simultaneous discharge of artillery, or of two or more bombs from an aircraft. **2** A sudden burst or burst: a *salvo* of hail. **3** Tribute; praise. [< Ital. *salva* a salute]

sal vo·lat·i·le (sal vō·lat'ə·lē) Ammonium carbonate; smelling salts. [NL, volatile salt]

SAM (sam) surface-to-air missile.

S. Am., S. Amer. South America; South American.

sam·a·ra (sam'ər·ə, sə·mâr'ə) *n.* An indehiscent winged fruit, as of the elm or maple. [L, elm seed]

sa·mar·i·um (sə·mâr'ē·əm) *n.* A metallic element (symbol Sm) of the lanthanide series. [NL < Col. *Samarski,* 19th-century Russian mining official]

sam·ba (sam'bə, säm'bä) *n.* A dance of Brazilian origin in two-four time. —*v.i.* To dance the samba. [< a native African name]

Sam Browne belt (sam' broun') A military belt, with one or two light shoulder straps running diagonally across the chest from right to left. [< Sir Samuel J. Browne, 1824–1901, British army general]

same (sām) *adj.* **1** Identical; equal: They both are the *same* price. **2** Exactly alike; not different: The two children have the *same* first name. **3** Aforementioned; just spoken of. **4** Equal in degree of preference; indifferent. **5** Unchanged: The old place looks the *same.* —**all the same 1** Nevertheless. **2** Equally acceptable or unacceptable. — **just the same 1** Nevertheless. **2** Exactly identical or corresponding; unchanged. —*pron.* The identical person, thing, event, etc. —*adv.* In like manner; equally: with *the.* [< ON *samr, sami*] —**same'ness** *n.*

sam·i·sen (sam'i·sen) *n.* A three-stringed Japanese musical instrument played with a plectrum.

sa·mite (sā'mīt, sam'īt) *n.* A rich medieval fabric of silk, often interwoven with gold or silver. [< Gk. *hexamitos* woven with six threads]

Sa·mo·an (sə·mō'ən) *adj.* Of or pertaining to Samoa, its people, their language, culture, etc. —*n.* **1** A native or citizen of Samoa. **2** The language of the Samoans.

sam·o·var (sam'ə·vär) *n.* A metal urn containing a tube for charcoal for heating water, as for making tea. [Russ. < *samo-* self + *varit* boil]

Sam·o·yed (sam'ə·yed') *n.* **1** One of a Mongoloid people inhabiting the Arctic coasts of Siberia. **2** A large Siberian dog with a thick white coat. —*adj.* Of or pertaining to the Samoyed people. Also **Sam'o·yede** (-yed'). —**Sam'o·yed'ic** *adj.*

Samovar

samp (samp) *n.* Coarsely ground Indian corn; also, a porridge made of it. [< Algon.]

sam·pan (sam'pan) *n.* Any of various small flat-bottomed boats used along rivers and coasts of China and Japan. [< Chin. *san* three + *pan* board]

sam·ple (sam'pəl) *n.* **1** A portion, part, or piece taken or shown as a representative of the whole. **2** An instance: This is a *sample* of his kindness. —*v.t.* **·pled, ·pling** To test or examine by means of a portion or sample. —*adj.* Serving as a sample: a *sample* dress. [< OF *essample* example]

Sampan

sam·pler (sam'plər) *n.* **1** One who tests by samples. **2** A device for removing a portion of a substance for testing. **3** A piece of needlework, designed to show a beginner's skill. [< L *exemplum* example]

Sam·son (sam'sən) In the Bible, a Hebrew judge of great physical strength, betrayed to the Philistines by Delilah.

sam·u·rai (sam'ōō·rī) *n. pl.* **·rai** Under the Japanese feudal system, a member of the soldier class of the lower nobility; also, the class itself. [Jap.]

san·a·tive (san'ə·tiv) *adj.* Healing; health-giving. [< L *sanare* heal]

san·a·to·ri·um (san'ə·tôr'ē·əm, -tō'rē-) *n. pl.* **·to·ri·ums** or **·to·ri·a** (-tôr'ē·ə, -tō'rē·ə) An institution for the treatment of chronic disorders, as mental illness, alcoholism, etc. [< LL *sanatorius* healthy]

sanc·ti·fy (sangk'tə·fī) *v.t.* **·fied, ·fy·ing 1** To set apart as holy; consecrate. **2** To free of sin; purify. **3** To render sacred or inviolable, as a vow. [< L *sanctus* holy + *facere* to make] —**sanc'ti·fi·ca'tion, sanc'ti·fi'er** *n.*

sanc·ti·mo·ni·ous (sangk'tə·mō'nē·əs) *adj.* Making an

ostentatious display or a hypocritical pretense of sanctity. **—sanc′ti·mo′ni·ous·ly** adv. **—sanc′ti·mo′ni·ous·ness** n.

sanc·ti·mo·ny (sangk′tə·mō′nē) n. Assumed or outward sanctity; a show of devoutness. [< L sanctimonia holiness]

sanc·tion (sangk′shən) v.t. 1 To approve authoritatively; confirm; ratify. 2 To countenance; allow. —n. 1 Final and authoritative confirmation; justification or ratification. 2 A formal decree. 3 A provision for securing conformity to law, as by the enactment of rewards or penalties or both. 4 pl. In international law, a coercive measure adopted by several nations to force a nation to obey international law, by limiting trade relations, by military force and blockade, etc. [< L sanctus, p.p. of sancire make sacred]

sanc·ti·ty (sangk′tə·tē) n. pl. **·ties** 1 The state of being sacred or holy. 2 Saintliness; holiness. 3 Something sacred or holy.

sanc·tu·ar·y (sangk′chōō·er′ē) n. pl. **·ar·ies** 1 A holy or sacred place, esp. one devoted to the worship of a deity. 2 The most sacred part of a place in a sacred structure; esp. the part of a church where the principal altar is situated. 3 A place of refuge: a wildlife sanctuary. 4 Immunity from the law or punishment. [< L sanctus holy] **—Syn.** 1 church, shrine, temple. 3 preserve, shelter.

sanc·tum (sangk′təm) n. pl. **·tums** or **·ta** (-tə) 1 A sacred place. 2 A private room where one is not to be disturbed. [L < sanctus holy]

sanc·tum sanc·to·rum (sangk′təm sangk·tôr′əm, -tō′rəm) 1 HOLY OF HOLIES. 2 A place of great privacy: often used humorously. [LL, holy of holies]

sand (sand) n. 1 A hard, granular rock material finer than gravel and coarser than dust. 2 pl. Stretches of sandy desert or beach. 3 pl. Sandy grains, as those of the hourglass. 4 Slang Endurance; grit. —v.t. 1 To sprinkle or cover with sand. 2 To smooth or abrade with sand or sandpaper. [< OE]

san·dal (san′dəl) n. 1 A foot covering, consisting usu. of a sole only, held to the foot by thongs or straps. 2 A light, openwork slipper. [< Gk. sandalion] **—san′daled** adj.

san·dal·wood (san′dəl·wŏŏd′) n. 1 The fine-grained, dense, fragrant wood of any of several East Indian trees. 2 The similar wood of other trees. 3 Any tree yielding this wood. [< Med. L sandalum sandalwood + WOOD]

Sandal

sand·bag (sand′bag′) n. 1 A bag filled with sand, used for building fortifications, for ballast, etc. 2 A small bag filled with sand and used as a club. —v.t. **·bagged, ·bag·ging** 1 To fill or surround with sandbags. 2 To strike or attack with a sandbag. **—sand′bag′ger** n.

sand·bank (sand′bangk′) n. A mound or ridge of sand.

sand·bar (sand′bär′) n. A ridge of silt or sand in rivers, along beaches, etc., formed by the action of currents or tides.

sand·blast (sand′blast′, -bläst′) n. 1 An apparatus for propelling a jet of sand, as for etching glass or cleaning stone. 2 The jet of sand. —v.t. To clean or engrave by means of a sandblast. **—sand′blast′er** n.

sand·box (sand′boks′) n. A box of sand for children to play in.

sand·er (san′dər) n. A device, esp. a machine powered by electricity, that smooths and polishes surfaces by means of a disk or belt coated with an abrasive: also **sanding machine.**

sand flea 1 CHIGOE. 2 Any of various tiny crustaceans that jump like fleas.

sand·hog (sand′hôg′, -hog′) n. One who works under air pressure, as in sinking caissons, building tunnels, etc.: also **sand hog.**

sand·lot (sand′lot′) n. A vacant lot in or near an urban area. —adj. Of or played in such a lot: sandlot baseball.

sand·man (sand′man′) n. In nursery lore, a mythical person supposed to make children sleepy by casting sand in their eyes.

sand·pa·per (sand′pā′pər) n. Strong paper coated with abrasive for smoothing or polishing. —v.t. To rub or polish with sandpaper.

sand·pi·per (sand′pī′pər) n. Any of certain small wading birds having long, thin bills and frequenting shores and marsh lands.

sand·stone (sand′stōn′) n. A rock consisting chiefly of quartz sand cemented with other materials.

Sandpiper

sand·storm (sand′stôrm′) n. A high wind by which clouds of sand or dust are carried along.

sand·wich (sand′wich, san′-) n. 1 Two or more slices of bread, having between them meat, cheese, etc. 2 Any combination of alternating dissimilar things pressed together. —v.t. To place between other persons or things. [< John Montagu, fourth Earl of Sandwich, 1718–92]

sandwich man Informal A man carrying boards, called **sandwich boards,** one in front and one behind, for the purpose of advertising or picketing.

sand·y (san′dē) adj. **sand·i·er, sand·i·est** 1 Consisting of or characterized by sand; containing, covered with, or full of sand. 2 Yellowish red: a sandy beard. **—sand′i·ness** n.

sane (sān) adj. **san·er, san·est** 1 Mentally sound; not deranged. 2 Proceeding from a sound mind. 3 Sensible; wise. [< L sanus whole, healthy] **—sane′ly** adv. **—sane′· ness** n.

San·for·ize (san′fə·rīz) v.t. **·ized, ·iz·ing** To treat (cloth) by a special process so as to prevent more than slight shrinkage. [Back formation < Sanforized, a trade name]

sang (sang) p.t. of SING.

sang-froid (säng′frwä′, Fr. säṅ·frwä′) n. Calmness amid trying circumstances; composure. [F, lit., cold blood]

san·gui·nar·y (sang′gwə·ner′ē) adj. 1 Attended with bloodshed. 2 Prone to shed blood; bloodthirsty. [< L sanguis blood] **—san′gui·nar′i·ly** adv. **—san′gui·nar′i·ness** n.

san·guine (sang′gwin) adj. 1 Of buoyant disposition; hopeful. 2 Having the color of blood; ruddy: a sanguine complexion. 3 Obs. Bloodthirsty; sanguinary. Also **san·guin·e·ous** (sang·gwin′ē·əs). [< L sanguis blood] **—san′· guine·ly** adv. **—san′guine·ness** n. **—Syn.** 1 ardent, confident, enthusiastic, optimistic. 2 rubicund.

San·he·drin (san·hed′rən, -hēd′-, san′hi·drin, san′i-) n. In ancient times, the supreme council and highest court of the Jewish nation. Also **Great Sanhedrin.** [< Heb.]

san·i·tar·i·an (san′ə·târ′ē·ən) n. A person skilled in matters relating to sanitation and public health.

san·i·tar·i·um (san′ə·târ′ē·əm) n. pl. **·i·ums** or **·i·a** (-ē·ə) 1 A health resort. 2 SANATORIUM. [< L sanitas health]

san·i·tar·y (san′ə·ter′ē) adj. 1 Relating to the preservation of health and prevention of disease: sanitary measures. 2 Free from filth; clean; hygienic. —n. pl. **·tar·ies** A public toilet. [< L sanitas health] **—san′i·tar′i·ly** adv.

sanitary napkin An absorbent pad used by women during menstruation.

san·i·ta·tion (san′ə·tā′shən) n. 1 The science or process of establishing sanitary conditions, esp. as regards public health. 2 The removal of sewage, garbage, etc.

san·i·ta·tion·man (san′i·tā′shən·man′) n. pl. **·men** (-mən) A person, esp. a municipal employee, whose work is the collection of refuse and trash.

san·i·tize (san′ə·tīz) v.t. **·tized, ·tiz·ing** 1 To make sanitary, as by scrubbing, washing, or sterilizing. 2 To make acceptable or unobjectionable, as by deleting offensive parts: a sanitized fairy tale. **—san′i·ti·zer** n.

san·i·ty (san′ə·tē) n. 1 The state of being sane or sound; mental health. 2 Sane moderation or reasonableness. [< L sanus healthy] **—Syn.** 1 rationality, saneness. 2 common sense, level-headedness, sensibleness.

sank (sangk) p.t. of SINK.

San Ma·ri·no (mä·rē′nō) n. A republic located in an enclave of NE Italy, 23 sq. mi., cap. San Marino.

sans (sanz, Fr. säṅ) prep. Without. [< OF sens, sanz]

sans·cu·lotte (sanz′kyŏŏ·lot′, Fr. säṅ·kü·lôt′) n. 1 A revolutionary: used by the aristocrats as a term of contempt for the poorly clad republicans who started the French Revolution of 1789. 2 Any revolutionary republican or radical. [F, lit., without knee breeches] —**sans′cu·lot′tic** *adj.* —**sans′cu·lot′tism** *n.*

san·se·vi·e·ri·a (san′sə·vir′ē·ə, -vi·ē′rē·ə) *n.* Any of a genus of succulent plants of the lily family with a cluster of tall, lance-shaped leaves. [< the Prince of *Sanseviero*, 1710–71, Italian scholar]

San·skrit (san′skrit) *n.* The ancient and classical language of the Hindus of India, belonging to the Indic branch of the Indo-Iranian subfamily of Indo-European languages: also **San′scrit.** [< Skt. *samskrita* well-formed]

sans ser·if (sanz ser′if) *Printing* A style of type without serifs.

San·ta Claus (san′tə klôz′) In folklore, a friend of children who brings presents at Christmas time: usu. represented as a fat, jolly old man in a red suit; St. Nicholas. [< dial. Du. *Sante Klaus* Saint Nicholas]

Santa Fe Trail The trade route, important from 1821 to 1880, between Independence, Missouri and Santa Fe, New Mexico.

sap[1] (sap) *n.* **1** The juices of plants, which contain and transport the materials necessary to growth. **2** Any vital fluid; vitality. **3** Sapwood. **4** *Slang* A foolish, stupid, or ineffectual person. [< OE *sæp*]

sap[2] (sap) *v.* **sapped, sap·ping** *v.t.* **1** To weaken or destroy gradually and insidiously. **2** To approach or undermine (an enemy fortification) by digging trenches. —*v.i.* **3** To dig a sap or saps. —*n.* A deep, narrow trench dug so as to approach or undermine a fortification. [< MF *sappe* a spade] —**Syn.** *v.* **1** debilitate, disable, enervate, enfeeble.

sap·head (sap′hed′) *n. Slang* A stupid person; simpleton. —**sap′head′ed** *adj.*

sa·pi·ent (sā′pē·ənt, sap′ē-) *adj.* Wise; sagacious: often ironical. [< L *sapere* know, taste] —**sa′pi·ence, sa′pi·en·cy** *n.* —**sa′pi·ent·ly** *adv.*

sap·ling (sap′ling) *n.* **1** A young tree. **2** A young person. [Dim. of SAP[1]]

sap·o·dil·la (sap′ə·dil′ə) *n.* **1** A large tropical American evergreen tree which yields chicle and an edible fruit. **2** Its apple-shaped fruit: also **sapodilla plum.** [< Nahuatl *zapotl*]

sap·o·na·ceous (sap′ə·nā′shəs) *adj.* Soapy. [< L *sapo* soap] —**sap′o·na′ceous·ness** *n.*

sa·pon·i·fy (sə·pon′ə·fī) *v.t.* **·fied, ·fy·ing** To convert (a fat or oil) into soap by the action of an alkali. [< L *sapo* soap + *facere* to make] —**sa·pon′i·fi·ca′tion, sa·pon′i·fi′er** *n.*

sap·per (sap′ər) *n.* A soldier employed in making trenches, tunnels, and underground fortifications. [< SAP[2]]

sap·phire (saf′īr) *n.* **1** Any one of the hard, transparent, colored varieties of corundum, esp. a blue variety valued as a gem. **2** Deep blue. —**star sapphire** A sapphire cut without facets, showing six rays on the dome. —*adj.* Deep blue. [< Gk. *sappheiros* a gemstone]

sap·py (sap′ē) *adj.* **·pi·er, pi·est 1** Full of sap; juicy. **2** *Slang* Immature; silly. **3** Vital; pithy. —**sap′pi·ness** *n.*

sap·ro·phyte (sap′rə·fīt) *n.* An organism that lives on dead or decaying organic matter, as certain bacteria, fungi, etc. [< Gk. *sapros* rotten + -PHYTE] —**sap′ro·phyt′ic** (-fit′ik) *adj.*

sap·suck·er (sap′suk′ər) *n.* A small woodpecker that taps trees and drinks sap.

sap·wood (sap′wŏŏd′) *n.* The new wood beneath the bark of a tree.

S.A.R. Sons of the American Revolution.

sar·a·band (sar′ə·band) *n.* **1** A stately Spanish dance in triple time, of the 17th and 18th centuries. **2** Music for this dance. Also **sar′a·bande.** [< Sp. *zarabanda*]

Sar·a·cen (sar′ə·sən) *n.* **1** Formerly, a Muslim enemy of the Crusaders. **2** An Arab. —*adj.* Of or pertaining to the Saracens. —**Sar′a·cen′ic** (-sen′ik) or **·i·cal** *adj.*

Sar·ah (sâr′ə) In the Bible, the wife of Abraham and the mother of Isaac.

Sa·ran (sə·ran′) *n.* A synthetic plastic material used as a textile fiber and as a transparent, moistureproof wrapping: a trade name.

sar·casm (sär′kaz·əm) *n.* **1** The use of keenly ironic or scornful remarks. **2** Such a remark. [< Gk. *sarkazein* tear flesh, speak bitterly] —**Syn. 2** gibe, sneer, taunt.

Yellow-bellied sapsucker

sar·cas·tic (sär·kas′tik) *adj.* **1** Characterized by or of the nature of sarcasm. **2** Taunting. Also **sar·cas′ti·cal.** —**sar·cas′ti·cal·ly** *adv.*

sarce·net (särs′net) *n.* A fine, thin silk, used for linings. [< OF *drap sarrasinois,* lit. Saracen cloth]

sar·co·carp (sär′kō·kärp) *n.* The fleshy, usu. edible part of a drupe. [< Gk. *sarx* flesh + *karpos* a fruit]

sar·co·ma (sär·kō′mə) *n. pl.* **·mas** or **·ma·ta** (-mə·tə) A malignant tumor originating in connective tissue. [< Gk. *sarkaein* become fleshy] —**sar·co′ma·tous** (-kō′mə·təs) *adj.*

sar·coph·a·gus (sär·kof′ə·gəs) *n. pl.* **·gi** (-jī) or **·gus·es 1** A stone coffin or tomb. **2** A large ornamental coffin of marble or other stone placed in a crypt or exposed to view. [< Gk. *sarx* flesh + *phagein* eat]

sard (särd) *n.* A deep brownish red variety of chalcedony, used as a gem. [< L *sarda*]

sar·dine (sär·dēn′) *n.* **1** A small fish preserved in oil as a delicacy. **2** The young of the herring or some like fish similarly prepared. [< Gk. *sarda* a kind of fish]

sar·don·ic (sär·don′ik) *adj.* Scornful or derisive; sneering; mocking; cynical. [< Gk. *sardanios* bitter, scornful] —**sar·don′i·cal·ly** *adv.* —**sar·don′i·cism** *n.*

sar·do·nyx (sär·don′iks, sär′də·niks) *n.* A variety of onyx, containing layers of light-colored chalcedony and sard. [< Gk. *sardios* sard + *onyx* onyx]

sar·gas·so (sär·gas′ō) *n.* Any of a genus of large, floating brown seaweed: also **sargasso weed, sar·gas′sum.** [< Pg. *sarga,* a kind of grape]

sa·ri (sä′rē) *n. pl.* **·ris** A length of cloth, constituting the principal garment of Hindu women, one end falling to the feet, and the other crossed over the bosom, shoulder, and sometimes over the head: also **sa′ree.** [< Skt. *śāṭī*]

sa·rong (sə·rong′) *n.* A rectangular piece of colored cloth worn as a skirt by both sexes in the Malay Archipelago. [< Malay *sārung*]

sar·sa·pa·ril·la (sas′pə·ril′ə, sär′sə·pə·ril′ə) *n.* **1** A tropical American vine with fragrant roots. **2** An extract of these roots, used as flavoring. **3** Any of various plants resembling sarsaparilla. [< Sp. *zarza* a bramble + *parilla* little vine]

sar·to·ri·al (sär·tôr′ē·əl, -tō′rē-) *adj.* **1** Pertaining to a tailor or his work. **2** Pertaining to men's clothes. [< L *sartor* tailor] —**sar·to′ri·al·ly** *adv.*

Sari

sash[1] (sash) *n.* An ornamental band or scarf, worn around the waist or over the shoulder. [< Ar. *shāsh* muslin, turban]

sash[2] (sash) *n.* A frame, as of a window, in which glass is set. —*v.t.* To furnish with a sash. [Alter. of CHASSIS, taken as a pl.]

sa·shay (sa·shā′) *v.i. Informal* To move or glide about, esp. ostentatiously. [< Fr. *chassé* a dance movement]

Sask. Saskatchewan.

sass (sas) *Informal n.* Impudence; back talk. —*v.t.* To talk to impudently. [Dial. alter. of SAUCE]

sas·sa·fras (sas′ə·fras) *n.* **1** A small North American tree related to laurel. **2** A flavoring agent made from the bark of its roots. [< Sp. *sasafrás*]

sas·sy (sas′ē) *adj.* **·si·er, ·si·est** *Informal* Saucy; impertinent. —**sas′si·ly** *adv.* —**sas′si·ness** *n.*

sat (sat) *p.t.* of SIT.

SAT Scholastic Aptitude Test.

Sat. Saturday; Saturn.

Sa·tan (sā′tən) In the Bible, the great adversary of God and tempter of mankind; the Devil. [< Heb. *sātān* an enemy] —**sa·tan·ic** (sā·tan′ik, sə-), **sa·tan′i·cal** *adj.* —**sa·tan′i·cal·ly** *adv.*

satch·el (sach′əl) *n.* A small bag for carrying books, clothing, etc. [< L *sacellus* little sack]

sate[1] (sāt) *v.t.* **sat·ed, sat·ing 1** To satisfy the appetite of. **2** To indulge with too much so as to weary or sicken; satiate. [< OE *sadian*] —**Syn. 1** gratify. **2** cloy, glut, stuff, surfeit.

sate[2] (sāt) *Archaic p.t.* of SIT.

sa·teen (sa·tēn′) *n.* A smooth, shiny cotton fabric resembling satin. [Alter. of SATIN]

sat·el·lite (sat′ə·līt) n. 1 A body held in orbit about a more massive one; a moon. 2 An artificial body propelled into orbit, esp. around the earth. 3 One who attends upon a person in power. 4 Any obsequious attendant. 5 A small nation dependent on a great power. [< L satelles an attendant]

sa·ti·a·ble (sā′shē·ə·bəl, -shə·bəl) adj. Capable of being satiated. —**sa′ti·a·bil′i·ty, sa′ti·a·ble·ness** n. —**sa′ti·a·bly** adv.

sa·ti·ate (sā′shē·āt) v.t. **·at·ed, ·at·ing** 1 To satisfy the appetite or desire of; gratify. 2 To fill or gratify excessively; glut. —adj. Filled to satiety; satiated. [< L satis enough] —**sa′ti·a′tion** n.

sa·ti·e·ty (sə·tī′ə·tē, sā′shē·ə·tē) n. pl. **·ties** The state of being satiated; surfeit. [< L satis enough]

sat·in (sat′ən) n. A fabric of silk, rayon, etc., with glossy face and dull back. —adj. Of or similar to satin; glossy; smooth. [< OF] —**sat′in·y** adj.

sat·in·wood (sat′ən·wŏŏd′) n. 1 The smooth, hard wood of various trees, used in cabinetwork. 2 Any tree yielding such wood.

sat·ire (sat′īr) n. 1 The use of sarcasm, irony, or wit in ridiculing and denouncing abuses, follies, customs, etc. 2 A literary work that ridicules in this manner. [< L satira]

sa·tir·i·cal (sə·tir′i·kəl) adj. 1 Given to or characterized by satire: a satirical writer. 2 Sarcastic; caustic; biting. Also **sa·tir′ic.** —**sa·tir′i·cal·ly** adv. —**sa·tir′i·cal·ness** n.

sat·i·rist (sat′ə·rist) n. 1 A writer of satire. 2 A person fond of satirizing or ridiculing.

sat·i·rize (sat′ə·rīz) v.t. **·rized, ·riz·ing** To subject to or criticize in satire. —**sat′i·riz′er** n.

sat·is·fac·tion (sat′is·fak′shən) n. 1 The act of satisfying, or the state of being satisfied. 2 The making of amends, reparation, or payment. 3 That which satisfies; compensation.

sat·is·fac·to·ry (sat′is·fak′tər·ē) adj. Giving satisfaction; answering expectations or requirements. —**sat′is·fac′to·ri·ly** adv. —**sat′is·fac′to·ri·ness** n. —**Syn.** adequate, gratifying, pleasing, sufficient.

sat·is·fy (sat′is·fī) v. **·fied, ·fy·ing** v.t. 1 To supply fully with what is desired, expected, or needed. 2 To please; gratify. 3 To free from doubt or anxiety; convince. 4 To give what is due to. 5 To pay or discharge (a debt, obligation, etc.). 6 To answer sufficiently or convincingly, as a question or objection. 7 To make reparation for; expiate. —v.i. 8 To give satisfaction. [< L satis enough + facere do] —**sat′is·fi′er** n. —**sat′is·fy′ing·ly** adv.

sa·to·ri (sä·tō′rē) n. The sudden change of consciousness which is the goal of Zen Buddhism. [Jap.]

sa·trap (sā′trap, sat′rap) n. 1 A governor of a province in ancient Persia. 2 Any petty ruler under a despot. 3 A subordinate ruler or governor. [< O Pers. shathraparan, lit., a protector of a province]

sa·trap·y (sā′trə·pē, sat′rə·pē) n. pl. **·trap·ies** The territory or the jurisdiction of a satrap. Also **sa·trap·ate** (sā′trə·pit, sat′rə-).

sat·u·rate (sach′ə·rāt) v.t. **·rat·ed, ·rat·ing** To soak or imbue thoroughly to the utmost capacity for absorbing or retaining. —adj. Saturated. [< L satur full] —**sat′u·ra·tor** or **sat′u·rat′er** n.

sat·u·rat·ed (sach′ə·rā′tid) adj. 1 Replete; incapable of holding more of a substance: a saturated solution. 2 Chem. Designating an organic compound having no free or multiple valence bonds available for direct union with additional atoms. 3 Tending to increase the cholesterol content of the blood: said of some edible fats.

sat·u·ra·tion (sach′ə·rā′shən) n. 1 A saturating or being saturated. 2 A massive concentration, in any given area, as of advertising, military force, etc., for a specific purpose: often used attributively: saturation bombing.

saturation point 1 The maximum possible degree of impregnation of one substance with another. 2 A condition in which a person has reached the limit of patience, toleration, etc.

Sat·ur·day (sat′ər·dē, -dā) n. The seventh or last day of the week; the day of the Jewish Sabbath. [< OE Sæternesdæg Saturn's day]

Sat·urn (sat′ərn) Rom. Myth. The god of agriculture. —n. The planet of the solar system sixth in distance from the sun. • See PLANET. —**Sa·tur·ni·an** (sə·tûr′nē·ən) adj. [< L Saturnus]

Sat·ur·na·li·a (sat′ər·nā′lē·ə) n.pl. (usu. construed as sing.) Any season or period of general license or revelry. —**sat′ur·na′li·an** adj.

Sat·ur·na·li·a (sat′ər·nā′lē·ə) n.pl. The feast of Saturn held in ancient Rome in mid-December, and marked by wild reveling and abandon. —**Sat′ur·na′li·an** adj.

sat·ur·nine (sat′ər·nīn) adj. 1 Having a grave, gloomy, or morose disposition or character. 2 In astrology, born under the supposed dominance of Saturn. [< L Saturnus Saturn] —**sat′ur·nine·ly** adv. —**sat′ur·nine′ness** n.

sat·yr (sā′tər, sat′ər) Gk. Myth. A wanton woodland deity with a man's body and goatlike legs. —n. A lascivious man. [< Gk. satyros] —**sa·tyr·ic** (sə·tir′ik) or **·i·cal** adj.

sat·y·ri·a·sis (sat′ə·rī′ə·sis) n. An abnormally strong, insatiable sexual drive in males. [< Gk. satyros a satyr]

sauce (sôs) n. 1 An appetizing, usu. liquid relish for food to improve its taste. 2 A dish of fruit pulp stewed and sweetened: cranberry sauce. 3 Informal Pert or impudent language. 4 Slang Alcoholic liquor. —v.t. **sauced, sauc·ing** 1 To flavor or dress with sauce. 2 Informal To be saucy to. [< L salsus salted]

sauce·pan (sôs′pan′) n. A pan, usu. of metal or enamel, with projecting handle, for cooking food.

sau·cer (sô′sər) n. 1 A small dish for holding a cup. 2 Any round, shallow thing of similar shape. [< OF sauce sauce]

sau·cy (sô′sē) adj. **·ci·er, ·ci·est** 1 Disrespectful to superiors; impudent. 2 Piquant; sprightly; amusing. —**sau′ci·ly** adv. —**sau′ci·ness** n.

Sau·di A·ra·bi·a (sou′dē ə·rä′bē·ə, sä·ŏŏ′dē) A kingdom

of N CEN. Arabia, 927,000 sq. mi., cap. Riyadh. —**Sau′di A·ra′bi·an** adj., n.

sauer·kraut (sour′krout′) n. Shredded and salted cabbage fermented in its own juice. [< G sauer sour + kraut cabbage]

Saul (sôl) In the Bible, the first king of Israel.

sau·na (sou′nə, sô′-) n. 1 A Finnish steam bath in which the steam is produced by running water over heated stones. 2 A bath in which the bather is exposed to very hot, dry air. 3 A room or enclosure for a sauna. [Finnish]

saun·ter (sôn′tər) v.i. To walk in a leisurely or lounging way; stroll. —n. 1 A slow, aimless manner of walking. 2 An idle stroll. [< ME santren muse] —**saun′ter·er** n. —**saun′ter·ing·ly** adv.

sau·ri·an (sôr′ē·ən) n. Any of the suborder of reptiles comprising the lizards. —adj. Pertaining to or having the characteristics of lizards. [< Gk. sauros a lizard]

---

add, āce, câre, pälm; end, ēven; it, īce; odd, ōpen, ôrder; tŏŏk, pōōl; up, bûrn; ə = a in above, u in focus; yōō = u in fuse; oil; pout; check; go; ring; thin; this; zh, vision. < derived from; ? origin uncertain or unknown.

-saurus *combining form Zool.* Lizard: *brontosaurus.* [< Gk. *sauros* a lizard]

sau·sage (sô′sij) *n.* Finely chopped and highly seasoned meat, commonly stuffed into a prepared animal intestine or other casing. [< L *salsus* salted]

sau·té (sô·tā′, sō-) *v.t.* **·téed, ·té·ing** To fry quickly in a little fat. —*n.* A sautéed dish. [F, p.p. of *sauter* to leap]

sau·terne (sô·tûrn′, sō-; *Fr.* sō·tern′) *n.* A sweet, white wine. [< *Sauternes,* district in sw France]

sav·age (sav′ij) *adj.* **1** Of a wild and untamed nature; not domesticated. **2** Fierce; ferocious. **3** Living in or belonging to the most primitive condition of human society; uncivilized. **4** Remote and wild: *savage* mountain country. —*n.* **1** A primitive or uncivilized human being. **2** A brutal and cruel person. —*v.t.* **sav·aged, sav·a·ging** To beat or maul cruelly. [< L *silva* a wood] —**sav′age·ly** *adv.* —**Syn.** *adj.* **1** undomesticated, feral. **2** brutal, bloodthirsty, barbarous. **3** uncultivated.

sav·age·ry (sav′ij·rē) *n. pl.* **·ries 1** The state of being savage. **2** Cruelty in disposition or action. **3** A savage act.

sa·van·na (sə·van′ə) *n.* A tract of level land covered with low vegetation; a treeless plain, esp. in or near the tropics: also **sa·van′nah.** [< Cariban]

sa·vant (sə·vänt′, sav′ənt; *Fr.* så·vän′) *n.* A person of exceptional learning. [F < L *sapere* be wise]

save[1] (sāv) *v.* **saved, sav·ing** *v.t.* **1** To preserve or rescue from danger, harm, etc. **2** To keep from being spent, expended, or lost. **3** To set aside for future use; accumulate: often with *up.* **4** To treat carefully so as to avoid fatigue, harm, etc.: to *save* one's eyesight. **5** To prevent by timely action: A stitch in time *saves* nine. **6** *Theol.* To deliver from the consequences of sin; redeem. —*v.i.* **7** To be economical. **8** To preserve something from harm, etc. **9** To accumulate money. [< L *salvus* safe] —**sav′er** *n.*

save[2] (sāv) *prep.* Except; but. —*conj.* **1** Except; but. **2** *Archaic* Unless. [< OF *sauf* being excepted, orig. safe]

sav·ing (sā′ving) *adj.* **1** That saves or rescues: *lifesaving* equipment. **2** Economical; frugal. **3** Holding in reserve; qualifying: a *saving* clause. —*n.* **1** Preservation from loss or danger. **2** Avoidance of waste; economy. **3** Any reduction in cost, time, etc.: a *saving* of 16 percent. **4** *pl.* Sums of money saved, esp. those deposited in a bank. —*prep.* **1** With the exception of; save. **2** With due respect for: *saving* your presence. —*conj.* With the exception of. —**sav′ing·ly** *adv.* —**sav′ing·ness** *n.*

savings account An account drawing interest at a savings bank.

savings bank An institution for receiving and investing savings and paying interest on deposits.

sav·ior (sāv′yər) *n.* One who saves. —**the Savior** Jesus Christ. *Brit. sp.* **sav′iour.**

sa·voir faire (så·vwär fâr′) Ability to see and to do the right thing; esp., sophisticated social poise. [F, lit., to know how to act]

sa·vor (sā′vər) *n.* **1** Taste and smell: a *savor* of garlic. **2** Specific or characteristic quality. **3** Relish; zest: The conversation had *savor.* —*v.i.* **1** To have savor; taste or smell: with *of.* **2** To have a specified savor or character: with *of.* —*v.t.* **3** To give flavor to; season. **4** To taste or enjoy with pleasure; relish. **5** To have the savor or character of. *Brit. sp.* **sa′vour.** [< L *sapere* taste, know] —**sa′vor·er** *n.* —**sa′·vor·ous** *adj.*

sa·vor·less (sā′vər·lis) *adj.* Tasteless; insipid.

sa·vor·y[1] (sā′vər·ē) *adj.* **1** Of an agreeable taste and odor; appetizing. **2** In good repute. —*n. pl.* **·vor·ies** A small, hot serving of tasty food, usu. eaten at the end of a dinner. *Brit. sp.* **sa′vour·y.** [< OF *savourer* to taste] —**sa′vor·i·ly** *adv.* —**sa′vor·i·ness** *n.* —**Syn.** *adj.* **1** flavorful, palatable, piquant, tasty, toothsome. **2** respectable.

sa·vor·y[2] (sā′vər·ē) *n.* A hardy, annual herb of the mint family used for seasoning. Also **summer savory.** [< OF *savoreie*]

sa·voy (sə·voi′) *n.* A variety of cabbage with wrinkled leaves and a compact head. [< F *(chou de) Savoie* (cabbage of) Savoy]

Sa·voy·ard (sə·voi′ərd, sav′oi·ärd′) *n.* An actor or actress in or an admirer or producer of the Gilbert and Sullivan operas. [< the *Savoy,* London theater]

sav·vy (sav′ē) *Slang v.i.* **·vied, ·vy·ing** To understand; comprehend. —*n.* Understanding; know-how. —*adj.* Having good sense or know-how. [Alter. of Sp. ¿ *Sabe (usted)?* Do (you) know?]

saw[1] (sô) *n.* **1** A cutting tool with pointed teeth arranged continuously along the edge of a blade or disk. **2** A tool or machine having such teeth: a power *saw.* —*v.* **sawed, sawed** or **sawn, saw·ing** *v.t.* **1** To cut or divide with or as with a saw. **2** To shape or fashion with a saw. **3** To make a motion as if sawing: The speaker *saws* the air. —*v.i.* **4** To use a saw. **5** To cut: said of a saw. **6** To be cut with a saw: This wood *saws* easily. [< OE *sagu*] —**saw′er** *n.*

saw[2] (sô) *n.* A proverbial or familiar saying; old maxim. [< OE *sagu*]

saw[3] (sô) *p.t.* of SEE[1].

saw·bones (sô′bōnz′) *n. Slang* A surgeon.

saw·buck (sô′buk′) *n.* **1** A frame consisting of two X-shaped ends joined by connecting bars, for holding sticks of wood for sawing. **2** *Slang* A ten-dollar bill: from the resemblance of X, Roman numeral ten, to the ends of a sawbuck.

Sawbuck *def. 1*

saw·dust (sô′dust′) *n.* Tiny particles of wood cut or torn out by sawing.

saw·fish (sô′fish′) *n. pl.* **·fish** or **·fish·es** Any of a genus of large tropical fishes related to rays and having an elongated snout with teeth on each edge.

saw·fly (sô′flī′) *n. pl.* **·flies** A hymenopterous insect having in the female a pair of sawlike organs for piercing plants, wood, etc., in which to lay eggs.

saw·horse (sô′hôrs′) *n.* A frame consisting of a long wooden bar or plank supported by four extended legs.

saw·mill (sô′mil′) *n.* **1** An establishment for sawing logs with power-driven machinery. **2** A large sawing machine.

sawn (sôn) A *p.p.* of SAW[1].

Sawhorse

saw·toothed (sô′tōotht′) *adj.* Having teeth or toothlike processes similar to those of a saw; serrate. Also **saw′tooth′** (-tōoth′).

saw·yer (sô′yər) *n.* One who saws logs, esp. a lumberman who fells trees by sawing, or one who works in a sawmill.

sax (saks) *n. Informal* A saxophone.

sax·i·frage (sak′sə·frij) *n.* Any of numerous perennial plants usu. having a basal rosette of leaves and growing in rocky places. [< L *(herba) saxifraga,* lit., stone-breaking (herb)]

Sax·on (sak′sən) *n.* **1** A member of a Germanic tribal group living in NW Germany in the early centuries of the Christian era. With the Angles and Jutes, the Saxons conquered England in the fifth and sixth centuries. **2** The language of the early Saxons. **3** An inhabitant of modern Saxony in Germany. —*adj.* Of or pertaining to the early Saxons, or to their language.

sax·o·phone (sak′sə·fōn) *n.* Any of a group of reed instruments having a straight metal body equipped with finger keys and terminating in a curved, conical bore. [< A. J. *Sax,* 1814–94, Belgian instrument maker] —**sax′o·phon′ist** *n.*

say (sā) *v.* **said, say·ing** *v.t.* **1** To speak. **2** To express in words; tell. **3** To state positively: *Say* which you prefer. **4** To recite; repeat: to *say* one's prayers. **5** To allege: They *say* that he lied. **6** To assume: He is worth, *say,* a million. —*v.i.* **7** To make a statement; speak. —**say nothing of** Without mentioning. —**that is to say** In other words. —*n.* **1** What one has said or has to say: Let him have his *say.* **2** *Informal* Right or turn to speak or choose: Now it is my *say.* —**the say** *Informal* Authority: Who has *the say* in this office? —*interj.* A hail or exclamation to command attention: also *Brit.* **I say!** [< OE *secgan*] —**say′er** *n.* —**Syn.** *v.* **1** articulate, pronounce, utter. **2** declare, affirm. **5** assert.

Saxophone

say·ing (sā′ing) *n.* **1** An utterance. **2** A maxim or saw. —**go without saying** To be so evident as to require no explanation.

say-so (sā′sō′) *n. Informal* **1** An unsupported assertion or decision. **2** Right or power to make decisions: He has the *say-so.*

Sb antimony (L *stibium*).

SBA Small Business Administration.

SbE south by east.

SbW south by west.

SC Security Council (of the United Nations); South Carolina (P.O. abbr.).

S.C. Signal Corps; South Carolina; Supreme Court.

Sc scandium; stratocumulus.

sc. he (or she) carved or engraved it (L *sculpsit*); namely (L *scilicet*); scale; scene; science; screw; scruple (weight).

s.c. small capitals (printing).

scab (skab) *n.* **1** A crust on a wound or sore. **2** A contagious disease of sheep. **3** Any of certain plant diseases marked by a roughened or warty exterior. **4** A worker who will not join a labor union. **5** A worker who does the job of a person on strike. —*v.i.* **scabbed, scab·bing** **1** To form or become covered with a scab. **2** To act or work as a scab. [< Scand.] —**scab′bi·ly** *adv.* —**scab′bi·ness** *n.* —**scab′by** *adj.* (**·i·er, ·i·est**)

scab·bard (skab′ərd) *n.* A sheath for a weapon, as for a bayonet or a sword. —*v.t.* To sheathe in a scabbard. [< OHG *scar* a sword + *bergan* hide, protect]

sca·bies (skā′bēz) *n.* A skin disease affecting man and various animals, caused by infestation by certain mites; the itch. [< L *scabere* to scratch, scrape] —**sca·bi·et·ic** (skā′bē·et′ik), **sca′bi·ous** (-əs) *adj.*

sca·bi·o·sa (skā′bē·ō′sə) *n.* Any of various plants related to the teasel, with showy, usu. prickly flowers. Also **sca′bious** (-əs). [< Med. L *(herba) scabiosa* herb for scabies]

sca·brous (skā′brəs) *adj.* **1** Roughened with minute points. **2** Difficult to handle tactfully. **3** Suggestive; salacious. [< L *scabere* to scratch] —**sca′brous·ly** *adv.* —**sca′·brous·ness** *n.*

scads (skadz) *n.pl. Informal* A large amount or quantity. [?]

scaf·fold (skaf′əld, -ōld) *n.* **1** A temporary elevated structure for the support of workmen, materials, etc., as in constructing, painting, or repairing a building. **2** A platform for the execution of criminals. **3** Any raised platform. —*v.t.* To furnish or support with a scaffold. [< OF *escadafaut*]

scaf·fold·ing (skaf′əl·ding) *n.* **1** A scaffold, or system of scaffolds. **2** The materials for constructing scaffolds.

scag (skag) *n. Slang* Heroin.

sca·lar (skā′lər) *adj.* Defined by a single number, as a quantity having only magnitude. —*n.* A scalar quantity. [< L *scala* a ladder]

scal·a·wag (skal′ə·wag) *n.* **1** *Informal* A worthless person; rascal. **2** A Southern white who became a Republican during the Reconstruction period: a contemptuous term. Also **scal′la·wag, scal′ly·wag.** [?]

scald[1] (skôld) *v.t.* **1** To burn with hot liquid or steam. **2** To cleanse or treat with boiling water. **3** To heat (a liquid) to a point just short of boiling. **4** To cook in a liquid which is just short of the boiling point. —*v.i.* **5** To be or become scalded. —*n.* **1** A burn due to a hot fluid or steam. **2** Surface injury of plant tissue due to various causes, as exposure to sun, fungi, etc. [< L *ex-* very + *calidus* hot]

scald[2] (skôld, skäld) *n.* SKALD. —**scal·dic** (skôl′dik, skäl′-) *adj.*

scale[1] (skāl) *n.* **1** One of the thin, horny, usu. overlapping, protective plates covering most fishes, reptiles, etc. **2** SCALE INSECT. **3** A specialized leaf, as of a pine cone. **4** A flaky coating on metal, as from corrosion, etc. **5** Any thin, scalelike piece, as of skin. —*v.* **scaled, scal·ing** *v.t.* **1** To strip or clear of scale or scales. **2** To form scales on; cover with scales. **3** To take off in layers; pare off. —*v.i.* **4** To come off in layers or scales; peel. **5** To shed scales. **6** To become incrusted with scales. [< OF *escale* a husk] —**scal′er** *n.*

scale[2] (skāl) *n.* **1** An object bearing accurately spaced

Ascending chromatic scale *def.* 6

marks for use in measurement, or the series of marks so used. **2** Any system of units of measurement. **3** A proportion used in representing distances, as on a map or blueprint. **4** *Math.* A system of numeration in which the successive places determine the value of digits, as the decimal system. **5** Any progressive or graded series; a graduation: the social *scale.* **6** *Music* A series of tones arranged in a sequence of ascending or descending pitches according to any of various systems of intervals. **7** *Phot.* The range of light values which may be reproduced by a photographic paper. **8** A succession of steps or degrees: a salary *scale.* **9** A relative degree or extent: to live on a modest *scale.* —*v.* **scaled, scal·ing** *v.t.* **1** To climb to the top of. **2** To make according to a scale. **3** To regulate or adjust according to a scale or ratio: with *up, down,* etc. —*v.i.* **4** To climb; ascend. **5** To rise, as in steps or stages: mountains *scaling* to the skies. [< L *scala* a ladder] —**scal′er** *n.*

scale[3] (skāl) *n.* **1** The bowl, scoop, or platform of a weighing instrument or balance. **2** *Usu. pl.* The balance itself. —**the Scales** LIBRA. —**turn the scales** To determine; decide. —*v.* **scaled, scal·ing** *v.t.* **1** To weigh in scales. **2** To amount to in weight. —*v.i.* **3** To be weighed. [< ON *skál* a bowl]

scale insect Any of numerous plant-feeding insects of which the adult female is sedentary under a scalelike, waxy shield.

sca·lene (skā′lēn, skā·lēn′) *adj. Geom.* Having no two sides equal: said of a triangle. [< Gk. *skalēnos* uneven] • See TRIANGLE.

scal·lion (skal′yən) *n.* **1** A young, tender onion with a small white bulb. **2** A shallot or leek. [< L *(caepa) Ascalonia* (onion) of Ashkelon, a Palestinian seaport]

scal·lop (skal′əp, skol′-) *n.* **1** Any of various mollusks having a hinged shell with radiating ribs and wavy edge. **2** The edible abductor muscle of certain scallops. **3** A scallop shell. **4** One of a series of semicircular curves along an edge, as for ornament. —*v.t.* **1** To shape the edge of with scallops for ornamentation. **2** To bake (food) in a casserole with a sauce, usu. topped with bread crumbs. [< MF *escalope* shell] —**scal′lop·er** *n.*

Scallop shell

scalp (skalp) *n.* **1** The skin of the top and back of the skull, usu. covered with hair. **2** A portion of this, cut or torn away as a trophy among certain North American Indians. —*v.t.* **1** To cut or tear the scalp from. **2** *Informal* To buy (tickets) and sell again at prices exceeding the established rate. **3** *Informal* To buy and sell again quickly to make a small profit. —*v.i.* **4** *Informal* To scalp bonds, tickets, etc. [< Scand.] —**scalp′er** *n.*

scal·pel (skal′pəl) *n.* A small, sharp, surgical knife. [< L *scalpere* to cut]

scal·y (skā′lē) *adj.* **scal·i·er, scal·i·est** **1** Having a covering of scales or flakes. **2** Of the nature of a scale. **3** Incrusted with a flaking deposit. —**scal′i·ness** *n.*

scamp[1] (skamp) *n.* A confirmed rogue; rascal. [< obs. *scamp* to roam] —**scamp′ish** *adj.* —**scamp′ish·ness** *n.*

scamp[2] (skamp) *v.t.* To perform (work) carelessly or dishonestly. [?] —**scamp′er** *n.*

scam·per (skam′pər) *v.i.* To run quickly or hastily. —*n.* A hurried flight. [< L *ex* out + *campus* a plain, battlefield] —**scam′per·er** *n.*

scam·pi (skam′pē) *n.pl.* Large shrimp, usu. served in a garlic sauce. [Ital.]

---

add, āce, câre, pälm; end, ēven; it, īce; odd, ōpen, ôrder; tŏŏk, pōōl; up, bûrn; ə = *a* in *above, u* in *focus;* yōō = *u* in *fuse;* oil; pout; check; go; ring; thin; ᵺis; zh, *vision.* < derived from; ? origin uncertain or unknown.

scan (skan) v. **scanned, scan·ning** v.t. **1** To examine in detail; scrutinize closely. **2** To pass the eyes over quickly; glance at. **3** To separate (verse) into metrical feet. **4** *Electronics* To cause a beam, as of light, electrons, microwaves, etc., to pass systematically over a surface or through a region. —v.i. **5** To scan verse. **6** To conform to metrical rules: said of verse. [< LL *scandere* scan verses] —**scan′ner** n.

Scan., Scand. Scandinavia; Scandinavian.

scan·dal (skan′dəl) n. **1** A discreditable action or circumstance offensive to public morals or feelings. **2** Injury to reputation. **3** General criticism that injures reputation; malicious gossip. **4** A person whose conduct arouses public censure. [< Gk. *skandalon* a snare] —**Syn.** 2 discredit, disgrace, disrepute. **3** calumny, defamation, slander.

scan·dal·ize (skan′dəl·īz) v.t. **·ized, ·iz·ing** To shock the moral feelings of; outrage. —**scan′dal·i·za′tion, scan′dal·iz′· er** n.

scan·dal·ous (skan′dəl·əs) adj. **1** Causing or being a scandal; disgraceful. **2** Consisting of evil or malicious reports. —**scan′dal·ous·ly** adv. —**scan′dal·ous·ness** n.

Scan·di·na·vi·a (skan′də·nā′vē·ə) n. The region of NW Europe occupied by Sweden, Norway, and Denmark; 315,-156 sq. mi; Finland, Iceland, and the Faroe Islands are often included: total area, 485,539 sq. mi. —**Scan′di·na′vi·an** adj., n.

scan·di·um (skan′dē·əm) n. A rare metallic element of low density. [< L *Scandia* Scandinavia]

scan·sion (skan′shən) n. The act or art of scanning verse to show its metrical parts.

scant (skant) adj. **1** Meager in measure or quantity. **2** Being just short of the measure specified: a *scant* half-hour; a *scant* five yards. —**scant of** Insufficiently supplied with: to be *scant* of breath from running. —v.t. **1** To restrict or limit in supply; stint. **2** To treat briefly or inadequately. —adv. *Regional* Scarcely; barely. [< ON *skammr* short] —**scant′ly** adv. —**scant′ness** n.

scant·ling (skant′ling) n. **1** A small beam or timber, esp. an upright timber in a structure. **2** Such timbers collectively. [< OF *eschantillon* specimen]

scant·y (skan′tē) adj. **scant·i·er, scant·i·est 1** Too little; not enough: a *scanty* meal. **2** Scarcely enough for what is needed; insufficient. [< SCANT] —**scant′i·ly** adv. —**scant′i·ness** n. —**Syn. 1** deficient, poor, sparse. **2** limited, restricted.

scape·goat (skāp′gōt′) n. **1** In the Bible, the goat upon whose head Aaron symbolically laid the sins of the people on the day of atonement, after which it was led away into the wilderness. *Lev.* 16. **2** Any person bearing blame for the misdeeds of others. —v.t. *Informal* To make a scapegoat of. [< ESCAPE + GOAT]

scape·grace (skāp′grās′) n. A mischievous or incorrigible person.

s. caps. small capitals (printing).

scap·u·la (skap′yə·lə) n. pl. **·las** or **·lae** (-lē) Either of the two large, flat bones of the upper back; shoulder blade. [< L *scapulae* shoulder blades]

scap·u·lar (skap′yə·lər) n. **1** A garment of certain religious orders consisting of two strips of cloth hanging down front and back. **2** Two small rectangular pieces of cloth connected by strings, worn as a badge of membership by certain religious orders. Also **scap′u·lar′y** (-ler′ē). [< L *scapula* shoulder]

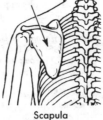

Scapula

scar (skär) n. **1** The mark left after the healing of a lesion. **2** Any lingering sign, as from hardship, misfortune, etc.: the *scars* of poverty. —v.t. & v.i. **scarred, scar·ring** To mark or become marked with a scar. [< LL *eschara* a scab]

scar·ab (skar′əb) n. **1** Any of various beetles, esp. a large, black beetle held sacred by the ancient Egyptians. **2** A gemstone or other ornament in the form of this beetle. Also **scar·a·bee** (skar′ə·bē). [< L *scarabaeus*] —**scar′a·boid** (-boid) adj.

scar·a·bae·us (skar′ə·bē′əs) n. pl. **·bae·us·es** or **·bae·i** (-bē′ī) SCARAB. Also **scar′a·be′us** —**scar·a·bae′id** adj., n.

scar·a·mouch (skar′ə·mouch, -mōōsh) n. **1** A boastful, cowardly person. **2** *Usu. cap.* A similar character in old Italian comedy. Also **scar′a·mouche**. [< Ital. *Scaramuccia*, lit., a skirmish]

scarce (skârs) adj. **scarc·er, scarc·est 1** Rare and unusual: *scarce* antiques. **2** Scant; insufficient. —**make oneself scarce** *Informal* To go or stay away. [< OF *eschars* scanty, insufficient] —**scarce′ness** n.

scarce·ly (skârs′lē) adv. **1** Only just; barely: so weary he could *scarcely* walk. **2** Rarely: he *scarcely* goes out now. **3** Certainly not; probably not: That's *scarcely* possible.

scar·ci·ty (skâr′sə·tē) n. pl. **·ties 1** Scantiness; insufficiency: a *scarcity* of truffles. **2** Rarity: the *scarcity* of genius.

scare (skâr) v. **scared, scar·ing** v.t. **1** To strike with sudden fear; frighten. **2** To drive or force by frightening: with *off* or *away.* —v.i. **3** To take fright; become scared. —**scare up** *Informal* To get together hurriedly; produce: *to scare up* a meal from leftovers. —n. A sudden fright; alarm. —adj. *Informal* Intended to provoke alarm or concern: *scare* tactics. [< ON *skiarr* shy] —**scar′er** n. —**scar′ing·ly** adv. —**Syn.** v. **1** alarm, startle, terrify. n. fright, panic.

scare·crow (skâr′krō′) n. **1** Any effigy set up to scare crows and other birds from growing crops. **2** A cause of false alarm. **3** A person who is ragged and tattered or thin and gangling.

scare·head (skâr′hed′) n. *Informal* A newspaper headline in large type for sensational news.

scarf¹ (skärf) n. pl. **scarfs 1** In carpentry, a lapped joint made as by notching two timbers at the ends, and bolting them together to form a single piece: also **scarf joint. 2** The notched end of either of the timbers so cut. —v.t. **1** To unite with a scarf joint. **2** To cut a scarf in. [ME]

Scarf joints

scarf² (skärf) n. pl. **scarfs** or **scarves** (skärvz) **1** A long and wide band, worn about the head, neck, shoulders, or waist. **2** A necktie or cravat with dangling ends. **3** A runner for a bureau or table. —v.t. To cover or decorate with a scarf. [< OF *escharpe*]

scar·i·fy (skar′ə·fī) v.t. **·fied, ·fy·ing 1** To make shallow scratches in, as the skin. **2** To criticize severely. **3** To stir the surface of, as soil. [< Gk. *skariphasthai* scratch an outline] —**scar′i·fi′er, scar′i·fi·ca′tion** n.

scar·la·ti·na (skär′lə·tē′nə) n. A mild form of scarlet fever.

scar·let (skär′lit) n. **1** A brilliant red, inclining to orange. **2** Cloth or clothing of a scarlet color. —adj. Brilliant red. [< Pers. *saqalāt* a rich, scarlet cloth]

scarlet fever An acute streptococcal infection marked by fever, sore throat, and a red rash.

scarlet letter A scarlet "A" which adulterous women were once condemned to wear.

scarlet runner A climbing bean with vivid red flowers and long seed pods. Also **scarlet runner bean.**

scarp (skärp) n. **1** Any steep slope. **2** A steep artificial slope, esp. the inner slope, about a fortification. —v.t. To cut to a steep slope. [< Ital. *scarpa*]

scarves (skärvz) A pl. of SCARF².

scar·y (skâr′ē) adj. **scar·i·er, scar·i·est** *Informal* **1** Easily scared. **2** Giving cause for alarm. —**scar′i·ness** n.

scat¹ (skat) v.i. **scat·ted, scat·ting** *Informal* To go away quickly: usu. in the imperative. [?]

scat² (skat) n. Jazz singing that employs improvised nonsense syllables. —v.i. **scat·ted, scat·ting** To sing scat. [?]

scathe (skāth) v.t. **scathed, scath·ing 1** To criticize severely. **2** *Archaic* To injure severely. [< ON *skatha*]

scathe·less (skāth′lis) adj. Without harm or injury.

scath·ing (skā′thing) adj. Blasting; withering: a *scathing* rebuke. —**scath′ing·ly** adv.

sca·tol·o·gy (ska·tol′ə·jē, skə-) n. **1** The scientific study of excrement. **2** Preoccupation with obscenity or with excrement, as in literature. [< Gk. *skōr, skatos* dung + -LOGY] —**scat·o·log·i·cal** (skat′ə·loj′i·kəl) adj. —**sca·tol′o·gist** n.

scat·ter (skat′ər) v.t. **1** To throw about in various places; strew. **2** To disperse; rout. **3** *Physics* To reflect (radiation) in more than one direction. —v.i. **4** To separate and go in different directions. —n. The act of scattering or the con-

dition of being scattered. [ME *scateren*] —**scat′ter·er** *n.* —
Syn. *v.* **1** disseminate, sow, spread, sprinkle. **2** drive away.
scat·ter·brain (skat′ər·brān′) *n.* A heedless, flighty person. —**scat′ter-brained′** *adj.*
scat·ter·site (skat′ər·sīt) *adj.* Of or describing housing sponsored by government, esp. for low-income groups, located in various communities to avoid ghettoization.
scaup (skôp) *n.* A North American wild duck related to the canvasback, having the head and neck black in the male: also **scaup duck.** [Obs. var. of SCALP + DUCK]
scav·enge (skav′inj) *v.* **·enged, ·eng·ing** *v.t.* **1** To remove filth, rubbish, and refuse from, as streets. —*v.i.* **2** To act as a scavenger. **3** To search for food. [Back formation < SCAVENGER]
scav·en·ger (skav′in·jər) *n.* **1** Any organism that feeds on refuse, carrion, etc. **2** A person who removes refuse or unwanted things, as a garbage collector or a junkman. [< AF *scawage* inspection]
sce·nar·i·o (si·nâr′ē·ō, -nä′rē·ō) *n. pl.* **·nar·i·os 1** The plot or outline of a dramatic work. **2** The written plot and arrangement of incidents of a motion picture. **3** An outline or plan of a projected series of actions or events. [< LL *scenarius* of stage scenes] —**sce·nar′ist** *n.*
scene (sēn) *n.* **1** A locality and all connected with it, as presented to view; a landscape. **2** The setting for a dramatic action. **3** The place and surroundings of any event, as in literature or art. **4** A division of an act of a play. **5** A specific incident or episode in a play, novel, motion picture, etc.: the ghost *scene* in *Hamlet.* **6** The painted canvas, hangings, etc., for the background for a play. **7** An unseemly display of anger or excited feeling, esp. in public. **8** *Slang* A place or realm of a currently popular activity: the country music *scene.* —**behind the scenes 1** Out of sight of a theater audience; backstage. **2** Privately; in secret. [< Gk. *skēnē* a tent, a stage]
scen·er·y (sē′nər·ē) *n. pl.* **·er·ies 1** The features of a landscape; view. **2** The painted backdrops, etc., used in the theater to represent a setting in a play.
sce·nic (sē′nik, sen′ik) *adj.* **1** Of or relating to beautiful natural scenery: a *scenic* spot. **2** In art, representing a situation, action, etc. **3** Relating to stage scenery. —**sce′·ni·cal·ly** *adv.*
scent (sent) *n.* **1** An odor. **2** The effluvium by which an animal can be tracked. **3** A clue aiding investigation. **4** A fragrant, fluid essence; perfume. **5** The sense of smell. —*v.t.* **1** To perceive by the sense of smell. **2** To form a suspicion of. **3** To cause to be fragrant; perfume. —*v.i.* **4** To hunt by the sense of smell. [< L *sentire* to sense]
scep·ter (sep′tər) *n.* **1** A staff or wand carried as the badge of command or sovereignty. **2** Kingly office or power. —*v.t.* To confer the scepter on; invest with royal power. Also, *esp. Brit.,* **scep′tre** (-tər). [< Gk. *skēptron* a staff]
scep·tic (skep′tik) *n.* SKEPTIC.
sched·ule (skej′ool, *Brit.* shed′yool) *n.* **1** A list specifying the details of some matter. **2** A timetable. **3** A detailed and timed plan for the steps in a procedure. —*v.t.* **·uled, ·ul·ing 1** To place in or on a schedule. **2** To appoint or plan for a specified time or date: He *scheduled* his appearance for five o'clock. [< LL *scedula*]
sche·ma (skē′mə) *n. pl.* **sche·ma·ta** (skē′mə·tə) A synopsis, summary, diagram, etc. [< Gk. *schēma*]
sche·mat·ic (skē·mat′ik) *adj.* Of or relating to a scheme, diagram, or plan. —*n.* A schematic diagram or drawing.
scheme (skēm) *n.* **1** A plan of something to be done; program. **2** An underhand plot: a *scheme* to defraud consumers. **3** A systematic arrangement: a color *scheme.* **4** An outline drawing; diagram. —*v.* **schemed, schem·ing** *v.t.* **1** To make a scheme for; plan. **2** To plan or plot in an underhand manner. —*v.i.* **3** To make schemes; plan. **4** To plot underhandedly. [< Gk. *schēma* a form, plan] —**schem′er** *n.*

Head of scepter

scher·zo (sker′tsō) *n. pl.* **·zos** or **·zi** (-tsē) *Music* A playful or light movement, as in a symphony. [Ital., a jest]
Schick test (shik) A test that indicates susceptibility to diphtheria if reddening of the skin occurs at the site of an injection of toxin. [< B. *Schick,* 1877–1967, Austrian physician]
schil·ling (shil′ing) *n.* The basic monetary unit of Austria.
schism (siz′əm, skiz′əm) *n.* **1** A division of a church into factions because of differences in doctrine. **2** A splitting into antagonistic groups. [< Gk. *schizein* to split]
schis·mat·ic (siz·mat′ik, skiz′-) *adj.* **1** Of or being a schism. **2** Promoting or guilty of schism. Also **schis·mat′·i·cal.** —*n.* One who makes or participates in a schism. —**schis·mat′i·cal·ly** *adv.* —**schis·mat′i·cal·ness** *n.*
schist (shist) *n.* Any crystalline rock that readily splits or cleaves. [< Gk. *schizein* to split] —**schist′ous, schist·ose** (shis′tōs) *adj.*
schizo- *combining form* Split; divided: *schizophrenia.* [< Gk. *schizein* to split]
schiz·oid (skit′soid) *adj.* Pertaining to or resembling schizophrenia. —*n.* One having schizoid characteristics.
schiz·o·phre·ni·a (skit′sō·frē′nē·ə) *n.* Mental illness characterized in varying degrees by irrational thinking, disturbed emotions, bizarre behavior, etc. [< SCHIZO- + Gk. *phrēn* mind] —**schiz′o·phren′ic** (-fren′ik) *adj., n.*
schle·miel (shlə·mēl′) *n. Slang* An inept, easily duped person. Also **schle·mihl′.** [Yiddish, an unlucky person]
schlep (shlep) *Slang v.* **schlepped, schlep·ping** *v.t.* **1** To drag awkwardly; lug. —*v.i.* **2** To drag something awkwardly. **3** To proceed wearily or heavily: to *schlep* uptown. —*n.* **1** A difficult journey. **2** A stupid, awkward person. Also **schlepp.** [Yiddish *shleppen* to drag] —**schlep′per** *n.*
schlock (shlok) *Slang n.* Shoddy, inferior merchandise. —*adj.* Of inferior quality; tawdry. [Yiddish] —**schlock′y** *adj.* (**·i·er, ·i·est**)
schmaltz (shmälts) *n. Slang* **1** Anything which is overly sentimental, as in music or literature. **2** Extreme sentimentalism. [< G *Schmalz,* lit., melted fat] —**schmaltz′y** *adj.* (**·i·er, ·i·est**)
schnapps (shnäps, shnaps) *n.* **1** A strong gin. **2** Any strong alcoholic liquor. Also **schnaps.** [G, a dram, a nip]
schnau·zer (shnou′zər) *n.* A breed of terrier having a wiry coat. [< G *Schnauze* snout]
schnor·kel (shnôr′kəl) *n.* SNORKEL.
schnoz·zle (shnoz′əl) *n. Slang* Nose. [< G *Schnauze*]
schol·ar (skol′ər) *n.* **1** A person eminent for learning. **2** An authority or specialist in an academic disicipline. **3** The holder of a scholarship. **4** One who learns under a teacher; a pupil. [< L *schola* school]

Schnauzer

schol·ar·ly (skol′ər·lē) *adj.* **1** Of or characteristic of a scholar: a *scholarly* mind. **2** Exhibiting great learning. **3** Devoted to learning. —*adv.* After the manner of a scholar. —**schol′ar·li·ness** *n.* —**Syn.** *adj.* **2** erudite, intellectual, learned, lettered. **3** bookish, studious.
schol·ar·ship (skol′ər·ship) *n.* **1** Learning; erudition. **2** A stipend or other aid given to a student to enable him to continue his studies.
scho·las·tic (skō·las′tik, skə-) *adj.* **1** Pertaining to or characteristic of scholars, education, or schools. **2** Pertaining to or characteristic of the medieval schoolmen. Also **scho·las′ti·cal.** —*n. Often cap.* **1** A schoolman of the Middle ages. **2** An advocate of scholasticism. [< Gk. *scholazein* devote leisure to study] —**scho·las′ti·cal·ly** *adv.*
scho·las·ti·cism (skō·las′tə·siz′əm, skə-) *n.* **1** *Often cap.* The systematized logic, philosophy, and theology of medieval scholars. **2** Any system of teaching which insists on traditional doctrines and forms.
school[1] (skool) *n.* **1** An educational institution. **2** The building or group of buildings in which formal instruction is given. **3** A period or session of an educational institu-

tion: *School begins tomorrow.* **4** The pupils and teachers in an educational institution. **5** A subdivision of a university devoted to a special branch of higher education: a medical *school.* **6** The training of any branch of the armed services: gunnery *school.* **7** A body of disciples of a teacher or a group of persons whose work shows a common style or influence: *a painting of the Flemish school.* **8** Any sphere or means of instruction: *the school of hard knocks.* **9** A group of people having similar opinions, patterns of behavior, interests, etc.: *He belongs to the old school.* — *v.t.* **1** To instruct in a school; train. **2** To subject to rule or discipline. [< Gk. *scholē* leisure, school]

school² (skōōl) *n.* A congregation of fish, whales, etc., that feed or swim together. —*v.i.* To come together in a school. [< MDu. *schōle*]

school board A legal board or committee in charge of public schools

school·book (skōōl′bŏŏk′) *n.* A book for use in school; textbook.

school·boy (skōōl′boi′) *n.* A boy attending school. —*adj.* Like or characteristic of a schoolboy.

school·fel·low (skōōl′fel′ō) *n.* A fellow pupil.

school·girl (skōōl′gûrl′) *n.* A girl attending school. — *adj.* Like or characteristic of a schoolgirl.

school·house (skōōl′hous′) *n.* A building in which a school is conducted.

school·ing (skōō′ling) *n.* **1** Instruction given at school. **2** The cost of educating and maintaining a student at a school. **3** The training of horses and riders.

school·man (skōōl′mən) *n. pl.* **·men** (-mən) One of the theologians of the Middle Ages.

school·marm (skōōl′märm′) *n. Informal* A woman schoolteacher, esp. one considered to be prudish.

school·mas·ter (skōōl′mas′tər, -mäs′-) *n.* A man who teaches in or is principal of a school.

school·mate (skōōl′māt′) *n.* A fellow pupil.

school·mis·tress (skōōl′mis′tris) *n.* A woman who teaches in or is principal of a school.

school·room (skōōl′rōōm′, -rŏŏm′) *n.* A room in which instruction is given.

school·teach·er (skōōl′tē′chər) *n.* One who teaches in a school below the college level.

schoon·er (skōō′nər) *n.* **1** A fore-and-aft rigged vessel having originally two masts, but later often three or more. **2** A large beer glass, holding about a pint. [< dial. *scoon* skim on water.]

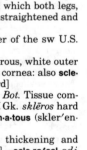

Schooner

schtick (shtik) *n.* SHTICK.

schuss (shŏŏs) *v.i.* To ski down a steep slope at high speed. —*n.* **1** A straight, steep ski course. **2** The act of skiing down such a course. [G, lit., a shot] — **schuss′er** *n.*

schwa (shwä, shvä) *n.* **1** A weak or obscure central vowel sound occurring in most of the unstressed syllables in English speech, as that of the *a* in *alone* or the *u* in *circus.* **2** The symbol (ə) for this sound. [< Heb. *shewa*]

sci. science; scientific.

sci·at·ic (sī·at′ik) *adj.* Pertaining to, in the area of, or affecting the hip. —*n.* A large leg nerve originating at the hip: also **sciatic nerve.** [< Gk. *ischion* hip, hip joint]

sci·at·i·ca (sī·at′i·kə) *n.* **1** Severe pain affecting the sciatic nerve. **2** Any painful affection of the hip and leg.

sci·ence (sī′əns) *n.* **1** Knowledge as of facts, phenomena, laws, and proximate causes, gained and verified by exact observation, organized experiment, and analysis. **2** Any of the various branches of such knowledge, as biology, chemistry, physics (**natural sciences**); economics, history, sociology (**social sciences**); agriculture, engineering (**applied sciences**). **3** Any department of knowledge in which the results of investigation have been systematized in the form of hypotheses and general laws subject to verification. **4** Expertness; skill: *the science of statesmanship.* **5** Originally, knowledge. [< L *scire* know]

Sci·ence (sī′əns) *n.* CHRISTIAN SCIENCE.

science fiction Novels and short stories dealing with actual or imaginary scientific developments and their effect on society or individuals. —**sci′ence-fic′tion** *adj.*

sci·en·tif·ic (sī′ən·tif′ik) *adj.* **1** Of, pertaining to, discovered by, derived from, or used in science. **2** Agreeing with the rules, principles, or methods of science; systematic. **3** Versed in science or a science. —**sci′en·tif′i·cal·ly** *adv.*

sci·en·tist (sī′ən·tist) *n.* One trained or learned in science or devoted to scientific study or investigation.

Sci·en·tist (sī′ən·tist) *n.* A Christian Scientist.

sci·en·tol·o·gy (sī′ən·tol′ə·jē) *n. Often cap.* A religious and psychotherapeutic cult purporting to solve personal problems, cure mental and physical disorders, and increase intelligence. [< L *scientia* science + -LOGY] —**sci′en·tol′o·gist** *n.*

sci-fi (sī′fī′) *Informal n.* Science fiction. —*adj.* Science-fiction.

scil·i·cet (sil′ə·set) *adv.* Namely; that is to say. [< L *scire licet* it is permitted to know]

scim·i·tar (sim′ə·tər) *n.* A curved sword or saber used by Turks. Also **scim′i·ter.** [MF < Pers. *shamshīr*]

scin·til·la (sin·til′ə) *n.* **1** A spark. **2** A trace; iota: *a scintilla of truth.* [L]

scin·til·late (sin′tə·lāt) *v.* **·lat·ed**, **·lat·ing** *v.i.* **1** To give off sparks. **2** To be witty and brilliant in conversation. **3** To twinkle, as a star. —*v.t.* To give off as a spark or sparks. [< L *scintilla* a spark] —**scin′til·la′ting·ly** *adv.* —**scin′til·la′tion** *n.* —**Syn.** 1, 2 glitter, glow, shine, sparkle.

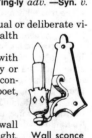

Scimitar

sci·o·lism (sī′ə·liz′əm) *n.* Pretentious, superficial knowledge. [< LL *sciolus* a smatterer] —**sci′o·list** *n.* —**sci′o·lis′tic** *adj.*

sci·on (sī′ən) *n.* **1** A child or descendant. **2** A bud or shoot from a plant or tree, used in grafting. [< OF *cion*]

scis·sion (sizh′ən, sish′-) *n.* **1** The act of cutting or splitting, or the state of being cut. **2** Any division. [< L *scissus,* p.p. of *scindere* to cut]

scis·sor (siz′ər) *v.t. & v.i.* To cut with scissors.

scis·sors (siz′ərz) *n.pl.* **1** A cutting implement with handles and a pair of blades pivoted face to face: sometimes a **pair of scissors.** **2** *(construed as sing.)* In wrestling, a hold secured by clasping the legs about the body or head of the opponent. [< LL *cisorium* a cutting instrument]

scissors kick In swimming, a kick in which both legs, bent at the knee, are thrust apart, then straightened and brought sharply together.

scis·sor·tail (siz′ər·tāl′) *n.* A flycatcher of the sw U.S. and Mexico having a forked tail.

scle·ra (sklēr′ə, sklir′ə) *n.* The firm, fibrous, white outer coat of the eyeball, continuous with the cornea: also **scle·rot·i·ca** (sklə·rot′i·kə). [< Gk. *sklēros* hard]

scle·ren·chy·ma (sklə·reng′kə·mə) *n. Bot.* Tissue composed of cells with hard, thick walls. [< Gk. *sklēros* hard + *enchyma* an infusion] —**scle·ren·chym·a·tous** (skler′en·kim′ə·təs, -ki′mə-) *adj.*

scle·ro·sis (sklə·rō′sis) *n.* Abnormal thickening and hardening of tissue. [< Gk. *sklēros* hard] —**scle·ro′sal** *adj.*

scle·rot·ic (sklə·rot′ik) *adj.* **1** Dense; firm, as the white of the eye. **2** Pertaining to or affected with sclerosis: also **scle·rosed** (-rōst′) [< Gk. *sklērotēs* hardness]

scoff (skôf, skof) *v.i.* **1** To speak with contempt or derision: often with *at.* —*v.t.* **2** To deride; mock. —*n.* **1** Words or actions of contempt. **2** A person or thing held in contempt. [ME *scof*] —**scoff′er** *n.* —**scoff′ing·ly** *adv.* —**Syn.** *v.* 1, 2 gibe, jeer, scorn, sneer, taunt.

scoff·law (skôf′lô, skof′-) *n.* A habitual or deliberate violator of traffic, safety, or public-health regulations.

scold (skōld) *v.t.* **1** To find fault with harshly. —*v.i.* **2** To find fault harshly or continuously. —*n.* One who scolds constantly: also **scold′er.** [< ON *skāld* a poet, satirist] —**scold′ing·ly** *adv.*

scol·lop (skol′əp) *n. & v.* SCALLOP.

sconce (skons) *n.* An ornamental wall bracket for holding a candle or other light. [< L *abscondere* to hide]

Wall sconce

scone (skōn, skon) *n.* **1** A thin oatmeal cake, baked on a griddle. **2** A teacake or soda biscuit. [? < MDu. *schoonbrot* fine bread]

scoop (skōōp) *n.* **1** The part of a dredge or steam shovel that lifts earth, sand, coal, etc. **2** A small shovellike implement for flour, sugar, ice cream, etc. **3** An implement for bailing, as water from a boat. **4** A spoon-shaped instrument for using in a cavity: a surgeon's *scoop.* **5** An act of scooping. **6** A scooping motion. **7** The amount scooped at once: a *scoop* of ice cream. **8** *Informal* A news story obtained and published ahead of rival papers. —*v.t.* **1** To take or dip out with a scoop. **2** To hollow out, as with a scoop; excavate. **3** *Informal* To heap up or gather in as if in scoopfuls; amass. **4** *Informal* To obtain and publish a news story before (a rival). [< MDu. *schope* a vessel for bailing out water] —**scoop'er** *n.*

scoop·ful (skōōp'fŏŏl') *n. pl.* **·fuls** As much as a scoop will hold.

scoot (skōōt) *v.i. Informal* To go quickly; dart off. —*n.* The act of scooting. [? < Scand.]

scoot·er (skōō'tər) *n.* **1** A child's vehicle consisting of a board mounted on two wheels and steered by a handle attached to the front axle, the rider standing with one foot on the board, using the other to push. **2** A similar vehicle powered by an internal-combustion engine and having a driver's seat: also **motor scooter.**

scope (skōp) *n.* **1** A range of view or action. **2** Capacity for achievement. **3** End in view; aim. **4** *Informal* A telescope, microscope, oscilloscope, etc. [< Gk. *skopos* a watcher]

-scope *combining form* An instrument for viewing, observing, or indicating: *microscope.* [< Gk. *skopos* a watcher]

sco·pol·a·mine (skō·pol'ə·mēn, -min, skō'pə·lam'ēn, -in) *n.* A depressant drug related to belladonna which blocks the formation of memories and various other functions of the brain. [< G. A. *Scopoli,* 1723–88, Italian naturalist]

-scopy *combining form* Observation; viewing: *microscopy.* [< Gk. *skopein* to watch]

scor·bu·tic (skôr·byōō'tik) *adj.* Of, like, or affected with scurvy. Also **scor·bu'ti·cal.** [< Med. L *scorbutus* scurvy] —**scor·bu'ti·cal·ly** *adv.*

scorch (skôrch) *v.t.* **1** To change the color, taste, etc., of, by slight burning. **2** To wither or shrivel by heat. **3** To criticize severely. —*v.i.* **4** To become scorched. **5** *Informal* To go at high speed. —*n.* **1** A superficial burn. **2** A mark caused by slight burning. [ME *scorchen*] —**scorch'ing·ly** *adv.*

scorched-earth policy (skôrcht'ûrth') The policy of destroying all crops, industrial equipment, dwellings, etc., before the arrival of an advancing enemy.

scorch·er (skôr'chər) *n.* **1** A person or thing that scorches. **2** *Informal* A very hot day. **3** *Informal* One who moves at great speed.

score (skôr, skōr) *n.* **1** The record of the winning points, counts, runs, etc., in competitive games. **2** A record of indebtedness; bill. **3** *Music* A printed or written copy of a musical composition in which all vocal and instrumental parts are shown on two or more connected staves one above another. **4** A group of 20. **5** *pl.* An indefinite large number. **6** A value assigned to an individual or group response to a test or series of tests, as of intelligence or performance. **7** *Slang* A success, esp. in making a purchase of narcotics. —**to pay off** (or **settle**) **old scores** To get even with someone for past wrongs, injuries, etc. —*v.* **scored, scor·ing** *v.t.* **1** To mark with notches, cuts, or lines. **2** To mark with cuts or lines for the purpose of keeping a tally. **3** To delete by means of a line drawn through: with *out.* **4** To make or gain, as points, runs, etc. **5** To count for a score of, as in games: A touchdown *scores* six points. **6** To rate or grade, as an examination paper. **7** *Music* **a** To orchestrate. **b** To arrange or adapt for an instrument. **8** *Informal* To criticize severely; scourge. **9** In cooking, to make superficial cuts in (meat, etc.). —*v.i.* **10** To make points, runs, etc., as in a game. **11** To keep score. **12** To make notches, cuts, etc. **13** To achieve a success. **14** *Slang* To purchase marihuana or narcotics. **15** *Slang* To succeed in having sexual intercourse with someone. [< ON *skor* notch] —**scor'er** *n.*

sco·ri·a (skôr'ē·ə, skō'rē·ə) *n. pl.* **·ri·ae** (-i·ē) **1** The refuse of melted metal or reduced ore. **2** Lava that is loose and cinderlike. [< Gk. *skōr* dung] —**sco'ri·a·ceous** (-ā'shəs) *adj.*

scorn (skôrn) *n.* **1** A feeling of contempt. **2** An object of supreme contempt. —*v.t.* **1** To hold in or treat with contempt; despise. **2** To reject with scorn; spurn. [< OF *escarn*] —**scorn'er, scorn'ful·ness** *n.* —**scorn'ful** *adj.* —**scorn'ful·ly** *adv.* —**Syn.** *n.* **1** disdain, scoffing. *v.* **1** contemn, detest.

Scor·pi·o (skôr'pē·ō) *n.* A constellation and the eighth sign of the zodiac; the Scorpion. Also **Scor·pi·us** (-əs). [< Gk. *skorpios*] • See ZODIAC.

scor·pi·on (skôr'pē·ən) *n.* **1** Any of an order of arachnids with long segmented tails bearing a poisonous sting. **2** In the Bible, a whip or scourge. [< Gk. *skorpios*]

Indian scorpion

Scorpion *n.* SCORPIO.

scot (skot) *n.* An assessment or tax. [< ON *skot*]

Scot (skot) *n.* A native of Scotland. • See SCOTCH.

Scot. Scotland; Scots; Scottish.

scotch (skoch) *v.t.* **1** To cut; scratch. **2** To wound so as to maim or cripple. **3** To quash or suppress: to *scotch* a rumor. —*n.* **1** A superficial cut; a notch. **2** A line traced on the ground, as for hopscotch. [?]

Scotch (skoch) *n.* **1** The people of Scotland collectively. **2** One or all of the dialects spoken by the people of Scotland. **3** Scotch whisky. —*adj.* Of or pertaining to Scotland, its inhabitants, or their dialects. • **Scotch, Scots, Scottish; Scot, Scotchman, Scotsman** Of the three proper adjectives, the form *Scotch* is accepted in Scotland only as applying to *Scotch plaid, Scotch terriers, Scotch whisky,* etc. In Scotland and northern England, the forms *Scots* and *Scottish* are preferred as applying to the people, language, culture, and institutions of Scotland: *Scots* or *Scottish English, the Scottish church.* In referring to an inhabitant of Scotland, *Scot* and *Scotsman* are preferred over the chiefly U.S. term *Scotchman.*

Scotch·man (skoch'mən) *n. pl.* **·men** (-mən) A Scot; Scotsman. • See SCOTCH.

Scotch tape A rolled strip of transparent adhesive tape: a trade name.

Scotch terrier A small terrier with compact body, short legs, and a grizzled coat.

Scotch whisky Whiskey made in Scotland from malted barley and having a rather smoky flavor. • Scotch whisky is traditionally spelled without the "e."

Scotch terrier

sco·ter (skō'tər) *n.* Any of several large ducks of northern regions, having black or dark brown plumage. [?< dial. E *scote,* var. of SCOOT]

scot-free (skot'frē') *adj.* **1** Free from any penalty, blame, or punishment. **2** Free from scot.

Scotland Yard 1 The headquarters of the London police: in full, **New Scotland Yard. 2** The London police force, esp. the detective bureau.

Scots (skots) *adj.* SCOTTISH. —*n.* The Scottish dialect of English. • See SCOTCH.

Scots·man (skots'mən) *n. pl.* **·men** (-mən) A Scot. • See SCOTCH.

Scot·ti·cism (skot'ə·siz'əm) *n.* A verbal usage or idiom peculiar to the Scottish people.

Scot·tish (skot'ish) *adj.* Pertaining to or characteristic of Scotland, its inhabitants, or their language. —*n.* **1** The dialect of English spoken in Scotland. **2** The people of Scotland collectively: with *the.* • See SCOTCH.

Scottish Gaelic The language of the Scottish Highlands.

Scottish terrier SCOTCH TERRIER. Also *Informal* **scot·tie** (skot'ē), **scot'ty.**

scoun·drel (skoun'drəl) *n.* An unscrupulous, dishonest person; villain. —*adj.* Villainous; base. [?] —**scoun'drel·ly** *adj.*

scour[1] (skour) *v.t.* **1** To clean or brighten by thorough washing and rubbing. **2** To remove dirt, grease, etc., from; clean. **3** To clear by means of a strong current of water; flush. —*v.i.* **4** To rub something vigorously so as to clean or brighten it. **5** To become bright or clean by rubbing. —*n.* **1** The act of scouring. **2** A cleanser used in scouring. **3** *Usu. pl.* A dysentery affecting cattle. [<OF *escurer*] —**scour′er** *n.* —**Syn.** *v.* **1** polish, scrub. **2** cleanse.

scour² (skour) *v.t.* **1** To range over or through, as in making a search. **2** To move or run swiftly over or along. —*v.i.* **3** To range swiftly about, as in making a search. [ME *scoure*]

scourge (skûrj) *n.* **1** A whip for inflicting suffering or punishment. **2** Any severe punishment. **3** Any means for causing suffering or death: the *scourge* of cholera. —*v.t.* **scourged, scourg·ing** **1** To whip severely; flog. **2** To punish severely; afflict. [<LL *excoriare* flay] —**scourg′er** *n.*

scout¹ (skout) *n.* **1** A person, plane, etc., sent out to observe and get information, as of the position or strength of an enemy in war. **2** The act of scouting. **3** A person in search of promising performers in athletics, entertainment, etc.: a talent *scout*. **4** A member of the Girl Scouts or the Boy Scouts. **5** A fellow; guy: usu. in the phrase **a good scout**. —*v.t.* **1** To observe or spy upon for the purpose of gaining information. —*v.i.* **2** To go or act as a scout. — **scout around** To go in search. [<L *auscultare* to listen] —**scout′er** *n.*

scout² (skout) *v.t. & v.i.* To reject with disdain. [<Scand.]

scout·mas·ter (skout′mas′tər, -mäs′-) *n.* The adult leader of a troop of Boy Scouts.

scow (skou) *n.* A large boat with a flat bottom and square ends, chiefly used to carry freight, garbage, etc. [<Du. *schouw*]

scowl (skoul) *n.* **1** A lowering of the brows, as in anger. **2** Gloomy aspect. —*v.i.* **1** To contract the brows in anger, sullenness, or disapproval. **2** To look threatening; lower. —*v.t.* **3** To affect or express by scowling. [?<Scand.]

scr. scrip; script; scruple (weight).

scrab·ble (skrab′əl) *v.* **·bled, ·bling** *v.i.* **1** To scratch, scrape, or paw. **2** To scribble. **3** To struggle or strive. —*v.t.* **4** To scrible on. **5** To scrape together. —*n.* **1** The act of scrabbling; a moving on hands and feet or knees. **2** A scrambling effort. [<Du. *schrabbelen*] —**scrab′bler** *n.*

scrag (skrag) *v.t.* **scragged, scrag·ging** *Informal* To wring the neck of; garrote. —*n.* **1** *Slang* The neck. **2** A lean, bony person or animal. [?<Scand.]

scrag·gly (skrag′lē) *adj.* **·gli·er, ·gli·est** Uneven; irregular; jagged: a *scraggly* beard.

scrag·gy (skrag′ē) *adj.* **·gi·er, ·gi·est** **1** SCRAGGLY. **2** Lean; scrawny. —**scrag′gi·ly** *adv.* —**scrag′gi·ness** *n.*

scram (skram) *v.i.* **scrammed, scram·ming** *Slang* To go away; leave quickly. [Short for SCRAMBLE]

scram·ble (skram′bəl) *v.* **·bled, ·bling** *v.i.* **1** To move by clambering or crawling. **2** To struggle in a disorderly manner; scuffle. **3** To strive for something in such a manner. —*v.t.* **4** To mix together haphazardly or confusedly. **5** To gather or collect hurriedly or confusedly. **6** To cook (eggs) with the yolks and whites stirred together. **7** *Telecom.* To encode (a message) so that a special decoder is needed to make it intelligible. —*n.* **1** A difficult climb, as over rough terrain. **2** A struggle for possession: a *scramble* for power. [?] —**scram′bler** *n.*

scrap¹ (skrap) *n.* **1** A small piece; fragment. **2** A small part of something written. **3** *pl.* Bits of unused food. **4** Old or refuse metal. —*v.t.* **scrapped, scrap·ping** **1** To break up into scrap. **2** To discard. —*adj.* Having the form of scraps: *scrap* metal. [<ON *skrap* scraps] —**Syn.** **1** bit, chip, segment, shard. **3** leftovers.

scrap² (skrap) *Informal v.i.* **scrapped, scrap·ping** To fight; quarrel. —*n.* A fight; quarrel; squabble. [?<SCRAPE, *n.* (def. 2)] —**scrap′per** *n.*

scrap·book (skrap′book′) *n.* **1** A blank book in which to paste pictures, cuttings from periodicals, etc. **2** A personal notebook.

scrape (skrāp) *v.* **scraped, scrap·ing** *v.t.* **1** To rub, as with something rough or sharp, so as to abrade. **2** To remove an outer layer thus: with *off, away*, etc. **3** To rub (a rough or sharp object) across a surface. **4** To rub roughly across or against (a surface). **5** To dig or form by scratching or scraping. **6** To gather or accumulate with effort or dif-

ficulty. —*v.i.* **7** To scrape something. **8** To rub with a grating noise. **9** To make a grating noise. **10** To draw the foot backward along the ground in bowing. **11** To manage or get along with difficulty. **12** To be very or overly economical. —*n.* **1** The act or effect of scraping; also, the noise made by scraping. **2** A difficult situation. **3** A quarrel or fight. **4** A scraping or drawing back of the foot in bowing. [<ON *skrapa*] —**scrap′er** *n.*

scrap·ing (skrā′ping) *n.* **1** The act of one who or that which scrapes. **2** The sound so produced. **3** *Usu. pl.* Something scraped off or together.

scrap·ple (skrap′əl) *n.* Cornmeal cooked with scraps of pork and spices and molded into a firm loaf to be sliced for frying.

scrap·py¹ (skrap′ē) *adj.* **·pi·er, ·pi·est** Composed of scraps; fragmentary. —**scrap′pi·ly** *adv.* —**scrap′pi·ness** *n.*

scrap·py² (skrap′ē) *adj.* **·pi·er, ·pi·est** *Informal* **1** Ready and willing to fight. **2** Strongly competitive; gritty; tough. — **scrap′pi·ly** *adv.* —**scrap′pi·ness** *n.*

scratch (skrach) *v.t.* **1** To tear or mark the surface of with something sharp or rough. **2** To scrape or dig with something sharp or rough. **3** To scrape lightly with the nails, etc., as to relieve itching. **4** To rub with a grating sound; scrape. **5** To write or draw awkwardly or hurriedly. **6** To erase or cancel by scratches or marks. **7** To withdraw (an entry) from a competition, race, etc. —*v.i.* **8** To use the nails or claws, as in fighting or digging. **9** To scrape the skin, etc., lightly, as to relieve itching. **10** To make a grating noise. **11** To manage or get along with difficulty. **12** To withdraw from a game, race, etc., —*n.* **1** A mark or incision made on a surface by scratching. **2** A slight flesh wound or cut. **3** The sound of scratching. **4** The line from which contestants start, as in racing. **5** *Slang* Money. —**from scratch** From the beginning; from nothing. —**up to scratch** *Informal* Meeting the standard or requirement. —*adj.* **1** Done by chance; haphazard. **2** Made for hurried notes, figuring, etc.: a *scratch* pad. **3** Chosen hastily and at random: a *scratch* team. [<MDu. *cratsen*] —**scratch′er** *n.*

scratch·y (skrach′ē) *adj.* **scratch·i·er, scratch·i·est** **1** Consisting of scratches: *scratchy* handwriting. **2** Making a scratching noise. **3** Causing itching: a *scratchy* sweater. —**scratch′i·ly** *adv.* —**scratch′i·ness** *n.*

scrawl (skrôl) *v.t. & v.i.* To write hastily or illegibly. —*n.* Irregular or careless writing. [?] —**scrawl′er** *n.*

scraw·ny (skrô′nē) *adj.* **·ni·er, ·ni·est** Lean and bony. [?] —**scraw′ni·ness** *n.*

scream (skrēm) *v.i.* **1** To utter a prolonged, piercing cry, as of pain, terror, or surprise. **2** To make a piercing sound: the wind *screamed* in the trees. **3** To laugh loudly or immoderately. **4** To use heated, hysterical language. —*v.t.* **5** To utter with a scream. —*n.* **1** A loud, shrill, prolonged cry or sound. **2** *Informal* A hugely entertaining person or thing. [<ON *skraema* to scare] —**scream′ing·ly** *adv.*

scream·er (skrē′mər) *n.* **1** One who or that which screams. **2** A South American wading bird, related to the ducks. **3** *Slang* A sensational headline in a newspaper.

screech (skrēch) *n.* A shrill, harsh cry; shriek. —*v.t.* **1** To utter with a screech. —*v.i.* **2** To shriek. [<ON *skrækja*] — **screech′er** *n.* —**screech′y** *adj.* (**·i·er, ·i·est**)

screech owl **1** Any of various small owls emitting a high-pitched wail. **2** The barn owl.

screed (skrēd) *n.* A prolonged spoken or written tirade; harangue. [<OE *scrēade*]

screen (skrēn) *n.* **1** Something that separates or shelters, as a light partition. **2** A coarse or fine metal mesh used for sifting, or as protection: a window *screen*. **3** Something that serves to conceal or protect: a smoke *screen*. **4** A surface, as a canvas or curtain, on which motion pictures and slides may be shown. **5** The surface of a cathode-ray tube, on which television pictures, computer information or graphics, etc., may be viewed. —**the screen** Motion pictures. —*v.t.* **1** To shield or conceal with or as with a screen. **2** To pass through a screen or sieve; sift. **3** To classify or scan for suitability, qualifications, etc.: to *screen* applicants for a job. **4** To project on a motion-picture screen. **5** To photograph (a motion picture); shoot. **6** To adapt (a play, novel, story, etc.) for motion pictures. —*v.i.* **7** To be suitable for representation as a motion picture. [<OF *escren*]

screen·ing (skrēn'ing) n. 1 A meshlike material, as for a window screen. 2 A showing of a motion picture. 3 pl. The parts of anything passed through or retained by a sieve; siftings.

screw (skrōō) n. 1 A device resembling a nail but having a slotted head and a tapering or cylindrical spiral for driving into wood, metal, plaster, etc., or for insertion into a corresponding threaded part. 2 A cylindrical socket with a spiral groove or thread 3 Anything having the form of a screw. 4 SCREW PRO-peller • See RUDDER. 5 A turn of or as of a screw. 6 Pressure; force.

a   b   c
Screws
a. wood screw.
b. thumbscrew.
c. round-headed screw.

7 Slang A prison guard. 8 Brit. Slang An old, worn-out, or bad-tempered horse. —**have a screw loose** Slang To be mentally deranged, eccentric, etc. —**put the screws on** (or to) Slang To exert pressure or force upon. —v.t. 1 To tighten, fasten, attach, etc., by a screw or screws. 2 To turn or twist. 3 To force; urge: to screw one's courage to the sticking point. 4 To contort, as one's features. 5 To practice oppression or extortion on; defraud. 6 To obtain by extortion. 7 Slang To act maliciously toward; harm. —v.i. 8 To turn as a screw. 9 To become attached or detached by means of twisting: with on, off, etc. 10 To twist or wind. 11 To practice oppression or extortion. —**screw up** Slang To botch; make a mess of: He screwed up his career. [< OF escroue nut] —**screw'er** n.

screw·ball (skrōō'bôl') n. 1 In baseball, a pitch thrown with a wrist motion opposite to that used for the outcurve. 2 Slang An unconventional or erratic person.

screw cap A cap or lid designed to screw onto the threaded top of a bottle, jar, or the like.

screw·driv·er (skrōō'drī'vər) n. A tool for turning screws.

screwed-up (skrōōd'up') adj. Slang 1 Disorganized or disorderly. 2 Mentally ill or emotionally distressed.

screw propeller An array of radial blades set at an angle on a rotary shaft to produce a spiral action in a fluid, used to propel ships, etc. • See RUDDER.

screw thread The spiral ridge of a screw or nut.

screw·y (skrōō'ē) adj. screw·i·er, screw·i·est Slang Irrational; eccentric. —**screw'i·ly** adv. —**screw'i·ness** n.

scrib·ble (skrib'əl) v. -bled, -bling v.t. 1 To write hastily and carelessly. 2 To cover with careless or illegible writing. —v.i. 3 To write carelessly or hastily. 4 To make illegible or meaningless marks. —n. 1 Hasty, careless writing. 2 Meaningless lines and marks; scrawl. [< L scribere write] —**scrib'bler** n. —**scrib'bly** adj.

scribe (skrīb) n. 1 One who copied manuscripts and books before printing was invented. 2 A clerk, public writer, or amanuensis. 3 An author: used humorously. 4 An ancient Jewish teacher of the Mosaic law. [< L scribere write] —**scrib'al** adj.

scrim (skrim) n. A lightweight, open-mesh, usu. cotton fabric, used for curtains, etc. [?]

scrim·mage (skrim'ij) n. 1 A rough-and-tumble contest; fracas. 2 In American football, a mass play from the line of scrimmage after the ball has been placed on the ground and snapped back, the play ending when the ball is dead. —**line of scrimmage** In football, the hypothetic line, parallel to the goal lines, on which the ball rests and along which the opposing linemen take position at the start of play. —v.t. & v.i. ·maged, ·mag·ing To engage in a scrimmage. [Var. of SKIRMISH]

scrimp (skrimp) v.i. 1 To be very economical or stingy. —v.t. 2 To be overly sparing toward; skimp. 3 To cut too small, narrow, etc. [?] —**scrimp'er** n.

scrim·py (skrim'pē) adj. ·i·er, ·i·est Skimpy or meager. —**scrimp'i·ly** adv. —**scrimp'i·ness** n.

scrim·shaw (skrim'shô) n. 1 The carving and engraving of usu. whalebone or whale ivory, as by American sailors. 2 An article so made. —v.t. 1 To make into scrimshaw by carving or engraving. —v.i. 2 To create scrimshaw. [?]

scrip (skrip) n. 1 Writing. 2 Any of various certificates showing that a person is entitled to receive something, as a fractional share of stock, a share of jointly owned property, etc. 3 A piece of paper money less than a dollar, formerly issued during emergencies in the U.S. [<SCRIPT]

Scrip. Scriptural; Scripture(s).

script (skript) n. 1 Handwriting; also, a particular style of

This line is in script.

handwriting. 2 Printed matter in imitation of handwriting. 3 A manuscript or text. 4 The written text of a play, TV show, etc. [<L scribere write]

scrip·ture (skrip'chər) n. 1 The sacred writings of any people. 2 Any authoritative book or writing. [<L scribere write] —**scrip'tur·al** adj. —**scrip'tur·al·ly** adv.

Scripture (skrip'chər) n. 1 Usu. pl. The books of the Old and New Testaments; the Bible; also **(the) Holy Scripture.** 2 A passage from the Bible.

scriv·en·er (skriv'ən·ər, skriv'nər) n. 1 A clerk or scribe. 2 A notary. [<L scribere write]

scrod (skrod) n. A young codfish, esp. when split and prepared for broiling. [<MDu. schrode]

scrof·u·la (skrof'yə·lə) n. Tuberculosis of the lymph glands. [<LL scrofa a breeding sow] —**scrof'u·lous** adj. —**scrof'u·lous·ly** adv. —**scrof'u·lous·ness** n.

scroll (skrōl) n. 1 A roll of parchment, paper, etc., esp. one containing or intended for writing. 2 The writing on such a roll. 3 Anything resembling a parchment roll, as a convoluted ornament or part. —v.t. To move one or more lines of copy off the top of a computer screen, so that additional lines may be displayed at the bottom, or vice versa. [<AF escrowe]

scroll saw A narrow-bladed saw for cutting thin sheets of wood into curved or convoluted shapes.

scrooge (skrōōj) n. A miserly, misanthropic person. [<Ebenezer Scrooge, a miserly character in Dickens' A Christmas Carol]

scro·tum (skrō'təm) n. pl. ·ta (·tə) or ·tums The pouch that contains the testes. [L] —**scro'tal** adj.

scrounge (skrounj) v.t. & v.i. scrounged, scoung·ing Slang 1 To hunt about and take (something); pilfer. 2 To mooch; sponge. [?] —**scroung'er** n.

scrub¹ (skrub) v. scrubbed, scrub·bing v.t. 1 To rub vigorously in washing. 2 To remove (dirt, etc.) by such action. —v.i. 3 To rub something vigorously in washing. —n. The act of scrubbing. [<MDu. schrobben] —**scrub'ber** n.

scrub² (skrub) n. 1 A stunted tree. 2 A tract of stunted trees or shrubs. 3 A domestic animal of inferior breed. 4 A poor, insignificant person. 5 In sports, a player not on the varsity or regular team. 6 A game of baseball contrived hastily by a few players. —adj. 1 Undersized or inferior. 2 Consisting of or participated in by untrained players or scrubs: scrub team. [Var. of SHRUB]

scrub·by (skrub'ē) adj. ·bi·er, ·bi·est 1 Of stunted growth. 2 Covered with or consisting of scrub or underbrush. —**scrub'bi·ly** adv. —**scrub'bi·ness** n.

scrub oak Any of various dwarf oaks.

scruff (skruf) n. The nape or outer back part of the neck. [Earlier scuff < ON skopt hair]

scruf·fy (skruf'ē) adj. ·i·er, ·i·est 1 Shabby; seedy. 2 Worthless. [<OE scruf scurf] —**scruf'fi·ly** adv. —**scruf'fi·ness** n.

scrump·tious (skrump'shəs) adj. Slang Elegant or stylish; splendid. [? Var. of SUMPTUOUS] —**scrump'tious·ly** adv.

scru·ple (skrōō'pəl) n. 1 Doubt or uncertainty about what one should do. 2 Reluctance arising from conscientious disapproval. 3 An apothecaries' weight of 20 grains. 4 A minute quantity. —v.t. & v.i. ·pled, ·pling To hesitate (doing) from considerations of right or wrong. [<L scrupus a sharp stone]

scru·pu·lous (skrōō'pyə·əs) adj. 1 Cautious in action for fear of doing wrong; conscientious. 2 Resulting from the exercise of scruples; careful. —**scru'pu·lous·ly** adv. —**scru'pu·los'i·ty** (-los'ə·tē), **scru'pu·lous·ness** n. —**Syn.** 1 ethical, honest, upright. 2 exact, precise.

scru·ti·neer (skrōō'tə·nir') n. 1 One who scrutinizes. 2

Brit. & Can. One who oversees a polling place, checking voters against the registry, etc.

scru·ti·nize (skrōō′tə·nīz) *v.t.* **·nized, ·niz·ing** To observe carefully; examine in detail. **—scru′ti·niz′er** *n.* **—scru′ti·niz′ing·ly** *adv.*

scru·ti·ny (skrōō′tə·nē) *n. pl.* **·nies** Close investigation; careful inspection. [< L *scrutari* examine]

scu·ba (skyōō′bə) *n.* A device worn by a free-swimming diver to provide a supply of air for breathing. [< *s(elf-) c(ontained) u(nderwater) b(reathing) a(pparatus)*]

scuba diving Swimming under water with the aid of a scuba. **—scuba diver**

scud (skud) *v.i.* **scud·ded, scud·ding** To move, run, or fly swiftly. **—n. 1** The act of scudding. **2** Light clouds driven rapidly before the wind. [?]

scuff (skuf) *v.i.* **1** To drag the feet in walking; shuffle. — *v.t.* **2** To scrape (the floor, ground, etc.) with the feet. **3** To roughen the surface by rubbing or scraping: to *scuff* one's shoes. **—n.** The act of scuffing; also, the noise so made. [? < ON *skūfa* shove]

scuf·fle (skuf′əl) *v.i.* **·fled, ·fling 1** To struggle roughly or confusedly. **2** To drag one's feet; shuffle. **—n.** A disorderly struggle; fracas. [? < Scand.] **—scuf′fler** *n.*

scull (skul) *n.* **1** A long oar worked from side to side over the stern of a boat. **2** A light oar, used in pairs by one person. **3** A small boat for sculling. **—v.t. & v.i.** To propel (a boat) by a scull or sculls. [ME *sculle*] **—scull′er** *n.*

scul·ler·y (skul′ər·ē) *n. pl.* **·ler·ies** A room where kitchen utensils are kept and cleaned. [< L *scutella* a tray]

scul·lion (skul′yən) *n. Archaic* A servant who scours dishes, pots, and kettles. [< OF *escouillon* a mop]

scul·pin (skul′pin) *n.* Any of a family of spiny fishes having a large head and fanlike pectoral fins. [< L *scorpaena,* a scorpionlike fish]

sculpt (skulpt) *v.t. & v.i. Informal* SCULPTURE.

sculp·tor (skulp′tər) *n.* A person who sculptures. **—sculp′tress** (-tris) *n. Fem.*

sculp·ture (skulp′chər) *n.* **1** The art of fashioning three-dimensional figures, busts, abstract pieces, etc., of stone, wood, clay, bronze, or other material. **2** A piece or group produced by sculpture. **—v.t. ·tured, ·tur·ing 1** To fashion, (stone, wood, metal, etc.) into sculpture. **2** To represent or portray by sculpture. **3** To embellish with sculpture. **4** To change (features on the surface of the earth) by erosion. **—v.i. 5** To work as a sculptor. [< L *sculpere* carve in stone] **—sculp′tur·al** *adj.* **—sculp′tur·al·ly** *adv.*

scum (skum) *n.* **1** A layer of impure or extraneous matter on the surface of a liquid. **2** Low, contemptible people. — *v.* **scummed, scum·ming** *v.t.* **1** To take scum from; skim. — *v.i.* **2** To become covered with or form scum. [< MDu. *schuum*] **—scum′mi·ness** *n.* **—scum′my** *adj.* (**·mi·er, ·mi·est**)

scup (skup) *n.* A small porgy of the E coast of the U.S. [< Algon.]

scup·per (skup′ər) *n.* A hole or gutter bordering a ship's deck, to let water run off. [? < OF *escope* a bailing scoop]

scup·per·nong (skup′ər·nong) *n.* **1** A light-colored grape of the S U.S. **2** A sweet wine made from this grape. [< the *Scuppernong* River in N.C.]

scurf (skûrf) *n.* **1** Loose scales thrown off by the skin, as dandruff. **2** Any scaly matter adhering to a surface. [< OE] **—scurf′i·ness** *n.* **—scurf′y** *adj.* (**·i·er, ·i·est**)

scur·ri·lous (skûr′ə·ləs) *adj.* Grossly offensive or indecent; coarse and abusive: a *scurrilous* attack. [< L *scurra* a buffoon] **—scur·ril·i·ty** (skə·ril′ə·tē) (*pl.* **·ties**), **scur′ri·lous·ness** *n.* **—scur′ri·lous·ly** *adv.*

scur·ry (skûr′ē) *v.i.* **·ried, ·ry·ing** To move or go hurriedly; scamper. **—n. pl. ·ries** The act or sound of scurrying. [?] — **Syn.** *v.* dart, dash, scoot, scuttle.

scur·vy (skûr′vē) A disease due to lack of vitamin C, marked by weakness, spotted skin, and bleeding gums. — *adj.* **·vi·er, ·vi·est** Low or contemptible. [< SCURF] **—scur′vi·ly** *adv.* **—scur′vi·ness** *n.*

scut (skut) *n.* A short tail, as of a rabbit or deer. [ME, a tail, a hare]

scutch·eon (skuch′ən) *n.* ESCUTCHEON.

scu·tel·late (skyōō·tel′it, skyōō′tə·lāt) *adj. Zool.* Covered with small plates or scales: also **scu′tel·lat·ed** (-lā′tid). [< L *scutum* a shield]

scu·tel·lum (skyōō·tel′əm) *n. pl.* **·la** (-ə) A small protective plate or scale, as on the tarsus of a bird. [< L *scutum* a shield] **—scu·tel′lar** *adj.*

scut·tle[1] (skut′l) *n.* **1** A small opening or hatchway with movable lid or cover, esp. in the roof or wall of a house, or in the deck or side of a ship. **2** The lid closing such an opening. **—v.t. ·tled, ·tling 1** To sink (a ship) by making holes below the water line. **2** To wreck or destroy. [< MF *escoutille* a hatchway]

scut·tle[2] (skut′l) *n.* A metal vessel or hod for coal. [< OE *scutel* a dish, platter]

scut·tle[3] (skut′l) *v.i.* **·tled, ·tling** To run in haste; scurry. — *n.* A hurried run or departure. [?] **—scut′tler** *n.*

scut·tle·butt (skut′l·but) *n.* **1** A drinking fountain aboard ship. **2** *Slang* Rumor; gossip. [Orig. *scuttled butt,* a lidded cask for drinking water]

scu·tum (skyōō′təm) *n. pl.* **·ta** (-tə) **1** A large shield carried by Roman foot soldiers. **2** *Zool.* A large, horny protective plate or scale: also **scute**. [L] **—scu·tate** (skyōō′tāt) *adj.*

Scyl·la (sil′ə) *Gk. Myth.* A sea monster who dwelt in a cave on the Italian coast opposite the whirlpool Charybdis. **—between Scylla and Charybdis** Between two equally menacing situations, one of which must be dealt with.

scythe (sīth) *n.* A tool composed of a long curved blade fixed at an angle to a long handle, used for mowing, reaping, etc. **—v.t. scythed, scyth·ing** To cut with a scythe. [< OE *sīthe*]

Scyth·i·a (sith′ē·ə) *n.* An ancient region of SE Europe, lying N of the Black Sea. **—Scyth′i·an** *adj., n.*

SD South Dakota (P.O. abbr.).

S.D., S. Dak. South Dakota.

SDR, S.D.R., SDRs, S.D.R.s Special Drawing Rights.

SE, S.E., se, s.e. southeast; southeastern.

Se selenium.

sea (sē) *n.* **1** The great body of salt water covering most of the earth's surface; the ocean. **2** A large body of salt water partly or wholly enclosed by land: the Adriatic *Sea.* **3** An inland body of water, esp. if salty: the *Sea* of Galilee. **4** The state of the ocean with regard to the course, flow, swell, or turbulence of the waves. **5** A heavy wave or swell. **6** Anything vast or boundless that resembles or suggests the sea. **—at sea 1** On the ocean. **2** Bewildered. **—follow the sea** To follow the occupation of a sailor. **—put to sea** To sail away from the land [< OE *sæ*]

sea anemone Any of various soft-bodied, sessile marine polyps with tentacles resembling the petals of a flower.

sea bass Any of various carnivorous food fishes of U.S. coastal waters.

Sea·bee (sē′bē′) *n.* A member of one of the construction battalions of the U.S. Navy. [< *c(onstruction) b(attalion)*]

sea·board (sē′bôrd′, -bōrd′) *adj.* Bordering on the sea. **—n.** The seashore or seacoast and the adjoining region. [< SEA + *board* a border < OE *bord*]

Sea anemone
a. tentacles contracted. b. extended.

sea bread HARDTACK.

sea breeze A breeze blowing from the sea toward land.

sea calf A spotted seal of the E U.S. coast.

sea·coast (sē′kōst′) *n.* The land on or close to the sea.

sea cow **1** Any of various large aquatic mammals, as the manatee or the dugong. **2** WALRUS.

sea cucumber Any of various cylindrical echinoderms having a rosette of tentacles at the mouth.

sea dog **1** SEAL[2]. **2** DOGFISH. **3** A sailor with long experience at sea.

sea eagle Any of various fish-eating birds related to the bald eagle.

sea·far·er (sē′fâr′ər) *n.* A sailor; mariner.

sea·far·ing (sē′fâr′ing) *n.* **1** The occupation of a sailor. **2** Traveling over the sea. **—adj.** Of, pertaining to, given to, or engaged in seafaring.

sea·food (sē′fōōd′) *n.* Edible saltwater fish or shellfish.

sea-girt (sē′gûrt′) *adj.* Surrounded by the sea.

sea·go·ing (sē′gō′ing) *adj.* **1** Designed or adapted for use on the ocean. **2** SEAFARING.

sea green Bluish green.

sea gull A gull, esp. one of a widely distributed gregarious species.

sea horse 1 Any of various small fishes found in warm seas, having a long curled tail and a head resembling that of a horse. **2** A walrus. **3** A mythical creature, half horse and half fish.

sea king A viking pirate chief of the Middle Ages.

seal[1] (sēl) *n.* **1** An impression made on a letter, document, etc., to prove its authenticity. **2** A wax wafer, piece of paper, etc., bearing such an authenticating impression. **3** A device with a raised or cut initial, word, or design, used to make such an impression. **4** A stamp, ring, etc., bearing such a device. **5** Something used to close or secure a letter, door, lid, wrapper, joint, passage, etc., firmly. **6** Anything that confirms, ratifies, or guarantees; pledge. **7** A sign or indication; token. **8** An ornamental stamp for packages, etc. —*v.t.* **1** To affix a seal to, as to prove authenticity or prevent tampering. **2** To stamp or otherwise impress a seal upon in order to attest to weight, quality, etc. **3** To fasten or close with a seal: to *seal* a glass jar. **4** To confirm the genuineness or truth of, as a bargain. **5** To establish or settle finally. **6** To secure, set, or fill up, as with plaster. [< L *sigillum* a small picture, seal] —**seal′a·ble** *adj.* —**seal′er** *n.*

Sea horse

Great Seal of the United States

seal[2] (sēl) *n.* **1** Any of various species of sea mammals with a short tail and four webbed flippers, with which it swims and waddles ashore. **2** The commercially valued fur of the **fur seal. 3** Leather made from the hide of a seal. —*v.i.* To hunt seals. [< OE *seolh*] —**seal′er** *n.*

sea legs The ability to walk aboard a ship in motion without losing one's balance or suffering from seasickness.

Seal

sea level The average level of the surface of the ocean.

sea lily CRINOID.

sealing wax A pigmented mixture of shellac and resin with turpentine that is fluid when heated but becomes solid as it cools: used to seal papers, etc.

sea lion One of various large, eared seals, esp. the California sea lion.

seal ring SIGNET RING.

seal·skin (sēl′skin′) *n.* **1** The pelt or fur of the fur seal, often dyed dark brown or black. **2** An article made of this fur. —*adj.* Made of sealskin.

Sea·ly·ham terrier (sē′lē·ham, -əm) One of a breed of terriers with short legs, a wide skull, square jaws, and a wiry white coat. [Orig. bred in *Sealyham,* Wales]

seam (sēm) *n.* **1** A visible line of junction between parts, as the edges of two pieces of cloth sewn together. • See PINK[2]. **2** A line, ridge, or groove marking joined edges, as of boards. **3** Any similar line, ridge, etc., as that formed by a scar, wrinkle, etc. **4** A thin layer or stratum, as of rock or ore. —*v.t.* **1** To unite by means of a seam. **2** To mark with a cut, furrow, wrinkle, etc. —*v.i.* **3** To crack open; become fissured. [< OE *sēam*] —**seam′er** *n.*

sea·man (sē′mən) *n. pl.* **·men** (-mən) **1** An enlisted man in the navy or in the coast guard, graded according to his rank. **2** A mariner; sailor. —**sea′man·like′** (-līk′) *adj.* — **sea′man·ly** *adj., adv.*

sea·man·ship (sē′mən·ship) *n.* The skill of a seaman in handling sea craft.

sea mew A gull, esp. the European mew.

sea·mount (sē′mount′) *n.* A submarine mountain.

seam·stress (sēm′stris) *n.* A woman whose occupation is sewing. [< OE *sēam* seam + -ST(E)R + -ESS]

seam·y (sē′mē) *adj.* **seam·i·er, seam·i·est 1** Like, formed by, or characterized by seams. **2** Showing an unworthy, unpleasant, or unpresentable aspect. —**seam′i·ness** *n.* — **Syn. 2** sordid, degraded, squalid, disagreeable.

sé·ance (sā′äns) *n.* **1** A session or sitting. **2** A meeting of persons seeking to receive communications from spirits of the dead. [F < OF *seoir* sit]

sea·plane (sē′plān′) *n.* An airplane that can take off from and land on the water.

sea·port (sē′pôrt′, -pōrt′) *n.* **1** A harbor or port accessible to seagoing ships. **2** A town or city located at such a place.

sea purse The leathery egg case of certain sharks, rays, etc.

sear (sir) *v.t.* **1** To wither; dry up. **2** To burn the surface of; scorch. **3** To burn or cauterize; brand. **4** To make callous; harden. —*v.i.* **5** To become withered; dry up. —*adj.* Dried or blasted; withered. —*n.* A scar or brand. [< OE *sēar* dry]

search (sûrch) *v.t.* **1** To look through or explore thoroughly in order to find something. **2** To subject (a person) to a search. **3** To examine with close attention; probe. **4** To penetrate or pierce: The wind *searches* my clothes. **5** To learn by examination or investigation: with *out.* —*v.i.* **6** To make a search. —*n.* **1** The act of searching. **2** An act of boarding and inspecting a ship in pursuance of the right to search. [< LL *circare* go round, explore] — **search′a·ble** *adj.* —**search′er** *n.*

search·ing (sûr′ching) *adj.* **1** Investigating thoroughly. **2** Keenly penetrating. —**search′ing·ly** *adv.* —**search′ing·ness** *n.*

search·light (sûrch′līt′) *n.* **1** An apparatus consisting of a powerful light equipped with a reflector and mounted so that it can be projected in various directions. **2** The light so projected.

search warrant A warrant authorizing a police officer to search a house or other specified place, as for stolen goods.

sea·scape (sē′skāp′) *n.* **1** A view of the sea. **2** A picture presenting such a view.

sea·shell (sē′shel′) *n.* The shell of a marine mollusk.

sea·shore (sē′shôr′, -shōr′) *n.* Land bordering on the sea.

sea·sick (sē′sik′) *adj.* Suffering from seasickness.

sea·sick·ness (sē′sik′nis) *n.* Nausea, dizziness, etc., caused by the motion of a ship at sea.

sea·side (sē′sīd′) *n.* SEASHORE.

sea·son (sē′zən) *n.* **1** A division of the year as determined by the earth's position with respect to the sun: spring, summer, autumn, and winter. **2** A period of time. **3** A period of special activity or when a specified place is frequented: usu. with *the:* the opera *season;* the Palm Beach *season.* **4** A fit or suitable time. **5** The time of and surrounding a major holiday. —**in season 1** At a time of availability and fitness, as for eating: Clams are *in season* during the summer. **2** In or at the right time. **3** Able to be killed or taken by permission of the law. **4** Ready to mate or breed: said of animals. —*v.t.* **1** To increase the flavor or zest of (food), as by adding spices, etc. **2** To add zest or piquancy to. **3** To render more suitable for use. **4** To make fit, as by discipline; harden. **5** To mitigate or soften; moderate. —*v.i.* **6** To become seasoned. [< LL *satio* sowing time] —**sea′son·er** *n.*

sea·son·a·ble (sē′zən·ə·bəl) *adj.* **1** Being in keeping with the season or circumstances. **2** Done or occurring at the proper or best time. —**sea′son·a·ble·ness** *n.* —**sea′son·a·bly** *adv.* —**Syn. 1** timely, well-timed. **2** opportune, favorable, propitious, advantageous.

sea·son·al (sē′zən·əl) *adj.* Of, pertaining to, characteristic of, or happening during a season or the seasons. — **sea′son·al·ly** *adv.*

sea·son·ing (sē′zən·ing) *n.* **1** The process by which something is rendered fit for use. **2** Something added to give relish; esp., a condiment. **3** Something added to increase enjoyment, give zest, etc.

season ticket A ticket entitling the holder to something specified, as train trips, admission to entertainments, etc., during a certain period of time.

seat (sēt) *n.* 1 The thing on which one sits; a chair, bench, stool, etc. 2 That part of a thing upon which one rests in sitting, or upon which an object or another part rests. 3 That part of the person which sustains the weight of the body in sitting; buttocks. 4 That part of a garment which covers the buttocks. 5 The place where anything is situated or established: the *seat* of pain, the *seat* of a government. 6 A place of abode, esp. a large estate. 7 The privilege or right of membership in a legislative body, stock exchange, or the like. 8 The manner of sitting, as on horseback. 9 A surface or part upon which the base of anything rests. —*v.t.* 1 To place on a seat or seats; cause to sit down. 2 To have seats for; furnish with seats: The theater *seats* only 299 people. 3 To put a seat on or in; renew or repair the seat of. 4 To locate, settle, or center: usu. in the passive: The French government is *seated* in Paris. 5 To fix, set firmly, or establish in a certain position, place, etc. [< ON *sæti*]

seat belt A strap or harness that holds a passenger firmly in the seat, as while riding in a car or airplane.

seat·ing (sē'ting) *n.* 1 The act of providing with seats; also, the arrangement of such seats. 2 Fabric for upholstering seats. 3 A fitted support or base; a seat.

SEATO (sē'tō) Southeast Asia Treaty Organization.

sea urchin Any of various echinoderms shielded within a spine-covered, rounded case.

sea wall A wall for preventing erosion of the shore by the sea or for breaking the force of waves. —**sea-walled** (sē'-wôld') *adj.*

sea·ward (sē'wərd) *adj.* 1 Going or situated toward the sea. 2 Blowing, as wind, from the sea. —*adv.* In the direction of the sea: also **sea'wards.** —*n.* A direction or position toward the sea, away from land.

sea·way (sē'wā') *n.* 1 A way or route over the sea. 2 An inland waterway that receives ocean shipping. 3 The headway made by a ship. 4 A rough sea.

sea·weed (sē'wēd') *n.* Any marine plant or vegetation, esp. any multicellular alga.

sea·wor·thy (sē'wûr'thē) *adj.* In fit condition for a sea voyage. —**sea'wor'thi·ness** *n.*

se·ba·ceous (si·bā'shəs) *adj.* 1 Of, pertaining to, or resembling fat. 2 Secreting sebum. [< L *sebum* tallow]

se·bum (sē'bəm) *n.* An oily substance secreted by special glands in the skin. [L, tallow]

sec (sek) *adj.* French Dry: said of wines. Also *Italian* **sec·co** (sek'kō).

SEC, S.E.C. Securities and Exchange Commission.

sec. second(s); secondary; secretary; section(s); sector.

se·cant (sē'kant, -kənt) *adj.* Cutting, esp. into two parts; intersecting. —*n.* 1 *Geom.* A straight line intersecting a given curve. 2 *Trig.* A function equal to the reciprocal of the cosine. [< L *secare* to cut]

se·cede (si·sēd') *v.i.* **·ced·ed, ·ced·ing** To withdraw formally from a union, fellowship, etc., esp. from a political or religious organization. [< L *se-* apart + *cedere* go] — **se·ced'er** *n.*

Ratio of AB to AD is the secant of angle BAD. AB is secant of arc CD.

se·ces·sion (si·sesh'ən) *n.* 1 The act of seceding. 2 *Usu. cap. U.S.* The withdrawal of the Southern States from the Union in 1860–61. —**se·ces'sion·al** *adj.* —**se·ces'sion·ism, se·ces'sion·ist** *n.*

Seck·el (sek'əl, sik'əl) *n.* A variety of small, sweet pear. Also **Seckel pear.** [< the Pennsylvania farmer who introduced it]

se·clude (si·klōōd') *v.t.* **·clud·ed, ·clud·ing** 1 To remove and keep apart from the society of others; isolate. 2 To screen or shut off, as from view. [< L *se-* apart + *claudere* to shut]

se·clud·ed (si·klōō'did) *adj.* 1 Separated; living apart from others. 2 Protected or screened. —**se·clud'ed·ly** *adv.* —**se·clud'ed·ness** *n.*

se·clu·sion (si·klōō'zhən) *n.* 1 The act of secluding, or the state or condition of being secluded; solitude; retirement. 2 A secluded place. —**se·clu'sive** *adj.* —**se·clu'sive·ly** *adv.* —**se·clu'sive·ness** *n.*

sec·ond¹ (sek'ənd) *n.* 1 A unit of time, 1/60 of a minute. 2 A unit of angular measure, 1/60 of a minute. 3 An instant; moment: Wait a *second.* [< Med. L *seconda (minuta)*, lit., second (minute), i.e., the result of the second sexagesimal division]

sec·ond² (sek'ənd) *adj.* 1 Next in order, authority, responsibility, etc., after the first. 2 Ranking next below the first or best. 3 Of lesser quality or value; inferior; subordinate. 4 Identical with another or preceding one; other. 5 *Music* Lower in pitch, or rendering a secondary part. —*n.* 1 The one next after the first, as in order, rank, importance, etc. 2 The element of an ordered set that corresponds to the number two. 3 An attendant who supports or aids another, as in a duel. 4 *Often pl.* An article of merchandise of inferior quality. 5 *Music* **a** The interval between any tone and another a whole step or half step away from or below it. **b** A subordinate part, instrument, or voice. 6 In parliamentary law, the act or declaration by which a motion is seconded: Do I hear a *second*? 7 *pl. Informal* A second portion of food. —*v.t.* 1 To act as a supporter or assistant of; promote; stimulate; encourage. 2 To support formally, as a motion, resolution, etc. —*adv.* In the second order, place, rank, etc. [< L *secundus* following]

sec·on·dar·y (sek'ən·der'ē) *adj.* 1 Of second rank, grade, or influence; subordinate. 2 Depending on, resulting from, or following what is primary. 3 Second in order of occurrence or development. 4 *Electr.* Of or pertaining to the output of a transformer. —*n. pl.* **·dar·ies** 1 One who or that which is secondary or subordinate. 2 *Electr.* A secondary circuit or coil. —**sec'on·dar'i·ly** *adv.*

secondary accent See ACCENT.

secondary education Education beyond the elementary or primary, and below the college, level.

secondary school A school providing secondary education.

second best One who or that which is next after the best. —**sec'ond-best'** *adj.*

second childhood A time or condition of dotage; senility.

sec·ond-class (sek'ənd·klas', -kläs') *adj.* 1 Ranking next below the first or best; inferior, inadequate, etc. 2 Of, pertaining to, or belonging to a class next below the first: *second-class* mail, *second-class* ticket, etc. —*adv.* By using second-class travel accommodations or second-class mail.

sec·ond-guess (sek'ənd·ges') *v.t.* 1 To use hindsight in criticizing (an action, decision, etc., or the person responsible for it). 2 OUTGUESS. —**sec'ond-guess'er** *n.*

sec·ond-hand (sek'ənd·hand') *adj.* 1 Previously owned, worn, or used by another; not new. 2 Received from another; not direct from the original source: *secondhand* information. 3 Of, pertaining to, or dealing in merchandise that is not new. —*adv.* Indirectly.

second hand The hand that marks the seconds on a clock or a watch.

second lieutenant See GRADE.

sec·ond·ly (sek'ənd·lē) *adv.* In the second place; second.

second nature An acquired trait or habit so ingrained as to seem innate.

sec·ond-rate (sek'ənd·rāt') *adj.* Second or inferior in quality, size, rank, importance, etc.; second-class. —**sec'·ond-rat'er** *n.*

second sight The supposed capacity to see objects not actually present, to see into the future, etc. —**sec'ond-sight'ed** *adj.*

sec·ond-sto·ry man (sek'ənd·stôr'ē, -stō'rē) *Informal* A burglar who enters a building through an upstairs window. Also **sec'ond-sto'ry-man.**

sec·ond-string (sek'ənd·string') *adj. Informal* 1 In sports, being a substitute rather than a regular or starting player. 2 SECOND-RATE.

second thought A reevaluation or reconsideration of something following one's initial response or decision.

second wind 1 The return of easy breathing after a period of exertion or exercise. 2 A renewed capacity for the continuation of any effort.

se·cre·cy (sē'krə·sē) *n. pl.* **·cies** 1 The condition or quality of being secret; concealment. 2 The character of being secretive.

se·cret (sē′krit) *adj.* **1** Kept separate or hidden from view or knowledge, or from all persons except the individuals concerned; unseen. **2** Affording privacy; secluded. **3** Good at keeping secrets; close-mouthed. **4** Unrevealed or unavowed: a *secret* partner. **5** Not revealed to everyone; mysterious; esoteric. —*n.* **1** Something known only by a few people. **2** Something that is not explained or is kept hidden; mystery. **3** An underlying reason; key. —**in secret** In privacy; in a hidden place. [< L *se-* apart + *cernere* to separate] —**se′cret·ly** *adv.*

sec·re·tar·i·at (sek′rə·târ′ē·it, -at) *n.* **1** A secretary's position. **2** The place where a secretary transacts business and keeps records. **3** The entire staff of secretaries in an office; esp., a department headed by a secretary-general.

sec·re·tar·y (sek′rə·ter′ē) *n. pl.* **·tar·ies 1** An employee who deals with correspondence, records, and clerical business for a person, business, committee, etc. **2** An official in a business, club, etc., who has overall responsibility for somewhat similar work. **3** An executive officer presiding over and managing a department of government. **4** A writing desk with a bookcase on top. [< L *secretum* a secret] —**sec′re·tar′i·al** (-târ′ē·əl) *adj.*

secretary bird A large, predatory African bird having a crest resembling quill pens stuck behind the ear.

secretary general *pl.* **secretaries general** A chief administrative officer, esp. the head of a secretariat.

sec·re·tar·y·ship (sek′rə·ter′ē·ship) *n.* The work or position of a secretary.

se·crete (si·krēt′) *v.t.* **·cret·ed, ·cret·ing 1** To remove or keep from observation; conceal; hide. **2** *Biol.* To form and release (an enzyme, hormone, etc.). [Alter. of obs. *secret*, to conceal] —**se·cre′tor** *n.*

se·cre·tion (si·krē′shən) *n.* **1** *Biol.* The cellular process by which materials are separated from blood or sap and converted into new substances: the *secretion* of milk, urine, etc. **2** The substance secreted. **3** The act of concealing or hiding.

se·cre·tive (sē′krə·tiv, si·krē′tiv) *adj.* **1** Having or showing a disposition to secrecy. **2** (si·krē′tiv) SECRETORY. —**se′-cre·tive·ly** *adv.* —**se′cre·tive·ness** *n.*

se·cre·to·ry (si·krē′tər·ē) *adj.* Of, pertaining to, causing, or produced by secretion (def. 1).

secret service A department of the government concerned with work of a secret nature.

Secret Service A division of the U.S. Treasury Department concerned with the suppression of counterfeiting, the protection of the President, etc.

sect (sekt) *n.* **1** A religious denomination, esp. a body of dissenters from an established or older form of faith. **2** Adherents of a particular philosophical system or teacher, esp. a faction of a larger group. [< L *sequi* follow]

sect. section; sectional.

sec·tar·i·an (sek·târ′ē·ən) *adj.* **1** Of, pertaining to, or characteristic of a sect. **2** Having devotion to or prejudice in favor of a sect. **3** Narrow-minded; limited; parochial. —*n.* **1** A member of a sect. **2** A person who is blindly devoted to a sect or factional viewpoint. —**sec·tar′i·an·ism′** *n.*

sec·ta·ry (sek′tər·ē) *n. pl.* **·ries** A member of a sect.

sec·tion (sek′shən) *n.* **1** The act of cutting; a separating by cutting. **2** A slice or portion separated by or as if by cutting. **3** A separate part or division, as of a book or chapter. **4** A distinct part of a country, community, etc. **5** *U.S.* An area of land one square mile in extent and constituting ¹⁄₃₆ of a township. **6** A portion of a railroad's right of way under the care of a particular crew of men. **7** In a sleeping-car, a space containing two berths. **8** A representation of an object, as if cut by an intersecting plane. —*v.t.* **1** To divide into sections. **2** To shade (a drawing) so as to designate a section or sections. [< L *sectus*, p.p. of *secare* cut]

sec·tion·al (sek′shən·əl) *adj.* **1** Of, pertaining to, or characteristic of a section. **2** Made up of sections. —**sec′tion·al·ly** *adv.*

sec·tion·al·ism (sek′shən·əl·iz′əm) *n.* Exaggerated concern for a particular section of a country rather than the whole. —**sec′tion·al·ist** *n.*

sec·tor (sek′tər) *n.* **1** *Geom.* A part of a circle bounded by two radii and the arc subtended by them. **2** *Mil.* **a** A part of a front in contact with the enemy. **b** Any of the subdivisions of a defensive position. **3** A distinct part, as of a society. —*v.t.* To divide into sectors. [< L *sectus*, p.p. of *secare* to cut] —**sec·to·ri·al** (-tôr′ē·əl, -tō′rē-) *adj.*

ACB is a sector of the circle.

sec·u·lar (sek′yə·lər) *adj.* **1** Of or pertaining to this world; temporal; worldly. **2** Not controlled by the church; civil; not ecclesiastical. **3** Not concerned with religion; not sacred: *secular* art. **4** Not bound by monastic vows, and not living in a religious community. **5** Of or describing a trend or process continuing for a long, indefinite period of time. —*n.* **1** A member of the clergy who is not bound by monastic vows and who does not live in a religious community. **2** A layman as distinguished from a member of the clergy. [< L *saeculum* generation, age]

sec·u·lar·ism (sek′yə·lər·iz′əm) *n.* **1** Regard for worldly as opposed to spiritual matters. **2** The belief that religion should not be introduced into public education or public affairs. —**sec′u·lar·ist** *n.* —**sec′u·lar·is′tic** *adj.*

sec·u·lar·ize (sek′yə·lə·rīz′) *v.t.* **·ized, ·iz·ing 1** To make secular; convert from sacred to secular possession or uses. **2** To make worldly. **3** To change (a regular clergyman) to a secular. —**sec′u·lar·i·za′tion** *n.*

se·cure (si·kyoor′) *adj.* **·cur·er, ·cur·est 1** Free from or not likely to be exposed to danger, theft, etc.; safe. **2** Free from fear, apprehension, etc. **3** Confident; certain. **4** In a state or condition that will not break, come unfastened, etc.: Is the door *secure?* **5** Reliable; steady; dependable: a *secure* job. —*v.* **·cured, ·cur·ing** *v.t.* **1** To make secure; protect. **2** To make firm, tight, or fast; fasten. **3** To make sure or certain; insure; guarantee. **4** To obtain possession of; get. —*v.i.* **5** To stop working: said of a ship's crew. **6** To berth; moor: said of a ship. [< L *se-* without + *cura* care] —**se·cur′a·ble** *adj.* —**se·cure′ly** *adv.* —**se·cure′ness, se·cur′er** *n.*

se·cur·i·ty (si·kyoor′ə·tē) *n. pl.* **·ties 1** The state of being secure; freedom from danger, risk, care, poverty, doubt, etc. **2** One who or that which secures or guarantees; surety. **3** *pl.* Written promises or something deposited or pledged for payment of money, as stocks, bonds, etc. **4** Defense or protection against espionage, attack, escape, etc. **5** Measures calculated to provide such defense or protection. **6** An organization or division of one charged with providing for safety and protection.

Security Council A permanent organ of the United Nations charged with the maintenance of international peace and security.

secy., sec'y. secretary.

se·dan (si·dan′) *n.* **1** A closed automobile having one compartment, front and rear seats, and two or four doors. **2** A closed chair, for one passenger, carried by two men by means of poles at the sides: also **sedan chair.** [?]

Sedan *def.* 2

se·date (si·dāt′) *adj.* Not disturbed by excitement, passion, etc. [< L *sedare* make calm, settle] —**se·date′ly** *adv.* —**se·date′ness** *n.* —**Syn.** calm, composed, staid.

se·da·tion (si·dā′shən) *n.* The reduction of sensitivity to pain, stress, etc., by administering a sedative.

sed·a·tive (sed′ə·tiv) *adj.* Tending to calm or soothe; esp., acting to allay nervousness or emotional agitation. —*n.* A sedative medicine.

sed·en·tar·y (sed′ən·ter′ē) *adj.* **1** Accustomed to sit much or to work in a sitting posture. **2** Characterized by sitting. **3** Remaining in one place; not migratory. **4** Attached or fixed to an object. [< L *sedere* sit] —**sed′en·tar′i·ly** *adv.* —**sed′en·tar′i·ness** *n.*

Se·der (sä′dər) *n. pl.* **Se·da·rim** (sə·där′im) or **Se·ders** In Judaism, a ceremonial dinner commemorating the Exodus, held on the eve of the first day of Passover, and traditionally on the eve of the second day by Jews outside of Israel. [< Heb. *sēdher* order]

sedge (sej) *n.* Any of a large family of grasslike plants growing in wet ground and usu. having triangular, solid stems and tiny flowers in spikes. [< OE *secg*] —**sedged, sedg′y** *adj.*

sed·i·ment (sed′ə·mənt) *n.* **1** Matter that settles to the bottom of a liquid; dregs; lees. **2** *Geol.* Fragmentary material deposited by water, ice, or air. [< L *sedere* sit, settle] **sed′i·men·ta′tion** *n.*

sed·i·men·ta·ry (sed′ə·men′tər·ē) *adj.* **1** Of, pertaining to, or having the character of sediment. **2** *Geol.* Designating rocks composed of compacted sediment. Also **sed′i·men′tal.**

se·di·tion (si·dish′ən) *n.* The incitement and act of resistance to or revolt against lawful authority. [< L *sed-* aside + *itio* a going]

se·di·tious (si·dish′əs) *adj.* **1** Of, pertaining to, or having the character of sedition. **2** Inclined to, taking part in, or guilty of sedition. —**se·di′tious·ly** *adv.* —**se·di′tious·ness** *n.*

se·duce (si·dyōōs′) *v.t.* **·duced, ·duc·ing 1** To lead astray, as from a proper or right course: *seduced* by quick profits. **2** To entice into wrong, disloyalty, etc.; tempt. **3** To induce to have sexual intercourse. [< L *se-* apart + *ducere* lead] —**se·duc′er** *n.* —**se·duc′i·ble** or **se·duce′a·ble** *adj.*

se·duc·tion (si·duk′shən) *n.* **1** The act of seducing or the condition of being seduced. **2** Something which seduces; an enticement. Also **se·duce′ment.**

se·duc·tive (si·duk′tiv) *adj.* Tending to seduce. —**se·duc′tive·ly** *adv.* —**se·duc′tive·ness** *n.*

sed·u·lous (sej′ŏŏ·ləs) *adj.* **1** Constant in application or attention; assiduous. **2** Diligent; industrious. [< L *se dolo* without guile] —**sed′u·lous·ly** *adv.* —**sed′u·lous·ness** *n.*

se·dum (sē′dəm) *n.* Any of a large genus of chiefly creeping or mat-forming plants with fleshy leaves, adapted to rocky terrain. [L, house leek]

see¹ (sē) *v.* **saw, seen, see·ing** *v.t.* **1** To perceive with the eyes; gain knowledge or awareness of by means of one's vision. **2** To perceive with the mind; comprehend. **3** To find out or ascertain; inquire about: *See* who is at the door. **4** To have experience or knowledge of; undergo: We have *seen* more peaceful times. **5** To encounter; chance to meet: I *saw* your husband today. **6** To have a meeting or interview with; visit or receive as a guest, visitor, etc.: The doctor will *see* you now. **7** To attend as a spectator; view. **8** To accompany; escort. **9** To take care; be sure: *See* that you do it! **10** In poker, to accept (a bet) or equal the bet of (a player) by betting an equal sum. —*v.i.* **11** To have or exercise the power of sight. **12** To find out; inquire. **13** To understand; comprehend. **14** To think; consider. **15** To take care; be attentive: *See* to your work. **16** To gain certain knowledge, as by awaiting an outcome: We will *see* if you are right. —**see about 1** To inquire into the facts, causes, etc., of. **2** To take care of; attend to. —**see through 1** To perceive the real meaning or nature of. **2** To aid or protect, as throughout a period of danger. **3** To finish. [< OE *sēon*]

see² (sē) *n.* **1** The official seat from which a bishop exercises jurisdiction. **2** The authority or jurisdiction of a bishop. [< L *sedes* a seat]

seed (sēd) *n.* **1** The ovule containing an embryo from which a plant may be reproduced. **2** That from which anything springs; source. **3** Offspring; children. **4** The male fertilizing element; semen; sperm. **5** Any small granular fruit, singly or collectively. —*v.t.* **1** To sow with seed. **2** To sow seed. **3** To remove the seeds from: to *seed* raisins. **4** To strew (moisture-bearing clouds) with crystals, as of dry ice, silver iodide, etc., in order to initiate precipitation. **5** In sports: **a** To arrange (the drawing for positions in a tournament, etc.) so that the more skilled competitors meet only in the later events. **b** To rank (a skilled competitor) thus. —*v.i.* **6** To sow seed. **7** To grow to maturity and produce or shed seed. —**go to seed 1** To develop and shed seed. **2** To become shabby, useless, etc.; deteriorate. [< OE *sæd*] —**seed′er** *n.* —**seed′less** *adj.*

seed·bed (sēd′bed′) *n.* **1** A protected bed of earth planted with seeds for later transplanting. **2** A place of early growth or nurture.

seed-case (sēd′kās′) *n.* SEED VESSEL.

seed coat The integument of a seed. • See EMBRYO.

seed leaf COTYLEDON.

seed·ling (sēd′ling) *n.* **1** Any plant grown from seed. **2** A very small or young tree or plant.

seed oyster A young oyster, esp. one transplanted from one bed to another.

seed pearl A small pearl, esp. one used for ornamenting bags, etc., or in embroidery.

seed plant A plant which bears seeds.

seed vessel A pericarp, esp. one that is dry, as a pod.

seed·y (sē′dē) *adj.* **seed·i·er, seed·i·est 1** Abounding with seeds. **2** Gone to seed. **3** Poor and ragged; shabby. **4** Feeling or looking wretched. —**seed′i·ly** *adv.* —**seed′i·ness** *n.*

see·ing (sē′ing) *conj.* Since; in view of the fact; considering.

Seeing Eye dog The name used for a dog trained to lead the blind, esp. one trained by an organization (**Seeing Eye**) in New Jersey: a trade name.

seek (sēk) *v.* **sought, seek·ing** *v.t.* **1** To go in search of; look for. **2** To strive; try to get. **3** To endeavor or try: He *seeks* to mislead me. **4** To ask or inquire for; request: to *seek* information. **5** To go to; betake oneself to: to *seek* a warmer climate. —*v.i.* **6** To make a search or inquiry. [< OE *sēcan*] —**seek′er** *n.*

seem (sēm) *v.i.* **1** To give the impression of being; appear. **2** To appear to oneself: I *seem* to remember her face. **3** To appear to exist: There *seems* no reason for hesitating. **4** To be evident or apparent: It *seems* to be raining. [< ON *sæma* honor, conform to]

seem·ing (sē′ming) *adj.* Having the appearance of reality but often not so: Her *seeming* nonchalance was solely due to three martinis. —*n.* Appearance; semblance; esp., false show. —**seem′ing·ly** *adv.* —**seem′ing·ness** *n.*

seem·ly (sēm′lē) *adj.* **·li·er, ·li·est 1** Befitting the proprieties; becoming; proper; decorous. **2** Handsome; attractive. —*adv.* Becomingly; appropriately. [< ON *sæmr* fitting] —**seem′li·ness** *n.*

seen (sēn) *p.p.* of SEE.

seep (sēp) *v.i.* To soak through pores or small openings; ooze. [< OE *sipian* soak] —**seep′y** *adj.*

seep·age (sē′pij) *n.* **1** The act or process of seeping; oozing; leakage. **2** The fluid that seeps.

seer (sē′ər *for def. 1;* sir *for def. 2*) *n.* **1** One who sees. **2** One who foretells events; a prophet. [< SEE¹ + -ER]

seer·suck·er (sir′suk′ər) *n.* A thin fabric, often striped, with crinkled surface. [< Pers. *shīr o shakkar,* lit., milk and sugar]

see·saw (sē′sô′) *n.* **1** A game or contest in which persons sit or stand on opposite ends of a board balanced at the middle and make it move up and down. **2** A board balanced for this sport. **3** Any up-and-down or back-and-fro movement, tendency, change, etc. —*v.t. & v.i.* To move on or as if on a seesaw. —*adj.* Moving up and down or to and fro. [Reduplication of SAW¹]

seethe (sēth) *v.* **seethed, seeth·ing** *v.i.* **1** To boil. **2** To foam or bubble as if boiling. **3** To be agitated, as by rage. —*v.t.* **4** To soak in liquid; steep. **5** *Archaic* To boil. —*n.* The act or condition of seething. [< OE *sēothan*]

seg·ment (seg′mənt) *n.* **1** A part cut off or distinct from the other parts of anything: a section. **2** *Geom.* A part of a line or curve lying between two of its points. —*v.t. & v.i.* To divide into segments. [< L *secare* to cut] —**seg·men·tal** (seg·men′tal) *adj.* —**seg·men′tal·ly** *adv.* —**seg·men·tar·y** (seg′mən·ter′ē) *adj.*

seg·men·ta·tion (seg′mən·tā′shən) *n.* **1** Division into segments. **2** The process of repeated cleavage whereby a complex organism develops from a single cell.

se·go (sē′gō) *n. pl.* **·gos 1** A perennial plant of the lily family, having bell-shaped flowers. **2** Its edible bulb. Also **sego lily.** [< Ute]

seg·re·gate (seg′rə·gāt) *v.* **·gat·ed, ·gat·ing** *v.t.* **1** To place apart from others or the rest; isolate. **2** To cause the separation of (a race, social class, etc.) from the general mass of society or from a larger group. —*v.i.* **3** To separate from a mass and gather about nuclei, as in crystallization. —*adj.* (-git) Separated or set apart from others; segregated.

[< L *se-* apart + *grex* a flock] **—seg're·ga'tive** *adj.* **—seg're·ga'tor** *n.*

seg·re·ga·tion (seg'rə·gā'shən) *n.* **1** A segregating or being segregated or process of segregating. **2** The act or policy of separating a race, social class, etc., from the general mass of society or from a larger group.

Seid·litz powders (sed'lits) An effervescent mixture of salts, used as a laxative. Also **Seidlitz powder.** [< similarity to spring water in *Seidlitz*, Czechoslovakia]

sei·gnior (sān·yôr', sān'yər) *n.* A man of rank, esp. a feudal lord. Also **sei·gneur** (sān'yər). [< L *senior* older] — **sei·gnio'ri·al** *adj.*

seign·ior·y (sān'yər·ē) *n. pl.* **·ior·ies** The territory, rights, or jurisdiction of a seignior.

seine (sān) *n.* Any long fishing net, having floats at the top edge and weights at the bottom. —*v.t. & v.i.* **seined, sein·ing** To fish or catch with a seine. [< Gk. *sagēnē* a fishing net]

seis·mic (sīz'mik, sīs'-) *adj.* Of, pertaining to, subject to, or produced by an earthquake or earthquakes. Also **seis'mal, seis'mi·cal.** [< Gk. *seismos* earthquake.]

seismo- *combining form* Earthquake: *seismograph.* [< Gk. *seismos* an earthquake]

seis·mo·gram (sīz'mə·gram, sīs'-) *n.* The record made by a seismograph.

seis·mo·graph (sīz'mə·graf, -gräf, sīs'-) *n.* An instrument for automatically recording the movements of the earth's crust. **—seis'mo·graph'ic** *adj.* — **seis·mog·ra·pher** (sīz·mog'rə·fər, sīs-), **seis·mog'ra·phy** *n.*

seis·mol·o·gy (sīz·mol'ə·jē, sīs-) *n.* The science dealing with earthquakes and related phenomena. **—seis·mo·log·ic**(sīz'mə·loj'ik,sīs'-) or **·i·cal** *adj.* **—seis'mo·log'i·cal·ly** *adv.* **—seis·mol'o·gist** *n.*

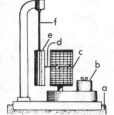

Seismograph
a. concrete base. b. clock. c. seismogram. d. stylus. e. weight. f. spring suspension.

seize (sēz) *v.* **seized, seiz·ing** *v.t.* **1** To take hold of suddenly and forcibly; clutch; grasp. **2** To grasp mentally; understand. **3** To take possession of by authority or right. **4** To take possession of by or as by force. **5** To take prisoner; capture. **6** To act upon with sudden and powerful effect; attack; strike. **7** To take advantage of immediately, as an opportunity. **8** *Naut.* To fasten or bind by turns of cord, line, or small rope; lash. —*v.i.* **9** To take hold or make use: usu. with *on* or *upon.* [< OF *saisir, seisir*] **—seiz'a·ble** *adj.* **—seiz'er** *n.*

sei·zure (sē'zhər) *n.* **1** The act of seizing or the state of being seized. **2** A sudden incapacitation, as by disease.

se·lah (sē'lə) *n.* A Hebrew word of unknown meaning in the Psalms, usu. considered as a direction to readers or musicians.

sel·dom (sel'dəm) *adv.* At widely separated intervals, as of time or space; infrequently; rarely. —*adj.* Infrequent; rare. [< OE *seldan*]

se·lect (si·lekt') *v.t.* **1** To take in preference to another or others; pick out; choose. —*v.i.* **2** To choose. —*adj.* **1** Chosen in preference to others. **2** Excellent; superior; choice. **3** Exclusive. **4** Very particular in selecting. [< L *se-* apart + *legere* choose] **—se·lect'ness, se·lec'tor** *n.*

se·lec·tee (si·lek'tē') *n.* One called up for military service under selective service.

se·lec·tion (si·lek'shən) *n.* **1** A selecting or being selected. **2** Anything selected. **3** *Biol.* Any process, natural or artificial, which determines the survival of specific characteristics.

se·lec·tive (si·lek'tiv) *adj.* **1** Of, pertaining to, or characterized by selection. **2** Having the power or tendency to select. **3** Having or characterized by good selectivity, as a radio receiver. **—se·lec'tive·ly** *adv.* **—se·lec'tive·ness** *n.*

selective service Compulsory military service according to specified conditions of age, fitness, etc. **—se·lec'·tive-ser'vice** *adj.*

se·lec·tiv·i·ty (si·lek'tiv'ə·tē) *n.* **1** The state or condition of being selective. **2** *Telecom.* That characteristic of a radio receiver or filter by which frequencies can be sharply discriminated.

se·lect·man (si·lekt'mən) *n. pl.* **·men** (-mən) One of a board of town officers, elected annually in New England, except in Rhode Island, to manage local affairs.

sel·e·nite (sel'ə·nīt) *n.* A crystalline form of gypsum. [< Gk. *selēnītēs (lithos)*, lit., moon(stone); so called because it was thought to wax and wane with the moon]

se·le·ni·um (si·lē'nē·əm) *n.* A nonmetallic element (symbol Se) of variable electrical resistance under the influence of light and having several allotropic forms. [< Gk. *selēnē* the moon]

self (self) *n. pl.* **selves** **1** One's own person known or considered as the subject of his own consciousness. **2** The distinct and characteristic individuality or identity of any person or thing. **3** Personal interest or advantage. —*adj.* **1** Being uniform or of the same quality throughout. **2** Of the same kind (as in material, color, etc.,) as something else: a coat with a *self* belt. —*pron.* Myself, yourself, himself, or herself. [< OE]

self- *combining form* **1** Of oneself or itself: *self-analysis.* **2** By oneself or itself: *self-employed.* **3** In oneself or itself: *self-absorbed.* **4** To, with, for, or toward oneself: *self-satisfied.* **5** In or of oneself or itself inherently: *self-evident.*

self-ab·ne·ga·tion (self'ab'ni·gā'shən) *n.* The complete putting aside of self-interest. **—Syn.** self-sacrifice, self-denial, self-control, self-restraint.

self-a·buse (self'ə·byo͞os') *n.* **1** The disparagement of one's own person or powers. **2** MASTURBATION.

self-ad·dressed (self'ə·drest') *adj.* Addressed to oneself.

self-as·sured (self'ə·sho͝ord') *adj.* Confident in one's own abilities. **—self'-as·sur'ance** *n.*

self-cen·tered (self'sen'tərd) *adj.* Concerned exclusively with oneself and one's own needs and desires.

self-com·mand (self'kə·mand', -mänd') *n.* SELF-CONTROL.

self-con·fi·dence (self'kon'fə·dəns) *n.* Confidence in oneself or in one's own unaided powers, judgment, etc. — **self'-con'fi·dent** *adj.* **—self'-con'fi·dent·ly** *adv.*

self-con·scious (self'kon'shəs) *adj.* **1** Uncomfortably conscious that one is observed by others; ill at ease. **2** Displaying such consciousness: a *self-conscious* giggle. **3** Conscious of one's existence. **—self'-con'scious·ly** *adv.* — **self'-con'scious·ness** *n.*

self-con·tained (self'kən·tānd') *adj.* **1** Keeping one's thoughts and feelings to oneself; impassive. **2** Exercising self-control. **3** Having within oneself or itself all that is necessary for independent existence or operation.

self-con·tra·dic·tion (self'kon'trə·dik'shən) *n.* **1** The contradicting of oneself or itself. **2** A statement, proposition, etc., that contradicts itself. **—self'-con'tra·dic'to·ry** *adj.*

self-con·trol (self'kən·trōl') *n.* Control of one's impulses, emotions, etc.

self-de·fense (self'di·fens') *n.* Defense of oneself, one's property, one's reputation, etc. **—self'-de·fen'sive** *adj.*

self-de·ni·al (self'di·nī'əl) *n.* The restraining of one's desires, impulses, etc. **—self'-de·ny'ing** *adj.*

self-de·ter·mi·na·tion (self'di·tûr'mə·nā'shən) *n.* **1** The principle of free will; decision by oneself without extraneous force or influence. **2** Decision by the people of a country or section as to its future political status. **—self'-de·ter'mined, self'-de·ter'min·ing** *adj.*

self-de·vo·tion (self'di·vō'shən) *n.* The devoting of oneself to the service of a person or a cause.

self-ed·u·cat·ed (self'ej'o͞o·kā'tid) *adj.* Educated through one's own efforts with little or no formal instruction. **—self'-ed'u·ca'tion** *n.*

self-es·teem (self'es·tēm') *n.* **1** A good or just opinion of oneself. **2** An overestimate of oneself; conceit.

self-ev·i·dent (self'ev'ə·dənt) *adj.* Requiring no proof of its truth or validity. **—self'-ev'i·dence** *n.* **—self'-ev'i·dent·ly** *adv.*

self-ex·ist·ence (self'ig·zis'təns) *n.* Existence that is independent, without external cause. **—self′-ex·ist′ent** *adj.*

self-ex·plan·a·to·ry (self′ik·splan′ə·tôr·ē, -tō′rē) *adj.* Explaining itself; needing no explanation.

self-ex·pres·sion (self′ik·spresh′ən) *n.* Expression of one's own personality or individuality, as in art.

self-fer·til·i·za·tion (self′fûr′təl·ə·zā′shən, -ī·zā′shən) *n.* Fertilization of an organism by its own sperm or pollen.

self-gov·ern·ment (self′guv′ərn·mənt, -ər·mənt) *n.* **1** Self-control. **2** Government of a country or region by its own people. **—self′-gov′ern·ing, self′-gov′erned** *adj.*

self-heal (self′hēl′) *n.* A weedy perennial herb reputed to cure disease.

self-im·age (self′im′ij) *n.* The image or idea one has of oneself or of one's position in life.

self-im·por·tance (self′im·pôr′təns) *n.* An excessively high appraisal of one's own importance; conceit. **—self′-im·por′tant** *adj.*

self-in·duced (self′in·d(y)ōōst′) *adj.* **1** Induced by oneself or by itself. **2** Produced by self-induction.

self-in·duc·tion (self′in·duk′shən) *n.* The production of an induced voltage in a circuit by the variation of the current in that circuit.

self-in·ter·est (self′in′trist, -in′tər·ist) *n.* Personal interest or advantage, or concern for it; selfishness. **—self′-in′ter·est·ed** *adj.*

self·ish (sel′fish) *adj.* **1** Motivated by personal needs and desires to the disregard of the welfare or wishes of others. **2** Proceeding from or characterized by undue concern for self. **—self′ish·ly** *adv.* **—self′ish·ness** *n.*

self·less (self′lis) *adj.* Having, showing, or prompted by a lack of concern for self. **—Syn.** unselfish, altruistic, self-sacrificing, self-denying.

self-load·ing (self′lō′ding) *adj.* Automatically reloading: said of a gun using the energy of recoil to eject and reload.

self-love (self′luv′) *n.* Love of oneself; the desire or tendency to seek to promote one's own well-being.

self-made (self′mād′) *adj.* **1** Having attained honor, wealth, etc., by one's own efforts. **2** Made by oneself.

self-pol·li·na·tion (self′pol′ə·nā′shən) *n.* Pollen transfer from stamens to pistils of the same flower, plant, or clone. **—self′-pol′li·na·ted** *adj.*

self-pos·ses·sion (self′pə·zesh′ən) *n.* The full possession or control of one's powers or faculties; presence of mind; self-control. **—self′-pos·sessed′** *adj.*

self-pres·er·va·tion (self′prez′ər·vā′shən) *n.* **1** The protection of oneself from injury or death. **2** The instinctive drive to protect oneself.

self-pro·nounc·ing (self′prə·noun′sing) *adj.* Having marks of pronunciation and stress applied to a word without phonetic alteration of the spelling.

self-re·li·ance (self′ri·lī′əns) *n.* Reliance on one's own abilities, resources, or judgment. **—self′-re·li′ant** *adj.* **—self′-re·li′ant·ly** *adv.*

self-re·spect (self′ri·spekt′) *n.* A proper respect for oneself, one's standing, position, etc. **—self′-re·spect′ing, self′-re·spect′ful,** *adj.* **—self′-re·spect′ful·ly** *adv.*

self-re·straint (self′ri·strānt′) *n.* Restraint imposed by the force of one's own will; self-control. **—self′-re·strained′** *adj.*

self-right·eous (self′rī′chəs) *adj.* Having or showing a high, usu. smug, opinion of one's own moral superiority. **—self′-right′eous·ly** *adv.* **—self′-right′eous·ness** *n.*

self-ris·ing (self′rī′zing) *adj.* Rising without the addition of leaven, as some flours.

self-sac·ri·fice (self′sak′rə·fīs) *n.* The subordination of one's self or one's personal welfare or wishes for others' good, for duty, etc. **—self′-sac′ri·fic′ing** *adj.*

self·same (self′sām′) *adj.* Exactly the same; identical. **—self′same′ness** *n.*

self-sat·is·fac·tion (self′sat′is·fak′shən) *n.* Satisfaction with one's own actions, characteristics, etc.; conceit. **—self′-sat′is·fied** *adj.* **—self′-sat′is·fy′ing** *adj.*

self-seek·ing (self′sē′king) *adj.* Given to the exclusive pursuit of one's own interests or gain. **—n.** Such a pursuit; selfishness. **—self′-seek′er** *n.*

self-ser·vice (self′sûr′vis) *adj.* Designating a particular type of café, restaurant, or store where patrons serve themselves.

self-serv·ing (self′sûr′ving) *adj.* Tending to justify or advance oneself, often at the expense of others.

self-start·er (self′stär′tər) *n.* **1** An engine or device with an automatic or semi-automatic starting mechanism; also, such a mechanism. **2** *Slang* One who requires no outside stimulus to start or accomplish work. **—self′-start′ing** *adj.*

self-styled (self′stīld′) *adj.* Characterized (as such) by oneself: a *self-styled* gentleman.

self-suf·fi·cient (self′sə·fish′ənt) *adj.* **1** Able to support or maintain oneself without aid or cooperation from others. **2** Having too much confidence in oneself. Also **self′-suf·fic′ing** (-sə·fī′sing). **—self′-suf·fi′cien·cy** *n.*

self-sup·port·ing (self′sə·pôrt′ing) *adj.* **1** Capable of supporting itself or its own weight. **2** Able to provide for oneself, as with money, lodging, clothing, etc.

self-will (self′wil′) *n.* Persistent adherence to one's own will or wish, esp. with disregard of the wishes of others; obstinacy. **—self′-willed′** *adj.*

self-wind·ing (self′wīn′ding) *adj.* Having an automatic winding mechanism, as some watches.

sell (sel) *v.* **sold, sell·ing** *v.t.* **1** To transfer (property) to another for a consideration; dispose of by sale. **2** To deal in; offer for sale. **3** To deliver, surrender, or betray in violation of duty or trust: often with *out*: to *sell* one's country. **4** *Informal* To cause to accept or approve something: They *sold* him on the scheme. **5** *Informal* To cause or promote the acceptance, approval, or sale of. **6** *Slang* To deceive; cheat. **—v.i.** **7** To engage in selling. **8** To be on sale or be sold. **9** To work as a salesperson. **10** To be popular with buyers, customers, etc. **—sell out 1** To get rid of (one's goods, etc.) by sale. **2** *Informal* To betray one's trust, cause, associates, etc. **—n.** **1** *Slang* A trick; joke; swindle. **2** An act or instance of selling. [< OE *sellan* give]

sell·er (sel′ər) *n.* **1** One who sells. **2** An item that is being sold, considered in reference to its sales.

sell-out (sel′out′) *n.* *Informal* **1** An act of selling out. **2** A performance for which all seats have been sold.

selt·zer (selt′sər) *n.* An artificially prepared mineral water that contains carbon dioxide. [< Seltzer]

Selt·zer (selt′sər) *n.* An effervescing mineral water. Also **Seltzer water.** [< Nieder *Selters,* a village in sw Prussia]

sel·vage (sel′vij) *n.* The edge of a woven fabric so finished that it will not ravel. Also **sel′vedge.** [< SELF + EDGE]

Sem. Seminary; Semitic.

se·man·tic (si·man′tik) *adj.* **1** Of or pertaining to meaning. **2** Of, relating to, or according to semantics. [< Gk. *sēmainein* signify]

se·man·tics (si·man′tiks) *n. pl. (construed as sing.)* **1** *Ling.* The study of the meanings of speech forms, esp. of the development and changes in meaning of words and word groups. **2** *Logic* The study of the relation between signs or symbols and what they signify. **—se·man′ti·cist** *n.*

sem·a·phore (sem′ə·fôr, -fōr) *n.* An apparatus for giving signals, as with movable arms, disks, flags, or lanterns. **—v.t.** To send by semaphore. [< Gk. *sēma* a sign + *pherein* carry] **—sem′a·phor′ic** (-fôr′ik, -for′ik) or **-i·cal** *adj.*

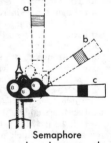

sem·blance (sem′bləns) *n.* **1** An outward, sometimes deceptive appearance; look. **2** A representation, likeness, or resemblance. **3** The barest trace; modicum. [< OF *sembler* seem]

se·men (sē′mən) *n.* The sperm-containing fluid of male animals. [< L *serere* sow]

Semaphore
a. clear. b. approach.
c. stop.

se·mes·ter (si·mes′tər) *n.* Either of the two periods of approximately 18 weeks into which an academic year is divided. [< L *sex* six + *mensis* month] **—se·mes′tral** *adj.*

semi- *prefix* **1** Partly; not fully: *semicivilized.* **2** Exactly half: *semicircle.* **3** Occurring twice (in the period specified): *semiweekly.* [< L]

sem·i·an·nu·al (sem′ē·an′yōō·əl, sem′ī-) *adj.* Occurring, issued, etc., twice a year or every six months. **—sem′i·an′·nu·al·ly** *adv.*

sem·i·breve (sem′ē·brēv′, sem′ī-) *n. Music* WHOLE NOTE.
sem·i·cir·cle (sem′i·sûr′kəl, sem′ē-) *n.* **1** A half-circle; an arc of 180°. **2** Anything formed or arranged in a half-circle. —**sem′i·cir′cu·lar** *adj.* —**sem′i·cir′cu·lar·ly** *adv.*
semicircular canal Any of three fluid-filled tubes in the inner ear which serve as the organ of balance. • See EAR.
sem·i·civ·i·lized (sem′ē·siv′ə·līzd, sem′ī-) *adj.* Partly civilized.
sem·i·co·lon (sem′i·kō′lən, sem′ē-) *n.* A mark (;) of punctuation, indicating a greater degree of separation than the comma but less than the period.
sem·i·con·duc·tor (sem′ē·kən·duk′tər, sem′ī-) *n.* **1** One of a class of crystalline solids, as germanium or silicon, having an electrical conductivity intermediate between conductors and insulators, used in making transistors and related devices. **2** A transistor or related device.
sem·i·con·scious (sem′ē·kon′shəs, sem′ī-) *adj.* Partly conscious; not fully aware or responsive. —**sem′i·con′·scious·ly** *adv.* —**sem′i·con′scious·ness** *n.*
sem·i·de·tached (sem′ē·di·tacht′, sem′ī-) *adj.* Joined to another on one side only, as two houses built side by side with one common wall.
sem·i·fi·nal (sem′ē·fī′nəl, sem′ī-) *adj.* Next before the final, as in a series of competitions. —*n.* **1** A semifinal match. **2** A semifinal round. —**sem′i·fi′nal·ist** *n.*
sem·i·flu·id (sem′ē·floo̅′id, sem′ī-) *adj.* Fluid, but thick and viscous. —*n.* A thick, viscous fluid.
sem·i·liq·uid (sem′ē·lik′wid, sem′ī-) *adj. & n.* SEMIFLUID.
sem·i·month·ly (sem′ē·munth′lē, sem′ī-) *adj.* Taking place, issued, etc., twice a month. —*n. pl.* **·lies** A publication issued twice a month. —*adv.* Twice monthly.
sem·i·nal (sem′ə·nəl) *adj.* **1** Of, pertaining to, or containing seed or semen. **2** Like seed in having or contributing to the potential for future development. [< L *semen* semen, seed] —**sem′i·nal·ly** *adv.* —**Syn. 2** original, originative, germinal, germinative.
sem·i·nar (sem′ə·när) *n.* **1** A group of students at a college or university, meeting regularly with a professor for informal discussion of research problems. **2** A course thus conducted. **3** A room in which such a course is conducted. **4** Any informal meeting to discuss a particular topic, problem, etc. [< L *seminarium* seed plot]
sem·i·nar·y (sem′ē·ner′ē) *n. pl.* **·nar·ies 1** A school of theology. **2** A boarding school, esp. for young women. **3** A place where anything is nurtured. [< L *seminarium* a seed plot]
sem·i·na·tion (sem′ə·nā′shən) *n.* **1** The act of sowing or spreading seeds. **2** Propagation. [< L *semen* a seed, semen]
sem·i·nif·er·ous (sem′ə·nif′ər·əs) *adj.* **1** Carrying or containing semen. **2** Seed-bearing.
Sem·i·nole (sem′ə·nōl) *n. pl.* **·noles** or **·nole** One of a Florida tribe of North American Indians of Muskhogean linguistic stock.
sem·i·of·fi·cial (sem′ē·ə·fish′əl, sem′ī-) *adj.* Having partial official authority or sanction; official to some extent. —**sem′i·of·fi′cial·ly** *adv.*
sem·i·per·me·a·ble (sem′ē·pûr′mē·ə·bəl, sem′ī-) *adj.* Selectively permeable; preventing passage of larger molecules, as membranes in osmosis.
sem·i·pre·cious (sem′ē·presh′əs, sem′ī-) *adj.* Designating a gem that is not as valuable as one classified precious.
sem·i·pri·vate (sem′ē·prī′vit, sem′ī-) *adj.* Partly private: said esp. of a hospital room with two, three, or four beds.
sem·i·pro (sem′ē·prō′, sem′ī-) *adj. & n.* SEMIPROFESSIONAL.
sem·i·pro·fes·sion·al (sem′ē·prə·fesh′ən·əl, sem′ī-) *adj.* **1** Taking part in a sport or other activity for pay but not on a full-time basis. **2** Engaged in by semiprofessional players. —*n.* A semiprofessional player, etc.
sem·i·qua·ver (sem′ē·kwā′vər, sem′ī-) *n.* SIXTEENTH NOTE.
sem·i·skilled (sem′ē·skild′, sem′ī-) *adj.* Partly skilled.
sem·i·sol·id (sem′ē·sol′id, sem′ī-) *adj.* Partly solid; highly viscous. —*n.* A semisolid substance.
Sem·ite (sem′īt, *esp. Brit.* sē′mīt) *n.* **1** A person consid-

ered as a descendant of Shem. **2** One of a people of sw Asia, now represented by the Jews and Arabs, but originally including the ancient Babylonians, Assyrians, Arameans, Phoenicians, etc.
Se·mit·ic (sə·mit′ik) *adj.* Of, pertaining to, or characteristic of the Semites or their languages. —*n.* **1** The Semitic family of languages. **2** Any of these languages, including Arabic, Hebrew, Amharic, Aramaic, etc.
Sem·i·tism (sem′ə·tiz′əm) *n.* **1** A Semitic word or idiom. **2** Semitic practices, opinions, or customs collectively. **3** Any political or economic policy favoring the Jews.
sem·i·tone (sem′ē·tōn′, sem′ī-) *n. Music* **1** The tone at an interval equal to half a tone in the standard diatonic scale. **2** Such an interval; a half step. —**sem′i·ton′ic** (-ton′·ik) *adj.*
sem·i·trop·i·cal (sem′ē·trop′i·kəl, sem′ī-) *adj.* Somewhat characteristic of the tropics.
sem·i·vow·el (sem′i·vou′əl) *n.* A vowellike sound used as a consonant, as (w), (y), and (r).
sem·i·week·ly (sem′ē·wēk′lē, sem′ī-) *adj.* Issued, occurring, done, etc., twice a week. —*n. pl.* **·lies** A publication issued twice a week. —*adv.* Twice a week.
sem·o·li·na (sem′ə·lē′nə) *n.* Coarse-ground wheat flour, used in making pasta. [< L *simila* fine flour]
sem·per fi·de·lis (sem′pər fi·dā′lis) *Latin* Always faithful: motto of the U.S. Marine Corps.
sem·per pa·ra·tus (sem′pər pə·rä′təs, -pə·rā′-) *Latin* Always prepared: motto of the U.S. Coast Guard.
sem·pi·ter·nal (sem′pə·tûr′nəl) *adj.* Enduring or existing to all eternity; everlasting. [< L *semper* always]—**sem′·pi·ter′nal·ly** *adv.* —**sem′pi·ter′ni·ty** *n.*
sen (sen) *n.* A Japanese coin or unit of currency, equal to 1/100 of a yen.
Sen., sen. senate; senator; senior.
sen·ate (sen′it) *n.* **1** *Usu. cap.* The upper branch of many national or state legislative bodies, as in the U.S. **2** A legislative body, as at a university; council. **3** A body of distinguished or venerable men often possessing legislative functions. **4** The highest governing body of the ancient Roman state. [< L *senatus*, lit., a council of old men]
sen·a·tor (sen′ə·tər) *n.* A member of a senate. —**sen′a·to′ri·al** *adj.* —**sen′a·to′ri·al·ly** *adv.* —**sen′a·tor·ship′** *n.*
send (send) *v.* **sent, send·ing** *v.t.* **1** To cause or enable to go: to *send* a messenger; to *send* one's daughter to medical school. **2** To cause to be conveyed; transmit; forward: to *send* a letter. **3** To cause to issue; emit or discharge, as heat, smoke, etc.: with *forth, out,* etc. **4** To drive by force; impel. **5** To cause to come, happen, etc.; grant: God *send* us peace. **6** To bring into a specified state or condition: The decision *sent* him into a panic. **7** To transmit, as an electric or magnetic signal. **8** *Slang* To thrill or delight. —*v.i.* **9** To dispatch an agent, messenger, or message. —**send for** To summon or order by a message or messenger. —**send packing** To dismiss abruptly or roughly. [< OE *sendan*] —**send′er** *n.*
send-off (send′ôf′, -of′) *n.* **1** The act of sending off; a start given to someone or something. **2** *Informal* A demonstration of friendship, enthusiasm, etc., toward someone beginning a new venture.
send-up (send′up′) *n. Brit. Slang* A parody; takeoff.
Sen·e·ca (sen′ə·kə) *n.* One of a tribe of North American Indians of Iroquoian stock, the largest tribe of the Five Nations, still living in New York and Ontario.
se·nes·cent (si·nes′ənt) *adj.* Growing old. [< L *senex* old] —**se·nes′cence** *n.*
sen·e·schal (sen′ə·shəl) *n.* A steward or major-domo in charge of the household of a medieval prince or noble. [< OF]
se·nile (sē′nīl, sen′īl) *adj.* Of, pertaining to, proceeding from, or characteristic of old age, esp. pertaining to or exhibiting certain mental infirmities often resulting from old age. [< L *senex* old] —**se′nile·ly** *adv.* —**se·nil·i·ty** (sə·nil′·ə·tē) *n.*
sen·ior (sēn′yər) *adj.* **1** Older in years; elder; after personal names (usu. abbreviated *Sr.*), to denote the elder of two related persons of the same name, esp. a father and

---

add, āce, câre, pălm; end, ēven; it, īce; odd, ōpen, ôrder; to̅o̅k, po̅o̅l; up, bûrn; ə = *a* in *above, u* in *focus*; yo̅o̅ = *u* in *fuse*; oil; pout; check; go; ring; thin; this; zh, *vision.* < derived from; ? origin uncertain or unknown.

his son. **2** Longer in service or superior in rank or dignity. **3** Of or pertaining to a senior or seniors. —*n.* **1** One older in years, longer in office, or more advanced in rank or dignity than another. **2** Any elderly person. **3** A member of a graduating class. [< L *senior* older]

senior citizen An elderly person, esp. one of or over the age of retirement.

sen·ior·i·ty (sēn·yôr′ə·tē, -yor′-) *n. pl.* **·ties 1** The state or condition of being senior. **2** The status or priority one achieves by length of service (as in a business firm).

sen·na (sen′ə) *n.* **1** A cathartic obtained from certain species of cassia. **2** Any of various cassia plants. [< Ar. *sanā*]

se·ñor (sā·nyôr′) *n. pl.* **·ño·res** (-nyō′rās) *Spanish* **1** A title of courtesy equivalent to *Mr.* or *Sir.* **2** A man; gentleman.

se·ño·ra (sā·nyō′rä) *n. Spanish* **1** A title of courtesy equivalent to *Mrs.* or *Madam.* **2** A woman; lady.

se·ño·ri·ta (sā′nyō·rē′tä) *n. Spanish* **1** A title of courtesy equivalent to *Miss.* **2** An unmarried woman; young lady.

sen·sa·tion (sen·sā′shən) *n.* **1 a** A mental event due to stimulation of a sense organ, as hearing, taste, etc. **b** The capacity to respond to such stimulation. **2** A state of mind induced by indeterminate stimuli: a *sensation* of fear. **3** A state of interest or excitement. **4** That which produces such a state of interest or excitement. [< L *sensus* sense]

sen·sa·tion·al (sen·sā′shən·əl) *adj.* **1** Of or pertaining to the senses or sensation. **2** Causing excitement; startling; thrilling. **3** Tending to shock, startle, etc., esp. by lurid or melodramatic details, techniques, etc. **4** *Informal* Excellent, great, etc. —**sen·sa′tion·al·ly** *adv.*

sen·sa·tion·al·ism (sen·sā′shən·əl·iz′əm) *n.* **1** *Philos.* The theory that all knowledge has a sensory basis. **2** The use of details, techniques, etc., that are intended to shock, or startle, as in literature, motion pictures, etc. —**sen·sa′tion·al·ist** *n.* —**sen·sa′tion·al·is′tic** *adj.*

sense (sens) *n.* **1** Any of the faculties of man and animals, specialized to receive and transmit external or internal stimuli, as sound, hunger, etc.; sight, touch, taste, hearing, and smell. **2** A perception or feeling produced by the senses. **3** A special capacity to perceive, appreciate, estimate, etc.: a *sense* of humor. **4** A somewhat vague perception or feeling; a *sense* of danger. **5** Rational perception or discrimination; awareness; realization: a *sense* of wrong. **6** Normal power of mind or understanding: The fellow has no *sense.* **7** That which is in accord with reason and good judgment: to talk *sense.* **8** Signification; meaning. **9** One of several meanings of the same word or phrase. **10** The opinion or judgment, as of a majority: the *sense* of the meeting. —*v.t.* **sensed, sens·ing 1** To perceive; become aware of. **2** *Informal* To comprehend; understand. [< L *sensus* perception, p.p. of *sentire* feel]

sense·less (sens′lis) *adj.* **1** Unconscious; incapable of feeling or perception. **2** Devoid of good sense, knowledge, or meaning: a *senseless* remark. **3** Without apparent cause or reason: a *senseless* crime. —**sense′less·ly** *adv.* —**sense′·less·ness** *n.*

sense organ A structure specialized to receive sense impressions, as the eye, nose, ear, etc.

sen·si·bil·i·ty (sen′sə·bil′ə·tē) *n. pl.* **·ties 1** The power to receive physical sensations. **2** A special susceptibility or sensitiveness to outside influences or mental impressions, as of pleasure or pain. **3** An awareness of and ability to respond to something (as an emotion or moral value). **4** Discriminating or excessive sensitivity in taste and emotion, with especial responsiveness to pathos.

sen·si·ble (sen′sə·bəl) *adj.* **1** Possessed of good mental perception; wise. **2** Capable of physical sensation; sensitive: *sensible* to pain. **3** Perceptible through the senses: *sensible* heat. **4** Perceptible to the mind. **5** Emotionally or mentally sensitive; aware. **6** Great enough to be perceived; appreciable. [< L *sensus,* p.p. of *sentire* feel, perceive] —**sen′si·ble·ness** *n.* —**sen′si·bly** *adv.*

sen·si·tive (sen′sə·tiv) *adj.* **1** Of or pertaining to the senses or sensation. **2** Receptive and responsive to sensations. **3** Responding readily to sensations, esp. of a particular kind: a *sensitive* ear. **4** Acutely receptive or responsive to the quality or strength of attitudes, feelings, or relationships. **5** Capable of appreciating aesthetic or intellec-

tual subtleties. **6** Easily irritated; tender: *sensitive* skin. **7** Hurt; sore. **8** Reacting excessively, as to an agent or substance: *sensitive* to insect bites. **9** Apt to take offense on slight provocation; touchy. **10** Capable of indicating very slight changes or differences; delicate: a *sensitive* barometer. **11** Readily fluctuating or tending to fluctuate: a *sensitive* stock market. [< L *sensus* sense] —**sen′si·tive·ly** *adv.* —**sen′si·tive·ness, sen′si·tiv′i·ty** *n.*

sensitive plant A tropical species of mimosa whose leaves close at a touch.

sen·si·tize (sen′sə·tīz) *v.t.* **·tized, ·tiz·ing 1** To make sensitive, esp., in photography, to make sensitive to light, as a plate or film. **2** *Med.* To make susceptible to an allergen. —**sen′si·ti·za′tion, sen′si·tiz′er** *n.*

sen·so·ri·um (sen·sôr′ē·əm, -sō′rē-) *n. pl.* **·ri·a** (-ē·ə) The entire sensory apparatus of an organism. [< L *sensus* sense]

sen·so·ry (sen′sər·ē) *adj.* **1** Of or pertaining to the senses or sensation. **2** AFFERENT. Also **sen·so·ri·al** (sen·sôr′ē·əl, -sō′rē-).

sen·su·al (sen′shōō·əl) *adj.* **1** Of or pertaining to the senses or their gratification; fleshly; carnal. **2** Unduly indulgent to the appetites or senses. **3** Caused by or preoccupied with bodily or sexual pleasure. [< L *sensus* perception] —**sen′su·al·ly** *adv.*

sen·su·al·ism (sen′shōō·əl·iz′əm) *n.* **1** Frequent or excessive indulgence in sensual pleasures. **2** *Philos.* A system of ethics holding that sensual pleasures are the highest good. —**sen′su·al·ist** *n.* —**sen′su·al·is′tic** *adj.*

sen·su·al·i·ty (sen′shōō·al′ə·tē) *n.* **1** The state of being sensual. **2** Sensual indulgence; lewdness; lasciviousness.

sen·su·al·ize (sen′shōō·əl·īz′) *v.t.* **·ized, ·iz·ing** To make sensual. *Brit. sp.* **sen′su·al·ise′.** —**sen′su·al·i·za′tion** *n.*

sen·su·ous (sen′shōō·əs) *adj.* **1** Of, pertaining or appealing to, or perceived or caused by the senses. **2** Keenly appreciative of or susceptible to the pleasures of sensation. —**sen′su·ous·ly** *adv.* —**sen′su·ous·ness** *n.*

sent (sent) *p.t.* & *p.p.* of SEND.

sen·tence (sen′təns) *n.* **1** A determination; opinion, esp. one expressed formally. **2** A final judgment, esp. one pronounced by a court. **3** The penalty pronounced upon a convicted person. **4** *Gram.* A word or group of words expressing a complete thought in the form of a declaration, a question, a command, a wish or an exclamation, usu. beginning with a capital letter and concluding with proper end punctuation. —*v.t.* **·tenced, ·tenc·ing** To pass sentence upon; condemn to punishment. [< L *sententia* opinion< *sentire* feel, be of opinion] —**sen′tenc·er** *n.* —**sen·ten·tial** (sen·ten′shəl) *adj.*

sen·ten·tious (sen·ten′shəs) *adj.* **1** Saying much in few words; terse; pithy. **2** Habitually using or full of aphoristic language. **3** Habitually using or full of moralistic language. [< L *sententia* opinion] —**sen·ten′tious·ly** *adv.* —**sen·ten′tious·ness** *n.*

sen·ti·ent (sen′shē·ənt, -shənt) *adj.* Possessing the powers of feeling or perception. [< L *sentire* feel] —**sen′ti·ence** *n.* —**sen′ti·ent·ly** *adv.*

sen·ti·ment (sen′tə·mənt) *n.* **1** Noble, tender, or refined feeling; delicate sensibility, esp. as expressed in a work of art. **2** A complex of opinions and feelings used as a basis for judgment or action. **3** A mental attitude, judgment, or thought often conditioned by feeling more than reason. **4** SENTIMENTALITY. **5** The meaning of something said, as distinguished from its expression. **6** A thought or wish phrased in conventional language, as a toast. [< L *sentire* feel]

sen·ti·men·tal (sen′tə·men′təl) *adj.* **1** Of, pertaining to, caused by, having, or showing sentiment. **2** Experiencing, displaying, or given to sentiment in an extravagant or maudlin manner. —**sen′ti·men′tal·ism, sen′ti·men′tal·ist** *n.* —**sen′ti·men′tal·ly** *adv.*

sen·ti·men·tal·i·ty (sen′tə·men·tal′ə·tē) *n. pl.* **·ties. 1** The state or quality of being overly sentimental, esp. in a superficial or maudlin way. **2** An expression of this.

sen·ti·men·tal·ize (sen′tə·men′təl·īz) *v.* **·ized, ·iz·ing** *v.t.* **1** To regard or treat with sentiment. —*v.i.* **2** To behave sentimentally.

sen·ti·nel (sen′tə·nəl) *n.* A guard, esp. a sentry. —*v.t.* **·neled** or **·nelled, ·nel·ing** or **·nel·ling 1** To watch over as a sentinel. **2** To protect or furnish with sentinels. **3** To station or appoint as a sentinel. [< LL *sentinare* avoid danger < *sentire* perceive]

sen·try (sen′trē) *n. pl.* **·tries** **1** A guard, esp. a soldier placed on guard to see that only authorized persons pass his post and to give warning of approaching danger. **2** The guard kept by a sentry. [? var. of SENTINEL]

Sep. September; Septuagint.

sep. sepal; separate; separated.

se·pal (sē′pəl) *n. Bot.* Any of the individual leaves of a calyx. [< NL *sepa* covering + *petalum* a petal] —**sep·a·line** (sep′-ə·lin, -līn), **sep′a·lous, se′paled, se′palled** *adj.*

Sepals of flower

sep·a·ra·ble (sep′ər·ə·bəl, sep′-rə-) *adj.* Capable of being separated or divided. —**sep′a·ra·bil′i·ty, sep′a·ra·ble·ness** *n.* —**sep′a·ra·bly** *adv.*

sep·a·rate (sep′ə·rāt) *v.* **·rat·ed, ·rat·ing** *v.t.* **1** To set apart; sever; disjoin. **2** To keep apart; divide: The Hudson River *separates* New York from New Jersey. **3** To divide into components, parts, etc. **4** To isolate or obtain from a compound, mixture, etc.: to *separate* the wheat from the chaff. **5** To consider separately; distinguish between. **6** *Law* To part by separation. —*v.i.* **7** To become divided or disconnected; draw apart. **8** To part company; sever an association. **9** To cease living together as man and wife. **10** To break up into component parts, as a mixture. —*adj.* (sep′ər·it, sep′rit) **1** Existing or considered apart from others; distinct; individual. **2** Detached; disunited. **3** Existing independently; not related. —*n.pl.* Garments to be worn in various combinations, as skirts and blouses. [< L *se-* apart + *parare* prepare] —**sep′a·rate·ly** *adv.* —**sep′a·rate·ness, sep′a·ra′tor** *n.* —**sep′a·ra′tive** (-rā′tiv, -ə·rə·tiv) *adj.*

sep·a·ra·tion (sep′ə·rā′shən) *n.* **1** The act or process of separating. **2** The state of being separated. **3** A gap or dividing line. **4** *Law* Relinquishment of cohabitation between husband and wife by mutual consent.

sep·a·ra·tist (sep′ər·ə·tist, sep′rə-) *n.* One who advocates or upholds separation, esp. political, racial, or religious separation. Also **sep′a·ra′tion·ist.** —**sep′a·ra·tism** *n.*

Sep·a·ra·tist (sep′ər·ə·tist, sep′rə-) *n. Can.* One who believes in or supports the withdrawal of a province, esp. Quebec, from Confederation.

Se·phar·dim (si·fär′dim) *n. pl.* The Spanish and Portuguese Jews or their descendants. Also **Se·phar′a·dim** (-ə·dim). [< Hebrew *sephārādhīm* < *Sephāradh, Obad.* 1:20, a country identified with Spain] —**Se·phar′dic** *adj.*

se·pi·a (sē′pē·ə) *n.* **1** A reddish brown pigment prepared from the ink of certain cuttlefish. **2** The color of this pigment. **3** A picture done in this color. —*adj.* Executed in or colored like sepia. [< Gk. *sēpia* cuttlefish]

se·poy (sē′poi) *n.* Formerly, a native Indian soldier in the British or other European army. [< Pers. *sipāh* army]

sep·sis (sep′sis) *n.* The presence of pathogenic microorganisms or their toxins in the blood or tissues. [< Gk. *sēpein* make putrid]

sep·ta (sep′tə) *n. pl.* of SEPTUM.

Sep·tem·ber (sep·tem′bər) *n.* The ninth month of the year, containing 30 days. [< L *septem* seven]

sep·te·nar·y (sep′tə·ner′ē) *adj.* Consisting of, pertaining to, or being seven. —*n. pl.* **·nar·ies** A group of seven things of any kind. [< L *septeni* seven each]

sep·ten·ni·al (sep·ten′ē·əl) *adj.* **1** Recurring every seven years. **2** Continuing or capable of lasting seven years. —**sep·ten′ni·al·ly** *adv.*

sep·tet (sep·tet′) *n.* **1** A group or set of seven, esp. seven musical performers. **2** *Music* A composition for such a group. Also **sep·tette′.** [< L *septem* seven]

sep·tic (sep′tik) *adj.* **1** Of, pertaining to, or caused by sepsis. **2** Productive of putrefaction; putrid. Also **sep′ti·cal.**

sep·ti·ce·mi·a (sep′tə·sē′mē·ə) *n.* BLOOD POISONING. Also **sep′ti·cae′mi·a.** [< Gk. *sēptikos* putrefactive + *haima* blood] —**sep′ti·ce′mic** (-sē′mik) *adj.*

septic tank A tank in which sewage is held until decomposed by anaerobic bacteria.

sep·til·lion (sep·til′yən) *n. & adj.* See NUMBER. [< L *sept(em)* + F *(m)illion* a million] —**sep·til′lionth** *adj., n.*

sep·tu·a·ge·nar·i·an (sep′tyōō·ə·jə·nâr′ē·ən, sep′tə·wäj′ə-) *n.* A person 70 years old, or between 70 and 80. [< L *septuaginta* seventy]

Sep·tu·a·ges·i·ma (sep′tə·wə·jes′ə·mə, -jā′zə-) *n.* The third Sunday before Lent. Also **Septuagesima Sunday.** [< L, seventieth]

Sep·tu·a·gint (sep′tyōō·ə·jint′, sep′tə·wə-) *n.* An ancient Greek version of the Old Testament, made between 280 and 130 B.C. [< L *septuaginta* seventy < a tradition that it was produced in 70 days by a group of 72 scholars]

sep·tum (sep′təm) *n. pl.* **·ta** (-tə) A partition between two masses of tissue or two cavities: the nasal *septum.* [< L *sepes* a hedge] —**sep′tal** *adj.*

sep·tu·ple (sep′tyōō·pəl, sep·tyōō′-) *adj.* **1** Consisting of seven; sevenfold. **2** Multiplied by seven; seven times repeated. —*v.t. & v.i.* **·pled, ·pling** To multiply by seven. —*n.* A number or sum seven times as great as another. [< L *septem* seven]

sep·ul·cher (sep′əl·kər) *n.* **1** A burial place; tomb; vault. **2** A receptacle for relics, esp. in an altar slab. —*v.t.* **·chered** or **·chred, ·cher·ing** or **·chring** To place in a grave; entomb; bury. Also **sep′ul·chre** (-kər). [< L *sepulcrum*]

se·pul·chral (si·pul′krəl) *adj.* **1** Of a sepulcher. **2** Dismal in color or aspect. **3** Low or melancholy in sound. —**se·pul′chral·ly** *adv.*

seq. sequel.

seq., seqq. the following (L *sequens, sequentia*).

se·quel (sē′kwəl) *n.* **1** Something which follows; a continuation; development. **2** A narrative which, though entire in itself, develops from a preceding one. **3** A consequence; result. [< L *sequi* follow]

se·quence (sē′kwəns) *n.* **1** The process or fact of following in space, time, or thought; succession or order. **2** Order of succession; arrangement. **3** A number of things following one another, considered collectively; a series. **4** An effect or consequence. **5** A section of motion-picture film presenting a single episode, without time lapses or interruptions. [< L *sequi* follow]

se·quent (sē′kwənt) *n.* That which follows; a consequence; result. —*adj.* **1** Following in the order of time; succeeding. **2** Consequent; resultant. [< L *sequi* follow]

se·quen·tial (si·kwen′shəl) *adj.* **1** Characterized by or forming a sequence, as of parts. **2** SEQUENT. —**se·quen·ti·al·i·ty** (si·kwen′shē·al′ə·tē) *n.* —**se·quen′tial·ly** *adv.* —**Syn. 1** consecutive, orderly, serial.

se·ques·ter (si·kwes′tər) *v.t.* **1** To place apart; separate. **2** To seclude; withdraw: often used reflexively. **3** *Law* To take (property) into custody until a controversy, claim, etc., is settled. **4** In international law, to confiscate and control (enemy property) by preemption. [< LL *sequestrare* remove, lay aside] —**se·ques′tered** *adj.*

se·ques·trate (si·kwes′trāt) *v.t.* **·trat·ed, ·trat·ing** SEQUESTER. —**se·ques·tra·tor** (sē′kwes·trā′tər, si·kwes′trā·tər) *n.*

se·quin (sē′kwin) *n.* A spangle or small coinlike ornament sewn on clothing. —*v.t.* **se·quined** or **se·quinned, se·quin·ing** or **se·quin·ning** To decorate with sequins. [< Ar. *sikka* a coining-die]

se·quoi·a (si·kwoi′ə) *n.* Either of two species of gigantic coniferous evergreen trees of the western U.S. [< *Sikwayi,* 1770?–1843, American Indian who invented the Cherokee alphabet]

Sequoia

ser. serial; series; sermon.

se·ra (sir′ə) A *pl.* of SERUM.

se·ra·glio (si·ral′yō, -räl′-) *n. pl.* **·glios** **1** That part of a sultan's palace where his harem lives. **2** The palace of a sultan. Also **se·rail** (se·rāl′). [< Ital. *serraglio* an enclosure]

se·ra·pe (se·rä′pē) *n.* A shawl or blanketlike outer garment worn in Latin America. [Sp.]

ser·aph (ser′əf) *n. pl.* **ser·aphs** or **ser·a·phim** (ser′ə·fim) An angel of the highest order, usu. represented as having six wings. [< Heb. *serāphīm,* pl.] —**se·raph·ic** (si·raf′ik) *adj.* —**se·raph′i·cal·ly** *adv.*

Ser·bo-Cro·a·tian (sûr′bō·krō·ā′shən) *n.* 1 The South Slavic language of Yugoslavia. 2 Any person whose native tongue is Serbo-Croatian. —*adj.* Of this language or people.

sere (sir) *adj.* Withered; dried up.

ser·e·nade (ser′ə·nād′) *n.* An evening piece, usu. the song of a lover beneath his lady's window. —*v.t. & v.i.* **·nad·ed, ·nad·ing** To entertain with a serenade. [< L *serenus* clear, serene] —**ser′e·nad′er** *n.*

Serape

ser·en·dip·i·ty (ser′ən·dip′ə·tē) *n.* The faculty of making fortunate discoveries by accident. [Coined by Horace Walpole (1754) after fairy tale characters] —**ser′en·dip′i·tous** *adj.*

se·rene (si·rēn′) *adj.* 1 Clear, bright, and fair; cloudless; untroubled. 2 Tranquil; calm; peaceful. 3 *Usu. cap.* Of exalted rank: used chiefly in royal titles: His *Serene* Highness. [< L *serenus*] —**se·rene′ly** *adv.* —**se·ren·i·ty** (si·ren′ə·tē), **se·rene′ness** *n.* —**Syn.** 2 composed, collected, placid.

serf (sûrf) *n.* 1 In feudal times, a person attached to the estate on which he lived. 2 Any person in servile subjection. [< L *servus* a slave] —**serf′dom, serf′age, serf′hood** *n.*

serge (sûrj) *n.* 1 A strong twilled woolen fabric woven with a diagonal rib on both sides. 2 A twilled silk or synthetic lining fabric. [< L *serica (lana)* (wool) of the Seres, an eastern Asian people]

ser·geant (sär′jənt) *n.* 1 See GRADE. 2 A police officer of rank next below a captain or lieutenant. 3 SERGEANT AT ARMS. [< L *servire* serve] —**ser′gean·cy, ser′geant·cy, ser′geant·ship** *n.*

sergeant at arms *pl.* **sergeants at arms** An officer in a legislative body, court, etc. who enforces order.

sergeant major *pl.* **sergeants major** See GRADE.

se·ri·al (sir′ē·əl) *adj.* 1 Of, like, or arranged in a series. 2 Published or presented in a series at regular intervals. 3 Of a serial or serials. 4 Of, pertaining to, or being atonal music consisting of a fixed series of tones based on the twelve-tone chromatic scale. —*n.* 1 A novel or other story regularly presented in successive installments, as in a magazine, on radio or television, or in motion pictures. 2 A periodical. —**se′ri·al·ly** *adv.*

se·ri·al·ism (sir′ē·əl·izm) *n.* Serial music. —**se′ri·al·ist** *n.*

se·ri·al·ize (sir′ē·əl·īz′) *v.t.* **·ized, ·iz·ing** To present in serial form. —**se′ri·al·i·za′tion** *n.*

serial number An identifying number assigned to a person, object, item of merchandise, etc.

se·ri·a·tim (sir′ē·ā′tim, ser′ē-) *adv.* One after another; in connected order; serially. [< L *series* series]

se·ries (sir′ēz) *n. pl.* **se·ries** 1 An arrangement or connected succession of related things placed in space or happening in time one after the other: a *series* of games; a *series* of lakes. 2 *Math.* The indicated sum of any finite set of terms or of an ordered infinite set of terms. 3 *Chem.* A group of related compounds or elements showing an orderly succession of changes in composition or structure. 4 *Electr.* An arrangement of electric devices in which the current flows through each in order. [L < *serere* join]

ser·if (ser′if) *n. Printing* A light line or stroke crossing or projecting from the end of a main line or stroke in a letter. [< L *scribere* write]

se·ri·o·com·ic (sir′ē·ō·kom′ik) *adj.* Mingling the comic with the serious. Also **se′ri·o·com′i·cal.** —**se′ri·o·com′i·cal·ly** *adv.*

se·ri·ous (sir′ē·əs) *adj.* 1 Grave and earnest in quality, feeling, or disposition; thoughtful; sober. 2 Being or done in earnest; not jesting or joking. 3 Involving much work, thought, difficulty, etc.: a *serious* problem. 4 Of grave importance; weighty. 5 Attended with considerable danger or loss: a *serious* accident. [< L *serius*] —**se′ri·ous·ly** *adv.* —**se′ri·ous·ness** *n.* —**Syn.** 1 sedate, staid, solemn, grim. 3 complex, complicated, involved, hard, troublesome.

ser·jeant (sär′jənt) *n. Brit.* SERGEANT.

ser·mon (sûr′mən) *n.* 1 A discourse, usu. based on a passage or text of the Bible, delivered as part of a church service. 2 Any serious talk or exhortation, as on duty, morals, etc. [< L *sermo* talk] —**ser·mon·ic** (sər·mon′ik) *adj.*

ser·mon·ize (sûr′mən·īz) *v.t. & v.i.* **·ized, ·iz·ing** To deliver sermons (to). —**ser′mon·iz′er** *n.*

Sermon on the Mount The discourse of Jesus found recorded in *Matt.* 5–7.

se·rol·o·gy (si·rol′ə·jē) *n.* The science of serums and their actions. [< SER(UM) + -LOGY] —**se·ro·log·i·cal** (sir′ə·loj′i·kəl) *adj.*

se·rous (sir′əs) *adj.* Pertaining to, producing, or resembling serum.

ser·pent (sûr′pənt) *n.* 1 A snake, esp. a poisonous or large one. 2 A treacherous person. [< L *serpere* to creep]

ser·pen·tine (sûr′pən·tīn, -tēn) *adj.* 1 Of or like a serpent. 2 Winding; zigzag. 3 Subtle; cunning. —*n.* A massive or fibrous, often mottled green or yellow, magnesium silicate.

ser·rate (ser′āt, -it) *adj.* Having sawlike teeth, as the margins of certain leaves. Also **ser′rat·ed.** [< L *serra* a saw] • See LEAF.

ser·ra·tion (se·rā′shən) *n.* 1 The state of being edged as with saw teeth. 2 A single projection of a serrate edge, or a series of such projections. Also **ser·ra·ture** (ser′ə·chər). [< L *serra* a saw]

ser·ried (ser′ēd) *adj.* Compacted in rows or ranks, as soldiers in company formation. [< LL *serrare* to lock]

se·rum (sir′əm) *n. pl.* **se·rums** or **se·ra** (sir′ə) 1 The fluid constituent of blood. 2 The serum of the blood of an animal which has developed immunity to a specific pathogen. 3 WHEY. 4 Any watery plant or animal secretion. [L, whey]

ser·vant (sûr′vənt) *n.* 1 A person employed to assist in domestic matters, sometimes living within the employer's house. 2 A government worker. [< OF *servir* to serve]

serve (sûrv) *v.* **served, serv·ing** *v.t.* 1 To work for as a servant. 2 To be of service to; wait on. 3 To promote the interests of; aid; help: to *serve* one's country. 4 To obey and give homage to: to *serve* God. 5 To satisfy the requirements of; suffice for. 6 To perform the duties connected with, as a public office. 7 To go through (a period of enlistment, term of punishment, etc.). 8 To furnish or provide, as with a regular supply. 9 To offer or bring food or drink to (a guest, etc.); wait on at table. 10 To bring and place on the table or distribute among guests, as food or drink. 11 To operate or handle; tend: to *serve* a cannon. 12 To copulate with: said of male animals. 13 In tennis, etc., to put (the ball) in play by hitting it to one's opponent. 14 *Law* **a** To deliver (a summons or writ) to a person. **b** To deliver a summons or writ to. 15 *Naut.* To wrap (a rope, stay, etc.), as with wire, cordage, etc., so as to strengthen or protect. —*v.i.* 16 To be a servant. 17 To perform the duties of any employment, office, etc. 18 To go through a term of service, as in the army or navy. 19 To offer or give food or drink, as to guests. 20 To wait on customers. 21 To be suitable or usable, as for a purpose; perform a function. 22 To be favorable, as weather. 23 In tennis, etc., to put the ball in play. —*n.* In tennis, etc.: **a** The delivering of the ball by striking it toward an opponent. **b** The turn of one who serves. [< L *servus* a slave]

serv·er (sûr′vər) *n.* 1 One who serves, as an attendant aiding a priest at low mass. 2 That which is used in serving, as a tray.

ser·vice (sûr′vis) *n.* 1 The act or occupation of serving. 2 The manner in which one serves or is served. 3 A division of employment, esp. of public or governmental employment: the diplomatic *service.* 4 Any branch of the armed forces. 5 A facility for meeting some public need: electric *service.* 6 Installation, maintenance, and repair provided for the buyer of something. 7 Assistance; aid; benefit: to be of *service.* 8 *Often pl.* A useful result or product of labor which is not a tangible commodity: a doctor's *services.* 9 *Often pl.* A public exercise of worship. 10 A religious or civil ritual: the marriage *service.* 11 The music for a liturgical office or rite. 12 A set of articles for a particular purpose: a tea *service.* 13 *Naut.* The protective wire, cordage, etc., wrapped around a rope. 14 *Law* The legal communication of a writ, process, or summons to a designated person. **15** In animal husbandry, the copulation of a female. —*adj.* **1** Pertaining to or for service. **2** Of, for, or used by servants or tradespeople: a *service* entrance. **3** Of, pertaining to, or belonging to a military service: a *service* flag. **4** For rough or everyday usage. —*v.t.* **·viced, ·vic·ing 1** To maintain or repair: to *service* a car. **2** To supply service to. **3** SERVE (def. 12). [< L *servus* a slave]

ser·vice·a·ble (sûr′vis·ə·bəl) *adj.* **1** That can serve a useful purpose; beneficial. **2** Capable of rendering long service; durable. —**ser′vice·a·ble·ness, ser′vice·a·bil′i·ty** *n.* —**ser′vice·a·bly** *adv.* —**Syn. 1** practical, practicable, utilitarian, helpful.

ser·vice·man (sûr′vis·man′) *n. pl.* **·men** (-men′) **1** A member of one of the armed forces. **2** A man who performs services of maintenance, supply, repair, etc.: also **service man.**

service station 1 A place for supplying motor vehicles with gasoline, oil, etc., and often for doing auto maintenance and repair work. **2** A place for adjusting, repairing, or supplying parts for electrical and mechanical appliances.

ser·vi·ette (sûr′vē·et′, -vyet′) *n.* A table napkin. [< MF *servir* serve]

ser·vile (sûr′vīl, -vil) *adj.* **1** Having the spirit of a slave; slavish; abject. **2** Of, pertaining to, or appropriate for slaves or servants: *servile* employment. [< L *servus* a slave] —**ser′vile·ly** *adv.* —**ser·vil′i·ty, ser′vile·ness** *n.* —**Syn. 1** obsequious, fawning, groveling, cowering, submissive, cringing.

serv·ing (sûr′ving) *n.* **1** A portion of food for one person. **2** The act of one who or that which serves. —*adj.* Used for dealing out food.

ser·vi·tor (sûr′və·tər) *n.* One who waits upon and serves another; an attendant; follower; servant.

ser·vi·tude (sûr′və·t(y)ōōd) *n.* **1** The condition of a slave; slavery; bondage. **2** Enforced service as a punishment for crime: penal *servitude*. [< L *servus* a slave]

ser·vo·mech·a·nism (sûr′vō·mek′ə·niz′əm) *n.* Any of various devices using feedback in which a small input is amplified and used to control a machine, operation, process, etc. [< L *servus* slave + MECHANISM]

ses·a·me (ses′ə·mē) *n.* An East Indian plant bearing edible, oily seeds (**sesame seed**) that yield an oil (**sesame oil**) used in cooking. [< Gk. *sēsamon*]

ses·qui·cen·ten·ni·al (ses′kwi·sen·ten′ē·əl) *adj.* Of or pertaining to a century and a half. —*n.* A 150th anniversary, or its celebration. [< L *sesqui*- one half more + CENTENNIAL]

ses·sile (ses′īl, -əl) *adj.* **1** *Bot.* Attached without a stalk, as a leaf. **2** *Zool. & Anat.* Attached at the base; sedentary. [< L *sessilis* sitting down, stunted] —**ses·sil′i·ty** *n.*

ses·sion (sesh′ən) *n.* **1** The sitting together of a legislative assembly, court, etc., for the transaction of business. **2** A single meeting or series of meetings of an assembly, court, etc. **3** In some schools, a term. **4** Any period of some specified activity: a *session* with the boss. [< L *sessus*, p.p. of *sedere* sit] —**ses′sion·al** *adj.* —**ses′sion·al·ly** *adv.*

ses·tet (ses·tet′) *n.* **1** The last six lines of a sonnet; also, any six-line stanza. **2** *Music* SEXTET. [< L *sextus* sixth]

set¹ (set) *v.* **set, set·ting** *v.t.* **1** To put in a certain place or position; place. **2** To put into a fixed, firm, or immovable position, condition, or state: to *set* brick; to *set* one's jaw. **3** To bring to a specified condition or state: *Set* your mind at ease; He *set* the barn afire; She has *set* her heart on being a doctor. **4** To restore to proper position for healing, as a broken bone. **5** To place in readiness for use: to *set* a trap. **6** To adjust according to a standard: to *set* a clock. **7** To adjust (an instrument, dial, etc.) to a particular calibration or position. **8** To place knives, forks, etc., on (a table) for a meal. **9** To bend the teeth of (a saw) to either side alternately. **10** To appoint or establish; prescribe: to *set* boundaries, regulations, fashions, etc. **11** To fix or establish a time for: We *set* our departure for noon. **12** To assign for performance, completion, etc.; to *set* a task. **13** To assign to some specific duty or function; appoint; sta-

tion: to *set* a guard. **14** To cause to sit. **15** To present or perform so as to be copied or emulated: to *set* the pace. **16** To give a specified direction to: He *set* his course for the Azores. **17** To put in place so as to catch the wind: to *set* the jib. **18** To place in a mounting or frame, as a gem. **19** To stud or adorn with gems: to *set* a crown with rubies. **20** To place (a hen) on eggs to hatch them. **21** To place (eggs) under a fowl or in an incubator for hatching. **22** To place (a price or value): with *by* or *on*: to *set* a price on an outlaw's head. **23** To arrange (hair), as with curlers, lotions, etc. **24** *Printing* **a** To arrange (type) for printing; compose. **b** To put into type, as a sentence, manuscript, etc. **25** *Music* To compose music for (words) or write words for (existing music). **26** To describe (a scene) as taking place: to *set* the scene in Monaco. **27** In the theater, to arrange (a stage) so as to depict a scene. **28** In some games, as bridge, to defeat. —*v.i.* **29** To go or pass below the horizon, as the sun. **30** To wane; decline. **31** To sit on eggs, as a fowl. **32** To become firm; solidify; congeal. **33** To become fast, as a dye. **34** To begin to move, as on a journey: with *forth, out, off,* etc. **35** To begin: *Set* to work. **36** To have a specified direction; tend. **37** To hang or fit, as clothes. **38** To mend, as a broken bone. **39** *Regional* To sit. **40** *Bot.* To begin development or growth, as a rudimentary fruit. — **set against 1** To balance; compare. **2** To make unfriendly to; prejudice against. —**set off 1** To put apart by itself. **2** To serve as a contrast or foil for; enhance. **3** To make begin; set in motion. **4** To cause to explode. —**set out 1** To display; exhibit. **2** To lay out or plan. **3** To begin a journey. **4** To begin any enterprise. **5** To plant. —**set to 1** To start; begin. **2** To start fighting. —**set up 1** To place in an upright or high position. **2** To raise. **3** To place in power, authority, etc. **4 a** To construct or build. **b** To put together; assemble. **c** To found; establish. **5** To provide with the means to start a new business. **6** To cause to be heard: to *set up* a cry. **7** To propose or put forward (a theory, etc.). **8** To cause. **9** To work out a plan for. **10** To claim to be. **11 a** To pay for the drinks, etc., of; treat. **b** To pay for (drinks, etc.). **12** To encourage; exhilarate. —**set upon** To attack; assail. —*adj.* **1** Established by authority or agreement; prescribed; appointed: a *set* time or method. **2** Customary; conventional: a *set* phrase. **3** Deliberately and systematically conceived; formal: a *set* speech. **4** Fixed and motionless; rigid. **5** Firm in consistency. **6** Fixed in opinion or disposition; obstinate. **7** Formed; built; made: deep-*set* eyes. **8** Ready; prepared: to get *set*. —*n.* **1** The act or condition of setting. **2** Permanent change of form, as by bending, pressure, strain, etc. **3** The arrangement, tilt, or hang of a garment, hat, sail, etc. **4** Carriage or bearing: the *set* of his shoulders. **5** The sinking of a heavenly body below the horizon. **6** The direction of a current or wind. **7** A young plant ready for setting out. **8** Inclination of the mind; bent. **9** *Psychol.* A temporary condition assumed by an organism preparing for a particular response or activity. **10** An arrangement of the hair, as by curling. **11** In tennis, a group of games completed when one side wins six games, or, if tied at five games, wins either two more games consecutively or wins a tie breaker. [< OE *settan* cause to sit]

set² (set) *n.* **1** A number of persons regarded as associated through status, common interests, etc.: a new *set* of customers. **2** A social group having some exclusive character; coterie; clique: the fast *set*. **3** A number of things belonging together or customarily used together: a *set* of instruments. **4** A group of books or periodicals issued together or related by common authorship, subject, etc. **5** In jazz performances, the music played during one period of time without an intermission; also, the period of time. **6** In the theatre, motion pictures, etc., the complete assembly of properties, structures, etc., required in a scene. **7** Radio or television receiving equipment assembled for use. **8** *Math.* Any collection of elements, objects, or numbers. [< L *secta* a sect]

se·ta (sē′tə) *n. pl.* **·tae** (-tē) *Biol.* A bristle or bristlelike process. [< L] —**se·ta·ceous** (si·tā′shəs), **se′tose** *adj.*

set·back (set′bak′) *n.* **1** A misfortune or reversal, as in

progress. 2 An indentation or steplike arrangement of the upper levels of a tall building.

Seth (seth) In the Bible, the third son of Adam.

set·off (set′ôf′, -of′) *n.* **1** Something that offsets, balances, or compensates for something else. **2** Something that contrasts with or sets off something else. **3** A counterclaim or the discharge of a debt by a counterclaim. **4** *Archit.* A ledge; offset.

set piece 1 Something, as a passage in literature, music, etc., aimed at creating a brilliant effect. **2** A fireworks display. **3** A piece of scenery for the stage.

set·screw (set′skroo′) *n.* **1** A screw so made that it can be screwed tightly against or into another surface to prevent movement. **2** A screw for regulating the tension of a spring or the opening of a valve.

set·tee (se·tē′) *n.* **1** A long wooden seat with a high back. **2** A sofa suitable for two or three people. [?< SETTLE]

set·ter (set′ər) *n.* **1** One who or that which sets. **2** One of a breed of medium-sized, silky-coated dogs trained to indicate the location of game birds while standing rigid.

set·ting (set′ing) *n.* **1** The position, degree, etc., at which something is set. **2** A frame or mounting, as for a jewel. **3** Physical environment or surroundings. **4** The scene, time, background, etc., as of a novel or play. **5** A number of eggs placed together for hatching. **6** The music composed for a poem, set of words, etc. **7** The tableware set out for one person.

set·tle (set′l) *v.* **·tled, ·tling** *v.t.* **1** To put in order; set to rights; to *settle* affairs. **2** To establish or fix permanently or as if permanently: He *settled* himself on the couch. **3** To calm; quiet: to *settle* one's nerves. **4** To cause (sediment or dregs) to sink to the bottom. **5** To make firm or compact: to *settle* dust or ashes. **6** To make clear or transparent, as by causing sediment or dregs to sink. **7** To make quiet or orderly: One blow *settled* him. **8**

Settle

To decide or determine finally, as an argument, legal case, etc. **9** To pay, as a debt; satisfy, as a claim. **10** To establish residents or residence in (a country, town, etc.). **11** To establish as residents. **12** To establish in a permanent occupation, home, etc. **13** *Law* To make over or assign (property) by legal act: with *on* or *upon*. —*v.i.* **14** To come to rest. **15** To sink gradually; subside. **16** To become clear by the sinking of sediment. **17** To become more firm by sinking. **18** To become established or located: The pain *settled* in his arm. **19** To establish one's abode or home. **20** To come to a decision; determine; resolve: with *on, upon,* or *with*. **21** To pay a bill, etc. —**settle down 1** To start living a regular, orderly life, esp. after a period of wandering or irresponsibility. **2** To become quiet or orderly. —*n.* A long, wooden, high-backed bench, usu. with arms and sometimes having a chest from seat to floor. [< OE *setl* a seat]

set·tle·ment (set′l·mənt) *n.* **1** The act of settling or the condition of being settled. **2** An area newly colonized. **3** A small, usu. remote village. **4** *Law* **a** The act of assigning property, money, etc., to someone. **b** That which is thus assigned. **5** An agreement or adjustment, as of differences. **6** An urban welfare institution that provides various educational or recreational services to a community or neighborhood: also **settlement house.**

set·tler (set′lər) *n.* **1** One who establishes himself in a colony or new country. **2** One who settles or decides.

set·tlings (set′lingz) *n.pl.* Dregs; sediment.

set-to (set′too′) *n.* A bout at fighting, arguing, etc.

set·up (set′up′) *n.* **1** A system or plan, as of a business operation, etc. **2** The arrangement or assembly of a machine, piece of equipment, etc. **3** The elements or circumstances of a situation or plan. **4** Carriage of the body; posture. **5** Ice, soda water, etc., provided for those who furnish their own liquor. **6** A table setting. **7** *Informal* **a** A contest or match arranged so as to result in an easy victory. **b** Anything easy to accomplish.

sev·en (sev′ən) *n.* **1** The sum of six plus one; 7; VII. **2** A set or group of seven members. [< OE *seofon*] —**sev′en** *adj., pron.*

seven deadly sins Pride, lust, envy, anger, covetousness, gluttony, and sloth.

sev·en·fold (sev′ən·fōld′) *adj.* **1** Seven times as many or as great. **2** Made up of seven; septuple. **3** Folded seven times. —*adv.* In sevenfold manner or degree.

seven seas All the oceans of the world.

sev·en·teen (sev′ən·tēn′) *n.* **1** The sum of 16 plus 1; 17; XVII. **2** A set or group of 17 members. —**sev′en·teen′** *adj., pron.*

sev·en·teenth (sev′ən·tēnth′) *adj. & adv.* Next in order after the 16th. —*n.* **1** The element of an ordered set that corresponds to the number 17. **2** One of seventeen equal parts.

sev·enth (sev′ənth) *adj. & adv.* Next in order after the sixth. —*n.* **1** The element of an ordered set that corresponds to the number seven. **2** One of seven equal parts. **3** *Music* The interval between any tone and the seventh tone above or below in the diatonic scale. —*adv.* In the seventh order, place, or rank: also, in formal discourse, **sev′enth·ly.**

seventh heaven The highest condition of happiness. [< the highest heaven according to certain ancient cosmologies]

sev·en·ti·eth (sev′ən·tē·ith) *adj. & adv.* Tenth in order after the 60th. —*n.* **1** The element of an ordered set that corresponds to the number 70. **2** One of seventy equal parts.

sev·en·ty (sev′ən·tē) *n. pl.* **·ties 1** The product of seven and ten; 70; LXX. **2** A set or group of 70 members. **3** *pl.* The numbers, years, etc., between 70 and 80. —**sev′en·ty** *adj., pron.*

sev·er (sev′ər) *v.t.* **1** To put or keep apart; separate. **2** To cut or break into two or more parts. **3** To break off; dissolve, as a relationship. —*v.i.* **4** To come or break apart or into pieces. **5** To go away or apart; separate. [< L *separare* separate] —**sev′er·a·ble** *adj.* —**sev′er·er** *n.*

sev·er·al (sev′ər·əl, sev′rəl) *adj.* **1** Being of an indefinite number, more than one or two, yet not large; divers. **2** Considered individually; single; separate. **3** Individually different; various or diverse. [< L *separ* separate]

sev·er·al·ly (sev′ər·əl·ē, sev′rəl·ē) *adv.* **1** Individually; separately. **2** Respectively.

sev·er·ance (sev′ər·əns, sev′rəns) *n.* The act of severing, or the condition of being severed.

severance pay Additional pay sometimes given to an employee who has been discharged.

se·vere (si·vir′) *adj.* **·ver·er, ·ver·est 1** Difficult; trying. **2** Unsparing; harsh; merciless: a *severe* punishment. **3** Conforming to rigid rules; extremely strict or accurate. **4** Serious and austere in disposition or manner; grave. **5** Austerely plain and simple, as in style, design, etc. **6** Causing sharp pain or anguish; extreme: *severe* hardship. —**se·vere′ness** *n.* [< L *severus*] —**se·vere′ly** *adv.*

se·ver·i·ty (si·ver′ə·tē) *n. pl.* **·ties** The quality or condition of being severe.

sew (sō) *v.* **sewed, sewed** or **sewn, sew·ing** *v.t.* **1** To make, mend, or fasten with needle and thread. **2** To enclose or secure by sewing. —*v.i.* **3** To work with needle and thread. —**sew up 1** To mend by sewing. **2** *Informal* **a** To achieve absolute control or use of. **b** To make or be totally successful. [< OE *siwan, siowian*]

sew·age (soo′ij) *n.* The waste matter carried off in sewers. [< SEW(ER) + -AGE]

sew·er (soo′ər) *n.* **1** A conduit, usu. laid underground, to carry off drainage and excrement. **2** Any large public drain. [< OF *seuwiere* a channel from a fish pond]

sew·er·age (soo′ər·ij) *n.* **1** A system of sewers. **2** Systematic draining by sewers. **3** SEWAGE.

sew·ing (sō′ing) *n.* **1** The act, business, or occupation of one who sews. **2** Material worked with needle and thread; needlework.

sewing circle A group of women meeting periodically to sew, usu. for some charitable purpose.

sewing machine A machine for stitching or sewing cloth, leather, etc.

sewn (sōn) A *p.p.* of SEW.

sex (seks) *n.* **1** Either of two divisions, male and female, by which organisms are distinguished with reference to the reproductive functions. **2** Males or females collectively. **3** The character of being male or female. **4** The activity or phenomena of life concerned with sexual desire or reproduction. **5** *Informal* Any act affording sexual gratification, as sexual intercourse. —*adj. Informal* SEX-UAL. [< L *sexus*]

sex·a·ge·nar·i·an (sek′sə·jə·nâr′ē·ən) *adj.* Sixty years old, or between sixty and seventy. —*n.* A person of this age. [< L *sexageni* sixty each]

Sex·a·ges·i·ma (sek′sə·jes′ə·mə, -jā′zə-) *n.* The second Sunday before Lent. [L, sixtieth]

sex·a·ges·i·mal (sek′sə·jes′ə·məl) *adj.* Of or based on the number 60. [< L *sexagesimus* < *sexaginta* sixty]

sex appeal A physical quality or charm which attracts sexual interest.

sex chromosome Either of a pair of chromosomes associated with the determination of sex in plants and animals.

sex·ism (seks′iz·əm) *n.* Prejudice or discrimination against women. [< SEX + -ISM, on analogy with *racism*] —**sex′ist** *n, adj.*

sex·less (seks′lis) *adj.* **1** Having no sex; neuter. **2** Without sexual interest or qualities. —**sex′less·ly** *adv.* —**sex′·less·ness** *n.*

sex linkage The presence on a sex chromosome of genes for certain nonsexual characteristics, resulting in the development of those characteristics in one sex only. —**sex·linked** (seks′lingkt′) *adj.*

sex·ol·o·gy (sek·sol′ə·jē) *n.* The study of human sexual behavior. —**sex·o·log·ic** (sek′sə·loj′ik) or **·i·cal** *adj.* —**sex·ol′o·gist** *n.*

sex·ploi·ta·tion (seks′ploi·tā′shən) *n.* The commercial exploitation of interest in sex, as by means of pornography. [Blend of SEX + EXPLOITATION]

sex·pot (seks′pot) *n. Slang* A very sexy woman.

sext (sekst) *n.* One of the canonical hours; the office for the sixth hour or noon. [< L *sex* six]

sex·tant (seks′tənt) *n.* An instrument for measuring the angular distance between two objects, as between a heavenly body and the horizon, used esp. in determining latitude at sea. [< L *sextus* sixth]

Sextant
a. eyepiece.

sex·tet (seks·tet′) *n.* **1** A group of six musical performers. **2** A musical composition for such a group. **3** Any collection of six persons or things. Also **sex·tette′**. [Alter. of SESTET]

sex·til·lion (seks·til′yən) *n. & adj.* See NUMBER. [< L *sex* six + F *(m)illion* a million]

sex·ton (seks′tən) *n.* An officer of a church having charge of maintenance and also of ringing the bells, overseeing burials, etc. [< Med. L *sacristanus* sacristan]

sex·tu·ple (sek·stÿoo′pəl, -stup′-, seks′too·pəl) *adj.* **1** Sixfold. **2** Multiplied by six; six times repeated. **3** *Music* Having six beats to the measure. —*v.t.* **·pled, ·pling** To multiply by six. —*n.* A number or sum six times as great as another. [< L *sextus* sixth] —**sex′tu·ply** *adv.*

sex·tu·plet (seks·tup′lit, -tÿoo′plit, seks′too·plit) *n.* **1** A set of six similar things. **2** One of six offspring produced at a single birth.

sex·u·al (sek′shoo·əl) *adj.* **1** Of, pertaining or peculiar to, characteristic of, or affecting sex, the sexes, or the organs or functions of sex. **2** Characterized by or having sex. [< L *sexus* sex] —**sex′u·al′i·ty** (-al′ə·tē) *n.* —**sex′u·al·ly** *adv.*

sexual intercourse 1 The sexual act, esp. between humans, in which the erect penis is introduced into the vagina for the ejaculation of semen and sexual gratification. **2** Any act of sexual connection, esp. between humans.

sex·y (sek′sē) *adj.* **sex·i·er, sex·i·est 1** *Informal* Provocative of sexual desire: a *sexy* dress; a *sexy* woman. **2** *Informal* Concerned in large or excessive degree with sex: a *sexy* novel. **3** *Slang* Interesting, exciting, or stimulating: Crime was the *sexiest* issue of the political campaign.

sf., sfz. sforzando.

sfor·zan·do (sfôr·tsän′do) *adj. & adv. Music* Accented with sudden explosive force. —*n.* A sforzando note or chord. Also **sfor·za′to** (-tsä′tō). [Ital. < *sforzare* to force]

sg. s.g. senior grade; specific gravity.

sgd. signed.

Sgt. Sergeant.

sh (sh) *interj.* An exclamation requesting silence.

sh. share; sheep; sheet; shilling.

Shab·bat (shä·bät′, shä′bəs) *n. pl.* **Shab·bat·im** (-bä′təm, -bô′səm) The Jewish Sabbath. [< Heb. *shabbāth*]

shab·by (shab′ē) *adj.* **·bi·er, ·bi·est 1** Threadbare, ragged. **2** Characterized by worn or ragged garments. **3** Mean; paltry. [< OE *sceabb* a scab] —**shab′bi·ly** *adv.* —**shab′bi·ness** *n.*

Sha·bu·oth (shä·voo′ōth, shə·voo′əs) *n.* The Jewish festival of Pentecost.

shack (shak) *n.* **1** A crudely built cabin or hut. **2** *Informal* A poorly built or designed house. —*v.i. Slang* To live or stay, usu. briefly, at a specific place. [?]

shack·le (shak′əl) *n.* **1** A bracelet or fetter for encircling and confining a limb or limbs. **2** *Usu. pl.* Any impediment or restraint. **3** One of various forms of fastenings, as a link for coupling railway cars. —*v.t.* **·led, ·ling 1** To restrain or confine with shackles; fetter. **2** To keep or restrain from free action or speech. **3** To connect or fasten with a shackle. [< OE *sceacul*] —**shack′ler** *n.*

Shackles

shad (shad) *n. pl.* **shad** Any of various anadromous fish related to the herring. [< OE *sceadd*]

shad·ber·ry (shad′ber′ē) *n. pl.* **·ries 1** SHADBUSH. **2** The fruit of the shadbush.

shad·bush (shad′boosh′) *n.* Any of various early-blooming shrubs with white flowers and edible purple berries. Also **shad′blow′** (-blō). [So called because it flowers when the shad appear in U.S. rivers]

shade (shād) *v.* **shad·ed, shad·ing** *v.t.* **1** To screen from light or heat. **2** To make dim with or as with a shadow; darken; **3** To screen or protect with or as with a shadow. **4** To cause to change, pass, blend, or soften, by gradations. **5 a** To represent (degrees of shade, colors, etc.) by gradations of light or shading. **b** To represent varying shades, colors, etc., in (a picture of painting). **6** To make slightly lower, as a price. —*v.i.* **7** To change or vary by degrees. —*n.* **1** Relative darkness caused by the interception or partial absence of rays of light. **2** A place having such relative darkness. **3** That part of a drawing, painting, etc. represented as being relatively dark or in shadow. **4** A gradation of darkness or blackness in a color. **5** A minute difference, variation, or degree: *shades* of meaning. **6** A screen or cover that partially or totally shuts off light: a lamp *shade.* **7** A ghost or phantom. **8** *pl. Slang* SUNGLASSES. —**in** (or **into**) **the shade 1** In or into a shady place. **2** In or into a condition of inferiority, defeat, obscurity, etc. [< OE *sceadu* a shade]

shad·ing (shā′ding) *n.* **1** Protective against light or heat. **2** The representation pictorially of darkness, color, or depth. **3** A slight difference or variation.

shad·ow (shad′ō) *n.* **1** A comparative darkness within an illuminated area caused by the interception of light by an opaque body. **2** The dark figure or image thus produced on a surface: the *shadow* of a man. **3** The shaded portion of a picture. **4** A mirrored image: to see one's *shadow* in a pool. **5** A phantom, ghost, etc. **6** A faint representation or indication; a symbol: the *shadow* to things to come. **7** A remnant; vestige: *shadows* of his former glory. **8** An insignificant trace or portion: not a *shadow* of evidence. **9** Gloom or a saddening influence. **10** An inseparable companion. **11** One who trails or follows another, as a detective or spy. **12** A slight growth of beard, esp. in the phrase **five o'clock shadow.** —*v.t.* **1** To cast a shadow upon; shade. **2** To darken or make gloomy. **3** To represent or foreshow dimly or vaguely: with *forth* or *out.* **4** To follow closely or secretly; spy on. **5** To shade in painting, drawing, etc. —*adj.* Of or pertaining to a shadow cabinet. [< OE *sceadu* a shade] —**shad′ow·er** *n.*

shad·ow·box (shad′ō·boks′) *v.i.* To spar with an imaginary opponent as a form of exercise. —**shad′ow·box′ing** *n.*

shadow box A small, open, framed cabinet, usu. hung on a wall to display knickknacks, etc.

shadow cabinet In the British or other parliamentary government, a group of opposition leaders who would assume specific cabinet positions if the government in power should fall.

shad·ow·y (shad′ō-ē) *adj.* **·ow·ier**, **·ow·i·est 1** Dark; shady. **2** Vague; dim. **3** Unreal; ghostly. —**shad′ow·i·ness** *n.*

shad·y (shā′dē) *adj.* **shad·i·er**, **shad·i·est 1** Full of shade; casting a shade. **2** Shaded or sheltered. **3** Morally questionable; suspicious. **4** Quiet; hidden. —**shad′i·ness** *n.*

shaft (shaft, shäft) *n.* **1** The long narrow rod of an arrow, spear, lance, harpoon, etc. **2** An arrow or spear. **3** Something hurled like or having the effect of an arrow or spear: *shafts* of ridicule. **4** A beam of light. **5** A long handle, as of a hammer, ax, etc. **6** *Mech.* A long and usu. cylindrical bar, esp. if rotating and transmitting motion. **7** *Archit.* **a** The portion of a column between capital and base. **b** A slender column, as an obelisk. **8** The stem of a feather. **9** The slender portion of a bone or the portion of a hair from root to the end. **10** A tall, narrow building or spire. **11** A narrow, vertical passage, as the entrance to a mine or an opening through a building for an elevator. **12** A conduit for the passage of air, heat, etc. **13** *Slang* Malicious or abusive treatment: with *the,* esp. in the phrases **get the shaft, give (someone) the shaft.** —*v.t. Slang* To act maliciously or abusively toward. [< OE *sceaft*]

shag (shag) *n.* **1** A rough coat or mass, as of hair. **2** A long, rough nap on cloth. **3** Cloth having a rough or long nap. **4** A coarse, strong tobacco: also **shag tobacco.** —*v.* **shagged, shag·ging** *v.t.* **1** To make shaggy or rough. —*v.i.* **2** To become shaggy or rough. [< OE *sceacga* wool]

shag·bark (shag′bärk′) *n.* **1** A species of hickory with rough, flaking bark. **2** Its edible nut. **3** Its wood.

shag·gy (shag′ē) *adj.* **·gi·er**, **·gi·est 1** Having, consisting of, or resembling rough hair or wool. **2** Covered with any rough, tangled growth; fuzzy. **3** Unkempt. —**shag′gi·ly** *adv.* —**shag′gi·ness** *n.*

sha·green (shə-grēn′) *n.* **1** An abrasive leather made of the skin of various sharks and rays. **2** A rough-grained rawhide. [< Turk. *sāghrī* horse's hide]

shah (shä) *n.* An eastern ruler, esp. of Iran. [< Pers.]

shake (shāk) *v.* **shook, shak·en, shak·ing** *v.t.* **1** To cause to move to and fro or up and down with short, rapid movements. **2** To affect by or as by vigorous action: with *off, out, from,* etc.: to *shake* out a sail; to *shake* off a tackler. **3** To cause to tremble or quiver; vibrate: The blows *shook* the door. **4** To cause to stagger or totter. **5** To weaken or disturb: to *shake* one's determination. **6** To agitate or rouse; stir: often with *up.* **7** *Informal* To get rid of or away from. **8** To clasp (hands) as a form of greeting, agreement, etc. **9** *Music* TRILL. —*v.i.* **10** To move to and fro or up and down in short, rapid movements. **11** To be affected by vigorous action: with *off, out, from,* etc. **12** To tremble or quiver, as from cold or fear. **13** To become unsteady; totter. **14** To clasp hands. **15** *Music* TRILL. —**shake down 1** To cause to fall by shaking. **2** To cause to settle by shaking. **3** To test or become familiar with (new equipment, etc.). **4** *Slang* To extort money from. —**shake up 1** To mix or blend by shaking. **2** To agitate or rouse; stir. **3** To jar or jolt. **4** To effect or cause rather extensive changes or reorganization in. **5** *Slang* To cause to lose one's composure; disconcert. —*n.* **1** The act or an instance of shaking: a *shake* of the hand. **2** A tight fissure in rock or timber. **3** *pl. Informal* A fit of bodily shaking or trembling: usu. with *the.* **4** MILKSHAKE. **5** *Informal* EARTHQUAKE. **6** *Informal* An instant; jiffy. **7** *Informal* A deal: to get a fair *shake.* **8** *Music* TRILL. —**give (someone or something) the shake** To get away from (someone or something). [< OE *scacan*]

shake·down (shāk′doun′) *n.* **1** A thorough search. **2** *Slang* Extortion of money. **3** A testing or becoming familiar with something, as with a new ship. —*adj.* For the purpose of testing mechanical parts or familiarizing personnel: a *shakedown* cruise.

shak·er (shā′kər) *n.* One who or that which shakes: a *saltshaker,* cocktail *shaker,* etc.

Shak·er (shā′kər) *n.* One of a sect practicing celibacy and communal living: so called from their trembling movements during religious meetings. —**Shak′er·ism** *n.*

Shake·spear·i·an (shāk·spir′ē-ən) *adj.* Of, pertaining to, or characteristic of Shakespeare, his work, or his style. —*n.* A specialist on Shakespeare or his writings. Also **Shake·spear′e·an.**

shake-up (shāk′up′) *n.* A rather extensive change or reorganization, as in a business office, etc.

shak·o (shak′ō, shāk′-, shäk′-) *n. pl.* **·os** A high, stiff military headdress, having a visor and an upright plume. [< Hung. *csákó*]

Shako

shak·y (shā′kē) *adj.* **shak·i·er, shak·i·est 1** Not firm or solid. **2** Not well founded, thought out, etc.: a *shaky* theory. **3** Not dependable or reliable. **4** Characterized by shaking. **5** Weak; unsound, as in body. —**shak′i·ly** *adv.* —**shak′i·ness** *n.*

shale (shāl) *n.* A rock resembling slate, with fragile, uneven layers. [< G *Schale* shale] —**shal′y** *adj.*

shall (shal) *v. p.t.* **should.** Used now only as an auxiliary, *shall* expresses: **1** Simple futurity: I *shall* go next week. **2** That which seems inevitable or certain: I know I *shall* never leave. **3** Determination, promise, threat, or command: They *shall* not pass; You *shall* pay for this; You *shall* have it. **4** In laws, resolutions, etc., that which is obligatory: It *shall* be required to have identification. [< OE *sceal* I am obliged] • **shall, will** The traditional rule is that to express simple futurity *shall* is used with the first person and the auxiliary *will* with the second and third. To express determination, obligation, command, etc., *will* is used with the first person and *shall* with the second and third. This rule is now widely ignored, both in speech and in writing. *Will,* by far the more common auxiliary, occurs with all subjects and in all contexts. *Shall* is still often used with the first person, less so with the second and third, where its use is likely to appear stilted.

shal·lop (shal′əp) *n.* An open boat propelled by oars or sails. [< Du. *sloep* sloop]

shal·lot (shə·lot′, shal′ət) *n.* **1** A mild, onionlike vegetable allied to garlic. **2** SCALLION. [< OF *eschalotte*]

shal·low (shal′ō) *adj.* **1** Lacking depth. **2** Not extending far inwards or outwards: a *shallow* room. **3** Lacking intellectual depth; superficial. —*n. Usu. pl. but construed as sing. or pl.* A shallow place in a body of water; shoal. —*v.t. & v.i.* To make or become shallow. [ME *schalowe*] —**shal′low·ly** *adv.* —**shal′low·ness** *n.*

shalt (shalt) *v.* Archaic second person singular, present tense of SHALL: used with *thou.*

sham (sham) *adj.* False; pretended; counterfeit; mock. —*n.* **1** A person who shams. **2** A hoax; deception. **3** An imitation; counterfeit. **4** Cheap artificiality or pretension. **5** A decorative cover or the like for use over a household article: a pillow *sham.* —*v.* **shammed, sham·ming** *v.t.* **1** To counterfeit; feign. —*v.i.* **2** To make false pretenses; feign something. [? dial. var. of SHAME]

sha·man (shä′mən, shā′-, sham′ən) *n.* A priest of shamanism. [< Skt. *śamana* ascetic]

sha·man·ism (shä′mən·iz′əm, shā′-, sham′ən-) *n.* **1** A religion of NE Asia holding that supernatural spirits, etc., work for the good or ill of mankind only through the shamans. **2** Any similar religion, such as that practiced by certain Indians of the American Northwest. —**sha′man·ist** *n.* —**sha′man·is′tic** *adj.*

sham·ble (sham′bəl) *v.i.* **·bled, ·bling** To walk with shuffling or unsteady gait. [?]

sham·bles (sham′bəlz) *n.pl. (usu. construed as sing.)* **1** SLAUGHTERHOUSE. **2** Any place of carnage or execution. **3** A place marked by great destruction, disorder, or confusion. [< OE *scamel* a bench.]

shame (shām) *n.* **1** A painful feeling caused by a sense of guilt, unworthiness, impropriety, etc. **2** Disgrace; humiliation. **3** A person or thing causing disgrace or humiliation. **4** Misfortune; outrage: It's a *shame* they didn't go. —**put to shame 1** To disgrace; make ashamed. **2** To surpass or eclipse. —*v.t.* **shamed, sham·ing 1** To cause to feel shame. **2** To bring shame upon; disgrace. **3** To impel by a sense of shame: with *into* or *out of.* [< OE *scamu*]

shame·faced (shām′fāst′) *adj.* **1** Showing shame; ashamed. **2** Bashful; modest. [< OE *scamfæst* abashed] —

shame·fac·ed·ly (shām′fā′sid·lē, shām′fāst′lē) *adv.* — **shame′fac′ed·ness** *n.*

shame·ful (shām′fəl) *adj.* 1 Bringing shame or disgrace; disgraceful; scandalous. 2 Indecent. —**shame′ful·ly** *adv.* —**shame′ful·ness** *n.* —**Syn.** 1 disreputable, dishonorable, ignoble, ignominious, base, despicable, contemptible, deplorable, vile, odious.

shame·less (shām′lis) *adj.* 1 Impudent; brazen; immodest. 2 Done without shame, indicating a want of decency. —**shame′less·ly** *adv.* —**shame′less·ness** *n.*

sham·my (sham′ē) *n.* CHAMOIS.

sham·poo (sham·pōo′) *v.t.* 1 To lather and wash (the hair and scalp) thoroughly. 2 To cleanse by rubbing. —*n.* The act or process of shampooing, or a preparation used for it. [< Hind. *chāmpnā* to press] —**sham·poo′er** *n.*

sham·rock (sham′rok) *n.* Any of several plants, with trifoliate leaves, accepted as the national emblem of Ireland, esp. the wood sorrel. [< Irish *seamar* trefoil]

shang·hai (shang′hī, shang·hī′) *v.t.* **·haied, ·hai·ing** 1 To drug or render unconscious and kidnap for service aboard a ship. 2 To cause to do something by force or deception. [< *Shanghai*]

Shamrock (wood sorrel)

Shan·gri-la (shang′grī·lä′) *n.* Any imaginary hidden utopia or paradise. [< *Shangri-la,* name of a utopian place in James Hilton's novel *Lost Horizon,* 1933]

shank (shangk) *n.* 1 The leg between the knee and the ankle. 2 The entire leg. 3 A cut of meat from the leg of an animal; the shin. 4 The stem, as of a tobacco pipe, key, anchor, etc. 5 The part of a tool connecting the handle with the working part; shaft. 6 The projecting piece or loop in the back of some buttons by which they are attached. 7 *Printing* The body of a type. 8 The narrow part of a shoe sole in front of the heel. • See SHOE. —**shank of the evening** *Informal* The early part of the evening. [< OE *sceanca*] —**shanked** *adj.*

shanks′ mare One's own legs as a means of conveyance.

shan′t (shant, shänt) Contraction of *shall not.*

shan·tung (shan′tung, shan·tung′) *n.* A fabric with a rough, nubby surface, originally made in China of silk, now often made of synthetic or cotton fiber. [< *Shantung,* China]

shan·ty¹ (shan′tē) *n. pl.* **·ties** A small, rickety shack or cabin. [< F (Canadian) *chantier* lumberer's shack]

shan·ty² (shan′tē) *n.* CHANTEY.

shape (shāp) *n.* 1 Outward form or contour. 2 Appearance of a body with reference only to its contour; figure. 3 Something that gives or determines shape, as a pattern or mold. 4 An assumed aspect or appearance; guise. 5 A developed or final expression or form: to put an idea into *shape.* 6 Any embodiment or form in which a thing may exist: the *shape* of a novel. 7 A ghost or phantom. 8 *Informal* The condition of a person or thing as regards health, orderliness, etc. —**in shape** In good physical condition or appearance. —**out of shape** In bad physical condition or appearance. —**take shape** To begin to have or assume definite form. —*v.* **shaped, shap·ing** *v.t.* 1 To give shape to; mold; form. 2 To adjust or adapt; modify. 3 To devise; prepare. 4 To give direction or character to: to *shape* one's course of action. 5 To put into or express in words. —*v.i.* 6 To take shape; develop; form: often with *up* or *into.* —**shape up** 1 To develop fully or appropriately; work out. 2 *Informal* To do, work, behave, etc., properly. [< OE *gesceap* creation] —**shap′er** *n.*

SHAPE (shāp) Supreme Headquarters Allied Powers, Europe.

shape·less (shāp′lis) *adj.* 1 Having no definite shape. 2 Lacking a pleasing shape or symmetry. —**shape′less·ly** *adv.* —**shape′less·ness** *n.*

shape·ly (shāp′lē) *adj.* **·li·er, ·li·est** Having a pleasing shape; well-formed. —**shape′li·ness** *n.*

shape-up (shāp′up′) *n.* The selection of a work crew, usu. on a day-to-day basis, from among a number of men assembled for a work shift.

shard (shärd) *n.* 1 A broken piece of a brittle substance, as of an earthen vessel. 2 *Zool.* A stiff covering, as the wing cover of a beetle. [< OE *sceard*]

share (shâr) *n.* 1 A portion alloted or due to a person or contributed by a person. 2 One of the equal parts into which the capital stock of a company or corporation is divided. 3 An equitable part of something used, done, or divided in common. —*v.* **shared, shar·ing** *v.t.* 1 To divide and give out in shares or portions; apportion. 2 To enjoy, use, participate in, endure, etc., in common. —*v.i.* 3 To have a part; participate: with *in.* 4 To divide something in equal parts: with *out* or *with.* [< OE *scearu*] —**shar′er** *n.*

share·crop·per (shâr′krop′ər) *n.* A tenant farmer who pays a share of his crop as rent for his land.

share·hold·er (shâr′hōl′dər) *n.* An owner of a share or shares of a company's stock.

sha·rif (shə·rēf′) *n.* SHERIF.

shark¹ (shärk) *n.* Any of a large order of mostly marine fishes having a cartilaginous skeleton, lateral gill slits, and a tough skin. —*v.i.* To fish for sharks. [?]

Great white shark

shark² (shärk) *n.* 1 A dishonest person, esp. a swindler. 2 *Slang* A person of exceptional skill or ability. [?< SHARK¹]

shark·skin (shärk′skin′) *n.* 1 Leather made of a shark's skin. 2 A summer fabric with a smooth surface. 3 A fabric with a pebbly surface.

sharp (shärp) *adj.* 1 Having a keen edge or an acute point; capable of cutting or piercing. 2 Not rounded; pointed; angular: *sharp* features. 3 Abrupt in change of direction: a *sharp* curve. 4 Distinct; well-defined: a *sharp* contrast. 5 Keen or quick in perception or discernment. 6 Keen or acute, as in seeing or hearing. 7 Shrewd, as in bargaining. 8 Quickly aroused; harsh: a *sharp* temper. 9 Heated; fiery: a *sharp* debate. 10 Vigilant; attentive: a *sharp* watch. 11 Quick; vigorous. 12 Keenly felt: *sharp* hunger pangs. 13 Intense or penetrating in effect; incisive to the point of being unsettling or wounding: a *sharp* look; a *sharp* tongue. 14 Shrill: a *sharp* sound. 15 Having an acid or pungent taste or smell. 16 *Slang* Stylishly dressed or well groomed. 17 *Music* Being above the proper or indicated pitch. —*adv.* 1 In a sharp manner. 2 Promptly; exactly: at 4 o'clock *sharp.* 3 *Music* Above the proper pitch. —*n.* 1 *Music* A character (♯) used on a natural degree of the staff to make it represent a tone a half-step higher; also, the tone so indicated. 2 A sewing needle of long, slender shape. 3 A cheat; sharper: a *cardsharp.* —*v.t.* 1 *Music* To raise in pitch, as by a half-step. —*v.i.* 2 *Music* To sing, play, or sound above the right pitch. [< OE *scearp*] —**sharp′ly** *adv.* —**sharp′ness** *n.*

sharp·en (shär′pən) *v.t.* & *v.i.* To make or become sharp. —**sharp′en·er** *n.*

sharp·er (shär′pər) *n.* A swindler; cheat.

sharp·ie (shär′pē) *n.* 1 A long, flat-bottomed sailboat having a centerboard and one or two masts. 2 *Informal* A shrewd, clever person, esp. in bargaining. [< SHARP]

sharp·shoot·er (shärp′shōo′tər) *n.* A skilled marksman. —**sharp′shoot′ing** *n.*

sharp-sight·ed (shärp′sī′tid) *adj.* Having keen vision. —**sharp′-sight′ed·ly** *adv.* —**sharp′-sight′ed·ness** *n.*

sharp-tongued (shärp′tungd′) *adj.* Bitter or caustic in speech.

sharp-wit·ted (shärp′wit′id) *adj.* Acutely intelligent; discerning.

Shas·ta daisy (shas′tə) A cultivated, daisylike variety of chrysanthemum having white-rayed flowers. [< Mt. *Shasta,* California]

shat·ter (shat′ər) *v.t.* 1 To break into pieces suddenly, as by a blow. 2 To break the health or well-being of, as the body or mind. 3 To damage or demolish. —*v.i.* 4 To break into pieces; burst. —*n. pl.* Shattered pieces or fragments, esp. in the phrase **in shatters.** [ME *scateren* to scatter]

shave (shāv) *v.* **shaved, shaved** or **shav·en, shav·ing** *v.i.* 1 To cut hair or beard close to the skin with a razor. —v.t. **2** To remove hair or beard from (the face, head, etc.) with a razor. **3** To cut (hair or beard) close to the skin with a razor: often with *off.* **4** To trim closely as if with a razor: to *shave* a lawn. **5** To cut thin slices or pieces from. **6** To touch or scrape in passing; graze; come close to. **7** *Informal* To lower or deduct from (a price, amount, etc.). —n. **1** The act or operation of shaving with a razor. **2** A thin slice or piece; shaving. **3** *Informal* The act of barely grazing something. [< OE *scafan*]

shav·en (shā′vən) A *p.p.* of SHAVE. —*adj.* **1** Shaved; also, tonsured. **2** Trimmed closely.

shav·er (shā′vər) n. **1** One who shaves. **2** An instrument for shaving: an electric *shaver*. **3** *Informal* A lad.

shave·tail (shāv′tāl′) n. *Slang* A second lieutenant, esp. one recently commissioned. [In allusion to young, unbroken army mules with bobbed tails]

Sha·vi·an (shā′vē·ən) n. An admirer of George Bernard Shaw, his writings, or his theories. —*adj.* Of or characteristic of George Bernard Shaw or his work.

shav·ing (shā′ving) n. **1** The act of one who or that which shaves. **2** A thin paring shaved from anything.

shawl (shôl) n. A wrap, as a square cloth, or large broad scarf, worn over the head or shoulders. [< Pers. *shāl*]

Shaw·nee (shô·nē′) n. One of a tribe of North American Indians of Algonquian stock, formerly living in Tennessee and South Carolina, now in Oklahoma. [< Algon.]

shay (shā) n. A light carriage; chaise. [Back formation < CHAISE, mistaking it for a plural]

she (shē) *pron.* **1** The female person or being previously mentioned or understood, in the nominative case. **2** Any woman. **3** Something personified as female: *She* is a great little car. —n. A female person or animal: often used in combination: a *she-lion.* [< OE *sēo*]

sheaf (shēf) n. *pl.* **sheaves** (shēvz) **1** Stalks of cut grain or the like, bound together. **2** Any collection of things, as papers, held together by a band or tie. —v.t. To bind in a sheaf; sheave. [< OE *scēaf*]

shear (shir) n. **1** Either of the blades of a pair of shears. **2** A cutting machine for sheet metal. **3** *Physics* **a** A deformation of a solid body, equivalent to a sliding over each other of adjacent layers. **b** A force or system of forces tending to cause this. **4** The act or result of shearing. —v. **sheared** (*Archaic* **shore**), **sheared** or **shorn**, **shear·ing** v.t. **1** To cut the hair, fleece, etc., from. **2** To remove by cutting or clipping: to *shear* wool. **3** To deprive; strip, as of power or wealth. **4** To cut or clip with shears or other sharp instrument: to *shear* a cable. —v.i. **5** To use shears or other sharp instrument. **6** To slide or break from a shear (def. 3). **7** To proceed by or as by cutting a way: with *through.* [< OE *sceran* to shear] —**shear′er** n.

shears (shirz) n.pl. Any large cutting or clipping instrument worked by the crossing of cutting edges. Also **pair of shears.**

shear·wa·ter (shir′wô′tər, -wot′ər) n. Any of various web-footed, far-ranging sea birds that usu. skim the water when flying.

sheath (shēth) n. **1** An envelope or case, as for a sword; scabbard. **2** *Biol.* Any structure that enfolds or encloses. [< OE *scæth*]

sheathe (shēth) v.t. **sheathed, sheath·ing** **1** To put into a sheath. **2** To plunge (a sword, etc.) into flesh. **3** To draw in, as claws. **4** To protect or conceal, as by covering: to *sheathe* plasterboard; to *sheathe* one's anger.

sheath·ing (shē′thing) n. **1** An outer covering, as of a building or ship's hull. **2** The material used for this. **3** The act of one who sheathes.

sheave¹ (shēv) v.t. **sheaved, sheav·ing** To gather into sheaves; collect.

sheave² (shēv) n. A grooved pulley wheel; also, a pulley wheel and its block. [ME]

sheaves (shēvz) n.pl. of SHEAF.

she·bang (shi·bang′) n. *Slang* Matter; concern; affair: tired of the whole *shebang.* [?]

shed¹ (shed) v. **shed, shed·ding** v.t. **1** To pour forth in drops; emit, as tears or blood. **2** To cause to pour forth. **3** To send forth or abroad; radiate: to *shed* light on a subject. **4** To throw off without allowing to penetrate, as rain; repel. **5** To cast off by natural process, as hair, skin, a shell, etc.

—v.i. **6** To cast off or lose hair, skin, etc., by natural process. **7** To fall or drop, as leaves or seed. —n. That which sheds, as a sloping surface or watershed. [< OE *scēadan* separate, part]

shed² (shed) n. **1** A small low building or lean-to, used for storage, etc. **2** A large hangarlike building, often with open front or sides. [Var. of SHADE]

she'd (shēd) Contraction of *she had* or *she would.*

shed·der (shed′ər) n. **1** One who sheds. **2** An animal that molts.

sheen (shēn) n. **1** A glistening brightness, as if from reflection. **2** Bright, shining attire. —v.i. To shine; gleam; glisten. [< OE *scēne* beautiful] —**sheen′y** *adj.*

sheep (shēp) n. *pl.* **sheep** **1** Any of a genus of woolly, medium-sized ruminants, esp. domesticated species grown for their fleece, flesh, and hide. **2** A meek or timid person. [< OE *scēap*]

Sheep

sheep·cote (shēp′kōt′) n. SHEEPFOLD. Also **sheep′cot′** (-kot′).

sheep dip Any insecticidal, medicinal, or cleansing solution used to bathe sheep.

sheep dog Any dog trained to guard and control sheep.

sheep·fold (shēp′fōld′) n. A pen for sheep.

sheep·herd·er (shēp′hûr′dər) n. A herder of sheep. —**sheep′herd′ing** n.

sheep·ish (shē′pish) *adj.* **1** Embarrassed; chagrined. **2** Meek; timid. —**sheep′ish·ly** *adv.* —**sheep′ish·ness** n.

sheep·skin (shēp′skin′) n. **1** A sheep's hide, or anything made from it, as parchment, an outdoor coat, etc. **2** A document written on parchment. **3** *Informal* A diploma.

sheep sorrel A low-growing weed related to buckwheat.

sheer¹ (shir) v.i. **1** To swerve from a course; turn aside. — v.t. **2** To cause to swerve. —n. **1** *Naut.* **a** The slight rise of the lengthwise lines of a vessel's hull. **b** A position of a vessel that enables it to swing clear of a single anchor. **2** A swerving course. [< SHEAR]

sheer² (shir) *adj.* **1** Having no modifying conditions; absolute; utter: *sheer* folly. **2** Exceedingly thin and fine: said of fabrics. **3** Perpendicular; steep: a *sheer* precipice. **4** Pure; pellucid. —n. Any very thin fabric used for clothes. —*adv.* **1** Entirely; utterly. **2** Perpendicularly. [ME *schere*] —**sheer′ly** *adv.* —**sheer′ness** n.

sheet (shēt) n. **1** A thin, broad, usu. rectangular piece of any material, as metal, glass, etc. **2** A broad, flat surface or expanse: a *sheet* of flame. **3** A large, usu. rectangular piece of cotton, linen, silk, etc., used as bedding. **4** A usu. rectangular piece of paper, used esp. for writing, printing, etc. **5** *Usu. pl. Printing* A printed signature for a book. **6** *Informal* A newspaper. **7** A sail: a literary use. **8** *Naut.* A rope or chain attached to the lower corner of a sail, used to regulate the angle of the sail to the wind. **9** The large, unseparated block of stamps printed by one impression of a plate. —v.t. To cover with, wrap in, or form into a sheet or sheets. —*adj.* Formed or cut into sheets: *sheet* metal. [< OE *scēte* linen cloth]

sheet anchor **1** An anchor used only in emergency. **2** A person or thing depended upon in an emergency.

sheet·ing (shē′ting) n. **1** Material for bed sheets. **2** Any material used for lining or covering a surface.

sheet metal Metal rolled and pressed into sheets.

sheet music Music printed on unbound sheets of paper.

sheik (shēk, shāk) n. The chief of an Arab tribe or family. Also **sheikh.** [< Ar. *shakha* grow old] —**sheik′dom, sheikh′·dom** n.

shek·el (shek′əl) n. **1** An ancient, esp. Hebrew unit of weight. **2** A coin having this weight. **3** *pl. Slang* Money; riches.

shel·drake (shel′drāk′) n. **1** Any of various Old World wild ducks with varicolored plumage. **2** MERGANSER. [< dial. E *sheld* dappled + DRAKE]

shelf (shelf) n. *pl.* **shelves** (shelvz) **1** A piece of material set horizontally into or against a wall, cabinet, closet, etc., to support articles. **2** The contents of a shelf. **3** Any flat projecting ledge, as of rock. **4** A reef; shoal. [< LG *schelf* set of shelves]

shell (shel) n. **1** The hard outer covering of a mollusk, lobster, egg, nut, etc. • See OYSTER. **2** Something like a shell in shape or function, as the outer framework of a building, a ship's hull, a hollow pastry or pie crust for filling, etc. **3** A sleeveless blouse or sweater. **4** A very light, long, and narrow racing rowboat. **5** A hollow metallic projectile filled with an explosive or chemical. **6** A metallic or paper cartridge case containing the powder, bullet, or shot for breechloading small arms. **7** Any case used to contain the explosives of fireworks. **8** A reserved or impersonal attitude: to come out of one's *shell*. —*v.t.* **1** To divest of or remove from a shell, husk, or pod. **2** To separate from the cob, as Indian corn. **3** To bombard with shells, as a fort. **4** To cover with shells. —*v.i.* **5** To shed or become freed from the shell or pod. **6** To fall off, as a shell or scale. [< OE *scell* shell] —**shell′er** *n.* —**shell′y** *adj.* (**·i·er**, **·i·est**)

she'll (shēl) Contraction of *she will* or *she shall*.

shel·lac (shə·lak′) *n.* **1** A purified lac in the form of thin flakes, used in varnish, insulators, etc. **2** A varnish made of shellac dissolved in alcohol. —*v.t.* **·lacked**, **·lack·ing 1** To cover or varnish with shellac. **2** *Slang* **a** To beat. **b** To defeat utterly. Also **shel·lack′**. [< SHELL + LAC¹]

shel·lack·ing (shə·lak′ing) *n.* *Slang* **1** A beating; assault. **2** A thorough defeat.

shell·back (shel′bak′) *n.* **1** A veteran sailor. **2** Anyone who has crossed the equator on a ship.

shell·bark (shel′bärk′) *n.* SHAGBARK.

shell·fire (shel′fīr′) *n.* The firing of artillery shells.

shell·fish (shel′fish′) *n. pl.* **·fish** or **·fish·es** An aquatic mollusk or crustacean, esp. if edible, as a clam, shrimp, etc.

shell game 1 A swindling game in which the victim bets on the location of a pea covered by one of three nutshells; thimblerig. **2** Any game in which the victim cannot win.

shell·proof (shel′pro̅o̅f′) *adj.* Built to resist the destructive effect of projectiles and bombs.

shell shock COMBAT FATIGUE. —**shell-shocked** (shel′·shokt′) *adj.*

shel·ter (shel′tər) *n.* **1** That which covers or shields from exposure, danger, etc. **2** The state of being covered, protected, or shielded. —*v.t.* **1** To provide protection or shelter for; shield, as from danger or inclement weather. —*v.i.* **2** To take shelter. [?] —**shel′ter·er** *n.*

shelve (shelv) *v.* **shelved**, **shelv·ing** *v.t.* **1** To place on a shelf. **2** To postpone indefinitely; put aside. **3** To retire. **4** To provide or fit with shelves. —*v.i.* **5** To incline gradually.

shelves (shelvz) *n. pl.* of SHELF.

shelv·ing (shel′ving) *n.* **1** Shelves collectively. **2** Material for the construction of shelves.

Shem (shem) In the Bible, the eldest son of Noah.

Shem·ite (shem′īt) *n.* SEMITE.

she·nan·i·gan (shi·nan′ə·gən) *n.* *Usu. pl. Informal* **1** Trickery; foolery. **2** Deceitful or underhanded actions. [?]

She·ol (shē′ōl) *n.* In the Old Testament, a place where the dead were believed to go. [< Heb. *shā′al* dig]

shep·herd (shep′ərd) *n.* **1** A keeper or herder of sheep. **2** Figuratively, a pastor, leader, or guide. —*v.t.* To herd, guide, protect, or direct, as a shepherd. [< OE *scēaphyrde*] —**shep′herd·ess** *n. Fem.*

shepherd dog SHEEP DOG.

shepherd's purse A common weed related to mustard, bearing small white flowers and pouchlike pods.

Sher·a·ton (sher′ə·tən) *adj.* Denoting a style of furniture characterized by simplicity and pleasing proportions. [< T. *Sheraton*, 1751–1806, English designer]

sher·bet (shûr′bit) *n.* **1** A frozen dessert, usu. fruit-flavored, made with water or milk, gelatin, etc. **2** Originally, a Turkish drink, made of fruit juice sweetened and diluted with water. Also **sher′bert** (-bərt). [< Ar. *sharbah* a drink]

she·rif (shə·rēf′) *n.* **1** A member of a princely Muslim family which claims descent from Mohammed. **2** The chief magistrate of Mecca. **3** An Arab chief. [< Ar. *sharíf* noble]

sher·iff (sher′if) *n.* **1** The chief law-enforcement officer of a county, who executes the mandates of courts, keeps order, etc. **2** In Canada, an official whose job is to enforce minor court orders, such as the eviction of persons for nonpayment of rent. [< OE *scīr-gerēfa* shire reeve] —**sher′·iff·dom** *n.*

sher·ry (sher′ē) *n. pl.* **·ries** A fortified wine originally made in Spain. [< *Xeres*, former name of Jerez, Spain]

she's (shēz) Contraction of *she is* or *she has*.

Shet·land pony (shet′lənd) A small, shaggy breed of pony originally bred on the Shetland Islands.

shew (shō) *n. & v. Archaic* SHOW.

shew·bread (shō′bred′) *n.* Unleavened bread formerly placed as an offering in Jewish temples.

SHF, S.H.F., shf, s.h.f. superhigh frequency.

shib·bo·leth (shib′ə·leth) *n.* A test word or pet phrase of a party; a watchword. [< Heb. *shibbōleth*, a word mispronounced by certain Hebrew spies, betraying them as aliens. *Judges* 12:4–6]

shied (shīd) *p.t. & p.p.* of SHY.

shield (shēld) *n.* **1** A broad piece of defensive armor, commonly carried on the left arm; a large buckler. **2** Anything that protects or defends. **3** Any of various devices that afford protection, as from machinery, electricity, radiation, etc. **4** Anything shaped like a shield, as a policeman's badge, decorative emblem, etc. **5** A heraldic escutcheon. —*v.t.* **1** To protect from danger; defend; guard. **2** To hide or screen from view. —*v.i.* **3** To act as a shield or safeguard. —**shield′er** *n.*

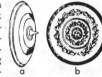

Shields.
a. Anglo-Saxon.
b. Greek.

shield·ing (shēld′ing) *n.* A protective device or screen: radiation *shielding.*

shi·er (shī′ər) Comparative of SHY.

shi·est (shī′ist) Superlative of SHY.

shift (shift) *v.t.* **1** To change or move from one position, arrangement, place, etc., to another. **2** To change for another or others of the same class. —*v.i.* **3** To change position, place, attitude, etc. **4** To manage or get along. **5** To evade; equivocate. —*n.* **1** The act of shifting. **2** A change in position, place, direction, etc. **3** A change in attitude, loyalty, etc. **4** An action or recourse taken in an emergency; expedient. **5** A trick or evasion. **6** GEARSHIFT. **7** A relay of workers or their period of work: the night *shift.* **8** A woman's dress that is not belted or fitted at the waist. **9** *Archaic* A chemise or undergarment. [< OE *sciftan* divide] —**shift′er** *n.*

shift·less (shift′lis) *adj.* **1** Unable or unwilling to work or accomplish something; inefficient or lazy. **2** Inefficiently or incompetently done. —**shift′less·ly** *adv.* —**shift′·less·ness** *n.*

shift·y (shif′tē) *adj.* **shift·i·er**, **shift·i·est 1** Characterized by or showing deceit or trickery. **2** Full of expedients; resourceful. —**shift′i·ly** *adv.* —**shift′i·ness** *n.*

shill (shil) *n. Slang* The ally of a sidewalk peddler or gambler who makes a purchase or bet to encourage onlookers to buy or bet. [?]

shil·le·lagh (shi·lā′lē, -lə) *n.* In Ireland, a stout cudgel made of oak or blackthorn. Also **shil·la′lah**, **shil·lea′lah**, **shil·le′lah**. [< *Shillelagh*, a town in Ireland famed for its oaks]

shil·ling (shil′ing) *n.* **1** A current silver coin of Great Britain, equal to five (new) pence or 1/20 of a pound. **2** A former colonial American coin, varying in value from 12 to 16 cents. [< OE *scilling*]

shil·ly-shal·ly (shil′ē·shal′ē) *v.i.* **·lied**, **·ly·ing** To act with indecision; vacillate. —*adj.* Irresolute; hesitating. —*n.* Weak or foolish vacillation; irresolution. —*adv.* In an irresolute manner. [Redupl. of *Shall I?*] —**shil′ly-shal′li·er** *n.*

shim (shim) *n.* A thin wedge of metal, wood, etc., used to fill out space. —*v.t.* **shimmed**, **shim·ming** To wedge up, fill out, or level by inserting a shim. [?]

shim·mer (shim′ər) *v.i.* To shine faintly; give off or emit a tremulous light; glimmer. —*n.* A tremulous shining or gleaming; glimmer. [< OE *scimerian*] —**shim′mer·y** *adj.*

shim·my (shim′ē) *n. pl.* **·mies 1** A jazz dance accompanied by shaking movements. **2** Undesired oscillation or vibration, as of automobile wheels. —*v.i.* **·mied**, **·my·ing 1** To vibrate or wobble. **2** To dance the shimmy. [Alter. of CHE-MISE]

shin (shin) *n.* **1** The front part of the leg below the knee; also, the shinbone. **2** The lower foreleg: a *shin* of beef. —*v.t. & v.i.* **shinned, shin·ning** To climb (a pole) by gripping with the hands or arms and the shins or legs: usu. with *up.* [< OE *scinu*]

shin·bone (shin′bōn′) *n.* TIBIA.

shin·dig (shin′dig) *n. Slang* A dance or noisy party. [?]

shine (shīn) *v.i.* **shone** or *(esp. for def. 5)* **shined, shin·ing 1** To emit light; beam; glow. **2** To show or be conspicuous. **3** To excel; be preeminent. —*v.t.* **4** To cause to shine. **5** To brighten by rubbing or polishing. —*n.* **1** Radiance; luster; sheen. **2** Fair weather; sunshine. **3** *Informal* A liking or fancy. **4** *Informal* A smart trick or prank. **5** A gloss or polish, as on shoes. [< OE *scīnan*]

shin·er (shī′nər) *n.* **1** One who or that which shines. **2** Any of various species of minnows with silvery scales. **3** *Slang* A black eye.

shin·gle[1] (shing′gəl) *n.* **1** A thin, tapering piece of wood or other material, used in courses to cover roofs. **2** A small signboard bearing the name of a doctor, lawyer, etc., and placed outside his office. **3** A short haircut. —*v.t.* **·gled, ·gling 1** To cover (a roof, building, etc.) with shingles. **2** To cut (the hair) short. [< L *scandula* a shingle] —**shin′gler** *n.*

shin·gle[2] (shing′gəl) *n.* **1** Rounded, stones, coarser than gravel, found on the seashore. **2** A place strewn with shingle, as a beach. [?] —**shin′gly** *adj.*

shin·gles (shing′gəlz) *n. pl. (construed as sing.)* A painful viral disease marked by inflammation of sensory nerves and blistering, chiefly affecting the torso. [< L *cingulum* girdle]

shin·ing (shī′ning) *adj.* **1** Emitting or reflecting a continuous light; gleaming. **2** Of unusual excellence; conspicuous. —**shin′ing·ly** *adv.*

shin·ny[1] (shin′ē) *n.* A game resembling hockey, or one of the sticks or clubs used by the players. Also **shin′ney.** [< *shin ye,* a cry used in the game]

shin·ny[2] (shin′ē) *v.i.* **·nied, ·ny·ing** *Informal* To climb using one's shins: usu. with *up.*

Shin·to (shin′tō) *n.* The primary religion of Japan, consisting chiefly in ancestor worship, and formerly in the worship of the Emperor as a divinity. Also **Shin′to·ism.** [< Chin. *shin* god + *tao* way] —**Shin′to·ist** *n.*

shin·y (shī′nē) *adj.* **shin·i·er, shin·i·est 1** Glistening; glossy; polished. **2** Full of sunshine; bright. —**shin′i·ness** *n.*

ship (ship) *n.* **1** Any large vessel suitable for deep-water navigation. **2** The crew and officers of such a vessel. **3** An aircraft or spacecraft. —*v.* **shipped, ship·ping** *v.t.* **1** To transport by ship. **2** To send by any means of transportation, as by rail, truck, or air. **3** To hire and receive for service on board a vessel, as sailors. **4** To draw (oars) inside a boat. *Naut.* To receive over the side: to *ship* a wave. —*v.i.* **6** To go on board ship; embark. **7** To enlist as a seaman. [< OE *scip*]

-ship *suffix* **1** The state or quality of: *friendship.* **2** Office, rank, or dignity of: *kingship.* **3** The art or skill of: *marksmanship.* [< OE *-scipe*]

ship biscuit A hard, crackerlike biscuit; hardtack.

ship·board (ship′bôrd′, -bōrd′) *n.* A ship. —**on shipboard** In or on a ship.

ship·build·er (ship′bil′dər) *n.* One who designs or works at building ships. —**ship′build′ing** *n.*

ship·load (ship′lōd′) *n.* A load that a ship can carry.

ship·mas·ter (ship′mas′tər, -mäs′-) *n.* The captain or master of a merchant ship.

ship·mate (ship′māt′) *n.* A fellow sailor.

ship·ment (ship′mənt) *n.* **1** The act of shipping. **2** Goods shipped; a consignment.

ship·per (ship′ər) *n.* One who ships goods.

ship·ping (ship′ing) *n.* **1** The act, process, or business of shipping goods. **2** Ships collectively, esp. with respect to nationality or tonnage.

ship·shape (ship′shāp′) *adj.* Trim; orderly; neat. —*adv.* In a seamanlike manner; neatly.

ship·worm (ship′wûrm′) *n.* Any of various wormlike marine mollusks that undermine wooden piers, ships, etc., by boring into them.

ship·wreck (ship′rek′) *n.* **1** A ship or parts of it after being wrecked. **2** The partial or total destruction of a ship at sea. **3** Utter destruction; ruin. —*v.t.* **1** To wreck, as a vessel. **2** To bring to disaster; destroy.

ship·wright (ship′rīt′) *n.* One whose work is to construct or repair ships.

ship·yard (ship′yärd′) *n.* An enclosure where ships are built or repaired.

shire (shīr) *n.* A territorial division of Great Britain; a county. [< OE *scīr*]

shirk (shûrk) *v.t.* **1** To avoid doing (something that should be done). —*v.i.* **2** To avoid work or evade obligation. —*n.* One who shirks: also **shirk′er.** [?]

shirr (shûr) *v.t.* **1** To gather (cloth) by parallel rows of small stitches. **2** To bake with crumbs in a buttered dish, as eggs. —*n.* A gathering of cloth made by shirring. [?]

shirt (shûrt) *n.* **1** A garment for the upper part of the body, usu. having a collar and cuffs and buttoning along the front. **2** UNDERSHIRT. —**lose one's shirt** *Slang* To lose everything. [< OE *scyrte* shirt, short garment]

shirt·ing (shûr′ting) *n.* Material used for making shirts, blouses, etc.

shirt-sleeve (shûrt′slēv′) *adj.* **1** Not wearing a jacket or coat; informally dressed: a *shirt-sleeve* audience. Also **shirt-sleeved. 2** Straightforward; plain; simple and direct in technique, approach, manner, etc.: *shirt-sleeve* diplomacy.

shirt·waist (shûrt′wāst′) *n.* A tailored blouse or shirt worn by women.

Shi·va (shē′və) SIVA.

shiv·er[1] (shiv′ər) *v.i.* To tremble, as with cold or fear. —*n.* The act of shivering; a shaking or quivering. —**shiv′er·y** *adj.* [ME *shiveren*]

shiv·er[2] (shiv′ər) *v.t. & v.i.* To break suddenly into fragments; shatter. —*n.* A splinter; silver. [ME *schivere*]

shlock (shlok) *n.* SCHLOCK. —**shlock′y** *adj.* (**·i·er, ·i·est**)

shoal[1] (shōl) *n.* **1** A shallow place in any body of water. **2** A bank or bar of sand, esp. one seen at low water. —*v.i.* To become shallow. [< OE *sceald* shallow]

shoal[2] (shōl) *n.* A thing or school, as of fish. —*v.i.* To gather in shoals. [< OE *scolu* shoal of fish.]

shoat (shōt) *n.* A young hog. [ME *shote*]

shock[1] (shok) *n.* **1** A violent collision or concussion; impact; blow. **2** The result of such a collision. **3** A sudden, severe effect on the mind or emotions; jolt: the *shock* of recognition. **4** Something causing such an effect. **5** An acute impairment of vital functions associated with failure of the circulatory system following grave trauma such as burns, poisoning, brain injury, massive bleeding, etc. **6** Involuntary muscular contraction caused by the passage of an electric current through the body. —*v.t.* **1** To disturb the emotions or mind of; horrify; disgust. **2** To subject to an electric shock. **3** To shake by sudden collison; jar. [< OF *choc*] —**shock′er** *n.* —**Syn.** *v.* **1** appall, take aback, surprise, astound.

shock[2] (shok) *n.* A number of sheaves of grain, stalks of corn, or the like, stacked for drying upright in a field. —*v.t. & v.i.* To gather (grain) into a shock or shocks. [ME *schokke*] —**shock′er** *n.*

shock[3] (shok) *adj.* Shaggy; bushy. —*n.* A coarse, tangled mass, as of hair. [?]

shock absorber *Mech.* A device designed to absorb the energy of sudden impacts, as in the suspension of an automobile.

shock·ing (shok′ing) *adj.* Causing sudden and violent surprise, horror, etc.: *shocking* news. —**shock′ing·ly** *adv.*

shock therapy A method of treating mental illness by inducing convulsions and unconsciousness with electric current or certain drugs. Also **shock treatment.**

shock wave *Physics* A powerful compression wave produced by a body moving faster than the speed of sound.

shod (shod) *p.t. & p.p.* of SHOE.

shod·dy (shod′ē) *n. pl.* **·dies 1** Reclaimed wool obtained by shredding waste materials. **2** Fiber or cloth manufactured of inferior material. **3** Vulgar display; sham. **4** Refuse; waste. —*adj.* **·di·er, ·di·est 1** Poorly made; inferior. **2** Made of or containing shoddy. **3** Cheaply pretentious; vulgar. **4** Nasty; mean: a *shoddy* remark. [?] —**shod′di·ly** *adv.* —**shod′di·ness** *n.* —**Syn.** *adj.* **1** tawdry, cheap, sloppy, second-rate.

shoe (shoo) *n.* **1** An outer covering, usu. of leather, for the human foot. **2** Something resembling a shoe in position or use. **3** A rim or plate of iron to protect the hoof of an animal. **4** The tread or outer covering of a pneumatic tire. **5** A braking device that stops or retards the motion of an object. —*v.t.* **shod** or **shoed, shoe·ing** To furnish with shoes or the like. [< OE *scōh*] —**sho'er** *n.*

Shoe
a. tongue. b. heel.
c. shank. d. vamp.

shoe·horn (shoo'hôrn') *n.* A smooth curved implement as of metal, horn, etc., shaped to aid in putting on a shoe.

shoe·lace (shoo'lās) *n.* A cord or string used to fasten a shoe.

shoe·mak·er (shoo'mā'kər) *n.* One who makes or repairs shoes. —**shoe'mak'ing** *n.*

shoe·shine (shoo'shīn') *n.* The waxing and polishing of a pair of shoes.

shoe·string (shoo'string) *n.* SHOELACE. —**on a shoe·string** With meager or inadequate financial resources.

shoe·tree (shoo'trē') *n.* A rigid form inserted in a shoe to hold its shape or to stretch it.

sho·far (shō'fär) A ram's horn used in Jewish ritual, sounded on solemn occasions. [< Heb. *shōphār*]

sho·gun (shō'gun) *n.* The hereditary commander in chief of the Japanese army until 1868. [< Chin. *chiang-chün* leader of an army] —**sho'gun·ate** (-it, -āt) *n.*

shone (shōn, shon) *p.t. & p.p.* of SHINE.

shoo (shoo) *interj.* Get away! —*v.t.* **1** To drive away by crying "shoo." —*v.i.* **2** To cry "shoo."

shoo-in (shoo'in') *n. Informal* One who is virtually certain to win, as an election.

shook (shook) *p.t.* of SHAKE.

shoot (shoot) *v.* **shot, shoot·ing** *v.t.* **1** To hit, wound, or kill with a missile discharged from a weapon. **2** To discharge (a missile or weapon): to *shoot* an arrow or a gun. **3** To send forth, as questions, glances, etc. **4** To pass over or through swiftly: to *shoot* rapids. **5** To photograph or film. **6** To thrust out; dart; flick: with *out:* He *shot* out an arm in gesture. **7** To push into or out of the fastening, as the bolt of a door. **8** To propel, discharge, or dump, as down a chute or from a container. **9** *Slang* To inject (a drug, esp. a narcotic). **10** In games: **a** To score (a goal, point, total score, etc.). **b** To play (golf, craps, pool, etc.). **c** To propel (a basketball, puck, marble, etc.) to attempt a score. **d** To cast (dice). —*v.i.* **11** To discharge a missile from a firearm, bow, etc. **12** To go off; discharge. **13** To move swiftly; dart. **14** To extend or project. **15** To put forth buds, leaves, etc. **16** To record photographically. **17** In games, to make a play by propelling the ball, puck, etc., in a certain manner. — **shoot at** (or **for**) *Informal* To strive for; seek to attain. — **shoot the works** *Informal* To risk everything. —*n.* **1** A young branch or growth; offshoot. **2** The process of early growth. **3** A narrow passage in a stream; a rapid. **4** An inclined passage down which anything may be shot. **5** The act of shooting; a shot. **6** A shooting match, hunting party, etc. [< OE *scēotan*] —**shoot'er** *n.*

shooting star METEOR.

shoot-out (shoot'out') *n.* A battle involving an exchange of gunfire.

shop (shop) *n.* **1** A place where goods and services are sold at retail: also **shoppe**. **2** A place for the carrying on of any skilled work: a machine *shop.* —**talk shop** To discuss one's work. —*v.i.* **shopped, shop·ping** To visit shops or stores to purchase or look at goods. [< OE *sceoppa* booth] —**shop'per** *n.* • **Shoppe** is an archaic spelling but is still used in the names of some establishments to suggest a quaint, old-fashioned character. However, the spelling *shop* has been in use since at least 1600, so it is hardly a novelty.

shop·keep·er (shop'kē'pər) *n.* One who owns or runs a shop.

shop·lift·er (shop'lif'tər) *n.* One who steals goods displayed for sale in a shop. —**shop'lift'ing** *n.*

shopping center A group of retail stores, restaurants, etc., including an ample parking area, usu. built as a unit and accessible chiefly by automobile.

shop steward A union worker elected to represent the union in conferences, etc., with management.

shop·worn (shop'wôrn', -wōrn') *adj.* **1** Soiled or damaged from having been handled or on display in a store. **2** Lacking freshness or originality: *shopworn* ideas.

sho·ran (shôr'an, shō'ran) *n.* A short-range electronic navigation system for ships and aircraft. [< *sho(rt) ra(nge) n(avigation)*]

shore[1] (shôr, shōr) *n.* **1** The land adjacent to an ocean, sea, lake, or large river. **2** Land, as distinguished from a body of water. [ME]

shore[2] (shôr, shōr) *v.t.* **shored, shor·ing** To prop, as a wall, by a vertical or sloping timber: usu. with *up.* —*n.* A beam set endwise as a prop, as against the side of a building. [ME *shoren*]

shore bird Any of various birds that feed and nest along the edges of lakes, oceans, rivers, etc.

shore·line (shôr'līn', shōr'-) *n.* The line or contour of a shore.

shore patrol A detail of the U.S. Navy, Coast Guard, or Marine Corps assigned to police duties ashore.

shore·ward (shôr'wərd, shōr'-) *adj. & adv.* Toward the shore. Also **shore'wards.**

shor·ing (shôr'ing, shō'ring) *n.* **1** The act of propping, as with shores. **2** Shores or their manner of use.

shorn (shôrn, shōrn) A *p.p.* of SHEAR.

short (shôrt) *adj.* **1** Having relatively little linear extension; not long. **2** Being below the average stature; not tall. **3** Having relatively little extension in time; brief. **4** Of no great distance: a *short* trip. **5** Less than the usual or standard duration, quantity, extent, etc.: on *short* notice; a *short* letter. **6** Having few items: a *short* list. **7** Not reaching or attaining a goal or requirement: an effort *short* of the mark. **8** Not retentive: a *short* memory. **9** Abrupt in manner; curt. **10** Having an inadequate supply: *short* of cash. **11** Quickly aroused or agitated: a *short* temper. **12** *Phonet.* **a** Of relatively brief duration. **b** Describing any vowel sound that contrasts with a long vowel, as the vowel sound in *mat* contrasted with that in *mate.* **13** In finance: **a** Not having in one's possession when selling, as stocks or commodities. **b** Describing a sale of stocks or commodities that the seller does not possess but anticipates procuring subsequently at a lower price for delivery as contracted. **14** In English prosody, unaccented. **15** Flaky or crisp: pastry made *short* with lard. —**for short** For brevity and ease of expression: The University of Connecticut is called Uconn *for short.* —**in short** In summary; briefly. —**in short order** Without delay; forthwith; promptly. —*n.* **1** Something short, as a garment, vowel, syllable, etc. **2** *pl.* Short trousers extending to the knee or above the knee. **3** *pl.* A man's undergarment resembling short trousers. **4** SHORT CIRCUIT. **5** SHORT SUBJECT. —*adv.* **1** Abruptly: to stop *short.* **2** In a curt manner. **3** So as to be short of a goal or mark. **4** By means of a short sale. — *v.t. & v.i.* **1** To give (someone) less than the amount due. **2** SHORT-CIRCUIT. [< OE *sceort*] —**short'ness** *n.*

short·age (shôr'tij) *n.* An inadequate supply; deficiency.

short·bread (shôrt'bred') *n.* A rich, dry cake or cooky made with shortening.

short·cake (shôrt'kāk') *n.* A dessert consisting of a cake or biscuit served with fruit and often topped with whipped cream.

short·change (shôrt'chānj') *v.t.* **·changed, ·chang·ing 1** To give less change than is due to. **2** To give less than what is rightfully due; cheat. —**short'chang'er** *n.*

short-cir·cuit (shôrt'sûr'kit) *v.t. & v.i.* To make a short circuit (in).

short circuit *Electr.* An electrical connection of low resistance or impedance, esp. when accidental or unintended.

short·com·ing (shôrt'kum'ing) *n.* A defect; imperfection.

short·cut (shôrt'kut') *n.* **1** A route between two places shorter than the regular way. **2** A means or method that saves time, effort, etc.

short·en (shôr′tən) *v.t.* **1** To make short or shorter; reduce; lessen. **2** To make flaky or crisp, as pastry. —*v.i.* **3** To become short or shorter. —**short′en·er** *n.*

short·en·ing (shôr′tən·ing, shôr′ning) *n.* **1** Edible fat, esp. as used in bakery products. **2** An abbreviation.

short·fall (shôrt′fôl′) *n.* **1** A failure to meet an expectation or requirement. **2** The amount or extent of such a failure: a *shortfall* of 20 percent.

short·hand (shôrt′hand′) *n.* **1** Any of various systems of recording speech by writing symbols, abbreviations, etc.; stenography. **2** Any method of quick communication. —*adj.* **1** Written in shorthand. **2** Using shorthand.

short-hand·ed (shôrt′han′did) *adj.* Not having a sufficient number of assistants or workmen.

short·horn (shôrt′hôrn′) *n.* One of a breed of cattle with short horns.

short-lived (shôrt′līvd′, -livd′) *adj.* Living or lasting but a short time.

short·ly (shôrt′lē) *adv.* **1** In a short time; soon. **2** In few words; briefly. **3** Curtly; abruptly.

short shrift Little or no mercy or delay in dealing with a person or disposing of a matter.

short·sight·ed (shôrt′sī′tid) *adj.* **1** NEARSIGHTED. **2** Resulting from or characterized by lack of foresight. —**short′-sight′ed·ly** *adv.* —**short′-sight′ed·ness** *n.*

short·stop (shôrt′stop′) *n.* In baseball, an infielder stationed between second and third bases.

short story A narrative prose story shorter than a novel or novelette.

short subject A relatively brief film, as a documentary or animated cartoon.

short-tem·pered (shôrt′tem′pərd) *adj.* Easily aroused to anger.

short-term (shôrt′tûrm′) *adj.* Payable a short time after issue, as securities.

short ton 2,000 pounds avoirdupois.

short wave A radio wave having a wavelength of about 100 meters or less. —**short′-wave′** *adj.*

short-wind·ed (shôrt′win′did) *adj.* Becoming easily out of breath. —**short′-wind′ed·ness** *n.*

Sho·sho·ne (shō·shō′nē) *n.* One of a large tribe of North American Indians, formerly occupying parts of Wyoming, Idaho, Nevada, and Utah. Also **Sho·sho′ni.**

Sho·sho·ne·an (shō·shō′nē·ən, shō′shə·nē′ən) *n.* The largest branch of the Uto-Aztecan linguistic family of North American Indians. —*adj.* Of or pertaining to this linguistic branch. Also **Sho·sho′ni·an.**

shot¹ (shot) *n.* **1** The act of shooting, as a firearm. **2** Something likened to a shot, as a cutting remark. **3** *pl.* **shot a** Any of the lead pellets that comprise ammunition for a shotgun; also, the pellets collectively. **b** A solid missile, as a ball of iron, fired from a cannon or other gun. **4** A solid metal ball thrown for distance in sports competitions. **5** The range of a projectile. **6** One who shoots; a marksman. **7** A single effort, attempt, or opportunity to do a specific thing: to have a *shot* at getting the job. **8** In certain sports and games, the act or manner of shooting the ball, puck, etc., as in attempting a score. **9** A conjecture; guess. **10** A hypodermic injection, as of a drug, or the dose so administered. **11** An action or scene recorded on film. **12** The taking of a photograph; also, a photograph. **13** A blast, as in mining. —**like a shot** Very quickly. —*adj.* **1** Having a changeable or variegated appearance: purple fabric *shot* with gold. **2** *Informal* Utterly exhausted or ruined; washed-up. [< OE *scot*]

shot² (shot) *p.t.* & *p.p.* of SHOOT.

shote (shot) *n.* SHOAT.

shot·gun (shot′gun′) *n.* A smoothbore gun, often double-barreled, adapted for the discharge of shot at short range. —*adj.* Coerced with, or as with, a shotgun.

Repeating shotgun

should (shŏŏd) **1** *p.t.* of SHALL. **2** An auxiliary expressing: **a** Obligation: You *should* write that letter. **b** Condition: If I *should* go, he would go too. **c** Futurity, as viewed from the past: She wondered how she *should* dress for the party. **d** Expectation: I *should* be at home by noon. **e** Politeness or modesty in requests or statements of doubt: I *should* hardly think so. [< OE *scolde,* p.t. of *sculan* owe]

shoul·der (shōl′dər) *n.* **1** The part of the trunk between the neck and the arm or forelimb. **2** The joint connecting the arm or forelimb with the body. **3** *pl.* The area of the upper back including both shoulders. **4** The shoulders considered as a support for burdens or the seat of responsibility. **5** The part of a garment designed to cover the shoulder. **6** The forequarter of an animal. **7** Something resembling a shoulder in form, as the broadened part of a bottle below the neck. **8** Either edge of a road or highway. —**straight from the shoulder** *Informal* Candidly; straightforwardly. —*v.t.* **1** To assume as something to be borne: to *shoulder* the blame. **2** To bear upon the shoulders. **3** To push with or as with the shoulder. —*v.i.* **4** To push with the shoulder. —**shoulder arms** To rest a rifle against the shoulder, holding the butt with the hand on the same side. [< OE *sculder* shoulder]

shoulder blade SCAPULA.

should·n't (shŏŏd′nt) Contraction of *should not.*

shout (shout) *n.* A sudden and loud outcry. —*v.t.* **1** To utter with a shout; say loudly. —*v.i.* **2** To utter a shout; cry out loudly. [ME *shouten*] —**shout′er** *n.*

shove (shuv) *v.t.* & *v.i.* **shoved, shov·ing 1** To push, as along a surface. **2** To press forcibly (against); jostle. —**shove off 1** To push along or away, as a boat. **2** *Informal* To depart. —*n.* The act of pushing or shoving. [< OE *scūfan*] —**shov′er** *n.*

shov·el (shuv′əl) *n.* A flattened scoop with a handle, as for digging, lifting earth, rock, etc. —*v.* **·eled** or **·elled, ·el·ing** or **·el·ling** *v.t.* **1** To take up and move or gather with a shovel. **2** To toss hastily or in large quantities as if with a shovel. **3** To clear or clean with a shovel, as a path. —*v.i.* **4** To work with a shovel. [< OE *scofl*] —**shov′el·er, shov′el·ler, shov′el·ful** *n.*

show (shō) *v.* **showed, shown** or **showed, show·ing** *v.t.* **1** To cause or permit to be seen; present to view. **2** To cause or allow (something) to be understood or known; explain. **3** To make known by behavior or expression; reveal: to *show* emotion. **4** To cause (someone) to understand or see; explain something to. **5** To confer; bestow: to *show* favor. **6** To make evident by the use of logic; prove. **7** To guide; lead, as into a room: Please *show* them in. **8** To enter in a show or exhibition. —*v.i.* **9** To become visible or known. **10** To appear; seem. **11** To make one's or its appearance. **12** To give a theatrical performance; appear. **13** In racing, to finish third or better. —**show off** To exhibit proudly; display ostentatiously. —**show up 1** To expose or expose, as faults. **2** To be evident or prominent. **3** To make an appearance. **4** *Informal* To be better than. —*n.* **1** A presentation, as of a film, television program, or live entertainment, for viewing by spectators. **2** An exhibition, as of merchandise or art. **3** A competition at which certain animals, as dogs, are displayed and judged. **4** Someone or something regarded as a spectacle to be viewed, as in wonder or amusement. **5** An act of showing; display or manifestation: a *show* of strength. **6** Pretense or semblance; also, ostentation: mere *show*. **7** A sign of metal, oil, etc., in a mining or drilling operation. **8** In racing, a finish of third place or better. [< OE *scēawian*] —**show′er** *n.* —**Syn.** *v.* **1** exhibit, manifest, display. **4** convince, teach. *n.* **1** viewing, showing. **5** mark, sign, indication.

show biz *Slang* SHOW BUSINESS.

show·boat (shō′bōt′) *n.* A boat on which an acting troupe gives performances in river towns.

show business The entertainment industry, esp. the theater, motion pictures, and television.

show·case (shō′kās′) *n.* A glass case for exhibiting and protecting articles for sale.

show·down (shō′doun′) *n.* *Informal* Any action that forces a resolution of an issue or dispute.

show·er (shou′ər) *n.* **1** A fall of rain, hail, or sleet, esp. of short duration. **2** A copious fall, as of tears, sparks, or other small objects. **3** A bath in which water is sprayed from an overhead nozzle: also **shower bath**. **4** A party for the giving of gifts, as to a bride. —*v.t.* **1** To sprinkle or wet with or as with showers. **2** To discharge in a shower; pour out. **3** To bestow upon in large numbers; overwhelm: to *shower* her with gifts. —*v.i.* **4** To fall as in a shower. **5** To take a shower bath. [< OE *scūr*] —**show'er·y** *adj.*

show·ing (shō'ing) *n.* **1** An act of presenting for public view, as a film. **2** A result of being shown, as in competition; record: a fine *showing.* **3** Presentation; statement, as of a subject.

show·man (shō'mən) *n. pl.* **·men** (-mən) **1** One who exhibits or produces shows. **2** One who is skilled at the art of effective performance. —**show'man·ship** *n.*

shown (shōn) *p.p.* of SHOW.

show·off (shō'ôf') *n.* One who makes a pretentious display of himself.

show·piece (shō'pēs') *n.* A prized object considered worthy of special exhibit.

show·place (shō'plās') *n.* A place exhibited or noted for its beauty, historic interest, etc.

show·room (shō'rōōm') *n.* A room for the display of merchandise.

show·y (shō'ē) *adj.* **show·i·er, show·i·est 1** Striking; splendid; brilliant. **2** Brilliant or conspicuous in a superficial or tasteless way; gaudy; meretricious. —**show'i·ly** *adv.* —**show'i·ness** *n.*

shpt. shipment.

shrank (shrangk) *p.t.* of SHRINK.

shrap·nel (shrap'nəl) *n. pl.* **·nel 1** A projectile for use against personnel, containing metal balls and a charge that expels them in mid-air. **2** Shell fragments. [< Henry *Shrapnel*, 1761–1842, British artillery officer]

shred (shred) *n.* **1** A long, irregular strip torn or cut off. **2** A fragment; particle. —*v.t.* **shred·ded** or **shred, shred·ding** To tear or cut into shreds. [< OE *scrēade* cutting] —**shred'der** *n.*

shrew (shrōō) *n.* **1** Any of numerous tiny mouselike mammals having a long pointed snout and soft fur. **2** A vexatious or nagging woman. [< OE *scrēawa*] —**shrew'ish** *adj.* —**shrew'ish·ly** *adv.* —**shrew'ish·ness** *n.*

Shrew

shrewd (shrōōd) *adj.* **1** Having keen insight, esp. in practical matters; clever; able. **2** Artful; sly. [< ME *shrew* malicious person] —**shrewd'ly** *adv.* —**shrewd'ness** *n.*

shriek (shrēk) *n.* A sharp, shrill cry or scream. —*v.i.* **1** To utter a shriek. —*v.t.* **2** To utter with a shriek. [< ON *skrækja*] —**shriek'er** *n.*

shrift (shrift) *n. Archaic* The act of shriving; confession. [< OE *scrift*]

shrike (shrīk) *n.* Any of various predatory birds with hooked bill and a slim tail. [< OE *scrīc* thrush]

shrill (shril) *adj.* **1** High-pitched and piercing, as a sound. **2** Emitting a sharp, piercing sound. **3** Harsh and immoderate: *shrill* criticism. —*v.t.* **1** To cause to utter a shrill sound. —*v.i.* **2** To make a shrill sound. [ME *shrille*] —**shrill'ness** *n.* —**shrill'y** *adv.* —**Syn. 1** penetrating. **3** intemperate, hysterical, bitter.

shrimp (shrimp) *n. pl.* **shrimp** or **shrimps 1** Any of numerous small, long-tailed crustaceans having ten legs and a fused head and thorax covered with a carapace, esp. various edible marine species. **2** *Informal* A small or insignificant person. [ME *shrimpe*]

Shrimp

shrine (shrīn) *n.* **1** A receptacle for sacred relics. **2** A sacred tomb or chapel. **3** A thing or spot made sacred by historic or other association. [< L *scrinium* case]

shrink (shringk) *v.* **shrank** or **shrunk, shrunk** or **shrunk·en, shrink·ing** *v.i.* **1** To draw together; contract as from heat, cold, etc. **2** To become less or smaller; diminish. **3** To draw back, as from disgust or horror; recoil: with *from.* —*v.t.* **4** To cause to shrink, contract, or draw together. —*n.* **1** The act of shrinking. **2** *Slang* A psychiatrist or psychoanalyst. [< OE *scrincan*] —**shrink'a·ble** *adj.* —**shrink'er** *n.*

shrink·age (shringk'ij) *n.* **1** The act or process of shrinking; contraction. **2** The amount lost by contraction. **3** Decrease in value; depreciation.

shrive (shrīv) *v.* **shrove** (shrōv) or **shrived, shriv·en** (shriv'-) or **shrived, shriv·ing** *Archaic v.t.* **1** To receive the confession of and give absolution to. —*v.i.* **2** To make confession. **3** To hear confession. [< OE *scrīfan*] —**shriv'er** *n.*

shriv·el (shriv'əl) *v.t. & v.i.* **·eled, ·el·ing** or **·elled, ·el·ling 1** To contract into wrinkles; shrink and wrinkle. **2** To make or become helpless or impotent; wither. [?]

shroud (shroud) *n.* **1** A cloth used to wrap a corpse for burial. **2** Something that envelops or conceals. **3** *Naut.* One of a set of ropes or wires stretched from a masthead to the sides of a ship, serving to strengthen the mast laterally. —*v.t.* **1** To clothe in a shroud. **2** To envelop or conceal; block from view. [< OE *scrūd* a garment]

shrove (shrōv) *p.t.* of SHRIVE.

Shrove·tide (shrōv'tīd') *n.* The three days immediately preceding Ash Wednesday, on which confession is made in preparation for Lent.

shrub (shrub) *n.* A woody perennial of low stature, usu. with several stems. [< OE *scrybb* brushwood] —**shrub'bi·ness** *n.* —**shrub'by** *adj.* (**·bi·er, ·bi·est**)

shrub·ber·y (shrub'ər·ē) *n. pl.* **·ber·ies** A group of shrubs, as in a garden.

shrug (shrug) *v.t. & v.i.* **shrugged, shrug·ging** To draw up (the shoulders), as in displeasure, doubt, surprise, etc. —*n.* The act of shrugging the shoulders. [?]

shrunk (shrungk) *p.t. & p.p.* of SHRINK.

shrunk·en (shrungk'ən) *p.p.* of SHRINK. —*adj.* Contracted and atrophied.

shtick (shtik) *n. Slang* Something contrived to make one's personality distinct or memorable, as an actor's characteristic mannerism or a comedian's routine. [< Yiddish < G *stück* piece, bit]

sh. tn. short ton.

shuck (shuk) *n.* **1** A husk, shell, or pod, as of corn. • See WALNUT. **2** A shell of an oyster or a clam. **3** *Informal* Something of little or no value: not worth *shucks.* —*v.t.* **1** To remove the husk or shell from (corn, oysters, etc.). **2** *Informal* To take off or cast off, as an outer covering. [?] —**shuck'er** *n.*

shucks (shuks) *interj. Informal* A mild exclamation of annoyance, disgust, etc.

shud·der (shud'ər) *v.i.* To tremble or shake, as from fright or cold. —*n.* A convulsive shiver, as from horror or fear. [ME *shudren*] —**Syn.** *v.* shiver, quake. *n.* tremor.

shuf·fle (shuf'əl) *v.* **·fled, ·fling** *v.t.* **1** To shift about so as to mix up or confuse; disorder. **2** To change the order of by mixing, as cards in a pack. **3** To move (the feet) along with a dragging gait. **4** To change or move from one place to another. —*v.i.* **5** To scrape the feet along. **6** To change position; shift ground. **7** To resort to indirect or deceitful methods; prevaricate. **8** To shuffle cards. —*n.* **1** A dragging of the feet. **2** The act of shuffling, as cards. **3** A deceitful or evasive course; artifice. [< LG *schuffeln*] —**shuf'fler** *n.*

shuf·fle·board (shuf'əl·bôrd', -bōrd') *n.* A game in which disks are slid by means of a pronged cue along a smooth surface toward numbered spaces.

shun (shun) *v.t.* **shunned, shun·ning** To keep clear of; avoid. [< OE *scunian*] —**shun'ner** *n.*

shunt (shunt) *v.t.* **1** To turn aside. **2** In railroading, to switch, as a train or car, from one track to another. **3** *Electr.* **a** To connect a shunt in parallel with. **b** To be connected as a shunt for or of. **4** To put off on someone else, as a task. —*v.i.* **5** To move to one side. **6** *Electr.* To be diverted by a shunt: said of current. **7** To move back and forth; shuttle. —*n.* **1** The act of shunting. **2** A railroad switch. **3** *Electr.* A conductor joining two points in a circuit and diverting part of the current. —**shunt'er** *n.*

shush (shush) *interj.* Keep quiet! —*v.t.* To try to quiet.

shut (shut) *v.* **shut, shut·ting** *v.t.* **1** To bring into such position as to close an opening. **2** To close (an opening) so as to prevent passage or movement in or out. **3** To close and fasten securely, as with a lock. **4** To keep from entering or leaving: with *out* or *in.* **5** To close, fold, or bring together, as extended parts: to *shut* an umbrella. —*v.i.* **6** To be or become closed or in a closed position. —**shut down 1** To cease from operating, as a factory. **2** To lower;

come down close: The fog *shut down.* —**shut off 1** To cause to stop operating: to *shut off* a light. **2** To separate: usu. with *from*: *shut off* from all companionship. —**shut out** In sports, to keep (an opponent) from scoring during the course of a game. —**shut up 1** *Informal* To stop talking or cause to stop talking. **2** To close all the entrances to, as a house. **3** To imprison; confine. —*adj.* **1** Made fast or closed. **2** *Regional* Freed, as from something disagreeable; rid: with *of.* [< OE *scyttan*]

shut·down (shut′doun′) *n.* The closing of a mine, industrial plant, etc.

shut-eye (shut′ī′) *n. Slang* Sleep.

shut-in (shut′in′) *n.* An invalid who has to stay at home. —*adj.* **1** Obliged to stay at home. **2** Inclined to avoid people.

shut·out (shut′out′) *n.* In sports, a game in which one side is prevented from scoring.

shut·ter (shut′ər) *n.* **1** A hinged screen or cover, as for a window. **2** *Phot.* A mechanism for momentarily admitting light through a camera lens to a film or plate. **3** One who or that which shuts. —*v.t.* To furnish, close, or divide off with shutters.

shut·tle (shut′l) *n.* **1** A device used in weaving to carry the weft to and fro between the warp threads. **2** A similar device in a sewing machine. **3** A system of transportation for moving goods or passengers in both directions between two nearby points; also, the vehicle, as a bus, train, or airplane, operating between these points, usu. frequently. —*v.t.* & *v.i.* **·tled, ·tling** To move back and forth frequently or like a shuttle. [< OE *scytel* missile]

shut·tle·cock (shut′l·kok′) *n.* A rounded piece of cork, with a crown of feathers, that is hit back and forth in the game of badminton.

shy¹ (shī) *adj.* **shy·er, shy·est,** or **shi·er, shi·est 1** Easily frightened or startled; timid. **2** Uneasy in the company of others; bashful; reserved. **3** Circumspect; watchful; wary. **4** Expressing or suggesting diffidence or reserve: a *shy* look. **5** *Informal* Having less than is called for or expected; short. —*v.t.* **shied, shy·ing 1** To start suddenly to one side, as a horse. **2** To draw back, as from doubt or caution: with *off* or *away.* —*n.* A starting aside, as in fear. [< OE *scēoh* timid] —**shy′ly** *adv.* —**shy′ness** *n.*

Shuttlecock

shy² (shī) *v.t.* & *v.i.* **shied, shy·ing** To throw with a swift, sidelong motion. —*n. pl.* **shies** A careless throw; a fling. [?]

shy·ster (shīs′tər) *n. Informal* Anyone, esp. a lawyer, who conducts his business in an unscrupulous or tricky manner. [?]

SI International System of Units (Le Système International d'Unités).

Si silicon.

Si·am (sī·am′) *n.* The former name for THAILAND. —**Si·a·mese** (sī′ə·mēz′, -mēs′) *adj., n.*

Siamese cat A breed of short-haired cat, typically fawn-colored or pale cream, with dark ears, tail, feet, and face, and blue eyes.

Siamese twins Any twins conjoined at birth. [< Eng and Chang (1811–74), conjoined twins born in Siam.]

sib (sib) *n.* **1** A blood relation, esp. a brother or sister. **2** Kinsmen collectively; relatives. —*adj.* Related by blood; akin. [< OE *sibb*]

sib·i·lant (sib′ə·lənt) *adj.* **1** Hissing. **2** *Phonet.* Describing those consonants which are uttered with a hissing sound, as (s), (z), (sh), and (zh). —*n. Phonet.* A sibilant consonant. [< L *sibilare* to hiss] —**sib′i·lance** *n.* —**sib′i·lant·ly** *adv.*

sib·ling (sib′ling) *n.* A brother or sister. [< OE, a relative]

sib·yl (sib′əl) *n.* **1** In ancient Greece and Rome, any of several women who prophesied future events. **2** A fortune-teller; sorceress. —**si·byl·ic** (si·bil′ik) or **si·byl′lic, sib′yl·line** (-īn) *adj.*

sic¹ (sik) *adv.* So; thus: used within brackets after something quoted, to indicate that the quotation is exactly reproduced, even though questionable or incorrect. [L]

sic² (sik) *v.t.* **sicked, sick·ing 1** To urge to attack: to *sic* a dog on a burglar. **2** To seek out or attack: used in the imperative esp. to a dog. [Var. of SEEK]

sick¹ (sik) *adj.* **1** Affected with disease; ill; ailing. **2** Of or used by sick persons. **3** Affected by nausea; nauseated. **4**

Sickly; weak: a *sick* laugh. **5** Mentally or emotionally upset or ill: *sick* with grief. **6** Disposed to find offensive or wearisome from being surfeited: with *of*: *sick* of hearing transistor radios in public places. [< OE *sēoc*] —**sick′ish** *adj.* —**sick′ish·ly** *adv.* —**sick′ish·ness** *n.*

sick² (sik) *v.t.* SIC².

sick·bay (sik′bā′) *n.* That part of a ship or naval base set aside for the care of the sick.

sick·bed (sik′bed′) *n.* The bed upon which a sick person lies.

sick·en (sik′ən) *v.t.* & *v.i.* To make or become sick or disgusted. —**sick′en·er** *n.*

sick·en·ing (sik′ən·ing) *adj.* Disgusting; nauseating. —**sick′en·ing·ly** *adv.*

sick headache MIGRAINE.

sick·le (sik′əl) *n.* A cutting or reaping implement with a long, curved blade mounted on a short handle. —*v.t.* **·led, ·ling** To cut with a sickle, as grass, hay, etc. [< OE *sicel*]

sick·le-cell anemia (sik′əl·sel′) A severe, hereditary anemia occurring among the offspring of parents who both have sickle-cell trait.

sickle-cell trait A tendency in erythrocytes to become deformed into a sickle shape and to clog small blood vessels, occurring chiefly among Negroes and due to the presence of a genetic hemoglobin abnormality inherited from one parent. Also **sickl·e·mi·a** (sik′əl·ē′mē·ə).

Sickle

sick·ly (sik′lē) *adj.* **·li·er, ·li·est 1** Habitually ailing; unhealthy; feeble. **2** Marked by the prevalence of sickness. **3** Nauseating; disgusting; sickening. **4** Of or characteristic of sickness: a *sickly* appearance. **5** Lacking in conviction; weak; unconvincing: a *sickly* excuse. **6** Faint; pallid. —*adv.* In a sick manner; poorly. —*v.t.* **·lied, ·ly·ing** To make sickly, as in color. —**sick′li·ly** *adv.* —**sick′li·ness** *n.*

sick·ness (sik′nis) *n.* **1** The state of being sick; illness. **2** A particular form of disease. **3** Nausea. **4** Any disordered and weakened state.

side (sīd) *n.* **1** Any of the boundary lines of a surface or any of the surfaces of a solid: the *side* of a box. **2** A boundary line or surface, distinguished from the top and bottom or front and back. **3** Either of the surfaces of an object of negligible thickness, as a sheet of paper or a coin. **4** The right half or the left half of a human body, esp. of the torso, or of any animal. **5** The space beside someone. **6** A lateral part of a surface or object: the right *side* of a room. **7** The lateral half of a slaughtered animal: a *side* of beef. **8** One of two or more contrasted surfaces, parts, or places: the far *side* of a river. **9** A slope, as of a mountain. **10** An opinion, aspect, or point of view: the conservative *side* of the issue. **11** A group of competitors or partisans of a point of view. **12** Family connection, esp. by descent through one parent: my father's *side.* —**on the side** In addition to the main part or chief activity. —**side by side 1** Alongside one another. **2** In a spirit of cooperation; together. —**take sides** To give one's support to one of two sides engaged in a dispute. —*adj.* **1** Situated at or on one side. **2** Being from one side: a *side* glance. **3** Incidental: a *side* issue. **4** Being in addition to the main dish: a *side* order. —*v.t.* To provide with a side or sides. —**side with** To range oneself on the side of; support, esp. in a dispute. [< OE]

side arms Weapons worn at the side, as pistols.

side·board (sīd′bôrd′, -bōrd′) *n.* **1** A piece of dining-room furniture for holding tableware. **2** *pl. Brit.* SIDEBURNS.

side·burns (sīd′bûrnz′) *n.pl.* **1** Whiskers grown on the cheeks; burnsides. **2** The hair growing on the sides of a man's face in front of the ears.

side·car (sīd′kär′) *n.* A one-wheeled passenger car attached to the side of a motorcycle.

side effect A secondary, often harmful effect, as of a drug.

side·kick (sīd′kik′) *n. Slang* A faithful subordinate or friend.

side·light (sīd′līt′) *n.* **1** A light coming from the side. **2** Incidental illustration or information.

side·line (sīd′līn′) *n.* **1** An auxiliary line of goods. **2** Any additional or secondary work differing from one's main job. **3** One of the lines bounding the two sides of an athletic field or court, as in football or tennis. **4** *pl.* The area just outside these lines. —*v.t.* **·lined, ·lin·ing** To make unfit or unavailable for active participation: Injuries *sidelined* him.

side·long (sīd′lông′, -long′) *adj.* Inclining or tending to one side; lateral. —*adv.* **1** In a lateral or oblique direction. **2** On the side.

side·man (sīd′man′) *n. pl.* **·men** (-men′) One of the supporting musicians, as distinguished from the featured performers, of a band, esp. a jazz band.

si·de·re·al (sī·dir′ē·əl) *adj.* **1** Of or relating to the stars. **2** Measured by means of the stars: *sidereal* time. [< L *sidus* star] —**si·de′re·al·ly** *adv.*

sid·er·ite (sid′ə·rīt) *n.* **1** A glassy ferrous carbonate mineral. **2** An iron meteorite. [< Gk. *sidēros* iron] —**sid′er·it′ic** (-rit′ik) *adj.*

side·sad·dle (sīd′sad′l) *n.* A saddle for a woman wearing skirts, designed to be ridden facing sideways, with both legs on the same side of the horse.

side·show (sīd′shō′) *n.* **1** A small show incidental to a major one, as in a circus. **2** Any subordinate issue or attraction.

side·split·ting (sīd′split′ing) *adj.* Provoking wild laughter; hilarious.

side·step (sīd′step′) *v.* **·stepped, ·step·ping** *v.i.* **1** To step to one side. **2** To avoid responsibility. —*v.t.* **3** To avoid, as an issue; dodge. —**side′step′per** *n.*

side step A step or movement to one side.

side·swipe (sīd′swīp′) *v.t. & v.i.* **·swiped, ·swip·ing** To strike or scrape along the side: to *sideswipe* a car while passing it. —*n.* **1** A glancing collision along the side. **2** *Informal* An oblique or parenthetical criticism.

side·track (sīd′trak′) *v.t. & v.i.* **1** To move to a siding, as a railroad train. **2** To divert from the main issue or subject. —*n.* A railroad siding.

side·walk (sīd′wôk′) *n.* A pavement at the side of the street for pedestrians.

side·ward (sīd′wərd) *adj.* Directed or moving toward or from the side; lateral. —*adv.* Toward or from the side: also **side′wards.**

side·ways (sīd′wāz′) *adv.* **1** From one side. **2** So as to incline with the side forward: Hold it *sideways.* **3** Toward one side; askance; obliquely. —*adj.* Moving to or from one side. Also **side′way′, side′wise′** (-wīz′).

side·wheel (sīd′ʰwēl′) *adj.* Describing a steamboat having a paddle wheel on either side. —**side′-wheel′er** *n.*

sid·ing (sī′ding) *n.* **1** A railway track by the side of the main track. **2** A material used to cover the side of a frame building, as paneling or shingles.

si·dle (sīd′l) *v.i.* **·dled, ·dling** To move sideways, esp. in a cautious or stealthy manner. —*n.* A sideways step or movement. [< obs. *sidling* sidelong] —**si′dler** *n.*

siege (sēj) *n.* **1** The surrounding of a town or fortified place in an effort to seize it, as after a blockade. **2** A steady attempt to win something. **3** A trying time: a *siege* of illness. —*v.t.* **sieged, sieg·ing** BESIEGE. [< L *sedere* sit]

si·en·na (sē·en′ə) *n.* **1** A yellowish brown pigment consisting of clay containing oxides of iron and manganese. **2** A yellowish brown color. **3** BURNT SIENNA. [< Ital. *(terra di) Siena* (earth of) Siena]

si·er·ra (sē·er′ə) *n.* A mountain range or chain, esp. one having a jagged outline. [< L *serra* a saw]

Si·er·ra Le·one (sē·er′rä lē·ōn′, sir′ə-) An independent member of the Commonwealth of Nations in w Africa, 27,925 sq. mi., cap. Freetown. • See map at AFRICA.

si·es·ta (sē·es′tə) *n.* A nap or rest taken in the afternoon. [Sp.< L *sexta (hora)* sixth (hour), noon]

sieve (siv) *n.* A utensil or apparatus for sifting, consisting of a frame provided with a bottom of mesh wire. —*v.t. & v.i.* **sieved, siev·ing** To sift. [< OE *sife* sieve]

sift (sift) *v.t.* **1** To pass through a sieve in order to separate the fine parts from the coarse. **2** To scatter by or as by a sieve. **3** To examine carefully. **4** To separate as if with a sieve; distinguish: to *sift* fact from fiction.

Sieve

—*v.i.* **5** To use a sieve. **6** To fall or pass through or as through a sieve: The light *sifts* through the trees. [< OE *siftan* sift] —**sift′er** *n.*

Sig., sig. signal; signature; signor.

sigh (sī) *v.i.* **1** To draw in and exhale a deep, audible breath, as in expressing sorrow, weariness, pain, or relief. **2** To make a sound suggestive of a sigh, as the wind. **3** To yearn; long: with *for.* —*v.t.* **4** To express with a sigh. —*n.* **1** The act of sighing. **2** A sound of sighing or one suggestive of sighing. [ME *sighen*] —**sigh′er** *n.*

sight (sīt) *n.* **1** The act or faculty of seeing; vision. **2** Something seen; an image perceived by the eye; spectacle: an inspiring *sight;* an ugly *sight.* **3** A view; glimpse: to catch *sight* of someone. **4** The range or scope of vision. **5** *Informal* Something remarkable or strange in appearance. **6** *Usu. pl.* A place or thing of particular interest, as to a tourist: seeing the *sights.* **7** A point of view; estimation. **8** Mental perception or awareness: Don't lose *sight* of the facts. **9** A device to assist aiming, as a gun or a leveling instrument. **10** An aim or observation taken with a telescope or other sighting instrument. —**at** (or **on**) **sight 1** As soon as seen. **2** On presentation for payment. —**out of sight 1** Beyond range of sight. **2** *Informal* Beyond expectation; too great or too much. **3** *Slang* Extraordinarily good. —*v.t.* **1** To catch sight of; discern with the eyes: to *sight* shore. **2** To look at through a sight, as a telescope; observe. **3** To adjust the sights of, as a gun. **4** To take aim with. —*v.i.* **5** To take aim. **6** To make an observation or sight. —*adj.* **1** Understood or performed on sight without previous familiarity or preparation: *sight* reading of music. **2** Payable when presented: a *sight* draft. [< OE *gesiht*]

sight·ed (sī′təd) *adj.* Having (a specified kind of) sight or vision: *far-sighted.*

sight·less (sīt′lis) *adj.* **1** Blind. **2** Invisible. —**sight′less·ly** *adv.* —**sight′less·ness** *n.*

sight·ly (sīt′lē) *adj.* **·li·er, ·li·est 1** Pleasant to the view; comely. **2** Affording a grand view. —**sight′li·ness** *n.*

sight·see·ing (sīt′sē′ing) *n.* The practice of going to see places or things of interest, as in touring. —*adj.* Engaged in or for the purpose of sightseeing. —**sight′se′er** *n.*

sig·ma (sig′mə) *n.* The 18th letter in the Greek alphabet (Σ, σ, ς).

sign (sīn) *n.* **1** Anything that directs the mind or attention toward something: a *sign* of aging; a *sign* of intelligence. **2** A telltale mark or indication; trace: the first *sign* of spring. **3** A motion or action used to communicate a thought, desire, or command. **4** A symbol; token: black armbands as a *sign* of grief. **5** A conventional written or printed symbol representing a word or relation: $ is a dollar *sign;* = is an equal *sign.* **6** Information, directions, advertising, etc., publicly displayed. **7** A structure on which such information is printed or posted. **8** An occurrence taken to be miraculous and proof of divine commission. **9** One of the twelve equal divisions of the zodiac. —*v.t.* **1** To write one's signature on, esp. in acknowledging or attesting to the validity of a document. **2** To write (one's name). **3** To indicate or represent by a sign. **4** To mark or consecrate with a sign, esp. with a cross. **5** To engage by obtaining the signature of to a contract. **6** To hire (oneself) out for work: often with *on.* —*v.i.* **7** To write one's signature. **8** To make signs or signals. —**sign off** To announce the end of a program from a broadcasting station and stop transmission. —**sign up** To enlist, as in a branch of military service. [< L *signum*] —**sign′er** *n.* —**Syn.** *n.* **2** vestige, evidence, spoor.

sig·nal (sig′nəl) *n.* **1** A sign or event agreed upon or understood as a call to action. **2** Any device, sound, gesture, etc., used to convey information or give direction or warning. **3** An event that incites to action or movement: His yawn was our *signal* to leave. **4** *Telecom.* A flow of energy that varies so as to transmit information. —*adj.* **1** Out of the ordinary; notable; distinguished. **2** Used to signal. —*v.* **·naled** or **·nalled, ·nal·ing** or **·nal·ling** *v.t.* **1** To inform or notify by signals. **2** To communicate by signals. —*v.i.* **3** To make a signal or signals. [< L *signum* sign] —**sig′nal·er** or **sig′nal·ler** *n.*

---

add, āce, câre, pälm; end, ēven; it, īce; odd, ōpen, ôrder; tŏŏk, pōōl; up, bûrn; ə = *a* in *above, u* in *focus;* yōō = *u* in *fuse;* oil; pout; check; go; ring; thin; this; zh, *vision.* < derived from; ? origin uncertain or unknown.

sig·nal·ize (sig′nəl·īz) *v.t.* **·ized, ·iz·ing** 1 To make notable or distinguished. 2 To point out with care.

sig·nal·ly (sig′nəl·ē) *adv.* In a signal manner; extraordinarily.

sig·nal·man (sig′nəl·mən) *n. pl.* **·men** (-mən) One who operates or is responsible for signals, as for a railroad.

sig·na·to·ry (sig′nə·tôr′ē, -tō′rē) *n. pl.* **·ries** One who has signed or is bound by a document, esp. a nation so bound. —*adj.* Being a signatory. [< L *signum* a sign]

sig·na·ture (sig′nə·chər) *n.* 1 The name of a person written by himself. 2 The act of signing one's name. 3 Any identifying mark or sign, as a musical theme to signal the beginning and end of a television show. 4 *Printing* **a** A distinguishing mark or number on the first page of each sheet of pages to be gathered as a guide to the binder. **b** A printed sheet that when folded and trimmed constitutes a section of a book, as 32 pages. 5 *Music* A symbol or group of symbols at the beginning of a staff, indicating time or key. [< L *signum* sign]

sign·board (sīn′bôrd′, -bōrd′) *n.* A board displaying a sign, as an advertisement.

sig·net (sig′nit) *n.* 1 A seal used instead of a signature on a document to indicate its official nature. 2 An impression made by or as if by a seal. —*v.t.* To mark wth a signet or seal. [< L *signum* sign]

signet ring A finger ring bearing a signet, as a monogram.

sig·nif·i·cance (sig·nif′ə·kəns) *n.* 1 Importance; consequence. 2 That which is signified or intended to be expressed; meaning. 3 The state or character of being significant. Also **sig·nif′i·can·cy.**

sig·nif·i·cant (sig·nif′ə·kənt) *adj.* 1 Having or expressing a meaning; esp., rich in meaning: *significant* details. 2 Important; momentous. —**sig·nif′i·cant·ly** *adv.* —**Syn.** 1 meaningful, suggestive. 2 weighty, consequential.

sig·ni·fi·ca·tion (sig′nə·fə·kā′shən) *n.* 1 That which is signified; meaning; sense; import. 2 The act of signifying; communication.

sig·nif·i·ca·tive (sig·nif′ə·kā′tiv) *adj.* 1 Signifying. 2 Conveying a meaning; significant.

sig·ni·fy (sig′nə·fī) *v.* **·fied, ·fy·ing** *v.t.* 1 To represent; mean; suggest. 2 To make known by signs or words; express. —*v.i.* 3 To have some meaning or importance; matter. [< L *signum* sign + -FY] —**sig′ni·fi′er** *n.*

sign language A system of communication by means of signs, largely manual.

si·gnor (sēn·yôr′) *n. pl.* **si·gno·ri** (-ē) or **si·gnors** *Italian* 1 A title of courtesy equivalent to *Mr.* or *Sir.* 2 A man; gentleman. Also **si·gnior′.** [< L *senior* senior]

si·gno·ra (sē·nyō′rä) *n. pl.* **si·gno·re** (-rā) or **·ras** *Italian* 1 A title of courtesy equivalent to *Mrs.* or *Madam.* 2 A woman; lady.

si·gno·ri·na (sē′nyō·rē′nä) *n. pl.* **·ri·ne** (-nā) or **·nas** *Italian* 1 A title of courtesy equivalent to *Miss.* 2 An unmarried woman; young lady.

sign·post (sīn′pōst′) *n.* A post bearing a sign.

Sikh (sēk) *n.* An adherent of a religion of India characterized by monotheism and the rejection of caste. —*adj.* Of or pertaining to the Sikhs. [Hind., lit., disciple] —**Sikh′ism** *n.*

si·lage (sī′lij) *n.* Succulent fodder stored in a silo.

si·lence (sī′ləns) *n.* 1 Absence of sound; stillness. 2 Abstinence from speech or from making any sound. 3 Failure to mention; oblivion; secrecy. —*v.t.* **·lenced, ·lenc·ing** 1 To make silent. 2 To stop the activity or expression of; put to rest. —*interj.* Be silent. [< L *silere* be silent]

si·lenc·er (sī′lən·sər) *n.* 1 A device attached to the muzzle of a firearm to muffle the report. 2 One who or that which imposes silence.

si·lent (sī′lənt) *adj.* 1 Not making any sound or noise; noiseless. 2 Not speaking; mute. 3 Disinclined to talk; taciturn. 4 Present but not audible: *silent* tears. 5 Characterized by the absence of comment: His statement was *silent* on that point. 6 Free from activity, motion, or disturbance. 7 Written but not pronounced, as the *e* in *bake*. 8 Not accompanied by a sound track: a *silent* film. [< L *silere* be silent] —**si′lent·ly** *adv.* —**si′lent·ness** *n.*

silent partner A partner who shares in the financing of an enterprise but has no part in its management.

sil·hou·ette (sil′ōō·et′) *n.* 1 A profile drawing or portrait having its outline filled in with uniform color, usu. black. 2 The outline of a solid figure. —*v.t.* **·et·ted, ·et·ting** To cause to appear in silhouette; outline. [< Étienne de *Silhouette*, 1709–1767, French minister]

Silhouette of Abraham Lincoln

sil·i·ca (sil′i·kə) *n.* The dioxide of silicon, occurring pure as quartz and as an important constituent of rocks, sand, and clay. [< L *silex, silicis* flint]

sil·i·cate (sil′ə·kāt, -i·kit) *n.* Any of various compounds consisting of an oxide of silicon and a metallic radical.

si·li·ceous (si·lish′əs) *adj.* Pertaining to or containing silica. Also **si·li′cious.**

si·lic·ic (si·lis′ik) *adj.* Pertaining to or derived from silica or silicon.

silicic acid Any of several gelatinous compounds of silica and water.

sil·i·con (sil′ə·kon′, -kən) *n.* A nonmetallic element (symbol Si) comprising about 25 percent of the earth's crust and forming many compounds analogous to those of carbon. [< L *silex, silicis* flint]

sil·i·cone (sil′ə·kōn′) *n.* Any of various synthetic compounds composed of chains of alternate silicon and oxygen atoms with hydrocarbon branches joined to the silicon.

sil·i·co·sis (sil′ə·kō′sis) *n.* A chronic lung disease due to inhalation of silica dust produced by stonecutting, etc.

silk (silk) *n.* 1 A soft, shiny fiber produced by various insect larvae, as silkworms, to form their cocoons. 2 Cloth or thread made of this fiber. 3 Anything resembling silk, as the fine strands of an ear of corn. 4 *Usu. pl.* A garment of silk, as the uniform of a jockey. —*adj.* Consisting of or like silk; silken. [< OE *seoloc*]

silk cotton The silky covering of the seeds of certain trees, used for filling cushions, etc.; kapok.

silk·en (sil′kən) *adj.* 1 Made of silk. 2 Like silk; glossy; smooth. 3 Suave; insinuating: *silken* speech. 4 Dressed in silk. 5 Luxurious.

silk-screen (silk′skrēn′) *adj.* Describing or made by a printing process which forces ink through the meshes of a silk screen prepared so that ink penetrates only in those areas to be printed. —*v.t.* To make or print by the silk-screen process.

silk-stock·ing (silk′stok′ing) *adj.* Marked by patrician elegance or extreme wealth. —*n.* A member of a silk-stocking social class.

silk·worm (silk′wûrm′) *n.* The larva of a moth that produces a dense silken cocoon.

silk·y (sil′kē) *adj.* **silk·i·er, silk·i·est** 1 Like silk; soft; lustrous. 2 Made or consisting of silk; silken. 3 Smooth or insinuating. —**silk′i·ly** *adv.* —**silk′i·ness** *n.*

sill (sil) *n.* 1 A horizontal member or beam forming the foundation, or part of the foundation, of a structure, as at the bottom of a casing in a building. 2 The horizontal part at the bottom of a door or window frame. [< OE *syll*]

sil·ly (sil′ē) *adj.* **·li·er, ·li·est** 1 Showing a lack of ordinary sense or judgment; foolish. 2 Trivial; frivolous. 3 *Informal* Stunned; dazed, as by a blow. —*n. pl.* **·lies** *Informal* A silly person. [< OE *gesǣlig* happy] —**sil′li·ly** or **sil′ly** *adv.* —**sil′li·ness** *n.*

si·lo (sī′lō) *n. pl.* **·los** 1 A pit or tower in which fodder is stored. 2 An underground structure for the housing and launching of guided missiles. —*v.t.* **·loed, ·lo·ing** To put or preserve in a silo. [< Gk. *siros* pit for corn]

silt (silt) *n.* 1 An earthy sediment consisting of extremely fine particles suspended in and carried by water. 2 A deposit of such sediment. —*v.t. & v.i.* To fill or become filled or choked with silt: usu. with *up.* [ME *sylte*] —**sil·ta·tion** (sil·tā′shən) *n.* —**silt′y** *adj.* **(·i·er, ·i·est)**

Si·lu·ri·an (si·lŏŏr′ē·ən, sī-) *adj. & n.* See GEOLOGY.

sil·van (sil′vən) *adj.* SYLVAN.

sil·ver (sil′vər) *n.* 1 A pale gray, lustrous, malleable metallic element (symbol Ag), having great electric and thermal conductivity and forming various photosensitive salts. 2 Silver regarded as a commodity or as a standard of currency. 3 Silver coin considered as money. 4 Articles, as tableware, made of or plated with silver; silverware. 5

A luster or color resembling that of silver. —*adj.* **1** Made of or coated with silver. **2** Resembling silver; having a silvery grey color. **3** Relating to, connected with, or producing silver. **4** Having a soft, clear, bell-like tone. **5** Designating a 25th wedding anniversary. **6** Favoring the use of silver as a monetary standard. —*v.t.* **1** To coat or plate with silver or something resembling silver. —*v.i.* **2** To become silver or white, as with age. [< OE *siolfor*] —**sil′·ver·er** *n.* —**sil′ver·ly** *adv.*

sil·ver·fish (sil′vər·fish′) *n. pl.* **·fish** or **·fish·es** Any of numerous silvery, wingless insects having bristles on the tail and long feelers, usu. found in damp and dark places.

silver fox **1** A fox with white-tipped black fur. **2** The fur, or a garment made of it.

silver nitrate The salt of silver and nitric acid, used in industry, photography, and in medicine as an antiseptic.

sil·ver·smith (sil′vər·smith′) *n.* A maker of silverware.

silver standard A monetary standard or system based on silver.

sil·ver·ware (sil′vər·wâr′) *n.* Articles made of or plated with silver, esp. tableware.

sil·ver·y (sil′vər·ē) *adj.* **1** Containing silver. **2** Resembling silver, as in luster or hue. **3** Having a soft, clear, bell-like tone. —**sil′ver·i·ness** *n.*

sim·i·an (sim′ē·ən) *adj.* Like or pertaining to the apes and monkeys. —*n.* An ape or monkey. [< L *simia* ape]

sim·i·lar (sim′ə·lər) *adj.* **1** Bearing resemblance to one another or to something else. **2** Having like characteristics, nature, or degree. **3** *Geom.* Shaped alike, but differing in measure. [< L *similis* like] —**sim′i·lar·ly** *adv.*

sim·i·lar·i·ty (sim′ə·lar′ə·tē) *n. pl.* **·ties** **1** The quality or state of being similar. **2** A point in which compared objects are similar.

sim·i·le (sim′ə·lē) *n.* A figure of speech expressing comparison or likeness by the use of such terms as *like* or *as*. [< L *similis* similar] • See METAPHOR.

si·mil·i·tude (si·mil′ə·t(y)ood) *n.* **1** Similarity; correspondence. **2** One who or that which is similar; counterpart. **3** A point of similarity. [< L *similis* like]

sim·i·tar (sim′ə·tər) *n.* SCIMITAR.

sim·mer (sim′ər) *v.i.* **1** To boil gently; be or stay at or just below the boiling point. **2** To be on the point of breaking forth, as with rage. —*v.t.* **3** To cook in a liquid at or just below the boiling point. —*n.* The state of simmering. [?]

si·mo·le·on (si·mō′lē·ən) *n. Slang* A dollar. [?]

Si·mon Le·gree (sī′mən li·grē′) A harsh or brutal taskmaster. [< a character in Harriet Beecher Stowe's *Uncle Tom's Cabin*, 1851]

si·mon-pure (sī′mən·pyŏŏr′) *adj.* Real; genuine; authentic. [< a character in Susanna Centlivre's play, *A Bold Stroke for a Wife*, 1718]

si·mo·ny (sī′mə·nē, sim′ə-) *n.* The purchase or sale of sacred things, as ecclesiastical preferment. [< *Simon* (Magus), who offered Peter money for the gift of the Holy Spirit *Acts* 8:9–24]

si·moom (si·mōōm′, sī-) *n.* A hot, dry, dustladen, exhausting wind of the African and Arabian deserts. Also **si·moon′** (-mōōn′). [< Ar. *samūm*]

simp (simp) *n. Slang* A simpleton.

sim·per (sim′pər) *v.i.* **1** To smile in a silly, self-conscious manner; smirk. —*v.t.* **2** To say with a simper. —*n.* A silly, self-conscious smile. —**sim′per·er** *n.* —**sim′per·ing·ly** *adv.*

sim·ple (sim′pəl) *adj.* **·pler**, **·plest** **1** Easy to comprehend or do: a *simple* problem or task. **2** Not complex or complicated. **3** Without embellishment; plain; unadorned: a *simple* dress. **4** Having nothing added; mere: the *simple* truth. **5** Not luxurious or elaborate: a *simple* meal. **6** Consisting of one thing; single. **7** Free from affectation; artless: a *simple* soul. **8** Weak in intellect; silly or foolish. **9** Of humble rank or condition; ordinary. **10** *Bot.* Not divided: a *simple* leaf. —*n.* **1** One who is foolish or ignorant; simpleton. **2** A medicinal plant. [< L *simplex*] —**sim′ple·ness** *n.* —**Syn.** **4** bare, sheer. **5** frugal, austere. **7** guileless, unsophisticated.

simple fraction A fraction in which both numerator and denominator are integers.

simple interest Interest computed on the original principal alone.

simple machine Any one of certain basic mechanical devices, as the lever, the wedge, the inclined plane, the screw, the wheel and axle, and the pulley.

sim·ple-mind·ed (sim′pəl·mīn′did) *adj.* **1** Weak in intellect; foolish or feeble-minded. **2** Artless or unsophisticated. —**sim′ple-mind′ed·ly** *adv.* —**sim′ple-mind′ed·ness** *n.*

simple sentence A sentence consisting of one independent clause, without subordinate clauses.

sim·ple·ton (sim′pəl·tən) *n.* A weak-minded or silly person.

sim·plic·i·ty (sim·plis′ə·tē) *n. pl.* **·ties** **1** The state of being simple; freedom from complexity or difficulty. **2** Freedom from ornament or ostentation. **3** Freedom from affectation; artlessness; sincerity. **4** Foolishness; stupidity.

sim·pli·fy (sim′plə·fī) *v.t.* **·fied**, **·fy·ing** To make more simple or less complex. —**sim′pli·fi·ca′tion, sim′pli·fi′er** *n.*

sim·plis·tic (sim·plis′tik) *adj.* Tending to ignore or overlook underlying questions, complications, or details. —**sim·plis′ti·cal·ly** *adv.*

sim·ply (sim′plē) *adv.* **1** In a simple manner. **2** Merely; only. **3** Really; absolutely: *simply* adorable.

sim·u·la·crum (sim′yə·lā′krəm, -lak′rəm) *n. pl.* **·cra** (-krə) **1** A likeness; image. **2** An imaginary or shadowy semblance. [< L, image]

sim·u·late (sim′yə·lāt) *v.t.* **·lat·ed**, **·lat·ing** **1** To make a pretense of; imitate, esp. to deceive. **2** To assume or have the appearance or form of, without the reality. [< L *similis* like] —**sim′u·la′tive** *adj.* —**sim′u·la′tor** *n.*

sim·u·la·tion (sim′yə·lā′shən) *n.* **1** The act of simulating. **2** Something given the form or function of another, as in order to test or determine capability; model.

si·mul·cast (sī′məl·kast′, -käst′) *v.t.* **·cast**, **·cast·ing** To broadcast by radio and television simultaneously. —*n.* A broadcast so transmitted.

si·mul·ta·ne·ous (sī′məl·tā′nē·əs, sim′əl-) *adj.* Occurring, done, or existing at the same time. [< L *simul* at the same time] —**si′mul·ta′ne·ous·ly** *adv.* —**si′mul·ta′ne·ous·ness, si′mul·ta·ne′i·ty** (-tə·nē′ə·tē) *n.*

sin (sin) *n.* **1** A transgression against moral or religious law or divine authority, esp. when deliberate. **2** The state of having thus transgressed; wickedness. **3** Any action or condition regarded as morally wrong or deplorable. —*v.* **sinned, sin·ning** *v.i.* **1** To commit a sin. **2** To do wrong. [< OE *synn*]

Si·nai (sī′nī), **Mount** The mountain where Moses received the law from God. *Ex.* 19.

since (sins) *adv.* **1** From a past time up to the present: traveling *since* last Monday. **2** At some time between the past and the present: He has *since* recovered from the illness. **3** Before now: long *since* forgotten. —*prep.* During the time following (a time in the past): Times have changed *since* you left. —*conj.* **1** During or within the time after which. **2** Continuously from the time when: She has been ill ever *since* she arrived. **3** Because of; inasmuch as. [< OE *siththan* afterwards]

sin·cere (sin·sir′) *adj.* **·cer·er**, **·cer·est** Free from hypocrisy, deceit, or calculation; honest; genuine: a *sincere* friend; *sincere* regrets. [< L *sincerus* uncorrupted] —**sin·cere′ly** *adv.* —**sin·cere′ness** *n.*

sin·cer·i·ty (sin·ser′ə·tē) *n.* The state or quality of being sincere; honesty of purpose or character; freedom from hypocrisy.

sine (sīn) *n.* A function of an acute angle in a right triangle expressible as the ratio of the side opposite the angle to the hypotenuse. [< L *sinus* a bend]

si·ne·cure (sī′nə·kyŏŏr, sin′ə-) *n.* A position or office providing compensation or other benefits but requiring little or no responsibility or effort. [< L *sine* without + *cura* care]

si·ne di·e (sī′nē dī′ē, sin′ā dē′ā) Without setting a date, as for another meeting; indefinitely: an adjournment *sine die*. [L, without a day]

si·ne qua non (sin′ə kwä nōn′, non′, sī′nē kwä non′) That which is absolutely indispensable; an essential element. [L, without which not]

sin·ew (sin′yoo) n. 1 TENDON. 2 Strength or power. 3 Often pl. A source of strength. —v.t. To strengthen, as with sinews. [< OE sinu, seonu] —sin′ew·less adj.

sin·ew·y (sin′yoo·ē) adj. 1 Of, like, or having sinews. 2 Having many sinews; tough. 3 Strong; brawny. 4 Vigorous; forceful.

sin·ful (sin′fəl) adj. Tainted with, full of, or characterized by sin. —sin′ful·ly adv. —sin′ful·ness n. —Syn. wicked, bad, immoral, evil.

sing (sing) v. sang or (now less commonly) sung, sung, sing·ing v.i. 1 To produce musical sounds with the voice. 2 To perform vocal compositions professionally or in a specified manner. 3 To produce melodious sounds, as a bird. 4 To make a continuous, melodious sound suggestive of singing, as a teakettle, the wind, etc. 5 To buzz or hum; ring: My ears are singing. 6 To be suitable for singing. 7 To relate or celebrate something in song or verse. 8 Slang To confess the details of a crime, esp. so as to implicate others. 9 To be joyous; rejoice. — v.t. 11 To perform (music) vocally. 12 To chant; intone. 13 To bring to a specified condition or place by singing: Sing me to sleep. 14 To relate, proclaim, praise, etc., in or as in verse or song. —n. Informal A singing, esp. by a group. [< OE singan] —sing′a·ble adj.

sing. singular.

singe (sinj) v.t. singed, singe·ing 1 To burn slightly. 2 To remove bristles or feathers from by passing through flame. 3 To burn the ends of (hair, etc.). —n. A slight or superficial burn; scorch. [< OE sengan] —sing′er n.

sing·er (sing′ər) n. 1 One who sings, esp. as a profession. 2 A poet. 3 A songbird.

Sin·gha·lese (sing′gə·lēz′, -lēs′) adj. Of or pertaining to a group of people in Sri Lanka or to their language. —n. 1 One of the Singhalese people. 2 Their language.

sin·gle (sing′gəl) adj. 1 Consisting of only one. 2 With no other or others; solitary; lone; alone. 3 Unmarried; also, pertaining to the unmarried state. 4 Of, pertaining to or involving only one person. 5 Consisting of only one part; simple. 6 Upright; sincere; honest. 7 Designed for use by only one person: a single bed. 8 Bot. Having only one row of petals, as a flower. —n. 1 One who or that which is single. 2 In baseball, a hit by which the batter reaches first base. 3 In cricket, a hit which scores one run. 4 pl. In tennis or similar games, a match with only one player on each side —v. ·gled, ·gling v.t. 1 To choose or select (one) from others: usually with out. —v.i. 2 In baseball, to make a single. [< L singulus] —sin′gle·ness n. —sin′gly adv.

sin·gle-breast·ed (sing′gəl·bres′tid) adj. Overlapping at the center of the front of the body just enough to allow for fastening by a single button or row of buttons.

single file A line of people, animals, etc., moving one behind the other. 2 In such a line: to walk single file.

sin·gle-foot (sing′gəl·foot′) n. The gait of a horse in which the sequence in which the feet leave the ground is right hind, right fore, left hind, left fore. —v.i. To go at this gait.

sin·gle-hand·ed (sing′gəl·han′did) adj. 1 Done or working alone; without assistance; unaided. 2 Having but one hand. 3 Capable of being used with a single hand. —sin′·gle-hand′ed·ly adv.

sin·gle-heart·ed (sing′gəl·här′tid) adj. Sincere and undivided, as in purpose, dedication, feeling, etc. —sin′gle-heart′ed·ly adv.

sin·gle-mind·ed (sing′gəl·mīn′did) adj. 1 Having only one purpose or end in view. 2 Free from duplicity; ingenuous; sincere. —sin′gle-mind′ed·ly adv. —sin′gle-mind′ed·ness n.

sin·gle-stick (sing′gəl·stik′) n. 1 A wooden, swordlike stick used in fencing. 2 The art or an instance of fencing with such sticks.

sin·gle·ton (sing′gəl·tən) n. 1 A single card of a suit originally held in the hand of a player. 2 Any single thing, distinct from two or more of its group.

sin·gle-track (sing′əl·trak′) adj. 1 Having only one track. 2 Having a limited scope, outlook, flexibility, etc.

sin·gle-tree (sing′gəl·trē′) n. WHIFFLETREE.

sing·song (sing′sông′, -song′) n. 1 Monotonous regularity of rhythm and rhyme in verse. 2 Verse characterized by such regularity. 3 A voice, speech tones, etc., characterized by a monotonous rise and fall of pitch. — adj. Having a monotonous rhythm or rise and fall of pitch.

sin·gu·lar (sing′gyə·lər) adj. 1 Being the only one of its type; unique; separate; individual. 2 Extraordinary; remarkable; uncommon: a singular honor. 3 Odd; not customary or usual. 4 Gram. Of, pertaining to, or being a word form which denotes one person or thing. —n. Gram. The singular number, or a word form having this number. —sin′gu·lar·ly adv. —sin′gu·lar·ness n. —Syn. 1 peculiar, distinctive. 3 strange, conspicuous.

sin·gu·lar·i·ty (sing′gyə·lar′ə·tē) n. pl. ·ties 1 The state or quality of being singular. 2 Something of uncommon or remarkable character.

sin·gu·lar·ize (sing′gyə·lə·rīz′) v.t. ·ized, ·iz·ing To make singular.

Sin·ha·lese (sin′hə·lēz′, -lēs′) adj., n. SINGHALESE.

sin·is·ter (sin′is·tər) adj. 1 Malevolent; evil: a sinister expression on the face. 2 Boding or attended with misfortune or disaster; inauspicious. 3 Of, pertaining to, or situated on the left side or hand. 4 Her. On the wearer's left, the spectator's right. [L, left, unlucky] —sin′is·ter·ly adv. —sin′is·ter·ness n.

sink (singk) v. sank or sunk, sunk (Obs. sunk·en), sink·ing v.i. 1 To go beneath the surface or to the bottom, as of water or snow. 2 To go down, esp. slowly or by degrees. 3 To seem to descend, as the sun. 4 To incline downward; slope gradually, as land. 5 To pass into a specified state: to sink into a coma. 6 To approach death: He's sinking fast. 7 To become less in force, volume, or degree: His voice sank to a whisper. 8 To become less in value, price, etc. 9 To decline in quality or condition; retrogress; degenerate: usu. with into or to. 10 To penetrate or be absorbed: The oil sank into the wood. 11 To be impressed or fixed, as in the heart or mind: I think that lesson will sink in. —v.t. 12 To cause to go beneath the surface or to the bottom: to sink a fence post. 13 To cause or allow to fall or drop; lower. 14 To cause to penetrate or be absorbed. 15 To make (a mine shaft, well, etc.) by digging or excavating. 16 To reduce in force, volume, or degree. 17 To debase or degrade. 18 To suppress or hide; restrain. 19 To defeat; ruin. 20 To invest. 21 To invest and subsequently lose. 22 To pay up; liquidate. 23 In certain sports, to cause (a ball or other object) to go through or into a receptacle or hole. —n. 1 A basinlike receptacle with a drainpipe and usu. a water supply. 2 A sewer or cesspool. 3 A place where corruption and vice gather or are rampant. 4 A hollow place or depression in a land surface, esp. one in which water collects or disappears by evaporation or percolation. 5 A body or mechanism by which matter or energy is absorbed or dissipated: a heat sink. [< OE sincan] —sink′a·ble adj. —Syn. 2 descend, dwindle, diminish, lessen.

sink·er (singk′ər) n. 1 One who or that which sinks. 2 A weight for sinking a fishing or sounding line. 3 Informal A doughnut.

sinking fund A fund accumulated to pay off a debt at maturity.

sin·less (sin′lis) adj. Having no sin; guiltless; innocent. —sin′less·ly adv. —sin′less·ness n.

sin·ner (sin′ər) n. One who has sinned.

Sino- combining form 1 Of or pertaining to the Chinese people, language, etc. 2 Chinese and: Sino-Tibetan. [< LL Sinae the Chinese]

Si·no-Ti·bet·an (sī′nō·ti·bet′n) n. A family of languages spoken over a wide area in CEN. and SE Asia, including the languages of China, Burma, Tibet, and Thailand.

sin·u·ate (sin′yoo·it, -āt) adj. 1 Winding in and out; wavy. 2 Bot. Having a strongly indented, wavy margin, as some leaves. —v.i. (sin′yoo·āt) ·at·ed, ·at·ing To curve in and out; turn; wind. [< L sinus curve] —sin′u·ate·ly adv. —sin′u·a′tion n.

sin·u·ous (sin′yoo·əs) adj. 1 Characterized by turns or curves; winding; undulating; tortuous: a sinuous path. 2 Devious; indirect; not straightforward. [< L sinus bend] — sin′u·ous·ly adv. —sin·u·os·i·ty (sin′yoo·os′ə·tē), sin′u·ous·ness n.

si·nus (sī′nəs) *n.* **1** Any of the natural cavities in the skull that contain air and usu. connect with the nostrils. **2** A dilated part of a blood vessel. **3** Any narrow opening leading to an abscess. **4** *Bot.* A recess or depression between two adjoining lobes, as of a leaf. [L, curve, hollow]

si·nu·si·tis (sī′nə·sī′tis) *n.* Inflammation of a sinus or the sinuses of the skull.

Si·on (sī′ən) *n.* ZION.

Siou·an (sōō′ən) *n. pl.* **Siouan** or **Siouans** **1** A large family of languages spoken by Indians who formerly inhabited parts of CEN. and E North America. **2** A member of any of the peoples speaking a language of this family. —*adj.* Of or pertaining to this language family.

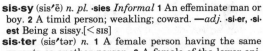

Sinuses
a. frontal.
b. maxillary.

Sioux (sōō) *n. pl.* **Sioux** One of a group of North American Indian tribes of Siouan linguistic stock formerly occupying parts of the Great Plains area in the Dakotas, Minnesota, and Nebraska.

sip (sip) *v.* **sipped, sip·ping** *v.t.* **1** To imbibe in small quantities. **2** To drink from by sips. **3** To take in; absorb. —*v.i.* **4** To drink in sips. —*n.* **1** A very small amount sipped. **2** The act of sipping. [< OE *sypian* drink in] —**sip·per** *n.*

si·phon (sī′fən) *n.* **1** A bent tube for transferring liquids from a higher to a lower level over an intervening barrier. **2** SIPHON BOTTLE. **3** *Zool.* A tubular structure in certain aquatic animals, as the squid, for drawing in or expelling liquids. —*v.t.* **1** To draw off by or cause to pass through or as through a siphon. —*v.i.* **2** To pass through a siphon. [< Gk. *siphōn*] —**si′phon·al** *adj.*

siphon bottle A bottle containing aerated or carbonated water, which is expelled through a bent tube in the neck of the bottle by the pressure of the gas when a valve in the tube is opened.

Siphon

sir (sûr) *n.* The conventional term of respectful address to a man: not followed by a proper name. [< SIRE]

Sir (sûr) *n.* A title of baronets and knights, used before the given name or the full name.

sire (sīr) *n.* **1** *Archaic* A father or forefather. **2** The male parent of an animal, esp. a domestic animal. **3** *Archaic* A man of high rank; also a form of address to a superior used esp. in addressing a king. —*v.t.* **sired, sir·ing** To beget; procreate: used chiefly of domestic animals. [< L *senior* older]

si·ren (sī′rən) *n.* **1** *Often cap. Gk. Myth.* One of a group of sea nymphs who lured sailors to destruction by their sweet singing. **2** A seductive, enticing woman. **3** A device for producing a series of loud tones, as for a warning, often consisting of a perforated rotating disk or disks through which sharp puffs of steam or compressed air are permitted to escape. —*adj.* Of or pertaining to a siren; seductive; enticing. [< Gk. *seirēn*]

Sir·i·us (sir′ē·əs) *n.* The Dog Star, the brightest star in the night sky, in the constellation of Canis Major. [< Gk. *seirios* scorching]

sir·loin (sûr′loin) *n.* A cut of meat, esp. of beef, from the upper portion of the loin. [< OF *sur-* above + *longe* loin]

si·roc·co (si·rok′ō) *n. pl.* **·cos** **1** A hot, dry, and dusty wind blowing from the Libyan deserts into s Europe, esp. to Italy, Sicily, and Malta. **2** Any hot or warm wind, esp. one blowing toward a center of low barometric pressure. [< Ar. *sharq* the east]

sir·up (sir′əp) *n.* SYRUP.

sis (sis) *n. Informal* Sister.

si·sal (sī′səl, -zəl, sis′əl) *n.* **1** A tough fiber obtained from the leaves of a species of agave. **2** The plant itself. Also **sisal hemp.** [< *Sisal,* town in Yucatán, Mexico]

sis·sy (sis′ē) *n. pl.* **·sies** *Informal* **1** An effeminate man or boy. **2** A timid person; weakling; coward. —*adj.* **·si·er, ·si·est** Being a sissy. [< SIS]

sis·ter (sis′tər) *n.* **1** A female person having the same parents as another person. **2** A female of the lower animals having one parent in common with another. **3 a** HALF SISTER. **b** SISTER-IN-LAW. **c** A foster sister. **4** A woman or girl allied to another or others by race, creed, a common interest, membership in a society, etc. **5** *Eccl.* A member of a sisterhood; nun. **6** *Chiefly Brit.* A head nurse in the ward or clinic of a hospital; also, any nurse. **7** A person or thing having similar characteristics to another. —*adj.* Bearing the relationship of a sister or one suggestive of sisterhood. [< OE *swostor*] —**sis′ter·ly** *adj.*

sis·ter·hood (sis′tər·hŏŏd) *n.* **1** A body of women united by some bond. **2** *Eccl.* A community of women forming a religious order. **3** The sisterly relationship.

sis·ter-in-law (sis′tər·in·lô′) *n. pl.* **sis·ters-in-law** **1** A sister of one's husband or wife. **2** A brother's wife. **3** A brother-in-law's wife.

Sis·y·phus (sis′ə·fəs) *Gk. Myth.* A king of Corinth, condemned in Hades forever to roll uphill a huge stone that always rolled down again.

sit (sit) *v.* **sat, sit·ting** *v.i.* **1** To rest on the buttocks or haunches; be seated. **2** To perch or roost, as a bird. **3** To cover eggs so as to give warmth for hatching. **4** To pose, as for a portrait. **5** To be in session; hold a session. **6** To occupy a seat in a deliberative body. **7** To have or exercise judicial authority. **8** To fit or hang: That dress *sits* well. **9** To rest; lie: an obligation that *sat* heavily on her. **10** To be situated or located. **11** BABY-SIT. —*v.t.* **12** To have or keep a seat or a good seat upon: to *sit* a horse. **13** To seat (oneself): *Sit* yourself down. —**sit in (on)** **1** To join; participate: to *sit in on* a game of cards or a business deal. **2** To attend or take part in a discussion or music session. **3** To take part in a sit-in. —**sit on (or upon)** **1** To belong to (a jury, commission, etc.) as a member. **2** To hold discussions about or investigate. **3** *Informal* To suppress, squelch, or delay action on or consideration of. —**sit out** **1** To remain until the end of. **2** To sit during or take no part in: They *sat out* a dance. **3** To stay longer than. —**sit up** **1** To assume a sitting position. **2** To maintain an erect posture while seated. **3** To stay up later than usual at night. **4** To be startled or show interest. [< OE *sittan*]

si·tar (si·tär′) *n.* A stringed instrument used in Hindu music, somewhat resembling the lute, having a long neck, a resonating gourd or gourds, and a variable number of strings, some of which are plucked, others vibrating sympathetically. [< Hind. *sitār*]

sit·com (sit′kom′) *n. Slang* A situation comedy. [< SIT(UATION) + COM(EDY)]

Sitar

sit-down (sit′doun′) *n.* **1** A strike during which strikers refuse to work or leave their place of employment until agreement is reached: also **sit-down strike.** **2** A form of civil disobedience in which demonstrators obstruct some activity by sitting down and refusing to move.

site (sīt) *n.* **1** A plot of ground used for or considered for some specific purpose. **2** The place, scene, or location of something: the battle *site.* [< L *situs* position]

sit-in (sit′in′) *n.* **1** SIT-DOWN (def. 2). **2** An organized demonstration in which a protesting group occupies an area prohibited to them, as by taking seats in a restricted restaurant, etc. —**sit′-in·ner** *n.*

sit·ter (sit′ər) *n.* One who sits, esp. a baby sitter.

sit·ting (sit′ing) *n.* **1** The act or position of one who sits. **2** An uninterrupted period of being seated, as for the painting of a portrait. **3** A session or term. **4** An incubation; period of hatching. **5** The number of eggs on which a bird sits at one incubation. That sits or is seated.

sitting duck *Informal* An easy target or victim.

sit·ting room (sit′ting·rōōm′, -rŏŏm′) LIVING ROOM.

sit·u·ate (sich′ōō·āt) v.t. ·at·ed, ·at·ing To place in a certain position; locate. [< L *situs* a place]

sit·u·at·ed (sich′ōō·ā′tid) adj. 1 Having a fixed location. 2 Placed in certain circumstances or conditions, esp. financially: He is well *situated*.

sit·u·a·tion (sich′ōō·ā′shən) n. 1 The way in which something is situated, relative to its surroundings; position; location. 2 A locality; site. 3 Condition as modified or determined by circumstances. 4 A salaried post of employment. 5 A combination of circumstances at a specific time; state of affairs. 6 An unusual, difficult, critical, or otherwise significant state of affairs. —**sit′u·a′tion·al** adj.

situation comedy A television or radio show typically centered about a few characters involved in comical situations and presented in separate episodes.

Si·va (sē′və, shē′-) The Hindu god of destruction and reproduction. —**Si′va·ism** n. —**Si′va·is′tic** adj.

six (siks) n. 1 The sum of five plus one; 6; VI. 2 A set or group of six members. —**at sixes and sevens** In a state of confusion and indecision. [< OE] —**six** adj., pron.

six-pack (siks′pak′) n. 1 A group of six cans or bottles packaged as a unit. 2 The contents of such a unit.

six·pence (siks′pəns) n. 1 A British coin worth six pence. 2 The sum of six pence.

six·pen·ny (siks′pen′ē, -pən·ē) adj. 1 Worth, or sold for sixpence. 2 Cheap; trashy. 3 Denoting a size of nails, usu. two inches long.

six-shoot·er (siks′shōō′tər) n. A revolver that will fire six shots without reloading.

six·teen (siks′tēn′) n. 1 The sum of 15 plus 1; 16; XVI. 2 A set or group of sixteen members. —**six′teen′** adj., pron.

six·teenth (siks′tēnth′) adj. & adv. Next in order after the 15th. —n. 1 The element of an ordered set that corresponds to the number 16. 2 One of 16 equal parts.

sixteenth note *Music* A note of one sixteenth of the time value of a whole note. • See NOTE.

sixth (siksth) adj. & adv. Next in order after the fifth. —n. 1 The element of an ordered set that corresponds to the number six. 2 One of six equal parts. 3 *Music* The interval between a tone and another five steps away in a diatonic scale.

sixth sense The power of intuitive perception, thought of as independent of the five senses.

six·ti·eth (siks′tē·ith) adj. & adv. Tenth in order after the 50th. —n. 1 The element of an ordered set that corresponds to the number 60. 2 One of sixty equal parts.

six·ty (siks′tē) n. pl. ·ties 1 The product of six and ten; 60; LX. 2 A set or group of 60 members. 3 pl. The numbers, years, etc., between 60 and 70. —**six′ty** adj., pron.

six·ty-fourth note (siks′tē·fôrth, -fōrth) *Music* A note of one sixty-fourth of the time value of a whole note. • See NOTE.

siz·a·ble (sī′zə·bəl) adj. Comparatively large. Also **size′a·ble.** —**siz′a·ble·ness** n. —**siz′a·bly** adv.

size¹ (sīz) n. 1 The dimensions of a thing as compared with some standard; physical magnitude or bulk. 2 Considerable amount, dimensions, etc. 3 One of a series of graded measures, as of hats, shoes, etc. 4 *Informal* State of affairs; true situation: That's the *size* of it. —v.t. **sized, siz·ing** 1 To arrange or classify according to size. 2 To cut or otherwise make (an article) to a required size. —**size up** *Informal* 1 To form an opinion of. 2 To meet specifications. [< OF *assise* ASSIZE]

size² (sīz) n. A liquid preparation used to give a smooth finish to cloth, paper, or other porous surface. —v.t. **sized, siz·ing** To treat with size. [? < SIZE¹]

size³ (sīz) adj. SIZED (def. 1).

sized (sīzd) adj. 1 Having graded dimensions or a definite size: usu. in combination: large-*sized*. 2 Arranged according to size.

siz·ing (sī′zing) n. 1 SIZE². 2 The act or process of adding size to a fabric, yarn, etc.

siz·zle (siz′əl) v. ·zled, ·zling v.i. 1 To emit a hissing sound under the action of heat. 2 To seethe with rage, resentment, etc. —v.t. 3 To cause to sizzle. —n. A hissing sound, as from frying. [Imit.]

S.J. Society of Jesus.

skald (skôld, skäld) n. A Scandinavian poet or bard of ancient times. [< ON *skáld* poet]

skate¹ (skāt) n. 1 A metal runner attached to a frame, with clamps or straps for fastening it to the sole of a boot or shoe, enabling the wearer to glide over ice. 2 A shoe or boot with such a runner permanently attached. 3 ROLLER SKATE. —v.i. **skat·ed, skat·ing** To glide or move over ice or some other smooth surface, on or as on skates. [< Du. *schaats*] —**skat′er** n.

skate² (skāt) n. Any of various flat-bodied, cartilaginous marine fishes with enlarged pectoral fins and ventral gill slits. [< ON *skata*]

Skate

skate·board (skāt′bôrd′, -bōrd′) n. A toy consisting of two pairs of skate wheels attached to a narrow board serving as a platform for riding. —**skate′board′er** n.

ske·dad·dle (ski·dad′l) *Informal* v.i. ·dled, ·dling To flee in haste. —n. A hasty flight. [?]

skeet (skēt) n. A variety of trapshooting in which clay targets, hurled in such a way as to resemble the flight of birds, are fired at from various angles. [?]

skein (skān) n. 1 A fixed quantity of yarn, thread, silk, wool, etc., wound in a loose coil. 2 Something like this: a *skein* of hair. [< OF *escaigne*]

skel·e·ton (skel′ə·tən) n. 1 The supporting framework of a vertebrate, composed of bone and cartilage. 2 Any framework constituting the main supporting parts of a structure. 3 A mere sketch or outline of anything. 4 A very thin person or animal. —**skeleton in the closet** A secret source of shame or discredit. —adj. Of, pertaining to, or like a skeleton. [< Gk. *skeletos* dried up] —**skel·e·tal** adj.

skeleton key A key having a large part of the bit filed away to enable it to open many simple locks.

skep·tic (skep′tik) n. 1 A person characterized by skepticism, esp. in regard to religion. 2 A person who advocates or believes in philosophical skepticism. *Chiefly Brit. sp.* **scep′tic.** [< Gk. *skeptikos* reflective]

skep·ti·cal (skep′ti·kəl) adj. Of, pertaining to, characteristic of, or marked by skepticism. *Chiefly Brit. sp.* **scep′ti·cal.** —**skep′ti·cal·ly** adv. —**skep′ti·cal·ness** n.

skep·ti·cism (skep′tə·siz′əm) n. 1 A doubting or incredulous state of mind. 2 Doubt about basic religious doctrines such as immortality, revelation, etc. 3 The philosophical doctrine that absolute knowledge in any given area is unattainable, and that relative certainty can be approximated only by a continuous process of doubt, criticism, and suspended judgment. *Chiefly Brit. sp.* **scep′ti·cism.**

sketch (skech) n. 1 A rough or undetailed drawing or design, often done as a preliminary study. 2 A brief plan, description, or outline. 3 A short literary or musical composition. 4 A short scene, play, comical act, etc. —v.t. 1 To make a sketch or sketches of. —v.i. 2 To make a sketch or sketches. [< Gk. *schedios* impromptu] —**sketch′er** n.

sketch·book (skech′bōōk′) n. 1 A pad or book of drawing paper for sketching. 2 A printed volume of sketches.

sketch·y (skech′ē) adj. **sketch·i·er, sketch·i·est** 1 Like or in the form of a sketch; roughly suggested without detail. 2 Incomplete; superficial. —**sketch′i·ly** adv. —**sketch′i·ness** n.

skew (skyōō) v.i. 1 To take an oblique direction. 2 To look sideways; squint. —v.t. 3 To give an oblique form or direction to. 4 To give a bias to; misrepresent; distort. —adj. 1 Placed, turned or running to one side; oblique; slanting. 2 ASYMMETRIC. —n. A deviation from straightness; an oblique direction or course. [< AF *eskiuer*]

skew·er (skyōō′ər) n. 1 A long pin of wood or metal, used for fastening meat while roasting. 2 Any of various articles of similar shape or use. —v.t. To run through or fasten with or as with a skewer. [?]

ski (skē, *Brit. also* shē) n. pl. **skis** 1 One of a pair of flat, narrow runners of wood, metal, or other material, worn clamped to boots for gliding over snow. 2 WATER SKI. —v. **skied, ski·ing** v.i. 1 To glide or travel on skis. —v.t. 2 To glide or travel over on skis. [Norw.< ON *skidh* snowshoe] —**ski′er** n.

skid (skid) n. 1 A log, plank, etc., often one of a pair, used to support or elevate something or as an incline on which heavy objects can be rolled or slid. 2 A low, movable platform that holds material to be moved, temporarily stored, etc. **3** A shoe, drag, etc., used to prevent a wheel from turning. **4** A runner used in place of a wheel in the landing gear of an airplane or helicopter. **5** The act of skidding. — **on the skids** *Slang* Rapidly declining in prestige, power, etc. —*v.* **skid·ded, skid·ding** *v.i.* **1** To slide instead of rolling, as a wheel over a surface. **2** To slide due to loss of traction, as a vehicle. **3** *Aeron.* To slip sideways when turning. —*v.t.* **4** To put, drag, haul, or slide on skids. **5** To brake or hold back with a skid. [?] —**skid′der** *n.*

skid row *Slang* An urban section frequented by vagrants, derelicts, etc.

skiff (skif) *n.* **1** A light rowboat. **2** A small, light sailing vessel. [< OHG *scif* ship]

skill (skil) *n.* **1** Ability or proficiency in execution or performance. **2** A specific art, craft, trade, or job; also such an art, craft, etc., in which one has a learned competence. [< ON *skil* knowledge]

skilled (skild) *adj.* **1** Having skill. **2** Having or requiring a specialized ability, as in a particular occupation, gained by training or experience.

skil·let (skil′it) *n.* A frying pan. [ME *skelet*] • See APPLIANCE.

skill·ful (skil′fəl) *adj.* **1** Having skill. **2** Done with or requiring skill. Also **skil′ful.** —**skill′fully** *adv.* —**skill′ful·ness** *n.*

skim (skim) *v.* **skimmed, skim·ming** *v.t.* **1** To remove floating matter from the surface of (a liquid): to *skim* milk. **2** To remove (floating matter) from the surface of a liquid: to *skim* cream from milk. **3** To cover with a thin film, as of ice. **4** To move lightly and quickly across or over. **5** To cause to bounce and ricochet swiftly and lightly, as a coin across a pond. **6** To read or glance over hastily or superficially. —*v.i.* **7** To move quickly and lightly across or near a surface; glide. **8** To make a hasty and superficial perusal; glance: with *over* or *through*. **9** To become covered with a thin film. —*n.* **1** The act of skimming. **2** That which is skimmed off. **3** A thin layer or coating. —*adj.* Skimmed: *skim* milk. [< OF *escume* scum, foam] —**skim′mer** *n.*

skim milk Milk from which the cream has been removed. Also **skimmed milk.**

skimp (skimp) *v.i.* **1** To provide too little; scrimp. **2** To keep expenses at a minimum. —*v.t.* **3** To do poorly, hastily, or carelessly. **4** To be stingy in providing for. —*adj.* Scant; meager. [?] —**skimp′ing·ly** *adv.*

skimp·y (skim′pē) *adj.* **skimp·i·er, skimp·i·est** Scanty; insufficient. —**skimp′i·ly** *adv.* —**skimp′i·ness** *n.*

skin (skin) *n.* **1** The membranous outer covering of an animal body. **2** The pelt or hide of an animal. **3** A vessel for holding liquids, made of the skin of an animal. **4** Any outside layer, coat, or covering resembling skin, as fruit rind. —**by the skin of one's teeth** *Informal* Very closely or narrowly; barely. —**get under one's skin 1** To provoke one. **2** To be a source of excitement, emotion, etc., to one. —**have a thick (thin) skin** To be very insensitive (or sensitive), as to insult, criticism, etc. —**save one's skin** *Informal* To avoid harm or death. —*v.* **skinned, skin·ning** *v.t.* **1** To remove the skin of; peel. **2** To cover with or as with skin. **3** To remove as if taking off skin: to *skin* a dollar from a roll of bills. **4** *Informal* To cheat or swindle. —*v.i.* **5** To become covered with skin. **6** To climb up or down; shin. [< ON *skinn*] —**skin·ner** *n.*

skin-deep (skin′dēp′) *adj.* **1** Penetrating only as deep as the skin. **2** Of little significance; superficial.

skin diving Underwater swimming in which the swimmer is equipped with a breathing apparatus, as a snorkel, goggles, and with various other equipment as foot fins, rubber garments, etc. —**skin diver**

skin·flint (skin′flint) *n.* One who tries to get or save money in any possible way. —**Syn.** miser, niggard, scrooge.

skink (skingk) *n.* One of a group of lizards with short limbs and smooth, flat, shiny scales. [< Gk. *skinkos,* a kind of lizard]

skin·ner (skin′ər) *n.* **1** One who strips or processes the skins of animals. **2** A dealer in skins. **3** *Informal* A mule driver.

skin·ny (skin′ē) *adj.* **·ni·er, ·ni·est 1** Consisting of or like skin. **2** Without sufficient flesh; too thin. **3** Lacking the

normal or desirable quality, quantity, size, etc. —**skin′ni·ly** *adv.* —**skin′ni·ness** *n.*

skin·ny-dip (skin′ē·dip′) *Informal v.i.* **·dipped, ·dip·ping** To swim in the nude. —*n.* A swim in the nude. —**skin·ny-dip·per** *n.*

skin-tight (skin′tīt′) *adj.* Fitting tightly to the skin, as a garment.

skip (skip) *v.* **skipped, skip·ping** *v.i.* **1** To move with springing steps, esp. by a series of light hops on alternate feet. **2** To be deflected from a surface; ricochet. **3** To pass from one point to another without noticing what lies between. **4** *Informal* To leave or depart hurriedly; flee. **5** To be advanced in school beyond the next grade in order —*v.t.* **6** To leap lightly over. **7** To cause to ricochet. **8** To pass over or by without notice. **9** *Informal* To leave (a place) hurriedly. **10** To fail to attend a session or sessions of (church, school, etc.) **11** To cause to be advanced in school beyond the next grade in order —*n.* **1** A light bound or spring, esp. any of a series of light hops on alternate feet. **2** A passing over without notice. [Prob. < Scand.]

skip·jack (skip′jak) *n.* Any of various fishes that jump above or play along the surface of the water.

skip·per[1] (skip′ər) *n.* **1** One who or that which skips. **2** Any of various insects that make erratic, skipping movements.

skip·per[2] (skip′ər) *n.* **1** The master or captain of a vessel, esp. of a small ship or boat. **2** One who is in charge of any endeavor. —*v.t.* To act as the skipper of (a vessel, etc.) [< Du. *schip* ship]

skirl (skûrl, skirl) *v.i.* **1** To shriek shrilly, as a bagpipe. —*v.t.* **2** To play on the bagpipe. —*n.* A high, shrill sound, as of a bagpipe. [< Scand.]

skir·mish (skûr′mish) *n.* **1** A minor fight or encounter, usu. an incident in a larger conflict. **2** Any unimportant dispute, argument, etc. —*v.i.* To take part in a skirmish. [< OF *eskermir* to fence, fight] —**skir′mish·er** *n.*

skirt (skûrt) *n.* **1** That part of a dress, gown, etc., that hangs from the waist down. **2** A separate garment for women or girls that hangs from the waist down. • See PLEAT. **3** Anything that hangs or covers like a skirt: the *skirt* of a dressing table. **4** *Slang* A girl; woman. **5** The margin, border, or outer edge of anything. **6** *pl.* The border, fringe, or edge of a particular area; outskirts. —*v.t.* **1** To lie along or form the edge of; to border. **2** To surround or border: with *with.* **3** To pass around or about, usu. to avoid crossing: to *skirt* the town. —*v.i.* **4** To be on or pass along the edge or border. [< ON *skyrt* shirt]

skit (skit) *n.* **1** A short theatrical sketch, usu. humorous or satirical. **2** A short piece of writing, humorous or satirical in tone. [?]

skit·ter (skit′ər) *v.i.* **1** To glide or skip along a surface lightly and quickly. **2** To draw a lure or baited hook along the surface of the water with a skipping or twitching movement. —*v.t.* **3** To cause to skitter.

skit·tish (skit′ish) *adj.* **1** Easily frightened, as a horse. **2** Very playful or lively. **3** Unreliable; fickle. [ME] —**skit′· tish·ly** *adv.* —**skit′tish·ness** *n.*

skit·tle (skit′l) *n.* **1** *pl. (construed as sing.)* A British version of the game of ninepins, in which a wooden disk or ball is thrown to knock down the pins. **2** One of the pins used in this game. —**beer and skittles** Carefree, unruffled enjoyment: usu. with a negative: Life is not all *beer and skittles.* [?]

skiv·vy (skiv′ē) *n. pl.* **·vies** *Slang* **1** A man's T-shirt. **2** *pl.* Men's underwear. [?]

skoal (skōl) *interj.* Good health, good luck, etc.: used as a toast. [< Dan. and Norw. *skaal* cup < ON *skāl* bowl]

Skr. Sanskrit.

Skt. Sanskrit.

sku·a (skyōō′ə) *n.* A predatory sea bird. Also **skua gull.** [< ON *skūfr*]

skul·dug·ger·y (skul·dug′ər·ē) *n.* Dishonesty; trickery; underhandedness. [?]

skulk (skulk) *v.i.* **1** To move about furtively or slily; sneak. **2** *Chiefly Brit.* To shirk; evade work or responsibility. —*n.* One who skulks. [< Scand.] —**skulk′er** *n.*

skull (skul) *n.* **1** The bony framework of the head of a vertebrate animal; the cranium. **2** The head considered as the seat of intelligence; mind. [< Scand.]

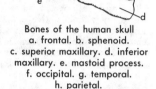

skull and crossbones A representation of the human skull over two crossed thighbones, used as a warning label on poison and, formerly, as an emblem of piracy.

skull·cap (skul′kap′) *n.* A cap closely fitting the skull and having no brim or peak.

Bones of the human skull
a. frontal. b. sphenoid.
c. superior maxillary. d. inferior
maxillary. e. mastoid process.
f. occipital. g. temporal.
h. parietal.

skunk (skungk) *n.* **1** A small nocturnal carnivore of North America, usu. black with a white stripe down the back, and ejecting an offensive odor when attacked. **2** *Informal* A low, contemptible person. —*v.t. Slang* To defeat, as in a contest, esp. to defeat so thoroughly as to keep from scoring. [< Algon. *seganku*]

skunk cabbage A stemless perennial herb growing in marshy terrain and having a strong, skunklike odor. Also **skunk′weed′** (-wēd′).

Skunk

sky (skī) *n. pl.* **skies 1** The blue vault that seems to bend over the earth; the firmament. **2** *Often pl.* The upper atmosphere, esp. in regard to its appearance: cloudy *skies*. **3** The celestial regions; heaven. **4** Climate; weather. —**out of a clear** (or **blue**) **sky** Without any warning. —**to the skies** Without reservations: to praise something *to the skies*. —*v.t.* **skied** or **skyed**, **sky·ing** *Informal* **1** To hit, throw, bat, etc., high into the air. **2** To hang, as a picture, esp. at an exhibition, above eye level. [< ON *skȳ* cloud]

sky blue A blue like the color of the sky; azure. —**sky′-blue′** *adj.*

sky·dive (skī′dīv′) *v.i.* **·dived, ·div·ing** To engage in skydiving. —**sky′div′er** *n.*

sky·div·ing (skī′dī′ving) *n.* The sport of jumping from an airplane and performing various maneuvers before opening a parachute.

sky·jack (skī′jak) *v.t.* HIJACK (def. 3). [< SKY + (HI)JACK] —**sky′jack′er** *n.*

sky·lark (skī′lärk′) *n.* A lark noted for singing as it flies. —*v.i.* To indulge in hilarious or boisterous frolic. —**sky′-lark′er** *n.*

sky·light (skī′līt′) *n.* A window facing skyward.

sky·line (skī′līn′) *n.* **1** The line where earth and sky appear to meet; horizon. **2** The outline of buildings, trees, etc., against the sky.

sky·rock·et (skī′rok′it) *n.* A rocket that is shot high into the air. —*v.t. & v.i.* To rise or cause to rise or ascend steeply, like a skyrocket, as wages, prices, etc.

sky·sail (skī′səl, -sāl′) *n. Naut.* A small sail above the royal in a square-rigged vessel.

sky·scrap·er (skī′skrā′pər) *n.* A very high building.

sky·ward (skī′wərd) *adv.* Toward the sky. Also **sky′-wards.** —**sky′ward** *adj.*

sky·writ·ing (skī′rī′ting) *n.* The forming of words in the air by the release of a substance, as a jet of vapor, from an airplane. —**sky′writ′er** *n.*

slab (slab) *n.* **1** A fairly thick, flat piece or slice, as of metal, stone, meat, etc. **2** An outer piece cut from a log. —*v.t.* **slabbed, slab·bing 1** To saw slabs from, as a log. **2** To form into a slab or slabs. [ME]

slack[1] (slak) *adj.* **1** Hanging loosely. **2** Careless; remiss; slovenly; slow. **3** Weak; loose: a *slack* mouth. **4** Lacking activity; not brisk or busy; slow or sluggish: a *slack* season. **5** Listless; limp: a *slack* grip. **6** Flowing sluggishly, as water. —*v.t.* **1** To make slack. **2** To slake, as lime. —*v.i.* **3**

To be or become slack. **4** To become less active or less busy: usu. with *off.* —*n.* **1** The part of anything, as a rope, that is slack. **2** A period of inactivity. **3** A cessation of movement, as in a current. —*adv.* In a slack manner. [< OE *slæc*] —**slack′ly** *adv.* —**slack′ness** *n.*

slack[2] (slak) *n.* A mixture of coal dust, dirt, and small pieces of coal left after coal has been screened. [ME *sleck*]

slack·en (slak′ən) *v.t. & v.i.* To make or become slack.

slack·er (slak′ər) *n.* One who shirks his duties, esp. one who avoids military service in wartime.

slacks (slaks) *n.pl.* Trousers, esp. for informal wear.

slag (slag) *n.* **1** *Metall.* The fused residue separated in the reduction of ores. **2** Volcanic scoria. —*v.t. & v.i.* **slagged, slag·ging** To form into slag. [< MLG *slagge*] —**slag′gy** *adj.*

slain (slān) *p.p.* of SLAY.

slake (slāk) *v.* **slaked, slak·ing** *v.t.* **1** To lessen the force of; quench: *slake* thirst or flames. **2** To mix (an oxide, as lime, etc.) with water; to hydrate. —*v.i.* **3** To become hydrated; said of lime. [< OE *slacian* retard]

slaked lime Calcium hydroxide produced by mixing calcium oxide and water.

sla·lom (slä′ləm, slā′-) *n.* In skiing, a race over a zigzag course laid out between upright obstacles. —*v.i.* To ski in or as in a slalom. [Norw.]

slam[1] (slam) *v.* **slammed, slam·ming** *v.t.* **1** To shut with violence and noise. **2** To put, dash, throw, etc., with violence. **3** *Slang* To strike with the fist. **4** *Informal* To criticize severely. —*v.i.* **5** To shut or move with force. —*n.* **1** A closing or striking with a bang; the act or noise of slamming. **2** *Informal* Severe criticism. [? < Scand.]

slam[2] (slam) *n.* **1** GRAND SLAM (def. 1). **2** LITTLE SLAM. [?]

slam-bang (slam′bang′) *Informal adv.* Vigorously, violently, or noisily. —*adj.* Vigorous, violent, or noisy.

slan·der (slan′dər) *n.* **1** The uttering of false statements or misrepresentations which defame and injure the reputation of another. **2** Such a statement. —*v.t.* **1** To injure by uttering a false statement, etc.; defame. —*v.i.* **2** To utter slander. [< L *scandalum* scandal] —**slan′der·er** *n.* • Popularly, *slander* and *libel* are used synonomously to mean defamation. Legally, however, *slander* refers to oral defamation and *libel* to defamation by any other means, as writing, pictures, effigies, etc.

slan·der·ous (slan′dər·əs) *adj.* **1** Uttering slander. **2** Containing or constituting slander. —**slan′der·ous·ly** *adv.* —**slan′der·ous·ness** *n.*

slang (slang) *n.* **1** A type of popular language comprised of words and phrases of a vigorous, colorful, or facetious nature, which are invented or derived from the unconventional use of the standard vocabulary. **2** The special vocabulary of a certain class, group, profession, etc.; argot; jargon. [?] —**slang′i·ness** *n.* —**slang′y** *adj.*

slant (slant) *v.t.* **1** To give a sloping direction to. **2** To write or edit (news or other literary matter) so as to express a special attitude or appeal to a particular group, interest, etc. —*v.i.* **3** To have or take an oblique or sloping direction. —*adj.* Sloping. —*n.* **1** A slanting direction, course, line, etc.; incline. **2** A point of view, esp. one that is personal or peculiar. [< Scand.] —**slant′ing** *adj.* —**slant′ing·ly** *adv.* —**slant′ing·ness** *n.*

slant·wise (slant′wīz′) *adj.* Slanting; oblique. —*adv.* At a slant or slope; obliquely. Also **slant′ways′** (-wāz′).

slap (slap) *n.* **1** A blow delivered with the open hand or with something flat. **2** The sound made by such a blow, or a sound like it. **3** An insult or rebuff. —*v.* **slapped, slap·ping** *v.t.* **1** To strike with the open hand or with something flat. **2** To put, place, throw, etc., violently or carelessly. —*adv.* **1** Suddenly; abruptly. **2** Directly; straight: *slap* into his face. [< LG *slapp*] —**slap′per** *n.*

slap-dash (slap′dash′) *adj.* Done or acting in a hasty or careless way. —*n.* Something done in a hasty or careless manner. —*adv.* In a slap-dash manner.

slap-hap·py (slap′hap′ē) *adj. Slang* **1** Confused or dazed, as by blows to the head. **2** Giddy or silly.

slap·jack (slap′jak) *n.* PANCAKE.

slap·stick (slap′stik′) *n.* **1** A flexible, double paddle formerly used in farces and pantomimes to make a loud report when an actor was struck with it. **2** The type of comedy which depends on farce, violent activity, etc. — *adj.* Using or suggestive of such comedy.

slash (slash) *v.t.* **1** To cut violently with or as with an edged instrument; gash. **2** To strike with a whip; lash; scourge. **3** To slit, as a garment, so as to expose ornamental material or lining in or under the slits. **4** To criticize severely. **5** To reduce sharply, as salaries. —*v.i.* **6** To make a long sweeping stroke with or as with something sharp; cut. —*n.* **1** The act of slashing. **2** The result of slashing; cut; slit; gash. **3** An ornamental slit cut in a garment. **4** An opening in a forest, covered with debris, as from cutting timber. **5** Such debris. [? < OF *esclashier* to break] —**slash′er** *n.*

slash·ing (slash′ing) *adj.* **1** Severely critical; merciless. **2** Spirited; dashing; impetuous. **3** *Informal* Tremendous; great. —*n.* A slash. —**slash′ing·ly** *adv.* —**slash′ing·ness** *n.*

slat (slat) *n.* Any thin, narrow strip of wood or metal; lath. —*v.t.* **slat·ted**, **slat·ting** To provide or make with slats. [< OF *esclat* splinter, chip]

slat (slāt) *n.* **1** A rock that splits readily into thin and even sheets or layers. **2** A piece, slab, or plate of slate used for roofing, writing upon, etc. **3** A list of candidates, as for nomination or election. **4** A dull bluish gray color resembling that of slate: also **slate gray.** —**a clean slate** A record unmarred by dishonor or dishonesty. —*v.t.* **slat·ed**, **slat·ing** **1** To cover with or as with slate. **2** To put on a political slate or a list of any sort. [< OF *esclat* a chip, splinter] —**slat′er** *n.* —**slat′y** *adj.* (**·i·er**, **·i·est**)

slat·tern (slat′ərn) *n.* An untidy or slovenly woman. [?]

slat·tern·ly (slat′ərn·lē) *adj.* Of, pertaining to, characteristic of, or fit for a slattern. —*adv.* In the manner of a slattern. —**slat′tern·li·ness** *n.* —**Syn.** *adj.* untidy, dowdy, frowzy, sluttish.

slaugh·ter (slô′tər) *n.* **1** The act of killing, esp. the butchering of animals for market. **2** The wanton or savage killing of one or more human beings, esp. of a great number in battle. —*v.t.* **1** To kill for the market; butcher. **2** To kill wantonly or savagely, esp. in large numbers. [< ON *slātr* butcher's meat] —**slaugh′ter·er** *n.* —**slaugh′ter·ous** *adj.* —**slaugh′ter·ous·ly** *adv.*

slaugh·ter·house (slô′tər·hous′) *n.* A place where animals are butchered.

Slav (släv, slav) *n.* A member of any of the Slavic-speaking peoples of E, SE, or CEN. Europe.

Slav. Slavic.

slave (slāv) *n.* **1** A person who is owned by and completely subject to another; one bound by slavery. **2** A person who is totally subject to some habit, influence, etc. **3** One who labors like a slave; drudge. **4** A machine or device that is controlled by another machine or device. **5** SLAVE ANT. —*v.i.* **slaved**, **slav·ing** To work like a slave; toil; drudge. [< Med. L *sclavus* Slav]

slave ant An ant enslaved by members of a slave-making ant species.

slave-driv·er (slāv′drī′vər) *n.* **1** An overseer of slaves at work. **2** Any severe or exacting taskmaster.

slave·hold·er (slāv′hōl′dər) *n.* An owner of slaves. —**slave′hold′ing** *adj. n.*

slav·er[1] (slā′vər) *n.* A person or a vessel engaged in the slave trade.

slav·er[2] (slav′ər) *v.i.* To dribble saliva; drool. —*n.* Saliva dribbling from the mouth. [? < ON *slafra*] —**slav′er·er** *n.*

slav·er·y (slā′vər·ē, slāv′rē) *n.* **1** The legalized social institution in which humans are held as property or chattels. **2** The condition of being a slave. **3** Submission to some habit, influence, etc. **4** Slavish toil; drudgery.

slave trade The business of dealing in slaves, esp. the procurement, transportation, and sale of black Africans.

slav·ey (slā′vē, slav′ē) *n. pl.* **slav·eys** *Chiefly Brit. Informal* A drudge, usu. a maidservant.

Slav·ic (slä′vik, slav′ik) *adj.* Of or pertaining to the Slavs or their languages. —*n.* A branch of the Indo-European language family including Byelorussian, Bulgarian, Czech, Polish, Serbo-Croatian, Slovene, Russian, and Ukrainian.

slav·ish (slā′vish) *adj.* **1** Of, pertaining to, or characteristic of a slave; servile. **2** Having no originality; imitative. —**slav′ish·ly** *adv.* —**slav′ish·ness** *n.*

slaw (slô) *n.* COLESLAW. [< Du. *sla,* short for *salade* salad]

slay (slā) *v.t.* **slew, slain, slay·ing 1** To kill violently; slaughter. **2** *Informal* To amuse, impress, etc., in an overwhelming way. [< OE *slēan*] —**slay′er** *n.*

slea·zy (slē′zē, slā′-) *adj.* **·zi·er**, **·zi·est 1** Lacking firmness of texture or substance. **2** Cheap in character or quality; shoddy, shabby, etc.: a *sleazy* novel; a *sleazy* dress. [?] —**slea′zi·ly** *adv.* —**slea′zi·ness** *n.*

sled (sled) *n.* **1** A vehicle on runners, designed for carrying people or loads over snow and ice. **2** A small sled used esp. by children for sliding on snow and ice. —*v.* **sled·ded, sled·ding** *v.t.* **1** To convey on a sled. —*v.i.* **2** To ride on or use a sled. [< MLG *sledde*] —**sled′der** *n.*

sled·ding (sled′ing) *n.* **1** The act of using or riding on a sled. **2** The conditions under which one uses a sled. **3** *Informal* The conditions under which one pursues any goal; going; progress.

sledge[1] (slej) *n.* A vehicle mounted on low runners for moving loads, esp. over snow and ice. — *v.t.* & *v.i.* **sledged, sledg·ing** To travel or convey on a sledge. [< MDu. *sleedse*]

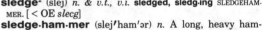

Sledge

sledge[2] (slej) *n.* & *v.t., v.i.* **sledged, sledg·ing** SLEDGEHAMMER. [< OE *slecg*]

sledge·ham·mer (slej′ham′ər) *n.* A long, heavy hammer, usu. wielded with both hands. —*v.t.* & *v.i.* To strike with or as with such a hammer. —*adj.* Like a sledgehammer; extremely powerful; crushing.

sleek (slēk) *adj.* **1** Smooth and glossy. **2** Well-groomed or well-fed. **3** Smooth-spoken and polished in behavior, esp. in a specious way. —*v.t.* **1** To make smooth or glossy; polish. **2** To soothe; mollify. [Var. of SLICK] —**sleek′ly** *adv.* —**sleek′ness** *n.*

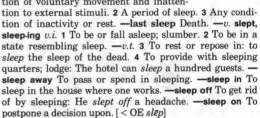

Sledge-hammers

sleep (slēp) *n.* **1** A natural, recurrent physiological state characterized by cessation of voluntary movement and inattention to external stimuli. **2** A period of sleep. **3** Any condition of inactivity or rest. —**last sleep** Death. —*v.* **slept, sleep·ing** *v.i.* **1** To be or fall asleep; slumber. **2** To be in a state resembling sleep. —*v.t.* **3** To rest or repose in: to *sleep* the sleep of the dead. **4** To provide with sleeping quarters; lodge: The hotel can *sleep* a hundred guests. — **sleep away** To pass or spend in sleeping. —**sleep in** To sleep in the house where one works. —**sleep off** To get rid of by sleeping: He *slept off* a headache. —**sleep on** To postpone a decision upon. [< OE *slēp*]

sleep·er (slē′pər) *n.* **1** One who or that which sleeps. **2** A railroad sleeping car. **3** A heavy beam resting on or in the ground, as a support for a roadway, rails, etc. **4** *Informal* Someone or something thought to be unpromising that unexpectedly attains value, importance, notoriety, etc.

sleeping bag A large, warmly-lined bag, usu. zippered and often padded, for sleeping in esp. outdoors.

sleeping car A passenger railroad car with accommodations for sleeping.

sleeping sickness 1 Any of several often fatal tropical diseases caused by protozoans transmitted by the bites of certain insects, as the tsetse fly in Africa, and marked by fever and progressive lethargy. **2** A form of encephalitis.

sleep·less (slēp′lis) *adj.* **1** Unable to sleep; wakeful; restless. **2** Marked by or giving no sleep. **3** Always active or moving. —**sleep′less·ly** *adv.* —**sleep′less·ness** *n.*

sleep·walk·er (slēp′wô′kər) *n.* A person who walks in his sleep; somnambulist. —**sleep′walk′ing** *n.*

sleep·y (slē′pē) *adj.* **sleep·i·er, sleep·i·est 1** Inclined to or ready for sleep; drowsy. **2** Lethargic, inactive, sluggish, or dull. **3** Conducive to sleep. —**sleep′i·ly** *adv.* —**sleep′i·ness** *n.*

sleet (slēt) *n.* **1** A mixture of snow or hail and rain. **2** Partly frozen rain. **3** A thin coating of ice, as on rails, wires, roads, etc. —*v.i.* To pour or shed sleet. [ME *slete*] —**sleet′y** *adj.*

sleeve (slēv) *n.* **1** The part of a garment that serves as a

---

add, āce, câre, pälm; end, ēven; it, īce; odd, ōpen, ôrder; tŏŏk, pōōl; up, bûrn; ə = *a* in *above, u* in *focus;* yōō = *u* in *fuse;* oil; pout; check; go; ring; thin; this; zh, *vision.* < derived from; ? origin uncertain or unknown.

covering for the arm. 2 *Mech.* A tube or tubelike part surrounding another part or into which another part fits. **—up one's sleeve** Hidden but at hand —*v.t.* **sleeved, sleev·ing** To furnish with a sleeve or sleeves. [< OE *slēfe*]

sleigh (slā) *n.* A light vehicle with runners, used esp. for transporting people on snow and ice. —*v.i.* To ride or travel in a sleigh. [< Du. *slee,* contraction of *slede* sledge[1]] **—sleigh'er** *n.*

sleight (slīt) *n.* 1 Deftness; skill; dexterity. 2 Craft; cunning. [< ON *slægdh* slyness]

Sleigh

sleight of hand 1 Skill in performing magical tricks or in juggling. 2 An instance of such skill in performing.

slen·der (slen'dər) *adj.* 1 Having a small width or circumference, in proportion to length or height; long and thin. 2 Having a slim figure; attractively slight. 3 Having slight force or foundation. 4 Small or inadequate. [ME *slendre*] **—slen'der·ly** *adv.* **—slen'der·ness** *n.*

slen·der·ize (slen'də·rīz) *v.t.* & *v.i.* **·ized, ·iz·ing** To make or become slender.

slept (slept) *p.t.* & *p.p.* of SLEEP.

sleuth (slōōth) *n.* 1 *Informal* A detective. 2 A bloodhound: also **sleuth'hound.** —*v.i.* To act as a detective. [< ON *slōdh* track]

slew[1] (slōō) *p.t.* of SLAY.

slew[2] (slōō) *n.* SLOUGH[1] (def. 2).

slew[3] (slōō) *n. Informal* A large number or amount. [< Ir. *sluagh*]

slew[4] (slōō) *v.* & *n.* SLUE[1].

slice (slīs) *n.* 1 A thin, broad piece cut off from a larger body. 2 A share or portion. 3 Any of various implements with a thin, broad blade, as a spatula. 4 **a** The course of a ball so hit that it curves in the direction of the dominant hand of the player who propels it. **b** The ball that follows such a course. —*v.* **sliced, slic·ing** *v.t.* 1 To cut or remove from a larger piece: often with *off, from,* etc. 2 To cut, separate, or divide into parts, shares, or thin, broad pieces. 3 To stir, spread, etc. with a slice. 4 To hit (a ball) so as to produce a slice. —*v.i.* 5 To cut with or as with a knife. 6 To slice a ball, as in golf. [< OHG *slizan* to slit] — **slic'er** *n.*

slick (slik) *adj.* 1 Smooth, slippery, or sleek. 2 *Informal* Deceptively clever; tricky; smooth. 3 Clever; deft; adept. 4 *Informal* Technically skillful but shallow and insignificant: a *slick* novel. 5 *Slang* Very good, attractive, enjoyable, etc. —*n.* 1 A smooth place on a surface of water, as from oil. 2 A film of oil on the surface of water. 3 *Informal* A magazine printed on glossy paper. —*adv. Slang* In a slick or smooth manner; deftly, cleverly, smoothly, etc. —*v.t.* 1 To make smooth, trim, or glossy. 2 *Informal* To make smart or presentable: often with *up.* [< OE *slician* make smooth]

slick·er (slik'ər) *n.* 1 A long, loose waterproof coat of oilskin. 2 *Informal* A clever, deceptive, crooked person.

slide (slīd) *v.* **slid, slid** or **slid·den, slid·ing** *v.i.* 1 To pass along a surface with a smooth movement. 2 To move smoothly over snow or ice. 3 To move or pass stealthily or imperceptibly. 4 To proceed in a natural way; drift: to let the matter *slide.* 5 To pass or fall gradually (into a specified condition). 6 To slip from a position: The cup *slid* off the saucer. 7 To slip or fall by losing one's equilibrium or foothold. 8 In baseball, to throw oneself along the ground toward a base. —*v.t.* 9 To cause to slide, as over a surface. 10 To move, put, enter, etc., with quietness or dexterity: with *in* or *into.* —*n.* 1 An act of sliding. 2 An inclined plane, channel, etc., on which persons, goods, logs, etc., slide downward to a lower level. 3 A small plate of glass on which a specimen is mounted and examined through a microscope. 4 A small plate of transparent material bearing a single image for projection on a screen. 5 A part or mechanism that slides, as the U-shaped portion of the tubing which is pushed in and out to vary the pitch of a trombone. 6 The slipping of a mass of earth, snow, etc., from a higher to a lower level. 7 The mass that slips down. [< OE *slīdan*] **—slid'er** *n.*

slide fastener ZIPPER.

slide rule A device consisting of a rigid ruler with a

central sliding piece, both graduated, used in calculation.

sliding scale A schedule affecting imports, prices, or wages, varying under conditions of consumption, demand, or market price.

slight (slīt) *adj.* 1 Of small importance or degree: a *slight* illness. 2 Slender in build: a *slight* figure. 3 Frail; fragile: a *slight* structure. —*v.t.* 1 To omit due courtesy toward or respect for: to *slight* a friend. 2 To do carelessly or thoughtlessly; shirk. 3 To treat as trivial or insignificant. —*n.* An act of discourtesy or disrespect. [< ON *slēttr* smooth] **—slight'er, slight'ness** *n.* **—slight'ly** *adv.*

sli·ly (slī'lē) *adv.* SLYLY.

slim (slim) *adj.* **slim·mer, slim·mest** 1 Small in thickness in proportion to height or length. 2 Slight; meager: a *slim* chance of survival. —*v.t.* & *v.i.* **slimmed, slim·ming** To make or become thin or thinner. [< Du. *slim* bad] **—slim'ly** *adv.* **—slim'ness** *n.*

slime (slīm) *n.* 1 Soft, moist, adhesive mud or earth; muck. 2 A mucous exudation from the bodies of certain organisms. 3 An offensive, digusting substance or quality. —*v.t.* **slimed, slim·ing** 1 To smear with or as with slime. 2 To remove slime from, as fishes. [< OE *slīm*]

slim·y (slī'mē) *adj.* **slim·i·er, slim·i·est** 1 Covered with slime. 2 Containing slime. 3 Filthy; foul. **—slim'i·ly** *adv.* **—slim'i·ness** *n.*

sling (sling) *n.* 1 A strap or pocket with a string attached to each end, for hurling a stone. 2 One of various devices for holding up an injured arm. 3 A device, as a band or chain, for lifting or moving heavy objects. 4 The act of slinging; a sudden throw. 5 A drink made of sugar, liquor, and water: a gin *sling.* —*v.t.* **slung, sling·ing** 1 To fling; hurl. 2 To move or hoist, as by a rope or tackle. 3 To suspend loosely in a sling. [? < ON *slyngva* hurl] **—sling'er** *n.*

sling·shot (sling'shot') *n.* A forked stick with an elastic strap attached to the prongs for hurling small missiles.

slink (slingk) *v.* **slunk** or **slinked, slink·ing** *v.i.* To move or go furtively or stealthily. [< OE *slincan*] **—slink'ing·ly** *adv.* — Syn. creep, steal, sneak, skulk.

slink·y (slingk'ē) *adj.* **slink·i·er, slink·i·est** 1 Sneaking; stealthy. 2 *Slang* Sinuous or feline in movement or form. **—slink'i·ly** *adv.* **—slink'i·ness** *n.*

slip[1] (slip) *v.* **slipped, slip·ping** *v.t.* 1 To cause to glide or slide. 2 To put on or off easily, as a loose garment. 3 To convey slyly or secretly. 4 To free oneself or itself from. 5 To unleash, as hounds. 6 To release from its fastening and let run out, as a cable. 7 To dislocate, as a bone. 8 To escape or pass unobserved: It *slipped* my mind. —*v.i.* 9 To slide so as to lose one's footing. 10 To fall into an error. 11 To escape. 12 To move smoothly and easily. 13 To go or come stealthily: often with *off, away,* or *from.* 14 To overlook: to let an opportunity *slip.* **—let slip** To say without intending to. **—slip one over on** *Informal* To take advantage of by trickery. **—slip up** *Informal* To make a mistake. —*n.* 1 A sudden slide. 2 A slight mistake. 3 A narrow space between two wharves. 4 A pier. 5 An inclined plane leading down to the water, on which vessels are repaired or constructed. 6 A woman's undergarment approximately the length of a dress. 7 A pillowcase. 8 A leash containing a device which permits quick release of the dog. 9 Undesired relative motion, as between a wheel and the road; also, the amount of this. **—give (someone) the slip** To elude (someone). [< MLG *slippen*]

slip[2] (slip) *n.* 1 A cutting from a plant for planting or grafting. 2 A small, slender person, esp. a youthful one. 3 A small piece of something, as of paper. —*v.t.* **slipped, slip·ping** To cut off for planting; make a slip or slips of. [< MDu. *slippe*]

slip·cov·er (slip'kuv'ər) *n.* A fitted cloth cover for a piece of furniture, that can be readily removed.

slip·knot (slip'not') *n.* 1 A knot so made that it will slip along the rope or cord around which it is formed. 2 A knot easily untied by pulling. Also **slip knot.**

slip·on (slip'on', -ôn') *adj.* 1 Designating a garment or accessory that can be easily donned or taken off. 2 Designating a garment, esp. a sweater, that is put on and taken off over the head: also **slip'o'ver** (-ō'vər). —*n.* A slip-on garment, glove, shoe, etc.

slip·per (slip'ər) *n.* A low, light shoe into or out of which the foot is easily slipped. **—slip'pered** *adj.*

slip·per·y (slip′ər·ē) *adj.* ·**per·i·er**, ·**per·i·est** 1 Having a surface so smooth that bodies slip or slide easily on it. 2 That evades one's grasp; elusive. 3 Unreliable; tricky. —**slip′per·i·ness** *n.*

slippery elm 1 A species of small elm with mucilaginous inner bark. 2 Its wood or inner bark.

slip·shod (slip′shod′) *adj.* 1 Wearing shoes or slippers down at the heels. 2 Slovenly; sloppy. 3 Performed carelessly: *slipshod* work.

slip·stream (slip′strēm′) *n. Aeron.* The stream of air driven backwards by the propeller of an aircraft.

slip-up (slip′up′) *n. Informal* A mistake; error.

slit (slit) *n.* A relatively straight cut or a long, narrow opening. —*v.t.* **slit, slit·ting** 1 To make a long incision in; slash. 2 To cut lengthwise into strips. 3 To sever. [ME *slitten*] —**slit′ter** *n.*

slith·er (slith′ər) *v.i.* 1 To slide; slip, as on a loose surface. 2 To glide, as a snake. —*v.t.* 3 To cause to slither. —*n.* A sinuous, gliding movement. [< OE *slidrian*] —**slith′er·y** *adj.*

sliv·er (sliv′ər) *n.* 1 A slender piece, as of wood, cut or torn off lengthwise; a splinter. 2 Corded textile fibers drawn into a fleecy strand. —*v.t. & v.i.* To cut or be split into long thin pieces. [< ME *sliven* to cleave] —**sliv′er·er** *n.*

slob (slob) *n.* 1 Mud; mire. 2 *Slang* A careless or unclean person. [< Ir. *slab*]

slob·ber (slob′ər) *v.t.* 1 To wet with liquids oozing from the mouth. 2 To shed or spill, as liquid food, in eating. —*v.i.* 3 To drivel; slaver. 4 To talk or act gushingly. —*n.* 1 Liquid spilled as from the mouth. 2 Gushing, sentimental talk. [ME *sloberen*] —**slob′ber·er** *n.* —**slob′ber·y** *adj.*

sloe (slō) *n.* 1 A small, plumlike, astringent fruit. 2 The shrub that bears it; the blackthorn. [< OE *slā*]

sloe gin A cordial with a gin base, flavored with sloes.

slog (slog) *v.t. & v.i.* **slogged, slog·ging** 1 To slug, as a pugilist. 2 To plod (one's way). —*n.* A heavy blow. [?] —**slog′ger** *n.*

slo·gan (slō′gən) *n.* 1 A catchword or motto adopted by a political party, advertiser, etc. 2 A battle or rallying cry. [< Scot. Gael. *sluagh* army + *gairm* yell]

slo·gan·eer (slō′gə·nir′) *Informal n.* One who coins or uses slogans. —*v.i.* To coin or use slogans.

sloop (slo͞op) *n.* A small sailboat with a single mast and at least one jib. [< Du. *sloep*]

slop[1] (slop) *v.* **slopped, slop·ping** *v.i.* 1 To splash or spill. 2 To walk or move through slush. —*v.t.* 3 To cause (a liquid) to spill or splash. 4 To feed (a domestic animal) with slops. —**slop over** 1 To overflow and splash. 2 *Slang* To show too much zeal, emotion, etc. —*n.* 1 Slush or watery mud. 2 An unappetizing liquid or watery food. 3 *pl.* Refuse liquid. 4 *pl.* Waste food or swill. [< ME *sloppe* mud]

Sloop

slop[2] (slop) 1 A loose outer garment, as a smock. 2 *pl.* Articles of clothing and other merchandise sold to sailors on shipboard. [ME *sloppe*]

slope (slōp) *v.* **sloped, slop·ing** *v.i.* 1 To be inclined from the level; slant downward or upward. 2 To go obliquely. —*v.t.* 3 To cause to slope. —*n.* 1 Any slanting surface or line. 2 The degree of inclination of a line or surface from the plane of the horizon. [< OE *aslupan* slip away] —**slop′er, slop′ing·ness** *n.* —**slop′ing·ly** *adv.*

slop·py (slop′ē) *adj.* ·**pi·er**, ·**pi·est** 1 Slushy; splashy; wet. 2 Watery or pulpy. 3 Splashed with liquid or slops. 4 *Informal* Messy; slovenly; careless. 5 *Informal* Maudlin; overly sentimental. —**slop′pi·ly** *adv.* —**slop′pi·ness** *n.*

slosh (slosh) *v.t.* 1 To throw about, as a liquid. —*v.i.* 2 To splash; flounder: to *slosh* through a pool. —*n.* Slush. [Var. of SLUSH]

slot (slot) *n.* 1 A long narrow groove or opening; slit. 2 A narrow depression cut to receive some corresponding part in a mechanism. 3 *Informal* An opening or position, as in

an organization, or a place in a sequence. —*v.t.* **slot·ted, slot·ting** To cut a slot or slots in. [< OF *esclot* the hollow between the breasts]

sloth (slōth, slôth, sloth) *n.* 1 Disinclination to exertion; laziness. 2 Any of several slow-moving, arboreal mammals of South America. [< SLOW]

sloth·ful (slōth′fəl, slôth′-, sloth′-) *adj.* Inclined to or characterized by sloth. —**sloth′ful·ly** *adv.* —**sloth′ful·ness** *n.* —**Syn.** lazy, indolent, sluggish, shiftless.

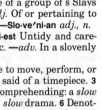

Three-toed sloth

slot machine A vending machine or gambling machine having a slot in which a coin is dropped to cause operation.

slouch (slouch) *v.i.* 1 To have a downcast or drooping gait, look, or posture. 2 To hang or droop carelessly. —*n.* 1 A drooping movement or appearance caused by depression or carelessness. 2 An awkward or incompetent person. [?] —**slouch′y** *adj.* (·**i·er**, ·**i·est**) —**slouch′i·ly** *adv.* —**slouch′i·ness** *n.*

slough[1] (slou; slo͞o *esp. for def.* 2) *n.* 1 A place of deep mud or mire. 2 A stagnant swamp, backwater, etc. 3 A state of great despair or degradation. [< OE *slōh*] —**slough′y** *adj.*

slough[2] (sluf) *n.* 1 Dead tissue separated and thrown off from living tissue. 2 The skin of a serpent that has been or is about to be shed. —*v.t.* 1 To cast off; shed. 2 To discard; shed, as a habit or a growth. —*v.i.* 3 To be cast off. 4 To cast off a slough or tissue. [ME *slouh*] —**slough′y** *adj.*

Slo·vak (slō′väk, slō′vak) *n.* 1 One of a Slavic people of NW Hungary and parts of Moravia. 2 The language spoken by the Slovaks. —*adj.* Of or pertaining to the Slovaks or to their language. Also **Slo·vak′i·an.**

slov·en (sluv′ən) *n.* One who is habitually untidy, careless, or dirty. [ME *sloveyn*]

Slo·vene (slō′vēn, slō·vēn′) *n.* One of a group of s Slavs now living in NW Yugoslavia. —*adj.* Of or pertaining to the Slovenes or to their language. —**Slo·ve′ni·an** *adj., n.*

slov·en·ly (sluv′ən·lē) *adj.* ·**li·er**, ·**li·est** Untidy and careless in appearance, work, habits, etc. —*adv.* In a slovenly manner. —**slov′en·li·ness** *n.*

slow (slō) *adj.* 1 Taking a long time to move, perform, or occur. 2 Behind the standard time: said of a timepiece. 3 Not hasty: *slow* to anger. 4 Dull in comprehending: a *slow* student. 5 Uninteresting; tedious: a *slow* drama. 6 Denoting a condition of a racetrack that retards the horses' speed. 7 Heating or burning slowly; low: a *slow* flame. 8 Not brisk; slack: Business is *slow*. —*v.t. & v.i.* To make or become slow or slower: often with *up* or *down*. —*adv.* In a slow manner. [< OE *slāw*] —**slow′ly** *adv.* —**slow′ness** *n.*

slow-mo·tion (slō′mō′shən) *adj.* 1 Moving or acting at less than normal speed. 2 Denoting a television or motion picture filmed at greater than standard speed so that the action appears slow in normal projection.

sludge (sluj) *n.* 1 Soft, water-soaked mud. 2 A slush of snow or broken or half-formed ice. 3 Muddy or pasty refuse, sediment, etc. [?] —**sludg′y** *adj.* (·**i·er**, ·**i·est**)

slue[1] (slo͞o) *v.* **slued, slu·ing** *v.t.* 1 To cause to swing, slide, or skid to the side. 2 To cause to twist or turn. —*v.i.* 3 To move sidewise. —*n.* The act of skidding or pivoting. [?]

slue[2] (slo͞o) *n. Informal* SLEW[3].

slue[3] (slo͞o) *n.* SLOUGH[1] (def. 2).

slug[1] (slug) *n.* 1 A bullet. 2 *Printing* **a** A strip of type metal between words or letters. **b** A metal strip bearing a line of type in one piece. 3 Any small chunk of metal; esp., one used in place of a coin in automatic machines.

slug[2] (slug) *n.* 1 Any of numerous land mollusks related to the snail, having an elongated body and a rudimentary shell. 2 The sluglike larvae of certain insects. [ME *slugge* a sluggard]

Slug

slug[3] (slug) *Informal n.* A heavy blow, as with the fist. —*v.t.* **slugged, slug·ging** To strike heavily, as with the fist. [?] —**slug′ger** *n.*

---

slug⁴ (slug) *n. Slang* A single drink, esp. of undiluted alcoholic liquor. [< Du. *sluck* a swallow]

slug·gard (slug′ərd) *n.* A person habitually lazy. —*adj.* Lazy; sluggish. [< SLUG²] —**slug′gard·ly** *adv.*

slug·gish (slug′ish) *adj.* 1 Having little motion; inactive; torpid. 2 Habitually idle and lazy. —**slug′gish·ly** *adv.* —**slug′gish·ness** *n.*

sluice (slōōs) *n.* 1 Any artificial channel for conducting water. 2 A device for controlling the flow of water; a floodgate: also **sluice gate.** 3 The water held back by such a gate. 4 Something through which anything issues or flows. 5 A sloping trough in which gold is washed from sand. —*v.* **sluiced, sluic·ing** *v.t.* 1 To drench or cleanse by a flow of water. 2 To wash in or by a sluice. 3 To draw out or conduct by or through a sluice. 4 To send (logs) down a sluiceway. —*v.i.* 5 To flow out or issue from a sluice. [< L *excludere* shut out]

sluice·way (slōōs′wā′) *n.* An artificial channel for the passage of water.

slum (slum) *n.* A squalid, dirty, overcrowded street or section of a city. —*v.i.* **slummed, slum·ming** To visit slums, as for reasons of curiosity. [?] —**slum′mer** *n.*

slum·ber (slum′bər) *v.i.* 1 To sleep lightly or quietly. 2 To be inactive; stagnate. —*v.t.* 3 To spend or pass in sleeping. —*n.* Quiet sleep. [< OE *slūma* sleep] —**slum′ber·er** *n.* —**slum′ber·ing·ly** *adv.*

slum·ber·ous (slum′bər·əs) *adj.* 1 Inviting to slumber. 2 Drowsy; sleepy. 3 Quiet; peaceful: a hot, *slumberous* afternoon. Also **slum·brous** (slum′brəs). —**slum′ber·ous·ly** *adv.* —**slum′ber·ous·ness** *n.*

slum·lord (slum′lôrd′) *n.* A landlord who derives high profits from run-down property, esp. housing. [< SLUM + (LAND)LORD]

slump (slump) *v.i.* 1 To fall or fail suddenly. 2 To stand, walk, or proceed with a stooping posture; slouch. —*n.* 1 The act of slumping. 2 A collapse or decline: a *slump* in the stock market. [Prob. < Scand.]

slung (slung) *p.t. & p.p.* of SLING.

slunk (slungk) *p.t. & p.p.* of SLINK.

slur (slûr) *v.t.* **slurred, slur·ring** 1 To slight; disparage; depreciate. 2 To pass over lightly or hurriedly. 3 To pronounce hurriedly and indistinctly. 4 *Music* **a** To sing or play as indicated by the slur. **b** To mark with a slur. —*n.* 1 A disparaging remark or insinuation. 2 *Music* **a** A curved line (‿ or ⌒) indicating that tones so tied are to be performed without a break between them. **b** The legato effect indicated by this mark. 3 A slurred pronunciation. [< ME *sloor* mud] —**slur′ring·ly** *adv.*

slurb (slûrb) *n. Slang* A suburban area so poorly planned and developed as to seem like a slum. [< SL(UM) + (SUB)URB]

slurp (slûrp) *v.t. & v.i. Slang* To sip noisily. [Imit.]

slush (slush) *n.* 1 Soft, sloppy material, as melting snow or soft mud. 2 Greasy material used for lubrication, etc. 3 Sentimental talk or writing. [ME *sloche*] —**slush′y** *adj.*

slush fund Money collected or spent for bribery, lobbying, political pressure, etc.

slut (slut) *n.* 1 A slatternly woman. 2 A sexually promiscuous woman; whore. 3 A female dog. [?] —**slut′tish** *adj.* —**slut′tish·ly** *adv.* —**slut′tish·ness** *n.*

sly (slī) *adj.* **sli·er** or **sly·er, sli·est** or **sly·est** 1 Artfully dexterous in doing things secretly. 2 Playfully clever; roguish. 3 Meanly or stealthily clever; crafty. 4 Done with or marked by artful secrecy: a *sly* trick. —**on the sly** In a stealthy way. [< ON *slægr*] —**sly′ly** *adv.* —**sly′ness** *n.*

Sm samarium.

smack¹ (smak) *n.* 1 A quick, sharp sound, as of the lips when separated rapidly. 2 A noisy kiss. 3 A sounding blow or slap. —*v.t.* 1 To separate (the lips) rapidly. 2 To kiss noisily. 3 To slap. —*v.i.* 4 To make a smacking noise, as in tasting, kissing, striking, etc.; slap. —*adv.* Directly; exactly: also **smack′-dab′** (-dab′). [< MDu. *smack* a blow]

smack² (smak) *v.i.* 1 To have a slight taste or flavor: usu. with *of.* 2 To have, keep, or disclose a slight suggestion: with *of.* —*n.* 1 A suggestive flavor. 2 A mere taste; smattering. [< OE *smæc* a taste]

smack³ (smak) *n.* A small sailing vessel used chiefly for fishing; esp. one having a well for fish in its hold. [< Du. *smak, smacke*]

smack⁴ (smak) *n. Slang* HEROIN.

smack·er (smak′ər) *n.* 1 One who or that which smacks. 2 *Slang* A dollar.

smack·ing (smak′ing) *adj.* Brisk; lively, as a breeze.

small (smôl) *adj.* 1 Not as large as other things of the same kind; little. 2 Being of slight degree, weight, or importance. 3 Ignoble; mean: a *small* nature. 4 Of humble background; poor. 5 Acting or transacting business in a limited way: a *small* shopkeeper. 6 Weak in characteristic properties: *small* beer. 7 Having little body or volume. 8 Not capital: said of letters. —**feel small** To feel humiliated or ashamed. —*adv.* 1 In a low or faint tone: to sing *small.* 2 Into small pieces. 3 In a small way; trivially. —*n.* 1 A small or slender part: the *small* of the back. 2 A small thing or quantity. [< OE *smæl*] —**small′ness** *n.*

small arms Arms that may be carried on the person, as a rifle, automatic pistol, or revolver.

small calorie See CALORIE.

small capital A capital letter cut slightly larger than the lower-case letters of a specified type and slightly smaller than the regular capital.

small fry 1 Small, young fish. 2 Young children. 3 Small or insignificant people or things.

small hours The early hours after midnight.

small-minded (smôl′mīn′did) *adj.* Having a petty mind; intolerant; ungenerous.

small potatoes *Informal* Unimportant, insignificant persons or things.

small·pox (smôl′poks′) *n.* An acute, highly contagious viral disease characterized by a rash that leaves pitted scars.

small talk Unimportant or casual conversation.

small-time (smôl′tīm′) *adj. Slang* Petty; unimportant: a *small-time* gambler.

smart (smärt) *v.i.* 1 To experience a stinging sensation. 2 To cause a stinging sensation. 3 To experience remorse, grief, hurt feelings, etc. —*v.t.* 4 To cause to smart. —*adj.* 1 Quick in thought; clever. 2 Impertinently witty. 3 Harsh; severe: a *smart* slap. 4 Brisk: to go at a *smart* pace. 5 Keen or sharp, as at trade; shrewd. 6 *Informal* or *Regional* Large; considerable: a *smart* crop of wheat. 7 Sprucely dressed. 8 Fashionable; chic. —*n.* 1 An acute stinging sensation, as from a scratch or an irritant. 2 Any mental or emotional suffering. [< OE *smeortan*] —**smart′ly** *adv.* —**smart′ness** *n.*

smart al·eck (al′ik) *Informal* A cocky, conceited person. —**smart-al·eck·y** (smärt′al′ik·ē) *adj.*

smart bomb *Slang* A bomb capable of being guided, as by a laser beam, to a target.

smart·en (smär′tən) *v.t.* 1 To improve in appearance. 2 To make alert or lively. —*v.i.* 3 To improve one's appearance: with *up.*

smart set Fashionable, sophisticated society.

smart·weed (smärt′wēd′) *n.* Any of several species of knotgrass having an acrid taste, growing usu. in wet soil.

smash (smash) *v.t.* 1 To break in many pieces suddenly. 2 To flatten; crush. 3 To dash or fling violently so as to break in pieces. 4 To strike with a sudden blow. 5 To destroy; ruin. 6 In tennis, to strike (the ball) with a hard, swift, overhand stroke. —*v.i.* 7 To be ruined; fail. 8 To move or be moved with force; collide. —**go to smash** *Informal* To be ruined; fail. —*n.* 1 An instance or sound of smashing. 2 Any disaster or sudden collapse, esp. financial ruin. 3 In tennis, a strong overhand shot. 4 *Informal* An outstanding public success. —*adj.* Outstandingly successful: a *smash* hit. [?] —**smash′er** *n.*

smash·ing (smash′ing) *adj.* 1 That smashes: a *smashing* blow. 2 *Informal* Extremely impressive; overwhelmingly good. —*interj. Chiefly Brit.* An exclamation expressing approval, enthusiasm, etc.

smash-up (smash′up′) *n.* A violent collision; a wreck.

smat·ter (smat′ər) *n.* A slight knowledge. [< ME *smateren* to dabble]

smat·ter·ing (smat′ər·ing) *n.* 1 A superficial or fragmentary knowledge. 2 A little bit or a few.

sm. c., sm. caps small capitals (printing).

smear (smir) *v.t.* 1 To rub or soil with grease, paint, dirt, etc. 2 To spread or apply in a thick layer or coating. 3 To harm the reputation of; slander. 4 *Slang* To defeat utterly. —*v.i.* 5 To become smeared. —*n.* 1 A soiled spot; stain. 2

A specimen, as of blood, tissue cells, etc., spread on a slide for microscopic examination. **3** A slanderous attack. [< OE *smeoru* grease] —**smear′y** *adj.* —**smear′i·ness** *n.*

smell (smel) *v.* **smelled** or **smelt, smell·ing** *v.t.* **1** To perceive by means of the nose and its olfactory nerves. **2** To perceive the odor of. **3** To test by odor or smell. **4** To discover or detect, as if by smelling. —*v.i.* **5** To give off a particular odor: to *smell* of roses. **6** To have an unpleasant odor. **7** To give indications of: to *smell* of treason. **8** To use the sense of smell. —*n.* **1** The sense by means of which odors are perceived. **2** That which is smelled; odor. **3** An unpleasant odor. **4** A faint suggestion; hint. **5** An act of smelling. [ME *smellen*] —**smel′ler** *n.* —**smel′ly** *adj.* (**·i·er, ·i·est**) —**Syn.** *n.* **2** aroma, fragrance, scent. **3** reek, stench, stink.

smelling salts A pungent preparation, as ammonium carbonate, used to relieve faintness, etc.

smelt[1] (smelt) *v.t. Metall.* **1** To reduce (ores) by fusion in a furnace. **2** To obtain (a metal) from the ore by a process including fusion. —*v.i.* **3** To melt or fuse, as a metal. [< MDu. *smelten* melt]

smelt[2] (smelt) *n. pl.* **smelts** or **smelt** Any of various small, silvery, anadromous or landlocked food fishes. [< OE]

smelt[3] (smelt) A *p.t. & p.p.* of SMELL.

smelt·er (smel′tər) *n.* **1** One engaged in smelting ore. **2** An establishment for smelting: also **smelt′er·y.**

smidg·en (smij′ən) *n. Informal* A tiny bit or part. [?]

smi·lax (smī′laks) *n.* **1** Any of a large genus of woody vines having oval leaves and globular fruit. **2** A twining plant of the lily family, with greenish flowers, used for bouquets, etc. [< Gk. *smilax* yew]

smile (smīl) *n.* **1** A pleased or amused expression of the face, formed by curling the corners of the mouth upward. **2** A favorable appearance or aspect: the *smile* of fortune. —*v.* **smiled, smil·ing** *v.i.* **1** To exhibit a smile; appear cheerful. **2** To show approval or favor: often with *upon.* —*v.t.* **3** To express by means of a smile. [ME *smilen.*] —**smil′er** *n.* —**smil′ing·ly** *adv.*

Smilax

smirch (smûrch) *v.t.* **1** To soil, as by contact with grime; smear. **2** To defame; dishonor: to *smirch* a reputation. —*n.* **1** A smutch; smear. **2** A moral stain. [ME *smorchen*]

smirk (smûrk) *v.i.* To smile in a self-complacent, affected manner. —*n.* An affected or artificial smile. [< OE *smercian*] —**smirk′er** *n.* —**smirk′ing·ly** *adv.*

smite (smīt) *v.* **smote, smit·ten** or **smote, smit·ing** *v.t.* **1** To strike (something) hard. **2** To strike a blow with (something); cause to strike. **3** To kill with a sudden blow. **4** To strike with disaster; afflict. **5** To affect or impress suddenly and powerfully. —*v.i.* **6** To strike a blow with or as if with sudden force. [< OE *smītan*] —**smit′er** *n.*

smith (smith) *n.* **1** One whose work is shaping metals, esp. a blacksmith. **2** A maker: used in combination: *gunsmith; wordsmith.* [< OE]

smith·er·eens (smith′ə·rēnz′) *n.pl. Informal.* Fragments produced as by a blow. Also **smith′ers.** [< Ir. *smidirin* a fragment]

smith·y (smith′ē, smith′ē) *n. pl.* **smith·ies** A blacksmith's shop.

smit·ten (smit′n) A *p.p.* of SMITE.

smock (smok) *n.* A loose outer garment worn to protect one's clothes. —*v.t.* To decorate (fabric) with smocking. [< OE *smoc*]

smock·ing (smok′ing) *n.* Shirred work; stitching that forms a gathered pattern.

smog (smog) *n.* A noxious mist resulting from the action of sunlight on atmospheric pollutants. [< SM(OKE) + (F)OG]

smoke (smōk) *n.* **1** The vaporous products of the combustion of an organic compound, as coal, wood, etc., charged with fine particles of carbon or soot. **2** Any system of solid particles dispersed in a gas. **3** The act of or time taken in smoking tobacco. **4** *Informal* A cigarette, cigar, or

Smocking

pipeful of tobacco. —*v.* **smoked, smok·ing** *v.i.* **1** To emit or give out smoke. **2** To emit smoke excessively, as a stove or lamp. **3** To inhale and exhale the smoke of tobacco. —*v.t.* **4** To inhale and exhale the smoke of (tobacco, opium, etc.). **5** To use, as a pipe, for this purpose. **6** To treat, cure, or flavor with smoke. **7** To drive away or force out of hiding by or as if by the use of smoke: *smoke* bees; *smoke* out the enemy. **8** To change the color of (glass, etc.) by darkening with smoke. [< OE *smoca*]

smoke·house (smōk′hous′) *n.* A building or room in which meat, fish, hides, etc., are smoked.

smoke·less (smōk′lis) *adj.* Having or emitting little or no smoke: *smokeless* powder.

smok·er (smō′kər) *n.* **1** One who smokes tobacco habitually. **2** A railroad car in which smoking is allowed. **3** A social gathering for men only.

smoke screen 1 A dense cloud of smoke emitted to screen an attack or cover a retreat. **2** Anything intended to conceal or mislead.

smoke·stack (smōk′stak′) *n.* An upright pipe through which combustion gases from a furnace are discharged into the air.

smok·y (smō′kē) *adj.* **smok·i·er, smok·i·est 1** Giving forth smoke, esp. excessively or unpleasantly. **2** Containing smoke: *smoky* air. **3** Like or suggestive of smoke: a *smoky* flavor. **4** Discolored by smoke. **5** Smoke-colored. —**smok′i·ly** *adv.* —**smok′i·ness** *n.*

smol·der (smōl′dər) *v.i.* **1** To burn showing little smoke and no flame. **2** To show suppressed feeling. **3** To exist in a latent state or inwardly. —*n.* A smoldering fire or thick smoke. *Brit. sp.* **smoul′der.** [ME *smolderen*]

smolt (smōlt) *n.* A young salmon on its first descent from the river to the sea. [ME]

smooch (smōōch) *v.i. Slang* To kiss and caress; neck. —**smooch′er** *n.* [?]

smooth (smōōth) *adj.* **1** Having no surface irregularities; continuously even. **2** Free from obstructions, shocks, or jolts. **3** Without lumps; well blended. **4** Free from hair. **5** Flowing or moving evenly and without interruption. **6** Mild-mannered; calm. **7** Suave and flattering, usu. in a deceitful way: a *smooth* talker. **8** Pleasant-tasting; mild: a *smooth* wine. **9** *Phonet.* Having no aspiration. —*adv.* Calmly; evenly. —*v.t.* **1** To make smooth or even on the surface. **2** To free from obstructions. **3** To soften the worst features of: usu. with *over.* **4** To make calm; mollify. —*v.i.* **5** To become smooth. —*n.* **1** The smooth portion or surface of anything. **2** The act of smoothing. [< OE *smōth*] —**smooth′er, smooth′ness** *n.* —**smooth′ly** *adv.* —**Syn.** *adj.* **1** glossy, polished, sleek. **6** collected, placid, unruffled. *v.* **3** extenuate, palliate. **4** soothe.

smooth·bore (smōōth′bôr′, -bōr′) *n.* A firearm with an unrifled bore: also **smooth bore.** —*adj.* Having no rifling: said of firearms.

smooth muscle Muscle tissue consisting of flat sheets of spindle-shaped cells, by which involuntary movement is effected in blood vessels, viscera, etc.

smor·gas·bord (smôr′gəs·bôrd; *Sw.* smœr′gŏs·bōrd) *n.* A Scandinavian buffet. Also **smör′gås·bord.** [Sw.]

smote (smōt) *p.t.* of SMITE.

smoth·er (smuth′ər) *v.t.* **1** To prevent (someone) from breathing. **2** To kill by such means; suffocate. **3** To cover, or cause to smolder, as a fire. **4** To hide or suppress: to *smother* a scandal. **5** To cook in a covered pan or under a blanket of some other substance. —*v.i.* **6** To be covered without vent or air, as a fire. **7** To be hidden or suppressed, as wrath. —*n.* That which smothers, as stifling vapor or dust. [< OE *smorian*] —**smoth′er·er** *n.* —**smoth′er·y** *adj.*

smudge (smuj) *v.* **smudged, smudg·ing** *v.t.* **1** To smear; soil. —*v.i.* **2** To be or become smudged. —*n.* **1** A smear; stain. **2** A smoky fire or smoke for driving away insects, preventing frost, etc. [? var. of SMUTCH] —**smudg′i·ly** *adv.* —**smudg′i·ness** *n.* —**smudg′y** *adj.* (**·i·er, ·i·est**)

smug (smug) *adj.* **smug·ger, smug·gest 1** Self-satisfied or extremely complacent. **2** Trim; neat; spruce. [?< LG *smuk* neat] —**smug′ly** *adv.* —**smug′ness** *n.*

smug·gle (smug′əl) *v.* **·gled, ·gling** *v.t.* **1** To take (merchandise) into or out of a country illegally. **2** To bring in or introduce illicitly or secretly. —*v.i.* **3** To engage in or practice smuggling. [< LG *smuggeln*] —**smug′gler** *n.*

smut (smut) *n.* **1** The blackening made by soot, smoke, etc. **2** Obscene writing, speech, or illustration. **3** Any of various fungus diseases of plants, characterized by patches of powdery black spores. **4** The parasitic fungus causing such a disease. —*v.t.* & *v.i.* **smut·ted, smut·ting** To make or become smutty. [< LG *schmutt* dirt]

smutch (smuch) *n.* A stain or smear. —*v.t.* To smear; smudge. [?] —**smutch·y** *adj.* (**·i·er, ·i·est**)

smut·ty (smut′ē) *adj.* **·ti·er, ·ti·est 1** Soiled with smut; stained. **2** Affected by smut: *smutty* corn. **3** Obscene; indecent. —**smut′ti·ly** *adv.* —**smut′ti·ness** *n.* —**Syn. 1** blackened, dirty. **3** coarse, earthy, suggestive.

Sn tin (L *stannum*).

Sn. sanitary.

snack (snak) *n.* A light meal. —*v.i.* To eat a snack. [< MDu. *snacken* to bite, snap]

snaf·fle (snaf′əl) *n.* A horse's bit without a curb, jointed in the middle. —*v.t.* **·fled, ·fling** To control with a snaffle. [?< Du. *snavel* muzzle]

sna·fu (sna-fōō′) *Slang adj.* In a state of utter confusion; chaotic. —*v.t.* **·fued, ·fu·ing** To put into a confused or chaotic condition. —*n.* A confused or chaotic situation. [< S(ITUATION) N(ORMAL) A(LL) F(UCKED) U(P)]

snag (snag) *n.* **1** A jagged or sharp protuberance, esp. the stumpy base of a branch left in pruning. **2** A snaggletooth. **3** The trunk of a tree fixed in a river, bayou, etc., which presents a danger to navigation. **4** Any hidden obstacle or difficulty. —*v.t.* **snagged, snag·ging** To injure, destroy, or impede by or as by a snag. [< Scand.] —**snag′gy** *adj.*

snag·gle·tooth (snag′əl-tōōth′) *n.* A tooth that is broken or out of alignment with the others. —**snag′gle-toothed′** (-tōōtht′, -tōōthd′) *adj.*

snail (snāl) *n.* **1** Any of numerous slow-moving, terrestrial or aquatic gastropod mollusks with a spiral shell. **2** A slow or lazy person. [< OE *snægl*]

snake (snāk) *n.* **1** Any of a large variety of limbless reptiles having a scaly body, no eyelids, and a specialized swallowing apparatus. **2** A treacherous person. **3** A flexible wire used to clean clogged drains, etc. —*v.* **snaked, snak·ing** *v.t. Informal* **1** To drag or pull forcibly; haul, as a log. —*v.i.* **2** To wind or move like a snake. [< OE *snaca*]

Snail

snake·bird (snāk′bûrd′) *n.* Any of several birds with a long sinuous neck, frequenting southern U.S. swamps.

snak·y (snā′kē) *adj.* **snak·i·er, snak·i·est 1** Of or like a snake. **2** Cunning; treacherous. **3** Full of snakes. **4** Winding; serpentine. — **snak′i·ly** *adv.* —**snak′i·ness** *n.*

Snakebird

snap (snap) *v.* **snapped, snap·ping** *v.i.* **1** To make a sharp, quick sound, as of twigs breaking. **2** To break suddenly with a crackling noise. **3** To close, fasten, etc., with a snapping sound. **4** To bite or snatch with a sudden, grasping motion: often with *up* or *at.* **5** To speak sharply: often with *at.* **6** To move or act with sudden, neat gestures: He *snapped* to attention. **7** To give way suddenly, as under mental pressure. —*v.t.* **8** To seize suddenly or eagerly; snatch: often with *up.* **9** To sever with a snapping sound. **10** To cause to make a sharp, quick sound. **11** To close, fasten, etc., with a snapping sound. **12** To take (a photograph). —**snap out of it** *Informal* **1** To recover quickly. **2** To change a mood, attitude, etc., quickly. —*n.* **1** The act of snapping or a sharp, quick sound produced by it. **2** A sudden breaking or release of anything or the sound so produced. **3** Any catch, fastener, etc., that closes or springs into place with a snapping sound. **4** A small, thin, crisp cake, esp. a gingersnap. **5** Brisk energy; zip. **6**

A brief spell: said chiefly of cold weather. **7** Any easy task or duty. **8** A snapshot. —*adj.* **1** Made or done suddenly: a *snap* judgment. **2** Fastening with a snap. **3** *Informal* Easy. —*adv.* Briskly; quickly. [< MDu. *snappen* bite at]

snap·drag·on (snap′drag′ən) *n.* Any of several varieties of plants having racemes of flowers with a saclike, double-lipped corolla.

snap·per (snap′ər) *n.* **1** One who or that which snaps. **2** Any of various voracious marine food fishes. • See RED SNAPPER. **3** A snapping turtle.

snapping turtle Any of various large voracious freshwater turtles having powerful jaws, a small plastron, and a tail with erect bony scales.

Snapping turtle

snap·pish (snap′ish) *adj.* **1** Apt to speak crossly. **2** Disposed to snap or bite, as a dog. —**snap′pish·ly** *adv.* —**snap′pish·ness** *n.*

snap·py (snap′ē) *adj.* **·pi·er, ·pi·est 1** *Informal* Brisk and energetic. **2** *Informal* Smart or stylish. **3** Snappish. — **snap′pi·ly** *adv.* —**snap′pi·ness** *n.*

snap·shot (snap′shot′) *n.* A photograph taken with a small, simple camera.

snare¹ (snâr) *n.* **1** A device, as a noose, for catching birds or other animals; a trap. **2** Anything that misleads, entangles, etc. —*v.t.* **snared, snar·ing 1** To catch with a snare; entrap. **2** To capture by trickery; entice. [< ON *snara*] — **snar′er** *n.*

snare² (snâr) *n.* **1** A cord that produces a rattling on a drumhead. **2** A snare drum. [< MDu. *snare* a string]

snare drum A small drum to be beaten on one head and having snares stretched across the other. • See DRUM.

snarl¹ (snärl) *n.* A sharp, angry growl. —*v.i.* **1** To growl harshly, as a dog. **2** To speak angrily and resentfully. — *v.t.* **3** To utter or express with a snarl. [< MLG *snarren* to growl] —**snarl′er** *n.* —**snarl′ing·ly** *adv.* —**snarl′y** *adj.*

snarl² (snärl) *n.* **1** A tangle, as of hair or yarn. **2** Any complication or entanglement. —*v.i.* **1** To become entangled or confused. —*v.t.* **2** To put into a snarl. [?< SNARL¹] —**snarl′er** *n.* —**snarl′y** *adj.*

snatch (snach) *v.t.* **1** To seize, take, grasp, etc., suddenly or eagerly. **2** To take or obtain as the opportunity arises: to *snatch* a few hours of sleep. —*v.i.* **3** To attempt to seize swiftly and suddenly: with *at.* —*n.* **1** A hasty grab or grasp: usu. with *at.* **2** A small amount; fragment: *snatches* of a conversation. [ME *snacchen*] —**snatch′er** *n.*

snatch·y (snach′ē) *adj.* **snatch·i·er, snatch·i·est** Interrupted; spasmodic.

sneak (snēk) *v.i.* **1** To move or go in a stealthy manner. **2** To act slyly or with cowardice. —*v.t.* **3** To put, give, move, etc., secretly or stealthily. **4** *Informal* To pilfer. — **sneak out of** To avoid (work, etc.) by sly means. —*n.* **1** One who sneaks; a stealthy, despicable person. **2** *pl. Informal* Sneakers. **3** A stealthy movement. —*adj.* Stealthy; covert: a *sneak* attack. [?] —**sneak′i·ly, sneak′ing·ly** *adv.* —**sneak′i·ness** *n.* —**sneak′y** *adj.* (**·i·er, ·i·est**)

sneak·er (snē′kər) *n.* **1** *pl.* Rubber-soled canvas shoes. **2** One who sneaks; a sneak.

sneer (snir) *n.* **1** A grimace of contempt or scorn. **2** A mean or contemptuous sound, word, etc. —*v.i.* **1** To show contempt or scorn by a sneer. **2** To express contempt in speech, writing, etc. —*v.t.* **3** To utter with a sneer. [ME *sneren*] —**sneer′er** *n.* —**sneer′ing·ly** *adv.* —**Syn.** *v.* **2** gibe, jeer, scoff, taunt.

sneeze (snēz) *v.i.* **sneezed, sneez·ing** To drive air forcibly and audibly out of the mouth and nose by a spasmodic involuntary action. —**not to be sneezed at** *Informal* Entitled to consideration; not to be ignored. —*n.* An act of sneezing. [ME *fnesen*] —**sneez′er** *n.*

snick·er (snik′ər) *n.* A half-suppressed or smothered laugh, usu. scornful. —*v.i.* **1** To utter a snicker. —*v.t.* **2** To utter or express with a snicker. [Imit.]

snide (snīd) *adj.* **snid·er, snid·est** Malicious; nasty. [?] — **snide′ly** *adv.* —**snide′ness** *n.*

sniff (snif) *v.i.* **1** To breathe through the nose in short, quick, audible inhalations. **2** To express contempt, etc., by sniffing: often with *at.* **3** To inhale a scent in sniffs. —*v.t.* **4** To inhale. **5** To smell or attempt to smell with sniffs. **6** To perceive as if by sniffs. —*n.* **1** An act or the sound of sniffing. 2 Something perceived by sniffing; an odor. [ME *sniffen*]

snif·fle (snif′əl) *v.i.* **·fled, ·fling** 1 To breathe through a partially obstructed nose noisily and with difficulty. 2 To snivel or whimper. —*n.* The act of sniffling, or the sound made by it. **—the sniffles** A clogged condition of the nose caused by a cold, allergy, etc. [Freq. of SNIFF] **—snif′fler** *n.*

snig·ger (snig′ər) *n.* SNICKER. —*v.i.* SNICKER. [Var. of SNICKER] **—Syn.** *n.,v.* giggle, smirk, snort, titter.

snip (snip) *v.* **snipped, snip·ping** *v.t.* 1 To clip, remove, or cut with a short, light stroke or strokes, as of shears: often with *off.* —*v.i.* 2 To cut with small, quick strokes. —*n.* 1 An act of snipping. 2 A small piece snipped off. 3 *Informal* A small or insignificant person. [< Du. *snippen*] **—snip′per** *n.*

snipe (snīp) *n. pl.* **snipe** or **snipes** Any of various marsh and shore birds having a long, flexible bill. —*v.i.* **sniped, snip·ing** 1 To hunt or shoot snipe. 2 To shoot at individuals, as of an enemy force, from a place of concealment. 3 To attack a person in an underhanded, malicious manner: with *at.* [< ON *snīpa*]

snip·er (snī′pər) *n.* One who shoots at individuals, as of an enemy force, from a place of concealment.

snip·pet (snip′it) *n.* 1 A small piece snipped off. 2 A small or insignificant person.

snip·py (snip′ē) *adj.* **·pi·er, ·pi·est** *Informal* 1 Supercilious; impertinent. 2 Fragmentary. **—snip′pi·ly** *adv.* **—snip′pi·ness** *n.*

snit (snit) *n. Informal* A state of irritability or agitation.

snitch (snich) *Slang v.t.* 1 To grab quickly; steal. —*v.i.* 2 To inform; tattle: usu. with *on.* [?]

sniv·el (sniv′əl) *v.i.* **·eled** or **·elled, ·el·ing** or **·el·ling** To cry in a snuffling manner. —*n.* The act of sniveling. [< OE (assumed) *snyflan*] **—sniv′el·er** or **sniv′el·ler** *n.*

snob (snob) *n.* 1 One who regards wealth and elevated social position as of paramount importance and who typically seeks to improve his station by associating with the rich or powerful or popular and by avoiding or behaving with condescension to those with whom association is inexpedient. 2 One who affects to be superior, as in taste or learning: an intellectual *snob.* [?] **—snob′ber·y** (*pl.* **·ies**), **snob′bish·ness** *n.* **—snob′bish** *adj.* **—snob′bish·ly** *adv.*

snood (snood) *n.* A small meshlike cap or bag worn by women to keep the hair in place at the back of the head. —*v.t.* To bind with a snood. [< OE *snōd*]

snoop (snoop) *Informal v.i.* To pry into things with which one has no business. —*n.* One who snoops. [< Du. *snoepen* eat goodies on the sly] **—snoop′er** *n.* **—snoop′y** *adj.* (**·i·er, ·i·est**)

snoot (snoot) *n. Informal* The nose or face. [Var. of SNOUT]

snoot·y (snoo′tē) *adj.* **snoot·i·er, snoot·i·est** *Informal* Haughty; snobbish. **—snoot′i·ly** *adv.* **—snoot′i·ness** *n.*

snooze (snooz) *Informal v.i.* **snoozed, snooz·ing** To sleep lightly; doze. —*n.* A short, light sleep. [?]

snore (snôr, snōr) *v.i.* **snored, snor·ing** To breathe with loud, snorting noises while asleep. —*n.* An act or sound of snoring. [Imit.] **—snor′er** *n.*

snor·kel (snôr′kəl) *n.* 1 A long ventilating tube capable of extending from a submerged submarine to the surface of the water. 2 A similar device used for underwater breathing. —*v.i.* To swim with a snorkel. [< G *Schnorchel*] **—snor′kel·er** *n.*

snort (snôrt) *v.i.* 1 To force the air violently and noisily through the nostrils, as a horse. 2 To express indignation, ridicule, etc., by a snort. —*v.t.* 3 To utter or express by snorting. —*n.* 1 The act or sound of snorting. 2 *Slang* A small drink of liquor. [ME *snorten*] **—snort′er** *n.*

snot (snot) *n.* 1 Mucus from or in the nose: a vulgar usage. 2 *Slang* A snotty person. [< OE *gesnot*]

snot·ty (snot′ē) *adj.* **·ti·er, ·ti·est** 1 Dirtied with snot: a vulgar usage. 2 *Slang* Contemptible; nasty. 3 *Slang* Impudent. **—snot′ti·ly** *adv.* **—snot′ti·ness** *n.*

snout (snout) *n.* 1 The projecting muzzle of a vertebrate. 2 Some similar anterior prolongation of the head, as that of a gastropod, skate, weevil, etc. 3 A person's nose, esp. a large one. [ME *snute*]

snow (snō) *n.* 1 Precipitation in the form of ice crystals formed from water vapor in the air when the temperature is below 32° F., usu. falling in irregular masses or flakes. 2 A fall of snow. 3 Flickering light or dark spots appearing on a television or radar screen. 4 *Slang* Cocaine. —*v.i.* 1 To fall as snow. —*v.t.* 2 To cause to fall as or like snow. 3 *Slang* To overpower with insincere or flattering talk. **—snow in** To close in or obstruct with snow.

Snow crystals

—snow under 1 To cover with snow. 2 *Informal* To overwhelm: *snowed under* with work. [< OE *snāw*]

snow·ball (snō′bôl′) *n.* 1 A small round mass of snow to be thrown. 2 A shrub related to honeysuckle, having globular clusters of sterile white flowers: also **snowball bush** or **tree.** —*v.i.* 1 To throw snowballs. 2 To gain in size, importance, etc. —*v.t.* 3 To throw snowballs at.

snow bank A large mound or heap of snow.

snow·ber·ry (snō′ber′ē) *n. pl.* **·ries** Any of various shrubs bearing white berries.

snow·bird (snō′bûrd′) *n.* 1 A junco. 2 SNOW BUNTING.

snow blindness A temporary or partial impairment of vision, caused by long exposure to the glare of snow. **—snow′-blind′** *adj.*

snow·bound (snō′bound′) *adj.* Forced to remain in a place because of heavy snow.

snow bunting A sparrowlike bird of northern regions, having white plumage with black or rust-colored markings.

snow·capped (snō′kapt′) *adj.* Having its top covered with snow, as a mountain.

snow·drift (snō′drift′) *n.* A pile of snow heaped up by the wind.

snow·drop (snō′drop′) *n.* A low, early-blooming bulbous plant bearing a single, white, drooping flower.

snow·fall (snō′fôl′) *n.* 1 A fall of snow. 2 The amount of snow that falls in a given period.

snow·flake (snō′flāk′) *n.* 1 A flake or crystal of snow. 2 Any of various plants allied to and resembling the snowdrop.

snow job *Slang* An attempt to overpower with a flow of insincere talk, esp. flattery.

snow line The limit of perpetual snow on the sides of mountains. Also **snow limit.**

snow·mo·bile (snō′mō·bēl) *n.* A motorized vehicle used for traveling over snow, ice, etc. **—snow′mo·bil′er, snow′·mo·bil′ing** *n.*

snow·plow (snō′plou′) *n.* Any large, plowlike device for removing snow from roads, railroad tracks, etc.

snow·shoe (snō′shoo′) *n.* A device, usu. a network of sinew in a wooden frame, to be fastened on the foot and used to prevent sinking in soft snow when walking. —*v.i.* **·shoed, ·shoe·ing** To walk on snowshoes.

Snowshoe

snow·slide (snō′slīd′) *n.* An avalanche of snow.

snow·storm (snō′stôrm′) *n.* A storm with a heavy fall of snow.

snow·y (snō′ē) *adj.* **·i·er, ·i·est** 1 Abounding in or covered with snow. 2 White as snow. **—snow′i·ly** *adv.* **—snow′i·ness** *n.*

snub (snub) *v.t.* **snubbed, snub·bing** 1 To treat with contempt or disdain. 2 To stop or check, as the movement of a rope in running out. —*n.* 1 An act of snubbing; a deliberate slight. 2 A sudden checking, as of a running rope or cable. —*adj.* Short and slightly turned-up: said of the nose. [< ON *snubba*] **—snub′ber** *n.* **—Syn.** *v.* 1 cut, high-hat, ignore, rebuff, slight.

snub-nosed (snub′nōzd′) *adj.* Having a snub nose.

snuff[1] (snuf) *v.t.* 1 To draw in (air, etc.) through the nose.

2 To smell; sniff. —*v.i.* **3** To snort; sniff. —*n.* An act of snuffing. [?< MDu. *snuffen*] —**snuf′fi·ness** *n.* —**snuf′fy** *adj.*

snuff[2] (snuf) *n.* The charred portion of a wick. —*v.t.* **1** To crop the snuff from (a wick). **2** To put out or extinguish: with *out.* [ME *snoffe*]

snuff[3] (snuf) *n.* **1** Pulverized tobacco to be inhaled into the nostrils. **2** The quantity of it taken at one time. —**up to snuff** *Informal* Meeting the usual standard, as in quality, health, etc. —*v.i.* To take or use snuff. [< Du. *snuf*]

snuf·fer (snuf′ər) *n.* **1** One who or that which snuffs (a candle). **2** *pl.* A scissorlike instrument for removing the snuff from a candle.

snuf·fle (snuf′əl) *v.* **·fled**, **·fling** *v.i.* **1** SNIFFLE. **2** To talk through the nose. —*v.t.* **3** To utter in a nasal tone. —*n.* An act of snuffling, or the sound made by it. —**the snuffles** THE SNIFFLES. See SNIFFLE. [Freq. of SNUFF[1]] —**snuf′fler** *n.*

snug (snug) *adj.* **snug·ger**, **snug·gest** **1** Comfortable and cozy. **2** Well-built and compact; trim: said of a ship. **3** Fitting closely, as a garment. —*v.* **snugged, snug·ging** —*v.t.* **1** To make snug. —*v.i.* **2** SNUGGLE. —**snug down** To prepare (a vessel) for a storm, as by lashing down movables. [?] —**snug′ly** *adv.* —**snug′ness** *n.*

snug·gle (snug′əl) *v.t.* & *v.i.* **·gled, ·gling** To nestle; cuddle; often with *up* or *together.* [Freq. of SNUG]

so[1] (sō) *adv.* **1** To this or that or such a degree; to this or that extent: Don't talk *so* much. **2** In this, that, or such a manner: Hold the flag *so.* **3** To such a great extent: I love him *so.* **4** Just as said, directed, suggested, or implied; consequently; therefore. **5** To an extreme degree; very: He is *so* tall. **6** About as many or as much as stated; thereabouts: I shall stay a day or *so.* **7** Too; also: and *so* do I. **8** According to the truth of what is sworn to or averred: *So* help me God. —*adj.* True: It isn't *so.* —*conj.* **1** With the purpose that: often with *that.* **2** As a consequence of which: He consented, *so* they went away. —*interj.* An expression of surprise, disapproval, triumph, etc. [< OE *swā*]

so[2] (sō) *n.* SOL.

So. South; southern.

soak (sōk) *v.t.* **1** To place in liquid till thoroughly saturated; steep. **2** To wet thoroughly; drench. **3** *Informal* To drink, esp. to excess. **4** *Slang* To charge exorbitantly. —*v.i.* **5** To remain or be placed in liquid till saturated. **6** To penetrate; pass: with *in* or *into.* **7** *Slang* To drink to excess. —**soak up 1** To take up; absorb. **2** *Informal* To take eagerly into the mind. —*n.* **1** The process or act of soaking, or state of being soaked. **2** Liquid in which something is soaked. **3** *Slang* A hard drinker. [< OE *socian*] —**soak′er** *n.* —**soak′ing·ly** *adv.*

so-and-so (sō′ən·sō′) *n. pl.* **·sos** An unnamed or undetermined person or thing: often a euphemism for offensive epithets.

soap (sōp) *n.* **1** *Chem.* A metallic salt of a fatty acid. **2** A cleansing agent consisting of a sodium or potassium salt of a fatty acid made by boiling a fat or oil with a lye. **3** *Slang* Money used for bribes. —**no soap** *Slang* It's not possible or acceptable. —*v.t.* To rub or treat with soap. [< OE *sāpe*] —**soap′i·ly** *adv.* —**soap′i·ness** *n.* —**soap′y** *adj.*

soap·ber·ry (sōp′ber′ē) *n. pl.* **·ries 1** A berrylike fruit containing a substance that forms a detergent lather with water. **2** Any of various related trees of s U.S. and tropical America that yield soapberries.

soap·box (sōp′boks′) *n.* Any box or crate used as a platform by street orators. —*adj.* Of or pertaining to such orators or oratory. —*v.i.* To make a speech to a street audience.

soap opera A daytime television or radio drama presented serially and usu. dealing with highly emotional domestic themes.

soap·stone (sōp′stōn′) *n.* STEATITE.

soap·suds (sōp′sudz′) *n.pl.* Soapy water, esp. when worked into a foam.

soar (sôr, sōr) *v.i.* **1** To float aloft through the air on wings, as a bird. **2** To sail or glide through the air. **3** To rise above any usual level: Prices *soared.* —*n.* **1** An act of soaring. **2** A range of upward flight. [< L *ex* out + *aura* breeze, air] —**soar′er** *n.* —**soar′ing·ly** *adv.*

sob (sob) *v.* **sobbed, sob·bing** *v.i.* **1** To weep with audible, convulsive catches of the breath. **2** To make a sound like a sob, as the wind. —*v.t.* **3** To utter with sobs. **4** To bring

to a specified condition by sobbing: to *sob* oneself to sleep. —*n.* The act or sound of sobbing. [Imit.] —**sob′bing·ly** *adv.*

so·ber (sō′bər) *adj.* **1** Moderate in or abstaining from the use of alcoholic beverages. **2** Not drunk. **3** Temperate in action or thought; rational. **4** Not frivolous; straightforward. **5** Solemn; serious: a *sober* expression. **6** Of subdued or modest color. —*v.t.* **1** To make sober. —*v.i.* **2** To become sober, as after intoxication: with *up.* [< L *sobrius*] —**so′ber·ly** *adv.* —**so′ber·ness** *n.* —**Syn.** *n.* **1** abstemious. **3** calm, dispassionate, staid, steady.

so·bri·e·ty (sō·brī′ə·tē) *n. pl.* **·ties 1** The state or quality of being moderate, serious, or sedate. **2** Abstinence from alcoholic drink.

so·bri·quet (sō′bri·kā, sō·bri·kā′) *n.* A fanciful or humorous appellation; a nickname. [F]

sob story *Slang* A sad personal narrative told to elicit pity or sympathy.

soc. socialist; society.

so-called (sō′kôld′) *adj.* **1** Popularly or generally named or known (by the following term): the *so-called* black market. **2** Called (by the following term): an ironic use, implying that the designated term is unjustified or unsuitable: his *so-called* wittiness.

soc·cer (sok′ər) *n.* A form of football in which the ball is propelled toward the opponents' goal by kicking or by striking with the body or head, but never with the hands. [Alter. of *association (football),* original name]

so·cia·ble (sō′shə·bəl) *adj.* **1** Inclined to seek company; friendly. **2** Characterized by or affording occasion for agreeable conversation and friendliness. —*n.* An informal social gathering. [< L *socius* friend] —**so′cia·bil′i·ty, so′cia·ble·ness** *n.* —**so′cia·bly** *adv.*

so·cial (sō′shəl) *adj.* **1** Of or pertaining to society or its organization: *social* questions. **2** Friendly toward others; sociable. **3** Living in a society: *social* beings. **4** Of or pertaining to public welfare: *social* work. **5** Pertaining to or characteristic of fashionable, wealthy people: the *social* register. **6** Living in communities: *social* ants. **7** Grouping compactly, as individual plants. **8** Partly or wholly covering a large area of land: said of plant species. —*n.* An informal social gathering. [< L *socius* ally]

social disease Venereal disease: a euphemism.

so·cial·ism (sō′shəl·iz′əm) *n.* **1** The theory of public collective ownership or control of the basic means of production, distribution, and exchange, with the avowed aim of operating for use rather than for profit. **2** A political system or party advocating or practicing this theory. —**so′cial·ist** *adj., n.* —**so′cial·is′tic** *adj.*

Socialist party A political party advocating socialism, esp. a U.S. party formed in 1901.

so·cial·ite (sō′shəl·īt) *n.* A person prominent in fashionable society.

so·cial·ize (sō′shəl·īz) *v.* **·ized, ·iz·ing** *v.t.* **1** To make friendly, cooperative, or sociable. **2** To put under group control; esp. to regulate according to socialistic principles. **3** To adopt for the uses and needs of society. —*v.i.* **4** To take part in social activities. *Brit. sp.* **so′cial·ise.** —**so′cial·i·za′tion** *n.*

socialized medicine The provision of comprehensive medical services at public expense.

social register A directory of persons prominent in fashionable society.

social science 1 The body of knowledge dealing with society, its members, organizations, interrelationships, etc. **2** Any of the fields into which this body of knowledge is divided, as economics, history, sociology, politics, etc.

social security A federal program of old-age pensions, unemployment benefits, disability insurance, survivors' benefits, etc., paid jointly by workers, employers, and the U.S. government.

social work Any of various activities for improving community welfare, as services for health, rehabilitation, counseling, recreation, adoptions, etc. Also **social service.** —**social worker**

so·ci·e·ty (sə·sī′ə·tē) *n. pl.* **·ties 1** A group of people, usu. having geographical boundaries and sharing certain characteristics, as language, culture, etc. **2** The people making up such a group. **3** The fashionable, usu. wealthy portion of a community. **4** A body of persons associated for a common purpose; an association, club, or fraternity. **5** Association based on friendship or intimacy: to enjoy the *society* of one's neighbors. [< L *socius* a friend]

Society of Friends A Christian religious group, founded in seventeenth-century England, noted for its repudiation of ritual and its opposition to military service and to violence.

Society of Jesus The Jesuits.

socio- *combining form* **1** Society; social: *sociology*. **2** Sociology; sociological: *socioeconomic*. [< F < L *socius* a companion]

so·ci·o·bi·ol·o·gy (sō′sē-ō-bī·ol′ə-jē) *n.* The study of social behavior in animals and humans, as determined by their biological characteristics.

so·ci·o·ec·o·nom·ic (sō′sē-ō-ek′ə·nom′ik, sō′shē-, -ē′kə-) *adj.* Based upon the interrelationship of social and economic factors. **—so′ci·o·ec′o·nom′i·cal·ly** *adv.*

so·ci·o·lin·guis·tics (sō′sē-ō-ling·gwis′tiks, sō′shē-) *n. pl.* (*construed as sing.*) The study of language as a social instrument and in its social context. [< SOCIO- + LINGUISTICS] **—so′ci·o·lin·guis′tic** *adj.* **—so′ci·o·lin·guis′ti·cal·ly** *adv.*

so·ci·ol·o·gy (sō′sē-ol′ə-jē, sō′shē-) *n.* The science dealing with the origin, evolution, and development of human society and its organization, institutions, and functions. **—so′ci·o·log′i·cal** *adj.* **—so′ci·o·log′i·cal·ly** *adv.* **—so′ci·ol′o·gist** *n.*

sock[1] (sok) *n.* A short stocking reaching part way to the knee. [< L *soccus* slipper]

sock[2] (sok) *Slang v.t.* To strike or hit, esp. with the fist. **—n.** A hard blow. [?]

sock·et (sok′it) *n.* A cavity into which a corresponding part fits: an electric light *socket;* the eye *socket.* [< OF *soc* a plowshare]

sock·eye (sok′ī′) *n.* A red salmon of the Pacific coast, highly valued as a food fish. [Alter. of Salishan *sukkegh*]

So·crat·ic method (sə-krat′ik, sō-) The method of instruction by questions and answers, as adopted by Socrates in his disputations, leading the pupil either to a foreseen conclusion or to contradict himself.

sod (sod) *n.* **1** Grassy surface soil held together by the matted roots of grass and weeds. **2** A piece of such soil. **—v.t.** **sod·ded, sod·ding** To cover with sod. [< MDu. *sode* piece of turf]

so·da (sō′də) *n.* **1** Any of several sodium compounds in common use, as sodium bicarbonate, carbonate, hydroxide, etc. **2** SODA WATER **3** A soft drink containing soda water and flavoring and sometimes ice cream. [< Ital. *soda (cenere)* solid (ash)]

soda ash Anhydrous sodium carbonate.

soda cracker A thin, crisp, usu. salted wafer of flour leavened with baking soda.

soda fountain **1** An apparatus from which soda water is drawn, usu. containing receptacles for syrups, ice, and ice cream. **2** A counter at which soft drinks and ice cream are dispensed.

soda jerk *Slang* A clerk who serves at a soda fountain.

so·dal·i·ty (sō-dal′ə·tē) *n. pl.* **·ties** A brotherhood or fraternity; esp., one for devotional or charitable purposes. [< L *sodalis* companion]

soda water An effervescent drink consisting of water charged under pressure with carbon dioxide, formerly generated from sodium bicarbonate.

sod·den (sod′n) *adj.* **1** Soaked; saturated. **2** Doughy; soggy, as undercooked bread. **3** Dull or stupid, as from drink. [ME *sothen,* pp. of *sethen* seethe] **—sod′den·ly** *adv.*

so·di·um (sō′dē-əm) *n.* A soft, silver-white, highly reactive metallic element (symbol Na) whose compounds are abundant in nature and essential to life. [< Med. L *soda* soda]

sodium bicarbonate A white crystalline compound that reacts with acids to liberate carbon dioxide; baking soda.

sodium carbonate The strongly alkaline sodium salt of carbonic acid, in crystalline hydrated form known as washing soda.

sodium chloride Common salt.

sodium cyanide A white, very poisonous salt of hydrocyanic acid, used in electroplating, as a fumigant, etc.

sodium hydroxide A white, deliquescent compound forming a strongly alkaline solution in water; caustic soda.

sodium hypochlorite An unstable compound of sodium, oxygen, and chlorine, used in weak aqueous solution as a laundry bleach.

sodium nitrate A white compound occurring naturally and produced synthetically, used as a fertilizer and in the manufacture of nitric acid and explosives.

sodium thiosulfate A crystalline compound of sodium, sulfur, and oxygen, used in photography as a fixing agent. Also, erroneously, **sodium hyposulfite.**

Sod·om (sod′əm) *n.* In the Bible, a city on the Dead Sea, destroyed with Gomorrah because of the wickedness of its people. *Gen.* 13:10.

sod·om·ite (sod′əm-īt) *n.* A person who practices sodomy.

sod·om·y (sod′əm-ē) *n.* Anal copulation, esp. between male persons or with animals. [< LL *Sodoma* Sodom]

so·ev·er (sō-ev′ər) *adv.* To or in any degree at all. • *Soever* is usu. added to *who, which, what, where, when, how,* etc., to form the compounds *whosoever,* etc., giving them emphasis or specific force. When used separately, as in "how great *soever* he might be," *soever* tends to sound stilted and literary.

so·fa (sō′fə) *n.* A long upholstered couch having a back and arms. [< Ar. *soffah* a part of a floor raised to form a seat]

soft (sôft, soft) *adj.* **1** Easily changed in shape by pressure. **2** Easily worked: *soft* wood. **3** Less hard than other things of the same kind: *soft* rock. **4** Smooth and delicate to the touch: *soft*

Sofa

skin. **5** Not loud or harsh: a *soft* voice. **6** Mild; gentle: a *soft* breeze. **7** Not glaring; subdued: *soft* colors. **8** Expressing mildness or sympathy: *soft* words. **9** Easily touched in feeling: a *soft* heart. **10** Out of condition: *soft* muscles. **11** *Informal* Weak-minded: *soft* in the head. **12** *Informal* Overly lenient: a judge *soft* on criminals. **13** Free from mineral salts that form insoluble compounds with soap: said of water. **14** Biodegradable: said of detergents. **15** Regarded as being nonaddicting and less harmful than hard narcotics: said of drugs, esp. marihuana. **16** *Phonet.* Describing *c* and *g* when articulated fricatively as in *cent* and *gibe.* **17** *Informal* Easy: a *soft* job. **—n.** That which is soft; a soft part or material. **—adv.** **1** Softly. **2** Quietly; gently. **—interj.** *Archaic* Hush! Stop!. [< OE *sôfte*] **—soft′ly** *adv.* **—soft′ness** *n.* **—Syn.** *adj.* **1** flexible, malleable, pliable. **5** low. **9** compassionate, kind, sympathetic.

soft·back (sôft′bak′, soft′-) *adj.* SOFT-COVER. **—n.** A soft-cover book.

soft·ball (sôft′bôl′, soft′-) *n.* **1** A variation of baseball requiring a smaller diamond and a larger, softer ball. **2** The ball used in this game.

soft-boiled (sôft′boild′) *adj.* Boiled so that the yolk and white are soft or semiliquid: said of eggs.

soft coal Bituminous coal.

soft-cov·er (sôft′kuv′ər, soft′-) *adj.* Designating a book having flexible sides, as of paper. Also **soft′bound′** (-bound′).

soft drink A nonalcoholic beverage, esp. a carbonated drink.

sof·ten (sôf′ən, sof′-) *v.t. & v.i.* To make or become soft or softer. **—sof′ten·er** *n.*

soft-heart·ed (sôft′här′tid, soft′-) *adj.* Full of kindness, tenderness, and compassion. **—soft′heart′ed·ly** *adv.*

soft palate The fleshy back part of the roof of the mouth. • See MOUTH.

soft-shell (sôft′shel′, soft′-) *adj.* Having a soft shell, as a crab after shedding its shell: also **soft′-shelled′.** **—n.** A crab that has shed its shell: also **soft-shelled crab.**

soft-soap (sôft′sōp′, soft′-) *v.t. Informal* To flatter.

soft soap **1** Fluid or semifluid soap. **2** *Informal* Flattery.

---

add, āce, cāre, pälm; end, ēven; it, īce; odd, ōpen, ôrder; tŏŏk, pōōl; up, bûrn; ə = *a* in *above, u* in *focus;*
yōō = *u* in *fuse;* oil; pout; check; go; ring; thin; ᵺis; zh, *vision.* < derived from; ? origin uncertain or unknown.

soft·ware (sôft′wâr′, soft′-) *n.* In a digital computer, any of the programs designed to control various aspects of the operation of the machine, such as input and output operations.

soft·wood (sôft′wood′, soft′-) *n.* **1** A coniferous tree or its wood. **2** Any light, loosely structured wood, or any tree with such wood.

soft·y (sôf′tē, sof′-) *n. pl.* **soft·ies** *Informal* **1** An extremely sentimental person. **2** A person who is easily taken advantage of. Also **soft′ie.**

sog·gy (sog′ē) *adj.* **·gi·er, ·gi·est 1** Saturated with water or moisture; soaked. **2** Heavy and wet: said of pastry. [< dial. E *sog* a swamp, bog] **—sog′gi·ly** *adv.* **—sog′gi·ness** *n.*

soil[1] (soil) *n.* **1** Finely divided rock mixed with decayed vegetable or animal matter, constituting the portion of the surface of the earth in which plants grow. **2** Region, land, or country. [< L *solium* a seat, mistaken for *solum* the ground]

soil[2] (soil) *v.t.* **1** To make dirty; smudge. **2** To disgrace; defile. **—v.i. 3** To become dirty. **—n.** A spot or stain. [< L *suculus,* dim. of *sus* a pig]

soi·rée (swä·rā′) *n.* An evening party or reception. Also **soi·ree′.** [F < *soir* evening]

so·journ (sō′jûrn, sō·jûrn′) *v.i.* To stay or live temporarily. **—n.** (sō′jûrn) A temporary residence or short visit. [< OF *sojourner*] **—so′journ·er** *n.*

sol (sōl) *n. Music* In solmization, the fifth note of a diatonic scale. [See GAMUT.]

Sol (sol) *Rom. Myth.* The god of the sun. **—n.** The sun. [L]

Sol. Solomon.

sol. solicitor; soluble; solution.

sol·ace (sol′is) *v.t.* **·aced, ·ac·ing 1** To comfort in trouble or grief; console. **2** To alleviate, as grief; soothe. **—n. 1** Comfort in grief, trouble, or calamity. **2** Anything that supplies such comfort. [< L *solacium*] **—sol′ac·er** *n.* **—Syn.** *v.* **2** assuage, ease, mitigate. *n.* **1** cheer, consolation.

so·lar (sō′lər) *adj.* **1** Of, from, reckoned by, or pertaining to the sun. **2** Using energy from the sun: *solar* heat. [< L *sol* sun]

solar energy 1 Energy emitted by the sun as radiation over the entire electromagnetic spectrum. **2** Radiation from the sun, esp. in the infrared range, technologically convertible to domestic and industrial uses.

so·lar·i·um (sō·lâr′ē·əm) *n. pl.* **·i·a** (-ē-ə) or **·ums** A room, porch, etc., in which people can sit in the sun. [L]

solar plexus 1 A network of sympathetic nerves serving the abdominal viscera. **2** *Informal* The pit of the stomach.

solar system The sun and the bodies that orbit it. • See PLANET.

sold (sōld) *p.t.* & *p.p.* of SELL.

sol·der (sod′ər) *n.* **1** An easily melted alloy used for joining metal parts. **2** Anything that unites or cements. **—v.t. 1** To unite or repair with solder. **2** To join together; bind. **—v.i. 3** To work with solder. **4** To be united by or as by solder. [< L *solidus* firm, hard] **—sol′der·er** *n.*

sol·dier (sōl′jər) *n.* **1** A person serving in an army. **2** An enlisted man in an army, as distinguished from a commissioned officer. **3** A brave, skillful, or experienced warrior. **4** One who serves a cause loyally. **—v.i. 1** To be or serve as a soldier. **2** To shirk: to *soldier* on the job. [< LL *solidus*] **—sol′dier·ly** *adj.* **—sol′dier·li·ness** *n.*

soldier of fortune A soldier willing to serve any government for money or adventure.

sol·dier·y (sōl′jər·ē) *n. pl.* **·ies 1** Soldiers collectively. **2** Military service.

sole[1] (sōl) *n.* **1** The bottom surface of the foot. **2** The bottom surface of a shoe, boot, etc. **3** The lower part or bottom of anything. **—v.t.** **soled, sol·ing** To furnish with a new sole, as a shoe. [< L *solea* a sandal]

sole[2] (sōl) *n.* Any of several marine flatfishes allied to the flounders, highly esteemed as food. [< L *solea* sole[1], fish]

sole[3] (sōl) *adj.* **1** Being the only one: a *sole* survivor. **2** Only: His *sole* desire was for sleep. **3** *Law* Unmarried; single. **4** Of or for only one person or group. **5** Acting or accomplished without another. [< L *solus* alone] **—sole′ness** *n.*

Sole

sol·e·cism (sol′ə·siz′əm) *n.* **1** A grammatical error or a violation of approved idiomatic usage. **2** Any impropriety or incongruity. [< Gk *soloikos* speaking incorrectly] **—sol′e·cist** *n.* **—sol′e·cis′tic** or **·ti·cal** *adj.*

sole·ly (sōl′lē) *adv.* **1** By oneself or itself alone; singly. **2** Completely; entirely. **3** Only.

sol·emn (sol′əm) *adj.* **1** Characterized by majesty, mystery, or power; awe-inspiring. **2** Characterized by ceremonial observances; sacred. **3** Marked by gravity; earnest. [< L *solemnis*] **—sol′emn·ly** *adv.* **—sol′emn·ness** *n.* **—Syn. 1** impressive. **3** grave, sedate, serious, somber.

so·lem·ni·ty (sə·lem′nə·tē) *n. pl.* **·ties 1** The state or quality of being solemn. **2** A solemn rite or observance.

sol·em·nize (sol′əm·nīz) *v.t.* **·nized, ·niz·ing 1** To perform according to legal or ritual forms: to *solemnize* a marriage. **2** To celebrate with formal ritual. **3** To make solemn, grave, or serious. **—sol′em·ni·za′tion, sol′em·niz′er** *n.*

so·le·noid (sō′lə·noid) *n. Electr.* A conducting wire in the form of a cylindrical coil, used to produce a magnetic field. [< Gk. *sōlēn* a channel + -OID] **—so′le·noi′dal** *adj.* **—so′le·noi′dal·ly** *adv.*

Solenoid

sol-fa (sōl′fä′) *Music v.t.* & *v.i.* **-faed, -fa·ing** To sing using the sol-fa instead of words. **—n. 1** The syllables used in solmization. **2** The act of singing them. [< Ital. *solfa.* See GAMUT.] **—sol′fa′ist** *n.*

sol·feg·gio (sōl·fej′ō) *n. pl.* **·feg·gi** (-fej′ē) or **·feg·gios** *Music* **1** A florid singing exercise using arbitrary vowels and consonants. **2** Solmization. [< Ital. *solfa* sol-fa]

so·lic·it (sə·lis′it) *v.t.* **1** To ask for earnestly; beg or entreat. **2** To seek to obtain, as by persuasion. **3** To entice (one) to an unlawful or immoral act. **—v.i. 4** To make a petition. [< L *sollicitare* agitate] **—so·lic′i·ta′tion** *n.*

so·lic·i·tor (sə·lis′ə·tər) *n.* **1** A person who solicits money for causes, subscriptions, etc. **2** The chief law officer of a city, town, etc. **3** In England, a lawyer who may appear as an advocate in the lower courts only. **—so·lic′i·tor·ship′** *n.*

Solicitor General *pl.* **Solicitors General 1** A law officer ranking below the Attorney General and assisting him. **2** The principal law officer in some of the states, corresponding to the Attorney General in others.

so·lic·i·tous (sə·lis′ə·təs) *adj.* **1** Full of anxiety or concern. **2** Full of eagerness. **—so·lic′i·tous·ly** *adv.* **—so·lic′i·tous·ness** *n.*

so·lic·i·tude (sə·lis′ə·t<del>y</del>ood) *n.* **1** The state of being solicitous. **2** That which makes one solicitous.

sol·id (sol′id) *adj.* **1** Having a definite shape and volume; resistant to stress; not fluid. **2** Filling the whole of the space occupied by its form; not hollow. **3** Of the same substance throughout: *solid* marble. **4** Three-dimensional. **5** Well-built; firm: a *solid* building. **6** United or unanimous: a *solid* base of support. **7** Financially safe; sound. **8** Continuous; unbroken: a *solid* hour. **9** Written without a hyphen: said of a compound word. **10** Carrying weight or conviction: a *solid* argument. **11** Serious; reliable: a *solid* citizen. **12** *Informal* Being on good terms: They were *solid* with the boss. **13** *Slang* Excellent. **14** *Printing* Having no leads or slugs between the lines; not open. **—n. 1** A mass of matter that has a definite shape which resists change. **2** A three-dimensional figure or object. [< L *solidus*] **—sol′id·ly** *adv.* **—so·lid′i·ty** (*pl.* **·ties**), sol′id·ness *n.*

solid angle The angle formed at the vertex of a cone or subtended at the point of intersection of three or more planes.

sol·i·dar·i·ty (sol′ə·dar′ə·tē) *n. pl.* **·ties** Unity of purpose, relations, or interests, as of a race, class, etc.

solid geometry The geometry of a space of three dimensions.

so·lid·i·fy (sə·lid′ə·fī) *v.t.* & *v.i.* **·fied, ·fy·ing 1** To make or become solid, hard, firm, or compact. **2** To bring or come together in unity. **—so·lid′i·fi·ca′tion** *n.*

solid state physics The physics of solid substances, esp. their properties and structure.

sol·i·dus (sol′ə·dəs) *n. pl.* **·di** (-dī) **1** A gold coin of the Byzantine Empire. **2** The sign (/) used to divide shillings from pence: 10/6 (10*s.* 6*d.*) or sometimes used to express fractions: 3/4. [L, solid]

so·lil·o·quize (sə·lil′ə·kwīz) *v.i.* **·quized, ·quiz·ing** To utter a soliloquy. **—so·lil′o·quist** (-kwist), **so·lil′o·quiz′er** *n.* **—so·lil′o·quiz′ing·ly** *adv.*

so·lil·o·quy (sə·lil′ə·kwē) *n. pl.* **·quies 1** A talking to oneself. **2** A speech made by an actor while alone on the stage, revealing his thoughts to the audience. [< L *solus* alone + *loqui* to talk]

sol·ip·sism (sol′ip·siz′əm) *n.* The theory that only knowledge of the self is possible, that, for each individual, only the self exists, and therefore that reality is subjective. **—sol′ip·sist** *n.* **—sol′ip·sis′tic** *adj.*

sol·i·taire (sol′ə·târ′) *n.* **1** A diamond or other gem set alone. **2** Any of various card games played by one person. [< L *solitarius* solitary]

sol·i·tar·y (sol′ə·ter′ē) *adj.* **1** Living, being, or going alone. **2** Made, done, or passed alone: a *solitary* life. **3** Remote; secluded. **4** Lonesome; lonely. **5** Single; one; sole: Not a *solitary* soul was there **—n. 1** *pl.* **·tar·ies** One who lives alone; a hermit. **2** *Informal* Solitary confinement in prison, usu. directed as a punishment. [< L *solus* alone] **—sol′i·tar′i·ly** *adv.* **—sol′i·tar′i·ness** *n.*

sol·i·tude (sol′ə·t/ᵒᵒd) *n.* **1** A being alone; seclusion. **2** Loneliness. **3** A deserted or lonely place. [< L *solus* alone] **—Syn. 1** privacy, retirement. **2** isolation, lonesomeness.

sol·mi·za·tion (sol′mə·zā′shən) *n. Music* The use of syllables as names for the tones of the scale, now commonly *do, re, mi, fa, sol, la, ti.* [< SOL + MI]

so·lo (sō′lō) *n. pl.* **·los** or **·li** (-lē) **1** A musical composition or passage for a single voice or instrument, with or without accompaniment. **2** Any of several card games, esp. one in which a player plays alone against others. **3** Any performance accomplished alone or without assistance. **—adj. 1** Performed or composed to be performed as a solo. **2** Done by a single person alone: a *solo* flight. **—v.i. ·loed, ·lo·ing** To fly an airplane alone, esp. for the first time. [< L *solus* alone] **—so′lo·ist** *n.*

Sol·o·mon (sol′ə·mən) In the Bible, king of Israel, successor to his father David. **—n.** Any very wise man.

Sol·o·mon's-seal (sol′ə·mənz·sēl′) *n.* Any of several perennial herbs of the lily family, having tubular greenish flowers.

so long *Informal* Good-by.

sol·stice (sol′stis) *n.* Either of the times of year when the sun is farthest from the celestial equator, either north or south. In the northern hemisphere the **summer solstice** occurs about June 22, the **winter solstice** about December 22. [< L *solstitium*] **—sol·sti·tial** (sol·stish′əl) *adj.*

sol·u·ble (sol′yə·bəl) *adj.* **1** Capable of being dissolved. **2** Capable of being solved or explained. [< L *solvere* solve, dissolve] **—sol′u·bil′i·ty, sol′u·ble·ness** *n.* **—sol′u·bly** *adv.*

sol·ute (sol′yᵒᵒt, sō′lᵒᵒt) *n.* The dissolved substance in a solution.

so·lu·tion (sə·lᵒᵒ′shən) *n.* **1** A homogeneous mixture of varying proportions, formed by dissolving one or more substances, whether solid, liquid, or gaseous, in another substance, usu. liquid but sometimes gaseous or solid. **2** The act or process by which such a mixture is made. **3** The act or process of explaining, settling, or solving a difficulty, problem, or doubt. **4** The answer or explanation reached in such a process. [< L *solutus*, pp. of *solvere* dissolve]

solve (solv) *v.t.* **solved, solv·ing** To arrive at or work out the correct solution or the answer to; resolve. [< L *solvere* solve, loosen] **—sol′va·ble** *adj.* **—sol′va·bil′i·ty, sol′ver** *n.*

sol·vent (sol′vənt) *adj.* **1** Having means sufficient to pay all debts. **2** Capable of dissolving. **—n. 1** That which solves. **2** A substance, usu. a liquid, capable of dissolving other substances. [< L *solvere* solve, loosen] **—sol′ven·cy** *n.*

Som. Somaliland.

So·ma·lia (sō·mä′lyə) *n.* A republic of E Africa, 262,000 sq. mi., cap. Mogadiscio. • See map at AFRICA. **—So·ma′li** (-lē) *adj., n.*

so·mat·ic (sō·mat′ik) *adj.* **1** Of or relating to the body; corporeal. **2** Of or pertaining to the walls of a body, as distinguished from the viscera. **3** Pertaining to those elements or processes of an organism which are concerned with the maintenance of the individual as distinguished

from the reproduction of the species: *somatic* cells. [< Gk. *sōma* body] **—so·mat′i·cal·ly** *adv.*

som·ber (som′bər) *adj.* **1** Dark; gloomy. **2** Somewhat melancholy; sad. *Brit. sp.* **som′bre.** [< F *sombre*] **—som′ber·ly** *adv.* **—som′ber·ness** *n.* **—Syn. 1** cloudy, dusky, murky.

som·bre·ro (som·brâr′ō) *n. pl.* **·ros** A broad-brimmed hat, usu. of felt, worn in Spain and Latin America. [< Sp. *sombra* shade]

Sombrero

some (sum) *adj.* **1** Of indeterminate quantity: Have *some* candy. **2** Of an unspecified number: It happened *some* days ago. **3** Not definitely specified: *Some* people dislike cats. **4** *Informal* Worthy of notice; extraordinary: That was *some* cake. **—pron. 1** A certain undetermined quantity or part: Please take *some.* **2** Certain ones not named: *Some* believe it is true. **—adv. 1** *Informal* Approximately; about: *Some* eighty people were present. **2** *Informal* Somewhat. [< OE *sum* some]

-some[1] *suffix of adjectives* Characterized by, or tending to be: *blithesome.* [< OE *-sum* like, resembling]

-some[2] *suffix of nouns* A group consisting of (a specified number): *twosome.* [< SOME]

some·bod·y (sum′bod′ē, -bəd·ē) *pron.* An unknown or unnamed person. **—n. pl. ·bod·ies** *Informal* A person of consequence or importance.

some·day (sum′dā′) *adv.* At some future time.

some·how (sum′hou′) *adv.* In some unspecified way.

some·one (sum′wun′, -wən) *pron.* Some person; somebody.

som·er·sault (sum′ər·sôlt) *n.* An acrobatic roll in which a person turns heels over head. **—v.i.** To perform a somersault. [< OF *sobresault*]

some·thing (sum′thing) *n.* **1** A thing not determined or stated. **2** A person or thing of importance. **3** An indefinite quantity or degree: He is *something* of an artist. **—adv.** Somewhat: *something* like his brother.

some·time (sum′tīm′) *adv.* **1** At some future time not precisely stated. **2** At some indeterminate time or occasion. **—adj. 1** Former: a *sometime* student at Oxford. **2** *Informal* Occasional; sporadic: a *sometime* thing.

some·times (sum′tīmz′) *adv.* At times; occasionally.

some·way (sum′wā′) *adv.* In some way; somehow: also **some way, some′ways′.**

some·what (sum′ʰwot′, -ʰwət) *adv.* To some degree. **—n.** An uncertain quantity or degree.

some·where (sum′ʰwâr′) *adv.* **1** In, at, or to some unspecified or unknown place. **2** At some unspecified time: *somewhere* around noon. **3** Approximately. **—n.** An unspecified or unknown place.

some·wheres (sum′ʰwârz′) *adv. Chiefly Regional* Somewhere.

som·nam·bu·late (som·nam′byə·lāt) *v.* **·lat·ed, ·lat·ing** *v.i.* To walk about while asleep. [< L *somnus* sleep + AMBULATE] **—som·nam′bu·la′tion** *n.*

som·nam·bu·lism (som·nam′byə·liz′əm) *n.* The act or state of walking during sleep. **—som·nam′bu·lant** (-lənt), **som·nam′bu·lis′tic** *adj.* **—som·nam′bu·list** *n.*

som·nif·er·ous (som·nif′ər·əs) *adj.* Tending to produce sleep; narcotic. [< L *somnus* sleep + -FEROUS]

som·no·lent (som′nə·lənt) *adj.* **1** Inclined to sleep; drowsy. **2** Tending to induce drowsiness. [< L *somnus* sleep] **—som′no·lence** or **·len·cy** *n.* **—som′no·lent·ly** *adv.*

son (sun) *n.* **1** A male child considered in his relationship to one parent or both. **2** Any male descendant. **3** One who occupies the place of a son, as by adoption, marriage, or regard. **4** Any male associated with a particular country, place, or idea: a *son* of liberty; a native *son.* **5** A familiar term of address to a young man or boy. **—the Son** Jesus Christ. [< OE *sunu*]

so·nant (sō′nənt) *Phonet. adj.* Voiced. **—n. 1** A voiced speech sound. **2** A syllabic sound. [< L *sonare* resound]

so·nar (sō′när) *n.* A system or device for using underwater sound waves for sounding, range finding, detection of submerged objects, communication, etc. [< *so(und) na(vigation and) r(anging)*]

so·na·ta (sə·nä′tä) *n. Music* An instrumental composition written in three or four movements. [< Ital. *sonare* to sound]

song (sông, song) *n.* **1** The act of singing. **2** Any melodious utterance, as of a bird. **3** A short musical composition for voice. **4** A short poem; a lyric or ballad. **5** Poetry; verse. — **for a song** At a very low price. —**song and dance** *Slang* A long, usu. repetitive statement or explanation, often untrue or not pertinent to the subject under discussion. [< OE]

song·bird (sông′bûrd′, song′-) *n.* Any of a large number of small, perching birds, having complex musical songs characteristic of each species.

Song of Solomon A book of the Old Testament, consisting of a dramatic love poem, attributed to Solomon. Also **Song of Songs.**

song sparrow A common North American sparrow noted for its song.

song·ster (sông′stər, song′-) *n.* **1** A person or bird given to singing. **2** A writer of songs. —**song′stress** (-stris) *n. Fem.*

son·ic (son′ik) *adj.* Of, pertaining to, determined, or affected by sound: *sonic* speed. [< L *sonus* sound]

sonic barrier *Aeron.* The effects, such as drag and turbulence, that hinder flight at or near the speed of sound.

son-in-law (sun′in·lô′) *n. pl.* **sons-in-law** The husband of one's daughter.

son·net (son′it) *n.* A poem of 14 lines in any of several fixed verse and rhyme schemes. [< Prov. *son* a sound]

son·net·eer (son′ə·tir′) *n.* A composer of sonnets. —*v.i.* To compose sonnets.

son·ny (sun′ē) *n. pl.* **·nies** *Informal* Little boy: a familiar form of address.

so·no·rous (sə·nôr′əs, -nō′rəs, son′ə·rəs) *adj.* **1** Productive or capable of producing sound vibrations. **2** Loud and full-sounding; resonant. **3** High-sounding: *sonorous* verse. [< L *sonare* resound] —**so·nor·i·ty** (sə·nôr′ə·tē, -nor-, son′·ôr′ə·tē), **so·nor′ous·ness** *n.* —**so·no′rous·ly** *adv.*

soon (sōōn) *adv.* **1** In the near future; shortly. **2** Without delay. **3** Early: He awoke too *soon.* **4** In accord with one's inclination; willingly: I would as *soon* go as not; I'd *sooner* quit than accept a demotion. —**had sooner** Would rather. —**sooner or later** Eventually; in time; sometime. [< OE *sōna* immediately]

soot (sŏŏt, sōōt) *n.* A black deposit of finely divided carbon from the incomplete combustion of wood, coal, etc. —*v.t.* To soil or cover with soot. [< OE *sōt*] —**soot′i·ness** *n.* — **soot′y** *adj.* (**·i·er, ·i·est**)

sooth (sōōth) *Archaic adj.* True; real. —*n.* Truth. —**in sooth** *Archaic* Truly. [< OE *sōth*] —**sooth′ly** *adv.*

soothe (sōōth) *v.* **soothed, sooth·ing** *v.t.* **1** To restore to a quiet or normal state; calm. **2** To mitigate, soften, or relieve, as pain or grief. —*v.i.* **3** To afford relief. [< OE *sōthian* verify] —**sooth′er** *n.* —**sooth′ing·ly** *adv.* —**Syn.** 1 compose, pacify, tranquilize. 2 allay, alleviate, ease.

sooth·say·er (sōōth′sā′ər) *n.* A person who claims to be able to foretell events. —**sooth′say′ing** *n.*

sop (sop) *v.* **sopped, sop·ping** *v.t.* **1** To dip or soak in a liquid. **2** To take up by absorption: often with *up.* —*v.i.* **3** To be absorbed; soak in. **4** To become saturated or drenched. —*n.* **1** Anything softened in liquid, as bread. **2** Anything given to pacify, as a bribe. [< OE *sopp*]

SOP, S.O.P. standard operating procedure; *(Mil.)* standing operating procedure.

sop. soprano.

soph·ism (sof′iz·əm) *n.* **1** A false argument seemingly correct but actually misleading. **2** A fallacy. [< Gk. *sophos* wise]

soph·ist (sof′ist) *n.* **1** A learned person; thinker. **2** One who argues cleverly and deviously. **3** *Often cap.* A member of a certain school of early Greek philosophy, preceding the Socratic school. **4** *Often cap.* One of the later Greek teachers of philosophy and rhetoric, skilled in subtle disputation. [< Gk. *sophos* wise] —**so·phis′tic** or **·ti·cal** *adj.* —**so·phis′ti·cal·ly** *adv.* —**so·phis′ti·cal·ness** *n.*

so·phis·ti·cate (sə·fis′tə·kāt) *v.* **·cat·ed, ·cat·ing** *v.t.* **1** To make less simple or ingenuous; render worldly-wise. **2** To

mislead or corrupt. —*v.i.* **3** To indulge in sophistry. —*n.* (-kit, -kāt) A sophisticated person. [< Gk. *sophos* wise] — **so·phis′ti·ca′tor** *n.*

so·phis·ti·cat·ed (sə·fis′tə·kā′tid) *adj.* **1** Worldly-wise. **2** Of a kind that appeals to the worldly-wise. **3** Very complicated in design, function, etc.: a *sophisticated* machine.

so·phis·ti·ca·tion (sə·fis′tə·kā′shən) *n.* **1** Worldly experience; urbanity, usu. with a loss of simplicity. **2** The state of being sophisticated. **3** Sophistry.

soph·is·try (sof′is·trē) *n. pl.* **·tries** **1** Subtly fallacious reasoning or disputation. **2** The art or methods of the Sophists.

soph·o·more (sof′ə·môr, -mōr) *n.* A second-year student in an American high school or college. —*adj.* Of or pertaining to second-year students or studies. [Earlier *sophomer* a dialectician< *sophom,* var. of SOPHISM]

soph·o·mor·ic (sof′ə·môr′ik, -mōr′-) *adj.* **1** Of, pertaining to, or like a sophomore. **2** Shallow and pretentious. **3** Immature; inexperienced. Also **soph′o·mor′i·cal.** —**soph′o·mor′i·cal·ly** *adv.*

-sophy *combining form* Knowledge or a system of knowledge: *philosophy.* [< Gk. *sophia* wisdom]

sop·o·rif·ic (sop′ə·rif′ik, sō′pə-) *adj.* **1** Causing or tending to cause sleep. **2** Drowsy; sleepy. —*n.* A medicine that produces sleep. [< L *sopor* sleep]

sop·ping (sop′ing) *adj.* Drenched; soaking.

sop·py (sop′ē) *adj.* **·pi·er, ·pi·est** Saturated and softened with moisture; soft and sloppy. —**sop′pi·ness** *n.*

so·pran·o (sə·pran′ō, -prä′nō) *n. pl.* **so·pran·os** or **so·pra·ni** (sə·prä′nē) **1** A part or singing voice of the highest range. **2** The music for such a voice. **3** A person having such a voice or singing such a part. —*adj.* Of or pertaining to a soprano voice or part. [< Ital. *sopra* above]

so·ra (sôr′ə, sō′rə) *n.* A grayish brown crake with a short yellow bill. Also **sora rail.** [?< N. Am. Ind.]

sor·cer·er (sôr′sər·ər) *n.* A wizard; magician.

sor·cer·ess (sôr′sər·es) *n.* A woman who practices sorcery; witch.

sor·cer·y (sôr′sər·ē) *n. pl.* **·cer·ies** Use of supernatural agencies; magic; witchcraft. [< L *sors* fate] —**sor′cer·ous** *adj.* —**sor′cer·ous·ly** *adv.*

sor·did (sôr′did) *adj.* **1** Of degraded character; vile; base. **2** Dirty; squalid. **3** Mercenary; selfish. [< L *sordidus* squalid] —**sor′did·ly** *adv.* —**sor′did·ness** *n.*

sore (sôr, sōr) *n.* **1** A place on an animal body where the skin or flesh is bruised, broken, or inflamed. **2** Anything that causes pain or trouble. —*adj.* **sor·er, sor·est** **1** Having a sore or sores; tender. **2** Pained or distressed. **3** Irritating; distressing. **4** Very great; extreme: in *sore* need of money. **5** *Informal* Offended; angry. —*adv. Archaic* Sorely. [< OE *sār*] —**sore′ness** *n.* —**Syn.** *n.* 1 cut, scrape, wound.

sore·head (sôr′hed′, sōr′-) *n. Informal.* A disgruntled person.

sore·ly (sôr′lē, sōr′-) *adv.* **1** Grievously; distressingly. **2** Greatly: His aid was *sorely* needed.

sor·ghum (sôr′gəm) *n.* **1** A canelike tropical grass cultivated for fodder and its sugary sap. **2** Syrup prepared from the sap of the plant. [< L *Syricus* of Syria, where originally grown]

so·ror·i·ty (sə·rôr′ə·tē, -ror′-) *n. pl.* **·ties** A women's organization having chapters at colleges, universities, etc. [< L *soror* a sister]

sor·rel[1] (sôr′əl, sor′-) *n.* Any of various plants with acid leaves. [< OF *sur* sour]

Sorghum

sor·rel[2] (sôr′əl, sor′-) *n.* **1** A reddish brown color. **2** An animal of this color. —*adj.* Reddish brown. [< OF *sor* a hawk with red plumage]

sor·row (sor′ō, sôr′ō) *n.* **1** Pain or distress because of loss, injury, misfortune, or grief. **2** An event that causes such pain or distress; affliction. **3** The expression of grief; mourning. —*v.i.* To feel or express sorrow; grieve. [< OE *sorg* care] —**sor′row·er** *n.*

sor·row·ful (sor′ə·fəl, sôr′-) *adj.* **1** Full of or showing sorrow or grief. **2** Causing sorrow: a *sorrowful* occasion. — **sor′row·ful·ly** *adv.* —**sor′row·ful·ness** *n.*

sor·ry (sor′ē, sôr′ē) *adj.* **·ri·er, ·ri·est 1** Feeling or showing regret or remorse. **2** Affected by sorrow; grieved. **3** Causing sorrow; melancholy. **4** Pitiable or worthless; paltry. [< OE *sārig* < *sār* sore] —**sor′ri·ly** *adv.* —**sor′ri·ness** *n.*

sort (sôrt) *n.* **1** A collection of persons or things characterized by similar qualities; a kind. **2** Character; nature. **3** Manner; way; style. **4** A person of a certain type: He's a good *sort.* —**of sorts** Of a poor or unsatisfactory kind: an actor *of sorts.* —**out of sorts** Slightly ill or ill-humored. —**sort of** *Informal* Somewhat. —*v.t.* To arrange or separate into grades, kinds, or sizes; assort. [< L *sors* lot, condition] —**sort′er** *n.*

sor·tie (sôr′tē) *n.* **1** A sudden attack by troops from a besieged place. **2** A single trip of an aircraft on a military mission. [< F *sortir* go forth]

S O S (es′ō-es′) **1** The international signal of distress in the Morse code (. . . – – – . . .), used by airplanes, ships, etc. **2** *Informal* Any call for assistance.

so-so (sō′sō′) *adj.* Passable; mediocre. —*adv.* Indifferently; tolerably. Also **so′so′, so so.**

sot (sot) *n.* A habitual drunkard. [< OE *sott* a fool] —**sot′·tish** *adj.* —**sot′tish·ly** *adv.* —**sot′tish·ness** *n.*

sot·to vo·ce (sot′ō vō′chē, *Ital.* sôt′tō vō′chā) Softly; in an undertone; privately. [Ital., lit., under the voice]

sou (sōō) *n.* **1** Any of several former French coins of varying value, esp. one equal to 12 deniers. **2** A coin equal to five centimes. [< LL *solidus,* a gold coin]

sou·brette (sōō-bret′) *n.* **1** The part of a frivolous or flirtatious young woman, often a maidservant, in a play or light opera. **2** An actress who portrays such parts. [< Prov. *soubret* shy] —**sou·bret′tish** *adj.*

sou·bri·quet (sōō′bri·kā, sōō·bri·kā′) *n.* SOBRIQUET.

souf·flé (sōō·flā′) *adj.* Made light and frothy, and fixed in that condition by heat: also **souf·fléed′** (-flād′). —*n.* A light, baked dish made of a sauce, beaten egg whites, and various flavorings and ingredients. [F < L *sub-* under + *flare* to blow]

sough (suf, sou) *v.i.* To make a sighing sound, as the wind. —*n.* A deep, murmuring sound. [< OE *swōgan* sound]

sought (sôt) *p.t. & p.p.* of SEEK.

soul (sōl) *n.* **1** That essence or entity of the human person which is regarded as being immortal, invisible, and the source or origin of spirituality, emotion, volition, etc. **2** The moral or spiritual part of man. **3** Emotional or spiritual force, vitality, depth, etc.: His acting lacks *soul.* **4** The most essential or vital element or quality of something: Justice is the *soul* of law. **5** The leading figure or inspirer of a cause, movement, etc. **6** Embodiment: the *soul* of generosity. **7** A person: Every *soul* trembled at the sight. **8** The disembodied spirit of one who has died. **9** Among U.S. Negroes: **a** The awareness of a black African heritage. **b** A strongly emotional pride and solidarity based on this awareness. **c** The qualities that arouse such feelings, esp. as exemplified in black culture and art. **10** SOUL MUSIC. **11** SOUL FOOD. —*adj.* Of or pertaining to soul (def. 9). [< OE *sāwol*]

soul brother A Negro male: used by other Negroes.

soul food Any of various Southern foods or dishes popular with American Negroes, as fried chicken, ham hocks, chitterlings, yams, etc.

soul·ful (sōl′fəl) *adj.* Full of emotion or feeling. —**soul′ful·ly** *adv.* —**soul′ful·ness** *n.* —**Syn.** deep-felt, heartfelt, deep, profound, moving, emotional.

soul kiss A kiss with the mouth open and the tongues touching.

soul·less (sōl′lis) *adj.* **1** Having no soul. **2** Without feeling or emotion; cold. —**soul′less·ly** *adv.* —**soul′less·ness** *n.*

soul music A type of popular music strongly emotional in character and influenced chiefly by the blues and gospel hymns.

soul-search·ing (sōl′sûrch′ing) *n.* A deep examination of one's motives, desires, actions, etc.

soul sister A Negro female: used by other Negroes.

sound[1] (sound) *n.* **1** Energy in the form of a disturbance, usually periodic, in the pressure and density of a fluid or the elastic strain of a solid, detectable by human organs of hearing when between about 20Hz and 20kHz in frequency. **2** The sensation produced by such energy. **3** Any noise, tone, voice, etc., of a specified quality or source: the *sound* of a door slamming shut. **4** Sounding or hearing distance; earshot: within *sound* of the battle. **5** Significance; implication: The story has a sinister *sound.* **6** Mere noise without significance: full of *sound* and fury. —*v.i.* **1** To give forth a sound or sounds. **2** To give a specified impression; seem: The story *sounds* true. —*v.t.* **3** To cause to give forth sound: to *sound* a bell; also, to give forth the sound of: to *sound* A on the violin. **4** To give a signal or order for or announcement of: to *sound* retreat. **5** To utter audibly; pronounce. **6** To make known or celebrated. **7** To test or examine by sound; auscultate. [< OF *son* < L *sonus*]

sound[2] (sound) *adj.* **1** Functioning without impairment; healthy. **2** Free from injury, flaw, or decay: *sound* timber. **3** Correct, logical, or sensible in reasoning, judgment, etc.: *sound* advice. **4** Not unorthodox; established: a *sound* belief. **5** Financially solid or solvent. **6** Stable; safe; secure: a *sound* investment. **7** Complete and effectual; thorough: a *sound* beating. **8** Deep; unbroken: *sound* sleep. **9** Legally valid. [< OE *gesund*] —**sound′ly** *adv.* —**sound′ness** *n.*

sound[3] (sound) *n.* **1** A long, narrow body of water connecting larger bodies of water or separating an island from the mainland. **2** The air bladder of a fish. [< OE *sund* sea and ON *sund* a strait]

sound[4] (sound) *v.t.* **1** To test the depth of (water, etc.), esp. by means of a lead weight at the end of a line. **2** To measure (depth) thus. **3** To explore or examine (the bottom of the sea, the atmosphere, etc.) by means of various probing devices. **4** To discover or try to discover the views and attitudes of (a person) by means of conversation, subtle questions, etc.: usu. with *out.* **5** To try to ascertain or determine (beliefs, attitudes, etc.) in such a manner. **6** *Surg.* To examine, as with a sound. —*v.i.* **7** To measure depth, as with a sounding lead. **8** To dive down suddenly and deeply, as a whale when harpooned. **9** To make investigation; inquire. —*n.* *Surg.* An instrument for exploring a cavity; a probe. —*adv.* Deeply: *sound* asleep. [< OF *sonder*] —**sound′a·ble** *adj.* —**sound′er** *n.*

sound barrier SONIC BARRIER.

sound effects In motion pictures, radio, on the stage, etc., the imitative sounds, as of rain, hoofbeats, fire, etc., produced by various methods.

sound·ing[1] (soun′ding) *adj.* **1** Giving forth a full sound; sonorous. **2** Noisy and empty. —**sound′ing·ly** *adv.*

sound·ing[2] (soun′ding) *n.* **1** Measurement of the depth of water. **2** *pl.* The depth of water as sounded. **3** Water of such depth that the bottom may be reached by sounding. **4** Measurement or examination of the atmosphere, space, etc. at various heights. **5** A sampling of public opinion.

sounding board 1 A structure over a pulpit or speaker's platform to amplify and clarify the speaker's voice. **2** A thin board, as the belly of a violin, used to increase the resonance of the sound: also **sound′board′**. **3** Any person, group, device, etc., used to propagate opinions. **4** A person or group on whom one tests the validity or effectiveness of something.

sound·less (sound′lis) *adj.* Making no sound; silent. —**sound′less·ly** *adv.* —**sound′less·ness** *n.*

sound·man (sound′man′) *n. pl.* **·men** (-men′) A man who has charge of sound effects.

sound·proof (sound′prōōf′) *adj.* Resistant to the penetration or spread of sound. —*v.t.* To make soundproof.

sound track That portion along the edge of a motion-picture film which carries the sound record.

soup (sōōp) *n.* **1** A food made of meat or fish, vegetables, etc., cooked and served, either whole or puréed, in water, stock, or other liquid. **2** *Slang* A heavy fog. **3** *Slang* Nitroglycerin. —**in the soup** *Slang* In difficulties; in a quandary. —**soup up** *Slang* To supercharge or otherwise modify (an engine) for high speed. [< F *soupe*]

soup·çon (sōōp-sôn′) *n.* A minute quantity; a taste. [F, lit., a suspicion]

soup·y (sōō′pē) *adj.* **soup·i·er, soup·i·est 1** Like soup in consistency. **2** Very foggy or cloudy. **3** Overly sentimental.

---

add, āce, câre, pälm; end, ēven; it, īce; odd, ōpen, ôrder; tŏŏk, pōōl; up, bûrn; ə = a in *above, u* in *focus;* yōō = *u* in *fuse;* oil; pout; check; go; ring; thin; this; zh, *vision.* < derived from; ? origin uncertain or unknown.

sour (sour) *adj.* **1** Sharp, acid, or tart to the taste, like vinegar. **2** Having an acid or rancid taste or smell as the result of fermentation. **3** Of or pertaining to fermentation. **4** Cross; morose: a *sour* smile. **5** Bitterly disenchanted. **6** Bad in quality, performance, etc.: an athlete gone *sour*. **7** Wrong or unpleasant in pitch or tone: a *sour* note. **8** Unpleasant. **9** Acid: said of soil. —*v.t.* & *v.i.* To become or make sour. —*n.* **1** Something sour. **2** A cocktail, made usu. with lemon juice, fruit garnishes, etc.: a whiskey *sour*. [< OE *sūr*] —**sour′ly** *adv.* —**sour′ness** *n.* —**Syn. 4** dour, acid, bitter, unhappy.

source (sôrs, sōrs) *n.* **1** That from which something originates or is derived. **2** A cause or agency: a *source* of joy. **3** The spring or fountain from which a stream of water originates. **4** A person, writing, or agency from which information is obtained. [< L *surgere* to rise]

sour cream A food product made of cream soured and thickened by the action of lactic acid bacteria.

sour·dough (sour′dō′) *n.* **1** Fermented dough for use as leaven in making bread. **2** A pioneer or prospector in Alaska or Canada: from the practice of carrying fermented dough to make bread.

sour grapes That which a person affects to despise, because it is unattainable: an allusion to Aesop's fable of the fox and the grapes.

sour·gum (sour′gum′) *n.* TUPELO.

sour·puss (sour′pŏŏs′) *n. Slang* A person with a sullen, peevish expression or disposition.

souse (sous) *v.t.* & *v.i.* **soused, sous·ing 1** To dip or steep in a liquid. **2** To pickle. **3** To make or become thoroughly wet. **4** *Slang* To make or get drunk. —*n.* **1** Pickled meats, esp. the feet and ears of a pig. **2** A plunge in water. **3** Brine. **4** *Slang* A drunkard. [< OHG *sulza* brine]

sou·tane (sōō·tän′, -tan′) *n.* CASSOCK. [< Ital. *sottana*]

south (south) *n.* **1** The general direction to the right of sunrise. **2** The point of the compass at 180°, directly opposite north. **3** A region or point lying in this direction. —*adj.* **1** Situated in a southern direction relatively to the observer or to any given place or point. **2** Facing south. **3** Belonging to or proceeding from the south. —*v.i.* To turn southward. —*adv.* **1** Toward or at the south. **2** From the south. —**the South 1** In the U.S., those states lying south of Pennsylvania and the Ohio River and east of the Mississippi. **2** The Confederacy. [< OE *sūth*]

South Africa A republic of s Africa, 472,359 sq. mi., cap. Pretoria, legislative center Cape Town.

South African A native or citizen of South Africa, esp. an Afrikaner. —*adj.* Of or pertaining to South Africa or its people.

South African Dutch AFRIKAANS.

South America The southern continent of the western hemisphere, about 6,900,000 square miles. —**South American**

south·bound (south′bound′) *adj.* Going southward.

south·east (south′ēst′, *in nautical usage* sou′ēst′) *n.* **1** The direction or compass point midway between south and east. **2** Any region lying in this direction. —*adj.* Of, pertaining to, toward, or from the southeast. —*adv.* Toward or from the southeast. —**south′east′ern, south′east′·ern·most** *adj.*

south·east·er (south′ēs′tər, *in nautical usage* sou′ēs′tər) *n.* A gale from the southeast.

south·east·er·ly (south′ēs′tər·lē, *in nautical usage* sou′·ēs′tər·lē) *adj.* & *adv.* **1** Toward the southeast. **2** From the southeast: said of wind.

south·east·ward (south′ēst′wərd) *adj.* & *adv.* Toward the southeast. —*n.* A southeastward point or direction — **south′east′ward·ly, south′east′wards** *adv.*

south·er (sou′thər) *n.* A strong wind from the south.

south·er·ly (sut͟h′ər·lē) *adj.* **1** Situated in or tending toward the south. **2** From the south: a *southerly* wind. —*adv.* Toward or from the south. —**south′er·li·ness** *n.*

south·ern (su͟th′ərn) *adj.* **1** Of, in, or facing the south. **2** From the south, as a wind. **3** *Often cap.* Of, from, or char-

acteristic of the South: *southern* cooking. —**south′ern·ly** *adv.* —**south′ern·most** *adj.*

Southern Cross A southern constellation having four bright stars in the form of a cross.

South·ern·er (su͟th′ərn·ər) *n.* A native or inhabitant of the s regions of the U.S.

Southern Hemisphere See HEMISPHERE.

southern lights AURORA AUSTRALIS.

Southern Yemen YEMEN, PEOPLE'S DEMOCRATIC REPUBLIC OF.

South Korea See KOREA.

south·land (south′land′) *n.* **1** A region situated to the south. **2** *Often cap.* The southern U.S. —**south′land′er** *n.*

south·paw (south′pô′) *Slang n.* **1** In baseball, a left-handed pitcher. **2** Any left-handed person or player. —*adj.* Left-handed.

South Pole The southern extremity of the earth's axis; the 90th degree of south latitude.

south-south·east (south′south′ēst′, *in nautical usage* sou′sou′ēst′) *n.* The direction or compass point midway between south and southeast. —*adj.* Of, pertaining to, toward, or from this direction. —*adv.* Toward or from this direction.

south-south·west (south′south′west′, *in nautical usage* sou′sou′west′) *n.* The direction or compass point midway between south and southwest. —*adj.* Of, pertaining to, toward, or from this direction. —*adv.* Toward or from this direction.

South Vietnam See VIETNAM.

south·ward (south′wərd, *in nautical usage* sut͟h′ərd) *adj.* Situated in or toward the south. —*adv.* In a southerly direction: also **south′ward·ly, south′wards.** —*n.* The direction of south; also, a region to the south.

south·west (south′west′, *in nautical usage* sou′west′) *n.* **1** The direction or compass point midway between south and west. **2** Any region lying in this direction. —*adj.* Of, pertaining to, toward, or from the southwest. —*adv.* Toward or from the southwest. —**the Southwest** The sw part of the U.S., generally including Oklahoma, Texas, New Mexico, Arizona, and southern California. —**south′·west′ern, south′west′ern·most** *adj.*

south·west·er (south′wes′tər, *in nautical usage* sou′·wes′tər) *n.* **1** A wind, gale, or storm from the southwest. **2** A waterproof hat of oilskin, canvas, etc., with a broad protective brim behind. Also **sou′′west′er.**

south·west·er·ly (south′wes′·tər·lē, *in nautical usage* sou′wes′·tər·lē) *adj.* & *adv.* **1** Toward the southwest. **2** From the southwest: said of wind.

south·west·ward (south′west′·wərd) *adj.* & *adv.* Toward the southwest. —*n.* A southwestward point or direction. — **south′west′ward·ly, south′west′wards** *adv.*

Southwester *def. 2*

sou·ve·nir (sōō′və·nir′, sōō′və·nir′) *n.* A token of remembrance; memento. [< L *subvenire* come to mind]

sov·er·eign (sov′rin, -ə·rən, -ərn, suv′-) *adj.* **1** Exercising or possessing supreme jurisdiction or power. **2** Free; independent; autonomous: a *sovereign* state. **3** Supremely excellent, great, or exalted. **4** Extremely potent or effective: a *sovereign* remedy. **5** Total; unmitigated: *sovereign* hate. **6** Of chief importance, supremacy, etc.: *sovereign* claims. —*n.* **1** One who possesses sovereign authority; a monarch. **2** A body of persons in whom sovereign power is vested. **3** An English gold coin equivalent to one pound sterling. [< L *super* above] —**sov′er·eign·ly** *adv.*

sov·er·eign·ty (sov′rin·tē, -ə·rən-, -ərn-, suv′-) *n. pl.* **·ties 1** The state or quality of being sovereign. **2** The ultimate, supreme power in a state. **3** A sovereign state. **4** The status or power of a sovereign.

so·vi·et (sō′vē·et, sō′vē·et′, sov′ē-, -ē·it) *n.* **1** In the Soviet Union, any of the elected legislative councils existing at various governmental levels. **2** Any of various similar socialist legislative councils. [< Russ. *sovyet* a council]

So·vi·et (sō′vē·et, sō′vē·et′, sov′ē-, -ē·it) *adj.* Of or pertaining to the Union of Soviet Socialist Republics. —*n.pl.* The Soviet people, esp. the officials of the government.

so·vi·et·ize (sō′vē·ə·tīz′, sov′ē-) *v.t.* **·ized**, **·iz·ing** To bring under a soviet form of government. —**so′vi·et·i·za′tion** *n.*

Soviet Russia 1 UNION OF SOVIET SOCIALIST REPUBLICS. **2** RUSSIAN SOVIET FEDERATED SOCIALIST REPUBLIC.

Soviet Union UNION OF SOVIET SOCIALIST REPUBLICS.

sow[1] (sō) *v.* **sowed, sown** or **sowed, sow·ing** *v.t.* **1** To scatter (seed) over land for growth. **2** To scatter seed over (land). **3** To disseminate; implant: to *sow* the seeds of distrust. —*v.i.* **4** To scatter seed. [< OE *sāwan*] —**sow′er** *n.*

sow[2] (sou) *n.* A female hog. [< OE *sū*]

sow·bel·ly (sou′bel′ē) *n. Informal* SALT PORK.

soy (soi) *n.* A dark brown salty liquid condiment made from fermented soybeans. Also **soy sauce.** [Japanese]

soy·bean (soi′bēn) *n.* **1** A small leguminous forage plant native to Asia. **2** Its edible bean, a source of oil, flour, and other products. Also, *esp. Brit.,* **soy·a** (soi′ə).

SP Shore Patrol; Submarine Patrol.

Sp. Spain; Spaniard; Spanish.

sp. special; specialist; species; specific; spelling; spirit(s).

s.p. without issue (L *sine prole*).

spa (spä) *n.* **1** Any locality frequented for its mineral springs. **2** A mineral spring. **3** A fashionable resort or resort hotel. [< *Spa,* a Belgian watering town]

space (spās) *n.* **1** The three-dimensional expanse that is considered as coextensive with the universe. **2** A limited or measurable distance or area, as that between or within points or objects. **3** A specific area designated for a particular purpose: landing *space.* **4** OUTER SPACE. **5** An interval or period of time. **6** One of the degrees of a musical staff between two lines. **7** *Printing* **a** A blank piece of type metal, used for spacing between lines, characters, etc. **b** The area occupied by such pieces. **8** Reserved accommodations, as on a ship or airliner. —*adj.* Of or pertaining to space, esp. to outer space. —*v.t.* **spaced, spac·ing 1** To separate by spaces. **2** To divide into spaces. [< L *spatium*] —**space′less** *adj.* —**spac′er** *n.*

space·craft (spās′kraft′, -kräft′) *n.* Any vehicle, manned or unmanned, designed for flight in outer space.

spaced-out (spāst′out′) *adj. Slang* Dazed or drugged, by or as by the use of narcotics.

space·flight (spās′flīt′) *n.* Flight in outer space.

space·ship (spās′ship′) *n.* Any vehicle designed to travel outside the earth's atmosphere.

space station A large, usu. manned satellite orbiting the earth and used for observation, experiments, as a relay station, etc.

space-time (spās′tīm′, -tīm′) *n.* A four-dimensional continuum in which each point is identified by three position coordinates and one coordinate of time. Also **space-time continuum.**

spa·cial (spā′shəl) *adj.* SPATIAL.

spac·ing (spā′sing) *n.* **1** The arrangement of spaces. **2** A space or spaces, as in a line of print.

spa·cious (spā′shəs) *adj.* **1** Of large or ample extent; not cramped or crowded; roomy. **2** Large or great in scale or scope. —**spa′cious·ly** *adv.* —**spa′cious·ness** *n.* —**Syn. 1** extensive, ample, sizable, capacious, commodious.

spack·le (spak′əl) *v.t.* **·led**, **·ling** To apply Spackle to.

Spack·le (spak′əl) *n.* A powder which, moistened to form a paste, is used for filling cracks, etc. before painting: a trade name.

spade[1] (spād) *n.* An implement used for digging in the ground, heavier than a shovel and having a flatter blade. —**call a spade a spade 1** To call a thing by its right name. **2** To speak the plain truth. —*v.t.* **spad·ed, spad·ing** To dig or cut with a spade. [< OE *spadu*] —**spade′ful** *n.* —**spad′er** *n.*

spade[2] (spād) *n.* **1** A figure, resembling a heart with a triangular handle, on a playing card. **2** A card so marked. **3** *Usu. pl.* The suit of cards so marked. [< Gk. *spathē* broad sword]

spade·work (spād′wûrk′) *n.* Any preliminary work necessary to get a project under way.

spa·dix (spā′diks) *n. pl.* **spa·di·ces** (spā′də·sēz) *Bot.* A spike of tiny flowers on a fleshy axis, usu. enclosed within a spathe. [L, branch torn from palm tree < Gk.]

spa·ghet·ti (spə·get′ē) *n.* **1** A thin, cordlike pasta. **2** Insulated tubing through which bare wire is passed, as in a radio circuit. [< Ital. *spago* a small cord]

Spain (spān) *n.* A nominal constitutional monarchy in sw Europe, 194,368 sq. mi., capital Madrid.

spake (spāk) *Archaic p.t.* of SPEAK.

span[1] (span) *v.t.* **spanned, span·ning 1** To measure, esp. with the hand with the thumb and little finger extended. **2** To extend in time across: His influence *spanned* two centuries. **3** To extend over or from side to side of: This road *spans* the continent. **4** To provide with something that stretches across or extends over. —*n.* **1** The distance or measure between two points, ends, or extremities: the *span* of an eagle's wing. **2** The space or distance between the supports of an arch, abutments of a bridge, etc. **3** The part that spans such a space or distance: the graceful *spans* of Brooklyn Bridge. **4** A period of time or duration: life *span.* **5** The extreme space over which the hand can be expanded, usu. considered to be nine inches. [< OE *spann* distance]

span[2] (span) *n.* A pair of matched horses, oxen, etc., used as a team. [< MDu. *spannen* join together]

span·gle (spang′gəl) *n.* **1** A small bit of brilliant metal foil, plastic, etc., used for decoration, esp. on theatrical costumes. **2** Any small sparkling object. —*v.* **·gled**, **·gling** *v.t.* **1** To adorn with or as with spangles; cause to glitter. —*v.i.* **2** To sparkle as spangles; glitter. [< MDu. *spang* a clasp, brooch] —**span′gly** *adj.*

Span·iard (span′yərd) *n.* A native or citizen of Spain.

span·iel (span′yəl) *n.* **1** A small or medium-sized dog having large pendulous ears and long silky hair. • See SPRINGER. **2** An obsequious follower. [< OF *espaignol* Spanish (dog)]

Span·ish (span′ish) *n.* **1** The language of Spain and many of the countries of the Western Hemisphere. **2** The people of Spain collectively: used with *the.* —*adj.* Of or pertaining to Spain, its people, their language, etc.

Spanish America Those countries of the Western Hemisphere in which Spanish is the common language. —**Span′ish-A·mer′i·can** *adj.*

Spanish American A native or inhabitant of Spanish America.

Spanish moss An epiphytic plant related to pineapple, growing in pendulous tufts on trees in s U.S. and tropical America.

spank (spangk) *v.t.* **1** To slap or strike, esp. on the buttocks with the open hand as a punishment. —*v.i.* **2** To move briskly. —*n.* A smack on the buttocks. [Imit.]

spank·er (spangk′ər) *n.* **1** One who spanks. **2** *Naut.* A fore-and-aft sail extended by a boom and a gaff from the mizzenmast of a ship or bark.

spank·ing (spangk′ing) *adj.* **1** Moving or blowing rapidly; swift; lively. **2** *Informal* Uncommonly large or fine. —*n.* A series of slaps on the buttocks. —*adv. Informal* Very: a *spanking* new bike. [?]

span·ner (span′ər) *n.* **1** One who or that which spans. **2** *Brit.* WRENCH.

spar[1] (spär) *n.* **1** *Naut.* A pole for extending a sail, as a mast, yard, or boom. **2** A similar heavy, round beam forming part of a derrick, crane, etc. **3** That part of an airplane wing which supports the ribs. —*v.t.* **sparred, spar·ring** To furnish with spars. [< ON *sparri* a beam]

spar[2] (spär) *v.i.* **sparred, spar·ring 1** To box, esp. with care and adroitness, as in practice. **2** To bandy words; wrangle. **3** To fight, as cocks, by striking with spurs. —*n.* The act or practice of boxing: also **spar′ring.** [< L *parare* prepare]

spar[3] (spär) *n.* Any of various vitreous, crystalline, easily cleavable, lustrous minerals. [< MDu.]

Spar (spär) *n.* A member of the women's reserve of the U.S. Coast Guard. Also **SPAR.** [< L *s(emper) par(atus)* always ready, the motto of the U.S. Coast Guard]

---

spare (spâr) v. **spared, spar·ing** v.t. 1 To refrain from injuring, molesting, or killing; treat mercifully. 2 To free or relieve (someone) from (pain, expense, etc.): *Spare* us the sight. 3 To use frugally; refrain from using or exercising. 4 To dispense or dispense with; do without: Can you *spare* a dime? —v.i. 5 To be frugal. 6 To be lenient or forgiving. —adj. **spar·er, spar·est** 1 That is over and above what is necessary, used, filled, etc.: *spare* time. 2 Held in reserve; additional; extra. 3 Thin; lean. 4 Not abundant or plentiful; scanty. 5 Not elaborate or fussy: a *spare* style of writing. —n. 1 A duplicate of something that has been saved for future use. 2 An extra tire usu. carried in or on a vehicle as a replacement in the event of a flat tire: also **spare tire.** 3 In bowling, the act of overturning all the pins with the first two balls; also, the score thus made. [< OE *sparian* to spare] —**spare′ly** adv. —**spare′ness, spar′er** n.

spare·ribs (spâr′ribz′) n.pl. A cut of pork ribs somewhat closely trimmed.

spar·ing (spâr′ing) adj. 1 Scanty; slight. 2 Frugal; stingy. —**spar′ing·ly** adv. —**spar′ing·ness** n.

spark (spärk) n. 1 An incandescent particle, esp. one thrown off by a fire. 2 Any similar glistening or brilliant point or particle. 3 A small trace or indication: a *spark* of wit. 4 Anything that kindles or animates. 5 *Electr.* The luminous effect of an electric discharge, or the discharge itself. —v.i. 1 To give off sparks. 2 In an internal-combustion engine, to have the electric ignition operating. —v.t. 3 To activate or cause: The shooting *sparked* a revolution. [< OE *spearca*] —**spark′er** n.

spar·kle (spär′kəl) v.i. **·kled, ·kling** 1 To give off flashes or bright points of light; glitter. 2 To emit sparks. 3 To effervesce, as certain wines, etc. 4 To be brilliant or vivacious. —n. 1 A spark; gleam. 2 Brilliance; vivacity. [Freq. of SPARK]

spar·kler (spär′klər) n. 1 One who or that which sparkles. 2 *Informal* A sparkling gem, as a diamond. 3 A thin, rodlike firework that emits sparks.

spark plug A device for igniting the charge in an internal-combustion engine by means of an electric spark.

spar·row (spar′ō) n. 1 Any of various small, plainly colored, passerine birds related to the finches, as the English sparrow. 2 Any of numerous similar birds, as the song sparrow. [< OE *spearwa*]

sparrow hawk 1 A small North American falcon with rufous back and tail. 2 A small European hawk.

sparse (spärs) adj. **spars·er, spars·est** Thinly spread or scattered; not dense: a *sparse* crowd. [< L *sparsus*, pp. of *spargere* sprinkle] —**sparse′ly** adv. —**sparse′ness, spar·si·ty** (spär′sə·tē) n.

Spar·ta (spär′tə) n. An ancient city in the Peloponnesus, s Greece, capital of ancient Laconia.

Spar·tan (spär′tən) adj. 1 Of Sparta or the Spartans. 2 Characterized by austerity, simplicity, self-denial, self-discipline, etc. 3 Heroically brave and enduring. —n. 1 A native or citizen of Sparta. 2 One of exceptional valor and fortitude. —**Spar′tan·ism** n.

spasm (spaz′əm) n. 1 A sudden, involuntary muscular contraction. 2 Any sudden action or effort. [< Gk. *spasmos* < *spaein* draw, pull]

spas·mod·ic (spaz·mod′ik) adj. 1 Of the nature of a spasm; intermittent; temporary; transitory. 2 Violent or impulsive. Also **spas·mod′i·cal.** —**spas·mod′i·cal·ly** adv.

spas·tic (spas′tik) adj. Of, pertaining to, or characterized by spasms. —n. A person afflicted with cerebral palsy or similar disability. —**spas′ti·cal·ly** adv.

spat[1] (spat) p.t. & p.p. of SPIT[1].

spat[2] (spat) n. 1 Spawn of a bivalve mollusk, esp. the oyster. 2 A young oyster, or young oysters collectively. [?]

spat[3] (spat) n. 1 *Informal* A petty dispute or quarrel. 2 A splash, as of rain; spatter. —v. **spat·ted, spat·ting** v.i. 1 To strike with a slight sound. 2 *Informal* To engage in a petty quarrel. —v.t. 3 To slap. [Imit.]

spat[4] (spat) n. A short gaiter worn over a shoe and fastened underneath with a strap. [Short for SPATTERDASH]

Spats[4]

spate (spāt) n. 1 A flood or overflow. 2 A large amount or incidence. 3 A sudden outpouring, as of words. [?]

spathe (spāth) n. *Bot.* A large bract or pair of bracts sheathing a flower cluster, as a spadix. [< Gk. *spathē* broad sword]

spa·tial (spā′shəl) adj. Of, involving, occupying, or having the nature of space. [< L *spatium* space] —**spa·ti·al·i·ty** (spā′shē·al′ə·tē) n. —**spa′tial·ly** adv.

spat·ter (spat′ər) v.t. 1 To scatter in drops or splashes, as mud or paint. 2 To splash with such drops; bespatter. 3 To defame. —v.i. 4 To throw off drops or splashes. 5 To fall in a shower, as raindrops. —n. 1 The act of spattering or the condition of being spattered. 2 The mark or soiled place caused by spattering. 3 The sound of spattering. 4 A small amount or number. [?< OE *spatlian* spit out]

spat·ter·dash (spat′ər·dash′) n. A knee-high legging worn as a protection from mud, esp. when riding.

spat·u·la (spach′oo·lə) n. A knifelike instrument with a dull, flexible, rounded blade, used to spread plaster, cake icing, etc. [L]

spav·in (spav′in) n. A laming disease of the hock joint of horses. [< OF *espavain*] —**spav′ined** adj.

spawn (spôn) n. 1 The eggs of fishes, amphibians, mollusks, etc., esp. in masses. 2 A great number of offspring: usu. derisive. 3 Any large quantity or yield. —v.i. 1 To produce spawn; deposit eggs or roe. 2 To come forth as or like spawn. —v.t. 3 To produce (spawn). 4 To give rise to; originate. [< L *expandere* expand]

spay (spā) v.t. To remove the ovaries from (a female animal). [< OF *espeer* cut with a sword]

S.P.C.A. Society for the Prevention of Cruelty to Animals.

speak (spēk) v. **spoke** (*Archaic* **spake**), **spo·ken** (*Archaic* **spoke**), **speak·ing** v.i. 1 To employ the vocal organs in ordinary speech; utter words. 2 To express or convey ideas, opinions, etc., in or as in speech: Actions *speak* louder than words. 3 To make a speech; deliver an address. 4 To converse. 5 To make a sound; also, to bark, as a dog. —v.t. 6 To express or make known in or as in speech. 7 To utter in speech: to *speak* words of love. 8 To use or be capable of using (a language) in conversation. —**so to speak** In a manner of speaking. —**speak for** 1 To speak in behalf of; represent officially. 2 To reserve or request: usu. used in the passive voice: Has that appointment been *spoken for?* [< OE *specan*] —**speak′a·ble** adj.

speak·eas·y (spēk′ē′zē) n. pl. **·eas·ies** A place where liquor is sold contrary to law, esp. such a place in the U.S. during prohibition.

speak·er (spē′kər) n. 1 One who speaks, esp. in public. 2 The presiding officer in a legislative body. 3 LOUDSPEAKER.

speak·ing (spē′king) adj. 1 Able to speak. 2 Of, pertaining to, or for speech. 3 Using a specified language: a French-*speaking* colony. 4 Vividly lifelike: the *speaking* image of his father. —n. 1 The act or technique of one who speaks. 2 Something spoken. —**speak′ing·ly** adv.

spear (spir) n. 1 A weapon consisting of a pointed head on a long shaft. 2 A similar instrument, barbed and usu. forked, as for spearing fish. 3 A leaf or slender stalk, as of grass. —v.t. 1 To pierce or capture with or as with a spear. —v.i. 2 To pierce or wound with or as with a spear. 3 To send forth spears, as a plant. [< OE *spere*] —**spear′er** n.

spear·head (spir′hed′) n. 1 The point of a spear or lance. 2 The person, group, etc., that leads an action or undertaking. —v.t. To be in the lead of (an attack, etc.).

spear·man (spir′mən) n. pl. **·men** (-mən) A man armed with a spear. Also **spears′man.**

spear·mint (spir′mint′) n. An aromatic herb similar to peppermint.

spe·cial (spesh′əl) adj. 1 Out of the ordinary; uncommon; unique; different: a *special* problem. 2 Designed for or assigned to a specific purpose, occasion, etc.: a *special* permit. 3 Memorable; notable: a very *special* occasion. 4 Extra or additional: a *special* bonus. 5 Intimate; esteemed; beloved: a *special* favorite. —n. 1 Something made, detailed for, or appropriated to a specific service, occasion, etc., as a train, newspaper edition, sales item, featured dish, etc. 2 A television show produced and scheduled for a single presentation only. [< L *species* kind, species] —**spe′cial·ly** adv. —**Syn.** adj. 1 peculiar, particular, distinctive, singular, original, unusual. **3** noteworthy, unforgettable, extraordinary, exceptional, rare.

special delivery Mail delivery by special courier for an additional fee.

Special Drawing Rights International monetary credit that can be drawn by member nations from the International Monetary Fund to be used in lieu of gold.

spe·cial·ist (spesh'əl·ist) *n.* A person devoted to one line of study, occupation, or professional work. —**spe'cial·ism** *n.* —**spe'cial·is'tic** *adj.*

spe·ci·al·i·ty (spesh'ē·al'ə·tē) *n. pl.* **·ties** *Chiefly Brit.* SPECIALTY.

spe·cial·ize (spesh'əl·īz) *v.* **·ized**, **·iz·ing** *v.i.* **1** To concentrate on one particular activity or subject. **2** To take on a form or forms adapted to special conditions or functions. —*v.t.* **3** To make specific or particular; particularize. **4** To adapt for or direct toward some special use or purpose. *Brit. sp.* **·ise**. —**spe'cial·i·za'tion** *n.*

spe·cial·ty (spesh'əl·tē) *n. pl.* **·ties 1** Something, as a trade, study, activity, etc., in which one specializes. **2** A product or article possessing a special quality, excellence, character, etc.: *Fish is the* specialty *of this restaurant.* **3** A special mark, quality, or characteristic. **4** The state of being special.

spe·cie (spē'shē) *n.* Coined money; coin. —**in specie 1** In coin. **2** In kind. [< L *(in) specie* (in) kind]

spe·cies (spē'shēz, -shiz) *n. pl.* **·cies 1** A category of animals or plants subordinate to a genus and comprising similar organisms usu. with the capacity of interbreeding only among themselves. **2** A group of individuals or objects having in common certain attributes and designated by a common name. **3** A kind; sort; variety; form. **4** *Eccl.* **a** The visible form of bread or of wine retained by the eucharistic elements after consecration. **b** The consecrated elements of the Eucharist. [L, kind]

spe·cif·ic (spi·sif'ik) *adj.* **1** Distinctly and plainly set forth; explicit. **2** Special; definite; particular; distinct: *He took no* specific *action.* **3** Belonging to or distinguishing a species. **4** Having some distinct medicinal or pathological property: a *specific* germ. **5** Designating a particular property, composition, ratio, or quantity serving to identify a given substance or phenomenon: *specific* gravity. —*n.* **1** Anything adapted to effect a specific result. **2** A medicine affecting a specific condition or pathogen. **3** *Usu. pl.* A particular item or detail. [< L *species* kind + -FIC] —**spe·cif'i·cal·ly** *adv.* —**spec·i·fic'i·ty** (spes'ə·fis'ə·tē) *n.*

spec·i·fi·ca·tion (spes'ə·fə·kā'shən) *n.* **1** The act of specifying. **2** A definite and complete statement, as in a contract; also, one detail in such a statement. **3** In patent law, the detailed description of an invention. **4** *Usu. pl.* A description of dimensions, types of material, capabilities, etc., of a device, building project, etc. **5** A single item in such a description.

specific gravity The ratio of the mass of a substance to that of an equal volume of some standard substance, water in the case of solids and liquids, and air or hydrogen in the case of gases.

spec·i·fy (spes'ə·fī) *v.t.* **·fied**, **·fy·ing 1** To mention or state in full and explicit detail. **2** To include as an item in a specification.

spec·i·men (spes'ə·mən) *n.* **1** A person or thing regarded as representative of a class. **2** A sample, as of blood, sputum, etc., for laboratory analysis. **3** *Informal* A person of a specified type or character. [< L *specere* look at]

spe·cious (spē'shəs) *adj.* Apparently good, right, logical, etc., but actually without merit or foundation: *specious* reasoning. [< L *speciosus* fair] —**spe'cious·ly** *adv.* —**spe'·cious·ness** *n.*

speck (spek) *n.* **1** A small spot or stain. **2** Any very small thing; particle. —*v.t.* To mark with specks. [< OE *specca*]

speck·le (spek'əl) *v.t.* **·led**, **·ling** To mark with specks. —*n.* A speck.

specs (speks) *n.pl. Informal* **1** EYEGLASSES. **2** Specifications. See SPECIFICATION (def. 4).

spec·ta·cle (spek'tə·kəl) *n.* **1** A grand or unusual sight or public display, as a pageant, parade, natural phenome-

non, etc. **2** An embarrassing or deplorable exhibition. **3** *pl.* EYEGLASSES. [< L *specere* see] —**spec'ta·cled** (-kəld) *adj.*

spec·tac·u·lar (spek·tak'yə·lər) *adj.* Of or like a spectacle; unusually wonderfully, exciting, etc. —*n.* Something spectacular, esp. a lavish television production. —**spec·tac'u·lar·ly** *adv.* —**spec·tac'u·lar'i·ty** (-lar'ə·tē) *n.*

spec·ta·tor (spek'tā·tər, spek·tā'-) *n.* **1** One who beholds; an eyewitness. **2** One who is present at and views a show, game, spectacle, etc. [L < *spectare* look at]

spec·ter (spek'tər) *n.* A phantom; apparition. Also *esp. Brit.* **spec'tre.** [< L *spectrum* vision]

spec·tra (spek'trə) A *pl.* of SPECTRUM.

spec·tral (spek'trəl) *adj.* **1** Pertaining to a specter; ghostly. **2** Pertaining to a spectrum. —**spec'tral·ly** *adv.*

spectro- *combining form* Spectrum: *spectroscope.*

spec·tro·gram (spek'trə·gram) *n.* A photograph or other record of a spectrum.

spec·tro·graph (spek'trə·graf, -gräf) *n.* A device for displaying and recording spectra.

spec·tro·scope (spek'trə·skōp) *n.* An instrument for sorting out into a spectrum the wavelengths in a beam of light or other radiation. —**spec'tro·scop'ic** (-skop'ik) or **·i·cal** *adj.* —**spec'tro·scop'i·cal·ly** *adv.*

spec·tros·co·py (spek·tros'kə·pē) *n.* **1** The science treating of the phenomena observed with the spectroscope. **2** The art of using the spectroscope.

spec·trum (spek'trəm) *n. pl.* **·tra** (-trə) or **·trums 1** The continuous band of colors observed when a beam of white light is diffracted, as by a prism, according to wavelength, ranging from red, the longest visible rays, to violet, the shortest. **2** Any array of radiant energy ordered according to a varying characteristic, as frequency, wavelength, etc. **3** A band of wave frequencies: the radio *spectrum.* **4** A series or range within limits: a wide *spectrum* of activities. [L, a vision]

spec·u·late (spek'yə·lāt) *v.i.* **·lat·ed**, **·lat·ing 1** To weigh mentally or conjecture; ponder; theorize. **2** To make a risky investment with hope of gain. [< L *speculari* look at, examine] —**spec'u·la'tor** *n.* —**spec'u·la·to'ry** (-lə·tôr'ē, -tō'rē) *adj.* —**Syn. 1** guess, presume, surmise, venture, hazard.

spec·u·la·tion (spek'yə·lā'shən) *n.* **1** The act of speculating or conjecturing. **2** A theory or conjecture. **3** An investment or business transaction involving risk with hope of large profit.

spec·u·la·tive (spek'yə·lə·tiv, -lā'tiv) *adj.* **1** Of, pertaining to, engaged in, or given to speculation or conjecture. **2** Strictly theoretical; not practical. **3** Engaging in or involving financial speculation. **4** Risky; doubtful. —**spec'u·la·tive·ly** *adv.* —**spec'u·la·tive·ness** *n.*

spec·u·lum (spek'yə·ləm) *n. pl.* **·la** (-lə) or **·lums 1** A mirror usu. of polished metal, used for telescope reflectors, etc. **2** *Med.* An instrument that dilates a passage of the body for examination. [L, mirror < *specere* see]

sped (sped) A *p.t. & p.p.* of SPEED.

speech (spēch) *n.* **1** The act of speaking; faculty of expressing thought and emotion by spoken words. **2** The power or capability of speaking. **3** That which is spoken; conversation; talk. **4** A public address. **5** A characteristic manner of speaking. **6** A particular language, idiom, or dialect: American *speech.* **7** The study or art of oral communication. [< OE *specan* speak]

speech·i·fy (spē'chə·fī) *v.i.* **·fied**, **·fy·ing** To make speeches: often used derisively. —**speech'i·fi'er** *n.*

speech·less (spēch'lis) *adj.* **1** Temporarily unable to speak because of physical weakness, strong emotion, etc.: *speechless* with rage. **2** Mute; dumb. **3** Silent; reticent. **4** Inexpressible in words: *speechless* joy. —**speech'less·ly** *adv.* —**speech'less·ness** *n.*

speed (spēd) *n.* **1** Rapidity of motion; swiftness. **2** Rate of motion: *speed* of light. **3** Rate or rapidity of any action or performance. **4** A transmission gear in a motor vehicle. **5** *Informal* A characteristic interest, life style, etc. **6** *Slang* An amphetamine drug, esp. methamphetamine. **7** *Archaic* Good luck; success: They wished him good *speed.* —*v.* **sped** or **speed·ed**, **speed·ing** *v.i.* **1** To move or go with speed. **2** To exceed the legal driving limit, esp. on highways. —*v.t.* **3** To promote the forward progress of: *speed* a letter. **4** To cause to move or go with speed. **5** To promote the success of. **6** To wish Godspeed to: *Speed* the parting guest. —**speed up** To accelerate in speed or action. —*adj.* Of, pertaining to, or indicating speed. [< OE *spēd* power]

speed·boat (spēd′bōt′) *n.* A motorboat capable of high speed.

speed·er (spē′dər) *n.* A person or thing that speeds; esp., a motorist who drives at a speed exceeding a safe or legal limit.

speed·om·e·ter (spi·dom′ə·tər) *n.* A device for indicating the speed of a vehicle.

speed·ster (spēd′stər) *n.* A speeder.

speed·up (spēd′up′) *n.* An acceleration in work, output, movement, etc.

speed·way (spēd′wā′) *n.* **1** A racetrack for automobiles or motorcycles. **2** A road for vehicles traveling at high speed.

speed·well (spēd′wel) *n.* Any of various herbs of the figwort family, usu. bearing blue or white flowers.

speed·y (spē′dē) *adj.* **speed·i·er, speed·i·est 1** Characterized by speed. **2** Without delay. —**speed′i·ly** *adv.* —**speed′·i·ness** *n.*

spe·le·ol·o·gy (spē′lē·ol′ə·jē, spel′ē-) *n.* **1** The scientific study of caves. **2** The exploration of caves. [< L *spelaeum* a cave + -LOGY] —**spe′le·o·log′i·cal** (-ə·loj′i·kəl) *adj.* —**spe′le·ol′o·gist** *n.*

spell[1] (spel) *v.* **spelled** or **spelt, spell·ing** *v.t.* **1** To pronounce or write the letters of (a word); esp., to do so correctly. **2** To form or be the letters of: C-a-t *spells* cat. **3** To signify; mean. —*v.i.* **4** To form words out of letters, esp. correctly. —**spell out 1** To read each letter of, usu. with difficulty. **2** To puzzle out and learn. **3** To make explicit and detailed. [< OF *espeler*]

spell[2] (spel) *n.* **1** A magical word or formula. **2** A state of enchantment. **3** An irresistible power or fascination. [< OE, story]

spell[3] (spel) *n.* **1** *Informal* A period of time, usu. of short duration. **2** *Informal* A continuing type of weather. **3** *Informal* A short distance. **4** *Informal* A fit of illness, debility, etc. **5** A turn of duty in relief of another. **6** A period of work or employment. —*v.t.* **1** To relieve temporarily from some work or duty. **2** *Austral.* To give a rest to, as a horse. —*v.i.* **3** *Austral.* To take a rest. [< OE *gespelia* a substitute]

spell·bind (spel′bīnd′) *v.t.* **·bound, ·bind·ing** To bind or enthrall, as if by a spell. —**spell′bind·er** *n.*

spell·bound (spel′bound′) *adj.* Enthralled or fascinated by or as by a spell. —**Syn.** astonished, amazed, aghast, agog, bewitched, enchanted, charmed.

spell·er (spel′ər) *n.* **1** One who spells. **2** A spelling book.

spell·ing (spel′ing) *n.* **1** The act of one who spells. **2** The art of correct spelling; orthography. **3** The way in which a word is spelled.

spelling bee A spelling competition.

spelt[1] (spelt) A *p.t. & p.p.* of SPELL[1].

spelt[2] (spelt) *n.* A species of wheat. [< OE]

spe·lun·ker (spē·lung′kər) *n.* An enthusiast in the exploration and study of caves; a speleologist. [< L *spelunca* a cave]

spend (spend) *v.* **spent, spend·ing** *v.t.* **1** To pay out or disburse (money). **2** To expend by degrees; use up. **3** To apply or devote, as thought or effort, to some activity, purpose, etc. **4** To pass: to *spend* one's life in jail. **5** To use wastefully; squander. —*v.i.* **6** To pay out or disburse money, etc. [< OE *aspendan*] —**spend′er** *n.*

spend·thrift (spend′thrift′) *n.* One who is wastefully lavish of money. —*adj.* Excessively lavish; prodigal.

spent (spent) *p.t. & p.p.* of SPEND. —*adj.* **1** Worn out or exhausted. **2** Deprived of force.

sperm[1] (spûrm) *n.* **1** The male fertilizing fluid; semen. **2** A male reproductive cell; spermatozoon. [< Gk. *sperma* a seed]

sperm[2] (spûrm) *n.* **1** SPERM WHALE. **2** SPERMACETI. **3** SPERM OIL.

-sperm *combining form Bot.* A seed (of a specified kind): gymnosperm. [< Gk. *sperma* a seed]

sper·ma·ce·ti (spûr′mə·sē′tē, -set′ē) *n.* A white, waxy substance separated from the oil contained in the head of the sperm whale, used for making candles, ointments, etc. [< L *sperma ceti* seed of a whale]

sper·mat·ic (spûr·mat′ik) *adj.* Of or pertaining to sperm or the male sperm-producing gland.

sper·ma·to·phyte (spûr′mə·tə·fīt′) *n.* Any seed-bearing plant; an angiosperm or a gymnosperm. [< Gk. *sperma* seed + *phylos* plant] —**sper′ma·to·phyt′ic** (-fit′ik) *adj.*

sper·ma·to·zo·on (spûr′mə·tə·zō′on) *n. pl.* **·zo·a** (-zō′ə) A male reproductive cell of an animal, which carries half the complement of genetic material normal for its species. [< Gk. *sperma* seed + *zōion* an animal] —**sper′ma·to·zo′al, sper′ma·to·zo′an, sper′ma·to·zo′ic** *adj.*

sperm oil A pale yellow lubricating oil obtained from the sperm whale.

sperm whale A large, toothed whale of warm seas, having a huge truncate head containing a reservoir of sperm oil.

Sperm whale

spew (spyoo) *v.i.* **1** To throw up; vomit. **2** To come or issue forth. —*v.t.* **1** To throw up; vomit. **2** To eject or send forth. —*n.* That which is spewed. [< OE *spīwan*]

sp. gr. specific gravity.

sphag·num (sfag′nəm) *n.* **1** Any of a genus of whitish gray mosses; peat moss. **2** This moss in dried form, used by florists for potting plants, etc. [< Gk. *sphagnos* kind of moss] —**sphag′nous** *adj.*

sphe·noid (sfē′noid) *n.* An irregular, wedge-shaped bone forming part of the orbit. —*adj.* Wedge-shaped. [< Gk. *sphēn* wedge] —**sphe·noi·dal** (sfi·noid′l) *adj.* • See SKULL.

sphere (sfir) *n.* **1** A round body in which every point on its surface is equidistant from the center; globe. **2** A planet, sun, star, etc. **3** CELESTIAL SPHERE. **4** The apparent outer dome of the sky. **5** The field or place of activity, experience, influence, etc.; scope; province. **6** Social rank or position. —*v.t.* **sphered, spher·ing 1** To place in or as in a sphere; encircle. **2** To set among the celestial spheres. **3** To make spherical. [< Gk. *sphaira* a ball]

-sphere *combining form* Denoting an enveloping spherical mass: *atmosphere.*

spher·i·cal (sfer′i·kəl) *adj.* **1** Shaped like a sphere; globular. **2** Pertaining to a sphere or spheres. Also **spher′ic.** —**spher′i·cal·ly** *adv.* —**spher′i·cal·ness** *n.*

sphe·roid (sfir′oid) *n.* A body having approximately the form of a sphere; an ellipsoid. —**sphe·roi′dal** (sfi·roid′l), **sphe·roi′dic** or **·di·cal** *adj.* —**sphe·roi′dal·ly** *adv.*

sphinc·ter (sfingk′tər) *n. Anat.* A ring of muscle serving to open and close an opening in the body. [< Gk. *sphingein* to close] —**sphinc′ter·al** *adj.*

sphinx (sfingks) *n. pl.* **sphinx·es** or **sphin·ges** (sfin′jēz) **1** *Egypt. Myth* A wingless monster with a lion's body and the head of a man, a ram, or a hawk. **2** *Gk. Myth.* Usu. *cap.* A winged monster with a woman's head and breasts and a lion's body, that destroyed those unable to guess her riddle. **3** A mysterious or enigmatical person. [< Gk.]

sphyg·mo·ma·nom·e·ter (sfig′mō·mə·nom′ə·tər) *n.* An instrument for measuring blood pressure. Also **sphyg·mom′e·ter** (-mom′ə·tər). [< Gk. *sphygmos* pulse + MANOMETER]

Sphinx *def.* 2

spi·cate (spī′kāt) *adj.* **1** Arranged in spikes: said of flowers. **2** Having a spur, as the legs of some birds. Also **spi′·cat·ed.** [< L *spica* spike]

spice (spīs) *n.* **1** An aromatic vegetable substance, as cinnamon, cloves, etc., used for flavoring. **2** Such substances collectively. **3** That which gives zest or adds interest. **4** An aromatic odor; an agreeable perfume. —*v.t.* **spiced, spic·ing 1** To season with spice. **2** To add zest or piquancy to. [< L *species* kind] —**spic′er** *n.*

spice·bush (spīs′boosh′) *n.* An aromatic deciduous shrub related to laurel. Also **spice′wood′** (-wood′).

spick-and-span (spik′ən·span′) *adj.* **1** Neat and clean. **2** Perfectly new, or looking as if new. Also **spic′-and-span′**. [Var. of SPIKE[1] + ON *spänn* chip]

spic·ule (spik′yōol) *n.* **1** A small, slender, sharp-pointed body; a spikelet. **2** *Zool.* One of the small, hard, needlelike growths supporting the soft tissues of certain invertebrates, as sponges. Also **spic·u·la** (spik′yə·lə). [< L *spicum* point, spike] —**spic′u·lar, spic′u·late** (-lāt, -lit) *adj.*

spic·u·lum (spik′yə·ləm) *n. pl.* **·la** (-lə) **1** SPICULE. **2** *Zool.* A small, pointed organ, as a spine of a sea urchin. [L]

spic·y (spī′sē) *adj.* **spic·i·er, spic·i·est** **1** Containing, flavored, or fragrant with spices. **2** Producing spices. **3** Full of spirit and zest; lively. **4** Somewhat improper or risqué. —**spic′i·ly** *adv.* —**spic′i·ness** *n.*

spi·der (spī′dər) *n.* **1** Any of numerous wingless arachnids capable of spinning silk into webs for the capture of prey. **2** A long-handled iron frying pan, often having legs. **3** Any of various devices with radiating, leglike projections. [< OE *spīthra*] — **spi′der·y** *adj.*

Garden spider

spider crab Any of various ocean crabs with long legs and spiny growths on the carapace.

spider monkey An arboreal Central and South American monkey with very long, slender limbs and a long prehensile tail.

spi·der·wort (spī′dər·wûrt′) *n.* Any of several plants with grasslike leaves and usu. blue, three-petaled flowers.

spiel (spēl) *Slang n.* An informal but purposeful speech or talk, usu. rehearsed, as by a politician or salesman. — *v.i.* To deliver a spiel. [< G *spielen* to play]

spi·er (spī′ər) *n.* One who spies.

spif·fy (spif′ē) *adj.* **·fi·er, ·fi·est** *Slang* Smartly dressed; spruce. —**spif′fi·ness** *n.* [?]

spig·ot (spig′ət, spik′-) *n.* **1** A plug for the bunghole of a cask. **2** A turning plug or valve fitting into a faucet; also, the faucet itself. [ME *spigote*]

spike[1] (spīk) *n.* **1** A very large, thick nail. **2** A slender, pointed piece of metal, as used along the top of an iron fence. **3** A projecting, pointed piece of metal in the soles of shoes to keep the wearer from slipping. **4** A very high, slender heel on a woman's shoe. **5** A straight, unbranched antler, as of a young deer. —*v.t.* **spiked, spik·ing** **1** To fasten with spikes. **2** To set or provide with spikes. **3** To block; put a stop to. **4** To pierce with or impale on a spike. **5** *Informal* To add alcoholic liquor to. [ME] —**spik′er** *n.* —**spik′y** *adj.*

spike[2] (spīk) *n.* **1** An ear of corn, barley, wheat, or other grain. **2** *Bot.* A flower cluster in which the flowers are closely attached to the stalk. [< L *spica* ear of grain]

spike·let (spīk′lit) *n. Bot.* A small spike.

spike·nard (spīk′nərd, -närd) *n.* **1** An ancient fragrant and costly ointment. **2** A perennial East Indian herb of the valerian family yielding this ointment. [< L *spica* spike + *nardus* nard]

spile (spīl) *n.* **1** A large timber or stake driven into the ground as a foundation; a pile. **2** A wooden spigot or plug used in a cask. **3** A spout driven into a sugar-maple tree to lead the sap to a bucket. —*v.t.* **spiled, spil·ing** **1** To pierce for and provide with a spile. **2** To drive spiles into. [< MDu., skewer]

spill[1] (spil) *v.* **spilled** or **spilt, spill·ing** *v.t.* **1** To allow or cause to fall or run out or over, as a liquid or a powder. **2** To shed, as blood. **3** *Naut.* To empty (a sail) of wind. **4** *Informal* To cause to fall, as from a horse. **5** *Informal* To divulge; make known, as a secret. —*v.i.* **6** To fall or run out or over: said of liquids, etc. —*n.* **1** The act of spilling. **2** That which is spilled. **3** *Informal* A fall to the ground, as from a horse or vehicle. **4** SPILLWAY. [< OE *spillan* destroy] —**spill′age, spill′er** *n.*

spill[2] (spil) *n.* **1** A slip of wood, or rolled strip of paper, used for lighting lamps, etc. **2** A splinter. **3** A slender peg, pin, or bar of wood, esp. for stopping up a hole. [Var. of SPILE[1]]

spill·way (spil′wā′) *n.* **1** A passageway in or about a dam to release the water in a reservoir. **2** The paved upper surface of a dam over which surplus water escapes.

spilt (spilt) A *pt. & p.p.* of SPILL[1].

spin (spin) *v.* **spun, spin·ning** *v.t.* **1** To draw out and twist into threads; also, to draw out and twist fiber into (threads, yarn, etc.). **2** To make or produce (a web or cocoon) as if by spinning. **3** To tell, as a story or yarn. **4** To protract; prolong, as a story by additional details: with *out.* **5** To cause to whirl rapidly. —*v.i.* **6** To make thread or yarn. **7** To extrude filaments of a viscous substance from the body: said of spiders, etc. **8** To whirl rapidly; rotate. **9** To seem to be whirling, as from dizziness. **10** To move rapidly. —*n.* **1** An act or instance of spinning. **2** A rapid whirling. **3** Any rapid movement or action. **4** A ride, as in an automobile. **5** The uncontrolled, spiral descent of an airplane after a stall. [< OE *spinnan*]

spin·ach (spin′ich) *n.* **1** An edible garden plant of the goosefoot family. **2** Its edible leaves. [< Ar. *isbānah*]

spi·nal (spī′nəl) *adj.* **1** Of or pertaining to the spine or spinal cord. **2** Of or pertaining to spines or a spiny process.

spinal column A series of hollow, articulated bones that enclose the spinal cord and form the axis of the skeleton of a vertebrate animal.

spinal cord The thick, soft cord of nerve tissue enclosed by the spinal column.

spin·dle (spin′dəl) *n.* **1** In hand spinning, a notched, tapered rod used to twist into thread the fibers pulled from the distaff. **2** The slender rod in a spinning wheel by the rotation of which the thread is twisted and wound on a spool or bobbin on the same rod. **3** A small rod or pin bearing the bobbin of a spinning machine. **4** A rotating rod, pin, axis, arbor, or shaft, esp. when small and bearing something that rotates: the *spindle* of a lathe. **5** The tapering end of a vehicle axle that enters the hub. **6** A small shaft passing through the lock of a door and bearing the knobs or handles. **7** Any decorative, often tapered rod, used in the back of a chair, etc. **8** A needlelike rod mounted on a weighted base, for impaling bills, checks, etc. —*v.* **·dled, ·dling** *v.i.* **1** To grow into a long, slender stalk or body. —*v.t.* **2** To form into or as into a spindle. **3** To provide with a spindle. [< OE *spinel*]

spin·dle-leg·ged (spin′dəl·leg′id, -legd′) *adj.* Having long, slender legs. Also **spin′dle-shanked′** (-shangkt′).

spin·dle-legs (spin′dəl·legz′) *n.* **1** Long, slender legs. **2** *Informal* A person having long, slender legs. Also **spin′-dle-shanks′** (-shangks′).

spin·dling (spind′ling) *adj.* SPINDLY.

spin·dly (spind′lē) *adj.* **·dli·er, ·dli·est** Of a slender, lanky growth or form, suggesting weakness.

spin·drift (spin′drift) *n.* Blown spray or scud. [Var. of SPOONDRIFT]

spine (spīn) *n.* **1** SPINAL COLUMN. **2** Any of various hard, pointed outgrowths on the bodies of certain animals, as the porcupine and starfish. **3** A thorny projection on the stems of certain plants, as the cactus. **4** The back of a bound book. **5** A projecting eminence or ridge. [< L *spina* spine, thorn]

spi·nel (spi·nel′, spin′əl) *n.* Any of various hard minerals, a red variety, the **ruby spinel,** being used as a gem. [< Ital. *spina* thorn]

spine·less (spīn′lis) *adj.* **1** Having no spine or backbone; invertebrate. **2** Lacking spines. **3** Having a very flexible backbone; limp. **4** Weak-willed; irresolute. —**spine′less·ness** *n.*

spin·et (spin′it) *n.* **1** A small harpsichord. **2** A small upright piano. **3** A small electronic organ. [< Ital. *spinetta*]

spin·na·ker (spin′ə·kər) *n. Naut.* A large jib-shaped sail set on the mainmast of a racing vessel, opposite the mainsail, and used when sailing before the wind. [?]

spin·ner (spin′ər) *n.* **1** One who or that which spins, as a spider or a machine. **2** In angling, a whirling spoon bait.

spin·ner·et (spin′ə·ret′) *n.* **1** An organ, as of spiders and silkworms, for spinning their silky threads. **2** A metal plate pierced with holes through which filaments of plastic material are forced, as in the making of rayon fibers.

spin·ning (spin′ing) *n.* **1** The action of converting fibers

add, āce, câre, pälm; end, ēven; it, īce; odd, ōpen, ôrder; tŏŏk, pōōl; up, bûrn; ə = *a* in *above, u* in *focus;* yōō = *u* in *fuse;* oil; pout; check; go; ring; thin; this; zh, *vision.* < derived from; ? origin uncertain or unknown.

into thread or yarn. **2** The product of spinning. —*adj.* That spins or is used in the process of spinning.

spinning jenny A machine for spinning more than one strand of yarn at a time.

spinning wheel A former household implement for spinning yarn or thread, consisting of a rotating spindle operated by a treadle and flywheel.

spin-off (spin′ôf′, -of′) *n.* **1** A secondary product, application, or result derived from another product or activity; by-product: industrial *spin-offs* from military technological research. **2** The distribution by a corporation to its stockholders of stocks or assets obtained from a subsidiary company. Also **spin′off′**.

Spinning wheel

spi·nose (spī′nōs) *adj.* Bearing, armed with, or having spines. Also **spi·nous** (-nəs). —**spi′nose·ly** *adv.* —**spi·nos′i·ty** (-nos′-ə·tē) *n.*

spin·ster (spin′stər) *n.* **1** A woman who has never married, esp. an elderly one. **2** A woman who spins; a spinner. [< SPIN + -STER] —**spin′ster·hood** *n.* —**spin′ster·ish** *adj.*

spin·y (spī′nē) *adj.* **spin·i·er, spin·i·est** **1** Having spines; thorny. **2** Difficult; perplexing. —**spin′i·ness** *n.*

spiny anteater ECHIDNA.

spir·a·cle (spir′ə·kəl, spī′rə-) *n.* **1** Any of numerous external openings through which air enters the tracheae of insects, etc. **2** The blowhole of a cetacean. [< L *spiraculum* airhole]

spi·ral (spī′rəl) *adj.* **1** Winding about and constantly receding from or advancing toward a center. **2** Winding and advancing; helical. **3** Winding and rising in a spire, as some springs. **4** Continuously increasing or developing. — *n.* **1** *Geom.* Any plane curve formed by a point that moves around a fixed center at a distance that is always increasing. **2** A curve winding like a screw thread. **3** Something wound as a spiral or having a spiral shape. **4** A continuously developing increase or decrease: price *spirals.* —*v.* **·raled** or **·ralled, ·ral·ing** or **·ral·ling** *v.t.* **1** To cause to take a spiral form or course. —*v.i.* **2** To take a spiral form or course. **3** To increase or decrease continuously or sharply, as prices, costs, etc. [< L *spira* coil] —**spi′ral·ly** *adv.* • The use of the intransitive verb (def. 3) without any accompanying modifier almost always means "to increase," as *Prices spiraled in June.* If "to decrease" is meant, an adverb should be used to prevent ambiguity, as *Prices spiraled downward in June.*

spi·rant (spī′rənt) *n. & adj. Phonet.* FRICATIVE. [< L *spirare* breathe]

spire (spīr) *n.* **1** The tapering or pyramidal roof of a tower; also, a steeple. **2** A slender stalk or blade. **3** The summit or tapering end of anything. —*v.* **spired, spir·ing** *v.t.* **1** To furnish with a spire or spires. —*v.i.* **2** To shoot or point up in or as in a spire. **3** To put forth a spire or spires; sprout. [< OE *spīr* stem] —**spired** *adj.*

Spire

spi·re·a (spī·rē′ə) *n.* Any of a genus of ornamental shrubs of the rose family, having small, white or pink flowers. Also **spi·rae′a.** [< Gk. *speira* coil]

spir·it (spir′it) *n.* **1** The animating principle of life and energy in man and animals. **2** SOUL (def. 1). **3** That part of a human being characterized by intelligence, emotion, will, etc.; the mind. **4 a** A supernatural being without a material body, as an angel, demon, etc. **b** Such a being regarded as having a certain character, abode, etc.: an evil *spirit.* **c** A supernatural being regarded as having a visible form, power of speech, etc.; ghost; specter. **5** A state of mind; mood; disposition: low *spirits.* **6** Vivacity, energy, courage, positiveness, etc.: to have *spirit.* **7** A characteristic or prevailing feeling, attitude, motivation, quality, etc.: in the *spirit* of fun; the *spirit* of the Reformation. **8** A person regarded with reference to any specific activity, characteristic, or temper: a

blithe *spirit.* **9** True intent or meaning: the *spirit* of the law. **10** Ardent loyalty or devotion: school *spirit.* **11** *pl.* A strong alcoholic liquor or liquid obtained by distillation. **12** *Usu. pl.* A distilled extract: *spirits* of turpentine. **13** *Usu. pl.* A solution of a volatile principle in alcohol; essence: *spirits* of ammonia. —**the Spirit** HOLY GHOST. — *v.t.* **1** To carry off secretly or mysteriously: with *away, off,* etc. **2** To infuse with spirit or animation; inspirit. —*adj.* **1** Of or pertaining to ghosts or disembodied entities. **2** Operated by the burning of alcohol: a *spirit* lamp. [< L *spiritus* breathing, breath of a god]

spir·it·ed (spir′it·id) *adj.* **1** Full of spirit; lively; animated. **2** Having a specific characteristic, temper, etc.: *high-spirited, mean-spirited.* —**spir′it·ed·ly** *adv.* —**spir′it·ed·ness** *n.*

spir·it·less (spir′it·lis) *adj.* Lacking enthusiasm, energy, or courage. —**spir′it·less·ly** *adv.* —**spir′it·less·ness** *n.*

spirit level An instrument for indicating the horizontal or perpendicular by reference to the position of a bubble of air in a tube of liquid.

spir·it·ous (spir′i·təs) *adj.* SPIRITUOUS.

spir·it·u·al (spir′i·chōo·əl, -ich·əl) *adj.* **1** Of or pertaining to spirit, as distinguished from matter. **2** Of or consisting of spirit; incorporeal. **3** Of, pertaining to, or affecting the highest or purest moral or intellectual qualities of man; not earthly or sensual. **4** Sacred or religious; not lay or temporal. **5** Supernatural. —*n.* **1** Anything pertaining to spirit or to sacred matters. **2** A religious folk song originating among the Negroes of the s U.S. —**spir′i·tu·al·ty** *n.* —**spir′i·tu·al·ly** *adv.* —**Syn.** *adj.* **3** otherworldly, unworldly, unearthly, pure, heavenly, angelic.

spir·it·u·al·ism (spir′i·chōo·əl·iz′əm) *n.* **1** The belief that the spirits of the dead can communicate with the living, usu. through the agency of a person called a medium. **2** *Usu. cap.* A religious movement based on this belief. **3** A philosophy that identifies ultimate reality as basically spiritual. —**spir′i·tu·al·ist** *n.* —**spir′i·tu·al·is′tic** *adj.*

spir·it·u·al·ize (spir′i·chōo·əl·īz′, -ich·ə·līz′) *v.t.* **·ized, ·iz·ing** **1** To make spiritual. **2** To treat as having a spiritual meaning or sense. *Brit. sp.* **·ise.** —**spir′i·tu·al·i·za′tion, spir′·i·tu·al·iz′er** *n.*

spir·it·u·el (spir′i·chōo·el′, *Fr.* spē·rē·tü·el′) *adj.* Characterized by esprit, or wit, and by the higher and finer qualities of the mind generally. [F] —**spir′i·tu·elle′** *adj. Fem.*

spir·it·u·ous (spir′i·chōo·əs, -ich·əs, -ət·əs) *adj.* Containing alcohol, esp. distilled alcohol. —**spir′i·tu·ous·ness** *n.*

spiro- *combining form* Spiral; coiled: *spirochete.* [< Gk. *speira* a coil]

spi·ro·chete (spī′rə·kēt) *n.* **1** Any of a genus of spiral-shaped bacteria usu. found in water. **2** Any similar microorganisms including those which cause syphilis, yaws, etc. Also **spi′ro·chaete.** [< Gk. *speira* coil + *chaitē* bristle] —**spi′ro·che′tal** *adj.* • See BACTERIUM.

spirt (spûrt) *n. & v.* SPURT.

spit[1] (spit) *v.* **spat** or **spit, spit·ting** *v.t.* **1** To eject (saliva, blood, etc.) from the mouth. **2** To throw off, eject, or utter by or as if by spitting: often with *out:* to *spit* out an oath. **3** To light, as a fuse. —*v.i.* **4** To eject saliva from the mouth. **5** To make a hissing noise, as an angry cat. **6** To fall in scattered drops or flakes, as rain or snow. —**spit on** *Informal* To treat with contempt. —*n.* **1** Spittle; saliva. **2** An act of spitting or expectorating. **3** A frothy, spitlike secretion of a spittle insect; also, a spittle insect. **4** A light, scattered fall of snow or rain. **5** *Informal* SPITTING IMAGE. [< OE *spittan*] —**spit′ter** *n.*

spit[2] (spit) *n.* **1** A pointed rod on which meat is skewered and roasted before a fire. **2** A point of low land, or a long, narrow shoal, extending into the water. —*v.t.* **spit·ted, spit·ting** To transfix or impale with or as with a spit. [< OE *spitu*]

spit·ball (spit′bôl′) *n.* **1** Paper chewed in the mouth and shaped into a ball for use as a missile. **2** In baseball, an illegal pitch of a ball moistened on one side with saliva, etc.

spite (spīt) *n.* **1** Malicious bitterness or resentment, usu. resulting in mean or vicious acts. **2** That which is done in spite. —**in spite of** (or **spite of**) In defiance of; notwithstanding. —*v.t.* **spit·ed, spit·ing** To show one's spite toward; vex maliciously; thwart. [Short for DESPITE] —**spite′ful** *adj.* —**spite′ful·ly** *adv.* —**spite′ful·ness** *n.*

spit·fire (spit′fīr′) *n.* A quick-tempered person.

spitting image *Informal* An exact likeness or counterpart. Also **spit and image.**

spit·tle (spit′l) *n.* **1** SALIVA. **2** SPIT¹ *n.* (def. 3). [< OE *spātl*]

spittle insect Any of various jumping insects whose nymphs excrete frothy matter.

spit·toon (spi-tōōn′) *n.* A receptacle for spit; a cuspidor.

spitz (spitz) *n.* One of a breed of small dogs with a tapering muzzle; a Pomeranian. Also **spitz dog.** [G, pointed]

spiv (spiv) *n. Brit. Informal* A flashy chiseler, sharper, or one who lives by his wits. [?]

splash (splash) *v.t.* **1** To dash or spatter (a liquid, etc.) about. **2** To spatter, wet, or soil with a liquid dashed about. **3** To make with splashes: to *splash* one's way. **4** To decorate or mark with or as with splashed colors. **5** To display prominently: His name was *splashed* all over the front page. —*v.i.* **6** To make a splash or splashes. **7** To move, fall, or strike with a splash or splashes. —*n.* **1** The act or noise of splashing liquid. **2** Something splashed, as a spot of liquid. **3** A small area or spot of color, light, etc. **4** A small amount; dash: a *splash* of bitters. **5** A brilliant or ostentatious display. —**make a splash** *Informal* To attract notice or become conspicuous, usu. briefly. [Var. of PLASH] —**splash′er** *n.* —**splash′y** *adj.* (·i·er, ·i·est)

splash·down (splash′doun′) *n.* The landing of a spacecraft, or a part of it, in the seas following its flight.

splat (splat) *n.* A thin, broad piece of wood, as that forming the middle of a chair back. [?]

splat·ter (splat′ər) *v.t. & v.i.* To spatter or splash. —*n.* A spatter; splash. [Blend of SPLASH and SPATTER]

splay (splā) *adj.* **1** Spread or turned outward. **2** Clumsily formed; ungainly. —*n. Archit.* A slanted surface or beveled edge. —*v.t.* **1** To make with a splay. **2** To open to sight; spread out. —*v.i.* **3** To spread out; open. **4** To slant; slope. [Var. of DISPLAY]

splay·foot (splā′foot′) *n.* **1** Abnormal flatness and turning outward of a foot or feet. **2** A foot so affected. —**splay′·foot′ed** *adj.*

spleen (splēn) *n. Anat.* **1** A highly vascular, ductless organ near the stomach of most vertebrates, which modifies, filters, and stores blood. **2** Ill temper; spitefulness: to vent one's *spleen.* [< Gk. *splēn*]

spleen·ful (splēn′fəl) *adj.* Irritable; peevish; ill-tempered. Also **spleen′ish, spleen′y.** —**spleen′ful·ly** *adv.*

splen·did (splen′did) *adj.* **1** Magnificent; imposing. **2** Conspicuously great or illustrious; glorious: a *splendid* achievement. **3** Giving out or reflecting brilliant light; shining. **4** *Informal* Very good; excellent: a *splendid* offer. [< L *splendere* to shine] —**splen′did·ly** *adv.* —**splen′did·ness** *n.* —**Syn. 1** majestic, dazzling, sublime, superb, grand. **2** outstanding, renowned, celebrated, marvelous.

splen·dif·er·ous (splen·dif′ər-əs) *adj. Informal* Exhibiting great splendor; very magnificent: a facetious usage.

splen·dor (splen′dər) *n.* **1** Exceeding brilliance or brightness. **2** Magnificence; greatness; grandeur. *Brit. sp.* ·**dour.** —**splen′dor·ous, splen′drous** *adj.*

sple·net·ic (spli-net′ik) *adj.* Fretfully spiteful; peevish; irritable. —*n.* A peevish person. —**sple·net′i·cal·ly** *adv.*

splen·ic (splen′ik, splē′nik) *adj.* Of or pertaining to the spleen.

splice (splīs) *v.t.* **spliced, splic·ing 1** To unite, as two ropes or parts of a rope, so as to form one continuous piece, by intertwining the strands. **2** To connect, as timbers, by beveling, scarfing, or overlapping at the ends. **3** *Slang* To join in marriage. —*n.* A joining or joint made by splicing. [< MDu. *splissen*] —**splic′er** *n.*

splint (splint) *n.* **1** SPLINTER. **2** A thin, flexible strip of split wood used for basket-making, chair bottoms, etc. **3** An appliance for supporting or immobilizing a part of the body. —

Splices
a. cut. b, c. long.

v.t. To confine, support, or brace, as a fractured limb, with or as with splints. [< MDu. *splinte*]

splin·ter (splin′tər) *n.* **1** A thin, sharp piece of wood, glass, metal, etc., split or torn off lengthwise; a sliver. **2** SPLINTER GROUP. —*v.t. & v.i.* **1** To split into thin sharp pieces or fragments; shatter; shiver. **2** To separate into smaller groups or factions. [< MDu.] —**splin′ter·y** *adj.*

splinter group A group or faction that has broken away from a parent group or organization, usu. because of disagreements.

split (split) *v.* **split, split·ting** *v.t.* **1** To separate into two or more parts by or as by force. **2** To break or divide lengthwise or along the grain. **3** To divide or separate: The mountains *split* the state down the middle. **4** To divide and distribute by portions or shares. **5** To divide into groups or factions. **6** To cast (a vote) for candidates of different parties. **7** To act upon as if by splitting or breaking: Thunder *split* the air. —*v.i.* **8** To break apart or divide lengthwise or along the grain. **9** To become divided through disagreement, etc. **10** To share something with others. **11** *Slang* To leave quickly or abruptly. —**split off 1** To break off by splitting. **2** To separate by or as by splitting. —**split up 1** To separate into parts and distribute. **2** To cease association; separate. —*n.* **1** The act of splitting. **2** The result of splitting, as a crack, tear, rent, etc. **3** A separation into factions or groups, usu. because of disagreements. **4** A sliver; splinter. **5** A share or portion, as of loot or booty. **6** A small, usu. six-ounce, bottle of wine, soft drink, etc. **7** A wooden strip, as of osier, used in weaving baskets. **8** A confection made of a sliced banana, ice cream, syrup, chopped nuts, and whipped cream. **9** A single thickness of a skin or hide split horizontally. **10** In bowling, the position of two or more pins left standing on such spots that a spare is nearly impossible. **11** An acrobatic trick in which the legs are fully extended to the front and back and at right angles to the body. **12** *Slang* A quick departure. —*adj.* **1** Divided or separated longitudinally or along the grain. **2** Divided, as to agreement, unanimity, etc.: a *split* ballot; a *split* decision. [< MDu. *splitten*] —**split′ter** *n.*

split infinitive A verbal phrase in which the sign of the infinitive "to" is separated from its verb by an intervening word, usu. an adverb, as in "to quickly return." • Although this construction is often condemned by purists, it is sometimes justified to avoid ambiguity or awkwardness.

split-lev·el (split′lev′əl) *adj.* Designating a type of dwelling in which the floors of adjoining parts are at different levels, connected by short flights of stairs. —*n.* A split-level dwelling.

split pea A dried, hulled pea that has split naturally into two parts, used mainly for soup.

split personality A psychological condition in which a person intermittently exhibits traits, mannerisms, attitudes, etc., of two or more unrelated personalities.

split second A very small instant of time. —**split′-sec′ond** *adj.*

split ticket A ballot on which the voter has distributed his vote among candidates of different parties.

split·ting (split′ing) *adj.* Acute or extreme in kind or degree: a *splitting* headache.

splotch (sploch) *n.* A spot or daub, as of ink, etc. —*v.t.* To soil or mark with a splotch or splotches. [?] —**splotch′y** *adj.*

splurge (splûrj) *Informal n.* **1** An ostentatious display. **2** An extravagant expenditure. —*v.i.* **splurged, splurg·ing 1** To show off; be ostentatious. **2** To spend money lavishly or wastefully. [?]

splut·ter (splut′ər) *v.i.* **1** To make a series of slight, explosive sounds, or throw off small particles, as meat frying in fat. **2** To speak hastily, confusedly, or incoherently, as from surprise or indignation. —*v.t.* **3** To utter excitedly or confused; sputter. **4** To spatter or bespatter. —*n.* A spluttering noise or utterance. [Blend of SPLASH and SPUTTER] —**splut′ter·er** *n.*

spoil (spoil) *v.* **spoiled** or **spoilt, spoil·ing** *v.t.* **1** To impair or destroy the value, usefulness, beauty, enjoyment, etc., of.

---

2 To weaken or impair the character or personality of, esp. by overindulgence. —*v.i.* **3** To lose normal or useful qualities; specifically, to become tainted or decayed, as food. —*n.* **1** *Usu. pl.* Plunder seized by violence; booty; loot. **2** *Usu. pl.* The jobs in government awarded by a winning political party to its faithful supporters. **3** An object of plunder. **4** Material removed in digging. [< L *spolium* booty] —**spoil′er** *n.* —**Syn.** *v.* **1** damage, injure, harm, mar, mutilate, disfigure, maim, botch, bungle. **2** indulge, humor. **3** decay, decompose, mold, rot, putrefy.

spoil·age (spoi′lij) *n.* **1** The act or process of spoiling. **2** Something spoiled. **3** Waste or loss due to spoilage.

spoils·man (spoilz′mən) *n. pl.* **·men** (-mən) One who works for a political party for spoils.

spoil·sport (spoil′spôrt′, -spōrt′) *n.* A person who spoils the pleasures of others.

spoils system The practice of giving public offices or other awards to supporters of a victorious political party.

spoke[1] (spōk) *n.* **1** One of the members of a wheel which brace the rim by connecting it to the hub. **2** One of the radial handles of a ship's steering wheel. **3** A rung of a ladder. —*v.t.* **spoked, spok·ing** To provide with spokes. [< OE *spāca*]

spoke[2] (spōk) *p.t.* & *a p.p.* of SPEAK.

spo·ken (spō′kən) *p.p.* of SPEAK. —*adj.* **1** Uttered as opposed to written. **2** Having a specified kind of speech: *smooth-spoken.*

spoke·shave (spōk′shāv′) *n.* A wheelwright's tool having a blade set between two handles, used with a drawing motion in rounding and smoothing wooden surfaces.

spokes·man (spōks′mən) *n. pl.* **·men** (-mən) One who speaks in the name and on behalf of another or others. — **spokes′wom′an** (-wōōm′ən) *n. Fem.*

spo·li·a·tion (spō′lē·a′shən) *n.* **1** The act of plundering or robbing. **2** The act of spoiling or damaging. [< L *spoliare* despoil] —**spo′li·a′tor** *n.*

spon·dee (spon′dē) *n.* A metrical foot consisting of two long or accented syllables. [< Gk. *spondeios (pous)* libation (meter)] —**spon·da′ic** (-dā′ik) *adj.*

sponge (spunj) *n.* **1** Any of a phylum of plantlike animals having a fibrous skeleton and growing underwater in large colonies. **2** The light, porous, extremely absorbent skeleton of such animals, used for bathing, cleaning, etc. **3** Any of various absorbent substances or materials used to clean, soak up liquids, etc. **4** Leavened dough. **5** A porous mass of metal, as platinum. **6** *Informal* SPONGER (def. 3). —**throw** (or **toss**) **up** (or **in**) **the sponge** *Informal* To yield; give up; abandon the struggle. —*v.* **sponged, spong·ing** *v.t.* **1** To wipe, wet, or clean with a sponge. **2** To wipe out; expunge; erase. **3** To absorb; suck in, as a sponge does. **4** *Informal* To get by imposing or at another's expense. — *v.i.* **5** To be absorbent. **6** To gather or fish for sponges. **7** *Informal* To be a sponger (def. 3): often with *off* or *on.* [< OE < Gk. *spongos*] —**spong′i·ness** *n.* —**spong′y** *adj.*

sponge cake A light cake of sugar, eggs, flour, etc., but containing no shortening.

spong·er (spun′jər) *n.* **1** One who uses a sponge, as for cleaning, etc. **2** A person or vessel that gathers sponges. **3** *Informal* A person who obtains something from others by taking advantage of their generosity, good nature, etc.

spon·son (spon′sən) *n.* **1** A curved projection from the hull of a vessel or seaplane, to increase its stability or surface area. **2** A similar protuberance on a ship or tank, for storage purposes or for the training of a gun. **3** An air tank built into the side of a canoe, to improve stability and prevent sinking. [?]

spon·sor (spon′sər) *n.* **1** A person who acts as surety for another, as in a loan, debt, etc. **2** A person or group who helps establish or finance something, as a club, activity, etc. **3** GODPARENT. **4** A business firm or enterprise that assumes all or part of the costs of a radio or television program which advertises its product or service. —*v.t.* To act as a sponsor for. [< L *spondere* to pledge] —**spon·so·ri·al** (spon·sôr′ē·əl, -sō′rē-) *adj.* —**spon′sor·ship** *n.*

spon·ta·ne·i·ty (spon′tə·nē′ə·tē, -nā-) *n. pl.* **·ties** **1** The state or quality of being spontaneous. **2** Something spontaneous, as an action, manner of behavior, etc.

spon·ta·ne·ous (spon·tā′nē·əs) *adj.* **1** Acting or arising naturally and without constraint from an inner impulse, prompting, or desire; not planned or contrived. **2** Apparently arising independently without external cause, stimulus, influence, or condition. **3** Produced without human labor; wild; indigenous. [< L *sponte* of free will] —**spon·ta′ne·ous·ly** *adv.* —**spon·ta′ne·ous·ness** *n.*

spontaneous combustion Ignition resulting from the accumulation of heat generated by slow oxidation.

spontaneous generation *Biol.* ABIOGENESIS.

spoof (spōof) *Informal v.t.* & *v.i.* **1** To deceive or hoax; joke. **2** To satirize in a good-natured manner. —*n.* **1** A deception; hoax. **2** A playful parody or satire. [< a game invented by A. Roberts, 1852-1933, English comedian]

spook (spōok) *Informal n.* A ghost; apparition; specter. — *v.t.* **1** To haunt (a person or place). **2** To frighten, disturb, or annoy. **3** To startle or frighten (an animal) into flight, stampeding, etc. [< Du.] —**spook′ish** *adj.*

spook·y (spōo′kē) *adj.* **spook·i·er, spook·i·est** *Informal* **1** Of or like a spook; ghostly; eerie. **2** Frightened; nervous; skittish. —**spook′i·ly** *adv.* —**spook′i·ness** *n.*

spool (spōol) *n.* **1** A cylinder having a projecting rim at each end, on which is wound thread, wire, etc., and a hole from one end to the other, as for mounting on a spindle. **2** The quantity of thread, wire, etc., held by a spool. **3** Anything resembling a spool in shape or purpose. —*v.t.* To wind on a spool. [< MLG *spole*]

spoon (spōon) *n.* **1** A utensil having a shallow, generally ovoid bowl and a handle, used in preparing, serving, or eating food. **2** Something resembling a spoon or its bowl. **3** A metallic lure attached to a fishing line: also **spoon bait**. **4** A wooden golf club with lofted face and comparatively short, stiff shaft. —*v.t.* **1** To lift up or out with a spoon. **2** To play or hit (a ball) with a weak shoving or scooping movement. —*v.i.* **3** To spoon a ball. **4** *Informal* To kiss and caress, as lovers. [< OE *spōn* chip]

spoon·bill (spōon′bil′) *n.* **1** A wading bird related to the ibis, having a spoon-shaped bill. **2** A duck having the bill broad and flattened; a shoveler. —**spoon′-billed′** *adj.*

spoon·drift (spōon′drift) *n.* SPINDRIFT. [< *spoon*, var. of SPUME + DRIFT]

spoon·er·ism (spōo′nə·riz′əm) *n.* The unintentional transposition of sounds or of parts of words in speaking, as in "half-*w*armed *f*ish" for "half-*f*ormed *w*ish". [< W. A. *Spooner*, 1844-1930, of New College, Oxford]

Spoonbill *def. 1*

spoon·feed (spōon′fēd′) *v.t.* **fed, ·feed·ing** **1** To feed with a spoon. **2** To pamper; spoil. **3** To present (information) in such a manner that little or no thought, initiative, etc., is required of the recipient. **4** To instruct or inform (a person or group) in this manner.

spoon·ful (spōon′fōol′) *n. pl.* **·fuls** As much as a spoon will hold.

spoon·y (spōo′nē) *adj.* **spoon·i·er, spoon·i·est** *Informal* Sentimental or silly, as in lovemaking. Also **spoon′ey.**

spoor (spōor) *n.* Footprints, droppings, or other traces of a wild animal. —*v.t.* & *v.i.* To track by or follow a spoor. [< MDu.]

spo·rad·ic (spə·rad′ik) *adj.* **1** Occurring infrequently; occasional. **2** Not widely diffused; occurring in isolated cases: a *sporadic* infection. Also **spo·rad′i·cal.** [< Gk. *sporas* scattered] —**spo·rad′i·cal·ly** *adv.* —**spo·rad′i·cal·ness** *n.* — **Syn.** **1** irregular, fitful, spasmodic, intermittent.

spo·ran·gi·um (spô·ran′jē·əm, spō-) *n. pl.* **·gi·a** (-jē·ə) A sac or single cell in which spores are produced. [< SPOR(O)- + Gk. *angeion* a vessel] —**spo·ran′gi·al** *adj.*

spore (spôr, spōr) *n.* **1** The reproductive body in plants that bear no seeds, as bacteria, algae, ferns, etc. **2** A minute body that develops into a new individual; any minute organism; a germ. —*v.i.* **spored, spor·ing** To develop spores: said of plants. [< Gk. *spora* seed, sowing] —**spo·ra·ceous** (spô·rā′shəs, spō-) *adj.*

spore case SPORANGIUM.

sporo- *combining form* Seed; spore: *sporophyte.*

spo·ro·phyll (spôr′ə·fil, spō′rə-) *n.* A leaf, or modified leaf, which bears sporangia. Also **spo′ro·phyl.**

spo·ro·phyte (spôr′ə·fīt, spō′rə-) *n.* The spore-bearing generation in plants which have a distinct reproductive phase.

spor·ran (spor′ən, spôr′-) *n.* A skin pouch, usu. with the fur on, worn in front of the kilt by Highlanders. [< Scots Gaelic *sporan*] • See KILT.

sport (spôrt, spōrt) *n.* 1 A diversion; pastime. 2 A particular game or physical activity pursued for diversion, esp. an outdoor or athletic game, as baseball, football, track, tennis, swimming, etc. 3 A spirit of jesting or raillery. 4 An object of derision; a laughingstock; butt. 5 An animal or plant that exhibits sudden variation from the normal type; a mutation. 6 *Informal* A gambler. 7 *Informal* One who lives a fast, gay, or flashy life. 8 A person characterized by his observance of the rules of fair play, or by his ability to get along with others: a good *sport.* 9 *Archaic* Amorous or sexual play. —*v.i.* 1 To amuse oneself; play; frolic. 2 To participate in games. 3 To make sport or jest; trifle. 4 To vary suddenly or spontaneously from the normal type; mutate. 5 *Archaic & Regional* To make love, esp. in a trifling manner. —*v.t.* 6 *Informal* To display or wear ostentatiously. —*adj.* Of, pertaining to, or fitted for sports; also, appropriate for casual wear: a *sport* coat: also **sports.** [Var. of DISPORT] —**sport′ful·ly** *adv.*

sport·ing (spôr′ting, spōr′-) *adj.* 1 Pertaining to, engaged in, or used in athletic games or field sports. 2 Characterized by or conforming to the spirit of sportsmanship. 3 Interested in or associated with gambling or betting. —**sport′ing·ly** *adv.*

sporting chance *Informal* A chance involving the likelihood of loss but also the possibility of success.

spor·tive (spôr′tiv, spōr′-) *adj.* 1 Relating to or fond of sport or play; frolicsome. 2 Interested in, active in, or related to sports. —**spor′tive·ly** *adv.* —**spor′tive·ness** *n.*

sports·man (spôrts′mən, spōrts′-) *n. pl.* **·men** (-mən) 1 One who pursues field sports, esp. hunting and fishing. 2 One who abides by a code of fair play. —**sports′man·like′, sports′man·ly** *adj.*

sports·man·ship (spôrts′mən·ship, spōrts′-) *n.* 1 The art or practice of field sports. 2 Honorable or sportsman-like conduct.

sports·wear (spôrts′wâr′, spōrts′-) *n.* Clothes made for informal or outdoor activities.

sports·wom·an (spôrts′wŏŏm′ən, spōrts′-) *n. pl.* **·wom·en** (-wim′in) A woman who participates in sports.

sport·y (spôr′tē, spōr′-) *adj.* **sport·i·er, sport·i·est** *Informal* 1 Relating to or characteristic of a sport. 2 Colorful; gay; loud, as clothes. —**sport′i·ly** *adv.* —**sport′i·ness** *n.*

spor·ule (spôr′yōōl, spor′-) *n.* A little spore. [Dim. of SPORE]

spot (spot) *n.* 1 A particular place or locality. 2 Any small portion of a surface differing as in color from the rest, as a mark, speck, blotch, etc. 3 A stain or blemish on character; a fault; a reproach. 4 A food fish of the Atlantic coast of the U.S. 5 One of the figures or pips with which a playing card is marked; also, a card having (a certain number of) such marks: the five *spot* of clubs. 6 *Slang* Paper money having a specified value: a ten *spot.* 7 *Chiefly Brit.* A portion or bit: a *spot* of tea. 8 *Informal* Place or allotted time, as on a list, schedule, etc. 9 *Informal* Position, job, or situation. 10 *Informal* SPOTLIGHT. 11 *Slang* NIGHTCLUB. 12 *Informal* A brief commercial or announcement, usu. scheduled between regular radio or television programs. —**hit the spot** *Slang* To gratify an appetite or need. —**in a spot** *Slang* In a difficult or embarrassing situation; in trouble. —**on the spot** 1 At once; immediately. 2 At the very place of occurrence. 3 *Slang* **a** In trouble, danger, difficulty, etc. **b** Accountable for some action, mistake, etc. —*v.* **spot·ted, spot·ting** *v.t.* 1 To mark or soil with spots. 2 To remove spots from. 3 To place or locate in or at a designated spot or spots. 4 To recognize or detect; identify; see. 5 To sully or disgrace, as the reputation of. 6 To schedule or list. 7 To shine a spotlight on. 8 *Informal* To yield (an advantage or handicap) to someone. —*v.i.* 9 To become marked or soiled with spots. 10 To make a stain or discoloration. —*adj.* 1 Paid or ready to be paid for at

once: *spot* cash. 2 Ready for instant delivery following sale. 3 Involving cash payment only. 4 Made or selected at random or according to a prearranged plan: a *spot* check. 5 Broadcast between regular programs: a *spot* announcement. 6 Televised or broadcast on the spot or from a specific spot. [< LG] —**spot′ta·ble** *adj.*

spot·check (spot′chek′) *v.t. & v.i.* To sample or examine at random or according to a prearranged plan.

spot·less (spot′lis) *adj.* 1 Free from spots, dirt, etc.: a *spotless* house. 2 Pure; unsullied: a *spotless* life. —**spot′less·ly** *adv.* —**spot′less·ness** *n.*

spot·light (spot′līt′) *n.* 1 A bright, powerful beam of light used to illuminate a person, group, building, etc. 2 A device that produces such a light. 3 Public notice or acclaim. —*v.t.* To light up or make prominent with or as with a spotlight.

spot·ted (spot′id) *adj.* 1 Discolored in spots; soiled. 2 Characterized or marked by spots.

spotted fever Any of various infectious diseases marked by fever and skin rash.

spot·ter (spot′ər) *n.* 1 In drycleaning, one who removes spots. 2 A detective hired to watch for theft, etc., as in a department store. 3 Anyone who keeps watch for something.

spot·ty (spot′ē) *adj.* **·ti·er, ·ti·est** 1 Having many spots. 2 Uneven or irregular, as in quality, performance, etc. —**spot′ti·ly** *adv.* —**spot′ti·ness** *n.*

spous·al (spou′zəl) *adj.* Pertaining to marriage. —*n.* Marriage; espousal.

spouse (spouz, spous) *n.* A partner in marriage; one's husband or wife. [< L *sponsus,* pp. of *spondere* to promise, betroth]

spout (spout) *v.i.* 1 To pour out copiously and forcibly, as a liquid under pressure. 2 To speak pompously, somewhat angrily, or at length. —*v.t.* 3 To cause to pour or shoot forth. 4 To utter pompously, somewhat angrily, or at length. —*n.* 1 A tube, trough, etc., for the discharge of a liquid. 2 A continuous stream of fluid. [ME *spoute*] —**spout′er** *n.*

spp. species (plural).

sprain (sprān) *n.* 1 A violent straining or twisting of the ligaments surrounding a joint. 2 The condition due to such strain. —*v.t.* To cause a sprain in. [< OF *espreindre* to squeeze]

sprang (sprang) A *p.t.* of SPRING.

sprat (sprat) *n.* Any of various small herringlike fish. [< OE *sprott*]

sprawl (sprôl) *v.i.* 1 To sit or lie with the limbs stretched out ungracefully. 2 To be stretched out ungracefully, as the limbs. 3 To move with awkward motions of the limbs. 4 To spread out in a straggling manner, as handwriting, vines, etc. —*v.t.* 5 To cause to spread or extend awkwardly or irregularly. —*n.* 1 The act or position of sprawling. 2 An unplanned or disorderly group, as of houses, spread out over a broad area: urban *sprawl.* [< OE *sprēawlian* move convulsively] —**sprawl′er** *n.*

spray[1] (sprā) *n.* 1 Liquid dispersed in fine particles. 2 An instrument for discharging small particles of liquid; an atomizer. 3 Something like a spray of liquid. —*v.t.* 1 To disperse (a liquid) in fine particles. 2 To apply spray to. —*v.i.* 3 To send forth or scatter spray. 4 To go forth as spray. [< MDu. *sprayen*] —**spray′er** *n.*

spray[2] (sprā) *n.* 1 A small branch bearing dependent branchlets or flowers. 2 Any ornament or pattern like this. [ME]

spread (spred) *v.* **spread, spread·ing** *v.t.* 1 To open or unfold to full width, extent, etc., as wings, sail, a map, etc. 2 To distribute over a surface, esp. in a thin layer. 3 To cover with something. 4 To force apart or farther apart. 5 To distribute over a period of time or among a group. 6 To make more widely known, active, etc.; promulgate or diffuse: to *spread* a rumor. 7 To set (a table, etc.), as for a meal. 8 To arrange or place on a table, etc., as a meal or feast. 9 To set forth or record in full. —*v.i.* 10 To be extended or expanded; increase in size, width, etc. 11 To be distributed or dispersed, as over a surface or area; scatter.

12 To become more widely known, active, etc. **13** To be forced farther apart; separate. —*n.* **1** The act of spreading. **2** The limit, distance, or extent of spreading, expansion, etc. **3** A cloth or covering for a table, bed, etc. **4** Something used for spreading: a cheese *spread.* **5** *Informal* A feast or banquet; also, a table with a meal set out on it. **6** A prominent presentation in a periodical. **7** Two pages of a magazine or newspaper facing each other and covered by related material; also, the material itself. —*adj.* Expanded; outstretched. [<OE *spraedan*] —**spread'er** *n.*

spread-ea·gle (spred'ē'gəl) *adj.* **1** Having the arms and legs spread wide apart. **2** Extravagant; bombastic: said of excessively patriotic oratory in the U.S. —*v.* **-ea·gled, -ea·gling** *v. t.* **1** To force to assume a spread-eagle position.

spread eagle **1** The figure of an eagle with extended wings, used as an emblem of the U.S. **2** Any position or movement resembling this, as a figure in skating.

spread·sheet (spred'shēt') *n.* A kind of computer program that processes numerical data for detailed financial calculations of various kinds.

spree (sprē) *n.* **1** A period of heavy drinking. **2** Any period of fun, activity, etc. [?]

sprig (sprig) *n.* **1** A shoot or sprout of a plant. **2** An ornament in this form. **3** An heir or offspring of a family, esp. a young man. [ME *sprigge*] —**sprig'ger** *n.*

spright·ly (sprīt'lē) *adj.* **-li·er, -li·est** Full of animation and spirits; vivacious; lively. —*adv.* Spiritedly; briskly; gaily. [<*spright,* var. of SPRITE] —**spright'li·ness** *n.*—*Syn. adj.* animated, brisk, bustling, cheerful, nimble, spry, quick.

spring (spring) *v.* **sprang** or **sprung, sprung, spring·ing** *v.i.* **1** To move or rise suddenly and rapidly; leap; dart. **2** To move suddenly as by elastic reaction; snap. **3** To happen or occur suddenly or immediately: An angry retort *sprang* to his lips. **4** To work or snap out of place, as a mechanical part. **5** To become warped or bent, as boards. **6** To rise above surrounding objects. **7** To come into

Springs

being: New towns have *sprung* up. **8** To originate; proceed, as from a source. **9** To develop; grow, as a plant. **10** To be descended: He *springs* from good stock. —*v.t.* **11** To cause to spring or leap. **12** To cause to act, close, open, etc., unexpectedly or suddenly, as by elastic reaction: to *spring* a trap. **13** To cause to happen, become known, or appear suddenly: to *spring* a surprise. **14** To leap over; vault. **15** To start (game) from cover; flush. **16** To explode (a mine). **17** To warp or bend; split. **18** To cause to snap or work out of place. **19** To force into place, as a beam or bar. **20** To suffer (a leak). **21** *Slang* To obtain the release of (a person) from prison or custody. —*n.* **1** *Mech.* An elastic device that yields under stress, and returns to normal form when the stress is removed. **2** Elastic quality or energy. **3** The act of flying back from a position of tension; recoil. **4** A cause of action; motive. **5** Any source or origin. **6** A flow or fountain, as of water. **7** The act of leaping up or forward suddenly; a jump; bound. **8** The season in which vegetation starts anew; in the north temperate zone, the three months of March, April, and May; in the astronomical year, the period from the vernal equinox to the summer solstice. —*adj.* **1** Of or pertaining to the season of spring. **2** Resilient; acting like or having a spring. **3** Hung on springs. **4** Coming from or housing a spring of water. [<OE *springan*]

spring·board (spring'bôrd', -bōrd') *n.* **1** A flexible board used to give impetus, as to a dive, acrobatic leap, etc. **2** Anything that gives impetus, as to an activity.

spring·bok (spring'bok') *n. pl.* **-bok** or **-boks** A small African gazelle noted for its ability to leap high in the air. Also **spring'buck'** (-buk'). [<Afrikaans]

spring chicken **1** A young chicken. **2** *Informal* A young person, esp. a girl: usu. with a negative: She's no *spring chicken.*

Springbok

spring·er (spring'ər) *n.* **1** One who or that which springs. **2** A young chicken. **3** A spaniel valuable for flushing game; also **springer spaniel.**

spring fever The listlessness that overtakes a person with the first warm days of spring.

spring tide **1** A high tide occurring about new moon and full moon. **2** Any great wave of feeling, etc.

Springer spaniel

spring·time (spring'tīm') *n.* **1** The season of spring. **2** Any early or youthful period. Also **spring'tide'** (-tīd').

spring·y (spring'ē) *adj.* **spring·i·er, spring·i·est 1** Elastic; resilient. **2** Having many water springs; wet. —**spring'i·ly** *adv.* —**spring'i·ness** *n.*

sprin·kle (spring'kəl) *v.* **·kled, ·kling** *v.t.* **1** To scatter in drops or small particles. **2** To scatter over or upon: *Sprinkle* the top with flour. —*v.i.* **3** To fall or rain in scattered drops. —*n.* **1** The act of sprinkling. **2** A small quantity. **3** A light rain. [ME *sprenkelen*] —**sprin'kler** *n.*

sprin·kling (spring'kling) *n.* **1** The act of one who or that which sprinkles. **2** A small amount or number: a *sprinkling* of people.

sprint (sprint) *n.* **1** The act of sprinting. **2** A short race run at top speed. **3** A brief period, as of speed. —*v.i.* To go or run fast, as in a sprint. [<Scand.] —**sprint'er** *n.*

sprit (sprit) *n.* A small spar reaching diagonally from a mast to the peak of a fore-and-aft sail. [<OE *sprēot* pole] • See SPRITSAIL.

sprite (sprīt) *n.* **1** A fairy, elf, or goblin. **2** A small, elflike person. **3** A ghost. [<L *spiritus*]

sprit·sail (sprit'səl, sprit'sāl') *n.* A sail extended by a sprit.

sprock·et (sprok'it) *n.* **1** A projection, as on the rim of a wheel, for engaging with the links of a chain. **2** A wheel bearing such projections: also **sprocket wheel.** [?]

sprout (sprout) *v.i.* **1** To put forth shoots; begin to grow; germinate. **2** To develop or grow rapidly. —*v.t.* **3** To cause to sprout. **4** To remove shoots from. —*n.* **1** A new shoot or bud on a plant. **2** Something like or suggestive of a sprout, as a young person. **3** *pl.* BRUSSELS SPROUTS. [<OE *sprūtan*]

a. spritsail. b. sprit.

spruce[1] (sproōs) *n.* **1** Any of a genus of evergreen trees of the pine family, having needle-shaped leaves and pendulous cones. **2** The wood of any of these trees. [<Med. L *Prussia* Prussia]

spruce[2] (sproōs) *adj.* **spruc·er, spruc·est** Smart, trim, and neat in appearance. —*v.* **spruced, spruc·ing** *v.t.* **1** To make spruce: often with *up.* —*v.i.* **2** To make oneself spruce: usu. with *up.* [<earlier *spruce,* a kind of superior Prussian leather] —**spruce'ly** *adv.* —**spruce'ness** *n.*

sprung (sprung) *p.p.* & *a p.t.* of SPRING.

spry (sprī) *adj.* **spri·er** or **spry·er, spri·est** or **spry·est** Quick and active; agile. [<Scand.] —**spry'ly** *adv.* —**spry'ness** *n.*

spt. seaport.

spud (spud) *n.* **1** A spadelike tool with narrow blade or prongs for uprooting weeds. **2** *Informal* A potato. —*v.t.* **spud·ded, spud·ding** To remove, as weeds, with a spud. [ME *spuddle*]

spume (spyoōm) *n.* Froth; foam; scum. —*v.i.* **spumed, spum·ing** To foam; froth. [<L *spuma* foam] —**spu'mous, spum'y** *adj.*

spu·mo·ni (spyoō·mō'nē) *n.* A frozen dessert of Italian origin, containing ice cream in layers of various colors and usu. candied fruit and nuts. Also **spu·mo'ne.** [<L *spuma* foam]

spun (spun) *p.t.* & *p.p.* of SPIN.

spunk (spungk) *n.* **1** A slow-burning tinder, as punk. **2** *Informal* Mettle; pluck; courage. [<L *spongia* sponge]

spunk·y (spungk'ē) *adj.* **spunk·i·er, spunk·i·est** *Informal* Spirited; courageous. —**spunk'i·ly** *adv.* —**spunk'i·ness** *n.*

spur (spûr) *n.* **1** Any of various pricking or goading instruments worn on the heel of a horseman. **2** Anything that incites or urges; incentive. **3** A part or attachment like a spur, as a steel gaff fastened to a gamecock's leg, a climbing iron used by linemen, etc. **4** A stiff, sharp spine on the legs or wings of certain birds. **5** A crag or ridge extending laterally from a mountain or range. **6** A branch of a railroad, lode, etc. **7** A buttress or other offset from a wall. **8** A brace reinforcing a rafter or post. **9** A tubular extension of a part of a flower, usu. containing the nectar. **—on the spur of the moment** Hastily; impulsively. **—win one's spurs** To gain recognition or reward, esp. for the first time. **—v.** spurred, spur·ring *v.t.* **1** To prick or urge with or as with spurs. **2** To furnish with spurs. **3** To injure or gash with the spur, as a gamecock. **—v.i.** **4** To spur one's horse. **5** To hasten; hurry. [< OE *spura*] **—spur'rer** *n.*

spurge (spûrj) *n.* Any of several flowering shrubs yielding a milky juice of bitter taste. [< OF *espurgier* to purge]

spu·ri·ous (spyŏŏr'ē·əs) *adj.* **1** Seemingly real or genuine, but actually not; false; counterfeit. **2** Illegitimate, as of birth. [< L *spurius*] **—spu'ri·ous·ly** *adv.* **—spu'ri·ous·ness** *n.*

spurn (spûrn) *v.t.* **1** To reject with disdain; scorn. **2** To strike with the foot; kick. **—v.i.** **3** To reject something with disdain. **—n.** The act or an instance of spurning. [< OE *spurnan*] **—spurn'er** *n.*

spurred (spûrd) *adj.* Wearing or having spurs.

spurt (spûrt) *n.* **1** A liquid gush of liquid. **2** Any sudden, short-lived outbreak, as of anger, energy, etc. **—v.i.** **1** To come out in a jet; gush forth. **2** To make a sudden, forceful effort. **—v.t.** **3** To squirt. [< OE *spryttan* come forth]

sput·nik (spŏŏt'nik, sput'-) *n.* An artificial earth satellite, esp. the first, called Sputnik I, launched in October, 1957, by the U.S.S.R. [Russ., lit., fellow traveler]

sput·ter (sput'ər) *v.i.* **1** To throw off solid or fluid particles in a series of slight explosions. **2** To speak excitedly and incoherently. **3** To make crackling or popping sounds, as burning wood, frying fat, etc. **—v.t.** **4** To throw off in small particles. **5** To utter excitedly or incoherently **—n.** **1** The act or sound of sputtering; esp. excited talk; jabbering. **2** That which is thrown out in sputtering. [< Du. *sputteren*] **—sput'ter·er** *n.*

spu·tum (spyŏŏ'təm) *n. pl.* **·ta** (-tə) Mucus from the respiratory tract, usu. mixed with saliva; expectorated matter. [< L *spuere* to spit]

spy (spī) *n. pl.* **spies 1** One who is hired to get secret information from or about an enemy, another government, etc.; a secret agent. **2** One who watches another or others secretly. **—v.** spied, spy·ing *v.i.* **1** To keep watch closely or secretly; act as a spy. **2** To make careful examination; pry: with *into*. **—v.t.** **3** To observe stealthily and usu. with hostile intent: often with *out*. **4** To catch sight of; see; espy. [< OF *espier* espy]

spy·glass (spī'glas', -gläs') *n.* A small telescope.

Sq. Squadron; Square (street).

sq. square; sequence; the following (L *sequentia*).

sq. ft. square foot; square feet.

sq. in. square inch(es).

sq. mi. square mile(s).

squab (skwob) *n.* **1** A young nestling pigeon about four weeks old. **2** A fat, short person. **—adj.** **1** Fat and short; squat. **2** Unfledged or but half-grown. [< Scand.]

squab·ble (skwob'əl) *v.i.* **·bled**, **·bling** To engage in a petty quarrel; bicker. **—n.** A petty quarrel. [< Scand.] **—squab'·bler** *n.*

squad (skwod) *n.* **1** A small group of persons organized to do a special job; esp., the smallest tactical unit in the infantry of the U.S. Army. **2** A team: a football *squad.* **—v.t.** **squad·ded, squad·ding 1** To form into a squad or squads. **2** To assign to a squad. [< L *quattuor* four]

squad car An automobile used by police for patrolling, and equipped with radiotelephone for communicating with headquarters.

squad·ron (skwod'rən) *n.* **1** An assemblage of war vessels smaller than a fleet. **2** A division of a cavalry regiment. **3** The basic unit of the U.S. Air Force, usu. consisting of two or more flights operating as a unit. **4** Any regularly arranged or organized group. **—v.t.** To arrange in a squadron or squadrons. [< Ital. *squadra* squad]

squal·id (skwol'id) *adj.* **1** Having a dirty, neglected, or poverty-stricken appearance. **2** Sordid; base. [< L *squalere* be foul] **—squal'id·ly** *adv.* **—squal'id·ness, squa·lid·i·ty** (skwo·lid'ə·tē) *n.* **—Syn. 1** foul, filthy, wretched, untidy.

squall¹ (skwôl) *n.* A loud, screaming outcry. **—v.i.** To cry loudly; scream; bawl. [< Scand.] **—squall'er** *n.*

squall² (skwôl) *n.* **1** A sudden, violent burst of wind, often accompanied by rain or snow. **2** A brief disturbance or commotion. **—v.i.** To blow a squall. [< Scand.] **—squall'y** *adj.* (**·i·er, ·i·est**)

squal·or (skwol'ər) *n.* The state of being squalid; wretched filth or poverty.

squa·ma (skwā'mə) *n. pl.* **·mae** (-mē) A thin, scalelike structure; a scale. [L] **—squa'mate** (-māt), **squa'mose, squa'mous** *adj.*

squan·der (skwon'dər) *v.t.* To spend (money, time, etc.) wastefully. **—n.** Prodigality; wastefulness. [?] **—squan'·der·er** *n.* **—squan'der·ing·ly** *adv.* **—Syn. v.** dissipate, waste, lavish, run through, throw away.

square (skwâr) *n.* **1** A parallelogram having four equal sides and four right angles. **2** Any object, part, or surface that is square or nearly so, as one of the spaces on a checkerboard. **3** An L- or T-shaped instrument by which to test or lay out right angles. **4** An open area bordered by streets or formed by their intersection. **5** A town or city block; also, the distance between one street and the next. **6** *Math.* The product of a number or element multiplied by itself. **7** *Slang* A person of excessively conventional tastes or habits. **—on the square 1** At right angles. **2** *Informal* Honest, fair, true, etc.; also, honestly, fairly, truly, etc. **—out of square** Not at right angles; obliquely. **—adj.** squar·er, squar·est **1** Having four equal sides and four right angles. **2** Approaching a square or a cube in form: a *square* box. **3** Forming a right angle: a *square* nook. **4** Adapted to forming squares or computing in squares: a *square* measure. **5** Being a square with each side of specified length: two inches *square.* **6** Perfectly adjusted, aligned, balanced, etc. **7** Even; settled: said of debts, etc. **8** Tied, as a score. **9** Honest; fair; just. **10** *Informal* Solid; full; satisfying: a *square* meal. **11** Broad; solid; muscular: a *square* build. **12** *Slang* Excessively conventional or conservative; not sophisticated. **13** *Naut.* At right angles to the mast and keel. **—v.** squared, squar·ing *v.t.* **1** To make square. **2** To shape or adjust so as to form a right angle. **3** To mark with or divide into squares. **4** To test for the purpose of adjusting to a straight line, right angle, or plane surface. **5** To bring to a position suggestive of a right angle: *Square* your shoulders. **6** To make satisfactory settlement or adjustment of: to *square* accounts. **7** To make equal, as a game score. **8** To cause to conform; adapt: to *square* one's opinions to the times. **9** To reconcile or set right. **10** *Math.* **a** To multiply (a number or element) by itself. **b** To determine the area of. **11** *Slang* To bribe. **—v.i.** **12** To be at right angles. **13** To conform; agree; harmonize: with *with.* **—square away 1** *Naut.* To set (the yards) at right angles to the keel. **2** To put into good order; make ready. **3** SQUARE OFF. **—square off** To assume a position for attack or defense; prepare to fight. **—square up** To adjust or settle satisfactorily. **—adv.** **1** So as to be square, or at right angles. **2** Honestly; fairly. **3** Directly; firmly. [< OF *esquarre*] **—square'ness, squar'er** *n.* • See PARALLELOGRAM.

square dance Any dance, as a quadrille, in which the couples form sets in squares.

square knot A common knot, formed of two overhand knots. • See KNOT.

square·ly (skwâr'lē) *adv.* **1** In a direct or straight manner: He looked her *squarely* in the eyes. **2** Honestly; fairly. **3** Plainly; unequivocally. **4** In a square form: *squarely* built. **5** At right angles (to a line or plane).

square measure A unit or system of units for measuring areas. • See MEASURE.

square-rigged (skwâr'rigd') *adj.* Having the principal sails extended by horizontal yards at right angles to the masts.

square-rig·ger (skwâr'rig'ər) *n.* A square-rigged ship.

square root *Math.* A number or element whose square is equal to a given quantity.

square sail A four-sided sail usu. rigged on a horizontal yard set at right angles to the mast.

square shooter *Informal* One who acts honestly and justly.

squash[1] (skwosh) *v.t.* **1** To squeeze or press into a pulp or soft mass; crush. **2** To quell or suppress. **3** *Informal* To silence or humiliate quickly and thoroughly; squelch. — *v.i.* **4** To be smashed or squashed. **5** To make a splashing or sucking sound. — *n.* **1** A crushed mass. **2** The sudden fall of a heavy, soft, or bursting body; also, the sound made by such a fall. **3** The sucking, squelching sound made by walking through ooze or mud. **4** Either of two games played on an indoor court with rackets and a ball. In one (**squash rackets**), a slow rubber ball is used; in the other (**squash tennis**), a livelier, smaller ball. **5** *Brit.* A fruit-flavored beverage. — *adv.* With a squelching, oozy sound. [< L *ex-* thoroughly + *quassare* crush] —**squash′er** *n.*

squash[2] (skwosh) *n.* **1** Any of various edible gourds usu. cooked and served as a vegetable. **2** The plant that bears it. [< Algon.]

squash·y (skwosh′ē) *adj.* **squash·i·er, squash·i·est 1** Soft and moist. **2** Easily squashed. —**squash′i·ly** *adv.* —**squash′·i·ness** *n.*

squat (skwot) *v.* **squat·ted** or **squat, squat·ting** *v.i.* **1** To sit on the heels or hams, or with the legs near the body. **2** To crouch or cower down, as to avoid being seen. **3** To settle on a piece of land without title or payment. **4** To settle on government land in accordance with certain government regulations that will eventually give title. — *v.t.* **5** To cause (oneself) to squat. — *adj.* **squat·ter, squat·test 1** Short and thick. **2** Being in a squatting position. — *n.* A squatting attitude or position. [< OF *esquatir*] —**squat′ter** *n.*

squat·ty (skwot′ē) *adj.* **·ti·er, ·ti·est** Short and thickset; squat.

squaw (skwô) *n.* An American Indian woman or wife.

squawk (skwôk) *v.i.* **1** To utter a shrill, harsh cry, as a parrot. **2** *Slang* To utter loud complaints or protests. — *n.* **1** A shrill, harsh cry. **2** *Slang* A shrill complaint. [Imit.] — **squawk′er** *n.*

squeak (skwēk) *n.* **1** A thin, sharp, penetrating sound. **2** *Informal* An escape, esp. in the phrase **a narrow** (or **close**) **squeak.** — *v.i.* **1** To make a squeak. **2** *Informal* To let out information; squeal. **3** To succeed or otherwise progress after narrowly averting failure: to *squeak* through. — *v.t.* **4** To utter or effect with a squeak. **5** To cause to squeak. [Prob. < Scand.] —**squeak′y** *adj.* (**·i·er, ·i·est**) —**squeak′i·ly** *adv.* —**squeak′i·ness** *n.*

squeal (skwēl) *v.i.* **1** To utter a sharp, shrill, somewhat prolonged cry. **2** *Slang* To turn informer; betray an accomplice or a plot. — *v.t.* **3** To utter with or cause to make a squeal. — *n.* A shrill, prolonged cry, as of a pig. [Imit.] — **squeal′er** *n.*

squeam·ish (skwē′mish) *adj.* **1** Easily disgusted or shocked. **2** Overly scrupulous. **3** Nauseated; also, easily nauseated. [< AF *escoymous*] —**squeam′ish·ly** *adv.* — **squeam′ish·ness** *n.*

squee·gee (skwē′jē) *n.* **1** An implement having a straight-edged strip of rubber, etc., used for removing water from window panes, etc., after washing them. **2** *Phot.* A smaller similar implement, often made in the form of a roller, used for pressing a film closer to its mount, etc. — *v.t.* **·geed, ·gee·ing** To use a squeegee on. [Var. of SQUEEZE]

squeeze (skwēz) *v.* **squeezed, squeez·ing** *v.t.* **1** To press hard upon; compress. **2** To extract something from by pressure: to *squeeze* oranges. **3** To get or draw forth by pressure: to *squeeze* juice from apples. **4** To force, push, maneuver, etc., by or as by squeezing: He *squeezed* his car into the narrow space. **5** To oppress, as with burdensome taxes. **6** To exert pressure upon (someone) to act as one desires, as by blackmailing. **7** To embrace; hug. — *v.i.* **8** To apply pressure. **9** To force one's way; push: with *in, through,* etc. **10** To be pressed; yield to pressure. — **squeeze by, through,** etc. *Informal* To avoid failure, defeat, trouble, etc., by the narrowest margin. — *n.* **1** The act or process of squeezing; pressure. **2** A handclasp; also, an embrace; hug. **3** A quantity of something, as juice, extracted or expressed. **4** The state or condition of being

squeezed; crush. **5** A time of trouble, scarcity, difficulty, etc. **6** SQUEEZE PLAY. **7** *Informal* Pressure exerted for the extortion of money or favors; also, financial pressure. [< OE *cwēsan* to crush] —**squeez′a·ble** *adj.* —**squeez′er** *n.*

squeeze play 1 In baseball, a play in which the batter bunts the ball so that a man on third base may score by starting while the pitcher is about to deliver the ball. **2** Any attempt or maneuver to realize some end or goal by coercion.

squelch (skwelch) *v.t.* **1** To crush; squash. **2** *Informal* To subdue utterly; silence, as with a crushing reply. — *v.i.* **3** To make or move with a splashing or sucking noise. — *n.* **1** A noise, as made when walking in wet boots. **2** A heavy fall or blow. **3** *Informal* A crushing retort or reply. [Imit.] —**squelch′er** *n.*

squib (skwib) *n.* **1** A brief news item. **2** A short witty or satirical speech or writing. **3** A broken firecracker that burns with a spitting sound. — *v.i.* **squibbed, squib·bing** *v.i.* **1** To write or use squibs. **2** To fire a squib. **3** To explode or sound like a squib. — *v.t.* **4** To attack with squibs; lampoon. [?]

squid (skwid) *n.* One of various ten-armed marine cephalopods with a long, slender body, ink sac, and broad caudal fins. [?]

squill (skwil) *n.* **1** A bulbous plant of the lily family. **2** Its bulb, containing various medicinal and poisonous alkaloids. [< Gk. *skilla* sea onion]

Squid

squint (skwint) *v.i.* **1** To look with half-closed eyes, as into bright light. **2** To look with a side glance; look askance. **3** To be cross-eyed. **4** To incline or tend: with *toward,* etc. — *v.t.* **5** To hold (the eyes) half shut, as in glaring light. **6** To cause to squint. — *adj.* **1** Affected with strabismus. **2** Looking obliquely or askance; indirect. — *n.* **1** An affection of the eyes in which their axes are differently directed; strabismus. **2** The act or habit of squinting. [?] —**squint′er** *n.*

squire (skwīr) *n.* **1** A knight's attendant; an armor bearer. **2** In England, the chief landowner of a district. **3** In the U.S., a title applied esp. to village lawyers and justices of the peace. **4** A gentleman who escorts a lady in public; a gallant. — *v.t.* **squired, squir·ing** To be a squire to (someone); escort. [Var. of ESQUIRE]

squirm (skwûrm) *v.i.* **1** To bend and twist the body; wriggle; writhe. **2** To show signs of pain or distress. — *n.* A squirming motion. [?] —**squirm′y** *adj.* (**·i·er, ·i·est**)

squir·rel (skwûr′əl *Brit.* skwir′əl) *n.* **1** Any of various slender rodents with a long bushy tail, living mainly in trees and feeding chiefly on nuts. The **red squirrel**, the **gray squirrel**, and the **fox squirrel** are North American types. **2** One of various related rodents, as the woodchuck, ground squirrel, etc. **3** The fur of a squirrel. — *v.t.* **squir·reled** or **·relled, squir·rel·ing** or **·rel·ling** To take away and hide (something) for possible use in the future: often with *away.* [< Gk. *skia* shadow + *oura* tail]

Gray squirrel

squirt (skwûrt) *v.i.* **1** To come forth in a thin stream or jet; spurt out. — *v.t.* **2** To eject (water or other liquid) forcibly and in a jet. **3** To wet or bespatter with a squirt or squirts. — *n.* **1** The act of squirting or spurting; also, a jet of liquid squirted forth. **2** A syringe or squirt gun. **3** *Informal* A youngster, esp. a mischievous one. [ME *swirten*] —**squirt′er** *n.*

squirt gun An instrument or toy shaped like a gun and used for squirting.

squish (skwish) *v.t. & v.i.* SQUASH[1]. — *n.* A squashing sound. [Var. of SQUASH[1]] —**squish′y** (**·i·er, ·i·est**) *adj.*

sq. yd. square yard(s).

Sr strontium.

Sr. Senior; Señor; Sir; Sister.

sr steradian.

Sra. Señora.

Sri Lank·a (srē langk′ə) An island south of India, an independent state of the Commonwealth of Nations, 25,-332 sq. mi., cap. Colombo: formerly Ceylon. •See map at INDIA.

S.R.O. standing room only.

Srta. Señorita.

SS, SS. Nazi special police (G *Schutzstaffel*).

SS, S.S., S/S steamship.

SS. Saints.

S.S. Sunday School; written above (L *supra scriptum*).

ss, ss., s.s. shortstop.

SSA, S.S.A. Social Security Administration.

SSB, S.S.B. Social Security Board.

SSE, S.S.E., sse, s.s.e. south-southeast.

S.Sgt., S/Sgt Staff Sergeant.

SSR, S.S.R. Soviet Socialist Republic.

SSS Selective Service System.

SST supersonic transport.

SSW, S.S.W., ssw, s.s.w. south-southwest.

St. Saint; Strait; Street.

St., st. statute(s); stratus (clouds).

st. stanza; stet; stitch; stone (weight); street.

s.t. short ton.

Sta. Santa; Station.

sta. station; stationary.

stab (stab) *v.* **stabbed, stab·bing** *v.t.* **1** To pierce with a pointed weapon; wound, as with a dagger. **2** To thrust (a dagger etc.), as into a body. **3** To penetrate; pierce. —*v.i.* **4** To thrust or wound with or as with a pointed weapon. —*n.* **1** A thrust or wound made with a pointed weapon. **2** A sharp painful or poignant sensation: a *stab* of grief. **3** *Informal* An effort; attempt. [ME *stabbe*] —**stab'ber** *n.*

sta·bile (stā'bil, -bīl) *adj.* **1** Stable; fixed. **2** *Med.* Not affected by moderate heat. —*n.* (stā'bēl) A piece of stationary abstract sculpture, usu. of sheet metal, wood, wire, etc. [< *stabilis*]

sta·bil·i·ty (stə-bil'ə-tē) *n. pl.* **·ties 1** The condition of being stable; steadiness. **2** Steadfastness of purpose or resolution; constancy. **3** *Physics* The ability of an object or system to resume equilibrium after a disturbance.

sta·bi·lize (stā'bə-līz) *v.* **·lized, ·liz·ing** *v.t.* **1** To make stable. **2** To keep from fluctuating, as currency: to *stabilize* prices. —*v.i.* **3** To become stable. —**sta'bi·li·za'tion** *n.*

sta·bi·liz·er (stā'bə-lī'zər) *n.* Something that stabilizes, esp. an auxiliary airfoil of an aircraft. • See AIRPLANE.

sta·ble¹ (stā'bəl) *adj.* **·bler, ·blest 1** Standing firmly in place; not easily moved, shaken, or overthrown; fixed. **2** Marked by firmness of purpose; steadfast. **3** Having durability or permanence; abiding. **4** Resistant to chemical change. **5** *Physics* Of, having, or exhibiting stability. [< L *stabilis*] —**sta'bly** *adv.* —**sta'ble·ness** *n.*

sta·ble² (stā'bəl) *n.* **1** A building for lodging and feeding horses or cattle. **2** Racehorses belonging to a particular owner; also, the personnel who take care of such racehorses. **3** *Informal* Those performers, writers, athletes, etc., who are under the same management or agency. — *v.t. & v.i.* **·bled, ·bling** To put or lodge in or as in a stable. [< L *stabulum*]

sta·ble·boy (stā'bəl-boi') *n.* A boy employed in a stable.

stac·ca·to (stə-kä'tō) *adj.* **1** *Music* Played, or to be played, with brief pauses between each note. **2** Marked by abrupt, sharp sounds or emphasis: a *staccato* style of speaking. —*adv.* So as to be staccato. —*n.* Something staccato. [< Ital. *staccare* detach]

stack (stak) *n.* **1** A large, orderly pile of unthreshed grain, hay, or straw, usu. conical. **2** Any pile or heap of things arranged somewhat neatly or systematically. **3** A group of rifles (usu. three) set upright and supporting one another. **4** *pl.* That part of a library where most of the books are shelved; also, the bookshelves. **5** A chimney; smokestack; also, a collection of chimneys or flues. **6** *Informal* A great amount; plenty. —*v.t.* **1** To gather or pile up in a stack. **2** To plan or arrange dishonestly beforehand so as to assure a certain result or outcome. **3** To assign (an airplane) to a pattern of designated altitudes while awaiting clearance to land: often with *up*. —**stack up 1** To total. **2** To compare: often with *against*. [< ON *stakkr*] —**stack'er** *n.*

sta·di·um (stā'dē-əm) *n. pl.* **·di·ums,** *for def.* **2 ·di·a** (-dē-ə) **1** A large modern structure for sports events, having seats arranged in tiers. **2** In ancient Greece and Rome: **a** A course for footraces, with banked seats for spectators. **b** A measure of length, equaling 606.75 feet. [< Gk. *stadion,* a measure of length]

staff (staf) *n. pl.* **staffs;** *also for defs.* **1–3 staves** (stāvz). **1** A stick or piece of wood carried for some special purpose, as an aid in climbing, as a cudgel, or as an emblem of authority. **2** A shaft or pole that forms a support or handle: the *staff* of a flag. **3** A stick used in measuring or testing, as a surveyor's leveling rod. **4** A group of people who function as assistants or advisors to a leader, director, president, etc. **5** A body of persons working together in some specific task, occupation, or enterprise: the hospital *staff;* the editorial *staff.* **6** *Mil.* A body of officers not having command but attached in an executive or advisory capacity to a military unit as assistants to the officer in command. **7** *Music* The five horizontal lines and the spaces between them on which notes are written. —*v.t.* To provide (an office, etc.) with a staff. [< OE *stæf* stick]

staff·er (staf'ər) *n.* A member of a staff, as of a periodical.

staff officer An officer serving on a military staff.

stag (stag) *n.* **1** The adult male of various deer, esp. the red deer. **2** A castrated bull or boar. **3** A man at a party, dance, etc., who is unaccompanied by a woman. **4** A social gathering for men only. —*adj.* Of or for men only. [< OE *stagga*]

Stag head

stage (stāj) *n.* **1** The platform on which plays, operas, etc., are given. **2** The area on the adjacent sides and in back of this platform, including the wings, backstage, etc. **3** The profession of acting: with *the.* **4** Any of the activities or occupations having to do with the theater or drama: with *the.* **5** Any raised platform or floor, esp. a scaffold for workmen. **6** A horizontal level, section, or story of a building. **7** The scene of, or plan of action for, an event or events. **8** A center of attention. **9** A distinct period or step in some development, progress, or process. **10** A water level: flood *stage.* **11** A regular stopping place on a journey, esp. a journey by stagecoach. **12** STAGECOACH. **13** The distance traveled between two stopping points; leg. **14** *Electronics* One of a series of modules through which a signal passes. **15** One of the series of propulsion units used by a rocket vehicle. —*v.t.* **staged, stag·ing 1** To put or exhibit on the stage. **2** To plan, conduct, or carry out: to *stage* a rally. **3** To organize, perform, or carry out so as to appear authentic, legitimate, or spontaneous, when actually not so: The entire incident was *staged* for the press photographers. [< OF *estage*]

stage·coach (stāj'kōch') *n.* A horse-drawn, passenger and mail vehicle having a regular route between towns.

stage·craft (stāj'kraft', -kräft') *n.* Skill in writing or staging plays.

stage door A door to a theater which leads to the stage or behind the scenes.

stage·hand (stāj'hand') *n.* A worker in a theater who handles scenery and props, etc.

stage-man·age (stāj'man'ij) *v.t.* **·aged, ·ag·ing 1** To be a stage manager for. **2** To direct, organize, or carry out so as to achieve maximum effectiveness, publicity, etc.

stage manager One who assists a director in the production of a play and, during its performance, superintends the stage area, actors, and technicians.

stage-struck (stāj'struk') *adj.* **1** Fascinated by the theater. **2** Longing to become an actor or actress.

stage whisper A loud whisper, as one uttered on the stage for the audience to hear.

stag·fla·tion (stag'flā'shən) *n. Econ.* Inflation combined with abnormally slow economic growth, resulting in high unemployment. [< *stag(nation)* + *(in)flation*]

stag·ger (stag'ər) *v.i.* **1** To move unsteadily; totter; reel. **2** To become less confident or resolute; waver; hesitate. — *v.t.* **3** To cause to stagger. **4** To affect strongly; overwhelm, as with surprise or grief. **5** To place in alternating rows or groups. **6** To arrange or distribute so as to prevent congestion or confusion: to *stagger* lunch hours. —*n.* The act of staggering. **—the (blind) staggers** Any of various diseases of domestic animals marked by staggering, falling, etc. [< ON *stakra*] **—stag′ger·er** *n.* **—stag′ger·ing·ly** *adv.*

stag·ing (stā′jing) *n.* **1** A scaffolding or temporary platform. **2** The act of putting a play, opera, etc., upon the stage. **3** The act of jettisoning a rocket stage from a space vehicle. **4** The business of running stagecoaches. **5** Traveling by stagecoach.

stag·nant (stag′nənt) *adj.* **1** Standing still; not flowing: said of water. **2** Foul from long standing. **3** Dull; inert; sluggish. [< L *stagnum* a pool] **—stag′nan·cy** *n.* **—stag′nant·ly** *adv.*

stag·nate (stag′nāt) *v.i.* **·nat·ed, ·nat·ing** To be or become stagnant. **—stag·na′tion** *n.*

stag·y (stā′jē) *adj.* **stag·i·er, stag·i·est** **1** Of or suited to the stage. **2** Excessively theatrical; artificial. **—stag′i·ly** *adv.* **—stag′i·ness** *n.*

staid (stād) *adj.* Sedate; sober; serious. [Orig. p.t. and p.p. of STAY¹] **—staid′ly** *adv.* **—staid′ness** *n.*

stain (stān) *n.* **1** A discoloration or spot from foreign matter. **2** A dye or thin pigment used in staining. **3** A moral blemish or taint. **—v.t.** **1** To make a stain upon; discolor; soil. **2** To color with a dye or stain. **3** To bring a moral stain upon; blemish. **—v.i.** **4** To take or impart a stain. [< OF *desteindre* to deprive of color] **—stain′a·ble** *adj.* **—stain′er** *n.*

stained glass Glass colored by the addition of pigments, usu. in the form of metallic oxides which are fused throughout the glass or burned onto its surface. **—stained′-glass′** *adj.*

stain·less (stān′lis) *adj.* **1** Without a stain. **2** Resistant to stain. **3** Made of stain-resistant materials. **—n.** Tableware made of stainless steel. **—stain′less·ly** *adv.*

stainless steel A corrosion-resistant steel alloyed with chromium and often other elements, esp. nickel.

stair (stâr) *n.* **1** A step, or one of a series of steps, for mounting or descending from one level to another. **2** *Usu. pl.* A series of steps. [< OE *stæger*]

stair·case (stâr′kās′) *n.* A flight of stairs, complete with the supports, balusters, etc.

stair·way (stâr′wā′) *n.* One or more flights of stairs.

stair·well (stâr′wel′) *n.* A vertical shaft enclosing a staircase.

stake (stāk) *n.* **1** A stick or post, as of wood or metal, sharpened for driving into the ground. **2** A post to which a person is bound to be burned alive; also, death by burning at the stake. **3** A post or stick set upright in the floor of a car or wagon, to confine loose material. **4** *Often pl.* Something wagered or risked, as the money bet on a race. **5** *Often pl.* A prize in a contest. **6** An interest or share, as in an enterprise. **7** GRUBSTAKE. **—at stake** In hazard or jeopardy. **—v.t.** **staked, stak·ing** **1** To fasten or support by means of a stake. **2** To mark the boundaries of with stakes: often with *off* or *out*. **3** *Informal* To wager; risk. **4** *Informal* To supply with money, equipment, etc.; back. [< OE *staca*]

sta·lac·tite (stə·lak′tīt′, stal′ək-) *n.* **1** An elongated, hanging cone of calcium carbonate formed by slow dripping from the roof of a cave. **2** Any similar formation. [< Gk. *stalaktitos* dripping] **—stal·ac·tit·ic** (stal′ək·tit′ik) or **·i·cal** *adj.*

sta·lag·mite (stə·lag′mīt′, stal′·əg-) *n.* **1** A usu. conical mound deposited on a cave floor by dripping from a stalactite. **2** Any similar formation. [< Gk. *stalagmos* a dripping] **—stal·ag·mit·ic** (stal′əg·mit′ik) or **·i·cal** *adj.* • See STALACTITE.

a. stalactite.
b. stalagmite.

stale (stāl) *adj.* **stal·er, stal·est** **1** Having lost freshness; slightly changed or deteriorated, as air, beer, old bread, etc. **2** Lacking in interest from age or familiarity; trite: a *stale* joke. **3** Lacking effectiveness, energy, spontaneity, etc., from too little or too much activity or practice. **—v.t. & v.i.** **staled, stal·ing** To make or become stale. [?] **—stale′ly** *adv.* **—stale′ness** *n.*

stale·mate (stāl′māt′) *n.* **1** In chess, a position in which a player can make no move without putting his king in check. The result is a draw. **2** Any tie, standstill, or deadlock. **—v.t.** **·mat·ed, ·mat·ing** **1** To put into a condition of stalemate. **2** To bring to a standstill. [< AF *estale* a fixed position + MATE²]

stalk¹ (stôk) *n.* **1** The stem or axis of a plant. **2** Any support on which an organ is borne, as a pedicel. **3** A supporting part or stem: the *stalk* of a quill. **4** Any stem or main axis, as of a goblet. [ME *stalke*] **—stalked, stalk′less** *adj.*

stalk² (stôk) *v.i.* **1** To approach game, etc., stealthily. **2** To walk in a stiff or haughty manner. **—v.t.** **3** To approach (game, etc.) stealthily. **4** To invade or permeate: Famine *stalked* the countryside. **—n.** **1** The act of stalking game. **2** A stalking step or walk. [< OE *bestealcian* move stealthily] **—stalk′er** *n.*

stalk·ing-horse (stô′king·hôrs′) *n.* **1** A horse behind which a hunter conceals himself in stalking game. **2** Anything serving to conceal one's intention.

stall (stôl) *n.* **1** A compartment in which a horse or bovine animal is confined and fed. **2** A small booth or compartment in a street, market, etc., for the sale or display of small articles. **3** A partially enclosed seat, as in the choir of a cathedral. **4** *Brit.* A seat very near the stage of a theater. **5** A small compartment, as for showering. **6** An evasive or delaying action. **7** A condition in which a motor temporarily stops functioning. **8** A condition in which an airplane loses the air speed needed to produce sufficient lift to keep it flying. **—v.t.** **1** To place or keep in a stall. **2** To bring to a standstill; halt the progress of. **3** To stop, usu. unintentionally, the operation or motion of. **4** To put (an airplane) into a stall. **5** To cause to stick fast in mud, snow, etc. **—v.i.** **6** To come to a standstill; stop, esp. unintentionally. **7** To stick fast in mud, snow, etc. **8** To make delays; be evasive: to *stall* for time. **9** To live or be kept in a stall. **10** *Aeron.* To go into a stall. [< OE *steall*]

stall-feed (stôl′fēd′) *v.t.* **-fed, -feed·ing** To feed (cattle) in a stall so as to fatten them. **—stall′-fed′** *adj.*

stal·lion (stal′yən) *n.* An uncastrated male horse. [< OHG *stal* stable]

stal·wart (stôl′wərt) *adj.* **1** Strong and robust. **2** Resolute: determined. **3** Brave; courageous. **—n.** **1** An uncompromising partisan, as in politics. **2** One who is stalwart. [< OE *stæl* place + *wierthe* worth] **—stal′wart·ly** *adv.* **—stal′wart·ness** *n.*

sta·men (stā′mən) *n. pl.* **sta·mens** or **stam·i·na** (stam′ə·nə) One of the pollen-bearing organs of a flower, consisting of a filament supporting an anther. [L, warp, thread] **—stam·i·nal** (stam′·ə·nəl) *adj.*

stam·i·na (stam′ə·nə) *n.* Strength and endurance, as in withstanding hardship or difficulty. [L, pl. of *stamen* warp, thread] **—stam′i·nal** *adj.*

stam·i·nate (stam′ə·nit, -nāt) *adj.* **1** Having stamens but no pistil, as male flowers. **2** Having stamens.

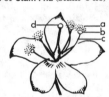

Stamen (a, b, c)
a. pollen. b. anther.
c. filament. d. pistil.

stam·mer (stam′ər) *v.t. & v.i.* To speak or utter with nervous repetitions or prolongations of a sound or syllable, and involuntary pauses. **—n.** The act or habit of stammering. [< OE *stamerian*] **—stam′mer·er** *n.*

stamp (stamp) *v.t.* **1** To strike heavily with the sole of the foot. **2** To bring down (the foot) heavily and noisily. **3** To affect in a specified manner by or as by stamping with the foot: to *stamp* out opposition. **4** To make, form, cut out, etc., with a stamp or die: often with *out*: to *stamp* out a circle from the steel. **5** To imprint or impress with a die, stamp, etc.: to *stamp* the date on a letter. **6** To fix or imprint permanently: The deed was *stamped* on his memory. **7** To characterize; brand: to *stamp* a story false. **8** To affix an official seal, stamp, etc., to. **9** To crush or pulverize, as ore. **—v.i.** **10** To strike the foot heavily on the ground. **11** To walk with heavy, resounding steps. **—n.** **1** The act of stamping. **2** A machine or tool, as a die, that cuts out or shapes a form. **3** An implement or device that imprints a design, character, mark, etc., on something; also, the design, character, mark, etc., so imprinted. **4** A printed device of paper to be attached to something to show that a tax or fee has been paid: a postage *stamp*. **5** TRADING STAMP. **6** A specific impression or effect: the *stamp* of genius. **7** Characteristic quality or form; kind; sort: I dislike men of his *stamp*. [ME *stampen*] —**stamp′er** *n.*

stam·pede (stam·pēd′) *n.* **1** A sudden starting and rushing off through panic: said primarily of a herd of cattle, horses, etc. **2** Any sudden, impulsive rush or movement of a crowd, as of a mob. **3** A spontaneous mass impulse, trend, or movement, as toward the support of a political candidate. **4** *Can.* RODEO. —*v.* **·ped·ed, ·ped·ing** *v.t.* **1** To cause a stampede in. —*v.i.* **2** To engage in a stampede. [< Am. Sp. *estampar* to stamp] —**stam·ped′er** *n.*

stamping ground A favorite or habitual gathering place.

stance (stans) *n.* **1** Mode of standing; posture, esp. with reference to the placing of the feet. **2** Attitude; point of view: a moral *stance*. [< L *stans* pr. p. of *stare* to stand]

stanch (stanch, stänch) *v.t.* **1** To stop or check the flow of (blood, tears, etc.). **2** To stop the flow of blood from (a wound). **3** To check or put an end to. —*adj.* STAUNCH. [< OF *estanchier* to halt] —**stanch′er** *n.* • The spelling *stanch* is usu. preferred for the verb in both England and the U.S., and *staunch* for the adjective. Many writers, however, use one or the other spelling for both.

stan·chion (stan′shən) *n.* **1** An upright bar forming a principal support. **2** A device that fits around a cow's neck, used to restrain movement in a stall. —*v.t.* **1** To provide, restrain, or support with stanchions. [< OF *estanchon*]

stand (stand) *v.* **stood, stand·ing** *v.i.* **1** To assume or maintain an erect position on the feet. **2** To be in a vertical position: The oars *stood* in the corner. **3** To measure a specified height when standing: He *stands* six feet. **4** To assume a specified position: to *stand* aside. **5** To be situated; have position or location; lie: The factory *stands* on a hill. **6** To have or be in a specified state, condition, or relation: We *stand* to gain everything by not fighting; He *stood* in fear of his life. **7** To assume an attitude for defense or offense: *Stand* and fight! **8** To maintain one's attitude, opinions, etc.: *Stand* firm. **9** To be or exist in a printed or written form: Photograph the letter just as it *stands*. **10** To remain unimpaired, unchanged, or valid: My decision still *stands*. **11** To collect and remain: Tears *stood* in her eyes. **12** To be of a specified rank or class: He *stands* third. **13** To stop or pause; halt. **14** *Naut.* To take a direction; steer. **15** *Brit.* To be a candidate, as for election. —*v.t.* **16** To place upright; set in an erect position. **17** To put up with; endure; tolerate. **18** To be subjected to; undergo: He must *stand* trial. **19** To withstand or endure successfully: to *stand* the test of time. **20** To carry out the duty of: to *stand* watch. **21** *Informal* **a** To treat: I'll *stand* you to a drink. **b** To bear the expense of: to *stand* a dinner. —**stand a chance** To have a chance. —**stand by 1** To stay near and be ready to help or operate. **2** To help; support. **3** To abide by; make good; adhere to. **4** To remain passive, as when help is needed. **5** *Telecom.* To keep tuned in, as for the continuance of an interrupted transmission. —**stand for 1** To represent; symbolize. **2** To put up with; tolerate. —**stand in for** To act as a substitute for. — **stand off 1** To keep at a distance. **2** To fail to agree or comply. **3** To put off; evade, as a creditor. —**stand on 1** To be based on or grounded in; rest. **2** To insist on observance of: to *stand on* ceremony. **3** *Naut.* To keep on the same tack or course. —**stand out 1** To stick out; project or protrude. **2** To be prominent or conspicuous. **3** To be outstanding, remarkable, etc. **4** To refuse to consent or agree. — **stand pat 1** In poker, to play one's hand as dealt, without drawing new cards. **2** To resist change. —**stand to reason** To conform to reason. —**stand up 1** To stand erect. **2** To withstand wear, criticism, analysis, etc. **3** *Slang* To fail, usu. intentionally, to keep an appointment with. —**stand up for** To side with; take the part of. —**stand up to** To confront courageously; face. —*n.* **1** The act or condition of standing, esp. of halting or stopping, as: **a** A stopping or halt, as in a retreat, to fight back or resist. **b** A stop for a performance, made by a theatrical company while on

tour; also, the place stopped at. **2** The place or location where one stands or is assigned to stand; position. **3** Any place where something stands: a taxi *stand*. **4** An opinion, attitude, point of view, etc.: to take a *stand*. **5** A structure upon which persons may sit or stand, as: **a** *Often pl.* A series of raised seats or benches, as at an athletic contest. **b** A platform: a reviewing *stand*. **c** A small platform in court from which a witness testifies. **6** A small table. **7** A rack or other structure for holding something: an umbrella *stand*. **8** A stall, counter, or the like where merchandise is displayed or sold. **9** A vertical growth of trees or plants. [< OE *standan*] —**stand′er** *n.*

stan·dard (stan′dərd) *n.* **1** A flag, ensign, or banner, used as an emblem of a government, body of men, head of state, etc. **2** A figure or image adopted as an emblem or symbol. **3** Something established and generally accepted as a model, example, or test of excellence, attainment, etc.; criterion. **4** Something established as a measure or reference of weight, extent, quantity, quality, or value. **5** In coinage, the established proportion by weight of pure gold or silver and an alloy. **6** The measurable basis of value in a monetary system. **7** An upright structure, timber, post, etc., used as a support. **8** A musical composition whose popularity has become firmly established over the years. **9** A plant growing on a vigorous, unsupported, upright stem. —*adj.* **1** Having the accuracy or authority of a standard; serving as a gauge or criterion. **2** Of recognized excellence, popularity, reliability, etc.: the *standard* repertoire of symphonies. **3** Not unusual or special in any way; ordinary; typical; regular: *standard* procedure; *standard* equipment. [< OF *estandard* banner]

stan·dard-bear·er (stan′dərd·bâr′ər) *n.* **1** The person who carries the flag or standard of a group, esp. of a regiment or other military body. **2** The official leader or representative of a group, as a presidential nominee.

standard gauge 1 A railroad track width of 56½ inches, considered as standard. **2** A railroad having such a gauge. —**stan′dard-gauge′** *adj.*

stan·dard·ize (stan′dər·dīz) *v.t.* **·ized, ·iz·ing** To make conform to, regulate, or test by a standard. —**stan′dard·i·za′tion, stan′dard·iz′er** *n.*

standard of living The average manner of day-to-day living of a country, group, or person, with reference to food, housing, clothing, comforts, etc.

standard time The official time for any region or country. Mean solar time is reckoned, east or west, from the meridian of Greenwich, England, each time zone comprising a sector of 15 degrees of longitude and representing a time interval of one hour. In the conterminous U.S., the four time zones, **Eastern Standard Time, Central Standard Time, Mountain Standard Time,** and **Pacific Standard Time** represent the 75th, 90th, 105th, and 120th meridians west of Greenwich, and are accordingly 5, 6, 7, and 8 hours earlier than Greenwich time. Therefore, noon in London corresponds to 7 A.M. in New York, 6 A.M. in Chicago, 5 A.M. in Denver, and 4 A.M. in San Francisco.

stand·by (stand′bī′) *n. pl.* **·bys 1** A person who can be relied on, as in an emergency. **2** Something that always pleases, is always effective, etc. **3** A person or thing waiting and ready to replace another person or thing; substitute.

stand·ee (stan·dē′) *n.* A person who must stand for lack of chairs or seats, as at a theater or on a train.

stand-in (stand′in′) *n.* **1** A person who substitutes for a motion-picture or television performer while lights are arranged, camera angles set, etc. **2** Any substitute for another person.

stand·ing (stan′ding) *adj.* **1** That is upright or erect. **2** Continuing for regular or permanent use; not special or temporary: a *standing* rule. **3** Stagnant; not flowing: *standing* water. **4** Begun or done while standing: a *standing* ovation; a *standing* high jump. **5** Not in use; idle: *standing* machinery. **6** Not movable. —*n.* **1** The act or condition of one who stands. **2** A place to stand in. **3** Relative place or position, as on a graded list of excellence, achievement, etc. **4** Reputation, esp. good reputation. **5** Duration; continuance: a feud of long *standing*.

standing room Place in which to stand, as in a theater when the seats are all occupied.

stand·off (stand′ôf′, -of′) *n.* **1** A draw or tie, as in a game. **2** A counterbalancing or neutralizing effect. —*adj.* **1** That stands off. **2** STANDOFFISH.

stand·off·ish (stand′ôf′ish) *adj.* Aloof; cool. —**stand′off′·ish·ly** *adv.* —**stand′off′ish·ness** *n.*

stand·out (stand′out′) *Informal n.* A person or thing that is unusually good or excellent. —*adj.* Unusually good or excellent.

stand·pat (stand′pat′) *adj. Informal* Resistant to change; conservative. —**stand′pat′ter, stand′pat′tism** *n.*

stand·pipe (stand′pīp′) *n.* A high vertical pipe or water tower, as at a reservoir, into which the water is pumped to create pressure.

stand·point (stand′point′) *n.* Point of view; position; stance.

stand·still (stand′stil′) *n.* A stopping; cessation; halt.

stand·up (stand′up′) *adj.* **1** Having an erect or vertical position: a *stand-up* collar. **2** Done, consumed, etc., while standing.

stan·hope (stan′hōp) *n.* A light, open, one-seated carriage. [< F. *Stanhope*, 1787–1864, English clergyman]

stank (stangk) *p.t.* of STINK.

stan·nic (stan′ik) *adj. Chem.* Of, pertaining to, or containing tin, esp. in its higher valence. [< L *stannum* tin]

stan·nous (stan′əs) *adj.* Of, pertaining to, or containing tin, esp. in its lower valence. [< L *stannum* tin]

stan·za (stan′zə) *n.* A certain number of lines of verse grouped together and forming a definite division of a poem. [Ital., room, stanza] —**stan·za·ic** (stan·zā′ik) *adj.*

sta·pes (stā′pēz) *n. pl.* **sta·pes** or **sta·pe·des** (stə-pē′dēz, stā′pə·dēz′) *Anat.* The innermost small bone of the middle ear of mammals. [LL, a stirrup] —**sta·pe·di·al** (stə-pē′dē·əl) *adj.*

staph (staf) *n.* STAPHYLOCOCCUS.

staph·y·lo·coc·cus (staf′ə·lō·kok′əs) *n. pl.* **·coc·ci** (-kok′sī, -sē, -ī, -ē) Any of a group of spherical bacteria occurring singly, in pairs, or in irregular clusters and often acting as infective agents. [< Gk. *staphylos* bunch of grapes + *kokkos* a berry] —**staph′y·lo·coc′cic** (-kok′sik, -kok′ik) *adj.* • See BACTERIUM.

sta·ple¹ (stā′pəl) *n.* **1** A principal commodity or product of a country or region. **2** A chief item, element, or main constituent of anything. **3** A product that is constantly sold and used, as sugar or salt. **4** Raw material. **5** The corded or combed fiber of cotton, wool, or flax, with reference to its length. **6** A source of supply; storehouse. —*adj.* **1** Regularly and constantly produced, consumed, or sold. **2** Main; chief. —*v.t.* **·pled, ·pling** To sort or classify according to length, as wool fiber. [< MDu. *stapel* market]

sta·ple² (stā′pəl) *n.* A U-shaped piece of metal or thin wire, having pointed ends and driven into a surface, as wood or paper, to serve as a fastening. —*v.t.* **·pled, ·pling** To fix or fasten by a staple or staples. [< OE *stapol* post]

sta·pler¹ (stā′plər) *n.* **1** A person who staples wool, etc. **2** A person who deals in staple goods.

sta·pler² (stā′plər) *n.* A device for driving staples into a surface.

star (stär) *n.* **1** *Astron.* Any of the numerous celestial objects that emit radiant energy, including visible light, generated by nuclear reactions. **2** Loosely, any of the luminous bodies regularly seen as points of light in the night sky. **3** A conventional figure having five or more radiating points. **4** Something resembling such a figure, as an emblem or device. **5** An asterisk (*). **6** A person of outstanding talent or accomplishment and a quality of personality that attracts wide public interest or attention. **7** A performer who plays the leading role in a play, opera, etc. **8** *Often pl.* Any of the planets or their configuration considered as influencing one's fate. **9** Fortune; destiny. —*v.* **starred, star·ring** *v.t.* **1** To set, mark, or adorn with stars. **2** To mark with an asterisk. **3** To present as a star in an entertainment. —*v.i.* **4** To be prominent or brilliant. **5** To play the leading part; be the star. —*adj.* **1** Of or pertaining to a star or stars. **2** Prominent; brilliant: a *star* football player. [< OE *steorra*] —**star′less, star′like** *adj.*

star·board (stär′bərd) *n.* The right-hand side of a vessel or aircraft as one faces the front or forward. —*adj.* Of, pertaining to, or on the starboard. —*adv.* Toward the starboard side. —*v.t.* To put, move, or turn (the helm) to the starboard side. [< OE *steorbord* steering side]

starch (stärch) *n.* **1** A complex, insoluble carbohydrate produced by photosynthesis and usu. stored in roots, tubers, seeds, etc. **2** A white, powdery substance consisting of purified starch extracted from potatoes, corn, etc. **3** Any starchy foodstuff. **4** A fabric stiffener made of starch suspended in water. **5** A stiff or formal manner. **6** *Informal* Energy; vigor. —*v.t.* To apply starch to; stiffen with or as with starch. [< OE *stearc* stiff]

starch·y (stär′chē) *adj.* **starch·i·er, starch·i·est 1** Stiffened with starch; stiff. **2** Primly formal or stiff. **3** Containing a large proportion of starch: a *starchy* vegetable. —**starch′·i·ly** *adv.* —**starch′i·ness** *n.*

star-crossed (stär′krôst′, -krost′) *adj.* Doomed; ill-fated: a *star-crossed* love affair.

star·dom (stär′dəm) *n.* **1** The status of a person who is a star. **2** Stars of the stage, screen, etc., collectively.

stare (stâr) *v.* **stared, star·ing** *v.i.* **1** To gaze fixedly, usu. with the eyes open wide, as from admiration, fear, or insolence. **2** To be conspicuously or unduly apparent; glare. —*v.t.* **3** To gaze fixedly at. **4** To affect in a specified manner by a stare: to *stare* a person into silence. —**stare down** To gaze back fixedly (at a person) until he turns his eyes away. —**stare one in the face** To be perfectly plain or obvious. —*n.* A steady, fixed gaze. [< OE *starian*] —**star′er** *n.*

star·fish (stär′fish′) *n. pl.* **·fish** or **·fish·es** Any of various radially symmetrical echinoderms with a star-shaped body having five or more arms.

star·gaze (stär′gāz′) *v.i.* **·gazed, ·gaz·ing 1** To gaze at or study the stars. **2** To daydream. —**star′gaz′·er** *n.*

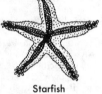

stark (stärk) *adj.* **1** Deserted; barren; bleak: a *stark* landscape. **2** Severe; difficult: *stark* measures. **3** With little or no ornamentation, color, etc.: a *stark* room. **4** Blunt; grim; pitiless: *stark* reality. **5** Complete; utter: *stark* madness. **6** Stiff or rigid, as in death. **7** Sharp and bare, as of outline. —*adv.* **1** In a stark manner. **2** Completely; utterly: *stark* naked. [< OE *stearc* stiff] —**stark′ly** *adv.* —**stark′ness** *n.*

Starfish

star·let (stär′lit) *n. Informal* A young movie actress being prepared for stardom.

star·light (stär′līt) *n.* The light given by a star or stars. —*adj.* Lighted by or only by the stars: also **star′lit′** (-lit′).

star·ling (stär′ling) *n.* **1** A chubby, gregarious, aggressive bird with iridescent black plumage, introduced from Europe and now common in North America. **2** Any of various related European birds. [< OE *stærling*]

star of David The six-pointed star used as a symbol of Judaism.

starred (stärd) *adj.* **1** Spangled or marked with stars. **2** Marked with an asterisk. **3** Affected by astral influence: used chiefly in combination: *ill-starred*. **4** Presented or advertised as the star of an entertainment.

star·ry (stär′ē) *adj.* **·ri·er, ·ri·est 1** Set or marked with stars. **2** Shining as or like stars. **3** Star-shaped. **4** Lighted by or abounding in stars. **5** Of, from, having to do with, or like stars. —**star′ri·ness** *n.*

Star of David

star·ry-eyed (stär′ē-īd′) *adj.* Excited by or given to fanciful thoughts of romance, adventure, etc.

Stars and Stripes The flag of the U.S., having 13 alternating horizontal stripes of red and white, and in the upper left-hand corner 50 white stars against a blue ground.

star-span·gled (stär′spang′gəld) *adj.* Spangled with stars or starlike spots or points.

Star-Spangled Banner 1 The flag of the U.S. **2** The national anthem of the U.S., with words written by Francis Scott Key in 1814.

start (stärt) *v.i.* **1** To make an involuntary, startled movement, as from fear or surprise. **2** To move suddenly, as with a spring, leap, or bound. **3** To begin an action, undertaking, trip, etc.: They *started* early on their vacation. **4** To become active, operative, etc.: School *starts* in the fall. **5** To be on the team, lineup, etc., that begins a game or contest. **6** To protrude; seem to bulge: His eyes *started* from his head. **7** To be displaced or dislocated; become loose, warped, etc. —*v.t.* **8** To set in motion, activity, etc.: to *start* an engine; to *start* a rumor. **9** To begin; commence: to *start* a lecture. **10** To put on the team, lineup, etc., that begins a game or contest: I'm *starting* the new players today. **11** To set up; establish. **12** To introduce (a subject) or propound (a question). **13** To displace or dislocate; loosen, warp, etc.: The collision *started* the ship's seams. **14** To rouse from cover; cause to take flight; flush, as game. **15** To draw the contents from; tap, as a cask. —**start up 1** To rise or appear suddenly. **2** To begin; come into being. **3** To begin the operation of (a motor, etc.). —**to start with** In the first place. —*n.* **1** A quick, startled movement or reaction. **2** A temporary or spasmodic action or attempt: by fits and *starts*. **3** A beginning or commencement, as of an action, undertaking, etc. **4** Advantage; lead, as in a race. **5** A place or time of beginning. **6** A loosened place or condition; crack: a *start* in a ship's planking. [ME *sterten*, start, leap]

start·er (stär′tər) *n.* **1** One who or that which starts, esp.. **a** A competitor or member of a team at the start of a race or contest. **b** A person giving the starting signal for a race or contest. **c** A person whose job is to see to it that buses, trolleys, etc., leave on schedule. **d** Any mechanical device that initiates movement in an engine or the like. **2** A substance or mixture that initiates a chemical reaction, esp. in food: a *starter* for bread.

star·tle (stärt′əl) *v.* **·tled, ·tling** *v.t.* **1** To arouse or excite suddenly; alarm. —*v.i.* **2** To be aroused or excited suddenly; take alarm. —*n.* A sudden fright or shock; a scare. [< OE *steartlian* to kick] —**star′tler** *n.*

star·tling (stärt′ling) *adj.* Rousing sudden surprise, alarm, or the like. —**star′tling·ly** *adv.*

star·va·tion (stär·vā′shən) *n.* **1** The act of starving. **2** The state of being starved. —*adj.* Insufficient to sustain life or to purchase basic necessities: a *starvation* diet; *starvation* wages.

starve (stärv) *v.* **starved, starv·ing** *v.i.* **1** To die or perish from lack of food. **2** To suffer from extreme hunger. **3** To suffer from lack or need: to *starve* for friendship. —*v.t.* **4** To cause to die of hunger. **5** To deprive of food. **6** To bring to a specified condition by starving: to *starve* an enemy into surrender. [< OE *steorfan* die] —**starv′er** *n.*

starve·ling (stärv′ling) *n.* A person or animal that is starving, starved, or emaciated.

stash (stash) *v.t. Informal* To hide or conceal (money or valuables), for future use or safe-keeping: often with *away.* —*n. Slang* **1** A place where things are stashed away. **2** Something stashed away. [?]

-stat *combining form* A device which stops or makes constant: *thermostat.* [< Gk. *-statēs* causing to stand]

state (stāt) *n.* **1** A mode or condition of being or existing: a *state* of war. **2** A particular physical or chemical stage or condition of something: Ice is the solid *state* of water. **3** Frame of mind: a *state* of utter peace. **4** Any extreme mental condition, as of excitement, nervousness, etc. **5** Social status or position. **6** A grand, ceremonious, or luxurious style of living or doing: to arrive in *state.* **6** A sovereign political community; nation. **7** A political and territorial unit within such a community: the *state* of Maine. —**lie in state** To be placed on public view before burial. —*adj.* **1** Of or pertaining to a state, nation, or government. **2** Intended for use on occasions of ceremony. —*v.t.* **stat·ed, stat·ing 1** To set forth explicitly in speech or writing; declare. **2** To fix; settle: to *state* terms. [< L *status* condition, state < *stare* to stand] —**state′hood** *n.* —**Syn.** **1** circumstances. **5** standing. *v.* **1** affirm, assert, aver.

state·craft (stāt′kraft′, -kräft′) *n.* The art of conducting affairs of state.

stat·ed (stā′tid) *adj.* **1** Regular; fixed. **2** Told; asserted: a *stated* fact. —**stat′ed·ly** *adv.*

state·house (stāt′hous′) *n. Often cap.* A building used for sessions of a state legislature. Also **state house.**

state·ly (stāt′lē) *adj.* **·li·er, ·li·est 1** Dignified; majestic: a *stately* mansion. **2** Slow; measured: a *stately* march. —*adv.* Loftily. —**state′li·ness** *n.* —**Syn. 1** imposing, grand, awesome, impressive.

state·ment (stāt′mənt) *n.* **1** The act of stating. **2** That which is stated. **3** A summary of assets and liabilities, showing the balance due. **3** A major or dominant idea expressed in the composition of a creative work, as in art, music, or design; motif. **4** The expression of such an idea.

state·room (stāt′rōōm′, -rŏŏm′) *n.* A small private bedroom on a passenger ship or railroad train.

state's evidence Testimony for the prosecution in a U.S. federal or state court, esp. that of a criminal against his accomplices. —**turn state's evidence** To offer state's evidence.

state·side (stāt′sīd′) *adj. Informal* Of or in the continental U.S. —*adv.* In or to the continental U.S.

states·man (stāts′mən) *n. pl.* **·men** (-mən) A person skilled in the science of government and prominent in national and foreign affairs. —**states′man·ly** *adv.* —**states′man·ship** *n.*

state socialism A political theory advocating government ownership of utilities and industries.

States' rights The powers not vested in the U.S. federal government by the Constitution nor prohibited by it to the states. Also **State rights.**

states·wom·an (stāts′wŏŏm′ən) *n. pl.* **·wom·en** (-wim′in) A woman skilled in the science of government and prominent in national and foreign affairs.

state·wide (stāt′wīd′) *adj. & adv.* Throughout a state.

stat·ic (stat′ik) *adj.* **1** Pertaining to bodies at rest or forces in equilibrium. **2** *Physics* Not involved in or with motion: *static* pressure. **3** *Electr.* Of or caused by stationary electric charges. **4** At rest; not active. **5** Of or pertaining to nonactive elements. **6** Dealing with fixed or stable conditions. Also **stat′i·cal.** —*n. Electronics* Electrical noise, esp. atmospheric, that interferes with radio communications. [< Gk *statikos* causing to stand] —**stat′i·cal·ly** *adv.*

stat·ics (stat′iks) *n.pl. (construed as sing.)* The mechanics of bodies at rest.

sta·tion (stā′shən) *n.* **1** A place where a person or thing usu. stands. **2** The headquarters of some official person or body of men: a police *station.* **3** A starting point or stopping place of a railroad or bus line. **4** A building for the accommodation of passengers or freight, as on a railroad or bus line; depot. **5** Social rank; standing. **6** *Mil.* The place to which an individual, unit, or ship is assigned for duty. **7** The installations of a radio or television broadcasting unit. —*v.t.* To assign to a station; set in position. [< L *stare* to stand]

sta·tion·ar·y (stā′shə·ner′ē) *adj.* **1** Remaining in one place. **2** Fixed; not portable. **3** Exhibiting no change of character or condition.

sta·tion·er (stā′shə·nər) *n.* A dealer in stationery and related goods. [< Med. L *stationarius* stationary, having a fixed location (for business)]

sta·tion·er·y (stā′shə·ner′ē) *n.* Paper, pens, pencils, ink, notebooks, and other related goods.

station wagon An automotive vehicle with one or more rows of seats behind the front seat and with a hinged tailgate for admitting luggage, etc.

stat·ism (stā′tiz·əm) *n.* A theory of government which advocates the concentration of economic planning, control, etc., in a centralized government. —**stat′ist** *n.*

sta·tis·tic (stə·tis′tik) *n.* Any element entering into a statistical statement. —*adj.* STATISTICAL.

sta·tis·ti·cal (stə·tis′tə·kəl) *adj.* **1** Of or pertaining to statistics. **2** Composed of statistics. —**sta·tis′ti·cal·ly** *adv.*

stat·is·ti·cian (stat′is·tish′ən) *n.* One skilled in collecting and tabulating statistical data.

sta·tis·tics (stə·tis′tiks) *n.pl.* **1** A collection of quantitative data or facts. **2** *(construed as sing.)* The branch of mathematics that deals with the collection and analysis of quantitative data. [< L *status* position, state]

stat·u·ar·y (stach′ōō·er′ē) *n. pl.* **·ar·ies** Statues collectively. —*adj.* Of or suitable for statues. [< L *statua* statue]

stat·ue (stach′ōō) *n.* A three-dimensional representation of a human or animal figure modeled in clay or wax, cast in bronze or plaster, or carved in wood or stone. [< L *status,* pp. of *stare* stand]

stat·u·esque (stach′ōō·esk′) *adj.* **1** Resembling a statue, as in grace or dignity. **2** Shapely; comely. —**stat′u·esque′ly** *adv.* —**stat′u·esque′ness** *n.*

stat·u·ette (stach′ōō·et′) *n.* A small statue. [F]

stat·ure (stach′ər) *n.* **1** The natural height of a body. **2** The height of anything, as a tree. **3** Status or reputation resulting from development or growth: artistic *stature.* [< L *status* condition, state]

sta·tus (stā′təs, stat′əs) *n.* **1** State, condition, or relation. **2** Relative position or rank. [< L *stare* to stand]

sta·tus quo (stā′təs kwō, stat′əs) The actual or existing condition or state. Also **status in quo.** [L]

stat·ute (stach′ōōt) *n.* **1** *Law* A legislative enactment. **2** An established law or regulation. [< L *statutus,* pp. of *statuere* constitute]

statute law The law as set forth in statutes.

statute mile MILE (def. 1).

statute of limitations A statute which imposes time limits upon the right of action in certain cases.

stat·u·to·ry (stach′ə·tôr′ē, -tō′rē) *adj.* **1** Pertaining to a statute. **2** Created by or based upon legislative enactment.

statutory rape See RAPE.

staunch (stônch, stänch) *adj.* **1** Firm in principle; constant; trustworthy. **2** Stout; seaworthy: a *staunch* ship. —*v.t.* STANCH. [< OF *estanchier* make stand] —**staunch′ly** *adv.* —**staunch′ness** *n.* —**Syn.** *adj.* **1** faithful, loyal, trusty. **2** sound, trim. • See STANCH.

stave (stāv) *n.* **1** A curved strip of wood, forming a part of the sides of a barrel, tub, or the like. **2** *Music* A staff. **3** A stanza; verse. **4** A rod, cudgel, or staff. **5** A rung of a rack or ladder. —*v.* **staved** or **stove, stav·ing** *v.t.* **1** To break or make (a hole) by crushing or collision. **2** To furnish with staves. —*v.i.* **3** To be broken in, as a vessel's hull. —**stave off** To ward off: to *stave off* bankruptcy. [< *staves,* pl. of STAFF]

Barrel stave

staves (stāvz) *n.* **1** A *pl.* of STAFF. **2** *pl.* of STAVE.

stay¹ (stā) *v.i.* **1** To stop; halt: *Stay* where you are. **2** To continue in a specified place or condition: to *stay* home; to *stay* healthy. **3** To remain temporarily as a guest or resident. **4** To tarry: I'll *stay* a few more minutes. **5** *Informal* To have endurance; last. **6** *Informal* To keep pace with a competitor, as in a race. —*v.t.* **7** To bring to a stop; halt. **8** To hinder; delay. **9** To put off; postpone. **10** To satisfy the demands of temporarily; appease: to *stay* the pangs of hunger. **11** To remain for the duration of: to *stay* the night. —*n.* **1** The act or time of staying: a week's *stay* at the beach. **2** A deferment or suspension of judicial proceedings: The court granted a *stay* of sentencing. **3** *Informal* Staying power; endurance. [< L *stare* stand] —**stay′er** *n.*

stay² (stā) *v.t.* To be a support to; prop or hold up. —*n.* **1** Anything which props or supports. **2** *pl.* A corset stiffened, as with steel strips or whalebone. [< OF *estayer*]

stay³ (stā) *Naut. n.* **1** A large, strong rope or wire, used to brace a mast or spar. **2** Any rope having a similar use. —*v.t.* **1** To support with a stay or stays. **2** To put (a vessel) on the opposite tack. —*v.i.* **3** To tack: said of vessels. [< OE *stæg*]

staying power The ability to endure.

stay·sail (stā′sāl′, -səl) *n. Naut.* A sail, usu. triangular, extended on a stay.

Ste. Sainte (female) (F *Sainte*).

stead (sted) *n.* Place of another person or thing as assumed by a substitute or a successor: My sister went in my *stead.* —**stand (one) in good stead** To give (one) good service, support, etc. [< OE *stede* place]

stead·fast (sted′fast′, -fäst′, -fəst) *adj.* **1** Firmly fixed in faith or devotion to duty. **2** Directed fixedly at one point, as the gaze. [< OE *stedefæst*] —**stead′fast′ly** *adv.* —**stead′· fast′ness** *n.*

stead·y (sted′ē) *adj.* **stead·i·er, stead·i·est 1** Stable; not liable to shake or totter: a *steady* ladder. **2** Unfaltering; constant: a *steady* light; *steady* loyalty. **3** Calm; unruffled: *steady* nerves. **4** Free from intemperance and dissipation: *steady* habits. **5** Regular: a *steady* customer. **6** Of a ship, keeping more or less upright in rough seas. —**go steady** *Informal* To date exclusively. —*v.t. & v.i.* **stead·ied, stead·y·ing** To make or become steady. —*interj.* Not so fast; keep calm. —*n. Slang* A sweetheart or constant companion. [< STEAD] —**stead′i·ly** *adv.* —**stead′i·ness** *n.*

steak (stāk) *n.* A slice of meat or fish, esp. of beef, usu. broiled or fried. [< ON *steik*]

steal (stēl) *v.* **stole, sto·len, steal·ing** *v.t.* **1** To take from another without right or permission. **2** To take or obtain in a subtle manner: He has *stolen* the hearts of the people. **3** In baseball, to reach (another base) without the aid of a hit or error: said of a base runner. —*v.i.* **4** To move quietly and stealthily: to *steal* away in the night. **5** To commit theft. **6** To move secretly or furtively. —*n. Informal* **1** The act of stealing or that which is stolen. **2** Any underhanded financial deal that benefits the originators. **3** A bargain: a *steal* at $3.99. [< OE *stelan*] —**steal′er** *n.* —**Syn.** *v.* **1** filch, pilfer, purloin. **4** skulk, slink.

stealth (stelth) *n.* Secret or furtive action, movement, or behavior. [< OE *stelan* steal]

stealth·y (stel′thē) *adj.* **stealth·i·er, stealth·i·est** Marked by stealth; designed to elude notice. —**stealth′i·ly** *adv.* —**stealth′i·ness** *n.*

steam (stēm) *n.* **1** Water in the form of a gas, esp. above the boiling point of the liquid. **2** The visible mist formed by sudden cooling of hot steam. **3** Any kind of vaporous exhalation. **4** Energy or power derived from hot water vapor under pressure. **5** *Informal* Vigor; force; speed. —**let off steam** To give expression to pent-up emotions or opinions. —*v.i.* **1** To emit steam or vapor. **2** To rise or pass off as steam. **3** To become covered with condensed water vapor: often with *up.* **4** To generate steam. **5** To move or travel by the agency of steam. —*v.t.* **6** To treat with steam, as in softening, cooking, cleaning, etc. —*adj.* **1** Of, driven, or operated by steam. **2** Producing or containing steam: a *steam* boiler; a *steam* pipe. **3** Treated by steam. **4** Using steam: *steam* heat. [< OE *stēam*] —**steam′i·ness** *n.* —**steam′y** *adj.* (**·i·er, ·i·est**)

steam·boat (stēm′bōt′) *n.* A boat propelled by steam.

steam engine An engine that derives its force from the pressure of hot steam.

steam·er (stē′mər) *n.* **1** A steamship or steamboat. **2** A pot or container in which something is steamed.

steam·fit·ter (stēm′fit′ər) *n.* A man who sets up or repairs steam pipes and their fittings. —**steam′fit′ting** *n.*

steam·roll·er (stēm′rōl′ər) *n.* **1** A machine having a heavy roller for flattening asphalt surfaces. **2** *Informal* Any force that ruthlessly overcomes opposition. —*v. Informal v.t.* **1** To crush ruthlessly. —*v.i.* **2** To move with crushing force. Also **steam′roll′.**

steam·ship (stēm′ship′) *n.* A large vessel used for ocean traffic and propelled by steam.

steam shovel A power-operated machine for digging and excavation.

ste·ap·sin (stē·ap′sin) *n.* A pancreatic enzyme that aids in the digestion of fat. [< STEA(RIN) + (PE)PSIN]

ste·ar·ic acid (stē·ar′ik, stir′ik) A fatty acid common in solid animal fats, used in making soap. Also **ste′a·rin.** [< Gk. *stear* suet]

ste·a·tite (stē′ə·tīt) *n.* Massive talc used in extensive beds and used for electric insulation. [< Gk. *stear, steatos* suet, tallow] —**ste′a·tit′ic** (-tit′ik) *adj.*

sted·fast (sted′fast′, -fäst′, -fəst) *adj.* STEADFAST.

steed (stēd) *n.* A horse; esp., a spirited horse. [< OE *stēda* studhorse]

steel (stēl) *n.* **1** Any of various alloys of iron containing carbon in amounts up to about 2 percent, often with other components that give special properties. **2** Something made of steel, as an implement or weapon. **3** Hardness of character. **4** *Can.* A railway track or line. —*adj.* **1** Made or composed of steel. **2** Adamant; unyielding. —*v.t.* **1** To cover with steel. **2** To make strong; harden: to *steel* one's heart against misery. [< OE *stēl*] —**steel′i·ness** *n.* —**steel′y** *adj.* (**·i·er, ·i·est**)

steel wool Steel fibers matted together for use in cleaning and polishing.

steel·work·er (stēl′wûr′kər) *n.* One who works in a steel mill.

steel·yard (stēl′yärd′, stil′yərd) *n.* A device for weighing, consisting of a scaled beam, a movable counterpoise, and hooks to hold the article to be weighed. Also **steel′·yards.**

steen·bok (stēn′bok, stān′) *n. pl.* **·bok** or **·boks** A small African antelope with short horns in the male. [< MDu. *steen* stone + *boc* buck]

steep[1] (stēp) *adj.* **1** Sloping sharply; precipitous. **2** *Informal* Exorbitant; high, as a price. —*n.* A cliff; a precipitous place. [< OE *stēap*] —**steep′ly** *adv.* —**steep′ness** *n.* —**Syn.** *adj.* **1** abrupt, high, sharp, sheer.

steep[2] (stēp) *v.t.* **1** To soak in a liquid, as for softening, cleansing, etc. **2** To imbue thoroughly: *steeped* in crime. —*v.i.* **3** To undergo soaking in a liquid. —*n.* **1** The process of steeping, or the state of being steeped. **2** A liquid or bath in which anything is steeped. [< ON *steypa* pour] —**steep′er** *n.*

Steenbok

steep·en (stē′pən) *v.t. & v.i.* To make or become steep or steeper.

stee·ple (stē′pəl) *n.* A lofty structure rising above the roof of a church, usu. having a spire. [< OE *stēpel*]

stee·ple·chase (stē′pəl·chās′) *n.* **1** A race on horseback across country. **2** A race over a course with hedges, rails, and water jumps. —**stee′ple·chas′er** *n.*

stee·ple·jack (stē′pəl·jak′) *n.* A man whose occupation is to climb steeples and other tall structures to inspect or make repairs.

steer[1] (stir) *v.t.* **1** To direct the course of (a vessel or vehicle). **2** To follow (a course). **3** To direct; guide; control. —*v.i.* **4** To direct the course of a vessel, vehicle, etc. **5** To undergo guiding or steering. **6** To follow a course: to *steer* for land. —**steer clear of** To avoid; keep away from. —*n. Slang* A tip; piece of advice. [< OE *stēoran*] —**steer′er** *n.*

steer[2] (stir) *n.* **1** A young castrated bovine. **2** Any male cattle raised for beef. [< OE *stēor*]

steer·age (stir′ij) *n.* That part of an ocean passenger vessel allotted to passengers paying the lowest fares.

steers·man (stirz′mən) *n. pl.* **·men** (-mən) One who steers a boat or a ship; a helmsman.

stein (stīn) *n.* A beer mug. [G]

stein·bok (stīn′bok) *n.* STEENBOK.

stel·lar (stel′ər) *adj.* **1** Of or pertaining to the stars; astral. **2** Chief; principal: a *stellar* role in a play. [< L *stella* star]

stel·late (stel′it, -āt) *adj.* Star-shaped; having rays pointing outward from a center. Also **stel·lat·ed** (stel′ā·tid). [< L *stella* star] —**stel′late·ly** *adv.*

St. El·mo's fire (sānt el′mōz) A luminous discharge of static electricity sometimes appearing on the superstructure of ships, on the tips of airplane wings, etc. Also **St. El·mo's light.**

stem[1] (stem) *n.* **1** The main ascending axis of a plant, serving to transport water and nutrients, to hold up the leaves to air and light, etc. **2** A subsidiary stalk supporting a fruit, flower, or leaf. **3** The slender upright support of a goblet, wine glass, vase, etc. **4** In a watch, the small projecting rod used for winding the mainspring. **5** *Music* The line attached to the head of a written musical note. **6** *Ling.* The unchanged element common to all the members of a given inflection. **7** The bow of a boat. —**from stem to stern 1** From one end of a ship to the other. **2** Throughout; thoroughly. —*v.t.* **stemmed, stem·ming** To remove the stems of or from. —**stem from** To be descended or derived. [< OE *stemm, stemn*] —**stem′mer** *n.*

stem[2] (stem) *v.t.* **stemmed, stem·ming 1** To stop, hold back, or dam up, as a current. **2** To make progress against, as a current, opposing force, etc. [< ON *stemma* stop]

stem·wind·er (stem′wīn′der) *n.* **1** A stemwinding watch. **2** *Slang* A very superior person or thing.

stem·wind·ing (stem′wīn′ding) *adj.* Wound, as a watch, by turning a knob at the outermost end of the stem.

stench (stench) *n.* A foul or offensive odor. [< OE *stenc*] —**stench′y** *adj.* —**Syn.** fetidness, miasma, reek, stink.

sten·cil (sten′səl) *n.* **1** A thin sheet or plate in which a written text or a pattern is cut through which applied paint or ink penetrates to a surface beneath. **2** Produced by stenciling. —*v.t.* **·ciled** or **·cilled, ·cil·ing** or **·cil·ling** To mark with a stencil. [< OF *estenceler*] —**sten′·cil·er** or **sten′cil·ler** *n.*

STENCIL

STENCIL

sten·o (sten′ō) *n. pl.* **sten·os 1** STENOGRAPHER. **2** STENOGRAPHY.

steno- *combining form* Tight; contracted: *stenography.* [< Gk. *stenos* narrow]

steno., stenog. stenographer; stenography.

ste·nog·ra·pher (stə·nog′rə·fər) *n.* One who is skilled in shorthand.

ste·nog·ra·phy (stə·nog′rə·fē) *n.* **1** The method of rapid writing by the use of contractions or arbitrary symbols; shorthand. **2** The act of using stenography. —**sten·o·graph·ic** (sten′ə·graf′ik) or **·i·cal** *adj.* —**sten′o·graph′i·cal·ly** *adv.*

sten·o·type (sten′ə·tīp) *n.* A keyboard-operated machine for recording on paper tape symbols representing speech.

sten·o·typ·y (sten′ə·tī′pē) *n.* A system of shorthand utilizing a keyboard-operated machine to record letters in various combinations that represent sounds, words, or phrases. —**sten′o·typ′ist** *n.*

sten·to·ri·an (sten·tôr′ē·ən, -tō′rē-) *adj.* Extremely loud. [< *Stentor,* a herald in the *Iliad,* famous for his loud voice] —**sten·to′ri·an·ly** *adv.*

step (step) *n.* **1** A change in location or position accomplished by lifting the foot and putting it down in a different place. **2** The distance passed over in making such a motion. **3** Any space easily traversed. **4** A stair or ladder rung. **5** A single action or proceeding regarded as leading to something. **6** A grade or degree: They advanced him a *step.* **7** The sound of a footfall. **8** A footprint; track. **9** *pl.* Progression by walking. **10** A combination of foot movements in dancing. **11** *Music* An interval approximately equal to that between the first two tones of a diatonic scale. —**in step 1** Walking or dancing evenly with another by taking corresponding steps. **2** Conforming; in agreement. —**out of step 1** Not in step. **2** Not conforming or agreeing. —**step by step** In slow stages. —**take steps** To adopt measures, as to attain an end. —**watch one's step** To be cautious. —*v.* **stepped, step·ping** *v.i.* **1** To move forward or backward by taking a step or steps. **2** To walk a short distance. **3** To move with measured, dignified, or graceful steps. **4** To move or act quickly or briskly. **5** To pass into a situation, circumstance, etc.: He *stepped* into a fortune. —*v.t.* **6** To take (a pace, stride, etc.). **7** To perform the steps of: to *step* a quadrille. **8** To place or move (the foot) in taking a step. **9** To measure by taking steps: often with *off.* **10** To cut or arrange in steps. —**step down 1** To decrease gradually. **2** To resign from an office or position; abdicate. —**step in** To begin to take part; intervene. —**step on** (or **upon**) **1** To tread upon. **2** To put the foot on so as to activate, as a brake or treadle. **3** *Informal* To reprove or subdue. —**step on it** *Informal* To hurry; hasten. —**step out 1** To go outside. **2** *Informal* To go out for fun or entertainment. **3** To step down. **4** To walk with long strides. —**step up** To increase; raise. [< OE *stæpe*] —**Syn.** *n.* **6** stage, level, position, notch.

step- *combining form* Related through the previous marriage of a parent or spouse, but not by blood: *stepchild.* [< OE *steop-*]

step·broth·er (step′bruth′ər) *n.* The son of one's stepparent by a former marriage.

step·child (step′chīld′) *n. pl.* **·chil·dren** The child of one's husband or wife by a former marriage.

step·daugh·ter (step′dô′tər) *n.* A female stepchild.

step-down (step′doun′) *adj.* **1** That decreases gradually. **2** *Electr.* Designating a transformer whose output voltage is less than its input voltage. **3** Designating a speed-reducing gear.

step·fa·ther (step′fä′thər) *n.* A man who has married one's mother after the decease or divorce of one's own father.

step-in (step′in′) *adj.* Put on, as undergarments or shoes, by being stepped into.

step·lad·der (step′lad′ər) *n.* A set of portable, usu. flat steps with a hinged frame at the back for support.

step·moth·er (step′muth′ər) *n.* A woman who has married one's father after the decease or divorce of one's own mother.

step·par·ent (step′pâr′ənt) *n.* A stepfather or stepmother.

steppe (step) *n.* **1** A vast plain devoid of forest. **2** One of the extensive plains in SE Europe and Asia. [< Russ. *step'*]

stepped-up (stept′up′) *adj. Informal* Speeded up; increased: *stepped-up* production.

step·per (step′ər) *n.* **1** One who or that which steps. **2** *Slang* A dancer.

step·ping·stone (step′ing·stōn′) *n.* **1** A stone forming a footrest, as for crossing a stream, etc. **2** That by which one advances or rises.

step·sis·ter (step′sis′tər) *n.* The daughter of one's stepparent by a former marriage.

step·son (step′sun′) *n.* A male stepchild.

step-up (step′up′) *adj.* **1** Increasing by stages. **2** Designating a transformer whose output voltage exceeds its input voltage. **3** Designating a speed-increasing gear. —*n.* An increase, as in intensity, amount, etc.

-ster *suffix of nouns* **1** One who makes or is occupied with: *songster.* **2** One who belongs or is related to: *gangster.* **3** One who is: *youngster.* [< OE *-estre*]

ster., stg. Sterling.

ste·ra·di·an (sti·rā′dē·ən) *n.* A solid angle with its vertex at the center of a sphere which encloses a surface equivalent to the square of the radius of the sphere: a unit of measure. [< Gk. *stereos* solid + RADIAN]

stere (stir) *n.* A cubic meter. [< Gk. *stereos* solid]

ster·e·o (ster′ē·ō, stir′-) *n. pl.* **·e·os** **1** A stereophonic record player, record, tape, etc. **2** Stereophonic sound. **3** STEREOTYPE (defs. 1 & 2). **4** A stereoscopic method; also, a steroscopic photograph. —*adj.* **1** STEREOPHONIC. **2** STEREOTYPED (def. 1). **3** Of or pertaining to the stereoscope; stereoscopic.

stereo- *combining form* Solid; firm; three-dimensional: *stereoscope.* [< Gk. *stereos* hard]

ster·e·o·phon·ic (ster′ē·ə·fon′ik, stir′-) *adj.* Of, for, or designating a system of sound reproduction in which two independent channels are used so as to present different sounds to each of a listener's ears. —**ster′e·o·phon′i·cal·ly** *adv.*

ster·e·o·scope (ster′ē·ə·skōp, stir′-) *n.* An instrument for presenting different images of an object to each eye, so as to produce a three-dimensional illusion. —**ster′e·o·scop′ic** (-skop′ik) or **·i·cal** *adj.* —**ster′e·o·scop′i·cal·ly** *adv.* —**ster·e·os·co·pist** (ster′ē·os′kə·pist, stir-) *n.*

ster·e·o·type (ster′ē·ə·tīp′, stir′-) *n.* **1** A printing plate cast in metal from a matrix molded from a raised surface, as type. **2** Anything made or processed in this way. **3** A conventional or hackneyed expression, custom, or mode of thought. —*v.t.* **·typed, ·typ·ing** **1** To make a stereotype of. **2** To print from stereotypes. **3** To give a fixed or unalterable form to. —**ster′e·o·typ′er, ster′e·o·typ′ist** *n.*

ster·e·o·typed (ster′ē·ə·tīpt′, stir′-) *adj.* **1** Produced from a stereotype. **2** Hackneyed; without originality.

ster·ile (ster′əl, *Chiefly Brit.* -īl) *adj.* **1** Having no reproductive power; barren. **2** Lacking productiveness: *sterile* soil. **3** Containing no microorganisms; aseptic: a *sterile* fluid. **4** Lacking vigor or interest; *sterile* prose. **5** Without results; futile: *sterile* hopes. [< L *sterilis*] —**ster′ile·ly** *adv.* —**ste·ril·i·ty** (stə·ril′ə·tē), **ster′ile·ness** *n.*

ster·il·ize (ster′əl·īz) *v.t.* **·ized, ·iz·ing** **1** To render incapable of reproduction, esp. by surgery. **2** To destroy microorganisms. **3** To make barren. —**ster′i·li·za′tion, ster′il·iz′er** *n.*

ster·ling (stûr′ling) *n.* **1** British money. **2** The official standard of fineness for British coins. **3** Sterling silver as used in manufacturing articles, as tableware, etc. **4** Articles made of sterling silver collectively. —*adj.* **1** Made of or payable in sterling: pounds *sterling.* **2** Made of sterling silver. **3** Having great worth; genuine: *sterling* qualities. [Prob. < OE *steorra* star + -LING]

sterling silver An alloy of 92.5 percent silver and usu. 7.5 percent copper.

stern¹ (stûrn) *adj.* **1** Marked by severity or harshness: a *stern* command. **2** Having an austere disposition: a *stern* judge. **3** Inspiring fear. **4** Resolute: a *stern* resolve. [< OE *styrne*] —**stern′ly** *adv.* —**stern′ness** *n.*

stern² (stûrn) *n.* **1** *Naut.* The aft part of a ship, boat, etc. **2** The hindmost part of any object. —*adj.* Situated at or belonging to the stern. [< ON *styra* steer] —**stern′most′** (-mōst′) *adj.*

ster·num (stûr′nəm) *n. pl.* **·na** (-nə) or **·nums** The structure of bone and cartilage that forms the ventral support of the ribs in vertebrates. [< Gk. *sternon* breast] —**stern·al** (stûr′nal) *adj.*

ster·nu·ta·tion (stûr′nyə·tā′shən) *n.* **1** The act of sneezing. **2** A sneeze or the noise produced by it. [< L *sternuere* to sneeze] —**ster·nu·ta·to·ry** (ster·nyōō′tə·tôr′ē, -tō′ri) *adj.*

stern-wheel·er (stûrn′ʰwē′lər) *n.* A steamboat propelled by one large paddle wheel at the stern.

ster·oid (ster′oid) *n.* Any of a large group of structurally similar organic compounds found in plants and animals, including many hormones and the precursors of certain vitamins. [< STER(OL) + -OID]

ster·ol (ster′ōl, -ol) *n.* Any of a class of steroids comprising solid, fat-soluble alcohols, as cholesterol. [Contraction of CHOLESTEROL]

ster·to·rous (stûr′tər·əs) *adj.* Characterized or accompanied by a snoring sound: *stertorous* breathing. [< L *stertere* to snore] —**ster′tor·ous·ly** *adv.* —**ster′tor·ous·ness** *n.*

stet (stet) Let it stand: a direction used in proofreading to indicate that a word, letter, etc., marked for omission is to remain. —*v.t.* **stet·ted, stet·ting** To mark for retention with the word *stet.* [< L *stare* to stand]

steth·o·scope (steth′ə·skōp) *n.* An apparatus for conducting sounds from the human body to the ears of an examiner. [< Gk. *stēthos* breast + -SCOPE] —**steth′o·scop′ic** (-skop′ik) *adj.* —**steth′o·scop′i·cal·ly** *adv.* —**ste·thos·co·py** (ste·thos′kə·pē) *n.*

stet·son (stet′sən) *n. Often cap.* A man's hat, usu. of felt, with a high crown and a broad brim, popular in the w U.S. [< *Stetson,* a trade name]

ste·ve·dore (stē′və·dôr, -dōr) *n.* One whose business is loading or unloading ships. —*v.t. & v.i.* **·dored, ·dor·ing** To load or unload (a vessel or vessels). [< L *stipare* compress, stuff]

stew (styōō) *v.t. & v.i.* **1** To boil slowly and gently. **2** *Informal* To worry. —*n.* **1** Stewed food, esp. a preparation of meat or fish and vegetables cooked by stewing. **2** *Informal* Mental agitation; worry. [< OF *estuver*]

stew·ard (styōō′ərd) *n.* **1** A person entrusted with the management of the affairs of others. **2** A person put in charge of services for a club, ship, railroad train, etc. **3** On shipboard, a person who waits on table and takes care of passengers' staterooms. **4** SHOP STEWARD. [< OE *stī* hall + *weard* ward, keeper] —**stew′ard·ship** *n.*

stew·ard·ess (styōō′ər·dis) *n.* A woman whose occupation is that of a steward, esp. one who is employed on an airplane to attend passengers.

stewed (styōōd) *adj.* **1** Cooked by stewing. **2** *Slang* Drunk.

stge. storage.

stick (stik) *n.* **1** A stiff shoot or branch cut or broken off from a tree or bush. **2** Any relatively long and thin piece of wood. **3** A piece of wood fashioned for a specific use: a walking *stick;* a hockey *stick.* **4** Anything resembling a stick in form: a *stick* of dynamite. **5** A piece of wood of any size, cut for fuel, lumber, or timber. **6** *Aeron.* The lever of an airplane that controls pitching and rolling. **7** A poke, stab, or thrust with a stick or pointed implement. **8** The state of being stuck together; adhesion. **9** *Informal* A stiff, inert, or dull person. —**the sticks** *Informal* An obscure rural district. —*v.* **stuck, stick·ing** *v.t.* **1** To pierce or penetrate with a pointed object. **2** To stab. **3** To thrust or force, as a sword or pin, into or through something else. **4** To force the end of (a nail, etc.) into something. **5** To fasten in place with or as with pins, nails, etc. **6** To cover with objects piercing the surface: a paper *stuck* with pins. **7** To impale; transfix. **8** To put or thrust: He *stuck* his hand into his pocket. **9** To fasten to a surface by or as by an adhesive substance. **10** To bring to a standstill: We were *stuck* in Rome. **11** *Informal* To smear with something sticky. **12** *Informal* To baffle; puzzle. **13** *Slang* To cheat. **14** *Slang* To force great expense, an unpleasant task, responsibility, etc., upon. —*v.i.* **15** To be or become fixed in place by being thrust in: The pins are *sticking* in the cushion. **16** To adhere; cling. **17** To come to a standstill; halt. **18** *Informal* To be baffled or disconcerted. **19** To hesitate; scruple: with *at* or *to*. **20** To persevere, as in a task or undertaking: with *at* or *to*. **21** To remain faithful, as to an ideal or bargain. **22** To protrude: with *out, through, up,* etc. —**be stuck on** *Informal* To be enamored of. —**stick around** *Slang* To remain near or near at hand. —**stick by** To remain loyal to. —**stick it out** To persevere to the end. —**stick up** *Slang* To stop and rob. —**stick up for** *Informal* To take the part of; defend. [< OE *sticca*]

stick·er (stik′ər) *n.* **1** One who or that which sticks. **2** A gummed label. **3** *Informal* Anything that confuses; a puzzle. **4** A prickly stem, thorn, or bur.

sticking plaster An adhesive material for covering slight cuts, etc.

stick·le (stik′əl) *v.i.* **·led, ·ling 1** To contend about trifles. **2** To hesitate for petty reasons. [< OE *stihtan* arrange]

stick·le·back (stik′əl·bak′) *n.* Any of various small, nest-building fresh- or salt-water fishes having sharp dorsal spines.

Stickleback

stick·ler (stik′lər) *n.* **1** One who insists upon exacting standards, as of behavior: with *for*: a *stickler* for punctuality. **2** A baffling problem.

stick·pin (stik′pin′) *n.* An ornamental pin for a necktie.

stick-to-it·ive·ness (stik′too′ə·tiv·nis) *n. Informal* Perseverance; diligence.

stick-up (stik′up′) *n. Slang* A robbery or hold-up.

stick·y (stik′ē) *adj.* **stick·i·er, stick·i·est 1** Adhering to a surface; adhesive. **2** Warm and humid. **3** *Informal* Unpleasant or complicated: a *sticky* situation. —**stick′i·ly** *adv.* —**stick′i·ness** *n.* —**Syn. 1** gluey, mucilaginous, viscous.

stiff (stif) *adj.* **1** Resistant to bending; rigid. **2** Not easily worked or moved: a *stiff* bolt. **3** Moving with difficulty or pain: a *stiff* back. **4** Not natural, graceful, or easy: a *stiff* bow. **5** Taut; tightly drawn: a *stiff* rope. **6** Strong and steady: a *stiff* breeze. **7** Thick; viscous: a *stiff* batter. **8** Harsh; severe: a *stiff* penalty. **9** High; dear: *stiff* prices. **10** Difficult; hard: a *stiff* examination. **11** Stubborn; unyielding: *stiff* resistance. **12** Awkward or noticeably formal; not relaxed or easy; wooden. **13** Strong; potent: a *stiff* drink. **14** Difficult; arduous: a *stiff* climb. —*n. Slang* **1** A corpse. **2** An awkward or unresponsive person. **3** A person; fellow: a working *stiff*. **4** A rough person. [< OE *stif*] —**stiff′ly** *adv.* —**stiff′ness** *n.*

stiff·en (stif′ən) *v.t. & v.i.* To make or become stiff or stiffer. —**stiff′en·er** *n.*

stiff-necked (stif′nekt′) *adj.* **1** Suffering from a stiff neck. **2** Stubborn; obstinate.

sti·fle (stī′fəl) *v.* **·fled, ·fling** *v.t.* **1** To kill by stopping respiration; choke. **2** To suppress or repress, as sobs. —*v.i.* **3** To die of suffocation. **4** To experience difficulty in breathing, as in a stuffy room. [ME *stuflen*] —**sti′fler** *n.* —**sti′fling·ly** *adv.*

stig·ma (stig′mə) *n. pl.* **stig·ma·ta** (stig·mä′tə, stig′mə·tə) or (*esp. for def. 2*) **stig·mas 1** A mark of disgrace. **2** *Bot.* That part of a pistil which receives the pollen. **3** *Biol.* Any spot or small opening. **4** A spot or scar on the skin. **5** *Med.* Any physical sign of diagnostic value. **6** *pl.* The wounds that Christ received at the Crucifixion. [L, mark, brand] —**stig·mat·ic** (-mat′ik) *adj.* —**Syn. 1** blemish, blot, stain.

stig·ma·tize (stig′mə·tīz) *v.t.* **·tized, ·tiz·ing 1** To characterize as disgraceful. **2** To mark with a stigma. *Brit. sp.* **stig′ma·tise.** —**stig′ma·ti·za′tion, stig′ma·tiz′er** *n.*

stile (stīl) *n.* A step, or series of steps, on each side of a fence or wall to enable one to climb over. [< OE *stigel*]

Stile

sti·let·to (sti·let′ō) *n. pl.* **·tos** or **·toes** A small dagger with a slender blade. —*v.t.* **·toed, ·to·ing** To pierce with a stiletto; stab. [< Ital. *stilo* dagger]

still¹ (stil) *adj.* **1** Being without movement; motionless. **2** Free from disturbance or agitation. **3** Making no sound; silent. **4** Low in sound; hushed. **5** Subdued; soft. **6** Dead; inanimate. **7** Having no effervescence: said of wines. **8** *Phot.* Not capable of showing movement. —*n.* **1** Absence of sound or noise. **2** *Phot.* A still photograph; esp. one taken on a motion-picture set, for advertising purposes. —*adv.* **1** Up to this or that time; yet: He is *still* here. **2** After or in spite of something; nevertheless. **3** In increasing degree; even yet: *still* more. **4** *Archaic or Regional* Always; constantly. —*conj.* Nevertheless. —*v.t.* **1** To cause to be still or calm. **2** To silence or hush. **3** To allay, as fears. —*v.i.* **4** To become still. [< OE *stille*] —**still′ness** *n.* —**Syn.** *adj.* **2** peaceful, tranquil, undisturbed. *v.* **1** soothe, tranquil-lize. **2** quiet.

still² (stil) *n.* **1** An apparatus for distilling liquids, esp. alcoholic liquors. **2** DISTILLERY. —*v.t. & v.i.* To distill. [< L *stilla* a drop]

Still²

still·born (stil′bôrn′) *adj.* Dead at birth. —**still′birth′** (-bûrth′) *n.*

still life *pl.* **lifes 1** In painting, the representation of inanimate objects. **2** A picture of such objects. —**still′-life′** *adj.*

Still·son wrench (stil′sən) A wrench resembling a monkey wrench, but with one serrated jaw capable of slight angular movement, so that the grip is tightened by pressure on the handle: a trade name. [< D. *Stillson*, its U.S. inventor in 1869]

Stillson wrench

still·y (stil′ē) *adj.* **·i·er, ·i·est** Quiet; calm. —*adv.* (stil′lē) Calmly; quietly.

stilt (stilt) *n.* **1** One of a pair of slender poles made with a projection above the ground to support the foot in walking. **2** A tall post or pillar used as a support for a dock or building. **3** Any of various shore birds with thin bills and long legs. [ME *stilte*]

stilt·ed (stil′tid) *adj.* Excessively formal or stuffy: *stilted* prose. —**stilt′ed·ly** *adv.* —**stilt′ed·ness** *n.*

stim·u·lant (stim′yə·lənt) *n.* **1** A drug that stimulates the rate or intensity of vital functions, esp. in the central nervous system. **2** Something that stimulates one to activity.

stim·u·late (stim′yə·lāt) *v.* **·lat·ed, ·lat·ing** *v.t.* **1** To rouse to activity; spur. **2** To increase action in by applying some form of stimulus: to *stimulate* the heart. **3** To affect by intoxicants. —*v.i.* **4** To act as a stimulus or stimulant. [< L *stimulus* a goad] —**stim′u·lat′er, stim′u·la′tor, stim′u·la′tion** *n.*

stim·u·la·tive (stim′yə·lā′tiv) *adj.* Having the power to stimulate. —*n.* Something that stimulates.

stim·u·lus (stim′yə·ləs) *n. pl.* **·li** (-lī, -lē) **1** Anything that rouses to activity, as a stimulant, incentive, etc. **2** Any agent that influences activity in an organism. [< L]

sting (sting) *v.* **stung, sting·ing** *v.t.* **1** To pierce or prick painfully: The bee *stung* me. **2** To cause to suffer sharp, smarting pain. **3** To cause to suffer mentally: to be *stung* with remorse. **4** To stimulate or rouse as if with a sting; goad. **5** *Slang* To overcharge. —*v.i.* **6** To have or use a sting, as a bee. **7** To suffer a sharp, smarting pain. **8** To suffer mental distress. —*n.* **1** A sharp offensive or defensive organ, as of a bee, capable of introducing an allergen or a venom into a victim's skin. **2** The act of stinging. **3** A wound made by a sting. **4** The pain caused by such a wound. **5** Any sharp, smarting sensation. **6** A keen stimulus; spur. [< OE *stingan*] —**sting'er** *n.* —**sting'ing·ly** *adv.*

sting ray Any of various flat-bodied fishes with a whiplike tail having one or more stinging spines. Also **sting'ray, sting·a·ree** (sting'ə·rē, sting'rē')

stin·gy (stin'jē) *adj.* **·gi·er, ·gi·est 1** Extremely penurious or miserly. **2** Scanty; meager: a *stingy* portion. [?] —**stin'gi·ly** *adv.* —**stin'·gi·ness** *n.* —**Syn. 1** avaricious, niggardly, parsimonious, tightfisted.

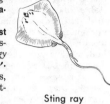

Sting ray

stink (stingk) *n.* A strong, foul odor; stench. —*v.* **stank** or **stunk, stunk, stink·ing** *v.i.* **1** To give forth a foul odor. **2** To be extremely offensive or hateful. —*v.t.* **3** To cause to stink. [< OE *stincan*] —**stink'er** *n.* —**stink'ing·ly** *adv.* —**stink'y** *adj.* (**·i·er, ·i·est**)

stink·bug (stingk'bug') *n.* Any of certain hemipterous insects with a sickening odor.

stink·weed (stingk'wēd') *n.* Any of various plants with foul-smelling flowers or leaves.

stint (stint) *v.t.* **1** To limit, as in amount. —*v.i.* **2** To be frugal or sparing. —*n.* **1** A task to be performed within a specified time: a weekly *stint.* **2** A bound; restriction. [< OE *styntan* stupefy] —**stint'er** *n.* —**stint'ing·ly** *adv.*

stipe (stīp) *n.* A stalklike support, esp. that of a fern frond, a pistil, or a mushroom cap. [< L *stipes* branch]

sti·pend (stī'pend, -pənd) *n.* A regular, fixed allowance or salary. [< L *stips* payment in coin + *pendere* weigh, pay out]

sti·pen·di·ar·y (stī·pen'dē·er'ē) *adj.* **1** Receiving a stipend. **2** Performing services for a fixed payment. —*n. pl.* **·ar·ies** One who receives a stipend.

stip·ple (stip'əl) *v.t.* **·pled, ·pling** To draw, paint, or engrave with dots. —*n.* **1** In painting, etching, etc., a method of representing light and shade by employing dots instead of lines. **2** The effect resulting from this method. **3** Stippled work. Also **stip'pling.** [< Du. *stip* dot] —**stip'pler** *n.*

stip·u·late (stip'yə·lāt) *v.* **·lat·ed, ·lat·ing** *v.t.* **1** To specify as the terms of an agreement, contract, etc. **2** To specify as a requirement for agreement. —*v.i.* **3** To demand something as a requirement or condition. [< L *stipulari* to bargain] —**stip'u·la·tor** *n.* —**stip'u·la·to·ry** (-lə·tôr'ē, -tō'rē) *adj.*

stip·u·la·tion (stip'yə·lā'shən) *n.* **1** The act of stipulating. **2** An agreement or contract.

stip·ule (stip'yōōl) *n.* One of a pair of leaflike appendages at the base of the petiole of certain leaves. [< L *stipula* stalk] —**stip'u·lar, stip'u·late, stip'u·lat'ed** *adj.*

stir[1] (stûr) *v.* **stirred, stir·ring** *v.t.* **1** To mix thoroughly by giving a circular motion to, as with a spoon, fork, etc.: to *stir* soup. **2** To cause to move, esp. slightly. **3** To move vigorously; bestir: *Stir* yourself! **4** To rouse, as from sleep, indifference, or inactivity. **5** To incite; provoke: often with *up.* **6** To affect strongly; move with emotion. —*v.i.* **7** To move, esp. slightly: The log wouldn't *stir.* **8** To be active; move about. **9** To take place; happen. **10** To undergo stirring: This molasses *stirs* easily. —*n.* **1** The act of stirring. **2** Movement. **3** Public interest; excitement. **4** A poke; nudge. [< OE *styrian*] —**stir'rer** *n.*

stir[2] (stûr) *n. Slang* A jail; prison. [?]

stir·ring (stûr'ing) *adj.* **1** Stimulating; inspiring. **2** Full of activity. —**stir'ring·ly** *adv.* —**Syn. 1** exciting, rousing. **2** animated, lively, sprightly.

stir·rup (stûr'əp, stir'-) *n.* **1** A loop of metal or wood suspended from a saddle to support a horseback rider's foot. **2** A similar device used as a support, as for a beam. [< OE *stigrāp* mounting rope] • See SADDLE.

stirrup bone STAPES.

stitch (stich) *n.* **1** A single passage of a threaded needle or other implement through fabric and back again, as in sewing. **2** A single turn of thread or yarn around a needle or other implement, as in knitting or crocheting. **3** Any individual arrangement of a thread or threads used in sewing: a chain *stitch.* **4** A sharp sudden pain. **5** *Informal* A garment: I haven't a *stitch* to wear. —**be in stitches** To

be overcome with laughter. —*v.t.* **1** To join together with stitches. **2** To ornament with stitches. —*v.i.* **3** To make stitches; sew. [< OE *stice* prick]

sti·ver (stī'vər) *n.* **1** A small Dutch coin, 1/20 of a guilder. **2** Anything of little value.

St. Johns·wort (sānt jonz'wûrt') Any of various small, woody perennials, usu. with yellow flowers. Also **Saint Johnswort, St. John's-wort.**

stk. stock.

sto·a (stō'ə) *n. pl.* **sto·ae** (stō'ē) or **sto·as** In Greek architecture, a covered colonnade, portico, cloister, or promenade. [Gk., porch]

stoat (stōt) *n. pl.* **stoats** or **stoat** The ermine, esp. in its brown summer coat. [ME *stote*]

stock (stok) *n.* **1** The goods a store or merchant has on hand. **2** A quantity of something acquired or kept for future use: a *stock* of provisions. **3** LIVESTOCK. **4** The original, as a man, race, or language, from which others are descended or derived. **5** A line of familial descent. **6** An ethnic group; race. **7** A related group of plants or animals. **8** A group of related languages; also, a language family. **9** The trunk or main stem of a tree or other plant. **10 a** A plant stem from which cuttings are taken for grafting. **b** A plant stem upon which a graft is made. **11** In finance: **a** The capital raised by a corporation through the sale of shares that entitle the holder to interest or dividends. **b** The part of this capital credited to an individual stockholder. **c** The certificate or certificates indicating this. **12** A fund or debt owed (as by a nation, city, etc.) to individuals who receive a fixed interest rate. **13** The part of a device that functions as a support and to which other parts are attached, as the wooden portion or handle of a firearm, whip, etc. **14** Raw material: paper *stock.* **15** The broth from boiled vegetables, meat, or fish, used in preparing soups, gravies, etc. **16** Something lacking life, feeling, or motion. **17** The group of plays produced by a theatrical company at one theater. **18** A broad, heavily starched band, formerly worn as a cravat. —**in stock** Available for purchase. —**out of stock** Not available; all sold out. —**stock in trade** One's abilities, talents, or resources. —**take stock 1** To take an inventory. **2** To size up a situation. —**take stock in** *Informal* To have trust or belief in. —**the stocks 1** A former device for public punishment consisting of a timber frame for confining the ankles, or the ankles and wrists. **2** The timber frame on which a ship or boat is built. —*v.t.* **1** To supply with cattle, as a farm. **2** To supply (a store) with merchandise. **3** To keep for sale: to *stock* avocados. **4** To supply with wildlife: to *stock* a pond. **5** To put aside for future use. **6** To provide with a handle or stock. —*v.i.* **7** To lay in supplies or stock: often with *up.* —*adj.* **1** Kept on hand: a *stock* size. **2** Banal; commonplace: a *stock* phrase. **3** Of or pertaining to the breeding and raising of livestock. **4** Employed in handling or caring for the stock: a *stock* clerk. **5** Of or pertaining to a stock or stocks (def. 9). [< OE *stocc*]

stock·ade (sto·kād') *n.* **1** A defense consisting of a strong, high barrier of upright posts, stakes, etc. **2** The area enclosed by such a barrier. **3** A similar area used to confine prisoners, esp. in military installations. —*v.t.* **·ad·ed, ·ad·ing** To surround or fortify with a stockade. [< OF *estaque* a stake]

stock·bro·ker (stok'brō'kər) *n.* One who buys and sells stocks or securities for others.

stock car 1 An automobile, usu. a sedan, modified for racing. **2** A railroad car used for transporting cattle.

stock company 1 An incorporated company that issues stock. **2** A theatrical company under one management that presents a series of plays.

stock exchange 1 A place where securities are bought and sold. **2** An association of stockbrokers.

stock farm A farm that specializes in the breeding of livestock.

stock·hold·er (stok'hōl'dər) *n.* One who holds stocks or shares in a company.

stock·i·net (stok'i·net') *n.* An elastic knitted fabric used chiefly for undergarments. [< STOCKING]

stock·ing (stok'ing) *n.* **1** A close-fitting knitted covering for the foot and leg. **2** Something resembling such a covering. [< STOCK, in obs. sense of "a stocking"]

stocking cap A long knitted cap, tapered and often having a pompon or tassel at the end.

stock·man (stok′mən) n. pl. ·men (-mən) 1 One who raises or owns livestock; a cattleman. 2 A man having charge of goods, as in a warehouse.

stock market 1 STOCK EXCHANGE. 2 The business transacted in such a place: The *stock market* was active.

stock·pile (stok′pīl′) n. A storage pile of materials or supplies. Also **stock pile.** —v.t. & v.i. ·piled, ·pil·ing To accumulate a supply or stockpile (of).

stock raising The breeding and raising of livestock.

stock·room (stok′rōōm′, -rŏŏm′) n. A room where reserve stocks of goods are stored.

stock·still (stok′stil′) adj. Completely motionless.

stock·y (stok′ē) adj. stock·i·er, stock·i·est Short and stout. —stock′i·ly adv. —stock′i·ness n.

stock·yard (stok′yärd′) n. A large yard with pens, stables, etc., where cattle are kept ready for shipping, slaughter, etc.

stodg·y (stoj′ē) adj. stodg·i·er, stodg·i·est 1 Dull; boring. 2 Indigestible; heavy. [?] —stodg′i·ly adv. —stodg′i·ness n.

sto·gy (stō′gē) n. pl. ·gies A long, slender, inexpensive cigar. Also **sto′gie.** [< *Conestoga*, Pennsylvania]

sto·ic (stō′ik) n. A person apparently unaffected by pleasure or pain. —adj. Indifferent to pleasure or pain; impassive: also **sto′i·cal.** [< STOIC] —sto′i·cal·ly adv. —sto′i·cal·ness n.

Sto·ic (stō′ik) n. A member of a school of Greek philosophy founded by Zeno about 308 B.C., holding the belief that wisdom lies in being superior to passion, joy, grief, etc. —adj. Of or pertaining to the Stoics or Stoicism. [< Gk. *Stoa*, the colonnade at Athens where Zeno taught]

sto·i·cism (stō′ə·siz′əm) n. Indifference to pleasure or pain.

Sto·i·cism (stō′ə·siz′əm) n. The doctrines of the Stoics.

stoke (stōk) v.t. stoked, stok·ing 1 To supply (a furnace) with fuel. 2 To stir up; intensify. —v.i. 3 To tend a fire. [Back formation < STOKER]

stoke·hole (stōk′hōl′) n. 1 The space about the mouth of a furnace; the fireroom. 2 The mouth of a furnace.

stok·er (stō′kər) n. 1 A person who tends a furnace or boiler. 2 A mechanical device for feeding coal to a furnace. [< Du. *stoken* stir a fire]

STOL, S.T.O.L. short takeoff and landing.

stole¹ (stōl) n. 1 *Eccl.* A long, narrow band, usu. of decorated silk or linen, worn about the shoulders by priests and bishops. 2 A fur, scarf, or garment resembling a stole, worn by women. [< Gk. *stolē* a garment] — **stoled** adj.

stole² (stōl) p.t. of STEAL.

sto·len (stō′lən) p.p. of STEAL.

stol·id (stol′id) adj. Expressing no feeling; impassive. [< L *stolidus* dull] —sto·lid·i·ty (stə·lid′ə·tē), stol′id·ness n. —stol′id·ly adv.

sto·ma (stō′mə) n. pl. sto·ma·ta (stō′mə·tə, stom′ə·tə) or sto·mas A small, mouthlike opening, esp. any of the minute epidermal breathing pores on a plant leaf. Also **sto′mate** (stō′māt′). [< Gk. *stoma* mouth] —sto′ma·tal adj.

Stole

stom·ach (stum′ək) n. 1 A pouchlike dilation of the alimentary canal, situated in most vertebrates next to the esophagus and serving as one of the principal organs of digestion. 2 Any digestive cavity, as of an invertebrate. 3 The abdomen; belly. 4 Desire for food; appetite. 5 Any desire or inclination. —v.t. 1 To put up with; endure. 2 To take into and retain in the stomach; digest. [< Gk. *stomachos*] —stom′ach·al adj. —sto·mach·ic (stō·mak′ik), sto·mach′i·cal adj., n. • See LIVER.

stom·ach·er (stum′ək·ər) n. A former article of clothing worn, esp. by women, over the breast and stomach.

stomp (stomp) v.t. & v.i. To stamp; tread heavily (upon).

—n. A jazz dance involving heavy stamping. [Var of STAMP] —stomp′er n.

stone (stōn) n. pl. stones or for def. 8 stone 1 ROCK (def. 3). 2 A small piece of rock, as a pebble. 3 A piece of shaped or hewn rock, as a gravestone. 4 A jewel; gem. 5 Something like a stone in shape or hardness: a *hailstone.* 6 An abnormal, hard concretion in the body. 7 The hard inner part of a drupe. 8 *Brit.* A measure of weight equal to 14 pounds. —cast the first stone To be the first to blame (someone). —leave no stone unturned To do everything within possibility. —adj. 1 Made of stone: a *stone* ax. 2 Made of coarse, hard earthenware: a *stone* bottle. —v.t. stoned, ston·ing 1 To hurl stones at. 2 To kill by throwing stones at. 3 To remove the stones or pits from. 4 To furnish or line with stone. [< OE *stān*] —ston′er n.

Stone Age The earliest known period of human cultural evolution, marked by the creation of stone implements.

stone-blind (stōn′blīnd′) adj. Completely blind.

stone-broke (stōn′brōk′) adj. *Informal* Without any money; having no funds. Also **ston′y-broke′.**

stone-crop (stōn′krop′) n. SEDUM.

stone-cut·ter (stōn′kut′ər) n. One who or that which cuts stone; esp. a machine for facing stone. —stone′cut·ting n.

stoned (stōnd) adj. *Slang* 1 Drunk. 2 Under the influence of a drug or narcotic.

stone-deaf (stōn′def′) adj. Completely deaf.

stone·ma·son (stōn′mā′sən) n. One whose trade is to prepare and lay stones in building. —stone′ma·son·ry n.

stone's throw (stōnz) 1 The distance a stone may be cast by hand. 2 A short distance.

stone·wall (stōn′wôl′) *Slang* v.i. 1 To act in a calculatedly obstructive way, as by lying or failing to respond to inquiry. —v.t. 2 To respond to in such a way.

stone·ware (stōn′wâr′) n. A very hard, glazed pottery, made from siliceous clay or clay mixed with flint or sand.

stone·work (stōn′wûrk′) n. 1 The art or process of cutting or setting stone. 2 Work built or made of stone. 3 pl. A place where stone is shaped. —stone′work′er n.

ston·y (stō′nē) adj. ston·i·er, ston·i·est 1 Abounding in stone or stones. 2 Made of or consisting of stone. 3 Hard as stone; unfeeling. 4 Like stone. 5 *Slang* Having no money. —ston′i·ly adv. —ston′i·ness n. —Syn. 3 chilly, cold, pitiless.

stood (stŏŏd) p.t. & p.p. of STAND.

stooge (stōōj) n. 1 *Informal* An actor who feeds lines to the principal comedian, acts as a foil for his jokes, etc. 2 Anyone who acts as or is the tool or dupe of another. —v.i. stooged, stoog·ing To act as a stooge: usu. with *for.* [?]

stool (stōōl) n. 1 A backless and armless seat intended for one person. 2 A low bench or portable support for the feet or for kneeling. 3 A seat or place used as a toilet. 4 The matter evacuated from the bowels; feces. 5 A stump or root from which suckers or sprouts shoot up. [< OE *stōl*]

stool pigeon 1 A living or artificial pigeon used to decoy others into a trap. 2 *Slang* An informer, as for the police.

stoop¹ (stōōp) v.i. 1 To lean the body forward and down. 2 To stand or walk with the upper part of the body habitually bent forward; slouch. 3 To bend: said of trees, cliffs, etc. 4 To lower or degrade oneself. —v.t. 5 To bend (one's head, shoulders, etc.) forward. —n. 1 A downward and forward bending of the body. 2 A habitual forward inclination of the head and shoulders. [< OE *stūpian*]

stoop² (stōōp) n. A small porch or platform at the entrance to a house. [< Du. *stoep*]

stop (stop) v. stopped, stop·ping v.t. 1 To bring (something in motion) to a halt: to *stop* an automobile. 2 To prevent the doing or completion of: to *stop* a revolution. 3 To prevent (a person) from doing something; restrain. 4 To withhold or cut off, as wages or supplies. 5 To cease doing: *Stop* that! 6 To check, as a flow of blood from a wound. 7 To obstruct (a passage, road, etc.). 8 To fill in or otherwise close, as a hole, cavity, etc. 9 To close (a bottle, barrel, etc.) with a cork, plug, etc. 10 To order a bank not to pay or honor: to *stop* a check. 11 *Music* To press down (a string) or close (a finger hole) to change the pitch of. 12 In boxing, etc., to parry. —v.i. 13 To come to a halt; cease progress or motion. **14** To cease doing something. **—stop off** To stop for a brief stay before continuing on a trip. **—stop over** *Informal* To stop briefly, as for a visit or a rest during a journey. **—n. 1** The act of stopping, or the state of being stopped. **2** That which stops or limits the range or time of a movement; an obstruction. **3** *Music* **a** The pressing down of a string or the closing of an aperture to change the pitch. **b** A key, lever, or handle for stopping a string or an aperture. **4** *Music* In an organ, a set of pipes producing tones of the same timbre. **5 a** *Brit.* A punctuation mark; a period. **b** In cables, etc., a period. **6** *Phonet.* **a** Complete blockage of the breath stream, as with the lips or tongue, followed by a sudden release. **b** A consonant so produced, as *p, b, t, d, k,* and *g.* **—put a stop to** To end; terminate. [< OE *-stoppian*] **—Syn** *v.* **2** deter, quash. **4** discontinue.

stop·cock (stop′kok′) *n.* A faucet or valve.

stop·gap (stop′gap′) *n.* A person or thing serving as a temporary substitute. **—adj.** Being a stopgap.

stop·o·ver (stop′ō′vər) *n.* The act of stopping over, or permission to stop over on a journey and continue later, using the ticket issued for the whole journey.

stop·page (stop′ij) *n.* **1** The act of stopping or the state of being stopped. **2** A blocking or obstruction.

stop·per (stop′ər) *n.* **1** One who or that which stops or brings to a stop. **2** A plug or cork for a container, as a bottle. **—v.t.** To secure or close with a stopper.

stop·ple (stop′əl) *n.* A stopper, plug, cork, or bung. **—v.t.** **·pled, ·pling** To close with or as with a stopple. [< ME *stoppen* stop]

stop·watch (stop′woch′) *n.* A watch with a hand indicating fractions of a second which may be stopped or started instantly, used for timing races, etc.

stor·age (stôr′ij, stō′rij) *n.* **1** The depositing of articles in a place for their safekeeping. **2** Space for storing goods. **3** A charge for storing. **4** A section of a computer in whch data is held for later use; memory.

storage battery A connected group of two or more electrolytic cells that can be reversibly charged and discharged.

store (stôr, stōr) *v.t.* **stored, stor·ing 1** To put away for future use. **2** To furnish or supply; provide. **3** To place in a warehouse or other place for safekeeping. **—n. 1** That which is stored or laid up against future need. **2** *pl.* Supplies, as of food, arms, or clothing. **3** A storehouse; warehouse. **4** A place where merchandise of any kind is kept for sale; a shop. **—in store** Set apart for the future; impending. **—set store by** To value or esteem. [< L *instaurare* restore, erect]

store·front (stôr′frunt′, stōr′-) *n.* **1** The front or facade of a store, usu. opening directly out onto a pedestrian sidewalk. **2** A public service or other facility, often temporary, situated on the site of a former store. **—adj.** Characteristic of or being a storefront.

store·house (stôr′hous′, stōr′-) *n.* A place in which goods are stored; depository.

store·keep·er (stôr′kē′pər, stōr′-) *n.* A person who keeps a retail store or who is in charge of supplies.

store·room (stôr′rōōm′, -rōōm′, stōr′-) *n.* A room in which things are stored.

sto·rey (stôr′ē, stōr′ē) *n. pl.* **·reys** *Chiefly Brit.* STORY[2].

sto·ried[1] (stôr′ēd, stōr′ēd) *adj.* Having or consisting of stories: a *six-storied* house.

sto·ried[2] (stôr′ēd, stōr′ēd) *adj.* **1** Having a notable history. **2** Ornamented with designs representing scenes from history or story.

stork (stôrk) *n.* A large wading bird with a long neck and long legs, related to the herons. [< OE *storc*]

storm (stôrm) *n.* **1** A disturbance of the atmosphere that creates strong winds, often with heavy precipitation of rain, snow, dust, etc. **2** Any heavy, prolonged precipitation of snow, rain, etc. **3** Anything similar to a storm: a *storm* of missiles. **4** A violent outburst: a *storm* of applause. **5** A violent and rapid assault. **—v.i. 1** To blow with violence; rain, snow,

White stork

hail, etc., heavily. **2** To be very angry; rage. **3** To rush with violence or rage: He *stormed* about the room. **—v.t. 4** To attack: to *storm* a fort. [< OE]

storm cellar An underground shelter adapted for use during cyclones, hurricanes, etc.

storm door An additional outer door used to conserve heat during cold weather.

storm petrel Any of certain petrels thought to portend storm.

storm troops A Nazi party militia unit, the *Sturmabteilung,* established in 1924. **—storm trooper**

storm window An extra window outside the ordinary one for greater insulation against cold.

storm·y (stôr′mē) *adj.* **storm·i·er, storm·i·est 1** Characterized by storms; turbulent. **2** Violent; rough. **—storm′i·ly** *adv.* **—storm′i·ness** *n.* **—Syn. 1** blustery, tempestuous. **2** disturbed, passionate, vehement.

stormy petrel 1 STORM PETREL. **2** A person thought to portend or foment trouble.

sto·ry[1] (stôr′ē, stōr′ē) *n. pl.* **·ries 1** A narrative or recital of an event, or a series of events. **2** A narrative intended to entertain a reader or hearer. **3** An account of the facts relating to a particular person, thing, or incident. **4** A news article in a newspaper or magazine. **5** The material for a news article. **6** An anecdote. **7** *Informal* A lie; falsehood. **8** The series of events in a novel, play, etc. **—v.t. ·ried, ·ry·ing 1** *Archaic* To relate as a story. **2** To adorn with designs representing scenes from history, legend, etc. [< L *historia*]

sto·ry[2] (stôr′ē, stōr′ē) *n. pl.* **·ries 1** A division in a building comprising the space between two successive floors. **2** All the rooms on one level of a building. [< Med. L *historia* story (painted on a row of windows)]

sto·ry·tell·er (stôr′ē·tel′ər, stōr′ē-) *n.* **1** One who relates stories or anecdotes. **2** *Informal* A prevaricator; fibber. **—sto′ry·tell′ing** *n., adj.*

stoup (stōōp) *n.* **1** *Eccl.* A basin for holy water at the entrance of a church. **2** A flagon, tankard, or large drinking glass. [< ON *staup* bucket]

stout (stout) *adj.* **1** Fat; thick-set. **2** Firmly built; strong: a *stout* fence. **3** Courageous: a *stout* heart. **4** Stubborn; unyielding: a *stout* denial. **—n. 1** A stout person. **2** *Usu. pl.* Clothing made for stout or big people. **3** A strong, very dark porter or ale. [< OF *estout* bold, strong] **—stout′ly** *adv.* **—stout′ness** *n.*

stout·heart·ed (stout′här′tid) *adj.* Brave; courageous. **—stout′heart′ed·ly** *adv.* **—stout′heart′ed·ness** *n.*

stove[1] (stōv) *n.* An apparatus, usu. of metal, in which fuel is consumed for heating or cooking. [< OE *stofa* a heated room]

stove[2] (stōv) A *p.t.* & *p.p.* of STAVE.

stove·pipe (stōv′pīp′) *n.* **1** A pipe for conducting the smoke from a stove to a chimney flue. **2** *Informal* A tall silk hat: also **stovepipe hat.**

stow (stō) *v.t.* **1** To place or arrange compactly; pack. **2** To fill by packing. **—stow away 1** To put in a place of safekeeping, hiding, etc. **2** To be a stowaway. [< OE *stōw* a place]

stow·age (stō′ij) *n.* **1** The act of stowing. **2** Space for stowing goods. **3** Charge for stowing goods. **4** The goods stowed.

stow·a·way (stō′ə·wā′) *n.* One who conceals himself on a ship, train, airplane, etc., to obtain free passage, to escape, or to cross a border illegally.

STP (es′tē′pē′) *n.* A hallucinogenic drug chemically related to mescaline and amphetamine. [< STP, a trade name for a gasoline additive supposed to increase engine power.]

STP standard temperature and pressure.

str. steamer; strait; string(s).

stra·bis·mus (strə·biz′məs) *n.* Inability to focus the eyes simultaneously on the same spot because of a disorder of the eye muscles. [< Gk. *strabizein* to squint] **—stra·bis′mal, stra·bis′mic** or **·mi·cal** *adj.*

strad·dle (strad′l) *v.* **·dled, ·dling** *v.i.* **1** To stand, walk, or sit with the legs spread apart. **2** To be spread wide apart: said of the legs. **3** *Informal* To appear to favor both sides of an issue. **—v.t. 4** To stand, walk, or sit with the legs on either side of. **5** To spread (the legs) wide apart. **6** *Informal* To appear to favor both sides of (an issue). **—n. 1** The act of straddling. **2** The distance between the legs in straddling. **3** *Informal* A noncommital position on an issue. [Freq. of STRIDE] —**strad′dler** *n.* —**strad′dling·ly** *adv.*

Strad·i·var·i·us (strad′i·vâr′ē·əs) *n.* One of the violins, cellos, etc., made by Antonio Stradivari (1644–1737), Italian violin maker.

strafe (strāf, sträf) *v.t.* **strafed, straf·ing 1** To attack (troops, emplacements, etc.) with machine-gun fire from low-flying airplanes. **2** To bombard or shell heavily. **3** *Slang* To punish. [< G *strafen* punish] —**straf′er** *n.*

strag·gle (strag′əl) *v.i.* **·gled, ·gling 1** To wander from the road, main body, etc.; stray. **2** To wander aimlessly about; ramble. **3** To occur at irregular intervals. [ME *straglen*] —**strag′gler** *n.* —**strag′gling·ly** *adv.* —**strag′gly** *adj.* (**·i·er, ·i·est**)

straight (strāt) *adj.* **1** Extending uniformly in the same direction without curve or bend. **2** Free from kinks; not curly, as hair. **3** Not stooped; erect. **4** Not deviating from truth, fairness, or honesty. **5** Free from obstruction; uninterrupted. **6** Correctly ordered or arranged. **7** Sold without discount for number or quantity taken. **8** *Informal* Accepting the whole, as of a plan, party, or policy: a *straight* ticket. **9** In poker, consisting of five cards forming a sequence. **10** Having nothing added: *straight* whiskey. **11** *Slang* Conforming to what is accepted as usual, normal, or conventional, esp. according to middle-class standards. **12** *Slang* HETEROSEXUAL. —*n.* **1** A straight part or piece. **2** The part of a racecourse between the winning post and the last turn. **3** In poker, a numerical sequence of five cards. **4** *Slang* A conventional person. **5** *Slang* HETEROSEXUAL. —*adv.* **1** In a straight line or a direct course. **2** Closely in line; correspondingly. **3** At once: Go *straight* to bed. **4** Uprightly: to live *straight*. **5** Correctly: I can't think *straight*. **6** Without restriction or qualification: Tell it *straight*. —**go straight** To reform after having led the life of a criminal. —**straight away** or **off** At once; right away. [< OE *streht,* pp. of *streccan* stretch] —**straight′ness** *n.*

straight angle An angle of 180°.

straight·a·way (strāt′ə·wā′) *adj.* Having no curve or turn. —*n.* A straight course or track. —*adv.* At once; straightway.

straight·en (strāt′n) *v.t.* **1** To make straight. —*v.i.* **2** To become straight. —**straighten out** To restore order to; rectify. —**straighten up 1** To make neat; tidy. **2** To stand in erect posture. **3** To reform. —**straight′en·er** *n.*

straight face A sober, expressionless, or unsmiling face. —**straight-faced** (strāt′fāst′) *adj.*

straight·for·ward (strāt′fôr′wərd) *adj.* **1** Candid; honest. **2** Proceeding in a straight course. —*adv.* In a straight course or direct manner: also **straight′for′wards** (-wərdz). —**straight′for′ward·ly** *adv.* —**straight′for′ward·ness** *n.* —**Syn.** **1** aboveboard, frank, open, sincere. **2** direct.

straight man *Informal* An entertainer who acts as a foil for a comedian.

straight-out (strāt′out′) *adj. Informal* **1** Unreserved; unrestrained. **2** Thorough; complete.

straight·way (strāt′wā′) *adv.* Immediately.

strain[1] (strān) *v.t.* **1** To pull or draw tight. **2** To exert to the utmost. **3** To injure by overexertion; sprain. **4** To deform in structure or shape as a result of stress. **5** To stretch beyond the true intent, proper limit, etc.: to *strain* a point. **6** To embrace tightly; hug. **7** To pass through a strainer. **8** To remove by filtration. —*v.i.* **9** To make violent efforts; strive. **10** To be or become wrenched or twisted. **13** To filter, trickle, or percolate. —**strain at 1** To push or pull with violent efforts. **2** To strive for. **3** To scruple or balk at accepting. —*n.* **1** An act of straining or the state of being strained. **2** Any very taxing demand on strength, emotions, etc.: the *strain* of city life. **3** Any violent effort or exertion. **4** The injury resulting from excessive tension or effort. **5** *Physics* The change of shape or structure of a body produced by the action of a stress. [< L *stringere* bind tight]

strain[2] (strān) *n.* **1** Line of descent, or the individuals, collectively, in that line. **2** Inborn or hereditary disposition; natural tendency. **3** A line of plants or animals selectively bred to perpetuate distinctive traits. **4** *Often pl.* A melody; tune. **5** Prevailing tone, style, or manner. [< OE *strēon* offspring]

strain·er (strā′nər) *n.* A utensil or device that filters, strains, or sifts.

strait (strāt) *n.* **1** *Often pl.* A narrow passage of water connecting two larger bodies of water. **2** Any narrow pass or passage. **3** *Often pl.* Distress; embarrassment: financial *straits.* —*adj. Archaic* **1** Narrow. **2** Strict. [< L *strictus,* p.p. of *stringere* bind tight.] —**strait′ly** *adv.* —**strait′ness** *n.*

strait·en (strāt′n) *v.t.* **1** To make strait or narrow; restrict. **2** To embarrass, or restrict, as in finances.

strait·jack·et (strāt′jak′it) *n.* **1** A jacket with long, closed sleeves for confining the arms of a violent patient or prisoner. **2** Anything that unduly confines or restricts. —*v.t.* To confine in or as if in a straitjacket.

strait-laced (strāt′lāst′) *adj.* **1** Formerly, tightly laced, as corsets. **2** Strict, esp. in morals or manners; prudish.

strand[1] (strand) *n.* A shore or beach, esp. on the ocean. —*v.t. & v.i.* **1** To drive or run aground, as a ship. **2** To leave or be left in difficulties or helplessness: *stranded* in a strange city. [< OE]

strand[2] (strand) *n.* **1** Any of the fibers, wires, or threads twisted or plaited together to form a rope, cable, cord, etc. **2** A single hair or similar filament. **3** Any of various ropelike objects: a *strand* of pearls. —*v.t.* To break a strand of (a rope). [ME *strond*]

strange (strānj) *adj.* **strang·er, strang·est 1** Previously unknown, unseen, or unheard of. **2** Peculiar; out of the ordinary: a *strange* experience. **3** Foreign; alien. **4** Out of place: to feel *strange* in a new school. **5** Inexperienced: *strange* to a new job. [< L *extraneus* foreign] —**strange′ly** *adv.* —**strange′ness** *n.* —**Syn.** **1** unfamiliar. **2** odd, queer, unusual. **4** unaccustomed.

stran·ger (strān′jər) *n.* **1** One who is not an acquaintance. **2** An unfamiliar visitor; guest. **3** A foreigner. **4** One unacquainted with something specified: with *to:* a *stranger* to higher mathematics.

stran·gle (strang′gəl) *v.* **·gled, ·gling** *v.t.* **1** To choke to death; throttle. **2** To repress; suppress. —*v.i.* **3** To suffer or die from strangulation. [< Gk. *strangalaein*] —**stran′gler** *n.*

stran·gle·hold (strang′gəl·hōld′) *n.* **1** In wrestling, an illegal hold which chokes one's opponent. **2** Anything that chokes freedom or progress.

stran·gu·late (strang′gyə·lāt) *v.t.* **·lat·ed, ·lat·ing 1** STRANGLE. **2** *Pathol.* To constrict so as to cut off circulation of the blood. [< L *strangulare*] —**stran′gu·la′tion** *n.*

strap (strap) *n.* **1** A long, narrow, and flexible strip of leather, webbing, etc., for binding or fastening things together. **2** A razor strop. **3** Something used as a strap: a shoulder *strap.* —*v.t.* **strapped, strap·ing 1** To fasten or bind with a strap. **2** To beat with a strap. **3** To sharpen or strop. **4** To embarrass financially. [Var. of STROP]

strap·hang·er (strap′hang′ər) *n. Informal* A standing passenger on a bus or train who keeps his balance by holding on to a strap, bar, etc.

strap·ping (strap′ing) *adj. Informal* Large and muscular; robust.

stra·ta (strā′tə, strat′ə) *n.pl.* of STRATUM.

strat·a·gem (strat′ə·jəm) *n.* **1** A maneuver designed to deceive or outwit an enemy. **2** Any device or trick for obtaining advantage. [< Gk. *stratēgēma* piece of generalship] —**Syn.** artifice, deception, ruse, trick.

stra·te·gic (strə·tē′jik) *adj.* **1** Of or based on strategy. **2** Important in strategy. **3** Having to do with materials essential for conducting a war. **4** Assigned to destroy important enemy installations: a *strategic* air force. Also **stra·te′gi·cal.** —**stra·te′gi·cal·ly** *adv.*

strat·e·gist (strat′ə·jist) *n.* One skilled in strategy.

strat·e·gy (strat′ə·jē) *n. pl.* **·gies 1** The science of planning and conducting military campaigns on a broad scale. **2** Any plan based on this. **3** The use of stratagem or artifice, as in business, politics, etc. **4** Skill in management. **5** An ingenious plan or method. [< Gk. *stratēgos* general]

strat·i·fy (strat′ə·fī) *v.* **·fied, ·fy·ing** *v.t.* **1** To form or arrange in strata or layers. —*v.i.* **2** To form in strata. **3** To be formed in strata. [< L *stratum* layer + -FY] —**strat'i·fi·ca'tion** *n.*

stra·to·cu·mu·lus (strāt'ō·kyōō'myə·ləs, strat'-) *n. pl.* **·li** (-lī) *Meteorol.* A type of dark, low-lying cloud, characterized by horizontal bases and high, rounded summits.

strat·o·sphere (strat'ə·sfir) *n. Meteorol.* The portion of the atmosphere beginning at about six miles above the earth, where a more or less uniform temperature prevails. —**strat·o·spher'ic** (-sfer'ik) or **·i·cal** *adj.*

stra·tum (strā'təm, strat'əm) *n. pl.* **·ta** (-tə) or **·tums** 1 A natural or artificial layer. 2 *Geol.* A more or less homogeneous layer of rock. 3 A level of society, having similar educational, cultural, and usu. economic backgrounds. [< L *stratus*, p.p. of *sternere* to spread]

Rock strata

stra·tus (strā'təs, strat'əs) *n. pl.* **·ti** (-tī) *Meteorol.* A low-lying, foglike cloud. [L, orig. p.p. of *sternere* to spread]

straw (strô) *n.* 1 A dry stalk of grain. 2 Stems or stalks of grain after being threshed, used for fodder, etc. 3 A mere trifle. 4 A slender tube made of paper, glass, etc., used to suck up a beverage. —**catch** (or **grab**) **at a straw** To try anything as a last resort. —**straw in the wind** A sign of the course of future events. —*adj.* 1 Made of or like straw, as in color. 2 Worthless; sham. [< OE *strēaw* straw]

straw·ber·ry (strô'ber'ē, -bər·ē) *n. pl.* **·ries** 1 Any of a genus of stemless perennials of the rose family, with trifoliolate leaves, usu. white flowers and slender runners by which it propagates: also **strawberry vine.** 2 Its edible fruit, consisting of a red, fleshy receptacle bearing many achenes. [< STRAW + BERRY]

strawberry blond A person having reddish blond hair.

straw boss *Informal* A worker acting as an assistant foreman.

straw vote An unofficial test vote.

stray (strā) *v.i.* 1 To wander from the proper course; roam. 2 To deviate from right or goodness; go astray. —*adj.* 1 Having strayed; straying: a *stray* dog. 2 Irregular; occasional: He made a few *stray* remarks. —*n.* A domestic animal that has strayed. [< L *extra vagare* wander outside] —**stray'er** *n.*

streak (strēk) *n.* 1 A long, narrow mark or stripe: a *streak* of lightning. 2 A trace or characteristic: a *streak* of meanness. 3 A layer or strip: meat with a *streak* of fat and a *streak* of lean. 4 *Informal* A period or interval: a winning *streak.* 5 *Slang* The act or an instance of streaking (*v.* def. 3). —**like a streak** *Informal* As rapidly as possible. —*v.i.* 1 To form a streak or streaks. 2 To move at great speed. 3 *Slang* To appear naked in a public place, usu. briefly and esp. while running, as for a thrill. —*v.t.* 4 To form streaks in or on. 5 *Slang* To appear naked in (a public place), usu. briefly and esp. while running, as for a thrill. [< OE *strica*] —**streak'y** *adj.* (**·i·er**, **·i·est**) —**streak'i·ly** *adv.* —**streak'er** *n.,* **streak'i·ness** *n.*

stream (strēm) *n.* 1 A current or flow of water, esp. a small river. 2 Any continuous flow or current: a *stream* of invective. —*v.i.* 1 To pour forth or issue in a stream. 2 To pour forth in a stream: eyes *streaming* with tears. 3 To proceed uninterruptedly, as a crowd. 4 To float with a waving movement, as a flag. 5 To move with a trail of light, as a meteor. 6 To come or arrive in large numbers. [< OE *strēam*] —**Syn.** *n.* 1 brook, course, creek, rill, rivulet.

stream·er (strē'mər) *n.* 1 An object that streams forth, or hangs extended. 2 A long, narrow flag or standard. 3 A stream or shaft of light. 4 A newspaper headline that runs across the whole page.

stream·let (strēm'lit) *n.* RIVULET.

stream·line (strēm'līn') *n.* 1 A line in a mass of fluid such that each of its tangents coincides with the local velocity of the fluid. 2 Any shape or contour designed to lessen resistance to motion of a solid in a fluid. —*adj.* 1 Designating an uninterrupted flow or drift. 2 Denoting a form or body designed to minimize turbulence in the flow of fluid around it. —*v.t.* **·lined, ·lin·ing** 1 To design with a streamline shape. 2 To make more up-to-date, esp. by reorganization.

stream·lined (strēm'līnd') *adj.* 1 STREAMLINE. 2 Improved in efficiency; modernized.

street (strēt) *n.* 1 A public way in a city, town, or village, usu. with buildings on one or both sides. 2 Such a public way as set apart for vehicles: Don't play in the *street.* 3 *Informal* The people living on a specific street. —*adj.* 1 Working in the streets: a *street* musician. 2 Opening onto the street: a *street* door. 3 Performed or taking place on the street: *street* crime. 4 Habituated to the ways of life in the streets, esp. in cities: *street* people. [< LL *strata (via)* paved (road)]

street Arab A homeless or outcast child who lives in the streets; gamin.

street·car (strēt'kär') *n.* A passenger car that runs on rails laid on the surface of the streets.

street people Young people, esp. of the late 1960s, usu. without a permanent residence and having a life style marked by the rejection of middle-class values and by the use of drugs.

street·walk·er (strēt'wô'kər) *n.* A prostitute who solicits in the streets. —**street'walk'ing** *n.*

strength (strength) *n.* 1 The quality or property of being physically strong: the *strength* of a weight lifter. 2 The capacity to sustain the application of force without yielding or breaking. 3 Effectiveness: the *strength* of an argument. 4 Binding force or validity, as of a law. 5 Vigor or force of style: a drama of great *strength.* 6 Available numerical force in a military unit or other organization. 7 Degree of intensity, as of color, light, or sound. 8 Potency, as of a drug, chemical, or liquor; concentration. 9 A support; aid: He is our *strength.* —**on the strength of** Relying on; on the basis of. [< OE *strang* strong] —**Syn.** 1 force, power, vigor. 2 solidity, tenacity, toughness.

strength·en (streng'thən) *v.t.* 1 To make strong. 2 To encourage; hearten. —*v.i.* 3 To become or grow strong or stronger. —**strength'en·er** *n.*

stren·u·ous (stren'yōō·əs) *adj.* Necessitating or marked by strong effort or exertion. [< L *strenuus*] —**stren'u·ous·ly** *adv.* —**stren'u·ous·ness** *n.*

strep throat (strep) A streptococcal throat infection.

strep·to·coc·cus (strep'tə·kok'əs) *n. pl.* **·coc·ci** (-kok'sī, -sē, -ī, -ē) Any of a large group of spherical bacteria that grow together in long chains, including a few pathogens. [< Gk. *streptos* twisted + COCCUS] —**strep'to·coc'cal** (-kok'-əl), **strep'to·coc'cic** (-kok'sik, -kok'ik) *adj.*

strep·to·my·cin (strep'tō·mī'sin) *n.* A potent antibiotic isolated from a mold. [< Gk. *streptos* twisted + *mykēs* fungus]

stress (stres) *n.* 1 Special weight, importance, or significance. 2 Physical or emotional tension. 3 *Mech.* A force tending to deform a body on which it acts. 4 Emphasis. 5 In pronunciation, the relative force with which a sound, syllable, or word is uttered. —*v.t.* 1 To subject to stress. 2 To accent, as a syllable. 3 To give emphasis or weight to. [< L *strictus*, p.p. of *stringere* draw tight] —**stress'ful** *adj.*

-stress *suffix of nouns* Feminine form of -STER: *songstress.*

stretch (strech) *v.t.* 1 To extend or draw out, as to full length or width. 2 To draw out forcibly, esp. beyond normal or proper limits. 3 To cause to reach, as from one place to another. 4 To put forth, hold out, or extend (the hand, an object, etc.). 5 To tighten, strain, or exert to the utmost: to *stretch* every nerve. 6 To adjust or adapt to meet specific needs, circumstances, etc.: to *stretch* the truth; to *stretch* food. 7 *Slang* To fell with a blow. —*v.i.* 8 To reach or extend from one place to another. 9 To become extended, esp. beyond normal limits. 10 To extend one's body or limbs, as in relaxing. 11 To lie down: usu. with *out.* —*n.* 1 An act of stretching, or the state of being stretched. 2 Extent to which something can be stretched. 3 A continuous extent of space or time: a *stretch* of woodland; a *stretch* of two years. 4 In racing, the straight part of the track. 5 *Slang* A term of imprisonment. —*adj.* Capable of being easily stretched, as clothing: *stretch* socks. [< OE *streccan* stretch] —**stretch'i·ness** *n.* —**stretch'y** *adj.*

stretch·er (strech'ər) *n.* 1 Any device for stretching: a shoe *stretcher.* **2** A portable, often webbed frame for carrying the injured, sick, or dead.

stretch-out (strech′out′) *n. Informal* A system of industrial operation in which employees are required to perform more work per unit of time worked, usu. without increase in pay.

strew (strōō) *v.t.* **strewed, strewed** or **strewn, strew·ing 1** To spread about at random; sprinkle. **2** To cover with something scattered or sprinkled. **3** To be scattered over (a surface). [< OE *strēawian*]

stri·at·ed (strī′ā·tid) *adj.* Striped, grooved, or banded: *striated* muscle. [< L *striatus*, p.p. of *striare* to groove] — **stri·a·tion** *n.*

strick·en (strik′ən) *adj.* **1** Struck down by injury, disease, calamity, remorse, etc. **2** Advanced or far gone, as in age: *stricken* in years. [< OE *stricen*, p.p. of *strican* to strike]

strict (strikt) *adj.* **1** Observing or enforcing rules exactly: a *strict* church. **2** Containing severe rules or provisions; exacting. **3** Harsh; stern: a *strict* teacher. **4** Exactly defined or applied: the *strict* truth. **5** Devout; orthodox: a *strict* Catholic. **6** Absolute: in *strict* confidence. [< L *strictus*, p.p. of *stringere* draw tight] —**strict′ly** *adv.* —**strict′· ness** *n.*

stric·ture (strik′chər) *n.* **1** Severe criticism. **2** Something that checks or restricts. **3** Closure or narrowing of a duct or passage of the body. [< L *strictus* strict]

stride (strīd) *n.* **1** A long and measured step. **2** The space passed over by such a step. —**hit one's stride** To attain one's normal speed. —**make rapid strides** To make quick progress. —**take (something) in one's stride** To do or accept (something) without undue effort or without becoming upset. —*v.* **strode, strid·den, strid·ing** *v.i.* **1** To walk with long steps, as from haste. —*v.t.* **2** To walk through, along, etc., with long steps. **3** To pass over with a single stride. **4** To straddle; bestride. [< OE *strīdan* to stride] —**strid′er** *n.*

stri·dent (strīd′nt) *adj.* Having a loud and harsh sound; grating. [< L *stridere* to creak] —**stri′dence, stri′den·cy** *n.* —**stri′dent·ly** *adv.*

strid·u·late (strij′ōō·lāt) *v.i.* **·lat·ed, ·lat·ing** To make a chirping, nonvocal noise, as a cricket, etc. [< L *stridere* to rattle, rasp] —**strid′u·la′tion** *n.* —**strid′u·la·to·ry** (-lə·tôr′ē, -tō′rē), **strid′u·lous** *adj.*

strife (strīf) *n.* **1** Angry contention; fighting. **2** Any contest or rivalry. **3** The act of striving; strenuous endeavor. [< OF *estriver* strive]

strike (strīk) *v.* **struck, struck** (*chiefly Archaic* **strick·en**), **strik·ing** *v.t.* **1** To hit with a blow; deal a blow to. **2** To crash into: The car *struck* the wall. **3** To deal (a blow, etc.). **4** To cause to hit forcibly: He *struck* his hand on the table. **5** To attack; assault. **6** To ignite (a match, etc.) **7** To form by stamping, printing, etc. **8** To announce; sound: The clock *struck* two. **9** To reach: A sound *struck* his ear. **10** To affect suddenly or in a specified manner: He was *struck* speechless. **11** To occur to: An idea *strikes* me. **12** To impress in a specified manner. **13** To attract the attention of: The dress *struck* her fancy. **14** To assume: to *strike* an attitude. **15** To cause to enter deeply or suddenly: to *strike* dismay into one's heart. **16** To lower or haul down, as a sail or a flag. **17** To cease working at in order to compel compliance to a demand, etc. **18** To make and confirm, as a bargain. —*v.i.* **19** To come into violent contact; crash; hit. **20** To deal or aim a blow or blows. **21** To make an assault or attack. **22** To sound from a blow or blows. **23** To be indicated by the sound of blows or strokes: Noon has just *struck.* **24** To ignite. **25** To lower a flag in token of surrender. **26** To take a course; start and proceed: to *strike* for home. **27** To cease work in order to enforce demands, etc. **28** To snatch at or swallow the lure: said of fish. —**strike camp** To take down the tents of a camp. —**strike down 1** To fell with a blow. **2** To incapacitate completely. — **strike dumb** To astonish; amaze. —**strike home 1** To deal an effective blow. **2** To have telling effect. —**strike it rich 1** To find a valuable pocket of ore. **2** To come into wealth or good fortune. —**strike off 1** To remove or take off by or as by a blow or stroke. **2** To deduct. —**strike oil**

1 To find oil while drilling. **2** *Slang* To meet with unexpected good fortune. —**strike out 1** To aim a blow or blows. **2** To cross out or erase. **3** To begin; start. **4** In baseball, to put out (the batter) by pitching three strikes. —**strike up 1** To begin to play, as a band. **2** To start up; begin, as a friendship. —*n.* **1** An act of striking. **2** In baseball, an unsuccessful attempt by the batter to hit the ball. **3** In bowling, the knocking down of all the pins with the first bowl. **4** The quitting of work by a body of workers to secure some demand from management. **5** A new discovery, as of oil or ore. **6** Any unexpected or complete success. **7** The sudden rise and taking of the bait by a fish. —**on strike** Refusing to work in order to secure higher pay, better working conditions, etc. [< OE *strīcan* stroke, move]

strike·break·er (strīk′brā′kər) *n.* One who takes the place of a worker on strike or who seeks to intimidate or replace the strikers with other workers. —**strike′break′ing** *n.*

strik·er (strī′kər) *n.* **1** One who or that which strikes. **2** An employee who is on strike.

strik·ing (strī′king) *adj.* **1** Notable; impressive: a *striking* girl. **2** On strike. **3** That strikes: a *striking* clock. —**strik′ing· ly** *adv.* —**strik′ing·ness** *n.*

string (string) *n.* **1** A slender line, thinner than a cord and thicker than a thread, used for tying parcels, lacing, etc. **2** A cord of catgut, nylon, wire, etc., for musical instruments, bows, tennis rackets, etc. **3** A stringlike formation, as of certain vegetables. **4** A series of things hung on a small cord: a *string* of pearls. **5** A connected series or succession, as of things, acts, or events. **6** A drove or small collection of stock, esp. of saddle horses. **7** *pl.* Stringed instruments, esp., the section of violins, cellos, etc., in a symphony orchestra. **8** In sports, a group of contestants ranked as to skill. **9** *Informal Often pl.* A condition or restriction attached to an offer or gift. —**on a string** Under control or domination. —**pull strings 1** To control the actions of others, usu. secretly. **2** To influence others to gain an advantage. —*v.* **strung, string·ing** *v.t.* **1** To thread, as beads, on or as on a string. **2** To fit with a string or strings, as a guitar or bow. **3** To bind, fasten, or adorn with a string or strings. **4** To tune the strings of (a musical instrument). **5** To brace; strengthen. **6** To make tense or nervous. **7** To arrange or extend like a string. **8** To remove the strings from (vegetables). —*v.i.* **9** To extend or proceed in a line or series. **10** To form into strings. —**string along** *Slang* **1** To cooperate with. **2** To deceive; cheat. **3** To keep (someone) on tenterhooks. —**string out** *Informal* To protract; prolong: to *string out* an investigation. —**string up** *Informal* To hang. [< OE *streng* string]

string bean 1 The unripe edible seed pod of several varieties of bean. **2** The plants bearing these pods. **3** *Informal* A tall, skinny person.

stringed instrument (stringd) A musical instrument provided with strings or wires, as a violin, guitar, etc.

strin·gent (strin′jənt) *adj.* **1** Rigid; severe, as regulations. **2** Hampered by scarcity of money: said of a market. **3** Convincing; forcible. [< L *stringens*, pr.p of *stringere* draw tight] —**strin′gen·cy, strin′gent·ness** *n.* —**strin′gent·ly** *adv.*

string·er (string′ər) *n.* **1** One who strings. **2** A heavy timber supporting other members of a structure. **3** A newsman employed on a free-lance basis, often in out-of-town or foreign locations. **4** A person having a specific rating as to excellence, skill, etc.: used in combination: a *second-stringer.*

string·halt (string′hôlt′) *n.* In horses, lameness marked by spasmodic movement of the hind legs.

string·y (string′ē) *adj.* **string·i·er, string·i·est 1** Of or like a string or strings: *stringy* hair. **2** Containing fibrous strings. **3** Forming in strings, as thick glue; ropy. **4** Tall and wiry in build. —**string′i·ly** *adv.* —**string′i·ness** *n.*

strip[1] (strip) *n.* **1** A narrow piece, comparatively long, as of cloth, wood, etc. **2** A number of stamps attached in a row. **3** A narrow piece of land used as a runway for airplanes. **4** A comic strip. [?]

strip[2] (strip) *v.* **stripped** or **stript, strip·ping** *v.t.* **1** To pull the covering, clothing, leaves, etc., from; lay bare. **2** To pull off (the covering, etc.). **3** To rob or plunder; spoil. **4** To make bare or empty. **5** To take away. **6** To deprive of something; divest. **7** To damage the teeth, thread, etc., of (a gear, bolt, etc.). —*v.i.* **8** To undress. [< OE *bestrȳpan* plunder]

stripe[1] (strīp) *n.* **1** A line, band, or long strip of material differing in color or finish from its adjacent surfaces. **2** Distinctive quality or character: *a man of artistic* stripe. **3** Striped cloth. **4** *pl.* Prison uniform. **5** A piece of material or braid on a uniform to indicate rank. —*v.t.* **striped, strip·ing** To mark with a stripe or stripes. [< MDu.]

stripe[2] (strīp) *n.* **1** A blow struck with a whip or rod. **2** A weal or welt on the skin caused by such a blow. [Prob. < LG]

strip·ling (strip′ling) *n.* A mere youth; a lad. [?]

strip mine A mine, esp. a coal mine, the seams of which are close to the surface of the earth and which is worked by stripping away the topsoil and the material beneath it. —**strip′-mine′** *v.t.* (**-mined, -min·ing**) —**strip miner**

strip·per (strip′ər) *n.* **1** One who or that which strips. **2** *Slang* A female performer of a striptease.

strip·tease (strip′tēz′) *n.* An act, usu. in burlesque, in which a female performer gradually disrobes before an audience. —**strip′teas′er** *n.*

strive (strīv) *v.i.* **strove, striv·en** (striv′ən) or **strived, striv·ing** **1** To make earnest effort. **2** To engage in strife; fight: *to* strive *against an enemy.* [< OF *estriver*] —**striv′er** *n.* — **Syn.** **1** endeavor, try. **2** contend, struggle.

strobe (strōb) *n.* **1** STROBOSCOPE. **2** An electronically controlled device that emits light in very brief, brilliant flashes, used in photography, in the theater, etc.: also **strobe light.**

strob·o·scope (strōb′ə·skōp) *n.* An instrument for studying the motion of an object by making the object appear to be stationary, as by periodic instantaneous illumination or observation. [< Gk. *strobos* twirling + -SCOPE] —**strob′o·scop′ic** (-skop′ik) or **·i·cal** *adj.* —**strob·os·co·py** (strō·bos′kə·pē) *n.*

strode (strōd) *p.t.* of STRIDE.

stroke (strōk) *n.* **1** The act or movement of striking. **2** One of a series of recurring movements, as of oars, arms in swimming, a piston, etc. **3** A rower who sets the pace for the rest of the crew. **4** A single movement of a pen or pencil. **5** A mark made by such a movement. **6** Any ill effect: *a* stroke *of misfortune.* **7** APOPLEXY. **8** A sound of a striking mechanism, as of a clock. **9** A sudden or brilliant mental act: *a* stroke *of wit.* **10** A light caressing movement; a stroking. —**keep stroke** To make strokes simultaneously, as oarsmen. —*v.t.* **stroked, strok·ing** **1** To pass the hand over gently or caressingly. **2** To set the pace for (a rowboat or its crew). [< OE *strācian* strike] —**strok′er** *n.*

stroll (strōl) *v.i.* **1** To walk in a leisurely manner; saunter. **2** To go from place to place. —*n.* A leisurely walk. [?]

stroll·er (strō′lər) *n.* **1** A small, light baby carriage, often collapsible. **2** One who strolls. **3** An actor who travels from place to place to perform.

strong (strông, strong) *adj.* **1** Physically powerful; muscular. **2** Healthy; robust: *a* strong *constitution.* **3** Resolute; courageous. **4** Mentally powerful or vigorous. **5** Especially competent or able: *strong* in mathematics. **6** Abundantly supplied: *strong* in trumps. **7** Solidly made or constituted: *strong* walls. **8** Powerful, as a rival or combatant. **9** Easy to defend: *a* strong *position.* **10** In numerical force: *an army 20,000* strong. **11** Well able to exert influence, authority, etc. **12** Financially sound: *a* strong *market.* **13** Powerful in effect: *strong* poison. **14** Not diluted or weak: *strong* coffee. **15** Containing much alcohol: *a* strong *drink.* **16** Powerful in flavor or odor: *a* strong *breath.* **17** Intense in degree or quality: *a* strong *light.* **18** Loud and firm: *a* strong *voice.* **19** Firm; tenacious: *a* strong *will.* **20** Fervid: *a* strong *desire.* **21** Cogent; convincing: *strong* evidence. **22** Distinct; marked: *a* strong *resemblance.* **23** Extreme: *strong* measures. **24** Emphatic: *strong* language. **25** Moving with great force: said of a wind, stream, or tide. **26** *Phonet.* Stressed. **27** *Gram.* Of verbs, indicating changes in tense by means of vowel changes, rather than by inflectional endings, as *drink, drank, drunk.* —*adv.* In a firm, vigorous manner. [< OE] —**strong′ly** *adv.* —**strong′ness** *n.*

strong-arm (strông′ärm′, strong′-) *Informal adj.* Using physical or coercive power: *strong-arm* tactics. —*v.t.* **1** To use physical force upon; assault. **2** To coerce; compel.

strong·box (strông′boks′, strong′-) *n.* A chest or safe for keeping valuables.

strong drink Alcoholic liquors.

strong·hold (strông′hōld′, strong′-) *n.* A strongly defended place; fortress.

strong·man (strông′man′, strong′-) *n. pl.* **·men** (-mən) A political leader having preeminent power, as from a military coup or other extralegal means.

strong-mind·ed (strông′mīn′did, strong′-) *adj.* **1** Having an active, vigorous mind. **2** Determined; resolute. — **strong′-mind′ed·ly** *adv.* —**strong′-mind′ed·ness** *n.*

strong-willed (strông′wild′, strong′-) *adj.* Having a strong will; obstinate.

stron·ti·um (stron′chē·əm, -chəm, -tē·əm) *n.* A metallic element (symbol Sr) chemically resembling calcium, used in pyrotechnics. [< *Strontian,* Argyll, Scotland, where first discovered] —**stron′tic** (-tik) *adj.*

strop (strop) *n.* A strip of leather on which to sharpen a razor. —*v.t.* **stropped, strop·ping** To sharpen on a strop. [< Gk. *strophos* band]

stro·phe (strō′fē), *n.* **1** In ancient Greece, the verses sung by the chorus in a play while moving from right to left. **2** A stanza of a poem. [< Gk. *strophē* a turning, twist] —**stroph·ic** (strof′ik, strō′fik) or **·i·cal** *adj.*

Strop

strove (strōv) *p.t.* of STRIVE.

struck (struk) *p.t. & p.p.* of STRIKE.

struc·tur·al (struk′chər·əl) *adj.* **1** Of, pertaining to, or characterized by structure. **2** Used in or essential to construction. —**struc′tur·al·ly** *adv.*

structural steel Rolled steel shaped and adapted for use in construction.

struc·ture (struk′chər) *n.* **1** That which is constructed, as a building. **2** Something based upon or organized according to a plan or design: *the political* structure *of a republic.* **3** The manner of such organization: *a hierarchical* structure. **4** The arrangement and relationship of the parts of a whole, as organs in a plant or animal, atoms in a molecule, etc. —*v.t.* **·tured, ·tur·ing** **1** To form or organize into a structure; build. **2** To conceive as a structural whole. [< L *structus,* p.p. of *struere* build]

stru·del (strood′l) *n.* A kind of pastry with a filling of fruit, nuts, etc. [G, lit., eddy]

strug·gle (strug′əl) *n.* **1** A violent effort or series of efforts. **2** A war; battle. —*v.i.* **·gled, ·gling** **1** To contend with an adversary in physical combat; fight. **2** To strive: *to* struggle *against odds.* **3** To make one's way by violent efforts: *to* struggle *through mud.* [ME *strogelen*] —**strug′gler** *n.* —**strug′gling·ly** *adv.*

strum (strum) *v.t. & v.i.* **strummed, strum·ming** To play idly or carelessly (on a stringed instrument). —*n.* The act of strumming. [Prob. Imit.] —**strum′mer** *n.*

strum·pet (strum′pit) *n.* A whore; prostitute. [ME]

strung (strung) *p.t. & p.p.* of STRING.

strung out *Slang* **1** Sick or in weakened health from prolonged use of drugs. **2** Addicted to narcotics.

strut (strut) *n.* **1** A proud or pompous step or walk. **2** A supporting piece in a framework, keeping two others from approaching nearer together. —*v.* **strut·ted, strut·ting** *v.i.* **1** To walk pompously and affectedly. —*v.t.* **2** To brace or support with a brace or strut. [< OE *strūtian* be rigid, stand stiffly] —**strut′ter** *n.* —**strut′ting·ly** *adv.*

strych·nine (strik′nīn, -nən, -nēn) *n.* A poisonous alkaloid obtained from nux vomica, used in medicine as a stimulant. Also **strych′ni·a** (-nē·ə) [< Gk. *strychnos* nightshade] —**strych′nic** *adj.*

stub (stub) *n.* **1** Any short remnant, as of a pencil, candle, cigarette, cigar, or broken tooth. **2** In a checkbook, the short piece on which the amount of a check is recorded and that remains when the check is detached. **3** A tree stump. —*v.t.* **stubbed, stub·bing** **1** To strike, as the toe, against a low obstruction or projection. **2** To clear or remove the stubs or roots from. [< OE *stubb*] —**stub′ber** *n.*

stub·ble (stub′əl) *n.* **1** The stubs of plants covering a field after reaping. **2** The field itself. **3** Any surface or growth resembling stubble, as short bristly hair or beard. [< L *stipula* stalk] —**stub′bly** *adj.* (**·bli·er, ·bli·est**)

stub·born (stub′ərn) *adj.* 1 Inflexible in opinion or intention. 2 Determined to have one's own way. 3 Not easily handled, bent, or overcome. 4 Characterized by perseverance or persistence: *stubborn* fighting. [ME *stoborne*] — **stub′born·ly** *adv.* —**stub′born·ness** *n.* —Syn. 1 opinionated, unyielding. 2 headstrong, obdurate, obstinate.

stub·by (stub′ē) *adj.* ·bi·er, ·bi·est 1 Short, stiff, and bristling: a *stubby* beard. 2 Short and thick: a *stubby* pencil. 3 Short and thick-set: a *stubby* man. —**stub′bi·ly** *adv.* —**stub′bi·ness** *n.*

stuc·co (stuk′ō) *n. pl.* ·coes or ·cos 1 Any plaster or cement used for the external coating of buildings. 2 Work done in stucco: also **stuc′co·work′**. —*v.t.* ·coed, ·co·ing To apply stucco to; decorate with stucco. [Ital.] —**stuc′co·er** *n.*

stuck (stuk) *p.t. & p.p.* of STICK.

stuck-up (stuk′up′) *adj. Informal* Conceited; very vain.

stud[1] (stud) *n.* 1 Any of a series of small knobs, round-headed nails, or small protuberant ornaments. 2 A small, removable button such as is used in a shirt front. 3 A post to which laths are nailed in a building frame. 4 STUD POKER. —*v.t.* stud·ded, stud·ding 1 To set thickly with small points, projections, or knobs. 2 To be scattered over: Daisies *stud* the meadows. 3 To support or stiffen by means of studs or upright props. [< OE *studu* post]

stud[2] (stud) *n.* 1 A collection of horses and mares for breeding, riding, hunting, or racing. 2 The place where they are kept. 3 A stallion. —**at stud** Available for breeding purposes: said of male animals. —*adj.* Of or pertaining to a stud. [< OE *stōd*]

stu·dent (st^yōōd′nt, -ənt) *n.* 1 A person engaged in a course of study, esp. in an educational institution. 2 One who closely examines or investigates. [< L *studere* be eager, apply oneself, study]

stud·horse (stud′hôrs′) *n.* A stallion kept for breeding. Also **stud horse.**

stud·ied (stud′ēd) *adj.* 1 Deliberately planned; premeditated: a *studied* insult. 2 Acquired or prepared by study. —**stud′ied·ly** *adv.* —**stud′ied·ness** *n.*

stu·di·o (st^yōō′dē·ō) *n. pl.* ·di·os 1 The workroom of an artist, photographer, etc. 2 A place where motion pictures are filmed. 3 A room or rooms where radio or television programs are broadcast or recorded. 4 A room or place in which music is recorded. [< L *studere* apply oneself, be diligent]

stu·di·ous (st^yōō′dē·əs) *adj.* 1 Given to or fond of study. 2 Considerate; careful; attentive. —**stu′di·ous·ly** *adv.* —**stu′di·ous·ness** *n.*

stud poker A game of poker in which the cards of the first round are dealt face down and the rest face up.

stud·y (stud′ē) *v.* stud·ied, stud·y·ing *v.t.* 1 To acquire a knowledge of: to *study* physics. 2 To examine; search into: to *study* a problem. 3 To scrutinize: to *study* one's reflection. 4 To memorize, as a part in a play. —*v.i.* 5 To apply the mind in acquiring knowledge. 6 To be a student. — **study up on** To acquire more complete information concerning. —*n. pl.* stud·ies 1 The process of acquiring information. 2 A particular instance or form of mental work. 3 A branch or department of knowledge. 4 A specific product of studious application: his *study* of plankton. 5 An examination or consideration of a problem, proposal, etc. 6 In art, a first sketch. 7 A careful literary treatment of a subject. 8 A room set aside for study, reading, etc. 9 A thoughtful state of mind: a brown *study.* 10 *Music* A composition designed to develop technique; an étude. [< L *studium* zeal] —Syn. *v.* 1 grasp, learn. 2 investigate, ponder, analyze.

stuff (stuf) *v.t.* 1 To fill completely; pack. 2 To plug. 3 To obstruct or stop up. 4 To fill with padding, as a cushion. 5 To fill (a fowl, roast, etc.) with stuffing. 6 In taxidermy, to fill the skin of (a bird, animal, etc.) with a material preparatory to mounting. 7 To fill too full; cram: He *stuffed* himself with cake. 8 To fill with knowledge, ideas, or attitudes, esp. unsystematically. —*v.i.* 9 To eat to excess. —*n.* 1 The material or matter out of which something is or may be shaped or made. 2 The fundamental element of anything: the *stuff* of genius. 3 *Informal* A

specific skill, field of knowledge, etc.: That editor knows her *stuff.* 4 Personal possessions generally. 5 Unspecified material, matter, etc.: They carried away tons of the *stuff.* 6 A miscellaneous collection of things. 7 Nonsense; foolishness. 8 Woven material, esp. of wool. 9 Any textile fabric. [< OF *estoffer* cram] —**stuff′er** *n.*

stuffed shirt *Informal* A pretentious, pompous person.

stuff·ing (stuf′ing) *n.* 1 The material with which anything is stuffed. 2 A mixture, as of crumbs with seasoning, used in stuffing fowls, etc. 3 The process of stuffing anything.

stuff·y (stuf′ē) *adj.* stuff·i·er, stuff·i·est 1 Badly ventilated. 2 Filled up so as to impede respiration: a *stuffy* nose. 3 Dull; uninspired: a *stuffy* speech. 4 Strait-laced; stodgy. — **stuff′i·ly** *adv.* —**stuff′i·ness** *n.*

stul·ti·fy (stul′tə·fī′) *v.t.* ·fied, ·fy·ing 1 To cause to appear absurd. 2 To make useless or futile. [< L *stultus* foolish + -FY] —**stul′ti·fi·ca′tion, stul′ti·fi′er** *n.*

stum·ble (stum′bəl) *v.* ·bled, ·bling *v.i.* 1 To miss one's step in walking or running; trip. 2 To speak or act in a blundering manner: The student *stumbled* through his recitation. 3 To happen upon something by chance: with *across, on, upon,* etc. 4 To do wrong; err. —*v.t.* 5 To cause to stumble. —*n.* The act of stumbling. [ME *stumblen*] —**stum′bler** *n.* — **stum′bling·ly** *adv.*

stum·bling·block (stum′bling·blok′) *n.* Any obstacle or hindrance.

stump (stump) *n.* 1 That portion of the trunk of a tree left standing when the tree is felled. 2 The part of a limb, etc., that remains when the main part has been removed. 3 *pl. Informal* The legs. 4 A place or platform where a political speech is made. 5 A short, thick-set person or animal. 6 A heavy step; a clump. —**take the stump** To electioneer in a political campaign. —**up a stump** In trouble or in a dilemma. —*adj.* 1 Being or resembling a stump. 2 Of or pertaining to political oratory or campaigning: a *stump* speaker. —*v.t.* 1 To reduce to a stump; lop. 2 To remove stumps from (land). 3 To canvass (a district) by making political speeches. 4 *Informal* To bring to a halt by real or fancied obstacles. 5 To stub, as one's toe. —*v.i.* 6 To walk heavily. [< MLG] —**stump′i·ness** *n.* —**stump′y** *adj.*

stun (stun) *v.t.* stunned, stun·ning 1 To render unconscious or incapable of action. 2 To astonish; astound. 3 To daze or overwhelm. —*n.* The act of stunning or the condition of being stunned. [< OF *estoner*]

stung (stung) *p.t. & p.p.* of STING.

stunk (stungk) *p.p.* and alternative *p.t.* of STINK.

stun·ner (stun′ər) *n.* 1 A person or blow that stuns. 2 *Slang* A person or thing of extraordinary qualities, such as beauty.

stun·ning (stun′ing) *adj.* 1 That stuns or astounds. 2 *Informal* Surprising; impressive; beautiful. —**stun′ning·ly** *adv.*

stunt[1] (stunt) *v.t.* To check the natural development of; dwarf; cramp. —*n.* 1 A check in growth, progress, or development. 2 A stunted animal or person. [< OE, dull, foolish] —**stunt′ed·ness** *n.*

stunt[2] (stunt) *Informal n.* 1 A sensational feat, as of bodily skill. 2 Any remarkable feat. —*v.i.* 1 To perform a stunt or stunts. —*v.t.* 2 To perform stunts with (an airplane, etc.). [?]

stunt man In motion pictures, a person employed to substitute for an actor when dangerous jumps, falls, etc., must be made.

stu·pe·fac·tion (st^yōō′pə·fak′shən) *n.* The act of stupefying or state of being stupefied.

stu·pe·fy (st^yōō′pə·fī′) *v.t.* ·fied, ·fy·ing 1 To dull the senses or faculties of; stun. 2 To amaze; astound. [< L *stupere* be stunned + -FY] —**stu′pe·fi′er** *n.*

stu·pen·dous (st^yōō·pen′dəs) *adj.* 1 Of prodigious size, bulk, or degree. 2 Astonishing; marvelous. [< L *stupere* be stunned] —**stu·pen′dous·ly** *adv.* —**stu·pen′dous·ness** *n.*

stu·pid (st^yōō′pid) *adj.* 1 Very slow in understanding; lacking in intelligence; dull-witted. 2 Affected with stupor; stupefied. 3 Dull and profitless; tiresome: to regard rote learning as *stupid.* 4 Resulting from slowness in understanding or a lack of intelligence. **5** *Informal* Annoying; bothersome: This *stupid* nail won't go in straight. [< L *stupidus* struck dumb] —**stu·pid·i·ty** (stʸo͞o·pid′ə·tē) (*pl.* ·ties) *n.*; **stu′pid·ness** *n.* —**stu′pid·ly** *adv.*

stu·por (stʸo͞o′pər) *n.* **1** Abnormal lethargy due to shock, drugs, etc. **2** Extreme intellectual dullness. [< L *stupere* be stunned] —**stu′por·ous** *adj.*

stur·dy (stûr′dē) *adj.* ·di·er, ·di·est **1** Possessing rugged health and strength. **2** Firm and resolute: a *sturdy* defense. [< OF *estourdir* stun, amaze] —**stur′di·ly** *adv.* —**stur′di·ness** *n.* —**Syn. 1** hardy, lusty, robust, vigorous. **2** determined, unyielding.

stur·geon (stûr′jən) *n.* Any of various large edible fishes of northern regions, valued as the source of caviar. [< Med. L *sturio*]

Sturgeon

stut·ter (stut′ər) *v.t.* & *v.i.* To utter or speak with spasmodic repetition, blocking, and prolongation of sounds and syllables. —*n.* The act or habit of stuttering. [Freq. of ME *stutten* stutter] —**stut′ter·er** *n.* —**stut′ter·ing·ly** *adv.*

St. Vi·tus's dance (sānt vī′təs·iz) CHOREA. Also **St. Vitus dance.** [< *St. Vitus,* third-century Christian child martyr]

sty[1] (stī) *n. pl.* **sties 1** A pen for swine. **2** Any filthy habitation. [< OE *stī, stig*]

sty[2] (stī) *n. pl.* **sties** A pustule on the edge of an eyelid. Also **stye.** [< OE *stīgan* rise + *ye* eye]

Styg·i·an (stij′ē·ən) *adj.* **1** Pertaining to or like the river Styx or the lower world. **2** Dark and gloomy.

style (stīl) *n.* **1** A fashionable manner or appearance: to be in *style.* **2** Fashion: the latest *style* in shirts. **3** A particular fashion in clothing. **4** A distinctive form of expression: a florid *style.* **5** An effective way of expression: His drawings have *style.* **6** Manner: a church in the Romanesque *style* of architecture. **7** A way of living or behaving: Domestic life is not his *style.* **8** A pointed instrument for marking or engraving. **9** An indicator on a dial. **10** *Printing* The typography, spelling, design, etc., used in a given published text. **11** *Bot.* The slender part of a carpel between stigma and ovary. **12** A system of arranging the calendar years so as to average that of the true solar year. Our calendar, adopted in 1752, is called **New Style,** while **Old Style** dates are 13 days earlier. —*v.t.* **styled, styl·ing 1** To name; give a title to: Richard I was *styled* "the Lion-Hearted." **2** To cause to conform to a specific style: to *style* a manuscript. [< L *stylus* writing instrument] —**styl′er** *n.*

style·book (stīl′bo͝ok′) *n.* A book setting forth rules of capitalization, punctuation, etc., for the use of printers, writers, and editors. Also **style manual.**

styl·ish (stī′lish) *adj.* **1** Having style. **2** Very fashionable. —**styl′ish·ly** *adv.* —**styl′ish·ness** *n.*

styl·ist (stī′list) *n.* **1** One who is a master of style: a literary *stylist.* **2** An adviser on or a creator of styles: a hair *stylist.* —**sty·lis′tic** *adj.* —**sty·lis′ti·cal·ly** *adv.*

styl·ize (stī′līz) *v.t.* ·ized, ·iz·ing To conform to or create in a distinctive or specific style. *Brit. sp.* **styl′ise.** —**styl′i·za′·tion** (stī′lə·za′shən), **styl′iz·er** *n.*

sty·lus (stī′ləs) *n. pl.* ·lus·es or ·li (lī) **1** An ancient instrument for writing on wax tablets. **2** A tiny, usu. jewel-tipped needle whose vibrations in tracing the groove in a phonograph record transmit sound. [L]

sty·mie (stī′mē) *n.* A condition in golf in which an opponent's ball lies in the line of the player's putt on the green. —*v.t.* ·mied, ·my·ing **1** To block (an opponent) by or as by a stymie. **2** To baffle or perplex. [?]

styp·tic (stip′tik) *adj.* Tending to halt bleeding; astringent: also **styp′ti·cal.** —*n.* A styptic substance. [< Gk. *stypsis* a contraction] —**styp·tic·i·ty** (stip·tis′ə·tē) *n.*

Sty·ro·foam (stī′rə·fōm) *n.* A lightweight, rigid, cellular material formed from a synthetic hydrocarbon polymer: a trade name.

Styx (stiks) *n. Gk. Myth.* The river across which the dead were ferried to Hades.

sua·sion (swā′zhən) *n.* The act of persuading: usu. in the phrase **moral suasion.** [< L *suadere* persuade] —**sua·sive** (swā′siv), **sua·so·ry** (swā′sər·ē) *adj.* —**sua′sive·ly** *adv.* —**sua′sive·ness** *n.*

suave (swäv) *adj.* Smooth and pleasant in manner, often superficially so. [< L *suavis* sweet] —**suave′ly** *adv.* —**suave′ness, suav′i·ty** (*pl.* ·ties) *n.*

sub (sub) *n. Informal* **1** SUBSTITUTE. **2** A subordinate or subaltern. **3** SUBMARINE. —*v.i.* **subbed, sub·bing** To act as a substitute for someone.

sub- *prefix* **1** Under; beneath; below: *subcutaneous.* **2** Almost; nearly: *subtropical.* **3** Further; again: *subdivide.* **4** Lower in rank or grade: *subordinate.* **5** Having less importance; secondary: *subtitle.* **6** Forming a further division: *subcommittee.* [< L *sub* under] • See TAXONOMY.

sub. subaltern; submarine; subscription; substitute; suburb; suburban.

sub·al·tern (sub·ôl′tərn, *esp. Brit.* sub′əl·tərn) *adj.* **1** *Brit. Mil.* Ranking below a captain. **2** Of inferior rank or position. —*n.* **1** A person of subordinate rank or position. **2** *Brit. Mil.* An officer ranking below a captain. [< L *sub-* under + *alternus* alternate]

sub·ant·arc·tic (sub′ant·ärk′tik, -är′tik) *adj.* Denoting or pertaining to a region surrounding the Antarctic Circle.

sub·arc·tic (sub·ärk′tik, -är′tik) *adj.* Denoting or pertaining to a region surrounding the Arctic Circle.

sub·a·tom·ic (sub′ə·tom′ik) *adj.* **1** Of or pertaining to the constituent parts of an atom. **2** Smaller than an atom.

sub·com·mit·tee (sub′kə·mit′ē) *n.* A small committee appointed from a larger committee for special work.

sub·con·scious (sub·kon′shəs) *adj.* **1** Only dimly conscious; not fully aware. **2** Not attended by full awareness, as an automatic action. —*n.* That portion of mental activity not in the focus of consciousness. —**sub·con′scious·ly** *adv.* —**sub·con′scious·ness** *n.*

sub·con·tract (sub·kon′trakt) *n.* A contract subordinate to another contract and assigning part of the work to a third party. —*v.t.* & *v.i.* (sub′kən·trakt′) To make a subcontract (for). —**sub·con·trac·tor** (sub′kon′trak′tər, sub′·kən·trak′-) *n.*

sub·cul·ture (sub′kul·chər) *n.* A group having specific patterns of behavior that set it off from other groups within a culture or society.

sub·cu·ta·ne·ous (sub′kyo͞o·tā′nē·əs) *adj.* Situated or applied beneath the skin. [< L *sub-* under + *cutis* skin] —**sub′cu·ta′ne·ous·ly** *adv.*

subd. subdivision.

sub·deb (sub′deb′) *n. Informal* **1** A young girl during the period before she becomes a debutante. **2** Any young girl of the same age.

sub·di·vide (sub′di·vīd′, sub′di·vīd′) *v.t.* & *v.i.* ·vid·ed, ·vid·ing **1** To divide again. **2** To divide (land) into lots for sale or improvement.

sub·di·vi·sion (sub′di·vizh′ən, sub′di·vizh′ən) *n.* **1** Division following upon division. **2** A part, as of land, resulting from subdividing.

sub·due (sub·dʸo͞o′) *v.t.* ·dued, ·du·ing **1** To gain dominion over, as by war or force. **2** To overcome by training, influence, or persuasion. **3** To repress (emotions, impulses, etc.). **4** To reduce the intensity of. [< L *subducere* lead away] —**sub·du′ed·ly** *adv.* —**sub·du′er** *n.* —**Syn. 1** conquer, subjugate, vanquish. **2** master, tame. **4** lessen, soften.

sub·group (sub′gro͞op′) *n.* A subdivision of a group.

sub·head (sub′hed′) *n.* **1** A heading or title of a subdivision of a chapter, etc. **2** A subordinate title. Also **sub′·head·ing.**

sub·hu·man (sub·ʰyo͞o′mən) *adj.* Less than or imperfectly human.

subj. subject; subjective; subjunctive.

sub·ja·cent (sub·jā′sənt) *adj.* Situated underneath; underlying. [< L *sub-* under + *jacere* to lie] —**sub·ja′cen·cy** *n.* —**sub·ja′cent·ly** *adv.*

sub·ject (sub′jikt) *adj.* **1** Being under the power of another. **2** Exposed: *subject* to criticism. **3** Having a tendency: *subject* to colds. **4** Conditional upon: *subject* to your consent. —*n.* **1** One who is under the governing power of another, as of a ruler. • See CITIZEN. **2** One who or that which is employed or treated in a specified way, as in an experiment. **3** The theme or topic of a discussion. **4** Something described or depicted in a literary or artistic work. **5** *Gram.* The word, phrase, or clause of a sentence about which something is stated or asked in the predicate. **6**

Music The melodic phrase on which a composition or a part of it is based. **7** A branch of learning. —*v.t.* (səb-jekt′) **1** To bring under dominion or control; subjugate. **2** To cause to undergo some experience or action. **3** To make liable; expose: *His inheritance was* subjected *to heavy taxation.* [< L *sub-* under + *jacere* throw] —**sub·jec′tion** *n.*

sub·jec·tive (səb-jek′tiv) *adj.* **1** Of or belonging to that which is within the mind and not subject to independent verification. **2** Expressing very personal feelings or opinions: a *subjective* piece of writing. **3** Highly influenced by the emotions or by prejudice. **4** *Med.* Of the kind of which only the patient is aware: said of symptoms. **5** *Gram.* Designating the case and function of the subject of a sentence. —**sub·jec′tive·ly** *adv.* —**sub·jec′tive·ness, sub·jec·tiv·i·ty** (sub′jek·tiv′ə·tē) *n.*

sub·join (sub·join′) *v.t.* To add at the end; affix. [< L *sub-* in addition + *jungere* join] —**sub·join′der** (-dər) *n.*

sub·ju·gate (sub′jŏō-gāt) *v.t.* **·gat·ed, ·gat·ing 1** To bring under dominion; conquer. **2** To make subservient or submissive. [< L *sub-* under + *jugum* a yoke] —**sub′ju·ga′tion, sub′ju·ga′tor** *n.*

sub·junc·tive (səb·jungk′tiv) *Gram. adj.* Of or pertaining to that mood of the finite verb that is used to express a future contingency, a supposition, or a wish or desire. —*n.* **1** The subjunctive mood. **2** A verb form or construction in this mood. [< L *subjunctus,* p.p. of *subjungere* subjoin] —**sub·junc′tive·ly** *adv.*

sub·lease (sub·lēs′) *v.t.* **·leased, ·leas·ing** To obtain or let (property) on a sublease. —*n.* (sub′lēs′) A lease of property from a tenant.

sub·let (sub·let′, sub′let′) *v.t.* **·let, ·let·ting 1** To let to another (property held on a lease). **2** To let (work that one has contracted to do) to a subordinate contractor. —*n.* Property, esp. dwellings, that is subleased or available for subleasing.

sub·li·mate (sub′lə·māt) *v.* **·mat·ed, ·mat·ing** *v.t.* **1** To refine; purify. **2** *Psychol.* To convert (a primitive impulse) into socially acceptable behavior. **3** *Chem.* SUBLIME. —*v.i.* **4** To undergo or engage in sublimation. —*adj.* Sublimated; refined. —*n. Chem.* The product of sublimation. [< L *sublimis* uplifted, sublime]

sub·li·ma·tion (sub′lə·mā′shən) *n.* **1** The act or process of sublimating. **2** *Chem.* A change of state from solid to vapor or from vapor to solid without liquefaction.

sub·lime (sə·blīm′) *adj.* **1** Characterized by or eliciting feelings of grandeur, nobility, or awe. **2** *Informal* Outstandingly excellent; supreme: a *sublime* meal. —*v.* **·limed, ·lim·ing** *v.t.* **1** To make sublime; ennoble. **2** *Chem.* To purify by the process of sublimation. —*v.i.* **3** *Chem.* To undergo sublimation. [< L *sublimis* lofty] —**sub·lime′ly** *adv.* —**sub·lim·i·ty** (sə·blim′ə·tē), **sub·lime′ness** *n.* —**Syn.** *adj.* **1** grand, magnificent, solemn. **2** noble.

sub·lim·i·nal (sub·lim′ə·nəl) *adj.* **1** Below or beyond the threshold of consciousness: a *subliminal* stimulus. **2** Too slight or weak to be felt or perceived. [< L *sub-* under + *limen* threshold] —**sub·lim′i·nal·ly** *adv.*

sub·ma·chine gun (sub′mə·shēn′) A lightweight, automatic or semi-automatic gun, designed for firing from the shoulder or hip.

sub·mar·gin·al (sub·mär′jən·əl) *adj.* **1** Below the margin. **2** Not productive enough to develop, cultivate, etc.: *submarginal* land.

sub·ma·rine (sub′mə·rēn′) *adj.* Existing, done, or operating beneath the surface of the sea. —*n.* (sub′mə·rēn) **1** A vessel, usu. a warship, designed to operate both on and below the surface of the water. **2** HERO (def. 5).

sub·max·il·lar·y (sub·mak′sə·ler′ē) *adj.* Of, pertaining to, or situated in the lower jaw. —*n. pl.* **·lar·ies** A submaxillary salivary gland, nerve, artery, etc.

sub·merge (səb·mûrj′) *v.* **·merged, ·merg·ing** *v.t.* **1** To place under or plunge into water. **2** To cover; hide. —*v.i.* **3** To sink or dive beneath the surface of water. [< L *sub-* under + *mergere* to plunge] —**sub·mer′gence** *n.*

sub·merse (səb·mûrs′) *v.t.* **·mersed, ·mers·ing** SUBMERGE. [< L *submergere* submerge] —**sub·mer′sion** *n.*

sub·mers·i·ble (səb·mûr′sə·bəl) *adj.* That may be sub-

merged. —*n.* SUBMARINE (def. 1). **2** Any of various, usu. small, underwater craft used for naval observation, scientific study, etc.

sub·mis·sion (səb·mish′ən) *n.* **1** A yielding to the power or authority of another. **2** Acquiescence or obedience. **3** The act of referring a matter of controversy to consideration, arbitration, etc. —**Syn. 1** surrender. **2** compliance, humbleness.

sub·mis·sive (səb·mis′iv) *adj.* Willing or inclined to submit; docile. —**sub·mis′sive·ly** *adv.* —**sub·mis′sive·ness** *n.*

sub·mit (səb·mit′) *v.* **·mit·ted, ·mit·ting** *v.t.* **1** To place under or yield to the authority of another. **2** To present for the consideration of others; refer. **3** To present as one's opinion; suggest. —*v.i.* **4** To give up; surrender. **5** To be obedient. [< L *sub-* under + *mittere* send] —**sub·mit′tal** *n.*

sub·nor·mal (sub·nôr′məl) *adj.* Below the normal; of less than normal intelligence, development, etc. —*n.* A subnormal individual. —**sub·nor·mal·i·ty** (sub′nôr·mal′ə·tē) *n.* —**sub·nor′mal·ly** *adv.*

sub·or·di·nate (sə·bôr′də·nit) *adj.* **1** Secondary; minor. **2** Lower in rank. **3** Subject or subservient to another. **4** *Gram.* Used within a sentence as a noun, adjective, or adverb: said of a clause. —*n.* One who or that which is subordinate. —*v.t.* (-nāt) **·nat·ed, ·nat·ing 1** To assign to a lower order or rank. **2** To make subject or subservient. [< L *sub-* under + *ordinare* to order] —**sub·or′di·nate·ly** *adv.* —**sub·or′di·nate·ness, sub·or′di·na′tion** *n.*

sub·orn (sə·bôrn′) *v. t.* **1** To bribe (someone) to commit perjury. **2** To incite or instigate to an evil act. [< L *sub-* secretly + *ornare* equip] —**sub·orn′er, sub·or·na·tion** (sub′ôr·nā′shən) *n.*

sub·poe·na (sə·pē′nə) *n.* A writ requiring a person to appear at court at a specified time and place. —*v.t.* **·naed, ·na·ing** To summon by subpoena. Also **sub·pe′na.** [< L *sub-* under + *poena* penalty]

sub·ro·gate (sub′rō·gāt) *v.t.* **·gat·ed, ·gat·ing** To substitute (one person, esp. one creditor) for another. [< L *sub-* in place of + *rogare* ask] —**sub′ro·ga′tion** *n.*

sub ro·sa (sub rō′zə) Confidentially; in secret. [L, under the rose, a symbol of silence]

sub·rou·tine (sub′rōō·tēn′) *n.* A part of a computer program, especially a sequence of instructions to perform a specific task.

sub·scribe (səb·skrīb′) *v.* **·scribed, ·scrib·ing** *v.t.* **1** To write, as one's name, at the end of a document; sign. **2.** To sign one's name to as an expression of assent. **3** To promise, esp. in writing, to pay or contribute (a sum of money). —*v.i.* **4** To write one's name at the end of a document. **5** To give approval; agree. **6** To promise to contribute money. **7** To pay in advance for a series of periodicals, tickets to performances, etc. with *to.* [< L *sub-* under + *scribere* write] —**sub·scrib′er** *n.*

sub·script (sub′skript) *adj.* **1** Written following and slightly beneath, as a small letter or number. —*n.* A subscript number, symbol, or letter, as the 2 in H_2O. [< L *subscriptus,* p.p. of *subscribere* subscribe]

sub·scrip·tion (səb·skrip′shən) *n.* **1** The act of subscribing; confirmation or agreement. **2** That which is subscribed; a signed paper or statement. **3** A signature written at the end of a document. **4** The total subscribed for any purpose. **5** The purchase in advance of a series of periodicals, tickets to performances, etc.

sub·sec·tion (sub·sek′shən, sub′sek′shən) *n.* A subdivision of a section.

sub·se·quent (sub′sə·kwənt) *adj.* Following in time, place, or order, or as a result. —**subsequent to** Following; after. [< L *sub-* next below + *sequi* follow] —**sub·se·quence** (sub′sə·kwəns), **sub′se·quen·cy, sub′se·quent·ness** *n.* —**sub′se·quent·ly** *adv.*

sub·serve (səb·sûrv′) *v.t.* **·served, ·serv·ing 1** To be of use or help in furthering (a process, cause, etc.); promote. **2** To serve as a subordinate to (a person). [< L *sub-* under + *servire* serve]

sub·ser·vi·ent (səb·sûr′vē·ənt) *adj.* **1** Servile; obsequious; truckling. **2** Adapted to promote some end or purpose, esp. in a subordinate capacity. —*n.* One who or that which subserves. **—sub·ser′vi·ent·ly** adv. **—sub·ser′vi·ent·ness, sub·ser′vi·ence, sub·ser′vi·en·cy** n.

sub·set (sub′set) n. Math. A set comprising some or all of the elements of another set.

sub·side (səb·sīd′) v.i. **·sid·ed, ·sid·ing 1** To sink to a lower level. **2** To become calm or quiet; abate. **3** To sink to the bottom, as sediment; settle. [< L sub- under + sidere to settle] **—sub·sid·ence** (səb·sīd′ns, sub′sə·dəns) n. **—Syn. 1** fall. **2** decrease, diminish, ebb, wane.

sub·sid·i·ar·y (səb·sid′ē·er′ē, -sid′ə·rē) adj. **1** Assisting; supplementary; auxiliary. **2** Of, pertaining to, or in the nature of a subsidy. —n. pl. **·ar·ies 1** One who or that which furnishes supplemental aid or supplies. **2** A business enterprise with over half of its assets or stock owned by another company. **—sub·sid·i·ar·i·ly** (səb·sid′ē·er′ə·lē) adv.

sub·si·dize (sub′sə·dīz) v.t. **·dized, ·diz·ing 1** To grant a regular allowance or financial aid to. **2** To obtain the assistance of by a subsidy. Brit. sp. **sub′si·dise.** **—sub′si·di·za′tion, sub′si·diz′er** n.

sub·si·dy (sub′sə·dē) n. pl. **·dies 1** Financial aid directly granted by government to a person or commercial enterprise whose work is deemed beneficial to the public. **2** Any financial assistance granted by one government to another. [< L subsidium auxiliary forces, aid < subsidere subside]

sub·sist (səb·sist′) v.i. **1** To continue to exist. **2** To remain alive; manage to live: to subsist on a meatless diet. **3** To continue unchanged; abide. [< L sub- under + sistere cause to stand] **—sub·sist′er** n.

sub·sis·tence (səb·sis′təns) n. **1** The act of subsisting. **2** That on which or by which one subsists; sustenance; livelihood. [< LL subsistentia < subsistere SUBSIST] **—sub·sis′·tent** adj.

sub·soil (sub′soil′) n. The stratum of earth just beneath the surface soil.

sub·son·ic (sub·son′ik) adj. Designating those sound waves beyond the lower limits of human audibility.

subst. substantive; substitute.

sub·stance (sub′stəns) n. **1** The material of which anything is made or constituted. **2** The essential meaning of anything said or written. **3** Material possessions; wealth; property. **4** The quality of stability or solidity: an argument lacking substance. **5** A distinct but unidentified kind of matter: a gaseous substance. **6** Essential components or ideas: The substance of the two arguments is the same. — **in substance 1** Essentially; chiefly. **2** Really; actually. [< L substare be present]

sub·stan·dard (sub·stan′dərd) adj. **1** Below an accepted standard; inferior: substandard housing. **2** Lower than the established legal standard. **3** Not conforming to the standard language usage of educated speakers and writers: "He don't want none" is substandard.

sub·stan·tial (səb·stan′shəl) adj. **1** Solid; strong; firm: a substantial bridge. **2** Of real worth and importance: a substantial profit. **3** Possessed of wealth or sufficient means. **4** Having real existence; not illusory. **5** Containing or conforming to the essence of a thing: in substantial agreement. **6** Ample and nourishing: a substantial meal. **—sub·stan′ti·al′i·ty** (-shē·al′ə·tē), **sub·stan′tial·ness** n. **—sub·stan′tial·ly** adv.

sub·stan·ti·ate (səb·stan′shē·āt) v.t. **·at·ed, ·at·ing 1** To establish by evidence; verify. **2** To give form or substance to. [< L substantia substance] **—sub·stan′ti·a′tion** n. **—sub·stan′ti·a′tive** adj.

sub·stan·tive (sub′stən·tiv) n. **1** A noun or pronoun. **2** A verbal form, phrase, or clause used in place of a noun. — adj. **1** Capable of being used as a noun. **2** Expressive of or denoting existence: The verb "to be" is called the substantive verb. **3** Having substance or reality. **4** Being an essential part or constituent. **5** Having distinct individuality. **6** Independent. [< L substantia substance] **—sub·stan·ti·val** (sub′stən·tī′vəl) adj. **—sub′stan·ti·val·ly, sub′stan·tive·ly** adv. **—sub′stan·tive·ness** n.

sub·sta·tion (sub′stā′shən) n. A subsidiary station, as for electric power or postal service.

sub·sti·tute (sub′stə·t(y)ōōt) v. **·tut·ed, ·tut·ing v.t. 1** To put in the place of another person or thing. **2** To take the place of. —v.i. **3** To act as a substitute. —n. One who or that which takes the place of another. —adj. Situated in or

taking the place of another: a substitute teacher. [< L sub- in place of + statuere set up]

sub·sti·tu·tion (sub′stə·t(y)ōō′shən) n. **1** The act of substituting, or the state of being substituted. **2** A substitute. **—sub′sti·tu′tion·al** adj. **—sub′sti·tu′tion·al·ly** adv.

sub·stra·tum (sub·strā′təm, -strat′əm) n. pl. **·stra·ta** (-strā′tə, -strat′ə) or **·stra·tums 1** An underlying stratum or layer, as of earth or rock. **2** A foundation or basis. [< L, p.p. neut. of substernere spread underneath] **—sub·stra′tal, sub·stra′tive** adj.

sub·struc·ture (sub′struk′chər, sub·struk′-) n. A structure serving as a foundation. **—sub·struc′tur·al** adj.

sub·ten·ant (sub·ten′ənt) n. A person who rents or leases from a tenant. **—sub·ten′an·cy** n.

sub·tend (səb·tend′) v.t. **1** Geom. To extend under or opposite to, as the chord of an arc or the side of a triangle opposite to an angle. **2** Bot. To enclose in its axil: A leaf subtends a bud. [< L sub- underneath + tendere stretch]

sub·ter·fuge (sub′tər·fyōōj′) n. Any plan or trick to escape something unpleasant. [< L subter- below, in secret + fugere flee, take flight]

sub·ter·ra·ne·an (sub′tə·rā′nē·ən) adj. **1** Situated or occurring below the surface of the earth. **2** Hidden. Also **sub′ter·ra′ne·ous.** [< L sub- under + terra earth] **—sub′ter·ra′ne·an·ly, sub′ter·ra′ne·ous·ly** adv.

sub·tile (sut′l, sub′til) adj. **1** Elusive; subtle. **2** Crafty; cunning. [< L subtilis] **—sub′tile·ly** adv. **—sub′tile·ness, sub·til·i·ty** (sub·til′ə·tē) n.

sub·ti·tle (sub′tīt′l) n. **1** A subordinate or explanatory title, as in a book, play, or document. **2** pl. In motion pictures, printed translations of foreign-language dialogue, usu. appearing at the bottom of the screen.

sub·tle (sut′l) adj. **sub·tler** (sut′lər, sut′l·ər), **sub·tlest 1** Not easily detected; elusive; delicate: a subtle aroma. **2** Characterized by or requiring keenness of mind, vision, hearing, etc.: subtle humor; subtle variations in sound. **3** Very skillful or ingenious: a subtle craftsman. **4** Not direct or obvious: a subtle hint. [< L subtilis fine] **—sub′tle·ness** n. **—sub′tly** adv.

sub·tle·ty (sut′l·tē) n. pl. **·ties 1** The state or quality of being subtle. **2** Something that is subtle.

sub·tract (səb·trakt′) v.t. & v.i. To take away or deduct, as a portion from the whole, or one quantity from another. [< L sub- away + trahere draw] **—sub·tract′er, sub·trac′tion** n. **—sub·trac′tive** adj.

sub·tra·hend (sub′trə·hend) n. Math. That which is to be subtracted from a number or quantity to give the difference.

sub·treas·ur·y (sub·trezh′ər·ē) n. pl. **·ur·ies 1** A branch office of the U.S. Treasury Department. **2** Any branch treasury. **—sub·treas′ur·er** n.

sub·trop·i·cal (sub·trop′i·kəl) adj. Of, pertaining to, or designating regions adjacent to the tropical zone. Also **sub·trop′ic.** **—sub·trop′ics** n.pl.

sub·urb (sub′ûrb) n. **1** A district or town adjacent to a city. **2** Outlying districts; environs. **—the suburbs** Residential areas near or within commuting distance of a city. [< L sub- near to + urbs a city]

sub·ur·ban (sə·bûr′bən) adj. Of or pertaining to a suburb or its residents.

sub·ur·ban·ite (sə·bûr′bən·īt) n. A resident of a suburb.

sub·ur·ban·ize (sə·bûr′bə·nīz′) v.t. **·ized, ·iz·ing** To make suburban or give a suburban character to. **—sub·ur′ban·i·za′tion** n.

sub·ur·bi·a (sə·bûr′bē·ə) n. **1** The social and cultural world of suburbanites. **2** Suburbs or suburbanites collectively.

sub·ven·tion (səb·ven′shən) n. A grant of money made, esp. by a government, to an institution, cause, or study; subsidy. [< L subvenire] **—sub·ven′tion·ar′y** (-er′ē) adj.

sub·ver·sion (səb·vûr′shən, -zhən) n. **1** The act of subverting; demolition; overthrow. **2** A cause of ruin. **—sub·ver′sion·ar′y** (-er′ē) adj.

sub·ver·sive (səb·vûr′siv) adj. Tending to subvert or overthrow. —n. A person regarded as desiring to weaken or overthrow a government, organization, etc. **—sub·ver′·sive·ly** adv. **—sub·ver′sive·ness** n.

sub·vert (səb·vûrt′) v.t. **1** To overthrow from the very foundation; destroy utterly. **2** To corrupt; undermine the principles or character of. [< L *subvertere* overturn] —**sub·vert′er** *n.*

sub·way (sub′wā) *n.* **1** A passage below the surface of the ground. **2** An underground railroad beneath city streets for local transportation; also, the tunnel through which it runs. **3** UNDERPASS.

suc·ceed (sək·sēd′) *v.i.* **1** To accomplish what is attempted or intended. **2** To come next in order or sequence. **3** To come after another into office, ownership, etc. —*v.t.* **4** To be the successor or heir of. **5** To come after in time or sequence; follow. [< L *succedere* go under, follow after] —**suc·ceed′er** *n.*

suc·cess (sək·ses′) *n.* **1** A favorable course or termination of anything attempted. **2** The gaining of position, fame, wealth, etc. **3** A person or thing that is successful. **4** The degree of succeeding: Did you have any *success* in getting an appointment? [< L *succedere* succeed] —**Syn. 1** achievement, satisfaction. **2** prosperity, eminence, station.

suc·cess·ful (sək·ses′fəl) *adj.* **1** Having achieved success. **2** Ending in success: a *successful* venture. —**suc·cess′ful·ly** *adv.* —**suc·cess′ful·ness** *n.*

suc·ces·sion (sək·sesh′ən) *n.* **1** The act of following consecutively. **2** A group of things that succeed in order; a series or sequence. **3** The act or right of legally or officially coming into a predecessor's office, possessions, position, etc. **4** A group or hierarchy of persons having the right to succeed. —**in succession** One after another. —**suc·ces′sion·al** *adj.* —**suc·ces′sion·al·ly** *adv.*

suc·ces·sive (sək·ses′iv) *adj.* Following in succession; consecutive. —**suc·ces′sive·ly** *adv.* —**suc·ces′sive·ness** *n.*

suc·ces·sor (sək·ses′ər) *n.* One who or that which follows in succession; esp. a person who succeeds to an office, position, or property.

suc·cinct (sək·singkt′) *adj.* Reduced to a minimum number of words; concise; terse. [< L *sub-* underneath + *cingere* girl] —**suc·cinct′ly** *adv.* —**suc·cinct′ness** *n.*

suc·cor (suk′ər) *n.* **1** Help rendered in danger, difficulty, or distress. **2** One who or that which affords relief. —*v.t.* To go to the aid of; help. *Brit. sp.* **suc′cour.** [< L *sub-* up from under + *currere* to run] —**suc′cor·er** *n.* —**Syn.** *n.* **1** aid, rescue, relief, support.

suc·co·tash (suk′ə·tash) *n.* A dish of corn kernels and beans, usu. lima beans, cooked together. [< Algon.]

suc·cu·bus (suk′yə·bəs) *n. pl.* **·bi** (-bī, -bē) One of a class of demons in female form fabled to have intercourse with sleeping men. [< LL *succuba* a strumpet]

suc·cu·lent (suk′yə·lənt) *adj.* **1** Juicy; full of juice. **2** *Bot.* Composed of fleshy, juicy tissue: a *succulent* leaf. **3** Absorbing; interesting. —*n.* A succulent plant. [< L *succus* juice] —**suc′cu·lence, suc′cu·len·cy** *n.* —**suc′cu·lent·ly** *adv.*

suc·cumb (sə·kum′) *v.i.* **1** To give way; yield, as to force or persuasion. **2** To die. [< L *sub-* underneath + *cumbere* lie]

such (such) *adj.* **1** Being the same or similar in kind or quality; of a kind mentioned or indicated: a book *such* as this; screws, bolts, and other *such* items. **2** Indicated but not specified: some *such* place. **3** Extreme in degree, quality, etc.: *such* an uproar. —**such as** As an example or examples of the kind indicated: flowers *such as* dandelions. —*pron.* **1** Such a person or thing or such persons or things. **2** The same as implied or indicated: *Such* was the result. —**as such** As the particular thing or kind it is, regardless of others: People *as such* deserve compassion. —*adv.* **1** So: *such* destructive criticism. **2** Especially; very: She's in *such* good spirits today. [< OE *swelc, swylc*]

such and such Understood to be specific but not specified: to consult *such and such* an expert.

such·like (such′līk′) *adj.* Of a like or similar kind. —*pron.* Persons or things of that kind.

suck (suk) *v.t.* **1** To draw into the mouth by means of a partial vacuum created by action of the lips and tongue. **2** To draw in or take up by suction. **3** To draw liquid or nourishment from with the mouth: to *suck* an orange or a lollipop. **4** To take and hold in the mouth as if to do this: to *suck* one's thumb. **5** To pull or draw into an association: with *in* or *into:* The lure of quick profits *sucked* him in. —

v.i. **6** To draw in liquid, air, etc., by suction. **7** To draw in milk from a breast or udder by sucking. **8** To make a sucking sound. —*n.* **1** The act or sound of sucking. **2** That which is sucked. [< OE *sūcan*]

suck·er (suk′ər) *n.* **1** One who or that which sucks. **2** Any of various freshwater fishes having thick, fleshy lips. **3** A mouth adapted for clinging and sucking, as that of a leech, tapeworm, etc. **4** *Slang* A person easily deceived. **5** *Bot.* An adventitious shoot. **6** A tube or pipe used for suction. **7** A lollipop. —*v.t.* **1** To strip (a plant) of suckers. —*v.i.* **2** To form or send out suckers or shoots.

Sucker *def.* 2

suck·le (suk′əl) *v.* **·led, ·ling** *v.t.* **1** To nourish at the breast; nurse. **2** To bring up; nourish. —*v.i.* **3** To suck at the breast. —**suck′ler** *n.*

suck·ling (suk′ling) *n.* An unweaned mammal.

su·cre (sōo′krā) *n.* The monetary unit of Ecuador.

su·crose (sōo′krōs) *n.* The sweet, soluble, crystalline carbohydrate familiar as the common white sugar of commerce, and consisting of fructose and glucose in chemical combination. [< F *sucre* sugar]

suc·tion (suk′shən) *n.* **1** The act or process of sucking. **2** The production of a partial vacuum in a space connected with a fluid or gas under reduced pressure. —*adj.* Creating or operating by suction.

suc·to·ri·al (suk·tôr′ē·əl, -tōr′-) *adj.* **1** Adapted for sucking or suction. **2** *Zool.* Living by sucking; having organs for sucking.

Su·dan (sōo·dan′) *n.* A republic of NE Africa, 967,500 sq. mi., cap. Khartoum. —**Su·da·nese** (sōo′də·nēz′) *adj., n.* • See map at AFRICA.

sud·den (sud′n) *adj.* **1** Happening quickly and without warning. **2** Causing surprise; unexpected: a *sudden* development. **3** Hurried; hasty; rash. —**all of a sudden** Without warning; suddenly. [< L *subitus,* p.p. of *subire* come or go stealthily] —**sud′den·ly** *adv.* —**sud′den·ness** *n.*

suds (sudz) *n.pl.* **1** Soapy water. **2** Froth; foam. **3** *Slang* Beer. [< MDu. *sudde, sudse* a marsh] —**suds′y** *adj.*

sue (sōo) *v.* **sued, su·ing** *v.t.* **1** To institute legal proceedings against, as for the redress of some wrong. **2** To prosecute (a legal action). —*v.i.* **3** To institute legal proceedings. **4** To seek to persuade someone by entreaty: with *for:* to *sue* for peace. [< AF *suer* pursue, sue] —**su′er** *n.*

suede (swād) *n.* Leather or a fabric having a napped surface. Also **suède.** [< F *gants de Suède* Swedish gloves]

su·et (sōo′it) *n.* The white, solid fatty tissue of beef, lamb, etc. [< L *sebum* fat] —**su′et·y** *adj.*

suf., suff. suffix.

suf·fer (suf′ər) *v.i.* **1** To feel pain or distress. **2** To sustain loss, injury, or detriment. **3** To undergo punishment, esp. death. —*v.t.* **4** To have inflicted on one; sustain, as an injury or loss: to *suffer* a fracture of the arm; to *suffer* a business reversal. **5** To undergo; pass through, as change. **6** To bear; endure: He never could *suffer* incompetence. **7** To allow; permit. [< L *sub-* up from under + *ferre* bear] —**suf′fer·a·ble** *adj.* —**suf′fer·a·bly** *adv.* —**suf′fer·er** *n.*

suf·fer·ance (suf′ər·əns, suf′rəns) *n.* **1** Permission given or implied by failure to prohibit. **2** The capacity for suffering or tolerating pain or distress. —**on sufferance** Tolerated or suffered but not encouraged.

suf·fer·ing (suf′ər·ing, suf′ring) *n.* **1** The state of anguish or pain of one who suffers. **2** The pain suffered; loss; injury.

suf·fice (sə·fīs′, -fīz′) *v.* **·ficed, ·fic·ing** *v.i.* To be sufficient or adequate. [< L *sub-* under + *facere* make]

suf·fi·cien·cy (sə·fish′ən·sē) *n. pl.* **·cies 1** The state of being sufficient. **2** That which is sufficient; esp., adequate means or income.

suf·fi·cient (sə·fish′ənt) *adj.* Being all that is needed; adequate; enough. [< L *sufficere* substitute, suffice] —**suf·fi′cient·ly** *adv.* —**Syn.** ample, satisfactory, fitting.

suf·fix (suf′iks) *n.* A letter or letters added to the end of a word or root, forming a new word or functioning as an inflectional element, as *-ful* in faithful and *-ed* in loved.

—*v.t.* To add as a suffix. [< L *suffixus,* p.p. of *suffigere* fasten underneath] —**suf′fix·al** *adj.*

suf·fo·cate (suf′ə·kāt′) *v.* **·cat·ed, ·cat·ing** *v.t.* **1** To kill by obstructing respiration in any manner. **2** To cause distress in by depriving of an adequate supply or quality of air. **3** To stifle or smother, as a fire. —*v.i.* **4** To die from suffocation. **5** To be distressed by an inadequate supply or quality of air. [< L *sub-* under + *fauces* throat] —**suf′fo·cat′ing·ly** *adv.* —**suf′fo·ca′tion** *n.* —**suf′fo·ca′tive** *adj.*

suf·fra·gan (suf′rə·gən, -jən) *n.* **1** An auxiliary or assistant bishop. **2** Any bishop subordinate to an archbishop. —*adj.* Assisting; auxiliary. [< L *suffragium* vote] —**suf′fra·gan·ship′** *n.*

suf·frage (suf′rij) *n.* **1** A vote in support of someone or something. **2** The right or privilege of voting; franchise. **3** Any short intercessory prayer. [< L *suffragium* a vote]

suf·fra·gette (suf′rə·jet′) *n.* A woman who advocates female suffrage. —**suf′fra·get′tism** *n.*

suf·fra·gist (suf′rə·jist) *n.* An advocate of suffrage, esp. for women.

suf·fuse (sə·fyōōz′) *v.t.* **·fused, ·fus·ing** To spread over, as with a fluid, light, or color. [< L *suffusus,* p.p. of *suffundere* pour underneath] —**suf·fu′sion** *n.* —**suf·fu′sive** *adj.*

sug·ar (shŏŏg′ər) *n.* **1** A sweet, crystalline foodstuff obtained chiefly from sugar cane and sugar beets; sucrose. **2** Any of a large class of mostly sweet and water-soluble carbohydrates widely distributed in plants and animals, as lactose, glucose, fructose, etc. —*v.t.* **1** To sweeten, cover, or coat with sugar. **2** To make less distasteful, as by flattery. —*v.i.* **3** To make maple sugar by boiling down maple syrup: usu. with *off.* **4** To form or produce sugar; granulate. [< Ar. *sukkar*] —**sug′ar·less** *adj.*

sugar beet A variety of beet cultivated as a commercial source of sugar.

sugar cane A tall tropical grass with a solid jointed stalk rich in sugar.

sug·ar-coat (shŏŏg′ər·kōt′) *v.t.* **1** To cover with sugar. **2** To cause to appear attractive or less distasteful. —**sug′ar-coat′ing** *n.*

sug·ar-cured (shŏŏg′ər·kyŏŏrd′) *adj.* Treated with a sweetened brine, as ham or pork.

sug·ar·plum (shŏŏg′ər·plum′) *n.* A small ball or disk of candy.

sug·ar·y (shŏŏg′ər·ē) *adj.* **1** Of, like, or composed of sugar; sweet. **2** Honeyed or complaisant; esp., excessively sweet or sentimental. —**sug′ar·i·ness** *n.*

sug·gest (səg·jest′, sə·jest′) *v.t.* **1** To bring or put forward for consideration, action, or approval; propose. **2** To arouse in the mind by association or connection: Gold *suggests* wealth. **3** To give a hint of; intimate: Her gesture *suggested* indifference. [< L *suggerere* carry underneath, suggest] —**sug·gest′er** *n.*

sug·gest·i·ble (səg·jes′tə·bəl, sə-) *adj.* **1** That can be suggested. **2** Responding readily to suggestions; easily led. —**sug·gest′i·bil′i·ty** *n.*

sug·ges·tion (səg·jes′chən, sə·jes′-) *n.* **1** The act of suggesting. **2** Something suggested. **3** A hint; trace; touch: a *suggestion* of irony. **4** An association of thoughts or ideas, esp. if based upon incidental or fortuitous similarities rather than a logical or rational relationship.

sug·ges·tive (səg·jes′tiv, sə-) *adj.* **1** Tending to suggest; stimulating thought or reflection. **2** Suggesting or hinting at something improper or indecent. —**sug·ges′tive·ly** *adv.* —**sug·ges′tive·ness** *n.*

su·i·cide (s/yōō′ə·sīd) *n.* **1** The intentional taking of one's own life. **2** One who takes or tries to take one's own life. **3** Personal or professional ruin brought on by one's own actions. [< L *sui* of oneself + *caedere* kill] —**su·i·ci·dal** (s/yōō′ə·sīd′l) *adj.* —**su′i·ci′dal·ly** *adv.*

su·i gen·e·ris (sōō′ī jen′ər·is, sōō′ē, gen′-) Of his (her, its) particular kind; unique. [L]

suit (s/yōōt) *n.* **1** A set of garments worn together; esp., a coat and trousers or skirt, made of the same fabric. **2** An outfit or garment for a particular purpose: a bathing *suit.* **3** A group of like things; a set. **4** Any of the four sets of thirteen cards each that make up a deck of cards. **5** A proceeding in a court of law for the recovery of a right or the redress of a wrong. **6** The courting of a woman. —**follow suit 1** To play a card identical in suit to the card

led. **2** To follow an example set by another. —*v.t.* **1** To meet the requirements of or be appropriate to; befit. **2** To please; satisfy. **3** To render appropriate; adapt. **4** To furnish with clothes. —*v.i.* **5** To agree; accord. **6** To be or prove satisfactory. **7** To put on a protective suit or uniform: with *up:* ballplayers *suiting up* before a game. [< OF *sieute* < L *sequi* follow]

suit·a·ble (s/yōō′tə·bəl) *adj.* Appropriate; proper; fitting. —**suit′a·bil′i·ty, suit′a·ble·ness** *n.* —**suit′a·bly** *adv.*

suit·case (s/yōōt′kās′) *n.* A case for carrying clothing, etc., esp. one that is flat and rectangular.

suite (swēt; *for def. 2, also* sōōt) *n.* **1** A set of things intended to go or be used together, as a number of connected rooms forming an apartment or leased as a unit in a hotel. **2** A set of matched furniture. **3** A company of attendants; a retinue. **4** *Music* An instrumental composition consisting of a series of short pieces. [< OF *sieute.* See SUIT.]

suit·ing (s/yōō′ting) *n.* Cloth used in making suits of clothes.

suit·or (s/yōō′tər) *n.* **1** One who institutes a suit in court. **2** A man who courts a woman. **3** A petitioner.

su·ki·ya·ki (sōō′kē·yä′kē, skē·yä′kē) *n.* A Japanese dish of thinly sliced meat and vegetables fried together and served with condiments. [Jap.]

Suk·koth (sŏŏk′ōth, sŏŏk′ōs) *n.* A Jewish holiday, originally a harvest festival, occurring in late September or in October. Also **Suk′kos, Suk′kot.** [< Hebrew *sūkōth* tabernacles, booths]

sulfa- *combining form Chem.* Sulfur; related to or containing sulfur. Also **sulf-, sulfo-.** [< SULFUR]

sul·fa drug (sul′fə) Any of various sulfonamide derivatives effective in the treatment of certain bacterial infections.

sul·fate (sul′fāt) *n.* A salt of sulfuric acid. —*v.* **·fat·ed, ·fat·ing** *v.t.* **1** To convert into a sulfate. **2** To treat with a sulfate or sulfuric acid. **3** *Electr.* To form a coating of lead sulfate on (the plate of a storage battery). —*v.i.* **4** To become sulfated. Also **sul′phate.** [< L *sulfur* sulfur] —**sul·fa′tion** *n.*

sul·fide (sul′fīd) *n.* A compound of sulfur with an element or radical. Also **sul′phide.**

sul·fite (sul′fīt) *n.* A salt or ester of sulfurous acid. Also **sul′phite.** —**sul·fit′ic** (-fit′ik) *adj.*

sul·fon·a·mide (sul·fon′ə·mīd, -mid) *n.* Any of a group of organic sulfur compounds containing a univalent amide radical.

sul·fur (sul′fər) *n.* **1** An industrially important, abundant nonmetallic element (symbol S), occurring in three allotropic forms and found in both free and combined states. **2** Any of various small yellow butterflies. Also, and for def. 2 always, **sul′phur.** —**sul′fur·y** *adj.*

sul·fu·rate (sul′fyə·rāt) *v.t.* **·rat·ed, ·rat·ing** SULFURIZE. —**sul′fu·ra′tion** *n.*

sulfur dioxide A colorless gas with a sharp odor, very soluble in water, used in manufacturing sulfuric acid, in bleaching, etc.

sul·fu·re·ous (sul·fyŏŏr′ē·əs) *adj.* **1** Of or like sulfur. **2** Greenish yellow.

sul·fu·ret (sul′fyə·ret) *v.t.* **·ret·ed** or **·ret·ted, ·ret·ing** or **·ret·ting** SULFURIZE. —*n.* SULFIDE.

sul·fu·ric (sul·fyŏŏr′ik) *adj.* Pertaining to or derived from sulfur, esp. in its higher valence.

sulfuric acid A colorless, exceedingly corrosive, syrupy liquid with a strong affinity for water, used extensively in the chemical industry.

sul·fur·ize (sul′fyə·rīz) *v.t.* **·ized, ·iz·ing** To impregnate, treat with, or subject to the action of sulfur. —**sul′fur·i·za′tion** *n.*

sul·fur·ous (sul′fər·əs, *for def. 1 esp.* sul·fyŏŏr′əs) *adj.* **1** Pertaining to or derived from sulfur, esp. in its lower valence. **2** Resembling burning sulfur; fiery. **3** Biting; vitriolic: *sulfurous* criticism. **4** Blasphemous, as language. —**sul′fur·ous·ly** *adv.* —**sul′fur·ous·ness** *n.*

sulfurous acid (sul·fyŏŏr′əs) An unstable acid formed by dissolving sulfur dioxide in water.

sulk (sulk) *v.i.* To be sullen in mood and tend to shun others. —*n.* A sulky mood or humor. [Back formation < SULKY]

sulk·y[1] (sul′kē) *adj.* **sulk·i·er, sulk·i·est** Sulking or tending to sulk. [? < OE *(ā)seolcan* be weak or slothful]—**sulk′i·ly** *adv.* —**sulk′i·ness** *n.*

sulk·y² (sul′kē) *n. pl.* **sulk·ies** A light, two-wheeled, one-horse vehicle for one person. [< SULKY¹; so called because one rides alone]

sul·len (sul′ən) *adj.* **1** Showing ill-humor, as from dwelling upon a grievance; morose; glum. **2** Depressing;

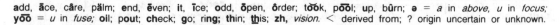

Sulky

somber: *sullen* clouds. **3** Slow; sluggish. **4** Melancholy; mournful. [< AF *solein* sullen, alone] —**sul′len·ly** *adv.* —**sul′len·ness** *n.* —**Syn. 1** gloomy, sad, sulky, moody.

sul·ly (sul′ē) *v.* **·lied, ·ly·ing** *v.t.* To mar the brightness or purity of; soil; defile. [< MF *souiller* to soil]

sulph- For all words so spelled, see SULF-.

sul·tan (sul′tən) *n.* A Muslim ruler. [< Ar. *sultān* a sovereign, dominion]

sul·tan·a (sul·tan′ə, -tä′nə) *n.* **1** A sultan's wife, daughter, sister, or mother. **2** A white, seedless variety of grape or raisin.

sul·tan·ate (sul′tən·āt, -it) *n.* **1** The authority of a sultan. **2** The domain of a sultan. Also **sul′tan·ship.**

sul·try (sul′trē) *adj.* **·tri·er, ·tri·est 1** Hot, moist, and still; close: said of weather. **2** Oppressively hot; burning. **3** Inflamed with passion. **4** Expressing or tending to excite sexual interest; sensual. [< obs. *sulter*, var. of SWELTER] —**sul′tri·ly** *adv.* —**sul′tri·ness** *n.*

sum (sum) *n.* **1** An amount of money. **2** The result obtained by the addition of numbers or quantities. **3** A problem in arithmetic. **4** The entire quantity, number, or substance; the whole: The *sum* of his effort came to naught. **5** Essence or core; summary: In *sum*, the issue is one of trust; the *sum* of an argument. **6** The highest or furthest point; summit. —*v.* **summed, sum·ming** *v.t.* **1** To present as a summary; recapitulate; summarize: usu. with *up.* **2** To add into one total: often with *up.* —*v.i.* **3** To give a summary; recapitulate: usu. with *up.* **4** To calculate a sum: often with *up.* [< L *summa (res)* highest (thing)]

su·mac (soo′mak, shoo′-) *n.* **1** Any of a genus of woody plants related to the cashew. **2** A species of sumac with hairy red fruit and compound leaves turning brilliant red in autumn: also **smooth sumac. 3** The dried and powdered leaves of certain species of sumac, used for tanning and dyeing. Also **su′mach.** [< Ar. *summāq*]

sum·ma cum lau·de (soom′ə koom lou′də, -dē, soo′mə, sum′ə kum lô′dē) *Latin* With the greatest praise: to be graduated *summa cum laude.*

sum·ma·rize (sum′ə·rīz) *v.t.* **·rized, ·riz·ing** To make a summary of. *Brit. sp.* **·rise.** —**sum′ma·ri·za′tion** *n.*

sum·ma ·ry (sum′ər·ē) *n. pl.* **·ries** A brief account of the substance or essential points of something spoken or written; recapitulation. —*adj.* **1** Giving the substance or essential points; concise. **2** Performed without ceremony or delay; instant: *summary* execution. [< L *summa.* See SUM.] —**Syn.** *n.* condensation, abridgment, epitome, précis, compendium. —**sum·ma·ri·ly** (sə·mer′ə·lē, sum′ər·ə·lē) *adv.*

sum·ma·tion (sum·ā′shən) *n.* **1** The act or operation of obtaining a sum; addition. **2** A sum or total. **3** A summing up of the main points of an argument, as the final speech in behalf of one of the parties in a court trial.

sum·mer (sum′ər) *n.* **1** The warmest season of the year, including, in the northern hemisphere, June, July, and August. **2** A year of life. **3** A bright or prosperous period. —*v.i.* **1** To pass the summer. —*v.t.* **2** To keep or care for through the summer. —*adj.* **1** Of, pertaining to, or occurring in summer. **2** Used or intended for use in the summer: a *summer* house. [OE *sumor, sumer*] —**sum′mer·y** *adj.*

sum·mer·sault (sum′ər·sôlt) *n. v.i.* SOMERSAULT.

summer squash Any of various small squashes with a soft rind, usu. eaten before they ripen.

sum·mer·time (sum′ər·tīm′) *n.* Summer; the summer season.

sum·mit (sum′it) *n.* **1** The highest part; the top; vertex.

2 The highest degree; maximum. **3** The highest level or office, as of a government or business organization. **4** A meeting of executives of the highest level, as heads of government. —*adj.* Of or involving those at the highest level: a *summit* conference. [< L *summus* highest]

sum·mit·ry (sum′it·rē) *n.* **1** Meetings of officials of the highest rank, as heads of government. **2** The use or dependency upon such meetings to solve international problems.

sum·mon (sum′ən) *v.t.* **1** To order to come; send for. **2** To call together; cause to convene, as a legislative assembly. **3** To order (a person) to appear in court by a summons. **4** To call forth or into action; arouse: usu. with *up*: to *summon* up courage. **5** To call on for a specific act. [< L *summonere* suggest, hint]—**sum′mon·er** *n.*

sum·mons (sum′ənz) *n. pl.* **sum·mons·es 1** An order or call to attend or act at a particular place or time. **2** *Law* **a** A notice to a defendant summoning him to appear in court. **b** A notice to appear in court as a witness or as a juror. [< OF *somondre* summon]

su·mo (soo′mō) *n.* A highly stylized form of wrestling popular in Japan. [< Japanese *sumō*]

sump (sump) *n.* A pit or reservoir in which liquids are received by drainage, as a cesspool. [< MDu. *somp, sump* a marsh]

sump·ter (sump′tər) *n.* A pack animal. [< OF *sometier* a driver of a pack horse]

sump·tu·ar·y (sump′choo·er′ē) *adj.* Limiting or regulating expenditure. [< L *sumptus* expenditure < *sumere* take]

sump·tu·ous (sump′choo·əs) *adj.* **1** Involving or showing lavish expenditure. **2** Luxurious; magnificent. [< L *sumptus* expense] —**sump′tu·ous·ly** *adv.* —**sump′tu·ous·ness** *n.*

sun (sun) *n.* **1** The star that is the gravitational center and the main source of energy for the solar system, about 93,000,000 miles distant from the earth, with a diameter of 864,000 miles and a mass 332,000 times that of the earth. **2** Any star, esp. one with a planetary system. **3** The light and heat from the sun; sunshine. **4** Anything brilliant and magnificent; a source of splendor. **5** A day or a year. —*v.* **sunned, sun·ning** *v.t.* **1** To expose to the light or heat of the sun. —*v.i.* **2** To bask in the sun; sun oneself. [< OE *sunne*]

Sun. Sunday.

sun·bathe (sun′bāth′) *v.i.* **·bathed, ·bath·ing** To bask in the sun. —**sun′·bath′er** *n.*

sun·beam (sun′bēm′) *n.* A ray or beam of the sun.

Sun·belt (sun′belt′) *n.* The southeastern and southwestern states of the U.S., ranging from Virginia south to Florida and west to California.

sun·bon·net (sun′bon′it) *n.* A wide-brimmed bonnet sometimes having a flap covering the neck.

sun·burn (sun′bûrn′) *n.* Injury to the skin by ultraviolet radiation from the sun. —*v.t. & v.i.* **·burned** or **·burnt** (bûrnt), **·burn·ing** To affect or be affected with sunburn.

sun·dae (sun′dē) *n.* Ice cream topped with crushed fruit, flavoring, syrup, nuts, etc. [? < *Sunday*]

Sun·day (sun′dē, -dā) *n.* The first day of the week; the Christian Sabbath. [< OE *sunnan dæg* day of the sun]

Sunday school A school meeting on Sundays for religious instruction, esp. of the young.

sun·der (sun′dər) *v.t. & v.i.* To break apart; sever. [< OE *syndrian, sundrian*]

sun·di·al (sun′dī′əl, -dīl) *n.* A device that shows the time of day by the shadow of a style or gnomon cast on a dial in sunlight.

sun·down (sun′doun′) *n.* SUN-SET (def. 2).

sun·dries (sun′drēz) *n. pl.* Various or miscellaneous articles. [< SUNDRY]

sun·dry (sun′drē) *adj.* Various; several; miscellaneous. [< OE *syndrig* separate]

sun·fish (sun′fish′) *n. pl.* **·fish** or

Sundial

·fish·es 1 Any of several North American freshwater perchlike fishes, usu. with narrow bodies. 2 Any of various large fishes of warm seas, having a deep compressed body.

sun·flow·er (sun′flou′ər) *n.* Any of a genus of tall plants with large leaves and large composite flower heads encircled with a ring of bright yellow ray flowers.

Sunflower

sung (sung) *p.p.* of SING.

sun·glasses (sun′glas′iz, -gläs′-) *n. pl.* Eyeglasses having colored lenses that protect the eyes from the glare of the sun.

sunk (sungk) *p.p. & a p.t.* of SINK.

sunk·en (sung′kən) A *p.p.* of SINK. —*adj.* 1 Lying at the bottom of a body of water. 2 Located beneath a surface. 3 Lower than the surrounding or usual level: *sunken* gardens. 4 Deeply depressed or fallen in: *sunken* cheeks.

sun·lamp (sun′lamp′) *n.* An electric lamp radiating ultraviolet rays, used esp. for the therapeutic treatments.

sun·less (sun′lis) *adj.* Dark; cheerless. —**sun′less·ness** *n.*

sun·light (sun′līt′) *n.* The light of the sun.

sun·lit (sun′lit′) *adj.* Lighted by the sun.

sun·ny (sun′ē) *adj.* ·ni·er, ·ni·est 1 Characterized by bright sunlight. 2 Filled with sunlight: a *sunny* room. 3 Cheerful; genial: a *sunny* smile. —**sun′ni·ly** *adv.* —**sun′ni·ness** *n.*

sun parlor A room enclosed in glass and having a sunny exposure. Also **sun porch, sun room.**

sun·rise (sun′rīz′) *n.* 1 The daily first appearance of the sun above the horizon. 2 The time at which the sun rises.

sun·set (sun′set′) *n.* 1 The apparent daily descent of the sun below the horizon. 2 The time at which the sun sets. 3 A final period or decline, as of life.

sun·shade (sun′shād′) *n.* Something used as protection from the sun, as a parasol or an awning.

sun·shine (sun′shīn′) *n.* 1 The direct light of the sun. 2 The light and warmth of sunlight. 3 Brightness or warmth, as of feeling. —**sun′shin′y** *adj.*

sun·spot (sun′spot′) *n.* One of many dark irregular spots appearing sometimes on the surface of the sun.

sun·stroke (sun′strōk′) *n.* Prostration and fever induced by heat and exposure to the sun. —**sun′struck′** (-struk′) *adj.*

sun·tan (sun′tan′) *n.* A darkened coloration of the skin induced by exposure to ultraviolet light. —**sun′tanned′** (-tand′) *adj.*

sun·up (sun′up′) *n.* SUNRISE.

sun·ward (sun′wərd) *adj.* Facing toward the sun. —*adv.* Toward the sun: also **sun′wards.**

sup¹ (sup) *v.t. & v.i.* **supped, sup·ping** To take (fluid food) a little at a time; sip. —*n.* A mouthful or sip of liquid or semiliquid food. [<OE *sūpan* drink]

sup² (sup) *v.* **supped, sup·ping** *v.i.* To eat supper. [<OF *soper*<*soupe* soup]

sup. above (L *supra*); superior, superlative; supplement; supplementary; supply.

su·per (sōō′pər) *adj.* 1 Surpassing others of its class, as in power or size: a *super* bomb; a *super* city. 2 *Informal* Outstanding; superb: a *super* performance. 3 *Slang* Great; wonderful: He's *super!* 4 More than normal or warranted. —*n.* 1 A superintendent (def. 2). 2 SUPERNUMERARY (esp. def. 2). 3 An article of superior size or quality.

super- *prefix* 1 Above in position; over: *superstructure.* 2 More than; above or beyond: *supersonic.* 3 More than normal or warranted; inordinate or inordinately: *superintelligent; superpatriot.* 4 Surpassing others in its class, as in power, size, or skill; superior: *superhighway.* 5 Extra: *supertax.* [<L *super* above, beyond] • See TAXONOMY.

su·per·a·ble (sōō′pər·ə·bəl) *adj.* That can be surmounted, overcome, or conquered. [<L *superare* overcome<*super* over] —**su′per·a·bil′i·ty** *n.* —**su′per·a·bly** *adv.*

su·per·a·bound (sōō′pər·ə·bound′) *v.i.* To abound to excess. [<L *super-* exceedingly + *abundare* overflow]

su·per·a·bun·dant (sōō′pər·ə·bun′dənt) *adj.* More than sufficient; excessive. [<LL *superabundare* to superabound] —**su′per·a·bun′dance** *n.* —**su′per·a·bun′dant·ly** *adv.*

su·per·an·nu·at·ed (sōō′pər·an′yōō·wāt′id) *adj.* 1 Re-

lieved of active work on account of age; retired. 2 Set aside or discarded as obsolete or too old. [<L *super* beyond + *annus* a year]

su·perb (sōō·pûrb′, sōō-) *adj.* 1 Extraordinarily good; excellent: a *superb* wine. 2 Having grand, impressive beauty; majestic: a *superb* cathedral. 3 Luxurious; elegant. [<L *superbus* proud] —**su·perb′ly** *adv.* —**su·perb′ness** *n.*

su·per·block (sōō′pər·blok′) *n.* A large block of commercial buildings or residences from which motor traffic is barred, often landscaped as a unit and joined by pedestrian walks.

su·per·car·go (sōō′pər·kär′gō) *n. pl.* ·goes or ·gos An officer on board ship in charge of the cargo and its sale and purchase.

su·per·charge (sōō′pər·chärj′) *v.t.* ·charged, ·charg·ing 1 To adapt (an engine) to develop more power, as by fitting with a supercharger. 2 To charge excessively, as with emotion.

su·per·charg·er (sōō′pər·chär′jər) *n.* A compressor for supplying extra air or fuel mixture to an internal-combustion engine.

su·per·cil·i·ous (sōō′pər·sil′ē·əs) *adj.* Haughtily contemptuous; arrogant. [<L *supercilium* eyebrow, pride] —**su′per·cil′i·ous·ly** *adv.* —**su′per·cil′i·ous·ness** *n.*

su·per·col·lid·er (sōō′pər·kə·līd·er) *n.* A very large particle accelerator.

su·per·con·duc·ting (sōō′pər·kən·duk′ting) *adj.* Having the property, when cooled to temperatures near absolute zero, of conducting electricity continuously without resistance: said of certain metals and alloys. —**su′per·con·duc′tive** *adj.* —**su′per·con·duc·tiv′i·ty** (-kon′duk·tiv′ə·tē), **su′per·con·duc′tor** *n.*

su·per·e·go (sōō′pər·ē′gō, -eg′ō) *n. pl.* ·gos *Psychoanal.* A largely unconscious element of the personality, acting principally as conscience and critic.

su·per·er·o·ga·tion (sōō′pər·er′ə·gā′shən) *n.* The performance of an act in excess of the demands or requirements of duty. [<L *super-* above + *erogare* pay out]

su·per·e·rog·a·to·ry (sōō′pər·ə·rog′ə·tôr′ē, -tō′rē) *adj.* 1 Of the nature of supererogation. 2 SUPERFLUOUS.

su·per·fi·cial (sōō′pər·fish′əl) *adj.* 1 Of, lying near, or on the surface: a *superficial* wound. 2 Of or pertaining to only the ordinary and the obvious; not profound; shallow. 3 Hasty; cursory: a *superficial* examination. 4 Apparent only; not real or genuine. [<L *super-* above + *facies* a face] —**su′per·fi·ci·al′i·ty** (-fish′ē·al′ə·tē), **su′per·fi′cial·ness** *n.* —**su′per·fi′cial·ly** *adv.*

su·per·fine (sōō′pər·fīn′) *adj.* 1 Of the best quality; very fine and delicate. 2 Unduly elaborate. —**su′per·fine′ness** *n.*

su·per·flu·i·ty (sōō′pər·flōō′ə·tē) *n. pl.* ·ties 1 The state of being superfluous. 2 That which is superfluous.

su·per·flu·ous (sōō·pûr′flōō·əs) *adj.* Exceeding what is needed; surplus. [<L *super-* above + *fluere* to flow] —**su·per′flu·ous·ly** *adv.* —**su·per′flu·ous·ness** *n.*

su·per·heat (sōō′pər·hēt′) *v.t.* 1 OVERHEAT. 2 To raise the temperature of (a vapor not in contact with its liquid) above the saturation point for a given pressure. 3 To heat (a liquid) above the boiling point without conversion into vapor. —**su′per·heat′er** *n.*

su·per·het·er·o·dyne (sōō′pər·het′ər·ə·dīn′) *adj. Electronics* Pertaining to or designating radio reception in which the incoming signals are converted to an intermediate frequency, and are then amplified and demodulated. —*n.* A radio receiver of this type. [<SUPER(SONIC) + HETERODYNE]

su·per·high·way (sōō′pər·hī′wā′) *n.* A highway for high-speed traffic, usu. with four or more lanes.

su·per·hu·man (sōō′pər·ʰyōō′mən) *adj.* 1 Above and beyond what is human; miraculous; divine. 2 Beyond normal human ability or power. —**su′per·hu′man·ly** *adv.*

su·per·im·pose (sōō′pər·im·pōz′) *v.t.* ·posed, ·pos·ing 1 To lay or impose something else. 2 To add as an incidental or superfluous feature. —**su′per·im·po·si′tion** (-im′pə·zish′ən) *n.*

su·per·in·duce (sōō′pər·in·dʸōōs′) *v.t.* ·duced, ·duc·ing To introduce additionally. [<L *super-* over + *inducere* lead in] —**su′per·in·duc′tion** (-duk′shən) *n.*

su·per·in·tend (sōō′pər·in·tend′) *v.t.* To have the charge and direction of; supervise. [<LL *super-* over + *intendere*

direct, aim at] **—su′per·in·ten′dence, su′per·in·ten′den·cy** n.

su·per·in·ten·dent (sōō′pər·in·ten′dənt) n. **1** One who has charge of an institution or undertaking; director. **2** One responsible for the maintenance and repair of a building. **—adj.** Superintending.

su·pe·ri·or (sə·pir′ē·ər, sōō-) adj. **1** Higher in rank, quality, or degree; better or excellent: superior vision; superior talent. **2** Greater in quantity: a superior supply. **3** Higher in relation to other things; upper. **4** Printing Set above the line, as 1 in x^1. **5** Serenely unaffected or indifferent: with to: superior to pettiness. **6** Affecting or suggesting an attitude of contemptuous indifference or disdain: superior airs. **—n. 1** One who is superior, as in rank or excellence. **2** The head of an abbey, convent, or monastery. [< L superus higher < super above] **—su·pe·ri·or·i·ty** (sə·pir′ē·ôr′ə·tē, -or′-, sōō-) n. **—su·pe′ri·or·ly** adv.

su·per·la·tive (sə·pûr′lə·tiv, sōō-) adj. **1** Being of the highest degree; most excellent or eminent. **2** Gram. Expressing the highest or extreme degree of the quality expressed by the positive degree of an adjective or adverb: "Wisest" is the superlative form of "wise." **3** Exaggerated. **—n. 1** That which is superlative. **2** The highest degree; apex. **3** Gram. **a** The superlative degree. **b** A form in the superlative degree. [< L superlatus excessive < super- above + latus carried] **—su·per′la·tive·ly** adv. **—su·per′la·tive·ness** n.

su·per·man (sōō′pər·man′) n. pl. **·men** (-men′) **1** A man of superhuman powers. **2** An intellectually and morally superior man.

su·per·mar·ket (sōō′pər·mär′kit) n. A large, chiefly self-service store selling food and household supplies.

su·per·nal (sōō·pûr′nəl) adj. **1** Heavenly; celestial. **2** Coming from above or from the sky. [< L supernus < super over] **—su·per′nal·ly** adv.

su·per·nat·u·ral (sōō′pər·nach′ər·əl, -rəl) adj. **1** Existing or occurring through some agency beyond the known forces of nature. **2** Of or concerning phenomena of this kind: supernatural tales. **3** Believed to be miraculous or divine. **4** Suggestive of ghosts, demons, or other agents unconstrained by natural law. **—n.** That which is supernatural. [< L super- above + natura nature] **—su′per·nat′u·ral·ism, su′per·nat′u·ral·ness** n. **—su′per·nat′u·ral·ist** adj., n. **—su′per·nat′u·ral·is′tic** adj. **—su′per·nat′u·ral·ly** adv.

su·per·nu·mer·a·ry (sōō′pər·nʸōō′mə·rer′ē) adj. **1** Being beyond a fixed or usual number. **2** Beyond a necessary number; superfluous. **—n.** pl. **·ar·ies 1** A supernumerary person or thing. **2** A stage performer without any speaking part. [< L super over + numerus a number]

su·per·pa·tri·ot (sōō′pər·pā′trē·ət, -ot) n. A person who is or claims to be a great patriot, often one whose patriotic fervor is marked by a readiness to regard dissent as unpatriotic or subversive. **—su′per·pa′tri·ot′ic** adj. **—su′per·pa′·tri·ot·ism** n.

su·per·pose (sōō′pər·pōz′) v.t. **·posed, ·pos·ing** To lay over or upon something else. **—su′per·pos′a·ble** adj. **—su′·per·po·si′tion** (-pə·zish′ən) n.

su·per·pow·er (sōō′pər·pou′ər) n. One of a few great, dominant nations characterized by superior economic or military strength and by large population.

su·per·sat·u·rate (sōō′pər·sach′ōō·rāt) v.t. **·rat·ed, ·rat·ing** To cause (a solution) to hold more of a solute than it can normally hold at the given temperature. **—su′per·sat′u·ra′tion** n.

su·per·scribe (sōō′pər·skrīb′) v.t. **·scribed, ·scrib·ing 1** To write or engrave on the outside or on the upper part of. **2** To address, as a letter. [< L super- over + scribere write] **—su′per·scrip′tion** (-skrip′shən) n.

su·per·script (sōō′pər·skript′) adj. Written above or overhead. **—n.** A letter, index, or other mark following and above a letter or figure, as in a^3 or c'. [< LL superscriptus, p.p. of superscribere superscribe]

su·per·sede (sōō′pər·sēd′) v.t. **·sed·ed, ·sed·ing 1** To take the place of, as by reason of superiority or right; replace. **2** To put something in the place of; set aside. [< L super- above + sedere sit] **—su′per·sed′er, su′per·se′dure** (-sē′jər) n.

su·per·son·ic (sōō′pər·son′ik) adj. **1** Of or capable of

moving at a speed greater than that of sound. **2** Moving at such a speed. **3** ULTRASONIC. **—su′per·son′i·cal·ly** adv.

su·per·star (sōō′pər·stär′) n. A public performer, as an actor, singer, or professional athlete, regarded as one of the best or most popular. **—su′per·star′dom** n.

su·per·sti·tion (sōō′pər·stish′ən) n. **1** An ignorant or irrational belief, often provoked by fear, and based upon assumptions of cause and effect contrary to known scientific facts and principles. **2** Any practice inspired by such belief. **3** Any unreasonable belief or impression. [< L superstitio excessive fear of the gods, amazement]

su·per·sti·tious (sōō′pər·stish′əs) adj. **1** Disposed to believe in or be influenced by superstitions. **2** Of, based upon, or manifesting superstition. **—su′per·sti′tious·ly** adv. **—su′·per·sti′tious·ness** n.

su·per·struc·ture (sōō′pər·struk′chər) n. **1** Any structure above the basement or considered in relation to its foundation. **2** Any structure built on top of another. **3** The parts of a ship's structure above the main deck.

su·per·tank·er (sōō′pər·tangk′ər) n. A very large tanker capable of carrying a vast cargo, as of oil.

su·per·tax (sōō′pər·taks′) n. An extra tax in addition to the normal tax; a surtax.

su·per·vene (sōō′pər·vēn′) v.i. **·vened, ·ven·ing** To follow closely upon something as an extraneous or additional circumstance. [< L super- over and above + venire come] **—su′per·ven′ient** (-vēn′yənt) adj. **—su′per·ven′tion** (-ven′·shən) n.

su·per·vise (sōō′pər·vīz) v.t. **·vised, ·vis·ing** To have charge of; direct. [< L super- over + videre see] **—Syn.** manage, run, oversee, superintend.

su·per·vi·sion (sōō′pər·vizh′ən) n. The act or process of supervising; direction, control, or guidance.

su·per·vi·sor (sōō′pər·vī′zər) n. **1** One who supervises; a superintendent or manager. **2** In education, an official supervising teachers and responsible for curricula, etc., in a particular subject. **—su′per·vi′sor·ship** n. **—su·per·vi·sor·y** (sōō′pər·vī′zər·ē) adj.

su·pine (sōō·pīn′, sə-) adj. **1** Lying on the back, or with the face turned upward. **2** Having no interest or care; listless. [< L supinus] **—su·pine′ly** adv. **—su·pine′ness** n.

supp., suppl. supplement; supplementary.

sup·per (sup′ər) n. **1** The last meal of the day; the evening meal. **2** A social event including the serving of supper: a church supper. [< OF soper sup] **—sup′per·less** adj.

sup·plant (sə·plant′, -plänt′) v.t. **1** To take the place of, as of something inferior or out of date; displace. **2** To take the place of (someone) by scheming, treachery, etc. **3** To replace (one thing) with another: to supplant naive expectations with realistic goals. [< L supplantare trip up] **—sup·plan·ta·tion** (sup′lan·tā′shən), **sup·plant′er** n.

sup·ple (sup′əl) adj. **sup·pler** (sup′lər, -əl·ər), **sup·plest 1** Easily bent; flexible; pliant: supple leather. **2** Agile or graceful in movement; limber. **3** Yielding readily to the wishes of others; compliant. **4** Servile; obsequious. **5** Quick to respond or adjust, as the mind; adaptable. **—v.t. & v.i. ·pled, ·pling** To make or become supple. [< L supplex, lit., bending under] **—sup·ple·ly** (sup′əl·ē, sup′lē) or **sup′ply** (sup′lē) adv. **—sup′ple·ness** n. **—Syn. 1** lithe, deft, nimble.

sup·ple·ment (sup′lə·mənt) n. **1** Something added that supplies a deficiency. **2** An addition to a publication, as a section providing additional information added to a book. **—v.t.** To make additions to; provide for what is lacking in. [< L supplere. See SUPPLY.] **—sup·ple·men·tal** (sup′lə·men′·təl) adj. • Both supplement and complement refer to something added to make up for a lack or deficiency. Complement (not to be confused with compliment, an expression of praise) emphasizes the correction or adjustment of something unfinished or imperfect, and often implies a balancing of elements: The design of the housing project called for low buildings to complement the high-rises. In the case of supplement, the fact of being added is more emphatic, and the expected result is one of improvement rather than completion: Student teachers supplemented the regular teaching staff, freeing them to give more individual help to slow learners.

---

add, āce, câre, pälm; end, ēven; it, īce; odd, ōpen, ôrder; tŏŏk, pōōl; up, bûrn; ə = a in above, u in focus; yōō = u in fuse; oil; pout; check; go; ring; thin; this; zh, vision. < derived from; ? origin uncertain or unknown.

sup·ple·men·ta·ry (sup'lə·men'tər·ē, -trē) *adj.* Added as a supplement; additional.

sup·pli·ant (sup'lē·ənt) *adj.* Entreating earnestly and humbly. —*n.* One who supplicates. [< L *supplicare* supplicate] —**sup'pli·ant·ly** *adv.* —**sup'pli·ant·ness** *n.*

sup·pli·cant (sup'lə·kənt) *n.* One who supplicates. —*adj.* Asking or entreating humbly. [< L *supplicare* supplicate]

sup·pli·cate (sup'lə·kāt) *v.* ·**cat·ed**, ·**cat·ing** *v.t.* 1 To ask for humbly or by earnest prayer. 2 To beg something of; entreat. —*v.i.* 3 To make an earnest request. [< L *sub*- under + *plicare* bend, fold] —**sup'pli·ca'tion** *n.* —**sup'pli·ca·to'ry** (-kə·tôr'ē, -tō'rē) *adj.*

sup·ply (sə·plī') *v.* ·**plied**, ·**ply·ing** *v.t.* 1 To make available; provide or furnish: to *supply* electricity to a remote area. 2 To furnish with what is needed: to *supply* an army with weapons. 3 To provide for adequately; satisfy. 4 To make up for; compensate for. 5 To fill (the place of another). —*v.i.* 6 To take the place of another temporarily. —*n. pl.* ·**plies** 1 That which is or can be supplied. 2 A store or quantity on hand. 3 *pl.* Accumulated stores, as for an army. 4 The amount of a commodity offered at a given price or available for meeting a demand. 5 The act of supplying. [< L *supplere* < *sub*- up from under + *plere* fill] —**sup·pli'·er** *n.*

sup·port (sə·pôrt', -pōrt') *v.t.* 1 To bear the weight of, esp. from underneath; hold in position; keep from falling, sinking, etc. 2 To bear or sustain (weight, etc.). 3 To provide money or necessities for; provide with the means of subsistence. 4 To give approval or assistance to; uphold. 5 To serve to uphold or corroborate; substantiate: His testimony *supports* our position. 6 To endure patiently; tolerate. 7 To provide with the means to endure; keep from collapsing or yielding: Faith *supported* her. 8 To carry on; keep up: to *support* a war. 9 In the theater, etc., to act in a subordinate role to. —*n.* 1 The act of supporting. 2 One who supports. 3 That which supports, as a brace or girdle for the body. [< L *sub*- up from under + *portare* carry] —**sup·port'a·ble** *adj.* —**sup·port'a·bly** *adv.* —**Syn.** 4 advocate, endorse, help, aid, assist. 5 verify, bear out. 6 bear, suffer. 7 sustain.

sup·port·er (sə·pôr'tər, -pōr'-) *n.* 1 One who or that which supports. 2 An elastic or other support for some part of the body.

sup·por·tive (sə·pôr'tiv, -pōr'-) *adj.* 1 Tending or intended to support. 2 Contributing importantly to the stability of one's physical or emotional health: *supportive* treatment. —**sup·por'tive·ly** *adv.*

sup·pose (sə·pōz') *v.* ·**posed**, ·**pos·ing** *v.t.* 1 To believe to be true or probable; presume. 2 To assume as true for the sake of argument or illustration. 3 To expect: I am *supposed* to follow. 4 To presuppose; imply: Mercy *supposes* a sense of compassion. —*v.i.* 5 To make a supposition. [< L *supponere* substitute, put under] —**sup·pos'a·ble** *adj.* —**sup·pos'a·bly** *adv.* —**sup·pos'er** *n.*

sup·posed (sə·pōzd') *adj.* 1 Accepted as genuine; believed. 2 Imagined only, instead of actually experienced. —**sup·pos·ed·ly** (sə·pō'zid·lē) *adv.*

sup·po·si·tion (sup'ə·zish'ən) *n.* 1 Something supposed; a conjecture or hypothesis. 2 The act of supposing. —**sup'po·si'tion·al** *adj.* —**sup'po·si'tion·al·ly** *adv.*

sup·pos·i·to·ry (sə·poz'ə·tôr'ē, -tō'rē) *n. pl.* ·**ries** A small mass of a usu. medicated substance that melts at body temperature, for introduction into a body cavity, as the rectum or vagina. [< LL *suppositorius* placed underneath or up < L *supponere* put under]

sup·press (sə·pres') *v.t.* 1 To put an end or stop to; crush, as a rebellion. 2 To stop or prohibit the activities of. 3 To withhold from knowledge or publication, as a book, news, etc. 4 To hold back or repress. 5 To stop or check (a hemorrhage, etc.). [< L *suppressus*, p.p. of *supprimere* press down] —**sup·press'er, sup·pres'sor** *n.* —**sup·press'i·ble, sup·pres'sive** *adj.*

sup·pres·sion (sə·presh'ən) *n.* 1 The act of suppressing, or the state of being suppressed. 2 The deliberate exclusion from consciousness of unacceptable ideas, memories, etc.

sup·pu·rate (sup'yə·rāt) *v.i.* ·**rat·ed**, ·**rat·ing** To discharge or generate pus. [< L *sub*- under + *pus, puris* pus] —**sup'·pu·ra'tion** *n.* —**sup'pu·ra·tive** (-rə·tiv, -rā'-) *adj.*

su·pra (soo'prə) *adv.* Above. [L]

supra- *prefix* Above; beyond: *supranational.* [< L *supra* above, beyond]

su·pra·na·tion·al (soo'prə·nash'ə·nəl) *adj.* Of or concerning several or a number of nations; involving more than one nation. —**su'pra·na'tion·al·ism** *n.* —**su'pra·na'tion·al·ist** *adj., n.*

su·pra·re·nal (soo'prə·rē'nəl) *adj.* Situated above the kidneys; adrenal. —*n.* An adrenal gland. [< L *supra*- above + *renalis* renal]

su·prem·a·cy (sə·prem'ə·sē, soo-) *n. pl.* ·**cies** 1 The state of being supreme. 2 Supreme power or authority.

su·preme (sə·prēm', soo-) *adj.* 1 Highest in power or authority; dominant. 2 Highest or greatest, as in degree; utmost: *supreme* devotion. 3 Ultimate; last and greatest. [< L *supremus,* superl. of *superus* < *super* above] —**su·preme'ly** *adv.* —**su·preme'ness** *n.*

Supreme Being God.

Supreme Court 1 The highest Federal court. 2 The highest court in many states.

Supreme Soviet The legislature of the Soviet Union.

supt. superintendent.

sur- *prefix* Over; beyond: *surtax.* [< OF *sur*- < L *super*-]

su·rah (soor'ə) *n.* A soft, usu. twilled, silk or silk and rayon fabric. [< *Surat,* India]

sur·base (sûr'bās') *n.* A border or molding above the top of a base, as of a pedestal.

sur·cease (sûr·sēs', sûr'sēs) *n.* Cessation; end. —*v.t. & v.i.* ·**ceased**, ·**ceas·ing** To end. [< AF *surseoir* to refrain < L *supersedere* to sit above]

sur·charge (sûr'chärj') *n.* 1 An additional amount charged or imposed. 2 An excessive burden, load, or charge. 3 OVERCHARGE. 4 A new valuation or something additional printed on a postage or revenue stamp. —*v.t.* (sûr·chärj') ·**charged**, ·**charg·ing** 1 OVERCHARGE. 2 To fill or load to excess. 3 To imprint a surcharge on (postage stamps). —**sur·charg'er** *n.*

sur·cin·gle (sûr'sing·gəl) *n.* A strap encircling the body of a horse, for holding a saddle, blanket, etc. [< SUR- + L *cingulum* a belt]

sur·coat (sûr'kōt') *n.* An outer coat or garment, esp., in the Middle Ages, one worn over armor.

surd (sûrd) *n.* 1 *Math.* An irrational number, esp. an indicated root, as $\sqrt{2}$. 2 *Phonet.* A voiceless speech sound. —*adj.* 1 *Math.* IRRATIONAL. 2 *Phonet.* VOICELESS. [< L *surdus* deaf, silent]

sure (shoor) *adj.* **sur·er, sur·est** 1 Not subject to uncertainty or doubt; beyond all question; indisputable. 2 Characterized by freedom from doubt or uncertainty; firm: *sure* convictions; a *sure* grasp of his subject. 3 Certain or confident; positive: I was *sure* I had seen her before. 4 Not liable to fail or disappoint; reliable; sound: a *sure* memory. 5 Bound to happen or be: a *sure* winner. 6 *Obs.* Safe; secure. —*adv. Informal* Surely; certainly. —**for sure** Certainly; beyond all question. —**to be sure** Indeed; certainly; quite so. [< L *securus*] —**sure'ness** *n.* —**Syn.** 1 unquestionable, unimpeachable, indubitable. 4 trustworthy, dependable, true.

Surcoat

sure-foot·ed (shoor'foot'id) *adj.* Not liable to fall or stumble. —**sure'-foot'ed·ly** *adv.* —**sure'-foot'ed·ness** *n.*

sure·ly (shoor'lē) *adv.* 1 In a sure manner. 2 Without doubt; certainly. 3 Really; certainly: used as an intensive to express strong probability: He *surely* knew that.

sure·ty (shoor'ə·tē, shoor'tē) *n. pl.* ·**ties** 1 The state of being sure; certainty. 2 Security against loss or damage. 3 One who assumes the debts, responsibilities, etc., of another; a guarantor. [< L *securus* secure] —**sure'ty·ship** *n.*

surf (sûrf) *n.* 1 The swell of the sea that breaks upon a shore. 2 The foam caused by the billows. —*v.i.* To ride the surf on a surfboard; engage in surfing. [?] —**surf'er** *n.*

sur·face (sûr'fis) *n.* 1 The outer part or face of an object. 2 That which has area but not thickness. 3 A superficial aspect; external appearance. —v. ·faced, ·fac·ing v.t. **1** To put a surface on; esp., to make smooth, even, or plain. **2** To cause to rise to the surface, as a submarine. —v.i. **3** To rise to the surface. **4** To come to public notice, esp. something formerly kept secret. [< SUR- + FACE] —sur′fac·er n.

sur·face-ac·tive (sûr′fis·ak′tiv) adj. Effective in changing the properties of a substance, esp. surface tension, at the area of contact with another substance: surface-active detergents.

surface tension That property of a liquid by which the surface molecules exert a strong cohesive force, thus forming an elastic skin that tends to contract.

sur·fac·tant (sûr·fak′tənt) n. A surface-active substance, as a detergent. [< SURF(ACE)-ACT(IVE) + -ANT]

surf·board (sûrf′bôrd′, -bōrd′) n. A long, narrow board used in surfing. —v.i. SURF. —surf′board·er n.

surf·boat (sûrf′bōt′) n. A boat of extra strength and buoyancy, for launching and landing through surf.

sur·feit (sûr′fit) v.t. **1** To feed or supply to fullness or to excess. —v.i. **2** To overindulge in food or drink. —n. **1** Excess in eating or drinking. **2** The result of such excess; satiety. **3** Any excessive amount: a surfeit of praise. [< OF surfaire overdo]

surf·ing (sûrf′ing) n. A water sport in which a person standing on a surfboard is borne by the surf toward the shore. Also **surf·rid·ing** (sûrf′rī′ding).

surg. surgeon; surgery; surgical.

surge (sûrj) v. surged, surg·ing v.i. **1** To rise and roll with a powerful, swelling motion, as waves. **2** To be tossed about by waves. **3** To move or go in a powerful, wavelike motion: The mob surged through the square. **4** To increase or vary suddenly, as an electric current. —n. **1** A large swelling wave; billow. **2** A great swelling or rolling movement, as of waves. **3** Electr. A sudden, transient rise in current flow. **4** Any sudden, sharp increase. [< L surgere]

sur·geon (sûr′jən) n. One who practices surgery. [< OF cirurgie surgery] —sur′geon·cy (-sē) n.

sur·ger·y (sûr′jər·ē) n. pl. ·ger·ies **1** The treatment of disease, injury, etc., by manual and operative means. **2** The branch of medicine concerned with surgical treatment. **3** A place where surgery is performed; an operating room. **4** Brit. A physician's office. [< Gk. cheirourgia a handicraft < cheir the hand + ergein to work] —sur·gi·cal (sûr′ji·kəl) adj. —sur′gi·cal·ly adv.

sur·ly (sûr′lē) adj. ·li·er, ·li·est Rude and ill-humored, esp. in response; gruff or insolent. [Earlier sirly like a lord < sir a lord] —sur′li·ly adv. —sur′li·ness n.

sur·mise (sər·mīz′) v. ·mised, ·mis·ing v.t. & v.i. To infer (something) on slight evidence; guess. —n. (sər·mīz′, sûr′mīz) A conjecture made on slight evidence; supposition. [< OF surmettre accuse < sur- upon + mettre put] —Syn. v. suppose, assume, conjecture.

sur·mount (sər·mount′) v.t. **1** To overcome; prevail over (a difficulty, etc.). **2** To mount to the top or cross to the other side of, as an obstacle. **3** To be or lie over or above. **4** To place something above or on top of; cap. [< L super- over + mons, montis a hill, mountain]

sur·name (sûr′nām′) n. **1** A last name; family name. **2** A name added to one's real name, as Ethelred the Unready. —v.t. (sûr′nām′, sûr·nām′) ·named, ·nam·ing To give a surname to; call by a surname. [< OF sur- above, beyond + nom a name]

sur·pass (sər·pas′, -päs′) v.t. **1** To go beyond or past in degree or amount; exceed or excel. **2** To be beyond the reach or powers of; transcend. —sur·pass′a·ble adj. —sur·pass′er n. —Syn. **1** eclipse, outdo, outstrip.

sur·pass·ing (sər·pas′ing, -päs′-) adj. Exceptional; excellent. —sur·pass′ing·ly adv.

sur·plice (sûr′plis) n. A loose white vestment with full sleeves, worn over the cassock by the clergy and choristers of some churches. [< Med. L superpellicium (vestimentum) an overgarment]

Surplice

sur·plus (sûr′plus) n. **1** That which remains over and above what is used or required. **2** Assets in excess of liabilities. —adj. Being in excess of what is used or needed. [< L super- over and above + plus more] —sur′plus·age (-ij) n.

sur·prise (sər·prīz′, sə-) v.t. ·prised, ·pris·ing **1** To cause to feel wonder or astonishment, esp. because unusual or unexpected. **2** To come upon suddenly or unexpectedly; take unawares. **3** To attack suddenly and without warning. **4** To lead unawares, as into doing something not intended: with into. —n. **1** The state of being surprised; astonishment. **2** Something that causes surprise, as a sudden and unexpected event. **3** A sudden attack or capture. [< L super- over + prehendere take] —sur·pris′er n.

sur·pris·ing (sər·prī′zing, sə-) adj. Causing surprise or wonder. —sur·pris′ing·ly adv. —Syn. amazing, startling.

sur·re·al·ism (sə·rē′əl·iz′əm) n. A 20th-century movement in art and literature characterized chiefly by the incongruous juxtaposition or use of dreamlike elements, in theory an expression of the unconscious mind. —sur·re′al·ist adj., n. —sur·re′al·is′tic adj. —sur·re′al·is′ti·cal·ly adv.

sur·ren·der (sə·ren′dər) v.t. **1** To yield possession of or power over to another because of demand or compulsion. **2** To give up or relinquish, esp. in favor of another; resign; abandon. **3** To give (oneself) over to a passion, influence, etc. —v.i. **4** To give oneself up, as to an enemy in warfare. —n. The act of surrendering. [< OF surrendre < sur- over + rendre give, render]

sur·rep·ti·tious (sûr′əp·tish′əs) adj. **1** Accomplished by secret or improper means; clandestine. **2** Acting secretly or by stealth. [< L subreptus, p.p. of subripere steal] —sur′rep·ti′tious·ly adv. —sur′rep·ti′tious·ness n.

sur·rey (sûr′ē) n. A vehicle having two seats facing forward and sometimes a top. [< Surrey, England]

Surrey

sur·ro·gate (sûr′ə·gāt, -git) n. **1** Someone or something taking the place of another; substitute. **2** In some U.S. states, a probate court judge. —v.t. (sûr′ə·gāt) ·gat·ed, ·gat·ing To put in the place of another; deputize or substitute. [< L subrogare < sub- in place of another + rogare ask]

sur·round (sə·round′) v.t. **1** To extend or place completely around; encircle or enclose. **2** To enclose on all sides so as to cut off communication or retreat. **3** To be or cause something to become a significant part of the environment or experience of: surrounded by lies; to surround oneself with the best legal talent. —n. Chiefly Brit. That which surrounds, as a border. [< LL super- over + undare rise in waves]

sur·round·ings (sə·roun′dingz) n.pl. The conditions, objects, etc., that constitute one's environment.

sur·tax (sûr′taks′) n. An extra or additional tax.

sur·tout (sər·tōō′, sûr′tōō) n. A man's long, close-fitting overcoat. [F < sur- above + tout all]

sur·veil·lance (sər·vā′ləns, -vāl′yəns) n. A careful watching of someone or something, usu. carried on secretly or discreetly: to keep a suspect under surveillance. [F < sur- over + veiller watch] —sur·veil′lant adj.

sur·vey (sər·vā′, sûr′vā) v.t. **1** To look at in its entirety; view comprehensively, as from a height. **2** To look at carefully and minutely; scrutinize. **3** To determine accurately the area, contour, or boundaries of according to the principles of geometry and trigonometry. **4** To make a survey of. —v.i. **5** To survey land. —n. (usu. sûr′vā) **1** The operation, act, process, or results of surveying land. **2** A systematic inquiry to collect data for analysis, used esp. for the preparation of a comprehensive report or summary. **3** The result of such an inquiry; a comprehensive report. **4** A general or overall view; overview: a *survey* of contemporary theater. [< L *super-* over + *videre* look]

sur·vey·ing (sər·vā′ing) *n.* **1** The science and art of surveying portions of the surface of the earth and representing them on maps. **2** The work of one who surveys.

sur·vey·or (sər·vā′ər) *n.* One who surveys, esp. one engaged in land surveying.

sur·viv·a·ble (sûr·vī′və·bəl) *adj.* Not precluding survival: a *survivable* accident. **—sur·viv·a·bil′i·ty** *n.*

sur·viv·al (sər·vī′vəl) *n.* **1** The act or fact of surviving; a continuation of life or existence. **2** The fact of living or lasting beyond another. **3** One who or that which survives.

sur·vive (sər·vīv′) *v.* **·vived, ·viv·ing 1** *v.i.* To live or continue beyond the death of another, the occurrence of an event, etc.; remain alive or in existence. **—v.t. 2** To live or exist beyond the death, occurrence, or end of; outlive or outlast. **3** To go on living after or in spite of: to *survive* a flood. [< L *super-* above, beyond + *vivere* live] **—sur·vi′vor, sur·viv′er** *n.*

sus·cep·ti·ble (sə·sep′tə·bəl) *adj.* **1** Readily affected; especially subject or vulnerable: with *to: susceptible* to infection; lax supervision *susceptible* to abuse. **2** Capable of being influenced or determined; liable: with *of* or *to: susceptible* of proof. **3** Easily affected in feeling or emotion; sensitive. [< L *suscipere* receive, undertake] **—sus·cep·ti·bil·i·ty** (sə·sep′tə·bil′ə·tē), **sus·cep′ti·ble·ness** *n.* **—sus·cep′ti·bly** *adv.* **—Syn. 1** unresistant, open. **2** admitting. **3** tender, impressionable.

sus·pect (sə·spekt′) *v.t.* **1** To think (a person) guilty without evidence or proof. **2** To have distrust of; doubt: to *suspect* one's motives. **3** To have an inkling or suspicion of; think possible. **—v.i. 4** To have suspicions. **—adj.** (sus′pekt, sə·spekt′) Suspected; exciting suspicion. **—n.** (sus′pekt) A person suspected, esp. of a crime. [< F *suspecter* < L *suspectus,* p.p. of *suspicere* look under, mistrust] **—sus·pect′er** *n.*

sus·pend (sə·spend′) *v.t.* **1** To bar for a time from a privilege or office as a punishment. **2** To cause to cease for a time; interrupt: to *suspend* telephone service. **3** To withhold or defer action on: to *suspend* a sentence. **4** To hang from a support so as to allow free movement. **5** To keep in suspension, as dust particles in the air. **—v.i. 6** To stop for a time. **7** To fail to meet obligations; stop payment. [< L *sub-* under + *pendere* hang]

sus·pend·er (sə·spen′dər) *n.* **1** One who or that which suspends. **2** *pl.* A pair of straps for supporting trousers. **3** *Brit.* A garter.

sus·pense (sə·spens′) *n.* **1** Anxiety caused by an uncertainty, as to the outcome of an event. **2** Excited interest caused by the progressive unfolding of events or information leading to a climax or resolution. **3** The state of being uncertain or indecisive. [< L *suspensus,* p.p. of *suspendere* suspend]

sus·pen·sion (sə·spen′shən) *n.* **1** The act of suspending, or the state of being suspended. **2** A temporary removal from office or position or withdrawal of privilege. **3** An interruption; cessation: *suspension* of normal procedure. **4** A deferment of action. **5** The state of hanging freely from a support. **6** A dispersion in a liquid or gas of insoluble particles that slowly settle on standing; also, a substance in this condition. **7** *Mech.* A system, as of springs or other absorbent parts, by which the chassis and body of a vehicle is insulated against shocks when moving. **8** *Music* The prolongation of one or more tones of a chord into the succeeding chord, causing a transient dissonance. **b** The note so prolonged.

suspension bridge A bridge having its roadway suspended from cables supported by towers and anchored at either end.

sus·pen·sive (sə·spen′siv) *adj.* **1** Tending to suspend or keep in suspense. **2** Suspending or deferring operation or effect: a *suspensive* veto. **—sus·pen′sive·ly** *adv.*

sus·pen·so·ry (sə·spen′sər·ē) *adj.* **1** Acting to support or sustain. **2** Suspending or delaying. **—n. pl. ·ries** Something that supports or sustains, esp. a truss for the scrotum.

sus·pi·cion (sə·spish′ən) *n.* **1** The act of suspecting; an uncertain but often tenacious feeling or belief in the likelihood of another's guilt, wrongdoing, etc., without evidence or proof. **2** *Informal* A slight amount; trace, as

of a flavor. **—v.t.** *Regional* To suspect. [< L *suspicere.* See SUSPECT.]

sus·pi·cious (sə·spish′əs) *adj.* **1** Tending to arouse suspicion; questionable. **2** Having or disposed to have suspicions. **3** Indicating suspicion. **—sus·pi′cious·ly** *adv.* **—sus·pi′cious·ness** *n.*

sus·tain (sə·stān′) *v.t.* **1** To keep up or maintain; keep in effect or being. **2** To maintain by providing with food and other necessities. **3** To keep from sinking or falling, esp. by bearing up from below. **4** To endure without succumbing; withstand. **5** To suffer, as a loss or injury; undergo. **6** To uphold or support as being true or just. **7** To prove the truth or correctness of; confirm. [< L *sub-* up from under + *tenere* to hold] **—sus·tain′a·ble** *adj.* **—sus·tain′er, sus·tain′ment** *n.* **—Syn. 7** corroborate, establish.

sus·te·nance (sus′tə·nəns) *n.* **1** The act or process of sustaining; esp., maintenance of life or health; subsistence. **2** That which sustains, as food. **3** Means of support; livelihood.

sut·ler (sut′lər) *n.* Formerly, a peddler or tradesman who followed an army to sell goods and food to the soldiers. [< Du. *soeteler*] **—sut′ler·ship** *n.*

sut·tee (su·tē′, sut′ē) *n.* **1** The former custom in which a Hindu woman willingly cremated herself on the funeral pyre of her husband: also **sut·tee′ism.** **2** The widow so cremated. [< Hind. *satī* < Skt., faithful wife, fem. of *sat* good, wise]

su·ture (sōō′chər) *n.* **1** The junction of two edges by or as by sewing. **2** *Anat.* The fusion of two bones at their edges, as in the skull. **3** *Surg.* **a** The act or operation of joining the edges of an incision, wound, etc. **b** The thread, wire, or other material used in this operation. **—v.t. ·tured, ·turing** To unite by means of sutures; sew together. [< L *sutus,* p.p. of *suere* sew] **—su′tur·al** *adj.* **—su′tur·al·ly** *adv.*

su·ze·rain (sōō′zə·rin, -rān) *n.* **1** A feudal lord. **2** A nation having paramount control over a locally autonomous state. [< L *susum* upwards] **—su′ze·rain·ty** *n.* (*pl.* **·ties**)

svelte (svelt) *adj.* **1** Slender; willowy: a *svelte* fashion model. **2** Sophisticated; smart; chic. [< Ital. *svelto* stretched, slender]

SW, S.W., sw, s.w. southwest; southwestern.

Sw. Sweden; Swedish.

swab (swob) *n.* **1** A soft, absorbent substance, as of cotton or gauze, usu. secured at the end of a small stick, for applying medication, cleansing a body surface, etc. **2** *Med.* A specimen of mucus, etc., taken for examination with a swab. **3** A mop for cleaning decks, floors, etc. **4** A cylindrical brush for cleaning firearms. **5** *Slang* An oaf; lout. **—v.t. swabbed, swab·bing** To clean or apply with a swab. [< MDu. *zwabben* swab] **—swab′ber** *n.*

swad·dle (swod′l) *v.t.* **·dled, ·dling 1** To wrap (an infant) in swaddling clothes. **2** To wrap with or as if with a bandage; swathe; bind. **—n.** A band or cloth used for swaddling. [< OE *swathian* swathe]

swaddling clothes Bands or strips of linen or cloth formerly wound around a newborn infant. Also **swaddling bands.**

swag (swag) *n.* **1** A curved decoration, as a hanging fastened at either end or a carved motif on a building. **2** *Slang* Property obtained by robbery or theft; plunder. **3** *Austral.* A bundle or pack containing belongings. **4** A swaying; a lurch. [? < Scand.]

swage (swāj) *n.* A tool or form for shaping metal by hammering or pressure. **—v.t. swaged, swag·ing** To shape (metal) with or as with a swage. [< OF *souage*]

swag·ger (swag′ər) *v.i.* **1** To walk with an air of conspicuous self-satisfaction and usu. of masculine vanity. **2** To behave in a blustering or self-satisfied manner. **3** To boast; brag. **—n. 1** A swaggering gait or manner. **2** Verve; dash; bravado. **—adj.** Showy or stylish; smart. [< SWAG] **—swag′ger·er** *n.* **—swag′ger·ing·ly** *adv.*

swagger stick A short, lightweight stick, usu. tipped with metal, carried by some military officers as a mark of elegance or authority.

Swa·hi·li (swä·hē′lē) *n. pl.* **·hi·li** or **·hi·lis 1** One of a Bantu people of Zanzibar and the adjacent coast. **2** The language of this people, now widely used in E and central Africa.

swain (swān) *n.* **1** A rustic youth. **2** A lover; wooer. [< ON *sveinn* a boy, servant]

swal·low[1] (swol′ō) *v.t.* **1** To cause (food, etc.) to pass from the mouth into the stomach by means of muscular action of the esophagus. **2** To take in or engulf in a manner suggestive of this; absorb; envelop: often with *up.* **3** To put up with or endure; submit to, as insults. **4** To refrain from expressing; suppress: to *swallow* one's pride. **5** To take back: to *swallow* one's words. **6** *Informal* To believe (something improbable or incredible) to be true. —*v.i.* **7** To perform the act or the motions of swallowing. —*n.* **1** The act of swallowing. **2** An amount swallowed at once; a mouthful. [< OE *swelgan* swallow] —**swal′low·er** *n.*

swal·low[2] (swol′ō) *n.* **1** Any of various small birds with short bill, long, pointed wings, and forked tail, noted for swiftness of flight and migratory habits. **2** A similar bird, as the swift. [< OE *swealwe*]

swal·low·tail (swol′ō-tāl′) *n.* **1** A man's dress coat with two long, tapering skirts or tails. **2** A butterfly having a tapering prolongation on each hind wing. —**swal′low-tailed′** *adj.*

swam (swam) *p.t.* of SWIM.

swa·mi (swä′mē) *n. pl.* **·mis** Master; lord: a Hindu title of respect, esp. for a religious teacher.

swamp (swomp, swômp) *n.* A tract or region of low land saturated with water; a bog. Also **swamp′land′** (-land′). — *v.t.* **1** To drench or submerge with water or other liquid. **2** To overwhelm with difficulties; crush; ruin. **3** To sink or fill (a boat) with water. —*v.i.* **4** To sink in water, etc.; become swamped. [?< LG] —**swamp′y** *adj.* (**·i·er, ·i·est**)

swamp fever MALARIA.

swan (swon, swôn) *n.* Any of several large, web-footed, long-necked birds allied to but heavier than the goose. [< OE]

swan dive A dive performed with the head tilted back and the arms held sideways and brought together as the water is entered.

swank (swangk) *n.* **1** Ostentatious display, as in taste or manner; swagger. **2** Stylishness; smartness. —*adj.* **1** Ostentatiously fashionable. **2** Stylish; smart. —*v.i. Slang* To swagger; bluster. [?< MHG *swanken* sway]

Trumpeter swan

swank·y (swangk′ē) *adj.* **swank·i·er, swank·i·est** *Informal* Ostentatiously or extravagantly fashionable. —**swank′i·ly** *adv.* —**swank′i·ness** *n.*

swan's-down (swonz′doun′, swônz′-) *n.* **1** The down of a swan, used for trimming, powder puffs, etc. **2** Any of various fine, soft fabrics, usu. with a nap. Also **swans′-down′.**

swan song A last work, utterance, or performance, as before retirement or death. [< the ancient fable that the swan sings a last song before dying]

swap (swop) *v.t. & v.i.* **swapped, swap·ping** *Informal* To exchange (one thing for another); trade. —*n.* The act or an instance of swapping. [< ME *swappen* strike (a bargain), slap] —**swap′per** *n.*

sward (swôrd) *n.* Land thickly covered with grass; turf. — *v.t.* To cover with sward. [< OE *sweard* a skin]

swarm[1] (swôrm) *n.* **1** A large number of bees moving together with a queen to form a new colony. **2** A hive of bees. **3** A large crowd or mass, esp. one in apparent overall movement; throng. —*v.i.* **1** To leave the hive in a swarm: said of bees. **2** To come together, move, or occur in great numbers: The crowd *swarmed* out of the stadium; gnats *swarming* about. **3** To be crowded or overrun; teem: with *with: swarming* with tourists. —*v.t.* **4** To fill with a swarm or crowd. [< OE *swearm*] —**swarm′er** *n.*

swarm[2] (swôrm) *v.t. & v.i.* To climb (a tree, etc.) by clasping with the hands and limbs. [?]

swart (swôrt) *adj.* Swarthy. [< OE *sweart*] —**swart′ness** *n.*

swarth·y (swôr′thē) *adj.* **swarth·i·er, swarth·i·est** Having a dark complexion; tawny. [Var. of obs. *swarty* < SWART] — **swarth′i·ly** *adv.* —**swarth′i·ness** *n.*

swash (swosh, swôsh) *v.i.* **1** To move with a splashing sound, as waves. —*v.t.* **2** To splash (water, etc.). **3** To splash or dash water, etc., upon or against. —*n.* The splash of a liquid. [Imit.] —**swash′er** *n.* —**swash′ing·ly** *adv.*

swash·buck·ler (swosh′buk′lər, swôsh′-) *n.* A swaggering soldier, adventurer, daredevil, etc. [< SWASH + BUCK-LER] —**swash′buck′ler·ing** *n.* —**swash′buck′ling** *adj., n.*

swas·ti·ka (swos′ti·kə) *n.* **1** A primitive ornament or symbol in the form of a cross with arms of equal length, bent at the ends at right angles. **2** Such a figure with the arms extended clockwise, used as the emblem of the Nazis. Also **swas′ti·ca.** [< Skt. *sú* good + *astí* being < *as* be]

Nazi swastika

swat (swot) *v.t.* **swat·ted, swat·ting** To hit with a sharp, quick, or violent blow. —*n.* A sharp, quick, or violent blow. [Var. of SQUAT] —**swat′ter** *n.* —**Syn** *v.* smack, strike, whack.

swatch (swoch) *n.* A strip, as of fabric, esp. one cut off for a sample. [?]

swath (swoth, swôth) *n.* **1** A row or line of cut grass or grain. **2** The space cut by a machine or implement in a single course. **3** A strip, track, row, etc. —**cut a wide swath** To make a fine impression. [< OE *swæth* a track]

swathe[1] (swāth, swäth) *v.t.* **swathed, swath·ing 1** To bind or wrap, as in bandages; swaddle. **2** To envelop; enwrap. —*n.* A bandage for swathing. [< OE *swathian*] —**swath′er** *n.*

swathe[2] (swāth, swäth) *n.* SWATH.

sway (swā) *v.i.* **1** To swing from side to side or to and fro; oscillate. **2** To bend or incline to one side. **3** To incline in opinion, sympathy, etc. **4** To control; rule. —*v.t.* **5** To cause to swing from side to side. **6** To cause to bend or lean to one side. **7** To cause (a person, opinion, etc.) to tend in a given way; influence. **8** To deflect or divert, as from a course of action. —*n.* **1** Power; influence. **2** A sweeping, swinging, or turning from side to side. [Prob. < ON *sveigja* bend] —**Syn.** *v.* **2** lean, veer. **4** govern, influence. *n.* **1** control, dominion.

sway·back (swā′bak′) *n.* A hollow or sagging condition of the back, as in a horse. —*adj.* Having such a back: also **sway′backed′** (-bakt).

Swa·zi·land (swä′zē·land) *n.* An independent kingdom of the Commonwealth of Nations in SE Africa, 6,704 sq. mi., cap. Mbabane. • See map at AFRICA.

swear (swâr) *v.* **swore, sworn, swear·ing** *v.i.* **1** To make a solemn affirmation with an appeal to God or some other deity or to something held sacred. **2** To make a vow. **3** To use profanity; curse. **4** *Law* To give testimony under oath. —*v.t.* **5** To affirm or assert solemnly by invoking sacred beings or things. **6** To promise with an oath; vow. **7** To declare or affirm, earnestly or emphatically: I *swear* he's a liar. **8** To take or utter (an oath). —**swear by 1** To appeal to by oath. **2** To have complete confidence in. —**swear in** To administer a legal oath to. —**swear off** *Informal* To promise to give up: to *swear off* drink. —**swear out** To obtain (a warrant for arrest) by making a statement under oath. [< OE *swerian*] —**swear′er** *n.*

swear·word (swâr′wûrd′) *n.* A word used in profanity or cursing.

sweat (swet) *v.* **sweat** or **sweat·ed, sweat·ing** *v.i.* **1** To exude or excrete salty moisture from the pores of the skin; perspire. **2** To exude moisture in drops. **3** To gather and condense moisture in drops on its surface. **4** To pass through pores or interstices in drops. **5** To ferment, as tobacco leaves. **6** To come forth, as through a porous surface; ooze. **7** *Informal* To work hard; toil; drudge. **8** *Informal* To suffer, as from anxiety. —*v.t.* **9** To exude (moisture) from the pores or a porous surface. **10** To gather or condense drops of (moisture). **11** To soak or stain with sweat. **12** To cause to sweat. **13** To cause to work hard. **14** *Informal* To force (employees) to work for low wages and under unfavorable conditions. **15** To heat (solder, etc.) until it melts. **16** To join, as metal objects with solder. **17** *Metall.* To heat so as to extract an element that is easily fusible; also, to extract thus. **18** To subject to fermentation, as hides or tobacco. **19** *Slang* To subject to torture or rigorous interrogation to extract information. —**sweat (something) out** *Slang* To wait through anxiously; endure. —*n.* 1 Moisture in minute drops on the skin. 2 The act or state of sweating. 3 Hard labor; drudgery. 4 *Informal* Impatience, anxiety, or hurry. [< OE *swætan*] —**sweat'i·ly** *adv.* —**sweat'i·ness** *n.* — **sweat'y** *adj.* (**·i·er, ·i·est**)

sweat·band (swet′band′) *n.* 1 A band, usu. of leather, inside a hat to protect it from sweat. 2 An absorbent cloth band worn over the forehead or around the wrist.

sweat·er (swet′ər) *n.* 1 One who or that which sweats. 2 A knitted or crocheted garment with or without sleeves.

sweat gland One of the numerous minute subcutaneous glands that secrete sweat.

sweat shirt A loose-fitting, usu. long-sleeved pullover of soft, absorbent material, sometimes hooded.

sweat·shop (swet′shop′) *n.* A place where work is done under poor conditions, for insufficient wages, and for long hours.

sweat·suit (swet′soot′) *n.* A sweat shirt and matching pants (**sweat pants**) worn esp. by athletes when warming up or just after competing.

Swed. Sweden; Swedish.

Swede (swed) *n.* A native or citizen of Sweden.

Swe·den (swe′dən) *n.* A constitutional monarchy of N Europe, 173,577 sq. mi., cap. Stockholm.

Swed·ish (swe′dish) *adj.* Of or pertaining to Sweden, the Swedes, or their language. —*n.* 1 The North Germanic language of Sweden. 2 The inhabitants of Sweden collectively: with *the.*

sweep (swep) *v.* **swept, sweep·ing** *v.t.* 1 To collect or clear away with a broom, brush, etc. 2 To clear or clean with a broom, etc.: to *sweep* a floor. 3 To touch or brush with a motion as of sweeping: to *sweep* the strings of a harp. 4 To pass over swiftly: The searchlight *swept* the sky. 5 To move, carry, bring, etc., with force: The flood *swept* the bridge away. 6 To move over or through with force: The gale *swept* the bay. 7 To drag the bottom of (a body of water, etc.). 8 To win totally or overwhelmingly. —*v.i.* 9 To clean a floor or other surface with a broom, etc. 10 To move or go strongly and evenly: The train *swept* by. 11 To walk with great dignity: She *swept* into the room. 12 To trail, as a skirt. 13 To extend with a long reach or curve: The road *sweeps* along the lake shore on the north. —*n.* 1 The act or result of sweeping. 2 A long stroke or movement: a *sweep* of the hand. 3 The act of clearing out or getting rid of. 4 An unbroken stretch or extent: a *sweep* of beach. 5 A total or overwhelming victory, as in an election. 6 The range, area, or compass reached by sweeping. 7 One who sweeps chimneys, streets, etc. 8 A curving line; flowing contour. 9 A long, heavy oar. 10 A long pole on a pivot, having a bucket suspended from one end, for use in drawing water. 11 *pl.* Sweepings. 12 *pl. Informal* Sweepstakes. [< OE *swāpan*] —**sweep′er** *n.*

Sweep *def. 10*

sweep·ing (swe′ping) *adj.* 1 Extending in a long line or over a wide area: a *sweeping* glance. 2 Covering a wide area; comprehensive: *sweeping* reforms. —*n.* 1 The action of one who or that which sweeps. 2 *pl.* Things swept up, as refuse. —**sweep′ing·ly** *adv.* —**sweep′ing·ness** *n.*

sweep·stakes (swep′staks′) *n. pl.* **·stakes** (construed as *sing.* or *pl.*) 1 A type of lottery in which all the sums staked may be won by one or by a few of the betters, as in a horse race. 2 A race, contest, etc., to determine the outcome of such a lottery. 3 A prize in such a lottery. Also **sweep′stake′.**

sweet (swet) *adj.* 1 Having a flavor like that of sugar, often due to the presence of sugar in some form. 2 Not salted, sour, rancid, or spoiled. 3 Gently pleasing to the senses; agreeable to the taste, smell, etc. 4 Agreeable or delightful to the mind or the emotions. 5 Having gentle, pleasing, and winning qualities. 6 Sound; rich; productive: said of soil. —*n.* 1 The quality of being sweet; sweetness. 2 Something sweet, agreeable, or pleasing. 3 *Usu. pl.* Confections, preserves, candy, etc. 4 A beloved person. 5 *Brit.* DESSERT. [< OE *swēte*] —**sweet′ly** *adv.* —**sweet′ness** *n.*

sweet alyssum A small plant related to mustard having spikes of fragrant white blossoms.

sweet·bread (swet′bred′) *n.* The pancreas (**stomach sweetbread**) or the thymus (**neck sweetbread** or **throat sweetbread**) of a calf or other animal, when used as food.

sweet·bri·er (swet′brī′ər) *n.* A species of rose with dense, prickly branches and fragrant leaves. Also **sweet′- bri′ar.**

sweet clover Any of several leguminous forage plants having fragrant white or yellow flowers.

sweet corn Any of several varieties of maize rich in sugar, cultivated for use as a vegetable.

sweet·en (swet′n) *v.t.* 1 To make sweet or sweeter. 2 To make more endurable; alleviate; lighten. 3 To make pleasant or gratifying. —**sweet′en·er** *n.*

sweet·en·ing (swet′n·ing) *n.* 1 The act of making sweet. 2 That which sweetens.

sweet flag A marsh-dwelling plant with sword-shaped leaves and a fragrant rhizome.

sweet gum 1 A large North American tree with maple-like leaves and bark exuding a fragrant gum. 2 The balsam or gum yielded by it.

sweet·heart (swet′härt′) *n.* 1 Darling: a term of endearment. 2 A lover.

sweetheart contract An agreement made between an employer and union officials, the terms of which are disadvantageous to union members. Also **sweetheart agreement.**

sweet·meat (swet′met′) *n. Usu. pl.* A highly sweetened food, as candy, cake, candied fruit, etc.

sweet pea A climbing leguminous plant cultivated for its fragrant, varicolored flowers.

sweet pepper A mild variety of capsicum used for pickling and as a vegetable.

sweet potato 1 A perennial tropical vine of the morning-glory family, with a fleshy tuberous root. 2 The sweet yellow or orange root, eaten as a vegetable.

sweet-talk (swet′tôk′) *Informal v.t.* 1 To persuade by coaxing or flattering. —*v.i.* 2 To flatter or coax someone. —**sweet talk**

sweet tooth *Informal* A fondness for candy or sweets.

sweet wil·liam (wil′yəm) A perennial species of pink with fragrant, closely clustered flowers. Also **sweet William.**

swell (swel) *v.* **swelled, swelled** or **swol·len, swell·ing** *v.i.* 1 To increase in size or volume, as by inflation with air or by absorption of moisture. 2 To increase in amount, degree, force, intensity, etc. 3 To rise above the usual or surrounding level, surface, etc. 4 To rise in waves or swells, as the sea. 5 To bulge. 6 *Informal* To become puffed up with pride. —*v.t.* 7 To cause to increase in size or volume. 8 To cause to increase in amount, degree, force, intensity, etc. 9 To cause to bulge. 10 To puff with pride. —*n.* 1 The act, process, or effect of swelling; expansion. 2 A long continuous wave without a crest. 3 A rise of, or undulation in, the land. 4 Any bulge or protuberance. 5 *Music* A crescendo and diminuendo in succession; also, the signs (< >) indicating it. 6 A device by which the loudness of an organ may be varied. 7 *Informal* A person who is very fashionable, elegant, or social. —*adj.* 1 *Informal* Very fashionable, elegant, or social. 2 *Slang* Very fine; first-rate; excellent. [< OE *swellan*] —**Syn.** *v.* 1 bulge, dilate, distend, enlarge, expand.

swell·ing (swel′ing) *n.* 1 The act or process by which a person or thing swells. 2 The condition of being swollen. 3 Something swollen, esp. an abnormal enlargement of a part of the body. —*adj.* That swells; increasing, bulging, puffing up, etc.

swel·ter (swel′tər) *v.i.* 1 To perspire or suffer from oppressive heat. —*v.t.* 2 To cause to swelter. —*n.* A sweltering condition; oppressive heat. [< OE *sweltan* die] **—swel′-ter·ing·ly** *adv.*

swept (swept) *p.t. & p.p.* of SWEEP.

swept·back (swept′bak′) *adj. Aeron.* Having the front edge (of a wing) tilted backward from the lateral axis, as an airplane.

swerve (swûrv) *v.t. & v.i.* **swerved, swerv·ing** To turn or cause to turn aside from a course; deflect. **—n.** The act of swerving; a sudden turning aside. [< OE *sweorfan* file or grind away]

swift¹ (swift) *adj.* **1** Moving with great speed; rapid; quick. **2** Capable of quick motion; fleet. **3** Happening, coming, finished, etc., in a brief time. **4** Quick to act or respond; prompt. **—adv.** In a swift manner. [< OE] **—swift′ly** *adv.* **—swift′ness** *n.*

swift² (swift) *n.* Any of various swallowlike birds with extraordinary powers of flight, as the chimney swift. [< SWIFT¹]

swig (swig) *n. Informal* A great gulp; deep draft. **—v.t. & v.i.** **swigged, swig·ging** *Informal* To take swigs (of). [?]

swill (swil) *v.t.* **1** To drink greedily or to excess. **2** To drench, as with water; rinse; wash. **3** To fill with, as drink. **—v.i.** **4** To drink greedily or to excess. **—n.** **1** Semiliquid food for domestic animals, as the mixture of edible refuse and liquid fed to pigs. **2** Garbage. **3** Unappetizing food. **4** A great gulp; swig. [< OE *swillan* to wash]

Chimney swift

swim¹ (swim) *v.* **swam** (*Regional* **swum**), **swum, swim·ming** *v.i.* **1** To move through water by working the legs, arms, fins, etc. **2** To float. **3** To move with a smooth or flowing motion. **4** To be flooded. **—v.t.** **5** To cross or traverse by swimming. **6** To cause to swim. **—n.** **1** The action or pastime of swimming. **2** The distance swum or to be swum. **3** The air bladder of a fish: also **swim bladder, swimming bladder. —in the swim** Active in current affairs, esp. those involved with fashion, socializing, etc. [< OE *swimman*] **—swim′mer** *n.*

swim² (swim) **swam** (*Regional* **swum**), **swum, swim·ming** *v.i.* **1** To be dizzy. **2** To seem to go round; reel. [< OE *swima* dizziness]

swimming hole A deep hole or pool in a stream, used for swimming.

swim·ming·ly (swim′ing·lē) *adv.* Easily and successfully.

swim·suit (swim′sōōt′) *n.* A garment designed to be worn while swimming.

swin·dle (swin′dəl) *v.* **·dled, ·dling** *v.t.* **1** To cheat; defraud. **2** To obtain by such means. **—v.i.** **3** To practice fraud. **—n.** The act or process of swindling. [< G *schwindeln* cheat] **—swin′dler** *n.* **—Syn.** *v.* **1** deceive, dupe, rook.

swine (swīn) *n. pl.* **swine** **1** A pig or hog: usu. used collectively. **2** A low, greedy, or vicious person. [< OE *swīn*] **—swin′ish** *adj.* **—swin′ish·ly** *adv.* **—swin′ish·ness** *n.*

swine·herd (swīn′hûrd′) *n.* A tender of swine.

swing (swing) *v.* **swung, swing·ing** *v.i.* **1** To move to and fro or backward and forward rhythmically, as something suspended. **2** To ride in a swing. **3** To move with an even, swaying motion. **4** To turn; pivot: We *swung* around and went home. **5** To be suspended; hang. **6** *Informal* To be executed by hanging. **7** *Slang* To be very up-to-date and sophisticated, esp. in one's amusements and pleasures. **8** *Informal* To sing or play with or to have a compelling, usu. jazzlike rhythm. **9** *Slang* To be sexually promiscuous. **—v.t.** **10** To cause to move to and fro or backward and forward. **11** To brandish; flourish: to *swing* an ax. **12** To cause to turn on or as on a pivot or central point. **13** To lift, hoist, or hang: They *swung* the mast into place. **14** *Informal* To bring to a successful conclusion: to *swing* a deal. **15** *Informal* To sing or play in the style of swing (*n.,* def. 8). **—n.** **1** The action process, or manner of swinging. **2** A free swaying motion. **3** A contrivance of hanging ropes with a seat on which a person may move to and fro through the air. **4** Freedom of action. **5** The arc or range of something that swings. **6** A swinging blow or stroke. **7**

A trip or tour: a *swing* through the west. **8** A type of jazz music played by big bands, achieving its effect by lively, compelling rhythms, contrapuntal styles, and arranged ensemble playing: also **swing music. —in full swing** In full and lively operation. [< OE *swingan* scourge, beat up]

swinge (swinj) *v.t.* **swinged, swinge·ing** *Archaic* To flog; chastise. [< OE *swengan* shake, beat] **—swing′er** *n.*

swinge·ing (swin′jing) *adj. Chiefly Brit. Informal* Very large, good, or first-rate. [< SWINGE]

swing·er (swing′ər) *n. Slang* **1** A lively and up-to-date person. **2** A person who indulges freely in sex.

swing·ing (swing′ing) *adj. Slang* **1** Lively and compelling in effect: a *swinging* jazz quartet. **2** Modern; modish.

swin·gle (swing′gəl) *n.* A large, knifelike wooden implement for beating and cleaning flax: also **swing′knife.** **—v.t.** **·gled, ·gling** To cleanse, as flax, by beating with a swingle. [< MDu. *swinghel*]

swin·gle·tree (swing′gəl·trē′) *n.* WHIFFLETREE.

swing shift An evening work shift, usu. lasting from about 4 p.m. to midnight. **—swing shifter**

swipe (swīp) *v.* **swiped, swip·ing** **—v.t.** **1** *Informal* To strike with a sweeping motion. **2** *Slang* To steal; snatch. **—v.i.** **3** To hit with a sweeping motion. **—n.** *Informal* A hard blow. [Var. of SWEEP]

swirl (swûrl) *v.t. & v.i.* To move or cause to move along in irregular eddies; whirl. **—n.** **1** A whirling along, as in an eddy. **2** A curl or twist; spiral. [ME *swyrl*] **—swirl′y** *adj.*

swish (swish) *v.i.* **1** To move with a hissing or whistling sound. **—v.t.** **2** To cause to swish. **—n.** **1** A swishing sound. **2** A movement producing such a sound. [Imit.]

Swiss (swis) *n.* **1** A citizen or native of Switzerland. **2** The people of Switzerland collectively: used with *the.* **—adj.** Of or pertaining to Switzerland or its people.

Swiss chard Chard.

Swiss cheese A pale yellow cheese with many large holes, originally made in Switzerland.

Swiss steak A cut of steak floured and cooked, often with a sauce of tomatoes, onions, etc.

Swit., Switz., Swtz. Switzerland.

switch (swich) *n.* **1** A small flexible rod, twig, or whip. **2** A tress of false hair, worn by women in building a coiffure. **3** A mechanism for shifting a railway train from one track to another. **4** The act or operation of switching, shifting, or changing. **5** The tuft of hair at the end of the tail in certain animals, as a cow. **6** *Electr.* A device used to start or stop a flow of current. **7** A blow with or as with a switch. **—v.t.** **1** To whip or lash. **2** To move, jerk, or whisk suddenly or sharply. **3** To turn aside or divert; shift. **4** To exchange: They *switched* plates. **5** To shift, as a railroad car, to another track. **6** *Electr.* To connect or disconnect with a switch. **—v.i.** **7** To turn aside; change; shift. **8** To swing back and forth or from side to side. **9** To shift from one track to another. [?] **—switch′er** *n.*

switch·back (swich′bak′) *n.* **1** A zigzag road or railroad up a steep incline. **2** *Brit.* ROLLER COASTER.

switch·board (swich′bôrd′, -bōrd′) *n.* A panel bearing switches or controls for several electric circuits, as a telephone exchange.

switch·man (swich′mən) *n. pl.* **·men** (-mən) One who handles switches, esp. on a railroad.

switch·yard (swich′yärd′) *n.* A railroad yard in which trains are stored, maintained, assembled, etc.

Swit·zer·land (swit′sər·lənd) *n.* A republic of CEN. Europe, 15,940 sq. mi., cap. Bern. • See map at ITALY.

swiv·el (swiv′əl) *n.* **1** A coupling or pivot that permits parts, as of a mechanism, to rotate independently. **2** Anything that turns on a pin or headed bolt. **3** A cannon that swings on a pivot: also **swivel gun.** **—v.** **·eled** or **·elled, ·el·ing** or **·el·ling** *v.t.* **1** To turn on or as on a swivel. **2** To provide with or secure by a swivel. **—v.i.** **3** To turn or swing on or as on a swivel. [< OE *swīfan* revolve]

swivel chair A chair whose seat turns freely on a swivel.

swob (swob) *n. & v.* **swobbed, swob·bing** SWAB.

swol·len (swō′lən) A *p.p.* of SWELL.

swoon (swōōn) *v.i.* To faint. **—n.** A fainting fit. [< OE *swōgan* suffocate]

swoop (swo͞op) v.i. **1** To drop or descend suddenly, as a bird pouncing on its prey. —v.t. **2** To take or seize suddenly; snatch. —n. The act of swooping. [< OE *swāpan* sweep]

swop (swop) n. & v. **swopped, swop·ping** SWAP.

sword (sôrd, sōrd) n. A weapon consisting of a long blade fixed in a hilt. —**at swords' points** Very unfriendly; hostile. —**cross swords 1** To quarrel; argue. **2** To fight. —**put to the sword** To kill with a sword. —**the sword 1** Military power. **2** War. [< OE *sweord*]

sword·fish (sôrd′fish′, sōrd′-) n. pl. **·fish** or **·fish·es** A large fish of the open sea having the upper jaw elongated into a swordlike process.

Swordfish

sword·grass (sôrd′gras′, -gräs′, sōrd′-) n. Any of several grasses or sedges with serrated or swordlike leaves.

sword·knot (sôrd′not′, sōrd′-) n. An ornamental tassel of leather, cord, etc., tied to a sword hilt.

sword play The act, technique, or skill of using a sword, esp. in fencing. —**sword′-play′er** n.

swords·man (sôrdz′mən, sōrdz′-) n. pl. **·men** (-mən) One skilled in the use of or armed with a sword, esp. a fencer. Also **sword′man.** —**swords′man·ship, sword′man·ship** n.

swore (swôr, swōr) p.t. of SWEAR.

sworn (swôrn, swōrn) p.p. of SWEAR.

swot (swot) n. & v. **swot·ted, swot·ting** SWAT.

swounds (zwoundz, zoundz) interj. ZOUNDS.

swum (swum) p.p. & regional p.t. of SWIM.

swung (swung) p.t. & p.p. of SWING.

syb·a·rite (sib′ə·rīt) n. A person devoted to luxury or sensuality; voluptuary. [< *Sybaris,* an ancient Greek city in southern Italy] —**syb·a·rit·ic** (sib′ə·rit′ik), **syb·a·rit′i·cal** adj. —**syb′a·rit′i·cal·ly** adv.

syc·a·more (sik′ə·môr, -mōr) n. **1** A medium-sized tree of Syria and Egypt allied to the fig. **2** Any of various plane trees widely distributed in North America. **3** An ornamental maple tree: also **sycamore maple.** [< Gk. *sykon* a fig + *moron* a mulberry]

syc·o·phant (sik′ə·fənt, -fant) n. A servile flatterer; toady. [< Gk. *sykon* fig + *phainein* to show] —**syc′o·phan·cy** (-sē) (pl. **·cies**) n. —**syc′o·phan′tic** (-fan′tik), **syc′o·phan′ti·cal** adj. —**syc′o·phan′ti·cal·ly** adv.

syl·la·bar·y (sil′ə·ber′ē) n. pl. **·bar·ies** A list of syllables; esp., a list of written characters representing syllables.

syl·lab·ic (si·lab′ik) adj. **1** Of, pertaining to, or consisting of syllables. **2** Phonet. Designating a consonant capable of forming a complete syllable, as *l* in *middle* (mid′l). **3** Having every syllable distinctly pronounced. Also **syl·lab′i·cal.** —n. Phonet. A syllabic sound. —**syl·lab′i·cal·ly** adv.

syl·lab·i·cate (si·lab′ə·kāt) v.t. **·cat·ed, ·cat·ing** SYLLABIFY. —**syl·lab′i·ca′tion** n.

syl·lab·i·fy (si·lab′ə·fī) v.t. **·fied, ·fy·ing** To form or divide into syllables. —**syl·lab′i·fi·ca′tion** n.

syl·la·ble (sil′ə·bəl) n. **1** Phonet. A word or part of a word uttered in a single vocal impulse. **2** A part of a written or printed word corresponding to the spoken division. **3** The least detail or mention: Please don't repeat a *syllable* of what you've heard here. —v. **·bled, ·bling** v.t. **1** To pronounce the syllables of. —v.i. **2** To pronounce syllables. [< Gk. *syn-* together + *lambanein* take]

syl·la·bus (sil′ə·bəs) n. pl. **·bus·es** or **·bi** (-bī) A concise statement or outline, esp. of a course of study. [< Gk. *sittyba* label on a book] —**Syn.** abstract, epitome, synopsis.

syl·lo·gism (sil′ə·jiz′əm) n. **1** Logic A form of reasoning consisting of three propositions. The first two propositions, called *premises,* have one term in common furnishing a relation between the two other terms, which are linked in the third, called the *conclusion.* Example: All men are mortal *(major premise);* kings are men *(minor premise);* therefore, kings are mortal *(conclusion).* **2** Reasoning that makes use of this form; deduction. [< Gk. *syn-* together + *logizesthai* infer] —**syl′lo·gis′tic, syl′lo·gis′ti·cal** adj. —**syl′lo·gis′ti·cal·ly** adv.

sylph (silf) n. **1** A being, mortal but without a soul, living in and on the air. **2** A slender, graceful young woman or girl. [< NL *sylphus*]

syl·van (sil′vən) adj. **1** Of, pertaining to, or located in a forest or woods. **2** Composed of or abounding in trees or woods. —n. A person or animal living in or frequenting forests or woods. [< L *silva* a wood]

sym. symbol; symmetrical; symphony.

sym·bi·o·sis (sim′bī·ō′sis, -bē-) n. An intimate and mutually advantageous partnership of dissimilar organisms, as of algae and fungi in lichens. [< Gk. *syn-* together + *bios* life] —**sym′bi·ot′ic** (-ot′ik) or **·i·cal** adj. —**sym′bi·ot′i·cal·ly** adv.

sym·bol (sim′bəl) n. **1** Something chosen to stand for or represent something else, as an object used to typify a quality, idea, etc.: The lily is a *symbol* of purity. **2** A character, mark, abbreviation, letter, etc., that represents something else. —v.t. **sym·boled** or **·bolled, sym·bol·ing** or **·bol·ling** SYMBOLIZE. [< Gk. *syn-* together + *ballein* throw]

sym·bol·ic (sim·bol′ik) adj. **1** Of, pertaining to, or expressed by a symbol. **2** Used as a symbol: with *of.* **3** Characterized by or involving the use of symbols or symbolism: *symbolic* poetry. Also **sym·bol′i·cal.** —**sym·bol′i·cal·ly** adv. —**sym·bol′i·cal·ness** n.

sym·bol·ism (sim′bəl·iz′əm) n. **1** The use of symbols to represent things; the act or art of investing things with a symbolic meaning. **2** A system of symbols or symbolical representation. **3** Symbolic meaning or character.

sym·bol·ist (sim′bəl·ist) n. One who uses symbols or symbolism, esp. an artist or writer skilled in the use of symbols.

sym·bol·is·tic (sim′bəl·is′tik) adj. Of or pertaining to symbolism or symbolists. —**sym′bol·is′ti·cal·ly** adv.

sym·bol·ize (sim′bəl·īz) v. **·ized, ·iz·ing** v.t. **1** To be a symbol of; represent symbolically; typify. **2** To represent by a symbol or symbols. **3** To treat as symbolic or figurative. —v.i. **4** To use symbols. *Brit. sp.* **sym′bol·ise.** —**sym′bol·i·za′tion, sym′bol·iz·er** n.

sym·me·try (sim′ə·trē) n. pl. **·tries 1** Corresponding arrangement or balancing of the parts or elements of a whole in respect to size, shape, and position on opposite sides of an axis or center. **2** The element of beauty and harmony in nature or art that results from such arrangement and balancing. **3** Math. An arrangement of points in a system such that the system appears unchanged after certain partial rotations. [< Gk. *syn-* together + *metron* a measure] —**sym·met′ric** (si·met′rik), **sym·met′ri·cal** adj. —**sym·met′ri·cal·ly** adv. —**sym·met′ri·cal·ness** n.

sym·pa·thet·ic (sim′pə·thet′ik) adj. **1** Pertaining to, expressing, or proceeding from sympathy. **2** Having a compassionate feeling for others; sympathizing. **3** Being in accord or harmony; congenial. **4** Of, proceeding from, or characterized by empathy. **5** Referring to sounds produced by responsive vibrations. Also **sym′pa·thet′i·cal.** —**sym′pa·thet′i·cal·ly** adv.

sympathetic nervous system The part of the autonomic nervous system that controls such involuntary actions as the dilation of pupils, constriction of blood vessels and salivary glands, and increase of heartbeat.

sym·pa·thize (sim′pə·thīz) v.i. **·thized, ·thiz·ing 1** To experience or understand the sentiments or ideas of another. **2** To feel or express compassion, as for another's sorrow or affliction: with *with.* **3** To be in harmony or agreement. *Brit. sp.* **sym′pa·thise.** —**sym′pa·thiz′er** n. —**sym′pa·thiz′ing·ly** adv.

sym·pa·thy (sim′pə·thē) n. pl. **·thies 1** The fact or condition of an agreement in feeling: The *sympathy* between husband and wife was remarkable. **2** A feeling of compassion for another's sufferings. **3** Agreement or accord: to be in *sympathy* with an objective. **4** Support; loyalty; approval: trying to enlist my *sympathies.* [< Gk. *syn-* together + *pathos* a feeling, passion] —**Syn. 1** affinity, concord. **2** commiseration, condolence, pity.

sympathy strike A strike in which the strikers support the demands of another group of workers. Also **sympathetic strike.**

sym·pho·ny (sim′fə·nē) n. pl. **·nies 1** A harmonious or agreeable mingling of sounds. **2** Any harmony or agreeable blending, as of color. **3** A composition for orchestra, consisting usu. of four extensive movements. **4** SYMPHONY ORCHESTRA. [< Gk. *syn-* together + *phōnē* a sound] —**sym·phon·ic** (sim·fon′ik) adj. —**sym·phon′i·cal·ly** adv.

symphony orchestra A large orchestra composed usu. of string, brass, woodwind, and percussion instruments.

sym·po·si·um (sim-pō′zē-əm) *n. pl.* **·si·ums, ·si·a** (-zē-ə) **1** A meeting for discussion of a particular subject or subjects. **2** A collection of comments, opinions, essays, etc. on the same subject. [< Gk. *syn-* together + *posis* drinking] — **sym·po′si·ac** (-ak) *adj.*

symp·tom (simp′təm) *n.* **1** An organic or functional condition indicating the presence of disease, esp. when regarded as an aid in diagnosis. **2** A sign or indication that serves to point out the existence of something else: *symptoms* of civil unrest. [< Gk. *syn-* together + *piptein* fall] — **symp′to·mat′ic** (-tə-mat′ik), **symp′to·mat′i·cal** *adj.* —**symp′·to·mat′i·cal·ly** *adv.* —Syn. 2 earmark, mark, signal, token.

syn- *prefix* With; together; associated; at the same time: *syncarp.* [< Gk. *syn* together]

syn. synchronize; synonym; synonymous; synonymy.

syn·a·gogue (sin′ə-gôg, -gog) *n.* **1** A place of meeting for Jewish worship and religious instruction. **2** A Jewish congregation or assemblage for religious instruction and observances. Also **syn′a·gog.** [< Gk. *synagōgē* an assembly]

syn·apse (sin′aps′, sə-naps′) *n.* The junction point of two neurons, across which a nerve impulse passes. Also **syn·ap·sis** (sə-nap′səs) *pl.* **·ap·ses** (-sēz). [< Gk. *syn-* together + *hapsis* a joining] —**syn·ap·tic** (-nap′tik) *adj.*

sync (singk) *n. & v.* **synced, sync·ing** SYNCH.

syn·carp (sin′kärp) *n.* A multiple or fleshy aggregate fruit, as the blackberry. [< Gk. *syn-* together + *karpos* a fruit] — **syn·car·pous** (sin-kär′pəs) *adj.*

synch (singk) *Slang v.i. & v.t.* **synched, synch·ing** To synchronize or cause to be synchronized. —*n.* Synchronization: usu. in phrases **in synch** and **out of synch.** [< SYNCHRONIZATION]

syn·chro·mesh (sing′krō·mesh′, sin′-) *n. Mech.* **1** A gear system in which parts are synchronized before engagement. **2** The synchronizing mechanism thus used.

Syncarp (blackberry)

syn·chro·nism (sing′krə·niz′əm, sin′-) *n.* **1** The state of being synchronous; concurrence. **2** A grouping of historic personages or events according to their dates. —**syn′chro·nis′tic, syn′chro·nis′ti·cal** *adj.* —**syn′chro·nis′ti·cal·ly** *adv.*

syn·chro·ni·za·tion (sing′·krə·nə·zā′shən) *n.* **1** The state of being synchronous. **2** The act of synchronizing, or the state of being synchronized.

syn·chro·nize (sing′krə·nīz, sin′-) *v.* **·nized, ·niz·ing** *v.i.* **1** To occur at the same time; coincide. **2** To move or operate in unison. —*v.t.* **3** To cause to operate synchronously: to *synchronize* watches. **4** To cause (the appropriate sound of a motion picture) to coincide with the action. **5** To assign the same date or period to; make contemporaneous. [< SYNCHRONOUS] —**syn′chro·niz′er** *n.*

syn·chro·nous (sing′krə·nəs, sin′-) *adj.* **1** Occurring at the same time; concurrent; simultaneous. **2** *Physics* Having the same period or frequency. **3** *Electr.* Normally operating at a speed proportional to the frequency of the current in the power line, as a motor. Also **syn′chro·nal.** [< Gk. *syn-* together + *chronos* time] —**syn′chro·nous·ly** *adv.* —**syn′chro·nous·ness** *n.*

syn·cline (sin′klīn) *n. Geol.* A trough or fold of stratified rock in which the layers dip downward on each side toward the axis of the fold. [< Gk. *syn-* together + *klinein* to incline] —**syn·cli′nal** (sin-klī′nəl) *adj.*

syn·co·pate (sing′kə-pāt, sin′-) *v.t.* **·pat·ed, ·pat·ing** **1** To contract, as a word, by syncope. **2** *Music* To treat or modify (a rhythm, melody, etc.) by syncopation. [< LL *syncope syncope*]

syn·co·pa·tion (sing′kə-pā′shən, sin′-) *n.* **1** The act of syncopating or state of being syncopated; also, that which is syncopated. **2** *Music* The suppression of an expected rhythmic accent by the continuation of an unaccented tone that begins just before it. **3** Any music featuring syncopation, as ragtime, jazz, etc. **4** Syncope of a word, or an example of it.

syn·co·pe (sing′kə-pē, sin′-) *n.* **1** The elision of a sound or syllable in the middle part of a word, as *e'er* for *ever.* **2** *Music* Syncopation. **3** Temporary loss of consciousness; fainting. [< Gk. *syn-* together + *koptein* to cut] —**syn′co·pal, syn·cop·ic** (sin-kop′ik) *adj.*

syn·cre·tize (sin′krə-tīz, sing′-) *v.t.* **·tized, ·tiz·ing** To attempt to blend and reconcile. [< Gk. *synkrētizein* combine] —**syn′cre·tism** *n.*

syn·dic (sin′dik) *n.* **1** The business agent of a university or other corporation. **2** A government official, as a civil magistrate, with varying powers in different countries. [< Gk. *syn-* together + *dikē* judgment] —**syn′di·cal** *adj.*

syn·di·cal·ism (sin′di·kəl·iz′əm) *n.* A social and political theory proposing the taking over of the means of production by federations of labor unions through the staging of general strikes, etc. [< F *(chambre) syndicale* a labor union] —**syn′di·cal·ist** *n.* —**syn′di·cal·is′tic** *adj.*

syn·di·cate (sin′də·kit) *n.* **1** An association of individuals united to negotiate some business or to engage in some enterprise, often one requiring large capital. **2** An association for purchasing feature articles, etc., and selling them again to a number of periodicals, as newspapers, for simultaneous publication. **3** The office or jurisdiction of a syndic; also, a body of syndics. —*v.t.* (-kāt) **·cat·ed, ·cat·ing** **1** To combine into or manage by a syndicate. **2** To sell for publication in many newspapers or magazines. [< F *syndic* syndic] —**syn′di·ca′tion, syn′di·ca′tor** *n.*

syn·drome (sin′drōm) *n.* **1** The aggregate of symptoms and signs characteristic of a specific disease or condition. **2** A group of traits regarded as being characteristic of a certain type, condition, etc. [< Gk. *syn-* together + *dramein* run] —**syn·drom·ic** (sin-drom′ik) *adj.*

sy·nec·do·che (si-nek′də·kē) *n.* A figure of speech in which a part stands for a whole or a whole for a part, a material for the thing made of it, etc., as *bronze* for a *statue.* [< Gk. *syn-* together + *ekdechesthai* take from]

syn·er·gism (sin′ər·jiz′əm) *n.* The mutually reinforcing action of separate substances, organs, agents, etc., which together produce an effect greater than that of all of the components acting separately. Also **syn′er·gy.** [< Gk. *synergos* working together] —**syn′er·gis′tic** or **·ti·cal** *adj.*

syn·fu·el (sin′fyōō′əl) *n.* Synthetic fuel.

syn·od (sin′əd, -od) *n.* **1** An ecclesiastical council. **2** Any assembly, council, etc. [< Gk. < *syn-* together + *hodos* a way]

sy·nod·i·cal (si-nod′i·kəl) *adj.* **1** Of, pertaining to, or of the nature of a synod; transacted in a synod. **2** *Astron.* Pertaining to the conjunction of two celestial bodies or to the interval between two successive conjunctions of the same celestial bodies. Also **syn·od·al** (sin′ə·dəl, si·nod′əl), **sy·nod′ic.** —**sy·nod′i·cal·ly** *adv.*

syn·o·nym (sin′ə-nim) *n.* **1** A word having the same or almost the same meaning as some other or others in the same language. **2** A word used in metonymy to substitute for another. [< Gk. *syn-* together + *onyma* a name] — **syn′o·nym′ic, syn′o·nym′i·cal** *adj.* —**syn′o·nym′i·ty** *n.*

sy·non·y·mous (si·non′ə·məs) *adj.* Being equivalent or similar to meaning. —**sy·non′y·mous·ly** *adv.*

sy·non·y·my (si·non′ə·mē) *n. pl.* **·mies** **1** The quality of being synonymous. **2** The study of synonyms. **3** The discrimination of synonyms. **2** A list or collection discriminating the meanings of synonyms or of allied terms.

sy·nop·sis (si·nop′sis) *n. pl.* **·ses** (-sēz) A general view or condensation, as of a story, book, etc.; summary. [< Gk. *syn-* together + *opsis* a view] —**Syn.** abridgment, abstract, digest, précis.

sy·nop·tic (si·nop′tik) *adj.* **1** Giving a general view. **2** Presenting the same or a similar point of view: said of the first three Gospels (**Synoptic Gospels**). Also **sy·nop′ti·cal.** —**sy·nop′ti·cal·ly** *adv.*

sy·no·vi·a (si·nō′vē·ə) *n.* The viscid, transparent, lubricating fluid secreted by a membrane in the interior of joints. [< Gk. *syn-* together + L *ovum* an egg] —**sy·no′vi·al** *adj.*

---

add, āce, câre, pälm; end, ēven; it, īce; odd, ōpen, ôrder; tŏŏk, pōōl; up, bûrn; ə = *a* in *above, u* in *focus;* yŏŏ = *u* in *fuse;* oil; pout; check; go; ring; thin; this; zh, *vision.* < derived from; ? origin uncertain or unknown.

syn·tax (sin′taks) *n.* **1** The arrangement and interrelationship of words in grammatical constructions. **2** The branch of grammar which deals with this. [< Gk. *syn-* together + *tassein* arrange] —**syn·tac·tic** (sin·tak′tik), **syn·tac′ti·cal** *adj.* —**syn·tac′ti·cal·ly** *adv.*

syn·the·sis (sin′thə·sis) *n. pl.* **·ses** (-sēz) **1** The assembling of separate or subordinate parts into a new form. **2** The complex whole resulting from this. **3** *Chem.* The building up of a compound by the direct union of its elements or of simpler compounds. [< Gk. *syn-* together + *tithenai* to place] —**syn′the·sist** *n.*

syn·the·size (sin′thə·sīz) *v.t.* **·sized**, **·siz·ing** **1** To unite or produce by synthesis. **2** To apply synthesis to. *Brit. sp.* **syn′the·sise.**

syn·the·siz·er (sin′thə·sīz′ər) *n.* Any of various complex electronic devices by which a musician can create and manipulate a wide variety of tones.

syn·thet·ic (sin·thet′ik) *adj.* **1** Of, pertaining to, or using synthesis. **2** Produced artificially by chemical synthesis. **3** Artificial; spurious. Also **syn·thet′i·cal.** —*n.* Anything produced by synthesis, esp. by chemical synthesis, as a material. [< Gk. *syn-* together + *tithenai* to place] —**syn·thet′i·cal·ly** *adv.*

syph·i·lis (sif′ə·lis) *n.* An infectious, chronic, venereal disease caused by a spirochete transmissible by direct contact or congenitally. [< *Syphilus,* a shepherd in a 16th-century Latin poem who had the disease] —**syph·i·lit·ic** (sif′ə·lit′ik) *adj., n.*

syphon (sī′fən) *n. & v.* SIPHON.

Syr. Syria; Syriac; Syrian.

syr. syrup (pharmacy).

Syr·i·a (sir′ē·ə) *n.* A republic of sw Asia, 72,234 sq. mi., cap. Damascus. • See map at JORDAN.

Syr·i·ac (sir′ē·ak) *n.* The language of the ancient Syrians, a dialect of Aramaic.

Syr·i·an (sir′ē·ən) *adj.* Of or pertaining to Syria, its people, or their language. —*n.* **1** A citizen or native of Syria. **2** The Arabic dialect spoken in modern Syria.

sy·rin·ga (si·ring′gə) *n.* **1** LILAC (defs. 1 and 2) **2** MOCK ORANGE. [< Gk. *syrinx* a pipe]

syr·inge (si·rinj′, sir′inj) *n.* **1** An instrument used to remove fluids from or inject fluids into body cavities. **2** HYPODERMIC SYRINGE. —*v.t.* **·inged**, **·ing·ing** To spray, cleanse, inject, etc. with a syringe. [< Gk. *syrinx* a pipe]

syr·inx (sir′ingks) *n. pl.* **sy·rin·ges** (sə·rin′jēz), **syr·inx·es** **1** A modification of the windpipe in songbirds serving as the vocal organ. **2** *pl.* PANPIPES. [Gk., a pipe] —**sy·rin·ge·al** (si·rin′jē·əl) *adj.*

syr·up (sir′əp) *n.* A thick, sweet liquid, as the boiled juice of fruits, sugar cane, etc. [< OF sirop < Turkish *sharbat* sherbet] —**syr′up·y** *adj.*

syst. system; systematic.

sys·tem (sis′təm) *n.* **1** A group or arrangement of parts, facts, phenomena, etc., that relate to or interact with each other in such a way as to form a whole: the solar *system;* the nervous *system.* **2** Any orderly group of logically related facts, principles, beliefs, etc.: the democratic *system.* **3** An orderly method, plan, or procedure: a betting *system* that really works. **4** A method of classification, organization, arrangement, etc.: books classified according to the Dewey decimal *system.* **5** The body, considered as a functional whole. —**the system** The dominant political, economic, and social institutions and their leaders, regarded as resistant to change or to effective influence. [< Gk. *systēma* an organized whole]

sys·tem·at·ic (sis′tə·mat′ik) *adj.* **1** Of, pertaining to, or characterized by system or classification. **2** Acting by or carried out with system or method; methodical. **3** Forming or based on a system. Also **sys′tem·at′i·cal.** —**sys′tem·at′i·cal·ly** *adv.* —**Syn. 2** orderly, organized, procedural, routine. **3** organizational, bureaucratic.

sys·tem·a·tize (sis′tə·mə·tīz′) *v.t.* **·tized**, **·tiz·ing** To make into a system; organize methodically. Also **sys′tem·ize.** *Brit. sp.* **sys′tem·a·tise′.** —**sys′tem·a·ti·za′tion**, **sys′tem·i·za′tion** *n.* —**sys′tem·a·tiz′er, sys′tem·iz′er** *n.*

sys·tem·ic (sis·tem′ik) *adj.* **1** Of or pertaining to a system; systematic. **2** Pertaining to or affecting the body as a whole: a *systemic* poison. —**sys·tem′i·cal·ly** *adv.*

systems analysis The technique of reducing complex processes, as of industry, government, research, etc., to basic operations that can be treated quantitatively and reordered into sequences amenable to control.

sys·to·le (sis′tə·lē) *n.* **1** The rhythmic contraction of the heart, esp. of the ventricles, that impels the blood outward. **2** The shortening of a syllable that is naturally or by position long. [< Gk. *syn-* together + *stellein* send] —**sys·tol·ic** (sis·tol′ik) *adj.*

T

T, t (tē) *n. pl.* **T's, t's** or **Ts, ts, tees** (tēz) **1** The 20th letter of the English alphabet. **2** Any spoken sound representing the letter *T* or *t.* **3** Something shaped like a T. —**to a T** Precisely; perfectly. —*adj.* Shaped like a T.

't Contraction of IT: used initially, as in *'tis,* and finally, as in *on't.*

-t Inflectional ending used to indicate past participles and past tenses, as in *bereft, lost, spent:* equivalent to *-ed.*

T Technician; temperature (absolute); tension (surface); time (of firing or launching).

T. tablespoon (s); Testament; Tuesday.

t. in the time of (L *tempore*); teaspoon(s); time; ton(s); transitive; troy.

Ta tantalum.

tab[1] (tab) *n.* A flap, strip, tongue, or projection of something, as a garment, file card, etc. —*v.t.* **tabbed, tab·bing** To provide with a tab or tabs. [?]

tab[2] (tab) *n. Informal* **1** A check or bill; also, the total cost of something. **2** Close watch: to keep *tabs* on someone's activities. [? Short for TABULATION]

tab. table(s); tablet(s).

tab·ard (tab′ərd) *n.* **1** Formerly, a short, sleeveless or short-sleeved outer garment. **2** A

Tabard *def. 3*

knight's cape or cloak, worn over his armor and emblazoned with his own arms. **3** A similar garment worn by a herald and embroidered with his lord's arms. [< OF]

Ta·bas·co (tə·bas′kō) *n.* A pungent sauce made from capsicum: a trade name.

tab·by (tab′ē) *n. pl.* **·bies 1** A silk taffeta, esp. one that is striped or watered. **2** A brown or gray domestic cat with dark stripes. **3** Any domestic cat, esp. a female. **4** A gossiping woman. —*adj.* **1** Of, pertaining to, or made of tabby. **2** Brindled. [< *Attabi,* a quarter of Baghdad where it was manufactured]

tab·er·na·cle (tab′ər·nak′əl) *n.* **1** A tent or similar temporary structure. **2** *Usu. cap.* In the Old Testament, the portable sanctuary used by the Israelites in the wilderness. **3** *Usu. cap.* The Jewish temple. **4** Any house of worship, esp. one of large size. **5** The human body as the dwelling place of the soul. **6** The ornamental receptacle for the consecrated eucharistic elements. [< L *taberna* shed] —**tab·er·nac·u·lar** (tab′ər·nak′yə·lər) *adj.*

ta·ble (tā′bəl) *n.* **1** An article of furniture with a flat top, usu. fixed on legs. **2** Such a table on which food is set for a meal. **3** The food served at a meal. **4** The persons present at a meal. **5** A gaming table, as for roulette. **6** A collection of related numbers, values, signs, or items of any kind, arranged for ease of reference or comparison, often in parallel columns. **7** A compact listing: *table* of contents. **8** A tableland; plateau. **9** Any flat horizontal rock, surface,

tableau 749 **tag**

etc. **10** A tablet or slab bearing an inscription. **—the Ta-bles** Laws inscribed on tablets, as the Ten Command-ments. **—turn the tables** To reverse a situation. **—**_v.t._ **·bled, ·bling 1** To place on a table. **2** To postpone discussion of (a resolution, bill, etc.). [< L _tabula_ board]

tab·leau (tab′lō, ta·blō′) _n. pl._ **·leaux** (-lōz) or **·leaus** (-lōz) **1** Any picture or picturesque representation. **2** A scene reminiscent of a picture, usu. presented by persons mo-tionless on a stage. [F, lit., small table]

ta·ble·cloth (tā′bəl·klôth′, -kloth′) _n._ A cloth covering for a table.

tab·le d'hôte (tab′əl dōt′, tä′bəl) _pl._ **tab·les d'hote** (tab′-əlz dōt′, tä′bəlz) A complete meal of several specified courses, served in a restaurant at a fixed price. [F, lit., table of the host]

ta·ble·land (tā′bəl·land′) _n._ A broad, level, elevated re-gion; a plateau.

ta·ble·spoon (tā′bəl·spoon′, -spoon′) _n._ **1** A measuring spoon with three times the capacity of a teaspoon. **2** A tablespoonful.

ta·ble·spoon·ful (tā′bəl·spoon·fool′, -spoon-) _n. pl._ **·fuls** The amount a tablespoon will hold; ½ fluid ounce.

tab·let (tab′lit) _n._ **1** A small, flat or nearly flat piece of some prepared substance, as a drug. **2** A pad, as of writing paper or note paper. **3** A small flat surface designed for or containing an inscription or design. **4** A thin leaf or sheet of ivory, wood, etc., for writing, painting, or drawing. **5** A set of such leaves joined together at one end. [< OF _tablete_, lit., small table]

table tennis A game resembling tennis in miniature, played indoors with a small celluloid ball and wooden paddles on a large table.

ta·ble·ware (tā′bəl·wâr′) _n._ Dishes, knives, forks, spoons, etc., used to set a table.

tab·loid (tab′loid) _n._ A newspaper, usu. one half the size of an ordinary newspaper, in which the news is presented concisely, often sensationally, and with many pictures. —_adj._ Compact; concise. [< TABL(ET) + -OID]

ta·boo (tə·boo′, ta-) _n. pl._ **·boos 1** A religious or social prohibition against touching or mentioning someone or something or doing something because such persons or things are considered sacred, dangerous, etc. **2** The prac-tice of such prohibitions. **3** Any restriction or ban based on custom or convention. —_adj._ Restricted, prohibited, or excluded by taboo, custom, or convention. —_v.t._ **1** To place under taboo. **2** To avoid as taboo. Also **ta·bu′.** [< Tongan]

ta·bor (tā′bər) _n._ A small drum on which a fife player beats his own accompaniment. Also **ta′bour.** [< Pers. _tabī-rah_ drum]

tab·o·ret (tab′ə·ret′, -rā′) _n._ **1** A small tabor. **2** A stool or small seat, usu. without arms or back. **3** A small table or stand. **4** An embroidery frame. Also **tab′ou·ret.**

tab·u·lar (tab′yə·lər) _adj._ **1** Of, pertaining to, or arranged in a table or list. **2** Computed from or with a mathematical table. **3** Having a flat surface. —**tab′u·lar·ly** _adv._

tab·u·late (tab′yə·lāt) _v.t._ **·lat·ed, ·lat·ing** To arrange in a table or list. —_adj._ Having a flat surface or surfaces; broad and flat. —**tab′u·la′tion, tab′u·la′tor** _n._

tac·a·ma·hac (tak′ə·mə·hak′) _n._ **1** A resinous substance with a strong odor, used in ointments and incense. **2** Any of the trees producing this substance. Also **tac′a·ma·hac′a** (-hak′ə), **tac′ma·hack′.** [< Nahuatl _tecomahca_]

ta·chom·e·ter (tə·kom′ə·tər) _n._ A device for indicating the speed of rotation of an engine, centrifuge, etc. [< Gk. _tachos_ speed + -METER]

tach·y·car·di·a (tak′i·kär′dē·ə) _n._ Abnormal rapidity of the heartbeat. [< Gk. _tachys_ swift + _kardia_ heart]

tac·it (tas′it) _adj._ **1** Existing, inferred, or implied without being directly stated. **2** Not spoken; silent. **3** Emitting no sound. [< L _tacitus,_ pp. of _tacere_ be silent] —**tac′it·ly** _adv._

tac·i·turn (tas′ə·tûrn) _adj._ Habitually silent or reserved. [< L _tacitus._ See TACIT.] —**tac·i·tur·ni·ty** (tas′ə·tûr′nə·tē) _n._ —**tac′i·turn·ly** _adv._ —**Syn.** uncommunicative, reticent.

tack (tak) _n._ **1** A small sharp-pointed nail, usu. with a relatively broad, flat head. **2** _Naut._ **a** A rope which holds down the lower outer corner of some sails. **b** The corner so held. **c** The direction in which a vessel sails when sailing closehauled, considered in relation to the position of its sails. **d** A change in a ship's direction made by a change in the position of its sails. **3** A policy or course of action. **4** A temporary fastening, as any of various stitches in sewing. —_v.t._ **1** To fasten or attach with tacks. **2** To secure temporarily, as with long stitches. **3** To attach as supple-mentary; append. **4** _Naut._ **a** To change the course of (a vessel) by turning into the wind. **b** To navigate (a vessel) to windward by making a series of tacks. —_v.i._ **5** _Naut._ **a** To tack a vessel. **b** To sail to windward by a series of tacks. **6** To change one's course of action. **7** ZIGZAG. [< OF _tache_ a nail] —**tack′er** _n._

tack·le (tak′əl) _n._ **1** A rope and pulley or combination of ropes and pulleys, used for hoisting or moving objects. **2** The rigging of a ship. **3** The equipment used in any work or sport; gear. **4** The act of tackling. **5** In football, either of two linemen stationed between the guard and end. —_v.t._ **·led, ·ling 1** To fas-ten with or as if with tackle. **2** To harness (a horse). **3** To undertake to master, accom-plish, or solve: _tackle_ a problem. **4** To seize suddenly and forcefully. **5** In football, to seize and stop (an opponent carrying the ball). [< MLG _taken_ seize] —**tack′ler** _n._

Tackles

tack·y¹ (tak′ē) _adj._ **tack·i·er, tack·i·est** Slightly sticky, as partly dried varnish. [< TACK, _v._]

tack·y² (tak′ē) _adj._ **tack·i·er, tack·i·est 1** _Informal_ Unfash-ionable; in bad taste. **2** Without good breeding; common. [?]

ta·co (tä′kō) _n. pl._ **·cos** A fried tortilla folded around any of several fillings, as chopped meat or cheese. [< Sp., wad]

tact (takt) _n._ **1** A quick or intuitive appreciation of what is fit, proper, or right; facility in saying or doing the proper thing. **2** A delicate sense of discrimination, esp. in aesthetics. [< L _tactus_ sense of touch, pp. of _tangere_ touch]

tact·ful (takt′fəl) _adj._ Having or showing tact. —**tact′ful·ly** _adv._ —**tact′ful·ness** _n._

tac·ti·cal (tak′ti·kəl) _adj._ **1** Of or pertaining to tactics. **2** Showing adroitness in planning and maneuvering. —**tac′·ti·cal·ly** _adv._

tac·ti·cian (tak·tish′ən) _n._ An expert in tactics.

tac·tics (tak′tiks) _n.pl._ **1** _(construed as sing.)_ The science and art of handling troops in securing military and naval objectives. **2** Any adroit maneuvering to gain an end. [< Gk. _taktikos_ suitable for arranging]

tac·tile (tak′təl, -tīl) _adj._ **1** Of, pertaining to, or having the sense of touch. **2** That may be touched; tangible. [< L _tactus._ See TACT.] —**tac·til·i·ty** (tak·til′ə·tē) _n._

tact·less (takt′lis) _adj._ Showing or characterized by a lack of tact. —**tact′less·ly** _adv._ —**tact′less·ness** _n._

tad·pole (tad′pōl) _n._ The aquatic larva of an amphibian, as a frog or toad, having gills and a tail. [< ME _tadde_ toad + _pol_ head, poll]

tael (tāl) _n._ **1** Any of several units of weight of E Asia. **2** A Chinese monetary unit. [< Pg. < Malay _tahil_]

taf·fe·ta (taf′ə·tə) _n._ A fine, glossy, somewhat stiff fabric woven of silk, rayon, nylon, etc. —_adj._ Made of or resembling taf-feta. [< Pers. _tāftah_]

Development of a tadpole

taff·rail (taf′rāl′) _n._ The rail around a vessel's stern. [< MDu. _tafereel_ panel, lit., small table]

taf·fy (taf′ē) _n. pl._ **taf·fies 1** A chewy confection made usu. of brown sugar or molasses, boiled down, and pulled until it cools. **2** _Informal_ Flattery; blarney. [?]

tag¹ (tag) _n._ **1** Something attached to something else, to identify, price, classify, etc.; a label. **2** A loose, ragged edge, esp. of a piece of cloth. **3** The metal sheath at the end of a lace, cord etc. **4** The final lines of a speech, song, or poem. —_v._ **tagged, tag·ging** _v.t._ **1** To supply, adorn, fit,

---

add, āce, câre, pälm; end, ēven; it, īce; odd, ōpen, ôrder; took, pool; up, bûrn; ə = _a_ in _above, u_ in _focus;_ yoo = _u_ in _fuse;_ oil; pout; check; go; ring; thin; this; zh, _vision._ < derived from; ? origin uncertain or unknown.

mark, or label with a tag. 2 *Informal* To follow closely or persistently. —*v.i.* 3 *Informal* To follow closely at one's heels: with *along, behind,* etc. [? < Scand.]

tag[2] (tag) *n.* A children's game in which a player, called "it," chases other players until he touches one of them, that person in turn becoming the one who must pursue another. —*v.t.* **tagged, tag·ging** To overtake and touch, as in the game of tag. [?]

Ta·ga·log (tə-gäl'əg, -gä'lôg) *n.* 1 A member of a people native to the Philippines. 2 The Austronesian language of this people, the official language of the Philippines.

tail[1] (tāl) *n.* 1 The rear end of an animal's body, esp. when prolonged to form a flexible appendage. 2 Anything similar in appearance, as a pigtail. 3 *Astron.* The luminous cloud extending from a comet. 4 The hind, back, or inferior portion of anything. 5 *Often pl. Informal* The reverse side of a coin. 6 A body of persons in single file. 7 A group of attendants; retinue. 8 *Aeron.* A system of airfoils placed some distance to the rear of the main bearing surfaces of an airplane. 9 *pl. Informal* A man's full-dress suit; also, a swallow-tailed coat. 10 *Informal* A person, as a detective, who follows another in surveillance. 11 *Informal* A trail or course, as one taken by a fugitive. —*v.t.* 1 To furnish with a tail. 2 To cut off the tail of. 3 To be the tail or end of. 4 To join (one thing) to the end of another. 5 To insert and fasten by one end. 6 *Informal* To follow secretly and stealthily; shadow. —*v.i.* 7 To form or be part of a tail. 8 *Informal* To follow close behind. 9 To diminish gradually: with *off.* —*adj.* 1 Rearmost; hindmost: the *tail* end. 2 Coming from behind: a *tail* wind. [< OE *tægl*]

tail[2] (tāl) *Law adj.* Restricted in some way, as to particular heirs: an estate *tail.* —*n.* A limiting of the inheritance of an estate, as to particular heirs. [< OF *taillié,* p.p. of *taillier* to cut]

tail·gate (tāl'gāt') *n.* A hinged or removable board or gate closing the back end of a truck, wagon, etc. Also **tail·board** (tāl'bôrd', -bōrd'). —*v.t.* & *v.i.* **·gat·ed, ·gat·ing** To drive too close for safety behind (another vehicle).

tail·light (tāl'līt') *n.* A warning light, usu. red, attached to the rear of a vehicle. Also **tail lamp.**

tai·lor (tā'lər) *n.* One who makes or repairs garments. —*v.i.* 1 To do a tailor's work. —*v.t.* 2 To fit with garments. 3 To make, work at, or style by tailoring. 4 To form or adapt to meet certain needs or conditions. [< LL *taliare* split, cut] —**tai'lor·ing** *n.*

tai·lor·bird (tā'lər·bûrd') *n.* Any of various small birds of Asia and Africa that stitch leaves together so as to conceal the nest. • See NEST.

tai·lor-made (tā'lər·mād') *adj.* 1 Made by or looking as if made by a tailor. 2 Right or suitable for a particular person, specific conditions, etc.

tail·piece (tāl'pēs') *n.* 1 Any endpiece or appendage. 2 In a violin or similar instrument, a piece of wood at the sounding-board end, having the strings fastened to it. 3 *Printing* An ornamental design at the end of a chapter or the bottom of a short page. 4 A short beam or rafter tailed into a wall.

tail·spin (tāl'spin') *n.* 1 *Aeron.* The uncontrolled descent of an airplane along a helical path at a steep angle. 2 *Informal* A sudden, sharp, mental or emotional upheaval.

tail wind A wind blowing in the same direction as the course of an aircraft or ship.

taint (tānt) *v.t.* 1 To affect with decay or contamination. 2 To render morally corrupt. —*v.i.* 3 To be or become tainted. —*n.* A cause or result of contamination or corruption. [< OF *teint,* pp. of *teindre* to tinge, color]

take (tāk) *v.* **took, tak·en, tak·ing** *v.t.* 1 To lay hold of; grasp. 2 To get possession of; seize; capture; catch. 3 To gain, capture, or win, as in a game or in competition. 4 To choose; select. 5 To buy. 6 To rent or hire; lease. 7 To subscribe to, as a periodical. 8 To assume occupancy of: to *take* a chair. 9 To assume the responsibilities of: to *take* office. 10 To accept into some relation to oneself: He *took* a wife. 11 To assume as a symbol or badge: to *take* the veil. 12 To subject oneself to: to *take* a vow. 13 To remove or carry off: with *away.* 14 To steal. 15 To remove by death. 16 To subtract or deduct. 17 To be subjected to; undergo: to *take* a beating. 18 To submit to; accept passively: to *take* an insult. 19 To become affected with; contract: He *took*

cold. 20 To affect: The fever *took* him at dawn. 21 To captivate; charm or delight: The dress *took* her fancy. 22 To react to: How did she *take* the news? 23 To undertake to deal with; contend with; handle: to *take* an examination. 24 To consider; deem: I *take* him for an honest man. 25 To understand; comprehend: I couldn't *take* the meaning of her remarks. 26 To hit: The blow *took* him on the forehead. 27 *Informal* To aim or direct: He *took* a shot at the target. 28 To carry with one: *Take* your umbrella! 29 To lead: This road *takes* you to town. 30 To escort. 31 To receive into the body, as by eating, inhaling, etc.: *Take* a deep breath. 32 To accept or assume as if due or granted: to *take* credit. 33 To require: it *takes* courage. 34 To let in; admit; accommodate: The car *takes* only six people. 35 To occupy oneself in; enjoy: to *take* a nap. 36 To perform, as an action: to *take* a stride. 37 To confront and get over: The horse *took* the hurdle. 38 To avail oneself of (an opportunity, etc.). 39 To put into effect; adopt: to *take* measures. 40 To use up or consume: The piano *takes* too much space. 41 To make use of; apply: to *take* pains. 42 To travel by means of: to *take* a train. 43 To seek: to *take* cover. 44 To ascertain by measuring, computing, etc.: to *take* a census. 45 To obtain or derive from some source. 46 To write down or copy: to *take* notes. 47 To obtain (a likeness or representation of) by photographing. 48 To conceive or feel: She *took* a dislike to him. 49 *Slang* To cheat; deceive. 50 *Gram.* To require by construction or usage: The verb *takes* a direct object. —*v.i.* 51 To get possession. 52 To engage; catch, as mechanical parts. 53 To begin to grow; germinate. 54 To have the intended effect: The vaccination *took.* 55 To gain favor, as a play. 56 To detract: with *from.* 57 To become (ill or sick). —**take after** 1 To resemble. 2 To follow in pursuit. —**take amiss** To be offended by. —**take back** To retract. —**take down** 1 To humble. 2 To write down. —**take for** To consider to be. —**take in** 1 To admit; receive. 2 To lessen in size or scope. 3 To include; embrace. 4 To understand. 5 To cheat or deceive. 6 To visit. —**take it** To endure hardship, abuse, etc. —**take off** 1 To mimic; burlesque. 2 To rise from a surface, esp. to begin a flight, as an airplane or rocket. 3 To leave; depart. 4 To begin: often used to refer to that point in an economic venture when growth becomes a self-generating and self-sustaining process. —**take on** 1 To hire; employ. 2 To undertake to deal with. 3 *Informal* To exhibit violent emotion. —**take over** To assume control of (a business, nation, etc.) —**take place** To happen. —**take to** 1 To become fond of. 2 *Informal* To adopt a way of doing, using, etc.: He has *taken* to walking to work. 3 To flee: to *take* to the hills. —**take up** 1 To make smaller or less; shorten or tighten. 2 To pay, as a note or mortgage. 3 To accept as stipulated: to *take up* an option. 4 To begin or begin again. 5 To occupy, engage, or consume, as space or time. 6 To develop an interest in or devotion to: to *take up* a cause. —**take up with** *Informal* To become friendly with; associate with. —*n.* 1 The act of taking or that which is taken. 2 *Slang* An amount of money received; receipts; profit. 3 A quantity collected at one time: the *take* of fish. 4 An uninterrupted run of the camera in photographing a movie or television scene. 5 A scene so photographed. 6 The process of making a sound recording. 7 A recording made in a single recording session. [< OE *tacan* < ON *taka*] —**tak'er** *n.* • See BRING.

take-home pay (tāk'hōm') Net wages after tax and other deductions.

take·off (tāk'ôf', -of') *n.* 1 *Informal.* A satirical representation; caricature. 2 The act of taking off, as in flight. 3 The place from which one takes off. 4 A point at which something begins.

take·o·ver (tāk'ō'vər) *n.* The act or an instance of taking over, esp. the assumption of power in a business, nation, etc.

tak·ing (tā'king) *adj.* Fascinating; captivating. —*n.* 1 The act of one who takes. 2 The thing or things taken; catch. 3 *pl.* Receipts, as of money. —**tak'ing·ly** *adv.* —**tak'ing·ness** *n.*

talc (talk) *n.* A soft mineral magnesium silicate, used in making talcum powder, lubricants, etc. —*v.t.* **talcked** or **talced, talck·ing** or **talc·ing** To treat with talc. [< Ar. *talq*]

tal·cum (tal'kəm) *n.* TALC.

talcum powder Finely powdered, purified, and usu. perfumed talc, used as a face and body powder.

tale (tāl) *n.* 1 A story that is told or written; a narrative of real or fictitious events. 2 An idle or malicious piece of gossip. 3 A lie. 4 *Archaic* A tally or amount; total. [< OE *talu* speech, narrative]

tale·bear·er (tāl′bâr′ər) *n.* One who gossips, spreads rumors, tells secrets, etc. —**tale′bear′ing** *adj., n.* —**Syn.** gossip, scandalmonger, newsmonger.

tal·ent (tal′ənt) *n.* 1 *pl.* A person's natural abilities. 2 A particular aptitude for some special work, artistic endeavor, etc. 3 A person, or people collectively with skill or ability. 4 Any of various ancient weights and denominations of money, used in ancient Greece, Rome, and the Middle East. [< L *talentum,* a sum of money] —**tal′ent·ed** *adj.*

ta·ler (tä′lər) *n.* A former German silver coin. [< G *Taler*]

tales·man (tālz′mən) *n. pl.* **·men** (-mən) One summoned to fill a vacancy in a jury when the regular panel has become deficient in number. [< ML *tales (de circumstantibus)* such (of the bystanders) + MAN]

tale·tel·ler (tāl′tel′ər) *n.* 1 RACONTEUR. 2 TALEBEARER. —**tale′tell′ing** *adj., n.*

ta·li (tā′lī) *n.pl.* of TALUS[1].

tal·i·pes (tal′ə·pēz) *n.* Congenital deformity of one or both feet. [< L *talus* ankle + *pes* foot]

tal·i·pot (tal′ə·pot) *n.* An East Indian palm crowned by large leaves often used as fans, umbrellas, etc. Also **talipot palm.** [< Skt. *tālī* fan palm + *pattra* leaf]

tal·is·man (tal′is·mən, -iz-) *n. pl.* **·mans** 1 An object, as a ring or amulet, supposed to ward off evil, bring good luck, etc. 2 Anything supposed to have a magical effect. [< LGk. *telesma* a sacred rite] —**tal′is·man′ic** (·man′ik) *adj.*

talk (tôk) *v.i.* 1 To express or exchange thoughts in audible words; speak or converse. 2 To communicate by means other than speech: to *talk* with one's fingers. 3 To chatter. 4 To confer; consult. 5 To gossip. 6 To make sounds suggestive of speech. 7 *Informal* To give information; inform. —*v.t.* 8 To express in words; utter. 9 To converse in: to *talk* Spanish. 10 To discuss: to *talk* business. 11 To bring to a specified condition or state by talking: to *talk* one into doing something. —**talk back** To answer impudently. —**talk down** To silence by talking. —**talk down to** To speak to patronizingly. —**talk shop** To talk about one's work. —*n.* 1 The act of talking; conversation; speech. 2 A speech, either formal or informal. 3 Report; rumor: *talk* of war. 4 A subject of conversation. 5 A conference or discussion. 6 Mere words; empty conversation, discussion, etc. 7 A special kind of speech; lingo: baseball *talk.* 8 Sounds suggestive of speech, as made by a bird or animal. [Prob. < OE *talian* reckon, tell]

talk·a·thon (tô′kə·thon′) *n. Informal* A prolonged session of talking, debating, etc. [< TALK + (MAR)ATHON]

talk·a·tive (tô′kə·tiv) *adj.* Given to or fond of much talking. —**talk′a·tive·ly** *adv.* —**talk′a·tive·ness** *n.* —**Syn.** garrulous, loquacious, voluble, windy.

talk·ie (tô′kē) *n.* Formerly, a motion picture with a sound track, as distinguished from a silent film.

talk·ing-to (tô′king·tōō′) *n. pl.* **·tos** *Informal* A scolding.

tall (tôl) *adj.* 1 Having more than average height; high. 2 Having a specified height: five feet *tall.* 3 *Informal* Extravagant; boastful; exaggerated: a *tall* story. 4 Large; extensive: a *tall* order. —*adv. Informal* Proudly: to walk *tall.* [< OE *getæl* swift, prompt] —**tall′ish** *adj.* —**tall′ness** *n.*

tal·lith (tal′ith, tä′lis) *n. pl.* **tal·li·thim** (tal′ə·sēm′, -thēm) A fringed shawl worn by Jewish men during morning prayer. [< Heb. *tallīth* cover]

tal·low (tal′ō) *n.* Solid, rendered animal fats, as of beef or mutton, refined for making candles, soaps, etc. —*v.t.* To smear with tallow. [< MLG *talg, talch*] —**tal′low·y** *adj.*

tal·ly (tal′ē) *n. pl.* **·lies** 1 A piece of wood on which notches or scores are cut as marks of number. 2 A score or mark. 3 A reckoning; account. 4 A counterpart; duplicate. 5 A mark indicative of number. 6 A label; tag. —*v.* **·lied, ·ly·ing** *v.t.* 1 To score on a tally; mark. 2 To reckon; count: often with *up.* 3 To register, as points in a game; score.

4 To cause to correspond. —*v.i.* 5 To make a tally. 6 To agree precisely: His story *tallies* with yours. 7 To keep score. 8 To score, as in a game. [< L *talea* rod, cutting] —**tal′li·er** *n.*

tal·ly·ho (tal′ə·hō′) *interj.* A huntsman's cry to hounds when the quarry is sighted. —*n.pl.* **·hos** 1 The cry of "tallyho." 2 A kind of coach drawn by four horses. —*v.t.* 1 To urge on, as hounds, with the cry of "tallyho." —*v.i.* 2 To cry "tallyho." [? < F *taïaut,* a hunting cry]

Tal·mud (tal′mud, täl′mōōd) *n.* The written body of Jewish civil and religious law. [< Heb. *talmūdh* instruction] —**Tal·mud′ic** or **·i·cal** *adj.* —**Tal′mud·ist** *n.*

tal·on (tal′ən) *n.* 1 The claw of a bird or other animal, esp. a bird of prey. 2 A human finger or hand thought of as resembling a claw. [< L *talus* heel] —**tal′oned** *adj.*

ta·lus[1] (tā′ləs) *n. pl.* **·li** (-lī) or **·lus·es** 1 The upper, pivotal bone of the ankle. 2 The entire ankle. [L, ankle]

ta·lus[2] (tā′ləs, tal′əs) *n.* 1 A slope, as of a tapering wall. 2 *Geol.* The sloping mass of rock fragments at the foot of a cliff. 3 The slope given to the face of a wall, as in a fortification. [F < L *talutium* slope bearing signs of the presence of gold]

tam (tam) *n.* TAM-O'-SHANTER.

ta·ma·le (tə·mä′lē) *n.* A Mexican dish made of ground meat seasoned with red pepper, rolled in cornmeal, wrapped in corn husks, and steamed. [< Nahuatl *tamalli*]

tam·a·rack (tam′ə·rak) *n.* 1 A species of larch common in N North America. 2 Its wood. [< Algon.]

tam·a·rind (tam′ə·rind) *n.* 1 A tropical tree of the bean family, with yellow flowers. 2 The edible fruit of this tree, a pod with acid pulp. [< Ar. *tamr hindi* Indian date]

tam·bour (tam′bōōr) *n.* 1 A drum. 2 A light wooden frame, usu. circular, esp. a set of two hoops between which fabric is stretched for embroidering. —*v.t. & v.i.* To embroider on a tambour. [< Ar. *tanbūr* drum]

tam·bou·rine (tam′bə·rēn′) *n.* A musical instrument like the head of a drum, with metal disks in the rim, played by striking it with the hand. [F, lit., small tambour]

tame (tām) *adj.* **tam·er, tam·est** 1 Having lost its native wildness; domesticated. 2 Docile; tractable; subdued; submissive. 3 Lacking in spirit; uninteresting; dull. —*v.t.* **tamed, tam·ing** 1 To make tame; domesticate. 2 To bring into subjection or obedience. 3 To tone down; soften. [< OE *tam*] —**tam′a·ble** or **tame′a·ble** *adj.* —**tame′ly** *adv.* —**tame′ness, tam′er** *n.*

tame·less (tām′lis) *adj.* Untamable or not tamed.

Tam·il (tam′əl) *n.* 1 A member of a Dravidian people of s India and N Sri Lanka. 2 Their language.

Tam·ma·ny (tam′ə·nē) *n.* A fraternal society in New York City (founded 1789) serving as the central organization of the city's Democratic party, located in **Tammany Hall.** [< *Tamanend,* a 17th c. Delaware Indian chief]

tam-o'-shan·ter (tam′ə·shan′tər) *n.* A Scottish cap with a round flat top, sometimes with a center pompon. [< the hero of a poem by Robert Burns]

tamp (tamp) *v.t.* 1 To force down or pack closer by repeated blows. 2 In blasting, to pack matter around a charge in order to increase the explosive effect. [Back formation < TAMPION] —**tam′per** *n.*

tam·per (tam′pər) *v.i.* 1 To meddle; interfere: usu. with *with.* 2 To make changes, esp. so as to damage, falsify, etc.: with *with.* 3 To use secret or improper measures, as bribery. [Var. of TEMPER] —**tam′per·er** *n.*

tam·pi·on (tam′pē·ən) *n.* A plug or cover for the muzzle of a gun. [< OF *tapon, tape* a bung]

tam·pon (tam′pon) *n.* A plug of absorbent material for insertion in a body cavity or wound to stop bleeding or absorb secretions. —*v.t.* To plug up, as a wound, with a tampon. [< OF *tapon, tape* a bung]

tan (tan) *v.* **tanned, tan·ning** *v.t.* 1 To convert into leather, as hides or skins, by treating with tannin. 2 To darken, as the skin, by exposure to sunlight. 3 *Informal* To thrash; flog. —*v.i.* 4 To become tanned. —*n.* 1 TANBARK. 2 TANNIN. 3 A yellowish brown color tinged with red. 4 A dark coloring of the skin, resulting from exposure to the sun. —*adj.*

1 Of the color tan. **2** Of, pertaining to, or used for tanning. [< Med. L *tanum* tanbark]

tan tangent.

tan·a·ger (tan′ə·jər) *n.* Any of a family of American songbirds related to finches and noted for the brilliant plumage of the male. [< Pg. *tangara* < Tupi] —**tan′a·grine** (-grēn) *adj.*

tan·bark (tan′bärk′) *n.* **1** The bark of certain trees used as a source of tannin. **2** Shredded bark from which the tannin has been removed, used on circus rings, racetracks, etc.

tan·dem (tan′dəm) *adv.* One behind the other. —*n.* **1** A team, as of horses, harnessed one behind the other. **2** A two-wheeled carriage drawn in such a way. **3** A bicycle with two or more seats one behind the other. —*adj.* Having parts or things arranged one behind another. [L, at length (of time)]

Tandem bicycle

tang (tang) *n.* **1** A sharp, penetrating taste, flavor or odor. **2** Any distinctive quality or flavor. **3** A trace or hint. **4** A slender shank or tongue projecting from the end of a sword blade, chisel, etc., for fitting into a handle, hilt, etc. [< ON *tongi* a point] —**tang′y** *adj.* (**·i·er**, **·i·est**)

tan·gent (tan′jənt) *adj.* **1** *Geom.* Coinciding at a point or along a line without intersection, as a curve and line, surface and plane, etc. **2** Touching; in contact. —*n.* **1** *Geom.* A line tangent to a curve at any point. **2** *Trig.* A function of an angle, equal to the quotient of its sine divided by its cosine. **3** A sharp change in course or direction. —**fly** (or **go**) **off on a tangent** *Informal* To make a sharp or sudden change, as in a course of action or train of thought. [< L *tangere* to touch] —**tan·gen·cy** (tan′jən·sē) *n.*

tan·gen·tial (tan·jen′shəl) *adj.* **1** Of, pertaining to, like, or in the direction of a tangent. **2** Touching slightly. **3** Divergent. —**tan·gen′ti·al·i·ty** (-shē·al′ə·tē) *n.* —**tan·gen′tial·ly** *adv.*

tan·ger·ine (tan′jə·rēn′, tan′jə·rēn′) *n.* **1** A variety of orange with a loose skin and easily separated segments. **2** A burnt orange color like that of the tangerine. [< *Tangier*, a city in Morocco]

tan·gi·ble (tan′jə·bəl) *adj.* **1** Perceptible by touch. **2** Not elusive or unreal; objective; concrete: *tangible* evidence. **3** Having value that can be appraised. —*n. pl.* Things having value that can be appraised. [< L *tangere* to touch] —**tan′gi·bil′i·ty, tan′gi·ble·ness** *n.* —**tan′gi·bly** *adv.*

tan·gle (tang′gəl) *v.* **·gled, ·gling** *v.t.* **1** To twist in a confused and not readily separable mass. **2** To ensnare as in a tangle; trap; enmesh. **3** To involve in such a way as to confuse, obstruct, etc. —*v.i.* **4** To be or become entangled. —**tangle with** *Informal* To become involved or fight with. —*n.* **1** A confused intertwining, as of threads or hairs; a snarl. **2** State of confusion or complication. **3** A state of bewilderment. [Prob. < Scand.] —**tan′gler** *n.*

tan·go (tang′gō) *n. pl.* **·gos** **1** A Latin American dance characterized by deliberate gliding steps and low dips. **2** The music for such a dance. —*v.i.* To dance the tango. [< Sp.]

tank (tangk) *n.* **1** A large vessel, basin, or receptacle for holding a fluid. **2** A natural or artificial pool or pond. **3** An armored combat vehicle that rides on treads and has mounted guns. **4** *Slang* A jail cell, esp. one for receiving prisoners. —*v.t.* To place or store in a tank. [? < Pg. *estanque*]

tank·age (tangk′ij) *n.* **1** The act or process of

U.S. Army tank

storing in tanks. **2** The price for storage in tanks. **3** The capacity or contents of a tank. **4** Slaughterhouse waste from which the fat has been rendered in tanks, used, when dried, as fertilizer or feed.

tank·ard (tangk′ərd) *n.* A large, one-handled drinking cup, often with a cover. [ME]

tank·er (tangk′ər) *n.* **1** A cargo ship for the transport of oil or other liquids. **2** A cargo plane used to carry gasoline and to refuel other planes in flight.

tank farm An area where oil is stored in tanks.

tan·ner (tan′ər) *n.* One who tans hides.

tan·ner·y (tan′ər·ē) *n. pl.* **·ner·ies** A place where leather is tanned.

tan·nic (tan′ik) *adj.* Of, pertaining to, or derived from tannin or tanbark.

tan·nin (tan′in) *n.* A yellowish, astringent substance extracted from tanbark, gallnut, etc., used in dyeing, tanning, etc. Also **tannic acid.** [< F *tanin* < *tanner* to tan]

tan·sy (tan′zē) *n. pl.* **·sies** Any of a genus of coarse perennial herbs, esp. a species with yellow flowers and pungent foliage. [< Gk. *athanasia* immortality]

tan·ta·lize (tan′tə·līz′) *v.t.* **·lized, ·liz·ing** To tease or torment by promising or showing something desirable and then denying access to it. *Brit. sp.* **·lise′.** [< TANTALUS] —**tan′ta·li·za′tion, tan′ta·liz′er** *n.* —**tan′ta·liz′ing·ly** *adv.*

tan·ta·lum (tan′tə·ləm) *n.* A hard, corrosion-resistant metallic element (symbol Ta). [< TANTALUS, from its inability to react with most acids]

Tan·ta·lus (tan′tə·ləs) *Gk. Myth.* A king who was punished in Hades by being made to stand in water that receded when he tried to drink and under fruit-laden branches he could not reach.

tan·ta·mount (tan′tə·mount) *adj.* Equivalent: with *to.* [< L *tantus* as much + OF *amonter* to amount]

tan·trum (tan′trəm) *n.* A violent fit of temper. [?]

Tan·za·ni·a (tan′zə·nē′ə) *n.* A republic of the Commonwealth of Nations in E Africa, 362,800 sq. mi., cap. Dar es Salaam. —**Tan′za·ni′an** *adj., n.* • See map at AFRICA.

Tao·ism (dou′iz·əm, tou′-) *n.* One of the principal religions or philosophies of China, founded in the sixth century B.C. by Lao-tse. [< Chin. *tao* way] —**Tao′ist** *adj., n.* —**Tao·is′tic** *adj.*

tap¹ (tap) *n.* **1** A spout through which liquid is drawn, as from a cask. **2** FAUCET. **3** A plug or stopper to close an opening, as in a cask. **4** Liquor drawn from a tap, esp. of a particular quality or brew. **5** A tool for cutting internal screw threads. **6** A point of connection for an electrical circuit. **7** The act or an instance of wiretapping. —**on tap 1** Contained in a cask; ready for tapping: beer *on tap.* **2** *Informal* Available; ready. —*v.t.* **tapped, tap·ping 1** To provide with a tap or spigot. **2** To pierce or open so as to draw liquid from. **3** To draw (liquid) from a container, body cavity, etc. **4** To make connection with: to *tap* a gas main. **5** To draw upon; utilize: to *tap* new sources of energy. **6** To make connection with secretly: to *tap* a telephone wire. **7** To make an internal screw thread in with a tap. [< OE *tæppa*]

tap² (tap) *v.* **tapped, tap·ping** *v.t.* **1** To touch or strike gently. **2** To strike gently with. **3** To make or produce by tapping. **4** To apply a tap to (a shoe) —*v.i.* **5** To strike a light blow or blows, as with the finger tip. **6** To walk with a light, tapping sound. **7** TAP-DANCE. —*n.* **1** The act or sound of striking gently. **2** Leather, metal, etc., affixed to a shoe sole or heel, for repair or tap-dancing. **3** *pl.* A military signal sounded on a trumpet or drum for the extinguishing of all lights in soldiers' quarters. [< OF *taper*]

ta·pa (tä′pä) *n.* **1** The inner bark of an Asian tree related to the mulberry. **2** A cloth made of this bark: also **tapa cloth.** [< native Polynesian name]

tap-dance (tap′dans′, -däns′) *v.i.* **-danced, -danc·ing** To dance a tap dance. —**tap′-danc′er** *n.*

tap dance A dance in which the dancer taps out a rhythm with the heels and toes of shoes.

tape (tāp) *n.* **1** A narrow strip of woven fabric. **2** Any long, narrow, flat strip of paper, metal, plastic, etc., as the magnetic strip used in a tape recorder. **3** TAPE MEASURE. **4** A string stretched across the finishing point of a racetrack and broken by the winner of the race. —*v.t.* **taped, tap·ing 1** To wrap or secure with tape. **2** To measure with a tape measure. **3** To record on magnetic tape. [< OE *tæppe* strip of cloth] —**tap′er** *n.*

tape deck An assembly of magnetic head, tape reels, and drive for tape recording and playback.

tape measure A tape marked in inches, feet, etc., for measuring. Also **tape·line** (tāp′līn′) *n.*

ta·per (tā′pər) *n.* **1** A slender candle. **2** A long wax-coated wick used to light candles, lamps, etc. **3** A weak light. **4** A gradual diminution of size in an elongated object; also, any tapering object, as a cone. **5** Any gradual decrease. —*v.t. & v.i.* **1** To make or become smaller or thinner toward one end. **2** To lessen gradually: with *off.* —*adj.* Growing smaller toward one end. [< OE]

tape-re·cord (tāp′ri·kôrd′) *v.t.* TAPE (*v.,* def. 3).

tape recorder An electromagnetic apparatus which can record sound on magnetic tape and play it back.

tap·es·try (tap′is·trē) *n. pl.* **·tries** **1** A heavy woven textile with a pictorial design, used for hangings, upholstery, etc. **2** Something like this, as in complexity of design. —*v.t.* **·tried, ·try·ing** **1** To hang or adorn with tapestry. **2** To depict or weave in a tapestry. [< Gk. *tapētion*, dim. of *tapēs* rug]

tape·worm (tāp′wûrm′) *n.* Any of various long flatworms parasitic in the intestines of man and various animals.

tap·i·o·ca (tap′ē·ō′kə) *n.* A starchy, granular foodstuff obtained from cassava, used in puddings, as a thickener for soups, etc. [< Tupi *tipioca*]

ta·pir (tā′pər) *n.* Any of various hoofed, herbivorous mammals of tropical America and SE Asia, having short stout limbs and a flexible snout. [< Tupi *tapy′ra*]

tap·room (tap′rŏŏm′, -rŏŏm′) *n.* BARROOM.

tap·root (tap′rŏŏt′, -rŏŏt′) *n.* A type of plant root having one main descending part. —**tap′root′ed** *adj.*

tar[1] (tär) *n.* A dark, usu. pungent, viscid mixture of hydrocarbons obtained by the dry distillation of wood, coal, etc. —*v.t.* **tarred, tar·ring** To cover with or as with tar. —**tar and feather** To smear with tar and then cover with feathers as a punishment. —*adj.* Made of, derived from, or resembling tar. [< OE *teru*]

tar[2] (tär) *n. Informal* A sailor. [Short for TARPAULIN]

tar·an·tel·la (tar′ən·tel′ə) *n.* **1** A lively Neapolitan dance. **2** Music for this dance. [< *Taranto,* a port in SE Italy]

ta·ran·tu·la (tə·ran′chŏŏ·lə, -tə·lə) *n. pl.* **·las** or **·lae** (-lē) **1** A large, hairy, venomous spider of S Europe. **2** Any of various large, hairy American spiders capable of inflicting a painful but not dangerous bite. [< *Taranto,* Italy]

Tarantula *def. 1*

tar·dy (tär′dē) *adj.* **·di·er, ·di·est** **1** Not coming, happening, etc., at the scheduled or proper time. **2** Moving, acting, etc., at a slow pace. [< L *tardus* slow] —**tar′di·ly** *adv.* —**tar′di·ness** *n.* —Syn. **1** late, dilatory, overdue, delayed. **2** slow, sluggish, leisurely, torpid.

tare[1] (târ) *n.* **1** In the Bible, a weed that grows among wheat, supposed to be the darnel. **2** Any one of various species of vetch. [?]

tare[2] (târ) *n.* **1** The deduction of the weight of a container, used to calculate the weight of its contents if the gross weight of the container and contents is determined. **2** The weight of the container. —*v.t.* **tared, tar·ing** To weigh, as a vessel or package, in order to determine the tare. [< Ar. *tarḥah*]

tar·get (tär′git) *n.* **1** An object presenting a usu. marked surface that is to be aimed and shot at, as in archery practice. **2** Anything that is shot at. **3** One who or that which is made an object of ridicule, criticism, etc.; butt. **4** A goal; objective. **5** A small round shield. —*v.t.* **1** To make a target of. **2** To establish as a goal. [< OF *targe* shield] —**tar′get·a·ble** *adj.*

tar·iff (tar′if) *n.* **1** A schedule of government-imposed duties to be paid for the importation or exportation of goods. **2** A duty of this kind, or its rate. **3** Any schedule of charges, prices, etc. —*v.t.* **1** To make a list of duties on. **2** To fix a price or tariff on. [< Ar. *ta′rif* information]

tarn (tärn) *n.* A small mountain lake. [< ON *tjörn*]

tar·nish (tär′nish) *v.t.* **1** To dim the luster of. **2** To sully, mar, debase, etc. —*v.i.* **3** To become tarnished. —*n.* **1** The condition of being tarnished; stain, blemish, loss of luster, etc. **2** The thin discolored film on the surface of tarnished metal. [< OF *ternir*] —**tar′nish·a·ble** *adj.*

ta·ro (tä′rō, tar′ō) *n. pl.* **·ros** Any of several tropical plants having starchy, edible rootstocks. [< native Polynesian name]

tar·ot (tar′ō, -ət, tar·ō′) *n.* Any of a set of old Italian figured playing cards, now used chiefly in fortunetelling.

tar·pau·lin (tär·pô′lin, tär′pə-) *n.* A waterproof material, esp. canvas, used as a covering for exposed objects. [?< TAR[1] + *palling,* pr.p. of PALL[1]]

tar·pon (tär′pon, -pən) *n. pl.* **·pon** or **·pons** A large game fish of the West Indies and the coast of Florida. [?]

tar·ra·gon (tar′ə·gon) *n.* **1** A European perennial plant allied to wormwood. **2** The fragrant leaves of this plant, used for seasoning. [< Ar. *tarkhun*]

tar·ry[1] (tar′ē) *v.* **·ried, ·ry·ing** *v.i.* **1** To put off going or coming; linger. **2** To remain in the same place; stay. **3** To wait. —*v.t.* **4** *Archaic* To wait for. [< L *tardare* to delay]

tar·ry[2] (tär′ē) *adj.* **tar·ri·er, tar·ri·est** Of, like, or covered with tar. —**tar′ri·ness** *n.*

tar·sal (tär′səl) *adj.* Of, pertaining to, or situated near the tarsus or ankle. —*n.* A tarsal part, as a bone.

tar·si·er (tär′sē·ər) *n.* A small, arboreal, nocturnal East Indian primate with large eyes and ears, long tail, and elongated digits. [< F < *tarse* tarsus]

tar·sus (tär′səs) *n. pl.* **·si** (-sī) **1** *Anat.* **a** The ankle. **b** In man, the seven bones of the ankle and heel. **2** *Zool.* **a** The shank of a bird's leg. **b** The distal part of the leg of certain arthropods. [< Gk. *tarsos* flat of the foot, any flat surface]

Tarsier

tart[1] (tärt) *adj.* **1** Having a sharp, sour taste. **2** Severe; caustic: a *tart* remark. [< OE *teart*] —**tart′ly** *adv.* —**tart′ness** *n.* —Syn. **1** acid, bitter. **2** cutting, biting, acrimonious, sarcastic.

tart[2] (tärt) *n.* **1** A small open pastry shell filled with fruit, jelly, custard, etc. **2** *Slang* A girl or woman of loose morality. [< OF *tarte*]

tar·tan (tär′tən) *n.* **1** A woolen plaid fabric, esp. one with a pattern distinctive to a particular clan of the Scottish Highlands. **2** A fabric made to look like this. **3** Any plaid. —*adj.* Made of or like tartan. [?< OF *tiretaine* linseywoolsey] • See PLAID.

tar·tar[1] (tär′tər) *n.* **1** A hard deposit of potassium tartrate that forms in wine casks. **2** A yellowish incrustation on teeth, chiefly calcium phosphate. [< Med. Gk. *tartaron*] —**tar·tar·e·ous** *adj.*

tar·tar[2] (tär′tər) *n.* A person of intractable or violent disposition.

Tar·tar (tär′tər) *n.* TATAR. —*adj.* Of or pertaining to the Tatars or Tatary.

tartar emetic A poisonous tartrate of antimony and potassium, used in medicine and in dyeing.

tar·tar·ic (tär·tar′ik, -tär′ik) *adj.* Pertaining to or derived from tartar or tartaric acid.

tartaric acid A white, crystalline organic acid present in grapes and other fruits.

Tar·ta·rus (tär′tər·əs) *Gk. Myth.* **1** The abyss below Hades where Zeus confined the Titans. **2** HADES (def. 2).

Tar·ta·ry (tär′tər·ē) *n.* TATARY.

task (task, täsk) *n.* **1** A piece of work, esp. one imposed by authority or required by duty or necessity. **2** Any unpleasant or difficult assignment; burden. —**take to task** To reprove; lecture. —*v.t.* **1** To assign a task to. **2** To burden. [< L *taxare* appraise]

task force **1** A military unit specially trained to execute a specific mission. **2** Any group assigned to handle a specific task.

task·mas·ter (task′mas′tər, täsk′mäs′tər) *n.* One who assigns tasks, esp. burdensome ones.

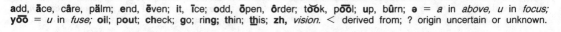

add, āce, câre, pälm; end, ēven; it, īce; odd, ōpen, ôrder; tŏŏk, pōōl; up, bûrn; ə = *a* in *above, u* in *focus;* yōō = *u* in *fuse;* oil; pout; check; go; ring; thin; this; zh, *vision.* < derived from; ? origin uncertain or unknown.

tas·sel (tas′əl) n. 1 A tuft of loosely hanging threads or cords used as an ornament for curtains, cushions, etc. 2 Something resembling a tassel, as the inflorescence on Indian corn. —v. ·seled or ·selled, ·sel·ing or ·sel·ling v.t. 1 To provide or adorn with tassels. 2 To form in a tassel or tassels. —v.i. 3 To put forth tassels, as Indian corn. [< OF, clasp]

taste (tāst) v. tast·ed, tast·ing v.t. 1 To perceive the flavor of (something) by taking into the mouth or touching with the tongue. 2 To eat or drink a little of. 3 To recognize by the sense of taste. 4 To experience. —v.i. 5 To recognize a flavor by the sense of taste. 6 To take a small quantity into the mouth: usu. with of. 7 To have experience or enjoyment: with of: taste of great sorrow. 8 To have a specified flavor when in the mouth: Sugar tastes sweet. —n. 1 The sensation associated with stimulation of the taste buds by foods or other substances. 2 The quality thus perceived; flavor. 3 A small quantity tasted. 4 A slight experience; sample. 5 Special fondness and aptitude; inclination: a taste for music. 6 Appreciation of the beautiful in nature, art, and literature. 7 Style or form with respect to the rules of propriety or etiquette. 8 Individual preference or liking. 9 The act of tasting. [< L taxare touch, handle, appraise]

taste bud Any of numerous clusters of receptors located on the tongue and capable of stimulation by sweet, salt, sour or bitter substances.

taste·ful (tāst′fəl) adj. Having, showing, or conforming to good taste. —taste′ful·ly adv. —taste′ful·ness n. —Syn. elegant, aesthetic, artistic, graceful.

taste·less (tāst′lis) adj. 1 Having no flavor; insipid; dull. 2 Uninteresting; dull. 3 Lacking or showing a lack of good taste. —taste′less·ly adv. —taste′less·ness n.

tast·er (tās′tər) n. 1 One who tastes, esp. to test the quality of something. 2 A device for testing or sampling, as the small, shallow, metal vessel used in testing wines.

tast·y (tās′tē) adj. tast·i·er, tast·i·est 1 Having a fine flavor. 2 Tasteful. —tast′i·ly adv. —tast′i·ness n.

tat (tat) v. tat·ted, tat·ting v.t. 1 To make (edging) by tatting. —v.i. 2 To make tatting. [Back formation < TATTING] —tat′ter n.

Ta·tar (tä′tər) n. 1 A member of any of the Mongolian and Turkic tribes that invaded much of w Asia and E Europe in the Middle Ages. 2 A member of a chiefly Turkic people now living in the Russian Soviet Federated Socialist Republic and Soviet Central Asia. 3 Any of the Turkic languages of the Tatars, as Uzbek. —adj. Of or pertaining to the Tatars or Tatary. —Ta·tar′i·an (tä·târ′ē·ən) adj., n. —Ta·tar′ic adj.

Ta·ta·ry (tä′tər·ē) n. A region of indefinite extent in Asia and E Europe invaded and inhabited by Tatars in the Middle Ages.

tat·ter (tat′ər) n. 1 A torn and hanging shred; rag. 2 pl. Ragged clothing. —v.t. 1 To tear into tatters. —v.i. 2 To become ragged. [< ON tǫturr rags]

tat·ting (tat′ing) n. 1 A kind of lace made by looping and knotting a single thread that is wound on a shuttle. 2 The act or process of making it. [?]

tat·tle (tat′l) v. ·tled, ·tling v.i. 1 To talk idly; chatter. 2 To tell secrets, plans, etc.; gossip. —v.t. 3 To reveal by gossiping. —n. Idle talk or gossip. [< MDu. tatelen] —tat′tler n.

tat·tle·tale (tat′l·tāl′) n. A talebearer; tattler. —adj. Revealing; betraying.

tat·too[1] (ta·tōō′) v.t. ·tooed, ·too·ing 1 To mark (the skin) in patterns with indelible pigments. 2 To mark the skin with (designs, etc.) in this way. —n. pl. ·toos 1 A pattern or design so made. 2 The act of tattooing or the condition of being tattooed. [< Polynesian] —tat·too′er n.

tat·too[2] (ta·tōō′) n. pl. ·toos 1 A continuous beating or drumming. 2 A signal by drum or bugle to soldiers to repair to quarters. —v.t. & v.i. ·tooed, ·too·ing To beat or rap on (a drum, etc.). [< Du. < tap tap, faucet + toe shut]

tau (tou) n. The nineteenth letter in the Greek alphabet (T, τ).

taught (tôt) p.t. & p.p. of TEACH.

taunt (tônt) n. A sarcastic, biting remark; insult; jibe. —v.t. 1 To reproach or challenge with sarcastic or contemptuous words. 2 To provoke with taunts. [? < OF tanter provoke] —taunt′er n. —taunt′ing·ly adv.

taupe (tōp) n. The color of moleskin; dark brownish gray. [< L talpa mole]

Tau·rus (tôr′əs) n. A constellation and the second sign of the zodiac; the Bull. [L, bull] • See zodiac.

taut (tôt) adj. 1 Stretched tight. 2 In proper shape; trim; tidy. 3 Tense; tight: taut muscles. [? < OE togian, to pull, tow] —taut′ly adv. —taut′ness n.

tau·tog (tô·tôg′, -tog′) n. Any of various blackish, edible fishes of the North American Atlantic coast. [< Algon.]

tau·tol·o·gy (tô·tol′ə·jē) n. pl. ·gies 1 Unnecessary repetition of the same idea in different words. 2 An instance of this. [< Gk. tautos identical + logos discourse] —tau·to·log·ic (tô′tə·loj′ik) or ·i·cal adj. —tau′to·log′i·cal·ly adv.

tav·ern (tav′ərn) n. 1 An inn. 2 A place licensed to sell liquor, beer, etc., to be drunk on the premises. [< OF < L taberna hut, booth]

taw (tô) n. 1 A game of marbles. 2 The line from which marble players shoot. 3 A fancy marble used for shooting. [?]

taw·dry (tô′drē) adj. ·dri·er, ·dri·est Pretentiously showy without taste or quality. [< St. Audrey, designating a cheap type of lace sold at St. Audrey's Fair at Ely, England] —taw′dri·ly adv. —taw′dri·ness n. —Syn. cheap, gaudy, meretricious, flashy.

taw·ny (tô′nē) adj. ·ni·er, ·ni·est Tan-colored; brownish yellow. —n. The color tan or brownish yellow. [< OF tanner to tan] —taw′ni·ness n.

tax (taks) n. 1 A compulsory contribution levied upon persons, property, or business for the support of government. 2 A heavy demand, as on one's powers or resources; a burden. —v.t. 1 To impose a tax on. 2 To settle or fix (amounts) chargeable in any judicial matter. 3 To impose a burden upon; task. 4 To charge; blame: usu. with with. [< L taxare estimate, appraise]

tax·a·ble (taks′ə·bəl) adj. Liable to be taxed: taxable income. —tax′a·bil′i·ty n.

tax·a·tion (tak·sā′shən) n. 1 The act of taxing. 2 The amount assessed as a tax. 3 Revenue raised from taxes.

tax·i (tak′sē) n. pl. tax·is or tax·ies TAXICAB. —v. tax·ied, tax·i·ing or tax·y·ing v.i. 1 To ride in a taxicab. 2 To move along the ground or on the surface of the water, as an airplane before taking off or after landing. —v.t. 3 To cause (an airplane) to taxi.

tax·i·cab (tak′sē·kab′) n. A passenger vehicle, usu. fitted with a taximeter, available for hire. [< TAXIMETER + CAB]

tax·i·der·my (tak′sə·dûr′mē) n. The art of stuffing and mounting the skins of dead animals to simulate their appearance when alive. [< Gk. taxis arrangement + derma skin] —tax′i·der′mal, tax′i·der′mic adj. —tax′i·der′mist n.

tax·i·me·ter (tak′si·mē′tər) n. An instrument for recording fares in a taxicab. [< F < taxe tariff + mètre a meter]

tax·on·o·my (tak·son′ə·mē) n. 1 The laws and principles of classification. 2 Biol. The systematic classification of plant and animal life into successive subgroups, as kingdom, phylum or division, class, order, family, genus, and species. [< Gk. taxis arrangement + nomos law] —tax·o·nom·ic (tak′sə·nom′ik) or ·i·cal adj. —tax′o·nom′i·cal·ly adv. —tax·on′o·mist n. • The prefixes sub-, meaning next below, and super-, meaning next above, are often used with the taxonomic categories specified in def. 2. Thus a suborder ranks next below an order but above a family (or a superfamily), whereas a superorder ranks above an order but below a class (or a subclass).

tax·pay·er (taks′pā′ər) n. One who pays or is liable to pay taxes.

TB, T.B., tb, t.b. tubercle bacillus; tuberculosis.

Tb terbium.

tbs. tbsp. tablespoon(s).

Tc technetium.

Te tellurium.

tea (tē) n. 1 An evergreen Asian plant having white flowers. 2 The prepared leaves of this plant, or an infusion of them used as a beverage. 3 A similar potable infusion of plant leaves or animal extract: beef tea. 4 Brit. A light evening or afternoon meal. 5 A social gathering at which tea is served. 6 Slang MARIHUANA. [< dial. Chinese t'e]

tea bag A small porous sack of cloth or paper containing tea leaves, which is immersed in water to make tea.

teach (tēch) v. **taught, teach·ing** v.t. **1** To give instruction to: *teach* a class. **2** To give instruction in: *teach* French. **3** To train by example, practice, or exercise. —v.i. **4** To act as a teacher; impart knowledge or skill. [< OE *tæcan*] —**teach′a·bil′i·ty, teach′a·ble·ness** n. —**teach′a·ble** adj.

teach·er (tē′chər) n. One who teaches, esp. as an occupation.

teach-in (tēch′in′) n. An extended meeting, as at a college or university, during which faculty and students participate in lectures, discussions, etc., on a controversial issue, esp. as a form of social protest.

teach·ing (tē′ching) n. **1** The act or occupation of a teacher. **2** That which is taught.

teaching machine Any of various mechanical devices that present educational material to a student, enabling him to learn at his own rate by a system of corrective feedback.

tea·cup (tē′kup′) n. **1** A small cup suitable for serving tea. **2** The amount a teacup will hold: also **tea′cup·ful** (-fŏŏl′)

teak (tēk) n. **1** A large tree of SE Asia yielding a hard, durable timber highly prized for furniture, etc. **2** The wood of this tree: also **teak′wood**. [< Pg. *teca* < Malayalam *tēkka*]

tea·ket·tle (tē′ket′l) n. A kettle with a spout, used for boiling water.

teal (tēl) n. Any of several small, short-necked, wild ducks. [ME *tele*]

team (tēm) n. **1** Two or more beasts of burden harnessed together. **2** A group of people working or playing together as a unit, esp. a group forming one side in a contest. —v.t. **1** To convey with a team. **2** To harness together in a team. —v.i. **3** To drive a team. **4** To form or work as a team: to *team* up. [< OE *tēam* offspring, team]

team·mate (tēm′māt′) n. A fellow player on a team.

team·ster (tēm′stər) n. One who drives a team or a truck, esp. as an occupation.

team·work (tēm′wûrk′) n. **1** Work done by a team. **2** Unity of action, as by the players on a team.

tea·pot (tē′pot′) n. A vessel with a spout, handle, and lid, in which tea is brewed and from which it is served.

tear[1] (târ) v. **tore, torn, tear·ing** v.t. **1** To pull apart, as cloth; rip. **2** To make by tearing: *tear* a hole in. **3** To injure or lacerate. **4** To divide or disrupt: a party *torn* by dissension. **5** To distress or torment: The sight *tore* his heart. —v.i. **6** To become torn or rent. **7** To move with haste and energy. —**tear down 1** To demolish, as a building. **2** To take apart, as a machine for repair. **3** *Informal* To attack or abuse verbally. —**tear into** To attack violently or with impetuous haste. —n. **1** The act of tearing. **2** A fissure made by tearing. **3** *Slang* A spree; frolic. **4** A rushing motion. **5** A violent outburst, as of anger. [< OE *teran*]

tear[2] (tir) n. **1** A drop of the saline liquid that normally lubricates the eyeball and in weeping flows from the eyes. **2** Something resembling this. **3** pl. Sorrow. **4** pl. The act of weeping: to burst into *tears*. —v.i. To fill with tears. [< OE *tēar*] —**tear′less, tear′y** adj.

tear·drop (tir′drop′) n. A tear. —adj. Shaped like a falling tear: a *teardrop* earring.

tear·ful (tir′fəl) adj. **1** Weeping. **2** Causing tears. **3** Accompanied by tears: a *tearful* confession. —**tear′ful·ly** adv. —**tear′ful·ness** n. —**Syn. 1** sobbing, crying, blubbering. **2** sad, pathetic, mournful.

tear gas (tir) A gas or other agent that causes the eyes to tear.

tear-jerk·er (tir′jûr′kər) n. *Slang* A story, play, film, etc., charged with sentimental sadness.

tea·room (tē′rŏŏm′, -rŏŏm′) n. A restaurant serving tea and other light refreshments.

tease (tēz) v. **teased, teas·ing** v.t. **1** To annoy or harass; pester. **2** To raise the nap, as with teasels. **3** To coax or beg. **4** To comb or card, as wool or flax. **5** To comb (hair) in such a way as to form fluffy layers. —v.i. **6** To annoy a person in a facetious or petty way. —n. **1** One who teases. **2** The act of teasing or the state of being teased. [< OE *tæsan* tease, pluck apart] —**teas′er** n. —**teas′ing·ly** adv.

tea·sel (tē′zəl) n. **1** Any of various coarse, prickly herbs having the flower heads covered with hooked bracts, esp. the **full·er′s teasel**. **2** The dried flower head of this plant, or a mechanical substitute, used to raise a nap on cloth. —v.t. **·seled** or **·selled, ·sel·ing** or **·sel·ling** To raise the nap of with a teasel. Also **tea′zel, tea′·zle**.[< OE *tæsel*]—**tea′sel·er** or **tea′·sel·er** n.

Teasel

tea·spoon (tē′spŏŏn′, -spŏŏn′) n. **1** A small spoon used for stirring tea, etc. **2** The amount a teaspoon will hold, ⅓ of a tablespoon: also **tea′spoon·ful** (-fŏŏl′).

teat (tit, tēt) n. **1** The protuberance on the breast or udder of most female mammals, through which milk is drawn; a nipple. **2** A small protuberance like a teat. [< OF *tete*]

teched (techt) adj. TETCHED.

tech·ne·ti·um (tek·nē′shē·əm) n. A synthetic radioactive metallic element (symbol Tc) occupying a former gap after molybdenum in the periodic table. [< Gk. *technētos* artificial]

tech·nic (tek′nik) n. TECHNIQUE. —adj. TECHNICAL.

tech·ni·cal (tek′ni·kəl) adj. **1** Of or pertaining to some particular art, science, or trade, esp. to the practical arts or applied sciences. **2** Of, characteristic of, used or skilled in a particular art, science, profession, etc. **3** Of, in, or exhibiting technique. **4** According to an accepted body of rules and regulations: a *technical* defeat. [< Gk. *technē* art] —**tech′ni·cal·ly** (-kə·lē, -klē) adv. —**tech′ni·cal·ness** n.

tech·ni·cal·i·ty (tek′ni·kal′ə·tē) n. pl. **·ties 1** The state or quality of being technical. **2** A technical point peculiar to some art, trade, etc. **3** A petty, formal, or highly specialized distinction or detail.

technical sergeant See GRADE.

tech·ni·cian (tek·nish′ən) n. One skilled in carrying out operations in a specific field.

tech·ni·col·or (tek′ni·kul′ər) n. Brilliant or realistic color. [< *Technicolor*] —**tech′ni·col′ored** adj.

Tech·ni·col·or (tek′ni·kul′ər) n. A process used in making color films: a trade name. Also **tech′ni·col·or**.

tech·nics (tek′niks) n.pl. (construed as sing.) The principles or study of an art or of the arts, esp. the industrial or mechanical arts.

tech·nique (tek·nēk′) n. **1** The way in which an artist, craftsman, scientist, etc., handles technical details or uses basic skills. **2** The degree of excellence in doing these things. **3** Any method of accomplishing something. [< Gk. *technikos* technical]

tech·noc·ra·cy (tek·nok′rə·sē) n. pl. **·cies** A government controlled by technicians, as scientists, engineers, etc. —**tech′no·crat** (tek′nə·krat) n. —**tech′no·crat′ic** adj.

tech·nol·o·gy (tek·nol′ə·jē) n. **1** The sum total of the technical means employed to meet the material needs of a society. **2** Applied science. **3** The technical terms used in a science, art, etc. [< Gk. *technē* skill + -LOGY] —**tech′no·log′ic** or **·i·cal** adj. —**tech′no·log′i·cal·ly** adv. —**tech·nol′o·gist** n.

tec·ton·ics (tek·ton′iks) n.pl. (construed as singular) **1** The science or art of constructing buildings or things. **2** The branch of geology relating to the continuing structural evolution of the earth's crust. [< Gk. *tektōn* carpenter] —**tec·ton′ic** adj. —**tec·ton′i·cal·ly** adv.

ted (ted) v.t. **ted·ded, ted·ding** To scatter or spread for drying, as newly mown grass. [? < ON *tethja* spread manure]

ted·dy bear (ted′ē) A toy bear. [< *Teddy,* a nickname of Theodore Roosevelt, 26th U.S. president, 1858–1919]

Te De·um (tē dē′əm) **1** An ancient Christian hymn beginning with the words *Te Deum*. **2** The music for this hymn. [< L *Te Deum (laudamus)* (we praise) Thee, O God]

te·di·ous (tē′dē·əs) adj. Fatiguing or boring, as because of lack of interest or repetitiousness. [< L *taedium* tedium] —**te′di·ous·ly** adv. —**te′di·ous·ness** n.

te·di·um (tē′dē·əm) n. The quality or state of being boring, wearisome, monotonous, etc. [< L *taedere* vex, weary]

tee[1] (tē) n. 1 The letter T. 2 Something resembling the form of the letter T. —adj. Shaped like a T.

tee[2] (tē) n. 1 A little peg or cone-shaped mound on which a golf ball is placed in making the first play to a hole. 2 In golf, the area from which a player makes his first stroke at the beginning of play for each hole. —v.t. & v.i. ·teed, tee·ing To place (the ball) on the tee before striking it. —tee off 1 To strike (a golf ball) in starting play. 2 To begin. 3 Slang To make angry or resentful.[?]

tee[3] (tē) n. In certain games, a mark toward which the balls, quoits, etc., are directed. [?<TEE[1]]

teem (tēm) v.i. To be full to overflowing; abound. [<OE tīeman]

teen·age (tēn′āj′) adj. Of, being in, or related to the years from 13 to 19 inclusive. —teen′ag′er n.

teens (tēnz) n. pl. 1 The numbers from 13 to 19 inclusive. 2 The years of one's age from 13 to 19 inclusive. [<OE tēne ten]

tee·ny (tē′nē) adj. ·ni·er, ·ni·est Informal Tiny. [Alter. of TINY]

teen·y·bop·per (tē′nē·bop′ər) n. Slang A modern, hip teen-ager of the 1960's, esp. a girl.

tee·pee (tē′pē) n. TEPEE.

tee shirt (tē) T-SHIRT.

tee·ter (tē′tər) v.i. 1 SEESAW. 2 To walk or move with a swaying or tottering motion. 3 To vacillate; waver. —v.t. 4 To cause to teeter. —n. SEESAW. [?<ON titra tremble]

tee·ter-tot·ter (tē′tər·tot′ər) n. SEESAW.

teeth (tēth) n. pl. of TOOTH.

teethe (tēth) v.i. teethed, teeth·ing To develop teeth; cut one's teeth.

tee·to·tal (tē′tōt′l) adj. 1 Of, pertaining to, or practicing total abstinence from alcoholic beverages. 2 Total; entire. [<TOTAL, with emphatic repetition of initial letter] —tee·to′tal·ism n. —tee·to′tal·ly adv.

tee·to·tal·er (tē·tōt′l·ər) n. One who abstains totally from alcoholic beverages. Also tee·to′tal·ist, tee·to′tal·ler.

Tef·lon (tef′lon) n. A tough, slippery, heat-resistant, chemically inert, synthetic polymer having many industrial and household applications: a trade name.

tel. telegram; telegraph; telephone.

tele- combining form 1 At, from, over, or to a distance; distant: telegraph. 2 Of, in, pertaining to, or transmitted by television: telecast. [<Gk. tēle far]

tel·e·cast (tel′ə·kast, -käst) v.t. & v.i. ·cast or ·cast·ed, ·cast·ing To broadcast by television. —n. A program broadcast by television.

tel·e·com·mu·ni·ca·tion (tel′ə·kə·myōō′nə·kā′shən) n. The technology of communicating at a distance, as in radio, television, telegraphy, etc. Also tel′e·com·mu′ni·ca′tions (construed as sing. or pl.).

tel·e·com·mut·ing (tel′ə·kə·myōōt′ing) n. Working at home by means of a home computer terminal connected by telephone line to a main computer.

tel·e·gram (tel′ə·gram) n. A message sent by telegraph.

tel·e·graph (tel′ə·graf, -gräf) n. Any of various devices, systems, or processes for transmitting messages to a distance, esp. by means of coded electric impulses conducted by wire. —v.t. 1 To send (a message) by telegraph. 2 To communicate with by telegraph. —v.i. 3 To transmit a message by telegraph. —te·leg·ra·pher (tə·leg′rə·fər) n.

tel·e·graph·ic (tel′ə·graf′ik) adj. 1 Of, pertaining to, or transmitted by the telegraph. 2 Concise, as a telegram. Also tel′e·graph′i·cal. —tel′e·graph′i·cal·ly adv.

te·leg·ra·phy (tə·leg′rə·fē) n. 1 The process of conveying messages by telegraph. 2 The technology used in doing this.

Te·lem·a·chus (tə·lem′ə·kəs) Gk. Myth. The son of Odysseus and Penelope, who helped his father kill his mother's suitors.

tel·e·mar·ket·ing (tel′ə·mär′kə·ting) n. The marketing of products and services over the telephone or on television.

te·lem·e·ter (tel′ə·mē′tər, tə·lem′ə·tər) n. An apparatus for indicating or measuring various quantities and for transmitting the data to a distant point. —v.t. & v.i. To transmit by telemeter. —te·lem′e·try n.

tel·e·ol·o·gy (tel′ē·ol′ə·jē, tē′lē-) n. 1 The study of final causes. 2 The belief that natural phenomena can be explained in terms of an overall design as well as by me-

chanical causes. 3 The study of evidence supporting this belief. 4 The explanation of nature in terms of utility or purpose. [<Gk. telos, teleos end + -LOGY] —tel′e·o·log′i·cal (-ə·loj′i·kəl) adj. —tel′e·ol′o·gist n.

te·lep·a·thy (tə·lep′ə·thē) n. The supposed communication of one mind with another by other than normal sensory means. —tel·e·path·ic (tel′ə·path′ik) adj. —tel′e·path′i·cal·ly adv. —te·lep′a·thist n.

tel·e·phone (tel′ə·fōn) n. An instrument for reproducing sound or speech at a distant point, using electric impulses transmitted by wire. —v. ·phoned, ·phon·ing —v.t. 1 To send by telephone, as a message. 2 To communicate with by telephone. —v.i. 3 To communicate by telephone. —tel′e·phon′ic (-fon′ik) adj. —tel′e·phon′i·cal·ly adv.

te·leph·o·ny (tə·lef′ə·nē) n. The technology of telephone communication.

tel·e·pho·to (tel′ə·fō′tō) adj. 1 Denoting a system of lenses which produces a large image of a distant object in a camera. 2 Of, pertaining to, or being telephotography.

tel·e·pho·to·graph (tel′ə·fō′tə·graf, -gräf) n. 1 A picture transmitted by wire or radio. 2 A picture made with a telephoto lens. —v.t. & v.i. To take or transmit (photographs) by telephotography. —tel′e·pho′to·graph′ic adj.

tel·e·pho·tog·ra·phy (tel′ə·fə·tog′rə·fē) n. 1 The technique of producing magnified photographs of distant objects. 2 The transmission of photographs or other visual material by radio or wire.

tel·e·proc·ess·ing (tel′ə·pros′es·ing) n. Data processing by a computer which collects data from distant locations by means of communications lines.

Tel·e·prompt·er (tel′e·promp′tər) n. A prompting device for television whereby a magnified script, unseen by the audience, is unrolled for a speaker or performer, line by line: a trade name.

tel·e·scope (tel′ə·skōp) n. An optical instrument for enlarging the image of a distant object. —v. ·scoped, ·scop·ing v.t. 1 To put together so that one part fits into another. 2 To shorten, condense, or compress. —v.i. 3 To slide or be forced one into another, as the cylindrical tubes of a collapsible telescope or railroad cars in a collision.

tel·e·scop·ic (tel′ə·skop′ik) adj. 1 Of, pertaining to, or done with a telescope. 2 Visible through or obtained by a telescope. 3 Visible only through a telescope. 4 Farseeing. 5 Having sections that slide within or over one another. Also tel′e·scop′i·cal.

te·les·co·py (tə·les′kə·pē) n. The technology of using or making telescopes. —tel′es·co·pist n.

Refracting telescope

tel·e·text (tel′ə·tekst′) n. A communications system that transmits information over a television broadcast signal, to be viewed on a television screen.

tel·e·thon (tel′ə·thon) n. A long telecast, usu. to raise funds for a charity. [<TELE- + (MARA)THON]

Tel·e·type (tel′ə·tīp) n. A teletypewriter: a trade name.

tel·e·type·writ·er (tel′ə·tīp′rī′tər) n. A telegraphic instrument resembling a typewriter, by which the work done on one is simultaneously typed on others, electrically connected but a distance away.

tel·e·view (tel′ə·vyōō) v.t. & v.i. To observe by means of television. —tel′e·view′er n.

tel·e·vise (tel′ə·vīz) v.t. & v.i. ·vised, ·vis·ing To transmit or receive by television.

tel·e·vi·sion (tel′ə·vizh′ən) n. 1 An optical and electric system for continuous transmission of visual images and sound that may be instantaneously received at a distance. 2 The technology of television transmission. 3 A television receiving set. 4 Television as an industry, an art form, or a medium of communications. 5 A show transmitted by television: to watch television.

tel·ex (tel′eks) n. 1 A communication system using teletypewriters connected by wire through exchanges which operate automatically. **2** A message sent by such a system. —*v.t.* To send by telex. [< TEL(ETYPEWRITER) + EX(CHANGE)]

tell (tel) *v.* **told, tell·ing** *v.t.* **1** To relate in detail; narrate, as a story. **2** To make known by speech or writing; express in words; communicate; utter; say. **3** To divulge; reveal; disclose: to *tell* secrets. **4** To decide; ascertain: I cannot *tell* who is to blame. **5** To distinguish; recognize: to *tell* right from wrong. **6** To command; direct; order: I *told* him to go home. **7** To let know; report to; inform. **8** To state or assure emphatically: It's cold out, I *tell* you! **9** To count; enumerate: to *tell* one's beads. —*v.i.* **10** To give an account or description: usu. with *of.* **11** To serve as indication or evidence: with *of:* Their rags *told* of their poverty. **12** To produce a marked effect: Every blow *told.* —**tell off 1** To count and set apart. **2** *Informal* To reprimand severely. —**tell on 1** To wear out; tire; exhaust. **2** *Informal* To tattle on; inform against. [< OE *tellan*] —**Syn. 1** recount, recite. **2** state, aver. **4** discriminate.

tell·er (tel′ər) *n.* **1** One who tells, as a story; narrator. **2** One who receives or pays out money, as in a bank. **3** One who counts, esp. one appointed to count votes.

tell·ing (tel′ing) *adj.* Producing a great effect. —**tell′ing·ly** *adv.* —**Syn.** striking, effective, impressive, forceful.

tell·tale (tel′tāl′) *adj.* Betraying or revealing. —*n.* **1** One who gives information about others; a tattler. **2** That which conveys information; an outward sign or indication. **3** An instrument or device for giving or recording information, as a time clock.

tel·lu·ri·um (te·lŏŏr′ē·əm, tel·yŏŏr′-) *n.* A rare, very poisonous, semimetallic element (symbol Te) resembling sulfur and selenium. [< L *tellus* the earth]

tel·ly (tel′ē) *n. pl.* **tel·lies** *Chiefly Brit. Informal* Television.

Tel·star (tel′stär′) *n.* Any of several U.S. comsats, the first of which was launched July 10, 1962.

te·mer·i·ty (tə·mer′ə·tē) *n.* Foolish boldness; rashness; foolhardiness. [< L *temeritas*] —**Syn.** audacity, heedlessness, recklessness, presumption, venturesomeness.

temp. temperature; temporary; in the time of (L *tempore*).

tem·per (tem′pər) *n.* **1** A fit of anger; rage. **2** A tendency to become easily angered. **3** State of mind or feeling; mood. **4** TEMPERAMENT (def. 1). **5** Equanimity; self-control: now only in the phrases **lose** (or **keep**) **one's temper. 6** The hardness and strength of a metal, esp. when produced by heat treatment. **7** Something used to temper a substance or mixture. —*v.t.* **1** To moderate or make suitable, as by adding another quality; free from excess; mitigate: to *temper* justice with mercy. **2** To bring to the proper consistency, texture, etc., by moistening and working: to *temper* clay. **3** To bring (metal) to a required hardness and elasticity by controlled heating and cooling. **4** To make experienced; toughen, as by difficulties, hardships, etc. **5** *Music* To tune (an instrument) by temperament. —*v.i.* To be or become tempered. [< L *temperare* combine in due proportion] —**tem′per·a·bil′i·ty** *n.* —**tem′per·a·ble** *adj.*

tem·per·a (tem′pər·ə) *n.* **1** An aqueous painting medium in which the pigment is laid down in a matrix of casein, size, egg, etc. **2** The method of painting in this medium; also a painting done in tempera. **3** A water-soluble paint used for posters. [< Ital. *temperare* to temper]

tem·per·a·ment (tem′pər·ə·mənt, -prə-) *n.* **1** The characteristic nature or disposition of a person. **2** A nature or disposition that is exceedingly dramatic, excitable, moody, etc. **3** *Music* The tuning of an instrument of fixed intonation to a slightly modified chromatic scale so that it is in tune for all keys. [< L *temperamentum* proper mixture]

tem·per·a·men·tal (tem′pər·ə·men′təl, -prə-) *adj.* **1** Of or pertaining to temperament. **2** Exceedingly excitable, moody, capricious, etc. **3** Unpredictable or erratic, as in performance. —**tem′per·a·men′tal·ly** *adv.*

tem·per·ance (tem′pər·əns) *n.* **1** Habitual moderation and self-control, esp. in the indulgence of any appetite. **2** The principle and practice of moderation or total abstinence from intoxicants. —*adj.* Of, relating to, practicing,

or promoting total abstinence from intoxicants. [< L *temperare* mix in due proportions]

tem·per·ate (tem′pər·it, tem′prət) *adj.* **1** Characterized by moderation or the absence of extremes; not excessive. **2** Calm; restrained; self-controlled. **3** Observing moderation or self-control, esp. in the use of intoxicating liquors. **4** Moderate as regards temperature; mild. [< L *temperare* mix in due proportions] —**tem′per·ate·ly** *adv.* —**tem′·per·ate·ness** *n.*

temperate zone Either of two zones of the earth, the one between the Tropic of Capricorn and the Antarctic Circle and the other between the Tropic of Cancer and the Arctic Circle. • See ZONE.

tem·per·a·ture (tem′pər·ə·chər, -prə-) *n.* **1** The degree of heat in the atmosphere as measured on a thermometer.

TEMPERATURE CONVERSION TABLE

This table provides approximate conversion figures from the Fahrenheit to the Celsius temperature scales and vice versa. On the Celsius scale, water boils at about 100° and freezes at about 0°. On the Fahrenheit scale, water boils at about 212° and freezes at about 32°. One Fahrenheit degree = 5/9° Celsius. To convert from Fahrenheit to Celsius, subtract 32 from the Fahrenheit reading, multiply by 5, and divide the product by 9. *Example:* 65°F − 32 = 33; 33 × 5 = 165; 165 ÷ 9 = 18.3°C. To convert from Celsius to Fahrenheit, multiply the Celsius reading by 9, divide the product by 5, and add 32. *Example:* 35°C × 9 = 315; 315 ÷ 5 = 63; 63 + 32 = 95°F.

Fahrenheit	Celsius	Fahrenheit	Celsius
500	260.0	0	−17.8
400	204.4	−10	−23.3
300	149.0	−20	−28.9
212	100.0	−30	−34.4
200	93.3	−40	−40.0
100	37.8	−50	−45.6
90	32.2	−60	−51.1
80	26.7	−70	−56.7
70	21.1	−80	−62.2
60	15.6	−90	−67.8
50	10.0	−100	−73.3
40	4.4	−200	−129.0
32	0.0	−300	−184.0
30	−1.1	−400	−240.0
20	−6.6	−459.4*	−273.0
10	−12.2		*Absolute zero.

Celsius	Fahrenheit	Celsius	Fahrenheit
500	932	0	32
400	752	−10	14
300	572	−20	−4
200	392	−30	−22
100	212	−40	−40
90	194	−50	−58
80	176	−60	−76
70	158	−70	−94
60	140	−80	−112
50	122	−90	−130
40	104	−100	−148
30	86	−200	−328
20	68	−273*	−459.4
10	50		*Absolute zero.

---

2 The degree or intensity of heat in a living body; also, the excess of this above the normal. **3** The intensity of heat or cold in any substance. [< L *temperatura* due measure]

tem·pered (tem′pərd) *adj.* **1** Having a particular kind of temper: used mostly in combination: *quick-tempered, ill-tempered.* **2** Moderated or changed by the addition of something else: love *tempered* with discipline. **3** *Music* Adjusted in pitch to some temperament. **4** Having the right degree of hardness, elasticity, etc.

tem·pest (tem′pist) *n.* **1** An extensive and violent wind, usu. attended with rain, snow, or hail. **2** A violent commotion or tumult. [< L *tempestas* space of time, weather < *tempus* time]

tem·pes·tu·ous (tem·pes′chŏŏ·əs) *adj.* Stormy; turbulent; violent. —**tem·pes′tu·ous·ly** *adv.* —**tem·pes′tu·ous·ness** *n.*

---

add, āce, câre, pälm; end, ēven; it, īce; odd, ōpen, ôrder; tŏŏk, pōōl; up, bûrn; ə = *a* in *above, u* in *focus;* yōō = *u* in *fuse;* oil; pout; check; go; ring; thin; this; zh, *vision.* < derived from; ? origin uncertain or unknown.

Tem·plar (tem′plər) *n.* KNIGHT TEMPLAR.

tem·plate (tem′plit) *n.* **1** A pattern, as of wood or metal, used as a guide in shaping or making something. **2** In building, a stout stone or timber for distributing weight or thrust. [< OF *temple* small timber]

tem·ple¹ (tem′pəl) *n.* **1** An edifice consecrated to the worship of one or more deities. **2** An edifice dedicated to public worship; esp., in the U.S.: **a** A synagogue. **b** A Mormon church. **3** Any usu. large or imposing building dedicated or used for a special purpose: a *temple* of learning. [< L *templum* temple]

tem·ple² (tem′pəl) *n.* The region on each side of the head above the cheek bone. [< L *tempus* temple]

tem·po (tem′pō) *n. pl.* **·pos** or **·pi** (-pē) **1** *Music* Relative speed at which a composition is played or is supposed to be played. **2** Characteristic rate of speed; pace. [< L *tempus* time]

tem·po·ral¹ (tem′pər·əl) *adj.* **1** Of or pertaining to the present as opposed to a future life. **2** Worldly; material, as opposed to spiritual. **3** Ephemeral; transitory, as opposed to eternal. **4** Of or relating to time. **5** *Gram.* Of, pertaining to, or denoting time: *temporal* conjunctions. [< L *tempus, temporis* time] **—tem·po·ral·i·ty** (tem′pə·ral′ə·tē), **tem′po·ral·ness** *n.* **—tem′po·ral·ly** *adv.*

tem·po·ral² (tem′pər·əl) *adj.* Of, pertaining to, or situated at the temple or temples of the head.

temporal bone The compound bone forming either side of the skull. • See SKULL.

tem·po·rar·y (tem′pə·rer′ē) *adj.* Lasting, to be used, etc., for a time only; not permanent. [< L *tempus, temporis* time] **—tem′po·rar′i·ly** *adv.* **—tem′po·rar′i·ness** *n.*

tem·po·rize (tem′pə·rīz) *v.i.* **·rized, ·riz·ing 1** To act evasively so as to gain time or put off commitment. **2** To comply with or yield to the situation, circumstances, etc.; compromise. [< L *tempus, temporis* time] **—tem′po·ri·za′·tion, tem′po·riz′er** *n.* **—tem′po·riz′ing·ly** *adv.*

tempt (tempt) *v.t.* **1** To attempt to persuade (a person) to do wrong, as by promising pleasure or gain. **2** To be attractive to; invite: Your offers do not *tempt* me. **3** To provoke or risk provoking: to *tempt* fate. **4** To incline or dispose: They were *tempted* to leave at once. [< L *temptare, tentare* test, try] **—tempt′a·ble** *adj.* **—tempt′er** *n.* **—tempt′ress** *n. Fem.*

temp·ta·tion (temp·tā′shən) *n.* **1** That which tempts. **2** The state of being tempted.

tempt·ing (temp′ting) *adj.* Alluring; attractive; seductive. **—tempt′ing·ly** *adv.* **—tempt′ing·ness** *n.*

tem·pu·ra (tem·pŏŏr′ə, tem′pŏŏr′ə, -pō·rä′) *n.* A Japanese dish of seafood or vegetables, dipped in batter and deep-fried. [Jap., fried food]

tem·pus fu·git (tem′pəs fyŏŏ′jit) *Latin* Time flies.

ten (ten) *n.* **1** The sum of nine plus one; 10; X. **2** A set or group of ten members. [< OE *tēne*] **—ten** *adj., pron.*

ten. tenement; tenor; tenuto (music).

ten·a·ble (ten′ə·bəl) *adj.* Capable of being held, maintained, or defended. [< L *tenere* to hold] **—ten′a·bil′i·ty, ten′a·ble·ness** *n.* **—ten′a·bly** *adv.*

te·na·cious (ti·nā′shəs) *adj.* **1** Having great cohesiveness; tough. **2** Adhesive; sticky. **3** Stubborn; obstinate; persistent. **4** Strongly retentive: a *tenacious* memory. [< L *tenax* holding fast] **—te·na′cious·ly** *adv.* **—te·na′cious·ness, te·nac·i·ty** (tə·nas′ə·tē) *n.*

ten·an·cy (ten′ən·sē) *n. pl.* **·cies 1** The holding of lands or estates by any form of title; occupancy. **2** The period of being a tenant. **3** The property occupied by a tenant.

ten·ant (ten′ənt) *n.* **1** A person who rents a house, land, etc., for his own use. **2** One who holds or possesses lands or property by any kind of title. **3** A dweller in any place; an occupant. **—v.t. 1** To hold as tenant; occupy. **—v.i. 2** To be a tenant. [< F *tenir* to hold] **—ten′ant·a·ble** *adj.*

tenant farmer One who farms land owned by another and pays rent either in cash or in a share of the crops.

ten·ant·ry (ten′ən·trē) *n. pl.* **·ries 1** Tenants collectively. **2** The state of being a tenant.

ten-cent store (ten′sent′) FIVE-AND-TEN-CENT STORE.

Ten Commandments In the Old Testament, the ten rules of conduct given by God to Moses on Mount Sinai.

tend¹ (tend) *v.i.* **1** To have an aptitude, tendency, or disposition; incline. **2** To lead or conduce: Education *tends* to

refinement. **3** To go in a certain direction. [< L *tendere* extend, tend]

tend² (tend) *v.t.* **1** To attend to the needs or requirements of; take care of; minister to: to *tend* children. **2** To watch over or be in charge of: to *tend* a store. **—v.i. 3** To be in attendance; serve or wait: with *on* or *upon*. **4** To give attention or care: with *to*. [Alter. of ATTEND]

ten·den·cy (ten′dən·sē) *n. pl.* **·cies 1** Inclination; propensity; bent: a *tendency* to lie. **2** A movement or course toward some purpose, end, or result. **3** The purpose or trend of a speech or story. [< L *tendere* extend, tend] **—Syn. 1** aptitude, proclivity, disposition, leaning, predilection.

ten·den·tious (ten·den′shəs) *adj.* Disposed to promote a particular view or opinion; lacking in detachment. **—ten·den′tious·ly** *adv.* **—ten·den′tious·ness** *n.*

ten·der¹ (ten′dər) *adj.* **1** Easily crushed, bruised, broken, etc.; delicate; fragile. **2** Easily chewed or cut: said of food. **3** Physically weak; not strong or hardy. **4** Youthful and delicate; not strengthened by maturity: a *tender* age. **5** Characterized by gentleness, care, consideration, etc.: a *tender* respect for the aged. **6** Kind; affectionate; loving: a *tender* father. **7** Sensitive to impressions, feelings, etc.: a *tender* conscience. **8** Sensitive to pain, discomfort, roughness, etc.: a *tender* skin. **9** Of delicate quality: a *tender* color. **10** Capable of arousing sensitive feelings; touching: *tender* memories. **11** Requiring deft or delicate treatment; ticklish; touchy: a *tender* subject. **—v.t.** To make tender; soften. [< L *tener*] **—ten′der·ly** *adv.* **—ten′der·ness** *n.*

ten·der² (ten′dər) *v.t.* **1** To present for acceptance, as a resignation; offer. **2** To proffer, as money, in payment of a debt, etc. **—n. 1** The act of tendering; an offer. **2** That which is offered as payment, esp. money. [< L *tendere* extend, tend] **—ten′der·er** *n.*

tend·er³ (ten′dər) *n.* **1** A boat used to bring supplies, passengers, and crew to and from a ship anchored near the shore. **2** A vessel that services ships at sea, lighthouses, seaplanes, etc. **3** A vehicle attached to the rear of a steam locomotive to carry fuel and water for it. **4** One who tends or ministers to.

ten·der·foot (ten′dər·fŏŏt′) *n. pl.* **·feet** (-fēt′) or **·foots 1** A newcomer, esp. to a rough or unsettled region. **2** Any inexperienced person or beginner. **3** A Boy Scout in the beginning group. **—adj.** Inexperienced.

ten·der·heart·ed (ten′dər·här′tid) *adj.* Compassionate; sympathetic. **—ten′der·heart′ed·ly** *adv.* **—ten′der·heart′ed·ness** *n.*

ten·der·ize (ten′də·rīz) *v.t.* **·ized, ·iz·ing** To make (meat) tender by some process or substance that softens the tough fibers and connective tissues. **—ten′der·iz′er** *n.*

ten·der·loin (ten′dər·loin′) *n.* **1** The tender part of the loin of beef, pork, etc., that lies parallel to the backbone. **2** *Often cap.* A city district noted for its high incidence of crime, corruption, and police leniency.

ten·don (ten′dən) *n.* One of the bands of tough, fibrous tissue attaching a voluntary muscle to a bone. [< Gk. *tenōn* a sinew < *tenein* stretch] **—ten′di·nous** *adj.*

ten·dril (ten′dril) *n.* One of the slender, threadlike, usu. coiling organs serving to attach a climbing plant to a supporting surface. [< OF *tendron* sprout] **—ten′driled** or **ten′drilled, ten′dril·ous** *adj.*

ten·e·ment (ten′ə·mənt) *n.* **1** A room, or set of rooms, designed for one family; apartment; flat. **2** TENEMENT HOUSE. **3** *Law* Anything, as land, houses, offices, franchises, etc., held of another by tenure. [< LL *tenementum* tenure < L *tenere* to hold] **—ten′e·men′ta·ry** (-men′tər·ē), **ten′e·men′tal** (-men′təl) *adj.*

tenement house A run-down building or house, usu. an apartment house, situated in a poor section of a city.

ten·et (ten′it, tē′nit) *n.* A principle, dogma, or doctrine, esp. one held by a group or profession. [L, he holds]

ten·fold (ten′fōld′) *adj.* **1** Made up of ten. **2** Ten times as many or as much. **—adv.** In a tenfold manner or degree.

Tenn. Tennessee.

ten·nis (ten′is) *n.* **1** A game in which two opposing players or pairs of players strike a ball with rackets over a low net on a court (**tennis court**), as of clay or synthetic materials, usu. outdoors. **2** An old form of tennis played in an interior space: also **court tennis.** [< AF *tenetz* take, receive, imperative of *tenir* hold]

ten·on (ten′ən) n. A projection on the end of a timber, etc., for inserting into a mortise to form a joint. —v.t. 1 To form a tenon on. 2 To join by a mortise and tenon. [< OF tenir to hold] • See MORTISE.

ten·or (ten′ər) n. 1 General intent or purport; substance: the tenor of the speech. 2 General course or tendency: the even tenor of their ways. 3 General character or nature. 4 A man's voice singing higher than a baritone and lower than an alto; also, a singer having, or a part to be sung by, such a voice. —adj. 1 Of or pertaining to a tenor. 2 Having a range of or similar to a tenor voice. [< L, a course < tenere to hold]

ten·pins (ten′pinz′) n.pl. 1 (construed as sing.) A game of bowling in which the players attempt to bowl down ten pins. 2 The pins.

tense[1] (tens) adj. **tens·er, tens·est** 1 Stretched tight; taut. 2 Under mental or nervous strain; apprehensive. 3 Phonet. Pronounced with the tongue and its muscles taut, as (ē) and (ᴏᴏ). —v.t. & v.i. **tensed, tens·ing** To make or become tense. [< L tensus, pp. of tendere to stretch] —tense′ly adv. —tense′ness n. —Syn. 2 anxious, nervous, restless, jittery, restive, fidgety.

tense[2] (tens) n. 1 Any of the forms of a verb that indicate when or how long the expressed action took place or the state of being existed. 2 A specific set of such verb forms: the past tense of to see. [< L tempus time, tense]

ten·sile (ten′sil, Brit. ten′sīl) adj. 1 Of or pertaining to tension. 2 Capable of tension. —ten·sil·i·ty (ten·sil′ə·tē) n.

tensile strength The resistance of a material to forces of rupture and longitudinal stress: usu. expressed in pounds or tons per square inch.

ten·sion (ten′shən) n. 1 The act of stretching or the condition of being stretched tight; tautness. 2 Mental or nervous strain or anxiety. 3 Any strained relation, as between governments. 4 Physics a A stress that tends to lengthen a body. b The condition of a body when acted on by such stress. 5 A device to regulate the tightness or tautness of something, esp. the thread in a sewing machine. 6 A condition of balance or symmetry produced by opposing elements, as in an artistic work. 7 Electric potential. —ten′sion·al adj.

ten·sor (ten′sər, -sôr) n. Any muscle that makes tense or stretches a part.

tent (tent) n. A shelter of canvas or the like, supported by poles and fastened by cords to pegs (called **tent pegs**) driven into the ground. —v.t. 1 To cover with or as with a tent. —v.i. 2 To pitch a tent; camp out. [< L tendere stretch]

ten·ta·cle (ten′tə·kəl) n. 1 Zool. Any of various long, slender, flexible appendages of animals, esp. invertebrates, functioning as organs of touch, motion, etc. • See SEA ANEMONE. 2 Bot. A sensitive hair, as on the leaves of some plants. [< L tentaculum < tentare to touch, try] —ten·tac′u·lar (ten·tak′yə·lər) adj.

ten·ta·tive (ten′tə·tiv) adj. 1 Not definite or final; subject to change. 2 Somewhat uncertain or timid: a tentative glance. [< L tentatus, pp. of tentare to try, probe] —ten′ta·tive·ly adv. —ten′ta·tive·ness n.

tent caterpillar The gregarious larva of several moths that form colonies in large silken webs in the branches of trees, etc.

ten·ter (ten′tər) n. A frame or machine for stretching cloth to prevent shrinkage while drying. [< L tentus extended]

ten·ter·hook (ten′tər·hŏok′) n. A sharp hook for holding cloth while being stretched on a tenter. —be on tenterhooks To be in a state of anxiety or suspense.

tenth (tenth) adj. & adv. Next in order after the ninth. —n. 1 The element of an ordered set that corresponds to the number ten. 2 One of ten equal parts.

ten·u·ous (ten′yŏo·əs) adj. 1 Without much substance; slight; weak: tenuous arguments. 2 Thin; slender. 3 Having slight density; rare. [< L tenuis thin] —ten′u·ous·ly adv. —ten′u·ous·ness, ten·u·i·ty (te·nyŏo′ə·tē, tə-) n.

ten·ure (ten′yər) n. 1 The act, right, length of time, or manner of holding something, as land, elected office, or a

position. 2 The permanent status of a teacher, civil servant, etc., after fulfilling certain requirements. [< L tenere to hold] —ten′ured, ten·u·ri·al (ten·yŏor′ē·əl) adj. —ten·u′ri·al·ly adv.

te·pee (tē′pē) n. A conical tent of the North American Plains Indians, usu. covered with skins.

tep·id (tep′id) adj. 1 Moderately warm, as a liquid. 2 Not enthusiastic. [< L tepere be lukewarm] —te·pid·i·ty (tə·pid′ə·tē), tep′id·ness n. —tep′id·ly adv.

te·qui·la (tə·kē′lə) n. A Mexican alcoholic liquor made from the maguey. [< Tequila, a district in Mexico]

ter., terr. terrace; territorial; territory.

ter·a·tism (ter′ə·tiz′əm) n. Biol. A monstrosity, esp. a malformed human or animal fetus. [< Gk. teras monster]

Tepee

ter·a·to·gen·ic (ter′ə·tō·jen′ik) adj. Tending to cause malformations, as in a developing fetus.

ter·bi·um (tûr′bē·əm) n. A rare-earth metal (symbol Tb). [< Ytterby, a town in Sweden] —ter′bic adj.

ter·cen·te·nar·y (tûr′sen·ten′ər·ē, -sent′ən·er′ē) adj. Of or pertaining to a 300th anniversary. —n. pl. ·nar·ies The 300th anniversary.

ter·gi·ver·sate (tər·jiv′ər·sāt, -giv′-) v.i. ·sat·ed, ·sat·ing 1 To be evasive; equivocate. 2 To change sides, attitudes, etc.; apostatize. [< L tergum back + versare to turn] —ter′gi·ver·sa′tor, ter′gi·ver·sa′tion n.

ter·i·ya·ki (ter′ē·yä′kē) n. A Japanese dish of meat or fish marinated in soy sauce, ginger, etc., then fried, broiled, or grilled. [< Jap.]

term (tûrm) n. 1 A word or expression used to designate some definite thing in a science, profession, art, etc.: a medical term. 2 Often pl. Any word or expression conveying some conception or thought: a term of reproach; to speak in general terms. 3 pl. The conditions or stipulations according to which something is to be done or acceded to: the terms of a contract; peace terms. 4 pl. Mutual relations; footing: usu. preceded by on or upon: to be on friendly terms. 5 Math. a The numerator or denominator of a fraction. b One of the units of an algebraic expression that are connected by the plus and minus signs. 6 Logic a In a proposition, either of the two parts, the subject and predicate, which are joined by a copula. b Any of the three elements of a syllogism. 7 A fixed or definite period of time, esp. of duration: a term of office. 8 A school semester or quarter. 9 End; conclusion. 10 Law a One of the prescribed periods of the year during which a court may hold a session. b A specific extent of time during which an estate may be held. c A space of time allowed a debtor to meet his obligation. 11 Med. The time for the normal termination of a pregnancy. —in terms of With respect to; as relating to. —v.t. To designate by means of a term; name or call. [< L terminus a limit]

term. terminal; termination; terminology.

ter·ma·gant (tûr′mə·gənt) n. A scolding or abusive woman; shrew. —adj. Violently abusive and quarrelsome; vixenish. [< ME < Termagant, an imaginary Muslim deity] —ter′ma·gan′cy n.

term·er (tûr′mər) n. A person serving or attending a certain term, as in a prison or school: used in combination: a second-termer.

ter·mi·na·ble (tûr′mə·nə·bəl) adj. That may be terminated; not perpetual. —ter′mi·na·bil′i·ty, ter′mi·na·ble·ness n. —ter′mi·na·bly adv.

ter·mi·nal (tûr′mə·nəl) adj. 1 Situated at or forming the end, limit, or boundary of something: a terminal bus station. 2 Situated at or occurring at the end of a series or period of time; final: a terminal experiment. 3 At, undergoing, or causing the termination of life: terminal cancer; a terminal patient. 4 Of or occurring regularly in or at the end of a term or period of time: terminal payments. 5

Borne at the end of a stem or branch. —*n*. **1** A terminating point or part; termination; end. **2 a** Either end of a railroad line, bus line, airline, etc. **b** A passenger or freight station located at these end points. **c** Any large passenger or freight station serving an area of considerable size. **3 a** A point in an electric circuit at which it is usual to make or break a connection. **b** A connector designed to facilitate this. **4** An electronic device by means of which a user may communicate with a computer, usually including a cathode-ray tube, a keyboard, and a printer. [<L *terminus* boundary] —**ter′mi·nal·ly** *adv*.

ter·mi·nate (tûr′mə·nāt) *v*. **·nat·ed, ·nat·ing** *v.t.* **1** To put an end or stop to. **2** To form the conclusion of; finish. **3** To bound or limit. —*v.i.* **4** To have an end; come to an end. [<L *terminus* a limit] —**ter′mi·na′tive** *adj*.

ter·mi·na·tion (tûr′mə·nā′shən) *n*. **1** The act of terminating or the condition of being terminated. **2** That which bounds or limits in time or space; close; end. **3** Outcome; result; conclusion. **4** The final letters or syllable of a word; a suffix. —**ter′mi·na′tion·al** *adj*.

ter·mi·na·tor (tûr′mə·nā′tər) *n*. **1** One who or that which terminates. **2** *Astron.* The boundary between the illuminated and dark portions of the moon or of a planet.

ter·mi·nol·o·gy (tûr′mə·nol′ə·jē) *n. pl.* **·gies** The technical terms relating to a particular subject, as a science, art, trade, etc. [<L *terminus* limit + -LOGY] —**ter′mi·no·log′i·cal** (-nə·loj′i·kəl) *adj*. —**ter′mi·no·log′i·cal·ly** *adv*.

ter·mi·nus (tûr′mə·nəs) *n. pl.* **·nus·es** or **·ni** (-nī, -nē) **1** The final point or goal; end; terminal. **2** Either end of a railroad or bus line, airline, etc.; also, a town or station located at either end [L]

ter·mite (tûr′mīt) *n*. Any of an order of whitish, soft-bodied insects resembling ants and noted for boring into and destroying wooden structures, furniture, etc. [<L *termes, termitis*]

tern (tûrn) *n*. Any of several birds resembling gulls, but smaller, with a sharply pointed bill and a deeply forked tail. [<Scand.]

ter·na·ry (tûr′nər·ē) *adj*. **1** Formed or consisting of three; grouped in threes. **2** Third in order, importance, etc. —*n. pl.* **·ries** A group of three; a triad. [<L *terni* by threes]

ter·pene (tûr′pēn) *n*. Any of various isomeric hydrocarbons contained in essential oils, resins, etc. [<*terp(entin)*, earlier form of TURPENTINE + -ENE]

Terp·sich·o·re (tûrp·sik′ə·rē) *Gk. Myth*. The Muse of dancing. [<Gk. *terpsis* enjoyment + *choros* dance]

terp·si·cho·re·an (tûrp′si·kə·rē′ən, -sə·kôr′ē-, -kō′rē-) *adj*. Of or relating to dancing. Also **terp′si·cho·re′al**.

ter·race (ter′is) *n*. **1** A raised level space, as of lawn, usu. with sloping sides; also, such levels collectively. **2** A raised street supporting a row of houses; also, the houses occupying such a street. **3** A flat roof, esp. of an Oriental or Spanish house. **4** An open, paved area connected to a house, apartment, or building, usu. with places for seating, plantings, etc. **5** A balcony. **6** A parklike area extending down the middle of a wide street or boulevard. **7** A relatively narrow step in the face of a steep natural slope. —*v.t.* **·raced, ·rac·ing** To form into or provide with a terrace or terraces. [<L *terra* earth]

ter·ra cot·ta (ter′ə kot′ə) **1** A hard, kiln-burnt clay, reddish brown and usu. unglazed, used for pottery, sculpture, etc. **2** A statue made of this clay. **3** A brownish red color. [Ital., lit, cooked earth]

ter·ra fir·ma (ter′ə fûr′mə) Solid ground, as distinguished from the sea or the air. [L]

ter·rain (te·rān′, ter′ān) *n*. **1** Battleground, or a region suited for defense, fortifications, etc. **2** A land area viewed with regard to some particular characteristic: marshy *terrain*. [<L *terrenus* earthen < *terra* earth]

Ter·ra·my·cin (ter′ə·mī′sin) *n*. An antibiotic effective against a wide variety of pathogenic organisms: a trade name.

ter·ra·pin (ter′ə·pin) *n*. **1** One of the several North American edible tortoises, esp. the diamond-back. **2** Its flesh. [<Algon.]

ter·rar·i·um (te·râr′ē·əm) *n. pl.* **·rar·i·ums** or **·rar·i·a** (-râr′ē·ə) **1** A glass enclosure for growing a collection of small plants. **2** A

Terrapin

vivarium for small land animals. [<L *terra* earth + -arium, on analogy with *aquarium*]

ter·res·tri·al (tə·res′trē·əl) *adj*. **1** Belonging to the planet earth. **2** Pertaining to land or earth. **3** Living on or growing in earth. **4** Belonging to or consisting of land, as distinct from water, air, etc. **5** Worldly; mundane. —*n*. An inhabitant of the earth. [<L *terra* land] —**ter·res′tri·al·ly** *adv*.

ter·ret (ter′it) *n*. One of two metal rings on a harness, through which the reins are passed. [<OF *touret* small wheel]

ter·ri·ble (ter′ə·bəl) *adj*. **1** Causing extreme fear, dread, or terror. **2** Severe; extreme: a *terrible* headache. **3** Awesome: a *terrible* burden of guilt. **4** Very bad; dreadful; awful: a *terrible* play. [<L *terribilis* < *terrere* terrify] —**ter′ri·ble·ness** *n*. —**ter′ri·bly** *adv*.

ter·ri·er (ter′ē·ər) *n*. Any of several breeds of small, active, wiry dogs, formerly used to hunt burrowing animals. [<L *terrarius* pertaining to earth]

ter·rif·ic (tə·rif′ik) *adj*. **1** Arousing great terror or fear; frightening. **2** *Informal* **a** Very great; extraordinary; tremendous. **b** Unusually good; excellent. —**ter·rif′i·cal·ly** *adv*.

ter·ri·fy (ter′ə·fī) *v.t.* **·fied, ·fy·ing** To fill with terror; frighten severely. [<L *terrere* frighten + -FY]

ter·ri·to·ri·al (ter′ə·tôr′ē·əl, -tō′rē-) *adj*. **1** Of or pertaining to a territory or territories. **2** Of, restricted to, or under the jurisdiction of a particular territory, region, or district. **3** *Often cap*. Organized or intended primarily for home defense: the British *Territorial* Army. —**ter′ri·to′ri·al·ism′**, **ter′ri·to′ri·al·ist** *n*. —**ter′ri·to′ri·al·ly** *adv*.

ter·ri·to·ri·al·i·ty (ter′ə·tôr′ē·al′ə·tē, -tō′rē-) *n*. Territorial condition, status, or position.

ter·ri·to·ry (ter′ə·tôr′ē, -tō′rē) *n. pl.* **·ries 1** The domain over which a nation, state, etc., exercises jurisdiction. **2** Any considerable tract of land; a region; district. **3** A region having a certain degree of self-government, but not having the status of a state or province. **4** A special sphere or province of activity, knowledge, etc. **5** A specific area used by or assigned to a person, group, etc.: a salesman's *territory*. [<L *terra* earth]

ter·ror (ter′ər) *n*. **1** Overwhelming fear. **2** A person or thing that causes extreme fear. **3** *Informal* A difficult or annoying person, esp. a child. **4** TERRORISM. [<L *terrere* frighten]

ter·ror·ism (ter′ə·riz′əm) *n*. The act or practice of terrorizing, esp. by violence committed for political purposes, as by a government seeking to intimidate a populace or by revolutionaries seeking to overthrow a government, compel the release of prisoners, etc. —**ter′ror·ist** *n*. —**ter′ror·is′tic** *adj*.

ter·ror·ize (ter′ə·rīz) *v.t.* **·ized, ·iz·ing 1** To reduce to a state of terror; terrify. **2** To coerce or intimidate through terrorism. —**ter′ror·i·za′tion, ter′ror·iz′er** *n*.

ter·ry (ter′ē) *n. pl.* **·ries** A very absorbent pile fabric in which the loops are uncut, used for towels, etc. Also **terry cloth**. [?]

terse (tûrs) *adj*. **ters·er, ters·est** Short and to the point; succinct. [<L *tersus*, pp. of *tergere* rub off, rub down] —**terse′ly** *adv*. —**terse′ness** *n*. —**Syn.** brief, concise, pithy, curt, laconic.

ter·tian (tûr′shən) *adj*. Recurring every other day: said of a fever or disease causing such a fever, as certain forms of malaria. [<L *tertius* third (recurring every third day, reckoned inclusively)]

ter·ti·ar·y (tûr′shē·er′ē, -shə·rē) *adj*. Third in point of time, importance, rank, or value. —*n. pl.* **·ar·ies** Any of the third row of wing feathers of a bird. [<L *tertius* third]

Ter·ti·ar·y (tûr′shē·er′ē, -shə·rē) *n. & adj*. See GEOLOGY.

tes·sel·late (tes′ə·lāt) *v.t.* **·lat·ed, ·lat·ing** To lay or adorn with small squares or mosaic tiles, as pavement. —*adj*. Adorned or laid with mosaic patterns: also **tes′sel·lat·ed**. [<L *tessellatus* checkered] —**tes′sel·la′tion** *n*.

tes·si·tu·ra (tes′i·tŏŏr′ə) *n*. The average range of a melody or vocal composition. [Ital., lit., texture]

test (test) *v.t.* **1** To subject to an examination or proof; try. —*v.i.* **2** To undergo or give an examination or test: usu. with *for*: to *test* for accuracy. **3** To receive a rating as a result of testing: The alcohol *tested* 75 percent. —*n*. **1** An examination or observation to find out the real nature of something or to prove or disprove its value or validity. **2** A method or technique employed to do this. **3** A criterion or standard of judgment or evaluation. **4** An undergoing of or subjection to certain conditions that disclose the character, quality, nature, etc., of a person or thing: a *test* of will. **5** A series of questions, problems, etc., intended to measure knowledge, aptitudes, intelligence, etc. **6** *Chem.* **a** A reaction by means of which a compound or ingredient may be identified. **b** Its agent or the result. [< L *testum* an earthen vessel < *testa* potsherd, shell] **—test'a·ble** *adj.* **—test'er** *n.*

Test. Testament.

tes·ta (tes'tə) *n. pl.* **·tae** (-tē) The outer, usu. hard and brittle coat of a seed. [L, shell]

tes·ta·ment (tes'tə·mənt) *n.* **1** The written declaration of one's last will: now usu. in the phrase **last will and testament. 2** A statement testifying to some belief or conviction; credo. **3** Proof; evidence: a *testament* to their courage. **4** In Biblical use, a covenant; dispensation. [< L *testari* testify] **—tes'ta·men'tal, tes'ta·men'ta·ry** (-men'tər·ē) *adj.*

Tes·ta·ment (tes'tə·mənt) *n.* Either of the two parts of the Bible, distinguished as the **Old** and the **New Testament.**

tes·tate (tes'tāt) *adj.* Having made a will before decease. [< L *testari* be a witness]

tes·ta·tor (tes·tā'tər, tes'tā·tər) *n.* One who has died leaving a will. [< L] **—tes·ta'trix** (-triks) *n. Fem.*

tes·ti·cle (tes'ti·kəl) *n.* One of the two sex glands of the male which secrete sex hormones and spermatozoa. [< L *testiculus*, dim. of *testis* testicle]

tes·ti·fy (tes'tə·fī) *v.* **·fied, ·fy·ing** *v.i.* **1** To make solemn declaration of truth or fact. **2** *Law* To give testimony; bear witness. **3** To serve as evidence or indication. **—v.t. 4** To bear witness to; affirm. **5** *Law* To state or declare on oath or affirmation. **6** To be evidence or indication of. **7** To make known publicly; declare. [< L *testis* witness + -FY] **—tes'ti·fi·ca'tion, tes'ti·fi'er** *n.*

tes·ti·mo·ni·al (tes'tə·mō'nē·əl) *n.* **1** A statement, often a letter, recommending the character, value, etc., of a person or thing. **2** An act, statement, event, etc., that gives public acknowledgment of esteem or appreciation. **—adj.** Pertaining to or constituting testimony or a testimonial.

tes·ti·mo·ny (tes'tə·mō'nē) *n. pl.* **·nies 1** An oral statement of a witness under oath in a court, usu. made in answer to questioning by a lawyer or judge. **2** Any public acknowledgment or declaration, as of a religious experience. **3** Proof of something; evidence. [< L *testimonium* < *testis* a witness]

tes·tis (tes'tis) *n. pl.* **·tes** (-tēz) TESTICLE. [L]

tes·tos·ter·one (tes·tos'tə·rōn) *n.* A natural or synthetic male sex hormone. [< TESTIS + STER(OL) + -ONE]

test-tube (tes'tyⁿōb') *adj.* **1** Experimental in nature. **2** Produced by artificial insemination.

test tube A tubular glass vessel used in making chemical or biological tests.

tes·ty (tes'tē) *adj.* **·ti·er, ·ti·est** Irritable; touchy. [< AF *testif* heady < OF *teste* head] **—tes'ti·ly** *adv.* **—tes'ti·ness** *n.* **—Syn.** irascible, peevish, petulant, querulous, snappish, crabby, grouchy.

tet·a·nus (tet'ə·nəs) *n.* An acute and often fatal infectious bacterial disease marked by spasmodic contraction of voluntary muscles, esp. the muscles of the jaw. [< Gk. *tetanos* spasm < *teinein* to stretch] **—te·tan·ic** (ti·tan'ik) *adj.*

tetched (techt) *adj. Regional* Slightly unbalanced mentally. [Alter. of *touched*]

tetch·y (tech'ē) *adj.* **tetch·i·er, tetch·i·est** Irritable; peevish; touchy. [< OF *teche* mark, quality] **—tetch'i·ly** *adv.* **—tetch'i·ness** *n.*

tête-à-tête (tāt'ə·tāt', *Fr.* tet·à·tet') *adj.* Confidential, as between two persons. **—n. 1** A confidential chat between two persons. **2** An S-shaped sofa on which two persons may face each other. **—adv.** In private or personal talk. [F, lit., head to head]

teth·er (teth'ər) *n.* **1** Something used to check or confine, as a rope for fastening an animal. **2** The limit of one's powers or field of action. **—at the end of one's tether** At the extreme limit of one's resources, patience, etc. [< Scand.]

tetra- *combining form* Four; fourfold: *tetrachloride.* [< Gk.]

tet·ra·chlo·ride (tet'rə·klôr'īd, -id, -klō'rīd, -rid) *n.* A compound containing four atoms of chlorine per molecule.

tet·ra·eth·yl lead (tet'rə·eth'il led) A poisonous organic antiknock compound.

tet·ra·he·dron (tet'rə·hē'drən) *n. pl.* **·drons** or **·dra** (-drə) A solid bounded by four plane triangular faces. [< Gk. *tetra-* four + *hedra* base] **—tet'ra·he'dral** *adj.*

Tetrahedron

te·tral·o·gy (te·träl'ə·jē, -tral'-) *n. pl.* **·gies 1** A group of four dramas presented together at the festivals of Dionysus at Athens. **2** Any series of four related novels, plays, operas, etc. [< TETRA- + -LOGY]

te·tram·e·ter (te·tram'ə·tər) *n.* In English verse, a line having four metrical feet. [< TETRA + -METER]

tet·rarch (tet'rärk, tē'trärk) *n.* **1** In the Roman Empire, the governor of one of four divisions of a province. **2** A subordinate ruler. [< Gk. *tetra-* four + *archos* ruler] **—tet·rar·chy** (tet'rär·kē, tē'trär-), **tet·rarch·ate** (tet'rär·kāt, -kit, tē'trär-) *n.*

tet·ra·va·lent (tet'rə·vā'lənt) *adj.* QUADRIVALENT. **—tet'·ra·va'lence, tet'ra·va'len·cy** *n.*

te·trox·ide (te·trok'sīd, -sid) *n.* Any oxide having four atoms of oxygen per molecule. [< TETR(A)- + OXIDE]

Teu·ton (tyⁿōt'n) *n.* **1** One of an ancient German tribe that dwelt in Jutland north of the Elbe, appearing in history as **Teu·to·nes** (tyⁿō'tə·nēz). **2** One belonging to any of the Teutonic peoples, esp. a German.

Teu·ton·ic (tyⁿō·ton'ik) *adj.* **1** Of or pertaining to the Teutons. **2** Of or pertaining to Germany or the Germans. **3** Of or pertaining to the peoples of northern Europe, including the English, Scandinavians, Dutch, etc. **—Teu·ton'i·cal·ly** *adv.*

Tex. Texan; Texas.

Texas leaguer In baseball, a looping fly ball that falls safe between an infielder and an outfielder.

text (tekst) *n.* **1** The actual or original words of an author or speaker, as distinguished from notes, commentary, illustrations, etc. **2** Any of the written or printed versions or editions of a piece of writing. **3** The main body of written or printed matter of a book or a single page, as distinguished from notes, indexes, illustrations, etc. **4** The words of a song, opera, etc. **5** A verse of Scripture, esp. when cited as the basis of a sermon. **6** Any subject of discourse; a topic; theme. **7** One of several styles of letters or types. **8** TEXTBOOK. [< L *textus* fabric, structure < *texere* to weave]

text·book (tekst'book') *n.* A book used as a standard work or basis of instruction in any branch of knowledge; schoolbook; manual.

tex·tile (teks'tīl, -til) *adj.* **1** Pertaining to weaving or woven fabrics. **2** Such as may be woven; manufactured by weaving. **—n. 1** A fabric, esp. if woven or knitted; cloth. **2** Material, as a fiber, yarn, etc., capable of being woven. [< L *textus* fabric. See TEXT.]

tex·tu·al (teks'choo·əl) *adj.* **1** Pertaining to, contained in, or based on a text. **2** Literal; word for word. **—tex'tu·al·ly** *adv.*

tex·ture (teks'chər) *n.* **1** The arrangement or characteristics of the threads, etc., of a fabric: a tweed having a rough *texture.* **2** The arrangement or characteristics of the constituent elements of anything, esp. as regards surface appearance or tactile qualities: the *texture* of bread. **3** The overall or characteristic structure, form, or interrelatedness of parts of a work of art, music, literature, etc.: the tightly-knit *texture* of his poems. **4** The basic nature or structure of something: the *texture* of rural life. [< L *textus* fabric. See TEXT.] **—tex'tur·al** *adj.* **—tex'tur·al·ly** *adv.*

T-group (tē'grⁿop) *n.* A group of people, often business or industrial personnel, who meet with a trained leader

---

add, āce, câre, pălm; end, ēven; it, īce; odd, ōpen, ôrder; tŏŏk, pōōl; up, bûrn; ə = a in *above*, u in *focus*; yⁿōō = u in *fuse*; oil; pout; check; go; ring; thin; this; zh, *vision*. < derived from; ? origin uncertain or unknown.

whose function is to guide them to a more insightful awareness of themselves and others through the free and uninhibited expression of their thoughts, feelings, prejudices, etc. [< *t(raining) group*]

-th[1] *suffix of nouns* **1** The act or result of the action: *growth.* **2** The state or quality of being or having: *health.* [< OE *-thu, -tho*]

-th[2] *suffix* Used in ordinal numbers: *tenth.* Also **-eth.** [< OE *-tha, -the*]

-th[3] See -ETH[1].

Th thorium.

Th., Thur., Thurs. Thursday.

Thai (tī) *n.* **1** *pl.* **Thai** or **Thais a** A native or citizen of Thailand. **b** A member of the majority ethnic group of Thailand. **2** Any one of a group of related languages used in Thailand. —*adj.* Of or pertaining to Thailand, its people, or their languages.

Thai·land (tī′land) *n.* A constitutional monarchy in SE Asia, 198,404 sq. mi., cap. Bangkok. • See map at INDO-CHINA.

thal·a·mus (thal′ə·məs) *n. pl.* **·mi** (-mī, mē) **1** A mass of gray matter at the base of the brain, involved in sensory transmission. **2** The receptacle of a flower. [< Gk. *thalamos* chamber] —**tha·lam·ic** (thə·lam′ik) *adj.*

Tha·li·a (thə·lī′ə, thä′lē·ə, thāl′yə) *Gk. Myth.* **1** The Muse of comedy and pastoral poetry. **2** One of the three Graces. [< Gk. *thallein* to bloom]

thal·li·um (thal′ē·əm) *n.* A soft, rare, highly poisonous metallic element (symbol Tl), used in rat poison, insecticides, and in making optical glass. [< Gk. *thallos* a green shoot; from the bright green line in its spectrum]

thal·lo·phyte (thal′ə·fīt) *n.* Any of a major division of plants without roots, stems, or leaves, comprising the bacteria, fungi, algae, and lichens. [< THALLUS + -PHYTE] —**thal′lo·phyt′ic** (-fit′ik) *adj.*

thal·lus (thal′əs) *n. pl.* **·lus·es** or **·li** (-ī) *Bot.* A plant body without true root, stem, or leaf, as in thallophytes. [< Gk. *thallos* a shoot]

than (than, *unstressed* thən) *conj.* **1** When, as, or if compared with: after an adjective or adverb to express comparison between what precedes and what follows: I am stronger *than* he (is); I know her better *than* (I know) him. **2** Except; but: used after *other, else,* etc: no other *than* you. **3** When: usu. used after *scarcely, hardly, barely:* Scarcely had we got settled *than* we had to leave. —*prep.* Compared to: used only in the phrases *than whom, than which:* An eminent judge *than whom* no other is finer. [< OE *thanne*] • The case of a word following *than* can be either nominative or objective, depending on the word's function in the elliptical clause introduced by *than: You owe him more money than I (owe him)* or *You owe him more money than (you owe) me.* However, in informal writing and speech, the objective case is acceptable following *than* whether or not it agrees with the ellipsis: *He is younger than me.*

thane (thān) *n.* **1** In Anglo-Saxon England, a man who ranked above an ordinary freeman but below an earl or nobleman and who held land of the king or a noble in exchange for military service. **2** The chief of a Scottish clan, a baron in the service of the king. [< OE *thegn*]

thank (thangk) *v.t.* **1** To express gratitude to; give thanks to. **2** To hold responsible; blame: often used ironically: We have him to *thank* for this mess. —**thank you** An expression of gratitude or in acknowledgment of a service rendered. [< OE *thancian*]

thank·ful (thangk′fəl) *adj.* Feeling or manifesting thanks or gratitude; grateful. —**thank′ful·ly** *adv.* —**thank′ful·ness** *n.*

thank·less (thangk′lis) *adj.* **1** Not feeling or expressing gratitude; ungrateful. **2** Not gaining or likely to gain thanks; unappreciated. —**thank′less·ly** *adv.* —**thank′less·ness** *n.*

thanks (thangks) *n.pl.* An expression of gratitude or appreciation. —*interj.* I thank you. —**thanks to 1** Thanks be given to. **2** Because of.

thanks·giv·ing (thangks′giv′ing) *n.* **1** The act of giving thanks. **2** A manner of expressing thanks, as a prayer, public celebration, etc.

Thanksgiving Day 1 In the U.S., the fourth Thursday in November, set apart as a legal holiday for giving

thanks for the year's blessings. Also **Thanksgiving. 2** In Canada, a similar holiday celebrated the second Monday in October.

that (that, *unstressed* thət) *adj. pl.* **those 1** Pertaining to some person or thing previously mentioned, understood, or specifically designated: *that* man. **2** Denoting something more remote in place, time, or thought than the thing with which it is being compared: This winter was colder than *that* one. —*pron. pl.* **those 1** As a demonstrative pronoun: **a** The person or thing implied, mentioned, or understood. **b** The thing further away or more remote: This will happen sooner than *that* will. **2** As a relative pronoun, *that* is used to introduce restrictive clauses and, as such, has a variety of meanings, as *who, whom, which, where, at which, with which,* etc.: The man *that* (whom) I saw is not here; The house *that* (which) you lived in was torn down. **3** Something: There is *that* to be said for him. —*adv.* **1** To that extent; so: I can't see *that* far. **2** *Informal* In such a manner or degree: It really is *that* bad! —*conj. That* is used primarily to connect a subordinate clause with its principal clause, with the following meanings: **1** As a fact that: introducing a fact: I tell you *that* it is so. **2** So that; in order that: I tell you *that* you may know. **3** For the reason that; because: She wept *that* she was growing old. **4** As a result: introducing a result, consequence, or effect: He bled so profusely *that* he died. **5** At which time; when: It was only yesterday *that* I saw him. **6** Introducing an exclamation: O *that* he would come! —**so that 1** To the end that. **2** With the result that. **3** Provided. [< OE *thæt*] • See WHO.

thatch (thach) *n.* **1** A covering of reeds, straw, etc., arranged on a roof so as to shed water. **2** Any of various palm leaves or coarse grasses so used. Also **thatching.** —*v.t.* To cover with a thatch. [< OE *thæc* cover] —**thatch′er** *n.* —**thatch′y** *adj.* (**thatch·i·er, thatch·i·est**)

thau·ma·tur·gy (thô′mə·tûr′jē) *n.* Magic; the performance or working of wonders or miracles. [< Gk. *thauma* wonder + *ergon* work] —**thau′ma·turge, thau′ma·tur′gist** *n.* —**thau′ma·tur′gic** or **·gi·cal** *adj.*

thaw (thô) *v.i.* **1** To melt or dissolve, as snow or ice. **2** To lose the effects of coldness or of having been frozen: often with *out.* **3** To rise in temperature so as to melt ice and snow: said of weather: It *thawed* last night. **4** To become less aloof, unsociable, rigid in opinions, etc. —*v.t.* **5** To cause to thaw. —*n.* **1** The act of thawing. **2** Warmth of weather such as melts things frozen. **3** A becoming less aloof, unsociable, etc. [< OE *thāwian*] —**thaw′er** *n.*

Th.B. Bachelor of Theology.

Th.D. Doctor of Theology.

the[1] (*stressed* thē; *unstressed before a consonant* thə; *unstressed before a vowel* thē, thi) *definite article. The* is opposed to the indefinite article *a* or *an,* and is used specifically: **1** When reference is made to a particular person, thing, or group: *The* children are getting restless; He left *the* room. **2** To give an adjective substantive force, or render a notion abstract: *the* quick and *the* dead; *the* doing of the deed. **3** Before a noun to make it generic: *The* dog is a friend of man. **4** With the force of a possessive pronoun: He kicked me in *the* (my) leg. **5** To give distributive force: equivalent to *a, per, each,* etc.: a dollar *the* bushel. **6** To designate the whole of a specific time period: in *the* Middle Ages; in *the* forties. **7** To designate a particular one as emphatically outstanding: usu. stressed in speech and italicized in writing: He is *the* officer for the command. **8** As part of a title: *The* Duke of York. **9** Before the name of a well-known place, thing, etc.: *the* Grand Canyon; *the* Eiffel Tower. [< OE]

the[2] (thə) *adv.* By that much; to this extent: *the* more, *the* merrier: used to modify words in the comparative degree. [< OE *thȳ*]

the·a·ter (thē′ə·tər) *n.* **1** A structure for the indoor or outdoor presentation of plays, operas, motion pictures, etc. **2** A place resembling such a structure, used for lectures, surgical demonstrations, etc. **3** The theatrical world and everything relating to it, esp.: **a** The legitimate stage, as distinguished from motion pictures, television, etc. **b** The works written for or the arts connected with the theater. **4** Theatrical effectiveness: The play was not good *theater.* **5** Any place that is the scene of events or action:

a *theater* of war operations. Also **the′a·tre.** [< Gk. *theatron* < *theasthai* behold]

the·a·ter-in-the-round (thē′ə·tər·in·thə·round′) *n.* A theater having a central stage and no proscenium, with seats surrounding the stage.

theater of the absurd A form of drama that concerns itself with the tragic or comic absurdities of man's condition and his futile efforts to deal with or resolve such absurdities.

the·a·tri·cal (thē·at′ri·kəl) *adj.* **1** Of or pertaining to the theater or things of the theater, as plays, actors, costumes, etc. **2** Dramatically effective or compelling. **3** Artificially dramatic, esp. in a pretentious or showy way. Also **the·at′ric.** —*n.pl.* Dramatic performances, esp. when given by amateurs. —**the·at′ri·cal·ism, the·at′ri·cal′i·ty** *n.* — **the·at′ri·cal·ly** *adv.*

the·at·rics (thē·at′riks) *n.pl.* **1** *(construed as sing.)* The art of the theater. **2** Exaggeratedly dramatic or showy behavior, mannerisms, etc.

thee (thē) *pron.* **1** The objective case of *thou.* **2** Thou: used generally by Quakers with a verb in the third person singular: *Thee* knows my mind. [< OE *thē*]

theft (theft) *n.* **1** The act or an instance of stealing; larceny. **2** That which is stolen. [< OE *thēoft*]

the·ine (thē′ən) *n.* The alkaloid identical with caffeine, found in tea. [< NL *thea* tea]

their (thâr) *pronominal adj.* The possessive case of the pronoun *they* used attributively; belonging or pertaining to them: *their* homes. [< ON *theirra* of them]

theirs (thârz) *pron.* **1** The possessive case of *they,* used predicatively; belonging or pertaining to them: That house is *theirs.* **2** The things or persons belonging or relating to them: our country and *theirs.* —**of theirs** Belonging or pertaining to them.

the·ism (thē′iz·əm) *n.* **1** Belief in a god or gods. **2** Belief in a personal God as creator and supreme ruler of the universe. [< Gk. *theos* god] —**the′ist** *n.* —**the·is·tic** or **·ti·cal** *adj.* —**the·is′ti·cal·ly** *adv.*

them (them, *unstressed* thəm) *pron.* The objective case of *they.* [< ON *theim*]

theme (thēm) *n.* **1** A main subject or topic, as of a poem, novel, play, speech, etc. **2** A short essay, often written as an exercise. **3** In a musical composition, a melodic, harmonic, or rhythmic subject or phrase, usu. developed with variations. **4** THEME SONG. [< Gk. *thema*] —**the·mat′ic** (-mat′ik) or **·i·cal** *adj.* —**the·mat′i·cal·ly** *adv.*

theme song **1** A musical motif recurring in a film, television presentation, etc. **2** The brief melody identifying a radio or television presentation, a dance band, etc.

them·selves (them′selvz′, *unstressed* thəm-) *pron.* A form of the third person, plural pronoun, used: **1** As a reflexive: They forced *themselves* to go. **2** As an intensive: They *themselves* are responsible. **3** As an indication of their normal, true, or proper selves: They were not *themselves* when they said it.

then (then) *adv.* **1** At that time. **2** Soon afterward; next in time: We dressed and *then* ate. **3** Next in space or order: Add the flour, *then* the butter. **4** At another time: often introducing a sequential statement following *now, at first,* etc.: At first she laughed, *then* she cried. —*conj.* **1** For that reason; as a consequence; accordingly: If we leave now, *then* you can go to bed. **2** In that case: I will *then,* since you won't. —*adj.* Being or acting in, or belonging to, that time: the *then* secretary of state. —*n.* A specific time already mentioned or understood; that time: We will be gone by *then.* [< OE *thanne*]

thence (thens) *adv.* **1** From that place. **2** From the circumstance, fact, or cause; therefore. **3** From that time; after that time. [< OE *thanon* from there]

thence·forth (thens′fôrth′, -fôrth′) *adv.* From that time on; thereafter. Also **thence′for′ward** (-fôr′wərd), **thence′· for′wards.**

theo- *combining form* God or a god: *theocracy.* [< Gk. *theos* a god]

the·o·cen·tric (thē′ə·sen′trik) *adj.* Having God for its center; proceeding from God.

the·oc·ra·cy (thē·ok′rə·sē) *n. pl.* **·cies** **1** A state, polity, or group of people that claims a deity as its ruler. **2** Government by a priestly class claiming to have divine authority, as in the Papacy. [< Gk. *theos* god + *krateein* rule] —**the· o·crat** (thē′ə·krat) *n.* —**the·o·crat·ic** (thē′ə·krat′ik) or **·i·cal** *adj.* —**the·o·crat′i·cal·ly** *adv.*

the·od·o·lite (thē·od′ə·līt) *n.* A surveying instrument having a small telescope for measuring angles. [?]

theol. theologian; theological; theology.

the·o·lo·gian (thē′ə·lō′jən) *n.* One versed in theology.

the·o·log·i·cal (thē′ə·loj′i·kəl) *adj.* Of, pertaining to, based on, or teaching theology. Also **the′o·log′ic.** —**the′o· log′i·cal·ly** *adv.*

the·ol·o·gize (thē·ol′ə·jīz) *v.* **·gized, ·giz·ing** *v.t.* **1** To devise or fit (something) into a system of theology. —*v.i.* **2** To reason theologically.

the·ol·o·gy (thē·ol′ə·jē) *n. pl.* **·gies** **1** The study of God, his attributes, and his relationship with man and the universe, esp. such studies as set forth by a specific church, religious group, or theologian. **2** The study of religion and religious doctrine, culminating in a synthesis or philosophy of religion. [< Gk. *theos* god + *logos* discourse]

the·o·rem (thē′ər·əm, thir′əm) *n.* **1** A proposition demonstrably true or so universally acknowledged as such as to become part of a general theory. **2** *Math.* A proposition to be proved or which has been proved. [< Gk. *theōrēma* sight, theory] —**the·o·re·mat·ic** (thē′ər·ə·mat′ik) *adj.*

the·o·ret·i·cal (thē′ə·ret′i·kəl) *adj.* **1** Of, relating to, or consisting of theory. **2** Existing only in theory; not applied; speculative; hypothetical. **3** Addicted to theorizing. Also **the′o·ret′ic.** —**the′o·ret′i·cal·ly** *adv.*

the·o·re·ti·cian (thē′ər·ə·tish′ən) *n.* One who theorizes. Also **the·o·rist** (thē′ər·ist).

the·o·rize (thē′ə·rīz) *v.i.* **·rized, ·riz·ing** To form or express theories; speculate. —**the′o·ri·za′tion, the′o·riz′er** *n.*

the·o·ry (thē′ər·ē, thir′ē) *n. pl.* **·ries** **1** A plan, scheme, or procedure used or to be used as a basis or technique for doing something. **2** A merely speculative or an ideal circumstance, principle, mode of action, etc.: often with *in:* In *theory,* the plan worked. **3** A body of fundamental or abstract principles underlying a science, art, etc.: a *theory* of modern architecture. **4** A proposed explanation or hypothesis designed to account for any phenomenon. **5** Loosely, mere speculation, conjecture, or guesswork. [< Gk. *theōria* view, speculation]

theos. theosophical; theosophist; theosophy.

the·os·o·phy (thē·os′ə·fē) *n.* **1** Any of several religious or philosophical systems claiming to have mystical insight into the nature of God and the universe. **2** *Usu. cap.* The religious system of a modern religious sect (**Theosophical Society**) that is strongly Buddhist or Brahmanic in character and claims to have and to be able to teach such mystical insights. [< Gk. *theos* god + *sophos* wise] —**the·o· soph·ic** (thē′ə·sof′ik) or **·i·cal** *adj.* —**the′o·soph′i·cal·ly** *adv.* —**the·os′o·phist** *n.*

ther·a·peu·tic (ther′ə·pyoo′tik) *adj.* **1** Having healing qualities; curative. **2** Pertaining to therapeutics. Also **ther′a·peu′ti·cal.** [< Gk. *therapeuein* serve, take care of] — **ther′a·peu′ti·cal·ly** *adv.*

ther·a·peu·tics (ther′ə·pyoo′tiks) *n.pl. (construed as sing.)* The branch of medicine that treats of remedies for disease. —**ther′a·peu′tist** *n.*

ther·a·py (ther′ə·pē) *n. pl.* **·pies** **1** The treatment of disease or any bodily disorder or injury by drugs, physical exercise, etc. **2** PSYCHOTHERAPY. [< Gk. *therapeuein* take care of] —**ther′a·pist** *n.*

there (thâr) *adv.* **1** In or at that place; in a place other than that of the speaker. **2** To, toward, or into that place; thither. **3** At that stage or point of action or proceeding. **4** In that respect, relation, or connection. —*n.* That place, position, or point: We moved it from *there* to here. [< OE *thær*] • *There* is also used: **a** As a pronominal expletive introducing a clause or sentence, the subject usually following the verb: *There* once lived three bears. **b** With independent phrases or clauses, as an equivalent of *that,* expressing encouragement, approval, etc.: *There's* a little dear. **c** As an exclamation expressing triumph, etc.: *There!* I told you so.

there·a·bouts (thâr′ə·bouts′, thâr′ə·bouts′) *adv.* Near that number, quantity, degree, place, or time; approximately. Also **there′a·bout′** (-bout′).

there·af·ter (thâr′af′tər, -äf′-) *adv.* **1** Afterward; from that time on. **2** Accordingly.

there·at (thâr′at′) *adv.* At that event, place, or time; at that incentive; upon that.

there·by (thâr′bī′, thâr′bī′) *adv.* **1** Through the agency of that. **2** Connected with that. **3** Conformably to that. **4** Nearby; thereabout. **5** By it or that; into possession of it or that: How did you come *thereby?*

there·for (thâr′fôr′) *adv.* For this, that, or it; in return or requital for this or that: We return thanks *therefor*.

there·fore (thâr′fôr′, -fōr′) *adv. & conj.* **1** For that or this reason. **2** Consequently: He did not run fast enough; *therefore* he lost the race.

there·from (thâr′frum′, -from′) *adv.* From this, that, or it; from this or that time, place, state, event, or thing.

there·in (thâr′in′) *adv.* **1** In that place. **2** In that time, matter, or respect.

there·in·af·ter (thâr′in·af′tər, -äf′-) *adv.* In a subsequent part of that (book, document, speech, etc.).

there·in·to (thâr′in·tōō′, thâr·in′tōō) *adv.* Into this, that, or it.

there·of (thâr′uv′, -ov′) *adv.* **1** Of or relating to this, that, or it. **2** From or because of this or that cause or particular; therefrom.

there·on (thâr′on′, -ôn′) *adv.* **1** On this, that, or it. **2** Thereupon; thereat.

there's (thârz) Contraction of *there is.*

there·to (thâr′tōō′) *adv.* **1** To this, that, or it. **2** In addition; furthermore. Also **there·un·to** (thâr′un′tōō, -un·tōō′).

there·to·fore (thâr′tə·fôr′, -fōr′, thâr′tə·fôr′, -fōr′) *adv.* Before this or that; previously to that.

there·un·der (thâr′un′dər) *adv.* **1** Under this or that. **2** Less, as in number. **3** In a lower or lesser status or rank.

there·up·on (thâr′ə·pon′, -pôn′, thâr′ə·pon′, -ə·pôn′) *adv.* **1** Upon that; upon it. **2** Following upon or in consequence of that. **3** Immediately following; at once.

there·with (thâr′with′, -with′) *adv.* **1** With this, that, or it. **2** Thereupon; thereafter; immediately afterward.

there·with·al (thâr′with·ôl′) *adv.* With all this or that; besides.

ther·mal (thûr′məl) *adj.* **1** Of, coming from, or having hot springs. **2** Of, relating to, or caused by heat. **3** Hot or warm: a *thermal* draft. **4** Aiding to conserve body heat: *thermal* fabrics. Also **ther′mic.** —*n.* A rising current of warm air in the atmosphere. [< Gk. *thermē* heat]

thermo- *combining form* Heat; of, related to, or caused by heat: *thermodynamics.* [< Gk. *thermos* heat, warmth]

ther·mo·dy·nam·ics (thûr′mō·dī·nam′iks, -di-) *n.pl.* *(construed as sing.)* The branch of physics that deals with the relations between heat, other forms of energy, and work. —**ther′mo·dy·nam′ic** or **·i·cal** *adj.* —**ther′mo·dy·nam′i·cist** (-nam′ə·sist) *n.*

ther·mo·e·lec·tric·i·ty (thûr′mō·i·lek′tris′ə·tē) *n.* Electricity generated by heat. —**ther′mo·e·lec′tric** or **·tri·cal** *adj.* —**ther′mo·e·lec′tri·cal·ly** *adv.*

ther·mo·gram (thûr′mə·gram) *n.* The record made by a thermograph.

ther·mo·graph (thûr′mə·graf, -gräf) *n.* **1** An instrument for detecting and recording temperature gradations across a surface. **2** A self-registering thermometer.

ther·mog·ra·phy (thər·mog′rə·fē) *n.* **1** The process of recording temperature variations with a thermograph. **2** A process that produces raised lettering on paper, as on stationery, by applying a powder to the lettering and then subjecting it to heat. —**ther·mo·graph·ic** (thûr′mə·graf′ik) *adj.*

ther·mom·e·ter (thər·mom′ə·tər) *n.* An instrument for measuring temperature, often consisting of a tube with a bulb containing a liquid which expands or contracts so that its height in the tube is proportional to the temperature. —**ther·mo·met·ric** (thûr′mō·met′rik) or **·ri·cal** *adj.* —**ther′mo·met′ri·cal·ly** *adv.*

ther·mo·nu·cle·ar (thûr′mō·n⁽ʸ⁾ōō′klē·ər) *adj.* *Physics*

Pertaining to or characterized by reactions involving the fusion of light atomic nuclei subjected to very high temperatures.

ther·mo·plas·tic (thûr′mō·plas′tik) *adj.* Becoming soft when heated, as certain synthetic resins. —*n.* A thermoplastic substance or material.

Ther·mop·y·lae (thər·mop′ə·lē) *n.* A narrow mountain pass in Greece; scene of a battle, 480 B.C., in which the Spartans held off the Persians and finally died to the last man rather than yield.

ther·mos (thûr′məs) *n.* A container having two walls separated by a vacuum which serves to retard transfer of heat to or from the contents. Also **thermos bottle.** [< *Thermos*, a trade name]

ther·mo·set·ting (thûr′mō·set′ing) *adj.* Permanently assuming a fixed shape when heated, as certain synthetic resins.

ther·mo·stat (thûr′mə·stat) *n.* An automatic control device used to maintain a desired temperature. [< THERMO- + Gk. *statos* standing] —**ther′mo·stat′ic** *adj.* —**ther′mo·stat′i·cal·ly** *adv.*

ther·mot·ro·pism (thər·mot′rə·piz′əm) *n.* *Biol.* Movement or growth in a direction determined by the location of a heat source. —**ther·mo·trop·ic** (thûr′mō·trop′ik) *adj.* —**ther′mo·trop′i·cal·ly** *adv.*

the·sau·rus (thi·sôr′əs) *n. pl* **·sau·ri** (-sôr′ī) or **sau·rus·es** **1** A book containing words and their synonyms grouped together. **2** A book containing words or facts dealing with a specific subject or field. [< Gk. *thēsauros* treasure]

these (thēz) *pl.* of THIS.

The·seus (thē′sōōs, -sē·əs) *Gk. Myth.* The chief hero of Attica, celebrated chiefly for killing the Minotaur, and for unifying Attica with Athens as its capital. —**The′se·an** (-sē·ən) *adj.*

the·sis (thē′sis) *n. pl.* **·ses** (-sēz) **1** A proposition, esp. a formal proposition advanced and defended by argumentation. **2** A formal treatise on a particular subject, esp. a dissertation presented by a candidate for an advanced academic degree. **3 a** *Logic* An affirmative proposition. **b** An unproved premise or postulate, as opposed to a hypothesis. [< Gk., a placing, proposition]

thes·pi·an (thes′pē·ən) *adj. Often cap.* Of or relating to drama; dramatic. —*n.* An actor or actress. [< *Thespis*, 6th-c. B.C. Gk. poet]

Thess. Thessalonians.

Thes·sa·lo·ni·ans (thes′ə·lō′nē·ənz) *n.pl. (construed as sing.)* Either of two epistles in the New Testament (**First** and **Second Thessalonians**) written by St. Paul to the Christians of Thessalonica.

Thes·sa·lo·ni·ca (thes′ə·lə·nī′kə, -lon′i·kə) *n.* An ancient city of N Greece.

the·ta (thā′tə, thē′tə) *n.* The eighth letter in the Greek alphabet (Θ, ϑ, θ).

thew (thyōō) *n.* **1** A sinew or muscle. **2** *pl.* Bodily strength or vigor. [< OE *thēaw* habit, characteristic quality]

they (thā) *pron.* **1** The persons, beings, or things previously mentioned or understood: the nominative plural of *he, she, it.* **2** People in general: *They* say that the fishing is excellent in this area. [< ON *their*]

they'd (thād) Contraction of *they had* or *they would.*

they'll (thāl) Contraction of *they shall* or *they will.*

they're (thâr) Contraction of *they are.*

they've (thāv) Contraction of *they have.*

T.H.I., T.-H.I. temperature-humidity index.

thi·a·mine (thī′ə·min, -mēn) *n.* Vitamin B₁, a compound found in cereal grains, liver, egg yolk, etc., and also made synthetically. Also **thi′a·min** (-min). [< THI(O)- + -AMINE]

thick (thik) *adj.* **1** Relatively large in depth or extent from one surface to its opposite; not thin. **2** Having a specified dimension of this kind, whether great or small: an inch *thick.* **3** Having the constituent or specified elements growing, packed, arranged, etc., close together: a field *thick* with daisies. **4** Viscous in consistency: a *thick* sauce. **5** Heavy; dense: a *thick* fog. **6** Foggy, hazy, smoky, etc. **7** Very dark; impenetrable: a *thick* gloom. **8** Indistinct; muffled; guttural, as speech. **9** Very noticeable; decided: a *thick* German accent. **10** *Informal* Dull; stupid. **11** *Informal* Very friendly; intimate. **12** *Informal* Going beyond what is tolerable; excessive. —*adv.* In a thick manner. —

n. The thickest or most intense time or place of anything: the *thick* of the fight. [< OE *thicce*] —**thick′ish** *adj.* — **thick′ly** *adv.* —**thick′ness** *n.*

thick·en (thik′ən) *v.t. & v.i.* **1** To make or become thick or thicker. **2** To make or become more intricate or intense: The plot *thickens*. —**thick′en·er** *n.*

thick·en·ing (thik′ən·ing) *n.* **1** The act of making or becoming thick. **2** Something added to a liquid to make it thicker. **3** That part which is or has been thickened.

thick·et (thik′it) *n.* A thick growth, as of underbrush. [< OE *thiccet* < *thicce* thick]

thick·head (thik′hed′) *n.* A stupid person. —**thick′head′·ed** *adj.* —**thick′head′ed·ness** *n.*

thick·set (thik′set′) *adj.* **1** Having a short, thick body; stocky. **2** Closely planted.

thick-skinned (thik′skind′) *adj.* **1** Having a thick skin, as a pachyderm. **2** Insensitive; callous to hints or insults.

thick-wit·ted (thik′wit′id) *adj.* Stupid; obtuse.

thief (thēf) *n. pl.* **thieves** (thēvz) One who takes something belonging to another, esp. secretly. [< OE *thēof*]

thieve (thēv) *v.* **thieved, thiev·ing** *v.t.* To take by theft; purloin; steal. —*v.i.* To be a thief; commit theft. [< OE *thēofian*]

thiev·er·y (thē′vər·ē) *n. pl.* **·er·ies** The practice or act of thieving; theft; also, an instance of thieving. —**thiev′ish** *adj.* —**thiev′ish·ly** *adv.* —**thiev′ish·ness** *n.*

thigh (thī) *n.* **1** The human leg between the hip and the knee. **2** The corresponding portion in other animals. [< OE *thēoh*]

thigh·bone (thī′bōn′) *n.* FEMUR. Also **thigh bone.**

thim·ble (thim′bəl) *n.* **1** In sewing, a pitted cover worn to protect the finger that pushes the needle. **2** Any similar device, esp. a ring on a rope to prevent chafing. [< OE *thȳmel* < *thūma* thumb]

thin (thin) *adj.* **thin·ner, thin·nest** **1** Having opposite surfaces relatively close to each other; being of little depth or width; not thick. **2** Lean and slender of figure. **3** Having the component parts or particles scattered or diffused; rarefied: a *thin* gas. **4** Not large or abundant, as in number: a *thin* audience. **5** Lacking thickness of consistency: a *thin* sauce. **6** Not dense or heavy: a *thin* fog. **7** Having little intensity or richness: a *thin* red. **8** Having little volume or resonance; shrill, as a voice. **9** Of a loose or light texture: *thin* clothing. **10** Insufficient; flimsy: a *thin* excuse. **11** Lacking essential ingredients or qualities: *thin* blood. **12** Meager; scant: *thin* hair. **13** Lacking vigor, force, substance, complexity, etc.; superficial; slight: *thin* humor. —*adv.* In a thin way: Slice the sausage *thin*. —*v.t. & v.i.* **thinned, thin·ning** To make or become thin or thinner. [< OE *thynne*] —**thin′ly** *adv.* —**thin′ness** *n.*

thine (thīn) *pron.* *Archaic* The things or persons belonging to thee: thou and *thine*. —*pronominal adj.* *Archaic* Thy: *thine* eyes. [< OE *thīn*]

thing (thing) *n.* **1** That which exists or is conceived to exist as a separate entity: all the *things* in the world. **2** That which is designated, as contrasted with the word or symbol used to denote it. **3** A matter or circumstance: *Things* have changed. **4** An act, deed, event, etc.: That was a shameless *thing* to do. **5** A procedure or step, as in an ordered course or process: the first *thing* to do. **6** An item, particular, detail, etc.: each *thing* on the schedule. **7** A statement or expression; utterance: to say the right *thing*. **8** An idea; opinion; notion: Stop putting *things* in her head. **9** A quality; attribute; characteristic: Kindness is a precious *thing*. **10** An inanimate object. **11** An object that is not or cannot be described or particularized: What kind of *thing* is that? **12** A person, regarded in terms of pity, affection, or contempt: that poor *thing*. **13** *pl.* Possessions; belongings: to pack one's *things*. **14** *pl.* Clothes; esp. outer garments. **15** A piece of clothing, as a dress: not a *thing* to wear. **16** A piece of literature, art, music, etc.: He read a few *things* by Byron. **17** The proper or befitting act or result: with *the:* That was not the *thing* to do. **18** The important point, attitude, etc.: with *the:* The *thing* one learns from travel is how to combat fatigue. **19** *Informal* A point; issue; case: He always makes a big *thing* out of

dividing up the bill. **20** *Informal* A strong liking, disliking, fear, attraction, etc.: to have a *thing* for tall girls. **21** *Law* A subject or property or dominion, as distinguished from a person. —**do one's (own) thing** *Slang* To express oneself by doing what one wants to do or can do well or is in the habit of doing. [< OE, thing, cause, assembly]

thing·a·ma·bob (thing′ə·mə·bob′) *n.* *Informal* THINGAMAJIG. Also **thing′um·a·bob′, thing′um·bob.**

thing·a·ma·jig (thing′ə·mə·jig′) *n.* *Informal* A thing the specific name of which is unknown or forgotten. Also **thing′um·a·jig′.**

think[1] (thingk) *v.* **thought** (thôt), **think·ing** *v.t.* **1** To produce or form in the mind; conceive mentally: to *think* evil thoughts. **2** To examine in the mind; meditate upon, or determine by reasoning: to *think* a plan through. **3** To believe; consider: I *think* him guilty. **4** To expect; anticipate: They did not *think* to meet us. **5** To bring to mind; remember; recollect: I cannot *think* what he said. **6** To have the mind preoccupied by: to *think* business morning, noon, and night. **7** To intend; purpose: Do they *think* to rob me? —*v.i.* **8** To use the mind or intellect in exercising judgment, forming ideas, etc.; engage in rational thought; reason. **9** To have a particular opinion, sentiment, or feeling: I don't *think* so. —**think of** (or **about**) **1** To bring to mind; remember; recollect. **2** To conceive in the mind; invent; imagine. **3** To have a specified opinion or attitude toward; regard. **4** To be considerate of; have regard for. — **think over** To reflect upon; ponder. —**think up** To devise, arrive at, or invent by thinking. —*n.* *Informal* The act of thinking. [< OE *thencan*] —**think′er** *n.*

think[2] (thingk) *v.i.* To seem; appear: now obsolete except with the pronoun as indirect object in the combinations *methinks, methought.* [< OE *thyncan* seem]

think·a·ble (thingk′ə·bəl) *adj.* **1** Susceptible of being thought; conceivable. **2** Possible.

think·ing (thingk′ing) *adj.* Using or given to using the mind; intellectually active. —*n.* **1** The act or process of using the mind to think. **2** A result of thought; opinion or position. —**think′ing·ly** *adv.*

think tank *Informal* **1** A group of people (**think tank·ers**), usu. academics, business executives, or government employees, organized for the investigation and study of social, scientific, and technological problems. **2** The place in which such a group works.

thin·ner (thin′ər) *n.* One who or that which thins, esp. a liquid added to a viscid substance to thin it.

thin-skinned (thin′skind′) *adj.* **1** Having a thin skin. **2** Easily offended; sensitive.

thio- *combining form* Containing sulfur: *thiosulfate.* [< Gk. *theion* sulfur]

thi·o·sul·fate (thī′ō·sul′fāt) *n.* Any salt of thiosulfuric acid, esp. sodium thiosulfate.

thi·o·sul·fu·ric acid (thī′ō·sul·fyŏŏr′ik) An unstable acid, known chiefly by its salts, which are used in bleaching and photography.

third (thûrd) *adj. & adv.* **1** Next in order after the second. **2** Being one of three equal parts. —*n.* **1** The element of an ordered set that corresponds to the number three. **2** One of three equal parts. **3** *Music* The interval between any tone and another two steps away in a diatonic scale. **4** In baseball, the third base. [< OE *thridda*]

third-class (thûrd′klas′, -kläs′) *adj.* **1** Ranking next below the second or second best. **2** Of, pertaining to, or belonging to a class next below the second: *third-class* mail. —*adv.* By third-class accommodations or mail.

third degree *Informal* Severe or brutal examination of a prisoner for the purpose of securing information or a confession.

third estate The common people, traditionally ranked after the nobility and the clergy.

third·ly (thûrd′lē) *adv.* Third.

third person The form of the pronoun, as *he, she, it,* to indicate the person or thing spoken of, or the grammatical form of the verb referring to such person or thing.

third rail An insulated rail on an electric railway for supplying current to the trains or cars.

third-rate (thûrd′rāt′) *adj.* **1** Third in rating or class. **2** Of poor quality; inferior.

third world 1 Any or all of the underdeveloped countries in the world, esp. such countries in Asia or Africa that are not aligned with either the Communist or non-Communist nations. **2** Those not resident in the countries of the third world but collectively identified with their peoples, as because of ideology, ethnic background, or disadvantaged status. Also **Third World.**

thirst (thûrst) *n.* **1** Discomfort or distress due to a need for water. **2** A craving or taste for any specified liquid: a *thirst* for alcohol. **3** Any longing or craving: a *thirst* for glory. — *v.i.* **1** To feel thirst; be thirsty. **2** To have an eager desire or craving. [< OE *thurst*] —**thirst′er** *n.*

thirst·y (thûrs′tē) *adj.* **thirst·i·er, thirst·i·est 1** Affected with thirst. **2** Lacking moisture; arid; parched. **3** Eagerly desirous. **4** *Informal* Causing thirst. [< OE *thurstig*] —**thirst′i·ly** *adv.* —**thirst′i·ness** *n.*

thir·teen (thûr′tēn′) *n.* **1** The sum of 12 plus 1; 13; XIII. **2** A set or group of 13 members. [< OE *thrēotēne*] —**thir′teen′** *adj., pron.*

thir·teenth (thûr′tēnth′) *adj. & adv.* Next in order after the 12th. —*n.* **1** The element of an ordered set that corresponds to the number 13. **2** One of 13 equal parts.

thir·ti·eth (thûr′tē·ith) *adj. & adv.* Tenth in order after the 20th. —*n.* **1** The element of an ordered set that corresponds to the number 30. **2** One of 30 equal parts.

thir·ty (thûr′tē) *n. pl.* **·ties 1** The product of three and ten. **2** A set or group of 30 members. **3** *pl.* The numbers, years, etc. from 30 to 40. [< OE *thrītig*] —**thir′ty** *adj., pron.*

thir·ty-sec·ond note (thûr′tē·sek′ənd) *Music* A note having one thirty-second of the time value of a whole note. • See NOTE.

this (this) *adj. pl.* **these 1** That is near or present, either actually or in thought: *This* house is for sale; I shall be there *this* evening. **2** That is understood or has just been mentioned: *This* offense justified my revenge. **3** That is nearer than or contrasted with something else: opposed to *that: This* tree is still alive, but that one is dead. —*pron. pl.* **these 1** The person or thing near or present, being understood or just mentioned: *This* is where I live; *This* is the guilty man. **2** The person or thing nearer than or contrasted with something else: opposed to *that: This* is a better painting than that. **3** The idea, statement, etc., about to be made clear: I will say *this:* he is a hard worker. —*adv.* To this degree; thus or so: I was not expecting you *this* soon. [< OE]

this·tle (this′əl) *n.* Any of various prickly plants with cylindrical or globular heads of composite flowers. [< OE *thistel*] —**this′tly** *adj.*

this·tle·down (this′əl·doun′) *n.* The silky fibers of the ripening flower of a thistle.

thith·er (thith′ər, thith′-) *adv.* To that place; in that direction. —*adj.* Situated or being on the other side; more distant. [< OE *thider*]

thith·er·to (thith′ər·tōō′, thith′-) *adv.* Up to that time.

Thistle

thith·er·ward (thith′ər·wərd, thith′-) *adv.* In that direction; toward that place. Also **thith′er·wards.**

tho (thō) *conj. & adv.* THOUGH.

thole (thōl) *n.* A pin or pair of pins serving as a fulcrum for an oar in rowing. Also **thole pin.** [< OE *thol*]

Tho·mism (tō′miz·əm) *n.* The theological and philosophical doctrines of St. Thomas Aquinas. [< St. *Thomas* Aquinas] —**Tho′mist** *adj., n.*

thong (thông, thong) *n.* **1** A narrow strip, usu. of leather, as for fastening. **2** A lash of a whip. [< OE *thwang* thong]

Thor (thôr, tôr) *Norse Myth.* The god of war and thunder and son of Odin.

tho·rax (thôr′aks, thō′raks) *n. pl.* **tho·rax·es** or **tho·ra·ces** (thôr′ə·sēz, thō′rə-) **1** The part of the body between the neck and the abdomen, enclosed by the ribs. **2** The middle segment between the head and abdomen of an insect. • See INSECT. [< Gk. *thōrax*] —**tho·rac·ic** (thō·ras′ik) *adj.*

tho·ri·um (thôr′ē·əm, thō′rē-) *n.* A rare, radioactive, metallic element (symbol Th) used as a fuel in certain nuclear reactors. [< THOR] —**tho′ric** *adj.*

thorn (thôrn) *n.* **1** A sharp, rigid outgrowth from a plant stem. **2** Any of various thorn-bearing shrubs or trees. **3** A cause of discomfort, pain, or annoyance. **4** The name of the Old English rune þ, equivalent to *th*, as in *thorn,* from which it derives its name. —*v.t.* To pierce or prick with a thorn. [< OE] —**thorn′less** *adj.*

thorn apple 1 JIMSONWEED. **2** HAW².

thorn·y (thôr′nē) *adj.* **thorn·i·er, thorn·i·est 1** Full of thorns; spiny. **2** Sharp like a thorn. **3** Full of difficulties or trials; painful; vexatious. —**thorn′i·ness** *n.*

tho·ron (thôr′on, thō′ron) *n.* A radioactive isotope of radon, resulting from the disintegration of thorium and having a half-life of 54.5 seconds.

thor·ough (thûr′ō, thûr′ə) *adj.* **1** Complete; exhaustive: a *thorough* search. **2** Attentive to details and accuracy; painstaking: a *thorough* worker. **3** Completely (such and such); through and through: a *thorough* nincompoop. [Emphatic var. of THROUGH] —**thor′ough·ly** *adv.* —**thor′ough·ness** *n.* —**Syn. 1** comprehensive, sweeping, out-and-out, total. **2** exact, precise, meticulous, careful, conscientious. **3** absolute, downright, utter, unmitigated, perfect.

thor·ough·bred (thûr′ə·bred′) *adj.* **1** Bred from pure stock; pedigreed. **2** Possessing or showing excellence, as in training, education, manners, culture, etc.; first-rate. —*n.* **1** A thoroughbred animal. **2** A person of culture and good breeding.

Thor·ough·bred (thûr′ə·bred′) *n.* A breed of English race horse, originally developed by mating Arabian stallions with English mares.

thor·ough·fare (thûr′ō·fâr′, thûr′ə-) *n.* **1** A much-frequented road or street through which the public have unobstructed passage. **2** A passage: now chiefly in the phrase **no thoroughfare.** [< OE *thurh* through + *faru* going]

thor·ough·go·ing (thûr′ō·gō′ing, thûr′ə-) *adj.* **1** Characterized by extreme thoroughness or efficiency. **2** Unmitigated; out-and-out.

those (thōz) *adj. & pron. pl.* of THAT. [< OE *thās*]

thou (thou) *pron.* The person spoken to, as denoted in the nominative case: archaic except in religious or poetic language, or in certain dialects. [< OE *thū*]

though (thō) *conj.* **1** Notwithstanding the fact that; although: *Though* he was sleepy, he stayed awake. **2** Granting that; even if: *Though* she may win, she will have lost her popularity. **3** And yet; still; however: I am well, *though* I do not feel very strong. —*adv.* Notwithstanding; nevertheless: It's not a good play, but I like it *though.* [< ON *thō*]

thought[1] (thôt) *n.* **1** The act or process of thinking. **2** The product of thinking, as an idea, concept, judgment, opinion, or the like. **3** Intellectual activity of a specific kind, time, place, etc.: Greek *thought.* **4** Consideration; attention; heed: Give the plan some *thought.* **5** Intention; plan; design: All *thought* of returning was abandoned. **6** Expectation; anticipation: He had no *thought* of finding her there. **7** A trifle; a small amount: Be a *thought* more cautious. [< THOUGHT²]

thought[2] (thôt) *p.t. & p.p.* of THINK. [< OE *thōht*]

thought·ful (thôt′fəl) *adj.* **1** Full of thought; meditative. **2** Showing, characterized by, or promoting thought. **3** Attentive; careful, esp. manifesting regard for others; considerate. —**thought′ful·ly** *adv.* —**thought′ful·ness** *n.*

thought·less (thôt′lis) *adj.* **1** Manifesting lack of thought or care; careless. **2** Not considerate of others. **3** Giddy; flighty. —**thought′less·ly** *adv.* —**thought′less·ness** *n.*

thou·sand (thou′zənd) *n.* **1** The product of ten times a hundred. **2** *Usu. pl.* An indefinitely large number. —*adj.* Consisting of a hundred times ten. [< OE *thūsend*] —**thou′sand·fold′** (-fōld′) *adj., adv.*

thou·sandth (thou′zəndth) *adj.* **1** Last in a series of a thousand. **2** Being one of a thousand equal parts. —*n.* **1** The element of an ordered set that corresponds to the number 1000. **2** One of a thousand equal parts.

thrall (thrôl) *n.* **1** A person in bondage; a slave; serf. **2** One controlled by a passion or vice. **3** Slavery. [< ON *thræl*]

thrall·dom (thrôl′dəm) *n.* **1** The state of being a thrall. **2** Any sort of bondage or servitude. Also **thral′dom.**

thrash (thrash) *v.t.* **1** To thresh, as grain. **2** To beat as if with a flail; flog; whip. **3** To move or swing with flailing, violent motions. **4** To defeat utterly. —*v.i.* **5** To move or swing about with flailing, violent motions. **6** To make one's way by thrashing. —**thrash out** (or **over**) To discuss fully and usu. come to a conclusion. —*n.* The act of thrashing. [Dial. var. of THRESH]

thrash·er[1] (thrash′ər) *n.* **1** One who or that which thrashes. **2** A machine for threshing grain. **3** THRESHER (def. 2).

thrash·er[2] (thrash′ər) *n.* Any of several long-tailed American songbirds resembling the thrushes and related to the mockingbirds. [?< THRUSH[1]]

thread (thred) *n.* **1** A very slender cord or line composed of two or more filaments, as of flax, cotton, silk, nylon, etc., twisted together. **2** A filament of metal, glass, etc. **3** A fine beam: a *thread* of light. **4** Something that runs a continuous course through a series or whole: the *thread* of his discourse. **5** *Mech.* The helical ridge of a screw. —*v.t.* **1** To pass a thread through the eye of: to *thread* a needle. **2** To string on a thread, as beads. **3** To cut a thread on or in, as a screw. **4** To make one's way through or over: to *thread* a maze. **5** To make (one's way) carefully. —*v.i.* **6** To make one's way carefully. **7** To fall from a fork or spoon in a fine thread: said of boiling syrup. [< OE *thrǣd*] —**thread′er** *n.*

thread·bare (thred′bâr′) *adj.* **1** Worn so that the threads show, as a rug or garment. **2** Clad in worn garments. **3** Commonplace; hackneyed. —**thread′bare′ness** *n.* —**Syn.** **2** shabby. **3** common, stale, stereotyped, trite.

thread·y (thred′ē) *adj.* **thread·i·er, thread·i·est** **1** Like a thread; stringy. **2** Forming threads, as some liquids. **3** Weak; lacking vigor: a *thready* pulse. —**thread′i·ness** *n.*

threat (thret) *n.* **1** A declaration of an intention to inflict injury or pain. **2** Any menace or danger. [< OE *threat* crowd, oppression]

threat·en (thret′n) *v.t.* **1** To utter threats against. **2** To be menacing or dangerous to. **3** To portend (something unpleasant or dangerous). **4** To utter threats of (injury, vengeance, etc.). —*v.i.* **5** To utter threats. **6** To have a menacing aspect; lower. —**threat′en·er** *n.* —**threat′en·ing·ly** *adv.*

three (thrē) *n.* **1** The sum of two plus one; 3, III. **2** A set or group of three members. [< OE *thrī*] —**three** *adj., pron.*

three-D (thrē′dē′) *adj.* THREE-DIMENSIONAL. —*n.* A technique, medium, or process giving the appearance of three dimensions to visual images. Also **3-D.**

three-deck·er (thrē′dek′ər) *n.* **1** A vessel having three decks or gun decks. **2** Anything having three levels.

three-di·men·sion·al (thrē′də·men′shən·əl) *adj.* **1** Of or having three dimensions. **2** Appearing to have depth as well as height and width.

three·fold (thrē′fōld′) *adj.* **1** Made up of three parts. **2** Having three times as many or as much. —*adv.* Triply; in a threefold manner.

three-mile limit (thrē′mīl′) A distance of three geographic miles from the shore line seaward, allowed by international law for territorial jurisdiction.

three·pence (thrip′əns, threp′-, thrup′-) *n. Brit.* **1** The sum of three pennies. **2** A small coin of Great Britain worth three pennies: also **thrip′pence** (thrip′əns).

three-ply (thrē′plī′) *adj.* Consisting of three thicknesses, strands, layers, etc.

three R's Reading, writing, and arithmetic.

three·score (thrē′skôr′, -skōr′) *adj. & n.* Sixty.

three·some (thrē′səm) *n.* **1** A group of three people. **2** A game played by three people; also, the players.

thren·o·dy (thren′ə·dē) *n. pl.* **·dies** An ode or song of lamentation; a dirge. Also **thren′ode** (-ōd) [< Gk. *thrēnos* lament + *ōidē* song] —**thre·nod·ic** (thri·nod′ik) *adj.* —**thren′o·dist** *n.*

thresh (thresh) *v.t.* **1** To beat stalks of (ripened grain) with a flail so as to separate the grain from the husks. —*v.i.* **2** To thresh grain. **3** To move or thrash about. —**thresh out** To discuss fully and to a conclusion. —**thresh over** To discuss over and over. [< OE *therscan*]

thresh·er (thresh′ər) *n.* **1** One who or that which threshes, esp. a machine for threshing. **2** A large shark having an extremely long tail: also **thresher shark.**

thresh·old (thresh′ōld, -hōld) *n.* **1** The plank, timber, or

stone lying under the door of a building; doorsill. **2** The entering point or beginning of anything: the *threshold* of the 20th century. **3** The minimum degree of stimulation necessary to produce a response or to be perceived. [< OE *therscold*]

threw (thrōō) *p.t.* of THROW.

thrice (thrīs) *adv.* **1** Three times. **2** Fully; extremely. [< OE *thriwa* thrice]

thrift (thrift) *n.* Care and wisdom in the management of one's resources; frugality. [< ON] —**thrift′less** *adj.* —**thrift′less·ly** *adv.* —**thrift′less·ness** *n.*

thrift·y (thrif′tē) *adj.* **thrift·i·er, thrift·i·est** **1** Displaying thrift or good management; frugal. **2** Prosperous; thriving. —**thrift′i·ly** *adv.* —**thrift′i·ness** *n.* —**Syn.** **1** economical, provident, prudent, saving.

thrill (thril) *v.t.* **1** To cause to feel a great or tingling excitement. —*v.i.* **2** To feel a sudden wave of emotion. **3** To vibrate or tremble; quiver. —*n.* **1** A feeling of excitement. **2** A thrilling quality. **3** A pulsation; quiver. [< OE *thyrlian* pierce] —**thrill′ing·ly** *adv.*

thrill·er (thril′ər) *n.* **1** One who or that which thrills. **2** *Informal* An exciting book, play, etc.

thrive (thrīv) *v.i.* **throve** (thrōv) or **thrived, thrived** or **thriv·en** (thriv′ən), **thriv·ing** **1** To prosper; be successful. **2** To flourish. [< ON *thrífast* reflexive of *thrífa* grasp] —**thriv′er** *n.* —**thriv′ing·ly** *adv.*

throat (thrōt) *n.* **1** The front part of the neck. **2** The passage extending from the back of the mouth and containing the epiglottis, larynx, trachea, and pharynx. **3** Any narrow passage resembling a throat. —**jump down one's throat** To scold or criticize with sudden violence. —**lump in the throat** A feeling of tightness in the throat, as from strong emotion. —**stick in one's throat** To be difficult or painful to say. [< OE *throte*]

Throat
a. soft palate. b. pharynx. c. epiglottis. d. esophagus. e. trachea.

throat·y (thrō′tē) *adj.* **throat·i·er, throat·i·est** Uttered in the throat; guttural. —**throat′i·ly** *adv.* —**throat′i·ness** *n.*

throb (throb) *v.i.* **throbbed, throb·bing** **1** To pulsate rhythmically, as the heart. **2** To feel or show emotion by trembling. —*n.* **1** The act or state of throbbing. **2** A pulsation, esp. one caused by excitement or emotion. [Imit.] —**throb′ber** *n.*

throe (thrō) *n.* **1** A violent pang or pain. **2** *pl.* The pains of death or childbirth. **3** Any agonized or agonizing activity. [< OE *thrawe*]

throm·bin (throm′bin) *n.* An enzyme in blood serum that promotes clotting. [< Gk. *thrombos* clot]

throm·bo·sis (throm·bō′sis) *n.* The formation of a blood clot inside the heart or a blood vessel. [< Gk. *thrombos* clot] —**throm·bot·ic** (-bot′ik) *adj.*

throne (thrōn) *n.* **1** The chair occupied by a king, pope, etc., on state occasions. **2** The rank or authority of a king, queen, etc. —*v.t. & v.i.* **throned, thron·ing** To enthrone; exalt. [< Gk. *thronos* seat]

throng (thrông, throng) *n.* **1** A closely crowded multitude. **2** Any numerous collection. —*v.t.* **1** To crowd into and occupy fully; jam. **2** To crowd upon. —*v.i.* **3** To collect or move in a throng. [< OE *gethrang*] —**Syn.** *n.* **1** crowd, host, jam, mass, press.

throt·tle (throt′l) *n.* **1** A valve controlling the supply of fuel or steam to the cylinders of an engine: also **throttle valve.** **2** The lever which operates the throttle valve: also **throttle lever.** —*v.t.* **·tled, ·tling** **1** To strangle, choke, or suffocate. **2** To silence, stop, or suppress. **3** To reduce or shut off the flow of (steam or fuel to the cylinders of an engine). **4** To reduce the speed of by means of a throttle. —*v.i.* **5** To suffocate; choke. [Dim. of ME *throte* throat] —**throt′tler** *n.*

through (thrōō) *prep.* **1** From end to end, side to side, or limit to limit of; into at one side, end, or point, and out of at another. **2** Covering, entering, or penetrating all parts of; throughout. **3** From the first to the last of: *through* the day. **4** Here and there upon or in. **5** By way of: He departed *through* the door. **6** By the instrumentality or aid of. **7** Having reached the end of: He got *through* his examinations. —*adv.* **1** From one end, side, surface, etc., to or beyond another. **2** From beginning to end. **3** To a termination or conclusion: to pull *through*. **4** Completely; entirely: He is wet *through*. —**through and through** Thoroughly; completely. —*adj.* **1** Going to its destination without stops: a *through* train. **2** Usable or valid for an entire trip: a *through* ticket. **3** Extending from one side or surface to another. **4** Allowing unobstructed or direct passage: a *through* road. **5** Finished: Are you *through* with my pen? [< OE *thurh*]

through·out (throo-out′) *adv.* Through or in every part. —*prep.* All through; everywhere in.

throve (thrōv) *p.t.* of THRIVE.

throw (thrō) *v.* **threw** (throo), **thrown**, **throw·ing** *v.t.* **1** To propel through the air by means of a sudden straightening or whirling of the arm. **2** To propel or hurl. **3** To put hastily or carelessly: He *threw* a coat over his shoulders. **4** To direct or project (light, shadow, a glance, etc.). **5** To bring to a specified condition or state: to *throw* the enemy into a panic. **6** To cause to fall: The horse *threw* its rider. **7** In wrestling, to force the shoulders of (an opponent) to the ground. **8** To cast (dice). **9** To make a (specified cast) with dice. **10** To shed; lose: The horse *threw* a shoe. **11** *Informal* To lose purposely, as a race. **12** To move, as a lever or switch. **13** *Slang* To give (a party, etc.). **14** In ceramics, to shape on a potter's wheel. —*v.i.* **15** To cast or fling something. —**throw away** **1** To cast off; discard. **2** To squander. —**throw cold water on** To discourage. — **throw off** **1** To reject; spurn. **2** To rid oneself of. **3** To do or utter in an offhand manner. **4** To emit; discharge. **5** To confuse; mislead. **6** To elude (a pursuer). —**throw oneself at** To strive to gain the affection or love of. —**throw oneself into** To take part in vigorously. —**throw oneself on** (or **upon**) To rely on utterly. —**throw open** **1** To open suddenly, as a door. **2** To free from restrictions or obstacles. —**throw out** **1** To emit. **2** To discard; reject. **3** To utter as if accidentally: to *throw out* hints. **4** In baseball, to retire (a runner) by throwing the ball to the base toward which he is advancing. —**throw over** **1** To overturn. **2** To jilt. —**throw together** To put together carelessly. — **throw up** **1** To vomit. **2** To erect hastily. **3** To give up. **4** *Informal* To mention (something) repeatedly and reproachfully; taunt. —*n.* **1** An act of throwing. **2** The distance over which a missile may be thrown: a long *throw*. **3** A cast of dice, or the resulting number. **4** A scarf or other light covering. **5** In wrestling, a flooring of one's opponent so that both his shoulders touch the mat simultaneously for ten seconds. [< OE *thrāwan* to turn, twist, curl] — **throw′er** *n.* —**Syn.** *v.* **1** fling, heave, hurl, pitch.

throw·back (thrō′bak′) *n.* **1** An atavism. **2** A throwing back.

thru (throo) *adj., adv. & prep.* THROUGH.

thrum (thrum) *v.* **thrummed, thrum·ming** *v.t.* **1** To play on (a stringed instrument), esp. idly; strum. **2** To drum on monotonously with the fingers. —*v.i.* **3** To strum a stringed instrument. —*n.* The sound made by thrumming. [Prob. imit.]

thrush[1] (thrush) *n.* Any of many species of migratory songbirds, usu. having long wings and spotted under parts, as the **hermit thrush**, the **wood thrush**, the robin, and the blue-bird. [< OE *thrysce*]

thrush[2] (thrush) *n.* A disease of the mouth, lips, and throat caused by a yeastlike fungus. [?]

thrust (thrust) *v.* **thrust**, **thrust·ing** *v.t.* **1** To push or shove with force. **2** To pierce with a sudden forward motion, as with a sword. **3** To interpose. —*v.i.* **4** To make a sudden push or thrust. **5** To force oneself on or ahead: to *thrust* through a crowd. —*n.* **1** A sudden and forcible push, esp. with a pointed weapon. **2** A vigorous attack; sharp onset. **3** A force that drives or propels. **4** Salient force or mean-

Wood thrush

ing: the *thrust* of his remarks. [< ON *thrȳsta*] —**thrust′er** *n.* —**Syn.** *v.* **1** lunge. **2** stab, stick. *n.* **4** import, intention, significance, sense, gist.

thru·way (throo′wā′) *n.* EXPRESSWAY.

thud (thud) *n.* **1** A dull, heavy sound. **2** A blow causing such a sound; a thump. —*v.i.* **thud·ded, thud·ding** To strike or fall with a thud. [< OE *thyddan* strike, thrust, press]

thug (thug) *n.* **1** Formerly, one of an organization of religious assassins in India. **2** Any assassin or ruffian. [< Skt. *sthaga* swindler]

thu·li·um (thoo′lē-əm) *n.* A metallic element (symbol Tm) of the lanthanide series. [< *Thule*, the northernmost limit of the habitable world in ancient geography]

thumb (thum) *n.* **1** The short, thick digit of the human hand. **2** A similar part in certain animals. **3** The division in a glove or mitten that covers the thumb. —**all thumbs** Clumsy with the hands. —**thumbs down** A signal of negation or disapproval. —**thumbs up** A signal of approval. —**under one's thumb** Under one's influence or power. — *v.t.* **1** To rub, soil, or wear with the thumb in handling. **2** To handle clumsily. **3** To run through the pages of (a book, etc.) rapidly. —**thumb a ride** To get a ride by signaling with the thumb. [< OE *thūma*]

thumb index A series of scalloped indentations cut along the front edge of a book and labeled to indicate its various sections. —**thumb′-in′dex** *v.t.*

thumb·nail (thum′nāl′) *n.* **1** The nail of the thumb. **2** Anything as small as a thumbnail. —*adj.* Very brief: a *thumbnail* sketch.

thumb·screw (thum′skroo′) *n.* **1** A screw to be turned by thumb and fingers. • See SCREW. **2** An instrument of torture for compressing the thumb or thumbs.

thumb·tack (thum′tak′) *n.* A broad-headed tack that may be pushed in with the thumb.

thump (thump) *n.* **1** A blow with a blunt or heavy object. **2** The sound made by such a blow; a thud. —*v.t.* **1** To beat or strike so as to make a heavy thud or thump. **2** *Informal* To beat or defeat severely. —*v.i.* **3** To strike with a thump. **4** To pound or throb, as the heart. [Imit.] —**thump′er** *n.*

thun·der (thun′dər) *n.* **1** The sound that accompanies lightning, caused by the explosive effect of the electric discharge. **2** Any loud noise resembling thunder. **3** A vehement or powerful utterance. —**steal one's thunder** To undermine the effectiveness of an opponent by anticipating his next move, argument, etc. —*v.i.* **1** To give forth peals of thunder: It is *thundering*. **2** To make a noise like thunder. **3** To utter vehement denunciations. —*v.t.* **4** To utter or express with a noise like thunder: The cannon *thundered* defiance. [< OE *thunor*] —**thun′der·er** *n.*

thun·der·bolt (thun′dər·bōlt′) *n.* **1** A lightning flash accompanied by a clap of thunder. **2** A person or thing acting with great force, speed, or destructiveness.

thun·der·clap (thun′dər·klap′) *n.* **1** A sharp, violent detonation of thunder. **2** Anything violent or sudden.

thun·der·cloud (thun′dər·kloud′) *n.* A dark, heavy mass of electrically charged cloud.

thun·der·head (thun′dər·hed′) *n.* A rounded mass of silvery cumulus cloud, often developing into a thundercloud.

thun·der·ous (thun′dər·əs) *adj.* Producing or emitting thunder or a sound like thunder. —**thun′der·ous·ly** *adv.*

thun·der·show·er (thun′dər·shou′ər) *n.* A shower of rain with thunder and lightning.

thun·der·storm (thun′dər·stôrm′) *n.* A local storm accompanied by lightning and thunder.

thun·der·struck (thun′dər·struk′) *adj.* Amazed, astonished, or confounded. Also **thun′der·strick′en** (-strik′ən).

Thur., Thurs. Thursday.

thu·ri·ble (thoor′ə·bəl) *n.* CENSER. [< L *thus, thuris* frankincense]

Thurs·day (thûrz′dē, -dā) *n.* The fifth day of the week. [< OE *Thunres dæg* day of Thor]

thus (thus) *adv.* **1** In this or that or the following way. **2** To such degree or extent; so: *thus* far. **3** In this case; therefore. [< OE]

thwack (thwak) *v.t.* To strike heavily with something flat; whack. —*n.* A blow with something flat. [Prob. imit.] — **thwack′er** *n.*

thwart (thwôrt) *v.t.* To obstruct (a plan, a person, etc.) as by interposing an obstacle; frustrate. —*n.* **1** An oarsman's seat extending athwart a boat. **2** A brace athwart a canoe. —*adj.* Lying, moving, or extending across something; transverse. —*adv. & prep.* Athwart. [< ON *thvert*, neut. of *thverr* transverse] —**thwart′er** *n.*

thy (thī) *pronominal adj.* Belonging or pertaining to thee: *Thy* kingdom come. [< OE *thīn* THINE]

thyme (tīm) *n.* **1** Any of various small shrubby plants of the mint family, having aromatic leaves. **2** The dried leaves of certain thyme plants, used for seasoning in cookery. [< Gk. *thymon*] —**thy·mic** (-mik), **thym′y** *adj.*

thy·mus (thī′məs) *n.* A ductless glandlike structure situated at the root of the neck and usu. becoming atrophied after early childhood. [< Gk. *thymos*] • See THYROID.

thy·roid (thī′roid) *adj.* **1** Of or pertaining to the cartilage of the larynx which forms the Adam's apple. **2** Of, pertaining to, or describing a large ductless gland situated near the larynx on each side of the trachea and secreting thyroxin. —*n.* **1** The thyroid cartilage. **2** The thyroid gland. [< Gk. *thyreoeidēs* shield-shaped]

thy·rox·in (thī-rok′sin) *n.* **1** A vital hormone, secreted by the thyroid gland, which regulates growth and metabolism. **2** A white, crystalline compound, obtained from the thyroid glands of animals and also made synthetically, used in the treatment of thyroid disorders. Also **thy·rox′ine** (-sēn, -sin).

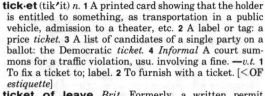

a. thyroid. b. thymus.

thyr·sus (thûr′səs) *n. pl.* **·si** (-sī, -sē) A staff wreathed in ivy and crowned with a pine cone or a bunch of ivy leaves, borne by Dionysus and the satyrs. [< Gk. *thyrsos*]

thy·self (thī-self′) *pron.* Emphatic or reflexive form of *thou:* I love thee for *thyself.*

ti (tē) *n. Music* In solmization, the seventh note of a diatonic scale. [Ital. See GAMUT.]

Ti titanium.

ti·ar·a (tē-âr′ə, -är′ə) *n.* **1** The pope's triple crown. **2** The upright headdress worn by the ancient Persian kings. **3** A jeweled head ornament or coronet worn by women on very formal or state occasions. [Gk., Persian headdress]

Ti·bet·an (ti-bet′n) *adj.* Of or pertaining to Tibet, the Tibetans, or to their language. —*n.* **1** An inhabitant or citizen of Tibet. **2** The language of Tibet.

tib·i·a (tib′ē-ə) *n. pl.* **tib·i·as** or **tib·i·ae** (tib′·ē-ē, -ē-ī) The inner and larger of the two bones of the leg below the knee; the shinbone. —**tib′i·al** *adj.*

Tibia

tic (tik) *n.* Any involuntary, recurrent muscular spasm. [F]

tick[1] (tik) *n.* **1** A light recurring sound made by a watch, clock, etc. **2** *Informal* The time elapsing between two ticks of a clock; an instant. **3** A mark, as a dot or dash, used in checking off something. —*v.i.* **1** To sound a tick or ticks. —*v.t.* **2** To mark or check with ticks. [Prob. imit.]

tick[2] (tik) *n.* **1** Any of numerous small, bloodsucking arachnids, parasitic on warm-blooded animals and often harboring and transmitting pathogenic microorganisms. **2** Any of certain usu. wingless parasitic insects. [< OE *ticia*]

tick[3] (tik) *n.* **1** The stout outer covering of a mattress; also, the material for such covering. **2** *Informal* Ticking. [< Gk. *thēke* a case]

Tick

tick[4] (tik) *n. Brit. Informal* Credit; trust: to buy merchandise on *tick.* [Short for TICK-ET]

tick·er (tik′ər) *n.* **1** One who or that which ticks. **2** Formerly, a telegraphic instrument that printed stock quotations on paper ribbon (**ticker tape**). **3** *Slang* The heart.

tick·et (tik′it) *n.* **1** A printed card showing that the holder is entitled to something, as transportation in a public vehicle, admission to a theater, etc. **2** A label or tag: a price *ticket.* **3** A list of candidates of a single party on a ballot: the Democratic *ticket.* **4** *Informal* A court summons for a traffic violation, usu. involving a fine. —*v.t.* **1** To fix a ticket to; label. **2** To furnish with a ticket. [< OF *estiquette*]

ticket of leave *Brit.* Formerly, a written permit granted to a convict to be at large before the expiration of his sentence.

tick·ing (tik′ing) *n.* A strong, closely woven cotton or linen fabric, used for mattress covering, awnings, etc. [< TICK[3]]

tick·le (tik′əl) *v.* **·led, ·ling** *v.t.* **1** To excite the nerves of by touching or scratching on some sensitive spot, producing a sensation resulting in spasmodic laughter or twitching. **2** To please: Compliments *tickle* our vanity. **3** To amuse or entertain; delight. **4** To move, stir, or get by tickling. —*v.i.* **5** To have a tingling sensation: My foot *tickles.* **6** To be ticklish. —*n.* **1** The sensation produced by tickling. **2** The touch or action producing such sensation. [ME *tikelen*]

tick·ler (tik′lər) *n.* **1** One who or that which tickles. **2** A memorandum book or file used as a reminder to attend to matters on certain dates in the future.

tick·lish (tik′lish) *adj.* **1** Sensitive to tickling. **2** Liable to be upset. **3** Easily offended; sensitive. **4** Requiring tact in handling; delicate: a *ticklish* situation. —**tick′lish·ly** *adv.* —**tick′lish·ness** *n.*

tick-tock (tik′tok′) *n.* The oscillating sound of a clock. —*v.i.* To make this sound. [Imit.]

tick·y tack·y (tik′ē tak′e) *Slang* **1** Shoddy, inferior materials: rows of little houses built of *ticky tacky.* **2** Dull, tedious uniformity. —**tick′y-tack′y** *adj.*

tid·al (tīd′l) *adj.* **1** Of, pertaining to, or influenced by the tides. **2** Dependent on the tide.

tidal wave 1 A great incoming rise of waters along a shore, caused by heavy winds and very high tides. **2** TSUNAMI. **3** A great upsurge, as of popular sentiment.

tid·bit (tid′bit′) *n.* A choice bit, as of food. [< dial. E *tid* a small object + BIT[1]]

tide (tīd) *n.* **1** The periodic rise and fall of the surface of the ocean caused by the gravitational attraction of moon and sun. **2** Anything that comes like the tide at flood. **3** The natural drift or tendency of events. **4** A current; stream: the *tide* of public feeling. **5** Season; time: *Easter-tide.* —**turn the tide** To reverse a condition completely. —*v.i.* **tid·ed, tid·ing** To ebb and flow like the tide. —**tide over 1** To give or act as temporary help, as in a difficulty. **2** To surmount. [< OE *tīd* a period, season]

tide·land (tīd′land′) *n.* **1** Land alternately covered and uncovered by the tide. **2** *Often pl.* Offshore land lying completely under the ocean, but within the limits of a nation's territorial waters.

tide·wa·ter (tīd′wô′tər, -wot′ər) *n.* **1** Water affected by the tide on the seacoast or in a river. **2** A region in which water is affected by the tide. —*adj.* Pertaining to or along a tidewater.

ti·dings (tī′dingz) *n.pl.* (*sometimes construed as sing.*) Information; news. [< OE *tīdung*]

ti·dy (tī′dē) *adj.* **·di·er, ·di·est 1** Neat in appearance; orderly: a *tidy* desk. **2** Keeping things in order: a *tidy* housekeeper. **3** *Informal* Moderately large: a *tidy* sum. **4** *Informal* Fairly good. —*v.t. & v.i.* **ti·died, ti·dy·ing** To put (things) in order. —*n. pl.* **·dies** An antimacassar. [< OE *tīd* time] —**ti′di·ly** *adv.* —**ti′di·ness** *n.* —**Syn.** *adj.* **1** shipshape, spruce, trim, well-kept.

tie (tī) *v.* **tied, ty·ing** *v.t.* **1** To fasten with cord, rope, etc., the ends of which are then knotted. **2** To draw the parts of together by a cord fastened with a knot: to *tie* one's shoes. **3** To form (a knot). **4** To form a knot in, as string. **5** To fasten, or join in any way. **6** To restrict; bind. **7 a** To equal (a competitor) in score or achievement. **b** To equal (a competitor's score). **8** *Informal* To unite in marriage. **9** *Music* To unite by a tie. —*v.i.* **10** To make a tie or connection. **11** To make the same score; be equal. —**tie down** To hinder;

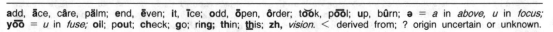

restrict. —**tie up 1** To fasten with rope, string, etc. **2** To wrap, as with paper, and fasten with string, cord, etc. **3** To moor (a vessel). **4** To block; hinder. **5** To be previously committed, so as to be unavailable: His money is *tied up* in real estate. —*n.* **1** A flexible bond or fastening secured by drawing the ends into a knot or loop. **2** Any bond or obligation. **3** In a contest, a draw; also, the point at which this occurs. **4** Something that is tied or intended for tying, as a shoelace, necktie, etc. **5** *Engin.* A structural member fastening parts together. **6** *Music* A curved line joining two notes of the same pitch to make them represent one tone. **7** One of a set of timbers laid crosswise on the ground as supports for railroad tracks. **8** *pl.* Low shoes with laces. [< OE *tīgan* bind] —**ti′er** *n.*

tie-dye (tī′dī′) *v.t.* **-dyed, -dye·ing** To create designs on fabric by tying parts of it in clumps that will not absorb the dye. —*n.* **1** The process of decorating fabrics by tie-dyeing. **2** Fabric so decorated; also, a design so made.

tie-in (tī′in′) *n.* Something that connects or associates.

tier (tir) *n.* A rank or row in a series of things placed one above another. —*v.t. & v.i.* To place or rise in tiers. [< OF, a sequence]

tierce (tirs) *n.* **1** Formerly, a third of anything. **2** The third canonical hour. [< OF, a third < L *tertius*]

tie-up (tī′up′) *n.* **1** A temporary stoppage of services, operations, progress of traffic, etc. **2** *Informal* Connection; linkage.

tiff (tif) *n.* A slight quarrel; a spat. —*v.i.* To be in or have a tiff. [?]

tif·fin (tif′ən) *Brit. n.* Midday luncheon. —*v.i.* To lunch. [< Anglo-Indian *tiffing* drinking]

ti·ger (tī′gər) *n.* **1** A large carnivorous feline of Asia, with black stripes on a tawny body. **2** A fiercely determined, spirited, or energetic person or quality. [< Gk. *tigris*] —**ti′·gress** *n. Fem.* —**ti′ger·ish, ti′grish** *adj.*

tiger beetle Any of certain active, usu. striped or spotted beetles having larvae that feed on other insects.

ti·ger·eye (tī′gər·ī′) *n.* A semiprecious stone, usu. shimmering yellow and brown. Also **ti′ger's-eye′.**

tiger lily Any of various lilies having orange flowers with recurved petals spotted with black. • See LILY.

tiger moth A stout-bodied moth with striped or spotted wings.

tight (tīt) *adj.* **1** Impervious to fluids; not leaky: often used in combination: *watertight.* **2** Firmly fixed or fastened in place; secure. **3** Fully stretched; taut: *tight* as a drum. **4** Strict; stringent: a *tight* schedule. **5** Fitting closely; esp. too closely: *tight* shoes. **6** *Informal* Difficult to cope with; troublesome: a *tight* spot. **7** *Informal* Stingy. **8** *Slang* Intoxicated. **9** Evenly matched: said of a race or contest. **10** Difficult to obtain because of scarcity or financial restrictions: said of money or of commodities. —*adv.* **1** Firmly; securely: Hold on *tight.* **2** With much constriction: The dress fits too *tight.* —**sit tight** To remain firm in one's position or opinion. [?< ON *thēttr* dense] —**tight′ly** *adv.* —**tight′ness** *n.*

tight·en (tīt′n) *v.t. & v.i.* To make or become tight or tighter. —**tight′en·er** *n.*

tight-fist·ed (tīt′fis′tid) *adj.* Stingy.

tight-lipped (tīt′lipt′) *adj.* **1** Having the lips held tightly together. **2** Reticent; uncommunicative.

tight·rope (tīt′rōp′) *n.* A tightly stretched rope on which acrobats perform. —*adj.* Pertaining to or performing on a tightrope.

tights (tīts) *n.pl.* A close-fitting garment for the lower torso and legs, worn by dancers, acrobats, etc.

tight·wad (tīt′wod′) *n. Slang* A miser.

tike (tīk) *n.* TYKE.

til·bur·y (til′ber·ē) *n. pl.* **·bur·ies** A light, two-wheeled carriage seating two persons. [< *Tilbury,* 19th-c. London coachmaker]

til·de (til′də, -dē) *n.* A sign (˜) used in Spanish over *n* to indicate the sound of *ny,* as in *cañon,* canyon. [Sp.< L *titulus* superscription, title]

tile (tīl) *n.* **1** A thin piece of baked clay, stone, etc., used for covering roofs, floors, etc., and as an ornament. **2** A thin piece of linoleum, plastic, cork, etc., for covering walls and floors. **3** A short earthenware pipe, as used in forming sewers. **4** Tiles collectively; tiling. **5** Any of the pieces in

the game of mah jong. —*v.t.* **tiled, til·ing** To cover with tiles. [< L *tegula* < *tegere* to cover] —**til′er** *n.*

til·ing (tī′ling) *n.* **1** The work of one who covers with tiles. **2** Tiles collectively. **3** Something made of or faced with tiles.

till¹ (til) *v.t. & v.i.* To put and keep (soil) in order for the production of crops, as by plowing, hoeing, etc.; cultivate. [< OE *tilian* strive, acquire] —**till′er** *n.*

till² (til) *prep & conj.* UNTIL. [< OE *til*] • *Till* and *until* have exactly the same meaning and may usu. be used interchangeably. However, *until* is the preferred form at the beginning of a sentence: *Until today, the weather has been bad; It won't be long till winter.*

till³ (til) *n.* **1** A money drawer behind the counter of a store. **2** The money in such a drawer; also, available cash. **3** Formerly, a drawer for holding valuables. [ME *tillen*]

till·age (til′ij) *n.* **1** The cultivation of land. **2** The state of being tilled. **3** Land that has been tilled. **4** Crops growing on such land. [< TILL¹ + -AGE]

till·er (til′ər) *n.* **1** A lever to turn a rudder. **2** A means of guidance. [< Med. L *telarium* a weaver's beam]

tilt (tilt) *v.t.* **1** To cause to rise at one end or side; slant. **2** To aim or thrust, as a lance. **3** To charge or overthrow in a tilt or joust. —*v.i.* **4** To incline at an angle; lean. **5** To contend with the lance; joust. **6** To argue; debate. —*n.* **1** A slant or slope. **2** The act of tilting something. **3** A medieval sport in which mounted knights, charging with lances, endeavored to unseat each other. **4** A quarrel or dispute. **5** *Can.* In certain provinces, a seesaw. —**at full tilt** At full speed. [ME *tylten* be overthrown, totter] —**tilt′er** *n.*

tilth (tilth) *n.* **1** The act of tilling; cultivation. **2** Cultivated land.

tim·bal (tim′bəl) *n.* A kettledrum. [< Ar. *at ṭabl* drum]

tim·bale (tim′bəl, *Fr.* tań·bál′) *n.* **1** A dish made of chicken, fish, cheese, or vegetables, mixed with eggs, sweet cream, etc., cooked in a drum-shaped mold. **2** A small cup made of fried pastry, in which food may be served. [F, timbal]

tim·ber (tim′bər) *n.* **1** Wood suitable for building or constructing things. **2** Growing or standing trees; forests. **3** A single piece of squared wood prepared for use or already in use. **4** Any principal beam in a ship. —*v.t.* To provide or shore with timber. [< OE] —**tim′ber·er** *n.*

timber hitch A knot by which a rope is fastened around a spar, post, etc.

tim·ber·land (tim′bər·land′) *n.* Land covered with forests.

timber line The boundary of tree growth on mountains and in arctic regions; the line above which no trees grow. —**tim′ber-line′** (-līn′) *adj.*

timber wolf The large gray wolf of northern forest areas. • See WOLF.

tim·bre (tam′bər, tim′-; *Fr.* tań′br′) *n.* The distinctive quality of sound, produced chiefly by overtones, that characterizes or identifies a singing voice, a musical instrument, or a voiced speech sound. [F < L *tympanum* a kettledrum]

tim·brel (tim′brəl) *n.* An ancient Hebrew instrument resembling a tambourine. [< OF *timbre,* a small bell]

time (tīm) *n.* **1** The general idea, relation, or fact of continuous or successive existence; the past, present, and future. **2** A definite moment, hour, period, etc.: The *time* is 3:30. **3** Epoch; era: the *time* of the Vikings. **4** The portion of duration allotted to some specific happening, condition, etc. **5** Leisure: He has no *time* to play golf. **6** Experience on a specific occasion: to have a good *time.* **7** A point in duration; occasion: Your *time* has come! **8** A period considered as having some quality of its own: *Times* are hard. **9** A system of reckoning or measuring duration: daylight-saving *time.* **10** A case of recurrence or repetition: three *times* a day. **11** *Music* The division of a musical composition into measures; meter. **12** Period during which work has been or remains to be done; also, the amount of pay due one: *time* and a half for overtime. **13** Rate of movement, as in dancing, marching, etc.; tempo. **14** Fit or proper occasion: This is no *time* to quibble. —**against time** As quickly as possible so as to finish within the allotted time. —**at the same time 1** At the same moment. **2**

Despite that; nevertheless. —**at times** Now and then. —**behind the times** Out-of-date; passé. —**for the time being** For the present time. —**from time to time** Now and then; occasionally. —**in good time 1** Soon. **2** At the right time. —**in time 1** While time permits or lasts. **2** Ultimately. —**keep time 1** To indicate time correctly, as a clock. **2** To make regular or rhythmic movements in unison with another or others. **3** To render a musical composition in proper time or rhythm. **4** To make a record of the number of hours worked by an employee. —**on time 1** Promptly. **2** Paid for, or to be paid for, later or in installments. —**time after time** Again and again. —*adj.* **1** Of or pertaining to time. **2** Devised so as to operate, explode, etc., at a specified time: a *time* bomb, *time* lock. **3** Payable at, or to be paid for at, a future date. —*v.t.* **timed, tim·ing 1** To record the speed or duration of: to *time* a race. **2** To cause to correspond in time: They *timed* their steps to the music. **3** To arrange the time or occasion for: He *timed* his arrival for five o'clock. **4** To mark the rhythm or measure of. [<OE *tīma*]

time·card (tīm′kärd′) *n.* A card for recording the arrival and departure times of an employee.

time clock A clock equipped to record times of arrival and departure of employees.

time exposure A long film exposure made by two separate manual operations of the shutter.

time-hon·ored (tīm′on′ərd) *adj.* Honored or accepted because of long-established usage or custom.

time·keep·er (tīm′kē′pər) *n.* **1** One who or that which keeps time. **2** TIMEPIECE.

time·less (tīm′lis) *adj.* **1** Eternal; unending. **2** Not assigned or limited to any special time, era, or epoch. —**time′less·ly** *adv.* —**time′less·ness** *n.*

time·ly (tīm′lē) *adj.* **·li·er, ·li·est** Being at a good or proper time. —**time′li·ness** *n.* —**Syn.** convenient, fitting, opportune, suitable.

time·piece (tīm′pēs′) *n.* A clock or watch.

tim·er (tī′mər) *n.* **1** A timekeeper. **2** A stopwatch. **3** A device similar to a stopwatch for timing various processes: a kitchen *timer*. **4** A device that begins operations in sequence or after measured intervals of time.

times (tīmz) *prep.* Multiplied by: four *times* two is eight.

time·serv·ing (tīm′sûr′ving) *adj.* Conducting oneself so as to conform to the demands and opinions of the times and of those in power, usu. for personal advantage. —*n.* The actions of a timeserving person. —**time′serv′er** *n.*

time-shar·ing (tīm′shâr′ing) *n.* The simultaneous use of a single large computer by many people at once, by means of individual terminals.

time signature A sign, usu. two numerals placed one above the other on a musical staff, to indicate meter.

time·ta·ble (tīm′tā′bəl) *n.* A schedule showing the times at which trains, boats, airplanes, buses, etc., arrive and depart.

time-worn (tīm′wôrn, -worn′) *adj.* Made worn and ineffective by long existence or use.

time zone One of the 24 established divisions or sectors into which the earth is divided for convenience in reckoning time: each sector represents 15 degrees of longitude, or a time interval of 1 hour.

tim·id (tim′id) *adj.* **1** Easily frightened; fearful. **2** Lacking self-confidence. [<L *timere* to fear] —**ti·mid·i·ty** (ti·mid′ə·tē), **tim′id·ness** *n.* —**tim′id·ly** *adv.* —**Syn.** **2** retiring, shrinking, shy, timorous.

tim·ing (tī′ming) *n.* The art or act of regulating the speed at which something is performed to secure maximum effects.

tim·or·ous (tim′ər·əs) *adj.* Fearful and anxious; timid. [<L *timor* fear] —**tim′or·ous·ly** *adv.* —**tim′or·ous·ness** *n.*

tim·o·thy (tim′ə·thē) *n.* A perennial fodder grass having its flowers in a dense cylindrical spike. Also **timothy grass**. [<*Timothy* Hanson, who took the seed from New York to the Carolinas about 1720]

Tim·o·thy (tim′ə·thē) A convert and companion of the apostle Paul. —*n.* Either of two epistles in the New Testament, written to Timothy by Paul.

tim·pa·ni (tim′pə·nē) *n. pl. (construed as sing. or pl.)* Kettledrums. [<Ital., pl. of *timpano* a kettledrum <L *tympanum* a drum] —**tim′pa·nist** *n.*

tin (tin) *n.* **1** A soft, silvery white, corrosion-resistant metallic element (symbol Sn) usu. found combined with oxygen; used in making alloys. **2** Tin plate. **3** *Chiefly Brit.* A can, as of preserved food. —*v.t.* **tinned, tin·ning 1** To coat or cover with tin, solder, or tin plate. **2** *Chiefly Brit.* To pack or preserve (food) in cans. —*adj.* Made of tin. [<OE]

tinc·ture (tingk′chər) *n.* **1** A medicinal solution, usu. in alcohol. **2** A tinge of color; tint. **3** A slight trace. [<L *tinctura* a dyeing]

tin·der (tin′dər) *n.* Any dry, readily combustible substance that will ignite on contact with a spark. [<OE *tynder*] —**tin′der·y** *adj.*

tin·der·box (tin′dər·boks′) *n.* **1** A box containing tinder, flint, and steel for starting a fire. **2** A highly flammable mass of material. **3** An excitable, temperamental person.

tine (tīn) *n.* A spike or prong, as of a fork or of an antler. [<OE *tind*] —**tined** *adj.*

tin·foil (tin′foil′) *n.* **1** Tin or an alloy of tin made into very thin sheets. **2** A similar sheeting made of rolled aluminum, commonly used as wrapping material.

ting (ting) *n.* A high metallic sound, as of a small bell.

tinge (tinj) *v.t.* **tinged, tinge·ing** or **ting·ing 1** To imbue with a faint trace of color. **2** To impart a slight trace of a quality to. —*n.* **1** A faint trace of added color. **2** A slight trace, as of a quality. [<L *tingere* to dye] —**Syn.** *n.* **1, 2** dash, hint, soupçon, tincture, touch.

tin·gle (ting′gəl) *v.* **·gled, ·gling** *v.i.* **1** To experience a prickly, stringing sensation. **2** To cause such a sensation. **3** To jingle; tinkle. —*v.t.* **4** To cause to tingle. —*n.* **1** A prickly, stinging sensation. **2** A jingle or tinkling. [Appar. var. of TINKLE] —**tin′gler** *n.* —**tin′gly** *adj.*

tin·horn (tin′hôrn′) *adj. Slang* Cheap, vulgar, and pretentious: a *tinhorn* politician. [With ref. to the fine appearance but poor sound of a tin horn]

tink·er (tingk′ər) *n.* **1** A mender of pots and pans, etc. **2** A clumsy workman; a botcher. **3** Work done hastily and carelessly. —*v.i.* **1** To work as a tinker. **2** To work in a clumsy, makeshift fashion. **3** To potter; fuss. —*v.t.* **4** To mend as a tinker. **5** To repair clumsily or inexpertly. [Var. of earlier *tinekere* a worker in tin]

tinker's damn *Slang* Any useless or worthless thing: usu. in the phrase **not worth a tinker's damn.** Also **tinker's dam.** [<TINKER + DAMN; with ref. to the reputed profanity of tinkers]

tin·kle (ting′kəl) *v.* **·kled, ·kling** *v.i.* **1** To produce slight, sharp, metallic sounds, as a small bell. —*v.t.* **2** To cause to tinkle. **3** To summon or signal by a tinkling. —*n.* A sharp, clear, tinkling sound. [Imit.] —**tin′kly (·kli·er, ·kli·est)** *adj.*

tin·ner (tin′ər) *n.* **1** A miner employed in tin mines. **2** A tinsmith.

tin·ni·tus (ti·nī′təs) *n.* A ringing, buzzing, or clicking sound in the ears, not caused by external stimuli. [<L *tinnire* to ring]

tin·ny (tin′ē) *adj.* **·ni·er, ·ni·est 1** Made of or containing tin. **2** Like tin in cheapness and brightness. **3** Having a thin, flat sound like that of tin being struck. —**tin′ni·ly** *adv.* —**tin′ni·ness** *n.*

Tin Pan Alley 1 A section of a city, esp. New York, frequented by musicians, song writers, and publishers of popular music. **2** The musicians, writers, publishers, etc., of popular music.

tin plate Sheet iron or steel plated with tin. —**tin′-plate′ (-plat·ed, -plat·ing)** *v.t.* —**tin′-plat′er** *n.*

tin·sel (tin′səl) *n.* **1** Very thin glittering bits of metal or plastic used for display and ornament. **2** Anything sparkling and showy, but with little real worth. —*adj.* **1** Made or covered with tinsel. **2** Like tinsel; superficially brilliant. —*v.t.* **·seled** or **·selled, ·sel·ing** or **·sel·ling 1** To adorn or decorate with or as with tinsel. **2** To give a false attractiveness to. [<L *scintilla* a spark]

tin·smith (tin′smith′) *n.* One who works with tin or tin plate.

tint (tint) *n.* **1** A variety of color; tinge: red with a blue *tint.* **2** A gradation of a color made by dilution with white. **3** A pale or delicate color. **4** In engraving, uniform shading produced by parallel lines or hatching. —*v.t.* To give a tint to. [< L *tinctus* a dyeing] —**tint′er** *n.*

tin·tin·nab·u·la·tion (tin′ti·nab′yə·lā′shən) *n.* The pealing, tinkling, or ringing of bells. [< L *tintinnare* to ring]

tin·type (tin′tīp′) *n.* An old type of photograph taken on a sensitized plate of enameled tin or iron.

tin·ware (tin′wâr′) *n.* Articles made of tin plate.

ti·ny (tī′nē) *adj.* **·ni·er**, **·ni·est** Very small; minute. [< obs. *tine* a small amount, bit] —**ti′ni·ness** *n.*

-tion *suffix of nouns* **1** Action or process of: *rejection.* **2** Condition or state of being: *completion.* **3** Result of: *connection.* [< L *-tio, -tionis*]

tip[1] (tip) *n.* A slanting position; a tilt. —*v.* **tipped, tip·ping** *v.t.* **1** To cause to lean; tilt. **2** To put at an angle: to *tip* one's hat. **3** To overturn or upset: often with *over.* —*v.i.* **4** To become tilted; slant. **5** To overturn; topple: with *over.* [ME *tipen* overturn] —**tip′per** *n.*

tip[2] (tip) *v.t.* **tipped, tip·ping** **1** To strike lightly; tap. **2** In baseball, to strike (the ball) a light, glancing blow. —*n.* A tap; light blow. [Prob. < LG *tippe*]

tip[3] (tip) *n.* **1** A small gift of money for services rendered. **2** A helpful hint. **3** A piece of confidential information: a *tip* on a horse race. —*v.* **tipped, tip·ping** *v.t.* **1** To give a small gratuity to. **2** *Informal* To give secret information to, as in betting, etc. —*v.i.* **3** To give gratuities. —**tip off** *Informal* **1** To give secret information to. **2** To warn. [? < TIP[2]] —**tip′per** *n.*

tip[4] (tip) *n.* **1** The point or extremity of anything tapering: the *tip* of the tongue. **2** A piece made to form the end of something, as a nozzle, ferrule, etc. **3** The uppermost part; top: the *tip* of a flagpole. —*v.t.* **tipped, tip·ping** **1** To furnish with a tip. **2** To form the tip of. **3** To cover or adorn the tip of. [Prob. < MDu., a point]

tip-off (tip′ôf′, -of′) *n.* *Informal* A hint or warning, usu. given confidentially.

tip·pet (tip′it) *n.* **1** Formerly, a long hanging strip of cloth attached to the sleeve or hood. **2** A covering, usu. of fur, velvet, etc., for the neck and shoulders, hanging well down in front. [Prob. dim. of TIP[4]]

tip·ple (tip′əl) *v.t. & v.i.* **·pled, ·pling** To drink (alcoholic beverages) frequently and habitually. —*n.* Liquor consumed in tippling. [< earlier *tipler* bartender]

tip·ster (tip′stər) *n.* *Informal* One who sells tips for betting, as on a race.

tip·sy (tip′sē) *adj.* **·si·er, ·si·est** **1** Mildly intoxicated. **2** Shaky; unsteady. [< TIP[1]] —**tip′si·ly** *adv.* —**tip′si·ness** *n.*

Tippet *def.* 1

tip·toe (tip′tō′, -tō′) *n.* The tip of a toe, or the tips of all the toes. —**on tiptoe 1** On one's tiptoes. **2** Expectantly; eagerly. **3** Stealthily; quietly. —*v.i.* **·toed, ·toe·ing** To walk on tiptoe; go stealthily or quietly. —*adv.* On tiptoe.

tip-top (tip′top′) *adj.* **1** At the very top. **2** *Informal* Best of its kind; first-rate. —*n.* The highest point. —**tip′-top′per** *n.*

ti·rade (tī′rād, tī·rād′) *n.* A prolonged declamatory outpouring, as of censure. [< Ital. *tirata* a volley]

tire[1] (tīr) *v.* **tired, tir·ing** *v.t.* **1** To reduce the strength of, as by exertion. **2** To reduce the interest or patience of, as with monotony. —*v.i.* **3** To become weary or exhausted. To lose patience, interest, etc. —**tire of** To become bored or impatient with. —**tire out** To weary completely. [< OE *tīorian*] —**Syn. 1** exhaust, fag, fatigue, wear out, weary.

tire[2] (tīr) *n.* **1** A band or hoop surrounding the rim of a wheel. **2** A tough, flexible tube, usu. of inflated rubber, set around the rims of the wheels of automobiles, bicycles, etc. —*v.t.* **tired, tir·ing** To put a tire on. *Brit. sp.* **tyre.** [Prob. < obs. *tire* to attire]

tired (tīrd) *adj.* Weary; fatigued. [Orig. pp. of TIRE[1]] —**tired′ly** *adv.* —**tired′ness** *n.*

tire·less (tīr′lis) *adj.* **1** Not becoming easily fatigued; untiring. **2** Ceaseless; *tireless* zeal. —**tire′less·ly** *adv.* —**tire′less·ness** *n.*

tire·some (tīr′səm) *adj.* Tending to tire, or causing one to tire; tedious. —**tire′some·ly** *adv.* —**tire′some·ness** *n.*

ti·ro (tī′rō) *n.* TYRO.

'tis (tiz) Contraction of *it is.*

tis·sue (tish′ōō) *n.* **1** Any light or gauzy textile fabric. **2** *Biol.* An aggregate of cells and intercellular material having a particular function: nerve *tissue.* **3** A network; chain: a *tissue* of lies. **4** TISSUE PAPER. **5** A disposable square of soft absorbent paper for use as a handkerchief, etc. [< OF *tistre* to weave]

tissue paper Very thin, unsized, translucent paper for wrapping delicate articles, protecting engravings, etc.

tit[1] (tit) *n.* A titmouse, titlark, etc.

tit[2] (tit) *n.* Teat; breast; nipple. [< OE *titt*]

ti·tan (tīt′n) *n.* Any person having gigantic strength or size; a giant. —**ti·tan′ic** *adj.* [< TITAN]

Ti·tan (tīt′n) *Gk. Myth.* One of a race of giant gods, who were succeeded by the Olympian gods. —**Ti·tan′ic** *adj.*

Ti·ta·ni·a (ti·tā′nē·ə, tī-, -tan′yə) In folklore, the queen of fairyland and wife of Oberon.

ti·ta·ni·um (tī·tā′nē·əm) *n.* A widely distributed lightweight metallic element (symbol Ti) resembling aluminum in appearance, used to make tough, heat-resistant alloys. [< L *Titani* the Titans]

tit·bit (tit′bit′) *n.* TIDBIT.

tit for tat Retaliation in kind; blow for blow. [?]

tithe (tīth) *n.* **1** One tenth. **2** *Usu. pl.* A tax of one tenth part of yearly income arising from lands and from the personal industry of the inhabitants, for the support of the clergy and the church. **3** A small part. **4** Loosely, any tax or levy. —*v.t.* **tithed, tith·ing 1** To give or pay a tithe, or tenth part of. **2** To tax with tithes. [< OE *tēotha, tēogotha* a tenth] —**tith′er** *n.*

ti·tian (tish′ən) *n.* A reddish yellow color much used by Titian, esp. in painting women's hair. —*adj.* Having the color titian. [< *Titian,* Venetian artist, 1477–1576]

tit·il·late (tit′ə·lāt) *v.t.* **·lat·ed, ·lat·ing 1** To cause a tickling sensation in. **2** To excite pleasurably. [< L *titillare* to tickle] —**tit′il·lat′er, tit′il·la′tion** *n.* —**tit′il·la′tive** *adj.*

tit·i·vate (tit′ə·vāt) *v.t. & v.i.* **·vat·ed, ·vat·ing** *Informal* To smarten; dress up. Also **tit′ti·vate.** [Earlier *tidivate* ? < TIDY, on analogy with *cultivate*] —**tit′i·va′tion, tit′i·va′tor** *n.*

tit·lark (tit′lärk′) *n.* A pipit. [ME *tit* a little thing + LARK]

ti·tle (tīt′l) *n.* **1** The name of a book, play, motion picture, song, etc. **2** A title page, as of a book. **3** A descriptive name; epithet. **4 a** An appellation showing rank, office, profession, station in life, etc. **b** In some countries, a designation of nobility or one conferred for unusual distinction. **5** In some sports, championship: to win the *title.* **6** *Law* **a** The legal right to own property. **b** Legal evidence of such a right. **c** A document setting forth such evidence. —*v.t.* **·tled, ·tling** To give a name to; entitle. [< L *titulus* a label, inscription]

ti·tled (tīt′ld) *adj.* Having a title, esp. of nobility.

title page A page containing the title of a work, its author, its publisher, etc.

title role The character in a play, opera, or motion picture for whom it is named.

tit·mouse (tit′mous′) *n. pl.* **·mice** (-mīs′) Any of numerous small birds related to the nuthatches. [< Me *tit-* little + *mose* < OE *mase* a titmouse]

ti·trate (tī′trāt) *v.t. & v.i.* **·trat·ed, ·trat·ing** To analyze (a substance) by titration. [< F *titrer*]

ti·tra·tion (tī·trā′shən, ti-) *n.* Quantitative analysis of a substance in solution by the completion of a specific reaction with a measured volume of a standard solution.

Titmouse

tit·ter (tit′ər) *v.i.* To laugh in a suppressed way. —*n.* The act of tittering. [Imit.] —**tit′ter·er** *n.* —**tit′ter·ing·ly** *adv.* —**Syn.** *v.* chuckle, giggle, snicker, snigger, snort.

tit·tle (tit′l) *n.* **1** The minutest quantity; iota. **2** A very small diacritical mark in writing, as the dot over an *i,* etc. [< L *titulus* title]

tit·tle-tat·tle (tit′l-tat′l) *n.* **1** Trivial talk; gossip. **2** An idle talker. —*v.i.* **·tled, ·tling** To gossip; chatter. [Reduplication of TATTLE]

tit·u·lar (tich′ŏŏ-lər, tit′yə-) *adj.* **1** Existing in name or title only: a *titular* ruler. **2** Pertaining to a title. **3** Having a title. [< L *titulus* a title] —**tit′u·lar·ly** *adv.*

Ti·tus (tī′təs) A disciple of the apostle Paul. —*n.* The epistle in the New Testament addressed to Titus and attributed to Paul.

tiz·zy (tiz′ē) *n. pl.* **·zies** *Slang* A bewildered or excited state of mind; a dither. [?]

TKO, T.K.O., t.k.o. technical knockout.

Tl thallium.

T.L. trade last.

T/L time loan.

Tm thulium.

TN Tennessee (P.O. abbr.).

Tn thoron.

tn. ton; train.

tng. training.

TNT, T.N.T. trinitrotoluene.

to (tŏŏ, *unstressed* tə) *prep.* **1** Toward or terminating in: going *to* town. **2** Opposite or near: face *to* face; Hold me *to* your breast. **3** Intending or aiming at: Come *to* my rescue. **4** Resulting in: frozen *to* death. **5** Belonging with; of: the key *to* the barn. **6** In honor of: Drink *to* our victory. **7** In comparison with: 9 is *to* 3 as 21 is *to* 7. **8** Until: five minutes *to* one. **9** For the utmost duration of: a miser *to* the end of his days. **10** Concerning: blind *to* her faults. **11** In close application toward: Get down *to* work. **12** For: The contest is open *to* everyone. **13** Noting action toward: Give the ring *to* me. **14** By: known *to* the world. **15** From the point of view of: It seems *to* me. **16** About; involved in: That's all there is *to* it. **17** On; against: Nail the sign *to* the post. **18** In: four quarts *to* a gallon. **19** Into: The house was reduced *to* ashes. —*adv.* **1** Forward: He wore his sweater back side *to*. **2** In a direction or position, esp. closed: Pull the door *to*. **3** Into a normal condition or consciousness: She soon came *to*. **4** Into action or operation: They fell *to* eagerly. —**to and fro** In opposite or different directions; back and forth. [< OE *tō*] • *To* is also used before a verb to indicate the infinitive: It is good *to* see you; You can go if you want *to* (go).

toad (tōd) *n.* **1** Any of various tailless, jumping, insectivorous amphibians resembling the frog but usu. having a warty skin and resorting to water only to breed. **2** A contemptible or loathsome person. [< OE *tādige*]

toad·fish (tōd′fish′) *n. pl.* **·fish** or **·fish·es** Any of a family of fishes with scaleless skin and a toadlike head.

toad·stool (tōd′stōōl′) *n.* An inedible or poisonous mushroom.

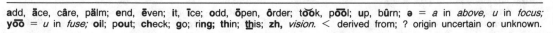

Toad

toad·y (tō′dē) *n. pl.* **toad·ies** An obsequious flatterer; a sycophant. —*v.t. & v.i.* **toad·ied, toad·y·ing** To act the toady (to). [< earlier *toad-eater*, a charlatan's attendant who pretended to eat toads] —**toad′y·ism** *n.*

to-and-fro (tōō′ən-frō′) *adj.* Moving back and forth or from one position to another. —*adv.* In a to-and-fro motion.

toast¹ (tōst) *v.t.* **1** To brown the outside of (a piece of bread, etc.) by heating in an oven, toaster, etc. **2** To warm thoroughly. —*v.i.* **3** To become warm or toasted. —*n.* Toasted bread. [< L *tostus* < *torrere* parch, roast]

toast² (tōst) *n.* **1** The act of drinking to someone's health or to some thing. **2** The person or thing thus named. —*v.t. & v.i.* To drink a toast or toasts (to). [< TOAST¹, from a custom of flavoring a drink with a spiced piece of toast] —**toast′er** *n.*

toast·er (tōst′ər) *n.* An electrical device for toasting bread.

toast·mas·ter (tōst′mas′tər, -mäs′tər) *n.* A person who, at public dinners, announces the toasts, calls upon the speakers, etc.

to·bac·co (tə-bak′ō) *n. pl.* **·cos** or **·coes 1** Any of various plants of the nightshade family, with large sticky leaves and yellow, white, or purple flowers. **2** The leaves of several of these plants, processed for smoking, chewing, etc. **3** The various products prepared from tobacco leaves, as cigarettes, cigars, etc. [< Sp. *tabaco*]

to·bac·co·nist (tə-bak′ə-nist) *n. Brit.* One who deals in tobacco.

To·bit (tō′bit) *n.* A book of the Apocrypha of the Old Testament. Also **To·bi·as** (tō-bī′əs).

to·bog·gan (tə-bog′ən) *n.* A long sledlike vehicle without runners, consisting of thin boards curved upward in front. —*v.i.* **1** To coast on a toboggan. **2** To descend swiftly: Wheat prices *tobogganed*. [< Algon.] —**to·bog′gan·er, to·bog′gan·ist** *n.*

Tobacco plant

to·by (tō′bē) *n. pl.* **·bies** *Often cap.* A mug or jug for ale or beer, often made in the form of an old man wearing a three-cornered hat. Also **toby jug.** [< *Toby*, dim. of the name *Tobias*]

toc·ca·ta (tə-kä′tə, *Ital.* tôk·kä′tä) *n.* An elaborate composition for piano, organ, etc. often preceding a fugue. [Ital., lit., a touching]

To·char·i·an (tō-kâr′ē-ən, -kär′-) *n.* **1** One of an ancient people who inhabited central Asia in the first Christian millennium. **2** The language of the Tocharians, two dialects of which are known.

to·coph·er·ol (tō-kof′ə-rōl, -rol) *n.* Vitamin E. [< Gk. *tokos* offspring + *pherein* to bear]

toc·sin (tok′sin) *n.* **1** A signal sounded on a bell; alarm. **2** An alarm bell. [< Prov. *tocar* to strike, touch + *senh* a bell]

to·day (tə-dā′) *adv.* **1** On or during this present day. **2** At the present time. —*n.* The present day or age. Also **to·day′.** [< OE *tō* + *daeg* day]

tod·dle (tod′l) *v.i.* **·dled, ·dling** To walk unsteadily and with short steps, as a little child. —*n.* The act of toddling. —**tod′dler** *n.*

tod·dy (tod′ē) *n. pl.* **·dies 1** A drink made with whiskey, brandy, etc., and hot water and sugar. **2** The fermented sap of certain East Indian palms (**toddy palms**). [< Skt. *tāla* a palm tree]

to-do (tə-dōō′) *n. Informal* A stir; fuss. —*Syn.* bustle, commotion, confusion, disturbance.

toe (tō) *n.* **1** One of the five digits of the foot. **2** The forward part of the foot. **3** That portion of a shoe, boot, sock, etc., that covers or corresponds to the toes. **4** Anything resembling a toe in contour, function, position, etc. —**on one's toes** Alert. —**tread on (someone's) toes** To trespass on (someone's) feelings, prejudices, etc. —*v.* **toed, toe·ing** *v.t.* **1** To touch or kick with the toes. **2** To furnish with a toe. **3** To drive (a nail or spike) obliquely. **4** To attach by nails driven thus. —*v.i.* **5** To stand or walk with the toes pointing in a specified direction: to *toe* out. —**toe the mark** (or **line**) **1** To touch a certain line with the toes preparatory to starting a race. **2** To conform to a discipline or a standard. [< OE *tā*]

toed (tōd) *adj.* **1** Having (a specified kind or number of) toes: used in combination: *pigeon-toed; three-toed.* **2** Fastened or fastening by obliquely driven nails. **3** Driven in obliquely, as a nail.

toe dance Dancing on the tips of the toes, as in ballet. —**toe′-dance′ (-danced, -danc·ing)** *v.i.* —**toe′-danc′er** *n.*

toe·hold (tō′hōld′) *n.* **1** In climbing, a small space which supports the toes. **2** Any means of entrance, support, or the like; a footing. **3** A hold in which a wrestler bends back the foot of his opponent.

toe·nail (tō′nāl′) *n.* **1** The nail growing on a toe. **2** A nail driven obliquely. —*v.t.* To fasten with obliquely driven nails.

tof·fee (tôf′ē, tof′ē) *n.* TAFFY. Also **tof′fy.**

tog (tog) *Informal n. pl.* Clothes. —*v.t.* **togged, tog·ging** To clothe: often with *up* or *out*. [< L *toga* toga]

to·ga (tō′gə) *n. pl.* **·gas** or **·gae** (-gī) **1** The loose, flowing outer garment worn in public by a citizen of ancient Rome. **2** Any robe characteristic of a calling. [< L < *tegere* to cover] —**to′· gaed** (tō′gəd) *adj.*

to·geth·er (tŏŏ-geth′ər, tə-) *adv.* **1** In company: We were sitting *together*. **2** In or into one group, mass, unit, etc.: They put the jigsaw puzzle *together*. **3** Into contact with each other: Glue these two pieces *together*. **4** Simultaneously: Let's sing it *together*. **5** With one another; mutually: They discussed it *together*. **6** In agreement or harmony: The tie and shirt go well *together*. **7** Considered collectively: He has more courage than all of us *together*. **8** Without cessation: He talked for hours *together*. —**get it all together** *Slang* To achieve a positive outlook on life; free oneself from anxiety. —**together with** Along with. [< OE *tōgædere*]

Roman toga

tog·ger·y (tog′ər-ē) *n. Informal* Clothing; togs.

tog·gle (tog′əl) *n.* **1** A pin, or short rod, properly attached in the middle, as to a rope, and designed to be passed through a hole or eye and turned. **2** A toggle joint. —*v.t.* **·gled**, **·gling** To fix, fasten, or furnish with a toggle or toggles. [?]

toggle joint A joint having a central hinge like an elbow, and operable by applying the force at the junction, thus changing the direction of motion.

toggle switch *Electr.* A switch connected to its actuating lever by a toggle joint loaded by a spring.

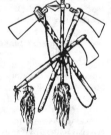
Toggle joint

To·go (tō′gō) *n.* A republic of w Africa, 21,500 sq. mi., cap. Lomé. —**To′go·lese′** (-lēs, -lēz) *adj., n.* • See map at AFRICA.

toil¹ (toil) *n.* **1** Fatiguing work; labor. **2** Any work accomplished by great labor. —*v.i.* **1** To work strenuously and tiringly. **2** To make one's way laboriously: to *toil* up a hill. —*v.t.* **3** To accomplish with great effort: to *toil* one's way. [< L *tudiculare* stir about] —**toil′er** *n.* —**Syn.** *v.* **1** drudge, labor, slave, travail.

toil² (toil) *n.* **1** *Archaic* A net, snare, or other trap. **2** *pl.* Anything that binds or entraps: the *toils* of remorse. [< L *tela* a web]

toi·let (toi′lit) *n.* **1** A fixture in the shape of a bowl, used for urination and defecation and equipped with a device for flushing and discharging with water. **2** A room containing such a fixture or fixtures. **3** PRIVY. **4** The act or process of bathing, grooming, and dressing oneself. **5** Formerly, a woman's attire or costume: also **toi·lette** (twa-let′). —*adj.* Used in dressing or grooming: *toilet* articles. [< F *toilette* orig. a cloth dressing gown, dim. of *toile* cloth]

toi·let·ry (toi′lit-rē) *n. pl.* **·ries** Soap, powder, cologne, etc., used in bathing and grooming oneself.

toilet water A scented liquid applied after the bath, after shaving, etc.

toil·some (toil′səm) *adj.* Involving hard work; laborious; difficult. —**toil′some·ly** *adv.* —**toil′some·ness** *n.*

toil·worn (toil′wôrn′, -wōrn′) *adj.* Exhausted by toil; showing the effects of toil.

To·kay (tō-kā′) *n.* **1** A large, sweet grape originally from Tokay, Hungary. **2** A wine made from it.

to·ken (tō′kən) *n.* **1** A visible sign; indication: This gift is a *token* of my affection. **2** Some tangible proof or evidence of one's identity, authority, etc. **3** A keepsake; souvenir. **4** A characteristic mark or feature. **5** A piece of metal issued as currency and having a face value greater than its actual value: a bus *token*. —**by the same token** Moreover; furthermore. —**in token of** As a sign or evidence of. —*adj.* **1** Having only the appearance of; nominal; minimal: *token* resistance; *token* integration. **2** Partial or very small: a *token* payment. [< OE *tācen*]

to·ken·ism (tō′kən-iz·əm) *n.* The policy of attempting to meet certain obligations or conditions by partial, symbolic, or token efforts.

To·khar·i·an (tō-kâr′ē-ən, -kär′-) *n.* TOCHARIAN.

told (tōld) *p.t. & p.p.* of TELL.

To·le·do (tə-lē′dō) *n. pl.* **·dos** A sword or sword blade from Toledo, Spain. Also **to·le′do.**

tol·er·a·ble (tol′ər·ə·bəl) *adj.* **1** Endurable; bearable. **2** Fairly good: *tolerable* health. [< L *tolerare* endure] —**tol′· er·a·ble·ness** *n.* —**tol′er·a·bly** *adv.*

tol·er·ance (tol′ər·əns) *n.* **1** The character, state, or quality of being tolerant. **2** Freedom from prejudice; open-mindedness. **3** The act of enduring, or the capacity for endurance. **4** An allowance for variations from specified measure, as of machine parts. **5** *Med.* Ability to withstand large or increasing amounts of a specified substance or stimulus.

tol·er·ant (tol′ər·ənt) *adj.* **1** Of a long-suffering disposition. **2** Indulgent; liberal. **3** *Med.* Resistant to the effects of a specific substance or stimulus. [< L *tolerare* endure] —**tol′er·ant·ly** *adv.*

tol·er·ate (tol′ə·rāt) *v.t.* **·at·ed**, **·at·ing** **1** To allow without opposition. **2** To concede, as the right to opinions or participation. **3** To bear or be capable of bearing. **4** *Med.* To be tolerant. [< L *tolerare* endure] —**tol′er·a′tive** *adj.* —**tol′· er·a′tion, tol′er·a′tor** *n.* —**Syn.** **1** permit. **3** endure, sustain.

toll¹ (tōl) *n.* **1** A tax or charge for some privilege granted, esp. for passage on a bridge or turnpike. **2** The right to levy such a charge. **3** A charge for a special service, as for a long-distance telephone call. **4** The number or amount lost, as in a disaster: The wreck took a *toll* of nine lives. —*v.t.* **1** To take as a toll. —*v.i.* **2** To exact a toll. [< OE]

toll² (tōl) *v.t.* **1** To sound (a church bell) slowly and at regular intervals. **2** To announce (a death, funeral, etc.) by tolling a church bell. **3** To call or summon by tolling. —*v.i.* **4** To sound slowly and at regular intervals. —*n.* **1** The act of tolling. **2** The sound of a bell rung slowly and regularly. [ME *tollen*] —**toll′er** *n.*

toll bridge A bridge at which toll for passage is paid.

toll call A long-distance telephone call.

toll·gate (tōl′gāt′) *n.* A gate at the entrance to a bridge, or on a road, at which toll is paid.

toll·keep·er (tōl′kē′pər) *n.* One who collects the tolls at a tollgate.

Tol·tec (tōl′tek, tol′-) *n.* Any of certain ancient Nahuatlan tribes that dominated Mexico about 900–1100 before the Aztecs. —*adj.* Of or pertaining to the Toltecs: also **Tol′tec·an.**

tol·u·ene (tol′yŏŏ·ēn) *n.* A hydrocarbon obtained from coal tar, used in making dyes, drugs, and explosives. Also **tol′u·ol** (-yŏŏ·wôl, -wōl).

tom (tom) *n.* **1** The male of various animals, esp. the cat. **2** Often cap. Slang UNCLE TOM. —*adj.* Male: a *tom* turkey.

tom·a·hawk (tom′ə·hôk) *n.* An ax used as a tool and as a war weapon by the Algonquian Indians. —*v.t.* To strike or kill with a tomahawk. [< Algon.]

to·ma·to (tə·mā′tō, -mä′-) *n. pl.* **·toes** **1** The pulpy edible berry, yellow or red when ripe, of a tropical American plant related to the potato, used as a vegetable. **2** The plant itself. **3** *Slang* An attractive girl or woman. [< Nah. *tomatl*]

tomb (tŏŏm) *n.* **1** A burial place; grave. **2** A tombstone or monument. —**the tomb** Death. —*v.t.* To entomb; bury. [< Gk. *tymbos* a mound]

North American Indian tomahawks

tom·boy (tom′boi′) *n.* A young girl who behaves like a lively, active boy. [< TOM + BOY] —**tom′boy·ish** *adj.* —**tom′boy·ish·ness** *n.*

tomb·stone (tŏŏm′stōn′) *n.* A stone, usu. inscribed, marking a place of burial.

tom·cat (tom′kat′) *n.* A male cat. —*v.i.* **·cat·ted**, **·cat·ting** *Slang* To engage in sexual relations indiscriminately: said of a man. [< *Tom*, hero of *The Life and Adventures of a Cat*, 1760, a popular anonymous work]

tome (tōm) *n.* A large, heavy book. [< Gk. *tomos* a fragment, volume]

tom·fool (tom′fŏŏl′) *n.* An idiotic or silly person. —*adj.* Foolish; stupid. [< *Tom Fool*, a name formerly applied to mental defectives]

tom·fool·er·y (tom′fŏŏl′ər·ē) *n. pl.* **·er·ies** Nonsensical behavior; silliness.

tom·my (tom′ē) *n. pl.* **·mies** A British soldier. Also **Tom′·my.** [Short for TOMMY ATKINS]

Tommy At·kins (at′kinz) A British private of the regular army. [< *Thomas Atkins*, a name used on British Army specimen forms]

Tommy gun *Informal* A type of submachine gun. [< J. *Thompson*, d. 1940, U.S. army officer]

to·mor·row (tə·môr′ō) *adv.* On or for the next day after today. —*n.* The next day after today. Also **to·mor′row.** [< OE *tō* to + *morgen* morning, morrow]

Tom Thumb 1 In English folklore, a hero as big as his father's thumb. 2 Any midget or dwarf.

tom·tit (tom′tit′) *n.* A titmouse or other small bird. [< the name *Tom* + TIT¹]

tom-tom (tom′tom′) *n.* Any of various drums, as of American Indian and African tribes, usu. beaten with the hands. [< Hind. *tamtam*, imit.]

-tomy *combining form* A cutting of a (specified) part or tissue: *lobotomy*. [< Gk. *tomē* a cutting]

ton (tun) *n.* 1 Any of several measures of weight; esp. the **short ton** of 2000 pounds avoirdupois; the **long ton** of 2240 pounds; or the **metric ton** of 1000 kilograms. 2 A unit for reckoning the displacement of vessels, equal to 35 cubic feet, or about one long ton of sea water: called **displacement ton.** 3 A unit for reckoning the freight capacity of a ship, usu. equivalent to 40 cubic feet of space: called **freight ton, measurement ton.** 4 A unit for reckoning the capacity of merchant vessels for purposes of registration, equivalent to 100 cubic feet or 2.832 cubic meters: called **register ton.** 5 *Informal* Any large amount, weight, etc. [Var. of TUN]

to·nal (tō′nəl) *adj.* 1 Of or pertaining to tone or tonality. 2 Having a keynote or tonic. —**to′nal·ly** *adv.*

to·nal·i·ty (tō·nal′ə·tē) *n. pl.* **·ties** 1 The existence of a keynote or tonic in music; also a key or mode. 2 The general color scheme or collective tones of a painting.

tone (tōn) *n.* 1 A vocal or musical sound; also, the quality of such a sound. 2 *Music* **a** A sound having a definite pitch, loudness, and timbre. **b** WHOLE STEP. 3 A predominating disposition; mood. 4 Characteristic tendency; quality: a want of moral *tone*. 5 Style or elegance: The party had *tone*. 6 Vocal inflection: a *tone* of pity. 7 The acoustical pitch, or change in pitch, of a phrase or sentence: A question is indicated by a rising *tone*. 8 The effect of light, shade, and color as combined in a picture. 9 A shade of a particular color: a deep *tone* of yellow. 10 Tonicity. —*v.* **toned, ton·ing** *v.t.* 1 To give tone to; modify in tone. 2 IN-TONE. —*v.i.* 3 To assume a certain tone or hue. 4 To blend or harmonize, as in tone or shade. —**tone down** 1 To subdue the tone of. 2 To moderate in quality or tone. —**tone up** 1 To raise in quality or strength. 2 To elevate in pitch. 3 To gain in vitality. [< Gk. *tonos* a pitch of voice, a stretching] —**ton′er** *n.*

tone·less (tōn′lis) *adj.* Lifeless; flat: a *toneless* voice. —**tone′less·ly** *adv.* —**tone′less·ness** *n.*

tong (tông, tong) *n.* 1 A Chinese association or closed society. 2 In the U.S., a former secret society composed of Chinese. [< Chin. *t'ang* a hall, meeting place]

Ton·ga (tong′gə) *n.* An independent kingdom in the Commonwealth of Nations situated on an archipelago E of Fiji, 270 sq. mi., cap. Nukualofa.

Ton·gan (tong′gən) *n.* 1 One of the Polynesian inhabitants of Tonga. 2 The language of Tonga.

tongs (tôngz, tongz) *n.pl.* (*sometimes construed as sing.*) An implement for grasping, holding, or lifting objects, consisting usu. of a pair of pivoted levers. Also **pair of tongs.** [< OE *tange*]

tongue (tung) *n.* 1 A muscular organ attached to the floor of the mouth of most vertebrates, important in masticating and tasting food, and in man as an organ of speech. • See MOUTH. 2 A similar organ in various insects, etc. 3 An animal's tongue, as of beef,

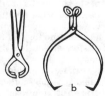

Tongs
a. blacksmith's.
b. ice.

prepared as food. 4 The power of speech: Have you lost your *tongue?* 5 Manner or style of speaking: a smooth *tongue.* 6 Utterance; talk. 7 A language or dialect. 8 Anything resembling a tongue in appearance, shape, or function. 9 A slender projection of land. 10 A long narrow bay or inlet. 11 A jet of flame. 12 A strip of leather for closing the gap in front of a laced shoe. • See SHOE. 13 The free or vibrating end of a reed in a wind instrument. 14 The clapper of a bell. 15 The harnessing pole of a horse-drawn vehicle. 16 The projecting edge of a tongue-and-groove joint. —**hold one's tongue** To keep silent. —**on the tip of one's tongue** On the verge of being remembered or uttered. —**with tongue in cheek** Facetiously, insincerely, or ironically. —*v.* **tongued, tongu·ing** *v.t.* 1 To use the tongue to attack or separate (notes) in playing a wind instrument. 2 To touch or lap with the tongue. 3 In carpentry: **a** To cut a tongue on (a board). **b** To join by a tongue-and-groove joint. —*v.i.* 4 To use the tongue to attack or separate notes in playing a wind instrument. 5 To extend as a tongue. [< OE *tunge*]

tongue-and-groove joint (tung′ən·grōōv′) In carpentry, a joint in which a projecting edge, or tongue, of one board is inserted into a corresponding groove of another board.

tongue-in-cheek (tung′ən·chēk′) *adj.* Said or meant insincerely, ironically, or facetiously.

tongue-tie (tung′tī′) *n.* Abnormal shortness of the membrane under the tongue, whereby its motion is impeded. —*v.t.* **·tied, ·ty·ing** 1 To deprive of speech or the power of speech. 2 To bewilder or amaze so as to render speechless.

Tongue-and-groove joint

tongue twister A word or phrase difficult to articulate quickly: "Miss Smith's fish-sauce shop" is a *tongue-twister.*

ton·ic (ton′ik) *adj.* 1 Having power to invigorate or build up; bracing. 2 Pertaining to tone or tones; in music, of the principal tone of a scale or tonal system. 3 *Physiol.* Of or pertaining to tension, esp. muscular tension. 4 *Pathol.* Rigid; unrelaxing: *tonic* spasm. 5 Of or pertaining to musical intonations or modulations of words, sentences, etc. 6 *Phonet.* Accented or stressed. —*n.* 1 *Med.* A medicine that promotes physical well-being. 2 Whatever imparts vigor or tone. 3 The basic tone of a key or tonal system. [< Gk. *tonos* sound, tone]

to·nic·i·ty (tō·nis′ə·tē) *n.* 1 The state of being tonic; tone. 2 The normal tension of muscle tissue. 3 Health and vigor.

to·night (tə·nīt′) *adv.* In or during the present or coming night. —*n.* The night that follows this day; also, the present night. Also **to·night′.** [< OE *tō* to + *niht* night]

ton·nage (tun′ij) *n.* 1 Weight, as expressed in tons. 2 Capacity, as of a vessel or vessels, expressed in tons. 3 A tax levied at a given rate per ton. [< OF *tonne* a ton, tun]

ton·neau (tu·nō′) *n. pl.* **·neaus** (-nōz′) or **·neaux** (-nōz′) The rear part of an early type of automobile enclosing the seats for passengers. [F, lit., barrel]

ton·sil (ton′səl) *n.* Either of two oval lymphoid organs situated on either side of the passage from the mouth to the pharynx. [< L *tonsillae* tonsils] —**ton′sil·lar, ton′sil·ar** *adj.* • See MOUTH.

ton·sil·lec·to·my (ton′sə·lek′tə·mē) *n. pl.* **·mies** Removal of the tonsils by surgery.

ton·sil·li·tis (ton′sə·lī′tis) *n.* Inflammation of the tonsils. —**ton′sil·lit′ic** (-lit′ik) *adj.*

ton·so·ri·al (ton·sôr′ē·əl, -sō′rē-) *adj.* Pertaining to a barber or to barbering: chiefly humorous. [< L *tonsor* a barber]

ton·sure (ton′shər) *n.* 1 The shaving of the head, or of the crown of the head, as of a priest or monk. 2 That part of a priest's or monk's head left bare by shaving. —*v.t.* **·sured, ·sur·ing** To shave the head of. [< L *tonsura* a shearing]

ton·tine (ton′tēn, ton·tēn′) *n.* A form of collective life annuity, the individual profits of which increase as the number of survivors diminishes, the final survivor taking the whole. —*adj.* Of or pertaining to such an annuity. [< Lorenzo *Tonti,* a 17th-c. Neapolitan banker]

to·nus (tō′nəs) *n. Physiol.* The slightly contracted state of a muscle at rest. [L, tone]

ton·y (tō′nē) *adj.* **ton·i·er, ton·i·est** *Informal* Aristocratic; fashionable. [< TONE]

too (tōō) *adv.* **1** In addition; also. **2** In excessive quantity or degree: *too* long. **3** Very; extremely: I am *too* happy for you. **4** *Informal* Indeed: an intensive: You are *too* going! [< OE *tō* to]

took (tŏŏk) *p.t.* of TAKE.

tool (tōōl) *n.* **1** A simple implement, as a hammer, saw, spade, chisel, etc., used in work. **2** A power-driven apparatus used for cutting, shaping, boring, etc. **3** The active part of such an apparatus. **4** *Often pl.* Something necessary to the performance of a profession, vocation, etc.: Paints and brushes are an artist's *tools.* **5** A person used to carry out the designs of another or others, esp. when such designs are unethical or unlawful. —*v.t.* **1** To shape or work with a tool. **2** To provide, as a factory, with machinery and tools. **3** In bookbinding, to ornament or impress designs upon with a tool. —*v.i.* **4** To work with a tool. **5** *Informal* To drive or travel in a vehicle: usu. with *along.* **6** To install, as in a factory, equipment, tools, etc; usu. with *up.* [< OE *tōl*] —**tool′er** *n.* —**Syn.** *n.* **1** appliance, device, instrument, utensil. **5** dupe, stooge.

tool·ing (tōō′ling) *n.* Ornamentation or work done with tools.

toot (tōōt) *v.i.* **1** To blow a horn, whistle, etc., with short blasts. **2** To give forth a short blast. —*v.t.* **3** To sound (a horn, etc.) with short blasts. **4** To sound (a blast, etc.). — *n.* **1** A short blast on a horn, whistle, etc. **2** *Slang* A drinking spree. [? < MLG *tūten*] —**toot′er** *n.*

tooth (tōōth) *n. pl.* **teeth** (tēth) **1** One of the hard, dense

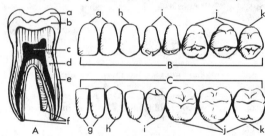

Teeth of human adult
A. cross-section of a molar. B. left upper jaw. C. left lower jaw. A.a. crown. b. enamel. c. pulp cavity. d. dentine. e. cement. f. roots. B. & C. g. incisors. h. canines. i. bicuspids. j. molars. k. wisdom teeth.

structures in the mouth of most vertebrates, used for seizing and chewing food, as offensive and defensive weapons, etc. **2** One of various hard bodies of the oral or gastric regions of invertebrates. **3** Something resembling a tooth in form or use, as a projection on a saw, comb, rake, or gearwheel. **4** Appetite or taste (for something): She has a sweet *tooth.* —**armed to the teeth** Completely or heavily armed. —**in the teeth of** Counter to or in defiance of. — **put teeth into** To make effective: to *put teeth into* a law. —**tooth and nail** With all one's strength and skill. —*v.t.* **1** To supply with teeth, as a rake or saw. **2** To give a serrated edge to; indent. —*v.i.* **3** To become interlocked, as gearwheels. [< OE *tōth*]

tooth·ache (tōōth′āk′) *n.* Pain in a tooth or in the nearby area.

tooth·brush (tōōth′brush′) *n.* A small brush used for cleaning the teeth.

toothed (tōōtht, tōōthd) *adj.* **1** Having (a specified type or number of teeth): used in combination: *sharp-toothed.* **2** Notched; serrated.

tooth·paste (tōōth′pāst′) *n.* A paste applied to a toothbrush and used in cleaning the teeth.

tooth·pick (tōōth′pik′) *n.* A small sliver, as of wood, used for removing particles of food from between the teeth.

tooth·some (tōōth′səm) *adj.* Having a pleasant taste. — **tooth′some·ly** *adv.* —**tooth′some·ness** *n.* —**Syn.** appetizing, delicious, savory, tasty.

too·tle (tōōt′l) *v.i.* **·tled, ·tling 1** To toot lightly or continuously, as on a flute, whistle, etc. —*v.t.* **2** To toot (a flute, whistle, etc.) lightly and continuously. —*n.* The sound of tootling. [Freq. of TOOT]

top[1] (top) *n.* **1** The uppermost or highest part: the *top* of a hill. **2** The higher or upper surface: the *top* of a bureau. **3** A lid or cover: a bottle *top.* **4** The roof of a vehicle, as an automobile. **5** The crown of the head. **6** *pl.* The aboveground part of a root vegetable. **7** The highest degree or reach: at the *top* of one's voice. **8** The most prominent place or rank: at the *top* of one's profession. **9** One who is highest in rank: the *top* of one's class. **10** The choicest or best part: the *top* of the crop. **11** The upper part of a shoe or boot. —**blow one's top** *Slang* To break out in a rage. —**from top to toe 1** From head to foot. **2** Completely. — **on top 1** Successful. **2** With success; victoriously. —**over the top** Over the upper edge of a trench so as to attack. —*adj.* **1** Of or pertaining to the top. **2** Forming or comprising the top. **3** Most important; chief: *top* authors. **4** Greatest in amount or degree: *top* prices; *top* speed. —*v.* **topped, top·ping** *v.t.* **1** To remove the top of; prune: to *top* a tree. **2** To provide with a top, cap, etc. **3** To form the top of. **4** To reach the top of; surmount: to *top* a wave. **5** To surpass or exceed: Can you *top* this? **6** In golf, tennis, etc., to hit the upper part of (the ball) in making a stroke. —*v.i.* **7** To top someone or something. —**top off** To complete, esp. with a finishing touch. [< OE]

top[2] (top) *n.* A toy of wood, plastic, metal, etc., with a point on which it is made to spin, as by the unwinding of a string. [< OE]

to·paz (tō′paz) *n.* **1** A yellow or brownish yellow crystalline mineral, valued as a gemstone. **2** A yellow sapphire. **3** A yellow variety of quartz resembling topaz. [< Gk. *topazos*]

top boot A boot with a high top, sometimes ornamented with materials different from the rest of the boot. —**top′-boot′ed** *adj.*

top·coat (top′kōt′) *n.* A lightweight overcoat.

top·drawer (top′drôr′) *adj. Informal* Of the highest quality, rank, or status.

top·flight (top′flīt′) *adj. Informal* Of the highest quality; outstanding; superior.

top·gal·lant (top′gal′ənt, tə·gal′ənt) *Naut. n.* The mast, sail, yard, or rigging immediately above the topmast and topsail. —*adj.* Pertaining to the topgallants.

top hat A man's formal hat, usu. black and made of silk, having a tall, cylindrical crown.

top·heav·y (top′hev′ē) *adj.* **·heav·i·er, ·heav·i·est 1** Too heavy at the top and liable to topple: a *topheavy* bookcase. **2** Having too many in positions of high rank, as an organization. —**top′heav′i·ly** *adv.* —**top′heav′i·ness** *n.*

top·ic (top′ik) *n.* **1** A subject treated of in speech or writing. **2** A theme for discussion. **3** A subdivision of an outline or a treatise. [< L *Topica,* title of a work by Aristotle] — **Syn. 1** issue, matter, point, question.

top·i·cal (top′i·kəl) *adj.* **1** Of or belonging to a place or spot; local. **2** Of or relating to matters of present or local interest; limited in relevance to a time or place. **3** Of or pertaining to a topic. **4** *Med.* Pertaining to a restricted area of the body. —**top′i·cal·ly** *adv.*

top kick *Slang* A top sergeant.

top·knot (top′not′) *n.* **1** A tuft or knot of hair or feathers on the top of the head. **2** A bow or other ornament worn as a headdress.

top·less (top′lis) *adj.* **1** Lacking a top. **2** Nude from the waist up. **3** Being without a covering for the breasts. **4** Presenting topless waitresses, dancers, etc., as a bar. **5** So high that no top can be seen. —**top′less·ness** *n.*

top·lev·el (top′lev′əl) *adj.* Of the highest rank or importance.

top·loft·y (top′lôf′tē) *adj.* **·i·er, ·i·est** Very proud or haughty. —**top′·loft′i·ness** *n.*

top·mast (top′mast′, -məst) *n. Naut.* The mast next above the lower mast.

top·most (top′mōst′) *adj.* Being at the very top.

top·notch (top′noch′) *adj. Informal* Best or highest, as in quality, merit, or performance. —**top′-notch′er** *n.*

to·pog·ra·phy (tə·pog′rə·fē) *n. pl.* **·phies 1** The art of representing on a map or chart the physical features of a place, as mountains, lakes, canals, usu. with indications of elevation. **2** The physical features of a region. **3** Topographic surveying. [< Gk. *topos* place + -GRAPHY] —**to·pog'ra·pher** *n.* —**top·o·graph·ic** (top'ə-graf'ik) or **·i·cal** *adj.* —**top'o·graph'i·cal·ly** *adv.*

top·per (top'ər) *n.* **1** One who or that which tops. **2** *Slang* One who or that which is of supreme quality. **3** *Informal* A top hat. **4** *Informal* A topcoat.

top·ping (top'ing) *adj.* **1** Towering high above. **2** Eminent; distinguished. **3** *Brit. Informal* Excellent; first-rate. —*n.* That which forms a top.

top·ple (top'əl) *v.* **·pled**, **·pling** *v.i.* **1** To fall, top foremost, by or as if by its own weight. **2** To seem to be about to fall; totter. —*v.t.* **3** To cause to totter or fall. **4** To cause to collapse; overthrow: to *topple* a government. [Freq. of TOP[1], *v.*]

tops (tops) *adj. Slang* Excellent; first-rate.

top·sail (top'sāl', -səl) *n. Naut.* **1** In a square-rigged vessel, a square sail set next above the lowest sail of a mast. **2** In a fore-and-aft-rigged vessel, a sail above the gaff of a lower sail.

top-se·cret (top'sē'krit) *adj.* Designating information requiring the strictest secrecy.

top sergeant *Informal* FIRST SERGEANT. See GRADE.

top·side (top'sīd') *n.* **1** The portion of a ship above the main deck. **2** *pl.* The side of a ship above the waterline. —*adv.* To or on the upper parts of a ship.

top·soil (top'soil') *n.* The surface soil of land.

top·sy-tur·vy (top'sē-tûr'vē) *adv.* **1** Upside down. **2** In utter confusion. —*adj.* **1** Being in an upset or disordered condition. **2** Upside-down. —*n.* A state of being topsy-turvy; disorder. [Earlier *topsy-tervy,* ? < TOP[1] + obs. *terve* overturn] —**top'sy-tur'vi·ly** *adv.* —**top'sy-tur'vi·ness** *n.*

toque (tōk) *n.* **1** A small, close-fitting, brimless hat worn by women. **2** TUQUE. [< Sp. *toca*]

To·rah (tôr'ə, tō'rə) *n.* In Judaism: **1** The Pentateuch. **2** A scroll, as of parchment, containing the Pentateuch. **3** The whole of Jewish law, including the Old Testament and the Talmud. [< Hebrew *tōrāh* an instruction, law]

torch (tôrch) *n.* **1** A stick of wood or some material dipped in tallow or oil and set ablaze at the end to provide a light that can be carried about. **2** Anything that illuminates or brightens. **3** A portable device giving off an intensely hot flame and used for burning off paint, melting solder, etc. **4** *Brit.* A flashlight. [< OF *torche*]

torch·bear·er (tôrch'bâr'ər) *n.* **1** One who carries a torch. **2** One who conveys knowledge, truth, etc. **3** A leader of a cause or movement.

torch·light (tôrch'līt') *n.* The light of a torch or torches. —*adj.* Lighted by torches.

torch song A popular love song, usu. melancholy and expressing hopeless yearning. —**torch singer**

tore (tôr, tōr) *p.t.* of TEAR[1].

tor·e·a·dor (tôr'ē-ə-dôr', tō'rē-) *n.* One who engages in a bullfight, esp. on horseback. [< Sp. < *toro* a bull]

to·ri·i (tôr'ē-ē, tōr'-) *n. pl.* **to·ri·i** The gateway of a Shinto shrine. [Jap.]

tor·ment (tôr'ment, -mənt) *n.* **1** Intense bodily pain or mental anguish. **2** A source of pain or anguish, or a persistent annoyance. **3** The inflicting of torture. —*v.t.* (tôr·ment') **1** To subject to intense or persistent physical or mental pain; make miserable. **2** To harass or vex. **3** To disturb; agitate; stir up. [< L *tormentum* a rack] —**tor·men'tor**, **tor·men'ter** *n.*

Japanese torii

—**Syn.** *n.* **1** agony, torture, suffering, misery.

torn (tôrn, tōrn) *p.p.* of TEAR[1].

tor·na·do (tôr·nā'dō) *n. pl.* **·does** or **·dos** **1** A whirling wind of exceptional force and violence, accompanied by a funnel-shaped cloud marking the narrow path of greatest destruction. **2** Any hurricane or violent windstorm. [Alter. of Sp. *tronada* a thunderstorm < *tronar* to thunder] —**tor·nad'ic** (-nad'ik) *adj.*

tor·pe·do (tôr·pē'dō) *n. pl.* **·does** **1** A self-propelled, tube-shaped underwater missile with an explosive warhead. **2** Any of various devices containing an explosive, as a submarine mine. —*v.t.* **·doed**, **·do·ing** **1** To damage or sink (a vessel) with a torpedo. **2** *Informal* To destroy utterly; demolish: Publicity could *torpedo* the agreement. **3** ELECTRIC RAY. [L, stiffness, numbness < *torpere* be numb]

torpedo boat A swift, lightly armed boat equipped to discharge torpedoes.

tor·pid (tôr'pid) *adj.* **1** Having lost sensibility or power of motion, partially or wholly, as a hibernating animal; dormant; numb. **2** Slow to act or respond; sluggish. **3** Apathetic; spiritless; dull. [< L *torpidus* < *torpere* be numb] —**tor·pid·i·ty** (tôr·pid'ə·tē), **tor'pid·ness** *n.* —**tor'pid·ly** *adv.*

tor·por (tôr'pər) *n.* **1** Complete or partial loss of sensibility or power of motion; stupor. **2** Apathy; listlessness; dullness. [< L *torpere* be numb] —**tor·po·rif·ic** (tôr'pə·rif'ik) *adj.*

torque (tôrk) *n.* That which causes or tends to cause twisting or rotational acceleration; the moment of a force. [< L *torquere* to twist]

tor·rent (tôr'ənt, tor'-) *n.* **1** A stream of liquid, esp. water, flowing rapidly and turbulently. **2** Any violent or tumultuous flow; a gush: a *torrent* of abuse. [< L *torrens,* lit., boiling, burning, pr.p. of *torrere* parch]

tor·ren·tial (tô·ren'shəl, to-) *adj.* **1** Of, like, or resulting in a torrent. **2** Resembling a torrent —**tor·ren'tial·ly** *adv.*

tor·rid (tôr'id, tor'-) *adj.* **1** Parched or hot from exposure to heat, esp. of the sun. **2** Intensely hot and dry; scorching. **3** Passionate. [< L *torridus* < *torrere* parch] —**tor·rid·i·ty** (tô·rid'ə·tē, to-), **tor'rid·ness** *n.* —**tor'rid·ly** *adv.*

torrid zone That part of the earth's surface on both sides of the equator between the tropics of Cancer and Capricorn. • See ZONE.

tor·sion (tôr'shən) *n.* **1** The act of twisting, or the state of being twisted. **2** *Mech.* Deformation or stress caused by twisting. [< L *tortus,* p.p. of *torquere* twist] —**tor'sion·al** *adj.* —**tor'sion·al·ly** *adv.*

tor·so (tôr'sō) *n. pl.* **·sos** or **·si** (-sē) **1** The trunk of a human body. **2** The part of a sculptured human figure corresponding to the trunk, esp. when the head and limbs are missing. [Ital., a stalk, trunk of a body]

tort (tôrt) *n. Law* Any civil wrong by act or omission for which a suit can be brought, exclusive of a breach of contract. [< L *tortus* twisted]

torte (tôrt, tôr'tə) *n. pl.* **tortes** or **tor·ten** (tôr'tən) A rich cake variously made of butter, eggs, fruits, and nuts. [G]

tor·til·la (tôr·tē'ə) *n.* A small, flat cake made of coarse cornmeal and baked on a griddle, common in Mexico. [Sp., dim. of *torta* a cake]

tor·toise (tôr'təs) *n.* A turtle, esp. one living on land. [< Med. L *tortuca*]

tortoise shell **1** The mottled yellow and brown shell of certain turtles, formerly used to make eyeglass frames, combs, etc. **2** A plastic imitation of this. —**tor'toise-shell'** *adj.*

Giant tortoise

tor·tu·ous (tôr'chōō·əs) *adj.* **1** Abounding in bends, twists, or turns; winding. **2** Not straightforward; devious: *tortuous* logic. [< L *tortus* twisted. See TORSION.] —**tor'tu·ous·ly** *adv.* —**tor'tu·ous·ness** *n.*

tor·ture (tôr'chər) *n.* **1** The infliction of extreme pain on one held captive, as in punishment, to obtain a confession or information, or to deter others from a course of action. **2** Intense physical or mental suffering; agony. **3** Something that causes severe pain. **4** *Informal* Something intensely annoying, embarrassing, or intolerable: Sitting through his speech was sheer *torture.* —*v.t.* **·tured**, **·tur·ing** **1** To inflict extreme pain upon; subject to torture. **2** To cause to suffer keenly in body or mind. **3** To twist or turn into an abnormal form; distort; wrench. [< L *tortura,* lit., a twisting < *tortus.* See TORSION.] —**tor'tur·er** *n.*

To·ry (tôr′ē, tō′rē) *n. pl.* **To·ries** **1** A historical English political party, opposed to the Whigs, now called the Conservative party. **2** One who adhered to the British cause at the time of the American Revolution. **3** A very conservative person: also **tory.** —**To′ry·ism** *n.*

toss (tôs, tos) *v.t.* **1** To throw, pitch, or fling about: *tossed* in a small boat on the open sea. **2** To throw or cast upward or toward another: to *toss* a ball. **3** To throw, esp. casually or indifferently: to *toss* clothes on a chair. **4** To remove from abruptly or violently: with *out:* He was *tossed* out of a job. **5** To throw (a coin) in the air to decide a question by comparing the side facing up, upon landing, with a previous call. **6** To lift with a quick motion, as the head. **7** To insert or interject casually or carelessly: to *toss* in impressive but irrelevant statistics. **8** To utter, write, or do easily or in an offhand manner: with *off.* **9** To bandy about, as something discussed. **10** To turn over and mix the contents of: to *toss* a salad. **11** To make restless; agitate. **12** To drink at one draft: often with *off.* —*v.i.* **13** To be moved or thrown about, as a ship in a storm. **14** To roll about restlessly or from side to side, as in sleep. **15** To go quickly or angrily, as with a toss of the head. **16** To toss a coin. —*n.* **1** The act of tossing, as a throw or pitch. **2** A quick movement, as of the head. **3** The state of being tossed. **4** TOSS-UP (def. 1). [Prob. < Scand.] —**toss′er** *n.* —**Syn.** *v.* **2** flip, flick, hurl. **12** quaff, swallow, gulp.

toss-up (tôs′up′, tos′-) *n.* **1** The tossing of a coin to decide a question. **2** An even chance.

tot[1] (tot) *n.* A little child; toddler. [Prob. < Scand.]

tot[2] (tot) *v.* **tot·ted, tot·ting** *Informal v.t.* **1** To add; total: with *up.* —*v.i.* **2** To add. [Short for TOTAL]

to·tal (tōt′l) *n.* The whole sum or amount. —*adj.* **1** Constituting or comprising a whole. **2** Complete: a *total* loss. —*v.* **·taled** or **·talled, ·tal·ing** or **·tal·ling** *v.t.* **1** To ascertain the total of. **2** To come to or reach as a total; amount to. **3** *Slang* To wreck completely; demolish, esp. a car. —*v.i.* **4** To amount: often with *to.* [< L *totus* all] —**to′tal·ly** *adv.*

to·tal·i·tar·i·an (tō·tal′ə·târ′ē·ən) *adj.* **1** Designating or characteristic of a government controlled exclusively by one party or faction that suppresses political dissent by force or intimidation and whose power to control the economic, social, and intellectual life of the individual is virtually unlimited. **2** Tyrannical; despotic. —*n.* An adherent of totalitarian government. —**to·tal′i·tar′i·an·ism** *n.*

to·tal·i·ty (tō·tal′ə·tē) *n. pl.* **·ties** **1** A total amount; aggregate; sum. **2** The state of being whole or entire.

tote (tōt) *Informal v.t.* **tot·ed, tot·ing** **1** To carry or bear on the person; transport; haul. **2** To carry habitually: He *totes* a gun. —*n.* **1** The act of toting. **2** A load or haul. [?] —**tot′er** *n.*

tote bag A large handbag for personal articles, carried esp. by women.

to·tem (tō′təm) *n.* **1** An animal, plant, or other natural object believed to be ancestrally related to a tribe, clan, or family group, and serving as its emblem, as among the North American Indians. **2** A representation of such an emblem. [< Algon.] —**to·tem·ic** (tō·tem′ik) *adj.* —**to′·tem·ism** *n.*

totem pole A pole carved or painted with totemic symbols, erected outside the houses of Indians along the NW coast of North America.

tot·ter (tot′ər) *v.i.* **1** To shake or waver, as if about to fall; be unsteady. **2** To walk unsteadily. —*n.* An unsteady or wobbly manner of walking. [Prob. < Scand.] —**tot′ter·er** *n.* —**tot′ter·ing·ly** *adv.* —**tot′ter·y** *adj.*

tou·can (tōō′kan, tōō·kän′) *n.* A fruit-eating bird of tropical America with brilliant plumage and a very large beak. [< Tupi *tucana*]

touch (tuch) *v.t.* **1** To place the hand, finger, or other body part in contact with; perceive by feeling. **2** To be or come in contact with. **3** To bring into contact with something else. **4** To hit or strike lightly; tap. **5** To lay the hand or hands on: Please don't *touch* the paintings. **6** To border on; adjoin. **7** To come to; reach: The temperature *touched* 90°. **8** To rival or equal: As a salesman, nobody could *touch* him. **9** To color slightly: The sun *touched* the clouds with gold. **10** To

Toucan

affect the emotions of, esp. so as to feel compassion or gratitude; move: She was *touched* by their concern for her health. **11** To hurt the feelings of. **12** To relate to; concern; affect: The war *touches* us all. **13** To have to do with, use, or partake of: He never *touches* anything stronger than ginger ale. **14** To affect injuriously; taint: vegetables *touched* by frost. **15** *Slang* To borrow money from. —*v.i.* **16** To touch someone or something. **17** To come into or be in contact. —**touch at** To stop briefly at (a port or place) in the course of a journey or voyage. —**touch down** To land after flight. —**touch off** **1** To cause to explode; detonate; fire. **2** To provoke or initiate, esp. a violent reaction. —**touch on** (or **upon**) **1** To relate to; concern: That *touches* on another question. **2** To treat or discuss briefly or in passing. —**touch up** To add finishing touches or corrections to, as a work of art or writing. —*n.* **1** The act or fact of touching; a coming into contact, as a tap. **2** The sense stimulated by touching; the tactile sense by which a surface or its characteristics, as of pressure or texture, may be perceived. **3** A sensation conveyed by touching: a silky *touch.* **4** Communication or contact: Let's keep in *touch.* **5** A distinctive manner or style, as of an artist, author, or craftsman: a master's *touch.* **6** Delicate sensitivity, appreciation, or understanding: a fine *touch* for collecting rare china. **7** Any slight or delicate detail that helps to finish or perfect something, as a work of art or writing: to apply the finishing *touches.* **8** A trace; hint: a *touch* of irony. **9** A slight attack; twinge: a *touch* of rheumatism. **10** A small quantity; dash: a *touch* of perfume. **11** The resistance to motion offered by the keys of a piano, typewriter, etc. **12** The manner in which something is struck or touched, as the keys of a piano. **13** *Slang* Borrowed money, or a request to borrow money. **14** *Slang* A person from whom money may be borrowed, esp. easily: a soft *touch.* [< OF *tochier*] —**touch′a·ble** *adj.* —**touch′er** *n.*

touch and go An uncertain, risky, or precarious state of things. —**touch′-and-go′** *adj.*

touch·back (tuch′bak′) *n.* In football, the act of touching the ball to the ground behind the player's own goal line when the ball was propelled over the goal line by an opponent.

touch·down (tuch′doun′) *n.* **1** A scoring play in football in which a player has possession of the ball on or over the opponent's goal line. **2** The act of touching down, as an aircraft or spacecraft.

tou·ché (tōō·shā′) *interj.* A term used in fencing to indicate a touch scored by one's opponent, and otherwise to acknowledge the wit or effectiveness of a point made in argument or conversation. [F]

touched (tucht) *adj.* **1** Affected emotionally; moved. **2** Slightly unbalanced in mind; crack-brained.

touch·ing (tuch′ing) *adj.* Appealing to the emotions; esp., inspiring tenderness or sympathy. —*prep.* With regard to; concerning. —**touch′ing·ly** *adv.* —**touch′ing·ness** *n.*

touch-me-not (tuch′mē·not′) *n.* Any of various plants, the ripe seed capsules of which explode when touched.

touch·stone (tuch′stōn′) *n.* **1** A dark stone formerly used to test the purity of gold by the color of the streak made on the stone by the metal. **2** Any criterion or standard by which quality or value may be tested.

touch·wood (tuch′wōōd′) *n.* PUNK[1] (def. 1).

touch·y (tuch′ē) *adj.* **touch·i·er, touch·i·est** **1** Apt to take offense on very little provocation. **2** Liable to cause hurt feelings or contention: a *touchy* subject. —**touch′i·ly** *adv.* —**touch′i·ness** *n.* —**Syn.** **1** sensitive, thin-skinned, volatile. **2** delicate, sensitive.

tough (tuf) *adj.* **1** Capable of bearing tension or strain without breaking, esp. because strong in texture or composition. **2** Difficult to cut or chew. **3** Strong in body or mind, esp. in resisting or enduring stress. **4** Requiring determined or intense effort; difficult: a *tough* assignment. **5** Resolute; unyielding; inflexible: a *tough* stand in the negotiations. **6** Severe; harsh: a *tough* punishment. **7** Given to or characterized by violence or rowdyism: a *tough* neighborhood. **8** *Informal* Unfortunate; regrettable. **9** *Slang* Great; fine. —*n.* A ruffian; rowdy. —*v.t.* *Informal* To manage to get through; endure: often with *out:* to *tough out* a recession. [< OE *tōh*] —**tough′ly** *adv.* —**tough′ness** *n.* —**Syn.** **5** uncompromising, stubborn, militant.

tough·en (tuf'ən) v.t. & v.i. To make or become tough or tougher. —**tough'en·er** n.

tou·pee (tōō·pā') n. A man's small wig worn to cover a bald spot. [< OF *toup, top* a tuft of hair]

tour (tōōr) n. 1 An excursion or journey, as for sightseeing. 2 A trip, usu. over a planned course, as to conduct business, present theatrical performances, etc. 3 A set period of time, as of service in a particular place; turn or shift. 4 A brief survey; circuit: a *tour* of the grounds. —v.t. 1 To make a tour of; travel. 2 To present on a tour: to *tour* a play. —v.i. 3 To go on a tour. [< OF *tor* a turn < L *tornus* a lathe]

tour de force (tōōr də fôrs') pl. **tours de force** (tōōr) A remarkable feat, as of skill, creativity, or industry. [F, lit., feat of strength]

touring car An old type of large, open automobile with a capacity for five or more passengers.

tour·ism (tōōr'iz·əm) n. 1 Recreational travel, considered esp. as an industry or source of income. 2 The organization and guidance of tourists. —**tour·is'tic** adj.

tour·ist (tōōr'ist) n. One who makes a tour or a pleasure trip. —adj. Of or suitable for tourists. —**tour'ist·y** adj.

tour·ma·line (tōōr'mə·lən, -lēn') n. A complex mineral with a vitreous to resinous luster, found in various colors and valued in its transparent varieties as a gemstone. Also **tour'ma·lin** (-lin). [< F]

tour·na·ment (tûr'nə·mənt, tōōr'-) n. 1 A series of competitive sports events or games for prizes or cash awards and often for a championship: a golf or bridge *tournament*. 2 In medieval times, a pageant in which two opposing parties of men in armor contended on horseback with blunted weapons, esp. lances. [< OF < *torneier* to tourney]

tour·ney (tûr'nē, tōōr'-) v.i. To take part in a tournament. —n. TOURNAMENT. [< OF *torneier*]

tour·ni·quet (tōōr'nə·kit, tûr'-) n. A device for controlling arterial bleeding by tightening a nooselike bandage. [< F *tourner* to turn]

tou·sle (tou'zəl) v.t. **·sled, ·sling** To disarrange or dishevel; rumple. —n. A tousled mass, esp. of hair. [Freq. of ME *tousen*]

tout (tout) *Informal* v.i. 1 To solicit patronage, customers, votes, etc. 2 To sell information, as to a bettor, about horses entered in a race. —v.t. 3 To solicit; importune. 4 To praise highly or proclaim: *touted* as the world's fastest human. 5 To sell information concerning (a race horse). —n. 1 One who touts. 2 One who solicits business. [< OE *tōtian, tȳtan* peep, look out]

tout à fait (tōō tá fe') *French* Entirely; quite.

tout de suite (tōōt swēt) Immediately; at once. [F]

tout en·sem·ble (tōō tän sän'bl') *French* All in all; everything considered.

tow[1] (tō) n. A short, coarse hemp or flax fiber prepared for spinning. [Prob. < OE *tōw-* spinning]

tow[2] (tō) v.t. To pull or drag, as by a rope or chain. —n. 1 The act of towing, or the state of being towed. 2 That which is towed, as a barge. 3 TOWLINE. —**in tow** 1 In the condition of being towed. 2 Drawn along as if being towed: a film star with her fans *in tow*. 3 Under one's protection or care: took the orphan *in tow*. [< OE *togian*]

tow·age (tō'ij) n. 1 The charge for towing. 2 The act of towing.

to·ward (tôrd, tōrd, tə·wôrd') prep. 1 In the direction of; facing. 2 With respect to; regarding. 3 In anticipation of or as a contribution to; for: He is saving *toward* his education. 4 Near in point of time; approaching: *toward* evening. 5 Tending or designed to result in. Also **to·wards'**. —adj. (tôrd, tōrd) Impending or imminent. [< OE *tō* to + -*weard* -ward] —**to·ward'ness** n.

tow·el (toul, tou'əl) n. A cloth or paper for drying anything by wiping. —v.t. **·eled** or **·elled, ·el·ing** or **·el·ling** To wipe or dry with a towel. [< OF *toaille*]

tow·el·ing (tou'ling, tou'əl·ing) n. Material for towels. Also **tow·el·ling.**

tow·er (tou'ər) n. 1 A structure very tall in proportion to its other dimensions, and either standing alone or forming part of a building. 2 A place of security or defense;

citadel. 3 Someone or something likened to a tower in strength or command. —v.i. To rise or stand like a tower; extend to a great height. [< L *turris*]

tow·er·ing (tou'ər·ing) adj. 1 Very high or very great: a *towering* figure in modern drama. 2 Rising to a high pitch of violence or intensity: a *towering* rage.

tow·head (tō'hed') n. 1 A head of very light-colored or flaxen hair. 2 A person having such hair. [< TOW[1] + HEAD] —**tow'head'ed** adj.

tow·hee (tō'ē, tō'hē) n. Any of various American finches related to the buntings and the sparrows. Also **towhee bunting.** [Imit.]

tow·line (tō'līn') n. A line, rope, or chain used in towing.

town (toun) n. 1 Any collection of dwellings and other buildings larger than a village and smaller than a city. 2 A closely settled urban district, as contrasted with less populated or suburban areas or with the open country. 3 A city of any size. 4 The inhabitants or voters of a town. 5 TOWNSHIP. 6 Those residents of a town who are not associated educationally or administratively with a college or university situated in the town: *town* and gown. —**go to town** *Slang* To work or proceed with dispatch; get busy. —**on the town** *Slang* On a round of bars, nightclubs, etc., in the city in search of diversion or excitement. —**paint the town red** *Slang* To go on a spree; carouse. —adj. Of, situated in, or for a town. [< OE *tūn, tuun* an enclosure, group of houses]

Towhee

town clerk An official who keeps the records of a town.

town crier Formerly, a person appointed to make proclamations through the streets of a town.

town hall A building in a town containing the public offices and often a place for meetings.

town house 1 A residence in a town or city, esp. when owned by one who also owns a house in the country. 2 A two- or three-story house, usu. for one family, contiguous to one or more similar houses.

town meeting A meeting of residents or voters of a town for the purpose of transacting town business.

town·ship (toun'ship) n. 1 In the U.S. and Canada, a territorial subdivision of a county with certain corporate powers of municipal government for local purposes. 2 In New England, a local political unit governed by a town meeting.

towns·man (tounz'mən) n. pl. **·men** (-mən) 1 A resident of a town. 2 A fellow citizen of a town. 3 A permanent resident of a town, as contrasted with a student or teacher in a school or college situated in the town.

towns·peo·ple (tounz'pē'pəl) n.pl. People who live in towns or in a particular town or city. Also **towns'folk'** (-fōk').

town·y (toun'ē) n. pl. **town·ies** *Informal* TOWNSMAN (def. 3). Also **town'ie.**

tow·path (tō'path', -päth') n. A path along a river or canal used by men, horses, or mules towing boats.

tow·rope (tō'rōp') n. A heavy rope or cable for towing.

tow truck (tō) A truck equipped to tow other vehicles.

tox·e·mi·a (tok·sē'mē·ə) n. The presence in the blood of toxins from a local source of infection. Also **tox·ae'mi·a.** [< TOX(IC) + Gk. *haima* blood] —**tox·e'mic** adj.

tox·ic (tok'sik) adj. 1 Poisonous. 2 Due to or caused by poison or a toxin. [< Gk. *toxicon (pharmakon)* (a poison) for arrows < *toxon* a bow] —**tox'i·cal·ly** adv. —**tox·ic'i·ty** (-sis'ə·tē) n.

toxico- *combining form* Poison; of or pertaining to poison or poisons: *toxicology*. Also **toxic-.** [< Gk. *toxicon* poison]

tox·i·col·o·gy (tok'sə·kol'ə·jē) n. The science that deals with poisons, their detection, antidotes, etc. —**tox'i·co·log'ic** (-kə·loj'ik) or **·i·cal** adj. —**tox'i·co·log'i·cal·ly** adv. —**tox'i·col'o·gist** n.

tox·in (tok'sin) n. 1 Any of various poisonous compounds produced by living organisms and acting as causative agents in many diseases. 2 Any toxic matter generated in living or dead organisms. [< TOX(IC) + -IN]

---

add, āce, câre, pälm; end, ēven; it, īce; odd, ōpen, ôrder; tŏŏk, pōōl; up, bûrn; ə = a in *above,* u in *focus;* yōō = u in *fuse;* oil; pout; check; go; ring; thin; this; zh, *vision.* < derived from; ? origin uncertain or unknown.

toy (toi) *n.* 1 Something designed or serving as a plaything for children. 2 Something trifling or unimportant. 3 An ornament; trinket. 4 A small animal, esp. one of a breed characterized by small size. —*v.i.* 1 To act or consider something without seriousness or conviction; trifle: to *toy* with an idea. 2 To use someone or something for one's amusement. 3 To act flirtatiously. —*adj.* 1 Designed as a toy. 2 Resembling a toy; esp., of miniature size: a *toy* dog. [Prob. < ME *toye* flirtation, sport] —**toy'er** *n.*

tp. township.

tpk. turnpike.

tr. translated; translation; translator; transpose; transitive; treasurer.

trace[1] (trās) *n.* 1 A vestige or mark left by some past event or by a person or thing no longer present. 2 An imprint or mark indicating the passage of a person or thing, as a footprint, etc. 3 A path or trail beaten down by men or animals. 4 A barely detectable quantity, quality, or characteristic. 5 A lightly drawn line; something traced. —*v.* **traced, trac·ing** *v.t.* 1 To follow the tracks or trail of. 2 To follow the course or development of, esp. by investigation of a series of events. 3 To find out or determine by investigation. 4 To follow (tracks, a course of development, etc.). 5 To draw; sketch. 6 To copy (a drawing, etc.) on a superimposed transparent sheet. 7 To form (letters, etc.) painstakingly. —*v.i.* 8 To have its origin; go back in time. 9 To follow a track, course of development, etc. [< OF *tracier* to trace] —**trace'a·bil'i·ty, trace'a·ble·ness** *n.* —**trace'a·ble** *adj.* —**trace'a·bly** *adv.* —**Syn.** 1 remnant, sign, aftermath, token, clue.

trace[2] (trās) *n.* One of two side straps or chains connected to a draft animal's harness and to the vehicle to be pulled. —**kick over the traces** To throw off control; become unmanageable. [< OF *trait* a dragging, a leather harness]

trac·er (trā'sər) *n.* 1 One who or that which traces. 2 An inquiry forwarded from one point to another, to trace missing mail, etc. 3 A substance, as a radioisotope, introduced into a system in minute amount as an indicator of the course of a process, reaction, disease, etc. 4 A bullet or shell that indicates its course by leaving a trail of smoke or fire.

trac·er·y (trā'sər-ē) *n. pl.* **·er·ies** 1 Ornamental stonework formed of branching lines, as in a Gothic window. 2 Any delicate ornamentation resembling this.

tra·che·a (trā'kē·ə) *n. pl.* **·che·ae** (-kē·ē, -kē·ī) or **·che·as** 1 In vertebrates, the duct by which air passes from the larynx to the bronchi and the lungs; the windpipe. 2 Any of the air passages in air-breathing arthropods. [< Gk. *(artēria) tracheia* a rough (artery)] —**tra'che·al** *adj.*

tra·che·ot·o·my (trā'kē·ot'ə·mē) *n. pl.* **·mies** *Surg.* An incision into the trachea. Also **tra'che·ost'·o·my** (-ost'ə·mē).

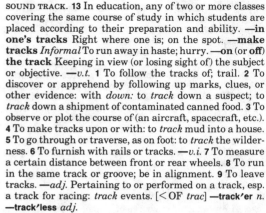

Trachea

tra·cho·ma (trə·kō'mə) *n.* A contagious virus disease of the eye characterized by granular excrescences on the inner surface of the eyelids. [< Gk. *trachōma* roughness] —**tra·chom·a·tous** (trə·kom'ə·təs) *adj.*

trac·ing (trā'sing) *n.* 1 The act of one who traces. 2 Something traced, as a copy made by tracing on transparent paper. 3 A record made by a self-registering instrument.

track (trak) *n.* 1 A mark or trail left by the passage of anything, as a series of footprints. 2 A path or way marked or worn out by the repeated passage of people, animals, or vehicles. 3 Any course or path, esp. one describing movement: the *track* of a missile or a comet. 4 A pair of parallel rails, usu. including the ties, that guide the wheels of a train, trolley, etc. 5 A usu. elliptical course for racing. 6 A sport in which footraces of various distances are held on a track. 7 TRACK AND FIELD. 8 A sequence of events; a succession of ideas. 9 Awareness of the progress or sequence; count; record: to lose *track* of an old friend; to keep *track* of expenses. 10 An endless metal belt, usu. one of a pair, by means of which certain vehicles are capable of moving over soft, slippery, or uneven surfaces. 11 The distance between the front or rear wheels of a vehicle, usu. measured from the center of the treads. 12 SOUND TRACK. 13 In education, any of two or more classes covering the same course of study in which students are placed according to their preparation and ability. —**in one's tracks** Right where one is; on the spot. —**make tracks** *Informal* To run away in haste; hurry. —**on** (or **off**) **the track** Keeping in view (or losing sight of) the subject or objective. —*v.t.* 1 To follow the tracks of; trail. 2 To discover or apprehend by following up marks, clues, or other evidence: with *down*: to *track* down a suspect; to *track* down a shipment of contaminated canned food. 3 To observe or plot the course of (an aircraft, spacecraft, etc.). 4 To make tracks upon or with: to *track* mud into a house. 5 To go through or traverse, as on foot: to *track* the wilderness. 6 To furnish with rails or tracks. —*v.i.* 7 To measure a certain distance between front or rear wheels. 8 To run in the same track or groove; be in alignment. 9 To leave tracks. —*adj.* Pertaining to or performed on a track, esp. a track for racing: *track* events. [< OF *trac*] —**track'er** *n.* —**track'less** *adj.*

track·age (trak'ij) *n.* 1 Railroad tracks collectively. 2 The right of one company to use the tracks of another. 3 The charge for this right.

track and field A sport consisting of footraces on a track and contests on a field, as in hurling, throwing, or leaping. —**track'-and-field'** *adj.*

trackless trolley TROLLEY BUS.

track record *Informal* A record of achievements.

tract[1] (trakt) *n.* 1 An extended area, as of land or water; stretch or expanse. 2 A system of parts or organs in an animal, having a distinct function: the alimentary *tract*. [< L *tractus* a drawing out < *trahere* draw]

tract[2] (trakt) *n.* A short treatise or pamphlet, as on religion or morals. [< L *tractatus* a handling]

tract·a·ble (trak'tə·bəl) *adj.* 1 Easily led or controlled; docile. 2 Readily worked or handled; malleable. [< L *tractare* handle, freq. of *trahere* draw] —**tract'a·bly** *adv.* —**tract'a·ble·ness, tract'a·bil'i·ty** *n.* —**Syn.** 1 manageable, compliant, mild, submissive.

trac·tile (trak'til, tīl) *adj.* That can be drawn out; ductile. [< L *tractus.* See TRACT[1].] —**trac·til'i·ty** *n.*

trac·tion (trak'shən) *n.* 1 The act of drawing, as by motive power over a surface. 2 The state of being pulled or drawn: to place a fractured limb in *traction*. 3 The power employed in pulling or drawing. 4 Adhesive or rolling friction, as of tires on a road. [< L *tractus.* See TRACT[1].] —**trac'tion·al, trac·tive** (trak'tiv) *adj.*

trac·tor (trak'tər) *n.* 1 A powerful, self-propelled vehicle used to pull farm machinery. 2 An automotive vehicle with a driver's cab, used to haul trailers, etc. 3 An airplane with the propeller or propellers situated in front of the lifting surfaces. [< L *tractus.* See TRACT[1].]

Tractor *def. 1*

trad (trad) *adj. Slang* Traditional: *trad* jazz.

trade (trād) *n.* 1 A business or occupation. 2 A skilled or specialized line of work, as a craft. 3 The people or companies engaged in a particular business. 4 The buying and selling or exchange of commodities; also, an instance of such commerce. 5 A firm's customers. 6 An exchange of personal articles; swap. 7 Any exchange of things or people having negotiable value: a baseball *trade*. 8 *Usu. pl.* TRADE WIND. —*adj.* 1 Of or pertaining to a trade. 2 Used by or intended for the members of a particular trade: a *trade* journal. —*v.t.* **trad·ed, trad·ing** 1 To give in exchange for something else. 2 To barter or exchange. —*v.i.* 3 To engage in commerce or in business transactions. 4 To make an exchange. 5 *Informal* To do one's shopping: with *at*: to *trade* at a store. —**trade in** To give in exchange as payment or part payment. —**trade off** To match or correlate, as incompatible elements or objectives, in the process of reaching a solution or compromise. —**trade on** To take advantage of. [< MLG, a track] —**trad'er** *n.*

trade-in (trād'in') *n.* Used merchandise accepted in payment or part payment for other, esp. new, merchandise.

trade-last (trād'last', -läst') *n. Informal* A favorable remark that one has heard and offers to repeat to the person complimented in return for a similar remark.

trade·mark (trād′märk′) *n.* **1** A name, symbol, design, device, or word used by a merchant or manufacturer to identify his product and distinguish it from that of others. **2** Any distinctive or characteristic feature. —*v.t.* **1** To label with a trademark. **2** To register and bring under legal protection as a trademark.

trade name **1** The name by which an article, process, etc., is designated in trade. **2** A name given by a manufacturer to designate a proprietary article, sometimes having the status of a trademark. **3** The name of a business concern.

trade-off (trād′ôf′, -of′) *n.* **1** A giving up of something, as an objective or advantage, in exchange for something else: a *trade-off* of higher pay for longer vacations. **2** The relationship that characterizes such an exchange; a compromise or adjustment between opposing elements or positions: the *trade-off* between taxation and improved public services.

trade school A school where practical skills or trades are taught.

trades·man (trādz′mən) *n. pl.* **·men** (-mən) A retail dealer; shopkeeper. —**trades′wom·an** *n. Fem.*

trade union LABOR UNION. Also **trades union.** —**trade un·ionism** —**trade unionist**

trade wind Either of two steady winds blowing toward the equator, one from the northeast on the north, the other from the southeast on the south side of the equatorial line.

trading post A building or small settlement in unsettled territory used as a station for barter, as for furs.

trading stamp A stamp of fixed value given as a premium with a purchase and exchangeable, in quantity, for merchandise.

tra·di·tion (trə·dish′ən) *n.* **1** The transmission of knowledge, opinions, customs, practices, etc., from generation to generation, esp. by word of mouth and by example. **2** The body of beliefs and usages so transmitted; also, any particular story, belief, or usage of this kind. **3** A custom so long continued that it has almost the force of a law. [< L *traditus,* p.p. of *tradere* deliver] —**tra·di′tion·al** *adj.* —**tra·di′tion·al·ly** *adv.*

tra·duce (trə·dyōōs′) *v.t.* **·duced, ·duc·ing** To misrepresent willfully the conduct or character of; defame; slander. [< L *traducere* transport, bring into disgrace] —**tra·duce′·ment, tra·duc′er** *n.*

traf·fic (traf′ik) *n.* **1** The passing of pedestrians, vehicles, aircraft, messages, etc., in a limited space or between certain points. **2** The people, vehicles, messages, etc., so moving. **3** The business of buying and selling commodities; trade. **4** Unlawful or improper trade: *traffic* in stolen goods. **5** The people or freight transported by a carrier, as a railroad. **6** The business of transportation. **7** Communication or contact; connection. —*v.i.* **·ficked, ·fick·ing** **1** To engage in buying and selling illegally: with *in:* to *traffic* in narcotic drugs. **2** To have dealings with *with.* [< MF < Ital. *traffico*] —**traf′fick·er** *n.*

traffic light A set of colored signal lights used to control the passage of automotive traffic.

tra·ge·di·an (trə·jē′dē·ən) *n.* **1** An actor of tragedy. **2** A writer of tragedies.

tra·ge·di·enne (trə·jē′dē·en′) *n.* An actress of tragedy.

trag·e·dy (traj′ə·dē) *n. pl.* **·dies** **1** A form of drama in which the protagonist comes to disaster, as through a flaw in character, and in which the ending is usu. marked by sorrow or pity. **2** A play, film, etc., of this kind. **3** Any tragic or disastrous incident or series of incidents. **4** *Informal* A misfortune. [< Gk. *tragōidia*]

trag·ic (traj′ik) *adj.* **1** Of or having the nature of tragedy. **2** Appropriate to or suggestive of tragedy: a *tragic* manner. **3** Causing or likely to cause suffering, sorrow, or death: a *tragic* accident. [< Gk. *tragikos* pertaining to tragedy] —**trag′i·cal·ly** *adv.*

trag·i·com·e·dy (traj′i·kom′ə·dē) *n. pl.* **·dies** **1** A drama having characteristics of both tragedy and comedy. **2** An

incident or series of incidents of this nature. —**trag′i·com′ic** or **·i·cal** *adj.* —**trag′i·com′i·cal·ly** *adv.*

trail (trāl) *v.t.* **1** To draw along lightly over a surface. **2** To drag or draw after: to *trail* oars; to *trail* an injured leg. **3** To follow the track of; trace: to *trail* game. **4** To be or come along behind. **5** To follow behind, as in pursuit or to keep under surveillance: to *trail* a suspect. —*v.i.* **6** To hang or extend loosely so as to drag over a surface. **7** To grow extensively and usu. irregularly along the ground or over rocks, etc. **8** To be or come along behind. **9** To move or walk heavily or ponderously; trudge. **10** To lag behind: to *trail* by 30,000 votes; to *trail* in the development of auto safety standards. **11** To flow or extend, as in a stream. —*n.* **1** The track left by something that has moved or been drawn or dragged over a surface. **2** The track, scent, etc., indicating the passage of someone or something. **3** The path worn by persons or by animals, esp. through a wilderness. **4** Something that trails or is trailed behind, as the train of a dress or the track of a meteor. **5** A sequence of results or conditions following after something: left a *trail* of broken hearts. [< AF *trailler* haul, tow a boat]

trail·er (trā′lər) *n.* **1** One who or that which trails. **2** A vehicle drawn by a cab or tractor having motive power. **3** A vehicle usu. drawn by an automobile or truck and equipped to serve as living quarters. **4** PREVIEW (def. 2).

trailing arbutus A prostrate evergreen shrub bearing clusters of fragrant pink flowers.

train¹ (trān) *n.* **1** A series of connected railway cars, often drawn by a locomotive. **2** Anything drawn along behind, as a trailing part of a skirt. **3** A line or group of followers; retinue. **4** A moving line of people, animals, vehicles, etc.; procession. **5** A series, succession, or set of connected things; sequence: a *train* of thought. **6** Something, as a period of time or set of circumstances, following after something else; aftermath: The argument left bitter feelings in its *train.* **7** *Mech.* A series of parts acting on each other, as for transmitting motion. —*v.t.* **1** To bring to a desired standard by careful instruction; esp., to guide in morals or manners. **2** To make skillful or proficient: to *train* soldiers. **3** To make obedient to orders or capable of performing tricks, as an animal. **4** To lead into taking a particular course; develop into a fixed shape: to *train* a plant on a trellis; to *train* the hair to lie flat. **5** To put or point in an exact direction; aim: to *train* a rifle or a gaze on someone. —*v.i.* **6** To undergo a course of training. [< OF *trahiner* to draw] —**train′a·ble** *adj.* —**train′er** *n.* —**Syn.** *v.* **1** educate, instruct, rear, bring up, mold.

train² (trān) *n. Can.* A large sled, having a shape like a toboggan. [< F *traineau* sled]

train·ee (trā·nē′) *n.* One who is being trainned, as a new employee.

train·ing (trā′ning) *n.* **1** Systematic instruction and drill. **2** The method or action of one who trains, as for an athletic contest.

train·man (trān′mən) *n. pl.* **·men** (-mən) A railway employee serving on a train.

traipse (trāps) *v.i.* **traipsed, traips·ing** To walk or wander about; gad. —*n.* The act of traipsing. [Prob. < OF *trapasser,* var. of *trespasser* trespass]

trait (trāt) *n.* A distinguishing feature or quality, as of character. [< L *tractus* a drawing out < *trahere* draw]

trai·tor (trā′tər) *n.* **1** One who commits treason. **2** One who betrays a trust or acts deceitfully and disloyally. [< L *tradere* betray] —**trai′tress** (-tris) *n. Fem.*

trai·tor·ous (trā′tər·əs) *adj.* **1** Of, constituting, or resembling treason. **2** Of or characteristic of a traitor; treacherous. —**trai′tor·ous·ly** *adv.* —**trai′tor·ous·ness** *n.*

tra·jec·to·ry (trə·jek′tər·ē) *n. pl.* **·ries** The path described by an object or body moving in space, as of a comet or a bullet. [< L *trajectus,* p.p. of *trajicere* throw over]

tram (tram) *n.* **1** *Brit.* STREETCAR. **2** An open vehicle running on rails, used to carry coal in a mine. Also **tram′car′** (-kär′). [< dial. *tram* a rail]

tram·mel (tram′əl) *n.* **1** *Usu. pl.* That which limits freedom or activity; hindrance. **2** A fetter or shackle, esp. one used in teaching a horse to amble. **3** An instrument for drawing ellipses. **4** An adjustable hook used to suspend cooking pots from a fireplace crane. **5** A net formed of three layers, the central one of finer mesh, to trap fish passing through either of the others: also **trammel net.** — *v.t.* **·meled** or **·melled, ·mel·ing** or **·mel·ling 1** To hinder or obstruct; restrict. **2** To entangle in or as in a snare; imprison. [< LL *tremaculum* net < L *tri-* three + *macula* a mesh] **—tram′mel·er** or **tram′mel·ler** *n.*

tramp (tramp) *v.i.* **1** To walk or wander about, esp. as a tramp or hobo. **2** To walk heavily or firmly. —*v.t.* **3** To walk or wander through. **4** To walk on heavily; trample. —*n.* **1** One who travels from place to place, usu. on foot and destitute and dependent on charity for a living. **2** The sound of heavy marching or walking. **3** A long stroll; hike. **4** A steam vessel that goes from port to port picking up freight wherever it can: also **tramp steamer. 5** *Slang* A sexually promiscuous woman. [ME *trampen*] **—tramp′er** *n.* — **Syn.** *n.* **1** vagrant, vagabond, hobo, bum.

tram·ple (tram′pəl) *v.* **·pled, ·pling** *v.i.* **1** To tread heavily, esp. so as to crush. **2** To injure or encroach upon someone or something by or as by tramping: with *on:* to *trample* on someone's rights. —*v.t.* **3** To tread heavily or ruthlessly on. —*n.* The sound of treading under foot. [< ME *trampen* tramp] **—tram′pler** *n.*

tram·po·line (tram′pə·lēn, tram′pə·lēn′) *n.* A heavy canvas stretched to a frame by springs and used for its resiliency in tumbling. Also **tram′po·lin.** [< Ital. *trampoli* stilts]

tram·way (tram′wā′) *n. Brit.* A streetcar line.

trance (trans, träns) *n.* **1** A state in which one appears to be unable to act consciously, as though hypnotized or governed by a supernatural force. **2** A dreamlike or sleepy state, as that induced by hypnosis. **3** A state of profound concentration marked by lack of awareness of one's surroundings; deep abstraction. [< OF *transir* pass, die]

tran·quil (trang′kwil) *adj.* **1** Free from agitation or disturbance; calm: a *tranquil* mood. **2** Quiet and motionless: a *tranquil* scene. [< L *tranquillus* quiet] **—tran′quil·ly** *adv.* **—tran′quil·ness** *n.* **—Syn. 1** relaxed, serene. **2** placid.

tran·quil·ize (trang′kwəl·īz) *v.t. & v.i.* **·ized, ·iz·ing** To make or become tranquil, esp. by using a drug. Also **tran′·quil·lize.** *Brit. sp.* **·lise.** **—tran′quil·i·za′tion** *n.*

tran·quil·iz·er (trang′kwəl·ī′zər) *n.* **1** One who or that which tranquilizes. **2** Any of various drugs that calm mental agitation without impairing consciousness. Also **tran′·quil·liz′er.**

tran·quil·li·ty (trang·kwil′ə·tē) *n.* The state of being tranquil; peacefulness; quiet. Also **tran·quil′i·ty.**

trans- *prefix* **1** Across; beyond; on the other side of: *transatlantic; transmigrate.* **2** Through: *transfix.* **3** Through and through; changing completely: *transform.* [< L *trans* across, beyond, over]

trans. transactions; transferred; transitive; translated; translation; translator.

trans·act (trans·akt′, tranz-) *v.t.* **1** To carry through; accomplish; do. —*v.i.* **2** To do business. [< L *transactus,* p.p. of *transigere* drive through, accomplish] **—trans·ac′tor** *n.*

trans·ac·tion (trans·ak′shən, tranz-) *n.* **1** The act or process of transacting. **2** Something transacted; esp., a business deal. **3** *pl.* Published reports, as of a society. **—trans·ac′tion·al** *adj.*

trans·at·lan·tic (trans′ət·lan′tik, tranz′-) *adj.* **1** Across or crossing the Atlantic Ocean: a *transatlantic* flight. **2** On the other side of the Atlantic.

trans·cend (tran·send′) *v.t.* **1** To go or pass beyond the limits of: knowledge that *transcends* reason. **2** To rise above in excellence or degree. —*v.i.* **3** To be surpassing; excel. [< L *trans-* beyond, over + *scandere* to climb]

tran·scen·dent (tran·sen′dənt) *adj.* **1** TRANSCENDENTAL (def. 1). **2** *Theol.* Existing apart from and above the material universe: said of God. [< L *transcendere* transcend] — **tran·scen′dence, tran·scen′den·cy** *n.* **—tran·scen′dent·ly** *adv.*

tran·scen·den·tal (tran′sen·den′təl) *adj.* **1** Rising above or going beyond ordinary limits; surpassing. **2** Beyond natural experience; supernatural. **3** Of or pertaining to transcendentalism. **—tran′scen·den′tal·ly** *adv.*

tran·scen·den·tal·ism (tran′sen·den′təl·iz′əm) *n.* The philosophical doctrine that man can attain knowledge which goes beyond or transcends appearances or sensory

phenomena. **—tran′scen·den′tal·ist** *adj., n.* **—tran′scen·den′·tal·is′tic** *adj.*

transcendental number An irrational number, such as pi, that cannot result from any finite set of algebraic equations having rational coefficients.

trans·con·ti·nen·tal (trans′kon·tə·nen′təl) *adj.* Extending or passing across a continent.

tran·scribe (tran·skrīb′) *v.t.* **·scribed, ·scrib·ing 1** To write over again; copy from an original. **2** To make a record of in handwriting or typewriting, as of something spoken. **3** To translate (shorthand notes, etc.) into standard written form. **4** To make a recording of for use in a later broadcast. **5** To adapt (a musical composition) for a change of instrument or voice. [< L *trans-* over + *scribere* write] **—tran·scrib′er** *n.*

tran·script (tran′skript) *n.* **1** Something transcribed, as from a stenographer's notes. **2** Any copy, esp., an official copy of a student's academic record. [< L *transcribere* transcribe]

tran·scrip·tion (tran·skrip′shən) *n.* **1** The act of transcribing. **2** Something transcribed; a copy; transcript. **3** A recording made for a later broadcast. **4** *Music* The adaptation of a composition for a different instrument or voice. **—tran·scrip′tion·al** *adj.*

tran·sept (tran′sept) *n.* A projecting part of a cruciform church crossing at right angles to the longer part and situated between the nave and choir; also, its projecting ends. [< L *transversus* transverse + *septum* an enclosure] **—tran·sep′tal** *adj.*

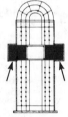

Transepts

trans·fer (trans·fûr′, trans′fər) *v.* **·ferred, ·fer·ring** *v.t.* **1** To carry, or cause to pass, from one person, place, etc., to another. **2** To make over possession of to another. **3** To convey (a drawing) from one surface to another. —*v.i.* **4** To transfer oneself. **5** To be transferred. **6** To change from one vehicle or line to another. —*n.* (trans′fər) **1** The act of transferring, or the state of being transferred. **2** That which is transferred, as a design conveyed from one surface to another. **3** A place, method, or means of transfer. **4** A ticket entitling a passenger on one vehicle to ride on another. **5** A delivery of title or property from one person to another. **6** A person transferred from one organization or position to another. [< L *trans-* across + *ferre* carry] **—trans·fer′a·bil′i·ty, trans·fer′ence, trans·fer′rer** *n.* **—trans·fer′a·ble, trans·fer′ra·ble** *adj.*

trans·fer·al (trans·fûr′əl) *n.* The act or an instance of transferring. Also **trans·fer′ral.**

trans·fig·u·ra·tion (trans′fig·yə·rā′shən) *n.* A change in shape or appearance. **—the Transfiguration 1** The supernatural transformation of Christ on the mount. **2** A festival commemorating this, August 6.

trans·fig·ure (trans·fig′yər) *v.t.* **·ured, ·ur·ing 1** To change the outward form or appearance of. **2** To make glorious. [< L *trans-* across + *figura* shape] **—trans·fig′ure·ment** *n.*

trans·fix (trans·fiks′) *v.t.* **1** To pierce through, as with a pointed implement; impale. **2** To fix in place by impaling. **3** To make motionless, as with horror, amazement, etc. [< L *trans-* through, across + *figere* fasten] **—trans·fix′ion** (-fik′shən) *n.*

trans·form (trans·fôrm′) *v.t.* **1** To change the form or appearance of. **2** To change the nature or character of; convert. **3** *Electr.* To subject to the action of a transformer. —*v.i.* **4** To be or become changed in form or character. [< L *trans-* over + *forma* a form] **—trans·form′a·ble, trans·form′a·tive** *adj.*

trans·for·ma·tion (trans′fər·mā′shən) *n.* **1** The act of transforming or the state of being transformed. **2** *Ling.* Any of the systematic processes by which grammatical sentences of a language may be derived from underlying constructions. **—trans′for·ma′tion·al** *adj.*

trans·form·er (trans·fôr′mər) *n.* **1** One who or that which transforms. **2** *Electr.* A device that couples electricity from one alternating-current circuit to another by electromagnetic induction, often with a change in the ratio of current to voltage and always with a small power loss.

trans·fuse (trans·fyōoz′) *v.t.* **·fused, ·fus·ing 1** To cause to flow or pass from one person or thing to another. **2** *Med.* **a** To transfer (blood, plasma, etc.) from one person or animal to another. **b** To give a transfusion to. **3** To pass into; permeate. [< L *transfusus,* p.p. of *transfundere*] —**trans·fus′er** *n.* —**trans·fus′i·ble, trans·fu·sive** (trans·fyōō′siv) *adj.*

trans·fu·sion (trans·fyōō′zhən) *n.* **1** The act or an instance of transfusing. **2** *Med.* The introduction of a fluid, as saline solution, blood, blood plasma, etc., into the blood stream.

trans·gress (trans·gres′, tranz-) *v.t.* **1** To disregard and go beyond the bounds of, as a divine or traditional law; violate. **2** To pass beyond or over (limits); exceed. —*v.i.* **3** To break a law; sin. [< L *transgressus,* p.p. of *transgredi* step across] —**trans·gres′sor** *n.*

trans·gres·sion (trans·gresh′ən, tranz-) *n.* The act or an instance of transgressing, esp. a sin.

tran·ship (tran·ship′) *v.t.* **·shipped, ·shipping** TRANSSHIP. —**tran·ship′ment** *n.*

tran·sient (tran′shənt, tranch′ənt, tranz′ē·ənt) *adj.* **1** Occurring or existing only for a time; not permanent; transitory. **2** Brief; fleeting; momentary. **3** Residing or staying in a place temporarily: a large *transient* population. —*n.* One who or that which is transient, esp. a temporary resident. [< L *transire* go across] —**tran′sience, tran′sien·cy** *n.* —**tran′sient·ly** *adv.* —**Syn. 1** temporary, passing. **2** ephemeral, fugitive, evanescent. **3** casual.

tran·sis·tor (tran·zis′tər, -sis′-) *n. Electronics* **1** A semiconductor device having three terminals and the property that the current between one pair of them is a function of the current between another pair. **2** A transistorized radio. [< TRANS(FER) (RES)ISTOR]

tran·sis·tor·ize (tran·zis′tər·īz, -sis′-) *v.t.* **·ized, ·iz·ing** To equip with transistors. —**tran·sis′tor·i·za′tion** *n.*

tran·sit (tran′sit, -zit) *n.* **1** The act of passing over or through; passage. **2** The process of change; transition. **3** The act of carrying across or through; conveyance. **4** Transportation, esp. for carrying large numbers of people, as in a city: public *transit.* **5** *Astron.* **a** The passage of one celestial body over the disk of another. **b** The passage of a celestial body across the meridian. **6** A surveying instrument resembling a theodolite. [< L *transire* go across]

tran·si·tion (tran·sish′ən, tranz-) *n.* **1** Passage from one place, condition, or stage to another; change. **2** Something, as a period of time or a situation, that leads from one stage or period to another. **3** *Music* A passage or modulation connecting sections of a composition. —**tran·si′tion·al** *adj.* —**tran·si′tion·al·ly** *adv.*

tran·si·tive (tran′sə·tiv) *adj.* **1** *Gram.* Having, requiring, or completed by a direct object: said of a verb. **2** Of or pertaining to transition. —*n. Gram.* A transitive verb. [< L *transitus* transit] —**tran′si·tive·ly** *adv.* —**tran′si·tive·ness, tran′si·tiv′i·ty** *n.*

tran·si·to·ry (tran′sə·tôr′ē, -tō′rē) *adj.* **1** Existing for a short time only; soon extinguished or annulled. **2** Brief; ephemeral. —**tran′si·to′ri·ly** *adv.* —**tran′si·to′ri·ness** *n.*

trans·late (trans·lāt′, tranz-, trans′lāt, tranz′-) *v.* **·lat·ed, ·lat·ing** *v.t.* **1** To change into another language. **2** To change from one form, condition, or place to another. **3** To explain in other words; interpret. **4** *Mech.* To change the position of in space, esp. without rotation. —*v.i.* **5** To change the words of one language into those of another, esp. as an occupation. **6** To admit of translation. [< L *translatus,* lit., carried across] —**trans·lat′a·ble** *adj.* —**trans·la′tor** *n.*

trans·la·tion (trans·lā′shən, tranz-) *n.* **1** The act of translating, or the state of being translated. **2** Something translated; esp., a reproduction of a work in a language different from the original. **3** *Mech.* Motion in which all the parts of a body follow identical courses. —**trans·la′tion·al** *adj.*

trans·lit·er·ate (trans·lit′ə·rāt, tranz-) *v.t.* **·at·ed, ·at·ing** To represent, as a word, by the characters of another alphabet. [< TRANS- + L *litera* a letter] —**trans·lit′er·a′tion** *n.*

trans·lu·cent (trans·lōō′sənt, tranz-) *adj.* Allowing the passage of light, but not permitting a clear view of any object. [< L *trans-* through, across + *lucere* to shine] —**trans·lu′cence, trans·lu′cen·cy** *n.* —**trans·lu′cent·ly** *adv.*

trans·mi·grate (trans·mī′grāt, tranz-, trans′mī-, tranz′·mī-) *v.i.* **·grat·ed, ·grat·ing** **1** To pass into another body, as the soul at death. **2** To migrate, as from one country or jurisdiction to another. —**trans·mi·gra·tion** (trans′mī·grā′·shən, tranz′-), **trans·mi′gra·tor** *n.* —**trans·mi′gra·to·ry** (-mī′·grə·tôr′ē, -tō′rē) *adj.*

trans·mis·si·ble (trans·mis′ə·bəl, tranz-) *adj.* Capable of being transmitted. —**trans·mis′si·bil′i·ty** *n.*

trans·mis·sion (trans·mish′ən, tranz-) *n.* **1** The act of transmitting, or the state of being transmitted. **2** That which is transmitted. **3** *Mech.* A device that transmits power from its source to its point of application, as from the engine of an automobile to the wheels. —**trans·mis′sive** *adj.*

trans·mit (trans·mit′, tranz-) *v.t.* **·mit·ted, ·mit·ting** **1** To send from one place or person to another; convey. **2** To pass on (a gene, a virus, etc.) from one organism to another. **3** To cause (light, sound, etc.) to pass through space or a medium. **4** To send out, as by means of radio waves. **5** To serve as a medium of passage for; conduct: Iron *transmits* heat. **6** *Mech.* To convey (force, motion, etc.) from one part or mechanism to another. [< L *trans-* across + *mittere* send] —**trans·mit′ta·ble** *adj.* —**trans·mit′tal, trans·mit′·tance** *n.*

trans·mit·ter (trans·mit′ər, tranz-) *n.* **1** One who or that which transmits. **2** The part of a telephone into which a person talks. **3** The part of a telegraph for sending messages. **4** *Telecom.* A device that modulates a carrier with a signal and sends the carrier forth, as in radio, telephony, or telegraphy.

trans·mog·ri·fy (trans·mog′rə·fī, tranz-) *v.t.* **·fied, ·fy·ing** To make into something altogether different; transform radically: often used humorously. [?] —**trans·mog′ri·fi·ca′·tion** *n.*

trans·mu·ta·tion (trans′myōō·tā′shən, tranz′-) *n.* **1** The act of transmuting, or the state of being transmuted. **2** The conversion of an atom of an element into an atom of a different element, as by radioactive decay, nuclear fission, etc. **3** The supposed conversion of a base metal into gold or silver. —**trans′mu·ta′tion·al, trans·mut·a·tive** (trans·myōō′tə·tiv, tranz-) *adj.*

trans·mute (trans·myōōt′, tranz-) *v.t.* **·mut·ed, ·mut·ing** To change in nature or form. Also **trans·mu′tate.** [< L *trans-* across + *mutare* to change] —**trans·mut′a·ble** *adj.* —**trans·mut′a·bil′i·ty, trans·mut′a·ble·ness, trans·mut′er** *n.* —**trans·mut′a·bly** *adv.*

trans·o·ce·an·ic (trans′ō·shē·an′ik, tranz′-) *adj.* **1** Crossing or traversing the ocean. **2** Lying beyond or over the ocean.

tran·som (tran′səm) *n.* **1** A horizontal piece framed across an opening; a lintel. **2** A small window above and often hinged to such a bar, usu. situated above a door. **3** The horizontal crossbar of a gallows or cross. [< L *transtrum* a crossbeam] —**tran′somed** *adj.*

transp. transportation.

trans·pa·cif·ic (trans′pə·sif′ik) *adj.* **1** Across or crossing the Pacific Ocean. **2** On the other side of the Pacific.

trans·par·en·cy (trans·pâr′ən·sē, -par′-) *n. pl.* **·cies** **1** The state or quality of being transparent. **2** Something whose transmission of light defines an image, esp. a piece of photographic film, often mounted as a slide and viewed by projecting its image on a screen or other surface.

trans·par·ent (trans·pâr′ənt, -par′-) *adj.* **1** Allowing the passage of light and of clear views of objects beyond. **2** Having a texture fine enough to be seen through; diaphanous. **3** Easy to understand. **4** Without guile; frank; candid. **5** Easily detected; obvious: a *transparent* lie. [< L *trans-* across + *parere* appear, be visible] —**trans·par′ent·ly** *adv.* —**trans·par′ence, trans·par′ent·ness** *n.*

tran·spi·ra·tion (tran′spə·rā′shən) *n.* A transpiring or exhalation, as the loss of water from a plant by evaporation.

tran·spire (trans·pīr′) *v.* **·spired, ·spir·ing** *v.t.* **1** To give off through permeable tissues, as of the skin and lungs or of

---

add, āce, câre, pälm; end, ēven; it, īce; odd, ōpen, ôrder; tŏŏk, pōōl; up, bûrn; ə = *a* in *above, u* in *focus;*
yōō = *u* in *fuse;* oil; pout; check; go; ring; thin; this; zh, *vision.* < derived from; ? origin uncertain or unknown.

leaf surfaces. —*v.i.* **2** To be emitted, as through the skin; be exhaled, as moisture or odors. **3** To become known. **4** To happen; occur. [< L *trans-* across, through + *spirare* breathe] • An accepted meaning of *transpire* is to become known or leak out: *It transpired that he had died penniless.* The word is more commonly used today, however, with the sense of "to happen": *We shall never know what transpired at that meeting.* The latter usage still strikes the more traditionally inclined as improper or ignorant. That judgment may be unduly harsh, but as a matter of style the usage is almost always inelegant and often pretentious.

trans·plant (trans·plant′) *v.t.* **1** To remove and plant in another place. **2** To remove and settle for residence in another place. **3** *Surg.* To transfer (an organ or tissue) from its original site to another part of the body or to another individual. —*v.i.* **4** To admit of being transplanted. —*n.* (trans′plant′) **1** That which is transplanted, as a seedling or an organ of the body. **2** The act of transplanting. —**trans′plan·ta′tion, trans·plant′er** *n.*

trans·port (trans·pôrt′, -pōrt′) *v.t.* **1** To carry or convey from one place to another. **2** To carry away with emotion, as with delight; enchant. **3** To banish to another country. —*n.* (trans′pôrt, -pōrt) **1** The act or a means of transporting; transportation. **2** A state of emotional rapture; intense delight. **3** A ship, train, truck, etc., used to transport troops, supplies, etc. **4** A system of transportation. **5** A deported convict. [< L *trans-* across + *portare* carry] — **trans·port′a·bil′i·ty, trans·port′er** *n.* —**trans·port′a·ble** *adj.*

trans·por·ta·tion (trans′pər·tā′shən) *n.* **1** The act of transporting. **2** A means of transporting or traveling. **3** The conveying of passengers or freight, esp. as an industry. **4** Money, a pass, etc., used for being transported.

trans·pose (trans·pōz′) *v.t.* **·posed, ·pos·ing 1** To reverse the order or change the place of: to *transpose* two numerals or a word in a sentence. **2** *Math.* To transfer (a term) from one side of an algebraic equation to the other with reversed sign. **3** *Music* To write or play in a different key. [< L *trans-* over + OF *poser* put] —**trans·pos′a·ble** *adj.* — **trans·po′sal, trans·pos′er, trans·po·si·tion** (trans′pə·zish′ən) *n.*

trans·sex·u·al (trans·sek′shoo·əl, -sek′shəl) *n.* A person who is genetically and physically of one sex but who identifies psychologically with the other and may seek treatment by surgery or with hormones to bring the physical sexual characteristics into conformity with the psychological preference. —*adj.* Of, for, or characteristic of transsexuals. —**trans·sex′u·al·ism** *n.*

trans·ship (trans·ship′) *v.t. & v.i.* **·shipped, ·ship·ping** To transfer from one conveyance or means of transport to another for further shipment. —**trans·ship′ment** *n.*

tran·sub·stan·ti·ate (tran′səb·stan′shē·āt) *v.t.* **·at·ed, ·at·ing 1** To change from one substance into another; transmute; transform. **2** *Theol.* To change the substance of (bread and wine) in the rite of transubstantiation.

tran·sub·stan·ti·a·tion (tran′səb·stan′shē·ā′shən) *n.* In the Roman Catholic and Eastern Orthodox churches, the conversion of the substance of the bread and wine of the Eucharist into that of Christ's body and blood.

trans·u·ra·ni·um (trans′yoo·rā′nē·əm, tranz′-) *adj.* Of or pertaining to elements having an atomic number greater than that of uranium. Also **trans′u·ran′ic** (-ran′ik).

trans·ver·sal (trans·vûr′səl, tranz-) *adj.* TRANSVERSE. — *n. Geom.* A straight line intersecting a system of lines.

trans·verse (trans·vûrs′, tranz-) *adj.* Lying or being across or from side to side. —*n.* (*also* trans′vûrs, tranz′-) That which is transverse. [< L *transversus* lying across] — **trans·verse′ly** *adv.*

trans·ves·tite (trans·ves′tīt, tranz-) *n.* One who wears the clothes of the opposite sex. [< L *trans-* over + *vestire* to clothe + -ITE] —**trans·ves′tism, trans·ves′ti·tism** (-ves′tə·tiz′əm) *n.*

trap¹ (trap) *n.* **1** A device for catching game or other animals, as a pitfall or a baited contrivance set to spring shut on being slightly jarred or moved. **2** A devious plan or trick by which a person may be caught or taken unawares. **3** A device for hurling clay pigeons into the air, used in trapshooting. **4** Any of various devices that collect residual material or that form a seal to stop a return flow

of noxious gas, etc., as a water-filled U- or S-bend in a pipe. **5** In golf, an obstacle or hazard: a sand *trap.* **6** TRAPDOOR. **7** A light, two-wheeled carriage suspended by springs. **8** *pl.* Percussion instruments, as drums, cymbals, etc. **8** *Slang* The mouth. —*v.* **trapped, trap·ping** *v.t.* **1** To catch in or as if in a trap. **2** To provide with a trap. **3** To stop or hold by the formation of a seal. **4** To catch (a ball) just as or after it strikes the ground. —*v.i.* **5** To set traps for game; be a trapper. [< OE *træppe*]

trap² (trap) *n. Geol.* A dark, fine-grained igneous rock, often of columnar structure, as basalt. Also **trap′rock′.** [< Sw. *trappa* a stair]

trap·door (trap′dôr′, -dōr′) *n.* A door, hinged or sliding, to cover an opening, as in a floor or roof.

tra·peze (tra·pēz′, trə-) *n.* A short swinging bar suspended by two ropes, for gymnastic exercises and acrobatic stunts. [< NL *trapezium* a trapezium]

tra·pe·zi·um (trə·pē′zē·əm) *n. p.* **·zi·ums** or **·zi·a** (-zē·ə) *Geom.* **1** A four-sided plane figure of which no two sides are parallel. **2** *Brit.* TRAPEZOID (def. 1). [< Gk. *trapeza* a table, lit., a four-footed (bench)]

Trapezium Trapezoid
def. 1 def. 1

trap·e·zoid (trap′ə·zoid′) *n. Geom.* **1** A quadrilateral of which two sides are parallel. **2** *Brit.* TRAPEZIUM (def. 1). [< Gk. *trapeza* a table + *eidos* a form] —**trap′e·zoi′dal** *adj.*

trap·per (trap′ər) *n.* One whose occupation is the trapping of fur-bearing animals.

trap·pings (trap′ingz) *n. pl.* **1** An ornamental covering or harness for a horse; caparison. **2** Adornments of any kind; embellishments. **3** The superficial signs or perquisites; marks: the *trappings* of success. [< ME *trappe*]

Trap·pist (trap′ist) *n.* A monk belonging to an ascetic order noted for silence. —*adj.* Of this order. [< *La Trappe,* France, site of the order's establishment in 1664]

trap·shoot·ing (trap′shoo′ting) *n.* The sport of shooting clay pigeons sent up from spring traps. —**trap′shoot′er** *n.*

trash (trash) *n.* **1** Worthless or waste matter; rubbish. **2** That which is broken or lopped off, as twigs and branches. **3** Foolish or idle talk. **4** Anything worthless, shoddy, or without merit: literary *trash.* **5** A person regarded as worthless or of no account. —*v.t. & v.i. Slang* To wreck or destroy (something) purposefully but often indiscriminately as an expression of alienation or rebellion. [?] — **trash′i·ness** *n.* —**trash′y** (·i·er, ·i·est) *adj.*

trau·ma (trou′mə, trô′-) *n. pl.* **·mas** or **·ma·ta** (-mə·tə) **1** Any physical injury resulting from force. **2** A severe emotional shock having a deep effect upon the personality. [< Gk., a wound] —**trau·mat·ic** (trou·mat′ik, trô-) *adj.* —**trau·mat′i·cal·ly** *adv.*

trau·ma·tize (trô′mə·tīz) *v.t.* **·tized, ·tiz·ing** To cause trauma to or in.

trav·ail (trə·vāl′, trav′āl) *n.* **1** Pain, anguish, or distress encountered in an effort or achievement. **2** Labor in childbirth. **3** Hard or wearisome labor. **4** Physical agony. —*v.i.* **1** To suffer the pangs of childbirth. **2** To toil; labor. [< OF < *travailler* to labor, toil]

trav·el (trav′əl) *v.* **trav·eled** or **·elled, trav·el·ing** or **·el·ling** *v.i.* **1** To go from one place to another or from place to place; make a journey or tour. **2** To proceed; advance. **3** To go about from place to place as a traveling salesman. **4** *Informal* To move with speed. **5** To pass or be transmitted, as light, sound, etc. **6** *Mech.* To move in a fixed path, as a machine part. **7** In basketball, to commit the infraction of failing to dribble while moving with the ball. —*v.t.* **8** To move or journey across or through: traverse. —*n.* **1** The act of traveling. **2** *Often pl.* A journey or tour, usu. extensive. **3** Passage to, over, or past a certain place. **4** Distance traveled, as by a machine part. [< OF *travailler* to travail]

trav·eled (trav′əld) *adj.* **1** Having made many journeys. **2** Frequented or used by travelers. Also **trav′elled.**

trav·e·logue (trav·ə·lôg, -log) *n.* **1** A documentary film about a traveled place. **2** A lecture or talk on travel, usu. illustrated pictorially. Also **trav′e·log.**

tra·verse (trə·vûrs′, tra-) *u.* **·ersed, ·ers·ing** *v.t.* **1** to pass over, across, or through. **2** To move back and forth over or along. **3** To examine carefully; scrutinize. **4** To oppose; thwart. **5** *Law* To make denial of. —*v.i.* **6** To move back and forth. **7** To move across; cross. —**trav·erse** (trav′ərs) *n.* **1** Something that traverses, as a crosspiece of a machine or structure. **2** Something serving as a screen or barrier. **3** The act of traversing or denying; a denial. —*adj.* (trav′·ərs) Lying or being across; transverse. [< L *transversus* transverse] —**tra·vers′a·ble** *adj.* —**tra·vers′al, tra·vers′er** *n.*

trav·erse rod (trav′ərs) A curtain rod equipped with a sliding mechanism for drawing a pair of curtains together or apart with a cord.

trav·es·ty (trav′is·tē) *n. pl.* **·ties 1** A grotesque imitation, as of a lofty subject; burlesque. **2** A distorted or absurd rendering or example, as if in mockery: a *travesty* of justice. —*v.t.* **·tied, ·ty·ing** To make a travesty of; burlesque; parody. [< Ital. *travestire* to disguise]

trawl (trôl) *n.* **1** A large net for towing on the bottom of the ocean by a fishing boat. **2** A stout fishing line, anchored and buoyed, from which many lines bearing baited hooks may be secured. —*v.i.* **1** To fish with a trawl. —*v.t.* **2** To drag, as a net, to catch fish. [?]

trawl·er (trô′lər) *n.* A boat used for trawling.

tray (trā) *n.* **1** A flat, shallow utensil with raised edges, used to hold or carry several or a number of articles, as dishes. **2** A tray and the articles on it. **3** A shallow, topless box serving as a compartment, as in a tool or sewing box. [< OE *trēg* a wooden board] —**tray′ful** (-fŏŏl′) *n.*

treach·er·ous (trech′ər·əs) *adj.* **1** Likely to betray allegiance or confidence; untrustworthy. **2** Of the nature of treachery; perfidious. **3** Apparently safe or secure, but in fact dangerous or unreliable: *treacherous* footing. — **treach′er·ous·ly** *adv.* —**treach′er·ous·ness** *n.*

treach·er·y (trech′ər·ē) *n. pl.* **·er·ies** Violation of allegiance, confidence, or faith; treason. [< OF *tricher* cheat]

trea·cle (trē′kəl) *n.* **1** Molasses, esp. that obtained in refining sugar. **2** Saccharine speech or sentiments. **3** Formerly, a compound used as an antidote for poison. [< Gk. *thēriakē* a remedy for poisonous bites] —**trea′cly** *adj.*

tread (tred) *v.* **trod, trod·den** or **trod, tread·ing** *v.t.* **1** To step or walk on, over, along, etc. **2** To press with the feet; trample. **3** To crush or oppress harshly. **4** To accomplish in walking or in dancing: to *tread* a measure. **5** To copulate with: said of male birds. —*v.i.* **6** To place the foot down; walk. **7** To press the ground or anything beneath the feet: usu. with *on.* —**tread water** In swimming, to keep the body erect and the head above water by moving the feet and arms. —*n.* **1** The act, manner, or sound of treading; a walking or stepping. **2** The part of a wheel or automobile tire that comes into contact with the road or rails. **3** The impression made by a foot, a tire, etc. **4** The horizontal part of a step in a stairway. [< OE *tredan*] —**tread′er** *n.*

tread·le (tred′l) *n.* A lever operated by the foot, usu. to cause rotary motion. —*v.i.* **·led, ·ling** To work a treadle. [< OE *tredel* < *tredan* tread] • See POTTER'S WHEEL.

tread·mill (tred′mil′) *n.* **1** A mechanism rotated by the walking motion of one or more persons or animals. **2** Monotonous routine; tedious and unrewarding effort.

treas. treasurer; treasury.

trea·son (trē′zən) *n.* **1** Betrayal, treachery, or breach of allegiance toward a sovereign or government. **2** A breach of faith; treachery. [< L *traditio* a betrayal, delivery] — **trea′son·ous** *adj.* —**trea′son·ous·ly** *adv.*

trea·son·a·ble (trē′zən·ə·bəl) *adj.* Of, involving, or characteristic of treason. —**trea′son·a·ble·ness** *n.* —**trea′son·a·bly** *adv.*

treas·ure (trezh′ər) *n.* **1** Riches accumulated or possessed, as a store of precious metals, jewels, or money. **2** Someone or something very precious. —*v.t.* **·ured, ·ur·ing 1** To set a high value upon; prize. **2** To lay up in store; accumulate. [< L *thesaurus*] —**Syn.** *v.* **1** cherish, esteem, value, venerate. **2** hoard.

treas·ur·er (trezh′ər·ər) *n.* **1** An officer authorized to receive, care for, and disburse revenues, as of a government, business corporation, or society. **2** A similar custodian of the funds of a society or a corporation.

treas·ure-trove (trezh′ər·trōv′) *n.* **1** *Law* Money, gold, etc., found hidden, the owner being unknown. **2** Any rich or rewarding discovery. Also **treasure trove.** [< AF *tresor* treasure + *trover* to find]

treas·ur·y (trezh′ər·ē) *n. pl.* **·ur·ies 1** A place of receipt and disbursement of public revenue or private funds. **2** The revenue or funds. **3** The place where a treasure is stored. **4** A department of government concerned with finances, the issuance of money, etc. [< OF *tresor* treasure]

treat (trēt) *v.t.* **1** To conduct oneself toward (a person, animal, etc.) in a specified manner. **2** To look upon or regard in a specified manner: They *treat* it as a childhood prank. **3** To give medical or surgical attention to. **4** To deal with in writing or speaking. **5** To depict or express artistically in a specified style. **6** To pay for the entertainment, food, or drink of. —*v.i.* **7** To deal with a subject in writing or speaking: usu. with *of.* **8** To carry on negotiations; negotiate. **9** To pay for another's entertainment. —*n.* **1** Something that gives unusual pleasure. **2** Entertainment of any kind furnished gratuitously to another. **3** *Informal* One's turn to pay for refreshment or entertainment. [< OF *tretier, traitier*] —**treat′er** *n.*

trea·tise (trē′tis) *n.* A formal, systematic, written exposition of a serious subject: a *treatise* on labor relations. [< OF *traitier*]

treat·ment (trēt′mənt) *n.* **1** The act, manner, or process of treating anything. **2** The therapeutic measures designed to cure a disease or abnormal condition.

trea·ty (trē′tē) *n. pl.* **·ties** A formal agreement or compact between two or more nations. [< OF *traitié*, p.p. of *traitier* treat]

treb·le (treb′əl) *v.t. & v.i.* **·led, ·ling** To multiply by three; triple. —*adj.* **1** Threefold. **2** *Music* **a** Of the highest range. **b** Soprano. —*n.* **1 a** *Music* A part or instrument of the highest range. **b** A soprano singer. **2** High, piping sound. [< L *triplus* triple] —**treb′ly** *adv.*

tree (trē) *n.* **1** A woody perennial plant having a distinct trunk with branches and foliage at some distance above the ground. **2** Any shrub or plant with a treelike shape or dimensions. **3** Something whose outline resembles the spreading branches of a tree, as a diagram: a genealogical *tree.* **4** A timber, post, or piece of wood used for a particular purpose. —*v.t.* **treed, tree·ing 1** To force to climb or take refuge in a tree: to *tree* an opossum. **2** *Informal* To get the advantage of; corner. [< OE *trēow*]

tree fern Any of various treelike ferns with woody trunks.

tree frog Any of various arboreal frogs having adhesive disks on the toes. Also **tree toad.**

tree·nail (trē′nāl′, tren′əl, trun′əl) *n.* A wooden peg or nail of dry, hard wood which swells when moist, used for fastening timbers.

tree of heaven AILANTHUS.

tree surgery The treatment of damaged trees by pruning, cementing cavities, etc. —**tree surgeon**

Trefoil
def. 2

tre·foil (trē′foil) *n.* **1** Any of various plants having threefold leaves, as clover. **2** An architectural ornament having the form of a three-lobed leaf. [< L *trifolium*]

trek (trek) *v.* **trekked, trek·king** *v.i.* **1** To move along with effort or slowly, esp. on foot. **2** To make a journey; travel. **3** In South Africa, to travel by ox wagon. —*v.t.* **4** To transport. **5** In South Africa, to draw (a vehicle or load): said of an ox. —*n.* **1** A journey or a stage in a journey. **2** The act of trekking. **3** In South Africa, an organized migration. [< Du. *trekken* draw, travel < MDu. *trecken*] —**trek′ker** *n.*

trel·lis (trel′is) *n.* A grating or lattice, often of wood, used as a screen or a support for vines, etc.

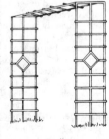

Trellis

—*v.t.* **1** To interlace so as to form a trellis. **2** To furnish with or fasten on a trellis. [<L *trilix* of three threads]

trem·a·tode (trem′ə·tōd, trē′mə-) *n.* Any of a class of parasitic flatworms, as the liver fluke. [<Gk. *trēma* a hole + *eidos* form] —**trem′a·toid** (-toid) *adj.*

trem·ble (trem′bəl) *v.i.* **·bled**, **·bling** **1** To shake involuntarily, as with fear or weakness. **2** To move slightly or vibrate, as from some jarring force: The building *trembled.* **3** To feel anxiety or fear. **4** To quaver, as the voice. —*n.* The act or state of trembling. [<LL *tremulus* tremulous] —**trem′bler** *n.* —**trem′bling·ly** *adv.* —**trem′bly** *adj.* — **Syn.** *v.* **2** quiver, shake, totter, quake.

tre·men·dous (tri·men′dəs) *adj.* **1** Extraordinarily large or extensive; enormous; great. **2** Causing astonishment by its magnitude, force, etc.; awe-inspiring. **3** *Informal* Wonderful; marvelous. [<L *tremendus* to be trembled at] —**tre·men′dous·ly** *adv.* —**tre·men′dous·ness** *n.*

trem·o·lo (trem′ə·lō) *n. pl.* **·los** *Music* **1** A rapid, periodic variation in the loudness of a tone. **2** The mechanism for causing this in organ tones. [Ital., trembling]

trem·or (trem′ər, trē′mər) *n.* **1** A quick, vibratory movement; a shaking. **2** Any involuntary quivering or trembling, as of a muscle. **3** A state of agitation or excitement, as in anticipation of something. [<OF *tremour* fear, a trembling]

trem·u·lous (trem′yə·ləs) *adj.* **1** Characterized or affected by trembling: *tremulous* speech. **2** Showing timidity and irresolution. **3** Characterized by mental excitement. Also **trem′u·lant.** [<L *tremulus*] —**trem′u·lous·ly** *adv.* —**trem′u·lous·ness** *n.*

tre·nail (trē′nāl, tren′əl, trun′əl) *n.* TREENAIL.

trench (trench) *n.* **1** A long narrow ditch, esp. one lined with a parapet of the excavated earth, to protect troops. **2** A long, narrow region much deeper than the adjacent surfaces, as along the ocean floor. —*v.t.* **1** To dig a trench or trenches in. **2** To fortify with trenches. **3** To cut deep furrows in. —*v.i.* **4** To cut or dig trenches. **5** To cut; carve. **6** To encroach. [<OF *trenchier* to cut] —**trench′er** *n.*

trench·ant (tren′chənt) *adj.* **1** Clear, vigorous, and effective: a *trenchant* rebuttal. **2** Cutting, as sarcasm; biting. **3** Incisive; sharp; keen: *trenchant* wit. **4** *Archaic* Cutting deeply and quickly: a *trenchant* sword. [<OF *trenchier*]

trench coat A raincoat with a belt, straps on the shoulders, and several pockets.

trench·er (tren′chər) *n.* A wooden plate or board used to serve food or as a surface for cutting it. [<OF *trenchier* to cut]

trench·er·man (tren′chər·mən) *n. pl.* **·men** (-mən) A person who eats heartily.

trench fever A relapsing fever transmitted by body lice.

trench foot A foot condition resembling frostbite, due to continued dampness and cold.

trench mouth A mildly contagious disease of the gums, and sometimes the larynx and tonsils, caused by a soil bacillus.

trend (trend) *n.* **1** A prevailing or probable tendency; predominant or likely course or direction; drift: a *trend* toward smaller families; investment *trends;* to study *trends* in education. **2** A popular preference or inclination: fashion *trends.* **3** The general course or direction, as of a coast; bent. —*v.i.* **1** To have or follow a general course or direction. **2** To exhibit a tendency; move: wheat prices *trending* upward. [<OE *trendan* to roll]

trend·y (tren′dē) *adj. Slang* **trend·i·er**, **trend·i·est** In step with current fashion; voguish. —*n. pl.* **trend·ies** *Chiefly Brit.* A trendy person or thing. —**trend′i·ness** *n.*

tre·pan (tri·pan′) *n.* **1** An early form of the trephine. **2** A large rock-boring tool —*v.t.* **·panned**, **·pan·ning** To use a trepan upon. [<Gk. *trypanon* a borer]

tre·phine (tri·fīn′, -fēn′) *n. Surg.* A cylindrical saw for removing a disk of tissue, as from the skull, cornea, etc. —*v.t.* **·phined**, **·phin·ing** To operate on with a trephine. [< L *tres fines* three ends]

trep·i·da·tion (trep′ə·dā′shən) *n.* **1** Tremulous agitation caused by fear; apprehension. **2** *Archaic* An involuntary trembling; tremor. [<L *trepidare* hurry, be alarmed]

tres·pass (tres′pəs, -pas′) *v.i.* **1** To violate the personal or property rights of another; esp., to go unlawfully onto another's land. **2** To go beyond the bounds of what is right

or proper; transgress. **3** To intrude; encroach: to *trespass* on one's privacy. —*n.* **1** *Law* **a** Any act accompanied by actual or implied force in violation of another's person, property, or rights. **b** An action for injuries sustained because of this. **2** Any transgression of law or moral duty. **3** An intrusion; encroachment. [<Med. L *trans-* across, beyond + *passare* to pass] —**tres′pass·er** *n.*

tress (tres) *n.* **1** A lock or curl of human hair. **2** *pl.* The hair of a woman or girl, esp. when long and worn loose [<OF *tresce*] —**tressed** (trest) *adj.*

tres·tle (tres′əl) *n.* **1** A beam or bar braced by two pairs of divergent legs, used to support tables, platforms, etc. **2** A braced framework functioning like a bridge in supporting a roadway or railway over a short span. [<L *transtrum* crossbeam]

trey (trā) *n.* A card, domino, or die having three spots or pips. [<L *tres* three]

tri- *prefix* **1** Three; threefold; thrice: *tricycle.* **2** *Chem.* Containing three atoms, radicals, groups, etc.: *trioxide.* **3** Occurring three times within a (specified) interval: *triweekly.* [<L *tri-* threefold]

tri·ad (trī′ad) *n.* **1** A group of three persons or things. **2** *Music* A chord of three tones, esp. a tone with its third and fifth. [<Gk. *trias<treis* three] —**tri·ad′ic** *adj., n.*

tri·al (trī′əl, trīl) *n.* **1** The examination in a court of law, often before a jury, of the facts of a case in order to determine its disposition. **2** The act of testing or proving by experience or use. **3** The state of being tried or tested. **4** An experience, person, or thing that puts strength, patience, or faith to the test. **5** An attempt or effort to do something. **6** Hardship; difficulty: the *trials* of poverty. — **on trial** In the process of being tried or tested. —**trial and error** The trying of one thing after another until something succeeds. —*adj.* **1** Of or pertaining to a trial or trials. **2** Made or used in the course of trying or testing. [<AF<*trier* to try] —**Syn.** *n.* **2** examination, experiment. **5** endeavor. **6** misfortune, trouble.

trial balance In double-entry bookkeeping, a draft of the debit and credit balances of each account in the ledger.

trial jury A jury of 12 persons impaneled to decide a civil or criminal case; petit jury.

tri·an·gle (trī′ang′gəl) *n.* **1** *Geom.* A figure, esp. a plane figure, bounded by three sides, and having three angles. **2** Something resembling such a figure in shape. **3** A situation involving three persons: the eternal *tri-*

Triangles
a. equilateral. b. isosceles.
c. scalene. d. right-angle.

angle. **4** *Music* A percussion instrument consisting of a resonant metal bar bent into a triangle and sounded by striking with a small metal rod. [<L *tri-* three + *angulus* an angle]

tri·an·gu·lar (trī·ang′gyə·lər) *adj.* **1** Pertaining to, like, or bounded by a triangle. **2** Concerned with or pertaining to three things, parties, or persons. —**tri·an′gu·lar′i·ty** (-lar′ə·tē) *n.* —**tri·an′gu·lar·ly** *adv.*

tri·an·gu·late (trī·ang′gyə·lāt) *v.t.* **·lat·ed**, **·lat·ing** **1** To divide into triangles. **2** To measure or determine by means of trigonometry. **3** To give triangular shape to. —*adj.* Marked with triangles. —**tri·an·gu·la′tion** *n.*

Tri·as·sic (trī·as′ik) *adj. & n.* See GEOLOGY. [<LL *trias* triad]

tri·ath·lon (trī′ath′lon) *n.* An athletic event comprising swimming, bicycle riding, and long-distance running. [<Gk. *tri-* three + *athlon* a contest]

tri·bal·ism (trī′bəl·iz′əm) *n.* Tribal organization, culture, or relations.

tribe (trīb) *n.* **1** A group of people, under one chief or ruler, united by common ancestry, language, and culture. **2** In ancient Israel, any of the 12 divisions of the Hebrews. **3** In ancient Rome, any of the three clans making up the Roman people. **4** A number of persons of any class or profession taken together: often contemptuous. **5** *Biol.* **a** A group of closely related genera. **b** Any group of plants or animals. [<L *tribus*] —**tri′bal** *adj.* —**tri′bal·ly** *adv.*

tribes·man (trībz′mən) *n. pl.* **·men** (-mən) A member of a tribe.

trib·u·la·tion (trib′yə·lā′shən) *n.* **1** A condition of distress; suffering. **2** The cause of such distress. [< L *tribulare* thrash] —**Syn. 1** misery, oppression, sorrow, trouble.

tri·bu·nal (trī·byōō′nəl, tri-) *n.* **1** A court of justice. **2** Any judicial body, as a board of arbitrators. **3** The seat set apart for judges, magistrates, etc. [< L *tribunus* tribune]

trib·une[1] (trib′yōōn, trib·yōōn′) *n.* **1** In ancient Rome, a magistrate chosen by the plebeians to protect them against patrician oppression. **2** Any champion of the people. [< L *tribunus*, lit., head of a tribe < *tribus* a tribe] —**trib′u·nar′y** (-yə·ner′ē), **trib′u·ni′tial** (-yə·nish′əl) *adj.*

trib·une[2] (trib′yōōn) *n.* A rostrum or platform. [< L *tribunal* a tribunal]

trib·u·tar·y (trib′yə·ter′ē) *adj.* **1** Supplying a larger body, as a stream flowing into a river. **2** Paying tribute. —*n. pl.* **·tar·ies** **1** A stream flowing into a larger one. **2** A person or state paying tribute. [< L *tributum.* See TRIBUTE.]

trib·ute (trib′yōot) *n.* **1** Money or other valuables paid by one state to another as the price of peace and protection, or by virtue of some treaty. **2** Any obligatory payment, as a tax. **3** Anything given that is due to worth, affection, or duty: a *tribute* of praise. [< L *tributum,* neut. p.p. of *tribuere* pay, allot]

trice (trīs) *v.t.* **triced, tric·ing** To raise with a rope: usu. with *up.* —*n.* An instant: only in the phrase **in a trice.** [< MDu. *trisen* to hoist]

tri·ceps (trī′seps) *n. pl.* **·cep·ses** (-sep·sēz) or **·ceps** The large muscle at the back of the upper arm which straightens the arm when it contracts. [L, three-headed]

tri·chi·na (tri·kī′nə) *n. pl.* **·nae** (-nē) or **·nas** A roundworm whose larvae cause trichinosis. [< Gk. *trichinos* of hair]

Triceps

trich·i·no·sis (trik′ə·nō′sis) *n.* A disease usu. resulting from eating undercooked infected pork and marked by encysted trichina larvae in the muscles. Also **trich′i·ni′a·sis** (-nī′ə·sis). —**trich′i·nosed** (-nōzd, -nōst), **trich′i·nous** (-ə·nəs) *adj.*

trick (trik) *n.* **1** A deception; a petty artifice. **2** A malicious or annoying act: a dirty *trick.* **3** A practical joke; prank. **4** A particular characteristic; trait: a *trick* of tapping her foot. **5** A peculiar skill or knack. **6** A feat of jugglery. **7** In card games, the whole number of cards played in one round. **8** A turn or spell of duty. **9** *Informal* A child or young girl. —**do** (or **turn**) **the trick** *Slang* To produce the desired result. —*v.t.* **1** To deceive or cheat; delude. —*v.i.* **2** To practice trickery or deception. [< OF *trichier* cheat] —**trick′er** *n.* —**Syn.** *n.* **1** ruse, stratagem, subterfuge, device.

trick·er·y (trik′ər·ē) *n. pl.* **·er·ies** The practice of tricks; artifice; wiles.

trick·le (trik′əl) *v.* **·led, ·ling** *v.i.* **1** To flow or run drop by drop or in a very thin stream. **2** To move, come, go, etc., bit by bit. —*v.t.* **3** To cause to trickle. —*n.* **1** The act or state of trickling. **2** A thin stream. [ME *triklen*]

trick·ster (trik′stər) *n.* One who plays tricks.

trick·y (trik′ē) *adj.* **trick·i·er, trick·i·est** **1** Given to tricks; crafty; deceitful. **2** Intricate; requiring adroitness or skill. —**trick′i·ly** *adv.* —**trick′i·ness** *n.*

tri·col·or (trī′kul′ər) *adj.* Having or characterized by three colors: also **tri′col′ored.** —*n.* The French national flag. *Brit. sp.* **tri′col′our.**

tri·corn (trī′kôrn) *n.* A hat with the brim turned up on three sides. —*adj.* Three-horned; three-pronged. [< L *tricornis* three-horned]

tri·cot (trē′kō, trī′kət) *n.* **1** A hand-knitted or woven fabric, or a machine-made imitation thereof. **2** A soft ribbed cloth. [< F *tricoter* knit]

tri·cus·pid (trī·kus′pid) *adj.* **1** Having three cusps or points, as a molar tooth: also **tri·cus′pi·date. 2** Having three segments, as the valve between the right auricle and right ventricle of the heart: also **tri·cus′pi·dal.** [< L *tricuspis* three-pointed]

tri·cy·cle (trī′sik·əl) *n.* A three-wheeled vehicle worked by pedals, esp. one used by children.

tri·dent (trīd′nt) *n.* A three-pronged implement or weapon, the emblem of Neptune (Poseidon). —*adj.* Having three teeth or prongs: also **tri·den·tate** (trī·den′tāt), **tri·den′tat·ed.** [< L *tri-* three + *dens* a tooth]

tried (trīd) *p.t. & p.p.* of TRY. —*adj.* **1** Tested; trustworthy. **2** Freed of impurities.

tri·en·ni·al (trī·en′ē·əl) *adj.* **1** Taking place every third year. **2** Lasting three years. —*n.* **1** A ceremony celebrated every three years. **2** A plant lasting three years. [< L *tri-* three + *annus* year] —**tri·en′ni·al·ly** *adv.*

tri·fle (trī′fəl) *v.* **·fled, ·fling** *v.i.* **1** To treat or speak of something as of no value or importance: with *with.* **2** To play; toy. —*v.t.* **3** To spend (time, money, etc.) idly and purposelessly: He *trifled* away his entire fortune. —*n.* **1** Anything of very little value or importance. **2** A dessert, popular in England, made of layers of macaroons or ladyfingers with sugared fruit, custard, and meringue or whipped cream. **3** A small amount: It costs only a *trifle.* —**a trifle** Slightly; to a small extent: a *trifle* short. [< OF *truffer* deceive, jeer at] —**tri′fler** *n.*

tri·fling (trī′fling) *adj.* **1** Frivolous. **2** Insignificant. —**tri′·fling·ly** *adv.*

tri·fo·cal (trī·fō′kəl) *adj. Optics* Of or describing a lens with three segments, for near, intermediate, and far vision respectively. —*n.* A trifocal lens.

tri·fo·li·ate (trī·fō′lē·it, -āt) *adj. Bot.* Having three leaves or leaflike processes. Also **tri·fo′li·at′ed.**

tri·fo·li·o·late (trī·fō′lē·ə·lāt′) *adj. Bot.* Having three leaflets, as a clover leaf.

tri·fo·ri·um (trī·fôr′ē·əm, -fō′rē-) *n. pl.* **·fo·ri·a** (-fôr′ē·ə, -fō′rē·ə) *Archit.* A gallery above the arches of the nave or transept in a church. [< L *tri-* three + *foris* a door] —**tri·fo′ri·al** *adj.*

trig[1] (trig) *adj.* **1** Characterized by tidiness; trim; neat. **2** Strong; sound; firm. —*v.t.* **trigged, trig·ging** To make trig or neat; often with *out* or *up.* [< ON *tryggr* true, trusty] —**trig′ly** *adv.* —**trig′ness** *n.*

Triforium

trig[2] (trig) *n.* TRIGONOMETRY.

trig., trigon. trigonometric; trigonometry.

trig·ger (trig′ər) *n.* **1** A lever of a gun activating the firing mechanism when moved by a finger. • See REVOLVER. **2** Any one of various devices designed to activate other devices or systems. —**quick on the trigger** **1** Quick to shoot a gun. **2** Quick-witted; alert. —*v.t. Informal* To cause or set off (an action). [< Du. *trekken* pull, tug at]

trigonometric functions *Math.* Any of various functions of an angle or arc, principally the sine, cosine, tangent, cotangent, secant, and cosecant.

trig·o·nom·e·try (trig′ə·nom′ə·trē) *n.* The branch of mathematics based on the use of trigonometric functions, as in studying the relations of the sides and angles of triangles. [< Gk. *trigōnon* a triangle + *metron* measure] —**trig·o·no·met·ric** (trig′ə·nə·met′rik) or **·ri·cal** *adj.* —**trig′o·no·met′ri·cal·ly** *adv.*

tri·he·dron (trī·hē′drən) *n. pl.* **·dra** (-drə) *Geom.* A figure having three plane surfaces meeting at a point. [< Gk. *tri-* three + *hedra* a base] —**tri·he′dral** *adj.*

tri·lat·er·al (trī·lat′ər·əl) *adj.* Having three sides. [< L *tri-* three + *latus, lateris* a side] —**tri·lat′er·al·ly** *adv.*

trill (tril) *v.t.* **1** To sing or play in a quavering or tremulous tone. **2** *Phonet.* To articulate with a trill. —*v.i.* **3** To utter a quavering or tremulous sound. **4** *Music* To execute a trill. —*n.* **1** A tremulous utterance of successive tones, as of certain insects or birds; a warble. **2** *Music* A quick alternation of two notes either a tone or a semitone apart. **3** *Phonet.* A rapid vibration of a speech organ, as of the tip of the tongue. **4** A consonant or word so uttered. [< Ital. *trillare*] —**trill′er** *n.*

tril·lion (tril′yən) *n. & adj.* See NUMBER. [< MF *tri-* three + *million* million] —**tril′lionth** *adj., n.*

tril·li·um (tril′ē·əm) *n.* Any of a genus of perennial plants of the lily family, bearing a whorl of three leaves and a solitary flower. [< L *tri-* three]

tri·lo·bate (trī·lō′bāt, trī′lə·bāt) *adj.* Having three lobes. Also **tri·lo′bal, tri·lo′bat·ed, tri·lobed** (trī′lōbd′).

tri·lo·bite (trī′lə·bīt) *n.* Any of various fossilized extinct marine arthropods found in abundance in Paleozoic rocks, characterized by two lengthwise grooves forming three ridges. [< Gk. *tri*- three + *lobos* a lobe] —**tri′lo·bit′ic** (-bit′ik) *adj.*

tril·o·gy (tril′ə·jē) *n. pl.* **·gies** A group of three literary or dramatic compositions, each complete in itself, but connected into a whole through theme and subject matter. [< Gk. *tri*- three + *logos* a discourse]

trim (trim) *v.* **trimmed, trim·ming** *v.t.* **1** To make neat by clipping, pruning, etc. **2** To remove by cutting: usu. with *off* or *away.* **3** To put ornaments on; decorate. **4** In carpentry, to smooth; dress. **5** *Informal* **a** To chide; rebuke. **b** To punish. **c** To defeat. **6** *Naut.* **a** To adjust (sails or yards) for sailing. **b** To cause (a ship) to sit well in the water by adjusting cargo, ballast, etc. **7** To bring (an airplane) to stable flight by adjusting controls. — *v.i.* **8** *Naut.* **a** To be or remain in equilibrium. **b** To adjust sails or yards for sailing. **9** To act so as to appear to favor opposing sides in a controversy. —*n.* **1** State of adjustment or preparation; fitting condition. **2** Good physical condition: in *trim* to play tennis. **3** *Naut.* Fitness for sailing. **4** *Naut.* Actual or comparative degree of immersion. **5** The moldings, etc., as about the doors of a building. **6** Ornament, as on a dress; trimming. **7** The attitude of an aircraft in flight. — *adj.* **trim·mer, trim·mest** Having a smart appearance; spruce. —*adv.* In a trim manner: also **trim′ly.** [< OE *trymman* arrange, strengthen] —**trim′ness** *n.* —**Syn.** *v.* **1** cut, lop. **2** pare. **3** adorn, garnish.

tri·mes·ter (trī·mes′tər, trī′mes·tər) *n.* **1** A three-month period; quarter, as of an academic year. **2** Any of the three three-month periods used to identify the progress of a pregnancy. [< L *trimestris* < *tri*- three + *mensis* a month] —**tri·mes′tral, tri·mes′tri·al** *adj.*

trim·e·ter (trim′ə·tər) *adj.* In prosody, consisting of three measures or of lines containing three measures. —*n.* A line of verse having three measures.

trim·ming (trim′ing) *n.* **1** Something added for ornament or to give a finished appearance or effect. **2** *pl. Informal* The proper accompaniments or condiments of an article or food. **3** Parts or pieces trimmed away. **4** A severe reproof or a chastisement. **5** *Informal* A defeat.

tri·month·ly (trī·munth′lē) *adj. & adv.* Done or occurring every third month.

Trin·i·dad and To·ba·go (trin′ə·dad, tō·bā′gō) An independent member of the Commonwealth of Nations on two islands N of Venezuela, 1,980 sq. mi., cap. Port-of-Spain.

Trin·i·tar·i·an (trin′ə·târ′ē·ən) *adj.* **1** Of or pertaining to the Trinity. **2** Holding or professing belief in the Trinity. —*n.* A believer in the doctrine of the Trinity. —**Trin′i·tar′i·an·ism** *n.*

tri·ni·tro·tol·u·ene (trī·nī′trō·tol′yōō·ēn) *n.* An explosive made by treating toluene with nitric acid. Also **tri·ni′tro·tol′u·ol** (-yōō·ōl, -ol). [< TRI- + NITRO- + TOLUENE]

trin·i·ty (trin′ə·tē) *n. pl.* **·ties** **1** The state or character of being three. **2** The union of three parts or elements in one; a triad. [< L *trinitas* a triad]

Trin·i·ty (trin′ə·tē) *n.* In Christian theology, the union in one divine nature of Father, Son, and Holy Spirit.

trin·ket (tring′kit) *n.* **1** Any small ornament, as of jewelry. **2** A trifle; trivial object. [< AF *trenquet*]

tri·no·mi·al (trī·nō′mē·əl) *adj.* **1** *Biol.* Of, having, or employing three terms or names. **2** *Math.* Expressed as a sum of three terms. —*n.* **1** *Math.* A trinomial expression in algebra. **2** A trinomial name. Also **tri·nom′i·nal** (-nom′ə·nəl). [< TRI- + (BI)NOMIAL] —**tri·no′mi·al·ly** *adv.*

tri·o (trē′ō) *n. pl.* **tri·os** **1** Any three things grouped or associated together. **2** *Music* **a** A composition for three performers. **b** A group of three musicians who perform trios. [< Ital. *tre* three]

tri·ox·ide (trī·ok′sīd) *n.* An oxide containing three atoms of oxygen per molecule.

trip (trip) *n.* **1** A journey; excursion. **2** A misstep or stumble. **3** An active, nimble step or movement. **4** A catch or similar device for starting or stopping a movement, as in a mechanism. **5** A sudden catch of the legs or feet to make

a person fall. **6** A blunder; mistake. **7** *Slang* **a** The hallucinations and other sensations experienced by a person taking a psychedelic drug. **b** Any intense, usu. personal experience. —*v.* **tripped, trip·ping** *v.i.* **1** To stumble. **2** To move quickly and lightly. **3** To make an error. **4** To run past the nicks or dents of the ratchet escape wheel of a timepiece. **5** *Slang* To experience the effects of a psychedelic drug: often with *out.* —*v.t.* **6** To cause to stumble or make a mistake: often with *up.* **7** To perform (a dance) lightly. **8** *Mech.* To activate by releasing a catch, trigger, etc. —**trip it** To dance. [< OF *treper, triper* leap, trample] —**Syn.** *n.* jaunt, tour, sojourn, voyage.

tri·par·tite (trī·pär′tīt) *adj.* **1** Divided into three parts. **2** Having three corresponding parts or copies. **3** Made between three persons: a *tripartite* pact. [< L *tri*- three + *partitus,* p.p. of *partiri* to divide] —**tri·par′tite·ly** *adv.* —**tri′par·ti′tion** (-tish′ən) *n.*

tripe (trīp) *n.* **1** A part of the stomach wall of a ruminant used for food. **2** *Informal* Contemptible or worthless stuff; nonsense. [< OF]

trip·ham·mer (trip′ham·ər) *n.* A heavy power hammer that is raised mechanically and allowed to drop by a tripping action.

tripl. triplicate.

tri·ple (trip′əl) *v.* **·led, ·ling** *v.t.* **1** To make threefold in number or quantity. —*v.i.* **2** To be or become three times as many or as large. **3** In baseball, to make a triple. —*adj.* **1** Consisting of three things united. **2** Multiplied by three; thrice said or done. —*n.* **1** A set or group of three. **2** In baseball, a fair hit that enables the batter to reach third base without the help of an error. [< Gk. *triploos* threefold] —**trip′ly** *adv.*

triple play In baseball, a play during which three men are put out.

trip·let (trip′lit) *n.* **1** A group of three of a kind. **2** Any of three children born at one birth. **3** *Music* A group of three notes that divide the time usu. taken by two. [< TRIPLE]

triple time *Music* A rhythm having three beats to the measure with the accent on the first beat.

trip·li·cate (trip′lə·kit) *adj.* Threefold; made in three copies. —*n.* One of three precisely similar things. —**in triplicate** In three identical copies. —*v.t.* (-kāt) **·cat·ed, ·cat·ing** To make three times; triple. [< L *triplicare* to triple] —**trip′li·cate·ly** *adv.* —**trip′li·ca′tion** *n.*

tri·pod (trī′pod) *n.* A three-legged frame or stand, as for supporting a camera, etc. [< Gk. *tri*- three + *pous* foot] —**trip·o·dal** (trip′ə·dəl), **tri·pod·ic** (tri·pod′ik) *adj.*

trip·per (trip′ər) *n.* **1** A person or thing that trips. **2** *Brit. Informal* A tourist or traveler. **3** *Mech.* A trip or tripping mechanism, as a cam, pawl, etc. **4** *Slang* A person who frequently uses psychedelic drugs.

trip·ping (trip′ing) *adj.* Light; nimble. —**trip′ping·ly** *adv.*

Tripod

trip·tych (trip′tik) *n.* **1** A picture, carving, or work of art on three panels side by side. **2** A writing tablet in three sections. [< Gk. *tri*- three + *ptyx, ptychos* a fold]

tri·reme (trī′rēm) *n.* An ancient warship with three banks of oars on each side. [< L *tri*- three + *remus* an oar]

tri·sect (trī·sekt′) *v.t.* To divide into three parts, esp., as in geometry, into three equal parts. [< TRI- + L *sectus,* p.p. of *secare* to cut] —**tri·sec′tion** (-sek′shən), **tri·sec′tor** *n.*

triste (trēst) *adj.* Sorrowful; sad. [F]

tri·syl·la·ble (trī·sil′ə·bəl) *n.* A word of three syllables. —**tri·syl·lab·ic** (trī·si·lab′ik) *adj.* —**tri′syl·lab′i·cal·ly** *adv.*

trite (trīt) *adj.* **trit·er, trit·est** Made commonplace or hackneyed by frequent repetition. [< L *tritus,* p.p. of *terere* to rub] —**trite′ly** *adv.* —**trite′ness** *n.* —**Syn.** stale, stereotyped, threadbare, cliché, shopworn, tired, stock.

trit·i·um (trit′ē·əm, trish′ē·əm) *n.* The radioactive hydrogen isotope of atomic mass 3, having a half-life of 12.5 years. [< Gk. *tritos* third]

tri·ton (trīt′n) *n.* A marine snail with a trumpet-shaped shell. [< TRITON]

Triton

Tri·ton (trīt′n) *Gk. Myth.* A sea god having a man's head and upper body and a dolphin's tail.

trit·u·rate (trich′ə·rāt) *v.t.* **·rat·ed, ·rat·ing** To reduce to a fine powder or pulp by grinding or rubbing; pulverize. — *n.* That which has been triturated. [< L *tritura* a rubbing, threshing < *tritus.* See TRITE.] *adj.* —**trit′u·ra·tor, trit′u·ra′tion** *n.*

tri·umph (trī′əmf) *v.i.* **1** To win a victory. **2** To be successful. **3** To rejoice over a victory; exult. —*n.* **1** A victory or conquest: a *triumph* of will power. **2** An important success: the *triumphs* of modern medicine. **3** Exultation over a victory. **4** In ancient Rome, a pageant welcoming a victorious general. [< Gk. *thriambos* a processional hymn to Dionysus] —**tri·um·phal** (trī·um′fəl) *adj.* —**tri·um′phal·ly** *adv.* —**tri·umph·er** *n.*

tri·um·phant (trī·um′fənt) *adj.* **1** Exultant for or as for victory. **2** Crowned with victory; victorious. —**tri·um′phant·ly** *adv.*

tri·um·vir (trī·um′vər) *n. pl.* **·virs** or **·vi·ri** (-və·rī′, -rē′) In ancient Rome, one of three men united in public office or authority. [< L *trium virorum* of three men] —**tri·um′vi·ral** *adj.*

tri·um·vi·rate (trī·um′vər·it, -və·rāt) *n.* **1** A group or coalition of three men who govern. **2** The office of a triumvir. **3** The triumvirs collectively. **4** A group of three persons; a trio. [< L *triumvir* triumvir]

tri·une (trī′yōōn) *adj.* Three in one: said of the Godhead. [< TRI- + L *unus* one] —**tri·un·i·ty** (trī·yōō′nə·tē) *n.*

tri·va·lent (trī·vā′lənt) *adj. Chem.* Having a valence or combining value of three. [< TRI- + L *valens,* pr.p. of *valere* be strong] —**tri·va′lence, tri·va′len·cy** *n.*

triv·et (triv′it) *n.* A short, usu. three-legged stand for holding cooking vessels in a fireplace, a hot dish on a table, or a heated iron. [< L *tri-* three + *pes, pedis* a foot]

triv·i·a (triv′ē·ə) *n.pl.* Insignificant or unimportant matters; trifles. [< L *trivialis* trivial]

triv·i·al (triv′ē·əl) *adj.* **1** Of little value or importance; insignificant. **2** *Archaic* Ordinary; commonplace. [< L *trivialis* of the crossroads, commonplace] —**triv′i·al·ism** *n.* —**triv′i·al·ly** *adv.* —**Syn. 1** slight, mean, paltry, inconsiderable, piddling.

triv·i·al·i·ty (triv′ē·al′ə·tē) *n. pl.* **·ties 1** The state or quality of being trivial. **2** A trivial matter.

triv·i·al·ize (triv′ē·ə·līz) *v.t.* **·ized, ·iz·ing** To treat as or make trivial; regard as unimportant. —**triv′i·al·i·za′tion** *n.*

tri·week·ly (trī·wēk′lē) *adj. & adv.* **1** Occurring three times a week. **2** Done or occurring every third week. —*n. pl.* **·lies** A triweekly publication.

tro·che (trō′kē) *n.* A small medicated lozenge, usu. circular. [< Gk. *trochiskos* a small wheel, a lozenge]

tro·chee (trō′kē) *n.* In prosody, a foot comprising a long and short syllable (‾ ◡), or an accented syllable followed by an unaccented one. [< Gk. *trochaios (pous)* a running (foot) < *trechein* to run] —**tro·cha·ic** (trō·kā′ik) *adj.*

trod (trod) *p.t. &* alternative *p.p.* of TREAD.

trod·den (trod′n) *p.p.* of TREAD.

trog·lo·dyte (trog′lə·dīt) *n.* **1** A prehistoric cave man. **2** A person with primitive habits. **3** A hermit. [< Gk. *trōglodytēs*] —**trog′lo·dyt′ic** (-dit′ik), **trog′lo·dyt′i·cal** *adj.*

Tro·jan (trō′jən) *n.* **1** A native of Troy. **2** A brave, persevering person. —*adj.* Of or pertaining to ancient Troy or to its people.

Trojan horse 1 *Gk. Myth.* During the Trojan War, a large, hollow wooden horse filled with Greek soldiers and brought within the walls of Troy, thus bringing about the downfall of the city. **2** *Mil.* The infiltration of military men into enemy territory to commit sabotage against industry and military installations.

Trojan War *Gk. Myth.* The ten years' war waged by the Greeks against the Trojans to recover Helen, the wife of Menelaus, who had been abducted by Paris.

troll¹ (trōl) *v.t.* **1** To sing in succession, as in a round. **2** To sing in a full, hearty manner. **3** To fish for with a moving lure, as from a moving boat. —*v.i.* **4** To roll; turn. **5** To sing a tune, etc., in a full, hearty manner. **6** To fish with a moving lure. —*n.* **1** A song taken up at intervals by several voices; round. **2** A rolling movement or motion. **3** In fishing, a spoon or other lure. [?] —**troll′er** *n.*

troll² (trōl) *n.* In Scandinavian folklore, a giant or dwarf living in caves or underground. [< ON]

trol·ley (trol′ē) *n. pl.* **·leys 1** A device that rolls or slides along an electric conductor to carry current to an electric vehicle. **2** A trolley car; also, a system of trolley cars. **3** A small truck or car suspended from an overhead track and used to convey material, as in a factory, mine, etc. —*v.t. & v.i.* To convey or travel by trolley. [< TROLL¹]

trolley bus A passenger conveyance operating without rails, propelled electrically by current taken from an overhead wire by means of a trolley.

trolley car A car arranged with a trolley and motor for use on an electric railway.

trol·lop (trol′əp) *n.* **1** A slatternly woman. **2** A prostitute. [?]

trom·bone (trom·bōn′, trom′bōn) *n.* A brass wind instrument of the trumpet family in the tenor range, usu. equipped with a slide for changing pitch. [< Ital. *tromba* a trumpet] —**trom·bon′ist** *n.*

Trombone

troop (trōōp) *n.* **1** A gathering of people. **2** A flock or herd, as of animals. **3** A unit of cavalry having 60 to 100 men and corresponding to a company in other military branches. **4** *pl.* Soldiers. **5** A unit of Boy Scouts or Girl Scouts. —*v.i.* **1** To move along as a group: shoppers *trooping* through a store. **2** To go: to *troop* across the street. —*v.t.* **3** To form into troops. [< LL *troppus* a flock] —**Syn. 1** company, crowd, multitude, throng.

troop·er (trōō′pər) *n.* **1** A cavalryman. **2** A mounted policeman. **3** A troop horse. **4** *Informal* A state policeman.

troop·ship (trōōp′ship′) *n.* A ship for carrying troops.

trope (trōp) *n.* **1** The figurative use of a word or phrase. **2** A figure of speech. **3** Figurative language in general. [< L *tropus* a figure of speech < Gk. *tropos* a turn]

tro·phy (trō′fē) *n. pl.* **·phies 1** Anything taken from an enemy and displayed or treasured in proof of victory. **2** A prize representing victory or achievement: a tennis *trophy.* **3** An animal skin, mounted head, etc., kept to show skill in hunting. **4** Any memento. [< Gk. *tropē* a defeat, turning] —**tro′phied** *adj.*

trop·ic (trop′ik) *n.* **1** *Geog.* Either of two parallels of latitude, the **tropic of Cancer** at 23° 27′ north of the equator and the **tropic of Capricorn** 23° 27′ south of the equator, between which lies the torrid zone. **2** *Astron.* Either of two corresponding parallels in the celestial sphere similarly named, and respectively 23° 27′ north or south from the celestial equator. **3** *pl.* The regions in the torrid zone. —*adj.* Of or pertaining to the tropics; tropical. [< Gk. *tropikos (kyklos)* the tropical (circle), pertaining to the turning of the sun at the solstice.]

-tropic *combining form* Having a (specified) tropism: *geotropic.* [< Gk. *tropos* a turn]

trop·i·cal (trop′i·kəl) *adj.* **1** Of, pertaining to, or characteristic of the tropics. **2** Of the nature of a trope or metaphor. —**trop′i·cal·ly** *adv.*

tropical fish Any of various small, usu. brightly colored fishes originating in the tropics and adapted to living in an aquarium (**tropical aquarium**) kept at a constant warm temperature.

tro·pism (trō′piz·əm) *n.* **1** A tendency in an organism to grow or move toward or away from a given stimulus. **2** An instance of such growth or movement. [< Gk. *tropē* a turning] —**tro·pis·tic** (trō·pis′tik) *adj.*

-tropism *combining form* A (specified) tropism: *phototropism.* Also **-tropy.**

trop·o·sphere (trōp′ə·sfir, trop′-) *n. Meteorol.* The region of the atmosphere extending from six to twelve miles above the earth's surface, characterized by decreasing temperature with increasing altitude. [< Gk. *tropos* a turning + SPHERE]

trot (trot) *n.* **1** The gait of a quadruped, in which each

add, āce, câre, pälm; end, ēven; it, īce; odd, ōpen, ôrder; tōōk, pōōl; up, bûrn; ə = *a* in *above, u* in *focus;* yōō = *u* in *fuse;* oil; pout; check; go; ring; thin; this; zh, *vision.* < derived from; ? origin uncertain or unknown.

diagonal pair of legs is moved alternately. **2** The sound of this gait. **3** A slow running gait of a person. **4** A little child. **5** *Informal* A literal translation of a foreign-language text, used by students, often dishonestly. **—the trots** *Slang* Diarrhea. —*v.* **trot·ted, trot·ting** *v.i.* **1** To go at a trot. **2** To go quickly; hurry. —*v.t.* **3** To cause to trot. **4** To ride at a trotting gait. **—trot out** *Informal* To bring forth for inspection, approval, etc. [< OHG *trottōn* to tread]

troth (trôth, trŏth) *n.* **1** Good faith; fidelity. **2** The act of pledging fidelity. **3** Truth; verity. **—plight one's troth** To promise to marry or be faithful to. [< OE *trēowth* truth]

Trot·sky·ism (trot′skē-iz′əm) *n.* The doctrines of Trotsky and his followers who opposed Stalin and believed that Communism to succeed must be international. [< L. *Trotsky*, 1879–1940, Russian Bolshevist leader] — **Trot′sky·ist, Trot′sky·ite** *n., adj.*

trot·ter (trot′ər) *n.* **1** One who or that which trots; a trotting horse, esp. one trained to trot in races. **2** *Informal* An animal's foot; a pig's *trotters.*

trou·ba·dour (trōō′bə-dôr, -dōr, -dŏŏr) *n.* One of a class of lyric poets, sometimes including wandering minstrels, flourishing in parts of France, Italy, and Spain during the 12th and 13th centuries. [< Prov. *trobador* < *trobar* compose, invent]

trou·ble (trub′əl) *n.* **1** The state of being distressed or worried. **2** A person, circumstance, or event that occasions difficulty or perplexity. **3** A condition of difficulty: to be in *trouble* at school; money *troubles.* **4** A disease or ailment: heart *trouble.* **5** Bother; effort: They took the *trouble* to drive me home. **6** Agitation; unrest: *trouble* in the streets. —*v.* **·led, ·ling** *v.t.* **1** To distress; worry. **2** To stir up or roil, as water. **3** To inconvenience. **4** To annoy. **5** To cause physical pain or discomfort to. —*v.i.* **6** To take pains; bother. [< OF *turbler* to trouble] **—troub′ler** *n.*

trou·ble·mak·er (trub′əl-mā′kər) *n.* One who habitually stirs up trouble for others.

trou·ble·shoot·er (trub′əl-shōō′tər) *n.* **1** A skilled workman able to analyze and repair breakdowns in machinery, electronic equipment, etc. **2** A person assigned to eliminate sources of difficulty or to mediate disputes, esp. in diplomacy and politics. **—troub′le·shoot′ing** *n.*

trou·ble·some (trub′əl·səm) *adj.* **1** Causing trouble; trying. **2** Difficult: a *troublesome* task. **—troub′le·some·ly** *adv.* **—troub′le·some·ness** *n.* **—Syn.** 1 burdensome, disturbing, galling, harassing.

troub·lous (trub′ləs) *adj.* **1** Uneasy; restless: *troublous* times. **2** Troublesome.

trough (trôf, trof) *n.* **1** A long, narrow receptacle for food or water for animals. **2** A similarly shaped receptacle, as for mixing dough. **3** A long, narrow depression, as between waves. **4** A gutter for rain water fixed under the eaves of a building. **5** *Meteorol.* An elongated region of relatively low atmospheric pressure. [< OE *trog*]

trounce (trouns) *v.t.* **trounced, trounc·ing** **1** To beat or thrash severely; punish. **2** *Informal* To defeat. [?]

troupe (trōōp) *n.* A company of actors or other performers. —*v.i.* **trouped, troup·ing** To travel as one of a company of actors or entertainers. [< OF *trope* troop]

troup·er (trōōp′ər) *n.* **1** A member of a theatrical company. **2** An older actor of long experience.

trou·sers (trou′zərz) *n.pl.* A two-legged garment, covering the body from the waist to the ankles or knees. [Blend of obs. *trouse* breeches and DRAWERS]

trous·seau (trōō′sō, trōō-sō′) *n. pl.* **·seaux** (-sōz, -sōz′) or **·seaus** A bride's outfit, esp. of clothing. [F < OF, dim. of *trousse* a packed collection of things]

trout (trout) *n.* Any of various fishes of the salmon family found mostly in fresh waters and esteemed as a game and food fish. [< OE *trūht*]

trow·el (trou′əl, troul) *n.* **1** A flat-bladed, sometimes pointed implement, used by masons, plasterers, and molders. **2** A small concave scoop with a handle, used in digging about small plants. —*v.t.* **·eled** or **·elled, ·el·ing** or **·el·ling** To apply, smooth, or dig

Trowels
a. garden. b. plastering. c. brick.

with a trowel. [< L *trulla,* dim. of *trua* a stirring spoon] **—trow′el·er** or **trow′el·ler** *n.*

troy (troi) *adj.* Measured or expressed in troy weight. [< *Troyes,* France; with ref. to a weight used at a fair held there]

troy weight A system of weights in which 12 ounces or 5,760 grains equal a pound, and the grain is identical with the avoirdupois grain. • See MEASURE.

tru·ant (trōō′ənt) *n.* **1** A pupil who stays away from school without leave. **2** A person who shirks responsibilities or work. **—play truant** **1** To be absent from school without leave. **2** To shirk responsibilities or work. —*adj.* **1** Being truant; idle. **2** Relating to or characterizing a truant. [< OF, a vagabond] **—tru·an·cy** (trōō′ən-sē) *n.* (*pl.* **·cies**)

truce (trōōs) *n.* **1** An agreement for a temporary suspension of hostilities; an armistice. **2** A temporary stopping, as from pain, etc.; respite. [< OE *truwa* faith, a promise]

Tru·cial States (trōō′shəl) A group of sheikdoms, bound by treaties with Great Britain, in E Arabia, 32,300 sq. mi.

truck[1] (truk) *n.* **1** Any of several types of strongly built motor vehicles designed to transport heavy loads, bulky articles, freight, etc. **2** A two-wheeled barrowlike vehicle for moving barrels, boxes, etc., by hand. **3** A small wheeled vehicle used for moving baggage, goods, etc. **4** A disk at the upper extremity of a mast or flagpole through which the halyards of signals are run. **5** A small wheel. —*v.t.* **1** To carry on a truck. —*v.i.* **2** To carry goods on a truck. **3** To drive a truck. [< Gk. *trochos* a wheel]

truck[2] (truk) *v.t. & v.i.* To exchange or barter. —*n.* **1** Commodities for sale. **2** Garden produce for market. **3** *Informal* Rubbish; worthless articles. **4** Barter. **5** *Informal* Dealings: I will have no *truck* with him. [< OF *troquer* to barter]

truck·age (truk′ij) *n.* **1** The conveyance of goods on trucks. **2** The charge for this. [< TRUCK[1]]

truck·er (truk′ər) *n.* One who drives or supplies trucks or moves commodities in trucks.

truck farm A farm on which vegetables are produced for market. **—truck farmer, truck farming**

truck·ing (truk′ing) *n.* The act or business of transportation by trucks.

truck·le (truk′əl) *v.* **·led, ·ling** *v.i.* **1** To yield or submit weakly: with *to.* **2** To move on rollers or casters. —*v.t.* **3** To cause to move on rollers or casters. —*n.* A small wheel. [< L *trochlea* system of pulleys] **—truck′ler** *n.*

truckle bed TRUNDLE BED.

truck·man (truk′mən) *n. pl.* **·men** (mən) **1** A truck driver. **2** One engaged in the business of trucking.

truc·u·lent (truk′yə-lənt) *adj.* Of savage character; cruel; ferocious. [< L *trux, trucis* fierce] **—truc·u·lence** (truk′yə-ləns), **truc′u·len·cy** *n.* **—truc′u·lent·ly** *adv.* **—Syn.** barbarous, brutal, fierce, ruthless, vicious.

trudge (truj) *v.i.* **trudged, trudg·ing** To walk wearily or laboriously; plod. —*n.* A tiresome walk or tramp. [?] **—trudg′er** *n.*

true (trōō) *adj.* **tru·er, tru·est** **1** Faithful to fact or reality. **2** Being real; genuine, not counterfeit: *true* gold. **3** Faithful to friends, promises, or principles; loyal. **4** Exact: a *true* copy. **5** Accurate, as in shape, or position: a *true* fit. **6** Faithful to the requirements of law or justice; legitimate: the *true* king. **7** Faithful to truth; honest: a *true* man. **8** Faithful to the promise or predicted event: a *true* sign. **9** *Biol.* Possessing all the attributes of its class: a *true* root. **10** *Music* Exactly in tune. **—come true** To turn out as hoped for or imagined. —*n.* The state or quality of being true; also, something that is true: usu. with *the.* **—in** (or **out of**) **true** In (or not in) line of adjustment. —*adv.* **1** In truth; truly. **2** Within proper tolerances: The wheel runs *true.* —*v.t.* **trued, tru·ing** To bring to conformity with a standard or requirement: to *true* a frame. [< OE *trēowe*] **—true′ness** *n.*

true bill *Law* A bill of indictment found by a grand jury to be sustained by the evidence.

true-blue (trōō′blōō′) *adj.* Staunch; faithful.

true·love (trōō′luv′) *n.* One truly beloved; a sweetheart.

truf·fle (truf′əl, trōō′fəl) *n.* Any of various fleshy underground edible fungi regarded as a delicacy. [< OF *truffe*]

tru·ism (trōō′iz-əm) *n.* An obvious or self-evident truth; a platitude.

trull (trul) *n.* A prostitute. [< G *Trolle*]

tru·ly (trōō′lē) *adv.* 1 In conformity with fact. 2 With accuracy. 3 With loyalty.

trump (trump) *n.* 1 In various card games, a card of the suit selected to rank above all others temporarily. 2 The suit thus determined. 3 *Informal* A fine, reliable person. —*v.t.* 1 To take (another card) with a trump. 2 To surpass; excel; beat. —*v.i.* 3 To play a trump. —**trump up** To invent for a fraudulent purpose. [Alter. of TRIUMPH]

trump·er·y (trum′pər·ē) *n. pl.* ·er·ies 1 Worthless finery. 2 Rubbish; nonsense. —*adj.* Having a showy appearance, but valueless. [< OF *tromper* to cheat]

trum·pet (trum′pit) *n.* 1 A soprano brass wind instrument with a flaring bell and a long metal tube. 2 Something resembling a trumpet in form. 3 A tube for collecting and conducting sounds to the ear; an ear trumpet. 4 A loud penetrating sound like that of a trumpet. —*v.t.* 1 To sound or publish abroad. —*v.i.* 2 To blow a trumpet. 3 To give forth a sound as if from a trumpet, as an elephant. [< OF *trompette*]

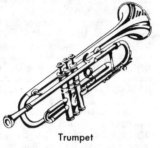

Trumpet

trum·pet·er (trum′pə·tər) *n.* 1 One who plays a trumpet. 2 One who publishes something loudly abroad. 3 A large South American bird, related to the cranes. 4 A large North American wild swan having a clarionlike cry: also **trumpeter swan.** • See SWAN. 5 A breed of domestic pigeons.

trun·cate (trung′kāt) *v.t.* ·cat·ed, ·cat·ing To cut the top or end from. —*adj. Biol.* Ending abruptly, as though cut off: a *truncate* leaf. [< L *truncare*] —**trun′cate·ly** *adv.* —**trun·ca·tion** (trung·kā′shən) *n.*

trun·cheon (trun′chən) *n.* 1 A short, heavy stick, esp. a policeman's club. 2 Any baton of office or authority. —*v.t.* To beat as with a truncheon; cudgel. [< OF *tronchon* a stump]

trun·dle (trun′dəl) *n.* 1 A small broad wheel, as of a caster. 2 The act, motion, or sound of trundling. 3 TRUNDLE BED. —*v.* ·dled, ·dling *v.t.* 1 To propel by rolling along: to *trundle* a wheelbarrow. 2 To haul or carry in a wheeled vehicle. —*v.i.* 3 To move ahead by revolving. 4 To progress on wheels. [< OE *trendel* a circle] —**trun′dler** *n.*

trundle bed A bed with very low frame resting upon casters, so that it may be rolled under another bed.

trunk (trungk) *n.* 1 The main stem or stock of a tree. 2 An animal or human body, apart from the head and limbs; the torso. 3 The thorax of an insect. 4 The main stem of a nerve, blood vessel, or lymphatic. 5 A main line of communication or transportation, as the circuit connecting two telephone exchanges. 6 A proboscis, as of an elephant. 7 A large box or case used for packing and carrying clothes or other articles. 8 *pl.* Very short, close-fitting trousers worn by swimmers, athletes, etc. 9 *Archit.* The shaft of a column. 10 A compartment in an automobile, opposite the end housing the motor, for carrying luggage, tools, etc. —*adj.* Being or belonging to a trunk or main body: a *trunk* railroad. [< L *truncus* stem, trunk]

trunk·fish (trungk′fish′) *n. pl.* ·fish or ·fish·es Any of a family of fishes characterized by a body covering of hard, bony plates.

truss (trus) *n.* 1 A supporting framework, as for a roof or bridge. 2 A bandage or support for a hernia. 3 A bundle or package. 4 *Naut.* A heavy iron piece by which a lower yard is attached to a mast. —*v.t.* 1 To tie or bind; fasten: often with *up.* 2 To support or brace (a roof, bridge, etc.) with trusses. 3 To fasten the wings of (a fowl) before cooking. [< OF *trousser, trusser* pack up, bundle] —**truss′er** *n.*

trust (trust) *n.* 1 A reliance on the integrity, veracity, or reliability of a person or thing. 2 Something committed to one's care for use or safekeeping. 3 The state or position

of one who has received an important charge. 4 Confident expectation; hope. 5 In commerce, credit. 6 *Law* a The confidence reposed in a person to whom the legal title to property is conveyed for the benefit of another. b The property or thing held in trust. c The relation subsisting between the holder and the property so held. 7 A combination of business firms formed to control production and prices of some commodity. —**in trust** In the charge or care of another or others. —**on trust** 1 On credit. 2 Without investigating: to accept a statement *on trust.* —*v.t.* 1 To rely upon. 2 To commit to the care of another; entrust. 3 To commit something to the care of: with *with.* 4 To allow to do something without fear of the consequences. 5 To expect; hope. 6 To believe. 7 To allow business credit to. —*v.i.* 8 To place trust or confidence; rely: with *in.* 9 To allow business credit. —**trust to** To depend upon; confide in. —*adj.* Held in trust: *trust* property. [< ON *traust,* lit., firmness] —**trust′er** *n.* —**Syn.** *n.* 1 confidence, credence, faith.

trus·tee (trus·tē′) *n.* 1 One who is entrusted with the property of another. 2 One of a body of persons, often elective, who hold the property and manage the affairs of a company or institution.

trus·tee·ship (trus·tē′ship) *n.* 1 The post or function of a trustee. 2 Supervision and control of a trust territory by a country or countries commissioned by the United Nations.

trust·ful (trust′fəl) *adj.* Disposed to trust. —**trust′ful·ly** *adv.* —**trust′ful·ness** *n.*

trust fund Money, securities, or similar property held in trust.

trust·ing (trus′ting) *adj.* Having trust; trustful. —**trust′ing·ly** *adv.* —**trust′ing·ness** *n.*

trust territory An area, usu. a former colonial possession, governed by a member state of the United Nations.

trust·wor·thy (trust′wûr′thē) *adj.* Worthy of confidence; reliable. —**trust′wor′thi·ly** (-wûr′thə·lē) *adv.* —**trust′wor′thi·ness** *n.*

trust·y (trus′tē) *adj.* trust·i·er, trust·i·est 1 Faithful to duty or trust. 2 Staunch; firm. —*n. pl.* trust·ies A trustworthy person; esp. a convict to whom special privileges are granted. —**trust′i·ly** *adv.* —**trust′i·ness** *n.*

truth (trōōth) *n. pl.* truths (trōōthz, trōōths) 1 The state or character of being true. 2 That which is true. 3 Conformity to fact or reality. 4 The quality of being true; fidelity; constancy. —**in truth** Indeed; in fact. [< OE *treowe* true]

truth·ful (trōōth′fəl) *adj.* 1 Conforming to fact; veracious. 2 Telling the truth. —**truth′ful·ly** *adv.* —**truth′ful·ness** *n.*

try (trī) *v.* tried, try·ing *v.t.* 1 To make an attempt to do or accomplish. 2 To make experimental use or application of: to *try* a new pen. 3 To subject to a test; put to proof. 4 To put severe strain upon; tax: to *try* one's patience. 5 To subject to trouble or tribulation. 6 To extract by rendering or melting; refine. 7 *Law* To determine the guilt or innocence of by judicial trial. —*v.i.* 8 To make an attempt; put forth effort. 9 To make an examination or test. —**try on** To put on (a garment) to test it for fit or appearance. —**try out** 1 To attempt to qualify: He *tried out* for the team. 2 To test the result or effect of. —*n. pl.* **tries** The act of trying; trial. [< OF *trier* sift, pick out] —**tri′er** *n.* • **try and, try to** These constructions are both standard in modern English: *Try and meet me at six; Try to finish your work on time.* However, *try to* is usu. preferable in precise, formal writing.

try·ing (trī′ing) *adj.* Testing severely; hard to endure. —**try′ing·ly** *adv.* —**try′ing·ness** *n.* —**Syn.** arduous, difficult, onerous, troublesome.

try·out (trī′out′) *n. Informal* A test of ability, as of an actor or athlete.

tryp·sin (trip′sin) *n.* A pancreatic enzyme that helps to digest proteins. [< Gk. *tripsis* a rubbing + (PEP)SIN] — **tryp′tic** (-tik) *adj.*

try square A device for marking off right angles and testing the accuracy of anything square.

tryst (trist, trīst) *n.* 1 An appointment to meet at a specified time or place. 2 The meeting place agreed upon. 3 The meeting so agreed upon. [< OF *triste, tristre* an appointed station in hunting]

tsar (zär, tsär) *n.* CZAR.

tset·se (tset′sē, tsē′tsē) *n.* Any of several bloodsucking flies of Africa, including species that carry and transmit pathogenic organisms to humans and animals. Also **tsetse fly.** [< Bantu]

T. Sgt., T/Sgt Technical Sergeant.

T-shirt (tē′shûrt′) *n.* A knitted cotton undershirt with short sleeves.

tsp. teaspoon(s); teaspoonful(s).

T-square (tē′skwâr′) *n.* A device used to measure out right angles or parallel lines, consisting usu. of a flat strip with a shorter head at right angles to it.

tsu·na·mi (tsoo-nä′mē) *n.* An immense wave generated by a submarine earthquake. [Jap. < *tsu* port, harbor + *nami* wave]

Tu., Tues. Tuesday.

tub (tub) *n.* 1 A broad, open-topped vessel of metal, wooden staves, etc., for washing and bathing. 2 A bathtub. 3 *Informal* A bath taken in a tub. 4 The amount that a tub contains. 5 Anything resembling a tub, as a broad, clumsy boat. 6 *Informal* A small cask. —*v.t. & v.i.* **tubbed, tub·bing** To wash or bathe in a tub. [< MDu. *tubbe*] —**tub′ber** *n.*

tu·ba (tyoo′bə) *n. pl.* **·bas** or **·bae** (-bē) A large bass instrument of the bugle family. [< L, a war trumpet]

tub·by (tub′ē) *adj.* **·bi·er, ·bi·est** Resembling a tub in form; round and fat. —**Syn.** chubby, chunky, corpulent, rotund.

tube (tyoob) *n.* 1 A long hollow cylindrical body of metal, glass, rubber, etc., generally used to convey or hold a liquid or gas. 2 Any device having a tube or tubelike part, as a telescope. 3 *Biol.* Any elongated hollow part or organ. 4 A subway or subway tunnel. 5 An electron tube. 6 A collapsible metal or plastic cylinder for containing paints, toothpaste, glue, and the like. —**the tube** *Slang* Television. —*v.t.* **tubed, tub·ing** 1 To fit or furnish with a tube. 2 To make tubular. [< L *tubus*] —**tu′bal** *adj.*

Tuba

tu·ber (tyoo′bər) *n.* 1 A short, thickened portion of an underground stem, as a potato. 2 A tubercle. [L, a swelling]

tu·ber·cle (tyoo′bər-kəl) *n.* 1 A small rounded eminence or nodule. 2 *Bot.* A small wartlike swelling, usu. due to symbiotic microorganisms, as on the roots of certain legumes. 3 *Pathol.* A small granular tumor within an organ. [< L *tuber* a swelling]

tubercle bacillus The rod-shaped bacterium that causes tuberculosis.

tu·ber·cu·lar (tyoo-bûr′kyə-lər) *adj.* 1 Affected with tubercles. 2 Tuberculous. —*n.* One affected with tuberculosis.

tu·ber·cu·lin (tyoo-bûr′kyə-lin) *n.* A substance derived from tubercle bacilli, used in a diagnostic test for tuberculosis. [< L *tuberculum* TUBERCLE + -IN]

tu·ber·cu·lo·sis (tyoo-bûr′kyə-lō′sis) *n.* A communicable disease caused by the tubercle bacillus and characterized by tubercles in the lungs or other organs or tissues of the body. —**tu·ber′cu·lous** (tyoo-bûr′kyə-ləs) *adj.*

tube·rose (tyoob′rōz′, tyoo′bə-rōs′) *n.* A bulbous plant of the amaryllis family, bearing a spike of fragrant white flowers. [< L *tuberosus* knobby < *tuber* a swelling]

tu·ber·ous (tyoo′bər-əs) *adj.* 1 Bearing projections or prominences. 2 Resembling tubers. 3 *Bot.* Bearing tubers: also **tu′ber·ose.** —**tu·ber·os·i·ty** (tyoo′bə-ros′ə-tē) *n.* (*pl.* **·ties**)

tub·ing (tyoo′bing) *n.* 1 Tubes collectively. 2 A piece of tube or material for tubes.

tu·bu·lar (tyoo′byə-lər) *adj.* 1 Having the form of a tube. 2 Of or pertaining to a tube or tubes.

tuck (tuk) *v.t.* 1 To thrust or press in the ends or edges of: to *tuck* in a blanket. 2 To wrap or cover snugly. 3 To thrust or press into a close place; cram. 4 To make tucks in, by folding and stitching. —*v.i.* 5 To contract; draw together. 6 To make tucks. —*n.* 1 A fold sewed into a garment. 2 Any inserted or folded thing. 3 A position in diving in which the knees are bent and the upper legs pressed against the chest. [< OE *tūcian* ill-treat, lit., tug]

tuck·er¹ (tuk′ər) *n.* 1 One who or that which tucks. 2 A

covering of muslin, lace, etc., formerly worn over the neck and shoulders by women. 3 A device on a sewing machine to make tucks.

tuck·er² (tuk′ər) *v.t. Informal* To weary completely; exhaust: usu. with *out.* [?]

Tu·dor (tyoo′dər) *adj.* 1 Of or pertaining to the English royal family (1485–1603) descended from Sir Owen Tudor. 2 Designating or pertaining to the architecture, poetry, etc., developed during the reigns of the Tudors.

Tues·day (tyooz′dē, -dā) *n.* The third day of the week. [< OE *tīwesdæg* day of Tiw, a god of war]

tuft (tuft) *n.* 1 A collection or bunch of small, flexible parts, as hair, grass, or feathers, held together at the base. 2 A clump or knot. —*v.t.* 1 To provide (a mattress, upholstery, etc.) with tightly drawn tufts or buttons to keep the padding in place. 2 To cover or adorn with tufts. —*v.i.* 3 To form or grow in tufts. [< OF *tuffe*] —**tuft′er** *n.*

tuft·ed (tuf′tid) *adj.* 1 Having or adorned with a tuft or crest. 2 Forming a tuft or dense cluster.

tug (tug) *v.* **tugged, tug·ging** *v.t.* 1 To pull at with effort; strain at. 2 To pull or drag with effort. 3 To tow with a tugboat. —*v.i.* 4 To pull strenuously: to *tug* at an oar. 5 To strive; struggle. —*n.* 1 A violent pull. 2 A strenuous contest. 3 A tugboat. 4 A trace of a harness. [< OE *tēon* tow] —**tug′ger** *n.* —**Syn.** *v.* 2 draw, haul, heave, lug.

tug·boat (tug′bōt′) *n.* A small, compact, ruggedly built vessel designed for towing or pushing barges and larger vessels.

tug of war 1 A contest in which a number of persons at one end of a rope pull against a like number at the other end. 2 A laborious effort; supreme contest. Also **tug-of-war** (tug′uv-wôr′, tug′ə-) *n.* (*pl.* **tugs-of-war**).

tu·i·tion (tyoo-ish′ən) *n.* 1 The act or business of teaching. 2 The charge or payment for instruction. [< L *tuitio* a guard, guardianship] —**tu·i′tion·al, tu·i′tion·ar·y** (-er′ē) *adj.*

tu·la·re·mi·a (too′lə-rē′mē-ə) *n.* An acute bacterial infection that can be transmitted to man from infected rabbits, squirrels, or other animals by the bite of certain flies or by direct contact. Also **tu′la·rae′mi·a.** [< *Tulare* County, California + Gk. *haima* blood]

tu·lip (tyoo′lip) *n.* 1 Any of numerous bulbous plants of the lily family, bearing variously colored cup-shaped flowers. 2 A bulb or flower of this plant. [< Turkish *tuliband* turban]

tulip tree A large North American forest tree related to magnolia, with greenish cup-shaped flowers.

tu·lip·wood (tyoo′lip-wood′) *n.* 1 The soft, light wood of the tulip tree. 2 Any of several ornamental cabinet woods. 3 Any of the trees yielding these woods.

tulle (tool, *Fr.* tül) *n.* A fine, silk, open-meshed material, used for veils, etc. [< *Tulle,* a city in sw France]

tum·ble (tum′bəl) *v.* **·bled, ·bling** *v.i.* 1 To roll or toss about. 2 To perform acrobatic feats, as somersaults, etc. 3 To fall violently or awkwardly. 4 To move in a careless or headlong manner; stumble. 5 *Informal* To understand; comprehend: with *to.* —*v.t.* 6 To toss carelessly; cause to fall. 7 To throw into disorder; rumple. —*n.* 1 The act of tumbling; a fall. 2 A state of disorder or confusion. [< OE *tumbian* fall, leap]

tum·ble·bug (tum′bəl·bug′) *n.* Any of several beetles that roll up a ball of dung to enclose their eggs.

tum·ble-down (tum′bəl·doun′) *adj.* Rickety, as if about to fall in pieces; dilapidated.

tum·bler (tum′blər) *n.* 1 A drinking glass without a foot or stem; also, its contents. 2 One who or that which tumbles, as an acrobat or contortionist. 3 One of a breed of domestic pigeons noted for turning somersaults during flight. 4 In a lock, a latch that engages and immobilizes a bolt unless raised by the key bit. 5 A revolving device the contents of which are tumbled about, as certain dryers for clothes.

tum·ble·weed (tum′bəl·wēd′) *n.* Any of various plants which break off in autumn and are driven about by the wind.

tum·brel (tum′bril) *n.* 1 A farmer's cart. 2 A rude cart in which prisoners were taken to the guillotine during the French

Tumbrel

Revolution. **3** A military cart for carrying tools, ammunition, etc. Also **tum′bril.** [< OE *tomberel*]

tu·me·fy (tʸoo′mə·fī) *v.t. & v.i.* **·fied, ·fy·ing** To swell or puff up. [< L *tumere* swell + *facere* make] **—tu·me·fac·tion** (tʸoo′mə·fak′shən) *n.*

tu·mes·cent (tʸoo·mes′ənt) *adj.* Swelling; somewhat tumid. [< L *tumescere* to swell up] **—tu·mes′cence** *n.*

tu·mid (tʸoo′mid) *adj.* **1** Swollen; enlarged, protuberant. **2** Inflated or pompous. [< L *tumidus* < *tumere* swell] **—tu·mid′i·ty, tu′mid·ness** *n.*

tum·my (tum′ē) *n. pl.* **-mies** *Colloq.* The stomach or abdomen.

tu·mor (tʸoo′mər) *n.* A local swelling on or in the body, esp. from growth of tissue having no physiological function. *Brit. sp.* **tu′mour.** [< L *tumere* to swell] **—tu′mor·ous** *adj.*

tu·mult (tʸoo′mult) *n.* **1** The commotion, disturbance, or agitation of a multitude; an uproar. **2** Any violent commotion. **3** Mental or emotional agitation. [< L *tumultus* < *tumere* swell] **—Syn.** ferment, hubbub, racket, turbulence.

tu·mul·tu·ous (tʸoo·mul′choo·əs) *adj.* **1** Characterized by tumult; disorderly; violent. **2** Greatly agitated or disturbed. **3** Stormy; tempestuous. **—tu·mul′tu·ous·ly** *adv.* **—tu·mul′tu·ous·ness** *n.*

tun (tun) *n.* **1** A large cask. **2** A varying measure of capacity for wines, etc., usu. equal to 252 gallons. **—***v.t.* **tunned, tun·ning** To put into a cask or tun. [< OE *tunne*]

tu·na (tʸoo′nə) *n. pl.* **tu·na** or **tu·nas** Any of various large marine food and game fishes related to mackerel. Also **tuna fish.** [Am. Sp., ult. < *thunnus* tunny]

tun·dra (tun′drə, toon′-) *n.* A rolling, treeless, often marshy plain of Siberia, arctic North America, etc. [Russ.]

tune (tʸoon) *n.* **1** A coherent succession of musical tones; a melody or air. **2** Correct musical pitch or key. **3** Fine adjustment: the *tune* of an engine. **4** State of mind; humor: He will change his *tune.* **5** Concord; agreement: to be out of *tune* with the times. **—sing a difficult tune** To assume a different style or attitude. **—to the tune of** *Informal* To the amount of: *to the tune of* ten dollars. **—***v.* **tuned, tun·ing** *v.t.* **1** To put into tune; adjust precisely. **2** To adapt to a particular tone, expression, or mood. **3** To bring into harmony or accord. **—***v.i.* **4** To be in harmony. **—tune in 1** To adjust a radio or television receiver to (a station, program, etc.). **2** *Slang* To become or cause to become aware, knowing, or sophisticated. **—tune out 1** To adjust a radio or television receiver to exclude (interference, a station, etc.). **2** *Slang* To turn one's interest or attention away from. **—tune up 1** To bring (musical instruments) to a common pitch. **2** To adjust (a machine, engine, etc.) to proper working order. [< ME *tone* tone] **—tun′er** *n.*

tune·ful (tʸoon′fəl) *adj.* Melodious; musical. **—tune′ful·ly** *adv.* **—tune′ful·ness** *n.*

tune·less (tʸoon′lis) *adj.* **1** Not being in tune. **2** Lacking in melody. **—tune′less·ly** *adv.* **—tune′less·ness** *n.*

tune-up (tʸoon′up′) *n.* A precise adjustment of an engine or other device.

tung oil (tung) A fast-drying oil extracted from the seeds of the subtropical **tung tree,** used in paints, varnishes, etc. [Chin. *t'ung* the tung tree]

tung·sten (tung′stən) *n.* A hard, heavy metallic element (symbol W), having a high melting point, used to make filaments for electric lamps and various alloys. [Sw. < *tung* weighty + *sten* stone]

tu·nic (tʸoo′nik) *n.* **1** Among the ancient Greeks and Romans, a loose body garment, with or without sleeves, reaching to the knees. **2** A modern outer garment gathered at the waist, as a short overskirt or a blouse. **3** A short coat worn as part of a uniform. **4** *Biol.* A mantle of tissue covering an organism or a part: also **tu′ni·ca** (-kə) [< L *tunica*]

tuning fork A fork-shaped piece of steel that produces a fixed tone when struck.

Tu·ni·sia (tʸoo·nē′zhə, -nish′ə, -nish′ē·ə) *n.* A republic of N Africa, 48,195 sq. mi., cap. Tunis. **—Tu·ni′sian** *adj., n.* • See map at AFRICA.

tun·nage (tun′ij) *n. Brit.* TONNAGE.

tun·nel (tun′əl) *n.* **1** An underground passageway or gallery, as for a railway or roadway. **2** Any similar passageway under or through something. **3** A burrow. **—***v.* **·neled** or **·nelled, ·nel·ing** or **·nel·ling** *v.t.* **1** To make a tunnel or similar passage through or under. **2** To proceed by digging or as if by digging a tunnel. **—***v.i.* **3** To make a tunnel. [< OF *tonne* a cask] **—tun′nel·er** or **tun′nel·ler** *n.*

tun·ny (tun′ē) *n. pl.* **·nies** or **·ny** TUNA. [< Gk. *thynnos*]

tup (tup) *n.* A ram, or male sheep. **—***v.t. & v.i.* **tupped, tup·ping** To copulate with (a ewe). [Prob. < Scand.]

tu·pe·lo (tʸoo′pə·lō) *n. pl.* **·los** Any of several North American gum trees having smooth, oval leaves and brilliant red autumn foliage. [< Muskhogean]

Tu·pi (too′pē′, too′pē′) *n. pl.* **Tu·pis** or **Tu·pi 1** A member of any of a group of South American Indian tribes comprising the N branch of the Tupian stock. **2** The language spoken by the Tupis: also **Tu·pi′-Gua·ra·ni′** (-gwä·rä·nē′).

Tu·pi·an (too·pē′ən) *adj.* Of or pertaining to the Tupis or their language. **—***n.* A large linguistic stock of South American Indians.

tup·pence (tup′əns) *n.* TWOPENCE.

tuque (tʸook) *n. Can.* A knitted stocking cap. [F (Canadian) < F *toque* < Sp. *toca*]

tur·ban (tûr′bən) *n.* **1** A head covering consisting of a sash or shawl, twisted about the head or about a cap, worn by men in the Orient. **2** Any similar headdress. [< Pers. *dulband* < *dul* a turn + *band* a band] **—tur′baned** (-bənd) *adj.*

tur·bid (tûr′bid) *adj.*. **1** Muddy or opaque: a *turbid* stream. **2** Dense; heavy: *turbid* clouds of smoke. **3** Confused; disturbed. [< L *turbidus* < *turbare* to trouble] **—tur′bid·ly** *adv.* **—tur′bid·ness, tur·bid·i·ty** (tûr·bid′ə·tē) *n.* • **turbid, turgid** Because these words sound alike, they are often confused: *Turbid* usu. refers to water, smoke, etc., so filled with sediment or particles as to be opaque. *Turgid* means abnormally swollen or inflated.

tur·bine (tûr′bin, -bīn) *n.* An engine consisting of one or more rotary units, mounted on a shaft and provided with a series of vanes, actuated by steam, water, gas, or other fluid under pressure. [< L *turbo* a whirlwind, top]

turbo- *combining form* Pertaining to, consisting of, or driven by a turbine: *turbojet.* [< L *turbo* a top]

tur·bo·fan (tûr′bō·fan′) *n. Aeron.* A jet engine with turbine-driven fans that augment its thrust.

tur·bo·jet (tûr′bō·jet′) *n. Aeron.* A jet engine that uses a gas turbine to drive the air compressor.

tur·bo·prop (tûr′bō·prop′) *n. Aeron.* A jet engine in which part of the thrust is produced by a turbine-driven propeller.

tur·bot (tûr′bət) *n. pl.* **·bot** or **·bots 1** A large, edible European flatfish. **2** Any of various flatfishes, as the flounder, halibut, etc. [< OF *tourbout*]

tur·bu·lent (tûr′byə·lənt) *adj.* **1** Violently disturbed or agitated: a *turbulent* sea. **2** Inclined to rebel; insubordinate. **3** Having a tendency to disturb. [< L *turbulentus* full of disturbance] **—tur′bu·lence, tur′bu·len·cy** *n.* **—tur′bu·lent·ly** *adv.* **—Syn. 1** stormy, tumultuous, wild. **2** obstreperous, unruly.

tu·reen (tʸoo·rēn′) *n.* A large, deep, covered dish, as for soup. [< F *terrine*]

turf (tûrf) *n. pl.* **turfs** (*Archaic* **turves**) **1** A mass of grass and its matted roots. **2** A plot of grass. **3** Peat. **4** *Slang* **a** A home territory, esp. that of a youthful street gang, defended against invasion by rival gangs. **b** Any place regarded possessively as the center of one's activity or interest: Philadelphia is his home *turf.* **—the turf 1** A racecourse. **2** Horse racing. **—***v.t.* To cover with turf; sod. [< OE]

turf·man (tûrf′mən) *n. pl.* **·men** (-mən) A man who is connected with horseracing.

tur·ges·cent (tur·jes′ənt) *adj.* Being or becoming swollen or inflated. [< L *turgere* swell] **—tur·ges′cence, tur·ges′cen·cy** *n.* **—tur·ges′cent·ly** *adv.*

tur·gid (tûr′jid) *adj.* **1** Unnaturally distended; swollen. **2** Using high-flown laguage; bombastic: *turgid* prose. [< L *turgere* swell] **—tur·gid·i·ty** (tər·jid′ə·tē), **tur′gid·ness** *n.* **—tur′gid·ly** *adv.* • See TURBID.

Turk (tûrk) *n.* A citizen or native of Turkey.

Turk. Turkey; Turkish.

tur·key (tûr′kē) *n. pl.* **·keys** **1** A large North American bird related to the pheasant, having the head naked and a spreading tail. **2** The edible flesh of this bird. **3** *Slang* A play or a motion picture that fails. [From mistaken identification with a guinea fowl originating in *Turkey*]

Turkey

Tur·key (tûr′kē) *n.* A republic of s Eurasia, 296,108 sq. mi., cap. Ankara.

turkey buzzard A black vulture of temperate and tropical America with a naked red head and neck. Also **turkey vulture.**

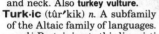

Turk·ic (tûr′kik) *n.* A subfamily of the Altaic family of languages. —*adj.* Pertaining to this linguistic subfamily, or to any of the peoples speaking its languages.

Turk·ish (tûr′kish) *n.* The language of Turkey. —*adj.* Of or pertaining to Turkey, its people, or their language.

Turkish bath A bath in which sweating is induced by exposure to high temperature, usu. in a room heated by steam.

Turkish Empire OTTOMAN EMPIRE.

Turkish towel A heavy, rough towel with loose, uncut pile. Also **turkish towel.**

tur·mer·ic (tûr′mər·ik, tyōō′mə·rik) *n.* **1** The orange-red, aromatic root of an East Indian plant; used as a condiment, dyestuff, etc. **2** The plant. **3** Any of several plants resembling turmeric. [? < F *terre mérite* deserving earth]

tur·moil (tûr′moil) *n.* Confused motion; disturbance; tumult. [?]

turn (tûrn) *v.t.* **1** To cause to rotate, as about an axis. **2** To change the position of, as by rotating: to *turn* a trunk on its side. **3** To move so that the upper side becomes the under: to *turn* a page. **4** To reverse the arrangement or order of; cause to be upside down. **5** To ponder: often with *over.* **6** To sprain or strain: to *turn* one's ankle in running. **7** To make sick or disgusted: The sight *turns* my stomach. **8** To shape in a lathe. **9** To give rounded or curved form to. **10** To give graceful or finished form to: to *turn* a phrase. **11** To perform by revolving: to *turn* cartwheels. **12** To bend, curve, fold, or twist. **13** To bend or blunt (the edge of a knife, etc.). **14** To change or transform: to *turn* water into wine. **15** To translate: to *turn* French into English. **16** To exchange for an equivalent: to *turn* stocks into cash. **17** To cause to become as specified: The sight *turned* him sick. **18** To make sour or rancid; ferment or curdle. **19** To change the direction of. **20** To change the direction or focus of (thought, attention, etc.). **21** To deflect or divert: to *turn* a blow. **22** To repel: to *turn* a charge. **23** To go around: to *turn* a corner. **24** To pass or go beyond: to *turn* twenty-one. **25** To compel to go; drive: to *turn* a beggar from one's door. —*v.i.* **26** To rotate; revolve. **27** To move completely or partially on or as if on an axis: He *turned* and ran. **28** To change position, as in bed. **29** To take a new direction: We *turned* north. **30** To reverse position; become inverted. **31** To reverse direction or flow: The tide has *turned.* **32** To change the direction of one's thought, attention, etc.: Let us *turn* to the next problem. **33** To depend; hinge: with *on* or *upon.* **34** To be affected with giddiness; whirl, as the head. **35** To become upset, as the stomach. **36** To change attitude, sympathy, or allegiance: to *turn* on one's neighbors. **37** To become transformed; change: The water *turned* into ice. **38** To become as specified: His hair *turned* gray. **39** To change color: said esp. of leaves. **40** To become sour or fermented, as milk or wine. —**turn against** To become or cause to become opposed or hostile to. —**turn down** **1** To diminish the flow, volume, etc., of: *Turn down* the gas. **2** *Informal.* **a** To reject or refuse, as a proposal, or request. **b** To refuse the request, proposal, etc., of. —**turn in** **1** To fold or double. **2** To bend or incline inward. **3** To deliver; hand over. **4** *Informal* To go to bed. —**turn off** **1** To stop the operation, flow, etc., of. **2** To leave the direct road; make a turn. **3** To deflect or

divert. **4** *Slang* To cause (a person) to lose interest in or liking for. —**turn on** **1** To set in operation, flow, etc.: to *turn on* an engine. **2** *Slang* To experience the effects of taking a psychedelic drug. **3** *Slang* To arrange for (someone) to take such a drug. **4** *Slang* To evoke in (someone) a profound or rapt response. —**turn out** **1** To turn inside out. **2** To eject or expel. **3** To bend or incline outward. **4** To produce or make. **5** To come or go out: to *turn out* for a meeting. **6** To prove (to be). **7** To equip or fit; dress. **8** *Informal* To get out of bed. —**turn over** **1** To change the position of. **2** To upset; overturn. **3** To hand over; transfer. **4** To do business to the amount of. **5** To invest and get back (capital). —**turn to** **1** To set to work. **2** To seek aid from. **3** To refer or apply to. —**turn up** **1** To fold the under side upward. **2** To incline upward. **3** To find or be found: to *turn up* new evidence. **4** To increase the flow, volume, etc., of. **5** To arrive. —*n.* **1** The act of turning, or the state of being turned. **2** A change to another direction or position: a *turn* of the tide. **3** A deflection from a course; a bend. **4** The point at which a change takes place: a *turn* for the better. **5** A rotation or revolution: the *turn* of a crank. **6** A regular time or chance in some sequence of action: It's his *turn* at bat. **7** Characteristic form or style. **8** Disposition; tendency: a humorous *turn.* **9** A deed: an ill *turn.* **10** A walk or drive: a *turn* in the park. **11** A round in a skein or coil. **12** *Music* An ornament in which the main tone alternates with the seconds above and below. **13** *Informal* A spell of dizziness or nervousness: The explosion gave me quite a *turn.* **14** A variation or difference in type or kind. **15** A short theatrical act. **16** A twist, as of a rope, around a tree or post. **17** A business transaction. —**at every turn** On every occasion; constantly. —**by turns** **1** In alternation or sequence: also **turn by turn.** **2** At intervals. —**in turn** One after another. —**out of turn** Not in proper order or sequence. —**to a turn** Just right: meat browned *to a turn.* —**take turns** To act, play, etc. in proper order. [< L *tornare* turn in a lathe < *turnus* a lathe] —**turn′er** *n.*

turn·a·bout (tûrn′ə·bout′) *n.* **1** The act of turning about so as to face the opposite direction. **2** An about-face in allegiance, opinion, etc.

turn·a·round (tûrn′ə·round′) *n.* **1** The time required for maintenance, refueling, discharging or loading cargo, etc., during a round trip of a ship, aircraft, etc. **2** A space, as in a driveway, large enough for the turning around of a vehicle. **3** A shift or reversal of a trend, procedure, development, etc.

turn·buck·le (tûrn′buk′əl) *n. Mech.* A threaded coupling that receives a threaded rod at each end so that it may be turned to regulate the distance between them.

turn·coat (tûrn′kōt′) *n.* One who goes over to the opposite side or party; a renegade.

turn·down (tûrn′doun′) *adj.* Folded down or able to be folded down, as a collar. —*n.* **1** A rejection. **2** A decline: a *turndown* in prices.

turn·ing (tûr′ning) *n.* **1** The art of shaping wood, metal, etc., in a lathe. **2** *pl.* Spiral shavings produced by turning wood or metal on a lathe. **3** A winding; bend.

turning point The point of decisive change, as in progress, decline, etc.

tur·nip (tûr′nip) *n.* **1** The fleshy, yellow or white edible root of certain plants related to cabbage. **2** Any of these plants. [< Earlier *turnepe*]

turn·key (tûrn′kē′) *n.* One who has charge of the keys of a prison; a jailer. —*adj.* Of, pertaining to, or being, by prearrangement with a buyer, a product or service in complete readiness for use when purchased: a *turnkey* housing project.

turn·out (tûrn′out′) *n.* **1** A turning out. **2** An assemblage of persons, as at a meeting: a good *turnout.* **3** A quantity produced; output. **4** Array; equipment; outfit. **5** A railroad siding. **6** A carriage or wagon with its horses and equipage.

turn·o·ver (tûrn′ō′vər) *n.* **1** An upset. **2** A change or revolution: a *turnover* in affairs. **3** A tart made by covering half of a circular crust with fruit, jelly, etc., and turning the other half over on top. **4** The amount of money taken in and paid out in a business within a given period. **5** The selling out and restocking of goods, as in a store. **6** The rate at which persons hired within a given period are replaced by others; also, the number of persons hired. —*adj.* Turning over, or capable of being turned over.

turn·pike (tûrn′pīk′) *n.* **1** A road on which there are, or formerly were, tollgates: also **turnpike road. 2** TOLLGATE. [ME *turnpyke* a spiked road barrier < TURN, *v.* + PIKE¹]

turn·stile (tûrn′stīl′) *n.* A kind of gate consisting of a vertical post and horizontal arms which by revolving permit persons to pass.

turn·stone (tûrn′stōn′) *n.* A ploverlike migratory bird that turns over stones when searching for food.

turn·ta·ble (tûrn′tā′bəl) *n.* **1** A rotating platform, usu. circular, on which to turn a locomotive or other vehicle around. **2** The revolving disk of a phonograph on which records are played.

tur·pen·tine (tûr′pən·tīn) *n.* **1** A resinous, oily liquid obtained from any of several coniferous trees. **2** The colorless essential oil (**oil of turpentine**) formed when turpentine is distilled, widely used in industry, medicine, and in mixing paints. —*v.t.* **·tined, ·tin·ing** To treat or saturate with turpentine. [< L *terebinthus* a Mediterranean tree]

tur·pi·tude (tûr′pə·t⁼ood) *n.* Inherent baseness; depravity. [< L *turpis* vile] —**Syn.** corruption, degeneracy, vileness, wickedness.

tur·quoise (tûr′koiz, -kwoiz) *n.* **1** A blue or blue-green stone, esteemed as a gemstone when highly polished. **2** A light, greenish blue: also **turquoise blue.** —*adj.* Light, greenish blue. [< MF *(pierre) turquoise* Turkish (stone)]

tur·ret (tûr′it) *n.* **1** A small projecting tower, usu. at the corner of a building. **2** *Mil.* A rotating armed structure containing guns and gunners, forming part of a warship or tank. **3** A structure for a gunner on a combat airplane, usu. enclosed in transparent plastic material. [< OF *tor* tower] —**tur′ret·ed** *adj.*

tur·tle (tûr′təl) *n.* **1** Any of numerous four-limbed, terrestrial or aquatic reptiles having a toothless beak and a soft body encased in a shell. **2** The edible flesh of certain turtles. —**turn turtle** To overturn; capsize. [? < Sp. *tortuga* < Med. L *tortuca* tortoise] • See SNAPPING TURTLE.

tur·tle·dove (tûr′təl·duv′) *n.* **1** A dove noted for its plaintive cooing. **2** The mourning dove. [< L *turtur* turtledove]

Turtle

tur·tle·neck (tûr′təl·nek′) *n.* **1** A pullover sweater or knitted shirt with a high, close-fitting, turnover collar. **2** Such a collar.

tusk (tusk) *n.* A long, projecting tooth, as in the boar, walrus, or elephant. —*v.t.* To use the tusks to gore, root up, etc. [< OE *tūx*]

tus·sah (tus′ə) *n.* **1** An Asian silkworm that spins large cocoons of brownish or yellowish silk. **2** The silk, or the fabric woven from it. [< Skt. *tasara* a shuttle]

tus·sle (tus′əl) *v.t. & v.i.* **·sled, ·sling** To scuffle or struggle. **2** To argue. —*n.* **1** A scuffle or struggle. **2** An argument. [Var. of TOUSLE]

tus·sock (tus′ək) *n.* A tuft or clump of grass or sedge. **2** A tuft, as of hair or feathers. [?] —**tus′sock·y** *adj.*

tut (tut) *interj.* An exclamation to express impatience.

tu·te·lage (t⁼ood′tə·lij) *n.* **1** The state of being under the care of a tutor or guardian. **2** The act or office of a guardian. **3** The act of tutoring; instruction. [< L *tutela* a watching, guardianship]

tu·te·lar·y (t⁼ood′tə·ler′ē) *adj.* **1** Watching over; protecting. **2** Of or pertaining to a guardian. Also **tu′te·lar.** —*n. pl.* **·ar·ies** A guardian spirit, divinity, etc.

tu·tor (t⁼ood′tər) *n.* **1** A private teacher. **2** A college teacher who gives individual instruction. **3** *Brit.* A college official entrusted with the tutelage and care of undergraduates assigned to him. —*v.t.* **1** To act as tutor to; train. **2** To treat sternly; discipline. —*v.i.* **3** To do the work of a tutor. **4** To be tutored or instructed. [< L, a watcher, guardian]

tu·to·ri·al (t⁼ood·tôr′ē·əl) *adj.* Of or involving tutors, or based upon their participation: the *tutorial* system. —*n.* A small class of students guided by a tutor.

tut·ti (t⁼oo′tē) *Music adj.* All: used to indicate that all performers take part. —*n.* A passage or section to be performed by all the voices and instruments together. [< Ital. *tutto* all]

tut·ti-frut·ti (t⁼oo′tē·fr⁼oo′tē) *n.* A confection, chewing gum, ice cream, etc., made or flavored with mixed fruits. —*adj.* Flavored with mixed fruits. [Ital., all fruits]

tu·tu (t⁼oo′t⁼oo; *Fr.* tü′tü) *n.* A short, projecting, layered skirt worn by ballet dancers. [F]

tux·e·do (tuk·sē′dō) *n. pl.* **·dos 1** A man's semiformal dinner or evening jacket without tails. **2** The suit of which the jacket is a part. Also **Tux·e′do.** [< *Tuxedo* Park, N.Y.]

TV (tē′vē′) *n.* TELEVISION.

TV terminal velocity.

TVA, T.V.A. Tennessee Valley Authority.

TV dinner A frozen meal in a partitioned tray, ready to be heated and served.

twad·dle (twod′l) *v.t. & v.i.* **·dled, ·dling** To talk foolishly and pretentiously. —*n.* Pretentious, silly talk. [?] —**twad′·dler** *n.*

twain (twān) *adj. & n. Archaic* Two. [< OE *twēgen* two]

twang (twang) *v.t. & v.i.* **twanged, twang·ing 1** To make or cause to make a sharp, vibrant sound. **2** To utter or speak with a harsh, nasal sound. —*n.* **1** A sharp, vibrating sound. **2** A sharp, nasal sound of the voice. **3** A sound resembling these. [Imit.] —**twang′y** *adj.* (**·i·er, ·i·est**)

tweak (twēk) *v.t.* To pinch and twist sharply. —*n.* A twisting pinch. [< OE *twiccan* twitch]

tweed (twēd) *n.* **1** A woolen fabric often woven in two or more colors to effect a check or plaid pattern. **2** *pl.* Clothes made of tweed. [< Scot. *tweel,* var. of TWILL]

twee·dle (twēd′l) *v.* **·dled, ·dling** *v.t.* **1** To play (a musical instrument) casually or carelessly. —*v.i.* **2** To produce a series of shrill tones. **3** To play a musical instrument casually or carelessly. —*n.* A sound so produced. [Imit. of the sound of a reed pipe]

tweet (twēt) *v.i.* To utter a thin, chirping note. —*n.* A twittering or chirping. [Imit.]

tweet·er (twē′tər) *n.* A loudspeaker specially designed to reproduce only high-frequency sounds.

tweeze (twēz) *v.t.* **tweezed, tweez·ing** *Informal* To handle, pinch, pluck, etc., with tweezers.

tweez·ers (twē′zərz) *n.pl.* (construed as *sing.* or *pl.*) Small pincers for picking up or extracting tiny objects. Also **pair of tweezers.** [< F *étui* a small case]

twelfth (twelfth) *adj. & adv.* Next in order after the 11th. —*n.* **1** The element of an ordered set that corresponds to the number 12. **2** One of 12 equal parts. [< OE *twelfta*]

Twelfth Day The twelfth day after Christmas; Epiphany.

twelve (twelv) *n.* **1** The sum of eleven plus one; 12; XII. **2** A set or group of 12 members. —**the Twelve** The twelve apostles. [< OE *twelf*] —**twelve** *adj., pron.*

Twelve Apostles The twelve original disciples of Jesus.

twelve·month (twelv′munth′) *n.* A year.

twelve-tone (twelv′tōn′) *adj. Music* Of, pertaining to, or composed in a system in which any series of all twelve tones of the chromatic scale is used as the basis of composition.

twen·ti·eth (twen′tē·ith) *adj. & adv.* Tenth in order after the tenth. —*n.* **1** The element of an ordered set that corresponds to the number 20. **2** One of 20 equal parts.

twen·ty (twen′tē) *n. pl.* **·ties 1** The sum of 19 plus 1; 20; XX. **2** A set or group of 20 members. **3** The numbers, years, etc., from 20 to 30. [< OE *twentig*] —**twen′ty** *adj., pron.*

twen·ty-one (twen′tē·wun′) *n.* BLACKJACK (def. 3).

twice (twīs) *adv.* **1** Two times. **2** In double measure; doubly. [< OE *twiga*]

twid·dle (twid′l) *v.* **·dled, ·dling** *v.t.* **1** To twirl idly; play with. —*v.i.* **2** To toy with something idly. **3** To be busy about trifles. —**twiddle one's thumbs 1** To rotate one's thumbs around each other. **2** To do nothing; be idle. —*n.* A gentle twirling. [Prob. < ON *tridla* stir] —**twid′dler** *n.*

twig (twig) *n.* A small shoot or branch of a woody plant. [< OE *twigge*]

---

add, āce, câre, pälm; end, ēven; it, īce; odd, ōpen, ôrder; t⁴ook, p⁴ool; up, bûrn; ə = *a* in *above, u* in *focus*; y⁴oo = *u* in *fuse*; oil; pout; check; go; ring; thin; t͟his; zh, *vision.* < derived from; ? origin uncertain or unknown.

twi·light (twī′līt′) *n.* **1** The light diffused over the sky after sunset and before sunrise. **2** The period during which this light prevails. **3** Any faint light; shade. **4** An obscure condition following the waning of past glory, achievements, etc. —*adj.* Pertaining or peculiar to twilight. [< OE < *twa* two + LIGHT]

twilight sleep A light anesthesia induced by morphine and scopolamine, formerly used in childbirth.

twill (twil) *n.* **1** Cloth woven in such a way as to produce diagonal, parallel ribs or lines. **2** The pattern formed by such weaving. —*v.t.* To weave (cloth) with a twill. [< OE *twili* a twilled fabric]

Twill

twin (twin) *n.* **1** Either of two young produced at the same birth. **2** Either of two persons or things greatly alike. —**the Twins** GEMINI. —*adj.* **1** Being a twin or twins: *twin* boys. **2** Being one of a pair of similar and closely related people or things. —*v.* **twinned, twin·ning** *v.i.* **1** To bring forth twins. **2** To be matched or equal. —*v.t.* **3** To bring forth as twins. **4** To couple; match. [< OE *twinn, getwinn*]

twine (twīn) *v.* **twined, twin·ing** *v.t.* **1** To twist together, as threads. **2** To form by such twisting. **3** To coil or wrap about something. **4** To encircle by winding or wreathing. —*v.i.* **5** To interlace. **6** To proceed in a winding course; meander. —*n.* **1** A string composed of two or more strands twisted together. **2** The act of twining or entwining. **3** A thing produced by twining. [< OE *twīn* a twisted double thread < *twa* two] —**twin′er** *n.* —**twin′ing·ly** *adv.*

twinge (twinj) *v.t. & v.i.* **twinged, twing·ing** To affect with or suffer a sudden pain. —*n.* **1** A sharp, darting, local pain. **2** A mental pang. [< OE *twengan* pinch] —**Syn.** *n.* **1** ache, cramp, throe.

twin·kle (twing′kəl) *v.* **·kled, ·kling** *v.i.* **1** To shine with fitful, intermittent gleams. **2** To be bright, as with amusement: Her eyes *twinkled*. **3** To wink or blink. **4** To move rapidly to and fro; flicker: *twinkling* feet. —*v.t.* **5** To cause to twinkle. **6** To emit (light) in fitful, intermittent gleams. —*n.* **1** A tremulous gleam of light; glimmer. **2** A quick or repeated movement of the eyelids. **3** An instant; a twinkling. [< OE *twinclian*] —**twin′kler** *n.*

twin·kling (twing′kling) *n.* **1** The act of something that twinkles. **2** A wink or twinkle. **3** An instant; moment. —**twink′ling·ly** *adv.*

twirl (twûrl) *v.t. & v.i.* **1** To whirl or rotate rapidly. **2** To twist or curl. **3** In baseball, to pitch. —*n.* **1** A whirling motion. **2** A curl; twist; coil. [?] —**twirl′er** *n.*

twist (twist) *v.t.* **1** To wind (strands, etc.) around each other. **2** To form by such winding: to *twist* thread. **3** To give a spiral shape to. **4** To deform or distort, esp. by means of torque. **5** To distort the meaning of. **6** To confuse; perplex. **7** To wreathe, twine, or wrap. **8** To cause to revolve or rotate. **9** To impart spin to (a ball) so that it moves in a curve. —*v.i.* **10** To become twisted. **11** To move in a winding course. **12** To squirm; writhe. —*n.* **1** The act, manner, or result of twisting. **2** The state of being twisted. **3** *Physics* A torsional strain. **4** A curve; turn; bend. **5** A wrench; strain, as of a joint or limb. **6** A peculiar inclination or attitude: a mind with a criminal *twist*. **7** An unexpected turn or development. **8** A variant or novel approach or method: a mystery novel with a new *twist*. **9** Thread or cord made of tightly twisted or braided strands. **10** A twisted roll of bread. **11** A spin given to a ball by a certain stroke or throw. [< OE *-twist* a rope]

twist·er (twis′tər) *n.* **1** One who or that which twists. **2** In baseball, a curve. **3** A tornado; cyclone.

twit (twit) *v.t.* **twit·ted, twit·ting** To taunt. —*n.* A taunting allusion; reproach. [< OE *ætwitan*] —**twit′ter** *n.* —**Syn.** *v.* gibe, jeer, scoff, tease.

twitch (twich) *v.t.* **1** To pull sharply; pluck with a jerky movement. —*v.i.* **2** To move with a quick, spasmodic jerk, as a muscle. —*n.* **1** A sudden involuntary contraction of a muscle. **2** A sudden jerk or pull. [ME *twicchen*]

twit·ter (twit′ər) *v.i.* **1** To utter a series of light chirping or tremulous notes, as a bird. **2** To titter. **3** To be excited.

—*v.t.* **4** To utter or express with a twitter. —*n.* **1** A succession of light, tremulous sounds. **2** A state of excitement. [Imit.]

'twixt (twikst) *prep.* Betwixt.

two (tōō) *n.* **1** The sum of one plus one; 2; II. **2** A set or group of two members. —**in two** Bisected; asunder —**put two and two together** To draw an obvious conclusion by considering the facts. [< OE *twā, tū*] —**two** *adj., pron.*

two-base hit (tōō′bās′) In baseball, a hit in which the batter reaches second base without benefit of an error. Also **two′-bag′ger** (-bag′ər).

two-bit (tōō′bit′) *adj. Slang* Cheap; small-time: a *two-bit* gambler.

two bits *Informal* Twenty-five cents.

two-by-four (tōō′bī-fôr′, -fōr′) *adj.* **1** Measuring two inches by four inches. **2** *Slang* Narrow or cramped: a *two-by-four* kitchen. —*n.* (tōō′bī-fôr′, -fōr′) A timber measuring two inches in thickness and four inches in width before finishing.

two-edged (tōō′ejd′) *adj.* **1** Having an edge on each side; cutting both ways. **2** Having a double meaning.

two-faced (tōō′fāst′) *adj.* **1** Having two faces. **2** Double-dealing; insincere. —**two′-fac′ed·ly** (-fā′sid·lē, -fāst′lē) *adv.* —**two′fac′ed·ness** *n.*

two·fer (tōō′fər) *n.* **1** An article sold at two for the price of one. **2** A free coupon entitling the holder to buy two theater tickets for the price of one.

two·fold (tōō′fōld′) *adj.* Double. —*adv.* In a twofold manner or degree; doubly.

two-hand·ed (tōō′han′did) *adj.* **1** Requiring the use of both hands at once. **2** Constructed for use by two persons: a *two-handed* saw. **3** Ambidextrous. **4** Having two hands. **5** Played by two people: a *two-handed* card game.

two·pence (tup′əns) *n. Brit.* **1** Two pennies. **2** A silver coin of the same value, now issued only for alms money on Maundy Thursday. **3** A trifle; small amount.

two·pen·ny (tup′ən·ē) *adj. Brit.* **1** Of the value of twopence. **2** Cheap; worthless.

two-ply (tōō′plī′) *adj.* **1** Woven double: a *two-ply* carpet. **2** Made of two strands or thicknesses of material.

two·some (tōō′səm) *n.* **1** Two persons together. **2** A game played by two persons. **3** The players.

two-step (tōō′step′) *n.* **1** A ballroom dance step in 2/4 time. **2** The music for it. —*v.i.* To do the two-step.

two-time (tōō′tīm′) *v.t.* **-timed, -tim·ing** *Slang* **1** To be unfaithful to. **2** DOUBLE-CROSS. —**two′-tim′er** *n.*

two-way (tōō′wā′) *adj.* **1** Permitting vehicles to go in opposite directions simultaneously: a *two-way* street. **2** Involving mutual or reciprocal exchanges, duties, obligations, etc.: a *two-way* agreement. **3** Involving two persons, groups, etc.: a *two-way* contest. **4** Capable of both sending and receiving communications: a *two-way* radio. **5** Made or fashioned so as to be used or worn in two ways: a *two-way* jacket.

twp. township.

TX Texas (P.O. abbr.).

-ty[1] *suffix of nouns* The state or condition of being: *sanity.* [< L *-tas*]

-ty[2] *suffix* Ten; ten times: used in numerals, as *thirty, forty,* etc. [< OE *-tig* ten]

Ty. Territory.

ty·coon (tī·kōōn′) *n.* **1** *Informal* A wealthy and powerful business leader. **2** A Japanese shogun. [< Japanese *taikun* a mighty lord]

ty·ing (tī′ing) *pr.p.* of TIE.

tyke (tīk) *n.* **1** A mongrel dog. **2** *Informal* A small mischievous child. [< ON *tik* bitch]

tym·pa·ni (tim′pə·nē) *n.pl.* TIMPANI.

tympanic membrane The membrane separating the middle ear from the external ear; the eardrum.

tym·pa·nist (tim′pə·nist) *n.* One who plays the timpani.

tym·pa·num (tim′pə·nəm) *n. pl.* **-na** (-nə) or **-nums 1** *Anat.* **a** The cavity of the middle ear lined with the tympanic membrane. **b** TYMPANIC MEMBRANE. **2** A drum. **3** *Archit.* **a** A recessed, usu. triangular, space bounded by the sides of a pediment or gable at the end of a building. **b** A similar space over a door or window, between the lintel and the arch. [< Gk. *tympanon* a drum] —**tym·pan·ic** (tim·pan′ik) *adj.*

typ., typo., typog. typographer; typographic; typography.

type (tīp) *n.* 1 A class or group having traits and characteristics in common: an old *type* of car. 2 A standard or model. 3 The characteristic plan, form, style, etc., of a given class or group. 4 A person, animal, or object embodying the characteristics of a class or group. 5 *Printing* a A piece or block of metal or of wood bearing, usu. in relief, a letter or character for use in printing. b Such pieces collectively. 6 Typewritten or printed letters and numerals. 7 The characteristic device on either side of a medal or coin. —*v.* **typed, typ·ing** *v.t.* 1 To represent; typify. 2 To determine the type of; identify: to *type* a blood sample. 3 TYPEWRITE. 4 To prefigure. —*v.i.* 5 TYPEWRITE. [< Gk. *typos* an impression, figure, type]

-type *combining form* 1 Representative form; stamp; type: *prototype*. 2 Used in or produced by duplicating processes or by type: *Linotype*. [< Gk. *typos* stamp]

type·face (tīp′fās) *n.* 1 A set of type of a particular design. 2 The face or impression of a type.

type·set·ter (tīp′set′ər) *n.* 1 One who sets type. 2 A machine for setting type. —**type′set′ting** *adj., n.*

type·write (tīp′rīt′) *v.t. & v.i.* **·wrote, ·writ·ten, ·writ·ing** To write with a typewriter.

type·writ·er (tīp′rī′tər) *n.* 1 A keyboard machine for producing characters, as letters, numbers, etc., that have the appearance of printer's type. 2 A typist.

ty·phoid (tī′foid) *adj.* 1 Pertaining to or resembling typhoid fever: also **ty·phoi′dal.** 2 Resembling typhus. —*n.* TYPHOID FEVER.

typhoid fever A serious infectious disease caused by a bacillus transmitted in contaminated water or food and characterized by high fever, severe intestinal disturbances, and prostration.

ty·phoon (tī·fōōn′) *n.* A violent tropical storm, occurring in the w Pacific. [< Chin. *tai feng,* lit., big wind]

ty·phus (tī′fəs) *n.* Any of a group of contagious rickettsial diseases marked by high fever, a rash, nervous and mental disorders, and extreme prostration. [< Gk. *typhos* smoke, a stupor] —**ty′phous** *adj.*

typ·i·cal (tip′i·kəl) *adj.* 1 Having the nature or character of a type: a *typical* schoolboy. 2 Characteristic or representative of a group, class, etc.: *typical* middle-class values. [< Gk. *typos* TYPE] —**typ′i·cal·ly** *adv.* —**typ′i·cal·ness** *n.*

typ·i·fy (tip′ə·fī) *v.t.* **·fied, ·fy·ing** 1 To represent by a type. 2 To serve as a characteristic example of. —**typ′i·fi·ca′tion** (-fə·kā′shən), **typ′i·fi′er** *n.*

typ·ist (tī′pist) *n.* 1 One who uses a typewriter. 2 A person whose work is operating a typewriter.

ty·po (tī′pō) *n. pl.* **ty·pos** *Informal* An error made by a printer or a typist. [< *typo(graphical error)*]

ty·pog·ra·pher (tī·pog′rə·fər) *n.* An expert in typography, esp. a printer or compositor.

ty·po·graph·i·cal (tī′pə·graf′i·kəl) *adj.* Of or pertaining to printing. Also **ty′po·graph′ic.** —**ty′po·graph′i·cal·ly** *adv.*

ty·pog·ra·phy (tī·pog′rə·fē) *n.* 1 The arrangement, style, and appearance of printed matter. 2 The act or art of composing and printing from types.

typw. typewriter; typewritten.

ty·ran·ni·cal (ti·ran′i·kəl, tī-) *adj.* Of or like a tyrant; despotic; arbitrary. Also **ty·ran′nic.** —**ty·ran′ni·cal·ly** *adv.* —**ty·ran′ni·cal·ness** *n.*

ty·ran·ni·cide (ti·ran′ə·sīd, tī-) *n.* 1 The slayer of a tyrant. 2 The slaying of a tyrant.

tyr·an·nize (tir′ə·nīz) *v.* **·nized, ·niz·ing** *v.i.* 1 To exercise power cruelly or unjustly. 2 To rule as a tyrant; have absolute power. —*v.t.* 3 To treat tyrannically; domineer. —**tyr′an·niz′er** *n.*

tyr·an·nous (tir′ə·nəs) *adj.* Despotic; tyrannical. —**tyr′an·nous·ly** *adv.* —**tyr′an·nous·ness** *n.*

tyr·an·ny (tir′ə·nē) *n. pl.* **·nies** 1 The office, power, or jurisdiction of a tyrant. 2 A government or ruler having absolute power; despot or despotism. 3 Power used in a cruel or oppressive manner. 4 Harsh rigor; severity. 5 A tyrannical act. [< L *tyrannus* a tyrant]

ty·rant (tī′rənt) *n.* 1 One who rules oppressively or cruelly; a despot. 2 Any person who exercises power or authority in a harsh, cruel manner. [< Gk. *tyrannos* a master, a usurper]

tyre (tīr) *n. Brit. sp.* of TIRE².

Tyre (tīr) *n.* A port and capital of ancient Phoenicia, now in sw Lebanon.

ty·ro (tī′rō) *n. pl.* **·ros** One who is beginning to learn or study something; novice. [< L *tiro* a recruit]

tzar (tsär) *n.* CZAR.

tzet·ze (tset′sē) *n.* TSETSE.

tzi·gane (tsē·gän′) *n.* A Gypsy, esp. a Hungarian Gypsy. [F < Hung. *czigány*]

U

U, u (yōō) *n. pl.* **U's, u's, Us, us** (yōōz) 1 The twenty-first letter of the English alphabet. 2 Any spoken sound representing the letter *U* or *u.* 3 Something shaped like a U. —*adj.* Shaped like a U.

U uranium.

U., u. uncle; union; unit; university.

U.A.R. United Arab Republic.

UAW, U.A.W. United Automobile Workers; (officially) United Automobile, Aerospace, and Agricultural Implement Workers of America.

u·biq·ui·tous (yōō·bik′wə·təs) *adj.* Existing, or seeming to exist, everywhere at once; omnipresent. —**u·biq′ui·tous·ly** *adv.* —**u·biq′ui·tous·ness** *n.*

u·biq·ui·ty (yōō·bik′wə·tē) *n.* The state of being or seeming to be everywhere at the same time; omnipresence, real or seeming. [< L *ubique* everywhere]

U-boat (yōō′bōt′) *n.* A German submarine. [< G *U-boot,* contraction of *Unterseeboot,* lit., undersea boat]

u.c. upper case (printing).

ud·der (ud′ər) *n.* A large, pendulous, milk-secreting gland having nipples or teats for the suckling of offspring, as in cows. [< OE *ūder*]

UFO (yōō′ef·ō′) *n. pl.* **UFOs, UFO's** Any of various unidentified flying objects alleged to have been seen traveling at speeds and following courses that would be impossible for any aircraft to duplicate. [< *u(nidentified) f(lying) o(bject)*]

U·gan·da (yōō·gan′də, ōō·gän′dä), *n.* An independent member of the Commonwealth of Nations in CEN. Africa, 93,981 sq. mi., cap. Kampala. • See map at AFRICA.

ugh (ug, ukh, u, ŏōkh, ŏō) *interj.* An exclamation of repugnance or disgust. [Imit.]

ug·li·fy (ug′lə·fī) *v.t.* **·fied, ·fy·ing** To make ugly. —**ug′li·fi·ca′tion** (-fə·kā′shən) *n.*

ug·ly (ug′lē) *adj.* **·li·er, ·li·est** 1 Distasteful in appearance; unsightly. 2 Distasteful to any of the senses. 3 Morally revolting or repulsive. 4 Bad in character or consequences, as a rumor or a wound. 5 Ill-tempered; quarrelsome. 6 Portending storms; threatening. [< ON *uggligr* dreadful < *uggr* fear] —**ug′li·ly** *adv.* —**ug′li·ness** *n.* —Syn. 1 homely, ill-looking, unlovely, unseemly. 2 repulsive, repellent, repugnant, revolting, abhorrent, disgusting. 5 ill-humored, irascible, irritable, testy, querulous.

ugly duckling Any ill-favored or unpromising child who unexpectedly grows into a beauty or a wonder. [< *The Ugly Duckling,* a story by Hans Christian Andersen]

U·gri·an (ōō′grē·ən, yōō′-) *n.* 1 A member of any of the Finno-Ugric peoples of Hungary and w Siberia. 2 UGRIC.

---

add, āce, câre, pälm; end, ēven; it, īce; odd, ōpen, ôrder; tŏōk, pōōl; up, bûrn; ə = *a* in *above, u* in *focus;* yōō = *u* in *fuse;* oil; pout; check; go; ring; thin; this; zh, *vision.* < derived from; ? origin uncertain or unknown.

—*adj.* Of or pertaining to the Ugrians or their languages.
U·gric (ōō′grik, yōō′-) *n.* A branch of the Finno-Ugric sub-family of languages including Magyar (Hungarian). — *adj.* UGRIAN.

UHF, U.H.F., uhf, u.h.f. ultrahigh frequency.

uit·land·er (īt′lan·dər, oit′-; *Afrikaans* œit′län·dər) *n. Often cap.* A foreigner; outlander. [Afrikaans]

U.K. United Kingdom.

u·kase (yōō·kās′, -kāz′, yōō′kās, ōō·koz′) *n.* **1** In imperial Russia, an edict or decree of the czar. **2** Any official decree. [<Russ. *ukaz*]

U·krain·i·an (yōō·krā′nē·ən, -krī′-) *adj.* Of or pertaining to the Ukraine, its people, or their language. —*n.* **1** A native or inhabitant of the Ukraine. **2** An East Slavic language spoken in the Ukraine.

u·ku·le·le (yōō′kə·lā′lē; *Hawaiian* ōō′kōō·lā′lä) *n.* A small, guitarlike musical instrument having four strings. [Hawaiian <*uku* insect + *lele* jump; from the movements of the fingers in playing]

ul·cer (ul′sər) *n.* **1** An open sore on skin or mucous membrane with disintegration of tissue. **2** Any evil or corrupt condition or vice. [<L *ulcus, ulceris*] —**ul′cer·ous** *adj.* —**ul′cer·ous·ly** *adv.*

ul·cer·ate (ul′sə·rāt) *v.t. & v.i.* ·at·ed, ·at·ing To make or become ulcerous. —**ul′cer·a′tion** *n.* —**ul′·cer·a′tive** *adj.*

Ukulele

-ule *suffix* Small; little: used to form diminutives: *granule.* [<L *-ulus*]

-ulent *suffix* Abounding in; full of (what is indicated in the main element): *opulent, truculent.* [<L *-ulentus*]

ul·na (ul′nə) *n. pl.* ·nae (-nē) or ·nas **1** The larger of the two bones of the forearm on the same side as the little finger. **2** The homologous bone in the foreleg of a quadruped. [< L, elbow] —**ul′nar** *adj.* • See HUMERUS.

ul·ster (ul′stər) *n.* A long, loose overcoat, sometimes belted at the waist, made originally of Irish frieze. [< *Ulster,* Ireland]

ult. ultimate; ultimately.

ul·te·ri·or (ul·tir′ē·ər) *adj.* **1** Not so pertinent as something else: *ulterior* considerations. **2** Intentionally unrevealed; hidden: *ulterior* motives. **3** Later in time, or secondary in importance; following; succeeding. **4** Lying beyond or on the farther side of a certain bounding line. [<L, compar. of *ulter* beyond] —**ul·te′ri·or·ly** *adv.*

ul·ti·ma (ul′tə·mə) *n.* The last syllable of a word. [<L, fem. of *ultimus* last]

ul·ti·mate (ul′tə·mit) *adj.* **1** Beyond which there is no other; maximum, greatest, utmost, etc. **2** Last; final, as of a series. **3** Most distant or remote; farthest. **4** Not susceptible of further analysis; elementary; primary. —*n.* The best, latest, most fundamental, etc., of something. [<L *ultimus* farthest, last, superl. of *ulter* beyond] —**ul′ti·mate·ness** *n.*

ul·ti·mate·ly (ul′tə·mit·lē) *adv.* In the end; at last; finally.

ul·ti·ma Thu·le (ul′tə·mə thōō′lē, tōō′lē) **1** In ancient geography, Thule, the northernmost habitable regions of the earth. **2** Any distant, unknown region. **3** The farthest possible point, degree, or limit.

ul·ti·ma·tum (ul′tə·mā′təm, -mä′-) *n. pl.* ·tums or ·ta (-tə) A final statement of terms, demands, or conditions, the rejection of which usu. results in a breaking off of all negotiations, a resorting to force, etc. [<L *ultimus* last, ultimate]

ul·ti·mo (ul′tə·mō) *adv.* In the month preceding the present month. [L]

ul·tra (ul′trə) *adj.* Going beyond the bounds of moderation; extreme. —*n.* One who holds extreme opinions. [<L, beyond, on the other side]

ultra- *prefix* **1** On the other side of; beyond in space: *ultramarine.* **2** Going beyond the limits or range of: *ultrasonic.* **3** Beyond what is usual or natural; extremely or excessively: *ultraconservative.*

ul·tra·high frequency (ul′trə·hī′) Any wave frequency between 300 and 3,000 megahertz.

ul·tra·ist (ul′trə·ist) *n.* One who goes to extremes in opinions, conduct, etc.; extremist. —*adj.* Radical; extreme: also **ul′tra·is′tic.** —**ul′tra·ism** *n.*

ul·tra·light (ul′trə·līt′) *adj.* Extremely light in weight. — *n.* An extremely lightweight airplane.

ul·tra·ma·rine (ul′trə·mə·rēn′) *n.* **1** A deep purplish blue pigment. **2** The color of ultramarine. —*adj.* Beyond or across the sea. [<L *ultra* beyond + *mare* sea]

ul·tra·mi·cro·scope (ul′trə·mī′krə·skōp′) *n.* A microscope in which objects too small to be seen by the transmitted light of an ordinary microscope are examined against a dark background by means of refracted light.

ul·tra·mi·cro·scop·ic (ul′trə·mī′krə·skop′ik) *adj.* **1** Too minute to be seen by an ordinary microscope. **2** Relating to the ultramicroscope. Also **ul′tra·mi′cro·scop′i·cal.**

ul·tra·mod·ern (ul′trə·mod′ərn) *adj.* Extremely modern, as in tastes, design, etc. —**ul′tra·mod′ern·ist** *n.*

ul·tra·son·ic (ul′trə·son′ik) *adj.* Pertaining to or designating sound waves having a frequency above the limits of audibility.

ul·tra·vi·o·let (ul′trə·vī′ə·lit) *adj.* Having wavelengths shorter than those of visible violet light and longer than those of X-rays.

ul·u·late (ul′yə·lāt′, yōol′yə·lāt′) *v.i.* ·lat·ed, ·lat·ing To howl, hoot, or wail. [<L *ululare*] —**ul′u·lant** *adj.*

U·lys·ses (yōō·lis′ēz) ODYSSEUS.

um·bel (um′bəl) *n.* A flower cluster having pedicels arising from a single point. [<L *umbella* a parasol, dim. of *umbra* shadow] —**um·bel·late** (um′bə·lit, -lāt), **um′bel·lat′ed** *adj.*

um·ber (um′bər) *n.* **1** A chestnut- to liver-brown iron oxide earth, used as a pigment. **2** The color of umber, either in its natural state (**raw umber**), or heated, so as to produce a reddish brown (**burnt umber**). —*adj.* **1** Of or pertaining to umber. **2** Of the color of umber. —*v.t.* To color with umber. [<F (*terre d'*)*ombre*<Ital. *ombra*<L *umbra* shade, shadow]

um·bil·i·cal (um·bil′i·kəl) *adj.* **1** Pertaining to or situated near the umbilicus. **2** Placed near the navel; central. —*n.* **1** A long, flexible tube that serves as a connecting device, conduit for air, power, communication, etc., for an astronaut or aquanaut when outside the craft. **2** A similar device used as a source of fuel, etc., for a spacecraft before launching. [<L *umbilicus* navel]

umbilical cord 1 The ropelike structure connecting the navel of a fetus with the placenta. **2** UMBILICAL (*n.*).

um·bil·i·cus (um′bə·lī′kəs, -bil′i-) *n. pl.* ·ci (-kī, -sī) **1** NAVEL. **2** A navel-shaped depression. [<L]

um·bra (um′brə) *n. pl.* ·bras or ·brae (-brē, -brī) **1** A shadow. **2** The cone of shadow cast at all times by a celestial body in the solar system. When the umbra of the moon strikes the earth, it creates an area of total solar eclipse. **3** The inner dark portion of a sunspot. [L, shadow]

um·brage (um′brij) *n.* **1** A feeling of anger or resentment, esp. in the phrase **take umbrage,** to have such feelings. **2** That which gives shade, as a leafy tree. **3** Shade or shadow. [<L *umbraticus* shady<*umbra* shade] —**um·bra′geous** (-brā′jəs) *adj.* —**um·bra′geous·ly** *adv.*

um·brel·la (um·brel′ə) *n.* **1** A light portable canopy on a folding frame, carried as a protection against sun or rain. **2** A usu. radial formation of military aircraft, used as a protective screen for operations on the ground or on water. **3** Something serving as a cover or shield, or as a means of linking together various things under a common name or sponsor: the expanding *umbrella* of nuclear power. [<L *umbella* parasol, dim. of *umbra* shadow]

umbrella tree A magnolia of the s U.S., with white flowers and umbrellalike whorls of leaves at the ends of the branches.

u·mi·ak (ōō′mē·ak′) *n.* A large, open boat made of skins on a wooden frame. Also **u′mi·ack.** [Eskimo]

Umiak

um·laut (ōōm′lout) *n.* **1** *Ling.* **a** The change in quality of a vowel sound caused by its partial assimilation to a vowel or semivowel (often later lost) in the following syllable. **b** A vowel which has been so altered, as *ä*, *ö*, and *ü* in German. **2** In German, the two dots (ö) put over a vowel modified by umlaut. —*v.t.* To modify by umlaut. [G, change of sound < *um* about + *laut* sound]

um·pir·age (um′pīr·ij, -pə·rij) *n.* The office, function, or decision of an umpire. Also **um′pire·ship.**

um·pire (um′pīr) *n.* **1** A person called upon to settle a disagreement or dispute. **2** In various games, as baseball, a person chosen to enforce the rules of the game and to settle disputed points. —*v.t. & v.i.* **·pired, ·pir·ing** To act as umpire (of or in). [Alter. of ME *noumpere*]

ump·teen (ump′tēn′) *adj.* *Slang* Indeterminately large in number; very many. —**ump′teenth′** *adj.*

UMW, U.M.W. United Mine Workers.

un-[1] *prefix* Used in forming adjectives, adverbs, and less often nouns, to indicate: **1** Not; opposed or contrary to: *unable, unmannerly.* **2** Lack of: *unease.* [< OE • See UN-[2].]

un-[2] *prefix* Used in forming verbs to indicate: **1** Reversal of an action: *untie.* **2** Removal from something: *unearth.* **3** Deprivation of a condition or quality: *unman; unnerve.* **4** Intensification: *unloose.* [< OE *un-, on-, and-*] • Beginning at the bottom of this page is a partial list of words formed with **un-**[1] and **un-**[2]. Other words formed with these prefixes, having strongly positive, specific, or special meanings, will be found in vocabulary place.

UN, U.N. United Nations.

un·a·ble (un·ā′bəl) *adj.* **1** Not able; incompetent. **2** Helpless; ineffectual.

un·ac·count·a·ble (un′ə·koun′tə·bəl) *adj.* **1** Impossible to be explained or accounted for; inexplicable. **2** Not responsible. —**un′ac·count′a·ble·ness** *n.* —**un′ac·count′a·bly** *adv.*

un·ac·cus·tomed (un′ə·kus′təmd) *adj.* **1** Not accustomed or familiar: usu. with *to: unaccustomed* to hard-ship. **2** Not common; strange: an *unaccustomed* sight. —**un′ac·cus′tomed·ness** *n.*

un·ad·vised (un′əd·vīzd′) *adj.* **1** Not having received advice. **2** Rash or imprudent. —**un′ad·vis′ed·ly** (-vī′zid·lē) *adv.* —**un′ad·vis′ed·ness** *n.*

un·af·fect·ed (un′ə·fek′tid) *adj.* **1** Not showing affectation; natural; sincere. **2** Not influenced or changed. —**un′·af·fect′ed·ly** *adv.* —**un′af·fect′ed·ness** *n.*

un-A·mer·i·can (un′ə·mer′ə·kən) *adj.* Not American, esp. not consistent with or opposed to the institutions, ideals, objectives, etc. of the U.S. —**un′-A·mer′i·can·ism** *n.*

u·nan·i·mous (yōō·nan′ə·məs) *adj.* **1** Sharing the same views or sentiments. **2** Showing or resulting from the assent of all concerned: the *unanimous* voice of the jury. [< L *unus* one + *animus* mind] —**u·na·nim·i·ty** (yōō′nə·nim′ə·tē) *n.* —**u·nan′i·mous·ly** *adv.*

un·ap·proach·a·ble (un′ə·prō′chə·bəl) *adj.* **1** Not easy to know or contact; aloof; reserved. **2** Inaccessible. —**un·ap·proach′a·bil′i·ty, un′ap·proach′a·ble·ness** *n.* —**un′ap·proach′·a·bly** *adv.*

un·armed (un·ärmd′) *adj.* Having no firearms, esp. on one's person.

un·as·sail·a·ble (un′ə·sāl′ə·bəl) *adj.* **1** That cannot be disproved or contested successfully. **2** Resistant to attack; impregnable. —**un′as·sail′a·ble·ness, un′as·sail′a·bil′i·ty** *n.* —**un′as·sail′a·bly** *adv.*

un·as·sum·ing (un′ə·sōō′ming) *adj.* Not pretentious; modest. —**un′as·sum′ing·ly** *adv.*

un·at·tached (un′ə·tacht′) *adj.* **1** Not attached. **2** Not connected with any particular group; independent. **3** Not married or engaged. **4** *Law* Not held or seized, as in satisfaction of a judgment.

un·a·vail·ing (un′ə·vā′ling) *adj.* Not effective; futile. —**un′a·vail′ing·ly** *adv.*

un·a·void·a·ble (un′ə·voi′də·bəl) *adj.* That cannot be avoided; inevitable. —**un′a·void′a·ble·ness** *n.* —**un′a·void′a·bly** *adv.*

---

unabashed	unarguable	unbloody	unchastity	unconfirmed	uncreated
unabated	unarm	unboastful	unchecked	uncongeal	uncredited
unabridged	unarmored	unboned	unchewed	uncongealed	uncritical
unaccented	unashamed	unbought	unchilled	uncongenial	uncross
unacceptable	unashamedly	unbound	unchivalrous	unconnected	uncrowded
unaccommodating	unasked	unbranched	unchlorinated	unconnectedly	uncrown
unaccompanied	unaspirated	unbranded	unchristened	unconquerable	uncrowned
unaccredited	unassailable	unbreakable	unclaimed	unconquerably	uncrystalline
unachievable	unassailably	unbreathable	unclassifiable	unconquered	uncrystallizable
unacknowledged	unassignable	unbridgeable	unclassified	unconscientious	uncrystallized
unacquainted	unassigned	unbridle	uncleaned	unconsecrated	uncultivated
unadorned	unassimilable	unbudging	unclear	unconsenting	uncultured
unadulterated	unassimilated	unburied	unclench	unconsidered	uncurbed
unadvisable	unassisted	unburnt	unclog	unconsoled	uncurdled
unaesthetic	unathletic	unbusinesslike	unclogged	unconsolidated	uncured
unaffiliated	unattainable	unbuttoned	unclouded	unconstituted	uncurl
unafraid	unattained	uncage	uncoated	unconstrained	uncurled
unaggressive	unattempted	uncalculating	uncock	unconsumed	uncursed
unaided	unattended	uncalendered	uncoerced	uncontaminated	uncurtained
unaligned	unattested	uncanceled	uncoined	uncontested	uncushioned
unalike	unattractive	uncared-for	uncollectable	uncontradicted	undamaged
unallied	unauthenticated	uncaring	uncollected	uncontrite	undamped
unalloyed	unauthorized	uncarpeted	uncollectible	uncontrollable	undated
unalluring	unavailable	uncastrated	uncolored	uncontrollably	undecayed
unalterable	unavenged	uncaught	uncombed	uncontrolled	undecaying
unaltered	unavowed	uncaused	uncomforted	unconversant	undecipherable
unambiguous	unavowedly	unceasing	uncommercial	unconverted	undeciphered
unambitious	unawakened	unceasingly	uncommissioned	unconvinced	undeclared
unamusing	unawed	uncensored	uncommitted	unconvincing	undeclinable
unannealed	unbacked	uncensured	uncompetitive	uncooked	undeclined
unannounced	unbaked	uncertified	uncomplaining	uncooperative	undecomposed
unanswerable	unbanked	unchallenged	uncompleted	uncoordinated	undecorated
unanswerably	unbaptized	unchangeable	uncomplicated	uncorked	undefaced
unanswered	unbeaten	unchanged	uncomplimentary	uncorrected	undefeated
unanticipated	unbelt	unchanging	uncomprehending	uncorroborated	undefended
unapparent	unbetrayed	unchangingly	uncomprehendingly	uncorrupt	undefiled
unappeasable	unbetrothed	unchaperoned	uncompressed	uncorrupted	undefinable
unappeased	unbleached	uncharged	uncompromised	uncounseled	undefined
unappetizing	unblemished	uncharted	uncomputed	uncountable	undeformed
unappreciative	unblest	unchartered	unconcealable	uncourteous	undelayed
unappropriated	unblinking	unchaste	unconcealed	uncourtly	undeliverable
unapproved	unblinkingly	unchastened	unconfined	uncovered	undelivered

---

un·a·ware (un′ə·wâr′) *adj.* 1 Not aware or cognizant, as of something specified. 2 Carelessly unmindful; inattentive; heedless. —*adv.* UNAWARES.

un·a·wares (un′ə·wârz′) *adv.* 1 Unexpectedly. 2 Without premeditation; unwittingly.

un·bal·ance (un·bal′əns) *v.t.* ·anced, ·anc·ing 1 To deprive of balance. 2 To disturb or derange mentally. —*n.* The state or condition of being unbalanced.

un·bal·anced (un·bal′ənst) *adj.* 1 Not in a state of equilibrium. 2 In bookkeeping, not adjusted so as to balance. 3 Lacking mental balance; unsound; erratic.

un·bar (un·bär′) *v.t.* ·barred, ·bar·ring To remove the bar from.

un·bear·a·ble (un′bâr′ə·bəl) *adj.* Not to be borne; intolerable; insufferable. —**un′bear′a·bly** *adv.*

un·beat·a·ble (un·bēt′ə·bəl) *adj.* 1 Not to be defeated. 2 *Slang* First-rate; excellent.

un·be·com·ing (un′bi·kum′ing) *adj.* 1 Not becoming or appropriate, as a dress. 2 Not fitting or decorous; improper. —**un′be·com′ing·ly** *adv.* —**un′be·com′ing·ness** *n.*

un·be·known (un′bi·nōn′) *adj.* Unknown: used with *to.* Also **un′be·knownst′** (-nōnst′).

un·be·lief (un′bi·lēf′) *n.* 1 Absence of positive belief; incredulity. 2 A refusal to believe; disbelief, as in religion.

un·be·liev·a·ble (un′bə·lēv′ə·bəl) *adj.* Too unusual or astonishing to be believed; incredible. —**un′be·liev′a·bly** *adv.* —**Syn.** inconceivable, untenable, staggering, improbable.

un·be·liev·er (un′bi·lē′vər) *n.* 1 One who does not believe; skeptic; doubter. 2 One who has no religious belief.

un·be·liev·ing (un′bi·lē′ving) *adj.* Doubting; skeptical. —**un′be·liev′ing·ly** *adv.* —**un′be·liev′ing·ness** *n.*

un·bend (un·bend′) *v.* ·bent, ·bend·ing 1 To relax, as from exertion or formality. 2 To straighten (something bent or curved). 3 To relax, as a bow, from tension. 4 *Naut.* To loose or detach, as a rope or sail. —*v.i.* 5 To become free of restraint or formality; relax. 6 To become straight or nearly straight again.

un·bend·ing (un·ben′ding) *adj.* 1 Not bending easily. 2 Resolute; firm. 3 Not relaxed socially; stiff. —**un·bend′ing·ly** *adv.* —**un·bend′ing·ness** *n.*

un·bi·ased (un·bī′əst) *adj.* Having no bias; not prejudiced; impartial. Also **un·bi′assed.** —**un·bi′ased·ly** *adv.* —**un·bi′ased·ness** *n.*

un·bid·den (un·bid′n) *adj.* 1 Not commanded or invited. 2 Spontaneous: *unbidden* thoughts.

un·blush·ing (un·blush′ing) *adj.* Not blushing; immodest; shameless. —**un·blush′ing·ly** *adv.*

un·born (un·bôrn′) *adj.* 1 Not yet born. 2 Of a future time or generation; future. 3 Not in existence.

un·bos·om (un·bŏŏz′əm, -bŏŏ′zəm) *v.t.* 1 To reveal, as one's thoughts or secrets: often used reflexively. —*v.i.* 2 To say what is troubling one; tell one's thoughts, feelings, etc.

un·bound·ed (un·boun′did) *adj.* 1 Having no bounds or limits; boundless. 2 Going beyond bounds; unrestrained. —**un·bound′ed·ly** *adv.* —**un·bound′ed·ness** *n.*

un·bowed (un·boud′) *adj.* 1 Not bent or bowed. 2 Not broken or subdued by defeat or adversity.

un·brace (un·brās′) *v.t.* ·braced, ·brac·ing 1 To free from bands or braces. 2 To free from tension; loosen. 3 To weaken.

un·bri·dled (un·brīd′ld) *adj.* 1 Having no bridle on. 2 Without restraint; unrestrained: an *unbridled* tongue.

un·bro·ken (un·brō′kən) *adj.* 1 Not broken; whole; entire. 2 Not violated: an *unbroken* promise. 3 Uninterrupted; continuous. 4 Not tamed or trained. 5 Not bettered or surpassed. 6 Not disarranged or thrown out of order.

un·bur·den (un·bûr′dən) *v.t.* 1 To free from a burden. 2 To relieve (oneself, one's mind, etc.) from cares, worries, etc. 3 To make known (one's cares, worries, guilt, etc.) in order to gain relief.

un·called-for (un·kôld′fôr′) *adj.* 1 Not needed; unnecessary. 2 Not justified by circumstances; unprovoked.

un·can·ny (un·kan′ē) *adj.* 1 Weird; unnatural; eerie. 2 So

undemocratic	undissected	unendurable	unexported	unforgetful	ungrammatical
undemonstrable	undisseminated	unenforceable	unexposed	unforgetting	ungrammatically
undemonstrative	undissolved	unenforced	unexpressed	unforgivable	ungranted
undenominational	undistilled	unenfranchised	unexpressive	unforgiven	ungratified
undependable	undistinguished	unengaged	unexpurgated	unforgiving	ungrounded
underived	undistracted	unengaging	unextended	unforgotten	ungrudging
underserved	undistributed	un-English	unextinguished	unformed	unguided
undeservedly	undisturbed	unenjoyable	unfaded	unformulated	unhackneyed
undeserving	undiversified	unenlightened	unfading	unforsaken	unhampered
undesignated	undiverted	unenlivened	unfallen	unfortified	unhang
undesigned	undivided	unenriched	unfaltering	unfought	unhanged
undesirable	undivorced	unenrolled	unfashionable	unfound	unharbored
undesirably	undocking	unenslaved	unfashionably	unfractured	unharmed
undesired	undogmatic	unentangled	unfastened	unframed	unharnessed
undesirous	undomesticated	unentered	unfathomable	unfranchised	unharrowed
undetached	undoubting	unenterprising	unfavored	unfree	unharvested
undetected	undramatic	unenthralled	unfeared	unfreedom	unhasty
undetermined	undramatized	unenthusiastic	unfearing	unfrozen	unhatched
undeterred	undrape	unenthusiastically	unfeasible	unfruitful	unhealed
undeveloped	undraped	unenviable	unfed	unfulfilled	unhealthful
undeviating	undreamed	unenvied	unfederated	unfunded	unheated
undifferentiated	undreamt	unenvious	unfelt	unfunny	unheeded
undiffused	undried	unequipped	unfeminine	unfurnished	unheedful
undigested	undrinkable	unerased	unfenced	unfussy	unheeding
undignified	undutiful	unerotic	unfermented	ungallant	unheedingly
undilated	undyed	unestablished	unfertilized	ungarnished	unhelpful
undiluted	uneatable	unethical	unfetter	ungenerous	unheralded
undiminished	uneaten	unexaggerated	unfettered	ungentle	unheroic
undimmed	uneconomic	unexalted	unfilled	ungentlemanly	unhesitating
undiplomatic	uneconomical	unexamined	unfilmed	ungently	unhesitatingly
undirected	unedifying	unexcavated	unfiltered	ungenuine	unhindered
undiscernible	uneducable	unexcelled	unfinished	ungifted	unhired
undiscerning	uneducated	unexchangeable	unfired	ungird	unhistoric
undischarged	unelectrified	unexcited	unfixed	ungirt	unhomogeneous
undisciplined	unembarrassed	unexciting	unflattered	unglazed	unhonored
undisclosed	unembellished	unexcused	unflattering	unglossed	unhousebroken
undiscouraged	unemotional	unexpanded	unflavored	unglove	unhoused
undiscoverable	unemotionally	unexpended	unfocus	ungloved	unhurried
undiscovered	unemphatic	unexpiated	unforbidden	unglue	unhurt
undiscriminating	unencumbered	unexpired	unforced	ungoverned	unhusk
undiscussed	unendangered	unexplainable	unfordable	ungraced	unhygienic
undisguised	unending	unexplained	unforeseeable	ungraceful	unhyphenated
undismayed	unendingly	unexploded	unforetold	ungraded	unhypocritical
undispelled	unendorsed	unexploited	unforfeited	ungrafted	unidentified
undisputed	unendowed	unexplored	unforged	ungrained	unidiomatic

good as to seem almost supernatural in origin: *uncanny* accuracy. —**un·can′ni·ly** *adv.* —**un·can′ni·ness** *n.*

un·cer·e·mo·ni·ous (un′ser·ə·mō′nē·əs) *adj.* 1 Not ceremonious; informal. 2 Abruptly rude or discourteous. —**un′cer·e·mo′ni·ous·ly** *adv.* —**un′cer·e·mo′ni·ous·ness** *n.*

un·cer·tain (un·sûr′tən) *adj.* 1 Not yet determined; indefinite: The date is *uncertain.* 2 Not to be relied upon; unpredictable: *uncertain* weather. 3 Not definitely or exactly known. 4 Not sure or convinced; doubtful; dubious. 5 Not constant; fitful; changeable. 6 Not clear, forceful, steady, etc.: His delivery of the speech was very *uncertain.* —**un·cer′tain·ly** *adv.*

un·cer·tain·ty (un·sûr′tən·tē) *n. pl.* ·**ties** 1 The state of being uncertain; doubt. 2 Something uncertain.

un·char·i·ta·ble (un·char′ə·tə·bəl) *adj.* Not forgiving or charitable, as in judgment; censorious. —**un·char′i·ta·ble·ness** *n.* —**un·char′i·ta·bly** *adv.*

un·char·ted (un·chär′tid) *adj.* 1 Not marked or charted on a map. 2 Not explored; unknown.

un·chris·tian (un·kris′chən) *adj.* 1 Not according with Christian principles, attitudes, etc. 2 Not Christian.

un·church (un·chûrch′) *v.t.* 1 To deprive of membership in a church; excommunicate. 2 To deny the status of a church to (a sect, etc.).

un·cir·cum·cised (un·sûr′kəm·sīzd) *adj.* 1 Not circumcised. 2 Not Jewish; Gentile.

un·civ·il (un·siv′əl) *adj.* Wanting in civility; discourteous; ill-bred. —**un·civ′il·ly** *adv.*

un·civ·i·lized (un·siv′ə·līzd) *adj.* 1 Not civilized; barbarous. 2 Uncouth; rude; gross. 3 Remote from civilization. —**Syn.** 1 savage, brutish, brutal, ferocious. 2 crude, cross, boorish, churlish, vulgar, coarse.

un·clad (un·klad′) *adj.* Without clothes; naked.

un·cle (ung′kəl) *n.* 1 The brother of one's father or mother. 2 The husband of one's aunt. 3 *Informal* An elderly man; used in direct address. 4 *Slang* A pawnbroker. [< L *avunculus* a mother's brother]

un·clean (un·klēn′) *adj.* 1 Not clean; foul. 2 Morally impure. 3 Ceremonially impure. —**un·clean′ness** *n.*

un·clean·ly[1] (un·klen′lē) *adj.* 1 Lacking cleanliness. 2 Morally impure. —**un·clean′li·ness** *n.*

un·clean·ly[2] (un·klēn′lē) *adv.* In an unclean manner.

Uncle Sam The personification of the government or the people of the U.S., represented as a tall, lean man with chin whiskers, wearing a plug hat, blue swallow-tailed coat, and red-and-white striped pants.

Uncle Tom *Informal* A Negro who acts in an obsequious or servile manner towards whites: a contemptuous term. —*v.i.* **Uncle Tommed, Uncle Tom·ming** To behave like an Uncle Tom. [< *Uncle Tom,* the faithful Negro slave in H. B. Stowe's *Uncle Tom's Cabin*] —**Uncle Tom′ism** *n.*

un·cloak (un·klōk′) *v.t.* 1 To remove the cloak or covering from. 2 To unmask; expose.

un·close (un·klōz′) *v.t. & v.i.* ·**closed,** ·**clos·ing** 1 To open or set open. 2 To reveal; disclose.

un·clothe (un·klōth′) *v.t.* ·**clothed** or ·**clad,** ·**cloth·ing** 1 To remove the clothes from; undress. 2 To divest; uncover.

un·com·fort·a·ble (un·kum′fər·tə·bəl, -kumf′tə·bəl) *adj.* 1 Not at ease; feeling discomfort. 2 Causing uneasiness; disquieting. —**un·com′fort·a·ble·ness** *n.* —**un·com′fort·a·bly** *adv.*

un·com·mon (un·kom′ən) *adj.* 1 Not usual or common. 2 Strange; remarkable. —**un·com′mon·ly** *adv.* —**un·com′mon·ness** *n.*

un·com·mu·ni·ca·tive (un′kə·myoo′nə·kə·tiv, -kāt′iv) *adj.* Not communicative; not disposed to talk, to give information, etc.; reserved; taciturn. —**un′com·mu′ni·ca·tive·ly** *adv.* —**un′com·mu′ni·ca·tive·ness** *n.*

un·com·pro·mis·ing (un·kom′prə·mī′zing) *adj.* Making or admitting of no compromise; inflexible; strict. —**un·com′pro·mis′ing·ly** *adv.* —**Syn.** resolute, steadfast, firm, indomitable, inexorable, tenacious, obstinate.

un·con·cern (un′kən·sûrn′) *n.* 1 Lack of anxiety, concern, or worry. 2 Lack of interest; indifference.

unilluminated	unintentional	unlisted	unmold	unorthodox	unplanted
unillumined	unintentionally	unlit	unmolested	unostentatious	unplayed
unillustrated	uninteresting	unliteral	unmollified	unostentatiously	unpleasing
unimaginable	uninterpreted	unliveliness	unmortgaged	unowned	unpledged
unimaginably	uninterrupted	unlively	unmotivated	unoxidized	unplowed
unimaginative	unintimidated	unlocked	unmounted	unpacified	unplucked
unimagined	unintoxicated	unlovable	unmourned	unpaginated	unplugged
unimbued	uninvited	unloved	unmoved	unpaid	unpoetic
unimitated	uninviting	unlovely	unmown	unpaired	unpoetical
unimmunized	uninvoked	unloving	unmuffle	unpalatable	unpointed
unimpaired	uninvolved	unlubricated	unmusical	unpardonable	unpolarized
unimpeded	unissued	unmagnified	unmuzzle	unpardonably	unpolished
unimportance	unitemized	unmanageable	unmuzzled	unparliamentary	unpolitical
unimportant	unjaded	unmanful	unnamable	unparted	unpolluted
unimposing	unjoined	unmanicured	unnameable	unpartisan	unpopulated
unimpressed	unjointed	unmannerly	unnamed	unpasteurized	unposted
unimpressionable	unjustifiable	unmarked	unnaturalized	unpatched	unpractical
unimpressive	unjustifiably	unmarketable	unnavigable	unpatented	unpredictable
unincorporated	unkennel	unmarred	unnavigated	unpatriotic	unpredictably
unindemnified	unkept	unmarriageable	unneeded	unpaved	unprejudiced
unindustrialized	unkindled	unmarried	unneighborly	unpeaceable	unpremeditated
uninfected	unkissed	unmasculine	unnoted	unpeaceful	unprepared
uninfested	unknowable	unmastered	unnoticed	unpedigreed	unprepossessing
uninflammable	unknowing	unmatched	unobjectionable	unpensioned	unpressed
uninflected	unlabeled	unmated	unobliging	unpeopled	unpretentious
uninfluenced	unlabored	unmatted	unobservant	unperceived	unpretentiously
uninformed	unladylike	unmeant	unobserved	unperfected	unpretentiousness
uninhabitable	unlamented	unmechanical	unobserving	unperforated	unpriced
uninhabited	unlash	unmedicated	unobstructed	unperformed	unprimed
uninhibited	unlasting	unmemorable	unobtainable	unpersuaded	unprinted
uninitiated	unlaundered	unmercenary	unobtrusive	unpersuasive	unprivileged
uninjured	unleaded	unmerited	unobtrusively	unperturbed	unprocessed
uninspired	unleased	unmethodical	unobtrusiveness	unphilosophical	unproductive
uninspiring	unlevel	unmilitary	unoffending	unphonetic	unprofitable
uninstructed	unlevied	unmilled	unoffered	unphotogenic	unprofitably
uninsurable	unlicensed	unmindful	unoiled	unphysical	unprogramed
uninsured	unlifelike	unmistaken	unopen	unpicturesque	unpromising
unintellectual	unlighted	unmixed	unopened	unpile	unpronounceable
unintelligent	unlikable	unmodified	unopposed	unpitying	unpropitious
unintelligible	unlikeable	unmodish	unoppressed	unplaced	unprosperous
unintelligibly	unlined	unmodulated	unordained	unplait	unprotected
unintended	unlink	unmoistened	unoriginal	unplanned	unproved

un·con·cerned (un'kən·sûrnd') *adj.* **1** Not anxious or worried. **2** Not interested; indifferent. —**un'con·cern'ed·ly** (-sûr'nid·lē) *adj.* —**un'con·cern'ed·ness** *n.*

un·con·di·tion·al (un'kən·dish'ən·əl) *adj.* Limited by no conditions; absolute. —**un'con·di'tion·al·ly** *adv.*

un·con·di·tioned (un'kən·dish'ənd) *adj.* **1** Not restricted; unconditional. **2** *Psychol.* Not acquired; natural.

un·con·scion·a·ble (un·kon'shən·ə·bəl) *adj.* **1** Unbelievably bad, wrong, inequitable, etc.: an *unconscionable* error. **2** Wholly unscrupulous. —**un·con'scion·a·ble·ness** *n.* —**un·con'scion·a·bly** *adv.*

un·con·scious (un·kon'shəs) *adj.* **1** Temporarily deprived of consciousness. **2** Not cognizant; unaware: with *of: unconscious* of his charm. **3** Not produced or accompanied by conscious effort; not intended or known: an *unconscious* pun. **4** Not endowed with consciousness or a mind. **5** Of or having to do with the unconscious. —*n.* That area of the psyche which is not in the immediate field of awareness and whose content may become manifest through dreams, morbid fears and compulsions, etc.: with *the.* —**un·con'scious·ly** *adv.* —**un·con'scious·ness** *n.*

un·con·sti·tu·tion·al (un'kon·sti·tv̄oo'shən·əl) *adj.* Contrary to or violating the precepts of a constitution. —**un'·con·sti·tu'tion·al'i·ty** *n.* —**un·con'sti·tu'tion·al·ly** *adv.*

un·con·ven·tion·al (un'kən·ven'shən·əl) *adj.* Not adhering to conventional rules, practices, etc.; informal; free. —**un'con·ven'tion·al'i·ty** *n.* —**un'con·ven'tion·al·ly** *adv.*

un·count·ed (un·koun'tid) *adj.* **1** Not counted. **2** Beyond counting; innumerable.

un·cou·ple (un·kup'əl) *v.t.* **·led, ·ling** **1** To disconnect or unfasten. **2** To set loose; unleash (dogs). —**un·coup'led** (-kup'əld) *adj.*

un·couth (un·kōōth') *adj.* **1** Marked by awkwardness or oddity; outlandish. **2** Coarse, boorish, or unrefined, as in manner or speech. [< OE *uncūth* unknown] —**un·couth'ly** *adv.* —**un·couth'ness** *n.*

un·cov·er (un·kuv'ər) *v.t.* **1** To remove a covering from.

2 To make known; disclose. —*v.i.* **3** To remove a covering. **4** To raise or remove the hat, as in token of respect.

unc·tion (ungk'shən) *n.* **1** The act of anointing, as for religious or medicinal purposes. **2** A substance used in anointing, as oil. **3** Anything that soothes or palliates. **4** A quality of speech, esp. in religious discourse, that awakens or is intended to awaken deep sympathetic feeling. **5** Excessive or affected sincerity or sympathy in speech or manner. [< L *unctio* < *ungere* anoint]

unc·tu·ous (ungk'chōō·əs) *adj.* **1** Like an unguent; greasy. **2** Greasy or soapy to the touch, as certain minerals. **3** Characterized by excessive or affected sincerity, sympathy, concern, etc. **4** Unduly smooth or suave in speech or manner. **5** Having plasticity, as clay. [< L *unctum* ointment, orig. neut. p.p. of *ungere* anoint] —**unc'tu·ous·ly** *adv.* —**unc'tu·ous·ness, unc'tu·os'i·ty** (-chōō·os'ə·tē) *n.*

un·cut (un·kut') *adj.* **1** Not cut. **2** In bookbinding, having untrimmed margins. **3** Not ground, as a gem. **4** Not shortened or abridged.

un·daunt·ed (un·dôn'tid, -dän'-) *adj.* Not daunted; fearless; intrepid. —**un·daunt'ed·ly** *adv.* —**un·daunt'ed·ness** *n.*

un·de·cid·ed (un'di·sī'did) *adj.* **1** Not having the mind made up; irresolute. **2** Not decided upon or determined. —**un'de·cid'ed·ly** *adv.*

un·de·ni·a·ble (un'di·nī'ə·bəl) *adj.* **1** That cannot be denied; indisputably true. **2** Unquestionably good; excellent: His reputation was *undeniable.* —**un'de·ni'a·bly** *adv.*

un·der (un'dər) *prep.* **1** Beneath; covered by: dust *under* the rug. **2** In a place lower than; at the foot or bottom of: *under* the hill. **3** Beneath the shelter of: *under* the paternal roof. **4** Beneath the concealment, guise, or assumption of: *under* a false name. **5** Less than in number, degree, age, value, or amount: *under* 10 tons. **6** Inferior to in quality, character, or rank. **7** Beneath the domination of; subordinate or subservient to: *under* the British flag. **8** Subject to the guidance, tutorship, or direction of: He studied *under* Mendelssohn. **9** Subject to the moral obligation of: a state-

unproven	unrelieved	unrevealed	unscholarly	unsinkable	unstitched
unprovided	unremarkable	unrevenged	unschooled	unsized	unstopped
unprovoked	unremarked	unrevised	unscientific	unskeptical	unstopper
unpruned	unremedied	unrevoked	unscratched	unslaked	unstrap
unpublishable	unremembered	unrewarded	unscreened	unsling	unstratified
unpublished	unremitted	unrhymed	unsealed	unsmiling	unstressed
unpunctual	unremorseful	unrhythmic	unseamed	unsmilingly	unstriated
unpunished	unremunerated	unrhythmical	unseasoned	unsmoked	unstriped
unpurified	unremunerative	unrighted	unseaworthy	unsnobbish	unstructured
unpuritanical	unrenewed	unripened	unseconded	unsocial	unstuck
unqualifying	unrented	unrisen	unsecret	unsoiled	unstudied
unquenchable	unrepaid	unroasted	unsecretive	unsold	unstuffed
unquestioning	unrepairable	unromantic	unsectarian	unsoldierly	unsubsidized
unrated	unrepaired	unromantically	unsecured	unsolicited	unsubstantiated
unratified	unrepealed	unroof	unseeing	unsolicitous	unsubtle
unreachable	unrepentant	unruled	unseen	unsoluble	unsuccessful
unreadable	unrepented	unsafe	unsegmented	unsolvable	unsuccessfully
unrealizable	unrepenting	unsafely	unselected	unsolved	unsuited
unrealized	unreplaced	unsafeness	unselective	unsorted	unsullied
unrebuked	unreplenished	unsaintly	unself-conscious	unsought	unsupportable
unreceipted	unreported	unsalability	unselfish	unsown	unsupported
unreceivable	unrepresentative	unsalable	unselfishly	unspecialized	unsuppressed
unreceived	unrepresented	unsalaried	unselfishness	unspecified	unsure
unreceptive	unrepressed	unsaleability	unsent	unspectacular	unsurmountable
unreciprocated	unrequested	unsaleable	unsentimental	unspent	unsurpassed
unreclaimed	unrequited	unsalted	unserviceable	unspilled	unsurprising
unrecognizable	unresented	unsalvageable	unset	unspiritual	unsurveyed
unrecognized	unreserve	unsanctified	unsew	unspoiled	unsurvivable
unreconciled	unresigned	unsanctioned	unsewn	unspoken	unsusceptible
unrecorded	unresistant	unsanitary	unsexual	unsponsored	unsuspected
unrecounted	unresisting	unsated	unshaded	unsportsmanlike	unsuspecting
unredeemed	unresistingly	unsatiated	unshakable	unstack	unsuspicious
unrefined	unresolved	unsatiating	unshaken	unstained	unswathe
unreflecting	unrespectful	unsatisfactorily	unshaven	unstamped	unswear
unreflective	unresponsive	unsatisfactory	unsheathed	unstandardized	unsweetened
unreformable	unresting	unsatisfied	unsheltered	unstarched	unswept
unreformed	unrestless	unsatisfying	unshod	unstarred	unsworn
unrefreshed	unrestrained	unsaved	unshorn	unstartling	unsymmetrical
unregistered	unrestrainedly	unsayable	unshrinkable	unstatesmanlike	unsympathetic
unregretted	unrestraint	unscaled	unshriven	unstemmed	unsympathetically
unregulated	unrestricted	unscanned	unshrouded	unstereotyped	unsystematic
unrehearsed	unretentive	unscarred	unshut	unsterile	untack
unrelated	unretracted	unscenic	unsifted	unsterilized	untactful
unrelaxed	unreturned	unscented	unsighted	unstick	untactfully
unrelievable		unscheduled	unsigned	unstimulating	untainted

ment *under* oath. **10** With the liability or certainty of incurring: *under* penalty of the law. **11** Subject to the influence or pressure of: *under* the circumstances. **12** Swayed or impelled by: *under* fear of death. **13** Driven or propelled by: *under* sail. **14** Included in the group or class of; found in the matter titled or headed: See *under* History. **15** Being the subject of: the matter *under* discussion. **16** During the period of; in the reign of. **17** By virtue of; authorized, substantiated, attested, or warranted by: *under* his own signature. **18** In conformity to or in accordance with; having regard to. **19** Planted or sowed with: an acre *under* wheat. —*adv.* **1** In or into a position below something; underneath. **2** In or into an inferior or subordinate condition, rank, etc. **3** So as to be covered or hidden. **4** Less in amount, value, time, etc.: We did it in ten minutes or *under*. —*adj.* **1** Situated or moving under something else; lower or lowermost: an *under* layer. **2** Subordinate; lower in rank or authority. **3** Less than usual, standard, or prescribed. **4** Held in subjection or restraint: used predicatively. [< OE]

under- *combining form* **1** Below in position; situated or directed beneath; on the underside: *undercarriage.* **2** Below or beneath another surface or covering: *undergarment.* **3** Inferior in rank or importance; subordinate: *undergraduate.* **4** Less than is usual or proper; not enough; insufficient(ly): *underdeveloped.* **5** At a lower rate; less in degree or amount: *underpay.*

un·der·a·chieve (un′dər·ə·chēv′) *v.i.* **·chieved, ·chiev·ing** To fail to achieve the approximate level of performance, esp. in school studies, commensurate with one's abilities as indicated by testing. —**un′der·a·chieve′ment, un′der·a·chiev′er** *n.*

un·der·act (un′dər·akt′) *v.t. & v.i.* To perform (a role, scene, etc.) in a somewhat less dramatic or emphatic way than might naturally be expected.

un·der·age (un′dər·āj′) *adj.* Not of a requisite or legal age.

untaken	untranslated	unwarlike
untalented	untrapped	unwarmed
untamable	untraveled	unwarned
untame	untraversed	unwarranted
untameable	untread	unwashed
untamed	untreatable	unwasted
untangled	untreated	unwatched
untaped	untried	unwavering
untapped	untrim	unwaveringly
untarnished	untrodden	unweakened
untasted	untroubled	unweaned
untaxable	untrustworthy	unwearable
untaxed	untuck	unweary
unteachable	untufted	unwearying
untechnical	untuned	unweathered
untempered	untuneful	unweave
untenable	unturned	unwed
untenanted	untwilled	unwedded
untended	untwisted	unweeded
untenured	untypical	unwelcome
untested	unusable	unwelded
untether	unutilized	unwhetted
unthatched	unuttered	unwhipped
untheatrical	unvaccinated	unwilled
unthinkable	unvalued	unwished
unthoughtful	unvanquished	unwithered
unthreshed	unvaried	unwitnessed
unthrifty	unvarying	unwomanly
unthrone	unvaryingly	unwooded
untilled	unveiled	unwooed
untinged	unventilated	unworkable
untired	unverifiable	unworked
untiring	unverified	unworkmanlike
untiringly	unversed	unworldly
untitled	unvitrified	unworn
untouched	unvocal	unworshiped
untracked	unvoiced	unwounded
untrained	unvolatilized	unwoven
untrammeled	unvulcanized	unwrinkled
untransferable	unwakened	unwrought
untransferred	unwalled	unyielding
untranslatable	unwanted	unzealous

un·der·arm (un′dər·ärm′) *adj.* **1** Situated, placed, or used under the arm. **2** UNDERHAND (def. 2). —*n.* ARMPIT.

un·der·bid (un′dər·bid′) *v.t.* **·bid, ·bid·ding 1** To bid lower than, as in a competition. **2** In bridge, to fail to bid the full value of (a hand). —**un′der·bid′der** *n.*

un·der·brush (un′dər·brush′) *n.* Small trees and shrubs growing beneath forest trees; undergrowth. Also **un′der·bush′** (-boŏosh′).

un·der·buy (un′dər·bī′) *v.t.* **·bought, ·buy·ing 1** To buy at a price lower than that paid by (another). **2** To pay less than the value for. **3** To buy less of (something) than is required.

un·der·car·riage (un′dər·kar′ij) *n.* **1** The framework supporting the body of a structure, as an automobile. **2** The principal landing gear of an aircraft.

Undercarriage *def. 2*

un·der·charge (un′dər·chärj′) *v.t.* **·charged, ·charg·ing 1** To make an inadequate charge for. **2** To load with an insufficient charge, as a gun. —*n.* (un′dər·chärj′) An inadequate or insufficient charge.

un·der·class·man (un′dər·klas′mən, -kläs′-) *n. pl.* **·men** (-mən) A freshman or sophomore.

un·der·clothes (un′dər·klōz′, -klōthz′) *n.pl.* UNDERWEAR. Also **un′der·cloth′ing.**

un·der·coat (un′dər·kōt′) *n.* **1** A coat worn under another. **2** A layer of paint, varnish, etc., beneath another layer; also, a protective coating applied to the undersurface of a vehicle: also **un′der·coat′ing.** —*v.t.* To provide with an undercoat (def. 2).

un·der·cov·er (un′dər·kuv′ər) *adj.* Secret; surreptitious; esp., engaged in spying.

un·der·cur·rent (un′dər·kûr′ənt) *n.* **1** A current, as of water or air, below another or below the surface. **2** A hidden drift or tendency, as of popular sentiments.

un·der·cut (un′dər·kut′) *n.* **1** The act or result of cutting away a part, section, etc., from the lower or under surface of something. **2** *Brit.* TENDERLOIN. **3** A notch cut in the side of a tree so that it will fall toward that side when sawed through. **4** In sports, a cut or backspin imparted to the ball by an underhand stroke. —*v.t.* (un′dər·kut′) **·cut, ·cut·ting 1** To cut away the underpart of. **2** To cut away a lower portion of so as to leave a part overhanging. **3** To work or sell for lower payment than (a rival). **4** In sports, to hit (a ball) with an oblique downward or underhand stroke so as to give the ball a backspin. **5** To lessen or destroy the effectiveness or impact of; undermine. —*adj.* **1** Having the parts in relief cut under. **2** Done by undercutting.

un·der·de·vel·oped (un′dər·di·vel′əpt) *adj.* **1** Not sufficiently developed. **2** Below a normal or adequate standard in the development of industry, resources, agriculture, etc.: an *underdeveloped* country.

un·der·dog (un′dər·dôg′, -dog′) *n.* **1** The one that is losing, has lost, or is at a disadvantage in a contest. **2** The weaker, subservient, or exploited person.

un·der·done (un′dər·dun′) *adj.* Not cooked to the fullest degree.

un·der·em·ployed (un′dər·əm·ploid′) *adj.* Employed only part of the time or for too few hours to assure an adequate income. —**un′der·em·ploy′ment** *n.*

un·der·es·ti·mate (un′dər·es′tə·māt) *v.t.* **·mat·ed, ·mat·ing** To put too low an estimate or valuation upon (things or people). —*n.* (-mit) An estimate below the just value, expense, opinion, etc. —**un′der·es′ti·ma′tion** *n.*

un·der·ex·pose (un′dər·ik·spōz′) *v.t.* **·posed, ·pos·ing** *Phot.* To expose (a film) to less light than is required for a clear image. —**un′der·ex·po′sure** (-spō′zhər) *n.*

un·der·feed (un′dər·fēd′) *v.t.* **fed, ·feed·ing** To feed insufficiently.

un·der·foot (un′dər·foŏot′) *adv.* **1** Beneath the feet; down on the ground. **2** In the way.

un·der·gar·ment (un′dər·gär′mənt) *n.* A garment to be worn beneath outer garments.

un·der·go (un′dər·gō′) *v.t.* **·went, ·gone, ·go·ing 1** To be subjected to; have experience of; suffer. **2** To bear up under; endure.

un·der·grad·u·ate (un′dər·graj′o͞o·it) *n.* A student of a university or college who has not taken the bachelor's degree. —*adj.* Of, being, or for an undergraduate.

un·der·ground (un′dər·ground′) *adj.* **1** Situated, done, or operated beneath the surface of the ground. **2** Done in secret; clandestine. **3** Of, relating to, or characterized by the underground (defs. 3 and 4), their works, actions, etc. —*n.* **1** That which is beneath the surface of the ground, as a passage or space. **2** *Brit.* SUBWAY. **3** A group secretly organized to resist or oppose those in control of a government or country: usu. with *the.* **4** An avant-garde movement in art, cinema, journalism, etc., generally considered to be in opposition to conventional culture or society and whose works are usu. experimental, erotic, or radical in style, content, or purpose: usu. with *the.* —*adv.* (un′dər·ground′) **1** Beneath the surface of the ground. **2** In or into hiding, secrecy, etc.

Underground Railroad A system of cooperation among antislavery people, before 1861, for assisting fugitive slaves to escape to Canada and the free states.

un·der·growth (un′dər·grōth′) *n.* UNDERBRUSH.

un·der·hand (un′dər·hand′) *adj.* **1** Done or acting in a sly or treacherously secret manner. **2** In certain sports, done or delivered with the hand and forearm lower than the elbow or shoulder. —*adv.* **1** In a secret, sly manner. **2** With an underhand motion.

un·der·hand·ed (un′dər·han′did) *adj. & adv.* UNDERHAND. —**un′der·hand′ed·ly** *adv.* —**un′der·hand′ed·ness** *n.*

un·der·lay (un′dər·lā′) *v.t.* ·**laid**, ·**lay·ing** **1** To place (one thing) under another. **2** To furnish with a base or lining. **3** To support or elevate with something placed beneath. —*n.* (un′dər·lā′) Something laid beneath something else, esp., in printing, a piece of paper, etc., placed under type, etc., in order to raise it.

un·der·lie (un′dər·lī′) *v.t.* ·**lay**, ·**lain**, ·**ly·ing** **1** To lie below or under. **2** To be the basis or reason for: What motives *underlie* his refusal to go? **3** To constitute a first or prior claim or lien over.

un·der·line (un′dər·līn′) *v.t.* ·**lined**, ·**lin·ing** **1** To mark with a line underneath; underscore. **2** To emphasize. —*n.* A line underneath a word or passage, as for emphasis.

un·der·ling (un′dər·ling) *n.* A subordinate; inferior.

un·der·ly·ing (un′dər·lī′ing) *adj.* **1** Lying under: *underlying* strata. **2** Basic; fundamental: *underlying* principles. **3** Not obvious, but implicit: *underlying* reasons.

un·der·mine (un′dər·mīn′, un′dər·mīn) *v.t.* ·**mined**, ·**min·ing** **1** To excavate beneath; dig a mine or passage under. **2** To weaken by wearing away at the base. **3** To weaken or impair secretly, insidiously, or by degrees.

un·der·most (un′dər·mōst′) *adj.* Having the lowest place or position.

un·der·neath (un′dər·nēth′) *adv.* **1** In a place below. **2** On the under or lower side. —*prep.* **1** Beneath; under; below. **2** Under the form or appearance of. **3** Under the authority of; in the control of. —*adj.* Lower. —*n.* The lower or under part or side. [< OE *underneothan*]

un·der·nour·ish (un′dər·nûr′ish) *v.t.* To provide with insufficient nourishment. —**un′der·nour′ished** *adj.* —**un′der·nour′ish·ment** *n.*

un·der·pass (un′dər·pas′, -päs′) *n.* A road, passageway, etc., that runs beneath something, esp. a road that passes under railway tracks or under another road.

un·der·pay (un′dər·pā′) *v.t.* ·**paid**, ·**pay·ing** To pay insufficiently.

un·der·pin·ning (un′dər·pin′ing) *n.* **1** Material or framework used to support a wall or building from below. **2** *Often pl.* Something used or functioning as a basis or foundation: the *underpinnings* of guilt in our society.

Underpass

un·der·play (un′dər·plā′) *v.t. & v.i.* **1** UNDERACT. **2** To behave, react to, etc., in a deliberately restrained manner.

un·der·priv·i·leged (un′dər·priv′ə·lijd) *adj.* **1** Deprived socially and economically of enjoying certain fundamental rights theoretically possessed by all members of a community or nation. **2** Of or pertaining to people who are underprivileged.

un·der·rate (un′dər·rāt′) *v.t.* ·**rat·ed**, ·**rat·ing** To rate too low; underestimate.

un·der·score (un′dər·skôr′, -skōr′) *v.t.* ·**scored**, ·**scor·ing** To draw a line below, as for emphasis; underline. —*n.* (un′dər·skôr′, -skōr′) A line drawn beneath a word, etc., as for emphasis.

un·der·sea (un′dər·sē′) *adj.* Being, carried on, or designed for use beneath the surface of the sea. —*adv.* (un′dər·sē′) Beneath the surface of the sea: also **un·der·seas** (un′dər·sēz′).

under secretary The assistant secretary of a principal secretary in government.

un·der·sell (un′dər·sel′) *v.t.* ·**sold**, ·**sell·ing** **1** To sell at a lower price than. **2** To present or promote, as a point of view or commodity, in an understated manner.

un·der·shirt (un′dər·shûrt′) *n.* A collarless undergarment, usu. without sleeves, worn beneath a shirt.

un·der·shoot (un′dər·sho͞ot′) *v.* ·**shot**, ·**shoot·ing** *v.t.* **1** To shoot short of or below (a target). **2** To land an airplane short of (the runway). —*v.i.* **3** To shoot or land short of the mark.

un·der·shot (un′dər·shot′) *adj.* **1** Propelled by water that flows underneath, as a water wheel. **2** Having a projecting lower jaw or teeth.

un·der·side (un′dər·sīd′) *n.* The lower or under side or surface.

un·der·signed (un′dər·sīnd′) *n.* The person or persons who have signed their names at the end of a document, letter, etc.

un·der·sized (un′dər·sīzd′) *adj.* Of less than the normal, legal, or average size.

Undershot water wheel

un·der·slung (un′dər·slung′) *adj.* Having the springs fixed to the axles from below, as certain automobiles.

un·der·stand (un′dər·stand′) *v.* ·**stood**, ·**stand·ing** *v.t.* **1** To come to know the meaning or import of. **2** To perceive the nature or character of: I do not *understand* her. **3** To have comprehension or mastery of: Do you *understand* German? **4** To be aware of; realize: She *understands* her position. **5** To have been told; believe: I *understand* that she went home. **6** To take or interpret: How am I to *understand* that remark? **7** To accept as a condition or stipulation: It is *understood* that the tenant will provide his own heat. —*v.i.* **8** To have understanding; comprehend. **9** To grasp the meaning, significance, etc., of something. **10** To believe or assume something to be the case. **11** To have a sympathetic attitude or tolerance toward something. [< OE *under-* under + *standan* stand] —**un′der·stand′a·ble** *adj.* —**un′der·stand′a·bly** *adv.*

un·der·stand·ing (un′dər·stan′ding) *n.* **1** An intellectual grasp of something; comprehension. **2** The power or capacity to think, acquire and retain knowledge, interpret experience, etc.; intelligence. **3** An agreement or settlement of differences. **4** An informal or confidential compact or agreement. **5** An individual viewpoint, interpretation, or opinion. **6** A sympathetic comprehension of or tolerance for the feelings, actions, attitudes, etc., of others. —*adj.* Possessing or characterized by comprehension, compassion, etc. —**un′der·stand′ing·ly** *adv.*

un·der·state (un′dər·stāt′) *v.t.* ·**stat·ed**, ·**stat·ing** **1** To state with less force than the actual truth warrants. **2** To state or describe in a deliberately restrained manner in order to achieve greater force or effectiveness. —**un′der·state′ment** *n.*

un·der·stat·ed (un′dər·stāt′əd) *adj.* Stated, executed, designed, etc., in an unemphatic, restrained, or simple manner.

un·der·stood (un′dər·sto͞od′) *p.t. & p.p.* of UNDERSTAND. —*adj.* **1** Grasped mentally; comprehended. **2** Taken for granted. **3** Agreed upon by all.

un·der·stud·y (un′dər·stud′ē) v.t. & v.i. **·stud·ied, ·stud·y·ing 1** To study (a part) in order to be able, if necessary, to substitute for the actor playing it. **2** To act as an understudy to (another actor). —n. pl. **·stud·ies 1** An actor or actress who can substitute for another actor in a given role. **2** A person prepared to perform the work or fill the position of another.

un·der·take (un′dər·tāk′) v.t. **·took, ·tak·en, ·tak·ing 1** To take upon oneself; agree or attempt to do. **2** To contract to do; pledge oneself to. **3** To guarantee or promise. **4** To take under charge or guidance.

un·der·tak·er (un′dər·tā′kər for def. 1; un′dər·tā′kər for def. 2) n. **1** One who undertakes any work or enterprise; esp. a contractor. **2** One whose business it is to prepare a dead person for burial and to conduct funerals.

un·der·tak·ing (un′dər·tā′king, esp. for def. 3; un′dər·tā′king) n. **1** The act of one who undertakes any task or enterprise. **2** The thing undertaken; an enterprise; task. **3** The business of an undertaker (def. 2). **4** An engagement, promise, or guarantee.

un·der·tone (un′dər·tōn′) n. **1** A low or subdued tone, esp. a vocal tone, as a whisper. **2** A subdued color, esp. one with other colors imposed on it. **3** A meaning, suggestion, quality, etc., that is implied but not expressed.

un·der·tow (un′dər·tō′) n. A flow of water beneath and in a direction opposite to the surface current, esp. such a flow moving seaward beneath surf.

un·der·val·ue (un′dər·val′yōō) v.t. **·ued, ·u·ing 1** To value or rate below the real worth. **2** To regard or esteem as of little worth. —un′der·val′u·a′tion n.

un·der·wa·ter (un′dər·wô′tər, -wot′ər) adj. **1** Being, occurring, used, etc., below the surface of a body of water: underwater research. **2** Below the water line of a ship. —adv. Below the surface of water.

under way 1 In progress: The meeting was already under way. **2** Into operation or motion: to get the fund drive under way.

un·der·wear (un′dər·wâr′) n. Garments worn underneath the ordinary outer garments.

un·der·weight (un′dər·wāt′) adj. Having less than the normal, desired, or permitted weight. —n. Weight less than normal, permitted, or desired.

un·der·went (un′dər·went′) p.t. of UNDERGO.

un·der·wood (un′dər·wŏŏd′) n. UNDERBRUSH.

un·der·world (un′dər·wûrld′) n. **1** The mythical abode of the dead; Hades. **2** The world of organized crime and vice.

un·der·write (un′dər·rīt′) v. **·wrote, ·writ·ten, ·writ·ing** v.t. **1** To write beneath or sign something, as a document. **2** To agree or subscribe to, esp. to agree to pay for (an enterprise, etc.). **3** In insurance: **a** To sign one's name to (an insurance policy), thereby assuming liability for certain designated losses or damage. **b** To insure. **c** To assume a risk or a liability for a certain sum) by way of insurance. **4** To engage to buy, at a determined price and time, all or part of the stock in (a new enterprise or company) that is not subscribed for by the public. —v.i. **5** To act as an underwriter; esp., to issue a policy of insurance.

un·der·writ·er (un′dər·rī′tər) n. **1** A person or company in the insurance business; also, an insurance employee who determines the risks involved, the amount of the premiums, etc., for a specific applicant or policy. **2** One who underwrites something.

un·de·sir·a·ble (un′di·zīr′ə·bəl) adj. Not desirable; objectionable. —n. An undesirable person. —un′de·sir′a·bil′i·ty n. —un′de·sir′a·bly adv.

un·do (un·dōō′) v.t. **·did, ·done, ·do·ing 1** To cause to be as if never done; reverse, annul, or cancel. **2** To loosen or untie. **3** To unfasten and open. **4** To bring to ruin; destroy. **5** To disturb emotionally. [< OE undōn] —un·do′er n.

un·do·ing (un·dōō′ing) n. **1** A reversal of what has been done. **2** Destruction; ruin; disgrace; also, the cause of such ruin or disgrace. **3** The action of unfastening, loosening, opening, etc.

un·done¹ (un·dun′) adj. **1** Untied; unfastened. **2** Ruined; disgraced. **3** Extremely disturbed or upset. [Orig. p.p. of UNDO]

un·done² (un·dun′) adj. Not done.

un·doubt·ed (un·dou′tid) adj. **1** Not doubted; assured; certain. **2** Not viewed with distrust; unsuspected. —un·doubt′ed·ly adv.

un·draw (un·drô′) v.t. & v.i. **·drew, ·drawn, ·draw·ing** To draw open, away, or aside.

un·dreamed-of (un·drēmd′uv′, -dremt′-) adj. Never imagined; wholly unforeseen: undreamed-of joy. Also **un·dreamt′-of** (-dremt′-).

un·dress (un·dres′) v.t. **1** To divest of clothes; strip. **2** To remove the dressing or bandages from, as a wound. **3** To divest of special attire; disrobe. —v.i. To remove one's clothing. —n. **1** The state of being nude or in only partial attire, as in undergarments, dressing robe, etc. **2** The military or naval uniform worn by officers when not in full dress.

un·due (un·dyōō′) adj. **1** Excessive; immoderate. **2** Not justified by law; illegal. **3** Not yet due, as a bill. **4** Not appropriate; improper.

un·du·lant (un′dyə·lənt, -jə-) adj. Undulating; fluctuating.

undulant fever A persistent bacterial disease usu. transmitted to man by contact with infected cattle and characterized by recurrent fever, exhaustion, neuralgic pains, etc.

un·du·late (un′dyə·lāt, -jə-) v. **·lat·ed, ·lat·ing** v.t. **1** To cause to move like a wave or in waves. **2** To give a wavy appearance or surface to. —v.i. **3** To move like a wave or waves. **4** To have a wavy form or appearance. —adj. (-lit, -lāt) Having a wavelike appearance, surface, or markings: also **un′du·lat′ed**. [< L unda wave]

un·du·la·tion (un′dyə·lā′shən, -jə-) n. **1** A waving or sinuous motion. **2** An appearance as of waves; a gentle rise and fall. —un′du·la·to′ry (-lə·tôr′ē, -tō′rē) adj.

un·du·ly (un·dyōō′lē) adv. **1** Excessively. **2** Improperly; unjustly.

un·dy·ing (un·dī′ing) adj. Immortal; eternal.

un·earned (un·ûrnd′) adj. **1** Not earned by labor, skill, etc. **2** Undeserved.

unearned increment An increase in the value of land or property independent of any efforts of the owner, as through an increase of population that creates demand.

un·earth (un·ûrth′) v.t. **1** To dig or root up from the earth. **2** To reveal; discover.

un·earth·ly (un·ûrth′lē) adj. **1** Not, or seemingly not, of this earth. **2** Supernatural; terrifying; weird; terrible. **3** Informal Ridiculous, absurd, preposterous, etc. —un·earth′li·ness n.

un·ease (un·ēz′) n. Mental or emotional discomfort, dissatisfaction, anxiety, etc.

un·eas·y (un·ē′zē) adj. **·eas·i·er, ·eas·i·est 1** Deprived of ease; disturbed; unquiet. **2** Not comfortable; causing discomfort. **3** Showing embarassment or constraint; strained. **4** Not stable or secure; precarious: an uneasy peace. —un·eas′i·ly adv. —un·eas′i·ness n.

un·em·ploy·a·ble (un′əm·ploi′ə·bəl) adj. Not employable because of illness, age, physical incapacity, etc. —n. An unemployable person.

un·em·ployed (un′əm·ploid′) adj. **1** Having no employment; out of work. **2** Not put to use or turned to account; idle. —**the unemployed** People who have no jobs. —un′em·ploy′ment n.

un·e·qual (un·ē′kwəl) adj. **1** Not equal in size, importance, weight, ability, duration, etc. **2** Inadequate; insufficient: with to. **3** Not balanced or uniform; variable; irregular. **4** Involving poorly matched competitors or contestants: an unequal contest. —un·e′qual·ly adv.

un·e·qualed (un·ē′kwəld) adj. Not equaled or matched; unrivaled. Also **un·e′qualled**.

un·e·quiv·o·cal (un′i·kwiv′ə·kəl) adj. Understandable in only one way; not ambiguous; clear. —un′e·quiv′o·cal·ly adv. —un′e·quiv′o·cal·ness n.

un·err·ing (un·ûr′ing, -er′-) adj. **1** Making no mistakes. **2** Certain; accurate; infallible. —un·err′ing·ly adv.

UNESCO (yōō·nes′kō) United Nations Educational, Scientific, and Cultural Organization.

---

add, āce, câre, pälm; end, ēven; it, īce; odd, ōpen, ôrder; tŏŏk, pōōl; up, bûrn; ə = a in above, u in focus; yōō = u in fuse; oil; pout; check; go; ring; thin; this; zh, vision. < derived from; ? origin uncertain or unknown.

un·es·sen·tial (un′ə·sen′shəl) *adj*. Not essential; not needed. —*n*. Something not essential; an extra.

un·e·ven (un·ē′vən) *adj*. 1 Not even, smooth, or level; rough. 2 Not straight, parallel, or perfectly horizontal. 3 Not equal or even, as in length, width, etc. 4 Not balanced or matched equally. 5 Not uniform; variable; fluctuating. 6 Not fair or just. 7 Not divisible by two without remainder; odd: said of numbers. —**un·e′ven·ly** *adv*. —**un·e′ven·ness** *n*.

un·e·vent·ful (un′i·vent′fəl) *adj*. Devoid of any noteworthy or unusual events or incidents; quiet. —**un′e·vent′·ful·ly** *adv*. —**un′e·vent′ful·ness** *n*.

un·ex·am·pled (un′ig·zam′pəld) *adj*. Without a parallel example; unprecedented; unique.

un·ex·cep·tion·a·ble (un′ik·sep′shən·ə·bəl) *adj*. That cannot be objected to; without any flaw; irreproachable. —**un′ex·cep′tion·a·bly** *adv*.

un·ex·cep·tion·al (un′ik·sep′shən·əl) *adj*. 1 Not unusual or exceptional; ordinary. 2 Subject to no exception.

un·ex·pect·ed (un′ik·spek′tid) *adj*. Coming without warning; not expected; unforeseen. —**un′ex·pect′ed·ly** *adv*. —**un′ex·pect′ed·ness** *n*. —**Syn**. unanticipated, sudden.

un·fail·ing (un·fā′ling) *adj*. 1 Giving or constituting a supply that never fails; inexhaustible: an *unfailing* spring. 2 Always fulfilling requirements or expectation. 3 Sure; infallible. —**un·fail′ing·ly** *adv*. —**un·fail′ing·ness** *n*.

un·fair (un·fâr′) *adj*. 1 Marked by injustice, deception, or bias; not fair. 2 Not honest or ethical in business affairs. —**un·fair′ly** *adv*. —**un·fair′ness** *n*.

un·faith·ful (un·fāth′fəl) *adj*. 1 Not faithful to or abiding by a vow, agreement, duty, etc.; disloyal. 2 Not accurate or exact; unreliable. 3 Not true to marriage vows; adulterous. —**un·faith′ful·ly** *adv*. —**un·faith′ful·ness** *n*.

un·fa·mil·iar (un′fə·mil′yər) *adj*. 1 Not knowing well or at all: with *with*: *unfamiliar* with his plays. 2 Not familiarly known; strange: an *unfamiliar* face. —**un′fa·mil′i·ar′·i·ty** (-mil′ē·ar′ə·tē) *n*. —**un′fa·mil′iar·ly** *adv*.

un·fast·en (un·fas′ən, -fäs′-) *v.t*. To untie or undo; loosen or open.

un·fa·vor·a·ble (un·fā′vər·ə·bəl) *adj*. 1 Not favorable; adverse. 2 Not propitious. —**un·fa′vor·a·bly** *adv*.

un·feel·ing (un·fē′ling) *adj*. 1 Not sympathetic; hard; callous. 2 Having no feeling or sensation. —**un·feel′ing·ly** *adv*. —**un·feel′ing·ness** *n*.

un·feigned (un·fānd′) *adj*. Not feigned; sincere; genuine. —**un·feign′ed·ly** (-fān′id·lē) *adv*.

un·fit (un·fit′) *v.t*. **·fit·ted** or **·fit**, **·fit·ting** To deprive of requisite fitness, skill, etc.; disqualify. —*adj*. 1 Not able to meet the requirements or needs; unsuitable. 2 Not physically or mentally sound or fit. 3 Not appropriate or proper for a given purpose. —**un·fit′ly** *adv*. —**un·fit′ness** *n*.

un·fix (un·fiks′) *v.t*. 1 To unfasten; loosen; detach. 2 To unsettle.

un·flag·ging (un·flag′ing) *adj*. Not diminishing or failing; tireless. —**un·flag′ging·ly** *adv*.

un·flap·pa·ble (un·flap′ə·bəl) *adj. Informal* Characterized by unshakable composure; imperturbable. —**un·flap′·pa·bil′i·ty** *n*.

un·fledged (un·flejd′) *adj*. 1 Not yet fledged, as a young bird. 2 Inexperienced or immature.

un·flinch·ing (un·flin′ching) *adj*. Done without shrinking; steadfast. —**un·flinch′ing·ly** *adv*.

un·fold (un·fōld′) *v.t*. 1 To open or spread out (something folded). 2 To unwrap. 3 To reveal or make clear, as by explaining or disclosing gradually. 4 To develop. —*v.i*. 5 To become opened; expand. 6 To become manifest or develop fully.

un·fore·seen (un′fôr·sēn′, -fōr-) *adj*. Unexpected.

un·for·get·ta·ble (un′fər·get′ə·bəl) *adj*. Difficult or impossible to forget; memorable. —**un′for·get′ta·bly** *adv*.

un·for·tu·nate (un·fôr′chə·nit) *adj*. 1 Not fortunate or lucky. 2 Causing, attended by, or resulting from misfortune; disastrous. 3 Not suitable or proper; bad; regrettable: an *unfortunate* thing to say. —*n*. One who is unfortunate. —**un·for′tu·nate·ly** *adv*. —**un·for′tu·nate·ness** *n*.

un·found·ed (un·foun′did) *adj*. 1 Not based on fact; groundless; baseless. 2 Not established.

un·fre·quent·ed (un′fri·kwent′id) *adj*. Rarely or never visited or frequented.

un·friend·ly (un·frend′lē) *adj*. 1 Not friendly or sympathetic. 2 Not favorable or propitious. —**un·friend′li·ness** *n*.

un·frock (un·frok′) *v.t*. 1 To remove a frock or gown from. 2 To depose, as a priest, from ecclesiastical rank.

un·furl (un·fûrl′) *v.t. & v.i*. 1 To unroll, as a flag; spread out. 2 To unfold. —**un·furled′** *adj*.

un·gain·ly (un·gān′lē) *adj*. 1 Awkward; clumsy. 2 Not attractive. —**un·gain′li·ness** *n*.

un·glued (un·glood′) *adj*. No longer glued together; separated. —**come unglued** *Slang* To become mentally or emotionally upset.

un·god·ly (un·god′lē) *adj*. 1 Without reverence for God; impious. 2 Unholy; sinful. 3 *Informal* Outrageous. —*adv. Informal* Outrageously. —**un·god′li·ness** *n*.

un·gov·ern·a·ble (un·guv′ər·nə·bəl) *adj*. That cannot be governed; wild; unruly. —**un·gov′ern·a·bly** *adv*.

un·gra·cious (un·grā′shəs) *adj*. 1 Lacking in graciousness of manner; unmannerly. 2 Not pleasing; offensive. —**un·gra′cious·ly** *adv*. —**un·gra′cious·ness** *n*. —**Syn**. 1 discourteous, rude, impolite, uncivil, ill-mannered, ill-bred.

un·grate·ful (un·grāt′fəl) *adj*. 1 Feeling or showing a lack of gratitude; not thankful. 2 Not pleasant; disagreeable. 3 Unrewarding; yielding no return. —**un·grate′ful·ly** *adv*. —**un·grate′ful·ness** *n*.

un·guard·ed (un·gär′did) *adj*. 1 Having no guard; unprotected. 2 Thoughtless; careless. 3 Without guile; direct; open. —**un·guard′ed·ly** *adv*.

un·guent (ung′gwənt) *n*. An ointment or salve. [< L *unguere* anoint] —**un′guen·tar′y** (-gwən·ter′ē) *adj*.

un·guis (ung′gwis) *n. pl*. **·gues** (-gwēz) A hoof, claw, nail, or talon. [L, nail]

un·gu·late (ung′gyə·lit, -lāt) *adj*. Having hoofs. —*n*. A hoofed mammal. [< L *ungula* hoof]

un·hand (un·hand′) *v.t*. To remove one's hand from; release from the hand or hands; let go.

un·hand·y (un·han′dē) *adj*. **·di·er**, **·di·est** 1 Hard to get to or use; inconvenient. 2 Clumsy; lacking in manual skill. —**un·hand′i·ly** *adv*.

un·hap·py (un·hap′ē) *adj*. **·pi·er**, **·pi·est** 1 Sad; depressed. 2 Causing or constituting misery, unrest, or dissatisfaction: *unhappy* circumstances. 3 Unfortunate; unpropitious. 4 Exhibiting lack of tact or judgment; inappropriate. —**un·hap′pi·ly** *adv*. —**un·hap′pi·ness** *n*.

un·health·y (un·hel′thē) *adj*. **·health·i·er**, **·health·i·est** 1 Lacking health, vigor, or wholesomeness; sickly. 2 Causing sickness; injurious to health. 3 Morally harmful. 4 Dangerous; risky. —**un·health′i·ly** *adv*. —**un·health′i·ness** *n*.

un·heard (un·hûrd′) *adj*. 1 Not perceived by the ear. 2 Not granted a hearing. 3 Obscure; unknown.

un·heard-of (un·hûrd′uv′, -ov′) *adj*. 1 Not known of before; unknown or unprecedented. 2 Outrageous; unbelievable.

un·hinge (un·hinj′) *v.t*. **·hinged**, **·hing·ing** 1 To take from the hinges. 2 To remove the hinges of. 3 To detach; dislodge. 4 To throw into confusion; unsettle, as the mind.

un·hitch (un·hich′) *v.t*. To unfasten.

un·ho·ly (un·hō′lē) *adj*. **·ho·li·er**, **·ho·li·est** 1 Not hallowed. 2 Wicked; sinful. 3 *Informal* Frightful; outrageous. —**un·ho′li·ly** *adv*. —**un·ho′li·ness** *n*.

uni- *combining form* One; single; one only: *unifoliate*. [< L *unus* one]

U·ni·ate (yoo′nē·at, -it) *n*. A member of any community of Eastern Christians that acknowledges the supremacy of the pope at Rome, but retains its own liturgy, ceremonies, and rites. —*adj*. Of the Uniates or their faith. Also **U′ni·at** (-it).

u·ni·cam·er·al (yoo′nə·kam′ər·əl) *adj*. Consisting of but one chamber, as a legislature.

UNICEF (yoo′nə·sef) United Nations Children's Fund. [< U(nited) N(ations) I(nternational) C(hildren's) E(mergency) F(und), its former name]

u·ni·cel·lu·lar (yoo′nə·sel′yə·lər) *adj*. Consisting of a single cell, as a protozoan.

u·ni·corn (yoo′nə·kôrn′) *n*. A mythical, horselike animal with

Unicorn

one horn growing from the middle of its forehead. [< L *unicornis* one-horned]

u·ni·cy·cle (yōō′nə·sī′kəl) *n.* A bicyclelike vehicle having only a single wheel propelled by pedals.

u·ni·form (yōō′nə·fôrm′) *adj.* 1 Being always the same or alike; not varying: *uniform* temperature. 2 Having the same form, color, character, etc. as others: a line of *uniform* battleships. 3 Being the same throughout in appearance, color, surface, etc.: a *uniform* texture. 4 Consistent in effect, action, etc.: a *uniform* law for all drivers. —*n.* A distinctive dress or suit worn, esp. when on duty, by members of the same organization, service, etc., as soldiers, sailors, postmen, etc. —*v.t.* To put into or clothe with a uniform. [< L *unus* one + *forma* form] —**u′ni·form·ly** *adv.*

u·ni·form·i·ty (yōō′nə·fôr′mə·tē) *n. pl.* **·ties** 1 The state or quality of being uniform. 2 An instance of it.

u·ni·fy (yōō′nə·fī) *v.t.* **·fied, ·fy·ing** To cause to be one; make uniform; unite. [< L *unus* one + *facere* make] —**u′ni·fi·ca′·tion** (-fə·kā′shən), **u′ni·fi′er** *n.*

u·ni·lat·er·al (yōō′nə·lat′ər·əl) *adj.* 1 Of, relating to, or affecting one side only; one-sided. 2 Made, undertaken, done, or signed by only one of two or more people or parties. 3 Growing on or turning toward one side only. —**u′ni·lat′er·al·ism** *n.* —**u′ni·lat′er·al·ly** *adv.*

un·im·peach·a·ble (un′im·pē′chə·bəl) *adj.* Not impeachable; beyond question as regards truth, honesty, etc.; faultless; blameless. —**un′im·peach′a·bly** *adv.*

un·im·proved (un′im·prōōvd′) *adj.* 1 Not improved; not bettered or advanced. 2 Having no improvements; not cleared, cultivated, or built upon. 3 Not made anything of; unused.

un·in·tel·li·gi·ble (un′in·tel′ə·jə·bəl) *adj.* Impossible to understand; incomprehensible. —**un′in·tel′li·gi·bil′i·ty** *n.* —**un′in·tel′li·gi·bly** *adv.*

un·in·ter·es·ted (un·in′tər·is·tid, -tris-) *adj.* Not interested; indifferent; unconcerned. • See DISINTERESTED.

un·ion (yōōn′yən) *n.* 1 The act or an instance of uniting two or more things into one, as: **a** A political joining together, as of states or nations. **b** Marriage; wedlock. 2 The condition of being united or joined; junction. 3 Something formed by uniting or combining parts, as: **a** A confederation, coalition, or league, as of nations, states, or individuals. **b** LABOR UNION. 4 A device for joining mechanical parts, esp. a coupling device for pipes or rods. 5 A college or university organization that provides facilities for recreation, meetings, light meals, etc.: also **student union.** 6 A device emblematic of union used in a flag or ensign, as the blue field with white stars in the flag of the U.S. —*adj.* Of, being, or relating to a union. —**the Union** The United States of America. [< L *unus* one]

un·ion·ism (yōōn′yən·iz′əm) *n.* 1 The principle of union. 2 Labor unions collectively; also, their principles and practices. —**un′ion·ist** *n.* —**un′ion·is′tic** *adj.*

Un·ion·ism (yōōn′yən·iz′əm) *n.* During the U.S. Civil War, the advocacy of political union between the States, as opposed to secession. —**Un′ion·ist** *n.*

un·ion·ize (yōōn′yən·īz) *v.* **·ized, ·iz·ing** *v.t.* To cause to join or to organize into a labor union. —*v.i.* To become a member of or organize a labor union. —**un′ion·i·za′tion** *n.*

Union Jack The British national flag.

Union of Soviet Socialist Republics A federal union of 15 republics in N Eurasia, 8,646,400 sq. mi., cap. Moscow.

union shop A factory, office, hospital, etc., in which only members of a labor union are employed.

union suit A one-piece, man's or boy's undergarment consisting of shirt and drawers.

u·nique (yōō·nēk′) *adj.* 1 Being the only one of its kind; single; sole. 2 Being without equal; unparalleled. 3 Very unusual or remarkable; exceptional, extraordinary, etc. [< L *unicus* < *unus* one] —**u·nique′ly** *adv.* —**u·nique′ness** *n.*

u·ni·sex (yōō′nə·seks′) *Informal adj.* For, appropriate to, or having characteristics of both sexes: *unisex* fashions. —*n.* The embodiment or integration of qualities, characteristics, etc., of both sexes, as in appearance, clothes, or activities.

u·ni·sex·u·al (yōō′nə·sek′shōō·əl) *adj.* 1 Of only one sex; dioecious: a *unisexual* plant. 2 *Informal* Of or having to do with unisex. —**u′ni·sex′u·al′i·ty** *n.* —**u′ni·sex′u·al·ly** *adv.*

u·ni·son (yōō′nə·sən, -zən) *n.* 1 A condition of perfect agreement and accord; harmony. 2 *Music* **a** The interval between tones of identical pitch. **b** The simultaneous sounding of the same tones by two or more parts. —**in unison** 1 So that identical tones are sounded simultaneously by two or more parts. 2 So that identical words or sounds are uttered simultaneously. 3 In perfect agreement. [< L *unisonus* having a single sound]

u·nit (yōō′nit) *n.* 1 A predetermined quantity, as of time, length, work, value, etc., used as a standard of measurement or comparison. 2 A fixed amount of work or classroom hours used in calculating a scholastic degree. 3 The quantity, as of a drug or antigen, required to produce a given effect or result. 4 A person or group considered both singly and as a constituent part of a whole: a military *unit.* 5 Something, as a mechanical part or device, having a specific function and serving as part of a whole: the electrical *unit* of a percolator. 6 *Math.* A quantity whose measure is represented by the number 1. —*adj.* Of or being a unit: the *unit* value of an article of merchandise. [Short for UNITY]

U·ni·tar·i·an (yōō′nə·târ′ē·ən) *n.* A member of a Protestant denomination which rejects the doctrine of the Trinity, but accepts the ethical teachings of Jesus and emphasizes complete freedom of religious opinion and the independence of each local congregation. —*adj.* Pertaining to the Unitarians, or to their teachings. —**U′ni·tar′i·an·ism** *n.*

u·ni·tar·y (yōō′nə·ter′ē) *adj.* 1 Of a unit or units. 2 Characterized by, based on, or pertaining to unity. 3 Having the nature of or used as a unit.

u·nite (yōō·nīt′) *v.* **u·nit·ed, u·nit·ing** *v.t.* 1 To join together so as to form a whole; combine. 2 To bring into close connection, as by legal, physical, marital, social, or other ties: to be *united* in marriage; allies *united* by a common interest. 3 To have or possess in combination: to *unite* courage with wisdom. 4 To cause to adhere; combine. —*v.i.* 5 To become or be merged into one; be consolidated by or as if by adhering. 6 To join together for action. [< L *unus* one]

u·nit·ed (yōō·nī′tid) *adj.* 1 Incorporated into one; combined. 2 Of or resulting from joint action. 3 Harmonious; in agreement. —**u·nit′ed·ly** *adv.* —**u·nit′ed·ness** *n.*

United Kingdom A constitutional monarchy located on several islands off the coast of N Europe, comprising Great Britain, Northern Ireland, and nearby islands, 94,284 sq. mi., cap. London.

United Nations 1 A coalition to resist the military aggression of the Axis Powers in World War II, formed of 26 national states in January, 1942. 2 An international organization of sovereign states (originally called the **United Nations Organization**) created by the United Nations Charter adopted at San Francisco in 1945.

United Kingdom

United States of America A federal republic including 50 states (49 in North America, and Hawaii, an archipelago in the Pacific Ocean), and the District of Columbia, 3,615,222 sq. mi., cap. Washington, D.C.

u·ni·ty (yōō′nə·tē) *n. pl.* **·ties 1** The state or quality of being one or united; oneness. **2** The product or result of being one or united. **3** Singleness of purpose or action. **4** A state of mutual understanding. **5** The quality or fact of being a whole through the unification of separate or individual parts. **6** In a literary or artistic production, a combination of parts that exhibits a prevailing oneness of purpose, thought, spirit, and style; also, the cohesive or harmonious effect so produced. **7** *Math.* **a** The number one. **b** The element of a number system that leaves any number unchanged under multiplication. [< L *unus* one]

Univ. Universalist; University.

univ. universal; universally; university.

u·ni·va·lent (yōō′nə·vā′lənt) *adj. Chem.* Having a valence or combining value of one; monovalent. **—u′ni·va′·lence, u′ni·va′len·cy** *n.*

u·ni·valve (yōō′nə·valv′) *adj.* Having the shell in one piece, as a snail. Also **u′ni·val′vate, u′ni·valved′.** **—n. 1** A mollusk having a univalve shell; a gastropod. **2** A shell of a single piece. **—u′ni·val′vu·lar** (-val′vyə·lər) *adj.*

u·ni·ver·sal (yōō′nə·vûr′səl) *adj.* **1** Prevalent or common everywhere or among all things or persons. **2** Of, applicable to, for, or including all things, persons, cases, etc., without exception. **3** Accomplished or interested in a vast variety of subjects, activities, etc.: Leonardo da Vinci was a *universal* genius. **4** Adapted or adaptable to a great variety of uses, shapes, etc. **5** *Logic* Including or designating all the members of a class. **—n. 1** *Logic* A universal proposition. **2** Any general or universal notion or idea. **3** A behavioral trait common to all men or cultures. **—u′ni·ver′sal·ly** *adv.* **—u′ni·ver′sal·ism, u′ni·ver′sal·ness** *n.*

u·ni·ver·sal·i·ty (yōō′nə·vər·sal′ə·tē) *n.* **1** The quality, condition, or an instance of being universal. **2** Limitlessness, as of range, occurrence, etc.

u·ni·ver·sal·ize (yōō′nə·vûr′səl·īz) *v.t.* **·ized, ·iz·ing** To make universal. **—u′ni·ver′sal·i·za′tion** *n.*

universal joint *Mech.* A coupling for connecting two shafts, etc., so as to permit angular motion in all directions. Also **universal coupling.**

u·ni·verse (yōō′nə·vûrs) *n.* **1** The aggregate of all existing things; the whole creation embracing all celestial bodies and all of space; the cosmos. **2** In restricted sense, the earth. **3** Something regarded as being a universe in its comprehensiveness, as a field of thought or activity. [< L *universus* turned, combined into one < *unus* one + *versus*, p.p. of *vertere* turn]

u·ni·ver·si·ty (yōō′nə·vûr′sə·tē) *n. pl.* **·ties 1** An educational institution for higher instruction, usu., in the U.S., an institution that includes an undergraduate college or colleges and professional schools granting advanced degrees in law, medicine, the sciences, academic subjects, etc. **2** The buildings, grounds, etc., of a university. **3** The students, faculty, and administration of a university.

un·just (un·just′) *adj.* Not legitimate, fair, or just; wrongful. **—un·just′ly** *adv.*

un·kempt (un·kempt′) *adj.* **1** Not combed: said of hair. **2** Not neat or tidy. **3** Without polish; rough. [< UN-[1] + *kempt* combed, p.p. of *kemb,* dial. var. of COMB]

un·kind (un·kīnd′) *adj.* Lacking kindness; unsympathetic; harsh; cruel. **—un·kind′ly** *adj.* **(·li·er, ·li·est)** & *adv.* **— un·kind′li·ness, un·kind′ness** *n.*

un·known (un·nōn′) *adj.* **1** Not known; not apprehended mentally; not recognized, as a fact or person. **2** Not determined or identified: an *unknown* substance. **—n.** An unknown person, thing, or quantity.

un·lace (un·lās′) *v.t.* **·laced, ·lac·ing** To loosen or unfasten the lacing of; untie.

un·law·ful (un·lô′fəl) *adj.* **1** Contrary to or in violation of law; illegal. **2** Not moral or ethical. **—un·law′ful·ly** *adv.* **— un·law′ful·ness** *n.*

un·learn (un·lûrn′) *v.t.* **·learned** or **·learnt, ·learn·ing 1** To dismiss from the mind (something learned); forget. **2** To attempt to abandon the habit of.

un·learn·ed (un·lûr′nid) *adj.* **1** Not possessed of or characterized by learning; illiterate; ignorant. **2** Characterized by lack of knowledge, professional skill, etc. **3** (un·lûrnd′) Not acquired by learning or study.

un·leash (un·lēsh′) *v.t.* To set free from or as from a leash: He *unleashed* his rage.

un·less (un·les′) *conj.* If it be not a fact that; except that: *Unless* we persevere, we shall lose. **—prep.** Save; except; excepting: with an implied verb: *Unless* a miracle, he'll not be back in time. [Earlier *onlesse (that)* in a less case < ON + LESS]

un·let·tered (un·let′ərd) *adj.* Not educated; not lettered; illiterate.

un·like (un·līk′) *adj.* Having little or no resemblance; different. —*prep.* 1 Not like; different from. 2 Not characteristic of: It's *unlike* her to complain. —**un·like′ness** *n.*

un·like·ly (un·līk′lē) *adj.* 1 Improbable. 2 Not inviting or promising success. —*adv.* Improbably. —**un·like′li·hood, un·like′li·ness** *n.*

un·lim·it·ed (un·lim′it·id) *adj.* 1 Having no limits in space, number, or time. 2 Not restricted or limited.

un·load (un·lōd′) *v.t.* 1 To remove the load or cargo from. 2 To take off or discharge (cargo, etc.). 3 To relieve of something burdensome or oppressive. 4 To withdraw the charge of ammunition from. 5 *Informal* To dispose of, esp. by selling in large quantities. —*v.i.* 6 To discharge freight, cargo, etc.

un·lock (un·lok′) *v.t.* 1 To unfasten (something locked). 2 To open; release. 3 To lay open; reveal or disclose. —*v.i.* 4 To become unlocked.

un·looked-for (un·lookt′fôr′) *adj.* Not anticipated; unexpected.

un·loose (un·lo͞os′) *v.t.* **·loosed, ·loos·ing** To make loose; set free; undo, release, etc. Also **un·loos′en** (-lo͞o′sən).

un·luck·y (un·luk′ē) *adj.* **·luck·i·er, ·luck·i·est** 1 Not favored by luck; unfortunate. 2 Resulting in or attended by ill luck; disastrous. 3 Likely to prove unfortunate; inauspicious. —**un·luck′i·ly** *adv.* —**un·luck′i·ness** *n.*

un·make (un·māk′) *v.t.* **·made, ·mak·ing** 1 To reduce to the original condition or form. 2 To ruin; destroy. 3 To deprive of rank, power, etc.

un·man (un·man′) *v.t.* **·manned, ·man·ning** 1 To cause to lose courage; dishearten. 2 To deprive of manly qualities; make weak or timid. 3 To castrate; emasculate.

un·man·ly (un·man′lē) *adj.* Not manly; weak, cowardly, effeminate, etc. —**un·man′li·ness** *n.*

un·mask (un·mask′, -mäsk′) *v.t.* 1 To remove a mask from. 2 To expose the true nature of. —*v.i.* 3 To remove one's mask or disguise.

un·mean·ing (un·mē′ning) *adj.* 1 Having no meaning: an *unmeaning* speech. 2 Having no expression: an *unmeaning* stare. —**un·mean′ing·ly** *adv.* —**un·mean′ing·ness** *n.*

un·men·tion·a·ble (un·men′shən·ə·bəl) *adj.* Not fit to be mentioned or discussed; embarrassing. —*n.pl.* Things not ordinarily mentioned or discussed, esp. undergarments. —**un·men′tion·a·ble·ness** *n.* —**un·men′tion·a·bly** *adv.*

un·mer·ci·ful (un·mûr′sə·fəl) *adj.* 1 Showing no mercy; cruel; pitiless. 2 Extreme; exorbitant. —**un·mer′ci·ful·ly** *adv.* —**un·mer′ci·ful·ness** *n.*

un·mis·tak·a·ble (un′mis·tā′kə·bəl) *adj.* That cannot be mistaken for something else; evident; obvious. —**un′mis·tak′a·bly** *adv.*

un·mit·i·gat·ed (un·mit′ə·gā′tid) *adj.* 1 Not relieved or lessened: *unmitigated* sorrow. 2 Absolute; thoroughgoing: an *unmitigated* liar. —**un·mit′i·gat′ed·ly** *adv.*

un·mor·al (un·môr′əl, -mor′-) *adj.* 1 Incapable of distinguishing between right and wrong; not guided by moral considerations. 2 Outside the realm of morality or ethics. —**un·mo·ral·i·ty** (un′mə·ral′ə·tē) *n.* • *Unmoral, amoral,* and *immoral* are alike in meaning not moral. However, *unmoral* and *amoral* are synonomous in referring to objects or acts (or people involved with such objects or acts) which stand outside the realm of morality whereas *immoral* infers a conflict with accepted standards of morality.

un·nat·u·ral (un·nach′ər·əl, -nach′rəl, un′-) *adj.* 1 Contrary to the norm. 2 Contrary to the common laws of morality or decency; monstrous; inhuman. 3 Contrived; artificial. —**un·nat′u·ral·ly** *adv.* —**un·nat′u·ral·ness** *n.*

un·nec·es·sary (un·nes′ə·ser′ē, un′-) *adj.* Not required; not necessary. —**un·nec′es·sar·i·ly** (un·nes′ə·sâr′ə·lē) *adv.*

un·nerve (un·nûrv′) *v.t.* **·nerved, ·nerv·ing** 1 To deprive of strength, firmness, courage, etc. 2 To make nervous.

un·num·bered (un·num′bərd) *adj.* 1 Not counted. 2 Innumerable. 3 Not numbered.

un·oc·cu·pied (un·ok′yə·pīd′, un′-) *adj.* 1 Empty; unin-

habited: an *unoccupied* house. 2 Idle; unemployed; at leisure.

un·of·fi·cial (un·ə·fish′əl) *adj.* Not official; not authoritative. —**un·of·fi′cial·ly** *adv.*

un·or·gan·ized (un·ôr′gən·īzd) *adj.* 1 Not organized. 2 Without form or structure. 3 Not unionized.

un·pack (un·pak′) *v.t.* 1 To open and take out the contents of. 2 To take out of the container, as something packed. —*v.i.* 3 To take the contents out of a suitcase, etc.

un·par·al·leled (un·par′ə·leld) *adj.* Without parallel; unmatched; unprecedented.

un·peg (un·peg′) *v.t.* **·pegged, ·peg·ging** To unfasten by removing the peg or pegs from.

un·peo·ple (un·pē′pəl) *v.t.* **·pled, ·pling** To depopulate; deprive of inhabitants.

un·per·son (un′pûr′sən) *n.* One reduced to a state of oblivion, as by official action or the loss of position, after a period of fame or public importance.

un·pin (un·pin′) *v.t.* **·pinned, ·pin·ning** 1 To remove a pin or pins from. 2 To unfasten by removing pins.

un·pleas·ant (un·plez′ənt) *adj.* Disagreeable; objectionable. —**un·pleas′ant·ly** *adv.* —**un·pleas′ant·ness** *n.*

un·plug (un·plug′) *v.t.* **·plugged, ·plug·ging** 1 To remove a plug from. 2 To remove an obstruction from, as a drain. 3 To break an electrical connection by pulling out a plug.

un·plumbed (un·plumd′) *adj.* Not measured or explored fully; unfathomed; unknown.

un·polled (un·pōld′) *adj.* 1 Not cast or registered: said of a vote. 2 Not canvassed in a poll.

un·pop·u·lar (un·pop′yə·lər) *adj.* Generally disliked, unaccepted, etc. —**un·pop′u·lar·ly** *adv.* —**un·pop′u·lar′i·ty** (-lar′ə·tē) *n.*

un·prac·ticed (un·prak′tist) *adj.* 1 Not skilled; inexperienced. 2 Not used or tried.

un·prec·e·dent·ed (un·pres′ə·den′tid) *adj.* Being without precedent; preceded by no similar case; novel.

un·prej·u·diced (un·prej′o͞o·dist) *adj.* 1 Free from prejudice or bias; impartial. 2 Not impaired, as a right.

un·prin·ci·pled (un·prin′sə·pəld) *adj.* Without moral principles; unscrupulous.

un·print·a·ble (un·prin′tə·bəl) *adj.* Not fit for printing, esp. because of profanity, obscenity, etc.

un·pro·fes·sion·al (un′prə·fesh′ən·əl) *adj.* 1 Not pertaining to, characteristic of, or belonging to a particular profession. 2 Violating the standards, ethical code, etc., of a profession. —**un′pro·fes′sion·al·ly** *adv.*

un·qual·i·fied (un·kwol′ə·fīd) *adj.* 1 Being without the proper qualifications; unfit. 2 Without limitation or restrictions; absolute: *unqualified* approval.

un·ques·tion·a·ble (un·kwes′chən·ə·bəl) *adj.* Too certain or sure to be open to question, doubt, etc.; indisputable. —**un·ques′tion·a·bly** *adv.*

un·qui·et (un·kwī′ət) *adj.* 1 Turbulent; agitated; tumultuous. 2 Disturbed physically, mentally or emotionally; restless; uneasy. —**un·qui′et·ly** *adv.* —**un·qui′et·ness** *n.*

un·quote (un·kwōt′) *v.t. & v.i.* **·quot·ed, ·quot·ing** To close (a quotation).

un·rav·el (un·rav′əl) *v.* **·eled** or **·elled, ·el·ing** or **·el·ling** *v.t.* 1 To separate the threads of, as a tangled skein or knitted article. 2 To unfold; explain, as a mystery or a plot. —*v.i.* 3 To become unraveled.

un·read (un·red′) *adj.* 1 Having read very little; uninformed; unlearned. 2 Not yet read or examined.

un·read·y (un·red′ē) *adj.* Not ready; unprepared, as for speech, action, etc. —**un·read′i·ly** *adv.* —**un·read′i·ness** *n.*

un·re·al (un·rē′əl, -rēl′) *adj.* 1 Having no reality, actual existence, or substance. 2 Not true or sincere; false. 3 Fanciful; imaginary. —**un·re·al·i·ty** (un′rē·al′ə·tē) *n.*

un·rea·son·a·ble (un·rē′zən·ə·bəl, -rēz′nə-) *adj.* 1 Acting without or contrary to reason. 2 Immoderate; exorbitant. —**un·rea′son·a·ble·ness** *n.* —**un·rea′son·a·bly** *adv.*

un·rea·son·ing (un·rē′zən·ing) *adj.* Marked by the absence of reason; irrational. —**un·rea′son·ing·ly** *adv.*

un·reel (un·rēl′) *v.t. & v.i.* To unwind from a reel.

un·re·gen·er·ate (un′ri·jen′ər·it) *adj.* 1 Not changed spiritually by regeneration; unrepentant. 2 Not convinced by or converted to a particular doctrine, theology, cause, etc. **3** Stubborn; recalcitrant.

un·re·lent·ing (un′ri·lent′ing) *adj.* **1** Not relenting; inflexible. **2** Not diminishing in pace, effort, speed, etc. —un′re·lent′ing·ly *adv.*

un·re·li·a·ble (un′ri·lī′ə·bəl) *adj.* Not to be relied upon; undependable. —un′re·li·a·bil′i·ty, un′re·li′a·ble·ness *n.* —un′re·li′a·bly *adv.*

un·re·lig·ious (un′ri·lij′əs) *adj.* **1** IRRELIGIOUS. **2** Not related to or connected with religion.

un·re·mit·ting (un′ri·mit′ing) *adj.* Incessant; not stopping or relaxing. —un′re·mit′ting·ly *adv.* —un′re·mit′ting·ness *n.*

un·re·served (un′ri·zûrvd′) *adj.* **1** Not qualified; unrestricted. **2** Not reticent; informal; open. **3** Not set aside, as seats. —un·re·serv·ed·ly (un′ri·zûr′vid·lē) *adv.* —un′re·serv′ed·ness *n.*

un·rest (un′rest′, un′rest′) *n.* **1** Restlessness, esp. of the mind. **2** Angry dissatisfaction, bordering on revolt.

un·rid·dle (un·rid′l) *v.t.* ·dled, ·dling To solve, as a mystery.

un·right·eous (un·rī′chəs) *adj.* **1** Not righteous; wicked; sinful. **2** Unfair; inequitable. —un·right′eous·ly *adv.* —un·right′eous·ness *n.*

un·ripe (un·rīp′) *adj.* **1** Not arrived at maturity; not ripe; immature. **2** Not ready; not prepared. —un·ripe′ness *n.*

un·ri·valed (un·rī′vəld) *adj.* Having no rival; peerless.

un·roll (un·rōl′) *v.t.* **1** To spread or open (something rolled up). **2** To exhibit to view. —*v.i.* **3** To become unrolled.

un·ruf·fled (un·ruf′əld) *adj.* **1** Not disturbed or agitated; calm. **2** Not ruffled; smooth.

un·ru·ly (un·rōō′lē) *adj.* Disposed to resist rule or discipline; ungovernable. —un·ru′li·ness *n.*

un·sad·dle (un·sad′l) *v.* ·dled, ·dling *v.t.* **1** To remove a saddle from. **2** To remove from the saddle. —*v.i.* **3** To take the saddle off a horse.

un·said (un·sed′) *adj.* Not said; not spoken.

un·sat·u·rat·ed (un·sach′ə·rā′tid) *adj.* **1** Capable of dissolving more solute. **2** Having at least one free or multiple valence bond available for direct union with an atom or radical: said of organic compounds.

un·sa·vor·y (un·sā′vər·ē) *adj.* **1** Having a disagreeable taste or odor. **2** Having no savor; tasteless. **3** Disagreeable or offensive, esp. morally. —un·sa′vor·i·ness *n.*

un·say (un·sā′) *v.t.* ·said, ·say·ing To retract (something said).

un·scathed (un·skāthd′) *adj.* Not injured.

un·scram·ble (un·skram′bəl) *v.t.* ·bled, ·bling *Informal* To resolve the confused, scrambled, or disordered condition of.

un·screw (un·skrōō′) *v.t.* **1** To remove the screw or screws from. **2** To remove or detach by withdrawing screws, or by turning. —*v.i.* **3** To become unscrewed or permit of being unscrewed.

un·scru·pu·lous (un·skrōō′pyə·ləs) *adj.* Not scrupulous; having no scruples; unprincipled. —un·scru′pu·lous·ly *adv.* —un·scru′pu·lous·ness *n.*

un·seal (un·sēl′) *v.t.* **1** To break or remove the seal of. **2** To open (that which has been sealed or closed).

un·search·a·ble (un·sûr′chə·bəl) *adj.* That cannot be searched into or explored; mysterious. —un·search′a·ble·ness *n.* —un·search′a·bly *adv.*

un·sea·son·a·ble (un·sē′zən·ə·bəl) *adj.* **1** Not suitable to the season: *unseasonable* weather. **2** Untimely; inopportune. —un·sea′son·a·ble·ness *n.* —un·sea′son·a·bly *adv.*

un·seat (un·sēt′) *v.t.* **1** To remove from a seat. **2** To throw (a rider) from a horse. **3** To deprive of office or rank; depose.

un·seem·ly (un·sēm′lē) *adj.* ·li·er, ·li·est Unbecoming, indecent, unattractive, or inappropriate. —*adv.* In an unseemly fashion. —un·seem′li·ness *n.*

un·set·tle (un·set′l) *v.* ·tled, ·tling *v.t.* **1** To move from a fixed or settled condition. **2** To confuse, upset, or disturb. —*v.i.* **3** To become unsettled. —un·set′tling·ly *adv.*

un·sex (un·seks′) *v.t.* To deprive of sex, sexual power, or the distinctive qualities of one's sex.

un·shack·le (un·shak′əl) *v.t.* ·led, ·ling **1** To unfetter; free from shackles. **2** To free, as from restraint.

un·sheathe (un·shēth′) *v.t.* ·sheathed, ·sheath·ing To take from or as from a scabbard or sheath; bare.

un·ship (un·ship′) *v.t.* ·shipped, ·ship·ping To unload from a ship or other vessel.

un·sight·ly (un·sīt′lē) *adj.* ·li·er, ·li·est Offensive to the sight; ugly. —un·sight′li·ness *n.*

un·skilled (un·skild′) *adj.* **1** Without special skill or training: an *unskilled* worker. **2** Requiring no special skill or training.

un·skill·ful (un·skil′fəl) *adj.* Lacking or not evincing skill; awkward; incompetent. Also **un·skil·ful.** —un·skill′ful·ly *adv.* —un·skill′ful·ness *n.*

un·snap (un·snap′) *v.t.* ·snapped, ·snap·ping To undo the snap or snaps of.

un·snarl (un·snärl′) *v.t.* To undo snarls; disentangle.

un·so·cia·ble (un·sō′shə·bəl) *adj.* **1** Not sociable; not inclined to seek the society of others. **2** Lacking or not conducive to sociability. —un·so·cia·bil·i·ty (un·sō′shə·bil′ə·tē), un·so′cia·ble·ness *n.* —un·so′cia·bly *adv.*

un·sol·der (un·sod′ər) *v.t.* **1** To take apart (something soldered). **2** To separate; divide.

un·so·phis·ti·cat·ed (un′sə·fis′tə·kā′tid) *adj.* **1** Showing inexperience or naiveté; artless. **2** Genuine; pure. **3** Not complicated; simple. —un′so·phis′ti·cat·ed·ly *adv.* —un′so·phis′ti·cat·ed·ness, un′so·phis′ti·ca′tion *n.*

un·sound (un·sound′) *adj.* **1** Not strong or solid: *unsound* construction. **2** Unhealthy in body or mind. **3** Untrue or logically invalid: *unsound* arguments. **4** Not deep; disturbed: said of sleep. —un·sound′ly *adv.* —un·sound′ness *n.*

un·spar·ing (un·spâr′ing) *adj.* **1** Not sparing or saving; lavish. **2** Showing no mercy. —un·spar′ing·ly *adv.* —un·spar′ing·ness *n.*

un·speak·a·ble (un·spē′kə·bəl) *adj.* **1** That cannot be expressed; unutterable: *unspeakable* joy. **2** Extremely bad or objectionable: an *unspeakable* crime. —un·speak′a·ble·ness *n.* —un·speak′a·bly *adv.*

un·sta·ble (un·stā′bəl) *adj.* **1** Lacking in stability or firmness; liable to move, sway, shake, etc. **2** Having no fixed purpose; easily influenced: an *unstable* character. **3** Emotionally unsteady. **4** Liable to change; fluctuating; variable: an *unstable* economy. **5** *Chem.* Easily decomposed, as certain compounds. —un·sta′ble·ness *n.* —un·sta′bly *adv.*

un·stead·y (un·sted′ē) *adj.* ·stead·i·er, ·stead·i·est Not steady, as: **a** Not stable; liable to move or shake. **b** Variable; fluctuating. **c** Undependable or irregular. —un·stead′i·ly *adv.* —un·stead′i·ness *n.*

un·stop (un·stop′) *v.t.* ·stopped, ·stop·ping **1** To remove a stopper from. **2** To open by removing obstructions; clear.

un·stop·pa·ble (un·stop′ə·bəl) *adj.* Impossible to stop or check. —un·stop′pa·bly *adv.*

un·strap (un·strap′) *v.t.* ·strapped, ·strap·ping To undo or loosen the strap or straps of.

un·string (un·string′) *v.t.* ·strung, ·string·ing **1** To remove from a string, as pearls. **2** To take the string or strings from. **3** To loosen the string or strings of, as a bow or guitar. **4** To make unstable or nervous.

un·struc·tured (un·struk′chərd) *adj.* Not having a definite organization or plan.

un·strung (un·strung′) *adj.* **1** Having the strings removed or loosened. **2** Emotionally upset.

un·stud·ied (un·stud′ēd) *adj.* **1** Not stiff or artificial; natural; unaffected. **2** Not acquainted through study.

un·sub·stan·tial (un′səb·stan′shəl) *adj.* **1** Lacking solidity or strength; unstable; weak. **2** Having no valid basis in fact. **3** Unreal; fanciful. —un′sub·stan′tial·ly *adv.* —un′sub·stan′ti·al′i·ty (-shē·al′ə·tē) *n.*

un·suit·a·ble (un·sōō′tə·bəl) *adj.* Not suitable; unfitting. —un·suit·a·bil·i·ty (un·sōō′tə·bil′ə·tē), un·suit′a·ble·ness *n.* —un·suit′a·bly *adv.*

un·sung (un·sung′) *adj.* **1** Not celebrated, as in song or poetry; obscure. **2** Not sung.

un·swerv·ing (un·swûr′ving) *adj.* **1** Not changing or wavering; consistent: *unswerving* loyalty. **2** Not swerving from a path or course. —un·swerv′ing·ly *adv.*

un·tan·gle (un·tang′gəl) *v.t.* ·gled, ·gling **1** To free from tangles; disentangle. **2** To clear up or straighten out (a perplexing or confused situation, etc.).

un·taught (un·tôt′) *adj.* **1** Not having been instructed; ignorant. **2** Known without having been taught; natural.

un·thank·ful (un·thangk′fəl) *adj.* **1** Not grateful. **2** Not appreciated. —un·thank′ful·ly *adv.* —un·thank′ful·ness *n.*

un·think·ing (un·thingk′ing) *adj.* Lacking thoughtfulness, care, or attention. —**un·think′ing·ly** *adv.* —**un·think′ing·ness** *n.*

un·thread (un·thred′) *v.t.* 1 To remove the thread from, as a needle. 2 To unravel; disentangle. 3 To find one's way out of, as a maze.

un·ti·dy (un·tī′dē) *adj.* ·di·er, ·di·est Not tidy; messy; disorderly. —**un·ti′di·ly** *adv.* —**un·ti′di·ness** *n.*

un·tie (un·tī′) *v.* ·tied, ·ty·ing *v.t.* 1 To loosen or undo, as a knot. 2 To free from that which binds or restrains. —*v.i.* 3 To become loosened or undone.

un·til (un·til′) *prep.* 1 Up to the time of; till: We will wait *until* midnight. 2 Before: used with a negative: The music doesn't begin *until* nine. —*conj.* 1 To the time when: *until* I die. 2 To the place or degree that: Walk east *until* you reach the river. 3 Before: with a negative: He couldn't leave *until* the car came for him. [< ME *und*- up to, as far as + TILL] • See TILL².

un·time·ly (un·tīm′lē) *adj.* Coming before time or not in proper time; premature or inopportune. —*adv.* Before time or not in the proper time; inopportunely.

un·to (un′tōō) *prep. Archaic* 1 To. 2 Until. [< ME *und*- up to, as far as + TO, on analogy with *until*]

un·told (un·tōld′) *adj.* 1 Not told, revealed, or described. 2 Of too great a number or extent to be counted or measured.

un·touch·a·ble (un·tuch′ə·bəl) *adj.* 1 Inaccessible to the touch; out of reach. 2 Forbidden to the touch. 3 Unpleasant, disgusting, or dangerous to touch. —*n.* In India, formerly, a member of the lowest caste.

un·to·ward (un·tôrd′, -tōrd′, -tə·wôrd′) *adj.* 1 Causing or characterized by difficulty or unhappiness; unfavorable. 2 Not easily managed; refractory. 3 Improper; unseemly. —**un·to·ward′ly** *adv.* —**un·to·ward′ness** *n.*

un·true (un·trōō′) *adj.* 1 Not true; false or incorrect. 2 Not conforming to rule or standard. 3 Disloyal; faithless. —**un·tru′ly** *adv.*

un·truth (un·trōōth′, un′trōōth′) *n. pl.* ·truths (-trōōths, -trōō͟thz) 1 The quality or character of being untrue. 2 Something that is not true; a falsehood; lie.

un·truth·ful (un·trōōth′fəl) *adj.* 1 Not truthful; not telling the truth. 2 Not consistent with the truth. —**un·truth′ful·ly** *adv.* —**un·truth′ful·ness** *n.*

un·tu·tored (un·tyōō′tərd) *adj.* Not educated; untaught.

un·twine (un·twīn′) *v.* ·twined, ·twin·ing *v.t.* 1 To undo (something twined); unwind by disentangling. —*v.i.* 2 To become undone.

un·twist (un·twist′) *v.t.* 1 To separate by a movement the reverse of twisting; untwine. —*v.i.* 2 To become untwined.

un·used (un·yōōzd′) *adj.* 1 Not used. 2 Never having been used. 3 Not accustomed: with *to.*

un·u·su·al (un·yōō′zhōō·əl) *adj.* Not usual; odd, rare, or extraordinary. —**un·u′su·al·ly** *adv.* —**un·u′su·al·ness** *n.*

un·ut·ter·a·ble (un·ut′ər·ə·bəl) *adj.* Too great, deep, etc., to be expressed or described in words. —**un·ut′ter·a·ble·ness** *n.* —**un·ut′ter·a·bly** *adv.*

un·var·nished (un·vär′nisht) *adj.* 1 Not varnished. 2 Not embellished or adorned; simple: the *unvarnished* truth.

un·veil (un·vāl′) *v.t.* 1 To remove the veil or covering from; disclose to view; reveal. —*v.i.* 2 To remove one's veil; reveal oneself.

un·war·rant·a·ble (un·wôr′ən·tə·bəl, -wor′-) *adj.* That cannot be justified; inexcusable; indefensible. —**un·war′rant·a·bly** *adv.*

un·war·y (un·wâr′ē) *adj.* ·war·i·er, ·war·i·est Not careful; incautious. —**un·war′i·ly** *adv.* —**un·war′i·ness** *n.* —**Syn.** careless, heedless, reckless, unguarded.

un·well (un·wel′) *adj.* Sick; ailing.

un·wept (un·wept′) *adj.* 1 Not lamented or wept for. 2 Not shed, as tears.

un·whole·some (un·hōl′səm) *adj.* 1 Harmful to physical, mental, or moral health. 2 Sickly in health or in appearance. —**un·whole′some·ly** *adv.* —**un·whole′some·ness** *n.*

un·wield·y (un·wēl′dē) *adj.* ·i·er, ·i·est Difficult to move, manage, or control, as because of great size or awkward shape. —**un·wield′i·ly** *adv.* —**un·wield′i·ness** *n.*

un·will·ing (un·wil′ing) *adj.* 1 Not willing; reluctant; loath. 2 Done, said, granted, etc., with reluctance. —**un·will′ing·ly** *adv.* —**un·will′ing·ness** *n.*

un·wind (un·wīnd′) *v.* ·wound, ·wind·ing *v.t.* 1 To reverse the winding of; untwist or wind off. 2 To disentangle. —*v.i.* 3 To become disentangled or untwisted. 4 To free oneself from tension or anxieties; relax.

un·wise (un·wīz′) *adj.* Acting with, or showing, lack of wisdom or good sense. —**un·wise′ly** *adv.*

un·wit·ting (un·wit′ing) *adj.* 1 Having no knowledge or awareness; ignorant; unconscious. 2 Not intentional. —**un·wit′ting·ly** *adv.*

un·wont·ed (un·wôn′tid, -won′-) *adj.* Not ordinary or customary; unusual; uncommon. —**un·wont′ed·ly** *adv.* —**un·wont′ed·ness** *n.*

un·wor·thy (un·wûr′t͟hē) *adj.* 1 Not worthy or deserving: often with *of.* 2 Not befitting or becoming: usu. with *of:* conduct *unworthy* of a gentleman. 3 Lacking worth or merit. 4 Not deserved or merited. —**un·wor′thi·ly** *adv.* —**un·wor′thi·ness** *n.*

un·wrap (un·rap′) *v.t.* ·wrapped, ·wrap·ping To take the wrapping from; open; undo.

un·writ·ten (un·rit′n) *adj.* 1 Not written down; traditional. 2 Having no writing upon it; blank.

unwritten law A law or rule of conduct, procedure, etc., whose authority stems from custom and tradition rather than from a written command, decree, or statute.

un·yoke (un·yōk′) *v.t.* ·yoked, ·yok·ing 1 To release from a yoke. 2 To separate; part.

up (up) *adv.* 1 Toward a higher place or level. 2 In or on a higher place. 3 To or at that which is literally or figuratively higher, as: **a** To or at a higher price: Barley is going *up.* **b** To or at a higher rank: people who have come *up* in the world. **c** To or at a greater size or amount: to swell *up.* **d** To or at a greater degree, intensity, volume, etc.: Turn *up* the radio. **e** To or at a place regarded as higher up: *up* north. **f** To a position above the horizon: when the sun comes *up.* **g** To a later point in time or life: from her childhood *up* to her teens. 4 In or into a vertical position; on one's feet. 5 Out of bed: to get *up.* 6 So as to be level or even (with) in time, degree, amount, etc.: *up* to the brim. 7 In or into commotion or activity: to be *up* in arms. 8 Into or in a place of safekeeping: to lay *up* provisions. 9 Completely; wholly: Houses were burned *up.* 10 In baseball, at bat. 11 In some sports: **a** In the lead. **b** Apiece; alike: said of a score. 12 So as to be compact, secure, etc.: Fold *up* the linen. 13 In or into view, existence, etc.: to bring *up* a subject; It will turn *up.* 14 *Naut.* Shifted to windward, as a tiller. 15 Into an aggregate number or quantity: Add *up* these figures. 16 To a source, conclusion, etc.: to follow *up* a rumor. —**be up against** *Informal* To meet with something to be dealt with. —**be up against it** *Informal* To be in trouble, usu. financial trouble. —**be up to** 1 *Informal* To be doing or about to do: What is he *up to?* 2 To be equal to or capable of: I'm not *up to* playing golf today. 3 To be incumbent upon: It's *up to* her to help us. —*adj.* 1 Moving or directed upward. 2 In, at, or to a high level, condition, etc.: Is the river *up* today? 3 Above the ground or horizon: The jonquils are *up.* 4 In a raised or erect position or condition: The new school is finally *up.* 5 At an end: Your time is *up.* 6 *Informal* Going on; taking place: What's *up?* 7 *Informal* Informed; up-to-date: *up* on the newest movies. 8 Characterized by or showing agitation or excitement: Tempers are *up.* 9 In baseball, at bat. 10 *Informal* Alert; ready: to be *up* for a meeting. —**up and doing** Busy; bustling. —**up for** 1 Being considered or presented for: *up for* reelection. 2 Charged with or on trial for: *up for* manslaughter. —*prep.* 1 To, toward, or at a higher point, position, etc., on or along: monkeys scampering *up* a tree; *up* the social ladder. 2 To or at a point farther above or along: The farm is *up* the road. 3 From the coast toward the interior of (a country). 4 From the mouth toward the source of (a river). —*n. Usu. pl.* 1 An ascent or upward movement. 2 A state of prosperity. —**on the up and up**

Slang Honest; genuine. —**ups and downs** Changes of fortune or circumstance. —*v.* **upped, up-ping** *Informal v.t.* **1** To increase; cause to rise: to *up* one's price. **2** To put, lift, or take up. —*vi.* **3** To rise. **4** To do quickly and abruptly: usu. followed by another verb: Then she *up* and left. [OE]

up-and-coming (up′ən-kum′ing) *adj.* Enterprising; energetic; promising.

u-pas (yōō′pəs) *n.* **1** A tall Asian and East Indian tree related to mulberry, with an acrid, milky, poisonous juice. **2** The sap of this tree, used to make arrow poison. [< Malay *(phon) upas* poison (tree)]

up-beat (up′bēt′; *for adj., also* up′bēt′) *n. Music* An unaccented beat, esp. the last beat in a measure. —*adj.* Optimistic; confident.

up-braid (up-brād′) *v.t* To reproach for some wrongdoing; scold. [< OE *up-* up + *bregdan* weave; twist] —**up-braid′er** *adj.* —**up-braid′ing-ly** *adv.* —**Syn.** admonish, chastise, rebuke, reprimand.

up-bring-ing (up′bring′ing) *n.* Rearing and training received during childhood.

up-chuck (up′chuk′) *Informal v.t. & v.i.* To vomit. —*n.* Vomit.

up-coun-try (up′kun′trē) *Informal n.* Inland country. —*adj.* In, from, or characteristic of inland places. —*adv.* (up′kun′trē) In, into or toward the interior.

up-date (up′dāt′) *v.t.* **-dat-ed, -dat-ing** To bring up to date, as a textbook or manual.

up-end (up′end′) *v.t. & v.i.* To stand on end.

up-front (up′frunt′) *adj. Colloq.* Out in the open; unconcealed.

up-grade (up′grād′; *for v., also* up′grād′) *n.* An upward incline or slope. —*vt.* **-grad-ed, -grad-ing** To raise to a higher rank, responsibility, value, importance, etc., as an employee or job.

up-heav-al (up-hē′vəl) *n.* **1** The act of upheaving, or the state of being upheaved. **2** A violent change or disturbance, as of the established social order.

up-heave (up-hēv′) *v.* **-heaved** or **-hove, -heav-ing** *v.t.* **1** To heave or raise up. —*v.i.* **2** To be raised or lifted.

up-hill (up′hil′) *adv.* Up or as up a hill or an ascent. —*adj.* **1** Going up hill or an ascent; sloping upward. **2** Attended with difficulty or exertion. **3** Situated on high ground. —*n.* (up′hil′) An upward slope; rising ground; a steep rise.

up-hold (up-hōld′) *v.t.* **-held, -hold-ing 1** To hold up; keep from falling or sinking. **2** To raise; lift up. **3** To aid, encourage, sustain, or confirm. —**up-hold′er** *n.*

up-hol-ster (up-hōl′stər) *v.t.* To fit, as furniture, with coverings, cushioning, springs, etc. [ult. < ME *upholder* tradesman] —**up-hol′ster-er** *n.*

up-hol-ster-y (up-hōl′stər-ē, -strē) *n. pl.* **-ster-ies 1** The materials used in upholstering. **2** The act, art, or business of upholstering.

UPI, U.P.I. United Press International.

up-keep (up′kēp′) *n.* **1** The act of keeping in good condition. **2** The state of being kept in good condition. **3** The cost of keeping in good condition.

up-land (up′lənd, -land′) *n.* High land, esp. such land located far from the sea. —*adj.* Pertaining to or situated in an upland.

up-lift (up-lift′) *v.t.* **1** To lift up, or raise aloft; elevate. **2** To put on a higher plane, mentally, morally, culturally, or socially. —*n.* (up′lift′) **1** The act of lifting up raising. **2** An elevation to a higher mental, spiritual, moral, or social plane. **3** A social movement aiming to improve, esp. morally or culturally. **4** A brassiere designed to lift and support the breasts. —**up-lift′er** *n.*

up-most (up′mōst′) *adj.,* UPPERMOST.

up-on (ə-pon′, ə-pôn′) *prep.* On: *upon* the throne. —*adv.* On: The paper has been written *upon.* • *Upon* no longer differs in meaning from *on,* but it is sometimes preferred for reasons of euphony. When *upon* has its original meaning of *up* + *on,* it is written and pronounced as two words: *Let's go up on the roof.*

up-per (up′ər) *adj.* **1** Higher, as in location or position. **2** Higher in station, rank, authority, etc.: the *upper* house. **3** *Geol. Usu. cap.* Being a later division of a specified period or series. —*n.* **1** Something that is above another similar or related thing, part, etc., as an upper berth. **2** That part of a boot or shoe above the sole. **3** *Slang* Any of

various drugs that stimulate the central nervous system, as amphetamines. —**on one's uppers** *Informal* **1** Having worn out the soles of one's shoes. **2** At the end of one's resources; destitute. [ME, orig. compar. of UP]

up-per-case (up′ər-kās′) *adj.* Of, in, or designating capital letters. —*v.t.* **-cased, -cas-ing** To set in capital letters.

upper case A case in which are kept capital letters and some auxiliary type for use in printing. **2** Capital letters.

upper class The socially or economically superior group in any society. —**up′per-class′** (-klas′, -kläs′) *adj.*

up-per-class-man (up′ər-klas′mən, -kläs′-) *n. pl.* **-men** (-mən) A junior or senior in a high school or college.

up-per-cut (up′ər-kut′) *n.* In boxing, a swinging blow directed upward, as to an opponent's jaw. —*v.t & v.i.* **-cut, -cut-ting** To strike with an uppercut.

upper hand The advantage; control.

Upper House The branch, in a bicameral legislature, where membership is more restricted, as the U.S. Senate.

up-per-most (up′ər-mōst′) *adj.* Highest in place, rank, authority, importance, etc.; foremost. —*adv.* In the highest place, rank, importance, etc.

Upper Vol-ta (vol′tə) A republic of w Africa, 105,900 sq. mi., cap. Ouagadougou. • See map at AFRICA.

up-pish (up′ish) *adj. Informal* UPPITY. —**up′pish-ly** *adv.* —**up′pish-ness** *n.*

up-pi-ty (up′ə-tē) *adj. Informal* Arrogant; snobbish; haughty. —**up′pi-ti-ness** *n.*

up-raise (up-rāz′) *v.t.* **-raised, -rais-ing** To lift up; elevate.

up-right (up′rīt′) *adj.* **1** Being in a vertical position; erect. **2** Righteous; just. —*n.* **1** The state of being upright: a post out of *upright.* **2** Something having an upright position, as a vertical timber. **3** An upright piano. **4** In a football, a goal post. —*adv.* In an upright position; vertically. [< OE *up-* up + *riht* right] —**up′right′ly** *adv.* —**up′right′ness** *n.*

upright piano A piano having the strings mounted vertically within a rectangular, upright case.

up-ris-ing (up′rī′zing) *n.* **1** The act of rising up; esp., a revolt or insurrection. **2** An ascent; upward slope; acclivity.

up-roar (up′rôr′, -rōr′) *n.* **1** A state of confusion, disturbance, excitement, tumult, etc. **2** A loud, boisterous noise; din. [< Du. *op-* up + *roeren* stir]

up-roar-i-ous (up-rôr′ē-əs, -rō′·rē-) *adj.* **1** Accompanied by or making uproar. **2** Very loud and boisterous. **3** Provoking loud laughter. —**up-roar′i-ous-ly** *adv.* —**up-roar′ous-ness** *n.*

up-root (up-rōōt′, -rŏŏt′) *v.t.* **1** To tear up by the roots. **2** To destroy utterly; eradicate. —**up-root′er** *n.*

up-set (up-set′) *v.* **-set, -set-ting** *v.t.* **1** To overturn. **2** To throw into confusion or disorder. **3** To disconcert, derange, or disquiet. **4** To defeat (an opponent favored to win): The amateur team *upset* the professionals. —*v.i.* **5** To become overturned. —*adj.* (*also* up′set′) **1** Overturned. **2** Physically ill or mentally disturbed. —*n.* (up′set′) **1** The act of overturning. **2** A physical or emotional disturbance. **3** A defeat of an opponent favored to win. —**up-set′ter** *n.*

up-shot (up′shot′) *n.* The outcome; result.

up-side (up′sīd′) *n.* The upper side or part.

upside down **1** So that the upper part is underneath: to turn a table *upside down.* **2** In or into disorder or confusion: to turn a room *upside down* looking for something.

up-si-lon (yōōp′sə-lon, up′sə-lon) *n.* The twentieth letter in the Greek alphabet (Υ, υ). [< Gk. *u* u + *psilon* simple]

up-stage (up′stāj′) *adj.* **1** Of or pertaining to the back half of a stage. **2** *Informal* Conceited; haughty; snobbish. —*adv.* Toward or at the back half of a stage. —*n.* That part of a stage farthest from the audience. —*v.* (up′stāj′) **-staged, -stag-ing 1** To force (a fellow actor) to face away from the audience by moving or remaining upstage. **2** To try to outdo (someone), as in a professional or social encounter.

up-stairs (up′stârz′) *adj.* Of or on an upper story. —*n.* The part of a building above the ground floor; an upper story or stories. —*adv.* To or on an upper story.

up-stand-ing (up′stan′ding) *adj.* **1** Standing up; erect. **2** Honest, straightforward, etc. —**up-stand′ing-ness** *n.*

up-start (up′stärt′) *n.* A person who has suddenly risen from a humble position to one of consequence; esp., such a person who behaves in a way that is presumptuous, arrogant, etc.

up·state (up′stāt′) *adj.* Of, from, or designating that part of a state lying outside, usu. north, of a principal city. — *n.* The outlying, usu. northern, sections of a state. —*adv.* In or toward the outlying or northern sections of a state. —**up′stat′er** *n.*

up·stream (up′strēm′) *adv.* & *adj.* Toward or at the upper part or source of a stream.

up·sweep (up′swēp′) *n.* **1** A sweeping up or upward. **2** A hairdo in which the hair is piled on the top of the head and held there by pins or combs.

up·swing (up′swing′) *n.* **1** A swinging upward. **2** An increase or improvement.

up·take (up′tāk′) *n.* **1** The act of lifting or taking up. **2** Mental comprehension; understanding.

up·thrust (up′thrust′) *n.* **1** An upward thrust. **2** A sharp upward movement of rock in the earth's crust.

up·tight (up′tīt′) *adj. Slang* Uneasy, anxious, or nervous. Also **up′-tight′, up tight.** —**up′tight′ness** *n.*

up-to-date (up′tə-dāt′) *adj.* **1** Extending to the present; including the latest information, data, etc.: an *up-to-date* census report. **2** Abreast of the latest fashions, ideas, outlook, etc. —**up′-to-date′ness** *n.*

up·town (up′toun′) *adj.* & *adv.* Of, in, to, or toward the upper part of a town or city. —*n.* An uptown area.

up·turn (up′tûrn′, up′tûrn′) *v.t.* To turn up or over. —*n.* (up′tûrn′) A turn upward, as to improved business conditions.

up·ward (up′wərd) *adv.* **1** In or toward a higher place, position, or part. **2** Toward a source or interior part. **3** In the upper parts. **4** To or toward a higher, greater, or better condition. Also **up′wards.** —**upward of** or **upwards of** Higher than or in excess of. —*adj.* Turned, directed toward, or located in a higher place. —**up′ward·ly** *adv.*

u·rae·mi·a (yōō·rē′mē·ə) *n.* UREMIA.

U·ral-Al·ta·ic (yōōr′əl·al·tā′ik) *n.* A family of languages of Europe and N Asia, comprising the Uralic and Altaic subfamilies. —*adj.* Of or pertaining to these languages or the peoples speaking them.

U·ral·ic (yōō·ral′ik) *n.* A family of languages comprising the Finno-Ugric and Samoyedic subfamilies. —*adj.* Of or pertaining to this linguistic family. Also **U·ra·li·an** (yōō·rā′lē·ən).

U·ra·ni·a (yōō·rā′nē·ə) *Gk. Myth.* The Muse of astronomy.

u·ra·ni·um (yōō·rā′nē·əm) *n.* A heavy, radioactive, metallic element (symbol U), found only in combination and in association with radium, used in the generation of atomic energy. [< URANUS]

U·ra·nus (yōōr′ə·nəs, yōōr·ā′nəs) *Gk. Myth.* The son and husband of Gaea (Earth) and father of the Titans, Furies, and Cyclopes. —*n.* The planet of the solar system seventh in distance from the sun. • See PLANET. —**U·ra′ni·an** *adj.*

ur·ban (ûr′bən) *adj.* **1** Of, pertaining to, characteristic of, constituting, or including a city. **2** Living or located in a city or cities. [See URBANE.]

ur·bane (ûr·bān′) *adj.* Characterized by or having refinement, esp. in manner; polite; courteous; suave. [< L *urbs, urbis* a city] —**ur·bane′ly** *adv.* —**ur·bane′ness** *n.*

ur·ban·ism (ûr′bən·iz′əm) *n.* **1** Life in the cities. **2** The study of urban life. **3** The advocacy of living in a city. —**ur′ban·ist** *n.* —**ur′ban·is′tic** *adj.*

ur·ban·ite (ûr′bən·īt) *n.* One who lives in a city.

ur·ban·i·ty (ûr·ban′ə·tē) *n. pl.* **·ties** **1** The character or quality of being urbane. **2** *pl.* Urbane acts or behavior; courtesies, amenities, etc.

ur·ban·i·za·tion (ûr′bə·nə·zā′shən) *n.* **1** The act or process of urbanizing an area or a rural group of people. **2** The quality or state of being urbanized. *Brit. sp.* **·i·sa′tion.**

ur·ban·ize (ûr′bən·īz) *v.t.* **·ized, ·iz·ing 1** To cause (an area) to assume the characteristics of a city. **2** To cause (people) to adopt an urban life style. *Brit. sp.* **·ise.**

ur·ban·ol·o·gy (ûr′bə·nol′ə·jē) *n.* The study of problems peculiar to cities. —**ur′ban·ol′o·gist** *n.*

urban renewal A program for rebuilding or replacing

substandard housing and improving public facilities in distressed urban areas.

urban sprawl The uncontrolled spread of urban housing, shopping centers, etc., into rural or undeveloped areas close to a city.

ur·chin (ûr′chin) *n.* **1** A roguish, mischievous child. **2** A ragged street child. **3** HEDGEHOG. **4** SEA URCHIN. [< L *ericius* hedgehog]

Ur·du (ōōr′dōō, ōōr·dōō′, ûr′dōō) *n.* An Indic language, a variety of Hindi that is the official language of Pakistan and is also spoken by some of the population of India.

-ure *suffix of nouns* **1** The act, process, or result of: *pressure.* **2** The condition of being: *exposure.* **3** The function, rank, or office of: *prefecture.* **4** The means or instrument of: *ligature.* [< L *-ura*]

u·re·a (yōō·rē′ə) *n.* A soluble colorless crystalline compound excreted in urine and also made synthetically; used in the making of plastics. [< L *urina* urine] —**u·re′al** *adj.*

u·re·mi·a (yōō·rē′mē·ə) *n.* A toxic condition of the blood due to the presence of substances ordinarily excreted by the kidneys. —**u·re′mic** *adj.*

u·re·ter (yōō·rē′tər, yōō·rē′-) *n.* The duct by which urine passes from the kidney to the bladder or the cloaca. [< Gk. *ourein* urinate] —**u·re·ter·al** (yōō·rē′tə·rəl), **u·re·ter·ic** (yōōr′ə·ter′ik) *adj.* • See KIDNEY.

u·re·thra (yōō·rē′thrə) *n. pl.* **·thrae** (-thrē), **·thras** The duct by which urine is discharged from the bladder and which, in males, carries the seminal discharge. [< Gk. *ouron* urine] —**u·re′thral** *adj.*

urge (ûrj) *v.* **urged, urg·ing** *v.t.* **1** To drive or force forward. **2** To plead with or entreat earnestly: He *urged* them to accept the plan. **3** To advocate earnestly: to *urge* reform. **4** To move or force to some course or action. —*v.i.* **5** To present or press arguments, claims, etc. **6** To exert an impelling or prompting force. —*n.* **1** A strong impulse to perform a certain act. **2** The act of urging. [< L *urgere* to drive, urge] —**Syn.** *v.* **1** impel, press. **2** exhort, importune.

ur·gen·cy (ûr′jən·sē) *n. pl.* **·cies 1** The quality of being urgent; insistence: the *urgency* of her plea. **2** Something urgent: to prepare for any possible *urgencies.*

ur·gent (ûr′jənt) *adj.* **1** Requiring prompt attention; pressing; imperative. **2** Eagerly importunate or insistent. [< L *urgere* drive] —**ur′gent·ly** *adv.*

-urgy *combining form* Development of or work with a (specified) material or product: *metallurgy.* [< Gk. *ergon* work]

u·ric (yōōr′ik) *adj.* Of, relating to, or derived from urine.

uric acid A white, odorless substance found in small quantity in urine.

u·ri·nal (yōōr′ə·nəl) *n.* **1** A fixture for men's use in urination; also, a place containing such a fixture or fixtures. **2** A receptacle for urine.

u·ri·nal·y·sis (yōōr′ə·nal′ə·sis) *n. pl.* **·ses** (-sēz) Chemical analysis of the urine.

u·ri·nar·y (yōōr′ə·ner′ē) *adj.* Of or pertaining to urine or to the organs concerned in its production and excretion.

u·ri·nate (yōōr′ə·nāt) *v.i.* **·nat·ed, ·nat·ing** To void or pass urine. —**u′ri·na′tion** *n.*

u·rine (yōōr′in) *n.* A usu. fluid substance secreted by the kidneys of vertebrates and some invertebrates and containing nitrogenous and saline wastes. [< L *urina*]

u·ri·no·gen·i·tal (yōōr′ə·nō·jen′ə·təl) *adj.* UROGENITAL.

urn (ûrn) *n.* **1** A vase, usu. having a foot or pedestal, variously used as a receptacle for the ashes of the dead, or ornament, etc. **2** A vase-shaped receptacle having a faucet, designed to make and serve tea, coffee, etc. [< L *urna*]

Urn

uro- *combining form* Urine; pertaining to urine or to the urinary tract: *urology.* [< Gk. *ouron* urine]

u·ro·gen·i·tal (yōōr′ō·jen′ə·təl) *adj.* Of or pertaining to the urinary and genital organs and their functions.

u·rol·o·gy (yŏŏ·rol'ə·jē) *n.* The branch of medicine relating to the urogenital or urinary system. —**u·ro·log·ic** (yŏŏr'·ə·loj'ik) or **-i·cal** *adj.* —**u·rol'o·gist** *n.*

u·ros·co·py (yŏŏ·ros'kə·pē) *n.* Examination of the urine, as for diagnosis. —**u·ro·scop·ic** (yŏŏr'ə·skop'ik) *adj.* —**u·ros'·co·pist** *n.*

Ur·sa Major (ûr'sə) *Astron.* The Great Bear, a large northern constellation containing seven conspicuous stars, including two which point to the polestar. [L]

Ursa Minor *Astron.* The Little Bear, a northern constellation including the polestar. [L]

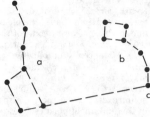

Ursa Major and Ursa Minor
a. Ursa Major. b. Ursa Minor.
c. Polaris.

ur·sine (ûr'sīn, -sin) *adj.* Of, pertaining to, or like a bear. [<L *ursus* bear]

ur·ti·car·i·a (ûr'tə·kâr'ē·ə) *n.* A skin eruption of systemic origin characterized by evanescent wheals and itching; hives. [<L *urtica* nettle] —**ur'ti·car'i·al, ur'ti·car'i·ous** *adj.*

Uru. Uruguay.

U·ru·guay (yŏŏr'ə·gwā, *Sp.* ōō'rōō·gwī) *n.* A republic of SE South America, 72,172 sq. mi., cap. Montevideo. —**U'ru·guay'an** *adj.*, *n.* • See map at ARGENTINA.

us (us) *pron.* The objective case of WE. [<OE *ūs*]

US, U.S. United States.

USA, U.S.A. United States of America; United States Army.

us·a·ble (yŏŏ'zə·bəl) *adj.* 1 Capable of being used. 2 That can be used conveniently. Also **use'a·ble.** —**us'a·ble·ness** *n.* —**us'a·bly** *adv.*

USAF, U.S.A.F. United States Air Force.

us·age (yŏŏ'sij, -zij) *n.* 1 The act or manner of using; treatment. 2 Customary or habitual practice; custom; habit. 3 The accepted and established way of using words, speech patterns, etc.

USCG, U.S.C.G. United States Coast Guard.

use (yŏŏz) *v.* **used, us·ing** *v.t.* 1 To put into service: to *use* a hammer. 2 To borrow; avail oneself of: May I *use* your pen? 3 To put into practice or employ habitually: to *use* diligence in business. 4 To conduct oneself toward; treat: to *use* one badly. 5 To partake of: He does not *use* tobacco. 6 To take advantage of; exploit: to *use* one's friends. 7 To expend, exhaust, or consume: usu. with *up.* —*v.i.* 8 To be accustomed: used in the past tense with an infinitive: We *used* to go to the theater regularly. —*n.* (yŏŏs) 1 The act of using, or the state of being used. 2 Function: He has lost the *use* of his legs. 3 Way or manner of using: to make good *use* of one's time. 4 Habitual practice or employment; custom; usage. 5 The ability or right to use, or the privilege of using. 6 Advantage; benefit; usefulness. 7 The purpose for which something is used. 8 *Law* The benefit or profit of property to which legal title is vested in another in trust for the beneficiary. —**have no use for** 1 To have no need of. 2 To have dislike or contempt for. —**in use** Being used or occupied. —**make use of** To have occasion to use; use. —**put to use** To utilize; employ. [<L *usus,* pp. of *uti* to use] —**us'er** *n.*

used (yŏŏzd) *adj.* 1 That has been employed in some way. 2 SECONDHAND. 3 Accustomed; experienced. —**used to** (yŏŏst) Accustomed to; habituated.

use·ful (yŏŏs'fəl) *adj.* Capable of being used; serviceable; helpful. —**use'ful·ly** *adv.* —**use'ful·ness** *n.*

use·less (yŏŏs'lis) *adj.* Being of or having no use; serving no function. —**use'less·ly** *adv.* —**use'less·ness** *n.*

us·er-friend·ly (yŏŏ'zər·frend'lē) *adj.* of a computer, program, software, etc., easy to use.

ush·er (ush'ər) *n.* 1 One who acts as doorkeeper, as of a court. 2 One who conducts persons to seats, etc., as in a church or theater. —*v.t.* 1 To act as an usher to; escort; conduct. 2 To precede as a harbinger; be a forerunner of. [<L *ostiarius* doorkeeper]

USM, U.S.M. United States Mail; United States Mint.

USMA, U.S.M.A. United States Military Academy.

USMC, U.S.M.C. United States Marine Corps; United States Maritime Commission.

USN, U.S.N. United States Navy.

USNA, U.S.N.A. United States Naval Academy.

USNG, U.S.N.G. United States National Guard.

USNR, U.S.N.R. United States Naval Reserve.

USO, U.S.O. United Service Organizations.

USS United States Ship, Steamer, or Steamship.

U.S.S. United States Senate.

USSR, U.S.S.R. Union of Soviet Socialist Republics.

usu. usual; usually.

u·su·al (yŏŏ'zhŏŏ·əl) *adj.* Such as occurs in the ordinary course of events; customary; common. [<L *usus* use] —**u'su·al·ly** *adv.* —**u'su·al·ness** *n.* —**Syn.** everyday, general, ordinary, prevalent.

u·su·fruct (yŏŏ'zə·frukt, yŏŏ'sə-) *n.* *Law* The right of using the fruits or profits of another's property. [<L *usus et fructus* use and fruit]

u·su·rer (yŏŏ'zhər·ər) *n.* One who practices usury. [<L *usura* use, usury]

u·su·ri·ous (yŏŏ·zhŏŏr'ē·əs) *adj.* 1 Practicing usury. 2 Of, relating to, or having the nature of usury. —**u·su'ri·ous·ly** *adv.* —**u·su'ri·ous·ness** *n.*

u·surp (yŏŏ·sûrp', -zûrp') *v.t.* To seize and hold (an office, rights, powers, etc.) without right or legal authority; take possesion of by force. [<L *usurpare* make use of, usurp]

u·sur·pa·tion (yŏŏ'sər·pā'shən, -zər-) *n.* The act of usurping, esp. the unlawful seizure of sovereign power.

u·su·ry (yŏŏ'zhər·ē) *n. pl.* **·ries** 1 The act or practice of lending money and charging interest that is excessive or unlawfully high. 2 Interest that is excessive or unlawfully high. [<L *usura* < *usus,* pp. of *uti* to use]

UT Utah (P.O. abbr.).

Ut. Utah.

u·ten·sil (yŏŏ·ten'səl) *n.* A vessel, tool, implement, etc., serving a useful purpose, esp. for domestic or farming use. [<L *utensilis* fit for use]

u·ter·ine (yŏŏ'tər·īn, -in) *adj.* 1 Of or pertaining to the uterus. 2 Born of the same mother, but having a different father. [<LL *uterinus* born of the same mother]

u·ter·us (yŏŏ'tər·əs) *n. pl.* **u·ter·i** (yŏŏ'tər·ī), **u·ter·us·es** The organ of a female mammal in which the fertilized ovum is deposited and develops until birth; womb. [L] • See OVARY.

u·til·i·tar·i·an (yŏŏ·til'ə·târ'ē·ən) *adj.* 1 Of or pertaining to utility; esp., placing utility above beauty, the amenities of life, etc. 2 Of, pertaining to, or advocating utilitarianism. —*n.* An advocate of utilitarianism.

u·til·i·tar·i·an·ism (yŏŏ·til'ə·târ'ē·ən·iz'əm) *n.* 1 The doctrine that holds usefulness to be the end and criterion of action. 2 The doctrine that the greatest happiness of the greatest number should be the sole end and criterion of all action.

u·til·i·ty (yŏŏ·til'ə·tē) *n. pl.* **·ties** 1 Fitness for some desirable, practical purpose; usefulness. 2 Fitness to supply the needs of people. 3 Something useful. 4 A public service, as a telephone system, gas, water, etc. 5 A company that provides such a service. [<L *utilis* useful < *uti* use]

u·til·ize (yŏŏ'təl·īz) *v.t.* **·ized, ·iz·ing** To make use of. *Brit. sp.* **u·til·ise.** —**u'til·i·za'tion, u'til·iz'er** *n.*

ut·most (ut'mōst) *adj.* 1 Of the highest or greatest degree. 2 Being at the farthest limit or most distant point; most remote; extreme. —*n.* The most possible. [<OE *ūtmost*]

U·to-Az·tec·an (yŏŏ'tō·az'tek·ən) *n.* One of the chief linguistic stocks of North American Indians formerly occupying NW and SW U.S., Mexico, and Central America. —*adj.* Of or pertaining to this linguistic stock.

u·to·pi·a (yŏŏ·tō'pē·ə) *n.* 1 Any state, condition, or place of ideal perfection. 2 A visionary, impractical scheme for social improvement. [<UTOPIA] —**u·to'pi·an** *adj.*, *n.* —**u·to'·pi·an·ism** *n.*

U·to·pi·a (yŏŏ·tō'pē·ə) *n.* An imaginary island described as the seat of a perfect social and political life in the book by Sir Thomas More, published in 1516. [<Gk. *ou* not + *topos* a place] —**U·to'pi·an** *adj.*, *n.*

u·tri·cle (yŏŏ'tri·kəl) *n.* A small sac or cavity. [<L *uter* skin bag] —**u·tric·u·lar** (yŏŏ·trik'yə·lər) *adj.*

ut·ter[1] (ut'ər) *v.t.* 1 To say, express, give out, or send forth, as in words or sounds. **2** To put in circulation; esp., to deliver or offer (something forged or counterfeit). [< ME *out* say, speak out] —**ut′ter·er** *n.*

ut·ter² (ut′ər) *adj.* **1** Complete; absolute; total: *utter* misery. **2** Unqualified; final: an *utter* denial. [< OE *ūttra*, orig. compar. of *ūt* out] —**ut′ter·ly** *adv.*

ut·ter·ance (ut′ər·əns) *n.* **1** The act of uttering. **2** A manner of speaking. **3** A thing uttered.

ut·ter·most (ut′ər·mōst′) *adj. & n.* UTMOST.

U-turn (yōō′tûrn′) *n.* A complete turn which reverses the direction of movement, as of a vehicle on a road.

u·vu·la (yōō′vyə·lə) *n. pl.* **·las** or **·lae** (-lē) The pendent fleshy portion of the soft palate in the back of the mouth. [LL, dim. of *uva* grape] • See MOUTH.

u·vu·lar (yōō′vyə·lər) *adj.* **1** Pertaining to the uvula. **2** *Phonet.* Articulated with the back of the tongue near the uvula. —*n. Phonet.* A uvular sound.

ux. wife (L *uxor*).

ux·o·ri·ous (uk·sôr′ē·əs, -sō′rē-, ug·zôr′ē-, -zō′rē-) *adj.* Excessively devoted to or dominated by one's wife. [< L *uxor* wife] —**ux·o′ri·ous·ly** *adv.* —**ux·o′ri·ous·ness** *n.*

Uz·bek (ōōz′bek, uz′-) *n.* **1** A member of a Turkic people living in the Uzbek S.S.R. **2** The Turkic language of the Uzbeks.

V

V,v (vē) *n. pl.* **V's, v's, Vs, vs** (vēz) **1** The 22nd letter of the English alphabet. **2** Any spoken sound representing the letter *V* or *v.* **3** Something shaped like a V. **4** In Roman notation, the symbol for five. —*adj.* Shaped like a V.

V vanadium; vector; velocity; victory; volume.

V.,v. volt; volume.

v. valve; verb; verse; version; versus; vicar; village; vocative; voice; voltage; von.

VA Virginia (P.O. abbr.).

VA, V.A. Veterans Administration.

Va. Virginia.

vacan·cy (vā′kən·sē) *n. pl.* **·cies 1** The state of being vacant; emptiness. **2** An apartment, room, etc., that is available for rent. **3** An unoccupied post, place, or office.

va·cant (vā′kənt) *adj.* **1** Containing or holding nothing; empty. **2** Not lived in or occupied. **3** Not being used; free: a *vacant* hour. **4** Being or appearing without intelligence: a *vacant* stare. **5** Having no incumbent, officer, or possessor. [< L *vacans* pr.p. of *vacare* be empty] —**va′cant·ly** *adv.* —**va′cant·ness** *n.* —**Syn. 1** blank, void. **4** vapid, dull, vacuous, witless, obtuse, blank.

va·cate (vā′kāt, vā·kāt′) *v.* **·cat·ed, ·cat·ing** *v.t.* **1** To make vacant, as a dwelling, position, etc. **2** To set aside; annul. —*v.i.* **3** To leave an office, dwelling, place, etc. **4** *Informal* To go away; leave. [< L *vacare* be empty]

va·ca·tion (vā·kā′shən) *n.* A time set aside from work, study, etc., for recreation or rest; a holiday. —*v.i.* To take a vacation. [See VACATE.] —**va·ca′tion·er, va·ca′tion·ist** *n.*

vac·ci·nate (vak′sə·nāt) *v.* **·nat·ed, ·nat·ing** *v.t.* **1** To inoculate with a vaccine as a preventive or therapeutic measure; esp., to inoculate against smallpox. —*v.i.* **2** To perform the act of vaccination. —**vac′ci·na′tor** *n.*

vac·ci·na·tion (vak′sə·nā′shən) *n.* **1** The act or process of vaccinating. **2** A scar produced at the site of inoculation with a vaccine.

vac·cine (vak·sēn′, vak′sēn) *n.* **1** The virus of cowpox, as prepared for inoculation to produce immunity to smallpox. **2** Any modified virus or bacterium used to give immunity against a specific disease. [< L *vaccinus* pertaining to a cow] —**vac′ci·nal** (-sə·nəl) *adj.*

vac·il·late (vas′ə·lāt) *v.i.* **·lat·ed, ·lat·ing 1** To move one way and the other; waver. **2** To waver in mind; be irresolute. [< L *vacillare* waver] —**vac′il·la′tion** *n.* —**vac′il·la·to′ry** (-ə·lə·tô′rē, -tō′rē) *adj.* —**Syn. 1** fluctuate, oscillate, sway.

va·cu·i·ty (va·kyōō′ə·tē) *n. pl.* **·ties 1** The state of being a vacuum; emptiness. **2** Vacant space; a void. **3** Lack of intelligence; stupidity. **4** An inane or stupid thing, statement, etc. [< L *vacuus* empty]

vac·u·ole (vak′yōō·ōl) *n.* A small cavity within a cell containing air or fluid or food particles. [< L *vacuus* empty]

vac·u·ous (vak′yōō·əs) *adj.* **1** Having no contents; empty. **2** Lacking intelligence; blank. [< L *vacuus*] —**vac′u·ous·ly** *adv.* —**vac′u·ous·ness** *n.*

vac·u·um (vak′yōō·əm, -yōōm) *n. pl.* **·u·ums** or **·u·a** (-yōō·ə) **1** *Physics* A space devoid, or nearly devoid, of matter. **2** A reduction of the pressure in a space below atmospheric pressure. **3** A void; an empty feeling. **4** *Informal* A vacuum cleaner. —*v.t. & v.i. Informal* To clean with a vacuum cleaner. [L, neut. of *vacuus* empty]

vacuum bottle THERMOS.

vacuum cleaner A machine for cleaning floors, carpets, etc., by means of suction.

vacuum pump A pump designed to remove gas or air from a sealed space.

vacuum tube *Electronics* An electron tube containing a negligible amount of gas.

va·de me·cum (vā′dē mē′kəm) Anything carried for constant use, as a guidebook, manual, etc. [L, go with me]

vag·a·bond (vag′ə·bond) *n.* **1** One who wanders from place to place without visible means of support; a tramp. **2** A shiftless, irresponsible person. —*adj.* **1** Wandering; nomadic. **2** Having no definite residence; irresponsible. **3** Driven to and fro; aimless. [< L *vagus* wandering] —**vag′a·bond′age, vag′a·bond′ism** *n.*

va·gar·y (vā′gə·rē, və·gâr′ē) *n. pl.* **·gar·ies** A wild fancy; extravagant notion. [< L *vagari* wander]

va·gi·na (və·jī′nə) *n. pl.* **·nas** or **·nae** (-nē) **1** The canal leading from the external genital orifice in female mammals to the uterus. **2** A sheath or sheathlike covering. [L, a sheath] —**vag·i·nal** (vaj′ə·nəl) *adj.*

va·gran·cy (vā′grən·sē) *n. pl.* **·cies 1** The condition of being a vagrant. **2** The offense of being a vagrant: arrested for *vagrancy.*

va·grant (vā′grənt) *n.* A person who wanders from place to place without a settled home or job and who exists usu. by begging or stealing; a tramp. —*adj.* **1** Wandering about aimlessly; wayward. **2** Pertaining to or characteristic of a vagrant. [< OF *wacrer* to walk, wander] —**va′grant·ly** *adv.* —**va′grant·ness** *n.*

vague (vāg) *adj.* **vagu·er, vagu·est 1** Lacking definiteness; not clearly stated: *vague* rumors; *vague* promises. **2** Indistinct; hard to perceive: *vague* shapes in the fog. **3** Not thinking or expressing oneself clearly. [< L *vagus* wandering] —**vague′ly** *adv.* —**vague′ness** *n.*

va·gus (vā′gəs) *n. pl.* **·gi** (-jī) *Anat.* Either of the pair of cranial nerves sending branches to the lungs, heart, stomach, and most of the abdominal viscera. Also **vagus nerve.** [L, wandering]

vain (vān) *adj.* **1** Having or showing excessive pride in oneself; conceited. **2** Unproductive; useless: *vain* efforts. **3** Without substantial foundation; unreal. —**in vain 1** To no purpose; without effect. **2** Irreverently: to take the Lord's name *in vain.* [< L *vanus* empty] —**vain′ly** *adv.* —**vain′ness** *n.* —**Syn. 1** boastful, egotistical, narcissistic.

vain·glo·ry (vān′glôr′ē, -glōr-, vān·glôr′ē) *n.* **1** Excessive or groundless vanity; boastfulness. **2** Empty, showy pomp. [< Med. L *vana gloria* empty pomp, show] —**vain·glo′ri·ous** *adj.* —**vain·glo′ri·ous·ly** *adv.* —**vain·glo′ri·ous·ness** *n.*

val·ance (val′əns, vā′ləns) *n.* **1** A drapery hanging from the tester of a bedstead. **2** A short, full drapery across the top of a window. [Prob. < OF *avaler* descend] —**val′anced** *adj.* • See CANOPY.

---

add, āce, câre, pälm; end, ēven; it, īce; odd, ōpen, ôrder; tōōk, pōōl; up, bûrn; ə = *a* in *above, u* in *focus;* yōō = *u* in *fuse;* oil; pout; check; go; ring; thin; <u>th</u>is; zh, *vision.* < derived from; ? origin uncertain or unknown.

vale[1] (vāl) n. VALLEY. [< L vallis]

va·le[2] (vä′lē) interj. Farewell. [L, lit., be in good health]

val·e·dic·tion (val′ə-dik′shən) n. 1 A bidding farewell. 2 VALEDICTORY. [< L valedicere say farewell]

val·e·dic·to·ri·an (val′ə-dik-tôr′ē-ən, -tō′rē-) n. A student, usu. the highest in scholastic rank, who delivers a valedictory at the graduating exercises of an educational institution.

val·e·dic·to·ry (val′ə-dik′tər-ē) adj. Pertaining to a leave-taking. —n. pl. ·ries A parting address, as by a member (ordinarily the first in rank) of a graduating class.

va·lence (vā′ləns) n. Chem. The combining capacity of an atom or radical as measured by the number of electrons gained or lost or shared in forming a bond with another atom or radical. [< L valens, pr.p. of valere be well, be strong]

val·en·tine (val′ən-tīn) n. 1 A card or small gift sent as a token of affection on Valentine's Day. 2 A sweetheart.

Valentine's Day February 14, a day observed in honor of St. Valentine, and on which valentines are sent to sweethearts, etc.

va·le·ri·an (və-lir′ē-ən) n. 1 Any of various plants with small pink or white flowers and a strong odor. 2 A sedative derived from the roots of some of these plants. [< Med. L valeriana]

val·et (val′it, val′ā, val·ā′) n. 1 A man's personal servant. 2 A manservant in a hotel who cleans and presses clothes. —v.t. & v.i. To act as a valet. [F < OF vaslet, varlet, dim. of vasal vassal]

val·e·tu·di·nar·i·an (val′ə·tyōō′də-nâr′ē-ən) n. 1 A chronic invalid. 2 A person unduly concerned about his health. —adj. 1 Infirm; ailing. 2 Unduly concerned about one's health. [< L valetudo, health, ill health < valere be well] —val′e·tu′di·nar′i·an·ism n.

Val·hal·la (val-hal′ə) n. Norse Myth. The great hall in which the souls of heroes, borne by the Valkyries, are received and feasted by Odin.

val·iant (val′yənt) adj. 1 Strong and intrepid; powerful and courageous. 2 Performed with valor; heroic. [< OF valoir be strong] —val′iant·ly adv. —val′i·an·cy or val′i·ance, val′iant·ness n.

val·id (val′id) adj. 1 Based on facts or evidence; sound: a valid argument. 2 Legally binding: a valid will. [< L validus powerful] —val′id·ly adv. —va·lid·i·ty (və-lid′ə-tē), val′id·ness n.

val·i·date (val′ə-dāt) v.t. ·dat·ed, ·dat·ing 1 To confirm by facts or authority. 2 To declare legally valid; legalize. —val′i·da′tion n.

va·lise (və-lēs′) n. A traveling bag; suitcase. [< Ital. valigia]

Val·kyr·ie (val-kir′ē, val′kir-ē) n. pl. ·ky·ries or ·ky·rie Norse Myth. One of the maidens who ride through the air and choose heroes from among those slain in battle, and carry them to Valhalla. Also Val′kyr (-kir). —Val·kyr′i·an adj.

val·ley (val′ē) n. 1 A long, wide area drained by a large river system: the Hudson valley. 2 Low land lying between mountains or hills. 3 Any hollow or depression shaped like a valley. [< L vallis]

val·or (val′ər) n. Marked courage; personal heroism; bravery. Brit. sp. val′our. [< L valere be strong] —val′or·ous adj. —val′or·ous·ly adv. —val′or·ous·ness n.

val·or·i·za·tion (val′ər-ə-zā′shən, -ī-zā′-) n. The maintenance by governmental action of an artificial price for any product. [< Pg. valor value] —val′or·ize (val′ə-rīz) v.t.

val·u·a·ble (val′yōō-ə-bəl, val′yə-bəl) adj. 1 Having financial worth, price, or value. 2 Very costly. 3 Worthy; estimable: a valuable friend. —n. Usu. pl. An article of value, as a piece of jewelry. —val′u·a·ble·ness n. —val′u·a·bly adv.

val·u·a·tion (val′yōō-ā′shən) n. 1 The act of estimating the value of something; evaluation. 2 Estimated value; appraisement. —val′u·a′tion·al adj.

val·ue (val′yōō) n. 1 The desirability or worth of a thing; merit: the value of self-discipline. 2 Something regarded as desirable, worthy, or right, as a belief or ideal. 3 Worth in money; market price. 4 A bargain. 5 Purchasing power: a decline in the value of the dollar. 6 Exact meaning: the value of a word. 7 Music The relative length of a tone. 8 Math. The number assigned to or represented by a symbol or expression. 9 In art, the relative lightness or darkness of a color. 10 The relation, as of light and shade, of one part to another in a work of art. —v.t. ·ued, ·u·ing 1 To assess; appraise. 2 To regard highly; prize. 3 To place a relative estimate of value upon: to value health above all else. [< L valere] —val′u·er n.

val·ue-add·ed tax (val′yōō·ad′id) A tax levied on each stage of a product's manufacture and marketing, from the raw material to the final retailer, the ultimate burden being placed on the consumer in the form of higher prices.

val·ued (val′yōōd) adj. 1 Highly esteemed: a valued friend. 2 Having a specified value: valued at ten dollars.

val·ue·less (val′yōō-lis) adj. Having no value; worthless. —val′ue·less·ness n.

valve (valv) n. 1 Mech. Any device used to block, direct, or otherwise control motion of a fluid. 2 Anat. A membranous structure inside a vessel or other organ, allowing fluid to flow in one direction only. 3 Zool. One of the parts of a shell, as of a clam, etc. 4 Bot. One of the parts into which a seed capsule splits. —v.t. valved, valv·ing To control the flow of by means of a valve. [< L valva leaf of a door]

val·vu·lar (val′vyə-lər) adj. 1 Pertaining to valves, as of the heart. 2 Having valves. 3 Having the form of a valve.

Gate valve in closed position (cross section)

va·moose (va-mōōs′) v.t. & v.i. ·moosed, ·moos·ing Slang To leave or depart hastily. Also va·mose′ (-mōs′) [< Sp. vamos let us go]

vamp[1] (vamp) n. 1 The piece of leather forming the upper front part of a boot or shoe. • See SHOE. 2 Something added to give an old thing a new appearance. —v.t. 1 To provide with a vamp. 2 To repair or patch. [< OF avant before + pied foot] —vamp′er n.

vamp[2] (vamp) Slang n. A seductive woman who entices and exploits men. —v.t. & v.i. To seduce (a man) by acting as a vamp. [Short for VAMPIRE]

vam·pire (vam′pīr) n. 1 In folklore, a reanimated corpse that rises from its grave at night to suck the blood of persons who are asleep. 2 A person who preys upon those of the opposite sex; esp. a woman who degrades or impoverishes her lover. 3 A bat of tropical America that drinks the blood of mammals: also vampire bat. 4 An insect- or fruit-eating bat mistakenly thought to suck blood: also false vampire. [< Slavic] —vam′pir·ism n.

van[1] (van) n. 1 A large covered wagon or truck for transporting furniture, household goods, etc. 2 Brit. A closed railway car for luggage, etc. [Short for CARAVAN]

van[2] (van) n. VANGUARD. [Short for VANGUARD]

va·na·di·um (və-nā′dē-əm) n. A rare, silver-white metallic element (symbol V), used to produce vanadium steel, a tough, resilient alloy. [L < ON Vanadīs, a name of the Norse goddess Freya]

Van Al·len belt (van al′ən) An extensive region of intense radiation consisting of charged atomic particles trapped by the earth's magnetic field and surrounding the earth in inner and outer belts. [< J. A. Van Allen, 1914–, U.S. physicist]

van·dal (van′dəl) n. One who engages in vandalism. [< VANDAL]

Van·dal (van′dəl) n. A member of a Germanic people that laid waste to Gaul, Spain, and North Africa in the fifth century and conquered Rome in 455.

van·dal·ism (van′dəl-iz′əm) n. Willful destruction or defacement of public or private property.

Van·dyke beard (van·dīk′) A small pointed beard. [< Anthony Van Dyck, 1599–1641, Flemish painter]

vane (vān) n. 1 A thin plate, pivoted on a vertical rod, to indicate the direction of the wind; a weathercock. 2 An arm or blade, as of a windmill, propeller, projectile, turbine, etc. 3 The web, or flat portion, of a feather. [< OE fana a flag] —vaned (vānd) adj.

Windmill vanes

van·guard (van'gärd) *n.* **1** The forward part of an advancing army. **2** The foremost position in a movement, trend, etc. **3** The leaders of a movement, trend, etc. [< OF *avant* before + *garde* guard]

va·nil·la (və·nil'ə) *n.* **1** Any of a genus of tall climbing orchids of tropical America. **2** The long seed capsule of one species: also **vanilla bean. 3** A flavoring extracted from these capsules or made synthetically. [< Sp. *vaina* sheath, pod] —**va·nil'lic** *adj.*

va·nil·lin (və·nil'in) *n.* The organic compound which gives vanilla flavoring its distinct odor and taste.

van·ish (van'ish) *v.i.* **1** To disappear; fade away. **2** To pass out of existence. [< L *evanescere* fade away] —**van'ish·er** *n.*

Vanilla
a. flower. b. bean.
c. pod.

vanishing point 1 In perspective, the point at which receding parallel lines appear to meet. • See PERSPECTIVE. **2** The point at which something approaches an end.

van·i·ty (van'ə·tē) *n. pl.* **·ties 1** Excessive pride in one's talents, looks, possessions, etc. **2** Worthlessness; futility. **3** Something that is worthless or futile. **4** A low table with an attached mirror, for use while dressing the hair or putting on makeup. **5** VANITY CASE. [< L *vanus* empty, vain]

vanity case A small case holding face powder, rouge, puff, mirror, etc. Also **vanity box.**

van·quish (vang'kwish, van'-) *v.t.* **1** To defeat in battle; conquer. **2** To suppress or overcome (a feeling): to *vanquish* fear. **3** To defeat in any encounter. [< L *vincere*] —**van'quish·er van'quish·ment** *n.* —**Syn. 1** beat, overcome, overpower, overwhelm, upset.

van·tage (van'tij) *n.* **1** Superiority, as over a competitor; advantage. **2** A position, place, situation, etc., that gives superiority or an advantage. [< OF *avantage* advantage]

vantage ground A position or condition which gives one an advantage.

van·ward (van'wərd) *adj. & adv.* Toward or in the front.

vap·id (vap'id, vā'pəd) *adj.* **1** Having lost sparkle and flavor. **2** Flat; insipid. [< L *vapidus* insipid] —**va·pid·i·ty** (və·pid'ə·tē), **vap'id·ness** *n.* —**vap'id·ly** *adv.*

va·por (vā'pər) *n.* **1** Moisture in the air; esp. visible floating moisture, as light mist. **2** Any cloudy substance in the air, as smoke. **3** The gaseous phase of any substance. **4** Something that is fleeting and unsubstantial. **5** A remedial agent applied by inhalation. —**the vapors** *Archaic* Depression of spirits. —*v.t.* **1** VAPORIZE. —*v.i.* **2** To emit vapor. **3** To pass off in vapor; evaporate. *Brit. sp.* **va'·pour.** [< L *vapor* steam] —**va'por·er** *n.*

va·por·ize (vā'pə·rīz) *v.t. & v.i.* **·ized, ·iz·ing** To convert or be converted into vapor. —**va'por·i·za'tion** *n.*

va·por·iz·er (vā'pə·rī'zər) *n.* **1** One who or that which vaporizes. **2** A device for boiling water or a medicated liquid to form a vapor for inhalation.

va·por·ous (vā'pər·əs) *adj.* **1** Of or like vapor; misty. **2** Emitting or forming vapor. **3** Whimsical; fanciful. —**va·por·os·i·ty** (vā'pə·ros'ə·tē), **va'por·ous·ness** *n.*

va·que·ro (vä·kā'rō) *n. pl.* **·ros** (-rōz, *Sp.* -rōs) A herdsman; cowboy. [< Sp. *vaca* cow]

var. variant; variation; variety; various.

var·i·a·ble (vâr'ē·ə·bəl, var'-) *adj.* **1** Having the capacity of varying; alterable. **2** Having a tendency to change; not constant. **3** Having no definite value as regards quantity. **4** *Biol.* Prone to deviate from a type. —*n.* **1** That which is liable to change. **2** *Math.* **a** A quantity that may be equal to any one of a specified set of numbers. **b** A symbol representing such a quantity. **3** A shifting wind. —**var'i·a·bil'i·ty, var'i·a·ble·ness** *n.* —**var'i·a·bly** *adv.* —**Syn.** *adj.* **2** fluctuating, unstable, unsteady, wavering.

variable zone TEMPERATE ZONE.

var·i·ance (vâr'ē·əns, var'-) *n.* **1** The act of varying or the state of being varied. **2** Discrepancy; difference. **3** A dispute; quarrel. **4** A license or official permission to do something contrary to official regulations. —**at variance** Not in agreement; disagreeing.

var·i·ant (vâr'ē·ənt, var'-) *adj.* **1** Varying; differing, esp. differing from a standard or type. **2** *Archaic* Variable; changeable. —*n.* **1** A person or thing that differs from another in form only. **2** One of several different spellings, pronunciations, or forms of the same word.

var·i·a·tion (vâr'ē·ā'shən, var'-) *n.* **1** The act or process of varying; modification. **2** The extent to which a thing varies. **3** A thing changed in form from others of the same type. **4** *Music* A repetition of a theme or melody with changes in key, rhythm, harmony, etc. **5** *Biol.* Deviation from the typical structure or function. —**var'i·a'tion·al** *adj.*

var·i·col·ored (vâr'i·kul'ərd, var'-) *adj.* Variegated in color; parti-colored.

var·i·cose (var'ə·kōs) *adj.* **1** Abnormally dilated, as veins. **2** Having or resulting from varicose veins: *varicose* ulcer. [< L < *varix* a varicose vein] —**var'i·cos'i·ty** (-kos'ə·tē) *n.*

var·ied (vâr'ēd, var'-) *adj.* **1** Consisting of diverse sorts; assorted. **2** Altered; changed. —**var'ied·ly** *adv.*

var·i·e·gate (vâr'ē·ə·gāt', var'-) *v.t.* **·gat·ed, ·gat·ing 1** To mark with different colors; dapple; streak. **2** To make varied; diversify. —*adj.* VARIEGATED. [< L *varius* various + *agere* to drive, do] —**var'i·e·ga'tion** *n.*

var·i·e·gat·ed (vâr'ē·ə·gā'tid, var'-) *adj.* **1** Varied in color, as with streaks or blotches. **2** Having or exhibiting different forms, styles, or varieties.

va·ri·e·ty (və·rī'ə·tē) *n. pl.* **·ties 1** Absence of sameness or monotony; diversity; variation; difference. **2** Sort; kind: a sweet *variety* of pickle. **3** A collection of diverse kinds; assortment: a *variety* of flowers. **4** A subdivision of a species. **5** Vaudeville: also **variety show.** [< L *varius* various]

va·ri·o·la (ver·ē·ō'lə, və·rī'ə·lə) *n.* SMALLPOX. [< L *varius* speckled] —**va·ri'o·lar** *adj.*

var·i·o·rum (vâr'ē·ôr'əm, -ō'rəm, var'-) *n.* **1** An edition of a work containing various versions of the text. **2** An edition of a work with notes by different critics or editors. —*adj.* Of or pertaining to such an edition. [< L *(cum notis) variorum* (with the notes) of various persons]

var·i·ous (vâr'ē·əs, var'-) *adj.* **1** Characteristically different from one another; diverse: *various* customs. **2** Being more than one and easily distinguishable; several: *various* friends. **3** Separate; particular; identifiable: He shook hands with *various* people. **4** Differing in nature or appearance; dissimilar. **5** Versatile; multifaceted. [< L *varius*] —**var'i·ous·ly** *adv.* —**var'i·ous·ness** *n.*

var·let (vär'lit) *n. Archaic* A scoundrel. [OF, a groom] —**var'let·ry** *n.*

var·mint (vär'mənt) *n. Regional* Any person or animal considered as troublesome, esp. vermin. [Alter. of VERMIN]

var·nish (vär'nish) *n.* **1** A solution of certain gums or resins in alcohol, linseed oil, etc., used to produce a shining, transparent coat on a surface. **2** The glossy, hard finish made by this solution when dry. **3** Any substance or finish resembling varnish. **4** Outward show; deceptive appearance. —*v.t.* **1** To cover with varnish. **2** To give a glossy appearance to. **3** To hide by a deceptive appearance; gloss over. [< Med. L *vernicium*, a kind of resin] —**var'nish·er** *n.*

var·si·ty (vär'sə·tē) *n. pl.* **·ties** *Informal* **1** *Brit.* UNIVERSITY. **2** The team that represents a university, college, or school in any competition. [Alter. of UNIVERSITY]

var·y (vâr'ē, var'-) *v.* **var·ied, var·y·ing** *v.t.* **1** To change the form, nature, substance, etc., of; modify. **2** To cause to be different from one another. **3** To diversify. **4** *Music* To systematically alter (a melody or other thematic element). —*v.i.* **5** To become changed in form, substance, etc. **6** To differ. **7** To deviate; depart: with *from.* **8** To alternate. **9** *Math.* To be subject to change. **10** *Biol.* To show variation. [< L *varius* various, diverse] —**var'y·ing·ly** *adv.*

vas (vas) *n. pl.* **va·sa** (vā'sə) *Biol.* A vessel or duct. [L, vessel, dish] —**va'sal** *adj.*

vas·cu·lar (vas'kyə·lər) *adj.* Of, pertaining to, or having vessels or ducts, as blood vessels, phloem tissue, etc. [< L *vasculum*, dim. of *vas* vessel] —**vas'cu·lar'i·ty** (-lar'ə·tē) *n.* —**vas'cu·lar·ly** *adv.*

vas def·er·ens (vas def′ər·ənz) The duct by which spermatozoa pass from the testicle to the penis. [<L *vas* vessel + *deferens* leading down]

vase (vās, vāz, väz) *n.* An urnlike vessel used as an ornament or for holding flowers. [<L *vas* vessel]

va·sec·to·my (və·sek′tə·mē) *n. pl.* **·to·mies** Surgical removal of a portion of the vas deferens, thus producing sterilization by preventing semen from reaching the seminal vesicles. [<VAS(O)- + -ECTOMY]

Vas·e·line (vas′ə·lēn, vas·ə·lēn′) *n.* PETROLATUM: a trade name.

vaso- *combining form* A vessel, esp. a blood vessel: *vaso-motor*. [<L *vas* a vessel]

vas·o·mo·tor (vas′ō·mō′tər) *adj.* Producing contraction or dilation of blood vessels.

vas·sal (vas′əl) *n.* 1 In feudalism, a man who held land from a superior lord to whom he rendered, in return, military or other service. 2 A person who is in a position that is subordinate, lowly, servile, slavish, etc. —*adj.* Of or pertaining to a vassal. [<LL *vassus* a servant]

vas·sal·age (vas′əl·ij) *n.* 1 The condition, duties, and obligations of a vassal. 2 A position of servitude, dependence, or subjection.

vast (vast, väst) *adj.* 1 Of great extent; immense: a *vast* desert. 2 Very great in number, quantity, or amount. 3 Very great in degree, intensity, or importance. [<L, waste, empty, vast] —**vast′ly** *adv.* —**vast′ness** *n.* —**Syn.** 1, 2 enormous, extensive, huge, tremendous.

vat (vat) *n.* A large vessel, tub, or cistern, esp. for holding liquids during some process, as heating, fermenting, etc. —*v.t.* **vat·ted, vat·ting** To treat in a vat. [<OE *fæt*]

VAT value-added tax.

Vat. Vatican.

vat dye Any of a class of fast dyes in which the color develops, as by oxidation in air, subsequent to treatment of the fabric in a usu. colorless dye solution. —**vat′dyed′** *adj.*

Vat·i·can (vat′ə·kən) *n.* 1 The papal palace in Vatican City, Rome. 2 The papal government.

Vatican City A sovereign papal state included in Rome. 108.7 acres.

vau·de·ville (vô′də·vil, vōd′vil) *n.* A theatrical entertainment consisting of short dramatic sketches, songs, dances, acrobatic feats, etc.; a variety show. [<F *(chanson de) Vau de Vire* (song of) the valley of the Vire river (in Normandy)]

vault¹ (vôlt) *n.* 1 An arched roof or ceiling, usu. of masonry. 2 Any vaultlike covering, as the sky. An arched passage or room. 4 An underground room or compartment for storage. 5 A place for keeping valuables: bank *vault*. 6 A burial chamber.—

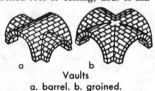

Vaults
a. barrel. b. groined.

v.t. 1 To cover with or as with a vault. 2 To construct in the form of a vault. [<OF *volte, vaute*]

vault² (vôlt) *v.i.* 1 To leap, as over an object, by the use of one's hands on the object or by the use of a pole. —*v.t.* 2 To leap over. —*n.* 1 The act of vaulting. 2 A leap. [<OF *volter* to leap, gambol] —**vault′er** *n.*

vault·ing¹ (vôl′ting) *n.* The construction that forms a vault.

vault·ing² (vôl′ting) *adj.* 1 That leaps or leaps over. 2 Unduly confident or presumptuous. 3 Used for leaping and leaping over.

vaunt (vônt, vänt) *v.i.* 1 To boast. —*v.t.* 2 To boast of. —*n.* A brag or boast. [<LL *vanitare* brag<L *vanus* empty, vain]

vb. verb; verbal.

V.C. Victoria Cross; Vietcong.

VCR Videocassette recorder, a recorder utilizing videotape to record programs, movies, etc., for replay by means of a television set.

VD, V.D., v.d. venereal disease.

VDT Video (or visual) display terminal, a computer terminal with attached keyboard for the display of data; cathode-ray tube; terminal.

veal (vēl) *n.* 1 A calf, esp. one grown or suitable for food.

2 The flesh of a calf as food. [<L *vitellus*, dim. of *vitulus* calf]

vec·tor (vek′tər) *n.* 1 *Math.* A quantity defined by its magnitude and direction. 2 *Med.* An insect or other living carrier of pathogenic organisms from one host to another. [<L, carrier<*vehere* carry]

Ve·da (vā′də, vē′-) *n.* Any of four collections of ancient Hindu sacred writings. [Skt., knowledge] —**Ve·da·ic** (vi·dā′ik), **Ve′dic** *adj.* —**Ve·da·ism** (vā′də·iz′əm, vē′-) *n.*

V-E Day (vē′ē′) May 8, 1945, the official date of the Allied victory in Europe in World War II.

veep (vēp) *n. Slang* A vice president, esp. the vice president of the U.S. [<*V.P.*, abbr. of vice president]

veer (vir) *v.i.* 1 To shift or turn in position or direction: The wind *veered* to the east. 2 To shift from one opinion, belief, etc., to another. —*v.t.* 3 To change the direction of. —*n.* A change in direction. [<F *virer* to turn]

veer·y (vir′ē) *n. pl.* **veer·ies** A melodious tawny thrush that breeds in CEN. North America. [Prob. imit.]

veg. vegetable; vegetation.

Ve·ga (vē′gə, vā′-) *n.* A bright star in the constellation Lyra. [<Ar. *(al-Nasr) al-Waqi* the falling (vulture)]

veg·e·ta·ble (vej′ə·tə·bəl, vej′tə-) *n.* 1 A plant, esp. one cultivated for food. 2 The edible part of a plant, raw or cooked. 3 *Informal* A person who is mindless, apathetic, or passive. —*adj.* 1 Pertaining to plants, as distinct from animals: the *vegetable* kingdom. 2 Derived from, of the nature of, or resembling plants. 3 Made from or pertaining to edible vegetables: *vegetable* soup. 4 *Informal* Showing little mental activity; apathetic, passive, etc. [<L *vegetus* vigorous, lively<*vegere* be lively]

veg·e·tal (vej′ə·təl) *adj.* 1 Of or pertaining to plants or vegetables. 2 Pertaining to nonreproductive aspects of plant life.

veg·e·tar·i·an (vej′ə·târ′ē·ən) *n.* A person whose diet is made up of vegetables, fruits, grain, nuts, and sometimes animal products, as milk, eggs, etc. —*adj.* 1 Pertaining to or advocating the eating of only vegetable foods. 2 Made up exclusively of vegetables, fruits, grain, etc. —**veg′e·tar′i·an·ism** *n.*

veg·e·tate (vej′ə·tāt) *v.i.* **·tat·ed, ·tat·ing** 1 To grow, as a plant. 2 To live in a monotonous, passive way.

veg·e·ta·tion (vej′ə·tā′shən) *n.* 1 The process or condition of vegetating. 2 Plant life in the aggregate.

veg·e·ta·tive (vej′ə·tā′tiv) *adj.* 1 Of or pertaining to vegetation and plant growth. 2 Growing or capable of growing as plants; productive. 3 VEGETABLE (def. 4). 4 Concerned with nonreproductive life processes.

ve·he·ment (vē′ə·mənt) *adj.* 1 Arising from or marked by strong feeling or passing. 2 Acting with great force; violent. [<L *vehemens, -entis* impetuous, rash] —**ve′he·mence, ve′he·men·cy** *n.* —**ve′he·ment·ly** *adv.* —**Syn.** 1 ardent, fervent, zealous, fierce. 2 energetic, forceful, intense, powerful.

ve·hi·cle (vē′ə·kəl, vē′hi-) *n.* 1 Any device for carrying or transporting persons or things, as a car, spacecraft, etc. 2 A neutral medium for administering a medicine, etc. 3 The medium with which pigments are mixed in painting. 4 Any means by which thoughts or ideas are transmitted or communicated. [<L *vehiculum*<*vehere* to carry, ride] —**ve·hic·u·lar** (vi·hik′yə·lər) *adj.*

veil (vāl) *n.* 1 A piece of thin and light fabric, worn over the face or head for concealment, protection, or ornament. 2 A piece of cloth, as a curtain, that covers, conceals, etc. 3 Anything that conceals or covers. —**take the veil** To become a nun. —*v.t.* 1 To cover with a veil. 2 To conceal, cover, hide, disguise, etc. [<L *velum* piece of cloth, sail]

veil·ing (vā′ling) *n.* 1 The act of covering with a veil. 2 Material for veils. 3 A veil.

vein (vān) *n.* 1 Any of the tubular vessels that convey blood to the heart. 2 One of the radiating supports of an insect's wing. 3 One of the slender vascular bundles that form the framework of a leaf. 4 LODE. 5 A long, irregular, colored streak, as in wood, marble, etc. 6 A distinctive tendency or disposition. —*v.t.* 1 To furnish or fill with veins. 2 To streak or ornament with veins. 3 To extend over or throughout as veins. [<L *vena* blood vessel]

Veining of maple leaf

veined (vānd) *adj.* 1 Having veins, esp. many veins. 2 Marked with streaks of another color: *veined* marble.

vein·ing (vā′ning) *n.* 1 A vein or network of veins. 2 A streaked or veined surface.

vein·let (vān′lit) *n.* A small vein.

ve·lar (vē′lər) *adj.* 1 Of or pertaining to a velum, esp. the soft palate. 2 *Phonet.* Formed with the back of the tongue touching or near the soft palate, as (k) in *cool.* —*n. Phonet.* A velar sound. [< L *velum* sail, curtain]

veld (velt, felt) *n.* In South Africa, open country having few shrubs or trees. Also **veldt.** [< MDu. *velt* field]

vel·lum (vel′əm) *n.* 1 Fine parchment made from the skins of calves; used for expensive binding, printing, etc. 2 A manuscript written on vellum. 3 Paper or cloth made to resemble vellum. [< OF *veel, viel* calf]

ve·loc·i·pede (və·los′ə·pēd) *n.* 1 An early form of bicycle or tricycle. 2 A child's tricycle. [< L *velox* swift + -PEDE]

ve·loc·i·ty (və·los′ə·tē) *n. pl.* **·ties** 1 Quickness of motion; speed; swiftness. 2 *Physics* A vector representing the rate of change of position of a body. [< L *velox* swift]

ve·lour (və·lŏŏr′) *n. pl.* **·lours** 1 A soft, velvetlike, cotton or wool fabric having a short, thick pile. 2 A type of felt with a velvety nap, used esp. for hats. Also **ve·lours** (və·lŏŏr′. [See VELURE.]

ve·lum (vē′ləm) *n. pl.* **·la** (-lə) 1 SOFT PALATE. 2 A thin membranous covering or partition. [L, veil]

ve·lure (və·lyŏŏr′) *n. Archaic* A heavy fabric resembling velvet, formerly used for hangings, etc. [< F *velours* < L *villosus* shaggy]

vel·vet (vel′vit) *n.* 1 A fabric of silk, rayon, nylon, etc., having on one side a short, smooth pile. 2 Something resembling velvet. 3 *Slang* Unexpected profit or gain. — *adj.* 1 Made of velvet. 2 Smooth and soft to the touch like velvet. [Ult. < L *villus* shaggy hair] —**vel′vet·y** *adj.*

vel·vet·een (vel′və·tēn′) *n.* 1 A fabric, usu. of cotton, with a short, close pile like velvet. 2 Clothes, esp. slacks, made of velveteen.

Ven. Venerable; Venice; Venus.

ve·na ca·va (vē′nə kā′və) *pl.* **ve·nae ca·vae** (vē′nē kā′vē) Either of the two great veins that deliver blood to the right auricle of the heart. [< L, hollow vein] • See HEART.

ve·nal (vē′nəl) *adj.* 1 Capable of being corrupted or bribed. 2 Characterized by corruption or bribery. [< L *venum* sale] —**ve·nal·i·ty** (vē·nal′ə·tē) *n.* —**ve′nal·ly** *adv.*

ve·na·tion (ve·nā′shən, vē-) *n.* 1 Veins collectively. 2 NERVATION. [< L *vena* a vein]

vend (vend) *v.t.* 1 To sell, as by peddling. 2 To sell by means of a vending machine. 3 To give expression to in public —*v.i.* 4 To sell merchandise. [< L *vendere*] —**Syn.** *v.t.* 1 dispense, hawk, market, peddle.

ven·dee (ven·dē′) *n.* The person or party to whom something is sold.

ven·det·ta (ven·det′ə) *n.* Private warfare or feud, as in revenge for a murder, injury, etc. [< L *vindicta* vengeance]

vend·i·ble (ven′də·bəl) *adj.* Salable; marketable. —*n.* A thing for sale. —**vend′i·bil′i·ty, vend′i·ble·ness** *n.* —**vend′i·bly** *adv.*

vending machine A machine that makes candy, stamps, etc., available when a coin is inserted.

ven·dor (ven′dər) *n.* 1 One who vends; seller. 2 VENDING MACHINE. Also **vender.**

ve·neer (və·nir′) *n.* 1 A thin layer, as of choice wood, upon a cheaper surface. 2 Mere surface or outside show: a *veneer* of politeness. —*v.t.* 1 To cover (a surface) with veneers. 2 To conceal, as something disagreeable or coarse, with an attractive and deceptive surface. [< G *furnieren* inlay < F *fournir* furnish] —**ve·neer′er** *n.*

ven·er·a·ble (ven′ər·ə·bəl) *adj.* Meriting or commanding veneration because of dignity, age, religious or historical associations, etc. [< L *venerari* revere] —**ven′er·a·bil′i·ty, ven′er·a·ble·ness** *n.* —**ven′er·a·bly** *adv.*

ven·er·ate (ven′ə·rāt) *v.t.* **·at·ed, ·at·ing** To regard with respect and deference; revere. [< L *venerari* revere]

ven·er·a·tion (ven′ə·rā′shən) *n.* 1 Profound respect combined with awe. 2 The act of worshiping; worship.

ve·ne·re·al (və·nir′ē·əl) *adj.* 1 Pertaining to or proceeding from sexual intercourse. 2 Communicated by sexual relations with an infected person: a *venereal* disease. 3 Pertaining to or curative of diseases so communicated. 4 Infected with syphilis, gonorrhea, or other venereal disease. [< L *Venus* goddess of love] —**ve·ne′re·al·ly** *adv.*

venereal disease Any of several diseases transmitted by sexual intercourse, as syphilis, gonorrhea, etc.

ven·er·y¹ (ven′ər·ē) *n.* The pursuit of sexual gratification. [< L *Venus,* goddess of love]

ven·er·y² (ven′ər·ē) *Archaic n. pl.* **·er·ies** The hunting of game; the chase. [< L *venari* to hunt]

Ve·ne·tian (və·nē′shən) *adj.* Pertaining to Venice or to its people. —*n.* A citizen or inhabitant of Venice.

Venetian blind A flexible window screen having movable, overlapping slats so fastened on webbing or tape as to exclude or admit light.

Ven·e·zue·la (ven′ə·zwā′lə, -zōō·ē′lə) *n.* A republic of N South America, 352,143 sq. mi, cap. Caracas. —**Ven′e·zue′lan** *adj., n.*

ven·geance (ven′jəns) *n.* The infliction of a deserved penalty; retributive punishment. —**with a vengeance** 1 With great force or violence. 2 Extremely; to an unusual extent. [< L *vindicare* defend, avenge]

venge·ful (venj′fəl) *adj.* Seeking to inflict vengeance; vindictive. —**venge′ful·ly** *adv.* —**venge′ful·ness** *n.*

ve·ni·al (vē′nē·əl, vēn′yəl) *adj.* So slight or trivial as to be overlooked, as a fault. [< L *venia* forgiveness, mercy] —**ve′ni·al·i·ty** (-al′ə·tē), **ve′ni·al·ness** *n.* —**ve′ni·al·ly** *adv.* —**Syn.** excusable, forgivable, pardonable.

ve·ni·re (vi·nī′rē) *n. Law* A panel of people from which a jury is selected. [< L *venire facias* that you cause to come]

ve·ni·re·man (vi·nī′rē·mən) *n. pl.* **·men** (-mən) A member of a venire.

ven·i·son (ven′ə·zən, -sən) *n.* The flesh of a wild animal, esp. a deer, used for food. [< L *venari* to hunt]

ve·ni, vi·di, vi·ci (vā′nē, vē′dē, vē′chē; wā′nē, wē′dē, wē′kē) *Latin* I came, I saw, I conquered: Julius Caesar's report to the Roman Senate of a victory.

ven·om (ven′əm) *n.* 1 The poison secreted by certain reptiles, insects, etc., which is transferred to a victim by a bite or sting. 2 Ill will; spite. [< L *venenum* poison] —**Syn.** 2 hate, malice, rancor, spitefulness.

ven·om·ous (ven′əm·əs) *adj.* 1 Able to give a poisonous sting. 2 Malicious; spiteful. —**ven′om·ous·ly** *adv.* —**ven′om·ous·ness** *n.*

ve·nous (vē′nəs) *adj.* 1 Of, pertaining to, contained, or carried in a vein or veins. 2 Designating the blood carried by the veins back to the heart and lungs. 3 Marked with or having veins: also **ve′nose.** [< L *vena* vein] —**ve′nous·ly** *adv.* —**ve·nos·i·ty** (vē·nos′ə·tē, və-), **ve′nous·ness** *n.*

vent (vent) *n.* 1 An outlet; means of escape. 2 An opening for the passage of liquids, gases, etc. 3 A slit in a garment, as a coat. 4 *Zool.* An opening through which wastes are eliminated. —**give vent to** To utter or express: to *give vent to* one's anger. —*v.t.* 1 To give expression to. 2 To permit to escape at a vent, as a gas. 3 To make a vent in. [< OF < *fendre* cleave < L *findere* split]

ven·ti·late (ven′tə·lāt) *v.t.* **·lat·ed, ·lat·ing** 1 To produce a free circulation of air in, as by means of open windows, doors, etc. 2 To provide with a vent. 3 To expose to examination and discussion. 4 To oxygenate, as blood. [< L *ventus* wind] —**ven′ti·la′tion** *n.* —**ven′ti·la′tive** *adj.*

ven·ti·la·tor (ven′tə·lā′tər) *n.* 1 One who or that which ventilates. 2 A device or opening for replacing stale air with fresh air.

ven·tral (ven′trəl) *adj.* Toward, near, in, or on the abdomen. [< L *venter, ventris* belly] —**ven′tral·ly** *adv.*

ven·tri·cle (ven′trə·kəl) *n.* Any cavity in the body, esp. either of the two lower chambers of the heart, from which blood is forced into the arteries. [< L *venter, ventris* belly] —**ven·tric·u·lar** (-trik′yə·lər) *adj.* • See HEART.

---

add, āce, cāre, pälm; end, ēven; it, īce; odd, ōpen, ôrder; tŏŏk, pōōl; up, bûrn; ə = *a* in *above, u* in *focus;* yōō = *u* in *fuse;* oil; pout; check; go; ring; thin; this; zh, *vision.* < derived from; ? origin uncertain or unknown.

ven·tril·o·quism (ven·tril′ə·kwiz′əm) *n.* The art of speaking in such a way that the sound seems to come from some source other than the person speaking. Also **ven·tril′o·quy** (-kwē). [< L *venter* belly + *loqui* speak] —**ven·tri·lo·qui·al** (ven′tra·lō′kwē·əl), **ven·tril′o·quis′tic** *adj.* —**ven′tri·lo′qui·al·ly** *adv.* —**ven·tril′o·quist** *n.* —**ven·tril′o·quize** (-kwīz) (·quized, ·qui·zing) *v.i. & v.t.*

ven·ture (ven′chər) *v.* ·tured, ·tur·ing *v.t.* 1 To expose to chance or risk; stake. 2 To run the risk of. 3 To express at the risk of denial or refutation: to *venture* a suggestion. 4 To place or send on a chance, as in a speculative investment. —*v.i.* 5 To take risk in going, coming, etc.: to *venture* into deep water. —*n.* 1 A risk; hazard. 2 An undertaking attended with risk. 3 That which is ventured, esp. property risk. —**at a venture** At random; haphazardly. [Alter. of ADVENTURE] —**ven′tur·er** *n.*

ven·ture·some (ven′chər·səm) *adj.* 1 Bold; daring. 2 Involving hazard; risky. —**ven′ture·some·ly** *adv.* —**ven′ture·some·ness** *n.*

ven·tur·ous (ven′chər·əs) *adj.* 1 Adventurous; bold. 2 Hazardous; risky; dangerous. —**ven′tur·ous·ly** *adv.* —**ven′·tur·ous·ness** *n.*

ven·ue (ven′yōō) *n. Law* 1 The place or neighborhood where a crime is committed or a cause of action arises. 2 The county or political division from which the jury must be summoned and in which the trial must be held. —**change of venue** The change of the place of trial, for good cause shown, from one county to another. [< OF *venir* come]

Ve·nus (vē′nəs) *Rom. Myth.* The goddess of love and beauty. —*n.* 1 A beautiful woman. 2 The planet of the solar system second in distance from the sun. •See PLANET.

Venus fly·trap (flī′trap′) An insectivorous plant of the SE U.S., with a basal rosette of leaves that entrap anything that touches certain sensitive hairs on their surface. Also **Ve′nus's-fly′trap** (vē′nəs·iz-).

ver. verse(s); version.

ve·ra·cious (və·rā′shəs) *adj.* 1 Speaking the truth; truthful. 2 True; accurate. [< L *verus* true] —**ve·ra′cious·ly** *adv.* —**ve·ra′cious·ness** *n.*

ve·rac·i·ty (və·ras′ə·tē) *n. pl.* ·ties 1 Honesty; truthfulness. 2 Accuracy; trueness. 3 That which is true; truth. [< L *verax*] — **Syn.** candor, frankness, integrity.

Venus flytrap

ve·ran·da (və·ran′də) *n.* An open porch, usu. roofed, along one or more sides of a building. Also **ve·ran′dah.** [< Pg. *varanda* railing, balustrade]

verb (vûrb) *n. Gram.* 1 One of a class of words which express existence, action, or occurrence, or that function as a copula or an auxiliary. 2 Any word or construction functioning similarly. [< L *verbum* word]

ver·bal (vûr′bəl) *adj.* 1 Of, in, or pertaining to words: a *verbal* contract; a *verbal* image. 2 Of, pertaining to, or concerned with words rather than the ideas they convey. 3 Word for word; verbatim; literal: a *verbal* translation. 4 *Gram.* **a** Partaking of the nature of or derived from a verb: a *verbal* noun. **b** Used to form verbs: a *verbal* prefix. 5 *Informal* Adept at using words, as in choice or range of vocabulary: She's very *verbal* for her age. —*n. Gram.* A noun directly derived from a verb, in English often having the form of the present participle, as, "There shall be *weeping* and *wailing* and *gnashing* of teeth"; also, an infinitive used as a noun, as, *"To err* is human": also **verbal noun.** [< L *verbum* word] —**ver′bal·ly** *adv.* •See ORAL.

ver·bal·ism (vûr′bəl·iz′əm) *n.* 1 A verbal phrase or expression. 2 A meaningless form of words; verbiage.

ver·bal·ist (vûr′bəl·ist) *n.* 1 One who is skilled in the use and meanings of words. 2 A person overly concerned with words rather than facts or concepts.

ver·bal·ize (vûr′bəl·īz) *v.* ·ized ·iz·ing *v.t.* 1 *Gram.* To change (a noun, etc.) into a verb. 2 To express in words. —*v.i.* 3 To speak or write verbosely. —**ver′bal·i·za′tion, ver′bal·iz′er** *n.*

ver·ba·tim (vər·bā′tim) *adj. & adv.* In the exact words; word for word. [< L *verbum* word]

ver·be·na (vər·bē′nə) *n.* Any of a genus of plants having

spikes of showy, often fragrant flowers. [< L, foliage, vervain]

ver·bi·age (vûr′bē·ij) *n.* 1 Use of too many words. 2 Manner of verbal expression. [< F *verbe* word]

ver·bose (vər·bōs′) *adj.* Using or containing an unnecessary number of words; wordy. [< L *verbum* word] —**ver·bose′ly** *adv.* —**ver·bose′ness, ver·bos′i·ty** (-bos′ə·tē) *n.* — **Syn.** garrulous, long-winded, prolix.

ver·bo·ten (vər·bōt′n, fər-) *adj. German* Forbidden.

ver·dant (vûr′dənt) *adj.* 1 Green with vegetation; fresh. 2 Immature in experience. [< F *verdoyer* grow green] —**ver′dan·cy** *n.* —**ver′dant·ly** *adv.*

ver·dict (vûr′dikt) *n.* 1 The decision of a jury in an action. 2 A conclusion expressed; an opinion. [< L *vere dictum* truly said]

ver·di·gris (vûr′də·grēs, -gris, -grē) *n.* 1 A green or greenish blue acetate of copper obtained by treating copper with acetic acid. 2 The blue-green crust formed by corrosion of copper, bronze, or brass in air, sea water, etc. [< OF *vert de Grece*, lit., green of Greece]

ver·dure (vûr′jər) *n.* 1 The fresh greenness of growing vegetation. 2 Green vegetation. [< F *verd* green]

verge[1] (vûrj) *n.* 1 The extreme edge; brink: on the *verge* of bankruptcy. 2 A bounding or enclosing line surrounding something. —*v.i.* **verged, verg·ing** 1 To be contiguous or adjacent. 2 To form the limit or verge. [< L *virga* twig]

verge[2] (vûrj) *v.i.* **verged, verg·ing** 1 To come near; approach: a remark *verging* on rudeness. 2 To tend; incline. [< L *vergere* to bend, turn]

ver·i·fi·ca·tion (ver′ə·fə·kā′shən) *n.* 1 The act of verifying, or the state of being verified. 2 A proof or confirmation, as by examination. —**ver′i·fi·ca′tive** *adj.*

ver·i·fy (ver′ə·fī) *v.t.* **·fied, ·fy·ing** 1 To prove to be true or accurate; confirm. 2 To test the accuracy or truth of. 3 *Law* To affirm under oath. [< L *verus* true + *facere* make] —**ver′i·fi′er** *n.* —**Syn.** 1 authenticate, corroborate, substantiate. 2 ascertain.

ver·i·ly (ver′ə·lē) *adv.* In truth; certainly. [< VERY]

ver·i·sim·i·lar (ver′ə·sim′ə·lər) *adj.* Appearing or seeming to be true; likely; probable. [< L *verus* true + *similis* like] —**ver′i·sim′i·lar·ly** *adv.*

ver·i·si·mil·i·tude (ver′ə·si·mil′ə·tyōōd) *n.* 1 Appearance of truth; likelihood. 2 That which resembles truth. [< L *verisimilitudo*]

ver·i·ta·ble (ver′ə·tə·bəl) *adj.* Genuine; true; real. [< F *vérité* truth] —**ver′i·ta·ble·ness** *n.* —**ver′i·ta·bly** *adv.*

ver·i·ty (ver′ə·tē) *n. pl.* ·ties 1 Truth; correctness. 2 A true statement; a fact. [< L *veritas* truth < *verus* true]

vermi- *combining form* A worm; of or related to a worm: *vermicide.* [< L *vermis* a worm]

ver·mi·cel·li (vûr′mə·chel′ē, -sel′ē) *n.* A food paste made into slender wormlike cords thinner than spaghetti. [Ital., lit., little worms]

ver·mi·cide (vûr′mə·sīd) *n.* Any substance that kills worms, esp. a drug destructive of intestinal worms. —**ver′mi·cid′al** *adj.*

ver·mi·form (vûr′mə·fôrm) *adj.* Like a worm in shape.

vermiform appendix A slender, wormlike sac protruding from the large intestine. •See INTESTINE.

ver·mi·fuge (vûr′mə·fyōōj) *n.* Any remedy that destroys intestinal worms. [< L *vermis* a worm + *fugare* expel]

ver·mil·ion (vər·mil′yən) *n.* 1 A brilliant, durable red pigment obtained from cinnabar or made synthetically. 2 An intense orange-red color. —*adj.* Of a bright orange-red color. —*v.t.* To color with vermilion. [< OF *vermeil*]

ver·min (vûr′min) *n. pl.* ·min 1 Noxious small animals or parasitic insects, as lice, worms, mice, etc. 2 *Brit.* Certain animals injurious to game, as weasels, owls, etc. 3 A repulsive person or persons. [< L *vermis* a worm] —**ver′min·ous** *adj.* —**ver′min·ous·ly** *adv.* —**ver′min·ous·ness** *n.*

ver·mouth (vər·mōōth′) *n.* A fortified white wine flavored with aromatic herbs. [< G *Wermuth* wormwood]

ver·nac·u·lar (vər·nak′yə·lər) *n.* 1 The native language of a locality. 2 The common daily speech of any people. 3 The specialized vocabulary of a profession or trade. 4 An idiomatic word or phrase. —*adj.* 1 Belonging to one's native land; indigenous: said of a language, idiom, etc. 2 Using the colloquial native tongue: *vernacular* poets. 3 Written in the language indigenous to a people: a *vernacu-*

lar translation of the Bible. [< L *vernaculus* domestic, native] —**ver·nac'u·lar·ly** *adv.*

ver·nal (vûr'nəl) *adj.* **1** Belonging to, appearing in, or appropriate to spring. **2** Youthful; fresh. [< L *vernus* belonging to spring] —**ver'nal·ly** *adv.*

vernal equinox The equinox that occurs on or about March 21.

ver·ni·er (vûr'nē·ər) *n.* A small, movable, auxiliary scale for obtaining fractional parts of the subdivisions of a main scale. Also **vernier scale.** [< Pierre *Vernier*, 1580–1637, French mathematician]

Ver·o·nal (ver'ə·nəl) *n.* BARBITAL: a trade name.

ve·ron·i·ca (və·ron'i·kə) *n.* SPEEDWELL. [< St. *Veronica*, a legendary follower of Christ]

ver·sa·tile (vûr'sə·til, -tīl) *adj.* **1** Having many aptitudes or talents. **2** Having many uses: a *versatile* fabric. **3** Movable in more than one direction, as the toe of a bird. **4** *Bot.* Turning about freely on the support to which it is attached: said of an anther. [< L *versare,* freq. of *vertere* turn] —**ver'sa·tile·ly** *adv.* —**ver'sa·til'i·ty** (-til'ə·tē) *n.*

verse (vûrs) *n.* **1** A single line of a poem. **2** A group of lines in a poem; stanza. **3** Metrical composition as distinguished from prose; poetry. **4** A specified type of metrical composition: iambic *verse.* **5** One of the short divisions of a chapter of the Bible. [< L *versus* a turning, a verse]

versed (vûrst) *adj.* Having ready skill and knowledge; proficient. [< L *versari* occupy oneself] —**Syn.** experienced, practiced, seasoned, skillful.

ver·si·fy (vûr'sə·fī) *v.* **·fied, ·fy·ing** *v.t.* **1** To turn prose into verse. **2** To narrate or treat in verse. —*v.i.* **3** To write poetry. —**ver·si·fi·ca·tion** (vûr'sə·fə·kā'shən), **ver'si·fi'er** *n.*

ver·sion (vûr'zhən, -shən) *n.* **1** A translation or rendition from one language into another. **2** A description of an event, occurrence, etc., from a personal viewpoint. [< Med. L *versio* a turning < L *vertere* to turn] —**ver'sion·al** *adj.*

vers li·bre (ver lē'br') *French* Free verse. —**vers li·brist** (lē'brist).

ver·so (vûr'sō) *n. pl.* **·sos 1** A left-hand page of a book, leaflet, etc. **2** The reverse of a coin or medal. [< L *verso (folio)* a turned (leaf)]

verst (vûrst) *n.* A Russian measure of distance equal to about two thirds of a mile. [< Russ. *versta*]

ver·sus (vûr'səs) *prep.* **1** In law, sports, and contests, against. **2** Considered as the alternative of: free trade *versus* high tariffs. [L, toward, turned toward]

ver·te·bra (vûr'tə·brə) *n. pl* **·brae** (-brē, -brā) or **·bras** Any of the individual bones of the spinal column. [L, a joint, vertebra < *vertere* to turn]—**ver'te·bral** *adj.*

ver·te·brate (vûr'tə·brit, -brāt) *adj.* **1** Having a backbone or spinal column. **2** Pertaining to or characteristic of vertebrates. **3** Pertaining to, having, or composed of vertebrae. —*n.* Any of a division of animals characterized by a spinal column, as fishes, birds, and mammals. [< L *vertebratus* jointed] —**ver'te·brat'ed** *adj.*

ver·tex (vûr'teks) *n. pl.* **·tex·es** or **·ti·ces** (-tə·sēz') **1** The highest point of anything; apex. **2** *Astron.* **a** ZENITH. **b** The point in the sky toward or from which a group of stars appears to be moving. **3** *Geom.* **a** The point of intersection of the sides of an angle. **b** The point farthest from the base. [L, the top < *vertere* to turn]

Human vertebrae
a. cervical.
b. thoracic. c. lumbar.

ver·ti·cal (vûr'ti·kəl) *adj.* **1** Perpendicular; upright. **2** Of or pertaining to the vertex. **3** Occupying a position directly overhead; at the highest point. **4** Of or pertaining to a business concern that undertakes a process from raw material to consumer: a *vertical* trust. —*n.* **1** A vertical

line, plane, or circle. **2** An upright beam or rod in a truss. —**ver'ti·cal·i·ty** (-kal'ə·tē), **ver'ti·cal·ness** *n.* —**ver'ti·cal·ly** *adv.*

vertical angle Either one of two angles which lie on opposite sides of two intersecting lines.

ver·tig·i·nous (vər·tij'ə·nəs) *adj.* **1** Affected by vertigo; dizzy. **2** Turning round; whirling. **3** Liable to cause giddiness. —**ver·tig'i·nous·ly** *adv.* —**ver·tig'i·nous·ness** *n.*

ver·ti·go (vûr'tə·gō') *n. pl.* **·goes** or **ver·tig·i·nes** (vər·tij'ə·nēz) A disorder in which a person or his surroundings seem to whirl about in such a way as to make the person dizzy and usu. sick. [L, lit., a turning around]

ver·vain (vûr'vān) *n.* A species of verbena supposedly having medicinal properties. [< L *verbena* verbena]

verve (vûrv) *n.* Enthusiasm or energy. [< L *verba,* pl. of *verbum* a word] —**Syn.** élan, liveliness, spirit, vigor.

ver·y (ver'ē) *adv.* **1** In a high degree; extremely: *very* generous. **2** Exactly: They both had the *very* same thought. —*adj.* **ver·i·er, ver·i·est 1** Absolute; complete: the *very* truth. **2** Suitable; right: the *very* tool we need. **3** Unqualified; complete: a *very* scoundrel. **4** Selfsame; identical: my *very* words. **5** The (thing) itself: used as an intensive: The *very* stones cry out. [< L *verus* true]

very high frequency Any wave frequency from 30 to 300 megahertz.

very low frequency Any wave frequency from 3 to 30 kilohertz.

ves·i·cant (ves'i·kənt) *adj.* Blister-producing. —*n.* That which produces blisters, esp. a chemical warfare agent which attacks the skin on contact or lung tissue if inhaled. [< L *vesica* a blister, bladder]

ves·i·cate (ves'i·kāt) *v.* **·cat·ed, ·cat·ing** *v.t.* **1** To raise blisters on. —*v.i.* **2** To blister, as the skin. —**ves'i·ca'tion** *n.*

ves·i·ca·to·ry (ves'i·kə·tôr'ē, və·sik'ə·tôr'ē, -tō'rē) *adj., n. pl.* **·ries** VESICANT.

ves·i·cle (ves'i·kəl) *n.* Any small bladderlike cavity, cell, cyst, or blister. [< L *vesica* a bladder] —**ve·sic·u·lar** (və·sik'yə·lar) *adj.* —**ve·sic'u·lar·ly** *adv.*

ves·per (ves'pər) *n. Archaic* EVENING. —*adj.* Of or pertaining to evening. [L, the evening star]

Ves·per (ves'pər) *n.* EVENING STAR. [L]

ves·pers (ves'pərz) *n.pl. Often cap. Eccl.* **1** The sixth in order of the canonical hours. **2** A service of worship in the late afternoon or evening.

ves·sel (ves'əl) *n.* **1** A hollow receptacle capable of holding a liquid, as a pot, tub, pitcher, etc. **2** A ship or large boat. **3** Any of several aircraft. **4** *Biol.* A duct or canal for containing or transporting a fluid. [< L *vas* a vessel]

vest (vest) *n.* **1** A short sleeveless jacket worn, esp. under a suit coat, by men. **2** A similar garment worn by women. **3** A vestee. **4** *Chiefly Brit.* UNDERSHIRT. —*v.t.* **1** To confer (ownership, authority, etc.) upon some person or persons. **2** To place ownership, control, or authority with (a person or persons). **3** To clothe or robe, as with church vestments. —*v.i.* **4** To clothe oneself, as in vestments. **5** To be or become legally vested, as property. [< L *vestis* clothing, a garment]

Ves·ta (ves'tə) *Rom. Myth.* The goddess of the hearth and the hearth fire.

ves·tal (ves'təl) *n.* **1** One of the virgin priestesses of Vesta: also **vestal virgin. 2** A chaste woman, esp. a virgin. —*adj.* **1** Of or relating to Vesta or her priestesses. **2** Chaste. [< L *Vesta* Vesta]

vest·ed (ves'tid) *adj.* **1** Wearing clothes, esp. church vestments. **2** Not dependent on any contingency; fixed; inalienable; absolute: a *vested* right.

vested interest 1 A special interest, as in an economic or political system or arrangement, often pursued by the holder at the expense of others. **2** A person or group that pursues such an interest.

vest·ee (ves·tē') *n.* A garment worn by women to fill in the neckline of a jacket, blouse, etc. [Dim. of VEST]

ves·ti·bule (ves'tə·byool) *n.* **1** A small antechamber leading into a building or another room. **2** An enclosed passage from one railway passenger car to another. **3** *Anat.* Any cavity leading to another cavity: the *vestibule* of the ear. —*v.t.* **·buled, ·bul·ing** To provide with a vestibule or vestibules. [< L *vestibulum* an entrance hall] —**ves·tib′u·lar** (-tib′yə·lər) *adj.*

ves·tige (ves′tij) *n.* **1** A trace of something absent, lost, or gone. **2** *Biol.* A remnant of an organ that is no longer functional. [< F < L *vestigium* a footprint] —**Syn. 1** hint, remnant, tinge, touch.

ves·tig·i·al (ves·tij′ē·əl) *adj.* Of, or of the nature of a vestige; surviving in small or degenerate form. —**ves·tig′i·al·ly** *adv.*

vest·ment (vest′mənt) *n.* **1** An article of clothing. **2** Any of several ritual garments of the clergy. [< L *vestire* clothe] —**vest·ment·al** (vest·men′təl) *adj.*

vest-pock·et (vest′pok′it) *adj.* **1** Small enough to fit in a vest pocket. **2** Much smaller than standard or usual size: a *vest-pocket* battleship.

vest-pocket park A small urban park, often on a vacant lot.

ves·try (ves′trē) *n. pl.* **·tries 1** In a church, a room where vestments are put on or kept. **2** A room in a church used for Sunday school, meetings, etc. **3** In the Anglican and Episcopal churches, a body administering the affairs of a parish or congregation. [< L *vestis* a garment]

ves·try·man (ves′trē·mən) *n. pl.* **·men** (-mən) A member of a vestry.

ves·ture (ves′chər) *n. Archaic* **1** Garments; clothing. **2** A covering or envelope. —*v.t.* **·tured, ·tur·ing** To cover or clothe. [< L *vestire* clothe] —**ves′tur·al** *adj.*

vet[1] (vet) *Informal n.* VETERINARIAN. —*v.t. & v.i.* **vet·ted, vet·ting** To treat (animals) as a veterinarian does. [Short for VETERINARIAN]

vet[2] (vet) *n. Informal* A veteran.

vet. veteran; veterinarian; veterinary.

vetch (vech) *n.* Any of a genus of trailing, leguminous vines grown for fodder. [< L *vicia*]

vet·er·an (vet′ər·ən, vet′rən) *n.* **1** An experienced soldier or an ex-soldier. **2** A member of the armed forces who has been in active service. **3** A person with long experience in an occupation, calling, etc. —*adj.* **1** Having had long experience or practice. **2** Of, pertaining to, or for veterans. [< L *vetus, veteris* old]

Veterans Day The fourth Monday in October, a U.S. holiday honoring the veterans of the armed forces, formerly celebrated November 11.

vet·er·i·nar·i·an (vet′ər·ə·nâr′ē·ən, vet′rə-) *n.* A practitioner of medical and surgical treatment of animals.

vet·er·i·nar·y (vet′ər·ə·ner′ē, vet′rə-) *adj.* Of, pertaining to, or designating the science or practice of preventing, curing, or alleviating the diseases and injuries of animals, esp. domestic animals. —*n. pl.* **·nar·ies** VETERINARIAN. [< L *veterinarius* pertaining to beasts of burden < *veterina* beasts of burden]

ve·to (vē′tō) *v.t.* **·toed, ·to·ing 1** To refuse approval of (a bill passed by a legislative body). **2** To forbid or refuse to consent to. —*n. pl.* **·toes 1** The right of one branch of government to cancel, prohibit, postpone, etc., the projects of another branch; esp., the right of a chief executive, as the president or a governor, to refuse to approve a legislative enactment by withholding his signature. **2** A message giving the reasons of a chief executive for refusing to approve a bill. **3** The exercise of the right to veto. **4** Any authoritative prohibition. [< L, I forbid] —**ve′to·er** *n.*

vex (veks) *v.t.* **1** To annoy by petty irritations. **2** To trouble or afflict. **3** To baffle, puzzle, or confuse. [< L *vexare* to shake] —**vex·ed·ly** (vek′sid·lē) *adv.* —**vex′ed·ness, vex′er** *n.* —**Syn. 1** chagrin, irritate, pester, pique.

vex·a·tion (vek·sā′shən) *n.* **1** The act of vexing, or the state of being vexed. **2** Trouble, annoyance, affliction, etc.

vex·a·tious (vek·sā′shəs) *adj.* Annoying; harassing. —**vex·a′tious·ly** *adv.* —**vex·a′tious·ness** *n.*

VFW, V.F.W. Veterans of Foreign Wars.

VHF, V.H.F., vhf, v.h.f. very high frequency.

VI Virgin Islands (P.O. abbr.).

V.I. Virgin Islands.

v.i. see below (L *vide infra*); verb intransitive.

vi·a (vī′ə, vē′ə) *prep.* **1** By way of; by a route passing through. **2** By means of. [< L *via* a way]

vi·a·ble (vī′ə·bəl) *adj.* **1** Capable of living and developing normally, as a newborn infant, a seed, etc. **2** Workable;

practicable: a *viable* plan. [< L *vita*] —**vi·a·bil′i·ty** *n.* —**vi′a·bly** *adv.*

vi·a·duct (vī′ə·dukt) *n.* A bridgelike structure, esp. a large one of arched masonry, to carry a road or railroad over a valley, section of a city, etc. [< L *via* a way + (AQUE)DUCT]

vi·al (vī′əl) *n.* A small bottle, usu. of glass, for medicines and other liquids. [< Gk. *phialē* a shallow cup]

vi·a me·di·a (vī′ə mē′dē·ə, vē′ə mä′-) *Latin* A middle way.

vi·and (vī′ənd) *n.* An article of food, esp. meat. **2** *pl.* Provisions; food. [< OF *viande*]

Viaduct

vi·at·i·cum (vī·at′ə·kəm) *n. pl.* **·ca** (-kə) or **·cums 1** *Often cap.* The Eucharist, as given on *the verge of death.* **2** The provisions needed for a journey. [L, traveling money < *via* a way]

vibes (vībz) *n.pl. (usu. construed as sing. for def. 2) Slang* **1** Vibrations. See VIBRATION (def. 3). **2** VIBRAPHONE.

vi·brant (vī′brənt) *adj.* **1** Having, showing, or resulting from vibration; resonant. **2** Throbbing; pulsing: *vibrant* with enthusiasm. **3** Energetic; vigorous. **4** *Phonet.* VOICED (def. 3). —*n. Phonet.* A voiced sound. [< L *vibrare* to shake] —**vi′bran·cy** (-sē) *n. (pl.* **·cies) —vi′brant·ly** *adv.*

vi·bra·phone (vī′brə·fōn) *n.* A musical instrument like the marimba in which a vibrato is produced by rotating disks in electrically powered resonators.

vi·brate (vī′brāt) *v.* **·brat·ed, ·brat·ing** *v.i.* **1** To move back and forth, as a pendulum. **2** To move back and forth rapidly. **3** To resound: The note *vibrates* on the ear. **4** To be emotionally moved. —*v.t.* **5** To cause to move back and forth. **6** To cause to quiver. **7** To send forth (sound, etc.) by vibration. [< L *vibrare* to shake]

vi·bra·tile (vī′brə·til, -tīl) *adj.* **1** Pertaining to vibration. **2** Capable of vibration. **3** Having a vibratory motion. —**vi′bra·til′i·ty** (-til′ə·tē) *n.*

vi·bra·tion (vī·brā′shən) *n.* **1** The act of vibrating; oscillation. **2** *Physics* **a** A periodic, back-and-forth motion of a particle or body. **b** Any physical process characterized by cyclic changes in a variable, as wave motion. **c** A single cycle of such a process. **3** *pl. Slang* One's emotional response to an aura felt to surround a person or thing, esp. when considered in or out of harmony with oneself. —**vi·bra′tion·al** *adj.*

vi·bra·to (vē·brä′tō) *n. pl.* **·tos** *Music* A cyclic variation in the pitch of a tone. [Ital. < *vibrare* vibrate]

vi·bra·tor (vī′brā·tər) *n.* **1** One who or that which vibrates. **2** An electrically operated massaging apparatus.

vi·bra·to·ry (vī′brə·tôr′ē, -tō′rē) *adj.* **1** Pertaining to, causing, or characterized by vibration. **2** That vibrates or is capable of vibration.

vi·bur·num (vī·bûr′nəm) *n.* **1** Any of a genus of shrubs or small trees related to honeysuckle. **2** The bark of several species, used medicinally. [L, the wayfaring tree]

Vic. Victoria.

vic. vicar; vicarage; vicinity.

vic·ar (vik′ər) *n.* **1** One who is authorized to perform functions in the stead of another; deputy. **2** In the Anglican Church, the priest of a parish of which the main revenues are appropriated by a layman, the priest himself receiving a salary. **3** In the Roman Catholic Church, a representative of a bishop or the pope. **4** In the Protestant Episcopal Church, the clergyman who is the head of a chapel. [< L *vicarius* a substitute < *vicis* a change]

vic·ar·age (vik′ər·ij) *n.* **1** The benefice, office, or duties of a vicar. **2** A vicar's residence.

vic·ar-gen·er·al (vik′ər·jen′ər·al, -jen′rəl) *n.* **1** In the Roman Catholic Church, a priest appointed by the bishop as assistant in administering a diocese. **2** In the Anglican church, an official assisting the bishop or archbishop.

vi·car·i·ous (vī·kâr′ē·əs, vi-) *adj.* **1** Suffered or done in place of another: a *vicarious* sacrifice. **2** Felt through identifying with another's experience: *vicarious* pleasure in his wife's talent. **3** Filling the office of or acting for another. **4** Delegated: *vicarious* authority. [< L *vicarius*] —**vi·car′i·ous·ly** *adv.* —**vi·car′i·ous·ness** *n.*

vice[1] (vīs) *n.* **1** Moral depravity; evil. **2** An immoral action, trait, etc. **3** A habitual, usu. trivial, failing or defect; short-coming. [<L *vitium* a fault] —**Syn. 1** corruption, dissoluteness, profligacy.

vice² (vīs) *n. & v.t.* **viced, vic·ing** *Chiefly Brit.* VISE.

vice³ (vī'sē) *prep.* Instead of; in place of. [<L *vicis* change]

vice- *prefix* One who acts for or takes the place of. [<L *vice*, abl. of *vicis* change]

vice admiral See GRADE. —**vice'-ad'mir·al·ty** (-mər-əl·tē) *n.*

vice-con·sul (vīs'kon'səl) *n.* A person who acts as a substitute for or a subordinate to a consul. —**vice-con·su·lar** (vīs'kon'sə·lər) *adj.* **vice-con·su·late** (vīs'kon'sə·lit), **vice'-con'sul·ship** *n.*

vice·ge·rent (vīs·jir'ənt) *n.* One duly authorized to exercise the powers of another; a deputy. —*adj.* Acting in the place of another. [<L VICE + *gerere* carry, manage] —**vice·ge'ren·cy** (-sē) *n. (pl. ·cies).*

vice president 1 An officer ranking next below a president, and acting, on occasion, in his place. **2** In the U.S. government, an officer of this rank designated by the Constitution to succeed the president if necessary. —**vice-pres·i·den·cy** (vīs'prez'·ə·dən·sē) (*pl. ·cies*) *n.* —**vice'-pres'i·den'·tial** (-prez'ə·den'shəl) *adj.*

vice·re·gal (vīs·rē'gəl) *adj.* Of or relating to a viceroy. —**vice·re'gal·ly** *adv.*

vice·re·gent (vīs'rē'jənt) *n.* A person who acts in the place of a regent when necessary. —*adj.* Of or pertaining to a vice-regent. —**vice'·re'gen·cy** *n.*

vice·roy (vīs'roi) *n.* One who rules a country, colony, or province by the authority of his sovereign. [<VICE- + F *roi* a king] —**vice·roy'al** (-roi'əl) *adj.* —**vice'roy'al·ty** (*pl. ·ties*), **vice'roy·ship'** *n.*

vice squad A police division charged with combating prostitution, gambling, and other vices.

vi·ce ver·sa (vī'sē vûr'sə, vī'sə vûr'sə, vīs'vûr'sə) With the relation of terms being reversed; conversely. [L]

vi·chy·ssoise (vē'shē·swäz', vē'shē·swäz', vish'-) *n.* A potato cream soup flavored with leeks, celery, etc., usu. served cold with a sprinkling of chives. [<*Vichy,* France]

Vi·chy water (vish'ē) **1** The effervescent mineral water from the springs at Vichy, France. **2** Any mineral water resembling it.

vi·cin·i·ty (vi·sin'ə·tē) *n. pl.* **·ties 1** A region adjacent or near; neighborhood. **2** Nearness; proximity. [<L *vicinus* nearby]

vi·cious (vish'əs) *adj.* **1** Corrupt in conduct or habits; depraved; immoral. **2** Of the nature of vice: *vicious* acts. **3** Unruly or dangerous, as an animal: a *vicious* dog. **4** Marked by evil intent; malicious; spiteful: a *vicious* lie. **5** Worthless or invalidated because defective; full of errors or faults: *vicious* arguments. **6** *Informal* Unusually severe or punishing: a *vicious* blow. **7** *Informal* Savage; heinous: a *vicious* crime. [<OF<L *vitiosus*<*vitium* a fault] —**vi'cious·ly** *adv.* —**vi'cious·ness** *n.*

vicious circle 1 The predicament that arises when the solution of a problem creates a new problem, etc. **2** *Logic* A fallacy in reasoning created when a conclusion is based upon a premise which depends upon the conclusion.

vi·cis·si·tude (vi·sis'ə·t^yood) *n.* **1** *Usu. pl.* Irregular changes or variations, as of conditions or fortune: the *vicissitudes* of life. **2** A change or alteration; also, the condition or quality of being changeable. [<L *vicis* a turn, change] —**vi·cis·si·tu·di·nary** (və·sis'ə·t^yood'ə·ner'ē), **vi·cis'·si·tu'di·nous** *adj.*

vic·tim (vik'tim) *n.* **1** A person injured or killed by circumstances beyond his control: a *victim* of a flood. **2** A sufferer from any diseased condition: a *victim* of arthritis. **3** One who is swindled; a dupe. **4** A living creature killed as a sacrifice to a deity. [<L *victima* a beast for sacrifice]

vic·tim·ize (vik'tim·īz) *v.t.* **·ized, ·iz·ing 1** to make a victim of; cause suffering to. **2** To cheat; dupe: *victimized* by loan sharks. —**vic·tim·i·za·tion** (vik'tə·mə·zā'shən) *n.* —**vic'·tim·iz'er** *n.*

vic·tor (vik'tər) *n.* One who wins any struggle or contest. —*adj.* Victorious: the *victor* nation. [<L *victus,* p.p. of *vincere* conquer]

vic·to·ri·a (vik·tôr'ē·ə, -tō'rē·ə) *n.* A low, light, four-wheeled carriage, with a folding top, a seat for two persons, and a raised driver's seat. [<*Victoria,* 1819–1901, Queen of England]

Victoria

Victoria Cross The highest British military decoration, awarded for outstanding valor.

Victoria Day In Canada, a national holiday celebrated on the first Monday preceding May 25th.

Vic·to·ri·an (vik·tôr'ē·ən, -tō'rē-) *adj.* **1** Of or relating to Queen Victoria of England, or to her reign. **2** Pertaining to or characteristic of the standards of morality and taste prevalent during that era. **3** Prudish; prim; priggish. —*n.* A person living during the time of Queen Victoria's reign; also, a person exhibiting the characteristic qualities, behavior, etc., of her era. —**Vic·to'ri·an·ism** *n.*

vic·to·ri·ous (vik·tôr'ē·əs, -tō'rē-) *adj.* **1** Having won victory; triumphant. **2** Characterized by or relating to victory. —**vic·to'ri·ous·ly** *adv.* —**vic·to'ri·ous·ness** *n.*

vic·to·ry (vik'tər·ē) *n. pl.* **ries 1** The overcoming of an enemy or adversary; triumph, as in war. **2** An overcoming of any difficulty or obstacle, considered as an achievement earned through effort. [<L *victor*]

vict·ual (vit'l) *n.* **1** Food fit for consumption by man. **2** *pl.* Food prepared for consumption. **3** *pl.* A supply of food; provisions. [<L *victualis* of food<*victus* food]

vi·cu·ña (vi·kōōn'yə, -kyōō'nə, vī-) *n.* **1** A small llamalike ruminant of the Andes having fine wool. **2** A textile made from this wool or some substitute: also **vicuña cloth.** Also **vi·cu'na.** [<Quechua]

Vicuña

vi·de (vī'dē, vē'dā') *v.* See: used to direct attention to: *vide* p. 36. [L, imperative sing. of *videre* see]

vi·de in·fra (vī'dē in'frə) *Latin* See below.

vi·de·li·cet (vi·del'ə·sit, vī-, vi·dā'·li·ket') *adv.* That is to say; namely. [L<*videre licet* it is permitted to see]

vid·e·o (vid'ē·ō) *adj.* **1** Of or pertaining to television, esp. to the picture. **2** Producing a signal convertible into a television picture: a *video* recording —*n.* **1** Television image or the electric signal corresponding to it. **2** Videotape. [L, I see]

vid·e·o·cas·sette (vid'ē·ō·kas·et') *n.* A cassette that contains videotape for recording programs, movies, etc.

vid·e·o·disc (vid'ē·ō·disk') *n.* A disc for recording both image and sound for replay through a television.

vid·e·o·tape (vid'ē·ō·tāp') *n.* A recording of a television program on magnetic tape. —*v.t.* **·taped, ·tap·ing** To make such a recording.

vi·de su·pra (vī'dē, sōō'prə) *Latin* See above.

vie (vī) *v.* **vied, vy·ing** *v.i.* To put forth effort to excel or outdo others. [<MF *envier* invite, challenge] —**vi'er** *n.*

Vi·en·nese (vē'ə·nēz', -nēs') *adj.* Of or pertaining to Vienna, its inhabitants, culture, etc. —*n. pl.* **·ese 1** A native or inhabitant of Vienna. **2** The German dialect spoken in Vienna.

Vi·et·nam (vē·et·näm') *n.* A country of SE Asia, cap. Hanoi; from 1954 to 1976 divided into: **Democratic Republic of Vietnam,** 63,344 sq. mi., cap. Hanoi: also **North Vietnam;** and **Republic of Vietnam,** 65,749 sq. mi., cap. Saigon: also **South Vietnam.** • See map at INDOCHINA.

Vi·et·nam·ese (vēet'nəm·ēz', vyet'-, -ēs') *adj.* Of or pertaining to Vietnam, its people, or their language. —*n. pl.* **·ese 1** A native or citizen of Vietnam. **2** The language of Vietnam.

view (vyōō) *n.* **1** The act of seeing or examining; survey; examination; inspection. **2** Range of vision. **3** Something seen: a *view* of the harbor. **4** A representation of a scene, esp. a landscape. **5** Something regarded as the object of action; purpose. **6** Opinion; judgment; belief: What are your *views* on this subject? **7** The immediate or forseeable future: no end in *view*. —**in view of** In consideration of. —**on view** Set up for public inspection. —**with a view to** With the aim or purpose of. —*v.t.* **1** To look at; behold. **2** To scrutinize; examine. **3** To survey mentally; consider. **4** To regard in a certain way. [< OF *veoir* see < L *videre*]

view·er (vyōō′ər) *n.* **1** One who views; esp., one who watches television. **2** A device for viewing, esp. one for viewing photographic transparencies.

view·less (vyōō′lis) *adj.* **1** That cannot be viewed. **2** Having no opinions. —**view′less·ly** *adv.*

view·point (vyōō′point′) *n.* The position from which one views or evaluates something; point of view.

vi·ges·i·mal (vī·jes′ə·məl) *adj.* **1** Of, pertaining to, or based on the number 20. **2** Twentieth. [< L *vicesimus*]

vig·il (vij′əl) *n.* **1** An act or period of keeping awake. **2** An act or period of keeping watch. **3** *Eccl.* **a** The eve of a holy day. **b** *pl.* Religious devotions on such an eve. [< L *vigil* awake]

vig·i·lance (vij′ə·ləns) *n.* The quality of being vigilant; alertness to threat or danger.

vigilance committee A body of men self-organized and without official legal sanction, with the professed purpose of maintaining order and punishing crime.

vig·i·lant (vij′ə·lənt) *adj.* Alert to danger; wary. [< L *vigilare* keep awake < *vigil* awake] —**vig′i·lant·ly** *adv.* —**Syn.** cautious, circumspect, heedful, watchful.

vig·i·lan·te (vij′ə·lan′tē) *n.* A member of a vigilance committee. —**vig′i·lant′ism** *n.*

vi·gnette (vin·yet′) *n.* **1** A short, subtly wrought picture in words; sketch. **2** A decorative design before the title page of a book, at the end or beginning of a chapter, etc. **3** An engraving, photograph, etc., that shades off gradually into the background. —*v.t.* **·gnet·ted**, **·gnet·ting** To finish, as an engraving or photograph, in the manner of a vignette. [< F *vigne* a vine]

vig·or (vig′ər) *n.* **1** Active bodily or mental strength; energy. **2** Vital or natural growth, as in a healthy plant. **3** Intensity or force. **4** Legal force; validity. *Brit. sp.* **vig′· our.** [< L < *vigere* be lively, thrive]

vig·or·ous (vig′ər·əs) *adj.* Possessing, characterized by, or done with vigor. —**vig′or·ous·ly** *adv.* —**vig′or·ous·ness** *n.*

vi·king (vī′king) *n.* *Often cap.* One of the Scandinavian sea rovers who harried the coasts of Europe from the eighth to the tenth centuries.

vil. village.

vile (vīl) *adj.* **vil·er**, **vil·est 1** Morally base; corrupt. **2** Disgusting; loathsome. **3** Very bad: *vile* food. [< L *vilis* cheap] —**vile′ly** *adv.* —**vile′ness** *n.*

vil·i·fy (vil′ə·fī) *v.t.* **·fied**, **·fy·ing** To speak of abusively or slanderously; defame. [< L *vilis* cheap + *facere* make] —**vil′i·fi·ca′tion** (-fə·kā′shən), **vil′i·fi′er** *n.* —**Syn.** denigrate, malign, revile, traduce.

vil·la (vil′ə) *n.* A house, usu. large and imposing, in the country or suburbs or at the seashore. [L, a country house, farm]

vil·lage (vil′ij) *n.* **1** A collection of houses in a rural district, smaller than a town but larger than a hamlet. **2** Such a settlement incorporated as a municipality. **3** The inhabitants of a village, collectively. [< L *villaticus* pertaining to a villa < *villa* a villa]

vil·lag·er (vil′ij·ər) *n.* One who lives in a village.

vil·lain (vil′ən) *n.* **1** One who has committed crimes or evil deeds; scoundrel: now often used humorously. **2** A character in a novel, play, etc., who is the opponent of the hero. **3** VILLEIN. [< OF *vilain* a farm servant]

vil·lain·ous (vil′ən·əs) *adj.* **1** Wicked; evil. **2** *Informal* Very bad; abominable. —**vil′lain·ous·ly** *adv.* —**vil′lain·ous·ness** *n.* —**Syn. 1** detestable, heinous, notorious, shameful.

vil·lain·y (vil′ən·ē) *n. pl.* **·lain·ies 1** The quality or condition of being villainous. **2** A villainous act; crime.

vil·lein (vil′ən) *n.* In feudal England, a member of a class of serfs who, by the 13th century, were regarded as freemen in their legal relations with all persons except their lord. [< OF *vilain.* See VILLAIN.] —**vil′lein·age, vil′len·age** *n.*

vil·lus (vil′əs) *n. pl.* **vil·li** (vil′ī, -ē) **1** *Anat.* Any of numerous tiny projections from mucous membrane, as the absorp-

tive processes in the small intestine. **2** *Bot.* Any of the soft hairs on the surface of certain plants. [L, a tuft of hair, shaggy hair] —**vil′lous** *adj.*

vim (vim) *n.* Force or vigor; energy; spirit. [L, accusative of *vis* power]

vin (van) *n.* *French* Wine.

vi·na·ceous (vī·nā′shəs) *adj.* **1** Of or pertaining to wine or grapes. **2** Wine-colored; red. [< L *vinum* wine]

vin·ai·grette (vin′ə·gret′) *n.* **1** An ornamental box or bottle for holding vinegar, smelling salts, etc. **2** Vinaigrette sauce. [< F *vinaigre* vinegar]

vinaigrette sauce A sauce made of vinegar and oil with herbs, onions, parsley, etc., served usu. on cold meats or fish.

Vin·cent's infection (vin′sənts) TRENCH MOUTH. Also Vincent's angina, Vincent's disease. [< J. H. *Vincent*, 1862–1950, French physician]

vin·ci·ble (vin′sə·bəl) *adj.* That can be conquered or overcome; conquerable. [< L *vincere* conquer] —**vin′ci·bil′i·ty, vin′ci·ble·ness** *n.*

vin·di·ca·ble (vin′də·kə·bəl) *adj.* That can be vindicated; justifiable.

vin·di·cate (vin′də·kāt) *v.t.* **·cat·ed**, **·cat·ing 1** To clear of accusation, censure, suspicion, etc. **2** To defend or maintain, as a right or claim, against challenge or attack and show to be just, right, and reasonable. **3** To provide justification for; justify. [< L *vindicare* avenge, claim] —**vin·di·ca·tive** (vin·dik′ə·tiv, vin′də·kā′tiv), **vin′di·ca·to′ry** (-kə·tôr′ē, -tō′rē) *adj.* —**vin′di·ca′tor** *n.*

vin·di·ca·tion (vin′də·kā′shən) *n.* **1** The act of vindicating, or the state of being vindicated. **2** A justification; defense.

vin·dic·tive (vin·dik′tiv) *adj.* Having or characterized by a vengeful spirit. [< L *vindicta* a revenge] —**vin·dic′tive·ly** *adv.* —**vin·dic′tive·ness** *n.* —**Syn.** retaliatory, revengeful, spiteful.

vine (vīn) *n.* **1** Any climbing plant. **2** The flexible stem of such a plant. **3** GRAPEVINE (def. 1). [< L *vinum* wine]

vin·e·gar (vin′ə·gər) *n.* **1** A variously flavored solution of acetic acid obtained by the fermentation of cider, wine, etc., and used as a condiment and preservative. **2** Acerbity, as of speech. [< OF *vin* wine + *aigre* sour] —**vin′e·gar·y** *adj.*

vin·er·y (vī′nər·ē) *n. pl.* **·er·ies** A building or area where vines are grown.

vine·yard (vin′yərd) *n.* An area devoted to the growing of grapevines. [< OE *wīngeard*] —**vine′yard·ist** *n.*

vingt-et-un (van·tā·œn′) *n.* BLACKJACK (def. 3). [F, twenty-one]

vin·i·cul·ture (vin′ə·kul′chər) *n.* The cultivation of grapes for making wine. [< L *vinum* wine] —**vin′i·cul′tur·al** *adj.*

vi·nous (vī′nəs) *adj.* **1** Pertaining to, characteristic of, or having the qualities of wine. **2** Caused by, affected by, or addicted to wine. [< L *vinum* wine] —**vi·nos·i·ty** (vī·nos′ə·tē) *n.*

vin·tage (vin′tij) *n.* **1** The yield of grapes or wine from a vineyard or wine-growing district for one season. **2** The harvesting of a vineyard and the making of wine; also, the season when these things are done. **3** Wine, esp. fine wine of a particular region and year. **4** The year or the region in which a particular wine is produced. **5** *Informal* The type or kind current at a particular time: a joke of ancient *vintage.* —*adj.* Of a fine vintage: *vintage* wines. [< OF *vendage* < L *vinum* wine + *demere* remove]

vint·ner (vint′nər) *n.* **1** A wine merchant. **2** A maker of wine. [< OF *vin* wine]

vin·y (vī′nē) *adj.* **·i·er**, **·i·est** Pertaining to, like, of, full of, or yielding vines.

vi·nyl (vī′nəl) *n.* An organic radical derived from ethylene and entering into the composition of numerous plastics. [< L *vinum* wine + -YL]

vi·ol (vī′əl, -ōl) *n.* Any of a family of stringed musical instruments, predecessors of the violin family. [< Med. L *vidula, vitula*]

vi·o·la (vē·ō′lə, vī-) *n.* A four-stringed musical instrument of the violin family, somewhat larger than the violin, and tuned a fifth lower. [Ital., orig., a viol]

vi·o·la·ble (vī′ə·lə·bəl) *adj.* That can or is likely to be violated. —**vi′o·la·ble·ness, vi′o·la·bil′i·ty** *n.* —**vi′o·la·bly** *adv.*

vi·o·la da gam·ba (vē·ō′lə·də·gäm′bə) An early bass of the viol family, held between the legs, and having a range similar to that of the cello. [Ital., viola of the leg]

vi·o·late (vī′ə·lāt) *v.t.* **·lat·ed, ·lat·ing** **1** To break or infringe, as a law, oath, agreement, etc. **2** To profane, as a holy place. **3** To break in on; interfere with: to *violate* one's privacy. **4** To ravish; rape. **5** To offend or treat contemptuously: to *violate* a person's beliefs. [< L *violare* use violence < *vis* force] —**vi′o·la′tion, vi′o·la′tor** *n.* —**vi′o·la′tive** *adj.* —**Syn. 2** desecrate, pollute. **3** disturb; interrupt.

vi·o·lence (vī′ə·ləns) *n.* **1** Physical force exercised to injure, damage, or destroy. **2** An instance of such exercise of physical force; an injurious or destructive act. **3** Intensity; severity; force: the *violence* of a tornado. **4** Injury or damage, as by irreverence, distortion, or alteration: editing that did *violence* to the original text.

vi·o·lent (vī′ə·lənt) *adj.* **1** Proceeding from or marked by great physical force or activity. **2** Caused by or exhibiting intense emotional or mental excitement; passionate: a *violent* rabble-rouser. **3** Characterized by intensity of any kind: *violent* heat. **4** Marked by the unjust or illegal exercise of force: to take *violent* measures. **5** Resulting from external force or injury; unnatural: a *violent* death. [< L *violentus* < *vis* force] —**vi′o·lent·ly** *adv.*

vi·o·let (vī′ə·lit) *n.* **1** Any of a widely distributed genus of perennial herbs, bearing irregular flowers usu. of a bluish purple color. **2** Any of several plants having violet-colored flowers. **3** A bluish purple color. —*adj.* Bluish purple. [< L *viola*]

vi·o·lin (vī′ə·lin′) *n.* **1** A musical instrument having four strings and a sounding box of wood, and played by means of a bow. **2** A violinist, esp. in an orchestra. [< Ital. *viola* a viola]

vi·o·lin·ist (vī′ə·lin′ist) *n.* One who plays the violin.

vi·ol·ist (vī′əl·ist) *n.* **1** One who plays the viol. **2** (vē·ō′list) One who plays the viola.

vi·o·lon·cel·lo (vī′ə·lən·chel′ō, vē′ə-) *n. pl.* **·los** CELLO. [< Ital. *violone* a bass viol, aug. of *viola*] —**vi′o·lon·cel′list** *n.*

VIP, V.I.P. *Informal* very important person.

vi·per (vī′pər) *n.* **1** Any of a family of venomous Old World snakes, including the African puff adder. **2** Any of a family of typically American poisonous snakes, the **pit vipers,** including the rattlesnake, copperhead, etc., which are characterized by a small depression between the nostril and the eye. **3** Any poisonous or allegedly poisonous snake. **4** A malicious, treacherous, or spiteful person. [< L *vipera*] —**vi·per·ine** (vī′pə·rīn) *adj.*

vi·per·ous (vī′pər·əs) *adj.* **1** Of, pertaining to, or composed of vipers. **2** Malicious, treacherous, or spiteful. —**vi′per·ous·ly** *adv.*

vi·ra·go (vi·rä′gō, -rā′-, vī-) *n. pl.* **·goes** or **·gos** A loud, ill-tempered woman; shrew; scold. [L, manlike woman]

vi·ral (vī′rəl) *adj.* Of, pertaining to, or caused by a virus.

vir·e·o (vir′ē·ō) *n. pl.* **·os** Any of various inconspicuous, insectivorous songbirds of North America. [L, a kind of small bird]

vir·es·cent (vī·res′ənt) *adj.* Greenish or becoming green. [< L *virescere* grow green] —**vi·res′cence** *n.*

vir·gin (vûr′jin) *n.* **1** A person, esp. a young woman, who has never had sexual intercourse. **2** A maiden or unmarried woman. —*adj.* **1** Being a virgin. **2** Consisting of virgins: a *virgin* band. **3** Pertaining or suited to a virgin; chaste; maidenly. **4** Uncorrupted; pure; clean: *virgin* whiteness. **5** Not hitherto used, touched, tilled, or worked upon: *virgin* forest. **6** Not previously processed or manufactured; new: *virgin* wool. **7** Occurring for the first time; initial: a *virgin* effort. [< L *virgo* a maiden]

Vir·gin (vûr′jin) VIRGIN MARY. —*n.* VIRGO.

vir·gin·al[1] (vûr′jin·əl) *adj.* **1** Of, pertaining to, like, or suited to a virgin; modest; maidenly. **2** Pure; pristine; unsullied. —**vir′gin·al·ly** *adv.*

vir·gin·al[2] (vûr′jin·əl) *n. Often pl.* A small, rectangular harpsichord with no legs. Also **pair of virginals.**

virgin birth *Usu. cap. Theol.* The doctrine that Jesus Christ was conceived by divine agency and born without impairment of the virginity of his mother Mary.

Virginal

Vir·gin·i·a cowslip (vər·jin′yə) A perennial herb of the E U.S. with clusters of blue or purple tubular flowers. Also **Virginia bluebell.**

Virginia creeper A woody vine of the grape family, with compound leaves, small green flowers, and inedible blue berries.

Virginia deer WHITE-TAILED DEER.

Virginia reel 1 A country dance performed by couples who stand initially in two parallel lines facing one another. **2** The music for such a dance.

vir·gin·i·ty (vər·jin′ə·tē) *n. pl.* **·ties 1** The state of being a virgin; maidenhood; virginal chastity. **2** The state of being fresh, untouched, etc.

Virgin Mary Mary, the mother of Jesus.

vir·gin's-bow·er (vûr′jinz·bou′ər) *n.* A species of clematis bearing white flowers in leafy clusters.

Vir·go (vûr′gō) *n.* A constellation and the sixth sign of the Zodiac; the Virgin. • See ZODIAC.

vir·gule (vûr′gyool) *n.* A slanting line (/) used to indicate a choice between two alternatives, as in the phrase *and/or.* [< L *virga* a rod]

vir·i·des·cent (vir′ə·des′ənt) *adj.* Greenish; turning green. [< L *viridis* green] —**vir′i·des′cence** *n.*

vir·ile (vir′əl, īl) *adj.* **1** Having the characteristics of manhood. **2** Having the vigor or strength of manhood. **3** Able to procreate. [< L *vir* a man] —**vi·ril·i·ty** (və·ril′ə·tē) *n.*

vi·rol·o·gy (və·rol′ə·jē, vī-) *n.* The study of viruses, esp. in relation to disease. —**vi·rol′o·gist** *n.*

vir·tu (vər·tōō′, vûr′tōō) *n.* **1** Rare, curious, or artistic quality: often in the phrase **objects (or articles) of virtu.** **2** A taste for or knowledge of such objects. **3** Such objects collectively. [< L *virtus*]

vir·tu·al (vûr′chōō·əl) *adj.* Being so in essence or effect, but not in form or fact. [< Med. L *virtualis* < L *virtus* strength] —**vir′tu·al′i·ty** (-al′ə·tē) *n.* —**vir′tu·al·ly** *adv.*

vir·tue (vûr′chōō) *n.* **1** General moral excellence; uprightness; goodness. **2** A particular moral excellence. **3** Any admirable quality or merit: Patience is a *virtue.* **4** Sexual purity; chastity. **5** Efficacy; potency, as of a medicine. —**by** (or **in**) **virtue of** By or through the force or authority of. —**make a virtue of necessity** To do willingly what one has to do anyhow. [< L *virtus* strength, bravery < *vir* man] —**Syn. 1** integrity, rectitude, righteousness, worthiness.

vir·tu·os·i·ty (vûr′chōō·os′ə·tē) *n. pl.* **·ties** The technical mastery of an art, as music.

vir·tu·o·so (vûr′chōō·ō′sō) *n. pl.* **·si** (-sē) or **·sos 1** A master of technique in some fine art, esp. in musical performance. **2** A knowledgeable collector or lover of curios or works of art. —*adj.* Of or characteristic of a virtuoso. [< LL *virtuosus* full of excellence]

vir·tu·ous (vûr′chōō·əs) *adj.* **1** Righteous; upright; dutiful. **2** Pure and chaste. —**vir′tu·ous·ly** *adv.* —**vir′tu·ous·ness** *n.*

vir·u·lent (vir′yə·lənt) *adj.* **1** Extremely harmful; noxious; deadly. **2** Severe and rapid in its progress: said of a disease. **3** Very infectious: said of a pathogenic microorganism. **4** Full of bitter hatred; hostile. [< L *virulentus* full of poison < *virus* a poison] —**vir′u·lence, vir′u·len·cy** *n.* —**vir′u·lent·ly** *adv.*

vi·rus (vī′rəs) *n.* **1** Any of a class of ultramicroscopic filter-passing pathogens capable of reproduction only within specific living cells. **2** Venom, as of a snake. **3** Any evil influence: the *virus* of greed. [L, poison, slime]

vis (vis) *n. pl.* **vi·res** (vī′rēz) Force. [L]

Vis., Visc., Visct. Viscount; Viscountess.

vi·sa (vē′zə) *n.* An official endorsement on a passport certifying that it has been examined and that the bearer may enter or pass through the country which has granted the endorsement. —*v.t.* **·saed, ·sa·ing 1** To put a visa on. **2** To give a visa to. [F< L < p.p. of *videre* see]

vis·age (viz′ij) *n.* **1** The face. **2** Appearance; aspect; look. [< L *visus* a look] —**vis′aged** *adj.*

vis-à-vis (vēz′ə·vē′, vēs-, -ä·vē′) *adj. & adv.* Face to face. —*prep.* **1** Opposite. **2** In relation to; toward. [F, face to face]

vis·cer·a (vis′ər·ə) *n.pl. sing.* **vis·cus** (vis′kəs) **1** The internal organs of the body, as the stomach, lungs, heart, etc. **2** Commonly, the intestines. [L, pl. of *viscus* an internal organ]

vis·cer·al (vis′ər·əl) *adj.* **1** Of or pertaining to the viscera. **2** Instinctive or emotional: a *visceral* reaction. —**vis′cer·al·ly** *adv.*

vis·cid (vis′id) *adj.* Glutinous in consistency; adhesive; syrupy; viscous. [< L *viscum* birdlime] —**vis·cid·i·ty** (vi·sid′ə·tē), **vis′cid·ness** *n.* —**vis′cid·ly** *adv.*

vis·cose (vis′kōs) *n.* A viscid substance produced from cellulose as a step in the manufacture of rayon, cellophane, etc. —*adj.* **1** VISCOUS. **2** Of, pertaining to, containing, or made from viscose.

vis·cos·i·ty (vis·kos′ə·tē) *n. pl.* **·ties 1** The property of fluids by which they offer resistance to flow or to change in the arrangement of their molecules. **2** The measure of this property.

vis·count (vī′kount) *n.* A nobleman ranking below an earl or count and above a baron. [< OF *visconte*] —**vis′count·cy, vis′count·ship, vis′count·y** *n.*

vis·count·ess (vī′koun·tis) *n.* The wife of a viscount, or a peeress holding the title in her own right.

vis·cous (vis′kəs) *adj.* **1** Greatly resistant to flow; of high viscosity. **2** VISCID. [< L *viscum* birdlime] —**vis′cous·ly** *adv.* —**vis′cous·ness** *n.*

vise (vīs) *n.* A clamping device, usu. of two jaws made to be closed together with a screw, lever, or the like, for grasping and holding a piece of work. —*v.t.* **vised, vis·ing** To hold, force, or squeeze in or as in a vise. [< OF *vis* a screw < L *vitis* vine]

vi·sé (vē′zā) *n., v.t.* **vi·séed** or **vi·séd, vi·sé·ing** VISA.

Vish·nu (vish′nōō) In Hindu theology, the second god of the trinity (Brahma, Vishnu, and Siva), known as "the Preserver."

Machinist's vise (cross section)

vis·i·bil·i·ty (viz′ə·bil′ə·tē) *n. pl.* **·ties 1** The fact, condition, or degree of being visible. **2** *Meteorol.* The clearness of the atmosphere in terms of the distance at which objects can be seen distinctly.

vis·i·ble (viz′ə·bəl) *adj.* **1** Capable of being seen. **2** That can be perceived mentally; evident. [< L *visus*, p.p. of *videre* see] —**vis′i·ble·ness** *n.* —**vis′i·bly** *adv.* —**Syn.** perceptible. **2** clear, distinct, obvious, plain.

Vis·i·goth (viz′ə·goth) *n.* A member of the western Goths, a Teutonic people that invaded the Roman Empire in the late fourth century and established a monarchy in France and Spain. —**Vis′i·goth′ic** *adj.*

vi·sion (vizh′ən) *n.* **1** The act or power of seeing; sense of sight. **2** That which is seen. **3** A beautiful person, landscape, etc. **4** A mental representation of external objects or scenes, as in sleep. **5** A conception in the imagination; mental image: *visions* of power and wealth. **6** The ability to perceive, discern, and anticipate; foresight; imagination. —*v.t.* To see in or as in a vision. [< L *visus*, p.p. of *videre* see] —**vi′sion·al** *adj.* —**vi′sion·al·ly** *adv.*

vi·sion·ar·y (vizh′ən·er′ē) *adj.* **1** Not founded on fact; existing in the imagination; imaginary. **2** Able or disposed to see visions; affected by fantasies; dreamy. **3** Impractical, speculative, utopian, etc. **4** Of, pertaining to, characterized by, or seen in a vision or visions. —*n. pl.* **·ar·ies 1** One who has visions. **2** One whose plans, projects, etc., are

unrealistic or impractical; dreamer. —**vi′sion·ar′i·ness** *n.*

vis·it (viz′it) *v.t.* **1** To go or come to see (a person) from friendship, courtesy, on business, etc. **2** To go or come to (a place, etc.), as for transacting business or for touring: to *visit* the Louvre. **3** To be a guest of; stay with temporarily: I *visited* them for several days. **4** To come upon or afflict. **5** To inflict upon. —*v.i.* **6** To pay a visit; call. **7** To stay with someone temporarily. **8** *Informal* To converse; chat. —*n.* **1** The act of visiting a person, place, or thing. **2** A social call or short stay. **3** *Informal* A friendly chat. **4** An official call, as for inspection, medical examination, etc. [< L *visare* < *visus*, p.p. of *videre* see]

vis·i·tant (viz′ə·tənt) *n.* **1** A visitor. **2** A migratory bird at a particular region for a limited period.

vis·i·ta·tion (viz′ə·tā′shən) *n.* **1** The act of visiting; esp., an official inspection, examination, etc. **2** A dispensation of punishment or reward, as by God. —**the Visitation 1** The visit of the Virgin Mary to her cousin, Elizabeth. *Luke* 1:39–56. **2** A church feast, observed on July 2, commemorating this event. —**vis′i·ta′tion·al** *adj.*

visiting card CALLING CARD.

vis·i·tor (viz′ə·tər) *n.* One who visits; guest.

vi·sor (vī′zər) *n.* **1** A projecting piece on a cap shielding the eyes. **2** In armor, the front piece of a helmet which protected the upper part of the face and could be raised or lowered. **3** A movable device over the inside of the windshield of a car, serving to reduce glare. [< OF *vis* face] —**vi′sored** (-zərd) *adj.*

vis·ta (vis′tə) *n.* **1** A view, esp. one seen through a long, narrow space, as along an avenue, between rows of trees, etc. **2** The space itself. **3** A mental view embracing a series of events. [Ital., sight < L *videre* see] —**vis′taed** (vis′təd) *adj.*

Visor *def. 2*

vis·u·al (vizh′ōō·əl) *adj.* **1** Of or pertaining to the sense of sight. **2** Perceptible by sight; visible. **3** Done or perceived by sight only. **4** Instructing through the sense of sight: *visual* aids. [< L *visus* a sight < *videre* see] —**vis′u·al·ly** *adv.*

visual aids Charts, diagrams, slides, motion pictures, etc., used as aids in teaching and lecturing.

vis·u·al·ize (vizh′ōō·əl·īz′, vizh′əl-) *v.* **ized, ·iz·ing** *v.t.* **1** To form a mental image of; picture in the mind. —*v.i.* **2** To form mental images. *Brit. sp.* **vis·u·al·ise.** —**vis′u·al·i·za′·tion, vis′u·al·iz′er** *n.*

vi·tal (vīt′l) *adj.* **1** Of or pertaining to life. **2** Essential to or supporting life. **3** Affecting life in a destructive way; fatal: a *vital* wound. **4** Of the utmost importance or interest. **5** Full of life; vigorous; energetic; dynamic. —*n.pl.* The organs necessary to life, as the brain, heart, etc. **2** The necessary parts of anything. [< L *vitalis* < *vita* life] —**vi′tal·ly** *adv.*

vi·tal·ism (vīt′l·iz′əm) *n.* The doctrine that the life and functions of a living organism depend upon a vital force that differs in kind from all chemical and physical forces. —**vi′tal·ist** *n.* —**vi′tal·is′tic** *adj.*

vi·tal·i·ty (vī·tal′ə·tē) *n.* **1** The power to live and develop. **2** Power of continuing in force or effect. **3** Physical or mental energy; vigor; strength.

vi·tal·ize (vīt′l·īz) *v.t.* **ized, ·iz·ing** To make vital; endow with life or energy; animate. —**vi′tal·i·za′tion, vi′tal·iz′er** *n.*

vital statistics Data relating to births, deaths, marriages, health, etc.

vi·ta·min (vī′tə·min) *n.* Any of a group of organic substances whose presence in the diet in minute quantities is essential for the maintenance of specific physiological functions. [< L *vita* life + AMINE] —**vi′ta·min′ic** *adj.*

vitamin A The fat-soluble vitamin essential to vision and occurring in all animal tissues and many vegetables.

vitamin B complex A varied group of water-soluble vitamins having distinct functions.

vitamin B$_1$ THIAMINE.

vitamin B$_2$ RIBOFLAVIN.

vitamin B$_6$ PYRIDOXINE.

vitamin B$_{12}$ A vitamin normally produced in the intestine and essential for the production of erythrocytes.

vitamin C ASCORBIC ACID.

vitamin D A substance essential in the formation of bone and the metabolism of calcium, occurring in fish-liver oils and formed from sterols in the skin when exposed to sunshine.

vitamin E An oily substance present in most foods and essential to fertility in experimental animals.

vitamin G RIBOFLAVIN.

vitamin H BIOTIN.

vitamin K₁ A vitamin, found in green leafy vegetables, which promotes the clotting of blood.

vitamin K₂ A form of vitamin K₁ prepared from fishmeal.

vitamin P A factor present in citrus juices that promotes the normal permeability of capillary walls.

vi·ti·ate (vish′ē·āt) *v.t.* **·at·ed, ·at·ing** **1** To impair the use or value of; spoil. **2** To debase or corrupt. **3** To render weak, ineffective, legally invalid, etc.: *Fraud vitiates a contract.* [< L *vitium* a fault] —**vi′ti·a′tion, vi′ti·a′tor** *n.*

vit·i·cul·ture (vit′ə·kul′chər, vī′tə-) *n.* The science and art of grape-growing; cultivation of grapes. [< L *vitis* a vine + CULTURE] —**vit′i·cul′tur·al** *adj.* —**vit′i·cul′tur·er, vit′i·cul′tur·ist** *n.*

vit·i·li·go (vit′ə·lī′gō) *n.* A skin disorder characterized by partial loss of pigment resulting in white spots. [L, a vesicular skin disease]

vit·re·ous (vit′rē·əs) *adj.* **1** Of, pertaining to, or like glass; glassy. **2** Obtained from glass. **3** Of or pertaining to the vitreous humor. [< L *vitrum* glass] —**vit′re·os′i·ty** (-os′ə·tē), **vit′re·ous·ness** *n.*

vitreous humor The transparent jellylike tissue that fills the eyeball. Also **vitreous body.**

vit·ri·fy (vit′rə·fī) *v.t. & v.i.* **·fied, ·fy·ing** To change into glass or a vitreous substance; make or become vitreous. [< L *vitrum* glass + *facere* make] —**vit′ri·fac′tion** (-fak′shən), **vit′ri·fi·ca′tion** *n.*

vit·ri·ol (vit′rē·ol, -əl) *n.* **1** Any sulfate of a heavy metal, as **green vitriol** (iron); **blue vitriol** (copper); **white vitriol** (zinc). **2** Sulfuric acid: also **oil of vitriol**. **3** Anything sharp or caustic, as sarcasm. —*v.t.* **·oled** or **·olled, ·ol·ing** or **·ol·ling** To subject (anything) to the agency of vitriol. [< L *vitrum* glass]

vit·ri·ol·ic (vit′rē·ol′ik) *adj.* **1** Of, like, or derived from vitriol. **2** Biting, sharp, or caustic: *vitriolic* remarks.

vit·tle (vit′l) *n.* VICTUAL.

vi·tu·per·ate (vī·tᵛo͞o′pə·rāt, vi-) *v.t.* **·at·ed, ·at·ing** To find fault with abusively; rail at; berate; scold. [< L *vituperare* blame, scold < *vitium* a fault + *parare* prepare] —**vi·tu′per·a′tion, vi·tu′per·a′tor** *n.* —**vi·tu′per·a′tive** *adj.* —**vi·tu′per·a′tive·ly** *adv.*

viv. *Music* lively (It. *vivace*).

vi·va (vē′vä) *interj.* Live; long live (the person or thing specified): used in acclamation. [Ital. < *vivere* live < L]

vi·va·ce (vē·vä′chā) *adv. Music* Lively; quickly; briskly. [< L *vivax*]

vi·va·cious (vi·vā′shəs, vī-) *adj.* Full of life and spirits; lively; active. [< L *vivax* < *vivere* live] —**vi·va′cious·ly** *adv.* —**vi·va′cious·ness** *n.* —**Syn.** animated, brisk, cheerful, sparkling, spirited.

vi·vac·i·ty (vi·vas′ə·tē, vī-) *n. pl.* **·ties** **1** The state or quality of being vivacious. **2** A vivacious act, expression, etc.

vi·var·i·um (vī·vâr′ē·əm) *n. pl.* **·var·i·a** (-vâr′ē·ə) or **·var·i·ums** A place for keeping or raising animals or plants for observation or research. Also **viv·a·ry** (viv′ər·ē). [< L *vivus* alive < *vivere* live]

vi·va vo·ce (vī′və vō′sē, vē′və vō′chā) By spoken word; orally or oral. [L]

vive (vēv) *interj. French* Live; long live (the person or thing specified): used in acclamation.

viv·id (viv′id) *adj.* **1** Having an appearance of vigorous life; lively; spirited. **2** Very strong; intense: said of colors. **3** Producing or suggesting lifelike images. **4** Producing a sharp impression on the senses: a *vivid* description. [< L *vividus* lively < *vivere* to live] —**viv′id·ly** *adv.* —**viv′id·ness** *n.*

viv·i·fy (viv′ə·fī) *v.t.* **·fied, ·fy·ing** **1** To give life to; animate; vitalize. **2** To make more vivid or striking. [< L *vivus* alive + *facere* make] —**viv′i·fi·ca′tion** (-fə·kā′shən), **viv′i·fi′er** *n.*

vi·vip·a·rous (vī·vip′ər·əs) *adj.* Bringing forth young that have developed from eggs within the mother's body. [< L *vivus* alive + *parere* bring forth] —**vi·vip′a·rous·ly** *adv.* —**vi·vip′a·rous·ness, viv·i·par·i·ty** (viv′ə·par′ə·tē) *n.*

viv·i·sect (viv′ə·sekt) *v.t.* **1** To perform vivisection on. —*v.i.* **2** To practice vivisection. —**viv′i·sec′tor** *n.*

viv·i·sec·tion (viv′ə·sek′shən) *n.* Cutting, dissection, or other operation on a living animal, esp. in experiments designed to promote knowledge of physiological and pathological processes. [< L *vivus* living, alive + *sectio* a cutting] —**viv′i·sec′tion·al** *adj.* —**viv′i·sec′tion·ist** *n., adj.*

vix·en (vik′sən) *n.* **1** A female fox. **2** A turbulent, quarrelsome woman; shrew. [< ME *fixen* a she-fox] —**vix′en·ish** *adj.* —**vix′en·ly** *adj., adv.*

viz, viz. namely (L *videlicet*).

viz·ard (viz′ərd) *n.* A mask or visor. [Alter. of VISOR]

vi·zier (vi·zir′) *n.* A high official of a Muslim country, as in the old Turkish Empire. Also **vi·zir′**. [< Ar. *wazīr* a counselor]

vi·zor (vī′zər) *n.* VISOR.

V-J Day (vē′jā′) Sept. 2, 1945, the official date of the Allied victory over Japan in World War II.

VL, V.L. Vulgar Latin.

VLF, V.L.F., vlf, v.l.f. very low frequency.

V-mail (vē′māl′) *n.* Mail transmitted overseas in World War II on microfilm, and enlarged at point of reception for final delivery. [< V(ICTORY) + MAIL¹]

V.M.D. Doctor of Veterinary Medicine (L *Veterinariae Medicinae Doctor*).

vo. verso.

voc. vocative.

vocab. vocabulary.

vo·ca·ble (vō′kə·bəl) *n.* A word viewed as a combination of sounds and letters apart from its meaning. [< L *vocabulum* a name, appellation < *vocare* to call]

vo·cab·u·lar·y (vō·kab′yə·ler′ē) *n. pl.* **·lar·ies** **1** A list of words or of words and phrases, esp. one arranged in alphabetical order and defined or translated; a lexicon; glossary. **2** All the words of a language. **3** All the words used or understood by a particular person, class, profession, etc. **4** The range of expression at a person's disposal, esp. in art. [< L *vocabulum.* See VOCABLE.]

vo·cal (vō′kəl) *adj.* **1** Of or pertaining to the voice or the production of the voice. **2** Having voice; able to speak or utter sounds: *vocal* creatures. **3** Composed for, uttered by, or performed by the voice: a *vocal* score. **4** Full of voices or sounds; resounding: The air was *vocal* with their cries. **5** Freely expressing oneself in speech: the *vocal* segment of the populace. [< L *vocalis* speaking, sounding] —**vo·cal·i·ty** (vō·kal′ə·tē), **vo′cal·ness** *n.* —**vo′cal·ly** *adv.*

vocal cords Two ligaments extending across the larynx, which, when tense, are caused to vibrate by the passage of air, thereby producing voice.

vo·cal·ic (vō·kal′ik) *adj.* **1** Of, pertaining to, or like a vowel sound. **2** Characterized by or consisting of vowel sounds.

vo·cal·ist (vō′kəl·ist) *n.* A singer.

vo·cal·ize (vō′kəl·īz) *v.* **·ized, ·iz·ing** *v.t.* **1** To make vocal; utter, say, or sing. **2** *Phonet.* **a** To change to or use as a vowel: to *vocalize* y. **b** To voice. —*v.i.* **3** To produce sounds with the voice, as in speaking or singing. **4** *Phonet.* To be changed to a vowel. —**vo′cal·i·za′tion, vo′cal·iz′er** *n.*

Vocal cords
a. open. b. closed.
c. voice. d. whisper.

vo·ca·tion (vō·kā′shən) *n.* **1** A stated or regular occupation. **2** A call to, or fitness for, a certain career. **3** The work or profession for which one has or believes one has a special fitness. [< L *vocare* to call] —**vo·ca′tion·al** *adj.* —**vo·ca′tion·al·ly** *adv.*

voc·a·tive (vok′ə·tiv) *Gram. adj.* In some inflected languages, denoting the case of a noun, pronoun, or adjective used in direct address. —*n.* **1** The vocative case. **2** A word in this case. [< L *vocare* to call]

vo·cif·er·ant (vō·sif′ər·ənt) *adj.* Vociferous; uttering loud cries. —**vo·cif′er·ance** *n.*

vo·cif·er·ate (vō·sif′ə·rāt) v.t. & v.i. ·at·ed, ·at·ing To cry out with a loud voice; shout. [< L vox a voice + ferre carry] —vo·cif′er·a′tion, vo·cif′er·a′tor n. —Syn. bawl, bellow, clamor, scream, yell.

vo·cif·er·ous (vō·sif′ər·əs) adj. Making or characterized by a loud outcry; noisy; clamorous. —vo·cif′er·ous·ly adv. —vo·cif′er·ous·ness n.

vod·ka (vod′kə) n. A colorless alcoholic liquor originally made in Poland and Russia, distilled from a mash, as of rye, wheat, or potatoes. [< Russ. voda water]

vogue (vōg) n. 1 Fashion or style. 2 Popular favor; popularity. [F, fashion, orig., rowing] —vogu′ish adj.

voice (vois) n. 1 The sound produced by the vocal organs of a vertebrate, esp. by a human being in speaking, singing, etc. 2 The quality or character of such sound: a melodious voice. 3 The power or ability to make such a sound: to lose one's voice. 4 Something suggesting the sound of vocal utterance: the voice of the wind. 5 Expressed opinion, choice, etc. 6 The right to express an opinion, choice, etc. 7 A person or agency by which the thought, wish, or purpose of another is expressed: This journal is the voice of the teaching profession. 8 Expression: to give voice to one's ideals. 9 Phonet. The sound produced by vibration of the vocal cords, as heard in the utterance of vowels and certain consonants, as b, d, and z. 10 A singer: Caruso was a great voice. 11 In a musical composition, a part for a singer or an instrument. 12 Gram. A form of a verb which indicates whether its subject is active or passive. —in voice Having the voice in good condition for singing and speaking. —lift up one's voice 1 To shout or sing loudly. 2 To protest. —with one voice With one accord; unanimously. —v.t. voiced, voic·ing 1 To put into speech; give expression to; utter. 2 Music To regulate the tones of, as the pipes of an organ. 3 Phonet. To utter with voice. [< L vox, vocis] • When the subject of a verb performs the action, the verb is in the active voice: My aunt baked a chocolate cake; Her father gave her a bicycle. When the subject of a verb is acted upon, the verb is in the passive voice: The chocolate cake was baked by my aunt; She was given a bicycle by her father.

voiced (voist) adj. 1 Having a voice or a specified kind of voice: often used in combination: high-voiced, soft-voiced. 2 Expressed by voice. 3 Phonet. Uttered with vibration of the vocal cords, as (b), (d), (z).

voice·less (vois′lis) adj. 1 Having no voice, speech, or vote. 2 Phonet. Produced without voice, as (p), (t), (s). — voice′less·ly adv. —voice′less·ness n.

voice-o·ver (vois′ō′vər) n. In motion pictures and television programs, the voice of a narrator or announcer speaking off camera.

voice·print (vois′print′) n. A graphic representation of the sound of a person's voice, consisting of a complex pattern of wavy lines corresponding to the various pitches used in the utterance.

void (void) adj. 1 Containing nothing; without content; empty. 2 Having no legal force or validity; not binding. 3 Producing no effect; useless. —void of Lacking; without. —n. 1 An empty space; vacuum. 2 The quality or condition of feeling empty, lonely, lost, etc. —v.t. 1 To make void or of no effect; annul. 2 To empty or remove (contents); evacuate. —v.i. 3 To eliminate waste from the body; urinate or defecate. [< L vacuus empty] —void′er, void′ness n. —void′ly adv.

voi·là (vwà·là′) interj. French There! behold! literally, see there.

voile (voil) n. A fine, sheer fabric, as of cotton, silk, wool, or rayon. [< OF veile veil]

vol. volcano; volume; volunteer.

vo·lant (vō′lənt) adj. 1 Flying, or capable of flying. 2 Agile; quick; nimble. 3 Her. Represented as flying, as a bird or bee. [< L volare to fly]

vol·a·tile (vol′ə·til; chiefly Brit. -tīl) adj. 1 Evaporating rapidly; capable of being vaporized. 2 Inconstant; changeable. 3 Transient; fleeting. [< L volatilis < volare fly] — vol′a·tile·ness, vol·a·til·i·ty (vol′ə·til′ə·tē) n.

vol·a·til·ize (vol′ə·til·īz′) v.t. & v.i. ·ized, ·iz·ing To pass off or cause to pass off in vapor. —vol′a·til·i·za′tion n.

vol·can·ic (vol·kan′ik) adj. 1 Of, pertaining to, produced by, or characterized by a volcano or volcanoes. 2 Like a

volcano; explosive; violent. —vol·can′i·cal·ly adv. —vol·can·ic·i·ty (vol′kə·nis′ə·tē) n.

vol·can·ism (vol′kən·iz′əm) n. The power or action of volcanoes.

vol·ca·no (vol·kā′nō) n. pl. ·noes or ·nos Geol. An opening in the earth's surface from which hot matter is or has been ejected, often surrounded by a hill or mountain of ejected material. [< L Vulcanus Vulcan]

vole (vōl) n. Any of various short-tailed, mouselike or rat-like rodents. [Short for earlier vole mouse field mouse]

vo·li·tion (və·lish′ən) n. 1 The act of willing; exercise of the will. 2 The power of willing; willpower. [< L velle to will] —vo·li′tion·al, vo·li′tion·ar·y (-ən·er·ē), vol·i·tive (vol′ə·tiv) adj. —vo·li′tion·al·ly adv.

vol·ley (vol′ē) n. 1 A simultaneous discharge of many guns. 2 A discharge of many bullets, stones, arrows, etc. 3 Any discharge of many things at once: a volley of oaths. 4 In tennis, the flight of the ball before it touches the ground; also, a return of the ball before it touches the ground. —v.t. & v.i. ·leyed, ·ley·ing 1 To discharge or be discharged in a volley. 2 In tennis, to return (the ball) without allowing it to touch the ground. [< MF voler to fly] —vol′ley·er n.

vol·ley·ball (vol′ē·bôl′) n. 1 A game in which a number of players on both sides of a high net use their hands to hit a ball back and forth over the net without letting it drop. 2 The ball used in this game.

vol·plane (vol′plān) v.i. ·planed, ·plan·ing To glide down in an airplane with the engine turned off. —n. An airplane glide. [< F vol plané gliding flight]

vols. volumes.

volt[1] (vōlt) n. A unit equal to the difference of electric potential which, when steadily applied to a conductor whose resistance is one ohm, will produce a current of one ampere. [< A. Volta, 1745–1827, Italian physicist]

volt[2] (vōlt) n. 1 In horse-training, a gait in which the horse moves sidewise round a center with the head turned out. 2 In fencing, a sudden leap to avoid a thrust. [< Ital. volta, p.p. fem. of volvere to turn]

volt·age (vōl′tij) n. Electromotive force expressed in volts.

vol·ta·ic (vol·tā′ik) adj. Pertaining to electricity developed through chemical action; galvanic.

voltaic battery A set of voltaic cells which operate as a unit.

voltaic cell A cell that generates electricity by a chemical reaction and that cannot be efficiently recharged.

volt·me·ter (vōlt′mē′tər) n. An instrument for measuring differences of electric potential.

vol·u·ble (vol′yə·bəl) adj. Having a flow of words or fluency in speaking; talkative. [< L volubilis easily turned < volutus, p.p. of volvere to turn] —vol′u·bil′i·ty (vol′yə·bil′ə·tē), vol′u·ble·ness n. —vol′u·bly adv.

vol·ume (vol′yōōm, -yəm) n. 1 A collection of sheets of paper bound together; a book. 2 A book that is part of a set. 3 A quantity or amount: a large volume of sales. 4 A measure of quantity in terms of space occupied, as cubic inch, cubic centimeter, liter, pint, etc. 5 Acoustics Fullness or quantity of sound or tone. —speak volumes To be full of meaning; express a great deal. [< L volumen a roll, scroll] —vol′umed adj.

vol·u·met·ric (vol′yə·met′rik) adj. Of, based on, or pertaining to measurement of substances by volume. Also vol′u·met′ri·cal. —vol′u·met′ri·cal·ly adv.

vo·lu·mi·nous (və·lōō′mə·nəs) adj. 1 Consisting of or capable of filling volumes: a voluminous correspondence. 2 Writing or speaking much. 3 Having great volume or bulk; large. [< L volumen a roll] —vo·lu·mi·nos·i·ty (və·lōō′mə·nos′ə·tē), vo·lu′mi·nous·ness n. —vo·lu′mi·nous·ly adv.

vol·un·tar·y (vol′ən·ter′ē) adj. 1 Done, made, or given by one's own free will or choice: a voluntary contribution. 2 Endowed with or exercising will or free choice. 3 Acting without constraint: a voluntary donor. 4 Subject to or directed by the will, as a muscle or movement. 5 Intentional; volitional: voluntary manslaughter. —n. pl. ·tar·ies 1 Voluntary action or work. 2 A solo, usu. on the organ, often improvised, played before, during, or after a church service. [< L voluntas will] —vol·un·tar·i·ly (vol′ən·ter′ə·lē, vol′ən·ter′-) adv. —vol′un·tar′i·ness n.

vol·un·teer (vol′ən·tir′) n. 1 One who enters into any service of his own free will. 2 One who voluntarily enters military service. —adj. 1 Of, pertaining to, or composed of volunteers; voluntary. 2 Serving as a volunteer. —v.t. 1 To offer or give voluntarily: to volunteer one's services. —v.i. 2 To enter or offer to enter into some service or undertaking of one's free will. [< OF voluntaire voluntary]

vo·lup·tu·ar·y (və·lup′chōō·er′ē) n. pl. ·ar·ies One addicted to luxury and sensual indulgence. [< L voluptas pleasure] —Syn. hedonist, sensualist, sybarite.

vo·lup·tu·ous (və·lup′chōō·əs) adj. 1 Pertaining to, inclining to, producing, or produced by sensuous or sensual gratification. 2 Devoted to the enjoyment of pleasures or luxuries. 3 Suggesting the satisfaction of sensual desire. [< L voluptas pleasure] —vo·lup′tu·ous·ly adv. —vo·lup′tu·ous·ness n.

vo·lute (və·lōōt′) n. 1 Archit. A spiral scroll-like ornament, as in Ionic capitals. 2 Zool. One of the whorls or turns of a spiral shell. 3 A spiral or twisted form. —adj. Having a spiral form; scroll-shaped. [< L voluta a scroll < p.p. of volvere to turn] —vo·lut′ed adj. —vo·lu′tion n.

Volute

vom·it (vom′it) v.i. 1 To disgorge the contents of the stomach; throw up. 2 To issue with violence from any hollow place; be ejected. —v.t. 3 To disgorge (the contents of the stomach). 4 To discharge or send forth copiously or forcibly: The volcano vomited smoke. —n. 1 The act of vomiting. 2 Matter ejected from the stomach in vomiting. [< L vomere] —vom′it·er n.

vom·i·tive (vom′ə·tiv) adj. Of, pertaining to, or causing vomiting. —n. EMETIC.

von (von; Ger. fōn, unstressed fən) prep. German Of; from: used in German and Austrian family names as an attribute of nobility.

voo·doo (vōō′dōō) n. 1 A primitive religion of African origin, found among Haitian and West Indian Negroes and the Negroes of the s U.S., characterized by belief in sorcery and the use of charms, fetishes, witchcraft, etc. 2 A person who practices voodoo. 3 A voodoo charm or fetish. —adj. Of or pertaining to the beliefs, ceremonies, etc., of voodoo. —v.t. To practice voodoo upon; bewitch. Also vou′dou. —voo′doo·ism, voo′doo·ist n. —voo′doo·is′tic adj.

vo·ra·cious (vô·rā′shəs, vō-, və-) adj. 1 Eating with greediness; ravenous. 2 Very eager, as in some desire; insatiable. 3 Immoderate: a voracious appetite. [< L vorax < vorare devour] —vo·ra′cious·ly adv. —vo·rac·i·ty (-ras′ə·tē), vo·ra′cious·ness n.

-vorous combining form Consuming; eating or feeding upon: omnivorous, carnivorous. [< L vorare devour]

vor·tex (vôr′teks) n. pl. ·tex·es or ·ti·ces (-tə·sēz) 1 A mass of rotating or whirling fluid, esp. one spiraling in toward a center; a whirlpool or whirlwind. 2 Something resembling a vortex, as an activity or situation from which it is difficult to escape. [< L, var. of vertex top, point] —vor′ti·cal (-ti·kəl) adj. —vor′ti·cal·ly adv.

vo·ta·ry (vō′tər·ē) n. pl. ·ries 1 One who is bound by vows, as a nun or priest. 2 One devoted to some particular worship, pursuit, study, etc. Also vo′ta·rist. —adj. 1 Of, pertaining to, or like a vow. 2 Consecrated by a vow. [< L votus, p.p. of vovere vow]

vote (vōt) n. 1 A formal expression of choice or opinion, as in electing officers, passing resolutions, etc. 2 That by which such choice or opinion is expressed, as the ballot, a show of hands, etc. 3 The number of ballots cast, hands raised, etc., to indicate such choice or opinion. 4 The votes of a specified group; also, the group itself. 5 The right to vote. 6 A voter. —v. vot·ed, vot·ing v.t. 1 To enact or determine by vote. 2 To cast one's vote for: to vote the Democratic ticket. 3 To elect or defeat by vote. 4 Informal To declare by general agreement: to vote a concert a success. —v.i. 5 To cast one's vote. —vote down To defeat or suppress by voting against. —vote in To elect. [< L votum a vow, wish, orig. p.p. neut. of vovere vow]

vot·er (vōt′ər) n. 1 A person who votes. 2 A person having the right to vote.

vo·tive (vō′tiv) adj. Performed, offered, lit, etc., as fulfillment of a vow, as an act of worship, in gratitude, etc. [< L votum. See VOTE.] —vo′tive·ly adv. —vo′tive·ness n.

vouch (vouch) v.i. 1 To give one's own assurance or guarantee: with for: I will vouch for their honesty. 2 To serve as assurance or proof: with for: The evidence vouches for his innocence. —v.t. 3 To bear witness to; attest or affirm. 4 To cite as support or justification, as a precedent, authority, etc. 5 To uphold by satisfactory proof or evidence; substantiate. [< L vocare call < vox, vocis a voice]

vouch·er (vou′chər) n. 1 A document that serves to vouch for the truth of something, or attest an alleged act, esp. the expenditure or receipt of money. 2 One who vouches for another; a witness.

vouch·safe (vouch′sāf′) v. ·safed, ·saf·ing v.t. 1 To grant, as with condescension; permit; deign. —v.i. 2 To condescend; deign. [< VOUCH + SAFE] —vouch′safe′ment n.

vous·soir (vōō·swär′) n. Archit. A wedge-shaped stone in an arch. [< OF vausoir, volsoir curvature of a vault]

vow (vou) n. 1 A solemn promise, as to God or a god. 2 A pledge of faithfulness: marriage vows. 3 A solemn and emphatic affirmation. —take vows To enter a religious order. —v.t. 1 To promise solemnly. 2 To declare with assurance or solemnity. 3 To make a solemn promise or threat to do, inflict, etc. —v.i. 4 To make a vow. [< L votum. See VOTE.] —vow′er n.

vow·el (vou′əl, voul) n. 1 Phonet. A voiced speech sound produced by the relatively unimpeded passage of air through the mouth. 2 A letter indicating such a sound, as a, e, i, o, or u. —adj. Of or pertaining to a vowel or vowels. [< L vocalis (littera) vocal (letter)]

vox pop. voice of the people (L vox populi).

vox po·pu·li (voks pop′yə·lī, -lē) The voice of the people; public sentiment. [L]

voy·age (voi′ij) n. 1 A journey by water, esp. by sea. 2 Any journey, as one by aircraft. —v. ·aged, ·ag·ing v.i. 1 To make a voyage; travel. —v.t. 2 To traverse. [< L viaticum] —voy′ag·er n. —Syn. n. 1 crossing, cruise, sail, trip.

vo·ya·geur (vwä·yä·zhœr′) n. pl. ·geurs (-zhœr′) Can. Formerly, a man engaged by a fur company to carry men, supplies, etc., between remote trading posts. [F]

vo·yeur (vwä·yûr′) n. One who is sexually gratified by looking at sexual objects or acts. [< F voir see] —vo·yeur′·ism n.

V.P. Vice President.

vs. versus.

v.s. see above (L vide supra).

VSS versions.

VT Vermont (P.O. abbr.).

Vt. Vermont.

v.t. verb transitive.

VTOL vertical takeoff and landing.

Vul., Vulg. Vulgate.

Vul·can (vul′kən) Rom. Myth. The god of fire and of metallurgy. —Vul·ca·ni·an (-kā′nē·ən) adj.

vul·can·ite (vul′kən·īt) n. A dark-colored, hard, vulcanized rubber. [< VULCAN]

vul·can·ize (vul′kən·īz) v.t. & v.i. ·ized, ·iz·ing To heat (natural rubber) with sulfur in order to increase strength and elasticity. [< VULCAN] —vul′can·i·za′tion, vul′can·iz′er n.

vul·gar (vul′gər) adj. 1 Lacking good manners, taste, etc.; coarse; unrefined. 2 Offensive or obscene in expression: a vulgar usage. 3 Of or pertaining to the common people; general; popular. 4 Written in or translated into the common language or dialect; vernacular. [< L vulgus the common people] —vul′gar·ly adv. —Syn. 1 boorish, crude, tasteless. 2 indecent, taboo. 3 ordinary, plebeian.

vul·gar·i·an (vul·gâr′ē·ən) n. A person of vulgar tastes or manners; esp., a wealthy person with coarse habits.

vul·gar·ism (vul′gə·riz′əm) n. 1 A word, phrase, or expression generally considered to be incorrect or coarse and indicative of ignorance or ill breeding on the part of the user. 2 VULGARITY.

---

add, āce, câre, pälm; end, ēven; it, īce; odd, ōpen, ôrder; tōōk, pōōl; up, bûrn; ə = a in above, u in focus; yōō = u in fuse; oil; pout; check; go; ring; thin; this; zh, vision. < derived from; ? origin uncertain or unknown.

vul·gar·i·ty (vul-gar′ə-tē) *n. pl.* **·ties 1** The state, quality, or character of being vulgar. **2** Something vulgar, as an act or expression.

vul·gar·ize (vul′gə-rīz) *v.t.* **·ized, ·iz·ing** To make vulgar. *Brit. sp.* **vul′gar·ise.** —**vul′gar·i·za′tion, vul′gar·iz′er** *n.*

Vulgar Latin The popular, informal speech of the ancient Romans, considered to be the chief source of the Romance languages.

vul·gate (vul′gāt) *adj.* Popular; accepted. —*n.* **1** Everyday speech. **2** A popularly accepted text. [< L *vulgare* make common < *vulgus* the common people]

Vul·gate (vul′gāt) *n.* A Latin version of the Bible, translated in the 4th century, since revised and used as the authorized version by Roman Catholics. —*adj.* Of or in the Vulgate.

vul·ner·a·ble (vul′nər-ə-bəl) *adj.* **1** That may be wounded; capable of being hurt. **2** Open to attack; assailable. **3** In contract bridge, having won one game of a rubber, and therefore subject to doubled penalities if contract is not fulfilled. [< L *vulnerare* to wound < *vulnus* a wound] —**vul′ner·a·bil′i·ty, vul′ner·a·ble·ness** *n.* —**vul′ner·a·bly** *adv.*

vul·pine (vul′pin, -pīn) *adj.* **1** Of or pertaining to a fox. **2** Like a fox; sly; crafty; cunning. [< L *vulpes* a fox]

vul·ture (vul′chər) *n.* **1** Any of various large birds related to hawks and falcons, having a naked head and dark plumage, and feeding on carrion. **2** Something or someone that preys upon others. [< L *vultur*] —**vul′tur·ous** *adj.*

Vulture

vul·va (vul′və) *n. pl.* **·vae** (-vē) The external genital parts of the female. [L, a covering, womb] —**vul′val, vul′var, vul′vi·form** (-və-fôrm) *adj.*

vy·ing (vī′ing) *pr.p.* of VIE. —*adj.* That vies or competes. —**vy′ing·ly** *adv.*

W

W, w (dub′əl-yōō, -yōō) *n. pl.* **W's, w's, Ws, ws** (dub′əl-yōōz, -yōōz) **1** The 23rd letter of the English alphabet. **2** Any spoken sound representing the letter *W* or *w*. **3** Something shaped like a W. —*adj.* Shaped like a W.

W tungsten (G *wolfram*).

W, W., w, w. watt; west; western.

w. warden; week(s); weight; wife; with; word; work.

WA Washington (P.O. abbr.).

wab·ble (wob′əl) *n., v.t. & v.i.* **·bled, ·bling** WOBBLE. [Var. of WOBBLE] —**wab′bler** *n.* —**wab′bly** *adj.*

Wac (wak) *n.* A member of the WAC, the women's division of the U.S. Army. [< *W(omen's) A(rmy) C(orps)*]

wack·y (wak′ē) *adj.* **wack·i·er, wack·i·est** *Slang* Extremely irrational or erratic; crazy. Also **whack′y.** [Prob. < WHACK] —**wack′i·ly** *adv.* —**wack′i·ness** *n.*

wad (wod) *n.* **1** A small compact mass of any soft or flexible substance, esp. as used for stuffing, packing, or lining. **2** A lump; mass: a *wad* of tobacco. **3** A small plug used to hold in a charge of powder in a muzzleloading gun. **4** A pasteboard or paper disk to hold powder and shot in place in a shotgun shell. • See CARTRIDGE. **5** Fibrous material for stopping up breaks, leakages, etc.; wadding. **6** *Informal* A large amount, esp. of money. **7** *Informal* A roll of banknotes. —*v.* **wad·ded, wad·ding** *v.t.* **1** To press (fibrous substances, as cotton) into a mass or wad. **2** To roll or fold into a tight wad, as paper. **3** To pack or stuff with wadding for protection, as valuables. **4** To place a wad in (a gun, etc.). **5** To hold in place with a wad. —*v.i.* **6** To form into a wad. [?] —**wad′der** *n.*

wad·ding (wod′ing) *n.* **1** Wads collectively. **2** Any substance used as wads.

wad·dle (wod′l) *v.i.* **·dled, ·dling 1** To walk with short steps, swaying from side to side. **2** To move clumsily; totter. —*n.* A clumsy rocking walk, like that of a duck. [Freq. of WADE] —**wad′dler** *n.* —**wad′dly** *adj.*

wade (wād) *v.* **wad·ed, wad·ing** *v.i.* **1** To walk through water or any substance more resistant than air, as mud, sand, etc. **2** To proceed slowly or laboriously: to *wade* through a lengthy book. —*v.t.* **3** To pass or cross, as a river, by walking on the bottom; walk through; ford. —**wade in** (or **into**) *Informal* To attack or begin energetically or vigorously. —*n.* An act of wading. [< OE *wadan* go]

wad·er (wā′dər) *n.* **1** One who wades. **2** A long-legged wading bird, as a snipe, plover, or stork. **3** *pl.* High waterproof boots or pants, worn esp. by anglers.

wa·di (wä′dē) *n. pl.* **·dies 1** In Arabia and N Africa, a ravine containing the bed of a watercourse, usu. dry except in the rainy season. **2** The stream of water flowing through a wadi. Also **wa′dy.** [< Ar. *wādī*]

Waf (waf, wäf) *n.* A member of the WAF, the women's division of the U.S. Air Force. [< *W(omen in the) A(ir) F(orce)*]

wa·fer (wā′fər) *n.* **1** A very thin crisp biscuit, cooky, or cracker; also, a small disk of candy. **2** *Eccl.* A small flat disk of unleavened bread, used in the Eucharist in some churches. **3** A thin hardened disk of dried paste, gelatin, etc., used for sealing letters, attaching papers, or receiving the impression of a seal. —*v.t.* To attach, seal, or fasten with a wafer. [< AF *wafre* < MLG *wafel*]

waf·fle[1] (wof′əl, wô′fəl) *n.* A batter cake, crisper than a pancake, baked in a waffle iron. [< Du. *wafel* a wafer]

waf·fle[2] (wof′əl, wô′fəl) *v.i.* **·fled, ·fling 1** *Chiefly Brit. Informal* To speak or write nonsense. **2** *Informal* To avoid giving a direct answer; hedge. —*n. Chiefly Brit. Informal* Nonsense; twaddle. [< obs. *woff, waff* to yelp]

waffle iron A utensil for cooking waffles, consisting of two indented metal griddles, hinged together, between which the waffle is baked.

waft (waft, wäft) *v.t.* **1** To carry or bear gently or lightly over air or water; float. **2** To convey as if on air or water. —*v.i.* **3** To float, as on the wind. **4** To blow gently, as a breeze. —*n.* **1** The act of one who or that which wafts. **2** A breath or current of air. **3** A passing sound or odor. **4** A waving motion. [< Du. *wachten* to guard] —**waft′er** *n.*

wag (wag) *v.* **wagged, wag·ging** *v.t.* **1** To cause to move lightly and quickly from side to side or up and down, as a dog's tail. **2** To move (the tongue) in talking. —*v.i.* **3** To move lightly and quickly from side to side or up and down. **4** To move busily in animated talk or gossip: said of the tongue. —*n.* **1** The act or motion of wagging: a *wag* of the head. **2** A droll or humorous person; wit. [Prob. < Scand.]

wage (wāj) *n.* **1** *Often pl.* Payment for service rendered, esp. such payment calculated by the hour, day, or week, or for a certain amount of work. **2** *Usu. pl. (construed as sing. or pl.)* Reward: the *wages* of sin. —*v.t.* **waged, wag·ing** To engage in and maintain vigorously; carry on: to *wage* war. [< AF *wagier* pledge] —**Syn.** *n.* **1** compensation, earnings, pay, remuneration.

wage earner One who works for wages.

wa·ger (wā′jər) *v.t. & v.i.* To bet. —*n.* **1** A bet. **2** The thing bet on. [< AF *wagier*] —**wa′ger·er** *n.*

wage·work·er (wāj′wûr′kər) *n.* An employee receiving wages. —**wage′work′ing** *n., adj.*

wag·ger·y (wag′ər-ē) *n. pl.* **·ger·ies 1** Mischievous joking. **2** A practical joke. [< WAG]

wag·gish (wag′ish) *adj.* **1** Being or acting like a wag; humorous. **2** Said or done as a joke. —**wag′gish·ly** *adv.* —**wag′gish·ness** *n.* —**Syn.** **1** droll, facetious, funny, jocose.

wag·gle (wag′əl) *v.* **·gled, ·gling** *v.t.* To wag; swing: The duck *waggles* its tail. —*n.* The act of waggling. [Freq. of WAG] —**wag′gling·ly** *adv.* —**wag′gly** *adj.* (**·i·er, ·i·est**)

Wag·ne·ri·an (väg-nir′ē-ən) *adj.* **1** Of or pertaining to Richard Wagner or to his music, style, or theories. **2** Specializing in the performance of Wagner's music. —*n.* One who admires the music or the theories of Richard Wagner.

wag·on (wag′ən) *n.* **1** Any of various four-wheeled, usu.

Wagon

horse-drawn vehicles for carrying heavy loads. **2** A child's open, four-wheeled cart, pulled and steered by a long handle. **3** PATROL WAGON. **4** STATION WAGON. **5** *Brit.* A railway freight car. **6** A stand on wheels or casters for serving food or drink: a tea *wagon.* —**on** (or **off**) **the (water) wagon** *Informal* Abstaining (or no longer abstaining) from alcoholic beverages. —**fix (someone's) wagon** *Slang* To even scores with; get revenge on. —*v.t.* To carry or transport in a wagon. *Brit. sp.* **wag′gon.** [< Du. *wagen*]

wag·on·er (wag′ən·ər) *n.* One whose business is driving wagons. *Brit. sp.* **wag·gon·er.**

wag·on·load (wag′ən·lōd′) *n.* The amount that a wagon can carry. *Brit. sp.* **wag·gon·load.**

wagon train A line of wagons traveling together.

wag·tail (wag′tāl′) *n.* Any of various birds that habitually jerk the tail, as certain pipits.

Wa·ha·bi (wä·hä′bē) *n.* A member of a strict orthodox Muslim sect. Also **Wah·ha′bi.** —**Wa·ha′bism, Wah·ha′bism** (-biz·əm) *n.*

waif (wāf) *n.* **1** A homeless, neglected person, esp. a child. **2** A stray animal. [Prob. < Scand.]

wail (wāl) *v.i.* **1** To grieve with mournful cries; lament. **2** To make a mournful, crying sound, as the wind. —*v.t.* **3** To mourn; lament. **4** To cry out in sorrow. —*n.* **1** A prolonged, high-pitched sound of lamentation. **2** Any mournful sound, as of the wind. [< ON *vei* woe] —**wail′er** *n.* —**wail′ful** *adj.* —**wail′ful·ly, wail′ing·ly** *adv.*

Wailing Wall A high wall in Jerusalem reputedly containing fragments of Solomon's temple and traditionally a place for Jews to pray and mourn.

wain (wān) *n.* An open, four-wheeled wagon for hauling heavy loads. [< OE *wægn, wæn*]

wain·scot (wān′skət, -skŏt, -skot) *n.* **1** A facing for inner walls, usu. of paneled wood. **2** The lower part of an inner wall, when finished with material different from the rest of the wall. —*v.t.* **·scot·ed** or **·scot·ted, ·scot·ing** or **·scot·ting** To face or panel with wainscot. [< MLG *wagen* a wagon + *schot* a wooden partition]

wain·scot·ing (wān′skət·ing, -skot-) *n.* **1** WAINSCOT. **2** Material for a wainscot. Also **wain′scot·ting.**

wain·wright (wān′rīt′) *n.* A maker of wagons.

waist (wāst) *n.* **1** The part of the body between the lower ribs and the hips. **2** The middle part of any object, esp. if narrower than the ends: the *waist* of a violin. **3** That part of a woman's dress covering the body from the waistline to the shoulders. **4** BLOUSE. **5** WAISTLINE (def. 2). [ME *wast*]

waist·band (wāst′band′) *n.* A band encircling the waist, esp. such a band inside a skirt or trousers.

waist·coat (wes′kit, wāst′kōt′) *n. Chiefly Brit.* VEST (def. 1).

waist·line (wāst′līn′) *n.* **1** The so-called line that encircles the middle of the waist. **2** That part of a garment covering this line or extending above or below it according to the dictates of fashion.

wait (wāt) *v.i.* **1** To stay in expectation, as of an anticipated action or event: with *for, until,* etc. **2** To be or remain in readiness. **3** To remain temporarily neglected or undone. **4** To perform duties of personal service; esp. to act as a waiter or waitress. —*v.t.* **5** To stay or remain in expectation of: to *wait* one's turn. **6** *Informal* To put off or postpone: Don't *wait* breakfast for me. —**wait on** (or **upon**) **1** To act as a clerk or attendant to. **2** To go to see; visit. **3** To attend as a result or consequence. —**wait up 1** To delay going to bed in anticipation of someone's arrival or

of something happening. **2** *Informal* To stop until someone catches up. —*n.* The act of waiting, or the time spent in waiting; delay. —**lie in wait** To remain hidden in order to make a surprise attack. [< AF *waitier*] —**Syn.** *v.* **1** abide, linger, remain, tarry.

wait·er (wā′tər) *n.* **1** A man employed to wait on table, as in a restaurant. **2** One who awaits something. **3** A tray for dishes, etc.

wait·ing (wā′ting) *n.* The act of one who waits. —**in waiting** In attendance, esp. at court.

waiting room A room for the use of persons waiting, as for a train, a doctor, etc.

wait·ress (wā′tris) *n.* A woman employed to wait on table, as in a restaurant.

waive (wāv) *v.t.* **waived, waiv·ing 1** To give up or relinquish a claim to. **2** To refrain from insisting upon or taking advantage of; forgo. **3** To put off; postpone; delay. [< OF *gaiver* abandon]

waiv·er (wā′vər) *n. Law* **1** The voluntary relinquishment of a right, privilege, or advantage. **2** The instrument which evidences such relinquishment. [< AF *weyver* abandon, waive]

wake[1] (wāk) *v.* **woke** or **waked, waked** (*Regional* **wok·en**), **wak·ing** *v.i.* **1** To emerge from sleep: often with *up.* **2** To be or remain awake. **3** To become aware or alert. **4** *Regional* To keep watch at night; esp., to hold a wake. —*v.t.* **5** To rouse from sleep or slumber; awake: often with *up.* **6** To rouse or stir up; excite. **7** To make aware; alert. **8** *Regional* To hold a wake over. —*n.* A vigil, esp. a watch over the body of a dead person through the night, just before the burial. [Fusion of OE *wacan* awaken and *wacian* be awake]

wake[2] (wāk) *n.* **1** The trail of turbulence left by a moving ship, aircraft, etc. **2** Any course passed over. —**in the wake of** Following close behind. [< ON *vök* an opening in ice]

wake·ful (wāk′fəl) *adj.* **1** Not sleeping or sleepy. **2** Watchful; alert. **3** Sleepless; restless: a *wakeful* time. —**wake′-ful·ly** *adv.* —**wake′ful·ness** *n.* —**Syn. 1** awake. **2** cautious, vigilant, wary.

wak·en (wā′kən) *v.t.* **1** To rouse from sleep; awake. **2** To rouse or urge to alertness or activity. —*v.i.* **3** To cease sleeping; wake up. [< OE *wacnian*] —**wak′en·er** *n.*

wake-rob·in (wāk′rob′in) *n.* **1** TRILLIUM. **2** JACK-IN-THE-PULPIT.

Wal·dorf salad (wôl′dôrf) A salad made of chopped celery, apples, walnuts, and mayonnaise. [< the first *Waldorf*-Astoria Hotel, New York City]

wale (wāl) *n.* **1** WELT (def. 1). **2** A ridge or rib on the surface of cloth, as on corduroy. **3** *Usu. pl.* One of several planks on the outer sides of a wooden ship. —*v.t.* **waled, wal·ing 1** To raise wales on by striking. **2** To manufacture (cloth) with ridges or ribs. [< OE *walu*]

walk (wôk) *v.i.* **1** To advance on foot in such a manner that one part of a foot is always on the ground, or, in quadrupeds, that two or more feet are always on the ground. **2** To go on foot for exercise or amusement. **3** To move in a manner suggestive of walking, as certain inanimate objects. **4** To act or live in some manner: to *walk* in peace. **5** In baseball, to advance to first base after being pitched four balls. —*v.t.* **6** To pass through, over, or across at a walk: to *walk* the floor. **7** To lead, ride, or drive at a walk: to *walk* a horse. **8** To force or help to walk. **9** To accompany on a walk: I'll *walk* you to school. **10** To bring to a specified condition by walking. **11** To cause to move with a motion resembling a walk: to *walk* a trunk on its corners. **12** In baseball, to allow to advance to first base by pitching four balls. —**walk away from 1** To outrun or outdo (someone). **2** To sustain little or no injury in an accident. —**walk off 1** To depart, esp. abruptly. **2** To get rid of (fat, etc.) by walking. —**walk off with 1** To win, esp. with little difficulty. **2** To steal. —**walk out** *Informal* **1** To go out on strike. **2** To depart suddenly. —**walk out on** *Informal* To forsake; desert. —**walk over 1** To defeat easily. **2** To treat with contempt. —*n.* **1** The act of walking, as for enjoyment. **2** Manner of walking; gait. **3** A place prepared for walking, as a sidewalk. **4** The distance covered or time spent in walking. **5** A piece of ground set apart for the feeding and exercise of domestic animals. **6** In baseball, the act of walking a batter; also, a being walked. —**walk of life** One's social or financial status. [< OE *wealcan* roll, toss] —**walk′er** n. —**Syn.** v. **1** saunter, step, stride, tread.

walk·a·way (wôk′ə·wā′) n. *Informal* A contest won without serious opposition. Also **walk′o·ver** (-ō′vər).

walk·ie-talk·ie (wô′kē·tô′kē) n. A portable radio transmitting and receiving set.

walking papers *Informal* Notice of dismissal from employment, office, etc.

walking stick 1 A staff or cane. **2** Any of various insects having legs and body resembling twigs.

walk-on (wôk′on′, -ôn′) n. A very small, usu. non-speaking role in a play, etc.

walk·out (wôk′out′) n. *Informal* A workmen's strike.

walk-up (wôk′up′) *Informal* n. **1** An apartment house or building of two or more stories having no elevator. **2** An apartment located higher than the ground floor in such an apartment house.

wall (wôl) n. **1** A continuous structure designed to enclose an area, to be the surrounding exterior of a building, or to be a partition between rooms or halls. **2** A fence of stone or brickwork, surrounding or separating yards, fields, etc. **3** *Usu. pl.* A barrier or rampart constructed for defense. **4** A sea wall; levee. **5** A barrier enclosing a cavity, vessel, or receptacle: the *wall* of the abdomen. **6** Something suggestive of a wall: a *wall* of bayonets. —**drive (push or thrust) to the wall** To force (one) to an extremity; crush. —**drive (or send) up the wall** *Informal* To make extremely nervous, tense, etc. —v.t. **1** To provide, surround, protect, etc., with or as with a wall or walls. **2** To fill or block with *up*: often with *up.* —adj. **1** Of or pertaining to a wall. **2** Hanging from, growing on, or built into a wall. [< OE *weall* < L *vallum* a rampart]

wal·la·by (wol′ə·bē) n. pl. **·bies** Any of various small to medium-sized kangaroos. [< Australian *wolaba*]

wall·board (wôl′bôrd′, -bōrd′) n. A material of varied composition pressed into sheets and used for walls, ceilings, etc.

wal·let (wol′it) n. A small, usu. folding case, as of leather, for holding paper money, cards, etc., and sometimes change, carried in a pocket or purse. [ME *walet*]

wall·eye (wôl′ī′) n. **1** An eye with a light-colored or white iris. **2** A kind of strabismus in which the eyes diverge. **3** Any of several walleyed fishes. [Back formation < WALL-EYED]

wall·eyed (wôl′īd′) adj. **1** Having a walleye or walleyes. **2** Having large, staring eyes, as certain fish. [< ON *vagl* a film on the eye + *auga* eye]

walleyed pike A large freshwater game fish of North America. Also **walleyed perch.**

wall·flow·er (wôl′flou′ər) n. **1** Any of various cultivated perennials related to mustard having fragrant yellow, orange, or red flowers. **2** *Informal* A person who because of unpopularity or shyness does not participate in some social activity, as a party or dance.

Wal·loon (wo·lōōn′) n. **1** One of a people of s Belgium and adjoining regions of France. **2** Their language, a dialect of French. —adj. Of or pertaining to the Walloons or their dialect.

wal·lop (wol′əp) *Informal* v.t. **1** To beat soundly; thrash. **2** To hit with a hard blow. —n. A hard blow. [< AF *waloper*] —**wal′lop·er** n.

wal·lop·ing (wol′əp·ing) *Informal* adj. Very large; whopping. —n. A beating; whipping or crushing defeat.

wal·low (wol′ō) v.i. **1** To roll about, as in mud, snow, etc. **2** To move with a heavy, rolling motion, as a ship in a storm. **3** To indulge oneself wantonly: to *wallow* in sensuality. —n. **1** The act of wallowing. **2** A depression or hollow made by wallowing. [< OE *wealwian*] —**wal′low·er** n.

wall·pa·per (wôl′pā′pər) n. Decorative paper for covering walls. —v.t. To cover with wallpaper.

Wall Street 1 A street in lower Manhattan, New York City, famous as the financial center of the U.S. **2** The U.S. financial world.

wall-to-wall (wôl′tə·wôl′) adj. Completely covering a floor: *wall-to-wall* carpeting.

wal·nut (wôl′nut′, -nət) n. **1** Any of various deciduous trees cultivated as ornamental shade trees and valued for their timber and their edible nuts. **2** The wood or nut of any of these trees. **3** The shagbark or its nut. **4** The color of the wood of any of these trees, esp. of the black walnut, a very dark brown: also **walnut brown.** [< OE *wealh* foreign + *hnutu* a nut]

Wal·pur·gis Night (väl·pŏŏr′gis) The night before May 1, thought to be the occassion of a gathering of witches for demonic rites and orgies. [< St. *Walpurga,* 8th-cent. English missionary in Germany]

wal·rus (wôl′rəs, wol′-) n. A very large, seallike mammal of arctic seas, with flexible hind limbs, projecting tusklike canines in the upper jaw, a bushy, bristly mustache on the muzzle, and a very tough hide. —adj. **1** Belonging or pertaining to a walrus. **2** Designating a type of bushy mustache drooping at the ends. [< Scand.]

Black walnut
a. shuck. b. nut.

waltz (wôlts) n. **1** A dance to music in triple time. **2** Music for or in the style of such a dance. —v.i. **1** To dance a waltz. **2** To move quickly: She *waltzed* out of the room. —v.t. **3** To cause to waltz. —adj. Pertaining to the waltz. [< G *walzen* to waltz, roll] —**waltz′er** n.

Walrus

wam·pum (wom′pəm, wôm′-) n. **1** Beads made of shells, formerly used as jewelry and currency among North American Indians. **2** *Informal* Money. [< Algon. *wampom(peag),* lit., a white (string of beads)]

wan (won) adj. **wan·ner, wan·nest 1** Pale, as from sickness; careworn. **2** Faint; feeble: a *wan* smile. [< OE *wann* dark, gloomy] —**wan′ly** adv. —**wan′ness** n. —**Syn. 1** ashen, livid, pallid. **2** weak.

wand (wond) n. **1** A slender, flexible rod waved by a magician. **2** Any rod symbolizing authority, as a scepter. **3** A musician's baton. [< ON *vöndr*]

wan·der (won′dər) v.i. **1** To travel about without destination or purpose; roam. **2** To go casually or by an indirect route; stroll. **3** To twist or meander. **4** To stray. **5** To deviate in conduct or opinion; go astray. **6** To be delirious. —v.t. **7** To wander through or across. [< OE *wandrian*] —**wan′der·er** n. —**wan′der·ing·ly** adv. —**Syn. 1** range, rove.

wan·der·lust (won′dər·lust′) n. An impulse to travel; restlessness. [< G *wandern* to travel + *Lust* joy]

wane (wān) v.i. **waned, wan·ing 1** To diminish in size and brilliance. **2** To decline or decrease gradually. **3** To draw to an end. —n. **1** A waning or decreasing. **2** The period of such decrease. —**on the wane** Decreasing; declining. [< OE *wanian* lessen]

wan·gle (wang′gəl) v. **·gled, ·gling** *Informal* v.t. **1** To obtain or make by indirect, manipulative, or dishonest methods; finagle. —v.i. **2** To resort to indirect, irregular, or dishonest methods. [?] —**wan′gler** n.

Wan·kel engine (väng′kəl, wäng′-) A light, compact type of internal-combustion engine having combustion chambers bounded by the wall of a shallow cylinder and the sides of a triangular piston that rotates in one direction inside it. Also **Wan′kel.** [< F. *Wankel,* 1902–, German inventor]

want (wont, wônt) v.t. **1** To feel a desire or wish for. **2** To wish; desire: used with the infinitive: to *want* to help. **3** To be deficient in, esp. to a required or customary extent. **4** To desire to see, speak to, arrest, etc.: He *wants* you on the phone; *wanted* by the police. **5** *Chiefly Brit.* To need; require. —v.i. **6** To have need: usu. with *for.* **7** To be needy or destitute. —n. **1** Lack; scarcity; shortage. **2** Poverty; destitution. **3** Something lacking; a need or craving. [Prob. < ON *vanta* be lacking] —**want′er** n. —**Syn.** n. **1** dearth, deficiency, insufficiency. **2** indigence, privation.

want ad *Informal* A classified advertisement, as in a newspaper, for something wanted, as an employee, a job, a lodging, etc.

want·ing (wŏn'ting, wôn'-) *adj.* 1 Missing; lacking: One juror is still *wanting.* 2 Not coming up to some standard, need, or expectation: He was found *wanting.* —**wanting in** Deficient in. —*prep.* 1 Lacking; without. 2 Less; minus.

wan·ton (wŏn'tən) *adj.* 1 Licentious; lewd; lustful. 2 Heartless or unjust; malicious: *wanton* savagery. 3 Unprovoked; senseless: a *wanton* murder. 4 Extravagant; unrestrained: *wanton* speech. 5 Not bound or tied; loose: *wanton* curls. 6 Capricious; frolicsome. —*v.i.* 1 To act in a wanton manner; be wanton. —*v.t.* 2 To waste or squander carelessly. —*n.* A lewd or licentious person. [< OE *wan* deficient + *tēon* bring up, educate] —**wan'ton·ly** *adv.* —**wan'ton·ness** *n.*

wap·i·ti (wŏp'ə·tē) *n. pl.* ·**tis** or ·**ti** A large North American deer; the American elk. [< Algon.] • See ELK.

war (wôr) *n.* 1 Armed strife or conflict between nations or states, or between different parties in the same nation. 2 Any act or state of conflict, struggle, or strife: a *war* against poverty. 3 Military science or strategy. —*v.i.* **warred, war·ring** 1 To wage war; fight or take part in a war. 2 To be in any state of active opposition. —*adj.* Of, pertaining to, used in, or resulting from war. [< OHG *werra* strife, confusion]

War Between the States CIVIL WAR.

war·ble (wôr'bəl) *v.* ·**bled, ·bling** *v.t.* 1 To sing (something) with trills and runs or with tremulous vibrations. —*v.i.* 2 To sing with trills, etc. 3 To make a liquid, murmuring sound, as a stream. 4 YODEL. —*n.* The act or sound of warbling. [< OF *werble* a warble]

war·bler (wôr'blər) *n.* 1 One who or that which warbles. 2 Any of a family of small, mostly Old World birds noted for their song. 3 Any of a large and varied family of small, migratory, New World birds, usu. having brilliant springtime plumage and distinctive songs.

war bonnet The ceremonial headdress of the North American Plains Indians.

war crime *Usu. pl.* Any of various crimes committed during or as a result of war, as maltreatment of prisoners, atrocities against civilians, genocide, etc. —**war criminal**

war cry A rallying cry or slogan used by combatants in a war, or by participants in any contest.

ward (wôrd) *n.* 1 In a hospital: **a** A large room for six or more patients. **b** A division for specific illnesses or groups of patients: the children's *ward.* 2 A division of a city for administrative or electoral purposes. 3 *Law* A person, as a minor, who is in the charge of a guardian or court. 4 The act of guarding or the state of being guarded. 5 A division or subdivision of a prison. 6 Any means of defense or protection. —*v.t.* To repel or turn aside, as a thrust or blow: usu. with *off.* [< OE *weardian* to watch, guard]

-ward *suffix* Toward; in the direction of: *upward, homeward.* Also **-wards.** [< OE *-weard*]

war dance A dance of certain tribes before going to war or in celebration of a victory.

war·den (wôr'dən) *n.* 1 A supervisor or custodian of something: a game *warden;* prison *warden.* 2 *Brit.* The head of certain colleges. 3 CHURCHWARDEN (def 1). [< AF *wardein*] —**war'den·ry** (*pl.* ·**ries**), **war'den·ship** *n.*

ward·er (wôr'dər) *n.* 1 A guard or sentinel. 2 *Chiefly Brit.* A prison official; warden. [< OF *guarder* guard, keep]

ward heeler *Slang* A hanger-on of a political boss in a ward or other local area, who does minor tasks, canvasses votes, etc.

ward·robe (wôrd'rōb') *n.* 1 A large upright cabinet for wearing apparel. 2 All the garments belonging to any one person. 3 The clothes for a particular season: a spring *wardrobe.* 4 The costumes of a theater, theatrical troupe, motion-picture company, etc.; also, the place where such costumes are kept. [< AF *warder* keep + *robe* a robe]

ward·room (wôrd'rōōm', -rŏŏm') *n.* 1 On a warship, the eating or living quarters allotted to the commissioned officers, excepting the commander. 2 These officers regarded as a group.

ward·ship (wôrd'ship) *n.* 1 The state of being a ward of a guardian or court. 2 Custody; guardianship.

ware (wâr) *n.* 1 Articles of the same class: used collectively in compounds: *glassware.* 2 *pl.* Articles for sale; merchandise. 3 Pottery; earthenware. [< OE *waru*]

ware·house (wâr'hous') *n.* 1 A storehouse for goods or merchandise. 2 *Chiefly Brit.* A large wholesale shop. —*v.t.* ·**housed** (-houzd'), ·**hous·ing** (-hou'zing) To place or store in a warehouse.

ware·house·man (wâr'hous'mən) *n. pl.* ·**men** (-mən) One who owns or works in a warehouse.

war·fare (wôr'fâr') *n.* 1 The waging or carrying on of war. 2 Struggle; strife.

war game 1 *pl.* Practice maneuvers imitating the conditions of actual warfare. 2 A simulated military conflict organized to test tactical procedures and concepts by discussion and analysis.

war·head (wôr'hed') *n.* The chamber in the nose of a bomb, guided missile, etc., containing an explosive, incendiary, or chemical charge.

war horse 1 A heavy horse used in warfare. 2 *Informal* A veteran of many struggles or contests, esp. political contests.

war·like (wôr'līk') *adj.* 1 Fond of or ready for war. 2 Relating to, used in, or suggesting war. 3 Threatening war. —**Syn.** 1 bellicose, belligerent. 2 martial, military.

war·lock (wôr'lok') *n.* 1 A male witch; sorcerer. 2 A magician or conjurer. [< OE *wær* a covenant + *lēogen* lie, deny]

warm (wôrm) *adj.* 1 Moderately hot; having heat somewhat greater than temperate: *warm* water; a *warm* climate. 2 Imparting heat: a *warm* fire. 3 Imparting or preserving warmth: a *warm* coat. 4 Having the natural temperature of most living persons or animals: *warm* blood. 5 Heated, as from exertion. 6 Ardent; enthusiastic; fervent: *warm* interest. 7 Lively; agitated: a *warm* argument. 8 Cordial; friendly: a *warm* welcome. 9 Amorous; loving: a *warm* glance. 10 Excitable; fiery: a *warm* temper. 11 Having predominating tones of red or yellow. 12 Recently made; fresh: a *warm* trail. 13 Near to finding a hidden object or fact, as in certain games. 14 *Informal* Uncomfortable by reason of annoyances or danger: They made the town *warm* for him. —*v.t.* 1 To make warm. 2 To make ardent or enthusiastic; interest. 3 To fill with kindly feeling. —*v.i.* 4 To become warm. 5 To become ardent or enthusiastic: often with *up* or *to.* 6 To become kindly disposed or friendly: with *to* or *toward.* —**warm up** 1 To warm. 2 To exercise the body, voice, etc., as before a game or performance. 3 To run an engine, etc., in order to attain correct operating temperature. —*n. Informal* A warming or being warm. [< OE *wearm*] —**warm'er, warm'ness** *n.* —**warm'ly** *adv.*

warm-blood·ed (wôrm'blud'id) *adj.* 1 Having a nearly uniform and warm body temperature, whatever the surrounding medium. 2 Enthusiastic; ardent; passionate.

warm-heart·ed (wôrm'här'tid) *adj.* Kind; affectionate.

warming pan A closed metal pan with a long handle, containing live coals or hot water, used for warming a bed.

war·mon·ger (wôr'mung'gər, -mong'-) *n.* One who favors or tries to incite war. —**war'mon'ger·ing** *adj., n.*

warmth (wôrmth) *n.* 1 The state, quality, or sensation of being warm. 2 Ardor or excitement of disposition or feeling. 3 Sympathetic friendliness, affection, or understanding. 4 The effect produced by warm colors.

warm-up (wôrm'up') *n.* The act or an instance of warming up.

warn (wôrn) *v.t.* 1 To make aware of possible harm; caution. 2 To advise; counsel. 3 To give notice in advance. 4 To notify (a person) to go or stay away. —*v.i.* 5 To give warning. [< OE *wearnian*] —**warn'er** *n.*

warn·ing (wôr'ning) *n.* 1 The act of one who warns or the state of being warned. 2 That which warns. —*adj.* Serving as a warning. —**warn'ing·ly** *adv.* —**Syn.** *n.* 2 admonition, advice, recommendation.

War of 1812 A war between the U.S. and Great Britain (1812–15).

War of Independence AMERICAN REVOLUTION.

warp (wôrp) *v.t.* **1** To turn or twist out of shape, as by shrinkage or heat. **2** To corrupt; pervert: a mind *warped* by bigotry. **3** *Naut.* To move (a vessel) by hauling on a rope or line fastened to something stationary. —*v.i.* **4** To become turned or twisted out of shape, as wood in drying. **5** To deviate from a correct or proper course: go astray. **6** *Naut.* To move by means of ropes fastened to a pier, anchor, etc. —*n.* **1** The state of being warped, twisted out of shape, or biased. **2** The threads that run the long way of a fabric, crossing the woof. **3** *Naut.* A rope or line used for warping. [< OE *weorpan* to throw] —**warp′er** *n.*

war paint 1 Paint applied to faces and bodies of primitive peoples as a sign of going to war. **2** *Informal* Cosmetics, as rouge, lipstick, etc. **3** *Informal* Official garb or regalia.

war·path (wôr′path′, -päth′) *n.* The route taken by an attacking party of American Indians. —**on the warpath 1** On a warlike expedition. **2** Ready for a fight; thoroughly angry.

war·plane (wôr′plān′) *n.* An airplane used in war.

war·rant (wôr′ənt, wor′-) *n.* **1** *Law* A judicial writ or order authorizing arrest, search, seizure, etc. **2** Something which assures or attests; guarantee. **3** That which gives authority for some course or act; sanction; justification. **4** A certificate of appointment given to a naval or military warrant officer. **5** A document giving a certain authority, esp. for the receipt or payment of money. —*v.t.* **1** To assure or guarantee the quality, accuracy, certainty, or sufficiency of: to *warrant* a title to property. **2** To guarantee the character or fidelity of; pledge oneself for. **3** To guarantee against injury, loss, etc. **4** To be sufficient grounds for; justify. **5** To give legal authority or power to; authorize. **6** *Informal* To say confidently; feel sure. [< AF *warant*] —**war′rant·er** *n.*

war·ran·tee (wôr′ən·tē′, wor′-) *n.* *Law* The person to whom a warranty is given.

warrant officer See GRADE.

war·ran·tor (wôr′ən·tôr, wor′-) *n.* *Law* One who makes or gives a warranty to another.

war·ran·ty (wôr′ən·tē, wor′-) *n. pl.* **·ties 1** *Law* A guarantee by the seller of property, a product, etc., that whatever is sold is or shall be as represented. **2** An official authorization or warrant. [< AF *warant* a warrant]

war·ren (wôr′ən, wor′-) *n.* **1** A place where rabbits live and breed. **2** Any building or area overcrowded with people. [< AF *warenne* a game park, a rabbit warren]

war·ri·or (wôr′ē·ər, wôr′yər, wor′-) *n.* A man engaged in or experienced in warfare or conflict.

war·ship (wôr′ship′) *n.* Any vessel used in naval combat.

wart (wôrt) *n.* **1** A small, usu. hard, benign excrescence on the skin, caused by a virus. **2** Any of various natural protuberances on certain plants and animals. [< OE *wearte*] —**wart′y** *adj.* (**·i·er**, **·i·est**)

wart hog An African wild hog having large tusks and warty excrescences on the face.

war whoop A yell, as made by American Indians, as a signal for attack, etc.

war·y (wâr′ē) *adj.* **war·i·er**, **war·i·est 1** Carefully watching and guarding. **2** Shrewd; wily. [< OE *wær*] —**war′i·ly** *adv.* —**war′i·ness** *n.*

Wart hog

was (woz, wuz, *unstressed* wəz) First and third person sing., past indicative of BE. [< OE *wæs*]

wash (wosh, wôsh) *v.t.* **1** To cleanse with water or other liquid, as by immersing, scrubbing, etc. **2** To wet or cover with water or other liquid. **3** To flow against or over: a beach *washed* by the ocean. **4** To remove or carry by the use or action of water: with *away, off, out,* etc. **5** To form or wear by erosion. **6** To purify, as gas, by passing through a liquid. **7** To coat with a thin layer of color. **8** To cover with a thin coat of metal. **9** *Mining* **a** To subject (gravel, earth, etc.) to the action of water so as to separate the ore, etc. **b** To separate (ore, etc.) thus. —*v.i.* **10** To wash oneself. **11** To wash clothes, etc., in water or other liquid. **12** To withstand the effects of washing: That calico will *wash.* **13** *Informal* To undergo testing successfully: That story won't *wash.* **14** To flow with a lapping sound, as waves. **15** To be carried away or removed by the use or action of

water: with *away, off, out,* etc. **16** To be eroded by the action of water. —**wash out** *Slang* To fail and be dropped from a course, esp. in military flight training. —*n.* **1** The act or an instance of washing. **2** A number of articles, as of clothing, set apart for washing. **3** Liquid or semiliquid refuse; swill. **4** Any preparation used in washing or coating, as a mouthwash. **5** A paint, as water color, spread lightly on a surface. **6** The breaking of a body of water upon the shore, or the sound made by this. **7** Erosion of soil or earth by the action of running water. **8** Material collected and deposited by water, as along a river bank. **9** Agitation or turbulence in water or air caused by something passing through it. **10** An area washed by a sea or river; a marsh; bog. **11** In the w U.S., the dry bed of a stream. —*adj.* Washable without injury: *wash* fabrics. [< OE *wascan*]

Wash. Washington.

wash·a·ble (wosh′ə·bəl, wôsh′-) *adj.* That can be washed without damage.

wash-and-wear (wosh′ən·wâr′, wôsh′-) *adj.* Designating a garment or fabric so treated as to require little or no ironing after washing.

wash·board (wosh′bôrd′, -bōrd′, wôsh′-) *n.* A board having a corrugated surface on which to rub clothes while washing them.

wash·bowl (wosh′bōl, wôsh′-) *n.* A basin or bowl used for washing the hands and face. Also **wash′ba·sin** (-bā′sən).

wash·cloth (wosh′klôth′, -kloth′, wôsh′-) *n.* A small cloth used for washing the body.

washed-out (wosht′out′, wôsht′-) *adj.* **1** Faded; pale. **2** *Informal* Exhausted; tired.

washed-up (wosht′up′, wôsht′-) *adj.* *Informal* **1** Finished; done with; through. **2** Exhausted.

wash·er (wosh′ər, wôsh′ər) *n.* **1** One who washes. **2** *Mech.* A small, flat, perforated disk of metal, rubber, etc., used to make a nut or joint tight. **3** WASHING MACHINE.

wash·er·wom·an (wosh′ər·wŏŏm′ən, wô′shər-) *n. pl.* **·wom·en** (-wim′in) LAUNDRESS.

wash·ing (wosh′ing, wô′shing) *n.* **1** The act of one who or that which washes. **2** Things (as clothing) washed or to be washed at one time. **3** A thin coating of metal: forks with only one *washing* of silver. **4** That which is obtained by washing: a *washing* of ore.

Washer
def 2

washing machine A machine that washes and usu. rinses automatically, used to clean clothes, linens, etc.

washing soda SODIUM CARBONATE.

Washington's Birthday (wash′ing·tənz, wô′shing-) The third Monday in February, a U.S. holiday observed in honor of the anniversary of George Washington's birth, February 22.

wash·out (wosh′out′, wôsh′-) *n.* **1** A considerable erosion of earth by the action of water; also, the excavation thus made. **2** *Slang* A hopeless or total failure.

wash·room (wosh′rŏŏm′, -rōŏm′, wôsh′-) *n.* A restroom or lavatory.

wash·stand (wosh′stand′, wôsh′-) *n.* **1** A stand for washbowl, pitcher, etc. **2** A bathroom sink.

wash·tub (wosh′tub′, wôsh′-) *n.* A usu. stationary tub used for laundry.

wash·wom·an (wosh′wŏŏm′ən, wôsh′-) *n. pl.* **·wom·en** (-wim′in) LAUNDRESS.

wash·y (wosh′ē, wô′shē) *adj.* **wash·i·er**, **wash·i·est 1** Watery; diluted. **2** Weak; feeble.

was·n't (woz′ənt, wuz′-) Contraction of *was not.*

wasp (wosp, wôsp) *n.* Any of numerous insects related to bees, having membranous wings, biting mouth parts, and effective stings, and including both social and solitary species. [< OE *wæsp*]

WASP (wosp, wôsp) *n.* *Slang* A white Protestant American, esp. one of N European ancestry. Also **Wasp.** [< *W(hite) A(nglo)-S(axon) P(rotestant)*] —**WASP′ish, Wasp′ish** *adj.*

wasp·ish (wos′pish, wôs′-) *adj.* **1** Of or like a wasp. **2** Irritable; bad-tempered. —**wasp′ish·ly** *adv.* —**wasp′ish·ness** *n.*

Thailand Dancers

—American President Lines

Prayer before a Buddhist statue in India

—California Texas Oil Co.

Dancing the Tarantella in Sicily
—Sheridan H. Garth

Women and children in the Belgian
Congo, Africa

A procession of virgins in Bali
—Sheridan H. Garth

A spring festival in Nidwalden, Switzerland, when
the cows are driven to upper Alpine pastures.
—Swiss Tourist

Croatian women of Yugoslavia dressed for church
in embroidered peasant costumes.

—Sheridan H. Garth

COSTUMES

Dryptosaurus

Agathaumus-Monoclonius

Allosaurus

Brontosaurus

Stegosaurus

Trachodon

DINOSAURS

Courtesy The American Museum of Natural History. Paintings (except Stegosaurus) by Charles R. Knight

EOHIPPUS — Eocene — Europe, North America. Size: from fox terrier to collie. Four toes on fore feet, 3 on hind feet.

HYPOHIPPUS — Middle Miocene — Asia, Europe, North America. Size: Shetland pony. Broad, hoofed middle toe with 2 side toes.

MESOHIPPUS — Oligocene — North America. Size: from coyote to sheep. Large middle toe with 2 slender side toes.

HIPPARION — Upper Miocene and Pliocene — Asia, Europe, North Africa, North America. Size: antelope.

EQUUS SCOTTI — Pleistocene — Asia, Africa, Europe, North America. Size: modern horse.

PLIOHIPPUS — Pliocene — North America. Size: nearly that of the modern horse. One-toed hoofed feet with vestigial side toes.

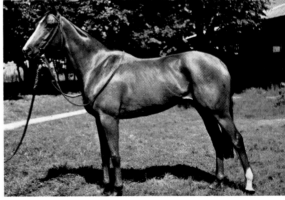

AMERICAN SADDLE HORSES

THE ENGLISH THOROUGHBRED

THE EVOLUTION OF THE HORSE

Paintings by Charles R. Knight

Courtesy The American Museum of Natural History

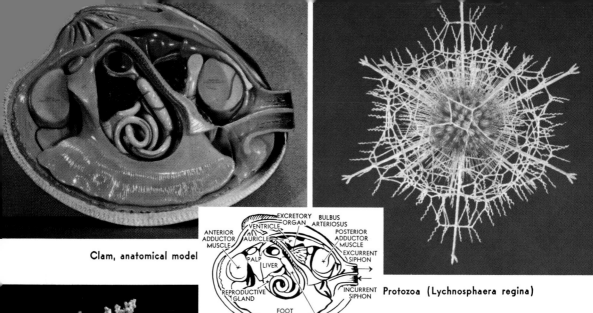

Clam, anatomical model

Labels on anatomical diagram: EXCRETORY ORGAN, BULBUS ARTERIOSUS, VENTRICLE, ANTERIOR ADDUCTOR MUSCLE, AURICLE, POSTERIOR ADDUCTOR MUSCLE, EXCURRENT SIPHON, PALP, LIVER, INCURRENT SIPHON, REPRODUCTIVE GLAND, FOOT, INTESTINE

Protozoa (Lychnosphaera regina)

Tridacna shell with coral growth

Sea Anemone

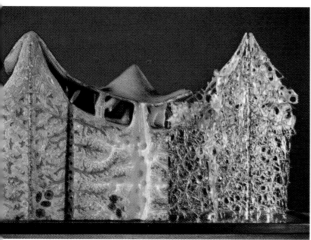

Sponge   *Courtesy The American Museum of Natural History*   Stalk Medusa (Halyclistis auricula)

INVERTEBRATES (Glass Models)

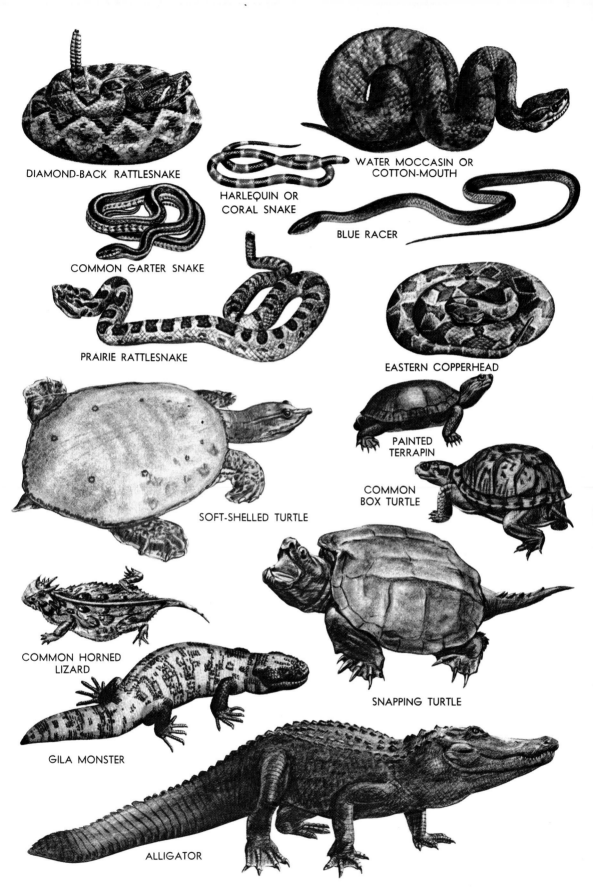

DIAMOND-BACK RATTLESNAKE

HARLEQUIN OR CORAL SNAKE

WATER MOCCASIN OR COTTON-MOUTH

BLUE RACER

COMMON GARTER SNAKE

PRAIRIE RATTLESNAKE

EASTERN COPPERHEAD

SOFT-SHELLED TURTLE

PAINTED TERRAPIN

COMMON BOX TURTLE

COMMON HORNED LIZARD

SNAPPING TURTLE

GILA MONSTER

ALLIGATOR

REPTILES OF NORTH AMERICA

Guilford L. Beck, Designer

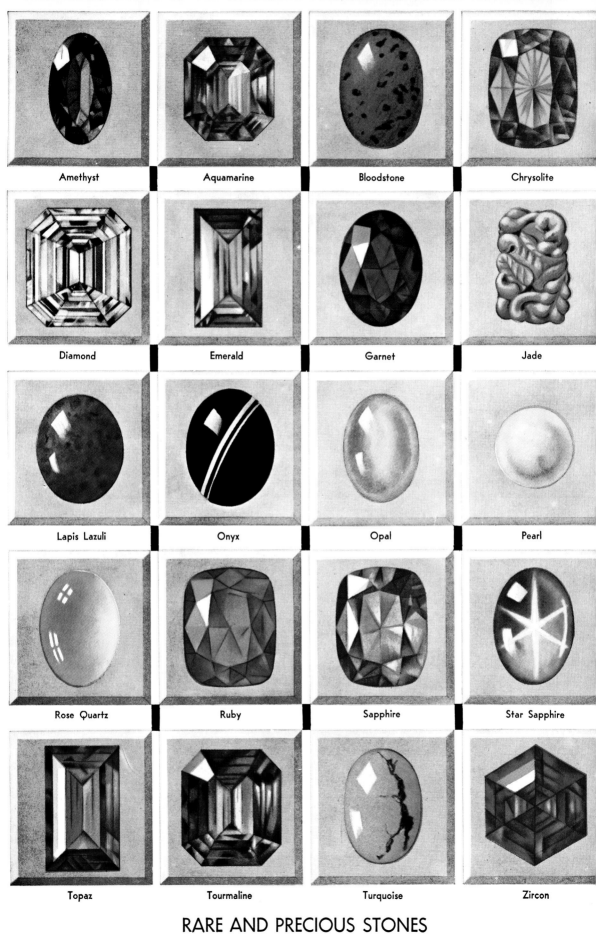

Amethyst	Aquamarine	Bloodstone	Chrysolite
Diamond	Emerald	Garnet	Jade
Lapis Lazuli	Onyx	Opal	Pearl
Rose Quartz	Ruby	Sapphire	Star Sapphire
Topaz	Tourmaline	Turquoise	Zircon

RARE AND PRECIOUS STONES

SHELLS

1. Polymita muscarum (Cuba)   2. Turbo petholatus (Philippines)   3. Pecten irradian (Senegal, Africa)   4. Vermetus spirata (Florida)   5. Polymita picta (Cuba)   6. Ianthina violacea (Australia)   7. Patella cymbiola (Madagascar)   8. Delphinula formosa (China)   9. Pterocera chiragra (Society Islands)   10. Ranella perca (Japan)   11. Haliotis excavata (Australia)   12. Pecten hericius (California)   13. Patella exarata (Sandwich Islands)   14. Spondylus gussoni (Sicily)   15. Balanus amphitrite (Florida)   16. Lima squamosa (Japan)   17. Eburna spirata (Ceylon)   18. Murex tenuispina (Eastern Seas)   19. Cypraea argus (Philippines)   20. Melongena corona (Gulf of Mexico)   21. Voluta ellioti (Australia)   22. Thais patula (Philippines)   23. Murex monodon (Australia)   24. Terebra suulata (Society Islands)   25. Conus episcopus (Ceylon)   26. Oliva porphyria (Panama)

Bronze face mask, Benin, West Africa

Mask of young man, Haida, Northwest Coast Indians, North America

Twisted face mask, Iroquois, Cayuga Tribe, New York State

Spirit Mask, Ibo Tribe, Southern Nigeria

Deer mask, Tibet

Devil dancer's mask, Ceylon

Pascola Dancers, Yaqui, Mexico

Noh Mask, Japanese Theatre

Dramatic Mask, Java

MASKS OF MANY LANDS
—Courtesy The American Museum of Natural History

wasp waist A very slim, narrow waist. —**wasp-waist-ed** (wosp′wās′tid, wôsp′-) *adj.*

was-sail (wos′əl, was′-, wo-sāl′) *n.* **1** An ancient toast, esp. to one's health. **2** The spiced drink, usu. ale and wine, prepared for a wassail. **3** An occasion of much drinking; a carousal. —*v.i.* **1** To take part in a wassail; carouse. —*v.t.* **2** To drink the health of; toast. [< ON *ves heill* be whole] —**was′sail-er** *n.*

Was-ser-mann test (wäs′ər-mən) A diagnostic test for syphilis, based on the detection of certain antibodies in the blood. Also **Wassermann reaction.** [< August von *Wassermann,* 1866–1925, German bacteriologist]

wast (wost, *unstressed* wəst) *Archaic* Were: used with THOU.

wast-age (wās′tij) *n.* That which is lost by leakage, waste, etc.

waste (wāst) *v.* **wast-ed, wast-ing** *v.t.* **1** To use or expend thoughtlessly; squander. **2** To make weak or feeble. **3** To use up; consume. **4** To fail to use or take advantage of, as an opportunity. **5** To lay waste; devastate. **6** *Slang* To kill; destroy. —*v.i.* **7** To lose strength, vigor, or bulk: often with *away.* **8** To diminish or dwindle gradually. **9** To pass gradually: said of time. —*n.* **1** Thoughtless or unnecessary expenditure, consumption, etc. **2** Failure to benefit or gain from something, as an opportunity. **3** A desolate or devastated place or region; wilderness; desert. **4** A continuous, gradual wearing away of strength, vigor, or substance. **5** Something discarded or rejected as worthless or unneeded, esp. tangled spun cotton thread. **6** Something that escapes without being used, as steam. **7** Garbage; rubbish; trash. **8** Something excreted from the body, as urine or excrement. —**lay waste** To destroy or devastate. —*adj.* **1** Cast aside as worthless; discarded. **2** Excreted from the body. **3** Not cultivated or inhabited; wild; barren. **4** Superfluous: *waste* energy. **5** Containing or conveying waste products. [< L *vastare* lay waste] —**wast′er** *n.* —**Syn.** *v.* **1** dissipate. **2** debilitate, enfeeble.

waste-bas-ket (wāst′bas′kit, -bäs′-) *n.* A container for paper scraps and other waste. Also **wastepaper basket.**

waste-ful (wāst′fəl) *adj.* **1** Prone to waste; extravagant. **2** Causing waste. —**waste′ful-ly** *adv.* —**waste′ful-ness** *n.*

waste-land (wāst′land′) *n.* A barren or desolate land.

waste-pa-per (wāst′pā′pər) *n.* Paper thrown away as worthless. Also **waste paper.**

waste pipe A pipe for carrying off waste water, etc.

wast-ing (wās′ting) *adj.* **1** Destructive; devastating. **2** Destructive to health; enfeebling.

wast-rel (wās′trəl) *n.* **1** A profligate; spendthrift. **2** An idler or loafer. [Dim. of *waster* one who wastes]

watch (woch, wôch) *v.i.* **1** To look attentively; observe closely. **2** To be on the alert. **3** To wait expectantly for something: with *for.* **4** To do duty as a guard or sentinel. **5** To keep vigil. —*v.t.* **6** To look at attentively; observe. **7** To keep informed concerning. **8** To be alert for; to *watch* one's opportunity. **9** To keep watch over; guard. —**watch out** To be careful. —*n.* **1** Close and continuous attention; careful observation. **2** Service as a guard or sentry. **3** The period of time during which a guard is on duty. **4** The person or persons set to guard or watch. **5** A small, portable timepiece worn on the wrist or carried in a pocket. **6** A vigil or wake. **7** *Naut.* **a** A spell of duty on board ship, usu. four hours. **b** The division of a crew on duty during such a period. [< OE *wæccan*] —**watch′er** *n.*

watch-case (woch′kās′, wôch′-) *n.* A metal covering for the mechanism of a watch.

watch-dog (woch′dôg′, -dog′, wôch′-) *n.* **1** A dog kept to guard a building or other property. **2** A person who keeps a vigilant lookout.

watch-ful (woch′fəl, wôch′-) *adj.* Watching carefully; vigilant; alert. —**watch′ful-ly** *adv.* —**watch′ful-ness** *n.*

watch-mak-er (woch′mā′kər, wôch′-) *n.* One who makes or repairs watches.

watch-man (woch′mən, wôch′-) *n. pl.* **-men** (-mən) A man employed to guard a building, etc., at night.

watch-tow-er (woch′tou′ər, wôch′-) *n.* A tower upon which a sentinel is stationed.

watch-word (woch′wûrd′, wôch′-) *n.* **1** PASSWORD. **2** A slogan or maxim.

wa-ter (wô′tər, wot′ər) *n.* **1** The colorless liquid that covers over 70 percent of the earth's surface, is capable of wetting and dissolving many different substances, and is an essential constituent of all organisms. **2** A chemical compound of hydrogen and oxygen which occurs as a solid, a liquid, or a vapor, depending upon its temperature. **3** *Often pl.* Any body of water, as a lake, river, or a sea. **4** Any liquid or liquid secretion of the body, as perspiration, tears, urine, etc. **5** Any preparation of water holding a substance in solution: mineral *water.* **6** An undulating sheen given to certain fabrics, as silk, etc. **7** In commerce and finance, stock issued without an increase of assets or earning power to back it. —**above water** Out of danger, debt, etc.; secure. —**hold water** To be logical, valid, or dependable. —**like water** Freely; prodigally. —**of the first water** Of the finest quality. —*v.t.* **1** To provide (land, plants, etc.) with water, as by sprinkling or irrigating. **2** To provide with water for drinking. **3** To dilute or weaken with water: often with *down.* **4** To give an undulating sheen to the surface of (silk, linen, etc.). **5** To enlarge the number of shares of (a stock company) without increasing the company assets in proportion. —*v.i.* **6** To secrete or discharge water, tears, etc. **7** To fill with saliva, as the mouth, from desire for food. **8** To drink water. [< OE *wæter*] —**wa′ter-er** *n.*

Water Bearer AQUARIUS.

wa-ter-bed (wô′tər-bed′, wot′ər-) *n.* A bed with a water-filled container serving as a mattress.

water bird Any bird living on or near water.

water bomber In Canada, an aircraft equipped to drop water on forest fires. Also **fire bomber.**

wa-ter-borne (wô′tər-bôrn′, -bōrn′, wot′ər-) *adj.* **1** Floating on water. **2** Transported in a ship, etc.

wa-ter-buck (wô′tər-buk′, wot′ər-) *n.* Either of two species of large African antelope, frequenting rivers, etc.

water buffalo A large, slow, oxlike animal of s Asia with curved horns, often domesticated as a draft animal.

water chestnut 1 The hard, nutlike, edible fruit of an aquatic plant native to Asia. **2** The plant itself: also **water cal-trop** (kal′trəp).

wa-ter-clock (wô′tər-klok′, wot′ər-) *n.* A device for measuring time by the fall or flow of water.

water closet TOILET (defs. 1 & 2).

wa-ter-col-or (wô′tər-kul′ər, wot′ər-) *n.* **1** A pigment or coloring matter prepared for painting with water as the medium. **2** A picture or painting done in watercolors. Also **water color.** —*adj.* Of or painted with watercolors.

wa-ter-cool (wô′tər-kōōl′, wot′ər-) *v.t.* To cool by means of water, as by a jacket or pipe.

water cooler A vessel or apparatus for cooling and dispensing drinking water.

wa-ter-course (wô′tər-kôrs′, -kōrs′, wot′ər-) *n.* **1** A stream of water, as a river or brook. **2** A channel for a stream of water.

wa-ter-craft (wô′tər-kraft′, -kräft′, wot′ər-) *n.* **1** Skill in sailing boats or in aquatic sports. **2** A boat or ship. **3** Boats and ships collectively.

wa-ter-cress (wô′tər-kres′, wot′ər-) *n.* An edible perennial herb of the mustard family, usu. growing in running water and cultivated for use as salad.

water cure HYDROPATHY.

wa-ter-fall (wô′tər-fôl′, wot′ər-) *n.* A fall of water over a precipice.

wa-ter-fowl (wô′tər-foul′, wot′ər-) *n. pl.* **-fowl** or **-fowls** A water bird, esp. a swimming game bird.

wa-ter-front (wô′tər-frunt′, wot′ər-) *n.* **1** Property abutting on or overlooking a natural body of water. **2** That part of a town which fronts on a body of water, usu. a commercial area of docks, warehouses, etc.

water gap A deep ravine in a mountain ridge giving passage to a stream.

water gas A poisonous fuel gas containing hydrogen and carbon monoxide produced by forcing steam over white-hot coke.

wa·ter·gate (wô′tər·gāt′, wot′ər-) n. FLOODGATE.

water gauge A gauge for indicating the level of water in a boiler, reservoir, etc.

wa·ter·glass (wô′tər·glas′, -gläs′, wot′ər-) n. 1 A drinking glass. 2 WATER GAUGE. 3 A glass-bottomed tube for examining objects lying under water. 4 A water-soluble silicate, as of sodium or potassium, used as an adhesive, for preserving eggs, etc. Also **water glass.**

water hole A pond or pool of water, esp. one used by animals for drinking.

water ice *Chiefly Brit.* SHERBET.

watering place 1 A place where water can be obtained, as a spring. 2 *Chiefly Brit.* A health resort having mineral springs; also, a pleasure resort near the water.

water jacket A casing containing water for cooling, as one surrounding a cylinder of an internal-combustion engine.

water level 1 The level of water in a body of water. 2 A ship's waterline.

wa·ter·lil·y (wô′tər·lil′ē, wot′ər-) n. pl. **·lil·ies** Any of various aquatic plants with large floating leaves and showy white or colored flowers.

wa·ter·line (wô′tər·līn′, wot′ər-) n. 1 *Naut.* **a** A line on the hull of a ship which shows where the water surface reaches. **b** Short, horizontal lines on a ship's hull which correspond with the surface of the water when the ship is unloaded, partly loaded, or fully loaded. 2 Any line or mark showing to what level water has risen.

Waterlily

wa·ter·logged (wô′tər·lôgd′, -logd′, wot′ər-) adj. 1 So saturated or filled with water as to be unmanageable and barely able to float, as a ship, etc. 2 Soaked with water.

Wa·ter·loo (wô′tər·lōō, wô′tər·lōō′) n. A decisive defeat, usu. in the phrase **meet one's Waterloo.** [< *Waterloo,* Belgium, scene of Napoleon's final defeat, 1815]

water main A main pipe in a system of pipes for carrying water, esp. one laid underground.

wa·ter·man (wô′tər·mən, wot′ər-) n. pl. **·men** (-mən) A boatman or oarsman.

wa·ter·mark (wô′tər·märk′, wot′ər-) n. 1 WATERLINE (def. 2). 2 A mark or design made in paper by pressure while the paper is still in a pulpy state; also, the metal pattern which produces these markings. —v.t. 1 To impress (paper) with a watermark. 2 To impress (a mark or design) as a watermark.

wa·ter·mel·on (wô′tər·mel′ən, wot′ər-) n. 1 A gourd cultivated for its large edible fruit, having a juicy, sweet, red or pink pulp. 2 The fruit.

water mill A mill operated by waterpower.

water moccasin A venomous, brownish pit viper, found along rivers, etc., of the SE U.S.

water nymph *Gk. & Rom. Myth.* A nymph dwelling in a stream, lake, etc.

water of crystallization Water that combines with certain salts to form usu. unstable hydrates of distinct crystalline structure. Also **water of hydration.**

water ouzel Any of various small diving birds related to thrushes.

water pipe 1 A pipe for carrying water. 2 HOOKAH.

water polo A game in which two teams of swimmers attempt to take or throw an inflated ball across each other's goal line.

wa·ter·pow·er (wô′tər·pou′ər, wot′ər-) n. The power derived from the kinetic energy of flowing or falling water, used for driving machinery.

wa·ter·proof (wô′tər·prōōf′, wot′ər-) adj. 1 WATERTIGHT. 2 Coated with some substance, as rubber, which prevents the passage of water. —n. 1 Waterproof fabric. 2 *Brit.* A raincoat or other waterproof garment. —v.t. To render waterproof.

water rat 1 MUSKRAT. 2 Any of various rodents that frequent lakes, streams, etc. 3 *Slang* A waterfront tough or thief.

wa·ter·shed (wô′tər·shed′, wot′ər-) n. 1 A ridge of high land that divides two areas drained by different river sys-

tems. 2 The whole region from which a river receives its supply of water. 3 A decisive turning point affecting outlook, actions, etc.

wa·ter·side (wô′tər·sīd′, wot′ər-) n. The shore of a body of water; the water's edge.

wa·ter·ski (wô′tər·skē′, wot′ər-) v.i. **-skied, -ski·ing** To glide over water on skilike runners (**water skis**) while being towed by a motorboat. —**wa′ter·ski′er** n.

water snake 1 Any of various harmless North American snakes that live chiefly in water. 2 Any aquatic snake.

wa·ter·soak (wô′tər·sōk′, wot′ər-) v.t. To saturate with water.

water softener A substance that removes dissolved minerals from water, as by precipitation, absorption, etc.

water spaniel A breed of spaniel having a water-resistant coat, used for retrieving waterfowl.

wa·ter·spout (wô′tər·spout′, wot′ər-) n. 1 A moving, whirling column of spray and mist, resulting from a tornado at sea, on a lake, etc. 2 A pipe for the free discharge of water.

water sprite A nymph, sprite, etc., living in water.

water table The surface marking the upper level of a water-saturated zone of permeable rock.

wa·ter·tight (wô′tər·tīt′, wot′ər-) adj. 1 So closely made that water cannot enter or leak through. 2 That cannot be misunderstood, found illegal or in error, etc.: a *watertight* contract. —**wa′ter·tight′ness** n.

water tower 1 A tank or tower, used as a reservoir and to maintain pressure in a system of water distribution. 2 A vehicular towerlike structure from which water can be played on a burning building from a great height.

water vapor The vapor of water, esp. below the boiling point, as in the atmosphere.

wa·ter·way (wô′tər·wā′, wot′ər-) n. A river, channel, or other stream of water, esp. when navigable by boats and ships.

water wheel A wheel designed to be turned by flowing water. • See UNDERSHOT.

water wings An inflatable device used to keep a beginning swimmer afloat.

wa·ter·works (wô′tər·wûrks′, wot′ər-) n.pl. A system of buildings, pipes, pumps, etc. for furnishing a water supply, esp. for a city.

wa·ter·worn (wô′tər·wôrn′, -wōrn′, wot′ər-) adj. Worn smooth by running or falling water.

wa·ter·y (wô′tər·ē, wot′ər·ē) adj. 1 Of, containing, or like water. 2 Diluted. 3 Overly liquid; thin. 4 Tearful. 5 Weak; vapid; insipid. —**wa′ter·i·ness** n.

watt (wot) n. A unit of power equivalent to one joule per second, or about ¹/₇₄₆ of a horsepower. [< J. *Watt,* 1736–1819, Scottish engineer]

watt·age (wot′ij) n. An amount of power, esp. electric power, expressed in watts.

watt·hour (wot′our′) n. Energy equivalent to one watt acting for one hour.

watt-hr. watt-hour(s).

wat·tle (wot′l) n. 1 A framework of poles and twigs woven together, used for walls, fences, etc. 2 The poles and twigs used for this. 3 A fold of skin, often wrinkled and brightly colored, hanging from the throat of a bird or lizard. 4 Any one of various acacias of Australia, Tasmania, and South Africa. —v.t. **·tled, ·tling** 1 To weave or twist, as twigs, into a network. 2 To form,, as a fence, by intertwining flexible twigs. 3 To bind together with wattles. [< OE *watul*]

Wattle of turkey

watt·me·ter (wot′mē′tər) n. An instrument for measuring electric power in watts.

wave (wāv) v. **waved, wav·ing** v.i. 1 To move freely back and forth or up and down, as a flag in the wind. 2 To signal by moving something back and forth or up and down. 3 To have an undulating shape or form: Her hair *waves.* —v.t. 4 To cause to wave: to *wave* a banner. 5 To flourish, as a weapon. 6 To give a wavy appearance to or form into waves: to *wave* one's hair. 7 To signal by waving something: He *waved* me aside. 8 To express by waving something: to *wave* farewell. —*n.* 1 A ridge or undulation moving on the surface of a liquid. 2 A similar undulation on a freely moving surface: *waves* in the tall grass. 3 A curve or curl in the hair. 4 A curved pattern or shape, as on watered silk. 5 A back-and-forth or up-and-down motion, as with the hand. 6 A more or less prolonged meteorological condition: a heat *wave.* 7 An upsurge of something: a crime *wave;* a *wave* of emotion. 8 A surging movement, as of a mass or group: a *wave* of refugees. 9 *Usu. pl.* A large body of water. 10 *Physics* A periodic disturbance propagated through a medium, characterized by a function of time that defines its frequency, amplitude, phase, and velocity. [< OE *wafian*] —**wav′er** *n.*

Wave (wāv) *n.* A member of the **WAVES,** the women's division of the U.S. Navy. [< *W(omen) A(ppointed for) V(oluntary) E(mergency) S(ervice)*]

wave·form (wāv′fôrm′) *n.* 1 The curve produced by recording, as on a graph, the varying dimensions of a wave through successive oscillations. 2 A mathematical formula for such a curve.

wave·length (wāv′length′) *n. Physics* The distance, along the line of propagation, between two points of like phase in consecutive cycles of a wave.

wave·let (wāv′lit) *n.* A little wave.

wa·ver (wā′vər) *v.i.* 1 To move one way and the other; flutter. 2 To be uncertain; vacillate. 3 To show signs of falling back or giving way; falter. 4 To flicker; gleam. —*n.* A wavering. [< OE *wafian* to wave] —**wa′ver·er** *n.* —**wa′·ver·ing·ly** *adv.* —**Syn.** 1 oscillate, quiver, shake. 2 hesitate.

wav·y (wā′vē) *adj.* **wav·i·er, wav·i·est** Full of waves or curves, as hair, lines, etc. —**wav′i·ly** *adv.* —**wav′i·ness** *n.*

wax[1] (waks) *n.* 1 BEESWAX. 2 Any of various pliable plant and animal substances that are insoluble in water, that burn in air, or otherwise resemble beeswax. 3 A solid mineral substance resembling wax, as paraffin. 4 SEALING WAX. 5 A waxlike commercial product, used for polishing furniture, floors, etc. —*v.t.* To coat or polish with wax. —*adj.* Made of or pertaining to wax. [< OE *weax*]

wax[2] (waks) *v.i.* **waxed, waxed** (*Archaic* **wax·en**), **wax·ing** 1 To increase in size: said esp. of the moon. 2 To become: to *wax* angry. [< OE *weaxan* grow]

wax bean A pale yellow variety of string bean.

wax·ber·ry (waks′ber′ē) *n. pl.* **·ries** 1 The wax myrtle, or bayberry. 2 Its fruit.

wax·en (wak′sən) *adj.* 1 Consisting of or covered with wax. 2 Pale; pallid: a *waxen* complexion.

wax myrtle Any of various North American shrubs or small trees having fragrant leaves and small berries covered with white wax, often used in making candles.

wax palm Either of two South American palms yielding waxes widely used to make polishes, cosmetics, etc.

wax paper Paper coated with paraffin to render it moistureproof. Also **waxed paper.**

wax·wing (waks′wing′) *n.* Any of various crested passerine birds having soft, mainly brown plumage, and red, waxy tips on the wings.

wax·work (waks′wûrk′) *n.* 1 Work produced in wax; esp., life-size figures of notable persons. 2 *pl.* An exhibition of such figures. —**wax′work′er** *n.*

wax·y (wak′sē) *adj.* **wax·i·er, wax·i·est** 1 Resembling wax in appearance, consistency, etc. 2 Pale; pallid, as wax. 3 Made of, abounding in, or polished with wax. —**wax′i·ness** *n.*

Cedar waxwing

way (wā) *n.* 1 Direction; route: Which *way* is the city? 2 A path, course, road, etc., leading from one place to another. 3 Space or room to advance or work: Make *way* for the king. 4 Distance in general: a little *way* off. 5 Direction in general: Look the other *way.* 6 Passage from one place to another: on our *way* to Europe. 7 A customary or habitual manner or style of acting or being: Do it her *way.* 8 A plan of action; procedure; method: In what *way* will you accomplish this? 9 Respect; point; particular: He erred in two

ways. 10 A course of life or experience: the *way* of sin. 11 Desire; wish: to get one's *way.* 12 *Informal* State or condition: to be in a bad *way.* 13 The range of one's experience or observation: An accident threw it in his *way.* 14 *Informal* Neighborhood or locality: out our *way.* 15 *Naut.* **a** Forward motion; headway. **b** *pl.* A tilted framework of timbers upon which a ship slides when launched. —**by the way** In passing; incidentally. —**by way of** 1 With the object or purpose of; to serve as: *by way of* introduction. 2 Through; via. —**give way (to)** 1 To yield or submit. 2 To collapse. —**go out of one's** (or **the**) **way** To inconvenience oneself. —**in the way** In a position that impedes or hinders. —**out of the way** 1 In a position so as not to hinder or impede. 2 Out of the usual or convenient location or route. 3 Unusual. 4 Improper; wrong: Has he done anything *out of the way?*—**under way** In motion; making progress. —*adv. Informal* All the distance to: He went *way* to Denver. [< OE *weg*]

way·bill (wā′bil′) *n.* A statement listing or giving instructions concerning the shipping of goods.

way·far·er (wā′fâr′ər) *n.* One who travels, esp. on foot. —**way′far′ing** *n., adj.*

way·lay (wā′lā′) *v.t.* **·laid, ·lay·ing** 1 To lie in ambush for and attack. 2 To accost on the way. —**way′lay′er** *n.*

way-out (wā′out′) *adj. Slang* FAR-OUT.

-ways *suffix of adverbs* In a (specified) manner, direction, or position: *noways, sideways.*

ways and means 1 Means or methods of accomplishing an end or defraying expenses. 2 In legislation, methods of raising funds for the use of the government: also **Ways and Means.**

way·side (wā′sīd′) *adj.* Pertaining to or near the side of a road. —*n.* The side or edge of the road or highway.

way station Any station between principal stations, esp. on a railroad.

way train A train stopping at way stations.

way·ward (wā′wərd) *adj.* 1 Willful; headstrong. 2 Not predictable; erratic. [< ME *awei* away + -WARD] —**way′ward·ly** *adv.* —**way′ward·ness** *n.* —**Syn.** 1 disobedient, perverse, refractory, stubborn. 2 capricious.

WbN west by north.

WbS west by south.

w.c. water closet; without charge.

W.C.T.U. Women's Christian Temperance Union.

we (wē) *pron. pl.* 1 The persons speaking or writing, or a single person writing or speaking when referring to himself and one or more others. 2 A single person denoting himself, as a sovereign, editor, writer, or speaker, when wishing to give his words a formal or impersonal character. [< OE]

weak (wēk) *adj.* 1 Lacking in physical strength, energy, or vigor; feeble. 2 Incapable of resisting stress or supporting weight: a *weak* wall. 3 Lacking in strength of will or stability of character. 4 Not effective, forceful, or convincing: *weak* reasoning. 5 Lacking in power, intensity, etc.: a *weak* voice. 6 Lacking a specified component or components in the usual or proper amount: *weak* tea. 7 Lacking the power or ability to function properly: a *weak* heart. 8 Lacking mental or intellectual capability. 9 Lacking skill, experience, etc.: a *weak* player. 10 Lacking in power, influence, or authority: a *weak* state. 11 Deficient in some specified thing or quality: *weak* in languages. 12 *Gram.* Denoting a verb in English or other Germanic languages that forms its past tense and past participle by adding *d* or *t* rather than by vowel changes. 13 *Phonet.* Unstressed; unaccented, as a syllable or sound. 14 In prosody, indicating a verse ending in which the accent falls on a word or syllable otherwise without stress. 15 Characterized by declining prices: said of the stock market. [< ON *veikr*] —**Syn.** 1 slight, puny, enfeebled, frail.

weak·en (wē′kən) *v.t. & v.i.* To make or become weak or weaker. —**weak′en·er** *n.* —**Syn.** debilitate, enervate, enfeeble, sap.

weak·fish (wēk′fish′) *n. pl.* **·fish** or **·fish·es** Any of various marine food fishes, esp. several troutlike species of E U.S. coastal waters.

---

add, āce, câre, pălm; end, ēven; it, īce; odd, ōpen, ôrder; tōŏk, pōōl; up, bûrn; ə = a in *above*, u in *focus;* yōō = u in *fuse;* oil; pout; check; go; ring; thin; this; zh, *vision.* < derived from; ? origin uncertain or unknown.

weak-kneed (wēk′nēd′) *adj.* 1 Weak in the knees. 2 Without resolution, strong purpose, or energy; spineless.

weak·ling (wēk′ling) *n.* A feeble person or animal. —*adj.* Weak.

weak·ly (wēk′lē) *adj.* ·li·er, ·li·est Sickly; feeble; weak. —*adv.* In a weak manner. —**weak′li·ness** *n.*

weak-mind·ed (wēk′mīn′did) *adj.* 1 Not resolute or firm; indecisive. 2 FEEBLE-MINDED. —**weak′mind′ed·ly** *adv.* —**weak′mind′ed·ness** *n.*

weak·ness (wēk′nis) *n.* 1 The state, condition, or quality of being weak. 2 A characteristic indicating feebleness. 3 A slight failing; a fault. 4 A strong liking or fondness; also, the object of such a liking.

weal[1] (wēl) *n. Archaic* A sound or prosperous condition. [< OE *wela*]

weal[2] (wēl) *n.* A welt, as from a blow. [Var. of WALE]

weald (wēld) *n. Chiefly Brit.* 1 A forest area. 2 An open region; down. [OE, a forest]

wealth (welth) *n.* 1 A large amount of money or property; riches. 2 The state of being rich. 3 Great abundance of anything: a *wealth* of learning. 4 *Econ.* **a** All material objects which have economic utility. **b** All property possessing a monetary value. [ME *welthe* < *wele* weal]

wealth·y (wel′thē) *adj.* **wealth·i·er, wealth·i·est** 1 Possessing wealth; affluent. 2 More than sufficient; abounding. —**wealth′i·ly** *adv.* —**wealth′i·ness** *n.* —**Syn.** 1 rich, prosperous, well-to-do, well-off.

wean (wēn) *v.t.* 1 To transfer (the young of any mammal) from dependence on its mother's milk to another form of nourishment. 2 To free from usu. undesirable habits or associations: usu. with *from.* [< OE *wenian* accustom] —**wean′er** *n.*

wean·ling (wēn′ling) *adj.* Freshly weaned. —*n.* A child or animal newly weaned.

weap·on (wep′ən) *n.* 1 Any implement of war or combat, as a sword, gun, etc. 2 Any means that may be used against an adversary. 3 Any defensive organ or part of an animal or plant, as a claw, tooth, thorn, etc. [< OE *wæpen*] —**weap′on·ry** (-rē) *n.*

wear (wâr) *v.* **wore, worn, wear·ing** *v.t.* 1 To have on the person as a garment, ornament, etc. 2 To have on the person habitually: He *wears* a derby. 3 To have in one's aspect; exhibit: He *wears* a scowl. 4 To have as a characteristic: She *wears* her hair short. 5 To display or fly: A ship *wears* its colors. 6 To impair or consume by use or constant action. 7 To cause by scraping, rubbing, etc.: to *wear* a hole in a coat. 8 To bring to a specified condition by wear: to *wear* a sleeve to tatters. 9 To exhaust; weary. —*v.i.* 10 To be impaired or diminished gradually by use, rubbing, etc. 11 To withstand the effects of use, handling, etc.: These shoes *wear* well. 12 To remain sound or interesting over a period of time: a friendship that *wore* well. 13 To become as specified from use or attrition: his patience is *wearing* thin. 14 To pass gradually: with *on* or *away.* 15 To have an unpleasant or exhausting effect. —**wear down** 1 To make or become less through friction, use, etc. 2 To tire out; exhaust. 3 To overcome the resistance of by constant pressure, harassment, etc. —**wear off** To diminish gradually. —**wear out** 1 To make or become worthless by use. 2 To waste or use up gradually. 3 To tire or exhaust. —*n.* 1 The act of wearing, or the state of being worn. 2 Material or articles of dress to be worn: often in combination: *foot-wear, underwear.* 3 Vogue; fashion. 4 Destruction or impairment from use or time. 5 Capacity to resist use or time; durability. —**wear and tear** Loss or damage from use over a period of time. [< OE *werian*] —**wear′er** *n.*

wear·ing (wâr′ing) *adj.* 1 Fatiguing; exhausting: a *wearing* day. 2 Capable of being, or designed to be, worn. —**wear′ing·ly** *adv.*

wearing apparel Clothing; garments.

wea·ri·some (wir′ē·səm) *adj.* Causing fatigue; tiresome. —**wea′ri·some·ly** *adv.* —**wea′ri·some·ness** *n.* —**Syn.** annoying, irksome, tedious, vexatious.

wea·ry (wir′ē) *adj.* ·ri·er, ·ri·est 1 Worn out; tired; fatigued. 2 Discontented or bored: usu. with *of: weary* of life. 3 Indicating or characteristic of fatigue: a *weary* sigh. 4 Causing fatigue; wearisome. —*v.t. & v.i.* ·ried, ·ry·ing To make or become weary. [< OE *wērig*] —**wea′ri·ly** *adv.* —**wea′ri·ness** *n.*

wea·sel (wē′zəl) *n.* 1 Any of certain small, slender, usu. nocturnal carnivorous mammals. 2 A sly or treacherous person. —*v.i.* ·seled, ·sel·ing *Informal* 1 To fail to fulfill a promise, etc.; renege: with *out.* 2 To speak ambiguously; equivocate. [< OE *wesle*]

Weasel

weath·er (weth′ər) *n.* 1 The general atmospheric condition, as regards temperature, moisture, winds, or related phenomena. 2 Unpleasant atmospheric conditions. —**keep one's weather eye open** *Informal* To be alert. —**under the weather** *Informal* 1 Ailing; ill. 2 Suffering from a hangover. 3 Drunk. —*v.t.* 1 To expose to the action of the weather. 2 To discolor, crumble, or otherwise affect by action of the weather. 3 To pass through and survive, as a crisis. 4 *Naut.* To pass to windward of: to *weather* Cape Fear. —*v.i.* 5 To undergo changes from exposure to the weather. 6 To resist the action of the weather. —*adj.* Facing the wind. [< OE *weder*]

weath·er-beat·en (weth′ər·bēt′n) *adj.* 1 Bearing or showing the effects of exposure to weather. 2 Tanned, wrinkled, etc., by or as if by exposure to weather, as a face.

weath·er·board (weth′ər·bôrd′, -bōrd′) *n.* CLAPBOARD. —*v.t.* To fasten weatherboards on.

weath·er·bound (weth′ər·bound′) *adj.* Detained by unfavorable weather, as a ship.

weath·er·cock (weth′ər·kok′) *n.* 1 A weathervane, properly one in the form of a cock. 2 A fickle person or variable thing.

weath·er·glass (weth′ər·glas′, -gläs′) *n.* An instrument for indicating the weather, esp. a barometer.

weath·er·man (weth′ər·man′) *n. pl.* ·men (-men′) *n.* A person who reports on daily weather conditions.

Weathercock

weather map *Meteorol.* A map or chart giving weather conditions for a given region and specified time.

weath·er·proof (weth′ər·prōof′) *adj.* Capable of withstanding snow, rain, wind, etc., without appreciable deterioration. —*v.t.* To make weatherproof.

weather station A station or office where meteorological observations are made.

weath·er·strip (weth′ər·strip′) *n.* A narrow strip of material to be placed over or in crevices, as at doors and windows, to exclude drafts, rain, etc. Also **weath′er·strip′-ping.** —*v.t.* ·stripped, ·strip·ping To equip or fit with weatherstrips.

weath·er·vane (weth′ər·vān′) *n.* A vane that indicates the direction in which the wind is blowing.

weath·er·wise (weth′ər·wīz′) *adj.* Experienced in observing or predicting the weather, public opinion, etc.

weath·er·worn (weth′ər·wôrn′, -wōrn′) *adj.* Worn by exposure to the weather.

weave (wēv) *v.* **wove** or *esp. for defs. 7, 8, & 11* **weaved, wo·ven** or *esp. for defs. 7, 8, & 11* **weaved, weav·ing** *v.t.* 1 To make (a fabric) by interlacing threads or yarns, esp. on a loom. 2 To interlace (threads or yarns) into a fabric. 3 To form by interlacing strands, strips, twigs, etc.: to *weave* a basket. 4 To produce by combining details or elements: to *weave* a story. 5 To twist or introduce into: to *weave* ribbons through one's hair. 6 To spin (a web). 7 To make by going from one side to another: to *weave* one's way through a crowd. 8 To direct (a car, etc.) in this manner. —*v.i.* 9 To make cloth, etc., by weaving. 10 To become woven or interlaced. 11 To make one's way by moving from one side to another. —*n.* A particular method, style, or pattern of weaving. [< OE *wefan*]

weav·er (wē′vər) *n.* 1 One who weaves. 2 A person whose job is weaving. 3 WEAVERBIRD.

weav·er·bird (wē′vər·bûrd′) *n.* Any of various finchlike birds of Asia, Africa, and Australia, that weave intricate nests.

web (web) *n.* 1 Fabric being woven on a loom. 2 The network of delicate threads spun by a spider or by certain insect larvae. **3** An artfully contrived trap or snare. **4** Any complex network of interwoven parts, elements, etc.: a *web* of lies; a *web* of highways. **5** *Zool.* A membrane connecting the digits, as in aquatic birds, frogs, etc. **6** The vane of a feather. **7** *Anat.* A membrane or tissue. **8** A plate or sheet, as of metal, connecting the ribs, frames, etc., of a structure. **9** *Archit.* The part of a ribbed vault between the ribs. **10** A large roll of paper, as for use in a web press. —*v.t.* **webbed, web·bing 1** To provide with a web. **2** To cover or surround with a web; entangle. [< OE]

webbed (webd) *adj.* **1** Having a web. **2** Having the digits united by a membrane.

web·bing (web′ing) *n.* **1** A woven strip of strong fiber, used for safety belts, upholstery, etc. **2** Anything forming a web or weblike structure.

we·ber (vā′bər, wē′bər) *n.* A unit equal to the magnetic flux that, interacting with a single turn of wire, induces a potential difference of one volt as it is uniformly reduced to zero in one second. [< W. E. *Weber*, 1804–91, German physicist]

web·foot (web′fŏŏt′) *n.* **1** A foot with webbed toes. **2** A bird or animal having such feet. —**web′-foot′ed** *adj.*

web press A printing press which is fed from a continuous roll of paper instead of sheets.

wed (wed) *v.* **wed·ded, wed·ded** or **wed, wed·ding** *v.t.* **1** To take as one's husband or wife; marry. **2** To join in wedlock. **3** To unite or join closely: He is *wedded* to his job. —*v.i.* **4** To take a husband or wife; marry. [< OE *weddian* to pledge]

we'd (wēd) Contraction of *we had* or *we would*.

Wed. Wednesday.

wed·ding (wed′ing) *n.* **1** The ceremony of a marriage. **2** The anniversary of a marriage: golden *wedding.* [< OE *weddian* to pledge]

wedge (wej) *n.* **1** A V-shaped piece of metal, wood, etc., used for splitting wood, raising weights, etc. **2** Anything in the form of a wedge. **3** Any action which facilitates policy, entrance, intrusion, etc. **4** An iron golf club with the face at an angle for lofting the ball. —*v.* **wedged, wedg·ing** *v.t.* **1** To force apart with a wedge. **2** To fix in place with a wedge. **3** To crowd or squeeze (something). —*v.i.* **4** To force oneself or itself in like a wedge. [< OE *wecg*]

wedg·ie (wej′ē) *n.* A woman's shoe having a wedge-shaped piece making a solid, flat sole from heel to toe.

Wedg·wood (wej′wŏŏd′) *n.* A fine English pottery, characterized by small, white, classical figures in cameo relief against a tinted background. [< J. *Wedgwood*, 1730–95, English potter]

wed·lock (wed′lok) *n.* The state of being married. [< OE *wedd* a pledge + *-lāc*, suffix of nouns of action]

Wednes·day (wenz′dē, -dā) *n.* The fourth day of the week. [< OE *Wōdnesdæg* day of Woden]

wee (wē) *adj.* **we·er, we·est** Very small; tiny. [< OE *wēg* a quantity]

weed[1] (wēd) *n.* **1** Any unwanted or unsightly plant, esp. one that hinders the growth of cultivated plants. **2** *Informal* **a** Tobacco. **b** A cigarette or cigar. **c** Marihuana; also, a marihuana cigarette. **3** A thin, ungainly person. —*v.t.* **1** To pull up and remove weeds from. **2** To remove (a weed): often with *out.* **3** To remove (anything regarded as harmful or undesirable): with *out.* **4** To rid of anything harmful or undesirable. —*v.i.* **5** To remove weeds, etc. [< OE *wēod*] —**weed′er** *n.*

weed[2] (wēd) *n.* **1** *Usu. pl.* Mourning garb, as that worn by widows. **2** A black band, as of crepe, worn by a man on his hat or sleeve as a token of mourning. [< OE *wæd* garment]

weed·y (wē′dē) *adj.* **weed·i·er, weed·i·est 1** Abounding in weeds. **2** Of or pertaining to a weed or weeds. **3** Gawky; lanky: a *weedy* youth. —**weed′i·ly** *adv.* —**weed′i·ness** *n.*

week (wēk) *n.* **1** A period of seven successive days, esp. one beginning with Sunday. **2** The period within a week devoted to work: a 35-hour *week.* —**week in, week out** Every week. [< OE *wicu, wice*]

week·day (wēk′dā′) *n.* **1** Any day of the week except Sunday. **2** Any day other than those of the weekend.

week·end (wēk′end′) *n.* The time from Friday evening or Saturday to the following Monday morning. —*adj.* Of, for, or on a weekend. —*v.i.* To pass the weekend. —**week′end′er** *n.*

week·ly (wēk′lē) *adj.* **1** Of, pertaining to, or lasting a week. **2** Done or occurring once a week. **3** Reckoned by the week. —*adv.* **1** Once a week. **2** Every week. —*n. pl.* **·lies** A publication issued once a week.

ween (wēn) *v.t. & v.i. Archaic* To suppose; guess; fancy. [< OE *wēnan* think]

weep (wēp) *v.* **wept, weep·ing** *v.i.* **1** To manifest grief or other strong emotion by shedding tears. **2** To mourn; lament: with *for.* **3** To give out or shed liquid in drops. —*v.t.* **4** To weep for; mourn. **5** To shed (tears, or drops of other liquid). —*n.* **1** The act of weeping, or a fit of tears. **2** An exhudation of liquid; moisture. [< OE *wēpan*] —**weep′er** *n.* —**Syn.** *v.* **1** cry, sob. **2** bewail, grieve.

weep·ing (wē′ping) *adj.* **1** That weeps. **2** Having branches that curve downward.

weeping willow A willow, originally from China, noted for its long, drooping branches.

wee·vil (wē′vəl) *n.* Any of numerous small beetles with elongated snoutlike heads, often having larvae destructive to cotton, grain, fruit, etc. [< OE *wifel* a beetle] — **wee′vil·y, wee′vil·ly** *adj.*

weft (weft) *n.* **1** The cross threads in a web of cloth; woof. **2** A woven fabric; web. [< OE]

Weeping willow

weigh (wā) *v.t.* **1** To determine the weight of. **2** To balance or hold in the hand so as to estimate weight. **3** To measure (a quantity or quantities of something) according to weight: with *out.* **4** To consider or evaluate carefully: to *weigh* one's words. **5** To raise or hoist: now only in the phrase **weigh anchor.** —*v.i.* **6** To have a specified weight: She *weighs* ninety pounds. **7** To have influence or importance: The girl's testimony *weighed* heavily with the jury. **8** To be burdensome or oppressive: with *on* or *upon:* What *weighs* on your mind? **9** *Naut.* **a** To raise anchor. **b** To begin to sail. —**weigh down 1** To press or force down by weight or heaviness. **2** To burden or oppress. —**weigh in** To be weighed before a fight or other athletic contest. [< OE *wegan* weigh, carry, lift] —**weigh′er** *n.*

weight (wāt) *n.* **1** The quality of having heaviness. **2** The measure of this quality, expressed indefinitely or in standard units: Its *weight* is ten pounds. **3** A piece of something, usu. metal, used as a standard unit in weighing: a three-pound *weight.* **4** Any unit of heaviness, as a pound, ounce, etc.; also, a system of such units. **5** *Physics* The force of gravity exerted on any object, equal to the mass of the object multiplied by its acceleration due to gravity. **6** Any mass weighing a definite amount: a four-pound *weight* of flour. **7** Any object having heaviness and used to balance things, exert downward force, etc., as a paperweight, a counterbalance in a machine, a dumbbell for exercising, etc. **8** Burden; pressure: the *weight* of responsibility. **9** Influence; importance; consequence: the great *weight* of this decision. **10** The larger or most valuable part: the *weight* of the data is negative. **11** The comparative heaviness of clothes, as appropriate to the season: summer *weight.* —**carry weight** To be important, significant, influential, etc. —**pull one's weight** To do one's share. —**throw one's weight around** *Informal* To use one's importance or influence in an overbearing or improper manner. —*v.t.* **1** To add weight to; make heavy. **2** To oppress or burden. **3** To adulterate or treat (fabrics or other merchandise) with cheap foreign substances. [< OE *wiht, gewiht*]

weight·less (wāt′lis) *adj.* **1** Having little or no heaviness. **2** Subject to little or no gravitational force. —**weight′·less·ly** *adv.* —**weight′less·ness** *n.*

weight·y (wā′tē) *adj.* **weight·i·er, weight·i·est 1** Having great importance; far-reaching; grave: a *weighty* decision.

2 Having power to move the mind; cogent; influential: a *weighty* argument. **3** Burdensome; onerous. **4** Having great weight; heavy. —**weight′i·ly** *adv.* —**weight′i·ness** *n.* —Syn. **1** momentous, serious, solemn.

weir (wir) *n.* **1** A dam placed in a stream to raise or divert the water. **2** A fence of twigs, rods, etc., in a stream, used to catch fish. [< OE *werian* dam up]

weird (wird) *adj.* **1** Manifesting or concerned with the supernatural; unearthly; uncanny. **2** Odd; bizarre; fantastic. [< OE *wyrd* fate] —**weird′ly** *adv.* —**weird′ness** *n.*

weird·o (wir′dō) *n. pl.* **·os** *Slang* A person who is strange or eccentric. Also **weird′ie, weird′y** (-dē) (*pl.* **·ies**).

welch (welch, welsh) *v.t. & v.i. Slang* WELSH. —**welch′er** *n.*

wel·come (wel′kəm) *adj.* **1** Admitted or received gladly and cordially. **2** Producing satisfaction or pleasure; pleasing: *welcome* tidings. **3** Made free to use or enjoy: She is *welcome* to our car. —*n.* The act of bidding or making welcome; a hearty greeting. —**wear out one's welcome** To come so often or to linger so long as no longer to be welcome. —*v.t.* **·comed, ·com·ing 1** To greet gladly or hospitably. **2** To receive with pleasure: to *welcome* advice. [< OE *wilcuma*] —**wel′come·ly** *adv.* —**wel′come·ness, wel′·com·er** *n.*

weld (weld) *v.t.* **1** To unite, as two pieces of metal, by the application of heat along the area of contact. **2** To bring into close association or connection. —*v.i.* **3** To be welded or capable of being welded. —*n.* The joining of pieces of metal by welding; also, the closed joint so formed. [Alter. of WELL[1]] —**weld′a·ble** *adj.* —**weld′er** *n.*

wel·fare (wel′fâr) *n.* **1** The condition of being happy, healthy, prosperous, etc.; well-being. **2** WELFARE WORK. **3** Money given to those in need; relief. —**on welfare** Receiving welfare (def. 3) from the government. [< ME *wel* well + *fare* a going]

welfare state A state or social system in which the government assumes a large measure of responsibility for the welfare of its members, as regards employment, health insurance, social security, etc.

welfare work Organized efforts by a government or other organization to improve the economic condition of the needy. —**welfare worker**

wel·kin (wel′kin) *n. Archaic* **1** The vault of the sky; the heavens. **2** The air. [< OE *wolcn, wolcen* a cloud]

well[1] (wel) *n.* **1** A hole or shaft sunk into the earth to obtain a fluid, as water, oil, or natural gas. **2** A place where water issues naturally from the ground. **3** A source of continued supply; fount: a *well* of learning. **4** A depression, cavity, or vessel used to hold or collect a liquid: an *inkwell.* **5** A deep vertical opening descending through floors of a building, as for light, ventilation, stairs, etc. — *v.i.* **1** To pour forth or flow up, as water in a spring. —*v.t.* **2** To gush: Her eyes *welled* tears. [< OE *weallan* boil, bubble up]

well[2] (wel) *adv.* **bet·ter, best 1** Satisfactorily; favorably: Everything goes *well.* **2** In a good or correct manner; expertly: to dance *well.* **3** Suitably; with propriety: I cannot *well* remain here. **4** Agreeably or luxuriously: He lives *well.* **5** Intimately: How *well* do you know him? **6** To a considerable extent or degree: *well* along in years. **7** Completely; thoroughly; fully: *well* aware. **8** Far: He lagged *well* behind us. **9** Kindly; graciously: to speak *well* of someone. —**as well 1** Also; in addition. **2** With equal effect or consequence: He might just as *well* have sold it. —**as well as 1** As satisfactorily as. **2** To the same degree as. **3** In addition to. —*adj.* **1** Suitable, fortunate, right, etc.: It is *well* you called first. **2** In good health. **3** Prosperous; comfortable. —*interj.* An exclamation used to express surprise, expectation, indignation, etc., or to preface a remark. [< OE *wel*] —Syn. *adv.* **2** excellently. **3** befittingly, properly. **4** comfortably. • *Well* often appears in combination with participles to form modifiers. When used after a verb such as *be, seem,* etc., such a modifier is written as two words: to be *well satisfied.* When placed before a noun, it must be hyphenated: a *well-kept* secret.

we'll (wēl) Contraction of *we shall* or *we will.*

well-ap·point·ed (wel′ə·poin′tid) *adj.* Properly equipped; excellently furnished.

well·a·way (wel′ə·wā′) *interj. Archaic* Woe is me! [< OE *wei lā wei*]

well-bal·anced (wel′bal′ənst) *adj.* **1** Evenly balanced, adjusted, or proportioned. **2** Sound mentally; sensible.

well-be·ing (wel′bē′ing) *n.* A condition of health, happiness, or prosperity.

well-born (wel′bôrn′) *adj.* Of good family.

well-bred (wel′bred′) *adj.* **1** Well brought up; polite. **2** Of good or pure stock: said of animals.

well-dis·posed (wel′dis·pōzd′) *adj.* Favorably or kindly disposed or inclined, as to a person, idea, etc.

well-done (wel′dun′) *adj.* **1** Performed skillfully or satisfactorily. **2** Thoroughly cooked.

well-fa·vored (wel′fa′vərd) *adj.* Of attractive appearance; comely; handsome.

well-fed (wel′fed′) *adj.* **1** Plump; fat. **2** Properly fed.

well-fixed (wel′fikst′) *adj. Informal* Affluent; well-to-do.

well-found (wel′found′) *adj.* Well equipped.

well-found·ed (wel′foun′did) *adj.* Based on fact or sound thinking: *well-founded* suspicions.

well-groomed (wel′grōōmd′) *adj.* **1** Carefully dressed and scrupulously neat. **2** Carefully curried, as a horse.

well-ground·ed (wel′groun′did) *adj.* **1** Adequately schooled in the elements of a subject. **2** WELL-FOUNDED.

well-heeled (wel′hēld′) *adj. Slang* Plentifully supplied with money.

well-known (wel′nōn′) *adj.* **1** Widely known. **2** Famous. **3** Thoroughly known.

well-man·nered (wel′man′ərd) *adj.* Courteous; polite.

well-mean·ing (wel′mē′ning) *adj.* **1** Having good intentions. **2** Done with or showing good intentions: also **well·meant′** (-ment′).

well-nigh (wel′nī′) *adv.* Very nearly; almost.

well-off (wel′ôf′, -of′) *adj.* **1** In comfortable circumstances; well-to-do. **2** Fortunate.

well-pre·served (wel′pri·zûrvd′) *adj.* Not showing many signs of age.

well-read (wel′red′) *adj.* Having a wide knowledge of literature or books; having read much.

well-round·ed (wel′roun′did) *adj.* **1** Having a good and balanced variety of elements: a *well-rounded* education. **2** Having many interests, abilities, etc.: a *well-rounded* person. **3** Fully formed: a *well-rounded* figure.

well-spo·ken (wel′spō′kən) *adj.* **1** Speaking fluently, suitably, or courteously. **2** Fitly or excellently said.

well·spring (wel′spring′) *n.* **1** The source of a stream, spring, etc. **2** A source of continual supply.

well-thought-of (wel′thôt′uv′, -ov′) *adj.* In good repute; esteemed; respected.

well-to-do (wel′tə·dōō′) *adj.* In prosperous or wealthy circumstances; affluent.

well-turned (wel′tûrnd′) *adj.* **1** Gracefully shaped; shapely. **2** Expressed in a graceful or felicitous manner: a *well-turned* phrase.

well-wish·er (wel′wish′ər) *n.* One who wishes well, as to another. —**well′-wish′ing** *adj., n.*

welsh (welsh, welch) *v.t. & v.i. Slang* To fail to pay a debt or fulfill an obligation. [?] —**welsh′er** *n.*

Welsh (welsh, welch) *adj.* Pertaining to Wales, its people, or their language. —*n.* **1** The people of Wales. **2** The Celtic language of Wales.

Welsh·man (welsh′mən, welch′-) *n. pl.* **·men** (-mən) A native or citizen of Wales.

Welsh rabbit Melted cheese cooked with milk, ale, or beer and served hot on toast or crackers. • The form *rarebit* was a later development and is the result of mistaken etymology.

welt (welt) *n.* **1** A raised mark on the skin, resulting from a blow or lashing; wale. **2** A strip of material, covered cord, etc., applied to a seam to cover or strengthen it. **3** In shoemaking, a strip of leather set into the seam between the edges of the upper and the outer sole. —*v.t.* **1** To sew a welt on or in; decorate with a welt. **2** *Informal* To flog severely, so as to raise welts. [ME *welte*]

wel·ter (wel′tər) *v.i.* **1** To roll about; wallow. **2** To lie or be soaked in some fluid, as blood. —*n.* **1** A rolling movement, as of waves. **2** A turmoil; commotion. [< MDu. *welteren*]

wel·ter·weight (wel′tər·wāt′) *n.* A boxer or wrestler whose weight is between 136 and 147 pounds. [< earlier *welter* a heavyweight + WEIGHT]

Welt·schmerz (velt′shmerts) n. Weariness of life; melancholy. [G, lit., world pain]

wen (wen) n. A cyst containing sebaceous matter, occurring on the skin, esp. on the scalp. [< OE *wenn*]

wench (wench) n. *Archaic* 1 A young woman; girl: now a humorous usage. 2 A young peasant woman; also, a female servant. 3 A prostitute; strumpet. [< OE *wencel* a child, servant]

wend (wend) v. **wen·ded** (*Archaic* **went**), **wend·ing** v.t. 1 To go on (one's way); proceed. —v.i. 2 *Archaic* To proceed; go. [< OE *wendan*]

went (went) p.t. of GO.

wept (wept) p.t. & p.p. of WEEP.

were (wûr, *unstressed* wər) Plural and second person singular past indicative, and past subjunctive singular and plural of BE. [< OE *wære, wæron*]

we're (wir) Contraction of *we are*.

wer·en't (wûrnt, wûr′ənt) Contraction of *were not*.

were·wolf (wir′woolf′, wûr′-) n. pl. **·wolves** (-woolvz′) In European folklore, a person changed into a wolf or having power to assume wolf form at will. Also **wer′wolf′**. [< OE *werwulf* man-wolf]

wert (wûrt, *unstressed* wərt) *Archaic* Were: used with *thou*.

west (west) n. 1 The general direction in which the sun appears at sunset. 2 The point of the compass at 270°, directly opposite east. 3 Any region lying in this direction. —**the West** 1 The countries lying west of Asia and Asia Minor, including Europe and the Western Hemisphere; the Occident. 2 In the U.S.: **a** Formerly, the region west of the Allegheny Mountains. **b** The region west of the Mississippi, esp. the NW part of this region. 3 The noncommunist countries of Europe and the Western Hemisphere. —*adj.* 1 To, toward, facing, or in the west; western. 2 Coming from the west: the *west* wind. —*adv.* In or toward the west; in a westerly direction. [< OE]

west·er·ly (wes′tər·lē) adj. & adv. 1 In, toward, or of the west. 2 From the west. —**west′er·li·ness** n.

west·ern (wes′tərn) adj. 1 Of, in, directed toward, or facing the west. 2 From the west. —n. *Often cap.* A type of fiction or motion picture using cowboy and pioneer life in the western U.S. as its material.

West·ern (wes′tərn) adj. 1 Of, from, or characteristic of the West. 2 Belonging or pertaining to the Roman Catholic Church, as distinguished from the Eastern Orthodox Church.

west·ern·er (wes′tər·nər) n. 1 One who is native to or dwells in the west. 2 *Usu. cap.* One who is native to or dwells in the western U.S.

Western Hemisphere See HEMISPHERE.

west·ern·ize (wes′tər·nīz) v.t. **·ized, ·iz·ing** To make western in characteristics, habits, etc. —**west′ern·i·za′tion** n.

Western Roman Empire The part of the Roman Empire w of the Adriatic, which existed as a separate empire from 395 until the fall of Rome in 476.

Western Sa·mo·a (sə·mō′ə) An independent state located in the w part of the islands of Samoa, 1,133 sq. mi., cap. Apia.

West Germany See GERMANY.

West·min·ster Abbey (west′min′stər) A Gothic church in Westminster, London, where English monarchs are crowned and many notable persons are buried.

west-north·west (west′nôrth′west′, *in nautical usage* west′nôr·west′) n. The direction midway between west and northwest. —adj. & adv. In, toward, or from this direction.

west-south·west (west′south′west′, *in nautical usage* west′sou·west′) n. The direction midway between west and southwest. —adj. & adv. In, toward, or from this direction.

west·ward (west′wərd) adj. & adv. Toward the west. —n. A westward direction or region.

west·wards (west′wərdz) adv. WESTWARD.

wet (wet) adj. **wet·ter, wet·test** 1 Moistened, saturated, or covered with water or other liquid. 2 Marked by showers or by heavy rainfall; rainy. 3 Not yet dry: *wet* varnish. 4 Permitting the manufacture and sale of alcoholic beverages: a *wet* county. 5 Preserved or bottled in a liquid. —**all wet** *Slang* Quite wrong; mistaken. —n. 1 Water; moisture; wetness. 2 Showery or rainy weather. 3 *Informal* One opposed to prohibition. —v.t. & v.i. **wet** or **wet·ted, wet·ting** To make or become wet. [< OE *wæt*] —**wet′ly** adv. —**wet′ness, wet′ter** n. —**Syn.** v. dampen, moisten, soak.

wet·back (wet′bak′) n. *Informal* A Mexican who enters the U.S. illegally, esp. by swimming or wading across the Rio Grande.

wet blanket One who or that which discourages any proceedings.

wet dream *Informal* A male's involuntary expulsion of semen during sleep, usu. accompanying an erotic dream.

weth·er (weth′ər) n. A castrated ram. [< OE]

wet·land (wet′land′) n. *Usu. pl.* Swamps, marshes, and other land areas with heavy soil moisture.

wet nurse A woman who is hired to suckle the child of another woman.

wet pack A therapeutic method consisting of wrapping the patient in wet sheets.

wet suit A skin-tight rubber garment worn by divers, surfers, etc., to retain body warmth in cold waters.

we've (wēv) Contraction of *we have*.

wf, w.f. wrong font (printing).

wh, wh., whr, whr., w.-hr. watt-hour(s).

whack (ʰwak) v.t. & v.i. *Informal* To strike sharply; beat; hit. —n. 1 *Informal* A sharp, resounding blow. 2 *Slang* A share; portion. —**have** (or **take**) **a whack at** *Slang* 1 To give a blow to. 2 To have a chance or turn at. —**out of whack** *Slang* Out of order. [?] —**whack′er** n.

whack·ing (ʰwak′ing) adj. *Chiefly Brit. Informal* Strikingly large; whopping.

whale[1] (ʰwāl) n. 1 Any of various very large, air-breathing marine mammals of fishlike form. 2 *Informal* Something extremely good or large: a *whale* of a party. —v.i. **whaled, whal·ing** To engage in the hunting of whales. [< OE *hwæl*]

Blue whale

whale[2] (ʰwāl) v.t. **whaled, whal·ing** *Informal* To beat; thrash; flog. [Prob. var. of WALE]

whale·back (ʰwāl′bak′) n. A freight steamer having a rounded bow and main deck, used on the Great Lakes.

whale·boat (ʰwāl′bōt′) n. A long, deep rowboat, sharp at both ends.

whale·bone (ʰwāl′bōn′) n. 1 The horny, pliable substance hanging in plates from the upper jaw of certain whales. 2 A strip of whalebone, used in stiffening corsets, etc.

whal·er (ʰwā′lər) n. A person or a ship engaged in whaling.

whal·ing (ʰwā′ling) n. The industry of capturing whales. —adj. *Slang* Huge; whopping.

wham·my (ʰwam′ē) n. pl. **·mies** *Slang* A jinx; hex: usu. in the phrase **put a** (or **the**) **whammy on.** [< *wham*, informal interjection imit. of the sound of a hard blow]

wharf (ʰwôrf) n. pl. **wharves** (ʰwôrvz) or **wharfs** 1 A structure of masonry or timber erected on the shore of a harbor, river, etc., alongside which vessels may lie to load or unload cargo, passengers, etc. 2 Any pier or dock. —v.t. 1 To moor to a wharf. 2 To deposit or store on a wharf. [< OE *hwearf* a dam]

wharf·age (ʰwôr′fij) n. 1 Charge for the use of a wharf. 2 Wharf accommodations for shipping.

wharf rat 1 A rat that inhabits wharves. 2 *Slang* One who loiters about wharves, esp. with criminal intent.

what (ʰwot, ʰwut) pron. 1 Which specific act, thing, name, value, etc.: *What* is going on? *What* is that? 2 That which: *What* followed is a mystery. 3 How much: *What* will it cost? —**and what not** And so forth. —**but what** But that. —**what have you** What is similar or need not be mentioned. —**what if** Suppose that. —**what's what** *Informal* The actual state of affairs. —**what with** Taking into consideration. —adj. 1 Which or which kind of: I know *what* things I want. **2** How surprising, great, etc.: *What* a genius! **3** How much: *What* cash has he? **4** Whatever: Take *what* books you may need. —*adv.* How or how much: *What* do you care? —*interj.* An expression of surprise, annoyance, etc.: *What!* They stole it! [< OE *hwæt*]

what·ev·er (ʰwot′ev′ər, ʰwut′-) *pron.* **1** Anything that: Say *whatever* you want to say. **2** No matter what: *Whatever* you cook will be good. **3** *Informal* What: usu. interrogative: *Whatever* are you doing? —*adj.* **1** No matter what or which: *Whatever* things are left, you can keep. **2** Of any kind, amount, etc.: He has no ability *whatever*.

what·not (ʰwot′not′, ʰwut′-) *n.* An ornamental set of shelves for holding bric-a-brac, etc.

what·so·ev·er (ʰwot′sō·ev′ər, ʰwut′-) *pron. & adj.* Whatever: a slightly more formal usage.

wheal (ʰwēl) *n.* A small raised area or pimple on the skin. [Alter. of WALE]

wheat (ʰwēt) *n.* **1** Any of a genus of cereal grasses, esp. cultivated species yielding spikes of edible grain. **2** Grains of these species collectively, constituting a staple food usu. ground into flour.

wheat·en (ʰwēt′n) *adj.* **1** Made of wheat. **2** Having the pale gold color of ripe wheat.

wheat germ The embryo of the wheat kernel, used as a vitamin source.

whee·dle (ʰwēd′l) *v.* **·dled, ·dling** *v.t.* **1** To persuade or try to persuade by flattery, cajolery, etc.; coax. **2** To obtain by cajoling or coaxing. —*v.i.* **3** To use flattery or cajolery. [?] —**whee′dler** *n.* —**whee′dling·ly** *adv.*

wheel (ʰwēl) *n.* **1** A solid disk or a circular rim connected to a hub by spokes or rays capable of rotating on a central axis and used to facilitate movement, as in vehicles, or to act with a rotary motion, as in machines. **2** Anything resembling or suggestive of a wheel. **3** An instrument or device having a wheel or wheels as its distinctive characteristic, as a steering wheel, a potter's wheel, a water wheel, etc. **4** *Informal* A bicycle. **5** An old instrument of torture or execution, consisting of a wheel to which the limbs of the victim were tied and then stretched or broken. **6** A turning or rotating movement; revolution. **7** *Usu. pl.* That which imparts or directs motion or controls activity: the *wheels* of democracy. **8** *Slang* A person of influence or authority: also **big wheel. 9** *pl. Slang* An automobile. —**at** (or **behind**) **the wheel 1** Steering a motor vehicle, motor boat, etc. **2** In charge or in control. —*v.t.* **1** To move or convey on wheels. **2** To cause to turn on or as on an axis; pivot or revolve. **3** To perform with a circular movement. **4** To provide with a wheel or wheels. —*v.i.* **5** To turn on or as on an axis; pivot. **6** To change one's course of action, attitudes, opinions, etc.: often with *about*. **7** To move in a circular or spiral course. **8** To move on wheels. —**wheel and deal** *Slang* To act freely, aggressively, and often unscrupulously, as in the arrangement of a business or political deal. [< OE *hwēol*]

wheel·bar·row (ʰwēl′bar′ō) *n.* A boxlike vehicle ordinarily with one wheel and two handles, for moving small loads. —*v.t.* To convey in a wheelbarrow.

wheel·base (ʰwēl′bās′) *n.* The distance separating the axles of the front and rear wheels, as an automobile, etc.

wheel·chair (ʰwēl′châr′) *n.* A mobile chair mounted between large wheels, for the use of invalids. Also **wheel chair.**

wheel·er (ʰwē′lər) *n.* **1** One who wheels. **2** WHEELHORSE (def. 1). **3** Something furnished with a wheel or wheels: a *side-wheeler.*

wheel·er-deal·er (ʰwē′lər-dē′lər) *n. Slang* One who wheels and deals. —**wheel′er-deal′er·ing** *n.*

wheel·horse (ʰwēl′hôrs′) *n.* **1** A horse harnessed next to the front wheels and behind other horses. **2** A person who works hard and dependably.

wheel·house (ʰwēl′hous′) *n.* PILOTHOUSE.

wheel·wright (ʰwēl′rīt′) *n.* A man whose business is making or repairing wheels.

wheeze (ʰwēz) *v.t. & v.i.* **wheezed, wheez·ing** To breathe

or utter with a husky, whistling sound. —*n.* **1** A wheezing sound. **2** *Informal* A trite joke. [Prob. < ON *hvæsa* hiss] —**wheez′er, wheez′i·ness** *n.* —**wheez′i·ly, wheez′ing·ly** *adv.* —**wheez′y** *adj.* (**·i·er, ·i·est**)

whelk[1] (ʰwelk) *n.* Any of various large, spiral-shelled, marine snails, some of which are edible. [< OE *weoloc*]

whelk[2] (ʰwelk) *n.* A pimple or pustule. [< OE *hwelian* suppurate]

whelm (ʰwelm) *v.t.* **1** To submerge. **2** To overpower; overwhelm. [ME *whelmen*]

whelp (ʰwelp) *n.* **1** One of the young of a dog, wolf, lion, or certain other carnivores. **2** A dog. **3** A worthless young fellow. —*v.t. & v.i.* To give birth (to): said of certain carnivores. [< OE *hwelp*]

Common whelp

when (ʰwen) *adv.* **1** At what or which time: *When* did you arrive? **2** Under what circumstances: *When* do I apply the brake? **3** At an earlier time: I knew them *when.* —*conj.* **1** At which: the time *when* we went on the picnic. **2** At which or what time: They watched till midnight, *when* they fell asleep. **3** As soon as: He laughed *when* he heard it. **4** Although: He walks *when* he might ride. **5** At the time that; while: *when* we were young. **6** If it should happen that: An employee is fired *when* he is caught stealing. **7** After which; then: We had just awakened *when* you called. **8** Considering that: Why bother to ask me *when* you already know the answer? —*pron.* What or which time: since *when; when.* —*n.* The time; date: to know the *when* and why of something. [< OE *hwanne, hwænne*]

whence (ʰwens) *adv.* From what place or source: *Whence* does he come? —*conj.* From what or out of which place, source, or cause: asked *whence* these sounds arise. [< OE *hwanne* when]

whence·so·ev·er (ʰwens′sō·ev′ər) *adv. & conj.* From whatever place, cause, or source.

when·ev·er (ʰwen′ev′ər) *adv. & conj.* At whatever time.

when·so·ev·er (ʰwen′sō·ev′ər) *adv. & conj.* WHENEVER.

where (ʰwâr) *adv.* **1** At or in what place, respect, or situation: *Where* is my book? *Where* am I at fault? **2** To what place or end. *Where* is this getting us? **3** From what place or source: *Where* did you get that hat? —*conj.* **1** At, in, or to which or what place: I know the hotel *where* they are. **2** At, in, or to the place, position, or situation in which: They are living *where* they are happiest. —*pron.* The place in which: from *where* we stood. —*n.* Place; locality. [< OE *hwǣr*]

where·a·bouts (ʰwâr′ə·bouts′) *adv.* Near or at what place; about where. —*n.pl. (construed as sing. or pl.)* The place in which a person or thing is.

where·as (ʰwâr′az′) *conj.* **1** Since the facts are such as they are; seeing that: often used in the preamble of a resolution, etc. **2** While on the contrary; when in truth. —*n. pl.* **·as·es** A clause or item beginning with the word "whereas."

where·at (ʰwâr′at′) *adv. Archaic* At what: *Whereat* are you angry? —*conj.* At which point.

where·by (ʰwâr′bī′) *adv. Archaic* By what; how. —*conj.* By which: a plan *whereby* we will win.

wher·e'er (ʰwâr′âr′) *adv. & conj.* WHEREVER.

where·fore (ʰwâr′fôr′, -fōr′) *adv. Archaic* For what reason; why: *Wherefore* didst thou doubt? —*conj.* **1** For which. **2** THEREFORE. —*n.* The cause; reason: the whys and *wherefores.* [< WHERE + FOR]

where·from (ʰwâr′frum′, -from′) *adv. & conj.* From which.

where·in (ʰwâr′in′) *adv.* In what way or regard: *Wherein* is the error? —*conj.* In which: a state *wherein* there is discord.

where·of (ʰwâr′uv′, -ov′) *adv. & conj.* Of which, whom, or what.

where·on (ʰwâr′on′, -ôn′) *adv. Archaic* On what or whom. —*conj.* On which: land *whereon* to build.

where·so·ev·er (ʰwâr′sō·ev′ər) *adv. & conj.* In, at, or to whatever place; wherever.

where·to (ʰwâr′tōō′) *adv. Archaic* To what place or end. —*conj.* To which or to whom. Also **where′un·to′.**

where·up·on (ʰwâr′ə·pon′, -ə·pôn′) *adv. Archaic* Upon

what; whereon. —*conj.* Upon which or whom; in consequence of which; after which: *whereupon* they took in sail.

wher·ev·er (ʰwâr′ev′ər) *adv. & conj.* In, at, or to whatever place or situation.

where·with (ʰwâr′with′, -with′) *adv. Archaic* With what: *Wherewith* shall I do it? —*conj.* With which; by means of which: *wherewith* we abated hunger. —*pron.* That with or by which: used with an infinitive: I have not *wherewith* to do it.

where·with·al (ʰwâr′with·ôl′, -with-) *n.* The necessary means or resources, esp. money: used with *the.*

wher·ry (ʰwer′ē) *n. pl.* **·ries** 1 A light, fast rowboat built for one person and used for racing or exercise. 2 *Brit.* A very broad, light barge. —*v.t. & v.i.* **·ried, ·ry·ing** To transport in or use a wherry. [?]

whet (ʰwet) *v.t.* **whet·ed, whet·ting** 1 To sharpen, as a knife, by friction. 2 To make more keen or eager; excite; stimulate, as the appetite. —*n.* 1 The act of whetting. 2 Something that whets. [< OE *hwettan*] —**whet′ter** *n.*

wheth·er (ʰweth′ər) *conj.* 1 If it be the case that: Tell us *whether* you are going or not. 2 In case; if: *whether* he lived or died, we never heard. 3 Either: He came in first, *whether* by luck or plan. —**whether or no** Regardless; in any case. [< OE *hwæther*]

whet·stone (ʰwet′stōn′) *n.* A fine-grained stone for whetting knives, axes, etc.

whew (ʰwyoo) *interj.* An exclamation of amazement, dismay, relief, etc.

whey (ʰwā) *n.* A clear liquid that separates from the curd when milk is curdled, as in making cheese. [< OE *hwæg*] —**whey′ey, whey′ish** *adj.*

whf. wharf.

which (ʰwich) *pron.* 1 What specific one or ones: *Which* are for sale? 2 The specific one or ones that: I know *which* I bought. 3 The thing, animal, or event designated earlier: used restrictively or nonrestrictively: The flood *which* wiped us out was last year; That car, *which* is not old, no longer runs. 4 *Archaic* The person or persons designated earlier: "Our Father, *which* art in heaven," 5 WHICHEVER: Use *which* you find most convenient. 6 A thing, situation, or fact that: He decided to go, *which* was lucky. —*adj.* 1 What specific one or ones: *Which* play did you see? 2 WHICHEVER: Take *which* one you want. 3 Being the one or ones designated earlier: The clock struck one, at *which* point he left. • See WHO. [< OE *hwelc, hwilc*]

which·ev·er (ʰwich′ev′ər) *pron. & adj.* 1 Any one (of two or of several): Select *whichever* (ring) you want. 2 No matter which: *Whichever* (song) you choose, sing it well. Also **which′so·ev′er.**

whiff (ʰwif) *n.* 1 A slight gust or puff of air. 2 A gust or puff of odor: a *whiff* of onions. 3 A sudden expulsion of breath or smoke from the mouth; a puff. —*v.t.* 1 To drive or blow with a whiff or puff. 2 To smoke, as a pipe. —*v.i.* 3 To blow or move in whiffs or puffs. 4 To exhale or inhale whiffs. [Imit.] —**whiff′er** *n.*

whif·fet (ʰwif′it) *n. Informal* 1 A trifling, useless person. 2 A small, snappish dog. [?]

whif·fle (ʰwif′əl) *v.* **·fled, ·fling** *v.i.* 1 To blow with puffs or gusts, as the wind. 2 To vacillate; veer. —*v.t.* 3 To blow or dissipate with a puff. [Freq. of WHIFF] —**whif′fler** *n.*

whif·fle·tree (ʰwif′əl·trē′) *n.* A horizontal crossbar, to the ends of which the traces of a harness are attached. [Var. of WHIPPLETREE]

Whig (ʰwig) *n.* 1 An American colonist who supported the Revolutionary War in the 18th century. 2 A member of an American political party opposed to the Democratic and succeeded by the Republican party in 1856. 3 A member of a political party (later the Liberal party) in England in the 18th and 19th centuries. —*adj.* Belonging to, consisting of, or supported by the Whigs. [Prob. short for *Whiggamore,* one of a body of 17th cent. Scottish insurgents] — **Whig′ger·y, Whig′gism** *n.* —**Whig′gish** *adj.*

while (ʰwīl) *n.* A period of time: a brief *while.* —**between whiles** From time to time. —**the while** At the same time. —**worth (one′s) while** Worth one′s time, labor, trouble, etc. —*conj.* 1 During the time that. 2 At the same time

that; although: *While* he found fault, he also praised. 3 Whereas: This man is short, *while* that one is tall. —*v.t.* **whiled, whil·ing** To cause to pass pleasantly: usu. with *away:* to *while* away the time. [< OE *hwīl*]

whiles (ʰwīlz) *Archaic or Regional adv.* Occasionally; at intervals. —*conj.* WHILE.

whi·lom (ʰwī′ləm) *Archaic adj.* FORMER. —*adv.* FORMERLY. [< OE *hwīlum* at times < *hwīl* a while]

whilst (ʰwīlst) *conj. Chiefly Brit.* WHILE.

whim (ʰwim) *n.* A sudden, capricious idea, notion, or desire; fancy. [Short for earlier *whim-wham* a trifle]

whim·per (ʰwim′pər) *v.i.* 1 To cry with plaintive broken sounds. —*v.t.* 2 To utter with or as if with a whimper. — *n.* A low, broken, whining cry. [Imit.] —**whim′per·er** *n.* — **whim′per·ing·ly** *adv.*

whim·si·cal (ʰwim′zi·kəl) *adj.* 1 Capricious; fanciful; unpredictable. 2 Odd; fantastic; quaint. —**whim·si·cal′i·ty** (-kal′ə·tē) (*pl.* **·ties**), **whim′si·cal·ness** *n.* —**whim′si·cal·ly** *adv.*

whim·sy (ʰwim′zē) *n. pl.* **·sies** 1 A whim; caprice. 2 Humor that is somewhat odd, fanciful, or quaint. Also **whim′sey.** [Prob. related to WHIM]

whine (ʰwīn) *v.* **whined, whin·ing** *v.i.* 1 To utter a high, plaintive, nasal sound expressive of grief or distress. 2 To complain in a fretful or childish way. 3 To make a steady, high-pitched sound, as a machine. —*v.t.* 4 To utter with a whine. —*n.* The act or sound of whining. [< OE *hwīnan* whiz] —**whin′er** *n.* —**whin′ing·ly** *adv.* —**whin′y** *adj.*

whin·ny (ʰwin′ē) *v.* **·nied, ·ny·ing** *v.i.* 1 To neigh, esp. in a low or gentle way. —*v.t.* 2 To express with a whinny. —*n. pl.* **·nies** A low, gentle neigh. [< WHINE]

whip (ʰwip) *v.* **whipped, whip·ping** *v.t.* 1 To strike with a lash, rod, strap, etc. 2 To punish by striking thus; flog. 3 To drive or urge with lashes or blows: with *on, up, off,* etc. 4 To strike in the manner of a whip: The wind *whipped* the trees. 5 To beat, as eggs or cream, to a froth. 6 To seize, move, jerk, throw, etc., with a sudden motion: with *away, in, off, out,* etc. 7 In fishing, to make repeated casts upon the surface of (a stream, etc.). 8 To wrap or bind about something. 9 To sew, as a flat seam, with a loose overcast or overhand stitch. 10 *Informal* To defeat; overcome, as in a contest. —*v.i.* 11 To go, move, or turn suddenly and quickly: with *away, in, off, out,* etc. 12 To thrash about in the manner of a whip: pennants *whipping* in the wind. 13 In fishing, to make repeated casts with rod and line. — **whip up** 1 To excite; arouse. 2 *Informal* To prepare quickly, as a meal. —*n.* 1 An instrument consisting of a lash attached to a handle, used for discipline or punishment. 2 A whipping or thrashing motion. 3 A member of a legislative body, as congress or parliament, appointed unofficially to enforce discipline, attendance, etc.: also **party whip.** 4 A dessert containing whipped cream or beaten egg whites, flavoring, sometimes fruit, etc. [ME *wippen*] —**Syn.** *v.* 1 beat, scourge, switch, thrash.

whip·cord (ʰwip′kôrd′) *n.* 1 A strong, hard-twisted cord, used in making whiplashes. 2 A twill fabric with a pronounced diagonal rib.

whip hand 1 The hand in which a person holds the whip while driving. 2 A position or means of advantage.

whip·lash (ʰwip′lash′) *n.* 1 The flexible striking part of a whip. 2 An injury to the neck, due to a sudden snapping back and forth of the head, as in automobile accidents: also **whiplash injury.**

whip·per·snap·per (ʰwip′ər·snap′ər) *n.* A pretentious but insignificant person, esp. a young person. [?]

whip·pet (ʰwip′it) *n.* A swift dog resembling an English greyhound in miniature, used in racing, etc. [?< WHIP]

whip·ping (ʰwip′ing) *n.* 1 The act of one who or that which whips; esp. a punishment by flogging. 2 Material, as cord or twine, used to whip or bind.

Whippet

whipping boy Anyone who receives blame deserved by another; scapegoat.

whipping post The fixture to which those sentenced to flogging are secured.

whip·ple·tree (ʰwip′əl·trē′) n. WHIFFLETREE.

whip·poor·will (ʰwip′ər·wil) n. A small nocturnal bird, allied to the goatsuckers, common in E North America. [Imit.]

whip·saw (ʰwip′sô′) n. A thin, narrow, two-man ripsaw. —v.t. ·sawed, ·sawed or ·sawn, ·saw·ing 1 To saw with a whipsaw. 2 To beat (an opponent) in two ways at the same time.

whip·stitch (ʰwip′stich′) v.t. To sew or gather with overcast stitches. —n. An overcast stitch.

whip·stock (ʰwip′stok′) n. A whip handle.

whir (ʰwûr) v.t. & v.i. whirred, whir·ring To fly or move with a buzzing sound. —n. 1 A whizzing, swishing sound. 2 Confusion; bustle. Also whirr. [Prob. < Scand.]

whirl (ʰwûrl) v.i. 1 To turn or revolve rapidly, as about a center. 2 To turn away or aside quickly. 3 To move or go swiftly. 4 To have a sensation of spinning: My head whirls. —v.t. 5 To cause to turn or revolve rapidly. 6 To carry or bear along with a revolving motion. —n. 1 A swift rotating or revolving motion. 2 Something whirling. 3 A state of confusion. 4 A round of activities, social events, etc. 5 Informal A short drive. 6 Informal A try. [Prob. < ON hvirfla revolve] —whirl′er n.

whirl·i·gig (ʰwûr′lə·gig′) n. 1 Any toy that spins. 2 A merry-go-round. 3 Anything that moves in a cycle. 4 A whirling motion. 5 Any of certain water beetles that move on the water in swift circles: also whirligig beetle. [< WHIRL + GIG]

whirl·pool (ʰwûrl′pool′) n. 1 An eddy or vortex where water moves in a rapid whirling motion, as from the meeting of two currents. 2 Anything resembling a whirlpool, esp. in movement.

whirl·wind (ʰwûrl′wind′) n. 1 A forward-moving column of air, with a rapid circular and upward spiral motion. 2 Anything resembling a whirlwind in movement, energy, or violence. —adj. Extremely swift or impetuous: a whirlwind courtship.

whish (ʰwish) v.i. To make or move with a whizzing sound. —n. Such a sound. [Imit.]

whisk (ʰwisk) v.t. 1 To brush or sweep off lightly: often with away or off. 2 To cause to move with a quick sweeping motion. 3 To beat with a quick movement, as eggs, cream, etc. —v.i. 4 To move quickly and lightly. —n. 1 A light sweeping or whipping movement. 2 A little bunch of straw, feathers, etc. for brushing. 3 A culinary instrument of wire loops for whipping (cream, etc.). [Prob. < Scand.]

whisk·broom (ʰwisk′broom′, -broom′) n. A small, short-handled broom for brushing clothing, etc.

whisk·er (ʰwis′kər) n. 1 pl. The hair of a man's beard, esp. the hair that grows on the cheeks. 2 A hair from the whiskers. 3 One of the long, bristly hairs near the mouth of some animals, as the cat, mouse, etc. [< WHISK] —whisk′-ered, whisk′er·y adj.

whis·key (ʰwis′kē) n. pl. ·keys or ·kies 1 An alcoholic liquor obtained by the distillation of a fermented mash of grain, as rye, corn, barley, or wheat. 2 A drink of whiskey. —adj. Pertaining to or made of whiskey. Also whis′ky. [< Ir. uisce beathadh, lit., water of life] • In the U.S. and Ireland, whiskey is usu. spelled with an e. Scotch and Canadian whisky, however, are traditionally spelled without the e.

whis·per (ʰwis′pər) n. 1 An act or instance of breathy speech with little or no vibration of the vocal chords. 2 An utterance made with such speech. 3 A secret communication; hint; insinuation. 4 Any low, rustling sound. —v.i. 1 To speak in a low, breathy way with little or no vibration of the vocal chords. 2 To talk cautiously or furtively; plot or gossip. 3 To make a low, rustling sound, as leaves. —v.t. 4 To utter in a whisper. 5 To speak to in a whisper. [< OE hwisprian] —whis′per·er n. —whis′per·ing·ly adv. —whis′-per·y adj.

whispering campaign An organized effort to discredit a person, group, cause, etc., by rumors and gossip.

whist (ʰwist) n. A game of cards from which bridge developed, played by four persons with a full pack of 52 cards. [Alter. of earlier whisk]

whis·tle (ʰwis′əl) v. ·tled, ·tling v.i. 1 To make a sound by sending the breath through the teeth or through puckered lips. 2 To make a sharp, shrill sound by forcing air, steam, etc., through a small opening. 3 To make a similar sound by swift passage through the air, as bullets, the wind, etc. 4 To make a shrill cry, as certain animals or birds. 5 To blow or sound a whistle. —v.t. 6 To produce (a tune) by whistling. 7 To call, manage, or direct by whistling. —n. 1 An instrument for making whistling sounds: a train whistle; a toy whistle. 2 A whistling sound. 3 The act of whistling. —wet one's whistle Slang To take a drink. [< OE hwistlian a shrill pipe] —whis′tler n.

whis·tle-stop (ʰwis′əl·stop′) Informal v.i. -stopped, -stop-ping To make whistle stops, esp. as part of a political campaign.

whistle stop Informal 1 A small town, at which formerly a train stopped only on signal. 2 Any of a series of brief stops at small communities during a tour, esp. one made by a political candidate.

whit (ʰwit) n. The smallest particle; speck: usu. with a negative: not a whit abashed. [< OE (ænig) wiht a little amount] —Syn. bit, grain, iota, jot, shred.

white (ʰwīt) adj. whit·er, whit·est 1 Having the color produced by reflection of all the rays of the solar spectrum, as the color of pure snow. 2 Light or comparatively light in color: white wine. 3 Bloodless; ashen: white with rage. 4 Very fair; blond. 5 Silvery or gray, as with age. 6 Snowy. 7 Wearing white clothing: white nuns. 8 Not malicious or harmful: a white lie. 9 Innocent; pure. 10 Unmarked by ink or print; blank. 11 Having a light-colored skin; Caucasian. 12 Of, pertaining to, or controlled by Caucasians: the white power structure. 13 Informal Fair; straightforward; honest. 14 Music Of, pertaining to, or being a tonal quality having accuracy of pitch but lacking resonance, color, and warmth. —n. 1 A white color. 2 The state or condition of being white; whiteness. 3 The white or light-colored part of something; esp., the albumen of an egg, or the white part of the eyeball. 4 Anything that is white or nearly white, as cloth, white wine, etc. 5 pl. A white uniform or outfit: the summer whites of the Navy. 6 A Caucasian. —v.t. whit·ed, whit·ing To make white; whiten. [< OE hwīt] —white′ly adv. —white′ness n.

white ant TERMITE.

white-bait (ʰwīt′bāt′) n. The young of various fishes, esp. of sprat and herring, served as a delicacy.

white birch A North American birch with white bark that peels off in papery sheets.

white-cap (ʰwīt′kap′) n. A wave with foam on its crest.

white cedar 1 A strong-scented evergreen tree of the cypress family, having small, scalelike leaves and growing in moist places. 2 Its soft, easily worked wood.

white clover A common variety of clover, with white flowers.

white coal Water power.

white-col·lar (ʰwīt′kol′ər) adj. Of, pertaining to, or designating usu. salaried employees, as office personnel, whose work does not often expose their clothes to soil or stain, thus enabling them to wear garments, as white shirts, etc., that are easily stained.

white corpuscle LEUKOCYTE.

whited sepulcher A corrupt or evil person who pretends to be good; hypocrite.

white elephant 1 A rare pale-gray variety of Asian elephant held sacred in E Asia. 2 Anything that is a burden and an expense to maintain.

white feather A symbol of cowardice. —show the white feather To show cowardice.

white-fish (ʰwīt′fish′) n. pl. ·fish or ·fish·es 1 Any of various silvery North American food fishes, living mostly in lakes. 2 Any of various other whitish or silvery fishes.

white flag A white flag or banner used as a signal of surrender.

white gold Gold alloyed with a white metal, usu. nickel and zinc, sometimes palladium, which gives the gold a platinumlike appearance.

white heat 1 The temperature at which metal, etc., becomes white with heat. 2 A state of intense emotion, enthusiasm, etc.

white-hot (ʰwīt′hot′) adj. So hot as to glow with white light.

White House, The 1 The official residence of the president of the U.S., at Washington, D.C. **2** The executive branch of the U.S. government.

white lead A poisonous white pigment composed of lead carbonate and hydrated lead oxide.

white lie A harmless, trivial lie.

white matter The whitish portion of the brain and spinal cord that is composed mainly of nerve fibers.

white meat Any light-colored meat, as the breast of chicken, turkey, etc.

whit·en (ʰwīt′n) *v.t.* & *v.i.* To make or become white or nearly white. —**whit′en·er** *n.* —**Syn.** blanch, bleach.

white noise Noise in which the average intensity at any frequency between two stated limits is constant.

white oak 1 Any of numerous oaks having gray or whitish bark. **2** The wood of any white oak.

white pepper Pepper ground from the white seeds inside black peppercorns.

white pine 1 A pine of E North America, with soft, bluish-green leaves in clusters of five. **2** The light, soft wood of this tree. **3** Any of several related pines.

White oak
a. leaves. b. blossom. c. acorn.

white poplar A large, rapidly growing tree valued for its ornamental leaves, which are green above and silvery-white below.

white potato The common potato.

White Russian BYELORUSSIAN.

white sauce A cooked sauce of flour, butter, milk, etc.

white slave A woman forced into or held in prostitution. —**white-slave** (ʰwīt′slāv′) *adj.* —**white slaver** —**white slavery**

white-tailed deer (ʰwīt′tāld′) A common North American deer, having a tail white on the underside.

white tie 1 A white bow tie, worn with men's formal evening dress. **2** The formal evening dress of men.

white·wash (ʰwīt′wosh′, -wôsh′) *n.* **1** A mixture of slaked lime and water used for whitening walls, etc. **2** A suppressing or hiding of faults and defects. **3** *Informal* A defeat in which the loser fails to score. —*v.t.* **1** To coat with whitewash. **2** To gloss over; hide. **3** *Informal* In games or sports, to defeat without allowing one's opponent to score. —**white′wash′er** *n.*

whith·er (ʰwith′ər) *adv. Archaic* To what place, condition, end, etc.: *Whither* are we bound? —*conj.* **1** To which place, condition, end, etc.: the village *whither* we went. **2** To whatever place, condition, end, etc.: Go *whither* you will. [< OE *hwider*]

whith·er·so·ev·er (ʰwith′ər·sō·ev′ər) *adv. Archaic* To whatever place.

whit·ing¹ (ʰwī′ting) *n.* A powdered white chalk used as a pigment, for polishing, etc.

whit·ing² (ʰwī′ting) *n.* **1** A small European food fish related to cod. **2** A silvery-scaled hake. **3** Any of several silvery fishes, esp. the **Carolina whiting,** common on the coast of the s U.S. [< MDu. *wit* white]

whit·ish (ʰwī′tish) *adj.* Somewhat white or very light gray. —**whit′ish·ness** *n.*

Whiting²

whit·low (ʰwit′lō) *n.* An inflammatory, festering lesion at the edge of a fingernail. [< WHITE + FLAW]

Whit·sun (ʰwit′sən) *adj.* Of, pertaining to, or for Whitsunday or Whitsuntide.

Whit·sun·day (ʰwit′sun′dē, -dā) *n.* The seventh Sunday after Easter; Pentecost. [< OE *Hwīta Sunnandæg,* lit., white Sunday < the white robes worn by recently baptized persons on that day]

Whit·sun·tide (ʰwit′sən·tīd′) *n.* The week that begins with Whitsunday. Also **Whitsun Tide.**

whit·tle (ʰwit′l) *v.* ·tled, ·tling *v.t.* **1** To cut or shave bits from (wood, a stick, etc.). **2** To make or shape by whittling. **3** To reduce or wear away a little at a time: with *down, off, away,* etc. —*v.i.* **4** To whittle wood. [< OE *thwitan* to cut] —**whit′tler** *n.* —**Syn.** *v.* **1** carve, trim, pare.

whiz (ʰwiz) *v.* whizzed, whiz·zing *v.i.* **1** To make a hissing and humming sound while passing rapidly through the air. **2** To move or pass with such a sound. —*v.t.* **3** To cause to whiz. —*n.* **1** The sound made by whizzing. **2** *Slang* Any person or thing of extraordinary excellence or ability. Also **whizz.** [Imit.] —**whiz′zer** *n.* —**whiz′zing·ly** *adv.*

whiz kid *Slang* A young person who is extraordinarily clever, talented, or successful. [Alter. of *Quiz Kid,* a panel member of a former quiz show made up of children]

who (hoo) *pron. possessive case* whose; *objective case* whom **1** Which or what person or persons: *Who* is she? They don't know *who* I am. **2** The person or persons that; whoever: *Who* insults my friends insults me. **3** That: used as a relative to introduce a clause: the man *who* mows our lawn. —**who's who** Who the most prominent people are. —**as who should say** As if one should say; so to speak. [< OE *hwa, hwā*] • **who, which, that** *Who* as a relative is usu. applied only to persons, *which* only to animals or to inanimate objects, *that* to persons or things.

WHO World Health Organization.

whoa (ʰwō) *interj.* Stop! stand still! [Var. of HO]

who·dun·it (hoo·dun′it) *n. Informal* A mystery story, play, etc. [< WHO + DONE + IT]

who·ev·er (hoo·ev′ər) *pron.* **1** Any one without exception; any person who. **2** No matter who.

whole (hōl) *adj.* **1** Containing all the parts necessary to make up a total; entire; complete. **2** Not broken, injured, defective, etc.; sound; intact. **3** Being the full amount, number, duration, etc.: He failed the *whole* class. **4** In or having regained sound health; hale. **5** Having the same parents: a *whole* brother. **6** *Math.* Integral; not mixed or fractional. —**as a whole** Altogether. —**on the whole** Taking all into consideration; in general. —*n.* **1** All the parts or elements making up a thing. **2** A complete unity or system. [< OE *hāl*] —**whole′ness** *n.*

whole·heart·ed (hōl′här′tid) *adj.* Done or undertaken with all earnestness, energy, dedication, etc. —**whole′-heart′ed·ly** *adv.* —**whole′heart′ed·ness** *n.*

whole note *Music* A note whose time value is the same as that of two half notes. • See NOTE.

whole number Any member of the set of numbers {. . . −3, −2, −1, 0, 1, 2, 3 . . .}; an integer.

whole·sale (hōl′sāl′) *n.* The sale of goods in large bulk or quantity, usu. for resale by retailers. —*adj.* **1** Pertaining to or engaged in such selling. **2** Made or done on a large scale or indiscriminately: *wholesale* murder. —*adv.* **1** In bulk or quantity. **2** Extensively or indiscriminately. —*v.t.* & *v.i.* ·saled, ·sal·ing To sell (something) in large quantity, usu. for resale by retailers. [< ME *by hole sale* in large quantities] —**whole′sal′er** *n.*

whole·some (hōl′səm) *adj.* **1** Tending to promote health: *wholesome* air or food. **2** Tending to promote mental or moral well-being: a *wholesome* play. **3** Healthy: *wholesome* red cheeks. [< WHOLE + -SOME] —**whole′some·ly** *adv.* —**whole′some·ness** *n.*

whole step An interval consisting of two semitones. Also **whole tone.**

whole-wheat (hōl′ʰwēt′) *adj.* **1** Made from the entire wheat kernel: *whole-wheat* flour. **2** Made from whole-wheat flour. Also **whole wheat.**

who'll (hool) Contraction of *who will* or *who shall.*

whol·ly (hō′lē, hōl′lē) *adv.* **1** Completely; totally. **2** Exclusively; only.

whom (hoom) *pron.* The objective case of WHO. [< OE *hwam*]

whom·ev·er (hoom·ev′ər) *pron.* The objective case of WHOEVER.

whom·so·ev·er (hoom′sō·ev′ər) *pron.* The objective case of WHOSOEVER.

whoop (hoop, ʰwoop, ʰwoop) *v.i.* **1** To utter loud cries, as of excitement, rage, or exultation. **2** To hoot, as an owl. **3** To make a loud, gasping intake of breath. —*v.t.* **4** To utter with a whoop or whoops. **5** To call, urge, chase, etc., with whoops. —**whoop it** (or **things**) **up** *Slang* **1** To celebrate in a noisy, riotous manner. **2** To arouse enthusiasm. — *n.* **1** A shout of excitement, joy, derision, etc. **2** A loud, convulsive intake of breath. **3** An owl's hoot. [Imit.]

whoop·ee (ʰwŏŏʹpē, ʰwŏŏpʹē) *Slang interj.* An exclamation of joy, excitement, etc. —**make whoopee** To have a noisy, festive time. [< WHOOP]

whooping cough A contagious respiratory disease of bacterial origin chiefly affecting children, marked in later stages by violent coughing.

whooping crane A large white North American crane having a whooplike cry.

whop·per (ʰwopʹər) *n. Informal* **1** Something large or remarkable. **2** An outrageous falsehood.

whop·ping (ʰwopʹing) *adj.* Unusually large, great, or remarkable.

whore (hôr, hōr) *n.* A woman who engages in sexual intercourse promiscuously; esp., a prostitute. —*v.i.* **whored**, **whor·ing 1** To have illicit sexual intercourse, esp. with a whore. **2** To be or act like a whore. [< OE *hōre*]

whorl (ʰwûrl, ʰwôrl) *n.* **1** The flywheel of a spindle. **2** *Bot.* A set of leaves, etc., distributed in a circle around a stem. **3** *Zool.* A turn of a spiral shell. **4** Any of the convoluted ridges of a fingerprint. [? < WHIRL] —**whorled** *adj.*

Whorl *def. 2*

whor·tle·ber·ry (ʰwûrʹtəl·ber′ē) *n. pl.* **·ries 1** A European shrub with edible blue-black berries. **2** Its fruit. **3** HUCKLEBERRY. [< OE *horta* whortleberry + BERRY]

whose (hōōz) The possessive case of WHO and often of WHICH. [< OE *hwæs*, genitive of *hwā* who]

who·so (hōōʹsō) *pron. Archaic* WHOEVER.

who·so·ev·er (hōōʹsō·evʹər) *pron.* WHOEVER.

why (ʰwī) *adv.* For what cause, purpose, or reason: *Why did you go?* —*conj.* **1** The reason or cause for which: I don't know *why* he went. **2** For or because of which: I know the reason *why* he went. —*n. pl.* **whys** A cause; reason. — *interj.* An exclamation expressing surprise, doubt, etc. [< OE *hwī, hwȳ*]

WI Wisconsin (P.O. abbr.).

W.I. West Indian; West Indies.

wick (wik) *n.* A strand of loosely twisted or woven fibers, as in a candle or lamp, acting by capillary attraction to convey fuel to a flame. [< OE *wēoca*] —**wick′ing** *n.*

wick·ed (wikʹid) *adj.* **1** Evil; depraved. **2** Mischievous; roguish. **3** Troublesome; painful: a *wicked* headache. [< OE *wicca* a wizard] —**wick′ed·ly** *adv.* —**wick′ed·ness** *n.* — **Syn. 1** malevolent, sinful, wrong. **2** devilish.

wick·er (wikʹər) *adj.* Made of twigs, osiers, etc. —*n.* **1** A pliant young shoot or rod; twig; osier. **2** WICKERWORK. [Prob. < Scand.]

wick·er·work (wikʹər·wûrk′) *n.* A fabric or texture, as a basket, made of woven twigs, osiers, etc.

wick·et (wikʹit) *n.* **1** A small door or gate often within a larger entrance. **2** A small opening in a door. **3** A small sluicegate at the end of a millrace. **4** In cricket: **a** Either of two arrangements of three upright rods set near together. **b** The level playing space between these. **c** A player's turn at bat. **5** In croquet, an arch, usu. of wire, through which one must hit the ball. [< AF *wiket*]

wick·et·keep·er (wikʹit·kē′pər) *n.* In cricket, the fielder stationed right behind the wicket.

wide (wīd) *adj.* **wid·er**, **wid·est 1** Having relatively great extent between sides. **2** Extended far in every direction; spacious: a *wide* expanse. **3** Having a specified degree of width: an inch *wide*. **4** Distant from the desired or proper point, issue, etc.: *wide* of the mark. **5** Having great scope, range, inclusiveness, etc.: a *wide* variety. **6** Loose; ample; roomy: *wide* trousers. **7** Fully open; expanded or extended: *wide* eyes. **8** *Phonet.* Formed with a relatively relaxed tongue and jaw: said of certain vowels. —*n.* In cricket, a ball bowled so as not to be within the batsman's reach. — *adv.* **1** To a great distance; extensively. **2** Far from the mark, issue, etc. **3** To the greatest extent; fully open. [< OE *wīd*] —**wide′ly** *adv.* —**wide′ness** *n.* —**Syn.** *adj.* **2** ample, broad, extensive, vast.

wide-an·gle lens (wīdʹang′gəl) A type of camera lens

designed to permit an angle of view wider than that of the ordinary lens.

wide-a·wake (wīdʹə·wāk′) *adj.* **1** Totally awake. **2** Alert.

wide-eyed (wīdʹīd′) *adj.* **1** With the eyes wide open. **2** Uninformed or unsophisticated.

wid·en (wīdʹn) *v.t. & v.i.* To make or become wide or wider. —**wid′en·er** *n.*

wide-o·pen (wīdʹō′pən) *adj.* **1** Opened wide. **2** *Informal* Remiss in the enforcement of laws which regulate gambling, prostitution, etc.: a *wide-open* city.

wide·spread (wīdʹspred′) *adj.* **1** Extending over a large space or territory. **2** Held, believed, indulged in, etc., by many people.

widge·on (wijʹən) *n.* Any of various river ducks having a short bill and wedge-shaped tail. Also **wig·eon.** [?]

wid·get (wijʹit) *n. Slang* **1** A product having a unique or ingenious feature; gadget. **2** Something unnamed and used as an example in a hypothetical situation. [Alter. of GADGET]

wid·ow (widʹō) *n.* **1** A woman who has lost her husband by death and has not remarried. **2** In some card games, an additional hand dealt to the table. **3** *Printing* A short line of type ending a paragraph at the top of a page or column; also, such a line at the end of any paragraph. —*v.t.* To make a widow of. [< OE *widewe*]

wid·ow·er (widʹō·ər) *n.* A man who has lost his wife by death and has not remarried.

widow's mite A contribution which, although small in amount, is all or even more than the giver can afford.

widow's peak A point of hair growing down from the hairline in the middle of the forehead.

width (width) *n.* **1** Dimension or measurement of an object taken from side to side, or at right angles to the length. **2** Something that has width: a *width* of cloth. [< WIDE]

width·wise (widthʹwīz) *adv.* In the direction of the width. Also **width′ways′.**

wield (wēld) *v.t.* **1** To use or handle, as a weapon or instrument. **2** To exercise (authority, power, influence, etc.). [Fusion of OE *wealdan* to cause and OE *wildan* to rule] — **wield′er** *n.*

wie·ner (wēʹnər) *n.* A kind of smoked sausage, similar to a frankfurter, made of beef and pork. Also **wie·ner·wurst** (wēʹnər·wûrst′). [Short for *wienerwurst* < G, Vienna sausage]

wife (wīf) *n. pl.* **wives** (wīvz) **1** A woman joined to a man in lawful wedlock. **2** *Archaic* A woman: now used in combination or in certain phrases: *housewife*, old *wives'* tales. —**take to wife** To marry (a woman). [< OE *wīf*] —**wife′· dom, wife′hood** *n.*

wife·ly (wīfʹlē) *adj.* **·li·er**, **·li·est 1** Of or like a wife. **2** Suitable to a wife.

wig (wig) *n.* A covering of real or artificial hair for the head. —*v.t.* **wigged**, **wig·ging 1** To furnish with a wig or wigs. **2** *Brit. Informal* To berate or scold. [Short for PERIWIG]

wig·gle (wigʹəl) *v.t. & v.i.* **·gled**, **·gling** To move or cause to move quickly from side to side; wriggle. —*n.* The act of wiggling. [< MLG *wiggelen*] —**wig′gly** *adj.* **(·gli·er, ·gli·est)**

Barrister's wig

wig·gler (wigʹlər) *n.* **1** One who or that which wiggles. **2** The larva of a mosquito.

wig·wag (wigʹwag′) *v.t. & v.i.* **·wagged**, **·wag·ging 1** To move briskly back and forth; wag. **2** To send (a message) by hand flags, torches, etc. —*n.* **1** The act of wigwagging. **2** A message sent by wigwagging. [< dial. E *wig* wiggle + WAG¹] —**wig′wag′ger** *n.*

wig·wam (wigʹwom, -wôm) *n.* A dwelling or lodge of certain North American Indians, commonly a rounded or conical framework of poles covered with bark, rush matting, or hides. [< Algon.]

Wigwam

wild (wīld) *adj.* **1** Living or growing in a natural state; not tamed, domesticated, or cultivated: *wild* animals; *wild* flowers. **2** Being in the natural state without civilized inhabitants or cultivation: *wild* prairies. **3** Uncivilized; primitive: the *wild* men of Borneo. **4** Undisciplined; unruly. **5** Morally dissolute; profligate. **6** Violent; turbulent: a *wild* night. **7** Reckless; imprudent: a *wild* speculation. **8** Unusually odd or strange; extravagant; bizarre: a *wild* imagination. **9** Eager and excited: *wild* with delight. **10** Frenzied; crazed: *wild* with fury. **11** Disorderly; disarranged: a *wild* mop of hair. **12** Far from the mark aimed at; erratic: a *wild* pitch. **13** In some card games, having its value arbitrarily determined by the dealer or holder. **14** *Slang* Terrific; great: The party was *wild*. **15** *Slang* Showy; jazzy: a *wild* necktie. —*n. Often pl.* An uninhabited or uncultivated place; wilderness: the *wilds* of Africa. —**the wild 1** The wilderness. **2** The free, natural, wild life. —*adv.* In a wild manner: to run *wild*. [< OE *wilde*] —**wild′ly** *adv.* —**wild′ness** *n.* —**Syn.** *adj.* **3** barbarous, savage. **7** irresponsible, rash. **8** fantastic.

wild boar An Old World hog often hunted as game.

wild carrot A weed from which the cultivated carrot is derived; Queen Anne's lace.

wild·cat (wīld′kat′) *n.* **1** Any of various undomesticated felines resembling the domestic cat, but larger and stronger, as the lynx, cougar, etc. **2** An aggressive, quick-tempered person. **3** An unattached locomotive, used on special work, as when sent out to haul a train, etc. **4** A successful oil well drilled in an area previously unproductive. **5** A tricky or unsound business venture, esp. a worthless mine. Also **wild cat.** —*adj.* **1** Unsound; risky; esp. financially. **2** Made, produced, or carried on without official sanction or authorization. **3** Not running on a schedule, as a locomotive. —*v.t. & v.i.* **·cat·ted, ·cat·ting** To drill for oil in (an area not known to be productive). —**wild′cat′-ter** *n.*

wildcat strike A strike unauthorized by regular union procedure.

wilde·beest (wīld′bēst, wil′də-) *n. pl.* **·beests** or **·beest** GNU. [< Du. *wild* wild + *beeste* a beast]

wil·der·ness (wil′dər·nis) *n.* **1** An uncultivated, uninhabited, or barren region. **2** A multitudinous and confusing collection of persons or things. [< OE *wilder* a wild beast + -NESS]

wild·fire (wīld′fīr′) *n.* A raging, destructive fire that is hard to extinguish. —**like wildfire** Very quickly; uncontrollably.

wild·flow·er (wīld′flou′ər) *n.* **1** Any uncultivated plant that bears flowers. **2** The flower of such a plant. Also **wild flower.**

wild·fowl (wīld′foul′) *n. pl.* **·fowl** or **·fowls** A wild bird, esp. wild duck, pheasant, etc., hunted as game. Also **wild fowl.**

wild-goose chase (wīld′gōōs′) Pursuit of the unknown or unattainable.

wild·life (wīld′līf′) *n.* Wild animals collectively.

wild oat 1 *Usu. pl.* Any of various uncultivated grasses. **2** *pl.* Indiscretions of youth, usu. in the phrase **sow one's wild oats.**

wild rice 1 A tall aquatic grass of North America. **2** The highly esteemed, edible grain of this plant.

Wild West The w U.S. in its early period of Indian fighting, lawlessness, etc. Also **wild West.**

wild·wood (wīld′wo͝od′) *n.* Natural forest land.

wile (wīl) *n.* **1** An act or a means of cunning deception. **2** Any trick or artifice. —*v.t.* **wiled, wil·ing** To lure, beguile, or mislead. —**wile away** To pass (time) pleasantly. [< OE *wīl*] —**Syn.** *n.* **2** machination, maneuver, ruse, stratagem.

wil·ful (wil′fəl) *adj.* WILLFUL.

will¹ (wil) *n.* **1** The power to make conscious, deliberate choices or to control what one does. **2** The act or experience of exercising this power. **3** A specific desire, purpose, choice, etc.: the *will* of the people. **4** Strong determination or purpose: the *will* to succeed. **5** Self-control. **6** Attitude or inclination toward others: ill *will*. **7** *Law* The legal declaration of a person's intentions as to the disposition of his estate after his death. —**at will** As one pleases. —**with a will** Energetically. —*v.* **willed, will·ing** *v.t.* **1** To decide upon; choose. **2** To resolve upon as an action or course. **3** *Law* To bequeath by a will. **4** To control, as a

hypnotized person, by the exercise of will. **5** To decree: The king *wills* it. —*v.i.* **6** To wish; desire: as you *will*. [< OE *willa*]

will² (wil) *v.* Present *sing. & pl.*: **will** (*Archaic* **thou wilt**); past: **would** (*Archaic* **thou would·est** or **wouldst**) As an auxiliary verb *will* is used with the infinitive without *to*, or elliptically without the infinitive, to express: **1** Futurity: They *will* arrive by dark. **2** Likelihood: You *will* be sorry. **3** Command; order: You *will* leave immediately. **4** Willingness or disposition: Why *will* you not tell the truth? **5** Capability or capacity: The ship *will* survive any storm. **6** Custom or habit: He *will* sit for hours and brood. **7** *Informal* Probability or inference: I expect this *will* be the main street. [< OE *willan*] • See SHALL.

willed (wild) *adj.* Having a will of a given character: used in combination: *weak-willed*.

will·ful (wil′fəl) *adj.* **1** Deliberate; intentional: *willful* disregard of the law. **2** Stubborn; headstrong: a *willful* child. —**will′ful·ly** *adv.* —**will′ful·ness** *n.*

wil·lies (wil′ēz) *n.pl. Slang* Nervousness; jitters: used with *the*. [?]

will·ing (wil′ing) *adj.* **1** Having the mind favorably inclined or disposed. **2** Readily and gladly acting, responding, doing, giving, etc. **3** Readily and gladly offered, done, given, etc. —**will′ing·ly** *adv.* —**will′ing·ness** *n.* —**Syn.** **3** accommodating, compliant, obliging.

will-o'-the-wisp (wil′ə-thə·wisp′) *n.* IGNIS FATUUS. [Earlier *Will with the wisp*]

wil·low (wil′ō) *n.* **1** Any of a large genus of shrubs and trees having usu. narrow leaves and flexible shoots often used in basketry. **2** The wood of a willow. **3** *Informal* Something made of willow wood, as a cricket bat. —*adj.* Made of willow wood. [< OE *wilige, welig*] • See WEEPING WILLOW.

wil·low·y (wil′ō-ē) *adj.* **·low·i·er, ·low·i·est 1** Tall and graceful. **2** Lithe; flexible; supple. **3** Abounding in willows. —**wil′low·i·ness** *n.*

will·pow·er (wil′pou′ər) *n.* Strength to direct or control one's actions or desires; determination.

wil·ly-nil·ly (wil′ē-nil′ē) *adj.* Being or happening whether one wants it or not. —*adv.* Willingly or unwillingly. [Earlier *will I, nill I* whether I will or not]

wilt¹ (wilt) *v.i.* **1** To lose freshness; droop or become limp. **2** To lose energy and vitality; become faint or languid. **3** To lose courage or spirit. —*v.t.* **4** To cause to wilt. —*n.* **1** The act of wilting or the state of being wilted. **2** A plant disease that causes wilting. [Prob. dial. var. of obs. *welk*]

wilt² (wilt) *Archaic* Will: used with *thou*.

Wil·ton (wil′tən) *n.* A kind of carpet having a velvety texture. Also **Wilton carpet, Wilton rug.** [< *Wilton*, England, where first made]

wi·ly (wī′lē) *adj.* **·li·er, ·li·est** Full of or characterized by wiles; sly; cunning. —**wi′li·ly** *adv.* —**wi′li·ness** *n.*

wim·ple (wim′pəl) *n.* A cloth wrapped in folds around the neck close under the chin and over the head, exposing only the face, worn by medieval women and still by certain nuns. —*v.* **·pled, ·pling** *v.t.* **1** To cover or clothe with a wimple. **2** To make or fold into pleats, as a veil. **3** To cause to move with slight undulations; ripple. —*v.i.* **4** To lie in plaits or folds. **5** To ripple. [< OE *wimpel*]

Wimple

win (win) *v.* **won, won, win·ning** *v.i.* **1** To gain a victory; be victorious in a contest, endeavor, etc. **2** To succeed in reaching or attaining a specified end or condition; get: often with *across, over, through,* etc. —*v.t.* **3** To be successful in; gain victory in: to *win* an argument. **4** To gain in competition or contest: to *win* the blue ribbon. **5** To gain by effort, persistence, etc.: to *win* fame. **6** To influence so as to obtain the good will or favor of: often with *over*. **7** To secure the love of; gain in marriage. **8** To succeed in reaching: to *win* the harbor. —**win out** *Informal* To succeed; triumph. —*n. Informal* A victory; success. [< OE *winnan* contend, labor] —**Syn.** *v.* **5** achieve, attain, earn, secure.

wince (wins) *v.i.* **winced, winc·ing** To shrink back; flinch. —*n.* The act of wincing. [< AF *wenchier*] —**winc′er** *n.*

---

winch (winch) *n.* **1** A windlass, particularly one turned by a crank and used for hoisting. **2** A crank with a handle for transmitting motion. [<OE *wince*] — **winch′er** *n.*

Win·ches·ter rifle (win′ches·tər) A type of repeating rifle, first produced in 1866: a trade name. Also **Winchester**.

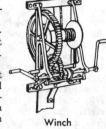
Winch

wind¹ (wind) *n.* **1** Any movement of air, esp. a natural horizontal movement. **2** Any powerful or destructive movement of air, as a tornado. **3** The direction from which a wind blows. **4** Air pervaded by a scent, as in hunting. **5** The power of breathing; breath: He lost his *wind*. **6** Idle chatter. **7** Bragging; vanity; conceit. **8** *pl.* The wind instruments of an orchestra; also, the players of these instruments. **9** The gaseous product of indigestion; flatulence. —**break wind** To expel gas through the anus. —**get wind of** To receive a hint or intimation of. —**how the wind blows** (or **lies,** etc.) What is taking place, being decided, etc. —**in the teeth of the wind** Directly against the wind: also **in the wind's eye.** —**in the wind** Impending; afoot. —*v.t.* **1** To follow by scent; to catch a scent of on the wind. **2** To exhaust the breath of, as by racing. **3** To allow to recover breath by resting. **4** To expose to the wind, as in ventilating. [<OE] —**Syn.** *n.* **1** blast, breeze, gale, gust, zephyr.

wind² (wind) *v.* **wound** *or* **wind·ed, wind·ing** *v.t.* **1** To coil (thread, rope, etc.) around some object or fixed core; twine. **2** To encircle or cover with something, as by coiling or wrapping: to *wind* a spool with thread. **3** To renew the motion of, as a clock, by turning a stem, key, etc. **4** To turn in a revolving motion: to *wind* a handle. **5** To cause to turn and twist. **6** To make (one's way) by a turning and twisting course. **7** To introduce carefully or deviously; insinuate: He *wound* himself into my confidence. **8** To raise or hoist, as by means of a capstan or windlass. —*v.i.* **9** To move in a turning, twisting course; meander. **10** To coil or twine about some central object or core. **11** To move in a circular or spiral course. **12** To proceed or gain an end carefully or deviously. —**wind down** To decrease or be decreased gradually; de-escalate: to *wind down* a war. —**wind up 1** To coil or wind round and round. **2** To excite; arouse. **3** To bring to conclusion or settlement: He *wound up* his affairs. **4** In baseball, to swing the arm preparatory to pitching. **5** To hoist. —*n.* **1** The act of winding, or the condition of being wound. **2** A bend, turn, or twist. [<OE *windan*] —**wind′er** *n.*

wind³ (wīnd, wind) *v.t.* **wind·ed** *or* **wound, wind·ing 1** To blow, as a horn; sound. **2** To give (a call or signal), as with a horn. [<WIND¹; infl. by WIND²]

wind·age (win′dij) *n.* **1** The rush of air caused by the rapid passage of an object, as a projectile. **2** Deflection of an object, as a bullet, from its natural course by wind. **3** *Naut.* The surface offered to the wind by a vessel.

wind·bag (wind′bag′) *n. Informal* An overly talkative person who says little of significance.

wind·blown (wind′blōn′) *adj.* **1** Tossed or blown by the wind. **2** Having a permanent direction of growth as determined by prevailing winds: said of plants and trees.

wind·borne (wind′bôrn′, -bōrn′) *adj.* Carried or transported by the wind.

wind·break (wind′brāk′) *n.* Anything, as a hedge, fence, etc., that protects from or breaks the force of the wind.

wind·break·er (wind′brā′kər) *n.* A sports jacket for outer wear, having a close-fitting or elastic waistband and cuffs. [<*Windbreaker,* a trade name]

wind·bro·ken (wind′brō′kən) *adj.* Having the heaves: said of a horse.

wind·chill factor (wind′chil′) **1** A measure of air temperature modified by the chilling effect of wind of a given velocity as felt on the surface of the skin. **2** The effect of wind in reducing perceived air temperature.

wind·ed (win′did) *adj.* **1** Out of breath. **2** Having a specified kind of wind or breath: used in combination: *short-winded.*

wind·fall (wind′fôl′) *n.* **1** Something, as ripening fruit, brought down by the wind. **2** A piece of unexpected good fortune.

wind·flow·er (wind′flou′ər) *n.* ANEMONE.

wind gauge An instrument for measuring the velocity of the wind; anemometer.

wind·hov·er (wind′huv′ər) *n. Brit.* KESTREL.

wind·ing (wīn′ding) *n.* **1** The act or condition of one who or that which winds; a turning or coiling. **2** A bend or turn, or a series of them. **3** Something that winds. —*adj.* **1** Turning spirally about an axis or core. **2** Having bends or lateral turns.

wind·ing sheet (wīn′ding) SHROUD (def. 1).

wind instrument (wind) A musical instrument whose sounds are produced by blowing air through it, esp. a portable one, as a flute, oboe, etc.

wind·jam·mer (wind′jam′ər) *n. Naut.* **1** A sailing vessel, as distinguished from a steamship. **2** A member of its crew.

wind·lass (wind′ləs) *n.* Any of several devices for hoisting or hauling, esp. one consisting of a drum turned by means of a crank so that the hoisting rope winds on the drum. [<ON *vinda* wind + *āss* a beam]

Differential windlass

wind·mill (wind′mil′) *n.* **1** A mill having at the top a system of adjustable slats, wings, or sails which, when turned by the wind, transmit power to a pump, millstone, or the like. **2** An imaginary wrong, evil, or foe: usu. in the phrase **tilt at windmills,** an allusion to Don Quixote's combat with windmills, which he mistook for giants. • See VANE.

win·dow (win′dō) *n.* **1** An opening in the wall of a building, etc., to admit light or air, usu. capable of being opened and closed, and including casements or sashes fitted with glass. **2** A windowpane or the sash or framework that encloses it. **3** Anything resembling or suggesting a window, as a transparent patch in certain envelopes. —*v.t.* To provide with a window or windows. [<ON *vindr* wind + *auga* an eye]

window box A box along a window ledge or sill, for growing plants.

window dressing 1 The act or art of arranging merchandise attractively in shop and store windows. **2** Any action, report, etc., designed to make something seem more attractive or plausible than it actually is.

win·dow·pane (win′dō·pān′) *n.* A pane of glass for a window.

window seat A seat in the recess of a window.

window shade A flexible covering for the inside of a window, used to regulate light.

win·dow·shop (win′dō·shop′) *v.i.* **-shopped, -shop·ping** To look at goods shown in store windows without buying them. —**win′dow-shop′per** *n.*

win·dow·sill (win′dō·sil′) *n.* The horizontal ledge at the bottom of a window opening.

wind·pipe (wind′pīp′) *n.* TRACHEA.

wind·row (wind′rō′) *n.* **1** A long row of hay or grain raked together preparatory to building into cocks. **2** A line of dust, surf, leaves, etc. swept together by wind. —*v.t.* To rake or shape into a windrow. —**wind′row′er** *n.*

wind·screen (wind′skrēn′) *n. Brit.* WINDSHIELD.

wind·shear (wind′shir′) *n.* A strong, rapid change in wind direction.

wind·shield (wind′shēld′) *n.* A transparent screen, as of glass, across and above the dashboard of motor vehicles, power boats, etc., providing protection from the wind.

wind·sock (wind′sok′) *n.* A large, conical bag, open at both ends, mounted on a pivot, and used to indicate the direction of the wind. Also **wind sock, wind sleeve.**

Wind·sor (win′zər) Name of the royal family of Great Britain since July 27, 1917.

Windsor chair A wooden chair, typically with a spindle back, slanting legs, and a flat or saddle seat.

Windsor knot A wide knot that can be used to tie a four-in-hand tie.

Windsor tie A wide, soft necktie tied in a loose bow.

wind·storm (wind′stôrm′) *n.* A violent wind, usu. with little or no precipitation.

wind·swept (wind′swept′) *adj.* Exposed to or propelled by the wind.

wind tunnel *Aeron.* A device in which the effects of artificially produced winds, as on airplane wings, can be studied.

wind·up (wīnd′up′) *n.* 1 The act of concluding. 2 A conclusion or culmination; end. 3 In baseball, the swing of the arm preparatory to pitching the ball.

wind·ward (wind′wərd) *adj.* 1 Of or toward the direction from which the wind blows. 2 Being on the side exposed to the wind. —*n.* The direction from which the wind blows. —*adv.* In the direction from which the wind blows.

wind·y (win′dē) *adj.* **wind·i·er, wind·i·est** 1 Of or abounding in wind; stormy; tempestuous: *windy* weather. 2 Exposed to the wind. 3 Suggestive of wind; boisterous; violent. 4 Flatulent. 5 Boastful, talkative, or pompous. 6 Idle; empty: *windy* talk. —**wind′i·ly** *adv.* —**wind′i·ness** *n.*

wine (wīn) *n.* 1 The fermented juice of the grape, used as an alcoholic beverage and in cooking. 2 The fermented juice of any of several other fruits or vegetables: dandelion *wine.* 3 The color of red wine. —*v.* **wined, win·ing** *v.t.* 1 To entertain or treat with wine. —*v.i.* 2 To drink wine. [< OE *wīn*]

wine·bib·ber (wīn′bib′ər) *n.* A person given to excessive drinking of wine. —**wine′bib′bing** *adj., n.*

wine cellar A storage space for wines; also, the wines stored.

wine-col·ored (wīn′kul′ərd) *adj.* Having the color of red wine.

wine·glass (wīn′glas′, -gläs′) *n.* A small goblet, usu. stemmed, from which to drink wine.

wine·grow·er (wīn′grō′ər) *n.* One who cultivates a vineyard and makes wine. —**wine′grow′ing** *adj., n.*

wine·press (wīn′pres′) *n.* An apparatus or a place where the juice of grapes is expressed. —**wine′press′er** *n.*

win·er·y (wī′nər-ē) *n. pl.* **·er·ies** An establishment where wine is made.

Wine·sap (wīn′sap′) *n.* An American variety of red winter apple.

wine·skin (wīn′skin′) *n.* A bag made of the entire skin of an animal, as a goat, used for containing wine.

wing (wing) *n.* 1 An organ of flight; esp. one of a pair of appendages of a bird or bat, adapted for flight. 2 An analogous organ in insects and some other animals. 3 Anything resembling or suggestive of a wing in form or function. 4 *Aeron.* The (or one of the) main supporting surface(s) of an airplane. 5 *Bot.* Any thin, winglike expansion of certain stems, seeds, etc. 6 A vane, as of a windmill. 7 Anything regarded as conferring the swift motion or rapture of flight: on *wings* of song. 8 Flight by or as by wings. 9 *Archit.* A part attached to a side, esp. a projection or extension of a building on the side of the main portion. 10 An annex or separate section of a large building: the surgical *wing* of a hospital. 11 Either of two sides, unseen by the audience, of a proscenium stage; also, a piece of scenery for the side of a stage. 12 Either of two sidepieces on the back of an armchair. 13 A side section of something that shuts or folds, as a screen. 14 A tactical and administrative unit of the U.S. Air Force, larger than a group. 15 *Mil.* Either division of a military force on either side of the center. 16 An analogous formation in certain outdoor games, as hockey or football. 17 Either of two extremist groups or factions in a political organization: the left *wing.* 18 A subsidiary group of a parent organization. 19 *Slang* An arm, esp., in baseball, a pitching or throwing arm. 20 *pl.* The insignia worn by certain qualified aircraft pilots, navigators, etc. —**on** (or **upon**) **the wing** 1 In flight. 2 Departing; also, journeying. —**take wing** To fly away. —**under one's wing** Under one's protection. —*v.t.* 1 To pass over or through in flight. 2 To accomplish by flying: the eagle *winged* its way. 3 To enable to fly. 4 To cause to go swiftly; speed. 5 To transport by flight. 6 To provide with wings for flight. 7 To supply with a side body or part. 8 To wound (a bird) in a wing. 9 To disable by a

minor wound. —*v.i.* 10 To fly; soar. —**wing it** *Slang* To act, do, arrange, etc., without advance preparation; improvise. [< ON *vængr*]

wing chair A large, upholstered armchair with a high back and side pieces designed as protection from drafts.

Wing chair

winged (wingd, wing′id) *adj.* 1 Having wings. 2 Passing swiftly. 3 Sublime; lofty.

wing·spread (wing′spred′) *n.* The distance between the tips of the fully extended wings, as of a bird, insect, or airplane. Also **wing′span′.**

wink (wingk) *v.i.* 1 To close and open the eye or eyelids quickly. 2 To draw the eyelids of one eye together, as in making a sign. 3 To emit fitful gleams; twinkle. —*v.t.* 4 To close and open (the eye or eyelids) quickly. 5 To move, force, etc., by winking: with *away, off,* etc. 6 To signify or express by winking. —**wink at** To pretend not to see. —*n.* 1 The act of winking. 2 The time necessary for a wink. 3 A twinkle. 4 A hint conveyed by winking. 5 A brief bit (of sleep): I had a *wink* after lunch. —**forty winks** A short nap. [< OE *wincian* close the eyes]

wink·er (wing′kər) *n.* 1 One who winks. 2 *Slang* EYELASH.

win·ner (win′ər) *n.* 1 One who or that which wins. 2 *Informal* Someone or something likely to succeed.

win·ning (win′ing) *adj.* 1 Successful in achievement, esp. in competition. 2 Capable of charming; attractive; winsome. —*n.* 1 The act of one who wins. 2 *Usu. pl.* That which is won, as money in gambling. —**win′ning·ly** *adv.* —**win′ning·ness** *n.*

win·ning·est (win′ing-əst) *adj. Informal* Most often winning: the *winningest* team in baseball.

win·now (win′ō) *v.t.* 1 To separate (grain, etc.) from the chaff. 2 To blow away (the chaff) thus. 3 To separate (what is valuable) or to eliminate (what is valueless): to *winnow* out the good or the bad. 4 To blow upon; cause to flutter. 5 To beat or fan (the air) with the wings. 6 To scatter by blowing; disperse. —*v.i.* 7 To separate grain from chaff. 8 To fly; flap. —*n.* 1 Any device used in winnowing grain. 2 The act of winnowing. [< OE *windwian* < *wind* the wind] —**win′now·er** *n.*

win·o (wī′nō) *n. pl.* **·noes** or **·nos** *Slang* A drunkard who habitually drinks wine, esp. cheap wine. [< WINE]

win·some (win′səm) *adj.* Charming; attractive. [< OE *wyn* joy] —**win′some·ly** *adv.* —**win′some·ness** *n.* —**Syn.** amiable, appealing, engaging, pleasant, winning.

win·ter (win′tər) *n.* 1 The coldest season of the year, extending from the end of autumn to the beginning of spring. 2 A time marked by lack of life, warmth, and cheer. 3 A year as including the winter season: a man of ninety *winters.* —*v.i.* 1 To pass the winter. —*v.t.* 2 To care for, feed, or protect during the winter: to *winter* plants. —*adj.* Pertaining to, suitable for, or characteristic of winter. [< OE] —**win′ter·er** *n.*

win·ter·green (win′tər-grēn) *n.* 1 A small evergreen plant bearing aromatic oval leaves, white, bell-shaped flowers and edible red berries. 2 A colorless, volatile oil extracted from the leaves of this plant or made synthetically, used as a flavor.

win·ter·ize (win′tə-rīz) *v.t.* **·ized, ·iz·ing** To prepare or put in condition for winter, as a motor vehicle, etc.

win·ter·kill (win′tər-kil′) *v.t. & v.i.* To die or kill by exposure to extreme cold: said of plants. —*n.* The act, process, or an instance of winterkilling.

winter solstice See SOLSTICE.

winter wheat Wheat planted before snowfall and harvested the following summer.

win·try (win′trē) *adj.* **·tri·er, ·tri·est** Of or like winter; cold, bleak, cheerless, etc. Also **win′ter·y** (-tər·ē). —**win′tri·ly** *adv.* —**win′tri·ness** *n.*

win·y (wī′nē) *adj.* **win·i·er, win·i·est** Having the taste, color, smell, etc., of wine.

wipe (wīp) *v.t.* **wiped, wip·ing** 1 To subject to slight friction or rubbing, usu. with some soft, absorbent material. 2 To remove by rubbing lightly: usu. with *away* or *off.* 3 To move or draw for the purpose of wiping: He *wiped* his hand across his brow. **4** To apply by wiping. —**wipe out 1** To kill or murder. **2** To destroy utterly; annihilate. **3** In surfing, to be overturned by a wave. —*n.* The act of wiping. [< OE *wīpian*] —**wip′er** *n.*

wire (wīr) *n.* **1** A slender rod, strand, or thread of metal. **2** Something made of wire, as a fence, a cord to conduct an electric current, etc. **3** WIREWORK. **4** A telephone or telegraph cable. **5** The telegraph system as a means of communication. **6** TELEGRAM. **7** The screen of a papermaking machine. **8** A line marking the finish of a race. —**get (in) under the wire** To conclude or achieve something at the very last moment. —**pull wires** *Informal* To use secret or private sources of influence to attain something. —*v.* **wired, wir·ing** *v.t.* **1** To fasten or bind with wire. **2** To furnish or equip with wiring. **3** To telegraph: to *wire* an order. **4** To place on wire, as beads. —*v.i.* **5** To telegraph. [< OE *wīr*] —**wir′er** *n.*

wire gauge 1 A gauge for measuring the diameter of wire. **2** A standard system of sizes for wire.

wire-haired terrier (wīr′hârd′) A fox terrier having a wiry coat. Also **wire′hair′** (-hâr′).

wire·less (wīr′lis) *adj.* **1** Without wire or wires; having no wires. **2** *Brit.* Radio. —*n.* **1** The wireless telegraph or telephone system, or a message transmitted by either. **2** *Brit.* Radio. —*v.t. & v.i. Brit.* To communicate (with) by radio.

Wire·pho·to (wīr′fō′tō) *n. pl.* **·tos** An apparatus and method for transmitting and receiving photographs by wire: a trade name.

wire·pull·er (wīr′pŏŏl′ər) *n.* **1** One who pulls wires, as of a puppet. **2** One who uses secret means to control others or gain his own ends; an intriguer. —**wire′pull′ing** *n.*

wire·tap (wīr′tap′) *n.* **1** A device used to make a connection with a telephone or telegraph wire to listen to or record the message transmitted. **2** The act of wiretapping. —*v.* **·tapped, ·tap·ping** *v.t.* **1** To connect a wiretap to. **2** To monitor by the use of a wiretap. —*v.i.* **3** To use a wiretap. —**wire′tap′per** *n.*

wire·work (wīr′wûrk′) *n.* A mesh or netting made of wire.

wir·ing (wīr′ing) *n.* An entire system of wire installed for the distribution of electric power, as for lighting, heating, sound, etc.

wir·y (wīr′ē) *adj.* **wir·i·er, wir·i·est 1** Lean, but tough and sinewy: said of persons. **2** Like wire; stiff; bristly. —**wir′i·ly** *adv.* —**wir′i·ness** *n.*

Wis., Wisc. Wisconsin.

wis·dom (wiz′dəm) *n.* **1** The ability to discern what is true or right and to make sound judgments based on such discernment. **2** Insight or intuition. **3** COMMON SENSE. **4** A high degree of knowledge; learning. **5** An accumulated body of knowledge, as in philosophy, science, etc. [< OE *wīs* wise] —**Syn. 1** sapience, sagacity. **4** enlightenment, erudition.

Wisdom of Solomon A book of the Old Testament Apocrypha, consisting of a hymn in praise of wisdom.

wisdom tooth The last tooth on either side of the upper and lower jaws in man. —**cut one's wisdom teeth** To acquire mature judgment. • See TOOTH.

wise¹ (wīz) *adj.* **wis·er, wis·est 1** Having or showing wisdom (def. 1). **2** Having or showing insight, intuition, common sense, or knowledge. **3** Shrewd; calculating; cunning. **4** *Informal* Aware of: *wise* to his motives. **5** *Slang* Arrogant; fresh: a *wise* guy. —**get wise** *Slang* **1** To learn the true facts about. **2** To become arrogant or fresh. —**wise up** *Slang* To make or become aware, informed, or sophisticated. [< OE *wīs*] —**wise′ly** *adv.* —**wise′ness** *n.*

wise² (wīz) *n.* Way of doing; manner; method: chiefly in the phrases **in any wise, in no wise,** etc. [< OE *wīse* manner]

-wise *suffix of adverbs & nouns* **1** In a (specified) way or manner: *nowise, likewise.* **2** In a (specified) direction or position: *lengthwise, clockwise:* often equivalent to *-ways.* **3** *Informal* With reference to: *Moneywise,* the job is worth considering. [< OE *wīse* manner, fashion]

wise·a·cre (wīz′ā′kər) *n.* A person who claims to know everything. [< MDu. *wijsseggher* a soothsayer]

wise·crack (wīz′krak′) *Slang n.* A smart, insolent, or

supercilious remark. —*v.i.* To utter a wisecrack. —**wise′·crack′er** *n.*

wish (wish) *n.* **1** A desire or longing, usu. for some definite thing. **2** An expression of such a desire; petition. **3** Something wished for. —*v.t.* **1** To have a desire or longing for; want: We *wish* to be sure. **2** To desire a specified condition or state for (a person or thing): I *wish* this day were over. **3** To invoke upon or for someone: I *wished* him good luck. **4** To bid: to *wish* someone good morning. **5** To request, command, or entreat: I *wish* you would stop yelling. —*v.i.* **6** To have or feel a desire; yearn; long: usu. with *for:* to *wish* for a friend's return. **7** To make or express a wish. —**wish on** *Informal* To impose (something unpleasant or unwanted) on a person. [< OE *wȳscan*] —**wish′er** *n.*

wish·bone (wish′bōn′) *n.* The forked bone situated in front of the sternum in most birds.

wish·ful (wish′fəl) *adj.* Having or indicating a wish or desire. —**wish′ful·ly** *adv.* —**wish′ful·ness** *n.*

wishful thinking A believing that what one wants to be true is true.

wish·y-wash·y (wish′ē·wosh′ē, -wôsh′ē) *adj. Informal* **1** Thin; diluted, as liquor. **2** Lacking in purpose, effectiveness, or strength.

wisp (wisp) *n.* **1** A small bunch, as of hay, straw, or hair. **2** A small bit; a mere indication: a *wisp* of vapor. **3** A slight, delicate thing: a *wisp* of a child. **4** WILL-O′-THE-WISP. [ME *wisp, wips*] —**wisp′y** *adj.* **(·i·er, ·i·est)**

wist (wist) *Archaic p.t. & p.p.* of WIT².

wis·te·ri·a (wis·tir′ē·ə, -târ′-) *n.* Any of a genus of woody twining shrubs of the bean family, with pinnate leaves, elongated pods, and showy clusters of blue, purple, or white flowers. Also **wis·tar·i·a** (wis·târ′ē·ə). [< C. *Wistar,* 1761–1818, U.S. anatomist]

wist·ful (wist′fəl) *adj.* **1** Wishful; yearning. **2** Musing; pensive. [Appar. < obs. *wistly* intently] —**wist′ful·ly** *adv.* —**wist′ful·ness** *n.*

Wisteria

wit¹ (wit) *n.* **1** The power of perceiving, reasoning, knowing, etc.; intelligence. **2** *pl.* **a** The mental faculties: to use one's *wits.* **b** Such faculties in relation to their state of balance: out of one's *wits.* **3** Practical intelligence; common sense. **4** The ability to perceive unexpected analogies or incongruities and to express them in an amusing or epigrammatic manner. **5** The ability to make jokes, amusing remarks, etc. **6** A person with wit (defs. 4 & 5). **7** Speech or writing characterized by wit (defs. 4 & 5). —**at one's wits' end** At the limit of one's devices and resources. —**live by one's wits** To make a living by using one's practical intelligence and resourcefulness, often in unscrupulous or fraudulent ways. [< OE]

wit² (wit) *v.t. & v.i.* Present indicative: I **wot,** thou **wost,** he, she, it **wot,** we, ye, they **wite(n);** *p.t.* and *p.p.* **wist;** *pr.p.* **wit·ting** *Archaic* To be or become aware (of); learn; know. —**to wit** That is to say; namely. [< OE *witan* know]

witch (wich) *n.* **1** A woman who practices sorcery or has supernatural powers, esp. to work evil. **2** An ugly old woman; a hag. **3** A bewitching or fascinating woman or girl. —*v.t.* **1** To work an evil spell upon; effect by witchcraft. **2** To fascinate or charm. —*v.i.* **3** DOWSE². [< OE *wicce* a witch, fem. of *wicca* a wizard]

witch·craft (wich′kraft′, -kräft′) *n.* **1** Black magic; sorcery. **2** Extraordinary influence or fascination.

witch doctor Among certain primitive peoples, a man skilled in counteracting evil spells.

witch·er·y (wich′ər·ē) *n. pl.* **·er·ies 1** Witchcraft; black magic; sorcery. **2** Power to charm; fascination.

witch hazel 1 Any of a genus of shrubs and small trees with usu. yellow flowers. **2** An extract derived from the bark and dried leaves of a certain witch hazel, used as a mild astringent. [< OE *wice* wych-elm + HAZEL]

witch hunt *Slang* An investigation or harassment of dissenters, often for the undeclared purpose of weakening political opposition.

witch·ing (wich′ing) *adj.* Having the power to enchant; bewitching. —**witch′ing·ly** *adv.*

with (with, with) *prep.* **1** In the company of: Walk *with* me. **2** Having; bearing: a hat *with* a feather. **3** Characterized or marked by: a man *with* brains. **4** In a manner characterized by; exhibiting: to dance *with* grace. **5** Among, into, near to, etc.: counted *with* the others. **6** In the course of: We forget *with* time. **7** From: to part *with* the past. **8** Against: to struggle *with* an adversary. **9** In the opinion of: That is all right *with* me. **10** Because of: faint *with* hunger. **11** In or under the care, supervision, etc., of: Leave the key *with* the janitor. **12** By means or aid of: to write *with* a pencil. **13** By the use, addition, etc., of: trimmed *with* lace. **14** As an associate, member, etc., of: worked *with* her sister; played *with* an orchestra. **15** In spite of: *With* all his money, he could not buy health. **16** At the same time as: to go to bed *with* the chickens. **17** In the same direction as: to drift *with* the crowd. **18** In regard to; in the case of: I am angry *with* them. **19** Onto; to: Join this tube *with* that one. **20** In proportion to: His fame grew *with* his achievements. **21** In support of: He voted *with* the Left. **22** Of the same opinion as: I'm *with* you there! **23** Having received or been granted: *With* your consent I'll go now. [< OE]

with- *prefix* **1** Against: *withstand*. **2** Back; away: *withhold*. [< OE *with* against]

with·al (with·ôl′, with-) *adv.* **1** Besides; in addition. **2** Notwithstanding; nevertheless. —*prep. Archaic* With: used at the end of the clause: a bow to shoot *withal*. [ME *with* + *alle* all]

with·draw (with·drô′, with-) *v.* **·drew, ·drawn, ·draw·ing** *v.t.* **1** To draw or take away; remove. **2** To take back, as an assertion or a promise. **3** To keep from use, sale, etc. —*v.i.* **4** To draw back; retreat. **5** To remove oneself; leave, as from an activity.

with·draw·al (with·drô′əl, with-) *n.* **1** The act or process of withdrawing. **2** The act or process of overcoming one's addiction to a habit-forming drug.

withdrawal symptom Any of the symptoms caused by the withdrawal of a physically addictive drug from an addict, as tremors, sweating, chills, vomiting, and diarrhea.

with·drawn (with·drôn′, with-) *adj.* **1** Not responsive socially or emotionally; introverted. **2** Isolated; remote.

withe (with, with, with) *n.* A willowy, supple twig, used to bind or wrap. [< OE *withthe*]

with·er (with′ər) *v.i.* **1** To become limp or dry, as a plant when deprived of moisture. **2** To waste, as flesh. —*v.t.* **3** To cause to become limp or dry. **4** To abash, as by a scornful glance. [ME *widren*] —**Syn.** **1** shrink, shrivel. **4** confuse, shame.

with·ers (with′ərz) *n.pl.* The highest part of the back of the horse, ox, etc., between the shoulder blades. [< OE *withre* resistance: so called because this part presses against the harness when a horse is pulling a load]

with·hold (with·hōld′, with-) *v.* **·held, ·hold·ing** *v.t.* **1** To hold back; restrain. **2** To refuse to grant, permit, etc. **3** To deduct (taxes, etc.) from a salary before payment. —*v.i.* **4** To refrain. —**with·hold′er** *n.*

withholding tax That part of an employee's wages or salary which is deducted as an installment on his income tax.

Withers

with·in (with·in′, with-) *adv.* **1** In the inner part; interiorly. **2** Inside the body, heart, or mind. **3** Indoors. —*prep.* **1** In the inner or interior part or parts of; inside: *within* the house. **2** In the limits, range, or compass of (a specified time, space, or distance): *within* a mile of here; *within* ten minutes' walk. **3** Not exceeding (a specified quantity): Live *within* your means. **4** In the reach, limit, or scope of: *within* my power. [< OE *with* with + *innan* in]

with-it (with′it) *adj. Slang* In touch with modern habits, fashions, trends, etc.; up-to-date.

with·out (with·out′, with-) *prep.* **1** Not having; lacking: *without* money. **2** In the absence of: We must manage *without* help. **3** Free from: *without* fear. **4** At, on, or to the outside of. **5** Outside of or beyond the limits of: living *without* the pale of civilization. **6** With avoidance of: He listened *without* paying attention. —*adv.* **1** In or on the outer part; externally. **2** OUTDOORS. [< OE *with* with + *ūtan* out]

with·stand (with·stand′, with-) *v.* **·stood, ·stand·ing** *v.t. & v.i.* To resist, oppose, or endure, esp. successfully. [< OE *with-* against + *standan* stand]

with·y (with′ē, with′ē) *n. pl.* **with·ies** WITHE.

wit·less (wit′lis) *adj.* Lacking in wit; foolish. —**wit′less·ly** *adv.* —**wit′less·ness** *n.*

wit·ness (wit′nis) *n.* **1** A person who has seen or knows something and is therefore competent to give evidence concerning it. **2** That which serves as or furnishes evidence or proof. **3** *Law* **a** One who has knowledge of facts relating to a given cause and is subpoenaed to testify. **b** A person who has signed his name to a legal document in order that he may testify to its authenticity. **4** Evidence; testimony. —**bear witness 1** To give evidence; testify. **2** To be evidence. —*v.t.* **1** To see or know by personal experience. **2** To furnish or serve as evidence of. **3** To give testimony to. **4** To be the site or scene of: This spot has *witnessed* many heinous crimes. **5** *Law* To see the execution of (an instrument) and subscribe to its authenticity. —*v.i.* **6** To give evidence; testify. [< OE *witnes* knowledge, testimony] —**wit′ness·er** *n.*

witness stand The platform in a courtroom from which a witness gives evidence.

wit·ted (wit′id) *adj.* Having (a specified kind of) wit: used in combination: *quick-witted*.

wit·ti·cism (wit′ə·siz′əm) *n.* A witty or clever remark. [< WITTY]

wit·ting·ly (wit′ing·lē) *adv.* Designedly; knowingly. [< WIT²]

wit·ty (wit′ē) *adj.* **·ti·er, ·ti·est** Having, displaying, or full of wit. [< OE *wittig* wise] —**wit′ti·ly** *adv.* —**wit′ti·ness** *n.*

wive (wīv) *v.t. & v.i.* **wived, wiv·ing** *Archaic* To marry (a woman). [< OE *wīf* a wife, woman]

wives (wīvz) *n. pl.* of WIFE.

wiz·ard (wiz′ərd) *n.* **1** A magician or sorcerer. **2** *Informal* A very skillful or clever person. —*adj.* Of or pertaining to wizards. [< OE *wīs* wise]

wiz·ard·ry (wiz′ərd·rē) *n.* The practice or methods of a wizard.

wiz·ened (wiz′ənd) *adj.* Shriveled; dried up. [< OE *wisnian*, dry up, wither]

wk. weak; week; work.

wks. weeks; works.

WL, w.l. water line; wave length.

W. long. west longitude.

WNW, W.N.W., wnw, w.n.w. west-northwest.

WO, W.O. wait order; Warrant Officer.

woad (wōd) *n.* **1** An Old World herb related to mustard. **2** The blue dye obtained from its leaves. [< OE *wād*] —**woad′ed** *adj.*

wob·ble (wob′əl) *v.* **·bled, ·bling** *v.i.* **1** To move or sway unsteadily. **2** To show indecision or unsteadiness; vacillate. —*v.t.* **3** To cause to wobble. —*n.* A wobbling motion. [? < LG *wabbeln*] —**wob′bler** *n.* —**wob′bling·ly** *adv.* —**wob′bly** *adj.* (**·bli·er, ·bli·est**)

woe (wō) *n.* **1** Overwhelming sorrow; grief. **2** Heavy affliction or calamity; disaster; suffering. —*interj.* Alas! [< OE *wā* misery]

woe·be·gone (wō′bi·gôn′, -gon′) *adj.* Having or exhibiting woe; mournful; sorrowful. —**Syn.** dejected, depressed, lugubrious, melancholy.

woe·ful (wō′fəl) *adj.* **1** Accompanied by or causing woe; direful. **2** Expressive of sorrow; doleful. **3** Paltry; miserable; mean; sorry. —**woe′ful·ly** *adv.* —**woe′ful·ness** *n.*

wok (wok) *n.* A Chinese cooking pan, as of iron, aluminum, or copper, with handles and a rounded bottom, usu. equipped with a separate metal ring to prevent tipping. [< Chinese]

Wok

woke (wōk) *p.t.* of WAKE¹.

wok·en (wō′kən) *Regional & alternative Brit. p.p.* of WAKE¹.

wold (wōld) *n.* An undulating tract of treeless upland. [< OE *wald* a forest]

wolf (woŏlf) *n. pl.* **wolves** (woŏlvz) **1** Any of various wild, carnivorous mammals related to the dog. **2** Any ravenous, cruel, or rapacious person. **3** *Slang* A man who zealously and aggressively pursues women. —**cry wolf** To give a false alarm. —**keep the wolf from the door** To avert want or starvation. —*v.t.* To devour ravenously: often with *down*. [< OE *wulf*]

Timber wolf

wolf·ber·ry (woŏlf′ber′ē) *n. pl.* **·ries** A shrub of the honeysuckle family, with pinkish, bell-shaped flowers and spikes of white berries.

wolf·hound (woŏlf′hound′) *n.* Either of two breeds of large dogs, the **Russian wolfhound** and the **Irish wolfhound,** formerly trained to hunt wolves.

wolf·ish (woŏlf′ish) *adj.* Of or like a wolf; rapacious; savage. —**wolf′ish·ly** *adv.* —**wolf′ish·ness** *n.*

wolf·ram (woŏl′frəm) *n.* TUNGSTEN. [G]

wolf·ram·ite (woŏl′frəm·īt) *n.* A grayish black or brown mineral, an important source of tungsten. [< G *Wolfram* tungsten]

wolfs·bane (woŏlfs′bān) *n.* A species of aconite, usu. with yellow flowers. Also **wolf′s-bane.**

wol·ver·ine (woŏl′və·rēn′) *n.* A rapacious carnivore related to weasels, with stout body and bushy tail. Also **wol′ver·ene′.** [< WOLF]

wolves (woŏlvz) *n. pl.* of WOLF.

wom·an (woŏm′ən) *n. pl.* **wom·en** (wim′in) **1** An adult human female. **2** The female part of the human race; women collectively. **3** Womanly character; femininity: usu. with *the.* **4** A female attendant or servant. **5** A paramour or mistress. **6** *Informal* A wife. —*adj.* **1** Of or characteristic of women. **2** Female: a *woman* lawyer. [< OE *wif* a wife + *mann* a human being] • See LADY.

wom·an·hood (woŏm′ən·hoŏd) *n.* **1** The state of a woman or of womankind. **2** Women collectively.

wom·an·ish (woŏm′ən·ish) *adj.* **1** For or characteristic of a woman; womanly. **2** Feminine or effeminate in nature, and according ill with the qualities associated with men. —**wom′an·ish·ly** *adv.* —**wom′an·ish·ness** *n.*

wom·an·ize (woŏm′ən·īz) *v.* **·ized, ·iz·ing** *v.t.* **1** To make effeminate or womanish. —*v.i.* **2** To have affairs with many women. —**wom′an·i·zer** *n.*

wom·an·kind (woŏm′ən·kīnd′) *n.* Women collectively.

wom·an·ly (woŏm′ən·lē) *adj.* Having the qualities natural, suited, or becoming to a woman; feminine. —**wom′an·li·ness** *n.*

womb (woŏm) *n.* **1** UTERUS. **2** A place where anything is engendered or brought into life. [< OE *wamb, womb* the belly]

wom·bat (wom′bat) *n.* Any of various burrowing Australian marsupials resembling a small bear. [< native Australian name]

Wombat

wom·en (wim′in) *n. pl.* of WOMAN.

wom·en·folk (wim′in·fōk′) *n.pl.* Women collectively: also **wom′en·folks′.**

won (wun) *p.t. & p.p.* of WIN.

won·der (wun′dər) *n.* **1** A feeling of mingled surprise, admiration, and astonishment. **2** One who or that which causes wonder. —*v.t.* **1** To have a feeling of curiosity or doubt in regard to. —*v.i.* **2** To be affected or filled with wonder; marvel. **3** To be curious or doubtful. —*adj.* Spectacularly successful: a *wonder* drug. [< OE *wundor*] —**won′der·er.** —**won′der·ing·ly** *adv.*

won·der·ful (wun′dər·fəl) *adj.* **1** Of a nature to excite wonder; astonishing. **2** Very good; excellent. —**won′der·ful·ly** *adv.* —**won′der·ful·ness** *n.*

won·der·land (wun′dər·land′) *n.* **1** A realm of imaginary wonders. **2** Any place of unusual beauty, astonishing sights, etc.

won·der·ment (wun′dər·mənt) *n.* **1** The emotion of wonder; surprise. **2** Something wonderful; a marvel.

won·drous (wun′drəs) *adj.* Wonderful; marvelous. —*adv.* Surprisingly. —**won′drous·ly** *adv.* —**won′drous·ness** *n.*

wont (wônt, wōnt) *adj.* Accustomed: He is *wont* to eat late. —*n.* Ordinary manner of doing or acting; habit. [< OE *gewunod,* p.p. of *gewunian* be accustomed]

won't (wōnt) Contraction of *will not.*

wont·ed (wun′tid, wōn′-) *adj.* **1** Commonly used or done; habitual. **2** Habituated; accustomed. —**wont′ed·ness** *n.*

woo (woō) *v.t.* **1** To make love to, esp. so as to marry. **2** To entreat earnestly; beg. **3** To seek. —*v.i.* **4** To pay court; make love. [< OE *wōgian*] —**woo′er** *n.*

wood (woŏd) *n.* **1** The hard, fibrous material between the pith and bark of a tree or shrub. **2** Trees or shrubs cut for use, as for building, fuel, etc. **3** *Usu. pl.* A large, dense growth of trees; forest. **4** Something made of wood, as a woodwind or certain golf clubs having a wooden head. —*adj.* **1** Made of wood; wooden. **2** Made for burning wood: a *wood* stove. **3** Living or growing in woods. —*v.t.* **1** To furnish with wood for fuel. **2** To plant with trees. —*v.i.* **3** To take on a supply of wood. [< OE *widu, wiodu*]

wood alcohol Methanol, esp. if obtained from wood tar.

wood·bine (woŏd′bīn) *n.* **1** A climbing European honeysuckle. **2** VIRGINIA CREEPER. [< OE *wudu* wood + *bindan* bind]

wood·block (woŏd′blok′) *n.* **1** A block of wood. **2** WOODCUT. Also **wood block.**

wood·chuck (woŏd′chuk) *n.* A hibernating marmot of North America; a groundhog. [Prob. < Algon.; infl. in form by WOOD and CHUCK]

Woodchuck

wood·cock (woŏd′kok′) *n.* **1** A European game bird related to the snipe. **2** A smaller related North American bird.

wood·craft (woŏd′kraft′, -kräft′) *n.* **1** Skill in knowing how to survive in the woods by making shelters, hunting game, etc. **2** The act or art of constructing articles of wood. —**wood′crafts′man** (*pl.* **·men**) *n.*

wood·cut (woŏd′kut′) *n.* **1** A block of wood engraved, as with a design, for making prints. **2** A print made from such a block.

wood·cut·ter (woŏd′kut′ər) *n.* One who cuts or chops wood. —**wood′cut′ting** *n.*

wood·ed (woŏd′id) *adj.* Abounding with trees.

wood·en (woŏd′n) *adj.* **1** Made of wood. **2** Stiff; awkward. **3** Dull; stupid. —**wood′en·ly** *adv.* —**wood′en·ness** *n.*

wood engraving 1 The art of cutting designs on wood for printing. **2** A block of wood with an engraving cut, as with a burin, into a surface that is perpendicular to the direction of the grain. **3** A print from such a block. —**wood engraver**

wood·en·head (woŏd′n·hed′) *n. Informal* A stupid person; blockhead. —**wood′en·head′ed** *adj.* —**wood′en·head′ed·ness** *n.*

wood·en·ware (woŏd′n·wâr′) *n.* Dishes, vessels, bowls, etc., made of wood.

wood·land (woŏd′lənd, -land′) *n.* Land covered with wood or trees; timberland. —*adj.* (-lənd) Belonging to or dwelling in the woods. —**wood′land′er** *n.*

wood louse Any of numerous small terrestrial flat-bodied crustaceans commonly found under old logs.

wood·note (woŏd′nōt′) *n.* A simple, artless, or natural song, call, etc., as of a woodland bird.

wood nymph A nymph of the forest.

wood·peck·er (woŏd′pek′ər) *n.* Any of a large family of birds having stiff tail feathers, strong claws, and a sharp bill for drilling holes in trees in search of wood-boring insects.

wood·pile (woŏd′pīl′) *n.* A pile of wood, esp. of wood cut in sizes for burning.

wood pulp Wood reduced to a pulp, used for making paper.

wood·shed (woŏd′shed′) *n.* A shed for storing firewood.

woods·man (woŏdz′mən) *n. pl.* **·men** (-mən) **1** A man who lives or works in the woods. **2** A man skilled in woodcraft.

Red-headed woodpecker

wood sorrel A creeping perennial woodland plant with cloverlike leaves containing oxalic acid. • See SHAMROCK.

woods·y (woŏd′zē) *adj.* **woods·i·er, woods·i·est** Of, pertaining to, or like the woods. —**woods′i·ness** *n.*

wood tar A tar produced by the dry distillation of wood.

wood thrush A large, common woodland thrush with reddish brown plumage, having a bell-like song. • See THRUSH[1].

wood turning The shaping of blocks of wood by means of a lathe. —**wood turner**

wood·wind (wood′wind′) n. 1 A musical wind instrument, as the flute, clarinet, bassoon, oboe, or saxophone. 2 pl. The woodwinds of an orchestra; also, the players of these instruments.

wood·work (wood′wûrk′) n. Things made of wood, esp. certain interior parts of a house, as moldings, doors, windowsills, etc. —**wood′work′er, wood′work′ing** n.

wood·worm (wood′wûrm′) n. A worm or larva dwelling in or that bores in wood.

wood·y (wood′ē) adj. **wood·i·er, wood·i·est** 1 Made of or containing wood. 2 Resembling wood. 3 Wooded; abounding with trees. —**wood′i·ness** n.

woof[1] (woof, woof) n. 1 The threads that are carried back and forth across the warp in a loom. 2 The texture of a fabric. [<OE ōwef]

woof[2] (woof) n. A low barking sound or growl, esp. of a dog. —v.i. To make such a sound. [Imit.]

woof·er (woof′ər) n. A loudspeaker designed to reproduce sounds of low frequency. [<WOOF[2] + -ER]

wool (wool) n. 1 The soft, durable fiber obtained from the fleece of sheep and some allied animals, as goats, alpacas, etc. 2 Yarn or fabric made of such fibers. 3 Garments made of wool. 4 Something resembling or likened to wool. —**pull the wool over one's eyes** To delude or deceive one. —adj. Made of or pertaining to wool or woolen material. [<OE wull]

wool·en (wool′ən) adj. 1 Of or pertaining to wool. 2 Made of wool. —n. Usu. pl. Cloth or clothing made of wool. Also **wool′en.**

wool·gath·er·ing (wool′gath′ər·ing) n. Idle daydreaming; absent-mindedness. —**wool′gath′er·er** n.

wool·grow·er (wool′grō′ər) n. A person who raises sheep for the production of wool. —**wool′grow′ing** adj.

wool·ly (wool′ē) adj. **·li·er, ·li·est** 1 Consisting of, covered with, or resembling wool. 2 Not clear or sharply detailed; fuzzy. 3 Resembling the roughness and excitement of the early American West, usu. in the phrase **wild and woolly.** —n. pl. **·lies** A garment made of wool, esp. woolen underwear. Also **wool′y.** —**wool′li·ness, wool′i·ness** n.

wooz·y (woo′zē) adj. **·i·er, ·i·est** Slang Befuddled, esp. with drink. [Prob. < wooze, var. of OOZE] —**wooz′i·ly** adv. —**wooz′i·ness** n.

word (wûrd) n. 1 A speech sound or combination of sounds which has come to signify and communicate a particular idea or thought, and which functions as the smallest meaningful unit of a language when used in isolation. 2 The letters or characters that stand for such a language unit. 3 Usu. pl. Speech; talk: hard to put into words. 4 A brief remark or comment. 5 A communication or message: Send him word. 6 A command, signal, or direction: Give the word to start. 7 A promise: a man of his word. 8 Rumor, gossip, or news: What's the latest word? 9 A watchword or password. 10 pl. The text of a song: words and music. 11 pl. Language used in anger, rebuke, etc.: They had words. —**in a word** In short; briefly. —**eat one's words** To retract what one has said. —**mince words** To be evasive or overly delicate in what one says. —**take one at his word** To believe literally in what another has said and act or respond accordingly. —**word for word** In exactly the same words; verbatim. —v.t. To express in a word or words; phrase. —**the Word** 1 LOGOS (def. 2). 2 GOSPEL (def. 1). 3 The Scriptures; the Bible. [<OE]

word·age (wûr′dij) n. 1 Words collectively. 2 The number of words, as in a novel. 3 VERBIAGE. 4 WORDING.

word·book (wûrd′book′) n. 1 A collection of words; vocabulary; lexicon; dictionary. 2 An opera libretto.

word·ing (wûr′ding) n. The style or arrangement of words; diction; phraseology.

word·less (wûrd′lis) adj. Having no words; dumb; silent.

word of mouth Spoken words; speech; oral communication. —**word-of-mouth** (wûrd′uv-mouth′) adj.

word order The sequence or arrangement of words in a sentence, phrase, or clause.

word·play (wûrd′plā′) n. 1 Clever repartee. 2 A play on words; pun.

word processing The computer-storage editing, transmittal, and reproduction of written information by means of a terminal, printer, memory, software, etc. —**word processor** n.

word·y (wûr′dē) adj. **word·i·er, word·i·est** 1 Expressed in many or too many words; verbose. 2 Of or pertaining to words; verbal. —**word′i·ly** adv. —**word′i·ness** n. —Syn. 1 long-winded, prolix, roundabout, redundant.

wore (wôr, wōr) p.t. of WEAR.

work (wûrk) n. 1 Continued physical or mental exertion or activity directed to some purpose or end; labor; toil. 2 Employment; job: to be out of work. 3 One's profession, occupation, business, trade, etc.: What is your work? 4 The place where one is employed or occupied professionally: She is at work. 5 An undertaking or task, often a part of one's job or occupation: to take work home; also, the amount of this that is accomplished or required: a day's work. 6 pl. A place where something is made, undertaken, etc.: often used in combination: the oilworks. 7 The material used or processed in manufacturing something. 8 Something that has been made, created, accomplished, etc., esp.: a An engineering structure, as a bridge. b A feat or deed: remembered for her good works. c Needlework or embroidery. d A product of the mind and imagination: the works of Beethoven. 9 Manner, quality, or style of doing something; workmanship. 10 pl. Running gear or machinery: the works of a watch. 11 The action of natural forces or the result of such action: the work of a storm. 12 Physics A transfer of energy between physical systems. —**the works** Slang 1 Everything belonging, available, etc. 2 Drastic or vicious treatment: to give someone the works. —**shoot the works** Slang 1 To risk everything. 2 To make a final, supreme effort. —v. **worked** (Archaic **wrought**), **work·ing** v.i. 1 To perform work; labor; toil. 2 To be employed in some trade or business. 3 To perform a function; operate: The machine works well. 4 To prove effective or influential: His stratagem worked. 5 To move or progress gradually or with difficulty: He worked up in his profession. 6 To become as specified, as by gradual motion: The bolts worked loose. 7 To move from nervousness or agitation: His features worked with anger. 8 To undergo kneading, hammering, etc.; be shaped: Copper works easily. 9 To ferment. —v.t. 10 To cause or bring about: to work a miracle. 11 To direct the operation of: to work a machine. 12 To make or shape by toil or skill. 13 To prepare, as by manipulating, hammering, etc.: to work dough. 14 To decorate, as with embroidery or inlaid work. 15 To cause to be productive, as by toil: to work a mine. 16 To cause to do work: He works his employees too hard. 17 To cause to be as specified, usu. with effort: We worked the timber into position. 18 To make or achieve by effort: to work one's passage on a ship. 19 To carry on some activity in (an area, etc.); cover: to work a sales territory. 20 To solve, as a problem in arithmetic. 21 To cause to move from nervousness or excitement: to work one's jaws. 22 To excite; provoke: He worked himself into a passion. 23 To influence or manage, as by insidious means; lead. 24 To cause to ferment. 25 Informal To practice trickery upon; cheat; swindle. 26 Informal To make use of for one's own purposes; use. —**work in** To insert or be inserted. —**work off** To get rid of, as extra flesh by exercise. —**work on** (or **upon**) 1 To try to influence or persuade. 2 To influence or affect. —**work out** 1 To make its way out or through. 2 To effect by work or effort; accomplish. 3 To exhaust, as a mine. 4 To discharge, as a debt, by labor rather than by payment of money. 5 To develop; form, as a plan. 6 To solve. 7 a To prove effective or successful. b To result as specified. 8 To exercise, train, etc. —**work over** 1 To repeat. 2 Slang To treat harshly or cruelly; beat up, torture, etc. —**work up** 1 To excite; rouse, as rage or a person to rage. **2** To form or shape by working; develop: to *work up* a new advertising campaign. **3** To make one's or its way. **4** To cause or bring about. [< OE *weorc*]

-work *combining form* **1** A product made from a (specified) material: *brickwork*. **2** Work of a (given) kind: *piecework*. **3** Work performed in a (specified) place: *housework*.

work·a·ble (wûr′kə-bəl) *adj.* **1** Capable of being worked, developed, etc. **2** Practicable, as a plan. —**work′a·bil′i·ty**, **work′a·ble·ness** *n.*

work·a·day (wûrk′ə-dā′) *adj.* **1** Of, pertaining to, or suitable for working days; everyday. **2** Commonplace; prosaic.

work·bench (wûrk′bench′) *n.* A bench for work, esp. that of a carpenter, machinist, etc.

work·book (wûrk′bŏŏk′) *n.* **1** A booklet based on a course of study and containing problems and exercises which a student works out directly on the pages. **2** A manual containing operating instructions. **3** A book for recording work performed or planned.

work·day (wûrk′dā′) *n.* **1** Any day, usu. not a Sunday or holiday, on which work is done. **2** The number of hours of one day spent in work. Also **working day.** —*adj.* WORKADAY.

work·er (wûk′kər) *n.* **1** One who or that which performs work. **2** A social insect, as a bee, ant, etc., that is sexually sterile and performs work for the colony. **3** A member of the working class.

work·fare (wûrk′fâr′) *n.* Welfare that is conditional upon assigned work or training by those receiving payments.

work·house (wûrk′hous′) *n.* **1** *Brit.* Formerly, a house for paupers able to work. **2** A prison in which petty offenders are put to work.

work·ing (wûr′king) *adj.* **1** Engaged actively in some employment. **2** That works, or performs its function: This is a *working* model. **3** Sufficient for use or action: They formed a *working* agreement. **4** Of, used in, or occupied by work: a *working* day. **5** Throbbing or twitching, as facial muscles. —*n.* **1** The act or operation of any person or thing that works. **2** *Usu. pl.* That part of a mine or quarry where excavation is going on or has gone on.

working capital That part of the finances of a business available for its operation or convertible into cash.

working class People who work for wages, esp. manual and industrial workers. —**work′ing-class′** *adj.*

work·man (wûrk′mən) *n. pl.* **·men** (-men′) **1** A male worker. **2** A man who earns his living by working with his hands or with machines. Also **work·ing·man** (wûr′king·man′).

work·man·like (wûrk′mən·līk) *adj.* Like or befitting a skilled workman; skillfully done. Also **work′man·ly.**

work·man·ship (wûrk′mən·ship) *n.* **1** The art or skill of a workman. **2** The quality of work. **3** The work produced.

work of art **1** A highly artistic product of the fine arts, esp. painting and sculpture. **2** Anything made or done with great beauty or skill.

work·out (wûrk′out′) *n.* **1** Any activity done to increase or maintain skill, physical fitness, etc. **2** Any instance of strenuous activity, disciplined work, etc.

work·room (wûrk′rŏŏm, -rŏŏm′) *n.* A room where work is performed.

work·shop (wûrk′shop′) *n.* **1** A building or room where any work is carried on; workroom. **2** A seminar or single session for training, discussion, etc., in a specialized field: a writers' *workshop*.

work·ta·ble (wûrk′tā′bəl) *n.* A table with drawers and other conveniences for use while working.

work·week (wûrk′wēk′) *n.* The total number of hours worked in a week; also, the number of required working hours in a week.

world (wûrld) *n.* **1** The earth. **2** The universe. **3** Any celestial body: Are there other inhabited *worlds*? **4** Often *cap.* A part of the earth: the *Old World*. **5** A specific time or period in history: the ancient *world*. **6** A division of existing or created things belonging to the earth; the animal *world*. **7** The human inhabitants of the earth; mankind. **8** A definite class of people having certain interests or activities in common: the scientific *world*. **9** Secular or worldly aims, pleasures, etc., as distinguished from religious or spiritual ones; also, those people who pursue such aims or pleasures. **10** Individual conditions or circum-

stances of a person's life: His *world* has changed. **11** A large quantity or amount: a *world* of trouble. —**come into the world** To be born. —**for all the world 1** In every respect. **2** For any reason. —**on top of the world** *Informal* Elated. —**out of this world** *Informal* Exceptionally fine; wonderful. [< OE *weorold*]

world·ly (wûrld′lē) *adj.* **·li·er, ·li·est 1** Pertaining to the world; mundane; earthly. **2** Devoted to secular, earthly things; not spiritual. **3** Sophisticated; worldly-wise. —*adv.* In a worldly manner. —**world′li·ness** *n.*

world·ly-mind·ed (wûrld′lē-mīn′did) *adj.* Absorbed in the things of this world. —**world′ly-mind′ed·ly** *adv.*

world·ly-wise (wûrld′lē-wīz) *adj.* Wise in the ways and affairs of the world; sophisticated.

world power A state or organization whose policies and actions have a worldwide influence.

World Series In baseball, the games played at the finish of the regular season between the champion teams of the two major U.S. leagues. Also **world series.**

World War I The war (1914–18) between the Allies and the Central Powers (Germany, Austria-Hungary, Turkey, and Bulgaria).

World War II The war (1939–45) between the United Nations and the Axis.

world-wea·ry (wûrld′wir′ē) *adj.* **·ri·er, ·ri·est** Weary of life and its conditions. —**world′-wea′ri·ness** *n.*

world·wide (wûrld′wīd′) *adj.* Extended throughout the world.

worm (wûrm) *n.* **1** *Zool.* Any of numerous limbless, elongated, soft-bodied invertebrate animals, including flatworms, roundworms, and annelids. **2** Any small animal resembling a worm, as a caterpillar, maggot, snake, shipworm, etc. **3** Something which suggests the inner, hidden gnawings of a worm: the *worm* of remorse. **4** A despicable or despised person. **5** Something conceived to be like a worm, as the thread of a screw. **6** *pl.* Any disorder due to parasitic worms in the intestines, etc. —*v.t.* **1** To move, proceed, insinuate, etc. (oneself or itself) in a wormlike manner: to *worm* one's way. **2** To draw forth by artful means, as a secret: with *out*. **3** To rid of intestinal worms. —*v.i.* **4** To move or progress slowly and stealthily. [< OE *wyrm*] —**worm′i·ness** *n.* —**worm′y** *adj.* (**·i·er, ·i·est**)

worm-eat·en (wûrm′ēt′n) *adj.* **1** Eaten or bored through by worms. **2** Worn-out or decayed.

worm gear A gear having teeth shaped so as to mesh with a threaded shaft.

worm·hole (wûrm′hōl′) *n.* The hole made by a worm or a wormlike animal. —**worm′holed′** *adj.*

worm·wood (wûrm′wŏŏd′) *n.* **1** Any of various European herbs or small shrubs related to the sagebrush, esp. a species yielding a bitter oil used in making absinthe. **2** Something that embitters or is unpleasant. [< OE *wermōd*]

Worm gear

worn (wôrn, wōrn) *p.p.* of WEAR. —*adj.* **1** Affected by wear, use, continuous action, etc.; frayed, damaged, etc. **2** Showing the effects of worry, anxiety, etc. **3** Hackneyed, as a phrase.

worn-out (wôrn′out′, wōrn′-) *adj.* **1** Used until without value or usefulness. **2** Thoroughly tired; exhausted.

wor·ri·some (wûr′i-səm) *adj.* Causing worry or anxiety.

wor·ry (wûr′ē) *v.* **·ried, ·ry·ing** *v.i.* **1** To be uneasy in the mind; feel anxiety. **2** To manage despite trials or difficulties; struggle: with *along* or *through*. —*v.t.* **3** To cause to feel uneasy in the mind; trouble. **4** To bother; pester. **5** To bite, pull at, or shake with the teeth. —*n. pl.* **·ries 1** A state of anxiety or uneasiness. **2** Something causing such a state. [< OE *wrygan* strangle] —**wor′ri·er, wor′ri·ment** *n.*

worse (wûrs) Comparative of BAD and ILL. —*adj.* **1** Bad or ill in a great degree; inferior. **2** Physically ill in a greater degree. **3** Less favorable, as to conditions, circumstances, etc. **4** More evil, corrupt, etc. —*n.* Someone or something worse. —*adv.* **1** In a worse manner, way, etc. **2** With greater intensity, severity, etc. [< OE *wyrsa*]

wors·en (wûr′sən) *v.t. & v.i.* To make or become worse.

wor·ship (wûr′ship) *n.* **1** Adoration, homage, etc., given to a deity. **2** The rituals, prayers, etc., expressing such adoration or homage. **3** Excessive or ardent admiration or love. **4** The object of such love or admiration. **5** *Chiefly Brit.* A title of honor in addressing certain persons of station. —*v.* ·**shiped** or ·**shipped**, ·**ship·ing** or ·**ship·ping** *v.t.* **1** To pay an act of worship to; venerate. **2** To have intense or exaggerated admiration or love for. —*v.i.* **3** To perform acts or have sentiments of worship. [< OE *weorthscipe* < *weorth* worthy] —**wor′ship·er, wor′ship·per** *n.* —**Syn.** *v.* **1** exalt, praise. **2** adore, dote on, idolize.

wor·ship·ful (wûr′ship·fəl) *adj.* **1** Feeling or giving great reverence, love, etc. **2** *Chiefly Brit.* Worthy of respect by reason of character or position: applied to certain dignitaries. —**wor′ship·ful·ly** *adv.* —**wor′ship·ful·ness** *n.*

worst (wûrst) Superlative of BAD and ILL. —*adj.* **1** Bad or ill in the highest degree. **2** Least favorable, as to conditions, circumstances, etc. **3** Most evil, corrupt, etc. —**in the worst way** *Informal* Very much. —*n.* Someone or something that is worst. —**at worst** Under the worst possible circumstances or conditions. —**get the worst of it** To be defeated or put at a disadvantage. —*adv.* **1** To the greatest or most extreme degree. **2** To the greatest or most extreme degree of inferiority, badness, etc. —*v.t.* To defeat; vanquish. [< OE *wyrsta*]

wors·ted (wŏŏs′tid, wûr′stid) *n.* **1** Woolen yarn spun from long staple, with fibers combed parallel and twisted hard. **2** A tightly woven fabric made from such yarn. —*adj.* Consisting of or made from such yarn. [< *Worsted*, former name of a parish in Norfolk, England]

wort¹ (wûrt) *n.* A plant or herb: usu. in combination: *liverwort*. [< OE *wyrt* a root, a plant]

wort² (wûrt) *n.* The unfermented infusion of malt that becomes beer when fermented. [< OE *wyrt* a root, a plant]

worth (wûrth) *n.* **1** Value or excellence of any kind. **2** The market value of something. **3** The amount of something obtainable at a specific sum: two cents' *worth* of candy. **4** Wealth. —*adj.* **1** Equal in value (to); exchangable (for). **2** Deserving (of): not *worth* going. **3** Having wealth and possessions to the value of: He is *worth* a million. —**for all it is worth** To the utmost. —**for all one is worth** With every effort possible. [< OE *weorth*]

worth·less (wûrth′lis) *adj.* Having no worth, usefulness, virtue, etc. —**worth′less·ly** *adv.* —**worth′less·ness** *n.*

worth·while (wûrth′hwīl′) *adj.* Sufficiently important to occupy the time; of enough value to repay the effort. —**worth′while′ness** *n.*

wor·thy (wûr′thē) *adj.* ·**thi·er**, ·**thi·est** **1** Possessing valuable or useful qualities. **2** Having such qualities as to deserve or merit some specified thing: *worthy* of the honor. —*n. pl.* ·**thies** A person of eminent worth: sometimes used humorously. —**wor′thi·ly** *adv.* —**wor′thi·ness** *n.*

-worthy *combining form* **1** Meriting or deserving: *trustworthy*. **2** Valuable as; having worth as: *newsworthy*. **3** Fit for: *seaworthy*.

wot (wot) *p.t., first and third person singular,* of WIT².

would (wŏŏd) *p.t.* of WILL, but used chiefly as an auxiliary to express: **1** Desire: They *would* like to go. **2** Condition: They *would* go if you asked them. **3** Futurity: He said he *would* bring it. **4** Determination: The dog *would* not let go. **5** Custom or habit: He *would* walk there every day. [< OE *wolde*, p.t. of *willan* will]

would-be (wŏŏd′bē′) *adj.* Desiring, professing, or intended to be: a *would-be* actress.

would·n't (wŏŏd′nt) Contraction of *would not*.

wound¹ (wŏŏnd) *n.* **1** A hurt or injury, esp. one in which the skin is torn, cut, etc. **2** A cutting or scraping injury to a tree or plant. **3** Any cause of pain or grief, as to the feelings, honor, etc. —*v.t. & v.i.* **1** To inflict a wound or wounds (upon). **2** To injure the feelings or pride of. [< OE *wund*] —**Syn.** *v.* **2** affront, hurt, offend, pique.

wound² (wound) *p.t. & p.p.* of WIND².

wove (wōv) *p.t. & a p.p.* of WEAVE.

wo·ven (wō′vən) *p.p.* of WEAVE.

wow (wou) *interj. Informal* An exclamation of wonder, surprise, pleasure, etc. —*n. Slang* A person or thing that is extraordinary, successful, etc. —*v.t. Slang* To cause to feel excitement, admiration, etc.

WPA, W.P.A. Works Progress Administration.

wrack (rak) *n.* **1** Ruin; destruction: esp. in the phrase **wrack and ruin. 2** Marine vegetation cast ashore by the sea, as seaweed. **3** A wrecked vessel; wreckage. —*v.t. & v.i.* To wreck or be wrecked. [Fusion of OE *wræc* punishment, revenge and MDu. *wrak* a wreck]

wraith (rāth) *n.* **1** An apparition of a person seen shortly before or shortly after his or her death. **2** Any specter; ghost. [?]

wran·gle (rang′gəl) *v.* ·**gled**, ·**gling** *v.i.* **1** To argue noisily and angrily. —*v.t.* **2** To argue; debate. **3** To get by stubborn arguing. **4** To herd or round up, as livestock. —*n.* An angry dispute. [ME *wranglen*] —**wran′gler** *n.*

wrap (rap) *v.* **wrapped** or **wrapt**, **wrap·ping** *v.t.* **1** To surround and cover by something folded or wound about. **2** To fold or wind (a covering) about something. **3** To surround so as to blot out or conceal: a mountain *wrapped* in clouds. **4** To fold or wind. —*v.i.* **5** To be or become twined, coiled, etc.: with *about, around,* etc. —**wrap up 1** To cover with paper, etc. **2** To put on warm garments. **3** *Informal* To conclude or finish. —**wrapped up in** Involved or absorbed in: *wrapped up in* his music. —*n.* **1** A garment folded about a person. **2** *pl.* Outer garments collectively. **3** A blanket. —**keep under wraps** To keep secret. [ME *wrappen*]

wrap·a·round (rap′ə·round′) *adj.* **1** Made so as to be wrapped around the body and then fastened: a *wraparound* skirt. **2** Designed so as to curve back on each side: a *wraparound* windshield. —*n.* Anything that encircles or curves back on each side.

wrap·per (rap′ər) *n.* **1** A paper enclosing a newspaper, magazine, or similar packet for mailing or otherwise. **2** A woman's dressing gown. **3** One who or that which wraps.

wrap·ping (rap′ing) *n. Often pl.* A covering or something in which an object is wrapped.

wrap-up (rap′up′) *n. Informal* **1** A summary or conclusion: a *wrap-up* of the news. **2** The final event, action, etc., in a connected series.

wrath (rath, räth; *Brit.* rôth) *n.* **1** Violent rage, anger, or fury. **2** An act done in violent rage. [< OE *wrǣth* wroth]

wrath·ful (rath′fəl, räth′-) *adj.* **1** Full of wrath; extremely angry. **2** Resulting from or expressing wrath. —**wrath′ful·ly** *adv.* —**wrath′ful·ness** *n.* —**Syn. 1** furious, apoplectic, mad, raging.

wreak (rēk) *v.t.* **1** To inflict or exact, as vengeance. **2** To give free expression to, as a feeling or passion. [< OE *wrecan* drive, avenge]

wreath (rēth) *n. pl.* **wreaths** (rēthz, rēths) **1** A band, as of flowers or leaves, commonly circular, as for a crown, decoration, etc. **2** Any curled or spiral band, as of smoke, snow, etc. [< OE *writha*] —**wreath·y** (rē′thē, -thē) *adj.*

wreathe (rēth) *v.* **wreathed**, **wreath·ing** *v.t.* **1** To form into a wreath, as by twisting or twining. **2** To adorn or encircle with or as with wreaths. **3** To envelop; cover: His face was *wreathed* in smiles. —*v.i.* **4** To take the form of a wreath. **5** To twist, turn, or coil, as masses of cloud.

wreck (rek) *v.t.* **1** To cause the destruction of, as by a collision. **2** To bring ruin, damage, or destruction upon. **3** To tear down, as a building; dismantle. —*v.i.* **4** To suffer destruction; be ruined. **5** To engage in wrecking, as for plunder or salvage. —*n.* **1** The act of wrecking, or the condition of being wrecked. **2** That which has been wrecked or ruined by accident, collision, etc. **3** The broken remnants or remains of something wrecked. **4** SHIPWRECK. **5** The ruined, usu. stranded hulk of a ship that has been wrecked. **6** A person who is ill or under great strain. [< AF *wrec* < Scand.]

wreck·age (rek′ij) *n.* **1** The act of wrecking, or the condition of being wrecked. **2** Broken remnants or fragments from a wreck.

wreck·er (rek′ər) *n.* **1** One who causes destruction of any sort. **2** One employed in tearing down and removing old buildings. **3** A person, train, car, or machine that clears away wrecks. **4** One employed to recover disabled vessels or wrecked cargoes.

wren (ren) *n.* **1** Any of numerous small, active, usu. brown birds having short rounded wings and tail and a thin, curved bill. **2** Any one of numerous similar birds. [<OE *wrenna*]

wrench (rench) *n.* **1** A violent twist. **2** A sprain or violent twist or pull in a part of the body. **3** A sudden surge of emotion, as of sorrow, pity, etc. **4** Any of various gripping tools for turning or twisting bolts, nuts, pipes, etc. — *v.t.* **1** To twist violently; turn suddenly by force. **2** To twist forcibly so as to cause strain or injury; sprain. **3** To cause to suffer. **4** To twist from the proper meaning, intent, or use. —*v.i.* **5** To give a twist or wrench [<OE *wrencan* to wrench]

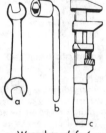

Wrenches *def.* 4
a. engineer's. b. offset. c. monkey.

wrest (rest) *v.t.* **1** To pull or force away by violent twisting or wringing; wrench. **2** To turn from the true meaning, intent, etc.; distort. **3** To seize forcibly. **4** To gain or extract by great effort. —*n.* **1** An act of wresting. **2** A key for tuning a piano, harp, etc. [<OE *wræstan*] —**wrest′er** *n.*

wres·tle (res′əl) *v.* ·**tled**, ·**tling** *v.i.* **1** To engage in wrestling. **2** To struggle, as for mastery; contend. —*v.t.* **3** To contend with (someone) in wrestling. **4** To throw (a calf) and hold it down for branding. —*n.* **1** The act or an instance of wrestling. **2** A hard struggle. [<OE *wræstlian*] —**wres′tler** *n.*

wres·tling (res′ling) *n.* A sport or exercise in which each of two unarmed contestants endeavors to throw the other to the ground or force him into a certain fallen position.

wretch (rech) *n.* **1** A vile or contemptible person. **2** A miserable or unhappy person. [<OE *wrecca* an outcast]

wretch·ed (rech′id) *adj.* **1** Sunk in dejection; profoundly unhappy. **2** Causing or characterized by misery, poverty, etc. **3** Unsatisfactory in ability or quality. **4** Despicable; contemptible. —**wretch′ed·ly** *adv.* —**wretch′ed·ness** *n.* —**Syn.** **1** distressed, miserable. **3** bad, paltry, worthless.

wrig·gle (rig′əl) *v.* ·**gled**, ·**gling** *v.i.* **1** To twist in a sinuous manner; squirm; writhe. **2** To proceed as by twisting or crawling. **3** To make one's way by evasive or indirect means. —*v.t.* **4** To cause to wriggle. **5** To make (one's way, etc.) by evasive or sly means. —*n.* The act or motion of one who or that which wriggles. [<MLG *wriggeln*] —**wrig′gly** *adj.*

wrig·gler (rig′lər) *n.* **1** Someone or something that wriggles. **2** A mosquito larva.

wright (rīt) *n.* One who builds or creates something: used in combination: *wheelwright; playwright.* [<OE *wyrhta*]

wring (ring) *v.* **wrung, wring·ing** *v.t.* **1** To squeeze or compress by twisting. **2** To squeeze or press out, as water, by twisting. **3** To acquire by forcible means. **4** To distress: Her plight *wrung* their hearts. **5** To twist violently: to *wring* his neck. —*v.i.* **6** To writhe or squirm with great effort. —*n.* A twisting or wringing. [<OE *wringan*]

wring·er (ring′ər) *n.* **1** One who or that which wrings. **2** A device used to press water out of fabrics after washing.

wrin·kle[1] (ring′kəl) *n.* **1** A small ridge, as on a smooth surface; a crease; fold. **2** A small fold or crease in the skin, usu. produced by age or by excessive exposure to the elements. —*v.* ·**kled**, ·**kling** *v.t.* **1** To make wrinkles in. —*v.i.* **2** To become wrinkled. [<OE *wrincle*] —**wrin′kly** *adj.*

wrin·kle[2] (ring′kəl) *n.* *Informal* A new or ingenious method, device, etc. [Prob. dim. of OE *wrenc* a trick]

wrist (rist) *n.* **1** The part of the arm that lies between the hand and the forearm; the carpus. **2** The part of a glove or garment that covers the wrist. [<OE]

wrist·band (rist′band′) *n.* **1** The band of a sleeve that covers the wrist. **2** A band for a wrist watch.

wrist·let (rist′lit) *n.* **1** A flexible band worn on the wrist for support or warmth. **2** A bracelet.

wrist pin *Mech.* A pin attaching a connecting rod to another part.

wrist watch A watch set in a band and worn at the wrist.

writ[1] (rit) *n.* **1** *Law* A written order, issued by a court, and commanding the person to do or not to do some act. **2** That which is written: now chiefly in the phrase **Holy Writ,** the Bible. [<OE *writan* write]

writ[2] (rit) *Archaic* or *Regional p.t.* & *p.p.* of WRITE.

write (rīt) *v.* **wrote** (or *Archaic* **writ**), **writ·ten·** (**or** *Archaic* **writ**), **writ·ing** *v.t.* **1** To trace or inscribe (letters, words, numbers, symbols, etc.) on a surface with pen or pencil. **2** To describe, set down, or signify in writing. **3** To communicate by letter. **4** To communicate with by letter. **5** To produce by writing; be the author or composer of. **6** To draw up; draft: to *write* a check. **7** To cover or fill with writing: to *write* two full pages. **8** To leave marks or evidence of: Anxiety is *written* on his face. **9** To underwrite: to *write* an insurance policy. **10** To store information in computer memory. —*v.i.* **11** To trace or inscribe letters, etc., on a surface, as of paper. **12** To communicate in writing. **13** To be engaged in the occupation of an author. —**write down 1** To put into writing. **2** To injure or depreciate in writing. —**write in 1** To insert in writing, as in a document. **2** To cast (a vote) for one not listed on a ballot by inserting his name in writing. —**write off 1** To cancel or remove (claims, debts, etc.) from an open account. **2** To acknowledge the loss or failure of. —**write out** To write in full or complete form. —**write up 1** To describe fully in writing. **2** To praise fully or too fully in writing. [<OE *writan*] • *Writ,* the archaic past participle of *write,* is now used chiefly in the phrase **writ large,** written or shown on a grand scale: *a name writ large in history.*

write-in (rīt′in) *n.* **1** The act of casting a vote for a candidate not listed on the ballot by writing in his name. **2** The name so written in. —*adj.* Of or pertaining to a write-in.

write-off (rīt′ôf, -of′) *n.* **1** A cancellation. **2** An amount canceled or noted as a loss. **3** A person or thing acknowledged to be a failure or a loss.

writ·er (rī′tər) *n.* **1** One who writes. **2** One who engages in literary composition as a profession.

write-up (rīt′up′) *n.* A written description or review.

writhe (rīth) *v.* **writhed, writh·ing** *v.t.* **1** To cause to twist or be distorted. —*v.i.* **2** To twist or distort the body, face, or limbs, as in pain. **3** To undergo suffering, as from embarrassment, sorrow, etc. —*n.* An act of writhing. [<OE *writhan*] —**writh′er** *n.*

writ·ing (rī′ting) *n.* **1** The act of one who writes. **2** HANDWRITING. **3** Anything written or expressed in letters, esp. a literary production. **4** A written form: put your request in *writing.* **5** The profession or occupation of a writer. —*adj.* **1** Used in or for writing: *writing* paper. **2** That writes.

writ·ten (rit′n) *p.p.* of WRITE.

wrong (rông) *adj.* **1** Not correct; mistaken. **2** Not appropriate: the *wrong* shoes for hiking. **3** Not morally or legally right. **4** Not in accordance with the correct or standard method: the *wrong* way to bake. **5** Not working or operating properly: What is *wrong* with the furnace? **6** Not meant to be seen, used, etc.: the *wrong* side of the fabric. **7** Not intended: a *wrong* turn. —**go wrong 1** To behave immorally. **2** To turn out badly; fail. **3** To take a wrong direction, etc. —*adv.* In a wrong direction, place, or manner; erroneously. —*n.* **1** That which is morally or socially wrong or unacceptable. **2** An injury or injustice. —**in the wrong** In error; wrong. —*v.t.* **1** To violate the rights of; inflict injury or injustice upon. **2** To impute evil to unjustly: You *wrong* him. **3** To seduce (a woman). **4** To treat dishonorably. [<Scand.] —**wrong′er, wrong′ness** *n.* —**wrong′ly** *adv.*

wrong·do·er (rông′doo′ər, rong′-) *n.* One who does wrong. —**wrong′do·ing** *n.*

wrong·ful (rông′fəl) *adj.* **1** Characterized by wrong or injustice; injurious; unjust. **2** Unlawful; illegal. —**wrong′ful·ly** *adv.* —**wrong′ful·ness** *n.*

wrong-head·ed (rông′hed′id) *adj.* Stubbornly holding to a wrong judgment, opinion, etc. —**wrong′-head′ed·ly** *adv.* —**wrong′-head′ed·ness** *n.*

wrote (rōt) *p.t.* of WRITE.

wroth (rôth) *adj.* Filled with anger; angry. [<OE *wrāth*]

wrought (rôt) *Archaic p.t.* & *p.p.* of WORK. —*adj.* **1** Beaten or hammered into shape by tools: *wrought* gold. **2** Made delicately or elaborately. **3** Made; fashioned; formed. — **wrought up** Disturbed or excited; agitated. [ME *wrogt,* var. of *worht,* p.p. of *wirchen* work]

wrought iron Strong, malleable, commercially pure iron.

wrung (rung) *p.t.* & *p.p.* of WRING.

wry (rī) *adj.* **wri·er, wri·est** **1** Bent to one side or out of position; contorted; askew. **2** Made by twisting or distorting the features: a *wry* smile. **3** Distorted or warped, as in interpretation or meaning. **4** Somewhat perverse or ironic: *wry* humor. —*v.t.* **wried, wry·ing** To twist; contort. [< OE *wrīgian* move, tend] —**wry'ly** *adv.* —**wry'ness** *n.*

wry·neck (rī'nek') *n.* **1** A bird allied to the woodpeckers, with the habit of twisting its head and neck. **2** A spasmodic twisting of the neck.

WSW, W.S.W., wsw, w.s.w. west-southwest.

wt, wt. weight.

WV West Virginia (P.O. abbr.).

W.Va. West Virginia.

WY Wyoming (P.O. abbr.).

wy·an·dotte (wī'ən·dot) *n.* One of an American breed of chicken. [< the *Wyandot* Indians, an Iroquoian tribe]

wych-elm (wich'elm') *n.* **1** A wide-spreading elm with large, dull-green leaves, common in N Europe. **2** Its wood. Also **witch-elm**. [< OE *wice* wych-elm + ELM]

Wyo. Wyoming.

X

X, x (eks) *n. pl.* **X's, x's, Xs, xs** (ek'siz) **1** The 24th letter of the English alphabet. **2** Any spoken sound representing the letter *X* or *x*. **3** In Roman notation, the symbol for 10. **4** An unknown quantity, result, etc. **5** A mark shaped like an X, representing the signature of one who cannot write. **6** A mark used in diagrams, maps, etc., to indicate or point out something. **7** A mark indicating one's answer on a test, one's choice on a ballot, etc. **8** A mark used to indicate a kiss. **9** A mark indicating "times" in multiplication: $4 \times 2 = 8$. **10** A mark indicating "by" in dimensions: $8\frac{1}{2} \times 11$ inches. **11** Something shaped like an X. —*v.t.* **x-ed** or **x'd, x-ing** or **x'ing 1** To mark with an *x*. **2** To cancel or obliterate with an *x:* usu. with *out.* —*adj.* Shaped like an X.

X Christ; Christian.

xan·thic (zan'thik) *adj.* **1** Having a yellow or yellowish color. **2** Of or pertaining to xanthin or xanthine. [< Gk. *xanthos* yellow]

xan·thin (zan'thin) *n.* A yellow pigment found in plants. Also **xan'tho·phyll** (-thə·fil). [< Gk. *xanthos* yellow]

xan·thine (zan'thēn, -thin) *n.* A white, crystalline, nitrogenous compound, contained in blood, urine, and other animal secretions. [< Gk. *xanthos* yellow]

Xan·thip·pe (zan·tip'ē) The wife of Socrates, renowned as a shrew. —*n.* A shrewish, ill-tempered woman.

xan·thous (zan'thəs) *adj.* Yellow. [< Gk. *xanthos*]

x-ax·is (eks'ak'sis) *n. Math.* A coordinate axis against which the variable *x* is plotted.

X chromosome The sex chromosome that occurs in pairs in the female and is coupled with a Y chromosome in the male of humans and most animals.

X.D., x.d., x-div. ex (without) dividend.

Xe xenon.

xe·bec (zē'bek) *n.* A small, three-masted Mediterranean vessel. [< Ar. *shabbāk*]

xe·non (zē'non) *n.* A heavy, colorless, gaseous element (symbol Xe) occurring in traces in the atmosphere and rarely forming compounds. [< Gk. *xenos* a stranger]

xen·o·pho·bi·a (zen'ə·fō'bē·ə, zē'nə-) *n.* Dislike or fear of strangers or foreigners. [< Gk. *xenos* a stranger + -PHOBIA] —**xen'o·phob'ic** *adj.*

xe·rog·ra·phy (zi·rog'rə·fē) *n.* A method of copying by which a colored powder is distributed by the action of light on an electrically charged plate to form a negative, which is then transferred thermally to a paper or other surface. [< Gk. *xēros* dry + -GRAPHY] —**xe·ro·graph·ic** (zir'ə·graf'ik) *adj.*

xe·roph·i·lous (zi·rof'ə·ləs) *adj.* Thriving under arid conditions: said of plants living in dry regions, as the cactus. [< Gk. *xēros* dry + *philos* loving]

xe·ro·phyte (zir'ə·fīt) *n. Bot.* A plant adapted to arid habitats. [< Gk *xēros* dry + *phyton* plant] —**xe'ro·phyt'ic** (-fit'ik) *adj.*

Xer·ox (zir'oks) *n.* A xerographic copying process: a trade name. —*v.t.* To make or reproduce by Xerox. —*adj.* Of, for, or reproduced by Xeroxing. Also **xer'ox.**

xi (zī, sī; *Gk.* ksē) *n.* The fourteenth letter of the Greek alphabet (Ξ, ξ)

X.I., x.i., x-int. ex (without) interest.

Xmas (kris'məs, eks'məs) *n.* CHRISTMAS. [< *X*, abbr. for *Christ* < Gk. *X*, chi, the first letter of *Christos* Christ + -MAS(S)]

X-ray (eks'rā') *n.* **1** An electromagnetic radiation having a wavelength shorter than that of ultraviolet light and longer than that of a gamma ray. **2** A photograph made with X-rays. —*adj.* Of, made by, or producing X-rays. —*v.t.* **1** To examine, diagnose, or treat with X-rays. —*v.i.* **2** To use X-rays. Also **X ray.**

x-ref. cross reference.

xy·lem (zī'ləm) *n.* The woody vascular bundles that serve as passageways for water in the roots, stems, and leaves of ferns and seed plants. [< Gk. *xylon* wood]

xy·lo·phone (zī'lə·fōn') *n.* A musical instrument consisting of an array of wooden bars graduated in length to produce a scale, played by striking the bars with two small mallets. [< Gk. *xylon* wood + *phōnē* sound] —**xy'lo·phon'ist** *n.*

Xylophone

Y

Y, y (wī) *n. pl.* **Y's, y's, Ys, ys** (wīz) **1** The 25th letter of the English alphabet. **2** Any spoken sound representing the letter *Y* or *y*. **3** Something shaped like a Y. —*adj.* Shaped like a Y.

-y¹ *suffix* Being, possessing, or resembling what is expressed in the main element: *stony, rainy.* [< OE *-ig*]

-y² *suffix* **1** Quality; condition: *victory.* **2** The place or establishment where something specified happens or is made: *bakery.* **3** The entire group or body of: *soldiery.* [< L *-ia* or < Gk. *-ia, -eia*]

-y³ *suffix* Little; small: *kitty:* often used to express endearment. [ME *-ie*]

Y (wī) *n. pl.* **Y's** or **Ys 1** YMCA or YWCA. **2** YMHA or YWHA.

Y yttrium.

y. yard(s); year(s).

yacht (yot) *n.* Any of various relatively small sailing or motor-driven ships built or fitted for private pleasure excursions or racing. —*v.i.* To cruise, race, or sail in a yacht. [< Du. *jaghte*, short for *jaghtschip* a pursuit ship]

yacht·ing (yot'ing) *n.* The act, practice, or pastime of sailing in or managing a yacht.

yachts·man (yots'mən) *n. pl.* **-men** (-mən) One who owns or sails a yacht.

---

add, āce, câre, pălm; end, ēven; it, īce; odd, ōpen, ôrder; tŏŏk, pōōl; up, bûrn; ə = *a* in *above*, *u* in *focus*; yōō = *u* in *fuse*; oil; pout; check; go; ring; thin; <u>th</u>is; zh, *vision*. < derived from; ? origin uncertain or unknown.

ya·hoo (yä′hoo͞, yä′-) *n.* An awkward or crude person; a bumpkin. [<*Yahoo*, one of a race of brutes in Swift's *Gulliver's Travels*, 1726]

Yah·weh (yä′we) In the Old Testament, a name for God. Also **Yah·ve, Yah·veh** (yä′ve). [<Heb. *YHWH*]

yak[1] (yak) *n.* A large, shaggy wild ox of CEN. Asia, often domesticated. [<Tibetan *gyag*]

yak[2] (yak) *Slang v.i.* **yakked, yak·king** To talk or chatter a great deal. —*n.* **1** Persistent chatter or talk. **2** A boisterous laugh. **3** Something, as a joke, causing such a laugh. Also (for *v.* and *n.* def. 1) **yak·e·ty-yak** (yak′ə·tē·yak′). [Imit.] —**yak′ker** *n.*

Yak

yam (yam) *n.* **1** The fleshy, edible, tuberous root of any of a genus of climbing tropical plants. **2** Any of the plants growing this root. **3** A variety of sweet potato. [<Pg. *inhame* < a native w African name]

yam·mer (yam′ər) *v.i. Informal* **1** To complain peevishly; whine; whimper. **2** To howl; roar; shout. —*v.t.* **3** To utter in a complaining or peevish manner.—*n.* The act of yammering. [<OE *geōmrian* to lament]

yang (yang) *n.* In Chinese philosophy, the male principle and element of the universe, source of life and heat and, with yin, co-creator of everything that is. [<Chin.]

yank (yangk) *v.t. & v.i.* To jerk or pull suddenly. —*n.* A sudden sharp pull; jerk. [?]

Yank (yangk) *n. & adj. Informal* YANKEE.

Yan·kee (yang′kē) *n.* **1** A native or citizen of the U.S. **2** A native or inhabitant of the northern U.S. **3** A native or inhabitant of New England. —*adj.* Of, like, or characteristic of Yankees. [?] —**Yan′kee·dom, Yan′kee·ism** *n.*

Yankee Doo·dle (do͞od′l) A song popular in the U.S. from pre-Revolutionary times.

yap (yap) *v.i.* **yapped, yap·ping 1** *Slang* To talk or jabber. **2** To bark or yelp, as a dog. —*n.* **1** A bark or yelp. **2** *Slang* Worthless talk; jabber. **3** *Slang* **a** A crude person. **b** The mouth. [Imit. of a dog's bark]

yard[1] (yärd) *n.* **1** A unit of length equal to 3 feet or 0.914 meter. **2** A long, slender spar set crosswise on a mast and used to support sails. [<OE *gierd* rod, yard measure]

yard[2] (yärd) *n.* **1** A plot of ground enclosed or set apart, as for some specific purpose: often in combination: *barnyard.* **2** The ground or lawn belonging and adjacent to a house, college, university, etc. **3** An enclosure used for building, selling, storing, etc.: often in combination: *shipyard; stockyard.* **4** An enclosure or piece of ground usu. adjacent to a railroad station, used for making up trains and for storage. —*v.t.* To put or collect into or as into a yard. [<OE *geard* an enclosure]

yard·age (yär′dij) *n.* The amount or length of something in yards.

yard·arm (yärd′ärm′) *n.* Either end of the yard of a square sail.

yard goods Fabric sold by the yard; piece goods.

yard·man (yärd′mən) *n. pl.* **·men** (-mən) A man employed in a yard, esp. in a railroad yard.

yard·mas·ter (yärd′mas′tər, -mäs′-) *n.* A railroad official having charge of a yard.

yard·stick (yärd′stik′) *n.* **1** A graduated measuring stick a yard in length. **2** Any measure or standard of comparison; criterion.

yar·mul·ke (yär′məl·kə) *n.* A skullcap traditionally worn by Jewish males in synagogues and often at school and in the home. Also **yar′mel·ke.** [Yiddish]

yarn (yärn) *n.* **1** Any spun fiber, as cotton, wool, or nylon, prepared for use in weaving, knitting, or crotcheting. **2** *Informal* A tale of adventure, often of doubtful truth. —*v.i. Informal* To tell a yarn or yarns. [<OE *gearn*]

yar·row (yar′ō) *n.* Any of a genus of perennial composite plants, esp. a common weed with finely divided, pungent leaves and clusters of small, usu. white flowers. [<OE *gearwe*]

yat·a·ghan (yat′ə·gan, -gən) *n.* A Turkish sword with a double-curved blade and without a handle guard. Also **yat′a·gan.**

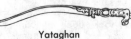

Yataghan

yaw (yô) *v.i.* **1** To move wildly or out of its course, as a ship when struck by a heavy sea. **2** To deviate from a flight path by rotating about a vertical axis: said of spacecraft, projectiles, etc. —*v.t.* **3** To cause to yaw. —*n.* **1** The action of yawing. **2** The amount of deviation in yawing. [?]

yawl (yôl) *n.* **1** A small, fore-and-aft rigged, two-masted sailboat. **2** A ship's small boat; jollyboat. [? <Du *jol*]

yawn (yôn) *v.i.* **1** To open the mouth wide, usu. involuntarily, with a full inhalation, as the result of drowsiness, boredom, etc. **2** To stand wide open: A chasm *yawned* below. —*v.t.* **3** To express or utter with a yawn. —*n.* **1** An act of yawning. **2** A wide opening. [<OE *geonian*] —**yawn′er** *n.*

Yawl def. 1

yawp (yôp) *v.i.* **1** To bark or yelp. **2** *Informal* To talk or shout loudly. —*n.* The act or sound of yawping. [Imit.] —**yawp′er** *n.*

yaws (yôz) *n. pl.* A contagious tropical disease marked by skin lesions. [<Cariban *yáya*]

y-axis (wī′ak′sis) *n. Math.* A coordinate axis along which the variable *y* is plotted.

Yb ytterbium.

Y chromosome The smaller of the unmatched pair of sex chromosomes found in the male of humans and most animals.

y·clept (i·klept′) *adj. Archaic* Called; named. Also **y·cleped′.** [<OE *geclypod*, p.p. of *clypian* call]

yd. yard(s).

ye[1] (thē, yē) *definite article Archaic* The. [< an incorrect transliteration of the Old English thorn, properly transliterated as *th*]

ye[2] (yē) *pron. Archaic* The persons addressed; you. [<OE *gē*]

yea (yā) *adv.* **1** Yes: used in voting orally. **2** *Archaic* Not only so, but more so. **3** *Archaic* In reality; verily: a form of introduction in a sentence. —*n.* **1** An affirmative vote. **2** One who casts such a vote. [<OE *gēa*]

ye·ah (ye′ə) *adv. Informal* Yes.

yean (yēn) *v.t. & v.i.* To bring forth (young), as a goat or sheep. [<OE (assumed) *geēanian*]

yean·ling (yēn′ling) *n.* The young of a goat or sheep. —*adj.* Young; newly born.

year (yir) *n.* **1** The period of time in which the earth completes a revolution around the sun: about 365 days, 5 hours, 49 minutes, and, in the Gregorian calendar, divided into 12 months beginning January 1 and ending December 31. **2** Any period of 12 months. **3** The period of time during which a planet revolves around the sun. **4** Any part of a year devoted to some activity: the school *year.* **5** *pl.* Any extended or past period of time: the *years* before automobiles. **6** *pl.* Length or time of life; age: active for his *years.* [<OE *gēar*]

year·book (yir′book′) *n.* A book published annually, usu. presenting information about the previous year.

year·ling (yir′ling) *n.* An animal between one and two years old. —*adj.* Being a year old.

year·long (yir′lông′, -long′) *adj.* Continuing through a year.

year·ly (yir′lē) *adj.* **1** Of a year. **2** Occurring once a year; annual. **3** Continuing for a year: a *yearly* subscription. —*adv.* Once a year; annually.

yearn (yûrn) *v.i.* **1** To desire something earnestly; long: with *for.* **2** To be deeply moved; feel sympathy. [<OE *giernan*] —**yearn′er** *n.* —**Syn.** **1** wish, want, covet, hunger, crave, pine for.

yearn·ing (yûr′ning) *n.* A strong emotion of longing or desire, esp. with tenderness.

year-round (yir′round′) *adj.* Continuing, operating, etc., throughout the entire year.

yeast (yēst) *n.* **1** Any of various single-celled fungi that produce ethyl alcohol and carbon dioxide in the process of fermenting carbohydrates. **2** A commercial preparation of certain yeasts, usu. in dry powdery form, used to leaven bread, make beer, etc. **3** Froth or spume. **4** Something causing mental or moral ferment. —*v.i.* To foam; froth. [<OE *gist*]

yeast·y (yēs'tē) *adj.* **yeast·i·er, yeast·i·est 1** Of or resembling yeast. **2** Causing fermentation. **3** Restless; unsettled. **4** Covered with froth or foam. **5** Light or unsubstantial. —**yeast'i·ness** *n.*

yegg (yeg) *n. Slang* A burglar, esp. one who cracks safes. Also **yegg'man.** [?]

yell (yel) *v.t. & v.i.* **1** To shout; scream. **2** To cheer. —*n.* **1** A sharp, loud cry, as of pain, terror, etc. **2** A rhythmic shout by a group, as in cheering an athletic team. [< OE *giellan*] —**yell'er** *n.*

yel·low (yel'ō) *adj.* **1** Of the color yellow. **2** Changed to a sallow color by age, sickness, etc.: a paper *yellow* with age. **3** Having a yellowish or light brown complexion. **4** Cheaply or offensively sensational: said of newspapers: *yellow* journalism. **5** *Informal* Cowardly; mean; dishonorable. —*n.* **1** The color of ripe lemons or, in the spectrum, the color between green and orange. **2** Any pigment or dyestuff having such a color. **3** The yolk of an egg. —*v.t. & v.i.* To make or become yellow. [< OE *geolu*] —**yel'low·ly** *adv.* —**yel'low·ness** *n.*

yel·low·bird (yel'ō·bûrd') *n.* Any of various birds with yellow plumage, as the goldfinch.

yellow fever An acute tropical disease caused by a virus transmitted by a mosquito and characterized by jaundice and other symptoms.

yel·low·ham·mer (yel'ō·ham'ər) *n.* **1** A European bunting with bright yellow and black plumage. **2** The flicker or golden-winged woodpecker. [? < OE *geolo* yellow + *amore*, a kind of bird]

yel·low·ish (yel'ō·ish) *adj.* Somewhat yellow.

yellow jack 1 A yellow flag indicating quarantine. **2** YELLOW FEVER.

yellow jacket Any of various social wasps with bright yellow markings.

yellow peril The supposed threat to the West from the power of the peoples of E Asia.

yellow pine 1 Any of various American pines, as the loblolly. **2** Their tough, yellowish wood.

yel·low·wood (yel'ō·wo͝od') *n.* Any of various trees having yellow or yellowish wood or yielding a yellow dye.

yel·low·y (yel'ō·ē) *adj.* Yellowish.

yelp (yelp) *v.i.* To utter a sharp or shrill cry. —*v.t.* To express by a yelp or yelps. —*n.* A sharp, shrill cry, as of a dog in distress. [< OE *gielpan* boast] —**yelp'er** *n.*

Yem·en Arab Republic (yem'ən) A country of sw Arabia, 75,000 sq. mi., cap. San'a. —**Yem·e·ni** (yem'ə·nē), **Yem'e·nite** (-nīt) *adj., n.*

Yemen, People's Democratic Republic of A republic on the s coast of Arabia, 110,000 sq. mi., cap. Madinat ash Sha'b. Also **Southern Yemen.** —**Yem'e·ni, Yem'e·nite** *adj., n.*

yen¹ (yen) *Informal n.* An ardent longing or desire. —*v.i.* **yenned, yen·ning** To yearn; long. [< Chin., opium]

yen² (yen) *n.* The basic monetary unit of Japan.

yen·ta (yen'tə) *n.* A female gossip or meddler. Also **yen'teh.** [Yiddish]

yeo·man (yō'mən) *n. pl.* **·men** (-mən) **1** A petty officer in the U.S. Navy or Coast Guard who performs clerical duties. **2** *Brit.* A farmer, esp. one who cultivates his own farm. **3** YEOMAN OF THE GUARD. **4** *Brit.* One of the attendants of a nobleman or of royalty. [? < OE *geong* young + *mann* a man]

yeo·man·ly (yō'mən·lē) *adj.* **1** Of or pertaining to a yeoman. **2** Brave; rugged. —*adv.* Like a yeoman; bravely.

Yeoman of the (Royal) Guard A member of the ceremonial bodyguard of the English royal household.

yeo·man·ry (yō'mən·rē) *n.* **1** Yeomen, as a group. **2** *Brit.* A home guard of volunteer cavalry, now part of the Territorial Army.

yeoman's service Faithful and useful support or service. Also **yeoman service.**

yep (yep) *adv. Informal* Yes.

yes (yes) *adv.* **1** As you say; truly; just so: a reply of affirmation or consent. **2** Moreover: She is willing, *yes* eager, to go. —*n. pl.* **yes·es** or **yes·ses** A reply in the affirmative. —*v.t. & v.i.* **yessed, yes·sing** To say "yes" (to). [< OE *gēa* yea + *sīe* it may be]

yes-man (yes'man') *n. pl.* **-men** (men') *Informal* A person who habitually agrees with the opinions or statements of others, esp. with those of his superiors.

yes·ter·day (yes'tər·dē, -dā') *n.* **1** The day preceding today. **2** The near past. —*adv.* **1** On the day last past. **2** At a recent time. [< OE *geostran* yesterday + *dæg* day]

yes·ter·year (yes'tər·yir') *n.* **1** Last year. **2** Recent years; recent past. **3** Time past; a past epoch: the peaceful days of *yesteryear.*

yet (yet) *adv.* **1** In addition; besides. **2** At some future time; eventually: he may *yet* succeed. **3** In continuance of a previous state or condition; still: I can hear him *yet.* **4** At the present time; now: Don't go *yet.* **5** After all the time that has or had elapsed: Are you not ready *yet?* **6** Up to the present time; heretofore: He has never *yet* lied to me. **7** Even: a *yet* hotter day. **8** Nevertheless: They are poor, *yet* happy. **9** As much as; even: He did not believe the reports, nor *yet* the evidence. —**as yet** Up to now. —*conj.* Nevertheless; but: I speak to you peaceably, *yet* you will not listen. [< OE *gīet*]

yew (yoo) *n.* **1** Any of a genus of evergreen trees and shrubs, with narrow, flat, dark green, poisonous leaves and red berrylike cones containing a single seed. **2** The hard, tough wood of the yew. [< OE *ēow, īw*]

Yid·dish (yid'ish) *n.* A language derived from 13th- and 14th-century Middle High German, now spoken primarily by Eastern European Jews and their relatives or descendants in other countries. It contains elements of Hebrew and the Slavic languages. —*adj.* Of, written, or spoken in Yiddish. [< G *jüdisch* Jewish]

yield (yēld) *v.t.* **1** To give forth by a natural process, or as a result of labor or cultivation: The field will *yield* a good crop. **2** To give in return, as for investment; furnish: The bonds *yield* five percent interest. **3** To give up, as to superior power; surrender; relinquish: often with *up:* to *yield* oneself up to one's enemies. **4** To give up one's possession of: to *yield* the right of way . —*v.i.* **5** To provide a return; produce; bear. **6** To give up; submit; surrender. **7** To give way, as to pressure or force. **8** To assent or comply, as under compulsion; consent: We *yielded* to their persuasion. **9** To give place, as through inferiority or weakness: with *to:* We will *yield* to them in nothing. —*n.* The amount yielded; product; result, as of cultivation, investment, etc. [< OE *gieldan* pay] —**yield'er** *n.*

yield·ing (yēl'ding) *adj.* **1** Productive. **2** Flexible; easily bent. **3** Obedient. —**yield'ing·ly** *adv.* —**yield'ing·ness** *n.*

yin (yin) *n.* In Chinese philosophy, the female principle and element of the universe, standing for darkness, cold, and death. [< Chin.]

yip (yip) *n.* A yelp, as of a dog. —*v.i.* **yipped, yip·ping** To yelp. [Imit.]

-yl *suffix Chem.* Used to denote a radical: *ethyl.* [< Gk. *hylē* wood, matter]

YMCA, Y.M.C.A. Young Men's Christian Association.

YMHA, Y.M.H.A. Young Men's Hebrew Association.

yock (yäk) *n. Slang* **1** A loud laugh or guffaw. **2** Something causing such a laugh. [Var. of YAK²]

yo·del (yōd'l) *v.t. & v.i.* **·deled** or **·delled, ·del·ing** or **·del·ling** To sing by changing the voice quickly from its low register to a falsetto and back. —*n.* Something yodeled, as a melody or refrain. Also **yo'dle.** [< G *jodeln*, lit., utter the syllable *jo*] —**yo'del·er, yo'del·ler, yo'dler** *n.*

yo·ga (yō'gə) *n.* **1** A Hindu mystical and ascetic discipline, the ultimate purpose of which is to gain spiritual illumination by means of a prescribed series of mental and physical exercises. **2** The exercises, esp. certain physical exercises, based on yoga techniques. [Skt., lit., union] —**yo'gic** (-gik) *adj.*

yo·gi (yō'gē) *n. pl.* **·gis** A person who practices yoga. Also **yo'gin** (-gən, -gin).

---

add, āce, câre, pälm; end, ēven; it, īce; odd, ōpen, ôrder; to͝ok, po͞ol; up, bûrn; ə = a in above, u in focus; yo͞o = u in fuse; oil; pout; check; go; ring; thin; ᵺis; zh, vision. < derived from; ? origin uncertain or unknown.

yo·gurt (yō′gərt) *n.* A semifluid food made of milk curdled with cultures of bacteria and sometimes flavored with fruit. Also **yo′ghurt.** [<Turk. *yōghurt*]

yoke (yōk) *n.* **1** A curved frame used for coupling draft animals, as oxen, usu. having a bow at each end to receive the neck of the animal. **2** Any of many similar contrivances, as a frame worn on the shoulder to balance pails of milk. **3** A pair of animals joined by a yoke. **4** Something that binds or connects; tie; bond: the *yoke* of marriage. **5** Any of various parts or pieces that connect or hold two things together. **6** Servitude; bondage. **7** A fitted part of a garment designed to support a plaited or gathered part, as at the hips or shoulders. —*v.* **yoked, yok·ing** *v.t.* **1** To attach by means of a yoke, as draft animals. **2** To join with or as with a yoke. —*v.i.* **3** To be joined or linked; unite. [<OE *geoc*]

Yoke *def. 1*

yoke·fel·low (yōk′fel′ō) *n.* A mate or companion, as in labor. Also **yoke′mate′** (-māt′).

yo·kel (yō′kəl) *n.* A country bumpkin.[?]

yolk (yōk, yōlk) *n.* **1** The yellow portion of an egg. **2** An oily exudation in unprocessed sheep's wool. [<OE *geolu* yellow] —**yolk′y** *adj.*

Yom Kip·pur (yom kip′ər, yōm, ki·pŏŏr′) The Jewish Day of Atonement, a holiday marked by prayer and fasting, celebrated in late September or in October.

yon (yon) *adj. & adv. Archaic & Regional* YONDER. [<OE *geon*]

yond (yond) *adj. & adv. Archaic & Regional* YONDER. [< OE *geond* across]

yon·der (yon′dər) *adj.* Being at a distance indicated or known. —*adv.* In that place; there. [<OE *geond,* yond]

yoo-hoo (yōō′hōō′) *interj.* A call used to attract the attention of someone

yore (yôr, yōr) *n.* Time long past: in days of *yore.* [<OE *geara* formerly]

York (yôrk) *n.* A royal house of England that reigned from 1461–85.

York·shire pudding (york′shir, -shər) A batter pudding baked in meat drippings.

you (yōō) *pron.* **1** The person or persons or the personified thing or things addressed: when used as a subject, always linked with a plural verb. **2** One; anyone: *You* learn by trying. [<OE *ēow,* dat. and acc. pl. of *ge* ye]

you'd (yōōd) Contraction of *you had* or *you would.*

you'll (yōōl) Contraction of *you will* or *you shall.*

young (yung) *adj.* **young·er** (yung′gər), **young·est** (yung′gist) **1** Being in the early period of life or growth; not old. **2** Not having progressed or developed far; newly formed: The day was *young.* **3** Pertaining to youth or early life. **4** Full of vigor or freshness. **5** Inexperienced; immature. **6** Denoting the younger of two persons having the same name or title; junior. **7** *Geol.* Having the characteristics of an early stage in the geological cycle: said of a river or of certain land forms. —*n.* **1** Young persons as a group. **2** Offspring, esp. of animals. —**with young** Pregnant. [< OE *geong*] —**young′ness** *n.* —**Syn. 4** lively, strong, active, spirited. **5** raw, green, unseasoned, uninitiated.

young·ber·ry (yung′ber′ē) *n. pl.* **·ries** A dark red berry resulting from crossing a blackberry and a dewberry. [< B. M. *Young,* U.S. horticulturist of late 19th c.]

young blood **1** Young people. **2** New, fresh ideas, attitudes, etc.

young·ish (yung′ish) *adj.* Rather young.

young·ling (yung′ling) *n.* **1** A young person, animal, or plant. **2** An inexperienced person. —*adj.* Young. [<OE *geongling*]

young·ster (yung′stər) *n.* A young person, esp. a child.

Young Turk One of a group bent on seizing control of or radically altering an organization, as a political party.

[Orig., a member of a 20th c. Turkish revolutionary party]

your (yôr, yōōr) *pronominal adj.* **1** Of, belonging to or pertaining to you: *your* fate. **2** Used before certain titles: *your* Majesty. [<OE *ēower,* genitive of *gē* ye]

you're (yŏŏr, yôr) Contraction of *you are.*

yours (yŏŏrz, yōōrz) *pron. (construed as sing. or pl.)* The things or persons belonging or pertaining to you: a home as quiet as *yours.* —**of yours** Belonging or relating to you. [ME *youres*]

your·self (yŏŏr·self′; yōŏr-) *pron. pl.* **·selves** (-selvz′) **1** The one who is you: used as a reflexive or emphatic form: Try not to hurt *yourself.* **2** Your normal, healthy, etc., condition: You are not *yourself* today. **3** ONESELF: It's best to take care of it *yourself.*

youth (yōōth) *n. pl.* **youths** (yōōths, yōōthz) **1** The state or condition of being young. **2** The period when one is young; that part of life between childhood and adulthood. **3** The early period of being or development, as of a movement. **4** A young person, esp. a young man. **5** Young people as a group: the nation's *youth.* [<OE *geoguth*]

youth·ful (yōōth′fəl) *adj.* **1** Of, pertaining to, or characteristic of youth. **2** Buoyant; fresh; vigorous. **3** Having youth; being still young. **4** Not far advanced; early; new. **5** *Geol.* Young. —**youth′ful·ly** *adv.* —**youth′ful·ness** *n.*

you've (yōōv) Contraction of *you have.*

yowl (youl) *v.i.* To howl; yell. —*n.* A loud, prolonged, wailing cry; a howl. [ME *youlen*]

yo-yo (yō′yō′) *n. pl.* **-yos** A wheellike toy with a deep central groove around which is looped a string on which the wheel can be spun in a variety of movements.[?]

yr. year(s); younger; your.

yrs. years; yours.

Y.T. Yukon Territory.

yt·ter·bi·um (i·tûr′bē·əm) *n.* A rare metallic element (symbol Yb) of the lanthanide series. [<*Ytterby,* Sweden]

yt·tri·um (it′rē·əm) *n.* A rare metallic element (symbol Y) similar to and usu. found with ytterbium. [<*Ytterby,* Sweden]

yuc·ca (yuk′ə) *n.* **1** Any of a large genus of liliaceous American plants usu. found in dry, sandy places, having a woody stem which bears a large panicle of white flowers emerging from a crown of sword-shaped leaves. **2** The flower of this plant. [<Sp. *yuca*< Taino]

Yucca

yuck (yuk) *n. Slang* **1** A loud laugh or guffaw. **2** Something causing such a laugh. —*v.i.* To laugh uproariously. [Imit.]

Yu·go·slav (yōō′gō·släv′) *adj.* Of Yugoslavia or its people: also **Yu′go·slav′ic.** —*n.* A native or citizen of Yugoslavia.

Yu·go·sla·vi·a (yōō′gō·slä′vē·ə) *n.* A republic of SE Europe, 98,538 sq. mi., cap. Belgrade. —**Yu′go·sla′vi·an** *adj., n.* • See map at BALKAN STATES.

yuk (yuk) *Slang n. & v.i.* **yukked, yuk·king** YUCK.

Yule (yōōl) *n.* Christmas or Christmas time. [<OE *geōl*]

yule log Formerly, a large log, place on the hearth as the foundation of the traditional Christmas Eve fire.

Yule·tide (yōōl′tīd′) *n.* Christmas time.

yum·my (yum′ē) *Informal adj.* **·mi·er, ·mi·est** Agreeable to the senses, esp. to the taste; delicious. —*n.* Something delicious. [Imit. of the sound made when something is pleasurable to the taste]

yup·pie (yup′ē) *n.pl.* **yup·pies** A young, usually urban, middle-class professional person. [<Y(OUNG) U(RBAN) P(ROFESSIONAL) + -IE]

YWCA, Y.W.C.A. Young Women's Christian Association.

YWHA, Y.W.H.A. Young Women's Hebrew Association.

Z

Z, z (zē, *Brit. & Can.* zed) *n. pl.* **Z's, z's, Zs, zs** (zēz, zedz) **1** The 26th letter of the English alphabet. **2** Any spoken sound representing the letter *Z* or *z.* **3** Something shaped like a Z. —*adj.* Shaped like a Z.

Z., z. zero; zone.

zai·bat·su (zī′bat·sōō′) *n. pl.* **zai·bat·su** The wealthy clique of Japan, representing four or five dominant families. [< Jap. *zai* property + *batsu* family]

Zaire (zīr′, zä·ir′) *n.* A republic of CEN. Africa, 904,754 sq. mi., cap. Kinshasa. • See map at AFRICA.

Zam·bi·a (zam′bē·ə) *n.* An independent member of the Commonwealth of Nations in CEN. Africa, 288,130 sq. mi., cap. Lusaka. • See map at AFRICA.

za·ny (zā′nē) *adj.* **·ni·er, ·ni·est** Absurdly funny; ludicrous. —*n. pl.* **·nies 1** In old comic plays, a clown who absurdly mimics the other performers. **2** Any ludicrous comic or buffoon. **3** A simpleton; fool. [< Ital. *zanni*] —**za′ni·ly** *adv.* —**za′ni·ness** *n.*

zap (zap) *Slang v.t.* **zapped, zap·ping 1** To kill. **2** To attack; hit; clobber. **3** To confront or impress suddenly and forcefully; astound; overwhelm. —*n.* **1** Vigorous effect; punch; vitality. **2** An attack or confrontation.

zeal (zēl) *n.* Ardor, as for a cause; fervor. [< Gk. *zēlos*] — **Syn.** enthusiasm, eagerness, devotion, passion, verve, spirit, heart.

zeal·ot (zel′ət) *n.* One who is zealous, esp. to an immoderate degree; partisan, fanatic, etc. —**zeal′ot·ry** *n.*

zeal·ous (zel′əs) *adj.* Filled with, marked by, or showing zeal; enthusiastic. —**zeal′ous·ly** *adv.* —**zeal′ous·ness** *n.*

ze·bec (zē′bek) *n.* XEBEC. Also **ze′beck.**

ze·bra (zē′brə, *Brit. & Can.* zeb′rə) *n.* Any of various African ponylike mammals having a whitish body with dark stripes. [Pg.] —**ze′brine** (-brēn, -brin), **ze′·broid** (-broid) *adj.*

ze·bu (zē′byōō) *n.* Any of various breeds of domesticated oxen of Asia and Africa, having a hump on the withers, a large dewlap, and short curved horns. [< Tibetan]

Zebra

Zech. Zechariah.

zed (zed) *n. Brit. & Can.* The letter *z.* [< Gk. *zēta*]

zeit·geist (tsīt′gīst) *n. Often cap.* The intellectual, moral, and cultural tendencies that characterize any age or epoch. [< G < *Zeit* time + *Geist* spirit]

Zen (zen) *n.* A form of Buddhism that originated in China and became widespread in Japan, that lays particular stress on deep meditation as a means of achieving an abrupt, intuitive, spiritual enlightenment. [< Jap. *zen* meditation]

Zend (zend) *n.* The ancient translation of and commentary on the Avesta. [< Pers., interpretation] —**Zend′ic** *adj.*

Zend-A·ves·ta (zend′ə·ves′tə) *n.* The sacred Zoroastrian writings including the Zend and the Avesta.

ze·nith (zē′nith) *n.* **1** The point of the celestial sphere that is exactly overhead. **2** The highest or culminating point; summit; acme. [< Ar. *samt (ar-rās)* the path (over the head)]

Zeph. Zephaniah.

zeph·yr (zef′ər) *n.* **1** The west wind. **2** Any soft, gentle wind. **3** Worsted or woolen yarn of very light weight: also **zephyr worsted.** [< Gk. *zephyros*]

zep·pe·lin (zep′ə·lin) *n.* A large, cigar-shaped dirigible. [< Count Ferdinand von *Zeppelin,* 1838–1917, German aircraft builder]

ze·ro (zir′ō, zē′rō) *n. pl.* **ze·ros** or **ze·roes 1** The numeral or symbol 0; a cipher. **2** *Math.* The element of a number system that leaves any element unchanged under addition, esp. a real number *0* such that $a + 0 = 0 + a = a$ for any real number *a.* **3** The point on a scale, as of a thermometer, from which measures are counted. **4** The temperature registered at the zero mark on a thermometer. **5** Nothing. **6** The lowest point: *Our hopes dropped to zero.* —*v.t.* **ze·roed, ze·ro·ing** To adjust (instruments) to an arbitrary zero point for synchronized readings. —**zero in 1** To move or bring into a desired position, as an airplane. **2** To adjust the sight of (a gun) or direct (ammunition) toward (a target). —**zero in on 1** To direct gunfire, bombs, etc. toward (a specific target). **2** To concentrate or focus one's energy, attention, efforts, etc., on. —*adj.* **1** Of, at, or being zero. **2** That limits vertical visibility to 50 feet or less: said of a cloud ceiling. **3** That limits horizontal visibility to 165 feet or less: said of conditions on the ground. [< Ar. *ṣifr*] • In popular usage the symbol for zero (0) is often rendered orally as (ō), as if it were the letter O.

zero hour 1 The time set for an attack. **2** Any critical moment.

zest (zest) *n.* **1** Agreeable excitement and keen enjoyment. **2** A quality that imparts such excitement. **3** Any piquant flavoring. [< F *zeste* lemon or orange peel] —**zest′·ful, zest′y** *adj.* **(·i·er, ·i·est)** —**zest′ful·ly** *adv.* —**zest′ful·ness** *n.* —**Syn. 1** delight, gusto, relish, pleasure, gratification, savor, thrill, kick.

ze·ta (zā′tə, zē′-) *n.* The sixth letter of the Greek alphabet. (Z,ζ)

Zeus (zōōs) *Gk. Myth.* The supreme deity.

zig·gu·rat (zig′ōō·rat) *n.* Among the Assyrians and Babylonians, a terraced temple tower pyramidal in form, each successive story being smaller than the one below. [< Assyrian *ziqquratu,* orig., a mountain top]

Ziggurat

zig·zag (zig′zag) *n.* **1** One of a series of sharp turns or angles. **2** A path or pattern characterized by such turns or angles going from side to side. —*adj.* Having a series of zigzags. —*adv.* In a zigzag manner. —*v.t. & v.i.* **·zagged, ·zag·ging** To move in zigzags. [< G *zickzack*]

zilch (zilch) *n. Slang* Nothing; zero. [Alter. of ZERO]

zil·lion (zil′yən) *n. Informal* A very large, indeterminate number: *a zillion things to do before the plane left.* [Imit. of *million, trillion,* etc.] —**zil′lionth** *adj.*

zinc (zingk) *n.* A bluish white metallic element (symbol Zn) occurring mostly in combination, extensively used in alloys, as bronze and brass, for galvanizing, and in electric batteries. —*v.t.* **zinced** or **zincked, zinc·ing** or **zinck·ing** To coat or cover with zinc; galvanize. [< G *zink*] —**zinc′ic** (-ik), **zinc′ous** (-əs), **zinck′y, zinc′y, zink′y** *adj.*

zinc ointment A medicated ointment containing zinc oxide.

zinc oxide A white powdery compound, used as a pigment and as a mild antiseptic.

zinc white Zinc oxide used as a pigment.

zing (zing) *Informal n.* **1** A high-pitched buzzing or humming sound. **2** Energy; vitality. —*v.i.* To make a shrill, humming sound.

zin·ni·a (zin′ē·ə, zin′yə) *n.* Any of various cultivated plants having opposite entire leaves and showy, composite flowers. [< J. G. *Zinn,* 1727–59, German botanist]

Zi·on (zī′ən) *n.* **1** A hill in Jerusalem, the site of the Temple of David and his successors. **2** The Jewish people. **3** Any place or community considered to be especially under God's rule, as ancient Israel. **4** The heavenly Jerusalem; heaven. [< Heb. *tsīyōn* a hill]

Zi·on·ism (zī′ən·iz′əm) n. A movement for a resettlement of the Jews in Palestine. —**Zi′on·ist** adj. & n.

zip (zip) n. 1 A sharp, hissing sound, as of a bullet passing through the air. 2 Informal Energy; vitality; vim. —v. **zipped, zip·ping** v.t. 1 To fasten with a zipper: often with up: to zip up a jacket. 2 To give speed and energy to. —v.i. 3 Informal To move or act with speed and energy. 4 To move with a sharp, hissing sound. [Imit.]

zip-code (zip′kōd′) v.t. -cod·ed, -cod·ing Sometimes cap. To provide (mail) with a zip code.

zip code (zip) A numerical code devised to identify each postal delivery area in the U.S. Also **ZIP Code, Zip Code**. [< z(one) i(mprovement) p(lan)]

zip·per (zip′ər) n. A sliding fastener with two rows of interlocking teeth. [< Zipper, a trade name]

zip·py (zip′ē) adj. ·pi·er, ·pi·est Informal Brisk; energetic.

zir·con (zûr′kon) n. 1 An adamantine, variously colored zirconium silicate, used as a gem in certain varieties. 2 A variety of this mineral having an artificially produced lustrous blue appearance. [< Ar. zarqūn cinnabar < Pers. zargūn golden]

zir·co·ni·um (zûr·kō′nē·əm) n. A metallic element (symbol Zr), used in heat-resistant alloys. [< ZIRCON] —**zir·con′·ic** adj.

zith·er (zith′ər, zith′-) n. A stringed instrument having a flat sounding board and 30 to 40 strings that are played by plucking. Also **zith′ern** (-ərn). [< Gk. kithara]

zlo·ty (zlô′tē) n. pl. ·tys or ·ty The basic monetary unit of Poland.

Zn zinc.

zo·di·ac (zō′dē·ak) n. 1 An imaginary belt encircling the heavens and extending about 8° on each side of the ecliptic, within which are the orbits of the moon, sun, and larger planets. It is divided into twelve parts, called **signs of the zodiac,** which formerly corre-

Zither

Signs of the zodiac (reading clockwise):
A. Vernal equinox: Aries, Taurus, Gemini.
B. Summer solstice: Cancer, Leo, Virgo.
C. Autumnal equinox: Libra, Scorpio, Sagittarius.
D. Winter solstice: Capricorn, Aquarius, Pisces.

sponded to twelve constellations. 2 Any complete circuit; round. [< Gk. (kyklos) zōdiakos (circle) of animals] —**zo·di·a·cal** (zō·dī′ə·kəl) adj.

zom·bie (zom′bē) n. 1 In voodoo cults, a snake deity. 2 The supernatural power by which a dead body is believed to be reanimated. 3 A corpse reactivated by such power. 4 Slang A person who looks weird or behaves eccentrically, mechanically, etc. 5 A strong cocktail made of several kinds of rum, fruit juices, and liqueurs. Also, esp. for defs. 1, 2, & 3, **zom′bi**. [< West African]

zo·nal (zō′nəl) adj. Of, pertaining to, exhibiting, or marked by a zone or zones; having the form of a zone. Also **zo′na·ry** (-nər·ē). —**zon′al·ly** adv.

zone (zōn) n. 1 One of five divisions of the earth's surface, bounded by parallels of latitude and named for the prevailing climate. These are the **torrid zone,** extending on each side of the equator 23° 27′; the **temperate** or **variable zones,** included between the parallels 23° 27′ and 66° 33′ on both sides of the equator; and the **frigid zones,** within the parallels 66° 33′ and the poles. 2 Ecol. A belt or area delimited from others by the charac-

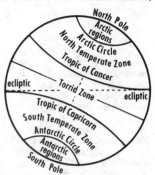

Terrestrial zones

ter of its plant or animal life, its climate, geological formations, etc. 3 A region, area, belt, etc., distinguished or set off by some special characteristic: a demilitarized zone; a residential zone; a no-parking zone. 4 An area, usu. circular, within which a uniform rate is charged for delivery of goods, telephone calls, etc. 5 In the U.S. postal system: a Any of the areas within which a uniform rate is charged for parcel post. b Any of the numbered postal districts in a city. 6 Geom. A portion of the surface of a sphere enclosed between two parallel planes. —v.t. **zoned, zon·ing** 1 To divide into zones; esp., to divide (a city, etc.) into zones which are restricted as to types of construction and activity, as residential, industrial, etc. 2 To encircle with a zone or belt. 3 To mark with or as with zones or stripes. [< Gk. zōnē a girdle] —**zoned** adj.

zonk (zongk) v.t. Slang To hit, esp. on the head; clobber; brain.

zonked (zongkt) adj. Slang Highly intoxicated or stimulated, as by alcohol or a drug: often with out. [?]

zoo (zōō) n. pl. **zoos** A park or place where wild animals are kept for exhibition. [Short for zoological garden]

zoo- combining form Animal: zoology. [< Gk. zōion an animal]

zo·o·ge·o·graph·ic (zō′ə·jē′ə·graf′ik) adj. Of, pertaining to, or engaged in zoogeography. Also **zo′o·ge′o·graph′·i·cal.** —**zo′o·ge′o·graph′i·cal·ly** adv.

zo·o·ge·og·ra·phy (zō′ə·jē·og′rə·fē) n. 1 The systematic study of the distribution of animals and of the factors controlling it. 2 The study of the relations between special animal groups and the land or aquatic areas in which they predominate. —**zo′o·ge·og′ra·pher** n.

zo·og·ra·phy (zō·og′rə·fē) n. The branch of zoology that describes animals; descriptive zoology. —**zo·og′ra·pher** or ·**phist** n. —**zo·o·graph·ic** (zō′ə·graf′ik) or ·**i·cal** adj.

zo·oid (zō′oid) n. 1 An entity, usu. very small, capable of movement and independent existence, as a spermatozoon. 2 An individual member of a compound organism, as in a sponge. —adj. Having essentially the nature of an animal: also **zo·oi·dal** (zō·oid′l). [< zo(o)- + -OID]

zool. zoological; zoologist; zoology.

zo·o·log·i·cal (zō′ə·loj′i·kəl) adj. 1 Of, pertaining to, or occupied with zoology. 2 Relating to or characteristic of animals. Also **zo′o·log′ic.** —**zo′o·log′i·cal·ly** adv.

zoological garden zoo.

zo·ol·o·gy (zō·ol′ə·jē) n. 1 The science that treats of animals with reference to their structure, functions, development, nomenclature, and classification. 2 The animal life of a particular area. 3 A scientific treatise on animals. [< zoo- + -LOGY]

zoom (zōōm) v.i. 1 To make a low-pitched but loud humming or buzzing sound, esp. when related to speed: The cars zoomed down the road. 2 To climb sharply upward, as an airplane. 3 To rise sharply, as prices. 4 To move a motion picture or TV camera rapidly or adjust the focus, as with a zoom lens, to make an image appear to come very close or become more distant: often with in or out. —v.t. 5 To cause to zoom. —n. The act of zooming. [Imit.]

zoom lens *Photog.* A lens, used chiefly on television and motion picture cameras, that permits the size of the image to be varied continuously without loss of focus.

zo·o·phyte (zō′ə-fīt) *n.* An invertebrate animal resembling a plant, as a coral or sea anemone. [< zoo- + Gk. *phyton* plant] —**zo′o·phyt′ic** (-fit′ik) or **·i·cal** *adj.*

zo·o·spore (zō′ə-spôr, -spōr) *n.* A motile, asexual spore of certain fungi and algae, usu. provided with cilia. [< zoo- + spore] —**zo′o·spor′ic** (-spôr′ik, -spor′ik), **zo·os·po·rous** (zō·os′pər·əs) *adj.*

zo·ri (zō′rē) *n.* A flat, thonged sandal of straw or rubber. [< Japanese]

Zo·ro·as·tri·an·ism (zō′rō·as′trē·ən·iz′əm) *n.* The religious system founded in ancient Persia by Zoroaster. It recognizes two creative powers, one good and the other evil, and teaches the final triumph of good over evil.

Zou·ave (zōō·äv′, zwäv) *n.* **1** A member of a unit of the French infantry wearing a brilliant Oriental uniform. **2** A member of any volunteer regiment wearing a similar uniform. [< Ar. *Zouaoua,* a tribal name]

zounds (zoundz) *interj.* An exclamation denoting astonishment. [Short for *God's wounds*]

Zr zirconium.

zuc·chet·to (tsōōk·ket′tō) *n. pl.* **·tos** A skullcap worn by ecclesiastics in the Roman Catholic Church, black for a priest, purple for a bishop, red for a cardinal, white for the pope. [Ital. < *zucchetta,* orig. a small gourd]

zuc·chi·ni (zōō·kē′nē) *n.* An elongated summer squash having a thin green skin. [< Ital. *zucca* a gourd, squash]

Zu·lu (zōō′lōō) *n. pl.* **Zu·lus** or **Zu·lu 1** A member of a Bantu nation of SE Africa. **2** The Bantu language of the Zulus. —*adj.* Of the Zulus or their language.

Zu·ñi (zōō′nyē) *n. pl.* **·ñi** or **·ñis 1** A member of a tribe of North American Indians, now living in New Mexico. **2** The language of this tribe.

zwie·back (zwī′bak, zwē′-, swī′-, swē′-, -bäk) *n.* A wheaten bread baked in a loaf and later sliced and toasted. [G, twice baked]

Zwing·li·an (zwing′lē·ən, tsving′-) *adj.* Of or pertaining to Huldreich Zwingli or his doctrines, esp. the doctrine that the Eucharist is simply a symbolic commemoration of the death of Christ. —*n.* A follower of Zwingli. —**Zwing′·li·an·ism** *n.*

zy·gote (zī′gōt, zig′ōt) *n.* **1** The product of the union of two gametes. **2** An individual developing from such a union. [< Gk. *zygon* a yoke] —**zy·got·ic** (zī·got′ik) *adj.*

zy·mase (zī′mās) *n.* A mixture of enzymes that promotes fermentation by breaking down glucose and related carbohydrates into alcohol and carbon dioxide. [< Gk. *zymē* leaven]

zy·mol·o·gy (zī·mol′ə·jē) *n.* The science of fermentation. [< Gk. *zymē* leaven + -LOGY] —**zy·mo·log·ic** (zī′mə·loj′ik) or **·i·cal** *adj.* —**zy·mol′o·gist** *n.*

zy·mot·ic (zī·mot′ik) *adj.* Of, pertaining to, or caused by fermentation. [< Gk. *zymōtikos*]

zy·mur·gy (zī′mûr·jē) *n.* The chemistry of fermentation as applied to brewing, making of yeast, and wine making. [< Gk *zymē* leaven + -URGY]

---

add, āce, câre, pälm; end, ēven; it, īce; odd, ōpen, ôrder; tŏŏk, pōōl; up, bûrn; ə = *a* in *above, u* in *focus;* yōō = *u* in *fuse;* oil; pout; check; go; ring; thin; this; zh, *vision.* < derived from; ? origin uncertain or unknown.

ENCYCLOPEDIC SUPPLEMENTS
Table of Contents

Abbreviations

This list of abbreviations and meanings is a selection of those commonly in use in printed works. There are many forms of abbreviations—capital letters or lower-case letters, periods or no periods, spaces between letters or no spaces, and so on. In this list abbreviations are given without periods. Most are given without spaces and the majority are in lower-case letters unless usage dictates otherwise.

Most of the words that the abbreviations represent are spelled here in lower-case letters, although they may appear elsewhere with initial capital letters. Abbreviations such as *mt* for *mount* usually begin with a capital letter when used with proper nouns—as in *Mt Shasta*.

In abbreviations of foreign words or phrases, such as those from French or Latin, the English meaning always appears first, followed by the word or phrase in the language of origin.

A

a abbreviation, about, acre, alto, ampere, are (measure), argent, assists (baseball), before (Lat. *ante*), year (Lat. *anno*)

A absolute (temperature), angstrom (unit), argon

AA Alcoholics Anonymous, antiaircraft, author's alteration

AAA American Automobile Association

AAAL American Academy of Arts and Letters

AAAS American Academy of Arts and Sciences, American Association for the Advancement of Science

AAE American Association of Engineers

AAF Army Air Forces

A and M Agricultural and Mechanical (College)

Aar Aaron

AARP American Association of Retired Persons

AAU Amateur Athletic Union

ab able-bodied (seaman), (times) at bat

Ab alabamine

AB adapter booster, airborne, Bachelor of Arts (Lat. *Artium Baccalaureus*)

ABA American Bar Association, American Booksellers Association

a&b assault and battery

abbr, abbrev abbreviation

ABC the alphabet, American Broadcasting Company, Audit Bureau of Circulation, Australian Broadcasting Commission

ab ex from without (Lat. *ab extra*)

ab init from the beginning (Lat. *ab initio*)

abl ablative

ABM antiballistic missile

abp archbishop, arterial blood pressure

abr abridged, abridgment

abs absent, absolute (temperature), absolutely, abstract

abstr abstract, abstracted

ac before meals (Lat. *ante cibum*)

a/c account, account current, air conditioning

Ac actinium

AC after Christ, Air Corps, alternating current

acad academic, academy

acc acceptance, accompanied, account, accountant

acc, accus accusative

ACC Air Coordinating Committee

accel accelerando, accelerate

acct account, accountant

ack acknowledge, acknowledgment

ACLU American Civil Liberties Union

ACP American College of Physicians

acpt acceptance

ACS American Chemical Society

A/cs Pay accounts payable

A/cs Rec accounts receivable

act active

ACT American College Test

actg acting

ACTH adrenocorticotropic hormone

ad advertisement, before the day (Lat. *ante diem*)

AD year of our Lord (Lat. *anno domini*)

ADA American Dental Association, Americans for Democratic Action

adc aide-de-camp

ADC aid to families with dependent children

add addenda, addendum, addition, additional, address

ad fin at the end, to one end (Lat. *ad finem*)

ad inf to infinity (Lat. *ad infinitum*)

adj adjacent, adjective, adjourned, adjunct, adjustment

Adj, Adjt adjutant

ad lib to the amount desired (Lat. *ad libitum*)

adm administrative, administrator, admitted

Adm admiral, Admiralty

adv adverb, adverbial, advertisement

ad val according to value (Lat. *ad valorem*)

advt advertisement

ae, aet, aetat of age (Lat. *aetatis*)

AEA Actors' Equity Association

AE and P ambassador extraordinary and plenipotentiary

AEC Atomic Energy Commission

AEF American Expeditionary Force

aeron aeronautics

af audio frequency

Af Africa, African

AF Air Force

AFAM, AF & AM Ancient Free and Accepted Masons

AFB Air Force Base

AFC American Football Conference, automatic frequency control

AFDC aid to families with dependent children

Afg, Afgh Afghanistan

AFL, AF of L American Federation of Labor

AFL-CIO American Federation of Labor–Congress of Industrial Organizations

AFM American Federation of Musicians

Afr Africa, African

AFT American Federation of Teachers

AFTRA American Federation of Television and Radio Artists

Ag August, silver (Lat. *argentum*)

AG adjutant general, attorney general, corporation (Ger. *aktiengesellschaft*)

agcy agency

agr, agri, agric agricultural, agriculture, agriculturist

agt agent, agreement

AHQ Army Headquarters

AI artificial intelligence, in the year of the discovery (Lat. *anno inventionis*)

AIDS acquired immuno-deficiency syndrome

AIM American Indian Movement

AK Alaska

aka also known as

AKC American Kennel Club

al other things (persons) (Lat. *alia, alii*)

Al aluminum

AL Alabama, aviation electronicsman

Ala Alabama

ALA American Library Association

Alas Alaska

Alb Albania, Albanian, Albany, Alberta

Alba Alberta

Ald, Aldm alderman

alg algebra

Alg Algeria, Algerian

ALP American Labor Party, Australian Labor Party

alt alteration, alternate, altitude, alto

Alta Alberta

alum aluminum

am ammeter, before noon (Lat. *ante meridiem*)

Am alabamine, America, American, americium

AM air mail, amplitude modulation, in the year of the world (Lat. *anno mundi*), Master of Arts (Lat. *Artium Magister*)

AMA American Management Association, American Medical Association

Amb ambassador

AMDG to the greater glory of God (Lat. *ad majorem Dei gloriam*)

AME African Methodist Episcopal

Amer America, American

AMG Allied Military Government (of Occupied Territory)

Am Ind American Indian
amp ampere, amperage
amp-hr ampere-hour
amt amount
amu atomic mass unit
AMVETS American Veterans (of World War II and the Korean War)
an anonymous, before (Lat. *ante*)
anal analogous, analogy, analysis, analytic(al)
anat anatomical, anatomy
anc ancient, anciently
and moderately slow (It. *andante*)
And Andorra
Ang Anglican, Angola
Angl Anglican, Anglicized
anim animated (It. *animato*)
ann annals, annual, annuities, annuity, years (Lat. *anni*)
anon anonymous
ans answer, answered
ant antenna, antiquarian, antiquity, antonym
Ant Antarctic, Antarctica
anthrop, anthropol anthropological, anthropology
antilog antilogarithm
antiq antiquarian, antiquities
A/O account of
AOL absent over leave
ap apothecary
Ap apostle, April
AP Associated Press, antipersonnel
APB all points bulletin
apmt appointment
APO Army Post Office
Apoc Apocalypse, Apocrypha, Apocryphal
app apparatus, apparent, appended, appendix, apprentice
appar apparatus, apparent
approx approximate, approximately
Apr April
APR annual percentage rate
APS Army Postal Service
apt apartment
aq aqueous, water (Lat. *aqua*)
AQ Achievement Quotient
ar argent, aromatic, arrival, arrive, in the year of the reign (Lat. *anno regni*)
Ar argon, silver (Lat. *argentum*)
Ar, Arab Arabia, Arabian, Arabic
AR Arkansas
Aram Aramaic
ARC American Red Cross, AIDS-related complex
arch archaic, archaism, archery, archipelago, architect
Arch, Archbp archbishop
archaeol archaeology
Archd archdeacon, archduke
archeol archeology

archit architecture
archt architect
arg argent, silver (Lat. *argentum*)
Arg Argentina, Argyll
arith arithmetic, arithmetical
Ariz Arizona
Ark Arkansas
Arm Armenia, Armenian
ArM Master of Architecture (Lat. *Architecturae Magister*)
ARM adjustable-rate mortgage
arr arrange, arranged, arrangements, arrival, arrive, arrived
art article, artificial, artist
ARV American Revised (Standard) Version (of the Bible)
as, asym asymmetric
As arsenic
AS Anglo-Saxon, antisubmarine
ASA American Standards Association
asb asbestos
ASCAP American Society of Composers, Authors and Publishers
ASCII American Standard Code for Information Interchange
ASE American Stock Exchange
ASEAN Association of South-East Asian Nations
asgd assigned
ASPCA American Society for the Prevention of Cruelty to Animals
assd assigned
assn association
assoc associate, association
asst assistant
Assyr Assyria, Assyrian
astr, astron astronomer, astronomical, astronomy
astrol astrologer, astrological, astrology
ASVAB Armed Services Vocational Apptitude Battery
at atmosphere, atomic
At astatine
AT antitank
ATC Air Transport Command
athl athlete, athletic, athletics
Atl Atlantic
atm atmosphere, atmospheric
at no atomic number
ATS Army Transport Service, Auxiliary Territorial Service
att, attn, atten attention
att, atty attorney
Atty Gen attorney general
ATV all-terrain vehicle
at wt atomic weight
au angstrom unit
Au gold (Lat. *aurum*)
AUC from (the year of) the building of the city (of

Rome) (Lat. *ab urbe condita*)
aud audible, audit, auditor
Aug August, Augustan, Augustus
Aus, Aust Austria
Aus, Austl Australia
AUS Army of the United States
auth authentic, author, authority, authorized
Auth Ver Authorized Version (of the Bible)
auto automatic, automotive
aux, auxil auxiliary
av according to value (Lat. *ad valorem*)
av, avdp avoirdupois
av, avg average
Av avenue
AV Authorized Version (of the Bible)
avc automatic volume control
Ave avenue
avg average
avn aviation
avoir avoirdupois
A/W actual weight, all water
AWL absent with leave
AWOL absent without leave
AWVS American Women's Volunteer Services
ax axiom, axis
az azimuth, azure
AZ Arizona

B

b bachelor, balboa (coin), base, base hit, baseman, bass, basso, bat, battery, bay, bench, bicuspid, bolívar (coin), boliviano (coin), book, born, brass, breadth, brother
B bacillus, Bible, bishop (chess), boron, British, brotherhood
B/- bag, bale
Ba barium
BA Bachelor of Arts (Lat. *Baccalaureus Artium*), British Academy
bach bachelor
bact, bacteriol bacteriological, bacteriologist, bacteriology
BAE Bachelor of Aeronautical Engineering, Bachelor of Arts in Education
BAg, BAgr Bachelor of Agriculture
BAgSci Bachelor of Agricultural Science
bal balance, balancing
Balt Baltic
Bap, Bapt Baptist
bapt baptized
bar barometer, barometric, barrel, barrister
BAR Browning automatic rifle
BAr, BArch Bachelor of Architecture

barit baritone
Bart baronet
BAS, BASc Bachelor of Agricultural Science, Bachelor of Applied Science
BASIC Beginner's All-purpose Symbolic Instruction Code
bat, batt battalion, battery
bb base(s) on balls
BBA, BBusAd Bachelor of Business Administration
BBB Better Business Bureau
BBC British Broadcasting Corporation
bbl barrel
BC Bachelor of Chemistry, Bachelor of Commerce, before Christ, British Columbia
BCD binary coded decimal
BCE Bachelor of Chemical Engineering, Bachelor of Civil Engineering, before Christian era
bch bunch
BCL Bachelor of Civil Law
BCP Book of Common Prayer
BCS Bachelor of Chemical Science
bd board, bond, bound, bundle
BD Bachelor of Divinity
B/D bank draft, bills discounted, brought down
bd ft board foot
bdg binding
bdl, bdle bundle
bds bundles, (bound in) boards
BDS Bachelor of Dental Surgery
Be beryllium
BE Bachelor of Education, Bachelor of Engineering, Bank of England, Board of Education
B/E bills of exchange
BEE Bachelor of Electrical Engineering
bef before
BEF British Expeditionary Force(s)
Bel, Belg Belgian, Belgium
Beng Bengal, Bengali
B ès L Bachelor of Letters (Fr. *Bachelier ès Lettres*)
B ès S Bachelor of Sciences (Fr. *Bachelier ès Sciences*)
bet, betw between
bev billion electron volts
bf bold face
BF Bachelor of Finance, Bachelor of Forestry
B/F brought forward
BFA Bachelor of Fine Arts
bg bag
BG brigadier general
BHE Bureau of Higher Education
bhp brake horsepower
Bi bismuth

Bib Bible, Biblical
bibl biblical, bibliographical
bibliog bibliography
bicarb bicarbonate of soda
b i d twice a day (Lat. *bis in die*)
biochem biochemistry
biog biographer, biographical, biography
biol biological, biologist, biology
BIOS basic input-output system
BIS British Information Services
BJ Bachelor of Journalism
bk bank, block, book
Bk berkelium
bkg banking
bkkpg bookkeeping
bklr black letter
bkpt bankrupt
bks barracks, books
bkt basket, bracket
bl bale, barrel, black, blue
BL, BLL Bachelor of Laws
B/L bill of lading
BLA Bachelor of Liberal Arts
bld bold face
bldg, blg building
BLE Brotherhood of Locomotive Engineers
B Lit, B Litt Bachelor of Letters, Bachelor of Literature (Lat. *Baccallaureus Litterarum*)
blk black, block
bln balloon
bls bales, barrels
BLS Bachelor of Library Science, Bachelor of Library Service, Bureau of Labor Statistics
blvd boulevard
bm board measure
BM Bachelor of Medicine (Lat. *Baccalaureus Medicinae*), Bachelor of Music (Lat. *Baccalaureus Musicae*), Bureau of Mines
BME Bachelor of Mechanical Engineering, Bachelor of Mining Engineering
BMechE Bachelor of Mechanical Engineering
BMEWS Ballistic Missile Early Warning System
BMR basal metabolic rate
BMus Bachelor of Music
Bn battalion
BN bank note
BNA Basel Anatomical Nomenclature (Lat. *Basle Nomina Anatomica*), British North America Act
bo back order, body odor, box office, branch office, broker's order, buyer's option
BO Board of Ordnance
B/O brought over
Boh Bohemia, Bohemian

Bol Bolivia, Bolivian
bor borough
bot botanical, botanist, botany, bottle
BOT Board of Trade
bp below proof, birthplace, bishop, blood pressure, boiling point
BP Bachelor of Pharmacy
BP, BPh, BPhil Bachelor of Philosophy (Lat. *Baccalaureus Philosophiae*)
B/P bill of parcels, bills payable
BPd, BPe Bachelor of Pedagogy
BPE Bachelor of Physical Education
BPH Bachelor of Public Health
BPI Bureau of Public Inquiries
BPOE Benevolent and Protective Order of Elks
br branch, brand, bridge, brief, brig, bronze, brother
Br Breton, Britain, British, bromine
BR Bill of Rights
B/R bills receivable
Braz Brazil, Brazilian
Brazil Brazilian
BRCS British Red Cross Society
B Rec bills receivable
brev brevet, brevetted
Br Hond British Honduras
Brig brigade, brigadier
Brig Gen brigadier general
Brit Britain, Britannia, Britannica, British
bro brother
bros brothers
bs balance sheet
BS Bachelor of Surgery
B/S bags, bales, bill of sale
BS, BSc Bachelor of Science (Lat. *Baccalaureus Scientiae*)
BSA Bachelor of Scientific Agriculture, Bibliographical Society of America, Boy Scouts of America
BSEd Bachelor of Science in Education
bsh bushel
BSS, BSSc, BS in SS Bachelor of (Science in) Social Sciences
Bt baronet
BT, BTh Bachelor of Theology
BTU, Bthu, btu British thermal unit
Btry battery
bu bureau, bushel, bushels
buck buckram
bul, bull bulletin
Bulg Bulgaria, Bulgarian
BV Blessed Virgin (Lat. *Beata Virgo*), farewell (Lat. *bene vale*)

BVM Blessed Virgin Mary (Lat. *Beata Virgo Maria*)
bvt brevet, brevetted
bx box
Bz benzine

C

c about (Lat. *circa*), candle, capacity (electrical), carton, case, catcher (baseball), cathode, Celsius, cent, centigrade, centime, centimeter, chapter, chief, child, cost, cubic
C calends, capacity (electrical), cape, carbon, cathode, Catholic, Celtic, century, Chancellor, chapter, church, Congress, Conservative, constant, copyright, Court, current, Roman numeral for 100
ca about (Lat. *circa*), cathode, centiare, chief accountant, claim agent, commercial agent, consular agent, controller of accounts
Ca calcium
CA California, Catholic Action, Central America, chronological age, Coast Artillery, Confederate Army
C/A commercial account, credit account, current account
CAA Civil Aeronautics Administration
CAB Civil Aeronautics Board
CAD computer-aided design, computer-aided drafting
CAF cost and freight; cost, assurance, and freight
CAI computer-aided instruction
cal calendar, calends, caliber, calomel, small calorie
Cal caliber, large calorie
Cal, Calif California
Cam camouflage
CAM computer-aided manufacturing
can canon, canto
Can Canada, Canadian
Canad Canadian
canc cancel, cancellation, cancelled
cant canton, cantonment
Cant Canterbury, Canticles, Cantonese
Cantab Cambridge (Lat. *Cantabrigia*)
cap capital, capitalize, chapter (Lat. *caput*)
CAP Civil Air Patrol
caps capital letters
Capt Captain
car carat
CAR Civil Air Regulations
Card Cardinal
CARE Cooperative for American Remittances Everywhere

cat catalog, catechism
CAT computerized axial tomography
cath cathedral
Cath Catholic
CATV community antenna television
cav cavalier, cavalry
CAVU ceiling and visibility unlimited
cb center of buoyancy, confined to barracks
Cb columbium, cumulonimbus
CB citizens band (radio), Construction Battalion, Bachelor of Surgery (Lat. *Baccalaureus Chiurgiae*)
CBC Canadian Broadcasting Corporation
CBD cash before delivery
CBOE Chicago Board Options Exchange
CBOT Chicago Board of Trade
CBS Columbia Broadcasting System
cc carbon copy, cash credit, cashier's check, chapters, chief clerk, circuit court, city council, city councilor, civil court, common councilman, company clerk, company commander, consular clerk, contra credit, copy, county clerk, county commissioner, county council, county court, cubic centimeter, current account (Fr. *compte courant*)
Cc cirrocumulus
CC cyanogen chloride (poison gas)
CCA Chief Clerk of the Admiralty, circuit court of appeals
CCC Civilian Conservation Corps; Commodity Credit Corporation
CCF Cooperative Commonwealth Federation (of Canada)
CCS Combined Chiefs of Staff
cd candela, cash discount, cord
Cd cadmium
CD certificate of deposit, civil defense, compact disc
C/D carried down
cd ft cord foot (feet)
CDR, Cdr commander
CDT central daylight time
Ce cerium
CE chemical engineer, chief engineer, Church of England, civil engineer, Council of Europe, Corps of Engineers
CEA Council of Economic Advisers
CEEB College Entrance Examination Board
Celt Celtic

cen, cent central, century

cent centered, centigrade, centimeter, one hundred (Lat. *centum*)

CERN European Council for Nuclear Research (Fr. *Centre Européen des Recherches Nucléaires*)

cert certificate, certify

certif certificate, certificated

cet par other things being equal (Lat. *ceteris paribus*)

Cey Ceylon

cf center field, center fielder, compare (Lat. *confer*)

Cf californium

CF cost and freight

C/F carried forward

CFI cost, freight, and insurance

cfm cubic feet per minute

CFR Code of Federal Regulations

cfs cubic feet per second

cg center of gravity, consul general

cg, cgm centigram

CG Coast Guard, commanding general

CGH Cape of Good Hope

cgs centimeter-gram-second

ch chain, champion, chargé d'affaires, check (chess), chestnut, chevronets, chief, child, children, chirurgeon, church, clearinghouse, courthouse, customhouse, of surgery (Lat. *chiurgiae*)

c-h, c-hr candle-hour

ch chaplain, chapter

Ch Chaldean, Chaldee, China, Chinese

CH Companion of Honor

Chanc chancelor, chancery

chap chaplain, chapter

char character, charter

ChB Bachelor of Surgery (Lat. *Chiurgiae Baccalaureus*)

ChE, CheE chemical engineer

chem chemical, chemist, chemistry

chg charge

chgd charged

Chin Chinese

ChJ chief justice

ChM Master of Surgery (Lat. *Chiurgiae Magister*)

chm checkmate

chm, chmn chairman

Chr Christ, Christian

chron, chronol chronological, chronology

Chron Chronicles

chs chapters

Ci cirrus

Cia company (Sp. *Compania*)

CIA Central Intelligence Agency

CIC Counter-Intelligence Corps

CID Criminal Investigation Division (Brit.)

Cie company (Fr. *compagnie*)

CIF cost, insurance, and freight

C in C, CINC, Cinc commander in chief

CIP cataloging in publication

CIO Congress of Industrial Organizations

cir, circ about (Lat. *circa, circiter, circum*), circular, circulation, circumference

cit citation, cited, citizen

civ civil, civilian

CJ body of law (Lat. *corpus juris*), chief judge, chief justice

ck cask, check, cook

cl carload, carload lots, center line, centiliter, civil law, claim, class, classification, clause, clearance, clergyman, clerk, cloth, craft loss (insurance)

Cl chlorine

clar clarinet

class classic, classical, classification, classified, classify

cler clerical

climatol climatological, climatology

clin clinic, clinical

clk clerk, clock

clm column

CLU chartered life underwriter

cm church missionary, circular mil, common meter, corresponding member

cm centimeter

Cm curium

CM court martial, Master of Surgery (Lat. *Chiurgiae Magister*)

Cmdr commander

CMG Companion (of the Order) of St. Michael and St. George

cml commercial

CMTC Citizens' Military Training Camp

Cn cumulonimbus

C/N circular note, credit note

CNN Cable News Network

CNO chief of naval operations

CNS central nervous system

c/o care of, carried over, cash order

Co cobalt, company, county

CO Colorado, commanding officer, conscientious objector

coad coadjutor

COBOL common business-oriented language

Cod codex

COD cash on delivery, collect on delivery

Codd codices

coef coefficient

C of C chamber of commerce

C of S chief of staff

cog, cogn cognate

col collected, collector, college, colonial, colony, color, colored, column

Col Colombia, colonel, Colorado, Colossians, Columbia

coll colleague, collect, collection, collective, collector, college, colloquial

collab collaborated, collaboration, collaborator

collat collateral

colloq colloquial, colloquialism, colloquially

Colo, Col Colorado

colog cologarithm

Coloss Colossians

com comedy, comic, comma, commentary, commerce, common, commonly, commune, communication, community

Com commission, commissioner, committee, commodore, communist

Com, Comdr commander, commodore

Com, Como commodore

comb combination

comdg commanding

Comdt Commandant

Com in Ch, Cominch Commander in Chief

coml commercial

comm commander, commentary, commerce, commercial, commissary, commission, committee, commonwealth, commutator

Como Commodore

comp companion, compare, compilation, compiled, complete, composition, compositor, compound, comprising

compar comparative

compt compartment, comptometer

Comr Commissioner

Com Ver Common Version (of the Bible)

con against (Lat. *contra*), concerto, conclusion, condense, conduct, connection, consols, consolidate, continued, wife (Lat. *conjunx*)

Con Conformist, Consul

conc concentrate, concentrated, concentration, concerning

Confed Confederate, Confederation

cong gallon (Lat. *congius*)

Cong Congregational, Congress, Congressional

conj conjugation, conjunction, conjunctive

Conn Connecticut

cons consecrated, conserve, consigned, consignment, consolidated, consonant, constable, constitution,

constitutional, construction, consul, consulting

consol consolidated

const constable, constant, constitution

constr construction, construed

cont containing, contents, continent, continue, contract, contraction, contrary, control

Cont Continental

contd continued

contemp contemporary

contg containing

contin continued, let it be continued (Lat. *continuetur*)

contr contract, contralto, control

contrib contribution, contributor

CONUS Continental United States

coop, co-op cooperative

cop copper, copyright, copyrighted

Cop Copernican, Coptic

cor corner, cornet, coroner, corpus, correct, corrected, correction, correlative, correspondence, correspondent, corresponding, corrupt

Cor Corinthians

corol, coroll corollary

corp, corpn corporation

Corp Corporal

corr correct, corrected, correspond, correspondence, correspondent, corresponding, corrupt, corrupted, corruption

correl correlative

corresp correspondence

cos companies, cosine, counties

COS cash on shipment

cosec cosecant

cosh hyperbolic cosine

cot cotangent

coth hyperbolic cotangent

covers coversed sine

cp candlepower, chemically pure, compare, court of probate

CP Canadian Press, Cape Province, center of pressure, Chief Patriarch, command post, Common Prayer, Communist Party

CPA certified public accountant

cpd compound

CPH Certificate in Public Health

Cpl corporal

cpm characters per minute, cost per million, cycles per minute

CPO chief petty officer

CPR cardiopulmonary resuscitation

cps characters per second, cycles per second

cpt counterpoint

CQ charge of quarters

cr created, credit, creditor, crescendo, creek, crown

Cr chromium

CR carriage return, Costa Rica

craniol craniological, craniology

craniom craniometry

cres, cresc crescendo

crim con criminal conversation

crit critic, critical, criticism

CRLF carriage return and line feed

crs credits, creditors

CRT cathode-ray tube

cryst crystalline, crystallography, crystals

cs capital stock, civil service

Cs cesium, cirrostratus

CS Christian Science, Christian Scientist, Confederate States

C/S case

CSA Confederate States of America

csc cosecant

CSC Civil Service Commission, Conspicuous Service Cross

csch hyperbolic cosecant

CSigO chief signal officer

CSIRO Commonwealth Scientific and Industrial Research Organization (Australia)

CSO chief staff officer

CSS Commodity Stabilization Service

CST central standard time

ct cent, certificate, county, court

Ct Connecticut, Count

CT central time, communications technician, computed tomography, Connecticut

CTC Citizens' Training Camp

ctg cartridge

ctn carton, cotangent

ctnh hyperbolic cotangent

ctr center

cts centimes, cents, certificates

cu cubic

Cu copper (Lat. *cuprum*), cumulus

cu cm cubic centimeter

cu ft cubic foot

cu in cubic inch

cur currency, current

cu yd cubic yard

cv, cvt convertible

CV Common Version (of the Bible)

cw continuous wave

CWO cash with order, chief warrant officer, commissioned warrant officer

CWS Chemical Warfare Service

cwt hundredweight (Lat. *centum* weight)

cy capacity, currency, cycles

cyc cyclopedia, cyclopedic

cyl cylinder

CYO Catholic Youth Organization

CZ Canal Zone

D

d date, daughter, day, dead, decree, degree, delete, democrat, democratic, deputy, diameter, died, director, dividend, dollar, door, dose, dyne, give (Lat. *da*), penny, pence (Lat. *denarius, denarii*)

D December, department, deuterium, Dutch, God (Lat. *Deus*), Lord (Lat. *Dominus*), Roman numeral for 500

da daughter, day

DA delayed action, dental apprentice, district attorney

DAB Dictionary of American Biography

DAE Dictionary of American English

DAH Dictionary of American History

Dak Dakota

Dan Daniel, Danish

Danl Daniel

DAR Daughters of the American Revolution

DARE Dictionary of American Regional English

dat dative

DAT Dental Apptitude Test

dau daughter

Dav David

DAV Disabled American Veterans

db daybook

db,dB decibel, decibels

DB Domesday Book

dba doing business as

DBE Dame (Commander of the Order) of the British Empire

dbh diameter at breast height (forestry)

DBib Douai Bible

dbl double

DC Dental Corps, direct current, Disarmament Commission, District of Columbia, Doctor of Chiropractic, from the beginning (Ital. *da capo*)

DCL Doctor of Canon Law, Doctor of Civil Law

DCM Distinguished Conduct Medal (Brit.)

DCS deputy clerk of sessions, Doctor of Christian Science, Doctor of Commercial Science

dd days after date, days' date, delivered, demand draft

DD Department of Defense, developmentally disabled, Doctor of Divinity (Lat. *Divinitatis Doctor*)

DDS Doctor of Dental Science, Doctor of Dental Surgery

DDSc Doctor of Dental Science

DE Delaware, destroyer escort, Doctor of Engineering, Doctor of Entomology

deb, deben debenture

Deb Deborah

dec deceased, declaration, declension, declination, decrease, decrescendo

dec, decim decimeter

Dec December

decd deceased

decl declension

decoct decoction

decresc decrescendo

ded, dedic dedication

def defective, defendant, defense, deferred, defined, definite, definition

deg degree

del delegate, delete, deliver, he or she drew it (Lat. *delineavit*)

Del Delaware

deliq deliquescent

Dem Democrat, Democratic

demon demonstrative

Den Denmark

denom denomination

dent dental, dentist, dentistry

dep departs, departure, deposed, deposit, depot

dep, dept department, deponent, deputy

Dep dependency

der, deriv derivation, derivative, derive, derived

dermatol dermatological, dermatologist, dermatology

desc descendant

descr descriptive, description

D ès L Doctor of Letters (Fr. *Docteur ès Lettres*)

D ès S Doctor of Sciences (Fr. *Docteur ès Sciences*)

det detach, detachment, detail

Deu, Deut Deuteronomy

devel development

DF dean of the faculty, defender of the faith (Lat. *Defensor Fidei*), direction finding, Federal District (Port. *Districto Federal;* Sp. *Distrito Federal*)

DFC Distinguished Flying Cross

dg decigram

DG by the grace of God (Lat. *Dei gratia*)

dh deadhead, designated hitter (baseball), that is to say (Ger. *das heisst*)

DHQ division headquarters

di, dia diameter

Di didymium

diag, diagr diagram

dial dialect, dialectic, dialectical

diam diameter

dict dictation, dictator, dictionary

diet dietetics

diff difference, different, differential

dil dilute

dim dimension

dim, dimin diminuendo, diminutive

din dinar

dioc diocesan, diocese

dipl diplomat, diplomatic

dir director

dis distance, distant

disc discount, discover, discovered

disch discharged

diss dissertations

dist discount, distance, distant, distinguish, distinguished, district

Dist Atty district attorney

distr distribute, distributed, distribution, distributive, distributor

div divergence, diversion, divide, divided, dividend, divine, division, divisor, divorced

Div divinity

dk deck, dock

DK disbursing clerk

dkg dekagram

dkl dekaliter

dkm dekameter

dks dekastere

dl deciliter

D/L demand loan

D Lit, D Litt Doctor of Letters, Doctor of Literature (Lat. *Doctor Litterarum*)

dlr dealer

DLS Doctor of Library Science

dm decameter, decimeter

Dm Deutschmark

DM deputy master, draftsman

DMB defense mobilization board

DMD Doctor of Dental Medicine (Lat. *Dentariae Medicinae Doctor*)

D Mus Doctor of Music

DN our Lord (Lat. *Dominus noster*)

DNA deoxyribonucleic acid

DNB Dictionary of National Biography (Brit.)

do ditto

DO Doctor of Osteopathy

DOA dead on arrival

doc document

DOD Department of Defence

DOE Department of Education, Department of Energy

dol dolce, dollar

dols dollars

dom domestic, dominion

Dom Dominica, Dominican
Dor Dorian, Doric
DOS disk operating system
DOT Department of Transportation
dow dowager
doz dozen
DP data processing, degree of polymerization, diametrical pitch, displaced person
DPH Doctor of Public Health
DPHy Doctor of Public Hygiene
DPh, DPhil Doctor of Philosophy
dpt department, deponent
DPW Department of Public Works
dr debtor, dram
Dr doctor, drive
DR dead reckoning, deposit receipt
dram pers dramatis personae
ds daylight saving, days after sight, decistere, document signed, (repeat) from this sign (It. *dal segno*)
Ds dysprosium
DS, DSc Doctor of Science
DSC Distinguished Service Cross
DSIR Department of Scientific and Industrial Research
DSM Distinguished Service Medal
DSO Distinguished Service Order (Brit.), district staff officer
dsp died without issue (Lat. *decessit sine prole*)
DSRD Department of Scientific Research and Development
DST daylight saving time, Doctor of Sacred Theology
dt delerium tremens, double time
DT dental technician
DT, DTh, DTheol Doctor of Theology
dts delerium tremens
Du duke, Dutch
dup, dupl duplicate
Dv, DV God willing (Lat. *Deo volente*)
DV Douai Version (of the Bible)
DVM Doctor of Veterinary Medicine
DVMS Doctor of Veterinary Medicine and Surgery
D/W dock warrant
DWI driving while intoxicated, Dutch West Indies
DWS Department of Water Supply
dwt dead weight tons, pennyweight (Lat. *denarius* weight)
DX distance, distant
Dy dysprosium
dyn, dynam dynamics
dz dozen

E

e east, eastern, erg, error
E earl, Earth, east, eastern, English
ea each
e and o e errors and omissions excepted
Eb erbium
EBCDIC Extended Binary Coded Decimal Interchange Code
EbN east by north
EbS east by south
EC Engineering Corps, Established Church, European Community
ECA Economic Cooperation Administration
ECAFE Economic Commission for Asia and the Far East
eccl, eccles ecclesiastical
Ecc, Eccl, Eccles Ecclesiastes
Ecclus Ecclesiasticus
ECE Economic Commission for Europe
ECG electrocardiogram
ECLA Economic Commission for Latin America
ECME Economic Commission for the Middle East
ecol ecological, ecology
econ economic, economics, economy
ECOSOC Economic and Social Council (of the United Nations)
ECSC European Coal and Steel Community
Ecua Ecuador, Ecuadorian
ed edited, edition, editor
EdB Bachelor of Education
EdD Doctor of Education
edit edited, edition, editor
EdM Master of Education
EDT eastern daylight time
educ education, educational
ee errors excepted
EE Early English, electrical engineer, electrical engineering, envoy extraordinary
EEC European Economic Community
EE&MP envoy extraordinary and minister plenipotentiary
EEG electroencephalogram
EEOC Equal Employment Opportunity Commission
EER energy efficiency rating
eff efficiency
efflor efflorescent
EFTA European Free Trade Association
EFTS electronic funds transfer system
eg for example (Lat. *exempli gratia*)
Eg Egypt, Egyptian
Egyptol Egyptology
EHF extremely high frequency

EHFA electric home and farm authority
EHV extra high voltage
EI, EInd East Indian, East Indies
EKG electrocardiogram
el elevated, elevation
ELD electroluminescent display
elec, elect electric, electrical, electrician
elem elementary, elements
elev elevation
ellipt elliptical
e long east longitude
elong elongation
Em, eman emanation (chemistry)
EM electrician's mate, engineer of mines, enlisted man
emb, embryol embryology
emf electromotive force
EMH educable mentally handicapped
Emp emperor, empire, empress
emph emphasis, emphatic
EMT emergency medical technician
emu electromagnetic units
emul emulsion
enc, encl enclosed, enclosure
ency, encyc, encycl encyclopedia
ENE east-northeast
eng engine, engineer, engineering, engraved, engraver, engraving
Eng England, English
EngD Doctor of Engineering
engin engineering
engr engineer, engraved, engraver, engraving
enl enlarged, enlisted
Ens ensign
ENT ear, nose, throat (physician)
entom, entomol entomological, entomology
env envelope
eo from office (Lat. *ex officio*)
EOM end of month
ep en passant (chess)
Ep, Epis, Epist Epistle, Epistles
EP extended play
EPA Environmental Protection Agency
Eph, Ephes Ephesians
Epis Episcopal
epil epilogue
EPU European Payments Union
eq equal, equalizer, equation, equator, equivalent
EQ educational quotient
equiv equivalent
er earned run
Er erbium
ER emergency room, King Edward (Lat. *Eduardus*

Rex), Queen Elizabeth (Lat. *Elizabeth Regina*)
ERA earned run average, Educational Research Association, Emergency Relief Administration, Equal Rights Amendment
ERIC Educational Resources Information Center
ERISA Employee Retirement Income Security Act
ERP European Recovery Program
erron erroneous, erroneously
ERV English Revised Version (of the Bible)
Es einsteinium
ESA Economic Stabilization Administration
ESC Economic and Social Council (of the United Nations)
eschat eschatology
Esd Esdras
ESE east-southeast
Esk Eskimo
ESL English as a second language
ESOP employee stock option plan
esp especially
ESP extrasensory perception
espec especially
Esq, Esqr esquire
est estate, estimated, estuary
Est Estonia
EST eastern standard time
estab established
Esth Esther
esu electrostatic unit
ET electronics technician, extraterrestrial
eta estimated time of arrival
et al and others (Lat. *et alii*), and elsewhere (Lat. *et alibi*)
etc and so forth, and others (Lat. *et ceteri, ceterae,* or *cetera*)
eth ether, ethical, ethics
Eth Ethiopia, Ethiopian, Ethiopic
ethnog ethnographical, ethnography
ethnol ethnological, ethnology
ETO European Theater of Operations
et seq and the following, and what follows (Lat. *et sequens, sequentes,* or *sequentia*)
ety, etym, etymol etymological, etymology
Eu europium
euphem euphemism, euphemistic
Eur Europe, European
ev electron volt
EV English Version (of the Bible)
EVA extra-vehicular activity (in space)

evac evacuation

evan, evang evangelical, evangelist

Evang Evangelical

evap evaporation

ex examination, examine, examined, example, except, excepted, exception, exchange, excursion, executed, executive

Ex, Exod Exodus

exam examination, examined, examinee, examinor

exc excellent, except, excepted, exception, excursion

Exc excellency

exch exchange, exchequer

excl exclusive

excl, exclam exclamation

exec executive, executor

Ex-Im Export-Import Bank

ex int without interest

ex lib from the library (of) (Lat. *ex libris*)

ex off from office (Lat. *ex officio*)

exp expenses, expiration, expired, export, exportation, exported, exporter, express

exper experimental

expt experiment

exptl experimental

exr executor

ext extension, external, extinct, extra, extract

Ez, Ezr Ezra

Eze, Ezek Ezekiel

F

f activity coefficent, farad, farthing, fathom, feet, female, feminine, fine, fluid (ounce), folio, following, foot, formed, forte, foul, franc, frequency, from, function (of), let it be made (Lat. *fiat*), strong (Lat. *forte*)

f/ f number (photography)

F Fahrenheit, February, fellow, fluorine, France, French, Friday, son (Lat. *filius*)

fa fire alarm, freight agent

FA field artillery, fine arts, food administration

FAA Federal Aviation Administration

FAAAS Fellow of the American Association for the Advancement of Science

fac facsimile, factor, factory

FACD Fellow of the American College of Dentists

FACP Fellow of the American College of Physicians

FACS Fellow of the American College of Surgeons

FAF financial aid form

Fah, Fahr Fahrenheit

FAIA Fellow of the American Institute of Architects

fam familiar, family

FAM, F&AM Free and Accepted Masons

FAO Food and Agriculture Organization (of the United Nations)

fas free alongside ship

FASA Fellow of the Acoustical Society of America

fasc a bundle (Lat. *fasiculus*)

fath fathom

fb freight bill, fullback

FBA Fellow of the British Academy

FBI Federal Bureau of Investigation

fbm feet board measure (board feet)

fc follow copy (printing)

Fc fractocumulus

FCA Farm Credit Administration

FCC Federal Communications Commission, Federal Council of Churches, first class certificate, Food Control Committee

FCDA Federal Civil Defense Administration

FCIC Federal Crop Insurance Corporation

fcp foolscap

FD defender of the faith (Lat. *Fidei Defensor*), fire department

FDA Food and Drug Administration, Food Distribution Administration

FDIC Federal Deposit Insurance Corporation

Fe iron (Lat. *ferrum*)

Feb, Febr February

FEB Fair Employment Board

fec he or she made it (Lat. *fecit*)

fed federal, federated, federation

fem female, feminine

FEPC Fair Employment Practices Commission

FERA Federal Emergency Relief Administration

feud feudal, feudalism

ff fixed focus, folios, following, fortissimo

ffa free foreign agent, free from alongside

FFA Future Farmers of America

FFS family financial statement

FFV First Families of Virginia

fg field goal

FGSA Fellow of the Geological Society of America

FHA Federal Housing Administration

FHLBB Federal Home Loan Bank Board

fhp friction horsepower

FICA Federal Insurance Contributions Act

fid fidelity, fiduciary

FIFO first in, first out

fig figuratively, figure

FIL Fellow of the Institute of Linguists

FILO first in, last out

fin finance, financial, finished

Fin Finland, Finnish

FIPS federal information processing standards

fl floor, florin, flower, fluid, flute

Fl Flanders, Flemish, fluorine

FL, Fla Florida

FLB Federal Land Bank

fl dr fluid dram

Flem Flemish

flex flexible

fl oz fluid ounce

fm fathom, from

Fm fermium

FM field manual, field marshal, frequency modulation

FMCS Federal Mediation and Conciliation Service

FmHA Farmers Home Administration

FNMA Federal National Mortgage Association ("Fannie Mae")

FO field officer, Foreign Office

fob free on board

FOE Fraternal Order of Eagles

fol folio, following

foll following

FOP Fraternal Order of Police

for foreign, forestry, free on rails

fort fortification, fortified

FORTRAN formula translator

fp fireplug, fire policy, floating policy, foolscap, footpound, forte piano (Ital.), forward pass, freezing point, fully paid

FPC Federal Power Commission

FPHA Federal Public Housing Administration

fpm feet per minute

FPO fleet post office

fps feet per second, footpound-second (system)

fr fragment, franc, from, right-hand page (Lat. *folio recto*)

Fr brother (Lat. *Frater*), father, France, francium, French, Friday, wife (Ger. *Frau*)

FRB Federal Reserve Bank, Federal Reserve Board

FRC Federal Radio Commission, Federal Relief Commission

FRCP Fellow of the Royal College of Physicians

FRCS Fellow of the Royal College of Surgeons

freq frequency, frequently, frequentitive

FRGS Fellow of the Royal Geographical Society

Fr Gui French Guiana

Fri Friday

Frl Miss (Ger. *Fräulein*)

FRS Federal Reserve System, Fellow of the Royal Society

FRSA Fellow of the Royal Society of Arts

frt freight

fs foot-second

Fs fractostratus

FS field service, fleet surgeon

FSA Farm Security Administration, Federal Security Agency

FSCC Federal Surplus Commodities Corporation

FSH follicle-stimulating hormone

FSLIC Federal Saving and Loan Insurance Corporation

FSP Food Stamp Program

FSR Field Service Regulations

ft feet, foot, fort, fortification, fortified

FT fire control technician

ft-c foot-candle

FTC Federal Trade Commission

FTE full-time equivalent

fth, fthm fathom

ft-l foot-lambert

ft-lb foot-pound

fur furlong

furl furlough

furn furnished, furniture

fut future

fv on the back of the page (Lat. *folio verso*)

FWA Federal Works Agency

fwd forward, front wheel drive

fwy freeway

FY fiscal year

FYI for your information

FZS Fellow of the Zoological Society

G

g conductance, gauge, gender, general, general intelligence, genitive, goal, goalie, goalkeeper, gold, gourde, grain, gram, grand, (specific) gravity, guide, guilder, guinea, gulf

G German, Germany, gram, (specific) gravity, gun

ga general average

Ga gallium, Georgia

GA Gamblers Anonymous, general agent, General Assembly, Georgia

Gael Gaelic

gal, gall gallon

Gal Galatians, Galen

galv galvanic, galvanism, galvanized

GAO General Accounting Office

GAR Grand Army of the Republic

GATT General Agreement on Tariffs and Trade

GAW guaranteed annual wage

gaz gazette, gazetteer

GB Great Britain

GBE (Knight or Dame) Grand (Cross) of the (Order of the) British Empire

GCA ground control approach (radar)

g-cal gram calorie

GCB (Knight) Grand Cross of the (Order of the) Bath

gcd greatest common divisor

gcf greatest common factor

GCI ground controlled interception (aircraft)

GCLH Grand Cross of the Legion of Honor

gcm greatest common measure

GCM general court martial

GCT Greenwich civil time

GCVO (Knight) Grand Cross of the (Royal) Victorian Order

Gd gadolinium

GD grand duchess, grand duchy, grand duke

gds goods

Ge germanium

geb born (Ger. *geboren*)

GED general equivalency diploma

gen gender, genera, general, generally, generator, generic, genitive, genus

Gen general, Genesis, Geneva, Genevan

geneal genealogical, genealogy

genit genitive

genl general

gent gentleman, gentlemen

geod geodesy, geodetic

geog geographer, geographic, geographical, geography

geol geologic, geological, geologist, geology

geom geometer, geometric, geometrical, geometry

ger gerund

Ger, Germ German, Germany

gest died (Ger. *gestorben*)

GFTU General Federation of Trade Unions

ggr great gross

GHA Greenwich hour angle

GHQ general headquarters

gi gastrointestinal, gill

GI general issue, government issue

Gib Gibralter

Gk Greek

gl glass, gloss

gld guilder

gloss glossary

gm gram

GM general manager, grand master, gunner's mate

Gmat Greenwich mean astronomical time

GmbH limited company (Ger. *Gesell-schaft mit beschränkter Haftung*)

Gmc Germanic

GMT Greenwich mean time

GNMA Government National Mortgage Association ("Ginnie Mae")

GNP gross national product

GO general orders

GOP Grand Old Party (Republican Party)

Goth gothic, Gothic

gov, govt government

Gov governor

GP general practitioner, Graduate in Pharmacy, general paresis

GPA grade point average

gpm gallons per minute

GPO General Post Office, Government Printing Office

gps gallons per second

GQ general quarters

gr grade, grain, gram, grammar, great, gross, group

Gr Grecian, Greece, Greek

GR King George (Lat. *Georgius Rex*)

grad graduate, graduated

gram grammar, grammarian, grammatical

GrBr, GrBrit Great Britain

GRE graduate record examination

gro gross

gr wt gross weight

GS general secretary, general staff, German silver, Girl Scouts

GSA General Services Administration, Girst Scouts of America

GSC General Staff Corps

GSO general staff officer

gt gilt, great

gtc good till canceled

gtd guaranteed

gtt a drop (Lat. *gutta*)

gu genitourinary

guar guaranteed

Guat Guatemala, Guatemalan

Guin Guinea

gun gunnery

guttat by drops (Lat. *guttatim*)

gv gravimetric volume

gym gymnasium, gymnastics

gyn, gynecol gynecological, gynecology

H

h harbor, hard, hardness, heavy sea, height, hence, high, hit, horns (music), hour, hundred, husband

h, hy henry (electricity)

H hydrogen, intensity of magnetic field

ha hectare, this year (Lat. *hoc anno*)

Hab Habakkuk

hab corp have the body (Lat. *habeas corpus*)

Hag Haggai

Hal halogen

hb halfback

Hb hemoglobin

HBM his or her Britannic majesty

HC House of Commons

hcap, hcp handicap

hcf highest common factor

HCL high cost of living

hd hand, head

hdbk handbook

hdkf handkerchief

hdqrs headquarters

He helium

HE high explosive, his eminence, his or her excellency

Heb, Hebr Hebrew

her heraldic, heraldry

herp, herpetol herpetology

HEW (Department of) Health, Education, and Welfare

hex hexachord, hexagon, hexagonal

hf half

Hf hafnium

HF high frequency

hfbd half-bound (bookbinding)

hfmor half-morocco (bookbinding)

hg hectogram, heliogram

Hg mercury (Lat. *hydrargyrum*)

HG High German, his or her grace, Home Guard

hgt height

HH his or her highness, his holiness

hhd hogshead

HHFA Housing and Home Finance Agency

HHS (Department of) Health and Human Services

HI Hawaii

HIH his or her imperial highenss

HIM his or her imperial majesty

Hind Hindi, Hindu, Hindustan, Hindustani

hist histology, historian, historical, history

HJ here lies (Lat. *hic jacet*)

HJS here lies buried (Lat. *hic jacet sepultus*)

hkf handkerchief

hl hectoliter

HL House of Lords, mustard-lewisite (poison gas)

HLBB Home Loan Bank Board

hm hectometer, in this month (Lat. *hoc menses*)

HM his or her majesty

HMO health maintenance organization

HMS his or her majesty's service (or ship or steamer)

HN nitrogen mustard gas

ho house

Ho holmium

HO head office, Home Office

HOLC Home Owners' Loan Corporation

hon honorably, honorary

Hon honorable

Hond Honduras

hor horizon, horizontal

horol horology

hort, hortic horticultural, horticulture

Hos Hosea

hosp hospital

hp high pressure, horsepower

HP high power

hp-hr horsepower-hour

hq look for this (Lat. *hoc quaere*)

HQ headquarters

hr home run, hour

HR mister (Ger. *Herr*)

HR home rule, House of Representatives

HRE Holy Roman Empire

HRH his or her royal highness

HRIP here rest in peace (Lat. *hic requiescat in pace*)

hrs hours

HS here is buried (Lat. *hic sepultus*), here lies (Lat. *hic situ*), high school, Home Secretary (Brit.), in this sense (Lat. *hoc sensu*)

HSH his or her serene highness

HSM his or her serene majesty

ht at this time (Lat. *hoc tempore*), heat, height, in or under this title (Lat. *hoc titulo*)

Hts heights

HUD (Department of) Housing and Urban Development

Hun, Hung Hungarian, Hungary

HV high voltage

HVAC heating, ventilation, and air conditioning

hw high water

hwm high water mark

hwy highway

hyd, hydros hydrostatics

hydraul hydraulic, hydraulics

hyg hygiene, hygroscopic

hyp, hypoth hypotenuse, hypothesis, hypothetical

I

i incisor, interest, intransitive, island

I iodine, island or islands, isle or isles, Roman numeral for 1

Ia, IA Iowa

IADB Inter-American Defense Board

IAEA International Atomic Energy Agency (of the United Nations)

ib, ibid in the same place (Lat. *ibidem*)

IBEW International Brotherhood of Electrical Workers

IBRD International Bank for Reconstruction and Development

IBT International Brotherhood of Teamsters (Chauffeurs, Warehousemen, and Helpers of America)

ICA International Cooperation Administration

ICAO International Civil Aviation Organization (of the United Nations)

ICBM intercontinental ballistic missile

ICC Indian Claims Commission, Interstate Commerce Commission

Ice, Icel Iceland, Icelandic

ICES International Council for the Exploration of the Sea

ICFTU International Confederation of Free Trade Unions

icth ichthyology

ICJ International Court of Justice (of the United Nations)

ICNAF International Commission for Northwest Atlantic Fisheries

ICU intensive care unit

icw interrupted continuous wave

id the same (Lat. *idem*)

ID Idaho, identification, infantry division, intelligence department, inside diameter

Ida Idaho

ie that is (Lat. *id est*)

IE Indo-European

IEP individualized education program

if intermediate frequency

IFCTU International Federation of Christian Trade Unions

IFF identification friend or foe (British radar device)

IFO identified flying object

IG amalgamation (Ger. *Interessengemeinschaft*), Indo-Germanic, inspector general

ign ignites, ignition, unknown (Lat. *ignotus*)

ihp indicated horsepower

IHS Jesus. Often taken to mean Jesus Savior of Mankind (Lat. *Iesus hominum salvator*) or in this sign (Lat. *in hoc signo*).

Il illinium

IL Illinois

ILA International Longshoremen's Association

ILGWU International Ladies' Garment Workers' Union

ill, illus, illust illustrate, illustrated, illustration, illustrator

Ill Illinois

illit illiterate

ILO International Labor Organization (of the United Nations)

ILS instrument landing system

IMCO Intergovernmental Maritime Consultative Organization (of the United Nations)

IMF International Monetary Fund (of the United Nations)

imit imitation, imitative

immun immunology

imp imperative, imperfect, imperial, impersonal, import, important, imported, importer, imprimatur, improper

Imp emperor (Lat. *imperator*)

imper imperative

imperf imperfect, imperforate

impers impersonal

impf imperfect

imp gal imperial gallon

impv imperative

in inch

IN Indiana

inbd inboard, inbound

inc inclosure, including, inclusive, income, incorporated, increase

inch, incho inchoative

incl inclosure, including

incog incognito

incorp incorporated

incorr incorrect

incr increased, increasing

ind independence, independent, index, indicated, indicative, indigo, indirect, industrial

Ind India, Indian, Indiana, Indies

IND in the name of God (Lat. *in nomine Dei*)

indecl indeclinable

indef indefinite

inden, indent indention

indic indicating, indicative, indicator

individ individual

induc induction

ined unpublished

in ex at length (Lat. *in extenso*)

in f at the end (Lat. *in fine*)

inf below (Lat. *infra*), inferior, infinitive, information

Inf infantry

infin infinitive

infl influence, influenced

init initial, in the beginning (Lat. *initio*)

inj injection

in-lb inch-pound

in lim at the outset (on the threshold) (Lat. *in limine*)

in loc in its place (Lat. *in loco*)

in loc cit in the place cited (Lat. *in loco citato*)

inorg inorganic

INRI Jesus of Nazareth, King of the Jews (Lat. *Iesus Nazarenus Rex Iudaeorum*)

ins inches, inspector, insular, insulated, insulation, insurance

INS International News Service

insc, inscr inscribe, inscribed, inscription

insep inseparable

insol insoluble

insp inspected, inspector

inst instant, instantaneous, instrument

Inst institute, institution

instr instruction, instructor, instrument

insur insurance

int intelligence, interest, interior, interjection, internal, interval, intransitive

intens insensitive

inter intermediate

interj interjection

internat international

interp interpreted, interpreter

Interpol International Police Organization

interrog interrogative

intr, intrans intransitive

in trans on the way (Lat. *in transitu*)

Int Rev Internal Revenue

introd introduction, introductory

inv invented, invention, inventor, invitation, invoice

invert invertebrate

invt inventory

Io ionium

IOBB Independent Order of B'nai B'rith

IOOF Independent Order of Odd Fellows

IOU I owe you

ip in passing (chess), innings pitched (baseball)

IPA International Phonetic Alphabet (association)

IPI International Press Institute

IPPC International Penal and Penitentiary Commission

IPR Institute of Pacific Relations

ips inches per second

iq the same as (Lat. *idem quod*)

IQ intelligence quotient

iqed what was to be proved (Lat. *id quod erat demonstrandum*)

Ir Ireland, iridium, Irish

IRA individual retirement account, Irish Republican Army

Iran Iranian, Iranic

IRBM intermediate range ballistic missile

Ire Ireland

IRO International Refugee Organization (of the United Nations)

irreg irregular, irregularly

IRS Internal Revenue Service

is island or islands, isle or isles

Is, Isa Isaiah

ISBN international standard book number

isl island, islands

iso isotropic

isom isometric

isoth isothermal

Isr Israel

ISSN international standard serial number

isth isthmus

it, ital italic, italics

It, Ital Italian, Italy

ITA Initial Teaching Alphabet

itin itinerant, itinerary

ITO International Trade Organization

ITU International Telecommunication Union, International Typographical Union

IU international unit

IWW Industrial Workers of the World

J

J joule (physics), judge, justice

ja joint account

Ja January

JA judge advocate

JAG judge advocate general

Jam Jamaica, Jamaican

Jan January

Jap Japan, Japanese

Jas James

JCAH Joint Commission on Accreditation of Hospitals

JCD Doctor of Canon Law (Lat. *Juris Canonici Doctor*), Doctor of Civil Law (Lat. *Juris Civilis Doctor*)

JCS joint chiefs of staff

jct, jctn junction

JD Doctor of Laws (Lat. *Jurum Doctor*)

Je June

Jer Jeremiah

jg junior grade

Jl July

Jn John

Jon Jonah

Jos Joseph, Joshua, Josiah

jour journal, journalist, journeyman

JP jet propulsion, justice of the peace
jr junior
Ju Judges
JUD Doctor of Civil and Canon Law (Lat. *Juris Utriusque Doctor*)
Judg Judges
Jul July
jun junior
Jun June
junc, junct junction
JurD Doctor of Law (Lat. *Juris Doctor*)
jursp jurisprudence
jus, just justice
juv juvenile
jv junior varsity
jwlr jeweler
Jy July

K

k calends (Lat. *kalendae*), capacity, carat, constant, kilo, kilogram, king, king (chess), knot (naut.), kopeck (coin), koruna (coin), krone (coin)
K potassium (Lat. *kalium*), strikeout
ka kathode (cathode)
kal kalends (calends)
Kan, Kans, Kas Kansas
KB king's bench, king's bishop (chess), knight bachelor
KBP king's bishop's pawn (chess)
kc kilocycle
KC king's counsel, knight commander, Knights of Columbus
kcal kilocalorie
KCB Knight Commander of the (Order of the) Bath
KCVO Knight Commander of the (Royal) Victorian Order
Ken Kentucky
kg keg, kilogram
KG Knight of the (Order of the) Garter
KGB Commission of State Security (Russ. *Komitet Godsudarvstvennoi Bezopasnost' i*)
Ki Kings (book of the Bible)
kilo kilogram, kilometer
kilog kilogram
kilol kiloliter
kilom kilometer
kingd kingdom
KKK Ku Klux Klan
kl kiloliter
km kilometer
kn kronen (coin)
KN king's knight (chess)
KNP king's knight's pawn (chess)
ko knockout
K of C Knights of Columbus
K of P Knights of Pythias

kop kopeck (coin)
KP king's pawn (chess), kitchen police, Knight (of the Order of St.) Patrick, Knight of Pythias
kr krona (coin), krone (coin)
Kr krypton
KR king's rook (chess)
KRP king's rook's pawn (chess)
KS Kansas
kt karat (carat), knight
KT Knights Templar
kv kilovolt
kva kilovolt-ampere
kvar reactive kilovolt-ampere
kw kilowatt
kwh kilowatt-hour
Ky, KY Kentucky

L

l book (Lat. *liber*), (games) lost, lake, land, lat, latitude, law, leaf, league, left, lempira, length, leu, lev, lex, line, link, lira, lire, lit, liter, low, place (Lat. *locus*)
L coefficient of inductance, Latin, length, lewisite, licentiate, Linnaeus, longitude
La lanthanum, Louisiana
LA Legislative Assembly, Library Association, local agent, Los Angeles, Louisiana
lab laboratory
lam laminated
Lam Lamentations
LAM Master of Liberal Arts (Lat. *Liberalium Artium Magister*)
LAN local area network
lang language
laryngol laryngological, laryngology
lat latitude
Lat Latin, Latvia
Latv Latvia
lb pound (Lat. *libra*)
LB Bachelor of Letters (Lat. *Litterarum Baccalaureus*), local board
lb ap apothecary pound
lb av avoirdupois pound
LBO leveraged buyout
lbs pounds
lb t troy pound
lc in the place cited (Lat. *loco citato*), left center, lower case
l/c letter of credit
LC Library of Congress
LCD liquid crystal display, lowest common denominator
lcl less than carload lot
lcm least common multiple, lowest common multiple
ld lead (printing)
Ld lord

LD Low Dutch
ldg landing, leading, loading
LDiv Licentiate in Divinity
ld lmt load limit
ldry laundry
LDS Latter-day Saints, Latter Day Saints, Licentiate in Dental Surgery
le left end
lea league, leather, leave
led ledger
LED light-emitting diode
leg legal, legate, legato, legislation
legis legislation, legislative, legislature
LEM lunar excursion module
L ès S Licentiate in Sciences (Fr. *Licencié ès Sciences*)
Lev, Levit Leviticus
lex lexicon
lf left field, left fielder, left forward, lightface (printing), low frequency
lg left guard
LG Low German
lg, lge large
LGk Late Greek
lgth length
lh left halfback, left hand
LH luteinizing hormone
LHA local hour angle
LHD Doctor of Humanities (Lat. *Litterarum Humaniorum Doctor*)
Li lithium
LI lithographer, Long Island
lib book (Lat. *liber*), librarian, library
Lib Liberal, Liberia
Lieut lieutenant
LIFO last in, first out
LILO last in, last out
lin lineal, linear
ling linguistics
linim liniment
Linn Linnaeus, Linnean
lino linotype
liq liquid, liquor
li qts liquid quarts
lit liter, literal, literally, literary, literature
LitB, LittB Bachelor of Letters or Bachelor of Literature (Lat. *Litterarum Baccalaureus*)
LitD, LittD Doctor of Letters or Doctor of Literature (Lat. *Litterarum Doctor*)
lith, litho, lithog lithograph, lithography
Lith Lithuania, Lithuanian
Lk Luke
ll leaves, lines
LL Late Latin, Legal Latin, Low Latin, lower left
LLB Bachelor of Laws (Lat. *Legum Baccalaureus*)
LLD Doctor of Laws (Lat. *Legum Doctor*)
LLM Master of Laws (Lat. *Legum Magister*)

LM Legion of Merit, Licentiate in Medicine, Licentiate in Midwifery, lunar (excursion) module
LMT local mean time
ln lane
LNG liquefied natural gas
loc local, location
local localism
loc cit in the place cited (Lat. *loco citato*)
log logarithm
long longitude
loq he, she, or it speaks (Lat. *loquitur*)
lox liquid oxygen
lp large paper, long playing, long primer, low pressure
LPG liquified petroleum gas
LPS Lord Privy Seal
LR living room, long run, lower right
LS left side, library science, Licentiate in Surgery, place of the seal (Lat. *locus sigilli*), long shot
lsc in the place cited above (Lat. *loco supra citato*)
LSCA Library Services and Construction Act
LSD landing ship, dock; lysergic acid diethylamide
LSS lifesaving service
LST landing ship, tank
lt left tackle
lt long ton
Lt Lieutenant
LTA Lawn Tennis Association
ltd limited
ltn long ton
LTh Licentiate in Theology
LtInf light infantry
Ltjg lieutenant, junior grade
LTL less than truckload lot
LTS launch telemetry station, launch tracking system
Lu lutetium
lubric lubricate, lubrication
Luth Lutheran
Lux Luxemburg
lv leave, leaves
lw low water
Lw Lawrencium
lwl load waterline
lwm low water mark
LXX Septuagint
lyr lyric, lyrical

M

m majesty, male, manual, mark, married, masculine, mass, measure, medicine, medium, member, meridian, meter, mile, mill, minim, minute, month, moon, morning, mountain, noon (Lat. *meridies*)
M handful (Lat. *manipulus*), master, medieval, middle, monsieur, of medicine (Lat.

medicinae), Roman numeral for 1,000

Ma masurium

MA machine accountant, Maritime Administration, Massachusetts, Master of Arts (Lat. *Magister Artium*), mental age, military academy

Mac, Macc Maccabees

MAC mean aerodynamic chord

Maced Macedonia, Macedonian

mach machine, machinery, machinist

Mad Madam

MADD Mothers Against Drunk Driving

Madm Madam

mag magazine, magnet, magnetism, magnitude

MAgr, MAgric Master of Agriculture

maj majority

Maj major

Mal Malachi, Malay, Malayan, Malta

malac malacology

Man manila (paper), Manitoba

Manch Manchukuo, Manchuria, Manchurian

manuf manufacture, manufactured, manufacturer, manufacturing

mar marine, maritime, married

Mar March

March marchioness

marg margarine, margin, marginal

Marq marquess, marquis

mas, masc masculine

MASH mobile Army surgical hospital

Mass Massachusetts

mat matinee, matins, maturity

MAT Master of Arts in Teaching, Miller Analogy Test

MATS Military Air Transport Service

math mathematical, mathematician, mathematics

matr, matric matriculate, matriculation

Matt Matthew

max maximum

Max Maximilian

MB Bachelor of Medicine (Lat. *Medicinae Baccalaureus*)

MBA Master of Business Administration

MBS Mutual Broadcasting System

mc megacycle, millicurie

MC Maritime Commission, master commandant, master of ceremonies, Medical Corps, member of Congress

MCAT Medical College Admission Test

MCh Master of Surgery (Lat. *Magister Chiurgiae*)

MCL Master of Civil Law

m/d memorandum of deposit, months' date

Md Maryland, mendelevium

MD Doctor of Medicine (Lat. *Medicinae Doctor*), Maryland, medical department, mentally deficient, Middle Dutch

MDS Master of Dental Surgery

mdse merchandise

MDT Mountain Daylight Time

MDu Middle Dutch

me marbled edged (bookbinding)

Me Maine, methyl

ME Maine, mechanical engineer, Methodist Episcopal, Middle English, military engineer, mining engineer

meas measurable, measure

mech, mechan mechanical, mechanics, mechanism

med medical, medicine, medieval, medium

MEd Master of Education

MedGk Medieval Greek

Medit Mediterranean

MedL Medieval Latin

meg megabyte, megacycle, megohm

megs megabytes

mem member, memoir, memorandum, memorial

memo memorandum

mensur mensuration

mep mean effective pressure

mer meridian, meridional

merc mercantile, mercurial, mercury

Messrs messieurs

met metaphor, metaphysics, meteorological, metronome, metropolitan

metal, metall metallurgical, metallurgy

metaph metaphor, metaphorical, metaphysics

metath metathesis, metathetical

meteor, meteorol meteorological, meteorology

meth method, methylated

Meth Methodist

meton metonymy

metrol metrological, metrology

metrop metropolitan

mev million electron volts

Mex Mexican, Mexico

mf fairly loud (It. *mezzoforte*), millifarad

mf, mfd microfarad

MF medium frequency, Middle French

mfg manufacturing

MFlem Middle Flemish

mfr manufacture, manufacturer

mg milligram

Mg magnesium

MG military government

Mgr manager, monseigneur, monsignor

mgt management

mh millihenry

MH Medal of Honor

MHG Middle High German

mi mile

MI Michigan

Mic Micah

Mich Michigan

micro microcomputer

micros microscope, microscopic, microscopy

MICU mobile intensive care unit

mid middle, midshipman

MidDan Middle Danish

MidSw Middle Swedish

mil mileage, military, militia, million

milit military

mimeo mimeograph, mimeographed

min mineralogical, mineralogy, minim, minimum, mining, minor, minute

mineral mineralogy

Minn Minnesota

mip marine insurance policy, mean indicated pressure

MIPS million instructions per second

MIr Middle Irish

MIRV multiple independently targetable reentry vehicle

misc miscellaneous, miscellany

MISL Major Indoor Soccer League

Miss Mississippi

mkk mark, markka

Mk mark

mkd marked

MKS meter-kilogram-second (system)

mkt market

ml millileter

ML Medieval Latin, Middle Latin, molder

MLA member of the Legislative Assembly, Modern Language Association

MLD minimum lethal dose

MLG Middle Low German

Mlle Mademoiselle (Fr.)

Mlles Mesdemoiselles (Fr.)

MLS Master of Library Science

mm milimeter, thousands (Lat. *millia*), with the necessary changes (Lat. *mutatis mutandis*)

MM machinist's mate, messieurs (Fr.)

Mme Madame (Fr.)

Mmes Mesdames (Fr.)

mmf magnetomotive force

mmfd micromicrofarad

mn the name being changed (Lat. *mutato nomine*)

Mn manganese

MN Minnesota

mo month, monthly

Mo Missouri, molybdenum, Monday

MO mail order, medical officer, Missouri, money order

mod moderate, moderato, modern

ModGr Modern Greek

ModL Modern Latin

Moham Mohammedan

MOI Ministry of Information

mol molecular, molecule

mol wt molecular weight

mon monastery, monetary

Mon Monday, monsignor

Mong Mongolia, Mongolian

monocl monoclinic

monog, monogr monograph

Mons monsieur

Monsig monsignor

Mont Montana

mor morocco (bookbinding)

Mor Moroccan, Morocco

MOR middle of the road

morn morning

morph morpheme, morphological, morphology

mort mortuary

mos months

MOS military occupational specialty

mot motor, motorized

mp melting point, moderately soft (It. *mezzo piano*)

MP Member of Parliament, military police

MPd Master of Pedagogy

MPE Master of Physical Education

mpg miles per gallon

mph miles per hour

MPPDA Motion Picture Producers and Distributors of America (Inc.)

Mr Mister

MR machinery repairman, mentally retarded, motivational research

MRA Moral Re-Armament

MRI magentic resonance imaging

Mrs Mistress

ms manuscript, months after sight

MS Master of Science (Lat. *Magister Scientiae*), mine sweeper, Mississippi, multiple sclerosis, sacred to the memory of (Lat. *memoriae sacrum*)

MSA Mutual Security Agency

MSc Master of Science

msg message

MSG master sergeant, monosodium glutamate

Msgr monsignor

MSgt master sergeant

msl mean sea level

mss manuscripts

MST Mountain Standard Time

mt mean time, metric ton, motor transport, mount, mountain, mountain time

Mt Matthew

MT Montana

mtg meeting, mortgage

mtge mortgage

mtl material, mean tidal level

mtn mountain

MTO Mediterranean Theater of Operations

Mt Rev most reverend

mts mountains

MU musician

mun municipal, municipality

mus museum, music, musician

MusB Bachelor of Music (Lat. *Musicae Baccalaureus*)

MusD Doctor of Music (Lat. *Musicae Doctor*)

MusM Master of Music (Lat. *Musicae Magister*)

mut mutilated, mutual

mv millivolt, softly (It. *mezzo voce*)

Mv mendelevium

MVA Missouri Valley Authority

MVD Ministry of Internal Affairs (Rus. *Ministerstvo Vnutrennikh Del*)

MVP most valuable player

MW most worshipful, most worthy

MY May

mya myriare

mycol mycological, micology

myg myriagram

myl myrialiter

mym myriameter

myth, mythol mythological, mythology

N

n born (Lat. *natus*), name, net, neuter, neutron, new, nominative, noon, normal, note, noun, number, our (Lat. *noster*)

N knight (chess), nationalist, navy, nitrogen, Norse, north, northern, November

Na sodium (Lat. *natrium*)

NA national army, North America

NAACP National Association for the Advancement of Colored People

NAB New American Bible

NAD National Academy of Design

Nah Nahum

NAm North American

NAM National Association of Manufacturers

NAS National Academy of Sciences, naval air station

NASA National Aeronautics and Space Administration

NASCAR National Association of Stock Car Auto Racing

NASL North American Soccer League

nat national, native, natural, naturalist

nathist natural history

natl national

NATO North Atlantic Treaty Organization

NATS National Air Transport Service

naut nautical

nav naval, navigable, navigation

navig nagivation, navigator

nb note well (Lat. *nota bene*)

Nb niobium

NB New Brunswick

NBA National Basketball Association, National Boxing Association

NBC Natinal Broadcasting Company

NbE north by east

NBS National Bureau of Standards

NbW north by west

nc nitrocellulose

NC no charge, no credit, North Carolina, nurse corps

NCAA National Collegiate Athletic Association

NCar North Carolina

NCE New Catholic Edition (of the Bible)

NCO noncommissioned officer

nd no date

Nd neodymium

ND, NDak North Dakota

Ne neon

NE Nebraska, New England, northeast, northeastern

NEA National Education Association

NEB New English Bible

Neb, Nebr Nebraska

nec not elsewhere classified

NEC National Electrical Code

NED New English Dictionary (Oxford English Dictionary)

neg negative, negatively

Neh Nehemiah

nei not elsewhere indicated

neol neologism

NEP New Economic Policy

nes not elsewhere specified, not elsewhere stated

Neth Netherlands

neur, neurol neurological, neurologic

neut neuter, neutral

Nev Nevada

Newf Newfoundland

NewTest New Testament

nf noun feminine

NF National Formulary, Newfoundland, no funds, Norman French

NFC National Football Conference

NFL National Football League

ng no good

NG national guard, New Guinea

NGk New Greek

NH New Hampshire

NHG New High German

nhp nominal horsepower

NHS National Health Service (Brit.)

Ni nickel

NI Northern Ireland

Nic, Nicar Nicaragua, Nicaraguan

Nig Nigeria, Nigerian

NIH National Institutes of Health

NIMH National Institute of Mental Health

NIRA National Industrial Recovery Act

NIre Northern Ireland

NJ New Jersey

NKVD People's Commissariat of Internal Affairs (Rus. *Narodnyi Komissariat Vnutrennikh Del*)

nl new line (printing), north latitude, not clear (Lat. *non liquet*), not far (Lat. *non longe*), not lawful (Lat. *non licet*)

NL New Latin

Nlat north latitude

NLRB National Labor Relations Board

nm nautical mile, noun masculine

NM, NMex New Mexico

NMR nuclear magnetic resonsance

NMSQT National Merit Scholarship Qualifying Test

NMU National Maritime Union

NNE north-northeast

NNW north-northwest

no north, northern, number

No nobelium

NOAA National Oceanic and Atmospheric Administration

nob for our part or on our part (Lat. *nobis*)

nol pros unwilling to prosecute (Lat. *nolle prosequi*)

nom nomenclature, nominal, nominative

nomin nominative

noncom noncommissioned (officer)

non cul not guilty (Lat. *non culpabilis*)

non dest notwithstanding (Lat. *non destante*)

non obs, non obst notwithstanding (Lat. *non obstante*)

non pros he or she does not prosecute (Lat. *non prosequitur*)

non seq it does not follow (Lat. *non sequitur*)

nor north, northern

Nor Norman, Norway, Norwegian

NORAD North American Air Defense Command

norm normal

Norw Norway, Norwegian

nos numbers

nov novelist

Nov November

NOW National Organization for Women, negotiable order of withdrawal

np net proceeds, new paragraph, no paging, no place (of publication)

Np neptunium

NP knight's pawn, neuropsychiatrist, no protest, notary public, unless before (Lat. *nisi prius*)

NPN nonprotein nitrogen

np or d no place or date

NPR National Public Radio

npt normal pressure and temperature

nr near

NRA National Recovery Administration, National Rifle Association

NRC National Research Council, Nuclear Regulatory Commission

ns near side (shipping), new series, new style, not specified

Ns nimbostratus

NS new style, Nova Scotia

NSC National Security Council

NSF National Science Foundation, not sufficient funds

NSPCA National Society for the Prevention of Cruelty to Animals

NSPCC National Society for the Prevention of Cruelty to Children

NSW New South Wales

nt net

NT New Testament, Northern Territory (Australia)

ntp normal temperature and pressure

NTSB National Transportation Safety Board

nt wt net weight

num number, numeral

Num, Numb Numbers

numis numismatic, numismatics

ny nonvoting (stock)

NV Nevada

NW northwest, northwestern

NWT Northwest Territories (Canada)

NY New York

NYC New York City

NYSE New York Stock Exchange
NZ New Zealand

O

o octavo, off, ohm, old, only, order, pint (Lat. *octavius*)
o- ortho-
O ocean, October, Ohio, old, Ontario, Oregon, oxygen
OAPC Office of Alien Property Custodian
OAr Old Arabic
OAS Organization of American States
OAU Organization of African Unity
ob he or she died (Lat. *obit*), in passing (Lat. *obiter*), obstetrical, obstetrics
Ob, Obad Obadiah
obb obbligato
obdt obedient
OBE Officer of the (Order of the) British Empire
ob-gyn obstetrician gynecologist, obstetrics gynecology
obit obituary
obj object, objection, objective
obl oblique, oblong
obs obscure, observation, observatory, obsolete, obsolescence
obsol obsolescent
ob s p died without issue (Lat. *obit sine prole*)
obstet obstetrical, obstetrics
obt obedient
obv obverse
oc in the work cited (Lat. *opere citato*)
o/c old charter, overcharge
Oc ocean
OC office of censorship, officer commanding, original cover
OCAS Organization of Central American States
occ occasion, occasionally, occident, occidental
occult occultism
OCD Office of Civilian Defense
oceanog oceanography
OCR optical character reading, optical character recognition
OCS office of contract settlement, officer candidate school
oct octavo
Oct October
octupl octuplicate
od olive drab, on demand, outside diameter
OD Doctor of Optometry, officer of the day, Old Dutch, Ordnance Department, overdraft, overdrawn
ODan Old Danish

ODu Old Dutch
OE Old English
OECD Organization for Economic Cooperation and Development
OED Oxford English Dictionary
OEEC Organization for European Economic Cooperation
OEM original equipment manufacture
OES office of economic stabilization, Order of the Eastern Star
OF Old French
off offered, office, official, officinal
OFM Order of Friars Minor
OG officer of the guard, original gum (philately)
OH Ohio
OHG Old High German
OHMS on his or her majesty's service
OIAA office of inter-American affairs
OIC office of information and culture (of the State Department)
OIr Old Irish
OIT office of international trade
OK, Okla Oklahoma
OL Old Latin
Old Test Old Testament
oleo oleomargarine
OM Order of Merit (Brit.)
OMB Office of Management and Budget
ON Old Norse
ONI Office of Naval Intelligence
ONormFr Old Norman French
onomat onomatopoeia, onomatopoeic
ONR Office of Naval Research
Ont Ontario
OOD officer of the day, officer of the deck
op operation, opposite, out of print, overprint, overproof, work (Lat. *opus*), works (Lat. *opera*)
OP observation post, Order of Preachers
OPA office of price administration
op cit in the work cited (Lat. *opere citato*)
OPEC Organization of Petroleum Exporting Countries
OPer Old Persian
ophthal ophthalmology
opp oppose, opposed, opposite
opt optative, optical, optics
OR operating room, Oregon
orat oratorical, oratory
orch orchestra, orchestral

ord ordained, order, ordinal, ordinance, ordinary, ordnance
ordn ordnance
Ore, Oreg Oregon
org organic, organism, organized
orig origin, original, originally
Ork Orkney (Islands)
ornith, ornithol ornithological, ornithologist, ornithology
orth orthopedic, orthopedics
Orth orthodox
Os osmium
OS Old Saxon, old style, ordinary seaman
OSA Order of Saint Augustine
OSB Order of Saint Benedict
osc oscillating, oscillator
OSerb Old Serbian
OSF Order of Saint Francis
OSHA Occupational Safety and Health Administration
OSl Old Slavic
OSp Old Spanish
OSRD Office of Scientific Research and Development
OSS Office of Strategic Services
osteo osteopath, osteopathy
OT Old Testament, on truck, overtime
OTC Officer's Training Corps
otol otology
OTS Officer Training School
ott octave (It. *ottava*)
OW one-way
OWI Office of War Information
Oxon Oxford (Lat. *Oxonia*)
oz ounce
oz ap apothecary ounce
oz av avoirdupois ounce
ozs ounces
oz t troy ounce

P

p after (Lat. *post*), by (Lat. *per*), by weight (Lat. *pondere*), first (Lat. *primus*), for (Lat. *pro*), in part (Lat. *partim*), page, part, participle, past, penny, perch (measure), period, perishable, peseta, peso, pint, pipe, pitcher, pole (measure), population, post, power, pressure, softly (It. *piano*)
p- para- (chemistry)
P bishop (Lat. *pontifex*), father (Fr. *père*, Lat. *pater*), parental, pastor, pawn (chess), pengö, people (Lat. *populus*), peso, phosphorus, piaster, pope (Lat. *papa*), president, pressure, priest, prince, prisoner, prompter (theater)

P- pursuit (military)
pa for the year (Lat. *pro anno*), paper, participial adjective, particular average (insurance), public address, yearly (Lat. *per annum*)
Pa Pennsylvania, protactinium
PA passenger agent, Pennsylvania, personal assistant, physician's assistant, power of attorney, press agent, private account, public address (system), purchasing agent
PABA para-aminobenzoic acid
Pac, Pacif Pacific
PAC Pan-American Congress, political action committee
p ae equal parts (Lat. *partes aequales*)
Pal Palestine
paleob paleobotany
paleog paleography
paleontol paleontology
palm palmistry
pam, pamph pamphlet
Pan Panama
p and h postage and handling
P and L profit and loss
pap paper
par paragraph, parallel, parenthesis
Par, Para Paraguay
paren parenthesis
parens parentheses
parl parliamentary
part participle, particular
pass everywhere (Lat. *passim*), passage, passenger, passive
pat patent, patented, patrol, pattern
PAT point after touchdown
patd patented
path, pathol pathology
Pat Off Patent Office
pat pend patent pending
PAU Pan American Union
PAYE pay as you earn, pay as you enter
payt payment
PB Pharmacopoeia Britannica, prayer book
PBA Public Buildings Administration
PBS Public Broadcasting Service, Public Buildings Service
PBX private branch (telephone) exchange
pc after meals (Lat. *post cibos*), percent, percentage, piece, postcard, price
p/c petty cash, price current
PC personal computer, police constable, post commander, Privy Council, professional corporation
PCA Progressive Citizens of America
PCB polychlorinated biphenyl

Pcs preconscious
pct percent
pd by the day (Lat. *per diem*), paid, potential difference
Pd palladium
PD per diem, phenyl dichloride, police department, postal district
PdB Bachelor of Pedagogy (Lat. *Pedagogiae Baccalaureus*)
PdD Doctor of Pedagogy (Lat. *Pedagogiae Doctor*)
PdM Master of Pedagogy (Lat. *Pedagogiae Magister*)
PDT Pacific Daylight Time
p/e price-earnings ratio
PE petroleum engineer, presiding elder, printer's error, probable error, Protestant Episcopal
ped pedal, pedestal, pedestrian
PEI Prince Edward Island
pen peninsula, penitent, penitentiary
PEN (International Association of) Poets, Playwrights, Editors, Essayists, and Novelists
Penn, Penna Pennsylvania
penol penology
per period, person
per an, per ann by the year (Lat. *per annum*)
perd, perden dying away (It. *perdendo*)
perf perfect, perforated, performer
perh perhaps
perm permanent
perp perpendicular, perpetual
pers person, personal
Pers Persia, Persian
persp perspective
pert pertaining
Peru, Peruv Peruvian
pet petroleum
petn petition
petrog petrography
petrol petrology
pf louder (It. *più forte*), pfennig (coin), power factor
pg page
PFC private first class
pfd preferred
pfg pfennig (coin)
Pg Portugal, Portuguese
PG past grand (master), paying guest, postgraduate
PGA Professional Golfers' Association
ph phrase
Ph phenyl
PH Purple Heart
phar, pharm pharmaceutical, pharmacist, pharmacy
PharB Bachelor of Pharmacy (Lat. *Pharmaciae Baccalaureus*)
PharD Doctor of Pharmacy (Lat. *Pharmaciae Doctor*)

PharM Master of Pharmacy (Lat. *Pharmaciae Magister*)
pharmacol pharmacology
PhB Bachelor of Philosophy (Lat. *Philosophiae Baccalaureus*)
PhC pharmaceutical chemist
PhD Doctor of Philosophy (Lat. *Philosophiae Doctor*)
phil philosopher, philosophical, philosophy
Phil Philippians, Philippines
Phila Philadelphia
philol philology
philos philosopher, philosophical, philosophy
phon phonetic, phonetics, phonology
phonet phonetic, phonetics
phot, photo, photog photograph, photographer, photographic, photography
photom photometrical, photometry
phr phrase
phren, phrenol phrenological, phrenology
PHS Public Health Service
phys physical, physician, physicist, physics
physiol physiological, physiology
Pi, pias piaster
pict pictorial, picture
pil pill (Lat. *pilla*)
pinx he or she painted (Lat. *pinxit*)
PIO public information officer
pizz plucked (music) (It. *pizzicato*)
pk pack, park, peak, peck
pkg package
pkt packet
PKU phenylketonuria
pl place, plate, plural
plat plateau, platform, platoon
plen plenipotentiary
plf, plff plaintiff
plu plural
plup, plupf pluperfect
plur plural, plurality
pm after death (Lat. *post mortem*), afternoon (Lat. *post meridiem*), postmortem
Pm promethium
PM pacific mail, past master, paymaster, police magistrate, postmaster, prime minister, provost marshall
pmk postmark
pmkd postmarked
pn promissory note
pneum pneumatic, pneumatics
png a person who is not acceptable (Lat. *persona non grata*)
PNG Papua New Guinea
pnxt he or she painted (Lat. *pinxit*)

po personnel officer, petty officer, postal order, post office, put-out
Po polonium
PO post office
POC port of call
pod pay on delivery
PoD Doctor of Podiatry
POD Post Office Department
POE port of embarkation, port of entry
poet poetic, poetical, poetry
pol, polit political, politics
Pol Poland, Polish
pol econ, polit econ political economy
pop popular, population
POP point of purchase
por pay on return
port portrait
Port Portugal, Portuguese
pos, posit position, positive
poss possession, possessive, possible, possibly
post postal
pot potential
POW prisoner of war
pp pages, parcel post, parish priest, past participle, postpaid, privately printed, very softly (It. *pianissimo*)
PP pellagra preventive (factor)
ppc to take leave (Fr. *pour prendre congé*)
ppd postpaid, prepaid
pph pamphlet
ppi policy proof of interest
PPI plan position indicator (radar)
ppl participle, past participle
ppm parts per million
ppp pianissimo
ppr present participle
pps additional postscript (Lat. *post postscriptum*), Parliamentary private secretary
ppv pay per view (television)
pq previous questions
PQ Province of Quebec
pr pair, pairs, paper, power, preferred, preposition, present, price, priest, prince, printing, pronoun
Pr praesodymium
PR proportional representation, public relations, Puerto Rico
preb prebend, prebendary
prec preceding
pred predicate, predication, predicative, prediction
pref preface, prefatory, preference, preferred, prefix
prelim preliminary
prem premium
prep preparation, preparatory, prepare, preposition
pres present, presidency, president, presumptive
Presb, Presbyt presbyter, Presbyterian

pret preterit
prev previous, previously
prim primary, primitive
prin principal, principally, principle
print printer, printing
priv private, privately, privative
prn whenever necessary (Lat. *pro re nata*)
pro professional
PRO Professional Review Organization, public relations officer
prob probable, probably, problem
proc proceedings, process, proclamation
prod produce, produced, product
prof professor
prog program, progress, progressive
prom promenade, promontory
pron pronoun, pronounced, pronunciation
pronom pronominal
prop proper, properly, property, proposition, proprietary, proprietor
propr proprietary, proprietor
pros prosody
Prot protectorate, Protestant
pro tem for the time being (Lat. *pro tempore*)
prov proverbial, providence, provident, province, provincial, provision, provost
Prov Proverbs
prox next (month) (Lat. *proximo*)
prs pairs
prtd printed
prtg printing
Prus, Pruss Prussia, Prussian
prv to return a call (Fr. *pour rendre visite*)
ps passenger steamer, permanent secretary, pieces, postscript, private secretary, prompt side (theater), pseudonym, public sale
Ps Psalms
PS police sergeant, Privy Seal, public school
PSAT Preliminary Scholastic Aptitude Test
pseud pseudonym
psf pounds per square foot
psi pounds per square inch
PSRO Professional Standards Review Organization
pss postscripts
PSS Psalms
PST Pacific Standard Time
psych, psychol psychological, psychologist, psychology
psychoanal psychoanalysis
pt for the time being (Lat. *pro tempore*), part, part time, payment, pint, point, port, post town, postal telegraph, preterit

Pt platinum

PT part time, physical training

pta peseta

PTA Parent-Teachers' Association

ptbl portable

ptg printing

pts parts, payments, pints

PTSA Parent-Teacher-Student Association

pty proprietary

Pu plutonium

pub public, publication, published, publisher

publ publication, published, publisher

pulv pulverized

punct punctuation

pur, purch purchaser, purchasing

pv par value, post village, priest vicar

PVC polyvinyl chloride

Pvt private

PW prisoner of war

PWA Public Works Administration

PWP Parents Without Partners

pwr power

pwt pennyweight

PX post exchange

pymt payment

Q

q quart, quarter, quarterly, quarto, query, question, queen

Q quarto, Quebec, queen (chess)

qb quarterback

QB Queen's Bench, queen's bishop (chess)

QBP queen's bishop's pawn (chess)

QC Quartermaster Corps, Queen's Counsel

qd as if he or she had said (Lat. *quasi dixisset*), as if one should say (Lat. *quasi dicat*), as if said (Lat. *quasi dictum*)

qe which is (Lat. *quod est*)

QED which was to be demonstrated (Lat. *quod erat demonstrandum*)

QEF which was to be done (Lat. *quod erat faciendum*)

QEI which was to be found out (Lat. *quod erat inveniendum*)

QID four times a day (Lat. *quater in die*)

ql as much as you please (Lat. *quantum libet*), quintal

Qld Queensland

qlty quality

QM quartermaster

QMC Quartermaster Corps

QMG quartermaster general

qn question

QN queen's knight (chess)

QNP queen's knight's pawn (chess)

QP queen's pawn (chess)

q pl, QP as much as you wish (Lat. *quantum placeat*)

Qq quartos

qqv which see (plural) (Lat. *quos vide*)

qr quarter, quarterly, quire

QR queen's rook (chess)

QRP queen's rook's pawn (chess)

qrs farthings (Lat. *quadrantes*), quarters, quires

qrtly quarterly

qs as much as suffices (Lat. *quantum sufficit*), quarter section

qt quantity, quart, quiet

qto quarto

qts quarts

qu quart, queen, query, question

quad quadrangle, quadrant, quadrat, quadrilateral, quadruple, quadruplet

quar, quart quarter, quarterly

Que Quebec

ques question

quin, quint quintuple, quintuplet

quor quorum

quot quotation, quoted

qv as much as you will (Lat. *quantum vis*), which see (Lat. *quod vide*)

qy query

R

r range, rare, received, recipe, residence, resides, retired, right, right-hand page (Lat. *recto*), rises, river, road, rod, roentgen, royal, rubber, ruble, run

R commonwealth (Lat. *res publica*), gas constant (chemistry), king (Lat. *rex*), queen (Lat. *regina*), rabbi, radical (chemistry), radius, railroad, railway, ratio, Réaumur, rector, redactor, Republican, resistance (electrical), respond or response (ecclesiastical), ring (chemistry), rook (chess), ruble, rupee, take (Lat. *recipe*)

Ra radium

RA rear admiral, regular army, right ascension, Royal Academy

rad radical, radio, radius, root (Lat. *radix*)

RAF Royal Air Force

ral, rall gradually slower (It. *rallentando*)

RAM random-access memory

R&D research and development

RAR radio acoustic ranging

Rb rubidium

rbi run batted in

RC Red Cross, reserve corps, Roman Catholic

RCAF Royal Canadian Air Force

RCCh Roman Catholic Church

rcd received

RCMP Royal Canadian Mounted Police

RCP Royal College of Physicians

rcpt receipt

RCS Royal College of Surgeons

Rct recruit

rd reduce, rix-dollar, road, rod, round

Rd Radium, road

RD research and development, rural delivery

re right end

Re rhenium, rupee

RE real estate, Reformed Episcopal, right excellent, Royal Engineers

REA Rural Electrification Administration

react reactance (electricity)

rec receipt, received, recipe, record, recorded, recorder, recording

recd received

recip reciprocal, reciprocity

recit recitative

rec sec recording secretary

rect receipt, rectified, rector, rectory

red reduced, reduction

redisc rediscount

redup, redupl reduplicated, reduplication

ref referee, reference, referred, refining, reformation, reformed

Ref Ch Reformed Church

refl reflection, reflective, reflectively, reflex, reflexive

refrig refrigeration

reg regent, regiment, region, register, registered, registrar, registry, regular, regularly, regulation, regulator

Reg queen (Lat. *regina*)

regt regent, regiment

REIT real estate investment trust

rel relating, relative, relatively, released, religion, religious

rel pron relative pronoun

rem remittance

REM rapid eye movement

rep repair, repeat, report, reporter, representative, reprint, republic

Rep representative, republic, Republican

repr representing, reprinted

Repub Republican

req required, requisition

res research, reserve, residence, resides, residue, resigned, resistance, resistor, resolution

resp respective, respiration, respondent

rest restaurant

Resurr Resurrection

ret retain, retired, returned

retd retained, returned

retrog retrogressive

rev revenue, reverse, reversed, review, revise, revised, revision, revolution, revolving

Rev Revelation, reverend

Rev Ver Revised Version (of the Bible)

rf radio frequency, range finder, rapid fire, right field, right fielder, right forward

RFA Royal Field Artillery

RFC Reconstruction Finance Corporation, Royal Flying Corps

RFD rural free delivery

rg right guard

RGB red-blue-green television tube

rh relative humidity, right halfback, right hand

Rh Rhesus (blood factor), rhodium

RH Royal highness

rhap rhapsody

rhbdr rhombohedral

rhet rhetoric, rhetorical

rhin, rhinol rhinology

rhomb rhombic

rhp rated horsepower

RI king and emperor (Lat. *rex et imperator*), queen and empress (Lat. *regina et imperatrix*), Rhode Island

rip supplementary (music) (It. *ripieno*)

RIP may he, she, or they rest in peace (Lat. *requiescat* or *requiescant in pace*)

RISC reduced instruction set computer

rit slow (It. *ritardando*)

riv river

rkva reactive kilovolt-ampere

rm ream, room

Rm Reichsmark

rms reams, rooms, root mean square

Rn radon

RN Royal Navy

RNA ribonucleic acid

RNR Royal Naval Reserve

RNWMP Royal Northwest Mounted Police

ro recto, rood

ROK Republic of Korea

rom roman (type)

Rom Roman, Romance, Romania, Romanian, Romans

ROM read-only memory

ROP record of production, run of press

rot rotating, rotation

ROTC Reserve Officers' Training Corps

roul roulette (philately)

roy royal

RP Reformed Presbyterian, Regius Professor

RPD Doctor of Political Science (Lat. *Rerum Politicarum Doctor*)

rpm revolutions per minute

RPO railway post office

rps revolutions per second

rpt report

rr very rarely (Lat. *rarissime*)

RR railroad, right reverend

RRB Railroad Retirement Board

rs reis, rupees

RS recording secretary, reformed spelling, revised statutes

RSFSR Russian Soviet Federated Socialist Republic

RSV Revised Standard Version (of the Bible)

rsvp please reply (Fr. *répondez s'il vous plaît*)

RSVP Retired Seniors Volunteer Program

rt right, right tackle

Rt Hon right honorable

Rt Rev right reverend

Rts rights

Ru Ruth, ruthenium

rub ruble

Rus, Russ Russia, Russian

RV recreational vehicle, Revised Version (of the Bible)

rva reactive volt-ampere

RW right worshipful, right worthy

ry railway

S

s buried (Lat. *sepultus*), fellow (Lat. *socius* or *sodalis*), lies (Lat. *situs*), sacral, saint, school, scribe, second, secondary, section, see, semi-, senate, series, set, shilling (Lat. *solidus*), sign, signed, silver, singular, sire, socialist, society, solo, son, soprano, southern, steel, stem, stere, stock, substantive, sun, surplus

s- symmetrical (chemistry)

S knight (chess) (Ger. *Springer*), sabbath, Saturday, Saxon, seaman, Senate, September, signature, Signor, south, southern, sulfur, Sunday

Sa samarium, Samuel

SA corporation (Fr. *société anonyme*), Salvation Army, seaman apprentice, sex appeal, South Africa, South America, South Australia

Sab sabbath

SAC Strategic Air Command

SADD Students Against Driving Drunk

SAE Society of Automotive Engineers

SAfr South Africa, South African

SALT strategic arms limitation talks

SAm, SAmer South America, South American

SAM surface-to-air missile

Sans, Sansk Sanskrit

S ap apothecary's scruple

SAR Sons of the American Revolution

Sask Saskatchewan

sat saturated, saturation

Sat Saturday, Saturn

SAT Scholastic Aptitude Test

sav savings

sb stolen base, substantive

Sb antimony (Lat. *stibium*)

SB Bachelor of Science (Lat. *Scientiae Baccalaureus*)

SBA Small Business Administration

SbE south by east

SbW south by west

sc he or she carved or engraved it (Lat. *sculpsit*), namely (Lat. *scilicet*), salvage charges, scale, scene, science, screw, scruple (weight), sized and calendered, small capitals (printing), supercalendered

Sc scandium, stratocumulus

SC Security Council (of the United Nations), Signal Corps, South Carolina, Supreme Court

Scan, Scand Scandinavia, Scandinavian

s caps small capitals (printing)

ScB Bachelor of Science (Lat. *Scientiae Baccalaureus*)

ScD Doctor of Science (Lat. *Scientiae Doctor*)

sch school, schooner

sched schedule

schol scholar, scholastic

sci science, scientific

sci fa show cause (Lat. *scire facias*)

scil namely (Lat. *scilicet*)

ScM Master of Science (Lat. *Scientiae Magister*)

Scot Scotland, Scots, Scottish

scr scrip, script, scruple (weight)

Script scriptural, scriptures

sculpt he or she carved it (Lat. *sculpsit*), sculptor

sd indefinitely (without date) (Lat. *sine die*), standard deviation

SD Doctor of Science (Lat. *Scientiae Doctor*), South Dakota, steward

SDR special drawing rights

SDS Students for a Democratic Society

Se selenium

SE southeast, southeastern

SEATO Southeast Asia Treaty Organization

sec according to (Lat. *secundum*), secant, second, secondary, secretary, section, sector

SEC Securities and Exchange Commission

sec-ft second-foot

sech hyperbolic secant

sec leg according to law (Lat. *secundum legem*)

sec reg according to rule (Lat. *secundum regulam*)

secs seconds, sections

sect section, sectional

secy secretary

seg segment

seismol seismology

sel selected, selection

Sem seminary, Semitic

sen senate, senator, senior

sent sentence

sep sepal, separate

Sep, Sept September, Septuagint

seq sequel

seq, seqq the following (Lat. *sequens, sequentia*)

ser serial, series, sermon

serv servant, service

sess session

sf, sforz with emphasis (It. *sforzando, sforzato*)

SFSR Soviet Federated Socialist Republic

sfz with emphasis (It. *sforzando, sforzato*)

sg senior grade, specific gravity

sgd signed

Sgt sergeant

sh share, sheet, shilling, shunt

SHAEF Supreme Headquarters, Allied Expeditionary Forces

Shak Shakespeare

SHAPE Supreme Headquarters Allied Powers (Europe)

SHF super-high frequency

shipt, shpt shipment

shtg shortage

sh tn short ton

Si silicon

SI international system of weights and measures (Fr. *Système International*), Staten Island

Sib Siberia, Siberian

SIDS sudden infant death syndrome

sig signal, signature, signor, signore, signori

sigill seal (Lat. *sigillum*)

sim simile

sin sine

sing singular

sinh hyperbolic sine

SIPC Securities Investment Protection Corporation

sist sister

sj under consideration (Lat. *sub judice*)

SJ Society of Jesus (Lat. *Societas Jesu*)

SJD Doctor of Juridicial Science (Lat. *Scientiae Juridicae Doctor*)

sk sack

Skr, Skt Sanskrit

sl without place (Lat. *sine loco*)

slan without place, date, or name (Lat. *sine loco, anno, vel nomine*)

S lat south latitude

Slav Slavic, Slavonian

sld sailed, sealed

slp without lawful issue (Lat. *sine legitima prole*)

SLR single-lens reflex (camera)

sm small

Sm samarium

SM Master of Science (Lat. *Scientiae Magister*), sergeant major, state militia

sm c, sm caps small capitals

smorz dying away (It. *smorzando*)

smp without male issue (Lat. *sine mascula prole*)

SMSA standard metropolitan statistical area

sn without name (Lat. *sine nomine*)

Sn tin (Lat. *stannum*)

so seller's option, strike out

So south, southern

soc socialist, society

sociol sociologist, sociology

sol solicitor, soluble, solution

Sol Solomon

soln solution

Som Somalia

son sonata

sop soprano

SOP standard operating procedure

SOPA senior officer present afloat

sos, sost, sosten sustained (It. *sostenuto*)

sp single phase, single pole, special, species, specific, specimen, spelling, spirit, without issue (Lat. *sine prole*)

Sp Spain, Spaniard, Spanish

SP shore patrol, shore police

SPAS Fellow of the American Philosophical Society (Lat. *Societatis Philosophiae Americanae Socius*)

SPCA Society for the Prevention of Cruelty to Animals

SPCC Society for the Prevention of Cruelty to Children

spec special, specification, speculation

specif specifically

spg spring

sp gr specific gravity

sp ht specific heat

sph spherical

spp species (plural)

SPQR government and people of Rome (Lat. *Senatus populusque Romanus*)

SPR Society for Psychical Research

spt seaport

sq sequence, square, the following (Lat. *sequentia*)

Sq squadron, Square (street)

sq ft square foot

sq in square inch

sq mi square mile

sq rd square rod

sq yd square yard

sr steradian

Sr senior, señor, sir, sister, strontium

Sra señora

SRO standing room only

Srta señorita

ss namely (in law) (Lat. *scilicet*), shortstop

SS saints, Silver Star, steamship, storm troopers (Ger. *Schutz-staffeln*), Sunday school, written above (Lat. *supra scriptum*)

SSA Social Security Act (Administration)

SSB Social Security Board

SSE south-southeast

SSgt staff sergeant

SSR Soviet Socialist Republic

SSS Selective Service System

SST supersonic transport

SSW south-southwest

st short ton, stand, stanza, statute, stet, stitch, stone (weight), street, strophe

St saint, straight, strait, stratus, street

sta station, stationary, stator

Sta saint (Sp. *Santa*), station

stac, stacc staccato

stan stanchion

Staph staphylococcus

stat immediately (Lat. *statim*), static, stationary, statistics, statuary, statute

STB Bachelor of Sacred Theology (Lat. *Sacrae Theologiae Baccalaureus*)

stbd starboard

std standard

STD Doctor of Sacred Theology (Lat. *Sacrae Theologiae Doctor*), sexually transmitted disease

Ste saint (Fr. *Sainte*)

steno, stenog stenographer, stenography

ster, stg sterling

St Ex stock exchange

stge storage

stip stipend, stipendiary, stipulation

Stir Stirling, Stirlingshire

stk stock

STOL short take-off and landing

stor storage

stp stamped

STP standard temperature and pressure

str steamer, strait, string

Strep streptococcus

stud student

sub subaltern, submarine, subscription, substitute, suburb, suburban, understand (or supply) (Lat. *subaudi*)

subd subdivision

subj subject, subjective, subjunctive

subs subscription, subsidiary

subseq subsequent, subsequently

subst substantive, substitute

succ successor

suf, suff suffix

sug, sugg suggested, suggestion

Sun, Sund Sunday

sup above (Lat. *supra*), superfine, superior, superlative, supplement, supplementary, supply, supreme

super superfine, superintendent, superior, supernumerary

superl superlative

supp, suppl supplement, supplementary

supr supreme

supt superintendent

sur surcharged, surplus

surg surgeon, surgery, surgical

surr surrender, surrendered

surv survey, surveying, surveyor, surviving

susp suspended

sv sailing vessle, under this word (Lat. *sub verbo*)

SV Holy Virgin (Lat. *Sancta Virgo*)

SW southwest, southwestern

Sw Sweden, Swedish

SWA, SWAfr South-West Africa

SWAT special weapons and tactics (team)

Swe, Swed Sweden, Swedish

Swit, Switz, Swtz Switzerland

syl, syll syllable

sym symbol, symmetrical, symphony

syn synchronize, synonym, synonymous, synonymy

syr syrup (pharmacy)

Syr Syria, Syriac, Syrian

syst system, systematic

T

t in the time of (Lat. *tempore*), tare, target, tea-

spoon, telephone, temperature, tempo, tenor, tense (grammar), terminal, territory, time, tome, ton, town, township, transit, transitive, troy (weight), volume (Lat. *tomus*)

T tablespoon, tantalum, technician, temperature (absolute), tension (surface), testament, time, trinity, Tuesday, Turkish

Ta tantalum

tab table, tablet

TAC Tactical Air Command, Technical Assistance Committee

tal qual as they come (or average quality) (Lat. *talis qualis*)

tan tangent

tanh hyperbolic tangent

TAP Technical Assistance Program

tart tartaric

taut tautological, tautology

tb trial balance

Tb terbium

TB tubercule bacillus, tuberculosis

tba to be announced

tbs, tbsp tablespoon, tablespoonful

tc tierce

Tc technetium

TC Trusteeship Council (of the United Nations)

tchr teacher

td touchdown

TD tank destroyer, tradesman, traffic director, Treasury Department

tdn total digestible nutrients

Te tellurium

tech technical, technological, techonology

technol technology

TEFL teaching English as a foreign language

tel telegram, telegraph, telegraphic, telephone

telecom telecommunication

teleg telegram, telegraph, telegraphic, telegraphy

temp in the time of (Lat. *tempore*), temperature, temporary

ten hold (It. *tenuto*), tenement, tenor

Tenn Tennessee

terr terrace, territorial, territory

term terminal, termination, terminology

test testamentary, testator

Test testament

tetr, tetrag tetragonal

Teut Teuton, Teutonic

Tex Texas, Texan

tfr transfer

tg type genus

TGIF thank God it's Friday

tgt target

Th thorium

Th Thursday

ThB Bachelor of Theology (Lat. *Theologiae Baccalaureus*)

ThD Doctor of Theology (Lat. *Theologiae Doctor*)

Th-Em thoron (thorium emanation)

theol theologian, theological, theology

theor theorem

theos theosophical, theosophist, theosophy

therm thermometer

thermochem thermochemical, thermochemistry

thermodynam thermodynamics

Thess Thessalonians, Thessaly

THI temperature-humidity index

Thu, Thurs Thursday

Ti titanium

t i d three times daily (Lat. *ter in die*)

tinct tincture

tit title

Tit Titus

tk truck

TKO technical knock-out

Tl thallium

TL trade last

T/L time loan

TLC tender loving care

tm true mean

Tm thulium

TMH trainable mentally handicapped

tn ton, train

Tn thoron

TN Tennessee

tng training

TNT trinitrotoluene, trinitrotoluol

to turn over, turnover

tonn tonnage

top, topog topographical, topography

tp title page, township, troop

tpke turnpike

tpr temperature, pulse, respiration

tps townships

tr tare, tincture, trace, train, transitive, translated, translation, translator, transpose, treasurer, trust

Tr terbium, troop

trag tragedy, tragic

trans transactions, transfer, transferred, transitive, translated, translation, translator, transportation, transpose, transverse

transf transfer, transference, transferred

transl translated, translation

transp transparent, transportation

trav traveler, travels

treas treasurer, treasury

trf transfer, tuned radio frequency

trfd transferred

tricl triclinic (crystal)

trig trigonometric, trigonomy

trim trimetric (crystal)

triple triplicate

trit triturate

trl trail

trop tropic, tropical, tropics

ts tensile strength

TSgt technical sergeant

tsp teaspoon, teaspoonful

Tu thulium

Tu Tuesday

TU trade union, training unit

TUC Trades Union Congress (Brit.)

Tue, Tues Tuesday

Turk Turkey, Turkish

TV television, terminal velocity

TVA Tennessee Valley Authority

twp township

TX Texas

Ty territory

typ, typo, typog typographer, typographic, typographer

typo typographic error

typw typewriter, typewritten

U

u and (Ger. *und*), uncle, university, upper

U uranium

UAW United Automobile (Aircraft, and Agricultural Implement) Workers (of America)

uc upper case (printing)

UCMJ Uniform Code of Military Justice

UFO unidentified flying object

UHF ultra-high frequency

UJD Doctor of Civil and Canon Law (Lat. *Utriusque Juris Doctor*)

UK United Kingdom

Ukr Ukraine

ult ultimate, ultimately

ult, ulto last month (Lat. *ultimo*)

UMT universal military training

UMW United Mine Workers

UN United Nations

unabr unabridged

unb, unbd unbound (bookbinding)

undsgd undersigned

undtkr undertaker

UNEDA United Nations Economic Development Administration

Unesco, UNESCO United Nations Educational, Scientific, and Cultural Organization

ung ointment (Lat. *unguentum*)

UNICEF United Nations Children's Fund (originally United Nations International Children's Emergency Fund)

Unit Unitarian, Unitarianism

univ universal, universally, university

Univ Universalist

unl unlimited

unm unmarried

unof unofficial

unp unpaged

unpub unpublished

UNREF United Nations Refugee Emergency Fund

UNRRA United Nations Relief and Rehabilitation Administration

UNRWA United Nations Relief and Works Agency

UNSCOB United Nations Special Committee on the Balkans

UP Union Pacific (railroad), United Press

UPC universal product code

UPI United Press International

UPS United Parcel Service

UPU Universal Postal Union (of the United Nations)

Ur uranium

urol urology

Uru Uruguay, Uruguayan

us as above (Lat. *ut supra*), in the place mentioned above (Lat. *ubi supra*)

US United States

USA United States Army, United States of America

USAF United States Air Force

USC&GS United States Coast and Geodetic Survey

USCG United States Coast Guard

USDA United States Department of Agriculture

USES United States Employment Service

USIA United States Information Agency

USM United States Mail, United States Marines, United States Mint

USMA United States Military Academy

USMC United States Marine Corps, United States Maritime Commission

USN United States Navy

USNA United States Naval Academy

USNG United States National Guard

USNR United States Naval Reserve

USO United Service Organizations

USOE United States Office of Education

USP United States patent, United States Pharmacopoeia

US Pharm United States Pharmacopoeia

USPHS United States Public Health Service

USPS United States Postal Service

USS United States Senate, United States Ship

USSCt United States Supreme Court

USSR Union of Soviet Socialist Republics

usu usual, usually

usw and so forth (Ger. *und so weiter*)

USW United Steel Workers

ut universal time, utility

Ut, UT Utah

UTC universal time coordinate

ut dict as directed (Lat. *ut dictum*)

ut sup as above (Lat. *ut supra*)

UTWA United Textile Workers of America

ux wife (Lat. *uxor*)

V

v against (Lat. *versus*), of (Ger. *von*), see (Lat. *vide*), valve, ventral, verb, verse, version, versus, vicar, vice-, village, vision, vocative, voice, volt, voltage, volume, volunteer, von

V vanadium, vector, velocity, venerable, victory, viscount, volume

va active verb, verbal adjective, volt-ampere

Va Virginia

VA Veterans Administration, Vicar apostolic, vice admiral, (Order of) Victoria and Albert, Virginia

vac vacuum

val valentine, valuation, value

var reactive volt-ampere, variant, variation, variety, various

Vat Vatican

VAT value-added tax

v aux auxiliary verb

vb verb, verbal

vb n verbal noun

VC Veterinary Corps, vice chairman, vice chancellor, vice consul, Victoria Cross

vd vapor density, various dates

Vd vanadium

VD venereal disease

VDT video display terminal

VDU video display unit

veg vegetable, vegetation

vel vellum (bookbinding)

Ven venerable, Venice, Venus

Venez Venezuela, Venezualan

vent ventilating, ventilation, ventilator

ver verse, version

vers versed sine, versine

vert vertebra, vertebrate, vertical

ves vessel, vestry, vesicle, vesicular

vet veteran, veterinarian, veterinary

veter veterinary

VFD volunteer fire department

VFR visual flight rules

VFW Veterans of Foreign Wars (of the United States)

vg for example (Lat. *verbi gratia*)

VG vicar general

VHF very high frequency

vi see below (Lat. *vide infra*), intransitive verb

Vi virginium

VI Virgin Islands

vic vicar, vicarage

Vic, Vict Victoria, Victorian

vil village

v imp impersonal verb

VIP very important person

v irr irregular verb

vis visibility, visual

Vis, Visc, Visct viscount, viscountess

VISTA Volunteers in Service to America

viv lively (music) (Lat. *vivace*)

viz namely (Lat. *videlicet*)

VL Vulgar Latin

VLF very low frequency

vm voltmeter

VMD Doctor of Veterinary Medicine (Lat. *Veterinariae Medicinae Doctor*)

vn, v neut neuter verb

vo verso

vocab vocabulary

vol volcano, volume, volunteer

volc volcanic, volcano

vols volumes

vox pop voice of the people (Lat. *vox populi*)

voy voyage

vp passive verb, various pagings, various places, voting pool (stocks)

VP vice president

vr reflexive verb

VR Queen Victoria (Lat. *Victoria Regina*)

V Rev very reverend

vs see above (Lat. *vide supra*), versus, vibration seconds (sound), volumetric solution

VS veterinary surgeon

VSS versions

vt transitive verb

Vt, VT Vermont

VTOL vertical take-off and landing

Vul, Vulg Vulgate
vulg vulgar, vulgarity
vv verses, vice versa, violins

W

w wanting, warden, warehousing, watt, week, weight, west, western, wide, width, wife, with, won, word, work
W tungsten (Ger. *wolfram*), Wales, Washington, watt, Wednesday, Welsh, west, western
WA Washington (state)
WAC Women's Army Corps
wae when actually employed
WAF Women in the Air Force
war warrant
WASP Women's Air Force Service Pilots
watt-hr watt-hour
WAVES Women Appointed for Voluntary Emergency Service
wb warehouse book, water ballast, westbound
W/B waybill
WbN west by north
WbS west by south
wc water closet, without charge
WCTU Women's Christian Temperance Union
Wed Wednesday
wf wrong font (printing)
WFlem West Flemish

WFTU World Federation of Trade Unions
WGmc, WGer West Germanic
wh, whr watt-hour
whf wharf
WHO World Health Organization (of the United Nations)
wi when issued (stocks), wrought iron
WI West Indies, West Indian, Wisconsin
WInd West Indies
Wis, Wisc Wisconsin
wk weak, week, work
wkly weekly
wks weeks, works
wl water line, wavelength
wldr welder
W long west longitude
wm wattmeter
wmk watermark
WMO World Meteorological Organization (of the United Nations)
WNW west-northwest
WO wait order, warrant officer
wp weather permitting, wire payment, word processing
WPA Work Projects Administration, Works Progress Administration
wpm words per minute
WRAC Women's Royal Army Corps
WRAF Women's Royal Air Force

WREN, WRNS Women's Royal Naval Service
wrnt warrant
WSW west-southwest
wt weight
WV, WVa West Virginia
WVS Women's Volunteer Service
WY, Wyo Wyoming

X

x symbol for an unknown quantity
X Christ, Christian, a ten-dollar bill, xenon
xc ex-coupon
xd unlisted (ex-directory), ex-dividend
Xe xenon
x-int ex-interest
Xmas Christmas
Xn Christian
Xnt Christianity
x ref cross-reference
x-rts ex-rights
Xtian Christian
Xty Christianity
xyl xylograph

Y

y yard, year, younger, youngest
Y Young Men's Christian Association, Young Men's Hebrew Association, Young Women's Christian Association, Young Women's Hebrew Association, yttrium
Yb ytterbium
yd yard
yds yards
Yid Yiddish
YM, YMCA Young Men's Christian Association
YM, YMHA Young Men's Hebrew Association
YPSCE Young People's Society of Christian Endeavor
yr year, younger, your
yrs years, yours
YSL Young Socialists' League
Yt yttrium
YT Yukon Territory
YW Young Women's Christian Association, Young Women's Hebrew Association
YWCA Young Women's Christian Association
YWHA Young Women's Hebrew Association

Z

z zone
Z zenith distance, zone
Zec, Zech Zechariah
Zep, Zeph Zephaniah
Z/F zone of fire
Zn zinc
zool zoological, zoologist, zoology
ZPG zero population growth
Zr zirconium

Gazetteer

This section lists all of the more important political divisions and geographical features of the world, and all the urban localities in the United States and Canada having a population of 15,000 or more. The population figures given for places in the United States are from the census of 1990; those for Canada are from the census of 1976. All other population figures are from the latest available official censuses or official estimates, usually 1990. Maps of virtually all countries and of other important geographical features may be found in the main section of this dictionary at the appropriate alphabetic place of entry.

Postal ZIP codes are included for places in the United States. These were not, however, available in all cases. The asterisk (*) following some ZIP codes indicates that the city is further divided into postal zones and that the number given does not adequately identify a post office. In such cases further information is available from local postal authorities.

In the table below the authorized post office abbreviations of U.S. states are listed.

Alabama	AL	Kentucky	KY	Ohio	OH
Alaska	AK	Louisiana	LA	Oklahoma	OK
Arizona	AZ	Maine	ME	Oregon	OR
Arkansas	AR	Maryland	MD	Pennsylvania	PA
California	CA	Massachusetts	MA	Puerto Rico	PR
Colorado	CO	Michigan	MI	Rhode Island	RI
Connecticut	CT	Minnesota	MN	South Carolina	SC
Delaware	DE	Mississippi	MS	South Dakota	SD
District of		Missouri	MO	Tennessee	TN
Columbia	DC	Montana	MT	Texas	TX
Florida	FL	Nebraska	NE	Utah	UT
Georgia	GA	Nevada	NV	Vermont	VT
Hawaii	HI	New Hampshire	NH	Virginia	VA
Idaho	ID	New Jersey	NJ	Virgin Islands	VI
Illinois	IL	New Mexico	NM	Washington	WA
Indiana	IN	New York	NY	West Virginia	WV
Iowa	IA	North Carolina	NC	Wisconsin	WI
Kansas	KS	North Dakota	ND	Wyoming	WY

The following abbreviations have been used throughout this section:

ab.	about	NW	northwest(ern)
adm.	administrative	penin.	Peninsula
betw.	between	pop.	population
boro.	borough	poss.	possession
cap(s).	capital(s)	prot.	protectorate
CEN.	central	prov.	province
co.	county	reg.	region
col.	colony	s	south(ern)
ctr.	center	SE	southeast(ern)
dept.	department	sq. mi.	square mile(s)
dist.	district	sw	southwest(ern)
div.	division	terr.	territory
E	east(ern)	twp.	township
ft.	feet	uninc.	unincorporated
isl(s).	island(s)	urb.	urban
mi.	mile(s)	vill.	village
mtn(s).	mountain(s)	w	west(ern)
N	north(ern)		
NE	northeaster(ern)		

Aachen city, w Germany; pop. 242,971.
Aarhus co., E Denmark; 310 sq. mi.; pop. 534,000.
— city, E Aarhus co.; cap.; pop. 244,839.
Aberdeen co., NE Scotland; 1,972 sq. mi.; pop. 324,574.
— city, SE Aberdeen co.; cap.; pop. 209,189.
— city, NE South Dakota 57401*; pop. 24,927.
— city, w Washington 98520; pop. 16,565.
Abidjan city, SE Ivory Coast; cap.; pop. 1,100,000.
Abilene city, CEN. Texas 79604*; pop. 106,654.
Acapulco city, sw Mexico; pop. 421,100.
Accra city, s Ghana; cap.; pop. 633,880.
Achaea dept., N Peloponessus, Greece; 1,146 sq. mi.; pop. 229,000; cap. Patras.
Aconcagua extinct volcano, CEN. Argentina; 22,831 ft.
Acre city, NE Israel; pop. 37,900.
Addis Ababa city, CEN. Ethiopia; cap.; pop. 1,125,340.
Addison vill. NE Illinois 60101; pop. 32,058.
Adelaide city, SE South Australia; cap.; pop. 933,350.
Aden former British col.; now part of Yemen.
— city, Yemen; pop. 318,000.
Aden, Gulf of inlet of Arabian Sea betw. Yemen and Somalia.
Aden Protectorate former group of Arab tribal districts comprising a British protectorate; now part of Yemen.
Adirondack Mountains mtn. range, NE New York.
Adrian city, SE Michigan 49221; pop. 22,097.
Adriatic Sea inlet of the Mediterranean Sea, E of Italy.
Aegean Sea inlet of the Mediterranean Sea betw. Greece and Asia Minor.
Afghanistan republic, sw Asia; 251,825 sq. mi.; pop. 15,592,000; cap. Kabul.
Africa second largest continent, s of Europe and w of Asia; 11,710,000 sq. mi.
Affton uninc. place, NE Missouri 63123; pop. 21,106.
Agaña city, w Guam 96910; cap.; pop. 896.
Agawam town, w Massachusetts 01001; pop. 27,323.
Agra city, N India; site of Taj Mahal; pop. 591,917.
Aguadilla town, NW Puerto Rico 00603*; pop. 20,879.
Aguascalientes state, CEN. Mexico; 2,499 sq. mi.; pop. 430,000.
— city, CEN. Aguascalientes state; cap.; pop. 247,800.
Agulhas, Cape cape, s South Africa; southernmost point of Africa.
Ahmedabad city, w India; former cap. of Gujarat; pop. 1,585,544.
Aisne river, N France; 175 mi. long.
Ajaccio city, w Corsica; cap.; birthplace of Napoleon; pop. 41,000.
Akron city, NE Ohio 44309*; pop. 223,019.
Alabama state, SE United States; 51,705 sq. mi.; pop. 4,062,608; cap. Montgomery.
Alameda city, w California 94501*; pop. 76,459.
Alamogordo town, s New Mexico 88310; site of the first atom bomb test; pop. 27,596.
Alaska state of the United States, NW North America; 591,004 sq. mi.; pop. 551,947; cap. Juneau.
Alaska, Gulf of inlet of the Pacific on the s coast of Alaska.
Alaska Highway road joining Dawson Creek, British Columbia and Fairbanks, Alaska; 1,527 mi.
Alaska Peninsula promontory of sw Alaska; ab. 400 mi. long.
Alaska Range mtn. range, CEN. Alaska.
Albania Balkan republic s of Yugoslavia; 11,100 sq. mi.; pop. 3,262,000; cap. Tirana.
Albany city sw Georgia 31701*; pop. 78,122.
— city, E New York 12207*; cap.; pop. 101,082.
— city, w Oregon 97321; pop. 29,462.

Albemarle Sound inlet of the Atlantic, NE North Carolina.
Alberta prov., W Canada; 255,290 sq. mi.; pop. 1,838,037; cap. Edmonton.
Albert Lea city, S Minnesota 56007; pop. 18,310.
Albuquerque city, NW New Mexico 87101*; pop. 384,736.
Alcan Highway *unofficial name of* Alaska Highway.
Alderney island, N Channel Islands; 3 sq. mi.
Aleppo city, NE Syria; pop. 878,000.
Aleutian Islands isl. group, SW of Alaska Peninsula.
Alexandria N Egypt; summer cap., pop. 2,409,000.
— city, CEN. Louisiana 71301*; pop. 49,188.
— city, NE Virginia 22313*; pop. 111,183.
Algeria republic, NW Africa; 919,595 sq. mi.; pop. 23,039,000; cap. Algiers.
Algiers city, N Algeria; cap.; pop. 1,507,241.
Alhambra city, SW California 91802*; pop. 82,106.
Alicante prov., E Spain; 2,264 sq. mi.; pop. 920,000.
— city, E Alicante prov.; cap.; pop. 235,868.
Alice city, S Texas, 78332; pop. 19,788.
Aliquippa boro., W Pennsylvania 15001; pop. 13,374.
Allahabad city N India; pop. 490,622.
Allegheny Mountains mtn. range of Appalachian system; extends from Pennsylvania through Virginia.
Allegheny River river, W New York and Pennsylvania; 325 mi. long.
Allen Park vill., SE Michigan 48101; pop. 31,092.
Allentown city, E Pennsylvania 18101*; pop. 105,090.
Alliance city, NE Ohio 44601; pop. 23,376.
Alma city, S Quebec, Canada; pop. 25,638.
Almaty city, SE Kazakstan; cap.; pop. 928,000.
Alps mtn. system, S Europe; extends from S coast of France to W coast of Slovenia.
Alsace reg. and former prov., NE France.
Alsace-Lorraine oft-disputed border reg., NE France; adjoins SW Germany.
Altadena uninc. place, SW California 91001; pop. 42,658.
Altai Mountains mtn. system, CEN. Asia.
Altamont uninc. place, S Oregon 97601; pop. 18,591.
Altamonte Springs city, CEN Florida 32715*; pop. 34,879.
Alton city, SW Illinois 62002; pop. 32,905.
Altoona city, CEN. Pennsylvania 16603*; pop. 51,881.
Altus city, SW Oklahoma 73521*; pop. 21,910.
Alum Rock uninc. place, SW California 95116; pop. 16,890.
Amarillo city, NW Texas 79105*; pop. 157,615.
Amazon river, N South America; 3,910 mi. long; carries the largest volume of water of all rivers.
America 1 The United States of America. 2 North and South America; the western Hemisphere.
American Samoa See Samoa.
Americus city, CEN. Georgia 31709; pop. 16,512.
Ames city, CEN. Iowa 50010*; pop. 47,198.
Amherst uninc. place, CEN. Massachusetts 01002*; pop. 17,824.
Amiens city, N France; pop. 131,476.
Amman city, CEN. Jordan; cap.; pop. 648,587.
Amoy isl. of China, Taiwan Strait.
— city, Amoy isl.; pop. 224,000.
Amritsar city, W Punjab, India; pop. 407,628.
Amsterdam city, W Netherlands; cap.; pop. 694,680.
— city, CEN. New York 12010; pop. 20,714.
Amur river, E Asia; 2,700 mi. long.
Anaheim city, SW California 92803*; pop. 266,406.
Anatolia penin. at W end of Asia; comprises most of Turkey.
Anchorage city, S Alaska 99510*; pop. 226,338.
Andalusia reg., S Spain.
Anderson city, CEN. Indiana 46011*; pop. 59,459.
— city, NW South Carolina 29621*; pop. 26,184.
Andes mtn. range, W South America; connects with the Rockies; more than 4,000 mi. long.
Andorra Co-principality betw. France and Spain; 181 sq. mi.; pop. 51,000.
— city, CEN. Andorra; cap.; pop. 2,000.
Andover town, NE Massachusetts 01810; pop. 29,152.
Angel Falls waterfall, SE Venezuela; more than 3,300 ft.
Angola republic, W Africa; 481,354; sq. mi.; pop. 10,002,000; cap. Luanda.
Anjou town, S Quebec, Canada; pop. 36,596.

Ankara city, CEN. Turkey; cap.; pop. 2,553,209.
Annandale uninc. place, NE Virginia 22003*; pop. 50,975.
Annapolis city, CEN. Maryland 21401*; cap.; site of U.S. Naval Academy; pop. 33,187.
Ann Arbor city, SE Michigan 48106*; pop. 109,592.
Anniston city, NE Alabama 36201*; pop. 26,623.
Ansonia city, SW Connecticut 06401; pop. 18,403.
Antarctica continent surrounding the South Pole; 5,405,000 sq. mi. Also **Antarctic Continent.**
Antarctic Circle parallel of latitude at 66° 33′ S; the boundary of the South Frigid Zone.
Antarctic Ocean parts of Atlantic, Pacific, and Indian oceans bordering on Antarctica.
Antarctic Zone region enclosed by the Antarctic Circle.
Antigua and Barbuda monarchy, island group of the West Indies; 171 sq. mi.; pop. 80,600; cap. St. John's.
Antilles islands of the West Indies excluding the Bahamas; comprises Greater Antilles: Cuba, Hispaniola, Jamaica, and Puerto Rico; and Lesser Antilles: Trinidad, the Windward Islands, the Leeward Islands, and other small islands.
Antioch city, S Turkey; pop. 91,511.
— city, W California 94509; pop. 62,195.
Antwerp city, N Belgium; pop. 1,105,000.
Apennines mtn. range of Italy s of Po valley.
Appalachian Mountains mtn. range E North America.
Appleton city, E Wisconsin 54911*; pop. 65,695.
Aquitaine reg., SW France.
Arabia penin., SW Asia, betw. the Red Sea and Persian Gulf.
Arabian Gulf See **Persian Gulf.**
Arabian Sea part of the Indian Ocean betw. Arabia and India.
Arab Republic of Egypt See **Egypt.**
Aragon reg., NE Spain.
Aral Sea salt inland sea, SW Kazakstan and NW Uzbekistan.
Ararat, Mount mtn., E Turkey; 17,011 ft.; traditional landing place of Noah's ark.
Arcadia dept., CEN. Peloponnesus, Greece; 1,168 sq. mi.; pop. 112,000; cap. Tripolis.
— city, SW California 91006*; pop. 48,290.
Archangel city, NW Russia; pop. 387,000.
Arctic Circle parallel of latitude at 66° 33′ N; the boundary of the North Frigid Zone.
Arctic Ocean sea, N of Arctic Circle, surrounding North Pole.
Arden-Arcade uninc. place, CEN. California 95825; pop. 92,040.
Ardmore city, S Oklahoma 73401; pop. 23,079.
Arecibo town, N Puerto Rico 00612*; pop. 48,586.
Argentina republic, S South America; 1,073,399 sq. mi.; pop. 23,364,431; cap. Buenos Aires.
Argonne ridge, N France; site of battles in World Wars I and II.
Arizona state, SW United States; 114,000 sq. mi.; pop. 3,677,985; cap. Phoenix.
Arkansas state, CEN. United States; 53,187 sq. mi.; pop. 2,362,239; cap. Little Rock.
Arlington town, E Massachusetts 02174; pop. 44,630;
— city, N Texas 76010*; pop. 261,721.
— city, NE Virginia 22210*; pop. 170,936.
— urb. co., NE Virginia; site of **Arlington National Cemetery,** containing tomb of the Unknown Soldier.
Arlington Heights vill., NE Illinois 60004*; pop. 75,460.
Armenia republic, SW Asia; 11,500 sq. mi.; pop. 3,074,000; cap. Yerevan.
Arnhem city, E Netherlands; pop. 127,846.
Aruba island member of the Netherlands, N of Venezuala; 75 sq. mi.; pop. 62,900; cap. Oranjestad.
Arvada town, CEN. Colorado 80001*; pop. 89,235.
Arvida city, CEN. Quebec, Canada; pop. 18,448.
Asbury Park city, E New Jersey 07712; pop. 16,799.
Ascension isl. poss. of Great Britain, South Atlantic; 34 sq. mi.; pop. 750.
Asheville city, W North Carolina 28801*; pop. 61,607.
Ashland city, NE Kentucky 41101; pop. 23,622.
— city, CEN. Ohio 44805; pop. 20,079.
Ashtabula city, NE Ohio 44004; pop. 21,633.
Asia, E part of Eurasian land mass; largest of the continents; 17,240,000 sq. mi.

Asia Minor penin. of extreme w Asia, comprising most of Turkey.
Aspen Hill uninc. place, NW Maryland 20906; pop. 44,494.
Astrakhan city, SE Russia; pop. 465,000.
Asunción city, SW Paraguay; cap.; pop. 607,706.
Aswan city, S Egypt; site of **Aswan Dam,** 1¼ mi. long; pop. 144, 377.
Athens city, SE Greece; cap.; pop. 2,885,737.
— city, CEN. Georgia, 30603*; pop. 45,734.
— city, SE Ohio 45701; pop. 21,265.
Atlanta city, CEN. Georgia 30301*; cap.; pop. 394,017.
Atlantic City city, SE New Jersey 08401*; pop. 37,986.
Atlantic Ocean ocean, extending from the Arctic to the Antarctic between the Americas and Europe and Africa.
Atlas Mountains mtn. range, NW Africa.
Attleboro city, SE Massachusetts 02703; pop. 38,383.
Auburn city, CEN. Alabama 36830*; pop. 33,830.
— city, SW Maine 04210; pop. 24,309.
— town, CEN. Massachusetts 01501; pop. 15,005.
— city, CEN. New York 13021; pop. 31,258.
— city, CEN. Washington, 98002*; pop. 33,102.
Auckland city, N North Island, New Zealand; pop. 775,000.
Augsburg city, S Germany; pop. 245,940.
Augusta city, E Georgia 30901*; pop, 44,639.
— city, S Maine 04330; cap.; pop. 21,325.
Aurora city, CEN. Colorado 80010*; pop. 222,103.
— city, NE Illinois 60507*; pop. 99,581.
Auschwitz, German name for Oswiecim, city, SW Poland; site of Nazi extermination camp in World War II; pop. 44,200.
Austin city, SE Minnesota 55912; pop. 21,907.
— city, CEN. Texas 78710*; cap.; pop. 465,622.
Austintown uninc. place, NE Ohio 44515; pop. 32,371.
Australasia isls. of the South Pacific, including Australia, New Zealand, and New Guinea.
Australia federal state, situated on an isl. continent in South Pacific; 2,966,200 sq. mi.; pop. 17,073,000; cap. Canberra.
Australia Capital Territory reg., SE Australia; 900 sq. mi.; contains Canberra, the capital; pop. 241,500.
Austria republic, CEN. Europe; 32,376 sq. mi.; pop. 7,623,000.
Austronesia isls. of the South Pacific, including Indonesia, Melanesia, Micronesia, and Polynesia.
Avignon city, SE France; pop. 90,786.
Avon river, CEN. England; 96 mi. long.
Azerbaijan prov., NW Iran: **Eastern Azerbaijan:** 25,908 sq. mi.; pop. 4,097,000; cap. Tabriz; **Western Azerbaijan:** 15,000 sq. mi.; pop. 1,915,000; cap. Orumiyeh.
Azerbaijan republic, W Asia; 33,400 sq. mi.; pop. 7,029,000; cap. Baku.
Azores three isl. groups of Portugal, E Atlantic; 922 sq mi.; pop. 335,000.
Azov, Sea of inlet of the Black Sea, S Russia and S Ukraine.
Azusa city, S California 91702; pop. 41,333.
Baden-Baden city, SW Germany; site of famous mineral springs; pop. 49,399.
Bad Lands arid plateau, South Dakota and Nebraska. also **Bad-lands.**
Baghdad city, CEN. Iraq; cap.; pop. 5,348,117.
Baguio city, Luzon, N Philippines; pop. 97,449.
Bahamas isl. republic SE of Florida; 5,382 sq. mi.; pop. 253,000; cap. Nassau.
Bahrain isl. monarchy, Persian Gulf near Saudi Arabia; 267 sq. mi.; pop. 503,000; cap. Manama.
Baikal freshwater lake, S Russia; 12,150 sq. mi.
Baker, Mount mtn., Cascade range, N Washington; 10,750 ft.
Bakersfield city, S California 93302*; pop. 105,611.
Baku city, SE Azerbaijan; cap.; pop. 1,800,000.
Balboa Heights adm. ctr. of Canal Zone, near Balboa; pop. 232.
Baldwin uninc. place, SE New York 11510; pop. 22,719.
— boro., SW Pennsylvania 15234; pop. 21,923.
Baldwin Park city, SW California 91706; pop. 69,330.
Balearic Islands isl. group, W Mediterranean; prov. of Spain; 1,936 sq. mi.; pop. 642,702; cap. Palma.
Bali isl. of Indonesia, E of Java; 2,243 sq. mi.
Balkan Mountains, mtn. range, Balkan penin.
Balkan Peninsula large penin. of SE Europe.
Balkan States countries of Balkan penin.: Albania, Bosnia-Herzegovina, Bulgaria, Croatia, Greece, Macedonia, Romania, Yugoslavia, and part of Turkey.
Baltic Sea inlet of the Atlantic in NW Europe.
Baltimore city, N Maryland 21233*; pop. 736,014.
Bamako city, CEN. Mali; cap.; pop. 646,163.
Banaras Hindu sacred city, NE India; pop. 553,000. Also **Benares.**
Bandar Seri Begawan city, N Brunei; cap.; pop. 37,000.
Bandung city, W Java, Indonesia; pop. 1,201,730.
Bangalore city, E Mysore, India; cap.; pop. 1,540,741.
Bangkok city, SW Thailand; cap.; pop. 3,133,834.
Bangladesh republic, S Asia; 55,598 sq. mi.; pop. 113,005,000; cap. Dacca.
Bangor city, CEN. Maine 04401; pop. 33,181.
Bangui city, SW Central African Republic; cap.; pop. 596,776.
Banjul city, W Gambia; cap.; pop. 45,600.
Barbados isl. monarchy, E Caribbean; 166 sq. mi.; pop. 267,000; cap. Bridgetown.
Barberton city, NE Ohio 44203; pop. 27,623.
Barcelona prov., NE Spain; 2,985 sq. mi.; pop. 3,975,000.
— city, S Barcelona prov.; cap.; pop. 1,902,713.
Barnstable town, SE Massachusetts 02630; pop. 30,898.
Barranquilla city, N Colombia; pop. 859,000.
Barrie city, S Ontario, Canada; pop. 34,389.
Barrington town, E Rhode Island 02806; pop. 15,849.
Barrow, Point extreme N point of Alaska.
Barstow city, E California 92311; pop. 21,472.
Bartlesville city, NE Oklahoma 74003*; pop. 34,256.
Basel city, N Switzerland; pop. 180,900.
Bataan prov. S Luzon, Philippines; 517 sq. mi.; pop. 116,000; cap. Balanga; occupies **Bataan Peninsula,** scene of World War II surrender of U.S. forces to the Japanese.
Batavia city, W New York 14020; pop. 16,310.
Bath co. boro., SW England; pop. 83,900.
Bathurst town, NE New Brunswick, Canada; pop. 16,301.
— Banjul; *the former name of.*
Baton Rouge city, CEN. Louisiana 70821*; cap.; pop. 219,531.
Battle Creek city, S Michigan 49016*; pop. 53,540.
Bavaria state, SE Germany; 27,241 sq. mi.; pop. 10,870,968; cap. Munich.
Bayamon town, N Puerto Rico 00619; pop. 184,854.
Bay City city, CEN. Michigan 48706*; pop. 38,936.
Bayonne city, NE New Jersey 07002; pop. 61,144.
Baytown city, S Texas 77520*; pop. 63,850.
Bay Village city, NE Ohio 44140; pop. 17,000.
Beaconsfield town, S Quebec, Canada; pop. 20,417.
Beaumont city, SE Texas 77701*; pop. 114,323.
Beaverton city, NW Oregon 97005*; pop. 53,310.
Beckley city, S West Virginia 25801*; pop. 18,296.
Bedford city, NE Ohio 44146; pop. 14,822.
Beijing. See **Peking.**
Beirut city, W Lebanon; cap.; pop. 200,000.
Belarus republic, E Europe; 80,155 sq. mi.; pop. 10,200,000; cap. Minsk.
Belém city, N Brazil; pop. 565,097.
Belfast co. boro., and port, SE N. Ireland; cap.; pop. 354,400.
Belgium monarchy, NW Europe; 11,783 sq. mi.; pop. 9,958,000; cap. Brussels.
Belgrade city E Yugoslavia; cap.; pop. 770,140.
Belize monarchy, NE Central America; 8,867 sq. mi.; pop. 189,000; cap. Belmopan.
Bell city, S California 90201; pop. 34,365.
Bellaire city, S Texas 77401; pop. 13,842.
Belle Glade city, SE Florida 33430; pop. 16,177.
Belleville city, SW Illinois 62220*; pop. 42,785.
— town, NE New Jersey 07109; pop. 34,213.
— city, SE Ontario, Canada; pop. 35,311.
Bellevue city, E Nebraska 68005; pop. 30,982.
— city, CEN. Washington 98009*; pop. 86,874.
Bellflower city, SW California 90706; pop. 61,815.
Bell Gardens city, SW California 90201; pop. 42,355.
Bellingham city, NW Washington 98225*; pop. 52,179.
Bellmawr boro., SW New Jersey 08031; pop. 12,603.
Bellmore uninc. place, SE New York 11710; pop. 16,438.
Bellwood vill., NE Illinois 60104; pop. 20,241.
Belmont city, CEN. California 94002; pop. 24,127.
— town, E Massachusetts 02178; pop. 24,720.
Beloit city, S Wisconsin 53511; pop. 35,573.

Bengal former prov., NE British India; divided (1947) into: East Bengal, now part of Bangladesh, and **West Bengal,** a state of India; 34,200 sq. mi.; pop. 49,788,000; cap. Calcutta.

Benghazi city, N Libya; pop. 170,000.

Benin republic, W Africa; 43,450 sq. mi.; pop. 4,741,000.

Benton city, CEN. Arkansas 72015; pop. 17,177.

Benton Harbor city, SW Michigan 49022; pop. 12,818.

Berea city, NE Ohio 44017; pop. 19,051.

Bergen city, SW Norway; pop. 209,000.

Bergenfield boro., NE New Jersey 07621; pop. 24,458.

Bering Sea part of the North Pacific betw. Alaska and Russia, joined to the Arctic by **Bering Strait.**

Berkeley city, W California 94701*; pop. 102,724.

– city, CEN. Missouri 63134; pop. 12,450.

Berkley city, SE Michigan 48072; pop. 16,960.

Berlin city, CEN. Germany; cap. prior to 1945 when divided into the British, French, Soviet, and US sectors. In 1949 the Soviet sector, **East Berlin,** was designated capital of East Germany. The remaining sectors formed **West Berlin,** associated with West Germany; when Germany was reunited in 1990, Berlin became the capital again in 1991; pop. 3,352,848.

– city, N New Hampshire 03570; pop. 11,824.

Bermuda isl. group, W Atlantic; British col.; 21 sq. mi.; pop. 59,330; cap. Hamilton.

Bern city, CEN. Switzerland; cap.; pop. 141,300. Also **Berne.**

Berwyn city, NE Illinois 60402; pop. 45,426.

Bessemer city, CEN. Alabama 35020*; pop. 33,497.

Bethany city, CEN. Oklahoma 73008; pop. 20,075.

Bethel Park boro., SW Pennsylvania 15102; pop. 33,823.

Bethesda uninc. area, W Maryland 20814*; pop. 62,936.

Bethlehem ancient town, W Jordan; birthplace of Jesus; pop. 25,000.

– city, E Pennsylvania 18016*; pop. 71,428.

Bettendorf city, CEN. Iowa 52722; pop. 28,132.

Beverly city, NE Massachusetts 01915; pop. 38,195.

Beverly Hills city, SW California, 90210*; pop. 31,971.

Bhutan monarchy, S Asia, between NE India and Tibet; 18,150 sq. mi.; pop. 1,442,000; cap. Thimphu.

Biddeford city, SW Maine 04005; pop. 20,710.

Big Spring city, W Texas 79720*; pop. 23,093.

Bikini atoll, Marshall Islands; 2 sq. mi.; site of US nuclear tests, July 1946.

Billerica town, NE Massachusetts 01821; pop. 37,609.

Billings city, CEN. Montana 59011*; pop. 81,151.

Biloxi city, SE Mississippi 39530*; pop. 46,319.

Binghamton city, CEN. New York 13902*; pop. 53,008.

Birkenhead co. boro., NW England; pop. 342,300.

Birmingham co. boro., CEN. England; pop. 1,033,900.

– city, CEN. Alabama 35203*; pop. 268,968.

– city, SE Michigan 48012*; pop. 19,997.

Biscay, Bay of inlet, of the Atlantic betw. W and SW France and N and NW Spain.

Bismarck city, CEN. North Dakota 58501*; cap.; pop. 49,256.

Bismarck Archipelago isl. group, Trust Territory of New Guinea; 19,200 sq. mi.

Bizerte city, N Tunisia; pop. 62,856.

Black Forest wooded mtn. reg., SW Germany.

Black Hills mtn. reg., SW South Dakota and NE Wyoming.

Black Sea inland sea betw. Europe and Asia, connects with the Aegean via the Bosporus, the Sea of Marmara, and the Dardanelles.

Blaine vill., E Minnesota 55433; pop. 38,975.

Bloomfield town, CEN. Connecticut 06002; pop. 19,483.

– city, NE New Jersey 07003; pop. 45,061.

Bloomington city, CEN. Illinois 61701; pop. 51,972.

– city, CEN. Indiana 47401*; pop. 60,633.

– city, E Minnesota 55420; pop. 86,335.

Bluefield city, S West Virginia 24701; pop. 12,756.

Blue Island city, NE Illinois 60406; pop. 21,203.

Blue Ridge Mountains, W part of the Appalachians.

Blytheville city, NE Arkansas 72315*; pop. 22,906.

Boardman uninc. place, NE Ohio 44512; pop. 38,596.

Boca Raton city, SE Florida 33432*; pop. 61,492.

Bogalusa city, SE Louisiana 70427; pop. 14,280.

Bogotá city, CEN. Colombia; cap.; pop. 4,067,000.

Bohemia former prov., W Czech Republic.

Boise city, SW Idaho 83707*; cap.; pop. 102,160.

Bolivia republic, CEN. South America; 424,164 sq. mi.; pop. 7,332,000; caps. Sucre (judicial), La Paz (admin).

Bologna prov., CEN. Italy; 1,429 sq. mi.; pop. 925,113.

– city, cap. of Bologna prov.; pop. 422,204.

Bombay city, W India; pop. 5,970,575.

Bonn city, W Germany; was cap. of West Germany; pop. 286,184.

Bordeaux city, SW France; pop. 201,000.

Borneo (Kalimantan) isl., betw. Java and South China seas; comprising North Borneo, Sarawak, Brunei, and Indonesian Borneo; 286,969 sq. mi.

Bosnia and Herzegovina country of the Balkan Penin.; 19,741 sq. mi.; pop. 4,029,000; cap. Sarajevo.

Bosporus strait, betw. the Black Sea and the Sea of Marmara.

Bossier City city, NW Louisiana 71111*; pop. 52,721.

Boston city, E Massachusetts 02205*; cap.; pop. 574,283.

Botany Bay inlet of the Pacific, s of Sydney, Australia.

Botswana republic, S Africa; 224,607 sq. mi.; pop. 1,295,000; cap. Gaborone.

Boucherville town, S Quebec, Canada; pop. 25,530.

Boulder city, CEN. Colorado 80302*; pop. 83,312.

Boulder Dam *the former name of* Hoover Dam.

Bountiful city, CEN. Utah 84010; pop. 36,659.

Bowie city, CEN. Maryland 20715; pop. 37,589.

Bowling Green city, S Kentucky 42101*; pop. 40,641.

– city, NW Ohio 43402*; pop. 28,176.

Boynton Beach city, SE Florida 33435*; pop. 46,194.

Bozeman city, SW Montana 59715*; pop. 22,660.

Bradenton city, W Florida 33506*; pop. 43,779.

Braintree city, E Massachusetts 02184; pop. 33,836.

Brampton town, SE Ontario, Canada; pop. 103,459.

Brandon city, SW Manitoba, Canada; pop. 34,901.

Branford town, CEN. Connecticut 06405; pop. 27,603.

Brantford city, SE Ontario, Canada; pop. 66,950.

Brasilia city, CEN. Brazil; cap.; pop. 750,000.

Brazil republic, NE and CEN. South America; 3,286,500 sq. mi.; pop. 150,368,000; cap. Brasilia.

Brazzaville city, SE Congo; cap.; pop. 596,200.

Brea city, SW California 92621; pop. 32,873.

Breed's Hill hill, near Bunker Hill. See **Bunker Hill.**

Bremen state, NW Germany, 156 sq. mi.; pop. 695,115;

– city, cap. of Bremen state; pop. 556,128.

Bremerhaven city, part of Bremen state, NW Germany; pop. 138,987.

Bremerton city, W Washington 98310*; pop. 38,142.

Brenner Pass Alpine pass, Austrian–Italian border.

Brentwood uninc. place, SE New York 11717; pop. 45,218.

Breslau Wroclaw: German name of city in Poland.

Brest city, NW France; pop. 166,826.

– city, SW Belarus; pop. 186,000.

Bridgeport city, SW Connecticut 06601*; pop. 141,686.

Bridgeton town, E Missouri 63044; pop. 17,779.

– city, SW New Jersey 08302; pop. 18,942.

Brighton co. boro. and resort, SW England; pop. 166,000.

Brisbane city, SE Queensland, Australia; cap.; pop. 1,240,300.

Bristol co. boro., SW England; pop. 408,000.

– city, CEN. Connecticut 06010; pop. 60,640.

– urb. twp., SE Pennsylvania 19007; pop. 10,405.

– town, E Rhode Island 02809; pop. 21,625.

– city, NE Tennessee 37620*; pop. 23,421.

Bristol Channel inlet of the Atlantic betw. Wales and SW England.

Britain see **Great Britain.**

British Columbia prov., W Canada; 358,971 sq. mi.; pop. 2,466,608; cap. Victoria.

British Guiana former British col., NE South America. See **Guyana.**

British Virgin Islands British col., E Greater Antilles; 59 sq. mi.; pop. 10,484; cap. Road Town.

British West Indies See **West Indies.**

Brittany reg., W France; former prov.

Brno city, CEN. Czech Republic; pop. 372,793.

Brockton city, E Massachusetts 02403*; pop. 92,788.

Brockville town, SE Ontario, Canada; pop. 19,903.

Bronx borough, N New York City, New York 10400*; pop. 1,203,789. Also **the Bronx.**

Brookfield vill., NE Illinois 60513; pop. 18,876.
— city, SE Wisconsin 53005; pop. 35,184.
Brookline town, E Massachusetts 02146; pop. 54,718.
Brooklyn (Kings) borough, SE New York City, New York 11200*; pop. 2,300,664.
Brooklyn Center vill., SE Minnesota 55429; pop. 28,887.
Brooklyn Park vill., SE Minnesota 55007; pop. 56,381.
Brook Park vill., N Ohio 44142; pop. 22,865.
Brossard city, S Quebec, Canada; pop. 37,641.
Browardale uninc. place, SE Florida 33311; pop. 6,257.
Brownsville uninc. place, NW Florida 33142; pop. 18,058.
— city, S Texas 78520*; pop. 98,962.
Brownwood city, CEN. Texas 76801*; pop. 18,387.
Brunei sultanate, NW Borneo; 2,226 sq. mi.; pop. 259,000; cap. Bandar Sari Begawan.
Brunswick city, NE Germany; pop. 261,669.
— city, SE Georgia 31520*; pop. 16,433.
— uninc. place, S Maine 04011; pop. 14,683.
— vill., N Ohio 44212; pop. 28,230.
Brussels city, CEN. Belgium; cap.; pop. 2,400,000.
Bryan city, CEN. Texas 77801*; pop. 55,002.
Bucharest city, S Romania; cap.; pop. 1,858,418.
Budapest city, CEN. Hungary; cap.; pop. 2,060,000.
Buena Park city, SW California 90622*; pop. 68,784.
Buenos Aires city, E Argentina; cap.; pop. 10,300,000.
Buffalo city, W New York 14240*; pop. 328,123.
Bulgaria republic, SE Europe; 42,855 sq. mi.; pop. 8,997,400; cap. Sofia.
Bull Run small stream, NE Virginia; site of Union defeats in the Civil War, 1861 and 1862.
Bunker Hill hill, Charlestown, Massachusetts, near which (on Breed's Hill) occurred the first organized engagement of the American Revolution, June 17, 1775.
Burbank city, SW California 91505*; pop. 93,643.
Burgundy reg., CEN. France.
Burkina Faso republic, W Africa; 105,869 sq. mi.; pop. 9,012,000; cap. Ouagadougou.
Burlingame city, CEN. California 94010*; pop. 26,801.
Burlington city, SE Iowa 52601*; pop. 27,208.
— town, NE Massachusetts 01803; pop. 23,302.
— city, CEN. North Carolina 27215*; pop. 39,498.
— city, NW Vermont 05401*; pop. 39,127.
— town, SE Ontario, Canada; pop. 104,314.
Burma See Myanmar.
Burma Road road betw. N Burma (Myanmar) and SW China; a World War II supply route.
Burnsville city, SE Minnesota 55337; pop. 51,288.
Burundi republic, CEN. Africa; *formerly part of* Ruanda-Urundi; 10,747 sq. mi.; pop. 5,451,000; cap. Bujumbura.
Butler city, W Pennsylvania 16001*; pop. 15,714.
Butte city, SW Montana 59701*; pop. 33,336.
Cádiz city, SW Spain; pop. 156,328.
Caguas town, CEN. Puerto Rico 00625*; pop. 87,218.
Cahokia vill. SW Illinois 62206; pop. 17,550.
Cairo city, NE Egypt; cap.; pop. 6,052,836.
Calais city, N France; pop. 78,820.
Calcutta city, NE India; pop. 3,148,746.
Calgary city, S Alberta, Canada; pop. 469,917.
Caticut *an alternate name of* Kozhikode.
California state, W United States; 158,706 sq. mi.; pop. 29,839,250; cap. Sacramento.
California, Gulf of inlet of the Pacific, W Mexico, betw. Lower California and the rest of Mexico.
Calumet City city, NE Illinois 60409; pop. 37,840.
Camarillo city, SW California 93010; pop. 52,303.
Cambodia (State of Kampuchia), republic, 70,238 sq. mi.; pop. 8,592,000; cap. Phnom Penh.
Cambridge city, SE England; site of Cambridge University; pop. 101,600.
— city, E Massachusetts 02138*; pop. 95,802.
Camden city, S Arkansas 71701; pop. 14,380.
— city, SW New Jersey 08101*; pop. 87,492.
Cameroon republic, W equatorial Africa; 179,714 sq. mi.; pop. 7,663,246; cap. Yaounde. Also **Cameroun.**
Campbell city, W California 95008; pop. 36,048.
Camp Springs uninc. place, SW Maryland 20748; pop. 16,392.

Canada independent member of the Commonwealth of Nations, N North America; 3,849,675 sq. mi.; pop. 22,992,604; cap. Ottawa.
Canal Zone US leased terr., CEN. Panama; extending five miles on either side of the Panama Canal.
Canary Islands isl. group of Spain near NW coast of Africa; 2,796 sq. mi.; pop. 1,410,655.
Canaveral, Cape, cape, E Florida 32920; pop. 8,014; site of the **John F. Kennedy Space Center,** a space research and missiles installation.
Canberra city, SE Australia; cap.; pop. 277,300.
Canea city, NW Crete; pop. 40,564. Also **Khania.**
Cannes city, SE France; pop. 70,527.
Canterbury co. boro., SE England; site of famous cathedral; pop. 34,512.
Canton city, S China; pop. 1,296,000.
— town, E Massachusetts 02021; pop. 18,503.
— city, NE Ohio 44701*; pop. 84,161.
Cap-de-la-Madeleine city, S Quebec, Canada; pop. 31,126.
Cape Girardeau city, SE Missouri 63701; pop. 34,438.
Cape Town city, S South Africa; legislative cap.; pop. 776,617. Also **Capetown.**
Cape Verde republic in the CEN. Atlantic Ocean, W of Cape Verde; 1,557 sq. mi.; pop. 339,000; cap. Praia.
Capri isl. near the W coast of Italy; 4 sq. mi.
Caracas city, N Venezuela; cap.; pop. 1,658,500.
Carbondale city, S Illinois 62901; pop. 27,033.
Cardiff co. boro., SE Wales; pop. 282,000.
Caribbean Sea part of the Atlantic betw. the West Indies and Central and South America.
Carlisle boro., S Pennsylvania 17013; pop. 18,419.
Carlsbad city, SE New Mexico 88220; pop. 24,952.
Carlsbad Caverns National Park area, SE New Mexico; contains **Carlsbad Caverns,** a series of limestone caves.
Carmichael uninc. place, CEN. California 95608; pop. 48,702.
Carnegie boro., SW Pennsylvania 15106; pop. 9,278.
Carol City uninc place, SE Florida, 33055*; pop. 53,331.
Caroline Islands isl. group in the Pacific, E of the Philippines; 463 sq. mi.
Carpathian Mountains mtn. range, CEN. and E Europe.
Carpentersville vill., NE Illinois 60110; pop. 23,049.
Carrara city, CEN. Italy; site of white marble quarries; pop. 70,227.
Carson city, SW California 90744; pop. 40,443.
Carson City city, W Nevada 89701*; cap.; pop. 40,443.
Carteret boro., NE New Jersey 07009; pop. 19,025.
Casablanca city, NW Morocco; pop. 1,506,373.
Cascade Range mtn. range in Oregon, Washington, and British Columbia.
Cashmere See Kashmir.
Casper city, CEN. Wyoming 82601; pop. 46,742.
Caspian Sea saltwater lake in CEN. Asia; 163,800 sq. mi.
Castile reg., N and CEN. Spain.
Castro Valley uninc. place, W California 94546; pop. 48,619.
Catalina Island *an alternate name of* Santa Catalina.
Catalonia reg. NE Spain.
Catania prov., E Sicily; 1,371 sq. mi.; pop. 1,029,515.
— city, Catania prov.; cap.; pop. 370,679.
Cataño town, N Puerto Rico 00638; pop. 26,318.
Catonsville uninc. place, CEN. Maryland 21228; pop. 35,233.
Catskill Mountains range of the Appalachians in SE New York.
Caucasus mtn. range betw. the Black and Caspian Seas.
— reg., W Asia, betw. the Black and Caspian Seas. Also **Caucasia.**
Cayey town, CEN. Puerto Rico 00633; pop. 40,927.
Cedar Falls city, CEN. Iowa 50613; pop. 36,322.
Cedar Grove twp., NE New Jersey 07009; pop. 12,053.
Cedar Rapids city, E Iowa 52401; pop. 108,751.
Celebes *the former name of* Sulawesi.
Center Point uninc. place, CEN. Alabama 35215; pop. 23,317.
Central African Republic republic, CEN. Africa; 240,324 sq. mi.; pop. 2,875,000; cap. Bangui.

Central America s part of North America, betw. Mexico and Colombia.

Central Falls city, NE Rhode Island 02863; pop. 17,637.

Centralia city, s Illinois 62801*; pop. 14,274.

Central Islip uninc. place, SE New York 11722; pop. 26,028.

Cerritos city, s California 90701; pop. 53,020.

Ceylon See **Sri Lanka.**

Chad, Lake lake, CEN. Africa; 8,000 sq. mi.

Chad, Republic of republic, CEN. Africa; 495,752 sq. mi.; pop. 5,678,000; cap. N'Djamena.

Chambersburg boro., s Pennsylvania 17201; pop. 16,647.

Champaign city, CEN. Illinois 61820; pop. 63,502.

Champlain, Lake lake, betw. New York and Vermont, extending into Canada; 600 sq. mi.

Changchun city, NE China; pop. 1,309,000.

Channel Islands British isl. group, English Channel near Normandy; includes Jersey, Guernsey, Alderney, and Sark; 75 sq. mi.

Chapel Hill town, CEN. North Carolina 27514*; pop. 38,719.

Charlesbourg city, s Quebec, Canada; pop. 63,147.

Charleston city, E Illinois 61920; pop. 20,398.

— city, SE South Carolina 29401*; pop. 80,414.

— city, CEN. West Virginia 25301*; cap.; pop. 57,287.

Charlotte city, CEN. North Carolina 28202*; pop. 395,934.

Charlotte Amalie city, s St. Thomas, U.S. Virgin Islands 00801*; cap.; pop. 12,220.

Charlottesville city, CEN. Virginia 22906*; pop. 40,341.

Charlottetown city, CEN. Prince Edward Island, Canada; cap.; pop. 17,063.

Chateauguay town, s Quebec, Canada; pop. 36,329.

Chatham city, s Ontario, Canada; pop. 38,685.

Chattanooga city, SE Tennessee 37401*; pop. 152,466.

Cheektowaga uninc. place, w New York 14225; pop. 84,387.

Chelmsford town, NE Massachusetts 01824; pop. 32,388.

Chelsea metropolitan boro., sw London, England; pop. 47,000.

— city, E Massachusetts 02150; pop. 25,431.

Cheltenham urb. twp., SE Pennsylvania 19012; pop. 35,509.

Cherbourg city, N France; pop. 32,536.

Chesapeake city, SE Virginia 23320*; pop. 151,976.

Chesapeake Bay inlet of the Atlantic in Virginia and Maryland.

Cheshire town, CEN. Connecticut 06410; pop. 25,684.

Chester co. boro., w Cheshire, England; cap.; pop. 61,370.

— city, SE Pennsylvania 19013*; pop. 41,856.

Cheviot Hills mtn. range, on the border betw. England and Scotland.

Cheyenne city, SE Wyoming 82001*; cap.; pop. 50,008.

Chicago city, NE Illinois 60607*; third largest city in the United States; pop. 2,783,726.

Chicago Heights city, NE Illinois 60411; pop. 33,072.

Chico city, CEN. California 95926*; pop. 40,079.

Chicopee city, sw Massachusetts 01021*; pop. 56,632.

Chicoutimi city, s Quebec, Canada; pop. 57,737.

Chihuahua state, N Mexico; 94,830 sq. mi.; pop. 2,000,000.

Chihuahua city, Chihuahua state, Mexico; cap.; pop. 369,500.

Chile republic, w South America; 292,153 sq. mi.; pop. 13,173,000; cap. Santiago.

Chillicothe city, CEN. Ohio 45601; pop. 21,923.

Chillum uninc. place, sw Maryland 20783; pop. 31,309.

China, People's Republic of republic, E and CEN. Asia; 3,696,100 sq. mi.; pop. 1,133,683,000; cap. Peking (Beijing).

China, Republic of (Taiwan) republic on Taiwan and several smaller isls.; 13,900 sq. mi.; pop. 20,221,000; cap. Taipei.

China Sea part of the Pacific bordering on China. See **East China Sea, South China Sea.**

Chino city, sw California 91710; pop. 59,682.

Chula Vista city, sw California 92010*; pop. 135,163.

Chungking city, CEN. China; cap. during World War II; pop. 1,900,000.

Cicero city, NE Illinois 60650; pop. 67,436.

Cincinnati city, sw Ohio 45234*; pop. 364,040.

Circassia reg., NW Caucasus, Russia.

Citrus Heights uninc. place, NE California 95610; pop. 107,439.

Clairton city, sw Pennsylvania 15025; pop. 9,656.

Claremont city, sw California 91711*; pop. 32,503.

Clark twp., NE New Jersey 07066; pop. 14,629.

Clarksburg city, N West Virginia 26301*; pop. 18,059.

Clarksdale city, NW Mississippi 38614; pop. 19,717.

Clarksville city, N Tennessee 37041*; pop. 75,494.

Clawson city, SE Michigan 48017; pop. 13,874.

Clayton city, E Missouri 63105; pop. 13,874.

Clearwater city, w Florida 33515*; pop. 98,784.

Cleburne city, CEN. Texas 76031; pop. 22,205.

Cleveland city, N Ohio 44101*; pop. 505,616.

— city, SE Tennessee 37311*; pop. 30,354.

Cleveland Heights city, N Ohio 44118; pop. 54,052.

Clifton city, NE New Jersey 07015*; pop. 71,742.

Clinton city, E Iowa 52732; pop. 29,201.

Clovis city, E New Mexico 88101; pop. 30,954.

Cocoa city, E Florida 32922*; pop. 17,722.

Cod, Cape penin, SE Massachusetts.

Coeur d'Alene city, N Idaho 83814; pop. 24,563.

Coffeyville city, SE Kansas 67337; pop. 12,917.

Cohoes city, E New York 12047; pop. 16,825.

College Park city, w Georgia 30337; pop. 20,457.

— city, w Maryland 20740*; pop. 21,927.

College Station city, CEN. Texas 77840*; pop. 52,456.

Collingswood boro., w New Jersey 08108; pop. 15,289.

Collinsville city, sw Illinois 62234; pop. 22,446.

Cologne city, w Germany; pop. 976,136.

Colombia republic, NW South America; 440,831 sq. mi.; pop. 32,978,000; cap. Bogotá.

Colombo city, w Sri Lanka; cap.; pop. 609,000.

Colón city, Caribbean end of the Canal Zone; an enclave of Panama; pop. 73,600.

Colonial Heights city, CEN. Virginia, 23834; pop. 16,064.

Colorado state, CEN. United States; 104,091 sq. mi.; pop. 3,307,912; cap. Denver.

Colorado River river flowing through Colorado, Utah, Arizona, California, and Mexico to the Gulf of California; length ab. 1,400 mi.

Colorado Springs city, CEN. Colorado 80901*; site of U.S. Air Force Academy; pop. 281,140.

Colton city, s California, 92324; pop. 40,213.

Columbia city, CEN. Missouri 65201*; pop. 69,101.

— city, CEN. South Carolina 29201*; cap.; pop. 98,052.

— city, CEN. Tennessee 38401*; pop. 28,583.

Columbia Heights city, E Minnesota 55421; pop. 18,910.

Columbia River river, sw Canada and NW United States; 1,200 mi. long.

Columbus, city, w Georgia 31902*; pop. 179,278.

— city, CEN. Indiana 47201*; pop. 31,802.

— city, E Mississippi 39701*; pop. 23,799.

— city, E Nebraska 68601; pop. 19,480.

— city, CEN. Ohio 43216*; cap.; pop. 632,910.

Commerce City town, CEN. Colorado 80022; pop. 16,466.

Comoros isl. republic in the Indian Ocean, NW of Madagascar; 719 sq. mi.; pop. 463,000; cap. Moroni.

Compton city, sw California 90220*; pop. 90,454.

Conakry city, w Guinea; cap.; pop. 197,267.

Concord city, w California 94520*; pop. 111,348.

— town, NE Massachusetts 01742; pop. 17,076.

— uninc. place, NE Missouri 63128; pop. 19,859.

— city, CEN. New Hampshire 03301*; cap.; pop. 36,006.

— city, CEN. North Carolina 28025; pop. 27,347.

Congo, Republic of the republic, CEN. Africa; 132,047 sq. mi.; pop. 2,326,000; cap. Brazzaville.

Congo, Democratic Republic of the republic, CEN. Africa; 905,446 sq. mi.; pop. 34,138,000; cap. Kinshasa.

Congo River river, CEN. Africa; 2,720 mi. long.

Connecticut state, NE United States; 5,018 sq. mi.; pop. 3,295,669; cap. Hartford.

Connersville city, E Indiana 47331; pop. 15,550.

Continental Divide ridge of the Rockies separating westflowing and east-flowing streams in North America.

Conway city, CEN. Arkansas 72032; pop. 26,481.

Coon Rapids vill., E Minnesota 55433; pop. 52,978.

Copenhagen city, E Denmark; cap.; pop. 1,343,916.

Copiague uninc. place, SE New York 11726; pop. 20,769.

Coral Gables city, SE Florida 33134; pop. 40,091.

Coral Sea part of the Pacific, E of Australia and New Guinea.

Cork co., sw Ireland; 2,880 sq. mi.; pop. 402,465.

— co. boro., CEN. Cork co.; cap.; pop. 138,267.

Corner Brook city, w Newfoundland, Canada; pop. 25,198.
Corning city, w New York 14830; pop. 11,938.
Cornwall city, sw Ontario, Canada; pop. 46,121.
Corona city, s California 91720; pop. 76,095.
Coronado city, s California 92118; pop. 26,540.
Corpus Christi city, s Texas 78408*; pop. 257,453.
Corsica isl., N Mediterranean; a dept. of France; 3,352. sq. mi.; pop. 244,600; cap. Ajaccio.
Corsicana city, CEN. Texas 75110; pop. 22,911.
Cortland city, CEN. New York 13045; pop. 19,801.
Corvallis city, w Oregon 97333*; pop. 44,757.
Costa Mesa city, sw California 92626*; pop. 96,357.
Costa Rica republic, Central America; 19,730 sq. mi.; pop. 3,015,000; cap. San José.
Côte d'Ivoire See **Ivory Coast.**
Côte-St.-Luc city, s Quebec, Canada; pop. 25,721.
Council Bluffs city, sw Iowa 51501*; pop. 54,315.
Coventry city and co. boro., CEN. England; pop. 339,300.
— town, CEN. Rhode Island 02816; pop. 31,083.
Covina city, sw California 91722*; pop. 43,207.
Covington city, N Kentucky 41011*; pop. 43,264.
Cranford urb. twp., E New Jersey 07106. pop. 22,624.
Cranston city, E Rhode Island 02910; pop. 76,060.
Crestwood city, E Missouri 63126; pop. 11,234.
Crete isl., E Mediterranean; adm. div. of Greece; 3,219 sq. mi.; pop. 502,165.
Crimea penin., SE Ukraine.
Croatia country of the Balkan Penin.; 21,829 sq. mi.; pop. 4,648,000; cap. Zagreb.
Crowley city, s Louisiana 70526; pop. 13,983.
Crystal vill., SE Minnesota 55428; pop. 23,788.
Cuba isl. republic, Caribbean Sea; 42,804 sq. mi. (with the Isle of Pines); pop. 10,603,000; cap. Havana.
Cudahy city, sw California 90201; pop. 22,817.
— city, sw Wisconsin 53110; pop. 18,659.
Culver City city, sw California 90230*; pop. 38,793.
Cumberland city, NW Maryland 21502*; pop. 23,706.
Cumberland Gap passage through Cumberland Mountains, betw. Tennessee and Virginia.
Cumberland River river, Kentucky and Tennessee; flows to Ohio River.
Cupertino city, w California 95014; pop. 40,263.
Curaçao isl., w Netherlands Antilles; 171 sq. mi.; pop. 147,388; cap. Willemstad.
Cutler Ridge uninc. place, SE Florida 33157; pop. 21,268.
Cuyahoga Falls city, NE Ohio 44222*; pop. 48,950.
Cyclades isl. group, s Aegean; a dept. of Greece; 1,023 sq. mi.; pop. 86,000; cap. Hermoupolis.
Cypress city, sw California 90630; pop. 42,655.
Cyprus isl. republic, E Mediterranean; 2,276 sq. mi.; pop. 568,000; cap. Nicosia.
Czech Republic republic, CEN. Europe; 30,452 sq. mi.; pop. 10,302,215; cap. Prague.
Dacca city, CEN. Bangladesh; cap.; pop. 5,300,000.
Dachau town, SE Germany; site of a Nazi concentration camp; pop. 34,162.
Dakar city, w Senegal; cap.; pop. 1,382,000.
Dallas city, N Texas 75260*; pop. 1,006,877.
Dalmatia coastal reg. Croatia; 4,954 sq. mi. pop. 750,000; cap. Split.
Dalton city, NW Georgia 30720; pop. 21,761.
Daly City city, w California 94017*; pop. 92,311.
Damascus city, sw Syria; cap.; pop. 1,156,000.
Danbury city, sw Connecticut 06810*; pop. 65,585.
Danube river, CEN. and E Europe; 1,770 mi. long.
Danvers town, NE Massachusetts 01923; pop. 24,174.
Danville city, E Illinois 61832; pop. 33,828.
— city, s Virginia 24541*; pop. 53,056.
Danzig *the former name of* Gdańsk.
Dardanelles strait, NW Turkey; connects Sea of Marmara with the Aegean.
Darien town, sw Connecticut 06820; pop. 18,196.
Darien, Gulf of inlet of the Caribbean, E coast of Panama.
Dartmouth town, SE Massachusetts 02714; pop. 27,244.
— city, s Nova Scotia, Canada; pop. 65,341.
Davenport city, E Iowa 52802*; pop. 95,333.
Davis city, CEN. California 95616; pop. 46,209.

Dayton city, sw Ohio 45401*; pop. 182,044.
Daytona Beach city, E Florida 32015*; pop. 61,921.
Dead Sea large salt lake on Israel–Jordan border; 1,292 ft. below sea level.
Dearborn city, SE Michigan 48120*; pop. 89,286.
Dearborn Heights city, SE Michigan 48127; pop. 60,838.
Death Valley desert basin, SE California; maximum depth 280 ft. below sea level.
Decatur city, N Alabama 35601*; pop. 48,761.
— city, CEN. Georgia 30030*; pop. 17,336.
— city, CEN. Illinois 62521*; pop. 83,885.
Deccan Plateau triangular tableland covering most of the penin. of India.
Dedham town, E Massachusetts 02026; pop. 23,782.
Deerfield vill., NE Illinois 60015; pop. 17,327.
Deerfield Beach town, SE Florida 33441; pop. 46,325.
Deer Park uninc. place, SE New York 11729; pop. 28,840.
Defiance city, NW Ohio 43512; pop. 16,768.
De Kalb city, N Illinois 60115; pop. 34,925.
Delaware state, E United States; 2,044 sq. mi.; pop. 668,696; cap. Dover.
— city, CEN. Ohio 43015; pop. 20,030.
Delaware River river separating Pennsylvania and Delaware from New York and New Jersey; 315 mi. long.
Del City city, CEN. Oklahoma 73115; pop. 23,928.
Delhi terr., CEN. India; 573 sq. mi.; pop. 5,116,000; contains New Delhi.
— city; Delhi terr.; cap.; pop. 3,706,558.
Delray Beach city, SE Florida 33444; pop. 47,181.
Del Rio city, sw Texas 78840; pop. 30,705.
Denison city, N Texas 75020; pop. 21,505.
Denmark monarchy, NW Europe; 16,633 sq. mi.; pop. 5,139,000; cap. Copenhagen.
Denton city, N Texas 76201; pop. 66,270.
Denver city, CEN. Colorado 80202*; cap.; pop. 467,610.
Depew vill., w New York 14043; pop. 17,673.
Des Moines city, CEN. Iowa 50318*; cap.; pop. 193,187.
Des Plaines city, NE Illinois 60016*; pop. 53,223.
Detroit city, SE Michigan 48233*; pop. 1,027,974.
Devil's Island rocky isl. off the coast of French Guiana; formerly a penal colony.
District of Columbia federal dist., E United States; coextensive with Washington, the capital; pop. 606,900.
Dixon city, N Illinois 61021; pop. 15,144.
Djibouti republic, E Africa; 8,950 sq. mi.; pop. 530,000; cap. Djibouti.
Dnepropetrovsk city, sw Ukraine; pop. 1,083,000. Also **Dnie-propetrovsk.**
Dnieper river, E Europe; 1,420 mi. long. Also **Dnepr.**
Dneister river, sw Ukraine; 876 mi. long. Also **Dnestr.**
Dodecanese isl. group, Aegean Sea; a dept. of Greece; 1,036 sq. mi.; pop. 120,000; cap. Rhodes.
Dolomite Alps E div. of the Alps, N Italy.
Dolton vill., NE Illinois 60419; pop. 23,930.
Dominican Republic republic, E Hispaniola; 18,704 sq. mi.; pop. 7,170,000; cap. Santo Domingo.
Don river, sw Russia; 1,222 mi. long.
Donets river, E Europe; 631 mi. long.
Dorval city, s Quebec, Canada; pop. 19,131.
Dothan city, SE Alabama 36301*; 53,589.
Douai town, N France; pop. 45,239.
Dover municipal boro., SE England; pop. 34,160.
— city, CEN. Delaware 19901; cap.; pop. 27,630.
— city, SE New Hampshire 03820; pop. 25,042.
Dover, Strait of strait at the E end of the English Channel; 21 mi. wide.
Downers Grove vill., NE Illinois 60515; pop. 46,858.
Downey city, sw California 90241*; pop. 91,444.
Dracut town, NE Massachusetts 01826; pop. 25,594.
Drayton Plains city, SE Michigan 48020; pop. 18,000.
Dresden city, s Germany; pop. 514,508.
Drummondville city, s Quebec, Canada; pop. 29,286.
Dublin city, E Ireland; cap.; pop. 544,586.
— city, CEN. Georgia 31021; pop. 16,312.
Dubuque city, E Iowa 52001*; pop. 57,546.
Duisburg city, w Germany; pop. 559,066.
Duluth city, NE Minnesota 55806*; pop. 85,493.

Dumont boro., NE New Jersey 07628; pop. 17,187.
Duncan city, S Oklahoma 73533; pop. 21,732.
Dundalk uninc. place, CEN. Maryland 21222; pop. 65,800.
Dundas town, S Ontario, Canada; pop. 19,179.
Dundee burgh, E Scotland; pop. 190,793.
Dunedin city, W Florida 33528; pop. 34,012.
Dunkerque town, N France; scene of evacuation of British forces in World War II, May–June 1940; pop. 83,163.
Dunkirk city, W New York 14048; pop. 13,989.
Dunmore boro., NE Pennsylvania 18512; pop. 15,403.
Durban city, SE South Africa; pop. 634,301.
Durham city, CEN. North Carolina 27701*; pop. 131,611.
Düsseldorf city, W Germany; pop. 594,770.
Dutch Guiana See Surinam.
Eagle Pass city, SW Texas 78852; pop. 20,651.
East Berlin See Berlin.
Eastchester uninc. place, SE New York 10709; pop. 18,537.
East Chicago city, NW Indiana 46312*; pop. 33,892.
East China Sea NE part of the China Sea.
East Cleveland city, NE Ohio 44112; pop. 33,096.
East Detroit city, SE Michigan 48021; pop. 35,283.
Easter Island isl. of Chile, South Pacific; known for stone monuments found there; 45 sq. mi.
East Germany See Germany.
East Hartford town, CEN. Connecticut 06108; pop. 50,452.
East Haven town, S Connecticut 06512; pop. 26,144.
East Indies **1** The isls. of the Malay Archipelago. **2** SE Asia. **3** Formerly, India. Also **East India.**
Eastlake city, NE Ohio 44094; pop. 21,161.
East Lansing city, CEN. Michigan 48823*; pop. 50,677.
East Liverpool city, E Ohio 43920; pop. 13,654.
East Los Angeles uninc. place, SW California 90022; pop. 126,379.
East Meadow uninc. place, SE New York 11554; pop. 36,909.
East Millcreek uninc. place, NE Utah 84101; pop. 21,184.
East Moline city, NW Illinois 61244; pop. 20,147.
Easton city, S Pennsylvania 18042; pop. 26,276.
East Orange city, NE New Jersey 07019*; pop. 73,552.
East Peoria city, CEN. Illinois 61611; pop. 21,378.
East Point city, CEN. Georgia 30044; pop. 34,402.
East Providence town, E Rhode Island 02914; pop. 50,380.
East Prussia former prov. of Prussia, NE Germany.
East Ridge town, SE Tennessee 37412; pop. 21,101.
East Saint Louis city, SW Illinois 62201*; pop. 40,944.
Eau Claire city, CEN. Wisconsin 54703*; pop. 56,856.
Ecuador republic, NW South America; 103,930 sq. mi.; pop. 10,782,000; cap. Quito.
Eden city, CEN. North Carolina 27288; pop. 15,238.
Edina city, SE Minnesota 55424; pop. 46,070.
Edinburg city, S Texas 78539; pop. 29,885.
Edinburgh city, E Scotland; cap.; pop. 420,169.
Edmond city, CEN. Oklahoma 73034; pop. 52,315.
Edmonds city, NW Washington 98020; pop. 30,744.
Edmonton city, CEN. Alberta, Canada; cap.; pop. 573,982.
Egypt republic, NE Africa; 385,229 sq. mi.; pop. 53,170,000; cap. Cairo: official name **Arab Republic of Egypt.**
Eire the Irish Gaelic name of Ireland.
Elba isl. betw. Italy and Corsica; sovereign under the exiled Napolean Bonaparte, 1814–15.
Elbe river, CEN. Europe; 725 mi. long.
Elbrus, Mount mtn., S Russia; 18,603 ft.
Elburz Mountains mtn. range N Iran.
El Cajon city, SW California 92020*; pop. 88,693.
El Centro city, S California 92243*; pop. 31,384.
El Cerrito city, W California 94530; pop. 4,490.
El Dorado city, S Arkansas 71730; pop. 23,146.
Elgin city, NE Illinois 60120; pop. 77,010.
Elizabeth city, NE New Jersey 07201*; pop. 110,002.
Elk Grove Village vill., NE Illinois 60007; pop. 33,429.
Elkhart city, N Indiana 46515*; pop. 43,627.
Ellis Island isl., upper New York Bay; former site of US immigration station, now a museum about immigration.
Elmhurst city, NE Illinois 60126; pop. 42,029.
Elmira city, S New York 14901*; pop. 33,724.
Elmont uninc. place, SE New York 11003; pop. 28,612.
El Monte city, SW California 91734*; pop. 106,209.
Elmwood Park vill., NE Illinois 60635; pop. 23,206.

El Paso city, W Texas 79940*; pop. 515,342.
El Salvador republic, W Central America; 8,124 sq. mi.; pop. 5,221,000; cap. San Salvador.
Elyria city, N Ohio 44035*; pop. 56,746.
Emporia city, CEN. Kansas 66801; pop. 25,512.
Enfield town, N Connecticut 06082; pop. 45,532.
England s part and largest political division of Great Britain; 50,363 sq. mi.; pop. 47,536,300; cap. London.
Englewood city, CEN. Colorado 80110; pop. 28,387.
— city, NE New Jersey 07631*; pop. 24,850.
English Channel strait, betw. England and France; 20–100 mi. wide.
Enid city, N Oklahoma 73701*; pop. 45,309.
Eniwetok atoll, Marshall Islands; U.S. nuclear weapons testing area.
Enterprise city, SE Alabama 36330*; pop. 20,123.
Epsom town, SE England; site of famous racecourse; pop. 72,000.
Equatorial Guinea republic, W Africa; 10,831 sq. mi.; pop. 350,000; cap. Malabo.
Erie city, NW Pennsylvania 16501*; pop. 108,718.
Erie, Lake southernmost of the Great Lakes; 9,940 sq. mi.
Erie Canal waterway betw. Albany and Buffalo, New York; integrated with New York State Barge Canal.
Eritrea country, E Africa; 48,263 sq. mi.; pop. 3,500,000; cap. Asmara.
Erivan see Yerevan.
Escondido city, SW California 92025*; pop. 108,635.
Essen city, W Germany; pop. 652,501.
Essex uninc. place, N Maryland 21221; pop. 40,872.
Estonia republic, E Europe; 17,400 sq. mi.; pop. 1,573,000; cap. Tallinn.
Ethiopia republic, E Africa; 423,517 sq. mi.; pop. 54,938,000; cap. Addis Ababa.
Etna, Mount volcano, E Sicily, Italy; 10,868 ft.
Euboea isl. of Greece in the Aegean; 1,457 sq. mi.
Euclid city, NE Ohio 44117; pop. 54,875.
Eugene city, W Oregon 97401*; pop. 112,669.
Euphrates river, SW Asia; 1,740 mi. long.
Eurasia large land mass comprising Europe and Asia.
Eureka city, NW California 95501*; pop. 27,025.
Europe continent comprising the W part of the Eurasian land mass; about 4,063,000 sq. mi.
Evanston city, NE Illinois 60204*; pop. 73,233.
Evansville city, SW Indiana 47708*; pop. 126,272.
Everest mtn., E Nepal; highest point of the earth's surface; 29,028 ft.
Everett city, E Massachusetts 02149; pop. 35,701.
— city, W Washington 98201*; pop. 69,961.
Everglades large swampy reg., S Florida.
Evergreen Park vill., NE Illinois 60642; pop. 20,874.
Exeter co. boro., CEN. Devonshire, England; cap; pop. 95,600.
Faeroe Islands isl. group of Denmark, North Atlantic; 540 sq. mi.; pop. 48,400; cap. Tórshavn.
Fairborn city, SW Ohio 45324; pop. 31,300.
Fairfax town, N Virginia 22030; pop. 19,622.
Fairfield city, CEN. California 94533; pop. 58,099.
— town, SW Connecticut 06430; pop. 53,418.
Fairhaven town, SE Massachusetts 02719; pop. 16,132.
Fair Lawn boro., NE New Jersey 07410; pop. 30,548.
Fairmont city, N West Virginia 26554*; pop. 20,210.
Fairview Park city, NE Ohio 44126; pop. 18,028.
Falkland Islands British col., South Atlantic; 4,618 sq. mi.; pop. 1,081; cap. Stanley.
Fall River city, SE Massachusetts 02722*; pop. 92,703.
Falls urb. twp., NE Pennsylvania 18615; pop. 36,083.
Falmouth town, E Massachusetts 02540; pop. 27,960.
Fargo city, SE North Dakota 58102*; pop. 74,111.
Faribault city, SE Minnesota 55021; pop. 17,085.
Farmers Branch city, N Texas 75234; pop. 24,250.
Farmington town, NW New Mexico 87401; pop. 33,997.
Fayetteville city, NW Arkansas 72701*; pop. 42,099.
— city, CEN. North Carolina 28302*; pop. 75,695.
Federal Republic of Germany See Germany.
Ferguson city, E Missouri 63135; pop. 22,286.
Ferndale city, SE Michigan 48220; pop. 25,084.

Fiji republic, South Pacific; comprises **Fiji Islands** (7,039 sq. mi.) and **Rotuma** (18 sq. mi.); pop. 740,000; cap. Suva.

Findlay city, CEN. Ohio 45840*; pop. 35,703.

Finland republic, N Europe; 130,559 sq. mi.; pop. 4,978,000; cap. Helsinki.

Finland, Gulf of part of the Baltic Sea betw. Finland and Russia.

Fitchburg city, N Massachusetts 01420*; pop. 41,194.

Flagstaff city, CEN. Arizona 86001*; pop. 45,857.

Flanders reg., N France and S Belgium.

Flint city, CEN. Michigan 48502*; pop. 140,761.

Floral Park vill., SE New York 11001*; pop. 15,947.

Florence city, CEN. Tuscany, Italy; cap.; pop. 417,487.

— city, NW Alabama 35630*; pop. 36,426.

— city, E South Carolina 29501; pop. 29,813.

Florence-Graham uninc. place, SW California 90001; pop. 48,662.

Florida state, SE United States; 58,664 sq. mi.; pop. 13,003,362; cap. Tallahassee.

Florida Keys isl. group SW of Florida.

Florissant city, E Missouri 63033*; pop. 51,206.

Fond du Lac town, N Wisconsin 54935; pop. 37,757.

Fontainebleau town, N France; site of a former royal residence; pop. 16,778.

Fontana city, CEN. California 92335; pop. 87,535.

Forest Park town, CEN. Georgia 30050; pop. 16,925.

— vill., NE Illinois 60130; pop. 14,918.

— city, SW Ohio 45405; pop. 18,609.

Forestville uninc. place, SW Maryland 20747; pop. 16,731.

Formosa *a former name of* Taiwan.

Fort Benning South uninc. place, W Georgia 31905; pop. 15,074.

Fort Collins city, N Colorado 80521*; pop. 87,758.

Fort Dodge city, CEN. Iowa 50501; pop. 25,894.

Forth, Firth of estuary of the Forth River; 51 mi. long.

Forth River river, SE Scotland; 65 mi. long.

Fort Knox military reservation, N Kentucky 40120*; site of the Federal gold bullion depository.

Fort-Lamy *the former name of* N'Djamena.

Fort Lauderdale city, SE Florida 33301*; pop. 149,377.

Fort Lee boro., NE New Jersey 07024; pop. 31,997.

Fort Myers city, SW Florida 33920*; pop. 45,206.

Fort Pierce city, E Florida 33454*; pop. 36,830.

Fort Smith city, W Arkansas 72901*; pop. 72,798.

Fort Thomas city, N Kentucky 41075; pop. 16,032.

Fort Walton Beach city, NW Florida 32548; pop. 21,471.

Fort Wayne city, NE Indiana 46802*; pop. 173,072.

Fort Worth city, N Texas 76101*; pop. 447,619.

Fostoria city, N Ohio 44830; pop. 14,983.

Fountain Valley city, SW California 92708; pop. 53,691.

Framingham town, E Massachusetts 01701; pop. 64,994.

France republic, W Europe; 210,026 sq. mi.; pop. 56,647,000; cap. Paris.

Frankfort city, CEN. Kentucky 40601; cap.; pop. 25,968.

Frankfurt am Main city, CEN. Germany; pop. 628,203.

Frankfurt an der Oder city, E Germany; pop. 77,175.

Franklin town, E Massachusetts 02038; pop. 22,095.

Franklin Park vill., NE Illinois 60131; pop. 18,485.

Franklin Square uninc. place, SE New York 11010; pop. 28,205.

Frederick city, NW Maryland 21701; pop. 40,148.

Fredericton city, CEN. New Brunswick, Canada; pop. 45,248.

Freeport city, NW Bahamas, on Grand Bahama Island; pop. 25,423.

— city, N Illinois 61032; pop. 25,840.

— vill., SE New York 11520; pop. 39,894.

Fremont city, N California 94536; pop. 173,339.

— city, E Nebraska 68025; pop. 23,680.

— city, N Ohio 43420; pop. 17,648.

French Guiana French overseas dept. NE South America; 33,399 sq. mi.; pop. 117,000; cap. Cayenne.

French Polynesia French overseas terr., South Pacific; comprises the Society, Marquesas, Gambier, and other islands; 1,550 sq. mi.; pop. 197,000; cap. Papeete.

French West Indies isls. comprising Guadaloupe and Martinique.

Fresno city, CEN. California 93706*; pop. 354,202.

Fridley city, E Minnesota 55421; pop. 28,335.

Friesland prov., N Netherlands; 1,295 sq. mi.; pop. 597,600; cap. Leeuwarden.

Frigid Zone See **North Frigid Zone, South Frigid Zone.**

Frisian Islands isl. group, North Sea near Germany, Denmark, and the Netherlands.

Fuji extinct volcano, Honshu, Japan; 12,389 ft.

Fullerton city, SW California 92631*; pop. 114,144.

Fundy, Bay of inlet of the Atlantic betw. Nova Scotia and New Brunswick and NE Maine.

Fuzhou city, SE China; pop. 710,000.

Gabon republic, W equatorial Africa; 103,347 sq. mi.; pop. 1,171,000; cap. Libreville.

Gadsden city, NE Alabama 35901*; pop. 42,523.

Gainesville city, N Florida 32601*; pop. 84,770.

— city, CEN. Georgia 30501*; pop. 17,885.

Galápagos Islands isl. group of Ecuador, South Pacific.

Galesburg city, W Illinois 61401; pop. 33,530.

Galicia reg., SE Poland and NW Ukraine.

— reg., NW Spain.

Galilee reg., N Israel.

Galilee, Sea of freshwater lake; betw. NE Israel, SW Syria, and NW Jordan; 64 sq. mi.

Gallipoli Peninsula penin., NW Turkey.

Galveston city, SE Texas 77550*; pop. 59,070.

Gambia, Republic of the, republic, W Africa; 4,127 sq. mi.; pop. 860,000; cap. Banjul.

Ganges river, N India and Bangladesh, sacred to Hindus; 1,560 mi. long.

Gardena city, SW California 90247*; pop. 49,847.

Garden City city, SE Michigan 48135; pop. 31,846.

— vill., SE New York 11530; pop. 21,686.

Garden Grove city, SW California 92640*; pop. 143,050.

Gardner city, N Massachusetts 01440; pop. 20,125.

Garfield city, NE New Jersey 07026; pop. 26,727.

Garfield Heights city, NE Ohio 44125; pop. 31,739.

Garland city, N Texas 75040*; pop. 180,650.

Gary city, NW Indiana 46401*; pop. 116,646.

Gascony reg., SW France.

Gastonia city, SW North Carolina 28052*; pop. 54,732.

Gatineau town, SW Quebec, Canada; pop. 73,479.

Gaza city, SW Israel; the **Gaza Strip,** the surrounding area; pop. 356,261.

Gdańsk port city, N Poland: formerly, as **Danzig,** cap. of the territory of the Free City of Danzig; pop. 449,200.

Gdynia city, NW Poland; pop. 232,500.

Geneva city, SW Switzerland; pop. 389,000.

— city, CEN. New York 14456; pop. 14,143.

Geneva, Lake of lake, SW Switzerland; 224 sq. mi.

Genoa city, NW Italy; pop. 714,641.

Georgetown city, N Guyana; cap.; pop. 187,056.

Georgia state, SE United States; 58,910 sq. mi.; pop. 6,508,419.

Georgia republic, W Asia; 26,900 sq. mi.; pop. 5,171,000; cap. Tbilisi.

German Democratic Republic See **Germany.**

Germany republic, CEN. Europe; divided 1949–90, into the **Federal Republic of Germany** (West Germany), cap. Bonn; and the **German Democratic Republic** (East Germany), cap. East Berlin. 137,820 sq. mi.; pop. 79,082,000; cap. Berlin.

Ghana republic W Africa; 92,098 sq. mi.; pop. 12,815,000; cap. Accra.

Ghent city, NW Belgium; pop. 241,695.

Gibraltar British col. on the Rock of Gilbraltar; 2.25 sq. mi.; pop. 29,760.

Gilbraltar, Rock of penin., S Spain; dominates the Strait of Gibraltar.

Gibraltar, Strait of strait, betw. Spain and Africa, W Mediterranean.

Gilbert Islands See **Kiribati.**

Glace Bay town, NE Nova Scotia, Canada; pop. 21,836.

Gladstone city, W Missouri 64118; pop. 26,243.

Glasgow burgh, SW Scotland; pop. 794,316.

Glastonbury city, CEN. Connecticut 06033; pop. 27,901.

Glen Burnie uninc. place, NE Maryland 21061; pop. 37,305.

Glen Cove city, SE New York 11542; pop. 24,149.

Glendale city, CEN. Arizona 85301*; pop. 148,134.

— city, SW California 91209*; pop. 180,038.

Glendora city, SW California 91740; pop. 47,828.

Glen Ellyn vill., NE Illinois 60137*; pop. 24,944.

Glens Falls city, E New York 12801; pop. 15,023.

Glenview vill., NE Illinois 60025; pop. 37,093.

Gloucester co. boro., CEN. Gloucestershire, England; cap.; pop. 91,300.

— city, NE Massachusetts 01930*; pop. 28,716.

Gloversville city, CEN. New York 12078; pop. 16,656.

Goa former Portuguese terr., W India; annexed by India in 1961; 1,394 sq. mi.; pop. 954,000; cap. New Goa.

Gobi Desert desert, CEN. Asia; 500,000 sq. mi.

Golden Gate strait betw. San Francisco Bay and the Pacific.

Golden Valley vill., SE Minnesota 55427; pop. 20,971.

Goldsboro city, CEN. North Carolina 27530; pop. 40,709.

Good Hope, Cape of promontory, SW South Africa.

Goshen city, N Indiana 46526; pop. 23,797.

Göteborg city, SW Sweden; pop. 434,699.

Gotland isl. of SE Sweden, Baltic Sea; 1,167 sq. mi.

Granada city, S Spain; pop. 229,108.

Granby city, S Quebec, Canada; pop. 37,132.

Grand Banks submarine shoal, North Atlantic; near Newfoundland.

Grand Canyon gorge of the Colorado River, NW Arizona; ab. 250 mi. long.

Grand Forks uninc. place, E North Dakota 58201*; pop. 49,425.

Grand Island city, CEN. Nebraska 68801; pop. 39,386.

Grand Junction city, W Colorado; 81501*; pop. 29,034.

Grand' Mère city, CEN. Quebec, Canada; pop. 15,999.

Grand Prairie city, N Texas 75051*; pop. 99,616.

Grand Rapids city, W Michigan 49501*; pop. 189,126.

Grandview city, W Missouri 64030; pop. 24,967.

Granite City city, SW Illinois 62040; pop. 32,862.

Great Barrier Reef coral reef off the coast of Queensland, Australia.

Great Bend city, CEN. Kansas 67530; pop. 15,423.

Great Britain principal isl. of the United Kingdom; comprises England, Scotland, and Wales; 94,248 sq. mi.; pop. 56,518,000; cap. London.

Great Divide See **Continental Divide.**

Greater Antilles See **Antilles.**

Great Falls city, CEN. Montana 59401*; pop. 55,097.

Great Lakes chain of five lakes, CEN. North America; on Canada–United States border; comprises Lakes Superior, Michigan, Huron, Ontario, and Erie; total 94,710 sq. mi.

Great Plains plateau, W North America; E of the Rockies.

Great Russia CEN. and NW reg. of Russia.

Great Salt Lake salt lake, NW Utah; ab. 2,000 sq. mi.

Great Slave Lake lake, S Northwest Territories, Canada; 11,170 sq. mi.

Great Smoky Mountains mtn. range, North Carolina and Tennessee.

Greece republic, SE Europe; 50,949 sq. mi.; pop. 10,038,000; cap. Athens.

Greeley city, N Colorado 80631*; pop. 60,536.

Green Bay city, E Wisconsin 54305*; pop. 96,466.

Greenbelt city, CEN. Maryland 20770; pop. 21,096.

Greendale vill., SE Wisconsin 53129; pop. 15,128.

Greenfield uninc. place, NW Massachusetts 01301*; pop. 18,666.

— town, SE Wisconsin 53220; pop. 33,403.

Greenfield Park town, S Quebec, Canada; pop. 18,430.

Greenland isl. territory of Denmark near NE North America; 840,000 sq. mi.; pop. 55,900.

Green Mountains mtn. range, CEN. Vermont.

Greensboro city, CEN. North Carolina 27420*; pop. 183,521.

Greensburg city, SW Pennsylvania 15601*; pop. 16,318.

Greenville city, W Mississippi 38701*; pop. 45,226.

— city, E North Carolina 27834*; pop. 44,972.

— city, NW South Carolina 29602*; pop. 58,282.

— city, NE Texas 75401; pop. 23,071.

Greenwich boro., SE London; former site of the Royal Observatory; location of prime meridian; pop. 218,000.

— town, SW Connecticut 06830*; pop. 58,441.

Greenwood city, CEN. Mississippi 38930; pop. 18,906.

— city, W South Carolina 29646*; pop. 20,807.

Grenada republic in the West Indies; 133 sq. mi.; pop. 101,000; cap. St. George's.

Gretna city, SE Louisiana 70053; pop. 17,208.

Griffin city, CEN. Georgia 30223; pop. 21,347.

Griffith town, NW Indiana 46319; pop. 17,916.

Grimsby town, S Ontario, Canada; pop. 15,567.

Grosse Pointe city, SE Michigan 48236; pop. 17,715.

Groves city, SE Texas 77619; pop. 16,513.

Guadalajara city, CEN. Mexico; pop. 1,813,100.

Guadalcanal isl., British Solomons; scene of an Allied invasion in World War II, 1943.

Guadeloupe French overseas dept., Lesser Antilles; 687 sq. mi.; pop. 380,000; cap. Basse-Terre.

Guam uninc. terr. of the United States, an isl. in the Marianas; 209 sq. mi. pop. 134,000; cap. Agaña.

Guantánamo city, SE Cuba, near, **Guantánamo Bay;** pop. 155,217.

Guatemala republic, N Central America; 42,042 sq. mi.; pop. 9,197,000.

— **City,** CEN. Guatemala; cap.; pop. 1,057,210.

Guayama town, SE Puerto Rico 00654; pop. 21,044.

Guayaquil city, W Ecuador; pop. 1,022,010.

Guelph city, S Ontario, Canada; pop. 67,538.

Guernica town, N Spain; object of a German bombing, 1937; pop. 11,704.

Guernsey one of the Channel Islands; 25 sq. mi.

Guiana coastal reg., NE South America. See **British Guiana, French Guiana, Guyana, Suriname.**

Guinea republic, W Africa; 94,900 sq. mi.; pop. 5,429,000; cap. Conakry.

Guinea, Gulf of large bay of the Atlantic off W Africa.

Guinea-Bissau republic, W Africa; 13,948 sq. mi.; pop. 973,000; cap. Bissau.

Gulfport city, SE Mississippi 39501*; pop. 40,775.

Gulf Stream A warm ocean current flowing from the Gulf of Mexico northeastward toward Europe.

Guyana republic, NE South America, 83,044 sq. mi.; pop. 756,000; cap. Georgetown.

Haarlem city, W Netherlands; pop. 158,291.

Hackensack city, NE New Jersey 07602*; pop. 37,049.

Haddonfield city, SW New Jersey 08033; pop. 11,628.

Hagerstown city, W Maryland 21740; pop. 35,445.

Hague, The city, W Netherlands; seat of government; pop. 443,845. Also **s'Gravenhage.**

Haifa city, NW Israel; pop. 229,300.

Haiti republic, W Hispaniola; 10,579 sq. mi.; pop. 5,862,000; cap. Port-au-Prince.

Halifax city, S Nova Scotia; Canada; cap.; pop. 117,882.

Hallandale city, SE Florida 33009; pop. 30,996.

Halle city, SW Germany; pop. 232,543.

Haltom City vill., N Texas 76117; pop. 32,856.

Hamburg state and city, N Germany; 288 sq. mi.; pop. 1,653,043.

Hamden town, S Connecticut 06514; pop. 52,434.

Hamilton city, CEN. Bermuda; cap.; pop. 2,060.

— city, SW Ohio 45012*; pop. 61,368.

— city, S Ontario, Canada; pop. 312,003.

Hammond city, NW Indiana 46320*; pop. 84,236.

Hampton city, SE Virginia 23660*; pop. 133,793.

Hampton Roads channel, SE Virginia; connects several rivers with Chesapeake Bay; scene of the engagement of the "Monitor" and the "Merrimack," 1862.

Hamtramck city, SE Michigan 48212; pop. 18,372.

Hanford city, CEN. California 93230*; pop. 30,897.

Hangzhou city, E China; pop. 933,000.

Hannibal city, NE Missouri 63401*; pop. 18,004.

Hannover city, CEN. Germany; pop. 535,834.

Hanoi city, CEN. Vietnam; cap; pop. 1,600,000.

Harare See **Salisbury.**

Harbin city, NE China; pop. 2,094,000.

Harlingen city, S Texas 78551*; pop. 48,735.

Harper Woods city, SE Michigan 48236; pop. 14,903.

Harrisburg city, CEN. Pennsylvania 17105*; cap; pop. 52,376.

Hartford city, CEN. Connecticut 06101*; cap.; pop. 139,739.

Harvey city, NE Illinois 60426; pop. 29,771.

Hastings city, S Nebraska 68901; pop. 22,837.

Hattiesburg city, SE Mississippi 39401*; pop. 41,882.
Havana city, W Cuba; cap.; pop. 1,961,674.
Haverford urb. twp., SE Pennsylvania 19083; pop. 52,371.
Haverhill city, NE Massachusetts 01831*; pop. 51,418.
Hawaii state of the United States, North Pacific; coextensive with the Hawaiian Islands; 6,471 sq. mi.; pop. 1,115,274; cap. Honolulu.
— largest of the Hawaiian Islands; 4,020 sq. mi.
Hawthorne city, SW California 90250; pop. 71,349.
— boro., NE New Jersey 07007; pop. 17,084.
Hays city, CEN. Kansas 67601; pop. 17,767.
Hayward city, W California 94544*; pop. 111,498.
Hazel Park city, SE Michigan 48030; pop. 20,051.
Hazleton city, E Pennsylvania 18201; pop. 24,730.
Hebrides isl. group off W coast of Scotland, ab. 3,000 sq. mi.
Heidelberg city, SW Germany; pop. 128,773.
Hejaz div., W Saudi Arabia; 150,000 sq. mi.; pop. 1,754,000; cap. Mecca.
Helena city, CEN. Montana 59601*; cap.; pop. 24,569.
Helicon mtn. range, CEN. Greece.
Helsinki city, S Finland; cap.; pop. 490,693.
Hempstead vill., SE New York 11551*; pop. 49,453.
Henderson city, NW Kentucky 42420; pop. 25,945.
— city, S Nevada 89015*; pop. 69,942.
Hermosa Beach city, SW California 90254; pop. 18,219.
Herzegovina See **Bosnia and Herzegovina.**
Hesse state, W Germany; 8,152 sq. mi.; pop. 5,576,085; cap. Wiesbaden.
Hialeah city, SE Florida 33010*; site of a famous racetrack; pop. 188,004.
Hibbing vill., NE Minnesota 55746; pop. 18,046.
Hickory city, CEN. North Carolina 28601*; pop. 28,301.
Hicksville uninc. place, SE New York 11802*; pop. 40,174.
Highland town, NW Indiana 46322; pop. 23,696.
Highland Park city, NE Illinois 60035*; pop. 30,575.
— city, SE Michigan 48203; pop. 20,121.
High Point city, CEN. North Carolina 27260*; pop. 69,496.
Hillcrest Heights city, S Maryland; pop. 17,136.
Hillside urb. twp., NE New Jersey 07205; pop. 21,044.
Hilo city, E Hawaii island, Hawaii 96720; pop. 37,808.
Himalayas mtn. range. CEN. Asia.
Hindustan 1 loosely, the reg. of the Ganges where Hindi is spoken. 2 loosely, India.
Hingham town, E Massachusetts 02043; pop. 19,821.
Hinsdale vill., NE Illinois 60521*; pop. 16,029.
Hiroshima city, SW Honshu isl., Japan; devastated by the first atom bomb used in war, Aug. 6, 1945; pop. 899,394.
Hispaniola isl., West Indies; ab. 30,000 sq. mi.; divided into Haiti and the Dominican Republic.
Hobart city, SE Tasmania, Australia; cap; pop. 170,200.
— city, NW Indiana 46342; pop. 21,822.
Hobbs city, SE New Mexico 88240; pop. 29,115.
Hoboken city, NE New Jersey 07030; pop. 33,397.
Ho Chi Minh City See **Saigon.**
Hoffman Estates city, NE Illinois 60172; pop. 46,561.
Hokkaido isl. of N Japan; ab. 29,000 sq. mi.
Holladay uninc. place, NW Utah 84117; pop. 22,189.
Holland See **Netherlands.**
— city, SW Michigan 49423*; pop. 30,745.
Hollywood area, NW Los Angeles, California; ctr. of US motion-picture industry.
— city, SE Florida 33022*; pop. 121,697.
Holyoke city, CEN. Massachusetts 01040*; pop. 43,704.
Homewood city, CEN. Alabama 35209; pop. 22,922.
— vill., NE Illinois 60430; pop. 19,278.
Honduras republic, NE Central America; 43,277 sq. mi.; pop. 4,674,000; cap. Tegucigalpa.
Hong Kong special administrative region, SE China; includes **Hong Kong Island**; 415 sq. mi.; pop. 5,841,000; cap. Victoria.
Honolulu city, SE Oahu, Hawaii 96815*; cap.; pop. 365,272.
Honshu isl. of GEN. Japan; 88,745 sq. mi.
Hood, Mount volcanic peak, Cascade Range, NW Oregon 11,245 ft.
Hoover Dam dam, Colorado River at the Arizona–Nevada border; 727 ft. high; 1,282 ft. long.
Hopewell city, SE Virginia 23860; pop. 23,101.

Hopkinsville city, SW Kentucky 42240; pop. 29,809.
Horn, Cape S extremity of South America.
Hot Springs city, CEN. Arkansas 71901; pop. 32,462.
Houma city, SE Louisiana 70360*; pop. 30,495.
Houston city, SE Texas 77013*; pop. 1,630,533.
Huber Heights city, SW Ohio 45424; pop. 38,696.
Hudson Center uninc. place, CEN. Massachusetts 01749; pop. 14,267.
Hudson Bay inland sea, N Canada; connected with the Atlantic by **Hudson Strait;** ab. 475,000 sq. mi.
Hudson River river, E New York; 306 mi. long.
Hull city, SW Quebec, Canada; pop. 61,039.
Hungary republic, CEN. Europe; 35,920 sq. mi.; pop. 10,437,000; cap. Budapest.
Huntington city, NE Indiana 46750; pop. 16,389.
— city, W West Virginia 25701*; pop. 54,844.
Huntington Beach city, SW California 92647*; pop. 181,519.
Huntington Park city, SW California 90255*; pop. 56,065.
Huntington Station uninc. place, SE New York 11746*; pop. 28,247.
Huntsville city, N Alabama 35804*; pop. 159,789.
— city, E Texas 77340*; pop. 27,925.
Huron, Lake one of the Great Lakes; betw. Michigan and Ontario; 23,010 sq. mi.
Hurst city, N Texas 76053; pop. 33,574.
Hutchinson city, CEN. Kansas 67501; pop. 39,308.
Hwang Ho river, N China; 2,900 mi. long.
Hyde Park public park, London, England.
Hyderabad city, CEN. India; pop. 1,607,396.
— city, SE Pakistan; pop. 600,796.
Iberia part of SW Europe containing Spain and Portugal.
Iceland isl. republic, North Atlantic; 39,699 sq. mi.; pop. 256,000; cap. Reykjavik.
Idaho state, NW United States; 83,564 sq. mi.; pop. 1,011,986; cap. Boise.
Idaho Falls city, SE Idaho 83402*; pop. 43,929.
Ijssel, Lake freshwater lake, CEN. Netherlands.
Illinois state, CEN. United States; 56,345 sq. mi.; pop. 11,466,682; cap. Springfield.
Imperial Beach city, SW California 92032; pop. 25,512.
Imperial Valley agricultural reg., SE California.
Independence city, W Missouri 64051*; pop. 112,301.
India republic, S Asia; 1,222,559 sq. mi.; pop. 853,373,000; cap. New Delhi.
Indiana state, CEN. United States; 36,185 sq. mi.; pop. 5,564,228; cap. Indianapolis.
— boro., CEN. Pennsylvania 15701; pop. 15,174.
Indianapolis city, CEN. Indiana 46206*; cap.; pop. 741,952.
Indian Ocean ocean betw. Africa, Asia, Australia, and Antarctica.
Indies See **East Indies, West Indies.**
Indochina 1 SE penin. of Asia. 2 Cambodia, Laos, Vietnam.
Indonesia republic, SE Asia; comprises over 100 isls. of the Malay Archipelago; 752,409 sq. mi.; pop. 180,763,000; cap. Jakarta.
Indus river, Tibet, Kashmir, and Pakistan; 1,800 mi. long.
Inglewood city, SW California 90306*; pop. 109,602.
Inkster vill. SE Michigan 48141; pop. 30,772.
Ionian Sea part of the Mediterranean betw. Greece and Sicily.
Iowa state, CEN. United States; 56,275 sq. mi.; pop. 2,787,424; cap. Des. Moines.
Iowa City city, E Iowa 52240*; pop. 59,738.
Iraklion city, N CEN. Crete; pop. 78,000. Also **Candia, Heraklion.**
Iran republic, SW Asia; ab. 636,372 sq. mi.; pop. 56,293,000; cap. Tehran.
Iraq republic, SW Asia; 169,975 sq. mi.; pop. 17,754,000; cap. Baghdad.
Ireland westernmost of the British Isles; 31,838 sq. mi.
— republic, S Ireland; 27,137 sq. mi.; pop. 3,614,000; cap. Dublin. See also **Northern Ireland.**
Irish Sea part of the Atlantic betw. Great Britain and Ireland.
Irkutsk city, S Russia; pop. 561,000.
Irondequoit uninc. place, W New York 14617; pop. 52,322.
Irrawaddy river, Tibet and Myanmar; 1,200 mi. long.
Irving city, N Texas 75061*; pop. 155,037.
Irvington town, NE New Jersey 07111; pop. 59,774.
Islamabad city, NE Pakistan; cap.; pop. 204,364.

Israel republic, E end of the Mediterranean; 7,992 sq. mi.; pop. 4,666,000; cap. Jerusalem.
Istanbul city, NE Turkey; pop. 6,748,435.
Italy republic, S Europe; 116,324 sq. mi.; pop. 57,512,000; cap. Rome.
Ithaca isl. of Greece, Ionian Sea; 36 sq. mi.
— city, CEN. New York 14850; pop. 29,541.
Ivory Coast (Côte d'Ivoire) republic, W Africa; 123,847 sq. mi.; pop. 12,657,000; cap. Abidjan.
Izmir city, W Turkey; pop. 1,762,849. Also **Smyrna.**
Jackson city, S Michigan 49201*; pop. 37,446.
— city, CEN. Mississippi 39205*; cap.; pop. 196,637.
— city, W Tennessee 38301*; pop. 48,949.
Jacksonville city, CEN. Arkansas 72076*; pop. 29,101.
— city, NE Florida 32201*; pop. 672,971.
— city, CEN. Illinois 62650*; pop. 19,324.
— city, E North Carolina 28540*; pop. 30,013.
Jakarta city, NW Java; cap. of Indonesia; pop. 7,829,000.
Jamaica isl. monarchy of the Greater Antilles; 4,244 sq. mi.; pop. 2,391,000; cap. Kingston.
Jamestown town, NW St. Helena; cap.; pop. 1,516.
— city, SW New York 14701; pop. 34,681.
— city, CEN. North Dakota 58401; pop. 15,571.
— restored vill., E Virginia 23081; site of the first English settlement in the present limits of the United States, 1607.
Jammu and Kashmir state, N India; subject of a territorial dispute with Pakistan; 85,806 sq. mi.; pop. 5,120,000; caps. Sringar and Jammu.
Janesville city, S Wisconsin 53545*; pop. 52,133.
Japan constitutional monarchy; E Asia; situated on a chain of isls.; 145,862 sq. mi.; pop. 123,692,000; cap. Tokyo.
Japan, Sea of part of the Pacific betw. Japan and the Asian mainland.
Java isl. of Indonesia; SE of Sumatra; 48,842 sq. mi.
Jefferson uninc. place, NE Virginia 22042; pop. 25,782.
Jefferson City city, CEN. Missouri 65101*; cap.; pop. 35,481.
Jefferson uninc. place, SE Louisiana 70121; pop. 14,521.
Jeffersonville city, SE Indiana 47130*; pop. 21,220.
Jennings city, E Missouri 63136; pop. 15,905.
Jericho vill., W Jordan; on the site of the ancient city.
Jersey one of the Channel Islands; 45 sq. mi.
Jersey City city, NE New Jersey 07303*; pop. 228,537.
Jerusalem city, E Israel; cap., pop. 493,500.
Jidda city, W Saudi Arabia; pop. 561,104.
Johannesburg city, NE South Africa; cap.; pop. 632,369.
Johnson City vill., S New York 13790; pop. 16,890.
— city, NE Tennessee 37601; pop. 49,381.
Johnstown city, CEN. Pennsylvania 15901*; pop. 28,134.
Joliet city, NE Illinois 60431*; pop. 76,836.
Joliette city, S Quebec, Canada; pop. 18,118.
Jonesboro city, NE Arkansas 72401; pop. 46,535.
Jonquière city, CEN. Quebec, Canada; pop. 60,691.
Joplin city, SW Missouri 64801*; pop. 40,961.
Jordan constitutional monarchy, W Asia; 34,443 sq. mi.; pop. 3,169,000; cap. Amman.
Jordan River river, CEN. Palestine; more than 200 mi. long.
Junction City city, CEN. Kansas 66441; pop. 20,604.
Juneau city, SE Alaska 99801; cap.; pop. 26,751.
Jungfrau mtn. peak, CEN. Switzerland; 13,653 ft.
Jura Mountains mtn. range, E France and W Switzerland.
Jutland penin., N Europe; comprises continental Denmark and part of Germany.
Kabul city, CEN. Afghanistan; cap.; pop. 1,424,400.
Kailua uninc. place, E Oahu, Hawaii 96734*; pop. 36,818.
Kalamazoo city, SW Michigan 49001*; pop. 80,277.
Kalimantan the Indonesian name of Borneo.
Kaliningrad city, extreme W Russia; pop. 361,000.
Kamchatka penin, E Russia, betw. The Bering and Okhotsk Seas.
Kampuchea, Roat (Cambodia) republic, SW Indochina peninsula, formerly **Khmer Republic**; 69,698 sq. mi.; pop. 8,592,000; cap. Phnom Penh.
Kaneohe uninc. place, E Oahu, Hawaii 96744; pop. 35,448.
Kankakee city, NE Illinois 60901; pop. 27,575.
Kannapolis uninc. place, CEN. North Carolina 28081; pop. 29,696.

Kansas state, CEN. United States; 82,277 sq. mi.; pop. 2,485,600; cap. Topeka.
Kansas City city, NE Kansas 66110*; pop. 149,767.
— city, W Missouri 64108*; pop. 435,146.
Karachi city, S Pakistan; former cap.; pop. 5,208,132.
Karelia autonomous republic, NW Russia; 66,560 sq. mi.; pop. 711,000; cap. Petrozavodsk.
Karnak vill., S Egypt; near the site of ancient Thebes.
Kashmir See **Jammu and Kashmir.**
Kathmandu city, CEN. Nepal; cap.; pop. 150,402.
Kauai one of the Hawaiian Islands; 551 sq. mi.
Kaunas city, CEN. Lithuania; pop. 377,000.
Kazakstan republic, CEN. Asia; 1,049,200 sq. mi.; pop. 15,654,000; cap. Alma-Ata.
Kazan city, NW Tatar Republic, E European Russia; cap.; pop. 1,002,000.
Kearney city, CEN. Nebraska 68847; pop. 24,396.
Kearns uninc. place, N Utah 84118; pop. 28,374.
Kearny town, NE New Jersey 07032; pop. 34,874.
Keene city, SW New Hampshire 03431; pop. 22,430.
Kelowna city, S British Columbia, Canada; pop. 51,955.
Kendall uninc. place, SE Florida 33156; pop. 87,271.
Kenmore vill., W New York 14217; pop. 17,180.
Kennedy, Cape the former name of Cape Canaveral.
Kenner city, SE Louisiana 70062; pop. 72,033.
Kennewick city, S Washington 99336; pop. 42,155.
Kenosha city, SE Wisconsin 53141*; pop. 80,352.
Kent city, NE Ohio 44240*; pop. 28,835.
— city, CEN. Washington 98031; pop. 37,960.
Kentucky state, CEN. United States; 40,409 sq. mi.; pop. 3,698,969; cap. Frankfort.
Kentucky River river, N Kentucky; 259 mi. long.
Kentwood city, SW Michigan 49508; pop. 37,826.
Kenya republic, E Africa; 224,961 sq. mi.; pop. 24,872,000; cap. Nairobi.
Kenya, Mount extinct volcano, CEN. Kenya; 17,058 ft.
Kettering city, SW Ohio 45429; pop. 60,569.
Key West southwesternmost of the Florida Keys.
— city, Key West Island, Florida 33040; pop. 24,832.
Kharkov city, NE Ukraine; pop. 1,464,000.
Khartoum city, CEN. Sudan; cap.; pop. 790,000.
Khmer Republic the former name of Cambodia.
Khyber Pass mtn. pass betw. Afghanistan and Pakistan; ab. 30 mi. long.
Kiel city, N Germany; pop. 250,750.
Kiel Canal ship canal betw. Kiel and the mouth of the Elbe; ab. 61 mi. long.
Kiev city, CEN. Ukraine; cap.; pop. 2,192,000.
Kilauea active crater, Mauna Loa volcano, Hawaii.
Kilimanjaro, Mount mtn., NE Tanzania; highest in Africa; 19,565 ft.
Killeen city, CEN. Texas 76540*; pop. 63,535.
Kimberley city, CEN. South Africa; pop. 105,258.
Kings borough Brooklyn, SE New York City, New York 11200*; pop. 2,300,664.
Kingsport city, NE Tennessee 37662*; pop. 36,365.
Kingston city, S Jamaica; cap.; pop. 524,638.
— city, SE New York 12401; pop. 23,095.
— boro., CEN. Pennsylvania 18704; pop. 14,507.
— city, SE Ontario, Canada; pop. 56,032.
Kingsville city, S Texas 78363*; pop. 25,276.
Kinshasa city, W Democratic Republic of the Congo; cap.; pop. 3,562,122.
Kinston city, CEN. North Carolina 28501; pop. 25,295.
Kiribati, republic including 3 isl. groups SW Pacific, comprising the Gilbert, Line, Phoenix Islands, and Banaba Island; 328 sq. mi.; pop. 71,000; cap. Bairiki.
Kirkland city, CEN. Washington 98033; pop. 40,052.
Kirksville city, N Missouri 63501; pop. 17,152.
Kirkwood city, E Missouri 63122; pop. 27,291.
Kitchener city, S Ontario, Canada; pop. 131,870.
Kitty Hawk vill., NE North Carolina; site of the first sustained airplane flight, by Wilbur and Orville Wright, 1903.
Klamath Falls city, S Oregon 97601*; pop. 17,737.
Klondike reg., NW Canada in the basin of the **Klondike River.**
Knoxville city, E Tennessee 37901*; pop. 165,121.
Kobe city, S Japan; pop. 1,367,392.

Kodiak Island isl., s Alaska; pop. 6,365.
Kokomo city, CEN. Indiana 46902*; pop. 44,962.
Kolonia city, cap. Micronesia; pop. 6,000.
Königsberg *the former German name of* Kaliningrad.
Korea penin., E Asia; 85,509 sq. mi.; divided into the **Democratic People's Republic of Korea** (North Korea) single-party republic; 47,250 sq. mi.; pop. 22,937,000; cap. Pyongyang; and the **Republic of Korea** (South Korea) multi-party republic; 38,259 sq. mi.; pop. 42,793,000; cap. Seoul.
Korea Strait strait, betw. the Sea of Japan and the East China Sea.
Kozhikode city, s India; pop. 333,979. Also **Calicut.**
Krakatoa isl. volcano betw. Sumatra and Java, Indonesia; site of most violent volcanic eruption of modern times, 1883.
Kraków city, s Poland; pop. 743,700.
Krasnodar city, sw Russia; pop. 620,000.
Krasnoyarsk city, CEN Russia; pop. 912,000.
Kuala Lumpur city, CEN. Malaysia; cap.; pop. 1,103,200.
Kunming city, sw China; pop. 1,085,100.
Kurdistan reg., NW Iran, NE Iraq, and SE Turkey; peopled largely by Kurds.
Kure city, sw Japan; pop. 234,550.
Kurile Island isl. group, SE Russia; 5,700 sq. mi.
Kuwait monarchy, NE Arabia; 6,880 sq. mi.; pop. 2,143,000.
— **City**, E Kuwait; cap.; pop. 44,224.
Kyoto city, sw Japan; pop. 1,470,564.
Kyrgyzstan republic, CEN Asia; 76,641 sq. mi.; pop. 4,291,000; cap. Bishkek.
Kyushu isl., s Japan; 16,247 sq. mi.; pop. 1,034,328.
Labrador terr., Newfoundland, Canada; ab. 110,000 sq. mi.; pop. 21,157.
— the penin. of North America betw. the St. Lawrence River and Hudson Bay.
La Canada-Flintridge uninc. place, sw California 91011; pop. 19,378.
Lachine city, s Quebec, Canada; pop. 41,503.
Lackawanna city, w New York 14218; pop. 20,585.
La Crosse city, w Wisconsin 54601*; pop. 51,003.
Ladoga, Lake lake, NW Russia; 7,100 sq. mi.
Lafayette uninc. place, w California 94549; pop. 23,501.
— city, CEN. Indiana 47901*; pop. 43,764.
— city, s Louisiana 70509*; pop. 94,440.
Lagos city, sw Nigeria; cap.; pop. 1,274,000.
La Grange city, w Georgia 30240; pop. 25,597.
— vill., NE Illinois 60525; pop. 15,362.
La Habra city, sw California 90631*; pop. 51,266.
Lahore city, E Pakistan; pop. 2,952,689.
Lake Charles city, sw Louisiana 70601*; pop. 70,580.
Lake District reg., NW England; contains 15 lakes.
Lake Forest city, NE Illinois 60045; pop. 17,836.
Lakeland city, CEN. Florida 33082*; pop. 70,576.
Lakewood city, sw California 90714*; pop. 73,557.
— city, CEN. Colorado 80215; pop. 126,481.
— uninc. place, E New Jersey 08701; pop. 26,095.
— city, N Ohio 44107, pop. 59,718.
Lake Worth city, SE Florida 33460; pop. 28,564.
La Marque city, SE Texas 77568; pop. 14,120.
La Mesa city, sw California 92041*; pop. 52,931.
La Mirada city, sw California 90638; pop. 40,452.
Lancaster city, sw California 93534*; pop. 97,291.
— city, CEN. Ohio 43130; pop. 34,507.
— city, SE Pennsylvania 17604*; pop. 55,551.
Lanzhou city, NW China; pop. 1,151,700.
Lansdale boro., SE Pennsylvania 19446; pop. 16,362.
Lansdowne–Baltimore Highlands uninc. place, CEN. Maryland 21227; pop. 15,509.
Lansing vill., NE Illinois 60438; pop. 28,086.
— city, CEN. Michigan 48924*; cap.; pop. 127,321.
Laos republic, NW Indochina; 91,430 sq. mi.; pop. 4,024,000.
La Paz city, w Bolivia; admin. cap.; pop. 1,049,800.
Lapland reg., N Norway, Sweden, and Finland, and NW Russia; inhabited by Lapps.
La Plata city, E Argentina; pop. 454,884.
LaPorte city, NW Indiana 46350; pop. 21,507.
La Puente city, sw California 91747*; pop. 36,955.
Laramie city, SE Wyoming 82070; pop. 26,687.
Laredo city, s Texas 78040*; pop. 122,899.

Largo city, w Florida 33540*; pop. 65,674.
La Salle city, s Quebec, Canada; pop. 76,713.
Las Cruces city, s New Mexico 88001*; pop. 62,126.
Las Vegas city, SE Nevada 89114*; pop. 258,295.
Latvia republic, E Europe; 24,900 sq. mi.; pop. 2,680,000; cap. Riga.
Laurel city, SE Mississippi 39440*; pop. 18,827.
Lurentian Mountains mtn. range, E Canada.
Lausanne city, w Switzerland; pop. 128,800.
Laval town, s Quebec, Canada; pop. 284,164.
Lawndale city, sw California 90260; pop. 27,331.
Lawrence town, CEN. Indiana 46226; pop. 26,763.
— city, E Kansas 66044*; pop. 65,608.
— city, NE Massachusetts 08142*; pop. 70,207.
Lawton city, sw Oklahoma 73501*; pop. 80,561.
Leavenworth city, NE Kansas 66048; pop. 38,495.
Lebanon republic, sw Asia; 3,950 sq. mi.; pop. 2,965,000; cap. Beirut.
— city, SE Pennsylvania 17042; pop. 24,800.
Leeds city and co. boro., CEN. England; pop. 451,845.
Lee's Summit city, w Missouri 64063; pop. 46,418.
Leeward Islands N isl. group, Lesser Antilles.
Leghorn city, NW Italy; pop. 176,757. Also **Livorno.**
Le Havre city, N France; pop. 196,000.
Leicester co. boro., CEN. England; pop. 328,835.
Leiden city, w Netherlands; pop. 109,254.
Leipzig city, CEN. Germany; pop. 545,307.
Lemon Grove city, sw California 92045; pop. 23,984.
Leningrad See **St. Petersburg.**
Leominster city, CEN. Massachusetts 01453; pop. 38,145.
Leopoldville *the former name of* Kinshasa.
Lesbos isl. of Greece off NW Turkey; 623 sq. mi.
Lesotho independent member of the Commonwealth of Nations; enclave in E South Africa; 11,720 sq. mi.; pop. 1,760,000; cap. Maseru.
Lesser Antilles See **Antilles.**
Lethbridge city, s Alberta, Canada; pop. 46,752.
Lévis city, s Quebec, Canada; pop. 17,819.
Levittown uninc. place, SE New York 11756; pop. 53,286.
Lewiston city, w Idaho 83501; pop. 28,082.
— city, sw Maine 04240; pop. 39,757.
Lexington city, CEN. Kentucky 40511*; pop. 204,165.
— town, NE Massachusetts 02173; pop. 28,974.
— city, CEN. North Carolina 27292; pop. 16,581.
Leyden See **Leiden.**
Leyte isl., E Philippines, 2,875 sq. mi.
Lhasa city, s Tibet, cap.; pop. 80,000.
Liberia republic, w Africa; 38,250 sq. mi.; pop. 2,595,000; cap. Monrovia.
Libreville city, w Gabon; cap.; pop. 352,000.
Libya socialist state, N Africa; 685,524 sq. mi.; pop. 4,206,000; cap. Tripoli.
Liechtenstein monarchy, CEN. Europe; 62 sq. mi.; pop. 28,000; cap. Vaduz.
Liège city, E Belgium pop. 196,825.
Lille city, N France; pop. 167,791.
Lilongwe city, CEN. Malawi; cap.; pop. 220,300.
Lima city, w Peru; cap.; pop. 5,659,200.
— city, w Ohio; 45802*; pop. 45,549.
Limerick co. boro., w Ireland; pop. 60,665.
Limoges city, CEN. France; pop. 133,000.
Lincoln city, CEN. Illinois 62656; pop. 15,418.
— city, SE Nebraska 68501*; cap.; pop. 191,972.
Lincoln Park city, SE Michigan 48146; pop. 41,832.
Linden city, NE New Jersey36,701; pop. 37,836.
Lindenhurst vill., SE New York 11757; pop. 26,879.
Lisbon city, w Portugal; cap; pop. 829,600.
Lithuania republic, E Europe; 25,200 sq. mi.; pop. 3,690,000; cap. Vilnius.
Little Rock city, CEN. Arkansas 72201*; cap.; pop. 175,795.
Littleton town, CEN. Colorado 80120*; pop. 33,685.
Livermore city, w California 94550*; pop. 56,741.
Liverpool co. boro., w England; pop. 544,861.
Livingston urb. twp., NE New Jersey 07039; pop. 26,609.
Livonia city, SE Michigan 48150*; pop. 100,850.
Lockport city, NW New York 14094; pop. 24,426.
Lodi city, CEN. California 95240*; pop. 51,874.
— boro., NE New Jersey 07644; pop. 22,355.

Lódz city, CEN. Poland; pop. 851,500.
Logan city, N Utah 84321; pop. 32,764.
Logan, Mount peak, SW Yukon Territory, Canada; 19,850 ft.
Logansport city, CEN. Indiana 46947; pop. 17,731.
Loire river, SE France; 620 mi. long.
Lombard vill., NE Illinois 60148; pop. 39,408.
Lomé city, S Togo; cap.; pop. 366,476.
Lomita city, SW California 90717; pop. 19,382.
Lompoc city, SW California 93436*; pop. 37,649.
London city and co., SE England; cap.; 1 sq. mil.; pop. 5,000 (the city proper): 117 sq. mi.; pop. 3,195,000 (the co.): 610 sq. mi.; pop. 6,677,928 (Greater London).
— city, Ontario, Canada; pop. 240,392.
Long Beach city, SW California 90801*; pop. 429,433.
— city, SE New York 11561*; pop. 33,510.
Long Branch city, E New Jersey 07740*; pop. 28,658.
Long Island isl., SE New York; 1,723 sq. mi.
Long Island Sound inlet of the Atlantic betw. Long Island and Connecticut.
Longmeadow town, S Massachusetts 01106; pop. 15,467.
Longmont city, N Colorado 80501; pop. 42,942.
Loungueuil city, SW Quebec, Canada; pop. 122,429.
Longview city, NE Texas 75601*; pop. 70,311.
— city, SW Washington 98632; pop. 31,499.
Lorain city, N Ohio 44052*; pop. 71,245.
Lorraine reg., E France.
Los Alamos uninc. place, CEN. New Mexico 87544; site of the development of the atom bomb; pop. 11,455.
Los Altos city, W California 94022; pop. 26,303.
Los Angeles city, SW California 90052*; pop. 3,485,398.
Los Gatos city, W California 95030*; pop. 27,357.
Louisiana state, S United States; 47,752 sq. mi.; pop. 4,238,216; cap. Baton Rouge.
Louisville city, N Kentucky 40201*; pop. 269,063.
Lourdes town, SW France; famous shrine; pop. 17,870.
Loveland city, N Colorado 80537; pop. 37,352.
Lowell city, NE Massachusetts 01853*; pop. 103,439.
Lower California penin., NW Mexico; betw. the Gulf of California and the Pacific. Also Baja California.
Lowlands areas of low elevation, E and S Scotland.
Luanda city, NW Angola; cap.; pop. 475,328.
Lubbock city, NW Texas 79408*; pop. 186,206.
Lübeck city, NE Germany; pop. 210,681.
Lucerne, Lake of lake, CEN. Switzerland; 44 sq. mi.
Lucknow city, CEN. Uttar Predesh, India; cap.; pop. 895,721.
Lüda city, NE China; pop. 1,185,000.
Ludlow town, S Massachusetts 01056; pop. 18,820.
Lufkin city, E Texas 75901*; pop. 30,206.
Lumberton city, S North Carolina 28358; pop. 18,601.
Lusaka city, CEN Zambia; cap.; pop. 870,030.
Lutherville-Timonium uninc. place, NE Maryland 21093; pop. 16,442.
Luxembourg, Grand Duchy of, monarchy; betw. Belgium, France, and Germany; 999 sq. mi.; pop. 379,000.
— city, CEN. Luxembourg; cap.; pop. 76,640. Also Luxemburg.
Luxor city, E Egypt; near the site of ancient Thebes; pop. 30,000.
Luzon isl., N Philippines; 40,420 sq. mi.
Lvov city, W Ukraine; pop. 790,000.
Lynbrook vill., SE New York 11563; pop. 19,208.
Lynchburg city, CEN. Virginia 24505*; pop. 66,049.
Lyndhurst urb. twp., NE New Jersey 07071; pop. 18,262.
— city, N Ohio 44124; pop. 15,982.
Lynn city, NE Massachusetts 01901*; pop. 81,245.
Lynnwood city, CEN. Washington 98036; pop. 28,695.
Lynwood city, SW California 90262*; pop. 61,945.
Lyon city, CEN. France; pop. 415,000.
Macao isl., Canton river delta, China.
— Portuguese special terr. comprising a penin. of Macao isl. and two small isls.; 6 sq. mi.; pop. 461,000.
— city; cap of Macao; pop. 461,000.
Macedonia reg., SE Europe; divided among Bulgaria, Greece, and Republic of Macedonia; 25,636 sq. mi.
— republic, Balkan Penin.; 9,928 sq. mi.; pop. 2,033,964; cap. Skopje.
Mackenzie river, NW Canada; 2,640 mi. long.

Mackinac, Straits of channel betw. Lakes Michigan and Huron; ab. 5 mi. wide and 40 mi. long.
Mackinac Island isl., Straits of Mackinac.
Macomb city, W Illinois 61455; pop. 19,952.
Macon city, CEN. Georgia 31201*; pop. 106,612.
Madagascar isl. republic, Indian Ocean off SE Africa; 226,662 sq. mi.; pop. 11,980,000; cap. Antananarivo: formerly called Malagasy Republic.
Madeira isl. group W of Morocco; an adm. dist. of Portugal; 306 sq. mi.; pop. 264,787; cap. Funchal.
Madera city, CEN. California 93637; pop. 29,281.
Madison boro., N New Jersey 07940; pop. 15,850.
— city, CEN. Wisconsin 53701*; cap.; pop. 191,262.
Madison Heights city, SE Michigan 48071; pop. 32,196.
Madisonville city, W Kentucky 42431; pop. 16,200.
Madras city, S India; pop. 3,276,622.
Madrid city, CEN. Spain; cap.; pop. 3,100,507.
Madura isl. of Indonesia E of Java; 1,762 sq. mi.
Magdeburg city, CEN. Germany; pop. 290,579.
Magellan, Strait of channel betw. the Atlantic and Pacific, separating the South American mainland from Tierra del Fuego.
Magnitogorsk city, S Russia; pop. 410,000.
Maine state, NE United States; 33,265 sq. mi.; pop. 1,233,223; cap. Augusta.
Main River river, CEN. Germany; 305 mi. long.
Majorca largest of the Balearic Islands; 1,405 sq. mi.
Malabar coastal reg., SW India. Also Malabar Coast.
Malacca city, W Malaysia; pop. 86,357.
Malacca, Strait of strait betw. Sumatra and the Malay Peninsula.
Málaga city, S Spain; pop. 566,330.
Malagasy Republic See Madagascar.
Malawi republic, SE Africa; 45,747 sq. mi.; pop. 8,831,000; cap. Lilongwe.
Malay Archipelago isl. group off SE Asia; includes isls. of Indonesia, Malaysia, and the Philippines.
Malay Peninsula S penin. of Asia; includes Malaya, Singapore, and part of Thailand.
Malaysia island monarchy including Malaya, Sarawak, and Sabah (North Borneo); 127,581 sq. mi.; pop. 17,886,000; cap. Kuala Lumpur.
Malden city, NE Massachusetts 02148; pop. 53,884.
Maldives isl. republic, Indian Ocean S of India; 115 sq. mi.; pop. 214,000; cap. Male.
Mali republic, W Africa; 478,841 sq. mi.; pop. 8,151,000; cap. Bamako.
Mallorca the Spanish name of Majorca.
Malta republic, CEN. Mediterranean; comprises the islands of Malta, Gozo, Comino, and two islets; 122 sq. mi.; pop. 353,000; cap. Valletta.
Mamaroneck vill., SE New York 10543; pop. 17,325.
Man, Isle of one of the British Isles, CEN. Irish Sea; 227 sq. mi.; pop. 61,723; cap. Douglas.
Managua city, SW Nicaragua; cap.; pop. 552,900.
Managua, Lake lake, SW Nicaragua; 390 sq. mi.
Manchester co. boro. and city, SE Lancashire, England; pop. 448,604.
— town, N Connecticut 06040*; pop. 51,618.
— city, S New Hampshire 03101*; pop. 99,567.
Manchuria former div., NE China.
Mandalay city, CEN. Myanmar; pop. 533,000.
Manhattan city, NE Kansas 66502*; pop. 37,712.
— borough (New York), isl., New York City, New York 10001*; pop. 1,487,536.
Manhattan Beach city, SW California 90266; pop. 32,063.
Manila city, SW Luzon, Philippines; pop. 1,879,000.
Manitoba prov., CEN. Canada; 246,512 sq. mi.; pop. 1,021,506; cap. Winnipeg.
Manitoba, Lake lake, SW Manitoba; 1,817 sq. mi.
Manitowoc city, E Wisconsin 54220*; pop. 32,520.
Mankato city, S Minnesota 56001*; pop. 31,477.
Mansfield city, NE Connecticut 06250; pop. 21,103.
— city, CEN. Ohio 44901*; pop. 50,627.
Maple Heights city, NE Ohio 44137; pop. 27,089.
Maple Shade urb. twp., SW New Jersey 08052; pop. 19,211.
Maplewood vill., E Minnesota 55109; pop. 30,954.
— urb. twp. NE New Jersey 07040; pop. 21,756.
Maracaibo city, NW Venezuela; pop. 1,206,726.

Maracaibo, Lake lake, NW Venezuela; ab. 5,000 sq. mi.
Marblehead town, NE Massachusetts 01945*; pop. 19,971.
Marietta city, NW Georgia; 30060*; pop. 44,129.
— city, SE Ohio 45750; pop. 15,026.
Marion city, CEN. Indiana 46952*; pop. 32,618.
— city, E Iowa 52302; pop. 20,403.
— city, CEN Ohio 43302; pop. 34,075.
Markham vill., NE Illinois 60426; pop. 13,136.
Marlborough city, CEN. Massachusetts 01752; pop. 31,813.
Marmara, Sea of sea betw. Europe and Asia, connecting the Bosporus and the Dardanelles. Also **Marmora.**
Marne river, NE France; 325 mi. long.
Marquesas Islands isl. group, French Polynesia; 492 sq. mi.
Marquette city, NW Michigan 49855; pop. 21,977.
Marrakech city, SW Morocco; provincial cap.; pop. 1,455,000.
Marrero uninc. place; SW Louisiana 70072; pop. 36,671.
Marseille city, SE France; pop. 801,000. Also **Marseilles.**
Marshall city, NE Texas 75670*; pop. 23,682.
Marshall Islands isl. republic in the W Pacific; 66 sq. mi.; pop. 25,000; cap. Jaluit.
Marshalltown city, CEN. Iowa 50158; pop. 25,178.
Marshfield city, E Massachusetts 02050; pop. 21,531.
Marshfield city, CEN. Wisconsin 54449; pop. 19,291.
Martinez city, W California 94553*; pop. 31,808.
Martinique isl. Lesser Antilles; French overseas dept.; 421 sq. mi.; pop. 360,000; cap. Fort-de-France.
Martinsville city, S Virginia 24112*; pop. 16,162.
Maryland state, E United States; 10,460 sq. mi.; pop. 4,798,622; cap. Annapolis.
Mason City city, N Iowa 50401*; pop. 29,040.
Mason-Dixon Line boundary betw. Pennsylvania and Maryland, surveyed by Charles Mason and Jeremiah Dixon in 1763; regarded as the division line for the North and the South, United States.
Massachusetts state, NE United States; 8,284 sq. mi.; pop. 6,029,051; cap. Boston.
Massapequa uninc. place, SE New York; 11758*; pop. 22,018.
Massapequa Park vill., SE New York 11762; pop. 18,044.
Massillon city, NE Ohio 44646; pop. 31,007.
Matsu isl. of the Republic of China, Taiwan Strait; 4 sq. mi.
Matterhorn mtn. in the Alps on the Swiss-Italian border; 14,701 ft.
Mattoon city, CEN. Illinois 61938; pop. 18,441.
Maui isl. of the Hawaiian Islands; 728 sq. mi.
Maumee city, NW Ohio 43537; pop. 15,561.
Mauna Loa active volcano, CEN. Hawaii (isl.); 13,675 ft.
Mauritania, Islamic Republic of republic, W Africa; 397,700 sq. mi.; pop. 2,000,000; cap. Nouakchott.
Mauritius island monarchy in the Indian Ocean, 788 sq. mi., pop. 1,080,000; cap. Port Louis.
Mayagüez city, W Puerto Rico 00708; pop. 82,703.
Mayfield Heights city, N Ohio 44124; pop. 19,847.
Mayotte dependency of France, isl. in the Mozambique Channel, off Madagascar, 144 sq. mi.; pop. 82,300; cap. Dzaoudzi.
Maywood city, SW California 90270; pop. 27,850.
— vill., NE Illinois 60153*; pop. 27,139.
McAlester city, CEN. Oklahoma 74501*; pop. 16,370.
McAllen city, S Texas 78501*; pop. 84,021.
McKeesport city, SW Pennsylvania 15134*; pop. 26,016.
McKinley, Mount peak, CEN. Alaska, highest in North America; 20,300 ft.
McKinney city N Texas 75069; pop. 21,283.
McLean uninc. place, NE Virginia 22101; pop. 38,168.
Mead, Lake reservoir formed by Hoover Dam in the Colorado River, Arizona and Nevada; 246 sq. mi.
Meadville city, NW Pennsylvania 16335; pop. 14,318.
Mecca city, W Saudi Arabia; birthplace of Mohammed and holy city to which Muslims make pilgrimages; pop. 550,000.
Medford city, NE Massachusetts 02155; pop. 57,407.
— city, SW Oregon 97501*; pop. 49,951.
Medicine Hat city, SE Alberta, Canada; pop. 32,811.
Medina city, W Saudi Arabia; a Muslim holy city and site of Mohammed's tomb; pop. 90,000.

Mediterranean Sea sea betw. Europe, Asia, and Africa; 965,000 sq. mi.
Mekong river, SE Asia; 2,500 mi. long.
Melanesia isls. of the W Pacific S of the Equator; ab. 60,000 sq. mi.
Melbourne city, S Victoria, Australia; cap.; pop. 3,002,300.
— city, E Florida 32901*; pop. 59,646.
Melrose city, NE Massachusetts 02176; pop. 28,150.
Melrose Park vill., NE Illinois 60160*; pop. 20,859.
Memphis city, SW Tennessee 38101*; pop. 610,337.
— ancient city, cap. of Egypt during the Old Kingdom, S of the Nile Delta.
Menlo Park city, W California 94025*; pop. 28,040.
Menomonee Falls vill., SE Wisconsin 53051*; pop. 26,840.
Mentor city, NE Ohio 44060; pop. 47,358.
Merced city, CEN. California 95340*; pop. 56,216.
Mercerville-Hamilton Square uninc. place, CEN. New Jersey 08619*; pop. 26,873.
Meriden city, CEN. Connecticut 06450; pop. 59,479.
Meridian city, E Mississippi 39301*; pop. 41,036.
Merrick uninc. place, SE New York 11566; pop. 23,042.
Merrillville city, NW Indiana 46410; pop. 27,257.
Merritt Island uninc. place, CEN. Florida 32952; pop. 32,886.
Mesa city, CEN. Arizona 85201*; pop. 288,091.
Mesabi Range range of hills, NE Minnesota; site of iron ore deposits.
Mesquite city, N Texas 75149; pop. 101,484.
Messina city, NE Sicily; pop. 272,119.
Metairie city, SW Louisiana 70004*; pop. 149,428.
Methuen city, NE Massachusetts 01844; pop. 39,990.
Meuse river, W Europe; 580 mi. long.
Mexico republic S North America; 756,066 sq. mi., pop. 81,883,000.
— **City,** CEN Mexico; cap.; pop. 8,236,960.
Mexico, Gulf of inlet of the Atlantic, among the United States, Mexico, and Cuba; 700,000 sq mi.
Miami city, SE Florida 33152*; pop. 358,548.
Miami Beach city SE Florida 33139; pop. 92,639.
Michigan state, N United States; 58,527 sq. mi.; pop. 9,328,784; cap. Lansing.
Michigan, Lake one of the Great Lakes; betw. Michigan and Wisconsin; 22,400 sq. mi.
Michigan City city, N Indiana 46360; pop. 33,822.
Micronesia, Federated States of, isl. republic of the W Pacific, N of the equator; 271 sq. mi.; pop. 108,000; cap. Kolonia.
Middle River uninc. place, N Maryland 21220; pop. 24,616.
Middletown city, CEN Connecticut; 06457; pop. 42,762.
— urb. twp., E New Jersey 07748; pop. 62,298.
— city, SE New York 10940; pop. 24,160.
— city, SW Ohio 45042; pop. 46,022.
— town, SE Rhode Island 02840; pop. 19,460.
Midi S reg. of France.
Midland city, CEN. Michigan 48640*; pop. 38,053.
— city, W Texas 79701*; pop. 89,443.
Midlands counties of CEN. England.
Midway Islands 2 isls. NW of Honolulu, under control of the U.S. Navy; 2 sq. mi.; scene of an important battle of World War II, June 1942.
Midwest City city, CEN. Oklahoma 73110; pop. 52,267.
Milan city, N Italy; pop. 1,464,127.
Milford city, SW Connecticut 06460; pop. 48,168.
— uninc. place, CEN. Massachusetts 01757; pop. 25,355.
Millbrae city, W California 94030; pop. 20,412.
Millburn urb. twp., NE New Jersey 07041; pop. 18,630.
Millington town, SW Tennessee 38053; pop. 17,866.
Millville city, S New Jersey 08332; pop. 25,992.
Milpitas city, W California 95035; pop. 50,686.
Milton town, E Massachusetts 02186; pop. 25,725.
Milwaukee city, SE Wisconsin 53203*; pop. 628,088.
Milwaukie city, NW Oregon 97222; pop. 18,692.
Mindanao isl. S Philippines; 36,537 sq. mi.
Mindoro isl., CEN. Philippines; 3,759 sq. mi.
Mineola vill., SE New York 11501*; pop. 18,994.
Minneapolis city, E Minnesota 55401*; pop. 368,383.
Minnesota state, N United States; 84,402 sq. mi.; pop. 4,387,029; cap. St. Paul.
Minnetonka vill., E Minnesota 55343; pop. 48,370.

Minorca one of the Balearic islands; 271 sq. mi.
Minot city, N North Dakota 58701*; pop. 34,544.
Minsk city, CEN. Belarus; cap.; pop. 1,612,000.
Miramar city, SE Florida 33023; pop. 40,663.
Mishawaka city, N Indiana 46544; pop. 42,608.
Mississippi state S United States; 47,689 sq. mi.; pop. 2,586,443; cap. Jackson.
Mississippi River river, CEN. United States; 2,350 mi. long.
Missoula city, W Montana 59801; pop. 33,351.
Missouri state, CEN. United States; 69,697 sq. mi.; pop. 5,137,804; cap. Jefferson City.
Missouri River river, CEN. United States; 2,470 mi. long.
Mobile city, SW Alabama 36601*; pop. 196,278.
Mobile Bay inlet of the Gulf of Mexico, SW Alabama.
Modesto city, CEN. California 95350*; pop. 164,730.
Mojave Desert arid reg. S California; ab. 15,000 sq. mi.
Moldova republic, E Europe; 13,000 sq. mi.; pop. 4,338,000; cap. Chişinău. Also **Moldavia.**
Moline city, NW Illinois 61265; pop. 43,202.
Molokai isl., CEN. Hawaiian Islands; 259 sq. mi.
Molucca Islands isl. group of Indonesia, betw. Sulawesi and New Guines; 33,315 sq. mi.
Monaco monarchy, SE France; 368 acres: pop. 29,000.
Moncton city, SE New Brunswick, Canada; pop. 55,934.
Mongolia republic (*formerly* **Outer Mongolia**). CEN Asia; 604,000 sq. mi.; pop. 2,116,000; cap. Ulan Bator.
— **Inner Mongolia** reg. N China, 454,600 sq. mi.; pop. 21,456,798; cap. Hohhot.
Monongahela River river, West Virginia and W Pennsylvania; 128 mi. long.
Monroe city, N Louisiana 71201*; pop. 54,909.
— city, SE Michigan 48161; pop. 22,902.
Monroeville boro., SW Pennsylvania 15145; pop. 29,169.
Monrovia city, E Liberia; cap.; pop. 421,000.
— city, SW California 91016; pop. 35,761.
Montana state, NW United States; 147,046 sq. mi.; pop. 803,655; cap. Helena.
Mont Blanc highest mountain of the Alps, on the French-Italian border; 15,781 ft.; site of tunnel, 7½ mi. long, connecting France and Italy.
Montclair city, SW California 91763; pop. 28,434.
— town, NE New Jersey 07042*; pop. 37,729.
Montebello city, SW California 90640; pop. 59,564.
Monte Carlo city, Monaco; pop. 10,000.
Montenegro constituent republic, S Yugoslavia; 5,333 sq. mi.; pop. 633,000; cap. Podgorića.
Monterey city, W California 93940*; pop. 31,954.
Monterey Park city, SW California 91754; pop. 60,738.
Monterrey city, NE Mexico; pop. 1,090,000.
Montevideo city, S Uruguay; cap.; pop. 1,311,976.
Montgomery city, CEN. Alabama 36104*; cap.; pop. 187,106.
Monticello estate and residence of Thomas Jefferson, near Charlottesville, Virginia.
Montmartre dist., N Paris; former artists' quarter.
Montpelier city, CEN. Vermont 05602*; cap.; pop. 8,247.
Montreal city, S Quebec, Canada; pop. 1,080,546.
Montreal-Nord city, S Quebec, Canada; pop. 97,250. Also **Montreal-North.**
Mont-Royal town, S Quebec, Canada; pop. 20,514.
Mont Saint Michel isl. off NW France; site of an ancient fortress and abbey.
Montville city, SE Connecticut 06353; pop. 16,673.
Moorhead city, W Minnesota 56560; pop. 32,295.
Mooreland city, CEN. Oklahoma 73852; pop. 18,761.
Moose Jaw city, S Saskatchewan, Canada; pop. 32,581.
Moravia reg., E Czech Republic.
Morgan City city, S Louisiana 70380; pop. 14,531.
Morgantown city, N West Virginia 26505*; pop. 25,879.
Morocco monarchy, NW Africa; ab. 177,117 sq. mi.; pop. 25,113,000; cap. Rabat.
Morristown town, CEN. New Jersey 07960; pop. 16,189.
— city, NE Tennessee 37814*; pop. 21,385.
Morton Grove vill., NE Illinois 60053; pop. 22,408.
Moscow city, W Russia; cap.; pop. 8,967,000.
Moselle river, NE France, Luxembourg, and W Germany; 320 mi. long.
Moss Point city, SE Mississippi 39563; pop. 18,998.

Mosul city, N Iraq; pop. 293,100.
Mountain Brook city, CEN. Alabama 35223; pop. 18,810.
Mountain View city, W California 94042*; pop. 67,460.
Mount Clemens city, SE Michigan 48046*; pop. 18,405.
Mountlake Terrace city, CEN. Washington 98043; pop. 19,320.
Mount Lebanon uninc. urb. twp., SW Pennsylvania 15228; pop. 33,362.
Mount Pleasant city, CEN. Michigan 48858; pop. 23,285.
Mount Prospect vill., NE Illinois 60056*; pop. 53,170.
Mount Vernon home and burial place of George Washington, near Washington, D.C.
— city, S Illinois 62864; pop. 16,988.
— city, SE New York 10551*; pop. 67,153.
Mozambique republic SE Africa; 313,661 sq. mi.; pop. 15,696,000; cap. Maputo.
Muncie city, E Indiana 47302; pop. 71,035.
Mundelein vill., NE Illinois 60060; pop. 21,215.
Munich city, SE Germany; pop. 1,211,617.
Munster town, NW Indiana 46321; pop. 19,949.
Murfreesboro city, CEN. Tennessee; 37130*; pop. 44,922.
Murmansk city, NW Russia; pop. 432,000.
Murray city, CEN. Utah 84107; pop. 31,282.
Murray River river, SE Australia; 1,600 mi. long.
Muscat and Oman: *the former name of* Oman.
Muscatine city, E Iowa 52761; pop. 22,881.
Muskegon city, W Michigan 49440*; pop. 40,283.
Muskogee city, E Oklahoma 74401*; pop. 37,708.
Myanmar military govt., *formerly* **Burma**, SE Asia; 261,228 sq. mi.; pop. 41,675,000; cap. Yangôn (Rangoon).
Mysore city, S India; pop. 355,685.
Nacogdoches city E Texas 75961*; pop. 30,872.
Nagasaki city, NW Kyushu island, Japan; largely destroyed by a U.S. atomic bomb, Aug. 9, 1945; pop. 445,854.
Nagoya city, CEN. Honshu isl., Japan; pop. 2,149,517.
Nagpur city, CEN. India; pop. 1,219,461.
Nairobi city, SW Kenya; cap.; pop. 1,103,600.
Namibia republic, SW Africa; 317,818 sq. mi.; pop. 1,302,000; cap. Windhoek.
Nampa city, SW Idaho 83651; pop. 28,365.
Nanjing city, E China; cap. 1928N37; pop. 2,022,500.
Nantes city, W France; pop. 245,000.
Nantucket isl. off SE Massachusetts; 57 sq. mi.; pop. 6,012.
Napa city, W California 94558*; pop. 61,842.
Naperville city, NE Illinois 60540; pop. 85,351.
Naples city, SW Italy; pop. 1,202,582.
Narragansett Bay inlet of the Atlantic, SE Rhode Island.
Nashua city, S New Hampshire 03060; pop. 67,865.
Nashville city, CEN. Tennessee 37202*; cap.; pop. 488,374.
Nassau city, New Providence, Bahamas Islands; cap.; pop. 101,503.
Natchez city, SW Mississippi 39120*; pop. 19,460.
Natchitoches city, CEN. Louisiana 71457; pop. 16,609.
Natick town, NE Massachusetts 01760*; pop. 30,510.
National City city, SW California 92050; pop. 54,249.
Naugatuck town, CEN. Connecticut 06770; pop. 30,625.
Nauru Republic, isl. W-CENT. Pacific just south of Equator (Oceania); 8 sq. mi., pop. 9,000; cap. Yaren.
Navarre reg. and former kingdom, N Spain and SW France.
Nazareth town, N Israel; scene of Christ's childhood; pop. 40,400.
Nebraska state, CEN. United States; 77,355 sq. mi.; pop. 1,584,617; cap. Lincoln.
Nederland city, SE Texas 77627; pop. 16,192.
Needham town, NE Massachusetts 02192; pop. 27,557.
Neenah city, CEN. Wisconsin 54956; pop. 23,219.
Negev desert reg., S Israel; 4,700 sq. mi. Also **Negeb.**
Nejd prov., CEN. Saudi Arabia; ab. 450,000 sq. mi.; cap. Riyadh.
Nepal republic betw. Tibet and India; 56,827 sq. mi.; pop. 19,000,000; cap. Kathmandu.

Netherlands monarchy, NW Europe; 16,026 sq. mi.; pop. 14,472,000; cap. Amsterdam; seat of government, The Hague.

Netherlands Antilles 3 isls. N of Venezuela and 3 in the Leeward Islands group; 308 sq. mi.; pop. 196,000; cap. Willemstad.

Netherlands Guiana See **Suriname.**

Nevada state, W United States; 110,561 sq. mi.; pop. 1,206,152; cap. Carson city.

New Albany city, S Indiana 47150; pop. 36,322.

Newark city, W California 94560; pop. 37,861.

— city, NW Delaware 19715*; pop. 25,098.

— city, NE New Jersey 07102*; pop. 275,221.

— city, CEN. Ohio 43055*; pop. 44,389.

New Bedford city, SE Massachusetts 02741*; pop. 99,922.

New Berlin city, SE Wisconsin 53151; pop. 33,592.

New Braunfels city, CEN. Texas 78130*; pop. 27,334.

New Brighton vill., E Minnesota 55112; pop. 22,207.

New Britain city, CEN. Connecticut 06050*; pop. 75,491.

New Brunswick city, CEN. New Jersey 08901*; pop. 41,711.

— prov., SE Canada; 27,834 sq. mi.; pop. 718,400; cap. Fredericton.

Newburgh city, SE New York 12550*; pop. 26,454.

Newburyport city, NE Massachusetts 01950; pop. 16,317.

New Caledonia isl. E of Australia; comprising with adjacent isls. a French overseas terr.; 7,233 sq. mi.; pop. 168,000; cap. Nouméa.

New Canaan city, SW Connecticut 06840; pop. 17,864.

New Castle city, E Indiana 47362; pop. 17,753.

— city, W Pennsylvania 16101*; pop. 28,334.

Newcastle upon Tyne city, NE England; pop. 203,591. Also **Newcastle, Newcastle on Tyne.**

New City uninc. place, SE New York, 10956; pop. 33,673.

New Delhi city, Delhi terr., India; cap. of India; pop. 273,036.

New England NE section of the United States, including Maine, New Hampshire, Vermont, Massachusetts, Rhode Island, and Connecticut.

Newfoundland prov., E Canada; comprising the island of **Newfoundland** (43,359 sq. mi.) and Labrador on the mainland; 143,510 sq. mi.; pop. 579,700; cap. St. John's.

New Georgia isl. group, British Solomon Islands; ab. 2,000 sq. mi.

New Guinea isl., N of Australia; 304,200 sq. mi. See **Papua New Guinea, West New Guinea.**

New Hampshire state, NE United States; 9,279 sq. mi.; pop. 1,113,915; cap. Concord.

New Haven city, S Connecticut 06510*; pop. 130,474.

New Hebride See **Vanuatu.**

New Hope city, SE Minnesota 55428; pop. 21,853.

New Iberia city, S Louisiana 70560*; pop. 31,828.

New Ireland volcanic isl. of the Bismarck Archipelago, S Pacific; 3,700 sq. mi.; pop. 70,800; part of Papua New Guinea.

Newington city, CEN. Connecticut 06111; pop. 29,208.

New Jersey state, E United States; 7,787 sq. mi.; pop. 7,748,634; cap. Trenton.

New Kensington city, W Pennsylvania 15068*; pop. 15,894.

New London city, SE Connecticut 06320; pop. 28,540.

Newmarket town S Ontario, Canada; pop. 24,795.

New Mexico state, SW United States; 121,593 sq. mi.; pop. 1,512,779; cap. Santa Fe.

New Milford boro., NE New Jersey 07646; pop. 15,990.

New Orleans city, SE Louisiana 70113*; pop. 496,938.

New Philadelphia city, CEN. Ohio 44663; pop. 15,698.

Newport city, N Kentucky 41071*; pop. 18,871.

— city, SE Rhode Island 02840*; pop. 28,227.

Newport Beach city, SW California 92660*; pop. 66,643.

Newport News city, SE Virginia 23607*; pop. 170,045.

New Rochelle city, SE New York 10802*; pop. 67,265.

New South Wales state, SE Australia; 309,500 sq. mi.; pop. 5,771,900; cap. Sydney.

Newton city, CEN. Iowa 50208; pop. 14,789.

— city, CEN. Kansas 67114; pop. 16,700.

— city, E Massachusetts 02158; pop. 85,585.

Newtown city, SW Connecticut 06470; pop. 20,779.

New Westminster city, SW British Columbia, Canada; pop. 36,393.

New York state, NE United States; 49,108 sq. mi.; pop. 18,044,505; cap. Albany.

— **City,** SE New York 10001*; divided into the five boroughs of the Bronx, Kings (Brooklyn), New York (Manhattan), Queens, and Richmond (Staten Island); 365 sq. mi.; pop. 7,322,564.

— borough (Manhattan), CEN. New York City, New York 10001*; pop. 1,487,536.

New York State Barge Canal waterway system, New York; connects the Hudson River with Lakes Erie, Champlain, and Ontario, 525 mi. long.

New Zealand monarchy, comprising a group of isls. SE of Australia; 104,454 sq. mi.; pop. 3,389,000; cap. Wellington.

Niagara Falls city, W New York 14302*; pop. 61,840.

— city, S Ontario, Canada; pop. 69,423.

Niagara River river betw. Ontario, Canada, and New York State, connecting Lakes Erie and Ontario; in its course occurs **Niagara Falls,** a cataract divided by Goat Island into the American Falls, ab. 167 ft. high and 1,000 ft. wide, and Horseshoe Falls on the Canadian side, ab. 160 ft. high and 2,500 ft. wide.

Nicaragua republic, Central America; 49,291 sq. mi.; pop. 3,871,000; cap. Managua.

Nicaragua, Lake lake, SW Nicaragua; 3,100 sq. mi.

Nice city, SE France; pop. 342,000.

Nicobar Islands isl. terr. of India; 19 isls. in the Bay of Bengal; 754 sq. mi.; pop. 22,000.

Nicosia city, CEN. Cyprus; cap.; pop. 166,900.

Niger river, W Africa; ab. 2,600 mi. long.

Niger, Republic of republic, CEN. Africa, 458,074 sq. mi.; pop. 7,800,000; cap. Niamey.

Nigeria, Federation of republic, W Africa; 356,669 sq. mi.; pop. 119,812,000; cap. Abuja.

Nile river, E Africa; 4,130 mi. long; the longest river in the world.

Niles vill., NE Illinois 60648; pop. 28,284.

— city, NE Ohio 44446; pop. 21,128.

Norfolk city, NE Nebraska 68701; pop. 21,476.

— city, SE Virginia 23501*; pop. 261,229.

Normal town, CEN. Illinois 61761; pop. 40,023.

Norman city, CEN. Oklahoma 73070*; pop. 80,071.

Normandy reg. and former prov., NW France.

Norridge vill., NE Illinois 60655*; pop. 14,459.

Norristown boro., SE Pennsylvania 19401*; pop. 30,749.

North Adams city, NW Massachusetts 01247*; pop. 16,797.

North America N continent of the Western Hemisphere; ⁄9,410,000 sq. mi. (including adjacent islands).

Northampton city, W Massachusetts 01060*; pop. 29,289.

North Andover town, NE Massachusetts 01845; pop. 22,792.

North Arlington boro., NE New Jersey 07032; pop. 13,790.

North Attleborough town, E Massachusetts 02760*; pop. 16,178.

North Bay city, CEN. Ontario, Canada; pop. 51,639.

North Bergen urb. twp., NE New Jersey 07047; pop. 48,414.

North Borneo See **Sabah.**

Northbrook vill., NE Illinois 60062*; pop. 32,308.

North Cape promontory, N Norway.

North Carolina state, SE United States; 52,669 sq. mi.; pop. 6,657,630; cap. Raleigh.

North Chicago city, NE Illinois 60064; pop. 34,978.

North Dakota state, N United States; 70,702 sq. mi.; pop. 641,364; cap. Bismarck.

Northern Ireland part of the United Kingdom in N reg. of Ireland; 5,452 sq. mi.; pop. 1,578,100; cap. Belfast.

Northern Territory reg., N Australia; 519,800 sq. mi.; pop. 156,500; cap. Darwin.

Northglenn city, CEN. Colorado 80233; pop. 27,195.

North Haven city, S Connecticut 06473; pop. 22,249.

North Highlands uninc. place, CEN. California 95660; pop. 42,105.

North Island isl., N New Zealand; 44,281 sq. mi.

North Kingston town, S Rhode Island 02852; pop. 23,786.

North Korea See **Korea.**

North Las Vegas city, SE Nevada 89030; pop. 47,707.

North Little Rock city, CEN. Arkansas 72114*; pop. 61,741.

North Miami city, SE Florida 33161; pop. 49,998.

North Miami Beach city, SE Florida 33160; pop. 35,359.

North Olmsted city, N Ohio 44070; pop. 34,204.
North Plainfield boro., NE New Jersey 07060; pop. 18,820.
North Platte city, CEN. Nebraska 69101*; pop. 22,605.
North Pole N extremity of the earth's axis.
North Providence town, NE Rhode Island 02908; pop. 32,090.
North Richland Hills town, N Texas 76118; pop. 45,895.
North Sea part of the Atlantic betw. Great Britain and Europe.
North Tonawanda city, SW New York 14120; pop. 34,989.
North Vancouver city, SW British Columbia, Canada; pop. 31,934.
Northwest Territories adm. div., N Canada; 1,271,442 sq. mi.; pop. 42,609.
Northwest Territory reg. awarded to the United States by Britain in 1783, extending from the Great Lakes S to the Ohio River and from Pennsylvania W to the Mississippi.
Norton Shores city, SW Michigan 49441; pop. 21,755.
Norwalk city, SW California 90650; pop. 94,279.
— city, SW Connecticut 06856*; pop. 78,331.
Norway monarchy, N Europe; 125,050 sq. mi.; pop. 4,246,000; cap. Oslo.
Norwich co. boro., E England; pop. 119,300.
— city, SE Connecticut 06360; pop. 37,391.
Nottingham co. boro., CEN. England; pop. 278,600.
Nova Scotia prov., E Canada; 20,402 sq. mi.; pop. 828,571; cap. Halifax.
Novato city, W California 94947; pop. 47,585.
Novaya Zemlya two isls., Arctic Ocean, NE Russia; ab. 35,000 sq. mi.
Novosibirsk city, SW Asian Russia, ab. 1,700 mi. E of Moscow; pop. 1,436,000.
Nürnberg city, CEN. Germany; pop. 484,184.
Nutley town, NE New Jersey 07110; pop. 27,099.
Oahu isl., CEN. Hawaiian Islands; 589 sq. mi.
Oak Forest city, NE Illinois 60452; pop. 26,203.
Oakland city, W California 94615*; pop. 372,242.
Oakland Park city, SE Florida 33308; pop. 1,743.
Oak Lawn vill., NE Illinois 60454*; pop. 56,182.
Oak Park vill., NE Illinois 60301*; pop. 53,648.
— city, SE Michigan 48237; pop. 30,462.
Oak Ridge city, E Tennessee 37830*; pop. 27,310.
Oakville town, S Ontario, Canada; pop. 68,950.
Ocala city, CEN. Florida 32670; pop. 42,045.
Oceania isls. of Melanesia, Micronesia, and Polynesia, and sometimes the Malay Archipelago and Australasia.
Oceanside city, SW California 92054*; pop. 128,398.
— uninc. place, SE New York 11572; pop. 32,423.
Oder river, CEN. Europe; 563 mi. long.
Odessa city, S Ukraine; pop. 1,115,000.
— city, W Texas 79760*; pop. 89,699.
Ogden city, N Utah 84401*; pop. 63,909.
Ohio state, CEN. United States; 41,330 sq. mi.; pop. 10,887,325; cap. Columbus.
Ohio River river, CEN. United States; 981 mi. long.
Oildale uninc. place, CEN. California 93308; pop. 26,553.
Okhotsk, Sea of inlet of the Pacific W of Kamchatka and the Kurile Islands.
Okinawa Japanese isl., largest of the Ryukyu Islands; 870 sq. mi.; pop. 1,161,000; cap. Naha.
Oklahoma state, CEN. United States; 69,956 sq. mi.; pop. 3,157,604; cap. Oklahoma City.
Oklahoma City city, CEN. Oklahoma 73100*; cap.; pop. 444,719.
Okmulgee city, CEN. Oklahoma 74447; pop. 13,441.
Okolona uninc. place, NW Kentucky 40219; pop. 18,902.
Olathe city, E Kansas 66061; pop. 63,352.
Old Bridge city, CEN. New Jersey 08857; pop. 22,151.
Olean city, SW New York 14760; pop. 16,946.
Olympia city, W Washington 98501*; cap.; pop. 33,840.
Olympus, Mount mtn., N Greece; regarded in Greek mythology as the home of the gods; 9,570 ft.
Omaha city, E Nebraska 68108; pop. 335,795.
Oman independent sultanate, SE Arabia; 120,000 sq. mi.; pop. 1,400,000; cap. Muscat.
Omsk city, S Russia; pop. 1,028,000.
Ontario city, SW California 91760*; pop. 133,179.
— prov., SE Canada; 344,090 sq. mi.; pop. 8,264,465; cap. Toronto.

Ontario, Lake easternmost of the Great Lakes; 7,540 sq. mi.
Opelika city, E Alabama 36801; pop. 22,122.
Opelousas city, CEN. Louisiana 70570; pop. 18,151.
Oporto city, W Portugal; pop. 335,700.
Opportunity uninc. place, E Washington 99214; pop. 22,326.
Orange former principality, now part of SE France.
— city, SW California 92667*; pop. 91,450.
— city, NE New Jersey 07050*; pop. 29,925.
— city, E Texas 77630*; pop. 19,381.
Orange River river, S Africa; 1,300 mi. long.
Oregon state, NW United States; 97,073 sq. mi.; pop. 2,853,733; cap. Salem.
— city, N Ohio 43616; pop. 18,334.
Orem city, CEN. Utah 84057; pop. 63,909.
Orillia town, S Ontario, Canada; pop. 24,412.
Orinoco river, Venezuela; ab. 1,700 mi. long.
Orkney Islands isl. group, N of Scotland, comprising **Orkney**, a co. of Scotland; 376 sq. mi.; pop. 18,134; cap. Kirkwall.
Orlando city, CEN. Florida 32802*; pop. 164,693.
Orléans city, CEN. France; pop. 106,246.
Osaka city, S Honshu, Japan; pop. 2,635,156.
Oshawa city, S Ontario, Canada; pop. 107,023.
Oshkosh city, E Wisconsin 54901*; pop. 55,006.
Oslo city, SE Norway; cap.; pop. 457,819.
Ossa mtn., E Greece; 6,490 ft. See **Pelion.**
Ossining vill., SE New York 10562; pop. 22,582.
Ostend city, NW Belgium; pop. 70,125.
Oswego city, N New York 13126; pop. 19,195.
Otranto, Strait of strait betw. the Adriatic and Ionian seas; ab. 43 mi. wide.
Ottawa city, N Illinois 61350; pop. 17,451.
— city, SE Ontario, Canada; cap. of Canada; pop. 304,462.
Ottumwa city, SE Iowa 52501; pop. 24,488.
Ouagadougou city, CEN. Burkina Faso; cap.; pop. 441,500.
Outremont city, S Quebec, Canada; pop. 27,089.
Overland city, E Missouri 63114; pop. 17,987.
Overland Park uninc. place, NE Kansas 66204; pop. 111,790.
Owatonna city, S Minnesota 55060; pop. 19,386.
Owensboro city, NW Kentucky 42301*; pop. 53,549.
Owen Sound city, S Ontario, Canada; pop. 19,525.
Owosso city, CEN. Michigan 48867; pop. 16,322.
Oxford co. boro., CEN. England; pop. 119,909.
— city, SW Ohio 45056; pop. 18,937.
Oxnard city, SW California 93030*; pop. 142,216.
Ozark Mountains hilly uplands, SW Missouri, NW Arkansas, and NE Oklahoma.
Pacifica city, W California 94044; pop. 37,670.
Pacific Ocean ocean betw. the American continents and Asia and Australia; extending betw. the Arctic and Antarctic regions; ab. 70 million sq. mi.
Padua city, NE Italy; pop. 222,163.
Paducah city, W Kentucky 42001*; pop. 27,256.
Pago Pago town, SE Tutuila, American Samoa 96920; pop. 2,450.
Painesville city, NE Ohio 44077; pop. 15,699.
Pakistan republic, S Asia; 307,374 sq. mi.; pop. 122,666,000; cap. Islamabad.
Palatine vill., NE Illinois 60067; pop. 39,253.
Palau Islands isl. group, W Caroline Island; 188 sq. mi.
Palermo city, NW Sicily, Italy; cap.; pop. 731,483.
Palestine terr., E Mediterranean; 10,434 sq. mi.; divided (1947) by the United Nations into Israel and a terr. that became part of Jordan.
Palma city, W Majorca; cap. of the Balearic Islands, pop. 287,389.
Palm Springs city, S California 92263*; pop. 40,181.
Palo Alto city, W California 94303*; pop. 55,900.
Palomar, Mount mtn., S California; 6,126 ft.; site of **Mount Palomar Observatory.**
Pampa city, N Texas 79065; pop. 19,959.
Panama republic, Central America; 29,157 sq. mi. (excluding Canal Zone); pop. 2,418,000.
— **City**, near the Pacific end of the Panama Canal; cap of Panama; pop. 411,500.
Panama, Isthmus of isthmus connecting North and South America.

Panama Canal ship canal connecting the Atlantic and the Pacific across Panama; completed (1914) by the United States on the leased Canal Zone; 40 mi. long.

Panama Canal Zone See **Canal Zone.**

Panama City city, NW Florida 32401*; pop. 34,378.

Panay isl., CEN. Philippines; 4,446 sq. mi.

Papal States region in CEN. and NE Italy over which the Roman Catholic Church formerly had temporal power.

Papua New Guinea independent monarchy in the Commonwealth of Nations, S Pacific, consisting of the E half of New Guinea; the isls. of the Bismarck Archipelago; Bougainville and Buka in the Solomon Isls.; and a number of smaller isls.; 178,704 sq. mi.; pop. 3,671,000; cap. Port Moresby.

Paradise uninc. place, SE Nevada 89109; pop. 84,818.

Paraguay republic, CEN. South America; 157,048 sq. mi.; pop. 4,279,000; cap. Asunción.

Paraguay River river, CEN. South America; ab. 1,300 mi. long.

Paramaribo city, N Surinam; cap.; pop. 175,000.

Paramount city, SW California 90723; pop. 47,669.

Paramus boro., NE New Jersey 07652; pop. 25,067.

Paraná river, CEN. South America; ab. 1,827 mi. long.

Paris city, N France; cap.; pop. 2,150,500.

— city, NE Texas 75460; pop. 24,699.

Parkersburg city, W West Virginia 26101*; pop. 33,862.

Park Forest vill., NE Illinois 60466; pop. 24,656.

Parkland uninc. place, CEN. Washington 98444; pop. 20,882.

Park Ridge city, NE Illinois 60068; pop. 36,175.

Parkville-Carney uninc. place N Maryland 21234; pop. 31,617.

Parma city, CEN. Italy; pop. 174,827.

— city, N Ohio 44129; pop. 87,876.

Parma Heights city, NE Ohio 44130; pop. 21,448.

Parnassus, Mount mtn., CEN. Greece; anciently regarded as sacred to Apollo and the Muses; 8,062 ft.

Parsippany-Troy Hills city, N New Jersey 07054; pop. 48,478.

Pasadena city, SW California 91109*; pop. 131,591.

— city, SE Texas 77501*; pop. 119,363.

Pascagoula city, SE Mississippi 39567; pop. 25,899.

Passaic city, NE New Jersey 07055*; pop. 58,041.

Patagonia reg. at the S tip of South America.

Paterson city, NE New Jersey 07510*; pop. 140,891.

Pawtucket city, NE Rhode Island 02860*; pop. 72,644.

Peabody city, NE Massachusetts 01960*; pop. 47,039.

Pearl City city, S Oahu, Hawaii 96782; pop. 30,993.

Pearl Harbor inlet, S Oahu, Hawaii; site of a U.S. naval base, bombed by Japanese, December 7, 1941.

Pearl River uninc. place, SE New York 10965; pop. 15,314.

Peekskill city, SE New York 10566; pop. 19,536.

Pekin city, CEN. Illinois 61554*; pop. 32,254.

Peking city, N China; cap.; pop. 9,540,000; Also **Beijing.**

Pelion mtn. range, SE Thessaly, Greece, In Greek mythology, the Titans attempted to reach heaven by piling Pelion on Ossa and both on Olympus.

Peloponnesus penin. betw. Aegean and Ionian Seas; one of the main divisions of S Greece; 8,603 sq. mi.; pop. 986,000.

Pembroke town, SE Ontario, Canada; pop. 14,927.

Pembroke Pines city, SE Florida 33023; pop. 65,452.

Penn Hills uninc. place; SW Pennsylvania 15235; pop. 51,430.

Pennine Alps SW div. of the Alps on the Swiss–Italian border.

Pennsauken urb. twp., W New Jersey 08110; pop. 34,733.

Pennsylvania state, E United States, 45,308 sp. mi.; pop. 11,924,710; cap. Harrisburg.

Pensacola city, NW Florida 32502*; pop. 58,165.

Penticton city, S British Columbia, Canada; pop. 21,344.

Peoria city, CEN. Illinois 61601*; pop. 113,504.

Persia *the former name of* Iran.

Persian Gulf inlet of the Arabian Sea betw. Iran and Arabia; also the **Arabian Gulf.**

Perth city, SW Western Australia; cap.; pop. 1,118,800.

Perth Amboy city, E New Jersey 08861*; pop. 41,067.

Peru republic, W South America; 496,225 sq. mi.; pop. 22,332,000; cap. Lima.

Petaluma city, W California 94952*; pop. 43,184.

Peterborough city, SE Ontario, Canada; pop. 59,683.

Petersburg city, SE Virginia 23803*; pop. 38,386.

Pharr city, S Texas 78577; pop. 32,921.

Phenix City city, E Alabama 36867; pop. 25,312.

Philadelphia city, SE Pennsylvania 19104*; pop. 1,585,577.

Philippines, Republic of the republic occupying the **Philippine Islands,** a Pacific archipelago SE of China; 115,800 sq. mi.; pop. 61,480,000; cap. Manila.

Phillipsburg city, W New Jersey 08865*; pop. 15,757.

Phnom Penh city, S CEN. Cambodia; cap.; pop. 564,000.

Phoenix city CEN. Arizona 85026*; cap.; pop. 983,403.

Picardy reg. and former prov., N France.

Pico Rivera city, SW California 90660; pop. 59,177.

Piedmont reg., E United States; extends from New Jersey to Alabama E of the Appalachians; ab. 80,000 sq. mi.

Pierre city, CEN. South Dakota 57501; cap.; pop. 12,906.

Pierrefonds town, S Quebec, Canada; pop. 35,402.

Pike's Peak mtn., CEN. Colorado; 14,110 ft.

Pikesville uninc. place, CEN. Maryland 21208; pop. 24,815.

Pine Bluff city, CEN. Arkansas 71601*; pop. 57,140.

Pinellas Park city, W Florida 33565; pop. 43,426.

Piqua city, W Ohio 45356; pop. 20,612.

Piraeus city, S Greece; pop. 187,362.

Pisa city, NW Italy; noted for its leaning tower; pop. 102,908.

Pittsburg city, W California 94565; pop. 47,564.

— city, SE Kansas 66762; pop. 17,775.

Pittsburgh city, SW Pennsylvania 15200*; pop. 369,879.

Pittsfield city, W Massachusetts 01201; pop. 48,622.

Placentia city, SW California 92670; pop. 41,259.

Plainfield city, NE New Jersey 07061*; pop. 46,567.

Plainview uninc. place, SE New York 11803; pop. 26,207.

— city, NW Texas 79072*; pop. 21,700.

Plainville city, CEN. Connecticut 06062; pop. 17,392.

Plano city, NE Texas 75074*; pop. 128,713.

Plantation city, NE Florida 33314; pop. 1,885.

Plant City city W Florida 33566; pop. 22,754.

Platte River river, S Nebraska; 310 mi. long.

Plattsburgh city, NE New York 12901; pop. 21,255.

Pleasant Hill uninc. place, W California 94523; pop. 31,585.

Pleasanton city, W California 94566; pop. 50,553.

Pleasure Ridge Park uninc. place, N Kentucky 40258; pop. 25,131.

Plum boro., SW Pennsylvania 15239; pop. 25,609.

Plymouth co. boro. and port, SW England; pop. 255,500.

Plymouth town, E Massachusetts 02360*; site of the first settlement in New England; pop. 45,608.

— vill., E Minnesota 55427; pop. 50,889.

Plymouth Colony colony of the shore of Massachusetts Bay founded by the Pilgrim Fathers in 1620.

Plymouth Rock rock at Plymouth, Massachusetts, on which the Pilgrim Fathers are said to have landed in 1620.

Pocatello city, Idaho 83201*; pop. 46,080.

Pointe-aux-Trembles city, S Quebec, Canada; pop. 55,618.

Pointe-Claire city, S Quebec, Canada; pop. 25,917.

Point Pleasant boro., E New Jersey 08742; pop. 18,177.

Poland republic, CEN. Europe; 120,727 sq. mi.; pop. 38,064,000; cap. Warsaw.

Polynesia isls. of Oceania, CEN. and SE Pacific; E of Melanesia and Micronesia.

Pomerania former province of Prussia, N Germany; now divided between Germany and Poland.

Pomona city, SW California 91766*; pop. 131,723.

Pompano Beach city, SE Florida 33060*; pop. 72,411.

Pompeii ancient city, S Italy; buried in the eruption of Mount Vesuvius, A.D. 79, now excavated.

Ponca City city N Oklahoma 74601*; pop. 26,359.

Ponce city, S Puerto Rico 00731; pop. 161,260.

Pontiac city, SE Michigan 48053*; pop. 71,166.

Poona city, W India; pop. 356,105.

Poplar Bluff city, SE Missouri 63901; pop. 16,996.

Popocatepetl dormant volcano, CEN. Mexico; 17,887 ft.

Po River river, N Italy; 405 mi. long.

Portage town, NW Indiana 46368; pop. 29,060.

— city, SW Michigan 49081; pop. 41,042.

Port Angeles city, NW Washington 98362; pop. 17,710.

Port Arthur city, SE Texas 77640*; pop. 58,724.

Port-au-Prince city, S Haiti; cap.; pop. 514,438.

Port Chester vill., SE New York 10573*; pop. 24,728.

Port Colborne town, S Ontario, Canada; pop. 20,536.

Port Huron city, E Michigan 48060*; pop. 33,694.
Portland city, SW Maine 04101*; pop. 64,358.
– city, NW Oregon 97208*; pop. 437,319.
Port-of-Spain city, NW Trinidad; cap. of Trinidad and Tobago; pop. 58,300. Also **Port of Spain.**
Porto-Novo city, SE Benin; cap.; pop. 104,000.
Port Said city, NE Egypt; at the Mediterranean end of the Suez Canal; pop. 400,000.
Portsmouth co. boro., S England; site of the chief British naval station; pop. 191,000.
– city, SE New Hampshire 03801*; pop. 25,925.
– city, S Ohio 45662; pop. 22,676.
– city, SE Virginia 23705*; pop. 103,907.
Portugal republic, SW Europe; 35,672 sq. mi.; pop. 10,388,000; cap. Lisbon.
Potomac River river through Maryland, West Virginia, and Virginia; 287 mi. long.
Potsdam city, CEN. Germany; scene of meeting of Allied leaders, 1945; pop. 126,262.
Pottstown boro., SE Pennsylvania 19464; pop. 21,831.
Pottsville city, CEN. Pennsylvania 17901; pop. 18,195.
Poughkeepsie city, SE New York 12601*; pop. 28,844.
Poznan city, W Poland; pop. 586,600.
Prague city, N Czech Republic; cap.; pop. 1,213,792.
Prairie Village city, NE Kansas 66208; pop. 23,186.
Pretoria city, CEN. South Africa; adm. cap.; pop. 443,059.
Prichard city, SW Alabama 36610; pop. 34,311.
Prince Albert city, CEN. Saskatchewan, Canada; pop. 28,631.
Prince Edward Island prov., NE Canada; 2,185 sq. mi.; pop. 118,229; cap. Charlottestown.
Prince George city, CEN. British Columbia, Canada; pop. 59,929.
Prince Rupert city, W British Columbia, Canada; pop. 14,754.
Provence reg. and former prov., SE France.
Providence city, NE Rhode Island 02904*; cap.; pop. 160,728.
Provo city, CEN. Utah 84601; pop. 86,835.
Prussia former state, N Germany; dissolved 1947.
Pueblo city, CEN. Colorado 81003*; pop. 98,640.
Puerto Rico isl., Greater Antilles; a Commonwealth of the United States 3,515 sq. mi.; pop. 3,187,570; cap. San Juan.
Puget Sound inlet of the Pacific, NW Washington.
Pullman city, SE Washington 99163*; pop. 23,478.
Punjab reg., NW India and E Pakistan.
P'yongyang city, W North Korea; cap.; pop. 2,000,000.
Pyrenees mtn. chain betw. France and Spain.
Qatar monarchy, E Arabia, W coast of the Persian Gulf; 4,400 sq. mi.; pop. 444,000; cap. Doha.
Quebec prov., E Canada; 523,859 sq. mi.; pop. 6,572,300.
– city, S Quebec prov., cap.; pop. 164,580.
Queens borough, E New York City, New York 11300*; pop. 1,951,598.
Queensland state, NE Australia; 666,900 sq. mi.; pop. 2,505,100; cap. Brisbane.
Quemoy Islands 2 isls. of the Republic of China in Taiwan Strait; 54 sq. mi.
Quezon City city, CEN. Philippines; cap.; pop. 1,587,140.
Quincy city, W Illinois 62301*; pop. 39,681.
– city, E Massachusetts 02169; pop. 84,985.
Quito city, CEN. Ecuador; cap.; pop. 1,233,865.
Rabat city, N Morocco; cap.; pop. 518,616.
Racine city, SE Wisconsin 53401*; pop. 84,298.
Rahway city, NE New Jersey 07065*; pop. 25,325.
Rainier, Mount extinct volcano, Cascade Range, SW Washington; 14,408 ft.
Raleigh city, CEN. North Carolina 27611*; cap.; pop. 207,951.
Rancho Cordova uninc. place, CEN. California 95670; pop. 48,731.
Randallstown uninc. place, NE Maryland 21133; pop. 26,277.
Randolph town, E Massachusetts 02368; pop. 30,093.
Rangoon (Yangôn) city, S Myanmar; cap.; pop. 2,500,000.
Rantoul vill., CEN. Illinois 61866; pop. 17,212.
Rapid City city, SW South Dakota 57701*; pop. 54,523.
Ravenna city, N Italy, famous for its art treasures and architecture; pop. 136,306.
Rawalpindi city, N Pakistan; pop. 794,843.
Raytown city, W Missouri 64133; pop. 30,601.

Reading town, NE Massachusetts 01867; pop. 22,539.
– city, SE Pennsylvania 19603*; pop. 78,380.
Recife city, NE Brazil; pop. 1,184,215.
Red Deer city, CEN. Alberta, Canada; pop. 32,184.
Redding city, N California 96001*; pop. 66,462.
Redlands city, SW California 92373*; pop. 60,394.
Redondo Beach city, SW California 90277*; pop. 57,102.
Red River river in Texas, Arkansas, and Louisiana; ab. 1,300 mi. long.
– river in N United States and S Canada; 540 mi. long.
Red Sea sea betw. Egypt and Arabia; 1,450 mi. long; ab. 170,000 sq. mi.
Redwood City city, W California 94064*; pop. 66,072.
Regina city, S Saskatchewan, Canada; cap.; pop. 149,593.
Reims city, NE France; site of a famous cathedral; pop. 181,000.
Reno city, W Nevada 89501*; pop. 133,850.
Renton city, CEN. Washington 98055; pop. 41,688.
Repentigny town, S Quebec, Canada; pop. 26,698.
Réunion French overseas dept.; isl. E of Madagascar; 970 sq. mi.; pop. 600,000; cap. Saint-Denis.
Revere city, E Massachusetts 02151; pop. 42,786.
Reykjavik city, SW Iceland; cap.; pop. 96,708.
Rheims *an alternate name of* Reims.
Rhine river, CEN. Europe; 810 mi. long.
Rhode Island state, NE United States; 1,212 sq. mi.; pop. 1,005,984; cap. Providence.
Rhodes isl. of the Dodecanese groups; 545 sq. mi.
Rhodesia See **Zimbabwe.**
Rhône river, Switzerland and SE France; 504 mi. long. Also **Rhone.**
Rialto city, S California 92376; pop. 72,388.
Richardson city, N Texas 75080*; pop. 74,840.
Richfield vill., E Minnesota 55423; pop. 35,710.
Richland city, S Washington 99352; pop. 32,315.
Richmond borough (Staten Island), SW New York City, New York 10300*; pop. 378,977.
– city, W California 94802*; pop. 87,425.
– city, E Indiana 47374; pop. 38,705.
– city, CEN. Kentucky 40475; pop. 21,155.
– city, CEN. Virginia 23232*; cap.; cap. of the Confederacy 1861–65; pop. 203,056.
Richmond Hill town, S Ontario, Canada; pop. 34,716.
Ridgewood urb. twp., NE New Jersey 07451*; pop. 24,142.
Rif mtn. range, N Morocco. Also **Riff.**
Riga city, CEN. Latvia; cap.; pop. 915,000.
Rijeka city, NW Croatia; pop. 132,933.
Rimouski town, E Quebec, Canada; pop. 27,897.
Rio de Janeiro city, SE Brazil; former cap.; pop. 5,603,388. Also **Rio.**
Rio de la Plata estuary of the Paraná and Uruguay rivers betw. Argentina and Uruguay; 170 mi. long.
Rio Grande river betw. Texas and Mexico; 1,890 mi. long.
Riverside city, SW California 92502*; pop. 226,505.
Riviera coastal strip on the Mediterranean from Hyeres, France to La Spezia, Italy.
Riviera Beach town, SE Florida 33404; pop. 27,639.
Roanoke city, W Virginia 24001*; pop. 96,370.
Roanoke Island isl. off North Carolina; 12 mi. long, 3 mi. wide.
Rochester city, SE Minnesota 55901; pop. 70,745.
– city, SE New Hampshire 03867; pop. 26,630.
– city, W New York 14603*; pop. 231,636.
Rockford city, N Illinois 61125*; pop. 139,426.
Rock Hill city, N South Carolina 29730*; pop. 41,643.
Rock Island city, NW Illinois 61201*; pop. 40,552.
Rockland town, E Massachusetts 02370; pop. 16,123.
Rockville city, CEN. Maryland 20850*; pop. 44,835.
Rockville Centre vill., SE New York 11570*; pop. 24,727.
Rocky Mount city, CEN. North Carolina 27801*; pop. 48,997.
Rocky Mountains mtn. system, W North America; extends from the Arctic to Mexico.
Rocky River city, N Ohio 44116; pop. 20,410.
Rolling Meadows city, NE Illinois 60008; pop. 22,591.
Romania republic, SE Europe; 91,700 sq. mi.; pop. 22,810,035; cap. Bucharest.

Rome city, w Italy; cap.; site of the Vatican City; cap. of the former Roman republic, the Roman Empire, and the States of the Church; pop. 2,816,474.
— city, NW Georgia 30161*; pop. 30,362.
— city, CEN. New York 13440*; pop. 44,350.
Rosario city, CEN. Argentina; pop. 810,000.
Rosedale uninc. place, NW Maryland 21237; pop. 18,703.
Roselle boro., NE New Jersey 07203 pop. 20,314.
Rosemead city, SW California 91770; pop. 51,638.
Roseville city, CEN. California 95678; pop. 44,685.
— city SE Michigan 48066; pop. 51,412.
— vill., SE Minnesota 55113; pop. 33,485.
Rostov-on-Don city, SW Russia; pop. 934,000.
Roswell city, SE New Mexico 88201*; pop. 44,654.
Rotterdam city, w Netherlands; pop. 1,576,232.
Rouen city, N France; site of a famous cathedral; scene of the burning of Joan of Arc; pop. 114,927.
Roumania an alternate form of Romania.
Rouyn city, w Quebec, Canada; pop. 17,678.
Royal Oak city, SE Michigan 48068*; pop. 65,410.
Rugby municipal boro., CEN. England; site of a boys' school; pop. 60,380.
Ruhr river, w Germany; 142 mi. long.
— reg. s of the Ruhr, an industrial and coal-mining district. 1,770 sq. mi.
Rumania an alternate form of Romania.
Russia federal republic, E Europe and N Asia; 6,592,800 sq. mi.; pop. 147,400,000; cap. Moscow.
Ruston city, N Louisiana 71270*; pop. 20,027.
Rutherford boro., NE New Jersey 07070*; pop. 17,790.
Rutland city, CEN. Vermont 05701; pop. 18,230.
Rwanda republic, CEN. Africa; 10,169 sq. mi.; pop. 7,232,000; cap. Kigali.
Rye city, SE New York, 10580; pop. 14,936.
Ryukyu Islands isl. group betw. Kyushu and Taiwan; 870 sq. mi.; pop. 1,161,000; chief isl. Okinawa; adm. by Japan.
Saar river, NE France and Germany; 152 mi. long.
Saar, The state, w Germany; 993 sq. mi.; pop. 1,051,000; cap. Saarbrücken.
Sabah part of Malaysia in N Borneo; 28,460 sq. mi.; pop. 1,176,400; cap. Kota Kinabalu.
Sacramento city, CEN. California; 95813*; cap.; pop. 369,365.
Sacramento River river, CEN. California; 382 mi. long.
Saginaw city, CEN. Michigan 48605*; pop. 69,512.
Sahara desert area, N Africa; ab. 3 million sq. mi. Also **Sahara Desert.**
Saigon city, s Vietnam; formerly cap. of South Vietnam; pop. 3,169,135; now called **Ho Chi Minh City.**
Saipan one of the Mariana isls.; 47 sq. mi.; captured from Japan by U.S. forces in World War II, 1944.
Saint, Sainte See entries beginning ST., STE.
Sakhalin isl. SE Russia; 29,700 sq. mi.; pop. 649,000; adm. ctr. Yuzhno-Sakhalinsk.
Salem city, NE Massachusetts 01970*; pop. 38,091.
— city, SE New Hampshire 03079; pop. 25,746.
— city, NW Oregon 97301*; cap.; pop. 107,786.
— town, CEN. Virginia 24153; pop. 23,756.
Salerno city, SW Italy; scene of a battle in World War II betw. Germans and Allied landing forces, 1943; pop. 153,091.
Salina city, CEN Kansas 67401*; pop. 42,303.
Salinas city, w California 93901*; pop. 108,777.
Salisbury city, SE Maryland 21801; pop. 20,592.
— city, CEN. North Carolina 28144; pop. 23,087.
— city, N Zimbabwe; cap.; pop. 633,000: Now called **Harare.**
Salonika city, NE Greece; pop. 345,799.
Salt Lake City city, CEN. Utah 84101*; cap.; pop. 159,936.
Salvador city, E Brazil; pop. 1,506,602.
— See **El Salvador.**
Salzburg city, w Austria; birthplace of Mozart; pop. 139,000.
Samar one of the Visayan isls., Philippines; 5,050 sq. mi.
Samarkand city, E Uzbekistan; pop. 481,000.
Samoa isl. group, SW Pacific; 1,173 sq. mi.; divided into **American** (or **Eastern**) **Samoa,** an uninc. terr. of the United States; 76 sq. mi.; pop. 27,159; cap. Pago Pago; and **Western Samoa,** an independent monarchy; 1,093 sq. mi.; pop. 165,000; cap. Apia.

Samos isl. of Greece, E Aegean; 184 sq. mi.
Samothrace isl. of Greece, NE Aegean; 71 sq. mi.
San Angelo city, CEN. Texas 76902*; pop. 84,474.
San Antonio city, CEN. Texas 78284*; site of the Alamo; pop. 935,933.
San Benito city, s Texas 78586; pop. 20,125.
San Bernardino city, SW California 92403*; pop. 164,164.
San Bruno city, w California 94066; pop. 38,961.
San Carlos city, w California 94070; pop. 26,167.
San Clemente city, s California 92672; pop. 41,100.
San Diego city, SW California 92109*; pop. 1,110,549.
San Dimas city, SW California 91773; pop. 32,397.
Sandusky city, N Ohio 44870*; pop. 29,764.
San Fernando city, SW California 91340*; pop. 22,580.
Sanford city, CEN. Florida 32771; pop. 32,387.
— city, SW Maine 04073; pop. 10,296.
San Francisco city, w California 94101*; pop. 723,959.
San Francisco Bay inlet of the Pacific, w California.
San Gabriel city, SW California 91776*; pop. 37,120.
San Joaquin River river, CEN. California; 317 mi. long.
San José city, CEN. Costa Rica; cap.; pop. 239,800.
San Jose city, w California 95101*; pop. 782,248.
San Juan city, NE Puerto Rico 00936*; cap.; pop. 431,227.
San Leandro city, w California 94577*; pop. 68,223.
San Lorenzo uninc. place, w California 94580; pop. 19,987.
San Luis Obispo city, w California 93401*; pop. 41,958.
San Marcos city, CEN. Texas 78666; pop. 28,743.
San Marino republic, an enclave in NE Italy; 24 sq. mi.; pop. 23,000.
— city, San Marino; cap.; pop. 2,343.
San Mateo city, w California 94402*; pop. 85,486.
San Pablo city, w California 94806; pop. 25,158.
San Rafael city, w California 94901*; pop. 48,404.
San Salvador city, s El Salvador; cap.; pop. 459,902.
— isl. CEN. Bahamas; site of Columbus' first landing in the western hemisphere, 1492.
Santa Ana city, SW California 92711*; pop. 293,742.
Santa Barbara city, SW California 93102*; pop. 85,571.
Santa Catalina isl. off SW California; 70 sq. mi.
Santa Clara city, w California 95050*; pop. 93,613.
Santa Cruz city, w California 95060*; pop. 49,040.
Santa Fe city, N New Mexico 87501*; cap.; pop. 55,859.
Santa Fe Trail trade route, important from 1821–80, betw. Independence, Missouri, and Santa Fe, New Mexico.
Santa Maria city, SW California 93454*; pop. 61,284.
Santa Monica city, SW California 90406*; pop. 86,905.
Santa Paula city, SW California 93060; pop. 25,062.
Santa Rosa city, w California 95402*; pop. 113,313.
Santee uninc. place, SW California 92071; pop. 52,902.
Santiago city, CEN. Chile; cap.; pop. 5,133,700. Also **Santiago de Chile.**
Santo Domingo city, s Dominican Republic; cap.; pop. 1,600,000.
São Paulo city, SE Brazil; pop. 10,063,000.
São Tomé and Principe republic, isls. off w Africa; 366 sq. mi.; pop. 121,000; cap. São Tomé.
— **São Tomé** city; cap. São Tomé isl.; 34,997.
Sapulpa city, CEN. Oklahoma 74066; pop. 18,074.
Sarajevo city, SE Bosnia-Herzegovina; cap.; scene of the assassination of Archduke Franz Ferdinand, June 28, 1914; pop. 415,631.
Sarasota city SW Florida 33578*; pop. 50,961.
Saratoga city, w California 95070; pop. 28,061.
Saratoga Springs city, CEN. New York 12866; pop. 25,001.
Sarawak part of Malaysia on NW Borneo; 48,050 sq. mi.; pop. 1,591,100; cap. Kuching.
Sardinia isl., CEN. Mediterranean; with adjacent isls. a reg. of Italy; 9,301 sq. mi.; pop. 1,617,215; cap. Cagliari.
Sarnia city, s Ontario, Canada; pop. 55,576.
Saskatchewan prov., CEN. Canada; 251,866 sq. mi.; pop. 1,000,300; cap. Regina.
Saskatoon city, CEN. Saskatchewan, Canada; pop. 177,641.

Saudi Arabia monarchy, N and CEN. Arabia; 865,000 sq. mi.; pop. 14,131,000; cap. Riyadh.

Saugus town, NE Massachusetts 01906; pop. 25,549.

Sault Ste. Marie city, CEN. Ontario, Canada; pop. 81,044.

Sault Sainte Marie Canals 3 canals that circumvent the rapids in the St. Marys River betw. Lakes Superior and Huron.

Savannah city, E Georgia 31401*; pop. 137,560.

Saxony reg. and former duchy, electorate, kingdom, and prov., CEN. Germany.

Sayreville boro., E New Jersey 08872; pop. 34,986.

Scandinavia reg. NW Europe; includes Sweden, Norway, and Denmark and sometimes Finland, Iceland, and the Faeroe Islands.

Scapa Flow sea basin and British naval base in the Orkney Islands, Scotland; 50 sq. mi.

Scarsdale town, SE New York 10583; pop. 16,987.

Schaumburg city, NE Illinois 60172; pop. 68,586.

Scheldt river, N France, Belgium and the Netherlands; 270 mi. long.

Schenectady city, E New York 12301*; pop. 65,566.

Schleswig-Holstein state, NE Germany; 6,069 sq. mi.; pop. 2,614,000; cap. Kiel.

Schuylkill River river, SE Pennsylvania; 130 mi. long.

Scituate city, NE Massachusetts 02066; pop. 16,786.

Scotch Plains urb. twp., NE New Jersey 07076; pop. 21,160.

Scotland a political div. and the N part of Great Britain; a separate kingdom until 1707; 30,418 sq. mi.; pop. 5,094,000; cap. Edinburgh.

Scottsdale city, CEN. Arizona 85251*; pop. 130,069.

Scranton city, NE Pennsylvania 18503*; pop. 81,805.

Seaford uninc. place, SE New York 11783; pop. 15,597.

Seal Beach city, SW California 90740; pop. 25,098.

Seaside city, W California 93955; pop. 38,901.

Seattle city, CEN. Washington 98109*; pop. 516,259.

Sebastopol See **Sevastopol.**

Security unic. place, CEN. Colorado 80911; pop. 18,768.

Sedalia city, CEN. Missouri 65301*; pop. 19,800.

Seguin city, CEN. Texas 78155; pop. 18,853.

Seine river, NE France; 482 mi. long.

Selma city, CEN. Alabama 36701*; pop. 23,755.

Semarang city, N Java, Indonesia; pop. 646,590.

Senegal river, NW Africa; ab. 1,000 mi. long.

Senegal, Republic of republic, NW Africa; 75,955 sq. mi.; pop. 7,277,000; cap. Dakar.

Seoul city, NW South Korea; cap.; pop. 8,114,000.

Sept-Iles city, E Quebec, Canada; pop. 30,617.

Serbia constituent republic, Yugoslavia; 34,116 sq. mi.; pop. 9,791,475; cap. Belgrade.

Sevastopol city, S Crimea, Ukraine; pop. 308,000.

Severn river, N Wales and W England; 210 mi. long.

Severna Park city, NE Maryland 21146; pop. 25,879.

Seville city, SW Spain; pop. 655,435.

Sèvres city, N France; pop. 21,149.

Seychelles isl. republic off E Africa; 175 sq. mi.; pop. 68,700; cap. Victoria.

Shaker Heights city, N Ohio 44120; pop. 30,831.

Shanghai city, E China; pop. 7,228,600.

Shannon river, CEN. Ireland; 224 mi. long.

Sharon city, W Pennsylvania 16146; pop. 17,493.

Shasta, Mount extinct volcano, Cascade Range, N California; 14,162 ft.

Shawinigan city, S Quebec, Canada; pop. 24,921.

Shawnee city, NE Kansas 66203*; pop. 29,653.

— city, CEN. Oklahoma 74801*; pop. 26,017.

Sheboygan city, E Wisconsin 53081; pop. 49,676.

Sheffield co. boro., CEN. England; pop. 544,200.

Shelby city, SW North Carolina 28150; pop. 14,669.

Shelton city, SW Connecticut 06484; pop. 35,418.

Shenandoah river, N Virginia and NE West Virginia; 170 mi. long.

Shenyang city, NE China; pop. 3,700,000; formerly called Mukden.

Sherbrooke city, S Quebec, Canada; pop. 76,804.

Sherman city, N Texas 75090; pop. 31,601.

Shetland Islands isl. group NE of the Orkney Islands, comprising **Shetland,** a co. of Scotland; 551 mi.; pop. 17,000; cap. Lerwick.

Shikoku isl., SW Japan; 7,248 sq. mi.

Shiloh national military park, SW Tennessee; scene of a Union victory in the Civil War, 1862; 6 sq. mi.

Shively city, N Kentucky 40216; pop. 15,535.

Shreveport city, NW Louisiana 71102*; pop. 198,525.

Shrewsbury city, CEN. Massachusetts 01545; pop. 24,146.

Siam *the former name of* Thailand.

Siam, Gulf of part of the South China Sea betw. the Malay Peninsula and Indochina.

Siberia reg., E Russia; ab. 5 million sq. mi.

Sicily isl. of Italy, CEN. Mediterranean; comprises with neighboring islands a reg. of 9,926 sq. mi.; pop. 5,006,684; cap. Palermo.

Sidney city, W Ohio 45365; pop. 18,710.

Sierra Leone republic, W Africa; 27,699 sq. mi.; pop. 4,151,000; cap. Freetown.

Sierra Nevada mtn. range, E California.

Silesia reg., CEN. Europe; divided betw. Czech Republic and Poland.

Silver Spring uninc. place, W Maryland 20907*; pop. 76,046.

Simi Valley city, SW California 93065; pop. 100,217.

Simla city, N India; pop. 55,368.

Simsbury city, CEN. Connecticut 06070; pop. 22,023.

Sinai penin., E Egypt, betw. the Mediterranean and the Red Sea.

Singapore isl. republic off the tip of the Malay Peninsula; 239 sq. mi.; pop. 2,718,000.

— city, S Singapore; cap.; pop. 2,390,800.

Sinkiang-Uigur Autonomous Region div. W China; 635,900 sq. mi.; pop. ab. 15,155,000; cap. Urumchi (Tihwa). Also formerly **Sinkiang.**

Sioux City city, W Iowa 51101*; pop. 80,505.

Sioux Falls city, SE South Dakota 57101*; pop. 100,814.

Skokie vill., NE Illinois 60076*; pop. 59,432.

Slidell town, SE Louisiana 70458; pop. 24,124.

Slovakia republic, CEN. Europe; 18,934 sq. mi.; pop. 5,310,154; cap. Bratislava.

Slovenia republic, Balkan Penin.; 7,819 sq. mi.; pop. 1,962,606; cap. Ljubljana.

Smyrna town, CEN. Georgia 30080; pop. 30,981.

— *an alternate name of* Izmir, Turkey.

Society Islands isl. group, French Polynesia; ab. 650 sq. mi.

Sofia city, W Bulgaria; cap.; pop. 1,047,920.

Solomon Islands isl. monarchy, SW Pacific; ab. 10,954 sq. mi.; pop. 319,000; cap. Honiara.

Somalia republic, E Africa; 246,000 sq. mi.; pop. 7,555,000; cap. Mogadishu. Also **Somali Democratic Republic.**

Somerset town, SE Massachusetts 02725; pop. 17,665.

Somerville city, E Massachusetts 02143; pop. 76,210.

Somme river, N France; 150 mi. long.

Soo Canals *informal name of* Sault Sainte Marie Canals.

Sorel city, S Quebec, Canada; pop. 19,666.

South Africa, Republic of republic, S Africa; 433,680 sq. mi.; pop. 30,797,000; seat of government Pretoria; seat of legislature Cape Town.

South America S continent of the Western Hemisphere; ab. 6,860,000 sq. mi.

Southampton co. boro., S England; pop. 207,800.

South Australia state, S Australia; 379,900 sq. mi.; pop. 1,425,000; cap. Adelaide.

South Bend city, N Indiana 46624*; pop. 105,511.

Southbridge uninc. place S Massachusetts 01550*; pop. 17,816.

South Carolina state, SE United States; 31,113 sq. mi.; pop. 3,505,707; cap. Columbia.

South Charleston city, CEN. West Virginia 25303; pop. 13,645.

South China Sea part of the Pacific betw. SE Asia and the Malay Archipelago.

South Dakota state, CEN. United States; 77,116 sq. mi.; pop. 699,999; cap. Pierre.

Southern Yemen See **Yemen.**

South Euclid city, NE Ohio 44121; pop. 23,866.

Southfield city, SE Michigan 48075*; pop. 75,728.

Southgate city, SE Michigan 48198; pop. 30,771.

South Gate city, SW California 90280; pop. 86,284.

South Hadley town, CEN. Massachusetts 01075; pop. 16,685.

South Holland vill, SE Illinois 60473; pop. 22,105.

Southington city, CEN. Connecticut 06489; pop. 38,518.
South Island one of the two main isls. of New Zealand; 58,093 sq. mi.
South Korea See **Korea.**
South Milwaukee city SE Wisconsin 53172; pop. 20,958.
South Orange vill., NE New Jersey 07079; pop. 16,390.
South Pasadena city, SW California 91030; pop. 23,936.
South Plainfield boro., NE New Jersey 07080; pop. 20,489.
South Pole s extremity of the earth's axis.
South Portland city, SW Maine 04106; pop. 23,163.
South St. Paul city, E Minnesota 55075; pop. 20,197.
South San Francisco city, W California 94080*; pop. 54,312.
South Sea Islands isls. of the South Pacific.
South Seas waters of the Southern Hemisphere, esp. the **South Pacific Ocean.**
South-West Africa formerly mandated terr., SW Africa; administered by the Republic of South Africa; now **Namibia.**
South Windsor city, CEN. Connecticut 06074; pop. 22,090.
Soviet Union *an alternate name of* Union of Soviet Socialist Republics (1922–91).
Spain monarchy, SW Europe; 194,885 sq. mi.; pop. 39,618,000; cap. Madrid.
Spanish America parts of the W hemisphere where Spanish is the predominant language.
Spanish Lake uninc. place, NE Missouri 63138; pop. 20,322.
Sparks city, W Nevada 89431; pop. 53,367.
Sparta city-state of ancient Greece, famous for its military power: sometimes called **Lacedaemon.**
Spartanburg city, NW South Carolina 29301*; pop. 43,467.
Spitsbergen See **Svalbard.**
Spokane city E Washington 99210*; pop. 177,196.
Springdale city, NW Arkansas 72764; pop. 29,941.
Springfield city, CEN. Illinois 62703*; cap.; pop. 105,227.
— city, SW Massachusetts 01101*; pop. 156,983.
— city, SW Missouri 63801*; pop. 140,494.
— city, CEN. Ohio 45501*; pop. 70,487.
— city, W Oregon 97477; pop. 44,683.
— uninc. place, SE Pennsylvania 19063; pop. 24,160.
Spring Valley vill., SE New York 10977; pop. 21,802.
Sri Lanka isl. republic s of India, formerly called Ceylon; 25,332 sq. mi.; pop. 16,109,000; cap. Colombo.
Stalingrad *the former name of* Volgograd.
Stamford city, SW Connecticut 06904*; pop. 108,056.
St. Ann city, E Missouri 63074; pop. 14,489.
Stanton city, SW California 90680; pop. 30,491.
State College boro., CEN. Pennsylvania 16801*; pop. 38,923.
Staten Island isl., SE New York City, at the entrance to New York Harbor.
— Richmond borough, SW New York City, New York 10300*; pop. 378,977.
Statesville city, CEN North Carolina 28677; pop. 17,567.
Staunton city, CEN. Virginia 24401; pop. 24,461.
St.-Bruno-de-Montarville town, CEN. Quebec, Canada; pop. 21,272.
St. Catharines city, s Ontario, Canada; pop. 123,351.
St. Charles city, E Missouri 63301*; pop. 54,555.
St. Clair, Lake lake betw. s Ontario and SE Michigan; 460 sq. mi.
St. Clair Shores vill., SE Michigan 48083*; pop. 68,107.
St. Cloud city, CEN. Minnesota 56301*; pop. 48,812.
St. Croix one of the Virgin Islands of the United States; 82 sq. mi.
Ste.-Foy city, s Quebec, Canada; pop. 71,237.
Sterling city, NW Illinois 61081; pop. 15,132.
Sterling Heights city, SE Michigan 48078*; pop. 117,810.
Ste.-Thérèse city, s Quebec, Canada; pop. 17,479.
Stettin *the German name for* Szczecin.
Steubenville city, E Ohio 43952; pop. 22,125.
Stevens Point city, CEN. Wisconsin 54481; pop. 23,006.
St. Helena isl., South Atlantic; British colony with Ascension Island and the Tristan da Cunha group as dependencies; 133 sq. mi.; pop. 5,147; cap. Jamestown; site of Napoleon's exile, 1815 to 21.
St. Hubert town, s Quebec, Canada; pop. 49,706.
St. Hyacinthe city, s Quebec, Canada; pop. 37,500.
Stillwater city, CEN. Oklahoma 74074*; pop. 36,676.
St. Jean city, s Quebec, Canada; pop. 34,363.

St. Jérôme city, s Quebec, Canada; pop. 25,175.
St. John one of the Virgin Islands of the United States; 19 sq. mi.
— city, s New Brunswick, Canada; pop. 85,976.
St. John's city, SE Newfoundland, Canada; cap.; pop. 86,576.
St. Joseph city, NW Missouri 64501*; pop. 71,852.
St. Kitts and Nevis monarchy isls. in the Lesser Antilles; 104 sq. mi.; pop. 44,100; cap. Basseterre.
St. Lambert city, s Quebec, Canada; pop. 20,318.
St. Laurent city, s Quebec, Canada; pop. 64,404.
St. Lawrence, Gulf of inlet of the Atlantic E Canada.
St. Lawrence River river, SE Canada; the outlet of the Great Lakes system; 1,900 mi. long.
St. Lawrence Seaway system of ship canals extending 114 miles along the St. Lawrence River from Montreal to Lake Ontario.
St. Leonard city, CEN. Quebec, Canada; pop. 78,452.
St. Louis city, E Missouri 63155*; pop. 396,685.
St. Louis Park vill., E Minnesota 55426; pop. 43,787.
Stockholm city, SE Sweden; cap.; pop. 1,629,631.
Stockton city, CEN. California 95204*; pop. 210,943.
Stoneham town, NE Massachusetts 02180; pop. 22,203.
Stonington city, NE Connecticut 06378; pop. 16,919.
Stoughton town, E Massachusetts 02072; pop. 26,777.
Stow vill., CEN. Ohio 44224; pop. 27,702.
St. Paul city, SE Minnesota 55101*; cap.; pop. 272,235.
St. Petersburg city, W Florida 33730*; pop. 893,629.
— city, NW Russia; pop. 5,020,000; called Leningrad, 1924–91.
Strasbourg city, NE France; pop. 253,834.
Stratford town, SE Connecticut 06497; pop. 49,389.
— city, s Ontario, Canada; pop. 25,657.
Stratford-on-Avon town, CEN. England; birthplace and burial place of Shakespeare; pop. 20,080.
Streamwood city, NE Illinois 60103; pop. 30,987.
Strongsville vill., N Ohio 44136; pop. 35,308.
St. Thomas one of the Virgin Islands of the United States; 28 sq. mi.; pop. 16,201.
— city, s Ontario, Canada; pop. 27,206.
Stuttgart city, SW Germany; pop. 581,989.
St. Vincent and the Grenadines monarchy isls. in the Windward Islands; 150 sq. mi.; pop. 115,000; cap. Kingstown.
Sucre city, CEN. Bolivia; judicial cap.; pop. 105,800.
Sudan reg., N Africa s of the Sahara.
Sudan, Republic of the republic, NE Africa; 966,757 sq. mi.; pop. 28,311,000; cap. Khartoum.
Sudbury city, CEN. Ontario, Canada; pop. 97,604.
Sudetenland border dists., W Czech Republic.
Suez city, NE Egypt; pop. 204,000.
Suez, Gulf of inlet of the Red Sea, NE Egypt.
Suez, Isthmus of strip of land joining Asia and Africa, betw. the Gulf of Suez and the Mediterranean.
Suez Canal ship canal across the Isthmus of Suez; 107 mi.
Suitland-Silver Hills uninc. place, CEN. Maryland 20023; pop. 35,111.
Sulawesi isl. of Indonesia, E of Borneo; 73,057 sq. mi.; pop. 11,341,000.
Sulu Archipelago isl. group, SW Philippines; 1,086 sq. mi.
Sumatra isl. of Indonesia s of the Malay Peninsula; 208,948 sq. mi.; pop. 22,934,000.
Summit city, NE New Jersey 07901; pop. 19,757.
Sumter city, CEN. South Carolina 29150*; pop. 41,943.
Sunnyvale city, W California 94086*; pop. 117,229.
Superior city, NW Wisconsin 54880*; pop. 27,134.
Superior, Lake largest of the Great Lakes; 31,820 sq. mi.
Surabaya city, NE Java, Indonesia; pop. 2,027,913.
Suriname republic, former Dutch colony NE coast of S. America; 63,251 sq. mi.; pop. 411,000; cap. Paramaribo.
Susquehanna river, New York, Pennsylvania, and Maryland; 444 mi. long.
Suwannee River river, Georgia and Florida; 250 mi. long.
Svalbard isl. group of Norway, Arctic Ocean; 23,958 sq. mi.: sometimes called **Spitsbergen.**
Swaziland republic, SE Africa; 6,704 sq. mi.; pop. 770,000; caps. Mbabane (admin.) and Lobamba (legislat.).

Sweden monarchy, NW Europe; 173,732 sq. mi.; pop. 8,529,000; cap. Stockholm.

Sweetwater Creek city, NW Florida 33601; pop. 13,909.

Swift Current city, SW Saskatchewan, Canada; pop. 14,264.

Switzerland federal state, CEN. Europe; 15,943 sq. mi.; pop. 6,756,000; cap. Bern.

Sydney city, NE Nova Scotia, Canada; pop. 30,645.

— city, E New South Wales, Australia; cap.; pop. 3,596,000.

Syracuse city, CEN. New York 13201*; pop. 163,860.

Syria republic, SW Asia; 71,498 sq. mi.; pop. 12,116,000; cap. Damascus.

Szczecin city, NW Poland; pop. 409,500. German name **Stettin.**

Tabriz city, NW Iran; pop. 971,482.

Tacoma city, W Washington 98402*; pop. 176,664.

Tahiti isl., Society group; 402 sq. mi.; pop. 85,000.

Tahoe, Lake lake E California and W Nevada; ab. 195 sq. mi.

Taipei city, N Taiwan; cap.; pop. 2,681,857.

Taiwan isl. off SE China; comprises with the Pescadores, the Republic of China; 13,900 sq. mi.; pop. 20,221,000; cap. Taipei; *formerly called* **Formosa.**

Tajikistan republic, CEN. Asia; 55,251 sq. mi.; pop. 5,112,000; cap. Dushanbe.

Takoma Park city W Maryland 20912; pop. 16,700.

Talledaga city, CEN. Alabama 35160; pop. 18,175.

Tallahassee city, N Florida 32303*; cap.; pop. 124,773.

Tallinn city, N Estonia; cap.; pop. 482,000.

Tallmadge city, NE Ohio 44278; pop. 14,870.

Tampa city, W Florida 33602*; pop. 280,015.

Tampico city, E Mexico; pop. 240,000.

Tanganyika, Lake lake, CEN. Africa; 12,700 sq. mi.

Tangier city, N Morocco; pop. 187,894.

Tanzania republic, E Africa, includes **Tanganyika** and **Zanzibar;** 364,217 sq. mi.; pop. 24,403,000; cap. Dar es Salaam.

Taranto city, SE Italy; pop. 247,681.

Tashkent city, E Uzbekistan; cap.; pop. 2,073,000.

Tasmania isl., SE Australia: comprises a state; 26,200 sq. mi.; pop. 437,300; cap. Hobart.

Taunton city, SE Massachusetts 02780*; pop. 49,832.

Taylor city, SE Michigan 48180; pop. 70,811.

Tbilisi city, SE Georgia; cap.; pop. 1,260,000.

Teaneck urb. twp., NE New Jersey 07666; pop. 37,825.

Tegucigalpa city, CEN. Honduras; cap.; pop. 551,606.

Tehran city, CEN. Iran; cap.; pop. 6,042,584.

Tel Aviv city, W Israel; includes Jaffa; pop. 317,800.

Tempe city, CEN. Arizona 85282*; pop. 141,865.

Temple CEN. Texas 76501; pop. 46,109.

Tennessee state, CEN. United States; 42,144 sq. mi.; pop. 4,896,641; cap. Nashville.

Tennessee River river, flowing through E Tennessee, N Alabama, W Tennessee, and SW Kentucky; 652 mi. long.

Terre Haute city, W Indiana 47808*; pop. 57,483.

Tewksbury city, NE Massachusetts 01876; pop. 27,266.

Texarkana city, SW Arkansas at the Arkansas-Texas line 75501; pop. 22,631.

— city, NE Texas; adjacent to and integrated with Texarkana, Arkansas 75501*; pop. 31,656.

Texas state S United States; 266,807 sq. mi.; pop. 17,059,805; cap. Austin.

Texas City city, SE Texas 77590*; pop. 40,822.

Thailand monarchy, SE Asia; 198,115 sq. mi.; pop. 56,217,000; cap. Bangkok: *formerly called* **Siam.**

Thames river, S England; 209 mi. long.

Thessaly div., CEN. Greece; 5,399 sq. mi.

Thetford Mines city S Quebec, Canada; pop. 20,784.

Thomasville city, S Georgia 31792; pop. 17,457.

Thorold town, S Ontario, Canada; pop. 14,944.

Thousand Islands group of ab. 1,500 isls. in the St. Lawrence River.

Thousand Oaks city, SE California 91360*; pop. 104,352

Thrace reg., E Balkan Peninsula.

Thunder Bay city, W Ontario, Canada; pop. 111,476.

Tiber river, CEN. Italy; 245 mi. long.

Tibet adm. div., W China; 471,700 sq. mi.; pop. 1,930,000; cap. Lhasa; formerly independent.

Tientsin city, NE China; pop. 4,300,000.

Tierra del Fuego isl. group, S South America, included in Chile and Argentina; 7,996 sq. mi. (Argentina), 19,480 sq. mi. (Chile).

Tiffin city, CEN. Ohio 44883; pop. 18,604.

Tigris river, SW Asia, ab. 1,150 mi. long.

Tijuana city, NW Lower California, Mexico; pop. 535,000.

Timbuktu town, CEN. Mali; pop. 11,900.

Timmins town, CEN. Ontario, Canada; pop. 44,747.

Timonium-Lutherville uninc. place, CEN. Maryland 21093; pop. 17,845.

Timor isl., SE Malay Archipelago; 11,965 sq. mi.; pop. 1,356,000; W Timor has been part of Indonesia since 1949.

Tirana city, CEN. Albania; cap.; pop. 238,100.

Tirol See Tyrol.

Titicaca, Lake lake betw. SE Peru and W Bolivia; 3,200 sq. mi.; elevation 12,500 ft.

Titusville city, E Florida 32870; pop. 39,394.

Tobago See **Trinidad and Tobago.**

Togo republic, W Africa; 21,925 sq. mi.; pop. 3,764,000; cap. Lomé.

Tokyo city, E Japan; cap.; pop. 8,278,116.

Toledo city, CEN. Spain; pop. 56,414.

— city, NW Ohio 43601*; pop. 332,943.

Tomsk city, S Russia; pop. 502,000.

Tonawanda city, W New York 14150*; pop. 17,284.

Tonga monarchy; isl. group, SE of Fiji; 301 sq. mi.; pop. 96,300; cap. Nuku'alofa.

Topeka city, NE Kansas 66603*; cap.; pop. 119,883.

Toronto city, S Ontario, Canada; pop. 633,318.

Torrance city, SW California 90510*; pop. 133,107.

Torrington city, SW Connecticut 06790*; pop. 33,687.

Toulon city, S France; pop. 168,000.

Toulouse city, S France; pop. 359,000.

Towson uninc. place, CEN. Maryland 21204; pop. 49,445.

Trafalgar, Cape headland, SW Spain; scene of a naval victory of Nelson over the French and Spanish, 1805.

Transcaucasia reg., part of Georgia, Armenia, and Azerbaijan; betw. the Caucasus mountains and Iran and Turkey.

Transvaal reg. NE South Africa; 101,352 sq. mi.

Traverse City city, NW Michigan 49684; pop. 15,155.

Trenton city, SE Michigan 48183; pop. 20,586.

— city, W New Jersey 08608*; cap.; pop. 88,675.

Trieste city, NE Italy; pop. 235,014.

Trinidad and Tobago isl. republic off N Venezuela; comprises isls. of **Trinidad;** 1,864 sq. mi., and **Tobago;** 116 sq. mi.; pop. 1,233,000; cap. Port-of-Spain.

Tripoli city, NW Lebanon; pop. 500,000.

— city, NW Libya; cap.; pop. 591,062.

Trois-Rivieres city, S Quebec, Canada; pop. 52,518.

Troy city, SE Michigan 48084; pop. 72,884.

— city, E New York 12180*; pop. 54,269.

— city, W Ohio 45373; pop. 19,478.

Trumbull city, SE Connecticut 06611; pop. 32,016.

Tucson city, SE Arizona 85726*; pop. 405,390.

Tulare city, CEN. California 93274; pop. 33,249.

Tullahoma city, CEN. Tennessee 37388; pop. 16,761.

Tulsa city, NE Oklahoma 74101*; pop. 367,302.

Tunis city, NE Tunisia; cap.; pop. 596,654.

Tunisia republic, N Africa; 59,664 sq. mi.; pop. 8,182,000; cap. Tunis.

Tupelo city, NE Mississippi 38801*; pop. 30,685.

Turin city, NW Italy; pop. 1,160,162.

Turkestan reg., CEN. Asia; extends from the Caspian Sea to the Gobi Desert.

Turkey republic, SW Asia; 300,948 sq. mi.; pop. 56,941,000; cap. Ankara. See **Anatolia.**

Turkmenistan republic, CEN. Asia; 188,500 sq. mi.; pop. 3,534,000; cap. Ashkhabad.

Tuscaloosa city, CEN. Alabama 35403*; pop. 77,759.

Tustin city, SW California 92680; pop. 50,689.

Tutuila chief isl., American Samoa; 53 sq. mi.

Tuvalu isl. country, SW Pacific, comprising nine coral atolls; about 10 sq. mi.; pop. 9,043; cap. Funafuti.

Twin Falls city, S Idaho 83301*; pop. 27,591.

Tyler city, E Texas 75702*; pop. 75,450.

Tyrol reg., W Austria and N Italy.

Ubangi river, CEN. Africa; 1,400 mi. long.

Uganda military republic, CEN. Africa; 93,100 sq. mi.; pop. 16,928,000; cap. Kampala.

Ukraine republic, E Europe; 233,100 sq. mi.; pop. 51,707,000; cap. Kiev.

Ulan Bator city, CEN. Mongolia; cap.; pop. 548,400.

Ulster former prov., N Ireland, of which the N part became Northern Ireland, 1925.

— prov., N Republic of Ireland; comprises the part of Ulster that remained after 1925; 3,093 sq. mi.; pop. 230,159.

Union urb. twp., NE New Jersey 07083*; pop. 50,024.

Union City city, NE New Jersey 07087; pop. 58,012.

Uniondale uninc. place, SE New York 11553; pop. 20,328.

Union of Soviet Socialist Republics federal union of 15 constituent republics occupying most of N Eurasia; 1922–91.

United Arab Emirates monarchy, E Arabia, composed of 7 emirates (*formerly* **Trucial States**); 30,000 sq. mi.; pop. 1,903,000; cap. Abu Dhabi.

United Arab Republic *the former name of* Egypt.

United Kingdom constitutional monarchy comprising Great Britain (England, Scotland, and Wales), Northern Ireland, the Isle of Man, and the Channel Islands; 94,248 sq. mi.; pop. 57,384,000; cap. London: officially **United Kingdom of Great Britain and Northern Ireland.**

United States of America federal republic, including 50 states (49 in North America, and Hawaii, an archipelago in the Pacific Ocean), and the District of Columbia (3,679,192 sq. mi.; pop. 248,709,873), and the Canal Zone, Puerto Rico, the Virgin Islands of the United States, American Samoa, and Guam, Wake, and other Pacific isls.; cap. Washington, coextensive with the District of Columbia.

University City city, E Missouri 63130; pop. 40,087.

University Heights city, N Ohio 44118; pop. 14,790.

University Park city, N Texas 76308; pop. 22,259.

Upland city, SW California 91786; pop. 63,374.

Upper Arlington city, CEN. Ohio 43221; pop. 34,128.

Upper Darby uninc. place, SE Pennsylvania 19082; pop. 84,054.

Upper Volta *the former name of* Burkina Faso.

Ural Mountains mtn. system in Russia, extending from the Arctic Ocean to Kazakstan.

Ural River river S Russia and W Kazakstan; 1,574 mi. long.

Urbana city, E Illinois 61801*; pop. 36,344.

Uruguay republic, SE South America; 68,037 sq. mi.; pop. 3,033,000; cap. Montevideo.

Uruguay River river, SE South America; 1,000 mi. long.

Utah state, CEN. United States; 84,899 sq. mi.; pop. 1,727,784; cap. Salt Lake City.

Utica city, CEN. New York 13503*; pop. 68,637.

Utrecht city, CEN. Netherlands; pop. 230,634.

Uzbekistan republic, CEN. Asia; 172,700 sq. mi.; pop. 19,905,000; cap. Tashkent.

Vacaville city, CEN. California 95688; pop. 71,479.

Val-d'Or town, W Quebec, Canada; pop. 19,915.

Valdosta city, S Georgia 31603*; pop. 39,806.

Valencia city, E Spain; pop. 732,491.

Vallejo city, W California 94590*; pop. 109,199.

Valleyfield city, S Quebec, Canada; pop. 29,716. Also **Salaberry de Valleyfield.**

Valley Forge locality, SE Pennsylvania, scene of Washington's winter encampment 1777–78.

Valley Station uninc. place, N Kentucky 40272; pop. 22,840.

Valley Stream vill., SE New York 11580*; pop. 33,946.

Valparaiso city, CEN. Chile; pop. 288,294.

— city, NW Indiana 46383; pop. 24,414.

Vancouver city, SW Washington 98660*; pop. 46,380.

— city, SW British Columbia, Canada; pop. 431,137.

Vancouver Island isl., off SW British Columbia, Canada; 12,408 sq. mi.

Vanuatu republic, isl. group member of the Commonwealth, SW Pacific, formerly **New Hebrides;** 4,707 sq. mi.; pop. 147,000; cap. Vila.

Vatican City sovereign papal state within Rome; includes the Vatican and St. Peter's Church; established June 10, 1929; 108.7 acres; pop. 1,000.

Venezuela republic, N South America; 352,144 sq. mi.; pop. 19,735,000; cap. Caracas.

Venice city, NE Italy; pop. 324,294.

Venice, Gulf of N part of the Adriatic.

Ventura city, S California 93002*; pop. 92,575.

Veracruz state, SE Mexico; 27,683 sq. mi.; pop. 6,171,000; cap. Jalapa; largest city Veracruz.

Verde, Cape westernmost point of Africa; a penin.; ab. 20 mi. long.

Verdun town, NE France; scene of several battles of World War I; pop. 23,621.

— city, S Quebec, Canada; pop. 68,013.

Vermont state, NE United States; 9,279 sq. mi.; pop. 564,964; cap. Montpelier.

Vernon city, NE Connecticut 06060; pop. 29,841.

Verona city, NE Italy; pop. 258,724.

Versailles city, N France; site of the palace of Louis XIV; scene of the signing of a treaty (1919) betw. the Allies and Germany after World War I; pop. 94,145.

Vesuvius active volcano, W Italy; 3,891 ft.

Vichy city, CEN. France; provisional cap. during German occupation, World War II; pop. 32,117.

Vicksburg city, W Mississippi 39180; pop. 20,908; besieged and taken by the Union Army in the Civil War, 1863.

Victoria state, SE Australia; 87,900 sq. mi.; pop. 4,321,500; cap. Melbourne.

— city, SW British Columbia; cap.; pop. 62,551.

— city, S Texas 77901*; pop. 55,076.

Victoria, Lake lake betw. Uganda, Tanzania, and Kenya; 26,828 sq. mi. Also **Victoria Nyanza.**

Victoria Falls cataract on the Zambesi River betw. Zambia and Zimbabwe; 343 ft. high; over a mile wide.

Victoriaville town, S Quebec, Canada; pop. 21,825.

Vienna city, NE Austria; cap.; pop. 1,482,825.

— town, NE Virginia 22180; pop. 14,852.

Vientiane city, CEN. Laos; adm cap.; pop. 377,409.

Vietnam republic, SW Indochina; 127,246 sq. mi.; pop. 66,128,000; cap. Hanoi; from 1954 to 1976 divided into **North Vietnam** and **South Vietnam,** with caps. at Hanoi and Saigon, respectively.

Villa Park vill., NE Illinois 60181; pop. 22,253.

Vilnius city, SE Lithuania; cap.; pop. 582,000. Also **Vilna, Vilnyus.**

Vincennes city, SW Indiana 47591; pop. 19,859.

Vineland boro., S New Jersey 08360; pop. 54,780.

Virginia state, E United States; 40,767 sq. mi.; pop. 6,216,568; cap. Richmond.

Virginia Beach city, SE Virginia 23458*; pop. 393,069.

Virgin Islands isl. group, West Indies E of Puerto Rico. See **British Virgin Islands.**

Virgin Islands of the United States uninc. terr., Virgin Islands; 136 sq. mi.; pop. 107,000; cap. Charlotte Amalie.

Visalia city, CEN. California 93279*; pop. 75,636.

Visayan Islands isl. group, CEN. Philippines; 23,621 sq. mi.

Vista city, SW California 92083; pop. 71,872.

Vistula river, CEN. and N Poland; 678 mi. long.

Vladivostok city, SE Russia; pop. 558,000.

Volga river, W Russia; 2,290 mi. long.

Volgograd city, W Russia; scene of a Russian victory over German forces in World War II, Sept. 1942 to Jan. 1943; pop. 999,000: from 1925–61 **Stalingrad.**

Volta river, E Ghana; 800 mi. long.

Vosges Mountains mtn., chain, E France.

Wabash river, W Ohio and Indiana; 475 mi. long.

Waco city, CEN. Texas 76701*; pop. 103,590.

Wade-Hampton uninc. place, NW South Carolina 29607; pop. 20,014.

Wahiawa city, CEN. Oahu, Hawaii 96786; pop. 17,386.

Waikiki beach on Honolulu harbor, SE Oahu, Hawaii.

Waipio city, Oahu, Hawaii 96786; pop. 11,812.

Wakefield town, E Massachusetts 01880*; pop. 24,825.

Wake Island coral atoll in the North Pacific; 4 sq. mi.; site of a U.S. naval and air base.

Wales penin., SW Britain; a principality of England; 8,019 sq. mi.; pop. 2,857,000.

Walla Walla city, SE Washington 99362; pop. 26,478.

Wallingford town, CEN. Connecticut 06492; pop. 40,822.

Walnut Creek city, w California 94596*; pop. 60,569.
Walpole town, E Massachusetts 02081; pop. 20,212.
Waltham city, E Massachusetts 02154; pop. 57,878.
Wantagh uninc. place, SE New York 11793; pop. 18,567.
Warminster uninc. place, SE Pennsylvania 18974; pop. 35,543.
Warner Robins city, CEN. Georgia 31093*; pop. 43,726.
Warren city, SE Michigan 48089*; pop. 144,864.
— city, NE Ohio 44481*; pop. 50,793.
Warrensville Heights vill., N Ohio 44122; pop. 15,745.
Warrington uninc. place, NW Florida 32507; pop. 16,040.
Warsaw city, CEN. Poland; cap.; pop. 1,651,200.
Warwick city, CEN. Rhode Island 02887*; pop. 85,427.
Washington state, NW United States; 68,139 sq. mi.; pop. 4,887,941; cap. Olympia.
— city, E United States; coextensive with the District of Columbia 20013*; pop. 606,900.
— city, sw Pennsylvania 15301; pop. 15,864.
Waterbury city, W Connecticut 06701*; pop. 108,961.
Waterford city, NE Connecticut 06385; pop. 17,930.
Waterloo vill., CEN. Belgium; scene of Napoleon's final defeat, June 18, 1815; pop. 24,536.
— city, CEN. Iowa 50701*; pop. 66,467.
— city, s Ontario, Canada; pop. 46,623.
Watertown city, SW Connecticut 06795; pop. 20,456.
— town, E Massachusetts 02172; pop. 33,284.
— city, N New York 13601; pop. 29,429.
— city, SE Wisconsin 53094; pop. 19,142.
Waterville city, CEN. Maine 04901*; pop. 17,173.
Waukegan city, NE Illinois 60085*; pop. 69,392.
Waukesha city, SE Wisconsin 53186*; pop. 56,958.
Wausau city, CEN. Wisconsin 54401*; pop. 37,060.
Wauwatosa city, SE Wisconsin 53213; pop. 49,366.
Waycross city, SE Georgia 31501; pop. 16,410.
Wayne vill., SE Michigan 48184; pop. 19,899.
— urb. twp., N New Jersey 07470*; pop. 47,025.
Waynesboro city, CEN. Virginia 22980; pop. 18,549.
Webster Groves city, E Missouri 63119; pop. 22,987.
Weimar city, SW Germany; pop. 62,803.
Weirton city, NW West Virginia 26062; pop. 22,124.
Welland city, s Ontario, Canada; pop. 45,047.
Welland Canal waterway betw. Lakes Erie and Ontario.
Wellesley town, E Massachusetts 02181; pop. 26,615.
Wellington city, CEN. New Zealand; cap.; pop. 135,400.
Wenatchee city, CEN. Washington 98801; pop. 21,756.
Weslaco city, s Texas 78596; pop. 21,877.
West Allis city, SE Wisconsin 53214; pop. 63,221.
West Bend city, SE Wisconsin 53095; pop. 23,916.
West Berlin See **Berlin.**
Westchester vill., NE Illinois 60153; pop. 17,701.
West Chester boro., SE Pennsylvania 19380; pop. 18,041.
West Covina city, SW California 91793*; pop. 96,086.
West Des Moines city, CEN. Iowa 50265; pop. 31,702.
Westerly city, SW Rhode Island 02891; pop. 21,605.
Western Australia state, W Australia; 975,100 sq. mi.; pop. 1,549,700; cap. Perth.
Western Sahara area on the W coast of Africa, claimed by Mauritania and Morocco; 102,703 sq. mi.; pop. 152,000.
Western Samoa See **Samoa.**
Westfield city, SW Massachusetts 01085; pop. 38,372.
— town, E New Jersey 07091*; pop. 28,870.
West Germany See **Germany.**
West Hartford town, CEN. Connecticut 06107; pop. 60,110.
West Haven town, s Connecticut 06516; pop. 54,021.
West Hollywood city, SW California 90069; pop. 36,118.
West Indies series of isl. groups separating the North Atlantic from the Caribbean, including Cuba, Jamaica, Hispaniola, Puerto Rico, the Bahamas, Trinidad and Tobago, and the Leeward and Windward Islands.
West Indies, the group of British cols. in the Caribbean, including the Leeward Islands (Antigua, St. Kitts-Nevis-Anguilla, Montserrat, and the British Virgin Islands) and the Windward Islands (St. Vincent, St. Lucia and Dominica).
West Lafayette city, CEN. Indiana 47906; pop. 25,907.
Westlake city, N Ohio 44145; pop. 27,018.
Westland city, SE Michigan 48185; pop. 84,724.
West Memphis city, E Arkansas 72301; pop. 28,259.

West Mifflin boro., SW Pennsylvania 15122; pop. 23,644.
Westminster city and metropolitan boro., London, England; site of the Houses of Parliament and Buckingham Palace; pop. 85,000.
— city, SW California 92863; pop. 78,118.
— city, CEN. Colorado 80030; pop. 74,625.
Westmont city, SE California 90047; pop. 31,044.
Westmount city, s Quebec, Canada; pop. 22,153.
West Orange town, NE New Jersey 07052; pop. 39,103.
West Palm Beach city, SE Florida 33401*; pop. 67,643.
West Pensacola uninc. place, SW Florida 32505; pop. 22,107.
West Point U.S. military reservation, SE New York 10996; seat of the U.S. Military Academy.
Westport city, SW Connecticut 06880; pop. 24,410.
West Saint Paul city, E Minnesota 55118; pop. 19,248.
West Seneca uninc. place, W New York 14224; pop. 47,866.
West Springfield town, s Massachusetts 01089; pop. 27,537.
West Virginia state, E United States; 24,231 sq. mi.; pop. 1,801,625; cap. Charleston.
West Warwick town, CEN. Rhode Island 02893; pop. 29,268.
Wethersfield town, CEN. Connecticut 06109; pop. 25,651.
Weymouth town, E Massachusetts 02188; pop. 54,063.
Wheaton city, NE Illinois 60187*; pop. 51,464.
Wheaton Glenmont uninc. place, CEN. Maryland 20902; pop. 53,720.
Wheat Ridge uninc. place, CEN. Colorado 80033; pop. 29,419.
Wheeling city, NW West Virginia 26003*; pop. 34,882.
Whitby Whitby town, s Ontario, Canada; pop. 28,173.
White Bear Lake city, E Minnesota 55110; pop. 24,704.
Whitehall city, CEN. Ohio 43213; pop. 20,572.
— boro., SW Pennsylvania 18052; pop. 14,451.
White Mountains range of the Appalachians, CEN. New Hampshire.
White Plains city, SE New York 10602*; pop. 48,718.
Whitney, Mount peak, E California; 14,496 ft.
Whittier city, SW California 90605*; pop. 77,671.
Wichita city CEN. Kansas 67202*; pop. 304,011.
Wichita Falls city, N Texas 76307*; pop. 96,259.
Wickliffe city, NE Ohio 44092; pop. 14,558.
Wight, Isle of isl. off the s coast of England; 147 sq. mi.
Wilkes-Barre city, NE Pennsylvania 18701*; pop. 47,523.
Wilkinsburg boro., sw Pennsylvania 15221; pop. 21,080.
Williamsburg city, E Virginia 23185; capital of Virginia (1699–1779); restored to colonial condition; pop. 11,530.
Williamsport city, CEN. Pennsylvania 17701; pop. 31,933.
Willoughby city, NE Ohio 44094; pop. 20,510.
Willowick city, NE Ohio 44094; pop. 15,269.
Wilmette vill., NE Illinois 60091; pop. 26,690.
Wilmington city, N Delaware; 19899*; pop. 71,529.
— city, NE Massachusetts 01887; pop. 17,654.
— city, SE North Carolina 28401*; pop. 55,530.
Wilson town, CEN. North Carolina 27893; pop. 36,930.
Wilson, Mount peak, sw California; 5,710 ft; site of a famous observatory.
Wilson Dam power dam in the Tennessee River at Muscle Shoals, NW Alabama; 137 ft. high, 4,862 ft. long.
Wimbledon town and municipal boro., s England; scene of international tennis matches; pop. 20,000.
Winchester town, E Massachusetts 01890; pop. 20,267.
Windham city, NE Connecticut 06280; pop. 22,039.
Windhoek city, CEN. Namibia; cap.; pop. 114,000.
Windsor municipal boro., s England; site of **Windsor Castle,** a residence of the English sovereigns; pop. 29,660: officially **New Windsor.**
— city, SE Ontario, Canada; pop. 196,526.
Windward Islands isl. group, s Lesser Antilles.
Winnipeg city, SE Manitoba, Canada; cap.; pop. 560,874.
Winnipeg, Lake lake, s Manitoba, Canada; 9,398 sq. mi.
Winona city, SE Minnesota 55987*; pop. 25,399.
Winston-Salem city, CEN. North Carolina 27102*; pop. 143,485.
Winter Haven city, CEN. Florida 33880*; pop. 24,725.
Winter Park city, CEN. Florida 32708; pop. 22,242.
Winthrop town, E Massachusetts 02152; pop. 18,127.
Wisconsin state, N United States; 56,153 sq. mi.; pop. 4,906,745.

Wisconsin Rapids city, CEN. Wisconsin 54494; pop. 18,245.
Woburn city, E Massachusetts 01808*; pop. 35,943.
Woodbridge urb. twp., NE New Jersey 07095; pop. 90,074.
Woodbridge city, NE Virginia 22193; pop. 26,401.
Woodland city, CEN. California 95695*; pop. 39,802.
Woodmere uninc. place, SE New York 11598; pop. 15,578.
Woodstock city, S Ontario, Canada; pop. 26,779.
Woonsocket city, NE Rhode Island 02895; pop. 43,877.
Wooster city, CEN. Ohio 44691*; pop. 22,191.
Worcester city, CEN. Massachusetts 01613*; pop. 169,759.
Worms city, SW Germany; pop. 73,505.
Worthington city, CEN. Ohio 43085; pop. 14,869.
Wroclaw city, SW Poland; pop. 637,400: *formerly called* **Breslau.**
Wuhan collective name for the cities of Hankow, Hanyang, and Wuchang, CEN. China; pop. 4,250,000.
Wuppertal city, W Germany; pop. 371,283.
Würzburg city, CEN. Germany; pop. 125,589.
Wyandotte city, SE Michigan 48192*; pop. 30,938.
Wyckoff urb. twp., NE New Jersey 07481; pop. 15,372.
Wyoming state, NW United States; 97,809 sq. mi.; pop. 455,975; cap. Cheyenne.
— city, W Michigan 49509; pop. 63,891.
Xenia city, CEN. Ohio 45385; pop. 24,664.
Yakima city, S Washington 98901*; pop. 54,827.
Yalta city, S Crimea; scene of a conference of Roosevelt, Churchill, and Stalin in February, 1945; pop. 81,000.
Yalu river forming part of the boundary betw. NE China and North Korea; 500 mi. long.
Yangôn See **Rangoon.**
Yangtze river flowing from Tibet to the East China Sea; 3,600 mi. long.
Yellow River *an alternate name of* Hwang Ho.
Yellow Sea inlet of the Pacific betw. Korean penin. and China; 400 mi. long, 400 mi. wide.
Yellowstone Falls 2 waterfalls of the Yellowstone River in Yellowstone National Park: **Upper Yellowstone Falls,** 109 ft.; **Lower Yellowstone Falls,** 308 ft.
Yellowstone National Park largest and oldest of the US national parks, largely in NW Wyoming; 3,458 sq. mi.; established 1872.
Yellowstone River river, NW Wyoming, SE Montana, and NW North Dakota; 671 mi. long.
Yemen, Republic of, republic, SW Arabia, formed by the joining of the former **People's Democratic Republic of Yemen (South Yemen)** and **The Yemen Arab Republic (North Yemen)** on May 22, 1990; 531,869 sq. mi.; pop. 11,546,000; cap. San'a.
Yerevan city, W Armenia; cap.; pop. 1,199,000.
Yokohama city, CEN. Honshu, Japan; pop. 2,773,322.
Yonkers city, SE New York 10701*; pop. 188,082.
York co. boro., CEN. Yorkshire, England; cap.; pop. 126,377.
— city, S Pennsylvania 17405*; pop. 42,192.
Yosemite Valley gorge in **Yosemite National Park** (1,183 sq. mi., established 1890), CEN. California; 7 mi. long, 1 mi. wide; traversed by the Merced River that forms **Yosemite Falls:** Upper Fall, 1,430 ft.; Lower Fall, 320 ft.; with intermediate cascades, 2,425 ft.
Youngstown city, NE Ohio 44501*; pop. 95,732.
Ypres town, NW Belgium; site of three major battles of World War I, 1914, 1915, 1917; pop. 21,000.
Ypsilanti city, SE Michigan 48197; pop. 24,846.
Yucaipa uninc. place, SW California 92399; pop. 32,824 .
Yucatán penin., SE Mexico and NE Central America; 70,000 sq. mi.
Yugoslavia republic, SE Europe; 39,448 sq. mi.; pop. 10,406,742; cap. Belgrade.
Yukon terr., NW Canada; 186,661 sq. mi.; pop. 26,000; cap. Whitehorse.
Yukon River river, NW Canada and CEN. Alaska; 1,770 mi. long.
Yuma city, SW Arizona 85364; pop. 54,923.
Zagreb city, CEN. Croatia; cap.; pop. 703,799.
Zaire See **Congo, Democratic Republic of the.**
Zambezi river, S Africa; 1,700 mi. long.
Zambia republic, CEN. Africa; 290,586 sq. mi.; pop. 8,456,000; cap. Lusaka.
Zanesville city, CEN. Ohio 43701*; pop. 26,778.
Zanzibar reg. of Tanzania off the coast of E Africa; comprises isls. of **Zanzibar** (640 sq. mi.) and **Pemba** (380 sq. mi.); pop. 354,000.
— city, W Zanzibar; cap.; pop.110,506.
Zealand isl. of Denmark betw. the Kattegat and the Baltic Sea; 2,709 sq. mi.
Zimbabwe republic, S Africa; 150,873 sq. mi.; pop. 9,369,000; cap. Harare.
Zion city, NE Illinois 60099; pop. 19,755.
Zululand reg. S South Africa; formerly a native monarchy; 10,362 sq. mi.; pop. 570,000.
Zurich city, NE Switzerland; pop. 345,159.
Zuyder Zee former shallow inlet of the North Sea, NW Netherlands; drainage projects have reclaimed much of the land and formed Lake Ijssel. Also **Zuider Zee.**

Grammar and Usage Handbook

Word Usage and Word Relationships

Agreement of Subject and Verb

It may seem needless to say that a singular subject takes a singular verb, while a plural subject takes a plural verb; however, when phrases or other elements come between the subject and the verb, the agreement may not be clear.

The small table around which the children play *was* in the hall.

The small tables owned by the church *were* in the hall.

The men, as well as the policeman, *were* aghast at the sight.

The following words are generally considered singular and take singular verbs: *each, either, neither, one, someone, anyone, everybody, nobody, somebody, much, anybody, everyone.*

The following words are plural and take plural verbs: *both, few, many, several.*

The following pronouns may be singular or plural depending on the meaning intended: *all, most, some, every, none, any, half, more.*

When one is referring to two or more persons who are of different sexes, or to a group of people whose gender one has no way of determining, the pronouns *they, them,* and *their* are often used to refer to *anyone, each, everybody,* etc., in order to avoid the awkward *he or she, him or her, his or her.*

Either—Or; Neither—Nor

Neither always takes *nor; either* takes *or.*

When a subject is compounded with *neither . . . nor* or *either . . . or,* the verb is normally singular if the nouns joined are singular, and plural if they are plural. If, however, one noun is singular and one plural, the verb agrees with the second or nearer subject.

Either Bill or Ralph *is* lying.

Neither she nor her sisters *skate* well.

Collective Nouns

A collective noun, such as *class, company, club, crew, jury, committee,* takes a singular verb when the whole is considered as a unit, and a plural verb when members of the whole are being considered separately.

The jury *has* deliberated for six hours.

The crew *were* near exhaustion after their many hours of exposure.

Some collective nouns, as *police* and *cattle,* are used only in the plural form; others, as *mankind* and *wildlife,* are generally used in the singular form.

The cattle *were* almost destroyed by the severe storm.

The New England wildlife *has* been protected.

Agreement of Pronoun with Its Antecedent

If the antecedent is singular, the pronoun is singular, if the antecedent is plural, the pronoun is likewise plural.

The *boy* did *his* best in the contest.

The *boys* in the school did *their* best.

The *boy* and the *girl* did *their* best.

Neither one of the boys did *his* best.

Capitalization

Conventions governing the use of capital letters are quite clear.

Capitalize the first word of every sentence.

The first person singular pronoun *I* and the vocative *O* are generally capitalized.

Unless style requires a different form, *a.m.* and *p.m.* are set in small letters without a space between them. Capital letters are used for B.C. and A.D. but, again, there is no space between them.

9:30 a.m.   10:30 p.m.

A.D. 1760 *or* 1760 A.D.

76 B.C.

Note: Although A.D. should technically precede the number of the year, popular usage permits it to follow the date. In printed matter B.C., A.D., a.m., and p.m. usually appear in small capitals (B.C., A.D., A.M., P.M.).

The first letter of a line of conventional poetry is capitalized. Much modern poetry, however, ignores this convention.

Hickory, dickory, dock
The mouse ran up the clock.

The first word after a colon should be capitalized only when it begins a complete sentence.

The candidate made only one promise: If elected, he would fight for better conditions.

The list contained these items: five pounds of flour, two dozen eggs, and a pound of butter.

Every direct quotation should begin with a capital,

except where the quoted passage is grammatically woven into the text preceding it.

> The announcer shouted, "There it goes, over the back wall for a home run!"
>
> The announcer shouted that the ball was going "over the back wall for a home run."

Capitalize the first letters of all important words in the titles of books, newspapers, magazines, chapters, poems, articles. Short conjunctions and prepositions are generally not capitalized.

> How to Win Friends and Influence People

Geographical divisions and regions require capitals.

> Arctic Circle   the Atlantic Seaboard
> the Orient   the Great Plains

Compass points are capitalized when they are part of a generally accepted name, but not when they denote direction or locality.

> Middle East   eastern New York
> Old South   Head west for twenty-five miles.

Capitalize names of streets, parks, buildings, but not the general categories into which they fall.

> Fifth Avenue
> Which avenue is widest?
> General Post Office
> We went to the post office.

Religions, religious leaders, the various appellations for God and the Christian Trinity require capitalization, as do all names for the Bible and its parts.

> the Father, the Son, and the Holy Ghost
> Virgin Mary, the Immaculate Virgin
> Yahweh, Jehovah, Saviour, Messiah
> Buddhism, Shintoism, Taoism
> New Testament
> Exodus
> Sermon on the Mount
> Ten Commandments

Capitalize the names of political parties, classes, clubs, organizations, movements, and their adherents. Use small letters for the terms that refer generally to ideology (bolshevism, fascism, socialism).

> Democratic Party
> the Right Wing
> Farm bloc
> Boy Scouts of America

Political Divisions are capitalized.

> Holy Roman Empire   the Colonies
> French Republic   Suffolk County
> the Dominion   Eighth Election District

Government bodies, departments, bureaus, and courts are capitalized.

> the Supreme Court   the Cabinet

> House of Representatives   Census Bureau
> Department of Labor   British Parliament

Capitalize the titles of all high-ranking government officials, and all appellations of the President of the United States. Many publishers, it should be pointed out, prefer small letters for titles that are not accompanied by the name of the official.

> President   Commander-in-Chief
> Secretary of State   Chief Justice
> Undersecretary   Prime Minister
> Ambassador to India   Minister of War

Capitalize the names of treaties, documents, and important events.

> Second World War   Declaration of Independence
> Treaty of Versailles   Boston Tea Party

Family designations, when used without a possessive pronoun, take a capital letter.

> I sent Mother home by taxi.
> I sent my mother home by taxi.

Capitalize seasons only when they are personified. All personifications require capitals.

> The frosty breath of Winter settled on the land.
> The voice of Envy whispered in her ear.
> Necessity is the mother of Invention.
> When Headquarters commands, we jump.
> He saw Mother Nature's grim visage.

Names and epithets of peoples, races, and tribes are capitalized.

> Caucasian   Sioux
> Negro   Cliff Dwellers

Articles and prepositions are generally capitalized in the names of Englishmen and Americans, and are not capitalized in French, Italian, Spanish, German, and Dutch names, unless otherwise specified by family usage.

> Thomas De Quincey   Ludwig van Beethoven
> Martin Van Buren   Leonardo da Vinci
> Fiorello La Guardia   San Juan de la Cruz

Capitalize the names of holidays and festivals.

> Christmas   Shrove Tuesday
> Yom Kippur   New Year's Day

Capitalize such parts of a book as Glossary, Contents, Index, and Preface.

Capitalize the first and last words in the salutation in business letters, and all titles.

> My dear Sir   Dear Doctor Brown
> My dear Reverend Lothrop   Dear Reverend Father

Capitalize only the first word of the complimentary close of a letter.

Very truly yours   Sincerely yours

Spelling

General Suggestions

When in doubt as to the correct spelling of a word, consult the dictionary; do not take anything for granted.

Keep a list of your spelling errors and study them.

Learn the most commonly misspelled words in the lists below.

Learn to spell by syllables, carefully pronouncing each syllable. Faulty spelling is often due to faulty pronunciation.

Use newly acquired words and make them part of your oral and written vocabulary.

Do not use the simplified or modern forms of spelling in business correspondence, as *thru* for *through*.

Learn some basic spelling rules such as the following.

cede, ceed, and sede endings According to the Government Style Manual, there is only one word which ends in *sede—supersede,* and three that end in *ceed— proceed, exceed, succeed.* All other words having this sound end in *cede—precede, secede, recede,* etc.

ie and ei a. After *c,* when the sound is long *e* (ē), the *e* usually precedes the *i: receive, deceive, ceiling, receipt.*

b. After most other letters, the *i* precedes the *e: thief, grief, believe, achieve, lien.*

c. When the sound is *not* long *e* (ē); and especially if the sound is long *a* (ā), the *e* precedes the *i: sleigh, veil.*

The exceptions must be learned, since they follow no rule: *neither, leisure, weird, seize.*

Beginnings and Endings of Words (Prefixes and Suffixes)

a. As a general rule, drop the final *e* in the base word when a suffix beginning with a vowel is added.

decide—deciding; write—writing; type—typist

b. As a rule, retain the final *e* in the base word when a suffix beginning with a consonant is added.

remote—remotely; care—carefully; infringe—infringement

c. In applying the rule for adding *ed* or *ing,* the accent (or lack of it) may serve as a guide. Words of one syllable (and most words of more than one syllable) that end in a single consonant (except *f, h,* or *x*), preceded by a single vowel, double the final consonant *if the accent falls on the last syllable.*

plan—planned, planning; whet—whetted, whetting

transfer—transferred, transferring; control—controlled, controlling

When the word is *not* accented on the last syllable, the consonant is usually not doubled.

travel—traveled, traveler; profit—profited, profiteer

d. When the endings *ness* and *ly* are added to a word not ending in *y,* the base word rarely changes. In most words ending in *y,* the *y* changes to *i* when *ly* is added.

natural—naturally; similar—similarly; genuine—genuineness; blessed—blessedness; hazy—hazily; body—bodily

If the base word ends in *n* and the suffix *ness* is added, the *n* is doubled.

sudden—suddenness; mean—meanness; vain—vainness

e. In regard to the word endings *ise, ize, yze,* the most common form is *ize,* but here the dictionary should be consulted if there is doubt.

legalize, fraternize, criticize, jeopardize

advertise, merchandise, surmise, enterprise

paralyze, analyze

In British English *ise* is sometimes used for *ize,* as *realise* for *realize.*

f. When adding the suffix *ful,* the *l* is single except when *ly* is also added *(fully).*

care—careful—carefully; hope—hopeful—hopefully

g. When the word beginnings (prefixes) *in, en, im, em, un, dis, mis, be, de, re, il,* and *over* are added to a word, the spelling of the word is not changed.

inactive, enjoy, impending, embrace, uneasy, dismiss, mistrust, beguile, degrade, retreat, illegal, overhaul

Forming the Plurals of Nouns

a. Most nouns form the plural by simply adding *s.*

table—tables; house—houses

b. Some nouns, especially those ending in *s,* form the plural by adding *es.*

class—classes; fox—foxes

c. Words ending in *y* preceded by a consonant form the plural by changing the *y* to *i* and adding *es.*

candy—candies; study—studies; secretary—secretaries

d. Words ending in *y* preceded by a vowel form the plural by adding *s* but without any other change in the word.

key—keys; boy—boys

e. Nouns ending in *o* preceded by a vowel form the plural by adding *s.*

rodeo—rodeos; radio—radios

When the *o* is preceded by a consonant, the plural is formed by adding *es.*

hero—heroes; torpedo—torpedoes

f. Nouns referring to music which end in *o* preceded by a consonant form the plural by simply adding *s*.

piano—pianos; oratorio—oratorios; contralto—contraltos; soprano—sopranos

g. Some few nouns follow none of the above rules but form the plural in an unusual way.

child—children; tooth—teeth; mouse—mice; ox—oxen

h. Compound nouns (more than one word) form the plural from the main word.

trade union—trade unions; father-in-law—fathers-in-law

i. When a solid compound ends in *ful*, the plural is formed at the end of the solid compound and not within the word.

basketful—basketfuls; pocketful—pocketfuls

j. When the words in compounds are of almost equal importance, both parts of the compound are pluralized.

head of department—heads of departments; woman operator—women operators

k. Words taken from another language sometimes form the plural as they would in the original language.

stratum—strata; addendum—addenda; datum—data

Summary of Spelling Rules

Problem	Rule	Examples	Exceptions

IE and **EI**	I before E, except after C.	ach*ie*ve, but c*ei*ling	1. Use *EI* when:
			  a. Sounded as *ā*: n*ei*ghbor, w*ei*gh
			  b. Sounded as *ī*: counterf*ei*t
			  c. Sounded as *ĭ*: h*ei*ght
			2. Use *IE* for almost all other sounds: fr*ie*nd, l*ie*utenant.
			3. If *i* and *e* do not form a digraph, rules do not apply: f*ie*ry, d*ei*ty.

Final Silent **E**	1. **Drop** before suffix beginning with a vowel. 2. **Retain** before suffix beginning with a consonant.	grieve—grievance absolute—absolutely	1. Retain *e* after soft *c* and soft *g* before suffixes beginning with *a* or *o*: peaceable, manageable.
Final **Y**	1. **Change** final *y* to *i* if *y* is **preceded** by a **consonant** and **followed** by any **suffix** except one beginning with *i*. 2. **Retain** final *y* if it is **preceded** by a **vowel.**	beauty—beautiful BUT carry—carrying boy—boys; valley—valleys	dry—dryness; sly—slyness. day—daily; pay—paid
Final Consonants	**Double** final consonants when: 1. Preceded by a single vowel 2. Followed by a suffix beginning with a vowel. 3. The consonant terminates a monosyllabic word. 4. The consonant terminates a polysyllabic word accented on the last syllable.	1. drop—dropped; beg—beggar 2. quit—quitting; swim—swimmer 3. hit—hitter; run—running 4. omit—omitted; transfer—transferred	Final consonant is not doubled if: 1. Accent shifts to preceding syllable when suffix is added: confer′—confer′ring BUT con′ference. 2. Final consonant is preceded by a consonant: start—started. 3. Final consonant is preceded by two vowels: beat—beating; boil—boiling.
k added to words ending in **c**	**Add** *k* to words ending in *c* before a suffix beginning with *e, i, y.*	frolic—frolicking—frolicked; picnic—picnicking—picnicked	
-cede **-ceed** **-sede**	Except for super*sede*, ex*ceed*, pro*ceed*, suc*ceed*, all words having this sound end in -*cede*.	accede, precede, recede, concede	

Plurals	1. Regular noun plurals add -*s* to the singular.
	2. Irregular plurals:
	  a. Add -*es* if noun ends in *o* preceded by consonant.
	  b. Change *y* to *i* and add -*es* if noun ends in *y* preceded by consonant.
	  c. Add -*s* if noun ends in *y* preceded by vowel.
		boy—boys; book—books
		
		a. echo—echoes; Negro—Negroes
		b. sky—skies; enemy—enemies
		c. play—plays; day—days
			a. piano—pianos; zero—zeros; solo—solos.

Possessives	1. Don't confuse contractions with possessive pronouns.
	
	2. Use no apostrophes with possessive or relative pronouns.
	3. If singular or plural noun **does not** end in *s*, add **apostrophe** and *s*.
	4. If singular or plural noun **does** end in *s*, add **apostrophe**
		Contraction Possessive
		1. it's (it is) its
		  they're their
		  (they are)
		2. *his, hers, ours, yours, theirs, whose*
		3. child's (Sing.), children's (Plur.)
		
		4. hostess' (Sing.), hostesses' (Plur.), princes' (Plur.)	

From *Business Letter Writing Made Simple*, revised ed., by Irving Rosenthal and Harry W. Rudman, Copyright © 1955, 1968 by Doubleday & Co., Inc.

Spelling Lists

List of Words Most Frequently Misspelled by High School Seniors

The list of words below* contains 149 words most frequently misspelled by high school seniors. These words and word-groups (those which are variants of the same word, as *acquaint* and *acquaintance*), were compiled by Dean Thomas Clark Pollock of New York University from 14,651 examples of misspelling submitted by 297 teachers in the United States, Canada and Hawaii. Each of the words represented was misspelled twenty times or more, and yet these words, comprising fewer than three per cent of the original list of 3,811 words, account for thirty per cent of the total misspellings.

NOTE: The trouble spots in each word are italicized. Numbers beside the words indicate how frequently each word is misspelled.

accom*mo*date	25	to*gether*	23	meant	21
excel*l*ent	25	de*s*cend	13	*where*	21
o*pp*ortunity	25	de*s*cend*ant*	9	chief	20
marry	4	du*r*ing	22	hero	10
mar*ries*	6	forty	22	hero*es*	9
mar*riage*	15	wom*a*n	22	heroine	1
		certain	21		
				lonely	20
char*a*cter	24	commi*t*	4	opinion	20
comple*te*	24	com*m*it*ted*	12	parl*ia*ment	20
fri*e*nd	24	com*m*it*ing*	5	pos*s*ess	20
tru*ly*	24	criticism	21	profes*s*or	20
accident*ally*	23	di*s*appear	21	rest*au*rant	20
do*e*sn't	23	exa*gg*erate	21	vill*ai*n	20

their	179	all right	91	*its*	52			
recei*ve*	163	separate	91	it'*s*	22			
too	152	unti*l*	88					
		privi*le*ge	82	occu*r*	9			
writer	11	defin*i*te	78	occu*r*red	52			
writing	81	*there*	78	occu*rr*ence	10			
written	13	beli*e*ve	77	occu*rr*ing	2			
describe	28	study	1	prob*ably*	33			
descri*p*tion	38	studi*e*d	3	speech	33			
		studi*es*	3	argument	32			
tragedy	64	study*ing*	34					
deci*de*	48	conven*ie*nce	5	*image*	3			
deci*s*ion	15	conven*ie*nt	33	*imag*ine	7			
				*imagi*nary	5			
occasion	54	differ*e*nce	15	*imag*ination	17			
occasion*ally*	8	differ*e*nt	23					
				qui*e*t	32			
succe*e*d	25	th*a*n	38	th*e*n	32			
succes*s*	22	athletic	37					
succes*s*ful	12	t*o*	37	pre*ju*dice	30			
		business	36	*s*ense	30			
int*e*rest	56			sim*i*lar	30			
beginn*i*ng	55	equip*p*ed	21					
		equip*m*ent	14	*your*	2			
im*m*ediate	3			you'*re*	28			
im*m*ediately	51	princip*al*	18					
		princip*le*	18	appear*a*nce	29			
coming	53			con*s*cious	29			
embarras*s*	48	*prophecy*	35	pleas*a*nt	29			
gramma*r*	47	*prophesy*	35					
		benefit	16	*stop*	1			
hum*o*r	2	benefi*c*ial	5	*stopped*	24			
hum*o*rous	45	benef*i*ted	11	*stopping*	4			
		benef*i*ting	1					
exist	3			sur*p*rise	29			
existence	43	develo*p*	34					
		environ*m*ent	34	*excite*	1			
lose	28	recom*m*end	34	*excited*	7			
losing	15	fascinate	33	*excitement*	13			
		finall*y*	33	*excit*ing	7			
disappoint	42							
rhythm	41	neces*s*ary	24	exper*ie*nce	28			
		neces*s*ity	9	government	27			
acquaint	17			laboratory	27			
acquaintance	9	for*eig*n	14	tri*e*d	27			
		for*eig*ners	9					
affect	26			famil*i*ar	21			
accept	25	performance	23	escape	21			

List of 100 Words Most Frequently Misspelled by College Freshmen

absence	effect	o'clock
accidentally	eighth	omitted
across	embarrassed	parallel
aggravate	environment	perhaps
all right	exercise	principal
amateur	February	principles
argument	forth	privilege
around	forty	proceed
athletic	fourth	pronunciation
believed	friend	quiet
benefited	government	quite
business	grammar	received
busy	grievance	recommend
capital	hadn't	referred
cemetery	height	relieve
choose	indispensable	rhythm
chosen	interested	schedule
coming	its	seize
committee	it's	separate
competition	knowledge	shining
conscientious	laboratory	stationery
conscious	latter	strength
coolly	literature	succeed
council	loose	superintendent
counsel	lose	supersede
criticism	losing	tragedy
deceive	maintenance	tries
definite	marriage	truly
desert	mischievous	villain
dessert	noticeable	Wednesday
dining	occasion	weird
disappointed	occurred	whether
doesn't	occurrence	woman
don't		

List of Words Frequently Misspelled on Civil Service Examinations

accident	municipal	society
all right	principal	simplified
auxiliary	principle	technicality
athletic	promotional	tendency
buoyant	president	their
catalogue		thousandth
career	precede	transferred

* The list compiled by Dr. Pollock appears in the *Teachers' Service Bulletin in English* (Macmillan, November, 1952).

comptroller
criticise
dividend

embarrass
expedient
government
inveigle
monetary

proceed
promissory
recommend
personnel
purchasable
responsibility
received
regrettable
supersede

transient
truly
villain

Wednesday
writ
whether
yield

Confusing Words

accept See EXCEPT.

addition, edition *Addition* means the process of joining together or finding the sum of. *Edition* refers to the form in which a book, magazine, or other literary work is published: first *edition*.

advice, advise *Advice* is the noun: to give *advice*. *Advise* is the verb: to *advise* a person.

affect See EFFECT.

all ready See ALREADY.

all right, alright *All right* is the only spelling to be used: It is *all right* to do so. The spelling *alright* is not yet considered acceptable and should not be used.

allude, elude *Allude* means to make indirect or casual reference: He *alluded* to one of Shakespeare's sonnets. *Elude* means to avoid or escape: The meaning *eludes* me.

already, all ready *Already* means before or by this time or the time mentioned: The group has *already* gone. *All ready* (two words) means that everyone is ready to do a given thing. We are *all ready* to go.

among, between. *Among* is used when referring to more than two persons or things. *Between* is usually preferable when referring to only two persons or things.

appraise, apprise *Appraise* means to make an official valuation of. *Apprise* means to notify or inform.

ascent, assent *Ascent* means rising, soaring, or climbing: the *ascent* of the mountain. *Assent* means agreement, consent, sanction: *assent* to a course of action.

between See AMONG.

can See MAY.

capital, capitol *Capital* means a city that is important in some special way: Albany is the *capital* of New York. *Capitol* means a building in which a State legislature meets: The *capitol* is on Chamber Street.

censor, censure *Censor* means (*n.*) an official examiner of manuscripts, plays, etc.; (*v.*) to act as a censor; delete; suppress. *Censure* means (*v.*) to express disapproval of; (*n.*) the expression of disapproval or blame.

census See SENSES.

cite, sight, site *Cite* means to mention or bring forward: to *cite* an incident. *Sight* (*n.*) means a view, a vision: a beautiful *sight*. *Site* means a place or location: the *site* of the church.

compliment, complement *Compliment* (*n.*) means praise or congratulation. *Complement* (*n.*) means one of two parts that mutually complete each other.

consul See COUNCIL.

council, counsel, consul *Council* (*n.*) means an assembly convened for consultation. *Counsel* (*n.*) means guidance, advice; also, a lawyer. *Consul* (*n.*) means an officer residing in a foreign country to protect his own country's interests.

creditable, credible *Creditable* means deserving credit or esteem; praiseworthy: a *creditable* project for reducing poverty. *Credible* means capable of being believed; reliable: a *credible* alibi.

decent, descent, dissent *Decent* means proper; respectable. *Descent* means the act of descending or going downward. *Dissent* means (*v.*) to disagree; (*n.*) a disagreement.

devise, device *Devise* (*v.*) means to invent, contrive, or plan. *Device* (*n.*) is something devised; invention; contrivance.

dissent See DECENT.

edition See ADDITION.

effect, affect *Effect*, common as both a noun and a verb, means (*v.*) to bring about; to cause or achieve: The treatments will *effect* an early cure; and (*n.*) result, outcome. *Affect*, in common use a verb only, means to influence or act upon: Fear *affects* the mind.

effective, effectual *Effective* means producing a desired result: *Effective* action averted the strike. *Effectual* means having the power to produce a desired result: *effectual* legal steps.

elicit, illicit *Elicit* means to bring to light: to *elicit* the truth. *Illicit* means unlawful or unauthorized.

elude See ALLUDE.

eminent, imminent *Eminent* means high in station; distinguished; prominent: an *eminent* statesman. *Imminent* means about to happen (said especially of danger): an *imminent* calamity.

except, accept *Except* (*v.*) means to take or leave out: to *except* no one from the restrictions. *Accept* means to receive or agree to; acknowledge: to *accept* an invitation.

formerly, formally *Formerly* means some time ago; once: He was *formerly* a judge. *Formally* means with formality or with regard to form: *formally* dressed.

illicit See ELICIT.

imminent See EMINENT.

lay, lie See not under LAY¹ in the body of this dictionary.

learn See TEACH.

lesson, lessen *Lesson* refers to instructive or corrective example. *Lessen* means to make less; decrease.

loose, lose *Loose* means not fastened or attached. *Lose* means to mislay or be deprived of.

may, can *May* expresses permission: The child *may* play in the yard. *Can* expresses ability to do: The child *can* do better than he is doing at present.

past, passed *Past* means (*adj.*) ended or finished: His hopes are *past;* and (*n.*) time gone by: He dreams of the *past*. *Passed*, the past tense and past particle of *pass*, means went (or gone) beyond or farther than: The car, which was going at high speed, *passed* him easily.

persecute, prosecute *Persecute* means to maltreat or oppress; to harass. *Prosecute*, generally used in a legal sense, means to bring suit against.

personal, personnel *Personal* pertains to a person: *personal* matters, *personal* opinions. *Personnel* pertains to a body or group of persons: *personnel* problem, *personnel* department.

practical, practicable *Practical* pertains to actual use and experience. *Practicable* means feasible or usable.

prosecute See PERSECUTE.

senses, census *Senses, the plural of sense,* refers to awareness and rationality or to the faculty of sensation: to come to one's *senses;* Her *senses* were dulled by the accident. *Census* refers to an official count of the people of a country or district, etc.

shall, will See note under SHALL in the body of this dictionary.

sight See CITE.

site See CITE.

stationery, stationary *Stationery* refers to writing supplies. *Stationary* means remaining in one place.

sweet, suite *Sweet* means having a taste like sugar. *Suite* refers to a set or series of things intended to be used together: *suite* of rooms, *suite* of furniture.

teach, learn *Teach* means to impart knowledge; *learn* means to acquire knowledge. The teacher *teaches;* the student *learns.*

will, shall See note under SHALL in the body of this dictionary.

Sample Business Letters

Letterhead

DOUBLEDAY & COMPANY, INC. *Publishers*

277 PARK AVENUE, NEW YORK, N.Y. 10017 TEL: 212 TA 6-2000

July 31, 19-- —————— Date Line

Inside Address —

Precision Book Stores, Inc.
1400 Michigan Avenue
Chicago, Ill. 60602

Attention: Mr. Frank Rowe

Salutation ———

Gentlemen:

We note, on examining your reorder of July 19, that

Body

and shall appreciate a prompt reply so that we might know how to proceed.

Very truly yours, ——————— Complimentary Close

John S. Poe —————— Signature

John S. Doe
Sales Manager

Reference Data ———

JSD:el
2 Encl.

This model letter includes in standard form all *the elements normally employed in the business letter.*

From *Business Letter Writing Made Simple,* revised ed., by Irving Rosenthal and Harry W. Rudman, Copyright © 1955, 1968 by Doubleday & Co., Inc.

The "Modified Block" Form

February 28, 19

Mr. John Jones
1492 Columbus Avenue
Louisville 3, Kentucky

Dear Mr. Jones:

I was very pleased to receive your prompt response to

and I look forward to seeing you on your next trip to the city.

Sincerely yours,

George Sabrin
George Sabrin

All the letter's contents, with the exception of the date, the complimentary close, the signature, are aligned on the left hand margin. This is still the most widely employed form.

Full Indention

19 Elm Street
Oswego, New York
April 5, 19

Mr. Gilbert Kahn
67 Wren Road
Miami, Florida 33138

My dear Mr. Kahn:

In undertaking the assignment you gave me when I was in your office last Thursday, I made it clear

nevertheless intend to do the best job I can.

Sincerely yours,

Lucille Graham
Lucille Graham

This form is all but obsolete, and there seems little doubt that in time it will cease entirely to be used.

Additional Sheets

Mr. John Jones—page 2—January 14, 19

therefore feel that we cannot accept the return of the merchandise at this late date. We like to cooperate

with all our accounts. . . .

It was necessary, because of its length, to continue this letter on an additional sheet. The additional sheet is headed by the addressee's name, the page number, and the date. There is the requisite minimum of three lines of text, in addition to complimentary close and signature.

The "Full Block" Form

February 28, 19

Mr. John Jones
1492 Columbus Avenue
Louisville 3, Kentucky

Dear Mr. Jones:

I was very pleased to receive your prompt response to my

and I look forward to seeing you on your next trip to the city.

Sincerely yours,

George Sabrin
George Sabrin

In the "full block" form all the letter's contents are aligned on the left hand margin.

Forms of Address

President of the United States

Address: Business: The President
The White House
Washington, D.C.
Social: The President
and Mrs. Roberts
The White House
Washington, D.C.
Salutation: Formal: Mr. President:
Informal: Dear Mr. President:
Closing: Formal: Most respectfully yours,
Informal: Sincerely yours,
In Conversation: Mr. President *or* Sir
Title of Introduction: The President *or* Mr. Roberts

Vice President of the United States

Address: Business: The Vice President
United States Senate
Washington, D.C.
Social: The Vice President
and Mrs. Hope
Home Address
Salutation: Formal: Mr. Vice President:
Informal: Dear Mr. Vice President:
Closing: Formal: Very truly yours,
Informal: Sincerely yours,
In Conversation: Mr. Vice President *or* Sir
Title of Introduction: The Vice President *or* Mr. Hope

Chief Justice of the United States

Address: Business: The Chief Justice
The Supreme Court
Washington, D.C.
Social: The Chief Justice
and Mrs. Page
Home Address
Salutation: Formal: Sir:
Informal: Dear Mr. Chief Justice:
Closing: Formal: Very truly yours,
Informal: Sincerely yours,
In Conversation: Mr. Chief Justice *or* Sir
Title of Introduction: The Chief Justice

Associate Justice of the Supreme Court

Address: Business: Mr. Justice Katsaros
The Supreme Court
Washington, D.C.
Social: Mr. Justice Katsaros
and Mrs. Katsaros
Home Address
Salutation: Formal: Sir:
Informal: Dear Mr. Justice Katsaros:
Closing: Formal: Very truly yours,
Informal: Sincerely yours,
In Conversation: Mr. Justice *or* Mr. Justice
Katsaros *or* Sir
Title of Introduction: Mr. Justice Katsaros

Cabinet Officer

Address: Business: The Honorable Gary George
Gussin
Secretary of the Treasury *or*
Attorney General of the United
States
Washington, D.C.
Social: The Secretary of the Treasury
and Mrs. Gussin
Home Address
or (for a woman cabinet member)
The Honorable Beatrice Schwartz
or (if she is married)
Mr. and Mrs. Henry Leo Woods
Salutation: Formal: Sir: *or* Dear Sir: *or* Madam:
Informal: Dear Mr. Secretary: *or*
Dear Madam Secretary:
Closing: Formal: Very truly yours,
Informal: Sincerely yours,
In Conversation: Mr. Secretary *or* Madam Secretary
or Mr. Attorney General *or*
Mr. (*or* Miss *or* Mrs.) Smith
Title of Introduction: The Secretary of the Treasury,
Mr. Smith *or*
The Attorney General of the
United States, Mr. Smith

Former President

Address: Business: The Honorable Alfred Edward
Work
Office Address
Social: The Honorable and Mrs. Alfred
Edward Work
Home Address
Salutation: Formal: Sir:
Informal: Dear Mr. Work:
Closing: Formal: Very truly yours,
Informal: Sincerely yours,
In Conversation: Mr. Work *or* Sir
Title of Introduction: The Honorable Alfred Edward
Work

United States Senator

Address: Business: The Honorable John Wandzilak
United States Senate
Washington, D.C.
Social: The Honorable and Mrs. John
Wandzilak
Home Address
or (for a woman senator)
The Honorable Marguerite
Sanders
or (if she is married)
Mr. and Mrs. John Row Doe
Salutation: Formal: Sir: *or* Madam:
Informal: Dear Senator Wandzilak:
Closing: Formal: Very truly yours,
Informal: Sincerely yours,
In Conversation: Senator *or* Senator Wandzilak *or*
Sir
Title of Introduction: Senator Wandzilak

Speaker of the House of Representatives

Address: Business: The Honorable Walter Fry
The Speaker of the House of
Representatives
Washington, D.C.
Social: The Speaker of the House of
Representatives and Mrs. Fry
Home Address
Salutation: Formal: Sir:
Informal: Dear Mr. Speaker:
Closing: Formal: Very truly yours,

Informal: Sincerely yours,
In Conversation: Mr. Speaker *or* Sir
Title of Introduction: The Speaker of the House of
Representatives *or*
The Speaker, Mr. Fry

Member of the House of Representatives

Address: Business: The Honorable Henry Cobb
Wellcome
United States House of
Representatives
Washington, D.C.
Social: The Honorable and Mrs. Henry
Cobb Wellcome
Home Address
or (for a woman member)
The Honorable Ann Davenport
or (if she is married)
Mr. and Mrs. John Knox Jones
Salutation: Formal: Sir: *or* Madam:
Informal: Dear Mr. Wellcome:
Closing: Formal: Very truly yours,
Informal: Sincerely yours,
In Conversation: Mr. Wellcome *or* Miss Davenport *or*
Mrs. Jones *or* Sir *or* Madam
Title of Introduction: Representative Wellcome

Ambassador of the United States

Address: Business: The Honorable John Wilson
Smith
The Ambassador of the United
States
American Embassy
London, England
Social: The Honorable and Mrs. John
Wilson Smith
Home Address
or (for a woman ambassador)
The Honorable Janet Lund
or (if she is married)
Mr. and Mrs. Joseph Leeds
Walker
Salutation: Formal: Sir: *or* Madam:
Informal: Dear Mr. Ambassador: *or* Dear
Madam Ambassador:
Closing: Formal: Very truly yours,
Informal: Sincerely yours,
In Conversation: Mr. Ambassador *or* Madam
Ambassador *or* Sir *or* Madam
Title of Introduction: The American Ambassador *or*
The Ambassador of the
United States

Minister Plenipotentiary of the United States

Address: Business: The Honorable James Lee Row
The Minister of the United States
American Legation
Oslo, Norway
Social: The Honorable and Mrs. James
Lee Row
Home Address
or (for a woman minister)
The Honorable Eugenia Carlucci
or (if she is married)
Mr. and Mrs. Arthur Johnson
Salutation: Formal: Sir: *or* Madam:

Informal: Dear Mr. Minister *or* Dear
Madam Minister:
Closing: Formal: Very truly yours,
Informal: Sincerely yours,
In Conversation: Mr. Row *or* Miss Carlucci *or*
Mrs. Johnson
Title of Introduction: Mr. Row, the American
Minister

Consul of the United States

Address: Business: Mr. John Smith
American Consul
Rue de Quelque Chose
Paris, France
Social: Mr. and Mrs. John Smith
Home Address
Salutation: Formal: Sir: *or* Dear Sir:
Informal: Dear Mr. Smith:
Closing: Formal: Very truly yours,
Informal: Sincerely yours,
In Conversation: Mr. Smith
Title of Introduction: Mr. Smith

Ambassador of a Foreign Country

Address: Business: His Excellency, Juan Luis Ortega
The Ambassador of Mexico
Washington, D.C.
Social: His Excellency
The Ambassador of Mexico and
Señora Ortega
Home Address
Salutation: Formal: Excellency:
Informal: Dear Mr. Ambassador:
Closing: Formal: Very truly yours,
Informal: Sincerely yours,
In Conversation: Mr. Ambassador *or* Sir
Title of Introduction: The Ambassador of Mexico

Minister of a Foreign Country

Address: Business: The Honorable
Carluh Matti
The Minister of Kezeah
Washington, D.C.
Social: The Honorable and Mrs. Carluh
Matti
Home Address
Salutation: Formal: Sir:
Informal: Dear Mr. Minister:
Closing: Formal: Very truly yours,
Informal: Sincerely yours,
In Conversation: Mr. Minister *or* Sir
Title of Introduction: The Minister of Kezeah

Governor of a State

Address: Business: The Honorable Joseph L. Marvin
Governor of Idaho
Boise, Idaho
Social: The Honorable and Mrs. Joseph L.
Marvin
Home Address
or (for a woman governor)
The Honorable Katherine Marvin
or (if she is married)
Mr. and Mrs. Walter O'Reilly
Salutation: Formal: Sir:
Informal: Dear Governor Marvin:

Closing: Formal: Very truly yours,
    Informal: Sincerely yours,
In Conversation: Governor Marvin *or* Sir *or* Madam
Title of Introduction: The Governor *or* The
                    Governor of Idaho

State Senators and Representatives are addressed
in the same manner as U.S. Senators and Representatives.

Mayor

Address: Business: Honorable Roger Shute
            Mayor of Easton
            City Hall
            Easton, Maryland
    Social: The Honorable
            and Mrs. Roger Shute
            Home Address
            or (for a woman mayor)
            The Honorable Martha Wayne
            or (if she is married)
            Mr. and Mrs. Walter Snow
Salutation: Formal: Sir: *or* Madam:
    Informal: Dear Mayor Shute:
Closing: Formal: Very truly yours,
    Informal: Sincerely yours,
In Conversation: Mr. Mayor *or* Madam Mayor
Title of Introduction: Mayor Shute

Judge

Address: Business: The Honorable Carson Little
            Justice, Appellate Division
            Supreme Court of the State of
              New York
            Albany, New York
    Social: The Honorable and Mrs. Carson
            Little
            Home Address
            or (for a woman judge)
            The Honorable Josefina Gonzalez
            or (if she is married)
            Mr. and Mrs. Rafael Montoya
Salutation: Formal: Sir:
    Informal: Dear Judge Little:
Closing: Formal: Very truly yours,
    Informal: Sincerely yours,
In Conversation: Mr. Justice *or* Madam Justice
Title of Introduction: Justice Little

Protestant Bishop

Address: Business: The Right Reverend John S.
            Bowman
            Bishop of Rhode Island
            Providence, Rhode Island
    Social: The Right Reverend and
            Mrs. John S. Bowman
Salutation: Formal: Right Reverend Sir:
    Informal: Dear Bishop Bowman:
Closing: Formal: Respectfully yours,
    Informal: Sincerely yours,
In Conversation: Bishop Bowman
Title of Introduction: Bishop Bowman

Protestant Clergyman

Address: Business: The Reverend David Dekker
            or (if he holds the degree)
            The Reverend David Dekker,
              D.D.
            Address of his church
    Social: The Reverend and Mrs. David
            Dekker
            Home Address
Salutation: Formal: Dear Sir:
    Informal: Dear Mr. (*or* Dr.) Dekker:
Closing: Formal: Sincerely yours,
    Informal: Sincerely yours,
In Conversation: Mr. (*or* Dr.) Dekker
Title of Introduction: Mr. (*or* Dr.) Dekker

Rabbi

Address: Business: Rabbi Paul Aaron Fine
            or (if he holds the degree)
            Dr. Paul Aaron Fine, D.D.
            Address of his synagogue
    Social: Rabbi (*or* Dr.) and Mrs. Paul
            Aaron Fine
            Home Address
Salutation: Formal: Dear Sir:
    Informal: Dear Rabbi (*or* Dr.) Fine:
Closing: Formal: Sincerely yours,
    Informal: Sincerely yours,
In Conversation: Rabbi (*or* Dr.) Fine
Title of Introduction: Rabbi (*or* Dr.) Fine

The Pope

Address: His Holiness Pope Paul VI
    or His Holiness the Pope
    Vatican City
Salutation: Your Holiness:
Closing: Your Holiness' most humble servant,
In Conversation: Your Holiness
Title of Introduction: *One is presented to:* His
                   Holiness *or* The Holy Father

Cardinal

Address: His Eminence Alberto Cardinal Vezzetti
    Archbishop of Baltimore
    Baltimore, Maryland
Salutation: Formal: Your Eminence:
    Informal: Dear Cardinal Vezzetti:
Closing: Your Eminence's humble servant,
In Conversation: Your Eminence
Title of Introduction: *One is presented to:* His
                   Eminence, Cardinal Vezzetti

Roman Catholic Archbishop

Address: The Most Reverend Preston Lowen
    Archbishop of Philadelphia
    Philadelphia, Pennsylvania
Salutation: Formal: Your Excellency: *or* Most
            Reverend Sir:
    Informal: Dear Archbishop Lowen:
Closing: Your Excellency's humble servant,
In Conversation: Your Excellency
Title of Introduction: *One is presented to:* The Most
                 Reverend
                 The Archbishop of Philadelphia

Roman Catholic Bishop

Address: The Most Reverend Matthew S. Borden
    Address of his church
Salutation: Formal: Your Excellency: *or* Most
    Reverend Sir:
    Informal: Dear Bishop Borden:
Closing: Formal: Your obedient servant,
    Informal: Sincerely yours,
In Conversation: Your Excellency
Title of Introduction: Bishop Borden

Monsignor

Address: The Right Reverend Monsignor Ryan
    Address of his church
Salutation: Formal: Right Reverend Monsignor:
    Informal: Dear Monsignor Ryan:
Closing: Formal: I remain, Right Reverend
    Monsignor, yours faithfully,
    Informal: Faithfully yours,
In Conversation: Monsignor Ryan
Title of Introduction: Monsignor Ryan

Priest

Address: The Reverend John Matthews (and the
    initials of his order)
    Address of his church
Salutation: Formal: Reverend Father:
    Informal: Dear Father Matthews:
Closing: Formal: I remain, Reverend Father, yours
    faithfully,
    Informal: Faithfully yours,
In Conversation: Father *or* Father Matthews
Title of Introduction: The Reverend Father
    Matthews

Member of Religious Order

Address: Sister Angelica (and initials of order) *or*
    Brother James (and initials)
    Address
Salutation: Formal: Dear Sister: *or* Dear Brother:
    Informal: Dear Sister Angelica: *or* Dear
    Brother James
Closing: Formal: Respectfully yours,
    Informal: Faithfully yours,
In Conversation: Sister Angelica *or* Brother James
Title of Introduction: Sister Angelica *or* Brother
    James

University Professor

Address: Business: Professor Robert Knowles
    Office Address
    Social: Professor *or* Mr.
    or (if he holds the degree)
    Dr. and Mrs. Robert Knowles
    Home Address
    or (for a woman professor)
    Professor or Miss (*or* Dr.)
    Catherine Stone
    or (if she is married)
    Mr. and Mrs. Wallace Bryant
Salutation: Formal: Dear Professor (*or* Dr.) Knowles:
    Informal: Dear Mr. (*or* Miss *or* Mrs. *or*
    Ms.) Knowles:
Closing: Formal: Very truly yours,

Informal: Sincerely yours,
In Conversation: Professor (*or* Dr. *or* Mr. *or* Miss
    or Mrs.) Knowles
Title of Introduction: Professor (*or* Dr.) Knowles

Physician

Address: Business: William L. Barnes, M.D. *or*
    Dr. William L. Barnes
    Office Address
    Social: Dr. and Mrs. William L. Barnes
    Home Address
Salutation: Dear Dr. Barnes:
Closing: Formal: Very truly yours,
    Informal: Sincerely yours,
In Conversation: Dr. Barnes
Title of Introduction: Dr. Barnes

Canada

Prime Minister

Address: Business: The Right Hon. John Smith,
    P.C., M.P.
    Prime Minister of Canada
    Parliament Building
    Ottawa, Ontario
    Social: The Hon. and Mrs. John Smith
    Home Address
Salutation: Formal: Sir: *or* Dear Sir:
    Informal: Dear Mr. Prime Minister: *or*
    Dear Mr. Smith:
Closing: Formal: Yours very truly,
    Informal: Yours very sincerely,
In Conversation: Mr. Prime Minister *or* Mr. Smith
    or Sir

Governor General—The Commonwealth

Address: Business: His Excellency
    John Smith (or his personal title)
    Government House
    Ottawa, Ontario
    Social: Their Excellencies
    The Governor General and
    Mrs. John Smith
    Home Address
Salutation: Formal: Sir: *or* Dear Sir:
    Informal: Dear Mr. Smith:
Closing: Formal: Your Excellency's obedient servant,
    Informal: Yours very sincerely,
In Conversation: Your Excellency

Former Prime Minister

Address: The Honourable (*or* Right Honourable)
    John Smith
    Home Address (*or* Office Address)

Cabinet Officer

Address: Business: The Hon. John Smith, P.C., M.P.
    Minister of Forestry
    Ottawa, Ontario
    Social: The Hon. and Mrs. John Smith
    Home Address
    or (for a woman cabinet member)
    The Hon. Mary Jones
    (*or, if she is married*)
    Mr. and Mrs. John Smith

Salutation: Formal: Sir: *or* Dear Sir: *or* Madam:
         or Dear Madam:
      Informal: Dear Mr. Smith; *or* Dear
         Mrs. Smith:
Closing: Formal: Yours very truly,
      Informal: Yours very sincerely,
In Conversation: Sir *or* Madam (*formally*); Mr. *or*
         Mrs. Smith *or* Mr. Minister
         (*informally*)

Judges

Judges of the following federal and provincial courts have the title The Honourable.

Supreme Court of Canada, Exchequer Court of Canada, Courts of appeal of the provinces of British Columbia, Manitoba, and Saskatchewan, Court of Chancery of the province of Prince Edward Island, Courts of Queen's Bench of the Provinces of Manitoba, Quebec, and Saskatchewan, Superior Court of the province of Quebec, Supreme courts of the provinces of Alberta, British Columbia, New Brunswick, Nova Scotia, Ontario, Prince Edward Island, and Newfoundland; and the territorial courts.

Address: Business: The Hon. Mr. Justice John Smith
      Social: The Hon. Mr. Justice John Smith
         and Mrs. Smith
Salutation: Formal: Sir:
      Informal: Dear Mr. Justice Smith:
Closing: Formal: Yours very truly,
      Informal: Yours very sincerely,
In Conversation: Sir (*formally*); Mr. Justice
         (*informally*)

Mayor

Address: His Worship
      The Mayor of St. Lazare
Salutation: Formal: Dear Sir:
      Informal: Dear Mr. Mayor:
Closing: Formal: Yours very truly,
      Informal: Yours very sincerely,
In Conversation: Sir (*formally*): Mr. Mayor
         (*informally*)

Member of Parliament

Address: John Smith, Esq., M.P.
      House of Commons
      Ottawa, Ontario
Salutation: Formal: Dear Sir: *or* Dear Madam:
      Informal: Dear Mr. (*or* Miss *or* Mrs.) Smith
Closing: Formal: Yours very truly,
      Informal: Yours very sincerely,
In Conversation: Sir *or* Madam (*formally*): Mr. (*or*
         Miss *or* Mrs.) Smith (*informally*)

The Library
Research Paper

by William W. Watt

What is research? In recent years the word has filtered out of the ivory tower and spread like an epidemic in the marketplace. Loose popular usage has worn the sharp edges from its meaning and threatened to deface its value. To many people *research* refers loosely to the act of looking up or checking up on anything, anywhere, in any way. Political polls, television ratings, the detection of factual errors in unpublished magazine articles, traffic counts at intersections, questionnaires on consumer habits, comparison shopping to price silk stockings—all are called *research*. The transitive verb ("I'll research it for you") appears to be catching up with the noun in popularity, and the well-drilled team is crowding out the lonely adventurer.

Though the weakening of a noble word may be disturbing, it is a useful reminder that the natural human passion for discovering, recording, and evaluating data is not—and never was—the special province of the academic expert in the library, laboratory, museum, geological quarry, or archaeological digging. The scholar's methods may be more systematic and his conclusions more profound. He may have a more sincere faith in the freedom that lies in the pursuit of truth for its own sake—in "pure" research. But he has no monopoly on the activity of research.

Of the infinite varieties, none is more generally useful than the experience that begins as a hunting expedition in a library and ends when the last period is typed on the finished paper. The library research paper is an inevitable academic assignment. Commonly known as the *term paper,* it regularly serves as a sort of commencement exercise at the end of the course or year. For the secondary school student who goes on to college, or for the college undergraduate who proceeds to graduate professional school, there is always another commencement, another beginning of a new research paper. But though the project may become increasingly ambitious and the process more complex, the essential discipline does not change with academic advancement. The basic rules remain the same. The student who forms scholarly habits of research in school will find them invaluable later, whether under the discipline of further formal education or the self-discipline of his vocation, his avocation, or a civic activity. Because the responsible adult is a student all his life, the word *student* will have no chronological limits in this article.

The experience of writing even a single research paper pays educational dividends to any serious student. It encourages him to develop a personal interest in a subject of his own choice. It offers an opportunity for genuine independent study. It introduces him to the resources of whatever library he is privileged to use. It shows him the excitement of tracking down knowledge that is not neatly packaged in a textbook or on a blackboard. It offers him the satisfaction of completing a task more thorough than any routine writing assignment. (The word *re-search* suggests thoroughness: a *searching again,* checking *and* double-checking.)

The task demands discriminating reading at various speeds and levels, accurate note-taking, intelligent summarizing, honest and systematic acknowledgement of intellectual indebtedness, and a more intricate organization than is ever required on a short composition. The process of separating truth from error and facts from judgments, of compiling and selecting evidence to support a credible conclusion, is a general application of *scientific* method; the problem of organizing the results on paper so that they will instruct and even intrigue a reader belongs to the province of *art*. In first-rate research the "two cultures" meet.

Ideally, then, the library research paper is the product of both critical thinking and creative writing. It should reflect the enthusiasm of an alert mind, not the methodological digging of a reluctant mole. But the most talented and enthusiastic student cannot even approach the ideal unless he is aware from the start that rigorous scholarly method (not pedantic methodology) is the foundation of success. To present an elementary understanding of that method is the purpose of this article.

Finding and Limiting a Subject

Unless the student has a specific assignment thrust upon him by a teacher, his first problem is to choose a subject for investigation. (He is luckier, of course, if the subject has chosen him.) Selecting a suitable subject should not be a haphazard process like rolling dice at random until the right combination pays off. As soon as the writer knows that he is faced with a research deadline—usually a comfortable number of weeks away—he should do some preliminary prowling in the library, along the open stacks if that is permitted, to see what, if anything, it contains within his spheres of general interest. If a teacher has restricted the choice to the limits of a single course, he should be on the alert for clues in the unfinished business of the required reading or class discussion. A good discussion in class is full of loose ends that need to be tied together or of questions that require more time and information to answer. A good teacher will always start more game than he can bring to earth; few mortals irritate him more than the student who, after weeks of classroom suggestions, both explicit and implicit ("This would make a good subject for a research paper") comes staggering toward the deadline still fumbling around for "something to write about."

The first rule for finding a subject is hallowed by age. Two thousand years ago the Roman poet Horace put it this way: "Choose a subject, ye who write, suited to your strength." This does not mean that a student should regard a research assignment only as another chance to ride a familiar hobby. It means that the beginner's reach should not so far exceed his grasp that he will quickly become bogged down in learned technicalities that defy translation.

The second rule is that even a subject well suited to the writer's taste and talent should be strictly limited in accordance with the proposed or required length of the paper. Overly ambitious intentions usually lead to unsuccessful research papers because the student cannot possibly treat his subject adequately within the allotted space and time.

The tentative choice of a subject may be nothing more than a general idea of the territory to be explored, but before the student has ventured far he should become aware of the boundaries so that he won't waste precious hours wandering off limits. Sometimes during the early stages of research a large, nebulous subject will rapidly assume a clearly defined shape, if only because of the limitations of a particular library. More often the reverse is true: a general topic divides and subdivides and the student, who thought he had focused on a subject, finds himself helplessly confused. It is best to limit the subject in advance and avoid this predicament, especially when there is a deadline to meet.

The problem of limiting a subject for research is no different in kind from the routine dilemma of channeling an ambitious idea into a short composition. The same writer who struggles to capture the significance of "Love" or "Ambition" or "The Beat Generation" in 500 words is just as likely to propose a research paper of 3,000 on "The Poetry of Robert Browning" or "The History of Television." Certainly "Browning's Dramatic Monologues" or "Educational Television" would be preferable. Making the necessary allowances for the experience of the writer and the resources of the library, "Browning's Dramatic Monologues on Renaissance Painters" or "Closed Circuit Television in the High School Science Class" would be even better. Nothing more quickly betrays the limitations of a writer's knowledge than his inability to limit his subject.

A more specific way of limiting is to begin with a definite *thesis*—a proposition to prove, perhaps even a side to defend in a hypothetical pro and con debate: to presume to show, for example, that Browning's failure to achieve success in the theater was largely the fault of the Victorian audience, or that classroom television costs more money than it's worth. Such a proposition gives direction to the research and provides a convenient mold for the paper. But the pre-fabricated thesis has caused many dangerous detours from the truth. When a writer has flown effortlessly to a conclusion, it is hard for him to persuade himself that he ought to go back and trudge over the land on foot. It is a human weakness, even among scholars, to warp the truth to accommodate a foregone conclusion, casually ignoring the stubborn facts that won't conform. Moreover, many useful subjects for research do not lend themselves to a thesis statement: they involve explanation, narrative, analysis, or revelation—but not necessarily proof. On the whole, unless a writer is already something of an expert on his subject at the start, he should postpone the choice of a thesis until he has done most of the digging.

He might, like a scientist, begin with a *working hypothesis,* a tentative proposition to serve as a guidepost. But he should always be careful not to mistake a hunch for a fact, or a prejudice for an opinion. Objectivity is at the heart of genuine scholarship. Any researcher would do well to remember Thomas Henry Huxley's definition of a tragedy: "the slaying of a beautiful hypothesis by an ugly fact."

Whatever the subject, there should be no misconceptions about the requirements of the job. Though no two subjects require identical treatment, *the final paper should make it clear that the writer has reflected on the material and marshaled it as evidence to support one or more convincing conclusions*. Many beginners honestly believe that research is only an exercise in genteel plagiarism: tracking down information and transferring it—in great chunks or little snippets—from print to typescript by way of hastily jotted notes—producing a result that could have been achieved more efficiently with a Gillette blade and a roll of Scotch tape. Many failing papers are little more than anthologies of unfamiliar quotations or patchwork quilts of paraphrase. To be sure, the novice is not required to aim at the goal of the ideal Ph.D. dissertation: "an original contribution to knowledge." He is not expected to be an authority on his subject and should not presume to be. Most of his material will have been carefully sifted by more experienced hands, but this does not exempt him from the duty of critical thinking. If he understands this from the start, he will not arbitrarily divide his labor into a physical act of compilation and a mental act of composition. From the first visit to the library he will be reflecting carefully upon the material, not just thoughtlessly jotting down notes. The final product will be a transfusion, not a series of transplants.

Using the Library

Because no two libraries are identical, no general instruction on "how to use the library" is custom-tailored to the individual in Azusa or Zanesville. The best way for a reader to get familiar with the machinery of a particular library is to make himself at home there. He should not stride directly to the delivery desk and say to whoever is in charge: "Do you have any books on closed circuit television?" Though the librarian—especially a trained reference librarian—may provide indispensable help at a later stage of the investigation, the student should begin with a declaration of independence. Given the run of the stacks in a small or middle-sized library, he can get off to a good start by going at once to the general territory of his subject (he can find *English Literature* or *American History* on a chart without memorizing the Dewey Decimal System). Wandering up and down the aisles from A to Z, he can get a preliminary view of the land by merely scanning the backbones of books.

But such freedom is not usually permitted in a large library, where the student may have to spend many minutes at the delivery desk waiting to receive the books he has requested. Moreover, a good research paper is not the end-product of aimless browsing. The student will save both himself and the librarian time and trouble by learning the names of the standard reference guides, where to find them, and how to use them. To do this is to practice one of the fundamental principles of research: *Always take pains in the present to avoid panic in the future*.

Regardless of the subject, three reference guides will probably prove indispensable: (1) the card catalogue; (2) a comprehensive encyclopedia: and (3) the *Reader's Guide to Periodical Literature*.

The Card Catalogue

The proper use of a card catalogue requires both imagination and persistence. (Serendipity—the ability to discover treasures that you are not looking for—is probably more of a reward for alertness and patience than a native gift.) In a complete catalogue any book in the library may be listed alphabetically on at least three cards:

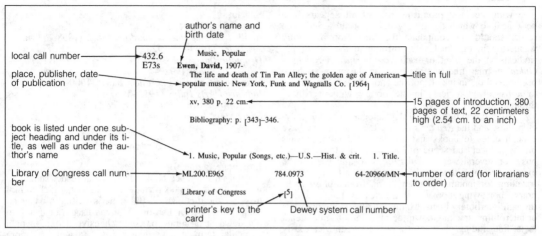

author's name and birth date

local call number — 432.6 E73s

Music, Popular

Ewen, David, 1907-
The life and death of Tin Pan Alley; the golden age of American popular music. New York, Funk and Wagnalls Co. ₍1964₎ — title in full

place, publisher, date of publication

xv, 380 p. 22 cm. — 15 pages of introduction, 380 pages of text, 22 centimeters high (2.54 cm. to an inch)

Bibliography: p. ₍343₎–346.

book is listed under one subject heading and under its title, as well as under the author's name

1. Music, Popular (Songs, etc.)—U.S.—Hist. & crit.   1. Title.

Library of Congress call number — ML200.E965   784.0973   64-20966/MN — number of card (for librarians to order)

Library of Congress   ₍5₎

printer's key to the card   Dewey system call number

by subject, author (last name first), and title. Other cards serve as cross-references.

For example, a student planning a paper on "Closed Circuit Television in the High School Science Class" might begin by looking up "Television." He should find a number of subject cards with this label at the top (probably typed in red), each alphabetically arranged by author. As he shuffles further, he should find other cards with more specific subject labels. "Television—apparatus and supplies" may interest him; "Television—law and legislation" may not. A group of books catalogued under "Television in education" certainly will. The student is on his way.

A single card, like a single dictionary entry, contains a wealth of information, some of which is essential for a bibliography. Consider the scope of the data on a typical subject card of the kind disseminated throughout the country by the Library of Congress (*above*).

A Comprehensive Encyclopedia

The reader digging for a research paper should ordinarily regard a complete encyclopedia as an indispensable guide, not an ultimate goal. The writer whose footnotes and bibliography show that he has quarried his material from a half dozen competing encyclopedias—however reputable—is easily identified as an explorer who has never left his safe home in the reference room.

For the conscientious student a good encyclopedia article has two main virtues: (1) it provides an authoritative and comprehensive view of a general subject, probably one in which he has staked out a more restricted claim; (2) it supplies bibliographical references which the student may not have discovered in the card catalogue. Let us take one possible example. The 1963 printing of the *Encyclopaedia Britannica* has an article on "Television" that runs to 19 large double-column pages, complete with photographs and diagrams. As the key to the contributors' initials reveals in the index volume, it is an authoritative article written by the Director of the Research Division of the Philco Corporation. But less than half a column is devoted to the applications of closed circuit TV in education. On the other hand, the article is followed by a list of six more extensive treatments of the general subject, any one of which might find a place in the student's final bibliography. Moreover, if the reader turns to "television" in the index volume, he will find

other references to "educational television" that do not appear in the general entry. By consulting several good encyclopedias on a subject the student may choose one which he feels will best help him construct a firm foundation for a research paper.

The *Reader's Guide*

Neither the card catalogue nor the most complete encyclopedia can pretend to give a comprehensive listing of magazine articles that have not been corralled in a book. Even in these days of prolific publishing, many interesting subjects of limited appeal have never been fully treated in book form. New developments, especially in science, are arriving and changing with such speed that even an encyclopedia publishing an annual supplement can never be completely up-to-date. On almost any subject of general interest the first place to hunt for magazine articles is the *Reader's Guide to Periodical Literature*.

The *Reader's Guide* has been indexing current contributions to the best-known American magazines since 1901 and now includes references to more than 125 publications. The semi-monthly issues (monthly in July and August) are conveniently bound in volumes that cover periods of one to four years. Articles are listed by author and subject. If a student's chosen subject relates to a specific event since 1901 ("The Hamlet of John Barrymore," "The Attack on Pearl Harbor"), he can begin at that date and work toward the present. If not, especially if he has no clues to authors, he should start with the subject entries in the most recent issues and hunt backward through the bound volumes. On looking up "Television," for example, in the volume for March 1963–February 1964, he would find three articles listed under "TELEVISION, Closed circuit" and twenty-one under "TELEVISION in education." (Any abbreviations in the entries can be understood easily by referring to a key at the front of the volume.) And these would be only a selection of the articles for one year in popular magazines: a glance at the *Education Index* (see below) would uncover many more in professional journals. It is no wonder that teachers turn gray when students report that they "can't find any material" on an obvious subject in an adequate library.

The reader with limited time and facilities cannot expect to locate every one of these articles. It is one of the inevitable frustrations of research to find that the article with the most promising title of all appears in a periodical to which the library does not subscribe. The reader should not compound the frustration by vainly wandering in the stacks. On turning to the list of periodicals at the front of each volume in the *Reader's Guide*, he may find that the ones on the premises have been ticked off in ink. If not, he should have easy access to a list of periodicals in the library without riffling through the card catalogue.

After consulting the card catalogue, several encyclopedias, and the *Reader's Guide*, the student may have enough clues to books and articles—depending always on the subject and scope of his research—to keep him busy for several weeks of digging. No amateur can be expected to play the scholar's game by all the rules—traveling for months, or even years, from library to library, borrowing books and articles at long distance through interlibrary loans, examining others on photostats or microfilms, tracking down the most infinitesimal detail to its final hiding place. But any reader can vicariously experience the excitement of such sleuthing on a smaller scale. Even the beginner should be familiar with more than three guides to research. Some of these tools can prove indispensable to him for detecting clues to possible sources of information on his topic.

Of the unnumerable research tools in a great library—including reference guides to reference books and bibliographies of bibliography—the following list contains only a generous sample.

Catalogues and Bibliographies
Books in Print (1948–   ). An annual author and title index to the *Publisher's Trade List Annual*. Lists the books still available from more than 1,100 American publishers. *Subject Guide to Books in Print* (1957–   ) lists them annually by subject.
Library of Congress Catalog (1942–   ). A complete catalogue by authors, showing facsimiles of the cards in the great library in Washington, D.C. A similar catalogue arranges books by subject.

Periodical Indexes
General
Book Review Digest (1905–   ). A monthly collection of excerpts from current book reviews indexed by author, subject, and title. It helps the reader to get a quick general picture of whether the first greetings were favorable, unfavorable, or lukewarm. More important, it directs him to reviews that he may want to read *in toto*.
International Index to Periodicals (1907–   ). A key to articles in scholarly journals that are not indexed in the *Reader's Guide*, which is limited to more popular magazines.
New York Times Index (1913–   ). A detailed index (now published twice a month) to a distinguished newspaper. Indispensable for a writer whose subject is related to any newsworthy event since the year before World War I. Even if the library does not have the complete file of the *Times* (now available in microfilm), he can make extensive use of the index to pin down exact dates, establish the chronological order of events, and find leads to news in any paper that may be available.
Poole's Index to Periodical Literature (1802–1906). Though much less thorough than the *Reader's Guide*, this annual subject index is a useful key to articles in English and American magazines in the nineteenth century.

Special
Agricultural Index (1916–   ).
Applied Science and Technology Index (1858–   ).
Art Index (1929–   ).
Dramatic Index (1909–   ).
Education Index (1929–   ).
Essay and General Literature Index (1900–   ).
Industrial Arts Index (1913–1957).
Public Affairs Information Service (1915–   ).
Short Story Index (1953–   ).

Dictionaries

Language (general)
Of all reference books, the general reader should be most familiar with his own desk dictionary, which to him may be "the dictionary." But if he is writing a paper on some aspect of English or American usage, or trying to pin down an accurate or comprehensive definition of a particular term at a particular time, he will find more complete or specialized information in the following works:

Dictionary of American English on Historical Principles. 4 vols. Chicago, 1936–1944. Supplemented by *A Dictionary of Americanisms*, 1951.
New *"Standard" Dictionary*. rev. ed. New York, 1959. A revision of an unabridged dictionary published by Funk and Wagnalls since 1913.
Oxford English Dictionary. 12 vols. and supplement. London and New York, 1933. When a writer is summoning up remembrance of things past, few records are more suggestive than the changing history of a word's meaning through the years. The great OED supplies such a record by citing the use of words in passages of prose and poetry, arranged in chronological order from the earliest occurrences. Once published as the *New English Dictionary* (NED).
Webster's Third New International Dictionary. Springfield, Mass., 1961. "Webster's Third" contains many new words and meanings not included in the second edition of the 1934 and illustrates them profusely in actual contexts. Based on recent linguistic theory, it records—often without restrictive labels—many usages that are widely frowned on.

Language (special)
Evans, Bergen and Cornelia. *A Dictionary of Contemporary American Usage*. New York, 1957.
Fowler, H. W. *A Dictionary of Modern English Usage*. London, 1926.
Nicholson, Margaret. *A Dictionary of American-English Usage*. New York, 1957. Based on Fowler.
Roget's International Thesaurus. 3rd ed., New York, 1962.
Webster's Dictionary of Synonyms. Springfield, Mass., 1942.

Biography
Dictionary of American Biography. 20 vols. and supplements. New York, 1928–   . The DAB contains lives of dead Americans.
Dictionary of National Biography. 22 vols. and supplements. London, 1885–   . The DNB has lives of dead Britons.
International Who's Who. London, 1936–   . Annual.
Kunitz, Stanley J. and Howard Haycraft. *Twentieth Century Authors*. New York, 1942. Supplement, 1945.
Webster's Biographical Dictionary. Springfield, Mass., 1943.

Who's Who. London, 1849–   . An annual dictionary of living Britons.

Who's Who in America. Chicago, 1899–   . A biennial dictionary of living Americans.

Encyclopedias and Surveys

General

There are many good, comprehensive encyclopedias which are following an editorial program of constant revision. Any good library should have several such encyclopedias of recent copyright. These encyclopedia publishers also supply yearbooks or supplemental material to make the most recent information promptly available to the researcher.

Special

Bailey, Liberty Hyde, ed. *Cyclopedia of American Agriculture.* 4 vols. New York, 1908–1909.

Baldwin, James M., and B. Rand, eds. *Dictionary of Philosophy and Psychology.* new ed. 3 vols. New York, 1949.

Bartlett's Familiar Quotations. 13th ed. Boston, 1955.

Blom, Eric., ed. *Grove's Dictionary of Music and Musicians.* 5th ed. 10 vols. London, 1954. Supplement, 1961.

Cambridge Ancient History. 17 vols., including plates. Cambridge, 1928–1939.

Cambridge Medieval History. 16 vols., including maps and plates. Cambridge, 1911–1936.

Cambridge Modern History. 2nd ed. 13 vols. and atlas. Cambridge, 1902–1926.

Cambridge Bibliography of English Literature. 5 vols. Cambridge, 1941. Supplement 1957.

Cambridge History of American Literature. 4 vols. New York, 1917–1921.

Cambridge History of English Literature. 15 vols. Cambridge, 1907–1927.

Catholic Encyclopedia. rev. ed. 17 vols. New York, 1936–

Dictionary of American History. rev. ed. 5 vols. and index. New York, 1946.

Encyclopedia of World Art. New York, 1958–   . In progress.

Feather, Leonard. *Encyclopedia of Jazz.* rev. ed. New York, 1960.

Fletcher, Sir Banister. *A History of Architecture.* 17th ed. New York, 1961.

Good, C. V. *Dictionary of Education.* 2nd ed. New York, 1959.

Harper's Encyclopedia of Art. 2 vols. New York, 1937. Re-issued as *New Standard Encyclopedia of Art,* 1939.

Hart, James D. *Oxford Companion to American Literature.* 3rd ed. New York, 1956.

Harvey, Sir Paul, ed. *Oxford Companion to Classical Literature.* 3rd ed. New York, 1956. *Oxford Companion to English Literature.* 3rd ed. New York, 1946.

Hastings, James, ed. *Encyclopedia of Religion and Ethics.* new ed. 13 vols. New York, 1951.

Kirk, Raymond E., and Donald F. Othmer. *Encyclopedia of Chemical Technology.* 15 vols. and supplements. New York, 1947–   .

Langer, William L., ed. *Encyclopedia of World History.* rev. ed. Boston, 1952.

McGraw-Hill Encyclopedia of Science and Technology. 15 vols. New York, 1960.

McLaughlin, Andrew C., and A. B. Hart, eds. *Cyclopedia of American Government.* 3 vols. New York, 1914.

Monroe, Walter S., ed. *Encyclopedia of Educational Research.* 3rd ed. by Chester Harris, New York, 1960.

Munn, Glenn G. *Encyclopedia of Banking and Finance.* rev. ed. L. Garcia. Boston, 1962.

Oxford History of English Literature. 12 vols. projected. Oxford, 1947–

Sarton, George. *Introduction to the History of Science.* 3 vols. Baltimore, 1927–1948.

Seligman, Edwin R. A., and A. Johnson, eds. *Encyclopedia of the Social Sciences.* 15 vols. New York, 1930–1935. Reissued in 8 vols., 1948.

Singer, Charles, ed. *History of Technology.* 5 vols. New York, 1956–1958.

Smith, Horatio, ed. *Columbia Dictionary of Modern European Literature.* New York, 1947.

Spiller, Robert E., ed. *A Literary History of the United States.* 3 vols. New York, 1948. rev. ed. 1 vol. 1953. Supplement by R. M. Ludwig, 1959.

Stevenson, Burton. *The Home Book of Quotations.* 9th ed. New York, 1959. Organized by subjects.

Thompson, Oscar, and N. Slonimsky, eds. *International Cyclopedia of Music and Musicians.* new ed. 3 vols. New York, 1940.

Tweney, C. F., and L. E. C. Hughes, eds. *Chamber's Technical Dictionary.* 3rd rev. ed. New York, 1958.

Universal Jewish Encyclopedia. 10 vols. and index. New York, 1939–1944.

Van Nostrand's Scientific Encyclopedia. 3rd ed. New York, 1958.

Yearbooks

In addition to the yearbooks made available by encyclopedia publishers, the following may be found useful.

American Year Book (1910–   ).
The New International Year Book (1907–   ).
Statesman's Year Book (1864–   ).
World Almanac and Book of Facts (1868–   ).

The Working Bibliography

At the very beginning of his search for materials the reader should be armed with a dependable pen and a supply of 3 x 5 index cards. (Pencils may smudge and encourage illegible scribbling; items jotted in notebooks or on miscellaneous scraps of paper are harder to organize and easier to overlook.) Though the search through the reference guides will turn up some material that will later prove unavailable or useless, it will pay at this stage to make a written record of every title that may conceivably bear on the chosen subject. When arranged in alphabetical form—with no more than one title on a card—these entries will form a tentative list of sources: a working bibliography. When the actual reading of sources begins, some of the cards will be jettisoned, and—as new references turn up in the reading—others will be added. The final bibliography, compiled after the paper is written, may have only a general family resemblance to its pioneering ancestor. But it is far less trouble to tear up a card that has not proved useful than to remember an unrecorded title or to return repeatedly to the reference guides.

To avoid trouble later on, the student should write down *the same facts in the same form* that will be required in the final bibliography. Authorities differ about the formal details, but if every researcher were permitted to follow his own fancy, whether through careless indifference or conscious resistance to tradition, the useful shorthand of scholarship would soon degenerate into chaos. The forms illustrated here for both bibliography and footnotes (pp. 1024–1026) are those recommended in *The MLA Style Sheet* (revised edition), compiled by William Riley Parker for the Modern Language Association after consulting with the editors of 109 journals and 34 university presses. No prudent beginner would ignore such an expert jury to accommodate his own whims. Accurate scholarly form demands *the right facts in the right order with the right punctuation*. Though the standard may seem pedantic to the novice, even the substitution of a semicolon for a colon is not acceptable.

Here are some sample entries for bibliography cards.

For a book with one author:

Galbraith, John K. *The Affluent Society*. Boston, 1958.

Notice that the entry contains four parts in the following order: (1) Author's name, last name first—for alphabetizing; (2) full title—underlined (italicized); (3) place of publication; (4) date of publication. Periods separate the parts except for the comma between place and date. A period also comes at the end of the entry. Unless a different form of an author's name is well known (Eliot T. S. or Maugham, W. Somerset), give the first name and any initials. Nobody wants to search through a large catalogue for Brown, J.

Some authorities insist on including the name of the publisher. It comes after the place of publication and is preceded by a colon and followed by a comma:

Galbraith, John K. *The Affluent Society*. Boston: Houghton Mifflin, 1958.

For a book with more than one author:

Sledd, James H., and Gwin J. Kolb. *Dr. Johnson's Dictionary*. Chicago, 1955.

Because the second name does not determine the alphabetical placing of the entry, it follows the normal order. If a book has more than two authors, it is sufficient to give the name of the first and add "and others."

For a periodical article:

Lippmann, Walter. "Cuba and the Nuclear Risk," *Atlantic,* CCXI (February 1963), 55–58.

The standard form has five parts in this order: (1) Author's name, last name first (the title comes first if the author is not known); (2) full title of article—in quotes; (3) name of periodical—underlined (italicized); (4) volume—in Roman numerals—and date—in parentheses; (5) page numbers. Except for the period after the author's name, the parts are separated by commas. Notice that this form differs from that of the *Reader's Guide*, where the entry reads:

Cuba and the nuclear risk. Atlan 211:55–8 F '63.

Such an abbreviated form should not be copied onto bibliography cards.

For a newspaper article:

New York *Times,* December 28, 1964, p. 6.

The place of publication is not ordinarily underlined, and the page number is preceded by the standard abbreviation for *page* (lower case p.). If a newspaper has two or more sections with separate paging, the section number is included after the date:

New York *Times,* January 3, 1965, sec. 4, p. 7.

For an encyclopedia article:

Fink, Donald G. "Television," *Encyclopaedia Britannica* (1963), XXI, 910A–913.

In addition to this minimum of information, the student should allow room in the upper left-hand corner of the card for the call number. This will save unnecessary trips to the card catalogue. If the library is large and unfamiliar and the stacks are open, it is helpful to add a further note about the location:

613.84 Neuberger, Maurine B. *Smoke Screen:*
N478s *Tobacco and the Public Welfare*. En-
(2nd floor, glewood Cliffs, N.J., 1963.
north stack)

Evaluating Sources

As soon as the student turns from the cards of his working bibliography to the actual pages of the sources, he can begin to evaluate the material. Often a quick glance at a book or article will assure him that it is not appropriate; the card, in this case, may be torn up at once. Though other sources will require more careful attention, the researcher should always be ready to change his reading pace, slowing down when the material is complicated or difficult, and speeding up when it is readily comprehensible. The independent reading for research will give him an incomparable opportunity to practice whatever he knows about the difference between skimming and thorough reading. Bacon's proverbial wisdom will become a practical reality: "Some books are to be tasted, others to be swallowed, and some few to be chewed and digested. . . ." "A man," said Samuel Johnson, "will turn over half a library to make one book." But not, the Doctor might have added, if the man plods through all the reading at the same unchanging pace.

Only a seasoned expert in a field can know for certain what authors to respect as authorities or disregard as quacks. But even the beginner can show some intelligent discrimination. The inexperienced reader can learn to evaluate sources just as the scholar does, by asking a few questions based on *external* and *internal evidence*. For example:

External Evidence
Who wrote the book or article? What's in a name? To a conscientious scholar, a great deal. If a name turns up again and again during the investigation—especially if others explicitly refer to the owner as an authority— it is a reasonable, though not a foolproof, assumption that he is more dependable than an obscure author. If the author has a pedigree in one or more standard biographical dictionaries, so much the better, though it must not be forgotten that the elect compile their own pedigrees. A Civil War historian in a great university probably knows more about the battle of Gettysburg than a feature writer commemorating the anniversary for a small town newspaper. A professional folklorist should have a more accurate knowledge of the history of the popular ballad than an itinerant guitar strummer.

Who published it? Though it is risky to make odious comparisons in the mushrooming world of publishing, a reader with some experience will be safer in trusting a reputable imprint of long standing than a new and untested brand name. A scholarly book published by a university press is probably a safer, if duller, guide to a specialized subject than a popular best-seller concocted for the trade. A sober account in the New York *Times* should be fitter to quote than a sensational exposé in a cheap tabloid.

When was it written? Is the material first-hand, second or third? A newspaper extra printed on December 8, 1941 might capture the confused excitement of the attack on Pearl Harbor, but an unbiased study published ten years later would probably be a more reliable source for the facts. An estimate of Winston Churchill published in 1919 would lack the perspective of a book written after the Battle of Britain. A student writing on a subject that is changing as swiftly as "Space Travel" or "Jet Propulsion" will naturally look for the latest word; a scholar delving into the past will be eager to uncover the earliest. The investigator with limited time and experience will lack the scholar's opportunities for tracking down a subject to its *primary sources*—burrowing beyond the printed page to the original manuscript. But he can share the scholar's desire for getting as near as possible to the first-hand truth of an event, the actual wording of a text or document. If he is writing about Shakespeare's treatment of the theme of mercy, he doesn't have to summarize a paraphrase of Portia's speech from a student cram book when a reputable text of *The Merchant of Venice* is close at hand. Nor should he quote a critic from the *Book Review Digest* when the original review is on a nearby shelf.

Internal Evidence

What does the actual text of the book or article reveal about the reliability of the author? The experienced reader will find it easier to answer such a question than the novices but it does not take much sophistication to distinguish between critical thinking and slanted writing (is the author's manner analytical or emotional, are the words neutral or loaded?); or between a distinterested search on all sides of the truth and an argument that is mere propaganda; or between a thorough investigation leading to conclusions founded on facts and a superficial survey resulting in unsupported conjectures.

Considering the amount of piffle on paper, no experienced reader has an ingenuous faith in the sanctity of print for its own sake. But many a reader who ought to know better, eager to accumulate evidence to support a thesis, will gather material at random without the slightest attention to the quality or reliability of his sources. The true scholar does not snap up ill-considered trifles; he is a discriminating reader and a natural skeptic. He not only wants to be shown, he insists on being convinced.

Taking Notes

It is sometimes convenient to jot down a general note about a book or article on one of the 3 x 5 bibliography cards. "A comprehensive survey with no recent evidence on the subject." "A jazzy sketch to amuse the reader, not inform him." But more specific or extensive notes should be on separate cards. Because they will not be shuffled in the same deck with the bibliography, these note cards need not be of the same size. Most scholars recommend 4 x 6 note cards (or slips of paper); some prefer half sheets (5½ x 8). Here convenience is more important than tradition. Note cards should be small enough to sort handily, large enough to allow room for legible notes, but not so large as to invite wholesale transcribing.

Note taking is a useful art, whether in routine reading, lectures, class discussions, or meetings of clubs and

---

II.2.a   "Social Balance"   Galbraith, 251-269

We ignore need for balance between private production and public services. Inadequate services in cities, blighted and polluted countryside, neglected education and recreation, inadequate housing -- vs. more and more cars, T.V. sets, comic books, switch-blade knives, gimmicks and gadgets. "Social balance," which would bring greater enjoyment to life, hindered by power of private advertising," "the truce on inequality," tendency to inflation.

[This published in 1958. How much progress since?]

committees. In research it assumes some of the dimensions of an exact science. The individual may eventually derive a personal method that suits him best. The following are some hints and warnings:

Do not take too many notes. Note-taking should be an aid to discriminating reading, not an opportunity for voluminous writing. The reader who postpones all his mental sorting until he begins to go through his note cards to write the paper is making his task unnecessarily difficult.

Restrict each note to one point on one side of the card. The definition of *point* is always arbitrary. It may be a sharp point like a brief direct quotation or a broad point like a short summary of a paragraph or a whole article. But do not clutter up a note with a miscellaneous scattering of quotations and reactions scribbled at random on both sides. The careful assignment of points to cards is another step in the winnowing process that accompanies research from start to finish. Organizing a research paper is not unlike playing a hand of bridge. If aces could not be quickly distinguished from deuces, or face-up cards from face-down, the game would be impossible.

Identify each card accurately at the top with a brief caption for the note and a key to the source, including the exact page number or numbers. If the complete information on that source appears as it should, on a bibliography card, all that is necessary on a note card is the author's name and the page—or, if he is responsible for more than one source, a short title: Muir, p. 61 or *The Present Age,* pp. 158–159. If a direct quotation extends from one page to another, carefully indicate the division with a slant line (/) at the appropriate point.

Taking notes with meticulous care. Note-taking is not jotting. Even when reading rapidly, come to a full stop at any important intersection. If necessary, look back and ahead to avoid the common distortion that comes from ripping a passage hastily out of its context. Remember that a careless glance may change *psychology* to *physiology,* and a single illegible word in a key quotation may later require an emergency trip to the library to revisit a book that somebody else has since withdrawn. Get it right the first time.

Take pains to distinguish between direct quotations and paraphrase and between the author's ideas and your own reactions to them. (The word *paraphrase* is used here in its general sense to mean any rewriting of another's material in your own words, whether it expands, contracts (summarizes), or keeps to the scale of the original.)

Nothing is more confusing and annoying to the reader of a research paper than the writer's failure to make these distinctions clear. Wholesale transgressions of this kind may represent conscious plagiarism. More often they result from ignorance of the meaning of research or of the rules of literary ethics. Because the problem sometimes arises at the writing stage, it is discussed in more detail on page 1024. But often a bad research paper—like a failing examination—can be traced back to poor or carelessly taken notes. Any passage taken word-for-word from the text, even a clause or unusual phrase, should appear in the notes in bold quotation marks. The student who "forgot to put in the quotes" is either dishonest, naive, or inexcusably careless. If the note-taker temporarily abandons direct quotations for paraphrase, he should carefully close the quotes and open them again when the paraphrase is finished. If he makes an independent comment of his own in the middle of a quotation or paraphrase, he should enclose it in square brackets [thus], not parentheses (thus). He might even go so far as to identify it with his own initials.

Take particular pains to copy quotations precisely.

Any scholar will quote much more than he finally uses, but even at the note-taking stage, it is wise to limit direct quotations to short passages *precisely* transcribed. Precisely means word for word, spelling for spelling (except for obvious typographical errors), punctuation mark for punctuation mark. Any omission from a quotation should be carefully identified with three spaced periods (. . .) followed by the period at the end of the sentence where appropriate. Every theater-lover is familiar with the way a press agent can play fast and loose with a critic's review. The reviewer may write: "My final judgment is that, except for the acting, the play is brilliant." With the dots carefully omitted, the advertisement reads: "My final judgment is that the play is brilliant." The scholar's rule is not pedantry, but simple honesty.

Examine each of the sample note cards carefully. The first note, conceivably for a paper on "The Economics of American Poverty," presents a brief summary of an entire chapter in John Kenneth Galbraith's *The Affluent Society.* (The code number in the upper left-hand corner has presumably been supplied later when the cards were organized to match an outline for the paper.) Because the phrases "Social Balance" and "the truce on inequality" are, at least in this context, Galbraith's own, they are put in quotation marks. The reader's reaction is carefully segregated in square brackets.

A passage of direct quotation has been sandwiched between two short pieces of paraphrase in the second note. Notice the slant line marking the transition from page 258 to 259, the parentheses (Galbraith's, not the note-taker's), the line under *minimum* to represent Galbraith's italics, and the three spaced periods to mark an omission from the quotation. Were the omission at the end of a sentence, a fourth spaced period would follow (. . . .).

The Outline

When a student has made the last of his notes and carefully read them all through to get a bird's eye view of the land, he is finally ready to plan the actual writing of the paper. Teachers of writing differ about the value of a formal outline for a short composition, but for a research paper of 2,000 words or more, some sort of blueprint is indispensable. Even the liveliest argument can't move ahead in a straight line without a well-articulated skeleton.

Though the traditional outline form can at times become a strait jacket for a writer, it has a number of virtues: (1) It tells the writer where he has been, where he is, and where he is going; (2) It reminds the writer that the reader demands the same information, suggesting the need for topic sentences (expressed or implied) and adequate transitions; (3) It avoids unnecessary repetition; (4) It emphasizes the importance of symmetry and proportion; (5) It requires the writer to coordinate his main points, subordinate his subpoints, and relegate trivia to limbo.

A formal outline should follow the accepted method of subordination:

I.
   A.
      1.
      2.
         a.
         b.
   B.

II. 3. 4   *Services*   Galbraith, pp. 258-259

Residential housing can't be limited to private sector. "It is improbable that the housing industry is greatly more incompetent or inefficient in the United States than in those countries -- Scandinavia, Holland, or (for the most part) England -- where slums have been largely eliminated and where <u>minimum</u> standards of cleanliness and comfort are well above our own. As the experience of these countries shows ... the housing industry functions well only in combination with a large, complex, and costly array of public services." Land purchase, clearance, city planning, zoning, research and architectural services, public assistance for poor.

The writer should use either a *topic outline* (limited to words or phrases) or a *sentence outline* (with complete sentences). According to strict rule, the two types should not be mixed. The sentence outline has the advantage of requiring specific assertions (which may turn into topic sentences) instead of ambiguous catchall topics. But with many kinds of material, sustaining a sentence outline is an artificial struggle.

Common errors in outlining should be strictly avoided; examples of these are given below.

The meaningless category

"Introduction," "Body," and "Conclusion," for example, are often too general to be useful. Oftentimes a writer can do better by ignoring the introduction entirely and plunging his pen right into the body.

Illogical coordination

I. Athletics
   A. Football
   B. Baseball
   C. Basketball
   D. Team sports

Improper subordination

Placing a topic under the wrong heading:

I. Athletics
   A. Football
   B. Baseball
     1. Good sportsmanship
Or putting a main point in a subordinate position:

I. School life
   A. Athletics

     1. Major sports
     2. Minor sports
   B. Classroom activities
     1. Discussion
     2. Learning

Single subdivision

If *I* is divided at all, it should have at least two subheads, A and B. If A is divided, it should have at least two subheads, 1 and 2. And so forth. The temptation to use a single subhead can be resisted by following a heading with a colon and a qualifying phrase. A. Athletics: a cause of student failure.

Here is a topic outline displaying the organization of this article: (Because details can be tucked in place as the writing progresses, a practical working outline might be simpler than this. The small bones are supplied here to help the reader in studying and reviewing the article.)

The Library Research Paper

I. The meaning of research
   A. A fashionable word
   B. A popular human activity
   C. The value of the research paper

II. Choosing and limiting a subject
   A. How and where to look
   B. Over-sized subjects
   C. Ways of reducing
     1. From general to specific
     2. The thesis: use and abuse
     3. The working hypothesis
   D. Keeping the end in view

III. Using the library
   A. Browsing in the stacks
   B. Consulting reference works

Writing the Paper

Except for the greater complexity of organization and the special problems of quotation, paraphrase, and proper acknowledgment, "writing up" the results of research is not essentially different from writing any other kind of paper. Whatever laws govern grammar and diction, spelling and punctuation, sentence and paragraph structure, none of them is suspended for research. The freedom to experiment with language may be more limited; the premium on clarity and accuracy is even higher. There is less room for the infinite riches of rhetoric: the drama and poetry of narrative and description are usually replaced by the humbler virtues of clear exposition. But good writing is good writing regardless of its habitat.

Illusions about research die hard. Even students who are convinced that the paper should be composed, not compiled, often assume that the art of composition requires a special style—freighted with *Academese*—and a special tone—impersonal, stuffy, and deadly dull.

Academese is only one kind of jargon. There is also *Pedagese,* the jargon of educationists, and *Scientese,* the jargon of would-be scientists, *Legalese, Commercialese,* and *Officialese.* All these dialects share the traits of jargon: involved sentence structure; unnecessary repetition and interminable circumlocution; a pseudotechnical vocabulary. Such writing has been called *gobbledygook* or—suggesting that it is often contrived to impress or even confuse—*bafflegab.* It might be better to revive the old-fashioned word *crabbed*—pronounced slowly with two syllables. A crabbed style suggests an animal that can move its imposing armaments forward only by slow, sideways slithering.

An expert talking to other experts will inevitably use the technical terms of his trade. Nobody writing on a technical subject, whether the propulsion of a rocket or the scansion of a poem, can entirely avoid technical language. But the problem is to explain it, not exploit it, to understand it, not merely parrot it. Genuine technical language is concise, concrete, and clear; it serves to identify and limit a phenomenon—a *paramecium,* not a *wiggly beasty, iambic pentameter,* not *words with a regular beat.* Pseudotechnical language is pulpy, abstract, and cryptic—*the intellectual confrontation in an interpersonal situation* instead of *the meeting of human minds.* The proliferation of such jargon by scholars does not make it scholarly.

The style and tone appropriate to a research paper will vary, of course, with the subject, the writer, and the intended reader. A style can be formal without being involved, or informal without being casual and careless. For the general writer who does not pretend to expert knowledge, the best advice on style is simply this: Relax but don't be lax; say simple things simply in your own language; do not write anything, even a quotation or a borrowed idea, in words that you do not understand yourself; be as concrete as possible; remember that, of all the virtues of good writing, the greatest is *clarity.*

The tone of a research paper can be serious without solemnity, dignified without stuffiness. The goal is not a charming personal essay; the reader is presumably interested in the subject, not the personality of the middle man. But the studied effort to be impersonal—and therefore ostensibly disinterested—often results in writing without either personality or interest. Though practice varies, it is better for a writer to use the first person, *I,* than to get tangled in the circumlocutions—the passive voice, for example—of the impersonal manner. Humor and irony may be useful if they grow naturally out of the subject instead of being thrust upon it. Irrelevant wisecracking is taboo. Jokes will not improve stale prose. The essential rule for tone is that all good writing more nearly reflects the living sound of a human voice, than the metallic chatter of a computer.

Quotation and Paraphrase Revisited

One special writing problem—anticipated in the discussion of note-taking—requires expansion here: the proper use of quotation and paraphrase. Make a careful comparison of the following samples:

(1) Short quotation

Leo Stein once said this about composition: "Every personal letter one writes, every personal statement one makes, may be creative writing if one's interest is to make it such."

(A short quotation in a research paper, as in any other paper, is introduced by a colon, or a comma, and carefully enclosed in quotation marks.)

(2) Long quotation

Talking about how to teach the proper use of language, Leo Stein said:

There is no difficulty in teaching them the routine of expression . . . but it is good to make them realize that there is no essential difference between them and those who write, except interest, use and purpose—that creativity in writing means nothing more than fitting words accurately and specifically to what one specifically and accurately intends. Shakespeare certainly intended more than most and had exceptional gifts, but anyone who has anything to say and wants to interest the receiver has a like object. Every personal letter one writes, every personal statement one makes, may be creative writing if one's interest is to make it such. Most people do not have this interest; what they write in ordinary communications is as dull as they can make it. They have never been taught to think of all writing as in its degree *writing* and all speaking *speaking,* and so they write in rubber stamps [clichés] and speak in the current routine of slang, as though writing and speaking were something reserved for the elect.

(Because the quotation is long—meaning, according to a common rule, five lines or more of typescript—it is set off in a separate paragraph, indented, and typed single-space without quotation marks. The student has represented Stein's italics (*writing, speaking*) by underlining. The three spaced periods in the first sentence stand for a deletion by the writer of the paper, and the bracketed word [clichés] in his addition.)

(3) Partial paraphase

Leo Stein maintains that creative writing is "nothing more than fitting words accurately and specifically to what one specifically and accurately intends." That Shakespeare had greater intentions and gifts does not, he insists, alter the rule. "Every personal letter one writers, every personal statement one makes, may be creative writing if one's interest is to make it such." A person who has no interest in writing or speaking, who mistakenly assumes that they are "reserved for the elect," will inevitably settle for dullness couched in clichés.

(To compress Stein's passage while preserving some of the original flavor, the writer of the paper uses an acceptable blend of paraphrase and direct quotation. Restricting the paraphrase to his own words and carefully setting off Stein's exact words in quotation marks, he weaves the two into a single tapestry.)

(4) Complete paraphrase

Leo Stein argues that creativity is not a special gift awarded to writers and speakers and denied to ordinary mortals. If he has something to say and is interested in saying it well, anyone, even in a personal letter, can be a creative writer.

(The summary, entirely in the student's own words, reproduces Stein's essential meaning but loses some of the flavor. It has the advantage of brevity.)

All four techniques are acceptable, depending on the purpose and scope of the paper. One *unacceptable* technique is far too common: a confusing mixture of the words of the source and the words of the student without proper distinction between them. It has been called *half-baked paraphrase.*

(5) Half-baked paraphrase

Stein says that students ought to be taught that people in general just don't bother to take advantage of their creativity, which only means in writing fitting words accurately and specifically to what one specifically and accurately intends. Shakespeare intended more than most and had exceptional gifts, but anyone who has anything to say and wants to interest the receiver has a like object. People in general are dull with words because they couldn't care less. They don't bother to think of all writing as in its degree writing and all speaking speaking, and so they use rubber stamps and slang.

(Though they are mixed clumsily with some comment of his own, the student has appropriated appreciable amounts of Stein's own wording without identifying it in quotation marks. A footnote or a bibliographical entry does not excuse this common practice. Whether it results from carelessness, laziness, or dishonesty, it is plagiarism.)

To quote or not to quote? No sacred formula answers the question. A historian working with original documents will resort to frequent quotation. A literary scholar cannot adequately analyze the work of a poet without reproducing excerpts from the poems, line by line, exactly as they appear in the original. But many inexperienced students quote too much: their research papers are merely collections of quotes loosely tethered by incidental interruptions. Generally speaking, direct quotation is useful to clinch an important point, to preserve some of the authentic flavor of the source, or to reproduce a passage that is particularly well written or peculiarly inept. A student should never quote at length unless the passage is especially important for his purpose.

Footnotes

Footnotes should be carefully supplied during the writing process, not superimposed later as an afterthought. In the first draft they can be included temporarily in the text itself. Even in the final draft, short notes may be conveniently inserted in the text in parentheses (*Hamlet* III, ii. 61–64) if the source is clearly identified and they do not clutter up the page with too many interruptions. Otherwise, footnotes are usually placed at the bottom of the page, not at the end of the paper. They are keyed to the text with Arabic numerals—not asterisks or other symbols—and should be numbered consecutively throughout the paper. The number in the text should be raised slightly above the line, and placed after any mark of punctuation and at the end—not the beginning—of any quotation, long or short. The number should not be enclosed in parentheses or followed by a period, either in the text or at the bottom of the page. At the foot of the page each note should begin with a capital letter on a new line—with the number raised and indented—and end with a period.

Occasionally a footnote is useful to supply an interesting detail or incidental comment that does not fit conveniently into the text. But in a research paper most footnotes are supplied to acknowledge specific borrowings from sources. Unlike the bibliography, which is a general listing of sources, they usually provide exact page references. With that exception, a complete footnote furnishes the same essential information as a bibliographical entry, but with a different system of punctuation and in a slightly different order.

A footnote is always used to acknowledge a direct quotation unless its exact source is made clear in the text or is familiar (like the Gettysburg Address) to any educated reader. But in spite of a common illusion, the student's responsibility does not end there. He should also use a footnote (1) to acknowledge the use of another writer's idea or opinion *even if it is completely paraphrased,* and (2) as a receipt for the loan of any facts, statistics, or other illustrative material that he has not acquired by original observation.

Here is a representative group of complete footnotes: (Compare them with the bibliographical entries on page 7, observing the differences in punctuation and order of their parts.)

For a book with one author:

[1]John K. Galbraith, *The Affluent Society* (Boston, 1958), p. 23.

For a book with more than one author:

[2]James H. Sledd and Gwin J. Kolb, *Dr. Johnson's Dictionary* (Chicago, 1955), pp. 49–50.

For a periodical article:

[3]Walter Lippman, "Cuba and the Nuclear Risk," *Atlantic,* CCXI (February 1963), 57.

For a newspaper article:

[4]New York *Times,* December 28, 1964, p. 6.

[4]New York *Times,* January 3, 1965, sec. 4, p. 7.

For an encyclopedia article:

[5]Donald G. Fink, "Television," *Encyclopaedia Britannica* (1963), XXI, 912.

Whenever a source is used for the first time, the student should give a complete footnote even though most of the information will be repeated in the bibliography. If, however, some of the details appear in the text—the author's name, for example, or the title—it is unnecessary to repeat them at the foot of the page. After the first footnote, an abbreviated form may be used if the complete note is not buried too far back. The easiest short form is the author's last name:

[6]Galbraith, p. 29.

If previous notes refer to more than one work by the same author, a shortened title should be added:

[7]Galbraith, *Affluent Society,* p. 29.

The popularity of the following Latin abbreviations is on the wane, partly because they have led to widespread misunderstanding. Though the writer may never

be required to use them, he should understand their meaning in the footnotes of others: (They are sometimes italicized because of their foreign origin.)

Ibid.	short for *ibidem,* meaning "in the same place." Refers to the same page of the same source cited in the footnote *immediately preceding.*
Ibid., p. 57.	another page of the same source cited in the footnote *immediately preceding.*
Galbraith, *op. cit.,* p. 59.	short for *opere citato,* meaning "in the work cited." Refers here to page 59 of the opus by Galbraith cited in a recent footnote. Obviously has no advantage over the use of the author's name alone or author and short title.
Op. cit., p. 59.	may be used if the author's name is made clear in the text.
Loc. cit.	short for *loco citato,* meaning "in the place cited"—that is, the same passage as in a recent footnote. Never used with a page number. Not used at all by many modern scholars.

Because documentation is intended to help the reader, not impress or confuse him, discretion is the better part of valor. If, for example, a number of short quotations from the same source appear in one paragraph of the paper, or if the writer is indebted to one authority for a tissue of small facts, it is unnecessary to present the reader with a whole flock of ibids. On occasion a single covering note may be sufficient:

[1]My main authority for the facts about the charge of the Light Brigade is Cecil Woodham-Smith, *The Reason Why* (New York, 1953), pp. 207–257.

As Frank Sullivan once observed, if you give a footnote an inch it will take a foot.

The student may find the following abbreviations useful in either footnotes or bibliography:

Abbreviations Commonly Used in Footnotes and Bibliographies

anon.—anonymous

c. or ca.—from Latin *circa,* meaning "about." Used with approximate dates (c. 1340).

cf.—compare (cf. p. 47). Should not be used interchangeably with *see* (see p. 79).

ch., chs., chap., chaps.—chapter(s)

col., cols.—column(s)

ed., eds.—editor(s), edition(s)

f., ff.—and the following page(s) or line(s). 76f. or 76ff. 76–78 and 76–87 are more exact.

l., ll.—line(s)

n., nn.—note(s). For example, p. 69, n. 3 refers to the third footnote on page 69. Also p. 69*n* (italicized without the period).

n.d.—no date. Inserted in square brackets when date of publication is not given.

no., nos.—number(s)

par., pars.—paragraph(s)

passim—here and there throughout the work

pseud.—pseudonym

rev.—review, reviewed (by), revised (by), revision

sc.—scene in a play. Unnecessary in short notes if acts are put in large Roman numerals, scenes in small Roman numerals, lines in Arabic (IV.iii.27–46).

sic—Latin for "thus" or "so." Inserted in square brackets to make a succinct comment on something in a quotation such as an error in logic or spelling [sic].

vol., vols.—volume(s)

The Final Bibliography

If exact indebtedness to sources is carefully acknowledged throughout the footnotes, a final bibliography may not be required. In scholarly publishing, a full-length book is usually supplied with one, an article is not. A teacher will often insist on a bibliography as an exercise in formal acknowledgment and a convenient map of the ground actually covered in preparing the paper. Ordinarily it should be no more than a *selected bibliography*. A complete inventory of all the discoverable sources may be useful to a specialist, but only an ingenuous student would expect extra credit for his ability to transcribe the card catalogue and the *Reader's Guide*. A selected bibliography contains only those items on the bibliography cards that have proved useful in writing the paper. The length of the list is roughly proportionate to the paper's scope. In a long list it may be convenient to have two or more groupings, separating books from articles, or sources of special importance from sources of general interest. For most research papers a single alphabetical listing is sufficient. Note that each entry in the following specimen contains the same information in the same order as on a bibliography card. If a book or article does not have an author, it is usually listed alphabetically under the first important word of the title.

Selected Bibliography

Ashworth, John. "Olivier, Freud, and Hamlet," *Atlantic,* CLXXXIII (May 1949), 30–33.

Brown, John R., "Theatrical Research and the Criticism of Shakespeare and His Contemporaries," *Shakespeare Quarterly,* XIII (1962), 451–461.

Hankins, John E. "Caliban the Bestial Man," PMLA, LXII (September 1947), 793–801.

Knight, G. Wilson. "The Embassy of Death: An Essay on Hamlet," *The Wheel of Fire* (London, 1949), 17–30.

Littleton, Taylor, and Robert R. Rea, eds. *To Prove a Villain: The Case of King Richard III.* New York, 1964.

Raysor, Thomas M., ed. *Coleridge's Shakespearean Criticism.* 2 vols. Cambridge, Mass. 1930.

"Shakespeare at 400," *Life,* LVI (April 24, 1964), 58–99.

Shakespeare, William. *The Complete Works,* ed. George Lyman Kittredge. Boston, 1936.

Tillyard, E. M. W. *The Elizabethan World Picture.* London, 1943.

Traversi, D. A. *An Approach to Shakespeare,* 2nd rev. ed. New York, 1956.

The Final Draft

The final draft of the research paper should be typed—double-spaced—on one side of heavy white paper (not onion skin) 8½ x 11 inches and unlined. Footnotes and long indented quotations should be single-spaced. Two spaces should appear between footnotes and three between the text and the first note. The pages should be numbered with Arabic numerals, either centered at the top or in the upper right-hand corner. Whether held in a binder or merely with a paper clip, the pages should be kept flat, not folded as in a shorter composition. Margins should be at least an inch wide all around. The title should appear on both the first page (about two inches from the top) and on a separate title page, which should also include the author's name, the date, and the name of the course, if any. Corrections in the final draft should be strictly limited, preferably made by neat erasing and retyping. A sloppy paper inevitably suggests a sloppy mind. Besides, it is absurd for the writer to stumble in haste over the final barrier after he has taken so long to come so far.

Greek and Latin Elements in English

Combining Forms

Greek/Latin	English	Example(s)
acantho-, Gk	spiny	acanthoid
acid-, acri-, acer-, acu-, L	keen, sharp, point	acrid, acerbic, acute
acme, Gk	culmination	acme
acous-, Gk	to hear	acoustic
acro-, Gk	tip, top	acrophobia
act-, -action, L	lead, drive, carry	interaction
actino-, Gk	light ray, radiate	actinoid
adeno-, Gk	gland	adenoid
adip-, L	fat	adipose
aeri-, L	air	aerie
aero-, Gk	air, aircraft, gas	aerobic, aerodrome
agit-, ag-, ig-, -act, L	to drive	agitate, agent, exigency, counteract
-agog, -agogue, Gk	leading	demagog, pedagogue
agon-, -agonist, Gk	contest, struggle	agony, antagonist
agri-, agro-, Gk	agriculture, field	agriculture, agronomy
alb-, L	white	albino, albumin
-algia, Gk	pain	neuralgia
alien-, alia-, alter-, L	foreign, strange, other	alienation, alternative
allo-, Gk	other	allotropy
alti, alto-, L	high, height	altimeter
amat-, ami-, amo-, -amour, L	love	amatory, amicable, paramour
ambi-, L	both	ambiguous
ambul-, L	to walk	ambulatory
amphi-, Gk	both	amphibian
amylo-, Gk	starch	amylopectin
andro-, -androus, anthropo-, Gk	man	android, polyandrous, anthropology
anemo-, Gk	wind	anemometer
angi-, angu- anx-, L	choking	angina, anguish, anxiety
angio-, Gk	vessel	angiosperm
Anglo-, L	English	Anglo-American
anima, L	breath, mind	animal, animate
ankylo-, Gk	bent	ankylosis
ann-, L	year	annual
antho-, Gk	flower	anthophore, anthology
aqua-, aque-, L	water	aquatic, aqueous
arbor-, L	tree, beam	arboretum
arch-, archi-, Gk	chief, primitive	architect
archeo-, Gk	ancient	archeology
-archy, Gk	govern	monarchy
arterio-, Gk	artery	arteriosclerosis
arthro-, arthri-, Gk	joint	arthropod, arthritis
articul-, L	joint	articulate

Greek/Latin	English	Example(s)
asco-, Gk	bag	ascospore
atmo-, Gk	air, breath, wind	atmosphere
audio-, L	hear	audiovisual
aug-, L	increase	augment
auto-, Gk	self	automatic
auro-, auriculo-, L	ear	auroventricular, auricle
aux-, Gk	strengthen	auxiliary
avi-, L	bird	aviation
bacci-, L	berry	baccivorous
bacteri-, Gk & L	bacterium	bacteriophage
ball-, Gk	to throw	ballistic
barb-, barbar-, L	beard	barber, barbarian
baro-, bari-, Gk	atmospheric pressure, weight	barometer, bariatrics
-base, bass-, L	low	abase, bassoon
basis, basi-, Gk	a step, foot	basic, basidium
bat-, L	to beat	battle
batho-, bathy-, Gk	deep, depth	bathos, bathysphere
bi-, bin-, L	two, double	bisect, binary
bibl-, biblio-, Gk	book	bible, bibliography
bio-, -biosis, Gk	life	biography, symbiosis
blasto-, -blast, Gk	bud, shoot	blastocele
blephar-, blepharo-, Gk	eyelid	blepharitis
bovi-, L	cattle	bovine
brachio-, -brace, Gk	arm	brachial
brachy-, Gk	short	brachycephaly
brady-, Gk	slow	bradycardia
branch-, Gk	fin, paw, limb	branching
branchio-, -branch, Gk	gills	branchiopod
brevi-, L	short	brevity
bronch-, broncho-, Gk	windpipe	bronchoscopy
bull-, L	bubble	bullet, ebullient
burs-, L	purse	bursar, bursitis
caco-, Gk	bad	cacophany
cad-, cid-, L	case, casualty, to fall	decadent, incident
cal-, chal-, L	to be hot	calorie, chaldron
calcul-, L	pebble, stone	calculate
calli-, Gk	fair, beautiful	calligraphy
camer-, L	chamber	bicameral
camp-, champ-, L	a plain	campus, champion
canal-, channel-, L	canal	canalization
cani-, L	dog	canine
cap-, capt-, cept-, L	to seize, take hold of	capable, capture, concept
capit-, cipit-, L	head	capital, occipital
carbo-, carboni-, -carbon, L	carbon	carboniferous, fluorocarbon
cardio-, Gk	heart	cardiovascular, cardiac
carn-, L	flesh	carnivorous
carpo-, -carpous, Gk	fruit	carpogonium, syncarpous
caus-, cus-, L	cause	causation, excuse
-cele, Gk	cavity, tumor, hernia, swelling	blastocele
-cene, Gk	recent	eocene
ceno-, Gk	common	cenocyte
centi-, cent-, L	hundred	centimeter, century
centr-, Gk & L	center	central
cephalo-, -cephalic, -cephalous, Gk	head, brain	microcephalic

Greek/Latin	English	Example(s)
cer-, cero-, Gk & L	wax	cerumin
cerebro-, L	brain	cerebrospinal
cervic-, cervico-, L	neck	cervical
chalc-, chalco-, Gk	copper	chalcedony
chemo-, Gk	chemical	chemotherapy
chilo-, Gk	lip	chiloplasty
chiro-, Gk	hand	chiropody
chloro-, Gk	green, chlorine	chlorophyll, chloromethane
chole-, cholo-, Gk	bile	cholesterol
chondro-, Gk	cartilage	chondritis
choreo-, choro-, Gk	dance	choreography, chorus
chromato-, chromo-, -chrome, Gk	color	chromatography
chron-, chrono-, Gk	time	chroni, chronograph
chryso-, Gk	gold	chrysolite
-cidal, -cide, L	to kill	suicidal, genocide
cine-, Gk	motion pictures	cinema
circ-, L	ring	circle, circus
cirri-, cirro-, L	curly	cirrostratus
cit-, L	incite	cite, solicit
clar-, L	clear	clarify, declare
claud-, claus-, clud-, clus-, L	to shut	claustrophobia, occlude
climato-, Gk	climate	climatology
clino, -cline, Gk & L	slope	clinometer, incline
cocci-, -coccus, Gk & L	berry-shaped, bacterium	streptococci
col-, cult-, L	to till	colony, culture
colo-, Gk	colon	colorectal
colori-, L	color	colorimeter
cono-, Gk	cone	conoid
contra-, counter-, L	against	contrast
copro-, Gk	dung	coprophagous
corn-, cornu-, L	horn	cornea, cornucopia
cosmo-, Gk	world, universe	cosmology
cost-, costo-, L	rib	costal
-cracy, -crat, Gk	govern	democracy
cred-, L	believe	credible, credit
cruci-, L	cross	crucial
cryo-, Gk	cold	cryogenic
crypto-, Gk	hidden	cryptogram
crystallo-, Gk	crystal	crystallography
cteno-, Gk	comb	ctenoid
cupri-, cupro-, L	copper	cupric, cuprous
curr-, curs-, cour-, L	to run	current, excursion, course
curvi-, curva-, L	curved	curvilinear, curvaceous
cyano-, cyani-, Gk	bluish, cyanogen	cyanotic, cyanide
cyclo-, -cyclic, -cycle, Gk	circle	cyclopentane, tricycle
cymo-, Gk	wave	cymoscope
cyst-, cysto-, Gk	bladder, cyst	cystic, cystotomy
cyto-, Gk	cell	cytoplasm
dactylo-, -dactyl, Gk	finger	pterodactyl
deca-, Gk	ten	decameron
deci-, L	a tenth	decile
demi-, L	half	demimonde

Greek/Latin	English	Example(s)
demn-, dam-, L	loss	condemn, indemnity, damn
demo-, Gk	people	democrat
dendro-, -dendron, Gk	tree	rhododendron
denti-, L	tooth	dentition
dermato-, derm-, dermo-, Gk	skin	dermatologist
deuter-, deutero-, Gk	second (adj.)	deuterium
dextro-, L	right	ambidextrous
di-, Gk	double	dimer
di-, dis-, L	apart	digress
digit-, digiti-, digito-, L	finger	digitigrade
dino-, Gk	terrible	dinosaur
diplo-, Gk	double	diploma, diplomacy
dodeca-, Gk	twelve	dodecahedron
dors-, dorsi-, dorso-, L	back	dorsoventral
-drome, -dromous, Gk	run	hippodrome
duo-, du-, L	two	dualism
duoden-, duodeno-, L	duodenum	duodenal
dyna-, dynamo-, Gk	power	dynamic, dynamometer
dys-, Gk	bad, difficult	dyslexia
echino-, Gk	spiny	echinoderm
ecto-, exo-, Gk	external, outside	ectomorphy, exogenous
electro-, Gk & L	electric	electromechanical
embryo-, Gk	embryo	embryology
-emia, Gk	blood condition or disease	septicemia
endo-, ento-, Gk	interior	endogenous
ennea-, Gk	nine	ennead
enter-, entero-, Gk	intestine	enteritis
eo-, Gk	early, earliest	eocene
equ-, equi-, L	equal, like, same	equate
erg-, Gk	work	ergon
erythro-, Gk	red	erythrocyte
ethn-, ethno-, Gk	nation	ethnocentric
eu-, Gk	good	euphoria
eury-, Gk	broad	eurycephalic
extra-, extro-, L	external	extraneous, extrovert
fac-, fec-, fic-, fact-, fect-, fict-, L	to do	fact, perfect, deficit
febri-, L	fever	febrile
-fend, -fense, L	to strike	defend
-fer, -ferous, L	bearing	transfer
ferro-, ferri-, L	iron	ferric
fibro-, L	fibrous	fibroid
fid-, L	faith	confidence
fin-, L	end	final, finance
fissi-, -fid, L	split	fission
-fix, L	to fix	prefix
flagr-, L	to burn	conflagration
flexi-, L	bent	flexible
flig-, -flict, L	to strike	profligate, inflict
fluo-, fluoro-, fluor-, L	fluorescence, fluorine	fluoride
flor-, flour-, L	flower	florist, flourish

Greek/Latin	English	Example(s)
fluv-, fluvi-, fluvio-, L	river	fluvial
foli-, folia-, folio-, L	leaf, leafy	foliation
form-, -form, L	form	formal, conform
fort-, forti-, L	strong	fortify
fract-, frang-, frag-, L	to break	fraction, frangible, fragment
fru-, fruit-, L	to enjoy	fruition
fug-, fuge-, -fugal, L	to flee	refugee, centrifugal
fund-, found-, L	bottom	fundament, profound
fungi-, L	fungus	fungicide
galacto-, Gk	milk	galactose
Gallo-, Gall-, L	French	Gallic
gameto-, Gk	gamete	gametophyte
gamo-, -gamy, Gk	union, sexual union	gamogenesis, oogamy
ganglio-, gangli-, Gk	ganglion	gangliated
gastro-, gastero-, Gk	stomach, abdomen	gastroenterology
gemm-, L	bud	gemmule
gen-, L	kin	genus
-gen, -genous, -geny, -gony, Gk	producing	oxygen, cosmogony
genito-, L	genital	genitourinary
geo-, Gk	earth	geography
geri-, geronto-, Gk	old age	geriatric, gerontology
-gerous, L	bearing	crystalligerous
giganto-, Gk	gigantic	gigantomachy
glauco-, Gk	light or blue-gray	glaucoma
glosso-, gloss-, Gk	tongue	glossary
glyco-, Gk	sweet	glycolysis
glypto-, -glyph, Gk	carved, carving	glyptodont, hieroglyphics
gnatho-, -gnathous, Gk	jaw	prognathous
-gon, gonio-, Gk	angle	polygon, goniometer
-gonium, Gk	seed	syngonium
gono-, Gk	reproduction	gonorrhea
-grade, -gress, L	walking, step	plantigrade, congress
grani-, L	grain	graniform
grapho-, -graph, -graphy, -gram, Gk	to write	polygraph
grat-, grate-, grati-, L	pleasing	gratitude
Greco-, L	Greek	Greco-Roman
greg-, L	a flock	aggregate, gregarious
gust-, gusta-, L	a tasting	disgust, gustatory
gymno-, gymn-, Gk	naked	gymnosophist, gymnast
gyneco-, gyneo- gyno-, Gk	woman, ovary	gynecology
gyro-, gyr-, Gk	circle	gyrate
hab-, hib-, L	to have	habit, inhibit
hagio-, hagi, Gk	sacred	hagiography
halo-, Gk	salt, sea	halogen, halophyte
haplo-, Gk	simple, single	haploid
hect-, hecto-, Gk	hundred	hectare
-hedral, -hedron, Gk	side	polyhedron
heli-, helico-, Gk	spiral	helicopter
helio-, Gk	sun	heliocentric
hema-, hemato-, hemo-, Gk	blood	hematocrit

Greek/Latin	English	Example(s)
hemi-, Gk	half	hemisphere
hepa-, hepat-, hepato-, Gk	liver	heparin
hepta-, Gk	seven	heptad
her-, L	heir	heredity
hernio-, L	hernia	herniotomy
hetero-, Gk	different	heteronym
hexa-, Gk	six	hexagon
hiero-, Gk	sacred	hieroglyph
hippo-, Gk	horse	hippocampus
histo-, Gk	tissue	histopathology
holo-, hol-, Gk	whole	hologram, holism
homo-, homeo-, homoio-, Gk	like, same	homoiothermy
horr-, -hor, L	to bristle	horrible, abhor
hum-, L	the ground	humus, humble
hyalo-, Gk	glass, glassy	hyaloid
hydro-, Gk	water	hydrotherapy
hygro-, Gk	wet	hygrometer
hylo-, Gk	matter, material	hylozoism
hymeno-, Gk	membrane	hymenopterous
hypno-, Gk	sleep	hypnosis
hystero-, hyster-, Gk	hysteria, uterus	hysterotomy, hysterical
i-, -it, L	to go	exit, itinerary
-iasis, Gk	disease	schistosomiasis
iatro-, -iatrics, -iatry, Gk	medicine	iatrogenic, psychiatry
ichth-, ichthyo-, Gk	fish	ichthyosaur
icono-, Gk	image	iconoclast
ideo-, Gk	idea	ideology
idio-, Gk	individual	idiosyncrasy
igni-, L	fire	ignition
ileo-, -ileac, L	ileum (small intestine)	ileocecal
ilio-, -iliac, L	ilium	sacroiliac
inguin-, inguino-, L	groin	inguinal
int-, L	within	intestine, internal
intra-, intro-, L	interior, inward	introduce
iodo-, Gk	iodine	iodoform
iso-, Gk	equal, like, same	isometric
-itis, Gk	inflammation	chondritis
jac-, -ject, L	to throw	adjacent, eject
jug-, junct-, -join, L	to join, yoke	conjugal, conjunction
jur-, jus-, L	to swear	jury, justify
juxta-, L	near	juxtaposition
kerato-, Gk	cornea, horn	keratin
kinesi-, kineto-, -kinesis, Gk	movement	psychokinesis
labi-, labio-, L	lip	labium
labor-, L	labor	elaborate
lac-, lec-, lic-, L	to entice	delectable
lacto-, L	milk	lactose
laryngo-, Gk	larynx	laryngoscope
lati-, L	broad	latitude
leg-, lect-, L	to collect, read	legible, recollect
lepid-, lepido-, Gk	scale, scaly	lepidopterous
-lepsy, -leptic, Gk	seizure	epilepsy

Greek/Latin	English	Example(s)
lept-, lepto-, Gk	small, think	leptophyllous
leuko-, Gk	white	leukocyte
levo-, L	left, left-sided	levotartaric
liber-, L	free	liberty
lig-, L	to bind	ligament, oblige
ligni-, lign-, L	wood	lignite
lin-, L	a line	delineate
lip-, lipo-, Gk	fat	lipoma
litera-, L	a letter	literature
litho-, -lith, Gk	stone	monolith
loc-, L	a place	local, locomotion
logo-, log-, Gk	speech, word	logic
-logy, -logical, Gk	science of	ecology
longi-, L	long	longitude
luci-, L	light	lucid
lumin-, lumini-, L	light	illuminate
lun-, luni-, L	moon	lunar
lympho-, lymphat-, lymphato-, L	lymph	lymphoma
lyo-, -lysis, -lyte, Gk	dissolving	electrolyte
-machy, Gk	fight	tauromachy
macro-, Gk	large	macrocosm
magneto-, L	magnet	magnetosphere
magni-, L	great, large	magnificent
mal-, L	bad	maladjustment
man-, main-, L	hand	manner, maintain
-mancy, -mantic, Gk	divining	chiromancy
-mania, -maniac, Gk	craving	monomania
mast-, masto-, Gk	breast	mastectomy
matri-, L	mother	matrilineal
medi-, medio-, L	middle	mediocre
medico-, L	medicine	medicolegal
mega-, megalo-, Gk	great	megalomania
melan-, melano-, Gk	black, dark	melanin
mem-, L	remembering	memoir
ment-, mon-, L	mind	mental, demonstrate
mero-, -mere, -merous, Gk	part, of parts	blastomere, trimerous
meso-, mes-, Gk	middle	mesozoic
metro-, -meter, -metry, Gk	measure	metrology, centimeter, telemetry
micro-, Gk	small	micron
milli-, L	thousand, thousandth	millipede
mir-, mar-, L	wonderful	miracle, marvel
miso-, mis-, Gk	hate	misanthrope
-mit, -miss, L	to send	emit, mission
mod-, L	manner	model, modify
mono-, Gk	one	monocle
mor-, mori-, mort-, L	to die	morgue, mortal
-morph, morpho-, -morphic, -morphous, Gk	form	endomorph, amorphous
mot-, mov-, L	to move	emotion, remove
moun-, L	hill	mound, mountain
muco-, muci-, L	mucus, slimy	mucilage
multi-, L	many	multifaceted
myco-, -mycete, Gk	fungus	ascomycete

Greek/Latin	English	Example(s)
myel-, myelo-, Gk	spinal cord	myelin
myo-, Gk	muscle	myocardial
myria-, Gk	very many	myriad
mytho-, Gk	myth	mythology
myxo-, Gk	slime	myxophobia
narco-, Gk	torpor	narcolepsy
nas-, naso-, L	nose	nasal
nati-, L	birth	nativity
necro-, Gk	corpse	necromancy
-nect, -nex, L	to bind	connect, annex
nemato-, Gk	thread	nematode
neo-, Gk	new	neo-Freudian
nephro-, Gk	kidney	nephron
neuro-, Gk	nerve	neuroanatomy
nitro-, nitr-, L	nitrogen	nitrate
noct-, nocti-, L	night	nocturnal
nomen-, nomin-, -noun, L	name	nomenclature, pronoun
nomo-, Gk	custom, law	nomothetic
noso-, -nose, -nosis, Gk	disease	diagnosis
not-, nit-, nis-, L	to get to know	notice, cognition
nota-, L	a mark	notary, notation
noto-, Gk	a back	notochord
nucleo-, L	nucleus	nucleotide
nudi-, L	bare	nudity
numer-, L	number	enumerate
nutr-, nur-, L	to nourish	nutrition, nurse
nycti-, nycto-, nyct-, Gk	night	nyctalopic
octa-, octo-, Gk & L	eight	octopus
oculo-, ocul-, L	eye	oculist
odonto-, -odont, Gk	tooth	odontology
odyno-, -odynia, Gk	pain	odynometer
-oid, -ode, Gk	like	spheroid
oleo-, L	oil	oleomargarine
oligo-, olig-, Gk	few	oligarchy
-oma, Gk	tumor	lymphoma
omni-, L	all	omnipotent
oneiro-, Gk	dream	oneiromancy
onto-, Gk	existence	ontology
oo-, Gk	egg	oogonium
ophio-, Gk	snake	ophiophobia
ophthalmo-, Gk	eye	ophthalmologist
-opia, Gk	vision defect	myopia
-opsis, Gk	appearance, sight	synopsis
orb-, L	a circle	orbit
orchido-, Gk	orchid	orchid
orchio-, orchi-, Gk	testicle	orchialgia
ord-, ordin-, L	order	ordain, subordinate
organo-, Gk	organ, organic	organometallic
ornitho-, Gk	bird	ornithology
oro-, L	mouth	oronasal
ortho-, Gk	correct, upright	orthopedic
-osis, Gk	disease	neurosis
ossi-, L	bone	ossify
oste-, osteo-, Gk	bone	osteoarthritis

Greek/Latin	English	Example(s)
pneumat-, pneumato-, Gk	breath	pneumatic
pneumo-, Gk	lung	pneumothorax
-pod, -podous, Gk	foot	arthropod
-poietic, Gk	making	hematopoietic
polio-, Gk	gray matter	poliomyelitis
poly-, Gk	many	polygyny
pon-, pos-, L	to place	opponent, position
popul-, pub-, L	people	popular, public
port-, L	to carry	portable
-prehend, L	to seize	apprehend
primi-, prim-, L	first	prime
procto-, Gk	rectum	proctoscope
proto-, Gk	first	prototype
pseudo-, Gk	false	pseudonym
psycho-, psych-, Gk	mind; spirit	psychology; psychic
psychro-, Gk	cold	psychrometer
ptero-, -pterous, -pter, Gk	wing	pterodactyl, helicopter
pulmo-, L	lung	pulmonary
punct-, pung-, L	to prick	puncture, pungent
pur-, L	pure	purity, puritan
-pute, L	clear	compute
py-, pye-, Gk	pus	pyorrhea
pyelo, Gk	pelvis	pyelogram
pyro-, pyr-, Gk	fire	pyromania, pyre
quadri-, quadru-, L	four	quadrilateral
quasi-, L	like, as if	quasi-serious
-quer, -quire, -quest, L	to seek	conquer, acquire, inquest
quin-, quinque-, quinqua-, L	five	quintuplet
radic-, L	root	radical
radio-, L	radiant energy, radio, radioactive	radioactivity, radioisotope
rat-, rati-, L	to suppose	ratio, ratify
recti-, L	straight	rectitude
recto-, L	rectum	rectoabdominal
reg-, res-, L	to rule	regal, resource
ren-, reni-, L	kidney	renal, reniform
rheo-, Gk	current	rheostat
rhino-, Gk	nose	rhinoceros
rhizo-, Gk	root	rhizome
rot-, rotat-, L	a wheel	rotor, rotate
-rrhea, -rrhagia, -rrhagic, -rrhage, Gk	flow	hemorrhage
-rupt, L	to break	interrupt
acchar-, saccharo-, Gk	sugar	saccharin
sacro-, L	sacrum	sacroiliac
sangui-, L	blood	sanguine
sapro-, Gk	decompose	saprophyte
sarco-, Gk	flesh	sarcophagus
scato-, Gk	dung	scatological
-scend, L	to climb	condescend
schisto-, Gk	to divide	schistosome
schizo-, Gk	to split	schizophrenia
sclero-, Gk	hard	sclerosis
-scope, -scopy, Gk	observation	microscope

Greek/Latin	English	Example(s)
oto-, Gk	ear	otology
ovi-, ovo-, ov-, L	egg	ovate
oxy-, Gk	oxygen; sharp	oxyacid; oxytone
pachy-, Gk	thick	pachyderm
paleo-, Gk	ancient	paleolithic
palmi-, palm-, L	palm	palmitic
pan-, panto-, Gk	all	pandemic, pantothenic
par-, per-, L	to prepare	apparatus, imperative
para-, Gk	near	paragraph
pari-, L	equal, like	par, disparity
-parous, L	bearing	viviparous
part-, -part, L	part	depart, partake
-pathy, patho-, Gk	disease, suffering	neuropathy, pathos
patri-, L	father	patrician
-ped, -pede, pedi-, L	foot	impede
peda-, pedo-, Gk	child	pedagogue
-pel, L	to drive	compel
pelvi-, L	pelvis	pelvic
-pend, -pond, L	to weigh	depend, ponder
penta-, Gk	five	pentagon
petro-, Gk	stone	petroglyph
-phage, phago-, -phagous, -phagy, Gk	eat	phagocyte
pharmaco-, Gk	drug	pharmacology
pharyngo-, Gk	pharynx	pharyngoscope
-phasia, Gk	speech defect	aphasia
pheno-, phanero-, -phany, Gk	visible	phenomenon
-philia, -phily, Gk	morbid love	pedophilia
philo-, -phile, Gk	love	philosophy, bibliophile
phleb-, phlebo-, Gk	vein	phlebitis
-phobia, Gk	fear	agoraphobia
-phone, phono-, -phony, Gk	sound	phonograph
photo-, Gk	light	photograph
phren-, phreno-, Gk	brain, mind	schizophrenic, phrenology
phyl-, phylo-, Gk	species	phylum, phylogeny
phyllo-, -phyllous, -phyll, Gk	leaf, leafy	chlorophyll
physio-, Gk	nature	physiocrat
-phyte, phyto-, Gk	plant (bot.)	phytoplankton
picr-, picro-, Gk	bitter	picric
piezo-, Gk	pressure	piezochemistry
pinna, pinni-, L	fin, web, leaf	pinnate, pinniped
pisci-, L	fish	pisciculture
plano-, L	flat	planoconvex
-plasia, -plasis, Gk	growth	hyperplasia
-plasm, Gk	material, matter	cytoplasm
-plast, Gk	cell	chloroplast
-plastic, -plasty, Gk	making, forming	rhinoplasty
platy-, Gk	flat	platypus
-plegia, Gk	paralysis	quadriplegia
plen-, L	to fill	plenty
pleur-, pleuro-, Gk	pleura, side	pleurisy
plic-, -plex, L	to fold	implicate, complex
plumb-, plumbo-, L	lead (metal)	plumbing

Greek/Latin	English	Example(s)
scoto-, Gk	darkness	scotoma
-scribe, scrip-, L	to write	describe, scripture
scyph-, Gk & L	cup	scyphiform
seb-, sebi-, sebo-, L	fat, fatty	sebaceous
-sect, -section, L	cut	bisect
sed-, sid-, -sess, siz-, L	to sit	sediment, residue, possess, size
seismo-, Gk	earthquake	seismograph
semi-, L	half	semiconductor
-sent, sent-, L	to feel	assent, sentiment
sept-, septi-, L	seven	septet
sequ-, sec-, L	to follow	sequence, second
sero-, L	serum	serous
serv-, -serve, L	a slave	servant, conserve
sex-, L	six	sexagenarian
sider-, sidero-, Gk	star	sidereal
-sign, L	a sign	assign, signal
silico-, L	silicon	silicosis
simil-, sem-, L	same	similar, resemble
simplici-, L	simple	simplicity
Sino-, L	Chinese	Sino-Soviet
sito-, -site, Gk	food, eat	parasite
socio-, L	society	socioeconomic
sol-, solit-, L	alone	sole, solitary
solu-, -solve, L	to loosen	solution, resolve
somato-, -soma, -some, Gk	body	chromosome
somn-, somni-, L	sleep	insomnia
-son, son-, L	sound	sonata
-sophy, -sopher, Gk	knowledge of	philosopher
spec-, -spect, L	to look	specimen, inspect
spectro-, L	spectrum	spectrogram
speleo-, spel-, Gk & L	cave	spelunker
spermo-, spermato-, -spermous, Gk	seed, spermatozoa	spermatozoid
-sphere, Gk	sphere	hemisphere
sphygmo-, Gk	pulse	sphygmomanometer
spiro-, spir-, Gk	spiral	spirogyra, spiral
spiro-, -spire, spir-, L	breath	spirometer, inspire, spirit
-stant, -sist, -stitute, -stance, L	to stand	constant, desist, institute, substance
-stat, Gk	to stop	thermostat, static
stato-, stat-, Gk	position	status
stell-, stelli-, L	star	stellar
steno-, Gk	narrow	stenosis
stereo-, Gk	solid	stereophonic
stetho-, Gk	chest	stethoscope
-stomy, Gk	surgical opening	ileostomy
-strict, -strain, L	to draw tight	constrict, restrain
-struct, L	to build	construct
sulfa-, sulfo-, L	sulfur	sulfonamide
sup-, sum-, L	above	superior, summit
tachy-, Gk	swift	tachyon
-tain, tang-, L	to touch	attain, tangible
tauro-, Gk	cattle	tauromachy
tauto-, Gk	same	tautology

Greek/Latin	English	Example(s)
taxo-, -taxis, -taxy, Gk	order	taxonomy
techno-, Gk	art, technical	technology
teg-, -tect, L	to cover	tegument, detect
tele-, teleo-, telo-, Gk	far, final	television, teleology
temp-, L	time	temporary
ten-, -tain, L	to hold	tenacity, contain
ter-, tre-, tri-, L	three	tercentenary
terato-, Gk	monster	teratology
termin-, L	end	exterminator
terr-, -ter, L	to scare	terror, deter
terri-, L	earth	territory
test-, -test, L	witness	testament, contest
tetra-, Gk	four	tetrad
-text, text-, L	to weave	context, textile
thanato-, Gk	death	thanatology
theo-, Gk	god	theology
thermo-, Gk	heat	thermometer
thio-, Gk	sulfur	Thiokol
thorac-, thoraco-, Gk	thorax	thoracic
thyro-, Gk	thyroid	thyroxin
tom-, -tome, tomo-, Gk	knife, cutting	tome, epitome, tomograph
tono-, Gk	tone	tonometer
topo-, Gk	place	topology
tot-, toti-, L	whole	totalitarian
toxico-, Gk	poison	toxicology
tracheo-, Gk	trachea	tracheotomy
-tract, treat-, L	to draw	extract, treatise
trib-, L	tribe	contribute
tricho-, Gk	hair	trichomonad
trop-, -troupous, -tropy, Gk	turned	tropism
tropho-, -trophy, Gk	nourishment	dystrophy
typhlo-, Gk	blind	typhlosis
typo-, Gk	type	typology
ultima-, ultra-, L	beyond	ultimate
uni-, L	one	unite
urethr-, urethro-, Gk	urethra	urethral
urin-, urino-, L	urine	urinary
uro-, -uria, Gk	urine	glycosuria
uter-, utero-, L	uterus	uterology
vagin-, vagino-, L	vagina	vaginectomy
val-, -vail, L	to be strong	valid, prevail
vari-, vario-, L	different	various
vaso-, L	vessel	vasodilation
vei-, -vey, veh-, L	to carry	vein, convey, vehicle
ven-, veni-, L	vein	venous
ven-, -vent, -vene, L	to turn	avenue, adventure, convene
ventr-, ventro-, L	abdomen	ventral
ver-, verit-, L	true	verdict, very, verity
vermi-, L	worm	vermiculite
-verse, -vert, vert-, L	to turn	adverse, revert, vertigo
via-, vio-, -vey, -voy, L	way	viaduct, obvious, convey, convoy

Greek/Latin	English	Example(s)
vic-, -vid, vis-, -view, -vise, L	to see	evident, visage, review, supervise
vice-, L	substitute	vice-president
vin-, vini-, L	wine, grapes	vineyard, viniculture
-vince, -vict, L	to conquer	convince, evict
vitr-, vitri-, L	glass	vitreous, vitriform
viv-, -vive, L	to live	vivacity, survive
voc-, -voke, L	voice	vocal, evoke
-volve, -volt, L	to roll	evolve, revolt
vor-, -vorous, L	eat	voracious, omnivorous
xeno-, Gk	foreign	xenophobia
xero-, Gk	dry	xerography
xylo-, Gk	wood	xylophone
zoo-, Gk	animal	zoology
zygo-, Gk	pair, yoke	zygote
-zyme, zymo-, Gk	fermentation	enzyme

Prefixes

Greek/Latin	English	Example(s)
a-, an-, Gk	not	amoral, anesthesia
ab-, a-, abs-, L	from, away, off, away from, down	abject, absent
ad-, a-, ac-, af-, ag-, al-, an-, ap-, ar-, as-, at-, L	to, toward	admit, align, accept, affinity, aggregate, alleviate, annex, appear, arrest, assimilate, attend
ana-, Gk	again	anadiplosis
ana-, Gk	according to, similar to	analog
ana-, Gk	thoroughly	anaphylaxis
ana-, Gk	up	analysis, anabolism
ana-, Gk	upon	anaclitic
ante-, Gk & L	before	antediluvian
anti-, Gk	against	antiaircraft
apo-, Gk	away from, off	apogee
cata-, cath-, cat-, Gk	down, away, in accordance with, against, very, completely	catacomb, catalog, catharsis, catabolism
cis-, L	on this side of	cisalpine
com-, co-, col-, con-, cor-, L	with, together, very, thoroughly	combat, collect, connect, correspond
contra-, L	against	contradict
de-, L	not	decentralize
de-, L	down	decline
dia-, Gk	through	diameter
dis-, di-, L	apart, not	disperse, disapprove, digress
en-, el-, em-, L	in, into	encounter, embed
endo-, Gk	within	endogenous
epi-, eph-, Gk	on, beside, among, outside, over, before	epilog, epitome, epiphenomenon
ex-, e-, ec-, ef-, Gk & L	out, off, from, beyond, not, thoroughly	exhale, exclude, exceed, efface
exo-, Gk	outside	exogenous
extra-, L	outside	extracurricular
hyper-, Gk	over, above, beyond	hyperactive
hypo-, Gk	under, beneath, less than	hypokinesis
in-, il-, im-, ir-, L	in, into, on	invade, induce
in-, il-, im-, ir-, L	not, against	inimical
inter-, L	between, among, together, mutual	intermix, interdependent
intra-, L	within	intramural
juxta-, L	next to	juxtapose

Greek/Latin	English	Example(s)
mal-, L	badly, evil	malcontent, maltreat
meta-, met-, Gk	after, beyond, changed, along with	metaphysics, metamorphosis
mis-, L	badly	misadventure
non-, L	not	nonchalant
ob-, oc-, of-, op-, L	against	obverse, oppress
para-, Gk	beside, beyond	parallel
per-, L	through, very, thoroughly	percussion
peri-, Gk	around, about, round, near	perimeter, perigee
post-, L	after	postpartum, postwar
pre-, L	before	premarital
preter-, L	beyond	preternatural
pro-, Gk	before	progestin
pro-, L	for	proslavery
pro-, Gk & L	forward	progress
pro-, L	substitute	pronoun
re-, L	again, back	rerun, return
retro-, L	back, backward	retrograde
sub-, suc-, suf-, sug-, sum-, sup-, sur-, sus-, L	under, less, subordinate, division	substance, subcategory, suffer
subter-, L	under, beneath, less than	subterfuge
super-, supra-, L	over, above, exceeding	superpose, suprarational
sym-, sy-, syl-, syn-, Gk	with, associated, simultaneous	symmetry, syllogism, synthesis
trans-, L	on that side of, across	transpose
ultra-, L	beyond, exceeding	ultraconservative

Suffixes of Adjectives

Greek/Latin	English	Example(s)
-able, -ive, L	tending to	irritable, restive
-able, -ile, -il, L	able to, able to be	teachable, ductile
-ac, L & Gk	affected by	maniac
-ac, -ic, Gk & L	pertaining to	iliac, manic
-aceous, -al, -ar, -ary, -ile, -il, -ine, -ory, Gk & L	pertaining to	curvaceous, dorsal, temporary, puerile, promissory
-al, -ate, -id, L	characterized by	jovial, ornate, flaccid
-an, L	coming from, originating in	European
-an, L	adhering to or following	Republican
-an, L	belonging to (in biology)	crustacean
-ant, -ent, L	doing, agency	errant, decadent
-escent, L	beginning to	obsolescent
-fic, -ficent, L	causing, making	terrific, magnificent
-ine, -in, -ing, -ive, -ory, L	like, of the nature of	bovine, charming, desultory
-ose, -ous, L	full of	verbose, aqueous

Suffixes of Nouns

Greek/Latin	English	Example(s)
-al, L	instance, nouns formed from adjs.	oval, signal
-al, L	act, action	recital
-ana, L	collection	Americana
-ance, -ence, -ancy, -ency, L	act, condition, concrete thing	assistance, violence, eminence

Greek/Latin	English	Example(s)
-arium, -ary, -orium, -ory, L	place	aquarium, apiary, auditorium, dormitory
-ary, L	practitioner	notary
-ate, L	office	episcopate
-ate, L	result	mandate
-cion, -sion, -ion, -tion, L	action, result, condition	ascension, demolition, condition
-ese, -ic, -ics, Gk	native art, system	Chinese, chiropractic, phonics
-ist, L	practitioner	psychiatrist
-ist, -ite, Gk	advocate, adherent	separatist, Jacobite
-ite, Gk	descendent of	Israelite
-ite, Gk	native	Canaanite
-ity, L	condition	acidity
-ium, L	chemical element	uranium
-ment, L	act, condition, instrument, result	movement, predicament, instrument
-mony, L	result	alimony
-or, L	practitioner	elector
-ory, L	instrument	depilatory
-trix, L	female practitioner	aviatrix
-tude, L	condition	negritude
-ure, L	action, office, result, instrument	divestiture, suture

Suffixes of Verbs

Greek/Latin	English	Example(s)
-ate, L	combine, combine with, treat with	associate, medicate
-esce, L	begin	coalesce
-fy, L	become, make	solidify, codify
-ize, Gk	become, make, practice, treat with	realize, canonize, idolize, simonize

Foreign Words and Phrases

A

à bas [Fr.], down, down with.

à beau jeu, beau retour [Fr.], one good turn deserves another; tit for tat.

ab extra [L.], from without.

ab imo pectore [L.], from the bottom of the heart.

ab incunabulis [L.], from the cradle.

ab initio [L.], from the beginning.

ab intra [L.], from within.

a bisogni si conoscono gli amici [It.], a friend in need is a friend indeed.

à bon chat, bon rat [Fr.], to a good cat, a good rat; tit for tat.

à bon marché [Fr.], cheap; a good bargain.

ab origine [L.], from the origin.

ab ovo [L.], from the egg; from the beginning.

ab ovo usque ad mala [L.], from the egg to the apples (as in Roman banquets); from beginning to end.

à bras ouverts [Fr.], with open arms.

abrégé [Fr.], an abridgment.

absens hæres non erit [L.], the absent one will not be heir; out of sight, out of mind.

absente reo [L.], the accused being absent.

absit invidia [L.], let there be no ill-will; envy apart.

absit omen [L.], may this not prove of (evil) omen.

ab uno disce omnes [L.], from one specimen judge of all the rest.

a buon vino non bisogna frasca [It.], good wine needs no bush.

ab urbe condita [L.], from the founding of the city, i.e. Rome (753 B.C.).

a capite ad calcem [L.], from head to heel.

à chaque saint sa chandelle [Fr.], to each saint his candle; honor to whom honor is due.

à cheval [Fr.], on horseback.

a che vuole, non mancano modi [It.], where there's a will there's a way.

à compte [Fr.], on account.

à corps perdu [Fr.], with breakneck speed.

à coup sûr [Fr.], of a certainty; without fail.

à couvert [Fr.], under cover.

a cruce salus [L.], salvation by the cross.

actionnaire [Fr.], shareholder in a company.

ad aperturam (libri) [L.], at the opening of the book; wherever the book opens.

ad arbitrium [L.], at will.

ad astra per aspera [L.], to the stars through hardship.

ad calendas Græcas [L.], at the Greek calends; i.e. never, as the Greeks had no calends in their mode of reckoning.

ad captandum vulgus [L.], to attract or please the rabble.

a Deo et rege [L.], from God and the king.

à dessein [Fr.], on purpose; intentionally.

à deux mains [Fr.], for two hands; two-handed; having a double office.

ad extremum [L.], to the last, or extremity.

ad finem [L.], to the end; at or near the end.

ad gustum [L.], to one's taste.

ad hominem [L.], to the man; to an individual's interests or passions.

adhuc sub judice lis est [L.], the case is still before the judge; the controversy is not yet settled.

a die [L.], from that day.

ad infinitum [L.], to infinity.

ad instar [L.], after the fashion of.

ad interim [L.], in the meanwhile.

ad internecionem [L.], to extermination.

à discrétion [Fr.], at discretion; without restriction.

ad libitum [L.], at pleasure.

ad majorem Dei gloriam [L.], for the greater glory of God.

ad modum [L.], in the manner of.

ad multos annos [L.], for many years.

ad nauseam [L.], to disgust or satiety.

adorer le veau d'or [Fr.], to worship the golden calf.

ad patres [L.], gathered to his fathers.

ad referendum [L.], for further consideration.

ad rem [L.], to the purpose; to the point.

à droite [Fr.], to the right.

adscriptus glebæ [L.], attached to the soil.

adsum [L.], I am present; here!

ad summum [L.], to the highest point.

ad unguem [L.], to the nail; to a nicety; exactly; perfectly.

ad unum omnes [L.], all to a man.

ad utrumque paratus [L.], prepared for either case or alternative.

ad valorem [L.], according to the value.

ad vitam aut culpam [L.], for life or fault; i.e. till some misconduct be proved.

ad vivum [L.], to the life; portrayed in a lifelike manner.

ægrescit medendo [L.], he becomes worse by the remedies used.

æquabiliter et diligenter [L.], equably and diligently.

æquo animo [L.], with an equal mind; with equanimity.

ære perennius [L.], more lasting than brass.

æs triplex [L.], triple brass; armor of adamant.

ætatis suæ [L.], of his (or her) age.

affaire d'amour [Fr.], a love affair.

affaire d'honneur [Fr.], an affair of honor; a duel.

affaire du cœur [Fr.], an affair of the heart.

affreux [Fr.], frightful; shocking.

à fleur d'eau [Fr.], on a level with the water.

à fond [Fr.], to the bottom; thoroughly; heartily.

a fortiori [L.], with stronger reason. See in Dict.

à gauche [Fr.], to the left.

à genoux [Fr.], on the knees.

age quod agis [L.], attend to what you are about.

à grands frais [Fr.], at great expense.

à haute voix [Fr.], aloud.

à huis clos [Fr.], with closed doors; secretly.

aide toi, et le ciel t'aidera [Fr.], help yourself, and Heaven will help you.

à la belle étoile [Fr.], under the stars; in the open air.

à la bonne heure [Fr.], in good time; very well, all right, as you please.

à l'abri [Fr.], under shelter.

à la campagne [Fr.], in the country.

à la carte [Fr.], according to the bill of fare at table.

à la dérobée [Fr.], by stealth.

à la française [Fr.], after the French mode.

à la mode [Fr.], according to the custom or fashion.

à la Tartuffe [Fr.], like Tartuffe, i.e. hypocritically.

al bisogno si conoscono gli amici [It.], friends are known in time of need.

à l'envi [Fr.], emulously; so as to vie.

alere flammam [L.], to feed the flame.

al fresco [It.], in the open air; cool.

alieni appetens, sui profusus [L.], greedy of other people's possessions, lavish of his own.

à l'improviste [Fr.], on the sudden.

alla vostra salute [It.], to your health.

allez-vous-en! [Fr.], away with you!

allons [Fr.], let us go; come on; come.

al piu [It.], at most.

alter ego [L.], another self.

alter idem [L.], another exactly similar.

alter ipse amicus [L.], a friend is the counterpart of oneself.

alterum tantum [L.], as much more.

à main armée [Fr.], by force of arms.

amantium iræ amoris integratio [L.], the quarrels of lovers are the renewal of love.

à ma puissance [Fr.], to the best of my power.

amar y saber no puede ser [Sp.], no one can love and also be wise.

a maximis ad minima [L.], from the greatest to the least.

âme de boue [Fr.], a soul of mud.

amende honorable [Fr.], satisfactory apology; reparation.

à merveille [Fr.], to a wonder; marvellously.

amici probantur rebus adversis [L.], friends are tested in adversity.

amicus humani generis [L.], a friend of the human race.

amicus Plato, sed magis amica veritas [L.], Plato is my friend, but truth is still more a friend to me.

amicus usque ad aras [L.], a friend even to the sacrificial altar, i.e. to the utmost extremity.

ami de cour [Fr.], a court friend; a false or unreliable friend.

à mon avis [Fr.], in my opinion.

amor patriæ [L.], love of country.

amour propre [Fr.], self-love; vanity.

ancient régime [Fr.], the ancient or former order of things.

anglicé [Fr.], in English; in the English language.

anguis in herba [L.], a snake in the grass; an unsuspected danger; a false friend.

animo et fide [L.], with courage and confidence.

anno ætatis suæ [L.], in the year of his or her age.

anno Christi [L.], in the year of Christ.

anno Domini [L.], in the year of our Lord.

anno humanæ salutis [L.], in the year of man's redemption.

anno mundi [L.], in the year of the world.

anno urbis conditæ [L.], in the year from the time the city (Rome) was founded (753 B.C.).

annuit cœptis [L.], He (God) has smiled on our

undertakings: motto, adapted from Virgil, on the reverse of the great seal of the United States.

annus mirabilis [L.], year of wonders; especially used in reference to the year 1666, in which occurred the great plague, and the great fire of London.

ante lucem [L.], before the dawn.

ante meridiem [L.], before noon.

à outrance [Fr.], to extremities.

à pas de géant [Fr.], with a giant's stride; with gigantic steps.

à peindre [Fr.], to be painted; worthy of the painter's art.

aperçu [Fr.], a general sketch or survey.

à perte de vue [Fr.], till beyond one's view.

à peu près [Fr.], nearly.

à pied [Fr.], on foot.

à point [Fr.], to a point; just in time; perfectly right.

a posse ad esse [L.], from possibility to reality.

appartement [Fr.], set of rooms on the same floor.

aprés moi le déluge [Fr.], after me the deluge.

a prima vista [It.], at first sight.

à propos de bottes [Fr.], apropos of boots; in an irrelevant manner; without rhyme or reason.

à propos de rien [Fr.], apropos of nothing; without reference to anything in particular; without a motive.

aquila non capit muscas [L.], an eagle does not catch flies.

arbiter bibendi [L.], ruler of the symposium; toastmaster.

arbiter elegantiarum [L.], a judge or supreme authority in matters of taste.

arcades ambo [L.], Arcadians both; fellows of the same stamp.

arcana cælestia [L.], celestial mysteries.

arcana imperii [L.], state secrets.

ardentia verba [L.], glowing language.

argent comptant [Fr.], ready money.

argumentum ad crumenam [L.], an argument to the purse, i.e. to one's interests.

argumentum ad hominem [L.], an argument to the individual man, i.e. to his interests and prejudices.

argumentum ad ignorantiam [L.], an argument intended to work on a person's ignorance.

argumentum ad judicium [L.], argument appealing to the judgment.

argumentum ad verecundiam [L.], argument appealing to modesty.

argumentum baculinum [L.], the argument of the cudgel; brute force.

ariston metron [Gr.], moderation is best.

arrectis auribus [L.], with ears pricked up; all attention.

arrière pensée [Fr.], mental reservation.

ars est celare artem [L.], it is true art to conceal art.

ars longa, vita brevis [L.], art is long, life is short.

Artium Magister [L.], Master of Arts.

asinus ad lyram [L.], an ass at the lyre; a stupid awkward fellow.

Athanasius contra mundum [L.], Athanasius against the world.

à tort et à travers [Fr.], at random; without consideration.

à toute force [Fr.], with all one's might.

à tout hasard [Fr.], at all hazards.

à tout prix [Fr.], at any price; at all costs.

at spes non fracta [L.], but hope is not crushed.

au bout de son Latin [Fr.], at the end of his Latin, at his wit's end; in a fix or quandary.

au contraire [Fr.], on the contrary.

au courant [Fr.], fully acquainted with matters; up to date.

audaces (or **audentes**) **fortuna juvat** [L.], fortune aids the bold.

au désespoir [Fr.], in despair.

audi alteram partem [L.], hear the other side.

audiatur et altera pars [L.], let the other side also be heard.

au fait [Fr.], well acquainted with; expert.

au fond [Fr.], at bottom; in reality.

auf Wiedersehen [G.], till we meet again; **au revoir.**

au grand sérieux [Fr.], in all seriousness.

au jour le jour [Fr.], from day to day; without thought of tomorrow; from hand to mouth.

au naturel [Fr.], in the natural state.

au pis aller [Fr.], at the worst.

aurea mediocritas [L.], the golden or happy mean.

au reste [Fr.], as for the rest.

au revoir [Fr.], adieu; until we meet again.

auri sacra fames [L.], the accursed craving for gold.

au sérieux [Fr.], seriously.

auspicium melioris ævi [L.], an auspice (or augury) of a better age (to come).

aussitôt dit, aussitôt fait [Fr.], no sooner said than done.

autant d'hommes, autant d'avis [Fr.], so many men, so many minds.

aut Cæsar aut nullus [L.], either Cæsar or nobody.

aut inveniam viam aut faciam [L.], I shall either find a way or make one.

autrefois acquit [Fr.], formerly acquitted; previously tried for the same offense and acquitted.

autre temps, autres mœurs [Fr.], other times, other manners.

au troisième [Fr.], on the third story.

aut vincere aut mori [L.], either to conquer or to die; victory or death.

aux armes! [Fr.], to arms!

auxilium ab alto [L.], help from on high.

avant-propos [Fr.], preliminary matter; preface.

avec permission [Fr.], with permission.

ave, Imperator! morituri te salutant [L.], hail, Emperor! those about to die (gladiators) salute thee.

a verbis ad verbera [L.], from words to blows.

avito viret honore [L.], flourishes on his ancestral honors.

à volonté [Fr.], at pleasure.

a vostra salute [It.] ⎫
à votre santé [Fr.] ⎬ to your health.
a vuestra salud [Sp.] ⎭

B

badaud [Fr.], a lounger in the streets; an idler.

badinage [Fr.], jocularity; chaff.

ballon d'essai [Fr.], a balloon sent up to ascertain the direction of the air-currents; hence, a device to test public opinion on any subject.

bas bleu [Fr.], a blue-stocking; a literary woman.

beatæ memoriæ [L.], of blessed memory.

beau idéal [Fr.], the ideal of perfection.

beauté du diable [Fr.], the devil's good looks; youthful freshness.

beaux esprits [Fr.], men of wit.

beaux yeux [Fr.], fine eyes; good looks.

bel esprit [Fr.], a person of wit or genius; a brilliant mind.

bella! horrida bella! [L.], wars! horrid wars!

bella matribus detestata [L.], wars hated by mothers.

bellum internecinum [L.], a war of extermination.

benedetto è quel male che vien solo [It.], blessed the misfortune that comes singly.

bene orasse est bene studuisse [L.], to have prayed well is to have striven well.

ben trovato [It.], well invented; cleverly fabricated or concocted.

bête noire [Fr.], a black beast; a bugbear.

bêtise [Fr.], a piece of stupidity; stupidity.

billet d'amour [Fr.], a love-letter.

bis dat qui cito dat [L.], he gives twice who gives quickly.

bis peccare in bello non licet [L.], it is not permissible to blunder twice in war.

bis pueri sens [L.], old men are twice boys.

bona fide [L.], in good faith.

bona fides [L.], good faith.

bon ami [Fr.], good friend.

bon avocat, mauvais voisin [Fr.], a good lawyer is a bad neighbor.

bon diable [Fr.], a good-natured fellow.

bon gré, mal gré [Fr.], with good or ill grace; willing or unwilling.

bon jour [Fr.], good day; good morning.

bon jour, bonne œuvre [Fr.], a good day, a good work; i.e. the better the day, the better the deed.

bonne bouche [Fr.], a delicate morsel, titbit.

bonne et belle [Fr.], good and handsome.

bonne foi [Fr.], good faith.

bon soir [Fr.], good evening.

bon vivant [Fr.], one fond of luxury and good living; a gourmet.

bon voyage! [Fr.], a good voyage (or journey) to you!

Borgen macht Sorgen [G.], borrowing makes sorrowing; who goes a-borrowing goes a-sorrowing.

breveté [Fr.], patented.

brevi manu [L.], with a short hand; extemporaneously.

brevis esse laboro obscurus fio [L.], if I labor to be brief, I become obscure.

brutum fulmen [L.], a senseless thunderbolt; striking blindly.

C

cadit quæstio [L.], the question falls; there is no further discussion.

cæca est invidia [L.], envy is blind.

cælum non animum mutant qui trans mare currunt [L.], they who cross the sea change their sky but not their feelings.

cætera desunt [L.], the rest is wanting.

cæteris paribus [L.], other things being equal.

campo santo [It.], a burying-ground—lit. "holy field."

candida Pax [L.], white-robed Peace.

cantabit vacuus coram latrone viator [L.], the penniless traveler will sing in the presence of the highwayman; i.e. a penniless man has nothing to lose.

cantate Domino [L.], sing unto the Lord.

cap à pié [L.], from head to foot.

caput mortuum [L.], lit. "dead head"; worthless residue.

cara sposa [It.], dear wife.

carent quia vate sacro [L.], because they have no sacred bard (to celebrate their praise).

carpe diem [L.], enjoy the present day; improve the time.

castello che dà orecchia si vuol rendere [It.], the fortress that parleys speedily surrenders.

casus belli [L.], that which causes or justifies war.

catalogue raisonné [Fr.], a catalogue arranged according to the subjects.

causa sine qua non [L.], an indispensable cause or condition.

cause célèbre [Fr.], a celebrated law case or trial.

caveat emptor [L.], let the buyer beware.

cave canem [L.], beware of the dog.

cavendo tutus [L.], safe by using caution.

cedant arma togæ [L.], let arms yield to the gown, that is, military authority to the civil power.

cela va sans dire [Fr.], that goes without saying; needless to say; that is a matter of course.

cela viendra [Fr.], that will come.

ce n'est pas être bien aise que de rire [Fr.], laughing is not always a sign that the mind is at ease.

ce n'est que le premier pas qui coûte [Fr.], it is only the first step that is difficult.

censor morum [L.], a censor of morals.

c'est à dire [Fr.], that is to say.

c'est le commencement de la fin [Fr.], it is the beginning of the end.

c'est magnifique, mais ce n'est pas la guerre [Fr.], it is magnificent, but it is not war; said by a French officer as he watched the Charge of the Light Brigade at Balaklava.

c'est selon [Fr.], that is according to circumstances; that is as may be.

c'est un autre chose [Fr.], that's quite another thing.

cetera desunt [L.], the rest is wanting; here there is a break.

ceteris paribus [L.], see cæteris.

chacun à son goût [Fr.], every one to his taste.

chacun tire de son coté [Fr.], every one inclines to his own side.

chapeau bras [Fr.], a cocked hat.

chapelle ardente [Fr.], the chamber in which a dead body lies in state.

chemin de fer [Fr.], iron road; a railway.

cherchez la femme [Fr.], look for the woman (to find where she has had a hand in the matter).

chère amie [Fr.], a dear (female) friend.

che sarà, sarà [It.], what will be, will be.

cheval de bataille [Fr.], a war-horse; what one chiefly relies on.

chevalier d'industrie [Fr.], lit. a knight of industry; a swindling or cheating rogue; one who lives by his wits.

chi tace confessa [It.], he who keeps silence confesses.

ci git [Fr.], here lies.

clarior e tenebris [L.], brighter from darkness or obscurity.

clarum et venerabile nomen [L.], an illustrious and venerable name.

cogito, ergo sum [L.], I think, therefore I exist.

comitas inter gentes [L.], politeness between nations.

comme il faut [Fr.], as it should be.

commune bonum [L.], a common good.

commune periculum concordiam parit [L.], common danger begets concord.

communibus annis [L.], on the annual average.

communi consensu [L.], by common consent.

compagnon de voyage [Fr.], a traveling companion.

componere lites [L.], to settle disputes.

compos voti [L.], having obtained one's wish.

compte rendu [Fr.], an account rendered; a report.

con amore [It.], with love; very earnestly.

conciergerie [Fr.], a doorkeeper's lodge; also name of an ancient prison at Paris.

concio ad clerum [L.], a discourse to the clergy.

concordia discors [L.], discordant concord.

concours [Fr.], a competition, as for a prize.

con diligenza [It.], with diligence.

conditio sine qua non [L.], a necessary condition.

con dolore [It.], with grief; sorrowfully.

confido et conquiesco [L.], I trust and am at peace.

conjunctis viribus [L.], with united powers.

conseil d'état [Fr.], a council of state; a privy-council.

consensus facit legem [L.], consent makes the law.

consilio et animis [L.], by wisdom and courage.

consilio et prudentia [L.], by wisdom and prudence.

constantia et virtute [L.], by constancy and virtue (or bravery).

consuetudo pro lege servatur [L.], custom or usage is held as law.

consule Planco [L.], when Plancus was consul; when I was a young fellow.

contra bonos mores [L.], against good manners or morals.

copia verborum [L.], rich supply of words.

coram nobis [L.], before us; in our presence.

coram non judice [L.], before one who is not a proper judge.

coram populo [L.], in presence of the people.

cordon bleu [Fr.], blue-ribbon; a cook of the highest excellence.

cordon sanitaire [Fr.], a line of guards to prevent the spreading of contagion or pestilence; a quarantine.

corps d'armée [Fr.], the body of an army; an army corps.

corps de garde [Fr.], a body of men in a guardroom; the room itself.

corps diplomatique [Fr.], a diplomatic body; a body of ambassadors and similar representatives.

corrigenda [L.], things to be corrected; a list of errors or imperfections.

corruptio optimi pessima [L.], a corruption of what is best is worst.

cos ingeniorum [L.], a whetstone for wits.

couleur de rose [Fr.], rose-color; an alluring aspect of circumstances.

coup [Fr.], a stroke.

coup de grâce [Fr.], a finishing stroke.

coup de main [Fr.], a sudden attack of enterprise.

coup de maître [Fr.], a master stroke.

coup de pied [Fr.], a kick.

coup de soleil [Fr.], sunstroke.

coup d'essai [Fr.], a first attempt.

coup d'état [Fr.], a sudden decisive blow in politics; a stroke of policy.

coup de théâtre [Fr.], a theatrical effect.

coup d'œil [Fr.], a rapid glance of the eye.

courage sans peur [Fr.], fearless courage.

coûte que coûte [Fr.], cost what it may.

crambe repetita [L.], cabbage warmed up a second time; i.e. the repetition of an old joke, a truism, etc.

credat Judæus Apella [L.], let Apella, the superstitious Jew, believe it, I won't; "tell that to the marines."

crede quod habes, et habes [L.], believe that you have it, and you have it.

credo quia absurdum [L.], I believe because it is absurd.

credo quia impossibele est [L.], I believe it because it is impossible.

crême de la crême [Fr.], cream of the cream; the very best or most select.

crescit amor nummi, quantum ipsa pecunia crescit [L.], the love of money increases as wealth grows.

crescit eundo [L.], it increases as it goes.

crescit sub pondere virtus [L.], virtue increases beneath oppression.

crimen falsi [L.], the crime of perjury.

crimen læsæ majestatis [L.], the crime of high treason; lese-majesty.

Croix rouge [Fr.], Red Cross.

crux [L.], a cross; puzzle; difficulty.

crux criticorum [L.], the puzzle of critics.

crux medicorum [L.], the puzzle of the doctors.

cucullus non facit monachum [L.], the cowl does not make the friar; i.e. don't trust to appearances.

cui bono? [L.], for whose advantage? to what end?

cui Fortuna ipsa cedit [L.], to whom Fortune herself yields.

cuilibet in arte sua credendum est [L.], everyone is to be trusted in his own special art.

culpam pœna premit comes [L.], punishment follows hard on crime.

cum bona venia [L.], with your good leave.

cum grano salis [L.], with a grain of salt; with some allowance.

cum multis aliis [L.], with many others.

cum notis variorum [L.], with the notes of various commentators.

cum privilegio [L.], with privilege or license from the authorities.

curiosa felicitas [L.], nice felicity of expression.

currente calamo [L.], with a running or rapid pen.

custos morum [L.], guardian of manners (or morals).

D

d'accord [Fr.], in agreement.

da locum melioribus [L.], give place to your betters.

dame d'honneur [Fr.], matron of honor.

dames de la halle [Fr.], women who sell articles in a market; market-women.

damnant quod non intelligunt [L.], they condemn what they do not understand.

dare pondus fumo [L.], to give weight to smoke; i.e. attach importance to matters of no consequence.

das Beste ist gut genug [G.], the best is good enough.

das Ewig-Weibliche zieht uns hinan [G.], the eternal-feminine draws us upwards.

data et accepta [L.], expenses and receipts.

data obolum Belisario [L.], give an obolus to Belisarius (a general of Justinian, said to have been neglected in his old age by that emperor and compelled to beg).

Davus sum non Œdipus [L.], I am Davus not Œdipus (who solved the riddle of the Sphinx); I am a bad hand at riddles.

de bon augure [Fr.], of good augury or omen.

de bonne grâce [Fr.], with good grace; willingly.

deceptio visus [L.], an optical illusion.

decet verecundum esse adolescentem [L.], it becomes a young man to be modest.

decies repetita placebit [L.], when ten times repeated it will still please.

decipimur specie recti [L.], we are deceived by the show of rectitude.

decori decus addit avito [L.], he adds distinction to his ancestral honors.

de die in diem [L.], from day to day.

de facto [L.], in point of fact; actual; actually.

dégagé [Fr.], free; easy; unconstrained.

de gustibus non est disputandum [L.], there is no disputing about tastes.

de haut en bas [Fr.], in a contemptuous or supercilious manner.

dei gratia [L.], by the grace of God.

de integro [L.], anew; over again from beginning to end.

déjeuner à la fourchette [Fr.], breakfast with a fork; a breakfast or luncheon with meat.

de jure [L.], from the law; by right.

de l'audace, encore de l'audace, et toujours de l'audace [Fr.], audacity, more audacity, and always audacity.

delenda est Carthago [L.], Carthage must be blotted out, or destroyed.

de luxe [L.], of luxury; made with unusual elegance.

de mal en pis [Fr.], from bad to worse.

de minimis non curat lex [L.], the law does not concern itself with trifles.

de mortuis nil nisi bonum [L.], (say) nothing but good of the dead.

de nihilo nihil fit [L.], from nothing nothing is made.

dénouement [Fr.], issue; solution.

de novo [L.], anew.

Deo adjuvante [L.], God assisting.

Deo duce [L.], God being the leader.

Deo favente [L.], God favoring.

Deo gratias [L.], thanks to God.

Deo juvante [L.], with God's help.

de omnibus rebus et quibusdam aliis [L.], concerning all things and certain others.

Deo non fortuna [L.], from God, not by chance.

Deo volente [L.], God willing.

de pis en pis [Fr.], from worse to worse.

de profundis [L.], out of the depths.

de retour [Fr.], having come back; returned.

de rigueur [Fr.], imperatively necessary; not to be dispensed with.

dernier ressort [Fr.], a last resource.

désagrément [Fr.], something disagreeable.

desipere in loco [L.], to jest or be jolly at the proper time.

désorienté [Fr.], having lost one's way; not knowing where to turn.

desunt cætera [L.], the remainder is wanting.

de trop [Fr.], too much; more than is wanted.

detur digniori [L.], let it be given to the more worthy.

detur pulchriori [L.], let it be given to the more (or most) beautiful.

Deus avertat! [L.], God forbid!

deus ex machina [L.], a god out of the machine; a deity introduced to bring about the dénouement of a drama; referring to the machinery and practice of the Greek and Roman stage.

Deus vobiscum! [L.], God be with you!

Deus vult [L.], God wills it.

di buona volontà sta pieno l'inferno [It.], hell is full of good intentions.

Dichtung und Wahrheit [G.], fiction and fact; poetry and truth.

dictum factum [L.], no sooner said than done.

dies non [L.], a day on which a law-court is not held.

Dieu est toujours pour les plus gros bataillons [Fr.], God is always on the side of the largest battalions; the leader with the largest army has the best chance of victory.

Dieu et mon droit [Fr.], God and my right.

Dieu vous garde [Fr.], God protect you.

digito monstrari [L.], to be pointed out with the finger (as a person of note).

dignus vindice nodus [L.], a difficulty worthy of powerful intervention.

dii majorum gentium [L.], gods of the superior class; the twelve higher gods of the Romans.

dii penates [L.], household gods.

diis aliter visum [L.], the gods decided otherwise; fate willed differently.

Dios me libre de hombre de un libro [Sp.], God deliver me from a man of one book.

di salto [It.], by leaps.

diseur de bons mots [Fr.], a sayer of good things; one noted for witty sayings.

disjecta membra [L.], scattered remains.

divide et impera [L.], divide and rule.

docendo discimus [L.], we learn by teaching.

dolce far niente [It.], sweet doing-nothing; sweet idleness.

Dominus vobiscum [L.], the Lord be with you.

domus et placens uxor [L.], home and a pleasing wife.

dorer la pilule [Fr.], to gild the pill.

double entendre [Fr.], incorrect for next.

double entente [Fr.], a double or equivocal meaning; a play on words.

do ut des [L.], I give that you may give; reciprocity.

doux yeux [Fr.], soft glances.

dramatis personæ [L.], the characters in the play.

droit au travail [Fr.], the right to live by labor.

droit des gens [Fr.], the law of nations.

drôle [Fr.], funny; a comic actor.

ducit amor patriæ [L.], love of country draws me.

dulce domum [L.], sweet home (or rather homeward).

dulce est desipere in loco [L.], it is pleasant to play the fool at times.

dulce et decorum est pro patria mori [L.], it is sweet and glorious to die for one's country.

dum spiro, spero [L.], while I breathe, I hope.

dum vivimus, vivamus [L.], while we live, let us live.

duomo [It.], a cathedral.

durante bene placito [L.], during good pleasure.

durante vita [L.], during life.

E

eau sucrée [Fr.], sweetened water: a French beverage.

ébauche [Fr.], a preliminary sketch; a rough outline.

ecce homo! [L.], behold the man!

ecce signum! [L.], behold the sign!

école [Fr.], a school.

e contra [L.], on the other hand.

édition de luxe [Fr.], a splendid and expensive edition of a book.

editio princeps [L.], the first printed edition of a book.

égarement [Fr.], bewilderment, mental confusion.

ego et rex meus [L.], I and my king.

eheu! fugaces labuntur anni [L.], alas! the fleeting years glide by.

elapso tempore [L.], the time having elapsed.

élève [Fr.], a pupil or student.

embarras de richesses [Fr.], an embarrassment of riches; an over-supply.

emeritus [L.], retired or superannuated after long service.

empressement [Fr.], promptitude; eagerness.

en ami [Fr.], as a friend.

en arrière [Fr.], in the rear; behind; back.

en attendant [Fr.], in the meantime.

en avant [Fr.], forward.

en badinant [Fr.], in sport; jestingly.

en cueros [Sp.], naked; unclothed.

en déshabillé [Fr.], in undress.

en Dieu est ma fiance [Fr.], my trust is in God.

en Dieu est tout [Fr.], in God are all things.

en effet [Fr.], in effect; substantially; really.

en famille [Fr.], with one's family; in a domestic state.

enfant gâté [Fr.], a spoiled child.

enfants perdus [Fr.], lost children; the soldiers forming a forlorn hope.

enfant terrible [Fr.], a terrible child, or one that makes disconcerting remarks.

enfant trouvé [Fr.], a foundling.

enfin [Fr.], in short; at last; finally.

en grand seigneur [Fr.], like a grandee or magnate.

en grande tenue [Fr.], in full dress, either official or evening.

en masse [Fr.], in a mass.

en passant [Fr.], in passing.

en pension [Fr.], in a boarding-house.

en plein jour [Fr.], in broad day.

en queue [Fr.], standing one behind another.

en rapport [Fr.], in harmony; in agreement.

en règle [Fr.], according to rules; in order.

en revanche [Fr.], in requital; in return.

en route [Fr.], on the way.

en suite [Fr.], in company; in a set.

entente cordiale [Fr.], cordial understanding, especially between two states.

entêté [Fr.], obstinate; self-willed.

entourage [Fr.], surroundings; adjuncts.

entr'acte [Fr.], the interval between the acts of a play.

entre deux feux [Fr.], between two fires.

entre deux vins [Fr.], between two wines; half-drunk.

entremets [Fr.], side dishes of dainties to be eaten between the serving of the joints.

entre nous [Fr.], between ourselves.

en vérité [Fr.], in truth; verily.

en vieillissant on devient plus fou et plus sage [Fr.], in growing old, men become more foolish and more wise.

eo animo [L.], with that mind or design.

eo nomine [L.], by that name.

epea pteroenta [Gr.], winged words.

Epicuri de grege porcus [L.], a swine from the herd of Epicurus; an Epicurean.

e pluribus unum [L.], one out of many; one composed of many.

epulis accumbere divum [L.], to sit down at the banquets of the gods.

e re nata [L.], according to the exigency.

errare humanum est [L.], to err is human.

esprit borné [Fr.], a narrow or contracted spirit.

esprit de corps [Fr.], the animating spirit of a collective body, as a regiment.

essayez [Fr.], try; make the attempt.

esse quam videri [L.], to be, rather than to seem.

est modus in rebus [L.], there is a method in all things.

esto quod esse videris [L.], be what you seem to be.

et cætera (or **et cetera**) [L.], and the rest.

et hoc genus omne [L.], and everything of the sort.

et id genus omne [L.], and everything of the kind.

et sequentes or **et sequentia** [L.], and those that follow.

et sic de cæteris [L.], and so of the rest.

et sic de similibus [L.], and so of the like.

et tu, Brute! [L.], thou also, Brutus!

eureka [Gr.], I have found it.

événement [Fr.], an event.

eventus stultorum magister [L.], fools must be taught by the result.

Ewigkeit [G.], eternity.

ex abrupto [L.], suddenly.

ex abundantia [L.], out of the abundance.

ex adverso [L.], on the opposite side; over against.

exæquo et bono [L.], agreeably to what is good and right.

ex animo [L.], heartily; sincerely.

ex auctoritate mihi commissa [L.], by virtue of the authority intrusted to me.

ex capite [L.], from the head; from memory.

ex cathedra [L.], from the chair or seat of authority; with high authority.

excelsior [L.], higher; that is, loftier or taller; not correctly used as an adverb.

exceptio probat regulam [L.], the exception proves (or tests) the rule.

exceptis excipiendis [L.], the due exceptions being made.

excerpta [L.], extracts.

ex concesso [L.], from what has been conceded or granted in argument.

ex curia [L.], out of court.

ex delicto [L.], from the crime.

ex dono [L.], by the gift.

exegi monumentum ære perennius [L.], I have reared a monument more lasting than brass.

exempla sunt odiosa [L.], examples are offensive.

exempli gratia [L.], by way of example.

ex facto jus oritur [L.], the law springs from the fact.

excitus acta probat [L.], the event justifies the deed.

ex mera gratia [L.], through mere favor.

ex mero motu [L.], from his own impulse; from his own free-will.

ex more [L.], according to custom.

ex necessitate rei [L.], from the necessity of the case.

ex nihilo nihil fit [L.], from, or out of, nothing, nothing comes; nothing produces nothing.

ex officio [L.], by virtue of office.

ex opere operato [L.], by outward acts.

ex pede Herculem [L.], from the foot (we recognize) a Hercules; we judge of the whole from the specimen.

experientia docet stultos [L.], experience instructs fools.

experimentum crucis [L.], the trial or experiment of the cross; an experiment of a most searching nature.

experto crede [L.], trust one who has had experience.

expertus metuit [L.], having experience, he fears it.

exposé [Fr.], statement; showing up.

ex post facto [L.], after the deed is done; retrospective.

expressis verbis [L.], in express terms.

ex professo [L.], professedly.

ex propriis [L.], from one's own resources.

ex quocunque capite [L.], for whatever reason.

ex tacito [L.], tacitly.

extinctus amabitur idem [L.], the same man when dead will be loved.

extrait [Fr.], extract.

extra muros [L.], beyond the walls.

ex ungue leonem [L.], from a claw (we may know) the lion.

ex uno disce omnes [L.], from one learn all; from this specimen judge of the rest.

ex usu [L.], by use.

ex vi termini [L.], by the force or meaning of the term or word.

ex voto [L.], according to one's prayer or vow.

F

faber suæ fortunæ [L.], the architect of his own fortune, a self-made man.

fâcheux [Fr.], vexatious; annoying; troublesome.

facies non omnibus una [L.], all have not the same face or features.

facile est inventis addere [L.], it is easy to add to things already invented.

facile princeps [L.], easily preëminent; indisputably the first; the admitted chief.

facilis descensus Averni [L.], the descent to the lower world is easy; the road to evil is easy.

facit indignatio versum [L.], indignation instigates the verse.

façon [Fr.], manner, style.

façon de parler [Fr.], manner of speaking.

facta non verba [L.], deeds not words.

fade [Fr.], insipid; tasteless.

fænum habet in cornu, longe fuge [L.], he has hay upon his horn (of old the sign of a dangerous bull), beware of him.

fæx populi [L.], the dregs of the people.

faire bonne mine [Fr.], to put a good face upon the matter.

faire l'homme d'importance [Fr.], to assume an air of importance.

faire mon devoir [Fr.], to do my duty.

faire sans dire [Fr.], to do, not to say; to act without ostentation.

fait accompli [Fr.], a thing already done.

falsi crimen [L.], the crime of forgery.

falsus in uno, falsus in omnibus [L.], false in one thing, false in all.

fama clamosa [L.], a current scandal; a prevailing report.

fama nihil est celerius [L.], nothing travels swifter than scandal.

fama semper vivat [L.], may his fame endure forever.

far niente [It.], the doing of nothing.

fas est et ab hoste doceri [L.], it is right to be taught even by an enemy.

Fata obstant [L.], the Fates oppose it.

Fata viam invenient [L.], the Fates will find a way.

faux pas [Fr.], a false step; a slip in behavior; a lapse from virtue.

fax mentis incendium gloriæ [L.], the passion for glory is the torch of the mind.

felicitas multos habet amicos [L.], prosperity has many friends.

femme couverte [Fr.], a married woman.

femme de chambre [Fr.], a chambermaid.

femme galante [Fr.], a gay woman; a courtesan.

femme seule (as a law term, **femme sole**) [Fr.], an unmarried woman.

fendre un cheveu en quatre [Fr.], to split a hair in four; to make a very subtle distinction.

festina lente [L.], hasten slowly.

fête champêtre [Fr.], an open-air festival or entertainment; a rural festival.

feu de joie [Fr.], a fire of joy; a bonfire; a fusillade as a sign of rejoicing.

feuilleton [Fr.], a fly-sheet; a novel or a story appearing in a newspaper.

fiat experimentum in corpore vili [L.], let the trial (or experiment) be made on a worthless subject.

fiat justitia, ruat cælum [L.], let justice be done though the heavens should fall.

fiat lux [L.], let there be light.

fide et amore [L.], by faith and love.

fide et fiducia [L.], by fidelity and confidence.

fide et fortitudine [L.], with faith and fortitude.

fidei coticula crux [L.], the cross is the touchstone of faith.

fidei defensor [L.], defender of the faith.

fideli certa merces [L.], to the faithful one reward is certain.

fide non armis [L.], by faith, not by arms.

fide, sed cui vide [L.], trust, but see whom.

fides et justitia [L.], fidelity and justice.

fides Punica [L.], Punic faith; treachery.

fidus Achates [L.], faithful Achates; i.e. a true friend.

fidus et audax [L.], faithful and bold.

filius nullius [L.], a son of nobody.

filius populi [L.], a son of the people.

filius terræ [L], a son of the earth; one of low birth.

fille de chambre [Fr.], a chambermaid.

fille de joie [Fr.], a woman of licentious pleasure; a prostitute.

fille d'honneur [Fr.], a maid of honor.

fin de siècle [Fr.], end of the (nineteenth) century.

finem respice [L.], look to the end.

finis coronat opus [L.], the end crowns the work.

flagrante bello [L.], during hostilities.

flagrante delicto [L.], in the actual commission of the crime.

flamma fumo est proxima [L.], flame is akin to smoke; where there is smoke there is fire.

flâneur [Fr.], a lounger.

flecti, non frangi [L.], to be bent, not broken.

flosculi sententiarum [L.], flowers of fine thoughts.

flux de bouche [Fr.], an inordinate flow of words; garrulity.

foi en tout [Fr.], faith in everything.

foi pour devoir [Fr.], faith for duty.

fons et origo [L.], the source and origin.

forensis strepitus [L.], the clamor of the forum.

forte scutum salus ducum [L.], a strong shield is the safety of leaders.

fortes fortuna juvat [L.], fortune helps the brave.

forti et fideli nihil difficile [L.], nothing is difficult to the brave and faithful.

fortiter et recte [L.], with fortitude and rectitude.

fortiter, fideliter, feliciter [L.], boldly, faithfully, successfully.

fortiter in re [L.], with firmness or resolution in acting.

fortunæ filius [L.], a spoiled child of fortune.

fortuna favet fortibus [L.], fortune favors the bold.

frangas, non flectes [L.], you may break but not bend (me).

fraus pia [L.], a pious fraud.

fripon [Fr.], a rogue; a knave; a cheat.

froides mains, chaud amour [Fr.], cold hands, warm heart.

front à front [Fr.], face to face.

fronti nulla fides [L.], there is no trusting to appearances.

fruges consumere nati [L.], born to consume fruits; born only to eat.

fugit irreparabile tempus [L.], irrecoverable time flies on.

fuimus Troes [L.], we were once Trojans (but Troy has been overthrown).

fuit Ilium [L.], Troy has been (but is now no more).

fulmen brutum [L.], a senseless thunderbolt; striking blindly.

fumum et opes, strepitumque Romæ [L.], the smoke, the show, and the noise of Rome.

functus officio [L.], having performed one's office or duty; hence, out of office.

furor arma ministrat [L.], rage provides arms.

furor loquendi [L.], a rage for speaking.

furor poeticus [L.], poetic fire.

furor scribendi [L.], a rage for writing.

fuyez les dangers de loisir [Fr.], avoid the dangers of leisure.

G

gage d'amour [Fr.], a pledge of love.

gaieté de cœur [Fr.], gaiety of heart.

Gallice [L.], in French.

garçon [Fr.], a boy; a waiter.

garde à cheval [Fr.], a mounted guard.

garde du corps [Fr.], a body-guard.

garde mobile [Fr.], a guard liable to general service.

gardez [Fr.], be on your guard; take care.

gardez bien [Fr.], take good care.

garde la foi [Fr.], keep the faith.

gaudeamus igitur [L.], therefore let us be joyful.

gaudet tentamine virtus [L.], virtue rejoices in temptation.

gaudium certaminis [L.], the joy of conflict.

genius loci [L.], the presiding spirit or genius of the place.

gens d'armes [Fr.], men at arms.

gens de condition [Fr.], people of standing.

gens d'église [Fr.], churchmen.

gens de guerre [Fr.], military men.

gens de lettres [Fr.], literary men.

gens de loi [Fr.], lawyers.

gens de même famille [Fr.], persons of the same family; birds of a feather.

gens de peu [Fr.], the meaner class of people.

gens togata [L.], civilians.

gentilhomme [Fr.], a gentleman.

genus irritabile vatum [L.], the irritable race of poets.

Germanice [L.], in German.

gibier de potence [Fr.], a gallowsbird.

giovine santo, diavolo vecchio [It.], a young saint, an old devil.

gitano [Sp.], a gypsy.

gli assenti hanno torto [It.], the absent are in the wrong.

gloria in excelsis [L.], glory to God in the highest.

gloria Patri [L.], glory be to the Father.

glückliche Reise! [G.], a pleasant journey!

gnothi seauton [Gr.], know thyself.

gobe-mouche [Fr.], a person who has no ideas of his own; a ninny; a trifler.

goût [Fr.], taste; relish.

goutte à goutte [Fr.], drop by drop.

grâce à Dieu [Fr.], thanks to God.

gradu diverso, via una [L.], the same road by different steps.

gradus ad Parnassum [L.], a step to Parnassus; aid in writing Greek or Latin verse.

grande chère et beau feu [Fr.], good cheer and a good fire; comfortable quarters.

grande fortune, grande servitude [Fr.], a great fortune is a great slavery.

grande parure ⎫ [Fr.], full
grande toilette ⎭   dress.

grand merci [Fr.], many thanks.

gratia placendi [L.], the delight of pleasing.

gratis dictum [L.], mere assertion.

graviora manent [L.], greater afflictions await us, more serious matters remain.

graviora quædam sunt remedia periculis [L.], some remedies are worse than the disease.

grex venalium [L.], a venal rabble.

grosse tête et peu de sens [Fr.], a large head and little sense.

grossièreté [Fr.], coarseness; vulgarity in conversation.

guerra al cuchillo [Sp.], war to the knife.

guerra cominciata, inferno scatenato [It.], war begun, hell unchained.

guerre à mort [Fr.], war to the death.

guerre à outrance [Fr.], war to the uttermost.

gutta cavat lapidem non vi, sed sæpe cadendo [L.], the drop hollows the stone by frequent falling, not by force.

H

habitué [Fr.], one who is in the habit of frequenting a place.

hac lege [L.], on this condition; with this restriction.

hæc olim meminisse juvabit [L.], it will delight us to remember this some day.

Hannibal ad portas [L.], Hannibal before the gates; the enemy close at hand.

hapax legomenon [Gr.], a word or expression occurring once only.

hardi comme un coq sur son fumier [Fr.], bold as a cock on his own dunghill.

haud longis intervallis [L.], at intervals of no great length.

haud passibus æquis [L.], not with equal steps.

haut goût [Fr.], high flavor; elegant taste.

helluo librorum [L.], a devourer of books; a bookworm.

heu pietas! heu prisca fides! [L.], alas for piety! alas for the ancient faith!

hiatus valde deflendus [L.], a hiatus or deficiency much to be regretted.

hic et nunc [L.], here and now.

hic et ubique [L.], here and everywhere.

hic jacet [L.], here lies.

hic labor, hoc opus est [L.], this is a laborious task; this is a toil.

hic sepultus [L.], here buried.

hinc illæ lacrimæ [L.], hence these tears.

hoc opus, hic labor est [L.], same as **hic labor, hoc opus est.**

hodie mihi, cras tibi [L.], mine today, yours tomorrow.

hoi polloi [Gr.], the many; the vulgar; the rabble.

hombre de un libro [Sp.], a man of one book.

hominis est errare [L.], to err is human.

homme d'affaires [Fr.], a businessman.

homme de bien [Fr.], a good man.

homme de lettres [Fr.], a man of letters.

homme d'épée [Fr.], a man of the sword; a soldier.

homme de robe [Fr.], a man in civil office; magistrate.

homme d'esprit [Fr.], a man of wit or genius.

homme d'état [Fr.], a statesman.

homo factus ad unguem [L.], a highly polished man; one finished to the highest degree.

homo homini lupus [L.], man is a wolf to man.

homo multarum litterarum [L.], a man of great learning.

homo sui juris [L.], a man who is his own master.

homo sum; humani nihil a me alienum puto [L.], I am a man; I count nothing that is human indifferent to me.

honi soit qui mal y pense [O. Fr.], shame to him who thinks evil of it; evil to him who evil thinks.

honores mutant mores [L.], honors change men's manners or characters.

honos habet onus [L.], honor brings responsibility.

horæ canonicæ [L.], prescribed hours for prayer; canonical hours.

horas non numero nisi serenas [L.], I number only hours of sunshine. (Motto for a sun dial.)

horresco referens [L.], I shudder as I relate.

horribile dictu [L.], horrible to relate.

hors de combat [Fr.], rendered unable any longer to fight.

hors de concours [Fr.], out of the competition.

hors de la loi [Fr.], in the condition of an outlaw.

hors de propos [Fr.], not to the point or purpose.

hors de saison [Fr.], out of season.

hors d'œuvre [Fr.], out of course; out of order.

hos ego versiculos feci, tulit alter honores [L.], I wrote these lines, another has borne away the honor.

hôtel de ville [Fr.], a townhall; municipal building of a town.

hôtel Dieu [Fr.], a hospital.

hôtel garni [Fr.], a furnished lodging.

humanum est errare [L.], to err is human.

hunc tu Romane caveto [L.], Roman, beware of that man.

hurtar para dar por Dios [Sp.], to steal for the purpose of giving to God (in alms).

I

ich dien [G.], I serve.

ici on parle Français [Fr.], French is spoken here.

idée fixe [Fr.], a fixed idea.

id genus omne [L.], all of that sort or description.

ignorantia legis neminem excusat [L.], ignorance of the law excuses no one.

ignoratio elenchi [L.], ignorance of the point in question; the logical fallacy of arguing to the wrong point.

ignoscito sæpe alteri, nunquam tibi [L.], forgive others often, yourself never.

ignoti nulla cupido [L.], no desire is felt for a thing unknown.

ignotum per ignotius [L.], the unknown (explained) by the still more unknown.

i gran dolori sono muti [It.], great griefs are silent.

il aboie après tout le monde [Fr.], he snarls at everybody.

il a la mer à boire [Fr.], he has the sea to drink up; i.e. all his powers will be taxed to succeed.

il a le diable au corps [Fr.], the devil is in him.

il conduit bien sa barque [Fr.], he steers his boat well; he knows how to get on.

il est plus aisé d'être sage pour les autres, que pour soi-même [Fr.], it is easier to be wise for others than for oneself.

il est plus honteux de se défier de ses amis, que d'en être trompé [Fr.], it is more disgraceful to suspect one's friends than to be deceived by them.

il faut attendre le boiteux [Fr.], it is necessary to wait for the lame man; we must wait for the truth.

il faut de l'argent [Fr.], money is needful.

Ilias malorum [L.], an Iliad of ills; a host of evils.

il n'a ni bouche ni éperon [Fr.], he has neither mouth nor spur; neither wit nor courage.

il n'appartient qu'aux grands hommes d'avoir de grands défauts [Fr.], only great men may have great faults.

il ne faut jamais défier un fou [Fr.], never defy a fool.

il ne faut pas éveiller le chat qui dort [Fr.], it is not wise to awake the cat that sleeps; let sleeping dogs lie.

il n'y a pas de héros pour son valet de chambre [Fr.], no man is a hero in the eyes of his valet.

il penseroso [It.], the pensive man.

il rit bien qui rit le dernier [Fr.], he laughs best who laughs last.

il sent le fagot [Fr.], he smells of the faggot; he is suspected of heresy.

il vaut mieux tâcher d'oublier ses malheurs, que d'en parler [Fr.], it is better to try to forget one's misfortunes, than to talk of them.

imitatores, servum pecus [L.], imitators, a servile herd.

immedicabile vulnus [L.], an incurable wound; irreparable injury.

imo pectore [L.], from the bottom of the breast.

impari Marte [L.], with unequal military strength.

impedimenta [L.], travelers' luggage; the baggage of an army.

imperium in imperio [L.], a state within a state, a government within another.

implicite [Fr.], by implication.

impos animi [L.], of weak mind.

in actu [L.], in act or reality.

in æternum [L.], forever.

in ambiguo [L.], in doubt.

in articulo mortis [L.], at the point of death; in the last struggle.

in bianco [It.], in blank; in white.

in camera [L.], in the chamber of the judge; in secret.

in capite [L.], in chief.

in cælo quies [L.], there is rest in heaven.

incredulus odi [L.], being incredulous I cannot endure it.

in curia [L.], in court.

inde iræ [L.], hence these resentments.

Index Expurgatorius [L.], a list of expurgated books (compiled by the Roman Catholic authorities).

Index Prohibitorius [L.], a list of prohibited books (prohibited to Roman Catholics).

in dubio [L.], in doubt.

in equilibrio [L.], in equilibrium; equally balanced.

in esse [L.], in being; in actuality.

in extenso [L.], at full length.

in extremis [L.], at the point of death.

infandum renovare dolorem [L.], to revive unspeakable grief.

in forma pauperis [L.], as a poor man or pauper.

in foro conscientiæ [L.], before the tribunal of conscience.

infra dignitatem [L.], below one's dignity.

in futuro [L.], in future; henceforth.

in hoc signo spes mea [L.], in this sign is my hope.

in hoc signo vinces [L.], under this sign or standard thou shalt conquer.

in limine [L.], at the threshold.

in loco [L.], in the place; in the passage mentioned; in the natural or proper place.

in loco parentis [L.], in the place of a parent.

in medias res [L.], into the midst of things.

in medio tutissimus ibis [L.], you will go safest in a middle course.

in memoriam [L.], to the memory of; in memory.

in necessariis unitas, in dubiis libertas, in omnibus caritas [L.], in things essential unity, in things doubtful liberty, in all things charity.

in nomine [L.], in the name of.

in nubibus [L.], in the clouds.

in nuce [L.], in a nutshell.

in omnia paratus [L.], prepared for all things.

inopem copia fecit [L.], abundance made him poor.

in ovo [L.], in the egg.

in pace [L.], in peace.

in partibus infidelium [L.], in parts belonging to infidels, or countries not adhering to the Roman Catholic faith.

in perpetuam rei memoriam [L.], in perpetual memory of the thing.

in perpetuum [L.], forever.

in petto [It.], within the breast; in reserve.

in pleno [L.], in full.

in posse [L.], in possible existence; in possibility.

in præsenti [L.], at the present moment.

in propria persona [L.], in one's own person.

in puris naturalibus [L.], purely in a state of nature; quite naked.

in re [L.], in the matter of.

in rerum natura [L.], in the nature of things.

in sæcula sæculorum [L.], for ages on ages.

in sano sensu [L.], in a proper sense.

in situ [L.], in its original situation.

in solo Deo salus [L.], in God alone is safety.

insouciance [Fr.], unconcern; careless indifference.

insouciant [Fr.], unconcerned; indifferent.

instar omnium [L.], equivalent to them all.

in statu quo [L.], in the former state; in the same state as before (some event).

in te, Domine, speravi [L.], in thee, Lord, have I put my trust.

inter alia [L.], among other things.

inter arma silent leges [L.], laws are silent in the midst of arms.

inter canem et lupum [L.], between dog and wolf; at twilight.

interdum vulgus rectum videt [L.], the rabble sometimes see what is right.

inter nos [L.], between ourselves.

inter pocula [L.], at one's cups.

in terrorem [L.], as a means of terrifying; by way of warning.

inter se [L.], among themselves.

inter spem et metum [L.], between hope and fear.

in totidem verbis [L.], in so many words.

in toto [L.], in whole; entirely.

intra muros [L.], within the walls.

in transitu [L.], in course of transit or passage.

intra parietes [L.], within walls; in private.

in usum Delphini [L.], for the use of the Dauphin; applied to editions of the classical authors.

in utramque fortunam paratus [L.], prepared for either fortune (or result).

in utroque fidelis [L.], faithful in both or each (of two).

in vacuo [L.], in empty space; in a vacuum.

inverso ordine [L.], in an inverse order.

in vino veritas [L.], there is truth in wine; truth is told under the influence of intoxicants.

invita Minerva [L.], against the will of Minerva; at variance with one's mental capacity; without genius.

ipse dixit [L.], he himself said it; a dogmatic saying or assertion.

ipsissima verba [L.], the very words.

ipso facto [L.], by the fact itself.

ipso jure [L.], by the law itself.

ira furor brevis est [L.], anger is a short madness.

ir por lana y volver trasquilado [Sp.], to go for wool, and come back shorn.

ita est [L.], it is so.

ita lex scripta [L.], thus the law stands written.

Italice [L.], in the Italian language.

J–K

Jacquerie [Fr.], French peasantry; a revolt of peasants.

jacta est alea [L.], the die is cast.

j'ai bonne cause [Fr.], I have a good cause.

jamais arrière [Fr.], never behind.

jamais bon coureur ne fut pris [Fr.], a good runner is never caught; an old bird is not to be caught with chaff.

januis clausis [L.], with closed doors.

je maintiendrai le droit [Fr.], I will maintain the right.

je me fie en Dieu [Fr.], I trust in God.

je ne sais quoi [Fr.], I know not what; a something or other.

je n'oublierai jamais [Fr.], I shall never forget.

je suis prêt [Fr.], I am ready.

jet d'eau [Fr.], a jet of water; a fountain.

jeu de main [Fr.], horseplay, practical joke.

jeu de mots [Fr.], a play on words; a pun.

jeu d'esprit [Fr.], a display of wit; a witticism.

jeu de théâtre [Fr.], stage-trick; clap-trap.

jeunesse dorée [Fr.], gilded youth; rich young fellows.

je vis en espoir [Fr.], I live in hope.

joci causa [L.], for the sake of a joke.

joli [Fr.], pretty; fine.

jour de fête [Fr.], a feast day.

jour de l'an [Fr.], New Year's day.

jubilate Deo [L.], rejoice in God; be joyful in the Lord.

jucundi acti labores [L.], accomplished labors are pleasant.

judex damnatur cum nocens absolvitur [L.], the judge is condemned when the offender is acquitted.

judicium Dei [L.], the judgment of God.

judicium parium, aut leges terræ [L.], the judgment of our peers or the laws of the land.

juge de paix [Fr.], a justice of peace.

juniores ad labores [L.], the younger men (are fittest) for labors.

jurare in verba magistri [L.], to swear to the words of a master.

jure divino [L.], by divine law.

jure humano [L.], by human law.

juris peritus [L.], skilled in the law; one who is learned in the law.

juris utriusque doctor [L.], doctor of both the civil and canon law.

jus canonicum [L.], the canon law.

jus civile [L.], the civil law.

jus divinum [L.], the divine law.

jus et norma loquendi [L.], the law and rule of speech.

jus gentium [L.], the law of nations.

jus gladii [L.], the right of the sword.

jus possessionis [L.], right of possession.

jus proprietatis [L.], the right of property.

jus summum sæpe summa malitia est [L.], law carried to extremes is often extreme wrong.

juste milieu [Fr.], the golden mean.

justum et tenacem propositi virum [L.], a man upright and tenacious of purpose.

kein Kreuzer, kein Schweizer [G.], no money no Swiss; a proverb of the time when the Swiss were common as mercenaries.

ktema es aei [Gr.], a possession for all time.

L

la beauté sans vertu est une fleur sans parfum [Fr.], beauty without virtue is like a flower without perfume.

labitur et labetur in omne volubilis ævum [L.], it glides on, and will glide on forever. See Rusticus expectat.

laborare est orare [L.], to work is to pray.

laborare et honore [L.], by labor and honor.

labor ipse voluptas [L.], labor itself is a pleasure.

labor omnia vincit [L.], labor conquers everything.

laborum dulce lenimen [L.], the sweet solace of our labors.

la bride sur le cou [Fr.], with rein on neck; at full speed.

la critique est aisée, et l'art est difficile [Fr.], criticism is easy, and art is difficult.

l'affaire s'achemine [Fr.], the business is progressing.

la fortune passe partout [Fr.], fortune passes everywhere; all suffer change or vicissitude.

l'allegro [It.], the merry man.

l'amour et la fumée ne peuvent se cacher [Fr.], love and smoke cannot conceal themselves.

lana caprina [L.], goat's wool; hence, a thing of little worth.

langage des halles [Fr.], the language of the markets, profane or foul.

la patience est amère, mais son fruit est doux [Fr.], patience is bitter, but its fruit is sweet.

lapis philosophorum [L.], the philosophers' stone.

la poverta è la madre di tutte le arti [It.], poverty is the mother of all the arts.

la propriété c'est le vol [Fr.], property is robbery.

lapsus calami [L.], a slip of the pen.

lapsus linguæ [L.], a slip of the tongue.

lapsus memoriæ [L.], a slip of the memory.

lares et penates [L.], household gods.

la reyne (or **le roy**) **le veult** [Norm. Fr.], the queen (or the king) wills it; the formula expressing the sovereign's assent to a bill.

l'argent [Fr.], money.

lasciate ogni speranza, voi ch'entrate [It.], abandon hope all ye who enter here.

lateat scintilla forsan [L.], perhaps a small spark may lie hid.

latet anguis in herba [L.], a snake lies hid in the grass.

Latine dictum [L.], spoken in Latin.

lauda la moglie e tienti donzello [It.], praise a wife and remain a bachelor.

laudari a viro laudato [L.], praised by one who is himself praised.

laudationes eorum qui sunt ab Homero laudati [L.], praises from those who were themselves praised by Homer.

laudator temporis acti [L.], one who praises time past.

laudum immensa cupido [L.], insatiable desire for praise.

laus Deo [L.], praise to God.

l'avenir [Fr.], the future.

la vertu est la seule noblesse [Fr.], virtue is the only nobility.

le beau monde [Fr.], the fashionable world.

le bon temps viendra [Fr.], the good time will come.

le coût ôte le goût [Fr.], the cost takes away the taste.

lector benevole [L.], kind or gentle reader.

le dessous des cartes [Fr.], the underside of the cards.

le diable boiteux [Fr.], the devil on two sticks or with crutches.

legalis homo [L.], a lawful person, i.e. one not outlawed, infamous, or excommunicated.

legatus a latere [L.], a papal ambassador.

le génie c'est la patience [Fr.], genius is patience.

le grand monarque [Fr.], the great monarch; a name applied to Louis XIV of France.

le grand œuvre [Fr.], the great work; the philosophers' stone.

le jeu ne vaut pas la chandelle [Fr.], the game is not worth the candle; the object is not worth the trouble.

le jour viendra [Fr.], the day will come.

le mieux est l'ennemi du bien [Fr.], the better is the enemy of the good.

le monde est le livre des femmes [Fr.], the world is woman's book.

le monde savant [Fr.], the learned world.

le mot de l'énigme [Fr.], the key to the mystery.

l'empire des lettres [Fr.], the republic (lit. empire) of letters.

leonina societas [L.], partnership with a lion.

le pas [Fr.], precedence in place or rank.

le point du jour [Fr.], daybreak.

le roi est mort, vive le roi! [Fr.], the king is dead, long live the king (his successor)!

le roi et l'état [Fr.], the king and the state.

le roi le veut [Fr.], the king wills it.

le roi s'avisera [Fr.], the king will consider or deliberate.

les absents ont toujours tort [Fr.], the absent are always in the wrong.

les affaires font les hommes [Fr.], business makes men.

les bras croisés [Fr.], with folded arms; idle.

les doux yeux [Fr.], tender glances.

lèse majesté [Fr.], high treason.

les extrêmes se touchent [Fr.], extremes meet.

les murailles ont des oreilles [Fr.], walls have ears.

les plus sages ne le sont pas toujours [Fr.], the wisest are not so always.

le style, c'est l'homme [Fr.], the style is the man.

l'état, c'est moi [Fr.], it is I who am the state.

l'étoile du nord [Fr.], the star of the north.

le tout ensemble [Fr.], the whole together.

lettre de cachet [Fr.], a sealed letter containing private orders; a royal warrant.

lettre de change [Fr.], bill of exchange.

lettre de créance [Fr.], letter of credit.

lettre de marque [Fr.], a letter of marque or reprisal.

levamen probationis [L.], relief from proving.

leve fit quod bene fertur onus [L.], the burden which is well borne becomes light.

le vrai n'est pas toujours vraisemblable [Fr.], the truth is not always probable; truth is stranger than fiction.

lex loci [L.], the law or custom of the place.

lex non scripta [L.], unwritten law; common law.

lex scripta [L.], statute (or written) law.

lex talionis [L.], the law of retaliation.

lex terræ [L.], the law of the land.

l'homme propose, et Dieu dispose [Fr.], man proposes, and God disposes.

libertas et natale solum [L.], liberty and one's native land.

liberum arbitrium [L.], free will.

libraire [Fr.], a bookseller.

licentia vatum [L.], the license of the poets; poetic license.

limæ labor et mora [L.], the labor and delay of the file; the slow and laborious polishing of a literary composition.

l'inconnu [Fr.], the unknown.

l'incroyable [Fr.], the incredible.

lingua franca [It.], the mixed language used between Europeans and Orientals in the Levant.

lis litem generat [L.], strife begets strife.

lit de justice [Fr.], a bed of justice; the throne of the king in the parliament of Paris; the sitting of that parliament when the king was present.

litem lite resolvere [L.], to settle strife by strife, to remove one difficulty by introducing another.

lite pendente [L.], during the trial.

littera scripta manet [L.], the written letter remains.

l'occasion fait le larron [Fr.], opportunity makes the thief.

loci communes [L.], common places.

loco citato [L.], in the place or passage cited.

locos y niños dicen la verdad [Sp.], fools and children speak the truth.

locum tenens [L.], one occupying the place of another; a substitute.

locus classicus [L.], a classical passage.

locus criminis [L.], place of the crime.

locus in quo [L.], the place in which.

locus pænitentiæ [L.], place for repentance.

locus sigilli [L.], the place of the seal on a document.

longe aberrat scopo [L.], he goes far from the mark.

longo intervallo [L.], by or with a long interval.

loyal devoir [Fr.], loyal duty.

loyal en tout [Fr.], loyal in everything.

loyauté m'oblige [Fr.], loyalty binds me.

loyauté n'a honte [Fr.], loyalty has no shame.

lucidus ordo [L.], a lucid arrangement.

lucri causa [L.], for the sake of gain.

lucus a non lucendo [L.], used as typical of an absurd derivation or explanation— **lucus**, meaning *grove*, is wrongly implied to be another form of **lucere**, meaning to *shine*.

ludere cum sacris [L.], to trifle with sacred things.

lupum auribus teneo [L.], I hold a wolf by the ears, i.e. I have caught a tartar.

lupus in fabula [L.], the wolf in the fable.

lupus pilum mutat, non mentem [L.], the wolf changes his coat, not his disposition.

lusus naturæ [L.], a sport or freak of nature.

M

ma chère [Fr.], my dear (fem.).

macte virtute [L.], go on or persevere in virtue.

ma foi [Fr.], upon my faith.

maggiore fretta, minore atto [It.], the more haste the less speed.

magister cæremoniarum [L.], master of the ceremonies.

magna civitas, magna solitudo [L.], a great city is a great solitude.

magnæ spes altera Romæ [L.], another hope of great Rome.

magna est veritas et prevalebit [L.], truth is mighty and will prevail.

magna est vis consuetudinis [L.], great is the force of habit.

magnanimiter crucem sustine [L.], bear the cross nobly.

magnas inter opes inops [L.], poor in the midst of great wealth.

magni nominis umbra [L.], the shadow of a great name.

magnum bonum [L.], a great good.

magnum vectigal est parsimonia [L.], economy is itself a great income.

magnum opus [L.], a great work.

magnus Apollo [L.], great Apollo, i.e. one of great authority.

maigre [Fr.], fasting. See in Dict.

main de justice [Fr.], the hand of justice; the sceptre.

maintien le droit [Fr.], maintain the right.

maison de campagne [Fr.], a country house.

maison de santé [Fr.], a private asylum or hospital.

maison de ville [Fr.], a town-house.

maître des basses œuvres [Fr.], literally, "master of low works"; i.e. a sewer-cleaner.

maître des hautes œuvres [Fr.], an executioner; a hangman.

maître d'hôtel [Fr.], a house-steward.

maladie du pays [Fr.], home-sickness.

mala fide [Fr.], with bad faith; treacherously.

mal à propos [Fr.], ill-timed. See in Dict.

mal de dents [Fr.], toothache.

mal de mer [Fr.], sea-sickness.

mal de tête [Fr.], headache.

malentendu [Fr.], a misunderstanding; a mistake.

male parta, male dilabuntur [L.], things ill gotten are consumed without doing any good.

malgré nous [Fr.], in spite of us.

malgré soi [Fr.], in spite of himself.

malheur ne vient jamais seul [Fr.], misfortunes never come singly.

mali exempli [L.], of a bad example.

mali principii malus finis [L.], bad beginnings have bad endings.

malis avibus [L.], with unlucky birds; with bad omens.

malo modo [L.], in a bad manner.

malo mori quam fœdari [L.], I would rather die than be debased.

malpropre [Fr.], slovenly; not neat and clean.

malum in se [L.], evil or an evil in itself.

malum prohibitum [L.], an evil prohibited; evil because prohibited.

malus pudor [L.], false shame.

manet alta mente repostum [L.], it remains deeply fixed in the mind.

manibus pedibusque [L.], with hands and feet.

manu forti [L.], with a strong hand.

manu propria [L.], with one's own hand.

Mardi gras [Fr.], Shrove Tuesday.

mare clausum [L.], a closed sea; a bay.

mariage de conscience [Fr.], a private marriage.

mariage de convenance [Fr.], marriage from motives of material interest rather than of love.

mariage de la main gauche [Fr.], left-handed marriage; a morganatic marriage.

Mars gravior sub pace latet [L.], a severer war lies hidden under peace.

más vale saber que haber [Sp.], better to be wise than to be rich.

más vale ser necio que porfiado [Sp.], better to be a fool than obstinate.

más vale tarde que nunca [Sp.], better late than never.

materfamilias [L.], the mother of a family.

materiam superabit opus [L.], the workmanship will prove superior to the material.

matre pulchra filia pulchrior [L.], a daughter more beautiful than her beautiful mother.

mauvaise honte [Fr.], false modesty.

mauvais goût [Fr.], bad taste.

mauvais sujet [Fr.], a bad subject; a worthless scamp.

maxima debetur puero reverentia [L.], the greatest reverence is due to a boy.

maximus in minimis [L.], very great in trifles.

mea culpa [L.], by my fault.

médecin, guéris-toi toi-même [Fr.], physician, heal thyself.

mediocria firma [L.], moderate or middle things are surest.

medio tutissimus ibis [L.], in a medium course you will be safest.

medium tenuere beati [L.], happy are they who have held the middle course.

mega biblion, mega kakon [Gr.], a great book is a great evil.

me judice [L.], I being judge; in my opinion.

memento mori [L.], remember death.

memor et fidelis [L.], mindful and faithful.

memoria in æterna [L.], in eternal remembrance.

mendacem memorem esse oportet [L.], a liar should have a good memory.

mens agitat molem [L.], mind moves matter.

mens legis [L.], the spirit of the law.

mens sana in corpore sano [L.], a sound mind in a sound body.

mens sibi conscia recti [L.], a mind conscious of its own rectitude.

meo periculo [L.], at my own risk.

meo voto [L.], according to my wish.

merum sal [L.], pure or genuine wit.

mésalliance [Fr.], marriage with one of a lower rank.

meum et tuum [L.], mine and thine.

mihi cura futuri [L.], my care is for the future.

mirabile dictu [L.], wonderful to relate.

mirabile visu [L.], wonderful to see.

mirabilia [L.], wonders.

mirum in modum [L.], in a wonderful manner.

mise en scène [Fr.], the getting up for the stage, or the putting on the stage.

miserabile vulgus [L.], a wretched crew.

miseris succurere disco [L.], I learn to succor the wretched.

mittimus [L.], we send; name of a writ in law. See in Dict.

mobile perpetuum [L.], perpetual motion.

modo et forma [L.], in manner and form.

modus operandi [L.], manner of working.

mole ruit sua [L.], it falls in ruins by its own weight.

mollia tempora fandi [L.], times favorable for speaking.

mon ami [Fr.], my friend.

mon cher [Fr.], my dear (masc.).

montani semper liberi [L.], mountaineers are always free men.

monumentum ære perennius [L.], a monument more lasting than brass.

more Hibernico [L.], after the Irish fashion.

more majorum [L.], after the manner of our ancestors.

more suo [L.], in his own way.

mors janua vitæ [L.], death is the gate of eternal life.

mors omnibus communis [L.], death is common to all.

mos pro lege [L.], custom or usage for law.

mot du guet [Fr.], a watchword.

mots d'usage [Fr.], words in common use.

motu proprio [L.], of his own accord.

mucho en el suelo, poco en el cielo [Sp.], much on earth, little in heaven.

muet comme un poisson [Fr.], dumb as a fish.

multa gemens [L.], with many a groan.

multum in parvo [L.], much in little.

mundus vult decipi [L.], the world wishes to be deceived.

munus Apolline dignum [L.], a gift worthy of Apollo.

muraglia bianca, carta di matto [It.], a white wall is the fool's paper.

murus aeneus conscientia sana [L.], a clear conscience is a firm wall.

mutare vel timere sperno [L.], I scorn to change or to fear.

mutatis mutandis [L.], with the necessary changes.

mutato nomine de te fabula narratur [L.], the name being changed the story is true of yourself.

muta est pictura poema [L.], a picture is a silent poem.

mutuus consensus [L.], mutual consent.

N

naissance [Fr.], birth.

natale solum [L.], native soil.

natura lo fece, e poi ruppe la stampa [It.], nature made him, and then broke the mould.

naturam expellas furca tamen usque recurret [L.], though you drive out Nature with a pitchfork, yet will she ever return.

natura non facit saltum [L.], nature does not make a leap; i.e. nature proceeds slowly.

naviget Anticyram [L.], let him sail to Anticyra (where he will get hellebore to cure him of madness).

nec cupias, nec metuas [L.], neither desire nor fear.

ne cede malis [L.], yield not to misfortune.

necessitas non habet legem [L.], necessity has no law.

nec mora, nec requies [L.], neither delay nor repose.

nec pluribus impar [L.], not an unequal match for numbers.

nec prece, nec pretio [L.], neither by entreaty nor by bribe.

nec quærere, nec spernere honorem [L.], neither to seek nor to contemn honors.

nec scire fas est omnia [L.], it is not permitted to know all things.

nec temere, nec timide [L.], neither rashly nor timidly.

née [Fr.], born; having as her maiden name.

nefasti dies [L.], days on which judgment could not be pronounced, nor assemblies of the people be held; hence, unlucky days.

ne fronti crede [L.], trust not to appearances.

négligé [Fr.], morning dress; an easy loose dress.

ne Jupiter quidem omnibus placet [L.], not even Jupiter pleases everybody.

nel bisogno si conoscono gli amici [It.], a friend in need is a friend indeed.

nemine contradicente [L.], no one speaking in opposition; without opposition.

nemine dissentiente [L.], no one dissenting; without a dissenting voice.

nemo bis punitur pro eodem delicto [L.], no one is twice punished for the same offence.

nemo me impune lacessit [L.], no one assails me with impunity.

nemo mortalium omnibus horis sapit [L.], no one is wise at all times.

nemo repente fuit turpissimus [L.], no one ever became a villain in an instant.

nemo solus sapit [L.], no one is wise alone (with no person to consult).

ne nimium [L.], avoid excess.

ne plus ultra [L.], nothing further; the uttermost point, perfection.

ne puero gladium [L.], intrust not a boy with a sword.

ne quid detrimenti respublica capiat [L.], lest the state receive any detriment.

ne quid nimis [L.], in nothing go too far.

nervi belli pecunia [L.], money is the sinews of war.

nervus probandi [L.], the sinews of the argument.

n'est-ce pas? [Fr.], is it not so?

ne sutor supra crepidam [L.], let not the shoemaker go beyond his last (properly sandal); let no one meddle with what lies beyond his range.

ne tentes, aut perfice [L.], either attempt it not or succeed.

netteté [Fr.], neatness.

ne vile fano [L.], let nothing vile be in the temple.

niaiserie [Fr.], silliness; simplicity.

nicht wahr? [G.], is it not so? am I not right?

ni firmes carta que no leas, ni bebas agua que no veas [Sp.], never sign a paper you have not read, nor drink water you have not examined.

nihil ad rem [L.], nothing to the point.

nihil (properly **nullum**) **quod tetigit non ornavit** [L.], he touched nothing without embellishing it.

nil admirari [L.], to be astonished at nothing.

nil conscire sibi nulla pallescere culpa [L.], to be conscious of no fault, and to turn pale at no accusation.

nil desperandum [L.], there is no reason for despair.

nil nisi cruce [L.], no dependence but on the cross.

ni l'un ni l'autre [Fr.], neither the one nor the other.

nimium ne crede colori [L.], trust not too much to looks (or externals).

n'importe [Fr.], it matters not.

nisi Dominus frustra [L.], unless God be with us all is in vain.

nitor in adversum [L.], I strive against opposition.

nobilitas sola est atque unica virtus [L.], virtue is the true and only nobility.

noblesse oblige [Fr.], rank imposes obligations; much is expected from one in good position.

no es oro todo lo quo reluce [Sp.], all is not gold that glistens.

no hay cerradura si es de oro la ganzúa [Sp.], there is no lock that a golden key will not open.

nolens volens [L.], willing or unwilling.

noli irritare leones [L.], do not irritate lions.

noli me tangere [L.], touch me not.

nolle prosequi [L.], to be unwilling to proceed. See in Dict.

nolo episcopari [L.], I do not wish to be made a bishop.

nom de guerre [Fr.], a war name; an assumed traveling name; pen name.

nom de plume [Fr.], an assumed name of a writer: an English expression formed from the French.

nomina stultorum parietibus hærent [L.], fools' names are stuck upon the walls.

non compos mentis [L.], not of sound mind.

non cuivis homini contingit adire Corinthum [L.], every man has not the fortune to go to Corinth.

non datur tertium [L.], there is not given a third one or a third chance.

non deficiente crumena [L.], the purse not failing; if the money holds out.

non est [L.], it is not; it is wanting or absent.

non est inventus [L.], he has not been found.

non est vivere sed valere vita [L.], life is not merely to live, but to be strong.

non far mai il medico tuo erede [It.], never make your physician your heir.

non ignara mali, miseris succurere disco [L.], not unacquainted with misfortune I learn to succor the wretched.

non libet [L.], it does not please me.

non liquet [L.], the case is not clear or proved.

non mi ricordo [It.], I do not remember.

non multa, sed multum [L.], not many things but much.

non nobis solum [L.], not to ourselves alone.

non nostrum est tantas componere lites [L.], it is not for us to settle such weighty disputes.

nonobstant clameur de haro [Fr.], notwithstanding the hue and cry.

non ogni fiore fa buon odore [It.], not every flower has a sweet perfume.

non omne licitum honestum [L.], not every lawful thing is honorable.

non omnia possumus omnes [L.], we cannot, all of us, do everything.

non omnis moriar [L.], I shall not wholly die.

non quis, sed quid [L.], not who but what, not the person but the deed.

non quo, sed quomodo [L.], not by whom, but in what manner.

non sequitur [L.], it does not follow.

non sibi, sed omnibus [L.], not for self, but for all.

non sibi, sed patriæ [L.], not for himself but for his country.

non sine numine [L.], not without divine aid.

non sum qualis eram [L.], I am not what I once was.

non tali auxilio [L.], not with such aid or help.

nonum prematur in annum [L.], let it be kept back (from publication) till the ninth year.

nosce te ipsum [L.], know thyself.

noscitur a (or **e**) **sociis** [L.], he is known by his companions.

nostro periculo [L.], at our risk.

nota bene [L.], mark well.

Notre Dame [Fr.], Our Lady.

n'oubliez pas [Fr.], don't forget.

nous avons changé tout cela [Fr.], we have changed all that.

nous verrons [Fr.], we shall see.

novus homo [L.], a new man; one who has raised himself from obscurity.

nuance [Fr.], shade; subtle variation.

nudis verbis [L.], in plain words.

nudum pactum [L.], a mere agreement, unconfirmed by writing.

nugæ canoræ [L.], melodious trifles.

nul bien sans peine [Fr.], no pains, no gains.

nulla dies sine linea [L.], not a day without a line; no day without something done.

nulla nuova, buona nuova [It.], no news is good news.

nulli secundus [L.], second to none.

nullius addictus jurare in verba magistri [L.], not bound to swear to the opinions of any master.

nullius filius [L.], a son of nobody; an illegitimate son.

nunc aut nunquam [L.], now or never.

nunquam minus solus, quam cum solus [L.], never less alone than when alone.

nunquam non paratus [L.], never unprepared; always ready.

nuptiæ [L.], nuptials; wedding.

O

obiit [L.], he, or she, died.

obiter dictum [L.], a thing said by the way.

obra de común, obra de ningún [Sp.], everybody's business is nobody's business.

obscurum per obscurius [L.], explaining an obscurity by something more obscure still.

observanda [L.], things to be observed.

obsta principiis [L.], resist the beginnings.

obstupui steteruntque comæ [L.], I was astonished and my hair stood on end.

occasio facit furem [L.], opportunity makes the thief.

occurrent nubes [L.], clouds will intervene.

oderint dum metuant [L.], let them hate provided they fear.

odi profanum vulgus [L.], I loathe the profane rabble.

odium medicum [L.], the hatred of physicians.

odium in longum jacens [L.], hatred long cherished.

odium theologicum [L.], the hatred of theologians.

œil de bœuf [Fr.], a bull's-eye.

œuvres [Fr.], works.

officina gentium [L.], the workshop of the world.

O fortunatos nimium sua si bona norint agricolas [L.], O too happy husbandmen if only they knew their own blessings.

ofrecer mucho especie es de negar [Sp.], to offer much is a kind of denial.

ogni bottega ha la sua malizia [It.], every shop has its tricks; tricks in all trades.

ogni medaglia ha il suo riverso [It.], every medal has its reverse side.

ogniuno per se, e Dio per tutti [It.], every one for himself, and God for all.

ohe! jam satis [L.], hold! enough.

ohne Hast, aber ohne Rast [G.], without haste, but without rest.

olet lucernam [L.], it smells of the lamp ("the midnight oil"); it is a labored production.

omen faustum [L.], a favorable omen.

omne ignotum pro magnifico [L.], whatever is unknown is held to be magnificent.

omnem movere lapidem [L.], to turn every stone; to leave no stone unturned; to make every exertion.

omne solum forti patria [L.], every soil is a brave man's country.

omne trinum perfectum [L.], every perfect thing is threefold.

omne tulit punctum qui miscuit utile dulci [L.], he gains the approval of all who mixes the useful with the agreeable.

omne vivum ex ovo [L.], every living thing comes from an egg (or germ).

omnia ad Dei gloriam [L.], all things for the glory of God.

omnia bona bonis [L.], all things are good to the good.

omnia mutantur, nos et mutamur in illis [L.], all things change, and we change with them.

omnia vincit amor [L.], love conquers all things.

omnia vincit labor [L.], labor overcomes all things.

omnis amans amens [L.], every lover is demented.

on commence par être dupe, on finit par être fripon [Fr.], one begins by being a fool, and ends in becoming a knave.

on connait l'ami au besoin [Fr.], a friend is known in time of need.

operæ pretium est [L.], it is worthwhile.

opprobrium medicorum [L.], the reproach of the doctors.

optimates [L.], men of the first rank. See in Dict.

opus operatum [L.], an effective work or operation. See **Opus,** in Dict.

ora et labora [L.], pray and work.

ora pro nobis [L.], pray for us.

orator fit, poeta nascitur [L.], an orator is made, a poet is born.

ore rotundo [L.], with round full voice.

ore tenus [L.], from the mouth merely.

origo mali [L.], origin of the evil.

oro è che oro vale [It.], that is gold that is worth gold; all is not gold that glitters.

O! si sic omnia [L.], O! if all things were so; O! if he had always so spoken or acted.

O tempora! O mores! [L.], O the times! O the manners!

otia dant vitia [L.], idleness occasions vice.

otiosa sedulitas [L.], idle industry; laborious trifling.

otium cum dignitate [L.], ease with dignity; dignified leisure.

otium sine litteris est mors [L.], leisure without literature is death.

oublier je ne puis [Fr.], I can never forget.

ouï-dire [Fr.], hearsay.

ou la chèvre est attachée, il faut qu'elle broute [Fr.], where the goat is tethered, there it must browse.

ouvrage de longue haleine [Fr.], a work of long breath; a work long in being accomplished; a long-winded or tedious business.

ouvrier [Fr.], a workman; an operative.

P

pabulum Acherontis [L.], food for Acheron, or the tomb.

pace [L.], by leave of; not to give offence to.

pace tua [L.], by your leave; with your consent.

pacta conventa [L.], the conditions agreed on.

pactum illicitum [L.], an illegal agreement.

padrone [It.], a master; a landlord.

pallida mors [L.], pale death.

palmam qui meruit ferat [L.], let him who has won the palm wear it.

palma non sine pulvere [L.], the palm is not won without dust; i.e. no success without exertion.

par accès [Fr.], by fits and starts.

par accident [Fr.], by accident or chance.

par accord [Fr.], by agreement; in harmony.

par avion [Fr], by airplane: French label for air mail.

par ci par là [Fr.], here and there.

par complaisance [Fr.], by complaisance.

par dépit [Fr.], out of spite.

pardonnez-moi [Fr.], pardon me; excuse me.

parem non fert [L.], he suffers no equal.

par excellence [Fr.], by way of eminence.

par exemple [Fr.], by example; for instance.

parfaitement bien [Fr.], perfectly well.

par faveur [Fr.], by favor; with the countenance of.

par force [Fr.], by force.

par hasard [Fr.], by chance.

pari passu [L.], with equal step; together.

paritur pax bello [L.], peace is produced by war.

par le droit du plus fort [Fr.], by the right of the strongest.

par les mêmes voies on ne va pas toujours aux mêmes fins [Fr.], by the same methods we do not always attain the same ends.

parlez du loup, et vous en verrez sa queue [Fr.], speak of the wolf, and you will see his tail; talk of the devil and he will appear.

parlez peu et bien si vous voulez qu'on vous regarde comme un homme de mérite [Fr.], speak little and well if you would be esteemed as a man of merit.

par manière d'acquit [Fr.], by way of acquittal; for form's sake.

par negotiis, neque supra [L.], neither above nor below his business.

par nobile fratrum [L.], a noble pair of brothers; two just alike; the one as good or as bad as the other.

parole d'honneur [Fr.], word of honor.

par oneri [L.], equal to the burden.

par parenthèse [Fr.], by way of parenthesis.

par pari refero [L.], I return like for like; tit for tat.

par précaution [Fr.], by way of precaution.

par privilège [Fr.], by privilege; license.

par rapport [Fr.], by reason of.

pars adversa [L.], the opposite party.

par signe de mépris [Fr.], as a token of contempt.

pars pro toto [L.], part for the whole.

parti [Fr.], a party; person.

particeps criminis [L.], an accomplice in a crime.

particulier [Fr.], a private person.—**en particulier,** in private.

partout [Fr.], everywhere; in all directions.

parturiunt montes, nascetur ridiculus mus [L.], the

mountains are in travail, a ridiculous mouse will be brought forth.

parva componere magnis [L.], to compare small things with great.

parva leves capiunt animas [L.], trifles captivate small minds.

parvenu [Fr.], a person of low origin who has risen suddenly to wealth or position.

parvum parva decent [L.], trifles become a little person.

pas [Fr.], a step.

pas à pas on va bien loin [Fr.], step by step one goes a long way.

passé [Fr.], past; out of date.

passe-partout [Fr.], a master-key, passport.

pas seul [Fr.], a dance performed by one person.

passim [L.], everywhere; throughout the book or writing referred to.

pasticcio [It.], patchwork.

paté de foie gras [Fr.], goose-liver paste.

pater patriæ [L.], father of his country.

patience passe science [Fr.], patience surpasses knowledge.

pâtisserie [Fr.], pastry; pastry shop.

patois [Fr.], a provincial dialect; the language of the lower classes.

patres conscripti [L.], the conscript fathers; Roman senators.

patriis virtutibus [L.], by ancestral virtues.

paucis verbis [L.], in a few words.

paulo majora canamus [L.], let us sing of somewhat higher themes.

pax in bello [L.], peace in war.

pax vobiscum [L.], peace be with you.

peccavi [L.], I have sinned.

peine forte et dure [Fr.], strong and severe punishment; a kind of judicial torture.

penchant [Fr.], a strong liking.

pensée [Fr.], a thought.

penetralia [L.], secret or inmost recesses.

per [L.], by; by means of; through.

per [It.], for; through; by.

per ambages [L.], by circuitous ways; hence, by allegory; figuratively; metaphorically.

per angusta ad augusta [L.], through trials to triumphs.

per annum [L.], by the year; annually.

per aspera ad astra [L.], through rough ways to the stars; through suffering to renown.

per baroniam [L.], by right of barony.

per capita [L.], by the head or poll.

per centum [L.], by the hundred.

per contante [It.], for cash.

per conto [It.], upon account.

per contra [L.], contrariwise.

per curiam [L.], by the court.

per diem [L.], by the day; daily.

perdu [Fr.], lost.

pereant qui ante nos nostra dixerunt [L.], deuce take

those who said our good things before us.

père de famille [Fr.], the father of a family.

pereunt et imputantur [L.], they (the hours) pass away and are laid to our charge.

per fas et nefas [L.], through right and wrong.

perfervidum ingenium Scotorum [L.], the intense earnestness of Scotsmen.

per gradus [L.], step by step.

periculum in mora [L.], there is danger in delay.

per interim [L.], in the meantime.

perjuria ridet amantium Jupiter [L.], at lovers' perjuries Jove laughs.

per mare per terras [L.], through sea and land.

per mese [It.], by the month.

permitte divis cetæra [L.], leave the rest to the gods.

per pares [L.], by one's peers.

per più strade si va a Roma [It.], there are many roads to Rome.

per saltum [L.], by a leap or jump.

per se [L.], by, or in, itself.

per stirpes [L.], by stocks.

per troppo dibatter la verità si perde [It.], truth is lost by too much controversy.

per viam [L.], by the way of.

petit chaudron, grandes oreilles [Fr.], little pitchers (have) big ears.

petitio principii [L.], a begging of the question.

petit-maître [Fr.], a fop.

peu-à-peu [Fr.], little by little; by degrees.

peu de chose [Fr.], a little thing; a trifle.

peu de gens savent être vieux [Fr.], few people know how to be old.

pezzo [It.], a piece; an Italian coin.

piccolo [It.], small.

pièce de résistance [Fr.], the chief dish of a meal; something substantial by way of entertainment; a substantial joint of meat.

pied-à-terre [Fr.], a resting-place; a temporary lodging.

pietra mossa non fa muschio [It.], a rolling stone gathers no moss.

pinxit [L.], he, or she, painted it.

pis aller [Fr.], the worst or last shift.

piuttosto mendicante che ignorante [It.], better be a beggar than be ignorant.

place aux dames [Fr.], make way for the ladies.

plebs [L.], common people; the multitude.

plein de soi-même [Fr.], full of himself.

plein pouvoir [Fr.], full power or authority.

pleno jure [L.], with full power or authority.

plus aloes quam mellis habet [L.], he has more gall than honey; sarcastic wit.

plus on est de fous, plus on rit [Fr.], the more fools, the more fun.

plus sage que les sages [Fr.], wiser than the wise.

poca barba, poca verguenza [Sp.], little beard, little shame.

poca roba, poco pensiero [It.], little wealth, little care.

poco a poco [It.], little by little.

poeta nascitur, non fit [L.], the poet is born, not made; nature, not study, must form the poet.

point d'appui [Fr.], point of support; prop.

poisson d'avril [Fr.], April fool (lit. April fish).

pondere, non numero [L.], by weight not by number.

pons asinorum [L.], an ass's bridge; a name given to the fifth proposition of the first book of Euclid.

populus vult decipi [L.], the populace wishes to be deceived.

possunt quia posse videntur [L.], they are able because they think they are.

post bellum auxilium [L.], aid after the war.

post cineres gloria venit [L.], after death comes glory.

post equitem sedet atra cura [L.], behind the rider sits black care.

poste restante [Fr.], to be left at the post office till called for: applied to letters.

post hoc ergo propter hoc [L.], after this, therefore on account of this; a non sequitur in argument.

post nubila jubila [L.], after sorrow joy.

post nubila Phœbus [L.], after clouds comes Phœbus, or the sun.

post obitum [L.], after death.

pour acquit [Fr.], received payment; paid; written at the bottom of a discharged account.

pour comble de bonheur [Fr.], as the height of happiness.

pour couper court [Fr.], to cut the matter short.

pour encourager les autres [Fr.], to encourage the others.

pour faire rire [Fr.], to excite laughter.

pour faire visite [Fr.], to pay a visit.

pour passer le temps [Fr.], to pass away the time.

pour prende congé [Fr.], to take leave: often abbreviated p.p.c. on visiting-cards.

pour se faire valoir [Fr.], to make himself of value.

pour tout potage [Fr.], all that one gets; all that a person is allotted.

pour y parvenir [Fr.], to attain the object.

præcognita [L.], things previously known.

præmonitus, præmunitus [L.], forewarned, forearmed.

præscriptum [L.], a thing prescribed.

prendre la balle au bond [Fr.], to catch the ball as it bounds.

prendre la lune avec les dents [Fr.], to take the moon by the teeth; to aim at impossibilities.

prends moi tel que je suis [Fr.], take me just as I am.

prenez garde [Fr.], beware; look out.

presto maturo, presto marcio [It.], soon ripe, soon rotten.

prêt d'accomplir [Fr.], ready to accomplish.

prêt pour mon pays [Fr.], ready for my country.

preux chevalier [Fr.], a brave knight.

prima donna [It.], the chief female vocalist. See in Dict.

primæ viæ [L.], the first passages; the chief canals of the body.

prima facie [L.], on first sight. See in Dict.

primo [L.], in the first place.

primo uomo [It.], the chief actor or vocalist.

primum mobile [L.], the souce of motion, the mainspring.

primus inter pares [L.], first among his peers.

principia, non homines [L.], principles, not men.

principiis obsta [L.], resist the beginnings.

prior tempore, prior jure [L.], first in time, first by right; first come, first served.

pro aris et focis [L.], for our altars and our hearths; for civil and religious liberty.

probatum est [L.], it is proved.

probitas laudatur, et alget [L.], honesty is praised, and is left to starve.

pro bono publico [L.], for the good of the public.

pro confesso [L.], as if conceded.

procul, O procul este, profani [L.], far, far hence, O ye profane!

pro Deo et ecclesia [L.], for God and the church.

pro et contra [L.], for and against.

profanum vulgus [L.], the profane rabble.

pro forma [L.], for the sake of form.

pro hac vice [L.], for this occasion.

proh pudor! [L.], for shame!

projet de loi [Fr.], a legislative bill.

prolétaire [Fr.], member of the lower classes; workingman.

pro memoria [L.], for a memorial.

pro nunc [L.], for the present.

propaganda [L.], the propagation of principles or views. See in Dict.

pro patria [L.], for our country.

propria quæ maribus [L.], things appropriate to males, men, or husbands (a fragment of a rule in old Latin grammars).

propriétaire [Fr.], an owner or proprietor.

pro rata [L.], according to rate or proportion.

pro rege, lege, et grege [L.], for the king, the law, and the people.

pro re nata [L.], for a particular emergency arising.

pro salute animæ [L.], for the health of the soul.

prosit! [L.], a health to you!

pro tanto [L.], for so much; for as far as it goes.

protégé [Fr.], one under the protection of another.

pro virili parte [L.], according to one's power; with all one's might.

prudens futuri [L.], thoughtful of the future.

publice [L.], publicly.

publiciste [Fr.], one who writes on national laws and customs; a publicist.

pugnis et calcibus [L.], with fists and heels; with all one's might.

punctum saliens [L.], a salient or prominent point.

Punica fides [L.], Punic or Carthaginian faith; treachery.

Q

quæ fuerunt vitia, mores sunt [L.], what were once vices are now customs.

quæ nocent, docent [L.], things which injure, instruct; we learn by what we suffer.

qualis ab incepto [L.], the same as at the beginning.

qualis rex, talis grez [L.], like king, like people.

qualis vita, finis ita [L.], as life is, so is its end.

quam diu se bene gesserit [L.], during good behavior.

quand même [Fr.], even though; nevertheless.

quand on ne trouve pas son repos en soi-même, il est inutile de le chercher ailleurs [Fr.], when a man finds no repose in himself, it is futile for him to seek it elsewhere.

quand on voit la chose, on la croit [Fr.], that which one sees he gives credit to.

quandoque bonus dormitat Homerus [L.], even good Homer sometimes nods; the wisest make mistakes.

quanti est sapere [L.], how desirable is wisdom or knowledge.

quantum libet [L.], as much as you please.

quantum meruit [L], as much as he deserved.

quantum mutatus ab illo! [L.], how changed from what he once was!

quantum sufficit [L.], as much as suffices; a sufficient quantity.

quantum vis [L.], as much as you wish.

que la nuit parait longue à la douleur qui veille! [Fr.], to sleepless grief how long must night appear.

quelque chose [Fr.], something; a trifle.

quelqu'un [Fr.], somebody.

quem deus vult perdere prius dementat [L.], whom a god would destroy he first drives mad.

quem di diligunt adolescens moritur [L.], he whom the gods love dies young.

querelle d'Allemand [Fr.], a German quarrel; a drunken affray.

qui a bu boira [Fr.], the tippler will go on tippling.

quid faciendum? [L.], what is to be done?

qui docet discit [L.], he who teaches learns.

quid pro quo [L.], one thing for another; tit for tat; value received.

quid rides? [L.], why do you laugh?

quién sabe? [Sp.] who knows?

quieta non movere [L.], not to disturb things at rest.

qui facit per alium facit per se [L.], he who acts by another acts by himself.

qu'il soit comme il est desiré [Fr.], let it be as desired.

qui m'aime, aime mon chien [Fr.], love me, love my dog.

qui n'a point de sens à trente ans, n'en aura jamais [Fr.], he who has no sense when thirty years old, will never have any.

qui n'a santé n'a rien [Fr.], he who lacks health lacks everything.

qui nimium probat, nihil probat [L.], he proves nothing who proves too much.

qui non proficit, deficit [L.], he who does not advance goes backward.

qui perd, péche [Fr.], he who loses, offends; an unsuccessful man is always deemed to be wrong.

quis custodiet ipsos custodes? [L.], who shall keep the keepers themselves?

qui s'excuse s'accuse [Fr.], he who excuses himself accuses himself.

qui tacet consentit [L.], he who is silent gives consent.

qui timide rogat, docet negare [L.], he who asks timidly invites denial.

qui transtulit sustinet [L.], he who transports, supports.

qui va là? [Fr.], who goes there?

qui vive? [Fr.], a challenge: "Who goes there?"

quoad hoc [L.], to this extent.

quo animo? [L.], with what intention?

quocunque jeceris stabit [L.], where-ever you throw it, it will stand.

quocunque modo [L.], in whatever manner.

quocunque nomine [L.], under whatever name.

quod avertat Deus! [L.], which may God avert!

quod bene notandum [L.], which may be especially noticed.

quod bonum, felix, faustumque sit! [L.], and may it be advantageous, fortunate, and favorable!

quod erat demonstrandum [L.], which was to be proved or demonstrated.

quod erat faciendum [L.], which was to be done.

quod non opus est, asse carum est [L.], what is not wanted (or is of no use to a person) is dear at a copper.

quod semper, quod ubique, quod ab omnibus [L.], what (has been believed) always, everywhere, by all.

quod vide [L.], which see; see that reference.

quo Fata vocant [L.], whither the Fates call.

quo jure [L.], by what right?

quo pax et gloria ducunt [L.], where peace and glory lead.

quorum pars magna fui [L.], of whom, or which, I was an important part.

quot homines, tot sententiæ [L.], many men, many minds.

R

raconteur [Fr.], a teller of stories.

railleur [Fr.], a jester; one addicted to raillery.

raison d'état [Fr.], a reason of state.

raison d'être [Fr.], the reason for a thing's existence.

rappel [Fr.], a recall.

rapprochement [Fr.], the act of bringing together.

rara avis in terris, nigroque simillima cygno [L.], a rare bird on earth, and very like a black swan (formerly believed to be nonexistent).

rari nantes in gurgite vasto [L.], swimming here and there on the vast sea.

Rathaus [G.], a townhall.

ratione soli [L.], as regards the soil.

re [L.], in the matter of; in reference to the question of.

Realschule [G.], a real school; a secondary German school giving an education more in modern subjects than in classics.

réchauffé [Fr.], lit. something warmed up; hence old literary material worked up into a new form.

recoje tu heno mientras que el sol luziere [Sp.], make hay while the sun shines.

reconnaissance [Fr.], survey. See Dict.

recte et suaviter [L.], justly and agreeably.

rectus in curia [L.], upright in court; with clean hands.

reçu [Fr.], received; a receipt.

recueil [Fr.], a collection.

reculer pour mieux sauter [Fr.], to go back in order to leap the better.

rédacteur [Fr.], an editor; one who edits or gives literary form to something.

redolet lucerna [L.], it smells of the lamp; it is a labored production.

reductio ad absurdum [L.], the reducing of a supposition or hypothesis to an absurdity.

regium donum [L.], a royal gift; the former annual grant of public money to the Presbyterian ministers of Ireland. See in Dict.

re infecta [L.], the business being unfinished.

relâche [Fr.], intermission; relaxation; respite.

relata refero [L.], I repeat the story as it was given me.

religieux [Fr], a monk or friar. See in Dict.

religio loci [L.], the religious spirit of the place.

rem acu tetigisti [L.], you have touched the matter with a needle; you have hit the thing exactly.

rem facias, rem; recte si possis, si non quocumque modo rem [L.], make money, money; honestly if you can, if not, make it anyhow.

remisso animo [L.], with mind remiss or listless.

remis velisque [L.], with oars and sails; using every endeavor.

remuda de pasturaje haze bizerros gordos [Sp.], change of pasture makes fat calves.

renascentur [L.], they will be born again.

rencontre [Fr.], an encounter; a hostile meeting.

renommée [Fr.], renown; celebrity.

renovate animos [L.], renew your courage.

renovato nomine [L.], by a revived name.

rentes [Fr.], funds; stocks.

répertoire [Fr.], a list; a stock of songs, dramas, etc., already prepared. See in Dict.

répondez s'il vous plait [Fr.], send an answer if you please.

répondre en Normand [Fr.], to give an evasive answer.

requiescat in pace [L.], may he (or she) rest in peace; **requiescant,** may they.

rerum primordia [L.], the first elements of things.

res angusta domi [L.], narrow circumstances at home.

res est sacra miser [L.], a sufferer is a sacred thing.

res gestæ [L.], things done; exploits.

res judicata [L.], a case or suit already settled.

respice finem [L.], look to the end.

respublica [L.], the commonwealth.

résumé [Fr.], a summary or abstract. See in Dict.

resurgam [L.], I shall rise again.

revanche [Fr.], revenge.

revenons à nos moutons [Fr.], let us return to our sheep; let us return to our subject.

re vera [L.], in truth; in actual fact.

revoir [Fr.], a meeting again; **au revoir,** good-bye until we meet again.

rez-de-chaussée [Fr.], the ground-floor.

rideau d'entr'acte [Fr.], the scene let down between the acts of a play.

ridere in stomacho [L.], to laugh secretly; to laugh in one's sleeve.

ride si sapis [L.], laugh, if you are wise.

rien n'arrive pour rien [Fr.], nothing comes for nothing.

rien n'est beau que le vrai [Fr.], there is nothing beautiful except the truth.

rifacimento [It.], a remaking. See Dict.

rigueur [Fr.], strictness; strict etiquette.

rira bien, qui rira le dernier [Fr.], he laughs well who laughs last.

rire entre cuir et chair [Fr.], **rire sous cape** [Fr.] } to laugh in one's sleeve.

risum teneatis, amici? [L], could you keep from laughing, friends?

rixatur de lana caprina [L.], he contends about goat's wool; he quarrels about trifles.

robe de chambre [Fr.], a morning-gown or dressing-gown.

robe de nuit [Fr.], a nightgown.

rôle [Fr.], a character represented on the stage. See in Dict.

rôle d'équipage [Fr.], the list of a ship's crew.

roué [Fr.], a man of fashion devoted to sensual pleasure. See in Dict.

rouge et noir [Fr.], red and black, a game of chance. See in Dict.

ruat cælum [L.], let the heavens fall.

rudis indigestaque moles [L.], a rude and undigested mass.

ruit mole sua [L.], it falls to ruin by its own weight.

ruse contre ruse [Fr.], trick against trick; diamond cut diamond.

ruse de guerre [Fr.], a stratagem of war.

rus in urbe [L.], the country in town.

rusticus expectat dum defluat amnis at ille labitur et labetur in omne volubilis ævum [L.], the rustic waits till the river flows past (and ceases to flow), but it glides on and will glide for all time.

S

sa boule est demeurée [Fr.], his bowl has stopped short of the mark; he has failed in his object.

sabreur [Fr.], a brave soldier distinguished for his use of his sabre.

sæpe stylum vertas [L.], often turn the style or pen (and make erasures with the blunt end on the waxen tablets); correct freely (if you wish to produce good literature).

saggio fanciullo è chi conosce il suo vero padre [It.], he is a wise child who knows his own father.

sal Atticum [L.], Attic salt; i.e. wit.

salle [Fr.], a hall; salle à manger, a dining-room; salle de batailles, a gallery or room decorated with pictures of martial subjects; salle de réception, a room in which visitors are received.

salon [Fr.], a saloon or drawing-room; a picture gallery.

salus populi suprema lex est [L.], the welfare of the people is the supreme law.

salve! [L.], hail!

salvo jure [L.], the right being safe; without prejudice to one's rights.

salvo pudore [L.], without offence to modesty.

salvo sensu [L.], the sense being preserved.

sang-froid [Fr.], coolness; indifference. See in Dict.

sang pur [Fr.], pure blood; of aristocratic birth.

sans cérémonie [Fr.], without ceremony or formality.

sans-culotte [Fr.], without breeches. See in Dict.

sans Dieu rien [Fr.], nothing without God.

sans façon [Fr.], without ceremony.

sans pain, sans vin, amour n'est rien [Fr.], without bread, without wine, love is naught.

sans pareil [Fr.], without equal.

sans peine [Fr.], without difficulty.

sans peur et sans reproche [Fr.], without fear and without reproach.

sans rime et sans raison [Fr.], without rhyme or reason.

sans souci [Fr.], without care.

sans tache [Fr.], without spot, stainless.

santé [Fr.], health; en bonne santé, in good health; maison de santé, a private hospital.

sapere aude [L.], dare to be wise.

sartor resartus [L.], the botcher repatched; the tailor re-tailored or mended.

sat cito, si sat bene [L.], soon enough done, if well enough done.

satis dotata si bene morata [L.], well enough dowered, if well principled.

satis eloquentiæ, sapientiæ parum [L.], eloquence enough, but little wisdom.

satis superque [L.], enough, and more than enough.

satis verborum [L.], enough of words; no more need be said.

sat pulchra, si sat bona [L.], she is handsome enough, if good enough.

sauce piquante [Fr.], a pungent sauce; a relish.

sauf et sain [Fr.], safe and sound.

sauve qui peut [Fr.], let him save himself who can.

savoir faire [Fr.], the knowing how to act; tact.

savoir vivre [Fr.], good-breeding; refined manners.

scandalum magnatum [L.], speech or writing defamatory to dignitaries.

scire facias [L.], cause it to be known. See in Dict.

scribendi recte sapere est et principium et fons [L.], the principle and source of good writing is to possess good sense.

scribimus indocti doctique [L.], learned and unlearned, we all write.

sdegno d'amante poco dura [It.], a lover's anger is short-lived.

séance [Fr.], See in Dict.

secrétaire [Fr.], a secretary; secrétaire d'état, a secretary of state.

secret et hardi [Fr.], secret and bold.

secundum artem [L.], according to art or rule; scientifically.

secundum naturam [L.], according to nature.

secundum ordinem [L.], in due order.

secundum usum [L.], according to practice.

sed hæc hactenus [L.], but so far, this will suffice.

seigneur [Fr.], a lord, nobleman; a seignior (which see in Dict.).

se jeter dans l'eau de peur de la pluie [Fr.], to cast oneself into the water out of fear of rain.

selon les règles [Fr.], according to rule.

selon lui [Fr.], according to him.

semel abbas, semper abbas [L.], once an abbot, always an abbot.

semel et simul [L.], once and together.

semel insanivimus omnes [L.], we have all, at some time, been mad.

semel pro semper [L.], once for all.

semper avarus eget [L.], the avaricious is always in want.

semper fidelis [L.], always faithful.

semper idem [L.], always the same.

semper paratus [L.], always ready.

semper timidum scelus [L.], guilt is always timid.

semper vivit in armis [L.], he lives always in arms.

sempre il mal non vien per nuocere [It.], misfortune does not always come to injure.

senatus consultum [L.], a decree of the senate.

senex bis puer [L.], the old man is twice a child.

se non è vero, è ben trovato [It.], if not true, it is cleverly invented (or fabricated).

sensu bono [L.], in a good sense.

sensu malo [L.], in a bad sense.

sequiturque patrem non passibus æquis [L.], he follows his father, but not with equal steps.

sero sed serio [L.], late, but seriously.

sero venientibus ossa [L.], those who come late shall have the bones.

serus in cælum redeas [L.], late may you return to heaven; may you live long.

servabo fidem [L.], I will keep faith.

servare modum [L.], to keep within bounds.

servus servorum Dei [L.], a servant of the servants of God.

sesquipedalia verba [L.], words a foot and a half long.

sic eunt fata hominum [L.], thus go the fates of men.

sic itur ad astra [L.], such is the way to the stars, or to immortality.

sic passim [L.], so here and there throughout; so everywhere.

sic semper tyrannis [L.], ever so to tyrants.

sic transit gloria mundi [L.], thus passes away the glory of this world.

sicut ante [L.], as before.

sicut patribus, sit Deus nobis [L.], as with our fathers, so may God be with us.

sic volo sic jubeo; stat pro ratione voluntas [L.], thus I will, thus I command; let my will stand for a reason.

sic vos non vobis [L.], thus you labor but not for yourselves.

si Deus nobiscum, quis contra nos? [L.], if God be with us, who shall stand against us?

si Dieu n'existait pas, il faudrait l'inventer [Fr.], if God did not exist, it would be necessary to invent him.

si diis placet [L.], if it pleases the gods.

siècle [Fr.], an age; siècle d'or, the golden age; siècles des ténèbres, the dark ages.

siesta [Sp.], a short nap during the heat of the day.

sile et philosophus esto [L.], be silent and pass for a philosopher.

silentium altum [L.], deep silence.

silent leges inter arma [L.], amidst arms, or in war, laws are silent, or disregarded.

similia similibus curantur [L.], like things are cured by like.

similis simili gaudet [L.], like is pleased with like.

si monumentum quæris circumspice [L.], if you seek his monument, look around you.

simplex munditiis [L.], elegant in simplicity.

sine cura [L.], without charge or care.

sine die [L.], without a day being appointed.

sine dubio [L.], without doubt.

sine mora [L.], without delay.

sine præjudicio [L.], without prejudice.

sine qua non [L.], without which, not.

si nous n'avions point de défauts, nous ne prendrions pas tant de plaisir à en remarquer dans les autres [Fr.], if we had no faults we should not take so much pleasure in remarking those of others.

si parva licet componere magnis [L.], if small things may be compared with great.

siste viator [L.], stop, traveler!

sit tibi terra levis [L.], light lie the earth upon thee.

sit ut est aut non sit [L.], let it be as it is, or not at all.

sit venia verbis [L.], may the words be excused.

si vis pacem, para bellum [L.], if you wish for peace, prepare for war.

sobriquet [Fr.], a nickname. See in Dict.

sœurs de charité [Fr.], sisters of charity.

soi-disant [Fr.], self-styled.

soi-même [Fr.], oneself.

sola nobilitas virtus [L.], virtue the only nobility.

solitudinem faciunt, pacem appellant [L.], they make a wilderness and call it peace.

sottise [Fr.], absurdity; foolishness.

sotto voce [It.], in an undertone.

soubrette [Fr.], a waiting-maid; an actress who plays the part of a waiting-maid, etc.

souffler le chaud et le froid [Fr.], to blow hot and cold.

sous tous les rapports [Fr.], in all respects or relations.

soyez ferme [Fr.], be firm; persevere.

spero meliora [L.], I hope for better things.

spes sibi quisque [L.], let every one hope in himself.

spirituel [Fr.], intellectual; witty.

splendide mendax [L.], nobly untruthful; untrue for a good object.

spolia optima [L.], the choicest of the spoils.

sponte sua [L.], of one's (or its) own accord.

spretæ injuria formæ [L.], the insult of despising her beauty.

stat magni nominis umbra [L.], he stands in the shadow of a mighty name.

stat pro ratione voluntas [L.], will stands in place of reason.

statu quo ante bellum [L.], in the state in which things were before the war.

status quo [L.], the state in which.

sta viator, heroem calcas [L.], halt, traveler, thou standest on a hero's dust.

stemmata quid faciunt? [L.], of what value are pedigrees?

sternitur alieno vulnere [L.], he is slain by a blow aimed at another.

stratum super stratum [L.], layer above layer.

studium immane loquendi [L.], an insatiable desire for talking.

Sturm und Drang [G.], storm and stress.

sua cuique voluptas [L.], every man has his own pleasures.

suaviter in modo, fortiter in re [L.], gentle in manner, resolute in execution (or action).

sub colore juris [L.], under color of law.

sub hoc signo vinces [L.], under this standard you will conquer.

sub judice [L.], still before the judge; under consideration.

sublata causa, tollitur effectus [L.], the cause being removed, the effect ceases.

sub pœna [L.], under a penalty.

sub prætexto juris [L.], under the pretext of justice.

sub rosa [L.], under the rose; secretly.

sub silentio [L.], in silence.

sub specie [L.], under the appearance of.

sub voce [L.], under such or such a word.

succès d'estime [Fr.], success of esteem; success with more prestige than profit.

sufre por saber y trabaja por tener [Sp.], suffer in order to be wise, and labor in order to have.

suggestio falsi [L.], suggestion of falsehood.

sui generis [L.], of its own or of a peculiar kind.

suivez raison [Fr.], follow reason.

summa summarum [L.], the sum total.

summum bonum [L.], the chief good.

summum jus, summa injuria [L.], the rigor of the law is the height of oppression.

sumptibus publicis [L.], at the public expense.

sum quod eris; fui quod es [L.], I am what you will be (dead), I was what you are (alive): inscription on tombstones.

sunt lacrimæ rerum [L.], there are tears for misfortune.

suo Marte [L.], by his own prowess.

suppressio veri, suggestio falsi [L.], a suppression of the truth

is the suggestion of a falsehood.

surgit amari aliquid [L.], something bitter arises.

sursum corda! [L.], lift up your hearts!

surtout pas de zèle! [Fr.], above all, no zeal!

suum cuique [L.], to each his own.

suus cuique mos [L.], every one has his particular habit.

T

tabagie [Fr.], a smoking-room.

table à manger [Fr.], a dining-table.

tableau vivant [Fr.], a living picture; the representation of some scene by groups of persons.

table d'hôte [Fr.], a public dinner at a hotel; a meal at a fixed price.

tabula rasa [L.], a smooth or blank tablet.

tâche sans tache [Fr.], a work (or task) without a stain.

tædium vitæ [L.], weariness of life.

taisez-vous [Fr.], be quiet; hold your tongue.

tam Marte quam Minerva [L.], as much by Mars as by Minerva; as much by courage as by skill.

tangere vulnus [L.], to touch the wound.

tantæne animis cælestibus iræ? [L.], can such anger dwell in heavenly minds?

tant mieux [Fr.], so much the better.

tanto buon che val niente [It.], so good as to be good for nothing.

tant pis [Fr.], so much the worse.

tant s'en faut [Fr.], far from it.

tantum vidit Virgilium [L.], he merely saw Virgil; he only looked on the great man.

Te, Deum, laudamus [L.], we praise Thee, O God (or rather, as God).

te judice [L.], you being the judge.

tel brille au second rang qui s'éclipse au premier [Fr.], a man may shine in the second rank, who would be eclipsed in the first.

tel est notre plaisir [Fr.], such is our pleasure.

tel maître, tel valet [Fr.], like master, like man.

tel père, tel fils [Fr.], like father, like son.

telum imbelle, sine ictu [L.], a feeble weapon thrown without effect.

tempora mutantur, nos et mutamur in illis [L.], the times are changing and we with them.

tempori parendum [L.], we must yield to the times.

tempus edax rerum [L.], time the devourer of all things.

tempus fugit [L.], time flies.

tempus ludendi [L.], the time for play.

tempus omnia revelat [L.], time reveals all things.

tenax propositi [L.], tenacious of his purpose.

tenez [Fr.], take it; hold; hark; look here.

tentanda via est [L.], a way must be attempted.

teres atque rotundus [L.], smooth and round; polished and complete.

terminus ad quem [L.], the term or limit to which.

terminus a quo [L.], the term or limit from which.

terræ filius [L.], a son of the earth.

terra firma [L.], solid earth; a secure foothold.

terra incognita [L.], an unknown or unexplored region.

tertium quid [L.], a third something; a nondescript.

tête de famille [Fr.], the head of the house; paterfamilias.

tête de fou ne blanchit jamais [Fr.], the head of a fool never becomes white.

tibi seris, tibi metis [L.], you sow for yourself, you reap for yourself.

tiens à la vérité [Fr.], maintain the truth.

tiens ta foi [Fr.], keep thy faith.

tiers-état [Fr.], the third estate. See in Dict.

timeo Danaos et dona ferentes [L.], I fear the Greeks even when they bring gifts.

tirailleur [Fr.], a sharpshooter; skirmisher. See in Dict.

toga virilis [L.], the manly toga; the dress of manhood.

to kalon [Gr.], the beautiful; the chief good.

tomava la por rosa mas devenia cardo [Sp.], I took her for a rose but she proved to be a thistle.

tombé des nues [Fr.], fallen from the clouds.

ton [Fr.], taste; fashion; high life.

to prepon [Gr.], the becoming (or proper).

tôt gagné, tôt gaspillé [Fr.], soon gained, soon spent.

tot homines, quot sententiæ [L.], so many men, so many opinions.

totidem verbis [L.], in just so many words.

toties quoties [L.], as often as.

totis viribus [L.], with all his might.

toto cælo [L.], by the whole heavens; diametrically opposite.

tôt ou tard [Fr.], sooner or later.

totus, teres, atque rotundus [L.], complete, polished, and rounded.

toujours perdrix [Fr.], always partridges; always the same thing over again.

toujours prêt [Fr.], always ready.

tour de force [Fr.], a feat of strength or skill.

tourner casaque [Fr.], to turn one's coat; to change sides.

tous frais faits [Fr.], all expenses paid.

tout-à-fait [Fr.], wholly; entirely.

tout-à-l'heure [Fr.], instantly.

tout au contraire [Fr.], on the contrary.

tout à vous [Fr.], wholly yours.

tout bien ou rien [Fr.], the whole or nothing.

tout comprende est tout pardonner [Fr.], to understand all is to forgive all.

tout court [Fr.], quite short; abruptly.

tout de même [Fr.], quite the same.

tout de suite [Fr.], immediately.

tout ensemble [Fr.], the whole together. See in Dict.

tout frais fait [Fr.], all expenses paid.

tout le monde est sage après le coup [Fr.], everybody is wise after the event.

tout mon possible [Fr.], everything in my power.

tout vient de Dieu [Fr.], all things come from God.

traducteur [Fr.], a translator.

traduction [Fr.], a translation.

traduttori traditori [It.], translators are traitors.

trahit sua quemque voluptas [L.], every one is attracted by his own liking.

transeat in exemplum [L.], may it pass into an example or precedent.

travaux forcés [Fr.], hard labor.

tria juncta in uno [L.], three joined in one.

tristesse [Fr.], depression of spirits.

Troja fuit [L.], Troy was; Troy is no more.

Tros Tyriusque mihi nullo discrimine agetur [L.], Trojan and Tyrian—there shall be no distinction so far as I am concerned.

trottoir [Fr.], the pavement; the footway on the side of a street or road.

trouvaille [Fr.], sudden good fortune; a godsend.

truditur dies die [L.], one day is pressed onward by another.

tu ne cede malis [L.], do not thou yield to evils.

tu quoque [L.], thou also; you're another.

tu quoque, Brute! [L.], thou also, Brutus!

tutor et ultor [L.], protector and avenger.

tutte le strade conducono a Roma [It.], all roads lead to Rome.

tuum est [L.], it is your own.

U

uberrima fides [L.], superabounding faith.

ubi bene, ibi patria [L.], where it is well, there is one's country.

ubi jus incertum, ibi jus nullum [L.], where the law is uncertain, there is no law.

ubi lapsus? [L.], where have I fallen?

ubi libertas, ibi patria [L.], where liberty is, there is my country.

ubi mel, ibi apes [L.], where honey is, there are the bees.

ubique [L.], everywhere.

ubique patriam reminisci [L.], to remember our country everywhere.

ubi supra [L.], where above mentioned.

Übung macht den Meister [G.], practice makes the master; practice makes perfect.

ultima ratio regum [L.], the last argument of kings; war.

ultima Thule [L.], remotest Thule; some far distant region.

ultimus Romanorum [L.], the last of the Romans.

ultra licitum [L.], beyond what is allowable.

ultra vires [L.], transcending authority.

una scopa nuova spazza bene [It.], a new broom sweeps clean.

una voce [L.], with one voice, unanimously.

una volta furfante e sempre furfante [It.], once a knave, always a knave.

un bienfait n'est jamais perdu [Fr.], an act of kindness is never lost.

un cabello hace sombra [Sp.], a single hair makes a shadow.

und so weiter [G.], and so forth.

une affaire flambée [Fr.], a gone case.

une fois n'est pas coutume [Fr.], one act does not constitute a habit.

un fait accompli [Fr.], an accomplished fact.

unguibus et rostro [L.], with claws and beak; tooth and nail.

unguis in ulcere [L.], a claw in the wound.

un je servirai [Fr.], one I will serve.

uno animo [L.], with one mind; unanimously.

un sot à triple étage [Fr.], an egregious fool.

un sot trouve toujours un plus sot qui l'admire [Fr.], a fool always finds a greater fool to admire him.

unter vier Augen [G.], under four eyes; between ourselves.

urbem lateritiam invenit, marmoream reliquit [L.], he (Augustus) found the city (Rome) brick, and left it marble.

urbi et orbi [L.], to the city (Rome) and the world.

usque ad aras [L.], to the very altars; to the last extremity.

usque ad nauseam [L.], so as to induce disgust.

usus loquendi [L.], usage in speaking.

ut ameris, amabilis esto [L.], that you may be loved, be lovable.

ut apes geometriam [L.], as bees practice geometry.

utcunque placuerit Deo [L.], as it shall please God.

utile dulci [L.], the useful with the pleasant.

utinam noster esset [L.], would that he were of our party.

ut infra [L.], as below.

uti possidetis [L.], as you now possess; each retaining what he at present holds.

ut pignus amicitiæ [L.], as a pledge of friendship.

ut prosim [L.], that I may do good.

ut quocunque paratus [L.], prepared for every event.

ut supra [L.], as above stated.

V—W—Z

vacuus cantat coram latrone viator [L.], the traveler with an empty purse sings in presence of the highwayman.

vade in pace [L.], go in peace.

væ victis [L.], woe to the vanquished.

vale (sing), **valete** (pl.) [L.], farewell.

valeat quantum valere potest [L.], let it pass for what it is worth.

valet anchora virtus [L.], virtue serves as an anchor.

valet de chambre [Fr.], a personal attendant; a body-servant.

valet de place [Fr.], a guide for visitors to a place.

valete et plaudite [L.], good-by and applaud us; said by Roman actors at the end of a piece.

variæ lectiones [L.], various readings.

variorum notæ [L.], the notes of various commentators.

varium et mutabile semper femina [L.], woman is ever a changeful and capricious thing.

vaudeville [Fr.], a ballad; a comic opera. See in Dict.

vaurien [Fr.], a worthless fellow.

vedi Napoli e poi muori [It.], see Naples and then die.

vehimur in altum [L.], we are carried out into the deep.

velis et remis [L.], with sails and oars; by every possible means.

vel prece, vel pretio [L.], with either entreaty or payment; for love or money.

veluti in speculum [L.], even as in a mirror.

venalis populus, venalis curia patrum [L.], the people are venal, and the senate is equally venal.

venenum in auro bibitur [L.], poison is drunk from golden vessels.

venia necessitati datur [L.], indulgence is granted to necessity; necessity has no law.

venienti occurrite morbo [L.], meet the coming of the disease; prevention is better than cure.

venit summa dies et ineluctabile tempus [L.], the last day has come, and the inevitable doom.

veni, vidi, vici [L.], I came, I saw, I conquered.

ventis secundis [L.], with favoring winds.

ventre à terre [Fr.], with belly to the ground; at full speed.

vera incessu patuit dea [L.], the real goddess was made manifest by her walk.

vera pro gratiis [L.], truth before favor.

vera prosperitá è non necessità [It.], it is true prosperity to have no want.

verbatim et litteratim [L.], word for word and letter for letter.

verbum sat sapienti [L.], a word is enough for a wise man.

verdad es verde [Sp.], truth is green.

veritas odium parit [L.], truth begets hatred.

veritas prevalebit [L.], truth will prevail.

veritas vincit [L.], truth conquers.

veritatis simplex oratio est [L.], the language of truth is simple.

vérité sans peur [Fr.], truth without fear.

ver non semper viret [L.], spring is not always green; as a punning motto of the Vernons, Vernon always flourishes.

vestigia nulla retrorsum [L.], no returning footsteps; no traces backward.

vexata quæstio [L.], a disputed question.

via [L.], by way of. See in Dict.

via crucis, via lucis [L.], the way of the cross, the way of light.

via media [L.], a middle course.

via militaris [L.], a military road.

via trita, via tuta [L.], the beaten path is the safe path.

vice [L.], in the place of. **Vice versa.** See in Dict.

vide et crede [L.], see and believe.

videlicet [L.], namely.

video meliora proboque deteriora sequor [L.], I see and approve the better things, I follow the worse.

videtur [L.], it appears.

vide ut supra [L.], see what is stated above.

vidi tantum [L.], I merely saw him.

vi et armis [L.], by force and arms; by main force; by violence.

vigilate et orate [L.], watch and pray.

vigueur de dessus [Fr.], strength from on high.

vilius argentum est auro, virtutibus aurum [L.], silver is less valuable than gold, and gold than virtue.

vincit amor patriæ [L.], the love of our country prevails.

vincit omnia veritas [L.], truth conquers all things.

vincit qui patitur [L.], he who endures conquers.

vincit qui se vincit [L.], he conquers who conquers himself.

vinculum matrimonii [L.], the bond of marriage.

vindex injuriæ [L.], an avenger of injury.

vino dentro, senno fuori [It.], when the wine is in, the wit is out.

vin ordinaire [Fr.], a cheap wine commonly used in wine-growing countries.

vires acquirit eundo [L.], as it goes it acquires strength (originally said of rumor).

Virgilium vidi tantum [L.], Virgil (or some great man) I merely saw.

virginibus puerisque [L.], for girls and boys.

vir sapit qui pauca loquitur [L.], he is a wise man who says but little.

virtus in actione consistit [L.], virtue consists in action.

virtus in arduis [L.], virtue or courage in difficulties.

virtus incendit vires [L.], virtue kindles strength.

virtus laudatur, et alget [L.], virtue is praised, and suffers from cold.

virtus millia scuta [L.], virtue (or valor) is a thousand shields.

virtus semper viridis [L.], virtue is always green.

virtus sola nobilitat [L.], virtue alone ennobles.

virtus vincit invidiam [L.], virtue overcomes envy or hatred.

virtute et fide [L.], by or with virtue and faith.

virtute et labore [L.], by or with virtue and labor.

virtute non astutia [L.], by virtue (or valor), not by craft.

virtute non verbis [L.], by virtue, not by words.

virtute officii [L.], by virtue of office.

virtute quies [L.], rest or quietude in virtue.

virtute securus [L.], secure through virtue.

virtuti, non armis, fido [L.], I trust to virtue, not to weapons.

virtutis amore [L.], from love of virtue.

virtutis fortuna comes [L.], fortune is the companion of valor or virtue.

virum volitare per ora [L.], to hover on men's lips; to be in everybody's mouth.

vis-à-vis [Fr.], opposite; face to face.

vis comica [L.], comic power or talent.

vis conservatrix naturæ [L.], the preservative power of nature.

vis consili expers mole rui sua [L.], strength without judgment falls by its own might.

vis inertiæ [L.], the power of inertia; dead resistance to force applied.

vis medicatrix naturæ [L.], the healing power of nature.

vis unita fortior [L.], united power is stronger.

vis vitæ [L.], the vigor of life.

vita brevis, ars longa [L.], life is short, art is long.

vitæ via virtus [L.], virtue, the way of life.

vitam impendere vero [L.], to stake one's life for the truth.

vita sine litteris mors est [L.], life without literature is death.

vivat regina! [L.], long live the queen!

vivat respublica! [L.], long live the republic!

vivat rex! [L.], long live the king!

viva voce [L.], by the living voice; orally.

vive la bagatelle! [Fr.], long live folly!

vive le roi! [Fr.], long live the king!

vive memor leti [L.], live ever mindful of death.

vivere est cogitare [L.], to live is to think.

vive ut vivas [L.], live that you may live.

vive, vale [L.], farewell, be happy.

vivida vis animi [L.], the living force of the mind.

vivit post funera virtus [L.], virtue survives the grave.

vivre ce n'est pas respirer, c'est agir [Fr.], life consists not in breathing, but in doing.

vix ea nostra voco [L.], I scarcely call these things our own.

vixere fortes ante Agamemnona [L.], brave men lived before Agamemnon; great men lived in previous ages.

vogue la galère! [Fr.], let come what may!

voilà! [Fr.], behold! there is; there are.

voilà tout [Fr.], that's all.

voilà une autre chose [Fr.], that's another thing; that is quite a different matter.

voir le dessous des cartes [Fr.], to see the under side of the cards; to be in the secret.

volens et potens [L.], willing and able.

volenti non fit injuria [L.], no injustice is done to the consenting person.

volo, non valeo [L.], I am willing, but unable.

volventibus annis [L.], as the years roll by.

vota vita mea [L.], my life is devoted.

vous y perdrez vos pas [Fr.], you will there lose your steps or labor.

vox et præterea nihil [L.], a voice and nothing more; sound but no sense.

vox faucibus hæsit [L.], his voice, or words, stuck in his throat; he was dumb from astonishment.

vox populi, vox Dei [L.], the voice of the people is the voice of God.

vraisemblance [Fr.], probability; apparent truth.

vulgo [L.], commonly.

vulnus immedicabile [L.], an irreparable injury.

vultus animi janua et tabula [L.], the countenance is the portal and picture of the mind.

vultus est index animi [L.], the countenance is the index of the mind.

Wahrheit gegen Freund und Feind [G.], truth in spite of friend and foe.

Wahrheit und Dichtung. See Dichtung.

Zeitgeist [G.], the spirit of the age.

zonam perdidit [L.], he has lost his purse; he is in straitened circumstances.

zum Beispiel [G.], for example.

Given Names

Masculine Names

Aar·on (âr′ən, ar′ən) ? Enlightener. [< Hebrew]
A·bel (ā′bəl) Breath. [< Hebrew]
A·bi·el ā′bē·el, ə·bī′əl) Strong father. [< Hebrew]
Ab·ner (ab′nər) Father of light. [< Hebrew]
A·bra·ham (ā′brə·ham; *Fr.* à·brà·àm′; *Ger.* ä′brä·häm) Exalted father of multitudes. [< Hebrew] Also *Sp.* **A·bra·hán** (ä′brä·än′). Dims. **Abe, A′bie.**
A·bram (ā′brəm; *Fr.* à·bräṅ′; *Sp.* ä· bräm′) Exalted Father. [< Hebrew]
Ab·sa·lom (ab′sə·ləm) The father is peace. [< Hebrew]
Ad·am (ad′əm) Red; man of red earth. [< Hebrew]
Ad·el·bert (ad′l·bûrt, ə·del′bûrt) Var. of ALBERT.
Ad·olph (ad′olf, ā′dolf) Noble wolf. [< Gmc.] Also *Dan., Du., Ger.* **A·dolf** (ä′dôlf), *Fr.* **A·dolphe** (à·dôlf′), *Ital., Sp.* **A·dol·fo** (*Ital.* ä·dôl′fō; *Sp.* ä·thôl′fō), *Lat.* **A·dol·phus** (ə·dol′·fəs), *Pg.* **A·dol·pho** (ə·thôl′fōō).
A·dri·an (ā′drē·ən) Of Adria: from the name of two Italian cities, or the Adriatic Sea. [< L] Also *Fr.* **A·dri·en** (à·drē·aṅ′), *Ital.* **A·dri·a·no** (ä′drē·ä′nō), *Lat.* **A·dri·a·nus** (ā′drē·ä′nəs).
Af·fon·so (ə·fôn′sōō) Pg. form of ALPHONSO.
Al·an (al′ən) Handsome [< Celtic] Also **Al′lan, Al′len.** Dim. **Al.**
Al·a·ric (al′ə·rik) All-ruler. [< Gmc.]
Al·as·tair (al′əs·tər) Scot. contr. of ALEXANDER. Also **Al′·is·ter.**
Al·ban (ôl′bən, al′-) White; of Alba: from the name of several Italian cities. [< L] Also **Al′bin.**
Al·bert (al′bûrt; *Fr.* àl·bâr′; *Ger., Sw.* äl′bert) Nobly bright. [< F < Gmc.] Also *Ital., Sp.* **Al·ber·to** (äl·ber′tō), *Lat.* **Al·ber·tus** (al·bûr′təs). Dims. **Al, Alb, Bert.**
Al·den (ôl′dən) Old friend. [OE]
Al·do (al′dō) Meaning uncertain. [< Gmc. or Hebrew]
Al·dous (ôl′dəs, al′-) From the old place. [OE] Also **Al′·dis, Al′dus.**
Al·ex·an·der (al′ig·zan′dər, -zän′-; *Du., Ger.* ä′lek·sän′dər) **Defender of men.** [< Gk.] Also *Fr.* **A·lex·an·dre** (à·lek·säṅ′dr′), *Modern Gk.* **A·le·xan·dros** (ä·lâ′ksän·drōs), *Ital.* **A·les·san·dro** (ä′läs·sän′drō), *Pg.* **A·le·xan·dre** (ə·lē·shaṅn′·drə), *Russ.* **A·le·ksandr** (ə·lyi·ksän′dər), *Sp.* **A·le·jan·dro** (ä′lä·hän′drō). Dims. **Al′ec, Al′eck, Al′ex, San′der, San′dy.**
A·lex·is (ə·lek′sis) Defender. [< Gk.]
Al·fon·so (äl·fôn′sō) Ital. and Sp. form of ALPHONSO. Also *Dan., Ger.* **Al·fons** (äl′fôns).
Al·fred (al′frid; *Ger.* äl′frät; *Fr.* àl·fred′) Elf counselor; hence, wise. [OE] Also *Ital.* **Al·fre·do** (*Ital.* äl·frä′dō; *Sp.* äl·frä′thō), *Lat.* **Al·fre·dus** (al·frē′dəs) or **Al·u·re·dus** (al′yōō·rē′dəs). Dims **Al, Alf, Fred.**
Al·ger (al′jər) Noble spear. [< Gmc.]
Al·ger·non (al′jər·nən) Mustached. [< OF] Dims. **Al·gie, Al′gy** (al′jē).
Al·len (al′ən) Var. of ALAN. Also **Al′lan.**
A·lon·zo (ə·lon′zō) Var. of ALPHONSO. Also *Ital., Sp.* **A·lon·so** (ä·lôn′sō).
Al·o·y·sius (al′ō·ish′əs) Lat. form of LOUIS. Also **A·lois** (ə·lois′).
Al·phon·so (al·fon′zō, -sō) Nobly ready. [< Sp. < Gmc.] Also *Fr.* **Al·phonse** (àl·fôṅs′). Dims. **Al, Alph, Al′phy.**
Al·va (al′və; *Sp.* äl′vä) White. [< L]
Al·vin (al′vin) Noble friend. [< Gmc.] Also **Al·win** (al′·win; *Ger.* äl′vēn), **Al′van,** *Fr.* **A·luin** (à·lwaṅ′), *Ital.* **Al·vi·no** (äl·vē′nō), *Sp.* **A·lui·no** (ä·lwē′nō).

Am·brose (am′brōz) Divine; immortal. [< Gk.] Also *Fr.* **Am·broise** (äṅ·brwàz′), *Lat.* **Am·bro·si·us** (am·brō′zhē·əs, -zē·əs).
A·me·ri·go (ä′mä·rē′gō) Ital. form of EMERY.
A·mos (ā′məs) Burden. [< Hebrew]
An·a·tole (an′ə·tōl; *Fr.* à·nà·tôl′) Sunrise. [< Gk.]
An·drew (an′drōō) Manly. [< Gk.] Also **An·dre·as** (an′·drē·əs, an·drē′əs; *Dan.* än·dres′; *Du., Ger.* än·drä′äs; *Lat.* an′drē·əs), *Fr.* **An·dré** (än·drā′), *Ital.* **An·dre·a** (än·drâ′ä), *Russ.* **An·drei** (än·drā′), *Sp.* **An·drés** (än·drās′). Dims. **An′·dy, Drew.**
An·gus (ang′gəs) Singular. [< Celtic]
An·selm (an′selm; *Ger.* än′zelm) Divine helmet. [< Gmc.] Also **An·sel** (an′səl), *Fr.* **An·selme** (äṅ·selm′), *Ital., Sp.* **An·sel·mo** (än·sel′mō), *Lat.* **An·sel·mus** (an·sel′məs).
An·tho·ny (an′thə·nē,-tə-) Inestimable: from the name of a Roman clan. Also **An·to·ny** (an′tə·nē). *Fr.* **An·toine** (äṅ·twän′) *Ger., Lat.* **An·to·ni·us** (*Ger.* än·tō′nē·ŏŏs; *Lat.* an·tō′·nē·əs), *Ital., Sp.* **An·to·nio** (än·tô′nyō). Dim. **To′ny.**
An·ton (än′tōn) Dan., Du., Ger. and Sw. form of ANTHONY.
Ar·chi·bald (är′chə·bôld) Nobly bold. [< Gmc.] Dims. **Ar′chie, Ar′chy.**
Ar·mand (är′mänd; *Fr.* àr·mäṅ′) Fr. form of HERMAN.
Ar·min·i·us (är·min′ē·əs) Lat. form of HERMAN.
Ar·nold (är′nəld; *Ger.* är′nôlt) Eagle power. [< Gmc.] Also *Fr.* **Ar·naud** (àr·nō′), *Ital.* **Ar·nol·do** (är·nôl′dō), *Sp.* **Ar·nal·do** (är·näl′thō). Dims. **Arn, Ar′nie.**
Ae·te·mas (är′tə·məs) He of Artemis. [< Gk.] Also **Ar′·te·mus.**
Ar·thur (är′thər; *Fr.* àr·tōōr′) He-bear; from a totemic or royal title suggesting valor, strength, and nobility. [< Celtic] Also *Ital.* **Ar·tu·ro** (är·tōō′rō). Dims. **Art, Art′ie.**
A·sa (ā′sə) Healer. [< Hebrew]
Ash·ley (ash′lē) Dweller among ash trees: from a surname. [< Gmc.]
Ath·el·stan (ath′əl·stan) Noble stone or jewel. [OE] Also **Ath′el·stane** (-stän).
Au·brey (ô′brē) Elf ruler. [< F < Gmc.]
Au·gus·tine (ô′gəs·tēn, ô·gus′tin) Dim. of AUGUSTUS. Also **Au·gus·tin** (ô·gus·taṅ′; *Fr.* ō·güs·taṅ′; *Ger.* ou′gŏŏs·tēn), *Ital.* **A·go·sti·no** (ä′gō·stē′nō), *Lat.* **Au·gus·ti·nus** (ô′gəs·tī′nəs), *Pg.* **A·gos·ti·nho** (ə·gōōsh·tē′nyōō), *Sp.* **A·gus·tin** (ä′gōōs·tēn′).
Au·gus·tus (ô·gus′təs) Venerable. [< L] Also **Au·gust** (ô′gəst; *Ger.* ou′gōōst), *Fr.* **Au·guste** (ō·güst′).
Au·re·li·us (ô·rē′lē·əs, ô·rēl′yəs) The golden one. [< L]
Aus·tin (ôs′tən) Contr. of AUGUSTINE.
A·ver·y (ā′vər·ē, ā′vrē) Courageous. [< Gmc.] Also **A·ver·il, A·ver·ill** (ā′vər·əl, ā′vrəl).

Bald·win (bôld′win) Bold friend. [< Gmc.] Also *Fr.* **Bau·doin** (bō·dwaṅ′).
Bal·tha·zar (bäl·thā′zər, -thaz′ər) Bel's or Baal's prince [< Chaldean], or splendid prince [< Persian]. Also **Bal·tha′sar** (-zər).
Bap·tist (bap′tist) Baptizer. [< Gk.] Also *Fr.* **Bap·tiste** (bà·tēst′).
Bar·na·bas (bär′nə·bəs) Son of consolation [< Hebrew], or prophetic son [< Aramaic]. Also **Bar·na·by** (bär′nə·bē). Dim. **Bar′ney.**
Bar·nard (bär′nərd) Var. of BERNARD.
Bar·ney (bär′nē) Dim. of BARNABAS or BERNARD.
Bar·ry (bar′ē) Spear; hence, straightforward. [< Celtic]

Bar·thol·o·mew (bär·thol′ə·myo͞o) Son of furrows. [< Hebrew] Also *Fr.* **Bar·thé·le·my** (bàr·tāl·mē′), *Ger.* **Bar·tho·lo·mä·us** (bär′tō·lō·mä′o͞os), *Ital.* **Bar·to·lo·me·o** (bär·tō′lō·mâ′ō), *Lat.* **Bar·thol·o·mae·us** (bär·tol′ə·mē′əs), *Sp.* **Bar·to·lo·mé** (bär·tō′lō·mā′). Dims. **Bart, Bat.**

Bas·il (baz′əl, bā′zəl) Kingly. [< Gk.]

Bax·ter (bak′stər) Baker. [< Gmc.]

Bay·ard (bā′ərd, bī′-, -ärd) From a surname. [< OF]

Ben·e·dict (ben′ə·dikt) Blessed. [< L] Also **Ben′e·dick,** *Fr.* **Be·noît** (bə·nwà′), *Ger.* **Be·ne·dikt** (bā′nä·dikt), *Ital.* **Be·ne·det·to** (bā′nä·dāt′tō) or **Be·ni·to** (bā·nē′tō), *Lat.* **Ben·e·dic·tus** (ben′ə·dik′təs), *Sp.* **Be·ni·to** (bā·nē′tō).

Ben·ja·min (ben′jə·mən; *Fr.* bań·zhá·mań′; *Ger.* ben′yä·mēn) Son of the right hand; hence, favorite son. [< Hebrew] Also *Ital.* **Ben·ia·mi·no** (ben′yä·mē′nō), *Sp.* **Ben·ja·mín** (ben′hä·mēn′). Dims. **Ben, Ben′jy, Ben′ny.**

Ben·net (ben′it) Var. of BENEDICT. Also **Ben′nett.**

Ber·nard (bûr′nərd, bər·närd′; *Fr.* ber·nàr′) Bear-brave: probably from a totemic title. [< Gmc.] Also *Ger.* **Bern·hard** (bern′härt), *Ital., Sp.* **Ber·nar·do** (*Ital.* Bär·när′dō; *Sp.* (ber·när′ħ̱ō), *Lat.* **Ber·nar·dus** (bər·när′dəs). Dims. **Bar′·ney, Ber′ney, Ber′nie.**

Bert (bûrt) Dim. of ALBERT, BERTRAM, GILBERT, HERBERT, and HUBERT. Also **Ber·tie** (bûr′tē).

Ber·tram (bûr′trəm) Bright raven. [< Gmc.] Also **Ber·trand** (bûr′trənd; *Fr.* ber·trän′). Dim. **Bert.**

Bill (bil) Dim. of WILLIAM. Also **Bil′ly.**

Bob (bob) Dim. of ROBERT. Also **Bob′bie, Bob′by.**

Bo·ris (bôr′is, bō′ris; *Russ.* bə·ryēs′) Warrior. [< Russ.]

Boyd (boid) Yellow-haired. [< Celtic]

Bri·an (brī′ən) Strong. [< Celtic] Also **Bry′an, Bry·ant** (brī′ənt).

Brice (brīs) Meaning uncertain. [? < Celtic] Also **Bryce.**

Bruce (bro͞os) From a Norman Fr. surname; orig. a place name.

Bru·no (bro͞o′nō) The brown one. [< Gmc.]

Bur·gess (bûr′jis) Citizen. [< Gmc.]

By·ron (bī′rən) From a Fr. surname; orig. a place name. Also **Bi′ron.**

Cad·wal·la·der (kad·wol′ə·dər) Battle arranger. [< Welsh] Also **Cad·wal′a·der.**

Cae·sar (sē′zər) Long-haired; ? symbolic title suggesting royalty or holiness. [< L] Also **Ce′sar,** *Fr.* **Cé·sar** (sā·zàr′), *Ital.* **Ce·sa·re** (chā′zä·rā).

Ca·leb (kā′ləb) Dog; hence, loyal. [< Hebrew]

Cal·vin (kal′vin) Bald: from a Roman name. [< L] Dim. **Cal.**

Carl (kärl) English form of KARL.

Car·ol (kar′əl) English form of CAROLUS.

Car·o·lus (kar′ə·ləs) Lat. form of CHARLES.

Car·y (kâr′ē) ? Dim. of CAROL. Also **Car′ey.**

Cas·per (kas′pər) English form of KASPAR. Also **Cas′par** (-pər).

Ce·cil (sē′səl, ses′əl) Blind: from the name of a Roman clan.

Ced·ric (sed′rik, sē′drik) War chief. [< Celtic]

Charles (chärlz; *Fr.* shàrl) Manly. [< F < Gmc.] Also *Ital.* **Car·lo** (kär′lō), *Lat.* **Car·o·lus** (kar′ə·ləs), *Sp.* **Car·los** (kär′lōs). Dims. **Char′ley, Char′lie, Chuck.**

Chaun·cey (chôn′sē, chän′-) Chancellor. [< OF]

Ches·ter (ches′tər) Dweller in camp; hence, soldier: from a surname. [< L] Dims. **Ches, Chet.**

Chris·tian (kris′chən; *Ger.* kris′tē·än) Christian. [< L < Gk.] Also *Fr.* **Chré·tien** (krā·tyań′). Dim. **Chris.**

Chris·to·pher (kris′tə·fər) Bearer of Christ. [< Gk.] Also *Fr.* **Chris·tophe** (krēs·tôf′), *Ger.* **Chris·toph** (kris′tōf), *Ital.* **Chri·sto·fo·ro** (krēs·tô′fō·rō), *Sp.* **Cris·tó·bal** (krēs·tō′·väl). Dims. **Chris, Kit.**

Clar·ence (klar′əns) From the name of an English dukedom.

Claude (klôd; *Fr.* klōd) Lame: from the name of a Roman clan. Also *Ital., Sp.* **Clau·di·o** (*Ital.* klou′dyō; *Sp.* klou′·ħ̱yō), *Lat.* **Clau·di·us** (klô′dē·əs).

Clay·ton (klā′tən) From an English surname; orig. a place name.

Clem·ent (klem′ənt) Merciful. [< L] Dim. **Clem.**

Clif·ford (klif′ərd) From an English surname; orig. a place name. Dim. **Cliff.**

Clif·ton (klif′tən) From an English surname; orig. a place name.

Clin·ton (klin′tən) From an English surname; orig. a place name. Dim. **Clint.**

Clive (klīv) Cliff; cliff-dweller: from an English surname.

Clyde (klīd) From a Scot. surname; orig. the river *Clyde.*

Col·in (kol′ən, kō′lən) Dove. [< Scot. < L]

Con·rad (kon′rad) Bold counsel. [< Gmc.]

Con·stant (kon′stənt; *Fr.* kôn·stän′) Var. of CONSTANTINE.

Con·stan·tine (kon′stən·tīn, -tēn) Constant; firm. [< L]

Cor·nel·ius (kôr·nēl′yəs; *Ger.* kôr·nä′lē·o͞os) ? Horn: from the name of a Roman clan. Dims. **Con, Con′nie, Neil.**

Craig (krāg) Crag; crag-dweller: from a Scot. surname.

Cris·pin (kris′pin) Curly-headed. [< L] Also *Lat.* **Cris·pi·nus** (kris·pī′nəs) or **Cris·pus** (kris′pəs).

Cur·tis (kûr′tis) Courteous. [< OF]

Cuth·bert (kuth′bərt) Notably brilliant. [OE]

Cyr·il (sir′əl) Lordly. [< Gk.]

Cy·rus (sī′rəs) The sun. [< Persian] Dim. **Cy.**

Dan (dan) Judge. [< Hebrew]

Dan·iel (dan′yəl; *Fr.* dà·nyel′; *Ger.* dä′nē·el) God is my judge. [< Hebrew] Dims. **Dan, Dan′ny.**

Da·ri·us (də·rī′əs) Wealthy. [< Persian]

Da·vid (dā′vid; *Fr.* dä·vēd′; *Ger.* dä′vēt) Beloved. [< Hebrew] Dims. **Dave, Da′vey, Da′vie, Da′vy.**

Dean (dēn) From an ancient religious or military title. [< OF < LL] Also **Deane.**

De·me·tri·us (di·mē′trē·əs) He of Demeter. [< Gk.] Also *Russ.* **Dmi·tri** (dmyē′trē).

Den·nis (den′is) Var. of DIONYSIUS. Also **Den′is,** *Fr.* **De·nis** or **De·nys** (də·nē′). Dim. **Den′ny.**

Der·ek (der′ik) Du. dim. of THEODORIC. Also **Der′rick, Dirck** (dûrk; *Du.* dirk), **Dirk.**

DeWitt (də·wit′) From a surname. Also **De Witt.**

Dex·ter (dek′stər) Right; right-handed; hence, fortunate or skillful. [< L]

Dick (dik) Dim. of RICHARD.

Dolph (dolf) Dim. of ADOLPH or RUDOLPH. Also **Dolf.**

Dom·i·nic (dom′ə·nik) Of the Lord. [< L] Also **Dom′i·nick.** Dim. **Dom.**

Don·ald (don′əld) World chief. [< Celtic] Dims. **Don, Don′nie.**

Doug·las (dug′ləs) Dark. [< Celtic] Dims. **Doug, Doug′ie.**

Drew (dro͞o) Skilled one [< Gmc.], or dim. of ANDREW.

Duane (dwān, do͞o·än′) Poem. [< Celtic]

Dud·ley (dud′lē) From an English surname; orig. a place name.

Duke (do͞ok, dyo͞ok) From the title. [< OF]

Dun·can (dung′kən) Brown warrior. [< Celtic]

Dun·stan (dun′stən) From an English place name.

Dwight (dwīt) Meaning uncertain. [< Gmc.]

Earl (ûrl) From the title. [OE] Also **Earle.**

Eb·en·e·zer (eb′ə·nē′zər) Stone of help. [< Hebrew] Dim. **Eb·en** (eb′ən).

Ed·gar (ed′gər) Rich spear; hence, fortunate warrior. [OE] Dims. **Ed, Ed′die, Ned.**

Ed·mund (ed′mənd; *Ger.* et′mo͞ont) Rich protector. [OE] Also **Ed·mond** (ed′mənd; *Fr.* ed·môn′). Dims. **Ed, Ed′die, Ned.**

Ed·ward (ed′wərd) Rich guardian. [OE] Also *Fr.* **É·dou·ard** (ā·dwàr′), *Ger.* **E·du·ard** (ā′do͞o·ärt), *Sp.* **E·duar·do** (ā·ħ̱wär′ħ̱ō). Dims. **Ed, Ed′die, Ned, Ted, Ted′dy.**

Ed·win (ed′win) Rich friend. [OE] Dims. **Ed, Ed′die.**

Eg·bert (eg′bərt) Bright sword; hence, skilled swordsman. [OE] Dims. **Bert, Bert′ie.**

El·bert (el′bərt) Var. of ALBERT.

El·dred (el′drid) Mature counsel. [OE]

El·e·a·zar (el′ē·ā′zər) God has helped. [< Hebrew] Also **El′e·a′zer.**

E·li (ē′lī) The highest one. [< Hebrew]

E·li·as (i·lī′əs) Var. of ELIJAH.

El·i·hu (el′ə·hyo͞o) Var. of ELIJAH.

E·li·jah (i·lī′jə) Jehovah is God. [< Hebrew]

El·i·ot (el′ē·ət)   God's gift.   [< Hebrew]   Also **El′li·ot, El′li·ott.**

E·li·sha (i·lī′shə)   God is salvation.   [< Hebrew]

El·lis (el′is)   Var. of ELIAS.

El·mer (el′mər)   Nobly famous. [OE]

El·ton (el′tən)   From an English surname; orig. a place name.

El·vin (el′vin)   Of the elves.   [OE]   Also **El·win** (el′win).

E·man·u·el (i·man′yōō·əl)   Var. of IMMANUEL.   Also **Em·man′u·el.**

Em·er·y (em′ər·ē)   Work ruler.   [< Gmc.]   Also **Em·er·ic** (em′ər·ik), **Em′o·ry.**

E·mile (ā·mēl′)   From the name of a Roman clan.   Also *Fr.* É·mile (ā·mēl′), *Ger.* **E·mil** (ā′mēl), *Ital.* **E·mi·lio** (ā·mē′lyō).

Em·mett (em′it)   Ant; hence, industrious.   [OE]   Also **Em′met.**

E·ne·as (i·nē′əs)   Praiseworthy.   [< Gk.]

E·noch (ē′nək)   Dedicated.   [< Hebrew]

E·nos (ē′nəs)   Man.   [< Hebrew]

En·ri·co (än·rē′kō)   Ital. form of HENRY.

E·phra·im (ē′frē·əm, ē′frəm)   Doubly fruitful.   [< Hebrew]

E·ras·mus (i·raz′məs)   Lovable.   [< Gk.]

E·ras·tus (i·ras′təs)   Lovable.   [< Gk.]   Dim. **Ras·tus** (ras′·təs).

Er·ic (er′ik)   Honorable king.   [< Scand.]   Also **Er′ich, Er′ik.**

Er·man·no (er·män′nō)   Ital. form of HERMAN.

Er·nest (ûr′nist)   Earnest.   [< Gmc.]   Also *Ger.* **Ernst** (ernst).   Dims. **Ern, Er′nie.**

Er·win (ûr′win)   Var. of IRVING.

Es·te·ban (äs·tā′bän)   Sp. form of STEPHEN.

E·than (ē′thən)   Firmness.   [< Hebrew]

Eth·el·bert (eth′əl·bûrt)   Nobly bright.   [OE]

Eth·el·red (eth′əl·red)   Noble council.   [< Gmc.]

É·tienne (ā·tyen′)   Fr. form of STEPHEN.

Eu·gene (yōō·jēn′)   Well-born.   [< Gk.]   dim. **Gene.**

Eus·tace (yōōs′tis)   Good harvest.   [< Gk]

Ev·an (eva′n)   Welsh form of JOHN.

Ev·e·lyn (ēv′lin, ev′ə·lin)   Ancestor.   [< OF < Gmc]

Ev·er·ard (ev′ər·ärd)   Strong as a boar.   [< Gmc.]   Also **Ev·er·art** (ev′ər·ärt).

Ev·er·ett (ev′ər·it)   Var. of EVERARD.   Also **Ev′er·et.**

E·ze·ki·el (i·zē′kē·əl, -kyəl)   God gives strength.   [< Hebrew]   Dim. **Zeke** (zēk).

Ez·ra (ez′rə)   Helper.   [< Hebrew]

Fë·dor (fyô′dər)   Russ. form of THEODORE.   Also **Fe·o·dor** (fyi·ô′dər).

Fe·li·pe (fā·lē′pā)   Sp. form of PHILIP.

Fe·lix (fē′liks)   Happy; fortunate.   [< L]

Fer·di·nand (fûr′də·nand; *Fr.* fer·dē·nän′; *Ger.* fer′dē·nänt)   Peaceful courage.   [< Gmc.]   Also *Sp.* **Fer·nan·do** (fer·nän′dō), **Her·nan·do** (her·nän′dō).   Dim. **Fer′die.**

Floyd (floid)   Var. of LLOYD.

Fran·cis (fran′sis, frän′-)   Free.   [< Gmc.]   Also *Fr.* **Fran·çois** (frän·swä′), *Ger.* **Franz** (fränts), *Ital.* **Fran·ce·sco** (frän·chä′skō), *Sp.* **Fran·cis·co** (frän·thēs′kō).   Dim. **Frank, Frank′ie.**

Frank (frangk)   Dim. of FRANCIS or FRANKLIN.   Also **Frank′ie.**

Frank·lin (frangk′lin)   Freeman.   [ME]   Dims. **Frank, Frank′ie.**

Fred (fred)   Dim. of ALFRED, FREDERICK, or WILFRED.   Also **Fred′die, Fred′dy.**

Fred·er·ick (fred′ər·ik, fred′rik)   Peace ruler.   [< Gmc.]   Also **Fred′er·ic, Fred′ric, Fred′rick,** *Fr.* **Fré·dé·ric** (frā·dā·rēk′), *Ger.* **Frie·drich** (frē′drikh), *Sp.* **Fe·de·ri·co** (fā′dā·rē′·kō).   Dims. **Fred, Fred′die, Fred′dy, Fritz.**

Fritz (frits)   Ger. dim. of FREDERICK.

Ga·bri·el (gā′brē·əl; *Fr.* gà·brē·el′; *Ger.* gä′brē·el)   Man of God.   [< Hebrew]   Dim. **Gabe** (gāb).

Ga·ma·li·el (gə·mā′lē·əl, -māl′yəl)   Reward of God.   [< Hebrew]

Gar·di·ner (gärd′nər, gär′də·nər)   From an English surname.   Also **Gar′de·ner, Gard′ner.**

Gar·ret (gar′it)   Var. of GERARD.   Also **Gar′rett.**

Gar·y (gâr′ē)   Dim. of GARRET.

Gas·par (gas′pər)   Var. of CASPER.   Also *Fr.* **Gas·pard** (gås·pär′).

Gas·ton (gas′tən; *Fr.* gås·tôn′)   Meaning uncertain.

Gau·tier (gō·tyā′)   Fr. form of WALTER.

Gene (jēn)   Dim. of EUGENE.

Geof·frey (jef′rē)   English form of Fr. *Geoffroi;* var. of GODFREY.   Dim. **Jeff.**

George (jôrj)   Earthworker; farmer.   [< Gk.]   Also *Fr.* **Georges** (zhôrzh), *Ger.* **Ge·org** (gā·ôrkh′), *Ital.* **Gior·gio** (jôr′jō), *Russ.* **Ge·or·gi** (gyi·ôr′gyi).   Dim. **Georg′ie, Geor′die.**

Ger·ald (jer′əld)   Spear ruler.   [< Gmc.]   Also *Fr.* **Gé·raud** (zhā·rō′) or **Gi·raud** (zhē·rō′).   Dims. **Ger′ry, Jer′ry.**

Ge·rard (ji·rärd′; *Brit.* jer′ärd)   Hard spear.   [< Gmc.]   Also *Fr.* **Gé·rard** (zhā·rär′), *Ger.* **Ger·hard** (gär′härt).   Dims. **Ger′ry, Jer′ry.**

Ge·ro·ni·mo (jä·rō′nē·mō)   Ital. form of JEROME.

Gia·co·mo (jä′kō·mō)   Ital. form of JAMES.

Gid·e·on (gid′ē·ən)   Hewer.   [< Hebrew]

Gi·e·ron·y·mus (jē′ə·ron′i·məs)   Lat. form of JEROME.

Gif·ford (gif′ərd, jif′-)   Meaning uncertain.   [< Gmc.]

Gil·bert (gil′bərt; *Fr.* zhēl·bâr′)   Bright wish.   [< Gmc.]   Dims. **Bert, Gil.**

Giles (jīlz)   From the name of the goddess Athena's shield; hence, shield or protection.   [< OF < Gk.]

Gio·van·ni (jō·vän′nē)   Ital. form of JOHN.

Giu·lio (jōō′lyō)   Ital. form of JULIUS.

Giu·sep·pe (jōō·zep′pä)   Ital. form of JOSEPH.

Glenn (glen)   From a Celtic surname; orig. a place name. Also **Glen.**

God·dard (god′ərd)   Divine resoluteness.   [< Gmc.]

God·frey (god′frē)   Peace of God.   [< Gmc.]   Also *Ger.* **Gott·fried** (gôt′frēt).

God·win (god′win)   Friend of God.   [OE]

Gor·don (gôr′dən)   From a Scot. surname.

Gra·ham (grā′əm)   From an English surname; orig. a place name.

Grant (grant)   From a Norman Fr. surname.

Greg·o·ry (greg′ər·ē)   Vigilant.   [< Gk.]   Dim. **Greg.**

Grif·fin (grif′in)   Var. of GRIFFITH.

Grif·fith (grif′ith)   Red-haired.   [< Celtic]

Gro·ver (grō′vər)   Grove-dweller.   [< Gmc.]

Gual·te·ri·o (gwäl·tä′rē·ō)   Sp. form of WALTER.

Gu·gliel·mo (gōō·lyel′mō)   Ital. form of WILLIAM.

Guil·laume (gē·yōm′)   Fr. form of WILLIAM.

Guil·ler·mo (gē·lyer′mō, gē·yer′mō)   Sp. form of WILLIAM.

Gus (gus)   Dim. of AUGUSTUS or GUSTAVUS.

Guy (gī; *Fr.* gē)   Leader   [< F < Gmc.]   Also *Ital.* **Gui·do** (gwē′dō).

Hal (hal)   Dim. of HAROLD or HENRY.

Ham·il·ton (ham′əl·tən)   From a surname.

Hank (hangk)   Dim. of HENRY.

Han·ni·bal (han′ə·bəl)   Grace of Baal.   [< Phoenician]

Hans (häns)   Ger. dim. of JOHANNES.   See JOHN.

Har·ley (här′lē)   From an English surname; orig. a place name.

Har·old (har′əld)   Chief of the army.   [OE < Scand.]   Dim. **Hal.**

Har·ry (har′ē)   Dim. of HAROLD or var. of HENRY.

Har·vey (här′vē)   Army battle.   [< F < Gmc.]

Hec·tor (hek′tər)   He who holds fast; defender.   [< Gk.]

Hen·ry (hen′rē)   Home ruler.   [< F < Gmc.]   Also *Du.* **Hen·drick** (hen′drik), *Fr.* **Hen·ri** (än·rē′), *Ger.* **Hein·rich** (hīn′rikh).   Dims. **Hal, Hank, Har′ry, Hen.**

Her·bert (hûr′bərt)   Glory of the army.   [OE]   Dims. **Bert, Bert′ie, Herb.**

Her·man (hûr′mən)   Man of the army.   [< Gmc.]   Also *Ger.* **Her·mann** (her′män).

Her·mes (hûr′mēz)   Of the earth.   [< Gk.]

Her·nan·do (er·nän′dō)   Sp. form of FERDINAND.

Hez·e·ki·ah (hez′ə·kī′ə)   God strengthens.   [< Hebrew]

Hil·a·ry (hil′ər·ē)   Joyful.   [< L]   Also *Fr.* **Hi·laire** (ē·lâr′).

Hi·ram (hī′rəm)   Honored brother.   [< Hebrew]   Dims. **Hi, Hy.**

Ho·bart (hō′bərt, -bärt)   Var. of HUBERT.

Hodge (hoj) Dim. of ROGER. Also **Hodg′kin.**
Ho·mer (hō′mər) Pledge, or blind one. [< Gk.]
Ho·no·ré (ô·nō·rā′) Honored. [< F < L]
Hor·ace (hôr′is, hor′-) Var. of HORATIO.
Ho·ra·ti·o (hə·rā′shē·ō) From the name of a Roman clan.
Ho·se·a (hō·zē′ə, -zā′ə) Salvation. [< Hebrew]
How·ard (hou′ərd) From an English surname. Dim. **How′ie.**
Hu·bert (hyōō′bərt) Bright spirit or mind. [< F < Gmc.]
Hugh (hyōō) Mind; intelligence. [< OF < Gmc.] Also **Hu·go** (hyōō′gō), Fr. **Hugues** (üg). Dim. **Hugh′ie.**
Hum·bert (hum′bərt) Bright support. [< OF < Gmc.]
Hum·phrey (hum′frē) Peaceful stake or support. [< OF < Gmc.] Also **Hum′frey, Hum′phry.**

I·an (ē′ən, ī′ən) Scot. form of JOHN.
Ich·a·bod (ik′ə·bod) ? Inglorious. [< Hebrew]
Ig·na·ti·us (ig·nā′shē·əs, -shəs) Fiery. [< Gk.] Also Fr. **I·gnace** (ē·nyàs′), Ger. **Ig·naz** (ig′näts), Ital. **I·gna·zio** (ē·nyä′tsyō).
Im·man·u·el (i·man′yōō·əl) God with us. [< Hebrew]
I·ra (ī′rə) Vigilant. [< Hebrew]
Ir·ving (ûr′ving) From a Scot. surname; orig. a place name. Also **Ir·vin** (ûr′vin).
Ir·win (ûr′win) Var. of IRVING.
I·saac (ī′zək) Laughter. [< Hebrew] Dim. **Ike** (īk).
I·sa·iah (ī·zā′ə, ī·zī′ə) Salvation of God. [< Hebrew]
Is·i·dore (iz′ə·dôr, -dōr) Gift of Isis. [< Gk.] Also **Is′a·dore, Is′a·dor, Is′i·dor.** Dim. **Iz·zy** (iz′ē).
Is·ra·el (iz′rē·əl) Contender with God. [< Hebrew]
I·van (ī′vən; Russ. i·vän′) Russ. form of JOHN.

Ja·bez (jā′biz) Sorrow. [< Hebrew]
Jack (jak) English form of Fr. **Jacques;** dim. of JOHN.
Ja·cob (jā·kəb) He who seizes by the heel; hence, successor. [< LL < Hebrew] Also Ger. **Ja·kob** (yä′kôb). Dims. **Jack, Jake** (jāk), **Jock** (jok).
Jacques (zhàk) Fr. form of JACOB. [< OF < LL]
James (jāmz) English form of Sp. **Jaime;** var. of JACOB. [< Sp. < LL] Also Sp. **Jai·me** (hī′mä). Dims. **Jam·ie** (jā′mē), **Jem, Jem′my, Jim, Jim′mie, Jim′my.**
Jan (yän)Du., Ger., and Pol. form of JOHN.
Já·nos (yä′nōsh) Hung. form of JOHN.
Ja·pheth (jā′fith) Enlarged; hence, powerful or honored. [< Hebrew] Also **Ja′phet** (-fit).
Jar·ed (jâr′id) Descent. [< Hebrew]
Jar·vis (jär′vis) From a Norman Fr. surname. Also **Jer·vis** (jûr′vis; Brit. Jär′vis).
Ja·son (jā′sən) Healer. [< Gk.]
Jas·per (jas′pər) Treasury lord [< OF, ? < Persian], or from the name of the jewel.
Jay (jā) ? Jay bird. [? < OF]
Jean (jēn; Fr. zhäṅ) French form of JOHN.
Jef·frey (jef′rē) Var. of GEOFFREY. Dim. **Jeff.**
Je·hu (jē′hyōō) Jehovah is he. [< Hebrew]
Jeph·thah (jef′thə) Opposer. [< Hebrew]
Jer·e·mi·ah (jer′ə·mī′ə) God's chosen. [< Hebrew] Also **Jer·e·my** (jer′ə·mē). Dim. **Jer′ry.**
Je·rome (jə·rōm′; Brit. jer′əm) Holy name. [< Gk.] Also Fr. **Jé·rôme** (zhä·rôm′), Sp. **Je·ró·ni·mo** (hä·rō′nē·mō).
Jer·ry (jer′ē) Dim. of GERALD, GERARD, JEREMIAH, or JEROME.
Jes·se (jes′ē) Meaning uncertain. [< Hebrew] Also **Jess.**
Je·sus (jē′zəs) English form of Lat. Josua; var. of JOSHUA.
Jeth′ro (jeth′rō) Abundant or excellent. [< Hebrew]
Jim (jim) Dim. of JAMES. Also **Jim′mie, Jim′my.**
Jo·ab (jō′ab) Jehovah is father. [< Hebrew]
Jo·a·chim (jō′ə·kim) Jehovah will judge. [< Hebrew] Also Sp. **Joa·quín** (hwä·kēn′)
João (hwouṅ) Pg. form of JOHN.
Job (jōb) Persecuted. [< Hebrew]
Jock (jok) Scot. form of JACK.
Joe (jō) Dim. of JOSEPH. Also **Jo′ey.**
Jo·el (jō′əl) Jehovah is God. [< Hebrew]
John (jon) God is good. [< Hebrew] Also Ger. **Jo·hann** (yō′hän) or **Jo·han·nes** (yō·hän′əs). Dims. **Jack, Jack′ie, Jack′y, Jock, John′nie, John′ny.**

Jon (jon) Var. of JOHN, or dim. of JONATHAN.
Jo·nah (jō′nə) Dove. [< Hebrew] Also **Jo·nas** (jō′nəs).
Jon·a·than (jon′ə·thən) God has given. [< Hebrew] Dims. **Jon, Jon′nie, Jon′ny.**
Jor·ge (Pg. zhôr′zhə; Sp. hôr′hä) Pg. and Sp. form of GEORGE.
Jo·seph (jōzəf; Fr. zhō·zef′; Ger. yō′zef) God shall give (a son). [< Hebrew] Also Lat. **Jo·se·phus** (jō·sē′fəs), Pg., Sp. **Jo·sé** (Pg. zhōō·ze′; Sp. hō·sä′). Dims. **Jo, Joe, Jo′ey.**
Josh·u·a (josh′ōō·ə) God is salvation. [< Hebrew] Also Fr. **Jo·sué** (zhō·zwä′), Lat. **Jos·u·a** (jos′ōō·ə). Dim. **Josh.**
Jo·si·ah (jō·sī′ə) God supports. [< Hebrew] Also Lat. **Jo·si·as** (jō·sī′əs).
Jo·tham (jō′thəm) God is perfection. [< Hebrew]
Juan (hwän) Sp. form of JOHN.
Ju·dah (jōō′də) Praised. [< Hebrew] Also **Jude** (jōōd; Fr. zhüd), Lat. **Ju·das** (jōō′dəs).
Jules (jōōlz; Fr. zhül) Fr. form of JULIUS.
Jul·ian (jōōl′yən) Var. of JULIUS.
Jul·ius (jōōl′yəs) Downy-beared; youthful: from the name of a Roman clan. Also Sp. **Ju·lio** (hōō′lyō). Dims. **Jule** (jōōl), **Jul·ie** (Jōō′lē)
Jun·ius (jōōn′yəs, jōō′nē·əs) Youthful: from the name of a Roman clan.
Jus·tin (jus′tin) Just. [< L] Also **Jus·tus** (jus′təs).

Karl (kärl) Ger. form of CHARLES.
Kas·par (käs′pär) Ger. form of JASPER.
Keith (kēth) From a Scot. surname; orig. a place name.
Kel·vin (kel′vin) From a Celtic surname.
Ken·neth (ken′ith) Handsome. [< Celtic] Dims. **Ken, Ken′nie, Ken′ny.**
Kent (kent) From an English surname; orig. a place name.
Kev·in (kev′ən) Handsome birth. [< Celtic]
Kit (kit) Dim. of CHRISTOPHER.
Kon′rad (kôn′rät) Ger. form of CONRAD.

La·ban (lā′bən) White. [< Hebrew]
La·fay·ette (lä′fē·et′, laf′ē·et′; Fr. à·fà·yet′) From a Fr. surname. Dim. **Lafe** (läf).
Lam·bert (lam′bərt) The land's brightness. [< F < Gmc.]
Lance (lans, läns) Of the land. [< Gmc.]
Lan·ce·lot (lan′sə·lot, län′-; Fr. läṅ·slō′) Fr. dim. of LANCE. Also **Laun·ce·lot** (lôn′sə·lot, lan′-, län′-).
Lars (lärz; Sw. lärs) Sw. form of LAURENCE.
Lau·rence (lôr′əns, lor′-) Laureled; hence, prophetic or poetic. [< L] Also **Law′rence,** Fr. **Lau·rent** (lō·räṅ′), Ger. **Lo·renz** (lō′rents). Dims. **Lar·ry** (lar′ē), **Lau·rie** (lô′rē) **Law·rie** (lôr′ē)
Laz·a·rus (laz′ə·rəs) God has helped. [< Hebrew] Also Fr. **La·zare** (là·zàr′), Ital. **Laz·za·ro** (läd′dzä·rō).
Le·an·der (lē·an′dər) Lion man. [< Gk.]
Lee (lē) From an English surname.
Leif (lēf) Loved one. [< Scand.]
Leigh (lē) From an English surname.
Lem·u·el (lem′yōō·əl) Belonging to God. [< Hebrew] Dim. **Lem.**
Le·o (lē′ō) Lion. [< L < Gk.]
Le·on (lē′on, -ən) Lion. [< L < Gk.] Also Fr. **Lé·on** (lā·ôṅ′).
Leon·ard (len′ərd) Lion-strong. [< Gmc.] Also Fr. **Lé·o·nard** (lā·ō·nàr′), Ger. **Le·on·hard** (lā′ōn·härt), Ital. **Le·o·nar·do** (lā′ō·när′dō). Dims. **Len, Len′ny.**
Le·on·i·das (lē·on′ə·dəs) Lionlike. [< Gk.]
Le·o·pold (lē′ə·pōld; Ger. lā′ō·pōlt) The people's strong one. [< Gmc.]
Le·roy (lə·roi′, lē′roi) Royal. [< OF]
Les·lie (les′lē, lez′-) From an English surname. Dim. **Les.**
Les·ter (les′tər) From an English surname; orig. the place name Leicester. Dim. **Les.**
Le·vi (lē′vī) He who unites. [< Hebrew]
Lew·is (lōō′is) Var. of LOUIS. Dims. **Lew, Lew′ie.**
Lin·coln (ling′kən) From an English surname.
Li·nus (lī′nəs) Meaning uncertain. [< Gk]
Li·o·nel (lī′ə·nəl, -nel) Young lion. [< F < L]
Lisle (līl) Var. of LYLE.
Llew·el·lyn (lōō·el′ən) Meaning uncertain. [< Welsh]
Lloyd (loid) Gray. [< Welsh]

Lo·ren·zo (lə·ren′zō; *Ital.* lō·ren′tsō; *Sp.* lō·rän′thō)   Var. of
   LAURENCE.
Lot (lot)   Veiled.   [< Hebrew]   Also **Lott.**
Lou·is (lōō′is, lōō′ē; *Fr.* lwē)   War famous.   [< OF < Gmc.]
   Also **Lew′is,** *Du.* **Lo·de·wijk** (lō′də·vīk), *Ger.* **Lud·wig**
   (lōōt′·vikh), *Ital.* **Lu·i·gi** (lōō·ē′jē), or **Lo·do·vi·co**
   (lō′dō·vē′kō), *Pg.* **Lu·iz** (lōō·ēsh′), *Sp.* **Lu·is** (lōō·ēs′).
   Dims. **Lew, Lou.**
Low·ell (lō′əl)   Beloved.   [OE]   Also **Lov·ell** (luv′əl).
Lu·cas (lōō′kəs)   Light.   [< L]
Lu·cian (lōō′shən)   Var. of LUCIUS.   [< L *Lucianus*]   Also
   Lu·cien (lōō′shən; *Fr.* lü·syań′).
Lu·ci·fer (lōō′sə·fər)   Light-bearer.   [< L]
Lu·cius (lōō′shəs)   Light.   [< L]
Lu·cre·tius (lōō·krē′shəs, -shē·əs)   Shining or wealthy.
   [< L]
Luke (lōōk)   English form of LUCAS.
Lu·ther (lōō′thər)   Famous warrior.   [< Gmc.]   Also *Fr.*
   Lo·thaire (lō·târ′), *Ital.* **Lo·ta·rio** (lo·tä′ryō).

Mac (mak)   Son.   [< Celtic]   Also **Mack.**
Mal·a·chi (mal′ə·kī)   Messenger.   [< Hebrew]
Mal·colm (mal′kəm)   Servant of (St.) Columbia.   [< Celtic]
Ma·nu·el (mä·nwel′)   Sp. form of IMMANUEL.
Mar·cel·lus (mär·sel′əs)   Dim. of MARCUS.   Also *Fr.*
   Mar·cel (màr·sel′), *Ital.* **Mar·cel·lo** (mär·chel′lō).
Mar·cus (mär′kəs)   Of Mars.   [< L]
Mar·i·on (mar′ē·ən, mâr′-)   Of Mary.   [< F]
Mark (märk)   English form of MARCUS.   Also *Fr.* **Marc**
   (màrk), *Ital.* **Mar·co** (mär′kō).
Mar·ma·duke (mär′mə·dōōk, -dyōōk)   Meaning uncertain.
   [? < Celtic]
Mar·shal (mär′shəl)   From the title.   [< Gmc.]   Also
   Mar′shall.
Mar·tin (mär′tən; *Fr.* màr·tań′; *Ger.* mär′tēn)   Of Mars.
   [< L]   Dims. **Mart, Mar′ty.**
Mar·vin (mär′vin)   Sea friend.   [< Gmc.]
Ma·son (mä′sən)   Stoneworker.   [< Gmc.]
Mat·thew (mat′yōō)   Gift of God.   [< Hebrew]   *Fr.*
   Ma·thieu (mà·tyœ′), *Ital.* **Mat·te·o** (mät·tä′ō), *Sp.* **Ma·te·o**
   (mä·tä′ō).   Dims. **Mat, Matt.**
Mat·thi·as (mə·thī′əs)   Var. of MATTHEW.   [< Gk.]
Mau·rice (mə·rēs′, môr′is, mor′is; *Fr.* mô·rēs′)   Moorish;
   dark.   [< F < L]
Max (maks; *Ger.* mäks)   Dim. of MAXIMILIAN.
Max·i·mil·ian (mak′sə·mil′yən; *Ger.* mäk′sē·mē·lē·än)
   Prob. coined by Frederick III from the Roman names
   Maximus and *Aemilianus.*   Dim. **Max.**
May·nard (mā′nərd, -närd)   Powerful strength.   [< Gmc.]
Mel·vin (mel′vin)   High protector.   [OE]   Dim. **Mel.**
Mer·e·dith (mer′ə·dith)   Sea protector.   [< Welsh]
Mer·vin (mû′vin)   Var. of MARVIN.
Mi·cah (mī′kə)   Who is like God?   [< Hebrew]
Mi·chael (mī′kəl; *Ger.* mi′khä·el)   Who is like God?
   [< Hebrew]   Also *Fr.* **Mi·chel** (mē·shel′), *Ital.* **Mi·che·le**
   (mē·kâ′·lā), *Sp., Pg.* **Mi·guel** (mē·gel′).   Dims. **Mike**
   (mīk), **Mick·ey** or **Mick·y** (mik′ē), **Mike·y** (mī′kē).
Mi·klós (mi′klōsh)   Hung. form of NICHOLAS.
Miles (mīlz)   Meaning uncertain.   [< Gmc.]   Also **Myles.**
Mi·lo (mī′lō; *Ital.* mē′lō)   Ital. var. of MILES.
Mil·ton (mil′tən)   From an English surname; orig. a place
   name.   [< Gmc.]   Dim. **Milt.**
Mitch·ell (mich′əl)   Var. of MICHAEL.   Dim. **Mitch.**
Mon·roe (mən·rō′, *Brit.* mun′rō)   From a Celtic surname;
   orig. a place name.
Mon·ta·gue (mon′tə·gyōō)   From a Norman Fr. surname;
   orig. a place name.   Dim. **Mon′ty.**
Mont·gom·er·y (mont·gum′ər·ē)   From a Norman Fr.
   surname; orig. a place name.   Dim. **Mon′ty.**
Mor·gan (môr′gən)   Sea-dweller.   [< Welsh]
Mor·ris (môr′is, mor′-)   Var. of MAURICE.
Mor·ti·mer (môr′tə·mər)   From a Norman Fr. surname; orig.
   a place name.   Dims. **Mort, Mor′ty.**
Mor·ton (môr′tən)   From an English surname; orig. a place
   name.   Dim. **Mort, Mor′ty.**
Mo·ses (mō′zis, -ziz)   ? Son.   [< Hebrew, ? < Egyptian]
   Dim. **Moe** (mō), **Moi·she** (moi′shə), **Mose** (mōz).
Moss (môs, mos)ˊ   Var. of MOSES.

Mur·dock (mûr′dok)   Seaman.   [< Celtic]   Also **Mur′doch.**
Mur·ray (mûr′ē)   From a Scot. surname, or var. of MAURICE.
Myles (Mīlz)   Var. of MILES.

Na·hum (nā′əm)   Consolation.   [< Hebrew]
Na·po·le·on (nə·pō′lē·ən)   Of the new city.   [< F < Gk.]
   Also *Fr.* **Na·po·lé·on** (nà·pô·lā·ôń′), *Ital.* **Na·po·le·o·ne**
   (nä·pō′lā·ō′nä).
Na·than (nā′thən)   Gift.   [< Hebrew]   Dims. **Nat.** (nat),
   Nate (nāt).
Na·than·iel (nə·than′yəl)   Gift of God.   [< Hebrew]   Also
   Na·than′a·el.   Dims. **Nat, Nate.**
Ned (ned)   Dim. of EDGAR, EDMUND, or EDWARD.   Also
   Ned′dy.
Ne·he·mi·ah (nē′hə·mī′ə)   Comfort of God.   [< Hebrew]
Neil (nēl)   Champion.   [< Celtic]   Also **Neal.**
Nel·son (nel′sən)   Neal's son: from an English surname.
Ne·ro (nir′ō)   Strong: from the name of a Roman clan.
Nev·ille (nev′il, -əl)   From a Norman Fr. surname; orig. a
   place name.   Also **Nev′il, Nev′ile, Nev′ill.**
New·ton (nōōt′n, nyōōt′n)   From an English surname; orig. a
   place name.
Nich·o·las (nik′ə·ləs)   The people's victory.   [< Gk.]   Also
   Nic′o·las, *Fr.* **Ni·co·las** (nē·kô·lä′), *Ital.* **Nic·co·lò**
   (nēk′kō·lô′), *Lat.* **Ni·co·la·us** (nik′ō·lä′əs), *Russ.* **Ni·ko·lai**
   (nyi·kə·lī′), *Sp.* **ni·co·lás** (nē′kō·läs′).   Dims. **Nick,**
   Nick′y.
Ni·gel (nī′jəl)   Noble.   [< Celtic]
No·ah (nō′ə)   Comfort.   [< Hebrew]
No·el (nō′əl)   Christmas.   [< OF < L]   Also *Fr.* **No·ël**
   (nō·el′).
Nor·bert (nôr′bərt)   Brightness of Njord.   [< Gmc.]
Nor·man (nôr′mən)   Northman.   [< Scand.]   Dim. **Norm.**

O·ba·di·ah (ō′bə·dī′ə)   Servant of God.   [< Hebrew]
Oc·ta·vi·us (ok·tā′vē·əs)   The eighth (born).   [< L]
O·laf (ō′ləf; *Dan., Norw.* ō′läf; *Sw.* ōō′läf)   Ancestor's
   heirloom.   Also **O′lav**   [< Scand.]
Ol·i·ver (ol′ə·vər)   Of the olive tree.   [< F < L]   Dims.
   Ol′lie, Ol′ly.
Or·lan·do (ôr·lan′dō; *Ital.* ôr·län′dō)   Ital. form of ROLAND.
Os·bert (ōz′bərt)   Divine brilliance.   [OE]
Os·car (os′kər)   Divine spear.   [OE]
Os·wald (oz′wəld, -wôld)   Divine power.   [OE]   Also
   Os′wold.
Ot·to (ot′ō; *Ger.* ôt′ō)   Rich.   [< Gmc.]
O·wen (ō′ən)   Young warrior   [< Welsh]

Pat·rick (pat′rik)   Patrician; aristocratic.   [< L]   Dims.
   Pad′dy, Pat, Patsy.
Paul (pôl; *Fr.* pôl; *Ger.* poul)   Little: from a given name of
   the Aemiliani, a Roman clan.   Also *Ital.* **Pa·o·lo** (pä′ō·lō),
   Lat. **Pau·li·nus** (pô·lī′nəs) or **Pau·lus** (pô′ləs), *Pg.* **Pau·lo**
   (pou′lōō), *Sp.* **Pa·blo** (pä′vlō).
Per·ci·val (pûr′sə·vəl)   Meaning uncertain.   [< OF]   Also
   Per′ce·val.
Per·cy (pûr′sē)   From a Norman Fr. surname; orig. a place
   name.
Per·ry (per′ē)   Of the pear tree: from an English surname.
Pe·ter (pē′tər; *Du., Ger., Norw., Sw.* pā′tər)   A rock.
   [< Gk.]   Also *Dan.* **Pe·der** (pā′thər), *Du.* **Pie·ter** (pē′tər),
   Fr. **Pierre** (pyâr), *Modern Gk.* **Pe·tros** (pâ′trôs), *Ital.* **Pie·tro**
   (pyä′trō), *Pg., Sp.* **Pe·dro** (*Pg.* pā′thrōō; *Sp.* pā′thrō), *Russ.*
   Pëtr (pyô′tər).   Dim. **Pete.**
Phi·lan·der (fi·lan′dər)   Lover of men.   [< Gk.]
Phi·le·mon (fi·lē′mən)   Loving.   [< Gk.]
Phil·ip (fil′ip)   Lover of horses.   [< Gk.]   Also *Fr.* **Phi·lippe**
   (fē·lēp′), *Ger.* **Phi·lipp** (fē′lip).   Dims. **Phil, Pip.**
Phin·e·as (fin′ē·əs)   Mouth of brass: prob. an oracular priest's
   title.   [< Hebrew]

Quen·tin (kwen′tin)   The fifth (born).   [< L]   Also **Quin·tin**
   (kwin′tən).
Quin·cy (kwin′sē)   ? var. of QUENTIN.   [< OF]

Ralph (ralf; *Brit.* räf)   Wolf-wise.   [< Gmc.]   *Fr.* **Ra·oul**
   (rà·ōōl′).

Ran·dal (ran′dəl) Shield wolf. [OE] Also **Ran′dall.**
Ran·dolph (ran′dolf) Shield wolf. [OE] Dim. **Ran′dy.**
Ra·pha·el (rā′fē·əl, raf′ē·əl) God has healed. [< Hebrew]
Ray (rā) Dim. of RAYMOND.
Ray·mond (rā′mənd; *Fr.* rā·môn′) Wise protection.
  [< Gmc.] Also **Ray′mund,** *Sp.* **Rai·mun·do** (rī·mōōn′dō)
  or **Ra·món** (rä·mōn′). Dim. **Ray.**
Reg·i·nald (rej′ə·nəld) Judicial ruler. [< Gmc.] Also *Fr.*
  Re·gnault (rə·nyō′) or **Re·naud** (rə·nō′), *Ital.* **Ri·nal·do**
  (rē·näl′dō), *Sp.* **Rey·nal·do** (rā·näl′thō). Dims. **Reg** (rej),
  Reg′gie, Rex.
Re·né (rə·nā′) Reborn. [< F < L]
Reu·ben (rōō′bin) Behold, a son! [< Hebrew] Dim.
  Rube.
Rex (reks) King [< L], or dim. of REGINALD.
Rey·nard (rā′nərd, ren′ərd) Brave judgment. [< Gmc.]
Reyn·old (ren′əld) Var. of REGINALD. [< OF]
Rich·ard (rich′ərd; *Fr.* rē·shàr′; *Ger.* riḳh′ärt) Strong king.
  [< OF < Gmc.] Also *Ital.* **Ric·car·do** (rēk·kär′dō), *Sp.*
  Ri·car·do (rē·kär′thō). Dims. **Dick, Dick′ie, Dick′y,**
  Rich, Rich′ie, Rick, Rick′y.
Ro·ald (rō′äl) Famous power. [< Norw. < Gmc.]
Rob·ert (rob′ərt; *Fr.* rô·bâr′) Bright fame. [< Gmc.] Also
  Ital., Sp. **Ro·ber·to** (rō·ber′tō). Dims. **Bob, Bob′by, Dob,**
  Dob′bin, Rob, Rob′bie, Rob′in.
Rod·er·ick (rod′ər·ik) Famous king. [< Gmc.] Also
  Rod′·er·ic, Rod·rick (rod′rik), *Fr.* **Ro·drigue** (rô·drēg′),
  Ital., Sp. **Ro·dri·go** (*Ital.* rō·drē′gō; *Sp.* rō·thrē′gō). Dims.
  Rod, Rod′dy.
Rod·ney (rod′nē) From an English surname; orig. a place
  name. Dim. **Rod.**
Ro·dolph (rō′dolf) Var. of RUDOLPH. Also **Ro·dol·phus**
  (rō·dol′fəs).
Rog·er (roj′ər; *Fr.* rô·zhā′) Famous spear. [< OF < Gmc.]
  Dims. **Hodge, Hodg′kin, Rodge.**
Ro·land (rō′lənd; *Fr.* rô·län′) Country's fame. [< Celtic <
  Gmc.] Also **Row′land.**
Rolf (rolf) Dim. of RUDOLPH. Also **Rolph.**
Rol·lo (rol′ō) Dim. of RUDOLPH.
Ron·ald (ron′əld; *Norw.* rô·näl′) Old Norse form of
  REGINALD.
Ro·ry (rôr′ē, rō′rē) Red. [< Celtic]
Ros·coe (ros′kō) From an English surname; orig. a place
  name.
Ross (rôs) From an English surname; orig. a place name.
Roy (roi) King. [< OF]
Ru·dolph (rōō′dolf) Famous wolf. [< Gmc.] Also
  Ru′·dolf, Ru·dol·phus (rōō·dol′fəs). *Fr.* **Ro·dolphe**
  (rô·dôlf′), *Ital.* **Ro·dol·pho** (rō·dôl′fō), *Sp.* **Ro·dol·fo**
  (rō·thôl′fō). Dims. **Rol′lo, Ru′dy.**
Ru·fus (rōō′fəs) Red-haired. [< L] Dim. **Rufe.**
Ru·pert (rōō′pərt) Var. of ROBERT. [< G] Also *Ger.*
  Ru·precht (rōō′preḳht).
Rus·sell (rus′əl) Red: from an English surname. [OE < OF]
  Dim. **Russ.**

Sal·o·mon (sal′ə·mən) Var. of SOLOMON.
Sam·son (sam′sən) The sun. [< Hebrew] Also **Samp′·son**
  (samp′sən, sam′-).
Sam·u·el (sam′yōō·əl) Name of God. [< Hebrew] Dims.
  Sam, Sam′my.
San·dy (san′dē) Dim. of ALEXANDER. Also **San·der**
  (san′·dər, sän′-).
Saul (sôl) Asked (of God). [< Hebrew]
Schuy·ler (skī′lər) Shelter. [< Du.]
Scott (skot) The Scot: from an English surname.
Seam·us (shā′məs) Irish form of JAMES.
Sean (shôn, shan) Irish form of JOHN.
Se·bas·tian (si·bas′chən) Venerable. [< Gk.]
Seth (seth) Appointed. [< Hebrew]
Sew·ard (sōō′ərd) ? Sow-herder: from an English surname.
Sey·mour (sē′môr, -mōr) From an English surname; orig. a
  place name. Dims. **Cy, Sy.**
Shawn (shôn) Irish form of JOHN. Also **Shaun.**
Shel·don (shel′dən) From an English surname; orig. a place
  name.

Shir·ley (shûr′lē) From an English surname; orig. a place
  name.
Sid·ney (sid′nē) St. Denis: from an English surname. Dim.
  Sid.
Sieg·fried (sēg′frēd; *Ger.* zēk′frēt) Victorious peace.
  [< Gmc.]
Sig·is·mund (sij′ə s·mənd, sig′-) Victorious protection.
  [< Gmc.]
Sig·mund (sig′mənd; *Ger.* zeḳh′mōōnt) Var. of SIGISMUND.
Si·las (sī′ləs) Meaning uncertain. [< Gk.] Dim. **Si** (sī).
Sil·va·nus (sil·vā′nəs) From the name of the Roman god of
  woods and crops.
Sil·ves·ter (sil·ves′tər) Of the woods; rustic. [< L]
Sim·e·on (sim′ē·ən) He who is heard (widely); hence,
  famous. [< Hebrew] Dim. **Sim** (sim).
Si·mon (sī′mən) Var. of SIMEON.
Sin·clair (sin·klâr′, sin′klâr) St. Clair: from a Norman Fr.
  surname.
Sol·o·mon (sol′ə·mən) Peaceful. [< Hebrew] Dim. **Sol.**
Stan·ley (stan′lē) From an English surname; orig. a place
  name. Dim. **Stan.**
Ste·phen (stē′vən) Crown. [< Gk.] Also **Ste′ven,** *Ger.*
  Ste·phan or **Ste·fan** (shte′fän), *Ital.* **Ste·fa·no** (stä′fä·nō),
  Russ. **Ste·pan** (styi·pän′). Dims. **Steve, Ste′vie.**
Stew·art (stooərt, styōō′-) Steward: from an English surname.
  Also **Stu′art.** Dims. **Stew, Stu.**
Sum·ner (sum′nər) Summoner: from an English surname.
Syd·ney (sid′nē) Var. of SIDNEY.
Syl·va·nus (sil·vā′nəs) Var. of SILVANUS.
Syl·ves·ter (sil·ves′tər) Var. of SILVESTER.

Taf·fy (taf′ē) Welsh dim. of DAVID.
Tad (tad) Dim. of THEODORE or THADDEUS.
Ted (ted) Dim. of EDWARD or THEODORE. Also **Ted′dy.**
Ter·ence (ter′əns) From the name of a Roman clan. Also
  Ter′rence. Dim. **Ter′ry.**
Thad·de·us (thad′ē·əs) Praised. [< Aramaic] Dims. **Tad,**
  Thad, Tha′dy, Thad′dy.
The·o·bald (thē′ə·bôld, tib′əld) The people's brave one.
  [< Gmc.]
The·o·dore (thē′ə·dôr, -dōr) Gift of God. [< Gk.] Also
  Fr. **Thé·o·dore** (tā·ô·dôr′), *Ger.* **The·o·dor** (tā′ō·dôr),
  Modern Gk. **The·o·do·ros** (thä·ô′thô·rôs), *Ital., Sp.*
  Te·o·do·ro (*Ital.* tā′ō·dô′rō; *Sp.* tā′ō·thô′rō). Dims. **Tad,**
  Ted, Ted′dy, Dode (dōd).
Thom·as (tom′əs; *Fr.* tô·mä′; *Ger.* tō′mäs) Twin.
  [< Aramaic] Also *Ital.* **Tom·ma·so** (tōm·mä′zō), *Sp.*
  To·más (tō·mäs′). Dims. **Tom, Tom′my.**
Thurs·ton (thûrs′tən) Thor's stone. [< Scand.]
Tim·o·thy (tim′ə·thē) Honor of God. [< Gk.] Also *Fr.*
  Ti·mo·thée (tē·mô·tā′), *Ital.* **Tim·mo·te·o** (tē·mô′tā·ō).
  Dims. **Tim, Tim′my.**
Ti·tus (tī′təs) Meaning uncertain. [< L]
To·bi·as (tō·bī′əs) God is good. [< Hebrew] Also
  To·bi·ah (tō·bī′ə). Dim. **To·by** (tō′bē).
Tod (tod) Fox: from an English surname. Also **Todd.**
To·ny (tō′nē) Dim. of ANTHONY.
Tris·tan (tris′tän; -tən) Confusion. [< Celtic] Also
  Tris·tram (tris′trəm). Dim. **Tris.**
Tyb·alt (tib′əlt) Var. of THEOBALD.

U·lys·ses (yōō·lis′ēz) ? Hater: Lat. form of Gk. *Odysseus.*
Um·ber·to (ōōm·ber′tō) Ital. form of HUMBERT.
Ur·ban (ûr′bən) Of the city. [< L]
U·ri·ah (yōō·rī′ə) God is light. [< Hebrew] Also **U·ri·as**
  (yōō·rī′əs).
U·ri·el (yōōr′ē·əl) Light of God. [< Hebrew]

Val·en·tine (val′ən·tīn) Strong; healthy. [< L] Dim. **Val.**
Van (van) From an English surname, or from the Ger. or Du.
  name element *von, van,* indicating residence or origin.
Va·si·li (və·syē′lyē) Russ. var. of BASIL.
Ver·gil (vûr′jəl) Var. of VIRGIL.
Ver·non (vûr′nən) Meaning uncertain. [< L or F] Dim.
  Vern.
Vic·tor (vik′tər; *Fr.* vēk·tôr′) Conqueror. [< L] Also *Ital.*
  Vit·to·rio (vit·tô′ryō). Dims. **Vic, Vick.**

Vin·cent (vin'sənt; *Fr.* vaṅ·säṅ') Conquering. [< L] Also *Ger.* **Vin·cenz** (vin'tsents), *Ital.* **Vin·cen·zo** (vēn·chen'tsō), *Sp.* **Vi·cen·te** (vē·thän'tā). Dims. **Vin, Vince, Vin'ny.**

Vir·gil (vûr'jəl) Flourishing: from the name of a Roman clan. Also **Ver'gil.** Dims. **Virge, Vir'gie.**

Viv·i·an (viv'ē·ən, viv'yən) Lively. [< F] Also **Viv·i·en** (viv'ē·ən; *Fr.* vē·vyäṅ').

Wal·do (wôl'dō, wol'-) Ruler. [< Gmc.]

Wal·lace (wol'is) Welsh(man): from a Scot. surname. Also **Wal'lis.** Dim. **Wal'ly.**

Wal·ter (wôl'tər; *Ger.* väl'tər) Ruler of the Army. [< Gmc.] Also *Ger.* **Wal·ther** (väl'tər). Dims. **Walt, Wal'ly.**

Ward (wôrd) Guard: from an English surname.

War·ren (wôr'ən, wor'-) From an English surname.

Wayne (wān) From an English surname. [? < Celtic]

Wes·ley (wes'lē; *Brit.* wez'lē) From an English surname; orig. a place name. Dim. **Wes.**

Wil·bur (wil'bər) Bright will. [< Gmc.] Also **Wil'ber.**

Wil·fred (wil'frid) Resolute peace. [< Gmc.] Also **Wil'frid.** Dim. **Fred.**

Wil·lard (wil'ərd) From an English surname.

Wil·liam (wil'yəm) Resolute protection. [< Gmc.] Also *Du.* **Wil·lem** (vil'əm), *Ger.* **Wil·helm** (vil'helm). Dims. **Bill, Bil'ly, Will, Wil'lie, Wil'ly.**

Wil·lis (wil'is) Willie's son: from an English surname.

Win·fred (win'frid) Friend of peace. [OE] Also **Win'frid.** Dims. **Win, Win'nie.**

Win·ston (win'stən) From an English surname; orig. a place name.

Wy·att (wī'ət) Dim. of GUY. [< OF]

Wys·tan (wis'tən) Battle stone. [OE]

Zach·a·riah (zak'ə·rī'ə) Remembrance of God. [< Hebrew] Also **Zach·a·ri·as** (zak'ə·rī'əs). Dims. **Zach** (zak), **Zack.**

Zach·a·ry (zak'ər·ē) Var. of ZACHARIAH.

Zeb·a·di·ah (zeb'ə·dī'ə) Gift of God. [< Hebrew]

Zeb·e·dee (zeb'ə·dē) Contr. of ZEBADIAH.

Zech·a·ri·ah (Zek'ə·rī'ə) Var. of ZACHARIAH.

Zeke (zēk) Dim. of EZEKIEL.

Zeph·a·ni·ah (zef'ə·nī'ə) Protected by God. [< Hebrew] Dim. **Zeph.**

Feminine Names

Ab·i·gail (ab'ə·gāl) Father's joy. [< Hebrew] Dims. **Ab'·by, Ab'bie.**

A·da (ā'də) Joyful; flourishing. [< Gmc.]

A·dah (ā'də) Beauty. [< Hebrew] Also **A'da.**

Ad·e·la (ad'ə·lə; *Sp.* ä·thä'lä) Noble. [< Gmc.] Also **A·dele** (ə·del'). *Fr.* **A·dèle** (à·del'), *Ger.* **A·de·le** (ä·dā'lə).

Ad·e·laide (ad'ə·lād) Nobility. [< Gmc.] Also *Fr.* **A·dé·la·ïde** (à·dā·là·ēd'), *Ger.* **A·del·heid** (ä'dəl·hīt), *Ital.* **A·de·la·i·de** (ä'd·lä'ē·dä). Dims. **Ad'die, Ad'dy.**

Ad·e·line (ad'ə·līn; *Fr.* àd·lēn') Of noble birth. [< Gmc.] Also **Ad'a·line, Ad·e·li·cia** (ad'ə·lish'ə), **Ad·e·li·na** (ad'ə·lī'nə). Dims. **Ad'die, Ad'dy.**

A·dri·enne (ā'drē·en; *Fr.* à·drē·en') Fem. of ADRIAN. [< F]

Ag·a·tha (ag'ə·thə) Good; kind. [< Gk.] Also *Fr.* **A·gathe** (à·gàt'), *Ger.* **A·ga·the** (ä·gä'tə). Dim. **Ag'gie.**

Ag·nes (ag'nis; *Ger.* äg'nes) Pure; sacred. [< Gk.] Also *Fr.* **A·gnès** (à·nyâs'). Dim. **Ag'gie.**

A·i·da (ä·ē'd, ä'də) From the heroine of Verdi's opera.

Ai·leen (ā·lēn'; *Irish* ī·lēn') Var. of EILEEN.

Ai·mée (ā·mā') French form of AMY.

Al·ber·ta (al·bûr'tə) Fem. of ALBERT. Also **Al·ber·ti·na** (al'bər·tē'nə), **Al·ber·tine** (al'bər·tēn).

Al·e·the·a (al'ə·thē'ə, ə·lē'thē·ə) Truth. [< Gk.]

Al·ex·an·dra (al'ig·zan'drə, -zän'-) Fem. of ALEXANDER. Also **Al·ex·an·dri·na** (al'ig·zan·drē'nə, -zän-), *Fr.* **A·lex·an·drine** (à·lek·sän·drēn'), *Ital.* **A·les·san·dra** (ä'läs·sän'drä), *Sp.* **A·le·jan·dra** (ä'lä·hän'drä) or **A·le·jan·dri·na** (ä'lä·hän·drē'nä). Dims. **A·lex·a** (ə·lek'sə), **Al·ex·in·a** (al'ig·zē'nə), **Al·ix** (al'iks), **San·dra** (san'drə).

A·lex·is (ə·lek'sis) Fem. of ALEX. Also **A·lex·i·a** (ə·lek'sē·ə).

Al·fre·da (al·frē'də) Fem. of ALFRED.

Al·ice (al'is; *Fr.* à·lēs'; *Ger.* ä·lē'sə; *Ital.* ä·lē'chä) Truth. [< OF < Gmc.] Also **Al'lis, Al'yce, Al'ys.** Dim. **Al'lie.**

A·li·cia (ə·lish'ə, ə·lish'ē·ə) Var. of ALICE. [< L]

A·line (ə·lēn', al'ēn) Var. of ADELINE.

Al·i·son (al'ə·sən) Of sacred memory. [< Gmc.] Also **Al'li·son.**

Al·ix (al'iks) Dim. of ALEXANDRIA.

Al·le·gra (ə·lā'grə) Spirited. [< Ital. < L]

Al·ma (al'mə) Providing; gracious. [< L]

Al·mi·ra (al·mī'rə) Lofty; princess. [< Arabic]

Al·the·a (al·thē'ə) Healer. [< Gk.]

Al·vi·na (al·vī'nə, al·vē'nə) Fem. of ALVIN.

Am·a·bel (am'ə·bel) Lovable. [< L] also **Am'a·belle.** Dim. **Mab** (mab).

A·man·da (ə·man'də) Lovable. [< L] Also *Fr.* **A·man·dine** (à·mäṅ·dēn'). Dim. **Man'dy.**

Am·a·ran·tha (am'ə·ran'thə) Immortal. [< Gk.]

Am·a·ryl·lis (am'ə·ril'əs) Country sweetheart. [< L]

A·mel·ia (ə·mēl'yə, ə·mē'lē·ə; *Ital.* ä·mā'lyä; *Sp.* ä·mä'lyä) Industrious. [< Gmc.] Also *Fr.* **A·mé·lie** (à·mā·lē'). Dim. **Mil'lie, Mil'ly.**

Am·i·ty (am'ə·tē) From the abstract noun.

A·my (ā'mē) Beloved. [< L]

An·as·ta·sia (an'ə·stā'zhə, -shə) Able to live again. [< L]

An·dre·a (an'drē·ə; *Ital.* än·drä'ä) Fem. of ANDREW.

An·ge·la (an'jə·lə) Angel. [< Gk.] Also **An·ge·li·na** (an'·jə·lē'nə, -lī'-), *Fr.* **An·gèle** (äṅ·zhel').

An·gel·i·ca (an·jel'i·kə; *Ital.* än·jä'lē·kä) Angelic. [< Gk.] Also *Fr.* **An·gé·lique** (äṅ·zhā·lēk').

A·ni·ta (ə·nē'tə) Dim. of ANNA. [< Sp.] Also **A·ni·tra** (ə·nē'trə).

Ann (an) Grace. [< Hebrew] Also *Sp.* **A·na** (ä'nä). Dims. **An'nie, Nan, Nan'cy, Ni'na.**

An·na (an'ə; *Ger.* ä'nä) Var. of HANNAH. Dim. **An'nie.**

An·na·bel (an'ə·bel) Gracefully fair. [< Hebrew] Also **An·na·bel·la** (an'ə·bel'ə), **An'na·belle.**

Anne (an) Var. of ANN.

An·nette (ə·net'; *Fr.* à·net') Dim. of ANNE. [< F]

An·the·a (an·thē'ə) Flowery. [< Gk.]

An·toi·nette (an'twə·net'; *Fr.* äṅ·twà·net') Fr. form of ANTONIA. Also *Ital.* **An·to·niet·ta** (än·tō·nyet'tä). Dims. **Net'tie, Net'ty, To'ni.**

An·to·ni·a (an·tō'nē·ə, an·tō'·nē'a) Fem. of ANTHONY. [< L] Also *Ital., Sp.* **An·to·ni·na** (än'tō·nē'nä).

A·pril (ā'prəl) From the name of the month.

Ar·i·ad·ne (ar'ē·ad'nē) Most pure. [< Gk.]

Ar·lene (är·lēn') Meaning and origin uncertain. Also **Ar·leen** (är·lēn'), **Ar·line** (är·lēn').

As·pa·sia (as·pā'zhə, -zhē·ə) Welcome. [< L < Gk.]

As·trid (as'trid) God's power. (< Scand.]

A·the·na (ə·thē'nə) From the name of the greek goddess of wisdom. Also **A·the·ne** (ə·thē'nē).

Au·drey (ô'drē) Noble might. [< OF < Gmc.]

Au·gus·ta (ô·gus'tə; *Ger.* ou·gōos'tä; *Ital.* ou·gōos'tä) Fem. of AUGUSTUS. Also **Au·gus·ti·na** (ô'gəs·tē'nə), **Au·gus·tine** (ô'gəs·tēn). Dims. **Gus'sie, Gus'ta.**

Au·re·lia (ô·rēl'yə) Golden. [< L]

Au·ro·ra (ô·rôr'ə, ô·rō'rə) From the name of the Roman goddess of the dawn.

A·va (ā'və) Meaning and origin uncertain.

Av·e·line (av'ə·lēn, -līn) Hazel. [< F]

A·vis (ā'vis) Bird. [< L]

Ba·bette (ba·bet') Fr. dim. of ELIZABETH.

Bap·tis·ta (bap·tis'tə) Fem of BAPTIST. Also *Ital.* **Bat·tis·ta** (bät·tēs'tä).

Bar·ba·ra (bär′bər·ə, -brə) Foreign; strange. [< Gk.]
Dims. **Bab, Bab′bie, Babs, Barb, Bar′bie, Bob′bie.**
Bath·she·ba (bath·shē′bə, bath′shi·bə) Daughter of the
promise. [< Hebrew]
Be·a·ta (bē·ā′tə) Blessed. [< L]
Be·a·trice (bē′ə·tris; *Ital*. bā′ä·trē′chä) She who makes
happy. [< L] Also **Be·a·trix** (bē′ə·triks; *Ger*. bā·ä′triks),
Fr. **Bé·a·trice** or **Bé·a·trix** (bā·ä·trēs′). Dims. **Bea, Bee,
Trix, Trix′ie, Trix′y.**
Beck·y (bek′ē) Dim. of REBECCA.
Be·lin·da (bə·lin′də) Serpent: title of an oracular priestess.
[< Gmc.] Dim. **Lin′da.**
Bel·la (bel′ə) Dim. of ARABELLA or ISABELLA. Also **Bell.**
Belle (bel) Beautiful. [< F]
Ben·e·dic·ta (ben′ə·dik′tə) Fem. of BENEDICT. Also *Ital*.
Be·ne·det·ta (bā′nä·dāt′tä), *Sp*. **Be·ni·ta** (bā·nē′tä).
Ber·e·ni·ce (ber′ə·nī′sē) Victorious. [< Gk.]
Ber·na·dette (bûr′nə·det′, *Fr*. ber·nà·det′) Fem. of
BERNARD. [< F]
Ber·nar·dine (bûr′nər·dēn) Fem. of BERNARD. [< F] Also
Ber·nar·di·na (bûr′nər·dē′nə).
Ber·nice (bər·nēs′, bûr′nis) Var. of BERENICE.
Ber·tha (bûr′thə; *Du*., *Ger*., *Sw*. ber′tä) Bright; famous.
[< Gmc.] Also *Fr*. **Berthe** (bert), *Ital*., *Sp*. **Ber·ta** (ber·tä).
Dims. **Ber′tie, Ber′ty.**
Ber·yl (ber′əl) From the name of the jewel.
Bess (bes) Dim. of ELIZABETH. Also **Bes′sie, Bes′sy.**
Beth (beth) Dim. of ELIZABETH.
Beth·el (beth′əl) House of God. [< Hebrew]
Bet·sy (bet′sē) Dim. of ELIZABETH.
Bet·ti·na (bə·tē′nə) Dim. of ELIZABETH. [< Ital.]
Bet·ty (bet′ē) Dim. of ELIZABETH. Also **Bet′te** (bet′ē, bet).
Beu·lah (byōō′lə) Married. [< Hebrew] Also **Beu′la.**
Bev·er·ly (bev′er·lē) From an English surname; orig. a place
name. Also **Bev′er·ley.** Dim. **Bev.**
Bid·dy (bid′ē) Dim. of BRIDGET.
Blanche (blanch, blänch; *Fr*. blänsh) White; shining. [< F
< Gmc.] Also **Blanch,** *Ital*. **Bian·ca** (byäng′kä), *Sp*.
Blan·ca (bläng′kä).
Bon·ny (bon′ē) Good. [< F] Also **Bon′nie.**
Bren·da (bren′də) Sword or torch. [< Gmc.]
Bridg·et (brij′it) High; august. [< Celtic] Also **Brig·id**
(brij′id, brē′id). Dims. **Bid′dy, Bri·die** (brī′dē).

Ca·mel·lia (kə·mēl′yə) From the name of the flower.
Ca·mil·ia (kə·mil′ə; *Ital*. kä·mēl′lä) Attendant at a sacrifice.
[< L] Also *Fr*. **Ca·mille** (kà·mēl′), *Sp*. **Ca·mi·la**
(kä·mē′lä).
Can·dice (kan′dis) Radiant. [< L] Also **Can·da·ce**
(kan′·də·sē, kan′dā′sē).
Can·di·da (kan′di·də) White; pure. [< L]
Ca·ra (kär′ə) Loved one. [< L]
Car·la (kär′lə) Fem. of CARLO.
Car·lot·ta (kär·lot′ə; *Ital*. kär·lôt′tä) Ital. form of
CHARLOTTE. Also *Sp*. **Car·lo·ta** (kär·lō′tä). Dims. **Lot′ta,
Lot′·tie, Lot′ty.**
Car·mel (kär′məl) Garden. [< Hebrew] Also **Car·mel·a**
(kär·mel′ə). Dim. **Car·me·li·ta** (kär′mə·lē′tə).
Car·men (kär′mən) Song. [< L]
Car·ol (kar′əl) From CAROL, masc., var. of CHARLES. Also
Car·o·la (kar′ə·lə), **Car′ole, Kar′ol.**
Car·o·line (kar′ə·līn, -lin; *Fr*. kà·rô·lēn′) Fem. of CHARLES.
Also **Car·o·lyn,** (kar′ə·lin), **Car·o·li·na** (kar′ə·lī′nə; *Ital*.,
Sp. kä′rō·lē′nä). Dim. **Car′rie.**
Cas·san·dra (kə·san′drə) From the name of the Trojan
prophetess in the *Iliad*. [< Gk.] Dims. **Cass, Cas′sie.**
Cath·er·ine (kath′ər·in, kàth′rin, *Fr*. ka·trēn′) Purity.
[< Gk.] Also **Kath′er·ine, Cath′a·rine, Cath·a·ri·na**
(kath′ə·rē′nə), *Ital*., *Sp*. **Ca·ta·ri·na** (kä′tä·rē′nä), or
Ca·te·ri·na (kä′·tä·rē′nä). Dims. **Cath′y, Kate, Kath′y,
Kath′ie, Ka′tie, Kay, Kit, Kit′ty.**
Cath·leen (kath′lēn, kàth·lēn′) Var. of KATHLEEN.
Ce·cil·ia (si·sil′yə, -sēl′yə) Fem. of CECIL. Also **Ce·cel′ia,
Ce·cile** (si·sēl′), **Cec·i·ly** (ses′ə·lē), *Fr*. **Cé·cile** (sā·sēl′).
Dims. **Cis, Cis′sie, Cis′sy.**
Ce·leste (si·lest′) Heavenly. [< F < L] Also **Ce·les·tine**
(si·les′tin, sel′is·tīn), *Fr*. **Cé·les·tine** (sā·les·tēn′).

Cel·ia (sēl′yə, sē′lē·ə; *Ital*. chā′lyä) From the name of a
Roman clan. Also *Fr*. **Cé·lie** (sā·lē′).
Cha·ris·sa (kə·ris′ə) Love; grace. [< Gk.]
Char·i·ty (char′ə·tē) From the abstract noun. Dim.
Cher′ry.
Char·lene (shär·lēn′) Fem. of CHARLES.
Char·lotte (shär·lət; *Fr*. shàr·lôt′; *Ger*. shär·lôt′ə) Fem. of
CHARLES. [< F] Dims. **Car′ry, Lot′ta, Lot′tie, Lot′ty.**
Cher·yl (cher′əl) Meaning and origin uncertain.
Chlo·e (klō′ē) Bud; sprout. [< Gk.]
Chris·ta·bel (kris′tə·bel) The fair anointed. [< L] Also
Chris′ta·bel′la, Chris′ta·belle.
Chris·ti·an·a (kris′tē·an′ə) Fem. of CHRISTIAN. Also *Ger*.
Chri·sti·a·ne (kris′tē·ä′nə)
Chris·ti·na (kris·tē′nə) Var. of CHRISTIANA. Also
Chris·tine (kris·tēn′; *Fr*. krēs·tēn′; *Ger*. kris·tē′nə). Dims.
Chris, Chris′sie, Chris′ta, Chris′tie, Ti′na.
Cic·e·ly (sis′ə·lē) Var. of CECILIA.
Cin·dy (sin′dē) Dim. of LUCINDA.
Claire (klâr) Var. of CLARA. [< F] Also **Clare.**
Clar·a (klar′ə, klâr′ə; *Ger*., *Sp*. klä′rä) Bright; illustrious.
[< L]
Clar·i·bel (klar′ə·bel) Brightly fair. [< L] Also
Clar′a·belle.
Cla·rice (klə·rēs′, klar′is) Derived from CLARA. Also
Cla·ris·sa (klə·ris′ə), **Cla·risse** (klə·rēs′).
Cla·rin·da (klə·rin′də) Derived from CLARA.
Clau·dette (klô·det′; *Fr*. klō·det′) Fem. of CLAUDE. [< F]
Clau·di·a (klô′dē·ə) Fem. of *Claudius*, Lat. form of CLAUDE.
Clem·en·tine (klem′ən·tēn, -tīn) Fem. of CLEMENT. [< F]
Cle·o·pat·ra (klē′ə·pat′rə, -pā′trə, -pä′trə) Celebrated of her
country. [< Gk.] Dim. **Cle·o** (klē′ō).
Cli·o (klī′ō, klē′ō) From the name of the Greek muse of
history.
Clo·til·da (klō·til′də) Famous in war. [< Gmc.] Also
Clo·thil′da, Clo·thil′de, *Fr*. **Clo·tilde** (klô·tēld′).
Co·lette (kō·let′; *Fr*. kô·let′) Fem. dim. of NICHOLAS.
[< F]
Col·leen (kol·ēn, ko·lēn′) Girl. [< Irish]
Con·stance (kon′stəns, *Fr*. kôn·stäns′) Constant; firm.
[< L] Dims. **Con′nie, Con′ny.**
Con·sue·lo (kən·swä′lō; *Sp*. kōn·swä′lō) Consolation.
[< Sp.]
Co·ra (kôr′ə, kō′rə) Maiden. [< Gk.]
Cor·del·ia (kôr·dēl′yə, -dē′lē·ə) Meaning uncertain. [< L]
Co·rin·na (kə·rin′ə) Maiden. [< Gk.] Also **Co·rinne**
(kə·rin′, -rēn′; *Fr*. kô·rēn′).
Cor·nel·ia (kôr·nēl′yə, -nē′lē·ə) Fem. of CORNELIUS. [< L]
Cris·ti·na (krēs·tē′nä) Ital. and Sp. form of CHRISTINA.
Crys·tal (kris′təl) From the common noun.
Cyn·thi·a (sin′thē·ə) Of Mount Cynthiuis: an epithet of the
Greek goddess Artemis; poetically ,the moon.

Dag·mar (dag′mär) Bright day. [< Dan.]
Dai·sy (dā′zē) From the name of the flower.
Dale (dāl) From the common noun.
Daph·ne (daf′nē) Laurel. [< Gk.]
Dar·leen (därl·lēn′) Beloved. [OE] Also **Dar·lene′,
Dar·line′.**
Dawn (dôn) From the common noun.
Deb·o·rah (deb′ər·ə, deb′rə) Queen bee. [< Hebrew]
Dims. **Deb, Deb′by.**
Deir·dre (dir′drə) From the name of a heroine of Irish myth.
Del·ia (dēl′yə) Of Delos: an epithet of the Greek goddess
Artemis. [< Gk.]
De·li·lah (di·lī′lə) Delicate; languid. [< Hebrew]
Del·la (del′ə) Var. of ADELA.
Del·phin·i·a (del·fin′ē·ə) Of Delphi. [< Gk.] Also *Fr*.
Del·phine (del·fēn′).
De·nise (də·nēz′, -nēs′) Fem. of *Denis*. Fr. form of DENNIS.
Des·i·ree (dez′ə·rē) Desired. [< F] Also *Fr*. **Dé·si·rée**
(dā·zē·rā′).
Di·an·a (dī·an′ə) From the name of the Roman goddess of
the moon. Also **Di·ane** (dī·an′; *Fr*. dyàn). Dim. **Di** (dī).
Di·nah (dī′nə) Judged. [< Hebrew]
Do·lo·res (də·lôr′is, -lō′ris; *Sp*. dō·lō′räs) Our Lady of

Sorrows: a title of the Virgin Mary. [< Sp.] Dim. **Lo·la** (lō′lə).

Dom·i·nique (dom′ə·nēk; *Fr.* dô·mē·nēk′) Fr. fem. of DOMINIC. Also **Dom·i·ni·ca** (dom′ə·nē′kə, də·min′ə·kə).

Don·na (don′ə) Lady. [< Ital.]

Do·ra (dôr′ə, dō′rə) Dim. of DOROTHY, EUDORA, or THEODORA.

Dor·cas (dôr′kəs) Gazelle. [< Gk.]

Do·reen (dô·rēn′, dôr′ēn, dō-) Irish dim. of DORA.

Do·rin·da (də·rin′də) Gift. [< Gk.]

Do·ris (dôr′is, dor′-) Dorian woman. [< Gk.]

Dor·o·thy (dôr′ə·thē, dor′-) Gift of God. [< Gk.] Also **Dor·o·the·a** (dôr′ə·thē′ə, dor′-; *Ger.* dō′rō·tā′ä), *Fr.* **Do·ro·thée** (dô·rô·tā′). Dims. **Doll, Dol′lie, Dol′ly, Do′ra, Dot, Dot′ty.**

Dru·sil·la (drōō·sil′ə) She who strengthens. [< L] Also **Dru·cil′la.**

E·dith (ē′dith) Prosperous in war. [OE] Also *Lat.* **Ed·i·tha** (ed′i·thə, ē′di·thə). Dim. **E·die** or **Ea·die** (ē′dē).

Ed·na (ed′nə) Rejuvenation. [< Hebrew]

Ed·wi·na (ed·wē′nə, -win′ə) Fem. of EDWIN.

Ef·fie (ef′ē) Dim. of EUPHEMIA.

Ei·leen (ī·lēn′) Irish form of HELEN.

E·ka·te·ri·na (yə·kə·tyi·ryē′nə) Russ. form of CATHERINE.

E·laine (i·lān′, ē·lān′) Var. of HELEN. [< OF] Also **E·layne′.**

El·ber·ta (el·bûr′tə) Fem. of ELBERT.

El·ea·nor (el′ə·nər, -nôr) Var. of HELEN. [< F] Also **El′i·nor, El·ea·no·ra** (el′ə·nôr′ə, -nō′rə, el′ē·ə-), *Fr.* **É·lé·o·nore** (ā·lā·ô·nôr′), *Ger.* **E·le·o·no·re** (ā′lā·ō·nō′rə), *Ital.* **E·le·o·no·ra** (ā′lā·ō·nō′rä). Dims. **El′la, El′lie, Nell, Nel′lie, Nel′ly.**

E·lec·tra (i·lek′trə) Shining; golden-haired. [< Gk.] Also **E·lek′tra.**

El·e·na (el′ə·nə, ə·lē′nə; *Ital.* â′lā·nä) Var. of HELEN. [< Ital.]

E·li·za (i·lī′zə) Dim. of ELIZABETH. Also *Fr.* **É·lise** (ā·lēz′)

E·liz·a·beth (i·liz′ə·bəth) Consecrated to God. [< Hebrew] Also **E·lis·a·beth** (i·liz′ə·bəth; *Ger.* ā·lē′zä·bet), *Fr.* **É·li·sa·beth** (ā·lē·zȧ·bet′), *Ital.* **E·li·sa·bet·ta** (ā·lē′zä·bät′tä). Dims. **Bess, Bes′sie, Beth, Bet′sy, Bet′te, Bet′ty, El′sa, El′sie, Lib′by, Li′sa, Liz, Liz′beth, Liz′zie, Liz′zy.**

El·la (el′ə) Dim. of ELEANOR. Also **El′lie.**

El·len (el′ən) Var. of HELEN.

E·lo·i·sa (ā′lō·ē′zä) Ital. form of LOUISE.

E·lo·ise (el′ō·ēz′, el′ō·ēz) Var. of LOUISE. [< F]

El·sa (el′sə; *Ger.* el′zä) Dim. of ELIZABETH. Also **El·sie** (el′·sē).

El·speth (el′spəth) Scot. form of ELIZABETH.

El·va (el′və) Elf. [< Gmc.]

El·vi·ra (el·vī′rä, -vir′ə) Elf ruler. [< Sp. < Gmc.]

Em·e·line (em′ə·līn, -lēn) Derived from EMILY. Also **Em′·me·line.**

Em·i·ly (em′ə·lē) Fem. of EMIL. Also **Em′i·lie,** *Fr.* **É·mi·lie** (ā·mē·lē′), *Ger.* **E·mi·li·e** (e·mē′lē·ə), *Ital., Sp.* **E·mi·lia** (ā·mē′lyä). Dim. **Em.**

Em·ma (em′ə) Grandmother. [< Gmc.] Dims. **Em, Em′·mie.**

E·nid (ē′nid) Chastity; purity. [< Celtic]

Er·i·ca (er′i·kə) Fem. of ERIC. Also **Er′i·ka.**

Er·ma (ûr′mə) Dim. of ERMENGARDE.

Er·men·garde (ûr′mən·gärd) Great guardian. [< Gmc.]

Er·men·trude (ûr′mən·trōōd) Great strength. [< Gmc.]

Er·nes·tine (ûr′nəs·tēn) Fem. of ERNEST.

Es·me·ral·da (es′mə·ral′də) Emerald. [< Sp.]

Es·telle (es·tel′) Star. [< L] Also **Es·tel·la** (es·tel′ə).

Es·ther (es′tər) Star. [< Pers.] Dims. **Es′sie, Het′ty.**

Eth·el (eth′əl) Noble. [< Gmc.]

Et·ta (et′ə) Dim. of HENRIETTA.

Eu·do·ra (yōō·dôr′ə, -dō′rə) Good gift. [< Gk.]

Eu·ge·nia (yōō·jē′nē·ə, -jēn′yə) Fem. of EUGENE. **Eu·ge·nie** (yōō·jē′nē), *Fr.* **Eu·gé·nie** (œ·zhā·nē′). Dims. **Gene, Ge′nie.**

Eu·la·li·a (yōō·lā′lē·ə, -lāl′yə) Fair speech. [< Gk.] Also **Eu·la·lie** (yōō′lə·lē; *Fr.* œ·lȧ·lē′).

Eu·nice (yōō′nis; *Lat.* yōō·nī′sē) Good victory. [< Gk.]

Eu·phe·mi·a (yōō·fē′mē·ə) Of good repute. [< Gk.] Also *Fr.* **Eu·phé·mie** (œ·fā·mē′). Dims. **Ef·fie** (ef′ē), **Phe′mie.**

E·va (ē′və; *Ger., Ital., Sp.* ā′vä) Var. of EVE. [< L]

E·van·ge·line (i·van′jə·lin, -lin, -lēn) Bearer of glad tidings. [< Gk.]

Eve (ēv; *Fr.* ev) Life. [< Hebrew]

Ev·e·lyn (ev′ə·lin; *Brit.* ēv′lin) Hazelnut. [< L] Also **Ev·e·li·na** (ev′ə·lī′nə, -lē′-).

E·vi·ta (ā·vē′tä) Sp. dim. of EVA.

Faith (fāth) From the abstract noun. Dim. **Fay.**

Fan·ny (fan′ē) Dim. of FRANCES. Also **Fan′nie.**

Faus·ti·na (fôs·tī′nə, -tē′-) Lucky. [< L] Also **Faus·tine** (fôs·tēn′; *Fr.* fōs·tēn′)

Fawn (fôn) From the name of the animal.

Fay (fā) Fairy or faith. [OF] Also **Fae, Faye.**

Fe·li·cia (fə·lish′ə, -lish′ē·ə, -lē′shə) Happy. [< L] Also **Fe·lice** (fə·lēs′), **Fe·lic′i·ty** (-lis′ə·tē)

Fern (fûrn) From the common noun.

Fer·nan·da (fer·nän′dä) Fem. of *Fernando,* Sp. form of FERDINAND.

Fi·del·ia (fi·dēl′yə, -dē′lē·ə) Faithful. [< L]

Fi·o·na (fē·ō′nə) Fair or white. [< Celtic]

Fla·vi·a (flā′vē·ə) Blonde. [<]

Flo·ra (flôr′ə, flō′rə) Flower. [< L]

Flor·ence (flôr′əns, flor′-; *Fr.* flô·räns′) Blooming. [< L] Dims. **Flo** (flō), **Flor·rie** (flôr′ē, flor′ē), **Flos·sie** (flos′ē).

Fran·ces (fran′sis, frän′-) Fem. of FRANCIS. Also *Fr.* **Fran·çoise** (frän·swȧz′) or **Fran·cisque** (frän·sēsk′), *Ital.* **Fran·ces·ca** (frän·chäs′kä). Dims. **Fan′nie, Fan′ny, Fran, Fran′cie, Frank, Fran′nie.**

Fran·cine (fran·sēn′) Derived from FRANCES. Also **Fran·cene′.**

Fred·er·i·ca (fred′ə·rē′kə, fred·rē′kə) Fem. of FREDERICK. Dim. **Fred′die.**

Frie·da (frē′də) Peace. [< G] Also **Fre′da.**

Ga·bri·elle (gä′brē·el′, gab′rē-; *Fr.* gȧ·brē·el′) Fem. of GABRIEL. Also **Ga·bri·el·la** (gä′brē·el′ə) Dim. **Ga·by** (gä·bē′).

Gail (gāl) Short for ABIGAIL. Also **Gale.**

Gay (gā) From the adjective.

Gen·e·vieve (jen′ə·vēv, jen′ə·vēv′) White wave. [< F < Celtic] Also *Fr.* **Ge·ne·viève** (zhen·vyev′).

Ge·nev·ra (ji·nev′rə) Var. of GUINEVERE. [< Ital.] Also **Ge·ne·va** (ji·nē′və).

Geor·gia (jôr′jə) Fem. of GEORGE.

Geor·gi·an·a (jôr′jē·an′ə) Fem. of GEORGE. Also **Geor·gi·na** (jôr·jē′nə), *Fr.* **Geor·gine** (zhôr·zhēn′) or **Geor·gette** (zhôr·zhet′).

Ger·al·dine (jer′əl·dēn) Fem. of GERALD. Dims. **Ger′ry, Jer′ry.**

Ger·maine (jər·mān′) German. [< F < L]

Ger·trude (gûr′trōōd, *Fr.* zher·trüd′) Spear maid. [< Gmc.] Also *Ger.* **Ger·trud** (ger′trōōt). Dims. **Ger′tie, Ger′ty, Tru′da, Tru′dy.**

Gil·ber·ta (gil·bûr′tə) Fem. of GILBERT. Also **Gil·ber·tine** (gil′bər·tēn), *Fr.* **Gil·berte** (zhēl·bert′)

Gil·da (gil′də) Servant of God. [< Celtic]

Gil·li·an (jil′ēl·ən, jil′yən) Var. of JULIANA.

Gi·nev·ra (ji·nev′rə) Var. of GUINEVERE. (< Ital.]

Gin·ger (jin′jer) From the plant name.

Gio·van·na (jō·vän′nä) Fem. of *Giovanni,* Ital. form of JOHN.

Gi·sele (zhē·zel′) Pledge or hostage. (< F < Gmc.] Also **Gi·selle′.**

Giu·lia (jōō′lyä) Ital. form of JULIA.

Glad·ys (glad′is) Welsh fem. form of CLAUDIUS.

Glen·na (glen′ə) Fem. of GLENN. Also **Glen·nis** (glen′is), **Gly·nis** (glin′is).

Glo·ri·a (glôr′ē·ə, glō′rē·ə) Glory. [< L]

Grace (grās) Grace; favor. [< L] Also **Gra·ci·a** or **Gra·ti·a** (grā′shē·ə, -shə).

Gret·a (gret′ə, grēt′ə; *Ger.* grä′tə) Dim. of MARGARET. [< G] Also **Gre·tel** or **Gre·thel** (grā′təl).

Gretch·en (grech′ən; *Ger.* grät′ᴋʜən) Dim. of MARGARET. [< G]

Gri·sel·da (gri·zel'də)   Stony or unbeatable heroine.
  [< Gmc.]   Also **Gris·sel** (gris'əl), **Griz·el** (griz'əl).
Gus·sie (gus'ē)   Dim. of AUGUSTA.   Also **Gus·ta** (gus'tə)
Gwen·do·lyn (gwen'də·lin)   White-browed.   [< Celtic]
  Also **Gwen'do·len, Gwen'do·line** (-lin, -lēn).   Dims.
  Gwen, Gwenn, Wen·dy (wen'dē).
Gwen·eth (gwen'ith)   Fair or blessed.   [< Celtic]   Also
  Gwen'ith, Gwyn·eth (gwin'ith), **Gyn·eth** (gin'ith).
Gwyn (gwin)   Fair or White.   [< Celtic]   Also **Gwynne**.

Han·nah (han'ə)   Grace.   [< Hebrew]   Also **Han'na**.
Har·ri·et (har'ē·ət)   Fem. of HARRY.   Dims. **Hat'tie, Hat'ty**.
Ha·zel (hā'zəl)   From the plant name.
Heath·er (heth'ər)   From the plant name.
Hed·da (hed'ə)   War.   [< Gmc.]
Hed·wig (hed'wig)   War.   [< Gmc.]
Hel·en (hel'ən)   Light; a torch.   [< Gk.]   Also *Fr.* **Hé·lène**
  (ā·len').   Dims. **Nell, Nel'lie, Nel'ly**.
Hel·e·na (hel'ə·nə)   Var. of HELEN.   Dim. **Le·na** (lē'nə).
Hel·ga (hel'gə)   Holy.   [< Gmc.]
Hé·lo·ïse (ā·lō·ēz')   Fr. form of ELOISE.
Hen·ri·et·ta (hen'rē·et'ə)   Fem. of HENRY.   Also *Fr.*
  Hen·ri·ette (än·ryet').   Dims. **Et'ta, Et'tie, Hat'tie,
  Hat'ty, Het'·ty, Net'tie, Ret'ta**.
Heph·zi·bah (hep'zə·bə)   She who is my delight.
  [< Hebrew]
Her·mi·o·ne (hər·mī'ə·nē)   Fem. of HERMES.
Hes·ter (hes'tər)   Var. of ESTHER.   Also **Hes'ther**.   Dim.
  Het'ty.
Het·ty (het'ē)   Dim. of ESTHER, HENRIETTA, or HESTER.
Hil·a·ry (hil'ər·ē)   Joyful.   [< L]
Hil·da (hil'də)   Battle maiden.   [OE]
Hil·de·garde (hil'də·gärd)   Guardian battle maiden.
  [< Gmc.]   Also **Hil'de·gard**.
Hol·ly (hol'ē)   From the plant name.
Ho·no·ra (hō·nôr'ə, -nō'rə)   Honor.   [< L]   Also
  Ho·no·ri·a (hō·nôr'ē·ə, -nō'rē·ə)   Dims. **No'ra, No'rah**.
Hope (hōp)   From the abstract noun.
Hor·tense (hôr'tens; *Fr.* ôr·täns')   Gardener: from the name
  of a Roman clan.   [< F < L]   Also *Lat.* **Hor·ten·si·a**
  (hôr·ten'shē·ə).

I·da (ī'də)   Happy; godlike.   [< Gmc.]
I·lo·na (i·lō'nə)   Radiantly beautiful.   [< Hung. < Gk.]
Il·se (il'sə; *Ger.* il'zə)   Dim. of ELIZABETH.   [< G]
Im·o·gene (im'ə·jēn)   Meaning and origin uncertain.   Also
  Im·o·gen (im'ə·jən).
I·na (ī'nə)   From the Lat. suffix for fem. names.
I·nez (ī'nez, ē'nez; *Sp.* ē·nāth')   Var. of AGNES.   [< Sp. &
  Pg.]
In·grid (ing'grid)   Daughter of Ing (a god in Gmc.
  mythology).   [< Gmc.]   Also **In·ga** (ing'gə).
I·rene (ī·rēn')   Peace.   [< Gk.]
I·ris (ī'ris)   Rainbow.   [< Gk.], or from the name of the
  flower.
Ir·ma (ûr'mə)   Var. of ERMA.
Is·a·bel (iz'ə·bel; *Sp.* ē'sä·bel')   Oath of Baal.   [< Hebrew]
  Also **Is·a·bel·la** (iz'ə·bel'ə), **Ital.** ē'zä·bel'lä), **Is·a·belle**
  (iz'ə·bel; *Fr.* ē·zä·bel'), **Is'o·bel**, *Fr.* **I·sa·beau** (ē·zä·bō').
  Dims. **Bell, Bel'la, Belle**.
Is·a·do·ra (iz'ə·dôr'ə, -dō'rə)   Fem. of ISIDORE.
I·vy (ī'vē)   From the plant name.

Jac·que·line (jak'wə·lin, -lēn, jak'ə-; *Fr.* zhä·klēn')   Fem. of
  Jacques, Fr. form of JACOB.   Dim. **Jac'kie**.
Jane (jān)   Var. of JOAN.   [< OF]
Jan·et (jan'it, jə·net')   Dim. of JANE.
Jan·ice (jan'is)   Var. of JANE.
Jas·mine (jaz'min, jas'-)   From the name of the flower.
Jean (jēn)   Var. of JOAN.   [< F]
Jeanne (jēn, *Fr.* zhän)   Fr. form of JOAN.
Jean·nette (jə·net')   Dim. of JEANNE.
Je·mi·ma (jə·mī'mə)   Dove.   [< Hebrew]
Jen·ni·fer (jen'ə·fər)   Var. of GUINEVERE.   Dims. **Jen'ny,
  Jin'ny**.
Jer·ry (jer'ē)   Dim. of GERALDINE.

Jes·si·ca (jes'i·kə)   Fem. of JESSE.   Dims. **Jess, Jes'sie,
  Jes'sy**.
Jew·el (jōō'əl)   From the common noun.
Jill (jil)   Short for JULIA.
Jo (jō)   Dim. of JOSEPHINE.
Joan (jōn, jō·an')   Fem. of JOHN.   Also **Jo·an·na** (jō·an'ə),
  Jo·anne (jō·an')
Joc·e·lyn (jos'ə·lin)   Playful; merry.   [< L]   Also **Joc'e·lin,
  Joc'e·line** (-lin).
Jo·han·na (jō·han'ə; *Ger.* yō·hän'ä)   Ger. form of JOAN.
Jo·se·pha (jō·sē'fə)   Var. of JOSEPHINE.
Jo·se·phine (jō'sə·fēn, -zə-)   Fem. of JOSEPH.   [< F]   Dims.
  Jo, Jo'sie, Jo'zy.
Joy (joi)   From the abstract noun.
Joyce (jois)   Joyful.   [< L]
Jua·na (wä'nə; *Sp.* hwä'nä)   Fem. of *Juan*, Sp. form of JOHN.
Jua·ni·ta (wä·nē'tə; *Sp.* hwä·nē'tä)   Sp. dim. of JUANA.
Ju·dith (jōō'dith)   Praised.   [< Hebrew]   Dim. **Ju'dy**.
Jul·ia (jōōl'yə)   Fem. of JULIUS.   Also **Ju·lie** (jōō'lē; *Fr.*
  zhü·lē').
Ju·li·an·a (jōō'lē·an'ə, -ä'nə)   Fem. of JULIAN.   Also *Fr.*
  Ju·li·enne (zhü·lyen').
Ju·li·et (jōō'lē·et, jōō'lē·et')   Dim. of JULIA.
June (jōōn)   From the name of the month.
Jus·ti·na (jus·tī'nə, -tē'-)   Fem. of JUSTIN.   Also **Jus·tine**
  (jus·tēn'; *Fr.* zhüs·tēn').

Kar·en (kâr'ən; *Dan., Norw.* kä'rən)   Var. of CATHERINE.
  [< Dan. & Norw.]
Kate (kāt)   Dim. of CATHERINE.   Also **Ka'tie**.
Kath·a·rine (kath'ə·rin, kath'rin)   Var. of CATHERINE.   Also
  Kath'er·ine, Kath'ryn.
Kath·leen (kath'lēn, kath·lēn')   Irish form of CATHERINE.
Kath·y (kath'ē)   Dim. of CATHERINE.
Ka·tri·na (kə·trē'nə)   Var. of CATHERINE.   Also **Kat·rine**
  (kat'rin, -rēn).   Dim. **Tri·na** (trē'nə).
Kay (kā)   Dim. of CATHERINE.
Kir·sten (kûr'stən; *Norw.* khish'tən, khir'stən)   Norw. form
  of CHRISTINE.
Kit·ty (kit'ē)   Dim. of CATHERINE.   Also **Kit**.
Kla·ra (klä'rä)   Ger. form of CLARA.

Lau·ra (lôr'ə)   Laurel.   [< L]   Also *Fr.* **Laure** (lôr).
  Dims. **Lau'rie, Lol'ly**.
Lau·ret·ta (lô·ret'ə)   Dim. of LAURA.   Also **Lau·rette'**.
Lau·rin·da (lô·rin'də)   Derived from LAURA.
La·verne (lə·vûrn')   From the name of the Roman goddess of
  spring and grain.
La·vin·i·a (lə·vin'ē·ə)   Purified.   [< L]
Le·ah (lē'ə)   Gazelle.   [< Hebrew]   Also **Le'a**.
Lei·la (lē'lä)   Dark night or dark beauty.   [< Arabic]
Le·na (lē'nə)   Dim. of HELENA or MAGDALENE.
Le·no·ra (lə·nôr'ə, -nō'rə)   Var. of ELEANOR.   Also **Le·nore**
  (lə·nôr').
Le·o·na (lē·ō'nə)   Fem. of LEO and LEON.   Also *Fr.* **Lé·o·nie**
  (lā·ô·nē').
Le·or·a (lē·ôr'ə, -ō'rə)   Var. of LEONORA.
Les·lie (les'lē, les'-)   From LESLIE. masc.   Also **Les'ley**.
Le·ti·tia (li·tish'ə)   Joy.   [< L]   Dim. **Let'ty** (let'ē).
Lib·by (lib'ē)   Dim. of ELIZABETH.
Li·la (lī'lə, lē'-)   Var. of LILLIAN.
Lil·i·an (lil'ē·ən, lil'yən)   Lily.   [< L]   Also **Lil'li·an**.
  Dims. **Lil, Lil'ly, Lil'y**.
Lil·y (lil'ē)   From the name of the flower; also, dim. of LILIAN.
Lin·da (lin'də)   Pretty   [< Sp.], or short for BELINDA or
  MELINDA.
Li·sa (lī'zə, lē')   Dim. of ELIZABETH.   Also **Li'za**, *Ger.* **Li·se**
  (lē'zə).
Li·sette (lē·zet')   Fr. dim. of ELIZABETH.   Also **Li·zette'**.
Liz·beth (liz'bəth)   Dim. of ELIZABETH.
Liz'zie (liz'ē)   Dim. of ELIZABETH.   Also **Liz'zy, Liz. Lo·is**
  (lō'is)   Desirable.   [< Gk.]
Lo·la (lō'lə; *Sp.* lō'lä)   Dim. of DOLORES.   [< Sp.]   Dim.
  Lo·li·ta (lō·lē'tə; *Sp.* lōl·lē'tä).
Lor·ene (lô·rēn')   Var. of LAURA.   Also **Laur·een',
  Laur·ene', Lor·een'**.

Lor·et·ta (lô·ret′ə, lō-) Dim. of LAURA. Also **Lor·ette** (lô·ret′).

Lo·rin·da (lô·rin′də, lə-) Var. of LAURINDA.

Lor·na (lôr′nə) Lost. [OE]

Lor·raine (lə·rān′) Var. of LAURA.

Lot·tie (lot′ē) Dim. of CHARLOTTE. Also **Lot′ta, Lot′ty.**

Lou·el·la (lōō·el′ə) Var. of LUELLA.

Lou·ise (lōō·ēz′) Fem. of LOUIS. [< F] Also **Lou·i·sa** (lōō·ē′zə). Dims. **Lou, Lou′ie, Lu, Lu′lu.**

Lu·cia (lōō′shə; *Ital.* lōō·chē′ä) Fem. of LUCIUS.

Lu·cille (lōō·sēl′) Var. of LUCIA [< F] Also **Lu·cile′.**

Lu·cin·da (lōō·sin′də) Derived from LUCY. Dim. **Cin·dy** (sin′dē).

Lu·cre·tia (lōō·krē′shə, -shē·ə) Fem. of LUCRETIUS. Also *Fr.* **Lu·crèce** (lü·kres′), *Ital.* **Lu·cre·zia** (lōō·krä′tsyä).

Lu·cy (lōō′sē) Var. of LUCIA. Also *Fr.* **Lu·cie** (lü·sē′).

Lu·el·la (lōō·el′ə) Meaning and origin uncertain. Also **Lou·el′la.**

Lu·i·sa (lōō·ē′zä) Ital. form of LOUISA. Also *Ger.* **Lu·i·se** (lōō·ē′zə).

Lu·lu (lōō′lōō) Dim. of LOUISE.

Lyd·i·a (lid′ē·ə) She of Lydia. [< Gk.]

Ma·bel (mā′bəl) Short for AMABEL. Dim. **Mab** (mab).

Mad·e·leine (mad′ə·lin, -lān, *Fr.* mà·dlen′) Var. of MAGDALENE. [< F] Also **Mad·e·line** (mad′ə·lin, -lēn).

Madge (madj) Dim. of MARGARET.

Mae (mā) Var. of MAY.

Mag (mag) Dim. of MARGARET. Also **Mag′gie.**

Mag·da·lene (mag′də·lēn, mag′də·lē′nē) Woman of Magdala. [< Hebrew] Also **Mag·da·len** (mag′də·lən), **Mag·da·le·na** (mag′də·lē′nə; *Sp.* mäg′thä·lā′nä). Dims. **Le·na** (lē′nə), **Mag·da** (mag′də).

Mai·sie (mā′zē) Dim. of MARGARET. [< Scot.]

Mal·vi·na (mal·vī′nə, -vē′-) Meaning and origin uncertain.

Ma·mie (mā′mē) Dim. of MARGARET.

Man·dy (man′dē) Dim. of AMANDA.

Mar·cel·la (mär·sel′ə) Fem. of MARCELLUS. Also *Fr.* **Mar·celle** (mär·sel′).

Mar·cia (mär′shə) Fem. of *Marcius*, var. of MARCUS.

Mar·ga·ret (mär′gə·rit, mär′grit) Pearl. [< Gk.] Also *Ger.* **Mar·ga·re·te** (mär′gä·rā′tə), *Ital.* **Mar·ghe·ri·ta** (mär′gä·rē′tä), *Ital.,* *Sp.* **Mar·ga·ri·ta** (mär′gä·rē′tä). Dims. **Gret′a, Gretch′en, Madge, Mag, Mag′gie, Ma′mie, Meg, Me′ta, Peg, Peg′gy, Ri′ta.**

Marge (märj) Dim. of MARJORIE. Also **Mar′gie, Marj.**

Mar·ger·y (mär′jər·ē) Var. of MARGARET.

Mar·got (mär′gō; *Fr.* màr·gō′) Var. of MARGARET. [< F] Also **Mar′go.**

Mar·gue·rite (mär′gə·rēt′; *Fr.* màr·gə·rēt′) Var. of MARGARET. [< F]

Ma·ri·a (mə·rī′ə, -rē′ə; *Ger., Ital.* mä·rē′ä) Var. of MARY. [< L] Also *Sp.* **Ma·rí·a** (mä·rē′ä).

Mar·i·an (mar′ē·ən, mâr′-) Var. of MARION.

Mar·i·anne (mâr′ē·an′) From MARY and ANNE. Also **Mar·i·an·na** (mâr′ē·an′ə).

Ma·rie (mə·rē′; *Fr.* mà·rē′) Var. of MARY. [< F]

Mar·i·et·ta (mâr′ē·et′ə, mar′-) Dim. of MARIA.

Mar·i·gold (mar′ə·gōld, mâr′-) From the name of the flower.

Mar·i·lyn (mar′ə·lin, mâr′-) Var. of MARY.

Mar·i·on (mar′ē·ən, mâr′-) Var. of MARY.

Mar·jo·rie (mär′jər·ē) Var. of MARGARET. Also **Mar′jo·ry.** Dims. **Marge, Mar′gie, Marj.**

Mar·lene (mär·lēn′; *Ger.* mär·lā′nə) Var. of MAGDALENE.

Mar·sha (mär′shə) Var. of MARCIA.

Mar·tha (mär′thə) Lady. [< Aramaic] Also *Fr.* **Marthe** (màrt), *Ital., Sp.* **Mar·ta** (mär′tä). Dims. **Mar′ty, Mat′tie, Mat′ty.**

Mar·y (mâr′ē) Meaning uncertain. [< Hebrew] Dims. **May, Min′nie, Mol′ly, Pol′ly.**

Ma·til·da (mə·til′də) Mighty battle maiden. [< Gmc.] Also **Ma·thil·da** (mə·til′də), *Ger.* **Ma·thil·de** (mä·til′də). Dims. **Mat′tie, Mat′ty, Pat′ty, Til′da, Til′lie, Til′ly.**

Maud (môd) Contr. of MAGDALENE. Also **Maude.**

Mau·ra (môr′ə) Irish form of MARY. Also **Maur·ya** (môr′·yə).

Mau·reen (mô·rēn′) Dim. of MAURA.

Ma·vis (mā′vis) From the name of the bird, or the Irish fairy queen Maeve or Mab.

Max·ine (mak·sēn′, mak′sēn) Fem. of MAX. [< F]

May (mā) Dim. of MARY.

Meg (meg) Dim. of MARGARET.

Mel·a·nie (mel′ə·nē) Black. [< Gk.]

Me·lin·da (mə·lin′də) Var. of BELINDA.

Me·lis·sa (mə·lis′ə) Bee. [< Gk.]

Mer·ce·des (mər·sā′dēz, -sē′-, mûr′sə·dēz; *Sp.* mer·thā′thäs) Mercies. [< Sp.]

Mer·cy (mûr′sē) From the abstract noun.

Me·ta (mā′tə, mē′-) Dim. of MARGARET. [< G]

Mi·gnon (min′yon, *Fr.* mē·nyôn′) Dainty. [< F]

Mil·dred (mil′drid) Moderate power. [OE] Dims. **Mil′·lie, Mil′ly.**

Mil·li·cent (mil′ə·sənt) Power to work. [< Gmc.] Also **Mil′i·cent.**

Mi·mi (mē′mē) Fr. dim. of WILHELMINA.

Mi·na (mē′nə) Dim. of WILHELMINA.

Mi·ner·va (mi·nûr′və) From the name of the Roman goddess of wisdom.

Min·na (min′ə) Dim. of WILHELMINA.

Min·nie (min′ē) Memory or love [< Gmc.]; also, dim. of MARY.

Mi·ran·da (mi·ran′də) Admirable. [< L]

Mir·i·am (mir′ē·əm) Var. of MARY. [< Hebrew]

Moi·ra (moi′rə) Var. of MAURA.

Mol·ly (mol′ē) Dim. of MARY. Also **Moll.**

Mo·na (mō′nə) Noble. [< Irish]

Mon·i·ca (mon′ə·kə) Adviser. [< L]

Mu·ri·el (myŏŏr′ē·əl) Myrrh. [< Gk.]

Myr·na (mûr′nə) Meaning and origin uncertain.

Myr·tle (mûrt′l) From the plant name.

Na·dine (nā·dēn′, nə-; *Fr.* nà·dēn′) Hope. [< F < Russ.]

Nan (nan) Dim. of ANN.

Nan·cy (nan′sē) Dim. of ANN.

Nan·nette (na·net′) Dim. of ANN. [< F] Also **Na·nette′.**

Na·o·mi (nā·ō′mē, nā′ō·mē) Pleasant. [< Hebrew]

Nat·a·lie (nat′ə·lē) Christmas child. [< L] Also *Russ.* **Nat·ta·sha** (nä·tä′shə).

Nell (nel) Dim. of ELEANOR, ELLEN, or HELEN. Also **Nel′·lie, Nel′ly.**

Net·tie (net′ē) Dim. of ANTOINETTE, HENRIETTA, or JEANNETTE. Also **Net′ty.**

Ni·cole (ni·kōl′; *Fr.* Nē·kôl′) Fem. of *Nicolas,* Fr. form of NICHOLAS.

Ni·na (nī′nə, nē′-) Dim. of ANN. [< Russ.]

Ni·ta (nē′tə; *Sp.* nē′tä) Dim. of JUANITA. [< Sp]

No·na (nō′nə) Ninth. [< L]

No·ra (nôr′ə, nō′rə) Dim. of ELEANOR, HONORA, LEONORA. Also **No′rah.**

No·reen (nôr′ēn, nô·rēn′) Irish dim. of NORA.

Nor·ma (nôr′mə) Pattern. [< L]

Oc·ta·vi·a (ok·tā′vē·ə) Fem. of OCTAVIUS.

Ol·ga (ol′gə) Holy. [< Russ. < Scand.]

O·live (ol′iv) Var. of OLIVIA.

O·liv·i·a (ō·liv′ē·ə) She of the olive tree: prob. an epithet of the goddess Athena. [< L] Dims. **Liv′i·a, Liv′ie.**

O·lym·pi·a (ō·lim′pē·ə) She of Olympus. [< L < Gk.]

O·pal (ō′pəl) From the name of the gem.

O·phel·ia (ō·fēl′yə) Help. [< Gk.]

Ot·ti·lie (ot′ə·lē) Fem. of OTTO. [< Ger.]

Pam·e·la (pam′ə·lə) ? Invented by Sir Philip Sidney Dim. **Pam.**

Pan·sy (pan′zē) From the name of the flower.

Pa·tience (pā′shəns) From the abstract noun.

Pa·tri·cia (pə·trish′ə) Fem. of PATRICK. Dims. **Pat, Pat′sy, Pat′ty.**

Paul·a (pô′lə) Fem. of PAUL.

Pau·lette (pô·let′) Fr. fem. dim. of PAUL.

Pau·line (pô·lēn′) Fem. of PAUL. [< F] Also *Lat.* **Pau·li·na** (pô·lī′nə).

Pearl (pûrl) From the name of the jewel.

Peg (peg) Dim. of MARGARET. Also **Peg′gy.**

Pe·nel·o·pe (pə·nel′ə·pē) Weaver. [< Gk.] Dim. **Pen′ny.**

Per·sis (pûr′sis) She of Persia. [< Gk.]

Phi·lip·pa (fi·lip′ə, fil′ə·pə) Fem. of PHILIP.

Phoe·be (fē′bē) Bright; shining: an epithet of Artemis. [< Gk.] Also **Phe′be.**

Phyl·lis (fil′is) Green bough or leaf. [< Gk.] Also **Phil′·lis.**

Pol·ly (pol′ē) Dim. of MARY.

Pop·py (pop′ē) From the name of the flower.

Por·tia (pôr′shə, pōr′-) Fem. of *Porcius,* name of a Roman clan. [< L]

Pris·cil·la (pri·sil′ə) Ancient. [< L]

Pru·dence (prōōd′ns) From the abstract noun. Dim. **Prue.**

Queen·ie (kwē′nē) Derived from QUEEN, used as dim. of REGINA.

Ra·chel (rā′chəl; *Fr.* rà·shel′) Ewe or lamb. [< Hebrew] Dims. **Rae, Ray.**

Ra·mo·na (rə·mō′nə) Fem. of *Ramón,* Sp. form of RAYMOND.

Re·ba (rē′bə) Short for REBECCA.

Re·bec·ca (ri·bek′ə) Ensnarer. [< Hebrew] Dim. **Beck′y.**

Re·gi·na (ri·jē′nə, -jī′-) Queen. [< L]

Re·née (rə·nā′, rā′nē, rē′nē) Reborn. [< F]

Rhe·a (rē′ə) From the name of the Greek goddess.

Rho·da (rō′də) Rose. [< Gk.]

Ri·ta (rē′tə) Dim. of *Margarita,* Ital. and Sp. form of MARGARET.

Ro·ber·ta (rə·bûr′tə) Fem. of ROBERT. Dims. **Bert, Bob′·bie, Bob′by.**

Rob·in (rob′in) From the name of the bird, or from the masc. name.

Ro·chelle (rə·shel′) Stone or small rock. [< F]

Ron·ny (ron′ē) Dim. of VERONICA. Also **Ron′nie.**

Ro·sa (rō′zə) Var. of ROSE. [< L]

Ro·sa·bel (rō′zə·bel) Beautiful rose. [< L]

Ro·sa·lie (rō′zə·lē) Little rose. [< L] Also **Ro·sal·ia** (rō·zāl′yə, -zā′lē·ə).

Ros·a·lind (roz′ə·lind) Fair rose. [< Sp.] Also **Ros·a·lin·da** (roz′ə·lin′də).

Ros·a·line (roz′ə·lin, -līn, -lēn, rō′zə-) Var. of ROSALIND. Also **Ros′a·lyn** (-lin).

Ros·a·mond (roz′ə·mənd, rō′zə-) Famous protector. [< Gmc.] Also **Ros′a·mund, Ro·sa·mun·da** (rō′zə·mun′də).

Ros·anne (rōz·an′) From ROSE and ANNE. Also **Ros·an·na** (rōz·an′ə), **Rose·anne′, Rose·an′na.**

Rose (rōz) From the name of the flower. Also **Ro·sa** (rō′zə; *Fr.* rō·zà′; *Ger.* rō′zä; *Ital.* rō′zä; *Sp.* rō′sä).

Rose·mar·y (rōz′mâr′ē, -mə·rē) From the plant name. Also **Rose·ma·rie** (rōz′mə·rē).

Row·e·na (rō·ē′nə) ? From the name of an ancient Celtic goddess.

Rox·an·a (rok·san′ə) Dawn of day. [< Persian] Also **Rox·an′na,** *Fr.* **Rox·ane** (rôk·sań′). Dim. **Rox′y.**

Ru·by (rōō′bē) From the name of the jewel.

Ruth (rōōth) Companion. [< Hebrew]

Sa·bi·na (sə·bī′nə) A Sabine woman. [< L]

Sa·die (sā′dē) Dim. of SARAH.

Sal·ly (sal′ē) Dim. of SARAH.

Sa·lo·me (sə·lō′mē) Peace. [< Hebrew]

San·dra (san′drə, sän′-) Dim. of ALEXANDRA.

Sar·ah (sâr′ə) Princess. [< Hebrew] Also **Sar·a** (sâr′ə). Dims. **Sa′die, Sal′ly.**

Sel·ma (sel′mə) Fair [< Celtic], or a fem. dim. of ANSELM.

Se·re·na (sə·rē′nə) Serene. [< L]

Shar·on (shar′ən, shâr′-) Of Sharon. [< Hebrew]

Shei·la (shē′lə) Irish form of CECILIA.

Shir·ley (shûr′lē) From an English surname; orig. a place name.

Sib·yl (sib′əl) Prophetess. [< Gk.] Also **Syb′il.**

Sid·ney (sid′nē) From an English surname. Also **Syd′ney.**

Sig·rid (sig′rid; *Ger.* zē′grit; *Norw.* sē′grē) Conquering counsel. [< Gmc.]

Sil·vi·a (sil′vē·ə) Var. of SYLVIA.

Si·mone (sē·mōn′) Fr. fem. of SIMON.

So·fi·a (sō·fē′ä) Ger., Ital., and Sw. form of SOPHIA.

Son·ia (sōn′yə) Russ. dim. of SOPHIA. Also **Son′ya.**

So·phi·a (sō·fī′ə, -fē′ə) Wise. [< Gk.] Also **So·phie** (sō′·fē; *Fr.* sô·fē′) Dims. **So′phie, So′phy.**

So·phro·ni·a (sə·frō′nē·ə) Prudent. [< Gk.]

Sta·cie (stā′sē) Orig. dim. of ANASTASIA. Also **Sta′cy.**

Stel·la (stel′ə) Star. [< L]

Steph·a·nie (stef′ə·nē) Fem. of STEPHEN. Also **Steph·a·na** (stef′ə·nə), *Fr.* **Sté·pha·nie** (stā·fà·nē′).

Su·san (sōō′zən) Var. of SUSANNAH. Dims. **Sue, Su′sie, Su′zy.**

Su·san·nah (sōō·zan′ə) Lily. [< Hebrew] Also **Su·san′·na, Su·zanne** (sōō·zan′; *Fr.* sü·zań′). Dims. **Sue, Su·ky** (sōō′kē), **Su′sie, Su′zy.**

Syb·il (sib′əl) Var. of SYBIL.

Syl·vi·a (sil′vē·ə) Of the forest. [< L] Also **Sil′vi·a.**

Tab·i·tha (tab′ə·thə) Gazelle. [< Aramaic]

Te·re·sa (tə·rē′sə, -zə); *Ital.* tā·rā′zä; *Sp.* tā·rā′sä) Var. of THERESA. [< Ital. & Sp.] Dims. **Ter′ry, Tess, Tes′sie.**

Thal·ia (thāl′yə, thal′-) Flourishing; blooming. [< Gk.]

The·a (thē′ə) Goddess. [< Gk.]

Thel·ma (thel′mə) ? Var. of SELMA.

The·o·do·ra (thē′ə·dôr′ə, -dō′rə) Fem. of THEODORE. Dims. **Do′ra, The′da, The′o.**

The·o·do·sia (thē′ə·dō′shə) Gift of God. [< Gk.]

The·re·sa (tə·rē′sə, -zə) She who reaps. [< Gk.] Also *Fr.* **Thé·rèse** (tā·râz′) Dims. **Ter′ry, Tess, Tes′sie.**

Til·da (til′də) Dim. of MATILDA.

Til·ly (til′ē) Dim. of MATILDA. Also **Til′lie.**

Ti·na (tē′nə) Dim. of CHRISTINA.

Tri·na (trē′nə) Dim. of KATRINA.

Trix·ie (trik′sē) Dim. of BEATRICE or BEATRIX. Also **Trix, Trix′y.**

Tru·dy (trōō′dē) Dim. of GERTRUDE.

U·na (yōō′nə) One. [< L]

Un·dine (un·dēn′, un′dēn) She of the waves. [< L]

U·ra·ni·a (yōō·rā′nē·ə) From the name of the Greek goddess of heaven, the muse of astronomy.

Ur·su·la (ûr′syə·lə, -sə-) Little she-bear. [< L]

Va·le·ri·a (və·lir′ē·ə) Fem. of *Valerius,* name of a Roman clan. Also **Val·er·ie** or **Val·er·y** (val′ər·ē), *Fr.* **Va·lé·rie** (và·lā·rē′). Dim. **Val.**

Va·nes·sa (və·nes′ə) Butterfly. [< Gk.]

Ve·ra (vir′ə) Faith [< Slavic], or truth [< L].

Ver·na (vûr′nə) Short for *Laverna,* var. of LAVERNE.

Ve·ron·i·ca (və·ron′i·kə) True image. [< LL] Also *Fr.* **Vé·ro·nique** (vā·rô·nēk′). Dim. **Ron′nie, Ron′ny.**

Vic·to·ri·a (vik·tôr′ē·ə, -tô′rē·ə) Victory. [< L] Also *Fr.* **Vic·toire** (vēk·twàr′). Dim. **Vick′y.**

Vi·o·la (vī′ō·lə, vī·ō′lə, vē-) Violet. [< L]

Vi·o·let (vī′ə·lit) From the name of the flower.

Vir·gin·ia (vər·jin′yə) Fem. of *Virginius,* name of a Roman clan. Also *Fr.* **Vir·gi·nie** (vēr·zhē·nē′). Dim. **Gin′ny.**

Viv·i·an (viv′ē·ən, viv′yən) Lively. [< L] also **Viv′i·en,** *Fr.* **Vi·vienne** (vē·vyen′).

Wan·da (wän′də) Shepherdess or roamer. [< Gmc.]

Wen·dy (wen′dē) Dim. of GWENDOLYN.

Wil·hel·mi·na (wil′hel·mē′nə, wil′ə-; *Ger.* vil′hel·mē′nä) Fem. of *Wilhelm,* Ger. form of WILLIAM. Dims. **Mi′na, Min′na, Wil′la, Wil′ma.**

Wil·la (wil′ə) Dim. of WILHELMINA.

Wil·ma (wil′mə) Dim. of WILHELMINA.

Win·i·fred (win′ə·frid, -frēd) White wave or stream. [< Welsh] Dim. **Win′nie.**

Yo·lan·a (yō·lan′də) Meaning uncertain. [? < OF] Also **Yo·lan′de** (-də).

Y·vonne (i·von′, ē-) Meaning uncertain. [< F]

Ze·no·bi·a (zi·nō′bē·ə) She who was given life by Zeus. [< Gk.]

Zo·e (zō′ē) Life. [< Gk.]

Business Law

Business law deals with legal rules and principles of primary interest to the business community. Because of the complexity of modern business, the laws affecting businesses necessarily reach into diverse areas. Many of the laws are difficult and technical. Nevertheless, the person going into business or already in business should gain at least some familiarity with basic regulations and principles.

Although not a substitute for legal advice, such basic knowledge of the law allows the business person to make intelligent decisions and to foresee problems that may actually require legal advice or assistance. The following material provides an introduction to key concepts of business law.

Establishing a Business: Formats

Typically, the person going into business wants to be the sole owner of a particular enterprise. The simplicity of sole ownership, or *sole proprietorship,* is attractive. Whether the owner plans to add partners or employees later, it is usually possible simply to "set up shop."

The two main alternatives to sole proprietorship are the *partnership* and the *corporation.* In the former, two or more persons work together in a business enterprise, often on the basis of a partnership agreement. With a corporation (a separate legal entity) one or more persons can conduct business operations without taking responsibility for the debts of the business. Both the partnership and the corporation can take variant forms while maintaining a basic organizational pattern.

The Sole Proprietorship

The person operating a sole proprietorship owns the business in his or her own name. But the business can operate under the owner's name or a trade or business name: for example, "Mary Jones DBA ("doing business as") Jones Dress Shoppe."

Many states require that the person going into business as a sole proprietor register an assumed or fictitious business name under state and county laws. Typically, such a law is called an Assumed Names Act. Specific information is usually required, including the business name and the names and addresses of all persons who have an interest in the business.

There are many advantages to creating a sole proprietorship. The owner can keep track of the business' progress from month to month or year to year. He or she can control operating costs and can often avoid much of the paperwork required by other business arrangements. The sole proprietor remains the boss. If the business stays small, fulltime employees may not be needed.

Partnerships

A partnership is somewhat more complicated than the sole proprietorship but is less complex than the corporation. Formed, by two or more persons, the partnership is considered a business entity but not a tax entity. In other words, each partner must pay taxes on all partnership income.

Some other factors identify the partnership. Each partner, for example, is responsible for the debts and credit arrangements contracted by any other partner. Thus, any member of the partnership can bind the business and all its partners to business contracts and transactions. Professional partnerships were once common, but today, because most state laws allow doctors, lawyers, accountants, and other professional people to incorporate, the professional corporation has become a more standard form of business association. All members of such corporations share in the tax benefits.

The partnership agreement is sometimes informal—even oral. But ideally, partners should decide the terms of their agreement with the aid of a lawyer (see below).

A partnership has many of the advantages of a sole proprietorship but may also face similar strictures or regulations. An assumed or fictitious name must be registered. Generally, the various states levy no taxes on the right to function as a partnership or franchise. In addition, the partnership does not have to keep the general records required of a corporation. Unlike a corporation, which can stay in business indefinitely, a partnership usually dissolves on the death, retirement, or withdrawal of a partner.

The four main types of partnerships, each of which is used in specific circumstances, are the limited partnership, the joint venture, syndication, and the joint stock company.

Limited Partnership

In a limited partnership some or most of the partners can avoid the unlimited liability that characterizes the general partnership. Usually, the limited partnership has one general partner and a number of limited partners. The general partner is liable for the debts of the partnership and often for supervising all operations; the limited partners are liable only to the extent that they have invested in the partnership.

In those states that have Uniform Limited Partnership acts, the persons establishing a limited partnership must file a certificate of registration, usually with the secretary of state. The certificate gives the name of the business, its location, the names of the limited partners, and the partners' liabilities, powers, privileges, and duties.

A typical limited partnership may buy, manage, and sell apartment houses, hotels, and other kinds of real estate. The partners invest capital in the business and receive shares of the profits according to the amounts invested. A hybrid between the general partnership and the corporation, the limited partnership does not have to file articles of incorporation. Nor is it required to keep minutes or other records of operations. The limited partnership must, however, file partnership tax returns.

The Joint Venture

When two or more persons agree to join in a single transaction or project their partnership is called a joint venture. The partners in a joint venture agree to control and manage the business together. They must also agree to share profits and losses, usually on the basis of each partner's ownership interest in the property or project.

Thus, for example, should two or more persons jointly buy and own property but for some reason do not share its profits or losses, this would not be considered a joint venture. A joint venture occurs only when the parties intend to do business as a *partnership*.

Syndication

A joint venture that involves a large number of individuals is usually known as a *syndicate*. As with all true joint ventures, syndication requires tax filing as a partnership.

A public offering to sell a syndicate share or interest in a property or business requires special legal handling. The Securities and Exchange Commission (SEC) has ruled that such sales to the public fall under securities laws.

Joint Stock Company or Association

Some partnerships operate under articles of association that provide for the issuance of a share of stock or certificate to each partner. The certificates represent each partner's interest. In such a joint stock company or association, the articles of association also provide that a group of partners, called the board of directors, will control the business. Individual partners cannot bind the other partners by entering into separate transactions in the name of the company or association. But participants in the association are responsible for all the legal debts and obligations incurred by the association as a whole.

Federal and state securities laws apply to sales of joint stock company shares or certificates. But, under the typical articles of association, individual partners can transfer their certificates without the consent of other participants. The articles normally specify how long the association will exist and provide that the death or withdrawal of any member will not affect the association.

The Corporation

Many consider the corporation the ideal way to organize a business. By law, the person or persons who own and operate the corporation are separate from it.

The corporation may be small or large. A small corporation is usually referred to as a *close,* or *closely held, corporation.* An individual may own all the stock in such a corporation and manage it alone or jointly with a few others.

But many corporations have hundreds or thousands of shareholders or stockholders. In either case the corporation files its own tax returns and pays its own taxes. Corporate meetings must be held and minutes kept for each meeting. To do business under an assumed name, the corporation—like the sole proprietorship or the partnership—must register according to state law.

The corporation, as a flexible form of business organization, generally has the following advantages:

• The persons who invest in the corporation have no liability for corporate debts or obligations beyond the amounts each has invested.

• By selling stock and securities the corporation can raise substantial sums to finance business programs and projects.

• By corporate charter, the corporation can exist "in perpetuity"—in effect, forever.

• Because the typical corporation of any size has a manager or board of directors who run day-to-day operations, the individual shareholders need not bother with the details of such operations.

The corporate format does have some disadvantages. For example, the corporation must pay taxes on its earnings. Later, when these earnings are distributed to shareholders as *dividends,* the shareholders must claim them in their own tax returns and pay additional taxes on them. Careful planning, however, can reduce or eliminate the hazards of such "double taxation." And many corporations find ways to enjoy other major tax advantages.

Another disadvantage of the corporation is that, as a separate legal entity, it must operate in accordance with specific laws and keep certain records. Some expense is involved in incorporating, and an application for a corporate charter must be accompanied by initial tax statements and other documentation in addition to the necessary filing fees.

Two other kinds of corporations or corporation-like business structures should be noted: the Subchapter S corporation and the business trust.

Subchapter S Corporations

The unique advantage of the Subchapter S structure is that such a business may operate as a corporation while following partnership tax regulations. This type of business organization, permitted under federal and most state laws, thus avoids corporate taxes while operating in corporate form.

All the income or losses of a Subchapter S corporation are taxed individually according to the amount invested by each shareholder. The shareholders have immunity from personal liability for the debts and obligations of the firm. At the same time they avoid double taxation. But a "Sub-S" corporation can have no more than 35 shareholders.

The Business Trust

The business trust is taxed as a corporation and enjoys many of the advantages of a corporation. It can be formed and operated under federal and most state tax laws. The death or withdrawal of a shareholder does not terminate the trust, nor do the shareholders have personal liability for the trust's debts and obligations.

Also known as a Massachusetts business trust or a common trust, the business trust has been defined as an unincorporated business organization. The trust document specifies that property is to be held and managed by the trustee for the benefit of beneficiaries who hold transferable certificates. The beneficiaries receive the profits from management of the property. The states that provide for the legal creation of business trusts generally require that a declaration of trust be filed before beneficiaries' shares can be sold or distributed. Transfers or sales of trust shares must take place in accordance with the securities laws of the various states.

Launching a Business: Documents and Procedures

"I'm forming a partnership with a close friend. Do I need an agreement in writing?"

This is a question that lawyers hear frequently. In nearly all cases the answer is Yes, definitely. Prospective partners may be members of the same family, old friends, or business associates, but the written agreement is nonetheless appropriate.

The reasons for drawing up such a partnership agreement are much the same as for preparation of a preincorporation agreement. Both help to build a foundation for the enterprise and to reduce the possibility of later misunderstandings and disagreements.

The Partnership Agreement

Most states have adopted what is called the Uniform Partnership Act to guide partners as they set up and conduct their businesses. Such an act has some common-sense provisions. For example, it may provide that if *no* partnership agreement exists, the partners will share equally in the business' profits. The law may also specify that each partner will, in the absence of an agreement, have an equal voice in the operation of the business.

An agreement in writing takes precedence over such legal provisions. The partners may specify in the agreement the percentage of profits each will receive or who will supervise which aspects of the business. For instance, Partner A may receive 60% of the profits and Partner B may supervise the business' sales force. Someone who brings special knowledge or expertise to the business, or who will have to work unusually long hours, may receive advance recognition. The agreement might also specify special compensation arrangements.

Other Terms of the Agreement

In general, the terms of a partnership should deal with basics as well as with the finer points of the business relationship. The basics include the name chosen for the business, the rights and duties of each partner, and the objectives of the business. The agreement can also make note of the investments or other assets contributed by each partner, such as real estate, vehicles, or office equipment.

The business name deserves some thought. Do not choose a name that could be confused with another company name already in use. It is important to select a name that will characterize the business, give it stature, or make it sound attractive or impressive. Some partnerships have names formed from partners' initials or names.

The agreement should typically indicate how long the partnership will last. If all partners feel it is appropriate, the partnership may be of indefinite duration. In such a case, the partnership will continue until it is dissolved by one or more of the partners or until one of them dies or withdraws.

Many partnership agreements state that the partnership will continue for five or ten years. At the end of the specified period the agreement can be renewed if desired.

Other clauses typically appear in partnership agreements. For example, the agreement gives the starting and ending dates of the partnership's fiscal year. Specific provisions may indicate how any partner can exercise the right to examine the partnership's books, make specific banking arrangements, and lay out procedures for hiring employees, with special attention in many cases to employment contracts.

Contribution of Capital

It is important that the partnership agreement indicate how much capital or other assets each partner has contributed. Insofar as possible, all such assets should be listed. They can include not only those items mentioned but leases, patent rights, and special equipment of one kind or another. All such items rank as *capital*.

In any partnership one partner may contribute one kind of capital whereas another may contribute another kind. The agreement should specify clearly what is being contributed and what its value is. Some evaluations may have to be made by rough estimate; in other cases an appraiser should be hired to place a value on a partner's noncash contribution.

The terms of the agreement should spell out, with dates or target times if possible, when partners' contributions are due. One partner may invest cash at the time the partnership comes into being; another may contribute funds a year later; a third may make working premises available from the time the partnership goes into business. A partner may agree to invest in the business the first $10,000 of his share of the partnership's profits. Another may loan money to the partnership under specified conditions of repayment. The conditions should include the interest rate to be charged.

Partners' Responsibilities and Powers

In most partnerships, the various partners perform different but complementary jobs. The roles to be played by the partners should be described in the agreement as clearly as possible.

Making such terms clear beyond the possibility of misunderstanding may be impossible. But the effort should be made. The management responsibilities and the amount of time to be devoted to each can obviously vary widely. Insofar as a determination of such details can be made, it should be.

Court cases involving partners frequently hinge on the question of whether one partner is devoting enough time and effort to the business. That fact alone suggests the importance of the advance thinking put into this part of the agreement. A number of related questions should receive attention. Is each partner to be allowed to engage in other business activities while also working for the partnership? To what extent? What other business activities? Will the partners be allowed to take part only in other activities that are completely different from the partnership business?

The answers to such questions may call for thought—in particular where the question of partners' participation in other businesses is concerned. Will a partner investing in and operating a business identical to that of the partnership be in competition with his or her partners? Such questions lie at the heart of many court decisions.

Profits and Losses

The most basic method of providing for equitable distribution of profits and losses is simple. The partners simply agree to distribute profits according to the investment of each partner in the business. A partner who contributes 25% of the funding for the partnership, receives 25% of the profits. He or she also bears 25% of the losses, if any.

That formula need not control in any given case. For any group of partners, another approach may be more appropriate. The important thing is that the partners work the formula out in advance and include it in the agreement. A special formula may work best. In one case three partners establishing a real estate management business agreed that in the first year Partner A would receive half of the first $50,000 in profits while partners B and C would receive $12,500 each. From that point on the partners would divide the profits equally.

Among other important financial questions, salaries and expense accounts rank high. Unless the agreement contains provisions on salaries, for example, no partner would be entitled to anything more than a share of the profits. Yet a salary might be appropriate if one partner is to spend more time on partnership business than the others. As for expense accounts, is any partner to have unlimited privileges? Will any partner receive advances from company funds to cover business travel and entertainment?

Dissolution of the Partnership

The terms of the partnership agreement should specify under what conditions dissolution may take place. Some examples suggest possibilities. In one case a partnership agreement provided that the business would continue if any of the four partners died or had to withdraw for health or other reasons. Thus, the agreement, in effect, ensured that a new partnership would take the place of the original one. The agreement also specified how the partner leaving the business, or that partner's family, would be compensated in case of death or withdrawal. The partnership share could, of course, have substantial value.

In another case a partnership agreement contained a buy–sell clause. That provision, common to most partnership agreements, specified the conditions under which the remaining partners could buy the share of a partner who was withdrawing for any reason. A method of establishing the value of a partnership share was also specified; an arbitrator familiar with business appraisals would be named to conduct an evaluation.

Such terms, in a sense, help to resolve legal problems in advance. They can, however, be even more specific. Some buy–sell provisions provide for a departing partner's right to select an arbitrator. The remaining partner or partners have the same right. After the two arbitrators have selected a third person to assist in the arbitration, the three jointly decide on the value of a partnership share. The decision is then final and binding.

A recommended way to make sure that surviving partners will be able to buy the share of a deceased or ailing partner is to buy life insurance on the lives of all the partners. The insurance provides the cash needed for the surviving partners to buy the deceased's share.

Corporate Agreements

Three friends have decided to go into business and incorporate. What now?

First, remember that state law controls the establishment of corporations. But different laws refer to the basic documents of incorporation in different ways. The *articles of incorporation* may, for example, be called the *articles of agreement* or *charter,* or the *certificate of incorporation.*

Second, in forming their corporation they will be making decisions regarding the ownership of the business, issuance of stock shares, contributions of the various owners, and other matters. As in the case of partnership agreements, the more thorough the answers to such questions are, the better the chance that the business will succeed.

There will be four directors. Because the state in which this corporation is formed requires a minimum of three directors, they have fulfilled a basic requirement. Many other states, as noted, would allow an individual to incorporate alone. But either way, as a group or singly, the procedures are essentially the same from state to state,

with one exception. An individual incorporating as a one-person firm would not prepare a preincorporation agreement, but for four persons incorporating together, such an agreement is a good idea even though it is not required by law.

The Preincorporation Agreement

The agreement serves as an opportunity for each of the associates to make all the key decisions in advance. They can focus on areas of agreement and areas of potential disagreement and can make sure they are thinking alike. In this way they build for future business success.

The preincorporation agreement contains much that can be found in the typical partnership agreement: the corporate name, the purposes of the business, and so on. But the preincorporation agreement should address other questions as well, such as the stock to be issued, the number of shares to be authorized, the price per share, and the number of shares each associate will buy. The agreement should also specify any restrictions on transfers of shares and the procedures under which the corporation would buy the shares of an associate who dies or decides to sell out.

If such procedures are listed, the method of funding the purchases of associates' shares should be noted. Life insurance offers one effective method of funding in case of death.

Information as to how the corporation will be managed and controlled should appear in the agreement. It is important to specify the number of directors, to agree on what work each associate will perform in the corporation, and to establish salary schedules.

The name of the corporation has legal status. Most states require that the name be different enough from others already in use to avoid confusion. Because a name that is identical or very similar to any existing one may be rejected by state authorities, it is advisable to check with the governmental agency responsible for the registry of names to make sure the desired choice is available. If the name is already being used, it may nevertheless be possible to use it or a variation of it anyway, by obtaining permission from the owner of the name. Such permission should be in writing.

Most states require that the business name include a word or abbreviation indicating that the business is incorporated. The words that appear most often are *Incorporated, Corporation, Company, Limited,* or their abbreviated forms: *Inc., Corp., Co.,* and *Ltd.*

The Articles of Incorporation

With the preincorporation agreement on paper, the articles of incorporation can follow. This is the document that actually establishes the corporation: the corporate charter, filed with a state agency and usually in a standard form according to instructions issued by the agency itself. The agency may be the office of the secretary of state. In some states the articles of incorporation have to be filed with the local county clerk as well.

Other information in the articles of incorporation parallels that of the preincorporation agreement to some extent. The corporate name appears, followed by a statement of corporate purposes. Whereas some states require only a statement that the new firm will engage exclusively in lawful activities, others need specific information. The statement should be worded broadly so that the corporation has reasonable latitude in its later selection of business activities.

The business purposes of many young corporations change with time. In such cases the corporations simply file an amendment to the articles of incorporation to broaden the range of corporate purposes.

The articles of incorporation state how many shares of stock will be issued, where the firm's main office will be, and who in the corporation can be served with lawsuit papers. Most states do not require that all the shares of stock be issued at once. For that reason many corporations issue only enough shares to cover immediate and foreseeable needs. In some states lawsuit papers have to be filed with the secretary of state, who then serves the corporate officer designated in the articles of incorporation.

Finally, the articles of incorporation should note the names and addresses of the incorporators. The period for which the corporation is formed should be given if it is not perpetual. The state collects a filing fee when the incorporators register the articles.

Normally, the beginning corporation faces five other basic challenges.

1. To draw up bylaws. Much more complete than the articles of incorporation, the bylaws detail the rights and powers of the corporate officers, shareholders, and directors. The bylaws also give a time and place for the annual meetings, specify how notices of meetings will be sent out, indicate what constitutes a quorum, make provision for special meetings, and state how shareholders can act without formal meetings.

The bylaws touch on other subjects as well. They note how many directors the corporation has—usually a president, secretary, and treasurer; who the directors are and how they are elected; and what their powers and responsibilities are. In other provisions the bylaws describe the stock certificates, name the person or persons authorized to sign contracts and insert the corporate books and records, and specify how the bylaws can be amended.

2. To adopt the bylaws and elect the first board of directors. This task falls to the shareholders of the new corporation, the persons holding ultimate power. In a meeting held after the state has approved the articles of incorporation, the shareholders adopt the bylaws and elect the corporation's first board of directors.

In a small corporation, the same people may be officers, directors, and shareholders. When they set the ground-rules under which the business will operate, they are in effect making rules for themselves. In a larger corporation, the shareholders set policy but do not take part in day-to-day operations. They meet at least annually—and more frequently if the need arises. The annual meetings provide opportunities to review the corporation's annual report, elect new directors or reelect incumbents, and vote on policy changes.

3. To hold the first directors' meeting. The directors of the new corporation usually meet for the first time after the incorporators' meeting. Among other items of business, the directors elect the corporate officers, consider and ratify contracts, and approve all management plans. The board of directors may also confirm corporate banking arrangements and authorize the issuance of stock.

4. To issue corporate stock. Once the stock has been paid for, the corporation issues certificates that show the name of the corporation, the number of shares that each certificate represents, the type of share, and the name of the individual shareholder. Usually, the corporate president and secretary sign the certificates. If the stock sale is restricted, this information generally appears on the back of each certificate.

5. To make a Subchapter S election. In this step the business founders decide whether they want to be treated, for federal tax purposes, as a Subchapter S corporation. To be eligible to make such an election, the firm cannot have more than 35 shareholders. It must also have only one class of stock. The election must be made during the first 75 days of the tax year. All the shareholders must agree that the election of Subchapter S status should be made.

The Factor of Control

Whether a new business starts as a partnership or corporation, the founders should carefully consider the question of control: of ways and means of maintaining the authority of the founders and protecting their interests in the business.

A number of considerations are involved, such as those framed in the following questions: Who will be allowed to buy, inherit, or otherwise gain ownership of partners' or other shares? How do the controlling parties ensure that they retain management and supervisory responsibility? Who might be admitted to the inner circle in the future?

Retention of control involves complex legal questions. These reinforce the contention that a lawyer should help prepare all the basic business documents. The type of business, the methods by which interests may be transferred to others, possible restrictions on such transfers, employment contracts—all are important. Particular questions may hinge on interpretations of state laws dealing with restrictions on transfers of shares, on transfers of business control, and on other questions.

Some widely used methods of retaining control include the following:

1. Restrictions on transfers of interest. In general, the law frowns on restraints on sales or on assignments of business or property rights. But shareholders in a corporation can, for example, agree on a stock transfer restriction. Under such an agreement, the other partners or shareholders have the right of first refusal before a business share or stock can be sold to a third party outside the business. Where multiple shares are for sale, the other shareholders can usually buy in proportion to the total number of shares each owns.

Stock transfer restrictions generally appear in corporate bylaws. They are also printed on share certificates. The printed restriction puts a prospective purchaser on legal notice that resale restrictions exist.

2. Employment Contracts. An employment contract, or a series of them, between a partnership and its partners or between a corporation and its officers ranks as another way to retain control of a business. The contract spells out the rights, duties, and obligations of both parties—company and individual. The contract may restrict the individuals' ownership rights.

An employment contract may have other purposes. It may, for example, help the owner of a business protect patents or inventions with which the employee becomes acquainted. The contract may also provide details on a complicated compensation plan, or protect against competition from the employee should he or she leave the firm's employment.

3. Voting Rights. As businesses grow and add employees, shareholders, and others, voting rights become extremely important. A majority of shareholders might, in a given case, try to assume control by changing the business' purpose, design, or basic direction. Various kinds of voting restrictions can be used to protect the business operation, among them these:

• A corporation may provide for voting and nonvoting stock, for voting rules that ensure that the minority group is represented on the board of directors, and for elections of different directors in specified years.

• Shareholder agreements may require that shareholders vote their stock in a certain way. Shareholders might, for example, be able to vote only for other shareholders for the board of directors. "Outsiders" would be excluded. It should be noted, however, that such restrictions on voting or transfers of shares could inhibit many investors from buying the company's stock.

• Using a voting trust agreement, a number of shareholders may join together to give a lesser number, called the trustees, the right to vote on all the shares. The trustees themselves can agree on how the votes will be cast.

• Where state laws permit, the charter and bylaws of a corporation may provide for special requirements on quorums and shareholder votes. For example, a two-thirds majority might be needed to change the business' bylaws.

• A corporation's bylaws, a partnership agreement, or a shareholder agreement might make arbitration an alternative where disagreements arise. The arbitration option would be invoked in case of a voting deadlock.

4. <u>Buy–Sell Agreements.</u> A buy–sell agreement among the shareholders of a corporation ensures that the corporation can buy the stock of a deceased stockholder. The estate of the deceased has to sell the stock; the corporation has an obligation to buy. To ensure the corporation's ability to repurchase such shares, the firm must have a *stock retirement program.* Under an alternative program, called a *cross-purchase plan,* other stockholders can buy the shares of the deceased.

Establishing a price for stock to be purchased from the estate of a deceased shareholder may or may not be a problem. If the shares are traded on a regional or national stock exchange, the price quotation for a given day determines the price. In a close corporation, however, the problem of evaluation becomes critical. A mandatory buy–sell agreement always outlines an effective method of determining the price of a share of stock. The methods include the appraisal, the book value, and various other methods.

5. <u>Partnership Buy–Sell Agreement.</u> Under a partnership buy–sell agreement, the estate of a deceased partner has an obligation to offer the decedent's partnership interest for sale to the surviving partner or partners. The agreement should specify the terms of the sale. Both the partners and their spouses should sign the agreement. In many cases, life insurance offers the best method of purchasing the partnership interest of a deceased partner.

Business Contracts

You decide to have your office painted. You sit down with Tom Johnson, a painter, to discuss cost. Tom says he can do the job for $550. He would have the work completed in exactly two weeks. You say, "It's a deal." With those words you have a legally binding contract. All the necessary elements are present:

• Parties competent to contract.
• An offer (Tom's indication that he can do the work at a certain price by a certain date).
• Acceptance (your agreement to pay the $550).
• Consideration. The two of you are exchanging things of value. You have promised to pay $550 and Tom has promised to paint your office.

The Four Elements

Obviously, business contracts are rarely as simple and straightforward as the above example. But all contracts have to share the basic elements or they will not be regarded as contracts under the law.

The requirement that the parties to the contract be competent has special meaning. The contracting parties cannot be minors, for example, under the laws of the state in which the contract is made. Also, the parties must be sane. They must be capable of handling their own affairs.

At the offer stage of contract formulation, the law presumes that one party to the arrangement can provide something of value. In the example, Tom the painter *offered* to paint your office. He told you what the work would cost. He did not say he could *probably* do the work for $550, or that he would need half of that sum down, with the rest to follow on completion of the job; he stated his price.

Your acceptance followed when you said, "It's a deal." Where the second element involves *mutuality of obligation,* the acceptance phase involves *legal consideration:* in this case, what you agree to pay. The legal consideration can be many things besides money or property. An exchange can involve services.

Another type of consideration is known as *detrimental reliance.* You would have created the possibility of such a consideration if you had said to five painters, "I will pay $500 if one of you will paint my office." A painter relies on your promise, paints your office, and can sue you for breach of contract if you do not pay the $500.

Legality of purpose has equally broad legal meanings. No contract is enforceable if its purpose is illegal. But what does illegal mean? If the contract calls for the performance of an immoral or statutorily illegal act, it is unenforceable. The same applies if it goes contrary to a state's public policy. Examples of the latter include contracts to restrain trade, to evade or oppose revenue laws, and to corrupt legislative or judicial bodies.

Breach of Contract

Whether written or oral, a contract that has the four basic elements is enforceable at law. Enforcement becomes an alternative in the case of a *breach of contract* by one party or the other. A lawsuit in such a case seeks to recover whatever damages are suffered because of the breach.

The Uniform Commercial Code (UCC), valid in all states except Louisiana, sets the standards of some key aspects of contract law. The UCC, for example, provides that a written agreement be produced in a breach-of-contract case involving the sale of goods for $500 or more. The agreement need not be extremely detailed. It has only to indicate that the parties agreed on the sale and that such-and-such a quantity was involved. The UCC requires inclusion of such other factors as price, time and place of delivery, and quality of the goods.

Article Two of the UCC deals with the sale or transfer of goods or personal property. It specifies that a "merchant" (a person with special knowledge, skills, and familiarity with a business) has special rights and obligations. He or she has a kind of professional status. Three principal rules apply:

• Between merchants, the law usually requires a written contract where goods valued at more than $500 are sold.

• A merchant's offer to buy or sell goods, made in

writing and signed by the merchant, must be held open for a "reasonable" or specified length of time—and is not revocable during that time.

• A definite, written, and timely expression of acceptance creates a contract between merchants.

Violation of any of the stated UCC rules creates a cause of action—a reason to sue. A successful plaintiff generally receives *compensatory damages*. Insofar as possible, these compensate the plaintiff for damages ensuing from the broken contract. But there are other kinds of damages:

• *Consequential damages,* awarded where a plaintiff proves that a breach of contract had secondary negative effects.

• *Liquidated damages,* awarded when, for example, delay in the delivery of services or goods resulted in day-by-day losses for a plaintiff.

• *Equitable relief* may be invoked by a court to compel a delinquent defendant to deliver on a promise in a contract. A defendant may be required to deliver, for example, a work of art or an item of jewelry as promised in a legal contract.

Required Written Contracts

Under the statutes of frauds enacted by all states, some contracts have to be in writing. Typically, a statute of frauds would require that contracts be written when:

• the ownership of real estate is changing hands;
• real estate is being leased for more than a year;
• someone promises to pay the debt of someone else;
• performance under the contract will take more than a year;
• someone is agreeing to pay a commission for the sale of real estate; or
• a sale of goods, or tangible personal property, is being transacted.

Ordinarily, a contract need not be a formal legal document. A memorandum may be enough. But it should give the names of the parties, information on the subject matter, and the important terms and conditions. The signatures of the contracting parties should appear on the memorandum even though both may not be required legally.

What happens when a statute of frauds states that a contract is required but the parties have proceeded under an oral agreement? A lawsuit may be possible anyway. A suit may be justified, for example, where the oral agreement has been partially performed.

Defenses in a Breach-of-Contract Suit

A defendant in a breach-of-contract suit can utilize any of a variety of defenses. He or she may, depending on the circumstances, claim any of the following:

• That no breach took place.
• That the plaintiff suffered no damages.
• That the contract is invalid because a basic element is missing.
• That the statute of frauds requires a written contract and none exists.
• That the contract is illegal or against public policy and is therefore illegal.
• That the other contracting party misrepresented the facts to induce the defendant to sign the contract.
• That the contracting parties made a mutual mistake that resulted in a misunderstanding of what was to be sold or done.

The Business
and the Consumer

Currently, the consumer protection movement is gathering momentum. Based on the concept that the consumer needs the protection of the law, the movement tries to prevent companies from exerting pressure on the consumer, or from taking advantage of him or her. Because the consumer is in fact vulnerable when buying goods, borrowing funds, or investing for financial gain, a business owner should know some basics of consumer law.

Consumers have protection today in a number of areas, including the following:

• methods by which goods are presented, including during sales and in advertising;
• packaging and labeling of goods;
• methods used in selling goods;
• credit sales; and
• protection of consumer defenses.

Many more such areas could be listed. But these are among the most important. Each can be discussed separately.

Deceptive Practices in Sales

Various government agencies have passed statutes, rules, and regulations that forbid or restrict deceptive practices in the sale of consumer goods. Endorsements by persons with high public exposure, for example, may not be false or misleading. In a typical case an athlete or movie star will state publicly (perhaps on television or radio) that a specific product is safe or of outstanding quality. If the product does not meet the described standards, the endorser has taken part in deception. A lawsuit may be the consumer's best remedy.

Even if not intended to do so, a company's advertising may in effect deceive potential buyers. The deception need not involve an intentionally fraudulent act; the only test today is whether the buyer was misled.

The Federal Trade Commission (FTC) repeatedly challenges advertisers regarding misleading or deceptive advertising. The FTC also tries to protect consumers in other ways. The Public Health Cigarette Smoking Act, for example, requires that a health warning appear on each package of cigarettes sold. Radio and TV can no longer carry cigarette advertising. Other forms of cigarette advertising have to display the health warning prominently.

In advertising goods for sale at retail, store owners and others once used various forms of deception. One, called the "bait and switch," involved ads for "specials" that were not in stock in sufficient quantity to meet anticipated demand—or that were not in stock at all. The advertiser counted on "baiting" the customer into the shop or store and then selling him or her some other item or items, usually at higher prices.

The laws of many states outlaw such practices. Such laws may also prohibit "going out of business" advertising when the business is not really being discontinued, "fire sales" when there has been no fire, or "lost our lease" sales when no lease has been lost.

Packaging and Labeling

Many federal laws have dealt in recent years with deception in labeling and packaging. Among the laws are the Fair Packaging and Labeling Act; the Fair Products

Labeling Act; and the Food, Drug, and Cosmetics Act. In addition, various state and federal laws have outlawed the use of such terms as "full," "jumbo size," and "giant size."

Legislation in existence also requires specifics on labels. Under the Fair Products Labeling Act, a product label must identify the type of product, the name and place of business of the manufacturer, the packer or distributor, the net quantity of all the contents, and the net quantity of one serving if the label also gives the number of servings. Both the FTC and the U.S. Department of Health and Human Services have authority to require additional information or disclosures on a label.

Other legislation establishes standards and protects consumers in various ways. Food, drugs, and cosmetics receive special attention. The federal Food and Drug Administration (FDA) regulates labeling and packaging of all such items. The FDA also has authority to prevent "quackery" in medicine and drugs and to investigate "miracle drug" claims.

Approval and Testing of Goods

Many products are sold with a guarantee, tag, or other indication that the products have been tested and approved by some agency or organization. The "seal of approval" or tag means that the product has been tested and approved for normal consumer use. The seller has violated a warranty made to the consumer and may be liable for fraud if the product has not actually been tested and approved.

Tests and approvals, or tests alone, may precede the sale of some products. Products involving fire and electrical safety features may undergo tests by manufacturers' associations or testing companies for insurance purposes. Successful testing means a product meets industry safety standards. Some private and industry testing agencies, including consumer organizations that publish test results in their own magazines, simply report what their tests have revealed. No conclusions are drawn.

Some magazines also accept product advertising that includes "money back" guarantees. The guarantee requires only that the price of a product be refunded or that it be replaced if the product is defective. If a consumer is injured by the defective item, the magazine or organization giving its approval may be liable under the expanding concept of *product liability*.

Controls on Methods of Selling Goods

Many laws today regulate the ways in which merchants can sell their goods. The goal is always the same: to prevent violations of consumer rights. But some laws also provide for means of punishing the fraudulent or unlawful merchant. In two areas in particular, fair disclosure of contract terms and sales by mail, legislative action has created a network of protections for buyers or consumers.

Fair Disclosure of Contract Terms

The Consumer Credit Protection Act, better known as the "Truth in Lending Act," was designed to let the consumer know exactly what the credit offered by a lender will cost. Knowing what one lender's rates are, the consumer can "comparison shop" for a better "deal." This is true whether the individual is taking out a mortgage loan to buy a house, buying furniture or an auto-mobile, paying for home improvements on the installment plan, or charging meals, gasoline, or repair costs.

The Truth in Lending Act does not apply if no interest or other charges are added to the basic cost of a given item. The Act does ensure the availability of information on the two key factors in the cost of credit— the finance charge, or the amount paid to obtain credit, and the annual percentage rate (APR), the percentage of interest paid over a year's time. The finance charge includes not only the interest to be paid but also any service, carrying, or other charges. The APR must be computed for the consumer on the total cost of credit.

The Truth in Lending Act deals also with advertising. Where an ad mentions one feature of credit, such as the amount of the down payment, it must also mention all the other important terms.

Mail-Order Sales

More and more businesses are offering goods and services through the mail. Federal laws protect the consumer from mail fraud. State statutes may also prohibit mail-order fraud or deceit. Because most mail-order sales involve small amounts, the consumer may find it difficult or impossible to recover losses.

In mail-order sales the consumer has the following rights:

• to know when shipment of the merchandise can be expected;
• to have the merchandise shipped within 30 days;
• to cancel an order when merchandise is not shipped within 30 days;
• to be notified of delays and to have a free means of replying, such as a postage-free postcard;
• to agree to a new shipping date; and
• to have any payment returned if 30 days elapse and the merchandise is not shipped.

Where a person receives free samples or items mailed by charitable organizations seeking contributions, the recipient can, as he or she wishes, regard the merchandise as a gift.

Control of Methods of Payment

Protective laws regulate the methods by which payments may be made or demanded by a creditor on a consumer sale. Some state laws provide that if a creditor accepts payment in a form other than cash or check, the creditor takes a chance. State laws may also provide that installment payments have to be applied to the oldest unpaid portions of a debt. The payment sent by a debtor who is three months delinquent on an open credit account must go toward payment of the oldest monthly charge.

Both federal and state laws regulate accelerated and "balloon" final payments. At one time unscrupulous creditors or lenders could make the last payment in a monthly series larger than the debtor could pay. The lender could then repossess the merchandise when the debtor defaulted. Most laws now specify that if the final payment is double the average of the earlier scheduled payments, the debtor has the right to refinance the final payment on terms similar to those of the original transaction.

Other Financial Areas

In many other money areas the laws protect the consumer without prejudicing the rights of the businessperson. Credit cards, for example, the symbols of the so-called "cashless society," can no longer be issued to per-

Business Law 989

sons who have not applied for them. Also, in case of loss of a credit card, the owner cannot be held liable for more than $50 for purchases made illegally by the finder. But such purchases must have been made before the owner has notified the company issuing the card. If they are made after that time, the card holder cannot be held liable at all.

In contract sales, the "fine print" on the reverse sides of some agreements once provided that the buyer waived some legal protections. Under some recent consumer statutes, however, the buyer cannot inadvertently waive all such defenses. Where a household appliance is defective, for example, under the consumer protection statutes of many states the buyer has the right to withdraw from the contract.

Wages and salaries make up another sensitive area.

In general, the laws provide that the right to earn a living and support one's family takes precedence over any right to garnish or attach a person's earnings.

Federal and state laws contain many other provisions designed to protect the consumer. For example, the methods by which debts may be collected are strictly controlled. Credit reporting, which affects the individual's credit rating and, often, his or her ability to get a job and to purchase needed items, falls under the provisions of the Fair Credit Reporting Act of 1970. The Act applies only to personal, household, and family credit, and not to business or commercial credit. Very importantly, the Act gives the person whose credit-worthiness is in question the right to find out the name and address of the reporting agency. The individual then has the right to have any errors in the report corrected.

Business Math

Business Math is, as the term implies, the math that meets the needs of business. It differs from the math used in our daily lives only in the respect that its methods have been adapted to the special requirements of business. The businessman wants to know at what price to sell an article in order to make a certain profit, how much he may deduct from a bill if he pays for an order in cash, whether it is to his advantage to invest his money in one kind of stock or another. These and other practical problems that the businessman faces constitute the bulk of our Business Math section. In addition, we present at the outset some helpful hints that will save time in performing the mathematical computation that is required in solving the business problems later in the section.

It is suggested that the steps given here in solving problems be followed exactly, and that all information required be written down and clearly labeled. Only later, when the methods of solution can be readily applied, should short cuts be taken and steps be performed without indicating them on paper.

Easy Methods of Calculation

Short Cuts in Addition

In adding a column of figures, speed and rapidity will be attained by following these suggestions:

1. Take a combination of numbers which adds to 10 and add them as 10.

Example

Add:

$$\begin{pmatrix} 8 & 7 & 5 \\ 2 & 8 & 6 \end{pmatrix}$$
$$2 \quad 8 \quad 4$$
$$2 \begin{pmatrix} 8 & 3 \end{pmatrix}$$
$$\begin{pmatrix} 2 & 2 & 2 \\ 8 & 9 & 5 \end{pmatrix}$$
$$\overline{2 \quad 8 \quad 4 \quad 5}$$

Add the right-hand column from the top down as follows: 5, 15, 25, carry 2.

Add the second column from the top down as follows: 2, 9, 17, 25, 35, 44, carry 4.

Add the third column from the top down as follows: 4, 14, 16, 18, 28.

2. Take any combination of numbers which total 10 or less and add them as that total. For example, add 2, 3, 4 as 9; add 2, 2, 3 as 7; add 1, 2, 3 as 6; add 2, 4, 2 as 8.

3. Add 9 as 10 and then subtract 1. For example, 65 + 9 = 75 − 1 = 74.

Short Cuts in Multiplication

1. To multiply an integer (whole number) by 10 or a power of 10. **Rule:** Add one zero to the number to be multiplied for each zero in the multiplier.

Example

65 × 10	= 650	Add 1 zero.
301 × 100	= 30,100	Add 2 zeros.
750 × 1000	= 750,000	Add 3 zeros.
236 × 10,000	= 2,360,000	Add 4 zeros.
185 × 100,000	= 18,500,000	Add 5 zeros.

2. To multiply an integer by 5. **Rule:** Multiply by 10; take ½ of the answer.

Example

$$650 \times 5$$
$$650 \times 10 = 6500$$
$$\text{½ of } 6500 = 3250, \text{ Answer}$$

3. To multiply an integer by 15. **Rule**: Multiply by 10: take ½ the answer and add both.

Example

$$786 \times 15$$
$$786 \times 10 = \quad 7860$$
$$\text{½ of } 7860 = \quad \underline{3930}$$
$$11,790, \text{ Answer}$$

4. To multiply an integer by 11. **Rule:** Multiply by 10; add the original number.

Example

$$295 \times 11$$
$$295 \times 10 = 2950$$
$$295$$
(original
number) $\quad \underline{295}$
$$3245, \text{ Answer}$$

5. To multiply an integer by 9. **Rule:** Multiply by 10; subtract the original number.

Example

```
293 × 9
293 × 10  = 2930
293
(original
number)   −  293
              2637, Answer
```

6. To multiply an integer by 50, 25, 12½. **Rule:** Multiply by 100; then multiply the answer by ½, ¼, or ⅛ as the case may be because 50, 25, and 12½ are ½, ¼, and ⅛ of 100 respectively.

Example 1

```
275 × 50
275 × 100     = 27,500
½ of 27,500   = 13,750, Answer
```

Example 2

```
326 × 25
326 × 100     = 32,600
¼ of 32,600   = 8150, Answer
```

Short Cuts in Division

1. To divide an integer by 10 or a power of 10. **Rule:** Move the decimal point in the number to be divided as many places to the left as there are zeros in the divisor.

Example 1

```
875 ÷ 10
875 ÷ 10  = 87.50, Answer
```

Example 2

```
$975.85 ÷ 1000
$975.85 ÷ 1000  = $.97585, Answer
```

Exercise

1. 800 × 10 =	**9.** 285 × 5 =
2. 900 × 50 =	**10.** 88 × 11 =
3. 1756 × 100 =	**11.** 99 × 9 =
4. 288 × 25 =	**12.** 1725 × 15 =
5. 300 × 15 =	**13.** 836 × 1000 =
6. 756 ÷ 10 =	**14.** 19.5 ÷ 10 =
7. 97.8 ÷ 100 =	**15.** 28.65 ÷ 100 =
8. 42.6 ÷ 1000 =	

Answers:

1. 8000	**9.** 1425
2. 45,000	**10.** 968
3. 175,600	**11.** 891
4. 7200	**12.** 25,875
5. 4500	**13.** 836,000
6. 75.6	**14.** 1.95
7. .978	**15.** .2865
8. .0426	

Devices for Checking the Four Fundamental Operations

Addition

Add the column from top to bottom. Write the answer. Check by adding the column from bottom to top.

Subtraction

Add the answer or remainder to the subtrahend. The result should equal the minuend.

Operation	Check
86 minuend	68 remainder
− 18 subtrahend	+ 18 subtrahend
68 remainder	86 minuend

Multiplication

Multiply the multiplicand by the multiplier. Then make the multiplicand the multiplier and the multiplier the multiplicand, and multiply.

Operation	Check
85 multiplicand	15 multiplicand
× 15 multiplier	× 85 multiplier
425	75
85	120
1275 product	1275 product

A second check is to divide the product by the multiplier. The answer should be the multiplicand. Or divide the product by the multiplicand and the answer should be the multiplier.

```
                 Check
                          85  multiplicand
      multiplier 15) 1275  product
                    120
                     75

                          15  multiplier
      multiplicand 85 ) 1275  product
                       85
                      425
                      425
```

Division

Multiply the answer or quotient by the divisor. The product should equal the dividend.

```
              Operation
                   416⅔ quotient
      divisor 18 ) 7500  dividend
                   72
                   30
                   18
                  120
                  108
                   12   = ⅔
                   18
```

```
               Check
              416⅔ quotient
                18  divisor
            3 ) 36
                12
              3328
               416
              7500    dividend
```

Percentage

The term "per cent" is derived from the Latin. It means "by the hundred." To illustrate, take the number 1 and divide it into 100 parts. Each part is 1/100 of 1 and may be expressed in three ways, as follows:

1. Common fraction—1/100.
2. Decimal fraction—.01.
3. Per cent—1%.

The value of percentage lies in its use as a basis of comparison in various business transactions. It acts as a common denominator to which everything may be reduced, thus enabling the comparison to be made.

Per Cent, Fractions, and Decimals

1. To change a decimal to per cent. **Rule:** Move the decimal point two places to the right and then write a per cent sign.

Example 1

Change .15 to per cent.
.15 = 15%

Example 2

Change .075 to per cent.
.075 = 7.5%

Example 3

Change 6 to per cent.
6.00 = 600%

2. To change a common fraction to per cent. **Rule:** Change the common fraction to a decimal; then change the decimal to a per cent.

Example 1

Change 3/8 to a per cent.

3/8 = 8) 3.000
.375
.375 = 37.5% or 37½%

Example 2

Change 17/19 to a per cent.

.89 9/19
17/19 = 19) 17.00
15 2
18 0
17 1
9/19

.89 9/19 = 89 9/19%

Exercise

Express the following as per cent:

1. ½	**6.** .0075
2. 4/3	**7.** .02½
3. 5/6	**8.** .3
4. 11/20	**9.** 15/28
5. .08	**10.** .006

Answers:

1. 50%	**6.** .75% or ¾%
2. 133⅓%	**7.** 2½%
3. 83⅓%	**8.** 3/10% or 30%
4. 55%	**9.** 53 4/7%
5. 8%	**10.** 3/5% or .6%

3. To change a per cent to a decimal. **Rule:** Move the decimal point two places to the left and take away the per cent sign.

Example 1

Express 17% as a decimal.
17% = .17

Example 2

Express 8.5% as a decimal.
08.5% = .085

Example 3

Express 525% as a decimal.
525% = 5.25

Example 4

Express .75% as a decimal.
75% = .0075

Exercise

Express the following per cents as decimals:

1. 2½%	**6.** .5%
2. 37½%	**7.** .05%
3. 650%	**8.** .25%
4. 7.5%	**9.** 16.75%
5. 18.8%	**10.** 123%

Answers:

1. .025	**6.** .005
2. .375	**7.** .0005
3. 6.50	**8.** .0025
4. .075	**9.** .1675
5. .188	**10.** 1.23

4. To change a per cent to a common fraction. **Rule:** Change the common fraction to a decimal; then to a per cent.

Example 1

Change 25% to a common fraction.
25% = .25
.25 = 25/100 = ¼, *Answer*

Example 2

Change 150% to a common fraction.
150% = 1.50
1.50 = 1½ or 3/2, *Answer*

Exercise

Change the following to common fractions:

1. 50%	**6.** 75%
2. 20%	**7.** 80%
3. 40%	**8.** 62½%
4. 33⅓%	**9.** 87½%
5. 16⅔%	**10.** 12½%

Answers:

1. ½	**6.** ¾
2. ⅕	**7.** ⅘
3. ⅖	**8.** ⅝
4. ⅓	**9.** ⅞
5. ⅙	**10.** ⅛

Problems in Percentage

In computing a problem in percentage, the number or quantity upon which the per cent is to be computed is called the *base*, the per cent is called the *rate*, and the product of the base and the rate is called the *percentage*. All problems in percentage fall into three groups or cases.

Case I. Given the base and the rate, to find the percentage. **Rule:** Base × Rate = Percentage.

Example 1

Find 25% of 7800.

        Change 25% to .25; then multiply:
        7800 × .25 = 1950, *Answer*

Example 2

Find 250% of 19,600.

        19,600 × 2½ = 49,000, *Answer*

Exercise

Find the percentage:

1. 15% of 980
2. 12½% of 640
3. 33⅓% of 999
4. 125% of 260
5. 18% of 480

6. ¾% of 1200
7. .75% of 1600
8. 2½% of 1640
9. 10% of 968
10. 19% of 200

Answers:

1. 147
2. 80
3. 333
4. 325
5. 86.4

6. 9
7. 12
8. 41
9. 96.8
10. 38

Case II. Given the base and the percentage, to find the rate. **Rule:** Divide the percentage by the base.

Example

17 is what per cent of 29?

$^{17}/_{29}$ = .58$^{18}/_{29}$ = 58$^{18}/_{29}$%

Exercise

1. 25 is what per cent of 800?
2. 16 is what per cent of 280?
3. 180 is what per cent of 36,000?
4. 17.5 is what per cent of 85.6?
5. 18.4 is what per cent of 2.86?

Answers:

1. 3⅛%
2. 5⁵⁄₇%
3. ½% or .5%
4. 20⁹⁵⁄₂₁₄%
5. 643⁵¹⁄₁₄₃%

Case III. Given the percentage and rate, to find the base. This is called the indirect case. **Rule:** Percentage divided by rate equals the base.

Example

18 is 3% of what number?

18 ÷ .03 = 600, *Answer*

Exercise

1. 25 is 20% of what number?
2. 180 is 50% of what number?
3. 27 is 75% of what number?
4. 260 is 80% of what number?
5. 1704 is 12% of what number?

Answers:

1. 125
2. 360
3. 36
4. 325
5. 14,200

Aliquot Parts

Arithmetical calculations may be made much easier if the aliquot parts of 100% are used. By an aliquot part is meant a number which can be divided into another number so that the answer will be a whole number. Thus 25% is an aliquot part of 100% because 100% divided by 25% equals 4. It would be well to memorize the aliquot parts of 100%, and multiples of these aliquot parts for greater ease and speed in performing problems.

Aliquot Parts of 100%

50% = ½	87½% = ⅞	70% = ⁷⁄₁₀
25% = ¼	1% = ¹⁄₁₀₀	80% = ⅘
75% = ¾	10% = ¹⁄₁₀	33⅓% = ⅓
6¼% = ¹⁄₁₆	20% = ⅕	66⅔% = ⅔
12½% = ⅛	30% = ³⁄₁₀	16⅔% = ⅙
37½% = ⅜	40% = ⅖	8⅓% = ¹⁄₁₂
62½% = ⅝	60% = ⅗	83⅓% = ⅚

Example

Find 37½% of 800.

⅜ of 800 = 300, *Answer*

Exercise

Compute the following, using aliquot parts:

1. 20% of 850
2. 87½% of 864
3. 12½% of 960
4. 75% of 1200
5. 33⅓% of 963
6. 10% of 786
7. 16⅔% of 282
8. 66⅔% of 1296

9. 80% of 9000
10. 8⅓% of 2460
11. 83⅓% of 288
12. 62½% of 1200
13. 6¼% of 3200
14. 5% of 870
15. 50% of 1900

Answers:

1. 170
2. 756
3. 120
4. 900
5. 321
6. 78.6
7. 47
8. 864

9. 7200
10. 205
11. 240
12. 750
13. 200
14. 43½
15. 950

Aliquot Parts of $1.00

It will be noticed that the aliquot parts of $1.00 are the same as those of 100%. Therefore the same fractional equivalents may be used at all times.

Example

Find cost of 840 yards of silks @ 62½¢ per yd.

        62½ = ⅝
      ⅝ of 840 = 525, *Answer*

Exercise

Compute the following, using aliquot parts:

1. 160 yds. @ 50¢
2. 980 yds. @ 10¢
3. 750 yds. @ 40¢
4. 138 lbs. @ 33⅓¢
5. 280 lbs. @ 62½¢
6. 1780 lbs. @ 60¢
7. 66⅔ lbs. @ 90¢
8. 16⅔ lbs. @ 48¢

9. 75 yds. @ 88¢
10. 40 yds. @ $2.50
11. 270 lbs. @ 66⅔¢
12. 726 ft. @ 16⅔¢
13. 6480 yds. @ 62½¢
14. 22½ lbs. @ 40¢
15. 256 ft. @ 6¼¢

In problems 7 to 10, the base and the rate may be interchanged so that problem 7 will read 90 lbs. @ 66⅔¢ and will be done in the same manner as problems 1 to 6.

Business Uses of Math

Discounts on Invoices

Invoices and Terms

After a sale is made, the seller sends an *invoice* to the buyer. On it is listed the date, terms, goods and quantity sold, the price of each item, the extensions, and the total. The terms are most important because they are the conditions of payment. Some examples of terms are:

C.O.D.—Collect or cash on delivery.
Cash—Cash is to be paid on the date of the sale.
On account—Payment to be made within a reasonable time after the end of the month.
E.O.M.—End of the month.
n/30—Net 30 days after the date of the invoice (net means no discounts).
2/10 n/30—2% discount if paid within 10 days after the date of the invoice, net after 10 days and within 30 days.
2/5 1/15 n/30—2% discount if paid within 5 days, 1% discount if paid after 5 days but within 15 days; net if paid after 15 days and within 30 days.

Trade and Cash Discounts

Discounts on invoices are of two kinds, cash discounts and trade discounts. Cash discounts are those mentioned under terms, an inducement to the customer to pay his bill ahead of time. The customer is the one who decides whether he will take advantage of the discount. Trade discounts differ from cash discounts because they are deducted, not by the customer, but by the seller.

Manufacturers and wholesalers print catalogues once or twice a year. They are expensive. In order to bring the catalogue price down to the market price, they send their customers discount sheets, on which they list discounts given on the catalogue price to bring it down to the market price. If the price drops, two or more trade discounts may be given.

Problem 1: The Rowe Co. offers to sell a dining room suite for $250 less 20%, 10%, and 10%. The Wilson Co. offers a similar suite for $260 less 40%. Which is the better offer and by how much?

Rowe Co.	
$250	List Price or Catalogue Price
50	Trade Discount 20%
$200	Balance
20	Trade Discount 10%
$180	Balance
18	Trade Discount 10%
$162	Net Cost

Wilson Co.	
$260	List Price
140	Trade Discount 40%
$156	Net Cost

$162	Net Cost—Rowe Co.
156	Net Cost—Wilson Co.
$6	Wilson Co. offer better.

Problem 2: The Domestic Rug Co. received an invoice on November 10 amounting to $1280 less 20%, and 5%, terms 3/10 n/60. The invoice was paid November 20. Find the amount of the payment.

$1280.00	List Price
256.00	Trade Discount 20%
$1024.00	Balance
51.20	Trade Discount 5% (½ of 10%)
$ 972.80	Balance
29.18	Cash Discount 3%
$ 943.62	Net Cost

Problem 3: A dealer purchased a bicycle for $32.40 less 33⅓%, terms 2/10 n/30, plus a freight charge of 90¢. The invoice was dated March 15 and paid March 25. Find the amount of the payment.

$32.40	List Price
10.80	Trade Discount 33⅓%
$21.60	Balance
.43	Cash Discount 2%
$21.17	Net Cost
.90	Freight Charge
$22.07	Total Cost

Note: The discounts are taken only on the invoice; they cannot be taken on the freight charge or any other buying expense.

Exercise

1. Find net cost of invoice of $1375 less 20% and 10%.
2. Find total cost of invoice of $45 less 20% and buying expense of $2.10.
3. Find net cost of invoice dated April 16, terms 2/10 n/30, amounting to $1500 less 20% and 10% and paid on April 26.
4. A dealer offeres a rug for $60 less 30% and 10%. Another offers the same quality for $60 less 40%. Which offer is better and how much?

Single Discount Equivalent to a Series of Trade Discounts

For ease in computation and for purposes of comparison, it is often desirable to find one discount that is equivalent to a series. The procedure is as follows: Consider the catalogue price as 100%. Multiply this by the first discount and subtract from 100%. Multiply this difference or balance by the second discount and subtract the answer from the balance. Continue this multiplication and subtraction until all the discounts have been taken. The answer will be the net cost. To find the single discount, subtract the net cost from 100%.

Problem: Find one discount equivalent to a series of 30%, 20% and 10%.

100%	List Price
30	Trade Discount 30%
70%	Balance
14	Trade Discount 20% (20% of 70%)
56.0%	Balance
5.6	Trade Discount 10% (10% of 56%)
50.4	Net Cost

100% List Price − 50.4% Net Cost = 49.6%, *Ans.*
Proof: 30% + 14% + 5.6% = 49.6%, *Answer*

Exercise

Find one discount equivalent to the following series:

1. 20% and 10%
2. 30% and 10%
3. 50% and 20%
4. 25% and 20%
5. 37½% and 24%

6. 20%, 10%, and 5%
7. 20%, 10%, and 10%
8. 50%, 25%, and 20%
9. 40%, 30%, 20%, and 10%
10. 50%, 25%, and 10%

Answers:
1. 28%
2. 37%
3. 60%
4. 40%
5. 52½%

6. 31.6%
7. 35.2%
8. 70%
9. 69.76%
10. 66.25%

Commissions

Salesmen are usually paid a percentage of their sales as compensation for their work. This percentage is called *commission.* Commissions are generally paid on the amount of the sales, although in some cases they are calculated on the quantity of merchandise sold. When a salesman is paid commission only, he is on a straight commission basis. If he receives a drawing account, the amount of the drawings is deducted from his total commission at the end of the accounting period, and the balance paid him at that time.

To encourage salesmen to greater efforts, commission may be paid on a graduated basis; that is for example, 10% commission on the first $20,000 of sales and 15% on all sales over $20,000. Inside salesmen are usually paid on a commission and salary basis. Very often, no commission is paid until a stated amount or quota has been sold; commission is then paid on sales over the quota. The problems that follow deal with each of these phases of selling.

Straight Commission

Problem 1: A salesman sells 2500 yards of silk at $2 per yard. His rate of commission is 2½%. Find his commission.

$$2500 \times \$2 = \$5000, \text{ Sales}$$
$$2\tfrac{1}{2}\% \text{ of } \$5000 = \$125, \text{ Commission}$$

Problem 2: A salesman sells 2500 yards of silk at $2 per yard. His rate of commission is 5¢ per yard. Find his commission.

$$2500 \text{ yards} \times 5\cent = \$125, \text{ Commission}$$

Note that in the first problem the commission was based on price whereas in the second problem it was based on quantity.

Salary and Commission

Problem: A salesman is offered a salary of $50 per week and a commission of 5% on all sales. His sales for the year are $36,000. Find his yearly earnings.

Time	Sales	5% Commission	Salary	Total
1 year	$36,000	$1800	$2600 (52 × $50)	$4400 *Answer*

Salary, Commission, and Quota

Problem: A salesman is offered a salary of $110 per month and a 6% commission on all sales over $2000 per month. In April, his sales were $1950; in May, $3250; in June, $3375. Find his total earnings.

Time	Salary	Sales	Quota Over $2000	6% Commission	Totals
April	$110	$1950	$ 0	$ 0	$110.00
May	110	3250	1250	75.00	185.00
June	110	3375	1375	82.50	192.50
Totals	$330	$8575	$2625	$157.50	$487.50 *Answer*

To check the answer, add the vertical totals, then the horizontal totals. The grand total must be the same.
Thus, vertically, 110 + 185 + 192.50 = 487.50
horizontally, 330 + 157.50 = 487.50

Salary, Graduated Commission, and Quota

Problem: Noll, a salesman, receives a salary of $200 per month, 1% commission on all sales, and 2% commission on all monthly sales over $3000. In January his sales were $6000; in February, $4500; in March, $7400. Find his total income for the three months.

Salary, Graduated Commission, and Quota Problem Table

Time	Salary	Sales	On All Sales Com. 1%	Quota Over $3000	Over $3000 Com. 2%	Totals
January	$200	$ 6000	$ 60	$3000	$ 60	$320
February	200	4500	45	1500	30	275
March	200	7400	74	4400	88	362
Totals	$600	$17,900	$179	$8900	$178	$957 Answer

To check the answer of the problem just solved, add the horizontal totals:

$$600 + 179 + 178 = 957.$$

Exercise

In doing these problems use the diagram method of the previous problems. The headings can be found very easily by reading the problem carefully and then heading each column as the problem indicates.

1. Find the commission a salesman receives if his sales are $6500 and the commission is 7%.
2. John Miller, a salesman, receives a monthly salary of $90 and 5% commission on all sales. In addition, he receives 2% on sales over $3000 in any single month. His sales in April were $3850 and in May $2700. Find his total earnings.
3. A salesman has offers of employment from two firms. Kolapep offers him a salary of $100 per month, a commission of 5% in total monthly sales and 2% additional commission on monthly sales in excess of $2000. Cocapep offers him a commission of 8% on the first $1000 of monthly sales, 10% on the next $1000 of monthly sales and 12% on all monthly sales in excess of $2000. If his average sales are $3500 a month, where would he earn more and how much more?
4. The Electric Supply Co. has an agency for the sale of vacuum cleaners. Their commission is $12.50 each for the first 50 cleaners; $15 each for the second 50 cleaners or part thereof; $17.50 each for all over 100 cleaners sold each month. In May, they sold 76 cleaners; in June, they sold 105 cleaners. Find their commission.

Answers:
1. $455
2. $524.50
3. Cocapep is better by $55
4. $2477.50

Commission Merchants

For those people who cannot do their own buying or selling, agents known as commission merchants will attend to all such transactions. They charge a commission for their services, in the same manner as do salesmen. After selling the merchandise, they submit a statement called an *account sales*. After buying the merchandise, they submit a statement called an *account purchase*.

Problem 1: Williams has 860 bushels of potatoes to sell. He can sell them at $2.10 a bushel, with no expense. However, he sends them to a commission merchant who sells 450 bushels at $2.60 and the remainder at $2.25 a bushel. The merchant charges 3¢ a bushel for storage, $36.80 for freight, 1% for insurance, and 3% commission.

A. Find the amount of the net proceeds remitted to Williams.

B. How much does Williams gain or lose by having the merchant sell the potatoes?

A.   **Income**

450 bu. @ $2.60	....	$1170.00
410 bu. @ $2.25	....	922.50
Total Proceeds	....	$2092.50

Charges

Storage (3¢ per bu., 860 bu.)	..	$25.80
Freight	....	36.80
Insurance (1% of $2092.50)	....	20.93
Commission (3% of $2092.50)	.	62.78
Total Charges	....	$ 146.31
Net Proceeds	....	$1946.19

B.   860 bu. @ $2.10 = $1806, Total Proceeds

$1946.19, Net Proceeds—Commission Merchant
 1806.00, Total Proceeds
$ 140.19, Gain by sending to commission merchant

Note: All charges or expenses must be subtracted on a sale.

Problem 2: Benton, a sugar broker, purchases 35,000 pounds of sugar for a candy manufacturer at 5.5¢ per pound. Benton's expenses and charges are: handling $23.40, freight 36¢ per hundredweight, commission 5%. Find the total cost of the sugar to the candy manufacturer.

35,000 lbs. sugar @ 5.5¢ per lb. = $1925, Cost

Charges

Handling	....	$ 23.40
Freight (36¢ per cwt.—35,000 lbs.	....	126.00
Commission (5% of $1925)	.....	96.25
Total Charges	....	$ 245.65
Total Cost	....	$2170.65

Note: All charges and expenses must be added on a purchase.

Exercise

1. Wilson, a commission merchant, receives 1500 bushels of potatoes to sell. He sold 635 bushels at $1.50; 475 bushels at $1.40; and the remainder at $1.30 a bushel. He charged a commission of 5%. His expenses were: freight charges $84.50, sorting and weighing $38.40, and storage charges of 3¢ per bushel. Find the net proceeds.
2. Harris purchased 50,000 feet of lumber for a builder at $60 per 1000 feet. Freight charges were $150, insurance 1%, trucking $75 and commission 4%. Find the total cost of the lumber to the builder.

3. A fruit farm shipped 100 crates (32 boxes per crate) of strawberries to a commission merchant. He sold 1280 boxes at $.20, 960 boxes at $.15 and the remainder at $.12 per box. Freight charges were $24, storage $22.66, cartage $15.60, commission 5%. Find the net proceeds.

Answers:
1. $1850.37   **2.** $3375   **3.** $427.18

Payrolls

Time Basis

Employees other than salesmen are usually paid on a time basis. So-called white-collar workers such as clerks, bookkeepers, and the like are paid on an annual, monthly, or weekly salary basis. Other workers, especially those who do manual labor, are paid on an hourly basis, with forty hours per week generally regarded as regular time, and everything over forty hours as overtime. In many organizations each employee has a time card on which an accurate record of his time may be kept.

Problem 1: Below is the time card of a worker showing the time he has worked for one week. His regular wage is $1.10 per hour for a 40 hour week.

Day	In	Out	In	Out
Monday	7:00	12:00	1:00	4:00
Tuesday	7:00	12:00	1:00	4:00
Wednesday	7:00	12:00	1:00	4:00
Thursday	7:00	12:00	1:00	4:00
Friday	7:00	12:00	1:00	4:00

A. Find his total wages for the week.
B. His employer deducts 3% for social security and $6.38 for withholding tax. What is his take-home pay?

A.

Day	Hours
Monday	8
Tuesday	8
Wednesday	8
Thursday	8
Friday	8
Total	40
	× 1.10
	$44.00, Total Wages

B. Total wages $44.00

Deductions
Social Security (3%) $1.32
Withholding Tax 6.38
                              7.70
Take-home pay $36.30

Problem 2: A mechanic is working in a factory where his regular time is 40 hours a week. He is paid time and a half (1½ times) for overtime. His regular wages are $1.50 per hour. Deductions are 3% for social security and $14.25 for withholding tax. Last week he worked 57 hours.

A. Find his total earnings.
B. Find his take-home pay.

A.

Total Time (Hours)	Regular Time (Hours)	1½ Over-Time (Hours)*
57	40	17
		× 1½
		8½
		17
		25½

*(One hour of overtime equals 1½ hours of regular time. Convert overtime to regular time by multiplying by the overtime rate.)

```
  40     Regular Allowance
 25½     Overtime Allowance
 65½     Total Hours
× $1.50  Rate
$98.25,  Total Wages
```

B. Total wages $98.25
Deductions
Social Security (3%) .... $ 2.95
Withholding Tax 14.25
                           17.20
Take-home pay $81.05

Exercise

1. William Randall, a machinist, worked last week as follows: Monday 8 hours, Tuesday 10 hours, Wednesday 11 hours, Thursday 9 hours, Friday 10 hours and Saturday 5 hours. His regular time is 40 hours per week, with time and a half for overtime. His hourly rate is $1.60 per hour. Deductions of 3% for social security taxes and $13.81 for withholding taxes are made.
a. Find his total wages.
b. Find his take-home pay.

2. Hawkins, a mechanic, worked 47 hours last week. His regular time is 40 hours with time and a half for overtime. His hourly rate is $1.40 per hour. Social security tax deduction was 3% and withholding tax was $11.67.
a. Find his total wages.
b. Find his take-home pay.

Answers:
1. *a.* $95.20   **2.** *a.* $70.70
    b. $78.53   *b.* $56.91

Piecework Wages

Another method of compensation depends not on the time worked but on the quantity or pieces which the worker produces. The wage is computed by multiplying the number of pieces by the rate per piece.

Problem: Harris, a dress operator, produces 108 pieces of work during the week. His rate per piece is 35¢. Find his total wages.

108 × .35 = $37.80, Total Wages

Deductions for social security and withholding tax are computed in the same manner as in time wages.

Averages

By an average is meant a figure which is typical of a group of numbers. Averages are useful in comparing groups of numbers. To find an average, add all the items and divide the total by the number of items.

Problem 1: A salesman's sales per week are $1500, $2000, $3000, $6000, and $2500. Find his average sales for the five weeks.

$$\begin{array}{r} \$1500 \\ 2000 \\ 3000 \\ 6000 \\ \underline{2500} \\ \$15,000 \end{array}$$

$15,000 ÷ 5 = $3000, Average Sales per Week

Problem 2: Clark's average sales for the last 8 weeks of the year were $362.15 a week. For the first 3 weeks of the new year, his sales per week were $415.16, $523.25, and $392.35. Find his average sales per week for the 11 weeks.

$362.15 × 8 = $2897.20, Total sales for 8 weeks

$$\begin{array}{r} 415.16 \\ 523.25 \\ \underline{392.35} \\ \$4227.96, \text{ Total sales for 11 weeks} \end{array}$$

$4227.96 ÷ 11 = $384.36, Average sales per week for 11 weeks

Exercise

1. The Acme Sales Co. had a contest for its salesmen. Potter's average sales for the last 8 weeks of the year were $340. For the first 4 weeks of the new year, his weekly sales were $376, $625, $429, and $374. Find his average weekly sales for the 12 weeks.
2. In the same contest, Wolcott's sales for the last 6 weeks averaged $425. For the first 4 weeks of the new year, his weekly sales were $500, $735, $658, and $695. Find his average weekly sales for the 10 weeks.

Answers:
1. $377   2. $513.80

Simple Interest

Basic Method of Calculation

Interest is the charge made for the use of money for a specified time. The money used is called the *principal*. The per cent is called the *rate*. The rule for calculating interest is:

Principal × Rate × Time = Interest

Problem 1: Find the interest on $600 for 1 year at 6%.

$600 × $\frac{6}{100}$ × 1 = $36, Interest

Problem 2: Find the interest on $1200 for 90 days at 4%.

$1200 × $\frac{4}{100}$ × $\frac{90}{360}$ = $12, Interest

Note that for purposes of easier and faster computation the year is considered to have 360 days, and each month, regardless of how many days it actually has, is considered to have only 30 days.

Exercise

Find the interest:

	Principal	Time	Rate %	Rate %	Rate %
1.	$1600	6 months	6	4	3
2.	1200	3 months	6	3	2
3.	2400	2 months	6	5	3
4.	720	60 days	6	1	4
5.	840	80 days	6	1	2
6.	480	40 days	6	5	4
7.	220	120 days	6	3	2
8.	180	9 months	6	8	4½
9.	2800	8 months	6	2	3
10.	960	30 days	6	4	3

Answers:

1.	$ 48	$32	$24
2.	18	9	6
3.	24	20	12
4.	7.20	1.20	4.80
5.	11.20	1.87	3.73
6.	3.20	2.67	2.13
7.	4.40	2.20	1.47
8.	8.10	10.80	6.08
9.	112	37.33	56
10.	4.80	3.20	2.40

The Sixty-Day Method

To find interest on sums of money when the time is less than a year, the *sixty-day method* is used. This method is based upon the fact that 60 days (2 months) are $\frac{1}{6}$ of one year. Therefore, if the annual interest rate is 6%, the interest charge for 60 days is $\frac{1}{6}$ of 6% or 1%. **Rule:** To find the interest on any sum of money for 60 days (2 months) take 1% of that amount.

Problem 1: Find the interest on $1200 for 60 days at 6%.

1% of $1200 = $12.00, Interest for 60 days
Proof: $1200 × $\frac{6}{100}$ × $\frac{60}{360}$ = $12.

Finding the interest for 60 days is the basis for computing interest for other periods of time. For example, the interest for 30 days is half of that for 60 days; for 15 days, a quarter; for 10 days, a sixth, etc.

Problem 2: Find the interest on $1200 at 6% for the days shown below:

Interest on $1200 for 60 days at 6%	= $12.00
Interest for 30 days (½ of 60)	= 6.00
Interest for 20 days (⅓ of 60)	= 4.00
Interest for 15 days (¼ of 60)	= 3.00
Interest for 12 days (⅕ of 60)	= 2.40
Interest for 10 days (⅙ of 60)	= 2.00
Interest for 6 days (⅒ of 60)	= 1.20

From this point, it is easy to find the interest for any number of days. Always find the interest for 60 days first. That is the base. Then, break up the days for which the interest is to be calculated into aliquot parts of 60 and add the interest for those days. The following illustrations will show just what is to be done:

Problem 3: Find the interest on $1800 for 90 days at 6%.

90 = 60 + 30.

Interest on $1800 for 60 days at 6%	= $18
Interest on $1800 for 30 days at 6%	= 9
Interest on $1800 for 90 days at 6%	= $27

Problem 4: Find the interest on $1500 for 47 days at 6%.

A. 47 = 20 + 20 + 6 + 1
   or
B. 47 = 30 + 15 + 2.

A.

Interest on $1500 for 60 days at 6% = $15.00	
Interest on $1500 for 20 days at 6% =	$5.00
Interest on $1500 for 20 days at 6% =	5.00
Interest on $1500 for 6 days at 6% =	1.50
Interest on $1500 for 1 day at 6% =	.25
Interest on $1500 for 47 days at 6% =	$11.75

B.

Interest on $1500 for 60 days at 6% = $15.00	
Interest on $1500 for 30 days at 6% =	$7.50
Interest on $1500 for 15 days at 6% =	3.75
Interest on $1500 for 2 days at 6% =	.50
Interest on $1500 for 47 days at 6% =	$11.75

Problem 5: Find the interest on $270 for 56 days at 6%.

A. 56 = 30 + 20 + 6.
   or
B. 56 = 20 + 20 + 12 + 4.
   or
C. 56 = 60 − 4.

A.

Interest on $270 for 60 days at 6% = $2.70	
Interest on $270 for 30 days at 6% =	$1.35
Interest on $270 for 20 days at 6% =	.90
Interest on $270 for 6 days at 6% =	.27
Interest on $270 for 56 days at 6% =	$2.52

B.

Interest on $270 for 60 days at 6% = $2.70	
Interest on $270 for 20 days at 6% =	$ .90
Interest on $270 for 20 days at 6% =	.90
Interest on $270 for 12 days at 6% =	.54
Interest on $270 for 4 days at 6% =	.18
Interest on $270 for 56 days at 6% =	$2.52

C.

Interest on $270 for 60 days at 6% = $2.70	
Interest on $270 for 4 days at 6% =	.18
Interest on $270 for 56 days at 6% = $2.52	

Note that it is also possible to use aliquot parts of the other numbers besides 60 as well. Thus in Problem 4*a*, 1 day is ⅙ of 6 days. Therefore ⅙ of $1.50 = $.25. In Problem 5*b*, 4 days are ⅕ of 20 days or ⅓ of 12 days. The interest can be computed by taking ⅕ of $.90 or ⅓ of $.54, the answer in each case being $.18.

Exercise

Find the interest:

	Principal	Time	Rate %
1.	$1600	80 days	6
2.	1800	3 months	6
3.	1200	75 days	6
4.	4000	46 days	6
5.	280	23 days	6
6.	970	38 days	6
7.	250.68	14 days	6
8.	168.95	4 months	6
9.	1280	53 days	6
10.	560.80	44 days	6

Answers:

1.	$21.33	5.	$1.07	9.	$11.31
2.	27.00	6.	6.14	10.	4.11
3.	15.00	7.	.58		
4.	30.67	8.	3.38		

To Find the Interest at 6% for Any Time in Days

Frequently the number of days in an interest problem cannot easily be divided into aliquot parts of 60, such as 29 days, 71 days, etc. In such cases another method may be used, as follows:

Rule:
1. Divide the principal by 1000.
2. Multiply the result by the number of days.
3. Divide the product by 6.

Problem: Find the interest on $150 for 29 days at 6%.

$$\frac{$150}{1000} = $.150$$

```
    $.150
      29
    1350
    300
6 ) 4350
    .725  Answer
```

The answer arrived at by this method may be checked by the first method:

Interest on $150 for 60 days at 6% = $1.50	
Interest on $150 for 30 days at 6% =	$.75
Interest on $150 for 1 day at 6% =	$.025
Interest on $150 for 31 days at 6% =	.775
Interest on $150 for 29 days at 6% = $ .725 or $.73	

Exercise

Do the examples in the preceding exercise, but use the above method.

To Find the Interest at Rates Other Than 6%

Rule:
1. Find the interest at 6%.
2. Multiply the answer by the desired rate.
3. Divide by 6.

Problem: Find the interest on $800 for 37 days at 4½%.

A.

Interest on $800 for 60 days at 6% = $8.00	
Interest on $800 for 30 days at 6% =	$4.00
Interest on $800 for 6 days at 6% =	.80
Interest on $800 for 1 day at 6% =	.133
Interest on $800 for 37 days at 6% =	$4.933

B.

```
    $4.933
       4½
   $22.1985
```

C.

```
6 ) 22.1985
    3.6997½ or $3.70, Answer
```

Another method may also be used. For 5% take ⅚ of the answer; for 4%, ⅔ (or 4/6); for 3%, ½ (or 3/6); for 2%, ⅓ (or 2/6) and for 1%, ⅙. Whichever method is used is a matter of one's own preference.

Exercise

Find the interest.

	Principal	Time	Rate %	Rate %	Rate %
1.	$1836	60 days	5	4	3
2.	680	26 days	4	3	2
3.	275	3 months	3	2	1
4.	368	6 months	2	1	5
5.	212.50	72 days	1	5	4
6.	505.80	90 days	5	4	3
7.	906	36 days	4	3	2
8.	412.76	45 days	3	2	1
9.	1300	18 days	2	1	5
10.	1560	52 days	1	5	4

Answers:

1.	$15.30	$12.24	$9.18
2.	1.97	1.48	.98
3.	2.06	1.38	.69
4.	3.68	1.84	9.20
5.	.43	2.13	1.70
6.	6.32	5.06	3.79
7.	3.62	2.72	1.81
8.	1.55	1.03	.52
9.	1.30	.65	3.25
10.	2.25	11.27	9.01

Bank Discount

Discounting One's Own Notes

When a businessman needs money, he borrows it at the bank. In return he will give the bank his written promise to repay the money at a certain time. This written promise is called a *promissory note*. The bank will charge interest on the loan which it will deduct in advance, giving the borrower the difference between the value of the note at maturity and the interest. This difference is called the *net proceeds*. When interest is deducted in advance, it is called *bank discount*, and the rate is called the *rate of bank discount*.

In order to find how much a borrower will actually receive on a loan, calculate the interest and subtract the amount from the principal.

Problem: A businessman borrows $1500 from a bank on his 60-day note at a discount rate of 6%. Find the net proceeds.

Interest on $1500
for 60 days at 6% = $15, Bank Discount

$1500 Maturity Value
  15 Bank Discount
$1485 Net Proceeds

Exercise

Find the net proceeds of the following notes:

	Note	Time of Discount	Rate of Discount %
1.	$1200	90 days	6
2.	680	45 days	6
3.	420	120 days	6
4.	1100	60 days	6
5.	975	30 days	6

Answers:

1.	$1182	3.	$ 411.60	5.	$970.12
2.	674.90	4.	1089		

Discounting Others' Notes

Frequently, a businessman who is in need of money has customers' notes and acceptances on hand. He may borrow on these.

Problem 1: Harry Williams has received a note of $600 from a customer. It is dated April 15 and runs for 90 days. On May 12, he needs money. He sells it to the bank or, to use the correct business term, he *discounts* the note. What are the net proceeds?

To do this problem, four steps must be performed.

1. Find the day the note is due (date of maturity).
2. Find how long the bank must wait for payment (term of discount).
3. Find the bank discount.
4. Find the net proceeds.

Date of Maturity

Apr.   30
     − 15
Apr.   15
May   31
June 30
July   14 Date of Maturity
     90 days

Term of Discount

May   31
     − 12
May   19
June 30
July   14
     63 days, Term of Discount

Bank Discount

$6.30 for 63 days (By previously indicated method)

Net Proceeds

$600.00 Maturity Value
    6.30 Bank Discount
$593.70 Net Proceeds

Note that in finding the date of maturity and the term of discount, the actual number of days is used.

Explanation of the Solution:

1. *Date of Maturity.* The date of maturity is 90 days from April 15. There are 30 days in April; 15 days have already passed, so we have 15 days left in April. In May there are 31, in June, 30 days. This gives us 76 days, leaving 14 more to make up the 90. We reach, then, July 14.
2. *Term of Discount.* Counting from the date the note was discounted, May 12, to the date of maturity, July 14, there are 63 days.
3. *Bank Discount.* The bank discount is found by finding the interest for the term of discount, 63 days.
4. *Net Proceeds.* Net proceeds are found by deducting the bank discount from the value at maturity.

When the time of the note is not in days, but in months, the date of maturity is found by counting months, and not days.

Problem 2: Find the net proceeds of a note of $1500, dated July 16, time 3 months, and discounted August 31.

Date of Maturity

July 16
Aug.
Sept.
Oct. 16 Date of Maturity
    3 months

Term of Discount

Aug. 31
   − 31
Aug. 0
Sept. 30
Oct. 16
    46 days, Term of Discount

Bank Discount

$11.50, for 46 days (By previously indicated method)

Net Proceeds

$1500.00 Maturity Value
   11.50 Bank Discount
$1488.50 Net Proceeds

Exercise

Find the net proceeds:

	Face Value	Date	Time	Rate %	Date of Discount
1.	$1200	Mar. 2	60 days	6	Apr. 7
2.	1800	Apr. 30	90 days	6	June 3
3.	240	Sept. 16	30 days	6	Sept. 25
4.	550	Jan. 20	1 mo.	6	Jan. 31
5.	728	Feb. 17	3 mo.	6	Apr. 12
6.	2800	May 4	2 mo.	6	June 6

Answers:
1.	$1195.20	3.	$239.16	5. $ 723.75
2.	1783.20	4.	548.17	6. 2786.93

Discounting Interest-Bearing Notes

The face value and the maturity value of a non-interest-bearing note are the same. In the case of an interest-bearing note, the face value and maturity value differ, because the interest must be added to the face value to arrive at the maturity value.

Problem 1: Find the maturity value of a 60-day note of $800 bearing interest at 3%.

Interest = $4

$800 Face Value
   4 Interest
$804 Maturity Value

To discount an interest-bearing note, the maturity value must be found, because the bank discount is computed on the maturity value, not the face value.

Problem 2: Find the net proceeds of a 60-day note of $1200, bearing interest at 4%, dated January 18 and discounted February 13.

Date of Maturity

Jan. 31
   − 18
Jan. 13
Feb. 28
Mar. 19, Date of Maturity
    60 days

Term of Discount

Feb. 28
   − 13
Feb. 15
Mar. 19
    34 days, Time of Discount

Interest and Maturity Value

$1200.00 Face
   9.00 Interest
$1209.00 Maturity Value

Bank Discount

$6.85 for 34 days (By previously indicated method)

Net Proceeds

$1209.00 Maturity Value
   6.85 Bank Discount
$1202.15 Net Proceeds

Note that there is a new step in this solution; namely, finding the maturity value. Otherwise the solution is the same as in the non-interest-bearing notes.

Exercise

Find the net proceeds:

	Face Value	Date	Time	Interest Rate %	Rate of Discount %	Date of Discount
1.	$ 900	Mar. 12	60 da.	6	6	Mar. 30
2.	1200	Dec. 28	3 mo.	6	6	Feb. 6
3.	2600	July 6	1 mo.	3	6	July 25
4.	750	Nov. 19	90 da.	4	6	Jan. 20
5.	960	Aug. 27	120 da.	2	6	Oct. 14

Answers:
1.	$ 902.64	3.	$2601.29	5. $954.80
2.	1207.85	4.	753.96	

Borrowing Money to Pay a Bill

A firm may buy goods and the discount for cash may be so great that it will be worthwhile borrowing the money to be able to take advantage of the discount. It is important, then, to be able to figure out how much can be gained by borrowing to pay for cash, and, also, whether it is actually worthwhile to do so.

Problem: On April 3, F. B. Clark bought goods for $1500, terms 2/10, n/30. He did not have the money to pay the invoice on April 13, so that he could take advantage of the discount. He therefore borrowed sufficient money to pay the bill on his 20-day interest-bearing note. Did he gain or lose and how much?

$1500 Amount of Invoice
   30 Cash discount 2%
$1470 Net Cost
    Interest on $1470 for 20 days
    at 6% = $4.90
$30.00 Cash Discount
   4.90 Interest
$25.10 Gain by borrowing

Note that he must borrow the amount of the *net cost*.

Exercise

1. A merchant bought goods for $3640, terms 3/10, n/90. To take advantage of the cash discount, he borrowed the money for 80 days at 6% and paid the bill. How much was gained by borrowing the money?
2. A merchant purchased goods for $1500 less 20% and 10%, terms 2/10, n/30. To take advantage of the cash discount, he borrowed the money for 20 days at 6% and paid the bill. How much was gained by borrowing?
3. The Hudson Co. bought goods for $2480 less 25%, terms 2/10, n/60. To take advantage of the cash discount, they borrowed the money at 6% for 50 days. How much was gained by borrowing?

Answers:
1. $62.12   2. $18.07   3. $22.01

Borrowing Money for Loan Companies

Small-loan companies are permitted by law to lend money, usually up to $300, and charge a stated rate per cent of interest on the unpaid balance. Payments on such loans are generally made in monthly installments.

Problem: A man borrows $300 from a finance company. The company charges 2% interest per month on the unpaid balance. Payments of $50 are to be made monthly. The loan is for 6 months. Find the total amount of interest paid.

Interest Period	Unpaid Balance	Interest at 2%	Payment
End of first month	$300	$6.00	$50
End of second month	250	5.00	50
End of third month	200	4.00	50
End of fourth month	150	3.00	50
End of fifth month	100	2.00	50
End of sixth month	50	1.00	50
Total Interest		$21.00	

Note that the interest is computed on the amount due at the end of each month. The unpaid balance at the end of the first month is $300 so the interest at 2% of $300 is $6. At the end of the next month the unpaid balance, reduced by $50, is $250, and the interest is $5, etc.

Problem: A man borrows $200 for 4 months. The interest charges are 2½% on the first $100, 2% on the balance. Find the interest charges.

Interest Period	Unpaid Balance	Interest Charges	Payment
End of first month	$200	$4.50	$50
End of second month	150	3.50	50
End of third month	100	2.50	50
End of fourth month	50	1.25	50
Total Interest		$11.75	

Computation:
2½% of $100 = $2.50; 2% of $100 = $2.00; Total $4.50
2½% of $100 = $2.50; 2% of $ 50 = $1.00; Total $3.50
2½% of $100 = $2.50
2½% of $ 50 = $1.25

Exercise

1. Gates borrows $240 from a credit union for 5 months. He repays the loan in five monthly installments of $48 each, plus interest charges of ¾% per month on the unpaid balance. Find the interest charges.

2. Brown borrows $150 from a finance company and will repay it in 5 monthly installments of $30 each. The company charges 2½% on the first $100, 2% on the balance. Find the interest charges.
3. Aarons borrows $150 from a finance company and will repay it in 6 monthly installments of $25 each. The company charges 2% on the unpaid balance. Find the interest charges.

Answers:
1. $5.40   2. $10.90   3. $10.50

Compound Interest

Compound interest is interest which has been added to the principal, to form a part of the new principal. For example, if Brown deposits $100 in a savings bank and at the end of the year he is credited with 2% interest, his new principal is $102. At the end of the next year, the bank will compute the interest upon $102. If this is done each year, the interest is compounded annually. Banks add interest at stated periods, such as at the end of a month, quarter year, half year, or year, and interest is said to be compounded monthly, quarterly, semi-annually, or annually. Banks use compound-interest tables to compute the compound interest. Below, it will be computed arithmetically. Interest is not computed on cents, but on dollars only.

Problem: On January 2, 1943, Clark deposited $500 in a savings bank. Interest at the rate of 2% per annum was compounded semi-annually. On January 2, 1944, Clark deposited an additional $400. Find how much he had on deposit July 1, 1944.

  $500.00 Principal Jan. 2, 1943
     5.00 Interest July 1, 1943 (2% per year, 1% for ½ year)
  $505.00 Principal July 1, 1943
     5.05 Interest Jan. 2, 1944
  $510.05 Principal Jan. 2, 1944
   400.00 Deposit Jan. 2, 1944
  $910.05 Principal Jan. 2, 1944
     9.10 Interest July 1, 1944
  $919.15 Principal July 1, 1944

Note that interest is computed and added before deposits are added or withdrawals deducted.

Exercise

1. A savings bank pays 2% interest on its deposits and adds the interest on June 1 and December 1 of each year. On June 1, 1944 H. Williams deposits $600. If he makes no deposits or withdrawals, how much will he have on deposit December 1, 1945?
2. A savings bank pays 1½% interest on its deposits and adds the interest on January 2 and July 1 of each year. On January 2, 1943 W. Harris deposits $600. He deposits $400 on July 1, 1943 and withdraws $100 on January 2, 1944. How much will he have on deposit July 1, 1944?

Answers:
1. $618.18   2. $918.87

Profits and Pricing

Per Cent of Profit

Businessmen, in order to stay in business, must operate at a profit. To do so, it is imperative that they have certain information on their operations. This information will be considered here.

Per Cent of Profit on Cost

The selling price of goods less the cost of goods is the entire or gross profit. The gross profit less the overhead is the net profit. By overhead is meant the expenses or cost of doing business, such as rent, salaries, supplies, etc. What the businessman wants to know very often is whether he is making a big enough profit in comparison to his cost.

Problem: Goods costing $500 are sold for $800. The overhead is $100. Find *A.* rate of gross profit on cost; *B.* rate of net profit on cost.

$800 Selling Price
 500 Cost
$300 Gross Profit
 100 Overhead
$200 Net Profit

A. $300/500 = 60\%$, Rate of Gross Profit on Cost
B. $200/500 = 40\%$, Rate of Net Profit on Cost

Per Cent of Profit on Sales

Many businessmen prefer to base their profit on sales and not on cost. The reasons are that the sales price is known at once whereas the cost must be looked up and because expenses and profits are compared with sales.

Problem: Goods costing $500 are sold for $800. The overhead is $100. Find *A.* rate of gross profit on sales; *B.* rate of net profit on sales.

$800 Selling Price
 500 Cost
$300 Gross Profit
 100 Overhead
$200 Net Profit

A. $300/800 = 37\frac{1}{2}\%$, Rate of Gross Profit on Sales
B. $200/800 = 25\%$, Rate of Net Profit on Sales

Exercise

	Selling Price	Cost	Gain	Rate of Gain on Cost	Rate of Gain on Sales
1.	$ 75	$ 60			
2.	48	32			
3.	25	15			
4.	60	30			
5.	150	100			

Answers:

	Gain	Rate of Gain on Cost %	Rate of Gain on Sales %
1.	$15	25	20
2.	16	50	33⅓
3.	10	66⅔	40
4.	30	100	50
5.	50	50	33⅓

Selling Prices

Find the Selling Price, Given the Cost and Percent of Profit on Cost

Having determined the rate of gain on cost, it will be easy to compute the selling price of similar articles with the same rate of profit or mark-up.

Problem: Goods cost $50. The rate of profit on cost is 20%. Find the sales price.

$50 Cost
 10 20% Rate of Profit on Cost 20%
$60 Sales Price

Exercise

Find the sales price.

	Cost	Rate of Gross Profit on Cost %
1.	$120	50
2.	264	16⅔
3.	180	33⅓
4.	290	40
5.	175	100

Answers:
1. $180	3. $240	5. $350
2. 308	4. 406	

Finding the Selling Price, Given the Cost and Per Cent of Profit on Sales

Here the rate of profit is figured on sales and not on cost. The procedure in finding the sales price differs because an indirect method is used.

Problem: A refrigerator is billed to a dealer at $75 less 20% and 10%. At what price should he sell the refrigerator to gain 20% of the sales price?

$75 List Price
 15 Trade Discount 20%
$60 Balance
  6 Trade Discount 10%
$54 Net Cost

Sales Price	100%	
Profit	20%	
Cost		$54

Sales Price	100%	$67.50
Profit	20%	$13.50
Cost	80%	$54.00

$54 ÷ .8 = $67.50 or $54 ÷ ⅘ =
$54 × 5/4 = $67.50, *Answer*

To prove, take 20% of the sales, $67.50. The profit is $13.50. Sales, $67.50, minus Profit, $13.50, equal $54, Cost.

In this type of problem, the unknown is the sales price. This is 100%. The profit on sales is known to be 20% of 100%, or 20%. The cost is known to be $54. Now, subtract 20% from 100% to get the cost: 80%. The cost also equals $54. The problem now is: $54 is 80% of what number? As done in Percentage, Percentage ÷ Rate = Base or 54 ÷ .8.

Finding the Selling Price, Given the Cost, the Per Cent of Profit and Overhead Based on Selling Price

Problem: A refrigerator is billed to a dealer at $75 less 20% and 10%. At what price should he sell the refrigerator to gain 20% on sales, if he gives his salesman a commission of 8% on sales and his overhead is 12% of sales?

$75   List Price
15   Trade Discount 20%
$60   Balance
6   Trade Discount 10%
$54   Net Cost

Sales Price		100%	
Commission	8%		
Overhead	12%		
Profit	20%	40%	
Cost			$54

Sales Price		100%	$90
Commission	8%		
Overhead	12%		
Profit	20%	40%	$36
Cost		60%	$54

$$\$54 \div .6 = 90 \text{ or}$$
$$\$54 \div \tfrac{3}{5} = 54 \times \tfrac{5}{3} = \$90, \textit{ Answer}$$

The procedure followed is as in the previous problem. Everything based on sales is placed in the middle of the diagram, totaled, and subtracted from the sales, 100%. The difference is the cost. The problem is the same as before: the net cost is a certain percentage of what number? Prove as before.

Exercise

1. A merchant bought rugs at $27 less 25%. At what price must he sell them to make a profit of 16⅔% on sales?
2. A druggist buys face powder at 50¢ per box. The wholesaler offers the druggist a discount of 10% and 5%, if he will buy a carton (36 boxes). The druggist accepts. At what price must he mark each box to make a profit of 33⅓% on cost?
3. A dealer buys radios at $150 less 20% and 10%. He has an expense of $6 per radio for delivery and installation. (This is a selling expense and must be added to sales price to get total sales price.)
   a. At what price must he sell each radio to gain 25% on the purchase price?
   b. At what price must he sell each radio to gain 25% on the sales price?
4. A dealer buys fountain pens at $36 per dozen less 25% and 20%. The overhead is 25% of sales. At what price must he sell each pen to gain 15% on the sales price?
5. In 1944 the Brown Rug Co. determined its sales price by basing the gross profit of 40% on cost. In 1945, the company decided to base the 40% gross profit on sales price.
   a. If a rug cost $6, what was the sales price in 1944?
   b. If the cost of the rug was $6 in 1945, what was the sales price in 1945?
   c. By what per cent was the gross profit decreased or increased in 1945 as compared with 1944.
6. A dealer ordered 24 thermometers at $45 a dozen, less 20%. He found 6 defective items and returned them. The buying expenses on the purchase were $2.16. (Add buying expenses to find total cost.) If he wished to make a profit of 30% on sales, and if the overhead was 10%, at what price was each thermometer sold?
7. A dealer purchased bicycles at $32.50 less 20% and 5%, plus a freight charge of 90¢ on each bicycle. If his overhead is 24% of sales, at what price must he sell each bicycle to make a profit of 12% of the sales price?

Answers:
1. $24.30   4. $3   6. $ 5.20
2. 57   5. a. 8.40   7. 40
3. a. 141   b. 10
   b. 150   c. 19½₁% Increase

Find the List or Marked Price, Given the Selling Price and the Trade Discount

Wholesalers who sell their goods subject to a trade discount must be able to compute the list or catalogue price so that they will receive the market price they desire. The procedure is the same as in the preceding problem.

Problem: A radio cost $150 and it is to be sold at a profit of 33⅓% on cost. At what price should it be listed in the catalogue, if there is a trade discount of 60% to be given?

First Step.—To Find the Sales Price:
$150   Cost
50   Profit 33⅓% on cost
$200   Selling Price

Second Step.—To Find the List Price:

List Price	100%	$500
Trade Discount	60%	$300
Selling Price	40%	$200

$$\$200 \div .40 = \$500, \text{ List Price or}$$
$$\$200 \div \tfrac{2}{5} = \$200 \times \tfrac{5}{2} = \$500, \text{ List Price}$$

Problem: A shoe store owner buys shoes at $7 a pair. He wants to make a profit of 20% on the sales price, after offering a discount of 12½% on the marked or list price. Find the marked price.

First Step–To Find the Sales Price:

Sales Price	100%	$8.75
Profit	20%	$1.75
Cost	80%	$7.00

$$\$7 \div .80 = \$8.75, \text{ Sales Price or}$$
$$\$7 \div \tfrac{4}{5} = \$7 \times \tfrac{5}{4} = \tfrac{35}{4} = \$8.75, \text{ Sales Price}$$

Second Step–To Find the List Price:

List Price	100%	$10.00
Trade Discount	12½%	$1.25
Sales Price	87½%	$8.75

$$\$8.75 \div .875 = \$10, \text{ List Price or}$$
$$\$8.75 \div \tfrac{7}{8} = \$8.75 \times \tfrac{8}{7} = \$10, \text{ List Price}$$

Exercise

1. A haberdasher buys hats at $40 per dozen less 25% and 20%. He wants to make a profit of 25% on the cost and to offer a trade discount of 16⅔% off the list price. Find the marked or list price.
2. A merchant buys gloves at $18 per dozen pairs. He wants to make a profit of 33⅓% on cost and offer a trade discount of 20% off the list price. Find the list price.
3. A dealer pays $60 less 30%, and 10% for a rug. Selling expenses are 7½% of the selling price. He sells the rug to gain 25% on the sales price, after allowing a trade discount of 20% off the marked price. Find the marked price.
4. It cost a manufacturer $17 to make a rug. At what price should he list the rug in his catalogue to make a profit of 15% on the sales price after allowing a trade discount of 33⅓% on the catalogue price?
5. A merchant buy rugs at $28 less 25%. What is the marked price if he wishes to make a profit of 20% on the selling price after allowing a discount of 40% on the marked price?
6. A merchant buys a desk for $80. He wants to make a profit of 25% on cost. At what price must he mark it to allow a discount of 20% off the marked price?
7. A dealer buys suits at $40 less 10%. He wants to make a profit of 25% on the selling price and allow a special discount of 16⅔% off the marked price. Find the marked price.
8. A merchant buys stoves for $40 less 20% and 10%. He wants to make a profit on 33⅓% on the selling price after allowing a 10% discount on the marked price. Find the marked price.

Answers:
1. $36 4. $ 30 7. $57.60
2. 30   5.   43.75 8. 48
3. 70   6. 125

Comparison of Profits

Very often a merchant will have a special sale on certain goods. He then wishes to make a comparison between the profit realized on the goods sold at the old price and the profit at the sale price.

Problem: During November a hardware dealer sold 24 coal stoves at $125 each. The net cost of each stove was $87.50. The overhead expense was $17.50 per stove. In December, he ran a special sale and reduced the sales price to $117.50 per stove, and sold 32 stoves. The overhead in December was $17.25 per stove.

   A. How much profit did the dealer make in November?
   B. How much profit did he make in December?
   C. What was the rate of increase or decrease?

This problem may be calculated by two methods: on the basis of one stove or the total number of stoves.

Calculation on 1 Stove

A. *November*

1 stove @ $125.00 each = $125.00 Sales Price
1 stove @ $ 87.50 each =   87.50 Cost
                          $ 37.50 Gross Profit
                            17.50 Overhead
                          $ 20.00 Net Profit
24 stoves @ $20.00 profit on ea. = $480, Total Profit
                                              Answer

B. *December*

1 stove @ $117.50 each = $117.50 Sales Price
1 stove @ $ 87.50 each =   87.50 Cost
                          $ 30.00 Gross Profit
                            17.25 Overhead
                          $ 12.75 Net Profit
32 stoves @ $12.75 profit on ea. = $408, Total Profit
                                              Answer

C. $480 Net Profit, November
        408 Net Profit, December
       $ 72 Decrease in Profit

       $ 72 Decrease   72
       $480 Net Profit, November = ——— =
                                      480
            15% Rate of Decrease, *Answer*

Calculation on Total Number of Stoves

A. *November*

24 stoves @ $125.00 each = $3000 Sales Price
24 stoves @ $ 87.50 each = 2100 Cost
                           $ 900 Gross Profit
24 stoves @ $ 17.50 each =   420 Overhead
                           $ 480 Net Profit,
                                      Answer

B. *December*

32 stoves @ $117.50 each = $3760 Sales Price
32 stoves @ $ 87.50 each = 2800 Cost
                           $ 960 Gross Profit
32 stoves @ $ 17.25 each =   552 Overhead
                           $ 408 Net Profit,
                                      Answer

C. $480 Net Profit, November
        408 Net Profit, December
       $ 72 Decrease in Profit

       $ 72 Decrease   72
       $480 Net Profit, November = ——— =
                                      480
            15% Decrease, *Answer*

Exercise

1. A merchant bought chairs at $15 each. He sold them at $25 each. During October his sales were 150 chairs. In November, he ran a special sale, reducing the sales price to $20 per chair. The sales increased to 400 chairs.
   a. How much was the profit in October?
   b. How much was the profit in November?
   c. What was the rate of increase or decrease in the profit?
2. The Home Appliance Co. bought washing machines at $130 less 30% each. During April, 15 machines were sold at $129 each. During May, each machine was sold at $117.50 each. As a result 30 machines were sold.
   a. During which month did the company make more profit and how much?
   b. What was the rate of increase or decrease in the profit?

Answers:
1. *a.* $1500
   b. $2000
   c. 33⅓%, Increase

2. *a.* $570
   b. $795
   c. 39 + % or 40%

Distribution of Partnership Profits

Profits are distributed among partners according to the arrangements set forth in the partnership contract. If no mention is made, the profits or losses are distributed equally.

There are three usual methods of division of profits. They are:

1. According to an agreed-upon ratio.
2. According to partnership investment ratio.
3. Allowing interest on investment, and then dividing the balance equally.

Problem: Vincent, Dugan, and Carver have invested $6000, $8000, and 12,000 respectively in their wholesale business. The first year their profit was $7800.

A. How much will each receive if they agree to divide their profits equally?
B. How much will each receive if they agree to divide their profits in proportion to their investments (capital ratio)?
C. How much will they receive if each partner is allowed 6% on his investment, and then the remaining profit is divided equally?

A. There are three partners.
   ⅓ of $7800 = $2600, each partner's share

B.

Partner	Invest-ment	Share according to Capital Ratio	Computation of Share	Share
Vincent	$ 6000	$\frac{6000}{2600}$	3/13 of $7800	$1800
Dugan	8000	$\frac{8000}{26000}$	4/13 of $7800	2400
Carver	12000	$\frac{12000}{26000}$	6/13 of $7800	3600
Totals	$26000	$\frac{26000}{26000}$	13/13 of $7800	$7800

C.

Partner	Invest-ment	6% Interest on Captial	⅓ of Remaining Profit	Share
Vincent	$6000	$360	$2080	$2440
Dugan	8000	480	2080	2560
Carver	12000	720	2080	2800
Totals	$26000	$1560	$6240	$7800 Total Profit

```
    $7800  Total Profit
     1560  Interest
3 ) 6240
    $2080
```

Exercise

1. Todd invested $12,000 and Olsen $15,000 in their business. They agreed to allow interest on their investments of 8% and divide the remaining profit equally.
   a. How much must the business earn in one year to cover the 8% interest?
   b. If the profit at the end of the year was $5380, how much did each receive?

2. Abbot invested $12,000, Johnson $16,000, and Moore his services. Out of the first year's profit of $9675, Abbot and Johnson were allowed 12½% interest on their investments, and Moore $1600 as salary. The remaining profit was divided equally. Find each partner's income for the year.

3. Davis and Lee invested $8000 and $4000 respectively in their business. At the end of the year their sales were $18,525, cost of goods sold was $12,200 and overhead expenses were $1522. If the profit was to be divided according to their capital ratio, find each partner's share of the profit.

4. Young and Harrington invested $6000 and $12,000 respectively in their business. The sales for the year 1944 were $28,440; cost of goods sold, $15,460; overhead, $3200.
   a. Find the net profit.
   b. The profits are to be shared in capital ratio. Find each partner's share.
   c. If each partner is allowed 6% on his investment and the profit which remains is to be shared equally, how much will each partner receive?

Answers:
1. *a.* $2160
   b. Todd $2570
      Olsen $2810

2. Abbot $3025
   Johnson $3525
   Moore $3125

3. Davis $3202
   Lee $1601

4. *a.* $9780
   b. Young $3260
      Harrington $6520

Corporation Stock

Definitions and Terms

Corporations issue stock as evidence of ownership in the corporation. When a corporation makes a profit, its directors distribute a part or all of this profit among the stockholders. This distribution of profit is called a *dividend*. All undistributed profit is called *surplus*.

The value imprinted on the face of the stock certificate is called its par value. The par value of the stock is usually $100, although stock may be issued at other par values, such as $50 or $25. Some corporations issue stock with no par value. The market price of stock is the price at which the stock is sold in the various stock markets.

In this section we take up some of the problems of computing dividends and buying and selling stock.

Computing Dividends on Stock

Problem: A corporation has a capital stock of $500,000, each share having a par value of $100. It declares a dividend of 9%. If the net profits for the year are $75,000, find the amount of the dividend and how much is left in surplus.

$500,000 \div \$100 = 5000$ shares
9% of $100 = \$9$, Dividend on 1 share
5000 shares $\times \$9 = \$45,000$, Dividend declared
$75,000 - \$45,000 = \$30,000$, Amount left in surplus

Problem: A corporation has a capital stock of $400,000 each share having par value of $100. Its net profit for the year is $60,000. The directors declare a dividend of 4%. Find *A.* the amount of the dividend; *B.* the amount added to surplus; *C.* the dividend received by a stockholder who owns 60 shares of stock.

A. $400,000 \div 100$ = 4000 shares
    4% of 100   = $4, dividend on 1 share

    4000×4 = $16,000, amount of dividend

B. $60,000 - \$16,000$ = $44,000 amount added to surplus

C. 60 shares @ $4 per share = $240, dividend received by stockholder

Exercise

(Where no par value is stated, assume it is $100.)

1. A corporation declares a semi-annual dividend of 5%. Find Mr. Jones' dividend if he owns 100 shares.
2. A corporation's capital stock is $600,000. It declares a dividend of 5%. Find the amount of the dividend declared.
3. The Lincoln Radio Co. has capital stock of $500,000. Its profit is $80,000. Its directors declare an annual dividend of 6%.
   a. What does the total annual dividend amount to?
   b. How much will go to surplus?
   c. If Harry Wells has 75 shares, how much dividend will he receive?
4. The Ocean Hardware Corp. has a capital stock of $200,000. It declares semi-annual dividends of 3%.
   a. Find the total annual dividend.
   b. Find how much Max Morse, who owns 50 shares, will receive annually.
5. Anthony Lamb has 50 shares of common stock and 12 shares of 8% preferred stock in a certain corporation. A quarterly dividend of 60¢ per share is paid on the common stock and the regular 8% dividend on the preferred. How much income annually will Mr. Lamb receive from his stock holdings?

Answers:
1. $500
2. $30,000
3. *a.* $30,000
   b. $50,000
   c. $450
4. *a.* $12,000
   b. $300
5. $216

Finding the Rate of Dividend

Problem: A corporation which has a capital stock of $400,000 has a net profit of $80,000 for the year. It decides to keep $20,000 in surplus and distribute the rest of the profits as dividends. Find the annual rate of dividend.

$80,000 Total Profit
$\underline{20,000}$ Surplus
$60,000 Dividend declared

$\dfrac{60,000 \text{ Dividend declared}}{400,000 \text{ Capital stock}} = 15\%$, Rate of dividend, *Answer*

Exercise

1. A corporation with capital stock of $300,000 has a net profit of $50,000. The directors declare a dividend of $30,000. Find the rate of dividend.
2. A corporation is capitalized at $200,000. It makes a profit of $45,000. If $15,000 is set aside for surplus, what will be the rate of dividend?
3. The Borax Corp, is capitalized at $500,000. At the end of the year it will pay $60,000 in dividends.
   a. Find the annual dividend rate.
   b. Find how much a person who has 50 shares will receive in dividends.
4. The Lastelle Corp., with capital stock of $1,000,000, earns $180,000 for the year. The directors declare a dividend of $120,000.
   a. Find the amount left in surplus.
   b. Find the annual rate of dividend on the stock.
   c. Find how much a stockholder who has 100 shares receives.

Answers:
1. 10%
2. 15%
3. *a.* 12%
   b. $600
4. *a.* $60,000
   b. 12%
   c. $1200

Buying and Selling Stock

Stock may be bought and sold at any stock exchange through the medium of a broker who is a member of that exchange. The broker charges a fee, called *brokerage*, for his services. In addition a state and a federal tax must be paid on all stock sold.

Problem: Harry Wilson bought 300 shares of stock at 56½ (i.e., $56.50) and sold it at 65. Brokerage each way was 25¢ a share and the total taxes were 4¢ per share. Find his net profit on the transaction.

Sale

300 shares @ $65 each   = $19,500 Sales Price
300 shares
  @ 25¢ each = $75 brokerage
300 shares
  @ 4¢ each = $\underline{\$12}$ tax $\underline{\quad 87\quad}$
                       $19,413 Net Proceeds

Purchase

300 shares @ $56.50 each = $16,950 Cost
300 shares @   25¢ each = $\underline{\quad\ 75}$ Brokerage
                           $17,025 Total Cost

$19,413 Net Proceeds of Sale
$\underline{17,025}$ Total Cost
$ 2,388 Net Profit

Exercise

1. Stock costing $50 per share was sold for $58 per share. Brokerage each way was 24¢ per share and the taxes on the sale amounted to 4¢ per share. Find the net profit.
2. Warren bought 100 shares of stock at 90 and sold them for 105. Brokerage each way was 24¢ per share and the taxes on the sale were 4½¢ per share. Find the net profit.

3. Harris bought 300 shares of stock at 98½¢ and sold them at 112½. If brokerage is 25¢ per share each way and the taxes on the sale were 4¢ per share, find the amount of the net profit.

Answers:
1. $7.48   **2.** $1447.50   **3.** $4038

Finding Profit on Sale of Stock, Dividends Having Been Received

Problem: Morris bought 300 shares of stock at 98 and sold them at 110, after holding them a year. During this time, he received 2 semi-annual dividends of 4%. Brokerage was 25¢ per share each way and taxes on the sale were 4¢. Find his total profit.

Sale
300 shares @ $110 each	= $33,000 Sales Price
300 shares	
@ 25¢ each = $75 broker-	
age	
300 shares	
@ 4¢ each = $12 tax	87
	$32,913 Net Proceeds

Purchase
300 shares @ $98 each =	$29,400 Cost
300 shares @ 25¢ each =	75 Brokerage
	$29,475 Total Cost

$32,913	Net Proceeds of Sale
28,475	Total Cost
$ 3,438	Net Profit on Sale

Dividends
4% of 100	=	$4 per share, dividend for ½ year
300 shares @ $4	=	1200, Dividend for ½ year
1200 × 2	=	2400, Dividend for 1 year

$ 3,438	Net Profit on Sale
2,400	Dividends
$ 5,838	Total Profit, *Answer*

Exercise

1. Harvey bought 50 shares of stock at 32, brokerage 24¢ per share. The stock pays a quarterly dividend of 1%. At the end of a year, he sold the stock at 40, brokerage 25¢ per share, tax 4¢ per share. Find his total profit on the transaction.
2. On February 1, M. King bought 70 shares of stock at 98½, brokerage 22¢ a share. On April 1 and again on October 1, he received a cash dividend of $2.50 a share. On November 1 he sold the stock at 112, brokerage 24¢ a share, tax 4¢ a share. What was King's profit?
3. Mr. Carson bought 10 shares of 7% preferred stock at $140 a share. He received dividends for one year and then sold the stock at $142 per share. Brokerage was 26¢ per share on the purchase, 27¢ per share on the sale, and there was a tax of 10¢ per share on the sale. Find his total gain on the transaction.

Answers:
1. $573.50   **2.** $1260   **3.** $83.70

Finding the Rate of Return on Investment

Problem: A share of stock, par value $100, is bought for $81. A dividend of 9% is declared on the stock. Find the rate of return.

9% of $100 = $9, Dividend on 1 share

$$\frac{\$ 9 \text{ Dividend}}{\$81 \text{ Cost of Stock}} = \frac{1}{9} = 11\frac{1}{9}\%, \text{ Rate of return}$$

Exercise

1. On January 2, 1945 J. Martin invested $3400 in aircraft stock at 42½ (including brokerage). During 1945 he received 4 quarterly dividends of 60¢ each on each share of stock. (To find the number of shares, divide the investment by the cost of 1 share.) Find the rate of return on his investment.
2. An industrial stock, which yields an annual dividend of 3%, sells at $60. A public utility stock is quoted at 90 and yields a dividend of 5%. (No brokerage charges).
   a. Find the rate of return on each.
   b. Which is the better investment and by how much?
3. H. G. Lee purchases 50 shares of American Telephone & Telegraph at 190, paying a dividend of 9% per year. (Disregard brokerage.) Find the rate of return.

Answers:
1. $5\frac{11}{17}\%$
2. *a.* Industrial 5%, utility $5\frac{5}{9}\%$
    b. Utility by $\frac{5}{9}\%$
3. $4\frac{14}{19}\%$

Bonds

Definitions and Interest

A bond is an indebtedness of a corporation. As a rule, the par value of bonds is $1000, unless otherwise stated. Bonds with a par value of less than $1000 are called baby bonds. Since bonds are evidence of debt, the corporation which issues the bonds pays interest on the bonds, usually semi-annually. The interest is called the *income* or *yield*.

Bonds are bought and sold through brokers on the stock exchanges. The price of bonds is shown in two figures, for example, 98½; however the price actually represents three figures, namely $985. Brokers charge a commission on the purchase and sale of each bond.

Bond problems, as a rule, follow the procedures set forth in the solution of stock problems, with one exception which will be shown below.

Purchase of Bonds with Accrued Interest

Since interest on bonds is usually paid semi-annually, it follows that when bonds are bought on a day which is not a day on which interest is due and payable, the buyer will have to refund to the seller the interest which has accumulated or accrued up to the date of the purchase.

Problem: Find the cost of 10 bonds, par value $1000, bought at 96 on February 1. The interest rate is 6%. Interest is payable on January 1 and July 1. Brokerage, $2.50 per bond.

Accrued interest on $1000 for 31 days	
from January 1 to February 1 at	
6% ....$	5.17
Brokerage	2.50
Price of 1 bond	960.00
Cost of 1 bond ....$	967.67
Cost of 10 bonds—$967.67 × 10	$9676.70, *Answer*

Exercise

1. Find the cost of 4 bonds, par value $1000, bought at 110 on March 28, interest rate 4%, interest due March 1 and September 1, brokerage $2.50 per bond.
2. Find the cost of 20 bonds, par value $1000, bought at 98 on February 18, interest rate 6%, interest due January 1 and July 1, brokerage $2.50 per bond.

Answers:
1. $4422   2. $19,810

Sale of Bonds with Accrued Interest

The procedure in the sale of bonds is the opposite of that in computing the purchase of bonds. The accrued interest is given to the seller because it is his. Therefore, the accrued interest is added on to the selling price and the commission deducted.

Problem: A man sold 10 bonds, par value $1000, for 98 on November 30. Interest on the bonds was at the rate of 6%; the interest was due on April 1 and October 1. Brokerage was $2.50 per bond.

Accrued interest on $1000 at 6% from
    October 1 to November 30; 60
    days ....$ 10.00
Price of 1 bond 980.00
Gross Proceeds ....$ 990.00
Brokerage, $2.50 ....   2.50
Net Proceeds for 1 bond ....$ 987.50
Net Proceeds for 10 bonds—
    $987.50 × 10 ....$9875.00, *Answer*

Exercise

1. Find the net proceeds of 5 bonds, par value $1000, sold for 105 on September 19. Interest at the rate of 6% is due on January 1 and July 1. Brokerage $2.50 per bond.
2. Find the net proceeds of 15 bonds, par value $1000, sold for 97½ on October 30. Interest at the rate of 4%, payable on February 1 and August 1. Brokerage is $2.50 per bond.

Answers:
1. $5304.15   2. $14,737.50

Fire Insurance

Computation of Premiums

Insurance is the protection of the insured against any money loss arising from destruction or damage to the insured property.

Problem: Conroy's place of business, valued at $7500, was insured for 60% of its value for one year. The 1-year rate was 15¢ per C (per hundred dollars). Find the amount of the premium.

60% of $7500   = $4500, Value of Policy
$4500 @ 15¢ per C = $6.75, Premium for 1 year

Suppose that in the above problem the insurance company offers Conroy a 3-year rate which is 2½ times the annual rate. Find the premium for the 3 years and the average annual premium on a 3-year policy.

$6.75, Premium for 1 year
$6.75 × 2½ = $16.88, Premium for 3 years
$1688 ÷ 3 = $5.62⅔ or $5.63, Average annual
                premium

Exercise

1. George Allen owns a building valued at $18,000. He insures it for 80% of its value at $1.65 per $100 for 3 years. He has a stock of goods worth $5250. He insures the stock at its inventory value at $1.20 per $100 for 1 year.
    a. Find the premium on the building.
    b. Find the premium on the stock.
    c. Find the total yearly cost of insurance.
2. Personal property valued at $5000 was insured for 80% of its value at the 3-year rate of $5.00 per M ($1000). Find the average yearly cost of insurance.
3. On January 1 a man received a bill for insurance as follows: car insurance for 1 year, $48.50; fire insurance for $6000 on his home at a 3-year rate of $8 per M, and insurance for $3000 on the contents at the 3-year rate of 50¢ per C.
    a. Find the total cost of the premiums to be paid.
    b. Find the average yearly cost of the insurance.

Answers:
1. a. $237.60   2. $6.66⅔ or $6.67
   b. $ 63.00   3. a. $111.50
   c. $142.20   b. $ 69.50

Eighty Per Cent Co-Insurance Clause

Experience has shown that a fire will seldom destroy a piece of property completely. Consequently, many people insure themselves only for a fraction of the value of the property. To encourage people to take greater precautions, the insurance companies have a clause in the policy which states that the insured will not be paid in full for a fire loss, unless he has insured himself for at least 80% of the value of the property. If he has insured himself for less than the stipulated 80%, he becomes a co-insurer with the insurance company and bears part of the loss.

Problem: A factory building valued at $24,000 was insured for $12,800 under an 80% co-insurance clause. A fire caused a loss of $6600. How much did the insurance company pay and how much of the loss did the insured bear?

The formula for determining the loss is:
$$\frac{\text{Policy}}{80\% \text{ of value of property}} \times \text{Loss}$$

Substituting:
$$\frac{\$12,800}{80\% \text{ of } \$24,000} = \frac{\$12,800}{\$19,200} = \frac{2}{3} \times \$6600$$
$$= \$4400 \text{ Company pays}$$

$6600 Loss
 4400 Company pays
$2200 Loss suffered by insured

Exercise

1. A house valued at $7500 was insured for $5000. The policy contained an 80% co-insurance clause. A fire caused a loss of $4200.
    a. How much did the insurance company pay?
    b. How much loss did the insured suffer?

2. Martin's house is valued at $6000. He insures it for $4800 under a policy containing an 80% co-insurance clause. A fire caused a loss of $3000.
   a. How much did Martin receive under his policy?
   b. How much loss did he suffer?
3. A residence valued at $9000 was insured for $6000 under a policy containing an 80% clause. A fire caused a loss of $3600.
   a. How much did the insurance company pay?
   b. What per cent of the fire loss was borne by the owner?

Answers:

1. *a.* $3500	**2.** *a.* $3000	**3.** *a.* $3000
b. $700	*b.* 0	*b.* 16⅔%

Reinsurance and Contributing Insurance

If a policy calls for a very large amount, the insurance company may share the risk with other companies by reinsuring the property with other companies. Thus, if a policy of $600,000 is issued, the company will reinsure the property with other companies for, say, $500,000. Thus, by reinsuring the company assumes a risk of only $100,000. Another method of sharing the risk is to have the owner of the property take policies with a number of companies. Then, when a loss occurs, each company will pay a pro-rata share.

Problem: A building is insured for $50,000 as follows: Phoenix Insurance Co., $10,000; Globe Insurance Co., $20,000; World Insurance Co., $20,000. There is a loss of $20,000. How much will each company pay?

Company	Policy	Pro-rata Share	Calculation of Share	Share
Phoenix	$10,000	$\frac{\$10,000}{50,000} = \frac{1}{5}$	⅕ of $20,000	$ 4000
Globe	20,000	$\frac{20,000}{50,000} = \frac{2}{5}$	⅖ of 20,000	8000
World	20,000	$\frac{20,000}{50,000} = \frac{2}{5}$	⅖ of 20,000	8000
Total	$50,000	$\frac{\$50,000}{50,000} = \frac{5}{5}$	5/5 of $20,000	$20,000

Note that this problem is solved in the same way as the partnership problem which involved pro-rata share of profits according to capital ratio.

Exercise

1. The Atlas Co. insured its building for $10,000 in three companies as follows: Star Insurance Co., $4500; Western Insurance Co., $3500, and United Insurance Co., $2000. A fire caused a partial loss of $2000. For how much is each company liable?
2. A building was insured in three companies as follows: National Co., $8000; Standard Co., $9000; Mutual Co., $3000. If a loss of $1620 occurred, for how much is each company liable?
3. A factory valued at $20,000 was insured in two companies, each policy having an 80% co-insurance clause. The policy in the Arrow Co. was for $4000 and in the Bow Co. for $10,000. There is a fire loss of $3200. How much must each company pay? (Note: The first step is to find the loss under the 80% clause; then distribute the loss between the two companies.)

Answers:

1. Star $900
Western $700
United $400

2. National $648
Standard $729
Mutual $243

3. Arrow $800
Bow $2000

Real Estate

Rent

People who wish to buy real estate are confronted by a number of problems. Among them are:

1. Is it cheaper to rent or to buy?
2. If the house is rented to a tenant, what will be the per cent of return on the investment?
3. If the house is rented to a tenant, how much rent should be charged?

Renting vs. Buying

Problem: Henry Clark is paying $35 a month rent for a cottage. He can buy it for $4900 by paying 10% of the purchase price in cash and giving a mortgage bearing 5% interest on the balance. His estimated annual expenses are: taxes $125, water charges $25, repairs $50, and insurance $2. If he can earn 2% interest on his cash investment in the bank, will it be cheaper to rent or to buy?

Rental

12 months @ $35 per mo. = $420 Rental per year

Purchase

$4900	Cost of House
490	Cash Payment 10%
$4410	Mortgage

Expenses

Interest on mortgage (5% of $4410)	$220.50
Taxes	125.00
Water charges	25.00
Repairs	50.00
Insurance	2.00
Interest on investment (2% of $490)	9.80
Total Expense	$432.30

$432.30	Total Expense
420.00	Rental
$ 12.30	Cheaper to Rent

Rate of Return on Investment

Problem: Vinson bought a house for $6700, giving $1200 cash as a down payment and a 5% mortgage for the balance. In addition to the mortgage interest, other annual expenses were: taxes $143, insurance $9, repairs $75, depreciation 2% of cost of house. He rented the house to a tenant for $60 per month. Find the rate of return on his cash investment.

Rental to Tenant

12 months @ $60 per mo. = $720, Rental

Annual Expense

$6700	Cost of House
1200	Cash Payment
$5500	Mortgage

Expenses

Interest on mortgage (5% of $5500)	$275.00
Taxes	143.00
Insurance	9.00
Repairs	75.00
Depreciation (2% of $6700)	134.00
Total Expenses	$636.00

$720 Rental
636 Expenses
$ 84 Net Income

$$\frac{84}{1200} = 7\% \text{ Return, } Answer$$

Note that the actual cash investment is the down payment of $1200.

How Much Rent to Charge a Tenant

Problem: Harris owns a house that cost $8500. His yearly taxes are $225, repairs $100, insurance $26, and water bill $20. What monthly rental, to the nearest dollar, must he charge to realize 6% on his investment?

Desired Income

6% of $8500 = $510 Desired Annual Income

Expenses

Taxes	$225
Repairs	100
Insurance	26
Water bill	20
Total expenses	$371

$510 Desired Income
371 Expenses
$881 Annual Rent to be charged

$881 ÷ 12 = $73.41⅔ or $74.00
per month (to the nearest dollar)

Since the expenses must be borne by the tenant, they are added to the desired income to calculate the rental to be paid by the tenant.

Exercise

1. Brown buys a house for $5500, paying $1000 cash and giving a 5% mortgage for the balance. He insures the house for $4500 at the rate 50¢ per C. Taxes amount to $85 and depreciation and repairs are estimated at 3% of the cost. Brown desires a 6% return on his cash investment. What monthly rent, to the nearest dollar, must he charge a tenant?
2. Bernard bought a house for $10,000, paying $3500 cash and giving a 5% mortgage for the balance. Besides the interest on the mortgage, his annual expenses were: Taxes $300, water $80, oil $250, insurance $110, depreciation $490. He rented the house to a tenant for $150 per month. Find the rate of return on his cash investment.
3. Altman is paying $4800 a year rent for the first floor of a building. He can buy the building for $60,000. He would then receive $3000 yearly in rent from the other two floors. His annual expenses would amount to: taxes $950, insurance $240, repairs and janitor service $1700. If money is worth 6% to him in his business (6% of $60,000 would be lost and therefore is considered an expense), how much would he gain or lose by buying the building?

Answers:
1. $47   2. 7%   3. $1310 saved

Real Estate Taxes

Finding the Tax Rate

A government, to maintain itself, must impose taxes. Chief among taxes are those imposed on real estate. To levy the tax equitably and fairly, a value is given each piece of real estate. This value is called the *assessed value* and the tax is levied on the *assessed valuation*. To find out the tax rate the rule to follow is:

$$\frac{\text{Money Needed or Expenses}}{\text{Assessed Valuation}} = \text{Tax Rate}$$

The tax rate may be expressed as a per cent, or mills per dollar (a mill is .001 cent) or dollars per C ($100) or M ($1000).

Problem: Property in the city of Newcastle is assessed at $9,850,000. The expenses for the year are estimated to be: street improvements, $18,600; salaries, $46,300; schools, $102,500; sewers, $7250; buildings, $13,750; interest on bonded debt, $1300. It is estimated that $1500 will be received from special licenses and $5000 from the state as aid for schools.

A. Find the tax rate correct to the nearest hundred thousandth (5 places).
B. Express this rate per $1000.

A.

Money Needed or Expenses

$ 18,600	Street improvements
46,300	Salaries
102,500	Schools
7,250	Sewers
13,750	Buildings
1,300	Interest on debt
$189,700	Total expense
6,500	Total income
$183,200	Net expense to be raised by taxes

Income

$1500	Special licenses
5000	State school aid
$6500	Total income

$189,700	Total expense
6,500	Total income
$183,200	Net expense to be raised by taxes

$$\frac{\$183,200}{\$9,850,000} = \$.01859 \text{ per dollar, } Answer$$

B. $.01859 × 1000 = $18.59 per M ($1000), *Answer*

Finding the Tax Rate

When an owner of real estate knows his assessed valuation and the tax rate, he can find how much tax he must pay by multiplying the assessed valuation by the tax rate.

Problem: In the above problem, how much will Jones pay if his house, worth $10,000, is assessed at 80% of its value?

80% of $10,000 = $8000, Assessed valuation
$8000 × .01859 (tax rate) or
$8000 × 18.59 per M ($1000) = $148.72 Tax

Exercise

1. Taxable property in a certain town is assessed at $4,540,000. It is estimated that $2500 will be received from special licenses and $75,300 in state aid for schools. The estimated yearly expenses are: wages, $55,000; schools, $52,800; buildings, $20,000; improvements, $8000; interest on bonds, $12,000.
   a. Find the tax rate (correct to 5 places) to yield income to pay the budget (expenses).
   b. Express this rate as a tax per M ($1000).
   c. Mr. Johnson's property is valued at $7500 and is assessed at 80% of its value. How much tax will Mr. Johnson pay?
2. The assessed valuation of taxable property in a school district is $9,450,000. The gross cost of operating the schools is $300,669.21. Income from state aid and non-resident tuition fees is $126,623.97.
   a. Find the tax rate (carry the decimal to five places).
   b. Express this rate as tax rate per M ($1000).
   c. John Sperry's house is valued at $12,000 and assessed for 75% of its value. Find the amount of Mr. Sperry's school tax.
3. In a certain city, the assessed valuation of taxable property is $63,143,000. The city's total budget to meet expenses is $1,896,190. Receipts from other sources will amount to $736,240.
   a. Find the tax rate (carry the decimal to five places).
   b. Express the rate as a tax rate per M ($1000).
   c. H. Groves' property, valued at $16,000, is assessed at 75% of its value. Find the amount of his tax.

Answers:
1.	a. .01541	2.	a. .01841	3.	a. .01837
	b. $15.41		b. $18.41		b. $18.37
	c. $92.46		c. $165.69		c. $220.44

Business Letter Writing

by Irving Rosenthal
and Harry W. Rudman

Appearance and Structure of the Business Letter

In your letters, just as in your clothes, a good appearance is vital to making a favorable first impression. And the first is usually the lasting impression. Therefore it pays to take pains with the looks of your business letters. Use good paper; see that the typing is neat, well spaced and free from erasures; and let no error slip through that you can possibly catch.

Paper

Use good stationery. A secretary, sorting her employer's mail, may put your letter into the heap for "second" instead of "first reading" if it is on recognizably cheap paper. Why run that risk?

Showy, expensive stationery should also be avoided. Certainly the reader may take notice of parchment textures, deckle edges, and other ostentation; but it may not be with the reactions you desire. Such paper may arouse suspicion or contempt. A paper stock suitable for diplomatic correspondence, ceremonial invitations, or graduation certificates is obviously out of place in business correspondence.

Moreover, the most expensive paper is not always the best for correspondence. It may take ink poorly and prevent even and legible typing.

Sizes

Use standard 8½ by 11 inch sheets for longer letters and half sheets, 5½ by 8½ inches, for shorter letters. A brief message on a half sheet will look better than the same message lost on a full-size sheet.

Sometimes the so-called "Baronial" size, 10½ by 7¼ inches, is used. But this is generally reserved for correspondence by executives, with their names and titles engraved and embossed on the letterheads.

Color

White will probably remain the favored color of business letters. But the trend to other colors, especially in sales correspondence, has been increasing. It has been found that the bright colors, such as yellow and red, are "attention getters." These are being used increasingly for just that purpose. Color may also be used for associative value. An air travel company may select sky blue for its stationery; a vacation resort, green.

The Letterhead

Your letterhead has two purposes. Because it is your identification, you want it to be attractive and impressive.

And because it supplies the reader with essential information about your company—name, address, telephone number, etc., you want it to be clear and readable.

Fussy lettering and fancy symbols, mistakenly intended to impress the reader, unfortunately produce a different effect. Like pretentiously expensive stationery they may evoke annoyance and ill will instead. In any case, if they serve to a make a letterhead hard to read at first glance, they may be considered unsatisfactory.

Below are some letterheads showing attractive lettering and symbols that are impressive and in good taste without sacrifice of clarity.

Bottom and Side-Margin Messages

Business stationery sometimes carries printed matter at the foot of the sheet or down the side margins. The foot-line (it is seldom longer than a line) is usually the motto or slogan of the firm or a special sales message. Such messages may also be printed on the side margins, usually the left-hand margin. Most marginal matter, however, consists of lists of officers, sponsors, or branches of the organization.

Additional Sheets

Whenever a letter is longer than one page, the extra sheets should be of the same paper stock but without the letterhead imprint. A continuation line carrying the name of the addressee (the person to whom the letter is addressed), the page number, and the date should be typed at the top of each additional page. See that a minimum of three lines of text, besides the complimentary close and the signature, appear on the final page of the letter. For the sake of appearance it will be worth retyping the preceding page, if necessary, to make that possible.

Framing

Good typography requires proper placement of type on the page so that it sits in its margins like a well-framed picture. Since typewriting is a form of typography, accordingly it follows the same rules. The typewriting on a letter should be so arranged that, within its margins, in the spacing of dateline, salutation, and closing lines, and in its paragraphing, it resembles a well-composed and well-framed picture.

To achieve this pleasing effect the typist does not have to be an artist. She need only follow her own orderly habits of care in her margins (which should be larger in a brief letter), in her paragraph spacing, and in her indentations.

From *Business Letter Writing Made Simple*, revised ed., by Irving Rosenthal and Harry W. Rudman, Copyright © 1955, 1968 by Doubleday & Co., Inc.

Indentations

When letters were hand-written, paragraph indentations were necessary for visual clarity. The universal use of the typewriter has tended to make indentations encumbrances instead of conveniences. Many business letters, today, dispense with them. It is becoming general practice to use line space separations instead. This device speeds up stenographic work and improves the appearance as well. But whichever practice is used, it should be employed uniformly throughout the letter.

Nevertheless, the change from indentations to line spaces for paragraph indications and other purposes has not been complete. Today four forms are in use: The "full block" form; a kind of transitional form called "modified block"; the old "full indentation" form; and a type used for special effects, called "hanging indentation."

Additional Sheets

Mr. John Jones—page 2—January 14, 19

therefore feel that we cannot accept the return of the

merchandise at this late date. We like to cooperate

with all our accounts. . . .

It was necessary, because of its length, to continue this letter on an additional sheet. The additional sheet is headed by the addressee's name, the page number, and the date. There is the requisite minimum of three lines of text, in addition to complimentary close and signature.

The "Full Block" Form

February 28, 19

Mr. John Jones
1492 Columbus Avenue
Louisville 3, Kentucky

Dear Mr. Jones:

I was very pleased to receive your prompt response to my

and I look forward to seeing you on your next trip to the city.

Sincerely yours,

George Sabrin
George Sabrin

In the "full block" form all the letter's contents are aligned on the left hand margin.

The "Modified Block" Form

February 28, 19

Mr. John Jones
1492 Columbus Avenue
Louisville 3, Kentucky

Dear Mr. Jones:

I was very pleased to receive your prompt response to

and I look forward to seeing you on your next trip to the city.

Sincerely yours,

George Sabrin
George Sabrin

All the letter's contents, with the exception of the date, the complimentary close, and the signature are aligned on the left hand margin. This is still the most widely employed form.

Full Indention

19 Elm Street
Oswego, New York
April 5, 19

Mr. Gilber Kahn
67 Wren Road
Miami, Florida 33138

My dear Mr. Kahn:

In undertaking the assignment you gave me when I was in your office last Thursday, I made it clear

nevertheless intend to do the best job I can.

Sincerely yours,

Lucille Graham
Lucille Graham

This form is all but obsolete, and there seems little doubt that in time it will cease entirely to be used.

The "Full Block" Form

The "full block" form is gaining in usage because of its simplicity. In the full block form everything under the letterhead—dateline, inside address, salutation, body of the letter, complimentary close and signature—is aligned along the left-hand margin.

The "Modified Block" Form

The "modified block" form is the style in widest use. Here certain parts of the letter, such as the date line, the complimentary close, and the signature, are aligned to the right to help balance the rest of the letter, which has a left-hand alignment.

Some companies use the full block form for short letters (where it makes a better appearance) and the modified block form for longer letters.

Full Indentation

As mentioned before, the fully indented letter is a survival of the period when letters were hand-written. The typewriter has rendered this form obsolete. Today only a small proportion of business correspondence is typed in the full indentation form.

In the full indentation form not only paragraphs are indented but also the separate lines in the inside address and other sequences of lines in salutations and complimentary closings.

Hanging Indentation

"Hanging indentation" is seldom seen in business correspondence other than sales-promotion letters. There, it is used to focus attention or attain a repetitive, "hammering-home" effect.

Punctuation and
Abbreviations

Along with the dropping of indentations there has been a tendency to do without unessential punctuation and to avoid abbreviations, especially in the inside address where these would necessitate punctuation. This economy is for improvement of appearance—lines without terminal punctuation marks look less fussy—and for speed and convenience. The typist, freed of the bother of punctuating and figuring out abbreviations, can turn out more letters a day.

A stark, attractive simplicity, characteristic of the full block form of business letter, is increasingly to be noticed in the modified block letter as well. Periods are being omitted from the end of the dateline and after ordinal numbers such as 43rd and 44th; and commas, from the ends of the inside address lines. It is now also allowable to omit the colon from the salutation and the comma from the complimentary close. Most letters, however, still retain these marks of punctuation.

Abbreviations of cities and states are being avoided. Such abbreviations as Mr. or initials for first names are being retained and are followed by periods.

The new, unpunctuated form, where all punctuation is omitted, is called "open punctuation." The practice of using some punctuation is termed "mixed punctuation." The old form is called "closed punctuation." See the examples below:

Open Punctuation
Mr. Ferdinand L. Shorey
12 West 44 Street
New York, N.Y. 10036
Dear Mr. Shorey
      Yours sincerely

Mixed Punctuation
Mr. Ferdinand L. Shorey,
12 West 44 Street,
New York, N.Y. 10036.
Dear Mr. Shorey:
      Yours sincerely,

Closed Punctuation
Mr. Ferdinand L. Shorey
12 West 44 Street
New York, N.Y. 10036
Dear Mr. Shorey:
      Yours sincerely,

Hanging Indention

Dear Sir:

If you've been reading COSMOS for years, I hope you'll forgive me for sending you a letter

you don't need—But you'll understand why I jumped at the chance to write a special

letter to a list (on which your name appears) of successful executives who have been

appointed to even more responsible posts.

For readers of COSMOS know that the busier a man is the more rewarding COSMOS can be.

And if you haven't yet discovered the added advantage of reading COSMOS for every

week's news, then I hope you'll look into it now.

It's a quick, reliable short-cut to information you'll use a dozen times a day. A readable, reli-

able report on the

It is to be noted that this form is not appropriate for normal business correspondence, but is widely used in the sales letter for the apparent reason that it readily strikes the eye, arrests attention.

Even in the past the use in the salutation of the semicolon or the colon and dash was incorrect. Such practices today are grossly illiterate. Do not use **Dear Mr. Shorey;** or **Dear Mr. Shorey:—**

Elements of the Letter

Business letters should have at least the following elements: the letterhead, dateline, inside address, salutation, body, complimentary close, two signatures (the name of the company typed out and the written signature of the writer), and the dictator's and typist's initials, the former, usually in capitals and the latter in small letters. In addition, depending upon the operating procedure of the writer's company, there may be a file number, an order number, or a subject line for the purpose of future reference; an "attention" line where the letter is directed to a particular person or department; notice of an enclosure; and a postscript.

The Dateline

Usually the dateline is typed at the right. In full block letters it may be typed flush with the left margin. Sometimes it is centered under the letterhead.

The customary sequence is month, day, and year: as April 5, 1971. Some logical persons have been advocating a usage, now standard in Great Britain and in our armed forces, of a progressive time-interval sequence—the shortest interval, the day, first, followed by the month, and then the year: as 5 April 1971. Although not common, this form is acceptable.

The Inside Address

Inside addresses are included in business letters for several practical purposes. The inside address serves as a ready identification since envelopes are usually thrown away; it helps in filing correspondence; and it can be used with window envelopes. It is also useful to the post office when checking misdirected letters or letters with no return address on the envelope.

The inside address usually consists of three lines: the name of the person or the firm, the street address, and the line carrying city, state, and zip code. In foreign mail a fourth line carries the name of the country. If the addressee is associated with a company, its name may appear under his as the second line.

Examples: Mr. Thomas Smith
24 West 98 Street
New York, N.Y. 10025

Mr. Alan May
16 Charing Cross
London, N.W. (Zone No.)
England

Mr. Thomas Smith
West Side Riding Academy
24 West 98 Street
New York, N.Y. 10025

The Salutation

Present-day usage for the normal salutation is the word **Dear** and the title and the name of the addressee: as **Dear Mr. Doe** or **Dear Mr. Roe.** In personal friendships between businessmen it is permissible for them to use first names or nicknames in salutations: as **Dear John** or **Dear Hank.** In formal address the expression, **My Dear Mr. Doe,** is often used.

Sales letters addressed to regular patrons may use terms like **Dear Customer, Dear Madam, Dear Subscriber,** etc. In mass mailings any general terms such as **Dear Sir, Dear Madam, Dear Friend, Dear Fellow Citizen, Dear Reader** or any other salutation considered appropriate may be used—or none at all.

Whenever open punctuation is used, the colon may be omitted after the salutation. But, as we have mentioned before, it is more customary to retain it. The colon-dash and the semicolon, however, are never correct.

There are special forms of address for persons of high rank in government, the armed forces, the church, and the professions. These will be found in Appendix D.

Body

The body of the letter is, of course, its most important part. In appearance it should be clearly typed, neatly spaced, and uniform in typographical construction.

Long paragraphs should be avoided. The paragraphs should not be so short, however, as to give any impression of talking down to the addressee. But in sales letters short paragraphs are almost always the rule, in order to sustain interest.

Underlining to indicate italics or to give emphasis is being displaced by capitalizing. Capitals are regarded as more readable, more emphatic, and more pleasing in appearance. Moreover, capitalizing makes for easier and more rapid typing. Titles of books and names of periodicals, however, should continue to be underlined or placed in quotation marks.

The contents of the body will be dealt with at greater length in the separate sections discussing the different types of business letters. Here we may generalize as follows:

The opening paragraph should be short and, unless there is a compelling negative reason, it should immediately introduce the subject of the letter or connect it with a previous development in the correspondence. The middle paragraphs should do the main job of the letter—expand on the subject in such a way as to persuade the addressee to act upon it in the manner you desire. Let it convince him that it will be proper for or advantageous to him to conclude the purchase or the agreement, or to make the postponement, the payment, or the adjustment you are seeking.

The closing paragraph should summarize your message and make clear the action you desire. Avoid wavering words like **hoping, wishing, trusting,** etc. Be positive. Say something like "We feel certain that you will agree that this is the most satisfactory solution." Avoid dangling participial endings, such as "Hoping we hear from you."

The Complimentary Close

Just as you open your letter with a word of friendly greeting, so you close it with a cordial expression—what is called the complimentary close. Some people propose dispensing with both, and recommended plunging into the letter without salutation and closing abruptly with the signature. But the convention is so firmly entrenched as to render it unlikely that this suggested procedure will take hold.

The customary forms are "Yours truly," "Yours sincerely," or "Yours very truly" where the relationship is formal. The terms "Yours sincerely," "Sincerely yours," "Faithfully yours," and "Cordially yours" express rising degrees of intimacy. "Respectfully yours" has gone out of fashion and is now generally restricted to correspondence with dignitaries or official superiors in formal situations.

The Signature

It is considered a discourtesy not to sign a letter personally. If this becomes an impossibility and a rubber stamp has to be used, it should be inked and imprinted in such a way as to resemble the true signature as closely as possible. If the writer's secretary signs for him, she should put her initials under the signature to make that fact clear.

New attitudes regarding the position of women do not seem to have penetrated into business correspondence, at least as regards their marital status. That has to be indicated in the signature. A married woman who wishes to use her maiden name in business should add her married name (Mrs.＿＿＿＿＿) in parentheses. A widow retains her married name unless she takes legal steps to resume her maiden name. A divorcee retains her former husband's surname but may not use his initials or his first name.

Where the company name is included in the signature, it is typed one or two lines below the complimentary close. Four spaces should be left for the writer's signature, and his name and company position should follow:

Yours sincerely,

Thomas Smith

THE JOHN JONES COMPANY
Sales Manager

To make sure that the signature is not misread, the name is often typed above or below it.

Yours sincerely,
THE JOHN JONES COMPANY

Thomas Smith

Thomas Smith
Sales Manager

Special Parts of the Business
Letter: File Numbers

In addition to the standard parts of the letter special requirements may call for additional lines or items. On traffic or mail order correspondence file or other reference numbers may appear, usually at the left of the dateline or under it.

Attention Line

When a letter is addressed to an individual in a firm but is not intended for him exclusively, or if it is intended to be routed to a certain department, a line is added to that effect. Letters are often addressed to the **attention** of an individual instead of to him directly so that, if he should be away, the letter will not be held up but will be acted upon by the person temporarily taking his place.

The attention line is usually put between the inside address and the salutation, and may be placed either at the left, as in the example below, or in the center of the line.

The John Jones Company
710 West 10 Street
New York, N.Y. 10011

Attention Mr. Thomas Smith, Sales Manager

Gentlemen:

Note that where the attention line is used, the salutation is **Gentlemen,** not **Dear Mr. Smith.**

Enclosure Line

The enclosure line in the letter is not for the addressee, who will be informed about the enclosure in the text of the letter. It is for the mailing clerk or the stenographer herself as a reminder to include the enclosure in the mailing. It should therefore be in an inconspicuous position. It is usually typed under the stenographer's initials, as an abbreviation: Encl.

Postscripts

Postscripts in business letters differ from those in personal letters, which are afterthoughts set down after the letters have been finished. In business correspondence, postscripts have a definite, planned function. They may emphasize a point made elsewhere in the letter, or they may make a special offer. They are more customary in sales letters than in other business correspondence, and are designed to draw special attention. Examples will be found in the section on sales letters.

Envelopes

As much care should be observed with the envelope as with the letter itself. It is the first part of the letter to be seen, and, as we have already observed, the first impression is important. It should, of course, be of the same paper stock as the letter. The address should be typed in such a way as to be in pleasing balance with the imprint on the top left-hand corner, if there is such an imprint; or it should be well framed on the front of the envelope if the return address is imprinted on the flap in back.

The two standard envelope sizes are the number 6¾ and the number 10. The latter is also called the "official size" envelope. It is long enough to hold the full standard letterhead width of 8½ inches. The number 6¾ size averages that number of inches in width. Envelopes used for Baronial size stationery average 7½ inches in width, enough to permit enclosure folded the full width of the sheet.

Folding the Letter and
Inserting Enclosures

Part of the appearance of the letter depends, of course, on the way it is folded and placed in the envelope. Here the convenience of the addressee also receives consideration. The letter should be folded so that he can open it with ease and read it with comfort.

For the number 10 or the long "official size" envelope, the letter should be folded from the bottom to a little over a third of the page. Crease the fold down firmly. Then fold the top third down over the bottom fold and crease firmly again. Then slip the folded letter into the envelope.

For the number 6¾ envelope, fold the letter from

Sample Business Letter

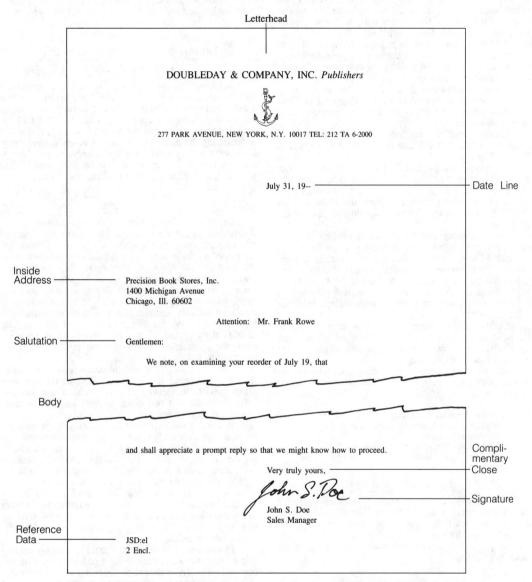

Letterhead

DOUBLEDAY & COMPANY, INC. *Publishers*

277 PARK AVENUE, NEW YORK, N.Y. 10017 TEL: 212 TA 6-2000

July 31, 19-- —————————————— Date Line

Inside Address —————————
Precision Book Stores, Inc.
1400 Michigan Avenue
Chicago, Ill. 60602

Attention: Mr. Frank Rowe

Salutation —————
Gentlemen:

We note, on examining your reorder of July 19, that

Body

and shall appreciate a prompt reply so that we might know how to proceed.
———————————— Compli-
mentary
Close

Very truly yours, ————————————

John S. Doe ————————— Signature

John S. Doe
Sales Manager

Reference Data ——————
JSD:el
2 Encl.

This model letter includes in standard form all *the elements normally employed in the*
business letter.

the bottom to about a quarter of an inch from the top. See that the sides are even when creasing. Now fold from the sides, first from right to left about a third of the way and then from left to right, creasing firmly after each of the two folds. Then enclose the letter with the last fold toward you. This will insure that when it is received the letter can be removed with the open end on top.

Checks, receipts, or other small enclosures should be placed inside the folds. If placed outside the folds, in the envelope, such vital items may be torn or cut when the envelope is opened; or they may be overlooked by the recipient and thrown away with the discarded envelope.

Letters mailed in window envelopes must be folded in a special way.

The Outside Address

Each year, according to post office records, some thirty million pieces of mail end up in the dead letter office. The chief reason is careless addressing.

The customary address form consists of four lines: the name and title of the addressee, street address or post office box number, city, state, and zip code. On all foreign mail the name of the country will, of course, replace the state, or be added as a fifth line.

Additional lines may be required for a province or department name in a foreign address, an apartment number, a company name in addition to the name of the individual addressee, an attention line if the letter is to be routed to a department of the company or to an individual in a department, or the specification, **Personal** or **Confidential,** where the letter is intended for private reading by the addressee.

Except where they are part of the address, such additional lines are typed in the lower left-hand corners of the envelopes.

No customary position has been settled upon for postal directions like **Air Mail** or % **S.S. America.** These may be written, rubber-stamped, or typed anywhere on the envelope, usually above the address. They should be conspicuous, but they should not obscure the address.

For readability and appearance the following positions have been found most satisfactory. In all cases start the address slightly below the vertical center of the envelope. On a number 6¾ envelope start slightly to the left of the horizontal center when using the block style. When using the indented style on this size of envelope start about one third the width of the envelope from the left.

On the larger number 10 envelope start slightly to the right of the horizontal center when using the block style. When using the indented style, start slightly to the left of the horizontal center.

Addresses of unusual size or envelopes with the return address on the flap in back may call for variations of these positions.

Professor Michael T. Kellogg
Bernard M. Baruch School of Business and
   Civil Administration
Lexington Avenue and Twenty-third Street
New York, N.Y. 10010

The Return Address

It is more convenient as well as more customary for the return address to appear on the front of the envelope than on the back flap. In any case make sure it appears somewhere on the envelope. This practice will be an additional precaution against the letter's ending up in the dead letter office.

Titles of Respect

It is customary to include certain titles of respect in the address. This courtesy extends to physicians after whose name M.D. usually appears, and to engineers (C.E., M.E., or E.E.). These abbreviations are professional as well as academic designations. Purely scholastic

titles like M.A. or non-professional titles like B.S. or Ph.B., etc., are omitted. In formal correspondence, however, higher degrees like D.D., LL.D., Ph.D., etc., may be used in the address.

Numbers and Abbreviations and Their Punctuation

It is the preferred usage to write out a numbered street or avenue—for example, **500 Fifth Avenue** or **223 East Thirty-third Street.** Where the number is above ninety-nine, it usually appears as a number: **2204 220th Street.** Do not abbreviate the name of the city, and avoid abbreviating the name of the state. The tendency is away from such abbreviations. Ordinal number-ending abbreviations like **th** and **rd** are not, today, followed by the period. Use 33rd and 34th, not 33rd. and 34th.

Zip Codes

On July 1, 1963, a new system of mail sorting and distribution called zip code was initiated by the Post Office Department. The zip code is a 5-digit number designed to cut down the steps required to move mail from the sender to the addressee, thereby holding down postal costs. The first three digits of the code identify sectional centers, which are main points of air, highway, and rail transportation, and the last two digits identify the post office or delivery station. In cities that previously had local postal zones, the first three digits of the zip code identify the city and the last two digits (which are generally the same as the former zone number) designate the branch post office or substation.

The first numeral of the zip code, 0 to 9, identifies one of ten national service areas. The second and third digits indicate the service area subdivision and the post office, and the last two digits identify the station from which the mail is delivered.

While the use of zip codes is optional but strongly recommended for first-class mail, it is *mandatory* for second-class and third-class bulk mailers, who must also presort and bundle their mail in accordance with detailed instructions that appear in the *Postal Manual.* Large-volume mailers should familiarize themselves with the regulations regarding zip codes by consulting the *Postal Manual* or their local post office, since failure to conform to the zip coding requirements can result in refusal of the post office to handle improperly zip-coded mail at the lower bulk rates.

Placement. The zip code should appear on the last line of both the address and return address following the city and state. There should be not less than two nor more than six spaces between the last letter of the state and the zip code, and no characters of any kind should follow the zip code:

Mr. Harold Jones
3025 Theresa Street
Arlington, Va.   22207

The Sales Letter

The concern of all business is to sell goods or services. Consequently all business letters are, directly or indirectly, sales letters.

Your best collection letter, for example, is one that does more than induce a delinquent customer to pay up.

It is the one that leaves him convinced, after the payment, that he has been dealing with a fair and considerate house with which he is glad to continue doing business.

Sales letters, as such, are distinguished from other business letters by the fact that their sales objective is not indirect but direct and, more or less, immediate. The qualifying phrase, "more or less," is used because some varieties of sales letters are not intended to make an immediate sale but rather to lead **gradually** to sales. And others are intended to pave the way for sales by other means.

Certain sales letters, for example, may be written to help a salesman make the sale. Others may be written to bring customers for your products to one of your dealers.

The most common and largest variety of sales letter is used in direct mail selling. Devices employed in that type of sales letter are presented in a later section; here we shall deal with the more general aspects of sales letters, and take up types of sales correspondence that are part of regular business operations.

Your Satisfied Customer

No selling job is ever over. The alert businessman keeps analyzing his accounts. Can A's volume be increased? B's orders show a slight decline over last year's; does that mean a decline in his business? Or is he sampling the ware of a competitor? Whatever his conclusion, the alert businessman sends off the appropriate letter.

In An Effort to Increase
Sales

Dear Mr. Martin:

I have been very pleased to note the steady increase in the frequency and size of your orders since we started doing business together. It is gratifying to know that your product is being well received in your area and that you are making money with it.

My reason for writing is twofold—to thank you for your patronage and to offer our cooperation in any way that will build your sales of our product even further. Under separate cover I am sending you some advertising aids that can be used in window and counter displays; mats for newspaper ads; and suggested spot announcements for your local radio station. Frank Moss, our representative in your territory, will drop in on you next Thursday to help you set up these displays and to offer his assitance in every way. If there is anything special you may need, don't hesitate to get in touch with me.

I look forward to the continuance of our pleasant, and I hope, mutually profitable relationship. With all good wishes, I am,

Sincerely yours,
Robert Johns

In An Effort to Retain
Good Will

Dear Mr. Burke:

Somewhere or other we read: "There are many good excuses for losing an order—but no excuse whatever for losing good will!"

That's why we're writing to you—not to ask why you preferred to place your recent order with somebody else, but to make sure it wasn't because of something which has lost us your good will as well.

If it was the latter, we'd be most grateful if you'd write us about it.

But regardless, we sincerely hope your new equipment gives you the kind of performance you expect of it—and that you won't hesitate to make use of
our nationwide service facilities should the need arise.

Next time, perhaps, it will be our good fortune to take care of your requirements.

Sincerely,
William H. Wolcott

The alert businessman never feels smug about his satisfied customers. He does not leave the initiative to them, content merely to take orders. He bears in mind those two business adages: "It costs less to keep a customer than to get one," and "Your customer is your competitor's prospect."

If he starts a new line, if he makes an improvement in one of his staples, if he has a plan for reducing the price to a customer by quantity shipping of combined orders, the alert businessman lets his satisfied customer know about it. He does not wait for the word to get around; he sees to it that it gets around. Keeping the satisfied customer posted is a good way of keeping them satisfied.

Dear Larry:

I hope this finds you well and your business booming. I think I have something that you ought to be able to go to town on.

I've just picked up a special lot of piece goods off-price that I'm going to cut tomorrow in Style 637, with which you have done so well. I plan to bring out the number at two dollars less than you have been paying, and I know it will fit in well with your January sale.

I can get a limited number of garments out of the lot, so I'd like to know how many you can use before I offer it to anyone else. We'll be able to ship within ten days.

All good wishes.

Sincerely yours,
Phil Nelson

Dear Mr. Forman:

When you were in the city several weeks ago, you mentioned the difficulties you were having in getting fast deliveries of merchandise shipped to you by us and by other manufacturers. I think I've come across something that can help you.

I have just had a conversation with Jack Bell of Vanguard Trucking, 247 Terhune Place, Jersey City, N.J., who runs a fleet of trucks through your territory. He told me that if you can work out an arrangement with a few other merchants near you to consolidate shipments, he will be glad to set aside one of his trucks to serve your group. If the amount of freight warrants it, he can provide daily overnight deliveries, and is confident he can cut your present transportation costs by forty per cent. I think its worth looking into, and I suggest you get in touch with Mr. Bell for more particulars.

Sincerely yours,
Robert Glass

Frequent Communication

Keep the contacts with your customers unbroken and, so far as you can, make the contacts personal. Some firms regard communication with their customers, once a month, a minimum requirement for good customer relations. They do not limit the correspondence to invoices and routine acknowledgments of orders and payments. To the routine mail they add interesting enclosures. And they take advantage of every suitable occasion to extend the contact. They avoid formalities and try to set up a personal relationship. For signatures they do not use only the firm name but rather the name of an officer of the firm, the head of a department, or a salesman.

Some concerns go about unobtrusively getting personal items about their customers and keep the data current. Birthdays are remembered. If a buyer gets married or has an addition to the family, the event is observed.

Many service firms such as laundries and cleaning establishments find it profitable to send their customers and prospective customers blotters bearing calenders and reminders of seasonal cleaning needs.

Department stores keep in touch with their charge-customers by sending them advance notices of sales, seasonal announcements, and letters about special services. Whatever your business is, there are sure to be occasions for getting in touch with your customers other than through routine notices and acknowledgments.

Special Customers

In every business there are customers who rate or demand special attention. Some should get it merely because the large volume of their business calls for every possible special and even personal consideration. Special and personal letters, if feasible, will be in order.

Others may have special needs. For example, dealers located in hot, moist regions may require special packaging or other measures to keep the wares they receive in good condition. Letters dealing with such special needs are in order.

Others may be merely fussy or eccentric. These may be hard to do business with and require special sales correspondence. If you decide that the volume of their business justifies it, carry on that additional correspondence with good grace.

Letters to Help
Your Salesmen

The salesman may be assisted, through letters, in two general ways. One type of letter prepares the ground for him—introduces him, mentions the new line he will demonstrate, some special offer he will explain in detail, etc.

Such help to a salesman may be needed for several reasons. One is the lingering effect of the fictional presentation of the salesman as an intrusive, high-pressure man with his toes wedged in the door sill, launched on a non-stop spiel. Even dealers who have good relations with salesmen and have found them helpful may think of those they know as exceptions and look for the obnoxious type in a new man. A letter can help the new man by presenting him in a friendly light, stressing the useful service he is to perform—the demonstration he will make or the plan he will explain, etc.

In such letters, however, take care not to tell the customer too much. Remember that the purpose is to introduce the salesman, not to substitute for his call. The letter should stimulate the customer's curiosity and leave it to the salesman to satisfy it. Similar letters can serve to bring customers to your show rooms, to exhibition booths, to dealers handling your products or services.

Letters sent between sales calls can strengthen the salesman-customer relationship. The seasonal nature of certain kinds of merchandise or the fact that salesmen will make only a few trips a year in the ordinary course, gives rise to considerable correspondence about reorders, substitutions, cancellations, returns, complaints, and the acknowledgments and adjustments these call for. As much of this correspondence as is practical should go out under the salesman's signature.

In addition it is frequently advisable to send out, also under the salesman's signature, letters advising the customer of new developments, new lines, new policies, etc.

Even in business the strongest bonds are personal, and a good salesman-customer relationship means a good relationship with the customer for the firm.

Testimonials

When enough time has elapsed for a new account to have tested your products and your business procedures, it is a good plan to write to the customer and ask whether he is satisfied and whether he has any suggestions or comments to make. This kind of inquiry should be the first step in the continuous keeping-your-customer-sold campaign that was mentioned earlier.

Such letters may evoke testimonials that will prove valuable in your promotion. And the letters will probably have the additional value of providing a running check on your business methods by revealing from time to time the need for changes.

Build up a testimonial file from the favorable letters your inquiries bring you. You can draw upon such a file when approaching prospects in the same area or in the same general line as the writers of the testimonials. The signer of the testimonial can say more for you than almost anything you can say for yourself.

> Dear Mr. Seaman:
>
> It is now eight months since we first started doing business together, and I note with satisfaction that the volume each month has been increasing nicely. At first, we were skeptical about the possibility of developing sales in your territory, because our product has been sold mainly in colder sections of the country. Your experience, therefore, has been gratifying.
>
> My purpose in writing is to find out whether you have any thoughts about how we can increase our volume to mutual advantage even further. As you can see, we're trying to work with you the best way we know how, and we'd appreciate hearing from you with any comments you may wish to make about our service and product. We like to receive brickbats as well as pats on the back. We can correct our faults—to the advantage of all concerned—only when they're pointed out.
>
> Sincerely yours,
> John Thomas

The Inquiry Letter

Answers to inquiries are a major part of business correspondence, and can be the most important type of sales letter. Those that are part of a direct-mail sales campaign will be dealt with in the next section. Here we touch upon the type of inquiry that originates in other ways.

Someone in the market for your sort of goods or services has looked up your firm in a trade directory; or has had it recommended to him by one of your customers with whom he is acquainted; or has heard of you in some other way. He writes to you for information. His inquiry to you may be the only one he is making. But the chances are that he is simultaneously asking for similar information from your competitors.

It is wise to assume that that is the case, and that your answer must stand the test of competition. Do your best to make your reply a sales letter that wins the inquirer's business.

Promptness is of the first importance. Your prospect will be quite as much sold by evidence of your alertness and efficiency as by what you may say.

Directness is also important. Give specific answers to the questions. If the questions are vague, don't follow that bad example; be specific about what you have to sell and thus you will probably answer effectively the questions your prospect has not been able to express.

Being specific does not mean being detailed. Leave the details to the catalogue or the other enclosures you send. A good sales letter is organized to have a certain impact. It cannot have that impact if it interrupts itself to go into minutiae.

Enclosures

Your postage outlay pays for an ounce per unit of reading matter. That ounce gives you leeway for several sheets besides your letter which—barring necessary exceptions—will usually be less than a page in length. Businessmen have found it profitable to take advantage of the full permissible weight by adding enclosures that reinforce the sales punch.

The enclosures can be particularly useful in supplying details which, if put into the body of the letter, might blunt its impact. If the prospect had to pause, while reading the letter, to take in details of measurement, construction, delivery schedules, etc., his interest would be too diffused for him to react as you would like him to.

Your letter should do two things. It should put the prospect into the buying mood and whet his interest so that he will want to look up the details. These can be furnished in an effective enclosure.

However, avoid a clutter of accompanying "literature." Some mailers believe in the more-the-better principle. But experience has shown that beyond a certain point **more** can become **too much.** Then, no matter how colorful and clever the enclosures are, they begin to clash with one another. They distract attention from the letter. They even become a nuisance to the recipient—and the letter may lose its effectiveness.

Moreover, the enclosures should not overshadow the letter. The letter itself should be attractive to look at, but above all its copy should be so carefully, sensibly, and effectively prepared that it produces the results desired.

It is generally advisable, when dealing with a smaller enclosure, to fold it into the letter so that it comes out along with the letter when the envelope is opened.

Dear Mr. Merton:

I am going to make this letter brief. I feel the enclosed brochure speaks for itself. But I am writing merely to let you know that the sales potential of the lamp described has been tested carefully in thirty selected stores similar to yours. Every one of them has come back with quick reorders. So we know WE HAVE SOMETHING YOU CAN DO WELL WITH.

We developed this item with a view to shooting for volume. We've brought it out at the lowest price possible, and we have complete confidence in its sales potential.

We all get a steady stream of mail across our desks, but I hope you will take a few minutes to study the brochure carefully, and to try out a sample order of the lamp. We'll let the selling talk for itself.

Sincerely yours,
Ivan Hubbell

Form Letters

Whatever the special function of the sales letter you write, make it personal if possible. If the volume of the correspondence makes this impractical, use forms and methods that will make it appear like a personal letter.

There are two main kinds of form letters—**complete** and **paragraph.** The complete form, even when it is individually typed and signed, is prepared in advance to cover certain standard needs.

Usually **complete form letters** are produced on a word processor or xeroxed, depending on the purpose they serve. Word processing is useful in letters where spaces can be provided to fill in dates, individual salutations, addresses, etc. In virtually all cases, the name of an individual, even in rubber stamp or stencil reproductions, is preferable in the signature to simply the name of the firm.

Complete form letters are usually identified by some combination of letters or initials under which they can be filed. Thus there may be a series of form letters with which catalogues are to be enclosed. These are keyed with the letter C and their numbers in the series. Then the secretary can be instructed to send out Form Letter C-4.

The greater flexibility of the **paragraph form letter** makes it possible to meet a larger number of calculable special situations. Such a letter is assembled from designated prepared passages kept on file in a "paragraph book." Some firms have several paragraph books with hundreds of paragraphs in each.

For illustration let us take a paragraph book containing ninety passages. Of these, one to ten may be devoted to letter openings; eleven to forty may consist of second paragraphs; forty-one to seventy may consist of third paragraphs; and the remaining twenty entries may be closings. Thus a typist may be instructed to use 7: 24: 51: 82, and will construct the letter from corresponding paragraphs in the paragraph book.

Structure of
the Sales Letter

In **sales letters** the same general principles of structure apply as in all business letters. But greater latitude is allowed in sales letters, just as greater latitude is allowed in the sales approach in general. You can be more unconventional and use more color and typographic tricks; and you will be pardoned a certain amount of puffing. Of course, if any one of these is carried to excess, it will prove self-defeating.

The salutation: One of the liberties that may be taken is with the salutation. In mass-mailings, where fill-in salutations and inside addresses are impossible, anonymous salutations such as **Dear Friend, Dear Sir** or **Dear Madame** may be used; or, if the list is a selected one permitting such specifications, **Dear Doctor, Dear Business Executive, Dear Fellow-Angler,** etc.

In some cases the salutation may be dispensed with and a flattering introductory phrase substituted for it, such as "To a Forward-Looking and Ambitious Young Businessman" or "To a Young Lady Who Keeps in Step with the Times." Or just a catchy headline like "Play Ball!" may be employed. However, these devices should be shunned in ordinary correspondence, and might be resorted to only where the multitude of identical letters is so great that individual salutations are impractical.

The opening: The opening is more crucial in a sales letter than in any other business correspondence. It is the sender's bid for attention; if it fails, the whole effort is wasted.

Some firms go to considerable trouble and expense in striving for attention-getting openings. In a conspicuous position on the letter they may have—stapled, glued on, or affixed in some other way—a small metal, cloth, or plastic object that pictorially symbolizes the opening line.

For example, one firm used a cord lasso, fastened to an upper corner of a letter so that the rope end touched the first line, to give animation to this opening: "Yes, we want to rope you in—and you'll be glad of it. . . ." Similarly a small aluminum bat glued to another letter helped to fix attention on this opening: "This is the season to go to bat for . . ."

Devices like these must be used with care for they are novelties that may appeal to some readers and by their "cuteness" irritate others. You may not be able to afford such expensive attention-getters; but still less can you afford a dull or lifeless opening. You can always attract attention with an imaginative thought and vivid words.

The question opening: One sure method is to put your opening in the form of a question. In that way you can take advantage of a quirk of human nature. We always react to a question as a challenge, and it is a rare person who does not feel the compulsion to make some response.

Of course the question should be provocative and relevant personally to the prospect, and should bring in the article or service being promoted.

This question opening was used by a home development company: "Are you over thirty, married, and a churchgoer?" Since the mailing list had been selected to concentrate on mature, married, churchgoing people, the reader was bound to answer "yes" and was thereby put in a receptive frame of mind to the rest of the proposition.

The striking statement: Another good type of opening is the **striking statement.** A good example is the one used, some twenty-five years ago, by the New York *Daily News* when it introduced itself and tabloid journalism to the metropolis. To its advertising prospects it sent a letter advising them to "Tell it to the Sweeneys" (through its pages) because "the Vanderbilts don't care." This was followed of course, with interesting material on the advantages of the mass market and its lower sales resistance.

Another example of the striking statement as an opening was the following, used in a letter to advertisers by a large woman's magazine: "Yes, men still carry on most of the nation's business—but their wives do still more of the buying!"

A proverb, too, can provide a good opening, especially when it is given an arresting new twist: "The early bird catches the worm—but was it wise for the worm to be early?"

Body of the letter: Having gained attention by your opening, you must next sustain interest while making sales points in the body of the letter.

The anecdote: Some writers have recourse to a story or anecdote for this purpose. An organization arranging outdoor exercise and entertainment for businessmen used this anecdote in a sales letter to its prospects:

"A vigorous man in his nineties was asked the secret of his longevity. 'Wal,' he replied, 'when my wife and I got married we agreed to do something to spare our nerves. If I was the grumpy one she'd go into the other room and take up her knittin'. And if she started to pick on me I'd put on my hat and go out for a walk. . . . So you see I been outdoors most of my life.'

"Being outdoors, that tried and true recipe for a long life and a healthy one, can be made easy for you by joining the _____Outdoors Club. (And equally easy for your wife as well, who won't be so inclined to pick on you if you include her.) Drive out in your own car or one of the Club's limousines will pick you up outside your office and bring you to the club grounds. Then you can swim, golf, swing a racket, walk or do anything else you like in clear sunlight and unpolluted country air."

Enclosures gave further details.

Facts and figures: Other writers rely on facts and figures. They support tempting descriptions of the article or service they are marketing with data giving the results of laboratory tests, consumption statistics, testimonials, guarantees, and other inducements.

Incidentally, experienced sales-letter writers advise that the core of the sales message should appear about two-fifths of the way down the letter.

The closing: In earlier business correspondence, in the days when businessmen dressed in frock coats and striped trousers like diplomats, it was considered proper to close sales letters with polite wishes like "hoping" or "trusting we shall hear from you." Such expressions tend to linger on. Usually they are left in mid-air as dangling participles. If you find them in your correspondence, pull out the blue pencil!

Sales letters now end with forceful suggestions for immediate action. They ask for the order; and they enforce it with all sorts of inducements, bargain offers, samples, free examination privileges, and a wide variety of other appeals.

Here is an example of the appeal of **exclusiveness:**

"There are many more than three thousand discriminating readers who will want this book, but only three thousand copies were printed. As this letter is being mailed, the day's orders reduce the number still available to 422. Better make sure of getting **your** free-examination copy by filling out and mailing the enclosed card **today.**"

The "You" Attitude again: Among the numerous factors that contribute to effective correspondence, the "you" attitude, referred to earlier, is paramount. The seller takes care not to show his anxiety to make a sale. What he stresses is the buyer's interests. The buyer will get a bargain; he will be guaranteed against dissatisfaction by the privilege of returning the merchandise; payment will be made easy for him by special terms, etc. In sales letters as much as in any other form of business correspondence be sure to consider the reader at all times.

The postscript: In that same frock-coat-and-striped-pants business era alluded to above, the postscript was frowned upon. It was considered unkempt—allowable, perhaps, in private correspondence, but distinctly incorrect in well-dressed business correspondence.

Today, however, few sales letters are without postscripts. As a typographical device, the postscript has won general adoption because of the special services it can perform. It can remove from the body of the letter, whose unity it might impair, some special matter which should be brought to the reader's attention. Or it can give a needed emphasis to something as no other method can.

"P.S. Special discount terms can be arranged" stands out in a postscript, yet does not interfere with other persuasions as it might if set in the body of the letter. And if you have already mentioned your booth at a convention, a postscript reminder can do a lot to draw visits there: for example, "P.S. We're looking forward to seeing you at booth 16. Ask for Mr. Elkin."

"Letters You Don't Have To Write"

A recent speech by Maxwell C. Ross, a well known sales promotion expert, listed **sixteen** ways letters can be used to create good will—and, eventually, sales. "There's just one prerequisite," he said; "the person using them has to be a nice guy, courteous, friendly, and above all, sincere."

Each is simply a friendly, personal letter that you send on some occasion when nobody would have thought very much about it if you hadn't sent the letter at all. They don't *have* to be written, but they create a tremendously favorable impression because they *are* written.

1. *You can use a letter to follow up a salesman's call.* You don't need to, for it isn't expected, but you'll be surprised at the reception it gets. You could start something like this: "John Smith told me today of the pleasant visit he had with you about your insurance program. I know that John will do a fine job for you." Then finish off in your own words.

2. *You can use letters to make appointments.* You say, "It's about time for me to sit down with you, Jim, and go over your insurance in the light of the new tax changes. I want to do this when you have the time for it, but it should be soon. I suggest that we get together late Friday afternoon. How would 4 o'clock be?" You don't need to say much more, but you'll be surprised at the nice reception you get.

3. *Whenever a customer or client has been promoted or changed jobs,* it's a nice gesture to send a letter like this—"Congratulations on your appointment to District Sales Manager. This is fine news, and I know you'll do a great job. If I can ever be of any help to you, please let me know."

4. *When a customer is ill,* there's no more appreciated time to get mail. All you need to say is—"I'm certainly sorry to hear that you are laid up for an operation. I hope it won't be many days before you're back at your desk." Add to that a book, or the loan of one, a magazine, or a box of candy, and the good will you build is far above the effort you take in doing it.

5. *When there is a death in the family.* If it's tactfully done a short message of sympathy can mean much.

6. *When a daughter or son gets married,* or *a new baby arrives.* These letters make no tangible effort to sell; they're simply good-will builders—the kind that some day will bring something nice to you because you went out of your way to do something nice for somebody else.

7. *When people buy a home,* write to them. You letter doesn't need to be long or fancy. Perhaps: "I hope you are enjoying your new home, and that you have recovered from the trials of moving." If you have something to sell, go ahead and mention it. Tell these folks you'd appreciate a chance to call when things are squared away. In some cases, an inexpensive gift like a small rosebush or a young tree creates far more good will than the cost.

8. *When a customer has a birthday.* Quite a few successful salesmen make a practice of keeping birthday lists and sending cards or letters. A personal letter is best, but if you use a card, write something in longhand on it.

9. *When people move to your town* a letter of welcome is an excellent source of new business. They don't know where to go for dry cleaning, laundry, milk—what service station to trade with, where to do their banking, or the nicer places to eat. So you write: "Welcome to Omaha. We know you'll like it here. If there is any way we can help you get settled, please let us know."

10. *When people move from your town,* it may seem a futile gesture to seem sorry—but the intangible good will you create may come back to you in unsuspected ways. And sometimes people *do* return. So you write: "I am sorry you are moving away from Lincoln. We will miss you as a customer, but should you ever return we'll be waiting to serve you again."

11. *When you read about a customer in the newspaper,* send him a letter. Clip the article, send it to him, and say: "I don't know whether your children keep a scrapbook of the nice things that happen to you, but just in case they do, here's an extra copy I clipped for you to give them." And if congratulations are deserved, give them!

12. *When a customer is elected to some office,* or honored in any other way, perhaps you would say: "I've heard some nice things about the work you've done for the Chamber of Commerce, so I was not surprised to see that you have been elected vice president for the coming year."

13. *When someone has done you a favor* he will appreciate a note from you. "Those two extra tickets got me off a rough spot. I hope I can repay the favor soon."

14. *When some product or service pleases you,* take time to write about it. "Quite often people write to you only with their complaints, but I wanted you to know how pleased I am with our new floor furnace, and with the courteous and efficient way your men installed it."

15. *When a serviceman comes home write to him* or to his parents if he lives at home. That's a small way to show your appreciation for all he has done for you and his country. Never again in his life will he so much *want* to be welcomed back; or want to feel that all he went through was not in vain.

16. *You can use letters to thank new and old customers for their orders.* Perhaps you do, but many don't. In Des Moines, a filling station operator sends a post card to new customers. All the card says is, "It was nice of you to stop at our station. I hope you'll come back often." That's all it needs to say.

Talent scout, G. L. Fultz, St. Louis' best dressed credit man, and staunch enemy of Whiskers and Goozle, says of the following assembled hogwash: "I know you will want to read this letter, for it's a dandy."

"Thank you very kindly (who was kind?) for your letter of November 12th, just received. I am sorry that our bookkeeping department (mass production) erroneously (new spelling) billed you for storage on the car that we handled for you. I am attaching corrected bill for which (?) I am sure you will find in order. Thanking you very kindly, we remain, very truly yours."

Miscellaneous Business Letters

Inquiries and Replies; Orders and Acknowledgments; Introduction and Recommendation;
Social Correspondence in Business, Inter-Office; Good Will; Payments By Mail.

Routine Letters

In terms of quantity the largest part of business correspondence consists of routine letters—inquiries, replies to inquiries, orders and remittances, acknowledgments, bills, etc. In these letters the writer needs little art; the basic requirements are to be clear and accurate.

Inquiry Letters

Inquiry letters and replies to inquiries should be concise, simple, and direct, except in cases that call for sensitivity, judgment, or tact. An inquiry about the price of an article need do no more than ask the price. But an inquiry about credit standing or about a job opportunity, and the answers to such inquiries, require care and tact. Similarly answers to inquiries in mail-order campaigns, where the objective is to produce sales, call for thought and skill.

In ordinary inquiries, however, the important thing, on the part of the inquirer, is to phrase his question simply, precisely, and inclusively so that he can be told just what he wants to know, without extraneous matter; and also all that he wants to know so that he does not have to send further letters to fill out details. Similarly, the important thing on the part of the correspondent in answering such inquiries is to make the reply full and precise so that the inquirer does not have to come back to him to have matters cleared up or filled out.

If the information sought is adequately covered in a catalogue or booklet, enclose it in your reply and use the letter to refer to the paragraphs or pages dealing explicitly with the matter inquired about.

To facilitate quick comprehension both of the inquiry and the reply it is advisable to present them as separate items, allowing an individual paragraph for each.

If either the question or the answer is to be kept confidential, do not rely on the other person to guess it. Say so. Examles:

Gentlemen:

We are organizing a summer camp for boys and are in the market for 24 two-occupant portable tents for camping out. We are undecided whether to use conventional canvas tents, with which we are familiar, or your new nylon tents. Would you be good enough:

To send us whatever literature you have available on the construction of your nylon tents, accessory equipment, etc.

To inform us of their suitability to the summer climate of the Catskill Mountains, where the camp is located.

To furnish comparative weights and costs between canvas and nylon.

To give us an idea of the durability of your product with estimates of how many years of service may be expected in ordinary use.

We shall appreciate your referring us to customers who have had experience with your tents in conditions approximating those of the boys' camp in the Catskills.

Sincerely yours,
Arthur Ives

Gentlemen:

We are in the market for a line of work pants. We should like to know—

What fabrics you make up.

What colors.

Minimum orders accepted per size.

Terms (including discount for cash).

Please send us a swatch catalogue with your reply.

Sincerely yours,
Bruce Samuelson

Gentlemen:

My wife and I will be in New York for the Christmas week vacation. We are people of modest means—I am an associate professor at the University here. We should like good (not lavish) hotel accommodations in Manhattan, but a little out of the immediate railroad-terminal district. We would like to take in the theater (dramas, not musicals). We enjoy good cooking, preferably without noisy entertainment.

Would your bureau book reservations such as we describe and provide information about restaurants?

Could you send us a selected list of hotels that would come within our description, listing locations and price ranges for rooms for two?

Could you list the well-reviewed plays and the price range for seats in medium locations. Fortunately our vision and hearing are good.

If you can provide such services, we will send you, by return mail, our first and alternate choices of hotel and theater reservations and a check for whatever sum you may require for deposit.

Sincerely yours,
Howard Carver

Answers to Inquiries

Dear Mr. Alexander:

We thank you for your letter of August 16 about our line of women's belts.

We wish to call your attention to the perforated pages in the back of the enclosed catalogue containing information on terms and convenient order forms.

Ours is a quality line. It is used for accessories by manufacturers serving exclusive shops, and is stocked by the New York Fifth Avenue stores.

We hope to have the pleasure of serving you.

Sincerely yours,
A. S. Cantor

Dear Mr. Jones:

Because of the decline in demand we have discontinued manufacture of the "union suit" type of men's underwear.

As the enclosed catalogue illustrates, we carry a full line of the currently popular types of men's underwear in a wide range of styles, colors, and prices.

We will be happy to serve you.

Sincerely yours,
V. A. Miles

Dear Mr. Hector:

Since your letter does not make clear what your speech defect is, we are unable to furnish a specific answer.

Our public speaking course has been designed to help shy people who are not sure of themselves to speak readily and effectively in public. If your defect is among those associated with shyness, we are confident that the course will help you overcome it.

But if the defect is organic, that may require surgical treatment. If it is a long-standing problem, such as chronic stuttering, that may call for pyschiatric treatment. We recommend that you try to determine the cause with the aid of a physician or professionally qualified person.

But common difficulties in speaking—such as inability to face an audience, lack of practice of organizing a speech, unfamiliarity with the techniques of preparing material, groping for words, difficulties over parliamentary rules, etc.,—can be overcome by our course of study.

If you do not find the answer you require, please try us again with the questions put in more specific terms.

Sincerely yours,
Marc Rafferty

A final note: Though answers to inquiries need not be elaborate, they should avoid stuffy over-formality. For example, instead of "Acknowledging yours of the 20th requesting a copy of our booklet, *Paint It Yourself,* we wish to advise you that the booklet is being mailed to you forthwith," write something like: "We are pleased to send you our booklet, *Paint It Yourself,* which you requested on May 20. Its suggestions have been useful to people of good taste who must keep within a modest budget." Or, instead of "Yours of September 10 received and contents noted. Be advised that the matter has been put into the hands of our Sales Department from whom you should hear shortly," write something like, "Our Sales Department has your inquiry of September 10 and is assembling material which should be helpful in answering your questions."

Orders

Many firms use printed order forms. If for some reason a letter is needed to accompany or precede the order to add some specific instructions about the order, make the letter concise and unmistakably clear.

Where the letter itself constitutes the order, care should be taken to make it direct, clear, and accurate. To facilitate this it is advisable to arrange the items in tabular form, giving a separate line to each. Details of color, size, material, price, identifying mark or number, etc., should be precisely stated. Manner of shipment should be specified—whether by mail, express, freight, etc.

If the goods are needed by a certain date, if method of payment is, in any way, to differ from the customary procedure, if delivery is to be made to an address other than the regular mailing address, anything requiring specific instructions should be made clear, and should be given a separate paragraph to prevent its being misunderstood or ignored.

Where remittance is enclosed, attention should be drawn to it and its nature specified—whether it is by check, money-order, express-order, draft, cash, or stamps.

Even in letters transmitting orders for goods, ordinary courtesy and tact should be observed. In his book *"Effective Letters in Business,"* Robert L. Shurter gives an example of a tactless order letter that drew a deservedly caustic reply: The letter—"Gents. Please send me one of them gasoline engines you show on page 785 and if it's any good I'll send you a check for it."

The reply—"Dear Mr. . . . Please send us the check and if it's any good we'll send you the engine."

Variations from ordinary punctuation are frequently used in orders. To compress items into single lines or a minimum number of lines, customary punctuation may be omitted and every possible abbreviation used. Names of separate articles are capitalized and also words that help to distinguish them from other kinds of goods of the same order. Thus Red will be capitalized to distinguish it from other colors an article may be manufactured in; or Wool to distinguish a garment in that fabric from garments in other fabrics. The objectives are conciseness and clarity and any typographic or grammatical means that promote these ends is justified.

Order Letters— Some Examples

Gentlemen:

Please rush to us to reach our stockroom next Thursday: 10 doz. Yo-yos, 50 checker sets, 50 anagram sets. This is for a special sales week which is going well. Our stock on these items is running out.

Our regular purchase order is being made out in the routine way and should reach you in a day or two; but please do not hold up delivery of this special order. A delay of even a few hours may mean lost sales.

Sincerely yours,
Kenneth Miller

Dear Mr. Bates:

The enclosed purchase order is in confirmation of the order we placed with you over the phone this morning. The order was phoned in to avoid delays. I must emphasize again that the shipment must reach us before October 4, when our sales will start.

Sincerely yours,
Seth Bellows

Gentlemen:

Please send us, for earliest possible delivery, the following goods selected from your latest catalogue. Charge my account.

3	doz.	Men's Nylon Hose, Black, asst. sizes @ $4.00	$12.00
3	doz.	Men's Nylon Hose, Blue, asst. sizes @ $4.00	12.00
3	doz.	Men's Nylon Hose, Brown, asst. sizes @ $4.00	12.00
1½	doz.	Men's Nylon Hose, Green, asst. sizes @ $4.00	6.00
4	doz.	Men's Cotton Hose, Black, Triangle Clocks @ $4.50	18.00
2	doz.	#61 Work Shirts, asst. sizes @ $9.00	18.00
2	doz.	Men's White Broadcloth Cotton Shirts, asst. sizes @ $16.00	32.00
			$110.00

Ship freight.

Sincerely yours,
Charles Bloom

Acknowledgments

Dear Mr. Thayer:

Thank you for your order of October 5. As you instructed, it will be shipped freight, via the D & W. The order is being made up today and will be at the yards tomorrow. It should reach you well within the time you specified.

Sincerely yours,
J. H. Hudson

Dear Mr. Jones:

We have just telegraphed you the following: "Cannot ship your order May 10. Goods not available." The telegram was sent to minimize any inconvenience this may cause you. We can supply the cheaper grade, #43, on the date required. The earliest we can supply the #41 grade specified in your order would be June 11. If the #43 grade is all right, please wire collect and we will ship immediately.

Sincerely yours,
Adam Pierce

Dear Mr. Poynter:

Thank you for your order of August 14.

Unfortunately your letter did not specify which color or colors, and which weight or weights, you wish. In our Queen's Taste stationery line the colors are Rose, Fern, Mauve, Beige, Robin's Egg, Canary, Russet, Shell White, and Alpine Snow. The weights are Tissue, Regular and Baronial. Probably our catalogue was not at hand when you made out your order. We are enclosing another giving samples of each color and weight.

A prompt reply will be to our mutual advantage.

Yours sincerely,
Eric Hunter

Dear Mr. Magnes:

Thank you for your order for Clover Danish Blue Cheese. It is being shipped out to you today.

We enclose a catalogue of our other products. Please note that with orders of $10.00 or more, customers may receive, free, their choice of a jar of Lingonberry or Currant preserves.

Yours sincerely,
Einar Toksvig

Follow-Ups on Orders

Sometimes orders are poorly attended to and it is necessary, strange as it may seem, to jog the attention of the supplier. Here, again, as emphasized in the section on **Complaints and Adjustments,** an irritable tone is inadvisable, even where loss or inconvenience has been caused by the delay. A calm letter will get quicker and more favorable attention and will enhance the writer's status as a considerate customer whose patronage is worth retaining. It is seldom necessary to write more than one reminder; but when that becomes necessary, a sharper tone is not always politic, especially where the writer has reasons of his own for maintaining business relations with the ineffecient firm. Examples:

Gentlemen:

Although our order #216 was acknowledged on June 2, and it is now near the end of the month, the air conditioners have not yet arrived. We have already undergone a hot spell and soon July will be upon us. I cannot understand the delay or your leaving us without an explanation for your delay in delivery of such a seasonal article. Up to now your deliveries have been prompt; and expecting delivery any day, I did not write to you. There is no question now that I shall lose some sales and I expect you to make up for the lost time, not to speak of the lost business, by shipping the goods by express at your expense. Please wire what you plan to do in the matter.

Sincerely yours,
Edward Hines

Answers to follow-ups on orders should be prompt, and they should be tactful even where the tone of the complaining letter is disagreeable. Give the reason for the delay, assure the customer that care will taken to avoid such delays in the future, and specify the date and the manner of the planned shipment.

Dear Mr. Osgood:

We regret the delay in shippping out your order #644, dated February 10.

You probably have read of the recent labor troubles in the lumber industry. These made it difficult for us to secure proper crating materials for the goods. Rather than risk damage in transit we held up the shipment until satisfactory crates were available. We have now managed to get some from another source of supply. Even though our shipping costs have risen, we feel the added expense, like the delay, is preferable to having the machinery arrive in poor condition.

Your order was shipped out today, express. We hope it reaches you in good time as, we are confident now, it will reach you in good order.

Sincerely yours,
Mark Lyons

Letters with Enclosures

When remittance such as checks, etc., or when invoices or special notices are enclosed, the number of enclosures should be stated in the letter. This is customarily done in a separate line, at the left margin, under the signature.

Gentlemen:

The enclosed check for $146.00 is in settlement of our account to date. We also enclose your bill. Please receipt and return it.

Sincerely yours,
Joseph Evans

2 enclosures

Gentlemen:

Thank you for your order #324 for a dozen Pop-Up Toasters. They were shipped today. The invoice is enclosed. We also enclose the catalogue on waffle irons requested in your letter.

Sincerely yours
Morton James

2 enclosures

Letters of Introduction

Letters of introduction should not be given thoughtlessly. Avoid them unless you can feel that it would actually be in the interest of both parties to get acquainted. Good-natured people often do harm when they mean to do good, by writing letters of introduction indiscriminately. The tenth "promising" young chap sent to glean advice in the field of his ambition from a busy executive is likely to get a discouraging brushoff.

Therefore, the first consideration in writing a letter of introduction is whether to write it at all. Having decided that the letter should be written, you might well consider several other elements. Since the best way to present letters of introduction is in person, the envelope containing the introduction should be unsealed and should bear the name of the person to whom it is addressed and, in the lower left-hand corner, the line "Introducing Mr. . . . ." This enables the recipient to welcome the caller by name and facilitates the relationship.

The letter should be brief and restrained. A long letter might impose an embarrassingly long wait on the caller while the letter is read. And extravagant statements about the caller, if they do not predispose the reader to skepticism, may evoke embarrassing comments of other sorts.

Sometimes there is a reason to mail the letter to the person addressed; for example, to allow him to appoint a time for the meeting. In that case a copy should be sent to the person being introduced so that he will be familiar with what has been said about him. Examples:

Dear Mr. Clements:

I hope you will have the time to see Mr. Wilbur, who was a student in my class this semester. You have several times expressed an interest in seeing "the cream of the crop" in each graduating class. It is because I can unreservedly place Mr. Wilbur in that category that I have suggested that he call on you.

Yours sincerely,
Roger Hessian

Dear Mr. Canning:

It gives me great pleasure to introduce to you Mr. Harvey Wright, who operates a large bottling plant in our city.

Mr. Wright is contemplating opening a branch in your city, and I could think of no one better for him to see than you for a quick survey of local conditions and prospects. My business association with Mr. Wright is now in its twelfth year and has led to a friendship which has enabled me to discover and appreciate his personal qualities.

I feel certain that any association this introduction may result in will be valued on both sides.

Yours sincerely,
Hiram Godkin

Letters of Recommendation

There are two main types of recommendation—the general recommendation "to whom it may concern," and the individual recommendation addressed to a specific person. The latter obviously is preferable, since the writer's personal acquaintance with the person addressed generally means that the letter will be given more attention than might otherwise be the case.

The best kind of recommendation is the one that performs a mutual service to the recommended person and the one to whom he is sent. So far as possible, therefore, it is well to find out beforehand whether and how the person about whom you are writing can be of service to the individual you are addressing.

Vital to any letter of recommendation is truthfulness and restraint. False statements are almost inevitably found out. In time they create handicaps that outweigh any temporary advantage that they gain for the person recommended. And exaggerated claims usually predispose the reader to skepticism and suspicion, and thus are often more injurious than helpful. Examples:

To Whom It May Concern:

Mr. Clarence Loman has been on our sales staff for the past eight years and has compiled an excellent sales record. He is a friendly person by nature and has won the friendship as well as the business patronage of his customers. We have convincing evidence of that from the letters we have received in response to the announcement of his retirement from traveling.

For reasons of health he cannot continue traveling, but he can serve in an inside position. We regret there is nothing of this kind available in our organization. He would make a crackerjack inside salesman and we can unreservedly recommend him to anyone in need of a person with real selling talents. It would take him no time to get a feeling of your stock and your methods; and to establish really friendly relations with customers. We are confident that he would be an asset to any firm that can use his services.

Very truly yours,
Martin Ullmann

Dear Mr. Carter:

I am taking the liberty of writing to you because I know that you sometimes give out manuscripts for first readings, and accepted manuscripts for preparations for the printer, to qualified young people, on a free-lance basis. I have heard that you do this, as a means of testing or training candidates for anticipated future openings in your editorial staff.

If that is the case, I feel that you will appreciate my sending Miss Ethel Willison to you. You have already become acquainted with her work and have even complimented her, without knowing it, when you complimented me on the excellent shape of the manuscript I turned in, and again, when I sent back corrected proofs. Miss Willison assisted me through all the stages of my book, and it is to her that I owe the smoothness and ease with which it went through all its stages.

Miss Willison has taken all the courses given here in preparation for a career in publishing and has applied what she learned, first on the college paper and, later, in helping other faculty members, as she has helped me, in preparing articles and books.

I am confident that she is just the kind of person you will look for when you are considering taking on a new editorial assistant. I take great pleasure in recommending her to you.

Sincerely yours,
David Proctor

Social Correspondence
in Business

Though the phrase "strictly business" symbolizes freedom from emotional involvements in or out of business, the words connote an attitude or a goal, rather than the reality of business itself. It would be unnatural to expect that human beings, who spend most of their waking hours in business, would not form personal relationships of varying degrees of closeness in the course of their business. The truth is that most of the friendships men form in their mature years arise out of business contacts. And friendly qualities are recognized as assets in business.

This is so generally understood that trade associations of businessmen have the fostering of friendly cooperation as their major aim. Generally, too, a business relationship would hardly be accounted good or secure if it failed to develop some measure of personal regard between heads or representatives of the two firms.

Consequently, there are many occassions for letters that should not be "strictly business," although they are essential to the conduct of business. Examples are given in the following pages:

Letters of Congratulations

Dear Mr. Leonard:

What a pleasure it was to see the item in *The Times* business section this morning about your promotion to the position of Sales-Manager. Actually I think I ought to write to the President of your concern, Mr. Tate, to congratulate him. He had the good sense to recognize a good man. From what I know about people in the field he couldn't have picked a better man. Congratulations on a well-deserved promotion.

Dear Mr. Slocum:

I don't know how others are reacting to the news in this morning's real-estate section, but I want to congratulate you on taking such a far-sighted and enterprising step. I have already heard some say that the site is too remote for such a development, but I put them with those who once thought Forty-second Street was too far outside the city. I think you have judged correctly that the site is directly in the path of the city's future growth.

Again, my congratulations and my best wishes for the success of a project which should serve the community as well as bring you well-deserved returns.

Admiringly yours,
Edmund Gates

Letters of Sympathy and Condolence

Dear Walter:

When your secretary called this morning to tell me that you wouldn't be able to keep our appointment because of your sudden illness, I was deeply disturbed. She told me that you were to spend some days in the hospital, under observation, to determine whether an operation will be necessary. I hope the tests indicate no such necessity and that you will be back in your office very soon and in condition to renew our postponed engagement.

Cordially yours,
Arthur Reinhardt

Dear Mrs. Rodd:

It was a hard blow to us, too, to hear of your husband's death. We missed him, very much, two years ago, when he retired. During our association with him over the twelve years that he was with us, all of us developed the highest regard for his wonderful qualities. We can fully understand how deeply you must feel his loss. But it must be a consolation to you that his last years were serene. We and his other friends feel grateful to you for having contributed so much to making him so happy.

Sincerely yours,
Charles U. Clifford

Dear George:

I was very sorry to receive the sad news of your great loss. I know that nothing anyone may say at a time like this can assuage your deep grief, but I hope that you will soon find abiding comfort in the high regard everyone had for your father's accomplishments, and in the good health, happiness, and achievements of those dear to you. I hope you will have no more sorrow for many years to come.

Sincerely yours,
Frank

Dear Mr. Cass:

I have just learned of the emergency appendicitis operation you have had to undergo. I had Miss Hale phone the hospital immediately and was reassured to hear that there were no complications and that you are getting along nicely.

That's fine and we want to keep it so. Therefore, I want it understood that no matter how good your recovery is, you are not to come back to the office until the doctor, on his most conservative estimate, tells you you may. And don't think of the office. This is an order!

In the meanwhile, to help you pass the time, there will be a package of books at the hospital. The well-read Miss Hale did the choosing and I think she has a good idea of your taste.

With all best wishes,
Robert E. Griffin

Accepting Invitations

Dear Mr. Canby:

It will be a pleasure to see you when I visit New York next month. Thank you for suggesting it. Indeed one of the prospects that made the trip so pleasing to me was the opportunity it might give me to become acquainted with you personally.

Sincerely yours,
Elmer Robinson

Dear Sir:

I consider it a great honor to be asked to speak at the Credit Men's Luncheon next month. Thank you very much.

I hope the enclosed data are what you need for the newspaper release. And I will be on hand an hour before the start of the luncheon, as you suggest, to talk over the details of the program.

Yours very truly,
Leon Hart

Declining Invitations

Dear Mr. Hopkins:

Unfortunately I will be out of town during the week of March 10 and will not be able, therefore, to be present at the reception celebrating the opening of your new store. Since I will not be there to offer my congratulations to you in person, permit me to do so here. And I wish to add my sincere best wishes for the success of the new store and the continued growth of your business.

Sincerely yours,
Anthony Asch

Dear Mr. Mann:

It is with deep regret that I must decline the great honor of organizing and heading the committee to arrange a reception for the Vice-President, who is to be one of the speakers at our coming convention. As you may have heard, Mr. Bixby, head of our Foreign Department, died suddenly last week. I have had to take over his duties temporarily, which for the present rules out any other activities for me. I will let you know as soon as I am free again for any service to the organization.

Sincerely yours,
Horace Seton

Resignations

Dear Sir:

I have just been appointed Coordinator of Sales for our firm. This will mean extensive traveling in order to keep in continual contact with our stores throughout the country. It will, therefore, be impossible for me to continue to serve as secretary of the club. And, so, with deep regret, I must tender my resignation from that office.

It has been a pleasure to serve the club during the past four years, and I have enjoyed and profited from the association with its able officers and members. Needless to say, I will be on hand for every get-together my new duties will permit.

Sincerely yours,
Edwin Robbins

Dear Sir:

I have agreed to serve on the Mayor's Committee for Emergency Housing. Since it may prejudice the value of the work I can do for the committee, if I continue as a member of the firm, I am submitting my resignation to take effect immediately.

This is a step I take not without regret, for the years I have been privileged to spend with the firm have been happy ones. But I feel that the opportunity afforded me by the Mayor to serve the community in so important a sphere of activity is one that I cannot pass up.

Sincerely yours,
Alan W. Furness

Inter-Office Correspondence

In concerns of any size a good many memos pass between departments, between the management and the staff, between individuals in different departments, etc. Thus the Stock Department may inform the Sales Department of the arrival of certain needed goods; or the management will send memoranda to department heads about certain changes of policy; or it may send a memo to the entire staff about price changes, the announcement of a special holiday, etc.; or a salesman may send a note to Shipping giving special instructions regarding the shipment of an order; or Promotion may send a memo to Sales and other departments concerned, reminding them of the start of a national advertising campaign so that they can prepare for the anticipated inquiries and orders.

Most firms provide printed forms and restrict inter-office correspondence to one subject only in order to encourage conciseness and clarity and to facilitate filing and reference. The printed forms also assure that the date, the department, the person, and the subject are clearly indicated. This makes salutations and signatures superfluous and they are omitted except in memoranda with a deliberately personal touch.

Although such notes are "stripped for action," the tone should nevertheless always be courteous. Inter-departmental feuds have often begun over tactless expression in such memoranda. And office morale has sometimes been damaged by an unintended curt note by management. Certain indispensible formalities of respect should be observed in inter-office correspondence as in other forms. Examples:

Form G-14	One Subject Only
Inter-Office Memo- randum	Made Simple Books Inc.
To:	From:
Department:	Department:
Subject:	Date:

To: Staffs	From: J. B. Wolcott
Department: Sales, Correspondence	Department: Man- agement
Subject: New Price List	Date: April 10, 1954

On May 1, our new price-list goes into effect. Copies should be in the hands of all our salesmen before the end of the week and in the hands of our dealers by April 28. Copies can be obtained from Miss Andrews.

To: Staffs	From: G. E. Ander- son
Department: All departments	Department: Per- sonnel
Subject: July 4 Holiday	Date: July 1, 1954

Since July 4, this year, falls on a Sunday, the office will be closed Monday, July 5, to allow a full holiday weekend.

To: Mr. Taylor, Mr. Green, Mr. Johns, Mr. Maxfield	From: Edward Earnshaw
Department: Sales, Shipping, Personnel, Accounting	Department: Promo- tion Date: February 10, 1954
Subject: Advertising campaign	

This weekend our special advertising campaign on our new Infra-Red cooker opens with full pages in the magazine supplements of metropolitan newspapers. There will be page ads in leading national magazines, along with other promotion: Most of the advertising will carry keyed coupons. Your departments should be prepared for the special load of mail that will come in. Just a reminder.

To: E. Dirksen	From: J. Meyers
Department: Shipping	Department: Sales Date: January 11,
Subject: Johnson Brothers order	1954

Dear Ed:

When Billing sends down the Johnson Brothers' order, please put a note on it to double wrap the shipment. Old Mr. Johnson complains that our wrapping paper isn't thick enough. The trouble is in his storeroom, which is a filthy damp place. So it'll be best to double wrap his stuff, or he'll come back at us with claims for spoilage. Hope it's not too much bother. Thanks.

Joe

Other types of memo forms frequently used are:

From the Desk of Frank Gannon
To:_____ Date:_____
To:_____ Date:_____
From:_____

It might be noted, in passing, that in large corporations or organizations, intra-company mail is frequently placed in heavy-stock envelopes that can be used over and over again. These envelopes have ruled lines on the outside, and the sender need merely place on the first free line the name and department of the person to whom the communication is addressed. That person in turn can use the same envelope by doing similarly the next time he wishes to dispatch a memo or some papers to another person in the organization.

Good-Will Letters

It should be enough, of course, to service customers promptly and efficiently. Yet it is human for them to want to be appreciated as well and to be given personal attention. If thanking a customer for his order has been overlooked, write him a special note of appreciation for his business.

Letting customers feel that they are "in" on your operations is another way of building their good will. If you are expanding your business, or promoting a man on your staff with whom your customers may have had occasion to become acquainted, or if you are making any operational change of interest to them, let your customers know about it.

If you are making gifts—calendars, personal memopads, initialed pencils, etc.,—to new customers, don't leave the old customers out. Give it to them, also.

There are also occasions and circumstances that might be used for the promotion of good will by drawing attention to them. We have already mentioned letters of congratulation and letters of sympathy and condolence. Watch significant dates in the lives or careers of customers, when it is possible or advisable—anniversaries of the concern, birthdays of the officers, marriages in their families, and send congratulations and appropriate gifts.

Send Christmas greetings to all customers, and mail them well in advance of the rush period, so that they don't come so late as to seem like afterthoughts.

Unusual occurrences may be made the occasion for a good-will note. Thus when Lever Brothers were constructing their striking New York building, they sent letters to all in the neighborhood within range of the sounds of construction, private families in nearby residential blocks as well as business neighbors, apologizing for the noise. They gave assurance that everything was being done to finish the building as soon as possible and that all avoidable construction sounds were being eliminated.

During the recent period of rapid and successive price boosts some firms notified their customers that they were not raising their prices though raw-material costs had risen; and others explained what they were doing to absorb part of the necessary price advances in operational economies.

Good will within an organization is as important as the good will of outside customers and neighbors. Well run concerns make use of their inter-office correspondence to keep up office morale through informational memoranda that make the staff feel they are part of what is happening: through announcements that will please the staff; and through personal notes of congratulation from management on pleasant occasions, such as the birth of children, the graduation of sons, etc.; and condolences in bereavements. Examples:

Dear Mr. Smythe:

The enclosed is the latest issue of our house organ, *Cuttings.* I am sure you will be interested in the piece on page twelve, on the old Smythe Tool Works which, I believe, were founded by your great-grandfather.

Would you like to get *Cuttings* regularly? I'd have it sent without asking if it weren't for my own experience. I groan at the amount of unsolicited mail I get from people who send it with the best of intentions; there aren't enough hours in the day to read everything that comes through the mail. So for that reason I have made it a policy to send *Cuttings* only if customers let us know that they want it. Incidentally, I shall be happy to send you as many copies of this issue as you may require.

Sincerely yours,
Gabriel Harcourt

Dear Mr. Connor:

It occurred to me, recently, that it was just about ten years ago that I entered your first order with our company in our order book. I was not then sales manager, of course—that came as the result of the good orders you and other friendly customers favored me with.

To make sure, I had my secretary look it up, and it turned out, sure enough, that our business connections did begin ten years ago, this month! That first order, incidentally, was for an assortment of our fans. Your latest order is for air conditioners! Time does move.

If we could get together, we'd be celebrating the glad occasion properly at Ludlow's or Keen's. But since that's not possible, here's the next best thing. Please join me in a glass of champagne of a kind I've found particularly palatable. A case of it should be in your office this morning if American Express is on its toes.

Your health and best wishes for ten more good years of business together.

Cordially,
Ed Schacht

Dear Mr. Alter:

We prepared a map for use by our office staff of the new city postal zones. It proved to be such a convenience that we decided to print up copies for our customers. Here's your copy and we hope you'll find it useful.

Sincerely yours,
Conrad Dietrichstein

Dear Mr. Freud:

As a customer of the Hooker Hat Company you will be interested to know that we have just completed negotiations which bring this fine firm into our organization. It was our desire to fill out our line of men's furnishings with a quality hat line, and Hooker was our choice.

We were glad, of course, that with so fine a product we could make the acquaintance of new customers appreciative of fine quality apparel for men.

We want to assure you that you will continue to receive the efficient service you have become accustomed to from the Hooker staff (which is being preserved intact), plus, we venture to add, special services made possible by the facilities of our larger organization.

On his next call your Hooker salesman will have our other lines of quality goods to offer you. We are mailing you our catalogue so that you may become acquainted with them. Any orders you wish to place from the catalogue will be credited to the salesman's account, and you will be billed on the same terms as in your account with Hooker.

Please let us know if there is any way that we can be of service to you. I look forward to the continuance of what I hope will be a pleasant and profitable relationship for us both.

Sincerely yours,
A. E. Handley

Dear Mr. Gates:

Thank you for your order number 112, which arrived this morning. It will be shipped today; the invoice is enclosed.

The same company is making a new line of waffle irons, and the introductory offer is so attractive we decided to call it to the attention of all our customers. We have tested the device and found it sturdy and efficient. We are enclosing a circular giving the details. Perhaps you'll want to take advantage of this offer.

Sincerely yours,
Morton James

2 enclosures

Dear Mr. Magnus:

Thank you for your order of Clover Danish Blue Cheese. It is being shipped to you today.

I think you will be interested in seeing a copy of a periodical we issue, *Good Cheer,* which contains recipes and notes about new European delicacies being introduced to American lovers of good foods. If you would like to receive it regularly, we shall be glad to put you on our mailing list.

Sincerely yours,
Gail Longinetti

1 enclosure

Requests for Charity

Although the solicitation of contributions for charity is a highly specialized, professional activity these days, businessmen frequently have occasion to sell theater tickets or to ask for donations for a pet organization. In such cases make your letter brief; leave the "selling" to the professional fund-raiser. You will get a check because the person you are writing to knows you, and values your friendship or patronage. Some examples:

Dear Mr. Adams:

    I am taking the liberty of sending you the enclosed advertising blank in behalf of the United Orphans League. I am very much interested in the organization and know of its good work and great need. I shall appreciate your check to the best of your ability. With many thanks and good wishes, I am,

Sincerely yours,

Sam Laury

Dear Ben:

    Enclosed are a couple of tickets for "Ah, Take the Cash." The seats are not so good, and I don't know anything about the show, but the cause is good. So I'd appreciate your taking the tickets and letting me have your check for $20 made out to the Community Chest. I hope you will enjoy the show and have the double satisfaction of knowing you've aided a worthy cause.

Sincerely yours,

Norman Rich

Although it is desirable to keep letters of this type short, they can vary in tone, length, and appeal if in the judgement of the writer, the nature of his relationship with the person to whom he is writing requires more than the semi-formal approach illustrated above.

Example of an
Acceptance Letter

Dear Mr. Bingham:

    I am happy to send you the enclosed check for the theater tickets you sent me. I know the cause is a good one, and I hope the project is a success. Keep up the good work.

Sincerely yours,

David K. Nelson

Words and Expressions to Avoid

Superfluous, Overformal, Flabby, Tactless, Hackneyed Language

According to our records—Often superfluous and can be omitted.

Acknowledge receipt of your letter—Overformal. Better, **We thank you for your letter.**

(Please) advise—Better **inform** or **tell** unless actually soliciting advice.

Agreeable to your letter—Old fashioned.

Along these lines—Better, **the gist of his remarks** or simply **like.**

Amount of, preceded by **in the, to the, for the**—Better say **check** or **remittance** for $_____.

(Please) arrange to return—Sufficient to say, **please return.**

As per your letter—**As per** is a legal term, therefore out of place in an ordinary letter. Better, **according to** or **as mentioned in.**

As stated above—Better to repeat what you stated, or **as I have mentioned.**

As yet—For **yet.**

Assuring you of—Old fashioned.

As to—Awkward.

At all times, at this time—Usually superfluous.

At hand—Usually superfluous.

Attached you will find—Overformal. Better, **we are attaching** or **we are enclosing.**

At the present time—**Now** is preferable.

At this writing—Formal. Better **now.**

At your earliest convenience, at an early date, at the earliest possible moment—Overformal. Better say **soon.**

Awaiting your favor—Better, **please let us hear from you soon.**

Beg—Relic of old-fashioned courtesy, now abandoned in business correspondence.

Claim—Avoid in the sense of **to assert** or **assertion;** might antagonize.

Communication—Formal. Better, **message, letter, report, inquiry,** etc.

Complaint—Aggressive sound. Usually better to say **request for adjustment.**

In compliance with your request—Overformal.

Contents noted—Superfluous.

(To) date—Overformal. "To date we have not received"—better, **we have not yet received.**

Deal—Improperly used for **transaction.**

It is desired that we receive—Inactive, weak, and long-winded. Better, **we want to receive** or **we'd appreciate receiving.**

We have duly investigated—**Duly** is superfluous.

Each and every—**Each** or **every** is sufficient by itself.

Early date—May mean two or three days or two or three weeks. Better be specific.

Enclosed please find—Better **here is** or **I enclose.**

Esteemed—Old-fashioned.

Even date—(meaning today). Better be specific. Say **your letter of this morning** or **of December _____ 19 _____.**

Event—Avoid "in the event that." **If** is preferable.

Favor—In sense of letter—old-fashioned, better say **your letter of _____.** Only proper, nowadays, when referring to a specific act of kindness.

For the reason that—**Because** is preferable.

Forward—**Send** or **ship** are preferable.

For your information—Superfluous. Omit.

Hand you—**Send out check** or **enclose our check** preferable.

Have for acknowledgement—Simpler to say "thanks."

Herewith—Superfluous.

Hoping—Weak and usually superfluous. Avoid, especially as dangling participle before complimentary close of letter.

Inasmuch as—Just say, **because.**

(We are) in receipt of—Overformal. Better, **we have received** or **thank you for.**

In order to—Just say **to.**

In reference to—Overformal, avoid. Better, **about.**

In regard to—Just say **about.**

In reply would wish to—Overformal, avoid.

Instant—Abbreviated as Inst., meaning the current month. A legal term, out of place in ordinary correspondence. Better name the month—instead of "the 5th Inst." say **October 5.**

In the nature of—Long-winded. Just say **like.**

It is the hope of the undersigned—for **I hope.**

Kindly let us know—Kindly is old fashioned. **Please let us know** is preferable.

Liberty (May we take the liberty to . . .)—Usually no

liberty involved. Preferable to be direct and say **may we.**

Line—Sometimes inaccurately used in sense of a business.

(To) lineup—Vague. Better say **try to interest, try to sell,** etc.

Lot—Often inaccurately used to indicate quantity. Watch it.

Miss—Avoid using alone. Always use with a name.

Must say—Avoid. Just say it.

Oblige—Antiquated.

Our Mr. . . .—Pretentious. If name does not sufficiently identify him, describe him as **Mr. . . . , our representative,** or **our Chicago manager,** etc.

Passive constructions—Avoid them. Recast when convenient into active construction. Instead of **The goods ordered by you have been shipped,** say **We have shipped the goods you ordered.**

Permit me to say—No permission needed; just say it.

Pertaining to—**About** is better.

Pleasure (We take pleasure in)—Overformal. Better, **We are sending** or **are glad to send.**

Posted—In sense of informed, is a poor usage. Better say **informed** or **well informed.**

Prior to—**Before** is better.

Pronoun—Should not be omitted because of risk of sounding curt. Avoid, "Goods received. Sending check today." Better say, "We have received the goods and are sending you our check today."

Proposition—Avoid using the term in the sense of task. "To ship this order during the Christmas rush will be a difficult proposition" is not as good as "To ship this order during the Christmas rush will be difficult."

Proximo—(Abbreviated as prox.) Meaning next month. Legal term, out of place in ordinary business correspondence. Say **next month.**

Pursuant to your order—Overformal. Better say **following your directions.**

Recent date—your letter of—Preferable, **your letter** or **your order of . . .** (give date).

Regret—When used the following way: **we regret very deeply,** or **most sincerely,** overformal. Better, **I'm sorry,** or **I regret.**

Replying, Regarding, Referring—Weak. Avoid hanging participles. The simple straight statement is usually more direct and forceful.

Return mail—Shopworn. Better, **this week.**

Same—Stilted. Instead of "We received the goods and found same satisfactory," "We received the goods and found them satisfactory."

State—Not as good as simple word **say** or some other expression. For example: Instead of as **stated above,** use **as we have said** or merely repeat the statement.

Thanking you in advance—A trite device; may antagonize as unwarranted.

Thank you again—Once is enough.

Trust—**Hope, believe, think,** etc. preferable.

Ultimo—(Abbreviation ult.) Meaning last month. A legal term, out of place in business correspondence. Better say, **last month.**

Under separate cover—Use sparingly. Better specify means of shipment, **we are sending you by parcel post.**

(The) Undersigned—Overformal. Preferable to say **I.**

Valued—Formal word. Avoid expressions like **your valued patronage.**

We—In place of **I,** is right only when emphasis is on action by the firm. Otherwise it is preferable to say **I.**

Wish to say—Say it.

Would say—Say it.

(The) Writer—Overformal. Don't hesitate to say **I.**

Glossary of Terms Commonly Used in Business and Formal Correspondence

Abstract of Title—Record summarizing deeds, mortgages, and other documents and transactions affecting title to a piece of real estate.

Accessory after the Fact—One who knowingly aids the criminal after a criminal act.

Accessory before the Fact—One who instigates or aids in a crime but takes no part in its commission.

Accommodation Paper—Negotiable paper bearing the endorsement of a person who thereby lends his credit to the maker of the paper.

Account—Right to transact business in a bank by depositing money or its equivalent therein; a salesman's customers; business transacted with a firm or an individual; right to conduct business with a firm by establishing credit; record of business transactions with a firm or an individual.

Accountant—One skilled in keeping the accounts of a firm and responsible for their accuracy. Certified Public Accountants (abbrev. CPA), corresponding to a Chartered Accountant in England, is one who has qualified for a certificate from the state and is consequently engaged to check on and certify the accuracy of a firm's books.

Account Sales—Record delivered by a broker or commission merchant to the owner of a consignment of goods, showing the amount and sale prices of goods sold and deductions for commissions and freight and other expenses.

Actuary—One whose profession is to calculate insurance risks and premiums.

Adjust (in insurance)—To determine the sum to be paid in settlement of a loss covered by a policy. **Adjustor, Adjuster**—one who makes the settlement in claims arising out of losses or complaints with the purpose of avoiding possible litigation.

Administrator, Administratrix—A person appointed by a court to settle an estate.

Advertising—Promotion of business through notices in the public prints, on posters, by radio, television, or other media. **Classified Advertising**—small advertisements listed alphabetically. **Display Advertising**—large advertisements usually using illustrations and type arrangements for effect. **Poster Advertising**—advertising on large cards posted in public places. **Outdoor Advertising**—very large advertising posted on roadside structures, on top of buildings, on sides of wall, etc. **Car Card Advertising**—small poster inserted in panels on cars, buses, railroad cars, etc. **Radio Advertising**—advertising over the radio with an "advertiser" paying the cost of programs as "sponsor." **Television Advertising**—advertising over television with an "advertiser" paying the cost of programs as "sponsor." **Mail Order Advertising**—advertising by mail or periodical advertisements, leading to purchases transacted by mail.

Affiant—A signer of an affidavit.

Affidavit—An attestation of the truth of a written statement.

Affiliate—A company in financial association with another.

Agent—Person or company acting for another person or company.

Agreement—Mutual consent to terms of trade or employment, usually in written form.

Allocation—Apportionment of goods in short supply so that all companies, when the government is the allocator, or all customers, when a company is the allocator, may secure a share assigned according to their regular consumption or their comparative immediate needs.

Allowance—A customary deduction from the gross weight of goods; in law, a sum in addition to regular taxable costs awarded by the court; a reduction in cost allowed the purchaser by the seller.

Amortization—Gradual liquidation of a mortgage or other debt by periodic payments in addition to interest.

Announcer—A person hired by a radio station or commercial sponsor to introduce radio programs and performers.

Annuity (in insurance)—Annual or periodic income to the insured for life or for a specified long term.

Appeal—Resort to a higher court for review of a lower court's decision in the hope of having it reversed, or the case retried.

Appraise—To set a value on goods, land, the estate of a deceased person; to estimate loss as by fire, etc.; **Appraisal**—act of appraising or the stated result of appraising; **Appraiser**—one designated by court or appointed by agreement to set a value on property.

Appreciate—To increase in value; **Appreciation**—a rise in value.

Arbitrage—Purchase of stock in one market for profitable resale in another.

Arbitration—Submission of a dispute to judgment by a third party agreed on by both parties to the dispute.

Arraignment—Formal summoning of accused into court where indictment is read to him and he is called upon to plead "guilty" or "not guilty."

Arrival Notice—Announcement by transportation company to consignee when shipment reaches destination.

Arson—Deliberate burning of a house (in some states, of any property); a statutory crime.

Assess—To set a value for taxation; to impose a fine; to impose a contribution as a "lodge assessment." **Assessment**—a valuation of property; a fine; an imposed contribution; **Assessor**—one appointed or elected to value property for taxation.

Asset Currency (in banking)—Currency secured exclusively by the general assets of the issuing bank as distinguished from that secured by special deposit of government bonds, commercial paper, etc.

Assets (Property)—In accounting, items on balance sheet of business showing book values of its resources as at a given date; **Fixed or Permanent Assets**—land, building, machinery, capital stock of another company which can be used repeatedly; **Current, Liquid or Floating Assets**—cash or materials which can be used only at one time; **Quick Assets**—cash or goods which can be immediately disposed of without loss.

Association—Organization of a large number of people

to transact business; if not incorporated, members are liable for its debts as in a partnership.

Attachment—Court order authorizing seizure of property, usually pending outcome of trial.

Auction—Public sale of property by competitive bidding of prospective buyers.

Auctioneer—A person whose job it is to conduct auction sales.

Audit—A verification of accounts; to make an audit.

Auditor—A person authorized to examine accounts.

Backlog—Amount of orders remaining to be filled.

Balance (in bookkeeping)—To prepare an accounting of assets and liabilities; the money in a bank account left after current withdrawals.

Balance Sheet—Statement of financial condition showing current assets and liabilities.

Bank—Institution where money or other property is deposited **A National Bank** is one organized under the National Bank Act; it functions as a commercial bank but may have trust and savings departments, depending on the laws of the state in which it operates. **A State Bank** is organized under state laws; it operates as a commercial bank, but may have trust and savings departments. **A Commercial Bank** does business primarily in short-term and seasonal loans to business organizations. **A Savings Bank** does business primarily in savings and their investment, but may also do commercial banking where state law permits. **A Trust Company** acts as fiduciary agent for trust funds of individuals or corporations; if part of commercial bank, trust funds are separate from bank funds. The **Federal Reserve Bank** is a banker's bank acting under the Federal Reserve Act as agent for the government in relations with other banks. The **Land Bank** lends money on real estate mortgages under terms of the Federal Farm Loan Act.

Bank Discount—Interest deducted in advance.

Banker—Officer of a bank. **Investment Banker** is one who supplies capital in securities, and finances transactions or advises on investments. **Private Banker** generally lends money to finance international projects, may also engage in commercial banking.

Bankruptcy—Condition of a company unable to meet its debts. In **Voluntary Bankruptcy,** the company petitions to be declared bankrupt; in **Involuntary Bankruptcy,** a creditor or group of creditors is the petitioner.

Bargain—Agreement or terms of a sale; purchase of material at an advantage.

Barter—Direct exchange of commodities without use of money.

Bear—One with a pessimistic attitude toward business; one who anticipates downswings in the market, as opposed to Bull.

Beneficiary—One in whose benefit a gift, trust fund income, or insurance money, is drawn.

Bequeath—To will personal property (property other than realty).

Bid—A possible offer at which goods will be supplied or work performed.

Big Board—A term for the New York Stock Exchange.

Bill—Account of or invoice for goods sold or work done. Abbreviations for "bill or exhcange," now chiefly designating piece of paper money.

Bill of Lading—Certificate drawn up and signed by transportation company, enumerating articles being shipped; acts as contract and receipt for shipment.

Binder—A sum of money or other valuable consideration binding parties to a contract.

Black Market—Trading that violates legal restrictions such as price ceilings, etc.

Blanket—Covering everything, rather than a specified item, such as blanket insurance, etc.

Block (in currency)—Legal prohibition or restriction of foreign credit, currency, securities or other property, usually during war; e.g., blocked currency.

Blue Chip—A stock regarded as an especially good investment.

Board of Directors—Group of persons directing affairs of a company, corporation, or association.

Board Room—Room in which Board of Directors meets; room in brokerage office containing board on which is posted records of transactions, prices, etc.

Board of Trade—Organization for advancement of business, usually of an industry or geographical area such as a town or state.

Bourse—The Paris Stock Exchange

Bond—An interest-bearing certificate of indebtedness; a bond differs from stock in not representing ownership. In actuality, bonds are long-term interest-bearing notes representing loans; or goods being manufactured, stored, or transported under care of bonded agencies.

Bonded Debt—Bond issue representing indebtedness.

Bonus—Extra goods shipped without charge on an order; sum given to employee in addition to contracted wages or salary.

Bookkeeper—One who keeps "books" or accounts of a company; generally distinguished from an accountant in having less formal training and lower status.

Book Value—Value given to assets on the books of owner, may be above or below current market value.

Boycott—Organized effort to prevent purchases of goods produced by a certain firm or industry and usually arising out of labor trouble.

Brand Name—Name of manufactured article registered to prevent copying.

Breach of Contract—Refusal to carry out terms of a contract in whole or in part.

Brief—Lawyer's statement of his client's case, containing legal citations supporting it.

Broker—Agent; one who buys or sells for another on commission.

Bucket Shop—A dishonest brokerage house where the customer's money is gambled with, against the customer's interest.

Budget—Plan for the expenditure of income.

Building and Loan Association—Association of investors whose savings are used to finance home construction and make loans on improved real estate.

Bull—One with optimistic attitude toward business; one who anticipates upswings in the market; opposite of Bear.

Bullion—Bars of gold and silver intended for coinage.

Business—Commercial transaction; organization conducting commercial transactions.

Business cycle—Recurrent succession of business fluctuations loosely divided into prosperity, crisis, liquidation, depression, recovery.

Call—Purchased rights to demand a certain amount of goods at a fixed price or within a fixed time; demand for payment of money as on a stock-holder, member of a mutual insurance company, etc., to pay installment of subscription to capital, or a contribution to meet losses.

Call Loan—One which may be terminated by either party at any time.

Call Money—Money that must be returned when demanded.

Cancel—To annul an order for goods or services.

Capacity—Calculated space of any form of container from warehouse or ship to carton.

Capital—A stock of accumulated wealth; amount of property and funds as distinguished from income.

Capitalism—An economic system in which capital plays a leading part in production and distribution.

Capitalist—One who uses capital for investment.

Capital Stock—Shares of a corporation considered as an aggregate.

Capital Surplus—Profits, such as from sale of stock above par value, other than earned surplus.

Carrier—A company transporting passengers or freight, e.g., railroad, airlines, bus or trucking company, etc.

Cartel—International combination allocating markets and supplies, and fixing prices in order to eliminate competitive buying and selling.

Catalogue—A list, usually with illustrations and textual description, of items for sale at announced prices.

Ceiling—Maximum wage, rent, etc., fixed by the government.

Certified Check—Bearing the signature or stamp of the cashier of the bank on which it is drawn. Its significance is that the sum has been withdrawn from the account of the drawer and the bank assumes responsibility for payment.

Chain Store—Branch of a large system of stores belonging to a single ownership.

Chamber of Commerce—A board of trade; an association to promote the commerce of a community, state or nation.

Charter—Certificate from the state approving the organization of a company and authorizing it to do business in the approved form.

Check—A standard form of written order to a bank to make a designated payment out of a depositor's balance.

Circulation—In a periodical, the number of purchasers by subscription or individual sales; in a store, movement of customers in and out.

Clearing House—Organization maintained by a banking group to exchange checks and adjust accounts among its members.

Closed Corporation—One in which all stock is privately held in a few hands; it usually may not be disposed of by holders without the consent of the other holders.

C.O.D.—Abbreviation for "cash on delivery." In C.O.D. transactions, goods must be paid for at the time of delivery.

Code—An arrangement of words, letters or other symbols to achieve secrecy or brevity in communication; a set of rules governing the conduct of a business.

Codicil—Addition to a will, modifying some provision in it.

Collateral—Property used as security for a loan.

Collective Bargaining—Negotiations between employers and a committee of their workers and/or representatives of the union.

Co-Maker—One who shares obligations of another by endorsing a contract.

Commercial Paper—Promissory notes of a large, reputable firm; dealt in by note brokers and sold to banks which discount them and, in that way, realize interest on them.

Commission—Percentage or allowance made to broker or agent for transacting business for another, e.g., salesman's commission.

Company—Association of persons for carrying on commercial or industrial enterprise; may be partnership, corporation or other joint enterprise.

Complaint (in law)—Statement of the cause of an action; the person initiating the complaint is called the complainant. In commerce, customer's charge of faulty goods, delivery or other service.

Comptroller—Auditor with the rank of executive.

Consign—To send or address goods by bill of lading, etc., to an agent in another place to be stored, sold or otherwise cared for.

Consignee—One to whom goods are shipped.

Consignment—Transaction in which purchase is not final; unsold goods may be returned to consignor.

Consumer—Ultimate purchaser or user of merchandise.

Contingent Order (in advertising)—Space in small circulation media to be paid for by returns from the advertisement.

Contract—Witnessed agreement, usually in writing, the terms of which are legally enforceable.

Contractor—One who specializes in a certain type of work; e.g., building contractor. **Sub-contractor**—one who performs part of a piece of work; e.g., plumbing sub-contractor.

Convenience Merchandise—Goods kept in a store for the convenience of certain customers.

Cooperative—A business enterprise or association with the object of producing, purchasing, selling, or occupying quarters at common savings to members by eliminating middle-man fees and profits.

Copy—Text of advertising; duplicate of an original letter or of an article of commerce. Ordinarily, carbon copy duplication for typing.

Copyright—Exclusive publication rights, now extended to cover plays, movie scenarios and movie films and radio and television scripts; other pieces of creative work are copyrighted **after** publication. Application must be made to Register of Copyrights, Library of Congress, Washington, D.C.

Corner—To secure such control of stock or commodities as to be able to dictate quotation prices.

Corporation—A business association operating on a state franchise and with liability limited to the amount of the investment.

Co-Sign—To assume joint responsibility in indebtedness by adding one's signature to the note of another.

Cottage Industry—One where operations are performed by workers at home.

Countermand—To reverse a personal order.

Courts—Where cases involving offenses against the law or claims protected by the law are tried. Courts where large claim cases are tried include Superior, Circuit, certain District, Chancery or County courts. Courts where small claim cases are tried are Justice courts, presided over by a Justice of the peace, and include Magistrate's court and certain District courts.

Covenant—Promise of some future action, made in contracts and other legal papers.

Coverage—The amount and type of protection against risks agreed on in an insurance policy.

Credit—Financial standing influencing sales to a concern on deferred payment; permission to defer payment for a certain period.

Creditor—One who extends credit; lender.

Credit Line—Amount of credit extended; e.g., "X's credit line is $2,000." Also, reproduction of signature, symbol or other acknowledgment in print to signify the originator or owner of writing, photographs or illustrations.

Credit Rating—Summary of credit line as published in Dun & Bradstreet or other credit house ratings and reports.

Cum Div—With dividend declared or pending.

Curb Market—The usual reference is to the American

Stock Exchange (formerly New York Curb Exchange), formerly conducted out-of-doors but now housed in a building of its own; it is the second largest stock market in the United States.

Custom—Generally accepted practice, company practice; customer's account.

Customer—Person or concern purchasing goods.

Cut—In printing, zinc etching, or copper or zinc halftone, usually reproducing a picture or hand-lettering.

Cutback—Reduction in production schedule; reduction in salary or other compensation.

Damage—Loss in merchandise, machinery, service, productive capacity or trade standing. Compensation for such damage may be claimed depending on the circumstances, in a court of law.

Dead Spot—Store location at point of little traffic.

Dead Stock—Unsaleable merchandise.

Debenture—Synonym for debt; documentary evidence of debt.

Debit and Credit Memoranda—Issued by companies to effect necessary adjustments in the course of business transactions.

Decontrol—Removal of government restrictions on prices, rents, etc.

Deduction—Sum or money subtracted from amount to be paid for goods or services.

Deed—Contract by which real estate is conveyed by one party to another; **Warranty Deed** contains a guarantee to clear title ownership; **Quick Claim Deed** relinquishes rights of former owner without guaranteeing clear title to purchaser; **Joint Tenancy Deed** transfers property to two or more owners with the provision that the survivor will own the entire property; **Trust Deed** is given as security for a debt and is a form of mortgage; **Tax Deed** is received by purchaser at a tax sale.

Defalcation—Misappropriation of money placed in trust; the sum misappropriated.

Default—To fail in fulfilling a contract or other financial obligation.

Deficit—Amount by which expenses exceed income, liabilities exceed assets, production falls below expectation.

Deflation—Decline in prices, volume of production, etc., usually accompanied by unemployment.

Delaware Corporation—A corporation chartered in Delaware to take advantage of low incorporation fees and tax rates.

Demand—Desire to purchase commodity together with capacity to pay for it.

Demand Bill or Draft—A bill payable at sight, or on demand.

Demand Item—Article in constant demand, which must be carried in stock constantly.

Demand Loan—Loan payable on demand.

Demand Note—Note payable on demand.

Demurrage—Charge by transportation company for detention of carriers beyond allotted time.

Deposit—Money or equivalent entrusted for safe-keeping with another, as in a bank; money given as partial payment in a transaction or as a binder in a contract.

Deposition—Testimony given by witness unable to appear in court.

Depreciation—Decline in value, usually as a result of loss through wear, neglect, exposure, etc. Machinery is usually calculated to suffer an annual depreciation of 10% in value through wear.

Depression—Deep and prolonged deline of industrial and general business activity.

Deteriorate—To spoil or lose quality with time, e.g.,

food and certain manufactured articles such as photographic film.

Detriment—Damage by intangible cause, such as injury to a firm's reputation through rumors.

Devise—To will property in real estate.

Director—Person entrusted with determining policies and decisions of a firm.

Disbursements—Payments to meet bills.

Discount—Allowance for cash or quick payment; **Trade Discounts** are discounts from wholesale prices allowed to customers and scaled according to amount of purchases and other considerations.

Distributor—Person or company through whom goods reach the consuming public; **Wholesale Distributors** supply **Retail Distributors** who serve the public directly.

Dividend—Money paid to shareholders or depositors as share of profits.

Dock Receipt—Signed by steamship company for freight delivered to dock.

Draft—Papers by which one party, usually the seller, orders another party, usually the buyer, to deliver to a third party, usually a bank, a sum to be credited to the account of the first party. Used to assure payment and to secure settlement of unpaid accounts, since rejection of a draft when presented by the bank is recorded and affects credit standing.

Drawee—Bank on which check or draft is drawn.

Drawer—Person who draws money from his bank account by check.

Dry Goods—Commodities made from fabrics.

Due Bill—In brokerage business, a type of IOU by broker, promising to deliver certain stocks not available at time of sale; also used for promised future delivery of dividends, etc.

Dummy—Sample of proposed book, magazine, or booklet to show size, format, and sample pages.

Dummy Corporation—One organized solely for intermediate purposes, and not for open business activity.

Duplicate—Copy or identical likeness, e.g., duplicate of bill.

Duty—Payment imposed by the government on goods imported, exported, or consumed, such as customs duties, excises, etc.

Earned Income—Income derived from wages, salary, or fees in return for labor, advice or management services.

Earned Surplus—Balance of profits and income remaining after deducting losses, dividends, and transfers to capital stock, etc.

Earnest Money—Deposit or binder; a sum of money paid to seal a bargain and to be deducted from purchase payment.

Economy—Organization of the production, distribution, and consumption of goods in a community.

Efficiency Engineer—A person whose profession it is to plan or change production methods to secure greater economy and efficiency.

Embezzle—To fraudulently appropriate to one's own use property entrusted to him.

Endorse (also Indorse)—To sign one's name as a payee or to indicate co-responsibility for payment on a check, bill, note, or other document.

Enterprise—In association with the word "free" or "private" has come to replace "capitalism" to differentiate the non-socialist from the socialist type of economy.

Entrepreneur—One who takes commercial risks; enterpriser.

Entry—Item in a business record.

Equity—In real estate, difference between value of property and owner's debt on it. In margin buying difference between market value of a stock and customer's indebtedness for its purchase.

Escrow—Papers or money in keeping of responsible third party such as a bank, held until certain conditions are fulfilled.

Estate—Property in lands or tenements, sometimes inaccurately used for property other than lands or tenements; total property left by a deceased person.

Estimate—Statement of amount of goods to be produced or stored or of sum for which certain work will be done.

Ex-Bonus
Ex-Coupon
Ex-Dividend
Ex-Interest
Ex-Privileges
Ex-Rights
} Earnings or privileges not included in the purchase of particular shares.

Exchange—Transfer of goods; place where business interests of a certain sort meet for transaction, e.g., stock exchange, cotton exchange, etc.

Executor (Executrix)—One designated to carry out terms of a will.

Execution—Carrying out a term of a will or a court order.

Expedite—To accelerate production or distribution of goods or rendering of service.

Expediter—One whose job it is to expedite or facilitate business and other transactions.

Export-Import Bank of Washington—Organized by the government in 1934 to facilitate foreign trade.

Express—Shipment by fast or unobstructed transportation; via Railway Express Agency.

Facsimile—Exact copy not necessarily of same size; photostat can serve as satisfactory facsimile.

Factor—Commercial agent who sells or buys goods for others on commission; commission agent.

Factor—Building where manufacture of goods is carried on.

Fail—To become insolvent.

Fee—Compensation for professional or special services; fixed charge for services of a public officer, e.g., sheriff's fee.

Feeder—Branch line in railroad, bus, or air transport that connects with trunkline.

Fee Simple—Unrestricted title to property.

Felony—Crime whose penalty is death or prison sentence.

Fiduciary—In trust; a fiduciary is a trustee.

Finance—Management of money matters.

Financial Rating—Financial information carried in directory such as *Moody's Manual.*

Firm—Correct meaning is partnership; in common usage, any business organization.

Fiscal—Relating to finance, e.g., U.S. fiscal year, period in which annual taxes are collected.

Fixtures—Fixed equipment in business or professional premises.

Foreclosure—Transfer of property to mortgagee when mortgagor defaults on interest payment.

Franchise—Special commercial rights granted by a city to operator of a public conveyance, e.g., a bus line; special rights granted by a manufacturer to a dealer.

Freight Bill—Prepared by transportation company and rendered to receiver or sender, depending on who is paying the freight charges.

Freight Claim—Also called "Loss and Damage Claim" or "Overcharge Claim," claim on transportation company for loss, damage or overcharge.

Fund—Cash or specified assets set aside for a specific purpose.

Funded Debt—Fund set up for payment of long-term indebtedness.

Funded Reserve—A reserve for which a fund has been invested to earn income.

Futures—In commodity exchange, contracts for subsequent delivery, as of a crop not yet harvested.

Garnishee—To take over property or money to satisfy a debt or a claim. A claimant may "garnishee" a defendant's wages.

Gold Standard—Rating of currency in terms of supposed value in gold.

Good will—Intangible asset resting on a special earning power gained through advertising, reputation, good business methods, favorable location, business standing, etc.

Gray Market—Trading by undercover methods, in between black market and regular market methods.

Gross—As a number, 12 dozen or 144; as an adjective, indicating a complete sum before deductions have been made, e.g., gross income before deductions of taxes, expenses, etc.

Handbill—Printed announcement handed out to passers-by.

Handicrafts—Goods produced by hand, e.g., certain pottery, woven goods, embroidery, basket work, etc.

Hedging—Stock trading in which sales or purchases are made to offset or "hedge" against possible loss in other transactions. "Puts and calls" are a form of hedging.

Heir—Person entitled by law or terms of a will to an inheritance.

High Pressure—To make sales of goods not actually needed or desired.

Holding Company—One organized to buy and hold stock of another company.

Holographic Will—One entirely in the handwriting of the testator, not valid in some states.

Huckster—One who prepares radio or television advertising, usually with methods of exaggerated showmanship.

Hypothecation—Pledging of collateral. Governments may "hypothecate" tax revenues as security for a loan. Property may be "hypothecated" for payment of a debt. Its earnings may be so used and the property remain with the debtor; but if payment is defaulted, the creditor may demand sale of the property to secure payment of the debt.

Identification—Driver's license, social security card or other document required as identification in check payments at stores, hotels, or other public places.

Implement—To find means to carry out an agreement.

Impulse Item—Something marketed to appeal to spontaneous decision of customer, usually novelties and luxuries as opposed to staples or necessities.

Income Group—Classification of people according to earnings.

Incorporate—To secure a charter of incorporation from a state, and to organize operations under its provisions.

Indemnify—To make secure against loss or damage; to make good a loss or damage.

Indenture—Sealed agreement of which each party concerned holds a signed copy.

Index—Stock market term referring to listed price quotations of securities traded on the market and analyzed for trends.

Indictment—Formal grand jury charge against a person accused of a major crime.

Industry—Collectively, manufacturing as contrasted to

agriculture; any branch of production, e.g., shoe industry, paper industry, etc.

Inflation—Rise in prices where income advance fails to keep up with prices.

Injunction—Court order restraining certain action.

Insert—Something added in a document; an enclosure in a mailing.

Insolvency—Inability to meet current financial obligations.

Installment—Periodic payment on a time-payment purchase. The British equivalent is "hire-purchase."

Institutional Advertising—Directed not at immediate sales but at increasing prestige leading to consideration of a company as an established institution.

Instrument—Person or document useful in accomplishing a stated purpose.

Interest—Payment by borrower for use of borrowed money measured in percentages and units of time; **simple** interest is payment on principal alone; **compound** interest is payment of accrued interest added to capital; **penal** interest is payment of special interest by defaulting debtor.

Interstate Commerce—Commerce across state boundaries.

Intestate—Descriptive of a property holder who dies without leaving a will. Division of property will then be made according to state inheritance laws.

Intrastate Commerce—Commerce within a state.

Inventory—Record of merchandise on hand and in stock rooms; **perpetual** inventory is one maintained by recording every sale and receipt of goods on an inventory card. Usually inventories are made at periodic intervals.

Investment—Money or other property risked with expectations of profit.

Investment Trust—Company whose business is investment in securities and bond issue, and which markets its own securities on the basis of these investments.

Invoice—A bill itemizing goods shipped and their prices.

IOU—Document bearing the letters "IOU" and a notation of a sum of money. If signed, an IOU has legal status as a debit account.

Island Counter—Table displaying or carrying goods for sale in such a position in a store that customers may walk around it.

Joint Stock Company—Large partnership with some of the features of a corporation.

Journal—Bookkeeping record in which transactions are first entered.

Judgment—Court decision; in a civil trial for damages, the sum awarded to the plaintiff.

Jury—Of two kinds. The **grand** jury consists of 12 to 23 persons who serve as an investigating body and dismiss or indict a suspect, depending on the evidence at hearings. Functions only in cases involving major crimes. **Petit** jury, an ordinary jury, usually consisting of 12 persons who hear civil suits and cases of minor law-breaking.

Kickback—Unauthorized payment out of wages, prices, or fees as extortion or bribery.

Know-How—Technical skill gained through training and experience.

Kraft—Strong brown paper used in packing for shipping.

Landlord—Owner of real estate; usually reference is to owner of specified building.

Layout—Sketch of a proposed advertisement, booklet, etc., in store merchandising, arrangement of merchandise.

Lease—A contract for the temporary conveyance of property, usually in consideration of rent.

Ledger—Account book. In larger sense, accounting in general.

Legacy—Inheritance through a will.

Legal Standard—Measure of value in gold or silver established by a government for the rating of its currency.

Legal Tender—Money that may lawfully be used in settlement of debts.

Lessee—Tenant under a lease.

Lessor—One who grants a lease.

Letters Patent—Document transferring title to public lands or rights to inventions (see Patent).

Liability—Indebtedness; **current** liabilities are short term debts such as taxes, accounts payable, etc., to be met within the year; **fixed** liabilities are long term debts such as mortgages, bonds, etc.; **deferred** liabilities are advance payments such as rent or interest before they come due.

Libel—Written statement held to be damaging to person or business about which it is made. To be distinguished from **slander,** which is a damaging statement made orally.

License—Legal permission to sell certain goods, e.g., a liquor license; or to practice a profession; or to sell goods on the street, e.g., a peddler's license, etc.

Lien—Legal right to property in payment of debt; usually has priority over other claims, e.g., tax lien, mechanics lien, etc.

Limit Order—Order to buy or sell stock at or above or below a specified price.

Line—Type of merchandise offered for sale, e.g., line of pearl buttons.

Liquid—Convertible into cash, e.g., liquid assets.

Liquidate—To convert assets into cash, generally in reference to business in financial difficulty and in need of ready cash.

List Price—Selling price as listed in catalogue.

Loan—Money lent on interest.

Lockout—Shutting out of employees during a labor dispute. Now illegal.

Logotype—Trademark or symbol used by a firm in its advertising.

Long and Short—To be **long** is to hold stock in expectation of a rise; to be **short** is to sell stocks one does not own, in a falling market, in expectation of buying them in at a still lower quotation and profiting from the difference.

Lots—In real estate, specified arrangement of ground; in the stock market, number of shares traded in. **Round** lots are those taken in round numbers, such as 100 shares; **odd** lots are transactions in lots under 100.

Maintenance of Membership—Clause in labor contract making it obligatory upon workers to keep in good standing in the union in order to retain jobs.

Malfeasance—Wrongful action: To be distinguished from **nonfeasance,** failure to perform an action agreed upon; and **misfeasance,** performance of an agreed action in such a way as to violate the rights of others.

Malice Aforethought—Intentional or planned injury.

Manifest—Invoice of a ship's cargo, for evidence at customs house.

Manufacture—Conversion of raw materials into a finished product, e.g., converting iron ore into steel plate.

Margin—Money deposited with a broker as security on stock purchases; thus margin may be forfeited if stock quotations take an adverse turn.

Markdown—Lowering of prices, usually to make sales for slow-moving goods.

Market—In general, the range for buying and selling; in particular, the range for buying and selling in a particular field, e.g., the stock market, the cotton market, etc.

Market Order—Order to sell at the market price of the day on which the order is issued.

Mark-Up—Amount added, in selling price, to wholesale price to cover overhead and profit.

Marshall Plan—Plan to extend economic aid abroad, initiated by George C. Marshall as United States Secretary of State in 1947.

Mass Market—The general public considered as potential consumers.

Mass Production—Large scale, mechanized production designed to lower production costs to permit purchase by the majority of potential consumers.

Maximum Hours—Limit of time workers may be employed without overtime payment.

Mediation—Resort to third party in disputes between employer and worker; not as conclusive as arbitration.

Melon—Extra dividend on stock, distributing surplus earnings or profits.

Merger—Consolidation of two or more companies into one.

Metes and Bounds—Dimensions and boundaries of a parcel of real estate.

Mill—A machine for grinding, pressing, stamping, or almost every repetitive process; a building or group of buildings containing manufacturing machinery.

Minimum Wage—Lowest limit of wages that may be paid to workers.

Minor—Person under legal age to assume certain responsibilities. The age varies—it is different for marriage, for business transaction, or for liability to criminal charges.

Model Change-Over—Reorganization of manufacturing process for the manufacture of a new model (sometimes called **mark**) of an article.

Monopoly—Exclusive control of an industry or some form of trade.

Morris Plan Company—Makes small personal loans for repayment in installments.

Mortgage—Transfer of rights in property as security for a loan or for other considerations. **Real estate** mortgages are on land and improvements upon it; **chattel** mortgages cover other forms of property; **crop** mortgage is a chattel mortgage on crops; a **first** mortgage is one which has priority in any claims on the property over subsequent mortgages (**second** and **third** mortgages, etc.)

Mortgage Certificates—Certificates for small shares of large first mortgages or first mortgage bonds. Issued by mortgage customers to investors.

National Advertising—Advertising in periodicals or over radio and television, nationwide in scope.

Negotiable—Salable or transferable as payment for debts.

Net—Sum, after deductions have been made, e.g., net income after expenses, taxes, etc. have been taken out.

Nonfeasance—see Malfeasance.

Notary Public—A person authorized by state law to witness and certify to the authenticity of signatures affixed to documents or statements in his presence.

Number—Item of manufacture; usually refers to item in a catalogue.

O.K.—With signature, constitutes endorsement or approval of something presented in writing. According to popular belief, from Old Kinderhook, birthplace of Martin van Buren, and used by his supporters in his campaign for the presidency.

Omnibus Clause—Section in a contract covering several items not specifically covered elsewhere in the document.

One Day Order—Order for stock transaction on a certain day, and cancelled if not executed on that day.

Open Order—Order for a stock transaction to be executed at any time and to hold good until notice of withdrawal is received. Also called GTC (Good till cancelled) order.

Option—First choice or right to obtain goods or services without competition for a specified period, e.g., ten days' option.

Order—Customer's itemized descripton of goods desired for purchase.

Overhead—Fixed expenses, such as rent, salaries, maintenance costs, etc.

Overstock—Goods in excess of current demand.

Over-the-Counter Trading—Trading by private dealers in securities not listed on the stock exchange.

Package—Combined merchandise and/or services, offered as a unit, in a "package deal," e.g., radio or television program in which script, actors, announcer, etc., are all provided as a unit in a "package program."

Pamphlet—Paper-covered booklet used as advertising or to convey information about a business.

Panic—Sudden widespread fright over financial situation causing artifical depression through sales of securities and other property.

Paper—Documents of any sort, negotiable notes, bills, etc.

Par—Normal or face value of securities.

Parcel—Package of goods; piece of property; to apportion merchandise in small lots to provide some supply to all accounts.

Parity—Rate of exchange at which different currencies acquire equal purchasing power.

Partnership—Defined in Uniform Partnership Act: "An association of two or more persons to carry on as coowners of a business for profit"; except in "limited partnership" in which liability of certain partners is restricted to the amount of capital contributed, partners are individually liable for debts contracted by the business.

Passbook—A book borne by customer, containing records of credit purchases; also bankbook.

Passing a Dividend—Failure to declare an expected dividend.

Patent—Right granted by the government for a term of seventeen years, for the exclusive production of an invented article or for an improvement of an article, not renewable.

Patent Attorney—One specializing in the preparation of patent applications and in the search to determine that the invention is new and does not infringe on previous patents.

Patent Office—Government bureau that registers patent applications and issues "letters patent," granting patent rights.

Patron—Customer.

Patronage—Business given by a customer.

Pattern (in industry)—A model made for duplication as in metal casting, dress manufacture, etc.

Pattern-Maker—One who makes patterns needed in industry.

Pay—to make an acceptable return, usually in money, for property delivered, or services rendered; remuneration such as wages or salaries.

Payee—Person to whom money has been, or is to be, paid.

Paymaster—One under whose management wage or salary payments are made.

Payroll—Paymaster's list of those entitled to wages or salary.

Peculation—Embezzlement.

Peg—To hold market prices at a set value by manipulating purchases or sales.

Pension—Payment made through grant, insurance, or other arrangement to person retired from employment, business, or public office.

"Percents"—Investments such as bonds or other securities, described by their interest rate, e.g., 3%.

Perpetual Trust—Trust estate with no prescribed duration.

Personal Property or Personal Estate—Property other than real estate.

Personnel—Employed staff.

Petition—Written application to a court instituting an action or requesting action upon a matter before it.

Petition in Bankruptcy—Written application by a debtor or his creditors that he be declared bankrupt.

Petty Cash—Cash fund used to make small payments.

Photo Engraving—Process of reproducing pictures through photography, where printing surface is in relief in contrast to lithography or gravure.

Photostat—Photographic process for reproducing documents, drawings, etc.; a document or drawing so reproduced.

Pica—12-point type, usually used on typewriters and in other print where readability is desired.

Picket—Person, during a strike, standing or walking back and forth before entrance of business to discourage non-striking employees or customers from entering.

Piece-Goods—Fabrics sold by pieces or fixed lengths.

Pilot Plant—A business operated to determine rates to be charged in its industry.

Pipeline—Piping over long distances used in the transportation of oil or gas.

Piracy—Infringement on copyrighted or patent property rights.

Pit—Section of Chicago Board of Trade where a specific commodity is traded; e.g., wheat pit.

Pivotal—A stock whose quotations influence the course of the market.

Planned Economy—Economical organization, usually of a state, in which production is arranged to prevent or reduce fluctuation and waste.

Plant—The building, machinery, etc., taken together that are used in a unit of industrial production.

Plantation—Large scale farming operation, carried on by hired labor; e.g., rubber plantation.

Plastics (in industry)—Synthetic materials mainly produced by molding process.

Pledge—Piece of property given as security for a loan.

Point—Unit used in quoting prices on stocks. In the United States, one point usually stands for $1 a share.

Point System—Method of wage payment by time units of work performed. Also called the "Bedaux System," from its originator.

Policy—Contract of insurance; guiding principles of a concern, usually determined or governed by a Board of Directors.

Pool—Merger of property or financial interests of a group, usually with the expectation of manipulating the market in its favor.

Portal-to-Portal Pay—Payment for time spent, as in mines, in passing to and from the entrance of the actual place of work.

Position—On produce exchanges, undertaking to make delivery in a given month; e.g., October position.

Possession—Such control of property as to give exclusive legal enjoyment of it.

Posthumous—Taking effect after death.

Power of Attorney—Legal authority to act for another, not as a lawyer, but to carry out transactions.

Practice—Professional service; e.g., legal practice; customary procedure of a firm.

Pre-Fab—A prefabricated article, usually a house or small industrial building, to facilitate speedy erection.

Preference Shop—One where, by agreement between union and management, preference is given to union members in employment, promotion, and tenure, but management may employ non-union workers if union cannot supply qualified personnel.

Preferred Stock—Issue which receives preference over common stock in dividends or distribution of assets.

Premium (in insurance)—Money or other consideration paid by the insured according to terms of contract. (In economics)—Greater value of one currency over another; additional payment for loan of money. (On the stock market)—Amount above par that securities are being quoted at; sum paid for an option.

Prepaid—Paid in advance.

Price—Value at which goods are exchanged or services rendered.

Pricing—Setting a price on goods.

Primary Markets—Markets in farm produce such as foods or fibers.

Principal—Actual party to transaction as distinguished from agent; money or other property on which interest is earned.

Priority—Precedence as in transportation, goods production, delivery of order, etc.

Privilege—Option on the sale or purchase of securities on specified items.

Probate—Proof established by legal procedures; e.g., probate of a will.

Process—A method of manufacture or of rendering services.

Production—Creation of goods having value to purchasers; e.g., agricultural production, industrial production.

Profit—What remains after production and sales costs have been deducted.

Profit and Loss—Accounting, after a given period, to determine condition of a business.

Promissory Note—Note undertaking payment of a debt at a specified time or occasion.

Promoter—One who initiates organization of a company, floating of securities, or other business undertaking.

Property—Things owned; real property is property in real estate, while personal property or personal estate refers to all other possessions of value.

Proprietor—Owner; one with legal right to possession.

Proxy—To act for another; one whose voting rights are entrusted to another, the usual reference being to voting of stock holders.

Public Domain—The field of property rights belonging to the public at large, such as manufacturing processes or literary properties not, or no longer, covered by patents and copyrights.

Public Utility—Company servicing the general public, such as a railroad, supplier of electricity, etc.

Put and Call—To "put" is to deliver, according to agreement, specified stock at a specified price to a buyer who receives a payment for this service. The privilege of "putting" may be sold to a third party. To "call" is to receive on demand specified stock at a specified price from a seller who is paid for this service. The privilege of "calling" may be sold to a third party.

Pyramid—To engage in transactions in banking or stock market, using gains as "margin" for further purchases or sales, in order to take continuous advantage of a market trend.

Qualified—Fit to do required work.

Quantity—Used relatively, usually in reference to goods in bulk, e.g., "These castings can be supplied in any reasonable quantity."

Quantity Theory of Money—Economic theory that changes in quantity of money in circulation affect price levels and currency values.

Query—To recheck a shipment, a shipper or an account; may refer to goods, invoices, personnel, etc. e.g., "Please query Hobson, rubber tape shipment overdue at warehouse."

Quit Claim—Document in legal form relinquishing some property right.

Quotations—Statements, oral or written, of market prices of stocks, bonds or commodities.

Quotation Board—Board in brokerage office on which market quotations are displayed.

Rebate—Repayment of a percentage of sum received in payment for goods or services. Rebate may be allowed for damage, delay, or savings in shipping costs, etc.

Receipt—Signed paper in evidence that goods or money has been received.

Receipts—Earnings of a business for a given period; e.g., "today's receipts."

Receiver—Person, firm, or bank appointed by courts to conduct a business declared bankrupt.

Recession—Decline in industrial activity, not so drastic as a depression.

Redemption—Payment of outstanding loans; e.g., redemption of a bond issue.

Referee—Appointed by court to hear evidence and render decision in business disputes.

Refund—Return of entire amount paid for goods or services, usually because of their unsatisfactory nature.

Reimburse—Repay money expended by another. An agent will be reimbursed for costs incurred during his operation.

Reorganization—Reestablishment of insolvent business with the consent of creditors and under court supervision, with the aim of avoiding receivership costs and forced sale losses.

Requisition—Order for supplies, materials, etc.

Rescued—Withdrawal of order or instructions.

Restrictive—Limiting. A restrictive covenant is a clause in a document setting certain conditions, as in real estate contracts restricting residence to certain races.

Retail Trade—Trade with consumers.

Retirement—Withdrawal from circulation, e.g., retirement of a currency.

Revenue—Source of income, usually referring to government income from taxation.

Revenue Bond—Short-term issue in anticipation of revenue payments.

Rigged Market—Subject to manipulation so that it does not reflect real values.

Rollback—Price reduction to previous levels, usually by government action.

Royalty—Share of profits paid by manufacturer to inventor (or owner of an invention), author, etc. or to his heirs.

Runaway—Removal of business to a region of low labor costs as an employer measure in labor trouble.

Sabotage—Obstruction, malicious waste of materials, or spoilage of product by workers during labor trouble.

Sales Engineering—Computing and adjusting installation and production costs from plans, as a means of promoting sales of equipment and machinery to a specific industry or factory.

Salvage—Goods rescued from shipwreck or other disaster.

Sample—A representative piece of an article offered for sale; e.g., swatch of cloth.

Scab—Opprobrious term, used in labor relations for person employed in place of strikers or refusing to strike with his fellow workers.

Schedule—Systematic listing of time for production or other performance in manufacturing, transportation, distribution, etc.

Search—To verify status of a property; e.g., mortgage title search, patent search, etc.

Seat—Membership in the Stock Exchange entitling one to share in its assets and privilege of trading there.

Security—(Chiefly used in the plural.) Stock certificates, bonds, or other documentary evidence of indebtedness giving the possessor the right to claim property secured by the document; **listed** security is one which, by meeting certain requirements, is listed for trading on the Stock Exchange.

Self-Mailer—Advertising message that can be sent by mail without enclosure in an envelope. A sticker or stamp is affixed to hold pages or folded edges together.

Shakeout—Minor decline in industrial activity in course of adjustment after inflation.

Shape-up—Hiring of dockworkers by selection of applicants at piers, usually arbitrarily, at the discretion of labor supervisor.

Shortage—Something missing from inventory or from cash, due to theft, loss, or error.

Silver Standard—Rating of currency in terms of a specified value in silver.

Sinking Fund—Fund continually added to and invested toward the payment of bonds or other maturing debts.

Sitdown Strike—One where striking employees stay in or at their places of work to prevent operation of machinery by others.

Slander—Oral statement held to be damaging to person or business about whom it is made. To be distinguished from libel, which is a damaging written statement.

Sleeper—Film, book, novel, or other property or article of trade that gains unexpected commercial success, doing better business than other items for which greater sales were anticipated.

Slowdown—Slowing down of work operations without actual walkout, as a worker tactic in labor dispute.

Smog—Saturation of air with smoke or other industrial exhausts leading to fog conditions.

Social Security—System and fund set up, under the Social Security Act, to insure security in old age. The fund is made up of compulsory contributions by employers and employees

Solicit—To seek business accounts.

Solvency—Capacity to meet financial obligations.

Specie—Metal (hard) money as distinguished from paper currency.

Specimen—Sample of minerals, ores, plants, or other things that are complete units of their kind.

Speculation—Buying or selling with chance of high profits and risk of considerable loss.

Spot Announcement (in radio advertising)—A commercial not part of a sponsored program.

Spot Delivery—In stock market, immediate delivery of stock.

Staple—An established product; e.g., oil is a staple of Texas.

Statement—List of unpaid items in a business account; a financial statement is a listing of assets and liabilities.

Statute of Limitations—Law setting time limit for legal action.

Stipulation—Condition specified in agreement or contract, usually something undertaken by buyer to bolster his credit.

Stock—Share of ownership in an incorporated business; supply of merchandise for sale; **common** stock is ordinary stock as distinguished from **preferred** stock, which takes precedence over it in distribution of assets or dividends; **guaranteed** stock is one whose dividends are guaranteed by another company.

Stockpile—Reserve supply of essential material.

Strike—Refusal by employees to work unless demands, generally for pay increases, vacations, and other benefits are met. Usually accompanied by picketing of the premises of the business affected.

Strike-Breaking—Coercive action with the intention of defeating strike action.

Sublease—To lease all or part of premises one has leased.

Sublet—To rent all or part of premises one has rented.

Subpoena—Court order served on witnesses summoning them to give testimony.

Subsidiary—A company, control of whose stock is held by another company.

Subsidy—Agreed sum paid, over and above market charges, to assure supply or service that would otherwise be unavailable because of lack of profit.

Substandard—Below standard quality.

Supermarket—Departmentalized branch in chain store system, where some departments may be rented as concessions, and doing a gross annual business of a specified figure, usually $100,000.

Supply—Amount of goods for sale at a given price.

Surplus—Oversupply; amount by which assets exceed liabilities and capital; amount of goods on hand above current demand.

Swindle—To defraud; dishonest business transaction.

Swindler—One who defrauds.

Swindle Sheet—Expense account, when padding or the possibility of padding is implied.

Syndicate—Group organized for special financing, such as purchase and resale of certain securities or underwriting of a stock issue, purchasing it at a discount.

Take-Home Pay—What is left of earnings after withholding tax and other deductions have been made.

Tariff—Schedule of duties imposed on importers and exporters.

Tax—To exact payment, usually payment exacted by government to provide revenue for its operations.

Tax Sale—Sale of a property to recover unpaid taxes.

Technological—Referring to technical processes or changes in industry; e.g., technological unemployment.

Tenant—Occupant of premises, generally one who pays rent for the occupancy.

Tenders—Sealed bids or offers for securities.

Terms—Terms of payment; prearranged conditions for payment of a debt; e.g., cash in 30 days, $5 down and $1 a week, etc.

Testator—One who makes a will.

Ticker—Machine in which messages are stamped on paper tape, used in reporting market quotations.

Tie-in Sale—Where additional product must be purchased to effect purchase of a certain article.

Title—All factors combined which accord right to exclusive possession of property.

Tool Engineering—New branch of engineering concerned with perfecting new machinery processes, equipment and use of raw material in preparation for production of a new product or a new model.

Tracer—Investigation designed to trace article undelivered by post office or transportation company; one who makes such an investigation.

Trade Acceptance—Bill of exchange governing purchase price, drawn by seller upon buyer whose endorsement constitutes "acceptance."

Trade Agreement—Agreement between employer and union, fixing wages, hours, working conditions.

Trade Edition or Trade Book—Edition designed for general public as distinguished from educational and professional use.

Trademark—Coined name, monogram, logotype, signature, picture, distinctively designed words or name, symbol, emblem or device, which may be registered in the Government Patent Office for exclusive use by the applicant. Registration term is 20 years and may be renewed.

Trade Name—Name or other symbol under which a firm does business and protected by common law against attempt to deceive customers by use of a similar name by a competing firm.

Trade Paper—Endorsed notes (two or more names) given in payment for merchandise; a periodical published in the interest of a certain branch of business.

Transcript—Letter-perfect copy of a document, which does not seek to reproduce exact appearance of original.

Travelers Checks—Issued by banks, travel agencies, American Express, and Western Union for the convenience of travelers.

Treasury Bills—Short-term government offerings, bearing no interest, but sold at a discount to buyers.

Treasury Certificates—Interest-bearing certificates of indebtedness issued in place of short-term bonds.

Trust—Holding of property by a responsible person or bank (trustee) for the good of another person (beneficiary).

Turnover—Number of times, within a specified period such as a year, in which a given commodity is sold out.

Upgrade—To advance an employee, a work process or a product in rank, earnings, price or quality.

Venue—Place where case is tried. **A change of venue** may be granted with the object of securing a fairer trial.

Volume—Amount of business done.

Voucher—A receipt or other proof of money paid, vouches for the accuracy of the terms of a transaction.

Wages—Payment for labor.

Waive—To voluntarily forego a right.

Warrant—Order for the payment of money or delivery of goods or documents; in banking, primarily written order for the payment of money.

Wash Sale—Fictitious trading to give an appearance of activity to inactive stocks.

Wharfage—Fee for use of piers.

Wholesale—Sale of goods to dealers for resale to retail merchants.

Will—Testament of a property-holder directing the distribution of his property after his death.

Window Dressing—Manipulations in financial statement to give it a more favorable appearance than is due.

Withholding Tax—Income tax payment deducted at source, as from wages, dividends, etc.

Without Prejudice—A contract term signifying that the agreement will not injure any prior or subsequent rights.

Zoning—Laws governing real estate, setting off special areas for special types of occupation; e.g., residence, business, hospitals, etc.

Wills and Estate Planning

Everyone should have an up-to-date will that reflects an estate plan adapted to individual needs and circumstances. The estate plan is a thoughtfully designed arrangement for the distribution of one's assets in such a way as to achieve maximum realization of the planner's objectives. These can include keeping taxes at a minimum; providing financial management for the benefit of a surviving widow and children; selection of a trusted relative, friend, or advisor as executor or guardian; and so on. An estate plan can be simple and inexpensive to draw up; for a larger estate or one with special problems the plan may be extremely complex.

Most persons or couples of reasonable means should have an estate plan—and a will or wills as integral parts of that plan. But whether it is part of an estate plan or not the will is ordinarily a written document that takes effect on the death of the testator, the legal term for the person making out a will. The will's purpose is to distribute one's worldly assets to those whom the testator desires or "wills" to have them.

The estate plan may deal with broader categories of assets than the will. The estate plan may, for example, have provisions covering gifts, insurance, and annuities, special types of contracts such as those providing for the purchase of a business by surviving associates, trusteeship arrangements, and other devices designed to accomplish the testator's purposes. The estate plan may also provide for changes in the estate to be made before the planner's death. The will generally takes effect only on the testator's death.

Estate Planning: Four Main Tools

You can make a beginning toward estate planning by considering the four main tools a planner can use. The four are trusts, lifetime gifts, joint ownership, and wills. Other tools are, of course, available, and each has a valid purpose. Under specific arrangements, for example, death benefits may be paid to named beneficiaries under pension plans, profit-sharing programs, IRAs, tax-sheltered annuities, and deferred compensation arrangements. Some estates use irrevocable living trusts or buy-sell agreements dealing with businesses.

Adding It Up. In general, property is anything you can own. Everything you own belongs in your estate. That includes both real property, or real estate, meaning both land and all the things that are permanently attached to the land, and personal property. The latter includes tangibles, those items that have bulk or substance, and intangibles, things without physical substance. Among common tangibles are furniture, an automobile, cameras, clothing, a boat, and so on. Intangibles are such items as stocks, bonds, life insurance policies, and bank deposits.

A first step in estate planning involves inventorying all your property of whatever kind. With each item you should note the value or estimated value. You should also indicate how the property is owned—outright, in joint tenancy, or otherwise.

Objectives. What do you want to accomplish when you plan your estate? Your objectives should be clear; they often determine what methods you will use to transfer your property, or specific parts of it, to your spouse, relatives, friends, charities, or other beneficiaries. At the least you will want to know who your heirs will be and what each heir will receive.

Some specific objectives help to shape estate plans. A property owner may want to provide financial support for dependents, including both money to live on and funds that would be available in emergencies. Nearly all estate planners hope to reduce such estate transfer costs as federal estate and state inheritance taxes, the expenses of administering the estate, and others. Very basically, a valid objective is to ensure that the estate will have sufficient assets to meet its obligations.

Other objectives may seem obvious. As noted, you will want to name the person or persons who will administer or settle your estate after your death—and under what terms. The disposition of closely held business interests should be provided for. Finally, property distribution should make up parts of the estate plan.

Tool 1: Trusts

As one of the key tools of estate planning, trusts play unique roles. Whatever the type of trust, and there are many kinds for persons in many economic categories, the typical trust instrument places *legal* title in one person, called the *trustee,* and *equitable* title in another person, the *beneficiary.* In each case the "person" may be an individual, a corporation, group, or organization. The *grantor* (or creator or settlor) who establishes the trust gives the trustee the right to hold and administer the trust *corpus,* or principle, for the benefit of the other person or entity.

Three main kinds of trusts are used by the estate planner: living, or *inter vivos* ("between the living"), trusts; testamentary trusts established by will; and insurance trusts. Living trusts are set up while the grantor is alive, and take effect at once. Testamentary trusts take effect on the grantor's death. The corpus of the insurance trust consists of funds from an insurance policy—or funds to be paid out under an insurance policy or policies—and, possibly, other property as well.

Why a trust? To some extent the reasons parallel those that justify estate planning itself. Among the reasons:

• To protect spendthrift heirs or other beneficiaries who may be mentally, physically, or emotionally unable to manage property. The trustee can have total management responsibility.

• To enable the trustee to use discretion and, often, expert knowledge in managing trust property for the benefit of heirs, the grantor, and family members or others.

• To have a device for giving or leaving property to minors with the assurance that the trustee will manage the property until the beneficiaries are old enough to handle the property themselves.

• To take all or part of your estate property out of probate and in that way to save your heirs the costs and delays of going through the probate process.

• To set up a useful tax-saving plan.

Tax Savings

Depending on your financial status and the complexity of the trust you want to set up, you could pay from $100 to $10,000 or more to an attorney to prepare your trust agreement. On average, you would pay about $300 to $500.

Such an expense could definitely be worth it. Remember that the federal government has provided that estates of $500,000 or less were to escape estate taxes in 1986. That figure was to rise to $600,000 in 1987 and subsequent years. In one case a couple had property worth $800,000, all in the husband's name. Assuming that the husband dies first, in 1987 or later, the entire estate passes to the wife. The so-called *marital deduction* allows whole estates of whatever kind to pass to a surviving spouse tax-free. But when the wife dies a different rule applies.

On the wife's death in 1987 or later, the federal exemption would apply only to the first $600,000 of the $800,000 estate. At rates in effect in 1986 the couple's heirs would pay $52,000 in estate taxes on the remaining $200,000.

This couple could have saved all $52,000 in federal taxes by establishing a trust. The couple would have had several choices, including these:

• A *bypass trust* that would set aside $600,000 of the husband's estate as the trust principle, with income from the trust and part of its principle going to the wife during her lifetime. The other $200,000 in the husband's estate would go directly, on his death, to the wife for her unrestricted use. On the wife's death the trust would dissolve and the entire estate would be distributed to the beneficiaries free of federal taxes.

• A *marital deduction trust*, with either of two kinds available: a general power of appointment trust or a so-called QTIP (qualified terminable interest property) trust. Again the couple's beneficiaries would pay no federal estate taxes on the death of the second spouse.

Under the general power of appointment trust, your spouse can decide after you die who will receive the trust's assets after he or she dies. The QTIP, by contrast, makes it possible for you to select the ultimate trust beneficiaries. With the QTIP you can make sure, if desired, that your spouse will not cut off your children by an earlier marriage. Otherwise the general power of appointment and the QTIP trust are virtually identical. Both, for example, qualify for the marital deduction and are included in the surviving spouse's estate. Both also produce income that must go to the surviving spouse.

• A *generation-skipping trust*, under which trust income goes to a grantor's children rather than to the wife and the principle goes to the grantor's grandchildren.

In many cases a grantor can use an *irrevocable life insurance trust* under which the proceeds from insurance policies are removed from the grantor's estate, to be distributed after the second spouse's death to the named beneficiaries. The spouse receives income from the trust until he or she dies.

Selecting the Trustee

The problem of selecting a trustee usually resolves into a choice between an individual and a corporation. The individual, whether the creator of the trust or someone else, might be closer to the trust beneficiaries than a corporate trustee—and might therefore be more responsive to the beneficiaries' needs. The individual might not even charge a fee. Under any circumstances, the person or persons serving as trustees could, as needed, obtain legal, investment, accounting, and other advice from experts.

The corporate trustee could offer different advantages. Such trustees are professional money and property managers. Unlike the individual trustee, they do not, usually, die or become incapacitated; personnel changes do not interrupt their services. Beyond that, they remain unbiased, independent of family pressures, and able to answer to charges of mismanagement. By comparison with the individual trustee who is also a trust beneficiary, the corporate trustee cannot incur personal income tax liabilities in administering trust property. A corporate trustee can, of course, act as cotrustee with an individual or individuals.

Tool 2: Gifts

Lifetime gifts function much like trusts. Essentially, they reduce the value of your estate and thus help to avoid estate taxes. An important difference, however, is that your surviving spouse has no access to the money you have given away. Thus most persons make certain that the surviving spouse will have enough income to live on after the first spouse's death.

In the 1980s the federal government liberalized the laws regulating gifts of property or money. In 1986 individuals could give up to $10,000 each to as many persons as they chose. For couples, the law allowed joint gifts of as much as $20,000 each to any number of donees. You need not report gifts of less than $10,000 to the Internal Revenue Service, but must (whether individual or couple) report all gifts exceeding that sum. After your death, the IRS will add up all the taxable gifts—those exceeding $10,000 per year per person—that you made during your lifetime and (if applicable) subtract the total from your $600,000 (1987) estate tax exemption.

Kinds of Gifts

You can give gifts in many different ways. A *charitable remainder trust* is actually a way to give assets to a charity while ensuring that you or your beneficiaries will receive the income from the gift property for a specified period. At the end of the period the trust dissolves and the charity receives the principle. Very wealthy persons may use a *GRIT* (grantor retained income trust) that sets aside part of the grantor's estate as a gift to a family member or friend. The grantor receives the income from the gift property for a specified period, whereupon it passes out of his or her estate and into the ownership of the beneficiary.

A third method of giving away assets operates on a principle opposite to that of the remainder trust. This *charitable lead trust* provides that a charity will receive the income from the specified property—but not the principle. When the trust ends, your heirs receive the principle. You arrange for a charitable lead trust in your will. Often, your estate enjoys even larger tax deductions than it would under a remainder trust.

Tool 3: Joint Ownership

Joint ownership of property offers both advantages and disadvantages that should be considered in estate planning. Joint ownership (a legal device that exists when two or more persons have ownership rights in property) allows that property to pass automatically to the other joint owner or owners *outside the probate estate* of the first owner to die. The device thus saves the time and expenses often involved in the probate process.

Other advantages may be noted. Some states levy lower inheritance taxes, or no taxes, where property is held jointly. Usually, too, the survivor receives jointly held property free of the claims of the creditors of a deceased joint owner.

Joint, Outright, and Community Property Ownership

Joint ownership is one of four basic ways in which real or personal property may be owned. The other three are outright ownership, community property ownership or rights, and tenancy in common. The three types of joint ownership or tenancy include:

Joint Tenancy with Right of Survivorship. Under joint tenancy with right of survivorship (WROS), the property interest of a descendant passes with his or her death to the surviving joint owner or owners. A married couple typically own their home jointly. When one dies, the property interest of that deceased passes to the survivor, who then owns the property outright in his or her own name.

A joint tenant can destroy the survivorship aspect of a joint tenancy. For example, if one joint tenant sells his or her share in property to a third party, that person and the remaining joint tenant own the property as tenants in common (see below).

Tenancy by the Entirety. A second form of joint tenancy is tenancy by the entirety. Some states provide for this special kind of joint ownership when a wife and husband own property jointly and exclusively. Tenancy by the entirety differs from joint tenancy with right of survivorship in three key ways: the former can only exist between husband and wife; in many states the survivorship rights can be terminated only with the consent of both parties; and, again depending on the laws of the particular state, the husband may have control over the property (and the right to any income from it) during their lifetimes.

Other Joint Interests. Where joint bank accounts or jointly owned government savings bonds are concerned, the owners may again have rights of survivorship. Thus family members commonly hold both types of property under this joint ownership arrangement. With a bank account, either party can make deposits or withdraw funds. On the death of one, the survivor becomes sole owner of the account by operation of law.

With savings bonds, a similar rule applies. Both joint owners have survivorship rights even though the bonds may be registered in co-ownership form and held in the name of "A" or "B." Either A or B could cash the bonds during the lifetime of the other.

Tenancy in Common

Under tenancy in common arrangements, no co-owner has survivorship rights: none acquires the interest of another in case of the other's death. Rather, the interest of a decedent goes to the decedent's heirs as if the interest had been owned outright. The survivor retains his or her share. Tenants in common can own proportionate interests in property—for example, 75 percent and 25 percent respectively.

In outright ownership, one person owns property exclusively in his or her name. Community property is discussed below.

Not a Will

Despite some advantages, joint ownership does not take the place of a will. In cases on record, couples owning property jointly, but having no wills, were involved in serious accidents. One spouse died instantly. The other survived by a few hours or days. The survivor could not make out a will. By law, the property passed to the surviving spouse on the death of the other. On the death of the second spouse, the property typically passed entirely to the second spouse's relatives.

Joint ownership may also produce results contrary to those intended, may save few or no taxes and other expenses, and may even increase taxes dramatically. The effects depend on state laws. But in many states lawyers cannot say for certain what the effects of joint tenancy may be. It may nonetheless be advisable to hold checking accounts and small savings accounts in joint ownership to provide the survivor with ready cash on the death of one joint owner; even if the account is frozen for a time it will normally become available well before the assets of the deceased's estate.

For sentimental or other reasons, a husband and wife usually own the family home jointly. Ownership of other assets should be based on sound legal advice—which also applies to the overall estate plan, including the will.

Joint Ownership—How Much?

No simple rules are available to indicate how much property should be held in joint tenancy. If the federal estate tax is not an important factor, a couple may hold all property jointly. But even if the couple's estate is large enough to be federally taxable, some joint ownership may be appropriate for the reasons noted.

The Economic Recovery Tax Act (ERTA) of 1981 produced some new rules on joint tenancies held by married couples. In particular, the act provided that only one-half of the value of the property held in a taxable joint tenancy is includable in the gross estate of the first spouse to die. This "fractional interest" applies regardless of whether the surviving spouse contributed to the purchase of the property.

As a caveat, joint ownership may actually result in a gift. This occurs where one joint owner has contributed all or a disproportionate share of the cost of purchasing property. If Mrs. Jones, for example, uses her own funds to buy corporate stock in her own and Daughter Joanne's name, and if the ownership is irrevocable, Mrs. Jones has made a gift, for federal tax purposes, to her daughter of one-half the value of the stocks. Her daughter has also gained some control over the stocks.

Different from Community Property

Property owned jointly should not be confused with community property. The latter exists in some western and southwestern states that follow Roman law rather than the English common law where property relationships between husbands and wives are concerned. In common-law states marriage gives husbands and wives certain rights in each other's property that often cannot be changed by a will. This is also true in community property states, but the rights are somewhat different.

In these states one-half the income earned during the marriage by either spouse belongs to the other. All property owned by the couple is presumably community property, of which each owns half. But property owned by either spouse before marriage and kept separate, with the income from such property also kept separate, and property acquired by one spouse individually, without contributions from the other spouse—for example, by gift or inheritance—are the separate properties of each spouse owning it.

In community property states married couples' wills cannot touch the separate property of either spouse or either spouse's share of the community property. But a couple can by contract agree on what is community property and what is the separate property of either. Such contracts take effect when written and signed. They are an essential tool of estate planning in community property states. But they do not obviate the need for a will any more than joint tenancy does.

The nine community property states are Arizona, California, Idaho, Louisiana, Nevada, New Mexico, Texas, Washington, and Wisconsin. In these states estate planners should be wary of making a person other than the spouse a joint owner of community property. As a rule, half the wife's or husband's share of the community property passes to the surviving spouse and the other half goes to the heirs named in the descendant's will. The surviving spouse may or may not be named as an heir.

Tool 4: Wills

As the fourth and most important tool used in estate planning, wills need always to be individualized to the creator's (or testator's) situation, estate, and desires. The written will is signed by the testator in the presence of witnesses; it operates at his or her death to distribute property according to specifications in the document itself. The law imposes certain obligations, including the primary duty to pay tax liabilities, debts, funeral expenses, and the costs of administration. The law also provides for a surviving spouse's legal rights in a decedent's estate and refuses to recognize, on public policy grounds, provisions discouraging marriage, wasting assets, or tying up wealth for unreasonable periods of time.

Wills may be short and simple or long and complex. But in all cases certain essential requirements must be met. The will must, for example, be signed and witnessed to be valid. For his or her own peace of mind, a testator should have a lawyer prepare the "last will and testament." "Do-it-yourself" wills, and wills written on standard forms, are generally inadvisable, largely because so many of them lead to legal problems later.

Advantages

A will allows you to dispose of your property to the persons you select, at the time you choose, in the amounts and proportions you specify. You can also indicate how your property will be protected and who will be responsible for its protection. Anyone who is 21 years of age and mentally capable of understanding the nature of a will can have one drawn up. In some states or under some conditions the age requirement is reduced or waived.

The cases of husbands and wives who sustained fatal injuries in a common disaster point up the importance of wills. Usually, the husband and wife have left their estates to each other. The deaths of both in the same accident could create difficulty, especially where the order in which the two died cannot be determined. For that reason most wills contain a common disaster clause providing for the distribution of family assets in the event of simultaneous deaths or deaths resulting from the same accident.

Selecting an Executor

Selecting the person who will oversee the distribution of your estate according to your will is as important as choosing a trustee. Many of the same principles apply.

The loyalty and ability of the executor may be the single most critical factor in ensuring effective and fair administration of your assets after your death: particularly in preventing losses and protecting the property you have left under your will.

Subject to the supervision of an appropriate court, the executor takes possession of the assets specified in the will, manages the estate as the deceased would have, pays debts, taxes, and expenses, retains legal counsel as required, and through counsel handles all the legal obligations and procedures incident to the "execution" of the will. The executor also accounts to the court and heirs for his or her stewardship and distributes the estate's assets according to the provisions of the will and applicable legal strictures. Business skill and judgment, diligence, and the capacity to attend to details and maintain proper records are essential qualities of the good executor.

As a testator, you can nominate the executor of your choice, and can also name alternates if desired. Often a testator appoints a surviving widow or trusted friend or relative. Testators often name their legal counsel as executor or co-executor. At your discretion as testator, you can name a corporate executor or trustee—usually the trust department of a bank. Such a selection means that your executor will have complete institutional facilities available, will enjoy permanence and freedom from personal and business distractions, and will be able to call on the staff and professional skills necessary to do the work properly. The widow, a relative, or a lawyer may be named coexecutor as a means of combining the close personal relationship of a trusted individual with the skills and facilities of the corporate executor.

Obviously, where a will establishes a trust, the bank trust officer or some equally qualified person is a logical choice as executor/trustee. The executor or trustee must be compensated for his or her services—except in the case of a relative or friend who serves out of a sense of duty or because he or she is a principal heir. Executors' fees are based on the size of the estate, but typically range from 1 or 1.5 percent to about 2.5 percent of the gross estate.

Preparation and Execution

Some statutory formalities govern the preparation of all wills. For example, as noted, wills must be in writing, must demonstrate the testator's intent to pass property to heirs, and may as a rule incorporate another document or other documents if the other documents exist when the will is drawn and if the will adequately identifies the additions. The only exceptions to the rule that wills must be written are *nuncupative,* or oral, wills. All wills have also to be signed, or given some visible mark intended as a signature—at the end of the will in some states and in other places in other jurisdictions.

Most states require that two witnesses *attest to,* or witness, the will's signature; some others require three witnesses. Where statutes require it, wills have to be published, with the testator stating that the will is his or her own. Witnesses generally sign in the presence of the testator and each other. No witness should be a beneficiary under the will. An attestation clause appearing before the witnesses' signatures states that all formalities have been complied with, but is not mandatory; the clause merely serves as evidence of proper execution.

Alteration, Revocation

A will can be either changed or revoked. But alteration or revocation has to take place before the death of the testator. The latter must sign any amendment, or codicil, in the presence of witnesses—exactly as when the original was executed.

Revocation may take place in a number of ways. Marking with intent to revoke, tearing up, or burning, or otherwise destroying a will effects revocation; so may the operation of law in given cases, or the testator's preparation and execution of a new will containing a specific clause of revocation or provisions that nullify or clash with provisions in an earlier document. Legal invalidation of a will may take place when a testator remarries, obtains a divorce along with agreement to a property settlement, or becomes a parent. State laws generally govern such invalidations.

Depending on the jurisdiction, destruction or revocation of a later will may revive an earlier one. But some states recognize revival only through republication—unless the intent appears otherwise.

Instructions and Disposition

A letter of instructions may provide a lawyer or executor with essential information and simplify the task of carrying out a testator's desires. Such a letter is not part of the will, and need not comply with any formal requirements. Its purpose is to furnish a detailed inventory of the estate's assets, give instructions regarding the locations of all needed documents—including birth, marriage, and military discharge records; social security card; insurance policies; a list of bank accounts and safe deposit boxes; title deeds; pension papers; and so on—and summarize instructions regarding liquidation of business affairs.

Other portions of the letter may indicate where the will is kept, detail funeral instructions, and state the testator's wishes concerning investment of the proceeds of the estate, the education of children or grandchildren, future plans for the widow or widower, and similar subjects. The will becomes a public record; the letter remains private, and can thus express hopes or suggestions on very private, personal matters.

Where to keep the will? The safe deposit box is the most appropriate place if it can be opened without undue delay after the testator's death. Alternatively, the will may be delivered to the executor or to the testator's lawyer, or kept in a safe place with personal papers at home. In no event should it be accessible to a "disappointed heir."

Intestacy

The person who dies *intestate*—without having made out a will—already has a kind of will: state laws governing intestacy. These laws comprise a "standard" will reflecting the legislature's conception of the deceased's probable objectives. Under intestacy laws, property left by a decedent passes to survivors according to rules fixed by the deceased's state of residence.

Such rules never operate as would an individual will made out according to a person's wishes. The rules frequently lead to serious shrinkage of the estate—and often to a distribution of assets quite different from what the deceased probably wanted. If the estate is large, long and costly litigation may follow the person's death. If the estate is small, it may be divided among various survivors in portions too small to help anyone. If the deceased leaves minor children, they will inherit part of the estate along with his widow.

The laws of intestacy provide in other ways for minor children. A guardian is usually appointed for the children, a process that involves expensive and time-consuming court proceedings. The guardian has to post a bond, renewable annually at a substantial premium. The guard-

ian is supervised by the court and must account to it annually, resulting in more expense and loss of time. All of these procedures are designed to protect the children—and none takes into consideration the fact that the guardian may be the children's mother and the deceased's widow.

Intestacy laws have other effects. They make it impossible for all assets to go to the widow if there are children too. Nor do the laws consider the needs of the deceased's parents if a widow or child survives. Children are treated equally even though their needs may be quite unequal. Under the laws, faithful, loving spouses and mere legal mates are treated exactly alike; so are helpless widows and surviving spouses who are capable in business affairs.

In brief, the time and expense involved in making out a will is infinitesimal in comparison with the problems that may come with intestacy. The "will you already have" is always inferior to the will you ought to have—even though the laws represent the state's best efforts to protect and provide for survivors.

Common Provisions

Intestacy laws work in parallel ways in specific situations. For example, where a husband leaves a widow but no children or parents, the widow inherits the entire estate—after deductions for various expenses that a proper will could have avoided. Where only the decedent's parents survive, the parents usually receive the whole estate—though in some states brothers and sisters also receive shares. As indicated, where a deceased leaves as survivors both wife and parents, the wife usually receives everything even if she is financially independent and the parents are aged and destitute. In a few states, however, the parents receive up to half of their son's estate regardless of the widow's needs.

If the wife and one child survive, each, usually, takes half the estate—but in some jurisdictions the child may take two-thirds or even virtually the entire estate under certain circumstances. Where the wife and two or more children survive, one-third of the estate generally goes to the wife and the remaining two-thirds are divided equally among the children.

The various state laws may, obviously, work great hardship or injustice. Further, the laws are subject to change without notification. A will, by contrast, can be changed only by the person making it out or under the circumstances already noted. A will should be reviewed from time to time, for example when a testator moves to another state; but the will remains the best available means of disposing of property after death.

What Law Governs?

The laws of the testator's state of legal residence determine the validity (or nonvalidity) of a will where personal property is involved. But because each state reserves the right to fix title to land situated within its boundaries, the law of the state where real property is located governs the validity and effect of the will respect to real estate.

All of this may affect the estate plan. A sound plan may call for avoidance of unnecessary ownership of real estate in states where the testator is a nonresident, particularly if there is any possibility that two or more states may claim a descendant as a resident and try to tax the entire estate rather than just the local real property. Most states, and indeed most countries of the world, cooperate with one another by recognizing as valid a will that is valid in the jurisdiction in which the will was made, the jurisdiction in which the testator was a resident, or—as regards real estate—the jurisdiction in which the property is located.

The extent of this cooperation may vary in given situations. The protocols governing such cooperation may, also, change. Thus it is desirable that the will be consistent with the requirements of the state of residence. Some unusual types of wills are recognized in only a few states; but a proper will drawn by legal counsel will be prepared in such a way as to meet the requirements of most if not all states.

Perpetual Calendar

Directions: Choose year you want in key below. Number opposite year is number of calendar to use for that year.

1776 9	1793....3	1810 ...2	1827 ...2	1844 9	1861...3	1878 3	1895...3	1912 9	1929 ...3	1946 ...3	1963...3	1980 ...10	1997....4
1777 4	1794....4	1811...3	1828 ...10	1845 4	1862...4	1879 4	1896..11	1913 4	1930 ...4	1947 4	1964...11	1981 5	1998....5
1778 5	1795....5	1812 ..11	1829 ...5	1846 5	1863...5	1880 ...12	1897....6	1914 5	1931 5	1948 ...12	1965...6	1982 6	1999....6
1779 6	1796...13	1813 ...6	1830 ...6	1847 6	1864..13	1881 7	1898...7	1915 6	1932 ..13	1949 7	1966...7	1983 7	2000...14
1780 ..14	1797....1	1814 ...7	1831 ...7	1848 ..14	1865....1	1882 1	1899...1	1916 ..14	1933 1	1950 1	1967...1	1984 8	2001....2
1781 2	1798....2	1815 ...1	1832 ...8	1849 2	1866...2	1883 2	1900...2	1917 2	1934 ...2	1951 2	1968...9	1985 3	2002....3
1782 3	1799....3	1816 ...9	1833 ...3	1850 3	1867...3	1884 ...10	1901...3	1918 3	1935 3	1952 ...10	1969...4	1986 4	2003....4
1783 4	1800....1	1817 ...4	1834 ...4	1851 4	1868..11	1885 5	1902...4	1919 4	1936 ..11	1953 5	1970...5	1987 5	2004...12
1784 ..12	1801....6	1818 ...5	1835 ...5	1852 ...12	1869...6	1886 6	1903...5	1920 ...12	1937 ...6	1954 6	1971...6	1988 ...13	2005....7
1785 7	1802....6	1819 ...6	1836 ..13	1853 7	1870...7	1887 7	1904..13	1921 7	1938 ...7	1955 7	1972...14	1989 1	2006....1
1786 1	1803....7	1820 ..14	1837 ...1	1854 1	1871...1	1888 8	1905...1	1922 1	1939 1	1956 8	1973...2	1990 2	2007....2
1787 2	1804....8	1821 ...2	1838 ...2	1855 2	1872...9	1889 3	1906...2	1923 2	1940 ...9	1957 3	1974...3	1991 3	2008...10
1788 ..10	1805....3	1822 ...3	1839 ...3	1856 ...10	1873...4	1890 4	1907...3	1924 ...10	1941 ...4	1958 4	1975...4	1992 ..11	2009....5
1789 5	1806....4	1823 ...4	1840 ...11	1857 5	1874...5	1891 5	1908..11	1925 5	1942 5	1959 5	1976...12	1993 6	2010....6
1790 6	1807....5	1824 ...12	1841 ...6	1858 6	1875...6	1892 ...13	1909...6	1926 6	1943 ...6	1960 ...13	1977...7	1994 7	2011....7
1791 7	1808...13	1825 ...7	1842 ...7	1859 7	1876..14	1893 1	1910...7	1927 7	1944 ..14	1961 1	1978...1	1995 1	2012....8
1792 8	1809....1	1826 ...1	1843 ...1	1860 8	1877...2	1894 2	1911...1	1928 8	1945 2	1962 2	1979...2	1996 9	2013....3

1 — 1989

JANUARY
S M T W T F S
1 2 3 4 5 6 7
8 9 10 11 12 13 14
15 16 17 18 19 20 21
22 23 24 25 26 27 28
29 30 31

FEBRUARY
S M T W T F S
1 2 3 4
5 6 7 8 9 10 11
12 13 14 15 16 17 18
19 20 21 22 23 24 25
26 27 28

MARCH
S M T W T F S
1 2 3 4
5 6 7 8 9 10 11
12 13 14 15 16 17 18
19 20 21 22 23 24 25
26 27 28 29 30 31

APRIL
S M T W T F S
1
2 3 4 5 6 7 8
9 10 11 12 13 14 15
16 17 18 19 20 21 22
23 24 25 26 27 28 29
30

MAY
S M T W T F S
1 2 3 4 5 6
7 8 9 10 11 12 13
14 15 16 17 18 19 20
21 22 23 24 25 26 27
28 29 30 31

JUNE
S M T W T F S
1 2 3
4 5 6 7 8 9 10
11 12 13 14 15 16 17
18 19 20 21 22 23 24
25 26 27 28 29 30

JULY
S M T W T F S
1
2 3 4 5 6 7 8
9 10 11 12 13 14 15
16 17 18 19 20 21 22
23 24 25 26 27 28 29
30 31

AUGUST
S M T W T F S
1 2 3 4 5
6 7 8 9 10 11 12
13 14 15 16 17 18 19
20 21 22 23 24 25 26
27 28 29 30 31

SEPTEMBER
S M T W T F S
1 2
3 4 5 6 7 8 9
10 11 12 13 14 15 16
17 18 19 20 21 22 23
24 25 26 27 28 29 30

OCTOBER
S M T W T F S
1 2 3 4 5 6 7
8 9 10 11 12 13 14
15 16 17 18 19 20 21
22 23 24 25 26 27 28
29 30 31

NOVEMBER
S M T W T F S
1 2 3 4
5 6 7 8 9 10 11
12 13 14 15 16 17 18
19 20 21 22 23 24 25
26 27 28 29 30

DECEMBER
S M T W T F S
1 2
3 4 5 6 7 8 9
10 11 12 13 14 15 16
17 18 19 20 21 22 23
24 25 26 27 28 29 30
31

2 — 1990

JANUARY
S M T W T F S
1 2 3 4 5 6
7 8 9 10 11 12 13
14 15 16 17 18 19 20
21 22 23 24 25 26 27
28 29 30 31

FEBRUARY
S M T W T F S
1 2 3
4 5 6 7 8 9 10
11 12 13 14 15 16 17
18 19 20 21 22 23 24
25 26 27 28

MARCH
S M T W T F S
1 2 3
4 5 6 7 8 9 10
11 12 13 14 15 16 17
18 19 20 21 22 23 24
25 26 27 28 29 30 31

APRIL
S M T W T F S
1 2 3 4 5 6 7
8 9 10 11 12 13 14
15 16 17 18 19 20 21
22 23 24 25 26 27 28
29 30

MAY
S M T W T F S
1 2 3 4 5
6 7 8 9 10 11 12
13 14 15 16 17 18 19
20 21 22 23 24 25 26
27 28 29 30 31

JUNE
S M T W T F S
1 2
3 4 5 6 7 8 9
10 11 12 13 14 15 16
17 18 19 20 21 22 23
24 25 26 27 28 29 30

JULY
S M T W T F S
1 2 3 4 5 6 7
8 9 10 11 12 13 14
15 16 17 18 19 20 21
22 23 24 25 26 27 28
29 30 31

AUGUST
S M T W T F S
1 2 3 4
5 6 7 8 9 10 11
12 13 14 15 16 17 18
19 20 21 22 23 24 25
26 27 28 29 30 31

SEPTEMBER
S M T W T F S
1
2 3 4 5 6 7 8
9 10 11 12 13 14 15
16 17 18 19 20 21 22
23 24 25 26 27 28 29
30

OCTOBER
S M T W T F S
1 2 3 4 5 6
7 8 9 10 11 12 13
14 15 16 17 18 19 20
21 22 23 24 25 26 27
28 29 30 31

NOVEMBER
S M T W T F S
1 2 3
4 5 6 7 8 9 10
11 12 13 14 15 16 17
18 19 20 21 22 23 24
25 26 27 28 29 30

DECEMBER
S M T W T F S
1
2 3 4 5 6 7 8
9 10 11 12 13 14 15
16 17 18 19 20 21 22
23 24 25 26 27 28 29
30 31

3 — 1985

JANUARY
S M T W T F S
1 2 3 4 5
6 7 8 9 10 11 12
13 14 15 16 17 18 19
20 21 22 23 24 25 26
27 28 29 30 31

FEBRUARY
S M T W T F S
1 2
3 4 5 6 7 8 9
10 11 12 13 14 15 16
17 18 19 20 21 22 23
24 25 26 27 28

MARCH
S M T W T F S
1 2
3 4 5 6 7 8 9
10 11 12 13 14 15 16
17 18 19 20 21 22 23
24 25 26 27 28 29 30
31

APRIL
S M T W T F S
1 2 3 4 5 6
7 8 9 10 11 12 13
14 15 16 17 18 19 20
21 22 23 24 25 26 27
28 29 30

MAY
S M T W T F S
1 2 3 4
5 6 7 8 9 10 11
12 13 14 15 16 17 18
19 20 21 22 23 24 25
26 27 28 29 30 31

JUNE
S M T W T F S
1
2 3 4 5 6 7 8
9 10 11 12 13 14 15
16 17 18 19 20 21 22
23 24 25 26 27 28 29
30

JULY
S M T W T F S
1 2 3 4 5 6
7 8 9 10 11 12 13
14 15 16 17 18 19 20
21 22 23 24 25 26 27
28 29 30 31

AUGUST
S M T W T F S
1 2 3
4 5 6 7 8 9 10
11 12 13 14 15 16 17
18 19 20 21 22 23 24
25 26 27 28 29 30 31

SEPTEMBER
S M T W T F S
1 2 3 4 5 6 7
8 9 10 11 12 13 14
15 16 17 18 19 20 21
22 23 24 25 26 27 28
29 30

OCTOBER
S M T W T F S
1 2 3 4 5
6 7 8 9 10 11 12
13 14 15 16 17 18 19
20 21 22 23 24 25 26
27 28 29 30 31

NOVEMBER
S M T W T F S
1 2
3 4 5 6 7 8 9
10 11 12 13 14 15 16
17 18 19 20 21 22 23
24 25 26 27 28 29 30

DECEMBER
S M T W T F S
1 2 3 4 5 6 7
8 9 10 11 12 13 14
15 16 17 18 19 20 21
22 23 24 25 26 27 28
29 30 31

4 — 1986

JANUARY
S M T W T F S
1 2 3 4
5 6 7 8 9 10 11
12 13 14 15 16 17 18
19 20 21 22 23 24 25
26 27 28 29 30 31

FEBRUARY
S M T W T F S
1
2 3 4 5 6 7 8
9 10 11 12 13 14 15
16 17 18 19 20 21 22
23 24 25 26 27 28

MARCH
S M T W T F S
1
2 3 4 5 6 7 8
9 10 11 12 13 14 15
16 17 18 19 20 21 22
23 24 25 26 27 28 29
30 31

APRIL
S M T W T F S
1 2 3 4 5
6 7 8 9 10 11 12
13 14 15 16 17 18 19
20 21 22 23 24 25 26
27 28 29 30

MAY
S M T W T F S
1 2 3
4 5 6 7 8 9 10
11 12 13 14 15 16 17
18 19 20 21 22 23 24
25 26 27 28 29 30 31

JUNE
S M T W T F S
1 2 3 4 5 6 7
8 9 10 11 12 13 14
15 16 17 18 19 20 21
22 23 24 25 26 27 28
29 30

JULY
S M T W T F S
1 2 3 4 5
6 7 8 9 10 11 12
13 14 15 16 17 18 19
20 21 22 23 24 25 26
27 28 29 30 31

AUGUST
S M T W T F S
1 2
3 4 5 6 7 8 9
10 11 12 13 14 15 16
17 18 19 20 21 22 23
24 25 26 27 28 29 30
31

SEPTEMBER
S M T W T F S
1 2 3 4 5 6
7 8 9 10 11 12 13
14 15 16 17 18 19 20
21 22 23 24 25 26 27
28 29 30

OCTOBER
S M T W T F S
1 2 3 4
5 6 7 8 9 10 11
12 13 14 15 16 17 18
19 20 21 22 23 24 25
26 27 28 29 30 31

NOVEMBER
S M T W T F S
1
2 3 4 5 6 7 8
9 10 11 12 13 14 15
16 17 18 19 20 21 22
23 24 25 26 27 28 29
30

DECEMBER
S M T W T F S
1 2 3 4 5 6
7 8 9 10 11 12 13
14 15 16 17 18 19 20
21 22 23 24 25 26 27
28 29 30 31

5 — 1987

```
JANUARY                    FEBRUARY
 S  M  T  W  T  F  S         S  M  T  W  T  F  S
             1  2  3         1  2  3  4  5  6  7
 4  5  6  7  8  9 10         8  9 10 11 12 13 14
11 12 13 14 15 16 17        15 16 17 18 19 20 21
18 19 20 21 22 23 24        22 23 24 25 26 27 28
25 26 27 28 29 30 31

MARCH                      APRIL
 S  M  T  W  T  F  S         S  M  T  W  T  F  S
 1  2  3  4  5  6  7                  1  2  3  4
 8  9 10 11 12 13 14         5  6  7  8  9 10 11
15 16 17 18 19 20 21        12 13 14 15 16 17 18
22 23 24 25 26 27 28        19 20 21 22 23 24 25
29 30 31                    26 27 28 29 30

MAY                        JUNE
 S  M  T  W  T  F  S         S  M  T  W  T  F  S
                1  2             1  2  3  4  5  6
 3  4  5  6  7  8  9         7  8  9 10 11 12 13
10 11 12 13 14 15 16        14 15 16 17 18 19 20
17 18 19 20 21 22 23        21 22 23 24 25 26 27
24 25 26 27 28 29 30        28 29 30
31

JULY                       AUGUST
 S  M  T  W  T  F  S         S  M  T  W  T  F  S
          1  2  3  4                           1
 5  6  7  8  9 10 11         2  3  4  5  6  7  8
12 13 14 15 16 17 18         9 10 11 12 13 14 15
19 20 21 22 23 24 25        16 17 18 19 20 21 22
26 27 28 29 30 31           23 24 25 26 27 28 29
                            30 31

SEPTEMBER                  OCTOBER
 S  M  T  W  T  F  S         S  M  T  W  T  F  S
       1  2  3  4  5                  1  2  3
 6  7  8  9 10 11 12         4  5  6  7  8  9 10
13 14 15 16 17 18 19        11 12 13 14 15 16 17
20 21 22 23 24 25 26        18 19 20 21 22 23 24
27 28 29 30                 25 26 27 28 29 30 31

NOVEMBER                   DECEMBER
 S  M  T  W  T  F  S         S  M  T  W  T  F  S
 1  2  3  4  5  6  7                1  2  3  4  5
 8  9 10 11 12 13 14         6  7  8  9 10 11 12
15 16 17 18 19 20 21        13 14 15 16 17 18 19
22 23 24 25 26 27 28        20 21 22 23 24 25 26
29 30                       27 28 29 30 31
```

6 — 1982

```
JANUARY                    FEBRUARY
 S  M  T  W  T  F  S         S  M  T  W  T  F  S
                1  2         1  2  3  4  5  6
 3  4  5  6  7  8  9         7  8  9 10 11 12 13
10 11 12 13 14 15 16        14 15 16 17 18 19 20
17 18 19 20 21 22 23        21 22 23 24 25 26 27
24 25 26 27 28 29 30        28
31

MARCH                      APRIL
 S  M  T  W  T  F  S         S  M  T  W  T  F  S
 1  2  3  4  5  6                        1  2  3
 7  8  9 10 11 12 13         4  5  6  7  8  9 10
14 15 16 17 18 19 20        11 12 13 14 15 16 17
21 22 23 24 25 26 27        18 19 20 21 22 23 24
28 29 30 31                 25 26 27 28 29 30

MAY                        JUNE
 S  M  T  W  T  F  S         S  M  T  W  T  F  S
                      1            1  2  3  4  5
 2  3  4  5  6  7  8         6  7  8  9 10 11 12
 9 10 11 12 13 14 15        13 14 15 16 17 18 19
16 17 18 19 20 21 22        20 21 22 23 24 25 26
23 24 25 26 27 28 29        27 28 29 30
30 31

JULY                       AUGUST
 S  M  T  W  T  F  S         S  M  T  W  T  F  S
                1  2  3      1  2  3  4  5  6  7
 4  5  6  7  8  9 10         8  9 10 11 12 13 14
11 12 13 14 15 16 17        15 16 17 18 19 20 21
18 19 20 21 22 23 24        22 23 24 25 26 27 28
25 26 27 28 29 30 31        29 30 31

SEPTEMBER                  OCTOBER
 S  M  T  W  T  F  S         S  M  T  W  T  F  S
          1  2  3  4                          1  2
 5  6  7  8  9 10 11         3  4  5  6  7  8  9
12 13 14 15 16 17 18        10 11 12 13 14 15 16
19 20 21 22 23 24 25        17 18 19 20 21 22 23
26 27 28 29 30              24 25 26 27 28 29 30
                            31

NOVEMBER                   DECEMBER
 S  M  T  W  T  F  S         S  M  T  W  T  F  S
 1  2  3  4  5  6                     1  2  3  4
 7  8  9 10 11 12 13         5  6  7  8  9 10 11
14 15 16 17 18 19 20        12 13 14 15 16 17 18
21 22 23 24 25 26 27        19 20 21 22 23 24 25
28 29 30                    26 27 28 29 30 31
```

7 — 1983

```
JANUARY                    FEBRUARY
 S  M  T  W  T  F  S         S  M  T  W  T  F  S
                      1            1  2  3  4  5
 2  3  4  5  6  7  8         6  7  8  9 10 11 12
 9 10 11 12 13 14 15        13 14 15 16 17 18 19
16 17 18 19 20 21 22        20 21 22 23 24 25 26
23 24 25 26 27 28 29        27 28
30 31

MARCH                      APRIL
 S  M  T  W  T  F  S         S  M  T  W  T  F  S
       1  2  3  4  5                        1  2
 6  7  8  9 10 11 12         3  4  5  6  7  8  9
13 14 15 16 17 18 19        10 11 12 13 14 15 16
20 21 22 23 24 25 26        17 18 19 20 21 22 23
27 28 29 30 31              24 25 26 27 28 29 30

MAY                        JUNE
 S  M  T  W  T  F  S         S  M  T  W  T  F  S
 1  2  3  4  5  6  7                  1  2  3  4
 8  9 10 11 12 13 14         5  6  7  8  9 10 11
15 16 17 18 19 20 21        12 13 14 15 16 17 18
22 23 24 25 26 27 28        19 20 21 22 23 24 25
29 30 31                    26 27 28 29 30

JULY                       AUGUST
 S  M  T  W  T  F  S         S  M  T  W  T  F  S
                1  2         1  2  3  4  5  6
 3  4  5  6  7  8  9         7  8  9 10 11 12 13
10 11 12 13 14 15 16        14 15 16 17 18 19 20
17 18 19 20 21 22 23        21 22 23 24 25 26 27
24 25 26 27 28 29 30        28 29 30 31
31

SEPTEMBER                  OCTOBER
 S  M  T  W  T  F  S         S  M  T  W  T  F  S
             1  2  3                           1
 4  5  6  7  8  9 10         2  3  4  5  6  7  8
11 12 13 14 15 16 17         9 10 11 12 13 14 15
18 19 20 21 22 23 24        16 17 18 19 20 21 22
25 26 27 28 29 30           23 24 25 26 27 28 29
                            30 31

NOVEMBER                   DECEMBER
 S  M  T  W  T  F  S         S  M  T  W  T  F  S
       1  2  3  4  5                  1  2  3
 6  7  8  9 10 11 12         4  5  6  7  8  9 10
13 14 15 16 17 18 19        11 12 13 14 15 16 17
20 21 22 23 24 25 26        18 19 20 21 22 23 24
27 28 29 30                 25 26 27 28 29 30 31
```

8 — 1984 (Leap Year)

```
JANUARY                    FEBRUARY
 S  M  T  W  T  F  S         S  M  T  W  T  F  S
 1  2  3  4  5  6  7                  1  2  3  4
 8  9 10 11 12 13 14         5  6  7  8  9 10 11
15 16 17 18 19 20 21        12 13 14 15 16 17 18
22 23 24 25 26 27 28        19 20 21 22 23 24 25
29 30 31                    26 27 28 29

MARCH                      APRIL
 S  M  T  W  T  F  S         S  M  T  W  T  F  S
             1  2  3         1  2  3  4  5  6  7
 4  5  6  7  8  9 10         8  9 10 11 12 13 14
11 12 13 14 15 16 17        15 16 17 18 19 20 21
18 19 20 21 22 23 24        22 23 24 25 26 27 28
25 26 27 28 29 30 31        29 30

MAY                        JUNE
 S  M  T  W  T  F  S         S  M  T  W  T  F  S
       1  2  3  4  5                           1
 6  7  8  9 10 11 12         3  4  5  6  7  8  9
13 14 15 16 17 18 19        10 11 12 13 14 15 16
20 21 22 23 24 25 26        17 18 19 20 21 22 23
27 28 29 30 31              24 25 26 27 28 29 30

JULY                       AUGUST
 S  M  T  W  T  F  S         S  M  T  W  T  F  S
 1  2  3  4  5  6  7                  1  2  3  4
 8  9 10 11 12 13 14         5  6  7  8  9 10 11
15 16 17 18 19 20 21        12 13 14 15 16 17 18
22 23 24 25 26 27 28        19 20 21 22 23 24 25
29 30 31                    26 27 28 29 30 31

SEPTEMBER                  OCTOBER
 S  M  T  W  T  F  S         S  M  T  W  T  F  S
                      1      1  2  3  4  5  6
 2  3  4  5  6  7  8         7  8  9 10 11 12 13
 9 10 11 12 13 14 15        14 15 16 17 18 19 20
16 17 18 19 20 21 22        21 22 23 24 25 26 27
23 24 25 26 27 28 29        28 29 30 31
30

NOVEMBER                   DECEMBER
 S  M  T  W  T  F  S         S  M  T  W  T  F  S
             1  2  3                           1
 4  5  6  7  8  9 10         2  3  4  5  6  7  8
11 12 13 14 15 16 17         9 10 11 12 13 14 15
18 19 20 21 22 23 24        16 17 18 19 20 21 22
25 26 27 28 29 30           23 24 25 26 27 28 29
                            30 31
```

9 — (Leap Year)

```
JANUARY                    FEBRUARY
 S  M  T  W  T  F  S         S  M  T  W  T  F  S
    1  2  3  4  5  6                1  2  3
 7  8  9 10 11 12 13         4  5  6  7  8  9 10
14 15 16 17 18 19 20        11 12 13 14 15 16 17
21 22 23 24 25 26 27        18 19 20 21 22 23 24
28 29 30 31                 25 26 27 28 29

MARCH                      APRIL
 S  M  T  W  T  F  S         S  M  T  W  T  F  S
                1  2            1  2  3  4  5  6
 3  4  5  6  7  8  9         7  8  9 10 11 12 13
10 11 12 13 14 15 16        14 15 16 17 18 19 20
17 18 19 20 21 22 23        21 22 23 24 25 26 27
24 25 26 27 28 29 30        28 29 30
31

MAY                        JUNE
 S  M  T  W  T  F  S         S  M  T  W  T  F  S
          1  2  3  4                           1
 5  6  7  8  9 10 11         2  3  4  5  6  7  8
12 13 14 15 16 17 18         9 10 11 12 13 14 15
19 20 21 22 23 24 25        16 17 18 19 20 21 22
26 27 28 29 30 31           23 24 25 26 27 28 29
                            30

JULY                       AUGUST
 S  M  T  W  T  F  S         S  M  T  W  T  F  S
    1  2  3  4  5  6                1  2  3
 7  8  9 10 11 12 13         4  5  6  7  8  9 10
14 15 16 17 18 19 20        11 12 13 14 15 16 17
21 22 23 24 25 26 27        18 19 20 21 22 23 24
28 29 30 31                 25 26 27 28 29 30 31

SEPTEMBER                  OCTOBER
 S  M  T  W  T  F  S         S  M  T  W  T  F  S
 1  2  3  4  5  6  7            1  2  3  4  5
 8  9 10 11 12 13 14         6  7  8  9 10 11 12
15 16 17 18 19 20 21        13 14 15 16 17 18 19
22 23 24 25 26 27 28        20 21 22 23 24 25 26
29 30                       27 28 29 30 31

NOVEMBER                   DECEMBER
 S  M  T  W  T  F  S         S  M  T  W  T  F  S
                1  2         1  2  3  4  5  6  7
 3  4  5  6  7  8  9         8  9 10 11 12 13 14
10 11 12 13 14 15 16        15 16 17 18 19 20 21
17 18 19 20 21 22 23        22 23 24 25 26 27 28
24 25 26 27 28 29 30        29 30 31
```

10 — (Leap Year)

```
JANUARY                    FEBRUARY
 S  M  T  W  T  F  S         S  M  T  W  T  F  S
       1  2  3  4  5                      1  2
 6  7  8  9 10 11 12         3  4  5  6  7  8  9
13 14 15 16 17 18 19        10 11 12 13 14 15 16
20 21 22 23 24 25 26        17 18 19 20 21 22 23
27 28 29 30 31              24 25 26 27 28 29

MARCH                      APRIL
 S  M  T  W  T  F  S         S  M  T  W  T  F  S
                      1            1  2  3  4  5
 2  3  4  5  6  7  8         6  7  8  9 10 11 12
 9 10 11 12 13 14 15        13 14 15 16 17 18 19
16 17 18 19 20 21 22        20 21 22 23 24 25 26
23 24 25 26 27 28 29        27 28 29 30
30 31

MAY                        JUNE
 S  M  T  W  T  F  S         S  M  T  W  T  F  S
             1  2  3         1  2  3  4  5  6  7
 4  5  6  7  8  9 10         8  9 10 11 12 13 14
11 12 13 14 15 16 17        15 16 17 18 19 20 21
18 19 20 21 22 23 24        22 23 24 25 26 27 28
25 26 27 28 29 30 31        29 30

JULY                       AUGUST
 S  M  T  W  T  F  S         S  M  T  W  T  F  S
       1  2  3  4  5                      1  2
 6  7  8  9 10 11 12         3  4  5  6  7  8  9
13 14 15 16 17 18 19        10 11 12 13 14 15 16
20 21 22 23 24 25 26        17 18 19 20 21 22 23
27 28 29 30 31              24 25 26 27 28 29 30
                            31

SEPTEMBER                  OCTOBER
 S  M  T  W  T  F  S         S  M  T  W  T  F  S
    1  2  3  4  5  6               1  2  3  4
 7  8  9 10 11 12 13         5  6  7  8  9 10 11
14 15 16 17 18 19 20        12 13 14 15 16 17 18
21 22 23 24 25 26 27        19 20 21 22 23 24 25
28 29 30                    26 27 28 29 30 31

NOVEMBER                   DECEMBER
 S  M  T  W  T  F  S         S  M  T  W  T  F  S
                      1         1  2  3  4  5  6
 2  3  4  5  6  7  8         7  8  9 10 11 12 13
 9 10 11 12 13 14 15        14 15 16 17 18 19 20
16 17 18 19 20 21 22        21 22 23 24 25 26 27
23 24 25 26 27 28 29        28 29 30 31
30
```

11 — (Leap Year)

```
JANUARY                    FEBRUARY
 S  M  T  W  T  F  S         S  M  T  W  T  F  S
          1  2  3  4                           1
 5  6  7  8  9 10 11         2  3  4  5  6  7  8
12 13 14 15 16 17 18         9 10 11 12 13 14 15
19 20 21 22 23 24 25        16 17 18 19 20 21 22
26 27 28 29 30 31           23 24 25 26 27 28 29

MARCH                      APRIL
 S  M  T  W  T  F  S         S  M  T  W  T  F  S
 1  2  3  4  5  6  7                  1  2  3  4
 8  9 10 11 12 13 14         5  6  7  8  9 10 11
15 16 17 18 19 20 21        12 13 14 15 16 17 18
22 23 24 25 26 27 28        19 20 21 22 23 24 25
29 30 31                    26 27 28 29 30

MAY                        JUNE
 S  M  T  W  T  F  S         S  M  T  W  T  F  S
                1  2             1  2  3  4  5  6
 3  4  5  6  7  8  9         7  8  9 10 11 12 13
10 11 12 13 14 15 16        14 15 16 17 18 19 20
17 18 19 20 21 22 23        21 22 23 24 25 26 27
24 25 26 27 28 29 30        28 29 30
31

JULY                       AUGUST
 S  M  T  W  T  F  S         S  M  T  W  T  F  S
          1  2  3  4                           1
 5  6  7  8  9 10 11         2  3  4  5  6  7  8
12 13 14 15 16 17 18         9 10 11 12 13 14 15
19 20 21 22 23 24 25        16 17 18 19 20 21 22
26 27 28 29 30 31           23 24 25 26 27 28 29
                            30 31

SEPTEMBER                  OCTOBER
 S  M  T  W  T  F  S         S  M  T  W  T  F  S
       1  2  3  4  5                  1  2  3
 6  7  8  9 10 11 12         4  5  6  7  8  9 10
13 14 15 16 17 18 19        11 12 13 14 15 16 17
20 21 22 23 24 25 26        18 19 20 21 22 23 24
27 28 29 30                 25 26 27 28 29 30 31

NOVEMBER                   DECEMBER
 S  M  T  W  T  F  S         S  M  T  W  T  F  S
 1  2  3  4  5  6  7                1  2  3  4  5
 8  9 10 11 12 13 14         6  7  8  9 10 11 12
15 16 17 18 19 20 21        13 14 15 16 17 18 19
22 23 24 25 26 27 28        20 21 22 23 24 25 26
29 30                       27 28 29 30 31
```

12 — (Leap Year)

```
JANUARY                    FEBRUARY
 S  M  T  W  T  F  S         S  M  T  W  T  F  S
             1  2  3         1  2  3  4  5  6  7
 4  5  6  7  8  9 10         8  9 10 11 12 13 14
11 12 13 14 15 16 17        15 16 17 18 19 20 21
18 19 20 21 22 23 24        22 23 24 25 26 27 28
25 26 27 28 29 30 31        29

MARCH                      APRIL
 S  M  T  W  T  F  S         S  M  T  W  T  F  S
    1  2  3  4  5  6                     1  2  3
 7  8  9 10 11 12 13         4  5  6  7  8  9 10
14 15 16 17 18 19 20        11 12 13 14 15 16 17
21 22 23 24 25 26 27        18 19 20 21 22 23 24
28 29 30 31                 25 26 27 28 29 30

MAY                        JUNE
 S  M  T  W  T  F  S         S  M  T  W  T  F  S
                      1            1  2  3  4  5
 2  3  4  5  6  7  8         6  7  8  9 10 11 12
 9 10 11 12 13 14 15        13 14 15 16 17 18 19
16 17 18 19 20 21 22        20 21 22 23 24 25 26
23 24 25 26 27 28 29        27 28 29 30
30 31

JULY                       AUGUST
 S  M  T  W  T  F  S         S  M  T  W  T  F  S
             1  2  3         1  2  3  4  5  6  7
 4  5  6  7  8  9 10         8  9 10 11 12 13 14
11 12 13 14 15 16 17        15 16 17 18 19 20 21
18 19 20 21 22 23 24        22 23 24 25 26 27 28
25 26 27 28 29 30 31        29 30 31

SEPTEMBER                  OCTOBER
 S  M  T  W  T  F  S         S  M  T  W  T  F  S
          1  2  3  4                        1  2
 5  6  7  8  9 10 11         3  4  5  6  7  8  9
12 13 14 15 16 17 18        10 11 12 13 14 15 16
19 20 21 22 23 24 25        17 18 19 20 21 22 23
26 27 28 29 30              24 25 26 27 28 29 30
                            31

NOVEMBER                   DECEMBER
 S  M  T  W  T  F  S         S  M  T  W  T  F  S
 1  2  3  4  5  6                     1  2  3  4
 7  8  9 10 11 12 13         5  6  7  8  9 10 11
14 15 16 17 18 19 20        12 13 14 15 16 17 18
21 22 23 24 25 26 27        19 20 21 22 23 24 25
28 29 30                    26 27 28 29 30 31
```

13　(Leap Year)　　　　1988

JANUARY
```
S  M  T  W  T  F  S
            1  2
 3  4  5  6  7  8  9
10 11 12 13 14 15 16
17 18 19 20 21 22 23
24 25 26 27 28 29 30
31
```

FEBRUARY
```
S  M  T  W  T  F  S
    1  2  3  4  5  6
 7  8  9 10 11 12 13
14 15 16 17 18 19 20
21 22 23 24 25 26 27
28 29
```

MARCH
```
S  M  T  W  T  F  S
       1  2  3  4  5
 6  7  8  9 10 11 12
13 14 15 16 17 18 19
20 21 22 23 24 25 26
27 28 29 30 31
```

APRIL
```
S  M  T  W  T  F  S
                1  2
 3  4  5  6  7  8  9
10 11 12 13 14 15 16
17 18 19 20 21 22 23
24 25 26 27 28 29 30
```

MAY
```
S  M  T  W  T  F  S
 1  2  3  4  5  6  7
 8  9 10 11 12 13 14
15 16 17 18 19 20 21
22 23 24 25 26 27 28
29 30 31
```

JUNE
```
S  M  T  W  T  F  S
          1  2  3  4
 5  6  7  8  9 10 11
12 13 14 15 16 17 18
19 20 21 22 23 24 25
26 27 28 29 30
```

JULY
```
S  M  T  W  T  F  S
                1  2
 3  4  5  6  7  8  9
10 11 12 13 14 15 16
17 18 19 20 21 22 23
24 25 26 27 28 29 30
31
```

AUGUST
```
S  M  T  W  T  F  S
    1  2  3  4  5  6
 7  8  9 10 11 12 13
14 15 16 17 18 19 20
21 22 23 24 25 26 27
28 29 30 31
```

SEPTEMBER
```
S  M  T  W  T  F  S
             1  2  3
 4  5  6  7  8  9 10
11 12 13 14 15 16 17
18 19 20 21 22 23 24
25 26 27 28 29 30
```

OCTOBER
```
S  M  T  W  T  F  S
                   1
 2  3  4  5  6  7  8
 9 10 11 12 13 14 15
16 17 18 19 20 21 22
23 24 25 26 27 28 29
30 31
```

NOVEMBER
```
S  M  T  W  T  F  S
       1  2  3  4  5
 6  7  8  9 10 11 12
13 14 15 16 17 18 19
20 21 22 23 24 25 26
27 28 29 30
```

DECEMBER
```
S  M  T  W  T  F  S
             1  2  3
 4  5  6  7  8  9 10
11 12 13 14 15 16 17
18 19 20 21 22 23 24
25 26 27 28 29 30 31
```

14　(Leap Year)

JANUARY
```
S  M  T  W  T  F  S
                   1
 2  3  4  5  6  7  8
 9 10 11 12 13 14 15
16 17 18 19 20 21 22
23 24 25 26 27 28 29
30 31
```

FEBRUARY
```
S  M  T  W  T  F  S
       1  2  3  4  5
 6  7  8  9 10 11 12
13 14 15 16 17 18 19
20 21 22 23 24 25 26
27 28 29
```

MARCH
```
S  M  T  W  T  F  S
          1  2  3  4
 5  6  7  8  9 10 11
12 13 14 15 16 17 18
19 20 21 22 23 24 25
26 27 28 29 30 31
```

APRIL
```
S  M  T  W  T  F  S
                   1
 2  3  4  5  6  7  8
 9 10 11 12 13 14 15
16 17 18 19 20 21 22
23 24 25 26 27 28 29
30
```

MAY
```
S  M  T  W  T  F  S
    1  2  3  4  5  6
 7  8  9 10 11 12 13
14 15 16 17 18 19 20
21 22 23 24 25 26 27
28 29 30 31
```

JUNE
```
S  M  T  W  T  F  S
             1  2  3
 4  5  6  7  8  9 10
11 12 13 14 15 16 17
18 19 20 21 22 23 24
25 26 27 28 29 30
```

JULY
```
S  M  T  W  T  F  S
                   1
 2  3  4  5  6  7  8
 9 10 11 12 13 14 15
16 17 18 19 20 21 22
23 24 25 26 27 28 29
30 31
```

AUGUST
```
S  M  T  W  T  F  S
       1  2  3  4  5
 6  7  8  9 10 11 12
13 14 15 16 17 18 19
20 21 22 23 24 25 26
27 28 29 30 31
```

SEPTEMBER
```
S  M  T  W  T  F  S
                1  2
 3  4  5  6  7  8  9
10 11 12 13 14 15 16
17 18 19 20 21 22 23
24 25 26 27 28 29 30
```

OCTOBER
```
S  M  T  W  T  F  S
 1  2  3  4  5  6  7
 8  9 10 11 12 13 14
15 16 17 18 19 20 21
22 23 24 25 26 27 28
29 30 31
```

NOVEMBER
```
S  M  T  W  T  F  S
             1  2  3  4
 5  6  7  8  9 10 11
12 13 14 15 16 17 18
19 20 21 22 23 24 25
26 27 28 29 30
```

DECEMBER
```
S  M  T  W  T  F  S
                1  2
 3  4  5  6  7  8  9
10 11 12 13 14 15 16
17 18 19 20 21 22 23
24 25 26 27 28 29 30
31
```

Word Processing Glossary

abbreviation document A document on which words or phrases are stored; each one is identified by a short code or abbreviation and can be called out and inserted into your main document by using that code or abbreviation only, rather than having to re-enter the entire word or phrase. For complicated words that are used often, use of an abbreviation document saves both time and typographical errors.

access To make something available to use; to access a document means to call it out for revision or printing.

application A specific task that your system can perform; you can "apply" the software/hardware parts of your system to achieve a desired result. Copying a document from one disk to another is a concrete application of one of your system's many possibilities.

automatic A function your system will perform repeatedly for you without specific prompting each time. An "automatic sheet feeder" feeds a new sheet of paper for each new page without your having to put the sheet into the system manually; "automatic page numbering" prints the proper page number on each sheet on a large job without your having to enter each page number separately.

automatic sheet feeder An optional piece of hardware that feeds single sheets of paper automatically to the printer. Most automatic sheet feeders have two trays and can feed the first sheet of a document from one tray, with all the rest of the sheets needed for that document being fed from the second tray. This feature permits the use of letterhead for the first page and blank sheets for all the following pages. Every automatic sheet feeder system has a manual feed option, so you can slip in a single job that bypasses the automatic feature.

backspace A key that moves the cursor backward one space at a time; in some systems the use of this key will delete the character the cursor backs over.

back up To move the cursor backward through the document without deleting copy.

backup copy A copy of an entire disk or documents on a disk that is made for safekeeping. Backup copies can also be made of program (systems or software) disks.

batch printing Lining up jobs in a queue (a waiting line) to print automatically one right after another. The creation or revision of other documents that are not in the printing queue can take place while the printing is going on.

bidirectional Pertaining to the ability to move in both directions. Most daisy wheel and thimble printwheels used on letter-quality printers and most matrix printheads move and print in both right-to-left and left-to-right directions. If your system can print superscripts and subscripts, the paper moves bidirectionally—first up and then down or first down and then up—when printing these characters.

block A storage space on a diskette that holds a certain number of characters. Each block holds the same number of characters. Your manufacturer can tell you how many characters are contained in the blocks in your system. Knowing this information is helpful in determining the total size of any document.

boilerplate Standard paragraphs used in your work. They can be filed by name or number and stored in a paragraph document to be called up for inclusion in a document whenever needed.

bold To overprint the same text with the same characters in order to make them appear slightly darker. Not all systems have the capability of printing each character twice.

breaking hyphen A hyphen that joins compound words ("long-standing") and will break if the first half of the compound word is at the end of a line ("long-"; "standing"). Entering a breaking hyphen may require a supershift, depending on the software program in your system.

brightness control The device on your system that allows you to lighten or darken the text that appears on your screen. It is especially useful if you work in a natural light setting in which the room's light varies from strong sunlight to early winter darkness.

carbon ribbon A better-quality printer ribbon. It normally is used only once, with each character striking at an unused spot on the ribbon, in contrast to a cloth ribbon that is used several times in a continuous loop. The carbon ribbon produces a darker, cleaner image.

carriage The mechanism in your printer that holds the printwheel or printhead and moves the printwheel (printhead) back and forth across the paper while printing is taking place. (Sometimes called a "carrier.")

carriage return (carrier return) *See* **return.**

center To position a word or phrase at the center of a line or centered on a tab stop. Once the centering location is determined and the centering commands are executed, the word or phrase will automatically center as it is entered.

character Any letter, number, space, command, or instruction that you enter into the system. You will normally see only the letters, punctuation marks, numbers, and spaces on the screen. If you enter a display or view mode, you will see all the other special characters you have entered that control the format of your document, such as hard returns, superscripts, tab stops, format changes, and so on. These normally invisible characters will not print out, but they do take up space on your disk.

cloth ribbon A printer ribbon that is on a continuous loop and can be reused until you decide it is printing too light to use any longer. A carbon ribbon is used only once and has to be replaced when it has run once through the printer.

code In some systems the supershift key is called "code." It needs to be pressed at the same time (or on some systems, just before) a coded character key is pressed to make the key perform its coded function. For example, the "u" key pressed alone results in a lowercase "u" being entered; shift + "u" results in an uppercase "U" being entered; and supershift (or code) + "u" results in the word last entered being underlined (if underlining a word is the function of the supershift + "u" key in your system).

column Vertically arranged blocks of text, usually found in tables or in newsletters or bulletins. Some systems will adjust the space between the columns automatically; some require you to tab to the space manually. Most systems will center columns around a center point, around a decimal, around a comma, or will print a column flush right or flush left.

communications The transferring of data to and from your word processing system to another computer system (word processor, data processor, intelligent copier, and so on) by cable or telephone. Communications requires special hardware (cable and/or modem) and software.

composite character A character that is produced by two or more characters one on top of the other.

continuous-form paper A long piece of paper that can go continuously through your printer. The paper is perforated at regular intervals so pages can be separated. This paper is pulled through the printer by a form-feed tractor.

copy (1) The content of your document; (2) to duplicate your document or disk on another disk, or to duplicate your document elsewhere on the same disk; (3) the duplicate of your document or disk.

create To start a new document. The first step is to give this new document a name, so you can later go back to it for revision or call it up for printing, or even instruct the system to erase it.

CRT An abbreviation of "cathode ray tube," another name for your screen (sometimes more technically called "video display" or VD).

cursor The indicator that shows where the next character to be entered will enter the system (sometimes a blinking underline or rectangle, sometimes a solid highlight).

cursor keys Some systems have keys with arrows that move the cursor up or down, right or left, depending on which key is pressed. If the key is held down, the cursor will continue to move in a given direction until the key is released. Other systems have keys with names that move the cursor forward or backward by character, by word, by sentence, by paragraph, or by page. Most systems have supershift combinations that enable you to move the cursor directly to a particular page in a long document, or to the start (top) or the end (bottom) of the document. By using "find" or "search" commands, you can move the cursor to particular words in your document.

cut To remove or copy part of a document (sometimes called "move"). In some systems you have to "paste" this part of the document elsewhere in the document; in other systems you have an option of "forgetting it," and thus deleting a sizable portion of the document at once rather than word by word or line by line.

date and time A time clock in the system. It must be set with the current date and time each time the system is turned on. Some systems can print the date and time from the clock onto a document, thus providing an automatic "stamp" as to when work was begun and/or ended. A system with a date and time feature will automatically keep track of the time spent working on each document.

decimal alignment The ability of the system to line up numbers in a column on a decimal point.

default The settings that are preassigned and will format and control the system unless you specifically enter different settings. The software manufacturer initially preassigns these settings, on the basis of the most widespread expected usage. You may enter new settings for a particular document: these will thereafter apply to that document unless you change the settings later. In some systems, you can enter new settings on the program diskette—creating your own default settings to which the system will automatically revert when not specifically told otherwise.

delete To remove (erase) characters, words, pages, documents, or entire disks. Deleted parts of a document normally cannot be retrieved (only if they are placed in the system's temporary memory can they be retrieved).

directory Another name for index: the system's list of documents that are stored on a disk.

disk A thin, flexible magnetic disk, enclosed in a rather stiff protective jacket. Depending on your system, it will be 5¼ inches in diameter or 8 inches in diameter. Some newer minisystems are appearing with disks that are 3 inches in diam-

eter. Documents and software programs are stored on disks. The amount of data that can be placed on a disk is not directly related to its diameter, but rather to the density of its formatting. (Often disks are called "diskettes.")

disk drives The recording and reading devices that are located on your screen console or in a separate disk drive unit. You place the disks into the slots in the disk drive, close the slot door or gate, and the system will automatically load the contents of the disks into the system for work. (In some systems, you need to instruct the system to load, or "boot," the program disk into the system.

disk name The name you assign a disk. It may be an actual name, an abbreviation, or an alphanumeric code. This name will thereafter be used in the system to gain access to the contents of the disk. You can change a disk name at any time.

display To show the contents of a disk on the screen. In a display mode, the hidden or invisible characters are also shown.

document A body of text of any length that you create, name, and store on a document disk.

document comment Some systems allow you to enter a comment about the document. This comment will serve as a reminder of some work function, deadline, or routing you need to remember. This comment will appear only on your screen: it will not be printed out, nor will it affect the formatting of the document. The document comment is a kind of electronic memo slip you can attach to your document, if you wish.

document name The name you give a document when you create it. That name is the means you have thereafter to gain access to the document for revision, copying, printing, or deletion.

document number Some systems will assign each document on a disk a number. That number does not change as you add or delete other documents on the disk.

double-density disk A disk that is initialized in such a way as to take considerably more data than a single-density disk. The amount varies from nearly double to over three times as much, depending on your system.

draft printer A high-speed matrix printer that prints out documents on continuous-form paper. You can use this printer for initial proofing and revision; its output is not as attractive as the output of a letter-quality printer.

duplicate To copy a document or disk elsewhere, but still leave the original intact.

edit To revise the text of a document.

edit keys The functional keys that allow you to instruct the system directly to perform functions relating to editing. Moving the cursor, going to a page or word, searching or finding, replacing, filing or ending, inserting required page ends, calling up view mode, are all typical functions performed directly by pressing edit keys.

elite Another name for a 12-pitch typeface; a 10-pitch typeface is sometimes called "pica."

end A term used in some systems for filing a document onto the document disk. Some systems require using a page end key to file each page as you proceed through the document, without having to file the entire document and then recall it again to continue work.

enter To put text and instructions into the system by pressing on keys. Some systems use the term "enter" to refer to their execute-an-instruction command.

erase To remove or delete text from a disk, making that space available for receiving new text. A system will normally have several methods of erasing text, ranging from single characters to documents to entire disks.

error message A brief message that may appear on your screen to tell you that you cannot perform a function the way you are trying to perform it. The message will usually prompt you to help you perform the function in a way that works in the system.

execute A command to the system to perform a function. You usually need to set the function up; when you execute the command, the function occurs. Some systems have a special "execute" or "enter" key; others use the return key as the execute key.

feature A function that your system is capable of performing. A spelling-hyphenation dictionary is an example of a feature.

field A distinctly identifiable part of your document that can be recalled and used by reference to its identity. For example, a list of addresses may include the state as a separate identifiable part or field. "State" is the field name, and "Iowa" or "IA" is a part of the field. When the field name is called up for use, the system will use "Iowa" or "IA."

file To store a document on a disk for future use. Also, "file" is another name for the document itself.

file name The name or alphanumeric code you have given the system to identify a particular document.

find A term used in some systems to define the search feature.

footer Text placed automatically at the bottom of each page, such as a document name, page number, date, or author's name.

format The layout of the page, using such specific instructions as margin width, tabs, number of lines, and line spacing.

global search and replace A feature that automatically searches out every instance of a string of characters in a document and replaces them with a different string of characters. You have told the system which word or phrase to search and which word or phrase to use as the replacement. The word "global" indicates this process occurs throughout the entire document without stopping, rather than moving from one instance to the next individually on your command.

go-to A feature that enables you to move quickly to a specific page (by page number) in a document.

hard copy A printout on paper of a document from your system.

hard return A return caused by pressing the return key rather than an automatic return (soft return) created by the system when a line turns over. The hard return will function wherever it appears, even though the document rearranges itself when text is added or deleted.

hard space A space made in combination with a supershift key; this space holds letters together as though it were a character itself. It is useful in ensuring that initials that are part of a person's name do not separate over two different lines.

hardware The physical equipment parts of a word processing system. Printers and keyboards are hardware.

header Text placed automatically at the top of each page, such as a document name, page number, date, or author's name.

highlight A feature that makes some text stand out on the screen. Highlighting may be by underlining, by brighter appearance of certain characters, or by lighting up the background behind characters, words, or blocks of text.

hyphenation Use of the character - at the end of a line to divide a word into syllables or between parts of compound words. Some systems can use a hyphenation dictionary to divide words automatically (though not always correctly). All systems differentiate between a hard hypen, which always appears and holds characters on either side together; a breaking hyphen, which always appears but will allow the characters that follow it to drop down to the next line if a line turnover is required; and an invisible hyphen, which is used in word division and will appear if at the end of a line but will not be printed if the word is elsewhere in the text.

index The list of documents on a document disk. The index can be viewed on the screen and printed out on paper.

initialize To prepare a disk to receive data. The data may be a software program or documents. The preparation may be for single- or double-density use, depending on your needs and the capabilities of your system.

insert To place text into a document between characters that are already in the document. The system will rearrange existing text around the new, inserted text.

justify To print a document with even right and left margins. Some systems have a "half-justify" option that makes the right-hand margin somewhat more even than a regular ragged right but not exactly even as in a justified right-hand margin. The system will require hyphenating when printing a justified right-hand margin, since the lines will spread so open as to be unattractive if there are too few characters on a line.

keyboard The hardware part that has keys for entering characters and commands. It is either part of the terminal or is connected to the terminal by a flexible cable.

keystroke One press of any key on the keyboard, including spaces, returns, and any command keys.

keystroke save A feature on some systems that allows you to put a certain number of characters into a temporary memory and play them back on command for any number of times until you replace them with a new set of characters. On other systems, this feature can be used with the cut-and-paste feature.

left justify A tab stop on which the first character of any entry in a column always lines up; the words or figures build toward the right.

left margin The place where all left-hand lines normally start to print. The placement of your left-hand margin on the paper is related to how you set up your margins when you format the page. You should learn how far in from the edge of the paper your left-hand margin should be for letterhead correspondence and use that setting routinely for correspondence work.

letter-quality printer Often referred to as an LQP. This printer uses an impact printing method with printwheels or thimbles to produce a quality of printing equal to or better than that produced by a good typewriter.

library A feature that enables you to store words, phrases, and even paragraphs elsewhere on a disk (in a library document) and to call them up for reproduction in the document you are working on by using a shorthand code of letters or numbers.

line counter Some systems show you which line you are working on at any given time. They normally count from the top of the page, so you have to calculate the number of top margin lines to figure out how far down the page you are at any line number.

line spacing The spacing between lines of print when your document prints out. Systems vary in their capability of ranging from single-line spacing (normally six lines to an inch) to increments of a single line or triple-line spacing. Half-line spacing or less is useful in printing superscripts and subscripts: if you can control your system to produce less than half-line spacing, your superscripts will not overlap the descenders on the line above when you are printing them in a single-spaced document.

list processing The feature that allows you to combine lists with a form (or shell) document in order to produce an original, personalized document that combines the individual features in the list with the copy in the form document.

load The term used in some systems to describe the function of placing your software program into the system's computer after you have turned the machine on.

lowercase The uncapitalized form of letters. The term is taken from earlier printing times when these letters were manually taken by typesetters one by one from a large compartmentalized drawer (called a "case") in which the uncapitalized letters were stored in the compartments located at the lower two-thirds of the case.

margin The space between any of the four edges of the paper and the place where your printing begins or ends. There are top, right, left, and bottom margins to each job.

math A feature that allows you to enter numbers together with numeric commands (addition, subtraction, multiplication, division, percentage) that will function in your job. Most often this feature is used in list processing and sorting work.

matrix printer A high-speed printer that prints dots instead of entire letters. The dots fit into a matrix, or pattern, to form the general shape of a letter or number. The more dots and the tighter the matrix, the more the matrix-produced letter looks like an impact-produced letter.

menu Choices listed on the screen from which you can select on option. You need to go to the proper menu to select a particular feature you want to make happen. Your manual illustrates all the possible menus you can call up and tells you how to call them up.

merge The act of combining elements from lists with a form document when list processing.

message Information, questions, or warnings that appear on your screen as a result of some condition that calls for a response from you. This condition may be due to the fact that you have asked the machine to do something it cannot do, or do it out of its own sequence, or it may be due to the printer running out of paper or ribbon, or needing a printwheel change.

module A piece of hardware that can be combined with other hardware pieces to form a working computer or word processing unit. Some modules are changeable; for instance, you can use more than one kind of printing module (printer) with a word processor. Or you can use more than one kind of keyboard (for instance, if you have a French-language software program, you could use a French-language keyboard without having to change any other elements in your system except to secure a French-language printwheel).

numeric keyboard Some systems use a special ten-key (0–9) section for numbers, configured in the same style as most calculators. Other systems use the 1–0 sequence of keys on an upper row in the main keyboard section.

operator A person who makes a word processing system function by entering characters and commands.

option Any one of the choices that can be selected by an operator from a menu.

originator A person who writes or dictates a document for word processing by a word processing operator.

overstrike To place a character over another character. If the same character overstrikes a character, the result is a slightly bolder appearance; if a different character overstrikes, the result is a combined character or a character with an accent mark. In legal work, many words are overstruck with a hyphen (as in "effective immediately") to show words that are proposed to be deleted from a legal document. Many word processing systems are able to actually delete those overstruck words in a revision after both parties have agreed to their deletion and the final document is being prepared.

page A section in a document marked off by a page end mark. This mark may be placed there automatically during pagination or it may be placed there manually. The system registers this area in the document as a page in its numbering system. The page may be full of type, partially full, or even completely empty.

page mark (page end mark) A character that instructs the system to end a page and to begin a new page with the next character. The page end mark may be placed automatically or manually. This mark is sometimes called a "new page" mark.

pagination The feature that divides a document into pages. You determine how many lines should be on a page when you enter the automatic pagination instructions, or you do so by entering a required page end mark at the place of your choice.

paper jam Paper has become wedged into the printer or feeder and needs to be manually removed.

paragraph Text of one or more lines that is separated from other text in the document by a paragraph marker (if your system has one and if you use it) or by two hard returns. In some systems, a number of printed paragraphs that you separate by a single hard return followed by a tab indent will be understood by the system's logic to be a single long paragraph if you try to move forward or backward by paragraphs. The system only recognizes the paragraph mark or two hard returns in sequence for its paragraph functioning.

paragraph document Copy—from a single word to an entire paragraph in length—that is stored in an alternate location, that is, not in the document you are working on, but can be inserted into your document either by a couple of manual keystrokes or by including a format command in your shell document.

paste To insert data that has been temporarily stored in a "paste" area or "keystroke save" area. The content of the data in the paste area does not change (and so can be used many times) until new data are stored in that area.

pica An often-used name for 10-pitch characters.

pitch The number of characters per horizontal inch. The pitches normally used in word processing are 10-pitch (sometimes called "pica"), 12-pitch (sometimes called "elite"), and 15-pitch. You need to instruct your system about which pitch you are using and make sure that you have the proper printwheel in the printer for that pitch setting.

platen The cylinder against which the printhead strikes to produce an impression.

printer The hardware unit that produces a paper copy of your document.

printhead The hardware device in the printer that produces matrix characters or that strikes a printwheel to produce impact characters.

printwheel A circular printing element, sometimes called a "daisy wheel" or a "thimble," depending on its shape.

program A software set of instructions that enables your system to perform word processing functions. You load your program into the system each time you turn the system on. Your manual explains how to enter commands into the system to make it perform functions that the program enables it to do. Most word processing programs are "packaged"; that is, they are prepared by the manufacturer and are licensed property. Generally, you are not able to change the content of a word processing program.

prompt A message that appears on your screen and requires a response from you.

proportional spacing Spacing between characters that is somewhat proportional to the amount of space taken up by each character (for instance, in proportional spacing, or PS, an "m" uses more space than an "I"). To use proportional spacing, your system must be able to use a PS print setting and you must have PS printwheels that are compatible with your system.

queue A waiting line. Sometimes you can have a queue of documents to be printed one after the other automatically, while you are editing yet a different document.

ragged right An uneven right-hand margin. Unless you justify a document, it will print out as you see it on the screen.

replace A feature of putting in new characters in the place of previously entered characters that now are deleted.

return Use of the return key ends a line at that point where it is pressed. The return key is also used in many systems to execute commands.

revision The work you do to change the contents of a document or the commands that control its appearance.

ribbon A narrow strip of carbon or cloth used in the printer against which the printwheel or printhead strikes to create an impression on the paper. In word processors, ribbons come in self-contained cartridges. Some ribbons made of cloth are in continuous-loop cartridges and can be used several times over; other ribbons can be used only once.

right justify A tab setting for the rightmost character in a column. All the other characters or numbers in the column will build out toward the left from the tab setting.

right margin The setting that controls the placing of rightmost characters on the page. If your document is ragged right, no character will extend beyond the right margin setting; if it is justified, all lines will end on the right margin setting (except possibly the last line of each paragraph).

screen The video screen on which your document and various menus, messages, and other information are displayed.

scroll To move the cursor forward or backward through a document, often resulting in the text of the document moving up or down the screen.

search To instruct the system to look for (find) a particular string of characters (a word or phrase), most often with a view to replacing those characters with others.

sentence The part of a document ending with a period, a question mark, or an exclamation mark. If your system advances or backs up by sentences, it will move from period to period (or the other sentence end marks). If there are several periods after initials (as in "F.D.R."), your system will read the text between each period as a sentence.

setting A location (margin setting) or command (typeface setting) you have put into a document or a program. Settings can be changed through appropriate menus.

shadow printing Some systems have the capability of overstriking characters with the same character moved slightly to one side of the original character, giving an impression of very bold printing.

shared printer A feature whereby more than one terminal can use the same printer.

shell A form document that permits the inclusion of variables taken from a list.

single density A method of formatting a disk to receive information that permits the storage of much less information per disk than double-density formatting. Systems that have double-density capability can normally read single-density diskettes, but single-density systems can read only single-density diskettes.

software Instructions on a program disk that tell the hardware (the physical equipment) what functions to perform and lead you through a series of menus to give the appropriate commands to make the system perform the functions you want. Software that works on your system to perform a wide variety of tasks can be purchased directly from your manufacturer or from companies that write software programs for your brand of equipment.

sort A feature that enables your system to organize lists in a wide variety of alphanumeric combinations. Each alphanumeric element in your sort is organized in either an ascending or a descending order (A to Z, 1 to 10000; or reverse).

spelling A feature that loads a spelling dictionary into the system to check the spelling of words in a document. The size of these dictionaries varies from 10,000 to 150,000 words, depending on the complexity of the software and the hardware. The larger the dictionary, the larger the working memory the system requires.

store To place (file) information on a disk, where it is available for recall and adjustment later. Depending on your system, print settings, lists, rulers or margins, paragraphs, phrases, and words can be stored in various ways for recall and inclusion in the content or formatting of a document.

subscript and superscript Characters printed off the main line of the text. Subscripts are generally printed half a line below the main line (H_2); superscripts above the main line (for footnote reference[5]).

swap Some systems have a special key function that exchanges a character with the character to its right. This is useful when correcting transpositions ("teh" instead of "the").

system The entire word processing unit, including all its hardware and software parts.

system page number The page number in a document assigned by the system for a given page. Each document begins with a system number of "1." If your document is the second one of a long work that is consecutively numbered, you may instruct the system to number the pages of the document beginning with another number, such as "38." In such a case, book or report page 38 will be system page 1, 39 will be 2, and so on. Depending on your system, you will need to use the system page number to "go to" or "print" a particular page (although some systems renumber all the pages in a document based on the initial page number you enter for the document).

systems disk The disk that holds the software program.

tab To enter a tab mark or to press the tab key to move the cursor over to the next tab mark.

temporary marker Markers that are automatically erased by the system when they are no longer needed. Some are entered by the system, such as a word-wrap return—as opposed to a hard return—that the system places at the end of each line when it drops down to the text line. If you rearrange the text, old word-wrap returns will be erased automatically, and new word-wrap returns entered automatically for the new lines, if line endings have been changed. The same happens to soft page end markers when lines are added or deleted.

text The part of a document that is normally displayed on the screen and printed out as the desired output. All the commands—both hard and soft—are considered not part of the text, even though they are essential to the word processing operation. The characters that show which commands have been entered can usually be seen only on the view (display) mode.

thousands separator On some systems a comma can be used in columnar work as a point on which numbers line up. The comma, in this case, separates the thousands position from the hundreds in large numbers.

top margin The number of lines between the top of the sheet of paper and the first line of printing.

typeface or typestyle The characters of a particular design of type appearance and size. A printwheel will contain characters of a single typestyle or typeface and of a single pitch. Light Italic is an example of a typeface, as are Boldface and Prestige.

underline To print with a line under the text for emphasis or as a substitute for italics. Each system has special function keys to make underlining easy.

update To revise text and bring the information on a disk to current status. It is especially important to update backup copies of disks, so you don't inadvertently use disks that are unlike the most recently revised printout.

uppercase The capitalized form of letters. The term is taken from earlier printing times when these letters were manually taken one by one by typesetters from a large compartmentalized drawer (called a "case") in which the capitalized letters were stored in compartments located at the upper third of the case.

variable Information, usually in a list or in a stored paragraph, that can be inserted automatically into a standardized form (shell) document.

view mode A special display of the document that shows all the commands as well as the text.

word A group of characters separated from adjoining groups by space. A punctuation mark is considered by the system to be part of the word it is attached to. The space following a word is also usually read by the system as being part of that word. When deleting the characters that make up a word, it is also necessary to delete the appropriate space, since the system does not do so automatically.

word processing The use of a computer system to create, edit, store, and print text. Dedicated word processors are computers in which many word processing functions are built into the construction of the hardware and the nature of the program in the software to perform the required tasks as rapidly and efficiently as possible.

word wrap A feature wherein a word that is entered and passes over the right-hand margin drops down to form the first word of the next line. This feature is performed automatically on word processors. Word wraps will be automatically readjusted by the system when line endings are changed due to text editing.

work station The screen/disk drive/computer/keyboard parts of your word processor considered as the place where you perform your word processing. The printer is not automatically a part of your work station, since you can share a printer with another work station.

Metrics Glossary

Ampere A unit for measuring the flow of electricity. Symbol: amp.

Area Amount of surface, measured in square units.

Are A metric surface measure, equal to 100 m². Symbol: a.

Atto- A prefix indicating one quintillionth of a given unit.

Barrel The amount contained in a barrel; especially the amount (as 31 gallons of fermented beverage or 42 gallons of petroleum) fixed for a certain commodity and used as a unit of measure for that particular commodity. Symbol: bbl.

Boardfoot A unit of quantity for lumber equal to the volume of a board 12 × 12 × 1 inches. Symbol: fbm.

Bushel A unit of dry capacity equal to 4 pecks (2150.42 in³) or 35.238 liters

Candela A unit for measuring the luminous intensity (amount) of a light produced by a light source.

Capacity See Volume.

Celsius The name of the scale for temperature commonly used in conjunction with the metric system. Also known as the Centigrade scale. In the Celsius scale, water boils at 100° C and freezes at 0° C, as opposed to 212° F and 32° F, respectively, in the Fahrenheit scale. Symbol: ° C.

Centare A metric surface measure equal to 1 m². Symbol: ca.

Centi- A prefix indicating one hundredth of a given unit.

Centigram One hundredth of a gram. Symbol: cg.

Centiliter One hundredth of a liter. Symbol: cl.

Centimeter One hundredth of a meter. One centimeter equals .3937 inch. Symbol: cm.

Chain A unit of measure equal to 66 feet (20.1168 meters). Symbol: ch.

Cubic unit symbols Examples: mm³, cm³, m³, etc., used to denote volume.

Customary unit Units of weights and measures currently in use in the United States, known also as English units. These include: inches, feet, yards, and miles for length; ounces, pounds, and tons for weight; pints, quarts, and gallons.

Deci- A prefix indicating one tenth of a given unit.

Decigram One tenth of a gram. Symbol: dg.

Deciliter One tenth of a liter. Roughly equal to .21 pint. Symbol: dl.

Decimeter Ten centimeters or one tenth of a meter. Symbol: dm.

Deka- A prefix indicating ten times a given unit.

Dekagram Ten grams. Symbol: dag.

Dekaliter Ten liters, roughly equivalent to 2.64 gallons. Symbol: dal.

Dekameter Ten meters. One dekameter roughly equals 10.91 yards. Symbol: dam.

Density The weight of any sample of a substance divided by the volume measure of that sample.

Dram A unit of avoirdupois weight equal to 27.343 grains or .0625 ounce (1.771 grams). Symbol: dr.

Fathom A unit of length equal to 6 feet (1.8288 meters) used for measuring the depth of water. Symbol: fath.

Femto- A prefix indicating one quadrillionth of a given unit.

Furlong A unit of distance equal to 220 yards (201.168 meters). No symbol.

Giga- A prefix indicating a billion times a given unit.

Gill A unit of liquid measure equal to .25 pint or 118.291 milliliters.

Grain A unit of weight equal to .002083 ounce (.0648 gram), originally based on the weight of a grain of wheat. Symbol: gr.

Gram A common metric unit of weight equal to one thousandth of a kilogram. Symbol: g.

Hectare The common unit of land measure in the metric system, equal to 100 acres or 10,000 square meters and equivalent to 2.471 acres. Symbol: ha.

Hecto- A prefix indicating one hundred times a given unit.

Hectogram One hundred grams. Symbol: hg.

Hectoliter One hundred liters. Symbol: hl.

Hectometer One hundred meters. Symbol: hm.

Hogshead A U.S. unit of capacity equal to 63 gallons (238.4809 liters). Symbol: hka.

Hundredweight A unit of weight (avoirdupois) commonly equivalent to 100 lbs. (45.359 kilograms) in the United States and 112 lbs (50.803 kilograms) in England. The former is known as the short hundredweight and the latter as the long hundredweight. Symbol: cwt.

Kelvin scale A temperature scale often used with the metric system and developed by the British physicist Lord Kelvin. The starting or zero point on the Kelvin scale is absolute zero (—273.15° C, —459.67° F)—the lowest theoretical temperature that a gas can reach. On this scale, water freezes at 273.15° K and boils at 373.15° K.

Kilo- A prefix indicating one thousand times a given unit.

Kilogram The standard unit of mass in the metric system. The kilogram is a cylinder of platinum-iridium alloy kept by the International Bureau of Weights and Measures near Paris. A duplicate kilogram is kept by the National Bureau of Standards in Washington and serves as the mass standard for the United States. One kilogram is approximately equal to 2.2 pounds. Symbol: kg.

Kiloliter One thousand liters. Symbol: kl.

Kilometer One thousand meters, equivalent to 3,280.8 feet or .621 mile. Symbol: km.

Link One of the standardized divisions of a surveyor's chain that is 7.92 inches (201.168 millimeters) long and serves as a measure of length. No symbol.

Liter The basic metric unit of liquid measure, equal to the volume of one kilogram of water at 4° C or one cubic decimeter. A liter is equivalent to 1.057 quarts. Symbol: l.

Lumen A unit for measuring the brightness of light when it reaches the surface of an object.

Mass The amount of material in an object, measured in kilograms (q.v.).

Mega- A prefix indicating one million times a given unit.

Meter The basic unit of length in the metric system. It is defined in terms of the wavelength of orange-red light emitted by a krypton-86 atom (1,650,763.73 such wavelengths to the meter). One meter equals 39.37 inches. Symbol: m.

Metric system A decimal system of weights and measures, adopted first in France and now in common use worldwide.

Metric ton One thousand kilograms, roughly equivalent to 2,200 pounds. Symbol: t.

Micron The millionth part of a meter. Symbol: μ.

Mile, International Nautical A unit of distance in sea and air navigation equal to 1.852 kilometers or 6,076.1033 feet.

Mill A unit of money (but not an actual coin) used primarily in accounting.

Milli- A prefix indicating one thousandth of a given unit.

Milligram   One thousandth of a gram. Symbol: mg.

Milliliter   One thousandth of a liter. Symbol: ml.

Millimeter   One tenth of a centimeter or one thousandth of a meter. Symbol: mm.

Minim   The smallest unit of liquid measure, the sixtieth part of a fluid dram, roughly equivalent to one drop.

Nano-   A prefix indicating one billionth of a given unit.

Ounce, avoirdupois   A unit of weight equal to 437.5 grains or .625 pound avoirdupois (28.349 grams). Symbol: oz. avdp.

Ounce, troy   A unit of weight equal to 480 grains or .833 pound troy (31.103 grams). Symbol: oz. tr.

Peck   A dry measure of 8 quarts or the fourth part of a bushel (8.89 liters).

Perimeter   The measure of the distance around a figure.

Pico-   A prefix indicating one trillionth of a given unit.

Pound, avoirdupois   A unit of weight and mass equal to 7,000 grains (.453 kilogram) divided into 16 ounces, used for ordinary commercial purposes. Symbol: lb. avdp.

Pound, troy   A unit of weight equal to 5,760 grains (.373 kilogram) divided into 12 ounces troy, used for gold, silver, and other precious metals. Symbol: lb. tr.

Radian   An arc of a circle equal in length to the radius of that circle. An angle emanating from the center of a circle that subtends (cuts off) such an arc is said to measure one radian. Measuring angles in radians is preferred with the metric system.

Rod   A unit of linear, 5.5 yards or 16.5 feet (5.0292 meters). A unit of surface measure 30.25 yd^2 (25.2901 m^2). No symbol.

Second   The sixtieth part of a minute of a degree, often represented by the sign ″ as in 13 15′ 45″, read as 13 degrees, 15 minutes, 45 seconds.

Specific gravity   The ratio of the density of a substance to the density of water at 4° C.

Square unit symbol   Example: mm^2, cm^2, m^2, etc.

Stere   A cubic measure equivalent to 35.315 cubic feet or 1.3080 cubic yards (1.001 m^3). Used to measure cordwood. No symbol.

Tera-   A prefix indicating a trillion times a given unit.

Ton, metric   See Metric ton.

Volume   The measure in cubic units of the amount of space inside any given container; also the measure of the amount such a container will hold. The latter is known as the *capacity* of the container and can be given in either units of liquid measure (see Liter, also Milliliter) or in cubic units.

Weight   The force of the earth's pull on an object. Weight, in the Metric system, is commonly measured in grams.

Units of Measurement–
Conversion Factors*

Units of Length

To Convert from **Centimeters**

To	Multiply by
Inches	0.393 700 8
Feet	0.032 808 40
Yards	0.010 936 13
Meters	**0.01**

To Convert from **Meters**

To	Multiply by
Inches	39.370 08
Feet	3.280 840
Yards	1.093 613
Miles	0.000 621 37
Millimeters	**1,000**
Centimeters	**100**
Kilometers	**0.001**

To Convert from **Inches**

To	Multiply by
Feet	0.083 333 33
Yards	0.027 777 78
Centimeters	**2.54**
Meters	**0.025 4**

To Convert from **Feet**

To	Multiply by
Inches	**12**
Yards	0.333 333 3
Miles	0.000 189 39
Centimeters	**30.48**
Meters	**0.304 8**
Kilometers	**0.000 304 8**

To Convert from **Yards**

To	Multiply by
Inches	**36**
Feet	**3**
Miles	0.000 568 18
Centimeters	**91.44**
Meters	**0.914 4**

To Convert from **Miles**

To	Multiply by
Inches	**63,360**
Feet	**5,280**
Yards	**1,760**
Centimeters	**160,934.4**
Meters	**1,609.344**
Kilometers	**1.609 344**

Units of Mass

To Convert from **Grams**

To	Multiply by
Grains	15.432 36
Avoirdupois drams	0.564 383 4
Avoirdupois ounces	0.035 273 96
Troy ounces	0.032 150 75
Troy pounds	0.002 679 23
Avoirdupois pounds	0.002 204 62
Milligrams	**1,000**
Kilograms	**0.001**

To Convert from **Avoirdupois Pounds**

To	Multiply by
Grains	**7,000**
Avoirdupois drams	**256**
Avoirdupois ounces	**16**
Troy ounces	14.583 33
Troy pounds	1.215 278
Grams	**453.592 37**
Kilograms	**0.453 592 37**
Short hundredweights	**0.01**
Short tons	**0.000 5**
Long tons	0.000 446 428 6
Metric tons	**0.000 453 592 37**

*All boldface figures are exact; the others generally are given to seven signficant figures.

In using conversion factors, it is possible to perform division as well as the multiplication process shown here. Division may be particularly advantageous where more than the significant figures published here are required. Division may be performed in lieu of multiplication by using the reciprocal of any indicated multiplier as divisor. For example, to convert from centimeters to inches by division, refer to the table headed "To Convert from *Inches*" and use the factor listed at "centimeters" (*2.54*) as divisor.

To Convert from **Kilograms**

To	Multiply by
Grains	15,432.36
Avoirdupois drams	564.383 4
Avoirdupois ounces	35.273 96
Troy ounces	32.150 75
Troy pounds	2.679 229
Avoirdupois pounds	2.204 623
Grams	**1,000**
Short hundredweights	0.022 046 23
Short tons	0.001 102 31
Long tons	0.000 984 2
Metric tons	**0.001**

To Convert from **Metric Tons**

To	Multiply by
Avoirdupois pounds	2,204.623
Short hundredweights	22.046 23
Short tons	1.102 311 3
Long tons	0.984 206 5
Kilograms	**1,000**

To Convert from **Grains**

To	Multiply by
Avoirdupois drams	0.036 571 43
Avoirdupois ounces	0.002 285 71
Troy ounces	0.002 083 33
Troy pounds	0.000 173 61
Avoirdupois pounds	0.000 142 86
Milligrams	**64.798 91**
Grams	**0.064 798 91**
Kilograms	**0.000 064 798 91**

To Convert from **Troy Ounces**

To	Multiply by
Grains	**480**
Avoirdupois drams	17.554 29
Avoirdupois ounces	1.097 143
Troy pounds	0.083 333 3
Avoirdupois pounds	0.068 571 43
Grams	**31.103 476 8**

To Convert from **Long Tons**

To	Multiply by
Avoirdupois ounces	**35,840**
Avoirdupois pounds	**2,240**
Short hundredweights	**22.4**
Short tons	**1.12**
Kilograms	**1,016.046 908 8**
Metric tons	**1.016 046 908 8**

To Convert from **Avoirdupois Ounces**

To	Multiply by
Grains	**437.5**
Avoirdupois drams	**16**
Troy ounces	0.911 458 3
Troy pounds	0.075 954 86
Avoirdupois pounds	**0.062 5**
Grams	**28.349 523 125**
Kilograms	**0.028 349 523 125**

To Convert from **Short Hundredweights**

To	Multiply by
Avoirdupois pounds	**100**
Short tons	**0.05**
Long tons	0.044 642 86
Kilograms	**45.359 237**
Metric tons	**0.045 359 237**

To Convert from **Short Tons**

To	Multiply by
Avoirdupois pounds	**2,000**
Short hundredweights	**20**
Long tons	0.892 857 1
Kilograms	**907.184 74**
Metric tons	**0.907 184 74**

To convert from **Troy Pounds**

To	Multiply by
Grains	**5,760**
Avoirdupois drams	210.651 4
Avoirdupois ounces	13.165 71
Troy ounces	**12**
Avoirdupois pounds	0.822 857 1
Grams	**373.241 721 6**

Units of Capacity, or Volume, Liquid Measure

To Convert from **Milliliters**

To	Multiply by
Minims	16.230 73
Liquid ounces	0.033 814 02
Gills	0.008 453 5
Liquid pints	0.002 113 4
Liquid quarts	0.001 056 7
Gallons	0.000 264 17
Cubic inches	0.061 023 74
Liters	**0.001**

To Convert from **Gills**

To	Multiply by
Minims	**1,920**
Liquid ounces	**4**
Liquid pints	**0.25**
Liquid quarts	**0.125**
Gallons	**0.031 25**
Cubic inches	**7.218 75**
Cubic feet	**0.004 177 517**
Milliliters	**118.294 118 25**
Liters	**0.118 294 118 25**

To Convert from **Cubit Meters**

To	Multiply by
Gallons	264.172 05
Cubic inches	61,023.74
Cubic feet	35.314 67
Liters	**1,000**
Cubic yards	1.307 950 6

To Convert from **Liquid Ounces**

To	Multiply by
Minims	**480**
Gills	**0.25**
Liquid pints	**0.062 5**
Liquid quarts	**0.031 25**
Gallons	**0.007 812 5**
Cubic inches	1.804 687 5
Cubic feet	0.001 044 38
Milliliters	29.573 53
Liters	0.029 573 53

To Convert from **Liters**

To	Multiply by
Liquid ounces	33.814 02
Gills	8.453 506
Liquid pints	2.113 376
Liquid quarts	1.056 688
Gallons	0.264 172 05
Cubic inches	61.023 74
Cubic feet	0.035 314 67
Milliliters	**1,000**
Cubic meters	**0.001**
Cubic yards	0.001 307 95

To Convert from **Cubic Inches**

To	Multiply by
Minims	265.974 0
Liquid ounces	0.554 112 6
Gills	0.138 528 1
Liquid pints	0.034 632 03
Liquid quarts	0.017 316 02
Gallons	0.004 329 0
Cubic feet	0.000 578 7
Milliliters	**16.387 064**
Liters	**0.016 387 064**
Cubic meters	**0.000 016 387 064**
Cubic yards	0.000 021 43

To Convert from **Minims**

To	Multiply by
Liquid ounces	0.002 083 33
Gills	0.000 520 83
Milliliters	0.061 611 52
Cubic inches	0.003 759 77

To Convert from **Liquid Quarts**

To	Multiply by
Minims	**15,360**
Liquid ounces	**32**
Gills	**8**
Liquid pints	**2**
Gallons	**0.25**
Cubic inches	**57.75**
Cubic feet	0.033 420 14
Milliliters	**946.352 946**
Liters	**0.946 352 946**

To Convert from **Liquid Pints**

To	Multiply by
Minims	**7,680**
Liquid ounces	**16**
Gills	**4**
Liquid quarts	**0.5**
Gallons	**0.125**
Cubic inches	**28.875**
Cubic feet	0.016 710 07
Milliliters	**473.176 473**
Liters	**0.473 176 473**

To Convert from **Cubic Feet**

To	Multiply by
Liquid ounces	957.506 5
Gills	239.376 6
Liquid pints	59.844 16
Liquid quarts	29.922 08
Gallons	7.480 519
Cubic inches	**1,728**
Liters	**28.316 846 592**
Cubic meters	**0.028 316 846 592**
Cubic yards	0.037 037 04

To convert from **Cubic Yards**

To	Multiply by
Callons	201.974 0
Cubic inches	**46,656**
Cubic feet	**27**
Liters	**764.554 857 984**
Cubic meters	**0.764 554 857 984**

To Convert from **Gallons**

To	Multiply by
Minims	**61,440**
Liquid ounces	**128**
Gills	**32**
Liquid pints	**8**
Liquid quarts	**4**
Cubic inches	**231**
Cubic feet	0.133 680 6
Milliliters	**3,785.411 784**
Liters	**3.785 411 784**
Cubic meters	**0.003 785 411 784**
Cubic yards	0.004 951 13

Units of Capacity, or Volume, Dry Measure

To Convert from **Liters**

To	Multiply by
Dry pints	1.816 166
Dry quarts	0.908 082 98
Pecks	0.113 510 4
Bushels	0.028 377 59
Dekaliters	**0.1**

To Convert from **Dekaliters**

To	Multiply by
Dry pints	18.161 66
Dry quarts	9.080 829 8
Pecks	1.135 104
Bushels	0.283 775 9
Cubic inches	610.237 4
Cubic feet	0.353 146 7
Liters	**10**

To Convert from **Cubic Meters**

To	Multiply by
Pecks	113.510 4
Bushels	28.377 59

To Convert from **Dry Pints**

To	Multiply by
Dry quarts	**0.5**
Pecks	**0.062 5**
Bushels	**0.015 625**
Cubic inches	**33.600 312 5**
Cubic feet	0.019 444 63
Liters	0.550 610 47
Dekaliters	0.055 061 05

To Convert from **Dry Quarts**

To	Multiply by
Dry pints	**2**
Pecks	**0.125**
Bushels	**0.031 25**
Cubic inches	**67.200 625**
Cubic feet	0.038 889 25
Liters	1.101 221
Dekaliters	0.110 122 1

To Convert from **Pecks**

To	Multiply by
Dry pints	**16**
Dry quarts	**8**
Bushels	**0.25**
Cubic inches	**537.605**
Cubic feet	0.311 114
Liters	8.809 767 5
Dekaliters	0.880 976 75
Cubic meters	0.008 809 77
Cubic yards	0.011 522 74

To Convert from **Bushels**

To	Multiply by
Dry pints	**64**
Dry quarts	**32**
Pecks	**4**
Cubic inches	**2,150.42**
Cubic feet	1.244 456
Liters	35.239 07
Dekaliters	3.523 907
Cubic meters	0.035 239 07
Cubic yards	0.046 090 96

To Convert from **Cubic Inches**

To	Multiply by
Dry pints	0.029 761 6
Dry quarts	0.014 880 8
Pecks	0.001 860 10
Bushels	0.000 465 025

To Convert from **Cubic Yards**

To	Multiply by
Pecks	86.784 91
Bushels	21.696 227

To Convert from **Cubit Feet**

To	Multiply by
Dry pints	51.428 09
Dry quarts	25.714 05
Pecks	3.214 256
Bushels	0.803 563 95

Units of Area

To Convert from **Square Centimeters**

To	Multiply by
Square inches	0.155 000 3
Square feet	0.001 076 39
Square yards	0.000 119 599
Square meters	**0.000 1**

To Convert from **Square Feet**

To	Multiply by
Square inches	**144**
Square yards	0.111 111 1
Acres	0.000 022 957
Square centimeters	**929.030 4**
Square meters	**0.092 903 04**

To Convert from **Square Meters**

To	Multiply by
Square inches	1,550.003
Square feet	10.763 91
Square yards	1.195 990
Acres	0.000 247 105
Square centimeters	**10,000**
Hectares	**0.000 1**

To Convert from **Square Yards**

To	Multiply by
Square inches	**1,296**
Square feet	**9**
Acres	0.000 206 611 6
Square miles	0.000 000 322 830 6
Square centimeters	**8,361.273 6**
Square meters	**0.836 127 36**
Hectares	**0.000 083 612 736**

To Convert from **Hectares**

To	Multiply by
Square feet	107,639.1
Square yards	11,959.90
Acres	2.471 054
Square miles	0.003 861 02
Square meters	**10,000**

To Convert from **Acres**

To	Multiply by
Square feet	**43,560**
Square yards	**4,840**
Square miles	**0.001 562 5**
Square meters	**4,046.856 422 4**
Hectares	**0.404 685 642 24**

To Convert from **Square Inches**

To	Multiply by
Square feet	0.006 944 44
Square yards	0.000 771 605
Square centimeters	**6.451 6**
Square meters	**0.000 645 16**

To Convert from **Square Miles**

To	Multiply by
Square feet	**27,878,400**
Square yards	**3,097,600**
Acres	**640**
Square meters	**2,589,988.110 336**
Hectares	**258.998 811 033 6**

Tables of
Weights and Measures

Linear Measure

Measure		Equivalents
1 inch		2.54 centimeters
12 inches	1 foot	0.3048 meter
3 feet	1 yard	0.9144 meter
5½ yards 16½ feet	1 rod (or pole or perch)	5.029 meters
40 rods	1 furlong	201.17 meters
8 furlongs 1,760 yards 5,280 feet	1 (statute) mile	1,609.3 meters
3 miles	1 (land) league	4.83 kilometers

Square Measure

Measure		Equivalents
1 square inch		6.452 square centimeters
144 square inches	1 square foot	929 square centimeters
9 square feet	1 square yard	0.8361 square meter
30¼ square yards	1 square rod (or square pole or square perch)	25.29 square meters
160 square rods or 4,840 square yards or 43,560 square feet	1 acre	0.4047 hectare
640 acres	1 square mile	259 hectares 2.59 square kilometers

Cubic Measure

Measure		Equivalents
1 cubic inch		16.387 cubic centimeters
1,728 cubic inches	1 cubic foot	0.0283 cubic meter
27 cubic feet	1 cubic yard (in units for cordwood, etc.)	0.7646 cubic meter
16 cubic feet	1 cord foot	
8 cord feet	1 cord	3.625 cubic meters

Chain Measure (for Gunter's, or surveyor's, chain)

Measure		Equivalents
7.92 inches	1 link	20.12 centimeters
100 links 66 feet	1 chain	20.12 meters
10 chains	1 furlong	201.17 meters
80 chains	1 mile (for engineer's chain)	1,609.3 meters
1 foot	1 link	0.3048 meter
100 feet	1 chain	30.48 meters
52.8 chains	1 mile	1,609.3 meters

Surveyor's (Square) Measure

Measure	Equivalents	
625 square links	1 square pole	25.29 square meters
16 square poles	1 square chain	404.7 square meters
10 square chains	1 acre	0.4047 hectare
640 acres	1 square mile	259 hectares
	1 section	2.59 square kilometers
36 square miles	1 township	9,324.0 hectares
		93.24 square kilometers

Nautical Measure

Measure	Equivalents	
6 feet	1 fathom	1.829 meters
100 fathoms	1 cable's length (ordinary)[1]	
10 cables' lengths	1 nautical mile	1.852 kilometers[2]
	6,076.10333 feet	
1 nautical mile	1.1508 statute miles[3]	
3 nautical miles	1 marine league	5.56 kilometers
	3.45 statute miles	
60 nautical miles	1 degree of a great circle of the earth	

Dry Measure

Measure	Equivalents		
1 pint		33.60 cubic inches	0.5505 liter
2 pints	1 quart	67.20 cubic inches	1.1012 liters
8 quarts	1 peck	537.61 cubic inches	8.8096 liters
4 pecks	1 bushel	2,150.42 cubic inches	35.2383 liters
1 British dry quart	1.032 U.S. dry quarts		

According to United States government standards, the following are the weights avoirdupois for single bushels of the specified grains: for wheat, 60 pounds; for barley, 48 pounds; for oats, 32 pounds; for rye, 56 pounds; for corn, 56 pounds. Some states have specifications varying from these.

Liquid Measure

Measure	Equivalents		
1 gill	4 fluid ounces (see next table)	7.219 cubic inches	0.1183 liter
4 gills	1 pint	28.875 cubic inches	0.4732 liter
2 pints	1 quart	57.75 cubic inches	0.9463 liter
4 quarts	1 gallon	231 cubic inches	3.7853 liters
4 British imperial quarts	1 imperial gallon	277.42 cubic inches	4.546 liters

The barrel in Great Britain equals 36 imperial gallons, in the United States, usually 31½ gallons.

Apothecaries' Fluid Measure

Measure	Equivalents		
1 minim		0.0038 cubic inch	0.0616 milliliter
60 minims	1 fluid dram	0.2256 cubic inch	3.6966 milliliters
8 fluid drams	1 fluid ounce	1.8047 cubic inches	0.0296 liter
16 fluid ounces	1 pint	28.875 cubic inches	0.4732 liter
1 British pint	20 fluid ounces		

See table immediately preceding for quart and gallon equivalents.

[1] In the U.S. Navy 120 fathoms or 720 feet equals 1 cable's length; in the British Navy, 608 feet equals 1 cable's length.
[2] By international agreement, 1954.
[3] The length of a minute of longitude at the equator. Also called geographical, sea, or air mile, and, in Great Britain, Admiralty mile.

Circular (or Angular) Measure

Measure	Equivalent
60 seconds (")	1 minute (')
60 minutes	1 degree (°)
90 degrees	1 quadrant 1 right angle
4 quadrants 360 degrees	1 circle

Avoirdupois Weight

Measure	Equivalents	
1 grain		0.0648 gram[1]
1 dram 27.34 grains		1.772 grams
16 drams 437.5 grains	1 ounce	28.3495 grams
16 ounces 7,000 grains	1 pound[2]	453.59 grams
100 pounds	1 hundredweight	45.36 kilograms
2,000 pounds	1 ton	907.18 kilograms

Troy Weight

Measure	Equivalents	
1 grain		0.0648 gram[1]
3.086 grains	1 carat	200 milligrams
24 grains	1 pennyweight	1.5552 grams
20 pennyweights 480 grains	1 ounce	31.1035 grams
12 ounces 5,760 grains	1 pound	373.24 grams

Apothecaries' Weight

Measure	Equivalents	
1 grain		0.0648 gram[1]
20 grains	1 scruple	1.296 grams
3 scruples	1 dram	3.888 grams
8 drams 480 grains	1 ounce	31.1035 grams
12 ounces 5,760 grains	1 pound	373.24 grams

[1]The grain is the same in all three tables of weight.
[2]In Great Britain, 14 pounds (6.35 kilograms) equals 1 stone, 112 pounds (50.80 kilograms) equals 1 hundred-weight, and 2,240 pounds (1,016.05 kilograms) equal 1 long ton.

Biographies

Aalto, (Hugo) Alvar (Henrik), 1898–1976, Finn. architect.

Aaron, Henry, 1934–, U.S. baseball player.

Abbott, George, 1887–1995, U.S. theatrical director & playwright.

—**Sir John Joseph Caldwell,** 1821–93, Can. statesman; Can. prime minister 1891–92.

—**William (Budd),** 1896–1974, U.S. comedian & actor.

Abd-el-Krim, 1885?–1963, Moorish leader in Rif region of Morocco.

Abd-ul-Baha, 1844–1921, Pers. religious leader; called **Abbas Effendi.**

Abdul-Jabbar, Kareem, b. Lew Alcindor, 1947–, U.S. basketball player.

Abel, I(orwith) W(ilbur), 1908–87, U.S. labor leader.

—**Rudolph,** 1902–72, Soviet spy.

Abélard, Peter, 1079–1142, Fr. theologian, philosopher, & teacher; also **Abailard.** See also HELOÏSE.

Abercombie, James, 1706–81, Brit. general.

Abernathy, Ralph David, 1926–90, U.S. clergyman & civil rights leader.

Abrams, Creighton W., Jr., 1914–74, U.S. general.

Abruzzi, Luigi Amedeo, Duca degli, 1873–1933, Ital. Arctic explorer.

Abzug, Bella Savitzky, 1920–98, U.S. politician & women's advocate.

Ace, Goodman, 1899–1982, U.S. comic writer & radio performer.

—**Jane,** 1900–74, U.S. radio performer, wife of prec.

Acheampong, Ignatius Kutu, 1931–79, African military officer; president of Ghana 1972–78.

Acheson, Dean Gooderham, 1893–1971, U.S. lawyer; secretary of state 1949–53.

Acton, John Emerich Edward Dalberg, Lord, 1843–1902, Eng. historian & author.

Adam, James, 1730–94, Scot. architect & furniture designer.

—**Robert,** 1728–92, Scot. architect; brother of prec.

Adams, Abigail Smith, 1744–1818, U.S. writer.

—**Ansel,** 1902–84, U.S. photographer.

—**Brooks,** 1848–1927, U.S. historian.

—**Charles Francis,** 1807–86, U.S. lawyer & diplomat; father of prec.

—**Franklin Pierce (F.P.A.),** 1881–1960, U.S. journalist.

—**Henry Brooks,** 1838–1918, U.S. historian & philosopher.

—**James Truslow,** 1878–1949, U.S. historian.

—**John,** 1735–1826, 2nd U.S. president 1797–1801; husband of Abigail.

—**John Quincy,** 1767–1848, 6th U.S. president 1825–29; son of prec. & father of Charles Francis.

—**Maude,** 1872–1953, U.S. actress.

—**Samuel,** 1722–1803, Amer. revolutionary leader.

—**Samuel Hopkins,** 1871–1958, U.S. author.

Adamson, Joy, 1910–80, Silesian naturalist & author.

Addams, Charles Samuel, 1912–88, U.S. cartoonist.

—**Jane,** 1860–1935, U.S. social worker.

Adderley, Julian Edwin (Cannonball), 1928–75, U.S. jazz musician.

Addinsell, Richard, 1904–77, Eng. film composer.

Addison, Joseph, 1672–1719, Eng. essayist & poet.

—**Thomas,** 1793–1860, Eng. physician.

Adenauer, Konrad, 1876–1967, Ger. statesman; first chancellor of W. Germany 1949–63.

Adler, Alfred, 1870–1937, Austrian psychiatrist.

—**Felix,** 1851–1933, U.S. educator & reformer.

—**Larry,** 1914–, U.S. musician.

—**Luther,** 1903–84, U.S. actor.

—**Mortimer Jerome,** 1902–, U.S. philosopher.

—**Richard,** 1921–, U.S. composer.

Adrian IV, b. Nicholas Breakspear, 1100?–59, pope 1154–59.

—**VI,** b. Adrian Florensz, 1459–1523, Du. pope 1522–23.

Adrian, Frederick 1903–59, U.S. fashion designer.

Aeschylus, 525–456 B.C., Gk. writer of tragedies.

Aesop, 6th c. B.C. Gk. writer of fables.

Aga Khan III, 1877–1957, Muslim spiritual leader.

—**IV,** 1936–, grandson & successor of prec.

Agassiz, Alexander, 1835–1910, U.S. zoologist.

—**(Jean) Louis (Rodolphe),** 1807–73, Swiss-born U.S. naturalist; father of prec.

Agee, James, 1909–55, U.S. author & critic.

Agnelli, Giovanni, 1921–, Ital. industrialist.

Agnew, Spiro Theodore, 1918–96, U.S. politician; U.S. vice president 1968–73; resigned.

Agnon, Shmuel Yosef, 1888–1970, Russ.-born Israeli author; Nobel Prize winner.

Agricola, Gnaeus Julius, A.D. 37–93, Roman general.

Agrippa, Marcus Vipsanius, 63–12 B.C. Roman statesman.

Agrippina, 13 B.C.–A.D. 33, mother of Caligula: called **the Elder.**

— A.D. 15?–59, mother of Nero: called **the Younger.**

Aguinaldo, Emilio, 1869–1964, Filipino statesman & revolutionary leader.

Aiken, Conrad Potter, 1889–1973, U.S. poet & author.

—**Howard H.,** 1900–73, U.S. mathematician.

Ailey, Alvin, 1931–89, U.S. choreographer.

Akbar, 1542–1605, Mogul emperor of Hindustan.

Akhmatova, Anna, 1888–1966, Soviet poet.

Akihito, 1933–, emperor of Japan.

Akuffo, Frederick William Kwasi, 1937–79, African military officer; president of Ghana 1978–79.

Alarón, Pedro Antonio de, 1833–91, Sp. playwright.

Alaric, 370?–410, king of the Visigoths; sacked Rome.

—**II,** ?–507, king of the Visigoths.

Albanese, Licia, 1913–, Ital. soprano active in U.S.

Albee, Edward, 1928–, U.S. playwright.

Albéniz, Isaac, 1860–1909, Sp. composer & pianist.

Albers, Josef, 1888–1976, Ger.-born U.S. painter.

Albert I, 1875–1934, king of Belgium 1909–34.

Albert, Prince, of Saxe-Coburg-Gotha, 1819–61, consort of Queen Victoria of England.

Albert, Carl Bert, 1908–, U.S. politician; speaker of House of Representatives 1971–77.

—**Eddie,** 1908–, U.S. actor.

Alberti, Leon Battista, 1404–72, Ital. architect & painter.

Albertson, Jack, 1910?–81, U.S. actor.

Albertus Magnus, Saint, 1200?–80, Ger. scholastic philosopher & theologian.

Albright, Ivan, 1897–1983, U.S. painter.

Albuquerque, Alfonso de, 1453–1515, Pg. viceroy in India.

Alcibiades, 450–404 B.C., Athenian general & politician.

Alcott, (Amos) Bronson, 1799–1888, U.S. educator.

—Louisa May, 1832–88, U.S. novelist; daughter of prec.

Alcuin, 735–804, Eng. theologian & scholar.

Alda, Alan, 1936–, U.S. actor.

Alden, John, 1599–1687, pilgrim at Plymouth Colony.

Aldrich, Nelson Wilmarth, 1841–1915, U.S. public official.

Aldrin, Edwin Eugene, Jr., 1930–, U.S. astronaut.

Aleichem, Sholem, pseud. of Solomon Rabinowitz, 1859–1916, Russ.-born U.S. author.

Aleixandre, Vicente, 1898–1984, Sp. poet; Nobel Prize winner.

Alemán Valdés, Miguel, 1902–83, Mexican statesman; president of Mexico 1946–52.

Alexander II, 1818–81, Russ. czar; emancipated serfs; assassinated.

Alexander III, 356–323 B.C., king of Macedonia & conqueror of Egypt & Asia Minor: called **the Great.**

Alexander VI, b. Rodrigo Lanzol y Borja, 1431–1503, pope 1492–1503.

Alexander Nevski, 1220?–63, Russ. military hero & saint.

Alexander Severus, 208?–235, Roman emperor 222–35.

Alexander, Grover Cleveland, 1887–1950, U.S. baseball player.

—Harold Rupert Leofric George (1st Earl Alexander of Tunis), 1891–1969, Brit. field marshal.

Alexanderson, Ernst F. W., 1878–1969, Swed.-born U.S. electrical engineer & inventor.

Alfieri, Count Vittorio, 1749–1803, Ital. playwright.

Alfonso XIII, 1886–1941, king of Spain 1902–31.

Alfred, 849–901, king of West Saxons: called **the Great.**

Alfvén, Hannes Olof Gösta, 1908–95, Swed. physicist; Nobel Prize winner.

Alger, Horatio, 1832–99, U.S. author.

Algren, Nelson, 1909–81, U.S. author.

Ali, Muhammad, b. Cassius Clay, 1942–, U.S. boxer.

Alinsky, Saul David, 1909–72, U.S. social reformer.

Allen, Ethan, 1737–89, Amer. revolutionary soldier.

—Fred, 1894–1956, U.S. humorist & radio performer.

—Frederick Lewis, 1890–1954, U.S. editor & historian.

—Gracie, 1906–64, U.S. actress & comedienne.

—Richard, 1760–1831, Amer. black religious leader.

—Stephen Valentine Patrick William (Steve), 1921–, U.S. comedian & author.

—Woody, 1935–, U.S. comedian, actor, author, & film director.

Allenby, Edmund Henry, 1861–1936, Brit. field marshal.

Allende Gossens, Salvador, 1908–73, president of Chile 1970–73.

Allgood, Sara, 1883–1950, Irish-born U.S. actress.

Allison, Fran, 1924?–89, U.S. actress.

Allport, Gordon Willard, 1897–1967, U.S. psychologist & author.

Allston, Washington, 1779–1843, U.S. painter.

Allyson, June, 1923–, U.S. actress.

Alma-Tadema, Sir Lawrence, 1836–1912, Dutch-born Eng. painter.

Alonso, Alicia, 1921–, Cuban ballerina.

Alpini, Prospero, 1553–1617, Ital. physician & botanist.

Alsop, Joseph, 1910–89, U.S. journalist & author.

—Stewart, 1914–74, U.S. journalist & author; brother of prec.

Altgeld, John Peter, 1847–1902, Ger.-born U.S. politician.

Altman, Benjamin, 1840–1913, U.S. merchant & art collector.

—Robert, 1925–, U.S. film director.

Alva, Fernando Alvarez de Toledo, Duke of, 1508–82, Sp. general in the Netherlands.

Alvarado, Pedro de, 1495?–1541, Sp. soldier in the New World.

Alvarez, Luis Walter, 1911–88, U.S. physicist; Nobel Prize winner.

Amado, Jorge, 1912–, Braz. author.

Amara, Lucine, 1927–, U.S. soprano.

Amati, Nicola, 1596–1684, Ital. violinmaker.

Ambler, Eric, 1909–, Eng. author.

Ambrose, Saint, 340?–397, bishop of Milan.

Ameche, Don, 1908–93, U.S. actor.

Amenhotep III, 14th c. B.C. king of Egypt; reigned ca. 1411–1375 B.C..

Amherst, Lord Jeffrey, 1717–97, Brit. governor-general of North America.

Amin Dada, Idi, 1925?–, Ugandan general; president of Uganda 1971–79.

Amis, Kingsley, 1922–1995, Brit. novelist.

Amory, Cleveland, 1917–, U.S. author & critic.

Ampère, André Marie, 1775–1836, Fr. physicist.

Amundsen, Roald, 1872–1928, Norw. explorer.

Anacreon, 572?–488 B.C., Gk. poet.

Anaxagoras, 500–428 B.C., Gk. philosopher.

Anaximander, 610–546? B.C., Gk. philosopher & astronomer.

Andersen, Hans Christian, 1805–75, Dan. writer of fairy tales.

Anderson, Carl David, 1905–91, U.S. physicist.

—Jack, 1922–, U.S. journalist.

—Dame Judith, 1898–1992, Austral.-born U.S. actress.

—Marian, 1902–93, U.S. contralto.

—Maxwell, 1888–1959, U.S. playwright.

—Sherwood, 1876–1941, U.S. author.

Andersson, Bibi, 1935–, Swed. actress.

André, John, 1751–80, Brit. major & spy in American Revolutionary War.

Andretti, Mario Gabriel, 1940–, Ital.-born U.S. auto racer.

Andrews A family of U.S. singers incl. three sisters: **La Verne,** 1916–67; **Maxine,** 1918–95, & **Patty,** 1920–.

—Julie, 1935–, Eng. actress & singer.

—Roy Chapman, 1884–1960, U.S. naturalist.

Andreyev, Leonid Nikolayevich, 1871–1919, Russ. author.

Andropov, Yuri Vladimirovich, 1914–84, general secretary U.S.S.R. communist party 1982–84.

Andros, Sir Edmund, 1637–1714, Brit. governor in North America.

Angela Merici, Saint, 1474?–1540, Ital. nun & founder of Ursuline order.

Angeles, Victoria de los, b. Victoria Gamez Cima, 1924–, Sp. soprano active in U.S.

Angelico, Fra, b. Giovanni da Fiesole, 1387–1455, Ital. painter.

Anglin, Margaret Mary, 1876–1958, Canadian actress active in U.S.

Ångstrom, Anders Jonas, 1814–74, Swed. physicist.

Anne, 1665–1714, queen of Great Britain 1702–14.

Anne of Cleves, 1515–57, Ger. princess; 4th wife of King Henry VIII of England.

Ann-Margret, b. Ann-Margret Olsson, 1941–, Swed.-born U.S. singer, actress.

Anouilh, Jean, 1910–87, Fr. playwright.

Anselm, Saint, 1033–1109, archbishop of Canterbury.

Ansermet, Ernest, 1883–1969, Swiss conductor.

Antheil, George, 1900–59, U.S. composer.

Anthony, Saint, ca. 250–350, Egyptian monk.

—of Padua, Saint, 1195–1231, Pg.-born Ital. Franciscan monk.

Anthony, Susan B(rownell), 1820–1906, U.S. women's suffragist.

Antisthenes, 444?–371? B.C., Gk. philosopher; founder of Cynic school.

Antonescu, Ion, 1882–1946, Rumanian general & dictator; premier of Romania 1940–44.

Antoninus Pius, A.D. 86–161, Roman emperor 131–61.

Antonio (Ruiz), 1921–, Sp. dancer.

Antonioni, Michelangelo, 1912–, Ital. film director.

Antony, Marc (L. Marcus Antonius), 83–30 B.C., Roman general & politician.

Apgar, Virginia, 1909–74, U.S. physician.

Apollinaire, Guillaume, pseud. of Wilhelm Apollinaris de Kostrowitzky, 1880–1918, Ital.-born Fr. author.

Appia, Adolphe, 1862–1928, Swiss theatrical producer & pioneer in stage lighting.

Appleton, Sir Edward Victor, 1892–1965, Brit. physicist; Nobel Prize winner.

Apuleius, Lucius, 2nd c. A.D. Roman satirist.

Aquinas, Saint Thomas, 1225?–74, Ital. theologian & philosopher.

Arafat, Yasir, 1929–, Palestinian leader.
Arcaro, George Edward (Eddie), 1916–97, U.S. jockey.
Archimedes, 287?–212 B.C., Gk. mathematician & inventor.
Archipenko, Alexander, 1887–1964, Russ.-born U.S. sculptor.
Arden, Elizabeth, 1884–1966, Can.-born U.S. businesswoman.
—Eve, 1912–90, U.S. actress.
Ardito Barletta Vallarina, Nicolás, 1938–, Panamanian statesman; president 1984–.
Ardrey, Robert, 1908–80, U.S. anthropologist & author.
Arendt, Hannah, 1906–75, Ger.-born U.S. political scientist & author.
Aretino, Pietro, 1492–1556, Ital. satirist.
Argentina, La, b. Antonia Mercé, 1888–1936, Argentine-born Spanish dancer.
Ariosto, Lodovico, 1474–1533, Ital. poet.
Aristarchus, 220?–150 B.C., Gk. grammarian.
—of Samos, 3rd c. B.C., Gk. astronomer.
Aristides, 530?–468 B.C., Athenian statesman & general: called **the Just.**
Aristippus, 435?–356? B.C., Gk. philosopher.
Aristophanes, 450?–380? B.C., Gk. playwright.
Aristotle, 384–322 B.C., Gk. philosopher.
Arius, 256?–336, Egyptian priest & theologian.
Arkin, Alan, 1934–, U.S. actor & director.
Arkwright, Sir Richard, 1732–92, Eng. inventor & industrialist.
Arlen, Harold, b. Hyman Arluck, 1905–86, U.S. composer.
Arliss, George, 1868–1946, Eng. actor active in U.S.
Armour, Philip Danforth, 1832–1901, U.S. industrialist.
Armstrong, Louis, 1900–71, U.S. jazz musician: called **Satchmo.**
—Neil Alden, 1930–, U.S. astronaut; first on the moon.
Arnaz, Desi, 1917–86, Cuban-born U.S. actor & producer.
Arno, Peter, 1904–68, U.S. cartoonist.
Arnold, Benedict, 1741–1801, Amer. revolutionary general & traitor.
—Matthew, 1822–88, Eng. poet & critic.
Aronson, Boris, 1900–80, Russ.-born stage designer & artist active in U.S.
Arp, Jean (or Hans), 1887–1966, Fr. sculptor & painter.
Arpad, ?–907, Hung. national hero.
Arrabal, Fernando, 1932–, Sp. playwright & author.
Arrau, Claudio, 1903–91, Chilean pianist.
Arrhenius, Svante August, 1859–1927, Swed. physicist & chemist.
Arrow, Kenneth Joseph, 1921–, U.S. economist; Nobel Prize winner.
Arroyo, Martina, 1937–, U.S. soprano.
Artaud, Antonin, 1896–1948, Fr. playwright & director.
Arthur, legendary 6th c. Brit. king.
Arthur, Chester Alan, 1829–86, 21st U.S. president 1881–85.
—Jean, 1905–91, U.S. actress.
Asch, Sholem, 1880–1957, Pol.-born U.S. Yiddish author.
Ashcroft, Dame Peggy, 1907–91, Eng. actress.
Ashe, Arthur Robert, Jr., 1943–93, U.S. tennis player.
Ashkenazy, Vladimir, 1937–, Russ. pianist active in U.S.
Ashton, Sir Frederick, 1904–88, Eng. choreographer.
Ashton-Warner, Sylvia, 1908–84, New Zealand author.
Ashurbanipal, 7th c. B.C. Assyrian king.
Asimov, Isaac, 1920–92, Soviet-born U.S. biochemist & author.
Asoka, ?–232 B.C., king of Magadha, India.
Aspasia, 470?–410 B.C., Gk. hetaera; consort of Pericles.
Asquith, Herbert Henry, 1852–1928, Brit. statesman; prime minister 1908–16.
Assad, Hafiz al, 1928–, president of Syria 1971–.
Astaire, Fred, 1899–1987, U.S. dancer, singer, & actor.
Aston, Francis William, 1877–1945, Eng. chemist & physicist.
Astor, John Jacob, 1763–1848, Ger.-born U.S. financier.
Astor, Lady, b. Nancy Langhorne, 1879–1964, U.S.-born Brit. politician; first woman member of House of Commons.
—Mary, 1906–87, U.S. actress & author.
Asturias, Miguel Angel, 1899–1974, Guat. author & diplomat; Nobel Prize winner.

Atahualpa, 1500?–33, last Inca king of Peru.
Atatürk, Kemal, 1881–1938, Turk. statesman; founded modern Turkey; president 1923–38.
Athanasius, Saint, 296?–373, Alexandrian bishop & theologian.
Atkinson, (Justin) Brooks, 1894–1984, U.S. drama critic & author.
Atlas, Charles, 1894–1972, Ital.-born U.S. physical culturist.
Attenborough, Richard, 1923–, Eng. actor & director.
Attila, 406?–453, king of the Huns.
Attlee, Clement Richard, Earl, 1883–1967, Eng. statesman; prime minister 1945–51.
Attucks, Crispus, 1723?–70, black patriot in the Amer. Revolution.
Atwood, Margaret, 1939–, Can. poet, novelist, & critic.
Auchincloss, Louis, 1917–, U.S. author.
Auden, W(ystan) H(ugh), 1907–73, Eng.-born U.S. poet.
Audubon, John James, 1785–1851, Haitian-born U.S. ornithologist & painter.
Auenbrugger, Leopold, 1722–1809, Austrian physician.
Auer, Leopold, 1845–1930, Hung. violinist & teacher.
Augustine, Saint, 354–430, early Christian church father; bishop of Hippo.
—Saint, ?–604, Roman monk sent to convert England to Christianity; first archbishop of Canterbury.
Augustus, b. Gaius Julius Caesar Octavianus, 63 B.C.–A.D. 14; first Roman emperor 27 B.C.–A.D. 14: also called **Octavian.**
Aug San Suu Kyi, 1945–, Burmese political leader, Nobel Prize winner.
Aurelian (L. Lucius Domitius Aurelianus), 212?–275, Roman emperor 270–75.
Auriol, Vincent, 1884–1966, Fr. statesman; president of France 1947–54.
Austen, Jane, 1775–1817, Eng. novelist.
Austin, Stephen Fuller, 1793–1836, U.S. politician & colonizer of Texas.
Autry, (Orvon) Gene, 1907–, U.S. actor, singer, & businessman.
Avedon, Richard, 1923–, U.S. photographer.
Averroes (Ar. ibn-Rushd), 1126–98, Sp.–Arab philosopher & physician.
Avicenna (Ar. ibn-Sina), 980–1037, Pers. philosopher & physician.
Ávila, Camacho, Manuel, 1897–1955, Mex. soldier, diplomat, & political leader; president 1940–46.
Avogadro, Amadeo, 1776–1856, Ital. chemist & physicist.
Axis Sally, b. Mildred Gillars, 1901–88, U.S.-born Ger. propagandist in World War II.
Ayub Khan, Mohammad, 1907–74, Pakistani politician; president of Pakistan 1958–69.

Baal Shem Tov, b. Israel Ben Eliezer, 1700?–60, Jewish religious leader in Poland; founder of Chassidism.
Babbage, Charles, 1792–1871, Eng. mathematician & inventor.
Babbitt, Irving, 1865–1933, U.S. scholar & critic.
—Milton, 1916–, U.S. composer.
Babel, Isaak Emmanuilovich, 1894–1941, Russ. author.
Baber, b. Zahir-ud-din Mohammed, 1480–1530, founder of the Mogul empire of India.
Babeuf, Francois, 1760–97, Fr. revolutionist.
Babson, Roger Ward, 1875–1967, U.S. statistician.
Bacall, Lauren, 1924–, U.S. actress.
Bach A family of Ger. composers & musicians incl **Johann Sebastian,** 1685–1750, & his sons: **Carl Philipp Emmanuel,** 1714–88; **Johann Christian,** 1735–82; & **Wilhelm Friedemann,** 1710–84.
Bacharach, Burt, 1929–, U.S. composer.
Bachauer, Gina, 1913–76, Gk. pianist.
Bache, Harold L., 1894–1968, U.S. business executive.
Backaus, Wilhelm, 1884–1969, Ger. pianist.
Bacon, Francis, 1561–1626, Eng. philosopher, essayist, & statesman.
—Francis, 1909–92, Irish-born Brit. painter.
—Roger, 1214?–92?, Eng. scientist & philosopher.
Baddeley, Hermione, 1906–86, Brit. actress.

Baden-Powell, Robert Stephenson Smyth, 1857–1941, Brit. general; founder of Boy Scouts.

Badoglio, Pietro, 1871–1956, Ital. general; premier of Italy 1943–44.

Baedeker, Karl, 1801–59, Ger. author & publisher.

Baekeland, Leo, 1863–1944, Belg.-born U.S. chemist & industrialist.

Baer, Karl Ernst von, 1792–1876, Russ. embryologist active in Germany.

Baeyer, Adolf von, 1835–1917, Ger. chemist, Nobel Prize winner.

Baez, Joan, 1941–, U.S. folk singer.

Baffin, William, 1584?–1622, Eng. navigator & explorer.

Bagnold, Enid, 1890–1981, U.S. author.

Bahaullah, Mirza Husayn Ali, 1817–92, Pers. religious leader.

Bailey, F. Lee, 1933–, U.S. lawyer.

—Mildred 1903–51, U.S. singer.

—Pearl Mae, 1918–90, U.S. singer.

Baird, John Logie, 1888–1946, Scot. inventor.

—William Britton (Bil), 1904–87, U.S. puppeteer.

Bairnsfather, Bruce, 1888–1959, Eng. cartoonist.

Baker, George (Father Divine), 1877?–1965, U.S. religious leader.

—George, 1915–75, U.S. cartoonist.

—Josephine, 1906–75, U.S. entertainer.

—Russell, 1925–, U.S. journalist & author.

Bakr, Ahmed Hassan al-, 1914–82, Iraqi military officer; president & prime minister of Iraq 1968–79.

Bakst, Leon Nikolaevich, 1866?–1924, Russ. painter & set designer.

Bakunin, Mikhail, 1814–76, Russ. anarchist leader.

Balaguer, Joaquin, 1902–, president of Dominican Republic 1966–78, 1986–96.

Balanchine, George, 1904–83, Russ.-born U.S. choreographer.

Balboa, Vasco Núñez de, 1475?–1519, Sp. explorer; discovered the Pacific Ocean.

Baldwin, James, 1924–87, U.S. author.

—Matthias William, 1795–1866, U.S. inventor.

—Stanley, 1867–1947, Eng. statesman; prime minister 1923–24, 1924–29, 1935–37.

Balenciaga, Cristobal, 1896?–1972, Sp. fashion designer active in France.

Balfour, Arthur James, Earl of, 1848–1930, Eng. statesman & philosopher; prime minister 1902–05.

Ball, Ernest, 1878–1927, U.S. composer.

—Lucille, 1911–89, U.S. actress & comedienne.

Ballard, Kaye, 1926–, U.S. actress.

Balmain, Pierre, 1914–82, Fr. fashion designer.

Balzac, Honoré de, 1799–1850, Fr. novelist.

Bancroft Anne, 1931–, U.S. actress.

—George, 1800–91, U.S. historian.

Bandaranaike, Sirimavo, 1916–, prime minister of Sri Lanka 1960–65, 1970–77.

Bankhead, Tallulah Brockman, 1903–68, U.S. actress.

Banneker, Benjamin, 1731–1806, U.S. astronomer, mathematician, & inventor.

Bannister, Sir Roger, 1929–, Eng. track runner & physician.

Banting, Sir Frederick Grant, 1891–1941, Can. physiologist.

Banton, Travis, 1874–1958, U.S. costume designer.

Banzer Suarez, Hugo, 1926–, Bolivian military officer; president of Bolivia 1971–78.

Bara, Theda, 1890–1955, U.S. actress.

Baraka, Amiri, b. (Everett) LeRoi Jones, 1934–, U.S. poet, playwright, & social activist.

Barber, Samuel, 1910–81, U.S. composer.

—Walter Lanier (Red), 1908–92, U.S. sports announcer.

Barbirolli, Sir John, 1899–1970, Eng. conductor.

Bardeen, John, 1908–91, U.S. physicist.

Bardot, Brigitte, 1934–, Fr. actress.

Barenboim, Daniel, 1942–, Argentine-born Israeli pianist & conductor.

Barkley, Alben William, 1877–1956, U.S. lawyer & politician; U.S. vice president 1949–53.

Bar Kokba, Simon, ?–A.D. 135, Jewish leader & self-proclaimed Messiah.

Barlach, Ernst Heinrich, 1870–1938, Ger. sculptor & author.

Barnard, Christian Neethling, 1922–, South African surgeon.

—Edward Emerson, 1857–1923, U.S. astronomer.

—Frederick Augustus Porter, 1809–89, U.S. educator.

Barnes, Djuna, 1892–1982, U.S. author & artist.

Barnet, Charlie, 1913–91, U.S. band leader.

Barnhart, Clarence L., 1900–93, U.S. lexicographer.

Barnum, P(hineas) T(aylor), 1810–91, U.S. showman & circus proprietor.

Baroja, Pio, 1872–1956, Sp. novelist.

Barrault, Jean-Louis, 1910–94, Fr. actor & stage director.

Barrie, Sir James Matthew, 1860–1937, Scot. author & playwright.

Barron, Clarence Walker, 1855–1928, U.S. financial editor & publisher.

Barrow, Clyde, 1909–34, U.S. criminal.

Barry, Gene, 1922–, U.S. actor.

—Philip, 1896–1949, U.S. playwright.

Barrymore A family of U.S. actors incl. **Ethel,** 1879–1959; **John,** 1882–1942; **Lionel,** 1878–1954; & **Maurice (Herbert Blythe),** 1847–1905, father of Ethel, John, & Lionel.

Barth, John Simmons, 1930–, U.S. author.

—Karl, 1886–1968, Swiss theologian.

Barthelme, Donald, 1931–89, U.S. author.

Barthes, Roland, 1915–80, Fr. author & critic.

Bartholdi, Frédéric Auguste, 1834–1904, Fr. sculptor.

Bartlett, John, 1820–1905, U.S. editor & publisher.

Bartók, Béla, 1881–1945, Hung. composer.

Bartolommeo, Fra, b. Baccio della Porta, 1472–1517, Ital. painter.

Bartolozzi, Francesco, 1727?–1815, Ital. engraver.

Barton, Bruce, 1886–1967, U.S. advertising executive & author.

—Clara, 1821–1912, U.S. civic worker; founder of the American Red Cross.

Baruch, Bernard Mannes, 1870–1965, U.S. financier & political adviser.

Barye, Antoine Louis, 1795–1875, Fr. sculptor, painter, & water colorist.

Baryshnikov, Mikhail, 1947–, Russ. ballet dancer & artistic director active in U.S.

Barzini, Luigi, 1908–84, Ital. author & statesman.

Barzun, Jacques, 1907–, Fr.-born U.S. educator & author.

Basehart, Richard, 1914–84, U.S. actor.

Basho, 1648–94, Jap. poet.

Basie, William (Count), 1904–84, U.S. jazz musician.

Basil, Saint (L. Basilius), 330?–379, bishop of Caesarea.

Baskerville, John, 1706–75, Eng. typographer.

Baskin, Leonard, 1922–, U.S. painter & illustrator.

Bass, Sam, 1851–78, U.S. outlaw.

Bassey, Shirley, 1937–, Welsh-born U.S. singer.

Bates, Alan, 1934–, Eng. actor.

Bateson, William, 1861–1926, Eng. biologist.

Batista y Zaldivar, Fulgencio, 1901–73, Cuban soldier & political leader; president 1940–44, 1952–59.

Batu Khan, ?–1255, Mongol leader.

Baudelaire, Charles Pierre, 1821–67, Fr. poet.

Baudouin, 1930–93, king of Belgium 1951–93.

Baugh, Samuel Adrian (Sammy), 1914–, U.S. football player.

Baum, L(yman) Frank, 1856–1919, U.S. author.

—Vicki, 1888–1960, Austrian-born U.S. author.

Baxter, Anne, 1923–86, U.S. actress.

Baylis, Dame Lilian, 1874–1937, Eng. theater manager.

Baylor, Elgin, 1934–, U.S. basketball player.

Beadle, George Wells, 1903–89, U.S. geneticist.

Bean, Roy, 1825?–1903, U.S. frontiersman.

Beard, Charles Austin, 1874–1948, & his wife **Mary Ritter,** 1876–1958, U.S. historians.

—Daniel Carter, 1850–1941, U.S. author; founder of the Boy Scouts of America.

—James, 1903–85, U.S. culinary expert & author.

Beardsley, Aubrey Vincent, 1872–98, Eng. artist & illustrator.

Beaton, Cecil, 1904–80, Eng. photographer & theatrical designer.

Beatrix, 1938–, queen of the Netherlands 1980–

Beatty, Clyde, 1905–65, U.S. animal trainer & circus performer.
—Warren, 1937–, U.S. actor, director, & screenwriter.
Beaumarchais, Pierre Augustin Caron de, 1732–99, Fr. playwright.
Beaumont, Francis, 1584–1616, Eng. playwright.
—William, 1785–1853, U.S. surgeon.
Beauregard, Pierre Gustave Toutant de, 1818–93, U.S. Confederate general.
Beauvoir, Simone de, 1908–86, Fr. author.
Beaverbrook, Lord, b. William Maxwell Aitken, 1879–1964, Can.-born Brit. publisher & politician.
Bechet, Sidney, 1897–1959, U.S. jazz musician.
Beck, C. C., 1910–, U.S. cartoonist.
Becket, Saint Thomas à, 1118–70, Eng. Catholic martyr; archbishop of Canterbury 1162–70.
Beckett, Samuel Barclay, 1906–89, Irish-born novelist & playwright.
Beckmann, Max, 1884–1950, Ger. painter.
Becquerel A family of Fr. physicists incl. **Alexandre Edmond,** 1820–91; **Antoine César,** 1788–1878, father of prec.; & **Antoine Henri,** 1852–1908, son of Alexandre.
Bede, Saint, 673–735, Eng. scholar, historian, & theologian; called **the Venerable Bede.**
Beebe, Charles William, 1877–1962, U.S. naturalist.
—Lucius Morris, 1902–66, U.S. journalist & author.
Beecham, Sir Thomas, 1879–1961, Eng. conductor.
Beecher, Henry Ward, 1813–87, U.S. clergyman & writer; brother of Harriet Beecher Stowe.
—Lyman, 1775–1863, U.S. clergyman; father of prec.
Beene, Geoffrey, 1927–, U.S. fashion designer.
Beerbohm, Sir Max, 1872–1956, Eng. author & caricaturist.
Beery, Noah, Jr., 1916–94, U.S. actor.
—Wallace, 1886–1949, U.S. actor; father of prec.
Beethoven, Ludwig van, 1770–1827, Ger. composer.
Begin, Menahem, 1913–92, Pol.-born Israeli statesman; prime minister of Israel, 1977–83; Nobel Prize winner.
Behan, Brendan Francis, 1923–64, Irish playwright.
Behn, Aphra, 1640–89, Brit. playwright, author, & poet.
Behrens, Peter, 1868–1940, Ger. architect.
Behring, Emil von, 1854–1917, Ger. bacteriologist.
Behrman, S(amuel) N(athaniel), 1893–1973, U.S. playwright.
Beiderbecke, Leon Bismarck (Bix), 1903–31, U.S. jazz musician.
Béjart, Maurice, 1928–, Fr. dancer, choreographer, & ballet-company director.
Belafonte, Harry, 1927–, U.S. singer.
Belasco, David, 1859–1931, U.S. theatrical producer & playwright.
Belinsky, Vissarion Grigorievich, 1811–48, Russ. critic & journalist.
Bell, Alexander Graham, 1847–1922, Scot.-born U.S. physicist; inventor of the telephone.
Bellamy, Edward, 1850–98, U.S. author.
—Ralph, 1904–92, U.S. actor.
Bellarmine, Saint Robert Francis Romulus, 1542–1621, Ital. Jesuit theologian.
Belli, Melvin, 1907–96, U.S. lawyer.
Bellinghausen, Fabian von, 1778–1852, Russ. admiral & explorer.
Bellini A family of Venetian painters incl. **Jacopo,** 1400?–70?, & his sons **Gentile,** 1429?–1507, & **Giovanni,** 1430?–1516.
—Vincenzo, 1801–35, Ital. operatic composer.
Belloc, Hilaire, 1870–1953, Eng. poet & author.
Bellow, Saul, 1915–, Can.-born U.S. novelist.
Bellows, George Wesley, 1882–1925, U.S. painter & lithographer.
Belmondo, Jean-Paul, 1933–, Fr. actor.
Belmont, August, 1816–90, Ger.-born U.S. financier.
Belmonte, Juan, 1892–1962, Sp. bullfighter.
Bemelmans, Ludwig, 1898–1962, Austrian-born U.S. author & illustrator.
Benavente, Jacinto, 1866–1954, Sp. playwright; Nobel Prize winner.
Ben Bella, Ahmed, 1918–, Algerian revolutionary leader; premier of Algeria 1962–65.

Benchley, Robert Charles, 1889–1945, U.S. humorist & author.
Bendix, Vincent, 1882–1945, U.S. inventor & manufacturer.
Benedict, Saint, 480–547, Ital. monk; founder of the Benedictine order.
Benedict, Ruth Fulton 1887–1948, U.S. anthropologist.
Benes, Eduard, 1884–1948, Czech statesman; president of Czechoslovakia 1935–38 & 1946–48.
Benét, Stephen Vincent, 1898–1943, U.S. poet & author.
—William Rose, 1886–1950, U.S. author & editor; brother of prec.
Ben-Gurion, David, 1886–1973, Russ.-born Israeli statesman; prime minister of Israel 1948–53 & 1955–63.
Benjamin, Judah Philip, 1811–84, U.S. lawyer & Confederate cabinet member.
Bennett, (Enoch) Arnold, 1867–1931, Eng. author.
—Floyd, 1890–1928, U.S. aviator.
—James Gordon, 1795–1872, Scot.-born U.S. journalist.
—Michael, 1943–, U.S. stage director & choreographer.
—Richard Bedford, 1870–1947, Can. statesman; prime minister 1930–35.
—Robert Russell, 1894–1981, U.S. composer.
—Tony, 1926–, U.S. singer.
Benny, Jack, 1894–1974, U.S. comedian.
Bentham, Jeremy, 1748–1832, Eng. jurist & philosopher.
Bentley, Eric Russell, 1916–, Eng.-born author & critic active in U.S.
Benton, Thomas Hart, 1889–1975, U.S. painter.
—William, 1900–73, U.S. businessman, publisher, & government official.
Berdyaev, Nikolai Alexsandrovich, 1874–1948, Russ.-born religious philosopher resident in France.
Berenson, Bernard, 1865–1959, Lithuanian-born U.S. art critic & writer.
Berg, Alban, 1885–1935, Austrian composer.
—Gertrude, 1899–1966, U.S. actress.
Bergen, Edgar John, 1903–78, U.S. ventriloquist & actor.
Berger, Frank M(ilan), 1913–, Czech-born U.S. pharmacologist.
—Hans, 1873–1941, Ger. neurologist & psychiatrist.
Bergerac, Cyrano de, 1619–55, Fr. poet & soldier.
Bergman, Ingmar, 1918–, Swed. film director.
—Ingrid, 1915–82, Swed.-born actress active in U.S.
Bergson, Henri Louis, 1859–1941, Fr. philosopher.
Beria, Lavrenti Pavlovich, 1899–1953, Soviet politician.
Bering, Vitus, 1680–1741, Dan. navigator.
Berio, Luciano, 1925–, Ital.-born composer active in U.S.
Berkeley, Busby, 1895–1976, U.S. film director & choreographer.
—George, 1685–1753, Irish-born Eng. prelate & philosopher.
Berle, Adolf Augustus, 1895–1971, U.S. diplomat & author.
—Milton, 1908–, U.S. comedian.
Berlin, Irving, 1888–1989, U.S. composer.
—Sir Isaiah, 1909–, Latvian-born Brit. historian.
Berlioz, Hector, 1803–69, Fr. composer.
Berman, Lazar, 1930–, Russ. pianist active in U.S.
Bernadette, Saint, b. Bernadette Soubirous, 1844–79, Fr. nun; called **Bernadette of Lourdes.**
Bernadotte, Folke, Count of Wisborg, 1895–1948, Swed. diplomat & mediator in Palestine; assassinated.
—Jean Baptiste Jules, 1763?–1844, Fr. general; king of Sweden & Norway as Charles XIV 1818–44.
Bernard, Claude, 1813–78, Fr. physiologist.
Bernard of Clairvaux, Saint, 1090–1153, Fr. Cistercian monk.
Bernbach, Willian, 1911–82, U.S. advertising executive.
Bernhardt, Sarah, 1844–1923, Fr. actress.
Bernini, Gian Lorenzo, 1598–1680, Ital. sculptor & architect.
Bernoulli A family of Swiss mathematicians & scientists incl. **Daniel,** 1700–82; **Jacques,** 1654–1705; & **Jean,** 1667–1748, father of Daniel & brother of Jacques.
Bernstein, Leonard, 1918–90, U.S. conductor, composer, & pianist.
Berra, Lawrence Peter (Yogi), 1925–, U.S. baseball player & manager.
Berrigan, Daniel, 1921–, U.S. priest, poet, & political activist.

—**Philip,** 1923–, U.S. priest & political activist; brother of prec.

Berry, Charles Edward (Chuck), 1926–, U.S. musician & singer.

Berryman, John, 1914–72, U.S. poet & critic.

Bert, Paul, 1833–86, Fr. physiologist.

Bertillon, Alphonse, 1853–1914, Fr. anthropologist & criminologist.

Bertolucci, Bernardo, 1940–, Ital. film director.

Berzelius, Baron Jöns Jakob, 1779–1848, Swed. chemist.

Besant, Annie Wood, 1847–1933, Eng. theosophist.

Bessel, Friedrich Wilhelm, 1784–1846, Ger. astronomer.

Bessemer, Sir Henry, 1813–98, Eng. engineer.

Betancourt, Romulo, 1908–81, president of Venezuela 1945–48 & 1959–64.

Bethe, Hans Albrecht, 1906–, Ger.-born U.S. physicist; Nobel Prize winner.

Bethune, Mary McLeod, 1875–1955, U.S. educator.

Betjeman, Sir John, 1906–84, Eng. poet; poet laureate 1972–84.

Bettelheim, Bruno, 1903–90, Austrian-born U.S. psychologist, educator, & author.

Betti, Ugo, 1892–1953, Ital. playwright.

Betz, Pauline, 1919–, U.S. tennis player.

Bevan, Aneurin, 1897–1960, Welsh labor leader & Brit. government official.

Bevin, Ernest, 1881–1951, Eng. labor leader & statesman.

Bhave, Acharya Vinoba, 1895–1982, Indian social reformer.

Bhumibol Adulyadej, 1927–, King of Thailand, 1946–.

Bhutto, Zulfikar Ali, 1928–79, president of Pakistan 1971–77; executed.

Bialik, Chaim Nachman, 1873–1934, Russ.-born Israeli poet.

Biddle, John, 1615–62, Eng. theologian.

—**Nicholas,** 1786–1844, U.S. financier.

Bienville, Sieur de, b. Jean Baptiste le Moyne, 1680–1768, Fr. colonial governor of Louisiana.

Bierce, Ambrose Gwinnett, 1842–1914?, U.S. author.

Bierstadt, Albert, 1830–1902, Ger.-born U.S. painter.

Biggs, E(dward George) Power, 1906–77, Eng.-born U.S. organist.

Bikila, Abebe, 1932–73, Ethiopian track runner.

Binet, Alfred, 1857–1911, Fr. psychologist.

Bing, Sir Rudolph, 1902–97, Austrian-born opera manager active in U.S. & Eng.

Bingham, George Caleb, 1811–79, U.S. painter.

Birdseye, Clarence, 1886–1956, U.S. inventor & industrialist.

Birendra Bir Bikram Shah Dev, 1945–, king of Nepal 1972–.

Bishop, Elizabeth, 1911–79, U.S. poet.

—**Joey,** 1918–, U.S. entertainer.

Bismarck, Prince Otto Eduard Leopold von, 1815–98, Ger. statesman; chancellor of German empire 1871–90.

Bizet, Georges, 1838–75, Fr. composer.

Björling, Jussi, 1911–60, Swed. tenor.

Bjørnson, Bjørnstjerne, 1832–1910, Norw. poet & author; Nobel Prize winner.

Black, Hugo La Fayette, 1886–1971, U.S. jurist; justice of the U.S. Supreme Court 1937–71.

—**Shirley Temple,** 1928–, U.S. actress & diplomat.

Blackett, Patrick Maynard Stuart, 1897–1974, Eng. physicist.

Black Hawk, 1767–1838, Sac Am. Ind. chief.

Blackmun, Harry Andrew, 1908–, U.S. jurist; justice of the U.S. Supreme Court 1970–.

Blackstone, Sir William, 1723–80, Eng. jurist.

Blackwell, Elizabeth, 1821–1910, Eng.-born U.S. physician.

Blaine, James Gillespie, 1830–93, U.S. statesman.

Blake, Eugene Carson, 1906–85, U.S. clergyman & social activist.

—**James Hubert (Eubie),** 1883–1983, U.S. pianist & songwriter.

—**William,** 1757–1827, Eng. poet & painter.

Blakelock, Ralph Albert, 1847–1919, U.S. landscape painter.

Blanc, Mel(vin Jerome), 1908–89, U.S. entertainer.

Blanda, George Frederick, 1927–, U.S. football player.

Blankers-Koen, Francina Eisje (Fanny), 1918–, Du. track & field athlete.

Blasco Ibáñez, Vicente, 1867–1928, Sp. author.

Blass, Bill, 1922–, U.S. fashion designer.

Blavatsky, Elena Petrovna, 1831–91, Russ. theosophist.

Blériot, Louis, 1872–1936, Fr. engineer & pioneer aviator.

Bleuler, Eugen, 1856–1939, Swiss psychiatrist.

Bligh, William, 1754–1817, Brit. naval officer.

Blitzstein, Marc, 1905–64, U.S. composer.

Bloch, Ernest, 1880–1959, Swiss-born composer active in U.S.

—**Konrad Emil,** 1912–, Ger.-born U.S. biochemist; Nobel Prize winner.

Block, Herbert Lawrence, 1909–, U.S. political cartoonist: called **Herblock.**

Bloomer, Amelia Jenks, 1818–94, U.S. social reformer.

Bloomfield, Leonard, 1887–1949, U.S. linguist & educator.

Blücher, Gebhard Leberecht von, 1742–1819, Prussian field marshal.

Bluford, Guion S., 1942–, U.S. astronaut.

Blum, Léon, 1872–1950, Fr. politician.

Blume, Judy, 1938–, U.S. author.

Boadicea, ?–A.D. 62, queen of a tribe of Britons; defeated by the Romans.

Boas, Franz, 1858–1942, Ger.-born U.S. anthropologist.

Boccaccio, Giovanni, 1313–75, Ital. writer.

Boccherini, Luigi, 1743–1805, Ital. composer.

Boccioni, Umberto, 1882–1916, Ital. sculptor & painter.

Bock, Jerry, 1928–, U.S. composer

Bode, Johann Elert, 1747–1826, German astronomer.

Bodenheim, Maxwell, 1893–1954, U.S. poet.

Bodoni, Giambattista, 1740–1813, Ital. printer & type designer.

Böhm, Karl, 1894–1981, Ger. conductor.

Boehme, Jakob, 1575–1624, Ger. theosophist & mystic.

Boethius, Anicius Manlius Severinus, 480?–524, Roman philosopher.

Bogarde, Dirk, 1920–, Brit. actor & director.

Bogart, Humphrey, 1899–1957, U.S. actor.

Bogdanovich, Peter, 1939–, U.S. film director.

Bohlen, Charles Eustis, 1904–74, U.S. diplomat.

Bohr, Aage Niels, 1922–, Dan. physicist; Nobel Prize winner.

—**Niels,** 1885–1962, Dan. physicist; Nobel Prize winner; father of prec.

Boileau-Despréaux, Nicolas, 1636–1711, Fr. poet & critic.

Boito, Arrigo, 1842–1918, Ital. composer & librettist.

Bok, Edward William, 1863–1930, Du.-born U.S. editor.

Bokassa, Jean-Bedel, 1922–96, African general; president of Central African Republic 1972–77; as **Bokassa I,** emperor of Central African Empire 1977–79.

Bolden, Charles (Buddy), 1868?–1931, U.S. jazz musician.

Boleyn, Anne, 1507?–36, second wife of Henry VIII of England; mother of Elizabeth I.

Bolger, Ray, 1904–1987, U.S. dancer & actor.

Bolívar, Simón, 1783–1830, South American revolutionary patriot & military leader.

Böll, Heinrich Theodor, 1917–85, Ger. author; Nobel Prize winner.

Boltzmann, Ludwig Edward, 1844–1906, Austrian physicist.

Bombeck, Erma, 1927–96, U.S. humorist.

Bonaparte, Napoleon, 1769–1821, Fr. general & emperor of France as Napoleon I 1805–14.

—**(Louis) Napoleon,** 1808–73, emperor of France as Napoleon III 1852–71; nephew of prec. Also **Buonaparte.**

Bonaventure, Saint, 1221–74, Ital. philosopher.

Bond, Julian, 1940–, U.S. politician & civil rights leader.

Bonheur, Rosa, 1822–99, Fr. painter.

Bonhoeffer, Dietrich, 1906–45, Ger. theologian.

Boniface VIII, b. Benedetto Gaetani, 1235?–1303, pope 1294–1303.

—**Saint,** 680?–755, Eng. missionary in Germany.

Bonnard, Pierre, 1867–1947, Fr. painter.

Bonney, William, 1859–81, U.S. outlaw: called **Billy the Kid.**

Boole, George, 1815–64, Eng. mathematician & logician.

Boone, Daniel, 1734–1820, Amer. frontiersman.

—**Pat,** 1934–, U.S. singer & actor.

Boorstin, Daniel J., 1914–, U.S. historian & author.

Booth, Edwin Thomas, 1833–93, U.S. actor.

—**John Wilkes,** 1838–65, U.S. actor; assassinated Abraham Lincoln; brother of prec.

—**Shirley,** 1907–, U.S. actress.

—**William,** 1829–1912, Eng. religious leader; founder of the Salvation Army.

Borah, William Edgar, 1865–1940, U.S. statesman.

Bordaberry, Juan Maria, 1928–, president of Uruguay 1972–76.

Borden, Gail, 1801–74, U.S. inventor.

—**Lizzie,** 1860–1927, U.S. alleged murderer.

—**Sir Robert Laird,** 1854–1937, Can. statesman; prime minister 1911–20.

Borg, Bjorn, 1956–, Swed. tennis player.

Borge, Victor, 1909–, Dan. pianist & entertainer active in U.S.

Borges, Jorge Luis, 1899–1986, Argentinian poet & author.

Borgia, Cesare, 1476–1507, Ital. military & religious leader.

—**Lucrezia,** 1480–1519, duchess of Ferrara & art patron; sister of prec.

Borglum, Gutzon, 1867–1941, U.S. sculptor.

Bori, Lucrezia, 1887–1960, Sp. soprano active in U.S.

Borlaug, Norman Ernest, 1914–, U.S. agronomist; Nobel Prize winner.

Borman, Frank, 1928–, U.S. astronaut & businessman.

Bormann, Martin Ludwig, 1900–45, Ger. Nazi politican.

Born, Max, 1882–1970, Ger. physicist; Nobel Prize winner.

Borodin, Alexander Porfirevich, 1834–87, Russ. composer.

Borromini, Francesco, 1599–1667, Ital. architect.

Bosch, Carl, 1874–1940, Ger. chemist & industrialist; Nobel Prize winner.

—**Hieronymus,** 1450?–1516, Du. painter.

Bose, Sir Jagadis Chandra, 1858–1937, Indian physicist & plant physiologist.

Boswell, James, 1740–95, Scot. author & lawyer; biographer of Samuel Johnson.

Botha, Louis, 1862–1919, Boer general; first prime minister of Union of South Africa.

—**Pieter Willem,** 1916–, South African politician; prime minister 1978–89.

Botticelli, Sandro, b. Allesandro di Mariano dei Filipepi, 1444?–1510, Florentine painter.

Botvinnik, Mikhail, 1911–, Russ. chess master.

Boucher, François, 1703–70, Fr. painter.

Boucicault, Dion, 1820?–90, Irish playwright & actor.

Bougainville, Louis Antoine de, 1729–1811, Fr. navigator.

Boulanger, Nadia Juliette, 1887–1979, Fr. composer & music teacher.

Boulez, Pierre, 1925–, Swiss-born composer & conductor active in U.S.

Boult, Sir Adrian, 1889–1983, Eng. conductor.

Boumédiene, Houari, 1927–78, Algerian army officer; president & premier of Algeria 1965–78.

Bourguiba, Habib ben Ali, 1903–, Tunisian statesman; president of Tunisia 1957–87.

Bourke-White, Margaret, 1906–72, U.S. photographer.

Bournonville, August, 1805–79, Danish dancer & choreographer.

Bouts, Dierick, 1420?–75, Du. painter.

Bovet, Daniel, 1907–92, Swiss-born Ital. pharmacologist.

Bow, Clara, 1905–65, U.S. actress.

Bowditch, Nathaniel, 1773–1838, U.S. mathematician & navigator.

Bowdler, Thomas, 1754–1825, Eng. physician & editor of Shakespeare's plays.

Bowell, Sir Mackenzie, 1823–1917, Eng-born Can. statesman; prime minister 1894–96.

Bowen, Elizabeth, 1899–1973, Irish-born Brit. author.

Bowes, Edward (Major), 1874–1946, U.S. radio personality.

Bowie, David, 1947–, Eng. actor & singer.

—**James,** 1796–1836, U.S. soldier & frontiersman.

Bowker, R(ichard) R(ogers), 1848–1933, U.S. editor & publisher.

Bowles, Chester, 1901–86, U.S. business executive & diplomat.

—**Jane Sydney Auer,** 1917–73, U.S. author.

—**Paul,** 1910–, U.S. author, composer, & musicologist; husband of prec.

Boyd, William (Bill), 1898–1972, U.S. actor.

Boyd Orr, Lord, 1880–1971, Brit. nutritionist & agricultural scientist; Nobel Prize winner.

Boyer, Charles, 1899–1978, Fr. actor.

Boyle, Kay, 1903–, U.S. author.

—**Robert,** 1627–91, Irish-born Brit. chemist & physicist.

Bradbury, Ray Douglas, 1920–, U.S. author.

Braddock, Edward, 1695–1755, Brit. general in N. America.

Bradford, William, 1590–1657, Eng.-born Pilgrim father & governor of Plymouth Colony.

Bradley, Milton, 1836–1911, U.S. manufacturer of games.

—**Omar Nelson,** 1893–1981, U.S. general.

—**Thomas,** 1917–, U.S. politician.

Bradstreet, Anne Dudley, 1612–72, Eng.-born Amer. poet.

Brady, Alice, 1892–1939, U.S. actress.

—**James Buchanan (Diamond Jim),** 1856–1917, U.S. financier & philanthropist.

—**Mathew,** 1823?–96, U.S. photographer.

Bragg, Sir William Henry, 1862–1942, Eng. physicist.

—**Sir (William) Lawrence,** 1890–1971, Austral.-born Eng. physicist; son of prec.

Brahe, Tycho, 1546–1601, Dan. astronomer.

Brahms, Johannes, 1833–97, Ger. composer.

Braille, Louis, 1809–52, Fr. educator.

Brailowsky, Alexander, 1896–1976, Russ.-born pianist active in U.S.

Bramante, b. Donato d'Angelo, 1444–1514, Ital. architect.

Brancusi, Constantin, 1876–1957, Rumanian sculptor.

Brand, Max, pseud. of Frederick Schiller Faust, 1892–1944, U.S. author.

Brandeis, Louis Dembitz, 1856–1941, U.S. jurist; justice of the U.S. Supreme Court 1916–39.

Brando, Marlon, 1924–, U.S. actor.

Brandt, Willy, 1913–, Ger. statesman; chancellor of W. Germany 1969–74.

Braque, Georges, 1882–1963, Fr. painter.

Brattain, Walter Houser, 1902–87, Chin.-born U.S. physicist; Nobel Prize winner.

Braudel, Fernand, 1902–85, Fr. historian & author.

Brautigan, Richard, 1935–84, U.S. author & poet.

Bream, Julian, 1933–, Eng. guitarist & lutenist.

Breasted, James Henry, 1865–1935, U.S. archaeologist.

Brecht, Bertolt, 1898–1956, Ger. playwright & poet.

Breckinridge, John Cabell, 1821–75, U.S. statesman & Confederate general; U.S. vice president 1857–61.

Brel, Jacques, 1929–78, Belg. singer & composer.

Brennan, Walter, 1894–1974, U.S. actor.

—**William Joseph, Jr.,** 1906–97, U.S. jurist; justice of the U.S. Supreme Court 1956–90.

Breslin, James (Jimmy), 1930–, U.S. journalist & author.

Bresson, Robert, 1907–, Fr. film director.

Breton, André, 1896–1966, Fr. poet & author.

Breuer, Josef, 1842–1925, Austrian physician.

—**Marcel,** 1902–81, Hung.-born architect active in U.S.

Brewster, William, 1567–1644, Eng.-born Pilgrim father.

Brezhnev, Leonid Ilyich, 1906–82, Soviet statesman; general secretary of the Communist Party of the Soviet Union 1966–82.

Brian Boru, 926–1014, king of Ireland 1002–14.

Briand, Aristide, 1862–1932, Fr. statesman & diplomat.

Brice, Fannie, 1891–1951, U.S. singer & comedienne.

Bricktop, b. Ada Beatrice Queen Victoria Louise Virginia Smith, 1894–1984, U.S. singer & entertainer.

Bridger, James, 1804–81, U.S. frontiersman & scout.

Bridges, Harry, 1901–90, Austral.-born U.S. labor leader.

—**Robert,** 1844–1930, Eng. poet.

Bridgman, Percy Williams, 1882–1961, U.S. physicist; Nobel Prize winner.

Bright, Richard, 1789–1858, Eng. physician.

Brill, A(braham) A(rden), 1874–1948, Austrian-born U.S. psychiatrist.

Brillat-Savarin, Anthelme, 1755–1828, Fr. writer on food & cooking.

Brinkley, David, 1920–, U.S. journalist & television news commentator.

Britten, (Edward) Benjamin, 1913–76, Eng. composer.

Broca, Pierre Paul, 1824–80, Fr. surgeon & anthropologist.

Brogan, Sir D(ennis) W(illiam), 1900–74, Eng. historian.

Brokaw, Tom (Thomas John), 1940–, U.S. journalist.

Bromfield, Louis, 1896–1956, U.S. author.

Bronk, Detlev W(ulf), 1897–1975, U.S. physiologist & educator.

Brontë An Eng. family incl. three sisters who were authors: **Anne,** 1820–49; **Charlotte,** 1816–55; **Emily (Jane),** 1818–48.

Bronzino, Il, b. Agnolo di Cosimo Allori, 1503?–74, Ital. painter.

Brook, Clive, 1887–1974, Eng. actor.
—**Peter,** 1925–, Eng. stage director & producer.

Brooke, Alan Francis, 1st Viscount Alanbrooke, 1883–1963, Brit. field marshal.
—**Edward William,** 1919–, U.S. senator.
—**Rupert,** 1887–1915, Eng. poet.

Brookings, Robert Somers, 1850–1932, U.S. businessman & philanthropist.

Brooks, Louise, 1905–85, U.S. actress.
—**Gwendolyn,** 1917–, U.S. poet.
—**Mel,** 1926–, U.S. author, actor, & film director.
—**Phillips,** 1835–93, U.S. bishop.
—**Van Wyck,** 1886–1963, U.S. critic & author.

Brosio, Manlio, 1897–1980, Ital. lawyer & diplomat.

Broun, (Matthew) Heywood (Campbell), 1888–1939, U.S. journalist & critic.

Browder, Earl Russell, 1891–1973, U.S. Communist Party leader.

Brown, Helen Gurley, 1922–, U.S. author & editor.
—**James,** 1933–, U.S. singer.
—**Jim,** 1936–, U.S. football player & actor.
—**Joe E.,** 1892–1973, U.S. comedian & actor.
—**John,** 1800–59, U.S. abolitionist.
—**Nacio Herb,** 1896–1964, U.S. songwriter.
—**Norman O(liver),** 1913–, Mexican-born U.S. author & educator.

Browne, Dik, 1917–89, U.S. cartoonist.
—**Sir Thomas,** 1606–82, Eng. physician & author.

Browning, Elizabeth Barrett, 1806–61, Eng. poet.
—**Robert,** 1812–89, Eng. poet; husband of prec.

Brown-Sequard, Charles E., 1817–94, Fr.-born Brit. physician & physiologist.

Brubeck, David Warren (Dave), 1920–, U.S. jazz musician & composer.

Bruce, Lenny, 1926–66, U.S. comedian.

Bruch, Max, 1838–1920, Ger. composer.

Bruckner, Anton, 1824–96, Austrian composer.

Brueghel A family of Flemish painters incl. **Peter,** 1525?–69 (known as **the Elder**), & his sons, **Peter,** 1564?–1638? (**the Younger**), and **Jan,** 1568–1625.

Bruhn, Erik, 1928–86, Dan. ballet dancer & choreographer.

Brumel, Valery, 1942–, Russ. track athlete.

Brummell, George Bryan (Beau), 1778–1840, Eng. man of fashion.

Brunelleschi, Filippo, 1377–1446, Florentine architect & sculptor.

Brunner, Emil, 1889–1966, Swiss theologian.

Bruno, Giordano, 1548?–1600, Ital. philosopher; burned as a heretic.

Brutus, Marcus Junius, 85–42 B.C., Roman republican leader; conspirator against Caesar.

Bryan, William Jennings, 1860–1925, U.S. statesman & orator.

Bryant, Sir Arthur Wynne Morgan, 1899–1985, Brit. historian.
—**William Cullen,** 1794–1878, U.S. poet.

Bryce, James, Viscount, 1838–1922, Eng. statesman & author.

Brynner, Yul, 1920–85, Russ.-born U.S. actor.

Brzezinski, Zbigniew, 1928–, Pol.-born U.S. educator and government official.

Buber, Martin, 1878–1965, Austrian-born Israeli Jewish philosopher & theologian.

Buchan, John, 1st Baron Tweedsmuir, 1875–1940, Scot. author & statesman; governor-general of Canada 1935–40.

Buchanan, Jack, 1891–1957, Scot.-born actor active in England & U.S.
—**James,** 1791–1868, 15th U.S. president 1857–61.

Buchman, Frank Nathan Daniel, 1878–1961, U.S. evangelist.

Buchner, Eduard, 1860–1917, Ger. organic chemist.

Buchwald, Art, 1925–, U.S. journalist & author.

Buck, Frank, 1884–1950, U.S. hunter & animal collector.
—**Pearl Sydenstricker,** 1892–1973, U.S. author.

Buckley, William Frank, Jr., 1925–, U.S. author & political commentator.

Buddha, Siddhartha Gautama, 563?–483? B.C., Indian religious teacher & philosopher; founder of Buddhism.

Budge, Donald, 1915–, U.S. tennis player.

Buffon, Comte Georges Louis Leclerc, 1707–88, Fr. naturalist.

Bujones, Fernando, 1942–, U.S. ballet dancer.

Bulfinch, Charles, 1763–1844, U.S. architect.

Bulgakov, Mikhail, 1891–1940, Russ. author & playwright.

Bulganin, Nikolai Aleksandrovich, 1895–1975, premier of the U.S.S.R. 1955–58.

Bull, Ole Bornemann, 1810–80, Norw. violinist.

Bülow, Hans von, 1830–94, Ger. conductor & pianist.

Bultmann, Rudolf Karl, 1884–1976, Ger. theologian.

Bulwer-Lytton, Edward George, 1803–73, Eng. playwright & author.

Bumbry, Grace, 1937–, U.S. mezzo-soprano.

Bunche, Ralph Johnson, 1904–71, U.S. educator & U.N. official; Nobel Prize winner.

Bundy, McGeorge, 1919–, U.S. government official & foundation executive.

Bunin, Ivan Alekseyevich, 1870–1953, Russ. poet & author; Nobel Prize winner.

Bunker, Ellsworth, 1894–1984, U.S. diplomat.

Bunsen, Robert Wilhelm, 1811–99, Ger. chemist.

Buñuel, Luis, 1900–1983, Sp. film director.

Bunyan, John, 1628–88, Eng. preacher & author.

Burbage, Richard, 1567?–1619, Eng. actor.

Burbank, Luther, 1849–1926, U.S. horticulturist.

Burchfield, Charles Ephraim, 1893–1967, U.S. painter.
—**Robert William,** 1923–, New Zealand-born Brit. lexicographer.

Burckhardt, Jacob Christoph, 1818–97, Swiss art historian.

Burger, Warren Earl, 1907–95, U.S. jurist; chief justice of the U.S. Supreme Court 1969–86.

Burgess, Anthony, 1917–93, Eng. author.
—**(Frank) Gelett,** 1866–1951, U.S. author & illustrator.

Burgoyne, John, 1722–92, Brit. general in American Revolutionary War; known as **Gentleman Johnny.**

Burke, Edmund, 1729–97, Irish-born Brit. orator, author, & statesman.

Burne-Jones, Sir Edward Coley, 1833–98, Eng. painter.

Burnett, Carol, 1936–, U.S. actress, singer, & comedienne.

Burney, Fanny, 1752–1840, Eng. author & diarist.

Burnham, Daniel H., 1846–1912, U.S. architect.

Burns, Arthur, 1904–87, Russ.-born U.S. economist.
—**George,** 1896–1996, U.S. actor & comedian.
—**Robert,** 1759–96, Scot. poet.

Burnside, Ambrose Everett, 1824–81, U.S. Civil War general.

Burr, Aaron, 1756–1836, Amer. lawyer & statesman; U.S. vice president 1801–05.

Burroughs, Edgar Rice, 1875–1950, U.S. author.
—**John,** 1837–1921, U.S. naturalist & author.
—**William,** 1914–97, U.S. author.

Burrows, Abe, 1910–85, U.S. author, playwright, & director.

Burton, Richard, 1925–84, Brit. actor.
—**Sir Richard Francis,** 1821–90, Eng. traveler & author.

Busch, Adolphus, 1839–1913, Ger.-born U.S. businessman & philanthropist.

Bush, George, 1924–, U.S. statesman; U.S. vice president 1981–89; 41st U.S. president 1989–93.
—**Vannevar,** 1890–1974, U.S. electrical engineer.

Bushman, Francis Xavier, 1883–1966, U.S. actor.

Bushmiller, Ernie, 1905–82, U.S. cartoonist.

Busoni, Ferruccio Benvenuto, 1866–1924, Ital. composer & pianist.

Butler, Nicholas Murray, 1862–1947, U.S. educator.
—**Samuel,** 1612–80, Eng. satirical poet.
—**Samuel,** 1835–1902, Eng. author.

Button, Richard Totten (Dick), 1929–, U.S. figure skater & TV commentator.

Buxtehude, Dietrich, 1637–1707, Dan.-born Ger. organist & composer.
Byrd, Richard Evelyn, 1888–1957, U.S. explorer.
—William, 1543–1623, Brit. composer.
Byron, George Gordon, Lord, 1788–1824, Eng. poet.

Caballe, Montserrat, 1933–, Sp. soprano.
Cabell, James Branch, 1879–1958, author.
Cable, George Washington, 1844–1925, U.S. author.
Cabot, John, b. Giovanni Caboto, 1451?–98, Ital. navigator & explorer.
Cabral, Pedro Alvares, 1460?–1526, Pg. navigator.
Cabrini, Saint Frances Xavier, 1850–1917, Ital.-born. U.S. nun; canonized 1946: known as **Mother Cabrini.**
Cadillac, Sieur Antoine de la Mothe, 1658–1730, Fr. explorer in N. America.
Cadmus, Paul, 1904–, U.S. painter.
Caedmon, 7th c. Eng. poet; first to be known by name.
Caesar, Gaius Julius, 100–44 B.C., Roman general, statesman, & historian; assassinated.
—Sid, 1922–, U.S. comedian & actor.
Caetano, Marcelo, 1906–80, Pg. lawyer; premier of Portugal 1968–74.
Cage, John, 1912–92, U.S. composer.
Cagliostro, Count Alessandro di, 1743–95, Ital. charlatan.
Cagney, James, 1899–1986, U.S. actor.
Cahn, Sammy, 1913–93, U.S. lyricist.
Calder, Alexander, 1898–1976, U.S. sculptor.
Calderón de la Barca, Pedro, 1600–81, Sp. poet & playwright.
Caldwell, Erskine, 1903–87, U.S. author.
—(Janet) Taylor, 1900–85, Eng.-born U.S. author.
—Sarah, 1928–, U.S. opera director & conductor.
—Zoe, 1933–, Austral. actress.
Calhoun, John Caldwell, 1782–1850, U.S. lawyer & politician; U.S. vice president 1825–32.
Caligula, b. Gaius Caesar, A.D. 12–41, Roman emperor 37–41; assassinated.
Calisher, Hortense, 1911–, U.S. author.
Callaghan, James, 1912, Eng. politician; prime minister 1976–79.
—Morley, 1903–90, Can. author.
Callas, Maria Meneghini, 1923–77, U.S. soprano.
Callisthenes, 360?–328? B.C., Gk. philosopher & historian.
Calloway, Cab(ell), 1907–94, U.S. singer & band leader.
Calvert, Sir George, 1580?–1632, Eng. statesman; founder of Maryland.
Calvin, John, 1509–64, Fr. Protestant reformer.
—Melvin, 1911–97, U.S. chemist; Nobel Prize winner.
Cambyses, ?–522 B.C., king of Persia; son of Cyrus.
Camões, Luiz Vaz de, 1524–80, Pg. poet.
Camp, Walter Chauncey, 1859–1925, U.S. football coach.
Campbell, Mrs. Patrick b. Beatrice Stella Tanner, 1865–1940, Eng. actress.
—Thomas, 1777–1844, Eng. poet.
Campin, Robert, 1375?–1444, Flem. painter.
Campion, Thomas, 1567–1620, Eng. poet & musician.
Camus, Albert, 1913–60, Algerian-born Fr. writer.
Canaletto, b. Antonio Canale, 1697–1768, Ital. painter.
Canary, Martha Jane, 1852–1903, U.S. frontierswoman: known as **Calamity Jane.**
Canby, Henry Seidel, 1878–1961, U.S. educator.
Candler, Asa, 1851–1929, U.S. industrialist.
Candolle, Augustine Pyrame de, 1778–1841, Swiss botanist.
Caniff, Milton, 1907–88, U.S. cartoonist.
Cannon, Joseph Gurney (Uncle Joe), 1836–1926, U.S. lawyer & politician.
—Walter Bradford, 1871–1945, U.S. physiologist.
Canova, Antonio, 1757–1822, Ital. sculptor.
Cantor, Eddie, 1892–1964, U.S. singer & actor.
Canute, 994?–1035, king of England, Denmark, & Norway.
Čapek, Karel, 1890–1938, Czech author & playwright.
Capet, Hugh, 940?–996, king of France 987–996.
Capone, Al(phonse), 1898–1947, U.S. criminal.
Capote, Truman, 1924–84, U.S. author.
Capp, Al, 1909–79, U.S. cartoonist.
Capra, Frank, 1897–1991, Ital.-born U.S. film director.

Captain Kangaroo, pseud. of Robert James Keeshan, 1927–, U.S. TV personality.
Caracalla b. Marcus Aurelius Antoninus Bassianus, A.D. 188–217, Roman emperor 212–17.
Caramanlis, Constantine, 1907–, Gr. statesman; prime minister, 1955–63 & 1974–80.
Caravaggio, Michelangelo Amerighi da 1573–1610, Ital. painter.
Cárdenas, Lázaro, 1895–1970, Mexican general; president of Mexico 1934–40.
Cardin, Pierre, 1922–, Ital.-born Fr. fashion designer.
Cardozo, Benjamin Nathan, 1870–1938, U.S. jurist; justice of U.S. Supreme Court 1932–38.
Carducci, Giosuè, 1835–1907, Ital. poet; Nobel Prize winner.
Carême, Marie Antoine, 1784–1833, Fr. chef & gastronome.
Carew, Thomas, 1595?–1645?, Eng. poet.
Carl XVI Gustaf, 1946–, king of Sweden 1973–.
Carlota, 1840–1927, Austrian-born empress of Mexico 1864–67.
Carlyle, Thomas, 1795–1881, Scot. author
Carman, (William) Bliss, 1861–1929, Can. poet & journalist active in U.S.
Carmichael, Hoaglund Howard (Hoagy), 1899–1981, U.S. songwriter.
Carnap, Rudolf, 1891–1970, Ger.-born U.S. philosopher.
Carné, Marcel, 1909–96, Fr. film director.
Carnegie, Andrew, 1835–1919, Scot.-born U.S. industrialist & philanthropist.
—Dale, 1888–1955, U.S. author & teacher of public speaking.
Carney, Art, 1918–, U.S. actor.
Carnot, Lazare Nicolas Marguerite, 1753–1823, Fr. revolutionary statesman & general.
—Nicolas Léonard Sadi, 1796–1832, Fr. physicist; son of prec.
Carol II, 1893–1953, king of Romania 1930–40; abdicated.
Carpaccio, Vittore, 1460?–1525?, Ital. painter.
Carracci A family of Ital. painters incl. **Lodovico,** 1555–1619, & his nephews **Agostino,** 1557–1602, & **Annibale,** 1560–1609.
Carranza, Venustiano, 1859–1920, Mexican revolutionist & statesman; president of Mexico 1915–20.
Carrel, Alexis, 1873–1944, Fr. surgeon & biologist.
Carreras, José, 1947–, Sp. tenor.
Carrington, Richard Christopher, 1826–75, Eng. astronomer.
Carroll, Charles, 1737–1832, Amer. revolutionary patriot.
—Lewis, pseud. of Charles Lutwidge Dodgson, 1832–98, Eng. mathematician & author.
Carson, Christopher (Kit), 1809–68, U.S. frontiersman.
—Johnny, 1925–, U.S. comedian & television personality.
—Rachel Louise, 1907–64, U.S. biologist & author.
Carter, Howard, 1873–1939, Eng. archaeologist.
—Elliott Cook, 1908–, U.S. composer.
—James Earl (Jimmy), 1924–, politician, 39th U.S. president 1977–81.
Cartier, Jacques, 1491–1557, Fr. explorer; discoverer of the St. Lawrence River.
Cartier-Bresson, Henri, 1908–, Fr. photographer.
Cartwright, Edmund, 1743–1823, Eng. inventor of the power loom.
Caruso, Enrico, 1873–1921, Ital. tenor.
Carver, George Washington, 1864?–1943, U.S. chemist & botanist.
—John, 1576?–1621, Eng.-born Amer. colonist; 1st governor of Plymouth colony.
—Raymond, 1938–88, U.S. author.
Cary, (Arthur) Joyce (Lunel), 1888–1957, Eng. author.
Casadesus, Robert, 1899–1972, Fr. pianist.
Casals, Pablo, 1876–1973, Sp. cellist & composer.
Casanova, Giovanni Jacopo, 1725–98, Ital. adventurer; known for his *Memoirs*.
Casement, Sir Roger, 1864–1916, Irish nationalist; hanged by the British for treason in World War I.
Casey, William J., 1913–87, U.S. public official.
Cash, Johnny, 1932–, U.S. singer & songwriter.
Caslon, William, 1692–1766, Eng. typographer.
Cassatt, Mary, 1845–1926, U.S. painter.

Cassini, Giovanni Domenico, 1625–1712, Fr. astronomer.
Cassiodorus, Flavius Magnus Aurelius, ?–575, Roman states-man & author.
Cassirer, Ernst, 1874–1945, Ger. philosopher.
Cassius Longinus, Gaius, ?–42 B.C., Roman general; conspir-ator against Caesar.
Catagno, Andrea del, ?–1457?, Ital. painter.
Castiglione, Count Baldassare, 1478–1529, Ital. statesman & author.
Castle, Irene, 1893–1969, U.S. dancer.
—**Vernon,** 1887–1918, Eng.-born U.S. dancer & aviator; hus-band of prec.
Castlereagh, Robert Stewart, Viscount, 1769–1822, Brit. statesman.
Castro (Ruz), Fidel, 1926–, Cuban revolutionary leader; dicta-tor of Cuba 1959–.
Catharine of Aragon, 1485–1536, first wife of Henry VIII of England; mother of Mary I.
Cather, Willa Sibert, 1876–1947, U.S. author.
Catherine II (Ekaterina Alekseevna), 1729–96, Ger.-born empress of Russia 1762–96: known as **Catherine the Great.**
Catiline (L. Lucius Sergius Catilina), 108?–62 B.C., Roman politician & conspirator.
Catlin, George, 1796–1872, U.S. painter & sculptor.
Cato, Marcus Porcius, 234–149 B.C., Roman statesman: known as **the Elder.**
—**Marcus Porcius,** 95–46 B.C., Roman statesman & philoso-pher; great-grandson of prec.: known as **the Younger.**
Catt, Carrie Chapman Lane, 1859–1947, U.S. suffragist.
Catton, (Charles) Bruce, 1899–1978, U.S. journalist & histo-rian.
Catullus, Gaius Valerius, 84?–54 B.C., Roman poet.
Cavafy, Constantinos, 1863–1933, Gk. poet.
Cavell, Edith, 1865–1915, Eng. nurse & patriot; executed by the Germans in World War I.
Cavendish, Henry, 1731?–1810, Eng. chemist & physicist.
Cavett, Dick, 1936–, U.S. TV personality & author.
Cavour, Count Camillo Benso di, 1810–61, Ital. statesman.
Caxton, William, 1422–91, first Eng. printer.
Cayce, Edgar, 1877–1945, U.S. photographer & psychic.
Cayley, Sir George, 1773–1857, Eng. engineer & aircraft de-signer.
Ceausescu, Nicolae, 1918–89, president of Rumania 1967–89.
Cecchetti, Enrico, 1850–1928, Russ. ballet teacher.
Cecil, Lord (Edward Christian) David, 1902–86, Eng. au-thor.
—**William, 1st Baron Burghley,** 1520–98, Eng. statesman.
Céline, Louis Ferdinand, 1894–1961, Fr. author.
Cellini, Benvenuto, 1500–71, Ital. sculptor & goldsmith.
Celsius, Anders, 1701–44, Swed. astronomer.
Cenci, Beatrice, 1577–99, Ital. noblewoman; executed for par-ricide.
Cerf, Bennett Alfred, 1895–1971, U.S. author & publisher.
Cervantes Saavedra, Miguel de, 1547–1616, Sp. novelist & playwright.
Cézanne, Paul, 1839–1906, Fr. painter.
Chabrier, Alexis Emmanuel, 1841–94, Fr. composer.
Chabrol, Claude, 1930–, Fr. film director.
Chadwick, Sir James, 1891–1974, Eng. physicist.
Chagall, Marc, 1887–1985, Russ.-born painter active in France.
Chaliapin, Feodor Ivanovich, 1873–1938, Russ. basso.
Chamberlain, (Arthur) Neville, 1869–1940, Eng. statesman; prime minister 1937–40.
—**Austen,** 1863–1937, Brit. statesman.
—**Owen,** 1920–, U.S. physicist; Nobel Prize winner.
—**Richard,** 1935–, U.S. actor.
—**Wilt(on Norman),** 1936–, U.S. basketball player.
Chambers, (Jay David) Whittaker, 1901–61, U.S. journalist.
Champion, Gower, 1921–80, U.S. dancer, choreographer, & stage director.
—**Marjorie (Marge),** 1925–, U.S. dancer.
Champlain, Samuel de, 1567?–1635, Fr. explorer in America.
Champollion, Jean François, 1790–1832, Fr. Egyptologist.
Chancellor, John, 1927–96, U.S. journalist & TV commenta-tor.
Chandler, Raymond, 1888–1959, U.S. author.

Chanel, Gabrielle (Coco), 1883?–1971, Fr. fashion designer.
Chaney, Lon, 1883–1930, U.S. actor.
Chang & Eng, 1811–74, Siamese-born conjoined twins resid-ing in U.S.; the original "Siamese twins."
Channing, Carol, 1923–, U.S. actress.
—**Edward,** 1856–1931, U.S. historian.
—**William Ellery,** 1780–1842, U.S. clergyman & social re-former.
Chaplin, Sir Charles Spencer (Charlie), 1889–1977, Eng.-born film actor & producer active in U.S.
—**Geraldine,** 1944–, U.S. actress; daughter of prec.
Chapman, George, 1559?–1634, Eng. playwright & transla-tor.
—**John,** 1774–1845, U.S. pioneer: called **Johnny Appleseed.**
Charcot, Jean Martin, 1825–93, Fr. neurologist.
Chardin, Jean Baptiste Siméon, 1699–1779, Fr. painter.
Chardonnet, Hilaire Bernigaud, Comte de, 1839–1924, Fr. chemist & inventor.
Charlemagne, 742–814, king of the Franks 768–814 & Holy Roman emperor 800–814: known as **Charles the Great.**
Charles I, 1600–49, king of England 1625–49; beheaded.
—**II,** 1630–85, king of England 1660–85; son of prec.
Charles V, 1337–80, king of France 1364–80: known as **Charles the Wise.**
Charles V, 1500–58, Holy Roman emperor; king of Spain as Charles I.
Charles XIV See BERNADOTTE, JEAN, BAPTISTE, JULES.
Charles Philip Arthur George, 1948–, Prince of Wales, heir apparent to the Brit. throne.
Charles, Jacques Alexandre César, 1746–1823, Fr. physicist.
Charpentier, Gustave, 1860–1956, Fr. composer.
Chase, Lucia, 1907–86, U.S. ballet dancer & ballet company director.
—**Mary Ellen,** 1887–1973, U.S. author & educator.
—**Salmon Portland,** 1808–73, U.S. statesman; chief justice of the U.S. Supreme Court.
Chateaubriand, François René, Vicomte de, 1768–1848, Fr. author & politician.
Chatterton, Ruth, 1893–1961, U.S. actress.
—**Thomas,** 1752–70, Eng. poet.
Chaucer, Geoffrey, 1340?–1400, Eng. poet.
Chávez, Carlos, 1899–1978, Mexican composer & conductor.
—**Cesar Estrada,** 1927–93, U.S. labor leader.
Chayefsky, Sidney (Paddy), 1923–81, U.S. playwright.
Cheever, John, 1912–82, U.S. author.
Chekhov, Anton Pavlovich, 1860–1904, Russ. playwright & author.
Chénier, André Marie de, 1762–94, Fr. poet.
Chennault, Claire Lee, 1890–1958, U.S. Air Force general.
Cheops, Egyptian king of the 4th dynasty ca. 2650 B.C.; built the Great Pyramid at Gizeh: also known as **Khufu.**
Chernenko, Konstantin Ustinovich, 1911–85, Soviet states-man; general secretary U.S.S.R. Communist Party 1984–85.
Cherenkov, Pavel Alekseevich, 1904–90, Soviet physicist.
Chernyshevski, Nikolai Gavrilovich, 1829–89, Russ. revolu-tionist & author.
Cherubini, (Maria) Luigi, 1760–1842, Ital. composer.
Chessman, Caryl (Whittier), 1921–60, U.S. criminal & au-thor; executed.
Chesterfield, Earl of, b. Philip Dormer Stanhope, 1694–1773, Eng. statesman & author.
Chesterton, Gilbert Keith, 1874–1936, Eng. author.
Chevalier, Maurice, 1888–1972, Fr. entertainer.
Chevrolet, Louis, 1878–1941, U.S. automobile manufacturer.
Chiang Ching, 1913–92, Chin. government official; wife of Mao Tse-tung.
—**Kai-shek,** 1886–1975, Chin. general & statesman; president of Republic of China (Taiwan) 1948–75.
—**Madame Chiang Kai-shek** See SOONG.
Chikamatsu Monzaemon, 1653?–1724, Jap. dramatist.
Child, Francis James, 1825–96, U.S. philologist & ballad ed-itor.
—**Julia McCormick,** 1912–, U.S. culinary expert & author.
Chippendale, Thomas, 1718–79, Eng. cabinetmaker.
Chirico, Giorgio di, 1888–1978, Ital. painter.
Chisholm, Shirley, 1924–, U.S. politician.

Chittenden, Russell Henry, 1856–1943, U.S. physiological chemist.

Chomsky, Noam, 1928–, U.S. linguist.

Chopin, Frédéric François, 1810–49, Pol. composer & pianist active in France.

—Kate, 1851–1904, U.S. author.

Chou En-Lai, 1898–1976, Chin. statesman.

Chrétien de Troyes, 12th c. Fr. poet.

Christensen, Lew, 1909–84, U.S. dancer, choreographer, & ballet company director.

Christians, Mady, 1900–51, Austrian actress.

Christie, Dame Agatha, 1890–1976, Eng. author.

Christoff, Boris, 1919–93, Bulgarian basso.

Christophe, Henri, 1767–1820, Haitian revolutionary leader; king of Haiti 1811–20.

Christopher, Saint, 3rd c. Christian martyr.

Christy, Howard Chandler, 1873–1952, U.S. painter & illustrator.

Chrysler, Walter Percy, 1875–1940, U.S. automobile manufacturer.

Chuang-tzu, 4th c. B.C. Chin. philosopher.

Churchill, Lord Randolph, 1849–95, Eng. statesman.

—Winston, 1871–1947, U.S. author.

—Sir Winston Leonard Spenser, 1874–1965, Eng. statesman & author; prime minister 1940–45 & 1951–55; Nobel Prize winner; son of Lord Randolph.

Chu Teh, 1886–1976, Chin. military leader.

Ciano, Count Galeazzo, 1903–44, Ital. diplomat.

Ciardi, John, 1916–86, U.S. poet & critic.

Cibber, Colley, 1671–1757, Eng. actor & poet.

Cicero, Marcus Tullius, 106–43 B.C., Roman statesman, orator, & writer.

Cimabue, Giovanni, 1240–1302, Florentine painter.

Cimarosa, Domenico, 1749–1801, Ital. composer.

Cimino, Michael, 1948–, U.S. film director.

Cincinnatus, Lucius Quinctius, 5th c. B.C. Roman general & statesman.

Claiborne, Craig, 1920–, U.S. journalist, author, & critic.

Clair, René, 1898–1981, Fr. film director.

Claire, Ina, 1892–1985, U.S. actress.

Clare, Saint, 1194–1253, Ital. nun.

Clark, Bobby, 1888–1960, U.S. comedian.

—(Charles) Joseph, 1939–, Can. statesman; prime minister of Canada, 1979–80.

—Dick, 1929–, U.S. TV personality.

—George Rogers, 1752–1818, U.S. soldier & frontiersman.

—James Beauchamp (Champ), 1850–1921, U.S. politician.

—Kenneth Bancroft, 1914–, U.S. psychologist.

—Sir Kenneth MacKenzie, 1903–83, Brit. art historian.

—Mark, 1896–1984, U.S. general.

—William, 1770–1838, U.S. explorer.

—(William) Ramsey, 1927–, U.S. lawyer & politician.

Clarke, Arthur Charles, 1917–, Eng. author.

—Kenny, 1914–1985, U.S. jazz musician.

Claude, Albert, 1899–1983, Belg. biologist.

Claude (de) Lorrain, b. Claude Gellée, 1600–82, Fr. painter.

Claudel, Paul Louise Charles, 1868–1955, Fr. author & diplomat.

Claudius I, born Tiberius Claudius Drusus Nero Germanicus, 10 B.C.–A.D. 54, 4th Roman emperor 41–54.

Clausewitz, Karl von, 1780–1831, Prussian general & writer on military science.

Clausius, Rudolf Julius Emanuel, 1822–88, Ger. physicist & mathematician.

Clavell, James, 1924–94, Brit. author.

Clay, Cassius Marcellus, 1810–1903, U.S. politician & abolitionist.

—Henry, 1777–1852, U.S. statesman & orator.

—Lucius DuBignon, 1897–1978, U.S. general & banker.

Cleary, Beverly, 1916–, U.S. author.

Cleaver, (Leroy) Eldridge, 1935–, U.S. author & political activist.

Clemenceau, Georges Benjamin Eugène, 1841–1929, Fr. statesman; premier of France 1906–09 & 1917–20.

Clemens, Samuel Langhorne, See TWAIN, MARK.

Clement VII, b. Guilio de' Medici, 1478–1534, pope 1523–34.

Clement of Alexandria, (L. Titus Flavius Clemens), A.D. 150?–220?, Gk. theologian.

Cleopatra, 69–30 B.C., queen of Egypt 51–30 B.C.

Cleveland, (Stephen) Grover, 1837–1908, 22nd & 24th U.S. president 1885–89 & 1893–97.

Cliburn, Harvey Lavan (Van), 1934–, U.S. pianist.

Clift, Montgomery, 1920–66, U.S. actor.

Clinton, De Witt, 1769–1828, U.S. lawyer & statesman.

Clive, Robert (Baron Clive of Plassey), 1725–74, Brit. general in India.

Clough, Arthur Hugh, 1819–61, Eng. poet.

Clovis, I, 466?–511, Frankish king.

Clurman, Harold, 1901–80, U.S. director & drama critic.

Cobb, Irvin Shrewsbury, 1876–1944, U.S. journalist & humorist.

—Lee J., 1911–76, U.S. actor.

—Ty(rus Raymond), 1886–1961, U.S. baseball player.

Cobbett, William, 1762–1835, Eng. political economist.

Cobden, William, 1804–65, Eng. statesman & economist.

Coca, Imogene, 1908–, U.S. comedienne & actress.

Cochise, ?–1874, Apache Am. Ind. chief.

Cochran, Jacqueline, 1912?–80, U.S. businesswoman & aviatrix.

Cockcroft, Sir John Douglas, 1897–1967, Eng. nuclear physicist; Nobel Prize winner.

Cocteau, Jean, 1889–1963, Fr. author & film director.

Cody, William Frederick, 1846–1917, U.S. plainsman, army scout, & showman: known as Buffalo Bill.

Coe, Frederick, 1914–79, U.S. TV producer & stage & film director.

Coffin, Robert Peter Tristram, 1892–1955, U.S. poet & author.

Cohan, George Michael, 1878–1942, U.S. theatrical producer, actor, & composer.

Cohn, Ferdinand Julius, 1828–98, Ger. botanist.

—Harry, 1891–1958, U.S. film executive.

Coke, Sir Edward, 1552–1634, Eng. jurist.

Colbert, Claudette, 1905–96, Fr.-born U.S. actress.

—Jean Baptiste, 1619–83, Fr. statesman.

Colby, William E., 1920–96, U.S. government official.

Cole, Nat "King", 1919–65, U.S. singer & pianist.

—Thomas, 1801–48, Eng.-born U.S. painter.

Coleman, Ornette, 1930–, U.S. jazz musician & composer.

Coleridge, Samuel Taylor, 1772–1834, Eng. poet.

Colet, John, 1466?–1519, Eng. theologian & scholar.

Colette, (Sidonie-Gabrielle Claudine), 1873–1954, Fr. author.

Colfax, Schuyler, 1823–85, U.S. statesman; U.S. vice president 1869–73.

Colgate, William, 1783–1857, U.S. businessman & philanthropist.

Collins, Joan, 1933–, Eng. actress active in U.S.

—Judy, 1939–, U.S. singer.

—Michael, 1890–1922, Irish revolutionist.

—(William) Wilkie, 1824–89, Eng. author.

Colman, Ronald, 1891–1958, Eng. actor active in U.S.

Colt, Samuel, 1814–62, U.S. inventor & firearms manufacturer.

Coltrane, John, 1926–67, U.S. jazz musician & composer.

Colum, Padraic, 1881–1972, Irish poet & playwright.

Columbus, Christopher, 1451–1506, Ital. navigator; discovered America.

Comaneci, Nadia, 1962–, Romanian gymnast.

Comden, Betty, 1919–, U.S. lyricist.

Commager, Henry Steele, 1902–98, U.S. historian.

Commoner, Barry, 1917–, U.S. biologist & educator.

Commons, John R., 1862–1945, U.S. economist & historian.

Como, Perry, 1913–, U.S. singer.

Compton, Arthur Holly, 1892–1962, U.S. physicist.

Compton-Burnett, Ivy, 1892–1969, Eng. author.

Comstock, Anthony, 1844–1915, U.S. social reformer.

Comte, Auguste, 1798–1857, Fr. philosopher.

Conant, James Bryant, 1893–1978, U.S. chemist, educator, & statesman.

Condon, Eddie, 1905–73, U.S. jazz musician.

—Edward Uhler, 1902–74, U.S. physicist.

Condorcet, Marie Jean Antoine Nicolas de Caritat, Marquis de, 1743–94, Fr. philosopher, mathematician, & politician.
Confucius, Latinized form of **Kung Fu-tse,** 551–478 B.C., Chin. philosopher & teacher.
Congreve, William, 1670–1729, Eng. playwright.
Connally, John Bowden, 1917–93, U.S. politician.
Connelly, Marc(us Cook), 1890–1980, U.S. playwright.
Connery, Sean, 1930–, Scot.-born U.S. actor.
Connolly, Cyril, 1903–74, Eng. critic & editor.
—**Maureen,** 1934–69, U.S. tennis player.
Connors, James Scott (Jimmy), 1952–, U.S. tennis player.
Conrad, Joseph, b. Teodor Jozef Konrad Korzeniowski, 1857–1924, Pol.-born Eng. author.
—**Paul,** 1924–, U.S. political cartoonist.
Constable, John, 1776–1837, Eng. painter.
Constantine I, ?–715, pope 708–715.
Constantine I, b. Flavius Valerius Aurelius, 272–337, first Christian emperor of Rome: called **the Great.**
Constantine II, 1940–, king of Greece 1964–67.
Coogan, John Leslie, Jr., (Jackie), 1914–84, U.S. actor.
Cook, Barbara, 1927–, U.S. singer & actress.
—**James,** 1728–79, Eng. naval officer & explorer.
Cooke, (Alfred) Alistair, 1908–, Eng.-born U.S. author, journalist, & TV narrator.
—**Jay,** 1821–1905, U.S. financier.
Cooley, Denton Arthur, 1920–, U.S. surgeon.
Coolidge, (John) Calvin, 1872–1933, 30th U.S. president 1923–29.
Cooper, Gary, 1901–61, U.S. actor.
—**Gladys,** 1888–1971, Eng. actress.
—**Jackie,** 1922–, U.S. actor & director.
—**James Fenimore,** 1789–1851, U.S. novelist.
—**Peter,** 1791–1883, U.S. manufacturer, inventor, & philanthropist.
Copernicus, Nicolaus, 1473–1543, Pol. astronomer.
Copland, Aaron, 1900–90, U.S. composer.
Copley, John Singleton, 1738–1815, U.S. painter.
Coppola, Francis Ford, 1939–, U.S. film director.
Coquelin, Benoît Constant, 1841–1909, Fr. actor.
Corbett, James John, 1866–1933, U.S. boxer.
Corbusier, Le, b. Charles Edouard Jeanneret, 1887–1965, Swiss architect active in France.
Corday, Charlotte, 1768–93, Fr. patriot; assassinated Marat.
Corelli, Arcangelo, 1653–1713, Ital. composer & violinist.
—**Franco,** 1924–, Ital. tenor.
Cori, Carl Ferdinand, 1896–1984, & his wife **Gerty Theresa Radnitz,** 1896–1957, Czech-born U.S. biochemists; Nobel Prize winners.
Corneille, Pierre, 1606–84, Fr. playwright.
Cornell, Ezra, 1807–74, U.S. financier & philanthropist.
—**Katherine,** 1898–1974, Ger.-born U.S. actress.
Corning, Erastus, 1794–1872, U.S. financier.
Cornwallis, Charles, Marquis, 1738–1805, Eng. general & statesman.
Coronado, Francisco Vásquez de, 1510?–54, Sp. explorer.
Corot, Jean Baptiste Camille, 1796–1875, Fr. painter.
Correggio, Antonio Allegri da, 1494–1534, Ital. painter.
Correll, Charles, 1890–1972, U.S. radio actor.
Corsaro, Frank, 1924–, U.S. opera director.
Cortázar, Julio, 1914–84, Argentine author.
Cortés, Hernando, 1485–1547, Sp. conqueror of Mexico.
Cosby, Bill, 1937–, U.S. comedian & actor.
Cosell, Howard, 1920–95, U.S. TV commentator.
Costa-Gavras, Henri, 1933–, Gk.-born French film director.
Costello, Lou, 1908–59, U.S. comedian & actor.
Cotton, John, 1584–1652, Eng.-born Puritan clergyman in America.
Coughlin, Charles Edward, 1891–1979, U.S. clergyman & political spokesman: called **Father Coughlin.**
Coulomb, Charles Augustin de, 1736–1806, Fr. physicist.
Couper, Archibald Scott, 1831–92, Scot. chemist.
Couperin, François, 1668–1733, Fr. composer.
Courbet, Gustave, 1819–77, Fr. painter.
Cournand, André Frédéric, 1895–1988, Fr.-born U.S. physiologist.
Courrèges, André, 1923–, Fr. fashion designer.
Court, Margaret Smith, 1942–, Austral. tennis player.

Cousin, Victor, 1792–1867, Fr. philosopher.
Cousins, Norman, 1912–90, U.S. editor & author.
Cousteau, Jacques-Yves, 1910–97, Fr. naval officer, underwater explorer, & filmmaker.
Cousy, Robert Joseph (Bob), 1928–, U.S. basketball player & coach.
Coverdale, Miles, 1488–1568, Eng. translator of the Bible.
Coward, Sir Noel, 1899–1973, Eng. playwright, composer, & actor.
Cowell, Henry Dixon, 1897–1965, U.S. composer.
Cowl, Jane, 1884–1950, U.S. actress.
Cowles, Gardner, Jr., (Mike), 1903–85, U.S. publisher.
Cowley, Abraham, 1618–67, Eng. poet.
—**Malcolm,** 1898–1989, U.S. critic.
Cowper, William, 1731–1800, Eng. poet.
Coxe, George Harmon, 1901–84, U.S. author.
Cozzens, James Gould, 1903–78, U.S. author.
Crabbe, George, 1754–1832, Eng. poet.
—**Larry (Buster),** 1908–83, U.S. swimmer & actor.
Craig, (Edward) Gordon, 1872–1966, Eng. director & stage designer.
Craigavon, James Craig, 1st Viscount, 1871–1940, Irish statesman; first prime minister of N. Ireland, 1921–40.
Craigie, Sir William Alexander, 1867–1957, Scot. philologist & lexicographer.
Cram, Ralph Adams, 1863–1942, U.S. architect & author.
Cranach, Lucas, 1472–1553, Ger. painter & engraver.
—**Lucas,** 1515–86, Ger. portrait painter; son of prec.: called **the Younger.**
Crane, (Harold) Hart, 1899–1932, U.S. poet.
—**Stephen,** 1871–1900, U.S. author & poet.
Cranko, John, 1928–73, South African-born choreographer & ballet-company director active in W. Germany.
Cranmer, Thomas, 1489–1556, archbishop of Canterbury; burned at the stake.
Crashaw, Richard, 1613–49, Eng. poet.
Crassus, Marcus Licinius, 115?–53 B.C., Roman politician.
Crater, Joseph Force, 1889–1937?, U.S. jurist.
Crawford, Cheryl, 1902–86, U.S. theatrical producer.
—**Joan,** 1908–77, U.S. actress.
Crazy Horse, b. Tashunca-Utico, 1849?–77, Sioux Am. Ind. chief.
Creasy, John, 1908–73, Eng. author.
Crespin, Régine, 1927–, Fr. soprano.
Crèvecoeur, Michel-Guillaume St. Jean de, 1735–1813, Fr.-born author active in America.
Crichton, James, 1560?–82, Scot. scholar & adventurer: called **the Admirable Crichton.**
—**Michael,** 1942–, U.S. physician, author, & film director.
Crick, Francis, 1916–, Eng. geneticist.
Cripps, Sir (Richard) Stafford, 1889–1952, Eng. lawyer & socialist statesman.
Crist, Judith, 1922–, U.S. film critic & journalist.
Croce, Benedetto, 1866–1952, Ital. philospher, statesman, critic, & historian.
Crockett, David (Davy), 1786–1836, U.S. frontiersman & congressman.
Croesus, 6th c. B.C. Lydian king famed for great wealth.
Cromwell, Oliver, 1599–1658, Eng. general & statesman.
—**Richard,** 1626–1712, Eng. general & statesman; son of prec.
Cronin, Archibald Joseph, 1896–1981, Eng. physician & author.
Cronkite, Walter Leland, Jr., 1916–, U.S. journalist & TV news commentator.
Cronyn, Hume, 1911–, Can.-born U.S. actor.
Crookes, Sir William, 1832–1919, Eng. physicist & chemist.
Crosby, Harry Lillis (Bing), 1904–77, U.S. singer & actor.
Cross, Milton, 1897–1975, U.S. opera commentator.
Crouse, Russel, 1893–1966, U.S. journalist & playwright.
Cruikshank, George, 1792–1878, Eng. illustrator & caricaturist.
Crumb, George, 1929–, U.S. composer.
Cukor, George, 1899–1983, U.S. film director.
Culbertson, Ely, 1893–1955, Romanian-born U.S. expert on the game of bridge.
Cullen, Countee, 1903–46, U.S. poet.

Cummings, Edward Estlin, 1894–1962, U.S. poet; usu. known as **e. e. cummings.**
Cunard, Sir Samuel, 1787–1865, Can. steamship executive.
Cunha, Tristão da, 1460?–1540, Pg. navigator & explorer.
Cunningham, Merce, 1922–, U.S. choreographer.
Cuomo, Mario, 1932–, U.S. politician.
Curie, Marie, b. Marja Sklodowska, 1867–1934, Pol.-born Fr. physicist & chemist.
—**Pierre,** 1859–1906, Fr. physicist; husband of prec.
Curley, James Michael, 1874–1958, U.S. politician.
Currier & Ives, A U.S. firm of lithographers established 1835 by **Nathaniel Currier,** 1813–88; later joined by **James Merritt Ives,** 1824–95.
Curry, John Steuart, 1897–1946, U.S. painter.
Curtis, Cyrus Hermann Kotzschmar, 1850–1933, U.S. publisher & philanthropist.
Curtiss, Glenn Hammond, 1878–1930, U.S. aviator & inventor.
Curtiz, Michael, 1888–1962, Hung.-born U.S. film director.
Curzon, Clifford, 1907–82, Brit. pianist.
Cushing, Harvey, 1869–1939, U.S. surgeon & author.
Cushman, Charlotte Saunders, 1816–76, U.S. actress.
Custer, George Armstrong, 1839–76, U.S. general.
Cuvier, Baron Georges Léopold, 1769–1832, Fr. naturalist.
Cynewulf, 8th c. Anglo-Saxon poet.
Cyril, Saint, 827–869, Gk. missionary & apostle to the Slavs.
Cyrus, ?–529 B.C., king of Persia 559–529 B.C.; founder of the Persian Empire: called **the Great.**
Czerny, Karl, 1791–1857, Austrian composer & pianist.

da Gama, Vasco, 1469?–1524, Pg. navigator.
Daguerre, Louis Jacques Mandé, 1787–1851, Fr. inventor.
Daimler, Gottlieb, 1834–1900, Ger. engineer & automobile manufacturer.
Daladier, Édouard, 1884–1970, Fr. statesman.
Daley, Richard Joseph, 1902–76, U.S. politician; mayor of Chicago 1955–76.
Dali, Salvador, 1904–89, Sp.-born painter active in U.S.
Dallapicola, Luigi, 1904–75, Ital. pianist & composer.
Dallas, George Mifflin, 1792–1864, U.S. statesman; U.S. vice president 1845–49.
Dalton, John, 1766–1844, Eng. chemist & physicist.
—**Robert,** 1867–92, U.S. outlaw.
Daly, (John) Augustin, 1838–99, U.S. playwright & theater manager.
D'Amboise, Jacques, 1934–, U.S. ballet dance & choreographer.
Damien de Veuster, Joseph, 1840–89, Belg. missionary to lepers in Hawaiian Islands: called **Father Damien.**
Damrosch, Leopold, 1832–85, violinist & conductor.
—**Walter Johannes,** 1862–1950, Ger.-born U.S. conductor; son of prec.
Dana, Charles Anderson, 1819–97, newspaper editor.
—**Richard Henry, Jr.,** 1815–82, U.S. lawyer & author.
Dane, Clemence, pseud. of Winifred Ashton, 1888–1965, Eng. author.
Daniel, Samuel, 1562?–1619, Eng. poet.
Danilova, Alexandra, 1904–97, Russ.-born ballerina active in U.S.
D'Annunzio, Gabriele, 1863–1938, Ital. author & adventurer.
Dante Alighieri, 1265–1321, Ital. poet.
Danton, Georges Jacques, 1759–94, Fr. revolutionary leader.
Da Ponte, Lorenzo, 1749–1838, Ital. librettist.
Dare, Virginia, 1587–?, first child born in America of Eng. parents.
Darío, Rubén, pseud. of Félix Rubén García-Sarmiento, 1867–1916, Sp. poet.
Darius I, 558?–486 B.C., king of Persia 521–486 B.C.: called **the Great.**
Darling, Ding, 1876–1962, U.S. political cartoonist.
Darnley, Henry Stewart, Lord, 1545–67, Scot. nobleman; second husband of Mary, Queen of Scots; assassinated.
Darrow, Clarence Seward, 1857–1938, U.S. lawyer.
Darwin, Charles Robert, 1809–82, Eng. naturalist; founder of evolutionary theory of natural selection.
—**Erasmus,** 1731–1802, Eng. physiologist & poet; grandfather of prec.

Daubigny, Charles François, 1817–78, Fr. painter.
Daudet, Alphonse, 1840–97, Fr. author.
—**Léon,** 1867–1942, Fr. journalist & author; son of prec.
Daumier, Honoré, 1808–79, Fr. painter & caricaturist.
David, 1030?–960? B.C., second king of Israel.
David, Gerard, 1450?–1523, Du. painter.
—**Hal,** 1921–, U.S. lyricist.
—**Jacques-Louis,** 1748–1825, Fr. painter.
Davidson, Jo, 1883–1952, U.S. sculptor.
Davies, Marion, 1897–1961, U.S. actress.
—**Robertson,** 1913–95, Can. novelist, playwright, & journalist.
Davis, Adelle, 1904–74, U.S. nutritionist & author.
—**Benjamin Oliver, Sr.,** 1877–1970, U.S. general; first black general in U.S. army.
—**Benjamin Oliver, Jr.,** 1912–, U.S. general; son of prec.
—**Elmer Holmes,** 1890–1958, U.S. radio news commentator.
—**Jefferson,** 1808–89, U.S. statesman; president of the Confederacy 1862–65.
—**Jim,** 1945–, U.S. cartoonist.
—**Miles,** 1926–91, U.S. jazz musician.
—**Richard Harding,** 1864–1916, U.S. war correspondent & author.
—**Ruth Elizabeth (Bette),** 1908–89, U.S. actress.
—**Sammy, Jr.,** 1925–90, U.S. singer & actor.
—**Stuart,** 1894–1964, U.S. painter.
Davy, Sir Humphry, 1778–1829, Eng. chemist.
Day, Clarence Sheperd, 1874–1935, U.S. author.
—**Doris,** 1924–, U.S. actress & singer.
—**Dorothy,** 1897–1980, U.S. journalist & social reformer.
Dayan, Moshe, 1915–81, Israeli soldier & statesman.
Day-Lewis, C(ecil), 1904–72, Irish-born Brit. poet & author.
Deacon, Richard, 1922–84, U.S. comic actor.
Dean, James, 1931–55, U.S. actor.
—**Jay Hanna (Dizzy),** 1911–74, U.S. baseball player.
DeBakey, Michael Ellis, 1908–, U.S. surgeon.
de Beauvior, Simone, 1908–86, Fr. author & philosopher.
De Broca, Philippe, 1935–, Fr. film director.
de Broglie, Louis Victor, Prince, 1892–1987, Fr. physicist.
Debs, Eugene Victor, 1855–1926, U.S. labor leader & socialist.
Debussy, Claude Achille, 1862–1918, Fr. composer.
Debye, Peter Joseph William, 1884–1966, Du.-born U.S. physicist & chemist.
Decatur, Stephen, 1779–1820, U.S. naval officer.
Dee, Ruby, 1923?–, U.S. actress.
Deere, John, 1804–86, U.S. inventor.
Defoe, Daniel, 1661?–1731, Eng. author.
De Forest, Lee, 1873–1961, U.S. inventor.
Degas, (Hilaire Germain) Edgar, 1834–1917, Fr. painter & sculptor.
De Gasperi, Alcide, 1881–1954, Ital. statesman; premier of Italy 1945–53.
de Gaulle, Charles André Joseph Marie, 1890–1970, Fr. general & statesman; president of France 1945–46 & 1959–69.
De Geer, Charles, 1720–78, Swed. entomologist.
de Ghelderode, Michel, 1898–1962, Belg. playwright.
de Havilland, Olivia, 1916–, U.S. actress born in Japan.
De Kalb, Johann, 1721–80, Ger. soldier; served in Amer. revolutionary army.
Dekker, Thomas, 1572?–1632?, Eng. playwright.
de Kooning, Willem, 1904–97, Du.-born U.S. painter.
De Kruif, Paul, 1890–1971, U.S. bacteriologist & author.
Delacroix, (Ferdinand Victor) Eugène, 1798–1863, Fr. painter.
de la Madrid Hurtado, Miguel, 1935–, president of Mexico 1982–89.
de la Mare, Walter, 1873–1956, Eng. poet & author.
de la Renta, Oscar, 1932–, Dom. Rep. fashion designer.
Delaunay, Robert, 1885–1951, Fr. painter.
de la Warr, Thomas West, Lord, 1577–1618, Eng. colonial administrator in America.
Delbrück, Max, 1906–81, Ger.-born U.S. molecular geneticist.
Delibes, (Clement Philibert) Lèo, 1836–91, Fr. composer.
Delius, Frederick, 1862–1934, Eng. composer.

Dellinger, John Howard, 1886–1962, U.S. radio engineer.
Dello Joio, Norman, 1913–, U.S. composer.
Del Monaco, Mario, 1915–82, Ital. tenor.
Delmonico, Lorenzo, 1813–81, Swiss-born U.S. restaurateur.
Delon, Alain, 1935–, Fr. actor.
Del Rio, Dolores, 1905–83, Mexican-born U.S. actress.
De Mille, Agnes George, 1908–93, U.S. dancer & choreographer.
—Cecil Blount, 1881–1959, U.S. film director; uncle of prec.
Democritus, 460?–352? B.C., Gk. philosopher.
Demosthenes, 384?–322 B.C., Athenian orator & patriot.
Dempsey, William Harrison (Jack), 1895–1983, U.S. boxer.
Demuth, Charles, 1883–1935, U.S. painter.
Deneuve, Catherine, 1943–, Fr. actress.
Deng Xiaoping, 1904–97, Chin. statesman; vice-premier Chin. Communist Party 1977–.
De Niro, Robert, 1945–, U.S. actor.
Denis, Saint, 3rd c., first bishop of Paris & patron saint of France.
De Quincey, Thomas, 1785–1859, Eng. author.
Derain, André, 1880–1954, Fr. painter.
Desai, Morarji, 1896–1995, Indian political leader; prime minister of India 1977–79.
Descartes, René, 1596–1650, Fr. mathematician & philosopher.
de Seversky, Alexander Prokofieff, 1894–1974, Russ.-born U.S. aeronautical engineer.
De Sica, Vittorio, 1902–74, Ital. film director and actor.
Desmoulins, Camille, 1760–94, Fr. revolutionist.
De Soto, Hernando, 1499?–1542, Sp. explorer.
Des Prez, Josquin, 1450?–1521, Du. composer.
Dessalines, Jean Jacques, 1758?–1806, Haitian military leader; emperor of Haiti as Jacques I.
De Sylva, Buddy, 1895–1950, U.S. lyricist.
De Valera, Éamon, 1882–1975, U.S.-born Irish statesman; president of Ireland 1959–73.
de Valois, Dame Ninette, 1898–, Irish-born ballerina, teacher, & impressario active in England.
De Voto, Bernard Augustine, 1897–1955, U.S. author & historian.
de Vries, Hugo, 1848–1935, Du. botanist.
De Vries, Peter, 1910–93, U.S. author.
Dewey, George, 1837–1917, U.S. admiral.
—John, 1859–1952, U.S. philosopher, psychologist, & educator.
—Melvil, 1851–1931, U.S. librarian.
—Thomas Edmund, 1902–71, U.S. lawyer & politician.
Dewhurst, Colleen, 1924–91, U.S. actress.
Diaghilev, Sergei Pavlovich, 1872–1929, Russ. ballet producer active in Paris.
Diamond, John Thomas (Legs), 1898–1931, U.S. criminal.
Dias, Bartholomeu, 1450?–1500, Pg. navigator.
Diaz, Porfirio, 1830–1915, Mexican general & statesman; president of Mexico 1884–1911.
Dickens, Charles, 1812–70, Eng. author.
Dickey, James, 1923–97, U.S. poet & author.
Dickinson, Emily Elizabeth, 1830–86, U.S. poet.
Diderot, Denis, 1713–84, Fr. critic, encyclopedist, & philosopher.
Didion, Joan, 1934–, U.S. author.
Didrikson, Babe, 1914–56, U.S. athlete.
Diefenbacker, John G., 1895–1979, Can. statesman; prime minister 1957–63.
Diem, Ngo Dinh, 1901–63, first president of S. Vietnam 1955–63; assassinated.
Dies, Martin, 1901–72, U.S. politician.
Diesel, Rudolf, 1858–1913, Ger. mech. engineer & inventor.
Dietrich, Marlene, 1901–92, Ger.-born film actress active in U.S.
Dietz, Howard, 1896–1983, U.S. lyricist & film executive.
Dillard, Harrison, 1923–, U.S. track runner.
Dillinger, John, 1903–34, U.S. criminal.
Dillon, C(larence) Douglas, 1909–78, U.S. government official.
DiMaggio, Joseph Paul (Joe), 1914–, U.S. baseball player.
Dinesen, Isak, pseud. of Baroness Karen Blixen-Finecke, 1885–1962, Dan. writer.

Diocletian, (L. Gaius Aurelius Valerius Diocletianus), 245–313, Roman emperor.
Diogenes, 412?–323? B.C., Gk. philosopher.
Dionysius the Areopagite, Saint, 1st c. A.D. Gk. mystic & theologian.
Dior, Christian, 1905–57, Fr. fashion designer.
Dioscorides, Pedanius, 1st c. A.D. Gk. physician & botanist.
Dirac, Paul Adrien Maurice, 1902–84, Eng. mathematician, physicist, & Nobel Prize winner.
Dirks, Rudolph, 1877–1968, U.S. cartoonist.
Dirksen, Everett McKinley, 1896–1969, U.S. politician.
Disney, Walt(er Elias), 1901–66, U.S. producer of animated & live films.
Disraeli, Benjamin, 1804–81, Eng. statesman & author; prime minister 1868 & 1874–80.
Di Stefano, Giuseppe, 1921–, Ital. tenor.
Dix, Dorothea Lynde, 1802–87, U.S. social reformer.
—Dorothy, pseud. of Elizabeth Meriwether Gilmer, 1870–1951, U.S. journalist.
Dixon, Jeremiah, ?–1777, Eng. astronomer & surveyor; with Charles Mason, established the Mason-Dixon line.
Djilas, Milovan, 1911–95, Yugoslav author.
Dobrynin, Anatoly, 1919–, Soviet diplomat.
Dobzhansky, Theodosius, 1900–75, Russ.-born U.S. geneticist.
Doctorow, E(dgar) L(aurence), 1931–, U.S. author.
Dodd, Frank Howard, 1844–1916, U.S. publisher.
Dodgson, Charles Lutwidge, See CARROLL, LEWIS.
Dohnányi, Ernst von, 1877–1960, Hung. composer.
Dolin, Sir Anton, 1904–83, Eng. ballet dancer & choreographer.
Dollfuss, Engelbert, 1892–1934, Austrian statesman; chancellor of Austria 1932–34; assassinated.
Dolly, Jenny, 1892–1941, & her sister **Rosie,** 1892–1970, Hung.-born vaudeville performers active in U.S.
Domenichino II, b. Domenico Zampieri, 1581–1641, Ital. painter.
Domingo, Placido, 1941–, Sp. tenor.
Dominic, Saint, 1170–1221, Sp. friar; founded the Dominican Order.
Donahue, Phil, 1935–, U.S. TV personality.
Donat, Robert, 1905–59, Eng. actor.
Donatello, b. Donato di Niccolò di Betto Bardi, 1386–1466, Ital. sculptor.
Donen, Stanley, 1924–, U.S. film director & producer.
Dönitz, Karl, 1891–1980, Ger. admiral.
Donizetti, Gaetano, 1797–1848, Ital. composer.
Donne, John, 1573?–1631, Eng. poet & clergyman.
Donovan, William Joseph (Wild Bill), 1883–1959, U.S. lawyer & military intelligence officer.
Dooley, Thomas Anthony, 1927–61, U.S. physician in Indochina.
Doolittle, Hilda (H.D.), 1886–1961, U.S. poet. active in Europe.
—James Harold, 1896–1993, U.S. aviator & Air Force general.
Doppler, Christian Johann, 1803–53, Austrian physicist & mathematician.
Dorati, Antal, 1906–88 Hung.-born U.S. conductor.
Doré, (Paul) Gustave, 1832–83, Fr. painter & engraver.
Dors, Diana, 1931–84, Brit. actress.
Doria, Andrea, 1466–1560, Ital. admiral & statesman.
Dorsey, James Francis (Jimmy), 1904–57, U.S. clarinetist & band leader.
—Thomas Francis (Tommy), 1905–56, U.S. trombonist & band leader; brother of prec.
Dos Passos, John, 1896–1970, U.S. author.
Dostoevski Fyodor Mikhailovich, 1821–81, Russ. author.
Dou, Gerard, 1613–75, Du. painter.
Doubleday, Abner, 1819–93, U.S. military officer; reputed inventor of baseball.
—Frank Nelson, 1862–1934, U.S. publisher.
Douglas, Aaron, 1900–79, U.S. painter.
—Helen Gahagan, 1900–80, U.S. actress, author, & politician.
—Kirk, 1918–, U.S. actor.
—Melvyn, 1901–81, U.S. actor; husband of Helen Gahagan.

—**Michael,** 1944–, U.S. actor, director, & producer; son of Kirk.

—**Norman,** 1868–1952, Eng. author.

—**Stephen Arnold,** 1813–61, U.S. senator; opposed Lincoln in campaign debates.

—**William Orville,** 1898–1980, U.S. jurist; justice of the U.S. Supreme Court 1939–75.

Douglass, Frederick, 1817–95, U.S. black leader & statesman.

Dove, Arthur Garfield, 1880–1946, U.S. painter.

Dow, Charles Henry, 1851–1902, U.S. economist & editor.

—**Herbert H.,** 1866–1930, Can.-born U.S. industrialist.

Dowland, John, 1563–1626, Eng. musician & composer.

Downes, (Edwin) Olin, 1886–1955, U.S. music critic.

Downing, Andrew Jackson, 1815–52, U.S. architect & landscape designer.

Doxiadis, Constantinos Apostolos, 1913–75, Gk. architect & urban planner.

Doyle, Sir Arthur Conan, 1859–1930, Eng. physician & author; creator of Sherlock Holmes.

D'Oyly Carte, Richard, 1844–1901, Eng. operatic producer.

Drabble, Margaret, 1939–, Eng. author.

Draco, 7th c. B.C. Gk. lawgiver & statesman.

Drake, Alfred, 1914–92, U.S. singer & actor.

—**Edwin Laurentine,** 1819–80, U.S. military officer & petroleum entrepreneur.

—**Sir Francis,** 1540–96, Eng. admiral & circumnavigator of the globe.

Draper, Henry, 1837–82, U.S. astronomer.

—**Ruth,** 1884–1956, U.S. monologuist.

Drayton, Michael, 1563–1631, Eng. poet.

Dreiser, Theodore, 1871–1945, U.S. author.

Dreisner, Samuel P., 1933–, U.S. chemist.

Dressler, Marie, 1869–1934, U.S. actress & comedienne.

Drew, John, 1826–62, Irish-born U.S. actor & his son **John,** 1853–1927, U.S. actor.

Dreyer, Carl Theodore, 1889–1968, Dan. film director.

Dreyfus, Alfred, 1859–1935, Fr. army officer.

Dreyfuss, Richard, 1947–, U.S. actor.

Driesch, Hans Adolf Eduard, 1867–1941, Ger. biologist & philosopher.

Drury, Allen, 1918–, U.S. author.

Dryden, John, 1631–1700, Eng. poet & playwright.

Duarte, José Napoleón, 1926–90, El Salvadoran politician; president 1984–89.

du Barry, Comtesse Marie Jeanne, 1746–93, mistress of Louis XV.

Dubček, Alexander, 1921–92, Czech politician; first secretary of the communist party of Czechoslovakia 1968–69.

Dubin, Al, 1891–1945, U.S. lyricist.

Dubinsky, David, 1892–1982, Russ.-born U.S. labor leader.

Dubois, William Edward Burghardt, 1868–1963, U.S. historian, black leader, & educator.

Du Bois-Reymond, Emil, 1818–96, Ger. physiologist.

Dubos, René, 1906–82, Fr. biologist.

Dubuffet, Jean, 1901–85, Fr. painter & sculptor.

Duccio di Buoninsegna, 1255?–1319, Ital. painter.

Duchamp, Marcel, 1887–1968, Fr. painter.

Duchin, Edwin Frank (Eddy), 1909–51, U.S. pianist & band leader.

Dufy, Raoul, 1877–1953, Fr. painter.

Dujardin, Felix, 1801–60, Fr. biologist.

Dukas, Paul, 1865–1935, Fr. composer.

Duke, Benjamin Newton, 1855–1929, & his brother **James Buchanan Duke,** 1856–1925, U.S. tobacco industrialists.

—**Vernon,** 1903–69, Russ.-born U.S. composer.

Dulles, Allen Welsh, 1893–1969, U.S. government official.

—**John Foster,** 1888–1959, U.S. statesman; secretary of state 1953–59; brother of prec.

Dumas, Alexandre (père), 1802–70, Fr. author & playwright.

—**Alexandre (fils),** 1824–95, Fr. author & playwright; son of prec.

Du Maurier, Daphne, 1907–89, Eng. author.

—**George Louis,** 1834–96, Fr.-born Eng. author & illustrator; grandfather of prec.

Dunant, Jean Henri, 1828–1910, Swiss philanthropist & founder of the Red Cross.

Dunbar, Paul Laurence, 1872–1906, U.S. poet.

Duncan, David Douglas, 1916–, U.S. photographer & author.

—**Isadora,** 1878–1927, U.S. dancer.

Dunham, Katherine, 1910–, U.S. dancer & choreographer.

Dunne, Irene, 1904–90, U.S. actress.

—**John Gregory,** 1932–, U.S. author & screenwriter.

Dunois, Comte Jean de, 1403?–68, Fr. general & companion of Joan of Arc; called the **Bastard of Orleans.**

Dunsany, Edward John Plunkett, Lord, 1878–1957, Irish poet & playwright.

Duns Scotus, Johannes, 1265–1308, Scot. monk & philosopher.

du Pont de Nemours, Pierre, 1739–1817, Fr.-born U.S. economist.

—**Eleuthère Irénée,** 1771–1834, Fr.-born U.S. industrialist; son of prec.

Du Pré, Jacqueline, 1945–87, Eng. cellist.

Dupré, Marcel, 1886–1971, Fr. organist.

Durand, Asher Brown, 1796–1886, U.S. painter.

Durant, William, 1861–1947, U.S. industrialist.

—**Will(iam James),** 1885–1981, U.S. historian & his wife **Ariel,** b. Ida Kaufman, 1898–1981, Russ.-born U.S. historian.

Durante, James Francis (Jimmy), 1893–1980, U.S. comedian & actor.

Duras, Marguerite, 1914–96, Fr. author.

Durbin, Deanna, 1921–, Can.-born U.S. actress.

Dürer, Albrecht, 1471–1528, Ger. painter & engraver.

Durkheim, Émile, 1858–1917, Fr. sociologist.

Durocher, Leo Ernest, 1906–91, U.S. baseball player & manager.

Durrell, Gerald Malcolm, 1925–95, Eng. zoologist & author.

—**Lawrence George,** 1912–90, Indian-born Eng. author & poet; brother of prec.

Dürrenmatt, Friedrich, 1921–90, Swiss playwright.

du Sable, Jean Baptiste Point, 1745–1818, U.S. pioneer trader & first settler of Chicago.

Duse, Eleanora, 1859–1924, Ital. actress.

Dutrochet, René, 1776–1847, Fr. biologist.

Dutton, Edward, 1831–1923, U.S. publisher.

Duvalier, François (Papa Doc), 1907–71, Haitian president 1957–71.

—**Jean-Claude,** 1951–, president of Haiti 1971–86; son of prec.

Duvall, Robert, 1931–, U.S. actor.

Duvivier, Julien, 1896–1967, Fr. film director.

Dvořák, Antonin, 1841–1904, Czech composer.

Dylan, Bob, 1941–, U.S. composer & singer.

Eads, James Buchanan, 1820–87, U.S. inventor.

Eagels, Joanne, 1894–1929, U.S. actress.

Eakins, Thomas, 1844–1916, U.S. painter & sculptor.

Eames, Charles, 1907–78, U.S. designer & film director.

Earhart, Amelia, 1898–1937, U.S. aviator.

Early, Jubal Anderson, 1816–94, U.S. Confederate general.

Earp, Wyatt, 1848–1929, U.S. frontier marshal.

Eastman, George, 1854–1932, U.S. inventor & industrialist.

—**Max Forrester,** 1883–1969, U.S. editor & author.

Eastwood, Clint, 1930–, U.S. actor & director.

Eaton, Cyrus Stephen, 1883–1979, U.S. financier.

Eban, Abba, 1915–, South African-born Israeli diplomat.

Ebbinghaus, Hermann, 1850–1909, Ger. experimental psychologist.

Eberhart, Richard, 1904–, U.S. poet.

Echeverría Alvarez, Luis, 1922–, president of Mexico 1970–76.

Eck, Johann, 1486–1543, Ger. theologian.

Eckhart, Johannes, 1260?–1327?, Ger. theologian & mystic: known as **Meister Eckhart.**

Eddington, Sir Arthur Stanley, 1882–1944, Eng. astronomer & astrophysicist.

Eddy, Mary Baker, 1821–1910, U.S. religious leader; founder of Christian Science.

—**Nelson,** 1901–67, singer & actor.

Edelman, Gerald Maurice, 1929–, U.S. biochemist.

Eden, Sir (Robert) Anthony, 1897–1977, Eng. statesman; prime minister 1955–57.

Ederle, Gertrude, 1906–, U.S. swimmer.

Edison, Thomas Alva, 1847–1931, U.S. inventor.
Edward, 1004?–66, king of England 1042–66: called **the Confessor.**
— 1330–76, Eng. warrior: known as **the Black Prince.**
—**VII,** 1841–1910, king of Great Britain 1901–10.
—**VIII,** 1894–1972, king of Great Britain 1936; abdicated; known as **Duke of Windsor** after abdication.
Edwards, Blake, 1922–, U.S. film director.
—**Jonathan,** 1703–58, Amer. theologian.
—**Ralph,** 1913–, U.S. TV personality.
Egbert, 775?–839, first king of all England 829–839.
Egk, Werner, 1901–83, Ger. composer.
Eglevsky, André, 1917–77, Russ.-born U.S. ballet dancer.
Ehrenberg, Christian G., 1795–1876, Ger. naturalist.
Ehrenburg, Ilya Grigorievich, 1891–1967, Soviet author.
Ehrlich, Paul, 1854–1915, Ger. bacteriologist.
—**Paul Ralph,** 1932–, U.S. biologist & author.
Eichmann, Adolf, 1906–62, Ger. Nazi official.
Eiffel, (Alexandre) Gustave, 1832–1923, Fr. engineer.
Eijkman, Christian, 1858–1930, Du. physician.
Einstein, Albert, 1879–1955, Ger.-born U.S. physicist.
—**Alfred,** 1880–1952, Ger.-born U.S. music critic.
Einthoven, Willem, 1860–1927, Du. physiologist.
Eiseley, Loren Corey, 1907–77, U.S. anthropologist & author.
Eisenhower, Dwight David, 1890–1969, U.S. general & 34th president 1953–61.
Eisenstaedt, Alfred, 1898–1995, Ger.-born photographer & author active in U.S.
Eisenstein, Sergei Mikhailovich, 1890–1948, Russ.-born Soviet film director & producer.
El Cid, b. Rodrigo Díaz de Bivar, 1044?–99, Sp. soldier & epic hero.
Eleanor of Aquitaine, 1122–1204, queen of France as the wife of Louis VII & queen of England as the wife of Henry II.
Elgar, Sir Edward, 1857–1934, Eng. composer.
Eliot, Charles William, 1834–1926, U.S. educator.
—**George,** pseud. of Mary Ann Evans, 1819–80, Eng. author.
—**John,** 1604–90, Amer. clergyman & missionary to Indians.
—**T(homas) S(tearns),** 1888–1965, U.S.-born Brit. poet, playwright, & critic.
Elizabeth I, 1533–1603, queen of England 1558–1603.
—**II,** 1926–, queen of Great Britain 1952–.
—**Angela Marguerite Bowes-Lyon,** 1900–86, queen of George VI of Great Britain & mother of Elizabeth II.
Elkin, Stanley, 1930–95, U.S. author.
Ellington, Edward Kennedy (Duke), 1899–1974, U.S. jazz composer, pianist, & band leader.
Elliott, Maxine, 1871–1940, U.S. actress.
—**Robert (Bob),** 1923–, U.S. comedian.
Ellis, (Henry) Havelock, 1859–1939, Eng. psychologist & author.
—**Perry Edwin,** 1940–86, U.S. fashion designer.
Ellison, Ralph, 1914–94, U.S. author.
Ellsworth, Lincoln, 1880–1951, U.S. polar explorer.
—**Oliver,** 1745–1807, U.S. jurist; chief justice of U.S. Supreme Court 1796–1800.
Elman, Mischa, 1891–1967, Russ.-born U.S. violinist.
Elssler, Fanny, 1810–84, Austrian dancer.
Elyot, Sir Thomas, 1490?–1546, Eng. scholar & diplomat.
Elzevir A family of Dutch printers including **Louis,** 1540?–1617; his son, **Bonaventure,** 1583–1652; and his grandson **Abraham,** 1592?–1652.
Emerson, Ralph Waldo, 1803–82, U.S. author, poet, & philosopher.
Emmet, Robert, 1778–1803, Irish nationalist & revolutionary.
Emmett, Daniel Decatur, 1815–1904, U.S. songwriter.
Endecott, John, 1589?–1665, Eng.-born Amer. colonist; first governor of Massachusetts Bay colony.
Empedocles, 495?–435? B.C., Gk. philosopher.
Enders, John Franklin, 1897–1985, U.S. bacteriologist; Nobel Prize winner.
Enesco, Georges, 1881–1955, Romanian composer.
Engels, Friedrich, 1820–95, Ger. socialist & author.
Ensor, James, 1860–1949, Belg. painter & printmaker.
Ephron, Nora, 1941–, U.S. author.
Epictetus, A.D. 50?–138?, Gk. philosopher.

Epicurus, 341?–270 B.C., Gk. philosopher.
Epstein, Sir Jacob, 1880–1959, U.S.-born Brit. sculptor.
Erasistratus, 304–250 B.C., Gk. physician & anatomist.
Erasmus, Desiderius, b. Gerhard Gerhards, 1466?–1536, Du. scholar & theologian.
Eratosthenes, 3rd c. B.C. Gk. mathematician & astronomer.
Erhard, Ludwig, 1897–1977, chancellor of W. Germany 1963–66.
Erickson, Arthur Charles, 1924–, Can. architect.
Ericsson, John, 1803–89, Swed.-born U.S. engineer & inventor.
—**Leif,** 11th c. Norw. explorer; son of Eric the Red.
Eric the Red, 10th c. Norw. explorer.
Erigena, Johannes Scotus, 815?–877?, Irish philosopher & theologian
Erikson, Erik Homburger, 1902–94, Ger.-born U.S. psychologist & author.
Erlander, Tage Frithiof, 1901–85, premier of Sweden 1946–69.
Erlanger, Joseph, 1874–1965, U.S. physiologist.
Ernst, Max, 1891–1976, Ger. painter active in France & U.S.
Ervin, Sam(uel) J., Jr., 1896–1985, U.S. politician.
Ervine, St. John Greer, 1883–1971, Irish Playwright & author.
Erving, Julius, 1950–, U.S. basketball player: called **Doctor J.**
Escoffier, Auguste, 1847–1935, Fr. chef & author.
Eshkol, Levi, 1895–1969, Russ.-born Israeli statesman; prime minister of Israel 1963–69.
Esposito, Philip Anthony, 1942–, Can.-born hockey player active in U.S.
Espriu, Salvador, 1913–85, Span. poet.
Essex, Robert Devereux, 2nd Earl of, 1566–1601, Eng. courtier & soldier; beheaded.
Esterhazy, Marie Charles Ferdinand Walsin, 1847–1923, Fr. army officer.
Esterházy, Miklós Jósef, 1714–90, Hung. prince & art patron.
Ethelred II, 968?–1016, king of England 978–1016: called **the Unready.**
Etherege, Sir George, 1634?–91, Eng. playwright.
Euclid, c. 300 B.C., Gk. mathematician.
Eugénie (Marie de Montijo de Guzmán), 1826–1920, Sp.-born empress of France as wife of Napoleon III.
Euler, Leonhard, 1707–83, Swiss mathematician.
Euripides, 479?–406? B.C., Gk. playwright.
Eustachio, Bartolommeo, 1524?–74, Ital. anatomist.
Evans, Sir Arthur John, 1851–1941, Eng. archaeologist.
—**Bergen,** 1904–78, U.S. author & educator.
—**Dame Edith,** 1888–1976, Eng. actress.
—**Gil,** 1912–88, Can.-born U.S. jazz musician.
—**Maurice,** 1901–89, Eng.-born U.S. actor.
—**Rowland, Jr.,** 1921–, U.S. journalist.
—**Walker,** 1903–75, U.S. photographer.
—**William J. (Bill),** 1929–80, U.S. jazz pianist & composer.
Evelyn, John, 1620–1706, Eng. diarist.
Everett, Edward, 1794–1865, U.S. clergyman, orator, & statesman.
Evers, (James) Charles, 1922–, U.S. politician & civil rights activist.
—**Medgar Wiley,** 1925–63, U.S. civil rights activist; murdered; brother of prec.
Evert, Chris(tine Marie), 1954–, U.S. tennis player.
Ewing, William Maurice, 1906–74, U.S. geologist.
Eysenck, Hans, 1916–97, Eng. psychologist.

Faber, John Eberhard, 1822–79, Ger.-born U.S. industrialist.
Fabergé, Peter Carl, 1846–1920, Russ. goldsmith & jeweler.
Fabiola, 1928–, Sp.-born queen of former King Baudouin of Belgium.
Fabius (Quintus Fabius Maximus Verrucosus Cunctator), ?–203 B.C., Roman general.
Fabre, Jean Henri, 1823–1915, Fr. entomologist.
Fabricius ab Aquapendente, Hieronymus, 1537–1619, Ital. surgeon & anatomist.
Fadiman, Clifton, 1904–, U.S. author & editor.
Fahd, 1923–, Saudi Arabian king & prime minister 1982–.
Fahrenheit, Gabriel Daniel, 1686–1736, Ger. physicist.

Fairbanks, Charles Warren, 1852–1918, U.S. statesman; U.S. vice president 1905–09.
—**Douglas,** 1883–1939, U.S. actor.
—**Douglas, Jr.,** 1909–, U.S. actor; son of prec.
Faisal ibn Abdul Aziz, 1904?–75, king of Saudi Arabia 1964–75; assassinated.
Falla, Manuel de, 1876–1946, Sp. composer.
Fälldin, Thorbjörn, 1926–, Swed. politician; prime minister of Sweden 1976–1978 & 1979–1982.
Fallopius, Gabriel, 1523–62, Ital. anatomist.
Faneuil, Peter, 1700–43, Amer. merchant.
Fanfani, Amintore, 1908–, premier of Italy 1958–59 & 1960–63.
Faraday, Michael, 1791–1867, Eng. physicist.
Fargo, William George, 1818–81, U.S. transportation entrepreneur.
Farley, James Aloysius, 1888–1976, U.S. politician.
Farmer, Fannie Merritt, 1857–1915, U.S. culinary expert, teacher, & author.
—**James Leonard,** 1920–, U.S. black civil rights leader.
Farouk I, 1920–65, king of Egypt 1936–52.
Farquhar, George, 1678–1707, Eng. playwright.
Farragut, David Glasgow, 1801–70, U.S. admiral.
Ferrar, Geraldine, 1882–1967, U.S. soprano.
Farrell, Eileen, 1920–, U.S. soprano.
—**James Thomas,** 1904–79, U.S. author.
—**Suzanne,** 1945–, U.S. ballerina.
Fassbinder, Rainer Werner, 1946–82, Ger. film & stage director.
Fast, Howard, 1914–, U.S. author.
Fatima, 606?–632?, daughter of Mohammed.
Fauchard, Pierre, 1678–1761, Fr. dentist; founder of modern dentistry.
Faulkner, William, 1897–1962, U.S. author.
Fauré, Gabriel Urbain, 1845–1924, Fr. composer.
Fawkes, Guy, 1570–1606, Eng. conspirator; participant in the Gunpowder Plot.
Fay, Frank, 1897–1961, U.S. actor.
Faye, Alice, 1915–, U.S. actress.
Febres-Cordero, León, 1931–, president of Ecuador 1984–88.
Feiffer, Jules, 1929–, U.S. cartoonist & author.
Feininger, Andreas, 1906–, Fr.-born U.S. photographer.
—**Lyonel Charles Adrian,** 1871–1956, U.S. painter; father of prec.
Feller, Robert William Andrew (Bob), 1918–, U.S. baseball player.
Fellini, Federico, 1920–93, Ital. film director.
Fénelon, François de Salignac de la Mothe-, 1651–1715, Fr. prelate & author.
Fenollosa, Ernest Francisco, 1853–1908, U.S. oriental scholar & author.
Ferber, Edna, 1885–1968, U.S. author.
Ferdinand V of Castile (and II of Aragon), 1452–1516, first king of united Spain 1474–1516; ruled jointly with his wife Isabella.
Ferencsik, Janos, 1907–84, Czech conductor.
Ferlinghetti, Lawrence, 1919–, U.S. poet.
Fermat, Pierre de, 1601–65, Fr. mathematician.
Fermi, Enrico, 1901–54, Ital. physicist active in U.S.
Fernandel, b.Fernand Contandin, 1903–71, Fr. actor.
Ferraro, Geraldine Anne, 1935–, U.S. statesman.
Ferrier, Sir David, 1843–1928, Scot. neurologist.
—**Kathleen,** 1912–53, Eng. contralto.
Fessenden, Reginald Aubrey, 1866–1932, Can.-born U.S. physicist & inventor.
Feuerbach, Ludwig Andreas, 1804–72, Ger. philosopher.
Feuermann, Emanuel, 1902–42, Pol.-born cellist active in U.S.
Feydeau, Georges, 1862–1921, Fr. playwright.
Feynman, Richard Phillips, 1918–88, U.S. physicist; Nobel Prize winner.
Fichte, Johann Gottlieb, 1762–1814, Ger. philosopher.
Fiedler, Arthur, 1894–1979, U.S. conductor.
—**Leslie,** 1917–, U.S. author & critic.
Field, Cyrus West, 1819–92, U.S. industrialist.
—**Eugene,** 1850–95, U.S. poet & journalist.
—**Marshall,** 1834–1906, U.S. businessman.

Fielding, Henry, 1707–54, Eng. author.
Fields, Dorothy, 1904–74, U.S. lyricist.
—**Gracie,** 1898–1979, Eng. singer & actress.
—**W.C.,** 1879–1946, U.S. film comedian.
Filene, Edward Albert, 1860–1937, U.S. businessman & social reformer.
Fillmore, Millard, 1800–74, 13th U.S. president 1850–53.
Fink, Mike, 1770?–1823, U.S. frontiersman.
Finlay, Carlos Juan, 1833–1915, Cuban physician.
Finney, Albert, 1936–, Eng. actor.
Firbank, Ronald, 1886–1926, Eng. author.
Firdausi, pseud. of Abdul Qasim Mansur, 940?–1020?, Persian epic poet.
Firestone, Harvey Samuel, 1868–1938, U.S. industrialist.
Fischer, Robert James (Bobby), 1943–, U.S. chess master.
Fischer-Dieskau, Dietrich, 1925–, Ger. baritone.
Fish, Hamilton, 1808–93, U.S. statesman.
Fishbein, Morris, 1889–1976, U.S. physician, author, & editor.
Fisher, Bud, 1884–1954, U.S. cartoonist.
—**Dorothy Canfield,** 1879–1958, U.S. author.
—**Fred,** 1875–1942, U.S. songwriter.
—**M(ary) F(rances) K(ennedy),** 1908–92, U.S. author.
Fiske, John, 1842–1901, U.S. philosopher.
—**Minnie Maddern,** 1865–1932, U.S. actress.
Fitch, John, 1743–98, Amer. inventor.
—**(William) Clyde,** 1865–1909, U.S. playwright.
Fitzgerald, Ella, 1918–96, U.S. jazz singer.
—**F(rancis) Scott (Key),** 1896–1940, U.S. author.
—**George F.,** 1851–1901, Irish physicist.
—**Geraldine,** 1914–, Irish-born U.S. actress.
FitzGerald, Edward, 1809–83, Eng. poet & translator.
Flagg, Ernest, 1857–1947, U.S. architect.
—**James Montgomery,** 1877–1960, U.S. painter, illustrator, & author.
Flagler, Henry Morrison, 1830–1913, U.S. business executive.
Flagstad, Kirsten, 1895–1962, Norw. soprano active in U.S.
Flaherty, Robert Joseph, 1884–1951, U.S. film director.
Flammarion, Camille, 1842–1925, Fr. astronomer & author.
Flaubert, Gustave, 1821–80, Fr. author.
Fleming, Sir Alexander, 1881–1955, Eng. bacteriologist.
—**Ian Lancaster,** 1908–64, Eng. author.
—**Victor,** 1883–1949, U.S. film director.
Flemming, Walther, 1843–1905, Ger. anatomist.
Fletcher, John, 1579–1625, Eng. playwright.
Flory, Paul John, 1910–85, U.S. physical chemist; Nobel Prize winner.
Flotow, Friedrich von, 1812–83, Ger. composer.
Flourens, Pierre Marie Jean, 1794–1867, Fr. anatomist & physiologist.
Flynn, Errol, 1909–59, Tasmanian-born actor active in U.S.
Foch, Ferdinand, 1851–1929, Fr. general; marshal of France.
Fodor, Eugene, 1940–, U.S. violinist.
Fokine, Michel, 1880–1942, Russ.-born U.S. choreographer.
Fokker, Anthony Herman Gerard, 1890–1939, Du.-born U.S. aircraft designer.
Folger, Henry Clay, 1857–1930, U.S. bibliophile.
Fonda, Henry, 1905–82, U.S. actor.
—**Jane,** 1937–, U.S. actress & political activist; daughter of prec.
—**Peter,** 1939–, U.S. actor; son of Henry.
Fontanne, Lynn, 1887–1983, Eng.-born U.S. actress.
Fonteyn, Dame Margot, 1919–91, Eng. ballerina.
Foot, Michael, 1913–, Brit. politician.
Forbes, Esther, 1891–1967, U.S. author & historian.
—**Malcolm,** 1919–90, U.S. publisher & sportsman.
Ford, Ford Madox, 1873–1939, Eng. author.
—**Gerald Rudolph,** 1913–, 38th U.S. president 1974–77.
—**Harrison,** 1942–, U.S. actor.
—**Henry,** 1863–1947, U.S. auto manufacturer.
—**John,** 1586?–1638?, Eng. playwright.
—**John,** 1895–1973, U.S. film director.
Foreman, George, 1949–, U.S. boxer.
Forester, C(ecil) S(cott), 1899–1966, Eng. author active in U.S.
Forman, Milos, 1932–, Czech film director active in U.S.

Forrest, Edwin, 1806–72, U.S. actor.

Forrestal, James Vincent, 1892–1949, U.S. banker & government official.

Forssman, Werner, 1904–79, Ger. surgeon; Nobel Prize winner.

Forster, E(dward) M(organ), 1879–1970, Eng. author.

Fortas, Abe, 1910–82, U.S. jurist; justice of U.S. Supreme Court 1965–69.

Fosdick, Harry Emerson, 1878–1969, U.S. clergyman & author.

Foss, Lukas, 1922–, Ger.-born U.S. composer & conductor.

Fosse, Bob (Robert Louis), 1927–87, U.S. choreographer and director.

Foster, Hal, 1892–1982, U.S. cartoonist.

—**John Stuart, Jr.,** 1922–, U.S. physicist.

Foster, Stephen Collins, 1826–64, U.S. composer.

Foucault, Jean Bernard Leon, 1819–68, Fr. physicist.

—**Michel,** 1926–84, Fr. philospher, historian, & author.

Fourdrinier, Henry, 1766–1854, & his brother **Sealy,** ?–1847, Eng. inventors & paper manufacturers.

Fourier, Charles, 1772–1837, Fr. utopian socialist.

—**François Marie Charles,** 1772–1837, Fr. socialist.

—**Jean Baptiste Joseph,** 1768–1830, Fr. mathematician & physicist.

Fowler, Henry Watson, 1858–1933, Eng. lexicographer.

Fox, George, 1624–91, Eng. preacher; founded the Society of Friends.

Foxx, James Emery (Jimmy), 1907–67, U.S. baseball player.

Foy, Eddie, 1856–1928, U.S. vaudeville performer.

Foyt, A(nthony) J(oseph), Jr., 1935–, U.S. auto racer.

Fra Angelico, b. Giovanni da Fiesole, 1400?–1455, Ital. painter.

Fracastoro, Girolamo, 1483–1553, Ital. physician.

Fragonard, Jean Honoré, 1732–1806, Fr. painter.

France, Anatole, pseud. of Jacques Anatole Thibault, 1844–1924, Fr. author.

Francesca da Rimini, ?–1285?, Ital. noblewoman; murdered by her husband.

Francescatti, Zino, 1902–91, Fr. violinist.

Francis I, 1494–1547, king of France 1515–47.

Francis of Assisi, Saint, 1182–1226, Ital. preacher; founder of Franciscan Order.

Francis, Arlene, 1908–, U.S. actress & TV personality.

Franck, César Auguste, 1822–90, Belg.-born Fr. composer.

—**James,** 1882–1964, Ger.-born U.S. physicist; Nobel Prize winner.

Franco, Francisco, 1892–1975, Sp. general; dictator of Spain 1939–75.

Frank, Anne, 1929–45, Ger.-born Du. diarist.

Frankfurter, Felix, 1882–1965, Austrian-born U.S. jurist; justice of U.S. Supreme Court 1939–62.

Franklin, Aretha, 1942–, U.S. singer.

—**Benjamin,** 1706–90, Amer. patriot, scientist, statesman, & diplomat.

—**Frederic,** 1914–, Eng.-born dancer & ballet company director active in U.S.

Franz Ferdinand, 1863–1914, archduke of Austria; assassinated.

Franz Josef I, 1830–1916, emperor of Austria 1848–1916.

Fraser, Dawn, 1939–, Austral. swimmer.

—**(John) Malcolm,** 1930–, prime minister of Australia 1975–83.

Fraunhofer, Joseph von, 1787–1826, Ger. optician & physicist.

Frazer, Sir James George, 1854–1941, Scot. anthropologist.

Frazier, Joe, 1944–, U.S. boxer.

—**Walt(er),** 1945–, U.S. basketball player.

Frederick I, 1121–90, king of Germany & Holy Roman emperor 1152–90: called **Barbarossa.**

Frederick II, 1194–1250, Holy Roman emperor, 1215–50.

Frederick II, 1712–86, king of Prussia 1740–86: called **the Great.**

Frederick IX, 1899–1972, king of Denmark 1947–72.

Frederick William, 1620–88, elector of Brandenburg: called **the Great Elector.**

Freed, Arthur, 1894–1973, U.S. film producer.

Frelinghuysen, Frederick Theodore, 1817–85, U.S. statesman.

Frémont, John Charles, 1813–90, U.S. military officer & explorer.

French, Daniel Chester, 1850–1931, U.S. sculptor.

Freneau, Philip Morin, 1752–1832, U.S. poet.

Frescobaldi, Girolamo, 1583–1643, Ital. composer.

Fresnel, Augustin Jean, 1788–1827, Fr. physicist.

Freud, Anna, 1895–82, Austrian neurologist; founder of modern theory of psychoanalysis.

—**Sigmund** 1856–1939, Austrian neurologist; founder of modern theory of psychoanalysis; father of prec.

Frick, Henry Clay, 1849–1919, U.S. industrialist & philanthropist.

Friedan, Betty, 1921–, U.S. author & feminist.

Friedman, Milton, 1912–98, U.S. economist; Nobel Prize winner.

Friendly, Fred W., 1915–98, U.S. radio & TV executive.

Fries, Elias Magnus, 1794–1878, Swed. botanist.

Friml, Rudolf, 1879–1972, Czech-born U.S. composer.

Frisch, Frank, 1898–1973, U.S. baseball player.

—**Karl von,** 1886–1982, Austrian zoologist.

Frobisher, Sir Martin, 1535?–94, Eng. navigator.

Froebel, Friedrich Wilhelm August, 1782–1852, Ger. educator.

Frohman, Charles, 1860–1915, U.S. theatrical manager.

Froissart, Jean, 1333?–1400, Fr. chronicler.

Fromm, Erich, 1900–80, Ger.-born U.S. psychoanalyst.

Frondizi, Arturo, 1908–95, Argentine politician; president of Argentina 1958–62.

Frontenac, Louis de Buade, Comte de, 1620–98, Fr. general & colonial administrator in N. America.

Frost, David, 1939–, Eng. TV personality active in U.S.

—**Robert Lee,** 1874–1963, U.S. poet.

Fry, Christopher, 1907–, Eng. playwright.

—**Roger Eliot,** 1866–1934, Eng. painter & art critic.

Fuchs, Klaus Emil Julius, 1912–88, Ger.-born Eng. spy in U.S.

Fuentes, Carlos, 1928–, Mexican author.

Fugger, Jacob, 1459–1525, Ger. merchant & banker.

Fulbright, J(ames) William, 1905–95, U.S. politician.

Fuller, Alfred Carl, 1885–1973, Can.-born U.S. business executive.

—**R. Buckminster,** 1895–1983, U.S. architect, designer, & author.

—**Charles,** 1939–, U.S. playwright.

—**(Sarah) Margaret,** 1810–50, U.S. social reformer.

Fulton, Robert, 1765–1815, U.S. inventor.

Funk, Isaac Kauffman, 1839–1912, U.S. publisher & lexicographer.

Furness, Betty, 1916–94, U.S. actress & TV personality.

Furnivall, Frederick James, 1825–1910, Eng. philologist.

Furtwängler, Wilhelm, 1886–1954, Ger. conductor.

Gabin, Jean, 1904–76, Fr. actor.

Gable, Clark, 1901–60, U.S. actor.

Gabo, Naum, 1890–1977, Russ.-born U.S. sculptor, painter, designer, & architect.

Gabor, Dennis, 1900–79, Hung.-born Brit. engineer; Nobel Prize winner.

Gaddis, William, 1922–, U.S. author.

Gadsden, James, 1788–1858, U.S. military officer & diplomat.

Gagarin, Yuri Alekseyevich, 1934–68, Soviet astronaut; first to orbit the earth.

Gage, Thomas, 1721–87, Eng. general & colonial governor of Massachusetts 1774–75.

Gainsborough, Thomas, 1727–88, Eng. painter.

Gaitskell, Hugh Todd Naylor, 1906–63, Eng. socialist leader.

Galanos, James, 1924–, U.S. fashion designer.

Galbraith, John Kenneth, 1908–, U.S. economist, diplomat, & author.

Gale, Zona, 1874–1938, U.S. author.

Galen, Claudius, A.D. 130?–200?, Gk. physician & writer.

Galileo Galilei, 1564–1642, Ital. astronomer, mathematician, & physicist.

Gallatin, (Abraham Alfonse) Albert, 1761–1849, Swiss-born U.S. financier & statesman.

Gallaudet, Thomas Hopkins, 1787–1851, U.S. educator.

Galli-Curci, Amelita, 1889–1963, Ital.-born U.S. soprano.

Gallup, George Horace, 1901–84, U.S. public opinion statistician.

Galsworthy, John, 1867–1933, Eng. author & playwright; Nobel Prize winner.

Galton, Sir Francis, 1822–1911, Eng. scientist.

Galvani, Luigi, 1737–98, Ital. physiologist.

Galway, James, 1939–, Brit. flutist.

Gambetta, Leon, 1838–82, Fr. statesman.

Gamio, Manuel, 1883–1960, Mexican anthropologist & archaeologist.

Gamow, George, 1904–68, Russ.-born U.S. physicist & author.

Gandhi, Indira Nehru, 1917–84, Indian stateswoman; prime minister of India 1966–77 and 1980–84; assassinated; daughter of Jawaharlal Nehru.

—Mohandas Karamchand, 1869–1948, Hindu nationalist leader & social reformer; assassinated: known as **Mahatma Gandhi.**

—Rajiv, 1944–91, Indian prime minister 1984–91.

Gannett, Frank E., 1876–1957, U.S. editor & publisher.

Ganz, Rudolph, 1877–1972, Swiss-born U.S. pianist, conductor, & composer.

Garamond, Claude, ?–1561, Fr. type founder.

Garand, John Cantius, 1888–1974, Can.-born U.S. inventor.

Garbo, Greta, 1905–90, Swed.-born actress active in U.S.

Garcia Lorca, Federico, 1899–1936, Sp. poet, playwright, & author.

García Márquez, Gabriel José, 1928–, Colombian novelist; Nobel Prize winner.

Garcilaso de la Vega, 1539?–1616, Peruvian historian: called **El Inca.**

Garden, Mary, 1874–1967, Scot.-born U.S. soprano.

Gardiner, Stephen, 1483?–1535, Eng. prelate & statesman.

Gardner, Erle Stanley, 1889–1970, U.S. author.

—Isabella Stewart, 1840–1924, U.S. social leader & art collector.

Garfield, James Abram, 1831–81, 20th U.S. president 1881; assassinated.

—John, 1913–52, U.S. actor.

Garibaldi, Giuseppe, 1807–82, Ital. patriot & general.

Garland, Hamlin, 1860–1940, U.S. author.

—Judy, 1922–69, U.S. singer & actress.

Garner, Erroll, 1923–77, U.S. jazz pianist.

—John Nance, 1868–1967, U.S. politician; U.S. vice president 1933–41.

Garnett, Constance Black, 1862–1946, Eng. translator.

—David, 1892–1981, Eng. writer; son of prec.

Garrick, David, 1717–79, Eng. actor & author.

Garrison, William Lloyd, 1805–79, U.S. abolitionist.

Garroway, Dave, 1913–82, U.S. TV personality.

Garvey, Marcus, 1887–1940, W. Indian black leader active in the U.S.

Gary, Elbert H., 1846–1927, U.S. industrialist.

Gascoigne, George, 1525?–77, Eng. poet.

Gaskell, Walter H., 1847–1914, Eng. biologist & neurologist.

Gates, Horatio, 1728?–1806, Amer. Revolutionary general.

—John Warne (Bet-a-Million), 1855–1911, U.S. financier.

Gatling, Richard Jordan, 1818–1903, U.S. inventor.

Gatti-Casazza, Giulio, 1869–1940, Ital. operatic manager active in U.S.

Gaudí i Cornet, Antonio, 1852–1926, Sp. architect & furniture designer.

Gauguin, Paul, 1848–1903, Fr. painter active in Tahiti after 1891.

Gauss, Karl Friedrich, 1777–1855, Ger. mathematician.

Gautier, Théophile, 1811–72, Fr. poet & critic.

Gay, John, 1685–1732, Eng. poet & playwright.

Gay-Lussac, Joseph Louis, 1778–1850, Fr. chemist.

Gaye, Marvin, 1939–84, U.S. musician & singer.

Gaynor, Janet, 1906–84, U.S. actress.

Gedda, Nicolai, 1925–, Swed. tenor.

Geddes, Norman Bel, 1893–1958, U.S. industrial & set designer.

Geer, Will, 1902–78, U.S. actor.

Gehrig, (Henry) Lou(is), 1903–41, U.S. baseball player.

Geiger, Hans W., 1882–1945, Ger. physicist.

Geisel, Ernesto, 1908–96, Brazilian military officer; president of Brazil 1974–79.

Geisel, Theodore, 1904–91, U.S. author: known as **Dr. Seuss.**

Gell-Mann, Murray, 1929–, U.S. physicist; Nobel Prize winner.

Genauer, Emily, 1911–, U.S. author, editor, & critic.

Genêt, Edmond Charles Édouard, 1763–1834, Fr. diplomat; first minister of France to the U.S. 1793–94: called **Citizen Genêt.**

—Jean, 1910–86, Fr. playwright & author.

Genghis Khan, 1162–1227, Mongol conqueror in Europe & Asia.

Geoffrey of Monmouth, 1100?–54, Eng. ecclesiastic & chronicler.

George I, 1660–1727, king of Great Britain 1714–27.

—II, 1683–1760, king of Great Britain 1727–60.

—III, 1738–1820, king of Great Britain 1760–1820.

—IV, 1762–1830, king of Great Britian 1820–30.

—V, 1865–1936, king of Great Britain 1910–36.

—VI, 1895–1952, king of Great Britain 1936–52.

George, Saint, ?–303?, Christian martyr; patron saint of England.

George, Grace, 1879–1961, U.S. actress.

—Henry, 1839–97, U.S. economist.

—Stefan, 1868–1933, Ger. poet.

Gerard, John, 1545–1612, Eng. botanist & barber-surgeon.

Géricault, (Jean Louis André) Théodore, 1791–1824, Fr. painter.

Gernreich, Rudi, 1922–85, Austrian-born U.S. fashion designer.

Gernsback, Hugo, 1884–1967, Luxembourg-born U.S. inventor & publisher.

Geronimo, 1829–1909, Apache Am. Ind. chief.

Gershwin, George, 1898–1937, U.S. composer.

—Ira, 1896–1983, U.S. lyricist; brother of prec.

Gesell, Arnold Lucius, 1880–1961, U.S. child psychologist.

Getty, Jean Paul, 1892–1976, U.S. business executive resident in England.

Getz, Stan, 1927–91, U.S. jazz musician.

Ghiberti, Lorenzo, 1378–1455, Florentine sculptor, painter, & goldsmith.

Ghirlandaio, Domenico, 1449–94, Ital. painter.

Giacometti, Alberto, 1901–66, Swiss-born sculptor & painter active in France.

Giannini, Amadeo Peter, 1870–1949, U.S. banker.

—Giancarlo, 1942–, Ital. actor.

Giap, Vo Nguyen, 1912–, N. Vietnamese general & political leader.

Gibbon, Edward, 1737–94, Eng. historian.

Gibbons, Floyd, 1887–1939, U.S. journalist & war correspondent.

Gibbs, J(osiah) Willard, 1839–1903, U.S. mathematician & physicist.

Gibran, Kahlil, 1883–1931, Lebanese poet & painter active in U.S.

Gibson, Althea, 1927–, U.S. tennis player.

—Charles Dana, 1867–1944, U.S. illustrator.

—William, 1914–, U.S. playwright & author.

Gide, André, 1869–1951, Fr. author & playwright; Nobel Prize winner.

Gielgud, Sir John, 1904–, Eng. actor & stage director.

Gierek, Edward, 1913–, first secretary of the Communist Party of Poland 1970–80.

Gieseking, Walter, 1895–1956, Fr.-born Ger. pianist.

Gigli, Beniamino, 1880–1957, Ital. tenor.

Gilbert, Cass, 1859–1934, U.S. architect.

—Sir Humphrey, 1539?–83, Eng. navigator.

—William, 1540–1603, Eng. physician & physicist.

—Sir W(illiam) S(chwenck), 1836–1911, Eng. poet, librettist, & lyricist.

Gilels, Emil Grigoryevich, 1916–85, Soviet pianist.

Gillespie, John Birks (Dizzy), 1917–93, U.S. jazz musician.

Gillette, William, 1855–1937, U.S. actor & playwright.

Ginastera, Alberto, 1916–83, Argentine composer.

Ginsberg, Allen, 1926–, U.S. poet.

Giordano, Umberto, 1867–1948, Ital. composer.

Giorgione II, b. Giorgio Barbarelli, c. 1478–1511, Venetian painter.

Giotto (di Bondone), 1266–1337, Florentine painter & architect.

Giovanni, Nikki, b. Yolande Cornelia Giovanni, Jr., 1943–, U.S. poet.

Giraudoux, Jean, 1882–1944, Fr. playwright.

Giscard d'Estaing, Valéry, 1926–, president of France 1974–81.

Gish, Dorothy, 1898?–1968, U.S. actress.

—Lillian, 1893–1993, U.S. actress; sister of prec.

Givenchy, Hubert de, 1927–, Fr. fashion designer.

Glackens, William James, 1870–1938, U.S. painter & illustrator.

Gladstone, William Ewart, 1809–98, Eng. statesman; prime minister 1868–74, 1880–85, 1886, & 1892–94.

Glaser, Donald Arthur, 1926–, U.S. physicist.

Glasgow, Ellen Anderson Gholson, 1874–1945, U.S. author.

Glazunov, Aleksandr Konstantinovich, 1865–1936, Russ. composer.

Gleason, Herbert John (Jackie), 1916–87, U.S. comedian & actor.

Glenn, John Herschel, 1921–, U.S. astronaut & politician.

Glière, Reinhold, 1875–1956, Russ. composer.

Glinka, Mikhail Ivanovich, 1804–57, Russ. composer.

Gluck, Alma, 1884–1938, Rumanian-born U.S. soprano.

—Christoph Willibald, 1714–87, Ger. composer.

Gobbi, Tito, 1915–84, Ital. baritone.

Godard, Jean-Luc, 1930–, Fr. film director.

Goddard, Henry Herbert, 1866–1957, U.S. psychologist.

—Robert Hutchings, 1882–1945, U.S. physicist.

Godey, Louis Antoine, 1804–78, U.S. magazine publisher.

Godfrey of Bouillon, 1061?–1100, Fr. crusader.

Godfrey, Arthur Michael, 1903–83, U.S. radio & TV personality.

Godkin, Edward Lawrence, 1831–1902, U.S. editor & publisher.

Godolphin, Sidney, 1st Earl of Godolphin, 1645–1712, Eng. statesman.

Godowsky, Leopold, 1870–1938, Pol. pianist.

Godunov, Boris Fyodorovich, 1551?–1605, czar of Russia 1598–1605.

Godwin, Gail, 1937–, U.S. author.

—Mary Wollstonecraft, 1759–97, Eng. feminist & author.

Goebbels, Paul Joseph, 1897–1945, Ger. Nazi propagandist.

Goering, Hermann Wilhelm, 1893–1946, Ger. Nazi politician.

Goes, Hugo van der, 1440?–82, Du. painter.

Goethals, George Washington, 1858–1928, U.S. military officer & engineer.

Goethe, Johann Wolfgang von, 1749–1832, Ger. poet, playwright, & statesman.

Gofman, John William, 1918–, U.S. physician & biophysicist.

Gogol, Nikolai Vasilevich, 1809–52, Russ. author.

Goldberg, Arthur Joseph, 1908–90, U.S. lawyer, jurist, & diplomat; U.S. Supreme Court justice 1962–65.

—Reuben Lucius (Rube), 1883–1970, U.S. cartoonist.

Golden, Harry Lewis, 1902–81, U.S. journalist & author.

Golding, William, 1911–93, Eng. author; Nobel Prize winner.

Goldman, Edwin Franko, 1878–1956, U.S. bandmaster & composer.

—Emma, 1869–1940, Lithuanian-born U.S. anarchist.

Goldoni, Carlo, 1707–93, Ital. playwright.

Goldsmith, Oliver, 1728–74, Eng. author.

Goldstein, Eugen, 1850–1931, Ger. physicist.

Goldwater, Barry, 1909–, U.S. senator & political leader.

Goldwyn, Samuel, 1882–1974, Pol.-born U.S. film producer.

Golgi, Camillo, 1844–1926, Ital. physician & histologist.

Gompers, Samuel, 1850–1924, U.S. labor leader.

Gomulka, Wladyslaw, 1905–1982, first secretary of the Communist Party of Poland 1956–70.

Goncourt, Edmond, 1822–96, & his brother **Jules,** 1830–70, Fr. diarists & authors.

Góngora, Luis de, 1561–1627, Sp. poet.

Gonzalez, Pancho, 1928–95, tennis player.

Goodall, Jane, 1934–, Eng. zoologist.

Goodenough, Florence Laura, 1886–1959, U.S. psychologist.

Goodhue, Bertram G., 1869–1924, U.S. architect.

Goodman, Benjamin David (Benny), 1909–86, U.S. musician.

—Paul, 1911–72, U.S. author & educator.

Goodrich, Benjamin Franklin, 1841–88, U.S. industrialist.

Goodson, Mark, 1916–92, U.S. TV producer.

Goodyear, Charles, 1800–60, U.S. inventor.

Goossens, Sir Eugene, 1893–1962, Brit. composer & conductor.

Gorbachev, Mikhail Sergeevich, 1931–, Soviet politician; general secretary U.S.S.R. communist party 1985–91, head of state 1988–90, and executive president 1990–91.

Gordimer, Nadine, 1923–, South African author; Nobel Prize winner.

Gordon, Charles George, 1833–85, Brit. military officer; called **Chinese Gordon.**

—Max, 1892–1978, U.S. theatrical producer.

—Ruth, 1906–1985, U.S. actress & author.

Goren, Charles Henry, 1901–91, U.S. bridge player & author.

Gorgas, William Crawford, 1854–1920, U.S. physician & sanitation engineer.

Göring, Hermann Wilhelm, 1893–1946, Ger. Nazi politician.

Gorki, Maxim, 1868–1936, Russ. author & playwright.

Gorky, Arshile, 1905–48, Turkish-born U.S. painter.

Gosden, Freeman, 1899–1982, U.S. radio actor.

Gottfried von Strassburg, 1170?–1220?, Ger. poet.

Gottschalk, Louis Moreau, 1829–69, U.S. pianist & composer.

Gottwald, Klement, 1896–1953, Czech communist leader.

Goudy, Frederic William, 1865–1947, U.S. type designer.

Gould, Chester, 1900–85, U.S. cartoonist.

—Glenn, 1932–82, Can. pianist.

—Jason (Jay), 1836–92, U.S. financier.

—Morton, 1913–96, U.S. composer & conductor.

—Shane, 1954–, Austral. swimmer.

Goulding, Ray, 1922–90, U.S. comedian.

Gounod, Charles François, 1818–93, Fr. composer.

Gourmont, Rémy de, 1858–1915, Fr. poet, author, & critic.

Gowon, Yakubu, 1934–, head of state of Nigeria 1966–75.

Goya, Francisco José de, 1746–1828, Sp. painter & etcher.

Graaf, Regnier de, 1641–73, Du. physician.

Grable, Betty, 1916–73, U.S. actress, singer, & dancer.

Gracchus, Gaius Sempronius, 153–121 B.C., & his brother **Tiberius Sempronius,** 163–133 B.C., Roman statesmen.

Grace, Princess, b. Grace Patricia Kelly, 1929–82, U.S.-born actress & wife of Prince Rainier III of Monaco.

Graham, Katharine, 1917–, U.S. publisher.

—Martha, 1894–1991, U.S. choreographer & dancer.

—Sheilah, 1905?–88, Eng.-born U.S. journalist & author.

—Thomas, 1805–69, Scot. physical chemist.

—William Franklin (Billy), 1918–, U.S. evangelist.

Grahame, Kenneth, 1859–1932, Eng. author.

Grainger, Percy Aldridge, 1882–1961, Austral.-born pianist & composer active in U.S.

Gram, Hans Christian Joachim, 1853–1938, Dan. bacteriologist.

Gramm, Donald, 1927–83, U.S. bass-baritone.

Granados, Enrique, 1867–1916, Sp. composer.

Grange, Harold (Red), 1903–91, U.S. football player.

Grant, Cary, 1904–86, Eng.-born U.S. actor.

—Ulysses S(impson), 1822–85, U.S. Civil War general & 18th U.S. president 1869–77.

Granville-Barker, Harley, 1877–1946, Eng. actor, playwright, & producer.

Grappelli, Stéphane, 1908–97, Fr. jazz violinist.

Grass, Günter Wilhelm, 1927–, Ger. author.

Gratian, (L. Flavius Gratianus) 359–383, Roman emperor 375–83.

Graves, Robert Ranke, 1895–1985, Eng. poet & author.

Gray, Asa, 1810–88, U.S. botanist.

—Harold, 1894–1968, U.S. cartoonist.

—Thomas, 1716–71, Eng. poet.

Graziano, Rocco (Rocky), 1922–90, U.S. boxer.
Greco, El, b. Domenikos Theotokopoulos, 1541?–1614?, Cretan-born painter active in Italy & Spain.
Greco, José, 1919–, Ital.-born U.S. dancer.
Greeley, Horace, 1811–72, U.S. editor & political leader.
Green, Adolph, 1915–, U.S. lyricist.
—Henrietta Robinson (Hetty), 1834–1916, U.S. financier.
—Henry, pseud. of Henry Vincent Yorke, 1905–73, Eng. author.
—John, 1908–89, U.S. songwriter.
—Martyn, 1899–1975, Eng. actor & singer active in U.S.
—William, 1873–1952, U.S. labor leader.
Greenberg, Henry (Hank), 1911–86, U.S. baseball player.
Greene, Graham, 1904–91, Eng. author.
—Nathanael, 1742–86, Amer. Revolutionary general.
—Robert, 1558–92, Eng. poet & playwright.
Greenstreet, Sydney, 1879–1954, Eng. actor active in U.S.
Gregory I, Saint, 540?–604, pope 590–640; known as the Great.
—XIII, 1502–85, pope 1572–85.
Gregory, Lady Augusta Persse, 1859?–1932, Irish playwright & theater director.
—Dick, 1932–, U.S. comedian & social activist.
Gresham, Sir Thomas, 1519?–79, Eng. financier.
Gretzky, Wayne, 1961–, Can.-born hockey player active in U.S.
Greuze, Jean Baptiste, 1725–1805, Fr. painter.
Grey, Beryl, 1927–, Eng. dancer & ballet company director.
—Lady Jane, 1537–54, Eng. noblewoman; beheaded.
—Zane, 1872–1939, U.S. author.
Grieg, Edvard Hagerup, 1843–1907, Norw. composer.
Griffith, D(avid) W(ark), 1875–1948, U.S. film director & producer.
Grigorovitch, Yuri, 1927–, Russ. choreographer & ballet company director.
Grimaldi, Francesco Maria, 1618–63, Ital. physicist.
Grimm, Jacob Ludwig Karl, 1785–1863, & his brother **Wilhelm Karl,** 1786–1859, Ger. philologists & collectors of fairy tales.
Gris, Juan, 1887–1927, Sp. painter.
Grisi, Carlotta, 1819–99, Ital. ballerina.
Grofé, Ferde, 1892–1972, U.S. composer & conductor.
Grolier de Servières, Jean, 1479–1565, Fr. diplomat & bibliophile.
Gromyko, Andrei Andreivich, 1909–89, Soviet economist & diplomat.
Groote, Gerhard, 1340–84, Du. religious reformer.
Gropius, Walter, 1883–1969, Ger. architect active in U.S. after 1937.
Gropper, William, 1897–1977, U.S. painter.
Grosz, George, 1893–1959, Ger. painter & illustrator.
Grotius, Hugo, 1583–1645, Du. jurist & statesman.
Grove, Sir George, 1820–1900, Eng. musicologist & author.
—Robert (Lefty), 1900–75, U.S. baseball player.
Groves, Leslie Richard, 1896–1970, U.S. general.
Grünewald, Matthias, 1480?–1528?, Ger. painter.
Guardi, Francesco, 1712–93, Ital. painter.
Guarneri, Giuseppe Antonia, 1687–1745, Ital. violin maker.
Gueden, Hilde, 1917–88, Austrian soprano.
Guest, Edgar A(lbert), 1881–1959, Eng.-born U.S. poet & journalist.
Guevara, Ernesto (Ché), 1928–67, Argentinian-born Cuban revolutionary leader.
Guggenheim A family of U.S. industrialists & philanthropists incl. **Meyer,** 1828–1905, & his sons **Benjamin,** 1865–1912; **Daniel,** 1856–1930; **Issac,** 1854–1922; **Murry,** 1858–1939; **Simon,** 1867–1941; **Solomon R.,** 1861–1949; & **William,** 1868–1941.
—Peggy, 1898–1979, U.S. art collector, patron, & author.
Guido d'Arezzo, 990?–1050?, Ital. monk & musician.
Guinness, Sir Alec, 1914–, Eng. actor.
Guitry, Sacha, 1885–1957, Fr. film director.
Gunther, John, 1901–70, U.S. author.
Gustaf VI, 1882–1973, king of Sweden 1950–73.
Gustavus Adolphus (Gustaf II), 1594–1632, king of Sweden 1611–32.
Guston, Philip, 1913–80, U.S. painter.

Gutenberg, Johann, 1400?–1468?, Ger. printer & reputed inventor of movable type.
Guthrie, Sir Tyrone, 1900–71, Eng. stage director active in U.S.
—Woodrow Wilson (Woody), 1912–67, U.S. folk singer.
Gwynne, Nell, 1650–87, Eng. actress; mistress of Charles II.

Haakon VII, 1872–1957, king of Norway 1905–57.
Haber, Fritz, 1868–1934, Ger. chemist.
Hachette, Louis, 1800–64, Fr. publisher & bookseller.
Hadrian (L. Publius Aelius Hadrianus), A.D. 76–138, Roman emperor, A.D. 117–138.
Haechkel, Ernst Heinrich, 1834–1919, Ger. biologist.
Hafiz, pseud. of Shams ud-din Mohammed, 14th c. Persian poet.
Hagen, Walter Charles, 1892–1969, U.S. golfer.
Haggard, Sir (Henry) Rider, 1856–1925, Eng. author.
Hahn, Otto, 1879–1968, Ger. physical chemist; Nobel Prize winner.
Haig, Alexander Meigs, Jr., 1924–, U.S. general and statesman; U.S. secretary of state 1981–82.
Haile Selassie, 1891–1975, emperor of Ethiopia 1930–74.
Hailey, Arthur, 1920–, Eng. author.
Hakluyt, Richard, 1552–1616, Eng. geographer & historian.
Halas, George Stanley, 1895–1983, U.S. football player, coach, and owner.
Halberstam, David, 1920–, U.S. journalist.
Haldane, J(ohn) B(urdon) S(anderson), 1892–1964, Eng. biologist.
—John Scott, 1860–1936, Eng. physiologist.
—Richard Burdon, 1856–1928, Eng. philosopher & statesman.
Hale, Edward Everett, 1822–1909, U.S. clergyman & author.
—George Ellery, 1868–1938, U.S. astronomer.
—Nathan, 1755–76, Amer. revolutionary officer; hanged as a spy by the British.
—Sarah Josepha, 1788–1879, U.S. editor, poet, & author.
Hales, Stephen, 1677–1761, Eng. botanist & chemist.
Halévy, Jacques, 1799–1862, Fr. composer.
—Ludovic, 1834–1908, Fr. playwright & author; nephew of prec.
Haley, Alex, 1921–92, U.S. author.
Halifax, Edward Frederick Lindley Wood, Earl of, 1881–1959, Eng. statesman & diplomat.
Hall, James Norman, 1887–1951, U.S. author.
Halley, Edmund, 1656–1742, Eng. astronomer.
Halliburton, Richard, 1900–39, U.S. explorer & author.
Hals, Frans, 1850?–1666, Du. painter.
Halsey, William Frederick, Jr. (Bull), 1882–1959, U.S. admiral.
Halsted, William Stewart, 1852–1922, U.S. surgeon.
Halston (Roy Halston Frowick), 1932–90, U.S. fashion designer.
Hambro, Carl Joachim, 1885–1964, Norw. statesman.
Hamilcar Barca, 270?–228 B.C., Carthaginian general; father of Hannibal.
Hamilton, Alexander, 1757–1804, West Indian-born Amer. statesman.
—Edith, 1867–1963, U.S. classicist & author.
—Lady Emma, 1761?–1815, mistress of Lord Nelson.
—Margaret, 1902–85, U.S. actress.
Hammarskjöld, Dag, 1905–61, Swed. statesman; secretary general of the U.N. 1953–61; Nobel Prize winner.
Hammerstein, Oscar, 1847?–1919, U.S. theatrical manager.
—Oscar II, 1895–1960, U.S. lyricist; nephew of prec.
Hammett, Dashiell, 1894–1961, U.S. author.
Hammurabi, 18th c. B.C., Babylonian king & lawgiver.
Hampden, John, 1594–1643, Eng. statesman.
—Walter, 1879–1955, U.S. actor.
Hampton, Lionel, 1913–, U.S. jazz musician.
—Wade, 1818–1902, U.S. politician & Confederate general.
Hamsun, Knut, 1859–1952, Norw. author.
Hancock, John, 1737–93, Amer. statesman.
Hand, Learned, 1872–1961, U.S. jurist.
Handel, George Frederick, 1685–1759, Ger. composer active in England.
Handler, Philip, 1917–81, U.S. educator.

Handlin, Oscar, 1915–, U.S. historian & sociologist.

Handy, W(illiam) C(hristopher), 1873–1958, U.S. jazz musician & composer.

Hanna, Marcus Alonzo (Mark), 1837–1904, U.S. businessman & politician.

Hannibal, 247–183 B.C., Carthaginian general; invaded Italy by crossing the Alps.

Hansard, Luke, 1752–1828, Eng. printer.

Hansberry, Lorraine, 1930–65, U.S. playwright.

Hanson, Howard, 1896–1981, U.S. composer & conductor.

Harbach, Otto Abels, 1873–1963, U.S. playwright & lyricist.

Harburg, E(dgar) Y. (Yip), 1898–1981, U.S. lyricist.

Harden, Sir Arthur, 1865–1940, Eng. biochemist.

Harding, Warren Gamaliel, 1865–1923, 29th U.S. president 1921–23.

Hardwick, Elizabeth, 1916–, U.S. author & critic.

Hardwicke, Sir Cedric Webster, 1893–1964, Eng. actor.

Hardy, Oliver Nowell, 1892–1957, U.S. comedian.

—Thomas, 1840–1928, Eng. author & poet.

Hargreaves, James, 1722?–78, Eng. inventor of the spinning jenny.

Harington, Sir John, 1561–1612, Eng. author & translator.

Harkness, Rebekah West, 1915–82, U.S. composer & ballet patron.

Harlan, John Marshall, 1833–1911, & his grandson **John Marshall Harlan II,** 1899–1971, U.S. jurists.

Harlow, Jean, 1911–37, U.S. actress.

Harold II, 1022?–66, last Saxon king of England 1066.

Haroun-al-Rashid, 764?–809, Caliph of Baghdad 786–809.

Harper, James, 1795–1869, & his brothers: **John,** 1797–1875, **(Joseph) Wesley,** 1801–70, & **Fletcher,** 1806–77, U.S. printers & publishers.

—William Rainey, 1856–1906, U.S. educator.

Harriman, Edward Henry, 1848–1909, U.S. industrialist.

—W(illiam) Averell, 1891–1986, U.S. businessman, statesman, & diplomat.

Harrington, (Edward) Michael, 1928–89, U.S. author.

Harriot, Thomas, 1560–1621, Eng. mathematician.

Harris, Frank, 1854–1931, Irish-born U.S. editor & author.

—Jed, 1900–79, Austrian-born U.S. theatrical producer.

—Joel Chandler, 1848–1908, U.S. author.

—Julie, 1925–, U.S. actress.

—Louis, 1921–, U.S. public opinion statistician.

—Robert, 1849–1919, Eng.-born Can. painter.

—Roy, 1898–1979, U.S. composer.

—Townsend, 1804–78, U.S. businessman & diplomat.

Harrison, Benjamin, 1833–1901, 23rd U.S. president 1889–93.

—George, 1943–, Eng. composer & musical performer.

—Rex, 1908–90, Eng. actor active in U.S.

—Ross Granville, 1870–1959, U.S. biologist.

—Wallace K., 1895–1981, U.S. architect.

—William Henry, 1773–1841, U.S. general & 9th U.S. president 1841; grandfather of Benjamin.

Hart, Johnny, 1931–, U.S. cartoonist.

—Lorenz, 1895–1943, U.S. lyricist.

—Moss, 1904–61, U.S. playwright.

—William S(urrey), 1872–1946, U.S. actor.

Harte, Francis Brett (Bret), 1836–1902, U.S. author.

Hartford, Huntington, 1911–, U.S. financier & art patron.

Hartley, Marsden, 1877–1943, U.S. painter.

Harvard, John, 1607–38, Eng. clergyman active in U.S.

Harvey, William, 1578–1657, Eng. physician & anatomist.

Hasek, Jaroslav, 1883–1923, Czech. author.

Hassam, Childe, 1859–1935, U.S. painter & etcher.

Hassan II, 1929–, king of Morocco 1961–.

Hassler, Hans Leo, 1564–1612, Ger. composer.

Hastings, Thomas, 1860–1929, U.S. architect.

—Warren, 1732–1818, Eng.statesman active in India.

Hauptmann, Gerhart, 1862–1946, Ger. author & playwright.

Haussmann, Baron Georges Eugène, 1809–91, Fr. prefect & city planner.

Havel, Vaclav, 1936–, Czech. dramatist and statesman; president of Czechoslovakia 1989–92. President of Czech Republic 1993–.

Hawking, Stephen William, 1942–, Eng. physicist.

Hawkins, Sir John, 1532–95, Eng. admiral.

Hawks, Howard, 1896–1977, U.S. film director.

Hawthorne, Nathaniel, 1804–64, U.S. author.

Hay, John Milton, 1838–1905, U.S. statesman & author; secretary of state 1898–1905.

Haya de la Torre, Victor Raúl, 1895–1979, Peruvian political leader.

Haydn, Franz Joseph, 1732–1809, Austrian composer.

Hayek, Friedrich August von, 1899–1922, Austrian-born Brit. economist; Nobel Prize winner.

Hayes, Helen, 1900–93, U.S. actress.

—Robert (Bob), 1942–, U.S. track runner & football player.

—Roland, 1887–1977, U.S. tenor.

—Rutherford Birchard, 1822–93, 19th U.S. president 1877–81.

Hays, Arthur Garfield, 1881–1954, U.S. lawyer.

Hayward, Leland, 1902–71, U.S. theatrical producer.

—Susan, 1919–75, U.S. actress.

Hayworth, Rita, 1918–87, actress.

Hazlitt, William, 1778–1830, Eng. author.

Head, Edith, 1907–81, U.S. costume designer.

Hearn, Lafcadio, 1850–1904, Gk.-born Irish author active in Japan.

Hearst, William Randolph, 1863–1951, U.S. publisher.

Heath, Edward, 1916–, Eng. politician; prime minister 1970–74.

Heatter, Gabriel, 1890–1972, U.S. journalist & radio commentator.

Heaviside, Oliver, 1850–1925, Eng. physicist & electrician.

Hecht, Ben, 1894–1964, U.S. journalist, author, & playwright.

Hefner, Hugh Marston, 1926–, U.S. editor & publisher.

Hegel, Georg Wilhelm Friedrich, 1770–1831, Ger. philosopher.

Heidegger, Martin, 1889–1976, Ger. philosopher.

Heiden, Eric, 1958–, Olympic speed skater.

Heifetz, Jascha, 1901–87, Lithuanian-born U.S. violinist.

Heine, Heinrich, 1797–1856, Ger. poet.

Heinlein, Robert Anson, 1907–1988, U.S. author.

Heinz, Henry John, 1844–1919, U.S. food processor.

Heisenberg, Werner, 1901–76, Ger. physicist; Nobel Prize winner.

Held, Anna, 1873?–1918, Fr.-born singer & actress active in U.S.

—John, Jr., 1889–1958, U.S. illustrator & author.

Heliogabalus, 204–222, Roman emperor 218–22.

Heller, Joseph, 1923–, U.S. author.

Hellinger, Mark, 1903–47, U.S. journalist & theatrical producer.

Hellman, Lillian, 1905–84, U.S. playwright.

Helmholtz, Hermann Ludwig Ferdinand von, 1821–94, Ger. physiologist & physicist.

Helmont, Jan Baptista van, 1577–1644, Flemish physician & chemist.

Héloïse, 1101?–64?, Fr. abbess; pupil, mistress, & later, wife of Abélard.

Helpmann, Sir Robert Murray, 1909–1986, Austral.-born dancer, choreographer, & actor active in Great Britain.

Helprin, Mark, 1947–, U.S. author.

Helvétius, Claude Adrien, 1715–71, Fr. philosopher.

Hemingway, Ernest, 1899–1961, U.S. author; Nobel Prize winner.

Henderson, (James) Fletcher, 1897–1952, U.S. jazz musician.

—Ray, 1896–1970, U.S. songwriter.

Hendrix, Jimi, 1942–70, U.S. musician & singer.

Hengist, 5th c. Jute invader of Great Britain.

Henie, Sonja, 1913–69, Norw.-born ice skater & actress active in U.S.

Henreid, Paul, 1908–92, Austrian actor active in U.S.

Henri, Robert, 1865–1929, U.S. painter.

Henry II, 1133–89, king of England 1154–89.

—IV, 1367–1413, king of England 1399–1413.

—V, 1387–1422, king of England 1413–22.

—VIII, 1491–1547, king of England 1509–47; established Church of England.

Henry IV (of Navarre), 1553–1610, king of France 1589–1610.

Henry the Navigator, 1394–1460, Pg. prince & promoter of navigation.

Henry, O., pseud. of William Sidney Porter, 1862–1910, U.S. author.

—Patrick, 1736–99, Amer. patriot, statesman, & orator.

Hensen, Victor, 1835–1924, Ger. marine biologist.

Henson, Jim (James Maury), 1936–90, U.S. puppeteer and director.

Henze, Hans Werner, 1926–, Ger. composer.

Hepburn, Audrey, 1929–93, Belg.-born actress active in U.S.

—Katharine, 1909–, U.S. actress.

Hepplewhite, George, ?–1786, Eng. furniture designer.

Hepworth, Dame Barbara, 1903–75, Eng. sculptor.

Heraclitus, ca. 5th c. B.C. Gk. philosopher.

Herbert, Frank, 1920–86, U.S. author.

—George, 1593–1633, Eng. poet & clergyman.

—Victor, 1859–1924, Irish-born U.S. composer.

—William, 1580–1630, Eng. statesman & poet.

Herder, Johann Gottfried von, 1744–1803, Ger. philosopher & author.

Heredia, José Maria de, 1842–1905, Cuban-born Fr. poet.

Herman, Jerry, 1932–, U.S. composer.

—Woodrow Charles (Woody), 1913–87, U.S. jazz musician.

Herod, 73?–4 B.C., king of Judea 37–4 B.C.: called **the Great.**

—Antipas, 4 B.C.–A.D. 40, governor of Galilee; son of prec.

Herodotus, 484?–424? B.C., Gk. historian.

Herophilus, 4th c. B.C., Gk. anatomist.

Herrick, Robert, 1591–1674, Eng. poet.

Herriman, George, 1881–1944, U.S. cartoonist.

Herschel, Sir William, 1738–1822, & his son **Sir John Frederick William,** 1792–1871, Eng. astronomers.

Hersey, John Richard, 1914–93, Chin.-born U.S. author.

Hershey, Milton Snavely, 1857–1945, U.S. businessman & philanthropist.

Herskovits, Melville Jean, 1895–1963, U.S. anthropologist.

Hertz, Gustav, 1887–1975, Ger. physicist; Nobel Prize winner.

Herzberg, Gerhard, 1904–, Ger.-born Can. physicist; Nobel Prize winner.

—Heinrich Rudolph, 1857–94, Ger. physicist.

Herzl, Theodor, 1860–1904, Hung.-born Austrian journalist; founder of the Zionist movement.

Hesburgh, Theodore Martin, 1917–, U.S. Roman Catholic priest & educator.

Hesiod, ca. 8th c. B.C., Gk. poet.

Hess, Dame Myra, 1890–1965, Eng. pianist.

—Victor Franz, 1883–1964, Austrian physicist.

—Walter Rudolf, 1881–1973, Swiss physiologist.

—(Walther Richard) Rudolf, 1894–1987, Ger. Nazi politician.

Hesse, Hermann, 1877–1962, Ger. author; Nobel Prize winner.

Heydrich, Reinhard, 1904–42, Ger. Nazi administrator: known as **the Hangman.**

Heyerdahl, Thor, 1914–, Norw. anthropologist & author.

Heyrovsky, Jaroslav, 1890–1967, Czech chemist; Nobel Prize winner.

Heyward, DuBose, 1885–1940, U.S. author.

Hiawatha, 16th c. Mohawk Am. Ind. chief.

Hickok, James Butler (Wild Bill), 1837–76, U.S. scout & marshal.

Hicks, Edward, 1780–1849, U.S. painter.

—Granville, 1901–82, U.S. author & critic.

Hidalgo y Costilla, Miguel, 1753–1811, Mexican priest & revolutionary.

Highet, Gilbert, 1906–78, Scot.-born U.S. author & educator.

Hilbert, David, 1862–1943, Ger. mathematician.

Hill, George Washington, 1884–1946, U.S. businessman.

—Graham, 1929–75, Eng. auto racer.

—Joe, 1872?–1915, Swed.-born U.S. labor organizer & songwriter.

Hillary, Sir Edmund, 1919–, New Zealand explorer & mountain climber.

Hillel, 60 B.C.?–A.D. 10, Babylonian teacher of biblical law.

Hiller, Wendy, 1912–, Eng. actress.

Hillman, Sidney, 1887–1946, Lituanian-born U.S. labor leader.

Hilton, Conrad Nicholson, 1887–1979, U.S. businessman.

—James, 1900–54, Eng. author.

Himmler, Heinrich, 1900–45, Ger. Nazi politician.

Hindemith, Paul, 1895–1963, Ger. composer active in U.S.

Hindenburg, Paul von, 1847–1934, Ger. field marshal; president of Germany 1925–34.

Hine, Lewis Wickes, 1874–1940, U.S. photographer.

Hines, Duncan, 1880–1959, U.S. food expert, author, & publisher.

—Earl (Fatha), 1905–83, U.S. jazz musician.

Hippocrates, 460?–377, B.C., Gk. physician.

Hires, Charles Elmer, 1851–1937, U.S. businessman.

Hirohito, 1901–89, emperor of Japan 1926–89.

Hiroshige, Ando, 1797–1858, Jap. painter.

Hirsch, Elray (Crazy Legs), 1923–, U.S. football player; Pro Football Hall of Fame, 1968.

Hirschfeld, Al(bert), 1903–, U.S. cartoonist.

Hirshhorn, Joseph, 1899–1981, Latvian-born U.S. mining executive, entrepreneur, & art collector.

Hiss, Alger, 1904–96, U.S. government official.

Hitchcock, Sir Alfred, 1899–1980, Eng. film director active in U.S.

—Henry-Russell, 1903–87, U.S. art historian.

Hitler, Adolf, 1889–1945, Austrian-born Nazi dictator of Germany 1933–45.

Hoban, James, 1762?–1831, Irish-born U.S. architect.

Hobart, Garret Augustus, 1844–99, U.S. statesman; U.S. vice president 1897–99.

Hobbema, Meindert, 1638–1709, Du. painter.

Hobbes, Thomas, 1588–1679, Eng. philosopher.

Hobby, Oveta Culp, 1905–95, U.S. journalist & government official.

Ho Chi Minh, 1890?–1969, president of N. Vietnam 1954–69.

Hodgkin, Dorothy Crowfoot, 1910–94, Brit. chemist; Nobel Prize winner.

Hoffa, James Riddle, 1913–75?, U.S. labor leader.

Hoffer, Eric, 1902–83, U.S. philosopher & author.

Hoffman, Malvina, 1887–1966, U.S. sculptor.

Hoffmann, E(rnst) T(heodor) A(madeus), 1776–1822, Ger. author & illustrator.

Hofmann, Hans, 1880–1966, Ger.-born U.S. painter.

—Josef Casimir, 1876–1957, Pol. pianist.

Hofmannsthal, Hugo von, 1874–1929, Austrian poet & playwright.

Hofstadter, Richard, 1916–70, U.S. historian.

Hogan, Ben W., 1912–97, U.S. golfer.

Hogarth, William, 1697–1764, Eng. painter & engraver.

Hokinson, Helen, 1899?–1949, U.S. cartoonist.

Hokusai, Katsushika, 1760–1849, Jap. painter & engraver.

Holabird, William, 1854–1923, U.S. architect.

Holbein, Hans, 1460?–1524, (called **the Elder**), and his son, **Hans,** 1497–1543, (**the Younger**), Ger. painters.

Hölderlin, (Johann Christian) Friedrich, 1770–1843, Ger. poet.

Holiday, Billie, 1915–59, U.S. jazz singer.

Holinshed, Raphael, ?–1580?, Eng. chronicler.

Holley, Robert W., 1922–93, U.S. biochemist.

Holliday, Judy, 1921–65, U.S. actress.

Holmes, Oliver Wendell, 1809–94, U.S. physician & poet.

—Oliver Wendell, Jr., 1841–1935, U.S. jurist; justice of U.S. Supreme Court 1902–32; son of prec.

Holst, Gustav Theodore, 1874–1934, Eng. composer.

Holyoake, Sir Keith Jacka, 1904–83, New Zealand statesman; New Zealand prime minister 1957 & 1960–72.

Home, Alexander Frederick Douglas, Lord, 1903–95, Brit. statesman; Brit. prime minister 1963–4.

Homer, ca. 8th c. B.C. Gk. epic poet.

Homer, Winslow, 1836–1910, U.S. painter.

Honecker, Erich, 1912–94, 1st secretary of German Democratic Republic Communist party 1971–76; general secretary 1976–89.

Honegger, Arthur, 1892–1955, Fr. composer.

Hood, Raymond, 1881–1934, U.S. architect.

Hooke, Robert, 1635–1703, Eng. philosopher & scientist.

Hooker, Thomas, 1586?–1647, Eng.-born clergyman; founder of Connecticut colony.

Hooton, Earnest Albert, 1887–1954, U.S. anthropologist.

Hoover, Herbert Clark, 1874–1964, 31st U.S. president 1929–33.
—**J(ohn) Edgar,** 1895–1972, U.S. criminologist; director of the FBI 1924–72.
Hope, Leslie Townes (Bob), 1903–, Eng.-born U.S. actor & comedian.
Hopkins, Gerard Manley, 1844–89, Eng. poet.
—**Harry Lloyd,** 1890–1946, U.S. politician & administrator.
—**Johns,** 1795–1873, U.S. financier & philanthropist.
—**Mark,** 1802–87, U.S. educator.
Hopkinson, Francis, 1737–91, U.S. lawyer & author.
Hoppe, William Frederick (Willie), 1887–1959, U.S. billiards player.
Hopper, Edward, 1882–1967, U.S. painter.
—**Hedda,** 1890–1966, U.S. actress & columnist.
Horace (L. Quintus Horatius Flaccus), 65–8 B.C., Roman poet.
Horne, Lena, 1917–, U.S. singer & actress.
—**Marilyn,** 1934–, U.S. mezzo-soprano.
Horney, Karen, 1885–1952, Ger.-born U.S. psychiatrist.
Hornsby, Rogers, 1896–1963, U.S. baseball player.
Horowitz, Vladimir, 1904–89, Russ.-born U.S. pianist.
Horsa, ?–455, Jute invader of Great Britain.
Houdini, Harry, 1874–1926, U.S. magician.
Houdon, Jean Antoine, 1741–1828, Fr. sculptor.
Houphouët-Boigny, Félix, 1905–93, president of Ivory Coast 1960–.
House, Col. Edward Mandell, 1858–1938, U.S. diplomat.
Houseman, John, 1902–89, U.S. producer, director, actor, & author for theater, TV, & films.
Housman, A(lfred) E(dward), 1859–1936, Eng. poet & classical scholar.
Houston, Sam(uel), 1793–1863, U.S. statesman & general; president of Republic of Texas 1836–38 & 1841–44.
Hovhaness, Alan, 1911–, U.S. composer.
Howard, Catherine, 1520?–42, 5th wife of King Henry VIII of England.
—**Henry, Earl of Surrey,** 1517?–47, Eng. soldier & poet.
—**Leslie,** 1893–1943, Eng. actor active in U.S.
—**Roy W.,** 1883–1964, U.S. editor & publisher.
—**Sidney Coe,** 1891–1939, U.S. playwright.
—**Trevor,** 1916–88, Eng. actor.
Howe, Elias, 1819–67, U.S. inventor of the sewing machine.
—**Gordon (Gordie),** 1928–, Can. hockey player.
—**Irving,** 1920–93, U.S. literary critic & author.
—**James Wong,** 1899–1976, Chin.-born U.S. cinematographer.
—**Julia Ward,** 1819–1910, U.S. suffragist & author.
—**Mark Anthony DeWolf,** 1864–1960, U.S. author.
—**Richard, Earl,** 1726–99, Eng. naval officer.
Howells, William Dean, 1837–1920, U.S. author & editor.
—**Herbert Norman,** 1892–1983, Brit. composer.
Hoxha, Enver, 1908–85, 1st secretary of Albanian Labor (Communist) Party 1945–85.
Hoyle, Edmond, 1672–1769, Eng. writer on games.
—**Sir Fred,** 1915–, Eng. astronomer.
Hu Yaobang, 1915–89, Chin. statesman; general secretary of Chin. Communist Party 1981–87.
Hua Guofeng, 1918?–, Chin. statesman; chairman of Chin. Communist Party 1976–81; premier 1976–80.
Hubble, Edwin Powell, 1889–1953, U.S. astronomer.
Hudson, Henry, ?–1611, Eng. explorer.
—**Rock,** 1925–85, U.S. actor.
Huggins, Sir William, 1824–1910, Eng. astronomer.
Hughes, Charles Evans, 1862–1948, U.S. jurist; chief justice of the U.S. Supreme Court 1930–41.
—**Howard Robard,** 1905–76, U.S. businessman.
—**(James) Langston,** 1902–67, U.S. author & poet.
Hugo, Victor Marie, 1802–85, Fr. poet, author, & playwright.
Huizinga, Johan, 1872–1945, Du. historian.
Hull, Cordell, 1871–1955, U.S. statesman; secretary of state 1933–44; Nobel Prize winner.
—**Robert Marvin (Bobby),** 1939–, Can. hockey player.
Humboldt, Baron (Friedrich Heinrich) Alexander von, 1769–1859, Ger. naturalist & traveler.
Hume, David, 1711–76, Scot. historian & philosopher.
Humperdinck, Engelbert, 1854–1921, Ger. composer.
Humphrey, Doris, 1895–1958, U.S. choreographer & dancer.

—**Hubert Horatio,** 1911–78, U.S. senator & political leader; U.S. vice president 1965–69.
Hunt, H(aroldson) L(afayette), 1889–1974, U.S. businessman.
—**(James Henry) Leigh,** 1784–1859, Eng. author.
—**Richard Morris,** 1827–95, U.S. architect.
Hunter, Alberta, 1895–1984, U.S. songwriter & singer.
—**John,** 1728–93, Eng. surgeon.
Huntington, Collis P., 1821–1900, U.S. railroad magnate.
—**Henry E.,** 1850–1927, U.S. railroad builder & philanthropist.
Huntley, Chester Robert (Chet), 1911–74, U.S. news analyst & commentator.
Hunyadi, János, 1387?–1456, Hung. soldier & national hero.
Hurok, Sol, 1888–1974, Russ.-born U.S. impresario.
Hurston, Zora Neale, 1903–60, U.S. author and anthropologist.
Husak, Gustav, 1913–91, general secretary of the Communist Party of Czechoslovakia 1969–87, & president 1975–89.
Huss John, 1369–1415, Bohemian religious reformer.
Hussein I, 1935–, king of Jordan 1952–.
Hussein, Saddam, 1937–, Iraqi politician; president of Iraq 1979–.
Husserl, Edmund, 1859–1938, Ger. philosopher; founder of phenomenology.
Huston, John, 1906–87, U.S. film director & actor.
—**Walter,** 1884–1950, Can.-born U.S. actor; father of prec.
Hutchins, Robert Maynard, 1899–1977, U.S. educator.
Hutchinson, Anne Marbury, 1591–1643, U.S. religious leader.
—**Thomas,** 1711–80, U.S. colonial administrator.
Huxley A family of Eng. scientists & writers incl. **Aldous Leonard,** 1894–1963, author; **Sir Julian Sorell,** 1887–1975, biologist, brother of prec.; **Thomas Henry,** 1825–95, biologist, grandfather of Aldous & Julian.
Huxtable, Ada Louise, 1921–, U.S. architecture critic & journalist.
Huygens, Christian, 1629–95, Du. mathematician, physicist, & astronomer.
Huysman, Joris Karl, 1848–1907, Fr. author.

Ibáñez, Carlos, 1877–1960, Chilean politician; president 1927–31 & 1952–58.
Ibert, Jacques, 1890–1962, Fr. composer.
ibn-Khaldun, 1332–1406, Arab historian.
ibn Saud, Abdul Aziz, 1880–1953, king of Saudi Arabia 1932–53.
Ibsen, Henrik, 1828–1906, Norw. playwright & poet.
Ickes, Harold LeClair, 1874–1952, U.S. lawyer & government official.
Ictinus, 5th B.C. Gk. architect.
Ikeda, Hayato, 1899–1965, premier of Japan 1960–64.
Ikhnaton, king of Egypt 1375–1358 B.C.: also known as **Akhnaton, Amenhotep IV.**
Indy, Vincent d', 1851–1931, Fr. composer.
Inge, William, 1913–73, U.S. playwright.
Ingenhousz, Jan, 1730–99, Du. physician & plant physiologist.
Ingersoll, Robert Green, 1833–99, U.S. lawyer, author, & lecturer.
Ingres, Jean Auguste Dominique, 1780–1867, Fr. painter.
Inman, Henry, 1801–46, U.S. painter.
Inness, George, 1825–94, U.S. painter.
Innocent III, b. Giovanni Latario de'Conti 1161–1216, pope 1198–1216.
Inönü, Ismet, 1884–1973, first premier of Turkey; president 1938–50.
Insull, Samuel, 1859–1938, Eng.-born U.S. utilities executive.
Ionesco, Eugene, 1912–94, Rumanian-born Fr. playwright.
Iqbal, Mohammed, 1873–1938, Moslem leader & national hero of Pakistan.
Irving, Sir Henry, 1838–1905, Eng. actor & theater manager.
—**John,** 1942–, U.S. novelist.
—**Washington,** 1783–1859, U.S. author.
Isaacs, Alick, 1921–67, Eng. biologist.
Isabella I, 1451–1504, queen of Castile & wife of Ferdinand V; sponsored the voyages of Columbus.

Isherwood, Christopher William Bradshaw, 1904–86, Eng.-born U.S. author.
Ismail Pasha, 1830–95, khedive of Egypt 1863–79.
Iturbi, José, 1895–1980, Sp. pianist & conductor active in U.S.
Ivan III, 1440–1505, grand duke of Muscovy & founder of Russ. Empire: called **the Great.**
—IV, 1530–84, grand duke of Muscovy & first czar of Russia: called **the Terrible.**
Ives, Burl, 1909–95, U.S. singer & actor.
—Charles Edward, 1874–1954, U.S. composer.

Jackson, Andrew, 1767–1845. U.S. general & 7th U.S. president 1829–37.
—Glenda, 1936–, Eng. actress.
—Henry M(artin), 1912–83, U.S. politician.
—Jesse, 1941–, U.S. black civil rights leader.
—Mahalia, 1911–72, U.S. gospel singer.
—Maynard, 1938–, U.S. politician.
—Michael, 1958–, U.S. singer & songwriter.
—Shirley, 1919–65, U.S. author.
—Thomas Jonathan (Stonewall), 1824–63, U.S. Confederate general.
Jacobs, Helen Hull, 1908–97, U.S. tennis player.
Jacquard, Joseph Marie, 1752–1834, Fr. inventor.
Jagger, Mick, 1944–, Eng. singer.
James I, 1566–1625, king of England 1603–25; also called **James VI** as king of Scotland 1567–1625.
—II, 1633–1701, king of England 1685–88; deposed.
James, Harry, 1916–83, U.S. bandleader.
—Henry, 1843–1916, U.S. author & critic active in England.
—Jesse Woodson, 1847–82, U.S. outlaw.
—William, 1842–1910, U.S. psychologist, philosopher, educator, & author; brother of Henry.
Jamison, Judith, 1944–, U.S. dancer.
Janáček, Leoš, 1854–1928, Czech composer.
Janis, Elsie, 1889–1956, U.S. actress.
Jannings, Emil, 1887?–1950, Swiss-born actor active in Germany.
Jansen, Cornelius, 1585–1638, Du. theologian.
Jacques-Dalcroze, Émile, 1865–1950, Swiss composer & educator.
Jarrell, Randall, 1914–65, U.S. poet.
Jaruzelski, Wojciech, 1923–, Pol. Communist Party leader 1981–89; president of Polish Peoples Republic 1989–90.
Jaspers, Karl, 1883–1969, Ger. philosopher.
Jastrow, Robert, 1925–, U.S. physicist.
Jaurès, Jean Léon, 1859–1914, Fr. socialist leader.
Jay, John, 1745–1829, Amer. statesman & first chief justice of the U.S. Supreme Court 1790–95.
Jean, Grand Duke, 1921–, ruler of Luxembourg 1964–.
Jeans, Sir James Hopwood, 1877–1946, Eng. mathematician, astronomer, physicist, & author.
Jeffers, (John) Robinson, 1887–1962, U.S. poet.
Jefferson, Joseph, 1829–1905, U.S. actor.
—Thomas, 1743–1826, Amer. statesman & 3rd. U.S. president 1801–09; drafted the Declaration of Independence.
Jellicoe, John Rushworth, (1st Earl Jellicoe), 1859–1935, Brit. admiral.
Jenner, Bruce, 1949–, U.S. decathlon athlete.
—Edward, 1749–1823, Eng. physician.
—William, 1815–98, Brit. physician.
Jenney, William LeBaron, 1832–1907, U.S. architect.
Jennings, Peter Charles, 1938–, Can.-born U.S. journalist.
Jensen, J. Hans, 1906–73, Ger. physicist; Nobel Prize winner.
Jenson, Nicholas, 1415?–80, Fr. printer & typographer.
Jerome, Saint, 340?–420; early Church father & religious scholar.
Jespersen, (Jens) Otto (Harry), 1860–1943, Dan. linguist.
Jessel, George Albert, 1898–1981, U.S. comedian.
Jesus, 6? B.C.–A.D. 29, religious leader & founder of Christianity; also called **Jesus Christ** & **Jesus of Nazareth.**
Jewett, Sarah Orne, 1849–1909, U.S. author.
Jiménez, Juan Ramón, 1881–1958, Sp. poet; Nobel Prize winner.
Joachim, Joseph, 1831–1907, Hung. violinist.

Joan of Arc, Saint, 1412–31, Fr. heroine; burned as a heretic: Fr. **Jeanne d'Arc**; also called **the Maid of Orleans.**
Jodl, Alfred, 1892?–1946. Ger. general.
Joffre, Joseph Jacques Césaire, 1852–1931, Fr. field marshal.
Joffrey, Robert, 1930–88, U.S. choreographer & ballet company director.
John, 1166?–1216, Eng. king 1199–1216; signed Magna Carta 1215.
John XXIII, b. Angelo Roncalli, 1881–1963, pope 1958–63.
John of Austria, Don, 1547–78, Sp.-born general.
John of the Cross, Saint, b. Juan de Yepis y Álvarez, 1542–91, Sp. mystic.
John of Gaunt, 1340–99, Eng. prince.
John, Augustus Edwin, 1878–1961, Eng. painter.
—Elton (Reginald Kenneth Dwight), 1947–, Eng. singer, songwriter.
John Paul I, b. Albino Luciani, 1912–78, pope 1978.
John Paul II, b. Karol Wojtyla, 1920–, pope 1978–.
Johns, Jasper, 1930–, U.S. painter & sculptor.
Johnson, Andrew, 1808–75, 17th U.S. president 1865–69.
—Dame Celia, 1908–82, Eng. actress.
—Harold (Chic), 1891–1962, U.S. comedian.
—Howard Deering, 1896?–1972, U.S. businessman.
—Jack Arthur, 1878–1946, U.S. boxer.
—James Weldon, 1871–1938, U.S. poet & author.
—John Harold, 1918–, U.S. publisher.
—(Jonathan) Eastman, 1824–1906, U.S. painter.
—Lyndon Baines, 1908–73, 36th U.S. president 1963–69.
Johnson, Philip Cortelyou, 1906–, U.S. architect.
—Samuel, 1709–84, Eng. author, critic, & lexicographer.
—Virginia Eshelman, 1925–, U.S. sex researcher.
—Walter Perry, 1887–1946, U.S. baseball player.
Joliot-Curie, Frèderic, 1900–58 & his wife, **Irène** (daughter of Marie & Pierre Curie), 1897–1956, Fr. physicists.
Jolliet, Louis, 1645–1700, Can. explorer in America. Also spelled **Joliet.**
Jolson, Al, 1886–1950, Russ.-born U.S. singer & actor.
Jones, Ernest, 1879–1958, Welsh-born Brit. psychoanalyst & author.
—Inigo, 1573–1652, Eng. architect & stage designer.
—James, 1921–77, U.S. author.
—James Earl, 1931–, U.S. actor.
—John Luther (Casey), 1864–1900, U.S. railroad engineer.
—John Paul, 1747–92, Scot.-born Amer. naval commander.
—Robert Tyre, Jr. (Bobby), 1902–71, U.S. golfer.
Jong, Erica, 1942–, U.S. author.
Jonson, Ben, 1572–1637, Eng. poet & playwright.
Joplin, Janis, 1943–70, U.S. singer.
—Scott, 1868–1917, U.S. jazz musician & composer.
Jordaens, Jacob, 1593–1678, Flemish painter.
Joseph, b. Hinmatonyalakit, 1840?–1904, Nez Percé Am. Ind. chief.
Josephine, 1763–1814, wife of Napoleon I & empress of France 1804–09.
Josephus, Flavius, A.D. 37–100?, Jewish historian.
Joule, James Prescott, 1818–89, Eng. physicist.
Jouvet, Louis, 1887–1951, Fr. actor & stage director.
Jowett, Benjamin, 1817–93, Eng. classical scholar.
Joyce, James, 1882–1941, Irish author & poet.
—William, 1906–46, U.S.-born Brit. traitor during World War II; executed: called **Lord Haw-Haw.**
Juan Carlos I, 1938–, king of Spain 1975–.
Juarez, Benito Pablo, 1806–72, Mexican patriot; president of Mexico 1867–72.
Juilliard, Augustus, 1836–1919, U.S. merchant, financier, & philanthropist.
Julian (L. Flavius Claudius Julianus), 331–363, Roman emperor: called **the Apostate.**
Juliana, 1909–, queen of the Netherlands 1948–80.
Julius II, b. Giuliano della Rovere, 1443–1513, pope 1503–13.
Jung, Carl Gustav, 1875–1961, Swiss psychologist.
Junkers, Hugo, 1859–1935, Ger. airplane designer.
Jussieu, Antoine Laurent de, 1748–1836, Fr. botanist.
Justinian I, 482–565, Byzantine emperor; codifier of Roman law.

Juvenal (L. Decimus Junius Juvenalis), A.D. 60?–140?, Roman poet.

Kabalevsky, Dmitri, 1904–87, Russ. composer.
Kádár, János, 1912–89, first secretary of the Communist party of Hungary 1956–88.
Kael, Pauline, 1919, U.S. film critic.
Kafka, Franz, 1883–1924, Czech-born Austrian author.
Kagawa, Toyohiko, 1888–1960, Jap. Christian social reformer & author.
Kahn, Albert, 1869–1942, U.S. architect.
—**Gus,** 1886–1941, U.S. lyricist.
—**Louis Isadore** 1901–74, Estonian-born U.S. architect.
—**Otto Herman,** 1867–1934, Ger.-born U.S. banker, art patron, & philanthropist.
Kaiser, Henry John, 1882–1967, U.S. industrialist.
Kalmar, Bert, 1884–1947, U.S. lyricist & librettist.
Kaltenborn, H(ans) V(on), 1878–1965, U.S. news commentator.
Kamehameha, 1758?–1819, king of Hawaii 1795–1819.
Kamerlingh Onnes, Heike, 1853–1926, Du. physicist.
Kander, John, 1927–, U.S. composer.
Kandinski, Vasili, 1866–1944, Russ. painter active in Germany.
Kanin, Garson, 1912–, U.S. playwright & stage director.
Kano A family of 15th-16th c. Jap. painters, incl. **Masanobu,** 1453–90, & his sons, **Motonobu,** 1476–1559, & **Yokinobu,** 1513–75.
Kant, Immanuel, 1724–1804, Ger. philosopher.
Kantor, MacKinlay, 1904–77, U.S. writer.
Kapitsa, Pyotr Leonidovich, 1894–1984, Russ. physicist & Nobel prize winner.
Karajan, Herbert von, 1908–89, Austrian conductor.
Karinska, Barbara, 1886–1983, Russ.-born U.S. costume designer & maker.
Karloff, Boris, 1887–1969, Eng.-born actor active in U.S.
Karsavina, Tamara, 1885–1978, Russ. ballerina.
Karsh, Yousuf, 1908–, Armenian-born Can. photographer.
Kasavubu, Joseph, 1910–69, first president of the Congolese Republic (now Zaire) 1960–65.
Kassem, Abdul Karim, 1914–63, Iraqi general; premier of Iraq 1958–63; executed.
Kastler, Alfred, 1902–84, Fr. physicist; Nobel prize winner.
Kaufman, George S., 1889–1961, U.S. playwright.
Kaunda, Kenneth David, 1924–, president of Zambia 1964–91.
Kawabata, Yasunari, 1899–1972, Jap. author.
Kay, Ulysses Simpson, 1917–95, U.S. composer.
Kaye, Danny, 1913–91, U.S. comedian & actor.
Kazan, Elia, 1909–, Turkish-born U.S. stage & film director & author.
Kazantzakis, Nikos, 1885–1957, Gk. poet & author.
Kean, Edmund, 1787–1833, Eng. actor.
Keaton, Buster, 1895–1966, U.S. film actor & director.
Keats, John, 1795–1821, Eng. poet.
Keeler, Ruby, 1910–93, Can.-born U.S. singer, dancer, & actress.
Kefauver, Estes, 1903–63, U.S. politician.
Keino, Kipchoge, 1940–, Kenyan track runner.
Keitel, Wilhelm, 1882–1946, Ger. field marshal.
Kekkonen, Urho Kaleva, 1900–86, president of Finland 1956–81.
Kekulé von Stradonitz, Friedrich August, 1829–96, Ger. chemist.
Keller, Helen Adams, 1880–1968, U.S. author & lecturer; blind and deaf from infancy.
Kelley, Clarence M., 1911–97, U.S. government official; director of the FBI 1973–77.
Kellogg, Frank Billings, 1856–1937, U.S. statesman; Nobel prize winner.
—**Will Keith,** 1860–1951, U.S. businessman.
Kelly, Alvin A. (Shipwreck), 1893–1952, U.S. flagpole sitter.
—**Ellsworth,** 1923–, U.S. painter & sculptor.
—**Emmett,** 1898–1979, U.S. circus clown.
—**Gene Curran,** 1912–96, U.S. dancer, singer, actor, choreographer, & film director.
—**George,** 1887–1971, U.S. playwright.

—**Walt(er),** 1913–73, U.S. cartoonist.
Kelvin, Lord (William Thompson), 1824–1907, Eng. physicist.
Kemble, Frances Anne (Fanny), 1809–93, Eng. actress.
Kempff, Wilhelm, 1895–1991, Ger. pianist.
Kempis, Thomas à, 1380–1471, Ger. mystic.
Kempton, (James) Murray, 1918–97, U.S. journalist & social critic.
Kendall, Edward Calvin, 1886–1972, U.S. biochemist; Nobel prize winner.
Kennan, George Frost, 1904–, U.S. statesman & author.
Kennedy A U.S. family prominent in politics, incl. **Joseph Patrick,** 1888–1969, businessman & diplomat, his wife **Rose Fitzgerald,** 1890–1995, & their sons, **Edward Moore,** 1932–, U.S. senator; **John Fitzgerald,** 1917–63, U.S. senator, 35th U.S. president 1961–63, assassinated; & **Robert Francis,** 1925–68, U.S. senator, assassinated.
Kennedy, Anthony M., 1936–, U.S. jurist; justice of the U.S. Supreme Court 1987–.
Kennelly, Arthur Edwin, 1861–1939, Indian-born U.S. electrical engineer.
Kenner, (William) Hugh, 1923–, Can. author & critic active in U.S.
Kenny, Elizabeth, 1886–1952, Austral. nurse & physiotherapist: called **Sister Kenny.**
Kent, Rockwell, 1882–1971, U.S. painter & illustrator.
Kenton, Stan, 1912–79, U.S. jazz musician.
Kenyatta, Jomo, 1893?–1978, African nationalist leader & first president of Kenya 1964–1978.
Keokuk, 1788?–1848, Sauk Am. Ind. leader.
Kepler, Johannes, 1571–1630, Ger. astronomer.
Kerensky, Alexander Feodorovich, 1881–1970, Russ. revolutionary leader & prime minister of Soviet provisional government 1917.
Kern, Jerome David, 1885–1945, U.S. composer.
Kerouac, Jack, 1922–69, U.S. author.
Kerr, Jean, 1923–, U.S. author & playwright.
—**Walter,** 1913–96, U.S. drama critic & author; husband of prec.
Kesey, Ken, 1935–, U.S. author.
Kesselring, Albert, 1887–1960, Ger. field marshal.
Ketcham, Hank, 1920–, U.S. cartoonist.
Kettering, Charles Franklin, 1876–1958, U.S. electrical engineer & inventor.
Key, Francis Scott, 1780?–1843, U.S. lawyer; wrote "The Star-Spangled Banner."
Keynes, John Maynard, 1883–1946, Eng. economist.
Khachaturian, Aram, 1903–78, Armenian-born Soviet composer.
Khama, Sir Seretse, 1921–80, president of Botswana 1965–80.
Khomeini, Ayatollah Ruhollah, 1899?–1989, Iranian religious and political leader.
Khorana, Har Gobind, 1922–, Indian-born U.S. biochemist.
Khrushchev, Nikita Sergeyevich, 1894–1971, premier of the Soviet Union 1953–64.
Kidd, Michael, 1919–, U.S. choreographer.
—**Captian William,** 1645?–1701, Eng. privateer & pirate; hanged.
Kieran, John Francis, 1892–1981, U.S. author & journalist.
Kierkegaard, Soren Aabye, 1813–55, Dan. philosopher & theologian.
Kiesinger, Kurt Georg, 1904–88, W. German politician; chancellor of W. Germany 1966–69.
Kilgallen, Dorothy, 1913–65, U.S. journalist.
Killy, Jean-Claude, 1943–, Fr. skier.
Kilmer, (Alfred) Joyce, 1886–1918, U.S. poet.
Kim Il Sung, 1912–94, Korean military leader; premier of N. Korea 1948–72, president 1972–94.
King, Billie Jean, 1943–, U.S. tennis player.
—**Coretta Scott,** 1927–, U.S. black civil rights leader; wife of Martin Luther, Jr.
—**Dennis,** 1897–1971, Eng. actor & singer.
—**Frank,** 1883–1969, U.S. cartoonist.
—**Martin Luther, Jr.,** 1929–68, U.S. clergyman & black civil rights leader; assassinated.
—**Stephen,** 1947–, U.S. author.

—**(William Lyon) Mackenzie,** 1874–1950, prime minister of Canada 1921–26, 1926–30 & 1935–48.

—**William Rufus Devane,** 1786–1853, U.S. statesman; U.S. vice president 1853.

Kingsley, Charles, 1819–75, Eng. clergyman & author.

—**Sidney,** 1906–95, U.S. playwright.

Kinsey, Alfred Charles, 1894–1956, U.S. zoologist; pioneered in studies of human sexual behavior.

Kipling, (Joseph) Rudyard, 1865–1936, Indian-born Eng. author.

Kipnis, Alexander, 1891–1978, Russ.-born U.S. basso.

—**Igor,** 1930–, Ger.-born U.S. harpsichordist; son of prec.

Kirchner, Ernst Ludwig, 1880–1938, Ger. painter.

Kirkland, Gelsey, 1953–, U.S. ballerina.

—**Lane,** 1922–, U.S. labor leader.

Kirkpatrick, Jeane, 1926–, U.S. diplomat & scholar.

Kirov, Sergei Mironovich, 1888–1934, Russ. revolutionary.

Kirstein, Lincoln, 1907–96, U.S. author, dance promoter, & ballet company director.

Kirsten, Dorothy, 1910–92, U.S. soprano.

Kissinger, Henry Alfred, 1923–, Ger.-born U.S. foreign-policy adviser; U.S. secretary of state 1973–77.

Kitchener, Horatio Herbert, (1st Earl Kitchener), 1850–1916, Brit. field marshal & statesman.

Kitt, Eartha, 1928–, U.S. singer.

Kittredge, George Lyman, 1860–1941, U.S. Shakespeare scholar & editor.

Klee, Paul, 1879–1940, Swiss painter.

Klein, Calvin, 1942–, U.S. fashion designer.

—**Lawrence Robert,** 1920–, economist; Nobel Prize winner.

Kleist, Heinrich von, 1777–1811, Ger. playwright.

Klemperer, Otto, 1885–1973, Ger. conductor.

Kliegl, Anton T., 1872–1927, & his brother **John H.,** 1869–1959, Ger.-born U.S. lighting experts.

Klimt, Gustav, 1862–1918, Austrian painter.

Kline, Franz Joseph, 1910–62, U.S. painter.

Klopstock, Friedrich Gottlieb, 1724–1803, Ger. poet.

Knievel, Robert (Evel), 1938–, U.S. motorcycle stunt man.

Knopf, Alfred Abraham, 1892–1984, U.S. publisher.

Knowles, John, 1926–, U.S. author.

Knox, John, 1507?–72, Scot. Protestant clergyman & religious reformer.

Koch, John, 1909–78, U.S. painter.

—**Robert,** 1843–1910, Ger. bacteriologist.

Kocher, Emil Theodor, 1841–1917, Swiss surgeon.

Kodály, Zoltan, 1882–1967, Hung. composer.

Koestler, Arthur, 1905–83, Hung.-born Eng. author.

Koffka, Kurt, 1886–1941, Ger.-born U.S. psychologist.

Kohl, Helmut, 1930–, chancellor of W. Germany, 1982–90; chancellor of Germany 1990–.

Kohler, Wolfgang, 1887–1967, Russ.-born U.S. psychologist.

Kokoschka, Oskar, 1886–1980, Austrian-born Brit. painter.

Kollwitz, Käthe, 1867–1945, Ger. painter, etcher, & lithographer.

Konoye, Prince Fumimaro, 1891–1945, premier of Japan 1937–39 & 1940–41.

Koo, V(i) K(uyuin) Wellington, 1887–1985, Chin. statesman & diplomat.

Kooweskoowe, b. John Ross, 1790–1866, Cherokee Am. Ind. leader.

Koppel, Ted (Edward James), 1940–, Eng.-born U.S. journalist.

Korda, Alexander, 1893–1956, Hung.-born Brit. film director.

Korngold, Erich Wolfgang, 1897–1957, Austrian-born U.S. composer, conductor, & pianist.

Korsakov, Sergei, 1853–1900, Russ. neurologist & psychiatrist.

Korzybski, Alfred Habdank Skarbek, 1879–1950, Pol.-born U.S. linguist.

Kosciusko, Thaddeus, 1746–1817, Pol. patriot in the Amer. Revolution.

Kosinski, Jerzy, 1933–91, Pol.-born novelist.

Kossel, Albrecht, 1853–1927, Ger. biochemist.

Kossuth, Lajos, 1802–94, Hung. patriot.

Kostelanetz, André, 1901–80, Russ.-born U.S. conductor.

Kosygin, Alexei Nikolayevich, 1904–80, Soviet statesman; premier of the Soviet Union 1964–80.

Koufax Sanford (Sandy), 1935–, U.S. baseball player.

Koussevitsky, Serge, 1874–1951, Russ.-born U.S. conductor.

Kovalevski, Alexander Onufriyevich, 1840–1901, Russ. embryologist.

Krafft-Ebing, Baron Richard von, 1840–1902, Ger. neurologist.

Kramer, Jack, 1921–, U.S. tennis player.

—**Stanley,** 1913–, U.S. film director.

Krebs, Sir Hans Adolf, 1900–81, Ger.-born Brit. biochemist; Nobel Prize winner.

Krehbiel, Henry Edward, 1854–1923, U.S. music critic.

Kreisky, Bruno, 1911–90, Austrian politician; chancellor of Austria 1970–83.

Kreisler, Fritz, 1875–1962, Austrian-born violinist.

Kresge, S.S., 1867–1966, U.S. merchant.

Kress, Samuel Henry, 1863–1955, U.S. businessman, art collector, & philanthropist.

Krips, Josef, 1902–74, Austrian conductor.

Krishna Menon, V(engalil) K(rishnan), 1896–1974, Indian statesman.

Kroc, Raymond A., 1902–84, U.S. restaurateur & businessman.

Krock, Arthur, 1886–1974, U.S. journalist.

Kroeber, Alfred Louis, 1876–1960, U.S. anthropologist.

Kropotkin, Prince Pyotr Alekseevich, 1842–1921, Russ. geographer & revolutionary.

Kruger, Paulus, 1825–1904, South African statesman; president of Transvaal 1883–1900.

Krupa, Gene, 1909–73, U.S. jazz musician.

Krupp, Alfred, 1812–87, Ger. munitions manufacturer.

Krupskaya, Nadezhda Konstantinovna, 1869–1939, Russ. social worker & revolutionist; wife of Nikolai Lenin.

Krutch, Joseph Wood, 1893–1970, U.S. critic & author.

Kubelik, Rafael, 1914–96, Czech conductor & composer.

Kublai Khan, 1216–94, founder of the Mongol dynasty of China.

Kubrick, Stanley, 1928–, U.S. film director.

Kühne, Willy, 1837–1900, Ger. physiologist.

Kun, Béla, 1885–1937, Hung. communist leader.

Küng, Hans, 1928–, Swiss theologian.

Kunitz, Stanley, 1905–, U.S. poet.

Kunstler, William M., 1919–95, U.S. lawyer.

Kurosawa, Akira, 1910–, Jap. film director.

Kurusu, Saburo, 1888–1954, Jap. diplomat.

Kusch, Polykarp, 1911–93, Ger.-born U.S. physicist & educator.

Kutuzov, Mikhail Ilarionovich, 1745–1813, Russ. field marshal.

Kuznets, Simon, 1901–85, Russ.-born U.S. economist; Nobel Prize winner.

Kyd, Thomas, 1558–94, Eng. playwright.

La Bruyère, Jean de, 1645–96, Fr. author.

LaChaise, François d'Aix de, 1624–1709, Fr. Jesuit priest.

Lachaise, Gaston, 1882–1935, Fr.-born U.S. sculptor.

Laemmle, Carl, 1867–1939, Ger.-born U.S. film producer.

Laënnec, René, 1781–1826, Fr. physician.

La Farge, Christopher Grant, 1862–1938, U.S. architect.

—**John,** 1835–1910, U.S. painter & stained-glass craftsman.

—**Oliver Hazard Perry,** 1901–63, U.S. anthropologist & author.

Lafayette, Marie Joseph du Motier, Marquis de, 1757–1834, Fr. general & patriot; served in Amer. revolutionary army.

Lafitte, Jean, 1780?–1825?, Fr. pirate active in U.S.

La Follette, Robert Marion, 1855–1925, U.S. senator & Progressive Party presidential candidate.

La Fontaine, Jean de, 1621–95, Fr. poet & writer of fables.

Lagerkvist, Pär, 1891–1974, Swed. author, poet, & playwrite.

Lagerlöf, Selma, 1858–1940, Swed. author; Nobel Prize winner.

Lagrange, Joseph Louis, 1736–1813, Fr. mathematician & astronomer.

La Guardia, Fiorello Henry, 1882–1947, U.S. politician; mayor of New York City 1934–45.

Lahr, Bert, 1895–1967, U.S. comedian & actor.

Laine, (Papa) Jack, 1873–1966, U.S. jazz musician.

Laing, R(onald) D., 1927–89, Scot. psychoanalyst & author.

Lalo, Victor Antoine Édouard, 1823–92, Fr. composer.

Lamarck, Jean Baptiste de Monet, Chevalier de, 1744–1829, Fr. naturalist.

Lamarr, Hedy, 1915–, Austrian-born U.S. actress.

Lamartine, Alphonse Marie Louis de Prat de, 1790–1869, Fr. poet.

Lamb, Charles, 1775–1834, Eng. author: pseud. **Elia.**

—**Mary,** 1764–1847, Eng. author; sister of prec.

—**Willis Eugene, Jr.,** 1913–, U.S. nuclear physicist; Nobel Prize winner.

L'Amour, Louis Dearborn, 1908–88, U.S. author.

Land, Edwin Herbert, 1909–91, U.S. inventor & industrialist.

Landau, Lev Davidovich, 1908–68, Soviet physicist; Nobel Prize winner.

Landers, Ann, pseud. of Esther Pauline Friedman, 1918–, U.S. columnist.

Landis, Kenesaw Mountain, 1866–1944, U.S. jurist & baseball commissioner.

Landon, Alf(red Mossman), 1887–1987, U.S. politician.

Landor, Walter Savage, 1775–1864, Eng. poet & author.

Landowska, Wanda, 1879–1959, Pol. harpsichordist active in U.S. after 1941.

Landru, Henri, 1869–1922, Fr. murderer; executed: known as **the modern Bluebeard.**

Landseer, Sir Edwin Henry, 1802–73, Eng. painter.

Landsteiner, Karl, 1868–1943, Austrian-born U.S. pathologist; Nobel Prize winner.

Lane, Burton, 1912–97, U.S. composer.

Lang, Andrew, 1844–1912, Scot. poet, scholar, & author.

—**Fritz,** 1890–1976, Austrian-born U.S. film director.

—**Paul Henry,** 1901–91, U.S. music critic.

Langdon, Harry, 1884–1944, U.S. vaudeville performer.

Lange, David Russell, 1942–, New Zealand statesman; prime minister 1984–89.

—**Dorothea,** 1895–1965, U.S. photographer.

Langer, Susanne, 1895–1985, U.S. philosopher & educator.

Langland, William, 1332?–1400, Eng. poet.

Langley, John Newport, 1851–1925, Eng. physiologist.

—**Samuel Pierpont,** 1834–1906, U.S. astronomer.

Langmuir, Irving, 1881–1957, U.S. chemist; Nobel Prize winner.

Langtry, Lillie, 1853–1929, Eng. actress.

Lanier, Sidney, 1842–81, U.S. poet.

Lankester, Sir Edwin Ray, 1847–1929, Eng. zoologist.

Lansky, Meyer, 1902–83, U.S. criminal.

Lanza, Mario, 1925–59, U.S. singer & actor.

Lao-tse, 604?–531? B.C., Chin. philosopher & mystic; founder of Taoism.

Laplace, Pierre Simon, Marquis de, 1749–1827, Fr. mathematician & astronomer.

Lapp, Ralph Eugene, 1917–, U.S. physicist.

Lardner, Ring(gold Wilmer), 1885–1933, U.S. author.

La Rochefoucauld, Duc François de, 1613–80, Fr. writer.

Larousse, Pierre Athanase, 1817–75, Fr.grammarian & lexicographer.

La Salle, Sieur Robert, Cavalier de, 1643–87, Fr. explorer.

Lashley, Karl Spencer, 1890–1958, U.S. psychologist.

Lasker, Albert Davis, 1880–1952, Ger.-born U.S. businessman & philanthropist.

—**Emmanuel,** 1868–1941, Ger. mathematician & chess master.

Laski, Harold Joseph, 1893–1950, Eng. political scientist.

Lasso, Orlando di, 1532?–94, Du. composer.

Laszlo, Ernest, 1899–1984, Hung. cinematographer.

Latimer, Hugh, 1485?–1555, Eng. Protestant martyr.

La Tour, Georges de, 1593–1652, Fr. painter.

Latrobe, Benjamin Henry, 1764–1820, Eng.-born U.S. architect & engineer.

Lattimore, Owen, 1900–89, U.S. author & oriental expert.

Lauder, Sir Harry, 1870–1950, Scot. singer.

Laue, Max Theodor Felix von, 1879–1960, Ger. physicist; Nobel Prize winner.

Laughton, Charles, 1899–1962, Eng.-born U.S. actor.

Laurel, (Arthur) Stan(ley), 1890–1965, Eng.-born U.S. comedian & actor.

Laurencin, Marie, 1885–1956, Fr. painter.

Laurents, Arthur, 1918–, U.S. playwright.

Laurier, Sir Wilfrid, 1841–1919, Can. statesman; prime minister 1896–1911.

Laval, Pierre, 1883–1945, Fr. lawyer & politician.

LaValliére, Louise LeBlanc, Duchesse de, 1644–1710, mistress of Louis XIV.

Laver, Rod(ney George), 1938–, Austral. tennis player.

Laveran, Charles Louis Alphonse, 1845–1922, Fr. physician; Nobel Prize winner.

Lavoisier, Antoine Laurent, 1743–94, Fr. chemist & physicist.

Lavrovsky, Leonid M., 1905–67, Soviet choreographer.

Law, Andrew Bonar, 1858–1923, Brit. statesman; prime minister 1922–23.

—**John,** 1671–1729, Scot. financier & speculator.

Lawes, Lewis Edward, 1883–1947, U.S. penologist.

Lawrence, David, 1888–1973, U.S. journalist.

—**D(avid) H(erbert),** 1885–1930, Eng. author & poet.

—**Ernest Orlando,** 1901–58, U.S. pysicist.

—**Gertrude,** 1898–1952, Eng. actress active in U.S.

—**Sir Thomas,** 1769–1830, Eng. painter.

—**Thomas, Edward,** 1888–1935, Welsh soldier, archaeologist, & author: known as **Lawrence of Arabia.**

Laxness, Halldór Kiljan, 1902–98, Icelandic author; Nobel Prize winner.

Layne, Robert, 1926–, U.S. football player.

Lazarus, Emma, 1849–87, U.S. poet & author.

Leacock, Stephen Butler, 1869–1944, Can. economist & humorist.

Leadbelly, b. Huddie Ledbetter, 1888?–1949, U.S. folk singer.

Leahy, William Daniel, 1875–1959, U.S. admiral.

Leakey, Louis Seymour Blazett, 1903–72, and his wife **Mary Nicol Leakey,** 1913–, Brit. anthropologists.

—**Richard E.,** 1944–, Kenyan anthropologist; son of prec.

Lean, Sir David, 1908–91, Eng. film director.

Lear, Edward, 1812–88, Eng. poet, painter, & illustrator.

—**William Powell,** 1902–78, U.S. engineer & manufacturer.

Leavis, F(rank) R(aymond), 1895–1978, Eng. critic.

Le Brun, Charles, 1619–90, Fr. painter.

Le Carré, John, pseud. of David J. M. Cornwell, 1931–, Eng. author.

Leconte de Lisle, Charles Marie, 1818–94, Fr. poet.

Lederberg, Joshua, 1925–, U.S. geneticist.

Lee, Ann, 1736–84, Eng. mystic; founder of the Shaker movement in America.

—**Francis Lightfoot,** 1734–97, Amer. revolutionary patriot.

—**Gypsy Rose,** 1914–70, U.S. stripteaser & author.

—**Harper,** 1926–, U.S. novelist.

—**Henry,** 1756–1818, Amer. revolutionary soldier & statesman: known as **Light-Horse Harry Lee.**

—**Peggy,** 1920–, U.S. singer.

—**Richard Henry,** 1732–94, Amer. revolutionary patriot.

—**Robert E(dward),** 1807–70, commander in chief of the Confederate Army; son of Henry.

—**Tsung-Dao,** 1926–, Chin.-born U.S. physicist.

Leeuwenhoek, Anton van, 1632–1723, Du. naturalist.

Le Gallienne, Eva, 1899–1991, Eng.-born U.S. actress.

—**Richard,** 1866–1947, Eng. author; father of prec.

Léger, Fernand, 1881–1955, Fr. painter.

Le Guin, Ursula, 1929–, U.S. author.

Lehár, Franz, 1870–1948, Austrian composer.

Lehman, Herbert Henry, 1878–1963, U.S. banker & politician.

Lehmann, Lili, 1848–1929, Ger. soprano.

—**Lotte,** 1888–1976, Ger. soprano.

Lehmbruck, Wilhelm, 1881–1919, Ger. sculptor.

Leibniz, Baron Gottfried Wilhelm von, 1646–1716, Ger. philosopher & mathematician.

Leicester, Robert Dudley, 1st Earl of, 1532?–88, Eng. courtier.

Leider, Frida, 1888–1975, Ger. soprano.

Leigh, Mitch, 1928–, U.S. composer.

—**Vivien,** 1913–67, Indian-born Eng. actress.

Leinsdorf, Erich, 1912–93, Austrian-born U.S. conductor.

LeMay, Curtis Emerson, 1906–90, U.S. air force officer.

Lemnitzer, Lyman L., 1899–1988, U.S. general.

Lenard, Phillip E. A., 1862–1947, Ger. physicist.

Lenclos, Ninon de, 1620–1705, Fr. courtesan & wit.

L'Enfant, Pierre Charles, 1754–1825, Fr. architect; planned Washington, D.C.

L'Engle, Madeleine, 1918–, U.S. author.

Lenglen, Suzanne, 1899–1938, Fr. tennis player.

Lenin, Nikolai, b. Vladimir Ilich Ulyanov, 1870–1924, Russ. revolutionary leader; premier of Soviet Union 1918–24.

Lennon, John, 1940–80, Eng. composer & musical performer.

Lenya, Lotte, 1900–81, Austrian singer & actress active in U.S.

Lenz, Heinrich F. E., 1804–65, Russ. physicist.

Leo I, Saint, 390?–461, pope 440–461: called **the Great**.

—III, Saint, 750?–816, pope 795–816.

—X, b. Giovanni de' Medici, 1475–1521, pope 1513–21.

Leonardo da Vinci, 1452–1519, Ital. painter, sculptor, architect, engineer, inventor, musician, scientist, & natural philosopher.

Leoncavallo, Ruggiero, 1858–1919, Ital. composer & librettist.

Leone, Giovanni, 1908–, Ital. politician; president of Italy 1971–78.

Leonidas, 5th c. B.C. Gk. military leader: king of Sparta 490?–480 B.C.

Leontief, Wassily W., 1906–, Russ.-born U.S. economist & author; Nobel Prize winner.

Leopardi, Count Giacomo, 1798–1837, Ital. poet.

Lepidus, Marcus Aemilius, ?–13 B.C., Roman statesman.

Lermontov, Mikhail Yurievich, 1814–41, Russ. poet & author.

Lerner, Alan Jay, 1918–86, U.S. playwright & lyricist.

—Max, 1902–92, Russ.-born U.S. author & journalist.

Le Roy, Mervyn, 1900–87, U.S. film director.

Lescaze, William, 1896–1969, U.S. architect.

Leschetizky, Theodor, 1830–1915, Russ. pianist & composer.

Lesseps, Count Ferdinand de, 1805–94, Fr. engineer; built Suez Canal.

Lessing, Doris, 1919–, Iranian-born Brit. author.

—Gotthold Ephraim, 1729–81, Ger. playwright & critic.

Lester, Richard, 1932–, Eng. film director.

Leutze, Emanuel Gottlieb, 1816–68, Ger.-born U.S. painter.

Levant, Oscar, 1906–72, U.S. pianist, composer, & author.

Levene, Phoebus A. T., 1869–1940, Russ.-born U.S. chemist.

—Sam, 1905–80, Russ.-born U.S. actor.

Levenson, Sam, 1911–80, U.S. humorist.

Leverholme, Viscount, b. William Hesketh Lever, 1851–1925, Brit. industrialist.

Leverrier, Urbain Jean Joseph, 1811–77, Fr. astronomer.

Levertov, Denise, 1923–97, Eng.-born U.S. poet.

Lévesque, René, 1922–87, Can. politician.

Levin, Ira, 1929–, U.S. author.

Levine, Jack, 1915–, U.S. painter.

—James, 1943–, U.S. conductor & music director.

—Joseph E., 1905–87, U.S. film producer.

Lévi-Strauss, Claude, 1908–, Belg.-born Fr. anthropologist.

Lewin, Kurt, 1890–1947, Ger.-born U.S. psychologist.

Lewis, Anthony, 1927–, U.S. journalist.

—Cecil Day See DAY-LEWIS, CECIL.

—C(live) S(taples), 1898–1963, Eng. author.

—Gilbert Newton, 1875–1946, U.S. chemist.

—Jerry, 1926–, U.S. actor & comedian.

—John L(lewellyn), 1880–1969, U.S. labor leader.

—Meriwether, 1774–1809, U.S. explorer.

—Oscar, 1914–70, U.S. sociologist & author.

—(Percy) Wyndham, 1884–1957, Eng. painter & author.

—Sinclair, 1885–1951, U.S. author.

Lewisohn, Ludwig, 1883–1955, Ger.born U.S. author & critic.

Lhevinne, Joseph, 1874–1944, Russ.-born U.S. pianist.

Li, Choh Hao, 1913–87, Chin.-born U.S. biochemist.

Libby, W(illard) F(rank), 1908–80, U.S. chemist; Nobel Prize winner.

Liberace, (Wladziu), 1919–87, U.S. pianist.

Lichtenstein, Roy, 1923–97, U.S. artist.

Liddell Hart, Basil Henry, 1895–1970, Eng. military scientist.

Lie, Trygve, 1896–1968, Norw. statesman; first secretary general of the U.N. 1946–53.

Liebig, Baron Justus von, 1803–73, Ger. chemist.

Lifar, Serge, 1905–86, Russ. dancer.

Ligeti, György, 1923–, Hung. composer.

Lilienthal, David Eli, 1899–1981, U.S. lawyer & administrator.

Lillie, Beatrice, 1898–1989, Can.-born comedienne & actress active in England & U.S.

Lilly, John C., 1915–, U.S. neurophysiologist & biophysicist.

Limón, José, 1908–72, Mexican-born U.S. dancer, choreographer, & dance company director.

Lincoln, Abraham, 1809–65, 16th U.S. president 1861–65; assassinated.

—Robert Todd, 1843–1926, U.S. statesman & lawyer; son of prec.

Lind, James, 1716–94, Scot. physician.

—Jenny, 1820–87, Swed. soprano.

Lindbergh, Anne Morrow, 1906–, U.S. author.

—Charles Augustus, 1902–74, U.S. aviator; made first transatlantic nonstop solo flight 1927; husband of prec.

Lindsay, Howard, 1889–1968, U.S. playwright.

—John Vliet, 1921–, U.S. politician.

—(Nicholas) Vachel, 1879–1931, U.S. poet.

Linklater, Eric, 1899–1974, Eng. author.

Linkletter, Art, 1912–, Can. radio & TV personality & author.

Linnaeus, Carolus, b. Karl von Linné, 1707–78, Swed. botanist & taxonomist.

Lin Biao, 1907–71, Chin. political leader.

Lin Yutang, 1895–1976, Chin. philologist & author.

Lipchitz, Jacques, 1891–1973, Lithuanian-born sculptor active in U.S.

Li Po, 700?–762, Chin. poet.

Lippi, Fra Filippo (Lippo), 1406?–69, & his son **Filippino,** 1457?–1504, Ital. painters.

Lippmann, Walter, 1889–1974, U.S. journalist.

Lippold, Richard, 1915–, U.S. sculptor.

Lipset, Seymour Martin, 1922–, U.S. sociologist.

Lipton, Sir Thomas Johnstone, 1850–1931, Irish merchant & yachtsman.

Lissajous, Jules A., 1822–80, Fr. physicist.

Lister, Joseph, 1827–1912, Eng. surgeon.

Liszt, Franz, 1811–86, Hung. composer & pianist.

Littlewood, Joan, 1916–, Eng. theater director.

Litvinov, Maxim Maximovich, 1876–1951, Russ. revolutionary & statesman.

Liu Shaoji, 1898–1973, Chin. government official.

Livingstone, David, 1813–73, Scot. missionary & explorer in Africa.

—Mary, 1916–83, U.S. radio personality.

Livy, (Titus Livius), 59 B.C.–A.D. 17, Roman historian.

Llewellyn, Richard, 1906–83, Brit. novelist & playwright.

Lloyd George, David, 1863–1945, Brit. statesman; prime minister 1916–22.

Lloyd, Harold Clayton, 1894–1971, U.S. actor & film producer.

Lobachevski, Nikolai Ivanovich, 1793–1856, Russ. mathematician.

Locke, John, 1632–1704, Eng. philosopher.

Lockwood, Belva Ann Bennett, 1830–1917, U.S. social reformer & suffrage leader.

Lodge, Henry Cabot, 1902–85, U.S. politician & diplomat.

Loesser, Frank, 1910–69, U.S. composer & lyricist.

Loewe, Frederick, 1904–88, Austrian-born U.S. composer.

Loewi, Otto, 1873–1961, Ger.-born U.S. pharmacologist.

Loewy, Raymond Fernand, 1893–1986, Fr.-born U.S. industrial designer.

Lofting, Hugh John, 1886–1947, Eng.-born U.S. author & illustrator.

Logan, Joshua, 1908–88, U.S. stage & film director, producer, & author.

Lomax, John Avery, 1867–1948, & his son **Alan,** 1915–, U.S. folk-song collectors.

Lombard, Carole, 1909–42, U.S. actress.

Lombardi, Vincent Thomas, 1913–70, U.S. football coach.

Lombardo, Guy Albert, 1902–77, Can.-born U.S. bandleader.

Lombrosso, Cesare, 1836–1909, Ital. criminologist & physician.

London, George, 1920–85, Can. bass-baritone.

—Jack, 1876–1916, U.S. author.

Long, Crawford Williamson, 1815–78, U.S. surgeon.

—Huey Pierce, 1893–1935, U.S. lawyer & politician; assassinated.

Longfellow, Henry Wadsworth, 1807–82, U.S. poet.

Longstreet, James, 1821–1904, U.S. Confederate general.

Lon Nol, 1913–85, Cambodian general; president of Kampuchea 1970–75.

Loos, Anita, 1888–1981, U.S. author.

Lopez Portillo, José, 1920–, president of Mexico 1976–1982.

Loren, Sophia, 1934–, Ital. actress.

Lorentz, Hendrik Antoon, 1853–1928, Du. physicist & author; Nobel Prize winner.

Lorenz, Konrad Zacharias, 1903–89, Austrian zoologist.

Lorre, Peter, 1904–64, Hung.-born actor active in U.S.

Losey, Joseph, 1909–84, U.S. film director active in England.

Louis IX (Saint Louis), 1214–70, king of France 1226–70.

—XIII, 1601–43, king of France 1610–43.

—XIV, 1638–1715, king of France 1643–1715; son of prec.

—XV, 1710–74, king of France 1715–74; great-grandson of prec.

—XVI, 1754–93, king of France 1774–92; guillotined; grandson of prec.

—XVIII, 1755–1824, king of France 1814–15 & 1815–24; brother of prec.

Louis Philippe, 1773–1850, king of France 1830–48.

Louis, Joe, 1914–81, U.S. boxer.

Lovecraft, H(oward) P(hillips), 1890–1937, U.S. author.

Lovelace, Richard, 1618–58, Eng. poet.

Lovell, Sir (Alfred Charles) Bernard, 1913–, Eng. astronomer.

Low, Sir David, 1891–1963, New Zealand-born Brit. cartoonist.

—Juliette Gordon, 1860–1927, U.S. founder of the Girl Scouts.

Lowell, Amy, 1873–1925, U.S. poet & critic.

—James Russell, 1819–91, U.S. poet & author.

—Percival, 1855–1916, U.S. astronomer; brother of Amy.

—Robert (Traill Spence, Jr.), 1917–77, U.S. poet.

Lowry, Malcolm, 1909–57, Eng. author.

Loy, Myrna, 1905–93, U.S. actress.

Loyola, Saint Ignatius, b. Iñigo do Oñez y Loyola, 1491–1556, Sp. soldier & priest; founder with Francis Xavier of the Society of Jesus.

Lubitsch, Ernst, 1892–1947, Ger.-born U.S. film director.

Lübke, Heinrich, 1894–1972, W. German government official; president of W. Germany 1959–69.

Lucas, George, 1944–, U.S. film producer, director, & writer.

Luce, Clare Boothe, 1903–87, U.S. writer & diplomat.

—Henry Robinson, 1898–1967, U.S. editor & publisher; husband of prec.

Luckman, Sidney, 1916–, U.S. football player.

Lucretius, 96?–55 B.C., Roman poet & philosopher.

Lucullus, Lucius Licinius, 1st c. B.C. Roman general & epicure.

Ludlum, Robert, 1927–, U.S. author.

Luening, Otto, 1900–96, U.S. composer.

Lugosi, Bela, 1882–1956, Romanian-born actor active in U.S.

Lukas, J. Anthony, 1933–, U.S. journalist.

—Paul, 1895–1971, Hung.-born actor active in U.S.

Lully, Jean Baptiste, 1633?–87, Ital.-born Fr. composer.

Lumet, Sidney, 1924–, U.S. film director.

Lumumba, Patrice, 1925–61, first prime minister of the Congolese Republic 1960–61; assassinated.

Lunt, Alfred, 1892–1977, U.S. actor.

Lupino, Ida, 1918–95, Eng.-born U.S. actress.

Luria, Salvador Edward, 1912–91, Ital.-born U.S. microbiologist.

Lusinchi, Jaime, 1924–, Venezuelan statesman; president 1984–88.

Luther, Martin, 1483–1546, Ger. monk, theologian, & leader of the Protestant Reformation.

Luthuli, Albert J., 1898–1967, South African civil rights leader.

Luxemburg, Rosa, 1871–1919, Ger. socialist leader.

Lwoff, André, 1902–94, Fr. microbiologist; Nobel Prize winner.

Lycurgus, 7th c. B.C. Spartan lawgiver.

Lyell, Sir Charles, 1797–1875, Eng. geologist.

Lyly, John, 1554?–1606, Eng. author.

Lynch, Charles, 1736–96, U.S. justice of the peace.

Lynd, Robert Staughton, 1892–1970, & his wife **Helen Merrell,** 1897–1982, U.S. sociologists.

Lysenko, Trofim Denisovich, 1898–1976, Soviet agronomist.

Maazel, Lorin, 1930–, Fr. conductor active in U.S.

Mabuse, Jan, b. Jan Gossaert, 1478–1533?, Flemish painter.

MacArthur, Charles, 1895–1956, U.S. playwright.

—Douglas, 1880–1964, U.S. general & commander in chief of Allies in sw Pacific, World War II.

Macaulay, Thomas Babington, 1800–59, Eng. historian, author, & statesman.

Macbeth, ?–1057, king of Scotland 1040–57.

Maccabeus, Judas, ?–150? B.C., Jewish patriot.

MacDiarmid, Hugh, pseud. of Christopher Murray Grieve, 1892–1978, Scot. poet.

MacDonald, George, 1824–1905, Scot. author.

—Dwight, 1906–82, U.S. critic & author.

—J(ames) E(dward) H(ervey), 1873–1932, Can. painter & poet.

—(James) Ramsey, 1866–1937, Eng. statesman.

—Jeanette, 1906–65, U.S. actress & singer.

—Sir John Alexander, 1815–91, Scot.-born Can. statesman; prime minister 1867–73 & 1878–91.

—John P., 1916–87, U.S. author.

MacDowell, Edward Alexander, 1861–1908, U.S. composer.

Macfadden, Bernarr, 1868–1955, U.S. physical culturist & publisher.

Mach, Ernst, 1838–1916, Austrian physicist.

Machiavelli, Niccolò, 1469–1527, Florentine statesman, political theorist, & author.

MacInnes, Helen, 1907–85, Scot. author.

MacIver, Robert Morrison, 1882–1970, Scot.-born U.S. sociologist.

Mack, Connie, 1862–1956, U.S. baseball player & manager.

Mackenzie, Alexander, 1822–92, Scot.-born Can. statesman; prime minister 1873–78.

—Sir Alexander, 1764–1820, Scot.-born Can. trader & explorer.

—William Lyon, 1795–1861, Scot.-born Can. insurgent leader.

MacLeish, Archibald, 1892–1982, U.S. poet.

MacLennan, Hugh, 1907–90, Can. author.

Macleod, John James Rickard, 1876–1935, Scot. physiologist.

MacMahon, Aline, 1899–1991, U.S. actress.

—Comte Marie Edmé Patrice, 1808–93, Fr. general; president of France 1873–79.

MacManus, Seumas, 1869–1960, Irish author, poet, & playwright.

MacMillan, Donald Baxter, 1874–1970, U.S. polar explorer.

—Sir Ernest, Campbell, 1893–1973, Can. conductor & composer.

—Kenneth, 1929–92, Scottish dancer, choreographer, & ballet company director.

—(Maurice) Harold, 1894–1987, Eng.statesman; prime minister 1957–63.

MacNeice, Louis, 1907–63, Irish-born Brit. poet.

MacNelly, Jeff, 1947–, U.S. political cartoonist.

Madison, Dolley, b. Dorothea Payne, 1768–1849, U.S. first lady & hostess.

—James, 1751–1836, 4th U.S. president 1809–17; husband of prec.

Maecenas, Gaius Cilnius, 73?–8 B.C., Roman statesman & patron of Horace & Virgil.

Maes, Nicolaes, 1632–93, Du. painter.

Maeterlinck, Maurice, 1862–1949, Belg. poet & playwright.

Magellan, Ferdinand, 1480–1521, Pg. explorer.

Magendie, François, 1783–1855, Fr. physiologist.

Maginot, Andre, 1877–1932, Fr. politician.
Magnani, Anna, 1908–73, Ital. actress.
Magritte, René, 1898–1967, Belg. painter.
Magsaysay, Ramón, 1907–57, Filipino statesman; president of the Philippines 1953–57.
Mahan, Alfred Thayer, 1840–1914, U.S. naval officer & historian.
Maharishi Mahesh Yogi, 1911?–, Indian guru.
Mahavira, Vardhamana Jnatiputra, ca. 6th c. B.C., Indian religious leader; founder of Jainism.
Mahler, Gustav, 1860–1911, Austrian composer & conductor.
Mailer, Norman, 1923–, U.S. author.
Maillol, Aristide, 1861–1944, Fr. sculptor.
Maimonides, 1135–1204, Sp. rabbi & philosopher.
Maintenon, Françoise d'Aubigné, Marquise de, 1635–1719, second wife of Louis XIV of France.
Maitland, Frederic William, 1850–1906, Eng. historian.
Major, John Roy, 1943–, Eng. statesman; prime minister of Great Britain 1989–.
Makarios III, 1913–77, Cypriot Greek Orthodox archbishop; president of Cyprus 1960–74 & 1875–77.
Makarova, Natalya, 1940–, Russ. ballerina active in U.S.
Malamud, Bernard, 1914–86, U.S. author.
Malan, Daniel F., 1874–1959, Afrikaner statesman.
Malcolm X, b. Malcolm Little, 1925–65, U.S. black leader; assassinated.
Malenkov, Georgi Maximilianovich, 1902–88, premier of the Soviet Union 1953–55.
Malibran, Maria Felicita, 1808–36, Sp. opera singer.
Malinowski, Bronislaw Kasper, 1884–1942, Pol.-born U.S. anthropologist.
Mallarmé, Stéphane, 1842–98, Fr. poet.
Malle, Louis, 1932–95, Fr. film director.
Mallon, Mary, 1870?–1938, U.S. domestic servant & typhoid carrier: called **Typhoid Mary.**
Malory, Sir Thomas, ?–1470?, Eng. writer; translated Arthurian legends into English.
Malpighi, Marcello, 1628–94, Ital. anatomist.
Malraux, André, 1901–76, Fr. author & government official.
Malthus, Thomas Robert, 1766–1834, Eng. political economist.
Mamet, David, 1947–, U.S. playwright.
Mamoulian, Rouben, 1897–1987, Russ.-born U.S. stage director.
Mancini, Henry, 1924–94, U.S. composer & pianist.
Manes, 216?–276?, Pers. prophet; founder of Manicheism.
Manet, Édouard, 1832–83, Fr. painter.
Maney, Richard, 1891–1968, U.S. press agent.
Mankiewicz, Joseph L., 1909–93, U.S. film director & screenwriter.
Mann, Horace, 1796–1859, U.S. educator.
—**Thomas,** 1875–1955, Ger.-born U.S. author; Nobel Prize winner.
Mannes, Marya, 1904–90, U.S. author & journalist.
Manolete, b. Manuel Laureano Rodríguez y Sánchez, 1917–47, Sp. bullfighter.
Mansart, Jules Hardouin, 1646?–1708, Fr. architect.
Mansfield, Katherine, 1888–1923, New Zealand-born Brit. author.
—**Michael Joseph (Mike),** 1903–, U.S. senator & ambassador.
—**Richard,** 1854–1907, Eng. actor active in U.S.
Mantegna, Andrea, 1431–1506, Ital. painter & engraver.
Mantle, Mickey Charles, 1931–95, U.S. baseball player.
Mantovani, Annunzio, 1905–80, Ital. conductor.
Manulis, Martin, 1915–, U.S. radio & TV producer.
Manutius, Aldus, b. Teobaldo Manucci, 1450–1515, Ital. printer & classical scholar.
Manzoni, Alessandro Francesco, 1785–1873, Ital. author.
Mao Zedong (Tse-tung), 1893–1976, Chin. statesman; chairman of Chin. Communist Party 1954–76.
Marat, Jean Paul, 1743–93, Fr. revolutionary leader; assassinated by Charlotte Corday.
Marble Alice, 1913–90, U.S. tennis player.
Marc, Franz, 1880–1916, Ger. painter.
Marceau, Marcel, 1923–, Fr. mime.
Marcel, Gabriel, 1889–1973, Fr. philosopher.

March, Fredric, 1897–1975, U.S. actor.
Marciano, Rocky, 1924–69, U.S. boxer.
Marconi, Guglielmo, 1874–1937, Ital. inventor of wireless telegraphy.
Marcos, Ferdinand Edralin, 1917–89, Filipino politician; president of the Philippines 1965–86.
Marcus Aurelius, A.D. 121–180, Roman emperor & philosopher.
Marcuse, Herbert, 1898–1979, Ger.-born U.S. philosopher.
Margaret, 1353–1412, queen of Denmark, Norway, & Sweden.
Margaret Rose, 1930–, Eng. princess, the sister of Queen Elizabeth II.
Margrethe II, 1940–, queen of Denmark 1972–.
Maria Theresa, 1717–80, queen of Hungary & Bohemia, & Holy Roman empress.
Marie Antoinette, 1755–93, Austrian-born queen of Louis XVI of France; guillotined.
Marignac, Jean de, 1817–94, Swiss chemist.
Marin, John Cheri, 1870–1953, U.S. painter.
Marini, Marino, 1901–80, Ital. sculptor.
Marion, Francis, 1732?–95, Amer. revolutionary commander: called **the Swamp Fox.**
Maris, Roger, 1934–85, U.S. baseball player.
Maritain, Jacques, 1882–1973, Fr. philosopher.
Markevich, Igor, 1912–83, Russ.-born Swiss conductor.
Markham, (Charles) Edwin, 1852–1940, U.S. poet.
Markova, Dame Alicia, 1910–, Eng. ballerina.
Marks, Johnny, 1909–85, U.S. composer.
Marlborough, John Churchill, Duke of, 1650–1722, Eng. general & statesman.
Marlowe, Christopher, 1564–93, Eng. playwright.
—**Julia,** 1866–1950, Eng.-born U.S. actress.
Marriner, Neville, 1925–, Brit. conductor.
Marquand, J(ohn) P(hillips), 1893–1960, U.S. author.
Marquette, Jacques, 1637–75, Fr. explorer of America.
Marquis, Don(ald Robert Perry), 1878–1937, U.S. journalist & humorist.
Marsh, Dame Ngaio, 1899–1982, New Zealand author.
—**Reginald,** 1898–1954, U.S. painter.
Marshall, George Catlett, 1880–1959, U.S. general & statesman; chief of staff of U.S. Army in World War II; Nobel Prize winner.
—**John,** 1755–1835, U.S. statesman & jurist; chief justice of the U.S. Supreme Court 1801–35.
—**Thurgood,** 1908–93, U.S. jurist; justice of the U.S. Supreme Court 1967–91.
Martel, Charles, 688?–741, Frankish king 715–741; grandfather of Charlemagne.
Martí, José (Julián), 1853–95, Cuban lawyer & revolutionary.
Martial (L. Marcus Valerius Martialis), A.D. 40?–104?, Roman poet.
Martin, John Joseph, 1893–1985, U.S. dance critic.
—**Mary,** 1913–90, U.S. singer & actress.
Martin du Gard, Roger, 1881–1958, Fr. author; Nobel Prize winner.
Martinelli, Giovanni, 1885–1969, Ital. tenor active in U.S.
Martini, Simone, 1283?–1344, Ital. painter.
Marvell, Andrew, 1621–78, Eng. poet.
Marx A family of U.S. actors & comedians; four brothers: **Arthur (Harpo),** 1893–1964; **Herbert (Zeppo),** 1901–79; **Julius (Groucho),** 1890–1977; **Leonard (Chico),** 1891–1961.
—**Karl,** 1818–83, Ger. socialist writer.
Mary I, 1516–58, queen of England 1553–58; known as **Bloody Mary** or **Mary Tudor.**
—**II,** 1662–94, queen of England 1689–94; co-ruler with her husband, William III.
Mary, Queen of Scots (Mary Stuart), 1542–87, queen of Scotland 1561–67; beheaded.
Masaccio, b. Tommaso Cassai, 1401–28, Florentine painter.
Masaryk, Jan Garrigue, 1886–1948, Czech diplomat & politician.
—**Thomas,** 1850–1937, first president of Czechoslovakia 1918–35; father of prec.
Mascagni, Pietro, 1863–1945, Ital. composer.
Masefield, John, 1878–1967, Eng. poet.

Maslow, Abraham, 1908–70, U.S. author & psychologist.

Mason, Charles, 1730–87, Eng. astronomer & surveyor; with Jeremiah Dixon, established Mason-Dixon line.

—James, 1909–84, Eng.-born actor active in U.S.

Massasoit, 1580?–1661, Am. Ind. chief of the Wampanoag tribes of Massachusetts.

Massenet, Jules, 1842–1912, Fr. composer.

Massey, Raymond, 1896–1983, Can.-born U.S. actor.

Massine, Leonide, 1896–1979, Russ.-born U.S. choreographer & dancer.

Masters, Edgar Lee, 1869–1950, U.S. poet.

—William Howell, 1915–, U.S. physician & sex researcher.

Masterson, William Barclay (Bat), 1853–1921, U.S. frontier peace officer & journalist.

Mastroianni, Marcello, 1924–96, Ital. actor.

Mata Hari, b. Margaretha Gertrud Zelle, 1876–1917, Du. dancer & spy.

Mather, Cotton, 1663–1728, Amer. theologian.

—Increase, 1639–1723, U.S. intellectual & pamphleteer; father of prec.

—Richard, 1596–1669, Eng.-born Amer. theologian; grandfather of Cotton.

Mathewson, Christopher (Christy), 1880–1925, U.S. baseball player.

Mathias, Robert Bruce (Bob), 1930–, U.S. decathlon athlete & politician.

Matisse, Henri, 1869–1954, Fr. painter.

Matsuoka, Yosuke, 1880–1946, Jap. statesman.

Maugham, W(illiam) Somerset, 1874–1965, Eng. author & playwright.

Mauldin, William H. (Bill), 1921–, U.S. cartoonist.

Maupassant, Guy de, 1850–93, Fr. author.

Maurer, Ion Gheorghe, 1902–, Romanian head of state 1958–61.

Mauriac, François, 1885–1970, Fr. author.

Maurois, André, pseud. of Émile Herzog, 1885–1967, Fr. author.

Mauser, Peter Paul, 1838–1914, & his brother, **Wilhelm,** 1834–82, Ger. inventors.

Maverick, Samuel Augustus, 1803–70, U.S. cattle rancher & public official.

Maxim, Sir Hiram Stevens, 1840–1916, U.S.-born Brit. inventor.

—Hudson, 1853–1927, U.S. inventor & explosives expert; brother of prec.

Maximilian, Ferdinand Joseph, 1832–67, Austrian archduke; emperor of Mexico 1864–67; executed.

Maxwell, Elsa, 1883–1963, U.S. columnist & noted hostess.

—James Clerk, 1831–79, Scot. physicist.

May, Elaine, 1932–, U.S. actress & film director.

—Rollo, 1909–94, U.S. psychoanalyst & philosopher.

Mayakovsky, Vladimir Vladimirovich, 1893–1930, Russ. poet & playwright.

Mayer, Jean, 1920–93, Fr. nutritionist active in U.S.

—Louis Burt, 1885–1958, Russ.-born U.S. film producer.

—Maria Goeppert, 1906–72, Ger.-born U.S. physicist; Nobel Prize winner.

Maynor, Dorothy, 1910–96, U.S. soprano.

Mayo, Charles Horace, 1865–1939, U.S. surgeon.

—William James, 1861–1939, U.S. surgeon; brother of prec.

—William Worrall, 1819–1911, U.S. physician; father of Charles Horace & William James.

Mays, Benjamin Elijah, 1894–1984, U.S. educator & theologian.

—Willie Howard, 1931–, U.S. baseball player.

Mazzini, Giuseppe, 1805–72, Ital. patriot & revolutionary.

Mboya, Thomas J. (Tom), 1930–69, Kenyan political leader.

McBride, Mary Margaret, 1899–1976, U.S. radio personality.

—Patricia, 1942–, U.S. ballerina.

McCarey, Leo, 1898–1969, U.S. film director.

McCarthy, Eugene Joseph, 1916–, U.S. politician.

—Joseph Raymond, 1908–57, U.S. politician.

—Mary, 1912–89, U.S. author & critic.

McCartney, Paul, 1942–, Eng. composer & musical performer.

McClellan, George Brinton, 1826–85, U.S. general.

McClintic, Guthrie, 1893–1961, U.S. theater director.

McClintock, Barbara, 1902–92, U.S. geneticist; Nobel Prize winner.

McClure, Samuel Sidney, 1857–1949, Irish-born U.S. editor & publisher.

McCormack, John, 1884–1945, Irish-born U.S. tenor.

—John William, 1891–1980, U.S. politician.

McCormick, Cyrus Hall, 1809–84, U.S. inventor of the reaping machine.

—Joseph Medill, 1877–1925, U.S. newspaper publisher.

—Robert Rutherford, 1880–1955, U.S. newspaper publisher; brother of prec.

McCullers, Carson, 1917–67, U.S. novelist.

McEnroe, John, 1959–, U.S. tennis player.

McGill, James, 1744–1813, Scot.-born Can. businessman & philanthropist.

McGinley, Phyllis, 1905–78, U.S. poet.

McGovern, George Stanley, 1922–, U.S. politician.

McGraw, John Joseph, 1873–1934, U.S. baseball player & manager.

McGuffey, William Holmes, 1800–73, U.S. educator.

McHugh, Jimmy, 1894–1969, U.S. composer.

McKenna, Siobhan, 1923–86, Irish actress.

McKim, Charles Follen, 1847–1909, U.S. architect.

McKinley, William, 1843–1901, 25th U.S. president 1897–1901; assassinated.

McKuen, Rod Marvin, 1933–, U.S. composer & poet.

McLaglen, Victor, 1886–1959, Eng. actor active in U.S.

McLuhan, (Herbert) Marshall, 1911–80, Can. educator & author.

McManus, George, 1884–1954, U.S. cartoonist.

McMillan, Edwin Mattison, 1907–91, U.S. chemist; Nobel Prize winner.

McNamara, Robert Strange, 1916–, U.S. government official & president of World Bank 1968–81.

McPherson, Aimee Semple, 1890–1944, Can.-born U.S. evangelist.

McQueen, Steve, 1930–80, U.S. actor.

Mead, Margaret, 1901–78, U.S. anthropologist.

Meade, George Gordon, 1815–72, U.S. Civil War general.

Meany, George, 1894–1980, U.S. labor leader; president of the AFL-CIO 1955–79.

Medawar, Sir Peter Brian, 1915–87, Eng. zoologist; Nobel Prize winner.

Medici, Catherine de, 1519–89, Florentine-born queen of Henry II of France.

—Cosimo I de, 1519–74, Duke of Florence & Grand Duke of Tuscany: called **the Great.**

—Emilio Garrastazú, 1905–85, Brazilian military officer; president of Brazil 1969–74.

—Lorenzo de, 1448?–92, Florentine prince, statesman, & patron of the arts: called **the Magnificent.**

Medill, Joseph, 1823–99, U.S. editor & publisher.

Mehta, Zubin, 1936–, Indian-born conductor active in the U.S.

Meighen, Arthur, 1874–1960, Can. statesman; prime minister 1920–21 & 26.

Meir, Golda, 1898–1978, Russ.-born Israeli stateswoman; prime minister of Israel 1969–74.

Meiss, Millard, 1904–75, U.S. art historian.

Meitner, Lise, 1878–1968, Ger. physicist.

Melanchthon, Philipp, 1497–1560, Ger. theologian & humanist.

Melba, Dame Nellie, 1861–1931, Austral. soprano.

Melchoir, Lauritz, 1890–1973, Dan. baritone.

Mellon, Andrew William, 1855–1937, U.S. financier & philanthropist.

Melville, Herman, 1819–91, U.S. author.

Memling, Hans, 1430–94, Flemish painter.

Menander, 343?–291?, b.c., Gk. playwright.

Mencken, H(enry) L(ouis), 1880–1956, U.S. author, editor, & critic.

Mendel, Gregor Johann, 1822–84, Austrian monk & botanist.

Mendeleyev, Dimitri Ivanovich, 1834–1907, Russ. chemist.

Mendelssohn, Felix, 1808–47, Ger. composer.

Mendès-France, Pierre, 1907–82, Fr. politician.

Mennin, Peter, 1923–83, U.S. composer & educator.

Menninger, Karl Augustus, 1893–90, U.S. psychiatrist.
Menotti, Gian Carlo, 1911–, Ital.-born U.S. composer.
Menuhin, Yehudi, 1916–, U.S. violinist.
Menzies, Sir Robert Gordon, 1894–1978, Austral. statesman.
Mercator, Gerhardus, 1512–94, Flemish geographer & cartographer.
Mercer, Johnny, 1909–76, U.S. lyricist.
—Mabel, 1900–84, Eng.-born U.S. singer.
Meredith, George, 1828–1909, Eng. author & poet.
Mergenthaler, Ottmar, 1854–99, Ger.-born U.S. inventor of the Linotype machine.
Mérimée, Prosper, 1803–70, Fr. author.
Merman, Ethel, 1909–84, U.S. singer & actress.
Merrick, David, 1912–, U.S. theatrical producer.
Merrill, Robert, 1919–, U.S. baritone.
Merton, Thomas, 1915–68, Fr.-born U.S. monk & author.
Merwin, W(illiam) S(tanley), 1927–, U.S. poet.
Mesmer, Friedrich Anton, 1734–1815, Austrian physician.
Messalina, Valeria, ?–A.D. 48, third wife of Emperor Claudius.
Messerschmitt, Willy, 1898–1978, Ger. aircraft designer & manufacturer.
Messiaen, Olivier, 1908–92, Fr. composer.
Messick, Dale, 1906–, U.S. cartoonist.
Mesta, Perle, 1891–1975, U.S. hostess & diplomat.
Mestrovic, Ivan, 1883–1962, Yugoslav-born U.S. sculptor.
Metaxas, Joannes, 1871–1941, Gk. general & dictator.
Metchnikoff, Élie, 1845–1916, Russ. zoologist & bacteriologist.
Metternich, Prince Klemens von, 1773–1859, Austrian statesman.
Meyer, Adolf, 1866–1950, Swiss-born U.S. psychiatrist.
—Joseph, 1894–1987, U.S. composer.
—Julius Lothar, 1830–95, Ger. chemist.
Meyerbeer, Giacomo, 1791–1864, Ger. composer active in France.
Meyerhof, Otto, 1884–1951, Ger. physiologist.
Meyerhold, Vsevolod Emilievich, 1874–1940, Russ. theatrical director & producer.
Michelangelo Buonarroti, 1475–1564, Ital. sculptor, architect, painter, & poet.
Michelet, Jules, 1798–1874, Fr. historian.
Michelson, Albert Abraham, 1852–1931, Ger.-born U.S. physicist; Nobel Prize winner.
Michener, James Albert, 1907–, U.S. author.
—Roland, 1900–91, Can. politician; governor-general of Canada 1967–74.
Midler, Bette, 1945–, U.S. singer & comedienne.
Mielziner, Jo, 1901–76, Fr.-born set designer active in U.S.
Mies van der Rohe, Ludwig, 1886–1969, Ger.-born U.S. architect.
Mikan, George Lawrence (Larry), 1924–, U.S. basketball player.
Miki, Takeo, 1907–88, prime minister of Japan 1974–76.
Mikoyan, Anastas Ivanovich, 1895–1978, president of U.S.S.R. 1964–65.
Milanov, Zinka, 1906–89, Yugoslav operatic soprano active in U.S.
Milburn, Rodney, 1950–, U.S. track athlete.
Milestone, Lewis, 1895–1980, U.S. film director.
Milhaud, Darius, 1892–1974, Fr. composer.
Mill, James, 1773–1836, Scot. philosopher, historian, & economist.
—John Stuart, 1806–73, Eng. philosopher & political economist; son of prec.
Millay, Edna St. Vincent, 1892–1950, U.S. poet.
Miller, Arthur, 1915–, U.S. playwright.
—Glenn, 1904–44, U.S. bandleader & arranger.
—Henry, 1891–1980, U.S. author.
—Joseph (Joe), 1684–1738, Eng. comedian.
—Perry Gilbert Eddy, 1905–63, U.S. scholar & critic.
—Samuel Freeman, 1816–90, U.S. jurist; justice of U.S. Supreme Court 1862–90.
Miles, Carl Wilhelm Emil, 1875–1955, Swed.-born U.S. sculptor.
Millet, Jean François, 1814–75, Fr. painter.

Millikan, Robert Andrews, 1868–1953, U.S. physicist; Nobel Prize winner.
Mills, Sir John, 1908–85, Eng. actor.
—Robert, 1781–1855, U.S. architect.
Milne, A(lan) A(lexander), 1882–1956, Eng. author.
—David, 1882–1953, U.S. painter.
Milnes, Sherril, 1935–, U.S. baritone.
Milstein, Nathan, 1904–92, Russ.-born U.S. violinist.
Miltiades, 540?–489?, B.C., Athenian general.
Milton, John, 1608–74, Eng. poet.
Mindszenty, Jozsef Cardinal, 1892–1975, Hung. Roman Catholic prelate.
Mingus, Charles (Charlie), 1922–79, U.S. jazz musician.
Minh, Duong Van, 1916–, S. Vietnamese general; president of S. Vietnam 1975; called **Big Minh.**
Minkowski, Hermann, 1864–1909, Russ.-born mathematician active in Germany.
Minnelli, Liza, 1946–, U.S. singer & actress.
—Vincente, 1913–86, U.S. film director, father of prec.
Minnesota Fats, b. Rudolf Walter Wanderone, Jr., 1913–96, U.S. pool player.
Minuit, Peter, 1580–1638, first Du. director-general of New Netherland (including New York).
Mirabeau, Gabriel Honoré de Riquetti, Comte de, 1749–91, Fr. revolutionary orator & statesman.
Miranda, Carmen, 1917–55, Pg.-born actress & singer active in U.S.
Miró, Joan, 1893–1983, Sp. painter.
Mishima, Yukio, 1925–70, Jap. novelist.
Mistral, Frédéric, 1830–1914, Fr. poet; Nobel Prize winner.
—Gabriela, 1889–1957, Chilean poet.
Mitchell, Arthur, 1934–, U.S. ballet dancer, choreographer, & ballet company director.
—John Newton, 1913–88, U.S. politician.
—Margaret, 1900–49, U.S. author.
—William (Billy), 1879–1936, U.S. general & air force advocate.
Mitford, Jessica, 1917–96, Eng. author.
—Nancy, 1904–73, Eng. author; sister of prec.
Mithridates, VI, ca. 132–63 B.C., king of Pontus: called **the Great.**
Mitropoulos, Dmitri, 1896–1960, Gk.-born U.S. conductor.
Mitterand, François, 1916–96, Fr. statesman; president 1981–95.
Mix, Thomas Edwin (Tom), 1880–1940, U.S. actor.
Mizoguchi, Kenji, 1898–1956, Jap. film director.
Möbius, August Ferdinand, 1790–1868, Ger. mathematician.
Mobutu Sese Seko, b. Joseph Desiré Mobutu, 1930–97, president of Zaire 1965–97.
Modigliani, Amadeo, 1844–1920, Ital. painter & sculptor active in France.
Modjeska, Helena Opid, 1840–1909, Pol.-born actress active in U.S.
Moffo, Anna, 1934–, U.S. soprano.
Mohammed, 570–632, Arabian religious & military leader, founder of Islam, & author of the Koran.
Mohammed Reza Pahlavi, 1919–1980, shah of Iran 1941–79.
Moholy-Nagy, Laszlo, 1895–1946, Hung. painter, designer, & photographer active in Germany & U.S.
Mohorovicic, Andrija, 1857–1936, Yugoslav geologist.
Moiseyev, Igor, 1906–, Russ. choreographer & dance company director.
Molière, pseud. of Jean Baptiste Poquelin, 1622–73, Fr. playwright.
Molnár, Ferenc, 1878–1952, Hung. playwright & author.
Molotov, Vyacheslav Mikhailovich, 1890–86, Soviet statesman; foreign minister of the Soviet Union 1939–49 & 1953–56.
Moltke, Count Helmuth von, 1800–91, Prussian field marshal.
Molyneux, Edward, 1894–1974, Eng. fashion designer.
Mommsen, Theodor, 1817–1903, Ger. historian.
Mondale, Walter Frederick, 1928–, U.S. statesman; U.S. vice president 1977–81.
Mondrian, Piet, 1872–1944, Du. painter.
Monet, Claude, 1840–1926, Fr. painter.

Moniz, Antônio Caetano de Abreu Freire Egas, 1874–1955, Pg. physiologist; Nobel Prize winner.

Monk, Thelonious, 1920–82, U.S. jazz musician.

Monmouth, James Scott, Duke of, 1649–85, Eng. rebel & claimant to throne; illegitimate son of Charles II.

Monnet, Jean, 1888–1979, Fr. political economist & statesman.

Monod, Jacques Lucien, 1910–76, Fr. biochemist & author.

Monroe, Harriet, 1860–1936, U.S. poet & editor.

—**James,** 1758–1831, 5th U.S. president 1817–25.

—**Marilyn,** 1926–62, U.S. film actress.

Montagu, Lady Mary Wortley, 1689–1762, Eng. letter writer.

—**(Montague Francis) Ashley,** 1905–, Eng.-born U.S. anthropologist.

Montaigne, Michel Eyquem de, 1533–92, Fr. author.

Montana, Bob, 1920–75, U.S. cartoonist.

Montand, Yves, 1921–91, Ital.-born Fr. actor & singer.

Montcalm, Joseph Louis, 1712–59, Fr. general.

Montefiore, Sir Moses Haim, 1734–1885, Ital.-born Brit. financier & philanthropist.

Montespan, Françoise Athenaïs Rochechouart, Marquise de, 1641–1707, mistress of Louis XIV of France.

Montesquieu, Baron de la Brède et de, title of Charles de Secondat, 1689–1755, Fr. jurist, philosopher, & historian.

Montessori, Maria, 1870–1952, Ital. educator.

Monteux, Pierre, 1875–1964, Fr.-born U.S. conductor.

Monteverdi, Claudio, 1567–1643, Ital. composer.

Montez, Lola, 1818–61, Irish-born dancer & adventuress.

Montezuma II, 1479?–1520, Aztec Indian emperor of Mexico 1502–20.

Montfort, Simon de, 1208?–65, Eng. statesman & soldier.

Montgolfier, Joseph Michel, 1740–1810, & his brother **Jacques Etienne,** 1745–99, Fr. inventors & balloonists.

Montgomery, Bernard Law, 1st Viscount, 1887–1976, Eng. field marshal.

—**Robert,** 1904–81, U.S. actor & producer.

Montherlant, Henri Millon de, 1896–1972, Fr. author.

Moody, Dwight Lyman, 1837–99, U.S. evangelist.

—**William Vaughn,** 1869–1910, U.S. playwright, poet, & literary historian.

Moore, Clement Clarke, 1779–1863, U.S. lexicographer & poet.

—**Douglas Stuart,** 1893–1969, U.S. composer.

—**George,** 1852–1933, Irish author, critic, & playwright.

—**Grace,** 1901–47, U.S. soprano & actress.

—**Henry,** 1898–1986, Eng. sculptor.

—**Marianne,** 1887–1972, U.S. poet.

—**Mary Tyler,** 1937–, U.S. actress.

—**Thomas,** 1779–1852, Irish poet.

—**Victor,** 1876–1962, U.S. actor.

Moorehead, Agnes, 1906–74, U.S. actress.

Moravia, Alberto, pseud. of Alberto Pincherle, 1907–90, Ital. author.

More, Sir Thomas, 1478–1535, Eng. statesman & writer; beheaded; canonized 1935.

Moreau, Gustave, 1826–98, Fr. painter.

—**Jeanne,** 1928–, Fr. actress.

Morgan, Helen, 1900–41, U.S. singer & actress.

—**Henry,** 1915–94, U.S. TV personality.

—**Sir Henry,** 1635?–88, Eng. buccaneer.

—**John Hunt,** 1825–64, U.S. Confederate cavalry officer.

—**J(ohn) Pierpont,** 1837–1913, U.S. financier.

—**Lewis Henry,** 1818–81, U.S. anthropologist.

—**Michèle,** 1920–, Fr. actress.

—**Thomas Hunt,** 1866–1945, U.S. geneticist; Nobel Prize winner.

Morgenthau, Henry, Jr., 1891–1967, U.S. government official.

Morison, Samuel Eliot, 1887–1976, U.S. historian.

—**Stanley,** 1889–1968, Eng. type designer.

Morisot, Berthe, 1841–95, Fr. painter.

Morita, Akio, 1921–, Jap. physicist & business executive.

Morley, Christopher Darlington, 1890–1957, U.S. author.

—**Edward Williams,** 1838–1923, U.S. chemist & physicist; Nobel Prize winner.

Morley, Robert, 1908–92, Eng. actor.

Morphy, Paul, 1837–84, U.S. chessmaster.

Morris, Gouverneur, 1752–1816, U.S. statesman & diplomat.

—**Robert,** 1734–1806, U.S. financier & statesman.

—**William,** 1834–96, Eng. painter, craftsman, & poet.

—**Wright,** 1910–, U.S. author.

Morrison, Toni, 1931–, U.S. author, editor; Nobel Prize winner.

Morse, Samuel Finley Breese, 1791–1872, U.S. artist & inventor of the telegraph.

Morton, Ferdinand Joseph (Jelly Roll), 1885–1941, U.S. jazz musician.

—**Julius Sterling,** 1832–1902, U.S. politician & nature lover.

—**Levi Parsons,** 1824–1920, U.S. statesman; U.S. vice president 1889–93.

—**William Thomas Green,** 1819–68, U.S. dentist.

Mosconi, Willie, 1913–93, U.S. billiards player.

Moseley, Henry Gwyn-Jeffreys, 1887–1915, Eng. physicist.

Moses, Anna Mary Robertson, 1860–1961, U.S. painter; called **Grandma Moses.**

—**Robert,** 1888–1981, U.S. public official.

Mosley, Sir Oswald Ernald, 1896–1980, Eng. fascist politician.

Mossadegh, Mohammed, 1881–1967, Pers. statesman; prime minister of Iran 1951–53.

Mössbauer, Rudolf Ludwig, 1929–, Ger.-born U.S. physicist; Nobel Prize winner.

Mostel, Sam (Zero), 1915–77, U.S. actor.

Moszkowski, Moritz, 1854–1925, Pol.-Ger. pianist & composer.

Motherwell, Robert, 1915–91, U.S. painter.

Mott, Charles Stewart, 1875–1973, U.S. industrialist.

—**Lucretia Coffin,** 1793–1880, U.S. social reformer.

Mountbatten, Louis, Earl, 1900–79, Eng. admiral & governor general of India 1947–48.

Moynihan, Daniel Patrick, 1927–, U.S. sociologist & government official.

Mozart, Wolfgang Amadeus, 1756–91, Austrian composer.

Mubarak, Hosni, 1929–, Egyptian statesman and president 1981–.

Mueller, Paul, 1899–1965, Swiss chemist; Nobel Prize winner.

Muggeridge, Malcolm, 1903–90, Eng. editor & author.

Muhammad, 570?–632, founder of Islamic religion.

Muhammad, Elijah, b. Elijah Poole, 1897–1975, U.S. religious leader.

Muir, John, 1838–1914, U.S. naturalist.

—**Malcolm,** 1885–1979, U.S. publisher & editor.

Muldoon, Robert David, 1921–92, New Zealand prime minister 1975–84.

Muller, Herman Joseph, 1890–1967, U.S. geneticist.

Müller, Paul, 1899–1965, Swiss chemist.

Mulligan, Gerald Joseph (Gerry), 1927–96, U.S. jazz musician.

Mulliken, Robert Sanderson, 1896–1986, U.S. chemist; Nobel Prize winner.

Mulroney, Martin Brian, 1939–, Can. statesman; prime minister 1984–93.

Mumford, Lewis, 1895–1990, U.S. author.

Munch, Charles, 1891–1968, Fr.-born U.S. conductor.

—**Edvard,** 1863–1944, Norw. painter.

Münchausen, Baron Karl Friedrich von, 1720–97, Ger. soldier & adventurer.

Muni, Paul, 1895–1967, U.S. actor.

Muñoz Marín, Luis, 1898–1980, governor of Puerto Rico 1948–64.

Munro, Hector Hugh, 1870–1916, Brit. author; known as **Saki.**

Murasaki, Lady, 11th c. Jap. novelist.

Murdoch, (Jean) Iris, 1919–, Irish-born Brit. author & philosopher.

—**Rupert,** 1931–, Austral.-born U.S. publisher.

Murieta, Joaquiin, ?–1853?, Mexican bandit in Amer. Southwest.

Murillo, Bartolomé Esteban, 1617–82, Sp. painter.

Murnau, Friedrich W., 1899–1931, Ger. film director.

Murphy, Audie, 1924–71, U.S. soldier & actor.

Murray, Arthur, 1895–1991, & his wife, **Kathryn,** 1906–, U.S. dancing teachers.
—**Sir James Augustus Henry,** 1837–1915, Eng. lexicographer.
—**John Courtney,** 1904–67, U.S. theologian.
—**Mae,** 1885–1965, U.S. actress.
Murrow, Edward R., 1908–65, U.S. news analyst.
Musial, Stan(ley Frank), 1920–, U.S. baseball player.
Muskie, Edmund Sixtus, 1914–96, U.S. politician.
Mussolini, Benito, 1883–1945, Ital. Fascist leader & premier; executed: called **Il Duce.**
Mussorgsky, Modest Petrovich, 1835–81, Russ. composer.
Mutsuhito, 1852–1912, emperor of Japan 1867–1912.
Muybridge, Eadweard, b. Edward James Muggeridge, 1830–1904, Eng.-born U.S. photographer.
Muzio, Claudia, 1889–1936, Ital. soprano.
Muzorewa, Abel Tendekayi, 1925–, African religious and political leader; prime minister of Zimbabwe 1979.
Myrdal, Alva Reimer, 1902–86, Swed. diplomat & sociologist.
—**Gunnar,** 1898–1987, Swed. sociologist & economist.
Myron, 5th c. B.C. Gk. sculptor.

Nabokov, Vladimir, 1899–1977, Russ.-born U.S. author.
Nader, Ralph, 1934–, U.S. lawyer & consumer advocate.
Nagurski, Bronko, 1908–90, Can.-born U.S. football player.
Nagy, Imre, 1895?–1958, premier of Hungary 1953–55; executed.
Naismith, James, 1861–1939, Can.-born U.S. athletic coach; originator of basketball.
Namath, Joseph William (Joe), 1943–, U.S. football player.
Nanak, 1469–1538, founder of the Sikh faith in India.
Nansen, Fridtjof, 1861–1930, Norw. Arctic explorer.
Napier, John, 1550–1617, Scot. mathematician.
Napoleon I and **III** See BONAPARTE.
Nash, Ogden, 1902–71, U.S. poet.
—**Thomas,** 1567–1601, Eng. playwright.
Nasser, Gamal Abdel, 1918–70, Egyptian revolutionary leader; president of the United Arab Republic 1958–70.
Nast, Thomas, 1840–1902, Ger.-born U.S. cartoonist.
Nathan, George Jean, 1882–1958, U.S. critic.
Nation, Carry Amelia, 1846–1911, U.S. temperance reformer.
Natwick, Mildred, 1908–94, U.S. actress.
Navratilova, Martina, 1956–, Czech tennis player.
Nazimova, Alla, 1879–1945, Russ.-born actress active in U.S.
Nebuchadnezzar II, ?–562? B.C., king of Babylon 605–562 B.C.; conqueror of Jerusalem.
Nefertiti, 14th c. B.C., Egyptian queen, 1367–1350 B.C..
Nehru, Jawaharlal, 1889–1964, Indian nationalist leader; prime minister of India 1947–64.
Neill, A(lexander) S(utherland), 1883–1973, Eng. educator & author.
Nelson, Viscount Horatio, 1758–1805, Eng. admiral.
—**(John) Byron,** 1912–, U.S. golfer.
—**Oswald George (Ozzie),** 1907–75, U.S. bandleader, actor, & TV producer.
—**Rick,** b. Eric Hilliard Nelson, 1940–85, U.S. singer & actor.
—**Willie,** 1933–, U.S. singer and songwriter.
Nemerov, Howard, 1920–91, U.S. poet.
Nemery, Gaafar al-, 1930–, Sudanese military officer; president of Sudan 1971–85.
Nenni, Pietro, 1891–1980, Ital. socialist leader & journalist.
Nernst, Hermann W., 1864–1941, Ger. physical chemist; Nobel Prize winner.
Nero, A.D. 37–68, Roman emperor 54–68.
Neruda, Pablo, 1904–73, Chilean poet; Nobel Prize winner.
Nerva, Marcus Cocceius, A.D. 35?–98, Roman emperor 96–98.
Nervi, Pier Luigi, 1891–1979, Ital. architect.
Neutra, Richard Joseph, 1892–1970, Austrian-born U.S. architect.
Nevelson, Louise, 1900–88, Russ.-born U.S. sculptor.
Nevins, Allan, 1890–1971, U.S. historian.
Newberry, John, 1713–67, Eng. publisher & bookseller.
—**Walter Loomis,** 1804–68, U.S. businessman & philanthropist.

Newcombe, John, 1944–, Austral. tennis player.
Newhouse, Samuel, 1895–1979, U.S. publisher.
Ne Win, U, 1911–, Burmese military leader; prime minister of Burma 1962–74; president 1974–81.
Newlands, John A. R., 1838–98, Eng. chemist.
Newman, Barnett, 1905–70, U.S. artist.
—**John Henry, Cardinal,** 1801–90, Eng. theologian & author.
—**Paul,** 1925–, U.S. actor.
Newton, Sir Isaac, 1642–1727, Eng. mathematician & physicist.
—**Robert,** 1905–56, Eng. actor.
Ngo Dinh Diem, 1901–63, South Vietnamese politician; president 1955–63; assassinated.
Nguyen Van Thieu, 1923–, South Vietnamese politician; president 1967–75.
Nicholas I, 1796–1855, czar of Russia 1825–55: called **the Great.**
—**II,** 1868–1918, czar of Russia 1894–1917; executed.
Nicholas, Saint, 4th c. prelate; patron saint of Russia, seamen, and children.
Nichols, Mike, 1931–, Ger.-born U.S. comedian & stage & film director.
Nicholson, Ben, 1894–1982, Eng. artist.
—**Jack,** 1937–, U.S. actor.
Nicklaus, Jack W., 1940–, U.S. golfer.
Nicolle, Charles J. H., 1866–1936, Fr. physician.
Nicolson, Sir Harold George, 1886–1968, Eng. diplomat, author, & journalist.
Niebuhr, Reinhold, 1892–1971, U.S. Protestant clergyman & theologian.
Nielsen, Carl, 1865–1931, Dan. composer.
Niemeyer Soares, Oscar, 1907–84, Brazilian architect.
Niemöller, Martin, 1892–1984, Ger. theologian.
Nietzsche, Friedrich Wilhelm, 1844–1900, Ger. philosopher & author.
Nightingale, Florence, 1820–1910, Eng. nurse in the Crimean War; considered the founder of modern nursing.
Nijinska, Bronislava, 1891–1972, Pol. dancer & choreographer.
Nijinsky, Vaslav, 1890–1950, Russ.-born ballet dancer & choreographer; brother of prec.
Nikolais, Alwin, 1912–93, U.S. choreographer & dance company director.
Nilsson, Birgit, 1918–, Swed. soprano.
Nimitz, Chester William, 1885–1966, U.S. admiral.
Nin, Anais, 1903–77, Fr.-born U.S. author.
Nirenberg, Marshall Warren, 1927–, U.S. biochemist.
Niven, David, 1910–83, Scot.-born actor active in U.S.
Nixon, Richard Millhouse, 1913–94, 37th U.S. president 1969–74; resigned.
Nizer, Louis, 1902–94, Eng.-born U.S. lawyer & author.
Nkrumah, Kwame, 1909–72, president of Ghana 1960–66.
Nobel, Alfred Bernhard, 1833–96, Swed. industrialist & philanthropist.
Nock, Albert Jay, 1870–1945, U.S. author.
Noguchi, Hideyo, 1876–1928, Jap. bacteriologist active in U.S.
—**Isamu,** 1904–88, U.S. sculptor.
Nolde, Emil, pseud. of Emil Hansen, 1867–1956, Ger. painter.
Nomura, Kichisaburo, 1877–1964, Jap. admiral & diplomat.
Nordenskjöld, Nils Adolf Erik, 1832–1901, Finn.-born Swed. polar explorer.
Nordica, Lillian, 1857–1914, U.S. soprano.
Norell, Norman, 1900–72, U.S. fashion designer.
Norman, Jessye, 1945–, U.S. soprano.
Normand, Mable, 1894–1930, U.S. actress.
Norris, (Benjamin) Frank(lin), 1870–1902, U.S. author.
—**George W.,** 1861–1944, U.S. politician.
Norstad, Lauris, 1907–88, U.S. general.
North, Alex, 1910–91, U.S. composer.
—**Lord Frederick,** 1732–92, Eng. statesman; prime minister 1770–82.
Norton, Charles Eliot, 1827–1908, U.S. author & educator.
Norworth, Jack, 1879–1959, U.S. lyricist.
Nostradamus, b. Michel de Notredame, 1503–66, Fr. physician & astrologer.
Novaes, Guiomar, 1895–1979, Brazilian pianist.

Novak, Robert David Sanders, 1931–, U.S. journalist.
Novalis, pseud. of Friedrich von Hardenberg, 1772–1801, Ger. poet.
Novarro, Ramon, 1899–1968, Mexican-born U.S. actor.
Novello, Ivor, 1893–1951, Eng. playwright, composer, & actor.
Novotna, Jarmila, 1911–94, Czech-born U.S. soprano.
Novotny, Antonin, 1904–75, president of Czechoslovakia 1957–68.
Noyes, Alfred, 1880–1958, Eng. poet.
Nu, U, 1907–95, prime minister of Burma 1948–58 & 1960–62.
Nureyev, Rudolf, 1938–93, Soviet-born ballet dancer & choreographer.
Nurmi, Paavo, 1897–1973, Finnish track runner.
Nyerere, Julius Kambarage, 1922–, African statesman & first president of Tanzania 1964–85.

Oakley, Annie, 1860–1926, U.S. markswoman.
Oates, Joyce Carol, 1938–, U.S. author.
—Titus, 1649–1705, Eng. conspirator.
Oberon, Merle, 1911–79, Tasmanian-born U.S. actress.
Oboler, Arch, 1909–87, U.S. writer.
Obote, (Apollo) Milton, 1924–, president of Uganda 1966–71 & 1980–85.
Obregón, Alvaro, 1880–1928, Mexican soldier & politician; president of Mexico 1920–24 & 1928; assassinated.
O'Brien, Lawrence Francis, 1917–90, U.S. politician & government official.
—Margaret, 1937–, U.S. actress.
—Pat(rick), 1899–1983, U.S. actor.
O'Casey, Sean, 1881–1964, Irish playwright.
Ochoa, Severo, 1905–93, Sp.-born U.S. biochemist.
Ochs, Adolph Simon, 1858–1935, U.S. newspaper publisher.
Ockham, William of, 1285?–1349?, Eng. philosopher.
O'Connell, Daniel, 1775–1847, Irish nationalist leader.
O'Connor, Flannery, 1925–64, U.S. author.
—Frank, pseud. of Michael John O'Donovan, 1903–66, Irish author.
—Sandra Day, 1930–, U.S. jurist; justice of U.S. Supreme Court, 1981–.
—Thomas P. (Tay Pay), 1848–1929, Irish journalist & nationalist.
O'Day, Anita, 1920–, U.S. jazz singer.
Odets, Clifford, 1906–63, U.S. actor & playwright.
Odetta, b. Odetta Holmes, 1930–, U.S. folk singer.
Oenslager, Donald, 1902–75, U.S. set designer.
Oersted, Hans Christian, 1777–1851, Dan. physicist.
Oerter, Alfred, 1936–, U.S. discus thrower.
O'Faoláin, Sean, 1900–91, Irish author.
Offenbach, Jacques, 1819–80, Ger.-born Fr. composer.
O'Flaherty, Liam, 1896–1984, Irish author.
Ogden, C(harles) K(ay), 1889–1957, Eng. psychologist & semanticist.
Ogilvy, David MacKenzie, 1911–, Eng. advertising executive active in U.S.
Oglethorpe, James Edward, 1696–1785, Eng. general & philanthropist; founder of Georgia colony.
O'Hara, John, 1905–70, U.S. author.
O'Higgins, Bernardo, 1778–1842, Chilean statesman.
Ohm, Georg Simon, 1787–1854, Ger. physicist.
Oistrakh, David Fyodorovich, 1908–74, Soviet violinist.
O'Keeffe, Georgia, 1887–1986, U.S. painter.
Olav V, 1903–91, king of Norway 1957–91.
Oldenburg, Claes Thure, 1929–, Swed.-born U.S. sculptor.
Oldfield, Berner Eli (Barney), 1878–1946, U.S. automobile racer.
Olds, Ransom Eli, 1864–1950, U.S. automobile manufacturer.
Oliphant, Patrick Bruce, 1935–, U.S. political cartoonist.
Oliver, Edna May, 1883–1942, U.S. actress.
—Joe (King), 1885–1938, U.S. jazz musician.
Olivier, Sir Laurence, 1907–89, Eng. actor & director.
Olmsted, Frederick Law, 1822–1903, U.S. landscape architect.
Olson, Charles, 1910–70, U.S. poet.
Omar Khayyám, ?–1123?, Pers. poet & astronomer.

Onassis, Aristotle Socrates, 1906–75, Turk.-born Gk. shipping magnate.
O'Neill, Eugene Gladstone, 1888–1953, U.S. playwright.
—Thomas Philip (Tip), 1912–94, U.S. statesman.
Onions, Charles Talbut, 1873–1965, Eng. lexicographer.
Onsager, Lars, 1903–76, Norw.-born U.S. physical chemist.
Oparin, Aleksandr Ivanovich, 1894–1980, Soviet biochemist.
Oppenheimer, J(ulius) Robert, 1904–67, U.S. physicist.
Ophuls, Max, 1902–57, Fr. film director.
Orczy, Baroness Emmuska, 1865–1947, Hung.-born Eng. author.
Orff, Carl, 1895–1982, Ger. composer.
Origen, A.D. 185?–254?, Gk. writer & church father.
Orlando, Vittorio Emanuele, 1860–1952, Ital. statesman; prime minister 1917–19.
Ormandy, Eugene, 1899–1985, Hung.-born U.S. conductor.
Orozco, José Clemente, 1883–1949, Mexican painter.
Orr, Robert Gordon (Bobby), 1948–, Can. hockey player.
Ortega y Gasset, José, 1883–1955, Sp. philosopher & author.
Orwell, George, pseud. of Eric Arthur Blair, 1903–50, Eng. author & social critic.
Osborne, John James, 1929–94, Eng. playwright.
Osceola, 1804–38, Seminole Am. Ind. chief.
Osler, Sir William, 1849–1919, Can. physician.
Osman I, 1259–1326, Turkish founder of the Ottoman Empire.
Ossietzky, Carl von, 1889–1938, Ger. journalist; Nobel Prize winner.
Ostwald, Wilhelm, 1853–1932, Ger. chemist; Nobel Prize winner.
Oswald, Lee Harvey, 1939–63, U.S. alleged assassin of President John F. Kennedy; murdered.
Otis, Elisha Graves, 1811–61, U.S. inventor.
O'Toole, Peter, 1932–, Irish actor.
Oursler, Fulton, 1893–1952, U.S. writer & editor.
Ouspenskaya, Maria, 1876–1949, Russ. actress active in U.S.
Outcault, Richard, 1863–1928, U.S. cartoonist.
Ovid (L. Publius Ovidius Naso), 43 B.C.–A.D. 17, Roman poet.
Owen, Robert, 1771–1858, Welsh social reformer.
—Wilfred, 1893–1918, Eng. poet.
Owens, Jesse, 1913–80, U.S. track athlete.
Owings, Nathaniel Alexander, 1903–84, U.S. architect.
Ozawa, Seiji, 1935–, Chin.-born conductor active in U.S.
Ozick, Cynthia, 1928–, U.S. author & critic.

Paar, Jack, 1918–, U.S. TV personality.
Pabst, Georg W., 1885–1967, Ger. film director.
Paderewski, Ignace Jan, 1860–1941, Pol. pianist, composer, & statesman.
Paganini, Niccolò, 1782–1840, Ital. violinist & composer.
Page, Geraldine, 1924–87, U.S. actress.
Paget, Sir James, 1814–99, Eng. surgeon & pathologist.
Pagnol, Marcel, 1895–1974, Fr. playwright & film producer.
Paige, Leroy David (Satchel), 1906–82, U.S. baseball player.
Paine, Thomas, 1737–1809, Eng.-born Amer. revolutionary patriot, political philosopher, & author.
Palestrina, Giovanni Pierluigi da, 1526?–94, Ital. composer.
Paley, Grace, 1922–, U.S. author.
—William Samuel, 1901–90, U.S. radio & TV executive.
Palladio, Andrea, 1508–80, Ital. architect.
Palme, Olof, 1927–86, prime minister of Sweden 1969–76 & 1982; assassinated.
Palmer, Arnold Daniel, 1929–, U.S. golfer.
—Daniel David, 1845–1913, Can. founder of chiropractic medicine.
—Potter, 1826–1902, U.S. merchant & real estate developer.
Palmerston, Henry John Temple, 3rd Viscount, 1784–1865, Eng. statesman; prime minister 1855–58 & 1859–65.
Pandit, Madame Vijaya Lakshmi, 1900–90, Indian diplomat & president of U.N. general assembly 1953–54.
Panini, 4th c. B.C. Indian Sanskrit grammarian.
Pankhurst, Emmeline Goulden, 1858–1928, Eng. suffragist.
Panofsky, Erwin, 1892–1968, Ger.-born U.S. art historian.
Papadopoulos, George, 1919–, Gk. military officer; premier of Greece 1967–73; president 1973.
Papandreou, George, 1888–1968, Gk. politician & opposition leader.

Papanicolaou, George Nicholas, 1883–1962, Gk.-born U.S. physician.
Papas, Irene, 1925–, Gk. actress.
Papp, Joseph, 1921–91, U.S. theatrical producer.
Paracelsus, pseud. of Theophrastus Bombastus von Hohenheim, 1493–1541, Swiss physician & alchemist.
Paré, Ambroise, 1510–90, Fr. surgeon.
Pareto, Vilfredo, 1848–1923, Ital. economist & sociologist.
Park Chung Hee, 1917–79, president of South Korea 1961–79.
—**Robert Ezra,** 1864–1944, U.S. sociologist.
Parker, Bonnie, 1910–34, U.S. criminal.
—**Charles Christopher, Jr.,** 1920–55, U.S. jazz musician: called **Bird.**
—**Dorothy,** 1893–1967, U.S. author.
—**Francis Wayland,** 1837–1902, U.S. educator.
Parkman, Francis, 1823–93, U.S. historian.
Parks, Bert, 1914–92, U.S. TV personality.
—**Gordon,** 1912–79, U.S. photographer & film director.
Parmigianino, II, b. Girolamo Mazzuoli, 1503–40, Ital. painter.
Parnell, Charles Stewart, 1846–91, Irish statesman.
Parr, Catherine, 1512–48, sixth wife of Henry VIII of England.
Parrington, Vernon Louis, 1871–1929, U.S. historian.
Parrish, Maxfield, 1870–1966, U.S. painter.
Parsons, Estelle, 1927–, U.S. actress.
—**Louella Oettinger,** 1893–1972, U.S. columnist.
—**Talcott,** 1902–79, U.S. sociologist.
Partridge, Eric H., 1894–1979, Eng. lexicographer & critic.
Pascal, Blaise, 1623–62, Fr. mathematician & philosopher.
Pasionaria, La (Dolores Ibarruri), 1895–1989, Sp. revolutionist & founder of Spain's Communist Party.
Pasolini, Pier Paolo, 1922–75, Ital. film director.
Pasternak, Boris, 1890–1960, Soviet poet & novelist; Nobel Prize winner.
Pasteur, Louis, 1822–95, Fr. chemist & bacteriologist.
Pastor, Antonio (Tony), 1837–1908, U.S. actor & theater manager.
Pater, Walter Horatio, 1839–94, Eng. essayist & critic.
Paton, Alan Stewart, 1903–88, South African author.
Patrick, Saint, 389?–461, Brit. missionary to and patron saint of Ireland.
Patterson, Eleanor Medill (Cissy), 1884–1948, and her brother **Joseph M.,** 1879–1946, U.S. publishers.
Patti, Adelina, 1843–1919, Sp.-born Ital. soprano.
Patton, George Smith, 1885–1945, U.S. general.
Pauker, Ana Rabinsohn, 1889?–1960, Romanian communist.
Paul, Saint, A.D.? –67?, b.Saul, a Jew of Tarsus who became the apostle of Christianity to the Gentiles; author of various New Testament books.
Paul VI, b. Giovanni Battista Montini, 1897–1978, pope 1963–78.
Pauli, Wolfgang, 1900–58, Swiss-Austrian physicist.
Pauling, Linus Carl, 1901–94, U.S. chemist.
Pausanias, 2nd c. A.D. Gk. traveler & geographer.
Pavarotti, Luciano, 1935–, Ital. tenor.
Pavese, Cesare, 1908–50, Ital. author.
Pavlov, Ivan Petrovich, 1849–1936, Russ. physiologist.
Pavlova, Anna, 1885–1931, Russ. ballerina active in France.
Paxinou, Katina, 1900–73, Gk. actress active in U.S.
Peabody, George, 1795–1869, U.S. businessman & financier.
Peale A family of U.S. painters incl. **Charles Willson,** 1741–1827; his brother **James,** 1749–1831; and **Rembrandt,** 1778–1860, son of Charles.
—**Norman Vincent,** 1898–1993, U.S. clergyman & author.
Pearson, Andrew Russell (Drew), 1897–1969, U.S. columnist.
—**Lester Bowles,** 1897–1972, Can. statesman; prime minister of Canada 1963–68.
Peary, Robert Edwin, 1856–1920, U.S. Arctic explorer.
Peck, Gregory, 1916–, U.S. actor.
—**Peckham, Rufus W.,** 1838–1909, U.S. jurist; justice of U.S. Supreme Court 1895–1909.
Peckinpah, Sam, 1925–84, U.S. film director.
Peel, Sir Robert, 1788–1850, Eng. statesman & founder of London & Irish police forces; prime minister 1834 & 1841–46.

Peerce, Jan, 1904–84, U.S. tenor.
Pegler, (James) Westbrook, 1894–1969, U.S. columnist.
Péguy, Charles, 1873–1914, Fr. poet & author.
Pei, I(eoh) M(ing), 1917–, Chin.-born U.S. architect.
Peirce, Benjamin, 1809–80, U.S. mathematician & astronomer.
—**Charles Sanders,** 1839–1914, U.S. philosopher & logician; son of prec.
Pélé, b. Edson Arantes do Nascimento, 1940–, Brazilian soccer player.
Pendergast, Thomas J., 1872–1945, U.S. politician.
Penfield, Wilder G., 1891–1976, U.S.-born Can. neurosurgeon.
Penn, Arthur, 1922–, U.S. film & stage director.
—**Irving,** 1917–, U.S. photographer.
—**William,** 1644–1718, Eng. Quaker; founder of Pennsylvania.
Penney, J(ames) C(ash), 1875–1971, U.S. merchant.
Pepin the Short, 714?–768, king of the Franks 751–768.
Pepys, Samuel, 1633–1703, Eng. author.
Percy, Sir Henry, 1364–1403, Eng. soldier: called **Hotspur.**
—**Walker,** 1916–90, U.S. author.
Pereira, William, 1909–85, U.S. architect.
Perelman, S(idney) J(oseph), 1904–79, U.S. author.
Peres, Shimon, 1923–, Israeli statesman; prime minister 1984–86, 1995–.
Peretz, Isaac Loeb, 1851–1915, Pol. poet & author.
Perez Rodrigues, Carlos Andres, 1922–, president of Venezuela 1974–78.
Pérez de Cuéllar, Javiera, 1920–, Peruvian diplomat and secretary-general of the U.N. 1982–91.
Pergolesi, Giovanni Battista, 1710–36, Ital. composer.
Pericles, ?–429 B.C., Athenian statesman & general.
Perkins, Frances, 1882–1965, U.S. social worker; first woman Cabinet member; secretary of labor 1933–45.
—**Maxwell,** 1884–1947, U.S. editor.
—**(Richard) Marlin,** 1905–86, U.S. zoo director.
Perlman, Itzhak, 1945–, Israeli violinist.
Perls, Frederick (Fritz), 1893–1970, Ger.-born U.S. psychologist.
Perón, Eva Duarte de, 1919–52, Argentine radio personality & political leader.
—**Juan Domingo,** 1895–1974, Argentinian political leader; president 1946–55 & 1973–74; husband of prec.
Perón, Maria Estela Isabel Martinez de, 1931–, president of Argentina 1974–76; wife of prec.
Perrault, Charles, 1628–1703, Fr. writer & compiler of fairy tales.
Perry, Antoinette, 1888–1946, U.S. stage actress, director, & producer.
—**Matthew Calbraith,** 1794–1858, U.S. commodore.
—**Oliver Hazard,** 1785–1819, U.S. naval commander; brother of prec.
Perse, St. John, pseud. of Alexis Saint-Léger Léger, 1887–1975, Fr. poet & diplomat; Nobel Prize winner.
Pershing, John Joseph, 1860–1948, U.S. general.
Perugino, II, b. Pietro Vannucci, 1446–1523, Ital. painter.
Perutz, Max Ferdinand, 1914–, Austrian-born Brit. physicist; Nobel Prize winner.
Pestalozzi, Johann Heinrich, 1746–1827, Swiss educator.
Pétain, Henri Philippe, 1856–1951, Fr. political leader; premier 1940–44.
Peter I, 1672–1725, czar of Russia 1689–1725: called **the Great.**
Peter, Saint, b. Simon, ?–A.D. 67?, 1st pope A.D. 42?–67?.
Peters, Roberta, 1930–, U.S. soprano.
Petipa, Marius, 1822–1910, Fr. dancer & choreographer active in Russ.
Peterson, Oscar, 1925–, U.S. jazz pianist.
—**Roger Tory,** 1908–96, U.S. ornithologist & author.
Petit, Roland, 1924–, Fr. dancer & choreographer.
Petrarch, Francesco, 1304–74, Ital. scholar & poet.
Petrie, Sir (William Matthew) Flinders, 1853–1942, Eng. archaeologist.
Petrillo, James Caesar, 1892–1984, U.S. labor leader.
Petronius, Gaius, A.D.?–66?, Roman satirist.

Peusner, Antoine, 1886–1962, Russ. painter & sculptor.

Pevsner, Sir Nikolaus, 1902–83, Ger.-born Brit. art historian.

Pham Van Dong, 1906–, premier of N. Vietnam 1955–87.

Phidias, 500?–432?, B.C., Gk. sculptor & architect.

Philby, Harold A. R., 1911–88, Eng.-born spy for the U.S.S.R.

Philip II, 382–336 B.C., king of Macedonia & conqueror of Thessaly & Greece; father of Alexander the Great.

Philip II, 1527–98, king of Spain 1556–98.

Philip, Prince (Duke of Edinburgh), 1921–, Gk.-born husband of Queen Elizabeth II.

Philip the Good, 1396–1467, Duke of Burgundy, 1419–67.

Philip (Metacomet), 1639?–76, sachem of the Wampanoag Amer. Indians.

Philippe, Gerard, 1922–57, Fr. actor.

Phillips, Wendell, 1811–84, U.S. orator & reformer.

Philo Judaeus, 20 B.C.?–A.D. 50?, Jewish Platonist philosopher.

Phyfe, Duncan, 1768–1854, Scot.-born U.S. cabinet maker.

Piaf, Edith, 1912–63, Fr. singer.

Piaget, Jean, 1896–1980, Swiss psychologist & author.

Piatigorski, Gregor, 1903–76, Ukrainian-born U.S. cellist.

Picabia, Francis, 1878–1953, Fr. painter.

Picard, Jean, 1620–82, Fr. astronomer.

Picasso, Pablo, 1881–1973, Sp. artist active in France.

Piccard, Auguste, 1884–1962, Swiss physicist.

Pickett, George Edward, 1825–75, U.S. Confederate general.

Pickford, Mary, 1893–1979, Can.-born U.S. actress.

Picon, Molly, 1898–1992, U.S. actress.

Pidgeon, Walter, 1897–1984, Can. actor.

Pierce, Franklin, 1804–69, 14th U.S. president 1853–57.

Piero della Francesca, 1418?–92, Ital. painter.

Pike, Zebulon Montgomery, 1779–1813, U.S. general & explorer.

Pilate, Pontius, 1st c. A.D. Roman governor of Judea A.D. 26?–36?; delivered Jesus to be crucified.

Pillsbury, Charles Alfred, 1842–99, U.S. businessman.

Pilsudski, Józef, 1867–1935, Pol. statesman.

Pindar, 522?–433, B.C., Gk. poet.

Pinel, Philippe, 1745–1826, Fr. physician & psychologist.

Pinero, Sir Arthur Wing, 1855–1934, Eng. playwright & actor.

Pinkerton, Allan, 1819–84, Scot.-born detective active in U.S.

Pinkham, Lydia Estes, 1819–83, U.S. businesswoman.

Pinter, Harold, 1930–, Eng. playwright.

Pinturicchio, b. Bernardino Betti, 1454–1513, Ital. painter.

Pinza, Ezio, 1892–1957, Ital.-born U.S. basso.

Pirandello, Luigi, 1867–1936, Ital. playwright & author.

Piranesi, Giovanni Battista, 1720–78, Ital. architect & engraver.

Pirenne, Henri, 1862–1935, Bel. historian.

Pisano, Giovanni, 1245–1314, Ital. sculptor.

—**Nicola,** 1220–84, Ital. sculptor; father of prec.

Piscator, Erwin, 1893–1966, Ger. theater director.

Pisistratus, ?–527 B.C., Gk. statesman.

Pissarro, Camille, 1830–1903, Fr. painter.

Piston, Walter, 1894–1976, U.S. composer.

Pitcher, Molly, b. Mary Ludwig, 1754–1832, Amer. revolutionary heroine.

Pitman, Sir Isaac, 1813–97, Eng. phoneticist; invented a system of shorthand.

Pitt, William, 1708–78, Eng. statesman.

—**William,** 1759–1806, Eng. prime minister 1783–1801 & 1804–06; son of prec.: called **the Younger.**

Pius XII, b. Eugenio Pacelli, 1876–1958, pope 1939–58.

Pizarro, Francisco, 1475?–1541, Sp. soldier & conqueror of Peru.

Planck, Max, 1858–1947, Ger. physicist.

Plath, Sylvia, 1932–63, U.S. poet resident in England.

Plato, 427?–327? B.C., Gk. philosopher.

Plautus, Titus Maccius, 254?–184 B.C., Roman playwright.

Plimpton, George Ames, 1927–, U.S. author & editor.

Plimsoll, Samuel, 1824–98, Eng. shipping reformer.

Pliny (L. Gaius Plinius Secundus), A.D. 23–79, Roman naturalist & writer: called **the Elder.**

— (L. Gaius Plinius Caecilius), A.D. 62–113, Roman statesman; nephew of prec.: called **the Younger.**

Plisetskaya, Maya, 1925–, Russ. ballerina.

Plotinus, 205?–270, Egyptian-born Roman philosopher.

Plummer, Christopher, 1929–, Can. actor active in U.S.

Plutarch, A.D. 46?–120?, Gk. historian.

Pocahontas, 1595?–1617, Am. Ind. princess; daughter of Powhatan.

Podgorny, Nikolai Viktorovich, 1903–83, Soviet politician; president of U.S.S.R. 1966–77.

Poe, Edgar Allan, 1809–49, U.S. author, critic, & poet.

Poincaré, Jules Henri, 1854–1912, Fr. mathematician.

—**Raymond,** 1860–1934, Fr. statesman; president 1913–20.

Poinsett, Joel Roberts, 1779–1851, U.S. diplomat & amateur botanist.

Poisson, Simeon D., 1781–1840, Fr. mathematician.

Poitier, Sidney, 1927–, U.S. actor.

Polanski, Roman, 1933–, Pol. film director active in U.S. .

Politian, b. Angelo Poliziano, 1454–94, Ital. classical scholar & poet.

Polk, James Knox, 1795–1849, 11th U.S. president 1845–49.

Pollaivollo, Antonio del, 1432?–98, Ital. sculptor & painter.

Pollock, Jackson, 1912–56, U.S. painter.

Polo, Marco, 1254?–1324?, Venetian traveler & author.

Polybius, 204?–122? B.C., Gk. historian.

Polycleitus, 5th c. B.C. Gk. sculptor & architect.

Pompadour, Jeanne Antoinette Poisson, Marquise de, 1721–64, mistress of Louis XV.

Pompey (L. Gnaeus Pompeius Magnus), 106–48 B.C., Roman general & statesman.

Pompidou, Georges Jean Raymond, 1911–74, president of France 1969–74.

Ponce de Leon, Juan, 1460–1521, Sp. discoverer of Florida.

Ponchielli, Amilcare, 1834–86, Ital. composer.

Pons, Lily, 1904–76, Fr.-born U.S. soprano.

Ponselle, Rosa Melba, 1897–1981, U.S. soprano.

Ponti, Carlo, 1913–, Ital. film director.

Pontiac, 1720?–1769, Ottowa Am. Ind. chief.

Pontormo, Jacopo da, b. Jacopo Carrucci, 1494–1557, Ital. painter.

Pope, Alexander, 1688–1744, Eng. poet & essayist.

—**John Russell,** 1874–1937, U.S. architect.

Porter, Cole, 1891–1964, U.S. composer & lyricist.

—**Katherine Anne,** 1890–1980, U.S. author.

Portman, John, 1924–, U.S. architect.

Post, Charles William, 1854–1914, U.S. breakfast-food manufacturer.

—**Emily Price,** 1873?–1960, U.S. writer on etiquette.

—**Marjorie Merriweather,** 1887–1973, U.S. philanthropist.

—**Wiley,** 1900–35, U.S. aviator.

Potemkin, Grigori Aleksandrovich, 1739–91, Russ. statesman & general.

Potok, Chaim, 1929–, U.S. author.

Potter, Beatrix, 1866?–1943, Eng. author & illustrator of children's books.

Poulenc, Francis, 1899–1963, Fr. composer.

Pound, Ezra Loomis, 1885–1972, U.S. poet resident in Italy.

Poussin, Nicholas, 1594–1665, Fr. painter.

Powell, Adam Clayton Jr., 1908–72, U.S. clergyman & politician.

—**Anthony,** 1905–, Eng. author.

—**Dick,** 1904–63, U.S. actor & singer.

—**Eleanor,** 1912–82, U.S. dancer & actress.

—**Hiram,** 1805–73, U.S. sculptor.

—**John Wesley,** 1834–1902, U.S. geographer & explorer.

—**Lewis Franklin, Jr.,** 1907–, U.S. jurist; justice of the U.S. Supreme Court 1972–87.

—**William,** 1892–1984, U.S. actor.

Power, Tyrone, 1913–58, U.S. actor.

Powhatan, 1550?–1618, Algonquin Am. Ind. chief.

Pratt, E(dwin) J(ohn), 1882–1964, Can. poet.

Praxiteles, 4th c. B.C. Athenian sculptor.

Prefontaine, Steven Roland, 1951–75, U.S. track runner.

Preminger, Otto Ludwig, 1906–86, Austrian-born U.S. film director & producer.

Prendergast, Maurice Brazil, 1859–1924, Can.-born U.S. painter & illustrator.

Presley, Elvis Aron, 1935–77, U.S. singer & actor.
Pretorius, Andries Wilhelmus Jacobus, 1799–1853, and his son **Marthinus Wessels,** 1819–1901, Du. colonizers & soldiers in South Africa.
Prévert, Jacques, 1900–77, Fr. poet.
Previn, André, 1929–, Ger.-born U.S. composer, conductor, & pianist.
Price, George, 1901–95, U.S. cartoonist.
—**Leontyne,** 1927–, U.S. soprano.
—**Vincent,** 1911–93, U.S. actor.
Priestley, J(ohn) B(oynton), 1894–1984, Eng. author.
—**Joseph,** 1733–1804, Eng. chemist.
Primrose, William, 1904–82, Scot.-born U.S. violinist.
Primus, Pearl, 1919–94, Trinidad-born dancer & choreographer active in U.S.
Prince, Harold, 1928–, U.S. theatrical producer & director.
Princip, Gavrilo, 1895–1918, Serbian political agitator & assassin of Archduke Franz Ferdinand.
Pritchett, V(ictor) S(awdon), 1900–, Eng. author.
Procter, William C., 1862–1934, U.S. industrialist.
Prokhorov, Alexander Mikhailovich, 1916–, Russ. physicist; Nobel Prize winner.
Prokofiev, Sergei Sergeyevich, 1891–1953, Soviet composer.
Proudhon, Pierre Joseph, 1809–65, Fr. author & political leader.
Proust, Joseph Louis, 1754–1826, Fr. chemist.
—**Marcel,** 1871–1922, Fr. author.
Ptolemy, 2nd c. A.D. Alexandrian astronomer, mathematician, & geographer.
Ptolemy I, 367?–283? B.C., Macedonian general of Alexander the Great & founder of the ruling dynasty of Egypt; king of Egypt 305–285 B.C..
—**II,** 309?–246 B.C., king of Egypt 285–246 B.C.; son of prec.
Pucci, Emilio, 1914–92, Ital. fashion designer.
Puccini, Giacomo, 1858–1924, Ital. operatic composer.
Pulaski, Count Casimir, 1748?–79, Pol. soldier & Amer. revolutionary general.
Pulitzer, Joseph, 1847–1911, Hung.-born U.S. publisher & philanthropist.
Pullman, George Mortimer, 1831–97, U.S. inventor.
Pupin, Michael Idvorsky, 1858–1935, Yugoslav-born U.S. physicist & inventor.
Purcell, Edward Mills, 1912–, U.S. physicist; Nobel Prize winner.
—**Henry,** 1658–95, Eng. composer.
Purkinje, Johannes Evangelista, 1787–1869, Czech physiologist.
Pushkin, Alexander Sergeyevich, 1799–1837, Russ. poet.
Putnam, George, 1814–72, U.S. publisher.
Puvis de Chavannes, Pierre, 1824–98, Fr. painter & muralist.
Puzo, Mario, 1920–, U.S. author.
Pyle, Ernest Taylor (Ernie), 1900–45, U.S. journalist & war correspondent.
—**Howard,** 1853–1911, U.S. author & illustrator.
Pynchon, Thomas, 1937–, U.S. author.
Pythagoras, 6th c. B.C. Gk. philosopher.

Qaddafi, Muammar al-, 1942–, Libyan military officer; head of state of Libya 1969–.
Quant, Mary, 1934–, Eng. fashion designer.
Quantrill, William Clarke, 1837–65, U.S. Confederate guerrilla leader.
Quarles, Benjamin Arthur, 1904–, U.S. historian.
Quasimodo, Salvatore, 1901–68, Ital. poet & critic; Nobel Prize winner.
Quayle, Anthony, 1913–89, Eng. actor.
—**Dan (James Danforth),** 1947–, U.S. statesman; U.S. vice president 1989–93.
Queen, Ellery, pseud. of cousins **Frederic Dannay,** 1905–82, & **Manfred Bennington Lee,** 1905–71, U.S. authors.
Queensbury, John Sholto Douglas, Marquis of, 1844–1900, Scot. boxing patron.
Quensnay, François, 1694–1774, Fr. economist.
Quercia, Jacopo della, 1378?–1438, Ital. sculptor.
Quezon y Molina, Manuel Luis, 1878–1944, Filipino statesman; first president of the Philippines 1935–44.

Quiller-Couch, Sir Arthur Thomas, 1863–1944, Eng. author; pseud. **Q.**
Quincy, Josiah, 1744–75, Amer. lawyer & revolutionary patriot.
Quinn, Anthony, 1915–, Mexican-born U.S. actor.
Quintero, Jose, 1924–, Panamanian-born U.S. stage director.
Quisling, Vidkun Abraham Lauritz, 1887–1945, Norw. traitor during World War II.

Rabelais, Françios, 1494?–1553, Fr. writer & satirist.
Rabe, David, 1940–, U.S. playwright.
Rabi, Isadore Isaac, 1898–1988, Austrian-born U.S. physicist.
Rabin, Yitzhak, 1922–95, prime minister of Israel 1974–77; 1992–95; assassinated.
Rachmaninoff, Sergei Vassilievich, 1873–1943, Russ.-born pianist, composer & conductor in U.S. after 1918.
Racine, Jean Baptiste, 1639–99, Fr. playwright.
Rackham, Arthur, 1867–1939, Eng. illustrator.
Radcliffe, Ann Ward, 1764–1823, Eng. author.
Raeburn, Sir Henry, 1756–1823, Scot. painter.
Raemaekers, Louis, 1869–1956, Du. cartoonist.
Raffles, Sir (Thomas) Stanford, 1781–1825, Eng. colonial administrator in East Indies.
Raft, George, 1895–1980, U.S. actor.
Raimondi, Marcantonio, 1475?–1534, Ital. engraver.
Raimu, b. Jules Auguste Muraire, 1883–1946, Fr. actor.
Rainier III (Louis Henri Maxence Bertrand de Grimaldi), 1923–, prince of Monaco.
Rains, Claude, 1889–1967, Eng.-born U.S. actor.
Raisa, Rosa, 1893–1963, Pol. dramatic soprano.
Raitt, John, 1917–, U.S. singer & actor.
Raleigh, Sir Walter, 1552–1618, Eng. statesman & poet; beheaded. Also **Ralegh.**
Ramakrishna, 1834–86, Hindu yogi.
Raman, Sir Chandrasekhara Venkata, 1888–1970, Indian physicist.
Rambert, Dame Marie, 1888–1982, Pol.-born ballet dancer, teacher, & impresario active in Great Britain.
Rameau, Jean Philippe, 1683–1764, Fr. composer.
Ramon y Cajal, Santiago, 1852–1934, Sp. histologist.
Rampal, Jean-Pierre, 1922–, Fr. flutist.
Ramsay, Sir William, 1852–1916, Scot. chemist.
Ramses A dynasty of Egyptian kings incl. **Ramses I,** founder of the dynasty in the 14th c. B.C., and **Ramses II,** ?–1225 B.C.
Rand, Ayn, 1905–82, Russ.-born U.S. author.
—**Sally,** 1904–79, U.S. dancer.
Randolph, A(sa) Phillip, 1889–1979, U.S. labor leader.
Ranjit Singh, 1780–1839, Indian ruler.
Rank, Otto, 1884–1939, Austrian psychoanalyst.
Rankin, Jeannette, 1880–1973, U.S. feminist & first U.S. congresswoman.
Ransom, John Crowe, 1888–1974, U.S. poet & educator.
Raphael, b. Raffaello Sanzio, 1483–1520, Ital. painter.
Rasmussen, Knud Johan Victor, 1879–1933, Dan. explorer & ethnologist.
Rasputin, Gregori Efimovich, 1871?–1916, Russ. mystic in the court of Czar Nicholas II; assassinated.
Rathbone, Basil, 1892–1967, South African-born U.S. actor.
Rathenau, Walter, 1867–1922, Ger. industrialist & statesman; assassinated.
Rather, Dan, 1931–, U.S. TV newscaster.
Rattner, Abraham, 1895–1978, U.S. painter.
Rauschenberg, Robert, 1925–, U.S. artist.
Ravel, Maurice Joseph, 1875–1937, Fr. composer.
Rawlings, Marjorie Kinnan, 1896–1953, U.S. author.
Rawls, Elizabeth Earle (Betsy), 1928–, U.S. golfer.
Ray, Man, 1890–1976, U.S. artist & photographer.
—**Satyajit,** 1922–92, Indian film director.
Rayburn, Sam(uel Taliaferro), 1882–1961, U.S. politician.
Rayleigh, John William Strutt, Baron, 1842–1919, Eng. physicist.
Read, Sir Herbert, 1893–1968, Eng. art critic & author.
Reagan, Ronald Wilson, 1911–, U.S. statesman; 40th U.S. president 1981–89.
Reasoner, Harry, 1923–91, U.S. journalist and television reporter.

Réaumur, René Antoine Ferchault de, 1683–1757, Fr. physicist.

Récamier, Jeanne Françoise Julie Adélaïde Bernard, 1779–1849, Fr. social leader & patron of literature.

Red Cloud, 1822–1909, Oglala Sioux Am. Ind. chief.

Redford, Robert, 1937–, U.S. actor.

Redgrave, Sir Michael, 1908–85, Eng. actor.

—Lynn, 1943–, Eng. actress; daugher of prec.

—Vanessa, 1937–, Eng. actress; sister of prec.

Redon, Odilon, 1840–1916, Fr. painter.

Reed, Sir Carol, 1906–76, Eng. film director.

—John, 1887–1920, U.S. journalist & poet.

—Oliver, 1938–, Eng. actor.

—Rex, 1940–, U.S. author, critic, & journalist.

—Walter, 1851–1902, U.S. Army surgeon & bacteriologist.

—Willis, 1942–, U.S. basketball player.

Regulus, Marcus Atilius, ?–249? B.C., Roman general.

Rehnquist, William Hubbs, 1924–, U.S. jurist; justice of the U.S. Supreme Court 1972–86; chief justice 1986–.

Reich, Wilhelm, 1897–1957, Austrian-born psychiatrist active in U.S.

Reichstein, Tadeus, 1897–96, Pol.-born Swedish chemist; Nobel Prize winner.

Reid, Ogden M., 1882–1947 U.S. newspaper publisher.

Reik, Theodor, 1888–1969, Austrian-born U.S. psychologist & author.

Reiner, Carl, 1922–, U.S. comedian & TV & film producer & director.

—Fritz, 1888–1963, Hung.-born U.S. conductor.

Reinhardt, Jean Baptiste (Django), 1910–53, Belg.-born jazz guitarist active in France.

—Max, 1873–1943, Austrian theatrical director & producer active in Germany & U.S.

Réjane, b. Gabrielle Réju, 1857–1920, Fr. actress.

Remarque, Erich Maria, 1898–1970, Ger.-born U.S. author.

Rembrandt Harmenszoon van Rijn, 1606–69, Du. painter & etcher.

Remington, Frederic, 1861–1909, U.S. painter & sculptor.

Renault, Mary, 1905–83, Eng. author.

Reni, Guido, 1575–1642, Ital. painter.

Renoir, Jean, 1894–1979, Fr. film director.

—Pierre Auguste, 1841–1919, Fr. painter; father of prec.

Renwick, James, 1818–95, U.S. architect.

Resnais, Alain, 1922–, Fr. film director.

Resnik, Regina, 1924–, U.S. mezzo-soprano.

Respighi, Ottorino, 1879–1936, Ital. composer.

Reston, James, 1909–95, Scot.-born U.S. journalist.

Reszke, Edouard de, 1853–1917, Pol. tenor.

—Jean de, 1850–1925, Pol. tenor; brother of prec.

Retz, Gilles de, 1404?–40, Fr. feudal lord & soldier; thought to be the original Bluebeard.

Reuter, Baron Paul Julius, 1816–99, Ger.-born Eng. news agency founder.

Reuther, Walter Philip, 1907–70, U.S. labor leader.

Revels, Hiram Rhoades, 1822–1901, U.S. clergyman, educator, & congressman.

Revere, Paul, 1735–1818, Amer. revolutionary patriot.

Revson, Charles Haskell, 1906–75, U.S. business executive.

Rexroth, Kenneth, 1905–82, U.S. author & critic.

Reynolds, Sir Joshua, 1723–92, Eng. painter.

—Richard S., Jr., 1908–80, U.S. business executive.

Reza Pahlevi, 1877–1944, shah of Iran 1925–41.

Rhee, Syngman, 1875–1965, first president of Republic of Korea 1948–60.

Rhine, Joseph Banks, 1895–1980, U.S. parapsychologist.

Rhodes, Cecil John, 1853–1902, Eng.-born South African financier & statesman.

Rhys, Jean, 1895–1979, British novelist.

Ribbentrop, Joachim von, 1893–1946, Ger. diplomat.

Ribera, Jusepe de, 1588–1652, Sp. painter & etcher: called Lo Spangnoletto.

Ribicoff, Abraham A., 1910–, U.S. politician.

Riboud, Jean, 1919–85, Fr. industrialist.

Ricardo, David, 1772–1823, Eng. political economist.

Rice, Elmer, 1892–1967, U.S. playwright.

—Grantland, 1880–1954, U.S. sportswriter.

—Thomas Dartmouth, 1808–60, U.S. minstrel show pioneer.

Richard, I, 1157–99, king of England 1189–99: called the Lion-Hearted.

—II, 1367–1400, king of England 1377–99.

—III, 1452–85, king of England 1483–85.

Richard, (Joseph Henri) Maurice, 1921–, Can. hockey player.

Richards, Dickinson Woodruff, 1895–1973, U.S. physician; Nobel Prize winner.

—I(vor) A(rmstrong), 1893–1979, Eng. critic & author.

Richardson, H(enry) H(obson), 1838–86, U.S. architect.

—Sir Owen Williams, 1870–1959, Eng. physicist.

—Sir Ralph, 1902–83, Eng. actor.

—Samuel, 1689–1761, Eng. novelist.

—Tony, 1928–91, Eng. film director.

Richelieu, Armand Jean du Plessis, Duc de, 1585–1642, Fr. cardinal & statesman.

Richler, Mordecai, 1931–, Can. author.

Richter, Conrad, 1890–1968, U.S. author.

—Hans, 1843–1916, Hung. conductor.

—Sviatoslav, 1914–97, Soviet pianist.

Richthofen, Manfred, Baron von, 1892–1918, Ger. military aviator: called the Red Baron.

Rickard, George Lewis (Tex), 1871–1929, U.S. boxing promoter.

Rickenbacker, Edward Vernon (Eddie), 1890–1973, U.S. aviator.

Ricketts, Howard Taylor, 1871–1910, U.S. pathologist.

Rickey, Branch, 1881–1965, U.S. baseball manager.

Rickover, Hyman George, 1900–86, U.S. admiral.

Ride, Sally Kirsten, 1951–, U.S. astronaut; first U.S. woman in space.

Riefenstahl, Leni, 1902–, Ger. film director.

Riemann, Georg Friedrich Bernhard, 1826–66, Ger. mathematician.

Riemenschneider, Tilman, 1460?–1531, Ger. sculptor.

Rienzi, Cola di, 1313–54, Ital. revolutionary statesman.

Riesman, David, 1909–, U.S. sociologist & author.

Riggs, Robert Larimore (Bobby), 1918–95, U.S. tennis player.

Riis, Jacob August, 1849–1914, Dan.-born U.S. journalist & social reformer.

Riley, James Whitcomb, 1849–1916, U.S. poet.

Rilke, Rainer Maria, 1875–1926, Czech-born Ger. poet.

Rimbaud, Arthur, 1854–91, Fr. poet.

Rimsky-Korsakov, Nikolai Andreyevich, 1844–1908, Russ. composer.

Rinehart, Mary Roberts, 1876–1958, U.S. author.

Ringling A family of U.S. circus owners incl. five brothers: Albert, 1852–1916; Alfred, 1861–1919; Charles, 1864–1926; John, 1866–1936; & Otto, 1858–1911.

Ripley, Robert LeRoy, 1893–1949, U.S. cartoonist.

Ristori, Adelaide, 1822–1906, Ital. actress.

Rittenhouse, David, 1732–96, U.S. astronomer & instrument maker.

Rivera, Diego, 1886–1957, Mexican painter.

Rivera y Orbaneja, Miguel Primo de, 1870–1930, Sp. general; dictator 1925–30.

Rivers, Larry, 1923–, U.S. artist.

Rizal, José Mercado, 1861–96, Filipino patriot.

Robards, Jason, Jr., 1922–, U.S. actor.

Robbe-Grillet, Alain, 1922–, Fr. author.

Robbins, Frederick Chapman, 1916–, U.S. physician; Nobel Prize winner.

—Harold, 1916–, U.S. author.

—Jerome, 1918–, U.S. dancer & choreographer.

Robert I, 1274–1329, king of Scotland 1306–29: called the Bruce.

Robert, Henry Martyn, 1837–1923, U.S. engineer, soldier, & parliamentarian.

Roberts, Elizabeth Madox, 1886–1941, U.S. poet & novelist.

—Granville Oral, 1918–, U.S. evangelist.

—Kenneth Lewis, 1885–1957, U.S. author.

—Owen Josephus, 1875–1955, U.S. jurist; justice of U.S. Supreme Court 1930–45.

Robertson, Oscar, 1938–, U.S. basketball player.

Robeson, Paul LeRoy, 1898–1976, U.S. singer & actor.

Robespierre, Maximilien François Marie Isidore de, 1758–94, Fr. revolutionary; guillotined.

Robinson, Bill (Bojangles), 1878–1949, U.S. dancer & actor.

—**Edward G.,** 1893–1973, Romanian-born U.S. actor.

—**Edwin Arlington,** 1869–1935, U.S. poet.

—**Jack Roosevelt (Jackie),** 1919–72, U.S. baseball player.

—**James H.,** 1863–1936, U.S. historian & educator.

—**Sir Robert,** 1886–1975, Brit. chemist; Nobel Prize winner.

—**Ray (Sugar Ray),** 1920–89, U.S. boxer.

Robson, Dame Flora, 1902–84, Eng. actress.

Rochambeau, Jean Baptiste Donatien de Vimeur, Comte de, 1725–1807, Fr. marshal; commanded Fr. allies in Amer. Revolution.

Roche, Kevin, 1922–, U.S. architect.

Rockefeller A family of U.S. oil magnates & philanthropists incl. **David,** 1915–, business executive; **John D(avison),** 1839–1937, grandfather of prec; **John D(avison), Jr.,** 1874–1960, son of prec; **Nelson Aldrich,** 1908–79, governor of New York 1958–73, vice president of the U.S. 1974–77, son of prec. & brother of David.

Rockne, Knute Kenneth, 1881–1931, Norw.-born U.S. football coach.

Rockwell, Norman, 1894–1978, U.S. painter & illustrator.

Rodgers, Richard, 1902–79, U.S. composer.

Rodin, Auguste, 1840–1917, Fr. sculptor.

Rodzinski, Artur, 1894–1958, Yugoslav-born U.S. conductor.

Roebling, John Augustus, 1806–69, Ger.-born U.S. engineer & bridge-builder.

—**Washington Augustus,** 1837–1926, U.S. engineer; son of prec.

Roebuck, Alvah Curtis, 1863–1948, U.S. businessman.

Roentgen, Wilhelm Konrad, 1845–1923, Ger. physicist; discoverer of X-rays; Nobel Prize winner.

Roethke, Theodore, 1908–63, U.S. poet.

Rogers, Carl R., 1902–87, U.S. psychologist.

—**Ginger,** 1911–95, U.S. actress.

—**James Gamble,** 1867–1947, U.S. architect.

—**Will(iam Penn Adair),** 1879–1935, U.S. humorist & actor.

Roget, Peter Mark, 1779–1869, Eng. physician & author.

Rolland, Romain, 1866–1944, Fr. author; Nobel Prize winner.

Rölvaag, Ole Edvart, 1876–1931, Norw.-born U.S. educator & author.

Romains, Jules, pseud. of Louis Farigoule, 1885–1972, Fr. author & playwright.

Romano, Giulio, 1499–1546, Ital. painter & architect.

Romanov, Mikhail Feodorovich, 1596–1645, czar of Russia 1613–45.

Romberg, Sigmund, 1887–1951, Hung.-born U.S. composer.

Rome, Harold, 1908–93, U.S. composer.

Rommel, Erwin, 1891–1944, Ger. general.

Romney, George, 1734–1802, Eng. painter.

Romulo, Carlos, 1901–85, Filipino statesman.

Ronsard, Pierre de, 1524–85, Fr. poet.

Rooney, Mickey, 1920–, U.S. actor.

Roosevelt, Anna Eleanor, 1884–1962, U.S. lecturer, author, stateswoman, & humanitarian.

—**Franklin Delano,** 1882–1945, 32nd U.S. president 1933–45; husband of prec.

—**Theodore,** 1858–1919, 26th U.S. president 1901–09.

Root, Elihu, 1845–1937, U.S. lawyer & statesman; Nobel Prize winner.

—**John Wellborn,** 1887–1963, U.S. architect.

Rorem, Ned, 1923–, U.S. composer.

Rorschach, Hermann, 1844–1922, Swiss psychiatrist.

Rosa, Salvator, 1615–73, Ital. painter & poet.

Rosay, Françoise, 1891–1974, Fr. actress.

Roscius, Quintus, 126?–62? B.C., Roman actor.

Rose, Billy, 1899–1966, U.S. theatrical producer & lyricist.

—**Leonard,** 1918–84, U.S. musician & teacher.

—**Pete(r Edward),** 1942–, U.S. baseball player.

Rosenberg, Alfred, 1893–1946, Nazi Ger. philosopher.

—**Julius,** 1918–53, & his wife **Ethel,** 1915–53, U.S. radicals; executed as spies for the U.S.S.R.

Rosenthal, Jean, 1912–69, U.S. theatrical lighting designer.

Rosenwald, Julius, 1862–1932, U.S. merchant & philanthropist.

Rosewall, Ken, 1934–, Austral. tennis player.

Ross, Betsy, 1752–1836, Amer. patriot; made first Amer. flag.

—**Diana,** 1944–, U.S. singer & actress.

—**Harold Wallace,** 1892–1951, U.S. editor.

—**Nellie Taylor,** 1876–1977, U.S. politician & public official; first U.S. woman governor.

—**Sir James Clark,** 1800–62, & his uncle **Sir John,** 1777–1856, Scot. polar explorers.

—**Sir Ronald,** 1857–1932, Brit. Nobel Prize winner.

Rossellini, Roberto, 1906–77, Ital. film director.

Rossetti, Christina Georgina, 1830–94, Eng. poet.

—**Dante Gabriel,** 1828–82, Eng. painter & poet; brother of prec.

Rossini, Gioacchino Antonio, 1792–1868, Ital. composer.

Rostand, Edmond, 1868–1918, Fr. playwright & poet.

Rostropovich, Mstislav Leopoldovitch, 1927–, Russ. cellist & conductor active in U.S.

Roszak, Theodore, 1907–81, U.S. sculptor.

Roth, Lillian, 1910–80, U.S. singer & actress.

—**Philip,** 1933–, U.S. author.

Rothko, Mark, 1903–70, Russ.-born U.S. painter.

Rothschild A family of Ger. bankers incl. **Mayer Amschel,** 1743–1812, & his sons: **Anselm Meyer,** 1773–1855; **James,** 1792–1868; **Karl,** 1788–1855; **Nathan Meyer,** 1777–1836; & **Solomon,** 1774–1855.

Rouault, Georges, 1871–1958, Fr. painter.

Rouget de Lisle, Claude Joseph, 1760–1836, Fr. poet, author, & composer.

Rousseau, Henri, 1844–1910, Fr. painter.

—**Jean Jacques,** 1712–78, Fr. philosopher & author.

Rowan, Carl T., 1925–, U.S. government official, ambassador, & journalist.

Rowlandson, Thomas, 1756–1827, Eng. artist & caricaturist.

Roxas y Acuña, Manuel, 1892–1948, Filipino statesman.

Royce, Josiah, 1855–1916, U.S. philosopher.

Rozsa, Miklos, 1907–95, Hung.-born composer.

Rubens, Peter Paul, 1577–1640, Flemish painter.

Rubenstein, Helena, 1882?–1965, Pol.-born U.S. businesswoman.

Rubinstein, Anton Gregor, 1829–94, Russ. pianist & composer.

—**Artur,** 1887–1982, Pol.-born pianist active in U.S.

Ruby, Harry, 1895–1974, U.S. composer.

Rudolf I, 1218–91, Holy Roman emperor 1273–91.

Rudolph, Paul, 1918–97, U.S. architect.

—**Wilma,** 1940–94, U.S. track runner.

Ruggles, Carl, 1876–1971, U.S. composer.

Ruisdael, Jacob van, 1628?–82, & his uncle **Salomon,** 1600?–70, Du. painters.

Ruiz Cortines, Adolfo, 1891–1973, Mex. president 1952–58.

Rundstedt, Karl Rudolf Gerd von, 1875–1953, Ger. field marshal.

Runyon, (Alfred) Damon, 1880–1946, U.S. author.

Rush, Benjamin, 1745–1813, U.S. physician.

Rusher, William A., 1923–, U.S. publisher.

Ruskin, John, 1819–1900, Eng. critic & author.

Russell, Sir Bertrand Arthur William, 1872–1970, Eng. mathematician & philosopher; Nobel Prize winner.

—**Charles Marion,** 1864–1926, U.S. artist.

—**Charles T.,** 1852–1916, U.S. founder of Jehovah's Witnesses.

—**Ken,** 1927–, Eng. film director.

—**Lillian,** 1861–1922, U.S. singer & actress.

—**Richard B.,** 1897–1971, U.S. politician.

—**Rosalind,** 1911–76, U.S. actress.

—**William Felton (Bill),** 1934–, U.S. basketball player & coach.

Rustin, Bayard, 1910–87, U.S. black civil rights leader.

Ruth, George Herman (Babe), 1895–1948, U.S. baseball player.

Rutherford, Sir Ernest, 1871–1937, New Zealand-born Eng. physicist; Nobel Prize winner.

—**Dame Margaret,** 1892–1972, Eng. actress.

Ruysbroeck, Jan van, 1293–1381, Flemish mystic & theologian.

Ryan, Nolan, 1947–, U.S. baseball player.

—**Robert,** 1909–73, U.S. actor.

—**Thomas Fortune,** 1851–1928, U.S. businessman.

Ryder, Albert Pinkham, 1847–1917, U.S. painter.

Ryun, James (Jim), 1947–, U.S. track runner.

Saarinen, Aline Bernstein, 1914–72, U.S. author & art critic.

—Eero, 1910–61, U.S. architect; husband of prec.

—Eliel, 1873–1950, Finnish-born U.S. architect; father of prec.

Sabbatai Zevi, 1626–76, Turkish-born Jewish mystic & self-proclaimed Messiah.

Sabin, Albert Bruce, 1906–93, Russ.-born U.S. physician & bacteriologist.

Sacajawea, 1787–1812, Soshone Am. Ind. guide and interpreter for the Lewis and Clark expedition.

Sacco, Nicola, 1891–1927, Ital. anarchist in the U.S.; executed with Bartolomeo Vanzetti for murder.

Sacher-Masoch, Leopold von, 1835–95, Austrian writer.

Sachs, Nelly, 1891–1970, Ger.-born Swed. poet; Nobel Prize winner.

Sackville-West, Victoria Mary (Vita), 1892–1962, Eng. author.

Sadat, Anwar, 1918–81, president of Egypt 1970–81; Nobel Prize winner; assassinated.

Sade, Comte Donatien Alphonse François, 1740–1814, Fr. author: known as **Marquis de Sade.**

Safire, William, 1929–, U.S. author & journalist.

Sagan, Carl Edward, 1934–96, U.S. astronomer.

—Françoise, pseud. of Françoise Quoirez, 1935–, Fr. author.

Sage, Margaret Olivia, 1828–1918, U.S. philanthropist.

—Russell, 1816–1906, U.S. financier; husband of prec.

Sahl, Mort, 1927–, Can.-born U.S. comedian.

Sainte-Beuve, Charles Augustin, 1804–69, Fr. poet, critic, & historian.

Saint Denis, Ruth, 1877?–1968, U.S. dancer, teacher, & choreographer.

Saint-Exupéry, Antoine de, 1900–44, Fr. author & aviator.

Saint-Gaudens, Augustus, 1848–1907, Irish-born U.S. sculptor.

Saint-Just, Louis Antoine Leon de, 1767–94, Fr. revolutionary.

Saint Laurent, Louis Stephen, 1882–1973, Can. statesman; prime minister 1948–57.

—Yves, 1936–, Fr. fashion designer.

Saint-Saëns, (Charles) Camille, 1835–1921, Fr. composer.

Saintsbury, George Edward Bateman, 1845–1933, Eng. critic.

Saint-Simon, Claude Henri de Rouvroy, Comte de, 1760–1825, Fr. philosopher & author.

—Louis de Rouvroy, Duc de, 1675–1755, Fr. statesman & author.

Saint-Subber, Arnold, 1918–, U.S. theatrical producer.

Sakel, Manfred, 1906–57, Austrian-born U.S. psychiatrist.

Sakharov, Andrei Dimitrievich, 1921–89, Soviet physicist; Nobel Prize winner.

Saki, pseud. of Hector Hugh Munro, 1870–1916, Scot. author.

Saladin, 1137?–93, sultan of Egypt & Syria.

Salant, Richard, 1914–93, U.S. radio & TV executive & lawyer.

Salazar, António de Oliveira, 1889–1970, Pg. statesman; premier 1928–68.

Salinger, J(erome) D(avid), 1919–, U.S. author.

Salisbury, Harrison E., 1908–93, U.S. journalist.

—Robert Arthur Talbot Gascoyne-Cecil, Marquess of, 1830–1903, Brit. statesman; prime minister 1885–86, 1886–92, & 1895–1902.

Salk, Jonas Edward, 1914–95, U.S. bacteriologist.

Sallust (L. Gaius Sallustius Crispus), 86–34 B.C., Roman historian & politician.

Salomon, Haym, 1740?–85, Amer. revolutionary patriot & banker.

Samoset, 1590?–1655, chief of Pemaquid Am. Ind.; friend of Pilgrims.

Samuelson, Paul, 1915–, U.S. economist & author.

Sand, George, pseud. of Amandine Aurore Lucie Dudevant, 1804–76, Fr. author.

Sandburg, Carl, 1878–1967, U.S. poet, biographer, & historian.

Sangallo, Antonio da, b. Antonio Cordiani, 1485–1546, Ital. architect.

—Giuliano da, 1445–1516, Ital. architect & sculptor.

Sanger, Fredrick, 1918–, Eng. chemist; Nobel Prize winner.

—Margaret, 1883–1966, U.S. pioneer in birth-control education.

San Martín, José de, 1778–1850, Argentinian-born S. Amer. revolutionary leader & general.

Sansovino, Jacopo, 1486–1570, Ital. sculptor & architect.

Santa Anna, Antonio Lopéz de, 1795–1876, Mexican soldier & politician.

Santayana, George, 1863–1952, Sp.-born U.S. philosopher & author.

Sapir, Edward, 1884–1939, U.S. anthropologist.

Sappho, 7th c. B.C. Gk. poet.

Saragat, Giuseppe, 1898–1988, Ital. president 1964–71.

Sarazen, Gene, 1902–, U.S. golfer.

Sardi, Vincent, 1885–1969, Ital.-born U.S. restaurateur.

Sardou Victorien, 1831–1908, Fr. playwright.

Sargent, John Singer, 1856–1925, U.S. painter.

Sarnoff, David, 1891–1971, Russ.-born U.S. radio & TV executive.

Saroyan, William, 1908–81, U.S. author.

Sarto, Andrea del, 1487–1531, Florentine painter.

Sartre, Jean Paul, 1905–80, Fr. philosopher, author, playwright, & critic.

Sasetta, ca. 1400–50, Ital. painter.

Sassoon, Siegfried, 1886–1967, Eng. poet.

—Vidal, 1928–, Eng.-born U.S. coiffeur.

Satie, Alfred Erik Leslie, 1866–1925, Fr. composer.

Sato, Eisaku, 1901–75, Jap. premier 1964–75.

Sa'ud Ibn Abdul, 1902–69, king of Saudi Arabia 1953–64.

Saul, Hebrew name of the apostle PAUL.

Saussure, Ferdinand de, 1857–1913, Swiss linguist.

Savonarola, Girolamo, 1452–98, Ital. monk & reformer; burned for heresy.

Sayao, Bidu, 1902–, Brazilian soprano active in U.S.

Sayers, Dorothy Leigh, 1893–1957, Eng. author.

Scalia, Antonin, 1936–, U.S. jurist; justice of the U.S. Supreme Court 1986–.

Scanderbeg, Iskender Bey, b. George Castriota, 1403?–68, Albanian chieftain.

Scarlatti, Alessandro, 1659–1725, and his son **Domenico,** 1685–1757, Ital. composers.

Schaller, George Beals, 1933–, U.S. zoologist.

Schary, Dore, 1905–80, U.S. film producer, writer, & director.

Scheff, Fritzi, 1879–1954, Austrian singer & actress active in U.S.

Schelling, Friedrich Wilhelm Joseph von, 1775–1854, Ger. philosopher.

Scherman, Thomas, 1917–79, U.S. conductor.

Schiaparelli, Giovanni Virginio, 1835–1910, Ital. astronomer.

—Elsa, 1890–1973, Ital.-born Fr. fashion designer.

Schick, Bela, 1877–1967, Hung.-born U.S. pediatrician.

Schiff, Dorothy, 1903–89, U.S. publisher.

—Jacob H., 1847–1920, U.S. businessman.

Schildkraut, Joseph, 1895–1964, Austrian actor.

Schiller, Johann Christoph Friedrich von, 1759–1805, Ger. poet & playwright.

Schipa, Tito, 1889–1965, Ital. tenor.

Schippers, Thomas, 1930–77, U.S. conductor.

Schirmer, Gustav, 1829–93, Ger.-born U.S. music publisher.

Schlafly, Phyllis Stewart, 1924–, U.S. women's liberation opponent.

Schlegel, August Wilhelm von, 1767–1845, Ger. author.

—Friedrich von, 1772–1829, Ger. philosopher & author; brother of prec.

Schleiden, Matthias Jakob, 1804–81, Ger. botanist.

Schlesinger, Arthur M., Sr., 1888–1965, and his son **Arthur M., Jr.,** 1917–, U.S. historians.

—James Rodney, 1929–, U.S. government official.

—John, 1926–, Eng. film director.

Schliemann, Heinrich, 1822–90, Ger. archaeologist.

Schmeling, Max(imilian), 1905–, Ger.-born boxer active in U.S.

Schmidt, Helmut, 1918–, chancellor of Federal Republic of Germany 1974–82.

Schnabel, Arthur, 1882–1951, Austrian-born pianist active in U.S.

Schnitzler, Arthur, 1862–1931, Austrian physician & playwright.

Schönberg, Arnold, 1874–1951, Austrian composer & conductor active in U.S.

Schonberg, Harold C., 1915–, U.S. music critic.

Schongauer, Martin, 1445?–91, Ger. painter & engraver.

Schopenhauer, Arthur, 1788–1860, Ger. philosopher.

Schrödinger, Erwin, 1887–1961, Austrian physicist; Nobel Prize winner.

Schubert, Franz Peter, 1797–1828, Austrian composer.

Schuller, Gunther, 1925–, U.S. composer.

Schultz, Dutch, b. Arthur Flegenheimer, 1902–35, U.S. criminal.

Schulz, Charles Monroe, 1922–, U.S. cartoonist.

Schuman, Robert, 1886–1963, Fr. statesman.

—**William Howard,** 1910–92, U.S. composer.

Schumann, Clara, 1819–96, Ger. pianist & composer.

—**Elisabeth,** 1885–1952, Ger. soprano.

—**Robert Alexander,** 1810–56,Ger. composer; husband of Clara.

Schumann-Heink, Ernestine, 1861–1936, Austrian contralto.

Schurz, Carl, 1829–1906, Ger.-born U.S. politician, military officer, & author.

Schütz, Heinrich, 1585–1672, Ger. composer.

Schwab, Charles Michael, 1862–1939, U.S. industrialist.

Schwann, Theodor, 1810–82, Ger. physiologist.

Schwartz, Delmore, 1913–66, U.S. poet & editor.

Schwarzkopf, Elisabeth, 1915–, Ger. soprano.

Schweitzer, Albert, 1875–1965, Alsatian medical missionary in Africa, musician, & theologian.

Scipio Africanus, Publius Cornelius, 237–183 B.C., Roman general: called **the Elder.**

Scofield, Paul, 1922–, Eng. actor.

Scopes, John Thomas, 1900–73, U.S. educator.

Scott, Dred, 1795–1858, U.S. slave.

—**George C.,** 1927–, U.S. actor & director.

—**Robert Falcon,** 1868–1912, Eng. Antarctic explorer.

—**Sir Walter,** 1771–1832, Scot. author & poet.

Scotti, Antonio, 1866–1936, Ital. baritone.

Scriabin, Alexander, 1872–1915, Russ. composer.

Scribe, Augustin Eugène, 1791–1861, Fr. playwright.

Scribner, family of U.S. publishers; **Charles,** 1821–71; his son, **Charles, Sr,** 1854–1930; and his grandson, **Charles, Jr.,** 1890–1952.

Scripps, Edward Wyllis, 1854–1926, U.S. newspaper publisher.

Seaborg, Glenn Theodore, 1912–, U.S. chemist; Nobel Prize winner.

Seabury, Samuel, 1729–96, U.S. religious leader.

Searle, Ronald, 1920–, Eng. cartoonist.

Sears, Richard Warren, 1862–1914, U.S. merchant.

Seeger, Pete, 1919–, U.S. folk singer.

Seferis, George, pseud. of Giorgios Seferiades, 1900–71, Gk. diplomat & poet.

Segal, George, 1924–, U.S. sculptor.

Segovia, Andrés, 1894–1987, Sp. guitarist.

Segrè, Emilio, 1905–89, Ital.-born U.S. physicist.

Sékou Touré, Ahmed, 1922–84, African political leader; first president of Guinea 1958–84.

Seldes, Gilbert Vivian, 1893–1970, U.S. author & critic.

Seleucus I, 358?–280 B.C., founder of Gk. dynasty in Syria.

Selfridge, Harry Gordon, 1857–1947, U.S.-born merchant & businessman active in Great Britain.

Sellers, Peter, 1925–80, Eng. actor.

Selznick, David, 1902–65, U.S. film director.

Semenov, Nikolai N., 1896–1986, Russ. chemist; Nobel Prize winner.

Semmelweis, Ignaz Philipp, 1818–65, Hung. physician.

Sendak, Maurice, 1928–, U.S. writer & illustrator.

Seneca, Lucius Annaeus, 3? B.C.–A.D. 65, Roman philosopher, statesman, & playwright.

Senghor, Léopold Sédar, 1906–, African poet & statesman; president of Senegal 1960–81.

Sennett, Mack, 1884–1960, Can.-born U.S. film director.

Sequoya, 1770?–1843, Cherokee Indian scholar.

Sergeyev, Konstantin, 1910–, Russ. choreographer & ballet company director.

Serkin, Rudolf, 1903–91, Czech-born U.S. pianist.

Serling, Rod, 1924–75, U.S. TV writer & producer.

Serra, Junípero, 1713–84, Sp. missionary in Mexico & California.

Service, Robert William, 1874–1958, Can. author.

Sesshu, 1420?–1506, Jap. painter.

Sessions, Roger, 1896–1985, U.S. composer & teacher.

Seton, Saint Elizabeth Ann, b. Elizabeth Bayley, 1774–1821, U.S. religious leader.

Seurat, Georges, 1859–91, Fr. painter.

Seuss, Dr., pseud. of Theodor Seuss Geisel, 1904–91, U.S. author & illustrator of children's books.

Sevareid, (Arnold) Eric, 1912–92, U.S. news analyst & radio & TV commentator.

Sevier, John, 1745–1815, U.S. soldier, frontiersman, & politician.

Sévigné, Marie de Rabutin-Chantal, Marquise de, 1626–96, Fr. writer.

Seward, William Henry, 1801–72, U.S. statesman; U.S. secretary of state 1861–69.

Sexton, Anne, 1928–74, U.S. poet.

Seymour, Jane, 1509?–37, third wife of Henry VIII of England.

Sforza, Count Carlo, 1872–1952, Ital. statesman.

Shackleton, Sir Ernest Henry, 1874–1922, Eng. Antarctic explorer.

Shah Jehan, 1592–1666, Mogul emperor of Hindustan 1628–58; builder of the Taj Mahal.

Shahn, Ben, 1898–1969, Lithuanian-born U.S. painter.

Shakespeare, William, 1564–1616, Eng. poet & playwright.

Shamir, Yitzhak, 1915–, Israeli statesman; prime minister 1983–84.

Shankar, Ravi, 1920–, Indian musician.

Shankara, c. 788–820, Indian philosopher.

Shapiro, Karl Jay, 1913–, U.S. poet.

Shapley, Harlow, 1885–1972, U.S. astronomer.

Shastri, Shri Lal Bahadur, 1904–66, Indian politician; prime minister of India 1964–66.

Shaw, Artie, 1910–, U.S. musician.

—**George Bernard.,** 1856–1950, Irish-born Brit. playwright, critic, & reformer; Nobel Prize winner.

—**Irwin,** 1913–84, U.S. author.

—**Robert,** 1927–78, Eng. actor, playwright, & author.

—**Robert Lawson,** 1916–, U.S. conductor & choral director.

Shawn, Edwin Meyers (Ted), 1891–1972, U.S. dancer & choreographer.

Shays, Daniel, 1747?–1825, Amer. revolutionary & rebel.

Shearer, Norma, 1905–83, Can.-born U.S. actress.

Shearing, George, 1919–, Eng.-born U.S. jazz musician.

Sheean, (James) Vincent, 1899–1975, U.S. journalist & author.

Sheen, Fulton John, 1895–1979, U.S. religious leader & author.

Shelley, Mary Wollstonecraft Godwin, 1797–1851, Eng. author.

—**Percy Bysshe,** 1792–1822, Eng. poet; husband of prec.

Shepard, Alan Bartlett, Jr., 1923–, U.S. astronaut.

—**Sam,** 1943–, U.S. playwright & actor.

Sheraton, Thomas, 1751–1806, Eng. furniture designer & cabinetmaker.

Sheridan, Ann, 1916?–67, U.S. actress.

—**Philip Henry,** 1831–88, U.S. Civil War general.

—**Richard Brinsley,** 1751–1816, Irish-born Brit. playwright & politician.

Sherman, James Schoolcraft, 1855–1912, U.S. statesman; U.S. vice president 1909–12.

—**Roger,** 1721–93, U.S. jurist & statesman.

—**William Tecumseh,** 1820–91, U.S. Civil War general.

Sherrington, Sir Charles Scott, 1857–1952, Eng. physiologist.

Sherwood, Robert Emmet, 1896–1955, U.S. playwright, journalist, & biographer.

Shinn, Everett, 1876–1953, U.S. painter & illustrator.

Shirer, William Lawrence, 1904–93, U.S. journalist & author.

Shockley, William Bradford, 1910–89, Eng.-born U.S. physicist.

Shoemaker, William Lee (Willie), 1931–, U.S. jockey.

Sholes, Christopher Latham, 1819–90, U.S. inventor.

Sholokhov, Mikhail Aleksandrovich, 1905–84, Soviet author; Nobel Prize winner.

Sholom, Aleichem, pseud. of Solomon Rabinowitz, 1859–1916, Russ.-born U.S. Yiddish author.

Shore, Dinah, 1917–94, U.S. singer & actress.

Short, Bobby, 1936–, U.S. singer.

Shorter, Frank, 1947–, Ger.-born U.S. track runner.

Shostakovich, Dmitri, 1906–75, Soviet composer.

Shubert A family of U.S. theater managers and producers incl. three brothers: **Lee,** 1875–1953; **Jacob J.,** 1880–1963; and **Sam S.,** 1876–1905.

Shultz, George Pratt, 1920–, U.S. educator; secretary of state 1982–88.

Shumlin, Herman, 1898–1979, U.S. theatrical producer & film director.

Shute, Nevil, 1899–1960, Eng. engineer & author.

Sibelius, Jean, 1865–1957, Finnish composer.

Siddons, Sarah Kemble, 1755–1831, Welsh actress.

Sidgwick, Nevil V., 1873–1952, Eng. chemist.

Sidney, Sir Philip, 1554–86, Eng. soldier, statesman, & poet.

Siegbahn, Karl Manne Georg, 1886–1978, Swed. physicist; Nobel Prize winner.

Siegel, Benjamin (Bugsy), 1906–47, U.S. criminal.

Sienkiewicz, Henryk, 1846–1916, Pol. author; Nobel Prize winner.

Siepi, Cesare, 1923–, Ital. basso.

Signorelli, Luca, 1441?–1523, Ital. painter.

Signoret, Simone, 1921–85, Fr. actress.

Sihanouk, King Norodom, 1922–, king of state of Cambodia 1964–70, 1993–.

Sikorsky, Igor Ivanovich, 1889–1972, Russ.-born U.S. aeronautical engineer.

Silliphant, Sterling, 1918–, U.S. playwright.

Sills, Beverly, 1929–, U.S. soprano & opera company director.

Silone, Ignazio, pseud. of Secondo Tranquilli, 1900–78, Ital. author.

Silvers, Phil, 1912–85, U.S. comedian.

Simenon, Georges, 1903–89, Belg.-born Fr. author.

Simeon Stylites, Saint, 390?–459, Syrian ascetic.

Simon, Michel, 1895–1975, Swiss actor active in France.

—**Neil,** 1927–, U.S. playwright.

—**Paul,** 1942–, U.S. singer & songwriter.

Simpson, George Gaylord, 1902–84, U.S. paleontologist.

—**O(renthal) J(ames),** 1947–, U.S. football player.

Sinatra, Francis Albert (Frank), 1915–, U.S. singer & actor.

Sinclair, Harry Ford, 1876–1956, U.S. businessman.

—**Upton Beall,** 1878–1968, U.S. author & politician.

Singer, Isaac Bashevis, 1904–91, Pol.-born U.S. author.

Singer, Isaac Merrit, 1811–75, U.S. inventor.

Siqueiros, David Alfaro, 1898–1974, Mexican painter & muralist.

Sisler, George, 1893–1973, U.S. baseball player.

Sisley, Alfred, 1839–99, Eng. painter active in France.

Sitting Bull, 1834?–90, Sioux Am. Ind. chief.

Sitwell A family of Eng. writers incl. **Dame Edith,** 1887–1964; and her brothers **Sir Osbert,** 1892–1969; and **Sir Sacheverell,** 1897–1988; all poets, essayists, critics, & authors.

Sjöström, Victor, 1879–1960, Swed. film director.

Skelton, John, 1460?–1529, Eng. poet.

—**Red,** 1913–97, U.S. actor & comedian.

Skinner, B(urrhus) F(rederic), 1904–90, U.S. psychologist.

—**Cornelia Otis,** 1901–79, U.S. actress & author.

—**Otis,** 1858–1942, U.S. actor; father of prec.

Skouras, Spyros Panagiotes, 1893–1971, U.S. film executive.

Skulnik, Menasha, 1898–1970, Pol.-born U.S. actor.

Sloan, John French, 1871–1951, U.S. painter.

Smetana, Bedřich, 1824–84, Czech composer.

Smith, Adam, 1723–90, Scot. economist.

—**Alfred Emanuel,** 1873–1944, U.S. politician.

—**Bessie,** 1894–1937, U.S. blues singer.

—**David,** 1906–65, U.S. sculptor.

—**Howard Kingsbury,** 1914–, U.S. radio & TV news commentator.

—**Ian Douglas,** 1919–, prime minister of Rhodesia 1964–79.

—**Capt. John,** 1579–1631, Eng. adventurer; president of the Virginia colony 1608.

—**Joseph,** 1805–44, U.S. founder of the Mormon church.

—**Kathryn Elizabeth (Kate),** 1909–86, U.S. singer.

—**Maggie,** 1934–, Eng. actress.

—**Margaret Chase,** 1897–1995, U.S. senator & congresswoman.

—**Oliver,** 1918–94, U.S. set designer, theatrical producer, & ballet company director.

—**Walter Wellesley (Red),** 1905–82, U.S. sports columnist.

—**William,** 1769–1839, Eng. geologist.

Smithson, James, 1765–1829, Eng. chemist & mineralogist.

Smollett, Tobias George, 1721–71, Eng. author.

Smuts, Jan Christiaan, 1870–1950, South African statesman & general.

Snead, Samuel J. (Sam), 1912–, U.S. golfer.

Snell, Peter, 1938–, New Zealand track runner.

Snow, Sir C(harles) P(ercival), 1905–80, Eng. author & physicist.

Socrates, 469?–399 B.C., Athenian philosopher & teacher.

Soddy, Frederick, 1877–1956, Eng. chemist; Nobel Prize winner.

Sodoma, II, b. Giovanni Antonio de'Bazzi, 1477?–1549, Ital. painter.

Soleri, Paolo, 1919–, Ital. architect active in U.S.

Solon, 638?–558? B.C., Athenian statesman & lawgiver.

Solti, Sir Georg, 1912–97, Hung.-born Brit. conductor active in U.S.

Solzhenitsyn, Alexander, 1918–, Russ. author resident in U.S., 1976–94; Nobel Prize winner.

Somoza Debayle, Anastasio, 1925–80, president of Nicaragua 1967–72 & 1974–79; assassinated.

Sondheim, Stephen, 1930–, U.S. composer & lyricist.

Sontag, Susan, 1933–, U.S. critic, author, & film director.

Soong A Chin. family active in politics & banking, incl. **T(se) V(en),** 1891–1971; and his sisters **Ching-ling,** 1890–1981, widow of Sun Yat-sen; and **Mei-ling,** 1897–, widow of Chiang Kai-shek.

Sophocles, 495?–406 B.C., Gk. playwright.

Sorel, Georges, 1847–1922, Fr. journalist & philosopher.

Sørensen, Søren P. L., 1868–1939, Dan. chemist.

Sorokin, Pitirim Aleksandrovich, 1889–1968, Russ.-born U.S. sociologist.

Sousa, John Philip, 1854–1932, U.S. composer & bandmaster.

Souter, David, 1939–, U.S. jurist; justice of the U.S. Supreme Court 1990–.

Southey, Robert, 1774–1843, Eng. poet.

Soutine, Chaim, 1893–1943, Lithuanian-born painter active in France.

Souvanna Phouma, Prince, 1901–84, prime minister of Laos, 1962–75.

Soyer, Moses, 1899–1974, & his twin brother **Raphael,** 1899–1987, Russ.-born U.S. painters.

Spaak, Paul-Henri, 1899–1972, Belg. lawyer & statesman; secretary general of NATO 1957–61; Belg. prime minister 1938, 1939, & 1946–49.

Spahn, Warren Edward, 1921–, U.S. baseball player.

Spalding, Albert Goodwill, 1850–1915, U.S. baseball player & sporting-goods manufacturer.

Spallanzani, Lazzaro, 1729–99, Ital. biologist.

Spark, Muriel, 1918–, Scot. author.

Spartacus, ?–71 B.C., Thracian leader of slaves in an uprising against Rome 73–71 B.C.

Spassky, Boris, 1937–, Russ. chess master.

Speaker, Tris, 1888–1958, U.S. baseball player.

Spellman, Francis Joseph, Cardinal, 1889–1967, U.S. religious leader.

Spencer, Herbert, 1820–1903, Eng. philosopher.

Spender, Sir Stephen, 1909–95, Eng. poet.

Spengler, Oswald, 1880–1936, Ger. philosopher.

Spenser, Edmund, 1552–99, Eng. poet.

Sperry, Elmer Ambrose, 1860–1930, U.S. inventor.

Spiegel, Samuel P., 1904?–85, U.S. film producer.

Spielberg, Steven, 1947–, U.S. film director & producer.
Spillane, Frank Morrison (Mickey), 1918–, U.S. author.
Spinoza, Baruch, 1632–77, Du. philosopher.
Spitz, Mark, 1950–, U.S. swimmer.
Spock, Benjamin, 1903–98, U.S. pediatrician & political activist.
Spode, Josiah, 1754–1827, Eng. potter.
Spohr, Ludwig, 1784–1859, Ger. composer, conductor, & violinist.
Springer, Axel, 1912–84, Ger. publisher.
Spyri, Johanna Heusser, 1827–1901, Swiss author.
Squanto, 1585?–1622, Am. Ind. friend of the Pilgrims.
Squibb, Edward Robinson, 1819–1900, U.S. physician & manufacturer.
Staël, Mme. Anne Louise Necker de, 1766–1817, Fr. writer.
Stagg, Amos Alonzo, 1862–1965, U.S. football coach.
Stalin, Joseph, b. Iosif Vissarionovich Djugashvili, 1879–1953, Soviet dictator 1927–53.
Standish, Miles, 1584?–1656, Eng.-born soldier & military leader of the Pilgrims in America.
Stanford, Leland, 1824–93, U.S. railroad builder & public official.
Stanislavsky, Constantin, 1863–1938, Soviet actor, director, producer, & teacher.
Stanley, Francis Edgar, 1849–1918, & his twin brother **Freelan Oscar,** 1849–1940, U.S. inventors & automobile manufacturers.
—**Sir Henry Morton,** 1841–1904, Eng. explorer & author.
—**Wendell Meredith,** 1904–71, U.S. biochemist.
Stanton, Elizabeth Cady, 1815–1902, U.S. suffragist.
—**Frank,** 1908–, U.S. radio & TV executive.
Stanwyck, Barbara, 1907–90, U.S. actress.
Stapleton, Maureen, 1925–, U.S. actress.
Stare, Frederick John, 1910–, U.S. nutritionist & biochemist.
Stark, Johannes, 1874–1957, Ger. physicist.
Starr, Ringo, b. Richard Starkey, 1940–, Eng. composer & musical performer.
Stassen, Harold Edward, 1907–, U.S. lawyer & politician.
Statler, Ellsworth Milton, 1863–1928, U.S. hotel executive.
Staudinger, Hermann, 1881–1965, Ger. chemist.
Stauffenberg, Count Claus Schenk von, 1907–44, Ger. staff officer; led abortive plot against Hitler.
Steegmuller, Francis, 1906–95, U.S. biographer.
Steele, Sir Richard, 1672–1729, Irish-born Eng. author & playwright.
Stefan, Joseph, 1835–93, Austrian physicist.
Stefansson, Vihjalmur, 1879–1962, Can. Arctic explorer.
Steffens, (Joseph) Lincoln, 1866–1936, U.S. journalist & author.
Steichen, Edward, 1879–1973, Luxembourg-born U.S. photographer.
Stein, Gertrude, 1874–1946, U.S. writer active in France.
Steinbeck, John Ernest, 1902–68, U.S. author; Nobel Prize winner.
Steinberg, Saul, 1914–, Romanian-born U.S. cartoonist.
—**William,** 1899–1978, Ger. conductor active in U.S.
Steinem, Gloria, 1934–, U.S. author, publisher, editor, & feminist leader.
Steiner, George, 1929–, Fr.-born U.S. critic.
—**Max,** 1888?–1971, Austrian-born U.S. film composer.
—**Rudolf,** 1861–1925, Austrian-born U.S. educator.
Steinmetz, Charles Proteus, 1865–1923, Ger.-born U.S. electrical engineer & inventor.
Steinway, Henry Englehard, 1797–1871, Ger.-born U.S. piano manufacturer.
Stella, Frank Philip, 1936–, U.S. painter.
Stendhal, pseud. of Marie Henri Beyle, 1783–1842, Fr. author.
Stengel, Charles Dillon (Casey), 1890–1975, U.S. baseball player & manager.
Stephens, James, 1882–1950, Irish poet & author.
Stephenson, George, 1781–1848, Eng. inventor.
Stern, Isaac, 1920–, Russ.-born U.S. violinist.
—**Otto,** 1888–1969, Ger.-born U.S. physicist.
Sternberg, Josef von, 1894–1969, U.S. film director.
Sterne, Laurence, 1713–68, Irish-born Brit. author.

Stetson, John Batterson, 1830–1906, U.S. hat manufacturer & philanthropist.
Steuben, Baron Friedrich Wilhelm von, 1730–94, Prussian army officer; served in Amer. Revolution.
Stevens, George, 1904–75, U.S. film director.
—**John Paul,** 1920–, U.S. jurist; justice of the U.S. Supreme Court 1975–.
—**Risé,** 1913–, U.S. mezzo-soprano.
—**Wallace,** 1879–1955, U.S. poet.
Stevenson, Adlai Ewing, 1835–1914, U.S. statesman; U.S. vice president 1893–97.
—**Adlai E(wing),** 1900–65, U.S. statesman; grandson of prec.
—**Robert Louis,** 1850–94, Scot. author.
Stevinus, Simon, 1548–1620, Belg. mathematician.
Stewart, Ellen, 1931–, U.S. theater director.
—**James,** 1908–97, U.S. actor.
—**Potter,** 1915–85, U.S. jurist; justice of the U.S. Supreme Court 1958–85.
Stiegel, Henry William, 1729–85, U.S. iron & glass manufacturer.
Stieglitz, Alfred, 1864–1946, U.S. photographer.
Still, Clyfford, 1904–80, U.S. painter.
—**William Grant,** 1895–1978, U.S. composer.
Stilwell, Joseph Warren, 1883–1946, U.S. general.
Stimson, Henry Lewis, 1867–1950, U.S. statesman.
Stockhausen, Karlheinz, 1928–, Ger. composer.
Stoker, Bram, 1847–1912, Irish author.
Stokowski, Leopold, 1882–1977, Eng.-born U.S. conductor.
Stone, Edward Durell, 1902–78, U.S. architect.
—**Harlan Fiske,** 1872–1946, U.S. jurist; chief justice of the U.S. Supreme Court 1941–46.
—**Irving,** 1903–89, U.S. author.
—**I(sidor) F(einstein),** 1907–89, U.S. journalist.
—**Lucy,** 1818–93, U.S. social reformer & women's suffragist.
Stoney, George J., 1826–1911, Irish physicist.
Stoppard, Tom, 1937–, Eng. playwright.
Story, Joseph, 1779–1845, U.S. jurist; justice of U.S. Supreme Court 1812–45.
Stoss, Veit, 1440?–1533, Ger. sculptor.
Stout, Rex Todhunter, 1886–1975, U.S. author.
Stowe, Harriet Beecher, 1811–96, U.S. author.
Strabo, 63? B.C.– A.D. 24?, Gk. geographer & historian.
Strachey, (Giles) Lytton, 1880–1932, Eng. author.
Stradivari, Antonio, 1644–1737, Ital. instrument maker.
Strand, Paul, 1890–1976, U.S. photographer.
Strasberg, Lee, 1901–82, Austrian-born U.S. drama teacher & actor.
Stratton, Charles Sherwood, 1838–83, U.S. midget: known as **General Tom Thumb.**
Straus, Isidor, 1845–1912, & his brother **Nathan,** 1848–1931, U.S. merchants & philanthropists.
—**Oskar,** 1870–1954, Austrian-born Fr. composer.
Strauss A family of Austrian composers incl. **Johann,** 1804–49 (called **the Elder**), and his sons: **Johann,** 1825–99 (**the Younger**); and **Josef,** 1827–70.
—**Levi,** 1829?–1902, U.S. clothing manufacturer.
—**Richard,** 1864–1949, Ger. composer & conductor.
Stravinsky, Igor Fyodorovich, 1882–1971, Russ.-born composer active in the U.S.
Streisand, Barbra, 1942–, U.S. singer & actress.
Strindberg, John August, 1849–1912, Swed. playwright & author.
Stroessner, Alfredo, 1912–, president of Paraguay 1954–89.
Stroheim, Erich von, 1885–1957, Austrian–born U.S. actor & film director.
Stroud, Robert, 1890–1963, U.S. convict & ornithologist.
Strougal, Lubomir, 1924–, premier of Czechoslovakia 1970–88.
Struve, Friedrich G. W., 1793–1864, Ger. astronomer.
—**Otto,** 1897–1963, Russ.-born U.S. astronomer.
Stuart, Charles Edward, 1720–88, pretender to the throne of Great Britain: called **Bonnie Prince Charlie & the Young Pretender.**
—**Gilbert Charles,** 1755–1828, U.S. painter.
—**James Edward,** 1688–1766, Eng. prince; father of Charles: called **the Old Pretender.**

—**James Ewell Brown (Jeb),** 1833–64, U.S. Confederate general.

Studebaker, Clement, 1831–1901, U.S. carriage manufacturer.

Sturges, Preston, 1898–1959, U.S. film director.

Stutz, Harry Clayton, 1876–1930, U.S. automobile manufacturer.

Stuyvesant, Peter, 1592–1672, last Du. governor of New Amsterdam (now New York).

Styne, Jule, 1905–94, Eng.-born U.S. composer.

Styron, William, 1925–, U.S. author.

Suckling, Sir John, 1609–42, Eng. poet.

Sucre, Antonio José de, 1795–1830, Venezuelan liberator of Ecuador & Bolivia; president of Bolivia 1826–28; assassinated.

Sudermann, Hermann, 1857–1928, Ger. playwright & novelist.

Suetonius, A.D. 69?–140, Roman author & biographer.

Suharto, Mohamed, 1921–, Indonesian general; president of Indonesia 1968–.

Sukarno, 1901–70, Indonesian statesman; first president of the republic of Indonesia 1945–67.

Suleiman I, 1496?–1566, Turkish sultan of the Ottoman Empire: called **the Magnificent.**

Sulla, Lucius Cornelius, 138–78 B.C., Roman general & reformer.

Sullavan, Margaret, 1911–60, U.S. actress.

Sullivan, Sir Arthur Seymour, 1842–1900, Eng. composer.

—**Ed(ward Vincent),** 1902–74, U.S. journalist & TV personality.

—**Harry Stack,** 1892–1949, U.S. psychiatrist.

—**John Lawrence,** 1856–1924, U.S. architect.

—**Louis Henri,** 1856–1924, U.S. architect.

Sully, Thomas, 1783–1872, Eng.-born U.S. painter.

Sully-Prudhomme, René François Armand, 1839–1907, Fr. poet; Nobel Prize winner.

Sulzberger, Arthur Hays, 1891–1968, U.S. publisher.

—**Arthur Ochs,** 1926–, U.S. publisher; son of prec.

Summerson, Sir John, 1904–, Eng. art historian.

Sumner, Charles, 1811–74, U.S. statesman & orator.

Sunday, William Ashley (Billy), 1862–1935, U.S. baseball player & evangelist.

Sun Yat-sen, 1865–1925, Chin. revolutionary leader & president of the republic of China 1912.

Suppé, Franz von, 1819–95, Austrian operetta composer.

Susann, Jacqueline, 1921–74, U.S. author.

Susskind, David, 1920–87, U.S. TV producer.

Sutherland, George, 1862–1942, U.S. jurist; justice of U.S. Supreme Court 1922–38.

—**Dame Joan,** 1926–, Austral. soprano.

Sutter, John Augustus, 1803–80, Ger.-born pioneer in California.

Suzuki, D(aisetz) T(eitaro), 1870–1966, Jap. Buddhist scholar.

—**Zenko,** 1911–, Jap. statesman and prime minister 1980–82.

Svoboda, Ludvik, 1895–1979, president of Czechoslovakia 1968–75.

Swanson, Gloria, 1899–1983, U.S. actress.

Swarthout, Gladys, 1904–69, U.S. mezzo-soprano.

Swedenborg, Emmanuel, 1688–1772, Swed. religious mystic, philosopher, & scientist.

Swift, Gustavus Franklin, 1839–1903, U.S. meat packer.

—**Jonathan,** 1667–1745, Irish-born Eng. satirist.

Swinburne, Algernon Charles, 1837–1909, Eng. poet & critic.

Swope, Herbert Bayard, 1882–1958, U.S. journalist.

Sydenham, Thomas, 1624–89, Eng. physician.

Sydow, Max von, 1929–, Swed. actor.

Symington, (William) Stuart, 1901–88, U.S. politician.

Synge, John Millington, 1871–1909, Irish playwright & poet.

Szell, George, 1897–1970, Hung.-born U.S. conductor.

Szent-Györgyi von Nagyrapolt, Albert, 1893–1986, Hung. chemist.

Szewinska, Irena, 1946–, Pol. track runner.

Szigeti, Joseph, 1892–1973, Hung. violinist.

Szilard, Leo, 1898–1964, Hung.-born U.S. physicist.

Szold, Henrietta, 1860–1945, U.S. Zionist; founder of Hadassah.

Tacitus, Gaius Cornelius, A.D. 55?–117?, Roman historian.

Taft, Robert Alphonso, 1889–1953, U.S. senator 1939–53.

—**William Howard,** 1857–1930, 27th U.S. president 1906–13; chief justice of the U.S. Supreme Court 1921–30; father of prec.

Tagliavini, Ferruccio, 1913–95, Ital. tenor.

Taglioni, Marie, 1804–84, Ital. ballerina.

Tagore, Sir Rabindranath, 1861–1941, Indian poet.

Tailleferro, Germaine, 1892–1983, Fr. composer.

Taine, Hippolyte Adolphe, 1828–93, Fr. philosopher & critic.

Takamine, Jokichi, 1854–1922, Jap. chemist & industrialist active in U.S.

Talese, Gay, 1932–, U.S. journalist & author.

Tallchief, Maria, 1925–, U.S. ballerina & dance company director.

Talleyrand-Périgord, Charles Maurice de, 1754–1838, Fr. statesman.

Tallis, Thomas, 1505?–85, Eng. composer.

Talma, François Joseph, 1763–1826, Fr. actor.

Talmadge, Norma, 1897–1957, U.S. actress.

Talvela, Martti, 1935–89, Finnish basso.

Tamayo, Rufino, 1899–1991, Mexican painter.

Tamerlane, 1336?–1405, Tartar conqueror of Asia. Also **Tamburlaine.**

Tamm, Igor Yevgenevich, 1895–1971, Soviet physicist; Nobel Prize winner.

Tanaka, Kakuei, 1918–93, premier of Japan 1972–74.

Tancred, 1078?–1112, Norman leader in the first crusade.

Tandy, Jessica, 1909–94, Eng.-born U.S. actress.

Taney, Roger Brooke, 1777–1864, U.S. jurist; chief justice of U.S. Supreme Court 1836–64.

Tanguay, Eva, 1878–1947, Can.-born U.S. actress.

Tanguy, Yves, 1900–55, Fr.-born U.S. artist.

Tanner, Alain, 1920–, Swiss film director.

—**Henry Ossawa,** 1859–1937, U.S. painter.

Tarbell, Ida Minerva, 1857–1944, U.S. author.

Tarkington, (Newton) Booth, 1869–1946, U.S. author.

Tarquin (L. Lucius Tarquinius Superbus), 6th c. B.C. king of Rome: called **the Proud.**

Tartini, Giuseppe, 1692–1770, Ital. violinist & composer.

Tasman, Abel Janszoon, 1603–59, Du. navigator & explorer.

Tasso, Torquato, 1544–95, Ital. poet.

Tate, John Orley Allen, 1899–1979, U.S. poet, critic, & biographer.

Tati, Jacques, 1908–82, Fr. actor, author, & film director.

Tatum, Art, 1901–56, U.S. jazz musician.

—**Edward Lawrie,** 1909–75, U.S. biochemist; Nobel Prize winner.

Tauber, Richard, 1892–1948, Austrian tenor.

Tawney, Richard, Henry, 1880–1962, Eng. economic historian.

Taylor, Deems, 1885–1966, U.S. composer & music critic.

—**Edward,** 1644?–1729, U.S. poet.

—**Elizabeth,** 1932–, Eng.-born U.S. actress.

—**James,** 1948–, U.S. singer & songwriter.

—**Laurette,** 1884–1946, U.S. actress.

—**Maxwell Davenport,** 1901–87, U.S. general.

—**Paul,** 1930–, U.S. dancer & choreographer.

—**Robert,** 1911–69, U.S. actor.

—**Zachary,** 1784–1850, U.S. general & 12th U.S. president 1849–50.

Tchaikovsky, Peter Ilyich, 1840–93, Russ. composer.

Tcheitchew, Pavel, 1898–1957, Russ.-born U.S. painter.

Teach, Edward, ?–1718, Eng. pirate: known as **Blackbeard.**

Teagarden, Jack, 1905–64, U.S. jazz musician & blues singer.

Teale, Edwin Way, 1899–1980, U.S. naturalist & author.

Teasdale, Sara, 1884–1933, U.S. poet.

Tebaldi, Renata, 1922–, Ital. soprano.

Tecumseh, 1768?–1813, Shawnee Am. Ind. chief.

Teilhard de Chardin, Pierre, 1881–1955, Fr. paleontologist, geologist, & philosopher.

Telemann, Georg Philipp, 1681?–1767, Ger. composer.

Teller, Edward, 1908–, Hung.-born U.S. physicist.

Temple, Shirley See BLACK, SHIRLEY TEMPLE.
Templeton, Alec, 1910–63, Welsh-born U.S. composer & musician.
Tenniel, Sir John, 1820–1914, Eng. illustrator.
Tennyson, Alfred, Lord, 1809–92, Eng. poet.
Tenzing Norgay, 1914–86, Nepalese Sherpa mountain climber.
Ter-Arutunian, Rouben, 1920–92, Soviet-born U.S. set & costume designer.
Ter Borch, Gerard, 1617–81, Du. painter.
Terence (L. Publius Terentius Afer), 190?–159 B.C., Roman playwright.
Teresa, Mother, b. Agnes Gonxha Bojaxhiu, 1910–97, Yugoslav-born Roman Catholic nun; founded Missionaries of Charity; Nobel Prize winner.
Tereshkova, Valentina Vladimirovna, 1937–, Russ. cosmonaut; first woman in space.
Terhune, Albert Payson, 1872–1942, U.S. author.
Terman, Lewis Madison, 1877–1956, U.S. psychologist.
Terrell, Mary Church, 1863–1954, U.S. civil rights leader.
Terry, Dame Ellen Alicia, 1847–1928, Eng. actress.
Terry-Thomas, 1911–90, Eng. comedian & actor.
Tertullian (L. Quintus Septimius Florens Tertullianus), A.D. 160?–230?, Roman theologian.
Tesla, Nikola, 1856–1943, Yugoslav-born U.S. inventor.
Tetley, Glen, 1926–, U.S. choreographer.
Tetrazzini, Luisa, 1874–1940, Ital. soprano.
Tetzel, Johann, 1465?–1519, Ger. Dominican monk.
Thackeray, William Makepeace, 1811–63, Eng. author.
Thalberg, Irving Grant, 1899–1936, U.S. film producer.
Thales, 640?–546 B.C., Gk. philosopher.
Thant, U., 1909–74, Burmese diplomat & secretary general of the U.N. 1962–71.
Tharp, Twyla, 1941–, U.S. dancer & choreographer.
Thatcher, Margaret Hilda, 1925–, Eng. political leader; prime minister 1979–90.
Thebom, Blanche, 1918–, U.S. mezzo-soprano.
Thiers, Louis-Adolphe, 1797–1877, Fr. author & statesman; president of Third Republic 1870–73.
Themistocles, 527?–460? B.C., Athenian general & statesman.
Theocritus, 3rd c. B.C. Gk. poet.
Theodora, ?–548, Byzantine empress; co-ruler with her husband, Justinian I.
Theodorakis, Mikis, 1925–, Gk. composer.
Theophrastus, 372?–287? B.C., Gk. philosopher & naturalist.
Theresa of Avila, Saint, 1515–82, Sp. Carmelite nun.
Theroux, Paul, 1941–, U.S. author.
Thespis, 6th c. B.C. Gk. poet & dramatist.
Thieu, Nguyen Van, 1923–, president of South Vietnam 1967–75.
Thomas, Ambroise, 1811–96, Fr. composer.
—**Danny,** 1914–91, U.S. entertainer & TV producer.
—**Dylan Marlais,** 1914–53, Welsh poet.
—**Lowell Jackson,** 1892–1981, U.S. news commentator & author.
—**Marlo,** 1943–, U.S. actress; daughter of Danny.
—**Norman Mattoon,** 1884–1968, U.S. socialist leader & author.
—**Seth,** 1785–1859, U.S. clock manufacturer.
—**Michael Tilson,** 1944–, U.S. conductor.
Thomas à Kempis, b. Thomas Hamerken, 1380?–1471, Ger. Christian writer.
Thomas of Erceldoune, 13th c. Scot. poet.
Thompson, Benjamin, Count Rumford, 1753–1814, Amer.-born Eng. statesman & scientist.
—**Dorothy,** 1894–1961, U.S. journalist.
—**Francis,** 1859–1907, Eng. poet.
—**J(ames) Walter,** 1847–1928, U.S. advertising executive.
Thomson, Sir George, 1892–1975, Eng. physicist.
—**Sir Joseph John,** 1856–1940, Eng. physicist; Nobel Prize winner; father of prec.
—**Sir John Sparrow David,** 1844–94, Can. statesman; prime minister 1892–94.
—**Thomas J.,** 1877–1918, U.S. painter.
—**Virgil,** 1896–1989, U.S. composer & music critic.
Thoreau, Henry David, 1817–62, U.S. author & naturalist.
Thorndike, Edward Lee, 1874–1949, U.S. psychologist.

—**Dame Sybil,** 1882–1976, Eng. actress.
Thorpe, James Francis (Jim), 1888–1953, U.S. football player & track athlete.
Thorvaldsen, Bartel, 1770–1844, Dan. sculptor.
Thucydides, 471?–399 B.C., Athenian statesman & historian.
Thurber, James Grover, 1894–1961, U.S. author & artist.
Thurmond, J. Strom, 1902–, U.S. politician.
Thurstone, Louis Leon, 1887–1955, U.S. psychologist.
Tibbett, Lawrence Mervil, 1896–1960, U.S. baritone.
Tiberius Claudius Nero Caesar, 42 B.C.–A.D. 37, Roman emperor A.D. 14–37.
Tiepolo, Giovanni Battista, 1696–1770, Venetian painter.
Tierney, Gene, 1920–91, U.S. actress.
Tiffany, Charles Lewis, 1812–1902, U.S. jeweler.
—**Louis Comfort,** 1848–1933, U.S. decorative designer; son of prec.
Tiglath-pileser III, ?–727 B.C., king of Assyria 745–727 B.C..
Tilden, William (Bill), 1893–1953, U.S. tennis player.
Tillich, Paul Johannes, 1886–1965, Ger.-born U.S. theologian.
Tillstrom, Burr, 1917–85, U.S. puppeteer.
Tinbergen, Jan, 1903–94, Du. economist; Nobel Prize winner.
—**Nikolaas,** 1907–88, Du. zoologist; brother of prec.
Tindemans, Leo, 1922–, premier of Belgium 1974–78.
Tintoretto, b. Jacopo Robusti, 1518–94, Venetian painter.
Tiomkin, Dimitri, 1894–1979, Russ.-born U.S. composer.
Tirso de Molina, pseud. of Gabriel Téllez, 1584–1648, Sp. playwright.
Titchener, Edward Bradford, 1867–1927, Eng.-born U.S. psychologist.
Titian, b. Tiziano Vecelli, 1477–1576, Venetian painter.
Tito, b. Josip Broz, 1892–1980, Yugoslav patriot & statesman; president of Yugoslavia 1963–80.
Tittle, Y(elverton) A(braham), Jr., 1926–, U.S. football player.
Titus Flavius Sabinus Vespasianus, A.D. 40?–81, Roman emperor 79–81.
Tobey, Mark, 1890–1976, U.S. painter.
Tocqueville, Alexis Charles Henri Maurice Clerel de, 1805–59, Fr. statesman & political writer.
Todd, Sir Alexander Robertus, 1907–97, Eng. chemist.
Todman, William, 1916–, U.S. TV producer.
Togliatti, Palmiro, 1893?–1964, Ital. communist leader.
Togo, Shigenori, 1882–1950, Jap. diplomat.
Tojo, Hideki, 1884–1948, Jap. general & politician.
Tokyo Rose, b. Iva d'Aquino, 1916–, U.S.-born propagandist for Japan in World War II.
Tolbert, William Richard, 1913–80, president of Liberia 1971–80.
Tolkien, J(ohn) R(onald) R(euel), 1892–1973, Eng. author.
Tolstoy, Count Leo Nikolayevich, 1828–1910, Russ. author & social reformer.
Tombaugh, Clyde William, 1906–97, U.S. astronomer.
Tomlin, Bradley Walker, 1899–1953, U.S. painter.
Tommasini, Vicenzo, 1880–1950, Ital. composer.
Tompkins, Daniel D., 1774–1825, U.S. statesman; U.S. vice president 1817–25.
Tone, Theobald Wolfe, 1763–98, Irish revolutionary.
Toomer, Jean, 1894–1967, U.S. author.
Torelli, Giacomo, 1608–78, Ital. stage designer.
Tormé, Mel(vin Howard), 1925–, U.S. singer.
Torquemada, Tomás de, 1420–98, Sp. monk & inquisitor.
Torre-Nilsson, Leopoldo, 1924–78, Argentine film director.
Torricelli, Evangelista, 1608–47, Ital. physicist.
Toscanini, Arturo, 1867–1957, Ital. conductor active in U.S.
Toulouse-Lautrec, Henri Marie Raymond de, 1864–1901, Fr. painter & lithographer.
Touré, Sékou, 1922–84, president of Guinea 1958–84.
Tourel, Jennie, 1910–73, Can.-born U.S. mezzo-soprano.
Toussaint L'Ouverture, Dominique François, 1743–1803, Haitian revolutionary leader & general.
Tovey, Donald Francis, 1875–1940, Eng. musicologist & composer.
Townes, Charles Hard, 1915–, U.S. physicist; Nobel Prize winner.
Townsend, Sir John S. E., 1868–1957, Irish physicist.
Toynbee, Arnold J(oseph), 1889–1975, Eng. historian.

Tracy, Spencer, 1900–67, U.S. actor.
Trajan (L. Marcus Ulpius Trajanus), A.D. 52?–117, Roman emperor 98–117.
Traubel, Helen, 1899–1972, U.S. soprano.
Traynor, Harold Joseph (Pie), 1899–1972, U.S. baseball player.
Tree, Sir Herbert Beerbohm, 1853–1917, Eng. actor-manager.
Treigle, Norman, 1927–75, U.S. basso.
Treitschke, Heinrich von, 1834–96, German historian and political writer.
Tremayne, Les, 1913–, Eng.-born U.S. radio actor.
Trevelyan, George Macaulay, 1876–1962, Eng. historian.
Trevino, Lee, 1939–, U.S. golfer.
Trigère, Pauline, 1912–, Fr.-born U.S. fashion designer.
Trilling, Diana Rubin, 1905–97, U.S. critic & author.
—Lionel, 1905–75, U.S. critic & author; husband of prec.
Trippe, Juan Terry, 1899–1981, U.S. airline pioneer.
Trollope, Anthony, 1815–82, Eng. author.
Trotsky, Leon, b. Lev Davidovich Bronstein, 1879–1940, Soviet revolutionary leader; assassinated.
Trudeau, Pierre Elliott, 1919–, Can. statesman; prime minister of Canada 1968–79 and 1980–84.
Trudeau, Garry, 1948–, U.S. cartoonist, satirist, & playwright.
Truffaut, François, 1932–84, Fr. film director.
Trujillo Molina, Rafael Leonidas, 1891–1961, Dominican general; president of the Dominican Republic 1930–38 & 1942–52; assassinated.
Truman, Harry S, 1884–1972, 33rd U.S. president 1945–53.
Trumbo, Dalton, 1905–76, U.S. author.
Trumbull, John, 1756–1843, U.S. painter.
Truth, Sojourner, b. Isabella Baumfree, 1797?–1883, U.S. social reformer.
Tshombe, Moise K., 1919–69, premier of Rep. of Congo.
Tsiolkovsky, Konstantin Eduardovich, 1857–1935, Russ. physicist.
Tsvett, Mikhail Semenovich, 1872–1920, Ital.-born Russ. botanist.
Tubman, Harriet, 1820?–1913, U.S. abolitionist.
—William V(acanarat) S(hadrach), 1895–1971, president of Liberia 1944–71.
Tuchman, Barbara, 1912–89, U.S. historian.
Tucker, Richard, 1915–75, U.S. tenor.
—Sophie, 1884–1966, Russ.-born U.S. singer & actress.
Tudor, Antony, 1908–87, Eng. choreographer.
Tu Fu, 712–770, Chin. poet.
Tugwell, Rexford Guy, 1891–1979, U.S. economist & political adviser.
Tune, Tommy, 1939–, U.S. dancer, choreographer, & stage director.
Tunney, James Joseph (Gene), 1897–1978, U.S. boxer.
Tupper, Sir Charles, 1821–1915, Can. statesman; prime minister 1896.
Tureck, Rosalyn, 1914–, U.S. pianist & harpsichordist.
Turgenev, Ivan Sergeyevich, 1818–83, Russ. author.
Turner, Frederick Jackson, 1861–1932, U.S. historian.
—John Napier, 1929–, Can. statesman; prime minister 1984.
—J(oseph) M(allord) W(illiam), 1775–1851, Eng. painter.
—Nat, 1800–31, U.S. slave; leader of an unsuccessful revolt.
—Tina, 1939–, U.S. singer.
Turpin, Dick, 1706–39, Eng. highwayman.
Tussaud, Mme. Marie Gresholtz, 1760–1850, Swiss-born wax modeler active in England.
Tutankhamen, 14th c. B.C. Egyptian king; tomb discovered 1922.
Twain, Mark, pseud. of Samuel Langhorne Clemens, 1835–1910, U.S. author.
Tweed, William Marcy (Boss), 1823–78, U.S. politician.
Twort, Frederick William, 1877–1950, Eng. bacteriologist.
Tyler, Anne, 1941–, U.S. author.
—John, 1790–1862, 10th U.S. president 1841–45.
—Wat, ?–1381, Eng. leader of Peasant Revolt against taxation.
Tyndale, William, 1484–1536, Eng. religious reformer; translated New Testament; executed for heresy.
Tyndall, John, 1820–93, Irish-born Eng. physicist.

Tzara, Tristan, 1896–1963, Rumanian poet & author; one of the founders of Dadaism.

Uccello, Paolo, b. Paolo di Dono, 1397–1475, Ital. painter.
Ulanova, Galina, 1910–98, Russ. ballerina.
Ulbricht, Walter, 1893–1973, E. German political leader; first secretary of Socialist Unity Party 1950–71.
Ullmann, Liv, 1939–, Norw. actress active in Sweden and the U.S.
Umberto I, 1844–1900, king of Italy 1878–1900.
Unamuno y Jugo, Miguel de, 1864–1936, Sp. philosopher & author.
Uncas, 1588?–1683, Mohegan Am. Ind. chief.
Undset, Sigrid, 1882–1949, Norw. author; Nobel Prize winner.
Unitas, John, 1933–, U.S. football player.
Untermeyer, Louis, 1885–1977, U.S. poet, editor, & critic.
Updike, John, 1932–, U.S. author.
Upjohn, Richard, 1802–78, Eng.-born U.S. architect.
Urban, Joseph, 1872–1933, Austrian-born U.S. architect & set designer.
Urey, Harold, 1893–1981, U.S. chemist; Nobel Prize winner.
Uris, Leon Marcus, 1924–, U.S. author.
Ussachevsky, Vladimir, 1911–90, U.S. composer born in Manchuria.
Ussher, James, 1581–1656, Irish archibishop.
Ustinov, Peter, 1921–, Eng. actor, director, producer, & author.
Utamaro, Kitagawa, 1753?–1806, Jap. printmaker.
Utrillo, Maurice, 1883–1955, Fr. painter.

Vail, Theodore N., 1845–1920, U.S. industrialist.
Valentine, Saint, 3rd c. Roman Christian martyr.
Valentino, Rudolph, 1895–1926, Ital.-born U.S. actor.
Valéry, Paul Ambroise, 1871–1945, Fr. poet & philosopher.
Vallee, Hubert Prior (Rudy), 1901–86, U.S. singer & actor.
Van Allen, James Alfred, 1914–, U.S. physicist.
Van Alstyne, Egbert, 1882–1951, U.S. composer.
Van Brocklin, Norman, 1926–83, U.S. football player & coach.
Vanbrugh, Sir John, 1664–1726, Eng. architect & playwright.
Van Buren, Abby, pseud. of Pauline Esther Friedman, 1918–, U.S. columnist.
—Martin, 1782–1862, 8th U.S. president 1837–41.
Vance, Cyrus Roberts, 1917–, U.S. secretary of state 1977–80.
—Vivian, 1912–79, U.S. actress.
Vancouver, George, 1758–98, Eng. navigator & explorer.
Van de Graaff, Robert Jemison, 1901–67, U.S. physicist.
Vandenberg, Arthur Hendrick, 1884–1951, U.S. journalist & politician.
Vanderbilt, Amy, 1908–74, U.S. writer on etiquette.
—Cornelius (Commodore), 1794–1877, U.S. capitalist & industrialist.
—Gloria, 1924–, U.S. poet, artist, & fabric designer.
Van der Waals, Johannes Diderik, 1837–1923, Du. physicist.
Van der Weyden, Rogier, 1399?–1464, Flemish painter.
Van Dine, S. S., pseud. of Willard Huntington Wright, 1888–1939, U.S. author.
Van Doren, Carl, 1885–1950, U.S. author.
—Mark, 1894–1972, U.S. author; brother of prec.
Van Druten, John William, 1901–57, Eng. playwright.
Van Dyck, Anton, 1599–1641, Flemish painter. Also **Van Dyke.**
Van Eyck, Hubert, 1366?–1426?, & his brother **Jan,** 1389?–1441?, Flemish painters.
van Gogh, Vincent, 1853–1890, Du. painter.
Van Heusen, James (Jimmie), 1913–90, U.S. composer.
Van Horne, Harriet, 1920–, U.S. journalist.
Van Leyden, Lucas, 1494?–1533, Du. engraver.
Van Peebles, Melvin, 1932–, U.S. playwright.
van't Hoff, Jacobus Henricus, 1852–1911, Du. physical chemist; Nobel Prize winner.
Vanzetti, Bartolomeo, 1888–1927, Ital. anarchist in the U.S.; executed with Nicola Sacco for murder.

Varda, Angés, 1928–, Fr. film director.
Vare, Glenna Collett, 1903–89, U.S. golfer.
Varése, Edgard, 1883–1965, Fr.-born U.S. composer.
Varnay, Astrid, 1918–, Swed.-born U.S. soprano.
Vasari, Giorgio, 1511–74, Ital. painter, architect, & writer.
Vauban, Sébastien Le Prestre, Marquis de, 1633–1707, Fr. military engineer & architect.
Vaughan, Henry, 1622–95, Eng. poet.
—**Sarah,** 1924–90, U.S. singer.
Vaughan Williams, Ralph, 1872–1958, Eng. composer.
Vaux, Calvert, 1824–95, Eng.-born U.S. landscape architect.
Veblen, Thorstein Bunde, 1857–1929, U.S. political economist & sociologist.
Veeck, William Louis, Jr. (Bill), 1914–86, U.S. sports promoter.
Vega, Lope de, 1562–1635, Sp. playwright & poet.
Velázquez, Diego Rodriguez de Silva y, 1599–1660, Sp. painter.
Venizelos, Eleutherios, 1864–1936, Ger. statesman.
Venturi, Robert, 1925–, U.S. architect.
Venuti, Giuseppe (Joe), 1903–78, U.S. jazz violinist.
Vercingetorix, 72?–46? B.C., Gallic chieftain defeated by Julius Caesar.
Verdi, Giuseppe, 1813–1901, Ital. composer.
Verga, Giovanni, 1840–1922, Ital. author.
Verlaine, Paul, 1844–96, Fr. poet.
Vermeer, Jan, 1632–75, Du. painter.
Verne, Jules, 1828–1905, Fr. author.
Vernier, Pierre, 1580?–1637, Fr. mathematician.
Veronese, Paolo, 1528–88, Venetian painter.
Verrazano, Giovanni da, 1480?–1528?, Ital. navigator.
Verrett, Shirley, 1931–, U.S. mezzo-soprano.
Verrocchio, Andrea del, 1435–88, Florentine sculptor & painter.
Verwoerd, Hendrik Frensch, 1901–66, prime minister of Republic of South Africa 1958–66; assassinated.
Vesalius, Andreas, 1514–64, Belg. anatomist.
Vesey, Denmark, 1762–1822, U.S. slave & insurrectionist.
Vespasian (L. Titus Flavius Sabinus Vespasianus), A.D. 9–79, Roman emperor 69–79.
Vespucci, Amerigo, 1454–1512, Ital. navigator.
Vickers, Jon, 1926–, Can. tenor.
Vico, Giovanni Battista (Giambattista), 1668–1744, Ital. philosopher & historian.
Victor Emmanuel II, 1820–78, king of Sardinia 1849–61 & first king of Italy 1861–78.
—**III,** 1869–1947, king of Italy 1900–46; grandson of prec.
Victoria, 1819–1901, queen of Great Britain 1837–1901.
Vidal, Gore, 1925–, U.S. novelist, playwright, & critic.
Vidor, King Wallis, 1895–1982, U.S. film director.
Vigny, Comte Alfred Victor de, 1797–1863, Fr. author.
Vigo, Jean, 1905–34, Fr. film director.
Villa, Francisco (Pancho), 1877–1923, Mexican revolutionary leader.
Villa-Lobos, Heitor, 1887–1959, Brazilian composer.
Villard, Henry, 1835–1900, U.S. journalist & financier.
Villella, Edward Joseph, 1936–, U.S. ballet dancer.
Villon, François, 1431–85?, Fr. poet.
Vincent de Paul, Saint, 1581?–1660, Fr. priest.
Viollet-le-Duc, Eugène Emmanuel, 1814–79, Fr. architect & restorer.
Virchow, Rudolf, 1821–1902, Ger. pathologist.
Virgil L. (Publius Vergilius Maro), 70–19 B.C., Roman poet. Also **Vergil.**
Virtanen, Artturi Ilmari, 1895–1973, Finnish biochemist.
Visconti, Luchino, 1906–76, Ital. film director.
Vishinsky, Andrei Yanuarievich, 1883–1954, Soviet jurist & diplomat.
Vishnevskaya, Galina, 1926–, Russ. soprano.
Vitruvius Pollio, Marcus, 1st c. B.C., Roman architect & engineer.
Vitti, Monica, 1933–, Ital. actress.
Vivaldi, Antonio, 1675?–1741, Ital. composer.
Vlaminck, Maurice de, 1876–1958, Fr. painter.
Volcker, Paul Adolph, 1927–, U.S. civil servant & administrator.

Volstead, Andrew John, 1860–1947, U.S. politician & prohibitionist.
Volta, Count Alessandro, 1745–1827, Ital. physicist.
Voltaire, b. François Marie Arouet, 1694–1778, Fr. writer & philosopher.
Von Braun, Wernher, 1912–77, Ger.-born U.S. aerospace engineer.
Von Fürstenberg, Diane, 1946–, Belg. fashion designer.
Von Karajan, Herbert, 1908–89, Austrian conductor.
Vonnegut, Kurt, Jr., 1922–, U.S. author.
Von Neumann, John, 1903–57, Hung.-born U.S. mathematician.
Von Sternberg, Josef, 1894–1969, Austrian-born U.S. film director.
Von Tilzer, Harry, 1878–1956, U.S. composer.
Voroshilov, Kliment Efremovich, 1881–1969, Soviet marshal & politician.
Vorster, Balthazar Johannes (John), 1915–83, prime minister of Republic of South Africa 1966–78.
Vought, Chance Milton, 1890–1930, U.S. aeronautical engineer & designer.
Vreeland, Diana, 1903?–89, U.S. fashion journalist.
Vuillard, (Jean) Édouard, 1868–1940, Fr. painter.

Wagner, George Raymond, 1915?–63, U.S. wrestler: known as Gorgeous George.
—**John Peter (Honus),** 1874–1955, U.S. baseball player.
—**Richard,** 1813–83, Ger. composer & critic.
—**Robert Ferdinand,** 1877–1953, U.S. politician.
Waite, Morrison Remick, 1816–88, U.S. jurist; chief justice of U.S. Supreme Court 1874–88.
Wajda, Andrzej, 1926–, Pol. film director.
Waksman, Selman Abraham, 1888–1973, Ukrainian-born U.S. microbiologist; Nobel Prize winner.
Wald, George, 1906–, U.S. biologist; Nobel Prize winner.
—**Lillian D.,** 1867–1940, U.S. social worker.
Waldheim, Kurt, 1918–, Austrian diplomat & secretary general of the U.N. 1972–1982.
Walesa, Lech, 1943–, Polish labor leader and statesman; president of Poland 1990–95.
Waley, Arthur, 1889–1966, Eng. oriental scholar & translator.
Walgreen, Charles Rudolph, 1873–1939, U.S. pharmacist & merchant.
Walker, Alice, 1944–, U.S. author.
—**James John (Jimmy),** 1881–1946, U.S. politician; mayor of New York City 1926–32.
—**Mort,** 1923–, U.S. cartoonist.
—**Nancy,** 1922–92, U.S. actress.
—**Ralph T.,** 1889–1973, U.S. architect.
Wallace, Alfred Russel, 1823–1913, Eng. naturalist.
—**DeWitt,** 1889–1981, U.S. publisher.
—**George Corley,** 1919–, U.S. governor & political leader.
—**Henry Agard,** 1888–1965, U.S. agriculturist & politician; U.S. vice president 1941–45.
—**Irving,** 1916–90, U.S. author.
—**Lew,** 1827–1905, U.S. author, diplomat, lawyer, & military leader.
—**Lila Bell Acheson,** 1889–1984, Can.-born U.S. publisher & patron of the arts; wife of DeWitt.
—**Mike,** 1918–, U.S. TV interviewer & commentator.
Wallenstein, Alfred Franz, 1898–1983, U.S. conductor.
Waller, Edmund, 1606–87, Eng. poet.
—**Thomas (Fats),** 1904–43, U.S. jazz musician.
Wallis, Hal Brent, 1899–1986, U.S. film producer.
Walpole, Horace, (4th Earl of Orford), 1717–97, Eng. author.
—**Sir Hugh Seymour,** 1884–1941, Eng. author.
—**Sir Robert,** 1676–1745, Eng. statesman; first prime minister of England 1721–42; father of Horace.
Walsh, Raoul, 1892–1980, U.S. film director.
Walter, Bruno, 1876–1962, Ger. conductor active in U.S.
Walters, Barbara, 1931–, U.S. TV personality.
Walther von der Vogelweide, 1170–1230, Ger. poet.
Walton, Ernest Thomas Sinton, 1903–95, Irish physicist; Nobel Prize winner.
—**Sir William Turner,** 1902–83, Eng. composer.
Wanamaker, John, 1838–1922, U.S. merchant.

Wanger, Walter, 1894–1968, U.S. film producer.
Wang Wei, 699–759, Chin. painter, poet, & musician.
Wank, Roland T., 1898–1970, U.S. architect.
Wankel, Felix, 1902–, Ger. engineer & inventor.
Warburg, Aby, 1866–1929, Ger. art historian.
—**James P.,** 1896–1969, U.S. financier.
—**Otto Heinrich,** 1883–1970, Ger. physiologist.
Ward, Aaron Montgomery, 1844–1913, U.S. merchant.
—**Artemus,** pseud. of Charles Farrar Browne, 1834–67, U.S. humorist.
—**Barbara (Lady Jackson),** 1914–81, Eng. economist & author.
—**Clara,** 1924–73, U.S. gospel singer.
Warfield, William Caesar, 1920–, U.S. baritone.
Warhol, Andy, 1927–87, U.S. painter & filmmaker.
Waring, Fred, 1900–84, U.S. bandleader.
Warmerdam, Cornelius, 1915–, U.S. pole vaulter.
Warner A family of U.S. film executives incl. three brothers: **Albert,** 1884–1967; **Harry Morris,** 1881–1957; & **Jack Leonard,** 1892–1978.
—**Glenn Scobey (Pop),** 1871–1954, U.S. football coach.
Warren, Earl, 1891–1974, U.S. jurist; chief justice of the U.S. Supreme Court 1953–69.
—**Harry,** 1893–1981, U.S. composer.
—**Leonard,** 1911–60, U.S. baritone.
—**Robert Penn,** 1905–89, U.S. poet & author.
Washington, Booker T(aliafero), 1856–1915, U.S. educator & author.
—**George,** 1732–99, Amer. general & statesman; first U.S. president 1789–97.
Wassermann, August von, 1866–1925, Ger. bacteriologist.
Waterfield, Robert Staton (Bob), 1920–83, U.S. football player & coach.
Waterman, Lewis Edson, 1837–1901, U.S. inventor & manufacturer.
Waters, Ethel, 1900–77, U.S. singer & actress.
—**McKinley Morganfield (Muddy),** 1915–83, U.S. blues singer & guitarist.
Watson, James Dewey, 1928–, U.S. biochemist; Nobel Prize winner.
—**John Broadus,** 1878–1958, U.S. psychologist.
—**Thomas John,** 1874–1956, U.S. businessman.
Watt, James, 1736–1819, Scot. engineer & inventor.
Watteau, Jean Antoine, 1684–1721, Fr. painter.
Watts, Alan Witson, 1915–73, Eng.-born U.S. religious philosopher & author.
—**André,** 1946–, Ger.-born U.S. pianist.
—**Isaac,** 1674–1748, Eng. theologian & poet.
Waugh, Evelyn Arthur St. John, 1903–66, Eng. author.
Wayne, Anthony, 1745–96, Amer. revolutionary general.
—**John,** 1907–79, U.S. actor.
Weaver, Robert Clifton, 1907–97, U.S. economist & government official.
—**Sylvester L., Jr. (Pat),** 1908–, U.S. TV executive.
Webb, Beatrice, 1858–1943, & her husband **Sidney,** 1859–1947; Eng. socialist reformers & economists.
—**Clifton,** 1896–1966, U.S. actor.
Weber, Carl Maria Friedrich Ernst von, 1786–1826, Ger. composer.
—**Max,** 1864–1920, Ger. economist & sociologist.
—**Max,** 1881–1961, Russ.-born painter.
Webern, Anton von, 1883–1945, Austrian composer.
Webster, Daniel, 1782–1852, U.S. statesman.
—**John,** 1580?–1625, Eng. playwright.
—**Margaret,** 1905–73, U.S. actress & stage director.
—**Noah,** 1758–1843, U.S. lexicographer.
Wechsler, David, 1896–1981, U.S. pyschologist.
—**James A.,** 1915–83, U.S. journalist & editor.
Wedekind, Frank, 1864–1918, Ger. playwright.
Wedgwood, Josiah, 1730–95, Eng. potter.
Wegener, Alfred L., 1880–1903, Ger. geologist.
Weidman, Charles, 1901–75, U.S. dancer & choreographer.
Weill, Kurt, 1900–50, Ger.-born U.S. composer.
Weingartner, Felix, 1863–1942, Austrian conductor.
Weismann, August, 1834–1914, Ger. biologist.
Weissmuller, John, 1904–84, U.S. swimmer & actor.

Weizmann, Chaim, 1874–1952, Russ.-born Israeli chemist & Zionist leader; first president of Israel 1949–52.
Welch, Joseph Nye, 1890–1960, U.S. lawyer.
—**Robert H. W., Jr.,** 1899–1985, U.S. manufacturer & political activist.
Welitsch, Ljuba, 1913–96, Bulgarian soprano.
Welk, Lawrence, 1903–92, U.S. bandleader.
Weller, Thomas Huckle, 1915–, U.S. biologist; Nobel Prize winner.
Welles, Orson, 1915–85, U.S. film director & actor.
Wellington, Arthur Wellesley, Duke of, 1769–1852, Irish-born Brit. statesman & general.
Wellman, William, 1896–1975, U.S. film director.
Wells, Henry, 1805–78, U.S. transportation entrepreneur.
—**H(erbert) G(eorge),** 1866–1946, Eng. author.
—**Mary,** 1928–, U.S. advertising executive.
Welty, Eudora, 1909–, U.S. author.
Wenceslaus, 1361–1419, king of Germany & Holy Roman emperor, 1378–1400 & king of Bohemia 1378–1419.
Wenrich, Percy, 1887–1952, U.S. composer.
Werfel, Franz, 1890–1945, Ger. author.
Wertheimer, Max, 1880–1943, Ger. psychologist.
Wertmüller, Lina, 1928–, Ital. film director.
Wesker, Arnold, 1932–, Eng. author & playwright.
Wesley, Charles, 1707–88, Eng. Methodist preacher & poet.
—**John,** 1703–91, Eng. clergyman; founder of Methodism; brother of prec.
West, Benjamin, 1738–1820, Amer. painter active in England.
—**Jerome Allen (Jerry),** 1938–, U.S. basketball player.
—**Jessamyn,** 1902–84, U.S. author.
—**Mae,** 1892–1980, U.S. actress.
—**Nathanael,** 1903–40, U.S. author.
—**Dame Rebecca,** pseud. of Cicily Isabel Fairfield, 1892–1983, Eng. author & critic.
Westinghouse, George, 1846–1914, U.S. inventor.
Westmore, Perc, 1904–70, U.S. cosmetician & businessman.
Westmoreland, William Childs, 1914–, U.S. general.
Weston, Edward, 1886–1958, U.S. photographer.
Weyden, Rogier van der, 1399?–1464, Flemish painter.
Weyer, Johann, 1515–88, Belg. physician.
Weyerhaeuser, Frederick, 1834–1914, Ger.-born U.S. businessman.
Wharton, Edith Newbold Jones, 1862–1937, U.S. author.
Wheatley, Phillis, 1753?–84, African-born Amer. poet.
Wheatstone, Sir Charles, 1802–75, Eng. physicist.
Wheeler, William Almon, 1819–87, U.S. statesman; U.S. vice president 1877–81.
Wheelock, John Hall, 1886–1978, U.S. poet.
Whistler, James Abbott McNeill, 1834–1903, U.S. painter active in England & France.
White, Byron Raymond, 1917–, U.S. jurist; justice of the U.S. Supreme Court 1962–93.
—**Edward Douglass,** 1845–1921, U.S. jurist; chief justice of U.S. Supreme Court 1910–21.
—**E(lwyn) B(rooks),** 1899–1985, U.S. author & editor.
—**George,** 1890–1968, U.S. theatrical producer & director.
—**Josh,** 1908–69, U.S. folk singer.
—**Patrick,** 1912–90, Eng.-born Austral. author; Nobel Prize winner.
—**Pearl,** 1889–1938, U.S. actress.
—**Ryan,** 1971–90, U.S. AIDS activist; succumbed to the disease after five years.
—**Stanford,** 1853–1906, U.S. architect.
—**T. H.,** 1906–64, Brit. author.
—**Theodore H.,** 1915–86, U.S. political analyst & author.
—**Walter Francis,** 1893–1955, U.S. civil rights leader & author.
—**William Allen,** 1868–1944, U.S. journalist & author.
Whitehead, Alfred North, 1861–1947, Eng. mathematician & philosopher active in U.S.
Whiteman, Paul, 1891–1967, U.S. conductor.
Whiting, Richard A., 1891–1938, U.S. composer.
Whitlam, Gough, 1916–, Austral. prime minister 1972–75.
Whitman, Marcus, 1802–47, & his wife **Narcissa Prentice,** 1808–47, U.S. missionaries & pioneers.
—**Walt(er),** 1819–92, U.S. poet & journalist.
Whitney, Cornelius Vanderbilt, 1899–1992, U.S. sportsman.

—**Eli,** 1765–1825, U.S. inventor.

Whittaker, Charles Evans, 1901–73, U.S. jurist; justice of U.S. Supreme Court 1957–62.

Whittier, John Greenleaf, 1807–92, U.S. poet.

Whitty, Dame May, 1865–1948, Eng. actress.

Wicker, Thomas Grey (Tom), 1926–, U.S. journalist & author.

Widor, Charles Marie, 1845–1937, Fr. organist & composer.

Wieland, Heinrich Otto, 1877–1957, Ger. chemist; Nobel Prize winner.

Wien, Wilhelm, 1864–1928, Ger. physicist.

Wiener, Norbert, 1894–1964, U.S. mathematician & logician.

Wieniawski, Henri, 1835–80, Pol. violinist & composer.

Wiesel, Elie, 1928–, Rumanian-born U.S. author; Nobel Prize winner.

Wiesner, Jerome Bert, 1915–94, U.S. engineer.

Wiggin, Kate Douglas Smith, 1856–1923, U.S. educator & author.

Wigglesworth, Michael, 1631–1705, U.S. pastor, physician, & poet.

Wightman, Hazel Hotchkiss, 1886–1974, U.S. tennis player.

Wigman, Mary, 1889–1973, Ger. dancer.

Wigner, Eugene Paul, 1902–95, Hung.-born U.S. physicist; Nobel Prize winner.

Wilberforce, William, 1759–1833, Eng. abolitionist & philanthropist.

Wilbur, Richard Purdy, 1921–, U.S. poet.

Wilcox, Ella Wheeler, 1850–1919, U.S. poet.

Wilde, Oscar Fingall O'Flahertie Wills, 1854–1900, Irish playwright & poet.

—**Patricia,** 1928–, Can.-born U.S. ballerina.

Wilder, Laura Ingalls, 1867–1957, U.S. author.

—**Samuel (Billy),** 1906–, Austrian-born U.S. film director.

—**Thornton Niven,** 1897–1975, U.S. author & playwright.

Wilhelm I, 1797–1888, king of Prussia 1861–88 & emperor of Germany 1871–88.

—**II,** 1859–1941, king of Prussia & emperor of Germany 1888–1918; grandson of prec.

Wilhelmina, 1880–1962, queen of the Netherlands 1890–1948.

Wilkes, John, 1727–97, Eng. political reformer.

Wilkins, Sir Hubert, 1888–1958, Austral. explorer, scientist, aviator, & photographer.

—**Maurice Hugh Frederick,** 1916–, Brit. biochemist; Nobel Prize winner.

—**Roy,** 1901–81, U.S. civil rights leader.

Willard, Frank, 1893–1957, U.S. cartoonist.

—**Jess,** 1883–1968, U.S. boxer.

William of Ockham, 1284?–1347?, Eng. philosopher & theologian.

William I, 1027–87, Norman invader of England; king of England 1066–87: known as **the Conqueror.**

—**III,** 1650–1702, king of England, Scotland, & Ireland 1689–1702; co-ruler with his wife Mary II 1689–94.

—**William I,** 1533–84, Prince of Orange; founder of the Dutch republic: known as **the Silent.**

Williams, Daniel Hale, 1853–1931, U.S. physician.

—**Edward Bennett,** 1920–88, U.S. lawyer.

—**Emlyn,** 1905–87, Welsh playwright & actor.

—**Esther,** 1923–, U.S. swimmer & actress.

—**Hiram King (Hank),** 1923–53, U.S. singer & composer.

—**Roger,** 1603?–83, Eng. clergyman; founder of Rhode Island.

—**Tennessee,** 1911–83, U.S. playwright.

—**Theodore Samuel (Ted),** 1918–, U.S. baseball player.

—**William Carlos,** 1883–1963, U.S. poet, author, & physician.

Williamson, Nicol, 1938–, Brit. actor.

Willis, Thomas, 1621–75, Eng. anatomist & physician.

Willkie, Wendell Lewis, 1892–1944, U.S. lawyer, businessman & politician.

Wills Moody, Helen, 1905–98, U.S. tennis player.

Willson, Meredith, 1902–84, U.S. playwright.

Willstätter, Richard, 1872–1942, Ger. chemist; Nobel Prize winner.

Willys, John North, 1873–1935, U.S. automobile manufacturer.

Wilson, Charles Erwin, 1890–1961, U.S. industrialist & government official.

—**Charles Thomson Rees,** 1869–1959, Scot. physicist; Nobel Prize winner.

—**Edmund,** 1895–1972, U.S. author, critic, & journalist.

—**Gahan,** 1930–, U.S. cartoonist.

—**Sir Harold,** 1916–95, Eng. politician; prime minister 1964–70 & 1974–76.

—**Henry,** 1812–75, U.S. vice president 1873–75.

—**Lanford,** 1937–, U.S. playwright.

—**Nancy,** 1937–, U.S. singer.

—**Samuel,** 1766–1854, U.S. merchant: known as **Uncle Sam.**

—**Teddy,** 1912–86, U.S. jazz musician.

—**(Thomas) Woodrow,** 1856–1924, 28th U.S. president 1913–21.

Winchell, Walter, 1897–1972, U.S. journalist & radio broadcaster.

Winchester, Oliver Fisher, 1810–80, U.S. firearms manufacturer.

Winckelmann, Johann Joachim, 1717–68, Ger. archaeologist.

Windaus, Adolf, 1876–1959, Ger. chemist.

Windsor, Duchess of, (Wallis Warfield Simpson), 1896–1986, U.S.-born wife of Edward VIII.

—**Duke of** See EDWARD VIII.

Winters, Jonathan, 1925–, U.S. comedian.

Winthrop, John, 1588–1649, Eng.-born Puritan; governor of Massachusetts.

Wise, Isaac Mayer, 1819–1900, Austrian-born U.S. religious leader; founder of Reform Judaism in the U.S.

—**Stephen Samuel,** 1874–1949, Hung.-born U.S. rabbi & Zionist leader.

Wister, Owen, 1860–1938, U.S. author.

Withers, Jane, 1917–, U.S. actress.

Wittgenstein, Ludwig, 1889–1951, Austrian philosopher active in England.

Wittkower, Rudolph, 1901–71, Ger.-born Brit. art historian.

Wodehouse, Sir P(elham) G(renville), 1881–1975, Eng.-born U.S. author.

Woffington, Margaret (Peg), 1714?–60, Irish actress.

Wöhler, Friedrich, 1800–82, Ger. chemist.

Wolf, Hugo, 1860–1903, Austrian composer.

Wolfe, James, 1727–59, Eng. general.

—**Thomas Clayton,** 1900–38, U.S. author.

—**Tom,** 1931–, U.S. journalist & author.

Wolff, Kaspar Friedrich, 1733–94, Ger. antomist.

Wolf-Ferrari, Ermanno, 1876–1948, Ital.-born Ger. composer.

Wolfflin, Heinrich, 1864–1945, Swiss art historian.

Wolfram von Eschenbach, 1170?–1220?, Ger. poet & knight.

Wollaston, William Hyde, 1766–1828, Eng. chemist & physicist.

Wollstonecraft, Mary, 1759–97, Eng. feminist & author.

Wolsey, Thomas, 1475?–1530, Eng. cardinal & statesman.

Wonder, Stevie, b. Stevland Morris, 1950–, U.S. singer, composer, & musician.

Wood, Grant, 1891–1942, U.S. painter.

—**Sam,** 1883–1949, U.S. film director.

Woodbridge, Frederick James Eugene, 1867–1940, Can.-born U.S. philosopher.

Woodcock, Leonard, 1911–, U.S. labor leader.

Woodhull, Victoria Clafin, 1838–1927, U.S. feminist.

Woods, Granville T., 1856–1910, U.S. inventor.

Woodson, Carter Goodwin, 1875–1950, U.S. historian.

Woodward, C(omer) Vann, 1908–, U.S. historian.

—**Joanne,** 1930–, U.S. actress.

—**Robert Burns,** 1917–79, U.S. chemist; Nobel Prize winner.

Woolf, (Adeline) Virginia (Stephen), 1882–1941, Eng. author & critic.

—**Leonard Sidney,** 1880–1969, Eng. author & critic; husband of prec.

Woollcott, Alexander, 1887–1943, U.S. journalist & critic.

Woolworth, Frank Winfield, 1852–1919, U.S. merchant.

Worcester, Joseph Emerson, 1784–1865, U.S. lexicographer.

Wordsworth, William, 1770–1850, Eng. poet.

Worth, Charles Frederick, 1825–95, Eng. fashion designer active in France.

Wouk, Herman, 1915–, U.S. author.

Wren, Sir Christopher, 1632–1723, Eng. architect.

Wright, Eizur, 1804–85, U.S. abolitionist.
—**Frances,** 1795–1852, U.S. lecturer & journalist.
—**Frank Lloyd,** 1867–1959, U.S. architect.
—**Mary Kathryn (Mickey),** 1935–, U.S. golfer.
—**Orville,** 1871–1948, & his brother **Wilbur,** 1867–1912, U.S. aviation pioneers.
—**Richard,** 1908–60, U.S. author.
Wrigley, William, Jr., 1861–1932, U.S. businessman.
Wunderlich, Fritz, 1930–66, Ger. tenor.
Wundt, Wilhelm, 1832–1920, Ger. physiologist & psychiatrist.
Wuorinen, Charles, 1938–, U.S. composer.
Wurster, William, 1895–1973, U.S. architect.
Wyatt, Sir Thomas, 1503–43, Eng. poet & diplomat.
Wycherley, William, 1640?–1716, Eng. playwright & poet.
Wycliffe, John, 1324?–84, Eng. religious reformer; translator of the Bible into English.
Wyeth, Andrew Newell, 1917–, U.S. painter.
—**N(ewell) C(onvers),** 1882–1945, U.S. painter & illustrator; father of prec.
Wyler, William, 1902–81, U.S. film director.
Wylie, Elinor Morton, 1885–1928, U.S. poet.
—**Philip,** 1902–71, U.S. author.
—**Wynn, Ed,** 1886–1966, U.S. comedian & actor.

Xanthippe, 5th c. B.C., wife of Socrates.
Xavier, Saint Francis, 1506–52, Sp. Jesuit missionary in the Orient; founder, with Ignatius of Loyola, of the Society of Jesus.
Xenakis, Iannis, 1922–, Romanian-born composer, architect, & engineer active in France.
Xenophon, 435?–355? B.C., Gk. historian & soldier.
Xerxes I, 519?–465 B.C., king of Persia 486–465 B.C..
—**II,** 450?–424 B.C., king of Persia 424 B.C.; son of prec.

Yale, Elihu, 1649–1721, Eng.-born Amer. merchant & philanthropist.
—**Linus, Jr.,** 1821–68, U.S. inventor & lock manufacturer.
Yamamoto, Isoroku, 1884–1943, Jap. admiral.
Yamasaki, Minoru, 1912–86, U.S. architect.
Yamashita, Tomobumi, 1885–1946, Jap. general.
Yang, Chen Ning, 1922–, Chin.-born U.S. physicist; Nobel Prize winner.
Yeager, Charles Elwood, 1923–, U.S. aviator & general.
Yeats, William Butler, 1865–1939, Irish poet, playwright, & essayist; Nobel Prize winner.
Yellen, Jack, 1892–1991, U.S. lyricist.
Yeltsin, Boris, 1931–, Russ. statesman; president of the Russ. S.S.R. 1990–.
Yerby, Frank Garvin, 1916–91, U.S. author.
Yerkes, Charles Tyson, 1837–1905, U.S. financier.
—**Robert Mearns,** 1876–1956, U.S. psychologist.
Yesenin, Sergey, 1895–1925, Russ. poet.
Yevtushenko, Yevgeny, 1933–, Russ. poet.
York, Alvin Cullum, 1887–1964, U.S. soldier: known as **Sergeant York.**
Yoshida, Shigeru, 1878–1967, Jap. prime minister 1946–54.
Youmans, Vincent, 1898–1946, U.S. composer.
Young, Andrew Jackson, Jr., 1932–, U.S. ambassador, mayor, & civil rights leader.
—**Brigham,** 1801–77, U.S. Mormon leader.
—**Denton True (Cy),** 1867–1955, U.S. baseball player.
—**Lester Willis,** 1909–59, U.S. jazz musician.

—**Loretta,** 1913–, U.S. actress.
—**Murat Bernard (Chic),** 1901–73, U.S. cartoonist.
—**Stark,** 1881–1963, U.S. author & magazine editor.
—**Thomas,** 1773–1829, Eng. physicist & physician.
—**Victor,** 1900–56, U.S. composer.
—**Whitney Moore, Jr.,** 1921–71, U.S. civil rights leader.
Younger, (Thomas) Cole(man), 1844–1916, U.S. outlaw.
Youngman, Henny, 1906–98, Eng.-born U.S. comedian.
Youskevitch, Igor, 1912–94, Russ.-born U.S. ballet dancer.
Yukawa, Hideki, 1907–81, Jap. physicist active in U.S.; Nobel Prize winner.
Yurka, Blanche, 1887–1974, U.S. actress.

Zadkine, Ossip, 1890–1967, Russ.-born Fr. sculptor.
Zaharias, Mildred Didrikson (Babe), 1914–56, U.S. athelete
Zangwill, Israel, 1864–1926, Eng. author & playwright.
Zanuck, Darryl, 1902–79, U.S. film producer.
Zapata, Emiliano, 1877?–1919, Mexican revolutionary leader.
Zatopek, Emil, 1922–, Czech track runner.
Zeeman, Pieter, 1865–1943, Du. physicist.
Zeffirelli, Franco, 1922–, Ital. stage, opera, & film director.
Zenger, John Peter, 1697–1746, Ger.-born Amer. journalist & publisher.
Zeno, 342?–270? B.C., Gk. philosopher: called **the Stoic.**
Zeppelin, Count Ferdinand von, 1838–1917, Ger. general & aviation pioneer.
Zernicke, Frits, 1888–1966, Du. physicist.
Zetterling, Mai, 1925–94, Swed. film actress & director.
Zhao Ziyang, 1919–, Chin. premier 1980–89.
Zhdanov, Andrei Aleksandrovich, 1896–1948, Soviet politician & general.
Zhivkov, Todor, 1911–, head of state of Bulgaria 1971–89.
Zhou Enlai, 1898–1976, Chin. statesman; premier & foreign minister of People's Republic of China 1949–76.
Zhukov, Georgi Konstantinovich, 1896–1974, Soviet marshal.
Ziegfeld, Florenz, 1869–1932, U.S. theatrical producer & playwright.
Zimbalist, Efrem, 1890–1985, Russ.-born U.S. violinist.
Zindel, Paul, 1936–, U.S. author.
Zinnemann, Fred, 1907–97, Austrian-born U.S. film director.
Zinoviev, Grigori Evseevich, 1883–1936, Soviet Communist leader.
Zinsser, Hans, 1878–1940, U.S. bacteriologist.
Zola, Emile, 1840–1902, Fr. author.
Zorach, William, 1887–1966, Lithuanian-born U.S. painter & sculptor.
Zorn, Anders Leonhard, 1860–1920, Swed. painter, etcher, & sculptor.
Zoroaster, ca. 6th c. B.C., Pers. founder of Zoroastrianism: also called **Zarathustra.**
Zsigmondy, Richard, 1865–1929, Ger. chemist.
Zukerman, Pinchas, 1948–, Israeli violinist, violist, & conductor active in U.S.
Zukor, Adolph, 1873–1976, Hung.-born U.S. film producer & executive.
Zurbarán, Francisco, 1598–1664, Sp. painter.
Zweig, Arnold, 1887–1968, Ger. author.
—**Stefan,** 1881–1942, Austrian-born Brit. author.
Zwingli, Huldreich, 1484–1531, Swiss religious reformer.
Zworykin, Vladimir Cosma, 1889–1982, Russ.-born U.S. engineer & inventor.